Webster's
New Explorer
Crossword
Puzzle
Dictionary

Webster's New Explorer Crossword Puzzle Dictionary

Third Edition

Created in Cooperation with the Editors of
MERRIAM-WEBSTER

FEDERAL
STREET
PRESS

A division of Merriam-Webster, Incorporated
Springfield, Massachusetts

Federal Street Press books are available for bulk purchase for sales promotion and premium use. For details, write the manager of special sales,
Federal Street Press, P.O. Box 281, Springfield, MA 01102.

This edition published by
Federal Street Press
A Division of Merriam-Webster, Incorporated
P.O. Box 281
Springfield, MA 01102

ISBN 978-1-59695-113-6

4th Printing RRD, Harrisonburg, VA 11/2013 NK

Printed in the United States of America

Preface

This dictionary has been thoroughly reviewed and updated from the Second Edition with over 10,000 additional entries. It contains more than 335,000 answer words and includes many terms and names that have only recently entered the general English vocabulary: recent slang (*plotz, himbo, crunk, bubkes*), sports stars (*A-Rod, Zidane*), computer languages (*SQL*), automobiles (*Mini, Prius*), Nobel Prize winners (*Pamuk, Yunus*), national currencies (*kroon, som, manat*), actors and actresses (*Alba, Falco*)—not to mention all the familiar words and names that show up with enough frequency in contemporary puzzle grids to have earned the name of "crosswordese": *asea, Oreo, aloe, A-one, espy, ciao, ta-ta, e'er, erose, amah, etui, Odie, tec, Tey, olio, ern, ASAP, Opie, ad-in, ecru, luau*, and a legion of others.

As crossword constructors continue to aim for ever fresher and cleverer clues and answers, we hope this updated reference will prove to be the indispensable tool for filling in those final few elusive letters in crosswords of all kinds for puzzlers of every ability and age.

Using This Book

The book is organized to make it easy to find answer words with a specific number of letters. Every answer word follows a numeral indicating the number of letters it contains. The answer words generally run up to 13 letters; an exception to this limit is made for multiword titles of works, to allow for those clues that omit one or two words from a title, perhaps enough for a five- or ten-letter answer.

As in any crossword dictionary, a single list of answer words will often include words representing various parts of speech. Thus, the entry for **fast** includes synonyms for the adjective (*rapid*), the noun (*diet*), and the verb (*abstain*), all in a continuous list. Puzzle clues are often intentionally ambiguous as to which meaning is intended, and listing all possible synonyms together represents the ideal format for the puzzle solver.

Since puzzle creators rarely provide a clue whose answer word shares the clue's root, such root-related words have generally been omitted from the answer lists. Thus, *singular* does not appear at **single**, *basal* does not appear at **basic**, and *papa* does not appear at **pop**. However, since clues do occasionally share a standard prefix (such as *re-* or *un-*) with an answer word, we have retained a number of clue/answer-word pairs of this kind (**redo**/*remodel*, **unsettle**/*unnerve*, etc.).

When one entry word simply adds a suffix to another entry word, as when **shared** follows **share**, the answer list for the suffixed entry word will usually omit any words that merely add the same suffix to a word in the un-suffixed word's list. For example, since **share** includes such answer words as *divide* and *prorate*, the list at **shared** omits *divided* and *prorated*. Therefore, the user who encounters a clue with a familiar suffix will occasionally want to look at a neighboring entry to be sure of finding all the possible synonyms.

When a personal name is entered as an answer term, the first name generally appears in parentheses and is ignored in the letter count. In cases where the first name is the one normally encountered—e.g., for historical figures such as *Napoleon* and *Galileo*, or fictional characters such as *Atticus* and *Scout Finch*—the last name is generally parenthesized instead. When a title begins with an article (*A*, *An*, or *The*), the article is parenthesized and omitted from the letter count. In a list of geographic entities (**river**, **bay**, **peak**, **mountain**, etc.), any generic term that forms part of a proper name (*River*, *Bay*, *Peak*, *Mount*, etc.) is similarly omitted from the letter count. If none of the answers as listed fits the blanks for a given clue, you should naturally check to see if adding a parenthesized or omitted element might produce the desired answer.

In the many entries that are broken into subentries, the subheadings often consist of a single word, which should usually be read as either preceding or following the main entry word. Thus, at **liquor**, the subheadings include **inferior** (which should be read as "inferior liquor") and **measure** (which should be read as "liquor measure"). The subentry **combining form** lists the kinds of word fragments, usually Greek or Latin in origin, that are commonly called roots (*omni*, *derm*, *giga*, etc.).

The dictionary is best used somewhat imaginatively. If you fail to find a clue word at its own entry, look up a synonym; only rarely will you fail to find one. If a clue takes a form such as *Basque game*, *white wine*, or *Italian tenor* and the dictionary provides no such entry, check at the entry for the generic term—**game**, **wine**, **tenor**, etc.

Webster's
New Explorer
Crossword
Puzzle
Dictionary

A

A1 **4** best, tops **5** prime **6** tip-top **7** optimal, perfect **8** splendid, superior, top-notch **9** excellent, first-rate, front-rank, matchless, top-drawer **10** blue-ribbon, first-class

Aaron *brother:* **5** Moses *father:* **5** Amram *sister:* **6** Miriam

aback **7** unaware **8** suddenly, unawares **10** by surprise **12** unexpectedly

abaft **4** back **5** after **6** astern, behind **8** rearward **9** sternward

abalone **7** mollusc, mollusk **9** gastropod

abandon **4** cede, drop, dump, ease, jilt, junk, play, quit **5** cease, chuck, ditch, leave, let go, scrap, yield **6** desert, disown, give up, laxity, maroon, reject, resign, strand, vacate **7** back out, bail out, cast off, discard, drop out, forsake, freedom, liberty, license, pull out, retreat **8** abdicate, give over, hand over, renounce, wildness, withdraw **9** looseness, repudiate, surrender, throw over **10** enthusiasm, exuberance, relinquish, wantonness **11** discontinue, leave behind, spontaneity, unrestraint **12** carelessness, heedlessness, intemperance, recklessness, unconstraint **13** impulsiveness

abandoned **4** free, lewd, lorn, wild **5** loose **6** gave up, jilted, vacant, wanton **7** cast off, corrupt, given up, outcast, uncouth **8** cast away, depraved, derelict, desolate, forsaken **9** cast aside, debauched, destitute, dissolute, lecherous, neglected, reprobate, shameless **10** degenerate, dissipated, friendless, lascivious, left behind, licentious, profligate, unoccupied **11** uninhibited **12** incorrigible, uncontrolled, unrestrained

abase **5** lower, shame **6** defame, demean, demote, grovel, humble, lessen, reduce **7** cheapen, degrade, devalue, put down **8** belittle **9** denigrate, discredit, disparage, downgrade, humiliate **10** depreciate, undervalue

abash **4** faze **5** mix up, shame, upset **6** dismay, puzzle, rattle **7** confuse, mortify, mystify **8** confound **9** discomfit, embarrass **10** discompose, disconcert

abashment **6** unease **7** chagrin **8** disquiet **9** confusion **12** discomfiture, discomposure

abate **3** ebb, end **4** ease, fade, fall, omit, slow, void, stem, wane **5** allay, annul, close, let up, quash, taper **6** deduct, lessen, negate, recede, reduce, relent, weaken **7** abolish, decline, deprive, die down, dwindle, ease off, nullify, slacken, subside **8** decrease, diminish, mitigate, moderate **9** alleviate, eradicate **10** invalidate

abatement **6** ebbing, rebate, waning **8** decrease, discount **9** declining, deduction, dwindling, exemption, lessening, reduction, shrinkage **10** diminution, subsidence **11** subtraction

abattoir **8** shambles

Abba ____ **4** Eban

abbey **6** friary **7** convent **8** cloister **9** monastery

abbot *female:* **6** abbess

abbreviate **3** cut **4** clip, trim **5** prune **6** cut out, reduce **7** abridge, curtail, cut back, shorten **8** compress, condense, contract, cut short, truncate

abbreviation **5** brief **6** digest, précis, sketch **7** acronym, cutting, outline **8** abstract, clipping, synopsis, trimming **10** abridgment, shortening **11** curtailment **12** condensation

ABC island **5** Aruba **7** Baranof, Bonaire, Curaçao **9** Admiralty, Chichagof

abdicate **4** cede, drop, quit **5** evade, forgo, leave, waive, yield **6** abjure, give up, reject, resign **7** abandon, cast off, discard **8** abnegate, disclaim, hand over, renounce, withdraw **9** repudiate, surrender **10** relinquish

abdomen **3** gut, pot **5** belly, tummy **6** middle, paunch **7** midriff, stomach **8** potbelly **9** bay window **10** midsection **11** breadbasket *depression:* **5** navel

abduct **4** grab, take **5** seize **6** kidnap, remove, snatch **8** carry off, draw away, take away **9** carry away, steal away **10** spirit away **11** make off with

Abduction from the Seraglio *character:* **5** Osmin, Selim **8** Belmonte, Pedrillo **9** Konstanze *composer:* **6** Mozart (Wolfgang Amadeus)

abecedarian **4** tyro **6** novice **7** amateur, dabbler, learner **8** beginner, initiate, neophyte **9**

beginning, smatterer **10** apprentice, dilettante, elementary **11** rudimentary **12** alphabetical

Abel *brother:* **4** Cain, Seth *father:* **4** Adam *mother:* **3** Eve *slayer:* **4** Cain

Abelard *son:* **9** Astrolabe *wife:* **7** Heloise

abele 6 poplar

aberrant 3 odd **7** deviant, strange, unusual **8** abnormal, atypical, peculiar, straying **9** anomalous, deviating, different, eccentric, irregular, unnatural, untypical **11** exceptional, nonstandard

aberration 4 slip **5** quirk **6** change, oddity **7** anomaly, mistake **8** mutation, straying **9** curiosity, deviation, exception, wandering **10** deflection, difference, distortion, divergence **11** abnormality, peculiarity **12** eccentricity, irregularity

abet 3 aid, egg **4** ally, back, help, prod, spur, urge **5** boost, egg on **6** assist, exhort, foment, incite, second, stir up **7** condone, endorse, forward, promote, support **8** advocate **9** encourage, instigate **11** countenance

abettor 4 aide, ally **6** backup, cohort, helper **7** inciter, partner **8** fomenter **9** accessory, supporter **10** accomplice, instigator **11** confederate, conspirator **12** collaborator

abeyance 4 lull, rest **5** break, lapse, pause **6** recess **7** respite, time-out, waiting **8** breather, interval **10** inactivity, quiescence, suspension **12** intermission, interruption

abeyant 7 dormant **8** deferred, inactive, recessed **9** postponed, quiescent, suspended **11** interrupted

abhor 4 hate **5** scorn **6** detest, loathe, reject, revile, vilify **7** contemn, despise, disdain, dislike **8** execrate **9** abominate, excoriate, repudiate

abhorrence 4 evil, hate **6** hatred, horror **7** disgust **8** aversion, distaste, loathing **9** repulsion, revulsion **10** repugnance **11** abomination, detestation

abhorrent 4 base, foul, vile **5** awful **6** horrid, odious **7** beastly, hateful, heinous **8** damnable, horrible, horrific **9** atrocious, execrable, invidious, loathsome, monstrous, obnoxious, repellent, repugnant, repulsive, revolting **10** abominable, deplorable, despicable, detestable, disgusting **12** contemptible **13** reprehensible

abide 4 bear, last, live, stay, wait **5** await, brook, dwell, exist, stand, tarry **6** accede, accept, comply, endure, keep on, linger, remain, reside, stay on, suffer **7** consent, hang out, inhabit, persist, sojourn, stomach, subsist, swallow, wait for **8** continue, live with, stand for, tolerate **9** put up with, withstand

abiding 4 fast, firm, sure **6** steady **7** durable, eternal, lasting, staying **8** constant, enduring, timeless **9** complying, perpetual, steadfast **10** continuing, persistent, persisting, unchanging **11** everlasting, unfaltering

abigail 4 maid

Abigail *brother:* **5** David *husband:* **5** David, Nabal *mother:* **5** Amasa *son:* **7** Chileah

ability 4 bent, gift **5** craft, flair, knack, might, savvy, skill **6** talent **7** aptness, command, faculty, know-how, mastery, prowess **8** aptitude, capacity, facility **9** adeptness, dexterity, expertise, handiness, ingenuity, potential **10** adroitness, capability, cleverness, competence, efficiency **11** proficiency **12** skillfulness **13** qualification

abject 3 low **4** base, mean, poor, vile **5** lowly, sorry **6** dismal, humble, shabby, sordid **7** debased, fawning, forlorn, ignoble, pitiful, servile **8** cast down, degraded, dejected, downcast, hopeless, pathetic, pitiable, rejected, resigned, wretched **9** afflicted, destitute, groveling, miserable, worthless **10** deplorable, obsequious, spiritless, submissive **11** deferential, downtrodden, subservient **12** contemptible, dishonorable, ingratiating

abjure 4 cede, deny **5** avoid, spurn **6** desert, disown, recall, recant, reject, refuse, revoke **7** abandon, disavow, decline, forsake, retract **8** disclaim, forswear, renounce, take back, withdraw **9** repudiate, surrender **10** relinquish **11** abstain from

ablaze 5 afire, aglow, fiery **6** aflame, alight, on fire **7** burning, flaming, excited, flaring, ignited, radiant

able 3 apt, fit **4** keen **5** adept, alert, sharp, smart **6** adroit, clever, expert, facile, suited **7** capable, skilled **8** skillful, talented **9** competent, effective, effectual, efficient, qualified **10** proficient **11** intelligent, resourceful **12** accomplished, enterprising

able-bodied 3 fit **4** hale **5** hardy, lusty, sound, stout **6** brawny, hearty, robust, strong, sturdy **7** capable **8** stalwart, vigorous **9** strapping

ablution 4 bath **6** laving **7** bathing, washing **8** lavation **9** cleansing, immersion **12** purification

abnegate 4 cede, deny, drop **5** forgo, waive, yield **6** abjure, give up, recant, revoke, vacate **7** disavow, gainsay **8** disallow, disclaim, forswear, renounce, withdraw **9** repudiate, surrender **10** contradict, contravene, relinquish

abnegation 6 denial **9** surrender **10** abstinence, self-denial **12** renouncement, renunciation

Abner *cousin:* **4** Saul *father:* **3** Ner *slayer:* **4** Joab

abnormal 3 odd **5** freak, outré, undue, weird **6** off-key **7** bizarre, deviant, strange, unusual **8** aberrant, atypical, freakish, peculiar **9** anomalous, divergent, eccentric, irregular, unnatural **11** heteroclite **13** preternatural

abnormality 4 flaw **6** oddity **7** anomaly **8** deviance **9** deviation, exception **10** aberration, difference **12** irregularity

abode 3 hut **4** home, nest, tent **5** house **7** address, lodging, sojourn **8** domicile, dwelling **9** residence **10** habitation *conical:* **5** tepee **6** teepee

abolish 3 end **4** undo, kill, void **5** abate, annul, erase, quash **6** cancel, negate, recall, repeal, revoke, vacate **7** destroy, nullify, rescind, retract, reverse, wipe out **8** abrogate, disallow, dissolve, overturn, prohibit **9** eliminate, eradicate, terminate **10** do away with, extinguish, invalidate

abolitionist 4 Mott (Lucretia), Weld (Theodore) **5** Brown (John), Child (Lydia), Lundy (Benjamin), Smith (Gerrit), Stowe (Harriet Beecher) **6** Birney (James), Lowell (James Russell), Parker (Theodore), Tappan (Arthur), Tubman (Harriet) **7** Lincoln (Abraham) **8** Douglass (Frederick), Garrison (William Lloyd), Phillips (Wendell), Whittier (John Greenleaf)

abominable 5 awful, nasty **6** cursed, horrid, odious **7** hateful, heinous **8** horrible, shocking, terrible, wretched **9** abhorrent, loathsome, offensive, repellent, repugnant, repulsive, revolting **10** deplorable, despicable, detestable, disgusting **12** contemptible

abominable snowman 4 yeti

abominate 4 damn, hate **5** abhor, curse, scorn **6** detest, loathe, revile **7** despise **8** execrate **9** repudiate

abomination 4 evil, hate **5** scorn **6** hatred, horror, plague **7** disdain, disgust, dislike **8** anathema, aversion, contempt, distaste, loathing **9** repulsion, revulsion **10** abhorrence, repugnance, repugnancy **11** detestation

aboriginal 5 first **6** native **7** ancient, endemic, primary **8** earliest, original, primeval **9** primitive **10** indigenous, primordial **13** autochthonous

aborigine 6 native **7** ancient **8** indigene **10** autochthon

abort 4 drop, halt, stop **5** check, expel, scrap, scrub **6** arrest, cancel **7** abandon, call off **8** cut short **9** interrupt, terminate

abortive 4 vain **5** empty **6** futile, unripe **7** failing, useless **9** fruitless, worthless **10** unavailing, unfruitful **11** ineffective, ineffectual **12** unproductive, unsuccessful

abound 4 flow, teem **5** burst, crawl, crowd, flood, swarm, swell **6** throng **8** overflow

abounding 4 full, rife **5** laden **6** filled, full of, jammed, packed **7** copious, profuse, replete, stuffed, teeming **8** abundant, swarming, thronged **9** alive with, bristling, plenteous, plentiful **11** overflowing

about 4 as to, back, in re, near, nigh, over, some **5** again, anent, circa, round **6** almost, around, nearby, nearly **7** apropos, close to, roughly **8** backward **9** as regards, in general, in reverse, regarding **10** as concerns, concerning, in regard to, more or less, relating to, relative to, respecting **11** dealing with, practically, referring to **12** with regard to **13** approximately, concerned with, in reference to, with respect to

about-face 4 turn **7** reverse **8** reversal **9** turnabout

above 3 o'er **4** atop, over, past **5** aloft, supra **6** beyond **8** overhead **9** exceeding *prefix:* **4** over **5** hyper, super, supra

above all 7 chiefly **9** primarily **10** especially **11** principally **12** particularly

aboveboard 4 free, open **5** frank **6** candid, honest, openly **7** frankly, up front **8** candidly, honestly, straight, truthful **10** truthfully, forthright, scrupulous

abracadabra 5 charm, magic **6** babble, jargon **9** gibberish **10** double talk, mumbo jumbo **11** incantation **12** gobbledygook **13** mystification

abrade 3 bug, irk, rub **4** burn, fret, gall, rasp, wear **5** annoy, chafe, erode, grate, graze, upset, weary **6** bother, ruffle, scrape **7** corrode, eat away, perturb, provoke, roughen **8** irritate, wear away, wear down **9** aggravate, grind down

Abraham *brother:* **5** Haran, Nahor *concubine:* **5** Hagar *father:* **5** Terah *grandfather:* **5** Nahor *grandson:* **4** Esau *nephew:* **3** Lot *son:* **5** Isaac, Medan, Shuah **6** Midian, Zimran **7** Ishmael *well:* **9** Beer-Sheba *wife:* **5** Sarah **7** Keturah

abrasion 5 chafe, scuff **6** scrape **7** chafing, erosion, grating, rubbing, scratch **8** friction, grinding, scraping, scuffing **10** irritation, scratching

abrasive 5 emery, rough, sharp **6** biting, pumice **7** wearing **8** annoying **9** smoothing, polishing **10** irritating **11** Carborundum, garnet paper

abreast 6 beside, next to, versed, with-it **7** versant **8** familiar, informed, up-to-date **9** au courant **10** acquainted, conversant

abridge 3 cut **4** pare, trim **5** limit, prune **6** lessen, narrow, reduce **7** curtail, cut back, shorten **8** boil down, compress, condense, cut short, diminish, restrict, truncate **9** summarize **10** abbreviate

abridgment 5 brief **6** digest **7** capsule, cutting, summary **8** abstract, synopsis **9** lessening, reduction, short form **10** diminution, shortening **11** compression, contraction, curtailment, restriction **12** abbreviation, condensation

abroad 4 afar, away **5** about **6** afield, astray, widely **7** touring **8** overseas **9** elsewhere, traveling

abrogate 3 end **4** undo, void **5** abate, annul, quash **6** cancel, negate, repeal, revoke, vacate **7** abolish, blot out, nullify, rescind, reverse **8** dissolve **9** discharge **10** extinguish, invalidate, obliterate

abrupt 4 curt **5** bluff, blunt, brief, brisk, gruff, hasty, sharp, sheer, short, steep **6** cut off, snippy, sudden **7** brusque, hurried **8** headlong **9** broken off, impetuous **10** unexpected **11** precipitate, precipitous **13** unceremonious

abruptness 10 brusquerie **12** precipitance

Absalom commander: 5 Amasa **father: 5** David **mother: 7** Maachah **sister: 5** Tamar **slayer: 4** Joab

abscess 4 boil, sore **5** botch, ulcer **6** lesion, pimple, trauma **7** blister, pustule **8** furuncle **9** carbuncle

abscond 4 bolt, flee, quit, skip **5** break, leave **6** decamp, escape, run off **7** run away, take off **8** slip away, sneak off **9** disappear, sneak away, steal away

absence 4 AWOL, lack, need, void, want **6** dearth, defect, vacuum **7** default, drought, failure, sick-out, vacancy **9** privation **10** deficiency, inadequacy **11** absenteeism, inattention **13** insufficiency

absent 4 away, AWOL, gone, lost **6** no-show **7** bemused, faraway, lacking, missing, omitted, wanting, without **8** distrait, heedless **9** elsewhere, forgetful **10** abstracted, distracted **11** inattentive, preoccupied

absentminded 4 lost **7** bemused, faraway **8** distrait, dreaming, heedless, unseeing **9** forgetful, oblivious, unheeding, unmindful **10** abstracted, distracted, unnoticing **11** inattentive, inconscient, preoccupied, unconscious, unobserving

absolute 4 full, pure, real, true **5** ideal, sheer, total, utter **6** actual, entire, simple, strict **7** eternal, factual, genuine, perfect, supreme, unmixed **8** autarkic, complete, despotic, flawless, infinite, outright, positive, ultimate, simplest, thorough, unflawed **9** arbitrary, autarchic, boundless, downright, embodying, imperious, masterful, sovereign, unalloyed, undiluted, unlimited **10** autocratic, autonomous, consummate, impeccable, monocratic, tyrannical **11** categorical, dictatorial, domineering, fundamental, independent, unequivocal, unmitigated, unqualified **12** indisputable, totalitarian, unrestrained, unrestricted **13** authoritarian, unconditional

absolutely 5 fully **6** wholly **7** utterly **8** entirely **9** doubtless, perfectly **10** completely, definitely, positively, thoroughly **11** doubtlessly **13** unequivocally

absolution 6 pardon **7** amnesty, freeing, release **9** releasing, remission **10** letting off **11** exculpation, exoneration, forgiveness **12** dispensation

absolutism 9 Caesarism, despotism **12** dictatorship

absolve 4 free **5** clear, let go, remit, spare **6** acquit, excuse, exempt, let off, pardon **7** forgive, release, relieve, set free **8** dispense **9** discharge, exculpate, exonerate, vindicate

absorb 4 bear, blot **5** imbue, learn, sop up, use up **6** assume, embody, endure, engage, imbibe, infuse, ingest, soak up, sponge, suck up, take in, take up **7** acquire, consume, drink in, engross, immerse, involve, receive, sustain **8** permeate **9** preoccupy, transform **10** assimilate **11** incorporate

absorbed 4 deep, into, lost, rapt **6** intent **7** engaged, wrapped **8** caught up, immersed, involved **9** engrossed, wrapped up **10** captivated, fascinated **11** preoccupied

absorbing 9 arresting, consuming **10** engrossing, intriguing **11** captivating, fascinating, interesting **12** monopolizing, preoccupying

abstain 4 curb, deny, diet, fast, keep, pass, stop **5** avoid, forgo, spurn **6** abjure, eschew, give up, pass up, refuse, reject **7** decline, forbear, refrain **8** abnegate, forswear, hold back, keep from, renounce, swear off, teetotal, withhold **9** constrain, do without **11** deny oneself

abstemious 5 sober **6** chaste, strict **7** ascetic, austere, sparing **9** abstinent, continent, temperate **10** restrained **11** self-denying

abstinence 6 denial **7** fasting **8** chastity, sobriety **9** soberness **10** continence, self-denial, temperance **12** renunciation **13** self-restraint

abstract 5 brief, ideal **6** detach, digest, précis **7** epitome, neutral, outline, shorten, summary, utopian **8** academic, breviary, condense, detached, notional, separate, synopsis **9** disengage, summarize **10** abridgment, conceptual, conspectus, disconnect, dissociate, impersonal **11** appropriate, impractical, speculative, theoretical **12** condensation, hypothetical, transcendent **13** disinterested

abstracted 4 lost, rapt **6** absent, intent **7** bemused, faraway **8** absorbed, distrait, heedless **9** engrossed, oblivious, unheeding, unmindful, unminding, withdrawn **11** inattentive, inconscient, preoccupied, unconscious **12** absentminded

abstruse 4 deep **5** heavy **6** knotty, occult **7** complex **8** esoteric, hermetic, involved, profound **9** difficult, intricate, recondite **11** complicated

absurd 5 balmy, comic, crazy, droll, inane, loony, potty, silly, wacky **6** insane **7** asinine, fatuous, foolish, idiotic **8** farcical **9** illogical, laughable, ludicrous **10** irrational, ridiculous **11** harebrained **12** preposterous, unreasonable

absurdity 5 farce, folly **7** inanity **8** nonsense **9** craziness, dottiness, silliness **11** foolishness, incongruity, witlessness **13** ludicrousness, senselessness

abundance 6 bounty, excess, plenty, riches, wealth **9** affluence, profusion **10** lavishness, prosperity **11** prodigality *Scottish:* **5** routh

abundant 4 full, lush, rich, rife **5** ample **6** filled, galore, lavish, plenty **7** aplenty, copious, crammed, crowded, liberal, profuse, replete **8** fruitful, prolific **9** abounding, bounteous, bountiful, extensive, luxuriant, plenteous, plentiful

abuse 3 mar **4** harm, hurt, rail **5** anger, decry, shame, spoil, wrong **6** damage, debase, deride, impair, injure, misuse, revile, vilify **7** calumny, corrupt, cursing, exploit, obloquy, oppress, profane **8** belittle, berating, derision, derogate, disgrace, ill-treat, maltreat, mistreat, swearing **9** blaspheme, contumely, desecrate, disparage, harshness, invective, manhandle, mishandle, persecute, profanity **10** defamation, depreciate, malignment, revilement, scurrility **11** disapproval **12** billingsgate, denunciation, vilification, vituperation

abusive 5 dirty, harsh **6** odious **7** corrupt **8** scurrile **9** injurious, insulting, invective, offending, offensive, truculent **10** calumnious, defamatory, scurrilous **11** blasphemous, castigating, opprobrious **12** calumniating,

contumelious, sharp-tongued, vituperative, vituperatory

abut 4 join, link **5** flank, touch, verge **6** adjoin, border, butt on **8** border on, neighbor **9** lie beside **11** butt against, communicate

abutting 4 next **6** beside, joined, next to **7** joining, verging **8** adjacent, next door, touching **9** adjoining, bordering, impinging **10** connecting, contiguous, juxtaposed **11** bordering on, coextensive, coterminous, neighboring **12** conterminous

abysmal 4 deep, vast **7** endless **8** infinite, profound, unending, wretched **9** boundless, cavernous, plumbless, soundless, unplumbed **10** bottomless, fathomless, unmeasured **11** illimitable, measureless **12** immeasurable, unfathomable

abyss 3 pit **4** gulf, hell, hole, void **5** abysm, chasm, depth, gorge, hades, Sheol **6** Tophet **7** fissure, Gehenna, inferno **8** crevasse, deepness **9** perdition **10** underworld

academia 10 university **12** professoriat

academic 3 don **5** pupil, tutor **6** closet, fellow, master **7** bookish, learned, scholar, student **8** abstract, gownsman, lecturer, pedantic **9** professor, scholarly **10** scholastic **11** book-learned, conjectural, impractical, speculative, theoretical **12** conventional, hypothetical

academic period 4 term **7** quarter **8** semester **9** trimester

academy 5 lycée **6** lyceum **7** college, society **9** institute **10** prep school **12** conservatory

Academy Award winner
picture:

1927-28: 5 Wings **1928-29: 14** Broadway Melody **1929-30: 25** All Quiet on the Western Front **1930-31: 8** Cimarron **1931-32: 10** Grand Hotel **1932-33: 9** Cavalcade **1934: 18** It Happened One Night **1935: 17** Mutiny on the Bounty **1936: 16** The Great Ziegfeld **1937: 15** Life of Emile Zola **1938: 20** You Can't Take It with You **1939: 15** Gone with the Wind **1940: 7** Rebecca **1941: 19** How Green Was My Valley **1942: 10** Mrs. Miniver **1943: 10** Casablanca **1944: 10** Going My Way **1945: 11** Lost Weekend (The) **1946: 19** Best Years of Our Lives (The) **1947: 19** Gentleman's Agreement **1948: 6** Hamlet **1949: 14** All the King's Men **1950: 11** All About Eve **1951: 15** American in Paris (An) **1952: 19** Greatest Show on Earth (The) **1953: 18** From Here to Eternity **1954: 15** On the Waterfront **1955: 5** Marty **1956: 26** Around the World in Eighty Days **1957: 20** Bridge on the River Kwai (The) **1958:**

4 Gigi **1959: 6** Ben-Hur **1960: 9** Apartment (The) **1961: 13** West Side Story **1962: 16** Lawrence of Arabia **1963: 8** Tom Jones **1964: 10** My Fair Lady **1965: 12** Sound of Music (The) **1966: 16** Man for All Seasons (A) **1967: 19** In the Heat of the Night **1968: 6** Oliver **1969: 14** Midnight Cowboy **1970: 6** Patton **1971: 16** French Connection (The) **1972: 9** Godfather (The) **1973: 5** Sting (The) **1974: 9** Godfather (Part Two, The) **1975: 25** One Flew over the Cuckoo's Nest **1976: 5** Rocky **1977: 9** Annie Hall **1978: 10** Deer Hunter (The) **1979: 14** Kramer vs. Kramer **1980: 14** Ordinary People **1981: 14** Chariots of Fire **1982: 6** Gandhi **1983: 17** Terms of Endearment **1984: 7** Amadeus **1985: 11** Out of Africa **1986: 7** Platoon **1987: 11** Last Emperor (The) **1988: 7** Rain Man **1989: 16** Driving Miss Daisy **1990: 16** Dances with Wolves **1991: 17** Silence of the Lambs (The) **1992: 10** Unforgiven **1993: 14** Schindler's List **1994: 11** Forrest Gump **1995: 10** Braveheart **1996: 14** English Patient (The) **1997: 7** Titanic **1998: 17** Shakespeare in Love **1999: 14** American Beauty **2000: 9** Gladiator **2001: 13** Beautiful Mind (A) **2002: 7** Chicago **2003: 14** Lord of the Rings (The) **2004: 17** Million Dollar Baby **2005: 5** Crash **2006: 8** Departed (The) **2007: 18** No Country for Old Men **2008: 18** Slumdog Millionaire **2009: 10** Hurt Locker (The)

actor:

1927-28: 8 Jannings (Emil) **1928-29: 6** Baxter (Warner) **1929-30: 6** Arliss (George) **1930-31: 9** Barrymore (Lionel) **1931-32: 5** Beery (Wallace), March (Fredric) **1932-33: 8** Laughton (Charles) **1934: 5** Gable (Clark) **1935: 8** McLaglen (Victor) **1936: 4** Muni (Paul) **1937: 5** Tracy (Spencer) **1938: 5** Tracy (Spencer) **1939: 5** Donat (Robert) **1940: 7** Stewart (James) **1941: 6** Cooper (Gary) **1942: 6** Cagney (James) **1943: 5** Lukas (Paul) **1944: 6** Crosby (Bing) **1945: 7** Milland (Ray) **1946: 5** March (Fredric) **1947: 6** Colman (Ronald) **1948: 7** Olivier (Laurence) **1949: 8** Crawford (Broderick) **1950: 6** Ferrer (José) **1951: 6** Bogart (Humphrey) **1952: 6** Cooper (Gary) **1953: 6** Holden (William) **1954: 6** Brando (Marlon) **1955: 8** Borgnine (Ernest) **1956: 7** Brynner (Yul) **1957: 8** Guinness (Alec) **1958: 5** Niven (David) **1959: 6** Heston (Charlton) **1960: 9** Lancaster (Burt) **1961: 6** Schell (Maximilian) **1962: 4** Peck (Gregory) **1963: 7**

Poitier (Sidney) **1964: 8** Harrison (Rex) **1965: 6** Marvin (Lee) **1966: 8** Scofield (Paul) **1967: 7** Steiger (Rod) **1968: 9** Robertson (Cliff) **1969: 5** Wayne (John) **1970: 5** Scott (George C.) **1971: 7** Hackman (Gene) **1972: 6** Brando (Marlon) **1973: 6** Lemmon (Jack) **1974: 6** Carney (Art) **1975: 9** Nicholson (Jack) **1976: 5** Finch (Peter) **1977: 8** Dreyfuss (Richard) **1978: 6** Voight (Jon) **1979: 7** Hoffman (Dustin) **1980: 6** De Niro (Robert) **1981: 5** Fonda (Henry) **1982: 8** Kingsley (Ben) **1983: 6** Duvall (Robert) **1984: 7** Abraham (F. Murray) **1985: 4** Hurt (William) **1986: 6** Newman (Paul) **1987: 7** Douglas (Michael) **1988: 7** Hoffman (Dustin) **1989: 8** Day-Lewis (Daniel) **1990: 5** Irons (Jeremy) **1991: 7** Hopkins (Anthony) **1992: 6** Pacino (Al) **1993: 5** Hanks (Tom) **1994: 5** Hanks (Tom) **1995: 4** Cage (Nicholas) **1996: 4** Rush (Geoffrey) **1997: 9** Nicholson (Jack) **1998: 7** Benigni (Roberto) **1999: 6** Spacey (Kevin) **2000: 5** Crowe (Russell) **2001: 10** Washington (Denzel) **2002: 5** Brody (Adrien) **2003: 4** Penn (Sean) **2004: 4** Foxx (Jamie) **2005: 7** Hoffman (Philip Seymour) **2006: 8** Whitaker (Forest) **2007: 8** Day-Lewis (Daniel) **2008: 4** Penn (Sean) **2009: 7** Bridges (Jeff)

actress:

1927-28: 6 Gaynor (Janet) **1928-29: 8** Pickford (Mary) **1929-30: 7** Shearer (Norma) **1930-31: 8** Dressler (Marie) **1931-32: 5** Hayes (Helen) **1932-33: 7** Hepburn (Katharine) **1934: 7** Colbert (Claudette) **1935: 5** Davis (Bette) **1936: 6** Rainer (Luise) **1937: 6** Rainer (Luise) **1938: 5** Davis (Bette) **1939: 5** Leigh (Vivien) **1940: 6** Rogers (Ginger) **1941: 8** Fontaine (Joan) **1942: 6** Garson (Greer) **1943: 5** Jones (Jennifer) **1944: 7** Bergman (Ingrid) **1945: 8** Crawford (Joan) **1946: 11** de Havilland (Olivia) **1947: 5** Young (Loretta) **1948: 5** Wyman (Jane) **1949: 11** de Havilland (Olivia) **1950: 8** Holliday (Judy) **1951: 5** Leigh (Vivien) **1952: 5** Booth (Shirley) **1953: 7** Hepburn (Audrey) **1954: 5** Kelly (Grace) **1955: 7** Magnani (Anna) **1956: 7** Bergman (Ingrid) **1957: 8** Woodward (Joanne) **1958: 7** Hayward (Susan) **1959: 8** Signoret (Simone) **1960: 6** Taylor (Elizabeth) **1961: 5** Loren (Sophia) **1962: 8** Bancroft (Anne) **1963: 4** Neal (Patricia) **1964: 7** Andrews (Julie) **1965: 8** Christie (Julie) **1966: 6** Taylor (Elizabeth) **1967: 7** Hepburn (Katharine)

1968: 7 Hepburn (Katharine) **9** Streisand (Barbra) **1969: 5** Smith (Maggie) **1970: 7** Jackson (Glenda) **1971: 5** Fonda (Jane) **1972: 8** Minnelli (Liza) **1973: 7** Jackson (Glenda) **1974: 7** Burstyn (Ellen) **1975: 8** Fletcher (Louise) **1976: 7** Dunaway (Faye) **1977: 6** Keaton (Diane) **1978: 5** Fonda (Jane) **1979: 5** Field (Sally) **1980: 6** Spacek (Sissy) **1981: 7** Hepburn (Katharine) **1982: 6** Streep (Meryl) **1983: 8** MacLaine (Shirley) **1984: 5** Field (Sally) **1985: 4** Page (Geraldine) **1986: 6** Matlin (Marlee) **1987: 4** Cher **1988: 6** Foster (Jodie) **1989: 5** Tandy (Jessica) **1990: 5** Bates (Kathy) **1991: 6** Foster (Jodie) **1992: 8** Thompson (Emma) **1993: 6** Hunter (Holly) **1994: 5** Lange (Jessica) **1995: 8** Sarandon (Susan) **1996: 9** McDormand (Frances) **1997: 4** Hunt (Helen) **1998: 7** Paltrow (Gwyneth) **1999: 5** Swank (Hilary) **2000: 7** Roberts (Julia) **2001: 5** Berry (Halle) **2002: 6** Kidman (Nicole) **2003: 6** Theron (Charlize) **2004: 5** Swank (Hilary) **2005: 11** Witherspoon (Reese) **2006: 6** Mirren (Helen) **2007: 9** Cotillard (Marion) **2008: 7** Winslet (Kate) **2009: 7** Bullock (Sandra)

accede 3 let **5** admit, agree, allow, grant, yield **6** accept, assent, comply, concur, give in, permit **7** agree to, approve, concede, consent **9** acquiesce, cooperate, subscribe

accelerando 6 faster **7** speed up **10** speeding up

accelerate 3 gun, rev **4** grow, roll **5** hurry, impel, rev up, speed **6** hasten, open up, step up **7** quicken, speed up **8** expedite, increase **9** fast-track **10** peel rubber

acceleration 7 speedup **8** hurrying, spurring **9** hastening, revving up **10** increasing, quickening, speeding up, stepping up

accent 4 beat, lilt, tone **5** acute, grave, meter, pulse, throb **6** rhythm, stress, weight **7** cadence **8** emphasis **9** diacritic, pulsation **10** inflection, intonation *Irish:* **6** brogue *Scottish:* **4** burr *Southern:* **5** drawl

accept 3 bow, buy, see **4** bear, gain, okay, take **5** admit, adopt, agree, catch, favor, go for, grasp, yield **6** accede, admire, affirm, assent, endure, follow, take in, take on **7** agree to, approve, believe, receive, respect, swallow, welcome **8** assent to, bear with, hold with, live with, stand for, tolerate **9** acquiesce, agree with, undertake **10** capitulate, comprehend, concur with, understand **11** acknowledge, countenance, subscribe to

acceptable 4 good, okay **6** decent, worthy **7** average, welcome **8** adequate, all right,

bearable, ordinary, passable, pleasing, standard, suitable **9** endurable, tolerable **10** sufficient **11** commonplace, respectable, supportable **12** satisfactory **13** unexceptional, unimpeachable

acceptably 4 well **5** amply **7** capably **8** properly, suitably **9** fittingly, tolerably **10** becomingly **11** competently **13** appropriately

acceptant 4 open **8** amenable, friendly, swayable **9** favorable, receptive, recipient, welcoming **10** open-minded, responsive **11** persuadable, persuasible, susceptible

acceptation 4 gist **5** point, sense **6** import **7** meaning, message, purport **9** intention **10** intendment **12** significance, significancy **13** signification, understanding

accepted 5 usual **6** common, normal, proper **7** correct, regular, routine **8** approved, everyday, expected, habitual, ordinary, orthodox, received **9** customary **10** accustomed, recognized, sanctioned **11** established, traditional **12** conventional

access 3 fit, way **4** adit, door, gust, pang, path, road, turn **5** burst, entry, get at, onset, route, sally, spell, throe **6** attack, avenue, entrée **7** contact, flare-up, ingress, passage, seizure **8** approach, entrance, eruption, increase, outburst **9** admission, explosion **10** admittance

accessible 4 near, open **5** handy **6** public, usable **8** possible **9** available, operative, reachable **10** attainable, employable, obtainable **11** practicable **12** approachable, unrestricted

accession 4 rise **5** raise **8** addition, approach, increase, outburst, taking on **9** accretion, adherence, increment, induction **10** admittance, assumption, attainment, succession **11** acquisition **12** augmentation, inauguration

accessory 3 aid **4** aide, prop, trim **5** extra, frill **6** helper **7** abettor, adjunct, fitting, insider, partner **8** addition, adjuvant, appendix **9** accretion, adornment, ancillary, appendage, assistant, associate, auxiliary, increment, secondary, tributary **10** accomplice, coincident, collateral, concurrent, decoration, incidental, subsidiary **11** appurtenant, concomitant, confederate, conspirator, subordinate, subservient **12** appurtenance, contributory **13** accompaniment, coconspirator, supplementary

accident 3 hap, lot **4** fate, luck, odds **5** fluke **6** chance, gamble, hazard, kismet, mishap **7** bad luck, destiny **8** calamity, casualty, fortuity, incident **9** mischance **10** misfortune **12** misadventure

accidental 3 odd **4** flat **5** fluky, sharp **6** casual, chance, flukey, random **7** unmeant **8** by chance, careless **9** chromatic, dependent, extempore, impromptu, unplanned, unwitting **10** coincident, contingent, fortuitous, unexpected, unforeseen, unintended **11** conditional, inadvertent **12** coincidental, uncalculated **13** unintentional

acclaim 4 hail, clap, laud **5** cheer, éclat, exalt, extol, glory, honor, kudos, roose **6** homage, praise, salute **7** applaud, approve, commend, glorify, magnify, ovation, root for **8** applause, plaudits **10** compliment

acclimate 5 adapt **6** adjust, change, harden, season **7** toughen **9** condition, habituate

accolade 4 bays, fame **5** award, badge, honor, kudos **6** praise **7** laurels, tribute **8** approval **10** decoration **11** distinction

accommodate 3 fit **4** hold, rent, suit **5** adapt, alter, board, defer, favor, house, humor, lodge, put up, yield **6** adjust, attune, bestow, billet, change, encase, harbor, modify, oblige, please, submit, tailor, take in **7** cater to, conform, contain, enclose, furnish, indulge, quarter, receive, shelter **8** accustom, allow for, domicile **9** entertain, harmonize, integrate, reconcile **11** domiciliate, make room for

accommodating 7 amiable, helpful, willing **8** gracious, obliging **9** adaptable **10** hospitable, solicitous, thoughtful **11** considerate, cooperative

accommodations 3 inn **4** digs, keep, room **5** hotel, lodge, motel **6** hostel **7** housing, lodging, shelter **8** hostelry, lodgment, quarters **9** residence **12** room and board

accompaniment 6 backup **7** adjunct **8** addition **9** accessory, associate, attendant, corollary **10** supplement **11** concomitant, enhancement **12** augmentation

accompany 4 join **5** bring, guide, pilot **6** attend, convoy, escort, go with **7** combine, conduct, consort **8** chaperon, come with **9** associate **10** appear with, go together **11** perform with

accompanying 8 incident **9** accessory, ancillary, attendant, attending, secondary **10** associated, coincident, collateral **11** concomitant

accomplice 4 aide, ally **5** aider **6** flunky, helper, stooge **7** abettor, partner **9** accessory, assistant, associate **11** confederate, conspirator, subordinate **13** coconspirator

accomplish 3 win **4** gain **5** reach, score **6** attain, effect, fulfil, rack up **7** achieve, execute, fulfill, perfect, pull off, realize,

succeed **8** bring off, carry out, complete **9** discharge **10** bring about

accomplished 4 able **5** adept **6** expert **7** skilled **8** finished, masterly, skillful, talented **9** practiced **10** proficient

accomplishment 3 act, art **4** deed, feat **5** craft, doing, skill **7** ability **9** adeptness, expertise **10** attainment, capability, completion **11** achievement, acquirement, proficiency

accord 4 deal, fuse, give, jibe, pact **5** agree, award, blend, chime, fit in, grant, match, merge, tally, union **6** affirm, assent, concur, confer, treaty **7** compact, concert, conform, empathy, entente, harmony, rapport **8** affinity, coincide, dovetail, sympathy **9** agreement, harmonize, reconcile **10** attraction, conformity, consonance, correspond, solidarity **11** concordance **13** understanding

accordant 8 agreeing **9** congruous, consonant **10** conforming, harmonious **13** correspondent

accordingly 2 so **4** duly, ergo, then, thus **5** hence **9** therefore, thereupon **12** consequently

accost 3 dog **4** call, dare, face, hail **5** annoy, beard, cross, front, hound, worry **6** bother, call to **7** affront, outface, outrage **8** approach, confront **9** challenge **10** buttonhole

accouchement 7 lying-in **8** childbed, delivery **10** childbirth **11** confinement, parturition

account 3 tab, use **4** bill, deem, note, rate, view **5** avail, basis, favor, score, story, track, value, worth **6** assess, client, esteem, reason, reckon, record, regard, report, repute **7** analyze, explain, expound, justify, recital, version **8** appraise, consider, customer, estimate **9** chronicle, narrative, rationale, reckoning, statement **11** explanation **13** consideration *book:* **6** ledger

accountable 6 liable **8** amenable **10** answerable **11** explainable, responsible

accounting 11 bookkeeping *method:* **4** FIFO, FILO, LIFO

accoutre 3 arm, rig **4** deck, gear **5** adorn, dress, equip, fix up, ready **6** attire, fit out, outfit, supply **7** appoint, furnish, prepare, provide, turn out **9** provision

accoutrement 3 kit **4** gear **6** outfit, tackle **7** regalia **8** tackling **9** accessory, apparatus, equipment, machinery, trappings **10** provisions **11** furnishings, habiliments **12** appointments **13** paraphernalia

accredit 2 OK **3** lay **4** okay **5** refer **6** assign, attest, charge, credit, enable **7** approve, ascribe, certify, commend, empower, endorse, license, warrant **8** sanction, validate, vouch for **9** attribute, authorize, recognize, recommend **10** commission, credential

accretion 4 rise **5** raise **6** growth **7** buildup **8** addition, increase **9** accession, appendage, increment **10** attachment **11** enlargement **12** accumulation, augmentation

accrue 4 grow **5** amass **6** gather, pile up **7** build up, collect, compile **8** increase **10** accumulate, amalgamate **11** agglomerate

accumulate 4 heap, grow, mass, pile **5** add to, amass, hoard, lay by, lay in, lay up, stock, store **6** accrue, garner, gather, pile up, rack up, roll up **7** acquire, backlog, collect, compile, lay down, stack up, store up **8** assemble, increase **9** stockpile

accumulation 4 bank, heap, mass, pile **5** hoard, stock, store, trove **6** growth **7** backlog, buildup, reserve **8** increase **9** accretion, amassment **10** collection **11** aggregation, enlargement

accumulative 6 heaped **7** growing **8** additive, additory **9** summative **10** collective, increasing **11** aggregative **12** augmentative

accuracy 8 veracity **9** certainty, exactness, precision **10** definition, exactitude **11** correctness, preciseness **12** definiteness

accurate 4 just, nice, true **5** exact, right **6** actual, dead on, proper, spot on **7** certain, correct, factual, precise **8** definite, reliable, rigorous **9** authentic, error-free, errorless **10** dependable

accursed 4 vile **6** odious **7** hateful **8** damnable **9** abhorrent, execrable, loathsome, offensive, repugnant, revolting **10** abominable, despicable, detestable

accusation 3 rap **6** charge **9** complaint **10** allegation, indictment **12** denunciation *false:* **7** calumny

accuse 3 tax **5** blame, brand **6** allege, charge, delate, finger, impute, indict **7** arraign, ascribe, censure, impeach **8** admonish, denounce, reproach **9** criminate, criticize, inculpate, reprobate **10** denunciate **11** incriminate

accustom 3 use **4** wont **5** adapt, inure **6** adjust, harden, season **7** conform **9** habituate **11** acclimatize, familiarize

accustomed 3 set **5** usual **6** normal **7** chronic, regular, routine **8** accepted, everyday, familiar, habitual, ordinary, standard **9** customary **10** habituated **11** commonplace, established, traditional **12** conventional

ace 3 bit, jot, pip, top **4** atom, hair, iota, mite, star **5** crumb, minim, pilot, point, score, speck **6** Bishop (Billy), bullet, defeat, master, winner **7** whisker **8** molecule, particle,

Red Baron **9** first rate, hole in one **10** Richthofen (Manfred von) **11** hairbreadth, tennis score **12** Rickenbacker (Eddie)

ace and face card 7 natural **9** blackjack

acedia 5 ennui **6** apathy **7** boredom, languor **8** lethargy

acerbate 3 vex **5** anger, annoy, peeve **6** madden **7** incense, inflame **8** embitter, irritate **9** aggravate **10** exasperate

acerbic 4 acid, sour, tart **5** acrid, harsh, rough, sharp **7** caustic, cutting, satiric **8** stinging **9** acidulous, corrosive, sarcastic **10** astringent

acerbity 7 acidity, sarcasm **8** acrimony, asperity, sourness, tartness **9** harshness, roughness, surliness **10** bitterness, causticity

Achates' companion 6 Aeneas

ache 3 yen **4** hurt, long, pain, pang, pine, pity, sigh **5** crave, smart, throb, yearn **6** hanker, hunger, stitch, suffer, thirst, twinge **8** yearning **11** commiserate *Scottish:* **6** stound

Achebe novel 15 Things Fall Apart

Acheron 5 Hades, river

achieve 2 do **3** get, win **4** gain **5** reach, score **6** attain, effect, finish, obtain, rack up, secure **7** acquire, execute, fulfill, get done, perform, realize, succeed **8** carry out, complete, conclude **9** actualize **10** accomplish

achievement 4 deed, feat **6** finish **7** exploit, success **10** attainment, completion **11** acquisition, tour de force

Achilles *adviser:* 6 Nestor *companion:* **9** Patroclus *father:* **6** Peleus *horse:* **7** Xanthus *lover:* **7** Briseis *mother:* **6** Thetis *slayer:* **5** Paris *victim:* **6** Hector *vulnerable part:* **4** heel

aching 4 hurt, sore **6** in pain **7** hurtful, hurting, painful **8** yearning **9** disturbed **10** afflictive, distressed **13** compassionate

acicular 5 acute, peaky, piked, sharp **6** peaked, pointy, spiked **7** pointed

acid 4 sour, tart **5** acerb **7** acerbic, acetose, caustic **8** stinging **9** corrosive, sarcastic, vitriolic *bleaching:* **6** oxalic *fatty:* **6** capric **7** caproic, stearic **8** caprylic *found in apples:* **5** malic *found in cranberries:* **7** benzoic *found in grapes:* **8** tartaric *found in lemons:* **6** citric *found in rhubarb:* **6** oxalic *found in sour milk:* **6** lactic *indicator:* **6** litmus *kind:* **5** amino, boric, iodic, malic, oleic **6** acetic, bromic, formic, nitric, oxalic, tannic **7** nitrous, silicic **8** carbolic, carbonic, muriatic, sulfuric **9** aqua regia **12** hydrochloric *neutralizer:* **4** base **6** alkali *tanning:* **6** tannic **8** catechin *vinegar:* **6** acetic

acidulous 3 dry **4** sour, tart **5** acerb, harsh, sharp **6** biting **7** acerbic, acetose, cutting, piquant, pungent **9** sarcastic

Acis *lover:* **7** Galatea *slayer:* **10** Polyphemus

acknowledge 3 own **4** avow, deem, tell, view **5** admit, agree, allow, grant, let on, own up **6** accede, accept, fess up, reveal **7** concede, confess, declare, divulge, profess **8** announce, consider, disclose, proclaim **9** recognize

acknowledgment 6 assent, avowal, credit, notice **9** admission **10** confession **11** affirmation, declaration, recognition

acme 3 cap, top **4** apex, peak **6** apogee, climax, summit, tiptop, vertex, zenith **8** capstone, pinnacle, ultimate **9** high point **10** perfection **11** culmination

acorn tree 3 oak

acoustic 5 aural **6** audile **8** auditory **9** unplugged

acquaint 4 clue, tell, warn **6** advise, fill in, inform, notify, orient, reveal **7** apprise, present **8** accustom, disclose **9** enlighten, introduce **11** familiarize

acquaintance 4 mate **5** amigo, crony, grasp **6** friend **7** comrade, contact **9** associate, colleague, companion **10** cognizance, experience **11** familiarity

acquainted 6 versed **7** abreast, in touch **8** familiar, informed, up-to-date **9** au courant **10** conversant

acquiesce 3 bow, yes **5** agree, allow, bow to, yield **6** accede, accept, assent, comply, concur, give in, submit **7** consent, go along **9** reconcile, subscribe

acquiescence 6 assent **7** consent **8** giving in, yielding **9** deference **10** acceptance, compliance, conformity, submission **11** resignation

acquiescent 6 docile **7** passive **8** resigned, yielding **10** submissive **11** unresistant, unresisting **12** nonresistant, nonresisting

acquire 3 add, buy, get, win **4** earn, form, gain, land **5** amass, annex **6** garner, obtain, pick up, secure, take on **7** bring in, collect, develop, procure **10** accumulate

acquirement 8 addition **9** accretion **11** acquisition

acquisition 4 gain **5** prize **7** winning **8** addition, learning, property, purchase **9** accretion

acquisitive 5 eager, itchy **6** grabby, greedy **8** covetous, desirous, grasping **10** avaricious

acquit 3 act **4** bear, free **5** carry, clear, let go **6** behave, deport, let off **7** absolve, comport, conduct, perform, release, set free **8** liberate **9** discharge, exculpate, exonerate, vindicate

acres 4 area, land **5** lands **6** estate **7** demesne, expanse, holding **8** property

acrid 4 acid, sour **5** harsh, nasty, sharp **6** biting, bitter **7** austere, burning, caustic, cutting, pungent **8** stinging **9** trenchant **10** astringent, irritating **11** acrimonious

acrimonious 3 mad **5** angry, cross, irate, sharp, testy **6** biting, bitter, cranky, ireful **7** acerbic, caustic, cutting **9** indignant, irascible, rancorous **11** belligerent, contentious, quarrelsome

acrimony 5 anger, spite **6** animus, malice, rancor **7** ill will **8** acerbity, asperity, mordancy **9** animosity, antipathy, harshness, virulence **10** bitterness **11** malevolence

Acrisius *daughter:* **5** Danaë *slayer:* **7** Perseus

acrobat 7 gymnast **9** aerialist, trapezist **11** funambulist

across 4 over **6** beyond **7** athwart **12** transversely *prefix:* **5** trans

act 3 law, run **4** bear, bill, deed, fake, feat, mime, play, pose, sham, work **5** bluff, feign, front, put-on, serve, stunt **6** affect, appear, behave, shtick **7** exploit, operate, perform, portray, pretend, routine, statute **8** function, pretense, simulate **9** officiate **10** masquerade **11** counterfeit, impersonate *wrongful:* **3** sin **4** tort **5** crime, error, fault **7** default, misdeed, offense

acting 6 pro tem **7** interim, playing **9** ad interim, dramatics, imitating, portrayal, temporary **10** pro tempore **12** entertaining

actinium symbol 2 Ac

action 4 case, deed, move, step, stir, suit, work **5** cause, doing **6** battle, bustle, combat **7** lawsuit, process, service **8** activity, behavior, conflict, fighting, function **9** execution, operation, procedure **10** engagement, proceeding **11** performance

action painter 5 Kline (Franz) **7** Pollock (Jackson) **9** de Kooning (Willem)

action painting 7 tachism

activate 4 stir, wake **5** rally, rouse, set up, waken **6** arouse, awaken, call up, turn on **8** energize, mobilize, motivate, vitalize **9** stimulate

active 4 busy, live, spry **5** agile, alert, alive, brisk, going **6** at work, in play, lively, moving **7** driving, dynamic, flowing, on the go, running, working **8** animated, bustling, emitting, erupting, spirited, vigorous **9** effective, energetic, operating, operative, sprightly **11** functioning, industrious **12** enterprising

activity 6 action, bustle, motion **7** process, pursuit, venture **8** exercise, exertion **10** exercising, liveliness **11** undertaking

actor 4 mime, star 5 mimic 6 mummer, player 7 artiste, trouper 8 thespian 9 performer 11 participant 12 impersonator
name: 3 Cox (Wally), Fox (James, Michael J.), Lee (Bruce), Lom (Herbert), Mix (Tom), Ray (Aldo) 4 Alda (Alan, Robert), Bean (Orson), Blue (Ben), Bond (Ward), Caan (James), Cage (Nicholas), Cobb (Lee J.), Coco (James), Culp (Robert), Dean (James), Depp (Johnny), Dern (Bruce), Duff (Howard), Egan (Richard), Falk (Peter), Ford (Glenn, Harrison), Foxx (Redd), Geer (Will), Gere (Richard), Grey (Joel), Hill (Arthur), Hope (Bob), Hurt (John, William), Ives (Burl), Kaye (Danny), Kean (Edmund), Keel (Howard), Ladd (Alan), Lahr (Bert), Lord (Jack), Lowe (Rob), Lunt (Alfred), Marx (Chico, Groucho, Harpo, Zeppo), Muni (Paul), Ngor (Haing S.), Peck (Gregory), Penn (Sean), Pitt (Brad), Raft (George), Reid (Wallace), Roth (Tim), Ryan (Robert), Shaw (Robert), Tati (Jacques), Tone (Franchot), Torn (Rip), Tune (Tommy), Wahl (Ken), Webb (Clifton, Jack), Wynn (Ed, Keenan), York (Michael) 5 Adler (Luther), Allen (Fred, Tim, Woody), Arkin (Adam, Alan), Asner (Ed), Autry (Gene), Ayres (Lew), Bacon (Kevin), Barry (Gene), Bates (Alan), Beery (Wallace), Benny (Jack), Berle (Milton), Boone (Richard), Booth (Edwin), Boyer (Charles), Brand (Neville), Burns (George), Caine (Michael), Candy (John), Chase (Chevy), Clift (Montgomery), Cosby (Bill), Dafoe (Willem), Davis (Clifton, Ossie, Sammy Jr.), Delon (Alain), Donat (Robert), Evans (Maurice), Ewell (Tom), Finch (Peter), Firth (Colin, Peter), Flynn (Errol), Fonda (Henry, Peter), Franz (Dennis), Gabin (Jean), Gable (Clark), Gould (Elliot), Grant (Cary, Hugh), Gwenn (Edmund), Hanks (Tom), Hardy (Oliver), Hauer (Rutger), Hawke (Ethan), Hayes (Gabby), Hogan (Paul), Irons (Jeremy), Jaffe (Sam), Jones (Dean, James Earl, Tommy Lee), Kazan (Elia), Keach (Stacy), Keith (Brian, David), Kelly (Gene), Kiley (Richard), Kline (Kevin), Kotto (Yaphet), Lamas (Fernando, Lorenzo), Lanza (Mario), Lewis (Jerry, Richard), Lloyd (Harold), Lorre (Peter), Lukas (Paul), Lynde (Paul), March (Fredric), Mason (James), McCoy (Tim), Mills (John), Mineo (Sal), Moore (Dudley, Roger, Victor), Neill (Sam), Nimoy (Leonard), Niven (David), Nolte (Nick), Olmos (Edward James), O'Neal (Patrick, Ryan), O'Shea (Milo), Payne (John), Perry (Luke,

Matthew), Pesci (Joe), Power (Tyrone), Price (Vincent), Pryce (Jonathan), Quaid (Dennis, Randy), Quinn (Aidan, Anthony), Rains (Claude), Reeve (Christopher), Scott (Campbell, George C., Randolph), Segal (George), Sheen (Charlie, Martin), Smits (Jimmy), Stack (Robert), Stamp (Terence), Sydow (Max von), Tracy (Spencer), Wayne (John), Wilde (Cornel), Wills (Chill), Woods (James), Young (Gig, Robert) 6 Abbott (Bud), Albert (Eddie), Ameche (Don), Arness (James), Backus (Jim), Balsam (Martin), Barker (Lex), Baxter (Warner), Beatty (Ned, Warren), Begley (Ed), Blades (Ruben), Bogart (Humphrey), Bolger (Ray), Brando (Marlon), Brooks (Albert, Mel), Burton (Richard), Caesar (Sid), Cagney (James), Cantor (Eddie), Cariou (Len), Carney (Art), Carrey (Jim), Carvey (Dana), Chaney (Lon), Cleese (John), Coburn (Charles, James), Colman (Ronald), Conrad (Robert, William), Conway (Tim, Tom), Coogan (Jackie), Cooper (Gary), Cotten (Joseph), Coward (Noël), Crabbe (Buster), Crenna (Richard), Cronyn (Hume), Crosby (Bing), Cruise (Tom), Culkin (Macaulay), Curtis (Tony), Dailey (Dan), Dalton (Timothy), Danson (Ted), Danton (Ray), Darren (James), De Niro (Robert), de Sica (Vittorio), De Vito (Danny), Dillon (Matt), Downey (Robert), Dullea (Keir), Duryea (Dan), Duvall (Robert), Ferrer (José, Mel), Fields (W.C.), Finney (Albert), Garcia (Andy), Garner (James), Gibson (Hoot, Mel), Glover (Danny), Graves (Peter), Greene (Lorne), Grodin (Charles), Harris (Ed, Richard), Harvey (Laurence), Hayden (Sterling), Heflin (Van), Heston (Charlton), Hingle (Pat), Holden (Bill), Hopper (Dennis, William), Howard (Leslie, Ron, Trevor), Hudson (Rock), Hunter (Jeffrey, Tab), Huston (John, Walter), Hutton (Jim, Timothy), Irving (Henry), Jacobi (Derek, Lou), Jagger (Dean), Keaton (Buster, Michael), Keitel (Harvey), Kilmer (Val), Knotts (Don), Landau (Martin), Landon (Michael), Laurel (Stan), Lemmon (Jack), Liotta (Ray), Lugosi (Bela), MacRae (Gordon), Malden (Karl), Martin (Dean, Steve), Marvin (Lee), Massey (Raymond), Mature (Victor), McCrea (Joel), Meeker (Ralph), Menjou (Adolphe), Mifune (Toshiro), Modine (Matthew), Morley (Robert), Mostel (Zero), Murphy (Audie, Eddie), Murray (Bill, Don), Neeson (Liam), Nelson (Ozzie), Newley (Anthony), Newman (Paul), O'Brian (Hugh), O'Brien (Edmund,

Pat), Oldman (Gary), O'Toole (Peter), Pacino (Al), Parker (Fess), Poston (Tom), Powell (Dick), Quayle (Anthony), Reeves (Keanu, Steve), Reiner (Carl, Rob), Reiser (Paul), Rennie (Michael), Ritter (John, Tex), Rogers (Roy, Wayne, Will), Romero (Cesar), Rooney (Mickey), Rourke (Mickey), Schell (Maximilian), Seagal (Steven), Sharif (Omar), Slezak (Walter), Snipes (Wesley), Spacey (Kevin), Spader (James), Swayze (Patrick), Taylor (Robert, Rod), Thomas (Danny, Richard), Turpin (Ben), Vallee (Rudy), Vaughn (Robert), Voight (Jon), Wagner (Robert), Walker (Robert), Warden (Jack), Wayans (Damon, Keenen Ivory), Weaver (Dennis, Fritz), Welles (Orson), Werner (Oskar), Wilder (Gene), Willis (Bruce) **7** Abraham (F. Murray), Andrews (Dana), Astaire (Fred), Aykroyd (Dan), Baldwin (Alec, Daniel, Stephen, William), Bellamy (Ralph), Bogarde (Dirk), Branagh (Kenneth), Bridges (Beau, Jeff, Lloyd), Bronson (Charles), Brosnan (Pierce), Brynner (Yul), Burbage (Richard), Bushman (Francis X.), Buttons (Red), Calhern (Louis), Calhoun (Rory), Cameron (Rod), Carroll (Leo G.), Chaplin (Charlie), Clooney (George), Connery (Sean), Connors (Chuck), Conried (Hans), Costner (Kevin), Crystal (Billy), Daniels (Jeff), da Silva (Howard), DeLuise (Dom), Dennehy (Brian), Donahue (Troy), Donlevy (Brian), Douglas (Kirk, Melvyn, Michael, Paul), Durante (Jimmy), Edwards (Vince), Feldman (Marty), Fiennes (Ralph), Freeman (Morgan), Garrick (David), Gazzara (Ben), Gielgud (John), Gleason (Jackie), Goodman (John), Gosling (Ryan), Gossett (Lou), Grammer (Kelsey), Granger (Farley, Stewart), Gulager (Clu), Hackman (Gene), Henreid (Paul), Hoffman (Dustin), Homolka (Oscar), Hopkins (Anthony), Hoskins (Bob), Janssen (David), Johnson (Ben, Don, Van), Jourdan (Louis), Jurgens (Curt), Karloff (Boris), Kennedy (Arthur, George), Klugman (Jack), Lawford (Peter), Leonard (Robert Sean, Sheldon), Lithgow (John), MacLane (Barton), Maharis (George), Mathers (Jerry), Matthau (Walter), McCarey (Leo), McGavin (Darren), McQueen (Steve), Milland (Ray), Mitchum (Robert), Montand (Yves), Morales (Esai), Navarro (Ramon), Newhart (Bob), O'Connor (Carroll, Donald), Olivier (Laurence), Palance (Jack), Paulsen (Pat), Peppard (George), Perkins (Anthony), Pickens (Slim), Pidgeon (Walter), Poitier (Sidney),

Preston (Robert), Randall (Tony), Redford (Robert), Rickman (Alan), Robards (Jason), Robbins (Tim), Robeson (Paul), Roberts (Pernell, Tony), Sanders (George), Savalas (Telly), Scourby (Alexander), Selleck (Tom), Sellers (Peter), Shatner (William), Shepard (Sam), Silvers (Phil), Sinatra (Frank), Skelton (Red), Skinner (Otis), Steiger (Rod), Stewart (James, Patrick), Stooges (Three), Tamblyn (Russ), Ustinov (Peter), Van Dyke (Dick, Jerry), Wallach (Eli), Widmark (Richard), Wilding (Michael), Winters (Jonathan), Woolley (Monty) **8** Banderas (Antonio), Barrault (Jean-Louis), Basehart (Richard), Belmondo (Jean-Paul), Berenger (Tom), Blackmer (Sidney), Borgnine (Ernest), Buchanan (Edgar), Buchholz (Horst), Chandler (Jeff), Costello (Lou), Crawford (Broderick, Michael), Cummings (Robert), Day-Lewis (Daniel), DiCaprio (Leonardo), Dreyfuss (Richard), Eastwood (Clint), Forsythe (John), Garfield (John), Goldblum (Jeff), Griffith (Andy), Guinness (Alec), Harrison (Noel, Rex), Hemmings (David), Holbrook (Hal), Holloway (Stanley), Houseman (John), Jannings (Emil), Kingsley (Ben), Langella (Frank), Laughton (Charles), Marshall (E.G., Herbert), McDowall (Roddy), McDowell (Malcolm), McGregor (Ewan), McLaglen (Victor), Meredith (Burgess), Rathbone (Basil), Redgrave (Michael), Reynolds (Burt), Ritchard (Cyril), Robinson (Edward G.), Sarrazin (Michael), Scofield (Paul), Seinfeld (Jerry), Stallone (Sylvester), Stroheim (Erich von), Sullivan (Barry), Travolta (John), Turturro (John), Van Damme (Jean-Claude), Von Sydow (Max), Whitaker (Forest), Whitmore (James), Williams (Robin) **9** Amsterdam (Morey), Barrymore (John, Lionel), Brandauer (Klaus Maria), Broderick (Matthew), Carnovsky (Morris), Carradine (David, John, Keith, Robert), Courtenay (Tom), Depardieu (Gérard), Fairbanks (Douglas), Fishburne (Larry), Franciosa (Anthony), Hardwicke (Cedric), Harrelson (Woody), Hyde-White (Wilfrid), Lancaster (Burt), MacMurray (Fred), Malkovich (John), Montalban (Ricardo), Nicholson (Jack), Pleasance (Donald), Robertson (Cliff, Dale), Strasberg (Lee), Tarantino (Quentin), Valentino (Rudolph), Zimbalist (Efrem) **10** Fitzgerald (Barry), Hasselhoff (David), Montgomery (Robert), Richardson (Ralph), Sutherland (Donald, Kiefer), Washington (Denzel)

11 Chamberlain (Richard), Greenstreet (Sydney), Mastroianni (Marcello), Trintignant (Jean-Louis) **13** Kristofferson (Kris)

actor's *quest:* **4** part, role *signal:* **3** cue

actress 3 Bow (Clara), Cox (Courtney), Day (Doris), Dee (Ruby, Sandra), Dru (Joanne), Gam (Rita), Loy (Myrna), May (Elaine), Rae (Charlotte) **4** Alba (Jessica), Ball (Lucille), Bara (Theda), Barr (Roseanne), Cass (Peggy), Cher, Coca (Imogene), Cruz (Penelope), Dahl (Arlene), Daly (Tyne), Dern (Laura), Diaz (Cameron), Dors (Diana), Down (Lesley-Ann), Duke (Patty), Duse (Eleonora), Eden (Barbara), Foch (Nina), Garr (Teri), Gish (Dorothy, Lillian), Grey (Jennifer), Gwyn (Nell), Hawn (Goldie), Holm (Celeste), Hunt (Helen, Linda, Marsha), Hurt (Mary Beth), Hyer (Martha), Ivey (Judith), Kahn (Madeline), Kerr (Deborah), Lake (Veronica), Lisi (Virna), Long (Nia, Shelley), Main (Marjorie), Mayo (Virginia), Neal (Patricia), Olin (Lena), Page (Geraldine), Raye (Martha), Rigg (Diana), Ross (Diana, Katharine), Rush (Barbara), Ryan (Meg, Peggy), Shue (Elisabeth), Weld (Tuesday), West (Mae), Wood (Natalie, Peggy), Wray (Fay), York (Susannah) **5** Adams (Maude), Aimee (Anouk), Allen (Joan, Gracie, Karen, Nancy), Alley (Kirstie), Arden (Eve), Astor (Mary), Bates (Kathy), Berry (Halle), Black (Karen), Bloom (Claire), Blyth (Ann), Booth (Shirley), Brice (Fanny), Britt (May), Bruce (Virginia), Buzzi (Ruth), Caron (Leslie), Close (Glenn), Crain (Jeanne), Danes (Claire), Davis (Bette, Geena, Judy), Dench (Judi), Derek (Bo), Dunne (Irene), Eggar (Samantha), Evans (Edith), Falco (Edie), Field (Sally), Fonda (Bridget, Jane), Gabor (Eva, Zsa Zsa), Garbo (Greta), Gless (Sharon), Grant (Lee), Greer (Jane), Grier (Pam), Hagen (Uta), Hasso (Signe), Hayek (Salma), Hayes (Helen), Heche (Anne), Henie (Sonja), Howes (Sally Ann), Jones (Cherry, Jennifer, Shirley), Kazan (Lainie), Kelly (Grace, Patsy), Kurtz (Swoosie), Lahti (Christine), Lange (Hope, Jessica), Leigh (Janet, Jennifer Jason, Vivien), Lenya (Lotte), Lewis (Juliette), Loren (Sophia), Mason (Marsha, Pamela), Meara (Anne), Miles (Sarah, Vera), Moore (Demi, Julianne, Mary Tyler, Terry), Naldi (Nita), North (Sheree), Novak (Kim), O'Hara (Maureen), Olson (Nancy), O'Neal (Tatum), Perez (Rosie), Picon (Molly), Pitts (Zasu), Reese (Della), Ricci (Christina),

Roman (Ruth), Ruehl (Mercedes), Ryder (Winona), Saint (Eva Marie), Scott (Lizbeth, Martha), Shire (Talia), Smith (Alexis, Maggie), Stone (Sharon), Storm (Gale), Swank (Hilary), Tandy (Jessica), Terry (Ellen), Tomei (Marisa), Tyler (Liv), Tyson (Cicely), Watts (Naomi), Welch (Raquel), Wiest (Dianne), Wyatt (Jane), Wyman (Jane), Young (Sean, Loretta) **6** Adjani (Isabelle), Angeli (Pier), Arthur (Beatrice, Jean), Ashley (Elizabeth), Bacall (Lauren), Bardot (Brigitte), Barkin (Ellen), Barrie (Wendy), Baxter (Anne), Bening (Annette), Bergen (Candice, Polly), Bisset (Jacqueline), Blaine (Vivian), Brooks (Louise), Bujold (Genevieve), Butler (Brett), Cannon (Dyan), Carter (Dixie, Lynda, Nell), Cooper (Gladys), Crouse (Lindsay), Curtin (Jane), Curtis (Jamie Lee), Danner (Blythe), Davies (Marion), Del Rio (Dolores), Dennis (Sandy), Diller (Phyllis), Draper (Ruth), Driver (Minnie), Dumont (Margaret), Duncan (Sandy), Durbin (Deanna), Duvall (Shelley), Ekberg (Anita), Ekland (Britt), Fabray (Nanette), Farmer (Frances), Farrow (Mia), Feldon (Barbara), Fisher (Carrie), Foster (Jodie), Garner (Peggy Ann), Garson (Greer), Gaynor (Mitzi), Gordon (Ruth), Grable (Betty), Grimes (Tammy), Hannah (Daryl), Harlow (Jean), Harper (Jessica, Tess, Valerie), Harris (Barbara, Julie, Rosemary), Hedren (Tippi), Hiller (Wendy), Hunter (Holly, Kim), Hussey (Ruth), Huston (Anjelica), Hutton (Betty), Irving (Amy), Keaton (Diane), Keeler (Ruby), Kidman (Nicole), Kinski (Nastassja), Knight (Shirley), Lamarr (Hedy), Lamour (Dorothy), Lasser (Louise), Laurie (Piper), Lillie (Beatrice), Louise (Tina), Lupino (Ida), MacRae (Sheila), Malone (Dorothy), Martin (Mary), Matlin (Marlee), McGraw (Ali), Merkel (Una), Merman (Ethel), Midler (Bette), Miller (Ann), Mirren (Helen), Monroe (Marilyn), Moreau (Jeanne), Moreno (Rita), Oberon (Merle), O'Brien (Margaret), Oliver (Edna May), Palmer (Lili), Paquin (Anna), Parker (Eleanor, Mary-Louise, Sarah Jessica, Suzy), Peters (Bernadette), Powers (Stephanie), Prowse (Juliet), Rainer (Luise), Rashad (Phylicia), Remick (Lee), Ritter (Thelma), Rivera (Chita), Rogers (Ginger), Scales (Prunella), Seberg (Jean), Sidney (Sylvia), Somers (Suzanne), Sommer (Elke), Spacek (Sissy), Streep (Meryl), Taylor (Elizabeth), Temple (Shirley), Theron (Charlize), Thomas (Marlo),

Tiffin (Pamela), Tomlin (Lily), Turner (Kathleen, Lana), Walker (Nancy), Warren (Lesley Ann), Watson (Emily), Weaver (Sigourney), Wilson (Marie), Winger (Debra), Wright (Teresa), Wynter (Dana) **7** Allyson (June), Andress (Ursula), Andrews (Julie), Aniston (Jennifer), Bassett (Angela), Bennett (Constance, Joan), Bergman (Ingrid), Binoche (Juliette), Blethyn (Brenda), Buckley (Betty), Bullock (Sandra), Burnett (Carol), Burstyn (Ellen), Colbert (Claudette), Collins (Joan, Pauline), Cornell (Katherine), Cushman (Charlotte), Darnell (Linda), DeCarlo (Yvonne), Delaney (Dana), Deneuve (Catherine), Dukakis (Olympia), Dunaway (Faye), Dunnock (Mildred), Fawcett (Farrah), Fleming (Rhonda), Fricker (Brenda), Gardner (Ava), Garland (Judy), Gershon (Gina), Gingold (Hermione), Goddard (Paulette), Grahame (Gloria), Grayson (Kathryn), Hayward (Susan), Heckart (Eileen), Hepburn (Audrey, Katharine), Hershey (Barbara), Jackson (Anne, Glenda, Kate), Langtry (Lillie), Learned (Michael), Lombard (Carole), MacGraw (Ali), Madonna, Magnani (Anna), Mangano (Silvana), McGuire (Dorothy), McKenna (Siobhan), McQueen (Butterfly), Meadows (Audrey, Jayne), Mimieux (Yvette), Miranda (Carmen), Mulgrew (Kate), Natwick (Mildred), Parsons (Estelle), Perlman (Rhea), Perrine (Valerie), Plummer (Amanda), Podesta (Rosanna), Portman (Natalie), Roberts (Julia), Russell (Jane, Rosalind, Theresa), Scacchi (Greta), Sevigny (Chloë), Shearer (Norma), Shields (Brooke), Siddons (Sarah), Simmons (Jean), Sorvino (Mira), Sothern (Ann), Stevens (Connie, Stella), Stritch (Elaine), Swanson (Gloria), Swinton (Tilda), Thaxter (Phyllis), Thurman (Uma), Tierney (Gene), Ullmann (Liv), Verdugo (Elena), Winfrey (Oprah), Winslet (Kate), Winters (Shelley), Withers (Jane), Woodard (Alfre) **8** Anderson (Judith, Loni, Melissa Sue), Arquette (Patricia, Rosanna), Ashcroft (Peggy), Bancroft (Anne), Bankhead (Tallulah), Basinger (Kim), Blondell (Joan), Byington (Spring), Caldwell (Zoe), Campbell (Mrs. Patrick), Channing (Carol, Stockard), Charisse (Cyd), Christie (Julie), Crawford (Joan), DeMornay (Rebecca), Dewhurst (Colleen), Dietrich (Marlene), Dressler (Marie), Fletcher (Louise), Fontaine (Joan), Fontanne (Lynn), Goldberg (Whoopi), Griffith (Melanie), Hayworth (Rita), Holliday (Judy), Lansbury (Angela),

Lawrence (Gertrude), Leachman (Cloris), Leighton (Margaret), Lindfors (Viveca), Lockhart (June), Lovelace (Linda), MacLaine (Shirley), McDaniel (Hattie), Mercouri (Melina), Minnelli (Liza), Nelligan (Kate), Neuwirth (Bebe), O'Donnell (Rosie), Pfeiffer (Michelle), Pickford (Mary), Prentiss (Paula), Redgrave (Lynn, Vanessa), Reynolds (Debbie), Roseanne, Rowlands (Gena), Sarandon (Susan), Shepherd (Cybill), Signoret (Simone), Spelling (Tori), Stanwyck (Barbara), Straight (Beatrice), Sullavan (Margaret), Talmadge (Norma), Thompson (Emma, Sada), Van Doren (Mamie), Vardalos (Nia), Williams (Esther), Woodward (Joanne) **9** Alexander (Jane), Barrymore (Drew, Ethel), Bernhardt (Sarah), Blanchett (Cate), Cardinale (Claudia), Christian (Linda), Clayburgh (Jill), Dandridge (Dorothy), DeGeneres (Ellen), Dickinson (Angie), Fairchild (Morgan), Henderson (Florence), Kellerman (Sally), Mansfield (Jayne), McDonnell (Mary), Moorehead (Agnes), O'Sullivan (Maureen), Pleshette (Suzanne), Plowright (Joan), Schneider (Romy), Singleton (Penny), Stapleton (Jean, Maureen), Strasberg (Susan), Streisand (Barbra), Struthers (Sally), Thorndike (Sybil), Vera-Ellen, Zellweger (Renée) **10** Ann-Margret, Lanchester (Elsa), Montgomery (Elizabeth), Richardson (Miranda, Natasha), Rossellini (Isabella), Rutherford (Margaret), Tushingham (Rita) **11** de Havilland (Olivia), McCambridge (Mercedes), Riefenstahl (Leni), Silverstone (Alicia), Steenburgen (Mary) **12** Bonham-Carter (Helena), Lollabrigida (Gina), Mastrantonio (Mary Elizabeth)

actual 4 echt, hard, live, real, true **5** exact **6** extant, living **7** certain, current, de facto, factual, genuine **8** absolute, bona fide, concrete, definite, existent, existing, material, physical, positive, tangible **9** authentic, objective, veritable **10** legitimate, phenomenal **12** indisputable

actuality 4 fact **5** being, truth **7** reality **9** existence, substance **10** embodiment **11** incarnation, materiality

actually 4 very **5** truly **6** indeed, in fact, really **7** de facto, no doubt **9** genuinely, in reality, veritably **10** absolutely

actuate 4 move, spur, stir **5** drive, impel, rouse **6** arouse, excite, propel, set off, turn on **7** provoke, trigger **8** activate, energize, mobilize, motivate, vitalize

act up 5 cut up **7** show off **9** misbehave **11** misfunction

acumen 3 wit **6** acuity, vision, wisdom **7** insight **8** keenness **9** acuteness, sharpness **10** astuteness, perception, shrewdness **11** discernment, penetration, percipience **12** perspicacity

acute 4 dire, keen **5** sharp **6** urgent **7** crucial, exigent, intense, pointed **8** critical, incisive, piercing, shooting, stabbing **9** knifelike, observant, trenchant **10** perceptive **11** penetrating, quick-witted, sharp-witted

ad ____ 3 hoc, lib, rem **7** hominem, interim, nauseam **9** infinitum

adage 3 saw **4** rule **5** axiom, maxim, motto **6** byword, saying, truism **7** proverb **8** aphorism, apothegm

adagio 4 slow **5** tempo

Adah *husband:* **4** Esau **6** Lamech *son:* **5** Jabal, Jubal **7** Eliphaz

Adam *grandson:* **4** Enos **5** Enoch *rib:* **3** Eve *son:* **4** Abel, Cain, Seth *wife:* **3** Eve **6** Lilith

Adam ____ 4 Bede **5** Smith

adamant 3 set **4** firm, hard **5** rigid, stiff, stone, tough **6** flinty **8** immobile, obdurate, resolute **9** immovable, unbending, unswaying **10** determined, inflexible, unbendable, unyielding **11** unbreakable

adapt 3 fit **4** suit **5** alter, shape, yield **6** adjust, change, modify, revise, square, tailor **7** arrange, conform, remodel **9** acclimate, habituate, reconcile **11** acclimatize, accommodate

adaptable 6 mobile, pliant, supple **7** ductile, plastic, pliable **8** flexible, moldable **9** malleable, versatile

adaptation 6 change **8** revision **9** reworking **10** adjustment, alteration **12** modification

ad astra per ____ 6 aspera

add 3 sum, tot **4** cast, foot, join, tote **5** affix, annex, count, tally, total, unite **6** append, attach, figure, reckon, tack on, take on **7** augment, compute, count up, enlarge, improve, include **8** compound, increase, totalize **9** build onto, calculate **10** supplement

Addams family 5 Gomez **7** Pugsley **8** Morticia **9** Grandmama, Wednesday **11** Uncle Fester *servants:* **5** Lurch, Thing

added 3 new **4** else, more **5** extra, fresh, other **7** another, farther, further **9** accessory **10** additional **13** supplementary

addendum 5 extra, rider **8** addition **10** supplement

adder 5 snake, viper **10** calculator **12** hognose snake

addict 3 fan, nut **4** bias, buff **5** hound, lover **6** abuser, devote, junkie, zealot **7** booster, devotee, fanatic, groupie, habitué **9** habituate, surrender **10** aficionado, enthusiast

addition 4 plus, rise **5** annex, extra, raise, rider **7** accrual, adjunct **8** addendum, appendix, increase **9** accession, accessory, accretion, extension, increment **10** supplement **11** enlargement **12** appurtenance, augmentation

additional see **added**

additionally 3 too **4** also, more, then **5** again **6** as well **7** besides, further **8** likewise, moreover **11** furthermore

additive 5 extra **8** extender **9** summative, substance

addle 5 mix up, spoil **6** muddle, puzzle **7** confuse, fluster, nonplus, perplex **8** befuddle, bewilder, confound, distract, throw off **9** dumbfound

add-on 3 ell **7** adjunct **9** accessory **11** enhancement

address 3 aim, air, set, URL **4** hail, send, tact, talk **5** apply, court, grace, greet, level, place, point, poise, remit, route, skill, speak, treat **6** call to, devote, direct, pursue, relate, salute, speech **7** bearing, consign, deliver, forward, know-how, lecture, oration, speak to, write to **8** appeal to, approach, converse, deal with, deftness, delivery, demeanor, dispatch, identify, location, petition, position, presence, transmit **9** attention, dexterity, diplomacy, expertise **10** adroitness, competence, directions, efficiency **11** comportment, designation, proficiency, savoir faire

adduce 3 lay **4** cite **5** claim, offer **6** allege, submit, tender **7** advance, present, proffer, propose, refer to, suggest **8** document **9** exemplify **10** illustrate

add up 3 sum **5** count, tally, total **6** amount, reckon **7** compute **9** make sense

add up to 4 mean **5** spell **6** amount, denote, import, intend **7** compute, connote, express, signify

adept 3 pro **4** able, deft, whiz **5** crack, savvy **6** adroit, expert, master, wizard **7** skilled **8** masterly, skillful, virtuoso **9** dexterous, masterful **10** proficient **11** crackerjack **12** professional

adequacy 5 might **6** enough **7** ability **8** capacity **10** capability, competence, sufficient **11** sufficiency **13** qualification

adequate 6 common, decent, enough **8** all right, passable, pleasing, standard, suitable **9** competent, sufficing **10** acceptable, sufficient **11** comfortable **12** satisfactory **13** unexceptional, unimpeachable

adequately 4 well **5** amply, right **6** enough **8** all right, passably, properly, suitably **9** fittingly, tolerably **12** sufficiently **13** appropriately

adhere 4 bond, glue **5** cling, paste, stick **6** attach, bind to, cement, cleave, cohere, fasten **7** stick to **8** hold fast

adherence 4 bond **5** cling **7** loyalty **8** adhesion, clinging, cohesion, fidelity, sticking **9** constancy **10** attachment **12** faithfulness

adherent 3 fan, ist **6** cohort, votary **7** devotee, sectary **8** disciple, follower, henchman, partisan, stalwart **9** satellite, supporter **10** aficionado

adhering 6 clingy, sticky **7** binding

adhesive 4 glue **5** epoxy, gluey, gooey, gummy, stamp, tacky **6** cement, clingy, gummed, sticky **7** holding, stickum **8** adhering, fastener, mucilage, sticking **9** attaching

adieu 3 bye **4** ciao, ta-ta **5** congé **6** bye-bye, so long **7** cheerio, good-bye, parting, toodles **8** farewell, toodle-oo **11** leave-taking

ad interim 6 acting, pro tem **9** temporary **10** pro tempore **11** temporarily

adios 4 by-by, ciao, ta-ta **5** adieu, later **6** bye-bye, so long **7** cheerio, goodbye, toodles **8** farewell, toodle-oo **10** hasta luego

adipose 3 fat **4** oily **5** fatty **6** greasy **7** fatlike

adit 3 way **4** door **5** entry **6** access, entrée, tunnel **7** ingress, passage **8** entrance **9** mine entry **10** passageway **12** mine entrance

adjacent 4 near **5** close **6** beside, nearby, next to **8** abutting, next door, touching **9** adjoining, alongside, bordering **10** contiguous, juxtaposed, near-at-hand **11** close-at-hand, neighboring **12** conterminous

adjoin 3 add **4** abut, link, line, meet **5** annex, touch, verge **6** append, attach, border, butt on, couple **7** connect, impinge **8** neighbor **11** communicate

adjourn 4 move, rise, stay **5** defer, delay **6** hold up, put off, recess, shelve **7** hold off, suspend **8** dissolve, hold over, postpone, prorogue **9** prorogate

adjudge 4 deem, rule **5** award, grant **6** decide, settle, umpire **7** mediate, referee **9** arbitrate

adjunct 5 added, affix **6** joined **8** addendum, addition, appanage, appendix, attached **9** accessory, accretion, appendage, assistant, associate, auxiliary **10** attachment **12** appurtenance

adjure 3 beg, bid **4** urge **6** exhort **7** beseech, entreat, command, implore, require **9** importune **10** supplicate

adjust 3 fit, fix, rig **4** suit, tune **5** adapt, order, right **6** accord, attune, modify, orient, settle, square, tailor, tune up **7** arrange, conform, correct, rectify, resolve **8** modulate, regulate **9** habituate, harmonize, reconcile **11** accommodate

adjutant 4 aide **6** deputy

adjuvant 4 aide **6** aiding, helper **8** enhancer, modifier **9** accessory, ancillary, assisting, auxiliary **10** collateral, subsidiary **11** appurtenant **12** contributory

ad-lib 9 extempore, improvise, impromptu **10** improvised, off-the-cuff, unprepared **11** extemporize, spontaneous, unrehearsed

Admetus father: 6 Pheres **wife: 8** Alcestis

administer 3 run **4** boss, deal, give, head **5** issue **6** direct, govern, head up, manage **7** conduct, control, deal out, deliver, dole out, execute, give out, mete out, oversee, perform, provide **8** carry out, dispense, share out **9** apportion, supervise **10** distribute, portion out

administration 6 régime **7** control **9** direction **10** governance, presidency **system of: 11** bureaucracy

administrator 4 boss, exec, head **5** chief **7** manager, officer **8** director, official, overseer **9** executive **10** supervisor

admirable 6 august, worthy **8** laudable **9** deserving, estimable, excellent, meritable **11** commendable, meritorious, outstanding **12** praiseworthy

admiral American: 4 Byrd (Richard), Sims (William) **5** Dewey (George), Stark (Harold) **6** Halsey (Bull), Nimitz (Chester) **7** Zumwalt (Elmo) **8** Farragut (David), Rickover (Hyman), Spruance (Raymond) **Chinese: 7** Zheng He **Confederate: 6** Semmes (Raphael) **Dutch: 5** Tromp (Maarten) **English: 5** Drake (Francis) **6** Nelson (Horatio), Rodney (George), Vernon (Edward) **7** Hawkins (John) **8** Beaufort (Francis), Jellicoe (John), Villiers (George) **11** Mountbatten (Louis) **fictional: 10** Hornblower (Horatio) **French: 10** Villeneuve (Pierre-Charles) **German: 4** Spee (Graf Maximilian von) **6** Dönitz (Karl), Raeder (Erich) **7** Doenitz (Karl), Tirpitz (Alfred von) **Japanese: 4** Togo (Hideki) **5** Yonai (Mitsumasa) **8** Yamamoto (Isoroku) **Spanish: 8** Menéndez (Pedro)

admiration 5 favor,**6** esteem, praise, regard **7** account, delight, respect **8** applause, approval, pleasure **9** affection **10** estimation **11** approbation **12** appreciation

admire 5 adore, honor, prize, value **6** esteem, praise, regard, relish, revere **7** adulate, applaud, approve, cherish, commend, respect **8** consider, treasure **9** delight in **10** appreciate

admirer 3 fan **4** beau, buff **7** booster, devotee, fancier **8** believer, follower, partisan **9** supporter **10** enthusiast

admission 3 way **4** door, gate **5** entry **6** access, assent, entrée **7** ingress **8** entrance **10** admittance, concession, confession **11** affirmation

admit 3 own **4** avow, take **5** agree, allow, enter, grant, let in, let on, lodge, own up **6** accept, fess up, harbor, permit, suffer, take in **7** concede, confess, receive, shelter, welcome **9** entertain, introduce, recognize **11** acknowledge

admix 5 blend, merge **6** mingle **7** combine **8** comingle, compound, immingle **9** commingle **11** intermingle

admixture 5 alloy, blend, combo **6** fusion **7** amalgam **8** compound **9** aggregate, composite **12** amalgamation

admonish 4 warn **5** alert, chide **6** lesson, monish, rebuke, talk to **7** caution, counsel, reprove, speak to **8** call down, forewarn, reproach **9** criticize, reprimand

admonition 3 tip **6** caveat, rebuke **7** caution, chiding, reproof, warning **8** reproach **9** criticism, reprimand **11** disapproval, forewarning

ado 4 fuss, stir **5** tizzy, whirl, worry **6** bother, bustle, flurry, hubbub, pother **7** concern, problem, trouble, turmoil **9** commotion, confusion **10** difficulty

adolescence 5 youth **7** puberty **8** minority **9** greenness **10** juvenility, pubescence **12** youthfulness

adolescent 4 teen **5** minor **6** teener **7** teenage **8** immature, preadult, teenager, youthful **9** pubescent

Adonai 3 God **4** YHWH **6** Elohim, Yahweh

Adonijah *brother:* **5** Amnon **7** Absalom, Chileab *father:* **5** David *mother:* **7** Haggith *slayer:* **7** Benaiah

Adonis *lover:* **5** Venus **9** Aphrodite *mother:* **5** Myrrh **6** Myrrha *slayer:* **4** boar

adopt 4 pick, take **5** raise **6** accept, affect, assume, choose, select, take on, take up **7** care for, embrace, endorse, espouse

adoption 6 choice **7** raising, support **8** espousal, taking in **9** embracing, selection **11** embracement

adorable 4 cute, dear **7** darling, lovable, winsome **8** charming, pleasing, precious **9** appealing **10** attractive, delightful

adoration 4 love **5** ardor, honor **6** esteem, praise **7** passion, worship **8** devotion, idolatry **9** adulation, affection, reverence **10** admiration **11** idolization

adore 4 love **5** honor, prize **6** admire, dote on, esteem, revere **7** cherish, idolize, respect, worship **8** dote upon, treasure, venerate **9** affection, delight in, reverence

adorn 4 deck, trim **5** fix up, grace **6** bedeck, enrich, pretty **7** dress up, enhance, enliven, furbish, garnish, smarten **8** beautify, decorate, ornament, prettify **9** embellish

adornment 5 decor, frill **6** finery **7** garnish **8** ornament, trimming **9** accessory, caparison **10** decoration **13** embellishment

ad rem 3 apt **7** apropos, fitting, germane **8** apposite, material, relevant **9** pertinent **10** applicable, relevantly, to the point **11** applicative, applicatory

adrift 4 asea, lost **5** at sea, loose **6** afloat **7** aimless, mixed up **8** confused, floating, unmoored **10** anchorless, bewildered **11** disoriented, purposeless

adroit 3 apt **4** able, deft **5** adept, canny, handy, savvy, smart **6** astute, clever, expert, nimble, shrewd **7** cunning, skilled **8** skillful, talented **9** dexterous, ingenious **11** intelligent, quick-witted, resourceful **13** perspicacious

adroitness 3 art **4** gift **5** craft, flair, knack, savvy, skill **7** address, cunning, know-how, prowess **8** deftness **9** adeptness, dexterity, expertise, ingenuity, readiness **10** cleverness, expertness **12** intelligence

adulation 7 acclaim, baloney, blarney, fawning, tribute, worship **8** applause, flattery, soft soap **10** overpraise **11** hero-worship **12** blandishment

adulatory 7 buttery, fawning **8** unctuous **9** kowtowing **10** flattering, obsequious, oleaginous **11** bootlicking, sycophantic

adult 4 aged, ripe **5** grown **6** mature **7** grown-up, matured, ripened **9** full-blown, full-grown **11** full-fledged

adulterate 3 cut **4** thin **5** alloy, dirty, taint, water **6** debase, defile, dilute, doctor, dope up, impair, weaken **7** cheapen, corrupt, defiled, degrade, devalue, diluted, falsify, pollute, tainted, thinned **8** degraded, denature, impurify, polluted, spurious **9** water down **10** tamper with **11** contaminate

adumbrate 3 dim, fog **4** bode, call, hint, mist, veil **5** augur, cloud **6** darken, shadow, sketch **7** becloud, bespeak, betoken, obscure, outline, portend, predict, presage, suggest **8** block out, disclose, forebode, forecast, foretell, indicate, intimate, prophesy **9** obfuscate, prefigure **10** foreshadow, overshadow **11** prefigurate **12** characterize

adumbration 4 hint, sign **5** shade, umbra **6** shadow **7** outline **8** penumbra **10** indication, intimation, suggestion

advance 3 aid **4** cite, help, lend, loan, move, rise **5** get on, march, money, raise, serve **6** assist, course, foster, mature, prefer, supply, uplift **7** deposit, develop, elevate, forward, furnish, further, headway, ongoing, present, proceed, promote, propose, upgrade **8** approach, get along, heighten, increase, progress **9** encourage, evolution, provision **10** accelerate, bring about **11** development, furtherance, improvement, progression **12** breakthrough

advanced 3 old **5** first **6** far out **7** forward, in front, leading, liberal, radical **8** far ahead, foremost **9** developed **10** precocious **11** broad-minded, progressive

advancement 4 gain, rise **5** boost **6** growth **7** headway **8** progress **9** elevation, promotion **10** betterment, preference **11** improvement, progression

advantage 4 boon, edge, gain, good, help, lead, odds **5** asset, avail, serve **6** better, profit **7** account, benefit, mastery **8** blessing, interest, leverage **9** allowance, head start, upper hand **10** ascendancy, domination, leadership, prosperity **11** superiority **12** running start

advantageous 4 good **6** timely, toward, useful **7** benefic, gainful, helpful **8** favoring, salutary **9** conducive, desirable, expedient, favorable, fortunate, promising **10** beneficial, profitable, propitious, worthwhile

advent 5 onset **6** coming **7** arrival **8** approach **9** beginning

adventitious 5 fluky **6** casual, chance, flukey **8** by chance **9** unplanned **10** accidental, contingent, fortuitous, incidental, unexpected

adventure 3 try **4** feat, risk, trip **5** quest, wager **6** chance, gamble, hazard **7** exploit **8** escapade **9** undertake **10** enterprise, experience

adventurous 4 bold, rash **5** brash, risky **6** daring **8** intrepid, reckless **9** audacious, dangerous, daredevil, foolhardy, hazardous, impetuous, imprudent **10** innovative **12** enterprising

adversary 3 con, foe **4** anti **5** enemy, rival **7** opposer **8** opponent, opposing **10** antagonist, competitor

adverse 3 bad **4** anti **7** counter, harmful, hostile, hurtful, opposed **8** contrary, damaging, negative, opposing, opposite **9** injurious **11** deleterious, detrimental, obstructive, unfavorable **12** antagonistic, antipathetic

adversity 4 dole **5** trial **6** misery, mishap **7** bad luck, bad news, trouble **8** bad break, distress, hard time, hardship **9** mischance,

suffering **10** difficulty, ill fortune, misfortune

advert 4 cite, note **5** refer **6** allude, notice, remark **7** bring up, mention, observe **8** indicate, point out

advertent 5 aware **7** heedful, mindful **9** attentive, intentive, observant, regardful

advertise 4 drum, hype, plug, puff, push, tout **5** boost, pitch **6** blazon, herald, inform, notify, report **7** advance, apprise, build up, declare, promote, publish, sponsor **8** announce, ballyhoo, proclaim **9** broadcast, publicize **10** annunciate, promulgate

advertisement 4 bill, plug, sign **5** blurb, flyer, promo **6** notice, poster, want ad **7** affiche **8** circular **9** billboard, broadcast, promotion, publicity **10** commercial **11** declaration, publication **12** announcement, proclamation

advertising award 4 Clio

advice 3 aid, tip **4** help, news, view, word **5** input **6** notice **7** caution, counsel, opinion, tidings, warning **8** guidance, teaching **10** admonition, suggestion **11** information, instruction **12** intelligence

advisable 4 wise **5** sound **6** seemly **7** politic, prudent **8** sensible, suitable, tactical **9** desirable, expedient, practical **10** worthwhile **11** recommended **12** advantageous

advise 3 tip **4** tell, tout, urge, warn **5** guide **6** clue in, confer, enjoin, fill in, inform, notify, tip off, wise up **7** apprise, caution, consult, counsel, suggest **8** acquaint, forewarn, instruct, point out **9** encourage, prescribe, recommend

advised 7 studied, weighed **8** designed, intended **10** calculated, considered, deliberate, thought out **11** intentional **12** premeditated

adviser 5 coach, guide **6** mentor **7** counsel, tipster **9** counselor **10** consultant, instructor

advisory 7 guiding, helping **9** educative **10** counseling **12** consultative **13** informational

advocacy 3 aid **6** urging **7** backing, defense, support **9** promotion

advocate 4 back, push, tout, urge **5** favor **6** backer, defend, preach, uphold **7** promote, propose, support **8** argue for, backstop, champion, exponent, plump for, side with **9** encourage, expounder, proponent, recommend, spokesman, supporter **11** countenance

Aeacus *father:* **4** Zeus *mother:* **6** Aegina *son:* **6** Peleus **7** Telamon

Aedon *brother:* **7** Amphion *sister-in-law:* **5** Niobe *son (victim):* **6** Itylus

Aeëtes *daughter:* **5** Medea *father:* **6** Helios

aegis 4 care, ward **5** armor, guard **6** charge,

shield **7** backing, control, defense, support **8** auspices, guidance, security **9** influence, patronage, safeguard **10** protection **11** sponsorship

Aegisthus *father:* **8** Thyestes *lover:* **12** Clytemnestra *mother:* **7** Pelopia *slayer:* **7** Orestes *victim:* **6** Atreus **9** Agamemnon

Aeneas *companion:* **7** Achates *father:* **8** Anchises *lover:* **4** Dido *mother:* **5** Venus **9** Aphrodite *son:* **5** Iulus **8** Ascanius *wife:* **6** Creusa **7** Lavinia

Aeneid *author:* **6** Vergil, Virgil *first words:* **16** arma virumque cano *hero:* **6** Aeneas

Aeolus *daughter:* **7** Alcyone **8** Halcyone *father:* **8** Poseidon

aeon 3 age **4** time **6** period **8** blue moon, duration

aerate 7 lighten, freshen, refresh **9** oxygenate, ventilate

aerial 4 high **5** lofty **6** flying, vapory **7** antenna, soaring **8** birdlike, elevated, ethereal, fanciful, towering, vaporous **9** pneumatic **10** impalpable **11** atmospheric, forward pass

aerie 4 nest **7** citadel, lookout **9** penthouse *resident:* **5** eagle **6** eaglet

aeroembolism 5 bends

aeronaut 4 Fogg (Phileas) **5** pilot **7** aviator **8** Zeppelin (Ferdinand, Graf von) **10** balloonist

Aerope *husband:* **6** Atreus *lover:* **8** Thyestes *son:* **8** Menelaus **9** Agamemnon

aery see **aerial**

Aesculapius *daughter:* **6** Hygeia **7** Panacea *father:* **6** Apollo *slayer:* **4** Zeus **7** Jupiter *teacher:* **6** Chiron *wife:* **6** Epione

Aeson *brother:* **6** Pelias *son:* **5** Jason

aesthete 4 buff **6** expert **7** devotee **9** authority **10** dilettante **11** appreciator, cognoscente, connoisseur

aesthetic 6 artful **8** artistic, creative, pleasing **9** beautiful, sensitive **10** attractive, harmonious

afar 5 apart **6** remote **7** distant

affable 4 kind, open, warm **6** at ease, genial, gentle, kindly, polite **7** amiable, cordial **8** friendly, gracious, obliging, pleasant, sociable **9** congenial, courteous

affair 4 case, love **5** amour, fling, worry **6** action, matter **7** concern, liaison, palaver, romance **8** business, function, interest, intrigue, occasion **9** dalliance, happening, procedure **10** proceeding **12** relationship

affect 3 act **4** fake, move, sham, stir, sway **5** act on, adopt, alter, bluff, fancy, feign, haunt, put on, touch **6** assume, change, strike **7** act upon, disturb, impress, inspire,

pretend **8** frequent, simulate **9** cultivate, influence

affectation 3 air **4** airs, pose, sham, show **6** facade **8** pretense **9** mannerism **10** pretension **13** artificiality

affected 5 apish, false, moved, phony, put-on **6** phoney **7** altered, assumed, changed, feigned, stilted **8** disposed, inclined, involved, mannered, precious, spurious **9** concerned, conscious, contrived, insincere, pretended, unnatural **10** artificial **11** overrefined, pretentious **13** self-conscious

affecting 3 sad **6** lively, moving **7** pitiful **8** exciting, poignant, touching **9** thrilling **10** disturbing, impressive **11** distressing, influential

affection 4 bias, love **5** trait **6** doting, liking, malady, virtue, warmth **7** ailment, concern, disease, emotion, feature, feeling, illness, leaning, passion, quality **8** devotion, disorder, fondness, interest, penchant, property, sickness, sympathy **9** attention, attribute, character, complaint, condition, sentiment **10** attachment, propensity, tenderness **12** predilection

affectionate 4 dear, fond, warm **6** caring, doting, loving, tender **7** devoted **8** friendly **11** sympathetic

affective 6 moving **7** emotive **8** stirring, touching **9** emotional

affectivity 7 emotion, feeling, passion **9** sentiment

affianced 7 engaged, pledged **8** intended, plighted, promised **9** betrothed, committed **10** contracted

affiche 4 bill, list **6** notice, poster **7** placard **8** handbill

affidavit 4 oath **9** testimony **11** affirmation, declaration

affiliate 4 ally, join **5** annex, unite **6** branch **7** combine, connect, partner **9** associate

affiliated 4 akin **5** bound **6** allied, joined, linked **7** kindred, related **9** connected, dependent **10** associated

affiliation 4 club **5** tie-in, union **6** hookup, league **7** cahoots, company, joining **8** alliance **10** connection, fellowship **11** association, combination, conjunction, partnership

affinity 6 simile **7** analogy, kinship, rapport **8** likeness, relation, sympathy **9** alikeness **10** attraction, similarity, similitude **11** resemblance **13** compatibility

affirm 3 say, yes **4** aver, avow, okay **5** state, swear, vouch **6** assent, assert, attest, depose, ratify, uphold **7** certify, confirm, declare, profess, protest, testify, witness **8** dedicate, validate **9** guarantee

affirmative 3 A-OK, aye, yea, yes **4** yeah **5** roger **6** assent, aye-aye, yessir **7** right on **8** approval, positive **9** affirming, approving, asserting, assertion, endorsing, favorable, ratifying **10** confirming, supporting **11** affirmation

affix 3 add, tag **4** bind, glue, join, nail, tack **5** annex, paste, put on, rivet, stick, tag on **6** append, attach, fasten, tack on **7** impress, stick on, subjoin **8** addition **9** appendage **10** attachment

afflict 3 try, vex **4** pain, rack **5** annoy, beset, harry, press, smite, worry, wound, wring **6** bother, burden, harass, harrow, injure, martyr, pester, plague, strike, suffer **7** agonize, anguish, torment, torture, trouble **8** distress

afflicted 6 pained, rueful, woeful **7** doleful, injured, unhappy, worried **8** dolorous, stricken, troubled, wretched **9** disturbed, miserable, sorrowful, tormented **10** distressed

affliction 3 woe **4** care **5** cross, grief, trial **6** ordeal, plague, sorrow **7** anguish, illness, scourge, torment, trouble **8** distress, hardship, sickness **9** adversity, heartache, infirmity **10** misfortune **11** tribulation

afflictive 3 sad **4** dire, sore **6** aching, bitter, woeful **7** galling, hurtful, hurting, painful **8** grievous, mournful **9** sorrowful **10** calamitous, deplorable, lamentable **11** distasteful, distressing, regrettable, troublesome, unfortunate, unpalatable **13** heartbreaking

affluence 5 means, worth **6** bounty, influx, plenty, riches, wealth **8** opulence, property, richness **9** abundance, plenitude, profusion, resources **10** prosperity

affluent 4 full, rich **5** flush **6** loaded **7** copious, flowing, moneyed, opulent, upscale, wealthy, well-off **8** abundant, well-to-do **9** bountiful, plentiful, tributary, well-fixed **10** prosperous, well-heeled

afford 4 able, bear, give **5** allow, grant, incur, offer, spare, stand **6** bestow, confer, donate, impart, manage, supply **7** furnish, present, support, sustain

affordable 5 cheap **6** modest **7** low-cost **8** bearable **10** manageable, reasonable **11** inexpensive

affray 3 row **5** clash, fight, melee, scrap **6** fracas, rumpus **7** dispute, quarrel, ruction, scuffle **8** disorder, skirmish

affront 3 vex **4** face, meet, slap, slur **5** abuse, anger, annoy, wrong **6** injury, insult, offend, slight **7** offense, outrage, put down **8** contempt, rudeness **9** aspersion, criticize, encounter, indignity

Afghanistan *capital:* **5** Kabul *city:* **5** Herat **8** Kandahar **12** Mazar-i-Sharif *ethnic group:* **7** Pashtun *language:* **4** Dari **6** Pashto *monetary unit:* **7** Afghani *neighbor:* **4** Iran **5** China **8** Pakistan **10** Tajikistan, Uzbekistan **12** Turkmenistan

aficionado 3 fan **4** buff **5** hound, lover **6** expert **7** admirer, devotee, habitué **10** enthusiast **11** appreciator

afield 4 afar, away, awry **5** amiss, badly, wrong **6** abroad, astray **8** straying **9** elsewhere, off course

afire 3 hot **5** aglow, fiery **6** ablaze, aflame, alight, red-hot **7** blazing, burning, excited, flaming, flaring, ignited, kindled **8** inflamed, in flames **9** energized, excitable **10** passionate **11** conflagrant

afloat 4 asea **5** at sea **6** adrift, buoyed **9** supported, sustained

afraid 4 wary **5** chary, jumpy, loath, scary, sorry, timid **6** averse, scared, trepid **7** anxious, fearful, uneager, worried **8** cautious, hesitant, skittish, timorous **9** concerned, regretful, reluctant, unwilling **10** frightened **11** disinclined **12** apprehensive

afresh 3 new **4** anew, over **5** again, newly **6** de novo, encore **8** once more, repeated **9** once again

Africa *country:* **4** Chad, Mali, Togo **5** Benin, Congo, Egypt, Gabon, Ghana, Kenya, Libya, Niger, Sudan, Zaire **6** Angola, Gambia, Guinea, Malawi, Rwanda, Uganda, Zambia **7** Algeria, Burundi, Comoros, Eritrea, Lesotho, Liberia, Morocco, Namibia, Nigeria, Senegal, Somalia, Tunisia **8** Botswana, Cameroon, Djibouti, Ethiopia, Tanzania, Zimbabwe **9** Cape Verde, Mauritius, Swaziland **10** Ivory Coast, Madagascar, Mauritania, Mozambique, Seychelles **11** Burkina Faso, Côte d'Ivoire, Sierra Leone, South Africa **12** Guinea-Bissau *ethnic group:* **3** Ibo **4** Akan, Arab, Baya, Boer, Copt, Fula, Issa, Jebu, Moor, Zulu **5** Bantu, Fulah, Galla, Hausa, Kongo, Mande, Pygmy, Swazi, Wolof, Xhosa **6** Berber, Fulani, Hamite, Herero, Kikuyu, Nubian, Somali, Tuareg, Ubangi, Yoruba **7** Ashanti, Bedouin, Bushman, Malinke, Swahili, Touareg **8** Egyptian, Mandingo **9** Hottentot *language:* **3** Ibo **4** Taal **5** Bantu, Galla, Hausa, Xhosa **6** Arabic, Berber, Somali, Yoruba **7** Amharic, Bambara, Swahili **8** Malagasy **9** Afrikaans

aft 6 astern **8** rearmost, rearward **9** sternward

after 4 back, hind, next, past, rear **5** below, later, since **6** astern, back of, behind, beyond, hinder **7** ensuing **8** hindmost **9** following, posterior, sternward **10** subsequent

after all 3 yet **5** still **6** at last, though **7** finally, however **8** in the end **11** nonetheless **12** nevertheless

aftereffect 5 issue **6** result, upshot **7** fallout, outcome **11** consequence, eventuality

afterlife 6 beyond **8** eternity **9** hereafter

aftermath 4 wake **6** effect, result, upshot **12** consequences, repercussion

afterward 4 next, soon, then **5** later **6** behind **7** by and by, thereon **8** latterly **9** hereafter **10** thereafter **12** subsequently

afterword 5 envoi **6** epilog **8** epilogue

Agag *kingdom:* **6** Amalek *slayer:* **6** Samuel

again 3 bis **4** also, anew, back, over **6** afresh, de novo, encore **8** once more

again and again 3 oft **4** much **5** often **8** ofttimes **10** frequently, oftentimes, repeatedly **11** continually

against 3 con **4** anti **6** contra, facing, versus **7** vis-à-vis **8** fronting, opposite, touching *prefix:* **4** anti **6** contra **7** counter

Agamemnon *avenger:* **7** Orestes *brother:* **8** Menelaus *daughter:* **7** Electra **9** Iphigenia *father:* **6** Atreus *slayer:* **9** Aegisthus *son:* **7** Orestes *wife:* **12** Clytemnestra

agape 4 love, open **6** amazed **7** yawning **8** wide open **9** astounded, love feast **10** astonished, confounded **11** dumbfounded, overwhelmed **13** thunderstruck

agate 3 taw **4** type **6** marble, quartz **7** shooter **8** type size

agave 4 aloe **5** yucca *drink:* **6** mescal, pulque *product:* **4** hemp **5** sisal

Agave *father:* **6** Cadmus *husband:* **6** Echion *mother:* **8** Harmonia *sister:* **3** Ino **6** Semele **7** Autonoë *son:* **8** Pentheus

age 3 eon, era **4** aeon, grow, span, time **5** epoch, ripen, stage **6** grow up, mature, mellow, period **7** develop **8** blue moon, division, interval, lifetime, majority, maturate **10** generation

aged 3 old **4** ripe, worn **5** cured, hoary, olden **6** mellow, senior **7** ancient, antique, elderly, matured, ripened **8** grown old, timeworn **9** developed, senescent, venerable **11** patriarchal **12** antediluvian

ageless 7 endless, eternal, lasting **8** dateless, enduring, immortal, timeless **9** immutable **11** everlasting

agency 4 firm **5** cause, force, means, organ, power **6** action, bureau, medium, office **7** company, channel, vehicle **8** activity, auspices, business, division, function, ministry **9** mechanism, operation **10** department, instrument **12** organization **13** establishment

agenda 5 slate **6** docket, lineup **7** program **8** calendar, schedule, to-do list **9** timetable *entry:* **4** item

Agenor *brother:* **5** Belus *daughter:* **6** Europa *father:* **7** Antenor, Neptune **8** Poseidon *mother:* **5** Libya *son:* **6** Cadmus

agent 3 fed, spy **4** G-man, narc, T-man, tool **5** actor, means, organ, proxy, spook **6** broker, deputy, factor, medium **7** channel, proctor, steward, vehicle **8** assignee, attorney, executor, minister, ministry **9** activator, go-between, middleman, operative **10** instrument, procurator

age-old 7 ancient, antique **9** venerable **10** immemorial **11** traditional

agglomerate 4 heap, mass, pile, rock **6** gather **7** cluster, collect **9** aggregate **10** collection **11** aggregation

agglomeration 4 heap **5** hoard, trove **7** cluster **9** aggregate, amassment, gathering **10** collection, cumulation **11** aggregation

aggrandize 4 hype **5** boost **6** beef up, expand, extend, praise **7** augment, build up, enhance, enlarge, ennoble, glorify, inflate, magnify **8** heighten, increase, multiply **11** distinguish

aggravate 3 vex **4** gall **5** anger, annoy, grate, mount, peeve, pique, rouse, upset **6** burn up, deepen, nettle, worsen **7** bedevil, disturb, enhance, inflame, magnify, perturb, provoke **8** heighten, increase, irritate **9** intensify **10** exacerbate

aggravation 4 pain **5** worry **6** bother **9** annoyance, worsening **11** provocation

aggregate 3 all, sum **4** body, bulk, floc **5** add up, gross, total, whole **6** amount, gather **7** collect **8** entirety, quantity, totality **9** composite **10** cumulative **11** agglomerate **12** conglomerate **13** agglomeration

aggregation 4 body, mass **5** crowd, group, hoard, total, trove **7** cluster, company **8** assembly **9** amassment, gathering **10** assemblage, collection, cumulation **11** agglomerate **12** accumulation

aggression 4 push, raid **5** fight, onset **6** attack **7** assault, offense **8** invasion **9** hostility, incursion, offensive, onslaught, pugnacity **10** assailment **12** belligerence **13** combativeness

aggressive 5 pushy **6** fierce, severe **7** hostile, scrappy, vicious, warlike **8** emphatic, forceful, militant **9** assertive, attacking, combative, energetic, intrusive, offensive **11** belligerent, contentious, domineering, hard-hitting **12** enterprising

aggrieve 4 hurt, pain **5** annoy, harry, upset, worry, wrong **6** harass, injure, plague **7** afflict, oppress, torment, trouble **8** distress **9** constrain, persecute

aghast 4 agog, awed **6** afraid, amazed, scared **7** anxious, fearful, shocked, stunned **8** appalled, dismayed, startled **9** awestruck, horrified, terrified **10** astonished, confounded, frightened **11** dumbfounded, overwhelmed **13** thunderstruck

agile 4 deft, spry **5** alert, brisk, catty, lithe, quick, zippy **6** active, adroit, limber, lively, nimble, supple **7** lissome **9** adaptable, dexterous, sprightly

agitate 4 move, rile, roil, rock, stir, toss **5** argue, churn, peeve, shake, upset **6** arouse, bother, excite, flurry, joggle, ruffle, stir up **7** discuss, dispute, disturb, fluster, perturb, provoke, tempest, trouble, unhinge **8** disquiet, irritate, unsettle **9** thrash out **10** discompose

agitation 4 flap, fuss, stir, to-do **5** clash **6** bustle, clamor, debate, flurry, lather, tumult **7** dispute, ferment, tempest, turmoil **9** commotion, confusion **10** turbulence **11** disturbance

agitator 5 rebel **6** shaker **7** inciter, stirrer **8** fomenter, inflamer **9** disrupter **10** instigator **11** provocateur

Aglaia see **Graces**

Aglauros *father:* **7** Cecrops *sister:* **5** Herse **9** Pandrosos

aglow 4 warm **5** afire **6** bright, aflame, alight **7** excited, radiant, shining **8** gleaming, luminous

agnate 4 akin, like **5** alike **6** allied, joined, linked **7** cognate, connate, kindred, kinsman, related, similar **8** relation, relative **9** analogous **10** affiliated **11** consanguine **13** corresponding

agnostic 7 doubter, skeptic **8** doubting **10** questioner, undogmatic **11** uncommitted **12** noncommittal

Agnus ___ **3** Dei

ago 4 back, gone, past, yore **5** since **6** before

agog 4 avid, keen **5** eager **6** roused **7** excited, fervent **8** desirous **9** expectant, impatient **12** enthusiastic

agon 5 clash **6** battle, strife **7** contest **8** conflict, struggle

agonize 4 fret, gall, hurt, pain, rack **5** chafe **6** harrow, squirm, suffer, writhe **7** afflict, torment, torture, trouble **8** distress, stew over, struggle **10** excruciate

agonizing 6 fierce **7** extreme, intense, painful, racking, tearing **9** harrowing, suffering, torturing, torturous **10** tormenting **12** excruciating

agony 4 pain **5** dolor, pangs **6** misery **7** anguish, passion, torment, torture **8** distress, outburst, struggle **9** suffering **10** affliction

agora 6 market **11** marketplace **12** meeting place

agrarian 5 rural **6** rustic **8** pastoral **10** campestral **12** agricultural

agree 3 buy, set, yes **4** jibe, okay, suit **5** admit, check, equal, fit in, match, tally **6** accede, accept, accord, assent, concur, settle, square **7** comport, concede, concert, concord, conform, consent **8** check out, coincide, dovetail **9** acquiesce, harmonize, recognize, subscribe **10** correspond **11** acknowledge

agreeable 4 nice, open **5** ready **7** affable, welcome, willing **8** amenable, in accord, pleasant, pleasing **9** approving, congenial, congruous, consonant, favorable, receptive **10** acceptable, compatible, concurring, consenting, consistent **11** pleasurable, sympathetic

agreed 3 aye, yea, yep, yes **4** okay **8** all right, of course **9** certainly **10** definitely, positively

agreement 4 bond, deal, pact **6** accord, assent, treaty **7** bargain, compact, concord, consent, entente, harmony **8** contract, covenant **9** concordat **10** acceptance, consonance **11** arrangement, concordance, concurrence

agree with 3 fit **4** suit **5** befit **6** assist, become **7** support **10** go together

agricultural 5 rural **7** bucolic **8** agrarian, pastoral

agriculture 7 farming, tillage **8** agronomy, ranching **9** husbandry **11** cultivation, soil culture

Agrippina *brother:* **8** Caligula *husband:* **8** Claudius *son:* **4** Nero

aground 5 stuck **6** ashore **7** beached **8** disabled, stranded *run:* **3** sew

ague 3 flu **5** chill, fever **7** malaria, shivers **9** influenza, shivering **10** blackwater

Ahab *daughter:* **8** Athaliah *father:* **4** Omri *prey:* **8** Moby-Dick *ship:* **6** Pequod *wife:* **7** Jezebel

Ahasuerus *kingdom:* **6** Persia *wife:* **6** Esther, Vashti

Ahaz *kingdom:* **5** Judah *son:* **8** Hezekiah *wife:* **3** Abi

Ahaziah *father:* **4** Ahab **5** Joram **7** Jehoram *kingdom:* **5** Judah **6** Israel *mother:* **7** Jezebel **8** Athaliah *sister:* **9** Jehosheba **11** Jehosobeath

ahead 4 ante, fore,on top **6** before, dormie, onward **7** earlier, forward, in front, leading, onwards **8** foremost, forwards, previous **9** in advance **10** beforehand

Ahinoam *father:* **7** Ahimaaz *husband:* **4** Saul **5** David *son:* **5** Amnon

Ah, Wilderness! *author* **6** O'Neill (Eugene)

aid 4 abet, care, hand, help, lift **6** assist, helper, relief, rescue, succor **7** backing, comfort, help out, support, sustain **8** befriend **9** assistant, attendant, subsidize **10** assistance, benefactor, mitigation **11** alleviation

Aida *composer:* **5** Verdi (Giuseppe) *father:* **8** Amonasro *lover:* **7** Radames *rival:* **7** Amneris

aide 4 ass't **6** deputy, helper, second **7** orderly **8** adjutant, sidekick **9** assistant, attendant, coadjutor **10** coadjutant, lieutenant

aikido 10 martial art

ail 4 ache, hurt, pain **5** upset, worry **6** bother **7** afflict, disturb, trouble **8** distress

ailing 3 ill, low **4** down, sick, weak **6** in pain, poorly, sickly, unwell **8** below par, diseased **9** enfeebled **10** indisposed **11** debilitated

ailment 6 malady, unrest **7** disease, ferment, illness, turmoil **8** disorder, disquiet, sickness, syndrome **9** affection, complaint, condition, infirmity **10** inquietude, uneasiness **11** disquietude, restiveness **12** restlessness

aim 3 end, try **4** cast, goal, head, mark, mean, plan, want, wish **5** angle, essay, focus, level, point, slant, train **6** aspire, design, desire, direct, intend, intent, object, strive, target, zero in **7** address, attempt, propose, purpose **8** ambition, endeavor **9** objective **11** contemplate

aimless 6 random **7** wayward **8** goalless **9** desultory, haphazard, hit-or-miss, irregular, pointless, unplanned **10** designless **11** purposeless

air 3 sky **4** aura, mien, mood, song, tune, vent **5** style **6** manner, melody, reveal, strain **7** bearing, divulge, express, feeling, quality **8** demeanor **9** broadcast, character, ventilate **10** atmosphere, deportment

aircraft 5 blimp, drone, plane **6** glider **7** airship, balloon, chopper **8** aerodyne, aerostat, airplane, jetliner, zeppelin **9** dirigible **10** helicopter *carrier:* **7** flattop *designer:* **6** Fokker (Anthony), Martin (Glenn) **7** Junkers (Hugo), Tupolev (Andrei) **8** Northrop (Jack), Sikorsky (Igor), Yakovlev (Alexander) **13** Messerschmitt (Willy)

airless 5 close **6** stuffy, sultry **8** stagnant, stifling **11** suffocating

airline 3 JAL, KLM, LOT, TWA **4** BOAC, El Al **5** Delta, Pan Am, USAir, Varig **6** Iberia, Qantas, Sabena, United, Virgin **7** Eastern,

JetBlue, Olympic **8** Aeroflot, Alitalia, American, Swissair **9** Aer Lingus, Air France, Lufthansa, Northwest, Southwest, U.S. Airways **11** Continental, Pan American

airman 3 ace **5** flier, flyer, pilot **6** flyboy **7** aviator **8** aeronaut

air movement 4 gust, wind **5** draft **6** breath, breeze **7** updraft **9** downdraft

air navigation system 5 loran, navar, radar

airplane 3 jet **5** avion **6** bomber **7** fighter **8** autogyro, transport **9** transport *A-bombdropper:* **8** Enola Gay *battle:* **8** dogfight *body:* **8** fuselage *engine:* **3** jet **6** fanjet **7** propjet **8** turbofan, turbojet **9** turboprop *engine casing:* **7** nacelle *engineless:* **6** glider *instrument:* **5** radar, radio **7** compass **9** altimeter, gyroscope **10** tachometer **11** transponder *maneuver:* **4** buzz, dive, loop, roll **8** nosedive **9** chandelle **10** barrel roll *movement:* **3** yaw **4** bank, spin **5** pitch **8** tailspin *part:* **3** fin **4** flap, nose, prop, tail, wing **5** cabin, wheel **6** engine, rudder **7** aileron **8** airscrew, elevator **9** empennage, propeller **10** stabilizer *pilotless:* **5** drone *safety machine:* **6** deicer *shelter:* **6** hangar *supersonic:* **3** SST *target:* **6** drogue *vapor:* **8** contrail

air plant 6 orchid **8** epiphyte **9** bromeliad, kalanchoe **11** Spanish moss **12** strangler fig

airport 5 field **7** helipad **8** heliport **9** aerodrome *abbreviation:* **3** ETA, ETD *building:* **8** terminal *flag:* **8** windsock *name:*
  Atlanta: 10 Hartsfield **Boston: 5** Logan
  Chicago: 5 O'Hare **6** Midway **Dublin: 7** Shannon **London: 7** Gatwick **8** Heathrow
  Los Angeles: 3 LAX **New York: 3** JFK **7** Kennedy **9** La Guardia **Paris: 4** Orly **8** DeGaulle **9** Le Bourget **Rome: 7** Da Vinci
  Washington: 6 Dulles, Reagan **8** National *part:* **5** apron, tower **6** runway **7** taxiway

Airport author 6 Hailey (Arthur)

airs 4 pose, show **5** front **6** vanity **7** hauteur **8** pretense **9** loftiness, mannerism, vainglory **10** pretension **11** affectation, insincerity, ostentation **13** artificiality

airship 3 jet **5** blimp, plane **8** zeppelin **9** dirigible

airtight 4 shut **6** closed, sealed **7** certain **8** hermetic, ironclad **10** impervious **11** impermeable, irrefutable **12** indisputable, invulnerable **13** incontestable

airy 4 open, rare, thin **5** blowy, fresh, gusty, light, lofty, proud, windy **6** aerial, bouncy, breezy, dainty, unreal **7** buoyant, gaseous, soaring, tenuous **8** affected, animated, delicate, ethereal, graceful, illusory, rarefied,

spirited, towering, vaporous, volatile **9** expansive, frivolous, pneumatic, resilient, sprightly, vivacious **10** diaphanous, ventilated **11** atmospheric, skyscraping **12** effervescent, high-spirited
Ajax 4 hero **5** Greek **7** warrior *father:* **6** Oileus **7** Telamon *opponent:* **6** Hector *participant:* **9** Trojan War
akin 4 like, same **5** alike **6** allied **7** kindred, related, similar, uniform **8** parallel **9** analogous, consonant **10** affiliated, comparable, compatible **11** consanguine **13** corresponding
Alabama *capital:* **10** Montgomery *city:* **5** Selma **6** Mobile **10** Birmingham, Huntsville, Tuscaloosa **12** Muscle Shoals *college, university:* **6** Auburn **8** Tuskegee *mountain:* **6** Cheaha *nickname:* **6** Cotton (State) **12** Heart of Dixie *river:* **6** Mobile **7** Alabama **9** Tombigbee *state bird:* **12** yellowhammer *state flower:* **8** camellia *state tree:* **12** longleaf pine
alacrity 8 dispatch **9** briskness, eagerness, quickness, readiness **10** enthusiasm, expedition, liveliness, promptness **11** promptitude, willingness **12** cheerfulness
Alamo *city:* **10** San Antonio *hero:* **5** Bowie (Jim) **6** Travis (William) **8** Crockett (Davy)
alamo 6 poplar **10** cottonwood
à la mode 4 chic, tony **6** trendy **7** dashing, stylish **8** up-to-date **9** exclusive **11** fashionable **12** with ice cream
alarm 3 SOS **4** bell, fear, horn **5** alert, dread, panic, scare, siren, spook, upset **6** dismay, excite, fright, signal, terror, tocsin **7** anxiety, disturb, red flag, startle, terrify, unnerve, warning **8** distress, frighten **9** terrorize **11** forewarning, trepidation **12** apprehension **13** consternation
alas 3 heu, woe **4** darn, drat **5** alack, oy vey **7** woe is me
Alaska *capital:* **6** Juneau *city:* **4** Nome **5** Sitka **6** Barrow **9** Anchorage, Fairbanks **10** Prudhoe Bay *island group:* **6** Kodiak **8** Aleutian, Pribilof *mountain, range:* **6** Brooks, Denali **8** McKinley, Wrangell *nickname:* **12** Last Frontier *park:* **6** Denali, Katmai *river:* **5** Yukon *state bird:* **9** ptarmigan *state flower:* **11** forget-me-not *state tree:* **11** sitka spruce
alb 4 gown **8** vestment
Albania *capital:* **6** Tirana, Tiranë *city:* **5** Korçë, Vlorë **6** Durrës **7** Shkodër *ethnic group:* **4** Gheg, Tosk *monetary unit:* **3** lek *neighbor:* **6** Greece **9** Macedonia **10** Montenegro *part of:* **7** Balkans *peninsula:* **6** Balkan *sea:* **8** Adriatic

albatross 5 check, goony, worry **6** burden, gooney **7** anxiety, seabird **9** hindrance, millstone, restraint **11** encumbrance
Albee play 7 Sandbox (The) **8** Seascape, Zoo Story (The) **9** Tiny Alice **13** American Dream (The) **14** Three Tall Women **16** A Delicate Balance **25** Who's Afraid of Virginia Woolf?
albeit 5 still, while **6** even if, much as, though **7** despite, whereas **8** although **10** even though
Alberta *capital:* **8** Edmonton *city:* **5** Banff **7** Calgary *lake:* **6** Claire, Louise **9** Athabasca *mountain, range:* **7** Rockies **8** Columbia *provincial flower:* **8** wild rose *river:* **4** Milk **5** Peace **9** Athabasca
Albion 7 England
album 3 ana **4** book **6** jacket, record **7** garland, omnibus **8** notebook, pictures, register **9** anthology, portfolio, scrapbook **10** collection, miscellany
Alcestis *father:* **6** Pelias *husband:* **7** Admetus *rescuer:* **8** Heracles, Hercules
alchemist 5 Faust **10** Paracelsus
alchemy 5 charm, magic **7** panacea, sorcery **8** wizardry **9** conjuring **10** necromancy
Alcina *sister:* **7** Morgana **10** Logistilla *victim:* **6** Rogero **8** Astolpho, Ruggiero
Alcinous *daughter:* **8** Nausicaa *wife:* **5** Arete
Alcmaeon *father:* **10** Amphiaraus *mother:* **8** Eriphyle *wife:* **10** Callirrhoe
Alcmene *husband:* **10** Amphitryon *son:* **8** Heracles, Hercules
alcohol 4 grog **5** booze, hooch, juice, sauce **6** hootch, liquor, red-eye, rotgut, tipple **7** spirits **8** home brew **9** aqua vitae, firewater, moonshine *name:* **4** amyl **5** butyl, cetyl, ethyl **6** glycol, methyl, sterol **7** butanol, ethanol, mannite, menthol **8** glycerin, glycerol, inositol, mannitol, methanol **9** isopropyl **11** cholesterol *used in perfumes:* **5** nerol **7** borneol **8** geraniol, linalool
alcoholic 4 hard **5** dipso, drunk **6** brewed **8** drunkard **9** distilled, fermented, inebriant, inebriate, spiritous **10** spirituous **11** dipsomaniac, inebriating **12** intoxicating
alcoholic drink see under **beverage**
Alcott novel 7 Jo's Boys **9** Little Men **11** Little Women
alcove 4 nook **5** niche **6** gazebo, recess **9** belvedere **11** summerhouse *Japanese:* **8** tokonoma
Alcyone *father:* **5** Atlas **6** Aeolus *husband:* **4** Ceyx *mother:* **7** Pleione *sisters:* **8** Pleiades
ale 3 nog **4** beer, nogg
aleatory 4 iffy **5** dicey, risky, shaky **6** chancy **9** hazardous, uncertain **10** contingent, pre-

carious, vulnerable 11 problematic, speculative 13 unpredictable
alehouse 3 bar, pub 6 bistro, saloon, tavern 7
taproom 8 beer hall 10 beer garden 11 rathskeller
alembic 5 still 6 filter 9 distiller
alert 3 SOS 4 keen, warn 5 alarm, quick,
ready, sharp, smart 6 brainy, bright, clever,
lively, notify, tip off, tocsin 7 heedful,
mindful, on guard, red flag, wakeful 8 animated, forewarn, open-eyed, vigilant,
watchful 9 attentive, mercurial, sprightly,
wide-awake 10 perceptive 11 intelligent,
quick-witted *Scottish:* 4 gleg 8 wakerife
Aleutian island 3 Fox 4 Adak, Atka, Attu,
Near 5 Amlia, Kiska 6 Unimak 8 Unalaska
9 Andreanof *town:* 11 Dutch Harbor
alewife 4 fish 7 herring 8 menhaden
Alexander *birthplace:* 5 Pella *conquest:* 4
Tyre 5 Egypt, Issus 6 Greece, Persia 7 Parthia 8 Granicus *father:* 6 Philip *general:* 9
Antipater *horse:* 10 Bucephalus *kingdom:*
9 Macedonia *mother:* 8 Olympias *teacher:*
9 Aristotle *wife:* 6 Roxana
alfalfa 3 hay 6 forage, legume 7 lucerne
alfresco 7 open-air, outdoor, outside 8 outdoors 9 out-of-door 10 out-of-doors
alga 6 desmid, diatom 7 seaweed *blue-green:*
6 nostoc *brown:* 4 kelp 5 fucus 8 rockweed
green: 9 chlorella *red:* 4 nori
algebra term 4 root 6 factor 8 binomial,
equation, monomial, variable 9 quadratic
10 polynomial
Algeria *capital:* 7 Algiers *city:* 4 Bône, Oran
6 Annaba 11 Constantine *coast:* 7 Barbary
desert: 6 Sahara *ethnic group:* 4 Arab 6
Berber *language:* 6 Arabic, Berber *monetary unit:* 5 dinar *mountain range:* 5 Atlas
12 Saharan Atlas *neighbor:* 4 Mali 5 Libya,
Niger 7 Morocco, Tunisia 10 Mauritania
Algren novel 17 Walk on the Wild Side (A)
19 Man with the Golden Arm (The)
Ali *son:* 5 Hasan 6 Husayn *wife:* 6 Fatima
alias 3 AKA 6 anonym, handle 7 moniker,
pen name 8 nickname 9 false name, pseudonym, stage name 10 also called, nom de
plume 11 nom de guerre
Ali Baba's spell 10 Open Sesame
alibi 4 plea 5 clear, cover, proof 6 answer, excuse 7 account, cover up, defense, pretext 9
assertion, exonerate 11 explanation
alien 6 exotic 7 foreign, opposed, strange 8
estrange, outsider, stranger, transfer 9 es-
tranged, extrinsic, foreigner, outlander 10
extraneous, outlandish 12 incompatible
alienate 4 part 5 repel 6 assign, convey, divide, offend, oppose 7 break up, turn off 8

disunify, disunite, estrange, separate, sign
over, transfer 9 disaffect
alienation 5 break 6 breach 7 discord,
divorce, rupture 8 division 10 conveyance,
separation 12 disaffection, estrangement
alight 4 land 5 fiery 6 arrive, bright, on fire,
settle 7 blazing, burning, deplane, descend,
detrain, flaming, flaring, get down, glowing, ignited, shining 8 dismount 9 touch
down 11 conflagrant
align 4 ally, join, line, true 5 agree, array, order, range 6 adjust, follow, line up 8 regulate 9 affiliate, associate 10 straighten
alike 4 akin, same 7 similar 8 parallel 9 analogous, consonant 10 comparable 13 corresponding
alikeness 6 simile 7 analogy 8 affinity, alliance, relation 9 closeness, semblance 10
comparison, connection, similarity, similitude 11 resemblance
aliment 4 eats, fare, feed, food, grub 7 nourish, nurture, sustain 9 nutriment 10 sustenance 11 nourishment
alimentary 9 nutritive 10 nourishing, sustain-
ing 11 nutritional *canal:* 7 enteron
alimony 4 keep 5 bread 6 living, upkeep 7
support 9 allowance, provision 10 livelihood, sustenance 11 maintenance, subsistence
alive 4 rife, spry 5 alert, awake, aware, brisk,
fresh, quick, ready, vital 6 active, extant,
living, moving, viable 7 animate, dynamic,
knowing, replete, running, teeming, working, zestful 8 animated, existent, existing,
sensible, sentient, swarming, thronged 9
abounding, breathing, cognizant, conscious, energetic, operative, sensitive,
wide-awake 11 functioning, overflowing
alkali 4 base, salt 9 substance 11 soluble salt
metal: 6 cesium, sodium 7 lithium 8 fran-
cium, rubidium 9 potassium 10 monovalent
opposite: 4 acid
alkaline 5 acrid, basic, salty 6 bitter 7 antacid, caustic, soluble 8 chemical *substance:* 3 lye 4 lime, soda 5 borax 6 potash
7 ammonia, antacid 8 pearl ash, saltwort 11
caustic soda
alkaloid 4 base *medicinal:* 5 ergot 7 codeine,
emetine, eserine, quinine 8 atropine, caffeine, lobeline, morphine 9 ephedrine,
quinidine, reserpine 11 scopolamine *narcotic:* 6 heroin 7 cocaine, codeine 8 morphine *poisonous:* 8 atropine, nicotine,
solanine 11 scopolamine
all 3 sum 4 each 5 every, gross, total, whole 6
entire, in toto, purely, wholly 7 exactly, totally, utterly 8 complete, entirety, everyone,

outright, totality **9** aggregate, everybody **10** altogether, everything *combining form:* **3** pan **4** omni, pant

all-around 7 general, overall, skilled **8** complete, sweeping, synoptic **9** adaptable, competent, many-sided, panoramic, universal, versatile **10** consummate, proficient **11** wide-ranging **12** encompassing **13** comprehensive

allay 4 balm, calm, ease, lull **5** abate, quell, quiet, still **6** lessen, reduce, settle, soothe, subdue **7** assuage, compose, lighten, mollify, quieten, relieve **8** decrease, diminish, mitigate, moderate **9** alleviate **11** tranquilize

all but 4 most, much, nigh **5** about **6** almost, nearly **8** as much as, in effect **9** just about, virtually **11** essentially, practically

All Creatures Great and Small *author* **7** Herriot (James)

allegation 5 claim **6** charge, report **9** assertion, statement **10** contention, profession **11** declaration

allege 3 say **4** avow, cite **5** claim, offer, state **6** adduce, assert, attest, charge, submit **7** advance, contend, declare, present, profess **8** maintain **10** put forward

alleged 7 accused, dubious, reputed, suspect **8** doubtful, so-called, supposed **9** described, pretended, purported, soi-disant **10** ostensible, self-styled **12** questionable

allegiance 4 duty **5** ardor, piety **6** fealty, homage **7** loyalty **8** devotion, fidelity **9** adherence, constancy, obedience **10** dedication, obligation **11** devotedness **12** faithfulness

allegiant 4 firm, true **5** liege, loyal **6** ardent, steady **7** devoted, dutiful, staunch **8** constant, faithful, resolute **9** steadfast **10** dependable

allegorical 5 moral **6** fabled **8** mythical, symbolic **9** legendary, spiritual **10** emblematic, exegetical, fictitious, figurative **12** iconographic, illustrative, metaphorical

allegory 4 myth, tale **5** fable, story **6** emblem, symbol **7** parable **8** apologue **9** symbolism **10** figuration **12** typification

allegro 4 fast **5** brisk **6** bouncy, lively **8** animated, spirited **9** sprightly

Allende *novel* **17** House of the Spirits (The)

allergy 5 dread **6** hatred **7** disgust, dislike **8** aversion, distaste, hay fever **9** antipathy, disliking, rejection, repulsion

alleviate 4 cure, ease **5** allay **6** lessen, reduce, remedy **7** assuage, lighten, mollify, relieve **8** decrease, diminish, mitigate

alleviation 4 ease **6** relief **7** decline **8** decrease, easement **9** lessening, reduction **10** diminution, mitigation

alley 4 lane, walk **6** marble, street **7** passage **10** backstreet

all-fired 7 totally, utterly **9** extremely **10** absolutely, completely **11** excessively

alliance 3 tie **4** axis, bloc, bond, pact **5** union **6** accord, league, treaty **7** compact, concord **8** affinity, relation **9** coalition **10** connection, federation **11** affiliation, association, combination, confederacy, conjunction, partnership, unification **12** relationship **13** confederation *international:* **3** CIS, OAS **4** APEC, EFTA, NATO, OECD, OPEC **5** ASEAN, CENTO, NORAD, SEATO **7** CARICOM **8** Interpol **10** Warsaw Pact

allied 4 akin **5** bound **6** agnate, joined, linked, united **7** cognate, connate, kindred, related, unified **8** in league **9** connected **10** affiliated, associated, connatural **11** consanguine

alligator 11 crocodilian *relative:* **4** croc **6** caiman, cayman **9** crocodile

alligator pear 7 avocado

all in 4 dead, used, worn **5** spent, tired **6** bushed, done in, used up **7** drained, far-gone, worn-out **8** depleted **9** dead tired, exhausted, washed-out

all in all 5 in all **6** mainly **7** en masse, largely **9** generally **10** altogether, by and large, on the whole

All in the Family *character:* **5** Edith (Bunker) **6** Archie (Bunker), Gloria **7** Michael *creator:* **4** Lear (Norman) *nickname:* **7** Dingbat **8** Meathead *setting:* **6** Queens **7** Astoria *star:* **6** Reiner (Rob) **7** O'Connor (Carroll) **9** Stapleton (Jean), Struthers (Sally) *theme song:* **16** Those Were the Days

allocate 4 give **5** allot, slice **6** assign, divide **7** dish out, divvy up, dole out, earmark, mete out, prorate **8** set apart **9** admeasure, apportion, designate **10** distribute

allocution 4 talk **5** spiel **6** sermon, speech **7** address, lecture, oration, oratory, pep talk **11** exhortation

allot 4 give **5** grant, share **6** accord, assign **7** deal out, divvy up, dole out, mete out **8** allocate, dispense, set aside **9** admeasure, apportion **10** distribute

allotment 3 cut, lot **4** bite, part **5** chunk, piece, quota, share, slice **6** ration **7** measure, portion **9** allowance, provision **13** apportionment

all-out 4 full **5** total **6** entire, utmost **7** maximum **8** absolute, complete, thorough **9** full-blown, full-scale, unlimited **12** totalitarian **13** thoroughgoing

all over 8 wherever **9** all around **10** everyplace, everywhere, far and near, far and wide, high and low, thoroughly, throughout **allow 3** let, lot, own **4** avow, give **5** admit, allot, brook, grant, leave, let on, stand **6** assign, endure, permit, suffer **7** concede, confess, consent, entitle, forbear, mete out **8** allocate, tolerate **9** apportion **11** acknowledge

allowance 3 aid, cut, lot, pay, sum **4** bite, edge, help, part, tare, tret **5** grant, leave, piece, quota, share, slice **6** amount, permit, ration **7** consent, measure, partage, portion, quantum, subsidy, vantage **8** handicap, pittance, quantity, sanction **9** advantage, allotment, head start, reduction **10** adjustment, allocation, assistance, concession, permission, sufferance, toleration **13** accommodation, apportionment, authorization

alloy 5 blend **6** fusion **7** amalgam, mixture **8** compound **9** admixture, composite **10** adulterant **11** interfusion **12** amalgamation, intermixture *brass-like:* **6** latten *copper-sulfur:* **6** niello *copper-tin:* **6** bronze *copper-zinc:* **5** brass **6** tombac *enamel-like:* **6** niello *gold-like:* **6** ormolu *gold-silver:* **8** electrum *iron-carbon:* **5** steel *iron-nickel:* **5** invar *mercury:* **7** amalgam *tin-lead:* **5** terne **6** pewter, solder *used in jewelry:* **6** tombac

all-powerful 6 mighty **7** supreme **8** absolute, almighty **10** invincible, omnipotent **11** controlling

all right 3 A-OK, aye, yea, yep, yes **4** good, okay, safe, well **5** A-okay **6** agreed, decent, proper, surely **7** average **8** adequate, of course, passable, passably, pleasing, standard, very well **9** agreeable, certainly, tolerable, tolerably **10** acceptably, adequately, definitely, positively, sufficient, well enough **12** satisfactory

all round see **all-around**

All the King's Men author 6 Warren (Robert Penn)

allude 4 hint **5** imply, point, refer **7** bring up, suggest **8** indicate, intimate

allure 4 draw, pull **5** charm, tempt **6** appeal, entice, lead on, seduce **7** attract, beguile, enchant, glamour, win over **8** charisma, inveigle, persuade **9** captivate, fascinate, magnetism, magnetize **10** attraction **11** enchantment, fascination

alluring 4 sexy **6** lovely **7** winning, winsome **8** charming, inviting, pleasing **9** appealing, beguiling, glamorous, seductive **10** appetizing, attractive, bewitching, enchanting **11** captivating, fascinating

ally 4 join **5** unite **6** friend, helper **7** comrade, partner **8** federate **9** accessory, affiliate, associate, auxiliary, bedfellow, colleague, supporter **10** accomplice **11** confederate **12** collaborator

almighty 4 very **6** hugely, mighty **7** awfully, godlike, supreme **8** absolute **9** extremely **10** invincible, omnipotent **11** all-powerful, exceedingly

almost 4 nigh **5** about **6** all but, nearly **8** as good as, as much as, not quite, well-nigh **9** just about, virtually **11** essentially, practically **13** approximately *Scottish:* **6** feckly

alms 4 gift **6** relief **7** present **8** donation, offering **10** assistance **11** benefaction, beneficence **12** contribution

aloe 9 emollient, succulent

Aloeus *father:* **7** Neptune **8** Poseidon *mother:* **6** Canace *son:* **4** Otus **9** Ephialtes *wife:* **9** Iphimedia

aloft 4 high, over **5** above **6** on high, upward **7** skyward **8** in flight, overhead

aloha 4 by-by, ciao, hail **5** hello, howdy **6** bye-bye, good-by, so long **7** good-bye, welcome **8** farewell, greeting **9** greetings *State:* **6** Hawaii

alone 4 only, sole, solo, stag **5** apart **6** singly, solely, unique, wholly **7** isolate, removed **8** detached, entirely, isolated, peerless, singular, solitary **9** matchless, unequaled, unmatched, unrivaled **10** nothing but, unequalled, unexampled, unexcelled **11** exclusively, unsurpassed **12** incomparable, unparalleled, unrepeatable **13** unaccompanied

aloneness 8 solitude **9** isolation, seclusion **10** uniqueness

along 3 too, yet **4** also, near, with **5** forth, there **6** as well, at hand, on hand, onward **7** besides, forward **8** likewise, moreover **11** furthermore **12** accompanying, additionally

alongside 6 beside, next to **8** touching **9** adjoining, bordering

aloof 3 shy **4** cold, cool **5** apart, proud **6** casual, chilly, frigid, offish, remote **7** distant, haughty, removed, stuck up **8** arrogant, detached, reserved, reticent, solitary **9** incurious, unbending, uncurious, withdrawn **10** disdainful, restrained, unfriendly, unsociable **11** constrained, indifferent, standoffish, unconcerned **12** uninterested **13** disinterested

alopecia 8 baldness

alp 4 peak **5** mount **8** mountain

alpaca 4 wool **5** cloth **6** mammal *habitat:* **4** Peru **5** Andes **7** Bolivia

alpha 4 dawn **5** first, start **6** outset **7** dawning, genesis, opening **9** beginning **12** commencement

alphabet 4 ABC's **7** letters *Arabic:* **2** ba, fa, ha, ra, ta, ya, za **3** ayn, dad, dal, gaf, jim, kaf, kha, lam, mim, nun, qaf, sad, sin, tha, waw, zay **4** alif, dhal, shin **5** ghayn *Greek:* **2** mu, nu, pi, xi **3** chi, eta, phi, psi, rho, tau **4** beta, iota, zeta **5** alpha, delta, gamma, kappa, omega, sigma, theta **6** lambda **7** epsilon, omicron, upsilon *Hebrew:* **2** he, pe **3** mem, nun, sin, taw, tet, vav, waw, yod **4** alef, ayin, beth, heth, kaph, koph, qoph, resh, shin, teth **5** aleph, gimel, lamed, sadhe, tsade, zayin **6** daleth, samekh *Old Irish:* **4** ogam **5** ogham *runic:* **7** futhark
Alpheus *beloved:* **8** Arethusa *father:* **7** Oceanus *form:* **5** river *mother:* **6** Tethys
Alpine *animal:* **4** ibex **7** chamois *dress:* **6** dirndl *house:* **6** chalet *lake:* **4** Como, Iseo **5** Garda **6** Geneva **7** Lucerne **8** Bodensee, Maggiore **9** Constance, Neuchâtel *pass:* **3** col **5** Cenis **7** Brenner, Simplon **9** St. Bernard *peak:* **5** Blanc, Eiger **7** Bernina **8** Jungfrau **10** Matterhorn *plant:* **9** edelweiss *primrose:* **8** auricula *resort:* **5** Davos **7** Bolzano, Zermatt **8** Chamonix, Grenoble, St. Moritz **9** Innsbruck **10** Interlaken **11** Saint Moritz *river:* **5** Rhine, Rhône *snowfield:* **4** firn, névé *stick:* **10** alpenstock *state:* **5** Tirol, Tyrol *tunnel:* **5** Blanc, Cenis **7** Arlberg, Simplon **10** St. Gotthard *wind:* **4** bora, föhn **5** foehn
already 4 even, once **5** by now, prior **6** before, by then **7** earlier, just now **8** formerly **9** before now **10** by this time, heretofore, previously
also 3 and, too **4** more, plus **5** again, along **6** as well **7** besides, further **8** likewise, moreover **9** along with, including, similarly **10** in addition **11** furthermore **12** additionally
also-ran 3 dud **5** loser **7** failure, wannabe, washout **8** defeated, runner-up
altar 6 shrine *boy:* **6** server **7** acolyte *cloth:* **4** pall **7** frontal *constellation:* **3** Ara *hanging:* **6** dorsal, dossal *platform:* **8** predella *screen:* **7** reredos *shelf:* **7** retable *site:* **4** apse, bema *vessel:* **5** cruet, paten **7** chalice **8** ciborium **10** monstrance
alter 3 fix **4** geld, spay, turn, vary **5** adapt **6** adjust, change, doctor, modify, mutate, neuter, revamp **7** remodel **8** castrate, moderate, modulate **9** refashion
alteration 4 turn **5** shift **6** change **8** mutation, revision **9** variation **10** adaptation, adjustment, changeover, conversion, remodeling, transition **12** modification
altercate 4 spat, tiff **5** argue, scrap **6** bicker, hassle **7** dispute, quarrel, wrangle **8** squabble **9** caterwaul

altercation 3 row **4** beef, flap, spat, tiff **5** brawl **6** blowup, combat, fracas, hassle **7** contest, dispute, quarrel, rhubarb, wrangle **8** argument, squabble **9** bickering **10** falling-out **11** controversy, embroilment
alternate 3 sub **5** proxy **6** backup, by turn, change, fill-in, rotate, second **7** another, relieve, stand-in **8** periodic, rotating **9** change off, fluctuate, recurrent, recurring, replacing, surrogate **10** equivalent, every other, periodical, substitute **11** every second, pinch hitter, replacement **12** intermittent
alternately 6 in lieu, rather **7** instead **10** preferably
alternative 5 other, proxy **6** backup, choice, option, second **7** another **8** atypical, druthers, election **9** different, selection, surrogate **10** preference, substitute **11** contingency, nonstandard, possibility
Althaea *father:* **8** Thestius *husband:* **6** Oeneus *son (victim):* **8** Meleager
although 4 when **5** still, while **6** albeit, even if, much as **7** despite, howbeit, whereas
altitude 6 height **8** eminence **9** elevation, high level
altitudinous 4 high, tall **7** eminent **8** elevated
alto 3 Day (Doris), Lee (Peggy) **4** Cher, Kitt (Eartha), Piaf (Edith) **5** Baker (Janet), Lenya (Lotte) **6** London (Julie), Merman (Ethel) **7** Clooney (Rosemary), Ferrier (Kathleen), Vaughan (Sarah) **8** Anderson (Marian), Dietrich (Marlene) **9** Forrester (Maureen) **10** Chookasian (Lili) **13** Schumann-Heink (Ernestine)
altogether 4 nude, well **5** fully, in all, quite **6** in toto, wholly **7** all told, en masse, exactly, totally, utterly **8** all in all, entirely **9** generally, perfectly **10** absolutely, by and large, completely, on the whole, thoroughly
altruism 7 charity **8** sympathy **10** compassion, generosity **11** benevolence **12** philanthropy, selflessness **13** unselfishness
altruistic 3 big **6** humane **8** generous **9** unselfish **10** benevolent, bighearted, charitable, open-handed **11** considerate, magnanimous, noble-minded **12** humanitarian **13** philanthropic
alum 4 grad **6** emetic **7** styptic **8** graduate **10** astringent
aluminum *source:* **7** bauxite *symbol:* **2** Al
always 3 e'er **4** ever **7** forever **8** evermore, for keeps **9** at any rate, endlessly, eternally **10** at all times, constantly, in any event, invariably **11** continually, forevermore, in perpetuum, perpetually, unceasingly **12** consistently, continuously

Amahl and the Night Visitors composer 7
Menotti (Gian Carlo)

amalgamate 3 mix **4** ally, fuse, meld, pool **5** admix, alloy, merge, unify, unite **6** mingle **7** combine **8** coalesce, compound, intermix **9** commingle, integrate **11** consolidate, intermingle

amalgamation 5 alloy, blend, union **6** fusion, merger **7** joining, melding, merging, mixture, uniting **8** alliance, compound **9** admixture, coalition, composite **10** commixture **12** intermixture **13** consolidation

Amalthea *form:* **4** goat *horn:* **10** cornucopia *nursling:* **4** Zeus

amanita 8 death cap, mushroom **9** fly agaric **10** death angel

amanuensis 6 scribe **7** copyist **9** scrivener, secretary **11** transcriber **12** stenographer

amass 4 bulk, heap, make, pile **5** hoard, lay up, store, uplay **6** accrue, garner, gather, pile up, roll up **7** acquire, collect, compile, round up, store up **8** assemble, cumulate **9** aggregate, stockpile **10** accumulate **12** come together

amassment 4 pile **5** clump, group, hoard, stack, stock, store, trove **7** cluster **8** assembly, quantity **9** gathering, stockpile **10** assemblage, collection, cumulation **11** aggregation **12** accumulation **13** agglomeration

amateur 4 tyro **6** layman, novice, tinker, votary **7** admirer, dabbler, devotee, learner **8** aspirant, beginner, neophyte, putterer **9** greenhorn, smatterer **10** apprentice, dilettante, enthusiast, uninitiate **11** abecedarian

amateurish 3 raw **5** green **6** simple **7** artless **8** dabbling, inexpert **9** deficient, unskilled, untutored **10** dilettante, unfinished, unpolished, unskillful **12** dilettantist, unproficient **13** inexperienced

amative see **amorous**

amatory 6 ardent, erotic, loving, tender **7** sensual **8** romantic **9** erogenous, seductive **10** passionate **11** aphrodisiac

amaze 4 daze **5** floor **6** wonder **7** astound, nonplus, perplex, startle **8** astonish, bewilder, blow away, bowl over, confound, surprise **9** dumbfound **10** admiration **11** flabbergast

amazement 3 awe **6** marvel, wonder **8** surprise **9** marveling **10** admiration, perplexity, wonderment **12** astonishment, bewilderment, confoundment

amazing 7 awesome **8** striking, stunning, wondrous **9** marvelous, startling, wonderful **10** astounding, impressive, miraculous, stu-

pendous, surprising **11** astonishing, bewildering, spectacular **12** breathtaking

Amazon 6 parrot **8** giantess **12** woman warrior *tributary:* **5** Negro (Rio)

ambassador 5 agent, envoy **6** legate **8** diplomat, emissary **9** messenger *papal:* **6** nuncio

amber 5 ocher, ochre, resin, rosin **6** orange, yellow **7** saffron

ambience 4 aura, mood, tone **6** flavor, medium, milieu **7** climate **10** atmosphere **11** environment **12** surroundings

ambient 5 music **6** milieu **7** general, setting **8** everyday **9** prevalent **10** atmosphere, prevailing **11** atmospheric, environment, mise-en-scène **12** encompassing, surroundings **13** environmental

ambiguity 5 doubt **6** enigma, puzzle **7** evasion **9** equivoque, obscurity, vagueness **11** incertitude, uncertainty **12** doubtfulness, equivocality, equivocation **13** double meaning

ambiguous 5 vague **6** opaque, unsure **7** cryptic, dubious, inexact, obscure, unclear **8** doubtful, puzzling, two-edged **9** enigmatic, equivocal, tenebrous, uncertain, unsettled **10** indefinite, inexplicit **11** problematic **12** inconclusive, questionable

ambit 4 area, room **5** field, limit, orbit, range, reach, scope, space, sweep **6** border, bounds, extent, limits, radius, sphere **7** breadth, circuit, compass, expanse, purview **8** boundary, confines **9** extension, perimeter, periphery **13** circumference

ambition 3 aim **4** goal, hope, itch, push, wish, zeal **5** ardor, dream, drive, vigor **6** desire, energy, hunger, spirit, target, thirst **7** avidity, craving, purpose **8** appetite, striving, yearning **9** eagerness, intention, objective **10** aspiration, enterprise, enthusiasm, get-up-and-go, initiative, pretension

ambitious 4 avid, bold, keen **5** eager, pushy **6** driven, hungry, intent **7** driving, zealous **8** aspiring, desirous, striving **9** energetic **10** aggressive **11** hard-working **12** enterprising, enthusiastic

ambivalent 5 mixed **6** unsure **7** warring **8** clashing, wavering **9** equivocal, uncertain, undecided **10** unresolved **11** fluctuating, vacillating **13** contradictory

amble 4 gait, walk **5** dally, drift, mosey **6** dawdle, linger, stroll, wander **7** meander, saunter

ambrosia 6 dainty, regale **7** dessert, perfume **8** delicacy, ointment

ambrosial 5 balmy, spicy, sweet **6** savory **7** scented **8** aromatic, fragrant, heavenly, luscious, perfumed, pleasing, redolent **9** deli-

cious **10** delectable, delightful **11** scrumptious
ambulate 4 hoof, move, pace, step, walk **5** tread, troop **6** foot it, hoof it **7** traipse
ambulatory 6 moving, on foot, roving **7** nomadic, roaming, walking **8** vagabond **9** itinerant **11** peripatetic
ambush 4 jump, lurk, trap **5** snare **6** assail, attack, entrap, lay for, waylay **7** assault, ensnare **8** surprise **9** ambuscade **11** concealment
ameliorate 3 fix **4** help, lift, mend **5** amend, raise **6** better, perk up, remedy, reform **7** elevate, enhance, improve, lighten, relieve, upgrade **8** mitigate **9** alleviate **10** convalesce, recuperate
amenable 4 open, tame **6** docile, liable, pliant, suited **7** plastic, pliable, subdued, subject, willing **8** biddable, in accord, obedient, yielding **9** adaptable, agreeable, complying, malleable, receptive, tractable **10** answerable, consenting, responsive, submissive **11** accountable, acquiescent, cooperative, responsible
amend 3 fix **4** help **5** alter, right **6** better, change, modify, reform, remedy, repair, revise, square **7** correct, improve, rectify **8** put right **9** meliorate **10** ameliorate
amendment 5 rider **6** change **7** codicil **8** addendum, revision **10** alteration, attachment, correction **11** enhancement, improvement **12** modification
amends 7 redress **8** reprisal **9** indemnity, quittance **10** recompense, reparation **11** restitution **12** compensation
amenities 5 mores **6** polish **7** decorum, manners **8** civility, courtesy **9** etiquette, propriety **12** social graces
amenity 5 charm, frill **6** luxury **7** comfort, quality **8** civility, courtesy, facility **9** advantage, etiquette, geniality, pleasance **10** affability, amiability, betterment, cordiality, enrichment, pleasantry, politeness **11** convenience, enhancement, improvement, sociability **12** agreeability, graciousness, pleasantness
ament 6 catkin
amerce 3 tax **4** dock, fine, levy **5** exact, mulct **6** punish **7** hit with, make pay **8** penalize
amercement 4 fine **5** mulct **7** damages, forfeit, penalty **10** assessment, punishment, reparation
American League *Baltimore:* **7** Orioles *Boston:* **6** Red Sox *Los Angeles:* **6** Angels (of Anaheim) *Chicago:* **8** White Sox *Cleveland:* **7** Indians *Detroit:* **6** Tigers *Kansas*

City: **6** Royals *Minnesota:* **5** Twins *New York:* **7** Yankees *Oakland:* **9** Athletics *Seattle:* **8** Mariners *Tampa Bay:* **9** Rays *Texas:* **7** Rangers *Toronto:* **8** Blue Jays
American Samoa *capital:* **8** Pago Pago *island, island group:* **4** Rose **5** Aunuu, Manua **6** Swains **7** Tutuila *language:* **6** Samoan
America's Cup winner 6 Ranger **7** Alinghi, Freedom **8** Columbia, Intrepid **9** Weatherly **10** Black Magic, Courageous
America, the Beautiful *music:* **4** Ward (Samuel Augustus) *words:* **5** Bates (Katherine Lee)
americium symbol 2 Am
Amfortas *father:* **7** Titurel *opera:* **8** Parsifal
amiability 7 amenity **9** geniality, pleasance **10** cordiality **11** sociability **12** complaisance, congeniality, friendliness, pleasantness, sociableness **13** agreeableness, enjoyableness
amiable 4 kind, warm **6** genial, gentle, kindly **7** affable, cordial, likable **8** cheerful, friendly, gracious, likeable, obliging, sociable **9** agreeable, congenial, courteous **10** responsive **11** complaisant, good-humored, good-natured, warmhearted
amicable 7 empathic, pacific **8** empathic, friendly, peaceful, sociable **9** congenial, peaceable **10** harmonious, like-minded, neighborly **11** sympathetic **13** understanding
amid 4 over **5** among, midst **6** during **7** amongst, between **10** throughout
amigo 3 pal **4** chum, mate, pard **6** friend **7** comrade, partner **8** sidekick **9** companion, confidant **12** acquaintance
amino acid 4 dopa **6** leucin, lysine, serine, toluid, valine **7** cystein, cystine, glycine, leucine, proline, toluide **8** cysteine, dopamine, histidin, thyroxin, toluidin, tyrosine
Amis, Kingsley *novel:* **8** Lucky Jim *son:* **6** Martin
Amis, Martin *father:* **8** Kingsley *novel:* **5** Money **10** Time's Arrow **11** Information (The) **12** London Fields
amiss 3 bad **4** awry, poor **5** badly, wrong **6** afield, astray, faulty, flawed **7** wrongly **8** erringly, faultily **9** defective, imperfect **10** improperly, mistakenly, out of place **11** erroneously, imperfectly, incorrectly, unfavorably **12** inaccurately **13** inappropriate
amity 5 union **6** accord, comity, unison **7** concert, concord, harmony **8** alliance, goodwill **9** agreement **10** cordiality, friendship, kindliness **11** concurrence **12** friendliness
Ammonite 6 Semite *god:* **6** Molech, Moloch
ammunition 4 ammo, shot **5** bombs **6** rounds,

shells **7** charges **8** armament, grenades, missiles, ordnance **10** cartridges **11** projectiles

Amneris's rival 4 Aïda

amnesty 6 pardon **7** freeing, release **8** immunity, reprieve **9** discharge **10** absolution **11** forgiveness **12** dispensation

Amnon *father:* **5** David *half sister:* **5** Tamar *mother:* **7** Ahinoam

amoeba 4 blob **8** rhizopod **9** protozoan

Amon *father:* **8** Manasseh *son:* **6** Josiah

Amonasro's daughter 4 Aïda

among 3 mid **4** amid **5** midst **6** amidst, within **7** between *other things:* **9** inter alia *prefix:* **5** inter

amorist 4 rake, wolf **5** lover, Romeo **7** Don Juan, gallant, playboy **8** Casanova, lothario, paramour **9** womanizer **12** heartbreaker

amorous 6 ardent, erotic, in love **7** amative, amatory, lustful **8** enamored, romantic **10** infatuated, passionate **11** aphrodisiac, impassioned

amorousness 4 love, lust **5** amour, ardor **6** desire **7** passion **9** eroticism

amorphous 7 unclear **8** formless, inchoate, nebulous, unformed, unshaped **9** shapeless, undefined **10** indistinct **11** nondescript **12** disorganized **13** characterless *mass:* **4** blob

amortize 5 repay **6** pay off, reduce **7** pay down **8** write off

amount 4 bulk, dose **5** add up, equal, price, total **6** dosage, matter, number, upshot **7** purport, quantum **8** quantity **9** aggregate, substance *owed:* **4** debt *small:* **3** bit, jot **4** atom, drop, iota, mite, whit **5** minim, spark, speck, trace **7** modicum, smidgen **8** molecule, particle **9** scintilla

amour 4 love **5** fling, lover **6** affair **7** liaison, passion, romance **8** intimacy, intrigue **9** dalliance **10** love affair **12** entanglement, relationship

amour propre 5 pride **6** egoism, vanity **7** conceit, egotism **8** self-love, vainness **9** vainglory **10** narcissism, self-esteem, self-regard **11** self-conceit, self-respect **12** pridefulness **13** conceitedness

amphetamines 5 speed **6** dexies, hearts, uppers **7** bennies, Dexoxyn **8** greenies, pep pills, Preludin **9** Dexedrine **10** Benzedrine, Methedrine

amphibian *burrowing:* **9** caecilian *genus:* **4** Hyla, Rana *legless:* **9** caecilian *tailed:* **3** eft **4** newt **10** salamander *tailless:* **4** frog, toad **8** bullfrog, tree toad **10** batrachian *wormlike:* **9** caecilian *young:* **7** tadpole **8** polliwog

Amphion *brother:* **6** Zethus *conquest:* **6** Thebes *father:* **4** Zeus *mother:* **7** Antiope *sister:* **5** Aedon *wife:* **5** Niobe

amphitheater 4 bowl **5** arena **7** stadium **8** coliseum **10** auditorium, hippodrome

Amphitrite *father:* **6** Nereus *husband:* **7** Neptune **8** Poseidon *mother:* **5** Doris *son:* **6** Triton

Amphitryon's wife 7 Alcmene

amphora 3 jar, jug, urn **4** ewer, vase **5** crock, flask **6** carafe, flagon, vessel

ample 4 wide **5** buxom, great, large, roomy **6** lavish, plenty, portly **7** copious, liberal, profuse **8** abundant, generous, handsome, spacious **9** bounteous, bountiful, capacious, expansive, extensive, plenteous, plentiful **10** commodious, sufficient **11** substantial

amplify 5 boost, raise, swell **6** dilate, expand, extend, jack up **7** augment, develop, distend, enhance, enlarge, inflate, magnify **8** increase **9** elaborate, intensify **10** supplement

amplitude 4 size **5** range, scale, scope, space **6** amount, extent, spread **7** bigness, breadth, expanse, stretch **8** distance, fullness, wideness **9** abundance, expansion, greatness, largeness, magnitude, roominess **12** spaciousness **13** capaciousness

amulet 4 juju, luck **5** charm **6** fetish, grigri, mascot **7** periapt **8** gris-gris, talisman **10** lucky piece, phylactery **11** rabbit's-foot

amuse 4 wile **5** charm, cheer **6** appeal, divert, engage, occupy, please, regale, tickle **7** animate, beguile, delight, enchant, enliven, gladden **8** distract, interest, recreate **9** entertain, fascinate

amusement 3 fun **4** play **7** delight, pastime **8** pleasure **9** diversion, enjoyment **10** recreation **11** distraction

amusing 3 fun **5** droll, funny **7** comical, risible **8** engaging, humorous, pleasing **9** diverting, enjoyable, laughable **12** entertaining

Amycus *father:* **7** Neptune **8** Poseidon *friend:* **8** Heracles, Hercules *mother:* **5** Melia

ana 5 album, varia **7** sayings **9** anecdotes, anthology **10** collection, miscellany **11** memorabilia, miscellanea

anabasis 5 march **7** advance, headway, retreat **8** progress **11** advancement, progression

anagogic 6 arcane, hidden, mystic, occult, secret **7** obscure **8** esoteric, mystical, telestic **9** spiritual **10** symbolical **11** allegorical

analects 5 album **6** digest **7** garland, omnibus **8** treasury **9** anthology, selection **10** compendium, miscellany **11** compilation, florilegium

analgesic 6 opiate **7** anodyne **10** anesthetic, painkiller

analogous 4 akin, like **5** alike **7** kindred, similar, related, uniform **8** parallel **9** consonant **10** comparable, equivalent, resembling

analogue 5 match **7** cognate **8** parallel **9** correlate **10** similarity **11** correlation, counterpart, equivalence **13** correspondent

analogy 6 simile **8** affinity, likeness, metaphor, parallel, relation **9** agreement, alikeness, semblance **10** comparison, similarity, similitude **11** correlation, equivalence, resemblance

analysis 5 assay, audit, proof, study **6** method, review, report, survey **7** finding, inquiry **8** division **9** breakdown, partition, statement **10** dissection, inspection, resolution, separation **11** examination **13** clarification

analytic 6 cogent, subtle **7** logical, testing **8** studious **9** organized **10** diagnostic, scientific, systematic **11** proposition, questioning **13** investigative, ratiocinative

analyze 4 part, test **5** assay, parse, study **6** divide **7** dissect, examine, inspect, resolve **8** classify, consider, separate **9** anatomize, break down, decompose, interpret **10** decompound, scrutinize **11** deconstruct, distinguish, investigate

Ananias 4 liar **9** falsifier **12** prevaricator *father:* **9** Nedebaeus *wife (coconspirator):* **8** Sapphira

anarchism 4 riot **6** theory **7** misrule **8** disorder **9** distemper, rebellion **11** lawlessness

anarchist 5 rebel **6** rioter **8** agitator, mutineer, provoker, revolter **9** dissident, insurgent **10** malcontent **11** provocateur **13** revolutionary *famous:* **6** Tucker (Benjamin), Zerzan (John) **7** Bakunin (Mikhail), Chomsky (Noam), Goldman (Emma), Stirner (Max) **8** Christie (Stuart), Proudhon (Pierre-Joseph) **9** Kropotkin (Peter)

anarchy 4 riot **5** chaos **7** misrule, mob rule, turmoil **8** disarray, disorder **9** confusion, distemper, mobocracy, rebellion **10** ochlocracy, revolution **11** lawlessness **13** nongovernment

anathema 3 ban **4** bane **5** curse, enemy, odium, taboo **6** pariah **7** bugbear, censure, malison, outcast, reproof **8** loathing **9** damnation, bête noire **10** black beast, execration **11** abomination, commination, detestation, imprecation, malediction **12** condemnation, denunciation

anathematize 3 ban **4** damn, oust **5** curse, expel **6** banish **7** condemn **8** denounce, execrate **9** objurgate, proscribe **13** excommunicate

anatomical depression 5 fossa, fovea

anatomical tube 3 vas **4** duct **5** canal

anatomist 5 Wolff (Kaspar) **6** Harvey (William) **8** Vesalius (Andreas)

anatomize 5 cut up **7** analyze, dissect **8** separate **9** break down, decompose

anatomy 5 frame, mummy **6** makeup **8** analysis, division, skeleton **9** framework, histology, structure **10** dissection, morphology, physiology **11** examination

Anaxo *brother:* 10 Amphitryon *daughter:* **7** Alcmene *father:* **7** Alcaeus *husband:* **9** Electryon

ancestor 8 forebear, foregoer **9** ascendant, precursor, prototype **10** antecedent, antecessor, forefather, forerunner, progenitor **11** predecessor **12** primogenitor

ancestral 6 family, inborn, inbred, lineal **7** genetic **8** familial **9** inherited **10** bequeathed, hereditary **11** consanguine, patrimonial *sequence:* **8** pedigree **9** bloodline, genealogy

ancestry 4 line, race **5** blood, breed, stock **6** family, origin, source **7** descent, history, kindred, lineage **8** heritage, pedigree **9** parentage **10** derivation, extraction

Anchises' son 6 Aeneas

anchor 4 moor **5** kedge **6** secure **7** grapnel, mooring **8** mainstay *network news:* **4** Daly (John), Hume (Brit) **5** Chung (Connie) **6** Brokaw (Tom), Couric (Katie), Gibson (Charles), Koppel (Ted), Lehrer (Jim), Murrow (Edward R.), Rather (Dan), Sawyer (Diane), Swayze (John Cameron) **7** Edwards (Douglás), Huntley (Chet), Walters (Barbara) **8** Brinkley (David), Cronkite (Walter), Jennings (Peter), Reasoner (Harry), Reynolds (Frank), Williams (Brian) **10** Chancellor (John) *part:* **3** arm **4** bill, ring **5** crown, fluke, shank, stock

anchorage 4 port **5** haven, roads **6** harbor, refuge, riding **7** mooring, shelter **9** harborage, roadstead

anchorite 5 loner **6** hermit **7** recluse **8** solitary

anchors ____ 6 aweigh

ancient 3 old **4** aged **5** hoary, olden **6** ageold, primal **7** antique, archaic, elderly **8** Noachian, old-timer, primeval, timeworn **9** venerable **10** primordial **12** antediluvian

ancient capital 4 Susa **5** Aksum, Balkh, Calah, Isker, Kalhu, Ninus, Pella, Petra, Sibir **6** Angkor, Bactra, Nimrud, Sardis **7** Babylon, Knossos, Memphis, Nineveh, Samaria, Shushan **10** Persepolis

ancient city *Asia Minor:* 4 Nice, Teos 5 Tyana 6 Edessa, Nicaea 7 Antioch 13 Halicarnassus *Babylonia:* 4 Sura 5 Agade, Akkad, Eridu, Larsa 7 Ellasar *Bengal:* 4 Gaur 9 Lakhnauti *Canaan:* 5 Gezer *Cyprus:* 7 Salamis *Egypt:* 5 Tanis 6 Thebes 7 Memphis 10 Heliopolis *Etruria:* 4 Veii *Euphrates River:* 7 Babylon *Greece:* 5 Crisa 6 Athens, Sparta 7 Calydon 10 Lacedaemon *Ionia:* 4 Myus, Teos 5 Chios, Samos 6 Priene 7 Ephesus, Lebedos, Miletus, Phocaea 8 Colophon, Erythrae 10 Clazomenae *Italy:* 5 Locri 7 Pompeii 8 Siracusa, Syracuse 11 Herculaneum *Latium:* 5 Gabii 9 Alba Longa *Mayan:* 4 Cobá 5 Tikal, Tulum, Uxmal 8 Palenque 11 Chichén Itzá *Nile River:* 5 Meroë *North Africa:* 5 Utica 8 Carthage *Palestine:* 4 Gaza 5 Ekron, Endor, Sodom 6 Beroea, Bethel, Gilead, Hebron 7 Jericho, Samaria 8 Ashkelon 9 Capernaum, Jerusalem *Peloponnesus:* 5 Tegea 6 Sparta 7 Corinth *Sumeria:* 4 Kish, Uruk 5 Erech, Larsa 6 Lagash *Turkey:* 5 Assos, Assus 9 Byzantium

ancient country *Adriatic coast:* 7 Illyria *Africa:* 10 Mauretania *Arabian Peninsula:* 5 Sheba *Asia:* 4 Aram 5 Media, Minni, Syria 7 Armenia, Ash Sham, Bactria *Asia Minor:* 5 Lydia, Mysia 6 Aeolis, Pontus 7 Cilicia, Phrygia 8 Bithynia *Balkan:* 7 Macedon 9 Macedonia *Black Sea:* 7 Colchis *Dead Sea:* 4 Edom *Euphrates River:* 9 Babylonia *Europe:* 4 Gaul 5 Dacia 6 Gallia *gold-rich:* 5 Ophir *Italy:* 6 Latium 7 Etruria *Nile valley:* 4 Cush *Peloponnesus:* 4 Elis 7 Arcadia *Syria:* 9 Phoenicia

ancient empire 6 Median 7 Hittite, Persian 8 Assyrian, Athenian, Chaldean, Seleucid 9 Ptolemaic 10 Babylonian

ancient kingdom *Anglo-Saxon:* 6 Wessex *Asia:* 4 Ghor, Ghur *Celtic:* 7 Cumbria *China:* 3 Shu *Euphrates valley:* 4 Hira 7 Al-Hirah *Greece:* 8 Pergamon, Pergamum *North Of Assyria:* 3 Van 6 Ararat, Urartu *Palestine:* 5 Judah 6 Israel *Persian Gulf:* 4 Elam *Portugal:* 7 Algarve *Spain:* 4 Leon 6 Aragon 7 Castile, Galicia, Granada, Navarre *Syria:* 4 Moab *Welsh:* 5 Powys *West Sahara:* 4 Gana 5 Ghana

ancient monument 6 sphinx 7 obelisk, pyramid

ancient royal forest 4 Dean 8 Sherwood

ancient town *Africa:* 4 Zama *Armenia:* 4 Dwin, Tvin *Asia Minor:* 4 Soli 5 Derbe, Issus, Soloi *Attica:* 6 Icaria *Black Sea:* 5 Olbia 9 Apollonia *Greece:* 4 Abae, Opus 8 Marathon *Italy:* 4 Elea, Luna 5 Cumae, Velia *Latium:* 5 Ardea, Cures *Macedonia:* 5 Pydna, Stobi 9 Apollonia *Peloponnesus:* 5 Asine *Persia:* 6 Hormuz 8 Harmozia *Sicily:* 5 Hybla *Spain:* 5 Munda *Tatar:* 5 Isker, Sibir *Wendish:* 5 Julin

ancilla 3 aid 4 aide, ally, hand, help 6 helper 9 assistant, attendant, supporter

ancillary 5 extra 8 adjuvant, incident 9 accessory, attendant, attending, auxiliary, satellite, secondary 10 additional, coincident, collateral, subsidiary, supporting 11 appurtenant, concomitant, subordinate, subservient 12 accompanying, contributory 13 supplementary

andante 4 slow 5 tempo 7 relaxed, walking 8 moderate

Anderson play 7 High Tor 8 Key Largo 9 Winterset 11 Valley Forge 14 What Price Glory

Anderson book 9 Poor White 12 Dark Laughter 13 Winesburg Ohio

Andes *grazer:* 5 llama 6 alpaca, guemal, huemal, vicuña 7 camelid, guanaco *native:* 4 Inca *peak:* 9 Aconcagua, Huascarán

andiron 7 firedog

Andorra *capital:* 7 Andorra *language:* 7 Catalan *liberator:* 11 Charlemagne *monetary unit:* 4 euro *monetary unit, former:* 6 peseta 11 French franc *mountain range:* 8 Pyrenees *neighbor:* 5 Spain 6 France *river:* 6 Valira

Andrea ____ 5 Doria 8 del Sarto

androgynous 7 epicene 8 bisexual 9 unisexual

android 5 robot 9 automaton

Andromache *husband:* 6 Hector *son:* 8 Astyanax, Molossus

Andromeda *father:* 7 Cepheus *husband:* 7 Perseus *mother:* 10 Cassiopeia *rescuer:* 7 Perseus

Andy Griffith Show *actor:* 6 Bavier (Francis), Howard (Ron), Knotts (Don), Nabors (Jim) *character:* 4 Opie (Taylor) 5 Gomer (Pyle) 6 Barney (Fife) 7 Aunt Bee

anecdote 4 tale, yarn 5 story 7 account, episode, recital 8 relation 9 narration, narrative 12 recollection, reminiscence

anemic 3 wan 4 pale, thin, weak 5 pasty 6 feeble, pallid, sickly, watery 7 insipid 8 ischemic 9 bloodless, colorless 10 spiritless

anemone 9 buttercup 10 windflower

anent 4 as to, in re 5 about, as for 7 apropos 8 touching 9 as regards 10 concerning 13 with respect to

anesthetic 6 opiate 7 anodyne 9 analgesic 10 painkiller, palliative *medical:* 5 ether 6 spinal 8 morphine, procaine 9 halothane, novocaine **10** benzocaine, chloroform, tetracaine **11** scopolamine *suffix:* **5** caine

anesthetize 4 numb, stun **6** benumb, deaden **8** etherize, knock out **9** narcotize **11** desensitize

anesthetized 4 dead, numb **5** inert **6** asleep, torpid **10** insensible **11** insensitive, unconscious

anew 4 over **5** again **6** afresh, de novo, lately, of late **8** once more, recently

angel 6 backer, cherub, patron, seraph, surety **7** sponsor **8** backer-up, guardian **9** celestial, guarantor, supporter **10** benefactor **11** underwriter *biblical:* **5** Uriel **7** Gabriel, Michael, Raphael *fallen:* **7** Lucifer *hierarchy:* **6** powers **7** thrones, virtues **8** cherubim, seraphim **9** dominions *Mormon:* **6** Moroni *of death:* **6** Azrael

Angel Clare's bride 4 Tess

angelic 4 holy, pure **5** godly **6** divine **7** saintly **8** cherubic, ethereal, heavenly **9** celestial **11** beneficient

Angelica *father:* 9 Galaphron *husband:* **6** Medoro *lover:* **7** Orlando

Angelou work 13 Heart of a Woman (The) **25** I Know Why the Caged Bird Sings

anger 3 ire, vex **4** bile, boil, burn, fume, fury, gall, huff, rage, rant, rave, rile **5** storm, upset, wrath **6** choler, dander, enrage, madden, nettle, offend, seethe **7** affront, bristle, dudgeon, incense, outrage, provoke, steam up, umbrage **8** acrimony **9** animosity, infuriate **10** antagonism, antagonize, exasperate

angle 3 aim, bow **4** axil, bend, bias, fish, hand, skew, turn **5** facet, slant **6** aspect, corner, crotch, dogleg **7** flexure, outlook, turning **9** direction, viewpoint **10** standpoint

angler 6 fisher **8** monkfish **9** fisherman, goosefish

Anglo-Saxon *assembly:* 4 moot **5** gemot **6** gemote *council:* **9** heptarchy *county:* **5** shire *court:* **4** moot **5** gemot **6** gemote *crown tax:* **4** geld *epic:* **7** Beowulf *free servant:* **5** thane, thegn *god:* **3** Ing *goddess of fate:* **4** Wyrd *historian:* **4** Bede *king:* **3** Ine, Ini **4** Edwy **5** Edgar, Edred **6** Alfred, Edmund, Edward, Egbert **8** Ethelred *kingdom:* **4** Kent **5** Essex **6** Mercia, Sussex, Wessex **10** East Anglia **11** Northumbria *king's council:* **5** witan *letter:* **3** edh, eth, wen, wyn **4** rune, wynn **5** thorn *nobleman:* **4** earl *poet:* **4** scop *prince:* **8** atheling *sheriff:* **5** reeve *slave:* **4** esne *warrior:* **5** thane, thegn

Angola *capital:* 6 Luanda *city:* **6** Huambo **7** Lubango **8** Benguela *exclave:* **7** Cabinda *language:* **10** Portuguese *monetary unit:* **6** kwanza *neighbor:* **5** Congo **6** Zambia **7** Namibia **11** South Africa *river:* **5** Congo

angora 3 cat **4** goat, hair, wool, yarn **6** mohair, rabbit

angry 3 hot, mad **4** sore **5** irate, riled, riley, upset, vexed, wroth **6** fuming, heated, ireful, wrathy **7** enraged, furious, riled up, teed off **8** choleric, incensed, inflamed, maddened, wrathful **9** indignant, irritated **10** aggravated, infuriated **11** acrimonious, exasperated

angst 4 fear **5** agita, worry **6** unease **7** anxiety, concern **8** disquiet, distress **10** insecurity **11** disquietude, fretfulness **12** apprehension

Anguilla *island, island group:* 3 Dog **4** Seal **5** Scrub **7** Leeward *location:* **10** West Indies *territory of:* **7** Britain

anguish 3 rue, woe **4** ache, care, dole, hurt, pain, pang **5** agony, dread, grief, throe, worry **6** misery, regret, sorrow, throes **7** anxiety, torment, torture **8** distress, hardship **9** heartache, suffering **10** affliction, heartbreak **12** wretchedness

angular 4 bony, edgy, lank, lean, thin **5** gaunt, lanky, spare, stiff **6** forked, skinny, zigzag **7** pointed, scraggy, scrawny **8** cornered, rawboned, ungainly **9** roughhewn **10** unfinished, ungraceful, unpolished

ani 6 cuckoo

anima 4 soul **6** psyche, spirit

animadversion 4 slam, slur **7** censure, obloquy **9** aspersion, criticism **10** accusation, imputation, reflection **11** insinuation **12** reprehension

animadvert 6 notice **7** observe **9** criticize

animal 5 beast, brute, feral **6** brutal, carnal, ferine **7** beastly, bestial, brutish, critter, fleshly, sensual, swinish, wilding **9** creature, wildling *antlered:* **3** elk **4** axis, deer **5** moose **7** caribou **8** reindeer *aquatic:* **3** eel **4** fish, frog, seal **5** otter, whale **6** dugong, sea cow, walrus **7** dolphin, manatee, octopus **8** bryozoan, porpoise **9** alligator, crocodile *arboreal:* **2** ai **4** bird **5** chimp, coati, koala, lemur, sloth **6** gibbon, monkey **7** opossum, tarsier **8** kinkajou, marmoset, squirrel **9** orangutan *burrowing:* **4** mole **5** brock, ratel **6** badger, gopher, marmot, rabbit **7** echidna **9** armadillo, groundhog, woodchuck *castrated:* **2** ox **5** capon, steer **6** barrow, wether **7** gelding *coat:* **3** fur **4** hair, hide **6** pelage *draft:* **2** ox **3** yak **4** mule, oxen (plural) **5** horse **6** donkey **8** elephant *exhibit:* **3** zoo *extinct:* **3** moa **4** dodo, urus **6** quagga **7** mammoth **8** dinosaur, eohippus, mastodon **9** trilobite *female:* **3** cow, dam, doe, ewe, hen, pen, roe, sow **4** mare, puss **5** bitch, goose, jenny, nanny, vixen **6** jennet **7** lioness *four-footed:* **9** quadruped *four-limbed:* **8** tetrapod *free-swimming:* **6** nekton *hibernating:* **4** bear, frog, toad **5** skunk, snake **7** polecat **8** chipmunk **9** groundhog, woodchuck *horned:* **2** ox **3** ram, yak **4** bull, goat, ibex, kudu **5** addax, bison, eland, rhino **6** cattle, koodoo **7** buffalo, gazelle, giraffe, unicorn **8** antelope *humped:* **2** ox **3** elk, yak **4** zebu **5** bison, camel, moose *imaginary:* **5** snark **6** Harvey **10** hippogriff *male:* **3** cob, ram, tom **4** boar, buck, bull, cock, stag, stud **5** billy, steer **6** gander **7** gobbler, rooster **8** bachelor, stallion *many-celled:* **8** metazoan *many-footed:* **9** centipede, millipede *meateating:* **9** carnivore *mythical:* **5** Hydra **6** dragon, kraken, sphinx **7** centaur, griffin, mermaid, Pegasus, unicorn **8** basilisk, Cerberus, Minotaur *one-celled:* **9** protozoan *Peruvian:* **5** llama **6** alpaca, vicuña *planteating:* **9** herbivore *skin disease:* **5** mange *spotted:* **4** axis, paca **6** calico, jaguar, ocelot **7** cheetah, leopard, piebald **8** skewbald **9** dalmatian *striped:* **4** kudu **5** tiger, zebra **6** koodoo, quagga *tender:* **8** herdsman *trail:* **3** pug **4** foil, slot **5** spoor *tusked:* **6** walrus **7** warthog **8** elephant *two-footed:* **5** biped *web-footed:* **4** duck, frog, toad **5** goose, otter **6** beaver **8** duckbill, platypus *young:* **3** cub, kid, kit, pup **4** calf, colt, fawn, foal, joey, lamb **5** bunny, chick, kitty, poult, shoat, stirk, whelp **6** cygnet, farrow, heifer, kitten, piglet **7** bullock, gosling, lambkin **8** suckling, yeanling, yearling **9** fledgling

animal behavior *study of:* **8** ethology

animal fat 4 suet **6** tallow

animalism 4 lust **7** abandon **8** vitality **9** carnality **10** sensualism, sensuality **11** lustfulness, physicality, unrestraint

animalize 4 warp **6** debase **7** corrupt, deprave, pervert, vitiate **9** brutalize **10** bestialize, demoralize

animal life 5 fauna

animal sound 3 arf, baa, bay, caw, coo, low, mew, moo **4** bark, bray, buzz, crow, hiss, hoot, howl, meow, purr, roar, yelp **5** bleat, chirp, croak, drone, growl, grunt, miaow, neigh, quack **6** bellow, gibber, gobble, warble **7** screech, twitter

animate 4 fire, live, move, spur, stir, urge **5** alert, alive, cheer, drive, exalt, impel, liven, nerve, spark, steel, vital **6** active, arouse, excite, inform, kindle, lively, living, moving, viable, vivify **7** actuate, chirk up, dynamic, enliven, hearten, inspire, quicken, refresh **8** activate, embolden, energize, in-

spirit, motivate, spirited, vitalize **9** breathing, encourage, energized, enhearten, make alive, stimulate **10** invigorate

animated 3 gay **4** keen **5** alert, alive, peppy, quick, vivid, vital **6** lively, living **7** dynamic, excited, vibrant, zestful **8** spirited, vigorous **9** activated, energetic, energized, exuberant, sprightly, vitalized, vivacious **12** high-spirited

animation 3 pep, vim, zip **4** brio, dash, élan, life, toon, zing **5** oomph, verve **6** energy, esprit, gaiety, spirit **7** cartoon, dynamic **8** dynamism, vitality, vivacity **10** liveliness *unit:* **3** cel **4** cell

animato 5 brisk, tempo **6** lively **8** spirited **9** energetic, sprightly

animosity 4 hate **5** venom **6** animus, enmity, hatred, rancor **7** dislike, ill will **8** acrimony **9** antipathy, hostility **10** antagonism, resentment

animus 4 plan, soul **6** design, enmity, intent, pneuma, psyche, rancor, spirit **7** dislike, ill will, meaning, purpose **9** antipathy, élan vital, hostility, intention **10** antagonism, intendment, opposition, vital force **11** disposition, malevolence

Anjou 4 pear *capital:* **6** Angers *native:* **7** Angevin

ankle 5 talus **6** tarsus

Anna Karenina *author:* **7** Tolstoy (Leo) *character:* **5** Dolly, Kitty, Levin (Konstantin), Stiva **6** Andrei (Karenin) **7** Vronsky (Count Alexei) **8** Ivanovna (Countess Lidia), Seriozha *film star:* **4** Bean (Sean) **5** Bloom (Claire), Garbo (Greta), Leigh (Vivien), March (Fredric), Reeve (Christopher) **6** Bisset (Jacqueline) **7** Connery (Sean), Marceau (Sophie) **10** Richardson (Ralph) *radio star:* **4** Peck (Gregory) **7** Bergman (Ingrid)

annals 6 record **7** account, history **8** archives, register **9** chronicle

annelid 4 worm **5** leech **9** earthworm

annex 3 add, arm, cop, ell, win **4** gain, hook, join, land, take, wing **5** add on, affix, seize, tag on **6** adjoin, append, attach, fasten, obtain, pick up, secure, tack on, take on **7** acquire, connect, preempt, procure, subjoin **8** accroach, addition, appendix, arrogate, superadd, take over **9** extension **10** attachment, commandeer, subsidiary, supplement **11** appropriate, expropriate, incorporate

Annie Oakley 4 comp, pass **10** free ticket, markswoman

annihilate 4 do in, kill, raze, rout, ruin, undo **5** abate, annul, crush, erase, quash, quell, wrack, wreck **6** murder, negate, quench, rub

out, squash, uproot, vanish **7** abolish, blot out, destroy, expunge, nullify, put down, root out, vitiate, wipe out **8** abrogate, demolish, massacre, suppress, vanquish **9** eradicate, extirpate, liquidate, slaughter **10** extinguish, invalidate, obliterate **11** exterminate

annihilation 7 killing **8** massacre **9** abolition **11** destruction, elimination, liquidation, termination **12** obliteration **13** extermination

anniversary *hundredth:* **9** centenary **10** centennial *tenth:* **9** decennial *thousandth:* **10** millennial

Anno ____ **6** Domini

annotate 5 gloss **6** remark **7** comment, explain **8** footnote **9** elucidate, interpret **10** commentate

announce 4 call, tell **5** augur, issue, sound, state **6** attest, blazon, herald, impart, report, reveal, signal **7** bespeak, declare, divulge, forerun, give out, portend, predict, presage, present, publish, release, signify, trumpet **8** disclose, forecast, foreshow, foretell, indicate, proclaim **9** advertise, broadcast, harbinger, make known, publicize **10** give notice, make public, promulgate **11** preindicate

announcement 4 news **5** promo **6** notice, report **7** message, release **8** briefing, bulletin **9** broadcast, statement **10** communiqué, disclosure **11** declaration, publication **12** proclamation, promulgation **13** advertisement, communication

announcer 2 DJ **5** emcee **6** deejay, herald, veejay **9** anchorman, voice-over **10** disc jockey, disk jockey, newscaster **11** anchorwoman, broadcaster, commentator **12** anchorperson, sportscaster

annoy 3 bug, irk, vex **4** bait, fret, gall, miff **5** chafe, chivy, harry, peeve, tease, upset, worry **6** badger, bother, harass, heckle, hector, molest, needle, nettle, pester, plague, ruffle **7** agitate, bedevil, disturb, hagride, perturb, provoke, tick off **8** distress, irritate **9** beleaguer *Scottish:* **4** fash

annoyance 4 drag, to-do **5** trial, upset, worry **6** bother, nettle, plague, strain **7** problem, trouble **8** distress, headache, irritant, nuisance, vexation **10** affliction, harassment, irritation **11** aggravation, botheration, disturbance, indignation, provocation **12** exasperation

annoying 5 pesky **8** tiresome **9** troubling, vexatious **10** disturbing, irritating **11** aggravating, distressing, troublesome **12** exasperating

annual 5 plant **6** flower, yearly **7** almanac **8** each year, yearbook, yearlong **9** every year

annul 4 undo, void **5** abate, erase, quash **6** cancel, delete, efface, negate, revoke, vacate **7** abolish, blot out, expunge, nullify, redress, rescind, retract, reverse, vitiate, wipe out **8** abrogate, dissolve **9** cancel out, discharge, frustrate **10** annihilate, counteract, extinguish, invalidate, neutralize, obliterate **11** countermand

annunciate see **announce**

anodyne 4 balm **5** bland **6** opiate, relief, remedy **7** soother **8** narcotic, nepenthe, painless, sedative **9** analgesic, calmative, innocuous, soporific **10** anesthetic, depressant, pain-killer, palliative **11** inoffensive, unoffending **12** tranquilizer

anoint 3 rub **4** daub, laud, name **5** anele, apply, bless, honor, smear **6** choose, hallow, ordain **7** confirm, massage **8** dedicate, sanctify, set apart, venerate **9** designate **10** consecrate

anomalous 3 odd **6** off-key **7** deviant, strange, unusual **8** aberrant, abnormal, atypical, peculiar **9** deviating, deviatory, divergent, irregular, unnatural, untypical **10** unexpected **11** heteroclite, incongruous, paradoxical **12** inconsistent **13** nonconforming, preternatural

anomaly 5 freak, quirk **6** oddity **7** paradox **9** departure, deviation, exception **10** aberration, divergence **11** abnormality, incongruity, peculiarity **12** idiosyncrasy, irregularity **13** inconsistency

anomie 4 flux **6** unrest **7** anxiety, inertia **10** alienation, insecurity **11** disquietude, instability, uncertainty **12** disaffection, estrangement, indifference, restlessness

anon 4 soon **5** later **7** by and by, shortly **8** directly, in a while **9** presently **10** before long **11** after a while

anonym 5 alias **6** handle **7** pen name **8** nickname **10** nom de plume **11** assumed name, nom de guerre

anonymous 7 unknown, unnamed **8** nameless, not named, unsigned **9** incognito **11** unspecified **12** unidentified, unrecognized

anorak 5 parka

another 3 new **4** else, more **5** added, fresh **7** farther, further, one more **9** different **10** additional **11** alternative, someone else **13** something else

anschluss 5 union **6** league **8** alliance **9** coalition **10** federation **11** confederacy **13** confederation

answer 4 fill, meet, plea, RSVP **5** atone, plead, rebut, reply, serve, solve **6** come in, refute, rejoin, result, retort, return **7** conform, defense, explain, fulfill, respond, satisfy **8** antiphon, rebuttal, response, solution **9** rejoinder **10** refutation **11** recriminate **13** countercharge

answerable 5 bound **6** liable **7** obliged, subject **8** amenable **9** compelled, duty-bound, obligated **11** accountable, constrained, responsible

ant 5 emmet **9** carpenter *relating to:* **6** formic

Antaean 4 huge **5** giant **6** heroic **7** mammoth, titanic **8** colossal, enormous, gigantic **9** cyclopean **10** gargantuan

Antaeus *father:* **7** Neptune **8** Poseidon *mother:* **4** Gaea *slayer:* **8** Heracles, Hercules

antagonism 3 con **6** animus, enmity, hatred, rancor **7** discord **8** conflict, friction **9** animosity, antipathy, hostility **10** antithesis, contention, dissension, opposition, resistance **11** contrariety **12** disagreement

antagonist 3 con, foe **4** anti **5** enemy, match **6** muscle **7** opposer **8** chemical, opponent **9** adversary, contender

antagonistic 4 anti **6** averse **7** adverse, hostile, opposed **8** clashing, contrary, inimical, opposing **9** bellicose, combative, rancorous, truculent **11** belligerent, conflicting, contentious **12** antipathetic

Antarctica sea 4 Ross **7** Weddell **8** Amundsen

ante 3 bet, pay, pot **4** cost, risk **5** level, pay up, price, put up, stake, wager **6** stakes **7** produce

anteater 8 aardvark, pangolin, tamandua

antecede 7 forerun, precede, predate **8** foredate, go before

antecedence 8 priority **10** precedence, precession, preference

antecedent 4 fore, line **5** cause, prior **6** former, reason **7** earlier **8** ancestor, anterior, forebear, foregoer, occasion, previous **9** condition, foregoing, precedent, preceding, precursor, prototype **10** forerunner, progenitor **11** determinant, predecessor

antedate 7 forerun, precede **11** anachronize

antediluvian 3 old **4** aged, fogy **5** hoary, passé **6** age-old, fogram, fossil, square **7** ancient, antique, archaic **8** mossback, Noachian, obsolete, outdated, outmoded, primeval, timeworn **9** out-of-date, primitive **10** antiquated, fuddy-duddy **12** old-fashioned **13** stick-in-the-mud

antelope 3 gnu, kob **4** guib, kudu, oryx, poku, puku, topi, tora **5** addax, bongo, eland, nyala, oribi, serow **6** dik-dik, duiker, impala, koodoo, lechwe, nilgai **7** blesbok,

chamois, gazelle, gemsbok, gerenuk, sassaby **8** bushbuck, reedbuck, steinbok **9** springbok, waterbuck **10** hartebeest *female:* **3** doe *genus:* **4** Oryx *male:* **4** buck *young:* **3** kid (see also **gazelle**)

antenna 4 wire **6** aerial, device, dipole, sensor **8** monopole, receiver

antennae 4 ears **11** sensitivity **13** receptiveness

anterior 4 past **5** prior **6** former **8** previous **9** foregoing, precedent, preceding **10** antecedent

anteroom 5 entry, foyer, lobby **6** alcove **9** vestibule

Anteros *brother:* **4** Eros *father:* **4** Ares, Mars *mother:* **5** Venus **9** Aphrodite *opposite:* **4** Eros

anthem 4 hymn, song **5** chant, paean, psalm **8** canticle

anthology 3 ana **5** album **6** digest, reader **7** garland, omnibus **8** analects, treasury **9** selection **10** assortment, collection, compendium, miscellany **11** compilation, florilegium

anthropoid 3 ape **4** saki, titi **5** biped **6** bonobo, gibbon, monkey, uakari **7** bipedal, gorilla, macaque, manlike, primate, tamarin, tarsier **8** capuchin, hominoid, humanoid, marmoset **9** orangutan **10** chimpanzee

anthropologist 4 Boas (Franz), Dart (Raymond), Mead (Margaret) **5** Sapir (Edward), Tylor (Edward Burnett) **6** Frazer (James George), Geertz (Clifford), Leakey (Louis), Morgan (Lewis Henry) **7** Bateson (Gregory), Kroeber (Alfred Louis) **8** Benedict (Ruth) **10** Malinowski (Bronisław) **11** Lévi-Strauss (Claude)

anti 3 con **6** averse **7** adverse, against, counter, opposed, opposer **8** contrary, opponent, opposing **9** adversary, opposed to **10** antagonist **12** antagonistic, antipathetic, in opposition

antiaircraft fire 4 flak

antibiotic 7 colicin **8** neomycin, viomycin **9** polymyxin **10** bacitracin, novobiocin, penicillin **11** bacteriocin, tyrothricin **12** streptomycin, tetracycline

antic 3 gag **4** dido, joke, lark, romp **5** caper, comic, prank, trick **6** frisky, frolic, lively **7** comical, foolish, playful **8** escapade, farcical, prankish, spirited **9** high jinks, laughable, ludicrous, sprightly **10** frolicsome, rollicking, shenanigan, tomfollery **11** mischievous, monkeyshine **12** monkeyshines **13** practical joke

anticipate 3 see **4** wait **5** await, check **6** divine, expect **7** counter, count on, foresee,

prepare, presage, prevent, wait for **8** forecast, foreknow, foretell **9** apprehend, forestall, prevision, visualize **10** prepare for
anticipation 7 inkling, outlook, promise **8** awaiting, forecast, prospect **9** awareness, foresight, foretaste **10** expectancy **11** expectation, realization **12** apprehension **13** visualization
Anticlea *father:* **9** Autolycus *husband:* **7** Laertes *son:* **7** Ulysses **8** Odysseus
antidote 4 cure, drug **6** remedy **7** negator **8** medicine **9** nullifier **10** corrective, counteract, preventive **11** counterstep, neutralizer **12** counteragent **13** counteractant, counteractive
Antigone *brother:* **9** Polynices **10** Polyneices *father:* **7** Oedipus *mother:* **7** Jocasta *sister:* **6** Ismene *uncle:* **5** Creon
Antigua and Barbuda *capital:* **7** St. Johns *island:* **7** Antigua, Barbuda, Redonda
Antilochus *father:* **6** Nestor *friend:* **8** Achilles *slayer:* **6** Memnon
antimony symbol 2 Sb
Antiope *father:* **6** Asopus *husband:* **5** Lycus **7** Theseus *queen of:* **7** Amazons *son:* **6** Zethus **7** Amphion **10** Hippolytus
antipasto 9 appetizer **11** hors d'oeuvre **12** hors d'oeuvres
antipathetic 5 loath **6** averse, loathe **7** adverse, hostile, opposed **8** aversive, clashing, contrary, inimical, opposing, opposite **9** abhorrent, loathsome, repellent, repugnant, repulsive **10** discordant, unfriendly **11** conflicting, distasteful, ill-disposed, uncongenial **12** antagonistic **13** contradictory
antipathy 4 hate **6** animus, enmity, hatred, rancor **7** allergy, dislike, ill will **8** aversion, distaste, loathing **9** animosity, hostility **10** abhorrence, antagonism, opposition, repellency
antiphon 5 psalm, reply, verse **6** answer, anthem, return **7** respond **8** response
antipodal 5 polar **7** adverse, counter, opposed, reverse **8** contrary, converse, opposite **9** diametric **11** conflicting, contrasting, diametrical **12** antithetical **13** contradictory
antipode 6 contra **7** counter, reverse **8** contrary, converse, flip side, opposite **9** other side **11** counterpole
antiquate 7 outdate, outmode **8** obsolete **9** obsolesce **12** superannuate
antiquated 3 old **4** aged **5** dated, fusty, hoary, moldy, passé **6** bygone, old hat **7** ancient, antique, archaic **8** obsolete, old-timey, outmoded **9** out-of-date **10** oldfangled, out-of-style **11** discredited, obsolescent **12** antediluvian, old-fashioned **13** inappropriate, superannuated

antique 3 old **4** aged **5** dated, hoary, olden, passé, relic **6** age-old, bygone, rarity **7** ancient, archaic, vintage **8** artifact, heirloom, old-timey, outdated, outmoded, timeworn **9** ancestral, objet d'art, out-of-date, venerable **10** antiquated, oldfangled **12** antediluvian, old-fashioned
antiseptic 6 iodine **7** alcohol, sterile **8** hygienic, peroxide, sanitary **9** boric acid, carvacrol, germicide, merbromin **10** gramicidin, sterilized **12** carbolic acid, disinfectant *pioneer:* **6** Lister (Joseph)
antisocial 7 ascetic, austere, hostile **8** eremitic, solitary **9** alienated, reclusive, withdrawn **10** unfriendly **11** standoffish **12** antagonistic, misanthropic
antithesis 3 con **6** contra **7** counter, reverse **8** antipode, antipole, contrary, contrast, converse, opposite **10** antagonism, opposition **11** counterpole
antithetical 5 polar **6** contra **7** counter, reverse **8** contrary, converse, opposite **9** antipodal, diametric **10** antipodean **11** diametrical **13** contradictory
antitoxin 4 sera (plural) **5** serum **11** neutralizer
antiwar 6 irenic **8** pacifist **10** nonviolent, pacifistic
Antony, Mark *defeat:* **6** Actium *friend:* **6** Caesar *lover:* **9** Cleopatra *wife:* **7** Octavia
anxiety 4 care, fear **5** agita, doubt, dread, panic, worry **6** unease **7** concern **8** distress, mistrust, suspense **9** self-doubt, suffering **10** uneasiness **11** disquietude, uncertainty **12** apprehension
anxious 4 avid, keen **5** eager **6** afraid, ardent, scared, uneasy **7** alarmed, fearful, worried **8** agitated, desirous, troubled, worrying **9** impatient, perturbed, terrified **10** breathless, disquieted, frightened **12** apprehensive
any 3 all **4** a bit, some **5** every **7** a little, several **8** whatever
anyhow 6 random **7** however **8** at random, randomly **9** hit-or-miss **10** carelessly, regardless **11** haphazardly **13** helter-skelter
anymore 3 now **5** today **8** nowadays **9** presently, these days
anyone 3 all **9** everybody
anything 5 aught
anytime 4 ever **8** whenever
anyway 4 ever, once **5** at all **7** however **12** nevertheless
anywise 5 at all
apace 4 fast **6** versed **7** abreast, flat-out, hastily, quickly, rapidly, swiftly **8** informed, up-

to-date, speedily **9** posthaste **12** lickety-split **13** expeditiously

Apache *chief:* **7** Cochise **8** Geronimo *subgroups:* **7** Cibecue **9** Jicarilla, Mescalero **10** Chiricahua

apart 5 alone, aside **6** singly **7** asunder, removed **8** detached, isolated, one by one **9** severally **10** separately **12** individually **13** independently, unaccompanied *prefix:* **3** dis

apart from 3 bar, but **4** save **6** except, saving **7** barring, besides **9** except for, excepting, excluding, other than, outside of **11** exclusive of

apartheid 8 division **9** partition **10** separation, separatism **11** segregation **12** separateness

apartment 4 flat, room **5** rooms, suite **6** rental **7** chamber, housing, lodging **8** building, dwelling **9** residence **10** maisonette **13** accommodation

apathetic 4 dull, flat, limp **5** inert **6** stolid, torpid **7** languid, passive, unmoved **8** sluggish **9** impassive, untouched **10** anesthetic, insensible, phlegmatic, spiritless **11** emotionless, indifferent, insensitive **12** unresponsive **13** disinterested

apathy 6 torpor **8** coldness, dullness, lethargy, obduracy, stoicism **9** aloofness, disregard, inertness, lassitude, passivity, stolidity, torpidity, unconcern **10** detachment, dispassion **11** callousness, disinterest, impassivity **12** heedlessness, indifference, listlessness **13** insensibility, insensitivity

ape 4 copy, mime, mock **5** mimic **6** bonobo, gibbon, parody, pongid, simian **7** copycat, emulate, gorilla, imitate, siamang, take off **8** simulate, travesty **9** burlesque, orangutan **10** anthropoid, caricature, chimpanzee **11** impersonate

aperçu 5 brief **6** digest, précis, sketch, survey **7** insight, outline **8** syllabus **10** compendium, impression

aperitif 3 kir **4** whet **5** drink **6** Pastis, Pernod, sherry **7** Campari, Cinzano **8** cocktail **9** appetizer

aperture 3 gap **4** hole, vent **5** chink **6** outlet **7** opening, orifice, pinhole

apery 7 mimicry **9** imitation

apex 3 cap, tip, top **4** acme, cusp, peak, roof **5** crest, crown, limit, point **6** apogee, climax, summit, vertex, zenith **8** capstone, pinnacle, ultimate **9** crescendo, sublimity **11** culmination, ne plus ultra **12** quintessence

aphorism 3 saw **4** rule **5** adage, axiom, maxim, moral **6** dictum, saying, truism **7** precept, proverb **8** apothegm

aphrodisiac 6 erotic **7** amative, amatory, amorous, lustful **8** excitant **10** passionate

Aphrodite *Roman counterpart:* **5** Venus *consort:* **4** Ares **6** Vulcan **10** Hephaestus *father:* **4** Zeus **7** Jupiter *goddess of:* **4** love *mother:* **5** Dione *sister:* **6** Athena **7** Artemis *son:* **4** Eros **6** Aeneas **7** Priapus

apiarist 9 beekeeper

apical 3 top **7** highest, topmost **8** loftiest **9** uppermost

apiculture 10 beekeeping

apiece 3 per **4** a pop, each **6** singly, to each **7** for each **8** one by one **9** per capita, severally **10** separately **12** individually, respectively

apish 5 phony, silly **6** phoney **7** slavish **8** affected **9** emulative, imitative **10** artificial

aplenty 4 full **5** ample **6** galore, indeed **7** copious, greatly **8** abundant, very much **9** extremely

aplomb 4 ease **5** poise **6** polish **8** coolness, easiness **9** assurance, certainty, certitude, composure **10** confidence, equanimity **11** nonchalance, savoir faire **12** self-reliance **13** self-assurance

apocalypse 6 augury, oracle, vision **8** disaster, prophecy **10** Armageddon, prediction, revelation

apocalyptic 4 dire **5** awful **7** baleful, baneful, fateful, fearful, ominous **8** Delphian, dreadful, oracular, terrible **9** appalling, climactic, grandiose, prophetic **10** foreboding, predicting **11** foretelling, prophetical, threatening **12** inauspicious *book:* **10** Revelation **11** Revelations

apocryphal 5 false, wrong **6** untrue **7** dubious **8** doubtful, spurious **9** incorrect, ungenuine **10** fictitious, inaccurate, unverified **11** unauthentic **12** questionable

apogee 4 acme, apex, peak **6** climax, summit, zenith **8** capstone, meridian, pinnacle **9** high point **11** culmination

Apollo 6 Helios **7** Phoebus *beloved:* **6** Cyrene, Daphne **8** Calliope *birthplace:* **5** Delos *father:* **4** Zeus **7** Jupiter *mother:* **4** Leto **6** Latona *oracle:* **6** Delphi *sister:* **5** Diana **7** Artemis *son:* **3** Ion **7** Orpheus *temple:* **6** Delphi

apologetic 5 sorry **6** rueful **8** contrite, penitent **9** regretful, repentant **10** remorseful **11** penitential **12** compunctious

apologia 4 plea **6** excuse, reason **7** defense **8** argument **11** elucidation, explanation **13** clarification, justification

apologize 5 atone **6** lament, regret, repent **7** confess **9** beg pardon **10** make amends

apologue 4 myth, tale **5** fable, story **7** parable **8** allegory

apology 4 plea **6** amends, excuse **7** redress,

regrets **8** mea culpa **9** admission, makeshift **10** concession, confession

apoplexy 4 esca **6** stroke

apostasy 7 perfidy **9** defection, desertion, disavowal, falseness, rejection **11** abandonment, repudiation **12** disaffection, renunciation

apostate 7 heretic, traitor **8** defector, deserter, recreant, renegade, turncoat **9** turnabout

apostatize 4 turn **6** defect, desert **7** abandon, forsake, sell out **8** renounce **9** repudiate

a posteriori 9 inductive

apostle 4 John, Jude, Paul **5** James, Judas, Peter, Silas, Simon **6** Andrew, Philip, Thomas **7** Matthew **8** Barnabas, disciple, follower, Matthias, preacher **9** missioner **10** colporteur, evangelist, missionary **11** Bartholomew **12** propagandist *of Germany:* **8** Boniface *of Ireland:* **7** Patrick *of the English:* **9** Augustine *of the French:* **5** Denis *of the Gauls:* **8** Irenaeus *of the Gentiles:* **4** Paul *of the Goths:* **7** Ulfilas *to the Indians:* **9** John Eliot

apothecary 7 chemist **8** druggist, pharmacy **9** drugstore **10** pharmacist

apothegm see **aphorism**

apotheosis 6 height **7** epitome **8** exemplar, ultimate **9** archetype, elevation **10** embodiment, exaltation **11** deification, ennoblement, idolization, lionization **12** enshrinement, quintessence **13** glorification

appall 3 awe **4** faze **5** alarm, shake, shock **6** dismay **7** horrify, outrage, overawe, perturb **8** confound, distress **10** disconcert **11** consternate

appalled 6 aghast **11** dumbfounded

appalling 5 awful **6** horrid **7** fearful **8** daunting, dreadful, horrible, horrific, shocking, terrible **9** atrocious, dismaying, frightful, loathsome **10** disgusting, formidable, horrifying

appanage 5 grant, right **7** adjunct **8** property **9** endowment, privilege **10** birthright, perquisite **11** prerogative

apparatus 4 gear, tool **5** gismo, gizmo **6** device, gadget, outfit, tackle, widget **7** utensil **8** matériel, tackling **9** equipment, implement, machinery **10** instrument **11** contraption **13** accouterments, accoutrements, paraphernalia

apparel 4 clad, duds, garb, gear, robe, suit, togs **5** adorn, array, dress, getup, habit **6** attire, clothe, livery, outfit **7** clothes, costume, garment, raiment, threads, vesture **8** clothing, enclothe, glad rags, vestment **9** embellish **11** habiliments

apparent 5 clear, overt, plain **6** patent **7** evident, obvious, seeming, visible **8** distinct, manifest, palpable **9** succedent **10** noticeable, observable **11** discernible, perceivable, perceptible

apparition 5 ghost, shade, umbra **6** shadow, spirit, vision, wraith **7** fantasm, phantom, specter **8** illusion, phantasm **10** appearance, phenomenon **13** hallucination

appeal 3 ask, beg, bid **4** call, lure, plea, pray, pull, suit, urge **5** apply, brace, charm, crave, plead **6** accuse, allure, charge, excite, invoke, sue for **7** attract, beseech, entreat, glamour, implore, request **8** call upon, charisma, entreaty, interest, intrigue, petition **9** fascinate, importune, magnetism, seduction **10** allurement, attraction, supplicate **11** application, fascination, imploration **12** drawing power, solicitation, supplication

appealing 8 alluring, charming, pleading, pleasant, pleasing **9** agreeable **10** attractive, bewitching, enchanting **11** captivating, fascinating

appear 4 look, loom, rise, seem, show **5** arise, issue, occur **6** arrive, emerge, show up, turn up **7** emanate **8** resemble **9** come forth **11** materialize

appearance 3 air **4** face, form, look, mien, pose, show **5** debut, dress, front, guise, image **6** advent, aspect, facade, manner **7** arrival, bearing, display, seeming **8** attitude, demeanor, illusion **9** semblance **10** impression, occurrence, simulacrum **11** countenance **13** manifestation

appease 4 calm, ease **5** allay, quiet **6** buy off, pacify, soothe **7** assuage, concede, content, gratify, mollify, placate, relieve, satisfy, sweeten **10** conciliate, propitiate

appellation 4 name **5** brand, label, nomen, style, title **7** moniker **8** cognomen **10** identifier **11** designation **12** denomination

append 3 add **5** add on, affix, annex, tag on **6** adjoin, attach, tack on **7** subjoin **10** supplement

appendage 3 arm, fin, leg, tab, tag **4** barb, flap, horn, limb, seta, tail, wing **5** extra **6** cercus, member **7** adjunct, antenna, elytron, stipule **8** pedipalp, pendicle, tentacle **9** accessory, auxiliary, extremity **10** attachment, collateral, incidental, projection, supplement **12** appurtenance, nonessential, protuberance

appendix 5 notes, rider **7** adjunct, codicil **8** addendum, addition **9** accessory, appendage **10** attachment, supplement **12** appurtenance

apperception 5 grasp **9** awareness **10** cognizance **11** realization, recognition **12** apprehension, assimilation **13** comprehension, introspection, understanding

appertain 4 bear **5** apply, refer **6** bear on, belong, relate **8** bear upon **10** be relevant **11** be connected, be pertinent

appetence 3 yen **5** taste **6** desire, hunger, relish, thirst **7** craving, longing, stomach **8** fondness

appetent 4 agog, avid, keen **5** eager **6** ardent **7** anxious, craving, lusting, thirsty **8** desirous, yearning **9** impatient **10** breathless

appetite 3 yen **4** bent, itch, lust, urge **5** taste **6** desire, hunger, liking, relish **7** craving, leaning, longing, passion, stomach **8** cupidity, fondness, gluttony, penchant, soft spot, voracity, weakness, yearning **9** hankering **10** preference, proclivity, propensity **11** inclination

appetizer 4 whet **5** snack **6** canapé, savory, tidbit **7** starter **8** aperitif, cocktail, stimulus **9** antipasto **11** amuse-bouche, hors d'oeuvre

appetizing 5 tasty **6** savory **8** saporous, tempting **9** agreeable, appealing, aperitive, flavorful, palatable, relishing, toothsome **10** delectable, flavorsome **11** scrumptious, tantalizing **13** mouth-watering

applaud 4 clap, hail, laud, root **5** bravo, cheer, extol **6** praise, rise to **7** acclaim, approve, commend **9** recommend **10** compliment

applause 4 hand **5** round **6** bravos, cheers, praise **7** acclaim, hurrahs, ovation, rooting **8** accolade, approval, cheering, clapping, plaudits **11** acclamation **12** commendation

apple 4 crab, Fuji, Gala, pome **6** Empire, Macoun, pippin, russet **7** Baldwin, costard, Duchess, Winesap **8** Braeburn, Cortland, greening, Jonagold, Jonathan, McIntosh **9** Delicious **10** Rome Beauty **11** Granny Smith, Gravenstein, Northern Spy, Transparent *dessert:* **5** crisp *juice:* **5** cider *sugar:* **4** ates **8** sweetsop

applejack 5 cider **6** brandy, liquor **8** calvados **9** hard cider

apple knocker see **rustic**

apple-polish 4 fawn **5** toady **6** kowtow **7** cater to, flatter, honey up, truckle **8** butter up **10** curry favor, ingratiate

apple-polisher 5 toady **6** yes-man **8** bootlick, groveler, lickspit **9** flatterer, sycophant **11** lickspittle

applesauce 5 hooey **6** bunkum **7** baloney, rubbish, twaddle **8** malarkey, nonsense **9** poppycock

appliance 6 device **7** utensil **9** implement **10** instrument **11** application *kitchen:* **4** oven **5** mixer, range, stove **6** fridge **7** blender,

toaster **9** can opener, microwave **10** dishwasher **12** refrigerator

applicability 3 use **7** account, fitness, utility **9** advantage, relevance **10** usefulness

applicable 3 apt, fit **4** just, meet **5** ad rem **6** seemly, suited, useful **7** apropos, fitting, germane **8** apposite, material, relevant, suitable **9** befitting, pertinent **10** felicitous **11** appropriate

applicant 6 seeker **7** hopeful **8** aspirant, inquirer **9** candidate, job-hunter, job-seeker

application 3 use **4** form, heed, plea, suit **5** study **6** appeal, debate, effort, letter **7** request **8** entreaty, exercise, exertion, industry, petition **9** assiduity, attention, diligence, operation, treatment **10** dedication **11** requisition, utilization

appliqué 5 decal

apply 3 dab, use **4** bend, give, turn, urge **5** press, put on, refer **6** accost, affect, appeal, assign, bear on, bestow, devote, direct, employ, engage, handle, relate, resort, take on **7** address, beseech, concern, entreat, execute, implore, involve, pertain, utilize **8** approach, bear upon, exercise, petition, set about **9** appertain, implement, importune, undertake **10** administer, buckle down

appoint 3 arm, fix, rig, set, tap **4** gear, name **5** equip **6** assign, decide, fit out, outfit, supply **7** dress up, furbish, furnish, provide, turn out **8** accouter, accoutre, accredit, delegate, nominate **9** authorize, designate, determine, embellish, provision **10** commission

appointment 3 job **4** date, meet, post, spot **5** berth, place, tryst **6** billet, choice, office **7** meeting **8** election, position **9** equipment, selection, situation **10** assignment, connection, engagement, rendezvous **11** arrangement, assignation, designation

appointments 7 fitting **8** equipage **9** equipment, trappings **11** furnishings **13** accouterments, accoutrements

apportion 3 cut, lot **4** give, mete, part **5** allot, allow, cut up, divvy, quota, serve, share, slice, split **6** assign, bestow, divide, parcel, ration **7** deal out, dish out, divvy up, dole out, measure, mete out, prorate, split up **8** allocate, dispense, separate, share out **9** admeasure, partition **10** administer, distribute

apportionment 3 cut, lot **4** part **5** piece, quota, share, slice, split **6** ration **7** measure, quantum **9** allotment, allowance **10** allocation, assignment

apposite 3 apt **4** just **5** ad rem **6** proper, suited, timely **7** apropos, fitting, germane, right on **8** material, on target, relevant, suitable **9** pertinent **10** applicable **11** appropriate

appositeness 7 aptness, fitness **9** relevance **10** pertinence, timeliness **11** suitability

appraisal 5 stock **6** rating, survey **7** pricing **8** estimate, judgment **9** valuation **10** assessment, estimation, evaluation

appraise 3 eye, fix, set **4** rate, size **5** assay, audit, gauge, judge, price, set at, value **6** assess, figure, size up, survey **7** adjudge, examine, inspect, measure, valuate **8** estimate, evaluate, look over **9** calculate, figure out

appreciable 5 clear, plain **6** marked **7** evident, obvious **8** apparent, clear-cut, concrete, manifest, material, palpable, sensible, tangible **10** detectable, measurable, noticeable, observable **11** discernible, perceptible, substantial **12** considerable

appreciate 4 gain, go up, grow, know, like, love, rise **5** enjoy, grasp, judge, prize, savor, value **6** admire, esteem, fathom, regard, relish **7** apprize, cherish, cognize, enhance, improve, inflate, realize, respect **8** evaluate, increase, treasure **9** apprehend, delight in, recognize **10** comprehend, understand

appreciation 4 gain, rise **6** growth, regard, thanks **7** tribute **8** increase, judgment **9** awareness, gratitude, inflation **10** evaluation, perception **11** recognition, sensitivity, testimonial **12** gratefulness

apprehend 3 nab **4** bust, fear, grab, know, nail, read, twig **5** catch, grasp, run in, seize, sense **6** absorb, accept, arrest, collar, detain, divine, fathom, pick up, take in **7** capture, catch on, cognize, compass, foresee, make out, preknow, realize **8** conceive **9** recognize, visualize **10** anticipate, appreciate, understand

apprehensible 5 clear, lucid, plain **7** evident, obvious **8** distinct, explicit, knowable, luminous **9** graspable **10** fathomable

apprehension 3 ken **4** care, fear, idea **5** alarm, angst, dread, grasp, pinch, worry **6** arrest, notion, pickup, unease **7** anxiety, capture, concern, seizure, thought **8** disquiet, judgment **9** agitation, awareness, detention, knowledge, misgiving, suspicion **10** conception, foreboding, perception, solicitude, uneasiness **11** disquietude, premonition **13** understanding

apprehensive 5 alive, awake, aware, sharp **6** afraid, astute, scared, uneasy **7** anxious, fearful, knowing, worried **8** sensible, sentient, troubled **9** cognizant, conscious, observant, sensitive **10** discerning, disquieted, insightful, perceptive

apprentice 4 bind, tiro, tyro **5** pupil **6** novice,

rookie **7** learner, starter, student, trainee **8** beginner, freshman, neophyte, newcomer **9** novitiate **10** tenderfoot

apprenticed 5 bound **7** obliged, pledged **8** articled **9** obligated **10** indentured

apprise 4 clue, post, tell, warn **6** advise, clue in, fill in, impart, inform, notify, reveal, wise up **7** let know **8** acquaint, announce, describe, disclose **9** make known **11** communicate

apprize 5 value **6** admire, esteem, regard, relish **7** cherish **8** hold dear, treasure **10** appreciate, rate highly

approach 4 near, nigh **5** reach, rival, verge **6** avenue, border, gain on **7** address, advance, apply to, attempt, descent **8** draw near, overture **11** approximate

approachable 7 affable **8** friendly, sociable **9** agreeable, congenial, reachable, receptive **10** accessible, attainable

approaching 6 coming **7** nearing **8** expected, imminent, oncoming, upcoming **11** forthcoming

approbate 4 back, like **5** favor **6** accept, assent, praise **7** applaud, approve, commend, consent, endorse, support **8** sanction **9** recommend **11** countenance

approbation 2 OK **3** nod **4** euge, okay **5** bravo, favor **6** esteem, praise **7** acclaim, consent, support **8** applause, approval, sanction **10** admiration, permission **11** endorsement, recognition **12** commendation

appropriate 3 apt, cop, due, fit **4** grab, just, lift, meet, take, true **5** allot, annex, claim, exact, filch, grasp, pinch, right, seize, steal, swipe, usurp **6** assign, assume, budget, devote, pilfer, proper, snatch, snitch, suited, timely, useful, worthy **7** apropos, desired, earmark, fitting, germane, merited, preempt, purloin **8** accroach, apposite, arrogate, deserved, eligible, entitled, relevant, rightful, set apart, set aside, suitable **9** befitting, opportune, pertinent, requisite **10** acceptable, admissible, applicable, commandeer, compatible, confiscate, convenient, felicitous, seasonable

appropriately 4 well **5** amply, aptly, right **8** properly, suitably **9** fittingly **10** acceptably, adequately, becomingly

appropriateness 3 use **5** order **7** account, aptness, fitness, service, utility **8** meetness **9** advantage, propriety, relevance, rightness **10** expediency, usefulness **13** applicability

appropriation 5 grant **7** funding, stipend, subsidy **9** allotment, allowance **10** allocation, assignment, earmarking, subvention

approval 2 OK **3** nod **4** okay **5** favor, leave,

say-so **6** assent **7** consent, go-ahead, license, support **8** applause, blessing, sanction, suffrage **10** acceptance, compliment, green light, permission **11** approbation, benediction, concurrence, endorsement **12** commendation, confirmation, ratification **13** authorization
approve 2 OK **4** okay **5** clear, favor, go for **6** accept, back up, praise, ratify, uphold **7** applaud, certify, commend, condone, confirm, endorse, initial, mandate, stand by, support, sustain **8** accredit, hold with, sanction **9** approbate, authorize, encourage **10** compliment **11** countenance
approximate 4 near **5** close, rough, touch **6** almost **7** similar, verge on **8** approach, ballpark, come near **10** resembling
approximately 4 most, nigh, or so **5** about, circa **6** all but, almost, nearly **7** close to **8** well-nigh **9** just about **10** more or less **11** practically
approximation 8 likeness, nearness **9** closeness **10** similarity **11** resemblance
appurtenance 7 adjunct **8** addition, appendix, ornament **9** accessory, apparatus, appendage **10** attachment **11** furnishings **13** accompaniment
appurtenant 5 extra **8** adjuvant **9** accessory, ancillary, auxiliary **10** additional, collateral, subsidiary **11** subordinate, subservient **12** accompanying, contributory
apricot 3 ume **4** ansu
a priori 8 provable, reasoned **9** deducible, deductive, derivable, inferable **11** inferential, presumptive
apron 5 stage **6** shield **7** garment **8** pinafore **9** extension
apropos 3 apt **4** as to, in re, meet **5** about, ad rem, anent, aptly, as for **6** proper, timely **7** fitting, germane, related **8** apposite, material, relevant, suitable, suitably, touching **9** as regards, opportune, pertinent, regarding **10** applicable, concerning, respecting **11** applicative, in respect to
apt 3 fit **4** just **5** alert, given, prone, quick, ready, savvy, smart **6** bright, clever, liable, likely, prompt, proper **7** apropos, fitting, germane, tending **8** apposite, disposed, inclined, relevant, suitable **9** befitting, pertinent, qualified **10** felicitous, responsive **11** appropriate, intelligent
aptitude 4 bent, gift **5** flair, knack, savvy **6** genius, liking, talent **7** ability, faculty, fitness **8** capacity, tendency **10** capability, cleverness, proclivity, propensity **11** disposition, inclination, suitability **12** predilection

aptness 4 bent, gift **5** flair, knack, skill **6** genius, talent **7** ability, faculty, fitness **8** tendency **9** propriety, readiness **10** capability, cleverness, expediency, likelihood **11** inclination, suitability **12** intelligence
aquanaut 5 diver **10** scuba diver
aquarium 4 tank **8** fish tank
aqua vitae 4 grog **5** booze, drink, hooch **6** brandy, cognac, liquor, tipple **7** alcohol, spirits **8** schnapps
aqueduct 5 canal **6** course **7** channel, conduit, passage **8** waterway **11** watercourse
aqueous 5 fluid **6** liquid, watery **9** liquefied
Aquila 5 eagle **13** constellation *star:* **6** Altair
Aquitaine 7 Guienne *queen:* **7** Eleanor
aquiver 5 shaky **7** quaking, shaking, trembly **9** shivering, trembling, tremulant, tremulous
Arab *chief:* **4** emir **5** sheik **6** sheikh, sultan *country:* **4** Iraq, Oman **5** Egypt, Libya, Qatar, Sudan, Syria, Yemen **6** Jordan, Kuwait **7** Algeria, Bahrain, Lebanon, Morocco, Tunisia **11** Saudi Arabia
arable 7 fertile **8** fruitful, tillable **10** cultivable, productive
Arachne *father:* **5** Idmon *form:* **6** spider *mother:* **6** Cyrene *rival:* **6** Athena **7** Minerva
arachnid 4 mite, tick **6** acarus, spider **8** scorpion **9** arthropod, phalangid, tarantula **10** harvestman **13** daddy longlegs
arbiter 3 ump **5** judge **6** expert, umpire **7** referee **8** mediator **9** authority, moderator **11** adjudicator
arbitrary 4 rash **6** chance, random **7** erratic, offhand, wayward, willful **8** fanciful, heedless **9** frivolous, impetuous, whimsical **10** capricious, subjective **10** irrational **12** unreasonable **13** discretionary
arbitrate 5 judge **6** settle, umpire **7** adjudge, mediate, referee **9** intervene **10** adjudicate **12** intermediate
arbitrator 5 judge **6** umpire **7** referee, settler **8** mediator **9** moderator **11** adjudicator
arbor 4 axle, beam **5** bower, frame, shaft **7** pergola, shelter, spindle
arc 3 bow, lob **4** arch, bend, path **5** curve, round **7** rainbow **9** curvation, curvature **11** measurement, progression
arcade 6 arches, loggia **7** gallery **10** passageway *game:* **8** Skee-Ball *pioneer:* **5** Atari
arcadia 4 Eden, Zion **6** heaven, utopia **7** Elysium, nirvana **8** paradise **9** fairyland, Shangri-la **10** wonderland
arcane 6 hidden, mystic, occult, opaque, secret **7** obscure, unknown **8** abstruse, esoteric **9** recondite **10** cabalistic, mysterious,

unknowable 11 inscrutable 12 impenetrable 13 unaccountable

Arcas *father:* 4 Zeus 7 Jupiter *mother:* 8 Callisto

arch 3 bow, coy, sly 4 bend, hump, pert 5 curve, fresh, saucy, vault 6 camber, cheeky, impish 7 playful, roguish, waggish 8 flippant, malapert 9 curvature 10 coquettish 11 mischievous *inner curve:* 6 soffit 8 intrados *kind:* 4 ogee 5 ogive, round, Tudor 6 lancet 7 rampart, trefoil 9 horseshoe, primitive, segmental 10 shouldered 11 equilateral 12 basket-handle *outer curve:* 8 extrados *part:* 6 impost 8 keystone, springer, voussoir

archaeological site *Africa:* 8 Zimbabwe 13 Great Zimbabwe *Britain:* 7 Avebury 9 Skara Brae, Sutton Hoo 10 Stonehenge *Cambodia:* 6 Angkor 9 Angkor Wat *Crete:* 7 Knossos *Egypt:* 4 Giza 5 Luxor 6 Abydos, Karnak, Naqada, Thebes 7 Memphis 9 El-Bahnasa 11 Oxyrhynchus *Greece:* 6 Delphi 7 Mycenae, Olympia *Guatemala:* 5 Tikal *Honduras:* 5 Copán *Indonesia:* 9 Borobudur *Iran:* 10 Persepolis *Iraq:* 4 Isin, Nuzi 6 Nimrud 7 Babylon, Nineveh, Samarra *Israel:* 7 Jericho *Italy:* 7 Pompeii 11 Herculaneum *Lebanon:* 6 Byblos 7 Baalbek *Mexico:* 5 Mitla, Tulum, Uxmal 8 Palenque 10 Monte Albán 11 Chichén Itzá *Peru:* 11 Machu Picchu *Syria:* 7 Palmyra *Tunisia:* 8 Carthage, Kairouan *Turkey:* 4 Troy 6 Knidos 8 Hisarlik, Pergamon 9 Hissarlik *Uzbekistan:* 9 Samarkand

archaeologist 4 Bell (Gertrude), Dart (Raymond) 5 Evans (Arthur) 6 Carter (Howard), Childe (V. Gordon), Kidder (Alfred), Petrie (Flinders) 7 Thomsen (Christian), Woolley (Leonard), Worsaae (Jens) 8 Breasted (James Henry), Goodyear (William) 10 Schliemann (Heinrich) 11 Champollion (Jean-François), Winckelmann (Johann)

archaic 3 old 5 dated, olden, passé 6 bygone 7 ancient, antique 8 obsolete, outdated 9 out-of-date, primitive, unevolved 10 antiquated 11 undeveloped 12 old-fashioned

archangel 5 Uriel 7 Gabriel, Michael, Raphael

arched 4 bent 5 bowed, round 6 curved 7 curving, rounded

archer 4 Tell (William) 5 Cupid 6 bowman 9 Robin Hood 11 Sagittarius

archery 9 toxophily

archetypal 5 ideal, model 7 classic, perfect, typical 9 classical, exemplary 10 consummate 12 paradigmatic, prototypical

archetype 4 idea 5 ideal, model 6 mirror 7 epitome, essence, example, pattern 8 exemplar, original, paradigm, standard 9 beau ideal, prototype 10 apotheosis, embodiment, protoplast 12 quintessence

archfiend 5 demon, devil, Satan 6 diablo 7 Lucifer

Archie *character:* 5 Betty, Lodge (Hiram) 6 Archie, Reggie 7 Andrews (Fred, Mary), Jughead 8 Veronica *creator:* 7 Montana (Bob) *Jughead's pet:* 6 Hot Dog *school:* 9 Riverdale *school staff:* 6 Grundy (Geraldine), Kleats (Coach) 7 Beazley (Miss), Clayton (Coach), Svenson (Mr.) 10 Flutesnoot (Prof.), Weatherbee (Mr. Waldo) *shop owner:* 7 Pop Tate

Archimedes 5 Greek 8 inventor *cry:* 6 eureka *discovery:* 5 screw 8 buoyancy 9 principle 11 water raiser

archipelago *Asian:* 5 Malay *Canada:* 6 Arctic *Japan:* 4 Goto 9 Gotoretto *Norway:* 11 Spitsbergen *Papua New Guinea:* 8 Bismarck 9 Louisiade *Philippines:* 4 Sulu *off Scotland:* 7 Orcades, Orkneys *United States:* 9 Alexander

architect 5 maker 7 creator 8 designer, inventor 9 generator 10 originator *American:* 3 Pei (I. M.) 4 Hood (Raymond), Kahn (Louis) 5 Gehry (Frank), McKim (Charles), Meier (Richard), Roche (Kevin), Stone (Edward Durell), Weese (Harry), White (Stanford) 6 Breuer (Marcel), Fuller (Buckminster), Graves (Michael), Morgan (Julia), Neutra (Richard), Rogers (Isaiah), Soleri (Paolo), Upjohn (Richard), Walter (Thomas), Warren (William), Wright (Frank Lloyd) 7 Burnham (Daniel), Gilbert (Cass), Johnson (Philip), Latrobe (Benjamin), Olmsted (Frederick Law), Renwick (James), Sturgis (John Hubbard), Venturi (Robert) 8 Bulfinch (Charles), Saarinen (Eero, Eliel), Sullivan (Louis), Thornton (William), Yamasaki (Minoru) 10 Richardson (Henry Hobson) *Austrian:* 4 Loos (Adolf) 6 Wagner (Otto) *Brazilian:* 8 Niemeyer (Oscar) *Canadian:* 6 Safdie (Moshe) *Dutch:* 8 Koolhaas (Rem), Rietveld (Gerrit) *English:* 4 Nash (John), Shaw (Richard), Wood (John), Wren (Christopher) 5 Jones (Inigo), Scott (George Gilbert), Wyatt (James) 6 Foster (Norman), Rogers (Richard), Street (George Edmund), Voysey (Charles) 7 Lutyens (Edwin) 8 Vanbrugh (John) *Finnish:* 5 Aalto (Alvar) 8 Saarinen (Eero, Eliel) *French:* 6 Perret (Auguste) 7 Garnier (Tony), L'Enfant (Pierre-Charles) 11 Le Corbusier 12 Viollet-le-Duc (Eugène) *German:* 7 Gropius (Walter) 8 Schinkel

(Karl) **10** Mendelsohn (Erich) *Israeli:* **6** Safdie (Moshe) *Italian:* **5** Nervi (Pier Luigi), Piano (Renzo) **6** Romano (Giulio), Soleri (Paolo) **7** Alberti (Leon Battista), Bernini (Gian Lorenzo), da Vinci (Leonardo), Orcagna, Peruzzi (Baldassare), Raphael, Vignola (Giacomo da) **8** Bramante (Donato), Leonardo (da Vinci), Palladio (Andrea), Sangallo (Giuliano da), Terragni (Giuseppe) **9** Borromini (Francesco), Sansovino (Jacopo) **12** Michelangelo *Japanese:* **5** Tange (Kenzo) **8** Yamasaki (Minoru) *Roman:* **9** Vitruvius *Scottish:* **10** Mackintosh (Charles Rennie) *Spanish:* **5** Gaudí (Antonio) *Swedish:* **7** Asplund (Erik Gunnar)

architecture 6 design, makeup **9** formation **11** composition **12** constitution, construction *ornament:* **4** boss, fret **5** gutta **6** finial, volute **7** cabling, console, crocket, diglyph **8** triglyph, vignette **9** arabesque, modillion *style:* **5** Doric, Ionic, Tudor **6** Gothic, Norman, Rococo **7** Baroque **8** Colonial, Georgian **9** Byzantine, Victorian **10** Corinthian, Romanesque

archive 4 file **6** record **7** collect, history, library, records **8** document, register **9** chronicle **10** collection, repository

archon 10 magistrate

arctic 3 icy **4** cold **5** chill, gelid **6** chilly, frigid, frosty, wintry **7** glacial, numbing **8** freezing, hibernal **11** hyperborean *animal:* **3** auk, fox **4** bear, hare, seal, vole **5** sable, whale **6** ermine, marten **7** caribou, lemming **8** reindeer **9** polar bear, ptarmigan *base:* **4** Etah **5** Thule **6** Barrow **11** Point Barrow *bird:* **3** auk *cetacean:* **7** narwhal *current:* **8** Labrador *dog:* **5** husky **7** Samoyed **8** malamute *explorer:* **4** Byrd (Richard), Cook (Frederick) **5** Bylot (Robert), Davis (John), Peary (Robert) **6** Baffin (William), Bering (Vitus), Henson (Matthew), Hudson (Henry), Nansen (Fridtjof), Nobile (Umberto) **7** Barents (Willem), Bennett (Floyd), Wilkins (George), Wrangel (Ferdinand) **8** Amundsen (Roald) **9** Ellsworth (Lincoln), Mackenzie (Alexander), MacMillan (Donald) **10** Stefansson (Vilhjalmus) *forest:* **5** taiga *jacket:* **5** parka **6** anorak *people:* **4** Lapp **5** Aleut, Inuit, Yakut **6** Eskimo, Tungus **7** Chukchi, Samoyed *sea:* **4** Kara **6** Laptev **7** Barents, Chukchi **8** Beaufort *transport:* **7** dogsled *treeless plains:* **6** tundra

ardent 3 hot **4** agog, avid, keen, true **5** eager, fiery, loyal **6** fervid, fierce, heated, intent, red-hot, strong, torrid **7** blazing, burning, devoted, earnest, fervent, flaming, glowing, intense, shining, staunch, zealous **8** constant, desirous, faithful, powerful, resolute, sizzling, vehement, white-hot **9** allegiant, impatient, impetuous, impulsive, perfervid, scorching, steadfast **10** breathless, hot-blooded, passionate **11** impassioned **12** enthusiastic

ardor 4 élan, fire, heat, zeal, zest, zing **5** gusto, verve, vigor **6** energy, fealty, fervor, spirit, warmth **7** avidity, loyalty, passion **8** devotion, fidelity **9** eagerness, intensity, vehemence **10** allegiance, enthusiasm, excitement **12** faithfulness

arduous 4 hard **5** harsh, rough, sheer, steep, tight, tough **6** severe, taxing, tiring, trying, uphill **7** labored **8** grueling, rigorous, toilsome **9** difficult, effortful, gruelling, laborious, punishing, strenuous **10** formidable **11** precipitate, precipitous

area 4 belt, turf, zone **5** field, place, range, realm, scene, space, tract **6** domain, locale, region, sector, sphere **7** expanse, stretch **8** district, locality, province, vicinity **9** bailiwick, territory **12** neighborhood *unit:* **3** ure **4** acre **7** hectare

arena 5 field, scene, stage **6** sphere **7** stadium, theater **8** activity, building, coliseum, province **10** hippodrome **12** amphitheater *level:* **4** tier

Ares Roman counterpart: 4 Mars *consort:* **9** Aphrodite *father:* **4** Zeus *mother:* **4** Enyo, Hera *sister:* **4** Eris *son:* **5** Remus **7** Romulus

arête 5 crest, ridge

Arethusa 5 nymph **6** spring **9** wood nymph *pursuer:* **7** Alpheus

argent 6 silver **7** silvern, silvery **9** whiteness

Argentina capital: 11 Buenos Aires *city:* **6** Paraná **7** Córdoba, La Plata, Rosario, Santa Fe **11** Mar del Plata *desert:* **9** Patagonia *language:* **7** Spanish *leader:* **5** Perón (Juan) *monetary unit:* **4** peso *mountain, range:* **5** Andes **9** Aconcagua *neighbor:* **5** Chile **6** Brazil **7** Bolivia, Uruguay **8** Paraguay *plain:* **6** Pampas *river:* **5** Plata (Río de la) **6** Paraná **8** Colorado **12** Río de la Plata *volcano:* **5** Maipo **9** Tupungato

Arges 7 Cyclops *brother:* **7** Brontes **8** Steropes *father:* **6** Uranus *mother:* **4** Gaea

argon symbol 2 Ar

Argonaut 4 hero **10** adventurer **13** paper nautilus *leader:* **5** Jason

argosy 4 ship **5** fleet **6** armada, supply **8** flotilla

argot 4 cant **5** idiom, lingo, slang **6** jargon, patois, patter **7** dialect **10** vernacular

arguable 4 moot **7** dubious **8** doubtful **9** debatable, in dispute, uncertain **10** disputable **11** contestable, problematic **12** questionable

argue 5 claim, clash, prove **6** assert, attest, bicker, debate, differ, induce, object, reason **7** agitate, canvass, contend, discuss, dispute, dissent, justify, protest, quarrel, quibble, stickle, testify, witness, wrangle **8** announce, conflict, consider, disagree, indicate, maintain, persuade, polemize, squabble **9** thrash out **10** polemicize **11** expostulate, remonstrate

argument 3 row **4** case, feud, flap, fuss **5** claim, proof, set-to, theme, topic **6** debate, dustup, hassle, motive, reason, rumpus, thesis **7** defense, dispute, polemic, sorites, subject, summary, wrangle **8** abstract, evidence, rebuttal **9** amplitude, assertion, discourse **10** contention, discussion, dissension, squabbling **11** controversy, disputation, embroilment **12** disagreement

argumentation 6 debate **7** dispute, oratory **8** forensic, rhetoric **9** dialectic, reasoning **10** discussion **11** controversy, disputation

argumentative 4 moot **9** in dispute, litigious, polemical **11** contentious, quarrelsome **12** disputatious, questionable **13** controversial

Argus *father:* **4** Zeus *mother:* **5** Niobe *slayer:* **6** Hermes

Argus-eyed 5 alert **8** watchful **9** all-seeing

argyle 4 sock **6** design **7** diamond, pattern **8** Campbell

aria 3 air, lay **4** hymn, lied, solo, song, tune **5** ditty **6** melody **7** descant

Ariadne *father:* **5** Minos *husband:* **7** Theseus *island home:* **5** Naxos *mother:* **8** Pasiphaë

arid 3 dry **4** drab, dull, sere **5** dusty, vapid **6** barren, boring, desert, dreary, jejune **7** bone-dry, insipid, parched, sterile, tedious, thirsty **8** droughty, lifeless, weariful **9** dry-asdust, infertile, unwatered, waterless, wearisome **10** lackluster, spiritless, unfruitful **12** moistureless **13** uninteresting

Ariel 6 spirit *master:* **8** Prospero

Aries 3 ram **13** constellation

aright 4 well **5** fitly **6** justly, nicely **8** decently, properly **9** correctly, fittingly, precisely **10** accurately, decorously

Ariosto *epic* **14** Orlando Furioso

arise 4 go up, lift, soar, wake **5** awake, begin, get up, issue, mount, occur, start **6** appear, ascend, aspire, come up, crop up, emerge, spring, uprear, wake up **7** emanate, proceed **8** commence **9** originate

Aristaeus *father:* **6** Apollo *mother:* **6** Cyrene *son:* **7** Actaeon *wife:* **7** Autonoë

aristocracy 5 elite, state **6** gentry, jet set **7** who's who **8** nobility, noblesse **9** beau

monde, blue blood, gentility, haut monde **10** government, patricians, patriciate, upper class, upper crust

aristocrat 9 blue blood, gentleman, patrician *ancient Greek:* **8** eupatrid *Russian:* **5** boyar **6** boyard

aristocratic 5 aloof, elite, noble **6** lordly **7** courtly, elegant, genteel, haughty, refined, stately **8** highborn, well-born, well-bred **9** dignified, exclusive, patrician **10** privileged, upper-class, upper-crust **11** blue-blooded

Aristophanes *play* **5** Birds (The), Frogs (The), Wasps (The) **6** Clouds (The), Plutus **10** Lysistrata

arithmetic 4 math **8** addition, counting, figuring **9** ciphering, reckoning **10** estimation **11** calculation, computation, mathematics

Arizona *capital:* **7** Phoenix *city:* **4** Mesa, Yuma **5** Tempe **6** Bisbee, Sedona, Tucson **8** Glendale, Prescott **9** Flagstaff **10** Scottsdale *mountain:* **9** Humphreys (Peak) *nickname:* **11** Grand Canyon (State) *park:* **15** Petrified Forest *river:* **4** Gila, Salt **8** Colorado *state bird:* **10** cactus wren *state flower:* **7** saguaro (cactus) *state tree:* **9** palo verde

ark 3 den **4** ship **5** chest, haven **6** adytum, asylum, refuge **7** convent, retreat, shelter **8** hideaway **9** safe house, sanctuary **10** repository, Torah chest *landfall:* **6** Ararat *wood:* **6** gopher **7** cypress

Arkansas *capital:* **10** Little Rock *city:* **4** Hope **9** Fort Smith, Pine Bluff **10** Hot Springs **11** Bentonville **12** Fayetteville *mountain, range:* **5** Ozark **8** Magazine *nickname:* **17** Land of Opportunity *river:* **3** Red *state bird:* **11** mockingbird *state flower:* **12** apple blossom *state tree:* **12** loblolly pine

arm 3 bay, ell, gun, rig **4** cove, gear, gulf, limb, wing **5** annex, bayou, equip, firth, force, inlet, power **6** fit out, harbor, muscle, outfit, slough, weapon **7** appoint, furnish, turn out **8** accouter, strength **9** extension *bone:* **4** ulna **6** radius **7** humerus *combining form:* **6** brachi **7** brachio *muscle:* **6** biceps **7** triceps

armada 4 navy **5** boats, fleet, force, group, ships **7** vessels **8** flotilla, warships

armadillo 4 apar, peba, tatu *relative:* **5** sloth **8** anteater, tamandua

armament 4 arms **5** armor **6** weapon **7** defense **8** ordnance, security, weaponry **9** munitions, safeguard **10** ammunition, protection

armamentarium 4 fund **5** stock, store **6** supply **9** inventory

armchair 6 remote **8** fauteuil **9** vicarious **11** theoretical

armed forces 4 army, navy **6** troops **7** marines **8** air force, military **10** servicemen
Armenia *capital:* **7** Yerevan *city:* **6** Gyumri **8** Vanadzor *lake:* **5** Sevan *monetary unit:* **4** dram *mountain, range:* **7** Aragats **8** Caucasus *neighbor:* **4** Iran **6** Turkey **7** Georgia **10** Azerbaijan *river:* **5** Araks
armistice 5 truce **9** agreement, cease-fire **10** suspension
armor 4 mail **5** aegis, cover, guard **6** shield **7** buckler **8** security **9** safeguard **10** protection *arm:* **8** brassard *body:* **7** cuirass *armpit:* **8** pallette *buttocks:* **5** culet *coat:* **7** hauberk **10** brigandine *face:* **5** visor **6** beaver *flexible:* **4** mail *foot:* **8** solleret *hand:* **7** gantlet **8** gauntlet *head:* **6** helmet *horse:* **4** bard **5** barde **8** chamfron *leg:* **6** greave **7** jambeau *mail:* **4** coif **7** hauberk *suit:* **7** panoply *thigh:* **4** tace **5** tasse **6** cuisse, tuille *throat:* **6** gorget
armory 4 dump **5** depot, plant, range, store **7** arsenal, factory **8** magazine **10** collection, storehouse
armpit 6 axilla **8** underarm *Scottish:* **5** oxter
arms 7 ensigns, warfare **8** weaponry
army 4 host **5** flock, horde **6** legion **7** militia **9** multitude *combat arm:* **5** armor **8** infantry **9** artillery *commission:* **6** brevet **7** reserve *Fort:* **3** Dix, Lee, Ord **4** Drum, Hood, Knox, Myer, Polk, Sill **5** Bliss, Bragg, Irwin, Lewis, McCoy, Meade, Riley, Story **6** Carson, Eustis, Gillem, Gordon, Greely, McNair, Monroe, Rucker **7** Belvoir, Benning, Detrick, Jackson, Ritchie, Shafter, Stewart **8** Buchanan, Campbell, Hamilton, Holabird, Huachuca, Monmouth **9** McClellan, McPherson **10** Richardson, Sam Houston, Wainwright **11** Leavenworth *law enforcer:* **2** MP *mascot:* **4** mule *meal:* **3** MRE **4** chow, mess *mine layer:* **6** sapper *NCO:* **8** corporal, sergeant *officer:* **5** major **7** captain, colonel, general, warrant **10** lieutenant *post:* **4** base, camp, fort *postal abbreviation:* **3** APO *ration:* **3** MRE *relating to:* **7** martial **8** military *school:* **3** OCS, OTS **7** academy **9** West Point *signaler:* **6** bugler *store:* **2** PX **10** commissary **12** post exchange *unit:* **5** corps, squad, troop **7** brigade, cavalry, company, platoon **8** division, regiment **9** battalion *vehicle:* **4** jeep, tank **6** Abrams, Humvee **7** Bradley **9** half-track
Arnaz, Desi *character:* **5** Ricky (Ricardo) *company:* **6** Desilu *mentor:* **6** Cougat (Xavier) *signature song:* **6** Babalu *star of:* **9** I Love Lucy *wife:* **4** Ball (Lucille), Lucy
aroma 4 balm, odor **5** scent, smell, spice **6**

flavor **7** bouquet, incense, perfume **9** fragrance, redolence
aromatic 5 balmy, spicy, sweet **6** savory **7** odorous, perfumy, pungent, scented **8** fragrant, perfumed, redolent **9** ambrosial
around 4 near, nigh **5** about, circa **6** nearby **7** through *prefix:* **4** ambi, peri **5** amphi **6** circum
around-the-clock 8 constant, unending **9** ceaseless, continual, incessant, perpetual, unceasing **10** continuous **11** unremitting **13** uninterrupted
arouse 4 fire, stir, wake, whet **5** alert, awake, pique, rally, waken **6** awaken, bestir, excite, fire up, foment, incite, kindle, work up **7** agitate, inflame **9** challenge, stimulate
arraign 3 tax, try **5** blame **6** accuse, charge, indict, summon **9** criminate, inculpate **11** incriminate
arrange 4 plan, sort **5** adapt, array, chart, order, score, unify **6** assort, codify, deploy, design, devise, lay out, line up, map out, scheme, set out, settle **7** dispose, marshal, prepare, work out **8** organize, sequence **9** blueprint, harmonize, integrate, methodize **10** bring about, categorize, instrument, symphonize, synthesize **11** choreograph, orchestrate, systematize
arrangement 5 array, order, setup **6** format, layout, lineup, series **8** grouping, ordering, sequence **9** structure **10** adaptation, deployment **11** disposition **12** distribution *floral:* **4** posy **7** bouquet, garland
arrant 4 rank **5** gross, total, utter **6** brassy, brazen **7** blatant, extreme, flat-out **8** absolute, complete, impudent, infernal, overbold **9** barefaced, downright, egregious, out-and-out, shameless, unabashed **10** immoderate, unblushing
arras 6 screen **7** drapery **8** curtains, tapestry
array 3 lot **4** clad, garb, pomp, show **5** adorn, batch, bunch, clump, dress, group, order **6** attire, bundle, clothe, draw up, finery, lineup, parade **7** apparel, arrange, cluster, display, dispose, garment, marshal, militia, panoply, raiment, variety **8** clothing, decorate, enclothe, organize, spectrum **9** formation **10** assortment **11** systematize
arrears 3 due **4** debt **5** claim, debit **7** deficit **9** liability **10** balance due, obligation **12** indebtedness
arrest 3 nab, tab, tag **4** bust, grab, halt, hold, jail, slow, snag, stay, stem, stop **5** block, catch, check, pinch, run in, seize, stall **6** collar, detain, haul in, lock up, pick up, pull in, retard, take in **7** capture, contain, seizure **8** imprison, obstruct, restrain **9** apprehend,

detention, interrupt **11** incarcerate **12** apprehension

arresting 6 marked, signal **7** salient **8** striking **9** affective, appealing, prominent **10** attractive, compelling, enchanting, impressive, noticeable, remarkable **11** conspicuous, eye-catching, outstanding

arrival 6 advent, coming **7** landing, success **8** entrance, incoming **9** emergence **10** appearance

arrive 4 come, land, show **5** get in, get to, reach **6** appear, show up, thrive, turn up **7** prosper, succeed **8** flourish

arriviste 7 parvenu, upstart **8** roturier **12** nouveau riche

arrogance 3 ego **4** airs, gall **5** brass, cheek, pride **6** hubris **7** conceit, disdain, hauteur **8** self-love **11** loftiness **11** haughtiness

arrogant 5 cocky, proud **6** lordly, snooty **7** haughty, pompous **8** cavalier, fastuous, insolent, superior **9** egotistic **10** disdainful, high-handed, peremptory **11** domineering, magisterial, overbearing **12** supercilious **13** high-and-mighty, self-important

arrogate 4 grab, take **5** annex, claim, seize, usurp **6** assume, demand **7** ascribe, preempt **8** accroach, take over **9** sequester **10** commandeer, confiscate **11** appropriate, expropriate

arrow 4 dart **5** shaft *poison:* **4** inée, upas **6** curare

arrowroot 5 plant, tuber **6** starch **7** coontie

Arrowsmith's wife 5 Leora

arroyo 3 gap **4** draw **5** brook, chasm, cleft, clove, creek, gorge, gulch, gully **6** coulee, ravine **7** channel **11** watercourse

Ars Amatoria poet 4 Ovid

arsenal 4 dump **5** depot, stock, store **6** armory, supply **7** factory, weapons **8** magazine, ordnance **9** stockpile **10** depository, repertoire, repository, storehouse

arsenic symbol 2 As

arson 6 firing **8** torching **9** pyromania **12** incendiarism

arsonist 5 firer, torch **7** firebug **10** incendiary

art 5 craft, skill **6** métier **7** finesse, know-how **8** artifice, painting, vocation **9** dexterity, expertise, sculpture **10** handicraft *botanical:* **6** bonsai *faddish:* **6** kitsch *style:* **2** op **3** pop **4** dada **6** cubist, rococo **7** fauvist, realist, surreal **8** abstract, futurist **9** classical **10** naturalist, surrealist **12** naturalistic, surrealistic **13** expressionist, impressionist

art deco 5 style **6** design *designer:* **4** Erté

Artemis *Roman counterpart:* 5 Diana *birthplace:* **5** Delos *brother:* **6** Apollo *father:* **4** Zeus *mother:* **4** Leto *priestess:* **9** Iphigenia

artery 3 way **4** duct, line, path, road, tube **5** aorta, track **6** avenue, course, street, vessel **7** carotid, channel, conduit, highway, passage, pathway **8** coronary **9** boulevard **12** thoroughfare

artful 3 sly **4** foxy, wily **5** adept, sharp, slick, smart, suave **6** adroit, astute, clever, crafty, shrewd, smooth, tricky **7** cunning **8** guileful, skillful **9** dexterous, ingenious **10** artificial, diplomatic

arthropod 3 bee, fly **4** crab, mite, moth, tick **6** beetle, insect, shrimp, spider **7** lobster **8** arachnid, barnacle, diplopod, myriapod, scorpion **9** butterfly, centipede, cockroach, millipede, trilobite **10** crustacean *body segment:* **6** somite, telson **8** metamere

Arthur see **King Arthur**

article 2 an **3** the **4** bind, item, part **5** essay, paper, piece, point, theme, thing **6** matter, object **7** element, feature, passage, section **10** particular **11** composition, stipulation *French:* **3** les, une *German:* **3** das, dem, den, der, des, die, ein **4** eine *Spanish:* **2** un **3** las, los, una

articled 5 bound **10** indentured

articulate 4 say **4** join, link, oral, talk **5** clear, hinge, joint, lucid, shape, speak, state, utter, vocal, voice **6** couple, fluent, prolix, relate, spoken, voiced **7** connect, express, jointed **8** coherent, definite, distinct, eloquent, vocalize **9** effective, enunciate, harmonize, integrate, pronounce, verbalize **10** coordinate, expressive **11** concatenate **12** intelligible, smooth-spoken

artifact 5 curio, relic **6** legacy, rarity, trophy **7** remnant, spin-off, vestige **8** creation, heirloom **9** by-product, handcraft, handiwork **10** handicraft **11** contrivance, fabrication

artifice 4 play, ploy, ruse, wile **5** craft, feint, guile, skill, trick **6** deceit, device, gambit **7** cunning, slyness **8** facility, foxiness, trickery, wiliness **9** adeptness, canniness, chicanery, duplicity, ingenuity, stratagem **10** adroitness, artfulness, cleverness, craftiness

artificial 4 fake, faux, mock, sham **5** bogus, dummy, faked, false, phony, put-on **6** ersatz, forced, hollow, unreal **7** assumed, feigned, in vitro, labored, man-made, plastic, pretend **8** affected, mannered, spurious **9** contrived, imitation, insincere, simulated, synthetic, unnatural **10** fabricated, factitious, fictitious, substitute

artillery 4 arms **5** canon, force **6** rocket **7** battery, bazooka, gunnery, weapons **8** cannonry, howitzer, ordnance, weaponry **9** munitions

artisan 6 worker **7** builder, workman **8** producer **9** carpenter, craftsman **12** craftsperson

artist 7 painter **8** sculptor, virtuoso *garb:* **5** smock *knife:* **7** spatula *medium:* **4** oil **5** paint **6** pastel **7** tempera **8** charcoal **10** watercolor *pigment board:* **7** palette *stand:* **5** easel *workshop:* **6** studio **7** atelier (see also **painter**)

artless 4 free, open, pure, true **5** crude, naive, plain **6** direct, honest, simple **7** genuine, natural, sincere, unaware **8** trusting **9** childlike, guileless, ingenuous, unstudied **10** aboveboard, forthright, unaffected, uncultured, unschooled **12** unartificial, unsuspicious

Art of Love poet 4 Ovid

arty 5 showy **6** pseudo **8** affected, imposing **9** overblown **11** pretentious **12** high-sounding

Aruba capital: 10 Oranjestad *language:* **5** Dutch **10** Papiamento *monetary unit:* **6** florin *part of:* **11** Netherlands

as 3 for, who **4** coin, like, that, when **5** being, since, which, while **6** though **7** because **11** considering, for instance

ASAP 4 stat **6** at once **11** immediately

as a rule 6 mainly, mostly **7** usually **8** commonly **9** generally **10** frequently, ordinarily

Ascanius 5 Iulus *father:* **6** Aeneas

ascend 4 go up, lift, rise, soar **5** arise, climb, crest, mount, scale **6** aspire, move up, occupy **7** lift off, take off **8** escalade, escalate, surmount

ascendancy 4 rule **5** power, reign **7** command, control, mastery **8** dominion **9** authority, dominance, influence, supremacy **10** domination, prepotency **11** preeminence, sovereignty **13** preponderance

ascendant 6 master, rising **7** regnant **8** ancestor, dominant, forebear, relative, superior **9** paramount, precursor, prevalent, sovereign **10** commanding, forefather, forerunner, prevailing, progenitor **11** controlling, overbearing, predecessor, predominant, predominate **12** preponderant, primogenitor

ascension 4 rise **6** rising **7** going up, scaling **8** climbing, mounting

ascent 4 ramp, rise **5** climb, grade, slope **6** rising **7** advance, incline **8** gradient, progress **9** acclivity, elevation, uplifting

ascertain 5 learn **7** catch on, find out, unearth **8** discover, make sure **9** determine, establish, figure out

ascetic 5 stoic **6** hermit, severe **7** austere, eremite, recluse **9** abstinent, anchoress, anchorite, mortified **10** abstemious, astringent, forbearing, restrained **11** disciplined, selfdenying *ancient Hebrew:* **6** Essene *Bud-*

dhist: **5** bonze *early Christian:* **7** stylite *Hindu:* **4** yogi **5** fakir, sadhu, Yogin *Muslim:* **4** Sufi

Asclepius see **Aesculapius**

ascribe 3 lay **4** cite **5** infer, refer **6** assign, charge, credit, impute **7** chalk up **8** accredit **9** attribute, reference **10** conjecture

Asenath husband: **6** Joseph *son:* **7** Ephraim **8** Manasseh

aseptic 4 cool, flat **5** clean **7** sterile **8** germfree, hygienic, sanitary **9** unfeeling **10** restrained, sterilized **11** emotionless, unemotional

asexual 6 agamic

as for 4 in re **5** about, anent **7** apropos **9** regarding **10** concerning, respecting **12** with regard to

as good as 4 nigh **6** all but, almost, nearly **8** in effect, well-nigh **9** basically, in essence, just about, virtually **11** essentially, practically

ash 4 soot, tree, wood **7** cinders, residue **8** clinkers

ashamed 6 abased, abject, guilty **7** abashed, humbled **8** contrite, penitent **9** chagrined, mortified, repentant **10** humiliated **11** discomfited, embarrassed

ashen 3 wan **4** gray, pale **5** faded, pasty, waxen **6** doughy, pallid, sallow, sickly **7** ghostly **8** blanched, bleached **9** bloodless, colorless **10** corpselike

Asher daughter: **5** Serah *father:* **5** Jacob *mother:* **6** Zilpah *son:* **4** Isui **6** Beriah, Ishuah, Jimnah

ashes 5 ruins **6** pallor **7** remains

ashy 3 wan **4** drab, pale **5** livid, waxen **6** doughy, leaden, pallid **7** ghastly, greyish **8** blanched **9** bloodless, colorless, washed-out **10** cadaverous

Asia country: **4** Laos **5** Burma, China, India, Japan, Korea, Nepal **6** Bhutan, Russia, Taiwan **7** Armenia, Georgia, Myanmar, Vietnam **8** Cambodia, Malaysia, Mongolia, Pakistan, Sri Lanka, Thailand **9** Indonesia, Kampuchea, Kazakstan, Singapore **10** Azerbaijan, Bangladesh, Kazakhstan, Kyrgyzstan, North Korea, South Korea, Tajikistan, Uzbekistan **11** Afghanistan, Philippines **12** Turkmenistan *ethnic group:* **3** Han, Lao, Tai **4** Arab, Kurd, Moor, Shan **5** Karen, Khmer, Malay, Tajik, Tamil, Uzbek **6** Burman, Lepcha, Manchu, Mongol, Sindhi **7** Baluchi, Bengali, Persian, Punjabi, Tibetan **8** Armenian, Assyrian, Javanese **9** Dravidian, Indo-Aryan, Sinhalese **10** Circassian, Montagnard, Singhalese *language:* **3** Lao **4** Ainu, Urdu **5** Hindi, Malay, Tamil,

Uzbek **6** Arabic, Bahasa, Korean, Nepali **7** Bengali, Burmese, Khalkha, Kurdish, Persian, Tibetan, Turkish **8** Armenian, Japanese, Javanese, Mandarin **9** Cambodian **10** Vietnamese

Asia Minor 8 Anatolia *country:* **6** Turkey *region:* **5** Ionia

Asian inland sea 4 Aral

Asian Sasquatch 4 yeti

aside 4 away **5** apart **7** tangent **8** away from **9** in reserve, privately **10** digression, discursion **11** parenthesis

aside from 3 bar, but **4** save **6** bating, except **7** barring, besides **9** excepting, excluding, other than, outside of

Asimov, Isaac *forte:* **5** sci-fi *work:* **6** I Robot **9** Nightfall **10** Foundation (Trilogy)

asinine 5 crazy, daffy, silly **6** absurd, simple **7** fatuous, foolish, idiotic, puerile, witless **8** mindless **9** brainless **10** irrational, ridiculous **11** nonsensical

ask 3 beg, bid **4** pray, quiz, seek **5** crave, exact, grill, plead, query **6** appeal, demand, desire, invite **7** beseech, call for, canvass, consult, enquire, entreat, examine, implore, inquire, request, require, solicit **8** petition, question **9** catechize, importune **10** supplicate **11** interrogate *Scottish:* **5** speer, speir

askance 8 sidelong, sideways **9** cynically, obliquely **10** critically, doubtfully, doubtingly, scornfully **11** skeptically **12** suspiciously **13** distrustfully, mistrustfully

asker 6 beggar, prayer, suitor **7** speaker **9** suppliant **10** petitioner, questioner, supplicant **11** supplicator

askew 4 awry **6** turned **8** cockeyed **9** crookedly

aslant 4 awry **5** askew **7** crooked **8** cockeyed, sideways, sidewise **9** obliquely

asleep 4 dead, idle, numb **5** inert **6** dozing, numbed **7** defunct, dormant, napping **8** benumbed, deadened, inactive, in repose, not alert, sluggish **9** senseless, unfeeling **10** insensible, slumbering, unanimated **11** indifferent, unconscious **12** anesthetized

as long as 3 for **5** since **6** seeing **7** because, whereas **8** provided **11** considering **12** provided that

as much as 6 all but, almost **8** well-nigh **11** essentially, practically

aspect 3 air **4** look, mien, side **5** angle, facet, phase, scene, slant **6** regard, status **7** bearing, seeming **8** exposure, position **9** direction **10** appearance **11** perspective

aspen 4 tree **6** poplar

asperity 5 rigor **8** acerbity, acrimony, grimness, hardness, hardship, mordancy, severity, tartness **9** harshness, roughness, sharpness **10** bitterness, difficulty, unevenness **12** irregularity, irritability

asperse 4 slur **5** libel, smear, sully **6** attack, defame, insult, malign, vilify **7** baptize, slander, tarnish, traduce **8** bad mouth, dishonor, sprinkle **9** denigrate, insinuate **10** calumniate

aspersion 4 muck, slam, slur **5** abuse **7** calumny, obloquy, slander **9** invective, stricture **10** defamation, detraction **11** denigration **12** vilification, vituperation **13** animadversion

asphalt 4 pave **7** bitumen, surface **8** blacktop, pavement

asphyxiate 4 kill **5** choke, drown **6** stifle **7** smother **8** strangle, throttle **9** suffocate

aspirant 6 seeker **7** hopeful, seeking **9** applicant, candidate, contender

aspiration 3 aim **4** goal, urge, wish **5** dream **6** desire, intent, object **7** craving, longing, passion, pursuit **8** ambition, striving, yearning **9** breathing, objective **10** pretension **13** ambitiousness

aspire 3 aim, try **4** long, pant, rise, seek, soar, want, wish **5** arise, mount, yearn **6** ascend, desire, hunger, strive, thirst

aspiring 7 longing, seeking, wanting, wishful **8** striving, vaulting, yearning **9** ambitious

as regards 4 in re **7** apropos **8** touching **10** concerning, respecting

ass 4 dolt, fool, jerk, moke, mule **5** burro, dunce, idiot **6** donkey, nitwit **8** bonehead, imbecile **10** nincompoop *female:* **5** jenny *male:* **4** jack *wild Asian:* **5** kiang **6** onager

assai 4 very

assail 4 bash, beat **5** abuse, beset, blast, pound, storm **6** attack, berate, buffet, charge, fall on, malign, oppugn, pummel, revile, strike, vilify **7** assault, bombard **8** fall upon, lambaste **9** break down

assassin 3 gun **5** bravo **6** gunman, hit man, killer **7** torpedo **8** murderer **9** cutthroat **10** hatchet man, triggerman *of Caesar:* **6** Brutus **7** Cassius *of Garfield:* **7** Guiteau (Charles Julius) *of J. F. Kennedy:* **6** Oswald (Lee Harvey) *of M. L. King:* **3** Ray (James Earl) *of Lincoln:* **5** Booth (John Wilkes) *of Marat:* **6** Corday (Charlotte) *of McKinley:* **8** Czolgosz (Leon) *of R. F. Kennedy:* **6** Sirhan (Sirhan)

assassinate 4 do in, kill, slay **6** finish, murder, rub out **7** bump off, execute, gun down, put away, take out **8** dispatch, knock off **9** eliminate, liquidate

assault 3 mug, war **4** raid **5** beset, fight, onset, set-to, storm **6** assail, attack, charge, fall on, strike, threat **7** aggress, besiege, mugging, offense **8** fall upon, invasion, storming **9** incursion, offensive, onslaught, violation **10** aggression

assay 3 try **4** rate, seek, test **5** judge, offer, prove, trial, value, weigh **6** assess, result, rating, strive, survey **7** analyze, attempt, examine, inspect, measure, valuate, venture **8** analysis, appraise, endeavor, estimate, evaluate, struggle **9** appraisal, undertake, valuation **10** assessment, evaluation, inspection **11** examination, measurement

assemblage 5 crowd, group **6** muster **7** company, turnout **8** audience **9** gathering **10** collection **11** aggregation, composition, convergence **12** congregation

assemble 4 call, form, make, mass, meet, mold **5** amass, build, clump, group, shape, unite **6** gather, muster, summon **7** cluster, collect, convene, convoke, fashion, marshal, produce, round up **8** congress, contrive **9** aggregate, forgather **10** accumulate, congregate **11** fit together, manufacture, put together **12** call together, come together **13** bring together

assembly 4 bevy **5** bunch, covey, crowd, flock, group, party, plena (plural), rally, set-up **6** muster, plenum, troupe **7** cluster, meeting **8** conclave **9** congeries, gathering **10** collection **11** association, fabrication, get-together, manufacture **12** congregation, construction *American Indian:* **6** powwow *ancient Greek:* **8** ecclesia *ancient Roman:* **7** comitia *Anglo-Saxon:* **4** moot **5** gemot **6** gemote **8** folkmoot, folkmote *ecclesiastical:* **5** synod **10** consistory *legislative:* **4** diet **6** senate **8** congress **10** parliament *place:* **4** hall, room **5** agora **10** auditorium *Russian:* **4** duma *witches':* **6** sabbat **7** sabbath

assent 2 OK **3** nod, yes, yup **4** okay, yeah **5** agree, uh-huh **6** accede, accord, concur, say yes **7** approve, consent, embrace **8** approval, sanction, thumbs-up **9** accession, acquiesce, admission, agreement, subscribe **10** acceptance, permission **11** affirmation, concurrence **12** acquiescence

assert 3 say **4** aver, avow **5** argue, claim, posit, state, utter, voice **6** adduce, affirm, allege, attest, avouch, defend, depose, insist, submit **7** advance, contend, declare, express, justify, profess, protest, publish, warrant **8** announce, maintain, proclaim **9** broadcast, postulate, predicate **10** promulgate

assertion 6 avowal **8** averment **9** affidavit, statement **10** allegation, avouchment, contention, deposition, disclosure, insistence,

profession **11** affirmation, attestation, declaration **12** asseveration **13** pronouncement

assertive 4 firm, sure **5** pushy **6** strong **7** assured, certain, decided, pushing **8** cocksure, emphatic, forceful, positive **9** confident, energetic, insistent **10** aggressive, resounding **11** affirmative, distinctive, self-assured **13** self-confident

assess 3 fix, tax **4** deem, levy, rate **5** assay, exact, judge, put on, set at, value, weigh **6** charge, figure, impose, reckon, survey **7** account, compute, subject, valuate **8** appraise, consider, estimate, evaluate **9** determine

assessment 3 fee, tax **4** duty, levy, toll **6** charge, impost, rating, tariff **8** estimate, judgment **9** appraisal, valuation **10** estimation, evaluation **12** appraisement

asset 4 boon, good, plus **5** merit **6** credit **7** benefit **8** blessing, resource **9** advantage **11** distinction *opposite:* **9** liability

assets 5 items, means, money **6** wealth **7** capital **8** bankroll, holdings, property **9** resources, valuables **11** possessions

asseverate 4 aver, avow **5** state **6** affirm, assert, attest, avouch, depose, insist **7** certify, contend, declare, profess **8** maintain, proclaim **9** pronounce

assiduous 4 busy **5** eager **6** active **7** moiling, zealous **8** diligent, sedulous, tireless **9** attentive, laborious **10** persistent, unflagging **11** hard-working, industrious **13** indefatigable

assiduously 4 hard **6** busily **9** earnestly, intensely **10** diligently, thoroughly **11** intensively **12** exhaustively, meticulously, persistently **13** painstakingly, unremittingly

assign 3 fix, lay, set **4** cede, deed, give, name **5** allot, allow, refer **6** charge, convey, credit, define, impute, remise, settle **7** appoint, ascribe, chalk up, earmark, lay down, mete out, specify, station **8** accredit, allocate, delegate, make over, relegate, sign over, transfer **9** admeasure, apportion, attribute, designate, establish, prescribe **10** pigeonhole

assignation 4 date **5** tryst **7** meeting **9** allotment **10** engagement, rendezvous **11** appointment, get-together

assignee 5 agent, proxy **6** deputy, factor **7** officer **8** attorney, delegate

assignment 3 job **4** beat, duty, post, task, work **5** chore, stint **6** office **8** homework, position, transfer **9** allotment **10** allocation, delegation, obligation **11** designation

assimilate 5 adapt, adopt, grasp, learn, liken, match **6** absorb, adjust, digest, equate, imbibe, soak up, take in, take up **7** blend in, compare, conform **8** parallel **10** comprehend, understand **11** incorporate

assimilation 8 taking in **9** awareness **10** absorption, conversion **11** mindfulness, recognition **12** apperception **13** consciousness, incorporation

assist 3 aid **4** abet, back, help, lift **5** boost, do for, serve, stead **6** relief, succor **7** backing, benefit, comfort, help out, secours, service, support, work for **8** benefact, work with **9** accompany, cooperate, open doors

assistance 3 aid **4** hand, help, lift **5** boost **6** relief, succor **7** backing, benefit, comfort, secours, service, subsidy, support **8** abetment **9** upholding **10** subvention, supporting **11** cooperation

assistant 3 aid **4** aide, ally, help **5** aider **6** backer, backup, deputy, flunky, helper, second **7** acolyte, ancilla, orderly **8** adjutant, henchman **9** attendant, auxiliary, coadjutor **10** accomplice, aide-de-camp, coadjutant, lieutenant **12** right-hand man

assistive 6 aiding, useful **7** helpful **10** beneficial **11** serviceable

assize 3 law **4** rule, writ **5** canon, edict **6** decree **7** finding, inquest, precept, statute, verdict **8** standard **9** ordinance, prescript **10** regulation

associate 3 pal **4** ally, chum, join, link, mate, pair, yoke **5** blend, buddy, crony, group, match, merge, unite **6** cohort, comate, couple, fellow, friend, hobnob, relate, worker **7** bracket, combine, compeer, comrade, conjoin, connect, consort, partner **8** confrere, coworker, employee, familiar, federate, identify, intimate **9** affiliate, bedfellow, colleague, companion, confidant, copartner, secondary **10** accomplice, amalgamate, compatriot, complement, confidante **11** concomitant, confederate, correlative **12** acquaintance **13** accompaniment

association 3 tie **4** band, bloc, bond, clan, club, crew, hint, tong **5** group, guild, order, tie-up, union **6** hookup, league **7** circuit, concert, linkage, linking, society **8** alliance, congress, overtone, relation, sodality, teamwork **9** coalition, undertone **10** conference, connection, federation, fellowship, fraternity, mental link, suggestion **11** affiliation, brotherhood, combination, conjunction, connotation, cooperation, implication, partnership **12** conjointment, organization, relationship, togetherness **13** collaboration

assort 5 class, group, order **6** codify, divide **7** arrange **8** classify, stratify **9** associate, designate, harmonize, methodize **10** categorize, distribute, pigeonhole **11** systematize

assorted 4 like **5** mixed **6** fitted, motley, suited, sundry, varied **7** adapted, diverse, matched, similar, various **9** different **11** diversified, conformable **12** conglomerate, multifarious **13** heterogeneous, miscellaneous

assortment 4 olio **5** array, group **6** choice, jumble, medley **7** mélange, mixture, variety **8** mishmash, mixed bag, pastiche **9** diversity, potpourri, selection **10** collection, hodgepodge, miscellany **11** gallimaufry

assuage 4 calm, cool, ease **5** allay, quiet **6** lessen, pacify, quench, reduce, soften, soothe, temper **7** appease, lighten, mollify, placate, relieve, sweeten **8** decrease, mitigate, moderate **9** alleviate **10** conciliate, propitiate

as such 5 per se **8** by itself **9** in essence, virtually **11** essentially **13** fundamentally, intrinsically

assumably 6 likely, surely **7** no doubt **8** probably **9** doubtless **10** most likely, presumably

assume 3 act, don **4** fake, sham, take **5** adopt, bluff, feign, posit, put on, seize, usurp **6** affect, draw on, expect, reckon, slip on, take in, take on, take up **7** believe, imagine, preempt, premise, presume, pretend, receive, suppose, suspect **8** accroach, arrogate, shoulder, simulate, take over **9** postulate, undertake **10** commandeer, presuppose, understand **11** appropriate, counterfeit

assumed 4 fake, sham **5** bogus, false, given, put on, tacit **6** made-up, phoney **7** feigned **8** affected, delusory, putative, spurious, supposed **9** deceptive, pretended, simulated **10** artificial, fictitious

assumption 5 posit **6** belief, thesis **7** conceit, premise, seizure, surmise **8** takeover **9** arrogance, postulate **10** acceptance, arrogation, conjecture, pretension, usurpation **11** expectation, supposition, undertaking **13** appropriation

assurance 3 say **4** oath, word **5** nerve, sayso, troth **6** aplomb, parole, pledge, safety, surety **7** promise, support, warrant **8** audacity, boldness, safeness, security, sureness, temerity, warranty **9** assertion, brashness, certainty, certitude, cockiness, composure, guarantee, hardiness, self-trust **10** brazenness, confidence, conviction, equanimity, profession **11** affirmation, presumption

assure 4 aver **5** bet on, cinch, swear **6** affirm, attest, ensure, insure, pledge, secure, soothe **7** certify, comfort, confirm, promise, satisfy **8** convince, persuade **9** guarantee **11** make certain

assured 3 set **4** cool **5** fixed **6** secure **7** certain, decided, settled **8** clear-cut, composed, definite, positive, sanguine **9** assertive, collected, confident, undoubted, unruffled **10** guaranteed, pronounced **11** beyond doubt, made certain, unflappable **13** imperturbable, self-confident, self-satisfied

assuredly 9 certainly, doubtless **10** positively **11** confidently, undoubtedly, without fail

assuredness 6 surety **9** certainty, certitude **10** confidence, conviction

Assyria *capital:* **5** Calah **7** Nineveh *city:* **5** Ashur, Assur *god:* **3** Sin **4** Asur, Nabu **5** Ashur, Nusku **6** Tammuz **7** Ninurta *goddess:* **6** Ishtar *king:* **3** Pul **6** Sargon **11** Sennacherib, Shalmaneser **12** Ashurbanipal *language:* **7** Aramaic *queen:* **9** Semiramis *river:* **6** Tigris *writing:* **9** cuneiform

astatine *symbol* **2** At

asterisk 4 star **6** symbol **9** character

astern 3 aft **4** baft, rear, tail **5** abaft **6** back of, behind **8** backward, rearmost, rearward

asteroid 5 Ceres

Asterope *father:* **5** Atlas *mother:* **7** Pleione *sisters:* **8** Pleiades

asthma 7 allergy **8** disorder

as to 4 in re **5** about, anent **7** apropos **9** regarding **10** concerning, respecting **11** according to

astonish 4 daze, stun **5** amaze, floor, shock **7** astound, stagger, startle, stupefy **8** blow away, bowl over, confound, dumfound, surprise **9** dumbfound, take aback **11** flabbergast

astonishing 7 amazing **8** stunning, wondrous **9** marvelous, startling, wonderful **10** astounding, miraculous, prodigious, staggering, stupendous, surprising **11** spectacular **12** breathtaking

astonishment 3 awe **5** shock **6** wonder **8** surprise **9** amazement, confusion **10** perplexity, wonderment **12** bewilderment, stupefaction **13** consternation

astound 4 daze, stun **5** amaze, shock **7** confuse **8** astonish, bewilder, confound, dumfound, surprise **9** dumbfound, overwhelm, take aback **11** flabbergast

Astraea *father:* **4** Zeus **7** Jupiter *mother:* **6** Themis

astral 6 dreamy, starry **7** exalted, highest, stellar **8** elevated, sidereal **9** celestial, topdrawer, unworldly, visionary **10** top-ranking **11** high-ranking **12** otherworldly

astray 4 awry **5** amiss, badly, wrong **6** adrift, afield **7** in error **9** off course *lead:* **6** seduce

astride 8 bridging, spanning **10** on each side, straddling

astringent 4 acid, keen **5** acerb, acrid, harsh, sharp, stern **6** biting, bitter, severe, strict **7** acerbic, ascetic, austere, caustic, cutting, puckery, pungent, styptic **8** incisive, stinging **10** irritating **11** contracting **12** constrictive

astrolabe successor 7 sextant

astrologer 5 Dixon (Jeane), Faust **9** stargazer, Zoroaster **11** horoscopist, Nostradamus

astrological aspect 5 trine **7** sextile **8** quartile **10** opposition **11** conjunction

astronaut 4 Ride (Sally) **5** Glenn (John), White (Edward), Young (John) **6** Aldrin (Buzz), Cooper (Gordon), Lovell (James), Worden (Alfred) **7** Bluford (Guion), Collins (Michael), Gagarin (Yuri), Grissom (Gus), Jemison (Mae), Schirra (Walter), Shepard (Alan), Yegorov (Boris) **8** Stafford (Thomas) **9** Armstrong (Neil), Carpenter (Scott), McAuliffe (Christa) **10** Tereshkova (Valentina)

astronomer *American:* **3** See (Thomas Jefferson) **5** Sagan (Carl) **6** Hubble (Edwin), Lowell (Percival) **7** Langley (Samuel), Newcomb (Simon), Shapley (Harlow) **8** Bowditch (Nathaniel), Mitchell (Maria), Tombaugh (Clyde) **9** Pickering (Edward) **11** Schlesinger (Frank) *Austrian:* **13** Schwarzschild (Karl) *Danish:* **5** Brahe (Tycho) *Dutch:* **4** Oort (Jan Hendrik) **6** Sitter (Willem de) **7** Huygens (Christiaan) *English:* **4** Ryle (Martin), Wren (Christopher) **6** Halley (Edmond), Lovell (Bernard) **7** Lockyer (Joseph), Parsons (William) **8** Herschel (Caroline, John, William) *French:* **6** Picard (Jean) **7** Laplace (Pierre-Simon de), Messier (Charles) *German:* **4** Wolf (Maximilian) **5** Vogel (Hermann) **6** Bessel (Friedrich), Kepler (Johannes), Müller (Johann), Struve (Otto) *Greek:* **12** Eratosthenes *Italian:* **7** Galileo (Galilei) **12** Schiaparelli (Giovanni) *Persian:* **11** Omar Khayyám *Polish:* **10** Copernicus (Nicolaus) *Swedish:* **7** Celsius (Anders) *Swiss:* **6** Zwicky (Fritz)

astute 3 sly **4** cagy, deep, foxy, keen, wily **5** cagey, canny, heady, quick, savvy, sharp **6** artful, clever, crafty, shrewd, tricky **7** cunning, knowing **8** guileful **9** insidious, sagacious **11** calculating **13** perspicacious

astuteness 3 wit **6** acumen **8** wiliness **9** canniness **10** craftiness **11** discernment, percipience **12** perspicacity

Astyanax *father:* **6** Hector *mother:* **10** Andromache

asunder 4 torn **5** apart, split **7** divided **9** into parts, separated

as usual 8 normally, wontedly **9** routinely **10**

habitually, ordinarily **11** customarily **12** consistently

as well 3 and, too, yet **4** also, even, just, more, plus **7** besides, further **8** likewise, moreover **9** along with, including, similarly **10** in addition **11** furthermore **12** additionally

as well as 3 and **4** plus **7** besides **9** along with **11** not counting **12** in addition to, together with

as yet 5 so far, to now **7** earlier, thus far **8** hitherto, until now **10** to this time **12** to the present

asylum 4 home, port **5** cover, haven **6** covert, harbor, refuge **7** retreat, shelter **8** hospital, security **9** harborage, safe house, sanctuary **10** protection, sanatorium **11** institution

asymmetric 6 uneven **7** not even, unequal **8** lopsided **9** irregular **10** unbalanced **12** overbalanced

Atalanta *husband:* **8** Melanion *suitor:* **10** Hippomenes

at all 4 ever, once **6** anyway **7** anytime **10** whatsoever

atavism 9 reversion, throwback **10** recurrence

ataxia 5 chaos, snarl **6** huddle, muddle **7** clutter **8** disarray, disorder **9** confusion

atelier 6 studio **8** workroom, workshop

Athamas *daughter:* **5** Helle *father:* **6** Aeolus *son:* **7** Phrixos, Phrixus **8** Learchus *wife:* **3** Ino **7** Nephele

Athena *Roman counterpart:* **7** Minerva *attribute:* **3** owl **5** Aegis **7** serpent *city:* **6** Athens *father:* **4** Zeus *names:* **4** Nike **6** Pallas **9** Parthenos *shield:* **5** Aegis *statue:* **9** Palladium *temple:* **9** Parthenon

athenaeum 6 museum **7** library **8** archives **10** repository

Athens *citadel:* **9** Acropolis *founder:* **7** Cecrops *last king:* **6** Codrus *lawgiver:* **5** Solon *marketplace:* **5** agora *rival:* **6** Sparta *senate:* **5** boule *temple:* **9** Parthenon

athirst 4 avid, keen **5** eager **6** ardent **7** anxious **8** desiring, desirous, yearning **9** impatient

athlete 4 jock **5** sport **6** player **7** acrobat, gymnast, tumbler **9** sportsman **10** competitor **11** sportswoman

athlete's foot 8 ringworm **10** tinea pedis

athletic 6 brawny, robust, sinewy **8** sporting, vigorous **9** strapping, strenuous *contest:* **4** agon, game **5** match *field:* **4** oval, ring, rink **5** arena, court **7** diamond, stadium **8** gridiron *prize:* **3** cup **5** medal **6** trophy, wreath

athletics 5 games, races **6** events, sports **7** contest **8** exercise **9** exercises **10** gymnastics, recreation **12** calisthenics

athwart 4 over **5** cross **6** across, beyond **9** crossways, crosswise, opposed to **12** transversely

Atlanta's civic center 4 Omni

Atlas *brother:* **10** Prometheus *daughter:* **5** Hyads **6** Hyades **8** Pleiades **10** Atlantides *father:* **7** Iapetus *mother:* **7** Clymene *race:* **5** Titan *wife:* **7** Pleione

at last 7 finally

Atli *wife (slayer):* **6** Gudrun

atmosphere 3 air **4** aura, mood, tone **6** medium, milieu **7** ambient, climate, feeling, quality **8** ambiance, ambience **11** environment, mise-en-scène **12** surroundings *stratum:* **9** exosphere **10** ionosphere, mesosphere **11** chemosphere, ozonosphere, troposphere **12** stratosphere, thermosphere *sun's:* **12** chromosphere

atmospheric 4 airy **6** aerial **8** ethereal

atoll 6 island *equatorial area:* **5** Baker *Indian Ocean:* **4** Male *Kiribati:* **4** Beru *Marshall Islands:* **6** Bikini **8** Eniwetok *Tuamotu:* **4** Anaa **5** Chain *Tuvalu:* **8** Funafuti

atom 3 bit, jot **4** iota, mite, whit **5** minim, speck, touch, trace **6** tittle **7** modicum, smidgen **8** particle **9** scintilla *charged:* **3** ion **5** anion *group:* **7** radical

atomic particle 3 ion **4** beta, muon, pion **5** alpha, boson, meson **6** baryon, hadron, lepton, proton **7** fermion, hyperon, neutron, nucleon **8** electron, mesotron, neutrino, positron, thermion *hypothetical:* **5** quark **6** parton

atomic weapon 5 A-bomb, H-bomb **6** Fat Man **9** Little Boy

atomize 4 nuke, ruin **5** smash, wreck **6** divide, rub out **7** break up, destroy, shatter **8** demolish, destruct, disperse, dynamite, fragment, nebulize **9** break down, devastate, pulverize **10** disconnect

at once 3 now, PDQ **4** ASAP, away, both, stat **6** pronto **8** directly, first off, right now, together **9** forthwith, instanter, instantly, right away **11** immediately, straightway **12** concurrently, straightaway

atone 3 pay **6** redeem, repair, repent **7** correct, expiate, rectify, redress, satisfy **10** compensate, make amends, recompense

atoner 8 penitent

atop 4 upon

Atossa *father:* **5** Cyrus *husband:* **6** Darius **7** Smerdes **8** Cambyses *son:* **6** Xerxes

at random 5 about **6** anyhow **7** anywise **8** by chance **9** aimlessly, haphazard **10** carelessly **11** any which way, haphazardly **12** accidentally **13** helter-skelter

at rest 4 dead **5** still **8** inactive, lifeless, reposing, sleeping, tranquil, unmoving **9** quiescent **10** motionless, stationary, untroubled **11** trouble-free

Atreus *brother:* **8** Thyestes *father:* **6** Pelops *mother:* **10** Hippodamia *slayer:* **9** Aegisthus *son:* **8** Menelaus **9** Agamemnon **11** Pleisthenes *victim:* **11** Pleisthenes *wife:* **6** Aerope

atrium 5 court, patio

atrocious 4 foul, vile **5** awful, cruel **6** brutal, horrid, odious, savage, wicked **7** heinous, noisome, obscene **8** barbaric, horrible, shocking, terrible **9** appalling, desperate, execrable, loathsome, monstrous, offensive, repulsive, revolting, sickening **10** abominable, despicable, detestable, disgusting, horrifying, outrageous, scandalous **12** contemptible

atrocity 4 evil **5** crime **6** horror, infamy **7** cruelty, outrage **8** enormity, savagery **9** barbarity, brutality **11** abomination, heinousness **13** monstrousness

atrophy 7 decline, wasting **9** decadence, waste away **10** devolution **11** declination **12** degeneration **13** deterioration

attach 3 fix, tie **4** bind, hook, link **5** affix, annex, latch, rivet, stick, unite **6** adhere, append, assign, fasten, secure **7** ascribe, connect **8** make fast **9** associate, attribute

attached 5 bound, fixed **7** sessile

attachment 3 tag, tie **4** bond, link, love **6** fealty **7** loyalty, seizure **8** addition, adhesion, devotion, fastener, fidelity, fondness **9** accessory, adherence, affection, connector, constancy **10** allegiance, connection **12** faithfulness

attack 4 bout, jump, raid, rush **5** beset, blitz, drive, fight, foray, onset, sally, siege, spasm, spell, storm, throe **6** access, ambush, assail, banzai, battle, charge, fall on, harass, have at, invade, irrupt, onrush, sortie, strike, tackle **7** aggress, assault, barrage, besiege, bombard, lay into, offense, seizure **8** fall upon, invasion, outbreak, paroxysm **9** beleaguer, incursion, offensive, onslaught, pugnacity **10** aggression, blitzkrieg

attain 3 get, win **4** gain **5** reach, score **6** arrive, come to, effect, make it, obtain, rack up **7** achieve, fulfill, pull off, realize, succeed **8** bring off, complete **10** accomplish

attainment 4 feat **6** finish **7** arrival **10** completion **11** achievement, acquirement, acquisition, fulfillment, realization

attempt 3 bid, try **4** seek, shot, stab **5** assay, crack, essay, offer, trial **6** attack, effort, strive, tackle **7** assault, venture **8** endeavor, striving, struggle **9** undertake **11** undertaking **12** make an effort

attend 3 aid, see **4** be at, go to, hear, heed, help, mark, mind, note **5** apply, catch, nurse, see to, serve, visit, watch **6** assist, convoy, doctor, drop in, escort, go with, harken, listen, notice, show up, turn up, wait on **7** be there, care for, conduct, hearken, oversee, pay heed, work for **8** chaperon, stay with, wait upon **9** accompany, chaperone, companion, look after, supervise **11** concentrate

attendant 4 aide, page **5** valet **6** escort, helper, lackey **7** orderly, servant **9** ancillary, assistant **10** bridesmaid, coincident **11** chamberlain, concomitant **12** accompanying *ancient Roman:* **6** lictor *in court:* **7** bailiff **8** tipstaff

attendants 5 suite, train **7** cortege, retinue **9** entourage

attendee 4 goer

attention 4 care, heed, mark, note **5** study **6** notice, regard, remark **7** amenity, command, concern, respect, service, thought **8** civility, courtesy, industry, scrutiny **9** assiduity, awareness, deference, diligence, gallantry, spotlight, treatment **10** absorption, cognizance, observance, politeness **11** application, mindfulness, observation, sensibility **12** deliberation **13** concentration, consciousness, consideration

attention getter 4 ahem **5** gavel

attentive 4 kind **5** alert, awake, aware, civil **6** intent, polite **7** all ears, devoted, gallant, heedful, mindful **8** gracious, obliging, open-eyed **9** advertent, courteous, observant, regardful **10** interested, respectful, solicitous, thoughtful **11** considerate **13** concentrating

attenuate 3 sap **4** rare, slim, thin **5** abate, blunt, reedy **6** lessen, rarefy, shrink, slight, stalky, subtle, twiggy, weaken **7** cripple, deflate, disable, reduced, slender, squinny, subtile, tenuous, unbrace **8** contract, enfeeble, mitigate, rarefied, tapering, wiredraw **9** constrict, dissipate, undermine **10** become thin, become fine, become less, debilitate

attest 4 aver, show **5** argue, prove, swear, vouch **6** adjure, affirm, assert, verify **7** certify, confirm, declare, display, exhibit, point to, support, sustain, swear to, testify, warrant, witness **8** announce, indicate, manifest **9** establish **10** asseverate **11** bear witness, demonstrate **12** authenticate

attestation 5 proof **7** witness **8** evidence **9** testament, testimony **10** validation **11** declaration, testimonial **12** confirmation

attic 4 loft, room **6** garret **7** storage **8** cockloft

Attica 6 Greece *division:* **4** deme

at times 9 sometimes 10 now and then, on occasion 11 now and again 12 occasionally

attire 4 clad, duds, garb, gear, togs, wear 5 array, drape, dress, getup, habit, tog up 6 clothe, enrobe, fit out, outfit 7 apparel, clothes, costume, garment, raiment, threads 8 clothing, garments, glad rags 11 habiliments

attitude 4 pose, view 5 angle, stand 6 manner, stance 7 bearing, mind-set, outlook, posture 8 carriage, demeanor, position, pretense 10 standpoint 11 inclination, perspective, point of view

attitudinize 4 mask, pose, sham 6 affect 7 pass for, pass off, posture, pretend, show off 10 masquerade

attorney 5 agent, proxy 6 deputy, factor, lawyer 7 counsel 8 advocate, assignee 9 barrister, counselor, solicitor 10 counsellor, legal eagle, mouthpiece

attract 4 draw, lure, wile 5 charm, court, tempt 6 allure, appeal, beckon, draw in, entice, invite, seduce 7 beguile, bewitch, enchant, solicit 8 appeal to, interest, intrigue, inveigle 9 captivate, fascinate, influence, magnetize

attraction 4 bait, call, draw, lure, pull 5 charm 6 allure, appeal, liking 8 affinity, cynosure, sympathy 9 affection, chemistry, magnetism, seduction 10 allurement 12 drawing power

attractive 4 cute, fair, sexy 5 bonny, dishy 6 comely, lovely, luring, pretty 7 Circean, likable, winsome 8 alluring, charming, engaging, enticing, fetching, handsome, inviting, magnetic, mesmeric, tempting 9 appealing, beauteous, beautiful, beckoning, glamorous, seductive 10 bewitching, enchanting 11 captivating, fascinating, good-looking, tantalizing 13 prepossessing

attractiveness 5 charm 6 appeal, beauty, glamor 7 glamour

attribute 3 lay 4 mark, sign 5 apply, facet, pin on, point, refer, trait 6 aspect, assign, charge, credit, emblem, impute, symbol, virtue 7 ascribe, connect, earmark, explain, feature, quality 8 accredit, classify, property 9 adjective, character, designate

attrition 3 rue 4 ruth, wear 6 sorrow 7 erosion, penance, remorse, rubbing, wearing 8 abrasion, friction, grinding 9 penitence, penitency, reduction, weakening 10 repentance 12 contriteness

attritional 5 sorry 6 rueful 8 contrite, penitent 9 regretful, repentant 10 apologetic, remorseful 11 penitential

attune 6 accord, adjust 7 balance, conform 9 harmonize, integrate, reconcile 10 coordinate, proportion 11 accommodate

Atwood novel 7 Cat's Eye 12 Oryx and Crake 13 Handmaid's Tale (The)

atypical 3 odd 5 queer 7 deviant, strange, unusual 8 aberrant, abnormal, peculiar 9 anomalous, deviative, different, divergent, irregular, unnatural 11 exceptional, heteroclite, nonstandard 13 preternatural

auberge 3 inn 5 hotel, lodge 6 hostel, tavern 7 hospice 8 hostelry 9 roadhouse 11 caravansary, public house

Auber opera 10 Fra Diavolo

auburn 4 rust 5 henna 6 russet 8 chestnut 11 burnt sienna 12 reddish-brown

Auchincloss novel 9 Embezzler (The) 13 East Side Story 14 Rector of Justin (The)

au courant 3 mod 4 up on 5 awake, aware, hep to, hip to, savvy 6 modern, modish, versed 7 abreast, current, in touch, knowing, stylish, versant, witting 8 familiar, informed, sentient, up-to-date 9 cognizant, conscious, plugged in 10 acquainted, conversant 11 fashionable 12 contemporary 13 up-to-the-minute

auction 4 sale, sell

audacious 4 bold, rash 5 brash, brave, cocky, risky, saucy 6 brazen, cheeky, daring 7 valiant 8 arrogant, fearless, impudent, insolent, intrepid, reckless, unafraid, uncurbed 9 daredevil, dauntless, foolhardy, shameless, undaunted, venturous 10 courageous, ungoverned, unhampered 11 adventurous, impertinent, temerarious, uninhibited, untrammeled, venturesome 12 unrestrained 13 adventuresome

audacity 4 gall 5 brass, cheek, moxie, nerve, spunk 6 mettle, spirit 7 courage 8 boldness, chutzpah, rashness, temerity 9 assurance, arrogance, brashness, cockiness, disregard, hardihood, hardiness, impudence, insolence 10 brazenness, effrontery 12 recklessness

audible 5 aural, clear, heard 8 distinct 9 auricular

audibly 5 aloud 7 aurally, clearly, out loud

audience 5 crowd, group, house 6 public 7 hearing, gallery, hearers, meeting 8 admirers, assembly, audition, devotees 9 clientele, following, gathering, interview, listeners 10 assemblage, spectators

audile see **auditory**

audio 5 sound

audit 4 scan 5 check, probe 6 go over, report, review, survey, verify 7 analyze, balance, checkup, examine, inspect 8 analysis, scrutiny 10 inspection, scrutinize 11 examination 13 investigation

audition 4 test 5 trial 6 tryout 7 hearing, reading

auditor 8 examiner, listener 9 inspector 10 accountant, controller 11 comptroller

auditory 5 aural 8 acoustic

Auel, Jean *novel:* 17 Clan of the Cave Bear (The) *series:* 14 Earth's Children

au fait 4 able 5 right 6 decent, proper, versed 7 abreast, capable, correct, versant 8 becoming, decorous, familiar, informed, relevant 9 befitting, competent, qualified 10 acquainted, conforming, conversant, to the point

au fond 8 at bottom 9 basically, in essence 11 essentially 13 fundamentally

Augean 9 difficult 10 formidable 11 distasteful *stable:* 3 sty 4 sink 5 filth, Sodom 7 cesspit 8 cesspool

auger 3 bit 5 borer, drill, screw 6 gimlet, trepan, wimble 9 corkscrew

Auge's son 8 Telephus

aught 3 all, nil, nix, zip 4 nada, zero 5 zilch 6 cipher 7 nothing 8 anything, goose egg 10 everything

augment 3 wax 4 grow, hike, rise 5 add to, boost, build, exalt, mount, raise 6 beef up, expand, extend 7 amplify, build up, develop, enhance, enlarge, magnify 9 intensify, reinforce 8 compound, heighten, increase, multiply 10 aggrandize, supplement 11 make greater

augmentation 4 rise 5 annex, extra, raise 7 adjunct, buildup 8 addition, increase 9 accession, accretion, increment 10 complement, enrichment 11 enhancement, enlargement

augur 4 bode, seer 6 herald, oracle 7 betoken, diviner, portend, predict, presage, promise, prophet, suggest 8 forebode, forecast, foreshow, foretell, indicate, prophesy, soothsay 9 adumbrate, foretoken, harbinger, predictor, prefigure 10 forecaster, foreshadow, foreteller, prophesier, soothsayer, vaticinate 11 Nostradamus 13 prognosticate

augury 4 omen, sign 5 token 6 herald 7 auspice, portent, presage, warning 8 bodement, forecast, prophecy 9 foretoken, harbinger 10 divination, forerunner, prediction, prognostic 11 forewarning

august 5 grand, noble, regal 6 lordly 7 eminent, stately 8 baronial, imposing, majestic, princely, splendid 9 dignified, grandiose 11 magnificent

auk 5 alcid 7 seabird *genus:* 4 Alca

au naturel 3 raw 4 nude 5 naked, plain 6 unclad 8 stripped 9 unclothed, undressed 10 stark naked

aunt *French:* 5 tante *German:* 5 Tante *Italian:* 3 zia *Japanese:* 6 obasan *Spanish:* 3 tía

aura 3 air 4 feel, glow, halo, mood, tone, vibe 5 aroma, vibes 6 nimbus 7 aureole, feeling, quality 8 ambience, mystique, radiance, stimulus 9 emanation, semblance, sensation 10 atmosphere

aural 6 audile 7 audible 8 acoustic, auditory 9 auricular

aureate 6 florid, golden 7 flowery, orotund 8 sonorous 9 bombastic, grandiose, overblown 10 euphuistic, rhetorical 11 declamatory 13 grandiloquent

aureole 4 aura, halo, ring 5 crown, light 6 circle, corona, nimbus 8 radiance

au revoir 4 by-by, ciao, ta-ta 5 adieu, adios 6 bye-bye, so long 7 good-bye 8 farewell 11 arrivederci

auricular see **aural**

Auriga star 7 Capella

aurora 4 dawn, morn 7 dawning, morning, sunrise 8 cockcrow, daybreak

Aurora Roman counterpart: 3 Eos *goddess of:* 4 dawn *husband:* 8 Tithonus *son:* 6 Memnon

auslander 5 alien 7 inconnu 8 outsider, stranger 9 foreigner

auspice 4 omen, sign 10 divination

auspices 5 aegis 6 charge 7 backing, support 8 guidance 9 influence, patronage 11 sponsorship, supervision

auspicious 5 lucky 6 bright, timely 7 hopeful 9 favorable, fortunate, opportune, promising, well-timed 10 propitious, prosperous 11 encouraging

Austen, Jane *novel:* 4 Emma 10 Persuasion 13 Mansfield Park 15 Northanger Abbey 17 Pride and Prejudice 19 Sense and Sensibility

Auster see **Notus**

austere 4 bare, cold, dour, firm, grim, hard 5 acrid, bleak, grave, harsh, plain, rigid, sharp, spare, stern 6 bitter, severe, simple, somber, strict 7 ascetic, serious, spartan 8 exacting 9 stringent, unadorned, unfeeling 10 astringent, restrained 11 self-denying

austerity 5 rigor 6 thrift 7 economy 8 acerbity, asperity, coldness, grimness, hardness, rigidity, severity 9 harshness, parsimony, privation, solemnity, spareness, sternness, stiffness 10 self-denial, simplicity, strictness, stringency 11 unadornment 13 self-restraint

Australia capital: 8 Canberra *city:* 5 Perth 6 Darwin, Sydney 8 Adelaide, Brisbane 9 Melbourne, Newcastle *desert:* 10 Great Sandy 13 Great Victoria *ethnic group:* 9

Aborigine *island:* **6** Fraser **8** Kangaroo, Melville, Tasmania *lake:* **4** Eyre *monetary unit:* **6** dollar *mountain, range:* **9** Ayers Rock **9** Kosciusko **13** Great Dividing *reef:* **12** Great Barrier *river:* **4** Swan **6** Murray **7** Darling **8** Flinders **11** Cooper Creek **12** Coopers Creek *strait:* **4** Bass **6** Torres

Austria *capital:* **6** Vienna *city:* **4** Graz, Linz **8** Salzburg **9** Innsbruck **10** Klagenfurt *lake:* **10** Neusiedler *monetary unit:* **4** euro *monetary unit, former:* **9** schilling *mountain:* **13** Grossglockner *mountain range:* **4** Alps *neighbor:* **5** Italy **7** Croatia, Germany, Hungary **8** Slovakia, Slovenia **11** Switzerland **13** Czech Republic, Liechtenstein *river:* **3** Ems **6** Danube

autarchy see **autocracy**

autarkic 4 free **8** separate **9** sovereign **10** autonomous, self-ruling **11** independent, self-reliant **13** self-governing

autarky 7 freedom **8** autonomy **12** independence, self-reliance

authentic 4 real, true **5** legit, pukka, right, solid, sound, valid **6** actual, trusty **7** certain, factual, for real, genuine **8** accurate, bona fide, credible, faithful, reliable **9** undoubted, veritable **10** convincing, dependable, legitimate, sure-enough **11** indubitable, trustworthy **12** questionless

authenticate 5 prove, vouch **6** adduce, attest, verify **7** bear out, certify, confirm, justify, voucher, warrant **8** accredit, notarize, validate **11** corroborate **12** substantiate

author 5 maker **6** penman, scribe, writer **7** creator **8** inventor, novelist, prosaist **9** generator **10** originator *American:* **3** Bly (Robert), Fox (Paula), Nin (Anaïs), Poe (Edgar Allan), Tan (Amy) **4** Agee (James), Baum (L. Frank), Buck (Pearl S.), Cain (James M.), Cook (Robin), Dana (Richard Henry), Fast (Howard), Ford (Richard), Grey (Zane), Jong (Erica), Mann (Thomas), Puzo (Mario), Rand (Ayn), Rice (Anne), Roth (Philip), Shaw (Irwin), Uris (Leon), West (Nathanael), Wouk (Herman) **5** Aiken (Conrad), Alger (Horatio), Banks (Russell), Barth (John), Benét (Stephen Vincent), Blume (Judy), Boyle (T. Coraghessan), Brown (Rita Mae), Clark (Mary Higgins), Crane (Hart, Stephen), Dunne (Dominick, John Gregory), Elkin (Stanley), Ellis (Bret Easton), Foote (Horton), Haley (Alex), Harte (Bret), Henry (O.), Jaffe (Rona), Jakes (John), James (Henry), Levin (Ira), Lewis (Sinclair), Lurie (Alison), Mason (Bobbie Ann), Oates (Joyce Carol), O'Hara (John), Ozick (Cynthia), Paine (Thomas),

Paley (Grace), Potok (Chaim), Price (Reynolds, Richard), Steel (Danielle), Stein (Gertrude), Stone (Irving), Stout (Rex), Stowe (Harriet Beecher), Turow (Scott), Twain (Mark), Tyler (Anne), Vidal (Gore), Welty (Eudora), White (Edmund, E. B., T. H.), Wolfe (Thomas, Tom), Wylie (Elinor) **6** Alcott (Louisa May), Asimov (Isaac), Auster (Paul), Bellow (Saul), Berger (Thomas), Bierce (Ambrose), Bowles (Paul), Cabell (James Branch), Capote (Truman), Cather (Willa), Chopin (Kate), Clancy (Tom), Conroy (Pat), Cooper (James Fenimore), Dickey (James), Didion (Joan), Ellroy (James), Ferber (Edna), French (Marilyn), Gaddis (William), Gaines (Ernest J.), Gilroy (Frank), Godwin (Gail), Hailey (Arthur), Harris (Frank, Joel Chandler), Hawkes (John), Heller (Joseph), Hersey (John), Hinton (S. E.), Holmes (Oliver Wendell), Hughes (Langston), Hunter (Evan), Irving (John, Washington), Jewett (Sarah Orne), Kidder (Tracy), Koontz (Dean), Krantz (Judith), L'Amour (Louis), L'Engle (Madeleine), Le Guin (Ursula K.), London (Jack), Mailer (Norman), McBain (Ed), Miller (Arthur, Henry, Joaquin, May), Morley (Christopher), Morris (Wright), Mosley (Walter), Norris (Frank), Parker (Dorothy), Piercy (Marge), Porter (Katherine Anne, William Sydney), Proulx (E. Annie), Runyon (Damon), Sarton (May), Sheehy (Gail), Singer (Isaac Bashevis), Smiley (Jane), Styron (William), Taylor (Peter), Updike (John), Walker (Alice), Waller (Robert James), Warren (Robert Penn), Wilder (Laura Ingalls, Thornton), Wilson (August, Edmund, Harriet, Lanford), Wister (Owen), Wright (James, Richard) **7** Baldwin (Faith, James), Beattie (Ann), Cheever (John), Clavell (James), Clemens (Samuel Langhorne), Collins (Jackie), Connell (Evan), Cozzens (James Gould), DeLillo (Don), Dreiser (Theodore), Ellison (Ralph), Erdrich (Louise), Farrell (James T.), Francis (Dick), Franzen (Jonathan), Gardner (Erle Stanley), Garland (Hamlin), Glasgow (Ellen), Goldman (William), Grafton (Sue), Grisham (John), Hammett (Dashiell), Heyward (DuBose), Howells (William Dean), Hurston (Zora Neale), Jackson (Shirley), Jarrell (Randall), Johnson (Diane, James), Keillor (Garrison), Kennedy (William), Kerouac (Jack), Kincaid (Jamaica), Lardner (Ring), Leonard (Elmore), Malamud (Bernard), Marquis (Don), Masters (Edgar Lee), McCourt

(Frank), Mumford (Lewis), Nabokov (Vladimir), O'Connor (Flannery), Pynchon (Thomas), Rexroth (Kenneth), Richter (Conrad), Roberts (Elizabeth Madox, Kenneth, Nora), Saroyan (William), Sheehan (Neil), Sheldon (Sidney), Theroux (Paul), Thoreau (Henry David), Thurber (James), Wallace (Lew), Wharton (Edith) **8** Anderson (Maxwell, Poul, Regina, Sherwood), Benchley (Peter), Bradbury (Ray), Bradford (Barbara Taylor), Caldwell (Erskine), Chandler (Raymond), Cornwell (Patricia), Crichton (Michael), Doctorow (E. L.), Faulkner (William), Kingston (Maxine Hong), Marquand (John P.), McCarthy (Cormac, Mary), McMillan (Terry), McMurtry (Larry), Melville (Herman), Michener (James), Mitchell (Donald Grant, Margaret, S. Weir), Morrison (Toni), Remarque (Erich Maria), Rinehart (Mary Roberts), Salinger (J. D.), Sandburg (Carl), Sinclair (Upton), Spillane (Mickey), Stockton (Frank R.), Vonnegut (Kurt), Wambaugh (Joseph) **9** Burroughs (Edgar Rice, John, William S.), Dos Passos (John), Hawthorne (Nathaniel), Hemingway (Ernest), Hillerman (Tony), Isherwood (Christopher), McCullers (Carson), Steinbeck (John), Wodehouse (P. G.), Woollcott (Alexander) **10** Cunningham (Michael), Fitzgerald (F. Scott), Kingsolver (Barbara), Tarkington (Booth) **11** Auchincloss (Louis), Matthiessen (Peter) *Argentinian:* **6** Borges (Jorge Luis) *Australian:* **4** West (Morris L.) **5** Stead (Christina), White (Patrick) **7** Clavell (James), Idriess (Ion) **8** Keneally (Thomas) **10** McCullough (Colleen), Richardson (Henry Handel) *Austrian:* **5** Kafka (Franz) **6** Handke (Peter) **7** Jelinek (Elfriede), Suttner (Bertha) **8** Bernhard (Thomas) **10** Schnitzler (Arthur) *Brazilian:* **6** Coelho (Paulo) *Canadian:* **3** Roy (Camille, Gabrielle) **5** Kirby (William), Moore (Brian), Munro (Alice) **6** Atwood (Margaret), Davies (Robertson) **7** Leacock (Stephen), Raddall (Thomas), Richler (Mordecai), Service (Robert), Shields (Carol) **8** Woodcock (George) **9** de la Roche (Mazo), MacLennan (Hugh) *Chilean:* **6** Donoso (José) **7** Allende (Isabel) *Chinese:* **5** Han Yu *Colombian:* **7** Márquez (Gabriel García) *Czech:* **5** Capek (Karel), Hasek (Jaroslav) **7** Kundera (Milan) *Danish:* **4** Rode (Helge), Wied (Gustav) **6** Jensen (Johannes Vilhelm) **7** Dinesen (Isak), Holberg (Ludwig) *Dutch:* **6** Vondel (Joost van den) *Egyptian:* **7** Mahfouz

(Naguib) *English:* **4** Amis (Kingsley, Martin), Dahl (Roald), Ford (Ford Madox, John), Lyly (John), Saki, Snow (C. P.), Ward (Mrs. Humphry), West (Rebecca) **5** Byatt (A. S.), Defoe (Daniel), Doyle (Authur Conan), Eliot (George, Thomas Stearns), Evans (Mary Ann), Frayn (Michael), Hardy (Thomas), James (Henry, P. D.), Lewis (C. S., Monk, Wyndham), Lowry (Malcolm), Milne (A. A.), Munro (H. H.), Powys (John Cowper, Llewelyn, Theodore Francis), Reade (Charles), Spark (Muriel), Waugh (Alec, Evelyn), Wells (Charles Jeremiah, H. G.), White (T. H.), Wilde (Oscar), Woolf (Leonard, Virginia), Young (Arthur, Edward, Francis Brett) **6** Ambler (Eric), Archer (Jeffrey), Austen (Jane), Belloc (Hilaire), Brontë (Anne, Charlotte, Emily), Bunyan (John), Butler (Samuel), Clarke (Arthur C.), Conrad (Joseph), Fowles (John), Graves (Robert), Greene (Graham, Robert), Hilton (James), Hudson (W. H.), Huxley (Aldous), Malory (Thomas), McEwan (Ian), O'Brian (Patrick), Orwell (George), Potter (Beatrix), Powell (Anthony), Sayers (Dorothy L.), Sterne (Laurence), Stoker (Bram), Storey (David), Walton (Izaak) **7** Ballard (J. G.), Burgess (Anthony), Burnett (Frances Hodgson), Carroll (Lewis), Clavell (James), Collins (Wilkie), Dickens (Charles), Dodgson (Charles), Durrell (Lawrence), Fleming (Ian), Follett (Ken), Forster (E. M.), Forsyth (Frederick), Golding (Louis, William), Kipling (Rudyard), Le Carré (John), Lessing (Doris), Lofting (Hugh), Maugham (Robin, W. Somerset), Murdoch (Iris), Naipaul (V. S.), Rendell (Ruth), Rowling (J. K.), Sassoon (Siegfried), Shelley (Mary Wollstonecraft, Percy Bysshe), Sitwell (Edith, Osbert, Sacheverell), Southey (Robert), Stewart (Mary), Surtees (Robert Smith), Tolkien (J. R. R.), Walpole (Horace, Hugh), Wyndham (John) **8** Christie (Agatha), Fielding (Henry), Forester (C. S.), Koestler (Arthur), Lawrence (D. H., T. E.), Macaulay (Rose, Thomas Babington), Meredith (George), Sillitoe (Alan), Smollett (Tobias), Strachey (Lytton), Trollope (Anthony), Zangwill (Israel) **9** De Quincey (Thomas), Du Maurier (Daphne, George), Goldsmith (Oliver), Isherwood (Christopher), Mansfield (Katherine), Masefield (John), Priestley (J. B.), Radcliffe (Ann), Stevenson (Robert Louis), Thackeray (William Makepeace), Wodehouse (P. D.) **10** Chesterton (Gilbert Keith), Galsworthy

(John), Richardson (Dorothy, Samuel) **12**
Quiller-Couch (Arthur Thomas) *Finnish:* **7**
Waltari (Mika) **9** Sillanpää (Frans Eemil)
French: **3** Nin (Anaïs) **4** Gide (André),
Hugo (Victor), Kock (Charles-Paul de),
Sade (Marquis de), Sand (George), Zola
(Emile) **5** Beyle (Marie Henri), Camus (Albert),
Dumas (Alexandre), Genet (Jean),
Sagan (Françoise), Staël (Germaine de),
Verne (Jules), Vigny (Alfred-Victor) **6**
Balzac (Honoré de), Daudet (Alphonse),
France (Anatole), Lesage (Alain-René,
Proust (Marcel), Sartre (Jean-Paul) **7** Cocteau
(Jean), Colette, Gautier (Léon, Théophile),
Malraux (André), Mauriac (Claude,
François), Maurois (André), Merimée
(Prosper), Rolland (Romain), Romains
(Jules), Simenon (Georges) **8** Beauvoir (Simone
de), Flaubert (Gustave), Marivaux
(Pierre), Rabelais (François), Stendhal, Voltaire
9 Giraudoux (Jean) **10** Maupassant
(Guy de), Saint-Simon (Duke de) **12**
Robbe-Grillet (Alain), Saint-Exupéry (Antoine
de) *German:* **4** Böll (Heinrich), Mann
(Thomas) **5** Grass (Gunter), Hesse (Hermann),
Kafka (Franz), Storm (Theodor),
Tieck (Ludwig), Zweig (Stefan) **6** Goethe
(Johann Wolfgang von), Toller (Ernst) **7**
Fontane (Theodor), Richter (Jean Paul),
Wieland (Christoph Martin) **8** Hoffmann
(E. T. A., Heinrich), Remarque (Erich Maria),
Schlegel (August Wilhelm von,
Friedrich von, Johann Elias) **9** Hauptmann
(Gerhart), Sudermann (Hermann) **10** Wassermann
(Jakob) *Greek:* **5** Homer **6** Hesiod,
Lucian, Pindar, Sappho **7** Plautus, Terence
8 Xenophon **9** Aeschylus, Euripedes, Herodotus,
Sophocles **10** Thucydides **11** Kazantzakis
(Nikos) *Hungarian:* **5** Jókai (Mór)
Icelandic: **7** Laxness (Halldór) *Indian:* **7**
Rushdie (Salman) *Irish:* **5** Behan (Brendan),
Doyle (Roddy), Joyce (James),
Moore (Brian), Synge (J. M.), Wilde (Oscar)
6 O'Brien (Edna), Stoker (Bram) **7**
Beckett (Samuel), O'Connor (Frank), Russell
(George William) **8** O'Faolain (Julia,
Sean), Stephens (James) **9** O'Flaherty
(Liam) *Italian:* **3** Eco (Umberto) **5** Verga
(Giovanni) **6** Silone (Ignazio) **7** Calvino
(Italo), Manzoni (Alessandro), Moravia
(Alberto) **9** Boccaccio (Giovanni), Vittorini
(Elio) **10** Pirandello (Luigi), Straparola (Gianfrancesco)
Japanese: **7** Mishima (Yukio)
8 Kawabata (Yasunari), Murakami (Haruki),
Murasaki (Shikibu) **9** Yokomitsu (Riichi),
Yoshikawa (Eiji) *Lebanese:* **6** Gibran
(Khalil) *Mexican:* **7** Fuentes (Carlos) *Nige-*

rian: **6** Achebe (Chinua) **7** Soyinka (Wole),
Tutuola (Amos) *Norwegian:* **3** Lie (Jonas) **6**
Hamsun (Knut), Undset (Sigrid) **7** Rolvaag
(Ole) **8** Bjornson (Bjornstjerne), Kielland
(Alexander) *Peruvian:* **11** Vargas Llosa
(Mario) *Polish:* **3** Lem (Stanislaw) **7** Reymont
(Wladyslaw) **8** Zeromski (Stefan) **10**
Gombrowicz (Witold) **11** Sienkiewicz
(Henryk) *Portuguese:* **6** Pessoa (Fernando)
8 Saramago (José) *Roman:* **4** Livy **5** Pliny,
Varro (Marcus Terentius) **7** Tacitus **8**
Apuleius **9** Petronius *Russian:* **5** Gogol
(Nikolai), Gorki (Maxim), Gorky (Maxim)
7 Chekhov (Anton), Pushkin (Alexander),
Tolstoy (Leo) **8** Andreyev (Leonid), Turgenev
(Ivan), Zamyatin (Yevgeny) **9** Ehrenburg
(Ilya), Lermontov (Mikhail),
Pasternak (Boris), Sholokhov (Mikhail) **10**
Dostoevsky (Fyodor) **11** Dostoyevsky (Fyodor),
Yevtushenko (Yevgeny) **12** Solzhenitsyn
(Alexander) *Scottish:* **3** Tey (Josephine)
4 Lang (Andrew) **5** Scott (Alexander, Walter)
6 Barrie (James M.), Buchan (John) **8**
Urquhart (Thomas) **9** Stevenson (Robert
Louis) *South African:* **5** Paton (Alan) **6** Fugard
(Athol) **7** Coetzee (J. M.) **8** Gordimer
(Nadine) *Spanish:* **6** Baroja (Pio) **7** Alarcón
(Pedro Antonio de) **9** Cervantes (Miguel
de) *Swedish:* **7** Johnson (Eyvind), Rydberg
(Viktor) **8** Lagerlöf (Selma) **10** Lagerkvist
(Pär), Strindberg (August) *Swiss:* **4** Wyss
(Johann Rudolf) **5** Spyri (Johanna) **6** Frisch
(Max) **9** Spitteler (Carl) *Trinidadian:* **7** Naipaul
(V. S.) *Welsh:* **4** Owen (Alun, Daniel,
Goronwy, John) **5** Evans (David, Evan),
Wynne (Ellis) *Yiddish:* **4** Asch (Sholem) **6**
Singer (Isaac Bashevis) **8** Aleichem
(Sholem)
authoritarian 5 harsh, rigid **6** despot, severe,
strict, tyrant **8** absolute, autocrat, despotic,
dictator, dogmatic **9** imperious, stringent **10**
absolutist, autocratic, oppressive, totalistic,
tyrannical **11** dictatorial, doctrinaire, domineering,
magisterial **12** totalitarian
authoritative 4 sure, true **5** legal, legit, sound
6 lawful, proven **7** factual **8** accepted, accurate,
approved, attested, dogmatic, official,
orthodox, reliable, verified **9** canonical, cathedral,
confirmed, imperious, trustable,
validated **10** autocratic, commanding, definitive,
dependable, documented, dominating,
ex cathedra, legitimate, sanctioned **11**
dictatorial, doctrinaire, domineering, irrefutable,
magisterial, overbearing, trustworthy
12 indisputable
authority 4 rule, sway **5** clout, force, power,
right, say-so **6** agency, charge, credit, ex-

pert, master, weight **7** command, control, grounds, license, mastery, warrant **8** citation, decision, dominion, prestige **9** influence, testimony **10** domination, governance, government, management **12** jurisdiction

authorization 4 okay, word **5** leave **6** permit **7** consent, go-ahead, license, mandate **8** approval, sanction **9** agreement, allowance, clearance **10** green light, permission, sufferance **11** approbation

authorize 3 let **4** okay, vest **5** allow **6** affirm, enable, invest, permit **7** approve, confirm, empower, endorse, entitle, license, qualify, warrant **8** accredit, sanction, vouch for **9** give leave, recognize **10** commission **11** countenance

auto see **automobile**

autobahn 7 highway **8** turnpike **10** expressway **12** superhighway

autobiography 4 life, vita **5** diary **6** memoir **7** account, journal **9** life story **11** confessions **13** reminiscences

autochthonous 6 native **7** endemic **8** original **10** aboriginal, indigenous

autocracy 7 czarism, tyranny **8** monarchy **9** despotism, monocracy **12** absolute rule, dictatorship

autocrat 4 czar, duce, emir, lord, raja, shah, tsar, tzar **5** mogul, rajah, ruler **6** caliph, despot, sultan, tyrant **7** magnate, monarch **8** dictator, oligarch, overlord **9** potentate, sovereign **10** absolutist

autocratic 7 haughty **8** absolute, arrogant, despotic **9** arbitrary, imperious, tyrannous **10** monocratic, tyrannical **11** dictatorial, domineering, overbearing

autodidactic 10 self-taught **12** self-educated

autograph 3 ink, pen **4** sign **5** write **7** endorse **8** original **9** signature, subscribe **11** endorsement, John Hancock

Autolycus *daughter:* **8** Anticlea *father:* **6** Hermes **7** Mercury

automated 7 robotic **9** by machine, motorized **10** electrical, electronic, mechanical, mechanized, programmed **12** computerized

automatic 6 reflex **8** habitual **9** impulsive, reflexive **10** mechanical, self-acting, unprompted **11** instinctive, involuntary, perfunctory, spontaneous, unmeditated *prefix:* **4** self

automaton 5 droid, golem, robot **7** android, machine **9** mechanism

automobile 3 bus, car **5** buggy, coupe, racer, sedan **6** beater, jalopy, tourer, wheels **7** clunker, flivver, hardtop, machine **8** dragster, motorcar, roadster, runabout **9** hatchback, limousine **10** rust bucket **11**

convertible *American:* **3** Geo, Reo **4** Cord, Dart, Ford, Fury, Jeep, Nash, Neon, Olds, Vega **5** Buick, Dodge, Eagle, Edsel, Essex, Focus, Pinto, T-bird **6** Cougar, DeSoto, Duster, Fraser, Hudson, Hummer, Impala, Kaiser, Model A, Model T, Saturn, Tucker, Willys **7** Charger, Cutlass, LaSalle, LeBaron, LeSabre, Lincoln, Maxwell, Mercury, Mustang, Packard, Pontiac, Rambler, Seville **8** Cadillac, Chrysler, Corvette, Eldorado, Franklin, Plymouth **9** Barracuda, Chevrolet, Hupmobile **10** Duesenberg, Oldsmobile, Studebaker **11** Continental, Pierce-Arrow, Thunderbird *British:* **2** MG **3** Jag **4** Mini **5** Lotus **6** Anglia, Arnage, Austin, Cooper, DeSoto, Jaguar, Morris **7** Bentley, Daimler, Hillman, Phantom, Sunbeam, Triumph **8** Vauxhall **9** Land Rover **10** Range Rover, Rolls-Royce **11** Aston Martin, Silver Ghost **12** Austin-Healey *French:* **5** Simca **7** Citroën, Peugeot, Renault *German:* **3** BMW **4** Audi, Benz, Golf, Opel **6** Beetle **7** Daimler, Maybach, Porsche, Quattro **8** Mercedes **10** Volkswagen **12** Mercedes-Benz *Italian:* **4** Fiat **6** Lancia **7** Bugatti, Ferrari **8** Maserati **9** Alfa-Romeo **11** Lamborghini *Japanese:* **5** Acura, Civic, Honda, Isuzu, Lexus, Mazda, Prius **6** Datsun, Altima, Maxima, Nissan, Subaru, Toyota **7** Corolla **8** Infiniti **10** Mitsubishi *Korean:* **3** Kia **6** Daewoo **7** Hyundai *Russian:* **4** Lada *Serbian:* **4** Yugo *Swedish:* **4** Saab **5** Volvo

automobile safety device 3 ABS **6** air bag **8** seat belt

automotive pioneer 4 Benz (Carl Friedrich), Ford (Henry), Olds (Ransom), Otto (Nikolaus), Pope (Albert) **5** Evans (Oliver), Rolls (Charles), Roper (Sylvester) **6** Cugnot (Nicholas Joseph), Duryea (Charles E., J. Frank), Lenoir (Etienne), Winton (Alexander) **7** Bugatti (Ettore), Citroën (André-Gustave), Daimler (Gottlieb), Peugeot (Armand), Stanley (Francis, Freelan) **8** Morrison (William) **10** Lanchester (Frederick William)

Autonoë *father:* **6** Cadmus *husband:* **9** Aristaeus *mother:* **8** Harmonia *sister:* **5** Agave *son:* **7** Actaeon

autonomous 4 free **8** autarkic, separate **9** sovereign **10** self-ruling **11** independent, self-reliant **12** self-governed, uncontrolled **13** self-contained, self-governing

autonomy 7 autarky, freedom **8** home rule, self-rule **11** sovereignty **12** independence

autopsy 6 assess **7** examine **8** evaluate,

necropsy **10** assessment, dissection, evaluation, postmortem **11** examination
auto racer 4 Foyt (A. J.), Hill (Graham) **5** Clark (Jim), Mears (Rick), Petty (Richard), Unser (Al, Bobby) **6** Carter (Pancho), Fangio (Juan), Vogler (Rich) **7** Brabham (Jack), Stewart (Jackie) **8** Andretti (Mario, Michael), Johncock (Gordon) **9** Earnhardt (Dale) **10** Rutherford (Johnny)
autumn 4 fall **6** season **8** maturity
auxiliary 4 aide **5** spare **6** backup, helper **7** reserve **8** adjutant, adjuvant **9** accessory, ancillary, assistant, coadjutor, secondary **10** accomplice, additional, collateral, subsidiary **11** appurtenant, subservient **12** contributory **13** complementary, supplementary
verb: 3 are, can, did, had, has, may, was **4** been, does, have, must, were, will **5** could, might, ought, shall, would **6** should
avail 3 aid, use **4** gain, good, help **5** asset, serve **6** profit **7** account, benefit, fitness, satisfy, service **9** advantage, relevance **10** usefulness **13** applicability
available 5 handy, on tap, ready, valid **6** at hand, on hand, usable **7** present, willing **8** prepared **9** qualified **10** accessible, attainable, convenient, obtainable, procurable **11** purchasable
avalanche 4 mass, rush **5** drown, flood, slide **6** deluge **7** overrun, smother **8** inundate, mudslide, overflow, rockfall **9** landslide, overwhelm, rockslide, snowslide **10** inundation **12** accumulation
Avalon 8 paradise
avant-garde 7 radical **8** advanced, contempo **10** innovative, pioneering **11** cutting-edge, leading-edge, progressive **12** experimental **13** up-to-the-minute
avarice 5 greed **7** avidity **8** cupidity, rapacity, voracity **10** greediness **12** covetousness
avaricious 6 grabby, greedy, stingy **7** miserly **8** covetous, esurient, grasping, ravenous **9** mercenary, rapacious **11** acquisitive
avatar 4 type **5** image **7** epitome **8** exemplar **9** archetype **10** apotheosis, embodiment, expression **11** incarnation, reification **13** manifestation *of Vishnu:* **4** Rama
avaunt 4 away **5** hence, leave, scram **6** beat it, depart, get out
ave 4 hail **8** farewell, greeting
avenge 5 repay, right **6** punish **7** get even, pay back, redress, requite **9** fight back, retaliate, vindicate
avenue 3 way **4** path, road **5** drive, means, route, track **6** access, artery, course, street **7** channel, parkway, pathway **8** approach **9** boulevard **10** passageway **12** thoroughfare

aver 4 avow **5** prove, state, swear **6** affirm, allege, assert, attest, avouch, depose, insist, verify **7** declare, profess, protest, testify, warrant **8** maintain **9** guarantee, predicate
average 3 par **4** fair, mean, norm, so-so **5** usual **6** common, divide, equate, figure, median, medium, middle, normal **7** balance, even out, typical **8** everyday, midpoint, moderate, ordinary **12** intermediate
averagely 4 so-so **6** enough, fairly, rather **8** passably **9** tolerably **10** moderately
averse 5 balky, loath **6** afraid **7** hostile, opposed, uneager **8** allergic, hesitant **9** reluctant, resistant, unwilling **10** indisposed **11** disinclined **12** antipathetic
aversion 4 fear, hate **5** dread **6** hatred, horror **7** allergy, disgust, dislike **8** disfavor, distaste, loathing **9** antipathy, disliking, repulsion, revulsion **10** abhorrence, antagonism, repugnance **11** abomination, detestation, displeasure **13** indisposition
aversive 8 ungenial **9** repellent, repugnant **11** uncongenial **12** antipathetic **13** unsympathetic
avert 4 foil, halt, turn, veer, ward **5** avoid, check, deter **6** thwart **7** deflect, fend off, forfend, obviate, prevent, rule out, ward off **8** go around, stave off, turn away **9** forestall, turn aside
avian 6 flying, winged **8** birdlike, ornithic
aviary 4 cage **8** birdcage, dovecote **9** birdhouse, enclosure
aviator 3 ace **4** Post (Wiley) **5** flier, pilot **6** airman, Cessna (Clyde), flyboy, Wright (Orville, Wilbur), Yeager (Chuck) **7** birdman, Earhart (Amelia) **8** aeronaut **9** bush pilot, Lindbergh (Charles) **10** Richthofen (Manfred von) **12** Rickenbacker (Eddie)
avid 4 agog, keen **5** eager **6** ardent, greedy, hungry **7** anxious, athirst, craving, fervent, thirsty, zealous **8** appetent, covetous, desirous, grasping **9** impatient **10** breathless, insatiable **12** enthusiastic
avidity 4 zeal **5** greed **6** fervor, thirst **7** avarice, craving **8** cupidity, keenness, rapacity **9** eagerness **10** greediness
Avis competitor 5 Hertz
____ **avis 4** rara
avocation 5 hobby **7** pastime, pursuit **8** sideline **9** amusement, diversion **10** recreation
avoid 4 bilk, duck, miss, shun, snub **5** annul, avert, dodge, elude, evade, shirk, skirt **6** bypass, divert, escape, eschew, pass up **7** abstain, prevent, refrain **8** preclude, sidestep, stay away, withdraw **9** keep clear **11** refrain from **12** keep away from
avoidance 5 dodge **6** escape **7** dodging, elu-

sion, evasion **8** escaping, escapism, eschewal, shirking, shunning **9** runaround **10** abstinence

avouch 3 own **4** aver, avow **5** admit, claim, state, swear **6** affirm, assert, depose, insist **7** certify, confess, confirm, declare, profess, testify **9** predicate, pronounce **11** acknowledge, corroborate

avow 3 own **4** aver **5** admit, allow, grant, let on, own up, state, swear **6** affirm, assert, avouch, depose **7** concede, confess, declare, profess, protest **8** disclose, maintain, proclaim **9** predicate **11** acknowledge

avowal 6 assent **9** admission, assertion, statement **10** profession **11** affirmation, attestation, declaration

avowedly 6 openly **7** frankly **8** candidly **9** allegedly **10** apparently, ostensibly, supposedly

await 4 bide, hope, stay **5** abide **6** expect **7** count on, look for **8** watch for **10** anticipate, hang around

awake 4 stir **5** alert, alive, aware, rouse **6** active, arouse, bestir, excite, revive, roused, stir up **7** animate, aroused, excited, on guard **8** activate, sensible, sentient, vigilant, watchful **9** attentive, cognizant, conscious, observant, stimulate, stirred up

award 4 gift, give, kudo **5** allot, badge, endow, grant, honor, kudos, medal, prize **6** accord, bestow, confer, donate, ribbon, trophy **7** concede, laurels, tribute **8** accolade, citation, donation **9** vouchsafe **10** blue ribbon, decoration, distribute **11** distinction *advertising:* **4** Addy, Andy, Clio *broadcasting:* **7** Peabody *cable:* **5** Telly *cartooning:* **6** Ignatz, Reuben *comic books:* **6** Eisner, Harvey *computing:* **6** Turing *horror writing:* **10** Bram Stoker *Internet:* **5** Webby *motion picture:* **5** Annie, Oscar **6** Razzie, Saturn **7** Academy **11** Golden Globe *mystery novel:* **5** Edgar **6** Agatha *record:* **6** Grammy *remodeling:* **9** Chrysalis *romance novel:* **4** Rita *science & technology:* **11** Enrico Fermi *science-fiction:* **4** Hugo **6** Nebula *software:* **5** Codie *television:* **4** Emmy *theater:* **4** Obie, Tony

aware 4 onto **5** alert, alive, awake **7** heedful, knowing, mindful, tuned in, witting **8** informed, sensible, sentient, vigilant **9** attentive, au courant, cognizant, conscious, observant **10** conversant, perceptive **12** apprehensive **13** knowledgeable

awash 4 full **6** afloat, filled, jammed, loaded, packed **7** brimful, covered, crammed, crowded, flooded, run-over, stuffed **8** brimming, chockful **9** chock-full **11** overflowing

away 3 far, fro, now, off, out **4** afar, gone **5** along, apart, aside, forth, hence **6** abroad, absent, afield, far off **7** distant, lacking, missing, not here **9** elsewhere **11** incessantly **12** continuously

away from 6 beyond

awe 5 alarm, amaze, scare **6** wonder **7** inspire, startle **8** astonish **9** amazement, reverence **10** veneration, wonderment **11** flabbergast **12** astonishment

aweless 4 bold **5** brave **7** valiant **8** fearless, intrepid, unafraid **9** dauntless, undaunted **10** courageous

awesome 3 rad **6** august **7** amazing, sublime **8** imposing, terrific, wondrous **10** formidable, impressive **11** astonishing **12** breathtaking **13** extraordinary

awful 3 bad **4** dire, very **5** nasty **6** odious **7** hateful, heinous **8** dreadful, horrible, horrific, shocking, terrible, terrific **9** appalling, atrocious, extremely, frightful, loathsome, offensive **10** deplorable, disgusting, formidable

awfully 4 much, very **6** hugely, vastly **7** greatly **8** terribly, whopping **9** extremely, immensely **10** dreadfully, enormously **11** exceedingly

awhile 7 briefly **8** for a time **11** temporarily

awkward 5 gawky, inept, messy, nerdy, splay **6** clumsy, gauche, klutzy, wooden **7** artless, gawkish, halting, lumpish, unhandy, unhappy **8** bumbling, bungling, tactless, ungainly **9** graceless, ham-handed, ill-chosen, inelegant, lumbering, maladroit **10** blundering, ungraceful, unskillful **11** heavy-handed, unfortunate **12** embarrassing, incommodious, inconvenient, infelicitous

awl 4 tool **7** piercer

awning 6 canopy **7** marquee **8** sunshade *ancient Roman:* **8** velarium

awry 5 amiss, askew, atilt, wrong **6** astray **7** askance, crooked **8** cockeyed **9** cock-a-hoop, crookedly *Scottish:* **5** agley

ax, axe 3 adz, can, hew **4** adze, boot, chop, fire, sack **6** bounce **7** boot out, chopper, cleaver, dismiss, hatchet, kick out **8** tomahawk **9** discharge, terminate *blade:* **3** bit *handle:* **5** helve

axillary 4 alar

axiom 3 law **4** rule **5** adage, maxim, moral, truth **6** dictum, truism **7** precept, theorem **8** aphorism, apothegm **9** postulate, principle **10** principium **11** fundamental

axiomatic 5 given **7** assumed, certain, obvious **8** accepted, absolute, manifest, provable **10** aphoristic, understood **11**

fundamental, indubitable, self-evident **12** unquestioned

axis 4 line, pole, stem **5** point, pivot **8** alliance **9** continuum, plant stem **11** partnership **12** straight line, turning point

axle 3 bar, pin, rod **4** beam **5** bogie, shaft **7** spindle, support

aye 3 yea, yep, yes **4** amen, okay, ever, vote **6** agreed, always **8** all right **11** affirmative, continually

Azerbaijan *capital:* **4** Baku *city:* **5** Gäncä **8** Sumqayit *exclave:* **8** Naxçivan **11** Nakhichevan *monetary unit:* **5** manat *neighbor:* **4** Iran **6** Russia **7** Armenia, Georgia *river:* **4** Kura **5** Araks *sea:* **7** Caspian

Azores *capital:* **12** Ponta Delgada *city:* **5** Horta *island:* **4** Pico **5** Corvo, Faial, Lajes **6** Flores **8** São Jorge, Terceura **9** São Miguel **10** Santa Maria *part of:* **8** Portugal

Aztec *capital:* **12** Tenochtitlán *conqueror:* **6** Cortés, Cortéz *emperor:* **9** Moctezuma, Montezuma *god:* **4** Xipe **6** Tlaloc **9** Xipetotec **12** Quetzalcoatl *hero:* **4** Nata *language:* **7** Nahuatl *temple:* **8** teocalli

azure 3 sky **4** blue **5** color **7** sky blue

B

baa 5 bleat

Babbitt 10 conformist, middlebrow, philistine *author:* **5** Lewis (Sinclair)

babble 3 gab, jaw, yak, yap **4** blab, chat, go on, gush, rant, rave **5** clack, prate, run on **6** burble, drivel, gibber, gossip, jabber, murmur, patter, piffle, rattle, yammer **7** blabber, blather, chatter, maunder, palaver, prattle, twaddle **8** nonsense, idle talk **9** gibberish **11** jabberwocky

babe 3 cub, tot **4** doll, girl **5** bairn, child, chick, cutie, toots, woman **6** infant, hottie **7** bambino, papoose, neonate, newborn **8** bantling, nursling

babel 3 ado, din, row **4** to-do **5** hoo-ha **6** bedlam, clamor, hubbub, jangle, outcry, racket, ruckus, tumult, uproar **7** clangor, discord, ferment, turmoil **8** brouhaha, clangour, foofaraw **9** cacophony, commotion, confusion **10** dissonance, hullabaloo, hurly-burly, turbulence **11** pandemonium **12** vociferation

baboon 3 oaf **4** clod, dolt, goon, lout **6** chacma, galoot, simian **7** palooka **8** lunkhead, mandrill, meathead **9** hamadryas

babushka 6 granny **7** bandana **8** bandanna, kerchief

baby 3 pet, tot **4** tiny **5** bairn, sissy, spoil **6** cocker, coddle, cosset, dote on, infant, pamper **7** bambino, cater to, indulge, neonate, newborn, papoose, toddler **8** bantling, dote upon, nursling, suckling, weanling **11** mollycoddle *ailment:* **5** colic, croup *bed:* **4** crib **6** cradle **8** bassinet *bedroom:* **7** nursery *breechcloth:* **6** diaper *cap:* **6** biggin, bonnet *carriage:* **4** pram **5** buggy **8** stroller **12** perambulator *doctor:* **12** pediatrician *food:* **3** pap **4** milk **6** pablum **7** pabulum *garment:* **7** rompers *Italian:* **7** bambino *napkin:* **3** bib *outfit:* **7** layette *powder:* **4** talc *shoe:* **6** bootee *Spanish:* **4** bebé, nene

baby grand 5 piano

babyhood 7 infancy **10** diaper days, immaturity

babyish 5 petty **7** foolish, puerile, spoiled **8** childish, immature, juvenile **9** infantile, infantine

Babylonian 6 lavish **9** luxurious *abode of the dead:* **5** Aralu *capital:* **7** Babylon *chaos:* **4** Apsu *city:* **5** Akkad **6** Cunaxa *crown prince:* **10** Belshazzar *division:* **5** Akkad, Sumer *first ruler:* **6** Nimrod *god:* **3** Bel **4** Adad, Addu, Enki, Enzu, Irra, Nabu, Nebo **6** Marduk, Tammuz **7** Shamash *goddess:* **4** Erua, Gula **5** Belit **6** Ishtar *hero:* **9** Gilgamesh *king:* **6** Sargon **9** Hammurabi **12** Ashurbanipal *priest:* **2** en *river:* **6** Tigris **9** Euphrates *tower:* **5** Babel **8** ziggurat *waters:* **4** Apsu **6** Tiamat *winged dragon:* **6** Tiamat

baccalaureate 6 degree **9** bachelor's **10** graduation

bacchanal 6 maenad see also **bacchanalia**

bacchanalia 4 bash, orgy **5** binge, revel, spree **6** bender, excess **7** blowout, carouse, debauch, revelry, wassail **8** carnival, festival, wingding **11** celebration, dissipation, merrymaking

bacchanalian 4 wild **7** drunken, riotous **8**

frenzied 9 debauched, orgiastic 12 intoxicating *cry* 4 evoe 5 evohe

Bacchus 8 Dionysus *attendant:* 6 maenad 9 bacchante *father:* 4 Zeus 7 Jupiter *lover:* 5 Venus 9 Aphrodite *mother:* 6 Semele *son:* 7 Priapus *staff:* 7 thyrsus

Bach, Johann Sebastian *birthplace:* 8 Eisenach *genre:* 5 fugue, motet, suite 6 sonata 7 cantata, chorale, partita, prelude, toccata 8 concerto, fantasia, oratorio, sinfonia *home:* 7 Leipzig *instrument:* 5 organ 11 harpsichord *musical style:* 7 baroque *religion:* 8 Lutheran

back 3 aft, aid 4 abet, fund, help, hind, rear 5 abaft, about, bet on, dorsa (plural), spine, stake, stern 6 assist, astern, dorsum, hinder, recede, uphold 7 endorse, finance, promote, retract, retreat, reverse, sponsor, support 8 advocate, bankroll, champion, rearward, side with 9 in reverse, posterior, retrocede, subsidize 10 retrograde *ailment:* 7 lumbago 10 rheumatism *muscle:* 3 lat 4 trap 8 rhomboid 9 trapezius *of an arthropod:* 6 tergum *of an insect:* 5 notum *of the neck:* 4 nape 6 scruff *prefix:* 4 post 5 retro *relating to:* 6 dorsal

back answer 3 lip 6 retort 7 riposte 8 comeback, repartee 9 rejoinder, wisecrack 10 return shot 11 parting shot

backbite 4 slam, slur 5 abuse, decry, knock, libel, smear, sully, taint 6 defame, defile, malign, vilify 7 asperse, put down, run down, slander, traduce 8 bad-mouth, belittle, besmirch, derogate, diminish 9 denigrate, discredit

backbiter 6 gossip 7 defamer, traitor 9 detractor, slanderer 10 talebearer

backbiting 5 abuse, smear, spite 6 gossip 7 abusing, calumny, obloquy, scandal, slander 8 libelous, smearing 9 aspersion, cattiness, gossiping, invective, maligning, traducing, vilifying 10 calumnious, defamation, defamatory, scandalous, slandering, slanderous 11 denigration 12 belittlement, depreciation, spitefulness, vituperation 13 disparagement

backbone 4 base, grit, guts, will 5 basis, moxie, nerve, spine, spunk 6 mettle, pillar, rachis 7 resolve, support 8 mainstay, tenacity 9 character, fortitude, framework, toughness, vertebrae 10 foundation, moral fiber, resolution 12 spinal column 13 determination, steadfastness

backbreaking 6 taxing, tiring 7 arduous, onerous 8 grueling, toilsome 9 fatiguing, gruelling, laborious, punishing, strenuous,

torturous, wearisome 10 burdensome, exhausting

backchat 6 banter, gossip 10 persiflage

backcomb 5 tease

backcountry 4 bush 6 sticks 7 boonies, outback 8 frontier, interior 9 boondocks 10 hinterland

backcourtman 5 guard

back down 4 balk 5 admit, demur, welsh, yield 6 beg off, bow out, cry off, give in, give up, recall, recant, renege 7 concede, disavow, retract, retreat 8 take back, withdraw 9 surrender, weasel out 10 chicken out

backdrop 6 milieu 7 climate, context, scenery, setting 8 stage set 10 atmosphere, background 11 environment, mise-en-scène 12 surroundings

backer 4 ally 5 angel 6 patron, surety 7 sponsor 8 advocate, defender, exponent, follower, investor, promoter 9 auxiliary, guarantor, proponent, supporter 10 bankroller, benefactor, meal ticket

backfire 4 fail 5 blast 6 fizzle, go awry 7 go amiss, go wrong 8 miscarry, ricochet 9 boomerang, discharge, explosion 10 disappoint, spring back 11 fall through 13 counteraction

backgammon *board section:* 5 table *piece:* 5 stone *wedge:* 5 point

background 4 base, tone 6 milieu 7 history, scenery, setting 8 heritage, training 9 education 10 experience, supporting 13 circumstances, qualification

backhanded 7 devious, oblique 8 indirect, derisive, sneering 9 insulting, sarcastic 10 roundabout 12 disingenuous 13 condescending *compliment:* 6 insult, slight 7 putdown 9 aspersion

backing 3 aid 4 help 5 aegis, funds 7 harmony, support 8 auspices 9 patronage, promotion 10 assistance 11 endorsement, sponsorship 13 accompaniment, encouragement

backland see **backcountry**

backlash 5 slack 6 recoil 8 kickback, reaction, response, ricochet 11 retaliation 12 repercussion

backlog 4 pile 5 hoard, stock, store 6 pile up, supply 7 nest egg, reserve 9 inventory, reservoir, stockpile 12 accumulation

back of 5 abaft 6 behind 9 following

back off see **back down**

back out 4 quit 5 leave, welsh, yield 6 beg off, desert, give up, renege 7 forsake 8 withdraw 9 surrender

backpack 4 gear, hike 5 tramp 6 duffel, ramble 8 knapsack, rucksack 9 haversack

backpedal see **back down**
backset see **setback**
backside 3 bum **4** butt, rear, rump, seat, tail, tush **5** fanny, hiney, stern **6** behind, bottom, breech, far end, heinie **8** buttocks, derriere, haunches **9** fundament, posterior **12** hindquarters
backslide 4 fall, sink, slip **5** lapse **6** return, revert **7** go wrong, regress, relapse **9** retrovert **10** degenerate, go downhill, recidivate **11** deteriorate
backstabbing 4 slur **5** smear **6** malice **7** calumny, scandal, slander **8** betrayal **9** treachery **10** defamation, detraction, traitorous **11** treacherous **12** belittlement, depreciation, vilification **13** disparagement
backstairs 6 covert, secret, sneaky, sordid **7** furtive **8** hush-hush **9** secretive **10** scandalous **11** clandestine, underhanded **13** surreptitious
backstop 5 fence **6** screen, uphold **7** bolster, support **8** advocate, champion, side with
back talk 3 lip **4** guff, sass **5** cheek, mouth, sauce **9** freshness, impudence, insolence **12** impertinence
backtrack 7 regress, retrace, retreat, reverse **8** turn tail
backward 4 dull, slow, rear **5** abaft, dense **6** averse, astern, behind, stupid **7** awkward, delayed, moronic **8** ignorant, inverted, rearward, retarded, reversed, stagnant **9** benighted, dim-witted, in reverse **10** half-witted, retrograde, slow-witted, uncultured **11** thickheaded, undeveloped **12** feebleminded, simpleminded, uncultivated **13** unprogressive
backwoods see **backcountry**
backwoodsman 4 hick, rube **5** swain, yokel **6** rustic **7** bumpkin, hayseed **9** hillbilly **10** clodhopper, country boy, provincial **11** mountaineer
bacon *side:* **6** flitch, gammon *slice:* **6** rasher
Bacon, Francis *work:* **12** Novum Organum
bacteria 5 cocci **6** coccus **7** bacilli, vibrios **8** bacillus, spirilla **9** spirillum *culture medium:* **4** agar *destroyer:* **10** antibiotic *pathogenic:* **5** E. coli
bacterial disease 6 plague, typhus **7** anthrax, leprosy, tetanus, typhoid **8** botulism, syphilis **9** gonorrhea, infection, pneumonia **10** diphtheria, meningitis **11** shigellosis
bacteriologist *American:* **6** Enders (John Franklin) **7** Noguchi (Hideyo), Theiler (Max) *British:* **7** Fleming (Alexander) *French:* **5** Widal (Fernand) **7** Nicolle (Charles-Jean-Henri), Pasteur (Louis) *German:* **4** Cohn (Ferdinand Julius), Koch

(Robert) **5** Klebs (Edwin) **7** Behring (Emil von), Ehrlich (Paul), Löffler (Friedrich) **10** Wassermann (August von) *Japanese:* **8** Kitasato (Shibasaburo) *Russian:* **11** Metchnikoff (Elie) *Swiss:* **6** Yersin (Alexandre-Emile-John)
bad 3 ill, low **4** evil, foul, sour **5** amiss, awful, lousy, wrong **6** crummy, putrid, rancid, rotten, sinful, wicked **7** harmful, hateful, hurtful, immoral, naughty, noisome, noxious, spoiled, tainted, vicious **8** damaging, dreadful, inferior, perverse, terrible, wretched **9** abhorrent, defective, execrable, injurious, loathsome, obnoxious, offensive, putrefied, reprobate, repulsive, sickening **10** disgusting, iniquitous **11** deleterious, detrimental, distasteful, intolerable **12** unacceptable **13** objectionable *comparative:* **5** worse *prefix:* **3** dys, mis *superlative:* **5** worst
bad blood 7 ill will **10** bitterness, ill feeling
Badebec *husband:* **9** Gargantua *son:* **10** Pantagruel
Baden 3 spa **6** resort **9** hot spring
badge 3 pin **4** arms, logo, mark, seal, sign **5** award, honor, kudos, medal, token **6** button, emblem, ensign **7** laurels **8** accolade, hallmark, insignia **10** coat of arms, decoration **11** distinction, purple heart
badger 3 bug, nag **4** bait, goad, ride **5** annoy, brock, chivy, harry, hound, ratel **6** chivvy, harass, hassle, heckle, hector, needle, pester, plague **7** torment **8** bullyrag **9** importune
Badger State 9 Wisconsin
badinage 4 play **6** banter, joking **7** jesting, joshing, kidding, ribbing, teasing **8** backchat, chitchat, repartee **9** cross talk **10** persiflage
badland 4 wild **5** waste, wilds **6** barren, desert **7** outback **8** wildness **10** wilderness **11** hill country
bad mark 3 gig **7** demerit
bad-tempered 4 dour, sour **5** cross, sulky, surly, testy **6** crabby, cranky, crusty, grumpy, ornery, sullen, touchy **7** grouchy, peevish **8** choleric, petulant **9** crotchety, dyspeptic, irascible, irritable, splenetic **10** ill-humored, ill-natured, unpleasant **11** quarrelsome **12** cantankerous, curmudgeonly, disagreeable, misanthropic
Baedeker 5 guide **6** manual **8** handbook **9** guidebook, vade mecum **10** compendium **11** enchiridion, travel guide
baffle 4 dash, foil **5** addle, block, floor, mix up, stump **6** bemuse, hinder, impede, muddle, puzzle, thwart **7** barrier, confuse, flummox, mystify, nonplus, perplex **8** befuddle,

bewilder, confound **9** deflector, dumbfound, frustrate **10** circumvent, disappoint, disconcert

bafflement 9 confusion **10** bemusement, perplexity **12** bewilderment

bag 3 cop, nab, kit, net, sag, win **4** flop, grip, hook, kill, land, nail, poke, sack, tote, trap **5** biddy, bulge, catch, crone, forgo, pouch, purse, seize, shoot, snare, steal, udder **6** beldam, collar, duffel, duffle, give up, secure, valise **7** abandon, acquire, capture, satchel **8** backpack, knapsack, reticule, suitcase **9** apprehend, haversack **12** protuberance

bagatelle 6 trifle, whimsy **9** plaything

baggage 4 gear **5** hussy, stuff, tramp, trull, wench **6** burden, things, wanton **7** carry-on, effects, jezebel, luggage, parcels, trollop **8** obstacle, matériel, slattern, strumpet **9** equipment, hindrance **10** impediment, prostitute **11** impedimenta **13** paraphernalia

baggy 5 loose

Baghdad *founder:* **6** Mansur *river:* **6** Tigris

bagnio 4 crib, stew **7** brothel, lupanar **8** bordello, cathouse **10** bawdy house, whorehouse

bagpipe *part:* **5** drone **7** bourdon, chanter *sound:* **5** skirl

Bahamas *capital:* **6** Nassau *island:* **3** Cat **5** Abaco **6** Andros, Inagua **7** Watling **9** Eleuthera, Mayaguana **11** Grand Bahama, San Salvador **13** New Providence *neighbor:* **4** Cuba

Bahrain *capital:* **6** Manama *island:* **6** Sitrah **7** Bahrain **10** Al Muharraq *language:* **6** Arabic *monetary unit:* **5** dinar *ruler:* **4** amir, emir **5** ameer, hakim

bail 3 bar, dip **4** bond, flee, lade **5** ladle, scoop **6** handle, pledge, surety **7** release **8** guaranty, security, warranty **9** guarantee **10** collateral **12** recognizance

bailiwick 4 area, turf, zone **5** field, realm **6** domain, sphere **7** demesne, purview, terrain **8** district, dominion, province **9** champaign, specialty, territory **10** discipline **12** jurisdiction

bailout 3 aid **6** relief, rescue **7** subsidy **11** benefaction, deliverance

bairn 3 kid, tot **4** babe, baby, tyke **5** child **6** infant

bait 3 nag, try, vex **4** lure, ride, trap **5** abuse, chase, chivy, decoy, harry, hound, leger, snare, taunt, tease, tempt, worry **6** allure, badger, come-on, entice, entrap, harass, heckle, hector, lead on, molest, pester, seduce **7** beguile, torment, torture **8** bullyrag, inveigle, ridicule **9** persecute, seduction,

sweetener **10** attraction, allurement, enticement, temptation *and switch:* **4** lure **5** trick **8** inveigle **10** substitute

bake 4 burn, char, cook, fire, kiln **5** broil, roast, toast **6** scorch **7** scallop, scollop, swelter

baked clay 7 ceramic

baker's dozen 8 thirteen

bakers' yeast 6 leaven **9** leavening

baking 3 hot **5** fiery **6** red-hot, torrid **7** burning **8** broiling, scalding, sizzling, white-hot **9** scorching *chamber:* **4** kiln, oven

baksheesh 3 tip **4** alms **5** bribe, favor **6** grease, reward **7** payment **8** gratuity **9** emolument **12** compensation

Balaam *beast:* **3** ass **6** donkey *father:* **4** Beor

balance 4 rest **5** level, poise, scale, weigh **6** adjust, excess, make up, offset, set off, square, stasis **7** harmony, remains, remnant, residue **8** atone for, equalize, outweigh, residual, residuum, symmetry **9** composure, congruity, equipoise, harmonize, remainder, stability **10** compensate, counteract, difference, equanimity, neutralize, proportion, steadiness **11** consistency, countervail, equilibrium, self-control **12** counterpoise

balanced 4 fair **5** equal **6** offset, stable, steady **7** equable, weighed **9** equitable, impartial **10** evenhanded, harmonized, stabilized

balcony 6 piazza **7** catwalk, gallery **8** platform **9** mezzanine *section:* **4** loge

bald 4 bare, nude **5** blunt, naked, plain, stark **6** barren, severe, shaven, smooth **8** glabrous, hairless, palpable, treeless **9** depilated, unadorned, uncovered **10** deforested, forthright **11** undisguised, unvarnished

baldachin 4 silk **6** canopy, fabric

Balder, Baldur *father:* **4** Odin *mother:* **5** Frigg **6** Frigga *slayer:* **3** Höd **4** Hoth, Loke, Loki **5** Hoder, Hothr *wife:* **5** Nanna

balderdash 3 rot **4** bosh, bull, bunk **5** bilge, crock, hooey **6** blague, bunkum, drivel **7** baloney, eyewash, garbage, hogwash, palaver, rubbish, twaddle **8** buncombe, claptrap, malarkey, nonsense, tommyrot **9** poppycock **10** tomfoolery **11** foolishness **13** horsefeathers

bald-faced 4 bold **6** arrant, brazen **7** blatant, defiant **8** impudent, insolent **9** audacious, shameless, unabashed **11** impertinent

baldness 8 alopecia **12** hairlessness

baldpate 7 widgeon **8** skinhead

Baldwin, James *essay:* **17** Nobody Knows My Name, Notes of a Native Son *novel:* **12** Fire Next Time (The) **13** Giovanni's Room

14 Another Country **21** Go Tell It on the Mountain *play:* **21** Blues for Mister Charlie

balefire 6 beacon

baleful 4 dire, evil **6** deadly, malign **7** direful, fateful, harmful, hostile, malefic, ominous **8** menacing, sinister **9** ill-boding, ill-omened, malignant **10** maleficent, malevolent, pernicious **11** apocalyptic, threatening **12** unpropitious

balk 3 bar, gag, jib, shy **4** beam, dash, foil, ruin **5** block, check, demur, plank, stall **6** baffle, boggle, desist, flinch, hinder, rafter, refuse, thwart **7** prevent, scruple, stumble **8** hang back, hesitate, obstruct **9** frustrate, hindrance **10** circumvent, disappoint

balky 5 loath **6** averse, ornery, mulish, unruly **7** froward, restive, wayward, willful **8** contrary, hesitant, perverse, stubborn **9** immovable, obstinate, reluctant **10** unreliable **11** intractable, wrongheaded **12** cross-grained, recalcitrant **13** uncooperative, unpredictable

ball 3 orb, wad **4** prom **5** dance, globe, round **6** sphere **8** spheroid *batted high:* **3** fly *batted straight:* **5** liner *high-arching:* **3** lob *of thread or yarn:* **4** clew *ornamental:* **6** pom-pom, pompon *tiny:* **7** globule

ballad 3 lay **4** poem, song *singer:* **8** minstrel **10** troubadour

ballast 4 load **5** poise **6** steady **7** balance, freight **8** balancer **9** stabilize, weigh down **10** dead weight, stabilizer **12** counterpoise **13** counterweight

ballerina 6 dancer **8** coryphée, danseuse **9** toe dancer **11** dancing girl *skirt:* **4** tutu see also **dancer**

ballet 4 Agon **6** Apollo, Jewels, Sylvia **7** Giselle, Orpheus **8** Bayadère (La), Coppélia, Firebird (The), Raimonda, Raymonda, Swan Lake, Sylphide (La) **9** Fancy Free, Petrushka, Sylphides (Les) **10** Don Quixote, Nutcracker (The), Petrouchka **12** Rite of Spring (The) *company:* **5** Kirov **7** Joffrey **8** Imperial *costume:* **4** tutu **6** tights **7** leotard *dancer:* **7** danseur **8** coryphée, danseuse **9** ballerina *for two:* **9** pas de deux *handrail:* **5** barre *jump:* **4** jeté **9** entrechat *knee bend:* **4** plié *position:* **6** pointe **8** attitude **9** arabesque *step:* **3** pas **8** glissade *turn:* **6** chaîné **9** pirouette

Ballets ____ 6 Russes

ball game see at **game**

Ballo in Maschera composer 5 Verdi (Giuseppe)

balloon sail 9 spinnaker

ball-shaped 7 globoid, globose **8** globular, spheroid **9** globulous, spherical

ball up 4 clew, daze **5** addle **6** fuddle, jumble,

muddle, puzzle, tangle **7** confuse, fluster **8** befuddle, bewilder, bollix up, confound, distract, throw off **9** disorient

ballyhoo 4 hype, tout **6** blazon, herald, hoopla, hubbub, tumult **7** promote, trumpet **8** brouhaha **9** commotion, publicity **12** extravaganza

balm 4 lull **5** aroma, cream, quiet, salve, scent, spice **6** chrism, relief, remedy, solace **7** anodyne, bouquet, comfort, incense, perfume, soother, unction, unguent **8** easement, ointment **9** emollient, fragrance, redolence **10** palliative **11** consolation, restorative

balmacaan 8 overcoat

balm of Gilead 6 poplar **7** soother **8** restorer **9** balsam fir **11** restorative **12** balsam poplar

balmy 4 calm, daft, mild, nuts, soft **5** crazy, loony, nutty, potty, silly, sweet, wacky **6** gentle, insane, smooth **7** cracked, foolish, lenient, summery **8** aromatic, deranged, fragrant, perfumed, peaceful, pleasant, pleasing, redolent, soothing, tropical **9** agreeable, ambrosial, temperate

baloney 3 rot **4** bosh, bull, bunk **5** bilge, hokum, hooey **6** bunkum, humbug **7** hogwash, rubbish **8** buncombe, claptrap, nonsense **9** poppycock **10** balderdash **11** foolishness

balsam poplar 9 tacamahac **12** balm of Gilead

Balthazar's gift 5 myrrh

Baltic city: 4 Riga **7** Tallinn **8** Helsinki **9** Stockholm *native:* **4** Lett, Sorb, Wend **7** Latvian **8** Estonian, Prussian **10** Lithuanian *state:* **6** Latvia **7** Estonia **9** Lithuania

Baltimore team 5 Blast, Colts **6** Ravens **7** Orioles

balustrade 4 rail **5** fence **7** railing **8** banister, handrail

Balzac character 4 Pons (Cousin) **5** Bette (Cousin) **6** Goriot (Père), Vidocq **7** Chabert (Colonel), Eugénie (Grandet), Grandet, Vautrin **8** Rubempré (Lucien de) **9** Birotteau, Rastignac (Eugène de) **13** Henri de Marsay

Bambi author 6 Salten (Felix)

bambino 3 kid, tot **4** babe, baby, tyke **5** bairn, child **6** cherub, Christ, infant, moppet, nipper **7** toddler

bamboozle 3 con **4** bilk, dupe, fool, gull, hoax, hose, scam **5** stump, trick **6** baffle, befool, diddle, puzzle **7** chicane, confuse, deceive, defraud, mislead, perplex, swindle **8** befuddle, confound, flimflam, hoodwink, throw off **9** frustrate **11** hornswoggle

ban 3 bar **5** curse, taboo **6** enjoin, forbid, outlaw **7** censure, exclude **8** anathema, prohibit, suppress **9** damnation, interdict, proscribe **10** injunction **11** forbiddance, malediction, prohibition, suppression **12** denunciation, interdiction, proscription

Ban *ally:* **6** Arthur *son:* **8** Lancelot

banal 4 blah, dull, flat **5** bland, corny, ho-hum, tired, trite, usual, vapid **6** common, jejune, stupid **7** clichéd, humdrum, insipid, prosaic, sapless, trivial **8** ordinary **9** hackneyed, quotidian, wearisome **10** namby-pamby, pedestrian, uninspired, wishy-washy **11** commonplace

banality 5 ennui **6** cliché, old saw, truism **7** bromide, inanity, old song **8** chestnut, monotony, prosaism **9** platitude **10** dreariness, shibboleth, triviality **11** commonplace, old chestnut, tediousness

banana 3 fei

banana-like fruit 8 plantain

banausic 4 blah, drab, dull, poky **6** dreary, earthy, stodgy **7** humdrum, mundane, routine, secular, sensual, tedious, worldly **8** everyday, material, plodding, temporal, workaday **9** practical, pragmatic **10** monotonous, pedestrian **11** acquisitive, utilitarian **13** materialistic, uninteresting

band 4 belt, bevy, club, crew, gang, gird, sash, tape **5** bunch, corps, covey, group, horde, party, strap, strip, troop, unite **6** concur, fillet, girdle, league, outfit, ribbon, team up, troupe **7** cluster, combine, company, coterie **8** cincture, engirdle, ensemble, symphony **9** cooperate, orchestra **10** federation *horizontal:* **4** fess *Mexican:* **8** mariachi *neck:* **6** torque *small:* **5** combo

bandage 4 bind **5** cover, dress, gauze, truss **6** swathe **7** plaster, swaddle **8** compress, dressing

bandanna 8 babushka, kerchief **9** headscarf **11** neckerchief

bandeau 3 bra **5** strip **6** fillet, ribbon, stripe **7** tube top **8** swimwear **9** brassiere

banderilla 4 dart

banderole 4 flag, jack **6** banner, burgee, colors, ensign, pennon, scroll **7** pennant **8** bannerol, standard, streamer

bandicoot 3 rat

bandit 6 outlaw, raider, robber, sacker **7** brigand, cateran, forager, ravager **8** marauder, pillager **9** cutthroat, desperado, holdup man, plunderer **10** freebooter, highwayman **11** bushwhacker

bandleader 7 maestro **9** conductor *famous:* **3** Rey (Alvino) **4** Shaw (Artie), Ward (Hedley), Welk (Lawrence) **5** Basie (Count), Brown (Les), Cugat (Xavier), Faith (Percy), Heath (Ted), James (Harry), Jones (Spike),

Kyser (Kay), Lewis (Ted), Lopez (Vincent), Owens (Buck), Prado (Pérez), Sousa (John Philip) **6** Cotton (Billy), Dorsey (Jimmy, Tommy), Duchin (Eddie, Peter), Herman (Woody), Hylton (Jack), Kenton (Stan), Miller (Glenn), Mingus (Charles), Waring (Fred) **7** Goodman (Benny), Trotter (John Scott) **8** Calloway (Cab), Giordano (Vince), Lombardo (Guy), Whiteman (Paul) **9** Ellington (Duke), Henderson (Fletcher), Mantovani

bandolier 4 belt, sash

bandwagon 3 fad **4** chic, mode, rage **5** craze, style, trend, vogue **7** fashion ·

bandy 3 bat **4** flip, swap, toss **5** argue, bowed **6** banter **7** discuss, shuffle **8** exchange **9** bowlegged, pass about **11** interchange

bane 3 woe **4** pest, ruin **5** curse, death, venom, virus **6** blight, burden, plague, poison **7** bugaboo, bugbear, scourge, torment, undoing **8** anathema, calamity, downfall, nuisance **9** bête noire, contagion, destroyer, ruination **10** affliction, pestilence **11** destruction

baneful 4 dire, evil **5** fatal **6** deadly **7** fateful, harmful, hurtful, malefic, noxious, ominous **9** ill-boding, ill-omened, injurious, malignant, pestilent, unhealthy **10** disastrous, pernicious **11** apocalyptic, deleterious, pestiferous, threatening **12** pestilential, unpropitious

bang 3 bat, box, hit, pop, rap **4** bash, beat, belt, blow, boom, bump, clap, peal, push, rape, shot, slam, sock, wham, whop **5** blast, burst, crack, crash, noise, pound, punch, smack, smash, sound, vigor, whack **6** fringe, report, strike, thrill, wallop **7** collide, exactly, resound **8** smack-dab, squarely **9** explosion **10** detonation

banger 7 athlete, sausage

Bangkok native 4 Thai

Bangladesh *capital:* **5** Dacca, Dhaka *city:* **6** Khulna **10** Chittagong *former name:* **6** Bengal *language:* **7** Bengali *monetary unit:* **4** taka *neighbor:* **5** Burma, India **7** Myanmar *river:* **5** Padma **6** Ganges, Jamuna **11** Brahmaputra

bangle 4 disk **5** charm **6** anklet, bauble **7** pendant, trinket **8** bracelet, wristlet

bang-up 3 ace **4** fine **5** dandy, primo, super **6** far-out, superb **7** capital **8** champion, fabulous, five-star, splendid, top-notch **9** excellent, first-rate **10** first-class **11** spectacular

banish 3 ban **4** oust **5** debar, eject, evict, exile, expel **6** deport, dispel, put out, run out **7** cast out, dismiss, exclude, shut out, turn out **8** drive out, relegate, send away **9** discharge, ostracize, rusticate, transport **10** expatriate **13** excommunicate

banishment 5 exile **7** banning **8** eviction **9** discharge, expulsion, ostracism **10** dispelling, relegation **11** deportation, dissolution **12** displacement

banister 3 bar **4** rail **7** railing **10** balustrade

bank 3 row **4** edge, heap, hill, mass, pile, rank, save, tier, tilt **5** amass, array, beach, coast, group, hoard, levee, marge, mound, pitch, shoal, shore, slope, stack, stash **6** coffer, dealer, invest, margin, rivage, strand **7** deposit, incline, lay away, pyramid **8** lakeside, lay aside, salt away, seafront, set aside, sock away, squirrel, treasury **9** riverside **10** repository, storehouse **11** credit union **12** squirrel away *machine:* **3** ATM

bank on 5 trust **7** believe

bankroll 4 back, fund **5** endow, funds, stake **6** pay for **7** capital, finance, sponsor, support **9** grubstake, subsidize **10** capitalize, underwrite

bankrupt 4 bare, bust, do in, ruin **5** break, drain, empty, strip, spent, use up, wreck **6** broken, divest, failed, fold up **7** deplete, deprive, exhaust, lacking, sterile **8** depleted, indebted **9** destitute, exhausted, pauperize, penniless **10** impoverish **12** impoverished

bankruptcy 4 lack, ruin **6** penury **7** failure **9** depletion, ruination, sterility, total loss **10** barrenness, exhaustion, insolvency **11** destitution, liquidation

banned 5 taboo **6** barred **7** illegal, illicit, tabooed **8** enjoined, verboten **9** forbidden **10** contraband, disallowed, prohibited, proscribed **11** interdicted

banner 4 flag, jack **6** burgee, ensign, pennon **7** pendant, pennant **8** banderol, gonfalon, standard, streamer **9** banderole *Roman:* **7** labarum **8** vexillum

bannerol see **banderole**

banquet 4 feed **5** feast, roast **6** dinner, regale, repast, spread

banquette 4 seat, sofa **5** bench, shelf **8** platform, sidewalk

Banquo 5 ghost *murderer:* **7** Macbeth

banshee 6 keener, wailer

bantam 3 wee **4** arch, fowl, mini, pert, runt, tiny **5** dwarf, saucy, small **6** cheeky, little, petite **8** insolent, malapert **9** combative, undersize **10** diminutive, undersized

banter 3 fun, kid, rag, rib, wit **4** fool, jest, jive, joke, josh, razz **5** chaff, dally, jolly, tease **7** jesting, joshing, kidding, mockery, ragging, razzing, ribbing, teasing **8** backchat, back talk, badinage, chitchat, drollery,

exchange, repartee **9** challenge, small talk **10** persiflage, pleasantry **11** give-and-take

bantling 4 babe, baby **5** bairn **6** infant **7** bambino, newborn, papoose

baptize 3 dip, dub **4** call, name, soak **5** douse, title **6** anoint, drench, purify **7** asperse, cleanse, entitle, immerse **8** christen, dedicate, initiate, sprinkle **9** designate **10** consecrate, denominate, regenerate

bar 3 ban, dam, pub, rod, tap **4** curb, dive, fess, halt, save, stop **5** block, court, estop, ingot, limit, stick, strip **6** bistro, except, impede, lounge, saloon, tavern **7** barrier, cantina, delimit, exclude, gin mill, rule out, taproom **8** alehouse, blockade, count out, obstacle, obstruct, restrict, tribunal **9** barricade, eliminate, honky-tonk, nightclub, roadhouse **11** obstruction, rathskeller **12** circumscribe, watering hole *type:* **3** raw **4** cash, fern, open, roll, tiki **6** sports

barb 3 dig **4** dart, hook **5** quill, shaft, thorn **6** zinger

Barbados *capital:* 10 Bridgetown *location:* **10** West Indies

barbarian 3 Hun **4** Goth, lout, rude, wild **5** beast, crude, brute **6** savage, Vandal **7** lowbrow, uncouth **8** Visigoth **9** foreigner, Ostrogoth, primitive **10** uncultured **11** uncivilized **12** uncultivated

barbaric 4 wild **5** crude, rough **6** brutal, coarse, savage **7** beastly, boorish, brutish, loutish, uncouth **8** churlish **9** atrocious, monstrous, primitive, unrefined **11** uncivilized

barbarism 8 malaprop, rudeness, solecism **9** vulgarism, vulgarity **10** coarseness, corruption **11** impropriety, malapropism **12** backwardness, unseemliness

barbarity 7 cruelty **8** atrocity, savagery **9** brutality, depravity **10** inhumanity, savageness **11** viciousness **12** ruthlessness **13** monstrousness

barbarous 4 base, fell, grim, rude, vile, wild **5** cruel, harsh **6** brutal, fierce, Gothic, savage, unholy, vulgar, wicked **7** brutish, Hunnish, inhuman, lowbrow, uncivil, ungodly, vicious, wolfish **8** backward, fiendish, inhumane, ruthless, sadistic **9** benighted, ferocious, graceless, heartless, merciless, monstrous, primitive, tasteless, truculent **10** abominable, outlandish, outrageous, philistine, unmerciful **11** unchristian, uncivilized **12** uncultivated

Barbary state 5 Tunis **7** Algiers, Morocco, Tripoli

barbecue 5 grill, roast **7** cookout, roaster

barber 3 bob, cut **4** clip, crop, trim **5** shave,

shear 6 shaver, tonsor 7 clipper, cropper 8 coiffeur 9 coiffeuse 10 beautician, haircutter 11 hairdresser, hair stylist

Barber of Seville *author:* 12 Beaumarchais (Pierre-Augustin de) *character:* 6 Figaro, Rosina, Rosine 7 Bartolo, Basilio 8 Almaviva, Bartholo *composer:* 7 Rossini (Gioacchino) 9 Paisiello (Giovanni)

bard 4 muse, poet, scop 5 skald 8 jongleur, minstrel 9 balladist 10 Parnassian, troubadour *fictitious:* 6 Ossian

Bard of Avon 11 Shakespeare (William)

bare 4 bald, mere, nude, void 5 empty, naked, shorn, stark, strip 6 barren, denude, devoid, expose, peeled, reveal, unclad, unveil, vacant 7 denuded, disrobe, emptied, exposed, uncover 8 bankrupt, disclose, stripped 9 unclothed, uncovered, undressed

barefaced 4 bald, bold, open 5 blunt, naked 6 arrant, brassy, brazen 7 blatant, glaring, obvious 8 flagrant, impudent, overbold 9 audacious, beardless, shameless, unabashed 10 unblushing 11 temerarious, unconcealed

barefoot 6 unshod 8 shoeless 9 discalced

bareheaded 7 hatless

barely 4 just 6 hardly, scarce 7 faintly 8 meagerly, scarcely

bargain 3 buy 4 bond, deal, pact, swap 5 agree, steal, trade, truck, value 6 barter, confer, dicker, haggle, higgle, palter, pledge 7 chaffer, compact, savings, traffic 8 closeout, contract, covenant, exchange, giveaway, good deal, huckster, markdown, transact 9 agreement, good value, negotiate, reduction 10 compromise, convention, loss leader, pennyworth 11 arrangement, transaction 13 understanding

barge 3 hoy 4 scow 5 clump, stump 6 lumber 7 galumph, stumble

baritone 4 Prey (Hermann) 5 Gobbi (Tito) 6 Bailey (Norman), London (George), Milnes (Sherrill), Terfel (Bryn), Warren (Leonard) 7 Hampson (Thomas), MacNeil (Cornell), Merrill (Robert), Tibbett (Lawrence) 8 Raimondi (Ruggero), Warfield (William)

barium symbol 2 Ba

bark 3 arf, bay, yap, yip 4 snap, woof, yelp 5 snarl 6 bellow *mulberry:* 4 tapa

barkeeper see bartender

barker 4 tout 5 shill 6 hawker 8 pitchman

Barlow epic 9 Columbiad

barman see bartender

Barmecidal 5 empty, false 6 unreal 7 fictive 8 apparent, illusive, illusory 9 imaginary 10 chimerical, ostensible 13 insubstantial

barn 6 stable *area of:* 4 loft 7 hayloft

barnacle 5 leech 7 sponger 8 hanger-on, nui-

sance, parasite 9 dependent, free rider 10 crustacean, freeloader

barnstorm 8 campaign

Barnum *elephant:* 5 Jumbo *midget:* 8 Tom Thumb *partner:* 6 Bailey

barnyard 4 foul, rude 5 crass, crude, dirty, nasty 6 coarse, earthy, filthy, ribald, smutty, vulgar 7 obscene, raunchy, uncouth 8 indecent 9 tasteless 10 indelicate 12 scatological

baron 4 lord, peer 5 mogul, noble 6 tycoon 7 kingpin, magnate 8 overlord 13 industrialist

baronial 5 ample, grand, noble 6 august, lordly 7 stately 8 imposing, majestic, princely 9 grandiose 10 commanding, impressive 11 magnificent, resplendent

baroque 6 florid, ornate, rococo 7 complex 8 dramatic 9 excessive, grotesque, irregular 10 flamboyant, ornamented 11 embellished, extravagant 12 ostentatious 13 overdecorated

Baroque *architect:* 4 Wren (Christopher) 7 Bernini (Gian Lorenzo), Guarini (Guarino), Maderno (Carlo) 9 Borromini (Francesco) *composer:* 4 Bach (Johann Sebastian) 5 Lully (Jean-Baptiste) 6 Handel (George Frideric), Rameau (Jean-Philippe), Schütz (Heinrich) 7 Corelli (Arcangelo), Purcell (Henry), Vivaldi (Antonio) 8 Albinoni (Tommaso), Couperin (François), Telemann (Georg Philipp) 9 Pachelbel (Johann), Scarlatti (Alessandro, Domenico) 10 Monteverdi (Claudio) *painter:* 4 Hals (Frans) 5 Steen (Jan) 6 Claude (Lorrain), Rubens (Peter Paul) 7 El Greco, Holbein (Hans), Poussin (Nicolas), Van Dyck (Anthony), Vermeer (Jan) 8 Carracci (Agostino, Annibale, Lodovico), Ter Borch (Gerard) 9 Rembrandt (van Rijn), Velázquez (Diego) 10 Caravaggio *sculptor:* 5 Puget (Pierre) 7 Bernini (Gian Lorenzo), Coustou (Guillaume, Nicholas), Pigalle (Jean-Baptiste) 8 Coysevox (Antoine), Girardon (François)

barrack 4 jeer, root 5 cheer, scoff, taunt 6 billet, casern, deride, hector 7 caserne 8 quarters

barrage 3 dam 4 fire, hail, mass 5 blitz, burst, salvo, storm, surge 6 deluge, shower, stream, volley 7 gunfire, torrent 8 drumfire, shelling 9 broadside, cannonade, crossfire, fusillade, onslaught 11 bombardment

barranca 4 bank 5 bluff, gully 6 arroyo

barrel 3 keg, tun, vat 4 butt, cask, drum, peck, race, rush, tear 5 hurry 6 firkin, hasten 8 hogshead *maker:* 6 cooper *part:* 4 hoop 5 stave *stopper:* 4 bung *support:* 6 gantry

barrelhouse 4 dive **5** hurry, joint **7** hangout **9** honky-tonk

barren 3 dry **4** arid, bare, poor **5** bleak, empty, stark, stony, waste **6** desert, devoid, effete, futile, fallow **7** badland, lacking, parched, sterile, wanting **8** desolate, heirless, impotent **9** childless, fruitless, infertile, unbearing, unfertile, wasteland **10** unfruitful, untillable **11** unrewarding **12** hardscrabble, unproductive, unprofitable

barricade 5 block, fence **7** barrier **8** blockade **9** roadblock *of trees:* **6** abatis

Barrie character 4 Hook (Capt.), John, Nana, Smee **5** Peter, Tommy, Wendy **7** Michael **8** Crichton **9** Tiger Lily **10** Tinker Bell **11** Captain Hook

barrier see **barricade**

barring 3 but **4** save **6** bating, except, saving **7** besides, without **9** aside from, excluding, excepting, outside of **11** exclusive of

barrio 4 slum, turf, ward **6** ghetto **7** quarter, section **8** district, precinct **12** neighborhood

barrister 6 lawyer **7** counsel **8** advocate, attorney **9** counselor

barroom 3 pub **6** lounge, saloon, tavern **7** gin mill, rum room, taproom **8** alehouse, beer hall, dramshop, drinkery, groggery, grogshop **9** beer joint, roadhouse **12** watering hole

bartender 7 tapster **8** boniface **10** mixologist **12** saloonkeeper

barter 4 swap **5** trade, truck **7** bargain, traffic **8** exchange

Bartered Bride composer 7 Smetana (Bedrich)

Barth novel 7 Chimera **12** Giles Goat-Boy **13** Sot-Weed Factor (The)

Baruch *father:* **6** Neriah, Zabbai *occupation:* **6** scribe

basal 5 basic, vital **6** bottom, lowest **7** minimal, primary, radical **8** simplest **9** beginning, essential, undermost **10** bottommost, elementary, primordial, underlying **11** fundamental, preliminary, rudimentary **12** foundational *layer:* **4** sima

base 3 bad, bed, fix, key, low **4** camp, evil, foot, fort, foul, home, mean, poor, post, prop, rest, root, seat, site, ugly, vile **5** build, cheap, dirty, found, hinge, lousy, lowly, nadir, plant, set up, sorry, stand **6** bottom, coarse, common, depend, derive, filthy, ground, humble, menial, origin, paltry, scurvy, shoddy, sleazy, sordid, source, trashy, wicked **7** bedrock, caitiff, essence, footing, ignoble, lowborn, low-down, pitiful, servile, squalid, support **8** beggarly, buttress, cowardly, garrison, inferior, ped-

estal, plebeian, recreant, unwashed, unworthy, wretched **9** construct, dastardly, degrading, establish, framework, loathsome, low-minded, predicate, principle **10** abominable, despicable, foundation, groundwork, substratum, unennobled **11** disgraceful, humiliating, ignominious **12** contemptible, meanspirited, substructure, underpinning

baseball *abbreviation:* **2** AB, AL, BA, BB, BI, CF, DH, DP, ER, FA, HR, IP, LF, LP, NL, RF, SB, SO, SS, WP **3** ERA, LOB, MVP, RBI *reputed founder:* **9** Doubleday (Abner) *glove:* **4** mitt *official:* **3** ump **6** umpire *pitch:* **4** drop, heat **5** curve, smoke **6** change, heater, sinker, slider, slurve **7** spitter **8** change-up, fadeaway, fastball, fork ball, knuckler, palm ball, spitball **9** brushback, screwball **11** knuckleball **12** change of pace, knuckle curve *player:* **6** batter **7** baseman, catcher, fielder, pitcher **9** infielder, shortstop **10** base runner, outfielder **11** left fielder **12** right fielder **13** center fielder *term:* **3** bag, bat, box, fan, fly, out, run, tag, tap, tip **4** balk, ball, base, bean, bunt, cage, deck, foul, hook, line, mitt, nono, pill, pole, save, walk **5** alley, apple, bench, bloop, clout, count, drive, error, flare, fungo, glove, homer, liner, mound, pop-up, slide, swing **6** assist, clutch, double, dugout, groove, ground, inning, inside, pop fly, pop-out, powder, putout, relief, rubber, runner, single, strike, triple, windup **7** battery, blooper, bullpen, cleanup, diamond, floater, fly ball, home run, infield, manager, outside, pickoff, rhubarb, sidearm, squeeze, stretch **8** baseline, beanball, delivery, foul ball, grounder, keystone, nohitter, outfield, pinch-hit, rosin bag, southpaw **9** full count, home plate, hot corner, line drive, sacrifice, strikeout, two-bagger **10** double play, frozen rope, ground ball, scratch hit, strike zone **11** knuckleball, pinch hitter, squeeze play, three-bagger (see also **American League, National League**)

baseballer 3 Ott (Mel) **4** Alou (Felipe, Jesús, Matty, Moises), A-Rod, Bell (George), Cobb (Ty), Cone (David), Dean (Dizzy), Fisk (Carlton), Ford (Whitey), Foxx (Jimmy), Kaat (Jim), Mays (Willie), Rice (Jim), Rose (Pete), Ruth (Babe), Ryan (Nolan), Sosa (Sammy) **5** Aaron (Henry), Anson (Cap), Banks (Ernie), Belle (Albert), Bench (Johnny), Berra (Yogi), Boggs (Wade), Bonds (Barry), Brett (George), Brock (Lou), Brown (Kevin), Carew (Rod), Clark (Will), Damon (Johnny), Davis

(Mark), Green (Shawn), Grove (Lefty), Gwynn (Tony), Henke (Tom), Jeter (Derek), Kiner (Ralph), Maris (Roger), Mauer (Joe), Paige (Satchel), Perez (Tony), Perry (Gaylord), Smith (Lee), Spahn (Warren), Staub (Rusty), Tiant (Luis), Viola (Frank), Weeks (Rickie), Young (Cy), Yount (Robin) **6** Dawson (Andre), Feller (Bob), Foster (George), Franco (John), Garvey (Steve), Gehrig (Lou), Gibson (Bob, Josh, Kirk), Gooden (Dwight), Herzog (Whitey), Hunter (Catfish), Koufax (Sandy), Lajoie (Nap), Maddux (Greg), Mantle (Mickey), Morgan (Joe), Murphy (Dale), Murray (Eddie), Musial (Stan), Palmer (Jim), Piazza (Mike), Pujols (Albert), Raines (Tim), Ripken (Cal), Seaver (Tom), Sisler (George), Sutter (Bruce), Sutton (Don), Thomas (Frank), Vaughn (Mo), Wagner (Honus), Walker (Larry) **7** Bagwell (Jeff), Canseco (José), Carlton (Steve), Clemens (Roger), Coleman (Vince), Collins (Eddie), Delgado (Carlos), Fingers (Rollie), Griffey (Ken), Hornsby (Roger), Hubbell (Carl), Jackson (Joe, Reggie), Johnson (Randy, Walter), Justice (David), Leonard (Buck), McGwire (Mark), Mondesi (Raul), Puckett (Kirby), Ramirez (Manny), Reardon (Jeff), Schmidt (Mike), Simmons (Al), Speaker (Tris) **8** Anderson (Sparky), Blyleven (Bert), Clemente (Roberto), DiMaggio (Joe), Guerrero (Vladimir), Martinez (Pedro), Mitchell (Kevin), Righetti (Dave), Robinson (Brooks, Frank, Jackie), Williams (Bernie, Ted), Winfield (Dave) **9** Alexander (Grover), Eckersley (Dennis), Gehringer (Charlie), Greenberg (Hank), Henderson (Rickey), Hernandez (Willie), Hershiser (Orel), Killebrew (Harmon), Mathewson (Christy), Mattingly (Don), Rodriguez (Alex), Sheffield (Gary) **10** Campanella (Roy), Conigliaro (Tony), Strawberry (Darryl), Valenzuela (Fernando) **11** Garciaparra (Nomar), Yastrzemski (Carl)

baseball team see **American League; National League**

baseboard 7 molding **8** skirting

baseless 4 idle, thin, vain **5** empty, false, wrong **6** feeble, flimsy **9** frivolous, pointless, senseless, unfounded, untenable **10** fallacious, gratuitous, groundless, inadequate, incredible, ungrounded **11** uncalledfor, unconfirmed, unnecessary, unsupported, unsustained, unwarranted **12** indefensible, contemptible, unpersuasive **13** unjustifiable

basement 6 bottom, cellar, ground **7** bedrock

10 foundation, groundwork, substratum **12** substructure

base on balls 4 walk

bash 3 bat, hit **4** belt, blow, fete, gala, slam, whop **5** blast, crack, crash, party, pound, smack, smash, thump, whack **6** attack, pummel, soiree, strike, wallop **7** blowout, shindig **8** wingding

Bashemath father: 7 Ishmael **husband: 4** Esau **sister: 8** Nebaioth

bashful 3 coy, shy **5** chary, mousy, timid **6** demure, modest **7** abashed, nervous **8** blushing, reserved, retiring, timorous **9** diffident, reluctant, shrinking, unassured **11** unassertive

basic 3 key **4** main **5** chief **6** bottom, innate, simple **7** capital, central, element, minimum, primary, radical **8** cardinal, inherent, rudiment **9** beginning, elemental, essential, intrinsic, primitive, principal, unadorned **10** elementary, underlying **11** fundamental **12** foundational

basically 6 au fond, mainly, mostly **7** at heart, chiefly, firstly, overall **8** in effect **9** generally, in essence, primarily

basic point 4 crux, gist, pith **5** heart **6** kernel **7** essence

basilica 6 church **7** minster **9** cathedral

basics 4 ABCs

basin 3 dip, pan, sag **4** bowl, sink **6** cirque, hollow **7** sinkage **8** sinkhole, washbowl **9** concavity **10** depression **liturgical: 5** stoup **7** piscina

basis 3 bed **4** crux, root, seat, seed **5** heart, nexus **6** bottom, ground, reason **7** bedrock, essence, footing, grounds, nucleus, premise, support, warrant **9** authority, postulate, principle **10** assumption, foundation, groundwork, substratum **11** fundamental, presumption **12** substructure, underpinning **13** justification

bask 3 sun **4** loll **5** glory, revel, relax **6** lounge, wallow, welter **7** indulge **8** sunbathe **9** luxuriate

basket 6 bushel, gabion **7** pannier **angler's: 5** creel **material: 5** osier **6** raffia

basketball inventor: 8 Naismith (James) **official: 6** umpire **7** referee **player: 5** cager, guard **6** center **7** forward **8** hoopster, swingman **10** point guard **team: 4** five **7** quintet **term: 3** gun, jam, key **4** cage, dunk, pass **5** board, hoops, lay-up, press, shoot, tip-in **6** freeze, screen, tap-off, tip-off, travel **7** dribble, keyhole, rebound, throw-in, time-out **8** alley-oop, jump ball, slam dunk **9** backboard, backcourt, field goal, free throw **11**

ball control (see also **National Basketball Association**)

basketballer 3 Bol (Manute) 4 Bird (Larry), Ming (Yao), Nash (Steve), Redd (Michael), Reed (Willis), West (Jerry, Mark) 5 Allen (Ray), Barry (Rick), Brand (Elton), Cousy (Bob), Davis (Baron), Ewing (Patrick), James (LeBron), Mikan (George), O'Neal (Shaq, Shaquille), Price (Mark) 6 Baylor (Elgin), Blount (Mark), Boozer (Carlos), Bryant (Kobe), Carter (Vince), Cowens (Dave), Duncan (Tim), Erving (Julius), Gervin (George), Jordan (Michael), Malone (Jeff, Karl, Moses), McAdoo (Bob), McHale (Kevin), Miller (Brad, Reggie), Parish (Robert), Pierce (Paul, Ricky), Pippin (Scottie), Rodman (Dennis), Skiles (Scott), Thomas (Kenny), Thorpe (Otis), Walton (Bill), Worthy (James) 7 Barkley (Charles), Billups (Chauncey), Dampier (Erick), Dawkins (Darryl), Edwards (James), Frazier (Walt), Garnett (Kevin), Hilario (Nene), Houston (Allan), Iverson (Allen), Jackson (Lauren), Jamison (Antawn), Johnson (Magic), McGrady (Tracy), Russell (Bill), Rollins (Tree), Taurasi (Diana), Wallace (Ben), Wilkins (Dominique) 8 Auerbach (Red), Cardinal (Brian), Havlicek (John), Magloire (Jamaal), Nowitzki (Dirk), Olajuwon (Akeem), Randolph (Zach), Robinson (David), Stockton (John), Thompson (Tina), Williams (Buck) 9 Donaldson (James), Ferdinand (Marie), Holdsclaw (Chamique), Robertson (Oscar) 10 Stojakovic (Predrag), Williamson (Corliss) 11 Abdul-Jabbar (Kareem), Chamberlain (Wilt)

Basmath's father 7 Solomon

Basque 6 bodice *cap:* 5 beret *game:* 6 pelota 7 jai alai *mountains:* 8 Pyrenees *province:* 5 Alava 7 Vizcaya 9 Guipúzcoa

bass 3 low 4 deep 6 singer 8 cabrilla *famous:* 5 Hines (Jerome), Pinza (Ezio), Ramey (Samuel), Siepi (Cesare), Tozzi (Giorgio) 6 Hotter (Hans), London (George), Morris (James) 7 Plishka (Paul), Robeson (Paul), Talvela (Martti) 8 Flagello (Ezio), Ghiaurov (Nicolai), Raimondi (Ruggero) 9 Chaliapin (Fyodor), Christoff (Boris)

Bassanio's beloved 6 Portia

bassinet 6 cradle, basket

bastard 5 cross 6 by-blow, hybrid 7 mongrel 9 love child 12 natural child *combining form:* 4 noth 5 notho

bastardize 4 warp 5 taint 6 debase, defile 7 corrupt, debauch, degrade, deprave, pervert, pollute, vitiate 9 brutalize 10 adulter-ate, bestialize, demoralize, depreciate 11 contaminate

baste 3 sew 4 beat, drub, lash, mill, pelt, rail, tack, whip 5 paste, scold 6 batter, berate, larrup, pummel, revile, stitch, thrash, wallop 7 bawl out, belabor, chew out, clobber, moisten, tell off, trounce, upbraid 8 bless out, chastise 9 dress down 10 tongue-lash

bastille 4 jail 6 prison 9 bridewell

bastinado 3 bat, rod 4 bash, beat, blow, cane, club 5 birch, crack, pound, smack, smash, stick, whack 6 cudgel, paddle, strike, switch, thwack, wallop 8 bludgeon 9 truncheon

bastion 5 tower 7 bulwark, citadel, parapet, rampart, redoubt 8 fastness, fortress 10 breastwork, stronghold 13 fortification

bat 3 bag, bop, hag 4 belt, biff, blow, bust, club, slam, sock, swat, whop, wink 5 biddy, blink, crone, smack 6 cudgel, thwack 7 meander 8 bludgeon 9 flying fox, truncheon 10 knobkerrie, shillelagh 11 pipistrelle ·

batch 3 lot, set 5 array, bunch, clump, crowd, group 6 bundle, clutch, parcel 7 cluster 8 quantity, shipment 10 assemblage, assortment, collection 11 aggregation 12 accumulation

bate 3 bar 4 omit 5 check 6 deduct, except, reduce 7 cut back, exclude, suspend 8 diminish, moderate, restrain, subtract

bateau 4 boat, dory 5 craft, skiff 6 dinghy, launch 7 shallop

bath 3 spa, tub 4 soak, wash 5 hydro, wells 6 shower 7 springs 8 ablution 13 watering place

bathe 3 dip, lap, lip, sop, tub, wet 4 bask, lave, soak, soap, swim, wash 5 clean, douse, flood, rinse, flush, souse, steep 6 shower 7 cleanse, immerse, pervade, suffuse 8 irrigate

bathetic 5 mushy, soppy, stale, tired, trite 6 drippy 7 clichéd, cloying, gushing, maudlin, mawkish 9 emotional, hackneyed, schmaltzy 10 lachrymose 11 commonplace, sentimental, stereotyped, tear-jerking 13 anticlimactic, overemotional, stereotypical

bathhouse 5 sauna 6 cabana

bathing suit 6 bikini, trunks 7 bandeau, maillot

bathos 7 letdown 8 banality, comedown 9 triteness 10 anticlimax

bathroom 3 lav, loo 4 john 5 privy 6 toilet 8 lavatory, outhouse

Bathsheba *father:* 5 Eliam *husband:* 5 David, Uriah *son:* 7 Solomon

bathtub gin 5 hooch 6 rotgut 7 bootleg 8 homebrew 9 moonshine 11 mountain dew

Batman *alias:* 13 Matches Malone *bat-signal:* 11 searchlight *butler:* 6 Alfred *creator:* 4 Kane (Bob) *film director:* 5 Nolan (Christopher) 6 Burton (Tim) *film star:* 4 Bale (Christian), West (Adam) 6 Carrey (Jim), DeVito (Danny), Keaton (Michael), Kilmer (Val) 7 Clooney (George), Thurman (Uma) 8 Meredith (Burgess), Pfeiffer (Michelle) 9 Nicholson (Jack) *secret identity:* 10 Bruce Wayne *setting:* 6 Gotham *sidekick:* 5 Robin *TV star:* 4 Ward (Burt), West (Adam) 8 McDowall (Roddy) *villain:* 5 Chill (Joe), Joker 7 Penguin, Riddler, Two-Face 8 Catwoman, Clayface, Deadshot, Mr. Freeze 9 Mad Hatter, Poison Ivy, Scarecrow

baton 3 rod 4 club, mace, wand 5 billy, staff, stick 6 cudgel 7 war club 8 bludgeon 9 billy club, truncheon 10 nightstick

____ **Bator** 4 Ulan

batrachian 4 frog, toad 9 amphibian

battalion 4 army, host, unit 5 force, horde 6 legion, throng, troops 8 squadron 10 contingent, detachment

batter 4 bash, beat, drub, hurt, maul, mush 5 baste, break, dough, paste, pound, wreck 6 bruise, buffet, bung up, hitter, mangle, pommel, pummel, thrash, wallop 7 assault, belabor, bombard, clobber, coating, contuse, cripple, lambast 8 demolish, lambaste

battery 3 lot, set 4 body, guns 5 abuse, array, batch, bunch, clump, group, suite 6 bundle, cannon, series 7 assault, beating, cluster 8 thumping 9 artillery, onslaught 10 energy cell 11 gunnery unit *terminal:* 5 anode 7 cathode

battle 4 fray 5 brush, clash, fight 6 action, assail, attack, combat, sortie 7 assault, contend, contest 8 conflict, skirmish, struggle 9 encounter, onslaught, scrimmage 10 engagement 11 hostilities

battle-ax 5 harpy, scold, shrew 6 virago 8 harridan 9 termagant, Xanthippe

Battle Born State 6 Nevada

battle cry 6 banzai

battlement 4 wall 7 barrier, bastion, bulwark, parapet, rampart 10 protection

battling 5 at war

batty 3 mad 4 daft, nuts, zany 5 barmy, crazy, kooky, loony, nutty, potty, wacky 6 crazed, cuckoo, insane, maniac, screwy, whacko 7 bananas, bonkers, cracked, idiotic, lunatic 8 deranged 9 bedlamite

bauble 3 toy 5 curio 6 gewgaw, trifle 7 bibelot, novelty, trinket, whatnot 8 gimcrack, ornament 9 objet d'art, plaything 10 knick-knack

Baucis's husband 8 Philemon

Bavaria 6 Bayern *capital:* 6 Munich *city:* 8 Augsburg, Bayreuth, Würzburg 9 Nuremberg *king:* 6 Ludwig *patron saint:* 6 Rupert

bawd 4 drab, moll, tart 5 madam, tramp, whore 6 floozy, harlot, hooker 7 trollop 8 strumpet 10 prostitute 11 nightwalker 12 streetwalker

bawdy 4 blue, lewd 5 crude, dirty 6 coarse, erotic, ribald, risqué, smutty, vulgar 7 obscene 8 indecent, prurient 9 lecherous, offensive, salacious 10 lascivious, libidinous, licentious, suggestive

bawdy house 4 crib, stew 6 bagnio 7 brothel, lupanar 8 bordello

bawl 3 cry, sob 4 howl, roar, rout, wail, weep, yell, yowl 5 shout 6 bellow, berate, boohoo, clamor, holler, outcry, scream, shriek, squall 7 blubber, bluster

bawl out 3 wig 4 lash 5 baste, scold 6 berate, rebuke 7 censure, chew out, condemn, tell off, upbraid 8 bless out, denounce, tear into 9 castigate, dress down, reprimand 10 tongue-lash

bay 3 arm 4 cove, gulf, howl, loch, nook, wail 5 award, bight, crown, firth, honor, inlet, niche 6 harbor, laurel, recess 7 garland, laurels 8 accolade 10 decoration *Aegean Sea:* 5 Anzac *Africa:* 6 Walvis *Alaska:* 7 Glacier *Antarctica:* 3 Ice 8 Amundsen *Argentina:* 6 Blanca *Atlantic Ocean:* 6 Baffin *Australia:* 5 Anson, Shark 6 Botany, Sharks 7 Repulse 9 Discovery *Baltic:* 4 Hano, Kiel 6 Danzig, Kieler 9 Pomerania 10 Pomeranian, Pommersche *Beaufort Sea:* 7 Prudhoe 9 Mackenzie *Brazil:* 9 Guanabara *Bristol Channel:* 10 Carmarthen *California:* 5 Morro 9 Monterey, San Diego *Canada:* 5 Fundy 6 Hudson 7 Repulse *Capetown:* 5 Table *Caribbean Sea:* 5 Limón 8 Chetumal *Central America:* 7 Fonseca *Cuba:* 10 Guantánamo *East River:* 8 Flushing *Egypt:* 6 Abu Qir *Eire:* 4 Clew 7 Brandon *English Channel:* 3 Tor 4 Lyme *Europe:* 6 Biscay *Florida:* 8 Biscayne *Greenland:* 6 Baffin 8 Melville *Gulf of Alaska:* 7 Resurrection *Gulf of California:* 5 Adair *Gulf of Guinea:* 5 Benin 6 Biafra *Gulf of Mexico:* 5 Tampa 6 Mobile 7 Aransas 8 Campeche, Sarasota 9 Matagorda, Pensacola 10 San Antonio, Terrebonne 11 Atchafalaya, Ponce de Leon 12 Apalachicola 13 Corpus Christi *Gulf of St. Lawrence:* 5 Bonne, Gaspé *Hawaii:* 5 Koloa, Lawai *Hong Kong:* 4 Deep *Honshu:* 3 Ise 5 Mutsu, Osaka, Owari, Tokyo 6 Atsuta, Sagami *Indian Ocean:* 6 Bengal *Indonesia:* 8 Humboldt *Irish Sea:* 4 Luce 7 Dundalk *Jamaica:* 4 Long *Japan:* 4 Tosa

Java Sea: 7 Batavia 8 Djakarta *Lake Erie:* 8 Sandusky *Lake Huron:* 7 Saginaw, Thunder *Lake Michigan:* 5 Green 13 Grand Traverse *Lake Ontario:* 11 Irondequoit *Lake Superior:* 5 Huron 8 Keweenaw 9 Whitefish *Long Island Sound:* 6 Oyster *Maine:* 5 Casco 7 Machias 9 Penobscot *Maryland-Virginia:* 10 Chesapeake 12 Chincoteague *Massachusetts:* 6 Boston 7 Cape Cod 8 Buzzards, Plymouth *New Brunswick:* 13 Passamaquoddy *Newfoundland:* 4 Hare 5 White 7 Fortune *New Jersey:* 5 Great 6 Newark 7 Raritan 8 Barnegat *New York:* 7 Jamaica *North Carolina:* 6 Onslow *Northwest Territories:* 5 Wager 7 Repulse 8 Franklin 9 Frobisher *Oregon:* 4 Coos *Puerto Rico:* 5 Sucia *Quebec:* 6 Ungava *Rhode Island:* 12 Narragansett *Sea of Japan:* 13 Peter the Great *South Carolina:* 4 Bull, Long *South China Sea:* 5 Subic, Subig 7 Camranh *Spain:* 5 Cadiz *Strait of Gibraltar:* 7 Tangier *Sydney:* 6 Botany *Tasmania:* 5 Storm *Texas:* 7 Trinity *Tyrrhenian Sea:* 6 Naples 7 Paestum *Wales:* 10 Caernarfon, Caernarvon *Washington:* 5 Dabob 6 Skagit *West Indies:* 5 Coral

bayou 5 creek, marsh 6 slough 9 everglade, tributary *Louisiana:* 5 Macon 9 Barataria, Lafourche 10 Terrebonne *Mississippi:* 9 Chickasaw

Bay State 13 Massachusetts

bay window 3 gut, pot 5 oriel, tummy 6 paunch 8 potbelly 9 beer belly, spare tire 11 corporation, breadbasket

bazaar 4 fair, mall, mart, souk 6 market 7 benefit 8 emporium, exchange 11 marketplace

bazooka's target 4 tank

be 4 live 5 exist

beach 4 bank 5 Cocoa, coast, Omaha, shore 6 Malibu, Pebble, strand, Venice 7 seaside, shingle, Waikiki 8 cast away, lakeside, littoral, seashore 9 lakeshore 10 Clearwater, Copacabana, oceanfront, run aground *resort:* 4 lido

____ **Beach** 3 Amy 4 Long, Palm, Vero 5 Dover, Miami, Omaha 6 Delray, Myrtle, Ormond 7 Daytona, Riviera, Waikiki 8 Imperial, Virginia

beached 6 ashore 7 aground 8 grounded, marooned, stranded 9 abandoned

beachhead 8 foothold

beachwear see bathing suit

beacon 4 buoy, sign 5 flare, guide 6 pharos, signal 7 bonfire, lantern 8 balefire 9 watchfire 10 lighthouse, signal fire 11 inspiration, transmitter 12 guiding light

bead 3 dab, dot, pea 4 blob, drop 6 bubble 7 driblet, globule 8 spherule

beak 3 neb, nib 4 bill, nose 5 snoot, snout, spout 6 pecker, schnoz 7 schnozz 8 mandible 9 proboscis, schnozzle

beaker 3 cup 6 carafe, goblet, vessel 8 decanter

beaklike part 7 rostrum

be-all and end-all 3 sum 4 pith, root, soul 5 total, whole 6 bottom 7 essence 8 entirety, sum total, totality 9 aggregate, substance 10 prime cause 12 quintessence

beam 3 bar, ray 4 balk, boom, burn, glow, grin, I-bar, spar 5 flare, flash, gleam, joist, plank, shaft, shine, shoot, smile, strut 6 girder, lintel, rafter, signal, streak, stream, timber 7 radiate 8 transmit 9 broadcast

beaming 6 bright, joyful, lucent 7 fulgent, lambent, radiant 8 animated, cheerful, luminous 9 brilliant, effulgent, refulgent 12 incandescent

bean 3 soy, wax 4 bush, conk, dome, fava, head, lima, mung, navy, pate, pole, poll, snap, soya 5 baked, brain, broad, horse, jelly, pinto 6 belfry, coffee, frijol, kidney, legume, noddle, noggin, noodle, string 7 jumping 9 headpiece 10 stringless *curd:* 4 tofu *of India:* 3 urd

beanery 4 café 5 diner, grill 9 hash house 10 coffee shop, restaurant 11 greasy spoon 12 luncheonette

beano 5 bingo

Bean Town 6 Boston

bear 3 lug 4 tote 5 abide, allow, beget, bring, brook, bruin, carry, stand, touch 6 accept, behave, convey, deport, endure, permit, suffer 7 comport, condone, conduct, deliver, stomach, support, sustain, swallow, undergo 8 engender, generate, shoulder, tolerate 9 procreate, propagate, reproduce, transport 10 bring forth 11 countenance *Alaskan:* 5 polar 6 Kodiak *Australian:* 5 koala *constellation:* 4 Ursa 9 Ursa Major, Ursa Minor *genus:* 5 Ursus *kind:* 3 sun 5 black, brown, honey, koala, polar, sloth 6 Kodiak 7 grizzly 10 spectacled *Kipling:* 5 Baloo 7 Adam-zad *relating to:* 6 ursine *young:* 3 cub

bearable 7 livable, tenable 8 adequate, passable 9 allowable, endurable, tolerable 10 acceptable, admissible, good enough, manageable, sufferable 11 supportable, sustainable

bearcat 5 panda

beard 4 dare, defy, face, fuzz 5 brave, front 6 goatee 7 outface, stubble, Vandyke 8 confront, imperial, whiskers **9** challenge, soul patch *on grain:* **3** awn

bearded 5 bushy, fuzzy, hairy **6** shaggy, tufted **7** bristly, goateed, hirsute, stubbly **8** unshaven **9** whiskered **11** bewhiskered

bear down 4 rout **5** crush, quell **6** burden, defeat, reduce, subdue **7** conquer, overrun, trample **8** overcome, vanquish **9** emphasize, overpower, overwhelm, subjugate

bearer 4 mule **5** envoy **6** coolie, porter, runner **7** carrier, courier **8** conveyor, emissary **9** go-between, messenger **11** internuncio

bear hug 6 clinch

bearing 3 air, set **4** look, mien, pose **5** poise **6** aspect, manner, stance **7** address, conduct, display, posture **8** attitude, behavior, carriage, delivery, demeanor, presence, relation **9** demeanour, direction **10** connection, deportment **11** comportment

bearish 4 curt **5** gruff, rough, terse, surly **6** cranky, ornery **7** anxious, dubious, prickly, uncouth **8** cautious, vinegary **9** crotchety, irascible **10** ill-humored **11** pessimistic **12** cantankerous

bearlike 6 ursine

bear out 4 show **5** prove **6** attest, uphold, verify **7** certify, confirm, justify **8** validate, vouch for **9** vindicate **11** corroborate, demonstrate **12** authenticate, substantiate

bear up 4 cope, fare, prop **5** brace, get by **6** endure, uphold **7** bolster, support, sustain **8** buttress, get along, maintain, underpin

beast 5 brute **6** animal **7** critter, monster, varmint **8** behemoth, creature, gargoyle

beastly 4 foul, mean, vile **5** awful, brute, feral, nasty **6** animal, brutal, odious **7** bestial, brutish, inhuman, ogreish, swinish **8** horrible, terrible **9** barbarous, revolting **10** abominable, detestable

beat 3 box, get, gyp, hit, lam, rap, tan, top **4** balk, belt, best, cane, dash, drub, drum, dump, flap, flog, foil, lash, lick, maul, pelt, rout, ruin, stir, tick, trim, whip, whop **5** baste, cheat, cozen, excel, forge, lay on, meter, outdo, paste, pound, pulse, punch, rhyme, route, scoop, scour, smear, spent, stick, stump, swing, throb, tread, tromp, whack, whisk **6** baffle, batter, better, buffet, cudgel, defeat, diddle, exceed, forage, hammer, larrup, muss up, patrol, pummel, rhythm, rounds, strike, thrash, thresh, thwart, wallop **7** belabor, clobber, circuit, conquer, exhaust, fashion, fatigue, lambast, lay down, prevail, pulsate, ransack, rough up, shellac, surpass, swindle, triumph, trounce **8** bewilder, bludgeon, Bohemian, lambaste, outshine, outsmart, outstrip,

overcome, precinct **9** exhausted, frustrate, palpitate, pulsation, shattered, transcend, vibration **10** circumvent, pistol-whip **11** oscillation

beating 4 rout **5** lumps **6** defeat, hiding, mayhem **7** assault, setback **9** hammering, pulsation, throbbing **11** palpitation, shellacking

beatitude 3 joy **5** bliss **7** delight, ecstasy, rapture **8** euphoria, gladness, rhapsody **9** happiness, transport **10** exaltation, joyfulness **11** blessedness **12** blissfulness

Beatles 4 John (Lennon), Paul (McCartney) **5** Ringo (Starr) **6** George (Harrison) **7** Fab Four *album:* **8** Revolver **9** Abbey Road, Sgt. Pepper **10** Rubber Soul *early:* **4** Best (Pete) **9** Quarrymen (The), Sutcliffe (Stuart) *manager:* **5** Klein (Allen) **7** Epstein (Brian) *producer:* **6** Martin (George) *wife:* **5** Linda **7** Yoko Ono

beatnik 5 rebel **6** hippie **7** radical **8** Bohemian **9** dissident **11** flower child **13** nonconformist

beat-up 6 shabby **7** rickety, worn-out **8** decrepit, tattered **9** crumbling **10** broken-down, ramshackle, tumble-down **11** dilapidated

beau 5 dandy, flame, lover, swain, wooer **6** steady, suitor **7** admirer, beloved **8** paramour, truelove, young man **9** boyfriend **10** sweetheart

Beau Brummell 3 fop **5** dandy, swell **7** coxcomb, gallant **8** macaroni **11** petit-maître **12** lounge lizard

beau ideal 5 guide, model **6** mirror **7** epitome, example, paragon, pattern **8** exemplar, paradigm, standard **9** archetype **12** quintessence

Beaumarchais hero 6 Figaro

beau monde 5 elite **6** gentry, jet set **7** society **8** smart set **10** glitterati, upper crust

beauteous see **beautiful**

beautiful 4 fair **5** bonny **6** comely, lovely, pretty **7** radiant **8** glorious, gorgeous, handsome, splendid, stunning **9** exquisite **10** attractive **11** good-looking, resplendent, well-favored

beautiful people 6 jet set **8** smart set **9** haut monde **10** glitterati **11** high society

beautify 4 deck, gild, trim **5** adorn, array, fix up, grace, prank, primp **6** bedeck, doll up **7** dress up, festoon, garland, garnish, gussy up, enhance, improve **8** decorate, ornament, prettify, spruce up **9** embellish, glamorize

beauty 5 asset, belle, dream, merit, peach **6** appeal, eyeful, looker, lovely **7** charmer, dazzler, stunner **8** knockout **9** eye-opener,

good looks **10** good-looker, loveliness **mark: 4** mole
beaver 6 castor, rodent **home: 5** lodge **project: 3** dam **skin: 4** plew **young: 3** kit, pup
Beaver State 6 Oregon
becalm 4 hush, lull, stop **5** allay, quiet, stall, still **6** arrest, pacify, sedate, settle, soothe, steady, subdue **7** assuage, compose, quieten **11** tranquilize
because 3 for, now **4** that **5** since **7** being as, whereas **8** being how, as long as, seeing as **10** inasmuch as
because of 4 over **5** due to **7** owing to, through **8** thanks to **10** by reason of **11** on account of
Beckett work 4 Not I, Play, Watt **6** Molloy, Murphy **7** Endgame **9** Happy Days, Unnamable (The) **10** Eleutheria, Malone Dies **14** Krapp's Last Tape **15** Waiting for Godot
beckon 3 bid, nod **4** lure, wave **6** allure, entice, invite, motion, signal, summon **7** attract
becloud 3 dim, fog **4** blur, hide, veil **5** addle, bedim, befog, cloak, muddy **6** impair, darken, muddle, puzzle, shroud **7** confuse, eclipse, obscure, perplex **8** befuddle **9** obfuscate **10** overshadow
become 3 fit, get, wax **4** grow, suit **5** befit **6** go with **7** enhance, flatter **8** turn into
becoming 3 apt **5** right **6** decent, proper, seemly **7** correct, fitting **8** decorous, suitable, tasteful **9** befitting **10** attractive, flattering, well-chosen **11** appropriate, comme il faut
bed 3 cot **4** base, bunk, crib, doss, sack, twin **5** basis, berth, layer **6** bottom, cradle, double, ground, Murphy, pallet **7** bedrock, stratum, trundle **8** rollaway **10** foundation, substratum **of India: 7** charpoy
bedaub 4 coat **5** cover, smear **6** smudge **7** overlay, plaster
bedazzle 4 daze **5** blind
bedcover 5 duvet, quilt **6** afghan, spread **7** blanket **8** coverlet **9** comforter **11** counterpane
bedeck 4 trim **5** adorn, array, prank **6** attire, bedaub, jazz up **7** appoint, bedizen, dress up, festoon, furbish, garland, garnish, gussy up **8** accouter, accoutre, beautify, decorate, ornament, prettify **9** embellish
bedevil 5 annoy, harry, spoil, tease, worry **6** harass, needle, nettle, pester, plague **7** hagride, provoke, torment, trouble **8** bewilder **10** exasperate
bedevilment 6 bother **7** torment, trouble **8** disorder, vexation **9** annoyance, confusion **10** irritation **11** aggravation **12** bewilderment

bedfellow 4 ally **5** crony **7** comrade **9** associate, colleague **10** compatriot **11** confederate **12** collaborator
bedim 3 fog **4** blur, mask, veil **5** befog, blear, cloud, gloom, shade **6** darken, muddle, shadow, shroud **7** becloud, confuse, eclipse, obscure **9** obfuscate
bedizen 4 deck, garb, gild **5** adorn, array, endue **6** doll up, dude up, invest, outfit, rig out **7** costume, dandify, dress up, garnish, gussy up, turn out **8** beautify, ornament **9** caparison, embellish
bedlam 3 ado **5** chaos, furor **6** asylum, clamor, furore, hubbub, tumult, uproar, welter **7** turmoil **8** foofaraw, madhouse, upheaval **9** commotion, maelstrom **10** hurlyburly **11** pandemonium
bedlamite 3 mad, nut **4** loon, nuts **5** batty, crazy, loony **6** insane, madman, maniac **7** cracked, lunatic **8** demented, deranged
bedouin 4 Arab **5** nomad
bedraggled 5 faded, seedy **6** shabby, ragtag, untidy **7** muddied, rundown, unkempt **8** decrepit, dripping, slovenly, tattered **10** disheveled, disarrayed, disordered, down-at-heel, ramshackle, threadbare **11** dilapidated
bedridden 6 laid up, shut-in **8** confined **12** hospitalized
bedrock 4 base, core, foot, root **5** axiom, basic, basis, floor, nadir **6** bottom, depths, ground **7** footing, support **10** foundation, groundwork, substratum **11** fundamental **12** substructure, underpinning
bedroom 7 boudoir, chamber
bedspread 8 coverlet **11** counterpane
bed-wetting 8 enuresis
bee food: 6 nectar **genus: 4** Apis **glue: 8** propolis **group: 5** swarm **6** colony **house: 4** hive **6** apiary **kind: 5** drone, mason, queen **6** mining, sewing, worker **8** quilting, spelling **9** carpenter **nest: 4** hive, skep **product: 3** wax **5** honey **relating to: 8** apiarian **wax cells: 9** honeycomb
beechnuts 4 mast
beef 4 crab, fuss, meat, veal **5** bitch, brawn, gripe **6** grouse, muscle **7** grumble **9** bellyache, complaint, grievance **cut: 3** rib **4** loin, rump, side **5** chuck, flank, plate, round, shank **7** brisket, sirloin **10** tenderloin **11** porterhouse **grade: 5** prime **6** choice **7** utility **8** standard **10** commercial **order: 4** rare **6** medium **8** well-done
beefcake 4 hunk, stud **5** himbo
beefeater 5 guard **6** sentry, warder, yeoman
beefy 5 bulky, burly, hefty, husky, meaty **6** brawny, fleshy, robust, stocky, sturdy **7**

massive 8 muscular, thickset 9 strapping 11 substantial

Beehive State 4 Utah

beekeeper 8 apiarist 12 apiculturist

beekeeping 10 apiculture

beeline 3 fly, nip, zip 4 race, whiz 5 hurry, speed 6 bullet, hasten, hustle, rocket 7 hotfoot 8 expedite, highball 10 make tracks 12 shortest path

Beelzebub 5 devil, fiend, Satan 6 diablo 7 Evil One, Lucifer, Old Nick, serpent 8 Apollyon 9 adversary, archfiend

beer 3 ale, IPA 4 bock, brew, suds 5 draft, lager, stout, weiss 6 porter 7 brewski, cerveza, pilsner 8 pilsener *vessel:* 3 mug 4 toby 5 stein 6 flagon, seidel 7 tankard 8 schooner 9 blackjack *drinking place:* 3 bar, inn, pub 6 saloon, tavern 7 taproom 8 alehouse 11 public house, rathskeller *ingredient:* 4 hops, malt 5 yeast 6 barley *maker:* 6 brewer *mythical inventor:* 9 Gambrinus *plant:* 7 brewery *Russian:* 5 kvass *Scottish:* 10 barley-bree

Beeri *daughter:* 6 Judith *son:* 5 Hosea

beet 5 chard 6 mangel, wurzel 10 Swiss chard *family:* 9 goosefoot

Beethoven, Ludwig van *birthplace:* 4 Bonn *opera:* 7 Fidelio *overture:* 6 Egmont 7 Leonore 10 Coriolanus *sonata:* 7 Tempest 8 Kreutzer 9 Moonlight, Waldstein 10 Pathétique 12 Appassionata *symphony:* 6 Choral, Eroica 8 Pastoral

beetle 3 bug, jut 5 bulge 6 insect, scarab, scurry 7 project 8 overhang, protrude, stand out, stick out *click:* 6 elater 7 firefly *dung:* 6 scarab 9 tumblebug *front wing:* 6 elytra (plural) 7 elytron *fruit-eating:* 8 curculio *insect-eating:* 7 ladybug 8 ladybird *kind:* 4 bean, dung, fire, June, stag 5 click, flour, grain, tiger, water 6 carpet, chafer, ground, May bug, museum 7 blister, cadelle, carabid, firefly, goldbug, goliath, June bug, vedalia 8 ambrosia, Japanese 9 longicorn, potato bug 10 cockchafer, rhinoceros *order:* 10 Coleoptera *ornament:* 6 scarab *snouted:* 6 weevil 7 billbug 8 curculio 9 wood borer *young:* 4 grub 5 larva 6 larvae (plural) 8 wireworm

beet soup 6 borsch 7 borscht

befall 3 hap 5 ensue, occur 6 betide, chance, follow, happen 7 come off, develop, fall out 8 happen to 9 come about, eventuate, transpire

befit 4 meet, suit 6 become, go with 9 agree with, chime with 10 accord with, be right for 11 be proper for

befitting 3 apt 4 just, meet 5 happy, right 6 decent, proper, seemly 7 correct 8 becoming, decorous, suitable 10 conforming, felicitous 11 appropriate, comme il faut

befog 3 dim 4 blur, hide, veil 5 bedim, blear, cloak, cloud, muddy 6 darken, puzzle 7 becloud, confuse, eclipse, envelop, obscure, perplex 8 bewilder, confound 9 obfuscate, overcloud 10 overshadow

befool 4 dupe, gull, hoax, play 5 cozen, trick 6 delude 7 chicane, deceive, mislead 8 hoodwink 9 bamboozle, victimize 11 hornswoggle

before 3 ere 4 ante, once, till, up to 5 ahead, until 6 facing, sooner, up till 7 ahead of, already, earlier, prior to 8 formerly 9 in advance, in front of, preceding 10 previously 11 in advance of *prefix:* 3 pre, pro 4 ante, fore

befoul 3 mar, tar 4 slur, soil 5 dirty, smear, spoil, sully, taint 6 defame, defile, malign, smudge 7 blacken, pollute, profane, spatter, tarnish, traduce 8 besmirch 9 bespatter, denigrate 10 adulterate 11 contaminate

befuddle 4 daze 5 addle, mix up 6 ball up, baffle, bemuse, muddle 7 confuse, fluster, perplex, stupefy 8 bewilder, confound, distract, throw off 9 disorient

befuddlement 3 fog 4 daze, haze, maze 5 mix-up 6 muddle, stupor 9 confusion 10 perplexity, puzzlement 11 distraction

beg 3 ask, bum, dun, nag, sue 4 pray, urge 5 apply, brace, cadge, crave, evade, hit on, mooch, plead, press, worry 6 adjure, appeal, call on, demand, invoke, pester 7 beseech, besiege, conjure, entreat, implore, request, solicit 8 petition, sidestep 9 importune, panhandle 10 supplicate

beget 4 bear, sire 5 breed, bring, cause, forge, hatch, spawn, yield 6 create, effect, father 7 produce 8 engender, generate, multiply, result in 9 procreate, propagate, reproduce 10 bring about

beggar 4 hobo, defy, ruin 5 tramp 6 bummer, cadger, fellow, pauper, prayer, sponge, suitor 7 moocher, sponger 8 bankrupt, deadbeat, vagabond 9 overwhelm, pauperize, schnorrer, suppliant 10 down-and-out, freeloader, impoverish, panhandler, petitioner, supplicant 11 bindle stiff, supplicator 12 street person

beggared 4 flat, poor 5 broke, needy 6 ruined 7 drained 8 bankrupt, dirt poor, indigent, strapped, wiped out 9 destitute, insolvent, penniless, penurious, tapped out 10 pauperized 11 impecunious, overwhelmed 12 dispossessed, impoverished

beggarly 3 low 4 base, mean, poor 5 cheap,

lowly, nasty, petty, sorry **6** cheesy, meager, measly, paltry, scanty, scurvy, shabby, shoddy, trashy **7** ignoble, miserly, pitiful, squalid **8** pitiable, inferior, wretched **9** miserable, niggardly **10** despicable, despisable **11** ignominious **12** contemptible, parsimonious

Beggar's Opera *music:* **7** Pepusch (John) *painting:* **7** Hogarth (William) *text:* **3** Gay (John)

beggarweed 6 dodder **9** knotgrass **11** tick trefoil

beggary 4 need, want **6** penury **7** bumming, cadging, poverty **8** mooching, pleading **9** indigence, neediness, pauperism, privation **10** meagerness, mendicancy **11** destitution, panhandling

begin 4 dawn, open, rise **5** arise, cause, dig in, enter, found, mount, set to, start **6** appear, attack, be born, broach, create, effect, emerge, get off, induce, invent, launch, spring, sprout, tackle, take up, tee off **7** break in, emanate, jump off, kick off, lead off, prepare, usher in **8** activate, commence, embark on, engender, initiate **9** establish, instigate, institute, introduce, originate **10** embark upon, inaugurate, issue forth **11** break ground

beginner 4 colt, tiro, tyro **6** newbie, new kid, novice, rookie **7** recruit, starter, student, trainee **8** freshman, neophyte, newcomer **9** fledgling, greenhorn, novitiate **10** apprentice, catechumen, tenderfoot **11** abecedarian

beginning 4 dawn, font, rise, root **5** alpha, basal, birth, fount, get-go, onset, start **6** day one, origin, outset, primal, source, spring **7** dawning, genesis, infancy, initial, kickoff, nascent, opening **8** creation, exordium, outstart, prologue, rudiment, simplest **9** elemental, emergence, inception, incipient **10** appearance, elementary, incipiency, initiative, initiatory, opening gun, rudimental **11** origination, rudimentary **12** commencement, inauguration, introductory

begird 3 hem **4** belt, bind, ring **5** beset, fence, hem in, round **6** circle, corral, girdle, immure **7** confine, enclose, wreathe **8** encircle, engirdle, surround **9** encompass **12** circumscribe

beg off 5 demur, welsh **6** bow out, cop out, opt out, pass up, refuse, renege **7** back out, bail out, decline, drop out, pull out **8** back down, withdraw

begone 5 leave, scram, split **6** beat it, decamp, depart, get out **7** buzz off, get lost, skiddoo, take off, vamoose **8** clear out,

hightail, shove off **9** skedaddle **10** make tracks

begrime 3 tar **4** foul, soil, spot **5** dirty, muddy, smear, spoil, sully, taint **6** defile, mess up, muck up, smirch, smooch, smudge, smutch **7** blacken, corrupt, pollute, tarnish **8** besmirch **11** contaminate

begrudge 4 envy **6** resent

beguile 3 con **4** draw, dupe, fool, hoax, lure, play, snow, wile **5** bluff, charm, fleet, trick **6** allure, beckon, betray, delude, divert, entice, humbug, lead on, seduce, take in **7** attract, bewitch, deceive, enchant, engross, exploit, finesse, mislead **8** distract, hoodwink, intrigue, maneuver **9** captivate, fascinate, while away **10** manipulate **11** double-cross

beguiling 4 wily **5** false **6** artful, subtle **8** alluring, deluding, delusive, delusory **9** deceitful, deceiving, deceptive, insidious, seductive **10** bewitching, chimerical, enchanting, fallacious, misleading **11** enthralling

Behan's autobiography 10 Borstal Boy

behave 3 act, run **5** carry, react **6** acquit, be good, deport, direct, manage **7** comport, conduct, disport, perform **8** function

behavior 3 act, air, way **4** mien, tone, ways **6** action, aspect, custom, habits, manner **7** bearing, conduct **8** demeanor, presence, response **10** deportment **11** comportment

behead 4 head, kill **7** execute **9** decollate **10** decapitate, guillotine

beheaded noblewoman 8 Jane Grey (Lady) **9** Catherine (Howard) **10** Anne Boleyn

behemoth 5 giant, jumbo, whale **7** goliath, mammoth, monster **8** colossus **9** leviathan **11** monstrosity

behemothic 4 huge **5** jumbo **7** mammoth, massive, titanic **8** colossal, gigantic, towering **9** Herculean, monstrous **10** gargantuan **11** elephantine

behest 3 say **4** will, wish, word, writ **5** edict, order **6** charge, demand, urging **7** bidding, command, dictate, mandate, precept, request **9** direction, enjoinder, ordinance, prescript, prompting **10** injunction **11** commandment, exhortation, instruction **12** solicitation

behind 3 can **4** late, next, rump **5** after, fanny **6** back of, bottom, heinie **7** backing **8** backside, buttocks, derriere, trailing **9** following, posterior **10** supporting **12** subsequent *to prefix:* **4** post **5** retro

behindhand 3 lax **4** late, slow **5** slack, tardy **6** in debt, remiss **7** belated, delayed, laggard, overdue **8** backward, careless, derelict **9** in

arrears, negligent, unmindful **10** delinquent, neglectful, unpunctual **11** undeveloped
behold 3 see **4** espy, note, view **6** descry, notice **7** discern, observe, witness *French:* **5** voilà *Latin:* **4** ecce
beholden 5 bound **7** obliged **8** grateful, indebted **9** duty-bound, obligated
beholder 4 seer **6** gawker, viewer **7** watcher, witness **8** observer, onlooker, passerby **9** bystander, spectator **10** eyewitness **12** rubbernecker
beige 3 tan **4** buff, ecru **7** vanilla
being 3 ens, man **4** body, esse, life, self, soul **5** human, stuff, thing **6** entity, matter, mortal, nature, object, spirit **7** essence **8** creature, existent, material **9** actuality, character, existence, personage, something, substance **10** individual **11** personality **12** essentiality **13** individuality *celestial:* **6** cherub, seraph
bejeweled 7 studded **8** sequined, spangled **9** encrusted **10** bespangled, gem-studded, ornamented
Bel *Sumerian counterpart:* **5** Enlil *wife:* **5** Belit **6** Beltis
Bel _____ **3** Air **5** Paese
bel _____ **5** canto **6** esprit
Bela *father:* **4** Beor **8** Benjamin *son:* **3** Ard
belabor 4 beat, drub, flog **5** baste, pound, scold **6** batter, berate, buffet, pummel, thrash, wallop **7** lambast, scourge, tell off, upbraid **8** chastise, lambaste, tear into **9** criticize, fulminate, overstate **10** flagellate **11** overexplain
Belarus *capital:* **5** Minsk *city:* **6** Homyel **7** Vitebsk **8** Mahilyow **9** Vitsyebsk *language:* **7** Russian **10** Belarusian **11** Belarussian *monetary unit:* **5** rubel, ruble **7** kapeyka *neighbor:* **6** Latvia, Poland, Russia **7** Ukraine **9** Lithuania *river:* **3** Bug **5** Neman **7** Dnieper, Pripyat
belated 4 late, slow **5** tardy **6** remiss **7** delayed, laggard, overdue **10** behindhand, behind time, unpunctual
Belau see **Palau**
belch 4 burp, emit, gush, spew, vent, void **5** eject, eruct, erupt, expel, issue, spout, spurt, vomit **6** hiccup, irrupt **7** explode, extrude **8** disgorge **10** eructation **11** expectorate
beldam 3 hag **5** crone **8** old woman
beleaguer 3 bug, dog, hem, nag, vex **4** gnaw **5** annoy, beset, harry, hound, siege, storm, tease, worry **6** assail, attack, badger, bother, fall on, harass, invest, pester, plague **7** bedevil, besiege, hagride, put upon, set upon, trouble **8** blockade, fall upon

belfry 7 steeple **8** carillon **9** bell tower, campanile *dweller:* **3** bat
Belgium *capital:* **8** Brussels *city:* **4** Gent **5** Ghent, Liège **7** Antwerp **9** Charleroi *ethnic group:* **7** Fleming, Flemish, Walloon *language:* **5** Dutch **7** Flemish *monetary unit:* **4** euro *monetary unit, former:* **5** franc *neighbor:* **6** France **7** Germany **10** Luxembourg **11** Netherlands *plain:* **8** Flanders *port:* **7** Antwerp **8** Oostende *river:* **4** Yser **5** Meuse **7** Schlede *sea:* **5** North *sleuth:* **6** Poirot (Hercule), Suchet (David)
belie 4 deny, hide, warp **5** color, twist **6** expose, doctor, garble **7** conceal, confute, distort, falsify, gainsay, pervert, trump up **8** confront, denounce, disagree, disguise, disprove, miscolor, misstate, negative **9** disaffirm, gloss over, repudiate **10** contradict, contravene, controvert **11** dissimulate **12** misrepresent
belief 3 ism **4** idea, mind, view **5** axiom, credo, creed, dogma, faith, hunch, tenet, trust **6** assent, avowal, credit, surety, theory, thesis **7** concept, feeling, opinion, precept, surmise, theorem **8** credence, doctrine, firmness, religion, sureness **9** assurance, certainty, certitude, intuition, postulate, principle, sentiment **10** acceptance, assumption, confidence, contention, conviction, hypothesis, impression, persuasion **11** supposition
believable 5 solid, sound, valid **6** cogent, likely **7** logical, tenable **8** credible, possible, probable, reliable **9** authentic, colorable, plausible **10** convincing, creditable, persuasive, reasonable **11** conceivable, trustworthy
believe 3 buy **4** deem, hold, know **5** lap up, think, trust **6** accept, affirm, assume, credit, expect, reckon **7** fall for, imagine, profess, suppose, suspect, swallow **8** conceive, consider **10** conjecture, presuppose, understand
belittle 3 cut, pan **5** abuse, decry, knock, scorn **6** deride, insult, jeer at, revile **7** cut down, put down, run down, sneer at **8** badmouth, derogate, diminish, discount, minimize, write off **9** criticize, discredit, disparage, dispraise, downgrade, underrate **10** depreciate, undervalue **13** underestimate
belittlement 5 abuse, scorn **7** calumny, jeering, scandal, slander **8** derision, ridicule **9** aspersion **10** backbiting, defamation, detraction **11** denigration **12** backstabbing, depreciation
Belize *capital:* **8** Belmopan *city:* **10** Belize City *ethnic group:* **4** Maya **5** Mayan *moun-*

tain: 8 Victoria *neighbor:* 6 Mexico 9 Guatemala *river:* 5 Hondo *sea:* 9 Caribbean
bell 4 peal 5 chime, knell 6 tocsin
belle 5 siren 6 beauty, eyeful 7 charmer 8 knockout, ornament 11 enchantress, femme fatale
Bellerophon *father:* 7 Glaucus 8 Poseidon *grandfather:* 8 Sisyphus *horse:* 7 Pegasus *victim:* 7 Chimera
belles lettres 10 literature
belletrist 8 novelist 4 poet 6 author, writer 9 dramatist 10 playwright
bellflower 9 campanula
___ **belli** 5 casus
bellicose 6 ornery 7 hawkish, hostile, martial, scrappy, warlike 8 factious, fighting, militant 9 assertive, combative, truculent 10 aggressive, pugnacious, rebellious 11 belligerent, contentious, hot-tempered, quarrelsome 12 disputatious, gladiatorial
belligerence 5 fight 6 attack, enmity, rancor, spleen 7 ill will 9 hostility, militancy, petulance, pugnacity 10 aggression, antagonism, truculence 11 bellicosity 12 churlishness 13 combativeness
belligerent 6 ardent, fierce 7 fighter, hostile, scrappy, soldier, warlike, warring, warrior 8 battling, churlish, fighting, invading, militant, opponent, petulant 9 aggressor, attacking, bellicose, combatant, combative, disputant, splenetic, truculent 10 aggressive, antagonist, pugnacious 11 contentious, hot-tempered, quarrelsome 12 antagonistic, disputatious
Bellini *opera:* 5 Norma 6 Pirata (Il) 8 Puritani (I) 10 Sonnambula (La) *sleepwalker:* 5 Amina
Bell Jar author 5 Plath (Sylvia)
bell metal 6 bronze
bellow 3 bay, cry, moo 4 bark, bawl, bray, howl, roar, rout, yowl 5 shout 6 clamor, holler 7 bluster
Bellow character 4 Rose (Billy) 5 Chick 6 Herzog (Moses E.) 7 Citrine (Charlie), Sammler (Arthur) 8 Humboldt, Fonstein (Harry) 9 Henderson 10 Ravelstein (Abe), Augie March
bell ringer 6 toller 9 Quasimodo 12 carillonneur 13 campanologist
bell ringing 11 campanology
bell-shaped 11 campanulate
bell sound 4 bong, boom, ding, dong, peal, ring, ting, toll 5 chime, clang, knell 6 tinkle
bell tower 6 belfry 7 clocher 8 carillon 9 campanile
___ **bellum** 4 ante, post
bellwether 4 dean, lead 5 doyen, guide, pilot

6 leader 7 pioneer 8 lodestar 9 harbinger 10 forerunner 11 trend setter
belly 3 gut, pot 5 tummy 6 paunch, venter 7 abdomen, midriff, stomach 9 bay window 10 front porch, midsection 11 breadbasket *Scottish:* 4 wame
bellyache 4 beef, carp, crab, fret, fuss, moan, yawp 5 bitch, bleat, colic, gripe, whine 6 grouse, snivel, squawk, yammer 7 grumble 8 complain 11 let off steam 12 collywobbles
bellyacher 4 crab 5 crank 6 griper, grouch, whiner 7 grouser 8 grumbler, sourpuss 10 complainer, crosspatch, malcontent 11 faultfinder
belly button 5 navel
belong 3 fit, set 4 suit, vest 5 agree, apply, befit, chime, fit in, match, tally 6 accord, attach, become, reside 7 pertain 9 correlate, harmonize 10 correspond
belongings 3 kit 4 gear 5 goods, stuff 6 assets, estate, legacy, things 7 baggage, effects 8 chattels, movables, property 9 patrimony 11 attachments, impedimenta, inheritance, possessions 13 appurtenances
beloved 3 gra, pet 4 baby, beau, dear, idol, love 5 flame, honey, lover, swain, sweet 6 adored, steady 7 darling, dearest, dear one, doted on, sweetie 8 favorite, idolized, ladylove, old flame, precious, truelove 9 boyfriend, cherished, inamorata, treasured 10 girlfriend, heartthrob, sweetheart, sweetie pie
below 5 infra, 'neath, under 7 beneath 10 underneath *prefix:* 3 sub 5 infra
belt 3 bat, bop 4 area, band, bash, biff, blow, gird, loop, ring, sash, slam, slug, sock, whap, whop, zone 5 smack, smash, strap, strip 6 begird, cestus, circle, engird, girdle, region, wallop 7 baldric, clobber, stretch 8 begirdle, ceinture, cincture, encircle, engirdle 9 bandoleer, bandolier, territory, waistband 10 cummerbund *celestial:* 6 zodiac
beltway 8 ring road
Belus *brother:* 6 Agenor *daughter:* 4 Dido *father:* 7 Neptune 8 Poseidon *mother:* 5 Libya *son:* 6 Danaus 7 Cepheus, Phineus 8 Aegyptus
belvedere 6 alcove, cupola, gazebo, pagoda 9 balcony, terrace 10 widow's walk 11 garden house, summerhouse, observatory
bemedaled 9 decorated 10 beribboned
bemired 4 miry, oozy 5 boggy, dirty, grimy, gummy, gunky, muddy, stuck 6 filthy, soiled, swampy 7 swamped
bemoan 3 rue 4 wail, weep 6 bewail, grieve, lament, oppose, regret 7 deplore 8 com-

plain, object to **10** sorrow over **12** disapprove of
bemuse 4 daze **5** addle **6** absorb, muddle,
puzzle **7** confuse, mystify, nonplus, perplex
8 bewilder, distract **10** disconcert
bemused 3 wry **4** lost **6** absent, remote **7** faraway **8** distrait **9** distraite **10** abstracted, distracted **11** preoccupied **12** absentminded **13**
lost in thought
bench 5 court **6** settee, settle, thwart **7** counter **8** platform **9** worktable *church:* **3** pew
outdoor: **6** exedra *upholstered:* **9** banquette
benchmark 4 norm **5** basis, gauge, guide,
model, scale **7** measure **8** exemplar, paradigm, standard **9** criterion, guideline, milestone, yardstick **10** touchstone
benchwarmer 5 scrub
bend 3 arc, bow, sag **4** arch, bank, cave, curl,
flex, hang, hook, lean, mold, sway, tend,
tilt, turn, veer, warp **5** angle, crook, curve,
round, shape, shift, stoop, twist, yield **6**
compel, corner, buckle, direct, double, fasten, kowtow, subdue, submit, zigzag **7** deflect, dispose, distort, flexure, turning **8**
lean over **9** curvature, deviation, genuflect
10 compromise, predispose
bendable 5 lithe **6** limber, pliant, supple
7 elastic, plastic, pliable **8** flexible,
moldable **9** malleable, tractable **11** manipulable
bender see **binge**
_____ **bene 4** nota
beneath 5 below, under *prefix:* **3** hyp, sub **4**
hypo **5** infra
_____ **Benedict 4** eggs
benediction 4 boon, okay **5** favor, grace **6** orison, thanks **7** benefit, benison, godsend **8**
approval, blessing **9** advantage **11** approbation **12** consecration, thanksgiving
benefaction 4 alms, care, fund, gift, help **5**
favor, grant **6** relief **7** charity, comfort,
handout, largess, service, subsidy **8** donation, largesse, oblation, offering, windfall **9**
endowment, patronage **10** assistance **12**
contribution, ministration
benefactor 5 angel, donor **6** backer, patron **7**
grantor, sponsor **9** supporter, sustainer **11**
contributor, underwriter
beneficence see **benefaction**
beneficent 4 kind **6** benign, caring, giving **8**
generous **10** altruistic, bighearted, charitable, ungrudging **11** kindhearted, magnanimous **13** compassionate, philanthropic
beneficial 4 good **5** brave, tonic **6** benign,
toward, useful **7** helpful **8** favoring,
salutary, valuable **9** favorable, healthful,
nurturing, wholesome **10** profitable, propi-

tious, salubrious **12** advantageous, constructive
beneficiary 4 heir **5** donee, payee **7** grantee,
heiress, legatee **8** assignee **9** inheritor, recipient
beneficiate 5 treat **6** reduce **7** prepare, process
benefit 3 aid **4** boon, gain, good, help, perk,
sake **5** avail, extra, favor, serve **6** assist, behalf, better, profit, relief, succor **7** account,
advance, charity, further, godsend, improve,
promote, relieve, welfare **8** blessing, interest **9** advantage, well-being **10** ameliorate,
fund-raiser, prosperity **11** good fortune **12**
contribute to
benevolence 4 boon, gift, help **5** amity,
favor, grant **6** comity, relief **7** caritas, charity **8** altruism, clemency, goodness, goodwill, humanity, kindness **10** compassion,
compliment, kindliness **11** magnanimity
benevolent 4 good, kind, warm **6** caring, do-
good, humane, kindly **7** helpful, liberal **8**
generous, tolerant **10** altruistic, beneficent,
bighearted, charitable, openhanded **11** considerate, magnanimous, warmhearted **12**
eleemosynary, humanitarian **13** compassionate, philanthropic, tenderhearted
Ben Hur author 7 Wallace (Lew)
benighted 6 obtuse, unread **8** backward, ignorant, untaught **9** untutored, unwitting **10**
illiterate, uneducated, uninformed, unlettered, unschooled **11** know-nothing **12** uncultivated **13** unenlightened, unprogressive
benign 4 kind, mild **6** genial, gentle, humane,
kindly, mellow **7** amiable, clement **8** gracious, harmless, merciful, pleasant **9** favorable, fortunate, healthful, temperate,
wholesome **10** auspicious, benevolent,
charitable, forbearing, propitious, remedi-
able **11** good-hearted **12** noncancerous
Benin *capital:* **9** Porto-Novo *city:* **7** Cotonou
coast: **5** Slave *ethnic group:* **3** Fon **6** Fulani, Yoruba *former name:* **7** Dahomey *language:* **3** Fon **6** French *monetary unit:* **5**
franc *neighbor:* **4** Togo **5** Niger **7** Nigeria
11 Burkina Faso *river:* **5** Ouémé
benison 5 grace **8** blessing **11** benediction **12**
consecration
Benjamin *brother:* **6**
Joseph *father:* **5** Jacob *mother:* **6** Rachel
bent 3 set **4** bias, gift **5** arced, bowed, flair,
knack **6** arched, curved, intent, talent **7** decided, faculty, leaning **8** aptitude,
capacity, penchant, resolute, resolved, tendency **10** determined, proclivity, propensity
11 disposition, inclination **12** predilection
benumb 4 daze, dull, stun **5** blunt, chill **6**

deaden, freeze **7** petrify, stupefy **8**
etherize, paralyze **10** immobilize **11**
desensitize
benumbed 4 cold **6** frozen **9** unfeeling **10** insensible **11** insensitive **12** anesthetized
Beowulf *drink:* **4** mead *monster:* **7** Grendel
bequeath 4 gift, will **5** endow, grant, leave **6**
bestow, commit, confer, devise, hand on,
impart, legate, pass on **7** furnish, present **8**
hand down, make over, transmit
bequest 3 lot **4** gift **5** share, trust **6** devise,
estate, legacy **7** portion **8** heritage **10** settlement **11** inheritance
berate 3 jaw **4** rail, rate **5** chide, scold **6** rail
at, rebuke, revile **7** bawl out, blister, chew
out, condemn, reprove, tell off, upbraid **8**
admonish, chastise, reproach **9** castigate,
criticize, reprimand **10** tongue-lash, vituperate
berceuse 7 lullaby **10** cradlesong
bereave 3 rob **4** lose **5** seize, strip **6** divest,
remove **7** deprive **8** take away **10** confiscate,
disinherit, dispossess **11** appropriate, requisition
bereaved 8 mourning **9** sorrowful, sorrowing
10 distressed **11** heartbroken **13** griefstricken
bereavement 3 rue, woe **4** loss **5** dolor, grief
6 misery, pining, regret, sorrow **7** anguish,
despair, remorse, sadness **8** grieving,
mourning **9** dejection, heartache **10** affliction, depression, desolation **11** deprivation,
despondency, lamentation, tribulation
bereft 4 lorn **5** shorn **6** devoid, robbed **7**
fleeced, forlorn, wanting **8** beggared,
deprived, desolate, divested, stricken,
stripped **9** destitute **10** despondent **12** disconsolate, dispossessed, impoverished
Bergen's dummy 7 Charlie (McCarthy) **8**
Mortimer (Snerd)
Berger novel 12 Little Big Man
Bergman role 4 Ilsa
berkelium symbol 2 Bk
berm 4 path **5** ledge, mound, shelf **8** shoulder
Bermuda *capital:* **8** Hamilton *territory of:* **7**
Britain
Bernice *brother:* **7** Agrippa *father:* **5** Herod
husband: **6** Polemo *lover:* **5** Titus **9** Vespasian
berry 3 haw **5** cubeb, fruit, grape **7** currant,
madrona, madrone **8** allspice **9** saskatoon
berserk 3 ape **4** amok **5** amuck, crazy **6**
crazed, insane **7** bonkers, lunatic **8** demented, deranged, frenzied
berth 3 bed, cot **4** dock, moor, pier, port,
post, quay, slip, spot **5** cabin, jetty, levee,
place, wharf **6** billet, office **8** position **9**

anchorage, situation **10** connection **11** appointment, compartment **13** accommodation
beryllium symbol 2 Be
beseech see **beg**
beset 3 dog, hem, try, vex **4** gird, ring **5**
harry, hem in, storm, worry **6** assail, attack,
badger, circle, fall on, harass, infest, pester,
plague, strike **7** assault, besiege, overrun,
trouble, torture **8** blockade, encircle, fall
upon, surround **9** beleaguer, encompass,
overswarm
besetment 3 nag **4** bane, pain, pest **5** curse,
trial **6** blight, bother, gadfly, pester, plague
7 torment **8** irritant, nuisance, vexation **9**
annoyance **10** affliction, botherment, holy
terror **11** aggravation, botheration
besetting 6 urgent **7** driving **8** dominant **9**
obsessive **10** compelling, persistent **11** omnipresent **12** overwhelming
beside 4 near, nigh **6** next to
besides 3 too **4** also, else, plus, save **5** added,
extra **6** and all, as well, beyond, except, to
boot **7** barring, farther, further, without **8** as
well as, likewise, moreover, more than **9**
aside from, along with, exceeding, excluding, other than, otherwise, outside of **10** in
addition **11** exclusive of, furthermore, not
counting **12** additionally, together with
besiege 3 nag **4** ring, trap **5** beset, hem in,
hound **6** assail, attack, circle, girdle, harass,
pester, plague **7** assault, confine, environ,
trouble **8** blockade, encircle, surround **9** beleaguer, encompass
besmear see **smear**
besmirch 4 blot, foul, slur, soil **5** dirty, libel,
stain, sully, taint **6** defile, damage, impugn,
malign **7** asperse, slander, tarnish **8** disgrace, dishonor
besom 5 broom
besotted 5 dotty, drunk **7** charmed, muddled,
smitten **8** enamored **9** enchanted **10** captivated, fascinated, infatuated, spellbound **11**
intoxicated
bespatter see **spatter**
bespeak 3 ask **4** book, hire, show **5** imply **6**
accost, attest, desire, evince, reveal **7** address, apply to, betoken, connote, lecture,
portend, request, reserve, signify, solicit,
suggest, testify, witness **8** announce, approach, foretell, indicate, intimate, petition
9 preengage **10** prearrange
bespoke 8 tailored **10** custom-made
best 3 gem, top **4** beat, pick, tops **5** cream,
elite, excel, model, one-up, outdo, pride,
prime, prize **6** choice, defeat, exceed, finest
7 conquer, leading, optimal, optimum, paragon, premium, supreme, surpass **8** exem-

plar, foremost, greatest, nonesuch, outshine, outstrip, overcome **9** matchless, nonpareil, number-one, paramount, transcend, unequaled **11** outstanding **12** incomparable *combining form:* **6** aristo

bestial 4 vile, wild **5** brute, cruel, feral **6** animal, brutal, carnal, fierce, malign, savage **7** beastly, brutish, inhuman, swinish, vicious **8** depraved, inhumane **9** ferocious **10** degenerate

bestialize 4 ruin, warp **5** abase **6** debase, defile **7** corrupt, debauch, degrade, deprave, pervert, pollute, subvert, vitiate, violate **9** brutalize **10** bastardize, demoralize

bestir 3 fly, rip **4** dash, flit, goad, race, rush, spur, stir, tear, urge, wake, whet **5** rally, rouse, scoot, waken, whirl **6** arouse, awaken, hasten, hustle, kindle **8** get going, scramble **9** challenge

bestow 4 give **5** apply, award, grant **6** confer, devote, donate, lavish **7** hand out, present **8** bequeath, give away *Scottish:* **7** propine

bestower 5 donor, giver **6** patron **7** donator **8** altruist **9** conferrer, patroness, presenter **10** benefactor **12** benefactress **13** good Samaritan

bestrew 3 dot, sow **6** pepper, shower **7** diffuse, disject, scatter, speckle, stipple **8** disperse, sprinkle **9** broadcast, interlard **10** distribute **11** disseminate

bestride 5 mount, tower **8** dominate, loom over, straddle **9** stand over

bet 3 pot **4** ante, game, play, risk, shot **5** put on, stake, wager **6** gamble, hazard, parlay, pledge **7** lay odds, venture *racing:* **6** exacta **8** perfecta, quinella, quiniela *taker:* **6** bookie

Betelgeuse 4 star *constellation:* **5** Orion

betel palm 5 areca

bête noire 4 bane, hate, ruin **5** trial **6** animus, horror **7** bugbear, nemesis, scourge, torment, undoing **8** anathema, aversion, downfall **9** ruination **10** black beast

bethink 4 cite, mind **6** call up, recall, remind, retain, review, revive **7** flash on **8** hark back, look back, remember, summon up **9** conjure up, recollect, reminisce **10** call to mind, retrospect

Bethuel *daughter:* **7** Rebekah *father:* **5** Nahor *mother:* **6** Milcah *son:* **5** Laban *uncle:* **7** Abraham

betide 4 fall **5** break, ensue, occur **6** befall, chance, happen **7** come off, develop, fall out **8** commence **9** come about, transpire

betimes 4 anon, soon **5** early **6** pronto, seldom, timely **7** too soon **8** directly, far ahead, fitfully, promptly **9** presently **10** before long, now and then, on occasion, seasonably **11** prematurely **12** occasionally, sporadically

betoken 4 bode, omen, show, warn **5** argue, augur **6** attest, denote, hint at **7** bespeak, point to, portend, presage, promise, signify, suggest, testify, witness **8** announce, forebode, evidence, foreshow, foretell, indicate, intimate, prophesy **9** prefigure **10** foreshadow **13** prognosticate

betray 4 dupe, jilt, trap **5** rat on, snare, spill, split **6** desert, entrap, evince, finger, inform, reveal, seduce, take in, tattle, tell on, turn in, unveil **7** abandon, beguile, deceive, divulge, forsake, let down, let slip, sell out, traduce **8** blurt out, denounce, disclose, discover, evidence, give away, manifest **10** apostatize, break faith **11** double-cross

betrayal 4 leak **7** perfidy, sellout, treason **8** exposure **9** duplicity, falseness, Judas kiss, treachery **10** disclosure, infidelity, revelation **13** faithlessness

betrayer 3 rat **4** fink, nark **5** Judas **6** snitch **7** stoolie, tattler, traitor **8** apostate, defector, informer, quisling, renegade, squealer, turncoat **10** talebearer, tattletale **11** backstabber, stool pigeon

betroth 3 wed **5** marry **6** pledge **7** espouse **8** affiance

betrothal 6 pledge **8** espousal **10** engagement

betrothed 6 fiancé **7** engaged, fiancée, pledged **8** intended, plighted, promised, wife-to-be **9** affianced, bride-to-be, spoken for **10** contracted **11** husband-to-be

better 4 fix, top, win **4** beat, help, mend, more, well **5** amend, cured, elder, excel, finer, outdo **6** exceed, fitter, repair **7** advance, correct, enhance, further, greater, improve, largest, mending, rectify, success, surpass, triumph, victory **8** greatest, improved, outshine, outstrip, stronger, superior, whip hand, worthier **9** advantage, desirable, excellent, healthier, improving, meliorate, preferred, transcend, upper hand **10** ameliorate, preferable, preferably, recovering, surpassing

bettor 7 gambler, wagerer

between 4 amid **5** among, twixt **6** within **7** betwixt *prefix:* **5** inter, intra

betweentimes 11 at intervals

bevel 4 bias, cant **5** angle, grade, slant, slope **7** chamfer, incline, oblique **8** diagonal

beverage 3 ade, nog, pop, tea **4** chai, cola, kava, maté, milk, soda **5** cider, cocoa, drink, juice, mocha, shake **6** coffee, eggnog, frappe, malted, nectar **7** potable, soda pop **8** lemonade, libation, potation **9** drinkable, milk shake *alcoholic:* **3** ale, gin, rum **4** beer, grog, mead, nipa, wine **5** cider, julep, negus, punch, stout, toddy, vodka **6** bishop, brandy, caudle, cooler, liquor, rickey, shandy, sherry, whisky **7** liqueur, martini, sangria, tequila, whiskey **8** cocktail, highball, sillabub, syllabub, vermouth *Arab:* **4** arak **6** arrack *Australasian:* **4** kava *Balkan:* **9** slivovitz *British:* **5** perry, stout **6** porter *carbonated:* **4** cola, soda **5** tonic **6** rickey **7** Perrier, seltzer, soda pop **8** club soda, root beer **9** ginger ale *central Asian:* **6** kumiss **7** koumiss *Dutch:* **7** schnaps **8** schnapps *from milk:* **5** kefir **6** kumiss **7** koumiss *Greek:* **4** ouzo **7** retsina *Hawaiian:* **3** 'ava *Irish:* **6** poteen **10** usquebaugh *Japanese:* **4** sake *medicinal:* **6** elixir, tisane *Mexican:* **6** pulque **7** tequila *of the gods:* **6** nectar *Oriental:* **4** arak, sake, saki **6** arrack *Russian:* **5** kefir, kvass, vodka *Scottish:* **6** scotch *South American:* **4** maté **5** yerba **9** yerba maté *Swedish:* **5** glogg *Turkish:* **4** raki *West Indies:* **3** rum see also **cocktail**

bevy 3 mob **4** band, club, crew, gang, herd, knot, pack **5** bunch, covey, crowd, drove, flock, group, horde, party, swarm **6** clutch, gaggle, troupe **7** cluster, company, coterie **8** assembly **9** menagerie, multitude **10** assemblage, collection

bewail 3 rue **4** keen, moan, weep **5** mourn **6** bemoan, grieve, lament, regret **7** deplore

beware 4 heed, mark, mind, note, shun **5** avoid, watch **6** attend, notice **7** look out **8** take heed, watch out

bewhiskered 5 bushy **7** bearded, goateed, hirsute, stubbly **8** unshaven

bewilder 3 fog **4** daze, stun **5** addle, amaze, befog, mix up, stump **6** baffle, ball up, bemuse, fuddle, muddle, puzzle, rattle **7** confuse, fluster, mystify, nonplus, perplex, stumble **8** befuddle, confound, distract **9** disorient, dumbfound **10** disconcert

bewilderment 3 awe **4** daze **6** wonder **8** surprise **9** amazement, confusion **10** perplexity, puzzlement **11** distraction **12** astonishment, discomfiture, stupefaction **13** consternation

bewitch 3 hex **4** draw, pull, snow, take, wile **5** charm, spell, trick **6** allure, dazzle, seduce, voodoo **7** attract, bedevil, beguile, control, delight, enchant, possess **8** demonize, ensorcel, enthrall, entrance, intrigue, overlook **9** captivate, enrapture, ensorcell, fascinate, hypnotize, magnetize, mesmerize, spellbind

Bewitched *character:* **6** Darrin, Endora **7** Maurice, Tabitha **8** Samantha **9** Aunt Clara *creator:* **4** Saks (Sol) *film director:* **6** Ephron (Nora) *film star:* **5** Caine (Michael)

6 Kidman (Nicole) **7** Ferrell (Will) **8** MacLaine (Shirley) *TV star:* **4** York (Dick) **7** Sargent (Dick) **9** Moorehead (Agnes) **10** Montgomery (Elizabeth)

bewitching 4 foxy **5** siren **7** magical **8** alluring, charming, engaging, enticing, magnetic, mesmeric **9** seductive **10** attractive **12** irresistible

bewitchment 3 hex **4** jinx **5** charm, magic, spell **6** trance **7** evil eye, sorcery **8** black art, wizardry **9** conjuring **10** necromancy **11** conjuration, enchantment, incantation, thaumaturgy

beyond 4 over, past **5** above, after **6** across, beside, yonder **7** besides, further, outside **8** as well as **9** afterlife, hereafter, otherwise **10** afterworld **12** over and above *prefix:* **4** meta, over, para **5** extra, hyper, super, trans, ultra **6** preter

Bhutan *capital:* **7** Thimphu *ethnic group:* **6** Bhutia **8** Assamese, Nepalese **9** Mongolian, Sharcrops *language:* **8** Dzongkha *monetary unit:* **8** ngultrum *mountain range:* **8** Himalaya **13** Great Himalaya *neighbor:* **5** China, India, Tibet *plain:* **5** Duars

bias 4 bend, bent, skew, sway, tilt, turn **5** angle, bevel, slant **7** beveled, bigotry, dispose, distort, incline, leaning, oblique, slanted **8** diagonal, penchant, slanting, tendency **9** crosswise, inclining, influence, prejudice, proneness, viewpoint **10** diagonally, favoritism, partiality, propensity, predispose, prepossess, proclivity, standpoint, transverse **11** disposition, inclination **12** one-sidedness, predilection **13** preconception

biased 6 racist, swayed, unfair, warped **7** bigoted, colored, partial, slanted **8** disposed, inclined, one-sided, partisan, slanting **9** jaundiced, sectarian, unneutral **10** influenced, interested, prejudiced **11** opinionated, predisposed, tendentious

bibelot 5 curio **6** bauble, gewgaw, trifle **7** memento, novelty, trinket, whatnot **8** gimcrack, ornament **9** objet d'art **10** knickknack

Bible *abbreviation:* **3** Col, Cor, Dan, Eph, Gal, Gen, Hab, Heb, Hos, Jas, Jer, Jon, Lam, Lev, Mal, Mic, Neh, Num, Pet, Rev, Rom, Sam, Tim, Tit **4** Deut, Ezek, Josh, Judg, Obad, Phil, Prov, Zech, Zeph **5** Chron, Thess **6** Eccles, Philem *Apocrypha book:* **5** Tobit **6** Baruch, Esdras, Esther, Judith **7** Susanna **8** Manasseh, Manasses **9** Maccabees *New Testament book:* **4** Acts, John, Jude, Luke, Mark **5** James, Peter, Titus **6** Romans **7** Hebrews, Matthew, Timothy **8** Philemon **9** Ephesians, Galatians **10** Colossians, Revelation **11** Corinthians, Philippians **13** Thessalonians *Old Testament book:* **3** Job **4** Amos, Ezra, Joel, Ruth **5** Hosea, Jonah, Kings, Micah, Nahum **6** Daniel, Esther, Exodus, Haggai, Isaiah, Joshua, Judges, Psalms, Samuel **7** Ezekiel, Genesis, Malachi, Numbers, Obadiah **8** Habakkuk, Jeremiah, Nehemiah, Proverbs **9** Leviticus, Zechariah, Zephaniah **10** Chronicles **11** Deuteronomy **12** Ecclesiastes, Lamentations **13** Song of Solomon *part:* **4** book **5** verse **7** chapter **9** testament *translator:* **4** Knox (Ronald Arbuthnott) **5** Eliot (John) **6** Jerome, Luther (Martin) **7** Erasmus (Desiderius), Tyndale (William), Zwingli (Huldrych) **8** Andrewes (Lancelot), Wycliffe (John) **9** Coverdale (Miles) *version:* **5** Douay **6** Coptic, Gothic, Syriac **7** Vulgate **9** Jerusalem, King James, Masoretic **10** New English, Septuagint

Biblical *animal:* **8** behemoth *ascetic order:* **6** Essene *battle:* **7** Jericho *battle site:* **10** Armageddon *charioteer:* **4** Jehu *city, town:* **4** Cana, Gaza, Tyre, Zoar **5** Endor, Golan, Haifa, Joppa, Sidon, Sodom **6** Asshur, Bethel, Emmaus, Gilgal, Hebron, Mizpah, Shiloh, Smyrna, Tarsus **7** Antioch, Baalbec, Bethany, Corinth, Ephesus, Ephraim, Jericho, Magdala, Nineveh, Samaria **8** Caesarea, Damascus, Gomorrah, Nazareth, Philippi, Tiberias **9** Beersheba, Bethlehem, Capernaum, Jerusalem *coin:* (see at **Hebrew**) *desert:* **5** Sinai *garden:* **4** Eden **8** Paradise *giant:* **7** Goliath *giant slayer:* **5** David *hill:* **4** Zion **7** Calvary *hunter:* **6** Nimrod *judge:* **3** Eli **4** Ehud **6** Gideon, Samson, Samuel **7** Deborah, Jephtha **8** Jephthah *king:* **3** Asa **4** Ahab, Amon, Elah, Jehu, Saul **5** David, Herod, Hiram **6** Josiah **7** Azariah, Menahem, Solomon **8** Hezekiah, Jeroboam, Manasseh, Rehoboam, Zedekiah **9** Zechariah **11** Jehoshaphat *land:* **3** Nod **4** Aram, Elam, Moab, Seba **5** Judah, Judea, Magog **6** Canaan, Goshen, Israel, Judaea **7** Chaldea, Galilee, Samaria **9** Palestine *land of plenty:* **6** Goshen *measure:* (see at **Hebrew**) *mountain:* **4** Nebo **5** Horeb, Sinai, Tabor **6** Ararat, Carmel, Gilboa, Gilead, Hermon, Moriah, Olivet, Pisgah **7** Lebanon *name:* **3** Asa, Bel, Dan, Eli, Eve, Gad, Ham, Ira, Job, Lot, Uri **4** Abel, Adam, Ahab, Amon, Boaz, Cain, Elam, Enos, Esau, Jael, Jehu, Joel, John, Lael, Leah, Levi, Mark, Mary, Mica, Moab, Noah, Omar, Onan, Paul, Reba, Ruth, Sara, Saul, Seth, Shem **5** Aaron, Abner, Amram, Asher, Caleb, David, Dinah, Elias, Enoch, Ethan, Hagar, Heman, Herod, Hosea, Isaac, Jacob, James, Jared, Jesse, Jonah, Jubal, Judah, Judas, Laban, Micah, Moses, Naomi, Peter, Rufus, Sarah, Sheba, Simon, Tamar, Tubal, Uriah, Uriel, Zadok **6** Ashhur, Balaam, Baruch, Canaan, Daniel, Elijah, Elisha, Esther, Gideon, Gilead, Hannah, Hebron, Isaiah, Israel, Jeshua, Jethro, Joanna, Joseph, Joshua, Josiah, Judith, Martha, Miriam, Nathan, Nimrod, Pasach, Philip, Pilate, Rachel, Reuben, Salome, Samson, Samuel, Simeon, Thomas, Tobias *patriarch:* (see at **Hebrew**) *people:* **6** Kenite, Levite **7** Amorite, Edomite, Elamite, Moabite **9** Israelite *plains:* **6** Sharon **7** Jericho *plotter:* **5** Haman *poem:* **5** psalm *pool:* **8** Bethesda *priest:* **3** Eli **4** Levi **5** Aaron, Annas **8** Caiaphas *Promised Land:* **6** Canaan *pronoun:* **2** ye **3** thy **4** thee, thou **5** thine *prophet:* (see **prophet**) *Psalmist:* **5** David *punishment:* **7** stoning *queen:* **5** Sheba **6** Esther **7** Jezebel *quotation:* **4** text *river:* **4** Nile **6** Jordan *sacred object:* **4** urim **7** thummin *scribe:* **6** Baruch *sea:* **3** Red **4** Dead **7** Galilee *sea monster:* **9** Leviathan *spice:* **5** aloes, myrrh **6** cassia **7** calamus **8** cinnamon **12** frankincense *spy:* **5** Caleb *strongman:* **6** Samson *temptress:* **3** Eve **7** Delilah *text set to music:* **8** oratorio *thief:* **8** Barabbas *tree:* **5** cedar *twin:* **4** Esau **5** Jacob *valley:* **4** Baca, Elah **6** Hinnon, Kidron, Shaveh, Siddim *weed:* **4** tare *witch's home:* **5** Endor

bibliography 4 list **7** catalog, history **8** book list **13** reference list

bibliopole 7 bookman **10** book dealer, bookseller

bibulous 6 spongy **7** thirsty **8** drinking **9** absorbent **10** absorptive

bicker 3 row **4** spar, spat, tiff **5** argue, clack, fight, scrap **6** gurgle, hassle **7** brabble, clatter, contend, dispute, fall out, flicker, quarrel, quibble, wrangle **8** squabble

bickering 3 row **4** at it, spat **5** brawl, run-in **6** blowup, fracas, hassle, ruckus, rumpus, strife **7** discord, dispute, quarrel, rhubarb, wrangle **8** squabble **11** altercation, embroilment

bicycle 4 bike *brake:* **7** caliper, coaster *for two:* **6** tandem *gear shift:* **10** derailleur *rider:* **6** cycler **7** cyclist *track:* **9** velodrome

bid 3 ask, say, try **4** call, tell, warn, wish **5** essay, greet, offer, order **6** amount, charge, direct, effort, enjoin, invite, render, summon, tender **7** attempt, command, proffer, request, require, venture **8** endeavor, instruct, proposal **10** invitation, submission **11** proposition

biddable 4 mild **6** docile, pliant **7** amiable,

pliable, willing **8** amenable, obedient, obliging **9** malleable, tractable **10** governable, manageable **11** acquiescent, cooperative, good-natured **13** accommodating

bidding 4 call, word **5** offer, order **6** behest, charge, demand, notice, tender **7** auction, command, dictate, mandate, request, summons **9** ordinance, summoning **10** injunction, invitation **11** commandment, instruction **12** proclamation

biddy 3 bag, bat, hag, hen **4** drab, trot **5** crone, witch **6** beldam **7** chicken

bide 4 live, stay, wait **5** await, dwell, tarry **6** hang in, linger, remain, reside **7** hang out, sojourn **8** continue, sit tight, tolerate **10** hang around **11** stick around

bier 10 catafalque

biff 3 bop, box, hit, jab, zap **4** bash, belt, blow, clip, ding, nail, slam, slug, sock, swat, whop **5** blast, catch, clout, pound, slosh, smack, thump, whack **6** strike, thwack, wallop

bifurcate 3 cut **4** fork **5** halve, split **6** bisect, branch, cleave, divide **8** separate **9** branch out **11** dichotomize, dichotomous

bifurcation 4 fork **6** branch **8** division **9** dichotomy, partition, radiation **10** separation

big 3 fat **4** full, hard, huge, main, mega, tall, vast **5** adult, ample, chief, great, grown, heavy, hefty, husky, large, lofty, major, proud, roomy **6** bumper, hugely **7** capital, copious, crammed, crowded, eminent, grown-up, hulking, leading, liberal, mammoth, massive, monster, notable, popular, replete, sizable, stuffed, swollen, weighty **8** colossal, enormous, generous, gracious, imposing, inflated, material, oversize, princely, spacious, swelling **9** capacious, chock-full, distended, extensive, heavy duty, humongous, important, momentous, overblown, paramount, ponderous, principal, prominent, unselfish **10** commodious, large-scale, preeminent, prodigious, voluminous **11** heavyweight, magnanimous, major-league, overflowing, significant, substantial **12** considerable **13** comprehensive, consequential *prefix:* **4** mega

big bang theorist 5 Gamow (George)

Big Bertha 6 cannon **8** howitzer *birthplace:* **5** Essen *manufacturer:* **5** Krupp

Big ____, Cal. 3 Sur

Big Dipper constellation: 9 Ursa Major *star:* **5** Alcor, Dubhe, Merak, Mizar

bigfoot 9 Sasquatch

biggety 4 bold, vain, wise **5** fresh, nervy, sassy **6** cheeky, snippy, snooty, uppity **7** forward, stuck-up **8** impudent, insolent,

puffed up, snobbish **9** conceited **11** smart-alecky **13** self-important

bighearted 6 giving **7** liberal **8** generous **9** forgiving **10** altruistic, benevolent, charitable, munificent, openhanded **11** magnanimous **13** compassionate

big house 3 can, jug, pen **4** coop, jail **5** clink, joint **6** cooler, lockup, prison **7** slammer **8** bastille, hoosegow, stockade **9** bridewell **11** reformatory **12** penitentiary

bight 3 arm, bay **4** cove, gulf **6** harbor

bigmouthed 4 loud, rude **8** boastful **10** boisterous

bigness 4 size **5** scale, scope **6** extent, volume **9** amplitude, immensity, magnitude **10** dimensions, importance

bigot 6 racist **8** jingoist **9** extremist, racialist **10** chauvinist **11** supremacist

bigoted 6 biased, narrow, unfair **9** hidebound, illiberal, sectarian **10** brassbound, intolerant, prejudiced **11** small-minded **12** narrow-minded

bigotry 4 bias **6** racism **9** apartheid, prejudice **10** xenophobia **11** intolerance

big shot 3 VIP **4** czar **5** celeb, mogul, nabob **6** fat cat, tycoon **7** kingpin, notable, pooh-bah **8** higher-up, luminary, top brass **9** celebrity, dignitary, personage **13** high-muck-a-muck

Big Ten team 4 Iowa (Hawkeyes) **6** Purdue (Boilermakers) **7** Indiana (Hoosiers) **8** Illinois (Fighting Illini), Michigan (Wolverines) **9** Minnesota (Golden Gophers), Ohio State (Buckeyes), Penn State (Nittany Lions), Wisconsin (Badgers) **12** Northwestern (Wildcats) **13** Michigan State (Spartans)

big-time 5 major **7** eminent, greatly, leading **8** renowned **9** high-level, important, paramount, prominent **10** large-scale **11** influential, major-league

big top 4 tent **6** circus

bigwig 3 VIP **5** heavy, mogul, nabob **6** honcho, kahuna **7** kingpin, magnate, notable **8** luminary, somebody **9** dignitary, personage **11** heavy hitter, muckety-muck **13** high-muck-a-muck

bijou 3 gem **5** jewel **8** gemstone

bijouterie 6 jewels **7** jewelry **8** trinkets **10** decoration

bike 5 cycle **7** scooter **10** motorcycle **12** motorscooter

bilge 3 rot **4** bull, bunk, guff **5** hooey, trash **6** bunkum **7** baloney, garbage, hogwash, malarky, rubbish, twaddle **8** claptrap, nonsense **9** poppycock, silliness **10** balderdash **11** foolishness

bilk 3 con, gyp **4** balk, beat, dash, duck, dupe,

foil, fool, hoax, hose, kite, milk, rook, ruin, scam, take 5 avoid, cheat, cozen, dodge, elude, evade, shake, shaft, skirt, stiff, trick 6 baffle, chisel, chouse, diddle, double, escape, eschew, fleece, rip off, sucker, thwart 7 deceive, defraud, prevent, swindle 8 flimflam, hoodwink, sidestep, stave off 9 frustrate 10 circumvent

bill 3 dun, fin, neb, nib, one, tab, ten 4 beak, bone, buck, chit, list, note, skin 5 check, fiver, score, visor 6 charge, damage, dollar, notice, poster, roster, tenner 7 account, charges, invoice, placard, program, sawbuck, smacker, ten-spot 8 Hamilton, mandible 9 greenback, reckoning, smackeroo, statement *part:* 4 cere

billet 3 bar, bed, gig, hut, job, rod 4 post, slab, spar, spot 5 berth, board, house, ingot, lodge, place, put up, stick, strip 6 bestow, canton, harbor, office 7 quarter 8 domicile, position, quarters, vocation 9 entertain, situation 10 assignment, connection, employment, encampment, livelihood, profession, occupation 11 appointment

billet-doux 8 mash note 10 love letter

billfold 6 wallet

billiards term 3 cue 4 foot, head, jaws, kiss, long, peas, pool, race, rack, spot 5 break, carom, chalk, count, masse 6 bridge, cannon, corner, crotch, inning, miscue, nurses, pocket, stance, string 7 bricole, cue ball, cushion, ferrule, kitchen, pyramid, scratch, shooter, snooker 8 apex ball, balkline, bank shot, cue stick, dead ball, jump shot, rotation, triangle 9 clean bank, eight ball 10 chuck nurse, head string, object ball 12 balance point

billingsgate 5 abuse 6 tirade 7 obloquy 9 contumely, invective 10 revilement, scurrility 12 vilification, vituperation

billion *British:* 8 milliard *combining form:* 4 giga

billionth *combining form:* 4 nano

bill of fare 4 menu 7 program 11 carte du jour

billow 4 mass, wave 5 bulge, cloud, surge, swell 6 puff up, roller 7 balloon, upsurge

Billy Budd *author:* 8 Melville (Herman) *character:* 4 Vere (Captain) 8 Claggert (John)

billy club 4 cane 5 baton 6 cudgel, paddle 8 bludgeon 9 bastinado, truncheon 10 knobkerrie, nightstick

bin 4 crib 5 frame, stall 6 bunker, hamper, trough 9 container 10 receptacle

binary 4 twin, dual 5 duple 6 double, duplex, paired 7 coupled, matched, twofold 9 dualistic

bind 3 tie 4 frap, gird, tape, wrap 5 chain, cinch, strap, tie up, truss 6 cement, commit, fasten, fetter, ligate, pinion 7 bandage, confine, enchain, shackle, trammel 8 enfetter, restrain 9 constrain, constrict, indenture

binder 4 file 5 cover 6 folder, jacket 7 wrapper 9 harvester

binding 8 required 9 mandatory, requisite 10 obligatory

bindlestiff 4 hobo

binge 3 jag 4 orgy, riot, soak, tear, time, toot 5 blast, booze, fling, party, revel, souse, spree, stint 6 bender 7 blowoff, blowout, carouse, debauch, rampage, revelry, shindig, splurge, surfeit, wassail 8 carousal, gluttony 9 bacchanal, brannigan 10 debauchery, indulgence 11 bacchanalia, celebration 12 intemperance

bingo 3 yes 5 beano 7 correct

biographer *American:* 5 Weems (Parson) 6 Parton (James) 7 Freeman (Douglas) 8 Bradford (Gamaliel), Sandburg (Carl) 10 McCullough (David) *English:* 6 Aubrey (John), Morley (John), Walton (Izaak) 8 Strachey (Lytton) *French:* 7 Maurois (André) *German:* 6 Ludwig (Emil) *Greek:* 8 Plutarch *Italian:* 6 Vasari (Giorgio) *Roman:* 9 Suetonius *Scottish* 7 Boswell (James)

biography 3 bio 4 life, obit, vita 5 diary, story 6 memoir 7 history, profile 8 obituary 11 confessions

biological category 5 class, genus, order 6 family, phylum 7 kingdom, species, variety 10 subspecies

bionomics 7 ecology

Bip's creator 7 Marceau (Marcel)

bird 2 io 3 ani, auk, daw, eme, emu, ern, iwa, jay, kea, mew, moa, owl, poe, tit, tui 4 Alca, Anas, chat, Chen, coot, crow, dove, duck, erne, guan, gull, hawk, ibis, iiwi, kite, kiwi, knot, koko, lark, loon, loro, lory, mina, moho, myna, Olor, Pavo, Pica, rail, rhea, rook, ruff, shag, skua, smew, sora, Sula, swan, teal, tern, Uria, wren, Xema 5 booby, brant, buteo, cahow, crake, crane, eagle, egret, finch, galah, goose, grebe, heron, junco, macaw, merle, murre, mynah, noddy, ousel, ouzel, owlet, pewee, pewit, pipit, quail, raven, robin, stilt, snipe, stork, swift, veery, vireo 6 avocet, barbet, bulbul, canary, chough, chukar, condor, corbie, cuckoo, curlew, drongo, dunlin, falcon, fulmar, gannet, godwit, grouse, hoopoe, jabiru, jacana, jaeger, kakapo, linnet, magpie, martin, merlin, mud hen, oriole, osprey, parrot, peahen, peewit, petrel, phoebe, plover, puffin, raptor, ratite, redleg, scoter, shrike, takahe, thrush, tomtit, toucan, towhee, trogon, turaco, turkey, verdin, wigeon, willet **7** anhinga, apteryx, bittern, blue jay, bunting, bustard, buzzard, catbird, chicken, courser, creeper, dovekie, flicker, goshawk, grackle, harrier, jacamar, jackdaw, kestrel, kinglet, lapwing, limpkin, mallard, marabou, moorhen, oilbird, ostrich, peacock, pelican, penguin, pintail, quetzal, redwing, sawbill, skimmer, skylark, sparrow, swallow, tanager, tattler, titlark, touraco, vulture, wagtail, warbler, waxbill, waxwing, widgeon **8** baldpate, bellbird, blackcap, bobolink, bobwhite, brantail, caracara, cardinal, cockatoo, curassow, dabchick, dotterel, flamingo, guacharo, hornbill, killdeer, lorikeet, lyrebird, marsh hen, moorfowl, murrelet, nightjar, nuthatch, oxpecker, parakeet, pheasant, Philomel, redshank, redstart, screamer, shoebill, shoveler, starling, thrasher, throstle, titmouse, tragopan, troupial, wheatear, whimbrel, wildfowl, woodcock, woodlark **9** accipiter, albatross, broadbill, cassowary, chaffinch, chickadee, cormorant, crossbill, francolin, gallinule, guillemot, gyrfalcon, kittiwake, merganser, nighthawk, owl parrot, partridge, phalarope, ptarmigan, razorbill, sandpiper, snakebird, spoonbill, stonechat, trumpeter, turnstone **10** bufflehead, chiffchaff, flycatcher, goatsucker, kingfisher, shearwater, sheathbill **11** lammergeier, nightingale **12** whippoorwill *class:* **4** Aves *colony:* **5** roost **7** rookery *combining form:* **5** ornis **6** ornith **7** ornitho **8** ornithes (plural) *extinct:* **3** moa **4** dodo **9** aepyornis, solitaire *mythical:* **3** roc **7** phoenix *relating to:* **5** avian **8** ornithic *sound:* **3** caw, coo **4** chip, crow, honk, hoot, peep **5** cheep, chirp, cluck, croak, quack, trill, tweet **6** squawk **7** screech, twitter *unfledged:* **4** eyas **5** chick **5** nestling

birdbrain 4 clod, dodo, dolt, goof, loon **5** dummy, dunce, idiot, moron, ninny **6** nitwit **7** airhead, dullard, halfwit **8** dumbbell, imbecile, meathead, numskull **9** dumb bunny, ignoramus, numbskull, simpleton **10** nincompoop **11** featherhead

birdcage 6 aviary
birdlife 8 avifauna
bird pepper 9 chiltepin
birds' eggs *study of:* **6** oology
birth 4 dawn, stem **5** arise, issue, onset, start **6** create, outset, spring **7** emanate, genesis, lineage, opening **8** delivery, generate, geniture, nascence, nascency, nativity, pedigree **9** beginning, originate **10** extraction **11** parturition **12** commencement

birth-control leader 6 Sanger (Margaret)
birth flower *April:* **5** daisy *August:* **9** gladiolus *December:* **10** poinsettia *February:* **8** primrose *January:* **9** carnation *July:* **8** sweet pea *June:* **4** rose *March:* **6** violet *May:* **15** lily of the valley *November:* **13** chrysanthemum *October:* **6** dahlia *September:* **5** aster
birthmark 4 mole **5** nevus, point, trait **7** feature **13** discoloration
Birth of a Nation director 8 Griffith (D. W.)
birthright 3 due, lot **6** legacy **7** bequest, portion **8** appanage, heirloom, heritage **9** patrimony **11** entitlement, inheritance
birthroot 8 trillium
birthstone *April:* **7** diamond **8** sapphire *August:* **7** peridot **8** sardonyx *December:* **6** zircon **9** turquoise *February:* **8** amethyst *January:* **6** garnet *July:* **4** ruby *June:* **5** agate, pearl **11** alexandrite *March:* **6** jasper **10** aquamarine, bloodstone *May:* **7** emerald *November:* **5** topaz *October:* **4** opal **10** tourmaline *September:* **8** sapphire **10** chrysolite
biscotti flavor 5 anise
biscuit 4 rusk, snap **6** cookie **7** cracker **8** cracknel, hardtack
bishop *district:* **7** diocese *headdress:* **5** miter, mitre *seat of office:* **3** see *skullcap:* **9** zucchetto *staff:* **7** crosier, crozier *throne:* **8** cathedra
bishopric 3 see **7** diocese
bismuth symbol 2 Bi
bison *European:* **6** wisent **7** aurochs *family:* **7** Bovidae *North American:* **7** buffalo
bistered 4 dark **5** brown, dusky, swart, tawny **6** brunet, tanned **7** swarthy **8** brunette **11** dark-skinned
bistro 3 bar, pub **4** café **5** joint **6** nitery, tavern **7** barroom, cabaret, hot spot, niterie, taproom **8** snack bar **9** coffee bar, nightclub, night spot **10** coffee shop **11** rathskeller **13** watering place
bit 3 dab, dot, end, jot, tad **4** atom, dash, drop, iota, lump, mite, part, rein, tick, time, whet **5** borer, flake, grain, minim, pinch, scrap, shard, shred, slice, space, speck, spell, trace, while **6** minute, moment, morsel, rather, second **7** portion, segment, smidgen, stretch, trickle **8** fraction, fragment, molecule, mouthful, particle, somewhat
bit by bit 6 evenly **9** by degrees, gradually, piecemeal **12** continuously **13** slow and steady
bitch goddess 7 success
bite 3 cut, eat, lot, nip **4** chaw, chew, edge, etch, food, gnaw, kick, meal, nosh, pain, part, rust, snap, tang, tapa, zest **5** champ,

chomp, erode, munch, piece, quota, share, slice, snack, stink, taste, tooth **6** crunch, morsel, nibble **7** corrode, eat away, eat into, engrave, portion **8** mouthful **9** masticate, occlusion

biting 3 raw **4** cold **5** bleak, crisp, harsh, nippy, sharp **6** bitter, severe **7** acerbic, caustic, cutting, mordant, satiric **8** freezing, incisive, piercing, scathing **9** sarcastic, trenchant **11** penetrating

bitter 4 acid, tart **5** acerb, acrid, harsh, sharp **6** severe **7** acerbic, caustic, galling, hostile, painful **8** grievous, virulent **9** rancorous, vitriolic **11** acrimonious

bitterness 4 gall **6** rancor **7** ill will **8** acridity, acrimony, asperity, coldness **9** animosity, antipathy **10** resentment

bittersweet 4 vine **8** poignant **10** nightshade

bitumen 3 tar **5** pitch **7** asphalt **8** blacktop

bivalve 4 clam, spat **6** cockle, mussel, oyster **7** geoduck, mollusc, mollusk, piddock, scallop **9** lampshell **10** brachiopod

bivouac 4 camp, tent **6** billet, encamp, laager, maroon **7** shelter, sojourn **10** encampment

bizarre 3 odd **5** antic, outré, queer, weird **7** curious, oddball, strange, uncanny, unusual **8** abnormal, atypical, freakish, peculiar, quixotic, singular **9** anomalous, eccentric, fantastic, grotesque, unearthly, unnatural **10** outlandish, outrageous **11** extravagant

bizarrerie 5 freak **6** oddity **7** anomaly, caprice, oddness **9** curiosity, weirdness **10** aberration

Bizet opera 6 Carmen

blab 3 gab, gas, jaw, yak **4** chat, leak, sing, talk, tell **5** run on, spill **6** babble, betray, burble, gabble, gossip, inform, jabber, reveal, snitch, squeal, tattle, tell on, yammer **7** blather, chatter, divulge, let slip, palaver, prattle **8** blurt out, disclose, give away, go public

blabber 3 gab, rat **4** chat, fink **5** clack, drool, prate **6** babble, canary, drivel, gabber, gabble, gossip, jabber, magpie, prater, ramble **7** blather, chatter, palaver, prattle, twaddle **8** idle talk, jabberer, prattler **9** chatterer **10** chatterbox, tattletale

blabbermouth 3 rat **4** fink **5** yenta **6** canary, gabber, gossip, magpie, prater, snitch **7** windbag **8** busybody, jabberer, prattler **10** chatterbox, talebearer, tattletale **11** stool pigeon

black 3 jet **4** ebon, inky, noir, onyx **5** ebony, raven, sable **6** pitchy **8** charcoal, funereal **9** pitch-dark *combining form:* **3** mel **4** atro, mela, melo **5** melam, melan **6** melano

blackball 3 bar **4** veto, shun, snub **5** block,

spurn **6** ice out, refuse, reject, strike **7** boycott, exclude, keep out, rule out **9** interdict, ostracize **11** vote against

black bass 7 sunfish

black beast see **bête noire**

Black Beauty author 6 Sewell (Anna)

black cohosh 7 bugbane

black crappie 7 sunfish **10** calico bass

black death 6 plague **13** bubonic plague

black diamond 4 coal **8** hematite **9** carbonado

blacken 3 dim, fog, ink **4** blot, burn, char, sear, slur, soil, soot **5** cloud, libel, shade, singe, smear, sully, taint **6** bruise, darken, defame, defile, malign, scorch, vilify **7** asperse, cloud up, eclipse, slander, traduce **8** besmirch, dishonor **10** calumniate

black eye 4 blot, onus, slur **5** stain **6** bruise, defeat, shiner, stigma **7** setback

blackfish 5 whale **6** tautog **10** pilot whale

Black Forest 11 Schwarzwald *city:* **10** Baden-Baden *peak:* **8** Feldberg *product:* **11** cuckoo clock *river:* **5** Rhein, Rhine **6** Danube, Neckar

black gold 3 oil **9** petroleum

blackguard 4 heel, punk **5** abuse, cheat, knave, rogue **6** rascal **7** hoodlum, lowlife, ruffian, villain **8** hooligan, scalawag **9** charlatan, miscreant, reprobate, scoundrel **10** delinquent, mountebank **11** rapscallion

blackhead 3 zit **4** spot **5** sebum **6** pimple **10** larval clam

blackjack 3 oak, sap **4** bash, club, cosh **6** coerce **7** pontoon, tankard **8** bludgeon **9** twenty-one, vingt-et-un **10** sphalerite

black lead 8 graphite

black letter 6 Gothic **7** Fraktur **10** Old English

blacklist 3 bar **4** oust **5** expel, purge, smear **6** banish, impugn **7** boycott, condemn, exclude, shut out **8** denounce **9** ostracize, proscribe **10** stigmatize

blackmail 5 bleed **6** extort, payoff **7** milking, squeeze **8** chantage, coercion **9** extortion, hush money, shake down

Blackmore novel 10 Lorna Doone

black out 4 edit, wipe **5** annul, erase, faint, swoon **6** cancel, censor, cut off, darken, delete, efface, excise **7** conceal, eclipse, expunge **8** collapse, make dark, sanitize, suppress **9** eradicate, expurgate **10** blue-pencil, obliterate

blackpoll 7 warbler

Black Prince 6 Edward

Black Sea *arm:* 4 Azov *city:* **5** Yalta **6** Odessa **9** Constanta *peninsula:* **6** Crimea **7** Crimean

Blackshirt 7 fascist

blacksmith 6 forger **7** farrier, striker **10** horseshoer

blacktail 8 mule deer

blackthorn 4 plum, sloe

black widow 6 spider

bladder 3 sac **4** cyst **5** pouch **7** blister, vacuole **7** vesicle *gall:* **9** cholecyst

blade 4 beau, buck, dude, edge, leaf, shiv **5** knife, sword **6** runner **9** swordsman

blah 4 bosh, dull, flat, tame **5** ho-hum, hooey, tired, vapid **6** boring, bunkum, dreary, humbug, stodgy **7** humdrum **8** banausic, lifeless, mediocre, nonsense, plodding **10** balderdash, lackluster, monotonous, pedestrian **11** indifferent, uninspiring **13** uninteresting

Blake work 5 Tiger (The), Tyger (The) **10** Book of Thel (The) **16** Songs of Innocence **17** Songs of Experience

blamable see **blameworthy**

blame 3 rap **4** onus **5** fault, guilt, knock **6** accuse, charge, finger, indict **7** censure, condemn **8** denounce, reproach **9** criticize, liability, reprehend, reprobate **10** accusation, imputation **11** culpability **12** condemnation, denunciation, reprehension
Scottish: **4** wite, wyte **6** dirdum

blameless 4 good, pure **5** clean, moral **7** perfect, upright **8** innocent, unguilty, virtuous **9** crimeless, exemplary, faultless, guiltless, honorable, lily-white, righteous, unsullied **10** immaculate, impeccable, inculpable **13** unimpeachable

blameworthy 3 lax **5** amiss **6** guilty, liable, sinful **7** at fault **8** criminal, culpable, derelict **9** negligent **10** answerable, censurable, delinquent, indictable, punishable **11** disgraceful, inexcusable, responsible **12** dishonorable **13** reprehensible, objectionable

blanch 4 fade, pale **5** quail, scald, start **6** bleach, shrink, whiten **7** decolor, lighten, parboil **8** etiolate

blanched 3 wan **4** ashy, pale **5** ashen, faded, livid, peaky, waxen, white **6** anemic, doughy, pallid, peaked **7** ghostly **9** bloodless, colorless, washed out **10** cadaverous

Blancheflor's beloved 6 Flores, Floris

bland 4 dull, flat, blah, mild, soft **5** balmy, banal, vapid **6** boring, gentle, pablum **7** insipid, restful, sapless **8** soothing **9** calmative **10** complacent, flavorless, monotonous, namby-pamby, wishy-washy **12** ingratiating **13** nonirritating

blandish 3 con, woo **4** coax, fawn, urge **5** cozen **6** cajole, stroke **7** blarney, flatter, wheedle **8** butter up, inveigle, soft-soap **9** importune, sweet-talk **10** curry favor

blandishment 3 oil **5** honey **7** blarney, eyewash, incense, promise **8** flattery, soft soap **9** adulation, seduction, sweet talk **10** allurement, compliment, inducement, sycophancy, temptation

blank 3 gap **4** bare, dull, seal, skip, void **5** chasm, dazed, empty, space **6** stupid, vacant, virgin **7** deadpan, obscure, vacuous **8** complete, omission, outright, spotless, unfilled **9** impassive **10** empty space, interstice, obliterate **11** featureless **12** inexpressive, unexpressive

blanket 4 bury, hide **5** cover, quilt, throw **6** afghan, stroud **7** overlay **8** coverlet, mackinaw, sweeping **9** comforter **10** overspread

blankness 6 vacuum **7** nullity, vacancy, vacuity **9** emptiness **10** desolation

blare 4 roar **5** blast, shout **6** clamor, jangle **7** trumpet

blaring 4 loud **5** sharp **6** brassy, shrill **7** clarion, jarring, roaring **8** blinding, piercing, strident **9** deafening, dissonant **10** stentorian **11** ear-piercing, penetrating, stentorious **12** earsplitting

blarney 3 con, oil **4** coax, bunk **5** charm, honey, hooey **6** bunkum, cajole, humbug **7** baloney, incense, wheedle **8** blandish, buncombe, cajolery, flattery, inveigle, nonsense, soft soap **9** adulation, sweet-talk **11** compliments **12** blandishment, inveiglement

blasé 4 cool **5** bored, jaded, sated **6** breezy **7** knowing, offhand, unmoved, worldly **9** apathetic, incurious, surfeited, unexcited **10** world-weary **11** indifferent, unconcerned, worldly-wise **12** disenchanted, uninterested **13** disillusioned, sophisticated

blaspheme 4 cuss **5** abuse, curse, swear **6** revile **7** pollute, profane **8** denounce, execrate **9** castigate, excoriate

blasphemous 6 coarse, sinful **7** godless, impious, obscene, profane, ungodly **10** irreverent **12** sacrilegious **13** disrespectful ·

blasphemy 3 sin **5** abuse, error **6** heresy **7** cursing, cussing, impiety, mockery **8** swearing **9** profanity, sacrilege, violation **10** execration, heterodoxy, iconoclasm **11** desecration, imprecation, irreverence, malediction, profanation

blast 3 din **4** bang, beat, blow, boom, clap, dash, gale, gust, kill, peal, ruin, slam, toot **5** blare, burst, crack, crash, salvo, shoot, smash, wreck **6** attack, blight, blow up, damage, squall, wallop **7** destroy, lambast, shatter, shrivel, trumpet **8** dynamite, lambaste, outburst 9 explosion, castigate, discharge, overwhelm, shock wave 10 annihilate, detonation

blat 4 bray 5 blurt 6 cry out 7 exclaim 8 blurt out

blatant 4 bald, loud 5 brash, clear, gaudy, naked, noisy, overt, saucy 6 arrant, brassy, brazen, crying, flashy, garish, patent, tawdry, vulgar 7 glaring, jarring, obvious 8 flagrant, immodest, impudent, insolent, manifest, overbold, strident 9 barefaced, clamorous, obtrusive, shameless, unabashed 10 boisterous, outrageous, scurrilous, unblushing, vociferous 11 conspicuous, loudmouthed, transparent 12 ear-splitting, obstreperous

blather 3 gab, gas, jaw, rot, yak 4 bosh, gush, rave, stir 5 bleat, drool, hokum, prate 6 babble, bunkum, drivel, effuse, gabble, jabber, natter, yammer 7 blabber, chatter, enthuse, palaver, prattle, rubbish, twaddle 8 chitchat, claptrap, idle talk, nonsense 9 commotion 10 balderdash, double-talk, flapdoodle 12 gobbledygook

blaze 4 burn, fire 5 burst, flame, flare, glare, shine 7 flare up 8 eruption, outburst 10 incandesce 13 conflagration *Scottish:* 3 low 4 lowe

blazer 6 marker, reefer 9 sport coat 10 sports coat 12 sports jacket

blazes 4 hell 5 abyss, Hades, Sheol 6 Tophet 7 Gehenna, inferno 9 perdition 11 netherworld

blazing 4 keen 5 afire, fiery 6 aflame, alight, ardent, fervid, on fire, red-hot 7 burning, fervent, flaming, flaring, furious, glowing, ignited, intense, lighted 8 dazzling, feverish, powerful, speeding, white-hot 9 brilliant, perfervid 11 conflagrant, impassioned 12 incandescent 13 scintillating

blazon 4 deck 5 adorn, sound 7 declare, display, publish, trumpet 8 announce, proclaim 9 advertise, broadcast 10 coat of arms, promulgate 11 ostentation

bleach 3 dim 4 fade, pale 5 white 6 blanch, blench, purify, whiten 7 decolor, launder, wash out 8 etiolate, peroxide, sanitize 9 whitewash

bleak 3 raw, sad 4 bare, cold, dour, drab, grim, wild 5 chill, drear, empty, harsh, stark 6 barren, chilly, dismal, dreary, gloomy, lonely, severe, somber, wintry 7 austere, exposed, joyless 8 blighted, desolate, funereal, hopeless 9 cheerless, windswept, woebegone 10 depressing, despondent, oppressive, melancholy

blear 3 dim, fog 4 blur, dull, mist, murk, veil 5 bedim, faint, vague 6 hidden, shroud 7 becloud, obscure, shadowy, unclear 10 indistinct

bleary 3 dim 5 all in, faint, filmy, fuzzy, milky, spent, tired, vague 6 pooped, sapped, used-up, wasted 7 blurred, drained, obscure, shadowy, unclear, worn-out 8 depleted 9 enervated, exhausted, washed-out 10 indistinct

bleat 3 baa 4 blat, carp, crab, fuss, yawp 5 gripe, whine 6 bellow, grouse, squawk, yammer 7 blather, grumble, whimper 8 complain 9 bellyache

bleed 3 sap, run 4 milk, ooze, pity, seep 5 drain, exude, leech, mulct 6 extort, fleece 7 diffuse, extract 9 blackmail 10 hemorrhage

blemish 3 mar 4 blot, flaw, harm, mark, maim, mole, scar, spot, vice, wart 5 fault, nevus, spoil, stain 6 blotch, damage, deface, defect, impair, injure, pimple, stigma 7 blacken, distort, freckle, pervert, tarnish, vitiate 8 impurity, mutilate, pockmark 9 birthmark 12 imperfection 13 disfigurement

blench 3 shy 4 balk, duck, fade 5 blink, cower, quail, quake, start, wince 6 flinch, purify, recoil, shrink, whiten 7 launder, shy away, squinch, tremble 8 draw back, etiolate 9 whitewash

blend 3 fit, mix 4 brew, fuse, meld, weld 5 admix, alloy, merge, unify, union, unite 6 commix, fusion, go with, hybrid, mingle 7 amalgam, combine, mélange, mixture 8 beverage, coalesce, compound, conflate, immingle, infusion, intermix, mishmash 9 admixture, commingle, composite, harmonize, integrate 10 amalgamate, commixture, consociation, synthesize 12 adulteration, amalgamation, intermixture

blender setting 3 mix 4 chop, whip 5 grate, mince, puree 7 liquefy

blesbok 8 antelope

bless 4 laud 5 exalt, extol, endow, favor, grace 6 anoint, bestow, hallow, praise, uphold 7 approve, beatify, glorify, magnify 8 enshrine, eulogize, make holy, sanctify 10 consecrate

blessed 4 holy 5 happy, lucky 6 joyous, sacred 7 saintly 8 beatific, hallowed 9 beatified, fortunate, venerated 10 inviolable, sacrosanct, sanctified 11 consecrated

blessedness 5 bliss 8 felicity, sanctity 9 beatitude, godliness, happiness 12 blissfulness

blessing 4 boon, good, okay 5 asset, favor, grace 6 assent, bounty, thanks 7 benefit, benison, consent, fortune, godsend, support 8 approval, good luck, windfall 9 advantage 10 invocation, permission 11 approbation, benediction, endorsement, good fortune, valediction 12 commendation, consecration, thanksgiving 13 encouragement

"____ bleu!" 5 Sacré

blight 3 mar, nip 4 bane, dash, ruin 5 blast, decay, spoil, wreck 6 canker, wither 7 disease, scourge, shrivel 9 withering 10 pestilence 13 deterioration

blimp 7 airship 8 zeppelin 9 dirigible

blind 4 boma, daze, dull 5 decoy, front, shade, shill 6 dazzle 7 eyeless, muddled, shutter 8 bedazzle, jalousie, unseeing 9 enclosure, sightless 10 visionless

blind alley 6 pocket 7 dead end, impasse 8 cul-de-sac, deadlock 9 stone wall 10 standstill 11 obstruction

blind god 4 Eros, Hodr, Hoth 5 Cupid, Hoder, Hodur, Hothr

blindworm 8 slowworm

blink 3 bat 4 wink 5 flash, yield 6 give in, squint 7 flicker, flutter, nictate, twinkle 9 nictitate 11 scintillate

blink at 4 omit 5 clear, let go 6 bypass, excuse, forget, ignore, slight 7 condone, connive, let pass, neglect 8 discount, overlook, pass over 9 disregard, exonerate, whitewash

blip 6 censor, screen 9 deviation, expurgate, radar spot 10 bowdlerize

bliss 3 joy 4 Zion 6 Canaan, heaven 7 ecstasy, elation, elysium, nirvana, rapture 8 empyrean, euphoria, paradise 9 beatitude, cloud nine, happiness 10 exaltation 11 blessedness

blissful 5 happy 6 divine, elated, joyful, joyous 8 beatific, ecstatic, euphoric 9 ambrosial, delighted, entranced, rapturous 10 delightful, entrancing

blissfulness 3 joy 7 ecstasy 8 euphoria 9 beatitude, happiness 10 exaltation 11 contentment

blister 4 bleb, flay, lash 5 blain, bulla, slash 6 assail, canker, scathe, scorch 7 lambast, scarify, scourge, vesicle 8 lambaste 9 castigate, excoriate

blithe 3 gay 4 boon 5 happy, jolly, merry, sunny 6 bouncy, casual, cheery, chirpy, jaunty, jocund, jovial 7 gleeful 8 carefree, careless, cheerful, chirrupy, gladsome, heedless, mirthful 9 lightsome, sprightly, unworried, vivacious 10 untroubled 11 thoughtless 12 lighthearted

blitz 4 raid, rush 6 attack 7 air raid, bombard, bombing 8 shelling 9 offensive, onslaught 10 mass attack 11 bombardment

blitzkrieg 6 attack 7 assault, bombing 9 offensive, onslaught 11 bombardment

blizzard 4 gale 6 squall 8 whiteout 9 snowstorm

bloat 5 bulge, swell 6 billow, expand, fatten, puff up 7 balloon, distend, enlarge, inflate 10 distension

bloated 5 puffy, tumid 6 puffed 7 pompous, swollen 8 arrogant, enlarged, inflated 9 distended, overblown, overlarge 11 pretentious 13 self-important

bloc 4 band, ring 5 cabal, party, union 6 clique, league 7 combine, faction 8 alliance 9 coalition 10 consortium, contingent, federation 11 association, combination 13 confederation

block 3 bar 4 clog, fill, hunk, Lego, plug, slab, stop, wall, wing 5 brick, choke, chunk, close, ingot 6 cut off, hinder, impede 7 barrier, congest, occlude, stopper 8 obstacle, obstruct 9 barricade, hindrance, intercept

blockade 3 bar 4 stop, wall 5 beset, hem in, siege 6 shut in 7 barrier, besiege 8 close off, encircle, obstruct, stoppage 9 barricade, beleaguer, blank wall, hindrance, roadblock 10 impediment 11 obstruction

blockage 3 bar 4 clog, halt 7 barrier 8 obstacle, stoppage 10 impediment 11 obstruction

blockbuster 4 bomb 11 spectacular

blockhead 3 oaf 4 clod, dolt, dope, fool 5 clunk, dummy, dunce, idiot, moron, ninny 6 nitwit 7 halfwit, jackass 8 clodpole, clodpoll, dumbbell, imbecile, numskull 9 ignoramus, lamebrain, numbskull, simpleton 10 nincompoop 12 featherbrain

blockheaded 4 dull, dumb 5 dense, thick 6 obtuse, stupid 7 doltish 9 brainless, dimwitted 10 slow-witted

block out 4 mark 5 chart, close, draft, frame 6 hinder, screen, sketch 7 obscure, outline, prepare, repress, shut off 8 indicate, obstruct 9 adumbrate, formulate

block up 3 dam 4 clog, fill, plug, stop 5 choke 7 congest

bloke 3 guy, man 4 chap, gent 6 fellow 9 gentleman

blond 4 fair, gold, pale 5 light, sandy, straw, tawny 6 flaxen, golden 7 towhead 8 platinum 9 champagne, towheaded 10 fairhaired 11 sandy-haired 12 honey-colored

blood 4 gore 7 descent, kindred, kinship, lineage 8 ancestry 10 extraction *cancer of:* 8 leukemia *cell:* 3 red 5 white 8 hemocyte, monocyte, platelet 9 corpuscle, leukocyte 10 lymphocyte 11 erythrocyte, granulocyte *clot:* 8 thrombus *coloring matter:* 10 hemoglobin *combining form:* 3 hem 4 hemo *dis-*

ease: 6 anemia 8 leukemia 10 hemophilia *factor:* 2 Rh *fluid part:* 5 serum 6 plasma *of the gods:* 5 ichor *particle in:* 7 embolus *poisoning:* 6 pyemia 7 toxemia 10 septicemia *pressure:* 8 systolic 9 diastolic *relating to:* 5 hemic *serum:* 6 plasma *study of:* 10 hematology *sugar:* 7 glucose

bloodbath 7 carnage, slaying 8 butchery, massacre 9 slaughter 10 decimation 12 annihilation 13 extermination

bloodless 3 wan 4 ashy, dull, pale, weak 5 ashen, waxen 6 anemic, feeble, pallid, sallow, torpid 8 listless 9 insensate, unfeeling 10 insensible, nonviolent 11 coldhearted, passionless, unemotional

bloodletting 4 gore 7 carnage, killing 8 butchery, shambles, violence 9 slaughter 10 phlebotomy 11 venesection

bloodline 6 family, strain 7 descent, lineage 8 ancestry, pedigree 10 family tree

bloodroot 7 puccoon

bloodshed 4 gore 7 carnage, killing 8 butchery 9 slaughter

bloodstained 4 gory 6 grisly 7 imbrued, wounded 8 sanguine 10 sanguinary 11 ensanguined, sanguineous

bloodstone 10 chalcedony

bloodsucker 3 ked 4 tick 5 lamia, leech 6 lizard, sponge 7 sponger, vampire 8 hanger-on, parasite, sheep ked 10 freeloader 12 lounge lizard

bloodthirsty 5 rabid 8 ravening, sanguine 9 cutthroat, homicidal, murdering, murderous, predatory, voracious 10 sanguinary 11 sanguineous

blood vessel 4 vein 5 aorta 6 artery 7 jugular 9 capillary *combining form:* 3 vas 4 angi, vasi, vaso 5 angio

bloody 4 gory, grim, very 5 cruel 6 damage, damned, deadly, grisly 7 blasted, hateful, imbrued, wounded 8 accursed, infernal, sanguine 9 cutthroat, homicidal, murdering, murderous 10 detestable, sanguinary 11 ensanguined, sanguineous 12 death-dealing, slaughtering

bloom 4 blow, glow, open, posy 5 blush 6 floret, flower, thrive, unfold 7 blossom, burgeon, coating, develop, dusting, prosper 8 flourish, rosiness 10 cloudiness, effloresce 13 discoloration

blooper 4 goof, slip, trip 5 boner, break, error, fluff, gaffe, lapse 6 boo-boo, bungle, howler, slipup 7 blunder, faux pas, fly ball, misstep, mistake, offense 8 solecism 9 indecorum, false step 11 impropriety 12 indiscretion

blossom 3 bud, wax 4 blow, glow, grow,

open, posy 5 bloom, blush, flush 6 expand, flower, mature, thrive, unfold 7 burgeon, develop, prosper 8 flourish, floweret, progress 10 effloresce, peak period 13 efflorescence

blot 4 blur, mark, onus, slur, smut, soil, spot 5 brand, odium, smear, speck, stain, sully 6 absorb, smudge, stigma 7 bestain, blemish, spatter, tarnish 8 black eye, discolor, disgrace 9 bespatter, moral flaw

blotch 4 mark, spot 5 stain 6 macula, macule, mottle, smudge 7 blemish, splotch 12 imperfection

blot out 4 raze, void 5 annul, crush, erase, quash, quell, scrub 6 cancel, delete, efface, squash 7 abolish, destroy, expunge 9 eliminate, eradicate, extirpate 10 annihilate, extinguish, obliterate 11 exterminate

blotto see **drunk**

blouse 5 middy, shell, shirt, smock, tunic 6 guimpe

bloviate 4 rail, rant, rave 5 mouth, orate, spout 7 bluster, carry on, declaim, inveigh, soapbox, talk big 8 harangue, perorate, sound off, splutter 9 hold forth 10 vociferate

blow 3 bop, fan, hit, jar 4 bang, bash, belt, biff, bump, cuff, damn, fail, gasp, gust, huff, pipe, puff, slam, slug, swat, toot, whop, wind 5 boast, botch, crack, drive, erupt, leave, pound, punch, shock, slosh, smack, smash, sound, spend, waste, whack 6 buffet, depart, impact, mishap, thwack, wallop 7 assault, breathe, chagrin, consume, debacle, explode, flutter, fritter, trumpet 8 calamity, disaster, flounder, knockout, squander 9 bombshell, collision, dissipate, throw away 10 concussion, misfortune, trifle away 11 catastrophe

blow-by-blow 4 full 5 fussy 6 minute 7 careful, precise 8 detailed, itemized, thorough 10 exhaustive, meticulous, scrupulous 13 thoroughgoing

blowhard see **boaster**

blow in 4 land 5 pop by 6 appear, arrive, drop by, show up, turn up 7 hit town 11 materialize

blowout 4 bash, fete, gala, riot, tear 5 binge, blast, break, party, split, spree 6 frolic, shindy 7 shindig, victory 8 carousal, flat tire 9 festivity

blowsy 5 dingy, ruddy 6 florid, frowsy, sloppy, untidy 7 flushed, healthy, unkempt 8 blooming, blushing 10 bedraggled

blow up 4 bomb, burn, fume, rage 5 bloat, burst, erupt, flare, go off, storm, swell 6 expand, lose it, seethe 7 bristle, distend, enlarge, explode, inflate, magnify, rupture, shatter **8** boil over, demolish, detonate, dynamite, heighten, mushroom **9** discredit, fulminate, overstate **10** aggrandize

blowy 4 airy, wild **5** fresh, gusty, windy **6** breezy, stormy **7** squally **8** blustery **9** windswept **11** tempestuous

blubber 3 cry, fat, sob **4** bawl, flab, keen, lard, pipe, wail, weep **5** flesh **6** snivel **7** carry on **8** whale fat

bludgeon 3 bat **4** club **5** baton, billy, bully **6** attack, cudgel, hector **7** bluster, war club **8** browbeat, bulldoze, bullyrag **9** bastinado, billy club, blackjack, strong-arm, truncheon **10** intimidate, nightstick *British:* **4** cosh

blue 3 low, sad, sea **4** cyan, down, glum, lewd, navy, racy **5** bawdy, ocean, royal, salty, spicy **6** cobalt, gloomy, risqué **7** naughty, profane, unhappy **8** dejected, downcast, indecent, off-color **9** depressed, woebegone **10** despondent, dispirited, melancholy, suggestive **11** downhearted *combining form:* **4** cyan **5** cyano *dark:* **4** anil **5** perse **6** indigo *dye:* **4** woad *grayish:* **5** merle, slate *greenish:* **4** aqua, cyan, teal **5** beryl **6** cobalt **7** azurite **9** turquoise *reddish:* **5** smalt **6** marine, purple, violet **7** cyanine, gentian, lobelia *sky:* **5** azure **8** cerulean

____ **Blue 3** Ben **9** Little Boy

blue blood 4 lady, lord, peer **5** elite, noble **6** aristo **7** royalty **8** nobleman **9** gentility, gentleman, patrician **10** aristocrat, noblewoman **11** gentle birth, gentlewoman

bluebonnet 4 Scot **11** Texas lupine

Blue Boy painter 12 Gainsborough (Thomas)

bluecoat 3 cop, law **4** fuzz **5** bobby **6** copper **9** constable, patrolman, policeman

Bluegrass State 8 Kentucky

Blue Grotto site 5 Capri

bluejacket 4 mate, salt, swab **5** limey **6** sailor, seaman **7** swabbie **9** sailorman

blue jeans 5 Levis **6** denims

blue moon 3 age, eon, era **4** aeon **5** epoch **7** dog's age **8** eternity, lifetime **10** generation

bluenose 4 prig, snob **5** prude **7** puritan **9** Mrs. Grundy, nice Nelly **10** goody-goody

bluenosed 4 prim **5** rigid **6** prissy, proper, square, stuffy **7** prudish **8** overnice, priggish **9** Victorian **10** scrupulous, tight-laced **11** puritanical, straitlaced

blue-pencil 3 cut **4** edit, trim **5** emend **6** cut out, delete, excise, remove, revise **7** clean up **8** boil down, cross out **9** strike out, tighten up

bluepoint 6 oyster

blueprint 3 map **4** cast, plan, plot **5** chart, draft, frame, model, trace **6** design, devise, rubric, scheme, set out, sketch **7** arrange, diagram, outline, picture, project **8** game plan, strategy **9** delineate **10** conception, rough draft **11** description

blue-ribbon 3 top **4** A-one **5** prime, prize **6** Grade A, tip-top **7** capital, premier, stellar **8** five-star, top-notch, superior **9** excellent, first-rate, top-drawer **10** first-class, top-quality, world-class **11** outstanding **12** prize-winning

blues 4 funk **5** dumps, gloom, grief **6** lament **7** sadness, trouble **8** doldrums, glumness **9** dejection, pessimism **10** depression, desolation, low spirits, melancholy, woefulness **11** despondency, melancholia, unhappiness **12** hopelessness, mournfulness

blues musician 3 Guy (Buddy) **4** Cray (Robert), King (Albert, B. B.), Wolf (Howlin') **5** Bland (Bobby "Blue"), Brown (Clarence "Gatemouth"), Dixon (Willie), Foley (Sue), Handy (W. C.), James (Elmore), Myers (Sam), Smith (Bessie), Wells (Junior) **6** Hooker (John Lee), Rainey (Gertrude "Ma"), Taylor (Koko), Turner (Joe), Walker (T-Bone), Waters (Ethel, Muddy) **7** Broonzy (Big Bill), Diddley (Bo), Collins (Albert), Hammond (John), Hopkins (Sam "Lightnin' "), Johnson (Robert), Rushing (Jimmy) **8** Burnside (R. L.), Copeland (Johnny) **9** Jefferson (Blind Lemon), Leadbelly, Ledbetter (Huddie) **10** Williamson (John Lee, Sonny Boy)

bluff 3 act, con **4** curt, fake, fool, jive, ruse, sham, show **5** blunt, cliff, feign, frank, gruff, rough, trick **6** abrupt, betray, candid, crusty, delude, direct, hearty, humbug **7** beguile, brusque, deceive, fake out, mislead, playact, pretend **8** headland, pretense **9** deception, outspoken, precipice, steep bank **10** escarpment, forthright, no-nonsense, promontory, subterfuge **11** counterfeit, double-cross, plainspoken, short-spoken **13** unceremonious

blunder 3 err **4** bull, gaff, goof, mess, muff, slip, trip **5** boner, botch, error, fluff, gaffe, gum up, lapse, lurch, misdo, snafu **6** bobble, bollix, bumble, bungle, foul up, fumble, goof up, howler, mess up, wander **7** balls-up, blooper, failure, faux pas, louse up, misstep, mistake, screw up, stumble **8** disaster, flounder **12** indiscretion, misadventure

blunderbuss 3 gun **4** dolt **5** klutz **6** galoot, lummox **7** bungler, firearm **8** bonehead, numskull **9** blockhead, numbskull **10** stumblebum **13** butterfingers

blunt 4 bald, calm, curt **5** allay, bluff, brief,

frank, gruff, plain, rough, terse **6** abrupt, benumb, candid, crusty, deaden, direct, lessen, obtuse **7** brusque, rounded, uncivil **8** enfeeble, not sharp, snippety **10** forthright **11** desensitize, insensitive, plainspoken, unvarnished **12** discourteous **13** unceremonious

blur 3 dim, fog **4** blot, dull, mist **5** befog, blear, cloud, muddy, smear, stain, taint **6** smudge, stigma **7** becloud, besmear, confuse, obscure, tarnish **8** besmirch, discolor *in printing:* **6** mackle

blurb 2 ad **4** hype, plug, puff **5** press, promo **6** notice **7** write-up **8** good word **9** promotion **12** commendation

blurry 4 hazy **5** vague **6** cloudy **7** clouded, unclear **9** undefined, unfocused **10** indistinct

blurt 4 blab, blat, bolt **5** spill **6** cry out, let out **7** divulge, exclaim, let slip, spit out **8** disclose, give away **9** ejaculate

blush 4 burn, glow, rose, view **5** bloom, color, flame, flush, rouge **6** mantle, pinken, redden, ruddle **7** blossom, crimson, redness, turn red **8** mantling, rosiness

bluster 4 bawl, crow, gust, huff, rage, roar, rout **5** blast, bully, prate, storm, strut, vaunt **6** bellow, clamor, hector, lean on **7** bombast, bravado, dragoon, roister, swagger, talk big **8** boasting, browbeat, bulldoze, bullyrag, domineer **9** gasconade **10** grandstand, intimidate **11** braggadocio

blustery 4 wild **5** blowy, gusty, rough **6** drafty, raging, raving, stormy **7** furious, squally, violent **9** truculent, turbulent **10** boisterous, tumultuous **11** tempestuous

boa 5 scarf, snake

Boadicea clan 5 Iceni

boar 3 pig **4** male **5** swine

board 4 fare, feed, food, lath, slab, slat **5** catch, get on, hop on, house, lodge, meals, panel, plank, put up, table **6** billet, embark **7** emplane, entrain, quarter **9** directors **11** directorate *artist's:* **7** palette *mystic:* **5** Ouija

boarder 5 guest **6** lodger, renter, roomer, tenant

board game see at **game**

boarding house 6 hostel **7** hospice, lodging, pension **8** pensione

boardwalk 7 gangway **9** esplanade, promenade

boast 3 own **4** blow, brag, crow, have, puff **5** exalt, exult, glory, mouth, prate, preen, strut, vaunt **6** parade **7** bluster, bombast, bravado, contain, enlarge, exhibit, inflate, possess, show off, swagger, talk big **9** gas-

conade **10** exaggerate, grandstand **11** rodomontade **12** exaggeration

boaster 6 gascon **7** egotist, peacock, showoff **8** big mouth, blowhard, braggart **11** braggadocio, rodomontade

boastful 4 vain **5** cocky **6** braggy **8** arrogant, braggart, puffed-up, vaunting **9** bigheaded, conceited, egotistic **11** egotistical, pretentious, swellheaded **12** vainglorious **13** swelled-headed *Scottish:* **6** vaunty

boat 3 ark, hoy, tug **4** dhow, dory, junk, pram, prau, proa, punt, scow, ship, yawl **5** balsa, barge, canoe, coble, ferry, kayak, ketch, scull, shell, skiff, sloop, smack, umiak, yacht **6** bateau, bugeye, caïque, cutter, dinghy, hooker, lateen, lugger, packet, sampan, vessel, wherry **7** caravel, coracle, cruiser, currach, curragh, gondola, inboard, lighter, pinnace, pirogue, pontoon, shallop, steamer, trawler, vedette, vidette **8** outboard, runabout, schooner, trimaran **9** catamaran, hydrofoil *bottom projection:* **4** keel *captain:* **5** pilot **6** master **7** skipper *dock, basin:* **6** marina *front end of:* **3** bow **4** fore, prow *on a ship:* **3** gig **6** launch **7** pinnace *race:* **7** regatta *rear end of:* **3** aft **5** stern *song:* **6** chanty, shanty **7** chantey **9** barcarole **10** barcarolle

boatman 3 tar **4** mate, swab **5** limey **6** Charon, sailor **7** mariner, oarsman, paddler **8** deckhand, water dog **9** gondolier, navigator

boat-shaped 8 scaphoid **9** navicular

Boaz's wife 4 Ruth

bob 3 jig, nod, rap, tap **4** buff, clip, crop, dock, trim **5** bunch, float **6** bounce, curtsy, jiggle, jounce, polish, trifle, wobble **7** cluster, curtsey, nosegay **8** shilling **9** genuflect

bobbery 3 ado, din, row **4** fray, riot **5** babel, noise **6** bedlam, hubbub, racket, ruckus, rumpus **7** ferment, ruction **9** commotion, confusion **10** hullabaloo, hurly-burly **11** disturbance, pandemonium

bobbin 4 pirn **5** quill, spool, wheel **7** spindle **8** cylinder

bobble 3 bob, dud **4** flub, goof, mess, muff **5** botch, error, fluff, gum up **6** ball up, bollix, bumble, bungle, flub up, fumble, goof up, muff up **7** blooper, failure, louse up, mistake

bobby 3 law **6** copper, peeler **7** officer **9** constable, patrolman, policeman

bobwhite 5 quail **9** partridge

Boccaccio *beloved:* **9** Fiammetta *tales:* **9** Decameron

bode 4 hint **5** augur **6** signal, warn of **7** betoken, portend, presage, promise, signify, suggest **8** foreshow, indicate **9** foretoken, prefigure **10** foreshadow

bodega 3 bar, pub **6** saloon **7** barroom, grocery **8** wineshop **12** general store

bodement 4 omen, sign **5** hunch **6** augury **7** portent, presage **8** prophecy **9** foretoken, harbinger **10** foreboding, intimation, prediction, prognostic **11** premonition **12** presentiment

bodiless 7 ghostly **8** ethereal, spectral **9** unfleshly **10** discarnate, immaterial, unphysical **11** disembodied, incorporeal, nonmaterial **12** apparitional **13** insubstantial

bodily 6 carnal **7** en masse, earthly, fleshly, sensual, somatic, totally **8** corporal, entirely, physical, visceral **9** corporeal **10** altogether, completely **11** unspiritual

bodkin 4 shiv **5** blade, knife, shank **6** dagger, lancet, needle **7** poniard **8** stiletto

____ **bodkins 4** odds

body 4 bulk, core, form, hull, mass, soma **5** frame, stiff, stock, torso **6** corpse, corpus **7** anatomy, cadaver, carcass, chassis, corpora (plural), remains **8** physique **9** aggregate, substance *combining form:* **4** dema, soma, some, somi (plural) **5** somat, somia, somus **6** somata (plural), somato *human:* **4** clay

body cavity 5 cecum, sinus **6** coelom **7** abdomen **8** hemocoel

body check 5 block

bodyguard 7 retinue **9** attendant, protector

body of water 3 bay, sea **4** cove, gulf, lake, pond, pool **5** bight, brook, creek, fiord, firth, fjord, inlet, ocean, river **6** harbor, lagoon, puddle, stream **7** channel, estuary **9** reservoir

body passage 4 duct, vein **5** canal **6** artery, meatus, ureter, vagina, venule, vessel **7** trachea, urethra **8** bronchus **9** arteriole, capillary, esophagus, intestine **10** bronchiole **13** bronchial tube, fallopian tube

body politic 5 state **6** nation **11** nation-state

boffo 3 gag, gas, hit **4** wild **5** laugh **6** scream **7** sold-out **8** smash-hit, smashing **10** successful **11** sensational

bog 3 fen **4** mire, quag **5** delay, marsh, swamp **6** impede, morass, muskeg, slough, slow up **8** quagmire **9** swampland

boggy 4 miry **5** mucky **6** marshy, quaggy, swampy **7** sloughy

Bogart, Humphrey *film:* **6** Sahara **7** Dead End, Sabrina **8** Big Sleep (The), Key Largo **10** Casablanca, High Sierra **11** Caine Mutiny (The) **12** African Queen (The) **13** Maltese Falcon (The) **15** Petrified Forest (The) **16** To Have and Have Not **24** Treasure of

the Sierra Madre (The) *wife:* **6** Bacall (Lauren)

bog down 4 flag, mire **5** choke, delay, stall **6** detain, falter, hang up, hinder, impede, retard, slow up **7** embroil, set back, slacken **8** encumber, keep back, obstruct, slow down **9** lose steam **10** decelerate

bogey 5 ghost, haunt, shade, spook **6** scarer, shadow, spirit, wraith **7** phantom, specter **8** phantasm, revenant **10** apparition

bogeyman 5 spook **7** bugbear, chimera, monster, phantom, specter, spectre **10** apparition

boggle 4 balk, mess, muff, stun **5** amaze, botch, fudge, gum up, shock, wreck **6** bollix, bungle, cobble, goof up, mess up, strain **7** astound, louse up, nonplus, stagger, stumble, stupefy **8** astonish, bewilder, bowl over, confound **9** dumbfound, mishandle, mismanage, overwhelm, take aback **11** flabbergast

boggy 4 miry **5** mucky **6** marshy, quaggy, swampy **7** sloughy

bogus 4 fake, mock, sham **5** false, phony, pseud, snide **6** ersatz, forged, pseudo **7** fictive, pretend **8** invented, specious, spurious **9** brummagem, concocted, imitation, pinchbeck, simulated, trumped up **10** artificial, fabricated, fraudulent, mendacious **11** counterfeit

Bohème, La *character:* **4** Mimi **7** Rodolfo *composer:* **7** Puccini (Giacomo) *setting:* **5** Paris

bohemian 4 arty, boho **5** artsy, gypsy, hippy **6** hippie **7** beatnik, dropout, oddball, offbeat **8** maverick, vagabond, wanderer **9** eccentric **10** avant-garde, free spirit, iconoclast, unorthodox **13** nonconformist

boil 3 jet **4** bolt, brew, burn, cook, dash, foam, fume, gush, moil, race, rage, rush, spew, spot, stew, vent **5** anger, churn, erupt, fling, froth, poach, shoot, storm, swirl **6** blow up, bubble, charge, canker, coddle, decoct, pimple, seethe, simmer **7** abscess, agitate, bristle, ferment, flare up, pustule, smolder **8** furuncle **9** carbuncle, discharge **10** effervesce **11** excrescence

boil down 4 pare, trim **6** amount, decoct, reduce **7** distill **8** compress, condense, simplify, truncate **9** summarize, synopsize **10** streamline **11** concentrate, encapsulate

boiler suit 8 coverall

boiling 3 hot **5** fiery **6** baking, red-hot, sultry, torrid **7** burning, febrile **8** agitated, roasting, scalding, sizzling, tropical **9** scorching **10** blistering

boil over 4 burn, fume, rage **5** erupt **6** blow up, bridle, see red, seethe **7** bristle, flare up

boisterous 4 loud, wild **5** noisy, rowdy **6** lively, stormy, unruly **7** blatant, raucous, riotous **8** strident **9** clamorous, convivial, turbulent **10** disorderly, disruptive, rollicking, tumultuous, uproarious, vociferous **11** loud-mouthed, tempestuous **12** high-spirited, obstreperous, rambunctious, ungovernable, unrestrained

Boito opera 11 Mefistofele

bold 4 edgy, free, pert, rude **5** bluff, brave, fresh, gutsy, nervy, sassy, saucy, sheer, showy, steep **6** arrant, brassy, brazen, bright, cheeky, daring, heroic **7** doughty, forward, glaring, obvious, valiant **8** cocksure, fearless, impudent, insolent, intrepid, resolute, unafraid, valorous **9** audacious, dauntless, intrusive, prominent, shameless, undaunted **10** courageous, pronounced **11** adventurous, impertinent, smart-alecky, venturesome **12** enterprising, presumptuous

boldness 4 gall, grit **5** drive, nerve, valor **6** aplomb, mettle, spirit **8** audacity, backbone, chutzpah, temerity **9** arrogance, challenge, hardihood, impudence, insolence **10** brazenness, disrespect, effrontery **11** discourtesy **12** impertinence

Bolero composer 5 Ravel (Maurice)

Bolivia *ancient culture:* **4** Inca **10** Tiahuanaco *capital:* **5** La Paz, Sucre *city:* **6** El Alto **9** Santa Cruz **10** Cochabamba *conqueror:* **7** Pizarro (Hernando) *Indian people:* **6** Aymara **7** Quechua *lake:* **5** Poopó **8** Titicaca *language:* **6** Aymara **7** Quechua, Spanish *monetary unit:* **9** boliviano *mountain, range:* **5** Andes **6** Sajama *neighbor:* **4** Peru **5** Chile **6** Brazil **8** Paraguay **9** Argentina *river:* **4** Beni **5** Abuna **6** Mamoré **7** Guaporé **9** Pilcomayo

bollix 4 flub, mess, muff, ruin **5** botch, gum up, mix-up, snafu, spoil, upset **6** bobble, bumble, bungle, foul up, fumble, goof up, jumble, mess up, muck up, muddle, muff up **7** balls-up, confuse, louse up, screw up **8** dishevel, disorder, scramble, unsettle **9** mishandle, mismanage

bolo 5 knife **7** machete

Bolshevik 3 Red **6** commie **7** comrade **8** Leninist, tovarich, tovarish **9** communist

bolshevism 7 Marxism **8** Leninism **9** communism

bolster 3 aid **4** buoy, gird, help, husk, prop **5** boost, brace, carry, cheer **6** assist, bear up, buoy up, pillow, upbear, uphold **7** bulwark, cushion, fortify, hearten, shore up, support, sustain **8** backstop, buttress, maintain **9** encourage, reinforce **10** strengthen **12** underpinning **13** reinforcement

bolt 3 bar, fly, rod, run **4** cram, dash, dart, flee, gulp, jump, lock, race, rush, tear, wolf **5** arrow, blurt, bound, chase, dowel, flush, rivet, scarf, scoot, shoot, skirr, slosh, start **6** charge, decamp, devour, gobble, guzzle, secure, spring **7** abscond, exclaim, hotfoot, make off, missile, rigidly, scamper, startle, take off **8** blurt out, hightail **9** skedaddle **10** make tracks, take flight **11** ingurgitate **13** thunderstroke

bomb 3 dud, hit **4** bust, dull, fail, flop, sink, zero **5** blast, blitz, lemon, loser, pound, shell **6** blow up **7** debacle, destroy, failure, home run, success, washout, wipe out **8** detonate, disaster, fall flat, long pass, long shot, spray can

bombard 4 pelt **5** blast, blitz, shell, storm **6** attack, assail, cannon, hammer, pepper, shower, strafe, strike **7** assault, barrage **8** catapult **9** cannonade

bombardment 4 hail **5** burst, salvo **6** attack, shower, volley **7** barrage, battery **8** drumfire **9** broadside, cannonade, fusillade, onslaught

bombardon 4 bass **8** bass tuba

bombast 4 rant **6** hot air **7** bluster, fustian, oration **8** rhapsody, tumidity **9** fancy talk, pomposity, turgidity **10** pretension **11** rodomontade

bombastic 5 wordy **6** prolix, turgid **7** aureate, flowery, orotund, pompous, swollen **8** inflated, puffed-up **9** overblown **10** euphuistic, rhetorical **11** declamatory, overwrought **12** magniloquent **13** grandiloquent

____ **Bombeck 4** Erma

bombed 4 high **5** drunk, fried, stiff, tight **6** blotto, stoned, wasted **8** comatose, tanked up **9** plastered **10** inebriated **11** intoxicated

bombinate 3 hum **4** buzz, purr, whir **5** drone, strum, thrum **6** bumble, rumble **7** grumble

bombshell 4 blow, jolt **5** shock **6** marvel **8** surprise **9** curveball, sensation **10** revelation **11** thunderbolt

Bonaduce role 5 Danny

bona fide 4 real, sure, true **5** valid **6** actual **7** earnest, genuine, sincere **8** sterling **9** authentic, undoubted, veritable **10** legitimate, sure-enough **11** indubitable, in good faith **13** authenticated

bona fides 6 candor **7** probity **8** goodwill **9** good faith, sincerity **10** reputation **11** reliability, sincereness

bonanza 4 mine **5** catch, hoard **7** pay dirt **8** Golconda, gold mine, treasure, treasury, windfall **12** extravaganza **13** treasure trove

bonbon 5 candy, sweet **7** fondant **9** sweetmeat, sugarplum **10** confection

bond 3 tie **4** bail, fuse, knot, link, pact, yoke **5** nexus **6** cement, fetter, pledge, surety **7** bargain, compact, linkage, promise, shackle, warrant **8** adhesive, affinity, cohesion, contract, covenant, guaranty, ligament, ligature, security, vinculum, warranty **9** adherence, agreement, coherence, guarantee **10** attachment, connection, connective, obligation

bondage 4 yoke **6** chains, thrall **7** durance, fetters, helotry, peonage, serfage, serfdom, slavery **9** captivity, detention, servitude, thralldom, vassalage, villenage **10** subjection **11** enslavement, subjugation **12** imprisonment

bondman 4 peon, serf **5** helot, slave **6** vassal

bondsman 4 peon, serf **5** helot, slave **6** surety **7** chattel

bone *ankle:* **4** tali (plural) **5** talus, tarsi (plural) **6** tarsus *arm:* **4** ulna **5** radii (plural), ulnae (plural) **6** radius **7** humerus *back:* **5** spine **8** vertebra **9** vertebrae (plural) *breast:* **7** sternum *calf:* **6** fibula *cavity:* **5** fossa *change into:* **6** ossify *cheek:* **5** malar **6** zygoma *chest:* **3** rib *collar:* **8** clavicle *combining form:* **4** oste **5** osteo *face:* **5** malar, nasal **7** frontal *finger:* **7** phalanx **8** phalange *foot:* **5** tarsi (plural) **6** tarsus **9** calcaneum, calcaneus **10** astragalus, metatarsus *hand:* **10** metacarpus *head:* **5** skull, vomer **7** cranium **8** parietal, sphenoid **9** occipital *heel:* **9** calcaneum, calcaneus *hip:* **5** ilium, pubis **6** pelvis **7** ischium *jaw:* **7** maxilla **8** mandible *kneecap:* **7** patella *leg:* **5** femur, tibia **6** fibula **7** patella *lower back:* **6** coccyx, sacrum *middle ear:* **5** anvil, incus **6** hammer, stapes **7** malleus, stirrup *pelvis:* **5** ilium *projection:* **7** mastoid *relating to:* **6** osteal *shin:* **5** tibia **6** tibiae (plural) *shoulder blade:* **7** scapula **8** scapulae (plural) *small:* **7** ossicle *substance:* **6** ossein *temporal process:* **7** mastoid *thigh:* **5** femur *toe:* **7** phalanx **8** phalange *U-shaped:* **5** hyoid *wrist:* **5** carpi (plural) **6** carpus

bonehead 4 clod **5** dunce, moron **6** cretin, dimwit, nitwit **7** halfwit **8** clodpole, clodpoll, lunkhead, numskull **9** ignoramus, lamebrain, numbskull **12** featherbrain

bonelike 7 osseous, osteoid

boner see **blooper**

bone up 4 cram **5** study **6** review, revise **8** pore over

bong 4 bell, dong, peal, ring, toll **5** chime, knell, sound **6** hookah, strike **7** resound **9** water pipe **11** reverberate

boniface 7 barkeep **8** publican, taverner **9** barkeeper, innkeeper **12** saloonkeeper

Bonjour Tristesse author 5 Sagan (Françoise)

bonkers 3 ape, mad, off **4** daft, loco, nuts, wild **5** batty, crazy, dotty, giddy, loony, potty **6** cuckoo, insane **7** bananas, haywire **8** demented, deranged, unhinged

bon mot 4 jest, quip **5** crack, sally **6** zinger **7** epigram, riposte **8** one-liner, repartee **9** witticism

bonny 4 fair, fine **6** comely, lovely, pretty **7** winsome **8** pleasing **9** beauteous, beautiful, excellent **10** attractive, delightful **11** good-looking

bon ton 4 élan **5** flair, style **6** gentry, jet set **7** fashion, society **8** elegance, smart set **9** haut monde, propriety **11** high society

bonus 4 gift, plus **6** reward **7** benefit, payment, premium **8** dividend **12** compensation **13** fringe benefit

bon vivant 7 epicure, flaneur, gourmet, trifler **8** aesthete, gourmand **10** aficionado, dilettante, gastronome **11** cognoscente, connoisseur **12** boulevardier, gastronomist, man-about-town

bony 4 lank, lean, thin **5** gaunt, lanky, spare **6** barren, skinny, twiggy **7** angular, osseous, scraggy, scrawny, starved **8** rawboned, skeletal, underfed **9** emaciated **10** cadaverous

boo 4 hiss, hoot, jeer, razz **6** bellow, deride, heckle, revile **7** catcall **9** raspberry, shout down

boob 3 oaf **4** dolt, dope, goof, goon, boor **5** chump, dunce, goose, ninny **6** breast, dumb ox **7** blunder, fathead, mistake, tomfool **8** lunkhead **9** simpleton **10** dunderhead, philistine

boo-boo see **blooper**

booby hatch 6 asylum, bedlam **8** bughouse, loony bin, madhouse, nuthouse **9** funny farm **11** institution

booby trap 4 mine **5** snare **6** hazard **7** pitfall, springe **8** deadfall, land mine

boodle 3 wad **4** bilk, haul, heap, loot, mint, perk, take **5** booty, prize, spoil **6** bundle, packet, payola, spoils **7** fortune, plunder, present **8** kickback **9** incentive **10** bribe money, inducement

book 4 list, text, tome **5** album, bible, codex, enter, folio, novel, tract **6** charge, engage, enroll, folder, line up, manual, octavo, quarto, record, script, volume **7** catalog, edition, reserve **8** hardback, inscribe, register, schedule, softback, treatise **9** hardcover, monograph, paperback, preengage **10** compendium **11** publication *binding:* **4** case, sewn, tape, Yapp **5** cloth **7** leather, perfect **9** hardcover *combining form:* **6** biblio *of* *hours:* 5 Horae *of Mass:* 6 missal *of psalms:* 7 psalter *part:* 4 head, mull, tail 5 board, cover, crash, envoy, hinge, joint, spine 6 gutter, lining 7 chapter, flyleaf, preface 8 appendix, fore edge, foreword 9 text block 10 dedication

bookie see **bookmaker**

bookish 5 nerdy 6 formal 7 erudite, learned 8 academic, cerebral, literary, pedantic, studious, well-read 9 scholarly 10 longhaired 12 intellectual, professorial

bookkeeping term 4 loss 5 asset, audit, check, debit, entry, yield 6 budget, credit, equity, income, ledger, margin, profit, return 7 account, accrual, balance, expense, invoice, revenue, voucher 8 discount, dividend, interest, write off 9 inventory, liability 10 appreciate, depreciate, fiscal year 11 double entry 12 amortization, appreciation, balance sheet, depreciation, variable cost

booklet 8 brochure, opuscule, pamphlet

bookmaker 6 binder, bookie, editor 7 printer 9 bet holder, oddsmaker, publisher

book of account 6 ledger, record 7 journal 8 register

bookplate 5 label 8 ex libris

bookstall 5 booth, kiosk 9 newsstand

boom 3 wax 4 bang, clap, grow, rise, slam, spar, wham 5 blast, boost, burst, crack, crash, sound, smash, swell 6 do well, expand, growth, rumble, thrive 7 explode, prosper, resound, thunder 8 flourish, kick hard, long beam 9 expansion 10 bull market, detonation, prosperity 11 reverberate *opposite:* 4 bust

boomerang 6 recoil 7 rebound 8 backfire, backlash, come back, kick back, ricochet 10 bounce back

booming 4 bass, deep 6 robust 7 roaring 8 affluent, resonant, sonorous, thriving 9 deafening 10 prospering, prosperous, successful 11 flourishing

boon 3 aid, gay 4 gift, good, help 5 asset, grant, favor, jolly, merry, token 6 blithe, bounty, jocund, jovial 7 benefit, festive, gleeful, godsend, largess, present 8 blessing, largesse, mirthful, windfall 9 advantage, convivial, privilege 10 indulgence 11 benediction, benefaction

boondocks 5 wilds 6 sticks 7 outback 8 backland, frontier 9 backwater, backwoods, provinces, rural area 10 hinterland 11 backcountry, countryside 12 back of beyond

boondoggle 4 cord, hoax, scam 5 fraud, hokum 6 hustle 7 fast one, hatband, lanyard, swindle 8 flimflam 10 fool around, mess around 11 horse around

boor 3 cad, oaf 4 lout, hick, rube 5 brute, chuff, churl, clown, yahoo, yokel 6 lummox, rustic 7 buffoon, bumpkin, hayseed, peasant 9 ignoramus, vulgarian 10 clodhopper, philistine, provincial

boorish 4 rude 5 crass, crude, rough 6 coarse, common, rugged, vulgar 7 apelike, ill-bred, loutish, lowbred, lumpish, uncivil, uncouth 8 churlish, cloddish, clownish, impolite, insolent, lubberly, swainish 9 graceless, offensive, tasteless, unrefined 10 philistine, provincial, robustious, uncultured, ungracious, unmannerly, unpolished, unsociable 11 bad-mannered, clodhopping, ill-mannered, uncivilized 12 discourteous, uncultivated 13 disrespectful

boost 3 aid 4 hike, lift, jump, plug, push, rise 5 raise, steal 6 assist, beef up, expand, extend, foster, jack up 7 advance, amplify, augment, elevate, magnify, promote, support 8 heighten, increase, shoplift 9 advertise, encourage, expansion, promotion 10 assistance 11 helping hand 13 encouragement

booster 3 fan 4 hypo, shot 6 backer, Jaycee, patron, rocket, rooter 7 vaccine 8 champion, defender, promoter, upholder 9 amplifier, expositor, injection, proponent, supporter 10 shoplifter 11 inoculation

boot 2 ax 3 axe, can 4 bang, fire, kick, sack 5 chuck, eject, evict, expel, start 6 bounce, thrill 7 dismiss, kick out, start up 8 throw out 9 discharge, dismissal, terminate *kind:* 5 wader 6 arctic, chukka, gaiter, galosh, mukluk 7 jodhpur, shoepac 8 balmoral, cothurni (plural), overshoe, shoepack 9 cothurnus 10 Wellington

Boötes star 8 Arcturus

booth 4 nook 5 berth, bower, kiosk, stall, stand 6 carrel 9 enclosure 11 compartment

bootleg 3 hot, run 5 hooch 6 pirate 7 illicit, smuggle 9 irregular, moonshine 10 bathtub gin, contraband 11 black market, mountain dew 12 unauthorized

bootless 4 vain 5 empty 6 futile, hollow 7 useless 8 abortive, impotent, nugatory 9 fruitless, valueless, worthless 10 profitless, unavailing 11 ineffective, ineffectual 12 unproductive, unprofitable, unsuccessful

bootlick 4 fawn 5 cower, crawl, creep, toady 6 cringe, grovel, kowtow, stroke 7 cater to, flatter, truckle 8 blandish 9 brownnose, importune, seek favor 10 curry favor 11 applepolish 12 bow and scrape

bootlicker 4 toad 5 toady 6 lackey, lapdog, minion, yes-man 7 doormat, spaniel 8 hanger-on 9 sycophant 11 lickspittle

booty 4 haul, lift, loot, pelf, swag, take **5** prize, spoil, yield **6** spoils **7** pillage, plunder, rear end, seizure, takings **8** buttocks

booze 4 brew, grog, swig **5** binge, drink, hooch, juice, quaff, sauce, souse, swill **6** guzzle, imbibe, liquor, rotgut, tank up, tipple **7** alcohol, carouse, put away, spirits, swizzle **8** cocktail, liquor up **9** aqua vitae, firewater, knock back, moonshine

boozehound 3 sot **4** lush, wino **5** drunk, hoser, souse **7** guzzler **8** drunkard **9** alcoholic, inebriate **11** dipsomaniac

bop 3 bat, box, hit, jab, pop, rap **4** bash, bean, belt, biff, boff, blow, clip, cuff, jive, slug, sock, swat, whop **5** clock, pound, smack, thump, whack **8** plant one

borax 4 junk

Bordeaux wine *district:* **5** Médoc **6** Graves *grape:* **6** Malbec, Merlot **8** Cabernet *name:* **5** Arsac, Ludon, Macau **6** Moulis **7** Labarde, Margaux, Pomerol **8** Cantenac, St. Julien, Pauillac **9** St. Emilion, St. Estèphe, St. Laurent *red:* **6** claret

bordello see **brothel**

border 3 hem, lip, rim **4** abut, brim, edge, join, line, pale, trim **5** bound, brink, flank, frame, limit, march, skirt, touch, verge **6** adjoin, bounds, butt on, define, fringe, limbus, margin, trench **7** contour, outline, selvage **8** approach, boundary, frontier, neighbor, sideline, surround **9** marchland, perimeter, periphery **11** butt against, communicate *heraldry:* **4** orle *inlaid:* **8** purfling *raised:* **7** coaming

bordereau 4 note **6** record **7** account **10** memorandum

bordering 4 nigh **5** close **6** almost, next to **7** meeting, verging **8** abutting, adjacent, touching **9** adjoining, alongside, close upon, impinging **10** approximal, contiguous, juxtaposed **11** coterminous, neighboring, practically

borderland 5 march **6** fringe, margin **8** frontier **9** marchland

borderline 4 pale **6** almost, nearly **7** dubious, unclear **8** boundary, doubtful, marginal, unstable **9** ambiguous, debatable, dubitable, equivocal, perimeter, uncertain, undecided, unsettled **11** demarcation, problematic **12** intermediate **13** indeterminate

border state 8 Delaware, Kentucky, Maryland, Missouri, Virginia

bore 3 irk **4** drag, drip, mine, peer, pill, ream, sink, tire, yawn **5** auger, drill, drone, gouge, prick, punch **6** burrow, pierce, tunnel **7** bromide, caliber, fatigue **8** diameter, puncture

9 penetrate, perforate, soporific **10** dullsville

boreal 3 icy **4** cold, cool **5** chill, gelid, polar **6** arctic, bitter, chilly, frosty, frigid, tundra **7** glacial, wintery **8** freezing, northern **9** northerly

Boreas *beloved:* **8** Orithyia *brother:* **5** Notus **8** Hesperus, Zephyrus *father:* **8** Astraeus *mother:* **3** Eos *son:* **5** Zetes **6** Calais

boredom 5 blahs, ennui **6** apathy, stupor, tedium, torpor **7** fatigue **8** doldrums, dullness, flatness, monotony **9** lassitude, weariness **11** incuriosity, tediousness **12** indifference

Borges work 5 Aleph (The) **10** Labyrinths

Borgia 4 Juan **6** Alonso, Cesare **7** Alfonso, Rodrigo **8** Lucrezia

boring 3 dry **4** arid, drab, dull, flat, zero **5** ho-hum, vapid **6** dreary, stodgy, tiring **7** humdrum, tedious **8** bromidic, drudging, lifeless, tiresome **9** wearisome **10** lackluster, lacklustre, monotonous, pedestrian, unexciting **13** uninteresting

boring tool 5 drill, auger **6** trepan

Boris Godunov composer 10 Mussorgsky (Modest) **11** Moussorgsky (Modest)

born 3 née **6** innate, native **8** destined, inherent **9** intrinsic **10** congenital, deep-seated *combining form:* **3** gen **4** gene **6** genous **7** genetic

borne by the wind 6 aeolic, eolian **7** aeolian

Borneo *ethnic group:* **4** Dyak **5** Dayak *mountain:* **8** Kinabalu *nation:* **6** Brunei *river:* **6** Rabang

Born Free *author:* **7** Adamson (Joy) *lion:* **4** Elsa

Borodin opera 10 Prince Igor

borough 4 town **5** burgh **7** village **8** township

bosh see **bunkum**

Bosnia-Herzegovina *capital:* **8** Sarajevo *language:* **7** Serbian **8** Croatian **13** Serbo-Croatian *monetary unit:* **4** mark **5** dinar *neighbor:* **6** Serbia **7** Croatia *part of:* **7** Balkans *sea:* **8** Adriatic

bosom 4 bust, core, soul, teat **5** chest, close, heart **6** breast **7** embrace **8** feelings, intimate **10** affections, conscience

bosomy 5 built, busty, buxom, curvy **6** chesty, zaftig **7** shapely, stacked **9** Junoesque **11** full-figured

boss 4 capo, head, stud **5** chief, neato **6** direct, honcho, leader, manage, master, survey, worthy **7** command, foreman, headman, oversee **8** director, employer, overlook, overseer, superior **9** chieftain, excellent, first-rate, supervise **10** supervisor, taskmaster **11** superintend *African:* **5** bwana

bossy 3 cow **4** calf **7** studded **8** despotic, imperial **9** arbitrary, assertive, imperious, masterful **10** autocratic, high-handed, imperative, oppressive, peremptory, tyrannical **11** controlling, dictatorial, domineering, magisterial, overbearing

botanist *American:* **4** Gray (Asa) **5** Sears (Paul B.) **6** Bailey (Liberty), Bessey (Charles), Carver (George Washington) **7** Bartram (John, William), Burbank (Luther) **9** Fairchild (David) *Austrian:* **6** Mendel (Gregor) *British:* **6** Sloane (Sir Hans) *Danish:* **7** Warming (Johannes) *Dutch:* **7** De Vries (Hugo) *French:* **7** Lamarck (Chevalier de) *German:* **4** Cohn (Ferdinand), Mohl (Hugo von) **5** Sachs (Julius von) *Irish:* **6** Harvey (William) *Scottish:* **5** Brown (Robert) *Swedish:* **8** Linnaeus (Carolus) *Swiss:* **6** Nägeli (Karl) **8** Candolle (Augustin)

botany branch 7 ecology **8** algology, bryology, mycology **9** phycology **10** morphology, palynology, physiology **11** hydroponics, paleobotany, pteridology, systematics **12** bacteriology

botch 4 blow, flop, flub, foul, goof, mess, muck, muff, ruin **5** fluff, gum up, misdo, mix-up, snafu, snarl, spoil **6** bobble, boggle, bollix, bumble, bungle, fiasco, fumble, goof up, mess up, muddle **7** balls-up, blunder, confuse, louse up, washout **8** bugger up, disaster, disorder, dishevel, mishmash, shambles **9** mishandle, mismanage, patchwork **10** discompose, hodgepodge, misconduct

botchy 5 messy **6** blowsy, blowzy, frowsy, frowzy, sloppy, untidy **7** chaotic **8** careless, confused, slapdash, slipshod, slovenly

both *combining form:* **3** his *prefix:* **4** ambi, amph **5** amphi

bother 3 ado, bug, irk, nag, vex **4** drag, fret, fuss, gall, pest, pain **5** annoy, eat at, harry, trial, upset **6** badger, flurry, harass, needle, pester, plague, ruffle **7** afflict, agitate, anxiety, bedevil, concern, disturb, fluster, perturb, provoke, torment, trouble **8** disquiet, headache, irritant, nuisance, vexation **9** aggravate, annoyance **10** discompose, exasperate, irritation **11** aggravation, intrude upon **12** exasperation **13** inconvenience

botheration 4 damn, pain, pest **5** trial **6** plague **7** torment **8** headache, irritant, nuisance, vexation **9** annoyance **10** difficulty, irritation **11** aggravation, provocation **12** exasperation **13** inconvenience

Botswana *capital:* **8** Gaborone *city:* **11** Francistown *desert:* **8** Kalahari *former name:* **12** Bechuanaland *language:* **6** Tswana *monetary unit:* **4** pula *neighbor:* **7** Namibia **8**

Zimbabwe **11** South Africa *river:* **5** Chobe **6** Molopo **7** Limpopo **8** Okavango

bottle 4 vial **5** cruet, cruse, flask, phial **6** ampule, carafe, fiasco, flacon, magnum, vessel **7** ampoule **8** decanter, jeroboam **9** container

bottle gourd 8 calabash

bottleneck 5 choke **6** hinder, impede, narrow **7** impasse **8** obstacle, obstruct, paralyze, slowdown, throttle **9** hindrance **10** choke point, congestion, traffic jam **11** obstruction

bottom 3 bum **4** base, boat, core, foot, root, pith, rump, seat, ship, sole, soul, tail, tush **5** basal, basic, basis, fanny, found, nadir **6** behind, breech, heinie, lowest, source **7** bedrock, essence, footing, primary, rear end **8** backside, buttocks, derriere, pedestal, pediment **9** establish, fundament, lowermost, posterior, predicate, principle, underbody, undermost, underside **10** foundation, nethermost, underbelly, underlying, underneath **11** fundamental, lowest point **12** undersurface

bottomless 4 deep, vast **7** abysmal, endless **8** baseless, enduring, profound, unending **9** boundless, unlimited **10** groundless, unfillable, ungrounded **11** everlasting, inestimable, never-ending **12** immeasurable, incalculable, unfathomable **13** inexhaustible

bottommost 4 last **5** least **6** lowest **7** deepest

bough 3 arm **4** limb **5** shoot **6** branch **8** offshoot

boulder 4 rock

boulevard 4 road **6** artery, avenue, street **7** terrace **8** main drag **9** esplanade, promenade **10** high street **12** thoroughfare

boulevardier 7 flaneur, trifler **9** bon vivant **10** aficionado, dilettante **11** cognoscente, connoisseur **12** man-about-town

bounce 2 ax **3** can, hop, pep, vim, zip **4** fire, jump, leap, oust, sack, zest **5** expel, vault, verve, vigor **6** energy, hurdle, spirit, spring **7** bluster, boot out, dismiss, kick out, rebound, saltate, sparkle **8** buoyancy, ricochet, vitality **9** animation, discharge, eliminate, terminate **10** ebullience, elasticity, liveliness

bounce back 5 rally **6** perk up, pick up, recoil, return, revive **7** cheer up, improve, rebound, recover **8** backfire **9** boomerang **10** recuperate, turn around

bounce off 5 carom **7** rebound **8** ricochet

bouncer 4 goon **5** guard **8** houseman, sentinel, watchman **9** muscleman

bouncing ball game 5 jacks

bouncy 3 gay **4** airy **5** peppy, perky **6** blithe, cheery, jaunty, jocund, lively **7** buoyant, elastic **8** animated, volatile **9** ebullient, en-

ergetic, expansive, exuberant, resilient,
sprightly **10** unsinkable **12** effervescent,
high-spirited **13** irrepressible
bound 3 end, hem, hop, rim **4** bolt, edge,
jump, leap, term, skip **5** caper, frisk, hem
in, limit, skirt, vault, verge **6** border,
bounce, define, demark, driven, finite,
fringe, gambol, hurdle, margin, spring,
sprint **7** confine, delimit, enclose, hotfoot,
limited, mark out, obliged, pledged, rebound, saltate **8** articled, beholden, confined, confines, enslaved, resolved, restrain,
surround **9** compelled, demarcate, obligated
10 determined, indentured, limitation **11** apprenticed, responsible **12** circumscribe
boundary 3 hem **4** mete, pale **5** ambit, limit **6**
limits, margin **7** compass, outline **8** confines, environs, purlieus **9** perimeter, precincts **10** borderline **11** demarcation **13**
circumference
bounder 3 cad, cur, dog **4** boor, worm **5**
knave, louse, rogue **6** rascal, rotter
boundless 4 vast **5** great **7** endless **8** infinite
9 excessive, limitless, unbounded, unlim-
ited **10** indefinite, unconfined, unmeasured
11 illimitable, measureless **12** immeasurable, unrestricted **13** inexhaustible, unsurpassable
bounteous 5 ample **6** benign, lavish **7** copious, liberal, profuse **8** abundant, generous,
handsome, prodigal **9** bountiful, capacious,
expansive, extensive, plenteous, plentiful,
unsparing **10** beneficent, big-hearted, freehanded, munificent, openhanded, voluminous **11** magnanimous, overflowing
bountiful see **bounteous**
bounty 5 grant, prize, yield **6** deluge, plenty,
reward, wealth **7** payment, premium **8**
plethora, richness **9** abundance, affluence,
plenitude, profusion **10** cornucopia, generosity, inducement, liberality, luxuriance,
prosperity **11** benevolence, copiousness **12**
compensation
Bounty captain: 5 Bligh (William) **event: 6**
mutiny **first mate: 9** Christian (Fletcher) **letters: 3** HMS
bouquet 4 balm, kudo, odor, posy **5** aroma,
kudos, scent, spice, spray **6** eulogy, medley
7 acclaim, corsage, essence, garland, incense, nosegay, perfume **8** accolade, encomium **9** fragrance, redolence **10**
compliment **11** arrangement, boutonniere
12 commendation
bourgeois 7 burgher **8** ordinary **10** conformist, philistine **11** middle-class **12** conventional
bourgeoisie 11 middle class, third estate

Bourne Identity author 6 Ludlum (Robert)
bout 3 jag, run **4** game, meet, term, tour, turn
5 match, round, shift, siege, spell, spasm,
spree, stint, throe, trick **6** attack **7** contest,
session **8** outbreak **9** smackdown **10** engagement
boutique 4 shop **8** emporium
bovine 2 ox **3** cow, yak **4** anoa, bull, calf,
gaur, neat, zebu **5** bison, steer, stirk **6** heifer,
placid, torpid, wisent **7** aurochs, banteng,
buffalo, bullock, cowlike **8** longhorn **genus:
3** Bos **sound: 3** low, moo
bow 3 arc, bob, dip, nod **4** arch, bend, knot,
lout, prow, turn **5** angle, crook, curve, debut, defer, hunch, round, stoop, yield **6** archer, congee, curtsy, give in, kowtow,
relent, salaam, salute, submit **7** concede,
curtsey, flexure, incline, rainbow, succumb,
turning **9** curvation, curvature, genuflect,
obeisance, surrender **10** capitulate **11** buckle
under **12** knuckle under **ornament: 10** figurehead
Bow, Clara 6 It girl
bowdlerize 4 blip, edit **6** censor, excise, purify, screen **7** abridge, cleanse, distort, launder **8** sanitize **9** expurgate **10** adulterate,
blue-pencil
bowed 4 bent **5** arced, bandy **6** arched,
curved **11** bandy-legged, curvilinear
bowel 3 gut **6** paunch **9** intestine
bower 5 arbor **6** anchor **7** enclose, pergola,
retreat **9** apartment
bowery 7 skid row
bowfin 4 amia **7** mudfish
bowl 5 arena, basin, jorum, mazer, stade,
tazza **6** tureen, vessel **7** stadium **8** coliseum
12 amphitheater
bowlegged 5 bandy
bowler 3 hat **5** derby **6** kegler
Bowl game 5 Super **Abilene: 5** Pecan **Anaheim: 7** Freedom **Atlanta: 5** Peach **Dallas: 6**
Cotton **El Paso: 3** Sun **Fresno: 10** California
Honolulu: 5 Aloha **Houston: 10** Bluebonnet
Jacksonville: 5 Gator **Memphis: 7** Liberty
Miami: 6 Orange **8** Carquest **Mobile: 6** Senior **New Orleans: 5** Sugar **Orlando: 13**
Florida Citrus **Pasadena: 4** Rose **San Diego: 7** Holiday **Shreveport: 12** Independence **Tampa: 10** Hall of Fame **Tempe: 6**
Fiesta **Tucson: 6** Copper
bowling 7 kegling **British: 8** skittles **Italian: 5**
bocce, bocci **6** boccie **term: 3** pin **4** hook,
lane, spot **5** curve, frame, spare, split **6** gutter, strike, string, turkey **7** duckpin **9** can-
dlepin
bowl over 3 awe, wow **4** daze, fell, stun **5**
floor, shock, throw **6** boggle, dismay **7** as-

tound, flatten, impress, stupefy 8 blow away, surprise 9 bring down, dumbfound, knock down, overwhelm 10 disconcert
bow out 4 exit, fold, quit 5 leave, welsh 6 beg off, give up, retire 8 withdraw 9 surrender ·
box 3 bin 4 case, cell, chop, cuff, duke, inro, loge, slap, sock, spar 5 booth, chest, clout, crate, fight, punch, smack, stall, trunk 6 buffet, carton, casket, coffer, coffin, encase, hopper, packet 7 confine, enclose, package 9 container, enclosure, rectangle 10 pĩgeonhole, receptacle 11 compartment
boxer 7 fighter, palooka 8 pugilist 9 flyweight 11 heavyweight, lightweight 12 bantamweight, middleweight, welterweight 13 featherweight *champ:* 3 Ali (Muhammad) 4 Bowe (Riddick) 5 Bruno (Frank), Jones (Roy), Lewis (Lennox), Louis (Joe), Moore (Archie), Tyson (Mike) 6 Hagler (Marvin), Hearns (Thomas), Holmes (Larry), McCall (Oliver), Moorer (Michael), Seldon (Bruce), Spinks (Leon, Michael), Tunney (Gene), Walker (Mickey) 7 Charles (Ezzard), Corbett (James), Dempsey (Jack), Douglas (Buster), Foreman (George), Frazier (Joe), Johnson (Jack), LaMotta (Jake), Leonard (Sugar Ray), Sharkey (Jack), Walcott (Joe), Willard (Jess) 8 de la Hoya (Oscar), Marciano (Rocky), Robinson (Sugar Ray), Sullivan (John L.) 9 Armstrong (Henry), Holyfield (Evander), Klitschko (Vitali, Wladimir), Patterson (Floyd), Schmeling (Max)
boxing 8 pugilism 10 fisticuffs 13 prizefighting *term:* 2 KO 3 jab, TKO 4 blow, bout, duck, foul, hook, kayo, ring, rope, spar 5 break, count, feint, glove, match, parry, punch, round, swing 6 bucket, canvas, corner 7 low blow, referee 8 heavy bag, knockout, uppercut 9 knockdown 11 punching bag
boy 3 lad, son, tad 5 gamin, puppy, sonny 6 laddie, nipper, shaver 9 shaveling, stripling, youngster *combining form:* 3 ped 4 paed, paid, pedo 5 paedo, paido *errand:* 5 gofer 8 lobbygow *French:* 6 garçon *Italian:* 7 ragazzo *Latin:* 4 puer *mischievous:* 6 urchin *Spanish:* 4 niño 8 muchacho
boyfriend 4 beau 5 swain 6 fiancé, old man, suitor 7 main man 9 inamorato
Boy Scout *founder:* 11 Baden-Powell (Robert) *gathering:* 8 jamboree *motto:* 10 be prepared *rank:* 4 Life (Scout), Star (Scout) 5 Eagle (Scout) 10 Tenderfoot *unit:* 5 troop 6 patrol
Boys Town *founder:* 8 Flanagan (Edward) *star:* 6 Crosby (Bing) *state:* 8 Nebraska
bozo 3 oaf 4 boob, clod, dodo, dolt, dope,

fool, goof, jerk, mutt, simp, yo-yo 5 chump, dummy, dunce, idiot, moron, ninny, noddy, stupe 6 dimwit, donkey, dum-dum, nitwit, noodle 7 airhead, dullard, pinhead 8 bonehead, clodpoll, dumbbell, dumbhead, imbecile, lunkhead, meathead, numskull 9 birdbrain, blockhead, ignoramus, lamebrain, numbskull, simpleton, thickhead 10 dunderhead, hammerhead, nincompoop 11 chowderhead, chucklehead, knucklehead
B.P.O.E. member 3 Elk
Brabantio's daughter 9 Desdemona
brabble 3 row 4 beef, feud, flap, riot, spat, tiff 5 argue, scrap, set to 6 bicker, blowup, fracas, grouse 7 dispute, fall out, palaver, quarrel, rhubarb, scuffle, wrangle 8 argument, squabble 9 altercate, bickering, brannigan, caterwaul, wrangling 10 falling-out 11 altercation, disputation, embroilment
brace 3 arm, bar, duo, tie 4 dyad, gird, pair, prop, stay 5 clamp, ready, shore, steel, strut, truss 6 accost, bear up, column, couple, demand, splint, steady, uphold 7 bolster, bracket, enliven, fortify, freshen, prepare, refresh, shore up, support, sustain, tighten, twosome 8 buttress 9 reinforce 10 cantilever, exhilarate, invigorate, strengthen 12 underpinning 13 underpropping
bracelet 6 bangle 7 manacle 8 wristlet
bracing 4 keen 5 brisk, crisp, fresh, nippy, sharp, tonic 6 biting, chilly 7 rousing 8 stirring 9 animating 10 energizing, quickening 11 restorative, stimulating, stimulative 12 exhilarating, invigorating
bracken 4 fern 5 brake, brush, scrub 11 undergrowth
bracket 3 arm 4 join, link, omit 5 brace 6 couple, relate, remove 7 combine, compare, conjoin, connect, embrace, enclose, include, support 8 buttress, encircle, leave out, put aside, set aside 9 associate, encompass 11 parenthesis 12 strengthener
brackish 4 sour 5 acrid, briny, salty 6 saline, salted 9 repulsive, sickening 10 nauseating
bract 4 leaf 5 glume 6 paleat, spathe 8 phyllary
brad 4 nail
Bradamant *brother:* 7 Rinaldo *husband:* 6 Rogero 8 Ruggiero
Bradbury, Ray *forte:* 5 sci-fi 7 fantasy *work:* 13 Dandelion Wine 14 Illustrated Man (The) 17 Martian Chronicles (The)
Brady Bunch *actor:* 4 Reed (Robert) 5 Davis (Ann B.), Olsen (Susan), Plumb (Eve) 6 Knight (Christopher) 8 Williams (Barry) 9 Henderson (Florence), McCormick (Maureen) 10 Lookinland (Mike) *character:* 3

Jan **4** Greg **5** Alice, Bobby, Cindy, Peter, Tiger **6** Marcia **9** Mike Brady *creator:* **8** Schwartz.(Sherwood)

brae 4 bank, hill **5** slope **8** hillside

brag 3 gas **4** blow, crow, puff **5** boast, mouth, prate, vaunt **7** show off, swagger, talk big **9** cockiness, gasconade **10** grandstand **11** rodomontade

braggadocio 6 hot air **7** boaster, bombast, bravado, conceit, puffery, swagger, windbag **8** blowhard, boasting, braggart, bragging **9** arrogance, cockiness, pomposity **10** cockalorum, pretension, swaggering **11** fanfaronade

braggart 6 blower **7** boaster, egotist, vaunter, windbag **8** big mouth, blowhard **9** big talker, know-it-all, swaggerer, vulgarian **11** braggadocio

Brahmin 8 highbrow **9** blueblood, patrician **10** aristocrat

braid 4 plat **5** plait, queue **7** galloon, pigtail **8** soutache **9** interlace **10** intertwine, interweave

brain 3 wit **4** bean, conk, mind **7** concuss **9** intellect **10** gray matter **12** intelligence *bone:* **5** skull **7** cranium *channel:* **4** iter *clot:* **10** thrombosis *gland:* **6** pineal **9** pituitary *layer:* **6** cortex *lobe:* **6** limbic, vermis **7** frontal **8** parietal, temporal **9** occipital *membrane:* **3** pia **4** dura **5** meninx **8** pia mater **9** arachnoid, dura mater *part:* **4** lobe **6** fornix **7** medulla **8** cerebrum, thalamus **9** sensorium, ventricle **10** cerebellum, hemisphere **12** diencephalon *relating to:* **8** cerebral **10** encephalic *ridge:* **4** gyri (plural) **5** gyrus *scan:* **3** EEG, MEG, MRI, PET *vertebrate:* **10** encephalon *wave record:* **3** EEG

brainchild 4 idea, opus, work **6** animus, scheme, theory **7** coinage **9** handiwork, invention **10** hypothesis, innovation **11** achievement, chef-d'oeuvre, contrivance

brainiac 3 wiz **4** whiz **6** genius **7** prodigy

brainless 3 dim **5** dense, silly, thick **6** simple, stupid **7** asinine, foolish, idiotic, moronic, vacuous, witless **9** dim-witted, nitwitted **10** acephalous **12** feebleminded

brainpower 3 wit **5** sense **6** smarts **8** aptitude, capacity, sagacity **9** intellect, mentality, mother wit **10** perception **11** discernment, penetration **12** intelligence **13** comprehension

brains 4 mind **6** smarts **9** intellect **12** intelligence

brainsick 3 mad **4** daft **5** batty, crazy, manic, potty **6** crazed, insane, mental **7** cracked, haywire, lunatic **8** aberrant, demented, deranged, maniacal, unhinged **9** bedlamite,

delirious, disturbed **10** disordered, incoherent, irrational, unbalanced

brainstorm 3 rap, jaw **4** idea **6** confer, huddle **7** discuss, dream up, think up **8** cogitate, mull over **9** mental fit **10** groupthink, kick around, toss around **11** inspiration, put together

brainteaser 5 poser, rebus **6** puzzle, riddle **7** stumper **9** conundrum **10** cryptogram

brainwashing 10 propaganda **11** mind control, reeducation

brainy 4 keen **5** quick, savvy, sharp, smart **6** adroit, astute, bright, clever **9** eggheaded, brilliant, sagacious **10** discerning, precocious **11** intelligent, quick-witted, readywitted **13** knowledgeable, perspicacious

brake 4 curb, slow, stop **5** block **6** damper, hinder, impede, retard, slough **7** barrier, bracken, slacken **8** blockade, obstacle, obstruct, slow down **9** deterrent, hindrance **10** constraint, decelerate **11** bracken fern

bramble 4 burr **5** brier, furze, gorse, hedge, shrub, thorn **6** nettle **7** thistle

branch 3 arm, leg **4** fork, limb, rami (plural), spur, wing **5** bough, ramus **6** office, ramify **7** chapter, diverge, outpost **8** division **9** tributary **10** subsidiary

branched 6 ramate, ramose

brand 4 blot, blur, logo, make, mark, onus, sear, slur, sort, spot, type **5** badge, class, odium, stain, stamp, sword, taint, torch **6** accuse, charge, impute, stigma, stripe **7** species, variety **8** black eye, disgrace, insignia, logotype **9** trademark **10** stigmatize

brandish 4 wave **5** flash, shake, sport, swing, wield **6** flaunt, parade **7** display, exhibit, show off **8** flourish

brand-new 4 mint **5** fresh **6** latest, unused, virgin **8** up-to-date **9** untouched **11** cutting-edge **13** inexperienced

brandy 4 marc, ouzo, raki **5** Pisco **6** cognac, grappa, kirsch, Metaxa **7** liqueur **8** Armagnac, calvados, digestif, eau-de-vie **9** applejack, framboise, slivovitz *cocktail:* **7** sidecar, stinger **9** Alexander

brannigan 3 row **4** bust, flap, spat, tiff **5** binge, fight, set-to, spree **6** bender, blowup, hassle, ruckus **7** brabble, discord, dispute, quarrel, wassail, wrangle **8** squabble **10** falling-out **11** altercation

brash 4 bold, flip, pert **5** cocky, gutsy, hasty, nervy, saucy **6** brassy, brazen, cheeky, madcap, uppish, uppity **7** brittle, forward **8** arrogant, cocksure, flippant, impudent, insolent, reckless, tactless **9** audacious, bumptious, ebullient, energetic, exuberant, hot-headed, impetuous, impolitic, maladroit, unabashed, untactful **10** ill-advised, incautious **11** overweening, thoughtless **12** high-spirited, presumptuous, undiplomatic, unrestrained **13** disrespectful, inconsiderate, irrepressible, self-assertive

brashness 4 gall, grit, guts **5** brass, cheek, crust, nerve, pluck **6** aplomb, daring, mettle, spirit **8** audacity, chutzpah, temerity **9** assurance **10** confidence, effrontery **11** presumption

brass 4 gall **5** cheek, nerve **8** audacity, chutzpah **9** brashness, impudence, insolence **10** confidence, effrontery **11** presumption **12** impertinence

brassbound 3 set **5** brash, rigid **6** brazen, narrow **7** adamant, bigoted, forward **8** obdurate **9** illiberal, presuming, obstinate, unbending **10** implacable, inflexible, intolerant, relentless, unswayable, unyielding **11** opinionated, small-minded, unrelenting **12** narrow-minded, presumptuous, single-minded **13** dyed-in-the-wool, self-asserting, self-assertive

brasserie 10 restaurant

brass hat 3 VIP **4** boss **5** elder **6** better, senior **7** big shot **8** big whell, higher-up, superior

brassica 4 kale, rape **5** colza **6** turnip **7** cabbage, mustard **8** broccoli, collards, kohlrabi, rutabaga **11** cauliflower

brass tacks 5 facts **7** details **11** nitty-gritty, particulars

brass worker 7 brazier

brassy see **brazen**

brat 3 imp **4** punk **6** urchin **10** holy terror

bravado 5 bluff **6** hot air **7** bluster, bombast **8** audacity, boasting, boldness, bragging, defiance, vaunting **9** gasconade **10** blustering, pretension, swaggering **11** braggadocio, grandiosity **12** boastfulness

brave 4 bold, dare, defy, face, game, meet, risk **5** beard, gutsy, hardy, manly, nervy, noble, stout **6** daring, heroic, manful, plucky, spunky, take on **7** defiant, doughty, gallant, valiant, venture **8** confront, face down, fearless, intrepid, reckless, resolute, spirited, splendid, stalwart, unafraid, valorous **9** audacious, challenge, dauntless, excellent, steadfast, undaunted, withstand **10** courageous **11** boldhearted, indomitable, lionhearted, undauntable, unflinching, venturesome **12** stouthearted **13** adventuresome

Brave New World author 6 Huxley (Aldous)

bravery 4 grit, guts **5** nerve, pluck, valor **6** daring, mettle, spirit **7** courage, heroism **8** audacity, boldness, temerity **9** derring-do,

fortitude, gallantry **11** intrepidity **12** fearlessness, intrepidness *false:* **7** bravado

bravo 3 olé **4** euge, rave, thug **5** cheer **6** encore, gunman, hit man, killer **7** ovation, plaudit, villain **8** applause, assassin **9** desperado

bravura 4 bold **5** showy **6** daring, florid, ornate **8** dazzling, skillful, virtuoso **9** brilliant

brawl 3 row **4** feud, flap, fray, fuss, maul, riot, spar, spat, tiff **5** clash, broil, fight, melee, scrap, set-to **6** affray, battle, bicker, dustup, fracas, rumble, tussle **7** bobbery, brabble, contend, quarrel, rhubarb, ruction, scuffle, wrangle **8** dogfight, skirmish, slugfest **9** fistfight, imbroglio, scrimmage **10** donnybrook, fisticuffs, free-for-all **11** altercation, disturbance

brawn 4 beef, meat, thew **5** clout, flesh, might, power, sinew **6** muscle **8** strength **9** puissance **10** headcheese

brawny 5 beefy, burly, husky, lusty, tough **6** robust, sinewy, stocky, strong, sturdy **8** athletic, muscular, powerful, thickset, vigorous **9** strapping, well-built **10** able-bodied

bray 4 mill **5** crush, grind, pound **6** bellow, hee-haw, pestle, powder **7** atomize, trumpet **9** pulverize

brazen 4 bold, loud **5** brash, gaudy, noisy, showy **6** arrant, brassy, cheeky **7** blatant, defiant, forward, glaring, jarring **8** flagrant, impudent, insolent **9** audacious, barefaced, obtrusive, shameless, unabashed **10** outrageous, procacious, unblushing **11** conspicuous, impertinent **12** contumelious, presumptuous **13** disrespectful

Brazil *capital:* **8** Brasília *city:* **5** Belém **6** Recife **8** Salvador, São Paulo **12** Rio de Janeiro **13** Belo Horizonte *discoverer:* **6** Cabral (Pedro) *island:* **6** Marajó **7** Caviana *language:* **10** Portuguese *monetary unit:* **4** real *neighbor:* **4** Peru **6** Guyana **7** Bolivia, Uruguay **8** Colombia, Paraguay, Suriname **9** Argentina, Venezuela **12** French Guiana *river:* **4** Pará **6** Amazon **8** Parnaíba **10** Alto Paraná **12** São Francisco *state:* **4** Acre, Pará **5** Amapá, Bahia, Ceará, Goiás, Piauí **6** Paraná

breach 3 gap **4** gash, hole, leap, open, rent, rift, slit **5** break, chasm, cleft, crack, split **6** hiatus, lacuna, schism **7** break in, discord, disrupt, fissure, infract, interim, opening, rupture, violate **8** aperture, disunity, division, fracture, infringe, interval, trespass **9** disregard, severance, violation **10** alienation, contravene, infraction, separation, transgress **11** delinquency, dereliction **12** disaffection, disobedience, estrangement, infringement, interruption **13** contravention, discontinuity, noncompliance, nonobservance, transgression

bread 3 bun **4** food, pita, rusk, wrap **5** bagel, money, scone, toast **6** living, muffin, sippet **7** biscuit, crouton, edibles, stollen **8** victuals, zwieback **9** provender **10** livelihood, provisions, sustenance **11** comestibles, maintenance, subsistence *communion:* **4** host **5** wafer **9** Eucharist *from heaven:* **5** manna *ingredient:* **4** meal **5** flour, yeast **6** leaven *Jewish:* **5** matzo **6** hallah, matzoh **7** challah *maker:* **5** baker *Scottish:* **7** bannock *spread:* **3** jam **4** oleo **5** jelly **6** butter **9** margarine *unleavened:* **5** matzo **6** matzoh

bread and butter 4 keep, work **6** basics, living **7** support **8** mainstay, victuals **10** employment, livelihood, occupation, sustenance **9** nutriment **11** maintenance, necessities, subsistence **12** alimentation

breadbasket 3 gut **5** belly, tummy **6** paunch **7** abdomen, stomach **8** potbelly **9** bay window, beer belly

breadth 4 area, size, span **5** range, reach, scope, space, sweep, width **6** extent, spread **7** compass, expanse, stretch **8** distance, fullness, latitude, vastness, wideness **9** amplitude, expansion, magnitude **10** liberality

break 3 gap **4** bust, dash, halt, knap, leak, luck, rest, rift, ruin, tame **5** burst, clear, crack, inure, sever, solve, spell **6** breach, chance, decode, divide, escape, exceed, hiatus, impair, lacuna, refute, relief, reveal **7** destroy, divulge, fall out, interim, lighten, opening, respite, rupture, shatter, surpass, suspend, take ten, time-out, violate **8** accustom, bankrupt, breather, decipher, disclose, division, downtime, fracture, good luck, interval, moderate, take five **9** interlude, interrupt **10** annihilate, controvert, impoverish **11** discontinue, disjunction, dislocation, opportunity, suspensions **12** intermission, interruption **13** discontinuity

breakable 4 weak **5** frail **6** flimsy **7** brittle, fragile, friable **8** delicate **9** frangible

breakaway 4 prop **7** escapee **8** offshoot, renegade, seceding

break down 4 fail, fold, sort, wilt **5** class, decay, index **6** cave in, digest, give in **7** analyze, crumble, crumple, give out, give way, go crazy, succumb **8** classify, collapse, dissolve **9** anatomize, decompose, fall apart **12** disintegrate

breakdown 5 crash, decay, smash, study, wreck **6** mishap **7** crack-up, debacle, failure, smashup **8** analysis, collapse, taxonomy **9** cataclysm, partition **10** disruption,

dissection, resolution **11** dysfunction, examination, prostration

breaker 4 wave **6** billow, comber, roller

Breakfast at Tiffany's author **6** Capote (Truman)

breakfront 7 cabinet **8** bookcase

break in 4 tame **5** train **6** breach, burgle, gentle, invade **7** intrude **8** initiate **9** condition, habituate, interfere, interpose, interrupt

breakneck 4 fast **5** fleet, hasty, quick, rapid, swift **6** racing, speedy, unsafe **8** meteoric **10** harefooted **11** precipitous

break off 3 end **4** drop, halt, kill, stop **5** abort, cease, scrub, sever **6** cancel, detach **7** curtail, scratch, suspend **8** cut short **9** terminate **11** discontinue

break out 4 bolt, flee **5** arise, erupt, flare **6** emerge, escape **7** explode **8** mushroom, separate

break through 5 burst **6** breach, emerge, pierce **7** rupture, surface **8** overcome **9** penetrate

breakthrough 4 find, gain, hike, leap, rise **5** boost **7** advance, radical, upgrade **8** advanced, increase, landmark **9** invention, milestone **10** avant-garde, innovation **11** cutting-edge, development, exceptional, progressive, quantum leap

break up 3 end **4** halt, knap, part **6** divide, sunder **7** destroy, disband, disjoin, disrupt, rupture, scatter, shatter **8** disperse, dissever, dissolve, disunite, separate **9** decompose, dismantle, pulverize, terminate **12** disintegrate

breakup 4 rift **5** split **7** divorce, parting **8** analysis **9** dispersal **10** dissection, separation **11** dissolution

breakwater 5 groin, jetty **7** seawall

breast 4 bosom, chest, heart *animal:* **7** brisket *combining form:* **3** maz **4** mast, mazo **5** masto, stern, steth **6** mastia (plural), sterno, stetho

breastbone 7 sternum

breast-feed 5 nurse **6** suckle **7** nourish

breastwork 7 barrier, bastion, bulwark, defense, parapet, rampart **9** barricade, earthwork **10** embankment **13** fortification, reinforcement

breath 4 gasp, gust, hint, puff **5** let-up, pause, trace, whiff **6** breeze **7** respite **10** exhalation, inhalation, suggestion

breathe 4 emit, sigh **5** exude, utter, voice **6** endure, exhale, expire, inhale, murmur **7** confide, express, give off, inspire, persist, radiate, respire, subsist, survive, whisper

breather 4 lull, rest, stay, vent **5** break, let-up, pause, spell **6** hiatus, recess **7** caesura, respite **8** downtime **9** remission **12** interruption

breathing *labored:* **7** dyspnea *normal:* **6** eupnea *rapid:* **8** polypnea

breathing apparatus 10 respirator *underwater:* **5** scuba

breathing orifice 4 nose **5** mouth **8** blowhole, spiracle

breathless 4 agog, avid, keen **5** eager **6** ardent **7** anxious, gasping, intense **8** gripping **9** expectant, impatient **11** short-winded **13** on tenterhooks

breathtaking 6 moving **7** awesome **8** dramatic, exciting, imposing, stunning, wondrous **9** panoramic, thrilling **10** impressive, staggering **11** astonishing, magnificent, spectacular **12** awe-inspiring, overwhelming **13** heart-stirring

Brecht play 4 Baal **13** Life of Galileo (The), Mother Courage **15** Seven Deadly Sins (The), Threepenny Opera (The) **20** Caucasian Chalk Circle (The)

breech 3 bum **4** duff, rear, rump, seat, tail **5** fanny **6** behind, bottom, heinie **7** keester, keister, rear end **8** backside, buttocks, derriere, haunches **9** fundament, posterior **12** hindquarters

breechclout 5 dhoti **9** loincloth

breed 3 ilk **4** bear, grow, kind, make, mate, race, rear, sire, sort, type **5** beget, brand, cause, class, cross, genus, hatch, likes, raise, stock, yield **6** couple, create, father, induce, nature, strain, stripe **7** bring up, develop, educate, lineage, nurture, produce, species, variety **8** copulate, engender, generate, mate with, multiply **9** cultivate, procreate, propagate, reproduce **10** discipline, extraction, give rise to, impregnate, inseminate

breeding 4 line **5** grace, taste **6** polish **7** culture, decorum, lineage, manners **8** ancestry, civility, courtesy, pedigree **9** genealogy, gentility, propriety **10** refinement, upbringing **11** cultivation

breeding ground 6 hotbed, origin **8** hothouse **10** forcing bed, mating spot **12** forcing house

breeze 3 zip **4** flit, sail, snap, waft **5** cinch, draft, waltz **6** zephyr **8** duck soup, kid stuff **10** child's play

breezy 4 airy, cool **5** fresh, gusty, windy **6** blithe, casual, drafty **7** offhand, relaxed **8** carefree, careless, detached, informal **9** easygoing **10** insouciant, nonchalant **11** unconcerned **12** devil-may-care, lighthearted

Breton 4 Celt

_____ **breve 4** alla

breviary 5 brief **6** digest, précis **7** epitome, essence, outline, rundown, summary **8** abstract, boildown, synopsis **9** reduction **10** abridgment, conspectus, prayer book **11** abridgement **12** condensation, divine office

brevity 7 economy **8** laconism **9** briefness, concision, crispness, pithiness, shortness, terseness **10** transience

brew 3 ale, tea **4** beer, loom, mull, plan, plot, suds **5** drink, lager, stout **6** cook up, foment, gather, impend, infuse, porter, scheme, stir up **7** concoct, ferment **8** contrive

briar 4 burr, pipe **5** furze, gorse, shrub, thorn **6** nettle **7** bramble, thistle

Briareus 7 Aegaeon *father:* **6** Uranus *mother:* **4** Gaea

bribe 3 buy, fix, sop **6** buy off, payoff, payola, square, suborn **7** corrupt **9** incentive **10** enticement, inducement, tamper with

bric-a-brac 6 curios **8** trinkets **9** ornaments **10** objets d'art **11** gingerbread, knickknacks **13** embellishment

brick 5 block, gaffe **7** blunder *layer:* **5** mason *laying:* **7** masonry *material:* **4** clay, marl *oven:* **4** kiln *row:* **6** course *sun-dried:* **5** adobe *toy:* **4** Lego *trough for carrying:* **3** hod

bridal 7 nuptial, spousal **8** conjugal **9** connubial **11** matrimonial *path:* **5** aisle

bridal wreath 6 spirea

bridewell 3 can, jug, pen **4** coop, jail **5** clink, joint **6** lockup, prison **7** slammer **8** bastille **12** penitentiary

bridge 4 join, link, span **5** unite **7** connect **8** overpass, traverse *great:* **8** Brooklyn **10** Golden Gate *kind:* **4** arch, draw, rope **5** swing, truss **7** bascule, covered, natural, pontoon, trestle, viaduct **10** cantilever, suspension *term:* **3** bid **4** book, east, pass, ruff, slam, suit, void, west **5** bonus, dummy, north, raise, south, trick, trump **6** double, renege, rubber **7** auction, finesse, no-trump, overbid **8** contract, jump call, redouble **9** grand slam, overtrick, singleton **10** little slam, undertrick, vulnerable

bridgelike game 5 whist **6** hearts

bridle 3 bit **4** curb, fume, rein, rule **5** check, flare, quell **6** govern, halter, hold in, manage, master, rein in, ruffle, seethe, subdue **7** bristle, control, flare up, inhibit, repress **8** hold back, moderate, restrain, suppress, withhold **9** constrain, deterrent, hackamore, restraint

brief 4 curt **5** pithy, short, terse **6** abrupt, digest, inform **7** brusque, concise, epitome, laconic, outline, passing, summary **8** abstract, breviary, fleeting, succinct, synopsis

9 momentary, transient 10 abridgment, conspectus 11 abridgement, compendious 12 condensation 13 short and sweet
briefs alternative 6 boxers
brig 3 can, jug, pen 4 coop, jail 5 clink 6 cooler, lockup, prison 7 slammer 8 stockade 9 guardroom 10 guardhouse
brigade 4 army, unit 5 force, group 6 troops 10 contingent, detachment
brigand 6 bandit, bummer, looter, pirate, raider 7 cateran, corsair, forager, rustler 8 marauder, pillager 9 buccaneer, plunderer 10 freebooter, highwayman
brigandage 7 pillage, sacking 10 despoiling, ransacking 11 depredation
bright 4 fair, keen 5 aglow, alert, clear, light, lucid, quick, shiny, smart, sunny, vivid 6 brainy, cheery, clever, lively, lucent 7 beaming, blazing, flaming, fulgent, glowing, lambent, lighted, radiant, shining 8 cheerful, dazzling, gleaming, luminous, lustrous, sunshiny 9 brilliant, effulgent, favorable, refulgent, sparkling 10 auspicious, glittering, precocious, propitious, shimmering 11 illuminated, intelligent, quick-witted 12 incandescent 13 scintillating
brighten 4 buoy 5 cheer, clear, shine 6 look up, perk up, polish, revive, solace 7 burnish, cheer up, clear up, enhance, enliven, furbish, gladden, hearten, improve 8 illumine 10 illuminate
brightness 5 éclat, shine 6 luster, lustre 8 radiance, splendor 10 brilliance, effulgence, luminosity *measure of:* 3 lux 5 lumen 6 candle 7 candela 10 foot-candle
brilliance see **brightness**
brilliant 6 ablaze, brainy, genius, lucent, superb 7 beaming, fulgent, lambent, radiant, shining, stellar 8 dazzling, luminous, masterly, striking 9 effulgent, ingenious, refulgent, sparkling 10 glittering 11 exceptional 12 incandescent
brilliantine 6 pomade 9 hair cream
brim 3 hem, lip, rim 4 edge, fill, well 5 brink, skirt, verge, visor 6 border, fill up, fringe, margin 7 run over 8 overflow, well over 9 perimeter, periphery 13 circumference
brimming 4 full 5 awash, flush 6 filled, jammed, loaded, packed 7 crammed, crowded, replete, stuffed, teeming, welling 8 bursting, overfull, suffused, swarming, swelling 9 chock-full, jam-packed 11 chockablock, running over
brimstone 6 sulfur
brine 3 sea 4 deep, main 5 ocean 8 seawater 9 salt water
bring 3 lug 4 lead, pack, tote 5 carry, fetch,

gross, yield 6 convey 7 attract, produce 9 transport
bring about 3 win 5 beget, cause 6 create, draw on, effect, secure 7 procure, produce, trigger 8 engender, generate, result in 10 accomplish, effectuate, give rise to
bring around 4 hook, sway, turn 7 convert, win over 8 convince, persuade, talk into 9 argue into, prevail on, sweet-talk 11 prevail upon
bring back 5 renew 6 recall, recoup, return, revive 7 recover, reprise, restore, salvage 8 retrieve, revivify 9 reinstate 10 repatriate 11 reestablish
bring down 3 bag, hew 4 drop, fell, raze 5 floor, level, shoot 6 defeat, depose, ground, humble, lay low, reduce 7 depress, flatten 8 demolish, overturn 9 humiliate, overthrow, prostrate, undermine
bring forth 4 bear 5 beget, yield 6 create, elicit, invent 7 deliver, produce 8 generate 9 propagate, reproduce 10 give rise to
bring forward 6 adduce, submit, tender, unveil 7 advance, present, produce, proffer 9 introduce
bring in 3 pay, net, win 4 draw, earn, gain, make, sell 5 fetch, gross, yield 6 garner, return, secure 7 acquire, be worth, realize 9 introduce
bring off 6 effect, finish, rescue 7 achieve, execute, realize, succeed 8 carry out 9 discharge, implement 10 accomplish, consummate, effectuate 12 carry through
bring out 4 cull 5 educe, utter, voice 6 elicit, reveal 7 declare, enhance, explain, extract 8 disclose, showcase 9 elucidate, highlight, introduce
bring together 3 mix, wed 4 herd, join, link, yoke 5 amass, batch, blend, group, marry, merge, rally, unify, unite 6 corral, muster 7 collect, compact, compile, convene, round up 8 assemble 9 aggregate, integrate, reconcile, stockpile 10 synthesize 11 consolidate
bring up 4 moot, rear 5 breed, raise, refer, teach, train, vomit 6 advert, allude, broach, foster, school 7 advance, educate, mention, nurture, propose, suggest, touch on 8 point out, instruct 9 cultivate, introduce 10 put forward 11 regurgitate
brink 3 hem, rim 4 bank, brim, edge 5 point, skirt, verge 6 border, fringe, margin 9 extremity, perimeter, periphery, threshold
briny 5 salty 6 saline
brio 3 pep, vim, zip 4 dash, élan, fire, life, zest, zing 5 ardor, flair, gusto, oomph, style, verve, vigor 6 bounce, esprit, fervor, spirit

7 panache, passion, sparkle **8** dynamism, vivacity **9** animation

brioche 4 roll

Briseis' lover 8 Achilles

brisk 4 busy, fast, keen, spry, yare **5** agile, fresh, nippy, quick, sharp, zippy **6** lively, nimble, snappy, speedy **7** bracing **8** animated, bustling, vigorous **9** energetic, sprightly **10** refreshing **11** stimulating **12** invigorating

bristle 4 boil, burn, fume, seta **5** anger, quill, setae (plural), spine **6** arista, chaeta, seethe **7** chaetae (plural) *Scottish:* **5** birse

bristle-like appendage 3 awn **4** seta **6** arista

British *air force:* **3** RAF *cathedral city:* **3** Ely **4** York **5** Ripon, Truro, Wells **6** Durham, Exeter **7** Chester, Lincoln **8** Coventry, Hereford, St. David's **9** Lichfield, Salisbury, Wakefield, Worcester **10** Canterbury, Gloucester *Channel Island:* **4** Sark **6** Jersey **8** Alderney, Guernsey *coin, current:* **5** pence (plural), penny, pound *coin, old:* **3** bob **5** crown, groat, noble **6** bawbee, florin, George, guinea, tanner, teston **8** farthing, shilling **9** halfcrown, halfpenny, sovereign **10** threepence *colony, former:* **4** Aden, Cape **5** Adana, Kenya, Malta, Natal **6** Ceylon, Cyprus, Gambia **7** Jamaica, Sarawak **9** Gold Coast, Singapore, Transvaal **10** Basutoland, New Zealand **11** Orange River, Sierra Leone **12** Bechuanaland *county:* **4** Avon, Kent, York **5** Derby, Devon, Essex, Gwent **6** Dorset, Durham, Oxford, Surrey, Sussex **7** Bedford, Cumbria, Norfolk, Rutland, Suffolk, Warwick **8** Cheshire, Cornwall, Hereford, Hertford, Somerset, Stafford **9** Berkshire, Cleveland, Hampshire, Lancaster, Leicester, Wiltshire, Worcester **10** Cumberland, Gloucester, Humberside, Lancashire, Merseyside, Shropshire **11** Westmorland **12** Lincolnshire *court, local:* **8** hustings *court, medieval:* **4** eyre *era:* **9** Edwardian, Victorian **11** Elizabethan *forest:* **5** Arden, weald **8** Sherwood *king, legendary:* **3** Lud **4** Beli, Bran **6** Arthur **7** Artegal, Belinus, Elidure **8** Brannius *language, ancient:* **6** Celtic, Cymric **9** Brythonic *legislature:* **10** Parliament *medical system:* **3** NHS *news agency:* **7** Reuters *nobleman:* **4** duke, earl, peer **5** baron **6** prince **8** marquess, viscount *order:* **6** Garter *people, early:* **5** Celts, Iceni, Jutes, Picts **6** Angles, Saxons *political party:* **4** Tory, Whig **6** Labour **12** Conservative *pope:* **8** Adrian IV *prince:* **5** Harry **6** Andrew, Edward **7** Charles, William *princess:* **4** Anne **5** Diana **8** Margaret *prison:* **5** Tower (of London) **7**

Newgate **8** Dartmoor *queen, ancient:* **8** Boadicea, Boudicca *resort:* **4** Bath **7** Margate **8** Brighton **9** Blackpool *royal house:* **4** York **5** Tudor **6** Stuart **7** Hanover, Windsor **9** Lancaster **11** Plantagenet *royal residence:* **7** Windsor **8** Balmoral **10** Buckingham *school:* **4** Eton **5** Rugby **6** Harrow **10** Winchester *school, military:* **9** Sandhurst *spa:* **4** Bath **5** Epsom **6** Buxton **7** Malvern, Matlock **8** Brighton **9** Harrogate **10** Cheltenham

British Columbia *capital:* **8** Victoria *city:* **6** Surrey **7** Burnaby **8** Richmond **9** Vancouver *mountain:* **11** Fairweather *provincial flower:* **7** dogwood (Pacific)

British Honduras 6 Belize

brittle 4 curt **5** crisp, frail, stiff **6** infirm **7** crumbly, fragile, friable **9** breakable, frangible, inelastic, irritable, sensitive **10** perishable, transitory

broach 3 tap **4** moot **6** open up **7** bring up, mention, propose, suggest **8** initiate **9** introduce **10** put forward

broad 4 wide **7** general, liberal **8** extended, generous, spacious, sweeping, tolerant **9** expansive, extensive *combining form:* **4** eury, lati, plat **5** platy

broadcast 3 air, sow **4** beam, show **5** radio, strew **6** blazon, report, spread **7** bestrew, declare, publish, scatter **8** announce, proclaim, televise, transmit **9** advertise, publicize **10** bruit about, promulgate **11** communicate, declaration, disseminate, publication **12** announcement, proclamation, promulgation, transmission

broaden 4 open **5** swell, widen **6** dilate, expand, extend, fatten, spread **7** amplify, augment, distend, enlarge, thicken **8** increase **10** supplement

broadloom 6 carpet

broad-minded 4 open **7** liberal **8** catholic, eclectic, flexible, tolerant, unbiased **9** accepting, indulgent, unbigoted **10** forbearing, undogmatic **11** progressive **12** unjudgmental, unprejudiced

broadsheet 7 tabloid **9** newspaper

broadside 4 hail **5** burst, salvo, sheet, storm **6** shower, volley **7** barrage, torrent **8** at random **9** cannonade, fusillade, laterally, obliquely **11** bombardment

broadtail 4 hawk **5** sheep **7** karakul **8** lambskin

Broadway backer 5 angel

Brobdingnagian 4 huge **5** giant, jumbo **7** hulking, immense, mammoth, massive, titanic **8** colossal, gigantic, towering **9** cyclopean, humongous, monstrous **10** gargantuan, prodigious **11** elephantine

brochette 4 spit **6** skewer
brochure 5 flier, flyer **7** booklet **8** pamphlet
brogue 4 lilt, shoe **6** accent, oxford **7** dialect
broil 3 row **4** bake, burn, char, cook, fray, riot, sear **5** brawl, clash, fight, grill, melee, roast, run-in, toast **6** affray, fracas, scorch, tumult **7** bobbery, rhubarb, ruction, swelter, wrangle **8** disorder, squabble **10** donnybrook, free-for-all **11** disturbance
broiling 3 hot **5** fiery **6** baking, red-hot, torrid **7** blazing, burning **8** ovenlike, scalding, sizzling, white-hot **9** scorching **10** blistering, oppressive, sweltering
broke 4 poor **5** needy, spent **6** busted, ruined **7** drained **8** bankrupt, beggared, dirt poor, indigent, strapped, wiped out **9** destitute, insolvent, out of cash, penniless, penurious, played out **10** cleaned out **11** impecunious
broke-in 4 tame **5** tamed **6** docile
broken 4 shot **5** tamed **6** beaten, busted, cut off, faulty **7** crushed, haywire, humbled, subdued **8** bankrupt, defeated, violated, weakened **9** depressed, disrupted, fractured, heartsick, shattered, sorrowful **11** discouraged, demoralized, interrupted **12** disconnected, disheartened **13** discontinuous
broken-down 7 rickety **8** battered, decaying, decrepit **9** crumbling, neglected **10** threadbare, ramshackle **11** debilitated, dilapidated **12** deteriorated
brokenhearted 7 crushed, unhappy **8** dejected, dolorous, hopeless, wretched **9** depressed, heartsick, sorrowful **10** despairing, despondent **12** inconsolable **13** grief-stricken
broker 5 agent **6** factor **8** diplomat, mediator **9** financier, go-between, middleman **10** interagent, interceder, matchmaker, negotiator **11** intercessor **12** intermediary **13** intermediator
brolly 8 umbrella **11** bumbershoot
bromide 4 bore, drip, lump, pill, yawn **5** drone, grind **6** cliché, old saw, truism **7** proverb **8** banality, chestnut, prosaism, sedative **9** platitude, soporific **10** shibboleth, triviality **11** commonplace, rubber stamp
bromidic 3 dry **4** arid, dull **5** banal, bland, dusty, stale, trite **6** boring **7** humdrum, insipid, tedious **8** shopworn, tiresome **9** dryasdust, moth-eaten, wearisome **10** monotonous, pedestrian, unoriginal **11** commonplace **13** unimaginative, uninteresting
bromine symbol 2 Br
bronco 5 horse **6** cayuse **7** mustang *Australian:* **6** brumby
Brontë *character:* **9** Catherine, Rochester **10** Heathcliff *novel:* **7** Shirley **8** Jane Eyre, Vil-

lette **16** Wuthering Heights *sisters:* **4** Anne **5** Emily **9** Charlotte
Bronx cheer 3 boo **4** hoot, jeer, razz **5** taunt **7** catcall **9** raspberry
brooch 3 pin **4** clip **5** clasp **8** fastener
brood 3 set, sit **4** fret, mope, muse, stew, sulk **5** cover, flock, gloom, hatch, worry **6** litter, ponder, repine **7** despond, progeny **8** children, meditate, ruminate **9** offspring
brook 4 bear, burn, gill, race, rill **5** abide, creek, stand **6** arroyo, endure, rillet, runnel, stream, suffer **7** rivulet, stomach, swallow **8** stand for, tolerate *Scottish:* **6** burnie
Brookner novel 10 Hotel du Lac
broom 5 besom, brush, shrub, sweep, whisk **7** heather
broth 5 stock **8** bouillon, consommé
brothel 4 crib, stew **6** bagnio **7** lupanar **8** bordello, cathouse **9** call house **10** bawdy house, whorehouse
brother 3 kin **4** monk **5** friar **7** comrade, sibling *French:* **5** frère *Italian:* **3** fra **5** frate **8** fratello *Latin:* **6** frater *relating to:* **9** fraternal *Spanish:* **7** hermano
brotherhood 4 club, gang **5** amity, guild, order, union **6** league **7** kinship, society **8** alliance, sodality **10** fellowship, fraternity, friendship **11** association, camaraderie, comradeship, confederacy **12** togetherness **13** consanguinity, secret society
brotherly 9 fraternal
Brothers Karamazov 4 Ivan **5** Mitya **6** Alexei, Alexey, Dmitri, Dmitry **7** Alyosha **10** Smerdyakov
brought up 4 bred **6** raised, reared
brouhaha 3 din **4** coil, flap, fuss, riot, to-do **5** babel, broil, hoo-ha, whirl **6** bedlam, clamor, fracas, furore, hubbub, hurrah, jangle, pother, racket, ruckus, rumpus, shindy, tumult, uproar **7** ferment **8** foofaraw **9** agitation, commotion **10** excitement, hullabaloo, hurly-burly **11** pandemonium
brow 3 top **4** mien **5** front, crest, crown **8** forehead **9** gangplank **10** expression **11** countenance
browbeat 3 cow **5** beset, bully, harry, press **6** badger, carp at, coerce, harass, hector, lean on **7** bluster, dragoon **8** bludgeon, bulldoze, bullyrag, domineer, overbear, pressure **9** tyrannize **10** intimidate
brown 4 sear **5** dusky, toast **6** scorch, tanned **7** swarthy *dark:* **5** mocha, sepia, umber **9** chocolate *grayish:* **3** dun **6** bister, bistre *light:* **3** tan **4** ecru, fawn **5** beige, hazel, khaki, tawny *moderate:* **4** teak **6** sienna *reddish:* **3** bay **4** roan **5** henna **6** auburn,

russet, sorrel, titian **8** chestnut *yellowish:* **6** bronze **12** butterscotch
Brown Bomber 5 Louis (Joe)
brown coal 7 lignite
brownie 3 elf, fay **5** fairy, pixie **6** sprite
Browning poem 8 Prospice, Sordello **11** Aurora Leigh, Pippa Passes **12** Rabbi Ben Ezra **13** Fra Lippo Lippi, My Last Duchess **14** How Do I Love Thee?
brown recluse 6 spider
brownshirt 4 Nazi **12** storm trooper
browse 4 crop, feed, scan, shop, skim **5** graze, munch **6** forage, nibble, peruse **7** dip into, pasture **8** glance at, look over **10** glance over **11** flip through, leaf through, look through, skim through **12** thumb through
Broz, Josip 4 Tito
bruin 4 bear
bruise 5 pound, wound **6** batter, damage, injure, injury **7** contuse **8** abrasion, discolor **9** contusion **13** discoloration
bruit about 6 blazon, gossip, report, spread **7** declare, publish **8** announce, proclaim **9** advertise, broadcast, circulate **10** annunciate, pass around, promulgate **11** blaze abroad
brume 3 fog **4** film, haze, mist, murk **5** vapor **6** miasma **8** haziness **11** obscuration
brummagem 4 fake, sham **5** bogus, false, gaudy, phony, showy **6** ersatz, pseudo, shoddy, tinsel, tawdry **7** chintzy **8** spurious **9** imitation, pinchbeck, tasteless **10** fabricated, fictitious **11** counterfeit, make-believe
brunch cocktail 5 shrub **6** mimosa **7** bellini **10** Bloody Mary **11** screwdriver
Brunei *capital:* 17 Bandar Seri Begawan *island:* **6** Borneo *language:* **5** Malay *neighbor:* **8** Malaysia *sea:* **10** South China
brunet 3 jet **4** dark, onyx **5** dusky, ebony, raven, sable, sooty, swart **6** swarth **7** swarthy **8** bistered, obsidian **10** dark-haired **11** brown-haired
Brunhild 5 queen **7** heroine **8** Valkyrie *husband:* **6** Gunnar **7** Gunther *lover:* **9** Siegfried
brunt 4 jolt **5** shock **6** burden, impact
brush 4 clip, kiss, skim **5** broom, clash, graze, run-in, scrap, scrub, shave, sweep, whisk **6** glance, scrape, tussle **7** contact, thicket **8** skirmish **9** encounter, shrubbery, sideswipe **11** undergrowth
brusque 4 curt, tart **5** bluff, blunt, brief, gruff, rough, short, surly, terse **6** abrupt, crusty, snippy **7** uncivil **8** impolite, snippety, succinct **10** peremptory, ungracious **11** ill-mannered **12** discourteous

brutal 4 hard **5** cruel, feral, harsh **6** rugged, savage, severe **7** beastly, bestial, callous, inhuman, swinish, vicious **8** barbaric, pitiless, ruthless, sadistic **9** barbarous, ferocious, merciless **10** relentless **11** cold-blooded, remorseless **12** bloodthirsty
brutalize 5 abuse **6** debase, harden **7** corrupt, debauch, deprave, pervert, roughen, subvert, vitiate **8** maltreat, mistreat **9** manhandle **10** bestialize
brute 4 ogre **5** beast, cruel, feral **6** animal, savage **7** beastly, bestial, inhuman, piggish, swinish, varmint **8** creature **10** troglodyte **11** instinctive
brutish 3 low **4** base, vile **5** crude, feral, gross, rough, stony **6** animal, carnal, coarse, scurvy, strong **7** beastly, bestial, boorish, inhuman, obscene, piggish, swinish, uncivil, uncouth **8** barbaric, degraded, depraved, inhumane, physical, sadistic **9** primitive, truculent, unrefined **11** animalistic, uncivilized
bryophyte 4 moss **8** hornwort **9** liverwort
Brythonic see **Cymric**
bubble 3 sac **4** blob, boil, dome, fizz, foam, moil **5** churn, froth, slosh, spume, swash **6** burble, gurgle, seethe, simmer **7** ferment, globule, vesicle **10** effervesce
bubbly 5 alive, fizzy, foamy, jolly, perky, sudsy **6** cheery, frothy, lively **7** buoyant, excited **8** animated, effusive **9** champagne, ebullient, exuberant, sparkling **10** carbonated
buccaneer 5 rover **6** cowboy, pirate, sea dog **7** corsair, sea wolf **8** picaroon, sea rover **9** sea robber **10** freebooter
buck 3 fop, guy, lad, lug **4** balk, bear, bill, chap, clam, dude, jerk, load, male, move, note, oner, pack, stag, tote, trip **5** cadet, carry, dandy, ferry, fight, money, pitch, repel, stark, throw, token **6** combat, dollar, fellow, oppose, resist, unseat **7** coxcomb, trestle **8** antelope, bank note, sawhorse, traverse **9** greenback, withstand, workhorse **10** completely **11** Beau Brummel
bucket 3 fly, run **4** pail, rush, whiz **5** hurry, speed **6** barrel, basket, hasten, hustle, vessel **9** clamshell **10** receptacle
Buckeye State 4 Ohio
buckle 4 bend, clip, fold, hasp, kink, warp **5** catch, clamp, clasp, heave, yield **6** cave in, fasten **7** contort, crumple, harness **8** collapse **9** fastening **10** coffee cake
buckle under 3 bow **4** cave, fold, give **5** defer, yield **6** cave in, submit **7** concede, succumb **8** collapse **9** surrender **10** capitulate **11** admit defeat

Buck novel 9 Good Earth (The)
buckram 4 taut **5** stiff **6** wooden **8** starched **9**
cardboard, unbending **10** inflexible **11** inter-
lining
bucks 4 kale **5** bread, dough, money, moola **6**
dinero, do-re-mi, moolah **7** lettuce **10**
greenbacks
buck up 4 buoy, lift **5** cheer, rally **6** solace **7**
comfort, console, gladden, improve, re-
fresh, smarten **8** brighten **9** encourage **10**
strengthen
____ **buco 4** osso
bucolic 5 rural **6** rustic **7** georgic, halcyon,
idyllic **8** agrarian, arcadian, pastoral **10**
campestral, provincial **11** countrified, picturesque
bud 4 germ, seed **5** gemma, spark **6** sprout **7**
burgeon **9** pullulate **10** primordium *combining form:* **5** blast **6** blasto
Buddha 7 Gautama **10** Siddhartha *dialogues:*
5 sutra *disciple:* **6** Ananda *enemy:* **4** Mara
Japanese: **5** Amida, Amita *mother:* **4** Maya
son: **6** Rahula *teachings:* **6** dharma *wife:* **9**
Yasodhara
Buddhist *chant:* **6** mantra *dialogues:* **5** sutra
enlightenment: **6** satori *evil spirit:* **4** Mara
fate: **5** karma *language:* **8** Pali **8** Sanskrit
monk: **4** lama **5** arhat, bonze *sacred city:* **5**
Lhasa *saint:* **5** arhat *scripture:* **5** sutra **6**
sutras **9** Pali canon *sect, tradition:* **3** Son,
Zen **4** Chan **5** Kegon **6** Huayan, Tendai **7**
Tiantai **8** Hinayana, Mahayana, Nichiren,
Pure Land **9** Theravada, Vajrayana *shrine:* **4**
tope **5** stupa **7** chorten *spell:* **6** mantra *spiritual leader:* **4** guru **9** Dalai Lama *state of
happiness:* **7** nirvana *temple:* **6** pagoda *title:* **7** mahatma *tree of enlightenment:* **2** bo
5 bodhi, pipal
buddy 3 mac, pal **4** chum, mate **5** crony **6** comate, fellow, friend **7** compeer, comrade,
partner **8** coworker, playmate, sidekick **9**
associate, companion **10** accomplice **11**
confederate
buddy-buddy 5 close, pally, thick, tight **6**
chummy **8** intimate **10** palsy-walsy **11** in-
separable
budge 4 move **5** shift, yield **7** give way
budgerigar 6 parrot **8** parakeet
budget 5 funds, means **6** amount, ration, supply **8** allocate, estimate **9** allowance, apportion, resources
buff 3 fan, fit, nut, rub, tan **4** ecru, fawn, sand,
wipe **5** beige, brush, fiend, freak, glaze,
gloss, lover, shine, toned **6** addict, expert,
polish, votary **7** admirer, burnish, devotee,
fanatic, fancier, furbish, groupie, habitué **8**
follower **9** yellowish **10** aficionado, alto-

gether, enthusiast **11** connoisseur, yellow-
brown
buffalo 4 anoa, arna, bilk, faze **5** bison, bovid, stump **6** baffle, muddle, rattle **7** carabao, confuse, defraud, flummox, fluster,
nonplus, perplex, swindle **8** befuddle, bewilder, confound, hoodwink **9** bamboozle,
dumbfound
buffalo grass 5 grama
buffer 6 screen, shield **7** buckler, bulwark,
cushion **8** absorber, mediator, polisher **9**
safeguard **10** protection **12** intermediary
buffet 3 box, hit, rap **4** beat, blip, blow, bump,
chop, cuff, drub, jolt, move, poke, slap,
sock **5** clout, drive, force, pound, punch,
smack, spank **6** batter, hammer, pummel,
thrash, wallop **7** belabor, clobber, counter,
lambast **8** lambaste, salad bar **9** sideboard
buffoon 3 wag **4** dolt, fool, goof, lout, zany **5**
antic, clown, comic, droll, dunce, joker, yokel **6** jester **7** bumpkin, dullard **8** bonehead
9 blockhead, harlequin **10** clodhopper **11**
merry-andrew
bug 3 fad, fan, irk, nag, nut, spy, tap, vex **4**
buff, flaw, fret, gall, germ, rage **5** annoy,
bulge, craze, fiend, freak, mania, peeve **6**
badger, bother, defect, insect, malady, needle, nettle, pester, plague, zealot **7** disease,
fanatic, microbe, provoke, wiretap **8** irritate, listen in, protrude, sickness **9** eavesdrop, infection, obsession **10** enthusiast **12**
imperfection **13** microorganism
bugaboo see **bugbear**
bugbear 4 bane, bogy, fear, ogre **5** bogey, bogie, poser **6** goblin, teaser **7** bugaboo, problem, specter, spectre **8** anathema,
bogeyman, phantasm **9** bête noire, booger-
man, boogeyman, hobgoblin **10** black beast
11 abomination
buggy 4 cart, tram **6** go-cart, jalopy **8** carriage
bugle *call:* **4** mess, taps **5** drill **6** sennet, tattoo **7** fanfare, retreat, tantara **8** assembly,
reveille *relative:* **6** cornet **7** trumpet **10**
flugelhorn *sound:* **5** blare
build 3 wax **4** body, form, make, mode, mold,
rise **5** boost, erect, forge, frame, habit,
mount, put up, raise, set up, shape, swell **6**
expand, figure **7** amplify, augment, compose, enlarge, fashion, magnify, produce,
upsurge **8** assemble, compound, engineer,
escalate, heighten, increase, multiply, physique **9** construct, establish, fabricate, institute, intensify, originate **10** accelerate,
inaugurate, strengthen **11** fit together, manufacture **12** conformation, constitution

builder 5 mason **9** carpenter **10** bricklayer, contractor
builder's knot 10 clove hitch
building 3 hut **5** house **7** edifice **8** dwelling **9** structure *addition:* **3** ell **4** wing **5** annex *block:* **4** Lego **5** brick *compartment:* **3** bay **4** room **6** office *connector:* **9** breezeway *farm:* **4** barn, crib, shed, silo *for apartments:* **8** tenement *for arms:* **7** arsenal *for gambling:* **6** casino *for grain:* **4** silo **7** granary **8** elevator *for horses:* **6** stable *for manufacture:* **4** shop **5** plant **7** factory *for music:* **10** auditorium *for sports:* **3** gym **4** bowl **5** arena **7** stadium **8** coliseum **9** gymnasium **10** hippodrome *material:* **4** iron, wood **5** adobe, brick, glass, steel, stone **6** cement **8** concrete *projection:* **3** bay, ell **4** wing **5** annex **6** dormer **7** cornice *round:* **7** rotunda
building kit 5 Legos **10** Erector set **11** Lincoln Logs
build up 4 hype, plug, puff **5** boost, brace, erect **6** accrue, expand, extend, praise **7** collect, develop, enhance, fortify, improve, promote **8** buttress, heighten, increase **9** advertise, construct, establish, intensify, publicize **10** accumulate, aggrandize, strengthen
buildup 4 hype, puff, to-do **6** growth, hoopla **8** increase, ballyhoo **9** accretion, expansion, promotion, publicity **10** escalation **11** development, enhancement, enlargement **12** accumulation, augmentation **13** strengthening
built-in 6 inborn, inbred, innate **8** included, inherent **9** essential, ingrained, intrinsic **10** congenital, deep-seated, indwelling **11** established, fundamental **12** constitutive, incorporated
bulb 4 leek, lily, sego **5** onion, tulip **6** allium, dahlia, garlic, squill **8** daffodil, hyacinth **9** amaryllis, narcissus *segment:* **5** clove
bulb-like bud 4 corm **5** tuber **7** rhizome
Bulgaria *capital:* 5 Sofia *city:* **4** Ruse **5** Stara, Varna **6** Burgas, Pleven, Zagora **7** Plovdiv *monetary unit:* **3** lev *mountain, range:* **6** Balkan, Musala **7** Rhodope *neighbor:* **6** Greece, Serbia, Turkey **7** Romania **9** Macedonia *part of:* **7** Balkans *river:* **6** Danube **7** Maritsa *sea:* **5** Black
bulge 3 bag, jut, sac, sag **4** blob, bump, edge, lump, poke **5** bloat, pouch, swell **6** beetle, billow, bubble, bug out, dilate, excess, expand **7** balloon, distend, inflate, project, puff out **8** overhang, protrude, stand out, stick out, swelling **9** allowance, head start **10** distension, projection, promontory, pro-

trusion **11** excrescence, protuberate **12** protuberance
bulk 4 body, core, heft, loom, mass **5** fiber, swell, total **6** amount, corpus, expand, volume **7** bigness, quantum **8** majority, quantity, stand out **9** aggregate, magnitude, substance
bulky 3 fat **5** beefy, hefty, husky, large, obese, stout **7** massive **8** cumbrous, unwieldy **9** corpulent, ponderous **10** cumbersome, overweight **11** substantial
bull 4 bunk, male, slip, toro, trip **5** boner, edict, error, fluff, force, hooey, lapse **6** bovine, bungle, decree, el toro **7** baloney, blooper, blunder, hogwash, mistake **8** nonsense **9** detective *combining form:* **4** taur **5** tauri, tauro
bulldoze 3 cow **4** move, push, raze **5** abash, bully, clear, cream, elbow, force, level, press, scare, shove **6** coerce, hector, hustle, jostle, lean on, menace, propel, thrust **7** bluster, clobber, dragoon, flatten, oppress, trounce **8** bludgeon, browbeat, bullyrag, demolish, domineer, restrain, shoulder **9** terrorize, tyrannize **10** intimidate, obliterate
bullet 3 ace **4** slug **6** dumdum, tracer **9** cartridge **10** projectile *size:* **7** caliber, calibre
bulletin 4 news **5** flash, scoop **6** notice, report **7** account, catalog, gazette, message, missive, release **8** briefing, calendar, dispatch, magazine, register **9** catalogue, statement **10** communiqué, periodical **12** announcement
bull fiddle 10 contrabass, double bass
bullfighter 6 torero **7** matador, picador **8** toreador **11** cuadrillero **12** banderillero *famous:* **6** Arruza **7** Ordóñez **8** Belmonte, Joselito, Manolete **9** Dominguin **10** El Cordobés
bullfighting *arena:* 5 plaza *cheer:* **3** olé *hero:* **6** torero **7** matador **8** toreador *lancer:* **7** picador *red cloth:* **6** muleta *Spanish:* **7** corrida *team:* **9** cuadrilla
bullheaded 6 mulish **7** adamant, willful **8** contrary, obdurate, perverse, stubborn **9** insistent, obstinate, pigheaded **10** headstrong, refractory, self-willed, unyielding **11** intractable, stiff-necked **12** intransigent, pertinacious, strong-willed
bullish 4 rosy **6** brawny, rising, upbeat **7** booming **9** advancing, expanding, favorable **10** optimistic
bully 3 cow **4** goon, pimp, punk, thug **5** abuse, heavy, meany, tease, tough **6** harass, hector, meanie, menace, pander, pick on, rascal **7** bluster, buffalo, dragoon, harrier, oppress, ruffian, torment, torture **8** bludgeon, browbeat, bulldoze, bullyrag, ha-

rasser, threaten **9** bulldozer, persecute, victimize, tormenter, tyrannize **10** browbeater, corned beef, intimidate, persecutor **11** intimidator

bullyrag see **bulldoze**

bulrush 4 reed, tule **5** sedge **7** cattail, papyrus

bulwark 4 wall **6** screen, shield **7** barrier, bastion, parapet, rampart, seawall **8** buttress, fortress, palisade **9** earthwork, safeguard **10** breakwater, breastwork, embankment, stronghold **13** fortification

bum 3 beg, vag **4** bust, hobo, idle, laze, lazy, loaf, loll, slug, wino **5** binge, cadge, drunk, hit up, idler, mooch, tramp **6** bottom, dawdle, loafer, loiter, lounge, slouch, unfair **7** depress, drifter, feel low, goof off, rear end, vagrant, wheedle **8** buttocks, derelict, fainéant, slugabed, sluggard, vagabond **9** do-nothing, goldbrick, importune, lazybones, panhandle, transient

bumbershoot 6 brolly **8** umbrella

bumble 3 mar **4** blow, flub, muff **5** botch, fluff, gum up, lurch **6** bobble, bollix, bungle, falter, fumble, mess up, muck up, rumble, slip up, teeter, totter **7** blunder, screw up, stagger, stumble **8** flounder

bumbling 5 inept, gawky **6** clumsy, gauche, klutzy **7** awkward, halting, unhandy **8** ungainly **9** all thumbs, graceless, ham-handed, incapable, maladroit, unskilled **11** heavy-handed, incompetent **13** butterfingers, uncoordinated

bummer 3 dud **4** drag, flop, hobo **5** tramp **6** beggar, cadger, downer, sponge, too bad **7** failure, forager, moocher, sponger **8** deadbeat, vagabond **9** tough luck **10** freebooter, panhandler, rotten luck, wet blanket

bump 3 bop, hit, jar, ram, rap, wen **4** bang, bash, bust, jolt, knot, lump, oust, slam **5** break, carom, clash, crack, crash, gnarl, knock, prang, shift, shock, shove, wound **6** demote, growth, impact, injury, jostle, jounce, nodule, remove, strike, wallop **7** collide, degrade, demerit, pothole, run into **8** demotion, dislodge, displace, swelling **9** carbuncle, collision, contusion, convexity **10** concussion, projection, protrusion **12** protuberance

bumpkin 3 oaf **4** boor, hick, lout, rube **5** clown, swain, yokel **6** rustic **7** hayseed, peasant **9** chawbacon, hillbilly, simpleton **10** clodhopper, country boy, countryman, provincial

bump off 3 ice **4** do in, kill, slay **5** erase, snuff **6** murder, rub out **7** butcher, execute, take out **8** knock off **9** eliminate, liquidate **11** assassinate

Bumppo, Natty *alias:* **7** Hawkeye **10** Deer-slayer, Pathfinder *creator:* **6** Cooper (James Fenimore)

bumptious 5 cocky, pushy **8** arrogant, impudent **9** audacious, obnoxious, obtrusive, officious **13** self-assertive

bumpy 5 jerky, nubby, ridgy, rough **6** bouncy, jouncy, knobby, knotty, patchy, pimply, uneven **7** jolting, nodular **9** difficult, irregular

bun 4 load, roll **6** pastry

bunch 3 lot, set, wen **4** band, bevy, bump, clot, crew, knot, lump, mass, push, slew **5** batch, clump, covey, crowd, flock, group, party, spray, stack, swell **6** bundle, circle, clutch, gather, huddle, parcel, throng **7** bouquet, collect, cluster **8** assembly, protrude, swelling **9** gathering **10** assemblage, assortment, collection, congregate **11** aggregation **12** accumulation

bunco steerer 3 gyp **6** con man **7** cheater, diddler, grifter, sharper **8** swindler **9** defrauder, trickster **12** double-dealer **13** confidence man

bundle 3 lot, pot, set, wad **4** bale, body, heap, mint, pack, pile, wrap **5** array, batch, bunch, clump, group, sheaf, truss **6** fardel, packet, parcel **7** cluster, fortune **8** fascicle **10** assortment

bung 4 plug **5** cecum, spile **7** stopper

bungalow 5 cabin, lodge **6** chalet **7** cottage

bungle 3 err **4** flub, goof, mess, muff, slip, trip **5** boner, botch, error, fluff, gum up, lapse, misdo, mix up, spoil **6** bollix, bumble, fiasco, foozle, foul up, fumble, goof up, mess up, muck up, muddle **7** blooper, blunder, failure, louse up, misstep, mistake, stumble **9** mishandle, mismanage

bungler 3 oaf **4** clod, dolt, goof **5** klutz **7** screw-up, tomfool **8** bonehead, goofball, shlemiel **9** blunderer, schlemiel **10** stumble-bum **11** blunderbuss, incompetent **13** butterfingers

bunglesome 6 clumsy, klutzy **7** awkward **8** bumbling **9** all thumbs **13** uncoordinated

bung up 4 beat, hurt **5** abuse, pound **6** batter, bruise, injure **7** contuse, disable **9** disfigure, manhandle

bunion 4 lump **8** swelling **10** protrusion, tumescence **11** enlargement

bunk 3 bed, cot, kip, rot **4** bosh, bull, guff, jazz **5** bilge, board, crash, hokum, hooey, house, lodge, put up **6** humbug, pallet, piffle **7** eyewash, baloney, hogwash, rubbish, twaddle **8** claptrap, domicile, flimflam, malarkey, nonsense, tommyrot **9** poppycock **10** balderdash

bunker 3 bin **6** dugout **7** bastion, chamber **8**

sand trap 10 embankment, stronghold 11 compartment

bunkum 3 rot 4 bosh, bull, guff, jazz 5 bilge, hokum, hooey 6 humbug, piffle 7 baloney, hogwash, rubbish, twaddle 8 claptrap, flim-flam, malarkey, nonsense, tommyrot 9 poppycock 10 balderdash

bunting 5 finch, flags 8 songbird 9 streamers

Bunyanesque 4 huge 5 giant, jumbo 7 mammoth, massive, titanic 8 behemoth, colossal, gigantic, towering 9 Herculean 10 gargantuan, prodigious

Bunyan's ox 4 Babe

buoy 4 lift, prop 5 boost, cheer, float, raise 6 assist, beacon, bear up, buck up, signal, solace, uphold, uplift 7 bolster, comfort, gladden, hearten, support, sustain 9 encourage

buoyancy 6 bounce, levity 7 jollity 8 airiness 10 ebullience, exuberance, exuberancy, liveliness, resilience 12 floatability 13 effervescence

buoyant 3 gay 4 airy 5 sunny 6 afloat, bouncy 7 elastic 8 cheerful, floating, volatile 9 expansive, floatable, resilient 10 unsinkable, weightless 12 effervescent, lighthearted

burble 3 gas, yak 4 blab, chat, gush, talk, wash 5 clack, plash, run on, slosh, swash 6 babble, bubble, gabble, gurgle, murmur, rattle, splash, yammer 7 chatter, prattle, sparkle

burden 3 tax, try 4 care, clog, core, duty, gist, haul, lade, load, onus, pile, pith, task, text 5 brunt, cargo, press, theme, weigh 6 amount, charge, chorus, cumber, hamper, lading, lumber, saddle, strain, stress, thrust, upshot, weight 7 afflict, anxiety, freight, oppress, payload, refrain, purport 8 encumber, handicap, obligate, overload, shiralee 9 millstone, substance, weigh down 10 deadweight 11 encumbrance

burdensome 5 tough 6 taxing, trying 7 arduous, exigent, irksome, onerous, weighty 8 crushing, exacting, grievous 9 demanding, difficult, fatiguing, ponderous 10 exhausting, oppressive 11 troublesome 12 backbreaking, unmanageable

bureau 4 unit 5 chest 6 agency 7 dresser, section 8 ministry 10 department, chiffonier 11 writing desk

bureaucrat 8 mandarin, minister, official 11 functionary 12 civil servant, officeholder

burg 4 city, town 7 borough 8 fortress 10 metropolis, walled town 12 municipality

burgee 4 flag 6 banner, ensign, pennon 7 pendant, pennant 8 standard, streamer

burgeon 4 blow, boom, open 5 bloom, build, mount, run up 6 emerge, expand, flower, sprout, thrive, unfold 7 augment, blossom, develop, enlarge, fill out, prosper, run riot 8 flourish, heighten, increase, multiply, mushroom, snowball 9 germinate 10 burst forth, effloresce

Burgess novel 7 Enderby 13 Earthly Powers 15 Clockwork Orange (A)

burghal 5 civic, urban 8 citified 9 municipal 12 metropolitan

burgher 7 citizen, denizen 8 townsman

burglar 4 yegg 5 thief *loot:* 4 swag

burglarize see **burgle**

burglary 5 heist, theft 7 larceny

burgle 3 rob 4 lift, loot 5 heist, steal, strip 6 rip off, thieve 7 despoil, plunder, ransack 9 break into, knock over 10 housebreak

burgomaster 5 mayor 10 magistrate

Burgundy wine *grape:* 5 Gamay 9 Pinot Noir 10 Chardonnay *red:* 8 Mercurey 10 Beaujolais *white:* 5 Rully 6 Chagny 7 Chablis 10 Montrachet 13 Pouilly-Fuissé

burial 4 tomb 5 grave 7 funeral 9 interment, obsequies, sepulcher, sepulchre, sepulture 10 entombment, inhumation *box:* 6 casket, coffin *ceremony:* 7 funeral, obsequy 9 obsequies *mound:* 6 barrow 7 tumulus *tomb:* 9 mausoleum, sepulcher, sepulchre

burial ground 8 boot hill, cemetery 8 boneyard, God's acre 9 graveyard 10 churchyard, necropolis 12 memorial park, potter's field *early Christian:* 8 catacomb

Burkina Faso *capital:* 11 Ouagadougou *ethnic group:* 3 Gur 5 Mossi 7 Voltaic *former name:* 10 Upper Volta *language:* 4 Moré 5 Dyula 6 French *monetary unit:* 5 franc *neighbor:* 4 Mali, Togo 5 Benin, Ghana, Niger 10 Ivory Coast *river:* 5 Volta (Black, Red) 6 Nazion 7 Mouhoun, Nakanbe 8 Red Volta 10 Black Volta

burlap 5 gunny 6 fabric 7 bagging, sacking *fiber:* 4 hemp, jute

burlesque 3 ape 4 mock, sham 5 farce, spoof 6 parody, satire, send-up 7 lampoon, mockery, mocking, takeoff 8 pastiche, skin show, travesty 10 caricature, distortion, girlie show, lampoonery

burly 4 hale 5 beefy, hefty, husky, tough 6 brawny, robust, strong, stocky 8 athletic, heavyset, muscular, powerful, stalwart, thickset, vigorous 9 strapping

Burma see **Myanmar**

burn 4 bake, char, cook, fire, fume, rage, sear 5 anger, blaze, broil, creek, flame, flare, gleam, roast, scald, singe, smart, smoke, sting, toast 6 ignite, kindle, scorch, seethe 7 bristle, combust, consume, cremate, flare up, inflame, radiate, smolder, swelter 8 smoulder 9 carbonize, cauterize 10 incinerate

burnable 8 volatile 9 flammable, ignitable 10 incendiary 11 combustible, inflammable

burned-out 4 beat, shot 5 spent, weary 6 sapped 7 drained, worn-out 8 consumed, fatigued 9 destroyed, exhausted, played-out 10 broken-down 11 debilitated 12 extinguished

burner 3 hob 4 ring

burning 3 hot 5 afire, aglow, fiery 6 ablaze, aflame, alight, ardent, fervid, heated, hectic, red-hot, torrid, urgent 7 blazing, fervent, fevered, glowing, ignited, kindled, searing 8 broiling, feverish, pressing, sizzling, white-hot 9 scorching 10 imperative, passionate 11 conflagrant, impassioned 12 incandescent *combining form:* 4 igni *malicious:* 5 arson

burnish 3 rub, wax 4 buff 5 glaze, gloss, scour, sheen, shine 6 luster, patina, polish, smooth 7 furbish, varnish 8 brighten

burnished 5 shiny 6 glossy, satiny, sheeny 7 lambent, radiant, shining 8 gleaming, lustrous, polished 9 brilliant 10 glistening 11 resplendent

burnsides 8 whiskers 9 sideburns 10 sideboards 11 dundrearies, muttonchops 12 side-whiskers

burp 5 belch, eruct, expel

burro 3 ass 6 donkey 7 jackass

Burroughs hero 6 Tarzan

burrow 3 den, dig 4 hole, lair, mine, nook, snug 5 delve, gouge, lodge 6 cavity, cuddle, nestle, nuzzle, tunnel 7 snuggle 10 excavation

burst 3 pop, run 4 bang, boom, clap, gush, gust, rive, rush, slam, wham 5 blast, crack, crash, erupt, flare, go off, lunge, sally, salvo, smash, spasm, split, storm, surge 6 access, blow up, emerge, irrupt, launch, plunge, shiver, spring, shower, volley 7 assault, barrage, dehisce, explode, flare-up, fly open, rupture, shatter, torrent 8 detonate, drumfire, eruption, fragment, outbreak, splinter, splitter 9 broadside, cannonade, explosion, fusillade, onslaught 11 bombardment

Burundi *capital:* 9 Bujumbura *ethnic group:* 4 Hutu 5 Tutsi *former name:* 6 Urundi *lake:* 10 Tanganyika *language:* 5 Rundi 6 French 7 Kirundi *monetary unit:* 5 franc *neighbor:* 5 Congo 6 Rwanda 8 Tanzania

bury 4 hide, sink, stow 5 cache, cover, embed, inter, plant, stash 6 absorb, entomb, inhume, mantle, shroud 7 blanket, conceal, cover up, implant, lay away, overlay, put away, secrete 8 ensconce, submerge

bus 5 clear 6 jitney 7 missile, trolley, vehicle 9 hand truck 10 spacecraft

bush 4 rose 5 lilac, shrub, wahoo 6 azalea, cassis, privet 7 currant, thicket, weigela 8 backland, barberry, hazelnut 9 backwater, backwoods, forsythia, manzanita 10 gooseberry, hinterland, wilderness 11 pussy willow 12 rhododendron

bushel 3 ton 4 heap, load, pile 6 basket, hamper 7 pannier

bush-league 5 minor 6 junior, two-bit 8 inferior, mediocre, small-fry 9 small-time 10 inadequate, second-rate 11 lightweight 13 insignificant

bushranger 6 outlaw 8 woodsman 12 frontiersman

bushwhack 4 trap 6 ambush, assail, attack, entrap, waylay 7 assault 8 surprise 9 blindside

bushwhacker 6 bandit, outlaw, raider, sniper 8 guerilla, woodsman 9 guerrilla 10 highwayman

bushy 5 bosky, fuzzy, hairy, leafy 6 fluffy, woolly 7 hirsute, unkempt 9 bristling, luxuriant, overgrown 10 disordered 11 flourishing

business 3 job 4 firm, line, work 5 trade 6 affair, custom, matter, métier, office, outfit, racket 7 calling, company, concern, pursuit, traffic 8 commerce, function, industry 9 patronage 10 employment, enterprise, livelihood, occupation 11 corporation 13 establishment *course:* 7 finance 8 modeling 9 marketing 10 accounting *expense:* 8 overhead *syndicate:* 6 cartel

businesslike 6 formal 7 orderly, serious 8 diligent, thorough 9 competent, efficient, practical, pragmatic 10 impersonal, methodical, no-nonsense, purposeful, systematic 11 disciplined, hardworking 12 professional

businessman 6 broker, dealer, trader, tycoon 7 magnate 8 investor, merchant 9 bourgeois, financier, tradesman, executive 10 capitalist, trafficker 12 entrepreneur, merchandiser 13 industrialist

busker 8 minstrel, musician 11 entertainer

buss 4 kiss, peck 5 smack 6 smooch 8 osculate

bust 3 bag, cop, dud, hit, jag, nab, net 4 bomb, bump, fail, flop, fold, raid, ruin, slug, sock, tear, tour 5 binge, bosom, break, broke, burst, catch, chest, crash, lemon, loser, punch, smash, spell, spree, stint, torso, trash 6 arrest, bender, breast, collar, demote, pick up 7 break up, carouse, degrade, demerit, destroy, exhaust, failure, rupture, wear out 8 bankrupt, demolish, fracture 9 apprehend, break down, destitute, downgrade, penniless 10 impoverish, police raid *opposite:* 4 boom bustle 3 ado, fly, run 4 flit, fuss, rush, stir, tear, teem, to-do 5 hurry, whirl, whisk 6 action, be busy, bestir, clamor, flurry, furore, hassle, hasten, hubbub, hustle, motion, pother, scurry, tumult, uproar 7 ferment, turmoil 8 activity, to-and-fro 9 commotion, whirlpool, whirlwind 10 hurly-burly, excitement, liveliness

bustling 4 busy, rife 5 brisk, fussy, peppy 6 active, hectic, lively 7 dynamic, festive, hopping, humming, jumping 8 animated, swarming, vigorous 9 energetic 10 tumultuous 11 hard-working, industrious

busty 5 ample, buxom, curvy 6 bosomy, chesty, zaftig 7 shapely, stacked 10 curvaceous, voluptuous 11 full-bosomed, well-rounded

busy 5 brisk, fussy, in use 6 active, at work, lively, on duty, tied up 7 crowded, engaged, hopping, humming, swamped, teeming, working 8 bustling, diligent, employed, hustling, meddling, occupied, overdone, sedulous 9 assiduous, congested, elaborate, energetic, intrusive, obtrusive, officious 10 meddlesome 11 distracting, impertinent, industrious, unavailable

busybody 5 prier, pryer, snoop, yenta 6 butt-in, gossip, old hen 7 meddler 8 informer, kibitzer, quidnunc 9 pragmatic 10 chatterbox, newsmonger, pragmatist, talebearer, tattletale 11 nosey parker, rumormonger 12 gossipmonger, rubbernecker, troublemaker

but 3 bar, yet 4 just, only, save 5 alone 6 except, merely, saving, unless 7 barring, besides, however 8 entirely 9 aside from, excepting, excluding, outside of 13 on the contrary

butcher 4 ruin, slay 5 botch, carve, clean, spoil, wreck 6 bollix, killer, mess up, slayer 7 cut meat, destroy, meat man 8 mutilate 9 slaughter 11 slaughterer

butcher-bird 6 shrike

butcherly 5 cruel 6 bloody, clumsy, savage 7 awkward 8 sadistic 9 ferocious, merciless 10 unskillful

butchery 7 carnage 8 abattoir, genocide, massacre 9 bloodbath, bloodshed, holocaust, slaughter 10 mass murder 12 annihilation 13 extermination

buteo 4 hawk 7 buzzard

butler 5 valet 7 steward 10 manservant

Butler, Samuel *novel:* 7 Erewhon 13 Way of All Flesh (The) *poem:* 8 Hudibras

butt 3 end, keg, tip, ram, tun, vat 4 base, cask, drum, dupe, join, push, rump, stub, tail 5 chump, fanny, patsy, stump, touch, verge 6 adjoin, barrel, border, bottom, fir-

kin, pigeon, sucker, target, thrust, victim 7 collide, fall guy, rear end, run into 8 derriere, hogshead, neighbor 9 cigarette, fundament, lie beside, pilgarlic, posterior, remainder 11 communicate, sitting duck 12 hindquarters 13 laughingstock

butter *artificial:* 4 oleo 9 margarine 13 oleomargarine *Indian:* 4 ghee *piece:* 3 pat *semifluid:* 4 ghee *tree:* 4 shea

butterball 5 blimp, whale 8 dumpling, elephant 10 bufflehead

butterfish 6 gunnel

butterfly 4 blue 5 diana, satyr, zebra 6 copper, morpho 7 admiral, buckeye, monarch, satyrid, skipper, sulphur, vanessa, viceroy 8 crescent, grayling, milkweed, victoria 9 aphrodite, metalmark, nymphalid, wood nymph 10 fritillary, hairstreak 11 swallowtail *bush:* 8 buddleia *fish:* 6 blenny, chiton 7 gurnard *larva:* 11 caterpillar *lily:* 8 mariposa *order:* 11 Lepidoptera *plant:* 8 oncidium *pupa:* 9 chrysalis *scientist:* 13 lepidopterist

butter up 4 coax 5 charm 6 cajole, kowtow, praise, stroke 7 adulate, beguile, blarney, flatter, massage, wheedle 8 blandish, bootlick, soft-soap 9 brownnose, sweet-talk 10 overpraise

butt in 6 kibitz, meddle 7 intrude, obtrude 8 busybody, overstep 9 interfere, interlope, interpose, interrupt

buttinsky 7 meddler 8 busybody, kibitzer, quidnunc 9 loudmouth 10 trespasser 12 troublemaker

buttocks 4 rear, rump, seat, tail 5 fanny, nates 6 behind, bottom, breech, heinie 7 hind end, hunkers, keister, rear end, tail end 8 backside, derriere, haunches 9 fundament, posterior

buttonball 8 sycamore 9 plane tree

button-down 6 square, stuffy 8 decorous, orthodox, straight 10 restrained 11 straitlaced, traditional 12 conservative, conventional

buttonhole 5 lobby 6 accost, chat up, detain, waylay 8 confront

buttonwood 8 sycamore 9 plane tree

buttress 4 pier, prop, stay 5 brace, carry, shore, strut, truss 6 back up, bear up, hold up, column, uphold 7 bolster, bulwark, fortify, shore up, support, sustain 9 reinforce, stanchion 10 strengthen 12 underpinning 13 fortification, reinforcement

buxom 5 ample, busty, curvy 6 bosomy, chesty, zaftig 7 shapely, stacked 10 curvaceous, voluptuous 11 full-bosomed, full-figured, well-rounded

buy 5 bribe **6** obtain, ransom, redeem **7** acquire, bargain, believe **8** purchase
buy back 6 ransom, recoup, redeem, regain **8** retrieve **10** repurchase
buyer 6 client, patron, vendee **7** shopper **8** consumer, customer **9** purchaser
buy off 3 fix, sop **5** bribe **6** settle **7** corrupt, silence **9** influence **10** manipulate, tamper with
buzz 3 fad, hum **4** call, fizz, high, hiss, news, purr, ring, talk, whir, whiz **5** craze, drone, hurry, rumor, strum, thrum, whirr, whish **6** bumble, fizzle, gossip, murmur, natter, report, rumble, sizzle, summon, wheeze, whoosh **7** chatter, scandal, whisper **8** sibilate **9** bombinate **11** reverberate, scuttlebutt
buzzard 5 buteo **7** vulture **13** turkey vulture
by 3 per, via **4** away, near, nigh, past **5** along, aside **6** at hand, beside, next to **7** through **9** alongside **10** incidental **11** according to **12** not later than
by and by 4 anon, soon **5** after, later **7** ere long, shortly **8** directly, latterly **9** afterward, presently **10** before long **12** subsequently
by and large 7 all told, broadly, en masse, overall, usually **8** all in all, normally **9** generally, typically **10** altogether, on the whole, ordinarily **11** principally
by dint of see **by means of**
bye-bye 4 ciao, ta-ta **5** adieu, adios **6** so long **7** cheerio, toodles **8** au revoir, farewell, sayonara, toodle-oo
bygone 3 old **4** dead, late, lost, once, past **5** dated, of old, olden **6** former, fossil, of yore, remote, whilom **7** antique, archaic, belated, defunct, extinct, old-time, onetime, quondam, vintage **8** departed, sometime, obsolete, outdated, outmoded, vanished **9** erstwhile, out-of-date **10** antiquated, oldfangled **12** antediluvian, old-fashioned

by means of 3 per, via **4** with **5** using **7** through **9** employing, utilizing
byname 6 handle **7** epithet, moniker **8** cognomen **9** sobriquet **10** diminutive, hypocorism **11** appellation
bypass 4 omit, skip **5** avoid, burke, shunt, skirt **6** detour, ignore **7** highway **8** go around, outflank, ring road, sidestep **10** circumvent, pass around **11** deviate from
by-product 5 yield **6** effect, result **7** outcome, residue, spin-off **8** offshoot **9** outgrowth **10** derivative, descendant **11** aftereffect, consequence **12** repercussion
Byron work 4 Cain, Lara **5** Beppo **6** Giaour (The), Werner **7** Corsair (The), Don Juan, Manfred **12** Childe Harold
bystander 6 gawker, viewer **7** watcher, witness **8** beholder, observer, onlooker, passerby **9** spectator **10** eyewitness **12** rubbernecker
by stealth 5 slyly **7** sub rosa **8** covertly, in secret, secretly **9** furtively, privately **10** under cover **11** insidiously **13** clandestinely
by virtue of see **by means of**
by way of see **by means of**
byword 3 saw **5** adage, axiom, maxim, motto, nomen **6** dictum, phrase, saying, slogan, truism **7** epigram, epithet, precept, proverb, refrain **8** aphorism, cognomen, nickname **9** platitude, prescript, sobriquet **10** hypocorism, shibboleth **11** catchphrase, commonplace, rallying cry
Byzantine 6 daedal, knotty **7** complex, devious **8** involved **9** elaborate, intricate **10** convoluted **11** complicated **12** labyrinthine **13** sophisticated, surreptitious *emperor:* **3** Leo **4** Zeno **5** Basil **6** Bardas, Justin, Phocas **7** Michael, Romanus **9** Heraclius, Justinian **10** Nicephorus, Theodosius *empress:* **3** Zoe **5** Irene **8** Theodora

C

cab 4 hack, taxi **6** jitney **7** hackney **8** carriage
cabal 3 mob **4** clan, club, plot, ring **5** coven, group, junta, mafia **6** cartel, circle, clique **7** coterie, faction, in-group **8** intrigue **9** camarilla **10** conspiracy **11** machination
cabaletta 4 aria, song

cabalistic 6 arcane, mystic, occult **8** esoteric **9** recondite **10** mysterious **11** inscrutable **12** impenetrable
caballero 6 knight **7** paladin **8** cavalier, horseman **9** chevalier
cabana 3 hut **5** shack **7** shelter

cabaret 4 café **6** bistro, nitery **7** hot spot **9** nightclub, nightspot **10** supper club **12** watering hole

cabbage 3 nab, nip **4** cash, hook, lift, palm **5** bread, dough, filch, kraut, money, moola, pinch, steal, swipe **6** dinero, do-re-mi, moolah, pilfer **7** purloin, scratch **10** greenbacks, sauerkraut *disease of:* **6** mildew, mosaic **7** root rot, yellows **8** blackleg, club root *family:* **4** cole, kale, rape **5** colza, savoy **6** turnip **7** collard, mustard **8** broccoli, colewort, kohlrabi, rutabaga **11** cauliflower *sliced:* **4** slaw

cabdriver 4 hack **5** cabby **6** cabbie

cabin 3 hut **4** camp, shed **5** berth, hovel, lodge, shack **6** cabana, chalet, lean-to, shanty **7** bivouac, cottage **9** stateroom

cabin cruiser 5 yacht **9** motorboat, powerboat

cabinet 4 case **6** bureau **7** armoire, chamber, commode, console, council, dresser **8** advisers, advisors, cupboard, ministry **9** presidium **10** chiffonier, collection, counselors

cabinetmaker *American:* **5** Eames (Charles, Ray), Phyfe (Duncan) **6** Belter (John Henry) **7** Goddard (John, Stephen, Thomas) **8** McIntire (Samuel), Townsend (Christopher, Edmund, James, Job, John) *English:* **4** Adam (James, Robert), Hope (Thomas), Kent (William) **8** Sheraton (Thomas) **11** Chippendale (Thomas), Hepplewhite (George) *French:* **6** Boulle (André-Charles) **8** Caffieri (Jacques, Jean-Jacques, Philippe), Cressent (Charles) *German:* **10** Weisweiler (Adam)

cable 4 rope, wire **5** braid, chain **6** stitch **8** transmit **9** telegraph

cabriolet 5 coupe **8** carriage

cache 4 bury, hide **5** cover, plant, stash, store, trove **6** memory, wealth **7** arsenal, conceal, lay away, nest egg, put away, reserve, secrete **8** ensconce, treasure **9** stockpile **10** accumulate **11** hiding place

cachet 4 rank, seal **5** motto, state **6** slogan, status **7** dignity, stature **8** approval, position, prestige, standing **11** consequence

cachinnate 4 crow, howl, roar **5** laugh, whoop **6** guffaw, shriek

cackle 3 gab, jaw **4** blab, chat, crow **5** clack, cluck **6** babble, burble, gabble, gaggle, gobble **7** blabber, blatter, chatter, prattle

cacoëthes 4 zeal **5** mania **6** desire **9** obsession

cacomistle 5 civet **7** raccoon **8** civet cat, ringtail

cacophonic 5 harsh **8** tuneless **9** dissonant, unmusical **10** discordant **11** unmelodious **12** unharmonious

cacophony 5 babel, noise **9** confusion, harshness **10** dissonance

cactus 5 nopal **6** cereus, cholla, mescal, peyote **7** opuntia, saguaro **11** prickly pear

cad 3 cur, dog, rat **4** boor, heel, lout, rake **5** creep, knave, louse, rogue **6** rascal, rotter **7** bounder **9** conductor, scoundrel

cadaver 4 body, mort **5** stiff **6** corpse **7** carcass, remains **8** deceased

cadaverous 5 ashen, gaunt, livid **6** pallid, wasted **7** deathly, ghastly, ghostly, shadowy **8** skeletal, spectral **9** deathlike, emaciated, ghostlike **10** corpselike

caddy 3 bin, box **4** aide **5** toter **6** casket **8** canister, tea chest

cadence 4 beat, flow, lilt **5** meter, pulse **6** rhythm **9** pulsation **10** conclusion, inflection, intonation

cadet 4 pimp **5** plebe **7** student, trainee **10** midshipman

cadge 3 beg, bum **5** mooch **6** hustle, sponge **8** freeload, scrounge **9** panhandle

cadmium symbol 2 Cd

Cadmus *daughter:* **3** Ino **5** Agave **6** Semele **7** Autonoë *father:* **6** Agenor *sister:* **6** Europa *victim:* **6** dragon *wife:* **8** Harmonia

cadre 4 cell, core **5** frame, staff **6** cohort **7** ingroup **9** framework

caducity 3 age **6** dotage, old age **8** senility **10** senescence **11** senectitude

Caesar *assassin:* **6** Brutus (Marcus Junius) **7** Cassius (Gaius) *battle:* **4** Zela **9** Pharsalus *conquest:* **4** Gaul **7** Britain *death date:* **4** Ides **11** Ides of March *eulogist:* **6** Antony (Marc) **7** Anthony (Mark) **8** Antonius (Marcus) *message:* **12** Veni vidi vici *river:* **7** Rubicon *utterance:* **4** Et tu **9** Et tu Brute *wife:* **7** Pompeia **8** Cornelia **9** Calpurnia

Caesarism 7 tyranny **9** authority, autocracy, despotism **10** absolutism **12** dictatorship

caesura 5 break, pause **12** interruption

café 5 diner **6** bistro, nitery **7** barroom, beanery, cabaret, hot spot **8** cookshop **9** lunchroom, nightclub, nightspot **10** coffee shop, restaurant, supper club **12** luncheonette, watering hole **13** watering place

café _____ 4 noir **5** latte **6** au lait, filtre **7** society

caftan 4 gown, robe **6** muumuu **12** dressing gown

cage 3 hem, pen **4** cell, coop, jail **5** score **6** aviary, corral, immure, lock up, shut in **7** close in, enclose, impound **8** imprison **9** enclosure **11** incarcerate

cagey 3 sly **4** foxy, wary, wily **5** canny, sharp **6** astute, clever, crafty, shrewd

cahier 6 record, report, review 7 journal 8 notebook

cahoots 6 hookup, league 8 alliance 9 collusion 10 complicity 11 partnership

caiman 9 crocodile 11 crocodilian

Cain *brother:* 4 Abel, Seth *father:* 4 Adam *land:* 3 Nod *mother:* 3 Eve *nephew:* 4 Enos *son:* 5 Enoch *victim:* 4 Abel

Caine Mutiny *author:* 4 Wouk (Herman) *character:* 5 Keith (Willie), Maryk (Steve), Queeg (Capt. Francis)

Cain novel 8 Serenade 13 Mildred Pierce 23 Postman Always Rings Twice (The)

cajole 3 con 4 coax, dupe 6 entice, seduce 7 beguile, blarney, deceive, wheedle 8 blandish, inveigle, maneuver, persuade, soft-soap 9 sweet-talk

cake 3 dry, set 4 coat, loaf, rime 5 cover, crust, torte 6 gâteau, harden, pastry 7 congeal, encrust, incrust 8 solidify *almond:* 8 macaroon *flat:* 5 cooky 6 cookie *oatmeal:* 4 farl 5 scone 7 bannock *ring-shaped:* 5 donut 6 jumble 8 doughnut *rum-soaked:* 4 baba *Scottish:* 4 farl 5 scone *shell-shaped:* 9 madeleine *topping:* 5 icing 8 frosting, streusel *twisted:* 7 cruller *without shortening:* 6 sponge

Cakes and Ale author 7 Maugham (W. Somerset)

cakewalk 4 romp, rout, snap 5 cinch, dance, strut 6 breeze, prance 8 pushover, walkover

calaboose 3 can 4 brig, coop, jail, tank 5 clink, pokey 6 cooler, lockup, prison 7 slammer 8 hoosegow 9 jailhouse

calamitous 4 dire 5 fatal 6 woeful 7 ruinous 8 grievous 10 disastrous, lamentable 11 cataclysmic, devastating, unfortunate 12 catastrophic 13 heartbreaking

calamity 4 ruin 5 wreck 7 tragedy 8 disaster, downfall 9 cataclysm 11 catastrophe, tribulation

calcium symbol 2 Ce

calculate 4 rely 5 assay, count, gauge, judge, solve, tally, tot up, value 6 assess, cipher, figure, intend, reckon 7 compute, measure, work out 8 appraise, estimate, evaluate, forecast 9 ascertain, determine, figure out

calculated 6 likely 7 planned 8 intended 9 worked out 10 deliberate 12 aforethought, premeditated

calculating 3 sly 4 wary, wily 5 canny, chary, sharp 6 artful, crafty, shrewd 7 careful, cunning, devious, politic 8 cautious, discreet, guileful, scheming 9 designing 11 circumspect

calculating device 6 abacus *Peruvian:* 5 quipu

calculation 8 analysis, counting, estimate, figuring, prudence 9 ciphering, reckoning 10 arithmetic, estimation, prediction 11 computation

Caledonia 8 Scotland

calendar 3 log 4 card, sked 6 agenda, docket 7 almanac, program 8 schedule 9 timetable *abbreviation:* 3 Apr, Aug, Dec, Feb, Fri, Jan, Mar, Mon, Nov, Oct, Sat, Sep, Sun, Tue, Wed 4 Sept 5 Thurs *ecclesiastical:* 4 ordo *unit:* 3 day 4 week, year 5 month

calenture 4 fire, zeal 5 ardor, fever 6 fervor 7 passion 10 enthusiasm

calf *hide:* 3 kip *leather:* 3 elk *meat:* 4 veal *stray:* 5 dogie *unbranded:* 8 maverick

Caliban 5 slave *master:* 8 Prospero *witch-mother:* 7 Sycorax

caliber 4 bore 5 class, gauge, grade, merit, value, worth 6 virtue 7 ability, quality, stature 8 diameter

calibrate 3 set 6 adjust, polish 7 measure 8 fine-tune, regulate 9 ascertain 11 standardize

California *capital:* 10 Sacramento *city:* 4 Napa 6 Fresno, Sonoma 7 Anaheim, Oakland, San Jose 8 San Diego, Santa Ana 9 Long Beach, Santa Cruz 10 Los Angeles 12 San Francisco *college, university:* 3 USC 4 UCLA 5 Mills 6 Pomona 8 Berkeley, Stanford, Whittier 9 Loma Linda 10 Golden Gate, Occidental, Pepperdine, Santa Clara *desert:* 6 Mohave *fault zone:* 10 San Andreas *lake:* 5 Owens, Tahoe 9 Salton Sea *lowest spot:* 11 Death Valley *motto:* 6 Eureka *mountain, range:* 5 Coast 6 Lassen (Peak), Shasta 7 Whitney 12 Sierra Nevada *nickname:* 6 Golden (State) *park:* 7 Sequoia 8 Yosemite 11 Kings Canyon 14 Channel Islands *river:* 10 Sacramento, San Joaquin *state bird:* 5 quail *state flower:* 11 golden poppy *state tree:* 7 redwood, sequoia *wine region:* 4 Napa 6 Sonoma

californium symbol 2 Cf

caliginous 3 dim 4 dark, dusk 5 dusky, foggy, misty, murky 6 gloomy 7 obscure, sunless 8 nebulous 9 lightless, tenebrous

Caligula *mother:* 9 Agrippina *predecessor:* 8 Tiberius *successor:* 8 Claudius

caliph's name 3 Ali 7 Abu Bakr

Calista's seducer 8 Lothario

calisthenics 7 workout 9 exercises

call 3 bid, cry 4 buzz, hail, lure, name, page, ring, yell 5 phone, pop in, shout, visit 6 bellow, come by, drop by, drop in, holler, salute, stop by, stop in, summon 7 convene, convoke, summons 8 estimate 9 designate, telephone

calla 4 lily
call down 5 chide, scold **6** rebuke **7** censure, reprove **8** admonish, reproach **9** reprimand
called 6 named **6** chosen, picked, yclept **7** ycleped **8** selected
caller 5 guest **6** suitor **7** visitor
call for 3 ask, beg **4** page, seek **5** crave, plead **6** demand, entail, pick up **7** beseech, entreat, implore, involve, require **11** necessitate
call forth 5 awake, educe, evoke, rouse **6** arouse, elicit **7** conjure, provoke **9** conjure up
calligrapher 6 penman, scribe **7** copyist **9** engrosser, scrivener
calligraphy 4 hand **6** script **7** writing **8** longhand **10** penmanship **11** handwriting
call in 5 phone **6** summon **7** convene, reclaim **8** retrieve, withdraw **9** repossess, telephone
calling 3 job **4** duty, work **5** craft, trade **6** career, métier **7** mission, pursuit, yelling **8** business, lifework, shouting, vocation **10** employment, obligation, occupation, profession
call in sick 7 book off
Calliope 4 Muse *father:* **4** Zeus **7** Jupiter *mother:* **9** Mnemosyne *son:* **7** Orpheus
Callisto *lover:* **4** Zeus **7** Jupiter *son:* **5** Arcas
Call It Sleep author 4 Roth (Henry)
call off 4 halt **5** abort, scrub **6** cancel, divert **8** distract
Call of the Wild *author:* **6** London (Jack) *dog:* **4** Buck
call on 5 visit **6** oblige **7** require
callosity 8 hardness **9** thickness
callous 5 stony **8** hardened, obdurate, uncaring **9** heartless, indurated, unfeeling **10** hard-bitten, hard-boiled **11** coldhearted, hardhearted, insensitive, unemotional **12** case-hardened, stonyhearted **13** unsympathetic
callow 3 raw **5** fresh, green, naive, young **7** puerile **8** immature, juvenile, youthful **9** unfledged **10** unseasoned **13** inexperienced, unexperienced
call up 5 draft, evoke **6** summon **8** mobilize, retrieve **9** conscript
calm 4 cool, ease, hush, lull **5** allay, peace, quiet, relax, salve, still **6** hushed, pacify, placid, poised, repose, sedate, serene, settle, smooth, soothe, stable, steady, stilly **7** appease, assuage, compose, halcyon, mollify, pacific, placate, restful, resting **8** composed, inactive, peaceful, reposing, serenity, tranquil **9** collected, composure, easygoing, impassive, possessed, quiescent, unruffled **10** phlegmatic, untroubled **11**

tranquility, tranquilize, unflappable **12** even-tempered, self-composed, tranquillity **13** imperturbable, self-possessed
calmative 8 quietive, relaxing, sedative **9** soporific **12** tranquilizer
calmness 4 lull **5** quiet **6** phlegm **8** coolness, serenity **9** composure, placidity, sangfroid **10** equanimity **11** tranquility **12** tranquillity
calumet 4 pipe **9** peace pipe
calumniate 5 libel, smear **6** defame, malign, vilify **7** asperse, slander, tarnish, traduce **8** besmirch **9** denigrate **10** scandalize
calumnious 8 libelous **9** maligning, traducing, vilifying **10** backbiting, defamatory, detracting, scandalous, slanderous
calumny 7 scandal, slander **9** aspersion **10** backbiting, defamation, detraction **11** denigration **12** backstabbing, belittlement, depreciation **13** disparagement
calvados 6 brandy **9** applejack
calvary 5 agony, cross, trial **6** misery, ordeal **7** anguish **8** distress **9** suffering **10** affliction, visitation **11** tribulation *inscription:* **4** INRI
Calvino work 11 Cosmicomics **15** Invisible Cities
Calypso *beloved:* **7** Ulysses **8** Odysseus *island:* **6** Ogygia
calyx part 3 cup **5** sepal
camaraderie 5 cheer **7** jollity **10** affability, fellowship **12** conviviality
camarilla 3 mob **4** camp, clan, ring **5** cabal, mafia **6** circle, clique **7** coterie, ingroup
Cambodia 9 Kampuchea *capital:* **9** Phnom Penh *city:* **10** Battambang **11** Kompong Cham *ethnic group:* **8** Mon-Khmer *lake:* **8** Tonle Sap *language:* **5** Khmer *leader:* **6** Pol Pot *monetary unit:* **4** riel *neighbor:* **4** Laos **7** Vietnam **8** Thailand *river:* **6** Mekong *ruin:* **9** Angkor Wat
camel *one-humped:* **9** dromedary *two-humped:* **8** Bactrian
camel-hair fabric 3 aba
camelopard 7 giraffe
Camelot 6 palace *lord:* **6** Arthur
Camembert 6 cheese
cameo 6 brooch, relief, walk-on **8** portrait
camera type 3 SLR, spy, TLR **5** video **7** digital, folding, pinhole **9** autofocus, single-use **10** viewfinder **11** rangefinder
cameraman 6 photog **7** lensman **12** photographer
Cameroon *capital:* **7** Yaoundé *ethnic group:* **4** Fang **5** Duala, Pygmy **6** Fulani **8** Bamileke *largest city:* **6** Douala *monetary unit:* **5** franc *neighbor:* **4** Chad **5** Congo, Gabon **7** Nigeria *river:* **5** Nyong **6** Sanaga

Camille's creator 5 Dumas (Alexandre)
Camino ____ **4** Real
camouflage 4 mask **5** cloak **7** conceal, deceive **8** disguise **9** dissemble **11** dissimulate
camp 3 hut **4** bloc, shed **5** cabin, lodge, shack **6** clique, shanty **7** bivouac, coterie, cottage, faction **10** settlement
campaign 4 push, race **5** blitz, drive, fight, lobby, stump **6** attack **7** agitate, canvass, crusade **8** movement, politick **9** barnstorm, offensive **10** engagement, expedition **11** electioneer, whistle-stop
campaigner 8 activist **9** candidate
campanile 6 belfry **8** carillon **9** bell tower
campesino 6 farmer **7** peasant
campestral 5 rural **6** rustic, sylvan **7** bucolic, country, idyllic **8** agrarian, pastoral **10** provincial **11** countrified
campus see **college**
Camus work 4 Fall (The) **5** Rebel (The) **6** Plague (The) **8** Caligula, Stranger (The)
can 3 may, tin **4** boot, fire, sack **5** let go, put up **7** dismiss **8** preserve **9** container, discharge **10** receptacle
Canaan 4 Zion **12** Promised Land *father:* **3** Ham *grandfather:* **4** Noah
Canaanite god 3 Mot **4** Baal **6** Molech, Moloch
Canada bay:* **5 Fundy, James **6** Baffin, Hudson, Ungava **8** Georgian **9** Frobisher *capital:* **6** Ottawa *city:* **6** London, Oshawa, Quebec, Regina, Surrey **7** Burnaby, Calgary, Halifax, Moncton, Toronto, Windsor **8** Edmonton, Hamilton, Montreal, Moose Jaw, Victoria, Winnipeg **9** Longueuil, North York, Saskatoon, Vancouver **10** Lethbridge, Thunder Bay **11** Fredericton, Scarborough **13** Charlottetown, Mississisauga *district:* **6** riding *explorer:* **6** Hudson (Henry) **7** Cartier (Jacques) **9** Champlain (Samuel de) *Indian people:* **4** Cree, Inuk **5** Blood, Haida, Huron, Inuit, Métis, Niska, Slave **6** Abnaki, Beaver, Eskimo, Micmac, Mohawk, Nootka, Ojibwa, Ojibwe, Ottawa, Piegan, Seneca, Stoney **7** Kutenai, Naskapi, Ojibway, Siksika, Wyandot **8** Algonkin, Chippewa, Iroquois, Kootenai, Kootenay, Kwakiutl, Salishan, Tsattine **9** Algonkian, Algonquin, Blackfeet, Blackfoot, Chipewyan, Tsimshian **10** Algonquian, Athapascan, Gros Ventre, Montagnais **11** Assiniboine *island, island group:* **5** Banks, Devon **6** Baffin **7** Belcher **8** Melville, Victoria **9** Anticosti, Ellesmere, Vancouver **10** Cape Breton **11** Southampton **12** Newfoundland, Prince Edward *lake:* **6** Louise **7** Nipigon **8** Reindeer, Winnipeg **9** Athabasca, Champlain, Great Bear **10** Great Slave *language:* **6** French **7** English *monetary unit:* **6** dollar *mountain, range:* **5** Coast, Logan, Rocky **10** Laurentian *national park:* **5** Banff, Fundy **6** Jasper **7** Glacier, Nahanni **8** Kootenay **9** Gros Morne **10** Grasslands, Point Pelee **11** Georgian Bay, Wood Buffalo *peninsula:* **5** Bruce, Gaspé **6** Ungava **8** Labrador *prime minister:* **4** King (W. L. Mackenzie) **5** Clark (Joe) **6** Abbott (John), Borden (Robert Laird), Bowell (Mackenzie), Harper (Stephen), Martin (Paul), Tupper (Charles), Turner (John) **7** Bennett (Richard Bedford), Laurier (Wilfrid), Meighen (Arthur), Pearson (Lester), Trudeau (Pierre Elliott) **8** Campbell (Kim), Chrétien (Jean), Mulroney (Brian), Thompson (John) **9** MacDonald (John), Mackenzie (Alexander), St. Laurent (Louis) **11** Diefenbaker (John) *province:* **3** Man., NWT, Ont., PEI, Que. **4** Alta, Sask. **6** Quebec **7** Alberta, Nunavut, Ontario **8** Manitoba **10** Nova Scotia **12** New Brunswick, Newfoundland (and Labrador), Saskatchewan **15** British Columbia **18** Prince Edward Island *provincial park:* **3** Gas **7** Rondeau **9** Garibaldi *river:* **3** Red **5** Liard, Slave, Yukon **6** Albany, Fraser, Nelson, Ottawa, Severn **8** Columbia, Saguenay **9** Athabasca, Churchill, Mackenzie **10** St. Lawrence *sea:* **8** Beaufort, Labrador *symbol:* **9** maple leaf *territory:* **5** Yukon **9** Northwest
Canadian insurgent 4 Riel (Louis)
canaille 3 mob **6** masses, rabble **8** riffraff, unwashed **9** hoi polloi **11** proletarian, proletariat
canal 4 duct **6** course **7** channel, conduit **8** aqueduct **11** watercourse *Africa:* **4** Suez **8** Ismailia *Belgium:* **6** Albert *Canada:* **7** Welland *Central America:* **9** Panama *China:* **7** Da Yunhe *Florida:* **10** Saint Lucie *Germany:* **4** Kiel **10** Nord-Ostsee *Greece:* **7** Corinth *Michigan:* **3** Soo *New York:* **4** Erie **6** Oswego **9** Champlain *Ontario:* **6** Rideau *Venice:* **5** Grand
canapé 6 morsel **9** appetizer **11** hors d'oeuvre *spread:* **4** paté *topper:* **3** roe **6** caviar
canard 3 fib, lie **4** tale, yarn **5** fraud, rumor, spoof **6** deceit **7** falsity, untruth **8** chestnut **9** falsehood
canary 3 rat **4** fink, wine **5** finch **6** snitch **7** rat fink, stoolie **8** informer, squealer **11** stool pigeon
Canary Islands 5 Ferro, Lobos, Palma **6** Gomera, Hierro **7** Inferno **8** Graciosa, Tenerife **9** Alegranza, Lanzarote
cancel 3 end **4** drop, lift, undo, x out **5** abort,

annul, erase, scrub 6 delete, efface, negate, offset, repeal, revoke 7 blot out, call off, destroy, expunge, nullify, rescind, wipe out 8 black out, deletion 9 terminate 10 invalidate, neutralize, obliterate

cancer 5 tumor 9 carcinoma 10 malignancy *treatment:* 5 chemo, X rays 9 radiation 12 chemotherapy

cancer-causing 12 carcinogenic *substance:* 10 carcinogen

candescent 7 glowing 8 dazzling 9 refulgent

Candia 5 Crete

candid 4 fair, just, open 5 blunt, frank, plain 6 honest 7 sincere 8 unbiased 9 equitable, guileless, impartial, objective 10 aboveboard, forthright, scrupulous, unreserved 11 openhearted, unconcealed, undisguised 12 unprejudiced 13 dispassionate

candidate 6 seeker 7 hopeful, nominee, stumper 8 aspirant 9 applicant, contender 10 campaigner, contestant *unlisted:* 7 write-in

Candide *author:* 8 Voltaire *lover:* 9 Cunegonde *tutor:* 8 Pangloss (Dr.) *valet:* 7 Cacambo

candle 5 taper 6 bougie *holder:* 6 sconce 7 menorah, pricket 9 girandole 10 candelabra 11 candelabrum *material:* 3 wax 4 wick 6 tallow 7 beeswax, stearin 8 paraffin *religious:* 6 votive 7 paschal

candlefish 8 eulachon *relative:* 5 smelt

candlelit service 5 vigil

candlepins 7 bowling

candor 7 honesty 8 fairness, openness 9 frankness, sincerity, whiteness 11 artlessness 13 guilelessness

candy 7 sweeten 9 sugarcoat 10 confection *kind:* 4 rock 5 fudge, lolly, sweet, taffy 6 bonbon, comfit, dragée, jujube, nougat, toffee 7 brittle, caramel, fondant, gumdrop, penuche, praline 8 licorice, lollipop, lollypop, marzipan, sourball 9 chocolate, jelly bean, nonpareil, sweetmeat 10 confection 12 butterscotch *medicated:* 7 lozenge 9 cough drop

cane 3 rod 4 beat, drub, flog, lash, reed, stem, swat 5 flail, grass, spank, staff, stave, stick, weave, whale 6 batter, buffet, cudgel, larrup, paddle, rattan, thrash, wallop 7 lambast, sorghum 8 lambaste 12 walking stick

Canea's land 5 Crete

canine 3 dog 4 tyke 5 hound, pooch

caning material 5 istle

Canis Major star 6 Sirius

Canis Minor star 7 Procyon

canker 4 rust, sore 5 stain 6 debase, infect 7

corrupt, debauch, deprave, pervert, vitiate 8 necrosis 10 demoralize

cankered 8 infested, infected

canker sore 5 ulcer 6 lesion 10 ulceration

cannabis 3 pot 4 hemp 5 bhang, ganja, grass 7 hashish 9 marijuana

canned 5 drunk, fired 6 potted 11 prerecorded

Cannery Row author 9 Steinbeck (John)

canniness 7 caution, cunning, slyness 8 prudence, wiliness 9 cageyness, foresight 10 artfulness, cleverness, craftiness, discretion, precaution, providence, shrewdness 11 forethought

cannon 6 pom-pom 8 howitzer, ordnance 9 artillery *part:* 5 chase 6 breech 8 cascabel, trunnion

cannonade 4 bomb 5 blitz, burst, salvo, shell 6 shower, volley 7 barrage, bombard 8 drumfire, shelling 9 broadside, fusillade 11 bombardment

cannonball 4 dive 5 speed 7 missile

cannoneer 6 gunner

cannon fodder 6 troops 8 infantry, soldiers

canny 3 sly 4 wary, wise 5 acute, cagey, chary, quick, sharp, smart 6 adroit, clever, frugal, saving, shrewd 7 cunning, knowing, prudent, thrifty 9 ingenious, provident 10 economical 11 quick-witted, sharp-witted 12 nimble-witted

canoe 6 dugout 7 pirogue *ancient:* 7 coracle *Eskimo:* 5 kayak, umiak

canon 3 law 4 list, rule 5 dogma, edict, round, tenet 6 decree 7 precept, statute 8 doctrine, standard 9 clergyman, criterion, ordinance 10 regulation

canonical 5 sound 6 lawful 7 classic 8 accepted, approved, official, orthodox, received 10 authorized, recognized, sanctioned 13 authoritative

canonical hour 4 none, sext 5 lauds, prime, terce 6 matins, tierce 7 vespers 8 compline

canonicals 9 vestments

canoodle 3 hug, pet 5 spoon 6 caress, cuddle, fondle

can opener 9 church key

canopy 5 cover, shade 6 awning, tester 7 marquee, shelter 8 covering, sunshade 9 baldachin 10 baldachino *canvas:* 4 tilt

cant 3 tip 4 heel, lean, list, tilt 5 angle, argot, bevel, idiom, lingo, piety, slang, slant, slope 6 humbug, jargon, patois, patter, speech 7 dialect, diction, incline, lexicon, palaver, recline 8 language, singsong 9 hypocrisy 10 dictionary, pharisaism, sanctimony, vernacular 11 inclination, insincerity 12 pecksniffery

cantaloupe 5 melon 9 muskmelon

cantankerous 4 dour, sour **5** cross, huffy, testy, waspy **6** crabby, cranky, crusty, grumpy, morose, ornery **7** bearish, crabbed, grouchy, peevish, prickly, waspish **8** cankered, liverish, petulant, snappish, stubborn, vinegary **9** crotchety, difficult, dyspeptic, irascible, irritable, obstinate **10** ill-natured, irritating, vinegarish **12** crossgrained

canter 3 bum **4** gait, hobo, lope **5** tramp **6** beggar **7** drifter, vagrant **8** derelict, vagabond **11** bindle stiff

Canterbury *Archbishop:* **3** Oda **6** Anselm, Becket (Thomas á), Parker (Matthew) **7** Cranmer (Thomas), Dunstan **9** Augustine

Canterbury Tales *author:* **7** Chaucer (Geoffrey) *character:* **4** host, monk **5** clerk, friar, reeve **6** knight, miller, parson, squire, yeoman **7** plowman, shipman **8** franklin, Griselda, manciple, merchant, pardoner, prioress, summoner **9** physician **10** wife of Bath *inn:* **6** Tabard

canticle 3 ode **4** hymn, song **6** Te Deum **10** Benedicite, Benedictus, Magnificat **12** Nunc Dimittis

canticles 11 Song of Songs **13** Song of Solomon

cantilever 4 beam **6** bridge **7** bracket, support

cantillate 4 sing **5** chant **6** intone, recite

cantina 3 bar, pub **6** saloon, tavern **7** barroom

canton 5 state **6** billet **7** quarter, section **8** district, division

cantor 5 hazan **6** singer **9** precentor

canvas 4 duck, sail, tarp, tent **7** tenting **8** painting **9** sailcloth, tarpaulin

canvasback 4 duck

canvass 3 con, vet **5** argue, study **6** debate, survey **7** discuss, dispute, examine, inspect, solicit **8** campaign **9** check over **10** scrutinize **11** electioneer **12** authenticate

canyon 4 Glen, Zion **5** Bryce, chasm, gorge, Grand, gulch, Hells **6** Copper, coulee, ravine, valley

cap 3 tam, top **4** best, coif **5** beret, cover, crest, crown, limit, trump **6** beanie, exceed, top off **7** calotte **9** culminate *clergyman's:* **7** biretta **9** zucchetto *hoodlike:* **4** coif *hunter's:* **7** montero *jester's:* **7** coxcomb **9** cockscomb *Jewish:* **8** yarmulke *knitted:* **5** toque, tuque **9** balaclava *military:* **4** kepi *mushroom:* **6** pileus *part:* **4** bill, brim, flap, peak **5** visor **7** earflap *Roman:* **6** pileus *Scottish:* **3** tam **8** balmoral **9** glengarry **11** tam-o'-shanter *Turkish:* **3** fez **6** calpac **7** calpack

capability 5 craft, means, skill **7** ability, potency **8** adequacy, aptitude, capacity, efficacy, facility **9** potential **10** competence, efficiency **12** potentiality **13** effectiveness, qualification

capable 3 apt **4** able **5** adept **6** adroit, au fait **9** competent, efficient, qualified **10** proficient **11** susceptible

capacious 4 wide **5** ample, roomy **7** sizable **8** abundant, spacious **9** extensive **10** commodious **11** substantial

capacitance *unit of:* **5** farad

capacity 4 bent, gift, rank, role, room **5** knack, range, reach, scope, skill, space **6** output, status, talent **7** ability, caliber, faculty **8** adequacy, aptitude, facility, position, standing **10** capability, competence **11** proficiency **13** qualification *unit of:* **4** gill, peck, pint **5** liter, litre, minim, quart **6** bushel, gallon **10** fluid ounce, milliliter

Capaneus *slayer:* **4** Zeus *wife:* **6** Evadne

caparison 5 adorn **6** finery **7** apparel, panoply, raiment **9** adornment, trappings

cape 4 cope, ness **5** cloak, point, talma **6** capote, mantle, tabard, tippet **7** manteau, pelisse **8** foreland, headland, mantelet, mantilla, pelerine **9** peninsula **10** promontory *clergyman's:* **8** mozzetta *papal:* **5** fanon, orale

Cape *Africa:* **4** Juby, Yubi **5** Blanc **6** Blanco **7** Agulhas *Alaska:* **3** Icy **4** Nome **11** Krusenstern *Algeria:* **3** Fer *Antarctica:* **3** Ann **4** Dart **5** Adare *Arctic:* **8** Nordkaap *Asia:* **5** Aniva *Australia:* **5** Byron, Otway, Sandy, Smoky **9** Arnhem **9** Van Diemen *Baffin Island:* **4** Dyer *Black Sea:* **5** Yasun *Borneo:* **4** Datu **6** Datoek *Brazil:* **4** Frio, Raso *California:* **9** Mendocino *Colombia:* **5** Aguja *Costa Rica:* **5** Velas *Crete:* **5** Plaka *Croatia:* **5** Ploca **6** Planka *Cuba:* **4** Cruz **5** Maisi *Denmark:* **4** Skaw **6** Skagen *Desolación Island:* **5** Pilar **6** Pillar *Djibouti:* **3** Bir *Egypt:* **5** Banas *England:* **8** Bolerium, Lands End *Florida:* **5** Sable **7** Kennedy **9** Canaveral *Greece:* **4** Busa **5** Gallo, Malea, Papas, Vouxa **6** Araxos, Maleas **7** Akritas *Guinea:* **5** Verga *Gulf of California:* **5** Lobos *Gulf of Guinea:* **5** Lopez *Gulf of Mexico:* **4** Rojo *Hawaii:* **5** Ka Lae **10** South Point **11** Diamond Head *Hispaniola:* **5** Beata *Honshu:* **3** Iro, Oma **5** Inubo, Kyoga, Nyudo *Indonesia:* **4** Vals **5** False *Japan:* **4** Esan, Nomo, Sata, Soya **5** Erimo, Kamui *Libya:* **3** Tin **4** Milh *Long Island Sound:* **10** Throgs Neck *Malay Peninsula:* **5** Bulat *Malaysia:* **4** Piai **5** Sirik *Massachusetts:* **3** Ann, Cod *Mediterranean:* **5** Ajdir *Mexico:* **4** Buey *Morocco:* **3** Sim **4** Guir, Rhir *Namibia:* **4** Fria *Newfoundland:* **5** Bauld *New Jersey:* **3** May

New Zealand: 5 Brett *North Carolina:* 4 Fear 7 Lookout 8 Hatteras *Northwest Territories:* 8 Bathurst *Nova Scotia:* 5 Canso 6 Breton *Oman:* 3 Nus 4 Hadd *Ontario:* 4 Hurd, Rich *Pakistan:* 5 Monze, Muari *Portugal:* 4 Roca *Puerto Rico:* 4 Rojo *Quebec:* 5 Gaspé *Red Sea:* 5 Kasar *Sicily:* 4 Boeo, Faro 7 Lilibeo, Passero, Pelorus *Solomon Islands:* 5 Zelee *Somalia:* 4 Asir 5 Assir, Hafun *South Africa:* 8 Good Hope *South America:* 4 Horn *Spain:* 3 Nao 4 Gata 5 Creus, Penas *Syria:* 5 Basit *Taiwan:* 5 O-Iuan 7 Garam Bi *Tierra del Fuego:* 5 Penas *Tunisia:* 5 Blanc *Turkey:* 3 Boz 4 Baba, Ince, Kara, Krio 6 Lectum 8 Bozburun 9 Inceburun, Karaburun *Vancouver Island:* 5 Scott *Virginia:* 5 Henry *Washington:* 5 Alava

Čapek, Karel coinage: 5 robot *play:* 3 R.U.R.

caper 4 dido, lark, leap, romp 5 antic, frisk, heist, prank, revel, shine, theft, trick 6 cavort, frolic, gambol, prance 7 roguery, rollick 8 escapade, mischief 10 shenanigan, tomfoolery 11 monkeyshine

Cape Verde capital: 5 Praia *city:* 7 Mindelo *island:* 3 Sal 4 Fogo, Maio 5 Brava 8 Boa Vista, São Tiago 10 São Vicente, São Nicolau, Santa Luzia, Santo Antão *language:* 7 Crioulo 10 Portuguese *monetary unit:* 6 escudo

capillary 4 tube 6 tubule 8 hairlike 11 blood vessel

capital 4 main 5 basic, chief, funds, major, prime 6 assets, lethal, wealth 8 cardinal 9 essential, excellent, financing, first-rate, principal, resources 10 first-class, investment, preeminent, underlying 11 fundamental, outstanding, predominant, wherewithal *Afghanistan:* 5 Kabul *Albania:* 6 Tirana, Tiranë *Alberta:* 8 Edmonton *Algeria:* 7 Algiers *Angola:* 6 Luanda *Antigua and Barbuda:* 7 St. John's 10 Saint John's *Argentina:* 11 Buenos Aires *Armenia:* 7 Yerevan *Assam:* 6 Dispur *Australia:* 8 Canberra *Austria:* 4 Wien 6 Vienna *Azerbaijan:* 4 Baku *Bahamas:* 6 Nassau *Bahrain:* 6 Manama *Bangladesh:* 5 Dacca, Dhaka *Barbados:* 10 Bridgetown *Belarus:* 5 Minsk *Belgium:* 8 Brussels *Belize:* 8 Belmopan *Benin:* 9 Porto-Novo *Bhutan:* 7 Thimphu *Bolivia:* 5 La Paz, Sucre *Bosnia and Herzegovina:* 8 Sarajevo *Botswana:* 8 Gaborone *Brazil:* 8 Brasília *Bulgaria:* 5 Sofia *Burkina Faso:* 11 Ouagadougou *Burma:* 6 Yangon 7 Rangoon *Burundi:* 9 Bujumbura *Cambodia:* 9 Phnom Penh *Cameroon:* 7 Yaoundé *Canada:* 6 Ottawa *Cape Verde:* 5 Praia

Central African Republic: 6 Bangui *Chad:* 8 N'Djamena *Chile:* 8 Santiago *China:* 6 Peking 7 Beijing *Colombia:* 6 Bogotá *Comoros:* 6 Moroni *Congo (Zaire):* 8 Kinshasa *Costa Rica:* 7 San José *Côte d'Ivoire:* 7 Abidjan 12 Yamoussoukro *Croatia:* 6 Zagreb *Cuba:* 6 Havana *Cyprus:* 7 Nicosia *Czech Republic:* 6 Prague *Denmark:* 10 Copenhagen *Dominica:* 6 Roseau *Dominican Republic:* 12 Santo Domingo *East Timor:* 4 Dili *Ecuador:* 5 Quito *Egypt:* 5 Cairo *El Salvador:* 11 San Salvador *Equatorial Guinea:* 6 Malabo *Eritrea:* 6 Asmara *Estonia:* 7 Tallinn *Ethiopia:* 10 Addis Ababa *Faeroe Islands:* 8 Tórshavn *Falkland Islands:* 7 Stanley *Fiji:* 4 Suva *Finland:* 8 Helsinki *France:* 5 Paris *French Guiana:* 7 Cayenne *Gabon:* 10 Libreville *Galápagos Islands:* 12 San Cristóbal *Gambia:* 6 Banjul *Georgia, Republic of:* 6 Tiflis 7 Tbilisi *Germany:* 6 Berlin *Ghana:* 5 Accra *Greece:* 6 Athens *Greenland:* 8 Godthaab *Grenada:* 9 St. George's 12 Saint George's *Guam:* 5 Agana *Guinea:* 7 Conakry *Guyana:* 10 Georgetown *Haiti:* 12 Port-au-Prince *Honduras:* 11 Tegucigalpa *Hungary:* 8 Budapest *Iceland:* 9 Reykjavík *India:* 8 New Delhi *Indonesia:* 7 Jakarta 8 Djakarta *Iran:* 6 Tehran 7 Teheran *Iraq:* 7 Baghdad *Ireland:* 4 Tara 6 Dublin *Israel:* 7 Tel-Aviv 9 Jerusalem *Italy:* 4 Rome *Jamaica:* 8 Kingston *Japan:* 5 Tokyo *Jordan:* 5 Amman *Kazakhstan:* 6 Astana 7 Alma-Ata *Kenya:* 7 Nairobi *Kiribati:* 6 Tarawa 11 South Tarawa *Korea, North:* 9 Pyongyang *Korea, South:* 5 Seoul *Kuwait:* 10 Kuwait City *Kyrgyzstan:* 7 Bishkek *Laos:* 9 Vientiane *Latvia:* 4 Riga *Lebanon:* 6 Beirut *Lesotho:* 6 Maseru *Libya:* 7 Tripoli *Liechtenstein:* 5 Vaduz *Lithuania:* 7 Vilnius *Macedonia:* 6 Skopje *Madagascar:* 12 Antananarivo *Malawi:* 8 Lilongwe *Malaysia:* 11 Kuala Lumpur *Maldives:* 4 Male *Mali:* 6 Bamako *Malta:* 8 Valletta *Manitoba:* 8 Winnipeg *Marshall Islands:* 6 Majuro *Mauritania:* 10 Nouakchott *Mauritius:* 9 Port Louis *Micronesia:* 7 Palikir *Moldova:* 8 Chişinău, Kishinev *Mongolia:* 9 Ulan Bator 11 Ulaanbaatar *Montenegro:* 7 Cetinje 9 Podgorica *Montserrat:* 8 Plymouth *Morocco:* 5 Rabat *Mozambique:* 6 Maputo *Myanmar:* 6 Yangon 7 Rangoon *Namibia:* 8 Windhoek *Nauru:* 5 Yaren *Nepal:* 8 Katmandu 9 Kathmandu *Netherlands:* 9 Amsterdam *Newfoundland:* 10 Saint Johns *New Zealand:* 10 Wellington *Nicaragua:* 7 Managua *Niger:* 6 Niamey *Nigeria:* 5 Abuja *Northern Ireland:* 7 Belfast

Northern Territory: 6 Darwin *North-West Frontier Province:* 8 Peshawar *Northwest Territories:* 11 Yellowknife *Norway:* 4 Oslo *Nova Scotia:* 7 Halifax *Oman:* 6 Muscat *Pakistan:* 9 Islamabad *Palau:* 5 Koror 10 Babelthuap *Papua New Guinea:* 11 Port Moresby *Paraguay:* 8 Asunción *Peru:* 4 Lima *Philippines:* 6 Manila *Poland:* 6 Warsaw *Portugal:* 6 Lisbon *Prince Edward Island:* 13 Charlottetown *Puerto Rico:* 7 San Juan *Qatar:* 4 Doha *Queensland:* 8 Brisbane *Réunion:* 7 St. Denis 10 Saint Denis *Romania:* 9 Bucharest *Russia:* 6 Moscow *Rwanda:* 6 Kigali *Saint Helena:* 9 Jamestown *Saint Kitts and Nevis:* 10 Basseterre *Saint Lucia:* 8 Castries *Samoa:* 4 Apia *Saskatchewan:* 6 Regina *Saudi Arabia:* 6 Riyadh *Scotland:* 9 Edinburgh *Senegal:* 5 Dakar *Serbia:* 8 Belgrade *Seychelles:* 8 Victoria *Shetland:* 7 Lerwick *Sicily:* 7 Palermo *Sierra Leone:* 8 Freetown *Sikkim:* 7 Gangtok *Sind:* 7 Karachi *Slovakia:* 10 Bratislava *Slovenia:* 9 Ljubljana *Solomon Islands:* 7 Honiara *Somalia:* 9 Mogadishu *South Africa:* 8 Cape Town, Pretoria 12 Bloemfontein *South Australia:* 8 Adelaide *South-West Africa:* 8 Windhoek *Spain:* 6 Madrid *Sri Lanka:* 7 Colombo *Sudan:* 8 Khartoum *Suriname:* 10 Paramaribo *Swaziland:* 7 Mbabane *Sweden:* 9 Stockholm *Switzerland:* 4 Bern 5 Berne *Syria:* 8 Damascus *Tahiti:* 7 Papeete *Taiwan:* 6 Taipei *Tajikistan:* 8 Dushanbe *Tanzania:* 6 Dodoma 11 Dar es Salaam *Tasmania:* 6 Hobart *Thailand:* 7 Bangkok *Tibet:* 5 Lhasa *Tirol:* 9 Innsbruck *Togo:* 4 Lomé *Tonga:* 9 Nuku'alofa *Trinidad and Tobago:* 11 Port-of-Spain *Tunisia:* 5 Tunis *Turkey:* 6 Ankara *Turkmenistan:* 8 Ashgabat 9 Ashkhabad *Tuvalu:* 8 Funafuti *Uganda:* 7 Kampala *Ukraine:* 4 Kiev *United Arab Emirates:* 8 Abu Dhabi *United Kingdom:* 6 London *Uruguay:* 10 Montevideo *Uttar Pradesh:* 7 Lucknow *Uzbekistan:* 8 Tashkent *Vanuatu:* 4 Vila *Venezuela:* 7 Caracas *Victoria:* 9 Melbourne *Vietnam:* 5 Hanoi *Wales:* 7 Cardiff *Western Australia:* 5 Perth *Yemen:* 4 Sana 5 Sanaa *Yugoslavia:* 8 Belgrade *Yukon:* 10 Whitehorse *Zambia:* 6 Lusaka *Zimbabwe:* 6 Harare

capitalist 6 backer, tycoon 7 magnate 8 investor 9 bourgeois, financier, plutocrat 12 entrepreneur

capitalistic 9 bourgeois

capitalize 4 back, fund 5 stake 6 profit 7 convert, finance, promote, sponsor, support 8 bankroll 9 grubstake, subsidize

capital sin see **deadly sin**

capitation 3 tax 7 payment, poll tax

Capitol Hill sound 3 aye, nay

capitulate 3 bow 4 cave 5 defer, yield 6 cave in, give in, give up, relent, submit 7 concede, succumb 9 acquiesce, surrender 12 knuckle under

capitulation 9 surrender 10 submission

capo 3 bar 4 boss, head 5 chief 9 godfather

capote 4 cope 5 cloak 6 mantle, tabard 7 manteau, pelisse 8 overcoat

Capote work 11 In Cold Blood 19 Breakfast at Tiffany's

capper 4 lure 5 blind, decoy, shill 6 climax, finale 8 clincher

capriccio 4 whim 5 caper, fancy, prank 6 notion, vagary, whimsy 7 impulse

caprice 3 bee 4 mood, vein, whim 5 fancy, freak, humor 6 foible, maggot, megrim, notion, vagary, whimsy 7 conceit 8 crotchet

capricious 4 iffy 5 flaky, moody 6 chancy, fickle 7 erratic, flighty, wayward 8 fanciful, unstable, variable, volatile 9 arbitrary, impulsive, mercurial, uncertain, whimsical 10 changeable, inconstant 12 effervescent, incalculable 13 temperamental, unpredictable

caprid 4 goat

capriole 4 leap 5 caper

capsize 4 keel, roll, sink 5 upset 7 founder, tip over 8 collapse, overturn, turn over

capstone 4 acme, apex, peak 6 apogee, climax, coping, summit, zenith 8 pinnacle 9 high point 11 culmination

capsule 6 canned, pocket, potted 7 compact, outline 9 condensed

capsulize 6 reduce 7 enclose 8 compress, condense 9 summarize, synopsize

captain 6 master 7 skipper *fictional:* 4 Ahab, Hook, Kirk, Nemo 5 Queeg 10 Hornblower *historical:* 4 Cook (James) 5 Bligh (William) *pirate:* 4 Kidd (William) 6 Morgan (Henry)

Captains Courageous author 7 Kipling (Rudyard)

caption 5 title 6 legend, rubric 7 cutline, heading 8 subtitle 9 underline

captious 5 testy 7 carping, peevish 8 caviling, contrary, critical, exacting, petulant, snappish 9 demanding, irritable 10 censorious, nit-picking 12 faultfinding, overcritical 13 hypercritical

captivate 4 draw, grip, hold, take 5 charm 6 allure, dazzle, enamor, please, ravish, seduce 7 attract, beguile, bewitch, delight, enamour, enchant, gratify 8 enthrall 9 enrapture, fascinate, hypnotize, infatuate, magnetize, mesmerize, spellbind

captivating 8 charming, enticing, fetching, magnetic, riveting **9** appealing, glamorous, seductive **10** bewitching, engrossing, intriguing **11** enthralling, fascinating

captive 5 bound, caged, taken **6** jailed **7** hostage **8** confined, detainee, internee, prisoner **10** enthralled, hypnotized, imprisoned

captivity 7 bondage, custody, slavery **9** detention **10** internment **11** confinement **12** imprisonment

capture 3 bag, get, nab, net, win **4** nail, take, trap **5** catch, lasso, prize, seize, snare **6** arrest, collar, entrap, occupy, secure **7** conquer, ensnare **8** preserve

Capuan 4 lush **5** plush **6** deluxe **7** opulent **8** luscious, palatial **9** luxuriant, luxurious, sumptuous **11** upholstered

car 4 auto, heap **5** buggy, coach, crate, sedan, wreck **6** beater, jalopy, junker, wheels **7** clunker, flivver **8** roadster **10** automobile, rattletrap, rust bucket *city:* **4** Aygo, Lupo **5** Matiz, Panda, Prime **6** Twingo **7** Picanto (see also **automobile**)

carafe 4 ewer **5** cruet **6** bottle, flacon, flagon **8** decanter

caravan 6 convoy, safari

caravansary 3 inn **4** khan **5** hotel, lodge, serai **6** hostel, tavern **10** campground

carbohydrate 5 sugar **6** starch **7** amylose, glucose, lactose, maltose, sucrose **8** fructose, glycogen **9** cellulose, galactose

carbolic acid 6 phenol

carbon 4 coal, coke, soot **8** charcoal, graphite, plumbago **9** lampblack

carbonate 6 aerate

carbon copy 4 dupe, twin **5** clone, ditto, mimeo, repro, Xerox **7** replica **8** knockoff **9** duplicate, facsimile **10** dead ringer **11** replication **12** reproduction

carbonize 4 burn, char, sear **5** singe, toast **6** scorch

carbuncle 4 boil, sore **5** ulcer **6** garnet, pimple **7** abscess, pustule **8** cabochon

carcass 4 body, hulk, mort **5** frame, shell, stiff **6** corpse **7** cadaver, remains **8** skeleton

carcinoid 5 tumor **8** neoplasm

carcinoma 5 tumor **6** cancer **8** neoplasm

card 3 wag, wit **4** menu, sked **5** joker **6** agenda, docket **7** program **8** calendar, comedian, humorist, schedule **9** timetable *fortune-telling:* **5** tarot *game:* **3** gin, loo, Uno, war **4** faro, fish, skat, solo, stud **5** monte, ombre, pitch, poker, rummy, whist **6** Boston, bridge, casino, écarté, euchre, fan-tan, hearts, piquet **7** auction, bezique, canasta, cooncan, old maid, primero **8** baccarat, Canfield, conquian, cribbage, gin rummy,

pinochle **9** blackjack, solitaire, twenty-one, vingt-et-un **11** chemin de fer *game authority:* **5** Hoyle (Edmond) *high:* **3** ace *low:* **5** deuce *performer's:* **3** cue *spot:* **3** pip *wild:* **5** deuce, joker

cardboard 5 stiff **6** unreal, wooden **7** bristol, buckram, stilted **8** lifeless **10** unlifelike **11** stereotyped, unrealistic

card-carrying 4 true **7** genuine **8** bona fide **9** authentic, certified **11** full-fledged

cardiac stimulant 7 ouabain **9** digitalis

cardinal 3 key **4** main **5** basic, chief, prime, vital **6** ruling **7** central, leading, pivotal, primary **9** essential, important, principal **10** overriding, overruling **11** fundamental **12** constitutive *point:* **4** east, west **5** north, south *suffix:* **4** teen *title:* **8** Eminence *virtue:* **7** justice **8** prudence **9** fortitude **10** temperance

care 4 fear, heed, mind, tend, ward **5** alarm, nurse, serve, trust, worry **6** attend, charge, effort, regard, regret, strain, stress, unease, wait on **7** anguish, anxiety, concern, custody, keeping **8** disquiet, handling **9** attention, curiosity, misgiving, oversight **10** management, solicitude **11** maintenance, safekeeping, supervision **12** guardianship **13** consideration

careen 4 race, sway, tilt **5** lurch, pitch, speed, swing, weave **6** repair, wobble **7** stagger

career 3 job **4** race, rush, tear, work **5** chase, speed **6** charge, course **7** calling, passage **8** lifework, vocation **9** encounter **10** livelihood, profession

care for 4 like, love, mind, tend **5** nurse, treat **6** attend, foster **7** cherish, nurture **8** preserve **9** cultivate, look after

carefree 4 wild **6** blithe, breezy, jaunty **8** reckless **10** insouciant, untroubled **12** happy-go-lucky, lighthearted **13** irresponsible

careful 4 safe, wary **5** chary, exact, fussy **7** dutiful, guarded, precise, prudent, studied **8** accurate, cautious, critical, discreet, gingerly, thorough **9** attentive, provident **10** deliberate, meticulous, particular, scrupulous **11** calculating, circumspect, considerate, foresighted, painstaking, punctilious **13** conscientious

carefully 6 warily **8** gingerly **10** cautiously, discreetly **12** meticulously, scrupulously **13** painstakingly, punctiliously

careless 3 lax **5** hasty, messy, slack **6** casual, remiss, sloppy, untidy **7** cursory, offhand, unkempt **8** feckless, heedless, reckless, slapdash, slipshod, slovenly **9** forgetful, negligent, oblivious, unheeding, unmindful, unstudied **10** disheveled, inaccurate, incautious, neglectful, unthinking, untroubled **11** inadvertent, inattentive, indifferent, perfunctory, spontaneous, thoughtless, unconcerned **12** uninterested, unreflective **13** irresponsible

caress 3 pat, pet, toy **4** kiss, love **5** dally, touch **6** coddle, cosset, cuddle, dandle, fondle, nuzzle, pamper, stroke **7** cherish, indulge **8** canoodle **10** endearment

caressive 7 calming **8** soothing

caretaker 6 warden **7** curator, janitor **9** custodian

careworn 3 wan **5** drawn, faded, jaded **7** haggard, pinched, wearied **8** fatigued, troubled **9** exhausted **10** distressed

cargo 4 haul, load **6** burden, lading **7** freight, payload **8** shipload, shipment **11** consignment

Caribbean country 4 Cuba **5** Haiti **7** Bahamas, Grenada, Jamaica **8** Dominica **10** Saint Lucia

caribe 7 piranha

caribou 4 deer **8** reindeer *kin:* **3** elk **6** wapiti

caricature 4 mock, sham **5** farce, phony **6** parody **7** cartoon, lampoon, mockery, take-off **8** travesty **9** burlesque **10** distortion, pasquinade **12** exaggeration

Carlsbad feature 4 cave **6** cavern

Carmen *author:* **7** Mérimée (Prosper) *composer:* **5** Bizet (Georges) *lover:* **7** Don José **9** Escamillo

carnage 4 gore **8** butchery, hecatomb, massacre **9** bloodbath, bloodshed, slaughter

carnal 4 lewd **6** animal, bodily, coarse, earthy, sexual, vulgar, wanton **7** earthly, fleshly, lustful, mundane, obscene, sensual, worldly **8** corporal, material, physical, sensuous, temporal **9** corporeal **10** lascivious

carnation 4 pink **5** color **6** flower

carnival 4 fair, fete **6** fiesta *attraction:* **4** ride **6** midway **8** sideshow **10** concession *character:* **5** shill **6** barker, hawker **7** grifter, spieler *game:* **8** Skee-Ball *New Orleans:* **9** Mardi Gras *performer:* **4** geek

carnivore 9 meat-eater **10** flesh-eater

carol 4 song **6** ballad *Christmas:* **4** noel

carom 6 bounce, glance **7** rebound **8** ricochet

Caron role 4 Gigi, Lili **5** Fanny

carotid's relative 5 aorta

carousal 3 bat, jag **4** bash, tear **5** binge, booze, drunk, fling, revel, spree **6** bender, frolic **7** blowout, debauch, shindig **8** wingding **9** brannigan *Scottish:* **6** splore

carouse 4 revel **6** cavort, frolic **7** roister *Scottish:* **4** birl

carp 3 nag **4** crab, fuss **5** bream, cavil, scold

6 peck at, pester **7** henpeck **8** complain, cyprinid, sea bream **9** complaint, criticize, find fault

carpe ____ **4** diem

carpenter 3 ant, bee **6** joiner, wright **7** builder, workman **10** woodworker

carpentry 7 joinery **10** timberwork *tool:* **3** saw **5** drill, plane **6** chisel, hammer **11** brace and bit, screwdriver

carper 6 critic, nagger **7** caviler, knocker **9** nitpicker **10** complainer, criticizer **11** faultfinder

carpet 3 mat, rug **4** Agra **5** Herat, Heriz, Koula, Ladik, Sarok, tapis **6** Herati, Kerman, Keshan, Kirman, Sarouk, Tabriz, Wilton **8** moquette **9** Axminster, broadloom

carpet beetle 10 buffalo bug

carping 7 blaming, railing **8** captious, critical **10** censorious **11** reproachful **12** faultfinding, overcritical

carrageen 7 seaweed **9** Irish moss

carrefour 5 plaza **6** square **10** crossroads

carriage 3 gig, rig **4** pose **5** coach **6** stance **7** posture, transit **8** attitude **9** transport **10** conveyance, deportment *American:* **5** buggy **8** rockaway **9** buckboard *attendant:* **6** flunky **7** footman *baby:* **4** pram **5** buggy **8** stroller **12** perambulator *driver:* **4** hack **5** cabby **8** coachman *folding top:* **6** calash *four-wheeled:* **4** trap **5** buggy, coupe **6** berlin, calash, fiacre, landau, surrey **7** droshky, hackney, phaeton **8** barouche, brougham, carryall, clarence, rockaway, sociable, stanhope, victoria **9** buckboard *Indian:* **6** gharry *man-drawn:* **8** rickshaw **10** jinricksha, jinrikisha *Russian:* **6** troika **7** droshky *stately:* **7** caroche *three-horse:* **6** troika *two-wheeled:* **3** gig **4** shay, trap **5** buggy, sulky, tonga **6** chaise, dennet, hansom **7** calèche, dogcart, tilbury **8** curricle **9** cabriolet *with attendants:* **8** equipage

carriage trade 5 elite **6** gentry **7** quality **9** blue blood, gentility **10** upper class, upper crust **11** aristocracy

carrick bend 4 knot

carrier 4 mule **5** envoy **6** bearer, porter, runner, vector **7** airline, courier, shipper, vehicle **8** conveyor, emissary **9** go-between, messenger, stretcher **11** internuncio, transporter

Carroll character 5 Alice, Bruno, snark **6** boojum, Sylvie **8** Dormouse, Red Queen **9** Mad Hatter, March Hare **10** Mock Turtle **11** White Rabbit **12** Humpty Dumpty

carrot 5 prize **6** reward **9** incentive **10** inducement

carry 3 get, lug **4** bear, haul, have, hump,

keep, move, pack, send, take, tote, wear **5** bring, ferry, fetch, range, stock **6** affect, bear up, convey, uphold **7** comport, conduct, portage, possess, support, sustain **8** buttress, transfer, transmit **9** influence, transport

carryall 4 tote **7** tote bag

carrying case 7 holdall, satchel

carry off 4 kill **6** abduct, kidnap, remove **7** achieve, destroy, execute, perform, realize **8** complete, conclude, dispatch, shanghai **10** accomplish, spirit away

carry on 3 run **4** go on, keep, rant, rave, wage **6** direct, endure, manage, ordain **7** conduct, operate, persist, prattle, proceed **8** continue, sound off **9** persevere

carry out 6 effect, govern, render **7** achieve, execute, fulfill, oversee, perform, realize **8** bring off, complete, finalize, transact **9** discharge, prosecute **10** accomplish, administer, effectuate **12** administrate

carry over 6 deduct **7** persist **8** postpone, transfer

carry through 4 last **5** abide **6** effect, endure **7** execute, perdure, perform, persist, survive **8** bring off, complete, continue **10** accomplish, effectuate

Carson work 11 Sea Around Us (The) **12** Silent Spring

cart 3 gig **4** dray, haul **5** buggy, carry **6** barrow, convey, schlep **7** schlepp, trundle, tumbrel, tumbril **8** carriage **9** transport **11** wheelbarrow *Indian:* **5** tonga *racing:* **5** sulky

____ carte **3** à la

____ Carte **5** D'Oyly

carte blanche 3 say **5** power, right, say-so **7** freedom, license **8** free hand, free rein **9** authority **10** blank check **11** prerogative

carte du jour 4 menu

cartel 4 bloc, OPEC, pool **5** trust **7** combine **9** syndicate **10** consortium **12** conglomerate

Carthaginian *goddess of the moon:* 5 Tanit **6** Tanith *queen:* **4** Dido **6** Elissa

cartilage 7 gristle

cartographer *English:* 5 Smith (William) *Flemish:* **6** Kremer (Gerhard) **8** Mercator (Gerardus), Ortelius *German:* **13** Waldseemüller (Martin) *Greek:* **7** Ptolemy *Italian:* **8** Vespucci (Amerigo)

cartography 9 mapmaking

carton 3 box **4** pack

cartoon 5 anime, manga **10** comic strip (see also **comic strip**)

cartoonist 3 Lee (Stan) **4** Arno (Peter), Auth (Tony), Capp (Al), Kane (Bob), Nast (Thomas), Szep (Paul) **5** Adams (Scott),

Block (Herbert), Booth (George), Chast (Roz), Crumb (R.), Davis (Jim), Gould (Chester), Hanna (Bill), Jones (Chuck), Kelly (Walt), Steig (William), Toles (Tom), Young (Chic) **6** Addams (Charles), Caniff (Milton), Conrad (Paul), Disney (Walt), Larson (Gary), Martin (Don), Peters (Mike), Schulz (Charles), Walker (Mort) **7** Barbera (Joe), Feiffer (Jules), Ketcham (Hank), Mauldin (Bill), Thurber (James), Trudeau (Garry) **8** Goldberg (Rube), Groening (Matt), Herblock, Hokinson (Helen), MacNelly (Jeff), Oliphant (Pat) **9** Fleischer (Max) **10** Hirschfeld (Al)

cartouche 5 frame **6** shield **9** cartridge

cartridge 4 case, tube **5** shell **8** cassette, cylinder **9** cartouche, container

cartwheel 4 coin **6** dollar, tumble **10** handspring

carve 3 cut, hew **4** chip, etch, form, hack **5** shape, slice **6** chisel, cleave, incise, sculpt **7** dissect, engrave, whittle **9** sculpture

Casablanca *actor:* 5 Lorre (Peter), Rains (Claude) **6** Bogart (Humphrey) **7** Bergman (Ingrid), Henreid (Paul) **11** Greenstreet (Sydney) *character:* **4** Ilsa (Lund), Rick (Blaine) **6** Laszlo (Victor) *director:* **6** Curtiz (Michael)

Casanova 4 rake, roué, wolf **5** Romeo **6** lecher, masher, tomcat **7** amorist, Don Juan, gallant, playboy, seducer **8** lothario, paramour **9** adulterer, ladies' man, libertine, womanizer **10** lady-killer, voluptuary **11** philanderer

cascade 4 fall, gush, lace, pour, spew **5** chute, falls, flood, spill **6** deluge, plunge, rapids, shower, tumble **7** Niagara, torrent **8** cataract **9** avalanche, waterfall **10** outpouring

Cascade Mountains peak 6 Lassen, Shasta **7** Rainier

case 3 box, con, vet **4** etui, hull, husk, skin, suit **5** cause, event, shell, trunk **6** action, sample, sheath **7** episode, examine, example, inspect, lawsuit **8** argument, covering, incident, instance, sampling, specimen **9** check over, condition, situation **10** occurrence, proceeding, scrutinize **11** eventuality **12** circumstance *grammatical:* **6** dative **8** ablative, genitive, vocative **9** objective **10** accusative, nominative, possessive

casebearer 5 larva **11** caterpillar

case-hardened 5 tough **7** callous **8** obdurate **9** indurated, insensate, toughened, unfeeling **11** insensitive **12** thick-skinned

casement 4 sash **6** window

Casey at the Bat poet 6 Thayer (Ernest Lawrence)

cash 4 coin, jack 5 bread, dough, money, scrip 6 dinero, redeem, wampum 7 cabbage, lettuce, scratch 8 currency 10 greenbacks, ready money 11 legal tender *machine:* 3 ATM

cashier 2 ax 3 axe, can 4 boot, fire, oust, sack 5 clerk, eject, expel, scrap 6 banker, bounce, bursar, reject, teller 7 boot out, discard, dismiss, kick out 8 jettison, throw out 9 discharge, eliminate, terminate, throw away 10 bookkeeper 11 bean counter, comptroller

cash in 3 die 4 conk, drop 5 croak 6 expire, pop off, redeem, retire 7 kick off, succumb 8 check out, drop dead, pass away, settle up 9 liquidate

casing 4 hull, husk, pipe, rind, skin, tire 5 frame, shell, space 7 wrapper 8 membrane

casino *attendant:* 6 dealer 8 croupier *game:* 4 faro 5 craps, monte, poker 6 tierce 8 baccarat, roulette 9 blackjack

cask 3 keg, tun 4 butt, drum, pipe 6 barrel, firkin 8 hogshead

casket 3 box 5 chest 6 coffer, coffin 8 jewel box

Caspian Sea *city:* 4 Baku *feeder:* 4 Kura, Ural 5 Volga

Cassandra 4 seer 7 prophet, seeress 8 doomster 9 doomsayer, pessimist, worrywart 10 prophetess *brother:* 7 Helenus *father:* 5 Priam *lover:* 9 Agamemnon *mother:* 6 Hecuba *slayer:* 12 Clytemnestra

cassava 4 yuca 5 yucca 6 manioc 7 tapioca

casserole 4 dish 5 crock 6 tureen

Cassiopeia 13 constellation *daughter:* 9 Andromeda *husband:* 7 Cepheus

Cassio's mistress 6 Bianca

cassock 4 robe 7 soutane 8 vestment

cassowary kin 3 emu, moa

cast 3 add, hue, sum, tot 4 drop, face, fire, form, hurl, kind, look, mold, shed, sort, tint, tone, toss, turn, type 5 color, fling, heave, leave, pitch, range, shade, shape, strew, throw, tinge, total, touch 6 actors, design, devise, direct, figure, nature, reject, slough, troupe, visage 7 arrange, company, quality, replica, scatter 8 abdicate, disperse, jettison, sprinkle 9 character, prognosis, throw away 10 appearance, conjecture, distribute, expression, prediction, strabismus, suggestion 11 countenance *a spell on:* 3 hex 5 charm 7 beguile, bewitch 8 enthrall 9 captivate, enrapture, fascinate, hypnotize, infatuate, mesmerize, spellbind *overboard:* 7 deep-six 8 jettison

cast about 4 hunt, seek 5 grope 6 search 7 seek out 8 contrive 9 search for, search out

castaway 5 leper, tramp 6 beggar, maroon, pariah 7 Ishmael, outcast, vagrant 8 deadbeat, derelict 10 Ishmaelite

cast down see **downcast**

caste 5 class 6 degree, estate, status 7 station 8 division, prestige

cast head 4 bust

castigate 4 beat, flay, rail, whip 5 baste, chide, scold, slash 6 berate, pummel, punish, rebuke, scorch, thrash 7 belabor, blister, chasten, chew out, lambast, reprove, scarify, scourge, upbraid 8 chastise, lambaste, penalize 9 criticize, dress down, excoriate, reprimand 10 discipline, tongue-lash

castigation 3 rod 6 rebuke 7 reproof 8 punition, scolding 10 correction, discipline, punishment 12 chastisement

castle 5 manor, villa 7 alcazar, château, citadel, mansion 8 fortress 10 stronghold *adjunct:* 4 moat *gate:* 10 portcullis *ledge:* 7 rampart *structure:* 6 turret *tower:* 4 keep 6 donjon *wall:* 6 bailey 10 battlement

cast off 5 fling, flung, let go, loose, untie 6 jilted, untied 7 unhitch 8 cut loose, forsaken, rejected, unfasten, unmoored 9 discarded, unhitched 10 left behind, unfastened

Castor *brother:* 6 Pollux 10 Polydeuces *constellation:* 6 Gemini *father:* 4 Zeus 9 Tyndareus *mother:* 4 Leda *sister:* 5 Helen *slayer:* 4 Idas

castor oil 8 laxative 9 cathartic, lubricant, purgative

cast out 4 oust 5 egest, eject, evict, exile, expel 6 banish, deport 7 discard 9 eliminate, ostracize

castrate 3 fix 4 geld, spay 5 alter, unman, unsex 6 neuter 7 unnerve 8 enervate, mutilate 9 sterilize 10 emasculate 11 desexualize

castrato singer 9 Farinelli

casual 5 light, minor 6 breezy, chance, random, remote 7 natural, offhand, relaxed, trivial, unfussy 8 detached, informal, laidback 9 easygoing, impromptu, irregular, uncurious, unplanned, unserious 10 accidental, contingent, fortuitous, improvised, incidental, insouciant, nonchalant, occasional 11 indifferent, low-pressure, spontaneous, unconcerned, unimportant 12 uninterested 13 disinterested, insignificant

casualty 4 prey 5 death 6 mishap, victim 8 accident, calamity, disaster, fatality 9 mischance 10 misfortune 11 catastrophe 12 misadventure

casuistry 7 sophism 9 deception, sophistry

12 equivocation, speciousness **13** deceptiveness

casus ___ **5** belli

cat 4 eyra, lion, lynx, pard, puma, puss **5** felid, kitty, liger, moggy, ounce, pussy, tabby, tiger, tigon **6** cougar, feline, jaguar, margay, mouser, ocelot, serval **7** caracal, cheetah, leopard, panther **10** jaguarundi **12** mountain lion *Alice's:* **5** Dinah *Born Free:* **4** Elsa *combining form:* **5** ailur **6** ailuro *disease:* **9** distemper *domestic:* **3** Mau, Rex **4** Manx **5** tabby **6** Angora, Birman, calico, exotic, Ocicat, Somali **7** bobtail, Burmese, Persian, Ragdoll, Siamese **8** longhair, Wirehair **9** Himalayan, Maine coon, shorthair, Tonkinese **10** Abyssinian *extinct:* **10** saber-tooth *fastest:* **7** cheetah *female:* **5** queen **7** lioness, tigress **9** grimalkin *genus:* **5** Felis *grinning:* **8** Cheshire *hybrid:* **5** liger, tigon **6** Bengal, Safari **7** Chausie **8** Savannah *lookalike:* **5** civet, genet **7** linsang *male:* **3** gib, tom *relating to:* **6** feline *sound:* **3** mew **4** hiss, meow, purr, roar **5** miaou, miaow **9** caterwaul *tailless:* **4** Manx *young:* **6** kitten

cataclysm 5 flood **6** deluge **7** Niagara, torrent, tragedy **8** calamity, cataract, disaster, flooding **10** inundation **11** catastrophe, devastation

cataclysmic 5 fatal **7** ruinous **10** calamitous, disastrous **11** devastating **12** catastrophic

catacomb 5 crypt, vault **8** cemetery **10** necropolis, undercroft

catafalque 4 bier

catalepsy 6 trance

catalog 4 list, roll **5** enter, index, tally **6** enroll, roster **7** itemize, program **8** classify, inscribe, register, roll call, schedule, syllabus **9** enumerate, inventory **10** prospectus *of books:* **11** bibliotheca *of saints:* **9** hagiology

catalyst 4 goad, spur **7** impetus, impulse **8** stimulus **9** incentive, stimulant **10** incitation, incitement, motivation

catamaran 4 boat, raft

catamount 4 lynx, puma **6** bobcat, cougar **7** panther, wildcat **12** mountain lion

cataract 5 falls, flood, rapid **6** deluge, rapids **7** cascade, Niagara, torrent **8** downpour **9** waterfall **10** inundation

catastrophe 3 woe **4** deluge, fiasco **7** debacle, tragedy **8** calamity, disaster, meltdown **9** cataclysm, emergency **11** devastation

catastrophic 5 fatal **6** deadly, tragic **7** ruinous **10** calamitous, disastrous **11** cataclysmic

Catawba 4 wine **5** river **6** Indian

catcall 3 boo **4** hiss, hoot, jeer, razz **9** criticism, raspberry **10** Bronx cheer

catch 3 bag, get, nab, net, see, wed **4** dupe, find, fool, grab, grip, gull, haul, hoax, hook, nail, snag, sock, spot, take, trap **5** block, clasp, clout, grasp, hit on, marry, reach, round, seize, smite, snare, stick, stump, trick, watch, whack **6** accept, anchor, arrest, clutch, collar, cut off, descry, detect, engage, entrap, fasten, flurry, follow, put out, rattle, secure, snatch, strike, take in, tangle, turn up **7** capture, confuse, deceive, disturb, ensnare, grapple, hit upon, perplex, receive **8** confound, contract, entangle, flimflam, fragment, hoodwink, kick over, meet with, overhaul, overtake **9** apprehend, bamboozle, embarrass, encounter, intercept **10** comprehend, understand **12** come down with

Catch-22 author 6 Heller (Joseph)

catchall term 3 etc. **4** et al. **5** and/or **7** and so on **10** and so forth

Catcher in the Rye *author:* **8** Salinger (J. D.) *character:* **9** Caulfield (Holden)

catcher's glove 4 mitt

catching 10 contagious, infectious **12** communicable

catch on 3 see **4** hear **5** learn **7** find out **8** discover **9** ascertain, determine, figure out

catchphrase see **catchword**

catch up 4 hold **6** gain on **7** close in, ensnare **8** entangle, enthrall **9** fascinate, mesmerize, spellbind

catchword 5 maxim, motto **6** slogan **10** shibboleth

catchy 6 fitful, spotty, tricky **7** erratic **8** sporadic **9** appealing, desultory, irregular, memorable, spasmodic

catechist 7 teacher

catechize 3 ask **4** quiz **5** grill, query, train **7** examine, inquire **8** instruct, question **9** inculcate **11** interrogate

catechumen 6 novice **7** convert, student, trainee **8** initiate, neophyte

categorical 7 certain, decided, express **8** absolute, clear-cut, definite, emphatic, explicit, positive **9** downright **10** definitive, forthright **11** unambiguous, unequivocal, unqualified

categorize 3 peg **4** sort **5** class, group **7** put down **8** classify, identify **10** pigeonhole

category 4 rank, tier **5** class, genre, grade, group, taxon **6** league **7** section **8** division, grouping **10** pigeonhole

catenation 4 link **5** chain **6** series, string **7** linkage **10** connection, succession

catercorner 9 obliquely, slantways, slantwise **10** cornerwise, diagonally caterpillar 5 larva 7 cutworm, webworm 8 armyworm, silkworm 10 casebearer

cater to 5 humor 6 pamper, supply 7 furnish, gratify, indulge

caterwaul 4 howl, meow, yowl 5 miaow 6 squall

catfish see **fish**

catharsis 5 purge, tonic 7 purging 8 curative 9 cleansing, purgation, purgative 10 lustration 11 expurgation, restorative 12 purification

cathartic 5 purge, tonic 8 curative 9 castor oil, purgative 11 restorative, therapeutic

Cathay 5 China

cathedral 5 duomo 6 church 8 basilica *feature:* 4 apse, nave 5 altar 6 chapel 7 chancel 10 clerestory 8 buttress, transept

cathedral city 3 Ely 4 Bath, York 5 Wells 6 Durham, Exeter, London, Oxford 7 Bristol, Chester, Lincoln, Norwich 8 Carlisle, Coventry, Hereford 9 Lichfield, Liverpool, Salisbury, Worcester 10 Canterbury, Chichester, Gloucester, Winchester 11 Westminster 12 Peterborough

Cather novel 8 Lost Lady (A) 9 My Antonia, One of Ours, O Pioneers 13 Song of the Lark 15 Professor's House (The) 16 Shadows on the Rock

catholic 5 broad 6 global 7 general, liberal 8 eclectic, tolerant 9 expansive, inclusive, undivided, universal, worldwide 10 ecumenical 12 cosmopolitan 13 comprehensive

catholicity 7 breadth 9 tolerance 10 liberality 11 magnanimity 12 universality

catholicon 6 elixir 7 cure-all, nostrum, panacea

catkin 5 ament

catlike 6 feline 7 furtive 8 stealthy

catnap 3 nap 4 doze 6 siesta, snooze 10 forty winks

catnip 3 nep

Cato *title:* 6 aedile, censor, consul 7 praetor, tribune 8 quaestor

cat's-paw 4 dupe, knot, pawn, tool 5 patsy 6 puppet, stooge

cattail 4 reed, rush

cattle 4 cows, kine, neat, oxen 7 bovines 9 livestock *breed:* 5 Angus, Devon, Kerry 6 Durham, Jersey, Sussex 7 Brahman, Hariana, Red Poll 8 Ayrshire, Galloway, Guernsey, Hereford, Highland, Holstein, Limousin, Longhorn 9 Charolais, Red Polled, Shorthorn, Simmental 10 Brown Swiss 11 Dutch Belted *catching rope:* 5 lasso 6 lariat *cry:* 3 low, moo *dehorn:* 4 poll *disease:* 4 loco 5 bloat 6 mad cow, nagana 7 anthrax, locoism, measles, murrain 8 blackleg, lumpy jaw, mastitis, staggers 10 rinderpest, Texas fever 11 brucellosis *dung:* 4 tath *extinct breed:* 9 Teeswater *family:* 7 Bovidae *feed:* 6 fodder, silage, stover *genus:* 3 Bos *goddess:* 6 Bubona *grazing land:* 5 range 6 meadow 7 pasture *group:* 4 herd 5 drove *herdsman:* 6 cowboy, drover, gaucho 7 vaquero 8 neatherd, wrangler 10 cowpuncher *identification:* 5 brand *pen:* 6 corral *round up:* 7 wrangle *stable:* 4 barn, byre *steal:* 6 rustle *wild flight:* 8 stampede

catty 4 mean 5 nasty 6 barbed, bitchy, feline 7 furtive, vicious 8 spiteful, stealthy 9 malicious 10 backbiting, malevolent

Caucasian *capital:* 4 Baku 6 Tiflis 7 Tbilisi, Yerevan *republic:* 7 Armenia, Georgia 10 Azerbaijan

Caucasus *peak:* 6 Elbrus *people:* 5 Osset

caucus 4 bloc, sect 5 cabal, lobby 6 parley, powwow 7 faction

caudal appendage 4 tail

caudillo 6 despot, tyrant 8 dictator 9 strongman

cauldron 3 pot 6 boiler, kettle 8 crucible

cause 4 case, make, root 5 evoke, hatch 6 compel, effect, elicit, induce, motive, origin, reason, source, spring 7 produce, provoke 8 engender, generate, movement 9 necessity, principle 10 antecedent, bring about, inducement, originator 11 determinant, precipitate 13 consideration

cause _____ 7 célèbre

causerie 4 chat 5 essay 6 column 7 article, feature 8 colloquy, dialogue 12 conversation

caustic 4 acid, keen, tart 5 acerb, acrid, sharp 6 biting, bitter, ironic 7 acerbic, cutting, mordant, pungent 8 scathing, stinging 9 corrosive, sarcastic, trenchant 10 astringent *solution:* 3 lye

cauterize 4 burn, numb, sear 6 deaden 11 anesthetize

caution 4 warn 6 caveat 7 warning 8 forewarn, monition, prudence 9 canniness, chariness, foresight, vigilance 10 admonition, discretion, providence 11 carefulness, forethought, forewarning 12 admonishment, discreetness

cautionary 7 warning 8 monitory 10 admonitory

cautious 4 wary 5 alert, cagey, canny, chary, leery 6 shrewd 7 careful, guarded, politic, prudent 8 discreet, gingerly, vigilant, watchful 9 judicious, provident 11 circumspect, considerate, foresighted

cavalcade 6 parade, series 7 cortege 8 sequence 10 procession, succession

cavalier 5 lofty, proud **6** casual, knight, lordly **7** gallant, haughty, offhand **8** arrogant, debonair, horseman, scornful, superior **9** caballero, gentleman **10** disdainful, dismissive, insouciant, nonchalant **12** aristocratic, supercilious

cavalryman 6 lancer **7** dragoon, trooper *Algerian:* **5** spahi *horse:* **5** waler *Prussian:* **5** uhlan *Russian:* **7** cossack *Turkish:* **5** spahi *weapon:* **5** lance, saber **7** carbine

cave 3 bow, den **4** bend, drop, give, grot, lair **5** antre, break, defer, yield **6** fold up, grotto, hollow, submit **7** crumple, knuckle, succumb **8** collapse **9** break down **10** capitulate, subterrane **11** buckle under **12** knuckle under, subterranean *dweller:* **3** bat **4** bear, lion **6** hermit **9** Cro-Magnon **10** troglodyte **11** Neanderthal *explorer:* **9** spelunker *formation:* **10** stalactite, stalagmite *France:* **7** Lascaux **10** Rouffignac *Iceland:* **7** Singing *Indiana:* **9** Wyandotte *Iraq:* **8** Shanidar *Kentucky:* **7** Mammoth *New Zealand:* **7** Waitomo *rock:* **8** dolomite **9** limestone *Scotland:* **7** Fingal's *South Africa:* **5** Cango *Spain:* **8** Altamira *study of:* **10** speleology

caveat 6 notice **7** caution, warning **8** monition **10** admonition **11** explanation, forewarning

caveat ____ **6** emptor

caveman 5 brute **6** savage **9** barbarian, Cro-Magnon **10** troglodyte

cavern 6 grotto **12** subterranean *Capri:* **10** Blue Grotto *Montana:* **13** Lewis and Clark *New Mexico:* **8** Carlsbad *Tennessee:* **10** Cumberland *Virginia:* **5** Luray

cavernous 4 vast **6** gaping, hollow **7** yawning

caviar 3 roe **4** eggs **6** relish *source:* **6** beluga **8** sturgeon

cavil 4 carp **7** nitpick, quibble **9** criticize, find fault

caviler 6 carper, critic **7** knocker **8** quibbler **10** criticizer **11** faultfinder

caviling 5 fussy **7** carping, finicky, nagging **8** captious, contrary, critical, exacting, niggling **10** censorious, nitpicking **12** faultfinding **13** hairsplitting

cavity 3 pit **4** bore, hole, void **5** decay, fossa **6** caries, hollow **7** vacuity **10** depression, interstice *body:* **5** antra (plural), sinus **6** antrum **8** follicle, hemocoel

cavort 4 leap, romp **5** caper, cut up, frisk, sport **6** frolic, gambol, prance **7** carry on, rollick **10** roughhouse **11** horse around

cavy 4 paca **6** rodent **9** guinea pig

caw 4 crow, yawp **6** squall, squawk

cay 3 key **4** isle, reef **5** islet **6** island

cayenne 6 pepper *genus:* **8** Capsicum

cayman see **caiman**

Cayman Islands *capital:* **10** George Town *discoverer:* **8** Columbus (Christopher) *territory of:* **7** Britain

Cayuga chief 5 Logan (James)

cease 3 die, end **4** halt, quit, stop **5** close **6** desist, ending, finish **8** conclude, give over, knock off, leave off **9** terminate **10** conclusion **11** discontinue, termination

cease-fire 5 truce **9** armistice **10** suspension

ceaseless 7 endless, eternal, nonstop **8** constant, immortal, unending **9** continual, incessant, perennial, perpetual, sustained, unabating **10** continuing, continuous **11** everlasting, never-ending, unremitting **12** interminable **13** uninterrupted

Cecrops' daughter 5 Herse **8** Aglauros, Aglaurus **9** Pandrosos, Pandrosus

cede 4 deed **5** grant, leave, yield **6** assign, convey, give up **7** abandon, concede **8** alienate, hand over, make over, part with, renounce, sign over, transfer **9** surrender, vouchsafe **10** relinquish

ceinture 4 belt, sash **6** girdle **9** waistband

Celaeno *father:* **5** Atlas *mother:* **7** Pleione *sisters:* **8** Pleiades

celebrate 4 fete, hold, hymn, keep, laud **5** bless, cry up, exalt, extol, honor, party, revel **6** praise **7** carouse, glorify, maffick, observe, perform, rejoice **8** eulogize **9** solemnize **11** commemorate

celebrated 5 famed, great, noted **6** famous **7** eminent, notable, partied **8** caroused, rejoiced, renowned **9** prominent, well-known **11** illustrious **13** distinguished

celebration 4 bash, fete, gala **5** beano, party **6** fiesta **7** blowout, jubilee, revelry **8** ceremony, festival, jamboree, wingding **10** observance

celebrity 3 VIP **4** fame, hero, lion, name, star **5** éclat, glory **6** renown, repute **7** notable **8** eminence, luminary, prestige, somebody **9** notoriety, personage, superstar **10** notability, prominence, reputation

celerity 4 pace **5** speed **8** alacrity, dispatch, rapidity, velocity **9** briskness, fleetness, quickness, swiftness **10** speediness

celestial 6 divine **7** blessed, elysian, sublime **8** beatific, empyreal, empyrean, ethereal, heavenly, Olympian, supernal **9** unearthly **12** otherworldly

celestial body 3 sun **4** moon, star **5** comet **6** meteor, nebula, planet **8** asteroid **9** satellite

Celestial Empire 5 China

celibate 5 unwed **6** chaste, single, virgin **8** virginal, virtuous **9** abstinent, continent

cell 4 room **5** cubby, zooid **6** alcove **7** chamber, cubicle **9** corpuscle, cubbyhole **11** compartment *blood:* **8** hemocyte *disease:* **6** cancer *division:* **7** meiosis, mitosis *fertilized egg:* **6** zygote *material:* **3** DNA, RNA **7** protein **9** chromatin, cytoplasm **10** protoplasm *nerve:* **6** neuron *part:* **4** gene **7** nucleus, vacuole **8** ribosome **9** centriole **10** chromosome *reproductive:* **3** egg **4** germ, ovum **5** sperm **6** gamete **8** gonidium

cellar 5 store **7** shelter **8** basement

cellist *American:* **2** Ma (Yo-Yo) **4** Rose (Leonard) **6** Lesser (Laurence), Parnas (Leslie) **7** Nelsova (Zara), Parisot (Aldo), Starker (Janos) **8** Schuster (Joseph) **10** Greenhouse (Bernard) *English:* **5** du Pré (Jacqueline) *French:* **8** Fournier (Pierre) *Russian:* **11** Piatigorsky (Gregor) **12** Rostropovich (Mstislav) *Spanish:* **6** Casals (Pablo)

cellophane 4 wrap **7** wrapper **8** wrapping **9** packaging

cell-phone sound 8 ringtone

celluloid 4 film **7** plastic

Celt 4 Gael, Scot **6** Breton **8** Irishman, Welshman **10** Cornishman, Highlander

Celtic *deity:* **4** Bran **5** Epona, Lugus, Macha **6** Brigit **8** Rhiannon **9** Cernunnos *festival:* **7** Beltane, Samhain *queen:* **8** Boadicea, Boudicca

cement 4 bind, glue, join **5** grout, unify, unite **6** mortar, secure **8** concrete *ingredient:* **4** lime **6** silica **7** alumina **8** magnesia, pozzolan **9** iron oxide, pozzolana

cemetery 8 boneyard, boot hill **8** God's acre **9** graveyard **10** churchyard, necropolis **12** burial ground, memorial park, potter's field *underground:* **8** catacomb

cenacle 7 coterie **9** Upper Room **12** retreat house

cenotaph 4 tomb **6** marker **8** memorial, monument

censer 8 thurible *carrier:* **8** thurifer

censor 3 ban, cut **4** blip, edit **5** bleep, purge **6** cut out, delete, excise, purify, screen **7** clean up **8** black out, restrict, suppress, withhold **9** expurgate, red-pencil **10** blue-pencil, bowdlerize

censorious 6 severe **7** carping **8** captious, critical **10** accusatory, condemning **11** reproachful **12** condemnatory, denunciatory, disapproving, faultfinding, overcritical, reprehending **13** hypercritical

censurable 5 wrong **6** guilty, sinful **7** heinous **8** blamable, blameful, culpable, improper, wrongful **9** incorrect **10** deplorable, despicable, detestable **11** blameworthy, disgrace-

ful, impeachable **12** unacceptable **13** discreditable, objectionable, reprehensible

censure 5 blame, chide, scold **6** berate, rebuke, strafe **7** condemn, reprove, upbraid **8** chastise, denounce, disallow, reproach **9** castigate, criticize, reprehend, reprimand, reprobate **10** disapprove

centaur 6 Chiron, Nessus

Centaurus star 4 Beta **5** Alpha

Centennial State 8 Colorado

center 3 hub, mid **4** axis, core, crux, mean, pith, root, seat **5** focus, heart, midst, pivot **6** inside, medial, median, middle, source **7** central, essence **8** interior, midpoint, omphalos **10** focal point **11** equidistant **12** intermediary, intermediate

centerboard 4 keel

centerfold 7 foldout **8** gatefold

centerpiece 7 epergne

central 3 hub, key, mid **4** main, mean **5** basic, chief, focal **6** medial, median, middle **7** leading, pivotal, primary, salient **8** cardinal, dominant, exchange, foremost, moderate **9** essential, paramount, principal **10** overriding **11** fundamental, outstanding, predominant **12** intermediate

Central African Republic *capital:* **6** Bangui *former name:* **11** Ubangi-Shari *language:* **5** Sango, Zande **6** French *monetary unit:* **5** franc *neighbor:* **4** Chad **5** Congo, Sudan **8** Cameroon

Central America *country:* **6** Belize, Panama **8** Honduras **9** Costa Rica, Guatemala, Nicaragua **10** El Salvador *language:* **7** Nahuatl, Spanish

centralize 5 focus, unify **11** concentrate, consolidate

centripetal 8 afferent, focusing, unifying **10** converging **11** integrative **12** centralizing **13** concentrating, consolidating

centurion 7 officer **9** commander

century plant 5 agave

cephalopod 5 squid **7** mollusc, mollusk, octopus **10** cuttlefish

Cepheus *daughter:* **9** Andromeda *kingdom:* **8** Ethiopia *wife:* **10** Cassiopeia

cerate 4 balm **5** cream, salve **6** chrism **7** unction, unguent **8** dressing, liniment, ointment **9** demulcent, emollient

Cerberus 5 guard **8** guardian, sentinel, watchdog *father:* **6** Typhon *form:* **3** dog *mother:* **7** Echidna

cereal 4 meal, mush, samp **5** gruel **6** farina **7** oatmeal **8** cornmeal, porridge *disease:* **4** bunt, smut **5** ergot *fungus:* **5** ergot *grass:* **3** rye **4** corn, oats, ragi, rice, teff **5** emmer, maize, spelt, wheat **6** barley, millet **7** sorghum **9** buckwheat *Russian:* **5** kasha

cerebral 6 mental **7** bookish **8** highbrow **9** scholarly **10** highbrowed **12** intellectual

cerebrate 5 think **6** reason **7** reflect **8** cogitate **9** speculate **10** deliberate

cerebration 7 thought **9** brainwork **10** cogitation, reflection **11** speculation **12** deliberation

ceremonial 6 august, formal, ritual, solemn **7** courtly, stately, studied **8** mannered, stylized **10** liturgical **11** ritualistic **12** conventional

ceremonious 6 formal, proper, seemly, solemn **7** courtly, stately **8** decorous, imposing, majestic **9** dignified, grandiose **10** impressive **11** punctilious **12** conventional

ceremony 4 form, pomp, rite **6** ritual **7** decorum, liturgy, service **8** protocol **9** formality **10** observance *Jewish:* **8** habdalah, havdalah **10** bar mitzvah, bat mitzvah *university:* **8** encaenia

Ceres *Greek counterpart:* **7** Demeter *daughter:* **10** Persephone, Proserpina, Proserpine *father:* **6** Cronus, Saturn *mother:* **3** Ops **4** Rhea

cerium *symbol* **2** Ce

certain 3 set **4** firm, sure, true **5** fixed **6** stated **7** assured, settled **8** credible, definite, destined, positive, provable, reliable, specific, surefire **9** authentic, confident, convinced **10** conclusive, dependable, guaranteed, inarguable, inevitable, infallible, stipulated, undeniable, verifiable **11** confirmable, indubitable, unavoidable **12** demonstrable, indisputable, well-grounded **13** incontestable, uncontestable

certainty 5 faith **6** surety **8** sureness **9** assurance, sure thing **10** confidence, conviction **12** definiteness

certificate 7 diploma, license, voucher **8** contract, document **9** affidavit **10** credential

certifier 6 notary **7** auditor **9** registrar

certify 2 OK **4** aver, avow, okay **5** state, swear, vouch **6** assert, assure, attest, verify **7** approve, confirm, endorse, license, testify, warrant, witness **8** accredit, guaranty, notarize **9** authorize, guarantee, recognize **10** commission **12** authenticate

Cervantes *character* **10** Don Quixote **11** Sancho Panza

cervid 3 elk **4** deer **5** moose **6** wapiti **7** caribou **8** reindeer

cesium *symbol* **2** Cs

cessation 3 end **4** halt, rest, stop **5** break, cease, close, letup, pause **6** ending, finish, freeze, hiatus, period, recess **7** respite **10**

conclusion, suspension **11** termination **12** interruption

cesspool 3 den, pit, sty **4** sink **5** sewer, Sodom **6** cloaca, gutter, pigsty **8** Gomorrah **12** Augean stable

cetacean 5 whale **7** dolphin **8** porpoise

Cetus *star* **4** Mira

Ceylon see **Sri Lanka**

cgs unit 3 erg **4** dyne, gram, phot **5** gauss, poise, stilb **6** second, stokes **7** lambert, maxwell, oersted **10** centimeter

Chablis 4 wine **8** Burgundy **9** white wine

Chad *capital:* **8** N'Djamena *city:* **4** Sarh **6** Abéché **7** Moundou *language:* **6** Arabic, French *monetary unit:* **5** franc *neighbor:* **5** Libya, Niger, Sudan **7** Nigeria **8** Cameroon *river:* **5** Chari **6** Logone

chafe 3 irk, rub, vex **4** fret, gall, peel, rage, skin, wear **5** annoy, erode **6** abrade, bother, scrape **7** provoke **8** irritate, vexation

chaff 3 kid, rag, rib **4** jest, joke, josh, razz **5** dregs, husks, tease **6** banter, debris, refuse **7** remains **8** detritus **9** sweepings

chaffer 6 barter, dicker, haggle, higgle, palter **7** bargain, chatter **8** exchange, huckster

chagrin 3 ire, irk, vex **5** abash, annoy, peeve, pique, upset **6** dismay **7** perturb **8** disquiet, distress, unsettle, vexation **9** annoyance, discomfit, displease, embarrass, humiliate, petulance **10** disappoint, discompose, disconcert, irritation **11** frustration, humiliation **12** discomfiture

chagrined 4 hurt **5** upset, vexed **6** shamed **7** ashamed **8** dismayed **9** disturbed, mortified, perturbed, unsettled **10** distressed, humiliated **11** discomposed, embarrassed **12** disappointed, disconcerted

chain 3 row **4** bind, bond, gyve **5** group, train, trust **6** cartel, catena, fetter, hobble, series, string, tether **7** combine, manacle, shackle **8** handcuff, sequence **9** syndicate **10** succession **11** concatenate, progression **12** conglomerate **13** concatenation *adjunct:* **8** sprocket *collar:* **6** torque *gang:* **6** coffle *ornamental:* **10** chatelaine *sound:* **5** clank

chain _____ 3 saw **4** gang, mail **5** store **6** letter **8** reaction

Chained Lady 9 Andromeda

chain store 6 big box

chair 4 seat **5** stool **6** rocker, settee, settle **7** preside *back:* **5** splat *bishop's:* **8** cathedra *designer:* **5** Eames (Charles, Ray) **6** Breuer (Marcel) *maker:* **5** caner *portable:* **5** sedan *reclining:* **6** chaise **12** chaise longue, chaise lounge *royal:* **6** throne *type:* **4** club, easy **6** morris **7** rocking **8** captain's, electric **9** di-

rector's, reclining **10** Adirondack, ladder-
back

chaise 4 sofa **5** chair, coach, divan **8** carriage

chalcedony 4 onyx, sard **5** agate, chert **6** jasper, quartz **9** carnelian, cornelian **10** bloodstone **11** chrysoprase

chalet 3 hut **4** camp **5** lodge **7** cottage

chalice 3 cup **5** grail **6** goblet *veil:* **3** aer

chalk out 5 draft **6** sketch **7** outline **8** block
out, rough out **11** skeletonize **12** characterize

chalk up 3 get, win **4** gain **6** attain, credit,
impute, obtain, secure **7** achieve, acquire,
ascribe, procure, realize **9** attribute

challenge 3 try **4** dare, defy, face, stir, wake **5**
brave, claim, demur, doubt, exact, rouse,
waken **6** arouse, awaken, demand, impugn,
invite, kindle **7** calling, dispute, protest, require, solicit, venture **8** confront, defiance,
demurral, demurrer, question, struggle **9**
objection, postulate, stimulate **10** difficulty,
insistence **12** remonstrance

challenger 5 rival **8** aspirant, opponent **9** adversary, contender **10** antagonist, competitor, contestant

chamber 4 cell, hall, room **5** haven, house **7**
cubicle **9** apartment, enclosure **11** compartment *burial:* **4** cist *ceremonial:* **4** kiva *underground:* **8** hypogeum

chambered seashell 8 nautilus

chamberlain 6 priest **7** officer, servant **9** attendant, treasurer

chameleon 6 lizard

chameleonic 6 fickle **7** protean **9** mercurial
10 changeable, inconstant

chamfer 5 bevel **6** groove

chamois 5 lizard **6** shammy **7** leather **8** antelope, ruminant *habitat:* **4** Alps *Old Testament:* **6** aoudad

chamois-like animal 4 goat, ibex

champ 3 gum **4** bite, chew, mash **5** gnash,
munch **7** trample **8** macerate, ruminate **9**
masticate

champagne 4 wine **6** bubbly *bucket:* **4** icer
center: **5** Reims **6** Rheims *type:* **3** sec **4**
brut

Champagne capital 6 Troyes

champaign 5 field, plain **7** expanse, terrain **11**
battlefield

champignon 6 fungus **8** mushroom

champion 4 back, hero **5** first, prime **6** uphold, victor, winner **7** capital, contend,
leading, paladin, premier, support, titlist **8**
advocate, defender, exponent, fight for,
foremost, medalist, unbeaten **9** excellent,
nonpareil, number one, principal, proponent, protector, supporter **11** illustrious,
outstanding, titleholder, white knight

championship 5 crown, title **6** laurel, trophy
7 contest, defense, laurels, pennant **8** advocacy **10** blue ribbon

chance 3 hap, hit, lot, odd **4** fate, luck, meet,
odds, risk, shot **5** break, fluke, light, wager
6 befall, casual, gamble, happen, hazard **7**
fortune, offhand, stumble, venture **8** accident, fortuity, occasion, prospect **9** advantage, transpire **10** accidental, fortuitous,
incidental, likelihood **11** contingency, opportunity, possibility, probability *even:* **6**
toss-up

chancellor 5 judge **8** minister **9** secretary
German: **4** Kohl (Helmut) **6** Brandt (Willy),
Erhard (Ludwig), Hitler (Adolf), Merkel
(Angela) **7** Schmidt (Helmut) **8** Adenauer
(Konrad), Bismarck (Otto von) **9** Schroeder
(Gerhard)

chancy 4 iffy **5** dicey, fluky, hairy, risky **6**
touchy, tricky **8** perilous, ticklish **9** dangerous, haphazard, hazardous, uncertain **10**
capricious, precarious **11** speculative, treacherous **12** incalculable **13** unpredictable

Chandler, Raymond *character:* **7** Marlowe
(Philip) *novel:* **8** Big Sleep (The) **11** Long
Good-Bye (The) **13** Murder My Sweet **16**
Farewell My Lovely *screenplay:* **10** Blue
Dahlia (The) **15** Double Indemnity

Chanel, _____ 4 Coco

change 3 fix **4** swap, turn, vary **5** add-on, alter, coins, money, morph, shift, trade **6** adjust, evolve, modify, mutate, reform,
remake, revamp, revert, revise, switch **7**
commute, convert, novelty, replace, reverse
8 exchange, mutation, revision, transfer **9**
alternate, deviation, diversify, fluctuate, refashion, transform, transmute, transpose,
variation **10** alteration, conversion, divergence, innovation, substitute **11** interchange, permutation, transfigure,
vicissitude **12** metamorphose, modification,
transmogrify **13** metamorphosis, transmutation *sudden:* **8** peripety **10** peripeteia

changeable 5 fluid **6** fickle, labile, pliant,
shifty **7** flighty, mutable, plastic, protean,
unfixed, varying **8** restless, shifting, slippery, ticklish, unstable, unsteady, variable,
volatile **9** adaptable, alterable, impulsive,
mercurial, uncertain, unsettled, whimsical
10 capricious, inconstant **11** chameleonic,
fluctuating, vacillating **13** kaleidoscopic,
temperamental, unpredictable

changeless 5 fixed **6** steady **7** abiding, regular, uniform **8** constant, enduring, resolute **9**
immutable, perpetual, steadfast, unvarying
10 invariable

change off 6 rotate **9** alternate

change of heart 8 reversal
change of life 9 menopause 11 climacteric
change of pace 5 pitch, shift 9 slow pitch
changeover 5 shift 10 alteration, conversion, transition
channel 3 way 4 band, duct, kyle, pass, path, pipe 5 agent, canal, carry 6 agency, convey, course, funnel, groove, gutter, medium, siphon, strait, trough, tunnel 7 conduct, conduit, passage, vehicle 8 aqueduct, pipeline, transmit 10 instrument 11 watercourse *Africa-Madagascar:* 10 Mozambique *Atlantic-Nantucket Sound:* 8 Muskeget *Atlantic-North Sea:* 7 English *Ellesmere-Greenland:* 7 Robeson *Ganges:* 5 Hugli 7 Hooghly *Hawaii:* 5 Kaiwi, Kauai *Japan:* 5 Bungo *Northwest Territories:* 9 M'Clintock *Pakistan:* 4 Nara *Scotland:* 5 Minch *Tierra del Fuego:* 6 Beagle *Tigris-Euphrates:* 11 Shatt al Arab *Virginia:* 12 Hampton Roads *West Indies:* 9 Old Bahama
channel bass 4 drum 7 red drum, redfish
Channel Islands *capital:* 8 St. Helier 11 St. Peter Port *dependency of:* 7 Britain *island:* 4 Herm, Sark 6 Jersey 8 Alderney, Guernsey
chanson 4 song
"Chanson ____" 6 Triste
chanson de ____ 5 geste
chant 4 sing, tune 5 drone 6 intone 8 vocalize 10 cantillate *Gregorian:* 9 plainsong 12 cantus firmus *Jewish:* 6 Hallel
chanteuse 6 singer 7 artiste 10 cantatrice
chanticleer 4 cock 7 rooster
chaos 5 havoc, snafu 6 bedlam, muddle 7 anarchy, clutter, entropy, turmoil 8 disarray, disorder 9 confusion 11 lawlessness, pandemonium
Chaos *daughter:* 3 Nox, Nyx 4 Gaea *son:* 6 Erebus
chaotic 7 jumbled, lawless 8 anarchic, confused, formless 9 amorphous, haphazard, scrambled 10 disordered, disorderly, topsy-turvy, tumultuous 11 harum-scarum, unorganized 12 disorganized 13 helter-skelter, unpredictable
chap 3 guy 4 gent 5 bloke 6 fellow
chaparral 5 scrub 7 thicket
chaparral cock 10 roadrunner
chapeau 3 hat 6 topper
chapel 6 bethel, church, shrine 7 chantry 9 sanctuary
chaperone 5 guide 6 attend, duenna, escort, matron 7 oversee 9 accompany, companion, supervise 11 superintend
chapfallen see **crestfallen**
chaplain 5 padre 6 pastor 8 minister, sky pilot

chaplet 5 crown 6 anadem, laurel, rosary, wreath 7 coronal, coronet, garland
chapter 4 unit 5 phase, stage 6 branch, period 7 episode, section 8 division 9 affiliate
char 4 burn, sear 6 scorch 9 carbonize
character 3 ilk 4 bent, case, cast, kind, mark, mind, name, rank, role, rune, sign, sort, type 5 ethos, state, trait 6 cipher, device, letter, makeup, nature, repute, status, symbol, temper, virtue 7 oddball, persona, quality, variety 8 eminence, identity, standing 9 attribute, eccentric, rectitude 10 reputation 11 disposition, personality, temperament *chief:* 4 hero 11 protagonist *defect:* 8 hamartia
character assassination 5 libel 7 calumny, scandal, slander 10 backbiting, defamation 12 backstabbing
characteristic 4 mark, sign 5 badge, point, token, trait 6 aspect, innate, normal, proper 7 feature, natural, quality, special, typical 8 especial, peculiar, property, specific, tendency 9 attribute, birthmark, component, mannerism, trademark 10 diagnostic, emblematic, individual, particular 11 distinction, distinctive, peculiarity, singularity 12 idiosyncrasy 13 idiosyncratic
characterize 4 mark 5 draft 6 define, sketch, typify 7 outline, portray 8 describe, identify 10 constitute, pigeonhole 11 distinguish, individuate, personalize 12 discriminate 13 differentiate, individualize
characterless 4 flat 5 mousy 7 humdrum, insipid, vacuous 8 mediocre 9 colorless 10 namby-pamby, wishy-washy 11 nondescript
charade 4 sham 5 farce, put-on 6 parody 8 disguise, pretense, travesty 9 deception 11 make-believe
chare see **chore**
charge 3 ask, bid, fee, lay, tab, tax 4 bill, care, cost, duty, fill, heap, kick, load, onus, race, rate, rush, task, tell, toll, warn 5 choke, debit, order, place, price, refer, trust 6 accuse, assign, attack, burden, credit, direct, enjoin, exhort, impugn, impute, indict, saddle, thrill 7 arraign, ascribe, bidding, command, conduct, entrust, expense, impeach, mandate, request, solicit 8 accredit, handling, instruct, price tag, reproach, stampede 9 attribute, committal, electrify, inculpate 10 accusation, allegation, commitment, injunction, management, obligation 11 incriminate, instruction, requirement, supervision
chargeable 6 liable 7 subject 11 accountable, responsible
chargeless 4 free 6 gratis 8 costless 10 gratuitous 13 complimentary

charger 5 horse, mount, steed **6** salver **7** courser, platter **8** trencher, warhorse

chariness 7 caution **8** prudence **9** integrity **10** discretion

chariot 8 carriage *four-horse:* **8** quadriga

charioteer 6 Auriga, driver

charisma 5 charm **6** allure, appeal, duende **7** glamour **9** magnetism **10** attraction **11** fascination

charitable 6 benign, giving, humane, kindly **7** clement, lenient, liberal **8** generous, merciful, obliging, tolerant **9** forgiving, indulgent **10** altruistic, beneficent, benevolent, forbearing, thoughtful **11** considerate, kindhearted, sympathetic **12** eleemosynary, humanitarian **13** philanthropic

charity 4 alms, love **5** grace, mercy **6** lenity, relief **7** caritas **8** altruism, clemency, donation, goodwill, leniency, offering **10** generosity, humaneness, kindliness **11** benefaction, beneficence, benevolence **12** contribution

charivari 5 babel, melee **6** jangle, jumble, medley, racket, ruckus, uproar **7** farrago **8** serenade, shivaree **9** cacophony, confusion **10** hodgepodge **11** celebration

charlatan 4 sham **5** bluff, faker, fraud, quack **6** con man **8** imposter, impostor, swindler **10** mountebank **11** quacksalver **13** confidence man

Charlemagne *brother:* **8** Carloman *capital:* **3** Aix **6** Aachen *father:* **5** Pepin *knight:* **6** Oliver, Roland **7** Olivier, Orlando, paladin **8** douzeper *nephew:* **6** Roland **7** Orlando *sword:* **7** Joyeuse *traitor:* **4** Gano **7** Ganelon

Charles's Wain 9 Big Dipper, Ursa Major

charleston 5 dance

Charlie and the Chocolate Factory author 4 Dahl (Roald)

Charlie Brown see **Peanuts**

Charlie McCarthy 5 dummy **6** stooge *friend:* **5** Snerd (Mortimer) *voice:* **6** Bergen (Edgar)

charm 3 hex **4** juju, lure, mojo, rune, take, wile **5** grace, quark, spell **6** allure, amulet, appeal, disarm, enamor, fetish, mascot, seduce, voodoo **7** attract, beguile, bewitch, enchant, glamour **8** enthrall, entrance, talisman, witchery **9** captivate, enrapture, ensorcell, fascinate, hypnotize, magnetism, mesmerize **10** allurement, attraction, phylactery, witchcraft **11** fascination, incantation **13** agreeableness

charmed 5 lucky **7** blessed **8** enamored **9** bewitched, enchanted, entranced, fortunate **10** captivated, fascinated, infatuated

charmer 4 roué **5** magus **6** wizard **7** seducer, warlock **8** conjurer, lothario, magician, sorcerer **9** enchanter **11** spellbinder

charming 7 winsome **8** adorable, alluring, inviting, magnetic **9** appealing, glamorous, seductive **10** attractive, delightful, enchanting, entrancing **11** captivating

Charon 7 boatman **8** ferryman *father:* **6** Erebus *mother:* **3** Nox *river:* **4** Styx

Charpentier opera 5 Médée **6** Louise

charpoy 3 bed, cot

chart 3 map **4** plan, plat, plot **5** graph, table **6** design, lay out, map out, sketch **7** arrange, diagram, outline, project **9** blueprint **10** tabulation

charter 3 let **4** deed, hire, rent **5** grant, lease **10** conveyance **12** constitution

Chartreuse 7 liqueur

chary 4 wary **5** cagey, canny **6** frugal, stingy **7** careful, guarded, miserly, prudent, sparing, thrifty **8** cautious, discreet, gingerly, hesitant **9** provident, reluctant **10** economical, restrained, suspicious, unwasteful **11** calculating, circumspect, constrained, disinclined

Charybdis 9 whirlpool *rock associated with:* **6** Scylla

chase 3 run **4** bolt, dash, game, hunt, prey, race, rush, tear **5** chivy, drive, eject, evict, hound, shoot, speed, trail **6** career, charge, course, follow, hasten, pursue, quarry **7** boot out, hunting, kick out, pursuit **8** run after, throw out

chase away 4 rout, shoo

chaser 4 wolf **6** masher **7** Don Juan **8** Casanova **9** ladies' man, womanizer **10** lady-killer **11** philanderer

chasm 3 gap **4** gulf, rift **5** abyss, cleft, clove, flume, gorge, gulch, split **6** ravine **8** crevasse

chasmal 6 gaping **7** echoing, yawning **9** cavernous

chassepot 5 rifle

chaste 4 pure **5** clean, moral **6** decent, modest, proper, seemly, vestal, virgin **7** austere, prudish **8** celibate, decorous, innocent, maidenly, platonic, spotless, virginal, virtuous **9** abstinent, continent, stainless, undefiled, unsullied **10** immaculate **11** unblemished

chasten 5 abase, scold **6** humble, punish, rebuke, refine, subdue **7** correct, upbraid **8** chastise **9** castigate, humiliate, reprimand **10** discipline

chastise 4 beat, flog, whip **5** scold **6** punish, rebuke, thrash **7** belabor, censure, chasten, correct, reprove, scourge, upbraid **9** castigate **10** discipline

chastisement 3 rod **7** reproof **8** punition **10** correction, discipline, punishment **11** castigation

chastity 6 purity, virtue **7** modesty **8** celibacy **9** innocence, integrity, virginity **10** abstention, continence, maidenhood

chasuble 8 vestment

chat 3 gab, jaw, rap, yak, yap **4** blab, gush, talk **5** prate, visit **6** babble, confab, gossip, jabber, natter, parley, patter, yak-yak **7** chatter, palaver, prattle, twaddle **8** causerie, colloquy, converse, dialogue, schmooze **9** tête-à-tête, yakety-yak **11** confabulate **12** conversation, tittle-tattle **13** confabulation

château 5 manor, villa **6** castle, estate **7** mansion **8** fortress **12** country house

chateaubriand 5 steak **10** tenderloin

Chateaubriand novel 4 René **5** Atala

chatelain 6 warden **8** governor **9** castellan

chatelaine 4 hook, wife **5** clasp **8** mistress

chattel 4 serf **5** slave **7** bondman **8** bondsman, property

chatter 3 gab, jaw, yak **4** blab, bull **5** prate **6** babble, gabble, gibber, gossip, jabber, natter, patter, yak-yak, yammer **7** blabber, blather, palaver, prattle, vibrate **9** small talk, yakety-yak **12** tittle-tattle

chatterbox 5 yenta **6** gabber, gossip, magpie, prater **7** blabber **8** jabberer, prattler **12** blabbermouth

chatty 5 gabby **7** voluble **9** garrulous, talkative **10** loquacious

Chaucer pilgrim 4 Cook, Monk **5** Clerk, Friar, Reeve **6** Miller, Parson, Squire **8** Franklin, Manciple, Merchant, Summoner **10** Nun's Priest, Wife of Bath

chauffeur 5 drive **6** driver **9** transport

chauvinism 6 sexism **8** jingoism **10** patriotism **11** nationalism

cheap 4 mean, poor **5** junky, tight **6** cheesy, common, cruddy, flashy, measly, paltry, shabby, shoddy, sleazy, stingy, tawdry, trashy **7** chintzy, cut-rate, low-cost, reduced, thrifty **8** inferior, trifling, uncostly **9** brummagem, low-priced **10** economical **11** inexpensive **12** contemptible, meretricious

cheapen 5 decry, lower **6** debase, reduce **7** devalue **8** mark down **9** devaluate, downgrade **10** depreciate, undervalue

cheapjack 5 junky **6** hawker, cheesy, cruddy, shoddy, sleazy, tawdry, trashy **7** haggler, higgler, packman, peddler **8** huckster, inferior, rubbishy **9** worthless

cheapskate 5 miser **7** niggard, scrooge **8** tightwad **9** skinflint **11** cheeseparer

cheat 3 con, gyp **4** bilk, burn, dupe, fool, gull, hoax, hose, milk, ream, rook, scam **5** bunco, cozen, crook, fraud, fudge, gouge, hocus, put-on, screw, shaft, short, slick **6** chisel, chouse, con man, deceit, delude, diddle, extort, fleece, humbug, rip-off, sucker, take in **7** beguile, chicane, deceive, defraud, diddler, mislead, sharper, shyster, swindle, two-time **8** flimflam, hoodwink, swindler, trickery **9** bamboozle, chicanery, deception, defrauder, imposture, overreach, trickster **11** double-cross **12** double-dealer **13** confidence man *on a check:* **4** kite

check 3 tab, try **4** bill, curb, halt, jibe, stay, stop, test, tick **5** block, brake, draft, prove, score, stall **6** accord, arrest, baffle, bridle, damage, desist, hold in, square, thwart, verify **7** compare, conform, control, examine, inhibit, repress, setback **8** dovetail, hold back, hold down, preclude, restrain, reversal, suppress **9** constrain, criterion, interrupt, restraint **10** correspond, inspection **11** examination **13** investigation

checkered 5 plaid **6** motley **7** mutable, spotted **9** patchwork, patterned **10** variegated **11** diversified

checklist 7 catalog **9** catalogue, inventory **11** enumeration

checkmate 4 beat **6** corner, defeat **7** outplay **8** vanquish **9** finish off

check out 3 die, eye **4** case **5** leave **6** assess **7** examine, inspect **8** appraise, evaluate, look over

check over 3 con, vet **4** scan **5** audit, study **6** review, survey **7** analyze, canvass, examine, inspect **10** scrutinize

checkup 4 exam **8** physical **10** inspection **11** examination

cheek 4 gall **5** brass, nerve **8** audacity, chutzpah, temerity **9** brashness, impudence, insolence **10** confidence, effrontery **11** presumption **12** impertinence

cheekbone 5 malar

cheeky 4 bold, flip, pert, wise **5** brash, cocky, fresh, nervy, sassy, saucy, smart **6** brazen **7** forward **8** flippant, impudent, insolent **11** impertinent, smart-alecky **12** presumptuous

cheep 4 peep **5** chirp, tweet **7** chirrup, chitter, twitter

cheer 3 olé, rah, yay **4** buoy, hail, root **5** bravo, huzza, nerve **6** buck up, gaiety, hoorah, hooray, hurrah, hurray, huzzah, rahrah, solace, spirit **7** animate, applaud, comfort, console, enliven, gladden, hearten **8** embolden, inspirit **9** animation, encourage **10** strengthen

cheerful 3 gay **4** glad, rosy **5** jolly, merry, perky, riant, sunny **6** blithe, bouncy, bright, chirpy, hearty, jaunty, jocund, lively **7**

beamish, buoyant, radiant **8** animated, carefree, chirrupy **9** vivacious **12** lighthearted

cheerio 3 bye **4** ciao, ta-ta **5** adieu **6** bye-bye, good-by, so long **7** good-bye, toodles **8** farewell, toodle-oo

cheerless 4 dour, drab, grim **5** bleak **6** dismal, dreary, gloomy, somber, sombre **7** forlorn, joyless **8** desolate, dolorous, funereal, mournful **9** dejecting **10** depressing, melancholy, oppressive, tenebrific **11** dispiriting

cheers 5 salud, skoal **6** cincin, l'chaim, prosit **7** l'chayim, sláinte **8** applause, approval, chinchin **9** bottoms up **10** jubilation **11** acclamation, approbation

Cheers *actor:* **4** Long (Shelley) **5** Alley (Kirstie), Wendt (George) **6** Danson (Ted) **7** Grammer (Kelsey), Perlman (Rhea) **8** Neuwirth (Bebe) **9** Harrelson (Woody) *character:* **3** Sam **4** Norm **5** Carla, Cliff, Diane, Ernie, Woody **6** Lilith **7** Frasier, Rebecca *creator:* **7** Burrows (James), Charles (Glen, Les)

cheery 5 happy, jolly, merry, sunny **6** blithe, bouncy, chirpy, lively, upbeat **7** buoyant, chipper, festive, gleeful **8** animated, carefree, gladsome **9** convivial, sparkling **12** lighthearted

cheese 3 pot **4** bleu, blue, jack **5** brick, cream **6** farmer **7** cottage, process, ricotta **9** smearcase *American:* **8** Longhorn **11** Liederkranz **12** Monterey Jack *Belgian:* **9** Limburger *curdling agent:* **6** rennet, rennin *Danish:* **7** Havarti *dish:* **6** fondue **7** rarebit, soufflé *Dutch:* **4** Edam **5** Gouda **6** Leyden *English:* **7** cheddar, Stilton **8** Cheshire **10** Lancashire *French:* **4** Brie **7** fromage, Livarot **9** Camembert, Reblochon, Roquefort **10** Neufchâtel **11** Pont l'Évêque, Port du Salut *German:* **6** Tilsit **7** Munster **8** Muenster, Tilsiter *Greek:* **4** feta *green:* **7** sapsago *Italian:* **6** Asiago, Romano **7** fontina, ricotta **8** Bel Paese, Parmesan, pecorino **9** provolone **10** Gorgonzola, mozzarella *lover:* **9** turophile *main ingredient:* **6** casein *Norwegian:* **9** Jarlsberg *pickled:* **4** feta **5** Ezine **8** Halloumi *protein:* **6** casein *Scottish:* **6** Dunlop, Orkney **7** kebbock, kebbuck *Swiss:* **6** Saanen **7** Gruyère, sapsago **8** Vacherin **10** Emmentaler **11** Emmenthaler *uncured:* **7** cottage *Welsh:* **10** Caerphilly

cheesecloth 5 gauze

cheeselike 6 caseic **7** caseous

cheeseparer 5 miser **7** niggard, scrooge **8** tightwad **9** skinflint **10** cheapskate, pinchpenny

cheeseparing 4 mean **5** chary, cheap, mingy, tight **6** frugal, shabby, stingy **7** chintzy, miserly, thrifty **8** grudging, skimping **9** niggardly, penurious **11** closefisted, tightfisted **12** parsimonious **13** penny-pinching

cheesy 4 poor **5** cheap **6** common, shabby, shoddy, sleazy, tawdry, trashy **7** caseous **8** rubbishy

Cheever, John *family:* **7** Wapshot *novel:* **8** Falconer **14** Wapshot Scandal (The) **16** Wapshot Chronicle (The) *story:* **7** Swimmer (The)

chef 4 cook

chef d'oeuvre 7 classic **9** showpiece **10** magnum opus, masterwork **11** masterpiece, tour de force

Chekhov, Anton *play:* **6** Ivanov **7** Seagull (The) **10** Uncle Vanya **12** Three Sisters **13** Cherry Orchard (The) *story:* **9** Black Monk (The)

chelonian 6 turtle **8** tortoise

chemical *agent:* **8** catalyst *combining power:* **7** valence *compound:* **4** acid, base, diol, enol, imid, oxim, salt, tepa, urea **5** amide, amine, diene, ester, imide, imine, indol, orcin, oxime, purin, pyran, salol, tolan, triol **6** alkali, benzin, benzol, diamin, emodin, guanin, halide, hydrid, indole, inulin, ionone, isatin, isolog, isomer, ketone, lactam, maltol, metepa, natron, nitril, pterin, purine, pyrone, pyrrol, quinol, retene, silane, skatol, tannin, tetryl, thiram, thymol, tolane, triene, trimer, uracil, ureide, yttria, zeatin **7** barilla, benzene, benzole, cumarin, diamide, diamine, diazine, diazole, diester, flavone, guanine, heptose, hydride, indamin, indican, indoxyl, isatine, levulin, metamer, monomer, naphtol, nitrile, orcinol, oxazine, phytane, picolin, polyene, polymer, pyrrole, quinoid, quinone, salicin, skatole, steroid, taurine, terpene, thiazin, thiazol, thymine, tolidin, triazin, urethan, uridine, vitamer, xylidin **8** cephalin, cyanamid, disulfid, elaterin, fluorene, furfural, guaiacol, hematein, hexamine, indamine, isologue, kephalin, lichenin, limonene, melamine, naloxone, naphthol, palmitin, phenazin, phosphid, phthalin, picoline, piperine, pristane, quinolin, resorcin, salicine, santonin, siloxane, sodamide, sorbitol, spermine, squalene, stilbene, strontia, tautomer, thiazine, thiazole, thiophen, thiotepa, thiourea, tolidine, triazine, triazole, triptane, tyramine, urethane, vanillin, warfarin, xanthene, xanthine, xanthone, xylidine, ytterbia, zaratite, zirconia (see also *element*) *quantity:* **4** mole *radical:* **4** acyl, amyl, aryl, cyan **5** allyl, butyl, ethyl, tolyl **6** acetyl, formyl, methyl, oxalic, phenyl, propyl, toluyl **7** benzoyl *reaction:* **5** redox *salt:* **5** niter, nitre, urate, ziram **6** haloid, humate, malate, oleate, phytin **7** ferrate, formate, gallate, maleate, pectate, persalt, picrate, tannate, toluate, zincate **8** fumarate, pyruvate, racemate, selenate, silicate, stearate, tartrate, thionate, titanate, valerate, vanadate, xanthate *suffix:* **3** ane, ase, ate, ein, ene, ide, ile, ine, ite, ium, oic, oin, one, ose, ous, yne **4** eine, idin, itol, oate, olic, onic **5** idine, onium, oside, ylene *warfare agent:* **7** tear gas **8** vesicant **10** mustard gas

chemin de fer 5 train **7** railway **8** railroad

chemise 4 slip

chemist 7 analyst **8** druggist **10** apothecary, pharmacist *American:* **4** Urey (Harold) **6** Remsen (Ira), Sumner (James) **7** Onsager (Lars), Pauling (Linus), Seaborg (Glenn) **8** Hoffmann (Roald), Langmuir (Irving), Mulliken (Robert), Richards (Theodore), Woodward (Robert) *Austrian:* **4** Kuhn (Richard) **5** Pregl (Fritz) *British:* **4** Abel (Frederick), Davy (Humphry), Todd (Alexander) **5** Boyle (Robert), Soddy (Frederick) **6** Dalton (John), Ramsay (William) **7** Faraday (Michael) **8** Smithson (James) **9** Priestley (Joseph), Wollaston (William) **10** Williamson (Alexander) *Dutch:* **8** van't Hoff (Jacobus) *French:* **5** Curie (Irene, Marie, Pierre) **7** Moissan (Henri), Pasteur (Louis) **8** Sabatier (Paul) **9** Gay-Lussac (Joseph), Lavoisier (Antoine), Berthelot (Marcellin) *German:* **5** Haber (Fritz) **6** Bunsen (Robert), Liebig (Justus von), Nernst (Walther), Wittig (Georg), Wohler (Friedrich) **7** Fischer (Emil, Ernst, Hans), Hofmann (August), Ostwald (Friedrich), Wallach (Otto), Wieland (Heinrich), Windaus (Adolf), Ziegler (Karl) **9** Zsigmondy (Richard) **10** Erlenmeyer (Richard), Staudinger (Hermann) **11** Willstatter (Richard) *Italian:* **5** Natta (Giulio) **8** Avogadro (Amedeo) *Russian:* **8** Semyonov (Nikolay), Zelinsky (Nikolay) **10** Mendeleyev (Dmitry) *Swedish:* **8** Svedberg (The, Theodor) **9** Berzelius (J. J.) *Swiss:* **6** Karrer (Paul), Werner (Alfred) (see also under **Nobel Prize winner**)

chemist's vessel 4 vial **5** flask, phial **6** ampule, beaker, mortar, retort **7** ampoule **8** crucible, test tube

chemoreceptor 8 taste bud

cheongsam 5 dress

Cheops 5 Khufu

cherish 4 keep, save **5** adore, guard, honor, nurse, prize, value **6** admire, cosset, defend, dote on, esteem, foster, harbor, relish, re-vere, shield **7** apprize, care for, nourish, nurture, shelter, worship **8** conserve, hold dear, preserve, treasure, venerate **9** cultivate, delight in, entertain, reverence, safeguard **10** appreciate

Cherokee *chief:* **4** Ross (John) *historian:* **7** Sequoia, Sequoya **8** Sequoyah

cherry *dark:* **4** bing *family:* **4** rose **8** Rosaceae *genus:* **6** Prunus *hybrid:* **4** Duke *sour:* **7** morello *sweet:* **4** bing **7** mazzard, oxheart *wild:* **7** mazzard **10** maraschino

cherry bomb 11 firecracker

Cherry Orchard author 7 Chekhov (Anton)

cherrystone 4 clam **6** quahog

Chersonese 9 peninsula

cherub 4 babe, baby **5** angel, child, cupid, putto **6** infant **7** bambino **8** amoretto, innocent

cherubic 4 cute, rosy **6** chubby **7** angelic **8** adorable, innocent

chess *champion:* **3** Tal (Mikhail) **4** Euwe (Max) **6** Karpov (Anatoly), Lasker (Emanuel) **7** Fischer (Bobby), Kramnik (Vladimir), Smyslov (Vassily), Spassky (Boris) **8** Alekhine (Alexander), Kasparov (Garry), Steinitz (Wilhelm) **9** Botvinnik (Mikhail), Petrosian (Tigran) **10** Capablanca (José) *draw game:* **9** stalemate *goal:* **4** mate **9** checkmate *move:* **6** castle, gambit *opening:* **6** gambit *piece:* **4** king, pawn, rook **5** queen **6** bishop, knight *risk:* **6** gambit *term:* **3** pin **4** draw, FIDE, file, fork, luft, rank **5** check **6** skewer **7** battery, capture, endgame **8** blockade, castling, diagonal **9** promotion

chest 3 box **4** arca, cist, kist **5** bosom, torso, trunk **6** breast, bureau, coffer, thorax **7** cabinet **8** cupboard, treasury **9** exchequer *combining form:* **5** stern **6** sterno, thorac

chesterfield 4 sofa **5** divan **8** overcoat **9** davenport

chestnut 4 tree **5** color, horse **6** cliché, marron **10** chinquapin *extract:* **6** tannin *water:* **4** ling

cheval glass 6 mirror

chevalier 5 noble **6** knight **8** horseman **9** caballero, gentleman

chevet 4 apse

chevron 6 stripe

chew 3 eat, gum **4** bite, gnaw **5** champ, chomp, munch **6** crunch, devour, nibble **7** consume **8** ruminate **9** masticate

chewing gum 6 chicle

chew out 3 jaw **5** scold **6** rebuke, revile **7** bawl out, reprove, tell off, upbraid **8** lambaste, reproach **9** castigate, criticize, reprimand **10** tongue-lash, vituperate

Chiang ____ 7 Kai-shek

chic 4 mode, rage, tony 5 nobby, smart, style, swank, swish, vogue 6 modish, trendy, with-it 7 dashing, elegant, fashion, stylish 8 elegance 10 dernier cri 11 fashionable

Chicago 7 Chi-Town 9 Windy City 10 Second City *newspaper:* 4 Trib 7 Tribune *team:* 4 Cubs 5 Bears, Bulls 8 White Sox 10 Black Hawks

chicane 4 dupe, fool, gull, hoax, ploy, ruse, wile 5 cavil, cheat, feint, fraud, trick 6 gambit 8 artifice, flimflam, hoodwink, trickery 9 bamboozle, deception, duplicity, stratagem, victimize 10 dishonesty, hanky-panky 13 double-dealing

chicanery 4 plot, ruse 5 fraud, trick 6 gambit 8 intrigue, trickery 9 deception, duplicity 10 subterfuge 11 machination, skulduggery

chichi 4 arty 5 gaudy, showy, swank 6 dressy, frills, frilly, la-di-da 7 splashy 8 affected, précieux, precious 10 flamboyant, preciosity 11 affectation, fashionable, overrefined, pretentious 12 ostentatious

chick 3 kid, tot 4 girl 5 child 6 moppet, nipper, pullet 7 toddler 8 juvenile 9 youngster

chickadee 8 titmouse *family:* 7 Paridae

chicken 4 fowl, funk 5 sissy, timid 6 coward, craven 7 dastard, gutless 8 cowardly, poltroon 11 lily-livered, yellowbelly 13 pusillanimous *breed:* 4 Java 6 Cochin 7 Cornish, Leghorn 9 Dominique, Orpington, Wyandotte 11 Jersey Giant, Rock Cornish *castrated:* 5 capon *cooking:* 5 fryer 7 broiler, roaster *disease:* 8 avian flu, pullorum 11 coccidiosis *female:* 3 hen 6 pullet *genus:* 6 Gallus *male:* 4 cock 7 rooster 8 cockerel *pen:* 4 coop 7 hennery 10 chick house *small:* 6 bantam *sound:* 6 cackle

chicken feed 6 bubkes, bupkes, bupkus 7 peanuts 8 pittance 11 chump change

chicken pox 9 varicella

chickpea 4 gram 8 garbanzo

chickweed 4 pink 7 potherb

chicle 3 gum 10 chewing gum

chicory 6 endive 7 witloof 9 radicchio

chide 3 kid 5 scold 6 berate, rebuke 7 chew out, lecture, reprove, upbraid 8 admonish, call down, reproach 9 castigate, reprimand

chiding 6 rebuke 7 reproof 8 reproach 9 reprimand 10 admonition 12 admonishment

chief 3 key 4 arch, boss, duce, emir, head, jefe, lion, main, star 5 first, major, prime 6 führer, honcho, leader, master, primal, ruling, sachem 7 fuehrer, headman, highest, leading, premier, primary 8 cardinal, champion, dictator, dominant, eminence, foremost 9 number-one, principal, prominent

10 preeminent 11 outstanding, predominant *prefix:* 4 arch

Chief Justice 3 Jay (John) 4 Taft (William Howard) 5 Chase (Salmon), Stone (Harlan Fiske), Taney (Roger), Waite (Morrison), White (Edward) 6 Burger (Warren), Fuller (Melville), Hughes (Charles Evans), Vinson (Fred), Warren (Earl) 7 Roberts (John) 8 Marshall (John), Rutledge (John) 9 Ellsworth (Oliver), Rehnquist (William)

chiefly 6 mainly, mostly 7 largely, notably, overall 9 generally, primarily 10 especially 11 principally 12 preeminently 13 predominantly

chief priest 7 primate

chiffchaff 4 bird 7 warbler

chiffonier 5 chest 6 bureau 7 armoire, dresser

chigger 4 mite 6 chigoe, red bug

chignon 3 bun 4 knot

chilblain 4 sore 8 swelling 12 inflammation

child 3 kid 4 brat 5 gamin, minor, youth 6 cherub, infant, moppet, nipper, shaver, urchin 7 bambino, toddler 8 juvenile, small fry 9 youngling, youngster *combining form:* 3 ped 4 paed, pedo 5 paedo *gifted:* 7 prodigy *homeless:* 4 waif *parentless:* 6 orphan *Scottish:* 5 bairn *spoiled:* 4 brat *young:* 3 tot 4 baby, tike, tyke 6 infant, kiddie, rug rat 8 bantling, weanling

childish 5 naive 7 puerile 8 arrested, immature, juvenile 9 infantile

childless 6 barren 7 sterile

childlike 5 naive 6 docile, filial 7 natural, puerile 8 innocent, trustful, trusting 9 ingenuous

children 4 kids, seed 5 brood, heirs, issue 6 scions 7 progeny 9 offspring, posterity 11 descendants

child's play 4 snap 5 cinch, setup 6 breeze, picnic 8 cakewalk, duck soup, kid stuff, pushover 11 piece of cake

Chile *capital:* 8 Santiago *city:* 6 Temuco 10 Concepción, Talcahuano, Valparaíso, Viña del Mar 11 Antofagasta *conqueror:* 7 Almagro (Diego de) 8 Valdivia (Pedro de) *desert:* 7 Atacama *island:* 6 Easter 13 Juan Fernández *lake:* 10 Llanquihue *language:* 7 Spanish *leader:* 7 Allende (Salvador) 8 Pinochet (Augusto) *monetary unit:* 4 peso *mountain range:* 5 Andes *neighbor:* 4 Peru 7 Bolivia 9 Argentina *passage:* 5 Drake *poet:* 6 Neruda (Pablo) 7 Mistral (Gabriela) *river:* 6 Bío-Bío *strait:* 8 Magellan

Chileab *father:* 5 David *mother:* 7 Abigail

chili con _____ 5 carne

Chilion *father:* 9 Elimelech *mother:* 5 Naomi

chill 3 ice, icy, raw 4 ague, cold, cool, hang 5

algid, gelid, nippy **6** arctic, formal, freeze,
frigid, frosty, wintry **7** distant, glacial, hostile **8** dispirit, freezing **10** demoralize, discourage, dishearten **11** emotionless,
refrigerate

chiller 7 shocker **8** thriller

chilling 5 frore, gelid, scary **6** frigid, frosty **8**
alarming **9** unnerving **10** disturbing, terrifying **11** distressing, frightening

chilly 3 raw **4** cold **5** algid, brisk, crisp, nippy
6 frigid **7** bracing, coldish, hostile **10** unfriendly

chilopod 9 centipede

chime 4 bell, bong, dong, peal, ring, toll,
tune **5** agree, clang, knell, sound **6** accord,
strike **7** concord, harmony **8** carillon **9**
agreement, harmonize **10** consonance, correspond

chime in 3 say **4** tell **5** state, utter **6** inject **7**
break in, declare **9** interrupt

chimera 5 dream, fancy **7** fantasy, figment,
monster, specter, spectre **8** illusion, phantasy **9** nightmare, pipe dream

Chimera father: 6 Typhon **mother: 7** Echidna
slayer: 11 Bellerophon

chimerical 6 absurd, unreal **7** fictive, utopian
8 delusive, delusory, fabulous, fanciful, illusory, mythical, spurious **9** ambitious, beguiling, deceptive, fantastic, fictional,
imaginary, visionary **10** far-fetched, fictitious, improbable, outlandish **11** extravagant, unrealistic **12** preposterous,
suppositious

chiming 8 harmonic **9** consonant **10** harmonious

chimney 3 lum **4** flue, tube, vent **5** stack **10**
smokestack **corner: 8** fireside **9** inglenook
output: 4 soot **5** fumes, smoke

chimpanzee 3 ape **7** primate **10** anthropoid
kin: 6 bonobo, gibbon **7** gorilla **9** orangutan

chin 3 gab, jaw, rap, yak **4** blab, chat, talk **5**
converse **hair: 5** beard **6** goatee **7** Vandyke
9 soul patch

china 6 dishes **7** ceramic **8** crockery **9** porcelain, tableware **11** earthenware **maker: 3**
Bow **5** Hizen, Imari, Spode **6** Doccia,
Sèvres **7** Bristol, Chelsea, Dresden, Limoges, Meissen **8** Caughley, Haviland, Wedgwood

China bay: 8 Hangzhou **capital: 7** Beijing
city: 4 Sian, Xi'an **5** Wuhan **6** Canton, Har-
bin, Mukden **7** Nanjing, Nanking, Tianjin **8**
Shanghai, Shenyang, Tientsin **9** Chongqing,
Guangzhou **desert: 4** Gobi **10** Taklimakan
dynasty: 3 Ch'i, Han, Qin, Sui, Wei, Yin **4**
Ch'en, Ch'in, Chou, Hsia, Ming, Qing,
Song, Sung, T'ang, Tsin, Yüan **5** Ch'ing,

Liang, Shang **6** Manchu, Mongol, Shu Han
emperor, legendary: 7 Huangdi, Huang-ti
ethnic group: 3 Han **feudal state: 3** Wei
gulf: 5 Bo Hai **heritage site: 9** Great Wall
island: 6 Hainan **8** Hong Kong **lake: 5** Tai
Hu **8** Hongze Hu, Poyang Hu **10** Dongting
Hu **language: 3** Han **8** Mandarin **leader: 3**
Mao (Tse-tung, Zedong) **8** Hu Jintao **9**
Kubla Khan, Mao Zedong, Sun Yat-sen **10**
Kublai Khan, Mao Tse-tung **12** Deng Xiaoping **13** Chiang Kai-shek, Teng Hsiao-
p'ing **monetary unit: 4** jiao, yuan **8**
renminbi **monetary unit, former: 4** tael
mountain, range: 6 Kunlun **8** Himalaya **9**
Altai Shan, Altay Shan, Himalayan **10**
Gongga Shan **old name: 6** Cathay **peninsula: 7** Leizhou **8** Liaodong, Shandong
province: 5 Anhui, Gansu, Hevei, Henan,
Hubei, Hunan, Jilin **6** Fujian, Shanxi, Yun-
nan **7** Guizhou, Jiangsu, Jiangxi, Qinghai,
Shaanxi, Sichuan **8** Liaoning, Shandong,
Szechuan, Szechwan, Zhejiang **9** Guang-
dong **12** Heilongjiang **region: 5** Macao, Tibet **6** Xizang **8** Hong Kong **10** Nei Monggol
12 Ningxia Huizu **13** Inner Mongolia, Xin-
jiang Uygur **river: 4** Amur **5** Chang, Huang,
Tarim **6** Mekong, Yellow, Zangbo **7** Salween, Yangtze

china clay 6 kaolin

chinchilla 3 fur **6** rodent

chine 5 crest, ridge, spine **7** hogback **8** backbone

Chinese aromatic root: 7 ginseng **bamboo: 7**
whangee **boat: 4** junk **6** sampan **bow: 6**
kowtow **broadsword: 3** dao **cabbage: 7** bok
choy, pak choi **calculator: 6** abacus **card
game: 6** fan-tan **cauterizing agent: 4** moxa
conveyance: 7 pedicab **8** rickshaw **10** jinricksha, jinrikisha **date: 6** jujube **dialect: 4**
Amoy **8** Mandarin **9** Cantonese, Pekingese
distance unit: 2 li **dog: 4** chow, Peke **8**
chow chow **9** Pekingese **fabric: 6** pongee,
tussah **8** shantung **feminine principle: 3** yin
food: 6 dim sum, lo mein, mantou, subgum,
wonton **8** chop suey, chow mein **9** fried rice
10 egg foo yong, egg foo yung, Peking
duck **11** egg foo young **fruit: 6** lichee, litchi,
lychee, loquat **7** kumquat **8** mandarin **gambling game: 6** fan-tan **gong: 6** tam-tam
gruel: 6 congee **healing art: 6** qigong **herb:
5** ramie **7** ginseng **idol: 4** joss **laborer: 6**
coolie **mandarin's residence: 5** yamen **masculine principle: 4** yang **money, silver: 5** sy-
cee **musical instrument: 3** kin **4** pipa **nurse:
4** amah **official: 8** mandarin **official seal: 6**
chop **oil: 4** tung **ox: 4** zebu **pagoda: 2** ta **penal system: 6** laogai **porcelain: 4** Ming **7**

celadon, Nankeen **8** mandarin **9** cloisonné *pottery:* **4** Kuan, Ming **5** Chien *prefix:* **4** Sino *puzzle:* **7** tangram *race:* **9** Mongoloid *religion:* **6** Taoism **8** Buddhism **12** Confucianism *sauce:* **3** soy *secret society:* **4** tong *sheep:* **5** urial *silkworm:* **6** tussah *tea:* **5** bohea, hyson **6** congou, oolong **8** souchong *temple:* **2** ta **6** pagoda **9** joss house *tree:* **4** tung **6** ginkgo, loquat **7** kumquat *unicorn:* **3** lin *vine:* **5** kudzu *vital energy:* **3** chi

chink 4 rift, slit **5** caulk, cleft, crack, split **6** cranny **7** crevice, fissure, opening **8** aperture

chinquapin 3 nut **8** chestnut

chintzy 5 cheap, gaudy, showy, tacky **6** flashy, garish, stingy, tawdry, vulgar **9** tasteless **12** meretricious

chip 4 flaw, nick **5** flake, notch, shard, slice, split, wafer, wedge **6** chisel, defect, paring, sliver **7** counter

chip in 6 ante up, kick in **7** pitch in **10** contribute **11** come through

chipper 4 spry **5** alert, brisk, perky, zesty **6** bright, lively, nimble **8** animated, spirited **9** sprightly, vivacious

chirk 4 buoy **5** cheer **7** animate, enliven, hearten **8** energize, inspirit **9** encourage **10** strengthen

chirography 6 script **8** longhand **10** penmanship **11** calligraphy, handwriting

chiromancy 9 palmistry

Chiron 7 centaur *father:* **6** Cronus *mother:* **7** Philyra *pupil:* **5** Jason **8** Achilles, Heracles, Hercules **9** Asclepius **11** Aesculapius

chiropody 8 podiatry

chiropractic founder 6 Palmer (Daniel)

chirp 4 chip, peep, sing **5** cheep, trill, tweet **6** warble **7** chirrup, twitter

chirpy 3 gay **5** sunny **6** blithe, cheery, sparky **7** buoyant, sparkly **8** cheerful, sunbeamy **9** lightsome

chirrup 4 chip, peep, sing **5** cheep, tweet **6** warble **7** chipper, twitter

chisel 3 gad, gyp, hew **4** beat, bilk, scam **5** carve, cheat, cozen, cut in, gouge, trick **6** butt in, diddle, fleece, horn in, sculpt **7** defraud, engrave, intrude, swindle

chit 3 IOU, kid **4** memo, note, slip **5** child **6** moppet **7** invoice, voucher **8** notation **9** youngster **10** memorandum

chitchat 3 gab **5** chaff **6** babble, banter, gossip **7** chatter, palaver, prattle **8** badinage **9** small talk **12** tittle-tattle

Chi-Town 7 Chicago

chitter 4 chip, peep, sing **5** cheep, chirp, tweet **6** warble **7** chatter, chirrup, twitter

chivalric see **chivalrous**

chivalrous 5 lofty, manly, noble **7** courtly, gallant, valiant **8** generous, gracious, knightly **9** honorable **10** benevolent, courageous **11** considerate, gentlemanly, magnanimous

chivy, chivvy 4 bait, ride **5** annoy, tease **6** badger, heckle, hector **7** torment **8** bullyrag

Chloe 11 shepherdess *beloved:* **7** Daphnis

chlordane 11 insecticide

chlorine symbol 2 Cl

Chloris *father:* **7** Amphion *husband:* **6** Neleus **8** Zephyrus *mother:* **5** Niobe *son:* **6** Nestor

chloroform 7 anodyne, solvent **10** anesthetic **11** anaesthetic

chockablock 4 full **6** jammed, loaded, packed **7** brimful, crammed, crowded, stuffed **9** jam-packed

chocolate 5 brown, cacao, cocoa

Chocolate Soldier composer 6 Straus (Oscar)

chocolate tree 5 cacao

choice 3 top **4** best, pick, rare, vote **5** cream, elite, prime, prize **6** chosen, dainty, option, rating, select **7** elegant, verdict **8** decision, delicate, druthers, election, judgment, selected, superior, volition **9** exquisite, selection **9** selection **10** preference **11** alternative **13** determination *even:* **6** toss-up

choir 6 chorus **7** chorale *area:* **4** loft **7** chancel, gallery *leader:* **6** cantor **8** choragus **9** precentor *member:* **9** chorister *section:* **4** alto, bass **5** tenor **7** soprano *vestment:* **4** gown, robe **5** cotta **8** surplice

choke 3 gag **4** clog, plug, stop **5** block, close **6** stifle **7** congest, occlude, silence, smother **8** obstruct, strangle, throttle **9** constrict, suffocate **10** asphyxiate

choking 8 quashing, stifling **10** repression, smothering, squelching, strangling **11** suppression

choleric 5 angry, fiery, irate **6** fierce, heated **7** enraged **8** incensed, wrathful **9** irascible, splenetic **10** infuriated **11** hot-tempered **13** quick-tempered

cholla 6 cactus **7** opuntia

Chomolungma 7 Everest (Mt.)

chomp 4 bite, chaw, chew **5** munch **6** crunch **9** masticate

choose 3 opt **4** cull, mark, pick, take, want **5** adopt, elect, favor **6** decide, desire, opt for, prefer, select **7** embrace, pick out **8** decide on, handpick **9** single out

choosy 5 fussy, picky **7** finical, finicky **9** finicking, selective **10** fastidious, particular, pernickety **11** persnickety

chop 3 cut, hew **4** dice, fell, hack, hash, seal, veer **5** cut up, grade, mince **7** quality

chop-chop 4 fast 5 quick 6 presto, pronto 7 quickly, rapidly 8 promptly, speedily 9 posthaste 12 lickety-split
chophouse 10 restaurant
Chopin, Frédéric *birthplace:* 6 Poland *instrument:* 5 piano *lover:* 4 Sand (George) *work:* 5 étude 7 mazurka, prelude 8 nocturne 9 polonaise 11 Minute Waltz
chopper 10 motorcycle
choppy 4 wavy 5 jerky, rough 6 ripply, stormy, uneven 7 erratic 8 variable 9 turbulent, unsettled
choral section 5 altos 6 basses, tenors 8 sopranos
choral work 5 motet 6 anthem 7 cantata, passion 8 oratorio
chord 5 triad 6 tetrad 7 harmony *sequence:* 7 cadence 11 progression
chore 3 job 4 duty, task 5 stint, trial 6 devoir, effort 7 routine 10 assignment, obligation 11 tribulation
choreograph 6 devise, direct, map out 7 arrange, compose 11 orchestrate
choreographer *American:* 4 Feld (Elliot), Holm (Hanya), Lang (Pearl) 5 Ailey (Alvin), Fosse (Bob), Tharp (Twyla) 6 Duncan (Isadora), Dunham (Katherine), Fokine (Michel), Graham (Martha), Morris (Mark), Taylor (Paul), Tetley (Glen) 7 de Mille (Agnes), Jamison (Judith), Joffrey (Robert), Martins (Peter), Massine (Leonide), Robbins (Jerome), St. Denis (Ruth), Tamiris (Helen), Weidman (Charles) 8 Champion (Gower, Marge), Humphrey (Doris), Nikolais (Alwin), Villella (Edward) 10 Balanchine (George), Cunningham (Merce) *Australian:* 8 Helpmann (Robert) *Cuban:* 6 Alonso (Alicia) *Danish:* 5 Bruhn (Erik) 7 Martins (Peter) 12 Bournonville (August) *English:* 5 Dolin (Anton), Tudor (Antony) 6 Ashton (Frederick), Weaver (John) 7 Markova (Alicia), Rambert (Marie) 8 de Valois (Ninette), Helpmann (Robert) 9 MacMillan (Kenneth) *French:* 5 Lifar (Serge) 6 Béjart (Maurice), Perrot (Jules), Petipa (Marius) 7 Camargo (Marie), Massine (Léonide), Noverre (Jean-Georges) *German:* 5 Jooss (Kurt) *Hungarian:* 5 Laban (Rudolf) *Mexican:* 5 Limón (José) *Russian:* 5 Lifar (Serge) 6 Fokine (Michel), Petipa (Marius) 8 Nijinska (Bronislava), Nijinsky (Vaslav)
chorography 3 map 7 mapping 8 features 9 mapmaking
chortle 5 laugh 6 giggle, guffaw, hee-haw, titter 7 chuckle, snicker
chorus 5 choir 7 refrain

chorus girl 7 chorine
chosen 4 pick 5 elect, elite, named 6 called, marked, pegged, picked, select 7 blessed 8 selected 9 appointed, delegated, exclusive
Chou _____ 5 En-lai
chouse 3 gyp 4 bilk, clip, dupe, herd 5 cheat, cozen, drive, trick 6 diddle, fleece 7 defraud, swindle 8 flimflam
chow 4 eats, feed, food, grub, meal, mess
chowchow 6 medley, relish 7 mélange
chowderhead 4 boob, clod, dodo, dolt, dope, fool 5 chump, dunce, idiot, noddy 6 dimwit, nitwit, noodle 7 halfwit, schnook 8 dumbbell, numskull 9 lamebrain, numbskull
chowhound 7 glutton 8 gourmand
chrism 3 oil 4 balm 5 cream, salve 6 cerate 7 unction, unguent 8 ointment
christen 3 dub 4 call, name, term 5 title 7 asperse, baptize, immerse 8 dedicate, sprinkle 9 designate
christening 7 baptism
Christian *denomination:* 6 Mormon, Quaker 7 Baptist, Friends 8 Anglican, Catholic, Lutheran, Moravian, Nazarene, Reformed 9 Calvinist, Episcopal, Mennonite, Methodist, Unitarian 10 Anabaptist 11 Pentecostal 12 Episcopalian, Presbyterian, Universalist *Eastern rite:* 5 Uniat 6 Uniate *Egyptian:* 4 Copt *love feast:* 5 agape *martyr, first:* 7 Stephen *symbol:* 3 IHS 4 fish, rood 5 cross 6 Chi-Rho 7 ichthus
Christiania 4 Oslo
Christian Science founder 4 Eddy (Mary Baker)
Christie, Agatha *character:* 6 Marple (Jane), Poirot (Hercule) *novel:* 14 Death on the Nile 16 Ten Little Indians 24 Murder on the Orient Express *play:* 9 Mousetrap (The) 24 Witness for the Prosecution
Christina's World painter 5 Wyeth (Andrew)
Christmas 4 Noel, Yule 8 Nativity, yuletide *crumpet:* 7 pikelet *song:* 4 noel 5 carol *symbol:* 7 Yule log
Christmas Carol, A *author:* 7 Dickens (Charles) *character:* 7 Scrooge (Ebenezer), Tiny Tim 8 Cratchit (Bob)
Christogram 6 Chi-Rho
Christopher Robin creator 5 Milne (A. A.)
chromatic 8 colorful 10 accidental
chromatin thread 7 spireme
chromium symbol 2 Cr
chromosome component 3 DNA 4 gene 8 telomere 10 centromere, chromomere
chronic 5 usual 6 wonted 7 routine 8 constant, enduring, habitual 9 ceaseless, confirmed, continual, customary, incessant,

perennial, perpetual, recurrent, recurring 10 accustomed, continuing, habituated, inveterate, persisting 11 unrelenting

chronicle 4 list, tale 6 annals, record, relate, report 7 account, history, narrate, recital, recount 8 describe 9 narration, narrative

chronicler 8 annalist, narrator, recorder, reporter 9 historian

chronograph 5 clock, watch 9 timepiece

chronology 5 annal 6 annals, record 7 history 8 calendar, register, schedule 9 timetable

chronometer 5 clock, watch 9 timepiece

chrysalis 4 pupa 8 covering

Chryseis *captor:* 9 Agamemnon *father:* 7 Chryses

Chrysippus *father:* 6 Pelops *slayer:* 6 Atreus 8 Thyestes

chthonic 6 Hadean, nether 7 hellish, satanic 8 accursed, infernal, plutonic 9 plutonian, Tartarean 10 sulphurous

chubby 5 hefty, husky, plump, podgy, pudgy, round, tubby 6 chunky, fleshy, portly, rotund, stocky, zaftig 8 plumpish, roly-poly

chuck 3 pat, tap 4 beef, cast, hurl, junk, oust, shed, toss 5 ditch, fling, heave, nudge, pitch, scrap, throw 6 give up, reject 7 abandon, boot out, discard, dismiss, kick out 8 jettison, throw out 9 throw away

chucker 7 bouncer

chuckle 5 laugh 6 giggle, guffaw, hee-haw, titter 7 chortle, snicker

chucklehead see chowderhead

chuff 3 oaf 4 boor, lout, rube 5 churl, clown, yahoo, yokel 7 bumpkin, hayseed 10 clodhopper

chum 3 pal 4 mate, pard 5 buddy, crony 6 friend, salmon 7 comrade 8 sidekick 9 companion

chummy 4 cozy 5 close, pally, palsy, thick 8 familiar, intimate 10 buddy-buddy, palsy-walsy

chump 3 oaf, sap 4 boob, dolt, dope, dupe, fool, goof, goon, gull, mark 5 booby, dummy, dunce, loser, patsy 6 pigeon, sucker, turkey 7 failure, fall guy, fathead 8 dolthead, lunkhead

chunk 3 sum, wad 4 clod, hunk, lump, slab 5 clump 6 nugget

chunky 5 beefy, dumpy, hefty, husky, plump, pudgy, squat, stout 6 chubby, fleshy, portly, rotund, stocky, stubby, stumpy 8 heavyset, thickset

church 4 cult, fane, kirk, sect 5 creed, faith 6 temple 7 minster 8 basilica, religion 9 cathedral, communion 10 tabernacle 12 denomination *adjunct:* 6 belfry 7 steeple 9 bell tower *basin:* 4 font 5 stoup *bench:* 3

pew *bishop's:* 9 cathedral *Buddhist:* 2 ta *calendar:* 4 ordo *caretaker:* 6 sexton *chapel:* 7 oratory *code:* 8 canon law *council:* 5 synod *court:* 4 rota 10 consistory *creed:* 6 Nicene 8 Apostles' *district:* 6 parish 7 diocese *father:* 5 Basil 6 Jerome, Justin, Origen 7 Ambrose, Clement 8 Ignatius 9 Augustine 10 Chrysostom, Tertullian, theologian *fund-raiser:* 5 bingo 6 bazaar, raffle *governing body:* 5 curia 7 classis 10 consistory, presbytery *head:* 4 pope 7 pontiff *law:* 5 canon *member:* 11 communicant *of a monastery:* 7 minster *officer:* 5 elder, vicar 6 beadle, deacon, sexton, verger, warden 9 presbyter, sacristan *part:* 4 apse, bema, loft, nave 5 aisle, altar, choir 6 vestry 7 chancel, gallery, narthex, steeple 8 sacristy, transept 9 baptistry, sanctuary 10 baptistery, clerestory *porch:* 6 parvis 7 galilee *reader:* 6 lector *recess:* 4 apse *response:* 4 amen *revenue:* 5 tithe *room:* 6 vestry 8 sacristy *Scottish:* 4 kirk *seats for clergy:* 7 sedilia *service:* 4 mass 6 matins 7 vespers 8 evensong 9 communion *small:* 6 chapel *tribunal:* 4 rota *vault:* 5 crypt

Churchill, Winston *daughter:* 4 Mary 5 Diana, Sarah *estate:* 8 Checkers *father:* 8 Randolph *gesture:* 5 V-sign *mother:* 6 Jennie (Jerome) *phrase:* 11 Iron Curtain *son:* 8 Randolph *trademark:* 5 cigar *wife:* 10 Clementine

church key 9 can opener

churchman 6 bishop, cleric, divine, parson, pastor, priest 8 minister, preacher, reverend 9 clergyman 12 ecclesiastic

churl 3 oaf 4 boor, clod, lout, rube 5 chuff, clown, yahoo, yokel 6 mucker 7 bumpkin, hayseed 10 clodhopper

churlish 4 base, curt, dour, rude 5 blunt, crude, gruff, surly 6 coarse, crusty, oafish, vulgar 7 boorish, brusque, loutish, lowbred, uncivil 8 cloddish, clownish 10 unmannerly 11 clodhopping, uncivilized 12 discourteous

churn 4 boil, foam, roil, stir 5 froth, swirl 6 bubble, seethe, simmer, stir up 7 agitate, ferment, smolder

chute 4 fall, ramp 5 falls, rapid, slide, spout 6 rapids 7 cascade, channel, descent 8 cataract 9 spinnaker, waterfall

chutzpah 4 gall 5 brass, cheek, moxie, nerve, spunk 8 audacity, temerity 10 effrontery

CIA predecessor 3 OSS

ciao 4 by-by, ta-ta 5 adieu, adios, aloha, hello, howdy 6 bye-bye, good-by, so long 7 cheerio, good-bye, toodles 8 farewell, toodle-oo 9 greetings

cicatrix 4 scar 13 scarification

Cicero *forte:* 7 oratory *speech:* 9 philippic *target:* 8 Catiline 10 Mark Antony
cicerone 4 guru 5 coach, guide, tutor 6 docent, escort, mentor 7 adviser 9 counselor, tour guide
Cid, El (Le) 4 epic, hero, play, poem 5 opera *composer:* 8 Massenet (Jules) *meaning:* 4 lord *name:* 4 Díaz (Rodrigo, Ruy) 5 Bivar *playwright:* 9 Corneille (Pierre) *sword:* 6 Colada, Tizona *wife:* 6 Jimena, Ximena
cigar 5 claro, stogy 6 corona, Havana, stogie 7 cheroot 8 panatela, perfecto *case:* 7 humidor *color:* 5 claro 6 maduro 8 colorado
cigarette 3 fag 4 butt 5 smoke 6 gasper 10 coffin nail
cilium 4 hair, lash 7 eyelash
Cimmerian 4 dark 5 dusky, murky 6 gloomy 7 hellish, shadowy, stygian 8 infernal, plutonic 9 plutonian
cinch 4 snap 5 girth, setup 6 assure, breeze, ensure, fasten, insure, picnic, secure, shoo-in 8 duck soup, kid stuff, pushover 9 certainty 10 child's play
cinchona bark extract 7 quinine
cincture 4 band, belt, sash 6 girdle 9 waistband
cinders 3 ash 4 coal, lava, slag 5 ashes, dross 6 embers 8 clinkers
cinema 4 film, nabe, show 5 flick, movie 6 movies 7 picture, theater, theatre 12 silver screen 13 motion picture
cinereous 4 ashy, gray, grey 5 ashen 7 ashlike
cinnabar 3 ore 7 mineral, pigment 9 vermilion *color:* 3 red
cinnamon bark 6 cassia
cinnamon stone 6 garnet 8 essonite
cipher 4 code, zero 5 aught, count, digit 6 figure, naught, nobody, number, reckon, symbol 7 compute, integer, numeral 8 estimate, monogram 9 calculate, nonentity 11 whole number
ciphering 8 figuring 9 computing, reckoning 10 arithmetic 11 calculation, computation
circa 4 near, nigh 5 about 6 approx., around 7 roughly 13 approximately
circadian 5 daily 6 cyclic 7 diurnal, regular 9 quotidian
Circe 5 siren, witch 9 sorceress 11 enchantress *brother:* 6 Aeëtes *father:* 3 Sol 6 Helios *home:* 5 Aeaea *lover:* 7 Ulysses 8 Odysseus *niece:* 5 Medea *son:* 5 Comus 9 Telegonus
Circean 6 luring 8 alluring, enticing, fetching, tempting 10 bewitching
circinate 6 coiled 7 rounded
circle 4 belt, gyre, hoop, loop, ring 5 crowd, cycle, group, orbit, wheel, whorl 6 clique, corona, girdle, gyrate, rotary, rotate 7 compass, coterie, cronies, friends, revolve, rondure 8 surround 9 encompass 10 associates, companions, revolution *bisector:* 8 diameter *colored:* 6 areola *combining form:* 3 gyr 4 cycl, gyro 5 cyclo *graph:* 8 pie chart *luminous:* 4 aura, halo 6 corona, nimbus 7 aureole *part:* 3 arc 6 sector 8 quadrant *small:* 4 disk 7 annulet
circlet 4 band, ring 6 bangle, diadem 8 bracelet, headband *for head or helmet:* 7 coronal
circuit 3 lap, way 4 loop, tour, trip, turn 5 ambit, cycle, orbit, round, route, track 6 course, hookup, league 7 compass, journey, pathway, travels 8 district, rotation 9 perimeter, periphery, round trip 10 revolution, roundabout 11 association, circulation 13 circumference
circuitous 7 devious, oblique, winding 8 circular, indirect, tortuous 10 collateral, convoluted, meandering, roundabout
circuit rider 5 judge 8 minister, preacher 9 clergyman
circular 4 bill 5 flier, flyer, round 7 annular, cycloid, discoid, handout, leaflet 8 handbill 9 throwaway *file:* 11 wastebasket *fort:* 8 martello *motion:* 4 eddy, gyre, spin 5 whirl 8 gyration, rotation 10 revolution *plate:* 4 disc, dish, disk
circularize 4 poll 6 survey 7 canvass 9 advertise, publicize
circulate 4 flow 6 rotate, spread 7 diffuse, radiate, revolve 8 disperse 9 propagate 10 distribute 11 disseminate
circulation 4 flow 6 spread 8 currency 9 diffusion 11 propagation 12 transmission 13 dissemination
circumciser 5 mohel
circumcision, Jewish 4 bris 9 Brit Milah
circumference 3 rim 5 ambit 6 border, bounds, limits, margin 7 circuit, compass 8 boundary, confines 9 perimeter, periphery
circumflex 9 diacritic
circumjacent 11 surrounding
circumlocution 8 pleonasm, verbiage 9 euphemism, loquacity, prolixity, verbosity, wordiness 10 redundancy 11 periphrasis, verboseness
circumnavigate 5 skirt 6 bypass, detour 8 sidestep
circumnavigator 4 Cook (James) 5 Drake (Francis) 8 Magellan (Ferdinand), van Noort (Olivier) 9 Cavendish (Thomas)
circumscribe 5 cramp, limit 6 fetter, hamper 7 confine, delimit, enclose, mark off, out-

line, trammel **8** restrict, surround **9** constrict

circumscribed 5 bound, fixed **6** finite, narrow, strait **7** bounded, cramped, limited, precise **8** confined, definite, hampered **10** restrained, restricted **11** determinate

circumscription 5 cramp, limit, stint **6** border, margin **8** boundary **9** perimeter, restraint, stricture **10** constraint, definition, limitation **11** confinement, restriction **12** ball and chain, delimitation

circumspect 4 safe, wary **5** chary **7** careful, guarded, prudent **8** cautious, discreet, gingerly **11** calculating

circumstance 4 fact, item **5** event, thing **6** detail, factor **7** adjunct, element, episode, feature **8** accident, incident, occasion **9** component, condition, happening **10** occurrence, particular **11** concomitant, constituent, eventuality *unforeseen:* **8** exigency **9** emergency

circumstantial 4 full **5** close, exact **6** strict **7** precise, replete **8** accurate, complete, detailed, thorough **9** elaborate, pertinent **10** blow-by-blow, ceremonial, exhaustive, incidental, particular

circumvent 5 avoid, dodge, elude, evade, hem in, skirt **6** bypass, detour **8** outflank, sidestep

circumvolution 4 gyre, turn **5** wheel, whirl **8** gyration, rotation **10** revolution

circus 4 ring **5** arena **6** big top **9** spectacle **12** amphitheater *animal:* **4** bear, flea, lion, seal **5** horse, tiger **8** elephant *attraction:* **5** freak **8** sideshow *owner:* **6** Bailey (James), Barnum (P. T.) **8** Ringling (Bros.) *performer:* **5** clown, tamer **7** acrobat, athlete, juggler, tumbler **9** aerialist, fire eater, strong man *worker:* **10** roustabout

Cisco Kid 9 caballero *actor:* **4** Beck (Jackson) **6** Baxter (Warner), Roland (Gilbert), Romero (Cesar) **7** Renaldo (Duncan) *horse:* **6** Diablo *sidekick:* **6** Pancho **7** Gordito

citadel 4 fort **7** redoubt **8** fastness, fortress **10** stronghold *of Carthage:* **5** Bursa, Byrsa *Russian:* **7** kremlin

citation 5 quote **6** eulogy **7** excerpt, mention, summons, tribute **8** accolade, encomium **9** panegyric, quotation, reference **12** commendation

cite 4 name, tell **5** offer, quote **6** adduce, recall, summon **7** arraign, mention, present, refer to, specify **8** point out, remember **9** recollect

citizen 7 burgess, burgher, subject **8** civilian, national, resident, townsman **10** inhabitant

Citizen Kane director 6 Welles (Orson)

citron 4 tree **5** melon

citrus family: **3** rue **8** Rutaceae *fruit:* **4** lime, ugli **5** lemon **6** citron, orange, pomelo **7** kumquat, tangelo **8** bergamot, mandarin, shaddock **9** tangerine **10** grapefruit

city 4 burg **5** urban **7** burghal **9** municipal **10** metropolis *combining form:* **5** polis *Eternal:* **4** Rome *fortress:* **7** citadel *French:* **5** ville *heavenly:* **4** Sion, Zion *Latin:* **4** urbs *Motor:* **7** Detroit *of Bells:* **10** Strasbourg *of Bridges:* **6** Bruges *of Brotherly Love:* **12** Philadelphia *of David:* **9** Jerusalem *official:* **5** mayor **7** manager **8** alderman **10** councilman *of God:* **6** heaven **8** paradise *of Gold:* **8** Eldorado *of Kings:* **4** Lima *of Lights:* **5** Paris *of Lilies:* **8** Florence *of Masts:* **6** London *of Rams:* **6** Canton *of Refuge:* **6** Medina *of Saints:* **8** Montreal *of Seven Hills:* **4** Rome *of the dead:* **10** necropolis *of Victory:* **5** Cairo *planner:* **8** urbanist *section:* **4** slum, ward **5** block, plaza **6** barrio, ghetto, square, uptown **8** business, downtown, red-light **11** residential *slicker:* **4** dude *windy:* **7** Chicago

city-state, Greek 5 Argos, polis **6** Athens, Delphi, poleis (plural), Sparta, Thebes **7** Corinth

city, town, village (see also **capital**) *Afghanistan:* **5** Balkh, Farah, Herat, Kushk **6** Konduz **8** Kandahar, Qandahar **9** Jalalabad *Alabama:* **3** Opp **4** Arab, Boaz, Elba **5** Selma **6** Athens, Dothan, Mobile **7** Decatur, Florala **8** Prichard **10** Birmingham, Huntsville, Scottsboro, Tuscaloosa **12** Muscle Shoals *Alaska:* **4** Nome **5** Kenai, Sitka **6** Barrow, Bethel, Kodiak, Valdez **9** Anchorage, Fairbanks, Ketchikan **11** Point Barrow *Albania:* **4** Fier **5** Berat, Korçë, Kukës, Vlorë *Alberta:* **4** Olds **5** Hanna, Leduc, Taber **7** Calgary **10** Lethbridge **11** Medicine Hat *Algeria:* **4** Bône, Oran **5** Batna, Blida, Médéa, Saïda, Sétif **6** Annaba, Bechar **11** Constantine *Angola:* **6** Huambo **7** Lubango **8** Benguela *Argentina:* **4** Azul, Goya **5** Junin, Lanus, Lujan, Merlo, Salta, Tigre **6** Parana **7** Córdoba, La Plata, La Rioja, Mendoza, Rosario, San Juan, Santa Fe **9** Catamarca **11** Bahía Blanca, Mar del Plata *Arizona:* **3** Ajo **4** Eloy, Mesa, Yuma **5** Globe, Tempe **6** Tucson **7** Sun City, Winslow **8** Glendale, Prescott **9** Flagstaff, Tombstone **10** Casa Grande, Scottsdale *Arkansas:* **4** Mena **5** Beebe, Cabot, Earle, Ozark, Wynne **9** Fort Smith, Pine Bluff, Texarkana **10** Hot Springs *Armenia:* **6** Gyumri **8** Vanadzor *Australia:* **3** Ayr **5** Dalby, Dubbo, Perth, Unley **6** Darwin, Sydney **8** Adelaide, Brisbane, Randwick **9** Bankstown, Blacktown, Gold Coast, Melbourne, Newcastle **10** Kalgoorlie, Parramatta, Sutherland, Wollongong **12** Alice Springs *Austria:* **4** Enns, Graz, Linz, Wels **5** Steyr, Traun **8** Salzburg **9** Innsbruck **10** Klagenfurt *Azerbaijan:* **5** Gäncä **8** Sumqayit **9** Kirovabad *Bahamas:* **8** Freeport *Bangladesh:* **5** Bogra, Pabna **6** Khulna, Sylhet **7** Barisal, Comilla, Jessore, Rangpur, Saidpur **10** Chittagong *Belarus:* **5** Brest, Gomel, Mozyr, Pinsk **6** Grodno, Homyel', Hrodna **7** Mogilev, Vitebsk **8** Babruysk, Mahilyow **9** Vitsyebsk *Belgium:* **3** Ath, Hal, Huy, Mol **4** Amay, Dour, Geel, Genk, Gent, Hoei, Luik, Mons, Vise **5** Aalst, Arlon, Diest, Evere, Ghent, Halle, Ieper, Jumet, Leuze, Liège, Namur, Ronse, Theux, Wavre, Ypres **6** Bruges, Brugge **7** Antwerp, Hasselt, Louvain **8** Oostende **9** Charleroi *Benin:* **5** Kandi **6** Abomey **7** Parakou *Bolivia:* **5** Oruro, Uyuni **6** Potosí **9** Santa Cruz **10** Cochabamba *Bosnia and Herzegovina:* **5** Bihac, Brcko, Jajce, Tuzla **6** Mostar, Zenica **9** Banja Luka *Botswana:* **4** Maun **5** Kanye **11** Francistown *Brazil:* **4** Codo, Pará **5** Bahia, Bauru, Belém, Ceara, Natal **6** Campos, Canoas, Caxias, Ilheus, Maceio, Manaus, Olinda, Recife, Santos **7** Aracaju, Caruaru, Goiania, Jundiai, Marilia, Niteroi, Pelotas, São Luis, Uberaba, Vitória **8** Campinas, Colatina, Curitiba, Londrina, Salvador, Santarém, São Paulo, Sorocaba, Teresina **9** Caratinga, Fortaleza, Guarulhos, Rio Grande **10** Guarapuava, Joao Pessoa, Juiz de Fora, Nova Iguaçu, Pernambuco, Petropolis, Piracicaba, Pôrto Velho, Santa Maria, Santo André, São Gonçalo, Uberlândia **11** Campo Grande, Caxias do Sul, Ponta Grossa, Pôrto Alegre **12** Montes Claros, Rio de Janeiro, Teófilo Otoni, Volta Redonda **13** Belo Horizonte *British Columbia:* **5** Comox **6** Surrey **7** Burnaby **8** Richmond **9** Vancouver *Bulgaria:* **3** Lom **4** Ruse **5** Varna, Vidin **6** Burgas **7** Plovdiv **11** Stara Zagora *Burma:* see **Myanmar** *California:* **4** Brea, Galt, Lodi, Ojai **5** Arvin, Azusa, Ceres, Chico, Chino, Dixon, Hemet, Indio, Norco, Ripon, Ukiah, Wasco, Yreka **6** Downey, Encino, Fresno, Oxnard, Pomona, Sonoma **7** Anaheim, Burbank, Compton, Fremont, Hayward, Modesto, Oakland, San Jose, Seaside, Soledad, Van Nuys **8** Berkeley, Glendale, Palo Alto, Pasadena, San Diego, Santa Ana, Stockton, Torrance, Yuba City **9** El Segundo, Hollywood, Long Beach, Menlo Park, Riverside, Sausalito **10**

Chula Vista, Culver City, Los Angeles, San Leandro, Santa Clara **11** Bakersfield, Laguna Beach, Pebble Beach, Redwood City, San Clemente, Santa Monica **12** Beverly Hills, Mission Viejo, Redondo Beach, San Francisco, Santa Barbara **13** San Bernardino, San Luis Obispo *Cambodia:* **8** Siem Reap **10** Battambang **11** Kompong Cham *Cameroon:* **4** Buea, Edea **5** Kribi, Lomie **6** Douala **7** Bamenda, Foumban **9** Bafoussam *Canada:* **4** York **5** Banff **6** London, Oshawa, Regina, St. John **7** Brandon, Burnaby, Calgary, Halifax, Iqaluit, Red Deer, St. John's, Sudbury, Toronto, Windsor **8** Hamilton, Montreal, Moose Jaw, North Bay, Victoria, Winnipeg **9** Dartmouth, Kitchener, Longueuil, North York, Saint John, Saskatoon, Vancouver **10** Lethbridge, Saint John's, Sherbrooke, Thunder Bay, Whitehorse **11** Fredericton, Medicine Hat, Mississauga, Scarborough, Yellowknife **12** Peterborough, Prince Albert, Prince George **13** Charlottetown, Trois-Rivières *Central African Republic:* **5** Bouar **7** Bambari *Chad:* **4** Sarh **6** Abéché *Chile:* **4** Lebu, Lota, Tomé **5** Ancud, Angol, Arica, Maipu, Penco, Rengo, Talca **6** Temuco **7** Copiapó, Iquiquè **8** Rancagua **10** Concepción, Talcahuano, Valparaíso **11** Antofagasta *China:* **4** Amoy, Jian, Luan, Xi'an, Yaan **5** Hefei, Jilin, Jinan, Lhasa, Qinan, Ssuan, Wuhan, Yibin, Yumen **6** Andong, Anqing, Anshan, Anshun, Anyang, Beihai, Canton, Dalian, Datong, Foshan, Fushun, Fuzhou, Guilin, Haikou, Handan, Harbin, Hohhot, Hoihao, Jilong, Luzhou, Mukden, Ningbo, Pengbu, Suzhou, Ürümqi, Xiamen, Xining, Xuzhou, Yanggu, Yichun, Yining, Zhangi, Zhaoan **7** Baoding, Changan, Chengdu, Dandong, Guiyang, Huainan, Jiamusi, Jiaxing, Kaifeng, Kunming, Lanzhou, Luoshan, Luoyang, Nanking, Nanjing, Nanning, Shantou, Tianjin, Taiyuan **8** Changchi, Changsha, Hangzhou, Hanzhong, Huangshi, Jiangmen, Shanghai, Shaoyang, Shenyang, Shenzhen, Zhenjing **9** Changchun, Chenjiang, Chongqing, Chungking, Guangzhou, Zhengzhou, Zhenjiang *Colombia:* **4** Buga, Cali **5** Bello, Mocoa, Neiva, Ocaña, Pasto, Tuluá, Tunja **6** Cúcuta, Ibagué **7** Ciénaga, Palmira, Pereira, Popayán **8** Medellín, Montería **9** Cartagena, Manizales **10** Santa Marta **11** Bucaramanga **12** Barranquilla *Colorado:* **6** Arvada, Aurora, Golden, Salida **7** Alamosa, Boulder, Durango, Greeley, La Junta **8** Brighton, Gunnison, Lakewood, Longmont, Loveland, Montrose, Thornton

9 Englewood, Estes Park, Leadville, Littleton, Rocky Ford, Telluride 10 Broomfield, Castle Rock 11 Fort Collins 13 Grand Junction *Congo (Zaire):* 4 Boma 6 Bukavu 7 Kolwezi 8 Bandundu 9 Kisangani 10 Lubumbashi 12 Stanleyville *Congo-Brazzaville:* 11 Pointe-Noire *Connecticut:* 6 Darien, Granby, Groton, Haddam 7 Danbury, Enfield, Meriden, Milford, Newtown, Norwalk, Norwich, Old Lyme, Pomfret, Windham 8 Guilford, New Haven, Simsbury, Stamford, Suffield, Westport 9 Greenwich, New Canaan, New London, Waterbury, Waterford 10 Bridgeport, Farmington, Kensington, Litchfield, New Britain, Ridgefield, Stonington, Torrington *Costa Rica:* 8 Alajuela 10 Puntarenas 11 Puerto Limón *Croatia:* 4 Pula 5 Sisak, Split, Zadar 6 Osijek, Rijeka 9 Dubrovnik *Cuba:* 5 Banes, Bauta 6 Bayamo 7 Holguín 8 Camagüey, Marianao, Matanzas, Santiago 10 Cienfuegos, Guantánamo 11 Pinar del Río *Cyprus:* 7 Kyrenia, Larnaca 8 Limassol 9 Famagusta *Czech Republic:* 4 Brno, Zlín 5 Plzen 7 Liberec, Olomouc, Ostrava 10 Bratislava *Delaware:* 5 Lewes 7 Seaford 10 Harrington, Wilmington, Winterthur *Denmark:* 5 Arhus, Skive, Vejle 6 Alborg, Odense, Viborg 13 Frederiksberg *Dominican Republic:* 4 Azua, Bani, Moca 5 Bonao, Nagua 8 Barahona, Santiago *Ecuador:* 4 Loja 5 Canar, Daule, Manta, Pinas 7 Machala 8 Riobamba 9 Guayaquil *Egypt:* 4 Giza, Idfu, Isna, Qena 5 Aswan, Asyut, Benha, Disuq, Girga, Luxor, Minuf, Tahta, Tanta 6 Helwan 7 El Arish, Zagazig 8 Damanhur, Damietta, El Faiyum, Ismailia, Port Said 10 Alexandria *Eire:* see **Ireland,** below *El Salvador:* 7 La Unión 8 Santa Ana 9 Sonsonate *England:* 4 Bath, Eton, Hove, Ryde, York 5 Brent, Brigg, Colne, Corby, Cowes, Derby, Dover, Egham, Eling, Esher, Eston, Goole, Leeds, Leigh, Lewes, Luton, Poole, Ryton, Wigan 6 Bexley, Bolton, Dudley, Durham, Exeter, Merton, Oldham, Oxford, Torbay, Warley, Welwyn 7 Bristol, Bromley, Croydon, Hackney, Ipswich, Malvern, Norwich, Salford, Seaford, Walsall 8 Abingdon, Basildon, Bradford, Brighton, Coventry, Hastings, Hatfield, Havering, Hertford, Kingston, Lewisham, Plymouth, Wallsend 9 Aylesbury, Blackpool, Cambridge, Islington, Leicester, Liverpool, Newcastle, Sheffield, Stratford 10 Birkenhead, Birmingham, Canterbury, Colchester, Manchester, Nottingham, Portsmouth, Sunderland 11 Bournemouth, Northampton, Southampton

12 Peterborough, Stoke-on-Trent, West Bromwich 13 Southend-on-Sea, Wolverhampton *Estonia:* 5 Narva, Pärnu, Tartu *Ethiopia:* 5 Aksum, Harer 6 Nazret 8 Dire Dawa *Finland:* 4 Kemi, Oulu, Pori 5 Espoo, Hango, Kotka, Lahti, Rauma, Turku, Vaasa 6 Vantaa 7 Tampere *Florida:* 5 Largo, Miami, Ocala, Ocoee, Oneco, Tampa 6 DeLand, Naples 7 Hialeah, Key West, Orlando, Sebring 8 Gulfport, Key Largo, Lakeland, Opa-Locka, Sarasota 9 Boca Raton, Bradenton, Fort Myers, Kissimmee, Palm Beach, Pensacola, Vero Beach 10 Clearwater, Cocoa Beach, Miami Beach, Punta Gorda, Titusville 11 Coral Gables, Gainesville, Key Biscayne, St. Augustine, Winter Haven 12 Apalachicola, Daytona Beach, Ft. Lauderdale, Jacksonville, Pompano Beach, St. Petersburg 13 Chattahoochee *France:* 3 Dax, Pau 4 Agde, Agen, Albi, Ales, Auch, Caen, Gien, Laon, Lyon, Metz, Nice, Orly, Rezé, Sens, Sète, Vire 5 Arles, Arras, Auray, Auton, Avion, Berck, Blois, Bondy, Brest, Creil, Digne, Dijon, Douai, Dreux, Flers, Gagny, Laval, Le Puy, Lille, Lunel, Lyons, Mâcon, Meaux, Melun, Muret, Nîmes, Niort, Noyon, Reims, Revin, Rodez, Rouen, Royan, Tours, Tulle, Vichy, Vitre 6 Amiens, Angers, Calais, Cannes, Dieppe, Evreux, Le Mans, Nantes, Nevers, Rennes, Rheims, Thiers, Toulon, Troyes 7 Ajaccio, Antibes, Avignon, Béthune, Bourges, Le Havre, Limoges, Lorient, Lourdes, Orléans, Roubaix 8 Beauvais, Besançon, Biarritz, Bordeaux, Chartres, Gentilly, Grenoble, Nanterre, Poitiers, Toulouse 9 Cherbourg, Dunkerque, Marseille, Perpignan 10 Marseilles, Strasbourg, Versailles 11 Carcassonne, Montpellier 13 Aix-en-Provence *Gabon:* 4 Oyem 5 Bitam 10 Port-Gentil 11 Franceville *Gambia:* 9 Serekunda *Georgia:* 4 Adel, Alma, Arco 5 Jesup, Macon, McRae 6 Albany, Athens 7 Augusta, Calhoun 8 Americus, Columbus, Marietta, Savannah, Valdosta 9 Brunswick *Georgia, Republic of:* 6 Batumi 7 Kutaisi, Rustavi, Sukhumi *Germany:* 3 Aue, Hof, Ulm 4 Bonn, Gera, Goch, Hamm, Jena, Kehl, Kiel, Köln, Marl, Suhl 5 Aalen, Ahlen, Borna, Bruhl, Calbe, Celle, Düren, Emden, Essen, Forst, Fulda, Furth, Gotha, Greiz, Hagen, Halle, Hanau, Herne, Hurth, Kleve, Lemgo, Lobau, Mainz, Trier 6 Aachen, Bremen, Coburg, Dachau, Dessau, Erfurt, Kassel, Lübeck, Munich 7 Cologne, Cottbus, Dresden, Hamburg, Hanover, Koblenz, Krefeld, Leipzig, München, Mun-

ster, Potsdam, Rostock, Zwickau **8**
Augsburg, Bayreuth, Chemnitz, Cuxhaven,
Dortmund, Duisburg, Freiburg, Hannover,
Mannheim, Nürnberg, Würzburg **9**
Bielefeld, Brunswick, Darmstadt, Frank-
furt, Göttingen, Karlsruhe, Magdeburg,
Nuremberg, Stuttgart, Wiesbaden, Wupper-
tal **10** Baden-Baden, Düsseldorf, Heidel-
berg, Regensburg **11** Brandenburg,
Bremerhaven, Saarbrücken **12** Braunsch-
weig **13** Gelsenkirchen *Ghana:* **4** Axim,
Keta, Tema **5** Lawra, Yendi **6** Kumasi
Greece: **3** Kos **4** Arta **5** Argos, Lamia,
Nemea, Volos **6** Sparta, Thebes **7** Corinth,
Khalkis, Larissa, Piraeus, Tríkala **8** Salon-
ika **12** Thessaloniki *Guatemala:* **5** Cobán **13**
Quezaltenango *Guinea:* **4** Labé **6** Kankan,
Kindia *Haiti:* **8** Gonaïves **10** Cap Haitien
Hawaii: **4** Aiea, Hilo, Laie **5** Kapaa, Lihue,
Maili **6** Kailua **7** Kaneohe, Waikiki, Wai-
luku *Honduras:* **5** Danlí **7** La Ceiba **12** San
Pedro Sula *Hong Kong:* **7** Kowloon *Hun-
gary:* **3** Ozd **4** Eger, Györ, Pécs **5** Abony,
Bekes **6** Szeged **7** Miskolc **8** Debrecen
Idaho: **4** Buhl **5** Nampa **6** Dubois, Moscow
7 Gooding, Payette, Rexburg **8** Caldwell **9**
Blackfoot, Pocatello, Sandpoint, Sun Val-
ley, Twin Falls **11** Coeur d' Alene, Grang-
eville *Illinois:* **6** DeKalb, Galena, Hardin,
Joliet, Macomb, Moline, Paxton, Peoria,
Skokie, Urbana **7** Chicago, Decatur, Glen-
coe, Oak Lawn, Oak Park, Tuscola,
Watseka, Wheaton **8** Carthage, Evanston,
Kankakee, La Grange, Monmouth, Rock-
ford, Vandalia, Waukegan **9** Belvidere, Ef-
fingham, Galesburg, Park Ridge, Yorkville
10 Belleville, Carbondale, Carrollton, Des
Plaines, Northbrook, Rock Island *India:* **3**
Mau **4** Agra, Ahwa, Bhuj, Durg, Gaya,
Kota, Mhow, Pune, Puri, Rewa, Tonk, Ziro
5 Adoni, Aimer, Akola, Alwar, Arcot, Ar-
rah, Banda, Barsi, Bidar, Bihar, Churu,
Damoh, Delhi, Dewas, Eluru, Gonda, Jalna,
Jammu, Karur, Miraj, Morvi, Nasik, Patan,
Patna, Poona, Sagar, Satna, Sikar, Simla,
Surat, Thana **6** Baroda, Bhopal, Bombay,
Cochin, Guntur, Howrah, Indore, Jaipur,
Jhansi, Kanpur, Madras, Meerut, Mysore,
Nagpur, Raipur, Rajkot, Ranchi, Ujjain **7**
Aligarh, Asansol, Belgaum, Bikaner, Burd-
wan, Cuttack, Gauhati, Gwalior, Jodhpur,
Kurnool, Lucknow, Madurai, Mathura, Nel-
lore, Patiala, Vellore **8** Amritsar, Bhatpara,
Calcutta, Dehra Dun, Kolhapur, Ludhiana,
Sholapur, Srinagar, Varanasi **9** Ahmadabad,
Allahabad, Bangalore, Hyderabad **10** Ah-
madnagar, Chandigarh, Trivandrum **11**

Pondicherry *Indiana:* **4** Gary **5** Berne,
Paoli, Vevay **6** Delphi, Kokomo, Marlon,
Muncie, Tipton **7** Bedford, Corydon,
Elkhart, La Porte, Winamac **8** Bluffton,
Kentland **9** Boonville, Fort Wayne, New Al-
bany, Rushville, South Bend, Vincennes **10**
Crown Point, Evansville, Logansport,
Scottsburg, Terre Haute, Valparaiso **11**
Bloomington *Indonesia:* **4** Pati **5** Ambon,
Bogor, Garut, Kudus, Medan, Tegal, Turen
6 Batang, Kediri, Madiun, Malang,
Manado, Padang **7** Bandung, Kendari **8** Se-
marang, Surabaja, Surabaya, Tjirebon **9**
Palembang, Pontianak, Surakarta **10** Peka-
longan **11** Tasikmalaja **12** Bandjarmasin
Iowa: **5** Onawa, Pella **6** Eldora, Harlan,
Keokuk, Le Mars, Red Oak **7** Allison, Ana-
mosa, Carroll, Clinton, Corydon, Denison,
Dubuque, Marengo, Osceola, Waverly **8**
Clarinda, Ida Grove, Waterloo **9** Davenport,
Fort Dodge, Indianola, Mason City, Musca-
tine, Oskaloosa, Sioux City, Storm Lake,
West Union, Winterset **10** Emmetsburg,
Rock Rapids, Spirit Lake **11** Cedar Rapids,
Fort Madison **13** Council Bluffs *Iran:* **3**
Qom, Qum **4** Amul, Arak, Khoi, Sari, Yazd,
Yezd **5** Ahvaz, Ahwaz, Babol, Rasht **6** Aba-
dan, Meshed, Shiraz, Tabriz **7** Esfahan,
Hamadan, Isfahan, Mashhad **9** Bakhtaran
Iraq: **3** Ana, Kut **4** Kufa **5** Al Kut, Amara,
Basra, Erbil, Hilla, Mosul, Najaf, Rutba **6**
Amarah, Hillah, Kirkuk, Ramadi, Rutbah **7**
Falluja, Samarra **8** Fallujah, Nasiriya **9** Na-
siriyah *Ireland:* **4** Athy, Birr, Cobh, Cork,
Naas, Tuam **5** Ennis, Sligo **6** Carlow, Gal-
way, Tralee **7** Dundalk, Kildare, Wexford,
Wicklow **8** Drogheda, Kilkenny, Limerick,
Monaghan **9** Castlebar, Killarney, Tipper-
ary, Waterford **10** Balbriggan *Israel:* **5**
Afula, Haifa, Holon, Jaffa **7** Rehovot **8**
Ashqelon, Nazareth, Ramat Gan **9** Beer-
sheba *Italy:* **4** Acri, Alba, Asti, Bari, Enna,
Este, Fano, Gela, Iesi, Lodi, Lugo, Pisa **5**
Adria, Agira, Anzio, Aosta, Arola, Cantù,
Capua, Carpi, Crema, Cuneo, Eboli,
Fermo, Fondi, Forli, Gaeta, Genoa, Imola,
Ivrea, Lecce, Lecco, Lucca, Massa, Melfi,
Menfi, Milan, Monza, Padua, Parma, Prato,
Siena, Turin **6** Ancona, Assisi, Foggia,
Mantua, Milano, Modena, Naples, Napoli,
Rimini, Torino, Venice, Verona **7** Bergamo,
Bologna, Bolzano, Brescia, Catania,
Firenze, Leghorn, Messina, Palermo, Peru-
gia, Pescara, Potenza, Ravenna, Salerno,
San Remo, Taranto, Trieste, Venezia **8**
Brindisi, Cagliari, Florence, La Spezia,
Piacenza, Siracusa, Syracuse *Ivory Coast:* **6**

Bouaké *Jamaica:* 6 May Pen 10 Montego Bay *Japan:* 3 Ina, Ise, Ito, Ota, Tsu, Ube, Uji, Yao 4 Ageo, Anan, Gifu, Hagi, Himi, Hofu, Iida, Joyo, Kaga, Kobe, Kofu, Kure, Miki, Mito, Naha, Nara, Noda, Oita, Otsu, Saga, Saku, Soka, Tosu, Ueda, Yono 5 Akita, Atami, Beppu, Chiba, Imari, Itami, Iwaki, Iwata, Izumi, Izumo, Kiryu, Kochi, Kyoto, Minoo, Odate, Ogaki, Okawa, Okaya, Omiya, Omuta, Osaka, Otaru, Oyama, Sabae, Saiki, Sakai, Sanjo, Suita, Tenri, Urawa 6 Akashi, Aomori, Himeji, Kadoma, Kurume, Matsue, Mitaka, Nagano, Nagoya, Numazu, Sasebo, Sendai, Suzuka, Toyama, Yonago 7 Fukuoka, Hitachi, Ibaraki, Imabari, Muroran, Niigata, Niihama, Nobeoka, Obihiro, Odawara, Okayama, Okazaki, Sapporo 8 Ashikaga, Fujisawa, Fukuyama, Hirakata, Hirosaki, Ichihara, Ichikawa, Kakogawa, Kamakura, Kanazawa, Kawasaki, Miyazaki, Nagasaki, Onomichi, Shizuoka, Takasaki, Toyonaka, Wakayama, Yamagata, Yokohama, Yokosuka 9 Hiroshima *Jordan:* 5 Aqaba, Irbid *Kansas:* 4 Gove, Iola 5 Colby, Hoxie, Lakin, Leoti, Paola, Pratt 6 Atwood, Beloit, Girard, Holton, Salina 7 Abilene, Emporia, Garnett, Kinsley, Wichita 8 Cimarron, Goodland, La Crosse, Sublette 9 Coldwater, Fort Scott, Great Bend, Oskaloosa 10 Hutchinson 11 Leavenworth 12 Council Grove, Overland Park 13 Medicine Lodge *Kazakhstan:* 5 Semey 6 Almaty, Aqtöbe, Guryev, Uralsk 7 Alma-Ata, Zhambyl 8 Balkhash, Chimkent, Dzhambul, Kyzl Orda, Pavlodar, Shymkent 9 Karaganda 10 Aktyubinsk *Kentucky:* 4 Inez 5 Cadiz, Hyden, McKee 6 Elkton, Harlan 7 Ashland, Campton, Greenup, Hindman, Paducah, Stanton 8 Fort Knox, Mayfield 9 Bardstown, Covington, Cynthiana, Lexington, Maysville, Owensboro, Pikeville, Pineville, Southgate, Vanceburg 10 Booneville, Hawesville, Louisville, Whitesburg 12 Bowling Green *Kenya:* 4 Embu 5 Nyeri 6 Kisumu, Nakuru 7 Mombasa *Kyrgyzstan:* 3 Osh 5 Naryn *Laos:* 5 Pakse 11 Savannakhet *Latvia:* 7 Jelgava, Liepaja 9 Ventspils 10 Daugavpils *Lebanon:* 4 Tyre 5 Sidon, Zahlé 7 Juniyah, Tripoli *Libya:* 4 Homs 5 Derna, Zawia 6 Tobruk 8 Benghazi, Misratah *Lithuania:* 6 Kaunas 8 Klaipeda *Louisiana:* 4 Jena 5 Amite, Arabi, Houma, Mamou, Norco, Rayne 6 Colfax, Edgard, Gretna, Minden, Ruston 7 Arcadia, Bastrop, Marrero, Oberlin 8 Bogalusa, De Ridder, Metairie, New Roads, Oak Grove,

Westwego 9 Abbeville, Chalmette, Hahnville, Leesville, New Iberia, Opelousas, Port Allen, Thibodaux, Winnfield, Winnsboro 10 New Orleans, Plaquemine, Shreveport 11 Lake Charles 12 Natchitoches *Macedonia:* 6 Bitola, Prilep, Tetovo *Maine:* 4 Saco 5 Orono 6 Auburn, Bangor, Gorham 7 Berwick, Kittery, Machias, Rumford 8 Lewiston, Portland, Rockland 9 Bar Harbor, Biddeford, Brunswick, Ellsworth, Kennebunk, Skowhegan, Wiscasset 11 Millinocket, Presque Isle 13 Kennebunkport *Malawi:* 5 Mzuzu, Zomba 8 Blantyre *Malaysia:* 4 Ipoh 5 Gemas, Klang 6 Kelang, Penang, Pinang 11 Johore Bahru *Mali:* 5 Kayes, Mopti, Ségou 7 Sikasso *Malta:* 10 Birkirkara *Maryland:* 5 Bowie 6 Denton, Elkton, Towson 8 Bethesda, Landover, Snow Hill 9 Baltimore, Rockville 10 Beltsville, Hagerstown 11 Chestertown, College Park, Leonardtown 12 Havre de Grace, Silver Spring *Massachusetts:* 5 Lenox, Salem 6 Boston, Dedham, Lowell, Malden, Monson, Natick, Saugus, Woburn 7 Amherst, Duxbury, Holyoke, Hyannis, Methuen, Needham, Swansea, Taunton, Walpole, Waltham, Wareham 8 Brockton, Chicopee, Falmouth, Plymouth, Rockport, Yarmouth 9 Brookline, Cambridge, Edgartown, Fall River, Fitchburg, Haverhill, Lexington, Nantucket, Worcester 10 Framingham, Gloucester, Greenfield, Leominster, New Bedford, North Adams, Pittsfield, Somerville 11 Northampton 11 Springfield 12 Provincetown, Williamstown *Mauritania:* 4 Atar 5 Kaedi 6 Dakhla *Mexico:* 4 León 5 Ameca, Choix, Tepic 6 Cancún, Celaya, Colima, Jalapa, Juárez, Mérida, Oaxaca, Puebla, Toluca, Tuxtla 7 Durango, Guasave, Morelia, Obregón, Reynosa, Tampico, Tijuana, Tlalpán, Torreón, Uruapan, Zapopan 8 Chetumal, Coyoacán, Culiacán, Ensenada, Mazatlan, Mexicali, Saltillo, Tuxtepec 9 Chihuahua, Fresnillo, Ixtacalco, Monterrey, Querétaro, Salamanca, Tapachula, Zacatecas 10 Cuernavaca, Hermosillo, Ixtapalapa, Xochimilco 11 Guadalajara, Nuevo Laredo 13 San Luis Potosí *Michigan:* 4 Alma, Holt 5 Flint, Ionia, L'Anse, Niles 6 Otsego, Paw Paw, Warren 7 Allegan, Corunna, Detroit, Gladwin, Livonia, Midland, Saginaw 8 Ann Arbor, Bessemer, Dearborn, Escanaba, Grayling, Hastings, Houghton, Muskegon, Sandusky 9 Cheboygan, Coldwater, Kalamazoo, Menominee, Port Huron, Ypsilanti 10 Charlevoix, Grand Haven 11 Battle Creek,

Grand Rapids *Minnesota:* 3 Ely 4 Mora 5 Anoka, Edina, Osseo 6 Aitkin, Benson, Duluth, Waseca, Windom, Winona 7 Glencoe, Hibbing, Mankato, Red Wing, St. Cloud, Wabasha 8 Brainerd, Elk River, Moorhead, Shakopee 9 Caledonia, Crookston, Faribault, Pipestone, Rochester, Saint Paul, Silver Bay 10 Park Rapids, Saint Cloud, Saint James, Saint Peter, Stillwater, Two Harbors 11 Bloomington, Fergus Falls, Long Prairie, Minneapolis, Worthington 12 Breckenridge, Granite Falls, Redwood Falls *Mississippi:* 4 Iuka 5 Amory 6 Biloxi, Leland, McComb, Purvis, Sardis, Sumner, Tupelo, Winona 7 Belzoni, Brandon, Okolona, Quitman, Wiggins 8 Gulfport, Hernando, Meridian, Paulding, Rosedale, Walthall 9 Greenwood, Indianola, New Albany, Pittsboro, Vicksburg 10 Batesville, Booneville, Brookhaven, Clarksdale, Ellisville, Greenville, Hazlehurst, Pascagoula, Port Gibson, Starkville, Waynesboro 11 Hattiesburg 12 Holly Springs *Missouri:* 3 Ava 4 Linn 5 Eldon, Hayti, Ladue, Rolla 6 Galena, Neosho, Potosi 7 Hermann, Ironton, Kennett, Linneus, Osceola, Palmyra, Sedalia, St. Louis 8 Gallatin, Hannibal 9 Boonville, Hartville, Hillsboro, Maryville, Pineville, Tuscumbia, Warrenton 10 Kansas City, Kirksville, Marble Hill, Marshfield, Perryville, Saint Louis, Springfield 11 Saint Joseph 12 Independence, Saint Charles *Moldova:* 5 Balti 7 Tighina 8 Tiraspol *Mongolia:* 5 Kobdo 6 Darhan 10 Choybalsan *Montana:* 5 Butte, Havre, Libby 6 Hardin, Polson 7 Bozeman 8 Billings, Missoula, Red Lodge 10 Great Falls *Montenegro:* 8 Titograd *Morocco:* 3 Fès 4 Safi, Salé, Taza 5 Nador, Oujda 6 Agadir, Meknès 7 Kenitra, Tangier 9 Marrakech, Marrakesh 10 Casablanca *Mozambique:* 5 Beira 7 Chimoio, Nampula 9 Quelimane, Quilimane *Myanmar:* 3 Pyu 4 Paan 5 Akyab, Bhamo, Chauk, Katha, Magwe, Minbu, Mogok, Tavoy 7 Bassein 8 Mandalay, Moulmein *Namibia:* 5 Outjo 6 Tsumeb 8 Oshakati 12 Keetmanshoop *Nebraska:* 3 Ord 5 Cozad, Omaha, Ponca, Tryon, Wahoo 6 Elwood, Gering, McCook, Minden, Wilber 7 Burwell, Fremont, Kearney, Kimball, Osceola, Tekamah 8 Beatrice, Fairbury, Hastings, Ogallala, Red Cloud, Schuyler, Tecumseh, Thedford 9 Fullerton, Papillion 10 Springview, Stockville 11 Grand Island, Hayes Center, North Platte, Plattsmouth *Netherlands:* 3 Ede, Epe, Oss 4 Echt, Tiel, Uden 5 Aalst, Assen, Breda, Delft, Emmen, Hague, Soest, Vaals, Venlo,

Vught, Weert, Weesp, Zeist 6 Arnhem 7 Haarlem, Tilburg, Utrecht 8 Enschede, Nijmegen, The Hague 9 Apeldoorn, Eindhoven, Groningen, Rotterdam, Zandvoort 10 Maastricht *Nevada:* 3 Ely 4 Elko, Reno 6 Fallon, Minden, Pioche 7 Tonopah 8 Las Vegas, Lovelock 9 Goldfield, Yerington 10 Winnemucca *New Brunswick:* 5 Minto 6 St. John 7 Moncton 9 Dalhousie, Saint John 10 Edmundston, Richibucto 12 Hopewell Cape, Perth Andover, Saint Andrews *Newfoundland:* 5 Burin 6 Wabana 10 Mount Pearl 11 Corner Brook *New Hampshire:* 5 Derry, Dover, Keene 6 Berlin, Exeter, Gorham, Nashua 7 Hanover, Laconia, Lebanon, Ossipee 8 Hinsdale, Seabrook 9 Littleton, Merrimack 10 Manchester, Portsmouth, Woodsville *New Jersey:* 4 Atco, Lodi 6 Camden, Newark, Nutley, Rahway, Rumson 7 Bayonne, Cape May, Clifton, Hoboken, Paramus, Passaic, Raritan, Teaneck 8 Freehold, Metuchen, Paterson, Vauxhall, Woodbury 9 Elizabeth, Glassboro, Lakehurst, Menlo Park, Montclair, Princeton, Riverside, Toms River 10 Asbury Park, Bloomfield, Cherry Hill, Hackensack, Jersey City, Morristown, Mount Holly, Perth Amboy, Piscataway, Plainfield, Somerville 11 Mays Landing 12 Atlantic City, New Brunswick 13 Palisades Park *New Mexico:* 4 Taos 5 Belen, Hobbs, Raton 6 Clovis, Deming, Grants 7 Roswell, Socorro 8 Estancia, Los Lunas, Portales 9 Carrizozo, Las Cruces, Los Alamos, Lovington, Tucumcari 10 Alamogordo, Bernalillo, Fort Sumner 11 Albuquerque *New York:* 4 Elma, Ovid, Troy 5 Depew, Ilion, Islip, Le Roy, Nyack, Olean, Owego, Utica 6 Attica, Cohoes, Delmar, Elmira, Hudson, Ithaca, Oneida 7 Batavia, Buffalo, Corning, Geneseo, Katonah, Mineola, Yonkers 8 Bay Shore, Cortland, Hyde Park, Kingston, Lockport, Ossining, Syracuse, 9 Greenport, Hempstead, Patchogue, Rochester, Scarsdale, Schoharie 10 Binghamton, Glens Falls, Huntington, Lackawanna, Lake George, Lake Placid, Mamaroneck, Massapequa, Mount Kisco, 11 Cooperstown, Plattsburgh, Port Chester, Saint George, Schenectady, Southampton, Watkins Glen, White Plains 12 Poughkeepsie *New Zealand:* 4 Hutt, Tawa 5 Levin, Taupo, Waihi 7 Dunedin, Manukau 8 Auckland 12 Christchurch *Nicaragua:* 4 León 5 Boaco, Rivas 6 Masaya 7 Granada *Nigeria:* 3 Aba, Ado, Ede, Ife, Ila, Iwo, Jos, Owo, Oyo 4 Kano, Ondo 5 Akure, Enugu, Gusau, Lagos, Okene, Zaria

6 Ibadan, Ilesha, Ilorin, Kaduna, Mushin, Sokoto **7** Onitsha, Oshogbo **8** Abeokuta **9** Maiduguri, Ogbomosho **12** Port Harcourt *North Carolina:* **4** Dunn **5** Ayden, Elkin, Erwin, Oteen, Sylva **6** Dobson, Durham, Lenoir, Manteo, Marlon, Shelby, Winton **7** Bayboro, Brevard, Edenton, Roxboro, Sanford, Tarboro **8** Asheboro, Beaufort, Gastonia, Hatteras, Snow Hill **9** Albemarle, Asheville, Charlotte, Kitty Hawk, Morganton **10** Chapel Hill, Greensboro, Smithfield, Wilkesboro **12** Murfreesboro, Winston-Salem *North Dakota:* **4** Mott **5** Cando, Fargo, Minot, Rolla **6** Amidon, Ashley, Bowman, Formon, Lakota, Linton, Medora, Mohall **8** Wahpeton, Washburn **9** Dickinson, Williston **10** Devils Lake, Grand Forks *Northern Ireland:* **5** Derry, Larne, Newry, Omagh **6** Antrim, Armagh **9** Bally-mena, Coleraine, Craigavon, Dungannon **10** Ballymoney **11** Ballycastle, Downpatrick, Enniskillen, Londonderry **13** Carrickfergus *North Korea:* **5** Haeju, Nampo **6** Wonsan **7** Hamhung, Kaesong, Sinuiju **8** Ch'ongjin, Kimchaek *Northwest Territories:* **6** Dawson **10** Whitehorse *Norway:* **4** Bodo **5** Hamar, Skien, Vardo **6** Bergen, Tromso **8** Kirkenes **9** Stavanger, Trondheim **10** Hammerfest **12** Kristiansand *Nova Scotia:* **5** Digby **6** Pictou **7** Arichat, Baddeck **8** Port Hood **9** Dartmouth, Kentville, Lunenburg, Shelburne, Westville **10** Antigonish **11** Guysborough *Ohio:* **4** Kent **5** Akron, Berea, Bryan, Carey, Eaton, Heath, Logan, Niles, Parma, Piqua, Solon, Xenia **6** Canton, Celina, Dayton, Elyria, Euclid, Kenton, Lorain, Marion, Medina, Sidney, Tiffin, Toledo **7** Ashland, Batavia, Bucyrus, Chardon, Findlay, Ironton, Oakwood, Pomeroy, Ravenna, Wauseon, Wooster **8** Conneaut, Marietta, Sandusky **9** Ashtabula, Cleveland, Coshocton, Mansfield **10** Cincinnati, Gallipolis, Zanesville **11** Chillicothe, Mount Gilead, Port Clinton **12** Steubenville *Oklahoma:* **3** Ada **4** Alva, Enid **5** Altus, Atoka, Sayre, Tulsa **6** Durant, El Reno, Guymon, Idabel, Lawton, Okemah, Poteau, Wewoka **7** Antlers, Ardmore, Cordell, Eufaula, Newkirk, Purcell, Sapulpa, Watonga **8** Anadarko, Okmulgee, Pawhuska, Sallisaw, Stilwell **9** Chickasha, Claremore, Frederick, McAlester, Wilburton **10** Stillwater, Tishomingo *Oman:* **3** Sur **6** Matrah **7** Salalah *Ontario:* **4** Ajax, Wawa, York **6** Barrie, Guelph, Kenora, London, Oshawa, Sarnia, Simcoe **7** Cobourg, Markham, Napanee, Sudbury, Windsor **8** Brampton, Cochrane, Goderich,

Hamilton, North Bay, Pembroke, Prescott **9** Brantford, Etobicoke, Kitchener, L'Original, Newmarket, North York, Owen Sound, Walkerton **10** Belleville, Brockville, Burlington, Haileybury, Parry Sound, Thunder Bay **11** Bracebridge, Fort Frances, Mississauga, Scarborough **12** Peterborough, St. Catharines *Oregon:* **5** Canby, Nyssa **6** Eugene **8** Coquille, La Grande, Portland, Roseburg **9** Clackamas, Corvallis, Gold Beach, Pendleton, The Dalles, Tillamook **10** Grants Pass **12** Klamath Falls *Pakistan:* **5** Bannu, Bhera, Kasur, Kohat **6** Gujrat, Lahore, Mardan, Multan, Quetta, Sukkur **7** Karachi, Sialkot **8** Lyallpur, Peshawar, Sargodha **9** Hyderabad **10** Bahawalpur, Faisalabad, Gujranwala, Rawalpindi *Papua New Guinea:* **3** Lae **10** Mount Hagen, Popondetta *Paraguay:* **3** Itá **4** Yuty **5** Luque, Pilar **7** Caacupé, Caazapa **9** Paraguarí **10** San Lorenzo *Pennsylvania:* **4** Erie, York **5** Avoca, Darby, Muncy, Paoli **6** Easton **7** Altoona, Bedford, Clarion, Hanover, Hershey, Latrobe, Reading, Ridgway, Sunbury **8** Carlisle, Edinboro, Hazleton, Montrose, Scranton, Somerset **9** Allentown, Ebensburg, Honesdale, Jim Thorpe, Lancaster, Lewisburg, Lock Haven, Meadville, New Castle, Wellsboro **10** Bloomsburg, Brookville, Carbondale, Clearfield, Gettysburg, McKeesport, Middleburg, Pittsburgh, Pottsville, Waynesburg **11** Valley Forge, Wilkes-Barre **12** Philadelphia, State College *Peru:* **3** Ica, Ilo **5** Ancon, Cuzco, Jauja, Junin, Lamas, Pisco, Piura, Tacna **6** Callao **8** Arequipa, Chiclayo, Chimbote, Trujillo *Philippines:* **3** Iba **4** Bago, Bais, Boac, Bogo, Cebu, Daet, Jolo, Lipa, Mati **5** Basco, Bulan, Cadiz, Danao, Davao, Digos, Gapan, Gubat, Iriga, Laoag, Ormoc, Pasay, Silay, Tagum, Vigan **6** Butuan, Iloilo, Quezon **7** Angeles, Bacolod, Basilan **8** Batangas, Calbayog, Caloocan **9** Zamboanga **10** Quezon City *Poland:* **4** Lodz, Nysa, Pila, Zary **5** Bytom, Bytow, Chelm, Kutno, Lomza, Luban, Lubin, Plock, Radom, Torun, Tychy **6** Elblag, Gdansk, Gdynia, Kalisz, Kielce, Krakow, Lublin, Poznan, Rybnik, Zabrze **7** Chorzow, Dabrowa, Gliwice, Rzeszow, Wroclaw **8** Gornicza, Katowice, Szczecin **9** Bialystok, Bydgoszcz, Sosnowiec, Walbrzych **11** Czestochowa *Portugal:* **4** Faro **5** Braga, Evora, Porto **6** Almada, Oporto, Queluz **7** Amadora **8** Barreiro, Santarém *Prince Edward Island:* **10** Summerside *Puerto Rico:* **5** Ponce **6** Caguas **7** Arecibo, Bayamón **8** Carolina,

Guaynabo, Mayagüez *Quebec:* 4 Alma 5 Amqui, Anjou, Gaspé, Laval, Lévis, Magog, Percé, Rouyn 6 Granby, Ham Sud, Matane, Ste.-Foy, Val d'Or 7 Bedford, Lachute 8 Beauport, Cap Santé, Joliette, Lac Brome, Maniwaki, Montreal, Rimouski, Roberval, Sept-Iles, Waterloo 9 Bécancour, Cookshire, Iberville, Inverness, La Malbaie, La Prairie, Longueuil, Montmagny, Sainte-Foy, Saint Jean, Tadoussac, Vaudreuil 10 Baie-Comeau, Chicoutimi 11 Beauharnois, Louiseville, Mont-Laurier 12 Charlesbourg 13 Trois-Rivières *Rhode Island:* 7 Newport, Rumford, Warwick 8 Apponaug, Coventry, Cranston, Tiverton, Westerly 9 Hopkinton, Pawtucket 10 Woonsocket 12 Narragansett *Romania:* 3 Dej 4 Aiud, Arad, Cluj, Deva, Husi, Iasi 5 Anina, Bacau, Buzau, Carei, Lugoj, Sibiu, Turda 6 Braila, Brasov, Galati, Oradea 7 Craiova 8 Ploiesti 9 Constanta, Timisoara 10 Cluj-Napoca *Russia:* 3 Kem, Ufa 4 Inta, Luga, Okha, Omsk, Orel, Orsk, Perm, Tula, Tura, Zima 5 Aldan, Artem, Chita, Ishim, Kansk, Kazan, Lysva, Onega, Penza, Pskov, Rzhev, Salsk, Serov, Sochi, Sokol, Tomsk, Tulun, Volsk, Yurga 6 Bratsk, Grozny, Kaluga, Kovrov, Kurgan, Rostov, Ryazan, Samara, Syzran, Tambov, Tyumen, Vyborg, Yelets 7 Irkutsk, Ivanovo, Izhevsk, Kalinin, Kolomna, Lipetsk, Magadan, Norilsk, Rybinsk, Saransk, Saratov, Shakhty, Vologda, Yakutsk, Zhdanov 8 Belgorod, Kemerovo, Kostroma, Murmansk, Nakhodka, Novgorod, Orenburg, Smolensk, Taganrog, Vladimir, Volzhski, Voronezh 9 Archangel, Astrakhan, Krasnodar, Stavropol, Ulyanovsk, Volgograd, 10 Dzerzhinsk 11 Arkhangel'sk, Chelyabinsk, Kaliningrad, Krasnoyarsk, Novosibirsk, Vladivostok 12 St. Petersburg 13 Yekaterinburg *Saskatchewan:* 8 Moose Jaw 9 Saskatoon 10 Assiniboia 12 Prince Albert *Saudi Arabia:* 4 Jauf, Taif 5 Jedda, Jidda, Mecca, Tabuk 6 Jeddah, Jiddah, Medina 8 Buraydah *Scotland:* 3 Ayr 4 Alva, Caol, Dyce, Oban 5 Alloa, Annan, Beith, Cowie, Cupar, Dalry, Ellon, Kelso, Kelty, Largs, Leven, Nairn, Patna, Troon 6 Dundee 7 Glasgow, Paisley 8 Aberdeen, Greenock, Hamilton 9 Inverness, Lockerbie 10 Kilmarnock 11 Dunfermline, John o' Groats *Senegal:* 5 Thiès 6 Kaolak 7 Kaolack 10 Saint-Louis *Serbia:* 3 Bor, Nis, Pec 4 Ruma 5 Becej, Cacak, Pirot, Sabac, Senta, Vrbas, Vrsac 7 Novi Sad 8 Subotica 10 Kragujevac *Slovakia:* 5 Nitra 6 Kosice, Presov, Zilina *Slovenia:* 4 Bled 5 Celje, Ko-

per, Kranj 7 Maribor *Somalia:* 3 Eil 5 Afgoi, Alula, Brava, Burao, Marka, Obbia 7 Berbera, Kismayu 8 Hargeysa, Kismaayo *South Africa:* 5 Brits, Ceres, De Aar, Nigel, Paarl 6 Benoni, Durban, Soweto 7 Springs 8 Boksburg, Mafeking 9 Germiston, Kimberley, Ladysmith, Uitenhage 10 East London 11 Krugersdorp, Vereeniging 12 Johannesburg 13 Port Elizabeth *South Carolina:* 5 Aiken, Cayce, Saxon 6 Sumter 7 Gaffney, Laurens, Manning, Pickens 8 Beaufort, Newberry, Rock Hill, Walhalla 9 Abbeville, Allendale, Greenwood, Kingstree, McCormick, Winnsboro 10 Charleston, Darlington, Greenville, Hilton Head, Orangeburg, Walterboro 11 Myrtle Beach, Spartanburg *South Dakota:* 7 Sturgis, Yankton 8 Deadwood, Elk Point 9 Brookings, Rapid City 10 Sioux Falls *South Korea:* 3 Iri 4 Yosu 5 Cheju, Masan, Mokpo, Pusan, Suwon, Taegu, Ulson, Wonju 6 Chinju, Chonju, Inchon, Kunsan, Taejon 7 Kwangju *Spain:* 4 Adra, Baza, Elda, Jaca, Jaén, León, Loja, Lugo, Olot, Reus, Vich, Vigo 5 Albox, Alcoy, Alora, Avila, Baena, Cádiz, Ceuta, Cieza, Ecija, Eibar, Elche, Gijón, Ibiza, Jodar, Lorca, Mahon, Oliva, Osuna, Palma, Ronda, Soria, Ubeda 6 Bilbao, Burgos, Cuenca, Huelva, Lérida, Málaga, Mérida, Murcia, Oviedo, Toledo 7 Almadén, Almería, Cáceres, Córdoba, Durango, Granada, Segovia, Sevilla, Seville, Tarrasa, Vitoria 8 Albacete, Alicante, La Coruña, Pamplona, Sabadell, Valencia, Zaragoza 9 Algeciras, Barcelona, Salamanca, Santander, Saragossa, Tarragona 10 Hospitalet, Valladolid 12 San Sebastián *Sri Lanka:* 5 Galle, Kandy 6 Jaffna 8 Dehiwala, Moratuwa 10 Batticaloa *Sudan:* 4 Juba 5 Kodok, Kosti 7 El Obeid, Kassala 8 Omdurman *Sweden:* 4 Lund, Täby, Umea 5 Falun, Gävle, Lulea, Malmö, Växjö, Visby 6 Orebro 7 Uppsala 8 Göteborg, Halmstad 9 Jönköping, Linköping 12 Kristianstad *Switzerland:* 3 Zug 4 Biel, Chur, Sion, Thun 5 Aarau, Arbon, Baden, Basel, Koniz 6 Geneva, Lugano, St. Gall, Zürich 7 Lucerne, Zermatt 8 Lausanne, Montreux, St. Moritz 9 Neuchâtel, Saint Gall 11 Saint Moritz *Syria:* 4 Hama, Homs 5 Idlib 6 Aleppo, Tartus 7 Latakia *Taiwan:* 5 Chia-i 6 T'ai-nan 7 Chi-lung, Hsin-chu 8 Feng-shan, Panch'iao, San-ch'ung, T'ai-chung 9 Kaohsiung *Tanzania:* 5 Lindi, Mbeya, Tanga 6 Arusha, Kigoma, Mwanza 8 Morogoro, Zanzibar 11 Dar es Salaam *Tennessee:* 5 Alcoa, Erwin, Rives 6 Loudon, Ripley, Selmer **7** Memphis, Waverly **8** Gallatin, Oak Ridge, Rutledge, Tazewell, Wartburg **9** Dandridge, Dyersburg, Jacksboro, Jonesboro, Knoxville, Lewisburg, Maryville **10** Cookeville, Crossville, Somerville, Waynesboro **11** Blountville, Chattanooga, Clarksville, Greeneville, McMinnville, Rogersville, Sevierville, Shelbyville **12** Elizabethton, Lawrenceburg, Madisonville, Murfreesboro *Texas:* **4** Azle, Waco **5** Alvin, Anson, Baird, Bowie, Bryan, Clute, Cuero, Emory, Ennis, Freer, Hondo, Marfa, Mexia, Olney, Pampa, Pecos, Pharr, Plano, Sealy, Vidor, Wylie **6** Belton, Boerne, Bonham, Burnet, Dallas, Denton, El Paso, Lamesa, Laredo, Linden, Lufkin, Odessa, Seguin **7** Abilene, Bandera, Denison, Houston, Kaufman, Lubbock, Midland, Wharton **8** Amarillo, Angleton, Beaumont, Eastland, Giddings, Gonzales, Granbury, Groveton, Hemphill, La Grange **9** Fort Worth, Galveston **10** Brownfield, Port Arthur, San Antonio, Sweetwater, Waxahachie **11** Brownsville, Littlefield, Nacogdoches, Weatherford **12** New Braunfels **13** Corpus Christi *Thailand:* **3** Nan, Tak **5** Phrae, Roi Et, Surin **8** Songkhla **9** Chiang Mai **10** Nonthaburi *Tunisia:* **4** Béja, Sfax **5** Gabès, Gafsa, Susah **6** Ariana **7** Bizerte, Safaqis *Turkey:* **5** Adana, Bursa, Izmir, Konya, Sivas **6** Edirne, Erzurm, Samsun **7** Antakya, Antalya, Antioch, Kayseri, Malatya **8** Istanbul **9** Eskisehir, Gallipoli, Gaziantep **10** Diyarbakir *Turkmenistan:* **8** Nebit Dag **9** Chardzhou, Dashhowuz *Uganda:* **5** Jinja, Mbale **7** Entebbe *Ukraine:* **4** Lviv, Lvov, Sumy **5** Lutsk, Rovno, Yalta **6** Odessa **7** Donetsk, Kharkiv, Kharkov, Kherson, Luhansk, Poltava **8** Mariupol, Vinnitsa, Zhitomir **9** Chernigov, Chernobyl, Krivoy Rog, Krivyy Rih, Nikolayev **10** Kirovograd, Sebastopol, Sevastopol, Simferopol, Zaporozhye *United Arab Emirates:* **5** Ajman, Dubai **6** Dubayy **8** Fujairah, Fujayrah *Uruguay:* **4** Melo **5** Minas, Pando, Rocha, Salto **6** Rivera **8** Paysandú **10** Las Piedras *Utah:* **3** Loa **4** Lehi, Orem **5** Manti, Ogden, Provo, Sandy **6** Dugway, Tooele **7** Parowan **8** Duchesne **9** Coalville **11** Saint George *Uzbekistan:* **5** Nukus **6** Kokand **7** Bukhara, Fergana **8** Andizhan, Chirchik, Namangan **9** Samarkand, Samarqand *Venezuela:* **4** Coro **5** Anaco, Cagua **6** Cumaná, Mérida, Petare **7** Cabimas, Guayana, Maracay **8** Valencia **9** Maracaibo **12** Barquisimeto, San Cristóbal *Vermont:* **5** Barre **7** Rutland **8** St. Albans **10** Bennington, Burlington, Middle-

bury **11** Brattleboro, Saint Albans, St. Johnsbury *Vietnam:* **3** Hue **4** Vinh **5** Da Lat, Hoi An, My Tho **6** Can Tho, Da Nang, Saigon **7** Bien Hoa, Nam Dinh, Qui Nhon **8** Haiphong, Nha Trang, Thanh Hoa **9** Long Xuyen *Virginia:* **4** Tabb **5** Luray **6** Grundy **7** Accomac, Boydton, Fairfax, Hampton, New Kent, Norfolk **8** Abingdon, Culpeper, Leesburg, Manassas, Montross, Nottoway, Powhatan, Tazewell **9** Arlington, Clintwood, Courtland, Eastville, Farmville, Lunenburg, Lynchburg **10** Alexandria, Appomattox, Front Royal, Hillsville, King George, Portsmouth, Rocky Mount **11** King William, Newport News **12** Prince George, Spotsylvania, Williamsburg *Wales:* **4** Rhyl **5** Neath, Risca, Tenby, Tywyn **7** Cwmbran, Denbigh, Harlech, Newport, Swansea **8** Aberdare, Bridgend **10** Caernarfon, Caernarvon, Llangollen **11** Aberystwyth *Washington:* **4** Omak **5** Brier, Camas, Kelso, Lacey, Pasco, Selah **6** Asotin, Colfax, Tacoma, Yakima **7** Ephrata, Everett, Prosser, Redmond, Seattle, Spokane **8** Bellevue, Chehalis, Colville, Okanogan **9** Montesano, Ritzville, Snohomish, Wenatchee **10** Bellingham, Coupeville, Ellensburg, Goldendale, Walla Walla, Waterville **11** Port Angeles *West Virginia:* **5** Nitro, Welch **6** Elkins, Hamlin, Hinton, Keyser, Ripley **7** Beckley, Weirton **8** Kingwood, Philippi, Wheeling **9** Pineville, Wellsburg **10** Buckhannon, Clarksburg, Huntington, Moorefield, Morgantown, Petersburg, Williamson **11** Harrisville, Martinsburg, Moundsville, Parkersburg **12** Harpers Ferry *Wisconsin:* **4** Kiel **5** Ripon, Tomah **6** Antigo, Barron, Oconto, Racine, Wausau **7** Baraboo, Chilton, Elkhorn, Hayward, Kenosha, Mauston, Merrill, Oshkosh, Shawano, Viraqua, Waupaca, Wautoma **8** Appleton, Green Bay, Kewaunee, La Crosse, Washburn, Waukesha, West Bend **9** Eau Claire, Ellsworth, Fond du Lac, Green Lake, Manitowoc, Marinette, Menomonie, Milwaukee, Sheboygan, Whitehall **10** Balsam Lake, Darlington, Dodgeville **12** Stevens Point *Wyoming:* **6** Casper, Lander **7** Laramie, Rawlins **8** Gillette, Kemmerer, Sheridan **10** Green River **11** Rock Springs *Yemen:* **4** Aden **5** Taizz **7** Hodeida, Mukalla **8** Hudaydah *Zambia:* **5** Kabwe, Kitwe, Mansa, Mbala, Mongu, Ndola **6** Kasama **7** Chipata *Zimbabwe:* **5** Gweru **6** Hwange, Kadoma, Kwekwe, Mutare, Umtali **7** Mashava **8** Bulawayo, Masvingo

civet 3 cat **5** rasse *Madagascar:* **5** fossa *relative:* **5** genet

civic 5 urban **6** public, social **8** communal, national, societal **9** municipal

civil 6 polite, public, seemly, urbane **7** affable, cordial, courtly, genteel, refined **8** decorous, gracious, mannerly, national, obliging, well-bred **9** courteous, political **10** diplomatic **12** well-mannered **13** accommodating

civilian clothes 5 mufti

civility 6 comity **7** amenity, decency, decorum, manners **8** courtesy **9** etiquette, gentility, propriety **10** politeness **11** correctness

civilization 7 culture

civilized 6 decent, proper, urbane **7** genteel, refined **8** decorous, mannerly, tasteful **9** courteous **10** cultivated **13** sophisticated

civil rights *organization:* **4** CORE, SCLC **5** NAACP *pioneer:* **4** King (Martin Luther) **5** Evers (Medgar), Parks (Rosa) **6** Du Bois (W. E. B.), Garvey (Marcus) **7** Jackson (Jesse) **8** Malcolm X, Marshall (Thurgood) **10** Washington (Booker T.)

Civil War *admiral:* **8** Buchanan (Franklin), Farragut (David) *battle:* **6** Shiloh **7** Bull Run **8** Antietam, Manassas **9** Mobile Bay, Nashville, Vicksburg **10** Cold Harbor, Gettysburg **11** Chattanooga, Chickamauga *general:* **3** Lee (Robert E.) **4** Hood (John Bell), Pope (John) **5** Bragg (Braxton), Buell (Don Carlos), Ewell (Richard Stoddart), Grant (Ulysses S.), Meade (George), Sykes (George) **6** Hooker (Joseph) **7** Forrest (Nathan Bedford), Jackson (Thomas "Stonewall"), Sherman (Thomas West, William Tecumseh) **8** Burnside (Ambrose), Johnston (Albert Sidney, Joseph Eggleston), Sheridan (Philip) **9** McClellan (George Brinton), Rosecrans (William), Schofield (John) **10** Beauregard (Pierre) *ship:* **7** Monitor **9** Merrimack *soldier:* **3** reb **4** yank **9** Billy Yank, Johnny Reb

civil wrong 4 tort

clabber 5 curds

clack 3 gab, jaw, yak **4** blab, chat **5** prate **6** babble, cackle, gabble, gossip, jabber, rattle **7** blabber, chatter, clatter, palaver, prattle **9** yakety-yak

clad 4 face, side, skin **5** dress, faced **6** clothe, decked, garbed, outfit **7** attired, clothed, covered, dressed, overlay, sheathe **8** costumed, overlaid, sheathed **9** outfitted

claim 4 call, dibs, hold, lien, plea, take **5** argue, exact, right, share, stake, title **6** adduce, allege, assert, defend, demand, insist **7** advance, call for, contend, declare, justify, profess, purport, require, solicit, warrant **8** interest, maintain **9** assertion, challenge, postulate, privilege **10** allegation, birthright **11** affirmation, declaration, prerogative, requisition **12** protestation

clairvoyance 3 ESP **7** insight **9** intuition, telepathy **10** sixth sense **11** penetration, second sight **12** precognition

clairvoyant 4 seer **5** sibyl **7** diviner **8** telepath **10** soothsayer

clam 4 buck **5** razor **6** dollar, quahog **7** bivalve, coquina, geoduck, mollusc, mollusk, smacker, steamer **11** cherrystone *genus:* **3** Mya

clamant 4 dire **6** crying, urgent **7** blatant, burning, exigent **8** pressing **9** insistent **10** compelling, imperative

clamber 5 climb, crawl, scale, swarm **8** scrabble, scramble, struggle

clammy 4 cool, dank, damp **5** close, moist, slimy **6** sticky

clamor 3 cry, din, row **4** bawl, roar, to-do **5** babel, hoo-ha, noise **6** bellow, demand, hoo-hah, hubbub, jangle, outcry, racket, ruckus, tumult, uproar **7** agitate, dispute, ferment, protest, turmoil **8** brouhaha, foofaraw, shouting **9** agitation, commotion **10** hullabaloo, hurly-burly **11** pandemonium

clamorous 5 noisy, vocal **6** crying, shrill, urgent **7** blatant, exigent, raucous, voluble **8** strident, vehement **9** insistent **10** boisterous, imperative, tumultuous, vociferous **11** importunate **12** obstreperous

clamp 4 grip, hold, vise **5** clasp, grasp **6** clench, clinch, clutch, fasten, secure **7** grapple

clamshell 6 bucket **7** grapple

clan 3 mob **4** camp, folk, ring, sept **5** cabal, house, stock, tribe **6** circle, clique, family **7** coterie, kindred, lineage **9** camarilla *emblem:* **5** totem

Clancy novel 12 Patriot Games **13** Sum of All Fears (The) **17** Hunt for Red October (The) **21** Clear and Present Danger

clandestine 6 covert, secret, sneaky **7** furtive, illicit, sub rosa **8** hush-hush, stealthy **10** undercover, under wraps **11** underhanded **12** hugger-mugger, illegitimate **13** surreptitious, under-the-table

clang 3 cry, din **4** ding, peal, slam **6** jangle **8** ding-dong

clangor 3 din **5** noise **6** clamor, jangle, racket, rattle, tumult, uproar **7** clatter, ringing **9** stridency **13** reverberation

clangorous 5 noisy **7** booming, rackety, ringing **8** clattery, sonorous **9** deafening **12** ear-splitting

Clan of the Cave Bear author 4 Auel (Jean M.)

clap 3 pat 4 bang, blow, boom, slam, slap 5 blast, burst, crack, crash, whack 6 strike 7 applaud 8 applause

claptrap 4 bull, bunk 5 cheap, hokum, showy, trash, tripe 6 bunkum, drivel, humbug, vulgar 7 baloney, eyewash, hogwash, twaddle 8 malarkey, nonsense 9 poppycock 10 balderdash, flapdoodle

Clara Bow 6 It girl

claret 3 red 4 wine 8 Bordeaux

clarify 5 clean, clear 6 define, filter, purify 7 analyze, cleanse, clear up, explain, resolve 8 simplify 9 elucidate 10 illuminate 13 straighten out

clarion 5 clear 7 ringing, rousing, trumpet 8 gleaming, stirring 9 brilliant

clarity 6 purity 8 accuracy, lucidity 9 clearness, limpidity, precision 10 exactitude, simplicity 12 transparency

Clarke novel 10 Earthlight 13 Childhood's End 19 Fountains of Paradise (The)

clash 4 bump, jolt 5 brawl, crash, melee, setto, smash 6 battle, fracas, impact, jangle 7 collide 8 conflict, mismatch, skirmish 9 collision, encounter 10 engagement 11 embroilment

clasp 3 hug, pin 4 clip, grip, hold 5 clamp, grasp, press 6 brooch, buckle, clench, clinch, clutch, enfold 7 embrace, grapple, squeeze 10 chatelaine

class 3 ilk 4 hold, kind, mark, part, rank, rate, sort, tier, type 5 allot, brand, caste, gauge, genre, genus, grade, grain, group, judge, order, score, stamp, style 6 assess, assign, assort, branch, course, league, nature, reckon, regard, stripe 7 bracket, caliber, quality, section, species, variety 8 appraise, category, consider, division, evaluate, grouping, separate 10 categorize, pigeonhole 11 description 12 denomination *middle:* 11 bourgeoisie *school:* 6 junior, senior 8 freshman 9 sophomore *working:* 11 proletariat

classic 5 ideal, model, prime 7 capital, typical, vintage 8 champion, enduring, standard, superior, top-notch 9 authentic, canonical, classical, excellent, exemplary, memorable, tradition 10 magnum opus, masterwork 11 chef d'oeuvre, masterpiece, tour de force, traditional 12 paradigmatic, prototypical 13 authoritative

classical 4 pure 5 Attic, Greek, ideal, Latin, Roman 7 ancient, fitting, Grecian, perfect, typical, vintage 8 Hellenic, standard, sterling 9 canonical, exemplary 10 consummate 11 traditional 13 authoritative

classical musician 4 Böhm (Karl), Hess (Myra), Lind (Jenny), Muti (Riccardo), Pons (Lily), Shaw (Robert) 5 Arrau (Claudio), Biggs (E. Power), Borge (Victor), Boult (Adrian), Davis (Colin), du Pré (Jacqueline), Gould (Glenn), Masur (Kurt), Mehta (Zubin), Melba (Nellie), Ozawa (Seiji), Patti (Adelina), Pinza (Ezio), Price (Leontyne), Ramey (Samuel), Sills (Beverly), Stern (Isaac), Szell (George) 6 Abbado (Claudio), Battle (Kathleen), Boulez (Pierre), Callas (Maria), Caruso (Enrico), Casals (Pablo), Galway (James), Levine (James), Maazel (Lorin), Midori, Norman (Jessye), Peters (Roberta), Previn (André), Rampal (Jean-Pierre), Rattle (Simon), Reiner (Fritz), Serkin (Peter, Rudolf), Terfel (Bryn), Tucker (Richard), Upshaw (Dawn), Walter (Bruno) 7 Bartoli (Cecilia), Beecham (Thomas), Bocelli (Andrea), Brendel (Alfred), Cliburn (Van), Corelli (Franco), Domingo (Plácido), Farrell (Eileen), Fiedler (Arthur), Fleming (Renée), Glennie (Evelyn), Haitink (Bernard), Heifetz (Jascha), Karajan (Herbert von), Menuhin (Yehudi), Nilsson (Birgit), Ormandy (Eugene), Perlman (Itzhak), Pollini (Maurizio), Sargent (Malcolm), Segovia (Andrés), Tebaldi (Renata) 8 Anderson (Marian), Argerich (Martha), Bergonzi (Carlo), Carreras (José), Flagstad (Kirsten), Horowitz (Vladimir), Kreisler (Fritz), Marriner (Neville), Oistrakh (David), Schnabel (Artur), Te Kanawa (Kiri), Zukerman (Pinchas) 9 Barenboim (Daniel), Bernstein (Leonard), Chaliapin (Feodor), Klemperer (Otto), Landowska (Wanda), Pavarotti (Luciano), Stokowski (Leopold), Toscanini (Arturo) 10 Rubinstein (Arthur), Sutherland (Joan), Tetrazzini (Luisa) 11 Furtwängler (Wilhelm), Kostelanetz (André), Schwarzkopf (Elisabeth) 12 Rostropovich (Mstislav)

classification 4 sort, type 5 genre, genus, grade, order 6 family, phylum, rating 7 sorting, species 8 category, division, grouping, ordering, taxonomy, typology 11 arrangement, cataloguing

classified 6 secret, sorted 7 divided, ordered 9 top secret 11 categorized 12 confidential

classified-ad abbreviation 3 ABS, AKC, APR, apt, brm, CDL, CPA, EDP, EOE, est, exc, exp, flr, FSH, FWD, gar, gdn, GWO, ISO, kit, LPN, lux, lwd, max, mgr, min, MLS, neg, OBO, opp, pkg, PWO, rec, ref, rep, sal, sep, sig, spd, TLC, wgn 4 appl, bldg, bdrm, bsmt, demo, flex, frpl, furn, HVAC, pass, pref, priv, prof, prop, temp, util, vacc, warr **5** specs (see also **real estate term**)

classify 4 rank, rate, sort **5** grade, group **6** assort **7** arrange **9** break down **10** categorize, pigeonhole

classy 4 chic, tony **5** swank **6** modish **7** dashing, elegant, refined, stylish **8** gracious, tasteful, well-bred **9** courteous **11** fashionable

clatter 4 to-do **6** clamor, hubbub, pother, rattle, tumult, uproar **7** turmoil **9** commotion **10** hurly-burly *Scottish:* **7** brattle

clattery 5 noisy **7** rackety **10** clangorous

Claudia's husband 6 Pilate

Claudio's beloved 4 Hero

Claudius *nephew:* **6** Hamlet *predecessor:* **8** Caligula *slayer:* **6** Hamlet **9** Agrippina *successor:* **4** Nero *wife:* **8** Gertrude **9** Agrippina

Clavell novel 6 Gai-Jin, Shogun, Tai-Pan **7** King Rat

claw 3 dig **4** nail, rake, tear **5** chela, talon, uncus **6** pincer, scrape, ungula **7** scratch

clay 3 cob **4** loam, lute, marl **5** argil, brick, earth, gault, loess, ocher, ochre **6** kaolin **10** terra-cotta *baked:* **4** tile **5** adobe, brick *box:* **6** saggar, sagger *building:* **5** adobe *ceramic:* **10** terra-cotta *constituent:* **6** silica **8** feldspar, silicate **9** kaolinite *in glass:* **4** tear *made of:* **7** fictile *porcelain:* **6** kaolin *red:* **8** laterite *rock:* **5** shale *tobacco pipe:* **6** dudeen *watery mixture:* **4** slip *white:* **6** kaolin

clay pigeon 6 target

clean 4 dust, fair, pure, swab, tidy, wash, wipe **5** bathe, fresh, groom, purge, scour, scrub, sweep **6** bright, chaste, decent, neaten, purify, spruce, vacuum, washed **7** clarify, launder, sinless **8** hygienic, innocent, sanitary, sanitize, spotless, unsoiled **9** blameless, faultless, sparkling, stainless, undefiled, unsullied, untainted, wholesome **10** antiseptic, immaculate **11** unblemished **12** spick-and-span

clean-cut 4 trim **7** defined, precise **8** definite, explicit, specific **9** wholesome **10** definitive **11** categorical, unambiguous, well-groomed

cleaner see **cleanser**

cleanhanded 8 innocent **9** blameless

clean-limbed 4 trim **7** shapely **8** handsome **10** statuesque

cleanse 4 lave, wash **5** purge, rinse **6** purify, refine **7** clarify, deterge, launder **8** lustrate, sanitize **9** disinfect, expurgate, sterilize

cleanser 3 lye **4** soap **9** detergent **10** antiseptic **12** disinfectant

cleansing 7 purging **8** ablution **9** catharsis,

purgation **10** lustration **11** expurgation **12** purification

clear 4 earn, fair, fine, pure **5** lucid, overt, plain, repay, solve, stark, sunny **6** acquit, limpid, secure, settle, simple **7** absolve, audible, clarify, clarion, defined, evident, legible, obvious, precise **8** apparent, definite, distinct **9** authorize, cloudless, elucidate, exculpate, exonerate, liquidate, meliorate, unblurred, unclouded, vindicate **10** ameliorate, illuminate, see-through **11** disentangle, open-and-shut, perceptible, transparent, unambiguous, unequivocal **12** unmistakable

clearance 3 gap **4** sale **7** go-ahead, removal **8** approval **10** green light, permission **13** authorization

clear away 6 remove **7** take out

clear out 6 crisp, exact, plain **7** decided, precise **8** definite, distinct, explicit, manifest **10** definitive, pronounced, undisputed **11** categorical, indubitable, unambiguous, unequivocal **12** unquestioned

clear-eyed 6 astute **9** judicious, observant **10** discerning, perceptive

clearheaded 4 calm, cool **10** perceptive

clearing 3 gap **5** field, glade **7** opening **10** settlement

clear out 5 scoot, scram, split **6** beat it, begone, bug off, decamp, depart **7** buzz off, skiddoo, take off, vamoose **8** shove off **9** drive away, skedaddle **10** hightail it

clear-sightedness 6 acuity, acumen **8** keenness, sagacity **10** astuteness, shrewdness **11** discernment, penetration, percipience **12** perspicacity

clear up 5 solve **6** cipher, unfold **7** clarify, dope out, explain, resolve, unravel **8** decipher **9** elucidate, figure out **10** illuminate

clearwing 4 moth

cleat 4 bitt **5** chock **6** batten **7** bollard, dolphin

cleavage 4 rift **5** chasm, cleft, split **6** schism **7** fissure **8** crevasse **9** splitting

cleave 3 cut, hew **4** chop, join, link, rend, rive **5** carve, cling, sever, slice, split, stick, unite **6** adhere, divide, sunder **7** combine **8** dissever, separate

cleft 3 gap **4** rift **5** chasm, chink, clove, crack, gorge, gulch, split **6** clough, ravine, schism **7** crevice, divided, fissure **8** cleavage

clemency 5 grace, mercy **6** lenity **7** caritas, charity **8** kindness, lenience, leniency, mildness **9** tolerance **10** compassion, gentleness, indulgence, sufferance, toleration **11** forbearance

clement 4 fair, kind, mild **5** balmy **6** benign,

humane, kindly **7** lenient **8** merciful, tolerant **9** indulgent **10** benevolent, charitable, forbearing **13** compassionate

clench 4 grip, grit, hold **5** clamp, clasp, grasp **6** clutch **7** grapple

Cleopatra *attendant:* **4** Iras **8** Charmian *brother:* **7** Ptolemy *husband:* **7** Ptolemy *killer:* **3** asp *lover:* **6** Antony (Marc), Caesar (Julius) **7** Anthony (Mark) *river:* **4** Nile

Cleopatra's Needle 7 obelisk

clepsydra 9 timepiece **10** water clock

clerestory 7 gallery

clergy 7 canonry **8** ministry **9** churchmen, diaconate, pastorate, rabbinate **10** priesthood **11** cardinalate **13** ecclesiastics

clergyman 5 clerk, padre, vicar **6** bishop, cleric, curate, divine, father, parson, pastor, priest, rector **7** dominie, prelate **8** chaplain, clerical, minister, preacher, reverend, shepherd, sky pilot **9** churchman, pulpiteer **10** evangelist, missionary, sermonizer **12** ecclesiastic *American:* **4** Hale (Edward Everett), King (Martin Luther, Thomas Starr) **5** Eliot (John), Moody (Dwight), Stone (Barton Warren), Weems (Parson) **6** Dwight (Timothy), Finney (Charles), Graham (Billy), Holmes (John Haynes), Hooker (Thomas), Mather (Cotton, Increase, Richard), Merton (Thomas), Parker (Samuel, Theodore), Sunday (John), Taylor (Edward, Graham, Nathaniel William) **7** Beecher (Henry Ward, Lyman), Edwards (Jonathan), Harvard (John), Russell (Charles Taze) **10** Muhlenberg (Frederick Augustus, Henry Melchior, John Peter Gabriel) *English:* **4** Ward (Nathaniel, Seth, William George) **5** Donne (John), Paley (William), Smith (Henry "Silver-Tongued," John "The Sebaptist," Sidney) **6** Cotton (John), Fuller (Andrew, Thomas), Taylor (Jeremy, Rowland), Wesley (Charles, John) **7** Cranmer (Thomas), Parsons (Robert) **8** Kingsley (Charles) **10** Whitefield (George) *home:* **5** manse **6** priory **7** rectory **8** vicarage **9** monastery, parsonage *traveling:* **12** circuit rider

cleric see **clergyman**

clerisy 8 literati **10** illuminati **13** intellectuals

clerk 7 cashier **8** salesman **9** secretary **10** accountant, bookkeeper **11** salesperson **12** stenographer

clever 3 apt, sly **4** able, deft, good, keen **5** adept, alert, canny, funny, handy, quick, savvy, sharp, smart, witty **6** adroit, astute, brainy, bright, crafty, expert, shrewd, tricky **7** amusing, capable, cunning, knowing, skilled **8** fanciful, humorous, pleasing,

skillful, talented **9** competent, dexterous, ingenious **10** proficient **11** intelligent, quick-witted, resourceful **12** entertaining

cliché 3 saw **6** truism **7** bromide **8** banality, buzzword, chestnut **9** platitude **10** shibboleth, stereotype **11** commonplace

clichéd 5 banal, bland, musty, stale, tired, trite, vapid **6** old-hat **7** humdrum, insipid, worn-out **8** bromidic, shopworn, timeworn **9** hackneyed **10** pedestrian, unoriginal **11** stereotyped **13** platitudinous, unimaginative

click 3 fit **4** snap, tick, work **5** agree, match **6** go over, pan out **7** come off, succeed

client 6 patron **7** patient, protégé **8** customer **9** dependent

clientele 4 fans **5** trade, train **6** custom, market, public **7** patrons, traffic **8** audience, patients, regulars, shoppers **9** customers **10** purchasers, supporters **12** constituency

cliff 4 crag **5** bluff, scarp **8** headland, palisade **9** precipice **10** escarpment

climacteric 4 apex, crux, cusp **5** acute **6** crisis **7** crucial **8** critical **9** menopause **11** culmination **12** change of life, turning point

climactic 4 peak **7** crucial, pivotal **8** critical, decisive, dramatic **9** momentous **10** definitive **11** culminating, determining

climate 6 medium, milieu **7** ambient **8** ambience **10** atmosphere **11** environment **12** surroundings

climax 3 cap **4** acme, apex, peak **5** crown **6** apogee, summit, top off **8** capstone, meridian, pinnacle **9** culminate **11** culmination

climb 4 go up, rise, soar **5** mount, scale, slope **6** ascend, ascent **7** clamber **8** escalate, increase

climbing 8 scandent

climbing device 3 cam, nut **5** biner, cinch, piton **7** crampon **9** carabiner

clinch 3 hug, ice **4** grip, hold, seal **5** clamp, clasp, grasp, sew up **6** clutch, decide, ensure, lock up **7** confirm, embrace, grapple, squeeze **8** nail down

clincher 4 tire **5** proof **6** kicker **7** quietus **9** deathblow **10** smoking gun **11** affirmation, attestation, coup de grâce **12** confirmation **13** corroboration

cling 4 bond **5** stick **6** adhere, cleave, clutch, hold on, linger **8** adhesion **9** adherence

clingstone 5 peach

clink 3 can, jug, pen **4** brig, cell, coop, jail, stir **5** pokey, pound **6** cooler, jingle, lockup, prison, tingle, tinkle **7** slammer **8** hoosegow **9** calaboose

clinker 3 dud **4** bomb, bust, flop, goof, slag **5** botch, brick, error, lemon, loser **6** bummer,

bungle, fiasco, howler, turkey **7** bloomer, blunder, failure, faux pas, mistake
clinkers 3 ash **4** slag **5** ashes **7** cinders
clinquant 5 gaudy **6** flashy, garish, tawdry, tinsel **8** specious **10** glittering **11** superficial
Clio see **Muse**
clip 3 bob, cut, mow, pin **4** crop, hasp, pare, snip, sock, trim **5** block, clasp, prune, punch, shave, shear, slash **6** broach, brooch, fleece, reduce **7** curtail, cut back, cut down, shorten **8** magazine, truncate **10** abbreviate, overcharge
clipped 3 cut, hit **4** curt, taut **5** brief, crisp, shorn, short, terse **6** abrupt, cut off, docked, pruned **7** blocked, clasped, cropped, trimmed **8** cut short, fastened **9** curtailed, shortened, truncated
clique 3 set **4** camp, clan, club, gang, ring **5** cabal, crowd, mafia **6** circle **7** coterie, faction, in-group **9** camarilla
cloak 4 cape, mask, robe, veil, wrap **5** cover, guise, talma **6** domino, facade, joseph, mantle, screen, shroud, veneer **7** blanket, conceal, curtain, dress up, manteau, obscure **8** disguise **9** dissemble, semblance **10** camouflage **11** dissimulate *ancient Greek:* **7** chlamys *ancient Roman:* **7** pallium *Arab:* **3** aba *fur:* **7** pelisse *hooded:* **6** capote **7** burnous **8** burnoose *liturgical:* **4** cope *Moroccan:* **8** djellaba *over armor:* **6** tabard **7** surcoat *Spanish:* **5** manta
clobber 4 belt, drub, flay, lick, slam, slug, sock, whip, whup **5** blast, brain, clout, cream, pound, smash **6** hammer, thrash, wallop **7** lambast, shellac, trounce **8** demolish, lambaste
clochard 3 bum, vag **4** hobo **5** tramp **6** beggar, canter **7** drifter, floater, moocher, vagrant **8** deadbeat, derelict, vagabond **9** transient **10** freeloader, panhandler **11** bindle stiff
cloche 3 hat **5** cover, toque, tuque
clock 4 time **9** timepiece **11** chronometer *water:* **9** clepsydra
clocklike 5 exact **6** minute, prompt, strict, timely **7** precise, regular **8** accurate, punctual, reliable, thorough **9** assiduous **10** dependable, meticulous, scrupulous **11** painstaking **13** conscientious
clockmaker 10 horologist
clockwise 6 deasil **7** dextral **11** right-handed
Clockwork Orange author 7 Burgess (Anthony)
clod 3 gob, wad **4** boob, dolt, dope, hunk, lump, soil **5** chump, chunk, clump, dummy, dunce, earth **6** dimwit **8** dumbbell **9** blockhead, lamebrain

cloddish 7 boorish, ill-bred, loutish, uncouth **8** churlish, clownish **9** unrefined **10** uncultured, unpolished **11** uncivilized
clodhopper 4 boor, boot, hick, lout **5** chuff, churl, clown, yokel **6** rustic **7** bumpkin, hayseed, redneck **9** chawbacon
clog 3 gum, jam, tax **4** fill, glut, load, plug, stop **5** block, choke, close, stuff **6** hamper, hinder **7** congest **8** encumber, obstruct, overload **10** impediment **11** encumbrance
cloisonné 6 enamel
cloister 5 abbey, court **6** arcade, garden **7** convent, retreat, seclude, shelter **9** courtyard, monastery, sequester
Cloister and the Hearth author 5 Reade (Charles)
cloistered 7 recluse **8** confined, hermetic, secluded **9** seclusive, withdrawn **11** sequestered
cloistered one 3 nun **4** monk
clone 4 copy **5** ditto **6** double, carbon **7** replica **9** duplicate, facsimile, replicate, reproduce **10** carbon copy, simulacrum **12** reproduction
Clorinda *beloved:* **7** Tancred *father:* **6** Senapo *guardian:* **6** Arsete *slayer:* **7** Tancred
close 3 end **4** near, nigh, shut, slam **5** block, cease, choke, humid, muggy, tight **6** ending, finale, finish, narrow, nearby, stuffy, sultry, windup, wrap up **7** airless, compact, crowded, stopper **8** adjacent, complete, conclude, finalize, intimate, obstruct, stifling **9** adjoining, cessation, condensed, terminate **10** conclusion, consummate, convenient, near-at-hand **11** constricted, neighboring, termination **12** confidential
closed-minded 4 deaf **6** narrow **8** obdurate **9** hidebound, obstinate, pigheaded, unbending **10** bullheaded, hardheaded **11** intractable
closefisted 5 cheap, mingy **6** frugal, stingy **7** miserly, thrifty **9** niggardly, penurious **13** penny-pinching
close in 3 hem **4** cage **5** fence, hedge **6** corral, immure **7** advance, confine, enclose, envelop, impound **8** approach, converge, encircle, enshroud, imprison, surround
close-knit 8 intimate
close match 6 toss-up
closemouthed 3 mum **4** mute **6** silent **7** laconic **8** reserved, reticent, taciturn **12** tightmouthed
closeness 8 intimacy
close off 4 clog, plug **5** block **6** stop up **7** isolate, occlude **8** insulate **9** segregate, sequester
closet 6 covert, inside, office, secret **7** cabinet, chamber, furtive, private **8** wardrobe

closing 3 end 4 last, stop 5 final 6 ending, finish, latest, period, windup, wrap-up 7 curtain 8 eventual, terminal, ultimate 9 cessation 10 concluding 11 termination

closure 3 cap, end, lid 6 ending, finish 8 fastener 9 cessation

clot 3 gel, set 4 curd, glob, jell, lump 5 clump 6 curdle, gelate 7 congeal 8 coagulum, thrombus 9 coagulate 10 gelatinize *combining form:* 6 thromb 7 thrombo

cloth see **fabric**

clothe 3 tog 4 deck, do up, garb, robe 5 array, cloak, couch, drape, dress, endow, endue, equip 6 attire, bedeck, outfit, swathe 7 apparel, costume, dress up 8 accouter

clothes 3 rig 4 duds, garb, rags, togs 5 array, dress, getup, habit 6 attire, outfit, things 7 apparel, costume, raiment, rigging, threads, toggery, vesture 8 garments, glad rags 9 vestments 11 habiliments *basket:* 6 hamper *civilian:* 5 mufti

clothes-moth genus 5 Tinea

clothespress 7 armoire 8 wardrobe

cloud 3 dim, fog, tar 4 blur, haze, mist, murk 5 addle, befog, brume, gloom, muddy, plume, smear, sully, taint 6 muddle, nebula, puzzle, shadow, smudge 7 besmear, confuse, obscure, perplex, tarnish 8 befuddle, besmirch, discolor, distract, overcast 9 obfuscate *type:* 4 nine 6 cirrus, nimbus 7 cumulus, stratus 11 altocumulus, altostratus 12 cirrocumulus, cirrostratus, cumulonimbus, interstellar, nimbostratus 13 stratocumulus

cloudburst 6 deluge, shower 7 monsoon, torrent 8 downpour, drencher, rainfall 10 outpouring

clouded 5 dusky, murky, shady 6 dreary, gloomy, somber, sombre 7 dubious, ominous, sunless, unclear 8 doubtful, overcast 9 ambiguous, equivocal, uncertain, unsettled 11 problematic

cloudless 4 fair, fine 5 clear, sunny 7 clarion 8 pleasant, rainless, sunshiny

cloud-like mass 6 nebula

cloud nine 5 bliss 6 heaven 7 ecstasy, elation, nirvana, rapture 8 euphoria

cloudy 4 dull, hazy 5 dusky, foggy, heavy, misty, murky, vague 6 gloomy, opaque, somber, sombre 7 louring, obscure, tainted, unclear 8 confused, darkened, lowering, nebulous, overcast 10 indistinct, vaporous

clout 3 box, hit, rag 4 blow, cuff, poke, pull, slam, slap, slug, sock, swat, sway 5 paste, power, punch, smack, smite, whack 6 strike 9 influence

clove 4 bulb 5 spice 7 chopped, severed

clove hitch 4 knot

clover 5 lotus 6 alsike, ladino, lucern 7 alfalfa, berseem, lucerne, melilot, trefoil 8 four-leaf, shamrock 9 lespedeza *family:* 3 pea *genus:* 9 Trifolium

clown 3 wag 4 bozo, mime, zany 5 cutup, joker, Punch 6 jester, mummer 7 buffoon 8 comedian, jokester 9 harlequin, prankster 11 merry-andrew *French:* 7 Pierrot *operatic:* 5 buffo *Spanish:* 8 gracioso

clownish 4 rude 6 clumsy, gauche, oafish 7 awkward, boorish, ill-bred, loutish, lumpish, uncouth 8 churlish, cloddish 9 unrefined

cloy 4 fill, glut, jade, pall, sate 5 gorge 6 sicken 7 satiate, surfeit 8 overfill

cloying 4 icky 5 gushy, mushy, sappy, soppy 6 sticky, sugary 7 fulsome, gushing, maudlin, mawkish 9 excessive, schmaltzy, sickening 10 disgusting, lovey-dovey, nauseating, saccharine 11 distasteful, sentimental

club 3 bat, sap 4 beat, cosh, frat, iron, mace 5 baton, billy, guild, lodge, order, union 6 cudgel, league 7 society 8 bludgeon, sodality, sorority 9 blackjack, truncheon 10 fellowship, fraternity, knobkerrie, nightstick 11 association, brotherhood *Australian:* 5 waddy *Irish:* 10 shillelagh *Maori:* 4 patu

clubfoot 7 talipes

cluck 4 dodo, dolt, dope, fool 5 dunce 6 dimwit, nitwit 7 pinhead

clue 3 cue 4 hint, idea, lead, sign, tell, warn 6 advise, inform, notify, notion, tip-off 7 inkling 8 evidence, telltale 10 indication, intimation, suggestion

Clue character 4 Plum (Prof.) 5 Green (Mr., Rev.) 7 Mustard (Col.), Peacock (Mrs.) 8 Scarlett (Miss)

clueless 4 lost 10 out to lunch

clump 3 gob, wad 4 clod, hunk, lump, mass, mess, plod 5 batch, bunch, chunk, group, stomp, tramp 6 bumble, bundle, lumber, parcel 7 cluster, galumph, stumble *of grass:* 4 tuft 6 tuffet 7 tussock

clumsy 5 bulky, gawky, inept, splay 6 clunky, gauche, klutzy, wooden 7 awkward, hulking, lumpish, uncouth, unhandy 8 bumbling, bungling, tactless, ungainly, unsubtle, unwieldy 9 all thumbs, graceless, ham-handed, inelegant, lumbering, maladroit 11 heavy-handed, inefficient *person:* 3 oaf 4 clod, goon, lout, slob 5 klutz 6 baboon, galoot, lummox 7 bumpkin, bungler, palooka 13 butterfingers

clunk 4 thud 5 clout, thump, whack 6 thwack, wallop

clunker 3 car 4 bomb, heap 5 crate, lemon, wreck 6 beater, jalopy, junker 7 stinker 10 rattletrap, rust bucket

cluster 3 lot, set 4 band, bevy, crew, knot, pack 5 array, batch, bunch, clump, covey, group 6 bundle, clutch, gather 7 collect, package 8 assemble, assembly 9 aggregate, associate, gathering 10 accumulate

cluster bean 4 guar

clutch 4 grab, grip, hold, keep 5 catch, clamp, clasp, grasp, pinch, seize 6 bundle, clench, clinch, snatch 7 cluster, grapple

clutter 4 hash, mash, mess, muss, ruck 5 chaos, snarl, strew 6 jumble, litter, muddle 7 mélange, rummage 8 disarray, disorder, mishmash, shambles 9 confusion 10 hodge-podge, hotchpotch

Clydesdale 5 horse 10 draft horse

Clymene *father:* 7 Oceanus *husband:* 7 Iapetus *mother:* 6 Tethys *son:* 5 Atlas 10 Epimetheus, Prometheus

Clytemnestra *brother:* 6 Castor, Pollux 10 Polydeuces *daughter:* 7 Electra 9 Iphigenia *father:* 9 Tyndareus *husband:* 9 Agamemnon *lover:* 9 Aegisthus *mother:* 4 Leda *slayer:* 7 Orestes *son:* 7 Orestes *victim:* 9 Agamemnon, Cassandra

Clytie *beloved:* 6 Apollo *form:* 9 sunflower 10 heliotrope

coach 3 bus, car, pro 5 drill, stage, train, tutor 6 chaise, mentor 7 prepare, trainer 8 carriage, instruct 10 instructor

coadjutor 3 aid 4 aide 6 bishop, deputy 9 assistant 10 aide-de-camp, lieutenant

coagulate 3 gel, set 4 clot, jell 6 curdle 7 congeal, jellify, thicken 8 coalesce, condense, solidify 10 gelatinize, inspissate 11 concentrate, consolidate

coal *carrier:* 3 hod 7 scuttle *distillate:* 3 tar *dust:* 4 culm, smut, soot 5 slack *element:* 6 carbon *fused leavings:* 4 slag 7 clinker *glowing:* 5 ember, gleed *hard:* 10 anthracite *lump:* 3 cob *miner:* 7 collier *region:* 4 Saar *residue:* 4 coke *soft:* 6 cannel 10 bituminous

coalesce 3 mix 4 fuse, join, link 5 blend, merge, unite 6 mingle 7 combine, conjoin 10 amalgamate

coalition 4 bloc, ring 5 party, union 6 fusion, league, merger 7 combine, melding, merging 8 alliance 9 anschluss 10 federation 11 affiliation, association, combination, confederacy, integration, unification 13 confederation, consolidation

coarse 3 raw 4 rude 5 bawdy, crass, crude, dirty, gross, harsh, rough, tacky 6 common, filthy, grainy, ribald, smutty, vulgar 7 boor-ish, obscene, raffish, raunchy, uncouth 8 granular, indecent 9 inelegant, roughneck, unrefined 10 uncultured 11 particulate 12 uncultivated

coast 4 bank 5 beach, drift, shore, slide 6 strand 7 seaside 8 littoral, seashore 9 freewheel *of Antarctica:* 4 Knox

coastal 7 seaside 8 littoral, riverine

coaster 4 sled, tray 6 trader

coat 5 crust, glaze, gloss, layer, parka, plate, tunic 6 blazer, duster, finish, jacket, patina, raglan, reefer, ulster, veneer 7 cutaway 8 covering, mackinaw, tegument 9 newmarket, redingote 10 integument, mackintosh 11 windbreaker 12 Prince Albert *animal:* 3 fur 4 hide, pelt, wool 6 pelage *fur-lined:* 7 pelisse *kind:* 3 pea, top 5 frock 6 trench *Levantine:* 6 caftan *of arms:* 5 crest 6 blazon, emblem, shield, tabard 8 blazonry 10 escutcheon *of egg white:* 5 glair 6 glaire *of mail:* 7 hauberk *soldier's:* 5 frock, tunic 6 capote *waterproof:* 7 slicker 10 mackintosh

coating 4 film, leaf, scum, skin 5 glaze, gloss, layer 6 finish, patina, veneer 7 dusting, lacquer, overlay, surface, varnish 8 covering *winter:* 3 ice 4 snow 5 sleet

coat rack *part* 3 leg, peg 4 base, hook 5 stand 6 hanger

coax 4 lure, urge 5 cable, press, tempt 6 cajole, entice, induce 7 blarney, wheedle 8 blandish, butter up, inveigle, persuade, softsoap 9 importune, sweet-talk

cob 3 ear 4 swan 5 adobe, horse

cobalt *symbol* 2 Co

cobble 4 make, mend 5 patch, stone 6 repair 11 paving stone

cobbler 3 pie 5 drink 8 cocktail 9 shoemaker *form:* 4 last *tool:* 3 awl

cobelligerent 4 ally

cobweb 3 net 4 mesh, trap 8 gossamer 9 confusion, spiderweb 12 entanglement

coccyx 8 tailbone

cochineal 3 dye 6 insect

cock 3 tap 4 boss, head, heap, hill, lord, mass, pile, rick, tilt 5 chief, mound, stack, strut, valve 6 faucet, honcho, leader, master, spigot 7 headman, hydrant, rooster, swagger 11 chanticleer

cock-a-hoop 4 awry 5 askew 7 askance, crooked 8 boastful, exultant, exulting, jubilant 9 triumphal 10 triumphant

Cockaigne 6 utopia 7 arcadia 9 Shangri-la 10 wonderland

cockalorum 7 bluster, bombast, bravado 8 blowhard, boasting, braggart, leapfrog 11 braggadocio

cockamamy 5 batty, crazy, daffy, flaky,

kooky, loony, nutty, wacky **6** absurd **9** ludicrous **10** incredible, ridiculous **11** harebrained

cock-and-bull story 5 crock **6** canard **7** whopper **9** fairy tale

cockcrow 4 dawn, morn **5** sunup **7** morning, sunrise **8** daybreak, daylight

cocker 4 baby **5** humor, spoil **6** coddle, cosset, pamper **7** indulge, spaniel **11** mollycoddle

cockeyed 4 awry **5** askew **8** lopsided **11** hare-brained

cockle 5 shell **6** dimple, furrow, groove, pucker, ripple **7** bivalve, mollusc, mollusk, wrinkle

cockleshell 4 boat

cockscomb see **coxcomb**

cocksure 5 brash **6** cheeky **9** bumptious **13** overconfident

cocktail 5 Bronx, drink, julep **6** Gibson, gimlet, mai tai, mimosa, mojito, Rob Roy, zombie **7** gin fizz, martini, sidecar, stinger **8** aperitif, daiquiri, pink lady, salty dog, sombrero **9** Cuba libre, manhattan, margarita, mint julep, rusty nail **10** Bloody Mary, Tom Collins, wallbanger **11** grasshopper, screwdriver, whiskey sour **12** black russian, cosmopolitan, old-fashioned *fruit:* **9** macedoine *gasoline:* **7** Molotov

Cocktail Party author 5 Eliot (T. S.)

cocky 4 bold, sure **5** brash, pushy, sassy, saucy **6** brassy, cheeky, jaunty **8** arrogant, impudent, insolent **9** conceited **10** swaggering **11** self-assured **12** enterprising **13** overconfident, self-confident

coconspirator 7 abettor **9** accessory **10** accomplice **11** confederate

coconut *husk fiber:* **4** coir *meat:* **5** copra

coda 5 envoi, envoy **6** ending, finale **7** summary **8** epilogue, follow-up **9** afterword **10** conclusion

coddle 4 baby **5** humor, spoil **6** cosset, pamper **7** cater to, indulge

code 6 cipher, symbol **7** encrypt **8** encipher *kind:* **3** PIN, zip **4** area **5** Morse, legal, penal *message in:* **10** cryptogram **11** cryptograph

code word see **communications code word**

codger 4 coot, fogy **5** fogey **6** duffer, fellow, fossil, geezer **7** old coot, old fogy **8** old fogey

codicil 5 rider **8** addendum, addition, appendix **10** postscript, supplement

codswallop see **nonsense**

coefficient 6 factor **7** measure **8** constant

coelenterate 5 coral **7** anemone, hydroid **9** cnidarian, jellyfish **10** sea anemone

coerce 3 cow **5** bully, force, impel, press **6** compel, menace, oblige **8** browbeat, bulldoze, dominate, pressure, threaten **9** blackjack, constrain, strong-arm, terrorize **10** intimidate

coercion 5 force **6** duress, menace, threat **8** pressure **10** compulsion, constraint

Coetzee novel 8 Disgrace

Coeur d'____ 5 Alene

coeval see **contemporary**

coexistent see **contemporary**

coffee 3 joe, mud **4** java **6** jamoke *alkaloid:* **8** caffeine *bean:* **3** nib *cake:* **6** kuchen *cup:* **9** demitasse *French:* **4** café *grinder:* **4** mill *kind:* **4** drip, java **5** decaf, latte, mocha **7** arabica, instant **8** espresso **9** Americano, macchiato **10** café au lait, cappuccino *maker:* **10** percolator *pot:* **3** urn

coffee shop 4 café **5** diner **8** snack bar **9** cafeteria, hash house, lunchroom **11** greasy spoon **12** luncheonette

coffer 5 chest **6** casket **8** treasury **9** exchequer, strongbox

coffin 3 box **4** kist **6** casket *carrier:* **6** hearse **10** pallbearer *nail:* **9** cigarette *stand:* **4** bier **10** catafalque

cogency 5 force, point, power, punch **7** potency **8** strength, validity **9** relevance **10** conviction, pertinence **13** effectiveness

cogent 5 solid, sound, valid **6** potent **7** telling, weighty **8** forceful, powerful, relevant **9** pertinent **10** compelling, convincing, meaningful, persuasive **11** influential, well-founded **12** well-grounded **13** consequential

cogitate 4 muse **5** think **6** ponder, reason **7** reflect **8** conceive, consider, meditate, mull over, ruminate **9** cerebrate, speculate **10** deliberate

cogitation 7 thought **10** meditation, reflection, rumination **11** cerebration, speculation **12** deliberation **13** consideration

cogitative 7 pensive **10** meditative, reflective, ruminative, thoughtful **11** speculative **13** contemplative

Cogito ____ sum 4 ergo

cognac 6 brandy

cognate 4 akin, like **5** alike **6** allied, common **7** kindred, related, similar **8** parallel **10** affiliated, associated

cognition 9 awareness, knowledge, sentience **10** perception

cognizance 4 heed, note **6** notice **9** attention, awareness, knowledge **12** jurisdiction

cognizant 5 aware **7** knowing, mindful **8** informed, sensible **9** conscious **13** knowledgeable

cognize 4 know **5** grasp **6** fathom **7** realize **8**

perceive 9 apprehend 10 appreciate, comprehend, understand

cognomen 4 name 5 alias, title 7 epithet, moniker, surname 8 nickname 11 appellation, appellative, designation 12 denomination

cognoscente 5 judge 6 critic, expert 7 epicure 8 aesthete 9 authority 10 specialist 11 connoisseur

cognoscible 8 knowable 10 fathomable 13 apprehensible

cogwheel 4 gear

cohere 4 fuse, join 5 agree, blend, cling, merge, stick, unite 6 accord 7 combine, comport, conform, connect 8 coalesce, dovetail 10 correspond 11 consolidate

coherence 4 bond 5 union, unity 8 adhesion, cohesion 9 agreement, congruity, integrity 10 conformity, connection, consonance, solidarity 11 consistency, integration

coherent 5 sound 7 logical, ordered, unified 8 rational 10 consistent, integrated, meaningful 11 coordinated

cohesion see **coherence**

coho 6 salmon 12 silver salmon

cohort 3 pal 4 ally, band, chum, crew, mate 5 buddy, crony, group 6 fellow, friend 7 comrade, partner 8 adherent, confrere, disciple, follower, henchman, sidekick 9 assistant, associate, colleague, companion, supporter 10 accomplice 11 demographic 12 collaborator

coif 3 cap, cut 4 hood, perm 6 hairdo 7 haircut 8 skullcap

coiffeur 6 barber 10 haircutter 11 hairdresser, hairstylist

coiffure 6 hairdo **aid:** 3 net, rat 5 snood

coil 4 curl, loop, ring, turn, wind 5 helix, twine, twist 6 rotate, spiral 7 entwine, revolve, wreathe 8 curlicue 9 corkscrew

coiled 6 spiral, volute 7 helical, voluted, whorled 9 circinate

coin 4 mint 6 invent, make up, strike **Afghanistan:** 3 pul 7 afghani **Albania:** 3 lek 9 quindarka **Algeria:** 5 dinar 7 centime **ancient Greek:** 4 obol **ancient Muslim:** 5 dinar **ancient Roman:** 8 denarius **Argentina:** 4 peso 7 centavo **Austria:** 4 euro 8 groschen 9 schilling **Bahrain:** 4 fils 5 dinar **Belgium:** 4 euro 5 franc 7 centime **Benin:** 5 franc 7 centime **Bhutan:** 7 chetrum 8 ngultrum **Bolivia:** 7 centavo 9 boliviano **Botswana:** 4 pula 5 thebe **Brazil:** 4 real 7 centavo 8 cruzeiro **Bulgaria:** 3 lev 8 stotinka **Burma:** 4 kyat **Burundi:** 5 franc 7 centime **Cameroon:** 5 franc 7 centime **Canada:** 6 loonie, toonie, twonie **Cape Verde Islands:** 6 escudo 7 centavo **Chile:** 4 peso 7 centavo **China:** 3 fen 4

jiao, yuan **Colombia:** 4 peso 7 centavo **Costa Rica:** 5 colón 7 centimo **Cuba:** 4 peso 7 centavo **Czech Republic:** 5 haler 6 koruna **defective:** 4 fido **Denmark:** 3 ore 5 krone **Dominican Republic:** 4 peso 7 centavo **Ecuador:** 5 sucre 7 centavo **edge:** 7 milling **Egypt:** 7 piastre **European gold:** 5 ducat **Finland:** 4 euro 5 penni 6 markka **former:** 3 ecu, mil, pie, sol, sou 4 anna, besa, doit, duit, fels, kran, para, pice, reis (plural) 5 fanam, litas, mohur, paisa, rupia, shahi, soldo, taler, toman 6 besant, centas, denier, heller, macuta, pagoda, tangka 7 santims, sapeque 8 maravedi, skilling 9 rigsdaler 10 Indian head, reichsmark 13 reichspfennig **France:** 3 ecu, sou 4 euro 5 franc 7 centime **Gambia:** 5 butut 6 dalasi **Germany:** 4 euro, mark 7 pfennig **Ghana:** 4 cedi 6 pesewa **Great Britain:** 3 bob 4 quid 5 crown, penny, pound 6 guinea 7 ha'penny 8 farthing, shilling, sixpence 9 halfpenny, sovereign 10 threepence **Greece:** 4 euro 6 lepton 7 drachma **Guatemala:** 7 centavo, quetzal **Guinea-Bissau:** 4 peso **Guyana:** 3 bit **Haiti:** 6 gourde 7 centime **Honduras:** 7 centavo, lempira **Hungary:** 5 pengo 6 filler, forint **Iceland:** 5 aurar (plural), eyrir, krona **India:** 3 pie 4 anna 5 paisa, rupee **Indonesia:** 3 sen 6 rupiah **Iran:** 4 rial 5 dinar **Iraq:** 4 fils 5 dinar **Ireland:** 4 euro 5 penny 8 farthing **Israel:** 5 agora 6 shekel **Italy:** 4 euro, lira 5 scudo **Japan:** 3 rin, sen, yen **Jordan:** 4 fils 5 dinar **Kenya:** 8 shilling **Korea, North and South:** 3 won 4 chon **Kuwait:** 4 fils 5 dinar **large:** 9 cartwheel **Lebanon:** 5 livre 7 piastre **Lesotho:** 4 loti 7 licente, lisente **Libya:** 5 dinar 6 dirham **Luxembourg:** 4 euro 5 franc **Macao:** 3 avo **Madagascar:** 5 franc **Malawi:** 6 kwacha 7 tambala **Mauritania:** 5 khoum 7 ouguiya **Mauritius:** 5 rupee **Mexico:** 4 peso 7 centavo **Moldova:** 3 leu **Monaco:** 4 euro 5 franc **Morocco:** 6 dirham **Mozambique:** 7 metical **Nepal:** 5 paisa, rupee **Netherlands:** 4 euro 6 florin, gulden 7 guilder **Nicaragua:** 7 centavo, córdoba **Nigeria:** 4 kobo 5 naira **Norway:** 3 ore 5 krone **Oman:** 4 rial 5 baiza **Pakistan:** 4 anna 5 paisa, rupee **Palestine:** 3 mil **Panama:** 6 balboa 9 centesimo **Papua New Guinea:** 4 kina, toea **Paraguay:** 7 centimo, guarani **Peru:** 3 sol 7 centimo **Philippines:** 4 peso, piso 7 sentimo **Poland:** 5 grosz, zloty **Portugal:** 4 euro 6 escudo 7 centavo **Qatar:** 5 riyal 6 dirham **Roman:** 6 aureus, bezant 7 solidus **Romania:** 3 ban, leu **Russia:** 5 kopek, ruble 6 kopeck **Samoa:** 4 sene, tala **San Marino:** 4 lira **Saudi Arabia:** 4 rial 6 halala **Scandinavia:** 3 ore

Seychelles: 5 rupee **Siam:** 3 att **side of a:** 7 obverse **Slovakia:** 5 haler 6 koruna **South Africa:** 4 rand 10 Krugerrand **Spain:** 4 euro 6 peseta 7 centimo **Sri Lanka:** 5 rupee **stamping metal:** 8 planchet **Suriname:** 6 florin, gulden 7 guilder **Swaziland:** 9 lilangeni **Sweden:** 3 ore 5 krona 8 skilling **Switzerland:** 5 franc 6 rappen **Syria:** 7 piastre **Tanzania:** 8 shilling **Thailand:** 4 baht 5 tical 6 satang **Timor:** 3 avo **Tonga:** 6 pa'anga, seniti **Tunisia:** 5 dinar **Turkey:** 4 lira, para 5 kurus **Uganda:** 8 shilling **United Arab Emirates:** 6 dirham **United Kingdom:** see **Great Britain United States:** 4 dime 5 penny 6 dollar, nickel 7 quarter 10 half-dollar **Uruguay:** 4 peso 9 centesimo **Vatican City:** 4 lira **Venezuela:** 7 bolivar **Virgin Islands:** 3 bit **Zambia:** 5 ngwee 6 kwacha

coinage 7 new word 8 creation, currency 9 invention, neologism 10 brainchild 11 contrivance

coincide 4 jibe 5 agree, equal, match, tally 6 accord, concur, square 7 comport, conform 8 dovetail 9 harmonize 10 correspond

coincident 7 similar 9 consonant 10 concurrent 11 concomitant, synchronous 12 accompanying, contemporary, simultaneous

coincidentally 8 by chance, together 12 accidentally, concurrently, fortuitously

coin-shaped 8 nummular

col 4 pass 5 ridge 6 saddle

____ **colada** 4 piña

colander's cousin 5 sieve 6 sifter 8 strainer

cold ____ 3 war 4 call, cash, cuts, feet, fish, sore, wave 5 cream, frame, front, patch, steel, sweat, water 6 turkey 7 comfort, storage 8 shoulder

cold 3 icy, raw 4 cool, dead, iced 5 aloof, chill, crisp, frore, gelid, nippy, polar 6 arctic, biting, chilly, frigid, frosty, frozen, wintry 7 bracing, glacial, shivery 8 chilling, comatose, freezing, lifeless 11 emotionless, passionless, unconscious, unemotional 12 unresponsive **combining form:** 4 cryo, kryo **common:** 6 coryza **symptom:** 5 cough, fever 6 sneeze 7 catarrh

cold-blooded 5 cruel 6 brutal 7 callous 8 hardened, obdurate, pitiless, ruthless 9 heartless, impassive, unfeeling 10 hardboiled, impersonal 11 ectothermic, emotionless, hard-hearted 12 matter-of-fact, stonyhearted 13 dispassionate, unimpassioned

cold feet 4 fear 5 alarm, doubt, dread, panic, worry 6 dismay, fright, terror 7 anxiety, jitters 8 timidity 9 cowardice 11 trepidation 12 apprehension

coldhearted see **cold-blooded**

cold-shoulder 3 cut 4 snub 6 ignore, slight 9 ostracize

cold storage 8 abeyance, dormancy 10 quiescence, suspension 12 intermission, interruption

cole 4 kale, rape 7 cabbage 8 brassica, broccoli, kohlrabi 11 cauliflower

Coleridge poem 9 Dejection, Kubla Khan 10 Christabel

Colette character 4 Gigi 5 Chéri 8 Claudine

colewort 4 kale 7 cabbage

colic 5 gripe 9 bellyache 11 stomachache 12 collywobbles

coliseum 4 bowl 5 arena, stade 6 circus 7 stadium

collaborate 6 team up 7 collude 8 conspire 9 cooperate

collaborator 4 ally 6 helper 7 abettor, partner, traitor 8 coworker, henchman, quisling 9 accessory, assistant, associate, auxiliary, colleague 10 accomplice 11 confederate, conspirator

collapse 4 cave, drop, fail, ruin 5 break, crash, plotz, smash, wreck 6 buckle, cave in, fold up 7 breakup, crack-up, crumple, debacle, deflate, failure, founder, give out, give way, pass out, shatter, smashup, succumb 8 condense, downfall 9 breakdown, cataclysm, fall apart, ruination 10 disruption 11 catastrophe, destruction, prostration 12 disintegrate

collar 3 bag, nab 4 grab, hook, nail, take 5 catch, seize 6 arrest, secure 7 capture 9 apprehend **armor:** 6 gorget **boy's:** 4 Eton **chain:** 4 torc 6 torque **jeweled:** 8 carcanet **lace-edged:** 6 rebato **metal:** 4 torc 6 torque **pleated:** 4 ruff

collarbone 8 clavicle

collate 5 group, order 7 arrange, collect, compare, compile 8 assemble, contrast, organize 9 integrate

collateral 4 bond 6 allied, lineal, pledge, surety 7 cognate, kindred, oblique, related, subject 8 indirect, parallel, security 9 accessory, ancillary, attendant, auxiliary, dependent, secondary, tributary 10 coincident, coordinate, reciprocal, subsidiary 11 concomitant, subordinate, subservient 12 accompanying, confirmatory, contributory 13 complementary, corresponding, corroborative

colleague 4 aide 6 cohort, fellow, helper 7 partner 8 confrere, coworker, teammate 9 assistant, associate, companion 10 compatriot 11 confederate 12 collaborator

collect 4 draw 5 amass, glean, group, infer,

raise **6** deduce, derive, gather, muster, prayer **7** build up, compile, compose, convene, dispose, marshal, round up **8** assemble, conclude, converge **10** accumulate, congregate, rendezvous

collected 4 calm, cool **5** quiet, still **6** poised, serene **7** assured **8** complete, composed, sanguine, tranquil **9** assembled, confident, unruffled **11** unflappable **13** imperturbable, self-possessed

collection 3 ana, kit, lot **4** band, bevy, crew, olio, ruck **5** bunch, crowd, hoard, trove **6** medley, muster **7** cluster, variety **8** assembly, caboodle **9** aggregate, anthology, congeries, gathering, stockpile **10** assemblage, assortment, cumulation, miscellany **11** aggregation **12** accumulation, congregation **13** agglomeration *miscellaneous:* **4** hash, olio **6** jumble, medley **7** mélange, mixture **8** mishmash, pastiche **9** potpourri **10** hodgepodge, hotchpotch, salmagundi **11** olla podrida *of anecdotes:* **3** ana *of animals:* **3** zoo **9** menagerie *of artistic works:* **6** museum **7** gallery *of clothes:* **8** wardrobe *of dried plants:* **9** herbarium *of literary pieces:* **8** analects **9** anthology *of reports:* **4** file **7** dossier *of trinkets:* **10** bijouterie

collective 5 joint **7** commune, kibbutz, kolkhoz **11** cooperative

collector *of bird's eggs:* **8** oologist *of books:* **11** bibliophile *of coins:* **11** numismatist *of fares:* **9** conductor *of phonograph records:* **10** discophile *of stamps:* **11** philatelist

colleen 4 girl, lass **6** maiden *country:* **4** Eire, Erin **7** Ireland

college 9 alma mater *building:* **3** gym, lab **4** dorm, hall *campus area:* **4** quad **10** quadrangle *class meeting:* **3** lab **7** lecture, seminar **8** tutorial, workshop *climber:* **3** ivy *degree:* **2** AA, AB, BA, BD, BS, CE, DD, MA, MM, MS **3** BLS, DST, MBA, MEd, MFA, MLS, PhD **5** LittD *graduate:* **6** àlumna, alumni (plural) **7** alumnae (plural), alumnus *official:* **4** dean **5** prexy **6** bursar, regent **7** proctor, provost **9** registrar *oldest in U.S.:* **7** Harvard *oldest women's in U.S.:* **12** Mount Holyoke *relating to:* **8** academic **10** collegiate *social group:* **4** frat **8** sorority **10** fraternity *song:* **9** alma mater *student class:* **4** soph **5** frosh **6** junior, senior **8** freshman **9** sophomore *teacher:* **3** don **4** prof **8** academic **9** professor *term:* **7** quarter, session **8** semester **9** trimester *VIP:* **4** BMOC *woman:* **4** coed

college team *Air Force:* **7** Falcons *Alabama:* **11** Crimson Tide *Arizona:* **8** Wildcats *Arizona State:* **9** Sun Devils *Arkansas:* **10** Ra-

zorbacks *Arkansas State:* **7** Indians *Army:* **6** Cadets *Auburn:* **6** Tigers *Baylor:* **5** Bears *Boston College:* **6** Eagles *Boston University:* **8** Terriers *Brigham Young:* **7** Cougars *Brown:* **5** Bears *California:* **11** Golden Bears *Central Michigan:* **9** Chippewas *Cincinnati:* **8** Bearcats *Citadel:* **8** Bulldogs *Clemson:* **6** Tigers *Colgate:* **10** Red Raiders *Colorado:* **9** Buffaloes *Colorado State:* **4** Rams *Columbia:* **5** Lions *Connecticut:* **7** Huskies *Cornell:* **6** Big Red *Dartmouth:* **8** Big Green *Davidson:* **8** Wildcats *Delaware State:* **7** Hornets *Drake:* **8** Bulldogs *Duke:* **10** Blue Devils *Eastern Kentucky:* **8** Colonels *Eastern Michigan:* **6** Eagles *Florida:* **6** Gators *Florida State:* **9** Seminoles *Fresno State:* **8** Bulldogs *Furman:* **8** Palidans *Georgia:* **8** Bulldogs *Georgia Tech:* **13** Yellow Jackets *Harvard:* **7** Crimson *Hawaii:* **15** Rainbow Warriors *Holy Cross:* **9** Crusaders *Houston:* **7** Cougars *Howard:* **6** Bisons *Idaho:* **7** Vandals *Idaho State:* **7** Bengals *Illinois:* **14** Fighting Illini *Illinois State:* **8** Redbirds *Indiana:* **8** Hoosiers *Indiana State:* **9** Sycamores *Iowa:* **8** Hawkeyes *Iowa State:* **8** Cyclones *Kansas:* **8** Jayhawks *Kansas State:* **8** Wildcats *Kent State:* **13** Golden Flashes *Kentucky:* **8** Wildcats *Lehigh:* **9** Engineers *Louisiana State:* **6** Tigers *Louisiana Tech:* **8** Bulldogs *Maine:* **10** Black Bears *Maryland:* **5** Terps **9** Terrapins *Massachusetts:* **9** Minutemen *Miami (Florida):* **10** Hurricanes *Miami (Ohio):* **8** Redskins *Michigan:* **10** Wolverines *Michigan State:* **8** Spartans *Minnesota:* **7** Gophers *Mississippi:* **6** Rebels *Mississippi State:* **8** Bulldogs *Missouri:* **6** Tigers *Montana:* **9** Grizzlies *Montana State:* **7** Bobcats *Navy:* **10** Midshipmen *Nebraska:* **11** Cornhuskers *Nevada:* **6** Rebels **8** Wolfpack *New Hampshire:* **8** Wildcats *New Mexico:* **5** Lobos *New Mexico State:* **6** Aggies *North Carolina:* **8** Tar Heels *North Carolina State:* **8** Wolfpack *Northeastern:* **7** Huskies *Northwestern:* **8** Wildcats *Notre Dame:* **13** Fighting Irish *Ohio State:* **8** Buckeyes *Ohio University:* **7** Bobcats *Oklahoma:* **7** Sooners *Oklahoma State:* **7** Cowboys *Oregon:* **5** Ducks *Oregon State:* **7** Beavers *Pennsylvania:* **7** Quakers *Pennsylvania State:* **12** Nittany Lions *Pittsburgh:* **8** Panthers *Princeton:* **6** Tigers *Purdue:* **12** Boilermakers *Rhode Island:* **4** Rams *Rice:* **4** Owls *Rutgers:* **14** Scarlet Knights *San Diego State:* **6** Aztecs *San Jose State:* **8** Spartans *South Carolina:* **9** Gamecocks *South Carolina State:* **8** Bulldogs *Southern California:*

7 Trojans **Southern Illinois:** 7 Salukis **Southern Methodist:** 8 Mustangs **Stanford:** 9 Cardinals **Syracuse:** 9 Orangemen **Temple:** 4 Owls **Tennessee:** 10 Volunteers **Tennessee State:** 6 Tigers **Tennessee Tech:** 12 Golden Eagles **Texas:** 9 Longhorns **Texas A&M:** 6 Aggies **Texas Christian:** 11 Horned Frogs **Texas Southern:** 6 Tigers **Texas Tech:** 10 Red Raiders **Toledo:** 7 Rockets **Tulane:** 9 Green Wave **UCLA:** 6 Bruins **UNLV:** 12 Runnin' Rebels **Utah:** 4 Utes **Utah State:** 6 Aggies **Vanderbilt:** 10 Commodores **Villanova:** 8 Wildcats **Virginia:** 9 Cavaliers **VMI:** 7 Keydets **VPI:** 8 Gobblers **Wake Forest:** 12 Demon Deacons **Washington:** 7 Huskies **Washington State:** 7 Cougars **West Virginia:** 12 Mountaineers **William & Mary:** 5 Tribe **Wisconsin:** 7 Badgers **Wyoming:** 7 Cowboys **Yale:** 4 Elis 8 Bulldogs

collide 3 hit, ram 4 bump 5 clash, crash, smash 6 impact, strike 7 impinge 8 conflict

collier 4 ship 5 miner 6 choker

Collins novel 9 Moonstone (The) 12 Woman in White (The)

collision 4 bump, jolt 5 clash, crash, shock, smash, wreck 6 impact 7 crack-up, smashup 10 concussion

collocate 7 arrange 8 position 9 juxtapose

collogue 6 confer, huddle, parley, powwow 7 consult

colloid 3 gel, sol 4 agar 7 mixture 8 hydrogel, hydrosol

colloquial 6 casual, vulgar 7 demotic 8 familiar, informal 9 idiomatic 10 vernacular

colloquium 5 forum 7 palaver, seminar 9 symposium 10 conference, roundtable

colloquy 4 chat, talk 5 forum 6 debate, parley 7 palaver, seminar 8 dialogue 9 symposium 10 conference, discussion, roundtable 12 conversation 13 confabulation

collude 4 plot 6 devise, scheme 7 connive 8 conspire, contrive, intrigue 9 machinate

collusion 4 plot 8 intrigue, skin game 10 conspiracy

collywobbles 5 colic, gripe 9 bellyache 11 stomachache

Colombia capital: 6 Bogotá **city:** 4 Cali 6 Ibagué 8 Medellín 9 Cartagena 12 Barranquilla **language:** 7 Spanish **liberator:** 7 Bolívar (Simón) **monetary unit:** 4 peso **mountain, range:** 5 Andes, Chita 6 Puracé, Tolima 9 Cristóbal **neighbor:** 4 Peru 6 Brazil, Panama 7 Ecuador 9 Venezuela **river:** 6 Chauca 7 Orinoco 9 Magdalena **sea:** 9 Caribbean

Colonel Blimp 4 fogy, Tory 5 fogey 6 fossil 7 old fogy 8 mossback, old fogey 10 fuddyduddy 11 reactionary

colonist 6 émigré, nester 7 evacuee, pilgrim, pioneer, settler 8 emigrant, squatter 9 immigrant 10 expatriate 11 homesteader

colonnade 4 stoa 9 peristyle

colony 7 outpost 9 satellite 10 settlement

color 3 dun, dye, hue, red, tan 4 aqua, blue, cast, ecru, glow, gold, gray, grey, jade, lime, navy, pink, puce, rose, teal, tint, tone 5 amber, azure, beige, belie, black, blush, brown, coral, ebony, flush, green, hazel, henna, ivory, khaki, lilac, mauve, ocher, ochre, olive, paint, peach, rouge, shade, stain, taupe, tinge, umber 6 auburn, bronze, canary, copper, indigo, maroon, orange, purple, redden, salmon, sienna, silver, violet, yellow 7 crimson, emerald, magenta, pigment, saffron, scarlet 8 chestnut, dyestuff, lavender, tincture 9 embellish, embroider, turquoise, vermilion 10 aquamarine, exaggerate, vermillion 12 pigmentation **band:** 5 facia, vitta 6 fascia **combining form:** 5 chrom 6 chromo 7 chromat 8 chromato **primary:** 3 red 4 blue 6 yellow **relating to:** 9 chromatic **secondary:** 5 green 6 orange, purple **soft:** 6 pastel

Colorado capital: 6 Denver **city:** 4 Vail 5 Aspen 6 Aurora, Pueblo 7 Boulder 8 Lakewood 11 Fort Collins **college, university:** 5 Regis 9 Fort Lewis **mountain, range:** 5 Longs (Peak), Pikes (Peak), Rocky 6 Elbert 7 Rockies **nickname:** 10 Centennial (State) **park:** 9 Mesa Verde **river:** 8 Arkansas 9 Rio Grande **state bird:** 11 lark bunting **state flower:** 9 columbine **state tree:** 10 blue spruce

colorant 3 dye 5 stain 7 pigment 8 dyestuff, tincture

colored 6 biased, warped 8 one-sided, partisan 9 jaundiced 10 prejudiced 11 tendentious

colorful 3 gay 5 gaudy, showy, vivid 6 bright, flashy, florid, garish, motley 7 splashy

coloring 4 cast, tint 5 front, tinge 6 facade, nuance 7 pigment 8 overtone 10 camouflage, complexion 12 embroidering 13 embellishment

colorless 3 wan 4 ashy, drab, dull, flat, pale 5 ashen, pasty, prosy, waxen, white 6 albino, doughy, pallid 7 insipid, neutral, prosaic 8 abstract, blanched, bleached 10 achromatic, lackluster

Color Purple author 6 Walker (Alice)

colossal 4 huge, vast 7 immense, mammoth, massive, titanic 8 enormous, gigantic, towering 9 cyclopean, monstrous 10 gargantuan, stupendous 11 astonishing, elephantine

colossus 5 giant, titan 6 statue 7 goliath, mammoth, monster 8 behemoth 9 leviathan

Colossus of ____ 6 Rhodes

colporteur 10 evangelist, missionary 12 propagandist

colt 4 foal, tyro 6 novice, rookie 8 beginner, freshman, neophyte, newcomer 9 fledgling 10 tenderfoot

coltish 6 frisky, impish 7 playful 10 frolicsome

Columbine *beloved:* 9 Harlequin *father:* 9 Pantaloon

columbium symbol 2 Cb

Columbus, Christopher *birthplace:* 5 Genoa *patron:* 8 Isabella 9 Ferdinand *ship:* 4 Niña 5 Pinta 10 Santa Maria *son:* 5 Diego *starting point:* 5 Palos

column 3 row 4 pier 5 shaft, stela 6 pillar 7 obelisk 8 pilaster *angle:* 5 arris *base:* 4 dado, ordo 5 socle 6 plinth 9 stylobate *bulge:* 7 entasis *female figure:* 8 caryatid *male figure:* 5 atlas 7 telamon 8 atlantes (plural) *style:* 5 Doric, Ionic 10 Corinthian *top:* 7 capital 8 chapiter

coma 6 stupor, torpor 8 blackout, hebetude, lethargy 9 lassitude

comate 3 pal 4 chum 5 buddy, crony 7 comrade, partner 9 associate, colleague, companion

comatose 5 dopey 6 stupid, torpid 7 out cold 8 sluggish 9 lethargic 10 insensible 11 unconscious

comb 4 rake, sift, sort 5 crest, curry, probe, scour, sweep, tease 6 search, winnow 7 ransack 8 untangle 10 straighten 11 investigate

combat 3 war 4 buck, duel, fray 5 fight, repel 6 action, battle, oppose, resist, strife 7 contend, contest, dispute 8 skirmish, struggle 9 withstand 11 controversy

combatant 7 battler, fighter, soldier, warrior 8 militant, opponent 9 adversary, aggressor, assailant, contender, disputant, mercenary 10 antagonist, challenger, competitor, contestant 11 belligerent

combative 6 feisty 7 scrappy, warlike 8 militant 9 agonistic, bellicose, truculent 10 aggressive, pugnacious 11 belligerent, contentious, quarrelsome 12 disputatious, militaristic

combativeness 9 pugnacity 10 aggression, truculence 11 bellicosity 12 belligerence

combe 4 dale, dell, glen, vale 6 dingle, valley

combination 3 mix 4 bloc, pool, ring 5 blend, union 6 fusion, hookup, merger 7 melding, merging 8 alliance 9 aggregate, coalition, composite, synthesis 10 connection 11 affiliation, association, conjunction, partnership, unification 13 consolidation

combine 3 add, mix, wed 4 band, bloc, fuse, join, link, pool, ring 5 blend, chain, group, marry, merge, trust, unify, union, unite 6 cartel, league, mingle 7 bracket, conjoin, connect, faction 8 coadjute, coalesce 9 associate, coalition, commingle, cooperate, integrate, syndicate 10 amalgamate 11 consolidate, incorporate 12 conglomerate *Japanese:* 8 keiretsu, zaibatsu *Korean:* 7 chaebol, jaebeol

combined action 7 synergy 9 synergism

combo 4 band, trio 5 group, nonet, octet 6 septet, sextet 7 quartet, quintet 8 ensemble

combust 4 burn 6 ignite, kindle 10 incinerate

combustible 4 edgy, fuel 8 burnable, volatile 9 excitable, flammable, ignitable 11 inflammable *material:* 3 gas, oil 4 coal, peat, wood 6 tinder

combustion 4 riot 7 burning 8 eruption, ignition, kindling 9 explosion, oxidation 13 thermogenesis

come 4 flow, hail, stem 5 arise, issue, occur 6 arrive, derive, show up, spring, turn up 7 advance, emanate, proceed 8 approach 9 originate *a cropper:* 4 fail, fall *across:* 4 find, meet 8 discover 9 encounter *apart:* 12 disintegrate *at:* 6 attack *away:* 5 leave 6 depart *before:* 7 precede *clean:* 7 confess *forth:* 5 issue 6 appear, emerge *forward:* 7 advance 9 volunteer *into:* 5 enter 7 acquire *near:* 5 verge 8 approach *round:* 5 rally 7 get well, recover *to pass:* 5 occur 6 happen *up:* 5 arise *upon:* 4 find, meet 8 discover 9 encounter

comeback 5 rally 6 answer, retort, return 7 rebound, revival, riposte 8 rebuttal, recovery, repartee, response 11 improvement 12 counterclaim, recuperation

come by 4 call 5 pop in, visit 6 drop in, look in 7 acquire, collect, inherit

comedian 3 wag, wit 4 card 5 clown, comic, droll, joker 6 jester 7 farceur 8 funnyman, humorist, jokester, quipster 11 entertainer *famous:* 3 Cho (Margaret), Fey (Tina), Nye (Louis) 4 Ball (Lucille), Chan (Jackie), Coca (Imogene), Cook (Peter), Dana (Bill), Foxx (Redd), Hope (Bob), Idle (Eric), Kaye (Danny), Leno (Jay), Marx (Chico, Groucho, Gummo, Harpo, Zeppo), Rock (Chris), Sahl (Mort), Wise (Ernie), Wood (Victoria) 5 Abbot (Bud), Allen (Gracie, Steve, Woody), Benny (Jack), Berle (Milton), Borge (Victor), Bruce (Lenny), Burns (George), Candy (John), Chase (Chevy),

Cosby (Bill), David (Larry), Guest (Christopher), Hardy (Oliver), Lewis (Jerry), Lloyd (Harold), Lopez (George), Maher (Bill), Meara (Anne), Moore (Dudley), Myers (Mike), Palin (Michael), Pearl (Minnie), Pryor (Richard), Rogen (Seth), Sales (Soupy) **6** Caesar (Sid), Carell (Steve), Carlin (George), Carrey (Jim), Carson (Johnny), Cleese (John), DeVito (Danny), Diller (Phyllis), Fields (W. C.), Gosden (Freeman), Izzard (Eddie), Keaton (Buster), Knotts (Don), Kovacs (Ernie), Laurel (Stan), Lehrer (Tom), Lemmon (Jack), Little (Rich), Martin (Dean, Steve), Midler (Bette), Murphy (Eddie), Murray (Bill), O'Brien (Conan), Radner (Gilda), Reiner (Carl), Rivers (Joan), Rogers (Will), Thomas (Danny), Tomlin (Lily), Turpin (Ben), Wayans (Damon, Keenan Ivory, Marlon, Shawn) **7** Aykroyd (Dan), Belushi (Jim, John), Buttons (Red), Burnett (Carol), Chaplin (Charlie), Colbert (Stephen), Crystal (Billy), Durante (Jimmy), Feldman (Marty), Freberg (Stan), Gleason (Jackie), Grammer (Kelsey), Hackett (Buddy), Keillor (Garrison), Matthau (Walter), Moranis (Rick), Newhart (Bob), Nielsen (Leslie), Paulsen (Pat), Rickles (Don), Russell (Mark), Sandler (Adam), Sedaris (Amy, David), Sellers (Peter), Silvers (Phil), Skelton (Red), Stewart (Jon), Stiller (Ben, Jerry), Winters (Jonathan) **8** Atkinson (Rowan), Costello (Lou), Goldberg (Whoopi), Grenfell (Joyce), Mulligan (Spike), O'Donnell (Rosie), Seinfeld (Jerry), Smothers (Dick, Tom), Williams (Robin), Youngman (Henny) **9** Carrot Top, DeGeneres (Ellen), Leguizamo (John), Letterman (David), Morecambe (Eric) **10** Poundstone (Paula) **11** Dangerfield (Rodney)

comedo 9 blackhead

comedown 4 dive, fall, ruin **5** crash **7** decline, descent, failure, setback **8** collapse **9** ruination

come down with 3 get **5** catch **7** develop **8** contract

comedy 5 farce, humor **6** levity **8** drollery, hilarity **9** drollness, slapstick, wittiness
show: **3** SNL **6** Hee-Haw **7** Laugh-In **9** Daily Show (The)

come forth 4 grow, rise **5** arise **6** appear **7** emanate

come in 5 enter, reply **6** answer **7** respond

comely 4 fair **5** bonny, sonsy **6** lovely, pretty, proper, sonsie **7** winsome **8** becoming, decorous, handsome, pleasing **9** beauteous, beautiful, befitting **10** attractive **11** good-looking

come off 4 fare, seem **5** click, occur **6** appear, go over, happen, pan out **7** develop, succeed **8** prove out **9** transpire

come-on 4 bait, lure, trap **5** decoy, snare **9** seduction **10** allurement, enticement, inducement, invitation, temptation **12** blandishment, inveiglement, solicitation

come out 4 leak **5** break, debut, end up **6** emerge **9** transpire

come out with 3 say **4** tell **5** state, utter **6** report **7** declare, deliver, publish, release **8** announce, proclaim

comestible 6 edible **7** eatable **8** esculent

comestibles 4 feed, food **6** viands **7** edibles **8** victuals **9** provender **10** provisions

comet 4 West **7** Halley's **8** Hale-Bopp, Kohoutek, McNaught **9** Hyakutake

come through 6 chip in, endure **7** pitch in, prevail, survive **8** transmit **10** contribute

come together 4 mass, meet **5** merge, swarm **6** gather, huddle **7** cluster, collect, combine, convene **8** assemble, converge **10** congregate

come upon 4 find **7** run into, uncover, unearth **8** bump into, discover, trip over **9** encounter, run across

comeuppance 3 due **5** lumps **7** deserts

comfort 3 aid **4** ease, help **5** cheer **6** assist, buck up, luxury, relief, solace, soothe, succor **7** amenity, cheer up, console, relieve, support **8** reassure, sympathy **10** assistance, sympathize **11** commiserate, consolation, contentment

comfortable 4 cozy, easy, homy, snug, soft **5** ample, cushy, homey, roomy **7** content, easeful, restful, well-off **8** adequate, homelike, pleasant, pleasing, spacious, well-to-do **9** agreeable, satisfied, well-fixed **10** commodious, prosperous, sufficient, well-heeled **11** substantial **12** satisfactory

comforter 4 down, pouf, puff **5** duvet, quilt **9** eiderdown

comfy 4 cozy, homy, snug **5** cushy, homey

comic 3 wag, wit **5** antic, droll, funny, joker **6** jester **7** risible **8** comedian, farcical, funnyman, humorist, jokester, quipster **9** laughable, ludicrous **10** ridiculous

comical 4 zany **5** droll, funny, goofy, silly **6** absurd **7** amusing, foolish, risible, waggish **8** farcical **9** laughable, ludicrous **10** ridiculous

comic strip 4 Pogo, Shoe **5** Hazel, Henry, Nancy **6** Archie, Popeye **7** Blondie, Dilbert, Far Side (The), Peanuts **8** Alley Oop, Andy Capp, Garfield, Krazy Kat, Li'l Abner, Superman **9** Betty Boop, Dick Tracy, Marmaduke, Mary Worth, Spider-Man, Yellow Kid

(The) **10** Doonesbury, Joe Palooka, Little Nemo **11** Bloom County, Brenda Starr, Flash Gordon, Hogan's Alley, Mutt and Jeff, Rex Morgan M.D., Steve Canyon **12** Beetle Bailey **13** Captain Marvel, Gasoline Alley, Prince Valiant *character:* **3** Arn, Jon, Kim, Liz, Owl, Roz **4** Asok, Elmo, Flip, Herb, Irma, Lizz, Loon, Lucy, Odie, Opus, Otto, Phil, Rube, Tess, Thun, Zero **5** Aleta, Alice, Bella, Betty, Carol, Cosmo, Foozy, Honey, Itchy, Lacey, Linus, Mammy, Ooola, Pappy, Patty, Percy, Phred, Plato, Porky, Rerun, Rocky, Rollo, Sally, Shmoo, Spike, Wally **6** Albert, Arlene, Belfry, Cookie, Doc Boy, Dottie, Frieda, Joanie, Junior, Lt. Flap, Lt. Fuzz, Marcie, Nermal, Pig-Pen, Reggie, Skyler, Sluggo, Snoopy, Vultan, Zipper, Zonker **7** Aunt May, Boopsie, Chalkie, Churchy, Dagwood, Dithers, Flattop, Florrie, Jughead, Mr. Butts, Mumbles, Phyllis, Portnoy, Skeezix, Tootsie, Wolf Gal **8** Black Cat, B. O. Plenty, Bull Pupp, Daisy Mae, Dr. Sivana, June Gale, Lana Lang, Lois Lane, Olive Oyl, Pete Ross, Shroeder, Veronica **9** Alexander, Brilliant, Chip Gizmo, Clark Kent, Dale Arden, Diet Smith, Gwen Stacy, Pat Patton, Pruneface, Uncle Duke **10** Aunt Fritzi, Betty Brant, Bill the Cat, Cutter John, Dragon Lady, Hans Zarkov, Hodge-Podge, Jimmy Olsen, Joe Btfsplk, Louise Lugg, Marryin' Sam, Miss Buxley, Perry White, Sam Catchem, Scott Sloan, Sgt. Snorkel, Walt Wallet **11** Happy Easter, Harry Osborn, Ignatz Mouse, Lola Granola, Mickey Dugan, Peter Parker, Steve Dallas, Summer Olson **12** Charlie Brown, Felicia Hardy, Gen. Halftrack, Gravel Gertie

coming 3 due **4** next **5** fated, onset **6** advent, future **7** arrival, ensuing, nearing **8** approach, expected, foreseen, imminent **9** following, impending **11** approaching *forth:* **7** issuant

comity 5 amity **7** concord, harmony **8** goodwill **10** friendship **11** benevolence, camaraderie **12** friendliness

comma 4 lull **5** pause **8** interval

command 3 bid **4** rule, sway **5** order **6** adjure, behest, charge, compel, direct, enjoin **7** bidding, conduct, control, dictate, mandate, mastery, precept **9** authority, direction, directive, expertise, ordinance **10** domination, imperative, injunction **11** instruction **12** jurisdiction *to go:* **4** mush **6** avaunt, begone **7** giddyap, giddyup *to stop:* **4** whoa **5** avast

commandeer 4 take **5** annex, seize, usurp **6** assume, hijack **7** preempt **8** accroach, arro-

gate **9** conscript, sequester **10** confiscate **11** appropriate, expropriate, requisition

commander 4 boss, head **6** honcho, leader, master **7** captain, general, headman, officer

commandment 3 law **4** fiat, rule **5** edict, order **6** decree **7** mitzvah, precept, statute

commedia dell' ____ **4** arte

comme il faut 6 decent, polite, proper, seemly **7** correct **8** becoming, decorous, suitable

commemorate 4 keep **7** observe **8** eulogize, monument **9** celebrate, solemnize **11** memorialize **13** monumentalize

commemorative 8 memorial **10** dedicatory **11** celebratory

commence 5 begin, start **6** launch, set out **7** kick off **8** embark on, initiate **10** embark upon, inaugurate

commencement 4 dawn **5** birth, onset, start **6** outset **7** dawning, genesis, opening **9** beginning, inception **10** graduation **12** inauguration

commend 4 hail, laud **5** extol **6** commit, kudize, praise, salute, tender **7** acclaim, applaud, approve, consign, entrust **8** hand over, relegate, turn over **10** compliment

commendable 6 worthy **8** laudable **9** admirable, deserving, estimable, meritable, venerable **10** creditable **11** meritorious **12** praiseworthy

commensurable see **commensurate**

commensurate 4 even **5** equal **10** comparable **11** coextensive **12** proportional **13** corresponding, proportionate

comment 4 note **5** opine **6** remark **7** mention, observe **8** critique, point out **9** criticism, interject **10** animadvert **11** observation **12** obiter dictum

commentary 5 gloss **6** review **8** analysis, critique, exegesis **9** editorial, narration, voiceover **10** annotation, exposition **11** explanation, observation **12** appreciation, obiter dictum

commerce 5 trade **7** contact, traffic **8** business, congress, dealings, exchange, industry **9** communion **11** interchange **13** communication

commercial 2 ad **6** advert **8** economic **10** mercantile **13** advertisement

commie 3 Red **5** pinko **6** bolshy **7** bolshie **9** Bolshevik

commination 5 curse **8** anathema **10** accusation, execration **11** imprecation, malediction **12** denunciation

commingle 3 mix **4** meld **5** blend, merge, unify **8** compound, intermix **9** integrate **10** amalgamate

comminute 4 bray 5 crush, grind 9 granulate, pulverize

commiserate 4 pity 7 condole, feel for 9 empathize 10 sympathize 13 compassionate

commiseration 4 pity, ruth 7 empathy 8 sympathy 10 compassion, condolence

commission 3 bid, fee 4 name 5 board, order, panel 6 agency, assign, charge, enable, engage, enjoin, enlist 7 appoint, command, council, empower, license, warrant 8 accredit, delegate, deputize 9 authorize, designate 10 delegation, deputation, percentage 11 certificate

commit 4 bind 5 allot, grant, refer 6 assign, convey, invest, ordain, pledge, record, reveal 7 achieve, consign, deposit, entrust, execute, perform, promise, pull off, trustee 8 allocate, carry out, hand over, obligate, relegate, turn over 10 accomplish, perpetrate

commitment 3 vow 4 bond, deal, duty 6 charge, devoir, pledge 7 promise 8 contract 9 agreement, assurance, guarantee 10 obligation 11 undertaking

committal see **commitment**

commixture 5 blend 6 fusion 7 amalgam, melange 8 compound, mingling 9 composite

commodious 4 wide 5 ample, roomy 8 spacious 9 capacious, expansive, luxurious 11 comfortable

commodities 5 goods, items, wares 8 articles, products 9 vendibles 11 merchandise

common 4 park 5 banal, daily, joint, plaza, trite, usual 6 mutual, normal, shared 7 general, generic, prosaic, regular, routine, typical 8 adequate, communal, conjoint, conjunct, déclassé, everyday, familiar, frequent, habitual, ordinary, standard, workaday 9 customary, prevalent, tolerable, universal 10 collective, pedestrian, prevailing, unexciting, widespread 12 conventional, run-of-the-mill, satisfactory 13 unexceptional, uninteresting

commonalty 3 mob 5 plebs 6 masses, people, plebes, public, rabble 7 commune 8 populace 9 hoi polloi, multitude, plebeians 11 proletariat, rank and file, third estate

commoners see **commonalty**

commonplace 5 banal, stale, tired, trite, usual 6 cliché, normal, truism 7 bromide, clichéd, humdrum, mundane, obvious, prosaic, regular, routine, typical 8 banality, bromidic, chestnut, everyday, habitual, mediocre, ordinary, well-worn, workaday 9 hackneyed, platitude, prevalent 10 pedestrian, shibboleth, stereotype, uneventful 11 stereotyped 12 conventional, run-of-the-mill, unremarkable 13 stereotypical, unexceptional, uninteresting

common sense 6 wisdom 8 judgment, prudence 10 shrewdness

Common Sense author 5 Paine (Thomas)

commotion 3 ado, din, row 4 flap, fuss, moil, riot, stew, stir, to-do 5 hoo-ha, storm, whirl 6 bustle, clamor, dither, flurry, fracas, furore, hoo-hah, hoopla, hubbub, hurrah, lather, outcry, pother, racket, ruckus, rumpus, shindy, tumult, uproar, upturn 7 ferment, tempest, turmoil 8 brouhaha, foofaraw 9 agitation, confusion 10 convulsion, hullabaloo, hurly-burly, turbulence 11 pandemonium

commove 5 rouse 6 excite 7 agitate, inspire, provoke 9 electrify, galvanize, stimulate

communal 5 civil, joint 6 common, mutual, public, shared 10 collective 11 socialistic

commune 10 collective *Israeli:* 7 kibbutz *Russian:* 3 mir 7 kolkhoz

communicable 8 catching 10 contagious, infectious 13 transmissible, transmittable

communicate 4 tell 6 convey, impart, inform, pass on, relate, reveal, signal 7 connect, contact, divulge 8 disclose, transmit 9 make known

communication 4 talk 7 contact, message, missive, talking 8 converse, exchange 9 directive 10 discussing, discussion 11 interchange, intercourse 12 conversation *means:* 2 IM, TV 3 Web 4 drum, mail, note 5 e-mail, media, phone, radio 6 letter, medium, pigeon, speech 8 Internet 9 telegraph, telephone 10 television

communications code word 4 Alfa, Echo, Golf, Kilo, Lima, Mike, Papa, Xray, Zulu 5 Alpha, Bravo, Delta, Hotel, India, Oscar, Romeo, Tango 6 Quebec, Sierra, Victor, Yankee 7 Charlie, Foxtrot, Juliett, Uniform, Whiskey 8 November

communicative 5 vocal 6 fluent, prolix 7 verbose, voluble 8 eloquent 9 expansive, garrulous, talkative 10 articulate, expressive, loquacious

communion 7 rapport, sharing 9 Eucharist, sacrament 10 connection, fellowship *cloth:* 8 corporal *cup:* 7 chalice *plate:* 5 paten

communism 7 Marxism 8 Leninism 10 bolshevism 12 collectivism

Communist 3 red 5 lefty, pinko 6 bolshy, Maoist 7 bolshie, comrade, Marxist 8 Leninist 9 Bolshevik, Stalinist 10 Bolshevist, Trotskyist

Communist leader *Chinese:* 3 Mao 4 Deng 5 Jiang 8 Hu Jintao 9 Mao Zedong 10 Jiang Zemin, Mao Tse-tung 12 Deng Xiaoping 13

Teng Hsiao-p'ing *Cuban:* **6** Castro (Fidel) *Russian:* **5** Lenin (Vladimir Ilyich) **6** Stalin (Joseph) **7** Kosygin (Aleksey), Trotsky (Leon) **8** Andropov (Yuri), Brezhnev (Leonid) **9** Chernenko (Konstantin), Gorbachev (Mikhail) **10** Khrushchev (Nikita)

community 4 town **7** enclave, society **12** neighborhood *closed:* **5** abbey **6** priory **7** convent, nunnery **8** cloister **9** monastery *ecological:* **10** biocenosis **11** biocoenosis

commute 5 alter **6** change, make up, modify, soften, travel **7** convert, curtail, shorten, shuttle **8** decrease, exchange, mitigate, transfer **9** transform, translate, transmute, transpose **10** compensate, substitute **11** interchange

Comoros *capital:* 6 Moroni *island:* **6** Mohéli **7** Anjouan **12** Grande Comore *language:* **6** Arabic, French **8** Comorian *monetary unit:* **5** franc *volcano:* **8** Karthala

compact 4 bond **5** close, dense, unify **7** bargain, bunched, crowded, pressed **8** compress, condense, contract, covenant **9** agreement, concordat **10** convention **11** concentrate, consolidate, transaction

compadre 3 pal **4** chum, mate **5** amigo, buddy, crony **6** cohort, friend **7** comrade, partner **8** confrere, sidekick, intimate **9** associate, colleague, companion

companion 3 pal **4** chum, mate **5** buddy, crony **6** cohort, escort, fellow **7** comrade, consort, partner **8** sidekick **9** associate, attendant, colleague

companionable 6 genial, social **7** affable, amiable **8** outgoing, sociable **9** agreeable, congenial, convivial **10** gregarious **11** good-natured

companionship 7 company, society **8** intimacy **10** fellowship **11** camaraderie

company 4 band, club, crew, firm, gang, team **5** corps, group, party, troop **6** circle, clique, guests, outfit, troupe **7** concern, coterie, retinue, society, visitor **8** assembly, business, ensemble, visitors **9** gathering **10** assemblage, enterprise, fellowship **11** association, camaraderie, corporation **12** congregation **13** companionship, establishment

comparable 4 akin, like **5** alike **6** agnate **7** similar, uniform **8** parallel **9** analogous **10** equivalent, homologous **12** commensurate **13** corresponding

comparative 4 near **8** relative **11** approximate

compare 5 liken, match **6** equate, relate **7** collate **8** contrast, parallel **9** correlate **10** assimilate

comparison 6 simile **7** analogy **8** affinity, contrast, likeness **9** collation, semblance **10** similarity, similitude **11** correlation, resemblance

compartment 3 bay **4** cell, nook, part, slot **5** berth, booth, niche, stall **6** alcove, carrel, locker **7** chamber, cubicle, section **8** division **9** cubbyhole **10** pigeonhole **11** subdivision

compass 3 hem **4** ring **5** ambit, field, grasp, orbit, range, reach, scope, sweep **6** bounds, circle, domain, extent, girdle, limits, radius, sphere **7** circuit, environ, purview **8** boundary, confines, environs **9** enclosure, extension, perimeter, periphery **13** circumference *kind:* **4** gyro **5** solar **8** magnetic *stand:* **8** binnacle

compassion 4 pity, ruth **5** mercy **7** charity, empathy **8** clemency, humanity, kindness, sympathy **10** condolence, humaneness **11** benevolence **13** commiseration, fellow feeling

compassionate 4 pity, warm **6** humane, tender **7** clement **8** merciful **10** benevolent, charitable, solicitous **11** commiserate, kindhearted, softhearted, sympathetic, warmhearted

compassionless 5 stony **7** callous **8** obdurate **9** heartless, unfeeling **11** coldblooded, hardhearted, ironhearted **12** stonyhearted

compass point 3 ENE, ESE, NNE, NNW, SSE, SSW, WNW, WSW **4** east, west **5** north, rhumb, south **7** bearing *Scottish:* **4** airt

compatible 6 proper **8** suitable **9** agreeable, congenial, congruous, consonant **10** consistent, harmonious, like-minded **11** appropriate, sympathetic

compatriot 7 paesano **8** confrere **9** associate, colleague, companion

compel 4 hale, urge **5** drive, force **6** coerce, impose, oblige **7** enforce **9** constrain

compelling 4 dire **5** acute **6** cogent, crying, urgent **7** clamant, exigent, telling, weighty **8** forceful, pressing **10** convincing, persuasive **11** importunate**12** well-grounded

compendious 5 brief, pithy, short **7** compact, concise, summary **8** succinct **9** condensed **11** abbreviated

compendium 4 list **5** brief, guide **6** aperçu, digest, manual, précis, sketch, survey **7** epitome, summary **8** abstract, Baedeker, handbook, overview, syllabus, synopsis **9** anthology, guidebook, vade mecum **10** abridgment, collection, conspectus **11** abridgement, compilation, enchiridion

compensate 3 pay **5** atone, repay **6** make up, offset, pay off, redeem, set off **7** balance, guerdon, requite, satisfy **8** outweigh **9** indemnify, reimburse **10** counteract, neutralize, recompense, remunerate **11** countervail

compensation 6 amends, reward, salary **7** damages, payment, redress **8** earnings, reprisal, requital, solatium **9** atonement, indemnity, quittance, repayment **10** recompense, reparation **11** restitution **12** remuneration *unexpected:* **4** gift **5** bonus **8** windfall

compete 3 vie **4** spar **5** fight **6** battle, strive **7** contend, contest **8** struggle

competence 5 skill **7** ability, know-how **8** adequacy, aptitude, capacity, facility **9** expertise **10** capability **11** proficiency, sufficiency **13** qualification

competent 3 fit **4** able **5** adept **6** au fait, decent, proper **7** capable, skilled **8** adequate **9** efficient, qualified **10** proficient, sufficient **12** satisfactory

competition 4 bout, game, meet, race **5** clash, fight, match, rival **6** strife **7** contest, matchup, rivalry **8** concours, conflict, striving, struggle, tug-of-war **10** antagonism, contention, tournament

competitor 5 enemy, rival **7** entrant **8** opponent **9** adversary **10** antagonist, contestant, opposition

compile 4 edit **5** amass **6** gather, select **7** build up, collate, collect **8** assemble **9** construct **10** accumulate **11** anthologize

complacency 5 pride **7** conceit **8** smugness **10** narcissism

complacent 4 smug **6** serene **7** assured **9** conceited, confident **11** self-assured, unconcerned **13** self-confident, self-contented, self-possessed, self-satisfied

complain 3 nag **4** beef, carp, crab, fret, fuss, moan, wail **5** gripe, grump, whine **6** grouch, grouse, lament, repine, yammer **7** grizzle, grumble, protest **9** bellyache

complainer 4 crab **5** crank **6** griper, grouch **7** grouser **8** grumbler, sourpuss **10** malcontent **11** faultfinder

complaint 4 beef **5** gripe **6** grouse, lament, malady **7** ailment, disease, protest **8** disorder, sickness, syndrome **9** condition, criticism, grievance, infirmity, objection **10** affliction, allegation **12** protestation

complaisant 4 easy, mild **7** amiable, lenient **8** generous, obliging **9** agreeable, compliant, easygoing, indulgent **11** deferential, good-humored, good-natured **12** good-tempered **13** accommodating

complement 4 crew, rest **9** correlate, remainder **10** supplement **11** counterpart

complete 3 end **4** done, full, halt **5** close, ended, total, utter, whole **6** entire, finish, intact, wind up, wrap up **7** achieve, fulfill, perfect, perform, plenary **8** absolute, conclude, finalize, finished, integral, round out, thorough **9** concluded, out-and-out, terminate **10** accomplish, consummate, exhaustive, unabridged **11** categorical, unmitigated **13** thoroughgoing

completed 4 done, over **5** ended **7** through **8** done with, executed, finished **9** concluded, fulfilled **10** terminated **11** consummated **12** accomplished

completely 4 A to Z **5** fully **6** wholly **7** totally, utterly **8** entirely **9** inside out, up and down **10** thoroughly

completion 3 end **6** finish, windup, wrap-up **8** fruition **10** conclusion

complex 6 daedal, knotty, system, varied **7** chelate, gordian, network **8** abstruse, compound, involved, syndrome, tortuous **9** aggregate, Byzantine, composite, elaborate, intricate **10** convoluted **11** complicated **12** conglomerate, labyrinthine **13** heterogeneous, sophisticated

complexion 3 hue **4** cast, tint, tone **5** color, humor, tinge **6** aspect, makeup, nature, temper **8** tincture **9** character **10** appearance, coloration **11** disposition, temperament **12** pigmentation **13** individuality

compliance 7 consent **8** docility **9** agreement, deference, obedience **10** acceptance, conformity, submission **11** amenability, flexibility, resignation **12** acquiescence, tractability

complicate 5 mix up, ravel, snarl **6** jumble, muddle, tangle **7** confuse, involve **8** confound, disorder, entangle **9** aggravate, convolute **10** disarrange, exacerbate

complicated 6 daedal, knotty **7** complex, gordian, tangled **8** abstruse, involved, tortuous **9** Byzantine, elaborate, intricate, recondite **10** convoluted **12** labyrinthine **13** heterogeneous, sophisticated

complicity 8 abetment **9** collusion **10** connivance **11** involvement

compliment 4 hail, kudo, laud **5** extol, honor, kudos **6** praise, salute **7** acclaim, applaud, bouquet, commend, regards, tribute **8** accolade, encomium **9** laudation, recommend **11** recognition **12** appreciation, commendation, congratulate

complimentary 4 free **6** gratis **8** costless **9** favorable, laudatory **10** chargeless, gratuitous **12** appreciative

comply 4 obey **5** yield **6** accede, submit **7** conform **9** acquiesce

component 4 part **5** piece **6** factor **7** element, segment **10** ingredient **11** constituent

comport 4 bear, jibe **5** agree, carry, fit in, match, tally **6** accord, acquit, behave, demean, square **7** conduct **8** coincide, dovetail **9** harmonize **10** correspond

comportment 3 air **4** mien **7** address, bearing, conduct **8** attitude, behavior, carriage, demeanor, presence

compose 4 calm, cool, form, lull, make **5** forge, quiet, relax, still, write **6** becalm, create, devise, draw up, indite, invent, make up, settle, solace, soothe **7** collect, console, contain, control **8** comprise **9** construct, fabricate, formulate, originate **10** constitute *type:* **3** set

composed 4 calm, cool **5** staid **6** poised, sedate, serene **9** collected, unruffled **11** unflappable **13** imperturbable, self-possessed

composer 6 scorer **8** melodist **9** balladist, songsmith, tunesmith **10** songwriter *American:* **3** Kay (Hershy, Ulysses) **4** Ager (Milton), Bock (Jerry), Cage (John), Hill (Edward Burlingame), Ives (Charles), Kern (Jerome), King (Carole), Lane (Burton), Monk (Thelonious), Work (Henry Clay) **5** Adams (John), Arlen (Harold), Beach (Amy), Blake (Eubie), Bland (James A.), Bloch (Ernest), Cohan (George M.), Friml (Rudolf), Glass (Philip), Gould (Morton), Grofé (Ferde), Handy (W. C.), Loewe (Frederick), Mason (Daniel Gregory, Lowell), Moore (Douglas), Reich (Steve), Rorem (Ned), Sousa (John Philip), Still (William Grant), Styne (Jule), Zappa (Frank) **6** Barber (Samuel), Berlin (Irving), Carter (Elliott), Cowell (Henry), Emmett (Daniel), Foster (Stephen), Hanson (Howard), Harris (Roy), Herman (Jerry), Joplin (Scott), Kander (John), McHugh (Jimmy), McKuen (Rod), Menken (Alan), Morton ("Jelly Roll"), Oliver ("King"), Parker (Charlie "Bird," Horatio), Piston (Walter), Porter (Cole), Previn (André), Seeger (Pete), Taylor (Deems), Varèse (Edgard), Warren (Harry) **7** Babbitt (Milton), Brubeck (Dave), Copland (Aaron), Gilbert (Henry F.), Gilmore (Patrick), Goldman (Edwin Franko), Herbert (Victor), Loesser (Frank), Mancini (Henry), Menotti (Gian Carlo), Rodgers (Richard), Romberg (Sigmund), Schuman (William), Thomson (Virgil), Tiomkin (Dimitri), Willson (Meredith), Youmans (Vincent) **8** Anderson (Leroy), Billings (William), Burleigh (Henry Thacker), Damrosch (Leopold, Walter), Gershwin (George), Hamlisch (Marvin), Herrmann (Bernard), Korngold (Erich Wolfgang), Kreisler (Fritz), Marsalis (Wyn-

ton), Schifrin (Lalo), Schuller (Gunther), Sessions (Roger), Sondheim (Stephen), Williams (John) **9** Bacharach (Burt), Bernstein (Elmer, Leonard), Donaldson (Walter), Ellington (Duke), Hovhaness (Alan), MacDowell (Edward) **10** Blitzstein (Marc), Carmichael (Hoagy), Gottschalk (Louis Moreau) *Argentinian:* **9** Ginastera (Alberto) *Australian:* **8** Grainger (Percy) *Austrian:* **4** Berg (Alban), Wolf (Hugo) **5** Haydn (Franz Joseph) **6** Czerny (Karl), Mahler (Gustav), Mozart (Leopold, Wolfgang Amadeus), Straus (Oscar), Webern (Anton) **7** Strauss (Eduard, Johann, Josef) **8** Bruckner (Anton), Schubert (Franz) **10** Schoenberg (Arnold) *Belgian:* **5** Ysaÿe (Eugène) **6** Franck (César) *Brazilian:* **5** Jobim (Antonio Carlos) **10** Villa-Lobos (Heitor) *Czech:* **3** Suk (Josef) **5** Friml (Rudolf) **6** Dvořák (Antonín) **7** Janáček (Leoš), Martinu (Bohuslav), Smetana (Bedřich) *Danish:* **7** Nielsen (Carl) *Dutch:* **9** Sweelinck (Jan Pieterszoon) *English:* **4** Arne (Thomas Augustine), Byrd (William) **5** Elgar (Edward), Holst (Gustav) **6** Delius (Frederick), Morley (Thomas), Tallis (Thomas), Walton (William), Wesley (Charles, Samuel) **7** Britten (Benjamin), Dowland (John), Gibbons (Orlando), Purcell (Henry), Tippett (Michael), Weelkes (Thomas) **8** Sullivan (Arthur) **9** Dunstable (John) **11** Lloyd Webber (Andrew) *Finnish:* **8** Palmgren (Selim), Sibelius (Jean) *Flemish:* **5** Dufay (Guillaume), Lasso (Orlando di) **6** Lassus (Orlande de) **8** Willaert (Adriaan) *French:* **4** Indy (Vincent d'), Lalo (Edouard) **5** Auber (Esprit), Bizet (Georges), Dukas (Paul), Fauré (Gabriel), Ibert (Jacques), Jarre (Maurice), Lully (Jean-Baptiste), Ravel (Maurice), Satie (Erik), Widor (Charles-Marie) **6** Boulez (Pierre), Campra (André), Franck (César), Gounod (Charles), Rameau (Jean-Philippe), Thomas (Ambroise) **7** Berlioz (Hector), Debussy (Claude), Delibes (Léo), Machaut (Guillaume de), Milhaud (Darius), Poulenc (Francis) **8** Chabrier (Emmanuel), Couperin (François, Louis), Honegger (Arthur), Massenet (Jules), Messiaen (Olivier) **9** Meyerbeer (Giacomo), Offenbach (Jacques) **10** Saint-Saëns (Camille) *German:* **4** Bach (C. P. E., Johann Christian, Johann Sebastian, Wilhelm Friedemann), Orff (Carl) **5** Bruch (Max), Gluck (Christoph Willibald von), Reger (Max), Spohr (Louis, Ludwig), Weber (Carl Maria von), Weill (Kurt) **6** Brahms (Johannes), Handel (George Frideric), Schütz (Hein-

rich), Vogler (Abt), Wagner (Richard) **7**
Hassler (Hans Leo), Strauss (Richard) **8**
Korngold (Erich Wolfgang), Schumann
(Robert), Telemann (Georg Philipp) **9**
Beethoven (Ludwig van), Buxtehude
(Dietrich), Hindemith (Paul), Meyerbeer
(Giacomo), Pachelbel (Johann) **10** Praeto-
rius (Michael) **11** Humperdinck (Engel-
bert), Mendelssohn (Felix), Stockhausen
(Karlheinz) *Hungarian:* **5** Léhar (Franz),
Liszt (Franz) **6** Bartók (Béla), Kodály (Zol-
tán), Ligeti (György) **8** Dohnányi (Erno)
Italian: **4** Peri (Jacopo), Rota (Nino) **5** Be-
rio (Luciano), Boito (Arrigo), Verdi
(Giuseppe) **6** Busoni (Ferruccio) **7** Bellini
(Vincenzo), Caccini (Giulio), Corelli (Ar-
cangelo), Martini (Padre), Puccini (Gia-
como), Rossini (Gioacchino), Salieri
(Antonio), Tartini (Giuseppe), Vivaldi (An-
tonio) **8** Albinoni (Tomaso), Clementi
(Muzio), Gabrieli (Andrea, Giovanni),
Mascagni (Pietro), Paganini (Niccolò), Re-
spighi (Ottorino) **9** Cherubini (Luigi),
Donizetti (Gaetano), Pergolesi (Giovanni
Battista), Scarlatti (Alessandro, Domenico),
Tommasini (Vincenzo) **10** Boccherini (Lu-
igi), Monteverdi (Claudio), Palestrina (G. P.
da), Ponchielli (Amilcare), Zingarelli (Nic-
colò) **11** Frescobaldi (Girolamo), Leoncav-
allo (Ruggero) **12** Dallapiccola (Luigi)
Japanese: **4** Taki (Rentaro) **5** Satoh
(Somei) **6** Tomita (Isao) **7** Ifukube (Akira)
9 Katsuhisa (Hattori), Takemitsu (Toru)
Mexican: **6** Chávez (Carlos) *Norwegian:* **5**
Grieg (Edvard) *Polish:* **6** Chopin (Frédéric)
7 Gorecki (Henryk) **10** Paderewski (Ignacy
Jan), Penderecki (Krzysztof), Wieniawski
(Henryk) **11** Lutoslawski (Witold), Szy-
manowski (Karol) *Romanian:* **6** Enescu
(Gheorghe, George) **7** Xenakis (Iannis) *Rus-
sian:* **6** Glinka (Mikhail) **7** Borodin (Alek-
sandr) **8** Glazunov (Aleksandr), Scriabin
(Aleksandr) **9** Balakirev (Mily), Prokofiev
(Sergey), Schnittke (Alfred) **10** Kabalevsky
(Dmitri), Mussorgsky (Modest), Rubinstein
(Anton), Stravinsky (Igor), Tcherepnin
(Nikolay) **11** Tchaikovsky (Pyotr Ilich) **12**
Khachaturian (Aram), Rachmaninoff
(Sergey), Shostakovich (Dmitry) *Spanish:*
5 Falla (Manuel de) **7** Albéniz (Isaac), Rodrigo (Joaquin) **8** Granados (Enrique), Victoria (Tomas Luis de) *Swiss:* **5** Bloch
(Ernest) **6** Martin (Frank) **8** Honegger (Ar-
thur) (see also **songwriter**)
composite **3** mix **5** blend **6** fusion, hybrid **7**
amalgam, complex, mixture **8** compound **11**
combination **12** amalgamation

composition **4** opus **5** essay, paper, theme **6**
design, layout, makeup **7** article **9** formation **11** arrangement **12** architecture, constitution, construction *choral:* **4** mass **5** motet
7 cantata, passion **8** oratorio *for eight:* **5** octet *for five:* **7** quintet *for four:* **7** quartet *for
nine:* **5** nonet *for one:* **4** aria, solo *for
seven:* **6** septet *for six:* **6** sextet *for three:* **4**
trio *for two:* **3** duo **4** duet *instrumental:* **3**
jig **4** reel **5** étude, fugue, gigue, march,
rondo, suite **6** sonata **7** caprice, partita, prelude, scherzo **8** concerto, fantasia, overture,
rhapsody, saraband, sinfonia, symphony,
tone poem **9** allemande, capriccio, sarabande **10** intermezzo *vocal:* **4** aria, lied,
mass, song **5** carol, chant, motet, opera,
round **6** arioso, ballad, chanty **7** cantata,
chanson, chantey, chorale, lullaby, requiem
8 berceuse, madrigal, oratorio **9** plainsong,
spiritual **10** plainchant
compos mentis **4** sane **5** lucid, sound **6** normal
composure **4** calm **5** poise **7** balance, dignity
8 calmness, coolness, evenness, serenity,
sobriety **9** sangfroid **10** equanimity **11** equilibrium
compound **3** mix **4** join, link **5** admix, alloy,
blend, union, unite **6** expand, extend, fusion, make up, mingle **7** amalgam, augment, complex, compost, enlarge, magnify,
mixture **8** coalesce, comingle, heighten, increase, intermix, multiply **9** admixture, aggravate, associate, commingle, composite,
intensify, synthesis **10** commixture, exacerbate **11** intermingle **12** amalgamation
aroma: **5** neral **6** citral **7** menthol **8** vanillin
chemical: (see at **chemical**) *protein:* **7** peptone
comprehend **4** know **5** catch, grasp **6** absorb,
accept, embody, fathom, take in **7** cognize,
compass, contain, discern, embrace, include, involve, subsume **8** comprise, perceive **9** encompass **10** appreciate,
understand
comprehensible **8** knowable **9** graspable **10**
fathomable **12** intelligible
comprehension **3** ken **5** grasp **6** uptake **9**
awareness, knowledge **10** cognizance, conception, perception **11** discernment **12** apperception **13** understanding
comprehensive **4** full, wide **5** broad **6** global
7 general, overall **8** catholic, complete,
sweeping **9** all-around, extensive, inclusive,
universal **10** exhaustive **12** all-inclusive, encyclopedic
comprehensiveness **5** range, reach, scope **7**
breadth **8** entirety, fullness, totality **9** amplitude

compress 3 jam **4** cram, push **5** crush, press **6** reduce, shrink, squash, squish, shrink **7** bandage, compact, squeeze **8** condense, contract **11** concentrate

comprise 4 form **6** make up **7** compose, contain, embrace, include, subsume **10** comprehend, constitute

compromise 4 mean, pact, risk **6** settle **7** bargain, compact **8** contract, endanger, trade off **9** agreement, middle way **10** concession, golden mean, jeopardize, settlement **12** middle ground

compulsion 4 itch, need, urge **5** drive, force **6** duress **8** coercion **9** necessity **10** constraint

compulsive 6 driven **7** driving **9** besetting, obsessive **12** irresistible, overwhelming

compulsory 7 binding **8** coercive, enforced, required **9** mandatory, requisite **10** imperative, obligatory

compunction 4 pang **5** demur, qualm **6** regret, unease **7** remorse, scruple **8** distress **9** hesitancy, misgiving **10** conscience, hesitation

compunctious 5 sorry **8** contrite, penitent **9** regretful, repentant **10** apologetic, remorseful **11** penitential

computation 8 figuring **9** ciphering, reckoning **10** arithmetic, estimation **11** calculation

compute 5 tally, total **6** cipher, figure, reckon **8** estimate **9** calculate, determine

computer 6 abacus, laptop **7** desktop **9** mainframe **10** calculator *code:* **5** ASCII *component:* **3** CPU **4** chip **5** mouse, tower **7** monitor **8** keyboard **9** hard drive *early:* **5** Eniac **6** Univac *expert:* **4** geek **6** techie *graphics application:* **3** CGI, FMV *information:* **4** data *instruction:* **5** macro *inventor:* **7** Babbage (Charles) *key:* **3** Alt, Esc, Tab **4** Ctrl **5** Enter, Shift *language:* **3** Ada, APL, SQL **4** Java, Lisp, Perl **5** ALGOL, BASIC, COBOL **6** Pascal **7** FORTRAN see also *programming language type:* **6** analog **7** digital

computer-game genre 3 FPS, RPG, RTS **6** action, puzzle, racing, sports **8** fighting, platform **9** adventure **10** simulation

comrade 3 pal **4** ally, chum, mate **5** buddy, crony **6** cohort, comate, fellow **7** consort **8** sidekick, tovarich, tovarish **9** associate, colleague, companion

con 3 gyp, vet **4** anti, bilk, coax, dupe, fool, hoax, rook, scam **5** cheat, fraud, learn, study, trick **6** cajole, fleece, gammon, inmate, survey **7** against, blarney, canvass, chicane, convict, deceive, defraud, examine, inspect, swindle, wheedle **8** blandish,

flimflam, hoodwink, inveigle, jailbird, memorize, negative, opponent, persuade, prisoner, soft-soap **9** bamboozle, check over, sweet-talk **10** antithesis, manipulate, scrutinize **11** hornswoggle **12** tuberculosis

concatenate 4 join, link **5** unite **7** connect

concavity 3 dip, sag **4** bowl, dent, sink **5** basin **6** crater, hollow, trough **7** sinkage **8** sinkhole **10** depression

conceal 4 bury, hide, mask, veil **5** cache, cloak, cover, stash **6** screen **7** obscure, secrete **8** ensconce, enshroud, palliate **10** camouflage

concealed 3 hid **5** privy **6** buried, covert, hidden, secret **8** obscured, shrouded, ulterior **11** clandestine

concede 3 own **4** avow, fold **5** admit, allow, award, grant, yield **6** accept, accord **7** confess **9** surrender, vouchsafe **10** capitulate, relinquish **11** acknowledge

conceit 4 idea, whim **5** fancy, pride **6** egoism, megrim, notion, vagary, vanity **7** caprice, egotism, thought **8** crotchet, metaphor, self-love, smugness, snobbery **9** self-pride, vainglory **10** narcissism, self-esteem **11** complacence, complacency, self-opinion, swelled head

conceited 4 vain **6** snobby, snooty, uppish, uppity **7** pompous, stuck-up **8** immodest, puffed up, snobbish **12** narcissistic, vainglorious

conceitedness 6 vanity **8** self-love **9** vainglory **10** narcissism

conceivable 8 possible **9** plausible, thinkable **10** imaginable, supposable

conceive 4 form **5** beget, fancy, grasp, think **6** devise, expect, ideate, ponder **7** dream up, feature, imagine, realize, suppose, suspect, think up **8** envisage, envision **9** formulate, originate, speculate, visualize **10** excogitate, mastermind

concentrate 4 mass **5** focus **6** gather, shrink **7** collect, compact **8** assemble, compress, condense, contract, converge **10** accumulate **11** consolidate

concentrated 5 thick **6** intent, strong **7** focused, intense **8** vehement **9** intensive, undiluted, undivided **12** undistracted

concentration 5 field, major, study **9** attention **10** absorption **11** application

concept 4 idea **5** image **6** notion, theory **7** conceit, thought **10** impression, perception

conception 4 idea **5** birth, image, start **6** notion, origin, outset, theory **7** conceit, genesis, thought **9** beginning **10** impression, perception

conceptual 5 ideal **8** abstract, notional **9**

imaginary, visionary **10** ideational **11** theoretical **12** hypothetical, intellectual
concern 4 care, firm, heed **5** doubt, worry **6** affair, bear on, bother, engage, gadget, matter, occupy, outfit, regard, unease **7** anxiety, company, disturb, involve, perturb, trouble **8** business, deal with, disquiet, interest, mistrust **9** attention, curiosity, misgiving, suspicion **10** enterprise, skepticism, solicitude, uneasiness **11** carefulness, contrivance, uncertainty **12** apprehension **13** consciousness, consideration, establishment
concerned 7 anxious, worried **8** affected, involved **10** implicated, interested
concerning 4 as to, in re **5** about, anent, as for **7** apropos **9** as regards, regarding **10** relating to, relative to, respecting
concert 5 agree, union **6** accord, concur, settle, soiree **7** arrange, concord, harmony, recital **8** coincide, musicale **9** agreement, cooperate, harmonize, negotiate **11** performance
concerted 5 joint **6** mutual, united **7** unified **8** combined **11** coordinated **13** collaborative
concert hall 5 arena, odeum **7** theater, theatre **10** auditorium
concession 5 favor, grant **8** giveback **9** admission, allowance, privilege **10** compromise **12** acquiescence
conch 5 shell **7** mollusc, mollusk
concierge 6 porter, warden **7** doorman, janitor **9** custodian **10** doorkeeper
conciliate 4 calm, ease **6** disarm, pacify, soothe **7** appease, assuage, mollify, placate, sweeten, win over **9** reconcile **10** propitiate
concise 5 brief, pithy, short, terse **7** compact, laconic, summary **8** abridged, succinct **9** condensed **10** compressed, contracted **11** compendious **13** short and sweet
conclave 5 synod **6** caucus, powwow **7** meeting, session **8** assembly **9** gathering **10** conference, consistory, convention **11** convocation
conclude 3 end **4** halt, stop **5** close, infer, judge **6** decide, deduce, derive, effect, figure, finish, gather, reason, settle, wind up, wrap up **7** collect, resolve **8** complete **9** determine, terminate
concluding 4 last **5** final **6** latest, latter **7** closing **8** eventual, terminal, ultimate
conclusion 3 end **4** stop **5** cease, close **6** ending, epilog, finale, finish, period, result, windup **7** closing, closure, outcome, verdict **8** decision, epilogue, judgment, sequitur **9** cessation, deduction, inference, summation **10** completion, denouement, resolution, set-

tlement **11** culmination, termination **13** determination *musical:* **4** coda *poetic:* **5** envoi
conclusive 4 last **5** final **6** cogent **8** deciding, decisive, ultimate **9** clinching **10** compelling, convincing, definitive, undeniable **11** determinant, determinate, irrefutable **12** irrefragable, unanswerable **13** determinative
concoct 3 mix **4** brew, cook **5** frame, hatch **6** cook up, create, devise, invent **7** dream up **8** conceive, contrive **9** fabricate, formulate, originate
concoction 4 brew, plan **5** blend **7** mixture, project **8** compound, creation **9** invention **11** combination, contrivance, fabrication, preparation
concomitant 7 adjunct **8** adjuvant **9** accessory, ancillary, associate, attendant, attending, companion, satellite **10** coincident, collateral **12** accompanying **13** accompaniment, supplementary
concord 4 pact **5** amity, peace, unity **6** accord, comity, treaty, unison **7** concert, entente, harmony, rapport **8** goodwill **9** agreement **10** consonance
concordant 8 agreeing **9** congruous, consonant **10** compatible, consistent, harmonious **11** appropriate
concourse 5 foyer **6** throng **7** joining, meeting **8** junction **9** gathering **10** confluence, crossroads
concrete 5 solid **6** actual **8** specific, tangible **10** particular **11** substantial *component:* **4** sand **5** water **6** gravel
concubine 7 hetaera, hetaira **8** mistress **9** courtesan, odalisque
concupiscence 4 lust **5** ardor **6** desire **7** lechery, passion **9** prurience, pruriency **11** lustfulness **13** lickerishness
concupiscent 3 hot **7** aroused, goatish, lustful **8** prurient **9** lecherous, lickerish, salacious **10** lascivious, libidinous, lubricious, passionate
concur 4 jibe **5** agree, unite **6** accord, assent **7** approve, combine, concord, consent, go along **8** coincide **9** cooperate, harmonize
concurrent 6 coeval **8** parallel **10** coexistent, coexisting, convergent, synchronic **11** synchronous **12** contemporary, simultaneous
concurrently 6 at once **8** together **12** coincidently
concuss 3 jar **4** rock, stun **5** shake, shock **7** agitate
concussion 3 jar **4** bump, jolt **5** clout, crash, shock **6** impact **7** jarring, jolting, shaking **8** pounding **9** agitation, collision
condemn 3 rap **4** damn, doom **5** blame, decry, knock, seize **7** censure, convict, de-

plore **8** denounce, sentence **9** criticize, deprecate, proscribe, reprehend, reprobate **10** denunciate

condensation 3 dew **5** brief **6** digest, précis **7** epitome, outline, summary **8** abstract, synopsis **9** reduction **10** abridgment, conspectus **11** abridgement

condense 5 sum up **6** digest, reduce, shrink **7** abridge, compact, shorten **8** boil down, compress, contract **9** constrict, epitomize, summarize, synopsize **10** abbreviate **11** concentrate, consolidate, precipitate

condensed 7 concise, summary **10** boiled down **11** compendious

condenser 9 capacitor

condescend 5 deign, stoop **6** unbend

condescending 5 lofty **6** lordly, snobby, snooty, uppish, uppity **7** haughty, pompous **8** affected, arrogant, cavalier, snobbish, superior **10** disdainful **11** patronizing, pretentious **12** supercilious

condign 3 apt, due, fit **4** fair, just **5** right **6** proper **7** fitting, merited **8** deserved, rightful, suitable **9** equitable, justified **11** appropriate

condiment 5 curry, sauce, spice **6** catsup, relish, tamari **7** chutney, ketchup, mustard **8** dressing, soy sauce **9** seasoning **10** mayonnaise

____ **con Dios! 4** Vaya

condition 5 shape, state, terms **6** fettle, malady, status **7** ailment, disease, fitness, proviso **8** syndrome **9** complaint, essential, exception, necessity, provision, requisite, situation **10** limitation, sine qua non **11** requirement, reservation, stipulation **12** prerequisite **13** qualification

conditional 7 reliant **8** relative **9** dependent, provisory, qualified, tentative, uncertain **10** contingent, restricted **11** provisional

condolence 3 rue **4** pity, ruth **6** solace **7** comfort **8** sympathy **10** compassion **13** commiseration

condonable 7 tenable **9** excusable, tolerable **10** acceptable, defensible, pardonable **11** justifiable

condone 5 remit **6** excuse, pardon **7** forgive **8** overlook

conduce 4 lead, tend **7** redound **10** contribute

conducive 7 helpful, leading, tending **9** favorable **10** beneficial, salubrious **11** efficacious, serviceable, stimulating **12** advantageous, contributory, instrumental **13** accommodating

conduct 3 act, run **4** bear, head, lead, show **5** guide, pilot, steer, usher **6** attend, behave, charge, convey, demean, deport, direct, escort, handle, manage **7** arrange, bearing, comport, control, manners, operate, oversee **8** behavior, demeanor, handling, shepherd, transmit **9** accompany, oversight, supervise **10** administer, deportment, management **11** comportment, supervision

conductor 5 guide **6** escort, leader **7** maestro **8** motorman **10** bandleader *American:* **4** Shaw (Robert) **5** Stock (Frederick), Szell (George) **6** Levine (James), Maazel (Lorin), Previn (André), Reiner (Fritz), Thomas (Theodore, Michael Tilson), Walter (Bruno) **7** Fennell (Frederick), Fiedler (Arthur), Monteux (Pierre), Ormandy (Eugene), Schwarz (Gerard), Slatkin (Leonard) **8** Damrosch (Leopold, Walter), Williams (John) **9** Bernstein (Leonard), Leinsdorf (Erich), Rodzinski (Artur), Steinberg (William), Stokowski (Leopold) **11** Kostelanetz (André), Mitropoulos (Dimitri) *Argentinian:* **7** Kleiber (Carlos) **9** Barenboim (Daniel) *Australian:* **7** Bonynge (Richard) *Austrian:* **4** Böhm (Karl) **6** Mahler (Gustav) **7** Karajan (Herbert von) **11** Weingartner (Felix) *Belgian:* **5** Ysaÿe (Eugene) *Canadian:* **6** Dutoit (Charles) **9** MacMillan (Ernest) *Czech:* **7** Kubelik (Jan, Rafael) *Dutch:* **7** Haitink (Bernard) **10** Mengelberg (Willem) *English:* **4** Wood (Henry) **5** Boult (Adrian), Davis (Colin) **6** Rattle (Simon) **7** Beecham (Thomas), Leppard (Raymond), Malcolm (George), Pinnock (Trevor), Sargent (Malcolm) **8** Goossens (Eugene), Marriner (Neville) **9** Mackerras (Charles) **10** Barbirolli (John) *Finnish:* **7** Salonen (Esa-Pekka) *French:* **5** Munch (Charles) **6** Boulez (Pierre), Prêtre (Georges) **7** Monteux (Pierre) *German:* **4** Muck (Carl, Karl) **5** Masur (Kurt) **6** Jochum (Eugen) **7** Kleiber (Erich) **9** Klemperer (Otto), Scherchen (Hermann) **10** Sawallisch (Wolfgang) **11** Furtwängler (Wilhelm), Mendelssohn (Felix) *Greek:* **11** Mitropoulos (Dimitri) *Hungarian:* **5** Seidl (Anton), Solti (Georg), Szell (George) **6** Doráti (Antal), Reiner (Fritz) **7** Nikisch (Arthur), Ormandy (Eugene), Richter (Hans) *Indian:* **5** Mehta (Zubin) *Italian:* **4** Muti (Riccardo) **6** Abbado (Claudio) **7** Chailly (Riccardo), Giulini (Carlo Maria) **8** Cantelli (Guido), Sinopoli (Giuseppe) **9** Toscanini (Arturo) *Japanese:* **5** Ozawa (Seiji) *Polish:* **9** Rodzinski (Artur) *Russian:* **7** Gergiev (Valery) **10** Temirkanov (Yuri) **12** Koussevitzky (Serge) *Spanish:* **6** Iturbi (José) *Swiss:* **8** Ansermet (Ernest) *Venezuelan:* **7** Dudamel (Gustavo) *stick:* **5** baton

conduit 4 duct, main, pipe **5** canal **6** course **7** channel **8** aqueduct, penstock, pipeline **11** watercourse

coney 4 pika **5** hyrax, lapin **6** rabbit **10** butterfish

confab 4 chat, talk **6** confer, huddle, parley, powwow **7** consult **8** collogue, colloquy, dialogue **10** conference, discussion **12** conversation, deliberation

confabulate see **confab**

confabulation see **confab**

confection see **candy**

confederacy 5 cabal, union **6** league **7** compact **8** alliance **9** coalition, syndicate **10** conspiracy, federation

confederate 3 reb **4** ally **5** rebel, unite **6** fellow **7** abettor, partner **9** accessory, associate, colleague, Johnny Reb **10** accomplice **11** conspirator **12** collaborator **13** coconspirator *admiral:* **6** Semmes *capital:* **8** Richmond *color:* **4** gray *general:* **3** Lee (Robert E.) **4** Hill (Ambrose), Hood (John Bell) **5** Bragg (Braxton), Ewell (Richard Stoddart), Price (Sterling), Smith (Edmund Kirby) **6** Morgan (John Hunt), Stuart (J. E. B.) **7** Forrest (Nathan Bedford), Hampton (Wade), Jackson (Thomas Jonathan "Stonewall"), Pickett (George) **8** Johnston (Albert Sidney, Joseph Eggleston) **9** Pemberton (John Clifford) **10** Beauregard (Pierre G. T.), Longstreet (James) *president:* **5** Davis (Jefferson) *soldier:* **9** butternut *spy:* **4** Boyd (Belle) *vice-president:* **8** Stephens (Alexander)

confederation see **confederacy**

confer 4 give, meet, talk **5** allot, award, grant, speak **6** accord, advise, bestow, confab, donate, huddle, parley, powwow **7** consult, discuss, present **8** collogue, converse **10** deliberate **11** confabulate

conference 4 talk **5** forum, synod **6** caucus, league, parley, powwow **7** meeting, palaver, seminar **8** assembly, colloquy, congress **9** symposium **10** colloquium, discussion, round-robin, roundtable **11** association, convocation **12** consultation, deliberation **13** confabulation

confess 3 own **4** avow, sing **5** admit, allow, grant, let on, own up **6** reveal **7** concede, divulge, profess **8** disclose **9** come clean **11** acknowledge

confession 5 creed **6** avowal **7** peccavi **9** admission, statement **10** disclosure

confidant 8 familiar, intimate

confide 4 tell **5** trust **6** bestow, commit, reveal **7** commend, consign, entrust, whisper **8** hand over, relegate, turn over

confidence 5 faith, poise, stock, trust **6** aplomb, surety **8** credence, reliance, sureness **9** assurance, certainty, certitude **10** conviction, equanimity *game:* **4** scam **5** bunco, bunko, grift, sting **7** swindle **8** flimflam

confidence man 3 gyp **5** shark **7** diddler, grifter, scammer, sharper, sharpie **8** swindler **9** charlatan, defrauder, trickster **11** bunco artist

confident 4 bold, sure **5** brash, brave, cocky **6** secure **7** assured, certain **8** cocksure, fearless, intrepid, positive, sanguine, unafraid **9** dauntless, undaunted **10** courageous, undoubtful **11** self-assured, self-reliant **13** self-assertive, self-possessed

confidential 5 close, privy **6** hushed, inside, secret **7** private **8** familiar, hush-hush, intimate **9** auricular **10** classified

configuration 4 cast, form **5** shape **6** figure, layout, makeup **7** contour, gestalt, outline, pattern **9** structure **12** conformation

confine 3 box, mew, pen **4** cage, coop, crib, jail, term **5** bound, cramp, hem in, limit **6** immure, intern, lock up, shut in, shut up **7** delimit, enclose, impound, put away **8** encircle, imprison, localize, restrict **9** constrain **11** incarcerate **12** circumscribe

confinement 7 custody, lying-in **8** childbed **9** captivity, detention, restraint **10** constraint **12** accouchement, imprisonment **13** incarceration

confines 6 bounds, limits **7** borders, compass **8** boundary, environs, purlieus **9** precincts **10** boundaries

confirm 3 fix, set **5** check, prove, vouch **6** attest, ratify, uphold, verify **7** approve, bear out, certify, concede, endorse, justify, support **8** buttress, check out, validate **9** ascertain, reinforce **10** strengthen **11** corroborate **12** authenticate, substantiate

confirmation 5 proof **7** support, witness **8** approval, evidence **9** testimony **10** validation **11** attestation, endorsement, testimonial **12** ratification, verification **13** certification, corroboration

confirmed 3 set **5** fixed, sworn **6** proven **7** chronic, settled **8** deep-dyed, definite, habitual, hardened, ratified **10** accustomed, deep-rooted, deep-seated, entrenched, habituated, inveterate, persistent **13** bred-in-the-bone, dyed-in-the-wool

confiscate 4 grab, take **5** annex, seize, usurp **7** escheat, impound, preempt **8** arrogate **9** sequester **10** commandeer **11** appropriate, expropriate

confiture 3 jam **8** conserve, preserve **9** marmalade, preserves

conflagrant 5 afire, fiery **6** ablaze, aflame, alight **7** blazing, burning, flaming

conflagration 3 war **4** fire **5** blaze **7** inferno **8** conflict **9** holocaust

conflate 3 mix **4** fuse, join, meld, weld **5** blend, merge, mix up **6** mingle, muddle **7** combine, confuse, mistake **8** coalesce, confound **9** commingle

conflict 3 row, war **4** bout, duel, rift, vary **5** brawl, clash, fight, melee, set-to **6** battle, combat, differ, fracas, strife **7** contend, contest, discord, dispute, rivalry, warfare **8** argument, disagree, mismatch, struggle, tug-of-war, variance **9** encounter, rencontre **10** contention, engagement **11** competition

conflicting 6 at odds **7** opposed, warring **8** clashing, contrary, opposing **9** dissonant **10** contending, discordant, discrepant **11** incongruent, incongruous, inconsonant **12** antagonistic, antipathetic, incompatible, inconsistent, inharmonious **13** contradictory

confluence 6 merger **7** joining, meeting, merging **8** junction **9** concourse, gathering **11** convergence

conform 3 fit **4** jibe, obey, suit **5** adapt, agree, fit in, match, yield **6** accord, adjust, attune, comply, follow, square, submit, tailor **8** dovetail **9** acquiesce, harmonize, reconcile **10** coordinate, correspond, proportion **11** accommodate

conformable 6 fitted, suited **7** adapted, matched **8** amenable, obedient, suitable **9** agreeable, compliant, congenial, consonant **10** submissive

conformation 4 cast, form **5** shape **6** figure **7** anatomy **9** structure **10** adaptation **11** arrangement **13** configuration

conforming 3 apt **6** decent, proper, seemly **7** correct, uniform **8** becoming, decorous, suitable **9** befitting, civilized **10** compatible, consistent **11** comme il faut

conformity 6 accord **7** decorum, harmony **9** agreement, coherence, congruity, obedience, orthodoxy **10** accordance, allegiance, compliance, consonance, observance, submission **11** consistency **12** acquiescence

confound 4 damn, faze **5** befog, mix up, stump **6** baffle, puzzle, rattle, refute **7** confuse, mistake, mystify, nonplus, perplex, stupefy **8** befuddle, bewilder, disprove **9** discomfit, dumbfound, embarrass, frustrate **10** controvert, disconcert **11** misidentify

confounded 5 utter **6** blamed, cursed, cussed, damned **7** blasted, blessed, doggone, shocked **8** absolute, accursed, dismayed, infernal, outright **9** consarned, dad-blamed, execrable, out-and-out **11** dumbfounded,

overwhelmed, unmitigated **13** thunderstruck

confrere see **colleague**

confront 4 defy, face, meet **5** beard, brave, cross **6** accost, breast, oppose, take on **9** challenge, encounter

confuse 3 fog **4** blur, daze, faze **5** abash, addle, befog, cloud, dizzy, mix up, muddy, stump, upset **6** baffle, ball up, bemuse, flurry, foul up, fuddle, garble, jumble, mess up, muddle, puzzle, rattle **7** agitate, becloud, derange, disrupt, distort, flummox, fluster, mislead, mistake, mystify, nonplus, perplex, perturb, snarl up **8** bedazzle, befuddle, bewilder, confound, disorder, disquiet, distract, throw off, unsettle **9** discomfit, disorient, embarrass **10** complicate, disarrange, discompose, disconcert **11** disorganize, misidentify **12** misrepresent

confused 4 lost **5** dazed, messy, muddy, muzzy, vague **6** addled **7** at a loss, chaotic, mixed up, muddled, puzzled **9** flustered, perplexed, unsettled **10** bewildered, nonplussed, topsy-turvy **11** disoriented **12** disconcerted

confusion 3 ado, din **4** flap, mess, stew **5** babel, chaos, havoc, mix-up, snafu, snarl **6** bedlam, dither, foul-up, hubbub, huddle, jumble, lather, muddle, tumult, unease **7** anarchy, clutter, turmoil **8** disarray, disorder, shambles **9** abashment, agitation, commotion, imbroglio **10** hullabaloo, perplexity, puzzlement, turbulence, uneasiness **11** derangement, disturbance, pandemonium **12** bewilderment **13** embarrassment

confute 4 deny **5** evert, rebut **6** defeat, negate **8** confound, disprove, puncture **10** controvert, disconfirm

congé 3 bow **5** adieu **6** good-by **7** good-bye, molding, parting, sendoff **8** farewell **9** dismissal **11** leave-taking

congeal 3 dry, gel, set **4** clot, jell **5** jelly **6** curdle, harden **7** stiffen, thicken **8** solidify **9** coagulate **10** gelatinize

congener 6 agnate **7** cognate, sibling **8** relation, relative

congenial 4 nice **6** social **7** affable, amiable, cordial, kindred, welcome **8** amicable, friendly, gracious, pleasant, pleasing, sociable, suitable **9** agreeable, congruous, consonant, favorable **10** compatible, consistent, gratifying, harmonious **11** cooperative, pleasurable, sympathetic **13** companionable

congenital 6 inborn, inbred, innate, native **7** natural **8** inherent **9** essential, ingrained, intrinsic **10** deep-seated, indigenous, indwelling

conger 3 eel

congeries 5 group 7 company 8 assembly 9 gathering 10 assemblage, collection 11 aggregation 12 congregation

congest 3 jam 4 clog, fill, plug, stop 5 block, choke, close, crowd 6 plug up 7 occlude 8 obstruct

conglobate 4 ball 6 sphere 8 ensphere 9 spherical

conglomerate 4 mass, pool 5 chain, group, mixed, trust 6 cartel, motley 7 chaebol, combine 8 keiretsu, zaibatsu 9 aggregate, syndicate 11 aggregation 12 multifarious 13 heterogeneous

conglomeration 5 hoard, trove 8 mishmash 9 aggregate 10 collection, cumulation, hodgepodge, miscellany 11 agglomerate, aggregation 12 accumulation

Congo, Democratic Republic of the *capital:* 8 Kinshasa *city:* 7 Kolwezi 9 Kisangani, Mbuji-Mayi 10 Lubumbashi *explorer:* 7 Stanley (Henry Morton) *former name:* 5 Zaire 12 Belgian Congo *lake:* 4 Kivu 5 Mweru 6 Albert, Edward 10 Tanganyika *language:* 6 French 7 English *monetary unit:* 5 franc *neighbor:* 5 Sudan 6 Angola, Rwanda, Uganda, Zambia 7 Burundi 8 Tanzania *river:* 4 Uele

Congo, Republic of *capital:* 11 Brazzaville *city:* 11 Pointe-Noire *former name:* 11 Middle Congo *language:* 6 French *monetary unit:* 5 franc *neighbor:* 5 Gabon 6 Angola 7 Cabinda 8 Cameroon

congratulate 4 laud 6 salute 10 compliment, felicitate

congregate 4 meet 5 swarm 6 gather, muster 7 collect, convene 8 assemble, converge 9 forgather 10 foregather, rendezvous

congregation 4 mass 5 crowd, flock, group 7 meeting 8 assembly, audience 9 gathering 10 assemblage, collection 11 churchgoers 12 parishioners

congress 4 diet 5 synod 6 league 7 meeting, society 8 assembly, conclave 10 convention, parliament 11 association, Capitol Hill, legislature

congressman 5 solon 7 senator 8 delegate, lawmaker 10 legislator

congruity 9 agreement, coherence 10 conformity 11 consistency

congruous 3 apt, fit 7 fitting 9 agreeable, befitting, congenial, consonant 10 compatible, concordant, consistent, harmonious 11 appropriate, sympathetic

conifer 3 fir, yew 4 pine 5 cedar, larch 6 spruce 7 cypress, hemlock, juniper 8 softwood 9 evergreen 10 arborvitae

conjectural 7 reputed 8 putative, supposed 11 speculative, theoretical 12 hypothetical, supposititious 13 suppositional

conjecture 5 guess, infer 6 assume, theory 7 presume, suppose, surmise, suspect 8 theorize 9 inference, speculate 11 hypothesize, proposition, speculation, supposition

conjoin 3 wed 4 band, link, yoke 5 unite 6 couple 7 combine, connect 8 federate 9 affiliate, associate, cooperate 11 consolidate

conjoint 6 common, mutual, public, shared, united 7 unified 8 combined, communal 9 concerted 10 collective 11 coefficient, cooperative, intermutual

conjointly 8 mutually, together

conjugal 6 wedded 7 marital, married, nuptial, spousal 8 hymeneal 9 connubial 11 matrimonial

conjugality 7 wedlock 8 marriage 9 matrimony

conjugate 4 fuse, join, link, pair, yoke 5 yoked 6 couple, joined, linked 7 bracket, combine, conjoin, connect, coupled 9 associate, connected

conjunct 5 joint 6 common, joined, mutual, shared, united

conjunction 2 as, if, or, so 3 and, but, for, nor, yet 4 lest, once, than, then, when 5 after, since, union, until, where, which, while 6 before, either, though, unless 7 because, however, neither, whereas, whether 8 alliance, although, moreover, whenever 9 therefore 10 connection 11 affiliation, association, combination, concurrence

conjuration 4 oath 5 charm, spell, trick 7 sorcery 10 adjuration, hocus-pocus, invocation 11 abracadabra, incantation

conjure 3 beg 4 urge 6 appeal, invoke, summon 7 beseech, entreat, imagine, implore 8 contrive 9 importune 10 supplicate

conjurer 4 mage, seer 5 magus 6 Magian, wizard 7 warlock 8 magician, sorcerer 9 enchanter, trickster 11 illusionist, necromancer

conjuring 5 magic 7 sorcery 8 wizardry 10 hocus-pocus, necromancy 11 abracadabra, legerdemain, thaumaturgy

conk 3 die, hit, rap 4 belt, swat 5 croak, faint, knock, thump, whack 8 knock out

con man see **confidence man**

connate 4 akin 6 allied, inborn, native 7 kindred, related 8 inherent 9 congenial, elemental, essential, ingrained, inherited, intrinsic 10 affiliated, congenital, indigenous, indwelling 11 consanguine

connect 3 tie, wed 4 ally, bind, join, link, yoke 5 marry, unite 6 attach, bridge, cou-

ple, fasten, relate **7** combine, conjoin **8**
transfer **9** affiliate, associate, interlock
Connecticut *capital:* **8** Hartford *city:* **4** Avon
6 Darien **8** New Haven, Stamford **9** Greenwich, New London, Waterbury **10** Bridge-
port *college, university:* **4** Yale **7** Trinity **8**
Wesleyan **9** Fairfield **10** Quinnipiac *nickname:* **6** Nutmeg (State) **12** Constitution
(State) *river:* **6** Thames **10** Housatonic **11**
Connecticut *state bird:* **5** robin (American)
state flower: **14** mountain laurel *state tree:*
8 white oak
connection 3 tie **4** bond, link **5** joint, nexus,
tie-in, union **6** hookup, splice **7** joining,
kinship, network **8** affinity, alliance, coupling, junction, juncture **9** coherence, communion, fastening **10** attachment,
catenation, continuity **11** affiliation, association, combination, conjunction, partnership **12** relationship
connective 2 or **3** and, nor, not **4** then **6** either **7** neither **8** syndetic **11** conjunction,
conjunctive
conniption 3 fit **4** bout, snit **5** furor, spasm,
spate, spell, throe **6** attack, frenzy **7** seizure,
tantrum **8** outburst, paroxysm **10** convulsion
connivance 8 intrigue **9** collusion **10** complicity, conspiracy
connive 4 plot, wink **5** blink **6** devise,
scheme, wink at **7** blink at, collude **8** conspire, contrive, intrigue **9** machinate
connoisseur 4 buff **6** expert **7** epicure, gourmet **8** aesthete, gourmand, highbrow **9** authority, bon vivant **10** dilettante,
gastronome **11** cognoscente
connotation 4 hint **7** meaning **8** overtone **9**
undertone **10** intimation, suggestion **11** association, implication **13** signification
connote 4 hint, mean **5** imply, spell **6** hint at,
intend **7** betoken, express, signify, suggest
8 indicate, intimate **9** insinuate
connubial 6 wedded **7** marital, married, nuptial, spousal **8** conjugal, hymeneal **11** matrimonial
connubiality 7 wedlock **8** marriage **9** matrimony **11** conjugality
conquer 4 beat, best, lick, tame, whip **5** crush
6 defeat, master, subdue **8** overcome, surmount, vanquish **9** checkmate, overpower,
overthrow, overwhelm, subjugate
conquest 3 win **4** rout **7** triumph, victory **9**
overthrow, seduction **11** subjugation
Conrad, Joseph *character:* **3** Jim **4** Axel,
Lena **5** Flora, Kurtz **6** Marlow, Verloc **7** Almayer **8** MacWhirr, Nostromo *work:* **5**
Youth **6** Chance **7** Lord Jim, Typhoon, Vic-

tory **8** Nostromo **11** Secret Agent (The) **13**
Almayer's Folly **15** Heart of Darkness
Conroy *novel* **10** Beach Music **11** Water Is
Wide (The) **12** Great Santini (The) **13**
Prince of Tides (The) **17** Lords of Discipline (The)
consanguineous 4 akin **6** agnate **7** cognate,
connate, kindred, related
conscience 5 demur, honor, qualm **6** ethics,
virtue **7** decency, remorse, scruple **8** morality, scruples, superego **9** integrity **10** contrition **11** compunction
conscienceless 6 amoral **7** immoral **9** unethical **12** unprincipled, unscrupulous
conscientious 4 fair, just, true **5** exact **6** honest **7** careful, dutiful, upright **8** diligent,
reliable, studious **9** honorable **10** high-
minded, meticulous, principled, scrupulous
11 hard-working, painstaking, punctilious
conscious 5 alive, awake, aware **7** knowing,
mindful, witting **8** sensible, sentient **9** attentive, cognizant **10** deliberate, perceptive
consciousness 4 heed, mind **6** regard **7** concern **9** alertness, awareness, knowledge **10**
cognizance, perception **11** realization, recognition
conscribe 5 draft, limit **6** call up, enlist, enroll, muster **7** recruit
conscript 5 draft, elect **6** called, choose, chosen, enlist, enroll, induct, select **7** drafted,
dragoon, impress, recruit, soldier **8** selected
consecrate 5 bless **6** anoint, devote, hallow,
ordain, pledge **8** dedicate, sanctify
consecrated 4 holy **6** sacred **7** blessed **8** hallowed **10** sanctified *oil:* **6** chrism
consecution see sequence
consecutive 4 next **5** later **6** serial **7** ensuing,
ordered, sequent **9** following, succedent **10**
sequential, subsequent, succeeding, successive **11** progressive **12** successional
consent 3 yes **4** okay **5** agree, allow, leave,
yield **6** accede, accord, assent, comply, concur, permit **7** approve, go-ahead **8** approval,
sanction **9** acquiesce, agreement, allowance, subscribe **10** compliance, permission
12 acquiescence **13** authorization, understanding
consequence 4 fame, note, rank **5** issue,
state **6** cachet, effect, import, moment, renown, repute, result, sequel, status, upshot,
weight **7** account, conceit, fallout, outcome,
stature **8** eminence, position, prestige, reaction **9** aftermath, magnitude **10** importance,
reputation **11** aftereffect, weightiness **12** repercussion, significance
consequent 5 later, sound **7** ensuing, logical
8 rational **9** deduction, following, resulting

consequential 3 big 5 major 7 serious, weighty 8 egoistic, indirect, material 9 conceited, egotistic, important, momentous 10 collateral, incidental, meaningful, subsidiary 11 significant, substantial 12 considerable 13 self-important

consequently 4 ergo, thus 5 hence 9 as a result, therefore, thereupon 10 inevitably 11 accordingly

conservation 4 care 7 control 9 attention, husbandry 10 management, protection 11 safekeeping 12 guardianship, preservation

conservative 4 tory 6 proper 7 diehard, old-line 8 cautious, discreet, old-guard, orthodox, rightist, standpat 9 right-wing, temperate 10 restrained 11 circumspect, reactionary, right-winger, standpatter, traditional

conservatory 6 school 7 academy, nursery 8 hothouse 10 greenhouse 11 music school

conserve 3 can, jam 4 keep, save 5 hoard, lay up, put up, skimp, store 6 keep up 7 husband, protect, support, sustain 8 maintain, set aside, withhold 9 confiture, economize, safeguard, sweetmeat

consider 3 see 4 deem, feel, mind, muse, note, rate, view 5 fancy, judge, sense, study, think, weigh 6 credit, look at, notice, ponder, reason, reckon, regard 7 account, believe, examine, imagine, inspect, reflect, respect, suppose 8 appraise, cogitate, conclude, envisage, meditate, mull over, ruminate 9 speculate, think over 10 deliberate, excogitate, scrutinize, think about 11 contemplate

considerable 3 big 5 ample, hefty, large, major 7 notable, sizable, weighty 8 material, sensible, sizeable 9 extensive, important, momentous, plentiful 10 large-scale, meaningful 11 respectable, significant, substantial 13 consequential

considerably 3 far 4 well 5 quite 6 rather 7 notably 8 somewhat 10 noticeably 11 appreciably 13 significantly, substantially

considerate 4 kind 6 kindly, polite, tender 7 amiable, careful, patient, tactful 8 discreet, generous, obliging 9 attentive 10 chivalrous, forbearing, solicitous, thoughtful 11 circumspect, complaisant, sympathetic, warmhearted 13 compassionate

consideration 3 fee 4 heed, tact 5 cause, favor, issue, study 6 esteem, factor, motive, reason, regard 7 account, concern, payment, respect, thought 8 kindness 9 attention, awareness 10 admiration, cogitation, discussion, reflection, solicitude 11 application, forbearance, mindfulness 12 deliberation

considered 7 advised, studied, weighed 8 studious 10 deliberate, thought-out 11 intentional 12 aforethought, premeditated

consign 4 give, send, ship 5 agree, allot, award, remit, yield 6 commit, convey, devote, submit 7 address, commend, confide, deliver, entrust, forward 8 dispatch, hand over, relegate, transmit, turn over 9 surrender

consist 3 lie 4 rest 5 abide, agree, dwell, exist, fit in 6 accord, inhere, reside 7 comport, conform, consort, subsist 8 dovetail 10 correspond

consistency 7 aptness, concord, density, fitness, harmony, texture 8 evenness, firmness, likeness 9 agreement, coherence, congruity, thickness, viscosity 10 conformity, consonance, similarity 11 suitability

consistent 4 even, true 6 steady 7 regular, uniform 8 constant 9 accordant, agreeable, congenial, congruous, consonant, unfailing, unvarying 10 compatible, conforming, dependable, invariable, unchanging 11 homogeneous, sympathetic, undeviating

consistently 8 wontedly 9 regularly, routinely 10 habitually, invariably 11 customarily

console 4 calm, case 5 cheer 6 buck up, solace 7 cabinet, comfort, hearten 9 sideboard

consolidate 3 mix, set 4 fuse, join, meld, pool 5 blend, merge, unify, unite 6 firm up, secure 7 compact, fortify 8 compress, condense, federate, solidify 9 integrate 10 amalgamate, strengthen 11 concentrate

consolidation 5 union 6 merger 7 melding, merging 9 coalition 11 combination, integration, unification 12 amalgamation

consonance 6 accord 7 concord, harmony 9 agreement, congruity, resonance 10 congruence

consonant 4 akin, like 6 agnate 7 musical, similar 8 blending, harmonic, resonant 9 congruous 10 compatible, harmonious 11 conformable 13 corresponding *kind:* 4 stop, surd 5 nasal, velar 6 atonic, voiced 7 lateral, palatal, spirant 8 alveolar, bilabial, unvoiced 9 fricative, voiceless

consort 3 set 4 mate, wife 5 agree, group, tally, unite 6 accord, attend, fellow, spouse, square, troupe 7 company, comport, conform, husband, partner 8 assembly, chaperon, dovetail 9 accompany, associate, companion, harmonize 10 correspond

consortium 4 bloc, club, ring 5 guild, trust, union 6 cartel, league 7 combine, society 8 alliance, congress 9 coalition, syndicate 10 federation 11 association 12 conglomerate

conspectus 5 brief 6 digest, précis, sketch,

survey 7 epitome, outline, summary 8 abstract, overview, synopsis 9 reduction 10 abridgment 11 abridgement 12 condensation

conspicuous 5 clear, overt, showy 6 marked, patent, signal 7 blatant, evident, glaring, notable, obvious, pointed, salient 8 apparent, distinct, flagrant, manifest, striking 9 arresting, egregious, notorious, obtrusive, prominent 10 celebrated, noticeable, pronounced, remarkable 11 eye-catching, illustrious, outstanding 12 ostentatious

conspiracy 4 plan, plot 5 cabal 6 scheme 8 intrigue 11 machination

conspirator 7 abettor, plotter, schemer 9 accessory, intriguer 10 accomplice 11 confederate

conspire 4 plot 5 cabal 6 scheme 7 collude, connive 8 intrigue 9 machinate

constable 6 deputy, lawman, warden 7 marshal, sheriff

constancy 5 faith 6 fealty 7 loyalty, resolve 8 adhesion, devotion, fidelity, firmness 9 adherence, diligence, endurance, fortitude 10 allegiance, attachment, dedication, resolution, steadiness 11 staunchness 12 faithfulness, perseverance 13 dependability, steadfastness

constant 4 even, fast, firm, true 5 fixed, loyal 6 dogged, stable, steady, trusty 7 abiding, chronic, endless, equable, lasting, nonstop, staunch, uniform 8 enduring, faithful, habitual, resolute, unending 9 ceaseless, confirmed, continual, immovable, immutable, incessant, obstinate, perpetual, steadfast, sustained, unceasing, unfailing, unmovable, unvarying 10 changeless, consistent, continuous, dependable, inflexible, invariable, inveterate, persistent, persisting, unchanging, unwavering 11 everlasting, inalterable, unalterable, unrelenting, unremitting 12 interminable, unchangeable

Constantine *birthplace:* 4 Nish *mother:* 6 Helena *son:* 7 Crispus *victim:* 6 Fausta 7 Crispus *wife:* 6 Fausta

constantly 4 ever 5 often 6 always 7 forever 9 eternally 10 frequently, invariably, repeatedly 11 incessantly, perpetually 12 continuously

constellation 5 group 7 pattern 10 assemblage, collection 11 arrangement *Altar:* 3 Ara *Archer:* 11 Sagittarius *Arrow:* 7 Sagitta *Balance:* 5 Libra *Bear, Great:* 9 Ursa Major *Bear, Little:* 9 Ursa Minor *Big Dipper:* 9 Ursa Major *Bird of Paradise:* 4 Apus *Bull:* 6 Taurus *Centaur:* 9 Centaurus *Chained Lady:* 9 Andromeda *Chameleon:* 10

Chamaeleon *Champion:* 7 Perseus *Charioteer:* 6 Auriga *Clock:* 10 Horologium *Colt:* 8 Equuleus *Crab:* 6 Cancer *Crane:* 4 Grus *Cross:* 4 Crux *Crow:* 6 Corvus *Crown:* 6 Corona *Cup:* 6 Crater *Dolphin:* 9 Delphinus *Dove:* 7 Columba *Dragon:* 5 Draco *Eagle:* 6 Aquila *Fishes:* 6 Pisces *Fly:* 5 Musca *Flying Fish:* 6 Volans *Furnace:* 6 Fornax *Graving Tool:* 6 Caelum *Great Bear:* 9 Ursa Major *Greater Dog:* 10 Canis Major *Hare:* 5 Lepus *Herdsman:* 6 Boötes *Horned Goat:* 11 Capricornus *Hunter:* 5 Orion *Indian:* 5 Indus *Keel:* 6 Carina *Lady in the Chair:* 10 Cassiopeia *Larger Bear:* 9 Ursa Major *Larger Dog:* 10 Canis Major *Lesser Dog:* 10 Canis Minor *Lion:* 3 Leo *Little Bear:* 9 Ursa Minor *Little Dipper:* 9 Ursa Minor *Little Fox:* 9 Vulpecula *Lizard:* 7 Lacerta *Lyre:* 4 Lyra *Mariner's Compass:* 5 Pyxis *Monarch:* 7 Cepheus *Net:* 9 Reticulum *Painter's Easel:* 6 Pictor *Pair of Compasses:* 8 Circinus *Peacock:* 4 Pavo *Pump:* 6 Antlia *Ram:* 5 Aries *Rescuer:* 7 Perseus *River Po:* 8 Eridanus *Sails:* 4 Vela *Scorpion:* 8 Scorpius *Serpent:* 7 Serpens *Serpent Holder:* 9 Ophiuchus *Sextant:* 7 Sextans *Shield:* 6 Scutum *Smaller Bear:* 9 Ursa Minor *Square:* 5 Norma *Stern:* 6 Puppis *Swan:* 6 Cygnus *Table:* 5 Mensa *Toucan:* 6 Tucana *Triangle:* 10 Triangulum *Twins:* 6 Gemini *Unicorn:* 9 Monoceros *Virgin:* 5 Virgo *Water Carrier:* 8 Aquarius *Water Monster:* 5 Hydra *Water Snake:* 6 Hydrus *Whale:* 5 Cetus *Winged Horse:* 7 Pegasus *Wolf:* 5 Lupus

consternate 5 alarm, daunt, shake, shock 6 appall, dismay 7 horrify, unnerve 8 distress

consternation 4 fear 5 alarm, dread, panic, shock 6 dismay, fright, horror, terror 11 trepidation 12 bewilderment

constituent 4 part 5 piece, voter 6 factor, member 7 element, portion 8 division, fraction 9 component, elemental, principal 10 ingredient

constitute 4 form, make 5 enact, found, set up, start 6 create, embody, make up 7 appoint, compose 8 complete, comprise, organize 9 establish, institute, represent

constitution 3 law 4 code 5 build, canon 6 design, makeup, nature 7 charter 8 physique 9 formation, structure 11 composition 12 architecture, construction

constitutional 4 walk 6 inborn, inbred, innate, lawful 7 built-in, organic 8 inherent 9 essential, ingrained, intrinsic 10 congenital, deep-seated

Constitution State 11 Connecticut

Constitution, U.S.S. 12 Old Ironsides

constitutive 5 vital 8 cardinal 9 essential 11 fundamental 12 constructive

constrain 3 bar 4 curb, deny, jail 5 chain, check, crush, force, impel, limit, press 6 bridle, coerce, compel, enjoin, oblige, secure, squash, squish 7 confine, deprive, inhibit, refrain, squeeze 8 compress, hold back, hold down, imprison, restrain, restrict 11 incarcerate

constraint 4 bond 5 check, force 6 duress 8 coercion, pressure 9 captivity, detention, restraint 10 compulsion, diffidence, inhibition, limitation, repression 11 confinement, restriction, suppression 13 embarrassment

constrict 4 curb 5 cramp, limit, pinch, strap 6 hamper, narrow, shrink 7 confine, inhibit, squeeze, tighten 8 compress, condense, contract, restrain, strangle, stultify 9 constrain 12 circumscribe

constrictor 3 boa 5 snake 6 muscle 8 anaconda 9 sphincter, strangler

construct 4 form, make 5 build, erect, forge, frame, put up, raise, set up, shape 6 create, devise 7 build up, compile, fashion, produce 8 assemble, engineer 9 establish, fabricate 11 manufacture, put together

construction 6 design, makeup 7 edifice, shaping 8 assembly, building 9 formation 10 fashioning 11 arrangement, engineering, fabrication, manufacture 12 architecture, constitution

constructive 6 useful 7 helpful, implied, virtual 8 implicit, positive, valuable 9 practical 10 beneficial

construe 5 educe, gloss, parse 6 induct 7 analyze, explain, expound 9 explicate, interpret 10 paraphrase, understand

consuetude 5 habit, usage 6 custom, manner 8 practice 10 convention

consult 3 ask 6 advise, confer, huddle, parley 7 examine, refer to 8 collogue, consider 11 confabulate

consume 3 eat, use 4 down, gulp, ruin 5 drain, drink, eat up, gorge, spend, use up, waste 6 absorb, devour, expend, finish, ingest, obsess, take up 7 deplete, destroy, engross, exhaust, put away, put down, swallow 8 squander 9 dissipate, finish off, polish off 10 annihilate, extinguish, monopolize, run through

consumer 4 user 5 buyer 6 client 7 shopper, end user 8 customer 9 purchaser

consumer advocate 5 Nader (Ralph)

consuming 6 ardent 7 fervent, intense 8 gripping, riveting 9 absorbing 10 engrossing 11 enthralling 12 monopolizing

consummate 3 end 4 ripe 5 close, crown,

ideal, utter 6 finish, superb, wind up, wrap up 7 achieve, perfect, supreme 8 absolute, complete, conclude, finished, flawless, peerless, ultimate 9 faultless, matchless, perfected, virtuosic 10 accomplish, impeccable, inimitable 11 superlative 12 accomplished 13 thoroughgoing

consumption 2 TB 3 use 5 decay, waste 6 intake 7 wasting 8 phthisis 9 depletion, ingestion 10 absorption 11 dissipation 12 tuberculosis

contact 4 meet 5 reach, touch 8 tangency, touching 9 closeness, communion, proximity 10 connection, contiguity 11 association, contingence 13 communication

contagion 3 pox 4 bane, meme 5 taint, venom, virus 6 miasma, plague, poison 7 disease, scourge 8 epidemic 9 infection, pollution 10 corruption, pestilence 13 contamination

contagious 6 catchy 8 catching, epidemic 9 spreading 10 infectious 12 communicable, pestilential 13 transmissible, transmittable

contain 4 hold, keep 5 check, house 6 embody, take in 7 collect, control, embrace, enclose, include, receive, repress, subsume 8 comprise, restrain 9 encompass 10 comprehend 11 accommodate

container 3 bag, bin, box, can, cup, jar, keg, mug, pod, pot, tin, tub, urn, vat 4 cage, case, cask, drum, etui, ewer, pail, sack, silo, tank, vase, vial, well 5 chest, crate, cruet, flask, glass, gourd, phial, pouch 6 basket, bottle, carafe, carton, casket, coffin, cooler, goblet, hamper, hatbox, holder, inkpot, shaker 7 bandbox, capsule, chalice, inkwell, package, pitcher, thermos 8 canister, catchall, decanter, envelope, hogshead, jerrican, puncheon 10 receptacle *liturgical:* 3 pyx 7 chalice 8 ciborium

contaminate 4 foul, soil 5 dirty, spoil, stain, sully, taint 6 befoul, debase, defile, infect, injure, poison 7 corrupt, deprave, pervert, pollute, profane, tarnish, vitiate 9 desecrate 10 adulterate

conte 4 tale 5 story 9 narrative

contemn 4 snub 5 abhor, scorn, spurn 6 deride 7 deplore, despise, disdain 8 ridicule 10 look down on

contemplate 3 eye 4 mull, muse, view 5 study, think, weigh 6 behold, debate, gaze at, intend, look at, ponder, regard 7 examine, inspect, propose, reflect 8 consider, gaze upon, look upon, meditate, mull over, ruminate, think out 9 think over 10 deliberate, excogitate, scrutinize

contemplation 5 study 6 musing 7 thought 8

thinking **9** intention, pondering **10** cogitation, meditation, reflection, rumination **11** cerebration, expectation, speculation **12** deliberation **13** consideration

contemplative 6 musing **7** pensive **10** cogitative, meditative, reflecting, reflective, ruminative, thoughtful **11** speculative **13** introspective

contemporary 3 new **6** coeval, extant, modern, recent **7** current, present, topical **8** existent, existing, up-to-date **9** au courant **10** coexistent, coexisting, coincident, concurrent, present-day, synchronic **11** synchronous **12** simultaneous

contempt 5 scorn, shame **7** despite, disdain, mockery **8** aversion, defiance, disfavor, disgrace, dishonor, distaste, ignominy **9** antipathy, discredit, disesteem, disrepute **10** disrespect, opprobrium, repugnance **12** disobedience, stubbornness

contemptible 3 low **4** base, mean, poor, vile **5** cheap, sorry **6** abject, odious, paltry, scummy, scurvy, shabby, sordid **7** hateful, ignoble, pitiful, squalid **8** inferior, pitiable, shameful, unworthy, wretched **9** abhorrent, loathsome **10** despicable, detestable, disgusting **11** ignominious **12** dishonorable

contemptuous 7 haughty **8** arrogant, derisive, scornful **10** disdainful **12** supercilious **13** condescending, disrespectful

contend 3 vie, war **4** aver, avow, cope, face, urge **5** argue, brawl, claim, fight **6** affirm, allege, assert, battle, charge, combat, debate, defend, insist, oppose, report, strive **7** compete, contest **8** confront, maintain, struggle **9** encounter, withstand

contender 5 match, rival **6** player **8** opponent **9** adversary, candidate, combatant **10** antagonist, challenger, competitor, contestant

_____ **contendere 4** nolo

content 4 cozy, gist **5** happy **6** at ease, serene **7** appease, gratify, meaning, placate, satisfy **9** gratified, satisfied, substance **11** comfortable **12** significance

contention 3 war **4** beef, feud **6** combat, rumpus, strife, thesis **7** discord, dispute, dissent, quarrel, rivalry, wrangle **8** argument, conflict, disunity, squabble **10** difference, dissension, dissidence **11** altercation, competition, controversy _Scottish:_ **5** sturt

contentious 5 fiery **7** carping, froward, peppery, scrappy, warlike **8** captious, caviling, contrary, militant, perverse **9** bellicose, combative, hotheaded, litigious, polemical, truculent **10** pugnacious **11** belligerent, quarrelsome **12** disputatious, faultfinding **13** argumentative, controversial

conterminous 10 coincident **11** coextensive

contest 3 vie **4** bout, duel, feud, fray, game, meet, race, tilt **5** clash, fight, match, repel, rival, trial **6** battle, combat, debate, oppose, resist, strife, strive **7** compete, dispute, rivalry, warfare **8** argument, conflict, endeavor, skirmish, struggle, tug-of-war **9** challenge, encounter, rencontre **10** engagement, tournament **11** competition

contestant 5 rival **7** also-ran, entrant, opposer, wannabe **8** opponent **9** adversary, contender **10** challenger, competitor

contiguity 9 adjacency, immediacy, proximity **11** propinquity

contiguous 4 next **8** abutting, adjacent, touching **9** adjoining, bordering **10** juxtaposed

continence 6 purity, virtue **8** chastity, sobriety **9** austerity **10** abnegation, abstinence, asceticism, chasteness, moderation, temperance **11** forbearance **12** renunciation **13** self-restraint

continent 4 Asia, mass **5** sober **6** Africa, chaste, Europe **8** celibate, mainland **9** abstinent, Australia, temperate **10** abstemious, Antarctica, restrained **11** abstentious **12** North America, South America _lost:_ **8** Atlantis

contingence 5 touch **7** contact **8** tangency, touching

contingency 4 pass **5** event, pinch **6** chance, crisis **8** exigency, juncture, occasion **9** emergency **10** likelihood **11** opportunity, possibility, probability, uncertainty

contingent 3 odd **4** band **5** group, party, troop **6** casual, chance, likely **7** reliant **8** possible, probable, relative **9** dependent, empirical, entourage, uncertain **10** accidental, delegation, deputation, detachment, fortuitous, incidental, unforeseen **11** conditional **13** unanticipated, unforeseeable, unpredictable

continual 6 steady **7** abiding, endless, nonstop, regular, running **8** constant, enduring, timeless, unbroken, unending **9** ceaseless, incessant, perpetual, perennial, recurrent, recurring, unceasing, unfailing, unvarying **10** persistent, persisting, relentless, unchanging, unflagging **11** everlasting, unremitting **12** interminable **13** uninterrupted

continually 4 ever **5** on end **6** always **7** forever **8** steadily, together **9** endlessly **10** constantly **11** incessantly, night and day **12** interminably, persistently, relentlessly, successively **13** consecutively

continuance 3 run **4** stay **5** delay **6** sequel **8** duration, survival **9** longevity **10** perma-

nence **11** adjournment, persistence **12** postponement, prolongation
continuation 3 run **4** coda **6** sequel **8** appendix, duration, epilogue **9** endurance, extension **10** resumption **11** persistence,
protraction **12** prolongation
continue 4 go on, last, stay **5** abide, renew,
run on, segue **6** endure, hang in, keep at,
keep on, keep up, pick up, push on, remain,
reopen, resume, retain, take up **7** carry on,
persist, press on, proceed, prolong, restart,
survive **8** maintain, postpone **9** carry over,
persevere **10** recommence
continuing 5 fixed **6** steady **7** abiding,
chronic, durable, eternal, lasting, ongoing **8**
constant, enduring, lifelong, stubborn **9**
long-lived, obstinate, perennial, prolonged,
steadfast, tenacious, unabating **10** inveterate, persistent, persisting **11** long-lasting
continuity 4 flow **6** script **8** duration, scenario, sequence **9** endurance **11** persistence,
progression
continuous see **continual**
continuously see **continually**
contort 4 knot, warp **5** twist, wring **6** deform,
wrench, writhe **7** distort, grimace, torture **9**
convolute, corkscrew, disfigure
contortionist 7 acrobat
contour 4 form, line **5** curve, lines, shape **6**
figure **7** outline, pattern, profile **9** lineament, lineation **10** silhouette **11** delineation
contra 6 facing, toward **7** against, counter, reverse, vis-à-vis **8** converse, fronting, opposite **10** conversely
contraband 3 hot **5** taboo **6** banned **7** bootleg,
illegal, illicit, smuggle **8** unlawful **9** forbidden **10** prohibited, proscribed **11** black market, bootlegging, trafficking
contract 4 bond, hire, pact, sink **5** catch, incur, lease **6** engage, induce, lessen, reduce,
shrink, treaty, weaken **7** abridge, acquire,
afflict, bargain, decline, dwindle, shorten,
shrivel **8** compress, condense, covenant, decrease, diminish **9** agreement, constrict,
succumb to **11** concentrate, transaction **12**
come down with *part:* **6** clause **7** article,
proviso
contraction 3 he'd, he's, I'll, it's, I've, tic **4**
ain't, can't, don't, flex, he'll, isn't, let's,
she'd, she's, won't, you'd **5** aren't, cramp,
didn't, hadn't, hasn't, she'll, spasm, they'd,
wasn't, you'll, you're, you've **6** haven't,
mustn't, needn't, they'll, they've, weren't **7**
couldn't, elision, mightn't, wouldn't **8**
shouldn't **9** reduction, shrinkage **10** abridgment **11** abridgement **12** abbreviation

heart's: **7** systole ***poetic:*** **3** e'en, e'er, o'er,
'tis **4** ne'er, 'twas **5** 'twere, 'twill
contradict 4 deny **5** belie, cross, rebut **6** impugn, negate, refute, take on **7** confute, dispute, gainsay **8** negative, traverse **9**
challenge, disaffirm
contradiction 6 denial **7** paradox **8** antinomy,
negation, rebuttal, variance **9** disparity **10**
gainsaying, opposition, refutation **11** discrepancy, incongruity **12** disagreement,
protestation **13** inconsistency
contradictory 7 counter, reverse **8** contrary,
converse, negating, opposite **9** antipodal **10**
antipodean, antithesis, nullifying **12** antithetical
contraption 3 rig **5** gizmo **6** device, doodad,
gadget **7** machine **9** apparatus, doohickey
11 contrivance
contrariety 10 antagonism, antithesis, opposition, perversity, unlikeness
contrariwise 9 vice versa **10** conversely, oppositely
contrary 5 balky **6** averse, ornery, unruly **7**
adverse, counter, froward, reverse, way-
ward **8** converse, opposite, perverse, stubborn **9** antipodal, diametric, dissident,
obstinate, vice versa **10** conversely, discordant, headstrong, oppositely, rebellious, refractory **11** conflicting, intractable,
wrongheaded **12** antagonistic, antipathetic,
antithetical, contumacious, cross-grained,
recalcitrant ***prefix:*** **7** counter
contrast 6 differ **7** collate, compare, diverge
8 conflict, disagree **9** disparity **10** comparison, difference, divergence **11** distinction,
distinguish
contravene 4 defy, deny **5** break, cross, fight
6 abjure, breach, disown, impugn, negate,
offend, oppose, reject **7** disobey, gainsay,
violate **8** disclaim, infringe, renege on **9**
disaffirm, go against, repudiate **10** contradict, transgress
contravention 6 breach **7** offense **8** trespass **9**
violation **10** infraction **12** infringement **13**
nonobservance, transgression
contretemps 3 row **4** slip, tiff **5** clash, run-in
6 dustup, mishap, slip-up **7** dispute, quarrel
8 argument **9** mischance **10** falling-out,
misfortune
contribute 3 add **4** give, help, tend **5** grant **6**
chip in, donate, kick in, submit, supply **7**
conduce, pitch in, redound **9** subscribe **11**
come through
contribution 4 alms, gift **5** input, share, tithe
7 charity, payment, present **8** donation, offering **11** benefaction, beneficence
contributory 8 adjuvant **9** accessory, ancil-

lary, auxiliary 10 collateral, subsidiary, supporting 11 appurtenant, subservient

contrite 5 sorry 8 penitent 9 regretful, repentant 10 apologetic, remorseful 11 penitential

contrition 3 rue 4 ruth 6 regret 7 penance, remorse 9 penitence 10 repentance 11 compunction 12 self-reproach

contrivance 4 ruse 6 device, gadget 7 gimmick 8 artifice 9 apparatus, expedient, invention, stratagem 10 brainchild 11 contraption

contrive 3 rig 4 fake, make, move, plan, plot 5 frame, hatch 6 cook up, devise, invent, make up, manage, scheme, vamp up, wangle 7 arrange, concoct, connive, develop, dream up, fashion, project, work out 8 cogitate, conspire, engineer, intrigue 9 construct, elaborate, fabricate, formulate, machinate

contrived 5 hokey 6 forced 7 labored 8 strained 9 concocted, insincere 10 artificial, engineered, fabricated, factitious

control 3 run 4 curb, rein, rule, sway 5 guide, power, steer 6 bridle, direct, govern, handle, manage, master, rein in, subdue 7 command, conduct, mastery, oversee, repress, reserve 8 dominate, dominion, regulate, restrain 9 authority, direction, restraint, supervise, supremacy 10 discipline, domination, management 11 supervision 12 jurisdiction

controlled 8 discreet, reserved 9 temperate 10 restrained

controversial 5 risky 6 touchy 7 awkward, charged, eristic 8 delicate, disputed, ticklish 9 explosive, litigious, polemical 11 contentious, problematic 12 disputatious 13 argumentative

controversy 3 row 5 clash 6 debate, rumpus, strife 7 dispute, quarrel, wrangle 8 argument, squabble 10 contention, falling-out 11 altercation, disputation, embroilment

controvert 4 deny 5 rebut 6 debate, oppose, oppugn, refute 7 confute, counter, dispute, gainsay 8 disprove, question 9 challenge, repudiate

contumacious 7 froward 8 contrary, insolent, mutinous, obdurate, perverse 9 obstinate 10 rebellious, refractory 11 disobedient, intractable 12 recalcitrant 13 insubordinate

contumacy 8 contempt, defiance 9 insolence 10 perversity 12 stubbornness 13 recalcitrance

contumelious 7 abusive 8 derisive, insolent, scornful 9 insulting, truculent 10 disdainful, scurrilous 11 opprobrious 12 vituperative

contumely 5 abuse 6 insult 7 affront, mockery, obloquy 8 contempt, ridicule, sneering 9 aspersion, invective 10 scurrility 12 vituperation

contuse 6 batter, bruise, injure 7 blacken

conundrum 5 poser 6 enigma, puzzle, riddle 7 baffler, mystery, problem, puzzler, stumper 10 puzzlement 13 Chinese puzzle

convalesce 4 heal, mend 7 improve, recover 10 recuperate

convene 4 call, meet 6 call in, gather, muster, summon 7 convoke, summons 8 assemble 9 forgather 10 congregate 12 come together

convenience 4 ease 7 amenity, benefit, comfort, leisure 8 facility 9 handiness 10 assistance 13 accessibility

convenient 3 fit 4 near 5 close, handy, ready 6 at hand, nearby, proper, useful 7 close by, helpful 8 suitable 9 available, immediate, opportune 10 accessible 11 appropriate, comfortable 12 advantageous

convent 5 abbey 6 priory 7 nunnery 8 cloister 9 monastery, sanctuary

convention 3 law 4 bond, code, pact, rule 5 canon, usage 6 accord, custom, treaty 7 compact, meeting, precept 8 assembly, congress, contract, covenant, practice, protocol 9 agreement, concordat, formality, gathering, propriety, tradition 11 convocation

conventional 5 trite, usual 6 formal, normal, proper, seemly, solemn, square 7 correct, regular, routine, typical 8 everyday, habitual, moderate, ordinary, orthodox, standard, straight 9 bourgeois, customary 10 button-down, conforming, prevailing, restrained, unoriginal 11 commonplace, traditional 12 conservative

conventionalize 5 adapt 7 conform 9 normalize

converge 4 join, meet 5 focus, merge, unite 11 concentrate 12 come together

conversant 8 familiar 9 au courant 10 acquainted 11 experienced

conversation 4 chat, talk 6 confab, debate, parley 7 palaver, talking 8 causerie, colloquy, dialogue, duologue, exchange, repartee 9 discourse, tête-à-tête 10 discussion 13 confabulation

conversation piece 5 curio 6 oddity 9 curiosity

converse 3 gab 4 chat, chin, talk 5 speak, visit 6 confer, contra, parley 7 chatter, counter, reverse 8 antipode, contrary, opposite 9 antipodal, diametric 10 antithesis 12 antithetical 13 contradictory

conversely 9 vice versa 10 oppositely 12 contrariwise

conversion 5 shift 6 change, switch 7 novelty, rebirth, turning **8** metanoia, mutation, reversal **9** about-face **10** alteration, change-over **11** permutation **12** modification, regeneration **13** metamorphosis, transmutation

convert 4 sway **5** alter **6** change, modify, redeem, reform, switch **7** commute, remodel **8** persuade, renovate **9** proselyte, transform, translate, transmute, transpose **11** transfigure **12** metamorphose, transmogrify *Christian:* **10** catechumen

convex 5 bowed, toric **6** arched, curved **7** bulging, curving, gibbous, rounded

convexity 4 arch **6** camber

convey 3 lug **4** bear, cart, cede, deed, pack, send, tell, tote **5** bring, carry, ferry **6** assign, impart, pass on **7** channel, conduct, consign, deliver, express, project **8** make over, sign over, transfer, transmit **9** transport **11** communicate

conveyance 3 car **4** auto, cart, deed, sled **5** coach, sedan, stage, title, wagon **7** charter, trailer, transit, vehicle **8** carriage, carrying **9** transport **10** automobile **12** transporting *public:* **3** bus, cab **4** taxi, tram **5** plane, train **6** subway **7** trolley **8** airplane, monorail, railroad, rickshaw **9** streetcar **10** jinricksha, jinrikisha

convict 5 felon, lifer **6** inmate, send up **7** condemn, put away **8** criminal, jailbird, prisoner, sentence, yardbird **10** find guilty

conviction 4 view **5** creed, faith **6** belief, surety **7** opinion **8** doctrine, sentence, sureness **9** assurance, certainty, certitude, sentiment **10** confidence, persuasion **12** condemnation

convince 6 assure, induce, prompt **7** satisfy, win over **8** persuade, talk into **9** influence, prevail on **11** bring around, prevail upon

convincing 5 solid, sound, valid **6** cogent **8** credible, faithful **9** plausible **10** believable, conclusive, persuasive, satisfying **11** trustworthy

convivial 3 gay **5** jolly, merry **6** hearty, jocund, jovial, lively, social **7** festive **8** mirthful, sociable **9** fun-loving, vivacious **10** gregarious **13** companionable

convocation 5 synod **7** council, meeting **8** assembly, conclave **9** gathering **10** assemblage **12** congregation

convoke 4 call **6** gather, invite, muster, summon **7** collect, convene **8** assemble **12** call together

convoluted 6 coiled **7** complex, tangled, winding **8** involved, tortuous **9** intricate **10** circuitous **11** anfractuous, complicated **12** labyrinthine

convoy 6 attend, escort **7** conduct **9** accompany

convulse 4 rock **5** shake **7** agitate, concuss **8** tetanize

convulsion 3 fit **5** spasm **6** attack, tumult, uproar **7** quaking, rocking, seizure, shaking **8** disaster, paroxysm, upheaval **9** commotion, trembling

cook 3 fix, fry **4** bake, boil, chef, heat, melt, stew **5** broil, grill, poach, roast, sauté, steam **6** braise, doctor, simmer **7** falsify, parboil, prepare, swelter

cookbook *abbreviation:* **3** tsp **4** tbsp *term:* **3** cup, fry, mix **4** bake, beat, boil, chop, pare, peel, roux, sift, stew, stir, toss, whip, zest **5** baste, blend, broil, cream, glaze, grate, grind, knead, mince, pinch, poach, roast, sauté, scald, steam, stock **6** blanch, braise, fillet, season, simmer **7** al dente, deglaze, parboil **8** dissolve, emulsify, julienne, marinate, meringue **10** caramelize

cooked 4 done, sham **5** bogus, faked, phony **6** made-up **7** altered **8** doctored, spurious **10** fictitious

cookery 7 cuisine *expert:* **3** Ray (Rachael), Yan (Martin) **4** Chen (Joyce), Kerr (Graham), Puck (Wolfgang), Root (Waverley) **5** Beard (James), Child (Julia), David (Elizabeth), Hines (Duncan), Pépin (Jacques), Smith (Jeff) **6** Bocuse (Paul), Carême (Marie-Antoine), Farmer (Fannie), Fisher (M. F. K.), Franey (Pierre), Waters (Alice) **7** Crocker (Betty), Ducasse (Alain), Stewart (Martha) **8** Bourdain (Anthony), Rombauer (Irma) **9** Claiborne (Craig), Escoffier (Auguste), Prudhomme (Paul)

cookie 4 Oreo, snap **5** wafer **7** biscuit, brownie **10** gingersnap

cooking *appliance:* **4** oven **5** mixer, range, stove **7** blender, toaster **9** microwave **10** rotisserie *implement:* **3** cup, pan, pot, wok **4** olla **5** ladle, sieve, spoon, whisk **6** grater, masher, sifter, tureen **7** griddle, skillet, spatula, steamer **8** colander, teaspoon **9** eggbeater, frying pan **10** rolling pin, tablespoon **12** measuring cup *measure:* **3** cup, tsp **4** tbsp **8** teaspoon **10** tablespoon *room:* **6** galley **7** kitchen

Cook Islands *capital:* **6** Avarua *dependency of:* **10** New Zealand *island:* **9** Rarotonga

cool 3 hep, hip, icy, rad **4** calm, cold, phat **5** abate, aloof, chill, funky, gelid, nippy **6** arctic, chilly, frigid, frosty, with-it **7** assured, compose, control, decline, distant, dwindle, repress, subside **8** composed, decrease, detached, diminish, reserved, suppress **9** collected, confident, impassive, unruffled **10**

nonchalant, phlegmatic, unsociable 11 indifferent, standoffish, unflappable 13 dispassionate, imperturbable, self-possessed

cooler 3 fan, jug, pen 4 brig, coop, jail 5 clink, pokey 6 fridge, icebox, lockup, prison 7 freezer, slammer 9 calaboose 11 refrigerant 12 refrigerator

cooling device 3 fan 6 fridge, icebox 7 freezer 12 refrigerator

coolness 5 chill, poise 6 aplomb, phlegm 7 reserve 9 composure, frigidity, sangfroid 10 dispassion, equanimity 11 nonchalance, self-control

coop 3 hem, jug, mew, pen 4 brig, cage, jail 5 cramp, fence, pokey 6 cooler, corral, lockup, prison, shut in 7 close in, confine, enclose, slammer 9 calaboose, enclosure

cooperate 5 agree, unite 6 concur, league 7 combine, conjoin, pitch in 8 coincide, conspire 11 collaborate, participate 12 work together

cooperation 8 alliance, teamwork 13 confederation

cooperative 5 joint 6 common, mutual, shared 8 coactive, conjoint, obliging 9 collegial, concerted 10 collective, synergetic 11 coordinated 13 accommodating, collaborative, uncompetitive *craft society:* 5 artel

Cooper hero 7 Hawkeye 10 Deerslayer, Pathfinder 11 Natty Bumppo

coordinate 4 mate, mesh 5 align, equal, match, order 6 adjust, relate 7 coequal, conform 8 organize, parallel 9 companion, correlate, harmonize, integrate, reconcile 10 proportion, reciprocal 11 accommodate, correlative, counterpart *system:* 9 Cartesian

coot 4 bird, fogy 5 fogey 6 codger, dotard, duffer, fellow, oddity, scoter, weirdo 7 oddball 9 character, eccentric

cootie 5 louse 9 body louse

cop 3 nab 4 lift, take 5 adopt, catch, filch, pinch, steal, swipe 6 pilfer 7 capture, officer 8 bluecoat 9 patrolman, policeman

copacetic 3 A-OK 4 fine, jake, okay 5 dandy, great, nifty 8 all right 9 excellent 12 satisfactory

cope 4 cape, hack 5 cloak, cover, get by, match, vault 6 canopy, endure, make do, manage, mantle 7 carry on, survive 8 vestment

copestone 5 crown

copious 4 lush, rich 5 ample 6 lavish, plenty 7 liberal, profuse, replete 8 abundant, generous 9 abounding, bounteous, bountiful, exuberant, luxuriant, plenteous, plentiful

Copland work 5 Rodeo 11 Billy the Kid 17 Appalachian Spring

cop-out 5 dodge 6 excuse 7 evasion, pretext, retreat

copper 4 cent, coin 5 metal, penny, token 9 butterfly, policeman *coating:* 6 patina *item:* 4 cent 5 penny 6 kettle *sulfate:* 7 vitriol 9 bluestone 11 blue vitriol *symbol:* 2 Cu

copperhead 5 snake, viper 8 pit viper

coppice 4 bosk, wood 5 copse, grove, woods 6 bosque, forest, growth 7 thicket 9 brushwood, underwood

copse see **coppice**

Copt 8 Egyptian

copula 4 bond, link 5 joint, union 7 coupler

copy 3 ape 4 echo, fake, mock, sham 5 clone, ditto, forge, mimic, model, repro 6 carbon, parrot, repeat 7 emulate, forgery, imitate, replica, takeoff 8 knockoff, likeness, simulate 9 duplicate, facsimile, imitation, replicate, reproduce 10 impression, simulacrum, simulation, transcribe, transcript 11 counterfeit, counterpart, reduplicate, replication 12 reproduction

copycat 3 ape 4 aper 5 mimic 6 parrot 8 imitator

copyist 5 clerk 6 scribe 8 imitator 9 engrosser 10 plagiarist 11 transcriber

copyread 4 edit

coquet 3 toy 4 fool, vamp 5 dally, flirt, tease 6 trifle

coquette 4 vamp 5 flirt, tease

coquettish 3 coy 6 fickle 9 frivolous, kittenish 11 flirtatious

coral 3 red 4 pink, rosy 5 polyp 9 limestone

coral reef 3 cay, key 5 atoll *off Australia:* 5 Wreck *world's largest:* 12 Great Barrier

cord 3 tie 4 band, lace, pile, rope, whip, yarn 5 cable, nerve, stack 6 strand, string, tendon *twisted:* 7 torsade

cordage 4 rope 5 ropes 7 rigging *fiber:* 4 bast, hemp, jute, pita 5 sisal

Corday's victim 5 Marat (Jean-Paul)

Cordelia *father:* 4 Lear *sister:* 5 Regan 7 Goneril

cordial 4 warm 6 genial, hearty, jovial, tender 7 affable, liqueur, sincere 8 cheerful, friendly, gracious, sociable 9 congenial, convivial, heartfelt 10 hospitable 11 sympathetic, warmhearted 12 wholehearted

cordiality 6 warmth 7 amenity 9 geniality 10 amiability 12 agreeability, friendliness

cordon 4 lace, line, ring 5 braid 6 circle, ribbon 7 barrier 8 espalier *bleu:* 4 chef, cook 6 ribbon 10 blue ribbon, decoration, master chef

core 3 hub, nub 4 base, crux, gist, meat, pith, root 5 basis, focus, heart, midst 6 center, depths, kernel, middle, upshot 7 essence, nucleus **8** interior, midpoint **9** substance **10** foundation

corium 5 cutis **6** dermis

cork 4 bark, plug, seal, stop **5** float **6** bobber **7** stopper, stopple

corker 4 lulu **5** beaut, dandy, dilly, doozy **6** doozie, killer **8** jim-dandy, knockout **9** humdinger **11** crackerjack **12** lollapalooza

corkscrew 4 coil, wind **5** helix, twist **6** spiral

cormorant 4 bird, shag **7** glutton

corn 5 grain, maize **6** hominy **9** granulate *bread:* **4** pone **7** bannock, hoecake *Indian:* **5** maize **6** mealie *kind:* **3** pop **5** flint, flour, sweet **6** Indian *pest:* **5** borer *piece:* **3** cob, ear **5** spike **6** kernel, nubbin

Corncracker State 8 Kentucky

corner 3 box, fix, jam, nab **4** hole, nook, trap, tree **5** angle, catch, coign, niche, seize **6** collar, cranny, dogleg, pickle, plight, recess, scrape **7** capture, dilemma, impasse, trouble **8** bottle up, monopoly **10** bring to bay **11** predicament **12** intersection *of eye:* **7** canthus

cornerstone 4 base **5** basis **7** support **8** rudiment **10** foundation, groundwork

cornet 4 cone, horn **7** officer, trumpet **10** instrument

Cornhusker State 8 Nebraska

cornice 3 cap **4** band, eave **5** crown **7** molding

cornmeal 4 masa, mush, samp **5** grits **6** hominy **7** hoecake *mush:* **7** polenta

cornucopia 4 cone, horn **6** bounty, plenty, wealth **9** abundance, profusion **12** horn of plenty

Cornwallis, Charles *adversary:* **6** Greene (Nathanael) *surrender site:* **8** Yorktown

corny 5 banal, sappy, stale, trite **6** old hat **7** clichéd, mawkish **8** shopworn **9** hackneyed, schmaltzy **11** sentimental, stereotyped

corollary 6 effect, result, sequel, upshot **8** parallel, sequence **9** resulting **10** associated, end product, equivalent **11** aftereffect, consequence *logical:* **9** inference

corona 4 aura, glow, halo **5** cigar, crown, glory **6** circle, nimbus **7** aureola, aureole

coroner 8 examiner

coronet 5 crown, tiara **6** anadem, circle, diadem, wreath **7** chaplet, circlet, garland **8** headband

Coronis *form:* **4** crow *son:* **9** Asclepius **11** Aesculapius

corporal 3 NCO **6** bodily, carnal **7** fleshly, somatic **8** physical

corporate 7 unified **8** combined **9** aggregate

corporeal 6 bodily, carnal, mortal **7** fleshly, somatic **8** material, physical, tangible **9** objective **10** phenomenal **11** substantial

corposant 11 St. Elmo's fire

corps 4 band, body **5** group, party, troop **6** outfit, troupe **7** company

corpse 4 body **5** bones, stiff **7** cadaver, carcass, carrion, remains *combining form:* **4** necr **5** necro

corpselike 4 ashy, dead **5** ashen, gaunt **6** wasted **7** deathly, ghastly, macabre **8** lifeless, skeletal **10** cadaverous

corpulence 7 fatness, obesity **9** adiposity, rotundity **10** fleshiness, overweight, portliness

corpulent 3 fat **5** bulky, gross, heavy, obese, plump, stout **6** fleshy, portly, rotund **7** porcine, weighty **9** overblown **10** overweight

corpus 4 body, bulk, core, mass **6** oeuvre **9** principal, substance **10** collection **11** compilation

corpuscle 4 cell **8** hemocyte, monocyte **9** blood cell, leukocyte **10** lymphocyte **11** erythrocyte, granulocyte

corral 3 mew, pen **5** fence **6** gather, shut in **7** close in, collect, confine, enclose, round up **8** surround **9** enclosure

correct 3 fit, fix **4** edit, just, mend, true **5** amend, emend, exact, right **6** adjust, dead on, decent, proper, punish, reform, remedy, repair, revise, seemly, spot on **7** chasten, fitting, improve, perfect, precise, rectify, redress **8** accurate, becoming, chastise, decorous, flawless, set right **9** castigate, faultless **10** conforming, discipline, impeccable, legitimate, meticulous, scrupulous **11** appropriate, comme il faut, punctilious **12** conventional *combining form:* **4** orth **5** ortho

correction 3 rod **6** rebuke **7** reproof **8** revision **9** amendment **10** adjustment, discipline, emendation, punishment **11** castigation

corrective 4 cure **6** remedy **8** antidote, punitive, remedial **10** beneficial **11** counterstep, restorative **12** counteragent **13** counteractive

correctness 7 decorum **8** accuracy, fidelity **9** precision, propriety **10** exactitude

correlate 5 match **6** analog **7** pendant **8** analogue, coincide, dovetail, parallel **9** harmonize **10** complement, correspond **11** counterpart

correlative 2 if, or **3** and, nor **4** both, then **6** either **7** neither, related **10** complement, reciprocal **11** counterpart **13** complementary, corresponding

correspond 4 jibe **5** agree, equal, match, write **6** accord, concur **7** comport, conform **8** dovetail **9** harmonize **11** communicate

correspondence 4 mail **7** analogy, letters **8** symmetry **9** agreement, congruity **10** conformity, similarity **11** consistency, correlation *mathematical:* **7** mapping **8** function

correspondent 5 match **6** analog, pen pal, writer **7** fitting **8** analogue, parallel, reporter, suitable **9** correlate **10** conforming, journalist **11** commentator, contributor, counterpart

corresponding 4 akin, like **5** alike **6** agnate **7** related, similar **8** matching, parallel **9** analogous, consonant **10** comparable **11** correlative

correspondingly 4 also **7** equally **8** likewise **9** similarly **11** analogously

corrida 9 bullfight *shout:* **3** olé

corridor 4 hall, lane, path **5** aisle, route, strip **6** artery, avenue **7** hallway, passage **10** passageway

corroborate 5 prove **6** uphold, verify **7** approve, bear out, certify, confirm, endorse, justify, support **8** document, validate **9** vindicate **12** authenticate, substantiate

corroborative 9 ancillary, auxiliary **10** collateral, supporting, supportive **12** confirmatory

corrode 4 rust **7** eat away, eat into, oxidize **8** wear away **9** undermine

corrosive 4 acid **5** acerb **6** biting **7** acerbic, caustic, cutting **9** sarcastic

corrosiveness 7 sarcasm **8** acerbity

corrugation 4 fold, ruck **5** plica, ridge **6** crease, furrow, groove **7** crinkle, wrinkle

corrupt 3 rot **5** bribe, decay, spoil, stain, taint, venal **6** befoul, debase, defile, molder, rotten, smirch **7** crooked, debauch, degrade, deprave, pervert, putrefy, tarnish, vitiate **8** bribable, degraded, depraved, infected, perverse **9** decompose, dishonest, miscreant, reprobate, unethical **10** bastardize, degenerate **12** unprincipled, unscrupulous **13** untrustworthy

corruptible 5 venal **7** buyable **8** bribable

corruption 4 vice **5** decay, fraud, graft **7** bribery, jobbery **9** barbarism, depravity, turpitude **10** immorality, wickedness **11** impropriety

corsair 5 rover **6** pirate **8** picaroon, sea rover **9** buccaneer, pickaroon, privateer **10** freebooter

corset 5 stays **6** bodice, girdle **7** support

Corsica *city:* **6** Bastia **7** Ajaccio *hero:* **8** Napoleon (Bonaparte) *patriot:* **5** Paoli (Pasquale)

cortege 5 train **6** parade **7** retinue **9** entourage **10** attendants, procession

cortex 4 bark, husk, peel, rind **6** casing **8** peridium

Cortland 5 apple

corundum 4 ruby **5** emery, topaz **7** emerald **8** abrasive, amethyst, sapphire

coruscate 5 flash, gleam, glint, shine **7** glisten, glitter, sparkle, twinkle **11** scintillate

corvid 3 jay **4** crow **5** raven **6** magpie **9** passerine

Corvino's wife 5 Celia

corybantic 3 mad **4** wild **5** rabid **6** crazed **7** frantic, furious **8** ecstatic, frenetic, frenzied **9** delirious

coryphée 6 dancer **8** danseuse **9** ballerina

Così Fan Tutte composer 6 Mozart (Wolfgang Amadeus)

cosine reciprocal 6 secant

cosmetic 4 kohl **5** blush, rouge **6** ceruse, lotion, makeup, powder **7** blusher, bronzer, mascara **8** lip gloss, lipstick **9** eye shadow **10** decorative, nail polish, ornamental **11** beautifying, superficial

cosmetologist 10 beautician

cosmic 4 huge, vast **7** immense **8** infinite **9** planetary, spiritual, unbounded, universal **12** astronomical, metaphysical

cosmopolitan 6 global, urbane **7** worldly **8** catholic, cultured, polished **9** civilized, universal, worldwide **10** cultivated, ecumenical **11** worldly-wise **13** sophisticated

cosmos 6 flower **8** creation, universe

Cossack *army:* **3** Don **4** Ural **5** Kuban *land:* **7** Ukraine *leader:* **5** Razin (Stenka) **6** ataman, hetman, Mazepa (Ivan) **7** Bulavin (Kondraty) **8** Pugachov (Yemelyan) *novel:* **10** Taras Bulba

cosset 3 pet **4** baby, lamb, love **5** humor, spoil **6** caress, cocker, coddle, cuddle, dandle, dote on, fondle, pamper **7** cater to, indulge **11** mollycoddle

cost 3 tab **4** rate, toll **5** price **6** charge, damage, outlay, tariff **7** expense, payment **8** price tag **9** sacrifice **11** expenditure **12** disbursement *business:* **8** overhead

Costa Rica *bay:* **8** Coronado *capital:* **7** San José *city:* **8** Alajuela **10** Puntarenas **11** Puerto Limón *discoverer:* **8** Columbus (Christopher) *language:* **7** Spanish *leader:* **5** Arias (Oscar) *monetary unit:* **5** colón *neighbor:* **6** Panama **9** Nicaragua *peninsula:* **3** Osa **6** Nicoya *river:* **7** San Juan *volcano:* **5** Barba, Irazú **9** Turrialba

costermonger 6 hawker **7** peddler **9** barrow boy

costive 4 mean, slow **5** bound, close, tight **6** frugal, stingy **7** miserly **9** penurious **10** hardfisted, pinchpenny **11** closefisted **12** cheeseparing, parsimonious

costless 4 free **6** gratis **10** gratuitous **13** complimentary

costly 4 dear, rich **5** fancy **6** lavish, pricey **7** opulent, premium **8** precious, splendid, valuable **9** expensive, luxurious, priceless **10** exorbitant, high-priced, invaluable **11** extravagant

costume 3 rig **4** duds, garb, mode **5** dress, getup, guise, habit, style **6** attire, outfit **7** apparel, clothes, fashion, threads, turnout, uniform **8** disguise, ensemble, garments **9** trappings

cot 3 bed, hut **4** camp **5** cabin, lodge, shack **6** shanty *wheeled:* **6** gurney

coterie 4 band, camp, clan, club, ring **5** cabal **6** circle, clique **7** in-group **9** camarilla

cotillion 4 ball, prom **5** dance *girl:* **3** deb **9** debutante

cottage 3 hut **4** camp **5** cabin, lodge, shack **6** shanty **8** bungalow *Russian:* **5** dacha *Swiss:* **6** chalet

cotton *cleaner:* **3** gin **6** linter *cloth:* **4** duck, jean, mull **5** baize, chino, denim, drill, khaki, scrim, terry, wigan **6** calico, canvas, chintz, dimity, muslin, oxford, sateen, velour **7** batiste, etamine, fustian, gingham, jaconet, nankeen, organdy, percale **8** corduroy, dungaree, moleskin, nainsook, tarlatan **9** grenadine, percaline, stockinet, swansdown **10** balbriggan **11** stockinette *cloth, Indian:* **5** surah **6** madras **7** dhurrie, khaddar *comb:* **4** card *fuzz remover:* **6** linter *highgrade:* **4** pima *measure:* **4** hank, pick, yard **5** count, skein *pad:* **7** pledget *pod:* **4** boll *refuse:* **5** flock *seed separator:* **3** gin *sheet:* **4** batt *thread:* **5** lisle

Cotton State 7 Alabama

cottonwood 5 alamo **6** poplar

cottony 4 soft **6** fluffy

____ **Coty 4** René

couch 3 den, put **4** lair, sofa, word **5** divan, lodge **6** burrow, chaise, daybed, lounge, phrase **7** express, lie down, recline **9** davenport, formulate **12** chesterfield

couch potato 7 slacker

cougar 3 cat **4** puma **7** panther **9** catamount **12** mountain lion

cough 4 hack, hawk

cough drop 6 troche **7** lozenge

cough up 3 pay **5** spend **6** lay out, pay out **7** deliver, dole out, fork out **8** fork over, hand over, shell out

couloir 5 chasm, gorge, gulch, gully **6** ravine

council 4 diet **5** board, junta **6** powwow, senate **7** cabinet, meeting **8** assembly, conclave, congress, ministry **10** conference, federation **12** consultation *ancient Greek:* **5** boule *church:* **5** synod **10** consistory *medieval English:* **4** moot **5** gemot **6** gemote **8** hustings *Muslim:* **5** divan *Russian:* **4** duma

6 soviet *secret:* **5** cabal, junto **9** camarilla *Spanish:* **7** cabildo

counsel 4 rede, urge, warn **6** advice, advise, charge, direct, enjoin, lawyer **7** consult, suggest **8** advocate, attorney **9** prescribe, recommend **10** advisement **12** deliberation *British:* **9** barrister, solicitor

count 3 add, sum, tot **4** bank, earl, mean, rely, tote **5** issue, score, tally, total, tot up, weigh **6** census, charge, depend, expect, figure, matter, number, reckon, result, tote up **7** compute, signify **8** estimate, militate, numerate, quantify **9** calculate, enumerate **10** allegation

countenance 3 mug **4** back, cast, face, look, mien, phiz **5** favor, go for **6** accept, aspect, visage **7** approve, commend, condone, endorse, support **8** advocate, features, hold with, sanction, tolerate **9** approbate, composure, encourage **10** expression **11** physiognomy

counter 3 bar, pit, vie **4** anti, desk **5** asset, check, match, polar, shelf, table **6** contra, offset, oppose **7** adverse, against, hostile, obverse, opposed, reverse **8** antipode, contrary, converse, opposing, opposite **9** antipodal, diametric **10** antipodean, antithesis, contravene **12** antagonistic, antipathetic, antithetical **13** contradictory

counteract 3 fix **4** foil **5** annul **6** cancel, negate, oppose, resist, thwart **7** balance, correct, nullify, prevent, rectify, redress **8** negative **9** cancel out, frustrate **10** balance out, neutralize

counteragent 4 cure **6** remedy **8** antidote **9** antitoxin, antivenin **10** corrective

counterbalance 6 cancel, make up, offset, redeem, set off **7** ballast, correct, even out, rectify, redress **8** equalize, outweigh **10** compensate

counterblow 7 revenge **8** reprisal, requital, revanche **9** vengeance **11** retaliation, retribution

counterclockwise 4 levo **12** levorotatory

counterfeit 4 copy, fake, hoax, sham **5** bluff, bogus, dummy, false, feign, forge, fraud, mimic, phony **6** affect, assume, deceit, ersatz, forged, pseudo **7** feigned, imitate, pretend **8** delusive, delusory, knock off, simulate, spurious **9** brummagem, deception, deceptive, fabricate, imitation, imposture, insincere, pinchbeck, pretended, simulated **10** fraudulent, misleading, simulacrum *prefix:* **5** pseud **6** pseudo

counterpane 4 pouf, puff **5** duvet **6** spread **8** bedcover, coverlet **9** bedspread, comforter, eiderdown

counterpart 4 like, twin **5** equal, match **6** analog, double **7** vis-à-vis **8** alter ego, analogue, parallel **9** correlate, duplicate **10** complement, coordinate, equivalent **11** correlative **13** correspondent

counterpoise 6 make up, offset, redeem, set off **7** balance, ballast **8** outweigh **9** stabilize **10** compensate

countersign 8 password **9** watchword

countervail 4 foil **6** cancel, offset, oppose, redeem, set off, thwart **7** balance, correct, nullify, rectify **8** outweigh **9** frustrate **10** compensate, neutralize

countless 6 legion, myriad, untold **7** umpteen **11** innumerable

Count of Monte Cristo 6 Dantès (Edmond) *author:* **5** Dumas (Alexandre)

count out 5 expel **6** except **7** exclude **9** disregard, eliminate

countrified 5 rural **6** rustic **7** bucolic **8** homespun, pastoral **10** campestral

country 4 home, land, soil **5** rural **6** nation, region, rustic, sticks **7** boonies, bucolic, outland **8** homeland, pastoral **9** backwoods, boondocks **10** campestral, fatherland, motherland, provincial *dance:* **3** jig **4** reel **10** strathspey *home:* **5** dacha, manor, ranch, villa **8** hacienda *music:* **9** bluegrass *road:* **4** lane, path **5** byway (see also **nation**)

country-music star 4 Cash (Johnny), Ford (Tennessee Ernie), Gill (Vince), Lynn (Loretta), Rich (Charlie), Tubb (Ernest) **5** Acuff (Roy), Autry (Gene), Black (Clint), Cline (Patsy), Davis (Skeeter), Jones (George), Owens (Buck), Pearl (Minnie), Pride (Charley), Swift (Taylor), Twain (Shania), Urban (Keith), Wells (Kitty), Wills (Bob) **6** Arnold (Eddy), Atkins (Chet), Brooks (Garth), Carter (A. P., June, Maybelle, Sara), Harris (Emmylou), Miller (Roger), Monroe (Bill), Nelson (Willie), Parton (Dolly), Ritter (Tex), Rogers (Kenny, Roy), Skaggs (Ricky), Travis (Randy), Tucker (Tanya), Twitty (Conway) **7** Haggard (Merle), Millsap (Ronnie), Paisley (Brad), Robbins (Marty), Rodgers (Jimmie), Wynette (Tammy) **8** Jennings (Waylon), McEntire (Reba), Williams (Hank) **9** Underwood (Carrie)

coup 4 blow, feat **5** upset **6** putsch, stroke **8** takeover **9** overthrow

coup de _____ 5 grâce

couple 3 duo, twa, two **4** bond, dyad, fuse, item, join, link, mate, pair, span, team, yoke **5** brace, hitch, marry, merge, unite **6** hook up, link up **7** bracket, combine, conjoin, connect, doublet, harness, twosome

coupler 4 link, ring **5** hitch, joint **6** hookup **7** shackle **8** ligature *railroad:* **7** drawbar

couplet 3 duo **4** dyad, pair **5** twins **7** distich, doublet, twosome

coupling 4 link, seam **5** joint, union **6** yoking **7** joining, pairing **8** junction, juncture **9** connector **10** connection

courage 4 dash, grit, guts **5** heart, moxie, nerve, pluck, spunk, valor **6** daring, mettle, spirit **7** bravery, heroism **8** audacity, backbone, boldness, firmness, temerity, tenacity, valiance, valiancy **9** assurance, fortitude, gallantry **10** resolution **11** doughtiness, intrepidity **12** fearlessness **13** dauntlessness

courageous 4 bold **5** brave, gutsy, nervy, stout **6** daring, heroic, manful, plucky, spunky, strong **7** doughty, gallant, valiant **8** fearless, intrepid, resolute, stalwart, unafraid, valorous **9** audacious, dauntless, tenacious, undaunted **11** venturesome **12** stouthearted

courier 5 envoy, gofer **6** legate, runner **8** emissary **9** go-between, messenger **11** internuncio

course 3 row, run, way **4** dart, dash, duct, flow, line, path, plan, race, road, rush, tack, tear **5** canal, chain, chase, class, hurry, orbit, order, range, route, scoot, scope, speed, surge, track, trend **6** career, design, hasten, hustle, manner, policy, polity, scheme, sequel, series, string, system **7** advance, channel, circuit, conduit, passage, pattern, program, regimen, routine, seminar **8** aqueduct, duration, progress, sequence, syllabus **9** procedure, racetrack **10** curriculum, succession **11** progression *curving:* **4** coil, curl, turn, wind **5** swing, twist **6** spiral **9** corkscrew *dinner:* **4** soup **5** salad **6** entrée **7** dessert **9** appetizer, blue plate

courser 4 bird **5** horse **7** charger **8** huntsman, warhorse

court 3 bar, woo **4** date, quad, yard **5** atria (plural), charm, motel, spark, suite, tempt **6** allure, atrium, homage, invite, palace, pursue **7** address, flatter, justice, retinue, romance, solicit **8** assembly, cloister, tribunal **9** captivate, curtilage, enclosure, entourage **10** magistrate, parliament, quadrangle **11** legislature *action:* **4** suit **5** trial **6** appeal, assize **7** hearing, inquest, lawsuit **10** proceeding *calendar:* **6** docket *call to:* **7** summons **8** subpoena **11** arraignment *circuit:* **4** eyre *crier's call:* **4** oyez *decision:* **6** assize **7** finding, verdict **8** judgment *ecclesiastical:* **4** rota **5** Curia **10** consistory *Indian:* **6** durbar *kind:* **4** moot **5** civil **6** county, family **7** circuit, customs, federal, supreme **8** chancery, criminal, district, juvenile, kangaroo, superior 9 appellate, municipal 11 territorial *medieval English:* 4 eyre, moot 5 gemot 6 gemote 8 hustings *of equity:* 8 chancery *officer:* 2 DA 5 clerk, crier, judge 7 bailiff, justice, marshal, sheriff 10 prosecutor *order:* 4 writ 5 edict 6 decree 7 summons 8 mandamus, subpoena *panel:* 4 jury *relating to:* 8 judicial 9 juridical *session:* 6 assize 7 sitting 8 sederunt

courteous 5 civil 6 polite 7 courtly, gallant, genteel 8 mannerly, well-bred 9 attentive 10 chivalrous, thoughtful 11 considerate 12 well-mannered

courtesy 7 amenity, decorum, manners, service 8 chivalry, civility 9 attention, etiquette, gallantry 10 cordiality, indulgence 11 courtliness 12 graciousness 13 attentiveness, consideration

court game see under **game**

courtly 5 noble 6 august, formal, urbane 7 elegant, gallant, refined, stately 8 gracious 9 dignified 10 chivalrous, flattering 11 ceremonious

courtship 4 suit 6 dating, wooing 7 romance 10 flirtation *former custom of:* 8 bundling

courtyard 4 quad 5 atria (plural), garth, patio 6 atrium 9 curtilage 10 quadrangle

cousin 3 kin 7 kinsman 8 relative

Cousteau, Jacques *ship:* 7 Calypso *vehicle:* 11 bathysphere

couturier 8 clothier, costumer, designer 10 dressmaker

cove 3 arm, bay 4 nook 5 bight, firth, inlet, niche 6 harbor, recess 9 concavity

covenant 3 vow 4 bond, pact 5 agree, swear 6 pledge, treaty 7 compact, promise 8 contract 9 agreement 10 convention

Covent Garden offering 5 opera 6 ballet

cover 3 cap, lid 4 bury, hide, hood, mask, veil, wrap 5 alibi, cloak, front, guise, stash, track 6 clothe, enfold, enwrap, facade, hiding, insure, refuge, screen, secure, shield, shroud, sleeve, travel 7 blanket, conceal, embrace, enclose, envelop, obscure, overlay, protect, secrete, shelter, write up 8 disguise, ensconce, enshroud, traverse 9 encompass, safeguard, sanctuary, superpose 10 overspread 11 concealment, superimpose *rooflike:* 6 awning, canopy *the eyes:* 4 loup 9 blindfold *the face:* 4 mask, veil *the head:* 4 hood *the mouth:* 6 muzzle *with asphalt:* 4 pave *with cloth:* 5 drape *with dirt:* 7 begrime, blacken 8 besmirch *with straw:* 6 thatch

coverall 8 jumpsuit 10 boilersuit

covered wagon 9 Conestoga

covering *anatomical:* 5 theca, velum 6 tegmen 7 velamen 8 tegument 10 integument *apex of roof:* 3 épi *close-fitting:* 6 sheath 9 sheathing *cloth:* 5 sheet *flap:* 9 operculum *for a book:* 4 case 6 jacket *for a cigar:* 7 wrapper *for a coffin:* 4 pall *for a corpse:* 6 shroud 8 cerement *for a package:* 7 wrapper *for concealment:* 10 camouflage *for food:* 4 cosy, cozy *for soil:* 5 mulch *metal:* 4 mail 5 armor *of a diatom:* 6 lorica *of a plant ovary:* 8 pericarp *of a seed:* 4 aril, case 5 testa *of fruits:* 4 peel, rind *of gloom:* 4 pall *of grain:* 4 hull, husk 5 chaff *shell-like:* 7 testudo 8 carapace *thin:* 4 film 6 patina, veneer *waterproof:* 4 tarp 9 tarpaulin

coverlet 4 pouf, puff 5 duvet 6 spread 8 bedcover 9 bedspread, comforter 11 counterpane

covert 4 lair 5 haven, privy 6 hidden, masked, refuge, secret, veiled 7 feather, furtive, retreat, shelter, sub-rosa, thicket 8 hush-hush, shrouded, stealthy 9 concealed, disguised, sanctuary, sheltered 10 undercover 11 camouflaged, clandestine, hiding place, underhanded 12 hugger-mugger 13 surreptitious, under-the-table

covertly 7 sub-rosa 9 by stealth 12 hugger-mugger

covet 4 want 5 crave 6 desire

covetous 4 avid, keen 5 itchy 6 grabby, greedy 7 envious 8 desirous, esurient, grasping, ravenous 9 rapacious, voracious 10 avaricious, gluttonous 11 acquisitive

covey 4 band, bevy, crew, nest 5 brood, bunch, flock, group, party, troop 6 gaggle, troupe 7 cluster, company

cow (see also **cattle**) 4 faze, kine (plural), neat 5 abash, bossy, bully, daunt 6 appall, bovine, dismay, hector, rattle 7 bluster, dragoon 8 bludgeon, browbeat, bulldoze, bullyrag 9 discomfit, embarrass, strong-arm 10 disconcert, intimidate *cud:* 5 rumen *French:* 5 vache *hornless:* 5 muley 7 pollard *mammary gland:* 5 udder *pen:* 6 corral *shed:* 4 barn, byre *Spanish:* 4 vaca *young:* 4 calf 5 stirk 6 heifer

coward 6 craven 7 caitiff, chicken, dastard, milksop, nebbish 8 poltroon, recreant 9 jellyfish 10 scaredy-cat 11 yellowbelly

_____ **Coward** 4 Noël

cowardly 5 timid, wimpy 6 afraid, craven, yellow 7 caitiff, chicken, fearful, gutless 8 poltroon, recreant, timorous 9 dastardly 11 lily-livered, milk-livered, poltroonish 12 apprehensive, fainthearted, poor-spirited, white-livered 13 pusillanimous

cowboy 5 rogue, waddy 6 drover, herder,

waddie 7 puncher, rancher 8 buckaroo, herdsman, maverick, wrangler 9 cattleman, ranch hand 10 cowpuncher 12 broncobuster *contest:* 5 rodeo *gear:* 5 cuffs, quirt, spurs 6 duster 7 bedroll, slicker, Stetson *legendary:* 9 Pecos Bill *leggings:* 5 chaps *movie:* 3 Mix (Tom) 4 Hart (William S.) 5 Autry (Gene), Wayne (John) 6 Gibson (Hoot), McCrea (Joel), Murphy (Audie), Ritter (Tex), Rogers (Roy, Will) 8 Cisco Kid, Eastwood (Clint) *rope:* 5 lasso, reata, riata 6 lariat *Spanish-American:* 6 charro, gaucho 7 vaquero

cowcatcher 5 pilot

cower 5 quail, wince 6 blench, cringe, flinch, recoil, shrink

cowfish 6 dugong, sea cow 7 grampus, manatee 8 sirenian

cowl 4 cape, hood 5 cloak 6 capote, domino, mantle 7 capuche

cowpox 8 vaccinia

cowpuncher see **cowboy**

coxcomb 3 fop 4 beau, buck, dude, fool 5 blood, dandy, swell 7 peacock 8 macaroni 9 exquisite 11 Beau Brummel 12 clotheshorse, fashion plate, lounge lizard

coy 3 shy 4 arch, cute, pert 5 saucy, timid 6 demure, modest 7 bashful, evasive, playful 8 blushing, decorous, skittish 9 diffident, kittenish 10 capricious, coquettish 11 flirtatious, mischievous 12 noncommittal

Coyote State 11 South Dakota

coypu 6 rodent *fur:* 6 nutria

cozen 3 gyp 4 bilk, scam 5 cheat, trick 6 diddle, fleece, take in 7 beguile, deceive, defraud, swindle, wheedle 8 flimflam 9 bamboozle 11 double-cross

cozy 4 safe, snug, soft 5 comfy, cushy, pally, tight 6 chummy, secure 8 familiar, intimate 11 comfortable

CPR expert 3 EMT

crab 3 nag 4 beef, fuss, yawp 5 gripe, sidle 6 grinch, griper, grouch, kvetch, squawk, yammer 7 decapod, grouser, growler 8 arthopod, complain, grumbler, sourpuss 9 bellyache, shellfish 10 bellyacher, complainer, crosspatch, crustacean, curmudgeon 11 faultfinder *claw:* 5 chela 6 nipper *constellation:* 6 Cancer *genus:* 3 Uca 6 Birgus 7 Limulus, Pagurus *kind:* 3 pea 4 blue, king, pine, rock 5 ghost, purse 6 hermit, spider 7 fiddler 9 Dungeness, horseshoe *king, horseshoe:* 7 limulus

crabbed 4 dour, glum, grim, sour 5 gruff, surly 6 crusty, gloomy, morose, sullen 9 illegible, irascible, saturnine, splenetic

crablike 8 cancroid

crabwise 8 sidelong, sideward, sideways 9 laterally

crack 3 gag, gap, rap, try 4 bang, barb, bash, belt, blow, boom, clap, flaw, jest, joke, open, peal, quip, rift, roll, shot, slam, slap, snap, stab, wham, whop 5 adept, break, burst, chink, cleft, crash, craze, knock, smack, smash, solve, split, whack, whirl, wreck 6 breach, cranny, decode, expert, master, moment, thwack, zinger 7 break up, crevice, decrypt, destroy, fissure, instant, shatter, skilled 8 crevasse, decipher, disorder, interval, masterly, skillful, superior 9 break into, excellent, interrupt, masterful, witticism 10 percussion, proficient

crackbrain 3 nut 4 kook 5 crank, wacko 6 cuckoo 7 dingbat, lunatic 9 ding-a-ling, fruitcake, screwball

crackdown 5 purge 8 quashing 10 repression 11 suppression

cracked 3 mad 4 daft, nuts 5 balmy, batty, crazy, daffy, loony, nutty 6 broken, crazed, cuckoo, insane, screwy 7 bonkers, lunatic, smashed 8 demented, deranged

cracker 5 wafer 6 hacker, rustic 7 biscuit, saltine, snapper 8 Georgian 9 Floridian

crackerjack 3 ace 4 lulu 5 dandy, nifty, sharp 6 corker, killer 8 jim-dandy, knockout 9 humdinger 12 lollapalooza

crackle 4 snap 7 glitter, sparkle, twinkle 9 crepitate 10 effervesce 13 effervescence

crackpot 3 nut 4 case, kook, loon 5 crank, loony, wacko 6 cuckoo, madman 7 dingbat, lunatic, oddball 9 ding-a-ling, eccentric, fruitcake, harebrain, screwball

crack-up, crack up 5 crash, smash, wreck 6 fiasco 7 debacle 8 accident, collapse, disaster 9 breakdown 11 catastrophe

cradlesong 7 lullaby 8 berceuse

craft 3 art, job 4 boat 5 guile, knack, skill, trade, wiles 6 career, deceit, métier 7 ability, calling, cunning, know-how, slyness 8 artifice, caginess, foxiness, vocation, wiliness 9 adeptness, canniness, dexterity, duplicity, expertise, ingenuity, technique 10 adroitness, artfulness, competence, occupation, profession, shrewdness 11 proficiency (see also **boat**)

craftiness 5 guile 7 cunning 8 artifice, subtlety

craftsman 5 smith 6 carter, carver, potter, weaver, wright 7 artisan, builder, cobbler, jeweler 9 carpenter 10 blacksmith

crafty 3 sly 4 foxy, keen, wily 5 acute, cagey, canny, sharp, slick 6 adroit, artful, astute, clever, shrewd, tricky 7 cunning, devious, fawning, vulpine 8 guileful, scheming, skillful, slippery **9** deceitful, designing, ingenious, insidious **11** calculating, duplicitous *Scottish:* **7** sleekit

crag 3 tor **4** hill **5** cliff

craggy 5 erose, harsh, rocky, rough **6** jagged, rugged, uneven

cram 3 jam, ram **4** bolt, fill, gulp, heap, load, pack, wolf **5** crowd, crush, drive, force, press, shove, study, stuff, wedge **6** gobble, review, squash, thrust **7** jam-pack, overeat, squeeze

crammed 4 full **5** awash, flush **7** brimful **8** brimming **9** chock-full

cramp 4 kink, pain, pang **5** crick, limit, spasm **6** hamper, stitch **7** confine, inhibit, shackle **8** confined, restrain, restrict **9** restraint, stricture **10** constraint, limitation **11** confinement, restriction

cramped 5 close, tight **6** narrow **9** confining, two-by-four

crane 4 bird, boom, rail **5** heron **7** derrick, stretch *arm:* **3** jib *genus:* **4** Grus *ship's:* **5** davit

Crane hero 12 Henry Fleming

cranium 5 skull **9** braincase

crank 3 nut **4** crab, kook **5** fancy **6** griper, grouch, notion, rotate, turn up, vagary **7** caprice, conceit, fanatic, grouser, oddball **8** crackpot, crotchet, grumbler, sourpuss **9** eccentric, screwball **10** bellyacher, crosspatch

cranky 5 cross, testy **6** crabby, crusty, cussed, grumpy, morose, ornery, tetchy, touchy **7** bearish, crabbed, peevish, prickly **8** contrary, petulant, tortuous, vinegary **9** crotchety, irascible, irritable, obstinate **10** bad-humored, ill-humored **12** cantankerous, disagreeable **13** unpredictable

cranny 3 gap **4** nook, slit **5** chink, crack, niche **6** corner **7** crevice

crash 3 din, jar, ram **4** bang, boom, bump, bust, clap, fail, fold, jolt, peal, slam, wham **5** blast, break, burst, crack, shock, smash, wreck **6** impact, pileup **7** collide, crack-up, debacle, decline, failure, smashup **8** accident, collapse **9** breakdown, collision **10** concussion

crass 4 rude **5** crude, gross **6** coarse, vulgar **7** boorish, loutish, uncouth **8** churlish **9** unrefined **13** materialistic

crate 3 box **4** heap **5** wreck **6** jalopy, junker **7** clunker

crater 3 pit **4** dent, hole, pock **5** crash **6** cavity, dimple, hollow, trough **7** caldera **8** collapse **10** depression *Hawaiian:* **7** Kilauea

cravat 3 tie **4** band **5** ascot, scarf **7** necktie

crave 3 ask, beg **4** need, want, wish **5** covet **6** demand, desire **7** call for, entreat, implore, long for, require **8** yearn for

craven 4 funk **6** abject, coward **7** caitiff, chicken, dastard, fearful, gutless, ignoble **8** cowardly, cringing, poltroon, recreant **9** dastardly **11** lily-livered, poltroonish, yellowbelly **13** pusillanimous, yellowbellied

craving 4 itch, lust, urge **6** desire, hunger, thirst **7** longing, passion **8** appetite, yearning **9** hankering

crawl 4 flow, inch, teem **5** creep, swarm **6** abound, grovel **7** slither, wriggle **9** pullulate

crawling 6 repent

craze 3 fad **4** chic, rage **5** crack, fever, furor, mania, trend, vogue **6** dement, enrage, frenzy, furore, madden **7** derange, fashion, unhinge **9** unbalance **10** dernier cri, enthusiasm

craziness 5 folly, mania **6** lunacy **8** hysteria, insanity **9** absurdity

crazy 3 fey, mad **4** amok, bats, daft, gaga, loco, nuts, wild, zany **5** balmy, barmy, batty, daffy, dotty, goofy, kooky, loony, loopy, nutty, rabid, silly, wacko, wacky **6** absurd, cuckoo, fruity, insane, mental, psycho, screwy, teched, whacky **7** berserk, bonkers, cracked, foolish, frantic, lunatic, meshuga, smitten, tetched, touched, unsound **8** cockeyed, crackpot, demented, deranged, frenetic, frenzied, maniacal, meshugge, unhinged **9** bedlamite, delirious, eccentric, fanatical, foolhardy, ludicrous, possessed, screwball, senseless **10** crackbrain, moonstruck, ridiculous, unbalanced **11** harebrained, nonsensical **12** preposterous *British:* **5** potty **6** scatty *Scottish:* **3** wud

creak 4 rasp **5** grate, grind **6** scrape, squeak, squeal **7** grating, screech **9** squeaking

creaky 4 aged **5** rusty **7** rickety, run-down, squeaky, unsound, worn-out **8** decrepit **9** tottering **10** broken-down, ramshackle

cream 3 top **4** balm, beat, best, drub, pick, whip, whup **5** blast, elite, prime, salve **6** cerate, choice, defeat, finest, thrash **7** clobber, destroy, trounce, unguent **8** lambaste, liniment, ointment

crease 4 fold, ruck **5** graze, plica, ridge **6** furrow, groove, rumple **7** crinkle, wrinkle

create 3 dub **4** form, make, sire **5** beget, build, cause, forge, found, hatch, set up, spawn, start **6** author, design, devise, father, invent **7** compose, concoct, develop, fashion, produce **8** conceive, engender, generate, occasion **9** construct, establish, fabricate, formulate, institute, originate **10** constitute

creation 5 birth, world **6** cosmos, nature **7**

genesis **8** universe **9** inception, macrocosm **10** conception **11** macrocosmos

creative 7 fertile **8** artistic, inspired, original **9** deceptive, demiurgic, ingenious, inventive **10** innovative, innovatory **11** imaginative **12** innovational

creator 3 god **6** author **8** inventor **9** architect, generator, patriarch **10** originator, progenitor

creature 3 man **5** beast, being, brute, human **6** animal, mortal, person **7** critter, varmint *fabled:* **3** elf, imp, orc, roc **4** ogre, puck, yeti **5** dwarf, fairy, ghost, giant, gnome, harpy, nymph, pixie, troll **6** dragon, goblin, gorgon, kraken, merman, Nessie, sphinx, sprite, wyvern **7** bigfoot, brownie, bugbear, centaur, chimera, gremlin, griffin, mermaid, monster, unicorn, vampire, wendigo, windigo **8** chimaera, minotaur, werewolf **9** hobgoblin, manticore, sasquatch **10** cockatrice, hippogriff, leprechaun (see also **monster**)

credence 5 faith, trust **6** belief, credit **8** reliance **9** sideboard **10** acceptance, confidence

credentials 6 papers **9** documents **10** references **12** certificates, testimonials **13** documentation

credenza 6 buffet **7** console **8** bookcase **9** sideboard

credible 5 solid, sound, valid **6** trusty **8** reliable **9** authentic, colorable, plausible **10** believable, convincing, persuasive, reasonable **11** trustworthy **12** satisfactory

credit 4 deem, feel **5** asset, faith, honor, refer, sense, think, trust **6** accept, assign, belief, charge, impute, notice, weight **7** ascribe, believe **8** consider, credence, prestige, reliance **9** attribute, authority, influence **10** confidence, reputation **11** recognition

creditable 6 worthy **8** laudable, reliable **9** colorable, deserving, estimable, plausible, reputable **10** believable **11** commendable, meritorious, respectable **12** praiseworthy

credo 5 canon, creed, dogma, tenet **6** belief, tenets **7** beliefs, precept **8** doctrine, ideology **9** catechism, principle

credulous 5 naive **6** unwary **8** gullible, trustful, trusting **9** believing **12** unsuspecting, unsuspicious **13** unquestioning

creed 4 sect **5** canon, dogma, faith, tenet **6** belief, church, tenets **7** beliefs, precept **8** doctrine, ideology, religion **9** catechism, communion, principle **12** denomination

creek 3 ria **4** burn, rill **5** brook **6** arroyo, rillet, runlet, runnel, stream **7** freshet, rivulet **8** brooklet **9** streamlet

creep 4 drag, edge, inch, jerk, lurk, slip **5** crawl, freak, glide, schmo, shirk, sicko, skulk, slide, slink, snake, sneak, steal **6** shmuck, sickie, spread, tiptoe, weirdo **7** gumshoe, oddball, pervert, schmuck, slither, wriggle **9** pussyfoot

creeping 6 repent **7** gradual **9** prostrate

creepy 5 eerie, weird **6** spooky **7** anxious, macabre, ominous, strange, uncanny **8** ghoulish, menacing, sinister **9** unnerving **10** disturbing, unpleasant, unsettling **11** hair-raising

crème de la crème 4 best **5** elect, elite **6** finest

Cremona family 5 Amati **8** Guarneri **10** Stradivari **12** Stradivarius

Creole *dish:* 5 gumbo **9** andouille, dirty rice, jambalaya *music:* **6** zydeco

Creon *daughter:* 6 Creusa, Glauce, Glauke *sister:* **7** Jocasta *son:* **6** Haemon *victim:* **8** Antigone

crescendo 4 acme, apex, peak, rise **5** crest, surge, swell **6** apogee, climax, growth, height, zenith **8** increase, pinnacle **9** high point **11** culmination

crescent-shaped 5 bowed **6** lunate, sickle **7** falcate *body or surface:* **4** lune **8** meniscus

crest 3 cap, top **4** acme, apex, comb, noon, peak, roof, tuft **5** arête, chine, crown, plume, ridge **6** apogee, climax, summit, vertex **7** hogback **8** pinnacle, surmount **9** high point **10** coat of arms, prominence **11** culmination *of a wave:* **8** whitecap

crestfallen 3 low **4** blue, down **6** droopy **8** dejected, downcast, drooping **9** depressed **10** dispirited **11** discouraged, downhearted **12** disappointed, disconsolate, disheartened

Crete *ancient city:* 7 Cnossus, Knossos **8** Phaistos *ancient name:* **6** Candia *capital:* **5** Canea *goddess:* **8** Dictynna **11** Britomartis *guard:* **5** Talos *king:* **5** Minos **9** Idomeneus *maze:* **9** labyrinth *monster:* **8** Minotaur *mountain:* **3** Ida *princess:* **7** Ariadne

cretin 3 oaf **4** boob, clod, dolt, dope, fool, lout **5** dumbo, dummy, dunce, idiot, moron **6** dimwit, nitwit **7** half-wit **8** imbecile, lunkhead, numskull **9** lamebrain, numbskull, simpleton

Creusa *brother:* 6 Haemon *father:* **5** Priam *husband:* **6** Aeneas *mother:* **6** Hecuba *sister:* **6** Glauce, Glauke *son:* **3** Ion **8** Ascanius

crevice 3 gap **4** seam, slit **5** chink, cleft, crack **6** cranny **7** fissure **8** cleavage **10** interstice

crew 4 band, bevy, gang, team **5** bunch, covey, group, party **6** rowers, rowing **7** company, sailors *leader:* **3** cox **8** coxswain

crib 3 bed, bin, box, hut, key **4** pony, trot **5** cheat, crate, hovel, shack, stall, steal, theft

6 cradle, crèche, manger, pilfer **7** barrier, brothel **8** bassinet, bedstead, bordello **9** enclosure **10** plagiarism, plagiarize

Crichton novel 11 Terminal Man (The) **12** Jurassic Park **15** Andromeda Strain (The)

cricket *period of play:* **7** innings *team:* **6** eleven *term:* **3** leg, off, rot **4** bowl **5** pitch **6** bowler, wicket, yorker **7** batsman, striker **9** fieldsman *turn at bat:* **4** over

crime 3 sin **4** evil, tort, vice **5** caper **6** breach, delict, felony **7** misdeed, offense **8** atrocity, iniquity **9** diablerie, violation **10** corruption, illegality, infraction, wrongdoing **11** misdemeanor **13** transgression *instructor:* **5** Fagin

Crimea *city:* **5** Kerch, Yalta **10** Sebastopol, Sevastopol, Simferopol *river:* **4** Alma *sea:* **4** Azov **5** Black *strait:* **5** Kerch

criminal 4 hood, thug **5** crook, felon, shady **6** outlaw **7** convict, corrupt, crooked, hoodlum, illegal, illicit, lawless, mobster **8** culpable, fugitive, gangster, jailbird, offender, scofflaw, unlawful, wrongful **9** desperado, felonious, miscreant, nefarious, racketeer, wrongdoer **10** delinquent, lawbreaker, malefactor, trespasser **12** illegitimate, transgressor *habitual:* **8** repeater **10** recidivist *intent:* **7** mens rea

criminate see **incriminate**

crimp 4 bend, curb, wave **5** frizz **6** crease, hamper, hold in **7** crinkle, inhibit, wrinkle **8** hold back, obstacle, restrain **9** constrain, restraint **10** impediment **11** obstruction

crimson 3 red **4** rose **5** blush, color, flush **6** redden

cringe 4 duck **5** cower, hunch, quail, wince **6** blench, flinch, recoil, shrink

crinkle 4 ruck **5** crimp, plica, ridge **6** crease, furrow, pucker, ruck up, rumple, rustle **7** crackle, crumple, scrunch, wrinkle **11** corrugation

crinkly 5 crepy **6** crepey, frizzy **7** frizzed **8** wrinkled

cripple 4 lame, maim **6** mangle **7** disable **8** mutilate, paralyze **9** hamstring, undermine **10** debilitate **12** incapacitate

crippled 4 halt, lame **6** maimed **7** gnarled, mangled **8** battered, deformed, disabled, weakened **9** enfeebled, misshapen, mutilated, paralyzed **11** debilitated, handicapped

crisis 4 crux, pass **5** pinch **6** climax, crunch, height, strait **7** impasse, straits **8** disaster, exigency, juncture, zero hour **9** emergency, extremity **10** crossroads **11** catastrophe, contingency **12** turning point

crisp 4 cold, cool, curl, deft, keen, neat, wavy **5** brisk, clean, crimp, curly, fresh, nippy, pithy, sharp, short **6** biting, chilly, lively, ripple, spruce **7** bracing, brittle, crunchy, cutting, wrinkle **8** clean-cut, clearcut, incisive **9** trenchant **11** stimulating **12** invigorating

crisscross 3 net **4** grid, mesh **5** weave **7** network, overlap **8** reticule **9** confusion, decussate, intersect, reticular **10** reticulate

criterion 4 norm **5** canon, gauge, ideal, model, tenet **7** measure, precept **8** exemplar, paradigm, standard **9** benchmark, yardstick **10** touchstone

critic 5 judge **6** carper, pundit **7** arbiter, caviler **8** caviller, censurer, quibbler, reviewer **9** belittler, nitpicker **10** disparager, mudslinger **11** commentator, connoisseur, faultfinder

critical 4 dire **5** acute, fussy **7** carping, crucial, finicky, pivotal, weighty **8** captious, caviling, decisive **9** desperate, important, momentous **10** belittling, censorious, conclusive, precarious **11** disparaging, significant **12** faultfinding **13** consequential, determinative, hairsplitting *study:* **6** examen **8** exegesis

criticism 4 flak, slap **5** blame, cavil, swipe **6** rebuke, review **7** censure, comment, opinion, reproof **8** analysis, judgment, reproach **9** appraisal, objection **10** assessment, commentary, evaluation, nitpicking **11** examination, observation **12** faultfinding

criticize 3 pan, rap **4** bash, carp, flay **5** blame, blast, cavil, chide, fault, judge, knock, roast, scold **6** assess, rebuke, review, scathe **7** blister, censure, condemn, nitpick, reprove **8** appraise, badmouth, chastise, denounce, evaluate, lambaste **9** castigate, disparage, dress down, excoriate, find fault, reprehend, reprimand, reprobate

critique see **criticism**

critter 5 beast **6** animal **7** varmint

Crius *father:* **6** Uranus *mother:* **4** Gaea *son:* **8** Astraeus

croak 3 die **6** cackle, cash in, expire, go west, squawk **7** go south, grumble, snuff it **8** check out

croaker 4 drum, fish, frog **6** doctor

croaky 5 gruff, husky, raspy **6** hoarse **8** gravelly

Croatia *capital:* **6** Zagreb *city:* **5** Split, Zadar **6** Osijek, Rijeka **9** Dubrovnik *monetary unit:* **4** kuna *neighbor:* **6** Bosnia, Serbia **7** Hungary **8** Slovenia *part of:* **7** Balkans *region:* **8** Dalmatia, Slavonia

crock 3 jar, lie, pot **4** tale **6** tureen **7** cripple, disable, fiction **9** break down **11** fabrication

crocked 3 lit **4** high **5** drunk, lit up, oiled, tipsy **6** bashed, blotto, bombed, juiced, potted, soaked, soused, stewed, stoned, tanked, wasted, zonked **7** drunken, pickled, pie-eyed, sloshed, smashed **9** plastered **10** inebriated, liquored up **11** intoxicated

crocodile 7 reptile *bird:* **6** plover *Indian:* **6** gavial **7** gharial *relative:* **9** alligator *South American:* **6** caiman, cayman *Southeast Asian:* **6** mugger

Croesus' kingdom 5 Lydia

croft 4 farm **5** field

crofter 4 hind **6** farmer

Cromwell, Oliver 13 lord protector *battle:* **6** Naseby **11** Marston Moor *party:* **10** Roundheads *regiment:* **9** Ironsides *son:* **7** Richard *victim:* **7** Charles (I)

crone 3 hag **4** trot **5** biddy, witch **6** beldam **7** beldame

Cronus 5 Titan **6** Saturn *daughter:* **4** Hera **6** Hestia **7** Demeter *father:* **6** Uranus *mother:* **4** Gaea *sister:* **4** Rhea **6** Cybele, Tethys *son:* **4** Zeus **5** Hades **7** Jupiter, Neptune **8** Poseidon *wife:* **4** Rhea **6** Cybele

crony 3 pal **4** chum **5** buddy **6** cohort **7** comrade **8** sidekick **9** associate, companion **10** accomplice **11** confederate

crook 3 bow **4** bend, flex, hook, wind **5** angle, curve, staff, thief **6** bandit, robber **7** burglar, crosier, hoodlum, pothook **8** criminal

crooked 4 awry **5** askew, lying, shady, venal **6** curved, errant, jagged, shifty, skewed, zigzag **7** bending, corrupt, devious, illegal, illicit, slanted **8** cockeyed, criminal, ruthless, tortuous, twisting **9** deceitful, dishonest, nefarious, underhand, unethical **10** fraudulent, mendacious, untruthful **11** duplicitous, underhanded **12** unscrupulous **13** double-dealing

croon 4 sing **6** murmur, warble

crooner 4 Cole (Nat "King"), Como (Perry) **5** Laine (Frankie), Tormé (Mel) **6** Crosby (Bing), Martin (Dean), singer, Vallee (Rudy) **7** Bennett (Tony), Sinatra (Frank) **8** Eckstine (Billy), vocalist, Williams (Andy)

crop 3 bob, cut, hew, lop, mow **4** chop, clip, pare, snip, trim **5** prune, shave, shear, stock, yield **6** gullet, handle, output **7** harvest, produce **8** fruitage, truncate **10** collection

croquet 5 roque

crosier 5 crook, staff

cross 3 mad **4** mule, rood, span **5** angry, surly, testy, trial **6** betray, bridge, crabby, cranky, grumpy, hybrid, negate, oppose, tetchy, touchy **7** athwart, calvary, grouchy, mongrel, peevish **8** captious, choleric, traverse **9** half blood, half-breed, hybridize, intersect, irascible, irritable, querulous,

splenetic **10** affliction, contradict, interbreed, transverse **12** cantankerous *a river:* **4** ford *bearer:* **8** crucifer *decoration:* **4** Iron **8** Victoria *kind:* **3** tau **4** ankh **5** Greek, Latin, papal **6** Celtic, fleury, formée, moline, pommée, potent **7** avellan, botonée, Calvary, Maltese, saltire **8** crucifix, fourchée, Lorraine, quadrate **11** patriarchal **12** Saint Andrew's **13** Saint Anthony's *section:* **5** slice

crossbow 8 arbalest, arbalist

crossbreed 4 mule **6** hybrid **7** bastard, mongrel **9** half blood, hybridize

cross-eye 6 squint **10** strabismus

crossing 8 junction, overpass, traverse **9** traversal, underpass **10** transverse **11** decussation, interchange, transversal **12** intersection

cross out 5 erase **6** cancel, delete, efface, excise **7** expunge

crosspatch 4 crab **5** crank, grump **6** griper, grouch **7** grouser **8** grumbler, sorehead, sourpuss **10** complainer, curmudgeon

crossroads 4 crux, pass **5** pinch **6** crisis, strait **8** exigency, juncture, zero hour **9** carrefour, emergency **11** contingency **12** intersection, turning point *goddess:* **6** Hecate, Hekate, Trivia

cross-shaped 8 cruciate **9** cruciform

crossways 6 aslant **7** athwart, oblique **8** diagonal **9** obliquely **10** diagonally, transverse **11** catercorner, cattycorner, kitty-corner **12** transversely

crotchet 3 bee **4** whim **5** fancy, freak, quirk, trick **6** foible, megrim, notion, vagary **7** caprice, conceit **11** quarter note **12** eccentricity

crotchety 5 testy **6** crabby, cranky, crusty, ornery, tetchy, touchy **7** bearish, peevish, prickly **8** contrary, snappish, vinegary **9** difficult, eccentric, irascible **10** vinegarish **11** ill-tempered **12** cantankerous, cross-grained

crouch 4 bend, duck **5** cower, hunch, squat, stoop **6** cringe, huddle, shrink **10** hunker down

croup 3 bum **4** butt, hack, rear, rump, seat, tail **5** cough, edema, whoop **6** behind **7** keister, rear end, tail end **8** backside, buttocks, derriere, haunches **9** posterior

croupier tool 4 rake

crow 4 blow, brag, puff **5** boast, exult, gloat, prate, vaunt **6** cackle **7** bluster **9** gasconade, humble pie *colony:* **7** rookery *cry:* **3** caw *family:* **6** corvid **8** Corvidae *genus:* **6** Corvus *relating to:* **7** corvine, corvoid *relative:* **3** daw, jay **4** rook **5** raven **6** chough, magpie **7** jackdaw, jaybird

crowbar 3 pry **5** jimmy, lever

crowd 3 jam, mob **4** army, bear, cram, fill, herd, host, mass, pack, pile, push, rout, ruck **5** bunch, crush, drove, flock, flood, group, horde, hurry, press, serry, shove, surge, swarm, troop **6** circle, clique, gaggle, huddle, jostle, legion, rabble, squash, squish, stream, throng **7** cluster, collect, company, coterie, squeeze **8** assembly **9** gathering, multitude **10** assemblage, collection **11** aggregation **12** congregation

crowded 4 full **5** awash, close, dense, thick, tight **6** loaded **7** brimful, compact, teeming **8** brimming, populous, swarming **9** chock-full, congested, jam-packed

crown 3 cap, top **4** acme, apex, peak, roof **5** cover, crest, tiara **6** climax, diadem, laurel, summit, top off, vertex, wreath, zenith **7** chaplet, coronal, coronet, garland, overlay, perfect **8** pinnacle, round off, surmount **9** culminate, finish off **10** consummate **11** culmination

crucial 4 dire **5** acute, vital **6** urgent **7** central, pivotal **8** critical, deciding, decisive **9** desperate, essential, important, momentous, necessary **10** imperative **11** climacteric, significant

crucible 4 test **5** trial **6** ordeal **8** acid test **10** melting pot

crucifix 4 rood **5** cross

crucifixion site 7 Calvary **8** Golgotha

crucify 4 rack **6** impale, martyr **7** mortify, pillory, torment, torture **10** excruciate

crud 3 goo **4** glop, gook, gunk, junk, muck **5** dreck, filth, slime, trash **6** debris, sludge **7** deposit, garbage, rubbish **12** incrustation

crude 3 raw **4** poor **5** crass, dirty, gross, rough **6** coarse, earthy, gauche, impure, ribald, risqué, vulgar **7** boorish, ill-bred, loutish, lowbred, obscene, obvious, raunchy, uncivil, uncouth **8** backward, cloddish, homespun, ignorant, indecent, inferior **9** elemental, graceless, inelegant, makeshift, primitive, rough-hewn, unrefined **10** amateurish, unfinished, unpolished

cruel 4 fell, grim, mean **5** harsh **6** brutal, fierce, savage **7** bestial, brutish, callous, heinous, vicious **8** inhumane, ruthless, sadistic **9** atrocious, barbarous, ferocious, heartless, merciless, monstrous, truculent **12** bloodthirsty

cruise 4 roam, rove, sail, surf, tour **5** drift, jaunt **6** junket, voyage **9** excursion

cruiser 4 boat **5** yacht **7** warship **8** squad car **9** patrol car, powerboat

crumb 3 bit, ort **4** iota **5** ounce, scrap, shred **6** morsel, sliver **7** smidgen **8** fragment, particle

crumble 5 decay **8** collapse **9** break down, decompose **11** deteriorate **12** disintegrate

crumbly 7 friable

crummy 4 poor **5** dingy, lousy, seedy, tacky **6** cruddy, flimsy, shoddy, sleazy **8** inferior

crumple 3 wad **4** cave **5** crimp **6** buckle, cave in, ruck up **7** crinkle, scrunch, wrinkle **8** collapse

crunch 4 chew **5** champ, chomp, grind, munch, sit-up **6** crisis **7** compute, process, squeeze **8** shortage, showdown

crusade 5 cause, drive **6** appeal **7** holy war **8** campaign, movement **9** offensive **10** expedition **11** undertaking

Crusader English: 7 Richard (Lionheart) **foe: 7** Saladin, Saracen **French: 5** Louis (IX) **6** Philip, Robert **7** Baldwin, Charles, Godfrey, Raymond, Raymund **8** Boniface, Montfort, Philippe, Theobald **German: 6** Conrad **9** Frederick, Friedrich **10** Barbarossa **Norman: 7** Tancred **8** Bohemund **preacher: 5** Peter (the Hermit), Urban (II) **7** Adhémar, Bernard **8** Innocent (III), Pelagius

crusading 11 evangelical **12** evangelistic

crush 3 jam, mob **4** cram, mash, pulp, push, ruin **5** crowd, drove, grind, horde, pound, press, quash, quell, smash, wreck **6** bruise, burden, defeat, reduce, squash, squish, subdue, throng **7** conquer, destroy, mortify, oppress, passion, put down, repress, scrunch, squeeze, squelch, squoosh, trample **8** bear down, beat down, demolish, overcome, suppress, vanquish **9** humiliate, multitude, overpower, overwhelm, pulverize, puppy love, subjugate **10** annihilate, extinguish, obliterate **11** infatuation

crust 4 cake, coat, rime, scab **7** coating, deposit **8** covering

crustacean 4 crab, flea **5** louse, prawn **6** isopod, shrimp, slater, sow bug **7** copepod, daphnia, decapod, lobster, pill bug **8** amphipod, barnacle, crawfish, crayfish, ostracod, sand flea **9** arthropod, beach flea, shellfish, water flea, wood louse **10** hermit crab, stomatopod, whale louse **11** branchiopod, fiddler crab **aggregate of: 5** krill **appendage: 7** pleopod **body segment: 6** somite, telson **8** metamere **claw: 5** chela **6** pincer **covering substance: 6** chitin **larva: 8** nauplius

crusty 4 curt **5** bluff, blunt, gross, gruff, short, surly **6** cranky **7** brusque, crabbed, prickly **8** choleric **9** irascible, irritable, saturnine, splenetic

crux 3 nub **4** core, gist, meat, pith **5** focus, heart **6** kernel, thrust **7** essence, purport **9** substance cry (see also **exclamation**) 3 sob 4 bawl, blub, call, howl, keen, mewl, moan, pule, wail, weep, yawp, yell, yelp, yowl 5 bleat, motto, mourn, shout, whine, whoop 6 boohoo, furore, holler, lament, scream, snivel, squall, squawk, squeak, squeal 7 blubber, screech, ululate, whimper 10 vociferate **bacchanals':** 4 evoe **calf:** 5 bleat **cat:** 3 mew 4 meow 5 miaow **cattle:** 3 low, moo **chick:** 4 peep 5 cheep **court:** 4 oyez **crane:** 5 clang **crow:** 3 caw **dog:** 3 arf 4 bark, woof **donkey:** 4 bray 6 hee-haw **duck:** 5 quack **frog:** 5 croak **goat:** 5 bleat **goose:** 4 honk 5 clang **hen:** 6 cackle **horse:** 5 neigh 6 nicker, whinny 7 whicker **lion:** 4 roar **owl:** 4 hoot **pig:** 4 oink 5 grunt **raven:** 3 caw 5 croak **rook:** 3 caw **sheep:** 5 bleat **songbird:** 5 chirp, tweet **turkey:** 6 gobble

cry down 5 decry 6 defame, deride, malign, revile, vilify 7 condemn 8 belittle, denounce, derogate, diminish 9 denigrate, deprecate, discredit, disparage 10 calumniate, depreciate 11 detract from, opprobriate

crying 4 dire 5 acute, vital 6 urgent 7 blatant, burning, clamant, exigent, heinous 8 flagrant, pressing, shocking 9 atrocious, clamorous, desperate, monstrous, notorious 10 compelling, imperative, outrageous, scandalous 11 importunate

crypt 5 vault 7 chamber 8 catacomb 9 mausoleum 10 undercroft

cryptic 5 vague 6 arcane, occult, opaque, secret 7 Delphic, obscure, unclear 8 abstruse, Delphian, esoteric, puzzling 9 ambiguous, enigmatic, recondite, tenebrous 10 mysterious, mystifying 12 unfathomable

crystal 4 lens 5 clear, lucid 6 limpid, lucent, quartz 8 clear-cut, luminous, pellucid 9 glassware, unblurred 11 translucent, transparent 12 transpicuous **gazer:** 4 seer 7 psychic 11 clairvoyant **set:** 5 radio

cry up 4 laud, puff 5 boost, extol 6 praise 7 acclaim

cub 3 pup 4 baby, tyro 6 novice, rookie 8 neophyte 9 offspring, youngster 10 apprentice

Cuba capital: 6 Havana **city:** 7 Holguín 8 Camagüey, Santiago 10 Guantánamo, Santa Clara **discoverer:** 8 Columbus (Christopher) **language:** 7 Spanish **leader:** 6 Castro (Fidel) 7 Batista (Fulgencio), Guevara (Che) **monetary unit:** 4 peso **sea:** 9 Caribbean

cubbyhole 5 niche 6 alcove, recess 7 cubicle

cube 4 dice 5 mince

Cub Scout rank: 4 Bear, Lion, Wolf 6 Bobcat 7 Webelos **unit:** 3 den 4 pack

Cuchulain father: 3 Lug 4 Lugh 5 Lugus **foe:** 4 Medb 5 Maeve **kingdom:** 6 Ulster **lord:** 9 Conchobar **mother:** 8 Dechtire **son:** 8 Conlaoch **victim:** 8 Conlaoch **wife:** 4 Emer

cuckoo 3 mad, nut 4 daft, kook, nuts 5 batty, crank, crazy, daffy, loony, loopy, nutty, potty, silly, wacko, wacky 6 crazed, fruity, insane, screwy, whacky 7 bonkers, cracked, idiotic, lunatic, nutcase 8 crackpot, demented 9 ding-a-ling, harebrain, screwball 12 crackbrained **bird:** 3 ani 8 keelbill

cucumber 4 pepo 7 gherkin

cuddle 3 hug, pet 4 neck, snug 5 spoon 6 burrow, caress, clinch, cosset, dandle, fondle, nestle, nuzzle 7 embrace, snuggle, squeeze 8 canoodle

cuddly 7 lovable, snuggly 8 huggable 11 embraceable

cudgel 5 bat, sap 4 club, cosh, mace 5 baton, billy 7 war club 8 bludgeon 9 bastinado, billy club, blackjack, truncheon 10 knobkerrie, nightstick, shillelagh

cue 3 key, nod, rod, tip 4 clue, hint, lead, prod, sign 5 alert 6 insert, notion, prompt, signal, tip-off 7 heads-up, inkling, warning 8 high sign, reminder, telltale 10 indication, intimation, suggestion

cuff 3 box, hit 4 belt, blip, clip, poke, slap, sock 5 clout, fight, punch, smack, whack 6 bangle, buffet, wallop 7 clobber, scuffle 8 bracelet, wristlet

cul-de-sac 5 pouch 6 pocket 7 dead end, impasse 10 blind alley 12 diverticulum

cull 4 pick, sift, thin 5 elect, glean 6 choose, garner, gather, select, winnow 7 extract, thin out

culminate 4 peak 5 crest 6 climax

culmination 3 top 4 acme, apex, peak 6 apogee, capper, climax, height, payoff, summit, zenith 8 capstone, pinnacle 11 ne plus ultra 12 consummation

culpability 4 onus 5 blame, fault, guilt

culpable 6 guilty, liable, sinful 7 at fault 8 blamable, blameful 10 censurable, delinquent 11 blameworthy, impeachable, responsible 13 reprehensible

cult 3 fad 4 sect 5 creed, faith 6 church 8 religion 10 persuasion 12 denomination

cultivable 6 arable 8 tillable

cultivate 4 farm, grow, tend, till 5 breed, nurse, raise 6 enrich, foster, refine 7 cherish, develop, further, improve, nourish, nurture, produce, promote 9 encourage, propagate

cultivated 6 urbane 7 genteel, refined 8 cultured, polished, well-bred

cultivation 6 polish 7 culture, tillage 8 breeding 10 refinement 11 development

culture 4 grow 5 taste 6 foster 7 nurture 9 cultivate, erudition, gentility 10 refinement 11 cultivation 12 civilization 13 enlightenment

cultured 6 urbane 7 erudite, genteel, learned, refined 8 educated, highbrow, literate, polished, well-bred 9 civilized 10 cultivated 11 enlightened

culture medium 4 agar

cum ____ salis 5 grano

cumber 4 clog, lade, load 6 burden, hinder, hobble, impede, saddle 7 clutter 8 handicap 9 hindrance

cumbersome 5 bulky, heavy, hefty 6 clumsy 7 awkward 8 unwieldy 9 lumbering, ponderous 10 slow-moving

cumshaw 3 fee, tip 5 bribe 6 payoff 7 present 8 gratuity, largesse 9 baksheesh, lagniappe, pourboire 10 perquisite

cumulate 4 heap 5 amass, hoard, lay up, store 6 garner, gather, pile up 7 collect, combine, store up 9 stockpile

cumulation 4 heap, mass, pile 5 cache, hoard, trove 9 stockpile 10 collection 11 aggregation 13 agglomeration

cumulative 8 additive, compound 9 summative 10 compounded, increasing

cunning 3 sly 4 cute, foxy, keen, wary, wily 5 acute, cagey, canny, craft, guile, savvy, sharp, skill, slick, smart 6 adroit, artful, astute, clever, crafty, deceit, shifty, tricky 7 finesse, know-how, slyness 8 artifice, caginess, deftness, facility, foxiness, guileful, slippery, subtlety, wiliness 9 adeptness, cageyness, canniness, dexterity, dexterous, duplicity, ingenious, ingenuity, insidious, sharpness, slickness 10 adroitness, artfulness, cleverness, craftiness, shiftiness, shrewdness, trickiness

cup 3 mug 4 toby 5 grail, jorum, stein 6 beaker, goblet, seidel 7 chalice, tankard 8 schooner *handle:* 3 ear, lug *holder:* 6 saucer *liturgical:* 3 ama 5 calix 7 chalice *Scottish:* 4 tass *small:* 6 noggin 8 cannikin, pannikin 9 demitasse *sports:* 5 Davis, Ryder, World 6 Curtis, Nextel 7 Stanley 8 America's, Wightman

cupbearer of the gods 4 Hebe 8 Ganymede

cupboard 5 ambry, cuddy 6 buffet, closet, larder, pantry 7 armoire, cabinet 8 credence, credenza 9 sideboard

Cupid 4 Amor, Eros 5 putto 6 cherub 8 amoretto *beloved:* 6 Psyche *brother:* 7 Anteros *father:* 6 Hermes 7 Mercury *mother:* 5 Venus 9 Aphrodite *title:* 3 Dan

cupidity 4 lust 5 greed 6 desire 7 avarice, avidity, craving, lechery, passion 8 rapacity, voracity 9 eagerness, esurience 10 greediness 11 infatuation 12 covetousness 13 rapaciousness

cupola 4 dome 5 vault 6 turret 7 furnace, lookout

cur 3 dog 4 mutt 7 mongrel

curate 6 cleric, priest 9 churchman, clergyman

curative 4 pill 5 tonic 6 elixir, relief, remedy 7 healing, nostrum, panacea, therapy 8 antidote, remedial, salutary, sanative, solution 9 healthful, medicinal, remedying, treatment, wholesome 10 beneficial, corrective 11 restorative, therapeutic 12 health-giving

curator 6 keeper, warden 9 caretaker, custodian 11 conservator

curb 3 bit 4 deny, rein 5 check, frame, leash, tie up 6 border, bridle, edging, fetter, hamper, hobble, hold in, rein in, subdue 7 abstain, contain, control, inhibit, refrain, repress 8 hold back, hold down, restrain, suppress, withhold 9 constrain, entrammel, restraint *British:* 4 kerb

curdle 4 clot, sour, turn 5 spoil 7 clabber, congeal, thicken 9 coagulate

curdling substance 6 rennet

cure 3 age, spa 4 heal, mend 5 treat 6 elixir, kipper, physic, pickle, relief, remedy 7 rectify, relieve, restore, therapy 8 antidote, medicant, medicine, preserve, recovery, solution 10 ameliorate, corrective 12 counteragent 13 counteractive

cure-all 6 elixir 7 nostrum, panacea 10 catholicon

curio 6 oddity, whimsy 7 novelty, whatsit 9 objet d'art

curiosity 5 freak 6 marvel, oddity, rarity, whimsy, wonder 7 anomaly, concern, novelty 8 interest, nonesuch

curious 3 odd 4 nosy 5 nosey, novel, queer, weird 6 exotic, prying, quaint, snoopy 7 bizarre, oddball, strange, unusual 8 meddling, peculiar, puzzling, singular 9 inquiring, intrusive 11 inquisitive, questioning

curium symbol 2 Cm

curl 4 coil, kink, wind 5 frizz, twine, twist 6 spiral 7 contort, crinkle, entwine, frizzle, ringlet, wreathe 9 corkscrew

curling *match:* 8 bonspiel *period of play:* 3 end *team:* 4 four *term:* 3 tee 4 hack, rink 5 house, stone

curly 4 wavy 5 kinky 6 frizzy

currency 4 cash, coin 5 dough, lucre, money, scrip 7 coinage 8 banknote 10 acceptance, prevalence **11** legal tender *unit:* see individual country

current 4 eddy, flow, flux, race, rush, tide **5** drift, flood, spate, tenor, trend **6** extant, modern, strain, stream **7** instant, ongoing, popular, present, regnant, topical **8** accepted, existent, existing, tendency, up-to-date **9** prevalent **10** present-day, prevailing, widespread **11** fashionable **12** contemporary *air:* **4** gale, gust, wind **5** blast, draft **6** breeze, squall, zephyr **7** cyclone, indraft, updraft **9** downdraft **10** slipstream *ocean:* **7** riptide **8** undertow **9** maelstrom, whirlpool *unit:* **3** amp **6** ampere

Currier's partner 4 Ives (James)

curry 4 beat, comb, seek, whip **5** groom **6** thrash

curse 3 hex, pox **4** bane, cuss, damn, evil, jinx, oath **5** swear **6** blight, plague, whammy **7** afflict, damning, malison, scourge, torment **8** anathema, cussword, execrate **9** bête noire, blaspheme, blasphemy, expletive, imprecate, profanity, swearword **10** affliction, execration, misfortune, pestilence **11** commination, imprecation, malediction, profanation **12** anathematize, denunciation

cursed 6 damned **7** blasted, dratted **8** damnable, infernal **9** execrable **10** confounded **13** blankety-blank

cursive 6 fluent, smooth **7** flowing, running

cursory 5 hasty, quick, rapid **6** casual **7** hurried, shallow, sketchy **8** careless **10** uncritical **11** perfunctory, superficial

curt 4 rude **5** bluff, blunt, brief, gruff, short, terse **6** abrupt, crusty **7** brusque, concise **8** succinct **10** peremptory

curtail 3 cut **4** clip, dock, trim **5** prune, slash **6** lessen, reduce **7** abridge, cut back, shorten **8** diminish, pare down, retrench, truncate **10** abbreviate

curtain 4 drop, veil **5** drape **6** screen **7** barrier *doorway:* **8** portiere *holder:* **3** rod *Indian:* **6** purdah *material:* **4** lace, silk **5** gauze **6** damask, velvet **8** chenille, jacquard *rod concealer:* **7** valance *sash:* **7** tieback *stage:* **4** drop **5** scrim **8** backdrop

curtains 3 end **4** ruin **5** death **6** demise, finish **7** decease **8** disaster

curtilage 4 quad, yard **5** court **8** cloister **9** courtyard, enclosure **10** quadrangle

curvaceous 5 buxom **7** rounded, shapely **9** Junoesque **10** statuesque, voluptuous **13** well-developed

curvature *of the spine:* **8** kyphosis, lordosis **9** scoliosis

curve 3 arc, bow **4** arch, bend, coil, curl, turn,

veer, wind **5** crook, round, swing, swirl, twist **6** convex, spiral, swerve **7** concave, flexure, rondure **9** corkscrew *of an arch:* **8** extrados, intrados *pitcher's:* **4** hook *plane:* **7** cycloid, limaçon **8** parabola, sinusoid, trochoid **9** hyperbola *S-shaped:* **3** ess **4** ogee **7** sigmoid

curved 4 bent **5** arced, bowed, round **6** arched, convex **7** arcuate, bending, embowed, falcate, rounded, sigmoid, sinuous, twisted *implement:* **6** sickle *molding:* **4** ogee *sword:* **5** kukri, saber, sabre **7** cutlass **8** scimitar

curvilinear see **curved**

curvy see **curvaceous; curved**

Cush *father:* **3** Ham *son:* **6** Nimrod

cushion 3 mat, pad **5** squab **6** absorb, buffer, pillow, soften **7** bolster, hassock, pillion **8** palliate, woolsack

cushy 4 cozy, easy, soft **11** comfortable, undemanding

cusp 3 tip **4** apex, edge, peak **5** point, verge **12** turning point

cuspid 6 canine **8** eyetooth

cuspidate 5 sharp **6** peaked, pointy **7** pointed

cuss 3 guy, man **4** chap, damn, dude, oath **5** curse, swear **6** fellow **9** expletive

cussed 4 dour **5** crude, gruff **6** crusty, cursed, grumpy, ornery **7** boorish, brusque, grouchy **8** churlish **9** obstinate **10** unyielding **11** contentious **12** antagonistic, cantankerous

cussword 4 oath **5** curse **9** expletive, swearword

custard 4 flan **7** pudding

custodian 5 super **6** keeper, porter, warden **7** curator, steward **8** guardian, overseer, watchdog, watchman **9** caretaker, concierge, protector **10** supervisor **11** conservator

custody 4 care, ward **5** guard, trust **6** charge **7** keeping **9** captivity, detention **10** caretaking, management, protection **11** confinement, safekeeping, supervision **12** guardianship

custom 3 use **4** norm **5** habit, mores (plural), trade, usage **6** groove, manner, praxis, ritual **7** folkway, precept, routine, traffic **8** business, habitude, practice **9** patronage **10** consuetude, convention

customary 5 usual **6** common, normal, wonted **7** general, regular, routine **8** accepted, everyday, familiar, frequent, habitual, ordinary, orthodox, standard **10** accustomed **11** established, traditional **12** conventional

custom-built 7 bespoke **10** tailor-made **11** made-to-order

customer 5 buyer 6 client, patron 7 shopper 8 consumer 9 purchaser *frequent:* 7 habitué
customized see **custom-built**
custom-made see **custom-built**
cut 3 bob, hew, lop, mow, saw 4 bite, chop, clip, crop, dice, dock, fell, gash, hack, nick, pare, reap, sawn, skip, slit, snip, snub, trim 5 carve, filet, lathe, lower, mince, notch, piece, prune, quota, sawed, sever, share, shave, shear, slash, slice, split, wound 6 cleave, delete, dilute, divide, excise, fillet, incise, reduce, scythe, sickle, sunder 7 abridge, curtail, dissect, portion, section, segment, shorten 8 division, separate, truncate 9 allotment, allowance, reduction 10 abbreviate *of beef:* 3 rib 4 loin, rump 5 chine, chuck, flank, roast, shank, steak, T-bone 6 saddle 7 brisket, sirloin 9 aitchbone 11 porterhouse
cut across 6 bisect 8 transect 9 transcend
cut-and-dried 5 stock 7 routine 9 formulaic 10 unoriginal 11 predictable 13 unimaginative
cutaneous 6 dermal
cutaway 4 coat, dive 5 tails
cut back 3 zag 4 clip, curb, dock, pare, trim 5 lower, prune, shave, slash 6 lessen, reduce 7 abridge, curtail, shorten 8 decrease, retrench, truncate 10 abbreviate
cut down 3 axe 4 chop, clip, fell, pare 5 lower, shave, slash 6 digest, reduce 7 abridge, shorten 10 abbreviate
cute 4 twee 6 dainty, pretty 7 cunning 8 affected 10 attractive 11 impertinent, smart-alecky
cut in 7 include, intrude, obtrude 9 introduce
cutlass 5 saber, sabre, sword 7 machete 8 scimitar
cut off 2 ax 3 axe, bar, end, lop 4 halt, kill, stop 5 abort, block, sever 6 disown 7 curtail, destroy, isolate, suspend 8 amputate, obstruct, renounce, separate, truncate 9 intercept, interrupt, terminate 10 disinherit 11 discontinue
cut out 3 end 4 halt 5 cease, leave, scram, usurp 6 beat it, delete, depart, escape, excise, remove, resect 7 defraud, deprive, take off 8 displace, supplant 9 eliminate, extirpate 10 disconnect
cutpurse 5 thief 10 pickpocket
cut short 3 bob 4 clip, crop, dock, halt, poll 5 abort, check, scrub, shear 7 abridge, curtail 8 break off 9 interrupt, terminate 10 abbreviate
cuttable 7 sectile 8 scissile
cutthroat 5 bravo 6 gunman, hit man, killer 7

torpedo 8 assassin, murderer 10 hatchet man, triggerman
cutting 5 acerb 7 acerbic 8 incisive, piercing 9 sarcastic, trenchant 11 penetrating *edge:* 5 blade *remark:* 3 dig 4 barb 5 taunt *tool:* 2 ax 3 axe, hob, saw 4 adze 5 knife, lathe, mower, plane, razor 6 reaper, scythe, shears, sickle 7 hatchet 8 scissors, tomahawk
cuttlefish 7 mollusc, mollusk 10 cephalopod *ink:* 5 sepia *relative:* 5 squid 7 octopus
cut up 4 dice, hash, romp 5 caper, clown, mince, slash 6 cavort 7 carry on, show off 9 misbehave 10 roughhouse
cutup 3 wag 4 zany 5 clown, joker 6 madcap 7 buffoon, farceur 8 jokester
cyan 4 blue
Cybele 4 Rhea *beloved:* 5 Attis *brother:* 6 Cronus *father:* 6 Uranus *husband:* 6 Cronus *mother:* 4 Gaea *son:* 4 Zeus 7 Jupiter, Neptune 8 Poseidon
cyber 5 wired 10 electronic
cybernetics founder 6 Wiener (Norbert)
cycle 3 age, lap, set 4 bike, loop, ring 5 chain, orbit, recur, round, wheel 6 course, period, series 7 circuit 8 rotation, sequence 9 vibration 10 revolution, succession, two-wheeler, velocipede 11 oscillation
cycle track 9 velodrome
cyclic 7 regular 8 periodic, repeated, rhythmic 9 iterative, recurring, repeating 10 isochronal 12 intermittent
cyclone 7 tornado, twister
cyclopean 4 huge 7 immense, mammoth, massive, titanic 8 colossal, enormous, gigantic 9 monstrous 10 gargantuan, tremendous 11 elephantine
Cyclops 5 Arges 7 Brontes 8 Steropes 10 Polyphemus
Cycnus *father:* 4 Ares, Mars *slayer:* 8 Heracles, Hercules
cygnet 4 swan *dam (mother):* 3 pen *sire (father):* 3 cob
Cygnus *form:* 4 swan *friend:* 7 Phaeton *star:* 5 Deneb
cylinder 4 drum, pipe, tube 5 spool 6 barrel, bobbin, platen, roller
cylindrical 6 terete 7 tubular 8 tubelike
Cymbeline *daughter:* 6 Imogen *son:* 9 Arviragus, Guiderius *son-in-law:* 9 Posthumus
Cymric 5 Welsh 6 Celtic 9 Brythonic *bard:* 8 Taliesin *Elysium:* 6 Annwfn
god: 5 Lludd *of Elysium:* 5 Arawn *of the dead:* 5 Pwyll *of the seas:* 3 Ler 4 Llyr 5 Dylan *of the sky:* 7 Gwydion *of the sun:* 4 Lleu, Llew *of the underworld:* 4 Gwyn

goddess: 3 Don 9 Arianrhod **magician:** 6 Merlin
Cymru 5 Wales
cynical 8 derisive, sardonic, scornful 12 misanthropic
Cynthia 4 Luna, moon 5 Diana 7 Artemis
cyprian 4 bawd, jade, slut, tart 5 hussy, tramp 6 floozy, harlot, hooker, wanton 7 jezebel, trollop 8 slattern, strumpet 10 prostitute
Cyprus capital: 7 Nicosia 8 Lefkosia **city:** 7 Larnaca 8 Limassol **language:** 5 Greek 7 Turkish **monetary unit:** 4 lira 5 pound **mountain:** 7 Olympus **port:** 9 Famagusta **sea:** 13 Mediterranean
Cyrano de Bergerac 4 poet 7 duelist 8 duellist **author:** 7 Rostand (Edmond) **beloved:** 6 Roxane 7 Roxanne **feature:** 4 nose **rival:** 9 Christian
Cyrus conquest: 5 Lydia, Media 7 Babylon

daughter: 6 Atossa **empire:** 7 Persian **father:** 8 Cambyses **son:** 8 Cambyses
cyst 3 sac, wen 4 sore 5 pouch, spore 6 growth 7 abscess, blister, capsule, vesicle 8 swelling
Cytherea 4 isle 5 Venus 6 island 9 Aphrodite
czar 5 chief, mogul 6 despot, honcho, tycoon, tyrant 7 emperor, kingpin, magnate 8 autocrat **Russian:** 4 Ivan 5 Basil, Boris, Peter 6 Alexis, Dmitry, Feodor, Fyodor, Vasily 7 Dimitri, Michael, Romanov 8 Nicholas, Romanoff, Theodore 9 Alexander 12 Boris Godunov **son:** 10 czarevitch **wife:** 7 czarina
czar's wife 7 czarina
Czech Republic capital: 6 Prague **city:** 4 Brno 7 Ostrava **monetary unit:** 6 koruna **neighbor:** 6 Poland 7 Austria, Germany 8 Slovakia **region:** 7 Bohemia, Moravia **river:** 4 Labe, Oder 5 March 6 Morava

D

dab 3 bit, pat 4 blob, blow, daub, peck, poke, spot 5 smear, touch 6 bedaub 7 besmear, plaster, splotch 8 flatfish
dabble 3 dip, dot, toy 4 fool, stud 5 fleck 6 dampen, fiddle, monkey, pepper, putter, splash, tinker 7 freckle, spatter, stipple 8 sprinkle 9 bespeckle, muck about 10 muck around
dabbler 4 duck, tyro 7 amateur 8 putterer, tinkerer 9 smatterer 10 dilettante
dabchick 5 grebe
dacha 5 villa 7 cottage 12 country house
dad 3 pop 4 papa 5 padre, pater 6 father, old man, parent
Dadaist 3 Arp (Jean), Ray (Man) 4 Ball (Hugo) 5 Ernst (Max), Grosz (George), Tzara (Tristan) 7 Duchamp (Marcel), Picabia (Francis) 10 Schwitters (Kurt)
daedal 6 knotty 7 complex 8 artistic, involved, skillful 9 elaborate, intricate 11 complicated 12 labyrinthine 13 sophisticated
Daedalus 7 builder 9 architect, artificer **construction:** 9 Labyrinth **father:** 6 Metion **son:** 6 Icarus **victim:** 5 Talos 6 Perdix
daffy see **daft**
daft 3 mad 4 loco, nuts 5 balmy, crazy, dopey, flaky, loony, nutty, potty, silly, wacko,

wacky 6 absurd, crazed, cuckoo, insane, screwy 7 cracked, foolish, idiotic, lunatic, witless 8 demented 10 unbalanced 11 harebrained
Dag father: 7 Delling **horse:** 9 Skinfaksi **mother:** 4 Nott
Dagda chief god of the: 5 Gaels, Irish **daughter:** 6 Brigit **instrument:** 4 harp **son:** 6 Aengus **wife:** 5 Boann
dagger 4 dirk, snee 5 skean, skene 6 bodkin, stylet 7 dudgeon, poniard 8 stiletto **handle:** 4 hilt **Malay:** 4 kris
_____ **Dahl** 5 Roald 6 Arlene
daikon 6 radish
daily 7 diurnal 8 everyday 9 circadian, quotidian **grind:** 7 rat race
dainty 5 goody, tasty, treat 6 choice, morsel, select, tidbit 7 elegant, fragile 8 delicacy, delicate, ethereal, graceful, kickshaw 9 exquisite, recherché 10 delightful
dairy 8 creamery
dais 5 stage 6 podium 7 rostrum 8 platform
daisy 5 oxeye 6 Shasta **British:** 10 moonflower **Scottish:** 5 gowan
Daisy Miller author 5 James (Henry)
Dakota dialect 5 Teton
Daksha's father 6 Brahma
dale 4 dell, glen, vale 6 dingle, valley

Dallas series *character:* 3 Liz, Ray 4 Jack, Jock, Lucy 5 April, Bobby, Cally, Cliff, Donna, James, Jenna 6 Carter 7 Clayton, J. R. Ewing, Kristin 8 Michelle, Sue Ellen 9 Miss Ellie *family:* 5 Ewing *ranch home:* 9 Southfork *star:* 4 Gray (Linda), Keel (Howard), Reed (Donna) 5 Davis (Jim), Duffy (Patrick), Rambo (Dack) 6 Crosby (Mary), Hagman (Larry), Howard (Susan), Kanaly (Steve), Tilton (Charlene), Wilson (Sheree) 7 Presley (Priscilla) 9 Bel Geddes (Barbara), Kercheval (Ken), Principal (Victoria)

dally 3 lag, pet, toy 4 drag, idle, play 5 delay, flirt, tarry 6 coquet, dawdle, diddle, linger, loiter, trifle 8 lollygag 9 hang about, waste time 10 fool around

dam 4 weir 5 block, check 7 barrier 8 hold back, restrain *major:* 4 Oahe 6 Hoover 7 San Luis 8 Fort Peck, Garrison, Oroville 10 Bonneville, Glen Canyon 11 Grand Coulee

damage 3 mar 4 blot, harm, hurt, loss, maim, ruin 5 abuse, burst, cloud, spoil, stain, wound 6 blight, deface, impair, injure, injury, mangle, ravage, scathe 7 blemish, destroy, marring, tarnish, vitiate 8 maltreat, mischief, mistreat, mutilate, sabotage 9 devastate, vandalism 10 impairment 11 devastation

damaged 4 hurt, rent 6 broken, busted, dinged, flawed, marred 7 injured, spoiled, totaled 8 battered, impaired, ruptured 9 blemished, fractured, imperfect, shattered 10 fragmented

damaging 6 nocent 7 harmful, hurtful, nocuous 9 injurious 11 deleterious, detrimental, prejudicial

dame 4 lady 5 woman 6 gammer, matron 7 dowager 9 matriarch

Damien's island 7 Molokai

Damkina's son 6 Marduk

damn 4 cuss, darn, doom, drat 5 curse, swear 7 condemn, doggone 8 execrate, sentence 9 imprecate 10 vituperate 12 anathematize

damnable 6 blamed, cursed, cussed 7 blasted, dratted 8 accursed, infernal 9 abhorrent, execrable 10 abominable, detestable

damned 5 utter 6 blamed, cursed, cussed, darned, dashed, doomed 7 awfully, blasted, doggone, dratted, goldarn 8 accursed, infernal 9 condemned 10 confounded 13 anathematized

Damocles' ____ 5 sword

Damon's friend 7 Pythias

damp 3 wet 4 dank, dewy 5 check, choke, humid, moist, musty 6 clammy 7 bedewed 8 humidify, humidity

dampen 4 cool, curb 5 chill 6 deaden 7 depress, moisten 8 diminish

damsel 3 gal 4 girl, lass, maid, miss 5 filly, wench 6 lassie, maiden

Dan *father:* 5 Jacob *mother:* 6 Bilhah *son:* 6 Hushim

Danaë *father:* 8 Acrisius *lover:* 4 Zeus *son:* 7 Perseus

Danaus *brother:* 8 Aegyptus *daughters:* 7 Danaïds 8 Danaïdes *father:* 5 Belus *founder of:* 5 Argos *grandfather:* 7 Neptune 8 Poseidon

dance 3 dip, hop, jig, tap 4 ball, flit, foot, heel, hoof, hula, juba, leap, lope, reel, step, trip 5 bamba, brawl, galop, gigue, hover, lindy, mambo, mixer, polka, rumba, stomp, swing, tread 6 ballet, bolero, boogie, Boston, cancan, chassé, foot it, formal, frolic, German, hoof it, rhumba, shimmy 7 beguine, coranto, courant, flicker, flitter, flutter, hoedown, one-step, shuffle 8 cakewalk, flamenco, galliard, glissade, rigadoon, rigaudon 9 allemande, cotillion, jitterbug, pas de deux *Argentinian:* 5 tango *art of:* 12 choreography *Austrian:* 7 ländler *ballroom:* 5 rumba, tango 6 cha-cha, rhumba 7 foxtrot, mazurka, two-step 8 merengue 9 cotillion 10 Charleston *Bohemian:* 5 polka *Brazilian:* 5 samba 6 maxixe 7 carioca, lambada 8 capoeira 9 bossa nova *combining form:* 5 chore 6 choreo, chorio *country:* 3 hay 4 reel 8 hornpipe *couple:* 5 polka 9 cotillion, malaguena 11 square dance *court:* 6 canary, pavane 8 saraband 9 allemande, sarabande *Cuban:* 5 conga, mambo, rumba 6 rhumba 8 habanera *designer:* 13 choreographer *English:* 6 morris *formal:* 4 ball, prom 9 cotillion *French:* 6 cancan 7 bourrée, gavotte 9 allemande 10 carmagnole *garment:* 4 tutu 7 leotard *Haitian:* 4 juba 8 merengue *Hawaiian:* 4 hula *Hungarian:* 7 czardas *Indian:* 6 nautch 7 bhangra *instrument:* 8 castanet *Israeli:* 4 hora *Italian:* 10 saltarello, tarantella, villanella 11 passacaglia *lively:* 3 jig 4 reel, trot 5 galop, gigue, polka, rumba 6 rhumba 7 bourrée 8 fandango, hornpipe, rigadoon, rigaudon 9 farandole, shakedown 10 Charleston, saltarello, tarantella *Maori:* 4 haka *movement:* 4 plié, step 8 capriole, glissade 9 pirouette *Muse of:* 11 Terpsichore *1920's:* 10 Charleston *Polish:* 5 polka 7 mazurka 9 polonaise *Polynesian:* 4 hula *ragtime:* 10 turkey trot *Scottish:* 3 bob 4 reel 5 fling 10 strathspey 11 schottische 13 Highland fling *shoes:* 5 pumps 8 slippers *slipper:* 7 toeshoe *slow:* 6 adagio, minuet, pavane 8 ha-

banera *Spanish:* 4 jota 6 bolero 7 zapateo 8
cachucha, chaconne, fandango, flamenco,
saraband 9 malaguena, sarabande 10 seguidilla *spectator:* 10 wallflower *springy:* 3 jig
square: 7 hoedown, lancers 9 cotillion,
quadrille *stately:* 5 pavan 6 pavane 8 saraband 9 polonaise, sarabande *step:* 3 pas
woman's: 6 cancan
dancer 6 hoofer 7 chorine, clogger, danseur,
stepper 8 coryphée, danseuse 9 ballerina,
chorus boy 10 cakewalker, chorus girl
American: 4 Feld (Elliot), Holm (Hanya),
Lang (Pearl), Tune (Tommy) 5 Ailey (Alvin), Fosse (Bob), Kelly (Gene), Shawn
(Ted), Tharp (Twyla), Watts (Heather) 6
Castle (Irene, Vernon), Duncan (Isadora),
Dunham (Katherine), Graham (Martha),
Morris (Mark), Taylor (Paul), Verdon
(Gwen) 7 Astaire (Adele, Fred), Bujones
(Fernando), de Mille (Agnes), Farrell (Suzanne), Gregory (Cynthia), Jamison (Judith), Joffrey (Robert), Kistler (Darci),
Martins (Peter), Massine (Leonide),
McBride (Patricia), Robbins (Jerome), St.
Denis (Ruth), Tamiris (Helen) 8 Champion
(Gower, Marge), d'Amboise (Jacques),
Humphrey (Doris), Kirkland (Gelsey),
LeClercq (Tanaquil), Mitchell (Arthur),
Nikolais (Alwin), Villella (Edward) 9
Tallchief (Maria) 10 Cunningham (Merce)
Cuban: 6 Alonso (Alicia) *Danish:* 5 Bruhn
(Erik) 7 Martins (Peter) 8 Tomasson
(Helgi) *English:* 5 Dolin (Anton), Somes
(Michael), Tudor (Antony) 7 Fonteyn (Margot), Markova (Alicia), Rambert (Marie) 8
de Valois (Ninette), Helpmann (Robert)
French: 5 Lifar (Serge) 6 Béjart (Maurice),
Perrot (Jules), Petipa (Marius) 7 Camargo
(Marie), Massine (Leonide) *German:* 5
Joоss (Kurt) *Italian:* 5 Grisi (Carlotta) *Mexican:* 5 Limón (José) *Russian:* 5 Lifar
(Serge) 6 Fokine (Michel), Petipa (Marius)
7 Massine (Leonide), Nureyev (Rudolf),
Pavlova (Anna), Ulanova (Galina) 8 Danilova (Aleksandra), Makarova (Natalia),
Nijinska (Bronislava), Nijinsky (Vaslav),
Vaganova (Agrippina) 9 Karsavina (Tamara), Semyonova (Marina) 11 Baryshnikov (Mikhail), Plisetskaya (Maya)
Scottish: 7 Shearer (Moira)
dancing 6 ballet 12 choreography *mania:* 9
tarantism
dandle 3 pet 4 play 6 caress, cosset, cradle,
cuddle, pamper
dandruff 5 scall, scurf
dandy 3 fop, pip 4 beau, buck, dude, fine,
lulu, toff 5 dilly, doozy, nifty, swell 6

doozie, peachy 7 coxcomb, foppish 8 terrific 9 excellent, first-rate, humdinger,
hunky-dory 11 Beau Brummel, crackerjack
12 lounge lizard
dang 4 damn, darn 6 cursed, cussed, damned,
darned 7 blasted, dratted, goldarn 8 infernal
10 confounded
danger 4 risk 5 peril 6 crisis, hazard, menace,
plight, threat 7 pitfall, trouble 8 distress,
jeopardy 9 emergency *signal:* 4 bell 5
alarm, siren 6 tocsin
dangerous 5 risky 6 unsafe 7 parlous 8 insecure, menacing, perilous, unstable 9 hazardous 10 precarious 11 threatening
dangle 4 hang 5 droop, swing 6 depend 7
suspend
Daniel ____ *pioneer:* 5 Boone *statesman:* 7
Webster
Danish *hero:* 5 Ogier *king:* 9 Christian, Frederick *queen:* 9 Margrethe
dank 3 wet 4 damp 5 humid, moist 6 clammy
8 dripping
Dante *beloved:* 8 Beatrice *birthplace:* 8 Florence *daughter:* 7 Antonia *deathplace:* 7
Ravenna *party:* 6 Guelph 7 Bianchi *patron:*
5 Scala *teacher:* 6 Latini *wife:* 5 Gemma
work: 5 canto 7 Inferno 8 Commedia, Paradiso 9 Vita Nuova 10 Purgatorio 12 Divine
Comedy (The)
Danton's *colleague* 5 Marat (Jean-Paul) 11
Robespierre (Maximilien)
Danzig 6 Gdańsk
Daphne *father:* 5 Ladon 6 Peneus *form:* 6
laurel 10 laurel tree *pursuer:* 6 Apollo 9
Leucippus
Daphnis' *lover* 5 Chloe
dapper 4 neat, trim 5 doggy, natty, sassy,
smart, swank 6 classy, jaunty, rakish,
snazzy, spiffy, spruce, sprucy 7 bandbox,
dashing, doggish, foppish, stylish 11 wellgroomed
dapple 4 spot 5 fleck, patch 6 mottle 7
speckle, stipple
dappled 4 pied 6 motley 7 flecked, mottled,
patched, piebald, spotted 8 brindled 10 variegated 11 varicolored
Dardanelles 10 Hellespont
Dardanus *descendants:* 7 Trojans *father:* 4
Zeus 7 Jupiter *mother:* 7 Electra
dare 3 try 4 defy, risk 5 beard, brave 6 hazard
7 attempt, venture 8 confront, defiance 9
challenge
daredevil see **daring**
darer 4 hero 6 risker
daring 4 bold, guts, rash 5 brash, brave,
gutsy, moxie, nerve, nervy, pluck, valor 6
heroic, plucky 7 bravery, courage, heroism

8 audacity, boldness, fearless, reckless **9** audacious, derring-do, fortitude, venturous **10** courageous **11** adventurous, venturesome **13** adventuresome

Darius *battle:* **8** Marathon *father:* **9** Hystaspes *country:* **6** Persia **7** Parthia *son:* **6** Xerxes *wife:* **6** Atossa

Darjeeling 3 tea

dark 3 dim **4** dusk, inky, murk **5** black, blind, cloud, dingy, dusky, ebony, murky, night, sable, shady, sooty, swart, umber, unlit, vague **6** brunet, cloudy, dismal, gloomy, opaque, somber, sombre, wicked **7** obscure, ominous, rayless, satanic, shadowy, stygian, subfusc, sunless, swarthy, unclear **8** bistered, brunette, infernal, sinister **9** enigmatic, lightless, secretive, tenebrous, unlighted **10** caliginous, indistinct, mysterious, mystifying, pitch-black **11** crepuscular **13** unilluminated *poetic:* **4** ebon

darken 3 dim **5** bedim, cloud, gloom, lower, shade, sully, umber **6** shadow **7** becloud, blacken, eclipse, obscure, tarnish **8** melanize, overcast **9** obfuscate, overcloud **10** overshadow *Scottish:* **5** gloam

dark-haired *female:* **8** brunette *male:* **6** brunet

darkness 4 dusk, evil, murk **5** black, gloom, night, shade **6** shadow **8** blackout **9** nightfall, obscurity

darkroom liquid 3 fix **8** emulsion, hardener

darling 3 gra, hon, pet **4** dear, duck, love **5** angel, deary, ducky, flame, honey, loved, sugar, sweet **7** beloved, dearest, sweetie **8** adorable, charming, favorite, precious **10** sweetheart, sweetie pie

darn 4 drat, knit, mend **5** patch **6** blamed, cursed, cussed, damned, shucks **7** blasted, doggone, dratted **8** infernal **9** embroider **10** confounded *French:* **3** zut

Darrow client 4 Debs (Eugene), Loeb (Richard) **6** Scopes (John) **7** Haywood (William), Leopold (Nathan)

dart 3 fly, run, zip **4** barb, bolt, buzz, dash, flit, leap, rush, sail, scud, skim, tear **5** arrow, bound, hurry, lance, pitch, scamp, scoot, shaft, shoot, skirr, spear, speed, spurt **6** glance, hasten, scurry, spring, sprint **7** javelin, missile, scamper *barbed:* **10** banderilla

D'Artagnan's friends 5 Athos **6** Aramis **7** Porthos **11** musketeers

Dartmouth location 5 Devon **7** Hanover **12** New Hampshire

darts term 3 leg **4** bust **5** split **6** double, flight, hockey, treble **8** bull's-eye

Darwin, Charles *colleague:* **7** Wallace (Alfred Russel) *ship:* **6** Beagle *theory:* **9** evolution, selection

dash 3 fly, nip, run **4** bolt, brio, cast, damn, dart, élan, foil, hurl, race, ruin, rush, slam, tear, zing **5** break, chase, flair, fling, pinch, smash, style, trace **6** esprit, hyphen, pizazz, scurry, splash, sprint, thrust, thwart **7** bravura, depress, destroy, pizzazz, shatter, smidgen, spatter **8** confound **9** animation, frustrate

dashboard reading 4 fuel **5** speed **7** mileage **8** pressure **11** temperature

dashing 4 bold **5** smart **6** dapper, jaunty, lively, modish **7** gallant, stylish **8** animated, spirited **11** adventurous, fashionable

Das Kapital author 4 Marx (Karl)

dassie 4 pika **5** coney, hyrax

dastard 6 coward, craven **7** chicken, quitter **8** poltroon, recreant **9** scoundrel

dastardly 3 low **4** base, mean **6** craven, yellow **8** cowardly, shameful, skulking **11** treacherous, underhanded **13** pusillanimous

data 4 info **5** facts, input **7** figures **9** documents **11** information *numerical:* **5** stats **10** statistics

date 3 age, era, woo **5** court, epoch, tryst **6** cutoff, escort **7** take out **8** deadline **9** accompany **10** engagement, rendezvous **11** anniversary, appointment, assignation

dated 3 old **5** passé **6** démodé, old hat **7** archaic, outworn **8** obsolete, outmoded **10** antiquated **12** old-fashioned **13** unfashionable *fashionably:* **5** retro

datum 4 fact

daub 4 blob, blot, spot **5** fleck, paint, smear **6** dapple, smudge, splash **7** besmear, dribble, plaster, speckle, splotch

daughter *Blythe Danner's:* **7** Paltrow (Gwyneth) *Bruce Dern's:* **5** Laura *Bush's:* **5** Jenna **7** Barbara *Carter's:* **3** Amy *Cash's:* **7** Rosanne *Cher's:* **8** Chastity (Bono) *Clinton's:* **7** Chelsea *Cole's:* **7** Natalie *Coppola's:* **5** Sofia *Danny Thomas's:* **5** Marlo *Debbie Reynolds's:* **6** Carrie (Fisher) *Eddie Fisher's:* **6** Carrie *Elizabeth II's:* **4** Anne *Elvis's:* **9** Lisa Marie *Fonda's:* **4** Jane *Ford's (Gerald):* **5** Susan *Freud's:* **4** Anna *Garland's:* **4** Liza (Minnelli) *Goldie Hawn's:* **10** Kate Hudson *Ingrid Bergman's:* **8** Isabella (Rossellini) *Janet Leigh's:* **8** Jamie Lee (Curtis) *Joel Grey's:* **8** Jennifer *Johnson's (Lyndon):* **4** Lucy **5** Linda *Jon Voight's:* **8** Angelina (Jolie) *Kennedy's (John F.):* **8** Caroline *Klaus Kinski's:* **9** Nastassja *Maureen O'Sullivan's:* **3** Mia (Farrow) *Naomi Judd's:* **7** Wynonna *Nat King Cole's:* **7** Natalie *Nixon's:* **5** Julie **6** Tricia *Pat Boone's:* **5** Debby *Ravi Shankar's:* **10** Norah Jones *Reagan's:* **5** Patti **7** Maureen *Richard Bur-*

ton's: 4 Kate **Ryan O'Neal's:** 5 Tatum **Sinatra's:** 5 Nancy **Tony Curtis's:** 8 Jamie Lee
Daughter of the Moon 7 Nokomis
daunt 3 cow 5 alarm, deter 6 dismay, subdue 7 terrify 8 frighten 10 disconcert, discourage, dishearten, intimidate
daunting 7 awesome 8 imposing 9 dismaying, unnerving 10 forbidding, formidable 11 dispiriting 12 discouraging, intimidating, overwhelming
dauntless 4 bold, game 5 brave 6 daring 7 gallant, valiant 8 fearless, unafraid 9 unfearful, unfearing 10 courageous 11 lionhearted 12 stouthearted
dauntlessness 4 guts 5 heart, nerve, pluck, spunk, valor 6 daring, mettle, spirit 7 bravery, cojones, courage 8 boldness 10 resolution 12 fearlessness
davenport 4 desk, sofa 5 couch, divan 6 daybed 12 chesterfield
David commander: 4 Joab 5 Amasa **companion:** 8 Jonathan **daughter:** 5 Tamar **father:** 5 Jesse **rebuker:** 6 Nathan **son:** 5 Amnon 7 Absalom, Solomon 8 Adonijah **song of:** 5 psalm **wife:** 6 Michal 7 Abigail, Ahinoam 9 Bathsheba
_____ **David** 4 Camp 5 Magen, Mogen 6 Star of
David Copperfield author: 7 Dickens (Charles) **character:** 4 Dora, Heep 5 Uriah 6 Barkis 8 Micawber, Peggotty 9 Murdstone 10 Steerforth
Da Vinci Code author 5 Brown (Dan)
davit 5 crane
dawdle 3 lag 4 idle, laze, loaf, loll 5 dally, delay, tarry 6 diddle, linger, loiter, lounge 8 lollygag 10 dillydally
dawn 4 morn 5 onset, sunup 6 aurora 7 morning, sunrise 8 cockcrow, daybreak, daylight 9 beginning 10 first light **goddess:** 3 Eos 6 Aurora **pertaining to:** 4 eoan
day abbreviation: 3 Fri, Mon, Sat, Sun, Thu, Tue, Wed 4 Thur, Tues 5 Thurs **before:** 3 eve **church calendar:** 5 feria **French:** 4 jour **German:** 3 Tag **holy:** 5 feast **hour:** 4 noon **Latin:** 4 dies **Spanish:** 3 día
daybreak 4 dawn, morn 5 sunup 6 aurora 7 dawning, morning, sunrise 8 cockcrow, daylight
daydream 4 muse 5 fancy 6 vision 7 fantasy, reverie 8 phantasy 9 fantasize 10 woolgather 13 woolgathering
daystar 3 Sol, sun 5 Venus 7 phoebus
daze 3 fog 4 haze, stun 5 amaze, blind 6 dazzle, stupor, trance 7 astound, confuse, stupefy 8 astonish, bedazzle, befuddle, confound 9 dumbfound

dazed 5 woozy 6 groggy, punchy 7 dazzled, stunned 8 confused 9 stupefied 10 punchdrunk
_____ **d'Azur** 4 Côte
dazzle 3 wow 4 stun 5 amaze, blind, éclat, glitz, shine 7 impress 8 astonish, bewilder, confound, outshine 9 overpower
dazzling 6 flashy, garish 7 radiant 8 splendid, stunning 9 brilliant 11 confounding, resplendent 12 overpowering
deacon 6 clergy, cleric, layman 8 reverend 9 churchman
dead 4 cold, gone, late 5 passé, slain, stiff 6 buried, fallen 7 defunct, done for, expired, extinct 8 deceased, departed, lifeless 9 senseless 10 corpselike 11 unconscious 12 extinguished
deadbeat 3 bum 5 idler 6 debtor, loafer, slouch 7 lounger, shirker, slacker 10 delinquent, malingerer
dead duck 5 goner 8 casualty, fatality
deaden 4 dull, kill, mute, numb, stun 5 blunt, quiet 6 benumb, dampen, lessen, muffle, obtund, reduce, stifle 7 smother, stupefy 8 suppress 11 anesthetize, desensitize
dead end 4 halt, stop 6 pocket, unruly 7 impasse 8 cul-de-sac, standoff 9 stalemate, terminate 10 blind alley, bottleneck, standstill
deadened 4 numb 6 asleep, dulled, killed, numbed 7 blunted 8 benumbed, impaired 12 anesthetized
deadeye 5 block 8 marksman 12 sharpshooter
deadfall 4 trap 7 springe 9 booby trap, mousetrap
deadliness 8 fatality 9 lethality, mortality
deadlock 3 tie 4 draw 7 impasse 8 standoff, stoppage 9 checkmate, stalemate 10 standstill
deadly 5 fatal, toxic 6 lethal, mortal 7 capital, killing 8 lethally, unerring 10 implacable 11 destructive, internecine 12 pestilential
deadpan 5 blank, empty 6 vacant 9 impassive 10 poker-faced 11 inscrutable 12 inexpressive, unexpressive
Dead Souls author 5 Gogol (Nikolay)
dead to rights 9 red-handed
deadweight 4 load 6 weight
deal 4 dole, sale, sell 5 allot, serve, shake, share, trade, treat 6 barter, dicker, parcel 7 bargain, deliver, dish out, dole out, mete out, package, portion, traffic, wrestle 8 contract, disburse, dispense, share out 9 agreement, apportion, negotiate 10 administer, compromise, distribute, measure out 11 arrangement, transaction 13 understanding

great: 4 gobs, heap, lots, tons 5 heaps, horde, loads, scads 6 oodles, plenty, stacks **out:** 8 disburse, dispense 9 apportion 10 administer, distribute **with:** 5 serve, treat 6 handle, regard 7 concern, involve

dealer 5 agent 6 broker, seller, trader, vendor 8 chandler, merchant, operator 9 tradesman 10 negotiator, trafficker 11 businessman, distributer, distributor 12 merchandiser **British:** 5 coper 6 draper, jobber, mercer 7 chapman

dealings 5 trade, truck 7 affairs, matters, traffic 8 business, commerce, concerns 11 intercourse 12 interactions, transactions, undertakings

dean 4 head 5 chief, doyen, elder 6 leader

dear 3 gra, pet 4 fond, lamb, love 5 honey, loved, sugar, sweet 6 costly, doting, loving, prized, scarce 7 beloved, darling, devoted, lovable, machree, querida, tootsie 8 favorite, precious, valuable 9 cherished, expensive, heartfelt, treasured 10 fair-haired, honeybunch, sweetheart 12 affectionate **French:** 4 cher 5 chère 6 chérie **Scottish:** 2 jo

dearth 4 lack, want 6 famine 7 absence, default, paucity 8 scarcity, shortage, sparsity 9 privation, scantness 10 deficiency, meagerness, scantiness

death 3 end 4 exit 6 demise, ending, expiry 7 decease, passing, quietus 8 casualty, curtains, fatality, necrosis, thanatos 9 bloodshed, departure 10 expiration, extinction, grim reaper 11 dissolution, termination 12 annihilation **after:** 10 posthumous **combining form:** 6 thanat 7 thanato **music:** 5 dirge, elegy 8 threnody **notice:** 4 obit 8 obituary 9 necrology **of tissue:** 8 gangrene **personification:** 10 grim reaper **put to:** 3 gas, hit, ice, zap 4 do in, hang, kill, slay 5 drown, lynch, snuff, waste 6 murder, poison, rub out 7 bump off, butcher, execute, smother, wipe out 8 blow away, dispatch, immolate, knock off, strangle, throttle 9 slaughter, suffocate 10 asphyxiate 11 assassinate, electrocute **rate:** 9 mortality **rites:** 7 funeral 8 exequies 9 interment, obsequies

Death in the Family author 4 Agee (James)

deathless 7 abiding, eternal, lasting, undying 8 enduring, immortal 11 everlasting 12 imperishable

deathlike see **deathly**

deathly 5 fatal 6 lethal, mortal 7 macabre, stygian 12 pestilential

debacle 4 rout 6 defeat, fiasco 7 breakup, failure 8 collapse, disaster 9 breakdown, cataclysm 10 disruption

debar 3 ban 4 stop 6 forbid, outlaw 7 exclude, prevent, rule out 8 preclude, prohibit 9 interdict

debark 4 land 6 alight, get off 11 decorticate

debase 3 mar 4 harm 5 lower, stain 6 damage, defile, demean, dilute, impair, reduce, weaken 7 cheapen, corrupt, degrade, devalue, pervert, pollute, vitiate 8 dishonor 9 undermine 10 adulterate, depreciate 11 contaminate

debatable 4 iffy, moot 7 dubious 8 arguable, doubtful 9 contested, uncertain, undecided 10 disputable, unresolved 11 problematic 12 questionable

debate 4 moot 5 argue, bandy, plead 7 contend, contest, discuss, dispute, quarrel, wrangle 8 argument, consider, forensic, question 9 dialectic, thrash out 10 controvert, toss around 11 application, controversy, disputation 12 deliberation 13 argumentation **again:** 6 rehash **art of:** 9 forensics **expert:** 7 eristic **place for:** 5 forum **side:** 3 con, pro

debauch 4 orgy, warp 6 seduce 7 corrupt, deprave, pervert, vitiate 9 bacchanal, brutalize 10 lead astray, saturnalia 11 bacchanalia

debauched 6 wanton 8 degraded, depraved, vitiated 9 corrupted, dissolute, libertine, perverted 10 degenerate, licentious

debilitate 3 sap 6 impair, weaken 7 cripple, disable 8 enfeeble 9 attenuate, undermine 10 devitalize

debilitated 4 weak 6 feeble, infirm, sapped 7 run-down, worn-out 8 weakened 9 enfeebled

debility 7 disease, malaise 8 weakness 9 infirmity 10 feebleness, infirmness, sickliness 11 decrepitude

Debir kingdom: 5 Eglon **slayer:** 6 Joshua

debit 4 bill, levy 6 charge 7 deficit 8 drawback 9 liability 11 encumbrance, shortcoming

debonair 5 suave 6 smooth, urbane 7 dashing, elegant 10 nonchalant 12 lighthearted

Deborah's husband 9 Lappidoth

debouch 5 empty, issue 6 emerge

debris 4 junk, slag 5 trash, waste 6 litter, refuse, rubble, spilth 7 garbage, rubbish 8 detritus, riffraff, wreckage **rock:** 5 scree, talus 8 colluvia 9 colluvium

debt 3 due, sin 6 arrear, red ink 7 arrears, default, deficit 8 mortgage, trespass 9 arrearage, liability 10 obligation 11 delinquency **acknowledgment:** 3 IOU 4 bill 5 check

debtless 7 solvent

debunk 6 expose, reveal, show up, unmask 7

lay bare, lay open, uncloak, uncover, undress **8** unshroud **9** demystify, discredit

Debussy's La ____ **3** Mer

debut 3 bow **5** entry **6** entree **7** come out, opening, present **8** entrance, premiere **9** beginning, coming out, introduce **12** introduction, presentation

decadence 5 decay **7** decline **10** degeneracy, regression **11** degradation **12** degeneration **13** deterioration

decadent 6 effete **7** debased **8** decaying, degraded, depraved **9** debauched, declining, dissolute **10** degenerate **13** self-indulgent

Decalogue 12 Commandments *verb:* **5** shalt

Decameron, The *author:* **9** Boccaccio (Giovanni) *heroine:* **8** Griselda

decamp 4 blow, bolt, exit, flee **5** leave, scram, split **6** beat it, begone, cut out, escape, get out, retire **7** abscond, make off, pull out, run away, skiddoo, take off, vamoose **8** clear out, withdraw **9** skedaddle

decant 4 pour **7** draw off, pour out **8** transfer

decanter 5 cruet, flask **6** bottle, carafe, flagon, vessel

decapitate 4 head **6** behead **9** decollate **10** guillotine

decapod 7 mollusc, mollusk **10** crustacean

decathlon champ 6 Jenner (Bruce), Morris (Glenn), O'Brien (Dan), Schenk (Christian), Sebrle (Roman), Toomey (Bill), Zmelik (Robert) **7** Doherty (Ken), Johnson (Rafer), Mathias (Bob) **8** Campbell (Milton), Thompson (Daley)

decay 3 rot **4** ruin, wane **5** spoil, waste **6** molder, wither **7** atrophy, crumble, decline, putrefy, rotting **8** putresce, spoilage **9** decompose **11** deteriorate **12** dilapidation, putrefaction **13** deterioration

decayed 6 putrid, rotted, rotten, ruined **7** carious, spoiled **8** decadent, moldered, overripe **9** putrefied **10** decomposed, degenerate

decease 3 die, end **4** fail, pass **5** death, dying, sleep **6** demise, depart, expire, finish, pass on, perish **7** passing, quietus, release, succumb **8** pass away **9** departure **10** expiration

deceased 4 body, dead, late **6** corpse **7** cadaver, carcass, expired, remains **8** departed, lifeless **9** inanimate

deceit 3 gyp **4** hoax, ruse, sham **5** fraud, guile, trick **6** humbug **7** swindle **8** artifice, flimflam, trickery **9** chicanery, deception, duplicity, imposture **10** dishonesty **13** double-dealing

deceitful 3 sly **4** wily **5** false, lying **6** crafty, sneaky, tricky **7** cunning, knavish, roguish **8** guileful, two-faced **9** deceptive, dishonest,

underhand **10** mendacious **11** underhanded **13** double-dealing

deceive 3 con **4** bilk, dupe, fool, gull, hoax **5** bluff, cozen, lie to, trick **6** delude, humbug, palter, take in **7** beguile, mislead, sandbag, two-time **8** flimflam, hoodwink **9** bamboozle, four-flush **11** double-cross

deceiving 5 false **6** tricky **8** deluding, delusive, delusory, guileful, two-faced **9** beguiling, deceptive **10** fallacious, misleading **11** duplicitous, underhanded

decelerate 4 slow **5** delay **6** retard, slow up **7** slacken **8** slow down

decency 7 decorum, dignity, fitness, modesty **8** civility **9** etiquette, propriety **10** conformity, seemliness

decennium 6 decade

decent 4 fair, good **5** right **6** honest, modest, proper, seemly **7** correct, fitting, upright **8** adequate, all right **9** competent, honorable, tolerable **10** acceptable, conforming, sufficient **11** comme il faut, presentable, respectable **12** satisfactory

deception 3 gyp, lie **4** gaff, hoax, hype, ruse, scam, sham, wile **5** cheat, feint, fraud, guile, put-on, trick **6** deceit, dupery, humbug, mirage **7** chicane, cunning, fallacy, fantasm, knavery, sophism **8** flimflam, illusion, intrigue, phantasm, trickery, trumpery, wiliness **9** casuistry, chicanery, duplicity, imposture, sophistry, treachery **10** dishonesty, hanky-panky, subterfuge

deceptive 5 false, phony **6** tricky **8** deluding, delusory, illusory, specious **9** beguiling, deceitful, deceiving **10** fallacious, misleading

decide 3 opt **4** rule, will **5** judge **6** settle **7** adjudge, resolve **8** conclude **9** determine **10** adjudicate

decided 3 set **4** firm **5** fixed **6** intent **7** assured, certain, obvious, settled **8** definite, resolute, resolved **10** determined, pronounced **11** established, unequivocal

decimate 4 raze, ruin **5** wreck **7** abolish, destroy, wipe out **8** demolish, massacre **9** slaughter **10** annihilate, obliterate **11** exterminate

decipher 4 read **5** break, crack, solve **6** decode, reveal **7** decrypt, resolve, unravel **8** unriddle **9** figure out, interpret, puzzle out, translate **12** cryptanalyze

decision 4 fiat **6** choice, ruling **7** finding, resolve, verdict **8** firmness, judgment, sentence **9** selection **10** conclusion, resolution, settlement **13** determination *rabbinical:* **9** responsum

decisive 3 set **7** crucial, settled **8** critical, resolute **10** conclusive, convincing, deter-

mined, imperative, peremptory **11** determining **12** unmistakable
deck 4 trim **5** adorn, array, dress, equip, floor, level, porch, prank **6** attire, blazon, clothe **7** apparel, appoint, festoon, furnish, garland, garnish, terrace **8** accouter, accoutre, beautify, decorate, emblazon, ornament, platform **9** embellish *chief:* **4** bos'n **9** boatswain *high:* **4** poop *lowest:* **5** orlop *out:* **5** array, fix up, slick, spiff, tog up **6** clothe, doll up **7** dress up, gussy up **8** spruce up *part:* **7** scupper
deckhand 3 gob **4** jack, swab **6** sailor, seaman **7** jack-tar, rouster, swabbie **10** bluejacket
declaim 4 rant **5** mouth, orate, speak **6** recite **7** deliver, lecture **8** bloviate, harangue, perorate **9** hold forth
declamatory 5 tumid, windy, wordy **6** florid, turgid **7** aureate, flowery, fustian, orotund, pompous, ranting, verbose **8** sonorous **9** bombastic, high-flown, overblown **10** euphuistic, oratorical, rhetorical **12** magniloquent **13** grandiloquent
declaration 5 edict **6** avowal, notice, report **7** promise **8** document, pleading **9** affidavit, manifesto, statement, testimony **10** confession, deposition, disclosure, expression, profession **11** affirmation, attestation **12** announcement, notification, proclamation **13** advertisement, pronouncement
declare 3 say, vow **4** aver, avow, tell, vent **5** claim, sound, state, swear, utter, voice **6** affirm, allege, assert, avouch, blazon, depone, depose, herald, insist, ordain, report, reveal **7** certify, confirm, deliver, divulge, express, profess, signify, testify **8** announce, disclose, indicate, maintain, manifest, proclaim, propound **9** advertise, broadcast, enunciate, predicate, pronounce **10** annunciate, asseverate, promulgate **11** come out with, disseminate *a saint:* **8** canonize *in cards:* **3** bid **4** meld *invalid:* **5** annul
declass 4 bump, bust **5** abase, lower **6** demote, reduce **7** degrade, set back **9** downgrade
déclassé 4 mean, poor **6** common, vulgar **7** ignoble, lowered **8** inferior, lowgrade, mediocre, middling **10** second-rate **11** secondclass
declension 5 class, slope **7** decline, descent **8** downfall **9** downgrade **10** inflection **12** dégringolade **13** deterioration
declination 3 ebb **5** slant, slide **6** ebbing **7** refusal, incline **8** downturn **9** downgrade **10** deflection **12** dégringolade, turning aside **13** deterioration

decline 3 dip, ebb, jib, rot, sag, set **4** balk, dive, drop, fade, fail, fall, flag, loss, sink, slip, wane **5** abate, avoid, demur, droop, lapse, lower, say no, slide, slope, slump, spurn **6** ebbing, go down, recede, refuse, reject, renege, waning, weaken, worsen **7** abstain, atrophy, descend, descent, devolve, dismiss, drop-off, dwindle, failure, falloff, forbear, refrain, relapse, sell-off, sinkage, subside **8** comedown, decrease, downfall, downturn, languish, lowering, turn down **9** backslide, decadence, downgrade, downslide, downswing, downtrend, reprobate, repudiate, weakening **10** degeneracy, degenerate, depression, devolution, disapprove, falling off **11** backsliding, deteriorate **12** degeneration, dégringolade **13** deterioration
declivitous 5 steep **6** sloped **7** pitched, sloping **8** inclined **9** inclining **10** descending
declivity 3 dip **4** drop, fall **5** slope **7** decline, descent **8** downturn, gradient **9** downgrade **11** inclination
decode see **decipher**
decollate 4 head, kill **6** behead **10** decapitate, guillotine
decolor 6 blanch, bleach, blench, whiten **7** wash out **11** achromatize
decompose 3 rot **5** decay, spoil, taint **6** fester, molder **7** analyze, break up, crumble, putrefy, resolve **8** dissolve, separate **9** anatomize, break down **12** disintegrate
decor 7 setting **8** backdrop, stage set **11** furnishings **13** ornamentation
decorate 4 do up, pink, trim **5** adorn, dress, frill **6** bedeck **7** bedizen, dress up, enhance, festoon, furnish, garnish **8** appliqué, beautify, emblazon, ornament **9** embellish *a border:* **6** purfle
decorated 6 ornate **7** adorned, honored, wrought **9** bemedaled, decked out, garnished **10** beribboned, ornamented **11** embellished
decoration 4 bays **5** award, badge, honor, kudos, medal **6** doodad, plaque **7** garnish, laurels **8** accolade, filigree, fretting, fretwork, frippery, furbelow, ornament, trimming, vignette **11** distinction *cutout:* **8** appliqué *furniture:* **4** buhl **6** boulle
decorous 3 fit **4** meet, prim **5** right **6** au fait, comely, decent, proper, seemly **7** correct, elegant, fitting **8** becoming, mannerly, suitable, tasteful **9** befitting, civilized, de rigueur, dignified **10** conforming **11** appropriate, respectable, well-behaved
decorously 5 fitly **7** rightly **8** decently, properly, suitably **9** correctly, fittingly **11** befittingly, respectably

decorousness 7 decency **8** civility **9** propriety, rightness **10** seemliness **11** correctness, orderliness **12** correctitude

decorticate 4 bare, bark, flay, hull, husk, pare, peel, skin **5** scale, scalp, shell, shuck, strip **6** denude **7** lay bare, pull off

decorum 5 order **7** decency, dignity, fitness, modesty **8** protocol **9** etiquette, propriety **10** properness, seemliness **11** correctness, orderliness **12** correctitude

decoy 4 bait, fake, lure **5** plant, shill, tempt **6** allure, capper, delude, entice, lead on, pigeon, seduce **7** deceive, mislead **8** inveigle **10** red herring

decrease 3 cut, ebb **4** bate, drop, ease, fall, loss, wane **5** allay, lower **6** lessen, reduce, shrink **7** abridge, curtail, cut back, cutback, cut down, decline, die down, drop off, dwindle, fall off, lighten, shorten, slacken, subside **8** diminish, downturn, moderate, rollback, taper off **9** abatement, alleviate, reduction **10** abbreviate, depreciate, diminution, falling off

decree 4 fiat, rule **5** canon, edict, enact, judge, order, ukase **6** behest, charge, dictum, impose, ordain, ruling **7** adjudge, appoint, bidding, command, declare, dictate, lay down, mandate, precept, statute **8** judgment, proclaim, sentence **9** directive, judgement, ordinance, prescribe, prescript, pronounce **10** adjudicate, injunction, regulation **11** declaration **12** adjudication, announcement, proclamation, promulgation **13** pronouncement *Muslim:* **5** fatwa

decrepit 4 aged, weak, worn **5** frail, seedy, tacky **6** creaky, feeble, infirm, senile, shabby, wasted, weakly **7** fragile, run-down, worn-out **8** battered, impaired, weakened **10** bedraggled, broken-down, down-at-heel, ramshackle **11** dilapidated

decrepitude 4 ruin **5** decay **7** frailty, wasting **8** collapse, debility, weakness **9** disrepair, infirmity **10** exhaustion, feebleness, infirmness **12** dilapidation, enfeeblement **13** deterioration

decretal 4 fiat, writ **5** edict, order, ukase **6** assize, dictum, letter, ruling **7** dictate **8** decision, judgment **11** declaration **13** pronouncement

decry 3 boo **4** bash, slam, slur **5** abuse **6** berate, malign, vilify **7** asperse, censure, condemn, degrade, devalue, put down **8** bad-mouth, belittle, denounce, derogate, reproach **9** criticize, deprecate, discredit, disparage, dispraise, reprehend, reprobate **10** depreciate, disapprove **11** rail against

decrypt see **decipher**

decumbent 4 flat **5** prone 6 supine **9** lying down, prostrate, reclining **10** horizontal

decussate 5 cross **8** crosscut **9** intersect **10** crisscross, intercross

dedicate 3 vow **5** bless **6** commit, devote, hallow, pledge **7** address **8** inscribe, restrict, set apart **10** consecrate

deduce 5 infer, judge, trace **6** derive, evolve, gather, reason, reckon **7** discern, make out, surmise **8** conclude **9** figure out

deduct 4 bate **5** abate, infer, judge **6** gather, remove **7** make out, take off, take out **8** conclude, knock off, perceive, subtract, take away

deduction 3 cut **4** tare **8** discount, illation, judgment, sequitur, write-off **9** abatement, inference, reasoning **10** conclusion **11** subtraction

deductive 7 a priori **8** dogmatic, illative, provable, reasoned **9** derivable, inferable **10** consequent **11** inferential **13** ratiocinative

deed 3 act **4** cede, fact, feat, pact **5** doing, title **6** action, assign, convey, escrow, remise **7** charter, exploit **8** alienate, contract, covenant, make over, sign over, transfer **9** adventure **10** conveyance, enterprise **11** achievement, performance, tour de force *brutal:* **8** atrocity *evil:* **3** sin **11** malefaction *good:* **7** mitzvah

deem 4 feel, hold **5** judge, think **7** account, adjudge, believe **8** consider

de-emphasize 8 downplay, minimize, play down **9** gloss over, soft-pedal, underplay **13** underestimate

deep 3 low **4** bass, rapt, sunk **5** abyss, grave, ocean **6** occult, orphic, secret **7** abyssal, obscure **8** abstruse, esoteric, hermetic, profound **9** engrossed, recondite **10** bottomless, fathomless, mysterious *combining form:* **5** bathy

deepen 6 darken, worsen **7** enhance, enlarge, magnify, thicken **8** heighten **9** aggravate, intensify **10** strengthen

deepness 5 abyss **9** intensity **10** profundity

deep-seated 6 inborn, inbred, innate **7** settled **8** inherent, lifelong, profound, stubborn **9** confirmed, ingrained, intrinsic **10** congenital, entrenched, indwelling, inveterate **11** established **12** long-standing **13** bred-in-the-bone, dyed-in-the-wool, thoroughgoing

deep-six 4 dump, toss **5** chuck, scrap **6** unload **7** discard **8** jettison **9** eliminate

deep water 7 trouble **8** distress **10** difficulty

deer 3 elk, roe **4** buck, musk, stag **5** moose **6** wapiti **7** caribou, venison *Asian:* **4** axis, maha **6** sambar **7** muntjac *British:* **4** hart *female:* **3** doe **4** hind *Japanese:* **4** sika *male:*

4 buck, hart, stag 7 roebuck *meat:* 5 jerky 7 venison *path:* 3 run 5 trail *red:* 7 brocket *relating to:* 7 cervine *track:* 4 slot 5 spoor *young:* 3 kid 4 fawn

Deere rival 4 Case, Ford, Toro 6 Kubota 7 Farmall

Deerslayer, The *author:* 6 Cooper (James Fenimore) *character:* 5 Harry (Hurry) 6 Hutter (Thomas), Judith (Hutter) 11 Natty Bumppo 12 Chingachgook

deface 3 mar 4 harm, ruin 6 damage, deform, impair, injure 9 disfigure, vandalize

de facto 6 actual, really 8 actually, existing

defalcation 7 default, failing, failure 10 embezzling, inadequacy, negligence 12 embezzlement

defamation 5 libel, smear 7 calumny, obloquy, slander 10 backbiting 11 traducement 12 backstabbing 13 disparagement

defamatory 8 libelous 9 maligning, traducing, vilifying 10 backbiting, calumnious, slanderous 11 denigrating

defame 5 abase, libel, smear 6 malign, vilify 7 asperse, blacken, blemish, slander, traduce 8 dishonor 9 denigrate, discredit 10 calumniate

default 4 fail 5 welsh 7 absence, exclude, failure, forfeit, neglect 9 selection

defeasance 4 deed 6 defeat 9 overthrow 11 termination

defeat 3 tan 4 beat, best, down, drub, edge, foil, lick, loss, rout, sink, undo, whip, whup 5 crush, outdo, skunk, swamp, upset, waste, whomp 6 outgun, reduce, subdue, wallop 7 beating, conquer, destroy, failure, licking, mow down, nose out, nullify, outplay, overrun, setback, shellac, trounce, wipe out 8 confound, knock out, outfight, outflank, overcome, vanquish, waterloo 9 frustrate, overpower, overthrow, overtrump, subjugate, thrashing, trouncing 10 obliterate 11 shellacking

defeatist 8 doomster 9 doomsayer, Gloomy Gus, pessimist, worrywart

defect 3 bug 4 flaw, lack, vice, want 5 botch, error, fault 6 damage, dearth, desert, foible, injury 7 blemish, default, failing 8 drawback, weakness 9 birthmark, deformity 10 apostatize, deficiency 11 shortcoming 12 imperfection, tergiversate *timber:* 4 knot *visual:* 6 myopia, squint 9 amblyopia, hyperopia 10 presbyopia, strabismus

defection 8 apostasy 9 desertion, forsaking, recreancy 10 disloyalty 11 abandonment

defective 5 amiss 6 broken, faulty, flawed 7 damaged, lacking, unsound, wanting 8 impaired 9 corrupted, deficient, imperfect 10

inaccurate, inadequate, incomplete 12 insufficient

defector 5 Judas 7 traitor 8 apostate, quisling, recreant, renegade, turncoat 9 turnabout 13 double-crosser

defend 4 back, hold, save 5 argue, cover, guard 6 screen, secure, shield, uphold 7 contend, justify, protect, support 8 advocate, champion, maintain, plead for, preserve 9 safeguard

defendable see **defensible**

defendant 7 accused, libelee 8 libellee

defender 7 paladin, tribune 8 advocate, champion, guardian 9 protector 11 white knight

defense 4 fort, ward 5 aegis, alibi, armor, guard 6 excuse, sconce, shield 7 bulwark, rampart, shelter 8 apologia, armament, fastness, fortress, muniment, security 9 safeguard 10 protection, stronghold 11 exculpation, explanation 13 justification *organization:* 4 NATO 5 ANZUS, NORAD, SEATO 10 Warsaw Pact

defenseless 4 open 7 exposed, unarmed 8 helpless, wide open 9 unguarded 10 vulnerable 11 unprotected

defensible 5 valid 7 tenable 8 passable 9 excusable, plausible 10 condonable, reasonable 11 justifiable

defer 3 bow 4 stay, wait 5 delay, remit, stall, table, yield 6 accede, hold up, put off, shelve, submit 7 hold off, lay over, put over, suspend 8 hold over, postpone, prorogue 9 acquiesce 13 procrastinate

deference 5 honor 6 esteem, homage, regard 7 respect 8 courtesy 9 obeisance 11 recognition

deferential 8 obliging 9 disarming, regardful 10 respectful 11 complaisant

defiance 4 dare 5 moxie 7 bravado 8 audacity, contempt 9 challenge, contumacy, impudence, insolence 10 brazenness, effrontery 12 contrariness, stubbornness

defiant 4 bold 5 brash, gutsy, sassy, saucy 6 brazen, cheeky, daring 8 arrogant, impudent, insolent 9 audacious, obstinate, resistant 10 refractory 12 recalcitrant

deficiency 4 flaw, lack, want 5 fault, minus 6 dearth 7 absence, blemish, demerit, failing, failure, paucity 8 scarcity, shortage, weakness 9 privation 10 inadequacy, scantiness 11 defalcation, shortcoming 12 imperfection *mental:* 6 idiocy 7 amentia *pigmentation:* 8 albinism

deficient 3 shy 5 minus, scant, short 6 faulty, flawed, meager, meagre, measly, scanty, scarce 7 failing, lacking, unsound, wanting

8 exiguous, impaired **9** defective, imperfect **10** inadequate, incomplete

deficit 4 lack, loss **6** red ink **8** shortage **10** impairment, inadequacy **12** disadvantage **13** insufficiency

defile 3 tar **4** foul, pass, rape, soil **5** dirty, gorge, march, shame, smear, spoil, stain, sully, taint **6** befoul, debase, ravish **7** besmear, corrupt, pollute, profane, tarnish, violate **8** deflower, dishonor **9** desecrate **11** contaminate

defiled 5 raped **6** impure **7** stained, unclean **8** profaned, polluted, ravished, violated **9** corrupted **10** deflowered, desecrated **12** contaminated

define 3 fix, hem, rim, set **4** edge **5** limit **6** assign, border, detail **7** clarify, delimit, lay down, mark off, mark out, outline, specify **9** delineate, demarcate, determine, establish **11** distinguish **12** characterize

definite 3 set **4** sure **5** clear, final, fixed, sharp, solid **7** certain, decided, express, precise, settled **8** clear-cut, distinct, explicit, specific **10** conclusive, pronounced **11** unambiguous, unequivocal **12** unmistakable

definiteness 8 accuracy, sureness **9** certainty, certitude, exactness, precision **10** exactitude

definitive 5 final **7** express **8** clear-cut, complete, explicit, settling, specific, ultimate **10** concluding, conclusive, exhaustive **11** categorical, determining, unambiguous **13** authoritative

deflate 4 dash **6** humble, reduce, shrink **7** devalue, put down **8** contract, ridicule **9** humiliate, shoot down

deflect 5 avert, parry **6** divert **7** deviate, diverge, hold off **9** turn aside

deflection 3 yaw **4** bend, tack, turn, veer **5** carom, curve, shift **6** double, swerve **7** bending, rebound, turning, veering **8** swerving **9** departure, deviation, diversion **10** divergence

deflower 4 rape **5** spoil **6** defile, ravish **7** despoil, violate **9** desecrate

Defoe, Daniel *character:* **6** Crusoe (Robinson), Friday, Roxana **12** Moll Flanders

deform 4 warp **5** spoil **6** deface **7** contort, distort **8** misshape **9** disfigure

deformed 4 awry, bent **5** askew, bowed **6** warped **7** buckled, crooked **8** crippled **9** contorted, misshapen, unshapely

deformity 4 flaw **6** defect **7** blemish **11** abnormality **12** imperfection, irregularity, malformation **13** disfigurement

____ **de France 3** Île

defraud 3 con, gyp **4** bilk, dupe, rook, scam **5**

cheat, cozen, mulct, trick **6** fleece, rip off **7** swindle **8** flimflam **9** bamboozle

deft 3 apt **4** able **5** adept, agile, handy **6** adroit, clever **7** skilled **8** dextrous, skillful **9** dexterous

deftness 5 knack, skill **7** address, prowess **8** facility **9** adeptness, dexterity **10** capability

defunct 4 cold, dead, late **5** kaput **7** extinct **8** deceased, departed, lifeless, vanished

defy 4 dare, face, gibe, jeer, mock **5** beard, brave, flout, stump **6** resist **7** affront, outdare, outface **8** confront **9** challenge, disregard, withstand

dégagé 6 breezy, casual **7** relaxed, unfussy **8** informal **9** easygoing **10** nonchalant, unreserved **13** unconstrained

degeneracy see **degeneration**

degenerate 4 sink **6** rotten, sunken, worsen **7** corrupt, debased, decayed, decline, descend, immoral, pervert, vicious, vitiate **8** decadent, degraded, depraved **9** backslide, dissolute **11** deteriorate

degeneration 7 atrophy, decline **8** downfall, lowering **9** decadence, depravity, downgrade **10** debasement, perversion, regression **12** dégringolade

degradation 4 fall **7** decline, descent **8** demotion **9** abasement, decadence, depravity, downgrade, reduction **10** corruption, debasement, degeneracy, perversion **11** downgrading **12** degeneration

degrade 4 bump, bust **5** abase, break, decry, lower **6** debase, demean, demote, impair, lessen, reduce **7** corrupt, declass, pervert, put down **8** belittle, cast down, derogate, diminish **9** decompose, discredit, disparage, downgrade, humiliate

degree 3 peg **4** heat, rank, rate, rung, step, term, tier **5** grade, honor, notch, order, pitch, point, ratio, scale, shade, stage, stair **6** amount, extent, status **7** measure, station **8** standing **9** dimension, gradation, intensity, magnitude **10** proportion *academic:* **2** BA, BS, MA, MD, MS **3** BFA, BSc, DDS, LLB, LLD, LLM, MBA, MFA, MSc, PhD **5** MPhil **7** master's **9** bachelor's, doctorate *highest:* **5** magna, summa **8** cum laude **13** magna cum laude, summa cum laude *seeker:* **9** candidate

dégringolade see **degeneration**

____ **de guerre 3** nom

dehydrate 3 dry **4** sear **5** parch **9** desiccate, exsiccate

Deianira *brother:* **8** Meleager *father:* **6** Oeneus *husband:* **8** Heracles, Hercules *mother:* **7** Althaea *victim:* **8** Heracles, Hercules

deific 5 godly **6** divine **7** godlike

deification 8 idolatry **10** apotheosis, glorifying **13** glorification

deify 5 exalt **7** glorify, idolize, worship **8** sanctify, venerate **11** apotheosize

deign 5 stoop **7** descend **9** vouchsafe **10** condescend

Deiphobus *brother:* **5** Paris **6** Hector *father:* **5** Priam *mother:* **6** Hecuba *wife:* **5** Helen

Deirdre *beloved:* **5** Noisi *father:* **5** Felim

deity 3 god **4** Lord **7** goddess, godhead, godhood **8** Almighty, divinity **12** supreme being (see also *god* and *goddess* at **Greek; Hindu; Norse; Roman**)

deject 5 chill, cloud, daunt **6** dampen, dismay **7** depress **8** dispirit **9** disparage **10** demoralize, discourage, dishearten

dejected 3 low, sad **4** blue, down, glum, sunk **6** bummed, gloomy, morose, somber, sombre **7** doleful, hangdog, humbled, unhappy **8** downcast, wretched **9** cheerless, depressed, woebegone **10** despondent, spiritless **11** crestfallen, downhearted **12** disconsolate, disheartened

dejection 5 dumps, gloom **7** despair, sadness **10** melancholy **11** despondency, unhappiness **12** mournfulness

Delaware *capital:* **5** Dover *city:* **10** Wilmington *nickname:* **5** First (State) **7** Diamond (State) *state bird:* **14** blue hen chicken *state flower:* **12** peach blossom *state tree:* **13** American holly

delay 3 lag **4** drag, hold, slow, stay, wait **5** dally, defer, stall, tarry, trail **6** dawdle, detain, hang up, hinder, holdup, impede, linger, loiter, put off, retard, slow up **7** bog down, hold off, respite, set back, slacken, suspend **8** hesitate, hold over, postpone, prorogue, reprieve, slow down **10** dillydally, moratorium, suspension **13** procrastinate

delaying 8 dawdling, dilatory **10** postponing, putting off

delectable 5 tasty, yummy **6** choice, savory **8** charming, heavenly, luscious, pleasing **9** ambrosial, delicious, enjoyable, exquisite, toothsome **10** delightful, enchanting **11** scrumptious **13** mouthwatering

delectation 3 fun, joy **4** zest **5** gusto **6** relish **7** delight **8** gladness, pleasure **9** enjoyment

delegate 4 name, send **5** agent, envoy, proxy **6** assign, depute, deputy, legate **7** appoint, consign, entrust **8** deputize, emissary, transfer **9** authorize, catchpole, designate, spokesman **10** commission, mouthpiece, procurator

delete 4 drop, omit, x out **5** erase, purge **6** cancel, censor, cut out, efface, excise, remove **7** blot out, destroy, expunge, take out, wipe out **8** black out, cross out **9** eliminate, eradicate, strike out **10** blue-pencil, obliterate

deleterious 3 bad **6** nocent **7** baneful, harmful, hurtful, nocuous, noxious, ruinous **8** damaging **9** injurious **10** pernicious **11** destructive, detrimental, mischievous, prejudicial

deletion 7 erasure, voiding **9** canceling **10** deficiency **11** elimination **12** cancellation

deliberate 4 chaw, cool, muse, pore, slow **5** chary, meant, study, think, weigh **6** chew on, ponder, reason **7** careful, heedful, planned, reflect, studied, willful, willing, witting **8** cautious, cogitate, consider, intended, measured, meditate, mull over, ruminate, talk over **9** cerebrate, conscious, unhurried **10** calculated, considered, purposeful, thought-out **11** circumspect, intentional **12** premeditated

deliberately 9 knowingly, on purpose, purposely, willfully, wittingly **11** consciously **12** purposefully **13** intentionally

deliberation 5 study **6** debate **7** thought **10** conference, discussion, reflection **13** consideration

Delibes, Léo *ballet:* **6** Sylvia **8** Coppélia, La Source *opera:* **5** Lakmé *waltz:* **5** Naila

delicacy 5 goody, treat **6** dainty, luxury, morsel, nicety, tidbit **7** frailty **8** kickshaw, fineness **9** fragility, precision **10** daintiness, difficulty, indulgence, stickiness **11** awkwardness **12** ticklishness

delicate 4 fine, lacy, twee, weak **5** frail **6** choice, dainty, flimsy, petite, queasy, sickly, slight, subtle, tender, touchy, tricky **7** elegant, fragile, refined, tactful, tenuous **8** ethereal, feathery, finespun, gossamer, graceful, pleasing, ticklish **9** exquisite, sensitive, squeamish **10** precarious

delicatessen 11 charcuterie

delicious 5 tasty, yummy **6** choice, divine, savory **8** heavenly, luscious **9** ambrosial, exquisite, toothsome **10** delectable, delightful **11** scrumptious **13** mouthwatering

delight 3 joy **4** glee **5** amuse, bliss, charm, enjoy, exult, glory, mirth, revel **6** divert, please, regale, relish **7** ecstasy, enchant, gladden, gratify, jollity, rapture, rejoice **8** enravish, entrance, fruition, hilarity, pleasure **9** delectate, enjoyment, enrapture, entertain **11** delectation *in:* **4** love **5** adore, enjoy, savor **6** admire, relish **7** cherish **10** appreciate

delighted 4 glad **5** happy **6** joyful **8** ecstatic, euphoric

delightful 5 yummy **6** dreamy, lovely **8**

charming, heavenly, luscious, pleasant, pleasing **9** congenial, enjoyable **10** delectable, enchanting, satisfying **11** captivating, fascinating, pleasurable, scrumptious **12** entertaining

Delilah's victim 6 Samson

DeLillo novel 5 Libra, Mao II **10** Underworld, White Noise

delimit 3 bar **5** bound, hem in **6** demark, define **7** confine, enclose **8** restrict **9** demarcate, determine **12** circumscribe

delineate 3 map **4** etch, limn **5** chart, image, trace **6** define, depict, detail, render **7** outline, picture, portray **8** describe, spell out **9** elucidate, interpret, represent **10** illustrate

delineation 5 draft, story **6** report **7** account, contour, drawing, outline, picture, profile **9** depiction, rendering **11** presentment

delinquency 4 debt **5** crime, fault, lapse **7** default, failure, misdeed, neglect, offense **8** omission **9** oversight **10** misconduct, nonpayment, wrongdoing **11** dereliction, misbehavior

delinquent 3 lax **5** slack **6** debtor **7** overdue **8** careless, offender **9** defaulter, in arrears, negligent **10** behindhand, neglectful

deliquesce 3 rot, run **4** flux, fuse, melt, thaw **5** decay **6** render, soften **7** liquefy, putrefy **8** dissolve, fluidize **9** decompose, disappear, waste away **12** disintegrate

delirious 3 mad **4** wild **5** crazy **6** crazed, insane, raving **7** frantic, lunatic **8** confused, demented, deranged, ecstatic, frenetic, frenzied, rambling **9** rapturous **10** bewildered, corybantic, distracted, irrational **11** lightheaded, overexcited, overwrought

delirium 5 furor, mania **6** fervor, frenzy **7** ecstasy, jimjams, rapture, seizure **8** dementia, hysteria **13** hallucination

delirium _____ 7 tremens

deliver 4 bear, deal, feed, find, give, hand, save, send, ship, sing, take **5** bring, serve, speak, state, throw, utter **6** convey, redeem, rescue, strike, supply **7** consign, present, produce, provide, set free, release **8** hand over, liberate, turn over **9** pronounce, surrender **10** bring forth, emancipate **11** come out with, come through

deliverance 6 rescue **7** freeing, opinion, release, verdict **8** decision **9** acquittal, discharge, salvation **10** absolution, liberation

Deliverance author 6 Dickey (James)

delivery 4 drop **5** birth, labor **6** rescue **7** address, bearing **8** birthing, shipment **9** elocution, rendition, salvation **10** childbirth, conveyance, liberation **11** consignment,

parturition, transferral **12** childbearing, transmission

dell 4 dale, glen, vale **6** dingle, hollow, valley

Delphic 4 dark **5** vatic **6** arcane, hidden, mantic, mystic, occult, veiled **7** cryptic, obscure **8** auguring, divining, esoteric, mystical, oracular **9** ambiguous, enigmatic, equivocal, prophetic, recondite, sibylline, vaticinal **10** mystifying, portentous **11** prophesying, prophetical

delta 5 plain **6** letter, symbol **7** deposit **8** triangle **9** increment

delude 3 con **4** dupe, fool, gull, hoax **5** bluff, cozen, trick **6** betray, humbug, juggle, take in **7** beguile, deceive, mislead **8** flimflam, hoodwink **11** double-cross

deluge 5 drown, flood, swamp **6** drench, engulf **7** Niagara, torrent **8** cataract, downpour, drencher, flooding, inundate, overflow **9** cataclysm, overwhelm **10** cloudburst, outpouring, inundation

delusion 4 hoax, sham **5** dream, fancy, snare **6** mirage **7** chimera, fallacy, fantasy, figment, phantom, specter **8** daydream, phantasm **9** deception **10** apparition **11** ignis fatuus **13** hallucination

delusive 5 false **8** fanciful, illusory, specious **9** beguiling, deceiving, deceptive, imaginary **10** chimerical, fallacious, misleading

delusory see delusive

deluxe 4 lush, posh **5** grand, plush, ritzy, swank **6** choice, costly, swanky **7** elegant, opulent **8** luscious, splendid **9** expensive, exquisite, luxuriant, luxurious, sumptuous **10** first class

delve 3 dig, dip **4** mine **5** probe **6** dredge, fathom, hollow, quarry, search, shovel **7** inquire **8** excavate *into:* **4** sift **5** probe **7** explore **8** prospect **11** investigate

delving 6 asking **7** inquest, inquiry, probing **8** research **9** inquiring, searching

demagnetize 7 degauss

demagogue 6 leader **7** inciter **8** agitator, fomenter **9** firebrand **10** instigator **11** provocateur **12** rabble-rouser

demand 3 ask, use **4** call, need, urge, want **5** claim, crave, exact, force, order **6** compel, direct, expect, insist **7** call for, request, require **11** requirement, requisition

demanding 4 hard **5** pushy, tough **6** taxing, trying **7** exigent, onerous, weighty **8** exacting, forceful, rigorous **9** assertive, difficult, insistent, strenuous, stringent **10** aggressive, burdensome, oppressive **11** challenging

demarcate 5 bound, limit **6** define, set off **7** delimit, mark off, outline **8** separate, set apart **9** delineate, determine **11** distinguish **12** circumscribe **13** differentiate

demarcation 9 outlining **10** border line, separation **11** distinction **12** delimitation

démarche 4 plan, ploy, ruse **5** feint **6** action, device, gambit, scheme, tactic **7** protest **8** artifice, maneuver, petition **9** stratagem **10** initiative **11** contrivance, machination

demean 4 bear **5** abase, carry, decry, lower **6** acquit, behave, debase, deport, humble **7** comport, conduct, degrade, detract **8** badmouth, belittle **9** disparage, humiliate

demeanor 3 air **4** look, mien **6** aspect, manner **7** address, bearing, conduct **8** behavior, carriage, presence **10** deportment **11** comportment

demented 3 mad **5** crazy, loony, nutty, wacko **6** crazed, insane, psycho **7** lunatic, unsound **8** deranged, frenzied, maniacal **9** delirious **10** hysterical, unbalanced **12** psychopathic

_____ **de mer 3** mal

demerit 4 mark **5** fault, stain **6** defect **7** blemish, penalty **9** downgrade **10** deficiency, punishment **11** shortcoming **12** imperfection

demesne 5 field, realm **6** domain, estate, region, sphere **7** terrain **8** dominion, province **9** bailiwick, champaign, territory *house:* **5** manor

Demeter see **Ceres**

demigod 4 diva, idol **8** superman **9** superstar

demise 3 die, end **4** drop, pass **5** death, dying, sleep **6** cash in, depart, ending, expire **7** decease, passing, quietus, release, silence, succumb **8** pass away **9** cessation, departure **10** expiration, extinction

demit 4 quit **6** bow out, give up, resign **8** abdicate, renounce, step down, withdraw

demiurgic 8 creative, original **9** formative, inventive **10** innovative **11** originative

demobilize 7 break up, disband, dismiss, scatter **8** disperse, separate **9** discharge, disengage, muster out

democratic 7 popular **8** populist **10** self-ruling **11** egalitarian **13** self-governing

Democrats' symbol 6 donkey

démodé 5 dated, passé **7** antique, archaic **8** old-timey, outdated **9** out-of-date **12** old-fashioned

demoiselle 6 damsel, lassie, maiden **10** damselfish

demolish 4 raze, ruin **5** crush, level, smash, total, wrack, wreck **7** destroy, flatten, wipe out **8** decimate, tear down **9** finish off **10** annihilate, obliterate

demolition 6 razing **8** leveling, wrecking **10** bulldozing **11** destruction **12** annihilation

demolition bomb 11 blockbuster

demon 3 imp **4** jinn **5** devil, fiend, genie, ghoul, jinni, Satan **7** hellion, incubus **9** archfiend *Arabic:* **5** afrit **6** afreet *female:* **5** lamia **7** succuba, succubi (plural) **8** succubae (plural), succubus

demonic 6 wicked **7** satanic **8** devilish, diabolic, fiendish, infernal **9** possessed **10** diabolical

demonize 6 malign, revile, vilify **7** bedevil, censure, slander **8** denounce **9** diabolize

demonstrate 3 try **4** mark, show, test **5** prove, rally **7** confirm, display, exhibit, explain, make out, protest **8** evidence, manifest, proclaim, validate **9** determine, establish **10** illustrate **12** authenticate

demonstration 4 expo, show, test **5** march, proof, rally, trial **6** picket **7** display, protest **9** spectacle **10** exhibition, exposition, validation **12** presentation **13** corroboration, manifestation

demonstrative 4 open **8** effusive, outgoing, specific **9** emotional, expansive, exuberant, outspoken **10** outpouring, unreserved, validating **12** affectionate, unrestrained **13** unconstrained

demoralize 5 chill, daunt, shake, unman, upset **6** dampen, debase, deject, rattle, weaken **7** corrupt, debauch, deprave, unnerve, vitiate **8** dispirit, psych out **9** undermine **10** discourage, dishearten

Demosthenes 6 orator *oration:* **9** Philippic

demote 4 bump, bust **5** lower **6** reduce **7** declass, degrade **9** downgrade

demulcent 4 balm **5** jelly, salve **7** unguent **8** liniment, ointment, soothing **9** softening

demur 5 qualm **6** object, oppose, resist **7** dispute, protest **8** hesitate, question **9** challenge, hesitancy, objection **10** hesitation, indecision, reluctance **11** compunction, remonstrate

demure 3 coy, shy **5** timid **6** modest **7** bashful **8** reserved, reticent, retiring **9** diffident **11** unassertive **12** self-effacing

demurral 7 protest **9** challenge, objection **12** remonstrance **13** remonstration

demurrer see **demurral**

den 4 base, cave, home, lair, nest, room **5** study **6** burrow, cavern, hollow **7** dayroom, hideout, sanctum **8** hideaway, playroom *rabbit:* **6** warren

denial 2 no **3** nay, nix **6** heresy **7** refusal **8** disproof, negation, rebuttal **9** disavowal, rejection **10** abnegation, gainsaying, refutation **11** repudiation **12** renunciation

denigrate 5 decry, libel, smear, stain, sully **6** darken, defame, defile, impugn, malign, vilify **7** asperse, devalue, put down, slander, tarnish, traduce **8** belittle, dishonor, tear down **9** discredit, disparage **10** calumniate, scandalize

denims 5 jeans **8** overalls **9** blue jeans, dungarees

denizen 5 liver **6** native **7** dweller, habitué, haunter, resider **8** habitant, occupant, resident **9** indweller, inhabiter **10** frequenter, inhabitant

Denmark *capital:* **10** Copenhagen *city:* **5** Århus **6** Ålborg, Odense **11** Helsingborg **13** Frederiksberg *island:* **3** Fyn **7** Falster, Zealand **8** Bornholm **9** Sjaelland *monetary unit:* **5** krone *neighbor:* **6** Sweden **7** Germany *part of:* **11** Scandinavia *peninsula:* **7** Jutland *possession:* **9** Greenland **12** Faroe Islands **13** Faeroe Islands *sea:* **5** North **6** Baltic *strait:* **5** Lille, Store **9** Langeland

denominate 3 dub **4** call, name, term **5** label, style, title **7** baptize, entitle **8** christen **9** designate

denomination 4 cult, name, sect **5** creed, faith, style, title **6** church **8** category, cognomen, religion **9** communion **10** persuasion *religious:* **5** Amish **6** Mormon **7** Baptist **8** Lutheran, Moravian, Reformed **9** Adventist, Episcopal, Mennonite, Methodist, Unitarian **11** Pentecostal **12** Presbyterian, Universalist **13** Roman Catholic

denotation 4 name, sign **5** sense **6** import **7** meaning **10** indication, signifying **11** designation **13** signification, specification

denote 4 mark, mean, name, show **5** spell **6** import **7** add up to, betoken, express **8** announce, indicate **9** designate, represent

denouement 6 effect, result, upshot **7** outcome **10** conclusion **11** consequence, culmination

denounce 3 rap **4** skin **5** blame, blast, decry, knock **6** rebuke, scathe **7** censure, condemn, upbraid **8** derogate, reproach **9** castigate, criticize, dress down, excoriate, reprehend, reprobate **10** denunciate, vituperate **11** incriminate **12** anathematize

de novo 4 anew, over **5** again, newly **6** afresh **8** once more **9** over again **11** from scratch

dense 4 dull, dumb **5** close, heavy, solid, thick, tight **6** obtuse, opaque, stupid **7** compact, crammed, crowded, doltish, serried **9** fatheaded, jam-packed **10** numskulled **11** blockheaded, numbskulled, thickheaded **12** impenetrable

dent 4 bash, ding, flaw, nick **5** tooth **6** dimple, hollow **10** depression, impression

dental addition 5 inlay, plate **6** braces, bridge **7** filling

denticulate 6 ridged **7** dentate, notched, serrate, serried, toothed **8** saw-edged, sawtooth, serrated **10** saw-toothed

dentin 6 enamel

dentine 5 ivory

denude 4 bare **5** strip **6** divest **7** disrobe, uncover, undress **8** unclothe

denunciate see **denounce**

deny 5 cross, rebut **6** disown, forbid, negate, refuse, refute, reject, renege **7** disavow, gainsay **8** abnegate, disallow, disclaim, forswear, renounce, traverse, withhold **9** disaffirm **10** contradict, contravene

depart 2 go **3** die **4** exit, flee, pass, quit **5** leave, scram, split **6** begone, decamp, demise, desert, escape, expire, go away, move on, pass on, perish, skidoo **7** decease, deviate, go forth, move out, pull out, skiddoo, take off, vamoose **8** pass away, shove off, slip away, withdraw **9** skedaddle, take leave

departing 6 egress, exodus **7** good-bye **8** farewell **9** desertion **11** leave-taking, valedictory

department 5 arena **6** branch, domain, sphere **7** section **8** category, division, province **9** bailiwick, territory **11** subdivision

departure 4 exit **5** adieu, break, congé, going **6** egress, exodus, flight **7** leaving **8** farewell **9** deviation, diversion **10** aberration, decampment, deflection, divergence, embarkment, setting-out, withdrawal **11** embarkation, leave-taking *of a ship:* **6** sortie *point:* **7** outport

dependable 4 sure, true **5** loyal, solid, tried **6** secure, steady, trusty **7** certain, staunch **8** accurate, constant, faithful, reliable, surefire **9** authentic, steadfast, unfailing **11** responsible, trustworthy **12** tried and true **13** authoritative *Scottish:* **6** sicker

dependence 4 need **5** faith, habit, stock, trust **8** reliance **9** addiction **11** contingency, habituation

dependent 5 child **6** minion, vassal **7** reliant, relying **9** secondary **10** contingent, equivalent **11** conditional, subordinate

depend on 5 bet on, trust **6** bank on, hang on, look to, rely on, turn on **7** build on, count on, hinge on, stand on, swear by

depict 4 draw, limn, show **5** image, paint **6** relate, render, sketch **7** express, picture, portray **8** describe **9** delineate, represent **10** illustrate

depiction 5 image **6** sketch **7** drawing, picture **9** portrayal, rendering **11** delineation, portraiture, presentment **12** illustration, presentation

deplete 3 sap **4** milk **5** bleed, drain, eat up,

depleted

empty, leech, use up **6** expend, lessen, reduce **7** consume, draw off, exhaust **8** decrease, diminish, draw down **9** undermine **10** run through

depleted 6 sapped, used up **7** drained, reduced **8** consumed, expended **9** exhausted, washed-out

deplorable 5 awful **6** rotten, woeful **8** dreadful, god-awful, grievous, terrible, wretched **9** execrable, miserable, sickening **10** calamitous, disastrous, lamentable **11** distressing, intolerable **12** contemptible, disreputable, heartrending **13** heartbreaking, reprehensible

deplore 3 rue **5** abhor, mourn **6** bemoan, bewail, grieve, lament, regret **7** condemn **8** denounce, object to **9** deprecate **10** disapprove

deploy 3 use **5** array **6** muster, unfold **7** arrange, display, dispose, marshal, utilize **8** position

_____ **de plume 3** nom

depone 5 state, swear **6** affirm, assert, attest **7** certify, confirm, declare, testify, warrant **11** corroborate **12** authenticate

deport 3 act **4** bear **5** carry, exile, expel **6** acquit, banish, behave, demean **7** conduct **8** displace, relegate **10** expatriate

deportee 2 DP **5** exile **8** expellee

deportment 3 air, set **4** mien, port **6** aspect, manner **7** address, bearing, conduct, manners **8** behavior, carriage, demeanor, presence

depose 4 aver, avow, oust **5** state, swear **6** affirm, assert, avouch, remove, topple, unmake **7** declare, profess, testify, uncrown **8** dethrone, displace, throw out, unthrone **9** overthrow

deposit 3 lay **4** bank, drop, dump, fund, lees, pawn, save, stow **5** cache, chest, dregs, place, put by, stash, store **6** settle **7** consign, grounds, lay away **8** put aside, security, sediment, sock away **9** settlings **11** precipitate **13** precipitation *alluvial:* **5** delta *black:* **4** soot *calcium carbonate:* **10** stalactite, stalagmite *containing gold:* **6** placer *eggs:* **5** spawn *geologic:* **7** horizon *glacial:* **4** till **5** drift, esker **7** moraine *loam:* **5** loess *mineral:* **4** lode **10** concretion *muddy:* **6** sludge *sand:* **4** bank **5** beach *sedimentary:* **4** silt *skeletal:* **5** coral *stream:* **8** alluvium, sediment *tooth:* **6** tartar

deposition 6 avowal **7** ousting, placing **9** affidavit, dismissal, testimony **10** testifying **11** attestation, declaration

depository 4 bank, dump, safe **5** attic, cache, depot, store, vault **7** archive, arsenal **8** magazine **9** warehouse **10** storehouse *for bones:* **7** ossuary

depot 4 dump **5** cache, store **6** armory, garage **7** arsenal, station **8** magazine, terminal, terminus **9** warehouse **10** depository, repository, storehouse **12** station house

deprave 4 warp **6** debase **7** corrupt, debauch, pervert, vitiate **9** brutalize **10** bastardize, bestialize, demoralize

depraved 3 bad, low **4** base, evil, ugly, vile **6** putrid, rotten, wanton, warped, wicked **7** bestial, corrupt, debased, immoral, twisted, vicious **8** degraded, perverse, vitiated **9** corrupted, debauched, miscreant, nefarious, perverted, reprobate **10** degenerate

depravity 4 vice **8** baseness **9** abasement, decadence **10** corruption, debasement, debauchery, degeneracy, immorality, perversion **12** degeneration

deprecate 7 frown on, put down **8** belittle, derogate, disfavor, object to, play down, pooh-pooh **9** disparage **10** disapprove **12** disapprove of

depreciate 4 drop, fall **5** abate, decry, erode, lower **6** lessen, reduce, slight **7** cheapen, devalue, put down **8** belittle, decrease, derogate, diminish, discount, mark down, write off **9** devaluate, disparage, downgrade, underrate **10** devalorize, undervalue **11** detract from

depreciation 8 discount **11** denigration **12** belittlement **13** disparagement

depreciative 9 slighting **10** derogatory, detracting, pejorative **11** disparaging, underrating **12** undervaluing

depredate 4 sack **5** waste **6** ravage **7** despoil, pillage, plunder **8** desolate, lay waste, prey upon, spoliate **9** desecrate, devastate, vandalize

depredation 4 sack **5** havoc **7** pillage, plunder, sacking **8** ravaging **9** marauding, ruination **10** spoliation **11** desecration, destruction, devastation **12** despoliation

depredator 6 looter, raider, vandal **7** forager, spoiler **8** marauder **9** plunderer **10** freebooter

depress 4 damp, dash, dent **5** chill, daunt, lower **6** dampen, deject, dismay, sadden **7** afflict, trouble **8** dispirit, enfeeble **9** disparage, weigh down **10** discourage, dishearten

depressed 3 low, sad **4** blue, down, glum, sunk **6** broody, gloomy, glumpy, lonely, somber **8** cast down, dejected, downcast **9** bummed out, flattened, woebegone **10** dispirited, lugubrious, melancholy, spiritless **11** crestfallen, downhearted, melancholic **12** disconsolate **13** disadvantaged

depressing 3 sad **5** bleak **6** dismal, dreary, gloomy, somber, sombre **7** joyless **8** funereal, mournful **9** saddening **10** melancholy, oppressive **11** melancholic **13** disheartening

depression 3 dip, low, pit, sag **4** bust, drop, funk, glen, hole, sink, vale **5** basin, blues, dolor, dumps, ennui, gloom, scoop, slump **6** cavity, crater, hollow, pocket, valley **7** cyclone, decline, sadness, sinkage **8** downturn, sinkhole **9** concavity, dejection **10** desolation, melancholy **11** melancholia, unhappiness *anatomical:* **5** fossa, fovea **6** foveae (plural) *geographic:* **7** Qattara *in ridge:* **3** col *in snow:* **8** sitzmark *small:* **4** dent **6** dimple

depressive 4 blue, dour, glum **6** woeful **7** doleful **8** downbeat, downcast, mournful **9** miserable, woebegone **10** despondent, melancholy **11** low-spirited

deprivation 4 lack, loss **6** denial **7** forfeit, removal **10** forfeiture **11** bereavement, divestiture **13** dispossession

deprive 3 rob **5** strip **6** divest **8** disseise, disseize **10** disinherit, dispossess *of brilliancy:* **4** dull **6** deaden *of courage:* **7** unnerve *of sensation:* **6** benumb

depth 4 base, drop, gulf **5** abyss, chasm, gorge **7** lowness **10** profundity *measure:* **6** fathom *of water:* **5** draft **7** draught

depthless 7 cursory, shallow, sketchy **10** uncritical **11** superficial

Dept. of ____ 5 Labor, State **6** Energy **7** Defense, Justice **8** Commerce, Interior, Treasury **9** Education **11** Agriculture

deputize 4 name **6** assign **7** appoint, empower, warrant **8** delegate **9** authorize, designate **10** commission

deputy 4 aide **5** agent, proxy **6** backup, factor **8** delegate **9** assistant, catchpole, surrogate

derange 4 muss **5** craze, upset **6** madden, mess up **7** confuse, perturb, unhinge **8** confound, disarray, disorder, distract, unsettle **9** interrupt, unbalance **10** discompose **11** disorganize

deranged 3 mad **4** loco **5** crazy, wacko **6** crazed, insane, maniac **7** berserk, bonkers, cracked, haywire, lunatic, unsound **8** demented, maniacal, unhinged **9** disturbed **10** disordered, flipped out, unbalanced

derangement 4 mess **5** chaos, mania **6** lunacy, muddle **7** madness **8** dementia, disorder, insanity **9** confusion, unbalance **10** hodgepodge **11** distraction, disturbance, psychopathy

derby 3 hat **4** race **7** contest **9** horse race

derelict 3 bum **4** hobo, lorn **5** tramp **6** remiss, shabby **7** drifter, outcast, run-down, uncouth, vagrant **8** careless, deserted, vagabond **9** abandoned, negligent **10** neglectful **11** dilapidated **12** disregardful, undependable **13** irresponsible

dereliction 5 fault **7** default, failure, neglect **9** deviation, disregard, oversight **11** abandonment, delinquency, shortcoming

deride 3 rag, rap **4** gibe, jeer, jibe, lout, mock, quiz, razz, twit **5** fleer, rally, scoff, scout, sneer, taunt **6** dump on, insult **7** catcall **8** ridicule

de rigueur 5 right **6** au fait, decent, proper **7** correct **8** becoming, decorous, required **9** essential, mandatory, requisite **10** compulsory, obligatory, prescribed **11** comme il faut

derision 5 abuse, scorn **7** disdain, mockery, ribbing **8** contempt, raillery, ridicule, scoffing **9** contumely, invective

derisive 7 abusive, jeering, mocking **8** sardonic, scoffing, scornful, taunting **9** insulting, sarcastic **10** disdainful **12** contemptuous

derivable 7 a priori **9** deducible, deductive, traceable **10** obtainable **11** extractable **12** attributable, determinable

derivation 4 root **6** origin, source **7** descent **8** ancestry **9** etymology **10** provenance, wellspring **11** origination, provenience

derivative 5 banal **7** spin-off **8** acquired, borrowed, offshoot **9** by-product, imitative, outgrowth, secondary **10** descendant, unoriginal

derive 3 get **4** draw, flow, rise, stem, take **5** adapt, arise, educe, infer, issue, trace **6** deduce, deduct, evolve, gather, obtain **7** descend, emanate, extract, proceed, work out **8** arrive at, conclude **9** formulate, originate

dernier cri 3 fad **4** chic, rage **5** craze, vogue **8** last word

derogate 5 decry **6** berate, dump on, insult **7** put down **8** bad-mouth, belittle, diminish, minimize, write off **9** disparage, dispraise **10** depreciate **11** detract from

derogatory 5 snide **8** decrying, scornful, spiteful **9** degrading, demeaning, maligning, slighting **10** belittling, detracting, disdainful, pejorative **11** disparaging **12** contumelious, depreciative

derrick 5 crane, davit, hoist

derriere 3 bum **4** beam, butt, rear, rump, seat, tail **5** fanny **6** behind, bottom **7** rear end **8** backside, buttocks **9** posterior

derring-do 4 guts **5** nerve, pluck, spunk, valor **6** daring, mettle **7** bravado, bravery, bravura, courage **8** boldness **9** gallantry **12** fearlessness **13** dauntlessness

dervish 4 monk, Sufi **9** mendicant *in Arabian*

Nights: 4 Agib **practice:** 7 dancing 8 whirling **wandering:** 5 fakir 8 calender

descant 4 sing 6 melody, remark, treble 7 comment, discuss, melisma, melodia, oration, soprano 9 discourse, expatiate 12 counterpoint

Descartes's axiom 13 cogito ergo sum

descend 4 dive, drop, fall, pass, sink 5 slide, stoop, swoop 6 alight, derive, go down, plunge, worsen 7 decline 8 come down, dismount 9 originate 10 degenerate, retrograde **by rope:** 6 rappel

descendant 4 heir 5 scion 7 progeny, spin-off 8 offshoot, relative 9 by-product, offspring, outgrowth 10 derivative

descendants 4 seed 5 brood, heirs, issue, spawn 6 litter 7 progeny 8 children 9 offspring, posterity 11 progeniture

descent 3 dip 4 drop, fall 5 birth, blood, slide, slope 6 origin, plunge, tumble 7 decline, drop-off, incline, lineage, sinkage 8 ancestry, comedown, gradient, pedigree 9 declivity, downgrade 10 derivation, devolution, extraction **airplane:** 8 approach **parachute:** 4 jump 7 bailout

describe 4 limn 6 denote, depict, recite, relate, render, report 7 explain, express, mark out, narrate, outline, picture, portray, recount 9 delineate, represent 10 illustrate 12 characterize

description 3 ilk 4 kind, sort, type 6 nature, report 7 account, picture, species 9 character, depiction, narrative, portrayal 10 recounting

descry 3 see 4 espy, spot 6 behold, detect, spy out, turn up 7 discern, find out, hit upon 8 discover, meet with, perceive 9 encounter, recognize

Desdemona father: 9 Brabantio **husband:** 7 Othello **slanderer:** 4 Iago **slayer:** 7 Othello

desecrate 4 sack 5 stain, sully, waste 6 befoul, debase, defile, ravage 7 corrupt, degrade, despoil, pillage, pollute, profane, violate 8 spoliate 9 depredate, devastate

desecration 5 abuse 7 impiety 9 blasphemy, sacrilege 10 debasement, defilement, spoliation 11 profanation 12 despoliation

desensitize 4 dull, numb 5 blunt 6 benumb, dampen, deaden, freeze, sedate 11 anesthetize

desert 4 flee, quit 5 leave, waste 6 barren, betray, decamp, defect, escape, go AWOL, maroon, strand 7 abandon, abscond, badland, forsake 8 renounce 9 repudiate, wasteland 10 apostatize, wilderness 12 tergiversate **African:** 5 Namib 6 Libyan, Nubian, Sahara 7 Arabian 8 Kalahari **Arizona:**

7 Painted **Asian:** 4 Gobi, Thar 6 Syrian 7 Kara-Kum 8 Kyzyl Kum, Qizilkum 10 Great Sandy **Australian:** 6 Gibson, Tanami 7 Simpson **basin bottom:** 5 playa **beast:** 5 camel 9 dromedary **California:** 6 Mohave, Mojave **Chilean:** 7 Atacama **clay:** 5 adobe **dweller:** 4 bedu 5 nomad 6 Beduin, Berber, Nubian 7 bedouin 8 Maghrebi, Maghribi **Egyptian:** 7 Arabian **fertile area:** 5 oases (plural), oasis **garb:** 3 aba 7 burnous 8 burnoose **hallucination:** 6 mirage **Israeli:** 5 Negev **region:** 3 erg **Saudi Arabia:** 7 Al-Nafud, An Nafud 10 Rub Al-Khali **travel group:** 7 caravan **wind:** 7 sirocco 8 scirocco

deserted 4 bare, lorn 6 barren, vacant 8 derelict, desolate, forsaken, solitary 9 abandoned, neglected 11 uninhabited

deserter 3 rat 4 AWOL 6 bolter 7 runaway 8 apostate, defector, fugitive, renegade, runagate, turncoat

desertion 7 perfidy 8 apostasy 9 defection, forsaking 11 abandonment, dereliction

deserts 3 due 6 reward 8 requital 9 reckoning 10 recompense 11 comeuppance

deserve 3 win 4 earn, gain, rate 5 merit 6 demand 7 justify, warrant

deserved 3 apt, due 4 just 5 right 7 fitting, merited 8 rightful, suitable 9 befitting 11 appropriate 13 rhadamanthine

deserving 3 due 6 worthy 8 laudable 9 admirable, estimable 10 creditable 11 commendable, meritorious, thankworthy 12 praiseworthy

desiccate 3 dry 5 dry up, parch, wizen 6 wither 7 shrivel 9 dehydrate 10 devitalize

desiderate 4 want, wish 5 covet, crave 6 desire 7 long for, wish for 8 yearn for

design 3 aim 4 cast, draw, form, mean, mind, plan, plot, will 5 chart, draft, frame, model, motif 6 create, device, devise, figure, intend, intent, invent, lay out, makeup, map out, motive, scheme, set out, sketch, tailor 7 arrange, diagram, drawing, execute, fashion, meaning, outline, pattern, prepare, project, propose, tracing 8 contrive, creation, game plan, intrigue, strategy, thinking 9 blueprint, construct, delineate, direction, formation, intention, invention 10 decoration, figuration 11 arrangement, composition 12 architecture, construction **book:** 8 vignette **carpet:** 3 gul 9 medallion **incised:** 8 intaglio **Indonesian:** 5 batik **inlaid:** 6 mosaic **intricate:** 9 arabesque **of squares:** 5 check **openwork:** 8 filigree **perforated:** 7 stencil **raised:** 8 repoussé **skin:** 6 tattoo **textile:** 8 polka dot **velvety:** 8 flocking

designate 3 dub, tap 4 call, name, pick, term

5 allot, elect, label, style, title **6** assign, choose, denote, depute, select **7** appoint, declare, earmark, reserve, signify, specify **8** allocate, christen, delegate, identify, set aside, stand for **9** apportion, stipulate **10** decide upon **11** appropriate **12** characterize

designation 4 name, sign **5** class, nomen, style, title **6** naming **8** cognomen, monicker **11** appellation

designed 7 devised, planned **8** intended, resolved **9** contrived, patterned **10** considered, deliberate, determined, thought-out **12** premeditated

designedly 9 expressly, knowingly, on purpose, purposely, willfully, wittingly **11** consciously, purposively **12** deliberately **13** intentionally

desirable 8 enviable, fetching **9** advisable, agreeable, preferred **10** attractive, beneficial **12** advantageous

desire 3 aim, yen **4** envy, eros, itch, lust, want, wish **5** covet, crave, fancy, go for, greed **6** pining, thirst **7** avarice, craving, long for, longing, passion **8** appetite, cupidity, petition, yearn for, yearning **9** eroticism, hankering, prurience, pruriency **10** aphrodisia, attraction, preference **11** inclination, lustfulness **13** concupiscence, lickerishness

desired 6 wanted **8** hoped-for **9** preferred, requested

desirous 4 avid **6** greedy **7** athirst, craving, envious, longing, wishful, wishing **8** covetous, grasping **10** solicitous

desist 4 halt, quit, stop **5** cease, yield **7** forbear, hold off, refrain **8** knock off, leave off, surcease **11** discontinue

desistance 3 end **4** halt, stop **5** cease, close **6** ending, finish, period **8** stoppage, stopping **9** cessation **10** conclusion **11** termination

desk 5 booth, stand, table **7** counter, lectern, rolltop **8** lapboard **9** secretary **10** escritoire *adjunct:* **8** inkstand, standish *item:* **3** pad **7** blotter, inkwell *library:* **6** carrel

desolate 4 bare, lorn, sack **5** alone, bleak, drear, stark, waste **6** barren, devoid, dismal, dreary, gloomy, ravage **7** despoil, forlorn, joyless, pillage, plunder **8** dejected, derelict, deserted, desolate, downcast, forsaken, lay waste, lifeless, lonesome, solitary, spoliate **9** abandoned, cheerless, deprecate, desecrate, destitute, devastate, sorrowful **10** despondent **11** dilapidated **12** inconsolable **13** disheartening

desolation 3 woe **4** ruin **5** gloom, grief, waste **6** misery, sorrow **7** anguish, despair, sadness **8** bareness **9** bleakness, dejection,

wasteland **10** loneliness **11** abandonment, devastation **12** wretchedness

despair 6 give up **8** lose hope

despairing 7 anxious, doleful, forlorn **8** dejected, desolate, hopeless, wretched **9** depressed **10** despondent **11** downhearted **12** disconsolate **13** brokenhearted

desperado 6 bandit, gunman, outlaw **7** bandito, brigand, convict, ruffian **8** criminal **9** cutthroat **10** gunslinger, highwayman, lawbreaker

desperate 4 bold, dire, rash **5** acute, risky **6** daring, futile **7** crucial, forlorn, frantic, useless, violent **8** critical, headlong, hopeless, reckless, shocking **9** foolhardy, impetuous **10** despondent, frustrated, outrageous, scandalous **11** climacteric, precipitate **12** overpowering **13** irretrievable

Desperate Housewives *actress:* **5** Cross (Marcia) **7** Hatcher (Teri), Huffman (Felicity) **8** Longoria (Eva), Sheridan (Nicollette) *creator:* **6** Cherry (Marc) *character:* **4** Bree (Van De Kamp), Edie (Britt), Mike (Delfino) **5** Betty (Applewhite), Orson (Hodge), Susan (Mayer) **7** Lynette (Scavo) **9** Gabrielle (Solis) *narrator:* **6** Strong (Brenda) *setting:* **8** Fairview **12** Wisteria Lane

desperation 5 agony **7** anguish, despair **8** distress **11** distraction **12** hopelessness, wretchedness

despicable 3 low **4** base, foul, grim, mean, ugly, vile **5** awful, cheap, gross, sorry **6** abject, scurvy, shabby, sordid **7** beastly, hateful, ignoble, pitiful **8** pitiable, shameful, wretched **9** degrading, loathsome **10** deplorable, detestable, disgusting **11** disgraceful, ignominious **12** contemptible, disreputable **13** reprehensible

despise 4 hate, shun, snub **5** abhor, avoid, scorn, spurn **6** detest, loathe, reject **7** contemn **8** execrate **9** abominate

despised one 6 pariah **7** outcast

despisement 4 hate **5** scorn **6** hatred, malice **7** disdain, ill will **8** aversion, contempt, loathing **9** antipathy, contumely **10** abhorrence **11** detestation

despite 8 although **11** in the face of **12** regardless of

despiteful 4 evil, mean **5** catty **6** bitchy, horrid, malign, odious, wicked **7** baleful, baneful, hostile, vicious **8** vengeful **9** malicious, rancorous, repellent **10** despicable, malevolent

despoil 4 sack **5** blast, strip, waste, wreck **6** denude, devour, maraud, ravage **7** pillage, plunder **8** desolate, spoliate **9** depredate, desecrate, devastate, strip away, vandalize 10 wreak havoc

despoiler 6 looter, sacker, vandal 7 ravager, wrecker 8 marauder, pillager 9 plunderer, spoliator 10 depredator, freebooter

despond 4 fret, mope, wilt 5 brood, droop, worry 6 give up, sorrow 8 languish 9 dejection 12 hopelessness

despondency 5 blues, dumps, gloom 6 misery, sorrow 7 anguish, despair, sadness 8 glumness 9 dejection 10 depression, melancholy 11 desperation, unhappiness 12 hopelessness

despondent 3 low, sad 4 blue, down, glum 7 doleful, forlorn 8 cast down, dejected, downcast, grieving, hopeless, mourning 9 depressed, desperate, heartsick, heartsore, sorrowful, woebegone 10 dispairing, dispirited, melancholy 11 discouraged, downhearted 12 disconsolate, disheartened

despot 4 czar, duce, tsar, tzar 5 ruler 6 tyrant 7 autarch, emperor 8 autocrat, dictator 9 oppressor, strong man

despotic 8 absolute 9 arbitrary, autarchic, imperious, tyrannous 10 autocratic, monocratic, tyrannical 11 dictatorial 12 totalitarian

despotism 7 czarism, tsarism, tyranny, tzarism 8 autarchy 9 autocracy 10 absolutism, domination 12 dictatorship

desquamate 4 pare, peel 5 scale 7 peel off 8 flake off, scale off 9 exfoliate

dessert 3 ice, pie 4 cake, flan, fool, tart 5 Betty, bombe, crepe, crisp, fruit, grunt, halva, Jell-O, melba, s'more, sweet, torte 6 afters, blintz, Danish, éclair, fondue, frappe, gâteau, halvah, hermit, junket, kuchen, mousse, pastry, sorbet, sundae, trifle 7 brownie, cobbler, compote, custard, gelatin, parfait, pudding, sabayon, sherbet, soufflé, spumoni, strudel 8 ambrosia, Bismarck, clafouti, crostata, flummery, ice cream, macaroon, meringue, napoleon, pandowdy, streusel, tiramisu, turnover 9 charlotte, cream puff, fruitcake, petit four, shortcake 10 blancmange, brown Betty, cheesecake, frangipane, icebox cake, peach Melba, zabaglione 11 baked Alaska, banana split, crème brûlée, gingerbread 12 hasty pudding, zuppa inglese *French:* 5 bombe 6 éclair, frappe, gâteau, mousse 7 parfait, sabayon 9 petit four 10 blancmange, frangipane *frozen:* 5 bombe 7 parfait, sherbet *German:* 6 kuchen 7 strudel *Italian:* 7 cannoli, spumoni 8 tiramisu 10 zabaglione 12 zuppa inglese *Turkish:* 5 halva 6 halvah

destination 3 aim, end, use 6 object, target 7 purpose 8 terminus 9 objective 10 appointing

destine 4 fate 6 assign, direct, intend 8 dedicate, set aside 9 designate, determine, preordain 10 foreordain 12 predetermine

destiny 3 lot 4 doom, fate 5 karma 6 design, future, kismet, Moirai 7 fortune, portion 8 prospect 9 hereafter 12 circumstance

destitute 4 bare, poor, void 5 broke, empty, needy 6 bereft, devoid, ruined 7 drained, lacking 8 bankrupt, depleted, dirt poor, divested, indigent, strapped, stripped 9 deficient, exhausted, penurious 10 bankrupted, stone-broke 11 impecunious 12 impoverished

destitution 6 penury 7 poverty 9 indigence, privation

destroy 3 axe, zap 4 doom, down, kill, nuke, raze, ruin, sack, slay, undo 5 crush, erase, quash, quell, smash, total, trash, waste, wrack, wreck 6 finish, lay low, mangle, ravage, rubble, rub out 7 abolish, atomize, despoil, expunge, nullify, pillage, shatter, wipe out 8 decimate, demolish, dispatch, dynamite, lay waste, pull down, snuff out, stamp out, tear down 9 devastate, dismantle, eradicate, extirpate, liquidate, pulverize 10 annihilate, extinguish, obliterate 11 exterminate

destroyer 4 bane, ruin 6 tin can, vandal 7 undoing, warship 8 downfall

destruction 4 loss, ruin 5 havoc 7 killing, sacking, undoing 8 downfall 9 ruination 10 extinction 11 devastation, liquidation 12 annihilation

destructive 7 baneful, harmful, ruinous 8 damaging 9 corrosive, injurious 10 shattering 11 deleterious, detrimental

desuetude 6 disuse 7 closure, neglect 9 cessation 11 abandonment

desultory 6 casual, chance, fitful, random, spotty 7 aimless, erratic, offhand, vagrant 8 shifting, slipshod, sporadic, wavering 9 haphazard, hit-or-miss, unplanned 10 capricious, digressive, disjointed 11 purposeless 12 unmethodical, unsystematic

detach 4 free, part, undo, wean 5 sever 6 cut off, remove, sunder 7 disjoin, divorce, release 8 separate, uncouple, withdraw 9 disengage 10 disconnect 12 disaffiliate

detached 5 alone, aloof, apart 6 remote 7 distant, neutral, removed, severed 8 abstract, isolated, separate, unbiased 9 incurious, withdrawn 10 impersonal 11 indifferent, unconcerned, unconnected 12 uninterested 13 disinterested, dispassionate, unaccompanied

detachment 5 squad 7 divorce, rupture 8 disunion, division 9 partition 10 neutrality, separation 11 dissolution

detail 4 item, list, part 5 point 6 assign, nicety, relate, report 7 appoint, article, element, itemize, listing, minutia, specify 8 allocate, spell out 9 enumerate, stipulate 10 assignment, particular 12 circumstance 13 particularize

detailed 4 full 6 minute 8 itemized, complete, thorough 10 blow-by-blow, exhaustive, meticulous, particular 13 thoroughgoing

detain 3 nab 4 bust, curb, hold, keep, mire, snag 5 check, delay, run in 6 arrest, collar, hang up, hinder, hold up, impede, pick up, retard, slow up 7 bog down, reserve, set back 8 hold back, keep back, restrain, slow down, withhold 9 apprehend 10 buttonhole *in conversation:* 10 buttonhole

detect 4 espy, find, spot 5 catch, dig up, hit on, scent, smell 6 descry, notice, turn up 7 discern, hit upon, uncover, unearth 8 discover, meet with 9 ascertain, encounter, ferret out, track down

detectable 6 patent 7 evident, visible 8 sensible, tangible 10 noticeable, observable 11 discernible, perceptible

detection 9 discovery 10 unearthing *system:* 5 radar, sofar

detective 3 tec 4 dick, G-man 6 shamus, sleuth 7 gumshoe 8 hawkshaw, informer, sherlock 9 inspector 10 private eye 12 investigator *fictional:* 3 Pym (Lucy) 4 Chan (Charlie), Gray (Cordelia), Moto (Mr.) 5 Banks (Alan), Bosch (Harry), Brown (Father), Dupin (Auguste), Lecoq, Lupin (Arsène), McGee (Travis), Morse (Inspector), Queen (Ellery), Rebus (John), Saint, Spade (Sam), Trent (Philip), Vance (Philo), Wolfe (Nero) 6 Alleyn (Roderick), Archer (Lew), Carter (Nick), Hammer (Mike), Holmes (Sherlock), Marple (Miss Jane), McCone (Sharon), Poirot (Hercule), Wimsey (Peter) 7 Cadfael (Brother), Campion (Albert), Charles (Nick, Nora), Maigret (Jules), Marlowe (Philip) 8 Drummond (Bulldog), Millhone (Kinsey) 9 Dalgliesh (Adam) 10 Robicheaux (Dave), Warshawski (V. I.) 11 Father Brown

detective-story writer 3 Poe (Edgar Allan), Tey (Josephine) 4 Carr (John Dickson), Knox (Ronald) 5 Blake (Nicholas), Block (Lawrence), Cross (Amanda), Doyle (Arthur Conan), Green (Anna Katherine), Innes (Michael), James (P. D.), Marsh (Ngaio), Queen (Ellery), Stout (Rex) 6 Bramah (Ernest), Buchan (John), Dexter (Colin), Hansen (Joseph), McBain (Ed), Mosley (Walter), Parker (Robert), Peters (Ellis), Sayers (Dorothy L.) 7 Bentley (E. C.), Biggers (Earl Derr), Collins (Wilkie), Francis (Dick), Freeman (Austin), Gardner (Erle Stanley), Grafton (Sue), Hammett (Dashiell), Hiaasen (Carl), Hornung (E. W.), Leonard (Elmore), Rendell (Ruth), Simenon (Georges), Van Dine (S. S.), Wallace (Edgar) 8 Chandler (Raymond), Christie (Agatha), Cornwell (Patricia), Gaboriau (Emile), Marquand (John), Mortimer (John), Paretsky (Sara), Rinehart (Mary Roberts), Spillane (Mickey) 9 Allingham (Margery), Highsmith (Patricia), Hillerman (Tony), Lockridge (Frances, Richard), Macdonald (John, Ross) 10 Chesterton (Gilbert Keith)

detent 4 pawl

detention 6 arrest 7 holding 10 internment 11 confinement 12 imprisonment

deter 5 avert, block 6 divert, hamper, hinder, impede, thwart 7 forfend, inhibit, obviate, prevent, rule out, shut out, ward off 8 dissuade, preclude, restrain, stave off 9 forestall, turn aside 10 discourage

deterge 4 wash 7 cleanse, wash off

detergent 4 soap 8 cleanser

deteriorate 3 rot 4 fade, fail, flag, sink, wear 5 decay, lapse, slide, spoil 6 weaken, worsen 7 decline, regress 8 languish 9 decompose, fall apart 10 debilitate, degenerate, depreciate, go downhill, retrograde, retrogress 12 disintegrate

deterioration 4 ruin 5 decay 6 ebbing, waning 7 atrophy, decline, erosion, failing, rotting 8 decaying, spoiling 9 crumbling, decadence, downgrade 10 debasement, degeneracy 12 degeneration, dégringolade

determinant 4 gene 5 agent, basis, cause, trait 6 factor, ground, reason 7 epitope, radical 9 attribute, influence

determinate 5 fixed 6 cymose 7 limited, precise, settled 8 constant, definite 10 definitive, restricted 11 established 13 circumscribed

determination 5 drive, spunk 6 fixing, mettle 7 finding, opinion, purpose, resolve, verdict 8 decision, firmness, judgment, tenacity 9 assurance, hardihood, impulsion, intention, resolving, willpower 10 conclusion, dedication, definition, doggedness, resolution, settlement 11 decidedness, intrepidity 12 perseverance, resoluteness, stubbornness 13 purposiveness

determine 3 fix, set 4 rule 5 bound, limit, prove 6 decide, figure, ordain, settle 7 control, delimit, find out, mark out, measure, preform, unearth 8 conclude, discover, regulate 9 ascertain, demarcate, establish, preordain, resolve on 10 delimitate, foreordain, predestine, predispose

determined 3 set **4** bent **5** fixed **6** driven, intent **7** decided, earnest, serious, settled **8** decisive, hellbent, resolute, resolved, stubborn **9** tenacious **10** persistent, purposeful, unwavering **11** established, persevering, unfaltering **12** foreordained, unhesitating

detest 4 hate **5** abhor, spurn **6** loathe **7** despise, dislike **8** execrate **9** abominate, repudiate

detestable 4 foul, vile **6** damned, horrid, odious **7** hateful, heinous **9** abhorrent, execrable, loathsome **10** abominable, despicable **12** contemptible

detestation 4 hate **6** hatred **8** anathema, aversion, loathing **9** repulsion, revulsion **10** abhorrence, execration, repugnance

dethrone 4 oust **6** depose **7** uncrown **8** displace

detonate 5 blast, burst, go off, spark **6** blow up, set off **7** explode **8** touch off

detonator 3 cap **4** fuse **9** explosive **11** blasting cap

detour 5 avoid, skirt **6** bypass **8** side trip **9** diversion

detract 6 divert, lessen, reduce **8** decrease, diminish, minimize **10** depreciate

detraction 9 aspersion, maligning, traducing **10** backbiting, belittling, derogation, slandering **11** denigration, deprecation, traducement **12** backstabbing, belittlement **13** disparagement

detractive 9 maligning, slighting, traducing, vilifying **10** defamatory, derogatory, pejorative **11** denigrating, disparaging **12** depreciative, depreciatory

detriment 4 harm, loss **6** damage, injury **7** marring **8** drawback **10** impairment **12** disadvantage

detrimental 3 bad, ill **7** adverse, harmful, hurtful, noxious **8** damaging, negative **9** injurious **11** deleterious, unfavorable

detritus 4 tufa, tuff **5** scree, talus **6** debris, rubble **7** remains **11** odds and ends

Detroit *county:* **5** Wayne *founder:* **8** Cadillac (Sieur de) *lake:* **4** Erie **10** Saint Clair *sobriquet:* **6** Motown **9** Motor City

de trop 5 extra, spare **7** too much, surplus **9** excessive, redundant **10** gratuitous **11** superfluous **13** supernumerary

Deucalion *father:* **10** Prometheus *kingdom:* **6** Phthia *mother:* **7** Clymene *son:* **6** Hellen *wife:* **6** Pyrrha

deuce 3 tie, two **4** card, draw **5** devil **7** dickens **10** even-steven

Deutschland über _____ 5 alles

Devaki's son 7 Krishna

_____ De Valera 5 Eamon

devaluate 5 abase, decry, lower **6** reduce, weaken **7** cheapen, degrade **8** mark down, write off **9** undermine, underrate, write down **10** depreciate

devaluation 7 decline **10** debasement, declension **11** declination

devalue see **depreciate**

devastate 4 raze, ruin, sack **5** waste **6** ravage **7** despoil, pillage, plunder **8** demolish, desolate, lay waste, overcome, spoliate **9** depredate, desecrate, overpower, overwhelm

devastation 4 loss, ruin **5** chaos, havoc, waste **6** ravage **7** pillage, plunder **8** disorder **9** confusion, ruination **10** demolition, desolation, spoliation **11** depredation

develop 3 age **4** form, grow **5** occur, reach, ripen **6** attain, dilate, emerge, evolve, expand, grow up, happen, mature, mellow, open up, thrive, unfold, unfurl **7** achieve, acquire, advance, burgeon, enlarge, expound, promote **8** flourish **9** actualize, elaborate, establish, transpire **11** come to light, materialize

development 5 phase **6** growth, result, spread **7** advance, buildup, outcome **8** ontogeny, progress, ripening **9** evolution, expansion, flowering, phylogeny, unfolding **10** maturation **11** elaboration, progression *of life:* **10** biogenesis

Devi 7 goddess *consort:* **5** Shiva *father:* **7** Himavat *name:* **3** Uma **4** Kali **5** Durga, Gauri **6** Chandi **7** Parvati

deviant 4 bent **5** kinky, queer **6** off-key **7** twisted, wayward **8** aberrant, abnormal, atypical, perverse **9** anomalous, different, divergent, irregular, unnatural **11** heteroclite

deviate 3 err, yaw **4** turn, vary, veer **5** sheer, stray **6** depart, swerve, wander **7** digress, diverge **8** aberrant **9** eccentric, turn aside

deviation 3 yaw **4** bend, tack, turn **5** error, shift **6** change **7** anomaly, turning, veering **8** variance **9** departure, diversion **10** aberration, alteration, deflection, divergence

device 4 ploy, tool **5** feint, gizmo, means, motif, motto, shift, thing, trick **6** dingus, doodad, emblem, figure, gadget, gambit, hickey, jigger, medium, motive, symbol, widget **7** gimmick, machine, utensil, whatnot, whatsit **8** artifice, creation, insignia **9** apparatus, appliance, doohickey, expedient, implement, invention, makeshift, mechanism, thingummy **10** instrument **11** contraption, contrivance, inclination, thingamabob, thingamajig, thingumajig *automatic:* **5** servo *binding:* **5** clamp *fastening:* **6** zipper *grasping:* **4** tong *heating:* **8** radiator *hoisting:* **5** crane, lewis **8** windlass *holding:* **4**

vise 5 clamp *paging:* 6 beeper *suction:* 4 pump

devil 3 imp 5 beast, cloot, demon, fiend, rogue, Satan, scamp 6 Belial, diablo, dybbuk, rascal, spirit 7 Clootie, dickens, Lucifer, Old Nick, serpent, tempter, villain 8 Apollyon, Mephisto, scalawag, succubus 9 archfiend, Beelzebub, cacodemon, scoundrel, skeezicks 10 blackguard, Old Scratch 11 rapscallion

devilfish 3 ray 5 manta 7 octopus 8 manta ray 10 cephalopod

devilish 3 bad 4 evil 6 cursed, wicked 7 demonic, hellish, roguish, satanic 8 accursed, damnable, diabolic, fiendish, infernal, sinister 9 nefarious 10 diabolical, iniquitous, villainous 11 mischievous

devil-may-care 4 rash, wild 6 rakish, sporty 7 raffish 8 rakehell, reckless 9 easygoing

devilry 7 knavery, roguery, sorcery, waggery 8 mischief 9 diablerie 10 wickedness, witchcraft 11 roguishness, waggishness 12 sportiveness

devious 3 sly 4 foxy, wily 6 artful, crafty, errant, erring, roving, shifty, sneaky, tricky 7 bending, crooked, cunning, curving, erratic, winding 8 aberrant, guileful, indirect, scheming, sneaking, twisting 9 deceptive, underhand, wandering 10 roundabout 11 out-of-the-way, underhanded

devise 4 form, plan, plot, will 5 chart, forge, frame, shape 6 cook up, create, design, invent, legacy, legate, scheme 7 arrange, bequest, concoct, connive, dope out, dream up, hatch up, project 8 bequeath, property 9 determine, formulate 11 inheritance

devitalize 3 sap 5 drain 6 deaden, weaken 7 exhaust 8 enfeeble, etiolate 9 desiccate 10 eviscerate

devoid of 7 lacking, wanting 8 free from

devoir 3 job 4 duty, task, work 5 chore, stint 6 charge 9 committal 10 assignment, commitment, obligation

devolution 5 decay 7 decline, passing 8 receding, transfer 9 conferral, decadence, recession, surrender 10 conveyance, declension, degeneracy, regression, relegation, transferal 11 degradation 12 degeneration, dégringolade, retrograding, transference 13 retrogression

devolve 4 give, pass 6 pass on 8 hand down, hand over, relegate, transfer 10 degenerate

devote 5 apply 6 commit, direct, donate, hallow 7 reserve 8 dedicate, give over, sanctify 9 confirm in, habituate 10 consecrate

devoted 4 dear, fond, true 5 loyal 6 ardent, caring, doting, fervid, loving 7 dutiful, fervent, zealous 8 constant, faithful 9 dedicated 10 thoughtful 12 affectionate

religiously: 6 oblate

devotee 3 fan, nut 4 buff 5 hound, lover 6 addict, votary, zealot 7 admirer, amateur, fanatic, fancier, habitué 8 follower 9 supporter 10 aficionado, enthusiast

devotion 4 love, zeal 5 ardor, piety 6 fealty, fervor, prayer, Rosary 7 loyalty, passion 8 fidelity, fondness 9 adherence, adoration, reverence 10 allegiance, attachment, dedication, enthusiasm 12 faithfulness

devour 3 eat 5 eat up, enjoy 6 absorb, feed on 7 consume, destroy, feast on, pillage 8 prey upon, wolf down 9 delight in, feast upon, polish off, swallow up 10 annihilate

devouring 4 avid 6 greedy 8 esurient, ravenous 9 voracious 10 gluttonous

devout 4 holy 5 godly, loyal, pious 6 ardent 7 earnest, fervent, serious, sincere, zealous 8 faithful, reverent 9 pietistic, prayerful, religious

devoutness 4 zeal 5 ardor, piety 9 reverence 10 commitment

dew 5 sweat, tears 8 moisture 11 precipitate 12 perspiration 13 precipitation

dewy 3 wet 4 damp, pure 5 fresh, moist, naive 7 artless, natural 8 innocent, wide-eyed 9 credulous, guileless, ingenuous, unworldly

dexter 5 right

dexterity 4 ease 5 craft, grace, skill 7 ability, aptness, know-how, prowess, sleight 8 deftness, facility 9 adeptness, expertise, readiness 10 adroitness, nimbleness, smoothness 12 skillfulness

dexterous 3 apt 4 able, deft 5 adept, agile, handy 6 adroit, artful, facile, nimble, smooth 7 skilled 8 masterly, skillful 10 proficient

____ **Dhabi** 3 Abu

diablerie 7 devilry, roguery, sorcery, waggery 8 deviltry, iniquity, mischief, satanism 9 devilment 10 black magic, wickedness, witchcraft, wrongdoing

diabolical 4 evil 5 awful 6 impish, wicked 7 beastly, demonic, heinous, hellish, puckish, roguish, satanic 8 demoniac, devilish, dreadful, fiendish, god-awful, hellborn, infernal, rascally, sinister 9 execrable, malicious, monstrous, nefarious 10 degenerate, demoniacal, horrendous, iniquitous, scandalous, villainous 11 mischievous

diabolism see **diablerie**

diacritic 5 acute, breve, grave, haček, tilde 6 accent, macron, umlaut 7 cedilla 8 dieresis 9 diaeresis 10 circumflex *Arabic:* 5 hamza 6 hamzah

diadem 5 crown, tiara **6** wreath **7** chaplet, coronal, coronet **8** headband

diagnose 4 spot **5** place **8** identify, pinpoint **9** determine, interpret, recognize **11** distinguish

diagnostic 8 analytic **10** analytical, expository, indicating, indicative **11** explanatory, exploratory **12** interpretive

diagonal 4 bias **5** bevel **6** biased **7** beveled, oblique, slanted **8** inclined, slanting **9** inclining, slantways, slantwise

diagonally 7 athwart **9** slantways, slantwise **10** cornerwise **11** catercorner, kitty-corner

diagram 3 map **5** chart, graph **6** design, layout, sketch **7** drawing, isotype **9** represent

dial 4 call, face, knob, tune, turn **5** phone **6** rotate **7** control **10** manipulate

dialect 4 cant, jive **5** argot, idiom, koine, lingo, slang **6** creole, jargon, patois, patter, pidgin, speech, tongue **8** language, localism **10** vernacular **11** regionalism, terminology **13** provincialism *Georgia:* **6** Gullah *London:* **7** cockney

dialectic 5 logic **6** debate **8** dialogue, forensic **9** reasoning **10** discussion **11** disputation **13** argumentation, investigation

dialogue 4 chat, talk **6** confer, parley, script **8** colloquy, converse **12** conversation **13** confabulation

diameter 4 bore **5** chord, width **7** breadth, caliber **8** bisector, wideness **9** broadness

diametric 7 counter, opposed **8** contrary, converse, opposite **12** antithetical **13** contradictory

diamond 3 gem **5** field, stone **7** rhombus *element:* **6** carbon *famous:* **4** Hope, Pitt **5** Sancy **6** Orloff, Regent **8** Braganza, Cullinan, Kohinoor **9** Excelsior **10** Great Mogul *holder:* **3** dop *inferior:* **4** bort *oval:* **9** briolette *pattern:* **6** argyle *playing card:* **7** lozenge *state:* **8** Delaware *surface:* **5** facet

Diana see **Artemis**

diapason 4 peal, stop **5** range, scale, scope **7** compass, measure **8** spectrum **10** tuning fork

diaper 5 nappy **7** pattern **8** ornament

diaphanous 5 filmy, gauzy, sheer, vague **6** flimsy **8** ethereal, gossamer **11** transparent **13** insubstantial

diaphragm 4 stop **6** septum **8** membrane **9** partition

diarist 4 Gide (André), Mann (Thomas) **5** Frank (Anne), Inman (Arthur Crew), Kahlo (Frida), Pepys (Samuel), Plath (Sylvia), Rorem (Ned), Scott (Walter), Swift (Jonathan), Woolf (Virginia) **6** Burney (Fanny), Evelyn (John) **7** Boswell (James), Thoreau (Henry David) **8** Robinson (Henry Crabb) **9** Lindbergh (Anne Morrow) **10** chronicler, journalist

diary 3 log **6** record **7** daybook, diurnal, journal, logbook **8** notebook, register **9** chronicle

diastase 6 enzyme **8** catalyst, reactant

diatribe 4 rant, rave **6** tirade **7** polemic **8** harangue, jeremiad **9** criticism, philippic **11** castigation **12** denunciation

dibs 4 gelt **5** claim, dough, money, title **6** rights **11** reservation

dice 4 cast, cube **5** bones, cubes, ivory, mince **11** devil's-bones *game:* **5** craps *losing throw:* **7** missout *singular:* **3** die *throw:* **7** boxcars **9** snake eyes

dicer 5 loser **6** risker **7** gambler

dicey 4 iffy **5** risky **6** chancy, tricky **8** ticklish **9** uncertain, whimsical **10** precarious **11** problematic, speculative **13** unpredictable

dichotomize 5 halve **7** dissect **8** hemisect **9** bifurcate

dichotomous 5 split **6** forked **7** pronged **9** bifurcate **10** bifurcated

dichotomy 7 forking **8** division **9** bisection, branching, splitting **11** bifurcation **13** contradiction

Dickens, Charles *birthplace:* **10** Portsmouth *captain:* **6** Cuttle *character:* **3** Ada (Clare), Pip, Tim **4** Dick (Mr.), Dora, Gamp (Sairey), Heep (Uriah), Nell **5** Drood (Edwin), Emily, Fagin, Lucie (Manette), Sikes (Bill) **6** Barkis, Bumble (Mr.), Carton (Sydney), Cuttle (Capt.), Darnay (Charles), Dombey (Fanny, Florence, Paul), Dorrit (Amy), Oliver (Twist) **7** Barnaby (Rudge), Dedlock (Lady), Defarge, Gargery (Joe), Manette (Dr.), Scrooge (Ebenezer), Tiny Tim **8** Cratchit (Bob), Havisham (Miss), Jarndyce (John), Magwitch (Abel), Micawber (Mr.), Nickleby (Nicholas), Peggotty (Clara, Daniel, Ham), Pickwick (Mr.) **9** Bill Sikes, Gradgrind (Mr.), Murdstone (Mr.), Pecksniff (Mr.), Uriah Heep **10** Chuzzlewit (Anthony, Jonas, Martin), Steerforth **11** Copperfield (David) *hero:* **6** Carton (Sydney) *nationality:* **7** English *pen name:* **3** Boz *villain:* **5** Fagin *work:* **9** Hard Times **10** Bleak House **11** Oliver Twist **12** Barnaby Rudge, Dombey and Son, Little Dorrit **14** Christmas Carol (A), Pickwick Papers (The) **15** Our Mutual Friend, Tale of Two Cities (A) **16** David Copperfield, Martin Chuzzlewit, Nicholas Nickleby **17** Great Expectations

dicker 4 deal, swap **5** argue, trade **6** barter,

haggle, higgle, palter **7** bargain, chaffer **8** contract, huckster **9** negotiate

dickey 10 shirtfront

Dickey novel 11 Deliverance

dictate 3 set **4** lead, rule, word **5** edict, order, tenet **6** behest, decree, direct, enjoin, govern, impose, ordain, recite **7** bidding, command, control, lay down, mandate, read off, summons **9** determine, direction, directive, prescribe, principle, pronounce, verbalize **10** injunction **12** prescription

dictative 5 bossy **8** despotic, dogmatic **9** imperious **10** peremptory **11** doctrinaire, magisterial **13** authoritarian

dictator 4 czar, duce, tsar, tzar **6** caesar, despot, tyrant **8** autocrat, martinet **9** oppressor, strongman *Chinese:* **3** Mao **9** Mao Zedong **10** Mao Tse-tung *German:* **6** Hitler (Adolf) *Italian:* **9** Mussolini (Benito) *military:* **8** caudillo *Russian:* **6** Stalin (Joseph) *Spanish:* **6** Franco (Francisco)

dictatorial 5 bossy **8** despotic, dogmatic **9** arbitrary, imperious, masterful **10** autocratic, iron-handed, peremptory, tyrannical **11** doctrinaire, domineering, overbearing **12** totalitarian **13** authoritarian

dictatorship 7 tyranny **9** autocracy, Caesarism, despotism, supremacy **10** absolutism

diction 6 phrase, speech **7** wordage, wording **8** delivery, language, parlance, phrasing, rhetoric, verbiage **9** elocution, verbalism **11** enunciation, phraseology

dictionary 7 lexicon **8** glossary, wordbook **10** repository **13** reference book *compiler:* **7** Johnson (Samuel), Webster (Noah) **13** lexicographer *geographical:* **9** gazetteer *of synonyms:* **8** thesauri (plural) **9** thesaurus

dictum 4 fiat **5** adage, axiom, edict, maxim, moral **6** ruling **7** mandate, opinion, precept, proverb **11** declaration **13** pronouncement

didactic 5 moral **6** teachy **7** donnish, preachy **8** advisory, edifying, pedantic, sermonic, teaching **9** hortative, pedagogic, teacherly **10** moralizing **11** informative, instructive

diddle 3 con, gyp, toy **4** beat, bilk, dupe, hoax, fool, idle, laze, loaf, loll, rook, scam **5** cheat, cozen, delay, drone, trick **6** chisel, chouse, dabble, dawdle, delude, fiddle, fleece, loiter, lounge, rope in, take in **7** deceive, defraud, goof off, mislead, swindle **8** flimflam, fool with, hoodwink, lollygag **9** bamboozle, overreach, victimize, waste time **10** dilly-dally, fool around, hang around

diddler 3 gyp **4** sham **5** cheat, faker, fraud, rogue **6** con man **7** grifter, shammer, sharper **8** swindler **9** con artist, defrauder,

trickster **11** flimflammer **12** double-dealer **13** confidence man

dido 4 jest, lark **5** antic, caper, curio, frill, prank **6** bauble, frolic, gewgaw, trifle, whimsy **7** bibelot, novelty, trinket **8** furbelow, gimcrack, kickshaw, mischief **9** bagatelle, plaything **10** knickknack, tomfoolery

Dido 6 Elissa *brother:* **9** Pygmalion *city founded by:* **8** Carthage *father:* **5** Belus **6** Mutton *husband:* **7** Acerbas **8** Sichaeus *lover:* **6** Aeneas

Dido and Aeneas composer 7 Purcell (Henry)

die 4 drop, fall, mold, pass, stop, wane **5** cease, croak **6** cash in, demise, expire, go west, matrix, pass on, peg out, perish, pop off **7** decease, go south, kick off, snuff it, succumb **8** cash it in, check out, drop dead, pass away **9** disappear **10** buy the farm **12** join the choir **13** kick the bucket *from hunger:* **6** starve *loaded:* **6** fulham

_____ **die 4** sine

diehard 7 devoted, fanatic **8** true-blue **9** dogmatist **10** determined **11** bitter-ender, doctrinaire, reactionary, standpatter **12** conservative, intransigent **13** stick-in-the-mud

_____ **diem 3** per **5** carpe

Dies _____ **4** Irae

diet 4 bant, eats, fare, fast, feed, menu **6** ration, reduce, regime **7** regimen **8** assembly, victuals **10** parliament **11** legislature, nourishment

Diet of _____ **5** Worms **6** Speyer, Spires **8** Augsburg

Dieu _____ **(British motto) 10** et mon droit

_____**-dieu 4** prie

differ 4 vary **5** demur **7** deviate **8** disagree

difference 3 gap **7** discord, dispute, dissent **8** conflict, contrast, variance **9** departure, deviation, disparity, otherness, variation **10** dissension, divergence, unlikeness **11** controversy, discrepancy, distinction **12** disagreement **13** dissimilarity

different 5 other **6** divers, single, sundry, unlike, varied **7** another, deviant, distant, diverse, several, special, unalike, unequal, unusual, various **8** discrete, distinct, peculiar, separate **9** disparate, divergent **10** dissimilar, individual, particular **11** contrasting, distinctive

differentiate 4 vary **5** adapt **6** change, modify **8** contrast, separate **9** diversify, transform **11** distinguish, individuate **12** characterize, discriminate

difficult 4 hard **5** tight, tough **6** thorny, uphill **7** arduous, awkward, labored, obscure, operose **8** exacting, perverse, puzzling, stubborn **9** demanding, effortful, herculean, laborious, strenuous **10** refractory **11** problematic

difficulty 3 ado, fix, jam **4** beef **4** pass, snag **5** hitch, nodus, pinch, rigor, worry **6** hang-up, hassle, pickle, plight, scrape, strait **7** dilemma, pitfall, problem, trouble **8** distress, hardship, hot water, obstacle, quandary, quagmire, question **9** adversity, challenge **10** impediment **11** aggravation, arduousness, predicament, vicissitude

diffidence 7 modesty, reserve, shyness **8** distrust, meekness, timidity **9** quietness, restraint, timidness **10** hesitation **11** bashfulness

diffident 3 shy **4** meek **5** timid **7** bashful **8** hesitant, reserved, retiring, timorous **9** reluctant, unassured **11** unassertive **12** self-effacing

diffuse 5 strew, vague, wordy **6** prolix, spread **7** scatter, verbose **8** disperse, rambling **9** broadcast, dispersed, propagate, scattered, spreading, spread out **10** distribute, longwinded, widespread **11** disseminate, distributed

diffusion 6 spread **7** osmosis **9** broadcast, dispersal, prolixity, spreading **10** dispersion, scattering **11** circulation, propagation **12** broadcasting, promulgation

dig 3 jab **4** barb, grub, hole, like, mine, poke, prod, root, site, stab **5** delve, ditch, enjoy, gouge, nudge, probe, scoop, spade, taunt **6** burrow, plunge, quarry, relish, rootle, shovel, thrust, trench, tunnel **7** explore, root out, unearth **8** excavate, prospect **10** excavation **11** investigate *up:* **6** exhume **7** unearth

digest 5 sum up **6** absorb, codify, précis **7** consume, stomach, summate, swallow **8** abstract, boil down, classify, compress, condense, syllabus, synopsis **9** summarize, summation, synopsize **10** abridgment **12** condensation

digger 4 plow **5** miner **6** shovel **7** soldier

digit 3 toe **5** thumb **6** cipher, figure; finger, number, pinkie **7** integer, numeral **9** character **11** whole number

dignified 4 prim **6** august, formal, proper, seemly **7** courtly, elegant, stately **8** cultured, decorous, ennobled, polished **9** distingué, patrician

dignify 5 adorn, exalt, grace, honor **7** ennoble, elevate, glorify, sublime **11** distinguish

dignitary 3 VIP **4** lion **5** chief, nabob **6** leader, worthy **7** notable **8** eminence, luminary **9** personage **10** notability **11** mucketymuck **13** high-muck-a-muck

dignity 4 rank **5** honor, merit, poise, pride, worth **6** cachet, status, virtue **7** address, decorum, gravity, hauteur, majesty, stature **8** grandeur, nobility, position, prestige, standing **9** propriety **10** augustness, seemliness **11** consequence, self-respect

digress 5 stray **6** depart, ramble, swerve, wander **7** deviate, diverge **8** divagate

digression 5 aside **7** episode, tangent **8** drifting, excursus, rambling, straying **9** deviation, wandering **10** deflection, divagation, divergence **11** parenthesis

dig up 4 find **6** expose, reveal **7** nose out, root out, uncover, unearth **8** discover **9** ferret out, run across, search out, track down

dik-dik 8 antelope

dike 3 dam **4** bank **5** ditch, drain, levee **7** barrier **8** causeway **10** embankment **11** watercourse

dilapidate 4 ruin **5** decay, wreck **7** break up, crumble, decline, neglect **9** break down, decompose, disregard **10** deliquesce **12** disintegrate

dilapidated 5 dingy, seedy **6** beat-up, ragtag, ruined, shabby **7** decayed, run-down **8** battered, crumbled, decrepit **9** crumbling **10** broken-down, down-at-heel, ramshackle **12** deteriorated

dilapidation 4 ruin **5** decay **7** atrophy **8** collapse, decaying **9** crumbling, decadence, disrepair **11** decrepitude **13** decomposition, deterioration

dilate 5 swell, widen **6** expand, extend **7** distend, enlarge, expound **9** discourse, expatiate

dilatory 4 idle, slow **5** slack, tardy **7** laggard **8** dallying, delaying, sluggish **9** leisurely, lingering, unhurried **11** time-wasting

dilemma 3 box, fix, jam **4** bind, hole, spot **6** choice, corner, pickle, plight, scrape **7** catch-22, problem **8** argument, quandary **10** difficulty **11** predicament

dilettante 4 tyro **7** amateur, dabbler **8** aesthete, putterer **9** smatterer

dilettantish see **amateurish**

diligence 4 zeal **8** industry **9** assiduity **10** commitment **11** application, persistence **12** perseverance, sedulousness **13** assiduousness

diligent 8 sedulous **9** assiduous **10** persistent, persisting, unflagging **11** hardworking, industrious, painstaking, persevering

dilly 3 pip **4** lulu **5** dandy, doozy, peach **6** corker, doozie, pippin, ripper, rouser **8** jimdandy, knockout **9** humdinger **10** ripsnorter **11** crackerjack

dillydally see **delay**

dilute 3 cut **4** thin, weak **5** water **6** watery,

weaken 8 diminish, weakened 9 attenuate, water down 11 watered-down

dim 4 dull, dumb, hazy, pale, slow 5 befog, blear, blind, cloud, dense, dusky, faint, muddy, murky, muted, thick, vague 6 bleary, gloomy, stupid 7 becloud, low beam, obscure, shadowy, subdued, unclear 9 tenebrous 10 ill-defined, indistinct, lackluster, lusterless 11 unpromising

dime novel 4 pulp 7 chiller, shocker 8 dreadful, thriller 12 bloodcurdler 13 penny dreadful

dimension 4 size 5 reach, scale, scope, width 6 aspect, extent, spread 7 compass, expanse, measure, quality 9 amplitude, magnitude

diminish 3 ebb 4 bate, wane 5 abate, peter, quell, taper 6 lessen, recede, reduce, subdue, temper, weaken 7 curtail, decline, dwindle, subside 8 belittle, decrease, minimize, moderate, restrain, taper off 9 attenuate, disparage, dispraise 10 depreciate 11 detract from

diminutive 3 wee 4 tiny 5 bitsy, dwarf, pygmy, small, teeny, weeny 6 bantam, little, midget, minute, peewee, petite, teensy 9 miniature, pint-sized, undersize 10 teenyweeny 11 lilliputian 12 teensy-weensy

____ **dimittis** 4 Nunc

dimple 3 pit 4 dent, dint, fret, nick 5 notch 6 ripple 8 pockmark 10 depression 11 indentation

dimwit 3 oaf 4 clod, dodo, dolt, dope, fool, simp, yo-yo 5 booby, chump, cluck, dummy, dunce, idiot, moron, stupe 6 dumdum 7 airhead, dullard, fathead, pinhead 8 bonehead, dumbbell, imbecile, lunkhead, meathead, numskull 9 birdbrain, blockhead, dumb bunny, dumb cluck, ignoramus, lamebrain, numbskull, simpleton 10 dunderhead, nincompoop 11 featherhead, knucklehead 12 featherbrain

dim-witted 4 dull, dumb, slow 6 stupid 7 doltish, foolish, idiotic, moronic 8 backward, imbecile, retarded 9 brainless, half-baked, imbecilic 11 birdbrained, lamebrained 12 feebleminded, simpleminded

din 3 row 4 roar 5 babel, clash, noise 6 bedlam, clamor, deafen, hubbub, racket, rattle, tumult, uproar 7 clangor, clatter, resound 8 brouhaha 9 commotion, stridency 10 hullabaloo, hurly-burly 11 pandemonium 13 clamorousness

Dinah *brother:* 4 Levi 6 Simeon *father:* 5 Jacob *mother:* 4 Leah

dine 3 eat, sup 4 feed 5 feast 6 eat out 7 banquet, nourish

diner 4 café 5 eater 6 eatery 7 canteen 8 snack bar 9 hash house 10 coffee shop, restaurant 11 greasy spoon 12 lunch counter, luncheonette, sandwich shop

Dinesen, Isak 6 Blixen (Karen) *work:* 11 Out of Africa 12 Winter's Tales 16 Seven Gothic Tales

ding 3 mar 4 dent, nick 5 clang 7 blemish

ding-a-ling 3 nut 4 kook, yo-yo 5 flake, loony, wacko 6 cuckoo, nitwit, weirdo 7 lunatic 8 crackpot 9 fruitcake, harebrain, lamebrain, screwball 10 crackbrain 12 scatterbrain

dinghy 5 skiff 7 rowboat, shallop 8 lifeboat, life raft, sailboat

dingle 4 dale, dell, glen, vale 6 ravine, valley

dingus 5 gizmo 6 doodad, gadget, jigger, widget 7 whatsit 9 doohickey, thingummy 11 thingamabob, thingamajig, thingumajig

dingy 4 foul, mean 5 dirty, seedy, tacky 6 filthy, grubby, grungy, scuzzy, shabby, soiled, sordid 7 run-down, squalid, sullied, unclean 8 begrimed

dinky 3 toy 4 tiny 5 small, teeny 9 undersize 10 locomotive

dinner 4 meal 5 feast 6 regale, repast, spread, supper 7 banquet 8 luncheon 9 collation 10 table d'hôte *course:* 4 meat, soup 5 salad 6 entrée 7 dessert 9 appetizer *jacket:* 3 tux 6 tuxedo

dinosaur 6 fossil 7 has-been 8 theropod 11 anachronism *fictional:* 8 Godzilla

dinosauric 4 huge 5 passé 6 bygone 7 extinct, mammoth 8 colossal, enormous, obsolete, outmoded 9 cyclopean, leviathan, out-of-date 10 antiquated, behemothic, fossilized, gargantuan, mastodonic, oldfangled 11 elephantine 12 antediluvian, old-fashioned, out-of-fashion 13 anachronistic

dint 4 nick 5 force, might, power 6 dimple, virtue 7 drive in, impress 10 impression 11 indentation

diocese 3 see 9 bishopric *Eastern Orthodox:* 7 eparchy *subdivision:* 6 parish

diode 9 rectifier 10 vacuum tube 12 electron tube *component:* 5 anode 7 cathode 9 electrode

Diomedes *city founded by:* 4 Arpi *father:* 4 Ares, Mars 6 Tydeus *foe:* 6 Aeneas, Hector *slayer:* 8 Heracles, Hercules *victim:* 6 Rhesus

Dione 5 Titan *cult partner:* 4 Zeus *daughter:* 5 Venus 9 Aphrodite *father:* 7 Oceanus *lover:* 4 Zeus *mother:* 6 Tethys

Dionysus see **Bacchus**

Dionyza's husband 5 Cleon

Dioscuri 5 twins 6 Castor, Gemini, Pollux *father:* 4 Zeus 9 Tyndareus *mother:* 4 Leda *sister:* 5 Helen

dip 3 sag **4** bail, draw, drop, duck, dunk, fall, lade, sink, skid, slip, slue, swim **5** basin, ladle, lower, pitch, sauce, scoop, slope, slump, spoon, stoop **6** go down, hollow, plunge **7** decline, descend, descent, falloff, immerse, sinkage **8** decrease, downturn, sinkhole, submerge, submerse **9** concavity, declivity, downswing, downtrend, immersion **10** depression

diphthong 7 digraph **8** ligature

diploma 6 degree **7** charter **8** document **9** sheepskin **10** credential

diplomacy 4 tact **7** address, finesse **8** delicacy **10** artfulness, discretion, statecraft **11** negotiation, savoir faire, tactfulness

diplomatic 4 deft **5** bland, suave **6** artful, astute, polite, smooth, urbane **7** courtly, politic, tactful **8** delicate, discreet **9** courteous **12** conciliating, conciliatory, paleographic **13** accommodating

diplomat's office 7 embassy, mission

diplopod 9 millipede

dipper 3 cup **4** bird **5** ladle, ouzel, scoop, stars **6** bucket **10** pickpocket, water ouzel

dippy 4 daft, zany **5** crazy, daffy, flaky, goofy, kooky, loony, nutty, silly, wacky **6** stupid **7** doltish, foolish, witless **9** half-baked **11** harebrained **12** preposterous

dipsomania 10 alcoholism

dire 4 grim **5** acute, awful **6** dismal, horrid, tragic, urgent, woeful **7** baleful, baneful, crucial, extreme, fateful, ominous, ruinous **8** alarming, critical, dreadful, grievous, horrible, horrific, menacing, shocking, sinister, terrible **9** appalling, desperate, frightful, illboding **10** calamitous, deplorable, depressing, foreboding, malevolent, oppressing, oppressive, pernicious **11** apocalyptic, distressing, threatening

direct 4 head, lead, show **5** apply, frank, guide, label, level, order, pilot, plain, point, route, steer, train **6** assign, charge, define, devote, divert, enjoin, escort, extend, govern, lineal, linear, manage, ordain, settle **7** address, carry on, command, conduct, control, genuine, nonstop, operate, oversee, preside, project, request **8** dispatch, instruct, regulate, shepherd, straight, unbroken, verbatim **9** determine, firsthand, immediate, prescribe **10** administer, contiguous, continuous, inevitable **11** categorical, undeviating, unequivocal, word for word *a helmsman:* **4** conn *proceedings:* **7** preside

direction 3 way **4** east, line, path, side, west **5** angle, north, point, south, trend **6** course, design **7** bearing, channel, command, purpose **8** guidance, tendency **9** clockwise,

oversight, viewpoint **10** management, standpoint, trajectory **11** instruction, supervision *blowing:* **7** leeward **8** windward *horizontal:* **7** azimuth *main line of:* **4** axis (see also **compass point**)

directive 4 fiat, memo, word, writ **5** edict, order, ukase **6** charge, decree, dictum, notice, ruling **7** bidding, command, dictate, mandate **8** deciding, managing **9** presiding **10** assignment, injunction, memorandum **11** instruction, supervising, supervisory **12** policy-making **13** communication, pronouncement

directly 3 due **4** anon, soon **5** right, spang **6** at once, pronto **7** bluntly, by and by, shortly **8** first off, in person, promptly, squarely, straight, verbatim **9** forthwith, instanter, instantly, presently, right away **10** face-to-face **11** immediately, straight off, straightway, word for word **12** contiguously, straightaway

director 4 boss, head **5** chief **6** leader, top dog **7** manager **8** overseer **9** conductor, organizer **10** head honcho, supervisor

directory 4 list **5** guide, index **6** folder **7** catalog **8** register **9** catalogue **11** compilation

dirge 6 lament **7** requiem **8** threnody **11** lamentation *Gaelic:* **8** coronach

dirigible 5 blimp **7** airship **8** zeppelin **9** steerable

dirk 4 shiv, stab **5** skean, skene, sword **6** bodkin, dagger, stylet **7** poniard

dirt 3 mud **4** clay, dust, land, loam, mire, muck, porn, smut, soil, spot **5** earth, filth, fraud, grime, stain **6** gossip, ground **7** chicane, squalor **9** chicanery, excrement, indecency **10** corruption, hanky-panky **11** pornography

dirt-poor 4 bust **5** broke **8** beggared, indigent **9** destitute, flat broke, penniless, penurious **10** stone-broke **12** impoverished

dirty 3 low, tar **4** base, foul, lewd, racy, smut, soil **5** bawdy, foggy, grimy, messy, mucky, muddy, murky, nasty, smear, sooty, stain, sully, taint **6** basely, befoul, coarse, debase, defile, filthy, grubby, impure, smudge, smutty, soiled, sordid, vulgar **7** begrime, corrupt, defiled, hateful, immoral, naughty, obscene, raunchy, smutchy, spotted, squalid, squally, sullied, tainted, tarnish, unclean, unkempt **8** begrimed, besmirch, indecent, off-color, polluted, unchaste, unwashed **9** ill-gotten, uncleanly **10** abominable, scandalous, scurrilous **11** distasteful, unlaundered **12** contaminated, scatological

Dis see **Pluto**

disability 7 ailment **8** drawback, handicap **9**

detriment, hindrance, infirmity, unfitness 10 affliction, impairment, impediment, incapacity 11 restriction, shortcoming 12 disadvantage

disable 3 sap 4 maim 5 spoil 6 hobble, weaken 7 cripple 8 enfeeble, handicap, paralyze, sabotage 9 hamstring, undermine 10 debilitate, immobilize 12 incapacitate *a racehorse:* 6 nobble

disabled 7 hobbled 8 crippled 9 arthritic, paralyzed, rheumatic 11 handicapped 13 incapacitated

disabuse 4 free 5 emend, purge 7 correct, deliver, rectify, redress, release, relieve 8 liberate, unburden 9 enlighten, undeceive 10 illuminate 11 disencumber, disillusion

disaccharide 7 lactose, maltose, sucrose

disaccord 3 jar, war 4 vary 5 brawl, clash 6 combat, debate, differ 7 contest, contend, dispute, dissent, quarrel 8 conflict, disagree 12 disharmonize

disadvantage 3 bar 4 harm, loss 6 burden, damage, hamper 7 barrier, setback 8 drawback, handicap, obstacle 9 detriment, hindrance, liability, prejudice 10 impairment, impediment, imposition, limitation 11 deprivation, obstruction

disadvantaged 7 lacking 8 deprived 11 handicapped

disaffect 4 wean 5 alien, repel 8 alienate, disquiet, disunite, estrange 10 antagonize

disaffirm 4 deny 5 annul, belie, cross 6 abjure, impugn, negate, refute, reject 7 confute, explode, gainsay, reverse 8 disclaim, disprove, negative, traverse 9 repudiate 10 contradict, contravene

disagree 4 vary 5 argue, clash 6 bicker, differ, divide, haggle 7 contend, contest, dispute, dissent 8 conflict

disagreeable 4 ugly 7 peevish 8 annoying, petulant 9 offensive 10 unpleasant 11 disobliging, distressing, ill-tempered

disagreement 5 clash 6 debate 7 discord, dispute, quarrel, wrangle 8 argument, conflict, squabble, variance 9 disparity 10 contention, difference, dissension, divergence, unlikeness 11 altercation, controversy, discrepancy, incongruity

disallow 4 deny, veto 5 debar 6 enjoin, forbid, refuse, reject 7 disavow, dismiss, exclude, rule out, shut out 8 disclaim, prohibit 9 interdict, proscribe, repudiate

disallowance 4 veto 5 taboo 6 denial 7 refusal 9 disavowal, dismissal, exclusion, rejection 11 prohibition, repudiation 12 interdiction, proscription

____-**disant** 3 soi

disappear 3 die 5 clear, leave 6 depart, die out, vanish 8 evanesce, fade away, melt away, pass away, slip away 9 evaporate, sneak away, steal away 13 dematerialize

disappoint 4 dash, foil, ruin 6 baffle, defeat, thwart 7 let down 9 frustrate 10 discourage, dishearten

disappointment 4 blow 6 bummer, defeat, downer 7 failure, letdown 8 comedown 9 bringdown 11 frustration

disapproval 4 veto 6 rebuke 7 censure, dislike, obloquy, reproof 8 reproach 9 criticism, objection, rejection *expression of:* 3 boo 4 hiss, hoot, jeer 7 catcall 9 raspberry 10 Bronx cheer, thumbs-down

disapprove 4 veto 6 oppose, reject, tut-tut 7 decline, dislike, dismiss, frown on 8 disfavor, turn down 9 dispraise

disarm 5 charm 6 allure 7 win over 8 sideline 9 captivate 10 neutralize

disarming 7 amiable, likable, winning, winsome 8 likeable 9 endearing 10 convincing, persuasive 11 insinuating 12 ingratiating

disarrange 4 mess 5 mix up, upset 6 jumble, mess up, mislay, muddle, muss up 7 confuse, disturb 8 disorder, displace, misplace, unsettle 10 discompose 11 disorganize

disarray 5 chaos 6 bedlam, jumble, mess up, muddle 7 clutter, undress 8 disorder, shambles, unsettle 9 confusion 10 discompose, dishabille

disassemble 6 detach 7 scatter 8 dismount, disperse, separate, take down, tear down 9 break down, come apart, dismantle, dismember, take apart

disassociate 5 sever, unfix 6 detach, sunder 7 back off 8 abstract, alienate, back down, disunite, liberate, separate, uncouple, withdraw 9 disengage 10 disconnect

disaster 3 woe 6 fiasco 7 debacle, failure, tragedy 8 calamity 9 cataclysm, ruination 11 catastrophe, devastation

disastrous 4 dire 5 fatal 6 tragic 7 fateful, ruinous 8 terrible 10 calamitous, horrendous 11 cataclysmic, destructive, devastating 12 catastrophic

disavow 4 deny 6 abjure, disown, impugn, negate, recant, reject 7 forsake, gainsay, retract 8 abnegate, disclaim, forswear, negative, renounce 9 repudiate

disband 3 end 4 part 5 sever 6 divide, sunder 7 break up, dissect, divorce, scatter 8 disperse, dissolve, separate

disbelieve 5 doubt, scorn, scout 6 eschew, reject 7 scoff at, suspect 8 discount, distrust, mistrust, question 9 discredit, repudiate

disbeliever 5 cynic 7 doubter, sceptic,

scoffer, skeptic **9** dissenter **10** questioner **11** freethinker

disbelieving 4 wary **5** leery **6** show-me **7** cynical, dubious **8** doubting **9** quizzical, skeptical **11** incredulous, mistrustful, questioning, unconvinced

disburden 4 shed **6** unlade, unload, unship, unstow **7** off-load, relieve **8** disgorge **9** discharge

disburse 3 pay **5** allot, issue **6** lay out, pay out, supply **7** deliver, dole out, furnish, mete out, provide **8** dispense, disperse **9** apportion, partition **10** distribute, measure out

disbursement 4 cost **5** funds **6** outlay **7** expense, payment **9** allotment **11** expenditure **12** distribution

discard 4 cast, drop, dump, junk, shed, toss, waif **5** chuck, ditch, eject, let go, scrap **6** reject **7** cast off, castoff, deep-six, wash out **8** get rid of, jettison, shuck off, throw out **9** throw away, toss aside

discarnate 8 bodiless, ethereal, spectral **9** asomatous, unfleshly **10** immaterial, unembodied, unphysical, wraithlike **11** disembodied, incorporeal, nonphysical **12** otherworldly **13** insubstantial

discern 3 see **4** espy, know, note **5** grasp, sense **6** behold, detect, divine, notice **7** glimpse, observe **8** identify, perceive **9** apprehend, ascertain, recognize **10** comprehend **11** distinguish **12** discriminate **13** differentiate

discernible 7 visible **8** apparent, palpable **10** detectable, noticeable, observable **11** appreciable, perceivable **12** recognizable

discerning 4 keen **5** acute, aware **6** astute **7** knowing **9** clear-eyed, insighted, observant, sagacious **10** insightful, perceptive **12** clearsighted **13** knowledgeable, perspicacious

discernment 6 acuity, acumen **7** insight **8** keenness, sagacity **9** intuition **10** astuteness, perception, shrewdness **11** penetration, percipience **12** perspicacity **13** comprehension, sagaciousness

discharge 2 ax **3** axe, can, pay **4** drop, emit, fire, free, gush, oust, quit, sack, spew, vent, void **5** annul, clear, demob, egest, eject, empty, expel, exude, let go, loose, pay up, quash, salvo, shoot, utter **6** bounce, excuse, exempt, let fly, let off, loosen, outlet, remove, settle, unbind, unload, vacate **7** absolve, boot out, barrage, cashier, deliver, dismiss, exclude, excrete, execute, fulfill, give off, kick out, manumit, off-load, release, relieve, removal, satisfy, unchain **9** abrogate, aquittal, dispense, displace, dissolve, ejection, emission, get rid of, liber-

ate, separate, throw off **9** acquittal, dismissal, eliminate, explosion, expulsion, muster out, pour forth, send forth, terminate, unshackle **10** deactivate, demobilize **11** exoneration, fulfillment *electrical:* **5** spark **6** leader **8** streamer **9** lightning

disciple 3 fan **6** minion **7** apostle, devotee, learner **8** adherent, follower, henchman, partisan, retainer **9** supporter **10** enthusiast

disciplinarian 8 enforcer, martinet **10** taskmaster **11** slave driver

disciplinary 8 punitive **9** punishing **10** corrective

discipline 4 curb, rule, will **5** check, drill, field, guide, order, teach, train **6** bridle, direct, ferule, method, punish, school, subdue **7** chasten, conduct, control, correct, educate **8** approach, chastise, instruct, penalize, restrain, training **9** castigate, obedience, subjugate, will-power **10** correction, punishment **11** castigation, self-control, self-mastery **12** chastisement **13** self-restraint

disclaim 4 deny **6** abjure, reject **7** disavow, gainsay, retract **8** disallow, forswear, renounce, traverse **9** repudiate **10** contradict

disclose 3 own **4** avow, tell **5** admit, spill **6** expose, impart, relate, report, reveal, unmask, unveil **7** display, divulge, uncover **8** discover, give away, unclothe **9** make known

disclosure 6 exposé **8** exposure **9** admission **10** revelation **11** declaration

discolor 3 tar **4** blot, dull, fade, smut, soil **5** smear, stain, sully, taint, tinge **6** defile, smudge **7** besmear, bestain, tarnish **8** besmirch

discoloration 4 spot **5** stain, taint **6** blotch, bruise, smudge **7** blemish **9** birthmark

discomfit 3 irk, vex **4** faze **5** abash, annoy, upset **6** baffle, bother, defeat, rattle, thwart **7** fluster, nonplus, perturb, unnerve **8** confound **9** embarrass **10** discompose, disconcert

discomfiture 5 upset **6** unease **8** disquiet **9** abashment, agitation, confusion **10** uneasiness **11** frustration **12** discomposure, perturbation **13** embarrassment, inconvenience

discomfort 3 irk, vex **4** ache, pain **5** annoy **6** bother, unease **7** malaise **8** vexation **9** annoyance **10** uneasiness **13** embarrassment

discommend 5 decry **7** censure, frown on, put down **8** admonish, disfavor, object to **9** criticize, deprecate, disesteem, disparage, reprehend **10** disapprove

discommode 3 irk, vex **5** annoy, upset **6** bother, burden, flurry, put out **7** disturb, fluster, perturb, trouble **8** encumber **9** aggravate, disoblige **13** inconvenience

discompose 3 irk, vex **5** annoy, harry, upset, worry **6** bother, dismay, flurry, harass, pester, plague, ruffle, untune **7** agitate, disturb, fluster, perturb, unhinge **8** disarray, disorder, unsettle **9** embarrass **10** disarrange **11** disorganize

discomposure 5 upset, worry **6** bother, unease **8** vexation **9** abashment, agitation, annoyance, confusion **10** discomfort, irritation, perplexity, uneasiness **11** disquietude **12** discomfiture, perturbation **13** consternation, embarrassment

disconcert 4 faze **5** abash, upset, worry **6** bemuse, bother, puzzle, rattle, ruffle **7** confuse, disturb, nonplus, perplex, perturb, trouble **8** bewilder, confound, disquiet **9** discomfit, embarrass, frustrate

disconfirm 4 deny **5** rebut **6** refute, negate **7** gainsay **8** abnegate, confound, disclaim, disprove **10** contradict, controvert

disconnect 3 cut, gap **5** break, sever, unfix **6** cut off, detach **7** disjoin **8** separate, uncouple **9** disengage **10** dissociate

disconnected 7 muddled **8** detached, separate **10** disjointed, incoherent, unattached **11** fragmentary, unorganized **13** discontinuous

disconsolate 3 low, sad **4** blue, down **5** bleak, drear **6** abject, dreary, gloomy, woeful **7** doleful, forlorn, joyless, unhappy **8** dejected, downcast, wretched **9** cheerless, depressed, miserable, sorrowful, woebegone **10** dispirited, melancholy **11** comfortless, crestfallen, downhearted

discontent 4 envy **7** malaise, unhappy **9** dysphoria **10** depression, inquietude, uneasiness **12** restlessness

discontented 5 upset **6** uneasy **7** annoyed, fretful, unhappy **8** restless **9** disturbed, irritated, perturbed **10** displeased **11** complaining, disgruntled, ungratified, unsatisfied **12** dissatisfied

discontinuation 3 end **4** stop **5** cease, close, pause **6** ending, finish **7** closing **8** abeyance **9** cessation **10** conclusion, desistance, moratorium, suspension **12** postponement

discontinue 3 end **4** halt, quit, stay, stop **5** cease, close, sever **6** desist, give up, wind up, wrap up **8** break off, close out, conclude, knock off, leave off, shut down, surcease **9** terminate

discontinuity 3 gap **4** hole, rent, rift **5** break, cleft, crack, split **6** breach, lacuna **7** fissure, opening, rupture

discontinuous 6 fitful **7** muddled **8** discrete, separate **9** spasmodic **10** incoherent, inco-

hesive **11** unconnected **12** disconnected, intermittent **13** nonsequential

discord 5 clash **6** enmity, rancor, strife **7** rupture **8** conflict, contrast, disunity, division, friction, mismatch, variance **9** animosity, antipathy, hostility **10** antagonism, contention, difference, dissension, dissidence, dissonance, opposition **12** inconsonance, polarization **13** inconsistency *goddess:* **3** Ate **4** Eris

discordant 5 harsh **6** at odds **7** grating, jarring **8** clashing, contrary, jangling, strident **9** dissonant, out of tune **10** cacophonic, unpleasant **11** cacophonous, conflicting, disagreeing, inconsonant, quarrelsome, unmelodious **12** unharmonious

discotheque 6 bistro, nitery **7** hot spot **9** dance club, nightclub, night spot

discount 4 agio **5** doubt, lower **6** deduct, ignore, rebate, reduce, slight **7** neglect, take off **8** belittle, derogate, decrease, diminish, knock off, mark down, markdown, minimize, overlook, roll back, rollback, subtract, take away **9** abatement, deduction, disregard, reduction, substract, underrate **13** underestimate

discountenance 4 faze **5** abash **6** rattle **7** frown on **8** confound, disfavor **9** deprecate, discomfit, embarrass **10** disapprove, disconcert, discourage

discourage 4 damp **5** daunt, check, chill, deter **6** dampen, deject, divert, hinder, impede **7** depress, inhibit, trouble **8** disfavor, dissuade, suppress **10** demoralize, dishearten

discouraging 5 bleak **7** unhappy **8** daunting **9** deterring, troubling **10** depressing **11** unfavorable, unpromising **12** unpropitious **13** disappointing, disheartening

discourse 4 talk **5** argue, essay, orate, speak, spiel, voice **6** sermon, speech, thesis **7** amplify, descant, enlarge, explain, expound, lecture **8** converse, harangue, perorate, rhetoric, speaking, treatise **9** expatiate, hold forth, monograph, sermonize, utterance **10** expression **11** interchange **12** conversation **13** verbalization *art of:* **8** rhetoric *religious:* **6** homily, sermon

discourteous 4 rude **6** unkind **7** boorish, brusque, ill-bred, uncivil, uncouth **8** impolite **10** ungracious, unmannerly **11** ill-mannered, impertinent **13** disrespectful

discover 4 espy, find, spot **5** learn **6** betray, detect, expose, reveal, unmask **7** divulge, find out, observe, unearth **8** come upon, perceive, proclaim, unshroud **9** ascertain, determine, encounter, make known **10** come across

discovery 4 find **5** trove **6** espial, strike **7** finding **8** locating, sighting **9** detection **10** revelation, unearthing

discredit 4 slur, ruin **5** doubt, shame **6** defame, malign, show up **7** asperse, degrade, put down, run down, slander, traduce **8** disgrace, ignominy **9** disparage, disrepute **10** disbelieve, opprobrium

discreditable 5 shady **6** shabby, shoddy **8** shameful, unworthy **9** degrading **10** inglorious **11** blameworthy, disgraceful, ignominious **12** contemptible, dishonorable, disreputable

discreet 4 wary **5** chary, muted, plain **6** modest, simple **7** careful, guarded, prudent, tactful **8** cautious, moderate **9** unadorned **10** controlled, reasonable, restrained **11** circumspect, considerate, unelaborate, unobtrusive **12** unnoticeable **13** unpretentious

discrepancy 3 gap **8** alterity, conflict, variance **9** disparity, otherness, variation **10** difference, divergence, divergency, unlikeness **12** disagreement **13** inconsistency

discrepant 6 unlike **7** diverse, varying **8** contrary **9** different, differing, disparate, divergent **11** conflicting, disagreeing **12** incompatible, inconsistent **13** contradictory

discrete 8 detached, distinct, separate **9** countable, different **10** individual **12** disconnected **13** discontinuous, noncontinuous

discretion 4 care, tact **7** caution, reserve **8** delicacy, judgment, prudence, wariness **9** canniness, chariness, restraint **13** judiciousness

discriminate 5 judge **6** assess **7** compare, discern, make out **8** contrast, disfavor, evaluate, perceive, separate **9** segregate, tell apart **11** distinguish **13** differentiate

discriminating 6 choosy, select **7** finical, finicky **8** eclectic **9** judicious, selective **10** discerning **11** prejudicial

discrimination 5 taste **6** acumen **7** bigotry, insight **8** inequity, judgment **9** prejudice **10** astuteness, favoritism, partiality, perception **11** discernment, intolerance, penetration

discriminatory 6 biased **7** partial, unequal **8** partisan **9** jaundiced **10** prejudiced **11** inequitable, predisposed

discursive 5 windy, wordy **6** chatty, prolix **7** diffuse, logical, verbose **8** rambling, tortuous **9** desultory **10** analytical, circuitous, digressive, long-winded, meandering **11** wide-ranging

discuss 4 moot **5** argue, weigh **6** debate, parley **7** canvass, expound **8** consider, converse, hash over, talk over **9** elucidate, expatiate, interpret, talk about, thrash out,

ventilate **10** deliberate, toss around *business:* **8** talk shop *lightly:* **5** bandy *thoroughly:* **7** exhaust

discussion 3 rap **4** chat, talk **6** confab, debate, parley, powwow **7** canvass, palaver **8** argument, colloquy **10** conference, rap session **11** bull session, ventilation **12** conversation, deliberation **13** confabulation

discus thrower 6 Alekna (Virgilijus), Marten (Maritza), Oerter (Al) **10** discobolus **11** Rashchupkin (Viktor)

disdain 5 abhor, scorn, scout, spurn **6** deride, refuse, reject, slight **7** contemn, despise, despite, hauteur, put down **8** aversion, belittle, contempt, disprize, misprize **9** antipathy **10** repugnance, undervalue

disdainful 5 aloof, proud **6** averse, lordly, sniffy, snooty, uppity **7** haughty **8** arrogant, cavalier, derisive, insolent, scorning, snobbish, spurning, superior, toplofty **11** overbearing **12** antipathetic, contemptuous, supercilious **13** high and mighty

disease 3 bug, ill **5** upset, virus **6** blight, malady **7** ailment, anthrax, illness, malaise, mycosis, purpura **8** debility, epidemic, myxedema, pandemic, sickness, syndrome, zoonoses (plural) **9** affection, black lung, contagion, ill health, infection, infirmity, sclerosis **10** affliction, blackwater, bronchitis, infirmness, sickliness *animal:* **5** mange, surra **6** rabies **7** bighead **8** enzootic, zoonosis **9** distemper, tularemia **10** rinderpest *blood:* **8** leukemia, leukoses (plural), leukosis *cabbage:* **8** clubroot *cattle:* **6** cowpox **7** foot rot, locoism, murrain **8** blackleg, vaccinia **9** vibriosis **10** rinderpest **11** brucellosis *cereal grass:* **4** bunt, smut **5** ergot *children's:* **5** mumps **7** measles, rubella **10** chicken pox **13** whooping cough *citrus tree:* **8** tristeza *classification:* **8** nosology *combining form:* **4** path **5** patho *communicable:* **3** flu **4** mono **5** mumps, polio **6** dengue, herpes, plague, rabies **7** bird flu, cholera, leprosy, malaria, measles, rubella, tetanus, typhoid **8** avian flu, impetigo **9** hepatitis, influenza **10** giardiasis **12** tuberculosis *deficiency:* **6** scurvy **7** rickets **8** beriberi, pellagra *disseminator:* **6** vector **7** carrier *eye:* **6** iritis **8** glaucoma, trachoma **9** retinitis *hair follicle:* **7** sycoses (plural), sycosis *heart:* **11** cardiopathy *horse:* **6** nagana, spavin **7** locoism, sarcoid **8** glanders **9** strangles *identification of:* **9** diagnosis *industrial:* **10** byssinosis *infectious:* **4** mono, yaws **6** dengue, typhus **7** leprosy, malaria, tetanus, typhoid **9** tularemia, vibriosis **10** rinderpest **13** whooping cough *liver:* **9** cirrhosis, hepatitis *livestock:* **7** locoism **9** vibriosis **10** rinderpest *lung:* **8** phthisic, phthisis **9** pneumonia **10** byssinosis **12** tuberculosis *lymph glands:* **8** scrofula *metabolic:* **4** gout *nervous system:* **4** kuru **6** rabies **10** diphtheria *of beets:* **8** heartrot *of mammals:* **6** rabies **7** malaria **9** distemper **10** babesiosis, rinderpest *parasitic:* **3** rot **4** smut **5** mange **7** malaria **8** hookworm, kala-azar **9** heartworm *plant:* **4** rust, scab, smut, wilt **5** blast, edema, scald, scurf, stunt **6** blight, blotch, canker, mosaic, streak **7** blister, crinkle, foot rot, frogeye, red leaf, root rot **8** clubroot, curly top, fusarium, gummosis, leaf curl, leaf roll, leaf rust, leaf spot, ring spot, root knot, stem rust **9** chlorosis, crown gall, white rust **10** blackheart, leaf scorch *poultry:* **8** leukosis *respiratory:* **6** asthma, coryza **10** byssinosis *sheep:* **3** gid **7** scrapie **9** vibriosis **10** bluetongue *silkworm:* **3** uji *skin:* **4** acne, yaws **5** favus, hives, lupus, mange, pinta, tinea **6** eczema, tetter **7** leprosy, prurigo, sarcoid, scabies, serpigo **8** impetigo, miliaria, pyoderma, ringworm, vitiligo **9** pemphigus, psoriasis **10** erysipelas **11** scleroderma *syphilitic:* **5** tabes *throat:* **5** croup, strep *thyroid:* **6** struma *tropical:* **4** yaws **5** pinta, sprue, surra **6** dengue **7** malaria **8** kala-azar *venereal:* **6** herpes **8** syphilis **9** chancroid, gonorrhea *viral:* **3** flu **4** AIDS, noma **5** Ebola, mumps, polio **6** dengue, grippe, herpes, rabies, zoster **7** bird flu, measles, rubella, rubeola, variola **8** avian flu, morbilli, shingles, smallpox **9** hepatitis, influenza, monkey pox, varicella **13** poliomyelitis

diseased 3 ill **6** ailing, infirm, sickly, unwell **7** fevered, unsound **8** feverish, infected

disembark 4 land **6** alight **7** deplane, detrain **8** go ashore

disembarrass 3 rid **4** free **7** release, relieve **8** liberate, unburden, untangle **9** extricate **11** disencumber, disentangle

disembodied 7 ghostly **8** ethereal, spectral **9** asomatous, unfleshly **10** immaterial, unphysical, wraithlike **11** incorporeal, nonmaterial, nonphysical **13** insubstantial

disembogue 4 flow, gush, pour, spew **5** empty **7** pour out **9** discharge

disembowel 3 gut **10** eviscerate, exenterate

disemploy 2 ax **3** axe, can **4** boot, fire, sack **7** cashier **9** discharge, terminate

disenchanted 5 blasé, jaded **6** soured **7** cynical **9** jaundiced **10** undeceived **11** worldly-wise **12** disappointed, dissatisfied **13** disenthralled, disillusioned

disencumber 3 rid **4** free **7** lighten, release,

relieve, sort out **8** free from, liberate, unburden **9** alleviate, disburden, extricate

disengage 4 free, part **5** loose, unfix **6** detach, opt out, unbind **7** back out, drop out, release, unloose **8** cut loose, liberate, separate, uncouple, unfasten, unloosen, withdraw **10** disconnect

disentangle 5 untie **6** detach **7** resolve, sort out, unravel, unsnarl, untwine **8** separate **9** extricate **10** unscramble **11** disencumber **13** straighten out

disenthrall 4 free **7** manumit, release **8** liberate **10** emancipate

disfavor 7 dislike **8** aversion, distrust, mistrust **9** deprecate, disesteem, disregard, disrepute **10** disrespect **11** disapproval **12** disadvantage, unpopularity

disfigure 3 mar **4** maim, scar **6** deface, defile, deform, impair, injure, mangle **7** blemish, distort **8** mutilate

disfranchise 3 bar **7** exclude **8** take away **9** deprive of **10** disentitle

disgorge 4 barf, spew **5** belch, eject, eruct, erupt, expel, vomit **6** give up, irrupt, spit up **7** release, throw up, upchuck **9** discharge

disgrace 5 odium, shame **6** stigma **7** attaint, mortify, obloquy **8** black eye, contempt, dishonor, ignominy, reproach **9** discredit, disrepute, humiliate **10** opprobrium, stigmatize **11** degradation, humiliation

disgraceful 7 ignoble **8** shameful **9** degrading **10** deplorable, inglorious, unbecoming **11** humiliating, ignominious, reproachful **12** dishonorable, disreputable

disgruntled 5 vexed **6** cranky, put out **7** annoyed, beefing, griping **8** grousing **9** irritated **10** discontent, displeased, ill-humored, malcontent **11** ungratified **12** discontented, malcontented

disguise 4 hide, mask, sham, veil **5** belie, cloak, feign, put on **6** facade **7** conceal, falsify, obscure **8** artifice, pretense **9** deception **10** camouflage, false front, pretension **12** misrepresent

disguised 6 masked, veiled **7** cloaked, feigned **9** incognito **10** undercover **11** camouflaged

disguisement 4 mask, veil **5** cloak, front **6** facade **8** pretense **9** deception **10** false front, pretention

disgust 6 nausea, offend, revolt, sicken **8** aversion, gross out, loathing, nauseate **9** antipathy, repulsion, revulsion **10** abhorrence, repugnance **11** abomination **13** squeamishness

disgusted 5 fed up **8** offended, repelled, repulsed, revolted, sickened **9** nauseated, squeamish **10** grossed out

disgusting 4 foul, icky, vile **5** gross, nasty, yucky **7** noisome **9** loathsome, offensive, repellent, repugnant, repulsive, revolting, sickening **10** nauseating

dish 4 bowl, buzz, food, talk, tray **5** plate **6** course, gossip, tureen **7** chatter, hearsay, platter, scandal, slander **9** casserole, container **11** scuttlebutt *baked:* **7** soufflé *baking:* **7** cocotte, scallop **9** casserole **12** scallop shell *cheese:* **6** fondue **7** ramekin, rarebit **8** raclette, ramequin *Chinese:* **6** dim sum, lo mein, subgum, wonton **8** chop suey, chow mein **10** egg foo yong, egg foo yung **11** egg foo young *deep:* **9** casserole *Hungarian:* **7** goulash *Italian:* **5** pasta, penne, pesto, pizza **6** scampi **7** cannoli, lasagna, polenta, ravioli **8** calamari, linguine, linguini, osso buco, rigatoni **9** foccaccia, manicotti **10** cannelloni, scaloppine, tortellini **11** saltimbocca *Japanese:* **5** sushi **7** sashimi, tempura **8** sukiyaki *Mexican:* **4** taco **5** chili **6** fajita, flauta, nachos, tamale **7** burrito, chalupa **8** frijoles **9** enchilada, guacamole **10** carne asada **11** chimichanga **12** refried beans **13** chili con carne *Middle Eastern:* **5** kebab, kibbe, kibbi **6** hummus, kibbeh **7** falafel **8** couscous, moussaka **10** shish kebab **11** baba ghanouj **12** baba ghanoush *principal:* **6** entrée *rice:* **5** pilaf **7** risotto *Scottish:* **5** brose **6** haggis *shallow:* **6** saucer *Thai:* **7** pad thai

disharmonize 3 jar, war **5** clash **6** jangle **7** discord **8** conflict, mismatch **9** disaccord

disharmony 6 strife **7** discord **8** conflict, disunion, disunity, friction, variance **9** cacophony **10** contention, difference, dissension, dissonance

dishearten 3 cow **5** chill, crush, daunt, shake **6** dampen, deject, dismay, sadden **7** depress, unnerve **8** dispirit, distress **10** demoralize, discourage, intimidate

dishes 4 ware *clay:* **7** pottery *porcelain:* **5** china

dishevel 5 touse **6** muss up, rumple, tousle **8** disarray, disorder **10** disarrange, discompose

disheveled 5 messy **6** mussed **7** unkempt **8** ill-kempt, uncombed

dishonest 5 false, lying, rogue, snide **6** tricky, unfair **7** corrupt, crooked, knavish **8** cheating, cozening, two-faced **9** deceitful, deceiving, deceptive, swindling **10** defrauding, fraudulent, mendacious, untruthful **13** double-dealing, untrustworthy

dishonesty 5 fraud, guile **6** deceit **7** falsity,

knavery, roguery **8** flimflam, pretense, trickery **9** chicanery, deception, duplicity, falsehood, hypocrisy **10** corruption **11** crookedness **13** double-dealing

dishonor see **disgrace**

dishonorable see **disgraceful**

dish out 5 ladle, serve **6** pile on, supply **7** deliver, present, serve up **8** allocate, disburse, dispense **10** distribute

disillusioned see **disenchanted**

disinclination 7 dislike **8** aversion, distaste **9** antipathy, objection **10** reluctance **13** indisposition, unwillingness

disinclined 5 loath **6** averse **7** opposed **8** hesitant **9** reluctant, resistant, unwilling **10** indisposed

disinfect 6 purify **8** sanitize **9** autoclave, sterilize **13** decontaminate

disingenuous 3 sly **4** foxy, wily **5** false **6** artful, crafty, tricky **7** cunning, devious, feigned **8** delusive, guileful, indirect, specious **9** deceitful, deceiving, deceptive, dishonest, insidious, insincere, sophistic **10** misleading **11** calculating, casuistical, sophistical

disinherit 6 cut off **7** bereave, exclude **9** deprive of, repudiate **10** dispossess

disintegrate 3 rot **4** turn **5** break, burst, decay, spoil, taint **6** molder **7** crumble, scatter, shatter **8** splinter **9** break down, decompose, fall apart **10** deliquesce

disinter 5 dig up **6** exhume, unbury **7** unearth **8** exhumate **9** resurrect

disinterest 6 apathy **7** neglect **8** coolness, lethargy **9** aloofness, disregard, unconcern **10** detachment, dispassion, neutrality **11** impassivity, inattention, insouciance, nonchalance, objectivity **12** indifference

disinterested 4 fair, just **5** aloof **6** candid **7** neutral **8** detached, unbiased **9** impartial, impassive, incurious, objective **10** evenhanded, impersonal, neglectful, nonchalant **11** inattentive, indifferent, unconcerned

disjoin 4 part **5** sever, unfix **6** detach, divide, sunder, unlink **7** break up, divorce **8** disunite, separate, uncouple, unfasten **9** disengage, take apart **10** dissociate **12** disaffiliate, disassociate

disjointed 7 jumbled, muddled **8** confused, inchoate, rambling **9** displaced **10** disordered, incoherent, incohesive **11** unconnected, unorganized **13** discontinuous

disk 4 puck **5** wafer **6** record *metal:* **4** slug *ornamental:* **6** bangle, sequin

dislike 4 shun **5** scorn, spurn **6** animus, oppose, reject, resent **7** deplore, frown on **8** aversion, disfavor, distaste **9** animosity, antipathy **10** alienation, disapprove, repugnance **11** disapproval

dislimn 3 dim **5** bedim **6** darken **7** becloud, obscure **9** obfuscate

dislocate 5 break **7** disrupt, unhinge **9** disengage **10** disconnect **13** disarticulate

dislodge 4 oust **5** eject, evict, expel **6** remove, uproot **8** displace, drive out, force out

disloyal 5 false **6** untrue **8** apostate, recreant **9** alienated, faithless **10** perfidious, traitorous, unfaithful **11** disaffected, treacherous

disloyalty 7 falsity, perfidy, treason **8** apostasy **9** falseness, recreancy, treachery **10** alienation, infidelity **12** disaffection **13** faithlessness

dismal 4 grim **5** bleak, drear **6** dreary, gloomy, horrid, somber, sombre **7** joyless **8** desolate, dreadful, funereal, lowering **9** atrocious, cheerless, depressed, tenebrous **10** depressing, depressive **11** dispiriting **12** discouraging **13** disheartening

dismantle 4 raze, undo **5** strip, unrig, wreck **6** denude, divest **7** break up, destroy **8** demolish, pull down, take down **9** break down, knock down, take apart **11** disassemble

dismay 4 faze, fear **5** abash, alarm, daunt, dread, panic, scare, shake, upset **6** appall, fright, horror, rattle **7** agitate, fluster, horrify, perturb, unnerve **8** affright, bewilder, confound, dispirit, distress, frighten **9** discomfit, dumbfound, embarrass **10** discompose, disconcert, discourage, dishearten **11** trepidation **12** perturbation **13** consternation

dismayed 5 upset **6** afraid, aghast, scared, shaken **7** fearful, shocked **9** disturbed

dismember 4 maim **5** cut up **7** disjoin, dissect **8** mutilate **9** dismantle, take apart

dismiss 2 ax **3** axe, can **4** drop, fire, oust, sack, shed **5** chuck, eject, evict, let go, scorn, spurn **6** bounce, depose, deride, lay off, reject, remove, retire, shelve, unseat **7** boot out, cashier, contemn, decline, disband, kick out, kiss off, turn off **8** displace, furlough, pooh-pooh, ridicule, throw out, turn away, turn down **9** discharge, repudiate, terminate **11** send packing

dismissal 5 congé **6** firing, layoff, ouster **7** removal **8** brush-off, bum's rush **9** discharge, expulsion **10** cashiering

dismount 6 alight, debark, get off **7** deplane, detrain **9** disembark **10** alight from **11** descend from

Disney, Walt 10 cartoonist *character:* **4** Gyro, Huey, Lady, Nemo **5** Ariel, Bambi, Daisy, Dewey, Dumbo, Goofy, Louie, Mulan, Pluto, Simba, Tramp **6** Beauty, Donald,

Mickey, Minnie, Mowgli **7** Aladdin, Scrooge **9** Gladstone, Pinocchio, Snow White **10** Beagle Boys, Clarabelle, Pocahontas *classic:* **5** Bambi, Dumbo **8** Fantasia **9** Pinocchio **10** Jungle Book (The) **15** Lady and the Tramp

disobedient 6 unruly **7** naughty, wayward, willful **8** contrary **10** headstrong, ill-behaved, rebellious, refractory **11** misbehaving, uncompliant **12** contumacious, noncompliant, obstreperous, recalcitrant **13** insubordinate

disoblige 5 annoy **6** bother, offend, put out **7** affront, disturb, trouble **9** displease, incommode **10** discommode **13** inconvenience

disorder 3 ill **4** mess, riot **5** chaos, havoc, mix up, snarl, upset **6** ataxia, hubbub, jumble, malady, mess up, muddle, muss up, ruckus, rumple, tumble, tumult, unrest, uproar **7** ailment, anarchy, clutter, confuse, disease, embroil, illness, misdeed, shuffle, turmoil **8** disarray, sickness, syndrome, unsettle, upheaval **9** affection, agitation, commotion, complaint, confusion, infirmity **10** affliction, turbulence, untidiness *mental:* **5** mania **8** delirium, insanity, neurosis, paranoia **9** psychosis **11** psychopathy **13** schizophrenia

disordered 6 roiled **7** chaotic, jumbled, muddled **8** confused, inchoate, shuffled **9** displaced **10** disjointed, dislocated, incoherent, incohesive **11** disarranged, unconnected, unorganized **13** discontinuous

disorderly 5 rowdy **6** unruly, untidy **7** jumbled, raucous, unkempt **8** confused **9** cluttered, offensive, turbulent **10** boisterous, topsy-turvy, tumultuous **12** disorganized, rambunctious, unsystematic

disorganize 5 upset **6** jumble, mess up **7** break up, confuse, derange, disband, disrupt **8** disorder, disperse, unsettle **10** disarrange

disoriented 4 lost **7** mixed up **8** confused **9** displaced, perplexed, unsettled **10** bewildered

disown 4 deny, dump **6** desert, reject **7** cast off, disavow **8** disclaim, renounce **9** repudiate

disparage 5 decry **6** defame, slight **7** condemn, degrade, devalue, dismiss, put down, run down **8** bad-mouth, belittle, derogate, discount, downplay, minimize, pooh-pooh **9** denigrate, deprecate, discredit, dispraise, downgrade, underrate **10** demoralize, depreciate, undervalue **11** detract from

disparagement 5 scorn **7** calumny, censure, despite, scandal, slander **8** contempt, despisal, reproach **9** aspersion, discredit, stricture **10** backbiting, defamation, derogation, detraction, diminution **11** degradation **12** backstabbing, depreciation **13** animadversion

disparate 6 at odds, divers, unlike, varied **7** diverse, unalike, unequal, various, varying **8** discrete, distinct, separate **9** different, divergent, unsimilar **10** dissimilar **11** distinctive, incongruous, inconsonant **12** incompatible, inconsistent

disparity 3 gap **8** contrast **9** imbalance **10** difference, divergence, divergency, inequality **11** discrepancy **13** disproportion, dissimilarity

dispassionate 4 calm, fair, just **7** neutral **8** composed, detached, unbiased **9** equitable, impartial, objective, unruffled **10** impersonal **11** unemotional **12** unprejudiced **13** disinterested

dispatch 4 kill, send, ship, slay **5** haste, hurry, scrag, speed **6** defeat, murder **7** bump off, execute, forward, killing, message, put away **8** alacrity, get rid of, shipment, transmit **9** dispose of, eliminate, swiftness **10** expedition, put to death, speediness **11** assassinate, promptitude

dispel 6 banish **7** cast out, scatter **8** disperse **9** clear away, dissipate, drive away

dispensable 5 minor **7** trivial **8** needless, unneeded **10** disposable, expendable, unrequired **11** superfluous, unessential, unimportant, unnecessary **12** nonessential

dispensary 6 clinic

dispensation 4 plan **5** favor, share **7** license, portion, service **8** bestowal, courtesy, kindness, ordering **9** allotment, exception, exemption, privilege, remission **10** indulgence, management **12** disbursement, distribution **13** apportionment, authorization

dispense 5 allot, apply, wield **6** assign, divide, excuse, exempt, ration, supply **7** absolve, deal out, deliver, dish out, dole out, furnish, give out, mete out, portion, provide, release **8** allocate, carry out, disburse, share out, transfer **9** apportion, discharge, partition **10** administer, distribute, measure out, portion out

disperse 3 sow **5** spray, strew **6** dispel, divide, spread, vanish **7** break up, diffuse, disband, radiate, scatter **9** broadcast, dissipate, partition, propagate **10** distribute

dispersion 6 spread **7** breakup, colloid **9** diffusion, spreading **10** scattering **11** dissipation **12** distribution **13** dissemination

dispirit 3 cow **5** chill, daunt **6** deject, dismay,

sadden **7** depress, oppress **8** distress **10** demoralize, discourage, dishearten

dispirited 3 low, sad **4** blue, down, glum **5** cowed **6** morose **7** daunted **8** cast down, dejected, dismayed, downcast, saddened **9** bummed out, depressed, oppressed, woebegone **10** distressed, melancholy **11** crestfallen, demoralized, discouraged, downhearted **12** disconsolate, disheartened

dispiriting 4 blue **6** dismal, dreary, gloomy **8** daunting, dolorous, funereal **9** cheerless, dismaying, saddening **10** depressing, oppressive **12** demoralizing, disconsolate, discouraging **13** disheartening

displace 4 oust, sack **5** exile, expel, usurp **6** banish, deport, depose, remove **7** succeed **8** dethrone, supplant **9** supersede, transport **10** expatriate, substitute

display 4 pomp, show **5** array, model **6** evince, expose, flaunt, lay out, parade, reveal, spread, unfold, unfurl, unveil **7** exhibit, panoply, present, showing, show off, trot out, uncover **8** brandish, evidence, manifest, showcase **9** showiness, spectacle **10** exhibiting, exhibition **11** demonstrate, ostentation **13** demonstration, manifestation

displeasing 6 vexing **7** irksome **8** annoying **10** bothersome, unpleasant **12** disagreeable **13** objectionable

displeasure 5 anger **8** aversion, disfavor, vexation **9** annoyance **10** discomfort, discontent, irritation, uneasiness **11** indignation, unhappiness **13** indisposition

disport 4 show **5** amuse **6** acquit, behave, divert, expose, flaunt, frolic, parade **7** conduct, display, exhibit, show off, trot out **9** entertain

disposal 5 order **7** removal **8** bestowal, chucking, jettison, ordering, transfer **9** clearance **10** allocation, assignment, demolition, discarding, regulation, relegation **11** arrangement, consignment, destruction, disposition **12** distribution, transference

dispose 4 bend, bias, rank **5** array, order, range **6** settle **7** arrange, incline, marshal, prepare **8** organize, regulate **9** make ready **11** systematize *of:* **4** dump, junk, sell **5** chuck, scrap **6** finish, handle, unload **7** deep-six, destroy, discard **8** deal with, throw out, transfer **9** eighty-six, eliminate **10** distribute

disposed 3 apt **4** fain, game **5** prone, ready **6** biased, minded **7** partial, willing **8** arranged, inclined **9** persuaded

disposition 4 bent, cast, mood, tone, type, vein **5** being, order, stamp **6** makeup, nature, temper **7** control, leaning, mind-set **8**

ordering, penchant, riddance, sequence, tendency, transfer 9 character, direction 10 management, proclivity, propensity, settlement 11 arrangement, inclination, personality, temperament 12 constitution, predilection 13 individuality *favorable:* 8 optimism *unfavorable:* 9 pessimism

dispossess 3 rob 4 oust 5 eject, evict, strip 6 divest 7 bereave, deprive

dispossession 4 loss 6 ouster 7 seizure 9 privation 10 divestment 11 deprivation, divestiture 13 expropriation

dispraise 3 pan 5 decry 6 censor, deride, dump on 7 put down, run down 8 bad-mouth, belittle, derogate 9 criticize, deprecate, discredit, disparage 10 depreciate, disapprove 11 detract from 12 depreciation

disproportion 8 imparity, mismatch 9 disparity 10 inequality, unevenness 12 lopsidedness

disproportionate 6 uneven 7 unequal 8 lopsided 10 unbalanced

disprove 5 belie, rebut 6 refute, negate 7 confute, explode 8 confound, overturn, puncture, traverse 9 discredit, overthrow 10 invalidate

disputable 4 iffy, moot 7 dubious 8 arguable, doubtful 9 debatable, uncertain, unsettled 10 unresolved 11 problematic 12 questionable 13 controversial

disputation 6 debate 8 argument, forensic, polemics 9 dialectic 11 controversy 13 argumentation

dispute 4 buck, duel, moot, tiff 5 argue, fight, rebut, repel 6 bicker, combat, debate, hassle, impugn, negate, oppose, refute, resist, rumpus, strife 7 confute, contend, contest, discuss, gainsay, quarrel, quibble, wrangle 8 argument, conflict, question, squabble 9 bickering, challenge, thrash out, withstand 10 contention, controvert, falling-out 11 altercation, controversy, embroilment

disputed 7 debated 8 arguable 9 contested, uncertain 12 questionable 13 controversial

disqualified 5 unfit 8 unfitted 10 ineligible, unequipped

disqualify 3 bar 5 debar 6 except 7 exclude, rule out, suspend 9 eliminate *as judge:* 6 recuse

disquiet 5 alarm, angst, upset, worry 6 bother, flurry, unease, unrest 7 agitate, anxiety, concern, disturb, ferment, fluster, perturb, trouble, turmoil 10 discompose, uneasiness 11 disturbance, restiveness 12 restlessness 13 Sturm und Drang

disquietude 4 care 5 worry 6 unease, unrest 7 anxiety, concern, ferment, turmoil 9 agita-

tion, misgiving 10 foreboding, uneasiness 11 nervousness, restiveness 12 apprehension, restlessness 13 Sturm und Drang

Disraeli, Benjamin *novel:* 5 Sybil 7 Lothair, Tancred 8 Endymion 9 Coningsby *opponent:* 4 Peel (Robert) 9 Gladstone (William) *queen:* 8 Victoria

disregard 4 skip 6 forget, ignore, slight 7 neglect, tune out 8 overlook 9 unconcern 12 heedlessness, indifference

disregardful 3 lax 5 slack 6 remiss 8 careless, derelict, heedless 9 forgetful, unheeding, negligent, unmindful 10 neglectful, regardless, unthinking 11 indifferent, unconcerned 12 absent-minded

disremember 6 forget

disreputable 4 basc 5 dingy, scamy, seedy, shady 6 scurvy, shabby, shoddy, sordid 7 run-down 8 decrepit, infamous, shameful 10 inglorious 11 dilapidated, disgraceful, ignominious 12 contemptible, unprincipled 13 discreditable, unrespectable

disrepute 5 odium, shame 7 obloquy 8 disfavor, disgrace, dishonor, ignominy 9 disesteem 10 opprobrium

disrespect 6 insult 7 disdain 8 boldness, contempt, rudeness 9 disregard, flippancy, impudence, insolence 10 incivility 11 discourtesy, presumption 12 impertinence, impoliteness

disrespectful 4 flip, rude 5 sassy, saucy 7 ill-bred, uncivil 8 flippant, impolite, impudent, insolent 10 ungracious 11 ill-mannered, impertinent 12 contemptuous, discourteous

disrobe 4 bare, peel 5 strip 6 denude, divest 7 undress 8 unclothe

disrupt 5 upset 6 mess up 7 break up, rupture 8 disorder, unsettle

dissatisfaction 6 dismay 9 annoyance, complaint 10 discontent, irritation, uneasiness 11 displeasure, frustration

dissatisfied 5 irked, vexed 7 annoyed, unhappy 8 bothered 10 begrudging, discontent, displeased, malcontent 11 complaining, disaffected, unfulfilled 12 disappointed, discontented, malcontented

dissect 5 probe, study 7 analyze, examine, inspect 9 anatomize, break down, take apart 10 scrutinize

dissection 7 autopsy 8 analysis, necropsy *of animals:* 7 zootomy

dissemble 4 hide, mask 5 cloak, feign 7 conceal, cover up, dress up, falsify 8 disguise, simulate 9 whitewash 10 camouflage 11 counterfeit

dissembler 4 fake 5 faker, fraud, phony 8 deceiver, imposter, impostor, pharisee **9** hypocrite, pretender

disseminate 3 sow **5** strew **6** blazon, spread **7** bestrew, diffuse, pass out, publish, scatter, send out **8** announce, disperse, proclaim **9** advertise, broadcast, circulate, propagate, publicize **10** promulgate

dissension 5 fight **6** strife **7** discord, dispute, faction, quarrel, wrangle **8** argument, clashing, conflict, disunity, friction, variance **9** bickering **10** contention, difference, quarreling **11** altercation, controversy **12** disagreement

dissent 5 demur **6** differ, heresy, object **7** protest **8** conflict, variance **9** misbelief **10** contention, difference, heterodoxy, opposition, resistance **11** unorthodoxy **12** nonagreement **13** nonconformism, nonconformity

dissenter 7 heretic **8** apostate, defector, deserter, partisan, recreant **10** schismatic, separatist **11** misbeliever, schismatist **13** nonconformist

dissertation 6 thesis **8** tractate, treatise **9** discourse, monograph **10** commentary, exposition **11** disputation **12** disquisition **13** argumentation

dissever 3 cut, hew **4** hack, part **5** carve, slice, split **6** cleave, detach, divide, sunder **7** disjoin, divorce **8** disjoint, disunite, separate, uncouple **10** disconnect

dissidence 6 heresy, schism, strife **7** discord, dispute, dissent, faction **8** conflict, friction, variance **10** contention, disharmony, dissension, heterodoxy, opposition **11** discordance, unorthodoxy **12** disagreement **13** nonconformism, nonconformity

dissident 7 heretic **8** partisan, recusant **9** differing, dissenter, heretical, heterodox, protestor **10** schismatic, separatist, unorthodox **11** contentious, disagreeing, misbeliever, nonbeliever, quarrelsome, schismatist **12** disputatious, unharmonious **13** nonconformist

dissimilar 6 unlike **7** diverse, unalike, unequal, various **8** distinct **9** different, disparate, divergent **13** heterogeneous

dissimilarity 8 contrast, variance **9** disparity, diversity, variation **10** difference, divergence, divergency, unlikeness **11** incongruity **13** heterogeneity, inconsistency

dissimulate see **dissemble**

dissimulation 5 fraud, guile, lying **6** deceit **7** cunning **8** artifice, flimflam, pretense **9** deception, duplicity, hypocrisy, mendacity, sophistry **10** craftiness, pharisaism **11** beguilement, smoke screen

dissipate 4 blow **5** use up, waste **6** burn up, spread, vanish **7** break up, scatter **8** disperse, evanesce, melt away, misspend, squander **9** evaporate, throw away **11** fritter away

dissipated 6 rakish, wanton, wasted **8** depraved **9** debauched, reprobate **10** degenerate, licentious, profligate **11** intemperate

dissociate 4 part **5** unfix **6** cut off, detach **7** disband, disjoin **8** alienate, disunite, estrange, separate, uncouple **9** disengage **10** disconnect

dissolute 3 lax **4** fast, wild **5** loose, slack **6** rakish, wanton **7** raffish, wayward **8** decadent, depraved **9** abandoned, debauched, indulgent, reprobate **10** degenerate, dissipated, licentious, profligate **12** unprincipled, unrestrained

dissolution 5 death, decay, split **6** demise **7** breakup, divorce, rupture, split-up **8** division **9** dispersal, partition **10** detachment, disbanding, profligacy **11** evaporation **12** liquefaction

dissolvable 7 soluble **8** meltable

dissolve 3 end **4** flux, melt, thaw, undo, void **5** annul, quash **6** recess, vacate, vanish **7** adjourn, break up, diffuse, liquefy **8** abrogate, disperse, evanesce, fade away, get rid of, melt away, prorogue, separate **9** decompose, dissipate, evaporate, prorogate, terminate, waste away **10** deliquesce, do away with **12** disintegrate

dissonance 6 strife **7** discord **8** clashing, conflict **9** cacophony, harshness **10** contention, difference, disharmony **11** incongruity **12** disagreement **13** inconsistency

dissonant 5 harsh **7** grating, jarring, raucous **8** strident **9** unmusical **10** cacophonic, discordant, inharmonic **11** cacophonous, conflicting, incongruous **12** incompatible, inharmonious

dissuade 5 deter **7** turn off **10** discourage, disincline

distaff 6 female **8** maternal

distance 4 area **5** ambit, lapse, orbit, range, reach, scope, space, sweep **6** course, degree, extent, length, radius, remove, spread **7** breadth, compass, expanse, horizon, mileage, reserve, spacing, stretch **8** interval **9** amplitude, disparity, expansion, extension **10** divergence, divergency, remoteness, separation **11** distinction *between levels:* **4** drop *between rails:* **4** gage *between supports:* **4** span *from bottom to top:* **6** height *geometric:* **8** altitude *greatest perpendicular:* **6** camber *measuring instrument:* **8** odometer **9** pedometer, telemeter **11** range finder *perpendicular:* 5 depth *shortest:* 7 beeline 12 straight line

distant 3 far, shy 4 afar, cold, cool 5 aloof, apart 6 absent, far-off, remote 7 faraway, haughty, obscure, removed, spacial, spatial 8 far-flung, isolated, outlying, reserved, secluded, solitary 9 separated, unsimilar, withdrawn 10 unsociable 11 out-of-the-way, sequestered, standoffish *combining form:* 3 tel 4 tele, telo

distaste 7 disgust, dislike 8 aversion, loathing 9 antipathy, hostility, revulsion 10 abhorrence, repugnance 13 indisposition

distasteful 8 unsavory 9 loathsome, obnoxious, offensive, repellent, repugnant, repulsive 10 abominable, unpleasant 11 displeasing, unpalatable 12 disagreeable, unappetizing 13 objectionable

distemper 6 malady 7 ailment, disease 8 disorder 9 contagion, strangles 10 affliction 11 derangement 13 panleucopenia

distend 5 bloat, bulge, swell, widen 6 dilate, expand, extend, puff up 7 amplify, augment, enlarge, inflate, stretch 8 increase, lengthen 10 stretch out

distill 6 refine 7 extract 8 boil down 11 concentrate, precipitate

distinct 4 sole 5 clear, lucid, plain 6 marked, patent, single, unique 7 audible, defined, diverse, evident, express, notable, obvious, special, unusual 8 apparent, clear-cut, definite, discrete, especial, explicit, manifest, palpable, peculiar, separate, specific 9 different, divergent 10 individual, noticeable, particular 11 categorical, unambiguous, uncquivocal 12 unmistakable

distinction 4 bays, rank 5 award, badge, grade, honor, kudos 6 nicety, renown 7 laurels 8 accolade, eminence, prestige 10 difference, divergence, divergency, prominence, unlikeness 11 differentia, peculiarity, preeminence, recognition 12 significance 13 dissimilarity

distinctive 6 proper, single, unique 7 special, unusual 8 peculiar, separate, singular 10 individual 13 idiosyncratic

distingué 6 classy, urbane 7 courtly, elegant, eminent, genteel, refined 8 cultured, decorous, highbrow, mannerly, polished, well-bred 9 dignified, high-class 10 cultivated 13 sophisticated

distinguish 4 mark, note, spot, view 5 honor, place 6 descry, notice, set off 7 dignify, make out, mark off, observe, pick out 8 classify, identify, perceive, separate 9 recognize, single out 10 categorize 12 charac-

terize, discriminate 13 differentiate, individualize

distinguished 5 famed, noted 6 famous 7 eminent, notable, stately 8 esteemed, imposing, renowned 9 dignified, prominent 10 celebrated 11 illustrious

distort 4 bend, skew, warp, wind 5 alter, color, twist 6 deform, garble 7 contort, falsify, pervert, torture 8 misstate 11 misconstrue 12 misinterpret, misrepresent

distortion 8 twisting 9 deformity

distract 5 addle, mix up 6 ball up, bemuse, divert, puzzle 7 confuse, fluster, mislead, perplex 8 befuddle, bewilder, confound, throw off 9 sidetrack, unbalance

distracted 8 confused, deranged, maddened, troubled 9 oblivious 10 nonplussed 11 disoriented, inattentive, preoccupied 12 absent-minded

distraction 5 upset 9 agitation, amusement, confusion, diversion 10 perplexity 12 interruption 13 entertainment

distrait 5 upset 7 anxious, bemused, faraway, worried 8 confused, deranged, harassed, maddened, troubled 9 tormented, withdrawn 10 abstracted, distracted, distraught 11 inattentive, preoccupied 12 absent-minded, apprehensive

distraught 5 upset 6 addled, crazed 7 anxious, frantic, muddled, rattled, shook up, unglued, worried 8 agitated, confused, demented, deranged, frenzied, harassed, troubled, worked up 9 flustered, perturbed, tormented, wigged-out 10 distressed, bewildered, freaked out, nonplussed 11 overwrought

distress 3 ail, irk, mar, try, vex, woe 4 ache, care, hurt, pain, pang, rack 5 agony, annoy, cross, dolor, grief, rigor, throe, trial, upset, worry 6 bother, grieve, harass, misery, pester, plague, sorrow, strain, strait, twinge 7 afflict, anguish, anxiety, exhaust, torment, torture, trouble 8 aggrieve, calamity, exigency, hardship 9 adversity, constrain, hard times, suffering 10 affliction, difficulty, heartbreak, misfortune, visitation 11 tribulation, vicissitude *call:* 6 Mayday *signal:* 3 SOS 5 alarm

distressing 4 dire 6 woeful 8 alarming, grievous, shocking 9 offensive 10 deplorable, lamentable 11 dispiriting, regrettable, unfortunate 13 heartbreaking

distribute 4 deal, mete 5 allot, place, strew 6 assign, assort, divide, donate, parcel, ration, spread 7 deal out, deliver, diffuse, dish out, divvy up, dole out, dribble, give out, hand out, mete out, prorate, radiate, scatter, slice up **8** allocate, classify, disburse, dispense, position, separate **9** apportion, circulate, partition, propagate, spread out **10** administer, measure out **11** disseminate

distribution 7 density **8** delivery, dividend, grouping, ordering, sequence **9** allotment, allotting, diffusion, dispersal, marketing, placement, spreading **10** dispersion, scattering **11** arrangement, probability, propagation **12** apportioning, dispensation **13** apportionment, dissemination

distributor 5 agent **6** broker, jobber **7** carrier **9** middleman **10** wholesaler **12** intermediate

district 4 area, ward **5** tract **6** barrio, locale, parcel, region, sector **7** borough, quarter, section **8** division, locality, precinct, vicinage, vicinity **11** subdivision **12** neighborhood *Danish:* **3** amt *ecclesiastical:* **5** synod **6** parish **7** diocese *Greek:* **4** deme *Indian:* **6** tahsil *judicial:* **7** circuit *London:* **4** Soho **7** Chelsea, Mayfair **9** Docklands, Greenwich, Southwark **10** Kensington, Piccadilly **11** Canary Wharf, Notting Hill **13** Knightsbridge *New York:* **4** Soho **7** Chelsea, Tribeca *theater:* **6** rialto

District of Columbia *college, university:* **6** Howard **8** American, Catholic **9** Gallaudet **10** Georgetown *motto:* **13** E Pluribus Unum *official bird:* **10** wood thrush *official flower:* **18** American Beauty rose

distrust 5 doubt **7** suspect **8** question, wariness **9** disbelief, discredit, misgiving, suspicion **10** disbelieve

distrustful 4 wary **5** chary, leery **7** cynical, dubious, jealous **8** doubtful, doubting **10** suspicious **12** questionable

disturb 4 faze **5** alarm, daunt, rouse, upset, worry **6** bother, harass, meddle, mess up, pester, stir up **7** agitate, break up, disrupt, fluster, perplex, trouble, unnerve **8** bewilder, distress, unsettle **9** incommode, interrupt **10** discompose, disconcert, tamper with **13** inconvenience, interfere with

disturbance 4 flap, fuss, stir, to-do **5** stink **6** clamor, hubbub, rumpus, tumult, unrest, uproar **7** bobbery, turmoil **8** disorder **9** agitation, commotion, confusion **10** alteration, disruption, turbulence **11** derangement, distraction **12** interruption *atmospheric:* **5** storm **7** cyclone, tornado **9** hurricane *mental:* **6** frenzy **8** delirium, neurosis **9** psychosis

disturbed 5 upset **6** insane, shaken **7** anxious, puzzled, rattled, worried **8** bothered, demented, deranged, troubled **9** concerned, psychotic, unsettled **10** distracted, distressed **12** disconcerted

disunion 7 divorce, rupture, split-up **8** division, severing, variance **9** partition **10** detachment, difference, separation **13** disconnection

disunite 4 part **6** divide, sunder **7** break up, disjoin, divorce, split up **8** dissever, separate, uncouple **9** disengage, fall apart **10** disconnect **12** disaffiliate

disunity 6 strife, schism **7** discord **8** conflict, division, variance **10** alienation, contention, disharmony, dissension **12** disaffection, disagreement, estrangement

disused 5 passé **8** obsolete, outdated, outmoded **9** abandoned, discarded **10** antiquated, superseded

ditch 3 dig, pit **4** drop, dump, foss, ha-ha, junk, moat **5** chuck, fosse, leave, scrap, swale **6** reject, trench, trough **7** abandon, cashier, discard, dismiss, forsake, foxhole **8** jettison, throw out **9** crash-land, dispose of, throw away **10** excavation

dither 4 fuss, stew **5** quake, shake, tizzy, waver **6** falter, flurry, quaver, shiver **7** flutter, tremble, twitter, whiffle **8** hesitate **9** agitation, commotion, confusion, vacillate **10** excitement, turbulence **12** shilly-shally

dithyramb 4 hymn, poem **5** chant

dithyrambic 6 ardent, fervid **9** perfervid, rhapsodic **10** boisterous, passionate **11** impassioned

ditto 4 copy, idem, same **5** clone, me too, mimeo, repro, Xerox **6** carbon, repeat **7** replica, reprint, similar **9** duplicate, facsimile, photocopy **10** carbon copy, mimeograph **11** replication **12** reproduction **13** reduplication

ditty 3 air, lay **4** song, tune **5** carol, chant **6** ballad

diurnal 5 daily **7** daytime **8** daylight **9** circadian, ephemeral, quotidian

diva 7 goddess **10** prima donna **11** leading lady

divagate 4 turn, veer **5** drift, stray **6** depart, ramble, wander **7** digress, diverge

divan 4 sofa **5** couch **6** settee **7** chamber, council **9** davenport **12** chesterfield

dive 3 bar, pub **4** dash, dump, hole, jump, leap **5** joint, lunge, pitch, sound, swoop **6** header, lounge, plunge, saloon, tavern **7** barroom, decline, descend, descent, hangout, plummet, taproom **8** submerge **9** honky-tonk, roadhouse **10** cannonball *type:* **4** pike, swan, tuck **6** gainer **7** cutaway **9** belly flop, jackknife

diver 4 loon

diverge 4 part, vary **5** stray **6** depart, differ, swerve **7** deflect, deviate, digress **8** disagree, separate **9** bifurcate, branch off, draw apart

divergence 7 parting **9** departure, deviation, differing **10** aberration, deflection, difference, digression, separation **11** disagreeing, discrepancy, distinction **12** disagreement

divergent 6 unlike **8** aberrant, abnormal, atypical **9** anomalous, different, differing, disparate, irregular **10** dissimilar

divers 6 sundry **7** several, various **8** assorted **9** different, disparate **13** miscellaneous

diverse 5 mixed **6** motley, sundry, unlike, varied **7** several, unalike, unequal, various, varying **8** assorted, discrete, distinct, manifold, separate **9** different, differing, disparate, multiform, multiplex, unsimilar **10** contrasted, dissimilar **11** contrasting, contrastive **12** multifarious **13** contradictory, miscellaneous *combining form:* **4** vari **5** vario *meanings:* **8** polysemy

diversion 5 sport **7** pastime, turning **8** pleasure, sideshow **9** amusement, deviation, enjoyment **10** aberration, deflection, recreation, red herring **11** distraction **13** entertainment

diversity 7 variety **10** assortment, difference, unlikeness **11** variegation **12** multiformity **13** dissimilarity, heterogeneity

divert 4 turn, veer **5** regale, swerve **7** beguile, deflect, delight, deviate, digress **8** distract, redirect **9** entertain, turn aside

divest 3 rid, rob **4** free **5** spoil, strip **6** denude **7** bereave, deprive, despoil, disrobe, undress **8** take away **9** dismantle **10** disinherit, dispossess

divide 3 cut **4** fork, part **5** allot, cut up, sever, share **6** assign, cleave, parcel, ration, schism, sunder **7** break up, dissect, divorce, dole out, isolate, prorate, quarter, share in, split up **8** allocate, classify, dispense, disunite, separate **9** apportion, branch out, partition, watershed **10** distribute, measure out **11** dichotomize, distinguish *into four parts:* **7** quarter *into three parts:* **7** trisect *into two parts:* **5** halve **6** bisect **9** bifurcate

divided 4 rent **5** cleft, riven, split **6** cloven **7** asunder, partite **8** ruptured

dividend 5 bonus, share **6** return, reward **7** benefit, guerdon, portion, premium **9** allotment **12** dispensation

divider 6 border, screen **9** partition

divination 6 augury **7** insight **8** prophecy **11** foretelling, soothsaying *by communication with the dead:* **10** necromancy *by figures:* **8** geomancy *by lots:* **9** sortilege *by numbers:* **10** numerology *by rods:* **7** dowsing **11** rhabdomancy *by stars:* **9** astrology

divine 4 holy **5** clerk, godly, infer **6** cleric, deduce, deific, intuit, parson, priest, sacred, superb **7** foresee, godlike **8** clerical, foreknow, foretell, heavenly, luscious, minister, preacher, prophesy, reverend **9** apprehend, churchman, clergyman, marvelous, religious, visualize **10** anticipate, conjecture, sanctified, superhuman, theologian **11** scrumptious **12** ecclesiastic

Divine Comedy *guide:* **6** Vergil, Virgil *poet:* **5** Dante (Alighieri) *section:* **5** canto **7** Inferno **8** Paradiso **10** Purgatorio

diviner 4 seer **5** augur, sibyl **6** oracle **7** palmist, prophet **8** haruspex **10** forecaster, prophetess, soothsayer

divinity 3 god **5** deity, fudge **7** goddess, godhead, godhood **8** theology

division 3 cut **4** part, unit **5** class, piece, slice, split **6** branch, moiety, parcel, schism, sector **7** breakup, discord, dissent, divorce, parting, portion, rupture, section, segment, split-up **8** category, conflict, district, disunion, disunity, variance **9** partition **10** detachment, difference, disharmony, dissidence, separation **11** dissolution **12** disagreement **13** apportionment *Bible:* **5** verse *book:* **7** chapter *British territorial:* **5** shire *building:* **4** wing *cell:* **7** meiosis, mitosis *city:* **4** ward **7** borough **8** precinct *contest:* **4** heat **6** inning, period *corolla:* **5** petal *country:* **5** state **6** canton **8** province **10** department, prefecture *family:* **4** side **6** branch *geologic time:* **3** eon, era **5** epoch **6** period *hospital:* **4** ward, wing *into two:* **9** bisection **11** bifurcation, bipartition *meal:* **6** course *music:* **3** bar **4** beat **7** measure **8** movement *opera, play:* **3** act **5** scena, scene *poem:* **5** canto, verse **6** stanza *population:* **7** segment, stratum *race:* **3** lap **4** heat *social:* **5** caste, class, tribe *state:* **6** county, parish *term:* **8** quotient *time:* **3** day, eon **4** week, year **5** month **6** decade, minute, moment, second **7** century, weekend **9** fortnight **10** millennium *tribal:* **4** clan *word:* **8** syllable *zodiac:* **4** sign

divisive 8 factious **11** disunifying

divorce 4 part **5** sever, split **6** divide, sunder **7** break up, breakup, disjoin, rupture **8** disjoint, dissever, disunion, disunite, separate **9** partition, severance **10** detachment, separation **11** dissolution

divot 3 sod **4** turf **5** clump

divulge 4 blab, leak, tell **5** spill **6** betray, expose, gossip, reveal, tattle **7** let slip, uncover **8** disclose, give away

Dixie *composer* **6** Emmett (Daniel D.)

dizziness 7 vertigo **9** giddiness

dizzy 5 addle, dazed, giddy, mix up, silly, tipsy **6** addled **7** confuse, dazzled, flighty, foolish, fuddled, muddled, puzzled, reeling **8** confused, swimming, whirling **9** befuddled, confusing **10** bewildered, confounded, distracted, exorbitant, immoderate, inordinate **11** extravagant, light-headed, vertiginous

Djibouti *language:* **6** Arabic, French *monetary unit:* **5** franc *neighbor:* **7** Eritrea, Somalia **8** Ethiopia *sea:* **3** Red

DNA *component:* **7** adenine, guanine, thymine **8** cytosine **10** nucleotide **11** deoxyribose *segment:* **4** exon, gene **7** cistron

doable 8 feasible, possible, workable **9** realistic **10** achievable, attainable **11** performable

do away with 3 end, nix, zap **4** kill, slay **5** annul, erase, whack **6** cancel, finish, murder, remove, repeal, revoke, rub out **7** abolish, bump off, deep-six, destroy, discard, expunge, rescind, squelch, wipe out **8** abrogate, blow away, demolish, dispatch, dissolve, massacre, stamp out **9** dispose of, eliminate, eradicate, extirpate, finish off, liquidate, slaughter **10** extinguish, obliterate **11** discontinue, exterminate

docent 5 guide **6** leader **7** teacher **8** lecturer **10** instructor

docile 4 tame **6** pliant **7** ductile, pliable **8** amenable, biddable, obedient, yielding **9** adaptable, compliant, teachable, tractable **10** submissive **11** acquiescent

dock 3 bob, cut **4** crop, fine, pier, quay, rump, slip **5** berth, jetty, levee, tie up, wharf **6** anchor, hangar, lessen, marina, reduce **7** abridge, landing, shorten **8** cut short, platform, truncate *worker:* **6** lumper **9** stevedore **12** longshoreman

docket 4 card **6** agenda, lineup, record **7** program **8** abstract, calendar, caseload, register, schedule **9** timetable

doctor 3 fix, vet **4** mend **5** adapt, alter, medic, treat **6** medico, repair **7** croaker, dentist, falsify, scholar, surgeon **8** sawbones **9** clinician, internist, physician **10** adulterate, specialist **11** medicine man, recondition, reconstruct *animal:* **3** vet **12** veterinarian *children's:* **12** pediatrician *famous:* **4** Koop (C. Everett), Weil (Andrew) **5** Galen, Spock (Benjamin) **6** Atkins (Robert), Chopra (Deepak), Ornish (Dean) **9** Kevorkian (Jack) **10** Schweitzer (Albert) **11** Hippocrates, Livingstone (David) *foot:* **10** podiatrist **11** chiropodist *heart:* **12** cardiologist *organization:* **3** AMA *teeth:* **7** dentist **10** exodontist *women's:* **12** gynecologist

Doctor of the Church 5 Basil **6** Jerome **7**

Ambrose, Gregory **9** Augustine **10** Athanasius

Doctorow novel 7 Ragtime **9** City of God (The) **10** Waterworks, World's Fair **12** Book of Daniel (The) **13** Billy Bathgate **18** Welcome to Hard Times

Doctor Zhivago *author:* **9** Pasternak (Boris) *character:* **4** Lara **7** Larissa *film director:* **4** Lean (David) *film star:* **6** Sharif (Omar) **8** Christie (Julie)

doctrinaire 5 rigid **8** dogmatic **9** obstinate **10** unyielding **11** domineering, magisterial **13** authoritarian

doctrine 3 ism **5** axiom, basic, canon, credo, creed, dogma, faith, tenet **7** precept **8** teaching **9** principle **11** fundamental

document 4 deed **5** paper **6** record **8** evidence, monument **9** testimony **10** instrument **11** certificate *travel:* **8** passport

dodder 4 limp **5** shake **6** falter, hobble, totter **7** shamble, shuffle, stagger, tremble **12** morning glory

doddering 5 shaky **6** doting, feeble, senile **7** fragile **8** unsteady, weakened **9** faltering

dodge 4 duck, jink, ploy, ruse, slip **5** avert, avoid, elude, evade, fence, parry, shirk, skirt, slide, trick **6** escape, scheme, weasel **7** evasion **8** sidestep **9** avoidance, deception, expedient

Dodger 5 Davis (Tommy) **6** Garvey (Steve), Karros (Eric), Koufax (Sandy), Piazza (Michael), Snider (Duke), Sutton (Don) **8** Newcombe (Don), Robinson (Jackie) **9** Hershiser (Orel) **10** Campanella (Roy) *field:* **7** Ebbetts *home:* **8** Brooklyn **10** Los Angeles *manager:* **6** Alston (Walter) **7** Lasorda (Tommy)

dodger 6 outlaw, screen **7** escapee **8** circular, deceiver, deserter, fugitive, handbill, runagate **9** throwaway

dodgy 4 iffy **5** fishy, vague **6** tricky **7** cryptic, obscure **8** doubtful, unproven **9** ambiguous, enigmatic, uncertain **10** indefinite, suspicious, unreliable **11** problematic **12** questionable **13** controversial

dodo 3 oaf **4** bird, boob, clod, dolt, dope, goof, yo-yo **5** chump, dummy, dunce, idiot, moron, ninny, noddy, stupe **6** dimwit, dumbass, nitwit **7** airhead, dullard, pinhead **8** bonehead, dumbbell, imbecile, lunkhead, meathead, numskull **9** birdbrain, blockhead, ignoramus, lamebrain, numbskull, simpleton **10** dunderhead, nincompoop **11** chowderhead, chucklehead

doe 4 deer **6** female, rabbit **8** kangaroo

doff 4 shed **6** remove **7** take off

dog 3 cur, pom, pug, pup, tag **4** alan, bird,

chow, fice, mutt, peke, puli, tail, tyke **5** Akita, boxer, canid, corgi, dhole, dingo, feist, frank, hound, husky, lemon, pooch, puppy, spitz, trail **6** Afghan, beagle, borzoi, bowwow, briard, canine, collie, detent, poodle, pursue, rascal, saluki, setter, shadow, Talbot, vizsla, wiener, wretch **7** andiron, basenji, harrier, Maltese, mastiff, mongrel, pointer, redbone, Samoyed, Scottie, sharpei, spaniel, terrier, whippet **8** Airedale, Brittany, elkhound, foxhound, inferior, keeshond, komondor, malamute, malemute, papillon, Pekinese, pinscher, sheepdog, Shiba Inu, spurious, wirehair **9** Chihuahua, dachshund, dalmation, deerhound, Great Dane, greyhound, Lhasa apso, Pekingese, retriever, schnauzer, wolfhound **10** bloodhound, Pomeranian, rottweiler, Weimaraner **11** basset hound, bullmastiff, frankfurter, wienerwurst **12** border collie, Newfoundland, Saint Bernard **13** cocker spaniel *Bush's:* **6** Millie *Buster Brown's:* **4** Tige *Charlie Brown's:* **6** Snoopy *command:* **3** sit **4** heel, stay *Dagwood's:* **5** Daisy *Dorothy's:* **4** Toto *family:* **7** Canidae *FDR's:* **4** Fala *fictional:* **3** Max **4** Buck, Lady **5** Astro, Pluto, Scamp, Tramp **6** Big Red **8** McBarker **9** Marmaduke, Old Yeller, Scooby-Doo, White Fang *"Garfield":* **4** Odie *genus:* **5** Canis *Grinch's:* **3** Max *L.B.J.'s:* **3** Her *monster:* **8** Barghest *movie:* **4** Asta, Lady, Toto **5** Benji, Tramp **6** Lassie **9** Beethoven, Old Yeller, Rin Tin Tin *name:* **4** Fido, Spot **5** Rover **6** Bowser *Nixon's:* **8** Checkers *Odysseus's:* **5** Argos *of Hades:* **8** Cerberus *Orphan Annio'o:* **5** Sandy *RCA:* **6** Nipper *Roy Rogers's:* **6** Bullet *Sgt. Snorkel's:* **4** Otto *sled command:* **4** mush *space traveler:* **5** Laika *Steinbeck's:* **7** Charley *television:* **4** King **5** Eddie, Tramp **6** Lassie, Murray **8** Wishbone **9** Rin Tin Tin *three-headed:* **8** Cerberus *tooth:* **4** fang *treat:* **4** bone *two-headed:* **6** Orthos *Wallace's:* **6** Gromit *Welsh:* **5** corgi *Wendy's:* **4** Nana *wild:* **5** dingo *young:* **3** pup **5** puppy, whelp
dog days 6 August **9** canicular
dogfight 3 row **4** fray **5** brawl, broil, melee, set-to **6** fracas, ruckus **7** ruction **10** donnybrook, free-for-all
dogfish 6 bowfin, burbot **8** mud puppy
dogged 7 adamant **8** obdurate, resolute, stubborn **9** insistent, steadfast, obstinate, tenacious, unbending **10** bullheaded, determined, hardheaded, persistent, persisting, unshakable, unyielding **11** persevering, unremitting **12** pertinacious
doggone 4 damn, dang, darn, rank **5** utter **6**

cursed, damned, darned **7** blasted, blessed, dratted **8** absolute, accursed, infernal, outright **9** out-and-out **10** confounded **11** unmitigated **13** blankety-blank
dogma 4 code, rule **5** canon, credo, creed, tenet **6** belief, gospel **7** precept **8** doctrine, ideology **9** orthodoxy, postulate, teachings **10** conviction, persuasion
dogmatic 8 oracular, orthodox **9** assertive, canonical, doctrinal **11** dictatorial, doctrinaire, magisterial, opinionated
Dog of Flanders author 5 Ouida
dog-paddle 4 swim
dog's age 3 eon **4** aeon **8** blue moon, eternity
Dog Star 6 Sirius
dogwood 6 cornel, Cornus **8** red osier
do in 4 kill, ruin, slay **5** cheat, wreck **6** defeat, finish, murder, rub out **7** blot out, bump off, destroy, execute, exhaust, frazzle, take out, wear out, wipe out **8** dispatch, knock off, knock out **9** eliminate, liquidate, prostrate, run ragged, shipwreck **11** assassinate
doing 3 act **6** action **8** activity *good:* **10** beneficent *evil:* **10** maleficent
do it 3 bit, jot **4** coin, damn, dram, drop, hoot, iota, mite, whit **8** trifle **8** particle
doldrums 5 blahs, blues, dumps, ennui, gloom, slump **6** apathy, tedium, torpor **7** boredom **9** dejection **10** depression, inactivity, quiescence, stagnation **12** listlessness
doleful 3 sad **4** down **7** forlorn, ruthful **8** cast down, dejected, dolorous, downcast, grieving, mournful, mourning **9** afflicted, cheerless, depressed, miserable, plaintive, sorrowful, sorrowing, woebegone **10** dispirited, lamentable, lugubrious, melancholy **11** crestfallen, downhearted **12** disconsolate
dole out 4 deal **5** allot **6** divide, parcel, ration **7** divvy up **8** disburse, dispense, disperse **9** apportion, partition **10** administer, distribute
doll 3 Ken **6** Barbie, figure, Kewpie, puppet **7** kachina **10** Betsy Wetsy, Raggedy Ann **11** Raggedy Andy *grotesque:* **8** golliwog
dollar 3 one **4** bill, buck, clam, oner, peso **5** taler **6** single **7** ringgit, smacker **8** simoleon **9** cartwheel, greenback
dollop 4 blob, glob, lump **7** portion
Doll's House, A author: 5 Ibsen (Henrik) *heroine:* **4** Nora
dolly 4 cart **7** stirrer **8** platform **10** locomotive
dolomite 6 marble **9** limestone
dolor 5 agony, grief **6** misery, sorrow **7** anguish, passion **8** distress **9** suffering **10** affliction
dolorous 6 rueful, woeful **7** ruthful **8** griev-

ous, mournful, wretched **9** afflicted, anguished, miserable, plaintive, sorrowful **10** lamentable, lugubrious, melancholy **13** heartbreaking

dolphin 5 whale **7** bollard **8** porpoise

dolt 3 ass, oaf **4** boob, clod, dodo, dork, fool, goof, goon, lout, yo-yo **5** booby, chump, dunce, idiot **6** nitwit **7** dullard, fathead, halfwit, jughead, saphead, schnook **8** bonehead, dumbbell, dummkopf, imbecile, lunkhead, meathead, numskull **9** blockhead, lamebrain, numbskull, simpleton **11** chowderhead

doltish 4 dull, dumb **5** dense, thick **6** oafish, obtuse, stupid **7** idiotic, moronic **8** ignorant, mindless **9** dim-witted, fatheaded, imbecilic

domain 4 fief, land, rule, turf **5** field, realm **6** estate, sphere **7** fiefdom, kingdom, terrain **8** dominion, province **9** bailiwick, territory

dome 4 head, hill, roof **5** mound **6** cupola **7** ceiling, stadium **8** mountain *shape:* **4** cone **5** onion

domestic 4 help, home, maid, tame **6** butler, family, native **7** servant **8** houseboy, internal, national **9** charwoman, household **10** indigenous **11** chambermaid

domesticate 4 tame **5** adapt, adopt, train **10** housebreak

domicile 3 pad **4** home **5** abode, house, lodge, put up **6** bestow, billet, harbor **7** quarter **8** dwelling, quarters **9** residence, residency **10** habitation

domiciliate 4 bunk, tame **5** house, lodge, put up **6** billet, harbor, reside **7** quarter

dominance 4 rule, sway **5** power **7** command, control **7** mastery **9** supremacy **10** ascendancy, prepotency **11** preeminence, sovereignty

dominant 4 main **5** chief, first, major **6** ruling **7** leading, supreme **8** foremost, powerful, reigning **9** ascendant, governing, number-one, paramount, prevalent, principal **10** commanding, preeminent, prevailing, surpassing **11** controlling, overbearing **12** preponderant

dominate 4 rule **5** reign **6** direct, govern, obsess **7** control, prevail, repress **8** bestride, hold sway, look down, loom over, overlook **9** subjugate, tower over, tyrannize **10** tower above

domination 4 rule, sway **5** might, power **7** command, control, mastery **9** authority, supremacy **10** ascendancy, prepotency, suzerainty **11** preeminence, sovereignty **13** preponderancy

dominator 4 boss, head **5** chief, ruler **6** honcho, leader, master, top dog **7** headman **8**

director, hierarch, kingfish **9** chieftain, commander

domineer 5 bully **6** hector **7** swagger **8** browbeat, bulldoze **9** tyrannize **10** intimidate

domineering 5 bossy **6** lordly **8** arrogant, despotic **9** imperious, masterful **10** autocratic, high-handed, oppressive, tyrannical **11** dictatorial, magisterial, overbearing

Dominica *capital:* **6** Roseau *discoverer:* **8** Columbus (Christopher) *location:* **10** West Indies *sea:* **9** Caribbean

Dominican Republic *capital:* **12** Santo Domingo *island:* **10** Hispaniola *language:* **7** Spanish *location:* **10** West Indies *monetary unit:* **4** peso *mountain:* **6** Duarte *neighbor:* **5** Haiti *sea:* **9** Caribbean

dominion 3 raj **4** rule, sway, turf **5** realm, power **6** domain, empery, empire, regnum, sphere **7** demesne, kingdom, terrain **8** province **9** ascendant, ownership, supremacy, territory **10** ascendancy, possession **11** preeminence, sovereignty

domino 4 bone, cape, mask **5** amice, cloak, visor **6** vizard **8** disguise *spot:* **3** pip

don 3 sir **4** lord **5** get on, put on, tutor **6** assume, fellow, take on **9** professor, undertake

Donalbain *brother:* **7** Malcolm *father:* **6** Duncan

donate 4 give **5** grant **6** bestow, chip in, supply **7** dish out, hand out, present, provide **8** give away, shell out, transfer **10** contribute

donation 3 aid **4** alms, gift **5** grant **7** bequest, handout **8** offering **9** endowment **11** benefaction, beneficence **12** contribution, philanthropy

Don Carlos *author:* **8** Schiller (Friedrich von) *composer:* **5** Verdi (Giuseppe) *father:* **6** Philip

done 4 over **5** all in, ended, ready, spent **6** bushed, gone by, used up **7** drained, dressed, far-gone, settled, through, worn-out **8** complete, depleted, finished, washed-up **9** completed, concluded, exhausted **10** terminated **12** accomplished *poetic:* **3** o'er

donee 7 grantee **8** receiver **9** recipient **11** beneficiary

done for 4 gone, sunk **5** kaput **6** beaten, doomed, ruined **7** wrecked **8** finished, stricken

done in 5 spent **6** bushed, effete, used up **7** drained, far gone, worn-out **8** depleted **9** exhausted, shattered, washed out

Don Giovanni *composer:* **6** Mozart (Wolfgang Amadeus) *conquest:* **4** Anna (Donna) **6** Elvira (Donna) **7** Zerlina *servant:* **9** Leporello

Donizetti, Gaetano *hero:* **7** Roberto (Devereux) *opera:* **5** Lucia (di Lammermoor) **10** Anna Bolena, La Favorita **11** Don Pasquale **12** Maria Stuarda

Don Juan 4 rake, roué, wolf **5** Romeo **6** chaser, masher **7** amorist, gallant, playboy, seducer **8** Casanova, lothario, paramour **9** ladies' man, libertine, womanizer **10** ladykiller, profligate **11** philanderer *drama:* **10** Stone Guest (The) *home:* **7** Seville *mother:* **4** Inez *poet:* **5** Byron (Lord) **7** Pushkin (Alexander)

donkey 3 ass **4** mule **5** burro **7** jackass *female:* **5** jenny **6** jennet

donkeywork 4 moil, toil **5** grind, labor **7** travail **8** drudgery

donnybrook 3 row **4** fray, riot **5** brawl, broil, fight, melee, set-to **6** fracas, ruckus, rumpus, tumult, uproar **7** dispute, quarrel, rhubarb, ruction **10** free-for-all **11** altercation

donor 5 giver, Type O **6** patron **7** granter, grantor **8** bestower **9** conferrer, presenter **10** benefactor **11** contributor

do-nothing 3 bum **4** slug **5** idler **6** loafer, slouch **7** goof-off, slacker **8** deadbeat, fainéant, layabout, slugabed, sluggard **9** lazybones, vegetable **11** couch potato

Don Pasquale composer 9 Donizetti (Gaetano)

Don Quixote *author:* **9** Cervantes (Miguel de) *beloved:* **8** Dulcinea *companion (squire):* **11** Sancho Panza *giant:* **8** windmill *home:* **8** La Mancha *horse:* **9** Rocinante, Rosinante, Rozinante

doodad 5 gizmo, thing **6** bauble, dingus, entity, gadget, gewgaw, jigger, widget **7** trinket, whatsit **8** gimcrack **9** doohickey, thingummy **10** attachment, decoration, knickknack **11** thingamabob, thingamajig, thingumajig

doodle 6 dabble, dawdle, fiddle, potter, putter, sketch, tinker, trifle **7** cartoon, drawing **8** scribble **10** mess around

doodlebug 7 ant lion, missile **8** buzz bomb

doohickey see **doodad**

doom 4 damn, fate, ruin **5** death **6** decree, demise, kismet **7** condemn, destiny, tragedy **8** calamity, disaster, judgment, sentence **11** catastrophe **12** annihilation, last judgment

doomful 4 dire **7** baleful, baneful, direful, fateful, malefic, ominous, unlucky **8** dreadful, ill-fated, sinister **10** foreboding, portentous **11** apocalyptic

doomsayer 7 killjoy **9** Cassandra, defeatist, Gloomy Gus, pessimist

____ **Doone 5** Lorna

door 3 way **4** adit, exit **5** entry **6** access, egress, entrée, portal **7** gateway, ingress, opening **8** entrance, entryway **9** admission **10** admittance **11** entranceway *rear:* **7** postern

doorkeeper 5 usher **6** porter **7** ostiary

doorway 5 entry **6** portal **8** entrance, entryway **11** entranceway

doozy 3 ace, pip **4** lulu **5** beaut, dandy, dilly, peach **6** corker **7** paragon **8** standout **9** humdinger **10** ripsnorter **10** phenomenon **11** crackerjack

dope 3 oaf **4** bozo, clod, dodo, dolt, drug, goof, info, news, yo-yo **5** chump, drugs, dummy, dunce, facts, idiot, moron, ninny, noddy, stupe **6** dimwit, doofus, dum-dum, heroin, nitwit, opiate, sedate, skinny **7** airhead, cocaine, details, dullard, lowdown, pinhead **8** bonehead, dumbbell, imbecile, lunkhead, meathead, narcotic, numskull **9** birdbrain, blockhead, ignoramus, lamebrain, marijuana, narcotize, numbskull, simpleton **10** dunderhead, nincompoop **11** anesthetize, chowderhead, chucklehead, information, preparation

doped 4 high **5** dazed **6** stoned, zonked **7** drugged, tuned-in **8** hopped-up, tripping, turned on, wiped out **9** spaced-out, strung out, stupefied **10** narcotized

dopey 4 dumb **5** silly **6** dulled, stupid, torpid **7** fatuous, fuddled, muddled **8** comatose, sluggish **9** lethargic, senseless, stupefied

Doris *brother:* **6** Nereus *daughters:* **7** Nereids *father:* **7** Oceanus *husband:* **6** Nereus

dormancy 5 sleep **6** repose **7** latency, slumber **8** abeyance, diapause, doldrums, downtime **9** torpidity **10** inactivity, quiescence, suspension **11** cold storage **12** intermission, interruption

dormant 5 inert **6** asleep, drowsy, fallow, latent, torpid **7** abeyant **8** comatose, inactive, sluggish **9** lethargic, potential, quiescent, suspended **10** slow-moving, slumbering

dormer 3 bay **4** nook **5** niche **6** window

dorsal 6 aboral **7** abaxial

____ **d'Orsay 4** Quai

dorsum 4 back

Dorus *brother:* **6** Aeolus *father:* **6** Hellen

dory 4 bark, boat **5** craft, skiff **6** barque, bateau **7** shallop **8** lifeboat

dose 3 fix, hit **4** dram, shot, slug **7** measure, portion **8** medicate, quantity

Dos Passos trilogy 3 U.S.A.

dossier 4 file **6** folder **9** portfolio

dot 4 mark, mote, stud **5** dower, dowry, point, speck **6** bestud, pepper, period **7** freckle, speckle, stipple **8** flyspeck, sprinkle **9** bespeckle **12** decimal point

dotage 8 senility 11 decrepitude, senectitude

dote on 5 adore, enjoy, fancy, prize 7 cherish, idolize 8 treasure 9 delight in

doting 4 dear, fond, gaga 6 loving 7 adoring, devoted 12 affectionate

dotted 4 semé, sown 6 spotty, strewn 8 punctate, stippled

dotty 4 gaga 5 crazy, loony, wacky 6 absurd, insane 7 foolish, smitten 8 enamored 9 eccentric 10 captivated, enraptured, infatuated 12 preposterous

double 4 copy, dual, fold, mate, tack, twin 5 clone, duple, image, match, twice 6 bifold, binary, duplex, paired, ringer 7 dualize, enlarge, magnify, replica, twofold 8 alter ego, geminate, increase 9 companion, dualistic, duplicate, look-alike, replicate 10 dead ringer, reciprocal, simulacrum, understudy 13 spitting image

double-barreled 4 dual 5 duple 6 bifold, binary, duplex, paired 7 twofold 9 dualistic

double bass 10 bull fiddle

double-cross 3 con 4 dupe 5 cheat, rat on, trick 6 betray, delude, humbug, juggle, take in 7 beguile, deceive, sell out, two-time 8 flimflam, hoodwink 9 four-flush

double dagger 6 diesis

double-dealer 3 gyp 5 cheat, knave 6 con man 7 cozener, diddler, sharper 8 deceiver, swindler 9 defrauder 11 flimflammer 13 confidence man

double-dealing 5 fraud 6 deceit 7 chicane 8 flimflam, trickery 9 chicanery, deceitful, deception, duplicity, two-timing 10 hankypanky 11 duplicitous

double-dome 7 egghead 8 Einstein, highbrow 10 pointy-head 12 intellectual

double-faced 9 deceitful, deceptive, equivocal, insincere 10 reversible 12 hypocritical 13 untrustworthy

doublet 3 duo 4 dyad, pair, span 5 brace 6 couple, jacket 7 twosome

double-talk 4 bosh, bunk 5 hokum, hooey 6 babble, bunkum, drivel, jabber 7 blather, hogwash, twaddle 8 flimflam, nonsense 9 gibberish, poppycock 10 balderdash 12 gobbledygook

double vision 8 diplopia

doubt 5 qualm 7 concern, dispute, dubiety, suspect 8 distrust, mistrust, question 9 challenge, disbelief, misgiving, suspicion 10 skepticism 11 dubiousness, incertitude, incredulity, uncertainty

doubtable 4 hazy, iffy, moot 7 dubious, suspect 8 arguable 9 ambiguous, debatable, equivocal, uncertain, undecided 10 disput-able, borderline, indefinite 11 problematic 12 questionable

doubter 5 cynic 6 Thomas 7 sceptic, skeptic 8 agnostic 10 Pyrrhonist, questioner, unbeliever 11 freethinker

doubtful 4 hazy, iffy, moot 5 fishy, shady, shaky 6 chancy, unsure 7 clouded, dubious, obscure, suspect, unclear 8 arguable, unlikely 9 ambiguous, debatable, dubitable, equivocal, uncertain, undecided, unsettled 10 borderline, disputable, improbable 11 problematic, speculative 12 questionable

doubtfulness 7 concern, dubiety 8 mistrust 9 ambiguity, misgiving, suspicion 10 indecision, skepticism, uneasiness 11 dubiousness, incertitude, uncertainty 13 indeterminacy

doubting Thomas see **doubter**

doubtless 6 likely, surely 7 certain, clearly 8 of course, probably 10 absolutely, definitely, positively, presumably 11 indubitably 12 indisputably 13 presumptively, unequivocally

douceur 3 tip 4 gift 5 bribe 7 present 8 gratuity 9 baksheesh

dough 4 cash 5 bread, money 6 dinero, moolah 7 cabbage, lettuce, scratch 8 currency 11 legal tender *inflator:* 5 yeast

doughboy 7 dogface 11 infantryman

doughty 4 bold 5 brave, gutsy, manly, stout 6 daring, heroic, plucky, spunky, strong 7 gallant, valiant 8 fearless, intrepid, resolved, stalwart, unafraid, valorous 9 dauntless, undaunted 10 courageous 12 stouthearted

doughy 3 wan 4 pale 5 pasty, waxen 6 pallid 8 blanched 9 colorless

do up 3 can, fix 4 mend, wash, wrap 5 clean, patch 6 clothe, doctor, fasten, repair, revamp 7 exhaust, festoon, launder, package, prepare, rebuild, wear out 8 decorate, gift wrap, ornament, overhaul 9 embellish 11 recondition, reconstruct

dour 4 glum, grim 5 bleak, harsh, rigid, stern, surly 6 gloomy, morose, severe, strict, sullen 7 austere, crabbed, peevish 9 obstinate, saturnine, stringent 10 forbidding, unyielding

douse 3 sop 4 duck, dunk, soak 5 bathe, drown, plash, slosh, souse 6 drench, put out, quench, splash, strike 7 immerse, slacken 8 inundate, saturate, snuff out, submerge, submerse 10 extinguish

dove 6 culver, pigeon 8 pacifist *call:* 3 coo *genus:* 7 Columba *pen:* 4 cote

dovecote 6 aviary 9 birdhouse

dovetail 3 fit 4 jibe, mesh 5 agree, match, tally 6 accord, splice, square 7 comport,

conform **8** check out **9** harmonize, interlock, intermesh **10** correspond
dovish 4 mild **6** gentle **7** antiwar, pacific **8** pacifist **9** peaceable **10** nonviolent, pacifistic **11** peace-loving **12** conciliatory
dowager 4 dame **5** widow **6** matron **9** matriarch **10** grande dame **11** grandmother
dowdy 4 drab **5** dated, frump, passé, seedy, tacky **6** blowsy, bygone, démodé, frowsy, frowzy, frumpy, old hat, shabby **7** rundown, unkempt **8** frumpish, outdated, outmoded, slattern, slovenly **9** out-of-date, unstylish **10** antiquated, bedraggled, slatternly **11** draggle-tail **12** old-fashioned **13** draggletailed
dowel 3 bar, peg, pin, rod **5** stick
dower 4 gift **5** endow, endue **6** legacy, talent **8** bequeath
dowitcher 5 snipe **9** sandpiper
do without 5 forgo, waive **6** abjure, eschew, give up, pass up **8** renounce
down 3 eat, fur, ill, low, off, sad **4** blue, fell, fuzz, lint, pile, sick **5** below, ended, floor, floss, fluff, level, lower, under **6** defeat, fallen, finish, lay low, nether **7** conquer, consume, destroy, flatten, swallow, unhappy **8** bowl over, complete, defeated, dejected, dispatch, feathers, finished, inferior, overcome, sluggish, surmount **9** completed, concluded, depressed, earthward, miserable **10** dispirited, groundward
down-and-out 5 broke, needy **6** hard-up, ruined **8** beggared, derelict, homeless **9** destitute, penniless, penurious **12** impoverished
down-and-outer 3 bum **6** beggar, pauper, wretch **7** have-not **9** mendicant **10** supplicant
down-at-heels 4 mean **5** dingy, ratty, seedy, tacky **6** ragged, ragtag, shabby, shoddy **7** ignoble, run-down, worn-out **8** decrepit, tattered **10** bedraggled, threadbare **11** dilapidated **12** deteriorated, disreputable
downbeat 3 low, sad **4** blue, glum **6** droopy, gloomy, morose **7** decline, doleful **8** dejected **9** depressed **10** dispirited, melancholy **11** discouraged, pessimistic **12** disconsolate, disheartened, heavyhearted
downcast 3 low, sad **4** blue, glum, sunk **5** moody, mopey **6** droopy, gloomy, morose **7** doleful, forlorn, unhappy **8** dejected, dismayed, listless, soul-sick, troubled **9** depressed, heartsick, heartsore, miserable, oppressed, woebegone **10** chapfallen, despondent, dispirited, distressed, melancholy, spiritless **11** crestfallen, discouraged, low-spirited **12** disconsolate, disheartened
downfall 4 bane, ruin **6** demise **7** decline, undoing **8** collapse, Waterloo **9** ruination **10**

devolution **11** declination, destruction **12** degeneration, dégringolade **13** deterioration
downgrade 4 bump, bust **5** abase, lower **6** demote **7** decline, demerit, descent, devalue **8** belittle, diminish, discount, minimize, relegate **9** denigrate, deprecate, devaluate, discredit, disparage, humiliate **10** depreciate, undervalue **12** degeneration, dégringolade **13** deterioration
downhearted see **downcast**
down-in-the-mouth see **downcast**
down payment 5 token **6** pledge **7** advance, deposit, earnest
downplay 8 belittle, discount, minimize, pooh-pooh **11** de-emphasize
downpour 6 deluge **7** monsoon **8** drencher **9** drenching, rainstorm **10** cloudburst, inundation **11** gully washer
downright 5 blunt, gross, total, truly, utter **7** blatant, flat-out **8** absolute, complete, explicit, positive, thorough **9** out-and-out **10** absolutely, sure-enough **11** indubitable, unequivocal, unmitigated, unqualified **13** thoroughgoing
downslide 3 dip, sag **4** drop, slip **5** slump **7** decline, drop-off, falloff **8** decrease **9** declivity, reduction
downstairs 6 cellar **8** basement
down-to-earth 8 rational **9** practical, pragmatic, realistic **10** hard-boiled, hardheaded, no-nonsense, reasonable **11** common-sense, plain-spoken **12** matter-of-fact **13** unpretentious, unsentimental
downtrend see **downslide**
downtrodden 6 abject, abused **9** oppressed **10** maltreated, mistreated, persecuted, tyrannized
downturn see **downslide**
downward 8 dropping **9** declining **10** descending
downy 4 soft **5** fuzzy **6** fleecy, fluffy **7** velvety **8** feathery *filler:* **5** eider
dowry 4 gift **6** talent *French:* **3** dot
doxy 4 bawd, drab, moll, slut, tart **5** wench **6** floozy, harlot **7** trollop **8** mistress, slattern **10** prostitute
doyen 4 dean, head **5** chief, maven **6** expert, leader, master, wizard **7** maestro **8** virtuoso **9** authority, patriarch **10** past master
Doyle's detective 6 Holmes (Sherlock)
D'Oyly Carte offering 8 operetta
doze 3 nap **5** sleep **6** catnap, drowse, nod off, snooze **7** drop off, slumber **8** drift off **10** forty winks
dozy see **drowsy**
DP 5 exile **6** émigré **7** evacuee, outcast, refu-

gee **8** deportee, emigrant, fugitive **10** expatriate

drab 4 dull, flat **5** bleak, brown, dingy, faded, mousy, muddy, olive, vapid **6** dismal, dreary, mousey **7** subfusc **8** lifeless **9** cheerless, colorless **10** lackluster **11** dispiriting

draconian 5 cruel, harsh, rigid **6** severe, strict **7** callous **8** ironclad, rigorous, ruthless **9** merciless, stringent **10** inflexible, ironfisted, ironhanded

Dracula author 6 Stoker (Bram)

draft 3 tap **4** dose, haul, plan, plot, pull, pump, swig **5** check, claim, drink, frame, press, swill **6** breeze, call up, demand, design, devise, enlist, enroll, induct, potion, scheme, select, siphon, sketch **7** compose, concoct, current, outline, portion, prepare, project, recruit **8** block out, contrive, rough out, skeleton, traction **9** adumbrate, allowance, blueprint, conscribe, conscript, fabricate, formulate, muster out **11** delineation, skeletonize *avoider:* **6** dodger *of a law:* **4** bill

drag 3 lug, tow, tug **4** bore, haul, puff, pull, swig **5** dally, delay, draft, shlep, tarry, trail **6** burden, dawdle, harrow, loiter, schlep, search, sledge **7** schlepp **8** friction, straggle **9** lag behind **13** procrastinate

dragging 4 beat, long **5** all in, spent, weary **6** pooped **7** drained, lengthy, tedious **8** drawn-out, extended, fatigued, overlong, sluggish, wiped out **9** exhausted, lethargic, long-drawn, pooped out, prolonged, washed-out, wearisome **10** protracted, slow-moving **12** interminable, long-drawn-out

draggle 3 lag **4** rove **5** stray, trail **8** straggle, trail off **10** fall behind

draggle-tail 4 bawd, drab, slut **5** wench, whore **6** harlot **8** slattern **10** prostitute **11** nightwalker **12** streetwalker

draggletailed 6 blowsy, frowsy, frowzy, sordid, untidy **8** slattern, sluttish **10** slatternly

dragnet 4 trap **5** snare, trawl **7** network

drag off 4 cart, haul

dragon 5 beast **8** basilisk **10** cockatrice *biblical:* **5** Rahab *Canaanite:* **3** Yam **4** Yamm **5** Lotan *Chinese:* **4** lung *French:* **8** Tarasque *genus:* **5** Draco *Greek:* **5** Ladon **9** Eurythion *slayer:* **4** Baal, Enki, Zeus **5** Indra **6** Cadmus, George (St.), Marduk, Sigurd **7** Beowulf, Jupiter, Michael (St.), Ninurta, Perseus **8** Margaret (St.) *Sumerian:* **3** Kur *Wagnerian:* **6** Fafnir

dragoon 3 cow **5** bully **6** badger, coerce, harass, hector **8** bludgeon, browbeat, bulldoze, bullyrag, threaten **9** persuade,

strong-arm, terrorize **10** cavalryman, intimidate

drain 3 dry, sap, tap **4** pump, sink, sump, swig, tire, vent, wear **5** bleed, draft, drink, empty, leech, sewer, swill, use up, weary **6** burden, gutter, siphon, trench **7** conduit, culvert, deplete, dwindle, draw off, exhaust, fatigue, outflow **8** bankrupt, draw down, wear down **9** discharge **10** impoverish **11** watercourse

drain away 3 ebb **4** drop, sink, wane **5** abate **6** lessen, reduce, remove **7** draw off, dwindle, retreat, subside **8** decrease, diminish, draw back, taper off, withdraw

drained 4 beat **5** all-in, spent, weary **6** bleary, pooped, used up **7** far-gone, worn-out **8** depleted, dragging, weakened, wiped out **9** exhausted, pooped out, washed-out

drainpipe 4 duct **5** sewer, spout **7** conduit **9** downspout

dram 3 bit, dab, nip, tot **4** atom, dash, drop, iota, jolt, mite, shot, slug, spot, swig, whit **5** crumb, grain, ounce, pinch, scrap, shred, snort, speck **6** morsel, sliver **7** modicum, smidgen, snifter, snippet, soupçon **8** particle

drama 4 play **7** pageant, theater, theatre, tragedy *award:* **4** Tony *former English:* **6** masque *Japanese:* **3** Noh *main part:* **8** epitasis *musical:* **5** opera **8** operetta, zarzuela *suspenseful:* **11** cliff-hanger

dramatic 5 vivid **8** striking, thespian **10** histrionic, theatrical *conflict:* **4** agon

dramatis personae 4 cast **5** parts, roles **6** actors, troupe **7** company **10** characters

dramatist 10 playwright *American:* **4** Hart (Moss), Inge (William), Rabe (David), Rice (Elmer), Uhry (Alfred) **5** Albee (Edward), Barry (Philip), Foote (Horton), Guare (John), Hecht (Ben), Mamet (David), Odets (Clifford), Parks (Suzan-Lori), Payne (John Howard), Simon (Neil) **6** Ferber (Edna), Gurney (A. R.), Henley (Beth), Miller (Arthur), Norman (Marsha), O'Neill (Eugene), Thomas (Augustus), Wilder (Thornton), Wilson (August, Lanford, Robert) **7** Hellman (Lillian), Kaufman (George S.), Kushner (Tony), Shanley (John Patrick), Shepard (Sam) **8** Anderson (Maxwell, Robert), Caldwell (Erskine), Connolly (Marc), Sherwood (Robert), Williams (Tennessee) **9** Chayefsky (Paddy), Fierstein (Harvey), Hansberry (Lorraine) **11** Hammerstein (Oscar), Wasserstein (Wendy) *Austrian:* **10** Schnitzler (Arthur) *Belgian:* **11** Maeterlinck (Maurice) *Czech:* **5** Havel (Vaclav) *English:* **3** Fry (Christopher), Gay (John) **4**

Gray (Simon), Hare (David), Rowe (Nicholas), Tate (Nahum) **5** Frayn (Michael), Milne (A. A.), Orton (Joe), Peele (George), Wilde (Oscar) **6** Barrie (James), Coward (Nöel), Dryden (John), Jonson (Ben), Pinero (Arthur Wing), Pinter (Harold), Steele (Richard), Storey (David) **7** Bennett (Alan), Delaney (Shelagh), Marlowe (Christopher), Marston (John), Osborne (John), Shaffer (Anthony, Peter), Webster (John) **8** Congreve (William), Rattigan (Terrence), Shadwell (Thomas), Stoppard (Tom), Tourneur (Cyril), Vanbrugh (John), Zangwill (Israel) **9** Ayckbourn (Alan), Churchill (Caryl), Goldsmith (Oliver), Middleton (Thomas), Wycherley (William) **11** Shakespeare (William) *French:* **5** Camus (Albert), Genet (Jean) **6** Musset (Alfred de), Racine (Jean), Sardou (Victorien), Sartre (Jean-Paul), Scribe (Eugène) **7** Anouilh (Jean), Ionesco (Eugène), Labiche (Eugène), Molière, Rostand (Edmond) **8** Marivaux (Pierre) Corneille (Pierre), Crébillon, Giraudoux (Jean) **12** Beaumarchais (P. A. Caron de) *German:* **5** Weiss (Peter) **6** Brecht (Bertolt), Goethe (Johann Wolfgang von), Kleist (Heinrich von) **8** Schiller (Friedrich von) **9** Hauptmann (Gerhart), Zuckmayer (Carl) *Greek:* **8** Menander **9** Aeschylus, Euripides, Sophocles **12** Aristophanes *Hindu:* **8** Kalidasa *Irish:* **4** Shaw (George Bernard) **5** Behan (Brendan), Friel (Brian), Synge (John Millington), Yeats (William Butler) **6** O'Casey (Sean) **7** Beckett (Samuel), Gregory (Lady Augusta) **8** Sheridan (Richard Brinsley) *Italian:* **5** Gozzi (Carlo), Verga (Giovanni) **7** Alfieri (Vittorio), Ariosto (Ludovico), Giacosa (Giuseppe), Goldoni (Carlo) **8** Trissino (Gian Giorgio) **9** D'Annunzio (Gabriele) **10** Metastasio (Pietro), Pirandello (Luigi) *Japanese:* **5** Zeami *Nigerian:* **7** Soyinka (Wole) *Norwegian:* **5** Ibsen (Henrik) **8** Bjornson (Bjornstjerne) *Roman:* **6** Seneca **7** Plautus, Terence *Romanian:* **7** Ionesco (Eugene) *Russian:* **7** Chekhov (Anton) **8** Zamyatin (Yevgeny) *South African:* **6** Fugard (Athol) *Spanish:* **4** Vega (Lope de) **5** Lorca (Federico García) **7** Alberti (Rafael), Arrabal (Fernando) **8** Quintero (Serafín, Joaquín) **9** Benavente (Jacinto) **11** García Lorca (Federico), Valle-Inclán (R. M. del) *Swedish:* **5** Sachs (Nelly) **10** Strindberg (August) *Swiss:* **6** Frisch (Max)

drape 4 fold, hang, roll **5** adorn, array, cloak, cover **6** clothe, enfold, enwrap, swathe,

wrap up **7** curtain, swaddle **8** enswathe, envelope, swathe in

drapery 7 curtain, hanging **8** curtains, hangings

drastic 4 dire **5** harsh **6** severe **7** extreme, radical **9** desperate **10** exorbitant

drat 4 damn, dang, darn **6** phooey, shucks **7** doggone

draw 3 gut, tie, tow, tug **4** etch, haul, limn, lure, puff, pull, pump **5** draft, drain, infer, judge, trace **6** allure, appeal, deduce, depict, derive, elicit, entice, extend, gather, indite, inhale, pencil, siphon, sketch **7** attract, deplete, exhaust, extract, outline, portray, prolong, spin out, win over **8** conclude, contract, convince, dead heat, deadlock, lengthen, protract, standoff **9** delineate, formulate, represent, stalemate **10** allurement, attraction, disembowel, eviscerate, exenterate *forth:* **5** educe **6** elicit **7** extract *from:* **4** milk, pump **5** bleed *together:* **3** tie **4** join, lace

draw back 4 duck **5** cower, quail, wince **6** blench, cringe, flinch, recoil, shrink **7** back off, retreat, take off **9** turn aside

drawback 4 flaw, snag **5** fault, hitch **6** defect, refund **7** failing, trouble **8** weakness **9** detriment, hindrance **10** deficiency, difficulty, impediment **11** shortcoming **12** disadvantage

draw down 4 milk **5** drain, spend, use up **6** expend, reduce **7** deplete, exhaust **8** decrease, diminish **9** reduction, siphon off

drawer 9 draftsman *for money:* **4** till

drawers 5 pants **6** undies **8** knickers, trousers **10** underpants

draw in 6 enmesh, entice, induce, prompt **7** involve, retract, win over **8** convince, persuade, pull back **9** prevail on **11** bring around, prevail upon

drawing 6 doodle, sketch **7** cartoon, outline

drawing power 4 lure, pull **6** allure, appeal **9** magnetism **10** attraction

drawn 4 taut, worn **6** peaked **7** fraught, haggard, pinched **8** careworn, fatigued, pictured, strained, stressed **9** attracted **10** delineated

drawn-out 4 long **7** lengthy, tedious **8** extended, overlong **9** prolonged **10** protracted

draw off 3 tap **4** pump **5** bleed, draft, drain **6** siphon

draw out 6 extend **7** prolong, stretch **8** elongate, lengthen, protract

draw up 4 balk, halt, lift, make, stop **5** array, draft, frame, order, raise, write **6** deploy, map out **7** compose, concoct, dispose, marshal, prepare, set down **8** organize, write out **9** formulate

dray 4 cart, drag **5** wagon **6** barrow, sledge **7** travois **9** stoneboat

dread 4 fear **5** alarm, panic **6** dismay, fright, horror, phobia, terror **7** anxiety **10** foreboding **11** trepidation **12** apprehension **13** consternation

dreadful 4 dire **5** awful **6** tragic **7** awesome, extreme, fearful, ghastly, heinous, hideous, ominous **8** alarming, horrible, horrific, shocking, terrible **9** appalling, frightful, revolting **11** distressing, frightening

dreadnought 10 battleship

dream 4 ache, long, wish **5** crave, fancy, ideal **6** aspire, bubble, desire, hanker, vision **7** chimera, fantasy, imagine, rainbow, reverie, specter, spectre **8** ambition, delusion, illusion, phantasm, phantasy **9** fantasize, nightmare **10** aspiration *divination by:* **11** oneiromancy *god:* **8** Morpheus *sleep:* **3** REM

dreamer 7 utopian **8** idealist **9** visionary **10** Don Quixote, lotus-eater **13** castle-builder

dreamlike 5 ideal, vague **6** unreal **7** shadowy, surreal **8** fanciful, illusory, nebulous **9** imaginary, visionary **12** otherworldly

Dream of Gerontius composer 5 Elgar (Edward)

dream up 5 frame, hatch **6** cook up, create, devise, invent **7** concoct, imagine **8** conceive, contrive, envisage, envision **9** formulate, visualize

dreamy 7 pensive **9** unworldly, visionary **10** idealistic **11** impractical **12** otherworldly

dreary 4 blah, drab, dull **5** bleak **6** boring, dismal, gloomy, somber, sombre **7** forlorn, humdrum, joyless, tedious **8** banausic, tiresome, wretched **9** cheerless **10** depressing, depressive, monotonous, oppressive, pedestrian **11** dispiriting

dreck 3 mud **4** junk, muck, slop **5** offal, swill, trash, waste **6** litter, refuse, sewage **7** garbage, rubbish **9** sweepings

dredge 3 dig **5** barge, scoop **6** deepen, dig out, gather **8** excavate, scoop out **9** hollow out, scrape out

dregs 4 lees, scum **5** trash **6** grouts **7** deposit, grounds, remains, residue **8** sediment **9** settlings **11** precipitate

drei 5 three

dreidel 3 top

Dreiser, Theodore *character:* **5** Clyde (Griffiths) **6** Carrie (Meeber), Eugene (Witla), Sondra (Finchley) **7** Roberta (Alden) **9** Hurstwood (George) **10** Cowperwood (Frank) *novel:* **5** Stoic (The), Titan (The) **6** Genius (The) **9** Financier (The) **12** Sister Carrie **14** Jennie Gerhardt **15** American Tragedy (An)

drench 3 sop **4** dunk, soak **5** douse, souse, steep, swill **6** deluge, seethe **7** immerse **8** inundate, saturate, submerge, waterlog

dress 3 gut **4** bind, clad, deck, doll, duds, garb, gown, sack, togs **5** adorn, align, A-line, array, frock, getup, guise, habit, smock, weeds **6** attire, bedeck, caftan, clothe, dirndl, enrobe, outfit, sacque **7** apparel, bandage, bedizen, chemise, clothes, costume, garment, garnish, raiment, threads, turnout, uniform **8** beautify, clothing, covering, decorate, ensemble, ornament, wardrobe **9** embellish, make ready **11** habiliments *a wound:* **7** bandage *designer:* **4** Dior (Christian), Erté, Head (Edith) **5** Blass (Bill), Bohan (Marc), Karan (Donna), Klein (Calvin), Prada (Miuccia), Pucci (Emilio), Quant (Mary), Worth (Charles Frederick) **6** Armani (Giorgio), Cardin (Pierre), Jacobs (Marc), Lauren (Ralph), Miyake (Issey), Poiret (Paul) **7** Balmain (Pierre), Cassini (Oleg), Halston, Lacroix (Christian), Mizrahi (Isaac), Versace (Gianni) **8** Galliano (John), Givenchy (Hubert) **9** Courrèges (André), de la Renta (Oscar), Gernreich (Rudi), Lagerfeld (Karl), St.-Laurent (Yves), Valentino **10** Balenciaga (Cristóbal) **12** Saint-Laurent (Yves), Schiaparelli (Elsa) *line:* **3** hem *mode of:* **5** habit *ordinary:* **5** mufti *oriental:* **9** cheongsam *part:* **5** skirt **6** bodice *South Seas:* **6** sarong

dress down 5 chide, scold **6** berate, rail at, rebuke, revile **7** bawl out, reprove, tell off, upbraid **8** admonish, chastise, reproach **9** castigate, reprimand **10** tongue-lash

dresser 5 chest **6** bureau **7** commode, highboy **10** chiffonier *gaudy:* **9** butterfly

dressing 5 sauce **6** catsup **7** bandage, catchup, ketchup **8** stuffing *salad:* **5** ranch **6** French **7** Italian, Russian **10** blue cheese **11** vinaigrette **12** green goddess

dressing room 6 vestry **8** vestiary

dressmaker 7 modiste **9** couturier **10** couturiere, seamstress

dress up 6 attire, clothe, rig out, tog out **7** apparel, deck out **8** beautify, disguise, prettify, trick out **9** embellish **10** camouflage

dressy 4 chic **5** showy, smart **6** classy, formal, frilly, ornate **7** duded up, elegant, stylish **9** rigged out

Dreyfus's defender 4 Zola (Emile) **6** Proust (Marcel)

dribble 4 drip, leak, weep **5** drool **6** bounce,

drivel, slaver **7** distill, drizzle, slobber, trickle **8** salivate, sprinkle

driblet 4 drop **6** gobbet **7** globule, smidgen **8** particle, pittance

dried grape 6 raisin

dried meat 5 jerky

dried plum 5 prune

drift 3 bat, gad **4** flow, flux, gist, roam, sail, skim, tide, waft, wash **5** amble, coast, creep, float, mosey, range, slide, stray, trend **6** bummel, linger, ramble, stream, stroll, wander **7** current, maunder, meander, meaning, saunter **8** movement, penchant, sideslip, tendency **9** deviation **10** propensity **11** disposition, inclination, progression **12** predilection

drifter 3 bum, vag **4** hobo **5** gypsy, nomad, tramp **7** floater, migrant, vagrant **8** derelict, vagabond **9** transient **11** beachcomber **12** rolling stone

drill 3 bit, dig **4** bore **5** auger, borer, punch, train **6** pierce, trepan, wimble **7** routine, wildcat, workout **8** exercise, practice, practise, rehearse **9** penetrate, rehearsal **10** discipline *command:* **6** at ease **8** left face **9** about face, attention, right face

drink 3 ade, lap, nip, sea, sip, tea **4** belt, brew, chug, deep, down, grog, gulp, soak, swig, tope, toss **5** booze, draft, drain, ocean, quaff, slurp, snort, swill, toast **6** absorb, brandy, cassis, cognac, embibe, guzzle, imbibe, jigger, liquid, liquor, pledge, potion, tank up, tipple, tisane **7** consume, potable, schnaps, spirits, swallow, swizzle, toss off **8** aperitif, beverage, libation, liquor up, schnapps **9** aqua vitae *after-dinner:* **6** frappé **7** cordial, liqueur *drugged:* **6** Mickey **10** Mickey Finn *honey:* **4** mead *hot:* **5** negus, toddy *liquor:* **5** booze, hooch **6** red-eye **9** firewater, moonshine *mixed:* **3** kir, nog **5** julep **6** Gibson, gimlet, mai tai, mimosa, mojito, rickey, Rob Roy, zombie **7** gin fizz, martini, sidecar, stinger **8** daiquiri, pink lady **9** alexander, Cuba libre, manhattan, margarita, mint julep, rusty nail **10** Bloody Mary, piña colada, Tom Collins **11** gin and tonic, grasshopper, screwdriver, whiskey sour **12** black Russian, old-fashioned *mixer:* **7** swirler *noisily:* **5** slurp *of liquor:* **4** dram, shot, slug **5** snort **6** bracer **8** highball *of the gods:* **6** nectar *soft:* **3** pop **4** cola, soda **5** tonic **7** soda pop **8** root beer **9** ginger ale **12** sarsaparilla *stimulating:* **6** bracer *Vedic ritual:* **4** soma (see also **beverage**)

drinkable 6 liquor **7** potable **8** beverage, libation, potation

drinking 8 potation *fountain:* **7** bubbler *glass:*

6 rummer **7** tumbler *horn:* **6** rhyton *spree:* **3** jag **4** tear, toot **5** binge, spree **6** bender **7** carouse **8** carousal

drip 4 leak, plop, weep **7** dribble, droplet, trickle **8** sprinkle

dripping 3 wet **5** runny, soppy **6** soaked, soused **7** drizzly, soaking, sopping **8** drenched **9** saturated **11** wringing-wet

drippy 5 mushy, rainy, sappy, sobby, soppy, soupy, teary, weepy **6** slushy, syrupy **7** drizzly, maudlin, mawkish, soaking, sopping, tearful **9** schmaltzy **11** sentimental

drive 3 pep, ram **4** goad, herd, push, spur, taxi, trip, urge **5** chase, force, guide, impel, jaunt, lunge, motor, moxie, oomph, pilot, pound, spunk, steer, surge, vigor **6** compel, convey, exhort, hammer, outing, plunge, propel, strike, thrust **7** actuate, impetus, operate, produce **8** ambition, mobilize, momentum, navigate, shepherd, vitality **9** chauffeur, excursion, urge along **10** enterprise, get-up-and-go, initiative, motivation *away:* **4** shoo **5** exile

drive away see **expel**

drivel 3 rot **4** bosh, bunk **5** drool, hokum, hooey, prate **6** babble, bunkum, gabble, jabber, slaver **7** baloney, blabber, blather, dribble, hogwash, prattle, rubbish, slobber, twaddle **8** claptrap, flimflam, nonsense, salivate **9** gibberish, poppycock **10** balderdash, double-talk, flapdoodle **12** blatherskite, gobbledygook

driver 4 hack, jehu **5** cabby **6** cabbie, cabman, hackie, mallet **7** hackman **8** coachman, motorist, muleteer, operator **9** chauffeur, dowitcher **10** taskmaster **11** tamping iron *of an elephant:* **6** mahout *Roman:* **10** charioteer *truck:* **8** teamster

driving 7 dynamic, powered **8** forceful, vigorous **9** energetic, inspiring **10** compelling

drizzle 4 mist, rain **7** dribble, spatter **8** droplets, sprinkle **10** sprinkling **13** precipitation

Dr. Jekyll and Mr. ____ 4 Hyde

droll 3 odd **5** comic, funny, nutty, witty **7** comical, risible **8** farcical, humorous **9** eccentric, laughable, ludicrous, whimsical

drollery 5 humor **6** comedy, joking, whimsy **7** jesting

dromedary 5 camel

drone 3 bee, hum **4** buzz, idle, laze, loaf, loll **5** idler **6** drudge, loiter, lounge, murmur, worker **7** bagpipe **8** aircraft, parasite **9** bombinate **10** pedal point

drool 4 gush, rave **5** froth **6** dote on, drivel, saliva, slaver **7** blather, dribble, enthuse, slobber **8** salivate **10** rhapsodize

droop 3 sag **4** fall, flag, hang, loll, sink, swag,

wilt **5** slump **6** dangle, slouch, weaken **7** decline, let down, subside **8** languish

droopy 4 blue, down, limp, weak **5** baggy **6** gloomy **7** doleful, languid, sagging, slouchy, wilting **8** cast down, dejected, downcast **9** depressed **10** dispirited **11** downhearted

drop 3 dip, nip, sag, tot **4** down, drib, dump, fall, fell, jilt, jolt, lose, omit, slip, slug, tear **5** cease, depth, lapse, lower, pitch, plump, scrub, slide, snort, speck, spend **6** cancel, cave in, demise, depart, expire, fumble, give up, go down, ground, plunge, reduce, smitch, topple, unload, vanish **7** abandon, decease, decline, deposit, descend, descent, distill, dribble, driblet, fall off, forfeit, give out, globule, pendant, plummet, trickle **8** bowl over, break off, collapse, comedown, downturn, keel over, nose-dive **9** declivity, discharge, downslide, downswing, downtrend, prostrate, reduction, terminate **10** depository

drop by 4 call **5** pop in, visit **6** stop in **8** come over

droplet 4 bead, drib, tear **7** globule

drop off 3 nap, sag **4** doze, fall, slip **5** slide, slump **6** catnap, drowse, lessen, snooze **7** decline, deliver, deposit, slacken **8** diminish, fall away, hand over **10** fall asleep

dropsical 5 puffy, tumid **6** turgid **7** swollen **8** inflated **9** edematous, tumescent

dropsy 5 edema **8** anasarca

dross 4 junk, scum, slag **5** dregs, offal, waste **6** debris, scoria **7** remains, residue, schlock **8** detritus, impurity, leavings

drossy 4 base **6** impure, scummy **7** trivial **8** inferior, unworthy **9** worthless

drought 4 lack, need, want **6** dearth **7** aridity, dryness **8** scarcity, shortage **10** deficiency

droughty 3 dry **4** arid, sere **7** bone-dry, dried up, parched, thirsty **10** desiccated

drove 3 mob **4** army, herd, host, mass, pack **5** crowd, flock, horde, troop **6** myriad, pushed, school, throng **7** phalanx **9** multitude

drover 6 cowboy **8** shepherd

drown 4 sink, soak **5** douse, flood, souse, swamp **6** deluge, drench, engulf **7** immerse, repress, smother **8** inundate, submerge **9** overpower, overwhelm, suffocate **10** asphyxiate, extinguish

drowse 3 nod **4** doze **5** sleep **6** catnap, snooze **7** doze off, drop off, shut-eye, slumber **10** forty winks

drowsy 4 dozy **5** dopey **6** droopy, sleepy, torpid **7** languid **8** indolent, sluggish **9** lethargic, somnolent, soporific **10** slumberous **13** lackadaisical

Dr. Seuss 6 Geisel (Theodor Seuss) *book:* **11** Cat in the Hat (The) **15** Green Eggs and Ham, Yertle the Turtle **19** Horton Hatches the Egg **26** How the Grinch Stole Christmas

drub 3 tan, wax, zap **4** bash, beat, club, deck, drum, flay, flog, lash, lick, mash, maul, pelt, trim, whip **5** baste, cream, crush, paste, pound, score, slash, smash, smear, spank, stamp, thump, wreck **6** batter, berate, bruise, buffet, deface, hammer, master, pummel, punish, revile, scorch, thrash, thresh, wallop **7** belabor, blister, censure, clobber, cripple, lambast, scourge, shatter, shellac, trounce **8** bulldoze, lambaste, lash into, outclass, outshine **9** castigate, excoriate, overwhelm

drubbing 4 loss, rout **6** defeat **7** setback **10** defeasance **11** shellacking

drudge 4 grub, hack, moil, peon, plod, slog **5** grind, slave **6** menial, slavey **7** grubber, plodder **8** dogsbody

drudgery 4 moil, toil **5** chore, grind **7** travail **9** grunt work **10** donkeywork **11** backbreaker

drudging 6 boring, tiring **7** irksome, tedious **8** dragging, tiresome **9** fatiguing, laborious, wearisome **10** monotonous

drug 4 dope, lull **5** sulfa **6** downer, ipecac, opiate, physic, poison, potion, remedy, statin **7** fen-phen, generic, stupefy **8** biologic, medicine, narcotic, nepenthe, relaxant, sedative **9** ibuprofen, medicinal, methadone **10** antibiotic, medicament, medication **11** thalidomide *addict:* **6** junkie *agent:* **4** narc *calming:* **8** sedative *experience:* **4** trip *illicit:* **3** ice, kif, LSD, pot **4** acid, coke, dope, hash, meth, scag, snow, weed **5** crack, grass, opium, smack, speed **6** heroin, peyote **7** cocaine, crystal, hashish **8** cannabis, goofball **9** mescaline **10** methadrine, psilocybin *seller:* **10** pharmacist *sleep-inducing:* **8** hypnotic **9** soporific **11** barbiturate

drugged 4 high **5** dazed, doped, dopey **6** flying, loaded, stoned, zonked **8** benumbed, hopped-up, turned on **9** spaced-out, stupefied **10** narcotized

druggist 7 chemist **10** apothecary, pharmacist

drugstore 8 pharmacy **10** apothecary

druid 4 Celt **6** priest **7** prophet *sacred object:* **3** oak **9** mistletoe

drum 3 keg, vat **4** beat, cask **5** conga, naker, tabor, thrum **6** barrel, tom-tom, tympan **7** tambour, timpani (plural), tympani (plural) **8** cylinder, timbales (plural) *Indian:* **5** tabla **8** mridanga *Irish:* **7** bodhran *large:* **4** bass *small:* **5** bongo, tabor **7** timbrel *string:* **5** snare

drumbeat 4 flam, roll, tuck **6** ruffle, tattoo **7** booming, pit-a-pat, rat-a-tat **8** rataplan

drumfire 5 salvo **6** volley **7** barrage, booming **9** broadside, cannonade, fusillade **11** bombardment

drumhead 4 skin **7** summary

drummer 4 Rich (Buddy) **5** Krupa (Gene), Roach (Max), Starr (Ringo), Watts (Charlie) **6** Blakey (Art), hawker, Puente (Tito), vendor **7** peddler **8** pitchman, salesman

drum up 6 invent **7** canvass, solicit **9** originate *interest:* **4** plug, tout **8** ballyhoo

drunk 3 lit, sot **4** lush, soak, wino **5** dipso, lit up, oiled, souse, tight, tipsy **6** blotto, boozer, juiced, soused, stewed, stinko, tiddly, wasted, zonked **7** crocked, guzzler, pie-eyed, sloshed, smashed, squiffy, tippler, tosspot **8** squiffed **9** inebriate, plastered **10** boozehound, inebriated **11** intoxicated

drunkard 3 sot **4** lush, soak, wino **5** dipso, rummy, souse, stiff, toper **6** bibber, boozer, soaker **7** guzzler, swiller, tippler, tosspot **9** alcoholic, inebriate, juicehead **10** boozehound **11** dipsomaniac

Drusilla *brother:* **8** Caligula *father:* **5** Herod **10** Germanicus *husband:* **5** Felix *mother:* **9** Agrippina *sister:* **8** Berenice **9** Agrippina

dry 3 set **4** arid, brut, dull, sere, sour, tart **5** baked, dusty, parch, stale, wizen **6** barren, desert, harden, stolid, thirst, wither **7** congeal, deadpan, parched, Saharan, shrivel, sterile, thirsty **8** rainless, solidify, tearless, teetotal, withered **9** anhydrous, dehydrate, desiccate, evaporate, unwatered **10** dehydrated, desiccated **11** unemotional **12** matter-of-fact **13** uninteresting *combining form:* **3** xer **4** xero *goods:* **6** linens, napery **8** clothing, textiles *out:* **5** sober **8** soberize *period:* **7** drought *wine:* **3** sec **4** brut

dryasdust 4 arid, dull **5** banal, inane, vapid **6** boring, stodgy **7** insipid, prosaic, tedious **9** wearisome **10** uninspired **13** uninteresting

dry measure 4 peck, pint **5** quart **6** bushel

Dryope *form:* **5** lotus *husband:* **9** Andraemon *sister:* **4** Iole

dry up 4 wilt **5** wizen **6** wither **7** deplete, exhaust, mummify, shrivel **9** desiccate, disappear, evaporate

dual 3 two **4** twin **5** duple **6** bifold, binary, double, duplex, paired **7** coupled, matched, twofold **8** matching **9** duplicate

dualistic 5 duple **6** bifold, binary, double, duplex, paired **7** twofold **9** Manichean **10** Manichaean

dualize 4 copy, dupe **5** clone **6** double **9** duplicate, replicate, reproduce

dub 4 call, name, term, trim **5** style, title **6**

duffer 7 baptize, bungler, entitle, fumbler **8** christen, nickname, rerecord **9** blunderer, designate **10** denominate

dubiety 5 doubt **7** concern **8** mistrust **9** confusion, suspicion **10** skepticism **11** incertitude, incredulity, uncertainty **12** doubtfulness

dubious 4 iffy **5** fishy **6** unsure **7** suspect, unclear **8** doubtful, hesitant, unlikely **9** equivocal, sceptical, skeptical, uncertain, undecided **10** improbable, unreliable **11** mistrustful, problematic, questioning, unconvinced, unpromising **12** questionable, undependable, undetermined

dubitable 5 fishy **7** suspect **8** doubtful, marginal **9** ambiguous, uncertain, unsettled **10** borderline **11** problematic **13** indeterminate

duce 5 ruler **6** despot, leader, tyrant **8** dictator **9** Mussolini (Benito), strongman

duck 3 bob, bow, dip, shy **4** bend, dive, dunk, shun **5** avoid, dodge, douse, elude, evade, fence, parry, shirk, stoop **6** escape, plunge **7** back out, immerse **8** sidestep, submerge, submerse **10** canvasback *Asian:* **5** Pekin **8** mandarin *dabbling:* **7** gadwall, mallard *diving:* **4** smew **7** pochard **9** merganser **10** bufflehead *Eurasian:* **4** smew *European:* **8** shelduck *genus:* **3** Aix **4** Anas *group:* **4** team **5** brace, flock, skein **6** flight *hunter's screen:* **5** blind *male:* **5** drake *red-wattled:* **7** Muscovy *river:* **4** teal **6** wigeon **7** pintail, widgeon *scaup:* **8** bluebill *sea:* **5** eider, scaup **6** scoter

duckbill 8 platypus **9** hadrosaur, monotreme

duck soup 4 easy, snap **5** cinch **6** breeze, picnic, simple **8** kid stuff, painless, pushover **10** child's play **11** piece of cake

ducky 4 cute **5** swell **6** lovely, peachy **7** darling **9** hunky-dory **10** peachy-keen

duct 4 flue, pipe, tube **5** canal **6** course, runway **7** channel, conduit **11** watercourse *anatomical:* **3** vas **4** vasa (plural)

ductile 6 pliant, supple **7** plastic, pliable **8** flexible, moldable **9** adaptable, compliant, malleable, tractable *metal:* **4** wire

ductless gland see **endocrine gland**

dud 3 dog **4** bomb, bust, flop **5** lemon, loser **6** bummer, misfit, turkey **7** debacle, failure, washout **8** abortion

dude 3 fop, guy **4** beau, buck, rake **5** blood, dandy **6** fellow **7** coxcomb **8** macaroni **9** exquisite **12** Beau Brummell, lounge lizard

dudgeon 3 ire **4** fury, huff, miff, rage **5** anger, pique, wrath **7** chagrin, offense, outrage, umbrage **8** vexation **10** resentment **11** indignation **12** exasperation

duds 3 rig **4** garb, gear, rags, togs **5** dress,

getup, weeds **6** attire, things **7** apparel, clothes, raiment, threads, toggery **8** clothing, garments **9** trappings, vestments **11** habiliments

due 4 debt, just, owed **5** lumps, owing **6** direct, earned, lawful, proper, unpaid **7** arrears, condign, deserts, merited, payable, payment, regular **8** adequate, deserved, expected, rightful, suitable **9** deserving, equitable, requisite, scheduled **10** obligatory, receivable, sufficient **11** appropriate, outstanding

duel 4 tilt **5** fight, joust **6** combat **7** contest, dispute **8** conflict **9** smackdown

duenna 8 chaperon **9** chaperone, companion, governess

duet *dancer's:* **9** pas de deux

due to 4 over **7** owing to, through **9** because of **11** considering

duff 3 can **4** buns, butt, rear, rump, tail, tush **5** fanny, slack **6** bottom **7** keester, keister, pudding, rear end **8** backside, buttocks, coal dust, derriere **10** leaf litter

duffer 4 boob, clod, dolt, dope, yo-yo **5** chump, dunce, klutz **6** dimwit, dum-dum, lubber, nitwit **7** dullard, fumbler, peddler, pinhead **8** bonehead, dumbbell, lunkhead, numskull **9** blockhead, ignoramus, numbskull, simpleton **10** nincompoop, stumblebum **11** incompetent

dugout 5 canoe **6** trench **7** piragua, pirogue, shelter

duiker 8 antelope

dukedom 5 duchy **6** domain

dulcet 5 sweet **7** melodic, tuneful **8** charming, cheerful, engaging, euphonic, pleasant, pleasing, soothing **9** agreeable, melodious **10** euphonious **11** mellifluous

dulcimer 6 zither **8** psaltery *Hungarian:* **8** cimbalom *Persian:* **6** santir **7** santour

dull 3 dim, dun, mat **4** arid, blah, blur, drab, flat, numb **5** blunt, dense, dusty, faded, hohum, inert, matte, muddy, muted **6** benumb, blurry, boring, deaden, dreary, gloomy, leaden, obtuse, stodgy, stupid **7** blunted, humdrum, insipid, muffled, prosaic, stupefy, subdued, tarnish, tedious **8** banausic, bromidic, deadened, discolor, lifeless, listless, monotone, plodding, sluggish **9** colorless, dim-witted, dryasdust, ponderous, wearisome **10** indistinct, lackluster, lusterless, monotonous, pedestrian **11** commonplace, desensitize, insensitive, thickheaded, thick-witted, unsharpened **12** simpleminded **13** uninteresting

dullard 3 oaf **4** bird, boob, bore, clod, dolt, dope, yo-yo **5** chump, dummy, dunce, idiot,

moron, ninny, noddy, stupe **6** dimwit, dumdum, nitwit **7** airhead, pinhead **8** bonehead, dumbbell, imbecile, lunkhead, meathead, numskull **9** birdbrain, blockhead, ignoramus, lamebrain, numbskull, simpleton **10** dunderhead **11** chowderhead, chucklehead

dullness 5 ennui **6** apathy, stupor, tedium, torpor **7** boredom, languor **8** hebetude, lethargy, monotony **9** bluntness, denseness, lassitude, stupidity, torpidity **12** indifference, listlessness, sluggishness

duly 8 properly, suitably **9** correctly, regularly **12** sufficiently **13** appropriately

duma 7 council **8** assembly, congress **11** legislature

Dumas character 5 Athos **6** Aramis, Dantès (Edmond) **7** Camille, Porthos **9** D'Artagnan

dumb 3 mum **4** dull, mute **5** dense, quiet, thick **6** deaden, obtuse, silent, stupid **7** doltish, foolish, idiotic, moronic **8** ignorant, taciturn, wordless **9** dim-witted, fatheaded, voiceless **10** speechless, tongue-tied **11** blockheaded, thick-witted **12** closemouthed, inarticulate, simple-minded

dumbbell see **dullard**

dumbfound 5 amaze **6** boggle, puzzle **7** astound, nonplus, perplex, stagger **8** astonish, bewilder, bowl over, confound, distract, surprise **9** take aback **11** flabbergast

dumbfounded 5 agape **6** amazed **7** puzzled, shocked **8** startled **9** astounded, perplexed, staggered, surprised **10** astonished, bewildered, bowled over, confounded, distracted, nonplussed, taken aback **13** thunderstruck

dummkopf 3 oaf **4** boob, clod, dodo, dolt, dope, fool, goof, jerk, mutt, simp, yo-yo **5** chump, dunce, idiot, moron, ninny, noddy, stupe **6** dimwit, donkey, nitwit, noodle **7** airhead, dullard, pinhead, schnook **8** bonehead, clodpoll, dumbbell, dumbhead, imbecile, lunkhead, meathead, numskull **9** birdbrain, blockhead, ignoramus, lamebrain, numbskull, simpleton, thickhead **10** dunderhead, hammerhead, nincompoop **11** chowderhead, chucklehead, knucklehead

dummy 4 boob, clod, dodo, dolt, mock, sham, yo-yo **5** chump, dunce, false, idiot, model, moron, ninny, noddy, stupe **6** dimwit, dumdum, effigy, ersatz, layout, mock-up, nitwit, puppet, stooge **7** airhead, dullard, manikin, pinhead, stand-in **8** bonehead, dumbbell, imbecile, lunkhead, mannekin, meathead, numskull **9** birdbrain, blockhead, ignoramus, imitation, lamebrain, numbskull, simpleton, simulated **10** artificial, dunderhead, fictitious, nincompoop, substitute **11** chowderhead, chucklehead

dump 4 drop, junk **5** chuck, depot, ditch, scrap **6** armory, midden, pigpen, pigsty, plunge **7** abandon, arsenal, deep-six, discard **8** jettison, landfill, magazine, throw out **9** stockpile, throw away **10** depository

dumpling 5 dough **8** quenelle **10** butterball

dumps 4 funk **5** blues, dolor, gloom, mopes, slump **7** sadness **8** doldrums **9** dejection **10** depression, gloominess, melancholy **11** despondency, unhappiness

dumpy 5 dingy, seedy, squat, stout **6** chubby, chunky, shabby, slummy, stocky, stubby, stumpy **7** run-down **8** heavyset, thickset **9** shapeless

dun 3 dim, fly **4** dull, drab, gray **5** annoy, brown, dusky, horse, murky, press **6** demand, gloomy, mayfly, needle, pester, plague, somber, sombre **9** ephemerid, importune

Duncan's slayer 7 Macbeth

dunce 3 oaf **4** boob, clod, dodo, dolt, dope, goof, mutt, simp, yo-yo **5** booby, chump, dummy, idiot, moron, ninny, noddy, stupe **6** dimwit, donkey, duffer, dum-dum, nitwit, noodle, stupid **7** airhead, dullard, fathead, pinhead **8** bonehead, clodpoll, dumbbell, imbecile, lunkhead, meathead, numskull **9** birdbrain, blockhead, ignoramus, lamebrain, numbskull, simpleton **10** dunderhead, hammerhead, nincompoop **11** chowderhead, chucklehead, knucklehead

Dunciad author 4 Pope (Alexander)

dundrearies 9 burnsides, sideburns **11** muttonchops **12** side-whiskers

dune 8 sandbank **area: 3** erg **5** beach, shore **6** desert

dung 4 muck **6** manure, ordure **9** excrement **beetle: 6** scarab **9** tumblebug

dungeon 4 jail **5** vault **6** prison **9** black hole, oubliette

dunghill 6 midden

dunk 3 dip, sop **4** soak **5** douse, drown, souse **6** drench **7** immerse **8** saturate, submerge, submerse

dunlin 9 sandpiper

duo 4 dyad, pair **5** brace **6** couple **7** doublet, twosome

dupe 3 con, kid, sap **4** butt, fool, gull, hoax, mark **5** cheat, chump, cozen, patsy, spoof, trick **6** befool, delude, double, outwit, pigeon, sucker **7** chicane, deceive, defraud, mislead **8** flimflam, hoodwink **9** bamboozle, victimize **11** double-cross, hornswoggle

dupery 3 con **4** scam, sham **5** cheat, fraud **6** deceit, humbug, hustle **7** chicane **8** cheating, flimflam, trickery **9** chicanery, deception, duplicity, imposture, swindling **10**

dishonesty, hanky-panky **11** hoodwinking **13** double-dealing, sharp practice

duple 4 dual, twin **6** bifold, binary, double, paired **7** coupled, doubled, twofold **9** dualistic

duplex see **duple**

duplicate 4 copy, fake, mate, redo, same, twin **5** clone, ditto, equal, match, mimeo, repro, Xerox **6** carbon, double **7** dualize, imitate, replica **8** knockoff **9** companion, facsimile, identical, imitation, look-alike, photocopy, replicate, reproduce **10** carbon copy, dead ringer, equivalent, reciprocal **11** counterfeit, counterpart, replication **12** reproduction

duplicitous 5 phony **6** shifty, sneaky **7** devious **8** delusive, guileful, scheming, sneaking, two-faced **9** deceitful, deceiving, deceptive, dishonest, underhand **10** fraudulent **11** underhanded **12** disingenuous **13** double-dealing

duplicity 5 fraud, guile **6** deceit **7** cunning, perfidy **8** scheming, trickery **9** chicanery, deception, treachery **10** dishonesty, doubleness **11** skulduggery **12** dissemblance, skullduggery **13** dissimulation, double-dealing

durability 4 wear **8** firmness **9** endurance, longevity, stability **10** permanence

durable 5 stout **6** stable, strong, sturdy **7** lasting **8** enduring **9** permanent, tenacious **10** dependable **11** long-lasting

durance 7 bondage **9** captivity, detention, restraint **11** confinement **12** enthrallment, imprisonment **13** incarceration

duration 3 run **4** term, time **6** extent, period **7** interim **8** interval **11** persistence

duress 5 force **6** menace, threat **8** bullying, coercion, menacing, pressure **9** restraint **10** compulsion, constraint **11** restriction **12** intimidation

during 4 amid **10** throughout

durra 7 sorghum **12** grain sorghum

Durrell work 4 Cleo **7** Justine **9** Balthazar **10** Mountolive **17** Alexandria Quartet

durum 5 wheat

dusk 4 dark **7** evening **8** darkness, eventide, gloaming, twilight **9** nightfall **12** semidarkness

dusky 3 dim **4** dark **5** murky, swart **6** brunet, gloomy, opaque, twilit **7** obscure, shadowy, swarthy **8** funereal, nubilous, overcast, twilight **9** tenebrous **10** caliginous **11** darkskinned

dust 4 grit, sand, sift, soot **5** ashes, grime **6** powder **8** sprinkle **10** besprinkle, sprinkling

dust-bowl victim 4 Okie

dustup 3 row **4** spat **5** fight, melee, run-in,

set-to 6 battle, fracas, hassle, tussle 7 dispute, quarrel, rhubarb, scuffle 8 argument, skirmish 9 bickering, brannigan 10 falling-out 11 altercation

dusty 3 dry 4 arid, dull 5 stale 7 parched, powdery, tedious, unswept

Dutch 7 trouble 8 hot water *African:* 9 Afrikaans *ceramics:* 5 delft *cheese:* 4 Edam 5 Gouda *dog breed:* 7 griffon 8 keeshond *painter:* 3 Dou (Gerrit, Gerard) 4 Cuyp (Aelbert Jacobsz), Gogh (Vincent van), Hals (Frans) 5 Bosch (Hieronymus), Hooch (Pieter de), Steen (Jan) 6 Rubens (Peter Paul) 7 de Hooch (Pieter), Hobbema (Meindert), van Gogh (Vincent), Vermeer (Jan) 8 Mondrian (Piet), Ruysdael (Jacob van, Salomon van), Terborch (Gerard) 9 de Kooning (Willem), Honthorst (Gerrit van), Rembrandt (van Rijn) *philosopher:* 7 Spinoza (Benedict de) *scholar:* 7 Erasmus (Desiderius)

Dutch South African 4 Boer

dutiful 7 devoted 8 faithful 9 compliant 10 respectful 13 conscientious

duty 3 job, tax, use 4 levy, onus, role, task, work 5 chare, chore, stint 6 burden, charge, devoir, impost, office, tariff 7 respect, service 8 function 10 allegiance, assessment, assignment, commitment, dedication, obligation

dwarf 4 runt 5 gnome, pygmy, stunt, troll 6 midget, peewee 7 manikin 8 Tom Thumb 9 miniature 10 diminutive, homunculus *in Snow White:* 3 Doc 5 Dopey, Happy 6 Grumpy, Sleepy, Sneezy 7 Bashful *Scottish:* 7 blastie

dwarfish 5 pygmy, small 6 midget 7 minikin, stunted 8 inferior, pint-size 9 miniature, pint-sized 10 diminutive, undersized

dweeb 4 dork, drip, geek, nerd, wimp, wuss 5 loser 7 nebbish

dwell 3 lie 4 bide, live, stay 5 abide, exist 6 locate, remain, repose, reside, settle 7 hang out

dweller 7 citizen, denizen, settler 8 habitant, occupant, resident 10 inhabitant

dwelling 3 pad 4 casa, digs, home, nest 5 abode, haunt, house 7 address, habitat, lodging 8 domicile, quarters 9 residence 10 brownstone, habitation *American Indian:* 4 tipi 5 hogan, tepee 6 pueblo, teepee, wigwam *clergyman's:* 5 manse 7 rectory 8 vicarage 9 parsonage *crude:* 3 hut 4 camp 5 cabin, hovel, shack 6 cabana, shanty 7 barrack 8 barracks *Eskimo:* 5 igloo *grand:* 5 manor, manse, villa 6 palace 7 château, mansion *Hindu:* 6 ashram *Navajo:* 5 hogan *Russian:* 5 dacha *small:* 3 cot, hut 5 cabin, hovel, shack 6 shanty 7 cottage 8 bungalow

dwindle 3 ebb 4 fade, fall, wane 5 abate, taper 6 lessen, recede, reduce, shrink, weaken, wither 7 decline, die away, die down, shrivel, slacken, subside 8 decrease, diminish, taper off 9 attenuate, drain away

dyad 3 duo, two 4 pair, yoke 5 brace, twins 6 couple 7 doublet, twosome

dye 4 tint 5 color, stain, tinge 7 pigment 8 colorant, pyronine, tincture *blue:* 4 woad 6 indigo 7 cyanine *plant:* 4 woad 5 sumac 6 madder *red:* 5 eosin, henna 6 kermes, ruddle 7 cudbear, fuchsin, magenta 8 alizarin, fuchsine, amaranth, safranin 9 cochineal, rhodamine, safranine 10 erythrosin *violet:* 6 archil *yellow:* 7 flavine 8 orpiment *yellowish red:* 7 annatto

dyed-in-the-wool 5 loyal, sworn 7 devoted, die-hard, old-line, settled, staunch 8 faithful, hard-core, orthodox, standpat, true-blue 9 confirmed, hard-shell, steadfast 10 deep-rooted, deep-seated, entrenched, inveterate, unwavering 11 established 13 bred-in-the-bone, thoroughgoing

dyewood 6 fustic 10 brazilwood

dying 6 demise 7 done for, quietus 8 moribund 9 departure 10 extinction, in extremis 12 annihilation

dynamic 7 driving, intense 8 forceful, forcible, powerful, vigorous 9 energetic, strenuous 10 compelling, energizing

dynamite 4 raze 5 blast 6 blow up 7 destroy, explode, shatter 8 demolish 9 explosive 10 annihilate *inventor:* 5 Nobel (Alfred)

dynamo 8 go-getter, live wire 9 generator 10 ball of fire 11 self-starter

dynasty *Chinese:* 3 Han, Qin, Sui 4 Hsia, Ming, Qing, Sung, Tang *Mongol:* 4 Yuan

Dynasty *series character:* 3 Ben, Dex 4 Adam, Dana 5 Blake, Sable 6 Alexis, Amanda, Fallon, Leslie, Monica, Steven 7 Claudia, Jeffery, Krystie 8 Samantha 9 Dominique *family:* 5 Colby 10 Carrington *setting:* 6 Denver *spin-off:* 6 Colbys (The) *star:* 5 Evans (Linda), James (John), Nader (Michael), Samms (Emma) 6 Corley (Al), Garber (Terri), Hunley (Leann), Martin (Pamela Sue) 7 Beacham (Stephanie), Carroll (Diahann), Cellini (Karen), Coleman (Jack), Collins (Joan), Thomson (Gordon) 8 Bellwood (Pamela), Cazenove (Christopher), Forsythe (John), Locklear (Heather), Oxenberg (Catherine), Scoggins (Tracy)

dysentery 4 flux 6 scours 8 diarrhea

dyslogistic 7 adverse 10 derogatory, pejorative 11 deleterious, disparaging, prejudicial, unfavorable

dyspepsia 5 gloom 6 dismay 7 chagrin, pyrosis 8 glumness 9 dejection, heartburn 10 gloominess 11 frustration, indigestion
dyspeptic 5 cross, surly 6 crabby, morose, ornery 9 irritable 10 ill-humored, ill-natured 11 disgruntled, ill-tempered

dysphoria 4 funk 5 blues, dumps, gloom, mopes 6 sorrow 7 sadness 9 dejection 10 depression, gloominess, melancholy 11 unhappiness 12 mournfulness, wretchedness 13 cheerlessness
dysprosium symbol 2 Dy`

E

each 3 all, per 4 a pop 5 every 6 apiece 8 everyone 9 per capita, everybody
eager 4 avid, keen 5 antsy, hyper, itchy, ready6 ardent, fervid, gung ho, intent, raring 7 anxious, athirst, earnest, fervent, restive 8 appetent, aspiring, desirous, restless, yearning 9 ambitious, hankering, impatient 10 breathless 12 enthusiastic
eagerness 4 urge, zeal, zest, zing 5 ardor, gusto 6 desire, fervor, spirit, thirst 7 avidity, craving, itching, longing 8 alacrity, ambition, appetite, fervency 9 intensity 10 enthusiasm, impatience
eagle 4 hawk 9 accipiter *nest:* 4 aery 5 aerie, eyrie *North American:* 4 bald 6 golden *sea:* 3 ern 4 erne 6 osprey
eagle-eyed 8 vigilant, watchful 9 attentive, observant 10 perceptive 12 sharp-sighted
ear 6 notice 7 auricle 9 attention *bone:* 5 anvil, incus 6 hammer, stapes 7 malleus, stirrup *canal:* 5 scala *combining form:* 3 aur, oto 4 auri, otic *doctor:* 9 otologist *inner:* 9 labyrinth *middle:* 8 tympanum *outer:* 5 pinna *part:* 4 drum, lobe 5 canal 6 tragus 7 cochlea *relating to:* 5 aural 9 auricular *science:* 7 otology
eardrum 8 tympanum
_____ **Earhart** 6 Amelia
earl 4 lord, peer 5 count, noble 8 nobleman, seigneur 9 patrician 10 aristocrat
earlier 3 ere, yet 4 once 5 as yet, so far 6 before, sooner 7 already, thus far 8 formerly, hitherto, previous 9 erstwhile, preceding 10 beforehand, heretofore, previously
earlier than 3 pre 6 before *Latin:* 4 ante
earliest 5 first, prime 6 maiden, primal 7 initial, pioneer, primary 8 original, primeval, pristine 10 aboriginal, primordial
earlike projection 3 lug
early 3 old 5 first, prior 6 primal, timely 7 ancient, betimes 8 original, previous, primeval, pristine, untimely 9 preceding, premature, primitive 10 antecedent, antiquated, precocious, primordial 11 prematurely *prefix:* 5 paleo
earn 3 bag, get, net, win 4 gain, make, rate, reap 5 amass, clear, gross, merit, score 6 attain, come by, obtain, pick up, rack up, secure, wangle 7 acquire, bring in, collect, deserve, harvest, procure, produce, realize, receive 8 pull down 9 bring home, knock down
earnest 3 vow 4 bond, busy, firm, keen, pawn, true, warm 5 grave, sober, token 6 active, ardent, intent, pledge, solemn, somber, surety 7 deposit, genuine, intense, serious, sincere, up front, warrant, zealous 8 contract, covenant, diligent, interest, security, sedulous, studious 9 assiduous, heartfelt 10 determined, no-nonsense, passionate, sobersided, thoughtful, unaffected 11 industrious 12 enthusiastic, wholehearted
earnestly 5 madly 7 for real, like mad
earnings 3 net, pay 4 gain 5 lucre, wages 6 EBITDA, income, profit, return, salary 7 profits 8 proceeds, take-home 9 emolument 10 bottom line
earring type 4 cuff, hook, hoop, stud 5 huggy, slave 6 clip-on, dangle 7 barbell, stick-on
ear shell see **abalone**
earshot 5 range, sound 7 hearing
earsplitting 4 loud 6 shrill 7 blaring, grating, raucous, roaring 8 piercing, strident 9 deafening, dissonant 10 screeching, stentorian 11 fullmouthed
earth 3 orb, sod 4 dirt, land, soil, turf 5 globe, world 6 ground, planet, sphere 7 dry land, terrain 8 creation 10 terra firma *brick:* 4 pisé 5 tapia *combining form:* 3 geo 4 geog 6 tellur 7 telluro *core:* 12 centrosphere *crust:* 4 sial, sima 11 lithosphere *god:* 3

Geb, Keb, Seb **5** Dagan *goddess:* **4** Erda, Gaea **5** Ceres, Nintu **6** Kishar **7** Demeter, Nerthus *pigment:* **5** ocher, ochre, umber **6** sienna *relating to:* **8** telluric **11** terrestrial *satellite:* **4** moon *science:* **7** geology **9** geography

earthenware 4 clay **5** china, delft **7** biscuit, faience, pottery **8** clayware, crockery, majolica **9** porcelain, stoneware **10** terra-cotta

earthlike 11 terrestrial

earthling 6 Terran

earthly 6 mortal **7** mundane, worldly **8** material, physical, temporal **9** corporeal **11** terrestrial

earthquake 5 shake, shock **6** tremor **7** temblor *measuring device:* **11** seismograph, seismometer *relating to:* **7** seismic *science:* **10** seismology **11** seismometry

earthwork 4 bank, berm, wall **7** bulwark, rampart **10** embankment **13** fortification

earthworm 7 annelid **12** night crawler

earthy 3 low **4** base, real **5** crude, dirty, dusty, gross, muddy, ocher, ochre, sandy **6** clayey, coarse, common, simple **7** mundane, worldly **8** temporal **9** corporeal, inelegant, practical, pragmatic, realistic, unrefined **10** hard-boiled, hardheaded, indelicate, uncultured, unpolished **11** terrestrial **12** matter-of-fact

earwax 7 cerumen

ease 3 aid **4** bate, calm, dull, free, help, rest **5** allay, loose, peace, poise, relax, slack **6** assist, deaden, loosen, relief, repose, soften **7** assuage, comfort, fluency, improve, leisure, lighten, mollify, relieve, slacken **8** calmness, deftness, diminish, dispatch, facility, idleness, mitigate, moderate, pleasure, serenity **9** abundance, affluence, alleviate, expertise, reduction, untighten, well-being **10** ameliorate, efficiency, facilitate, inactivity, moderation, prosperity, relaxation, smoothness **11** alleviation, contentment, nonchalance, spontaneity *off:* **3** ebb **4** bate, fade, fall, flag, wane **5** abate, let up, loose, relax, slack **6** lessen, loosen, relent, unbend, unwind **7** die away, die down, slacken, subside **8** diminish, loosen up, moderate **9** untighten

easel 4 desk **5** frame, stand **7** support **9** workbench, worktable

easement 6 relief **7** comfort **10** mitigation, palliative **11** alleviation, consolation, restorative **13** mollification

easily 6 simply **7** handily, lightly, readily **8** facilely, smoothly **11** dexterously, efficiently **12** effortlessly

East 4 Asia **6** Levant, Orient

Easter 5 Pasch *relating to:* **7** paschal *symbol:* **3** egg **4** lamb, lily **5** bunny **6** rabbit

Easter Island 7 Rapa Nui

eastern 8 oriental **9** Levantine *countries:* **6** Orient *European:* **4** Slav

East Indies *country:* **8** Malaysia **9** Indonesia, Singapore *plant:* **2** da

East Timor *capital:* **4** Dili *neighbor:* **9** Indonesia

easy 3 lax **4** calm, cozy, mild, soft, snug **5** basic, clear, comfy, cushy, light, loose, naive, plain **6** facile, fluent, placid, polite, secure, serene, simple, smooth **7** amiable, evident, lenient, obvious, patient, relaxed **8** apparent, composed, familiar, graceful, gullible, informal, obliging, peaceful, pleasant, sociable, tolerant, trusting **9** collected, forgiving, indulgent **10** charitable, effortless, elementary **13** uncomplicated

easygoing 3 lax **4** calm, cool, lazy **5** quiet **6** breezy, casual, dégagé, folksy **7** affable, offhand, patient, relaxed, unfussy **8** amenable, carefree, down home, flexible, indolent, informal, laid-back, together, tranquil **9** apathetic, indulgent, unhurried **10** nonchalant, permissive, unaffected **11** comfortable, complaisant, low-pressure, pococurante, unconcerned, unflappable **12** devil-may-care, even-tempered, happy-go-lucky

easy mark 3 sap **4** butt, dupe, fool, gull **5** chump, patsy, sport **6** pigeon, softie, sucker, turkey, victim **7** fall guy **8** pushover **9** soft touch **11** sitting duck

eat 3 sup, vex **4** bite, chow, dine, gnaw, meal, nosh, pick, take, wolf **5** erode, feast, gorge, graze, lunch, mouth, munch, scarf, scoff, scour, snack, use up **6** devour, feed on, gobble, ingest, inhale, nibble, pester, pick at, pig out, take in **7** banquet, consume, corrode, gorge on, swallow, torment **8** chow down, dissolve, take food, wear away **9** breakfast, decompose, masticate, partake of, polish off **10** break bread, gormandize, nibble away

eatable 6 edible **8** esculent, harmless **9** palatable **10** comestible, digestible

eatery 4 café **5** diner, grill **10** coffee shop, restaurant **11** greasy spoon **12** luncheonette

eating place 3 pub **4** café, mess **5** diner, grill, joint **6** bistro, tavern **7** automat, beanery, canteen, commons, dinette, tearoom **8** cookshop, messroom, pizzeria, snack bar **9** brasserie, cafeteria, chophouse, hash house, lunchroom, trattoria **10** coffee shop, restaurant, steak house **11** greasy spoon **12** luncheonette

eavesdrop 3 bug, tap **4** lurk **5** snoop **7** monitor **8** listen in, overhear

ebb 4 drop, fade, fall, flag, tide, wane **5**

abate, droop, let up **6** lessen, recede, reduce, relent, shrink, wither **7** decline, descent, die away, die down, ease off, retreat, slacken, subside **8** decrease, diminish, languish, moderate, withdraw **10** retrograde

Eblis 5 Satan *son:* **3** Tir **4** Awar **5** Dasim **8** Zalambur

ebon, ebony 3 jet **4** inky **5** black, jetty, raven, sable **6** brunet **8** brunette, jet-black **9** pitch-dark **10** pitch-black

ebullience 3 vim, zip **4** brio, élan, zing **5** gusto **6** gaiety **7** abandon, elation **8** buoyancy, vitality, vivacity **9** animation **10** enthusiasm, exuberance, liveliness **11** high spirits **13** effervescence

ebullient 5 brash, zingy, zippy **6** bouncy, bubbly, elated, frothy, geeked, pumped, raring **7** boiling, excited, gleeful, gushing, vibrant **8** hopped-up **9** sprightly, vivacious **11** exhilarated **12** enthusiastic, high-spirited **13** irrepressible

eccentric 3 odd, nut **4** coot, kook **5** crank, crazy, droll, flaky, freak, funky, funny, goofy, kooky, nutty, outré, queer, wacky, weird **6** far out, oddity, quaint, quirky, screwy, weirdo, whacko, whacky **7** bizarre, deviant, erratic, heretic, oddball, offbeat, strange, unusual **8** aberrant, abnormal, bohemian, cockeyed, crackpot, goofball, maverick, peculiar, singular, uncommon **9** anomalous, character, deviating, fantastic, fruitcake, grotesque, irregular, off-center, screwball, whimsical **10** elliptical, off-balance, unbalanced, uncentered **11** exceptional **13** idiosyncratic, nonconformist

eccentricity 4 kink **5** quirk, twist **8** crotchet, quiddity **9** deviation, weirdness **10** aberration **11** strangeness **12** idiosyncrasy

ecclesiastic see **clergyman**

ecclesiastical 4 holy **5** papal **6** church, sacred **8** churchly, clerical, pastoral, priestly **9** apostolic, canonical, episcopal, spiritual, synagogal **10** churchlike, pontifical, rabbinical, sacerdotal **11** ministerial, patriarchal, theological **12** episcopalian, evangelistic, tabernacular

ecdysiast see **stripteaser**

echelon 3 row **4** file, line, rank, tier **5** grade, group, level, order, queue **6** string **7** chevron **9** formation

echidna 8 anteater **9** monotreme **13** spiny anteater

Echidna *father:* **7** Phorcys **8** Chrysaor *mother:* **4** Ceto **10** Callirrhoë *offspring:* **5** Hydra **6** dragon, Orthus, Sphinx **7** Chimera **8** Cerberus, Chimaera

echinoderm 6 urchin **7** crinoid, sea star **8** starfish **9** coelomate, sea urchin **11** sea cucumber

echo 3 ape **4** mime, ring **5** evoke, mimic, trace **6** mirror, parrot, repeat, result, reverb, second **7** imitate, iterate, reflect, resound, revoice, vestige **8** resonate, response **9** duplicate, imitation, reiterate **10** reflection, repetition **11** reverberate **12** repercussion **13** reverberation

Echo 5 nymph, oread *beloved:* **9** Narcissus

echoic 7 mimetic **9** imitative **10** derivative **12** onomatopoeic **13** onomatopoetic

éclat 4 bang, dash, fame, pomp **5** glory, honor, kudos **6** luster, lustre, praise, renown, repute **7** acclaim, display, laurels, stardom, success **8** applause, eminence, prestige, standing **9** celebrity, notoriety, publicity **10** brilliance, brilliancy, exaltation, prominence, reputation **11** distinction, ostentation

eclectic 5 broad, fussy, mixed, picky **6** choosy, select, varied **7** diverse, finicky, mingled **8** assorted, catholic, elective **9** inclusive, selective **10** discerning, fastidious, particular **11** diversified **12** dilettantish, multifarious **13** heterogeneous

eclipse 3 dim **5** bedim, cloud, cover, excel, outdo, shade **6** darken, exceed, shadow **7** becloud, decline, obscure, surpass **8** downfall, outshine **9** adumbrate, obfuscate, overcloud **10** extinguish, overshadow *phenomenon:* **5** umbra **6** corona, shadow **7** annulus **8** penumbra **11** Diamond Ring **12** Bailey's Beads

eclogue 3 ode **4** idyl, poem **5** idyll, lyric **8** pastoral

ecological 5 green **8** bionomic *community:* **5** biome

ecology 9 bionomics **11** environment

economic 6 fiscal **8** material, monetary **9** budgetary, financial, pecuniary **10** mercantile, profitable *doctrine:* **12** laissez-faire *system:* **9** communism, socialism **10** capitalism **11** syndicalism **12** mercantilism

economical 4 mean **5** canny, close, spare, tight **6** frugal, saving, stingy **7** careful, miserly, prudent, sparing, thrifty **8** skimping **9** efficient, niggardly, penny-wise, penurious, provident, scrimping **10** unwasteful **12** cheeseparing, parsimonious **13** penny-pinching

economist *American:* **5** Arrow (Kenneth), Simon (Herbert, Julian), Solow (Robert), Tobin (James) **6** Becker (Gary), George (Henry), Thurow (Lester), Veblen (Thorstein), Walker (Amasa), Weaver (Robert) **7** Krugman (Paul), Kuznets (Simon), Stigler

(George), Volcker (Paul) **8** Friedman (Milton), Stiglitz (Joseph) **9** Galbraith (John Kenneth), Greenspan (Alan), Samuelson (Paul) **10** Schumpeter (Joseph) *Austrian:* **5** Hayek (Friedrich von), Mises (Ludwig von) *Canadian:* **7** Leacock (Stephen) *Dutch:* **9** Tinbergen (Jan) *English:* **3** Sen (Amartya) **4** Mill (John Stuart) **5** Coase (Ronald), Hayek (Friedrich von), Pigou (Arthur) **6** Engels (Friedrich), Keynes (John Maynard) **7** Bagehot (Walter), Malthus (Thomas), Ricardo (David) *French:* **3** Say (Jean-Baptiste) **6** Monnet (Jean), Turgot (Anne-Robert-Jacques), Walras (Léon) **7** Quesnay (François) *German:* **4** Marx (Karl) **5** Weber (Max) **6** Engels (Friedrich) **7** Schacht (Hjalmar) *Indian:* **3** Sen (Amartya) *Scottish:* **4** Mill (James) **5** Smith (Adam) *Swedish:* **6** Myrdal (Gunnar) *Swiss:* **8** Sismondi (Simonde de)

economize 4 save **5** skimp, stint **6** manage, scrimp **7** husband **8** conserve **10** cut corners **12** pinch pennies

economy 6 saving, thrift **8** prudence, skimping **9** concision, frugality, husbandry, parsimony, restraint, scrimping **10** discretion, efficiency, providence, stinginess **11** carefulness, conciseness, miserliness, thriftiness **13** niggardliness

Eco novel 9 Baudolino **13** Name of the Rose (The) **17** Foucault's Pendulum

ecru see **beige**

ecstasy 3 joy **5** bliss **6** frenzy, heaven, trance **7** delight, elation, madness, rapture **8** euphoria, paradise, rhapsody **9** beatitude, transport **10** exaltation, joyfulness **11** blessedness, derangement, enchantment, high spirits, inspiration **12** blissfulness, exhilaration, intoxication **13** seventh heaven

ecstatic 6 elated, joyful **7** gleeful **8** euphoric, exultant, jubilant, thrilled **9** delirious, delighted, entranced, overjoyed, rapturous, rhapsodic **11** exhilarated, transported

ectothermic 11 cold-blooded

Ecuador *capital:* **5** Quito *city:* **6** Ambato, Cuenca **7** Machala **9** Guayaquil *Indian people:* **7** Quechua *island group:* **9** Galápagos *language:* **7** Spanish *monetary unit:* **5** sucre *mountain range:* **5** Andes *neighbor:* **4** Peru **8** Colombia *volcano:* **6** Sangay **7** Cayambe **8** Cotopaxi **10** Chimborazo

ecumenical 6 cosmic, global **7** general, generic **8** catholic **9** inclusive, planetary, universal, worldwide **12** all-inclusive, cosmopolitan **13** comprehensive

ecumenical council 4 Lyon **5** Basel, Lyons, Trent **6** Nicene **7** Ephesus, Ferrara, Lateran, Vatican **8** Florence **9** Chalcedon, Constance

eczema 6 tetter

edacious see **voracious**

eddy 4 purl **5** swirl, twirl, whirl, whorl **6** vortex **8** backwash **9** backwater, maelstrom, whirlpool **11** counterflow

edema 5 croup, tumor **6** dropsy **8** anasarca, swelling *treatment:* **8** diuretic

Eden 6 heaven, utopia **7** arcadia, elysium **8** paradise *river:* **5** Gihon **6** Pishon **8** Hiddekel **9** Euphrates

edentate 5 sloth **8** aardvark, anteater, pangolin **9** armadillo, toothless

Edessa's king 5 Abgar

edge 3 cut, end, hem, lip, rim **4** bank, bite, brim, cusp, draw, ease, hone, inch, lead, limb, line, pink, side, whet, worm **5** arris, bound, brink, bulge, force, ledge, picot, point, ridge, sidle, skirt, sting, strop, verge **6** border, fringe, margin, nosing **7** acidity, contour, chamfer, outline, serrate, sharpen, vantage **8** acerbity, acridity, boundary, emborder, handicap, keenness, surround, thinness **9** acuteness, advantage, extremity, harshness, head start, perimeter, periphery, sharpness, threshold, upper hand **10** causticity, shrillness, stringency **11** astringency **12** incisiveness **13** effectiveness

edge city 5 exurb **6** suburb

edged 4 acid, tart **5** acerb, acute, sharp **6** barbed, strong **7** acerbic, cutting **8** incisive, piercing

edge in 6 inject **9** interject, interpose, insinuate **10** infiltrate **11** interpolate

edging 3 hem **4** lace **5** braid, frill, limit **6** border, fringe, lacing, margin, piping **7** flounce, selvage **8** rickrack, selvedge, trimming

edgy 3 hip **5** funky, nervy, sharp, tense, testy, wired **6** daring, touchy, uneasy **7** excited, keyed up, offbeat, restive, uptight **8** Bohemian, out-there, renegade, restless, skittery, skittish, volatile **9** excitable, impatient, irascible, irritable **10** high-strung, outlandish **11** provocative

edible 8 esculent **9** palatable **10** comestible *root:* **3** oca, yam **4** beet, taro, yuca **6** carrot, daikon, ginger, jicama, potato, radish, turnip, wasabi **7** burdock, cassava, ginseng, malanga, parsnip, salsify **8** celeriac, galangal, kohlrabi, rutabaga **11** horseradish, sweet potato *seed:* **3** nut, pea **4** bean **6** peanut

edibles 4 chow, eats, feed, food, grub **6** viands **7** aliment, goodies, nurture **8** victuals

9 provender **10** provisions, sustenance **11** comestibles

edict 3 law **4** bull, fiat, rule **5** canon, order, ukase **6** decree, dictum, ruling **7** command, dictate, mandate, precept, statute **9** directive, manifesto, ordinance, prescript **10** injunction, regulation **12** proclamation **13** pronouncement *Islamic:* **5** fatwa *papal:* **4** bull **8** decretal

Edict of ____ **5** Milan, Worms **6** Nantes

edifice 4 pile **8** building, erection **9** structure

edify 5 teach **6** better, fill in, illume, inform, update, uplift **7** educate, elevate, enhance, improve **8** illumine, instruct **9** elucidate, enlighten **10** illuminate

edit 3 cut **4** cull, omit **5** adapt, alter, amend, emend, fix up **6** delete, doctor, excise, polish, redact, refine, review, revise, reword, select **7** abridge, compile, correct, rewrite **8** annotate, assemble, condense, copyread, fine-tune **9** proofread, rearrange **10** blue-pencil, bowdlerize

editing term 4 dele, stet **5** caret **7** jump cut

edition 4 copy, form **5** issue, print **7** reissue, reprint, version **8** printing, variorum **10** impression, reprinting **12** reproduction

editor 8 redactor **9** scrivener, wordsmith **10** copyreader **11** proofreader

Edmonton player 5 Oiler

Edomite's ancestor 4 Esau

educate 4 rear **5** brief, coach, drill, edify, nurse, teach, train, tutor **6** inform, school **7** explain, nurture **8** instruct **9** brainwash, enlighten **10** discipline **12** indoctrinate

education 7 culture, tuition **8** breeding, coaching, guidance, learning, literacy, pedagogy, teaching, training, tutelage, tutorage, tutoring **9** erudition, knowledge, schooling, tutorship **11** instruction, learnedness, scholarship **13** enlightenment

educational 11 informative, instructive **13** informational, instructional *institution:* **6** school **7** academy, college **10** university **12** conservatory

educator 5 tutor **7** teacher **9** professor **10** instructor *American:* **4** Mann (Horace) **5** Dewey (John) **6** Butler (Nicholas Murray), Conant (James Bryant), Harris (William Torrey) **7** Barnard (Henry), Beecher (Catharine), Peabody (Elizabeth) **8** Hutchins (Robert Maynard), McGuffey (William) **10** Washington (Booker T.) *Czech:* **8** Comenius (John Amos) *English:* **6** Arnold (Thomas) **7** Spencer (Herbert) *German:* **7** Froebel (Friedrich), Herbart (Johann) *Italian:* **10** Montessori (Maria) *Swiss:* **10** Pestalozzi (Johann Heinrich)

educe 4 drag, draw, milk, pull **5** evoke, wrest, wring **6** derive, elicit, evince, evolve, extort, obtain, secure **7** distill, draw out, extract, procure **8** bring out **10** excogitate

eel 5 moray, siren **6** conger **7** hagfish, lamprey, sniggle *young:* **5** elver

eelpout 6 blenny, burbot **10** muttonfish

eely 5 slimy **6** slippy, wiggly **7** elusive, wriggly **8** slippery, slithery **9** wriggling

eerie 5 scary, weird **6** creepy, spooky **7** bizarre, strange, uncanny **8** chilling, spectral **9** fantastic, grotesque, unearthly **10** mysterious **11** frightening, hair-raising **12** otherworldly

efface 4 dele, x out **5** annul, erase **6** cancel, delete, rub out **7** blot out, destroy, expunge, scratch, wipe out **8** black out, wear away **9** eliminate, eradicate, extirpate **10** obliterate

effect 3 end **4** make **5** cause, enact, event, fruit **6** create, draw on, induce, intent, invoke, render, result, upshot **7** achieve, execute, fulfill, outcome, perform, produce, realize, turn out **8** bring off, carry out, conceive, generate **9** actualize, aftermath, discharge, implement, outgrowth **10** accomplish, bring about, conclusion, denouement **11** consequence **12** carry through, ramification, repercussion

effective 4 able **5** sound, valid **6** causal, cogent, direct, potent, useful **7** capable, operant **8** adequate **9** competent, operative **10** compelling, convincing, productive

effectiveness 5 clout, force, point, power, vigor **6** weight **7** cogency, potency **8** strength, validity **10** capability

effects 4 gear **5** goods, stuff **6** things **8** chattels, movables, property **9** equipment, moveables, trappings **10** belongings **11** impedimenta, possessions **13** accoutrements

effectual 5 sound, valid **6** potent, strong, useful **7** capable **8** decisive, powerful, workable **10** conclusive, fulfilling, productive **11** influential, practicable **13** authoritative, determinative

effectuate see **effect**

effeminate 5 sissy **6** swishy **7** epicene **9** sissified **10** old-maidish

effervescence 5 giddy **7** fizzing, foaming, sparkle **8** bubbling, buoyancy, vivacity **9** animation **10** ebullience, ebullition, exuberance, exuberancy, liveliness **12** exhilaration

effervescent 3 gay **4** airy **5** jolly **6** bouncy, bubbly, lively **7** boiling, buoyant, excited **8** animated, mirthful, volatile **9** sparkling, sprightly, vivacious **10** carbonated **12** high-spirited **13** irrepressible

effete 4 soft, weak **5** frail, spent **6** barren **6**

sickly **7** decayed, drained, sterile, worn-out **8** decadent, decaying, delicate, depleted, fatigued, pampered **9** declining, dissolute, enfeebled, exhausted, infertile, washed-out **10** degenerate, unfruitful **11** debilitated

efficacious 6 active, potent, strong **8** forceful, powerful, puissant **9** operative **10** productive **11** influential

efficacy see **effectiveness**

efficiency see **effectiveness**

efficient 4 able **5** adept **6** expert **7** capable, elegant, skilled **8** economic, masterly, skillful **9** competent **10** economical, productive

effigy 3 guy **4** icon, idol **5** dummy, image **6** figure **7** waxwork **8** likeness

effloresce 4 blow **5** bloom, burst **6** flower, sprout **7** blossom, burgeon **9** bear fruit

effluvium 3 air **4** odor, reek **5** smell, vapor, waste **6** miasma **7** exhaust **8** effusion, emission **9** by-product, discharge, emanation **10** exhalation

efflux see **effluvium**

effort 3 job, try **4** feat, push, task, toil, work **5** chore, essay, force, labor, might, nisus, pains, sweat, while **6** energy, strain **7** attempt, travail, trouble, venture **8** endeavor, exertion, industry, struggle **11** application, elbow grease

effortful 4 hard **6** tiring, uphill **7** arduous, labored, operose **8** exacting, toilsome **9** ambitious, difficult, laborious, strenuous **11** challenging

effortless 4 easy **5** adept, light, ready **6** expert, facile, fluent, simple, smooth **8** masterly, skillful **10** proficient **11** undemanding

effrontery 4 face, gall **5** brass, cheek, nerve **8** audacity, boldness, chutzpah, temerity **9** arrogance, assurance, brashness, hardihood, impudence, insolence **10** brazenness **11** presumption **12** impertinence

effulgence 4 glow **5** blaze, glory **6** luster, lustre **8** radiance, splendor **9** splendour **10** brightness, brilliance, brilliancy, luminosity

effulgent 5 vivid **6** bright, lucent **7** beaming, glowing, lambent, radiant, shining **8** dazzling, glorious, luminous, lustrous, splendid **9** brilliant **11** resplendent **12** incandescent

effuse 4 flow, gush, pour, shed **5** exude, issue **6** stream **7** emanate, enthuse, flow out, radiate

effusive 5 gushy **6** lavish, sloppy, smarmy **7** cloying, fulsome, gushing, profuse, verbose **9** expansive, exuberant **10** loquacious, outpouring, unreserved **11** extravagant **12** enthusiastic, unrestrained **13** demonstrative, unconstrained

eft 4 newt **6** triton **10** salamander

e.g. 3 say **10** for example **11** for instance **13** exempli gratia

egad 6 zounds **7** criminy **8** gadzooks **11** odds bodkins

egg 3 ova (plural) **4** ovum, seed **5** ovule *case:* **5** shell **7** ootheca *combining form:* **3** ovi, ovo *dish:* **6** omelet **8** omelette *fertilized:* **6** zygote **7** oospore *fish:* **3** roe **6** caviar *French:* **4** oeuf *immature:* **6** oocyte *louse:* **3** nit *part:* **4** yolk **5** glair, shell, white *shaped:* **5** ovate, ovoid *white:* **5** glair **7** albumen

egghead 6 pundit **8** highbrow **10** double-dome **12** intellectual

egg on 4 goad, prod, spur, urge **5** prick, rally **6** arouse, exhort, excite, incite, prompt, stir up **7** agitate **9** instigate, stimulate

eggplant 6 purple **9** aubergine **10** nightshade

egg-shaped 4 oval **5** ovate, ovoid **7** oviform

Eglah *husband:* 5 David *son:* **7** Ithream

eglantine 7 dog rose **10** sweetbriar, sweetbrier

Eglantine *father:* 5 Pepin *husband:* **9** Valentine

Eglon *king:* 5 Debir *slayer:* **4** Ehud

ego 4 self **5** pride **6** vanity **7** conceit **10** self-esteem

egocentric 7 selfish **9** conceited **10** self-loving **11** self-seeking **12** narcissistic, self-absorbed, self-affected, self-centered, self-involved, vainglorious **13** individualist, self-conceited, self-concerned, self-indulgent

egoism 5 pride **6** vanity **7** conceit **8** self-love **9** self-glory, self-pride, vainglory **10** narcissism, self-regard **11** selfishness, self-opinion

egoistic 4 smug, vain **7** selfish **9** conceited **12** self-absorbed, self-centered **13** self-concerned, self-contented, self-satisfied

egomaniacal 12 self-exalting, vainglorious

egotism 5 pride **6** vanity **7** conceit **8** boasting, bragging, self-love, vainness, vaunting **9** arrogance, pomposity, self-glory, self-pride, vainglory **10** narcissism, self-esteem **11** megalomania, self-opinion **12** boastfulness **13** conceitedness

egotistic 4 vain **5** cocky, proud **7** selfish, stuck-up **8** arrogant, boastful, inflated, puffed-up **9** conceited **11** pretentious, self-serving **12** self-absorbed, self-centered, self-involved **13** self-concerned, self-satisfied

egregious 4 rank **5** gross, stark **6** arrant, brazen **7** blatant, glaring, heinous **8** flagrant, infamous, outright, shocking **9** atrocious, notorious, shameless **10** deplorable, outrageous **11** conspicuous

egress, egression 4 door, exit 5 issue, leave 6 depart, escape, exodus, outlet 7 doorway, exiting, opening, passage 9 departure, emergence

egret 5 heron, wader

Egypt *ancient city:* 6 Thebes 7 Memphis *capital:* 5 Cairo *city:* 4 Giza 8 Port Said 10 Alexandria *dam:* 5 Aswan *desert:* 6 Libyan 7 Arabian, Western *gulf:* 4 Suez 5 Aqaba *lake:* 6 Nasser *language:* 6 Arabic *leader:* 5 Sadat (Anwar el-) 6 Nasser (Gamal Abdul) 7 Mubarak (Hosni) *monetary unit:* 5 pound *neighbor:* 5 Libya, Sudan 6 Israel *oasis:* 4 Siwa 6 Dakhla, Kharga 7 Farafra *peninsula:* 5 Sinai *river:* 4 Nile *sea:* 3 Red 13 Mediterranean

Egyptian *burial jar:* 7 canopic *Christian:* 4 Copt *cross:* 4 ankh *dynasty:* 5 Saite, Xoite 6 Hyksos, Tanite, Theban 7 Persian, Thinite 8 Memphite 9 Bubastite, Ethiopian 10 Diospolite *flower:* 5 lotus

god:
  chief: 6 Amen-Ra **crocodile-headed:** 5 Sebek **falcon-headed:** 4 Ment 5 Horus, Mentu 6 Sokari 7 Sokaris **ibis-headed:** 5 Thoth 6 Dhouti **jackal-headed:** 6 Anubis **of creation:** 4 Ptah 5 Phtha **of day:** 5 Horus **of death:** 6 Anubis **of earth:** 3 Geb, Keb, Seb **of evil:** 3 Set 4 Seth 5 Sebek **of life:** 4 Amen, Amon 5 Ammon **of magic:** 5 Thoth 6 Dhouti **of Memphis:** 4 Ptah 5 Phtha 6 Sokari 7 Sokaris **of the heavens:** 5 Horus **of the morning sun:** 5 Horus 7 Khepera **of the sun:** 4 Aten, Aton 5 Amen-Ra **of Thebes:** 4 Amen 6 Khensu, Khonsu **of the underworld:** 6 Osiris **of war;** 4 Ment 5 Mentu **of wisdom:** 5 Thoth 6 Dhouti **ram-headed:** 4 Amen, Amon 5 Ammon, Khnum 6 Khnemu **snake:** 4 Apep 5 Apepi

goddess:
  cat-headed: 4 Bast 5 Pakht **cow-headed:** 5 Athor 6 Hathor **lioness-headed:** 4 Bast 5 Pakht 6 Sekhet **of fertility:** 4 Isis **of love and mirth:** 5 Athor 6 Hathor **of motherhood:** 4 Apet, Isis **of Thebes:** 3 Mut **of the heavens:** 3 Nut **queen of the gods:** 4 Sati **vulture-headed:** 3 Mut 7 Nekhebt 8 Nekhebet *king:* (see **king** entry) *language:* 6 Arabic, Coptic *native:* 4 Arab, Copt 5 Nilot *queen:* 9 Cleopatra, Nefertiti *sacred bird:* 4 ibis 5 bennu *sacred bull:* 4 Apis *solar disk:* 4 Aten *sultan:* 7 Saladin *symbol of life:* 4 ankh *talisman:* 6 scarab *underworld:* 4 Aaru, Duat 6 Amenti *wind:* 7 khamsin, sirocco

eider 4 down, duck 7 sea duck

eidetic 5 exact, vivid 7 perfect, precise 8 absolute, lifelike

eidolon 4 icon 5 ghost, ideal, image, model, shade 6 mirage, vision, wraith 7 epitome, fantasm, figment, paragon, phantom, specter, spectre 8 exemplar, illusion, paradigm, phantasm 9 archetype, prototype 10 apparition

eight *combining form:* 4 octa, octo *group of:* 5 octad, octet 6 octave

eight bells 4 noon

eighteen-wheeler 3 rig 4 semi 11 semitrailer

eighth note 6 quaver

eighty-six 4 boot, junk, toss 5 chuck, eject, evict, scrap 6 bounce 7 discard, kick out 8 get rid of, jettison, throw out

Einstein, Albert *birthplace:* 3 Ulm *theory:* 10 relativity

einsteinium *symbol* 2 Es

Eire see Ireland

Eisenhower, Dwight 3 Ike *home:* 7 Abilene *wife:* 5 Mamie

eject 4 boot, bump, dump, fire, oust, sack, spew 5 chuck, evict, expel 6 banish, bounce 7 boot out, cast out, dismiss, kick out 8 disgorge, throw out 9 discharge

eke out 6 extend 7 augment, enhance, fill out, squeeze, stretch 8 increase 10 supplement

elaborate 4 busy 5 fancy, showy 6 daedal, dressy, evolve, expand, knotty, minute, ornate, refine, unfold 7 amplify, build up, careful, clarify, comment, complex, develop, discuss, elegant, enlarge, explain, expound, profuse, work out 8 detailed, involved, overdone, thorough 9 Byzantine, decorated, embellish, extensive, interpret, intricate 10 overworked 11 complicated, embellished, extravagant, painstaking 12 labyrinthine

Elaine *father:* 6 Pelles *lover:* 8 Lancelot 9 Launcelot *son:* 7 Galahad

Elam *capital:* 4 Susa 7 Shushan *father:* 4 Shem *king:* 12 Chedorlaomer

élan 3 pep, vim, zip 4 brio, dash, fire, life, zeal, zest, zing 5 ardor, flair, gusto, oomph, verve, vigor 6 energy, esprit, fervor, spirit 7 impetus 8 vivacity 9 animation, eagerness, intensity 10 enthusiasm

élan vital 4 soul 5 anima 6 animus, pneuma, psyche, spirit

elapse 4 go by, pass 6 expire, run out, slip by 8 pass away

elastic 6 bouncy, limber, pliant, rubber, supple 7 ductile, pliable, rubbery, springy 8 animated, flexible, moldable, stretchy, volatile 9 adaptable, expansive, malleable, resilient

10 extendable, extensible, rubber band, rubberlike **11** stretchable

elate 4 buoy **5** cheer, exalt, flush, set up **6** excite, perk up, uplift **7** cheer up, delight, enliven, gladden, gratify, hearten, inspire, overjoy **8** brighten, embolden, inspirit, spirit up **9** encourage **10** exhilarate, invigorate

elated 4 glad, high **5** happy **7** exalted, excited **8** ecstatic, euphoric, exultant, gladsome, jubilant **9** enraptured **10** enraptured **11** exhilarated, intoxicated, on cloud nine **12** high-spirited

elation 3 joy **4** glee **7** delight, ecstasy, rapture **8** buoyancy, euphoria **9** happiness, transport **10** exaltation, excitement, jubilation **12** exhilaration, intoxication

Elbe tributary 4 Eger, Iser, Ohre **5** Saale **6** Moldau, Vltava

elbow 4 push **5** joint, nudge, shove **6** hustle, jostle

eld 4 yore **6** old age **8** old times

elder 6 senior **8** old-timer **9** patriarch, presbyter **10** golden-ager

elderliness 3 age **6** dotage, old age **8** caducity **10** senescence **11** senectitude

elderly 3 old **4** aged, gray **5** aging, hoary **7** ancient **9** declining, venerable

eldritch 5 eerie, weird **6** creepy, spooky **7** uncanny

Eleanor's husband 7 Henry II **8** Franklin

elect 3 opt, tap **4** name, pick **5** co-opt, saved **6** choice, choose, chosen, decide, opt for, ordain, picked, vote in **7** resolve, vote for **8** destined, nominate, ordained, redeemed **9** delivered, designate, determine, exclusive, single out **10** designated, singled out

election 6 ballot, choice, voting **7** primary **8** choosing, decision **9** balloting **10** preference, referendum **11** alternative

electioneer 5 stump **7** canvass **8** campaign, politick **9** barnstorm

elective 6 chosen **8** optional **9** voluntary **11** sympathetic **13** discretionary, noncompulsory, nonobligatory

Electra brother: 7 Orestes **father: 9** Agamemnon **husband: 7** Pylades **mother: 12** Clytemnestra **sister: 9** Iphigenia **victim: 9** Aegisthus **12** Clytemnestra

electric appliance: 3 fan **4** iron, oven **5** clock, drier, dryer, mixer, range, stove **6** stereo, washer **7** blender, freezer, toaster **10** dishwasher, television **12** refrigerator **coil: 5** tesla **8** solenoid **device: 4** coil, fuse, plug **6** dynamo, magnet, switch **7** battery **8** resistor, rheostat, varistor **9** amplifier, capacitor, condenser, generator **11** transformer **gener-**

ator: 6 dynamo **particle: 3** ion **unit: 3** amp, ohm **4** volt, watt **5** farad, henry, joule **6** ampere **7** coulomb, faraday **8** kilowatt

electric current kind: 2 AC, DC **4** AC/DC **6** direct **11** alternating **power: 7** wattage **strength: 8** amperage

electricity 5 juice, spark **7** current **9** galvanism, lightning **kind: 6** static **7** current

electrify 3 jar **4** jolt, stun **5** amaze, power, shock **6** charge, excite, thrill **7** astound, enthuse, inflame, provoke, stagger, startle **8** astonish, energize

electrode 6 dynode **negative: 7** cathode **positive: 5** anode

electron 3 ion **7** polaron **stream: 10** cathode ray **tube: 6** triode **7** tetrode **8** dynatron, klystron

Electryon brother: 6 Mestor **daughter: 7** Alcmene **father: 7** Perseus **mother: 9** Andromeda **wife: 5** Anaxo

eleemosynary 6 humane **8** generous **10** altruistic, beneficent, benevolent, charitable, munificent, openhanded **12** humanitarian **13** philanthropic

elegance 4 chic, pomp, tone **5** charm, grace, style, taste **6** luxury, polish **7** culture, dignity **8** chicness, poshness, richness, splendor, urbanity **9** gentility, precision **10** ornateness, refinement **11** cultivation **12** tastefulness

elegant 4 chic, fine, posh **5** fancy, grand, noble, swank **6** choice, classy, dainty, lovely, modish, ornate, swanky, urbane **7** courtly, genteel, opulent, refined, stately, stylish **8** cultured, polished, splendid, tasteful **9** exquisite, luxurious, recherché, sumptuous **10** cultivated **11** fashionable

elegiac 7 pensive **8** dactylic **9** lamenting, sorrowful **10** melancholy

elegy 4 poem, song **5** dirge **6** lament, monody **8** threnody

_____ **eleison 5** Kyrie

Elektra composer 7 Strauss (Richard)

element 4 item, part **5** basic, facet, piece, point **6** aspect, detail, factor, member, sector **7** article, feature, portion, section **8** division, particle, rudiment **9** component, essential, principle **10** ingredient, particular **11** constituent, fundamental **chemical: 3** tin **4** gold, iron, lead, neon, zinc **5** argon, boron, radon, xenon **6** barium, carbon, cerium, cesium, cobalt, copper, curium, erbium, helium, indium, iodine, nickel, osmium, oxygen, radium, silver, sodium **7** arsenic, bismuth, bohrium, bromine, cadmium, calcium, dubnium, fermium, gallium, hafnium, hassium, holmium, iridium, krypton, lithium, mercury, niobium, rhenium, rhodium, silicon, sulphur, terbium, thorium, thulium, uranium, yttrium **8** actinium, aluminum, antimony, astatine, chlorine, chromium, europium, fluorine, hydrogen, illinium, lutecium, masurium, nitrogen, nobelium, platinum, polonium, rubidium, samarium, scandium, selenium, tantalum, thallium, titanium, tungsten, vanadium **9** americium, berkelium, beryllium, columbium, germanium, lanthanum, magnesium, manganese, neodymium, neptunium, palladium, plutonium, potassium, ruthenium, strontium, tellurium, virginium, ytterbium, zirconium **10** dysprosium, gadolinium, lawrencium, meitnerium, molybdenum, seaborgium **11** californium, einsteinium, mendelevium, phosphorous **12** darmstadtium, praseodymium **13** rutherfordium, protoactinium

elemental 3 key **4** pure **5** basal, basic, crude, prime **6** inborn, innate, primal, simple **7** central, connate, primary, radical **8** cardinal, inherent, integral, intimate, simplest **9** beginning, essential, ingrained, intrinsic, primitive **10** deep-seated, primordial, underlying **11** fundamental **13** uncomplicated

elementary 4 easy **5** basal, basic **6** simple **7** initial **9** beginning, essential, primitive **10** rudimental, underlying **11** fundamental, preliminary, rudimentary **12** introductory

elemi 9 resin **9** oleoresin

elephant 5 Babar **6** Horton, tusker **9** pachyderm *boy:* **4** Sabu *driver:* **6** mahout *enclosure:* **5** kraal *extinct:* **7** mammoth **8** mastodon *female:* **3** cow *group:* **4** herd *keeper:* **6** mahout *male:* **4** bull *maverick:* **5** rogue *nose:* **5** trunk **9** proboscis *seat:* **6** howdah *sound:* **6** bellow **7** trumpet *tooth:* **4** tusk *tusk:* **5** ivory *young:* **4** calf

elephant-headed god 6 Ganesa, Ganesh **7** Ganesha

elephantine 4 huge **6** clumsy **7** awkward, hulking, mammoth, massive **8** colossal, enormous, gigantic **9** graceless, humongous, monstrous, ponderous **10** gargantuan, mastodonic, prodigious, ungraceful **11** heavy-footed

Elephant Man 7 Merrick (Joseph)

elevate 4 lift, rear, rise **5** boost, elate, erect, exalt, hoist, raise **6** buoy up, jack up, lift up, pick up, uplift **7** advance, dignify, ennoble, glorify, hearten, improve, inspire, promote, upgrade **8** heighten **10** exhilarate

elevated 4 high **5** grand, lofty, moral, noble **6** aerial, formal, superb **7** ethical, refined, soaring, stately, sublime **8** eloquent, majestic, virtuous **9** dignified, grandiose, highflown, honorable, righteous

elevation 4 hill, rise **5** boost **6** ascent, height, uplift **7** advance, raising **8** altitude, mountain **9** acclivity, promotion, upgrading **10** apotheosis, preference, preferment **11** advancement, ennoblement *indication:* **9** benchmark

elevator 4 cage, lift, silo **5** hoist *maker:* **4** Otis

elf 5 fay, imp **4** peri, puck **5** fairy, gnome, pixie, troll **6** goblin, sprite **7** brownie, gremlin **10** leprechaun

elfin 5 antic **6** frisky, impish **7** implike, playful, puckish **8** pixieish **11** mischievous

Elgin _____ 7 Marbles

Eli 4 Yale **5** Yalie

Eli _____ 4 Yale **5** Lilly **7** Whitney

Elia 4 Lamb (Charles)

Eliab _brother:_ 5 David *daughter:* **7** Abihail *father:* **5** Helon, Pallu *son:* **6** Abiram, Dathan

Eliada _father:_ 5 David *son:* **5** Rezon

Eliam's daughter 9 Bathsheba

elicit 5 educe, evoke **6** derive, evince, extort **7** extract, provoke **8** bring out **9** call forth, draw forth

elide 4 fail, omit, skip **6** cut off, excise, forget, ignore, remove, slight **7** abridge, curtail, neglect **8** condense, cross out, discount, overlook, pass over, suppress **9** disregard, strike out

eligible 3 fit **6** fitted, likely, nubile, seemly, suited, worthy **7** capable **8** entitled, suitable **9** desirable, qualified **10** acceptable **11** appropriate **12** marriageable

Elihu _____ 4 Root, Yale

Elijah 5 Elias **7** prophet **8** Tishbite *father:* **5** Harim **7** Jeroham

Elimelech's wife 5 Naomi

eliminate 3 bar **4** bate, drop, oust, void **5** debar, egest, eject, erase, evict, expel, purge **6** delete, except, remove **7** abolish, discard, dismiss, exclude, expunge, obviate, rule out, take out **8** count out **9** clear away, eradicate, liquidate **11** exterminate

Eliot, George _lover:_ 5 Lewes (George Henry) *novel:* **6** Romola **8** Adam Bede **11** Middlemarch, Silas Marner **13** Daniel Deronda **14** Mill on the Floss (The) *pseudonym of:* **5** Evans (Mary Ann)

Eliot, T. S. _character:_ 8 Prufrock (J. Alfred) *play:* **13** Cocktail Party (The) **20** Murder in the Cathedral *poem:* **9** Gerontion, Hollow Men (The), Waste Land (The) **12** Ash Wednesday, Four Quartets

Eliphaz *father:* 4 Esau *mother:* 4 Adah *son:* 5 Teman

Elisabeth *husband:* 9 Zacharias *son:* 4 John (the Baptist)

Elisha *father:* 7 Shaphat *servant:* 6 Gehazi

Elisheba *brother:* 7 Nahshon *father:* 9 Amminadab *husband:* 5 Aaron *son:* 5 Abihu, Nadab 7 Eleazar, Ithamar

elite 3 top 4 best, pick 5 A-list, cream, elect, pride, prime, prize 6 choice, flower, gentry, select 7 quality, society 9 exclusive, gentility, patrician 10 upper class, upper crust 11 aristocracy 12 aristocratic

elixir 4 balm, cure 6 potion 7 arcanum, cureall, nostrum, panacea, philter, philtre 10 catholicon

Elizabeth I 6 Oriana 8 Gloriana

elk 4 deer 5 moose 6 sambar, wapiti 7 red deer

ell 3 arm 4 wing 5 annex, elbow, joint 8 addition 9 extension

ellipse 4 oval 5 curve, orbit

elliptical 5 brief, ovate, short 6 gnomic 7 concise, cryptic, laconic, obscure, summary 9 condensed, enigmatic 11 abbreviated

Ellison *work* 10 Juneteenth 12 Invisible Man

elm 5 wahoo

elocution 7 diction, oratory 8 delivery, rhetoric 11 declamation, speechcraft

elongate 4 draw 6 extend 7 draw out, lengthy, spin out, stretch 8 extended, lengthen 10 lengthened

elope 4 flee 6 escape, run off 7 abscond, run away 9 steal away

eloquence 5 force, power 6 fervor, spirit 7 fluency, oratory, passion 8 rhetoric 10 expression 12 expressivity, forcefulness

eloquent 5 lofty 6 ardent, fervid, fluent, moving 7 fervent, voluble 8 elevated, forceful, powerful, stirring 9 affecting 10 articulate, expressive, impressive, meaningful, passionate, persuasive, rhetorical 11 impassioned, sententious 12 smooth-spoken 13 silver-tongued

El Salvador *capital:* 11 San Salvador *city:* 8 Santa Ana 9 San Miguel *ethnic group:* 5 Pipil *lake:* 8 Ilopango *language:* 7 Spanish *monetary unit:* 5 colón 6 dollar *neighbor:* 8 Honduras 9 Guatemala *river:* 5 Lempa

else 5 if not 7 besides, further 9 otherwise 10 additional 11 differently 12 additionally

elucidate 7 clarify, clear up, explain, expound 8 annotate, spell out 9 exemplify, explicate, interpret 10 illuminate, illustrate

elude 4 defy, duck, flee, foil 5 avert, avoid, dodge, evade 6 baffle, escape, outwit, thwart 8 confound 9 frustrate 10 circumvent

elusive 6 subtle, tricky 7 evasive, phantom 8 baffling, fleeting, fugitive, slippery 10 evanescent, intangible, mysterious 13 insubstantial

elute 7 extract

elver 3 eel

elvish *see* **elfin**

Elysium 5 bliss 6 heaven 7 nirvana 8 empyrean, paradise

elytron 4 wing

emaciated 4 bony, lean, thin 5 gaunt 6 skinny, wasted 7 scrawny, starved, wizened 8 skeletal, underfed 10 cadaverous

emaciation 5 tabes 7 atrophy 8 marasmus 10 starvation 11 attenuation

e-mail abbreviation 3 AKA, BAK, BBL, BRB, BTW, FYI, HTH, IMO, IOW, KIT, LOL, NRN, OBO, POV, PDQ, TIA, UKW 4 ASAP, BCNU, BION, FWIW, GMTA, GTGB, IMHO, TTYL, YMMV

emanate 4 emit, flow, rise, stem 5 arise, exude, issue 6 derive, emerge, spring 7 come out, give off, give out, proceed, radiate 9 come forth, originate 10 derive from

emanation 4 aura, flow 6 efflux 8 effusion, emission 9 effluence

emancipate 4 free 5 let go, loose 6 loosen, redeem, unbind 7 manumit, release, set free, unchain 8 liberate, unfetter 9 discharge, unshackle 11 enfranchise

emancipation 7 release 10 liberation 11 deliverance

emancipator 5 Moses 7 Lincoln (Abraham) 9 deliverer, liberator

emasculate 3 fix 4 geld 5 alter, unman 6 neuter, soften, weaken 7 unnerve 8 castrate, enervate, unstring 10 debilitate, devitalize

embalm 7 mummify, perfume 8 preserve

embankment 4 berm, bund, dike, quay 5 levee, mound 6 escarp

embargo 3 ban, bar 5 edict, order 8 blockade, stoppage 10 impediment 11 prohibition

embark 5 board, enter, start 6 set out 7 set sail 8 commence

embarrass 4 faze 5 abash, upset 6 flurry, hamper, hinder, impede, rattle 7 confuse, flummox, fluster, mortify, nonplus, perturb 8 confound, distress 9 discomfit, humiliate 10 complicate, discomfort, discompose, disconcert

embarrassment 5 shame, upset 7 chagrin 8 distress 9 confusion 10 discomfort 11 humiliation 12 discomfiture, perturbation 13 mortification

embassy 5 envoy 7 mission 8 legation 10 ambassador, delegation, deputation

embay 4 trap 5 catch, seize 7 capture 8 encircle, surround

embed 3 fix, set 4 bury, root 5 infix, inlay, lodge 7 implant, ingrain 8 entrench

embellish 3 pad 4 deck, gild, trim 5 adorn, color 6 bedeck, blazon, emboss, enrich 7 amplify, dress up, enhance, festoon, garnish 8 beautify, decorate, ornament 9 elaborate, embroider 10 exaggerate 11 romanticize

embellishment 7 garnish, gilding, melisma, mordent 8 coloring, ornament 9 fioritura, floridity, hyperbole 10 decoration 11 elaboration 12 embroidering, exaggeration 13 ornamentation

ember 3 ash 4 coal 6 cinder

embezzle 4 loot 5 filch, steal 6 pilfer 7 purloin 8 peculate 9 defalcate

embitter 4 sour 6 poison 7 envenom 9 acidulate

emblazon 4 laud 5 extol 7 glorify 8 inscribe 9 celebrate

emblem 4 arms, flag, logo, mace, seal, sign 5 badge, brand, crest, image, token 6 banner, device, symbol 7 pennant 8 colophon, hallmark, insignia, monogram, standard 9 attribute, trademark 10 coat of arms

emblematic 8 symbolic 10 figurative, indicative 11 allegorical 12 illustrative, metaphorical

embodiment 6 avatar 7 epitome 8 exemplar 9 archetype 11 incarnation 13 manifestation

embody 5 reify 6 evince, mirror, typify 7 compose, contain, exhibit, realize, subsume 8 manifest 9 actualize, encompass, epitomize, exemplify, incarnate, integrate, objectify, personify, represent, symbolize 10 constitute, illustrate 11 emblematize, externalize, hypostatize, incorporate, materialize 12 substantiate

embolden 5 steel 7 fortify, hearten, inspire 8 inspirit 9 encourage 10 strengthen

embolus 4 clog, clot

embosom 3 hug 7 embrace, enclose, envelop, shelter

embouchure 10 mouthpiece

embowel 3 gut 4 draw 10 eviscerate, exenterate

embrace 3 hug 4 hold, lock, love, wrap 5 admit, adopt, clasp, cling, press 6 accept, cradle, cuddle, embody, enfold, fondle, nuzzle, take in, take on, take up 7 bear hug, cherish, contain, embosom, enclose, entwine, envelop, espouse, include, receive, snuggle, squeeze, subsume, welcome 8 comprise, encircle 9 encompass 10 comprehend 11 accommodate, incorporate 12 encirclement

embrangle see **embroil**

embrocation 5 salve 7 unguent 8 liniment

embroider 3 pad, sew, tat 4 gild 5 color 6 expand, overdo, play up, stitch 7 amplify, build up, enhance, garnish, magnify, stretch 8 decorate, ornament 9 dramatize, elaborate, embellish 10 exaggerate 11 hyperbolize, romanticize

embroidery 6 crewel 7 cutwork, orphrey 8 bargello, couching, smocking, tapestry 10 crewelwork, needlework 11 needlepoint

embroil 4 mire 6 tangle 7 confuse, ensnare, involve 8 disorder, entangle 9 implicate

embroilment 4 tiff 6 fracas 7 dispute, quarrel, wrangle 8 squabble 9 bickering 10 falling-out 11 altercation, controversy

embryo 3 bud 4 germ, seed 5 fetus, spark 7 nucleus 8 blastula, gastrula

emend 4 edit 5 alter, right 6 polish, revise 7 correct, improve, rectify, retouch

emerald 3 gem 5 beryl, green, stone 8 gemstone

Emerald Isle 4 Eire, Erin 7 Ireland

emerge 4 flow, loom, rise, stem 5 arise, issue 6 appear, derive, evolve, spring 7 come out, debouch, develop, emanate, proceed, surface 9 originate, transpire 11 come to light, materialize

emergency 3 fix 4 hole, pass 5 pinch 6 climax, clutch, crisis, crunch, strait 7 squeeze 8 accident, exigency

emeritus 7 retired

Emerson, Ralph Waldo essay: 12 Self-Reliance **forte:** 5 essay **friend:** 7 Thoreau (Henry David) **home:** 7 Concord

emery 6 powder 8 abrasive, corundum

emetic 8 vomitive 9 cathartic, purgative

émeute 4 riot 6 mutiny, revolt, rising, tumult 8 outbreak, upheaval, uprising 9 rebellion 12 insurrection

emigrant 7 pioneer, settler 8 colonist 10 expatriate

émigré 2 DP 5 alien, exile, expat 7 evacuee, migrant, refugee 8 colonist 10 expatriate

Emilia husband: 4 Iago 7 Palamon **slayer:** 4 Iago

eminence 3 VIP 4 fame, peak, rise 5 honor, power 6 bigwig, esteem, height, leader, renown, repute 7 dignity, notable 8 altitude, big-timer, luminary, prestige, standing 9 authority, dignitary, elevation, greatness, loftiness 10 importance, projection, prominence, promontory, reputation 11 distinction, superiority

eminent 4 high 5 famed, grand, great, large, lofty, noble, noted 6 august, famous 7 exalted, notable 8 esteemed, renowned, towering 9 important, well-known 10 celebrated, noteworthy, projecting **11** conspicuous, illustrious, outstanding, prestigious **13** distinguished

eminently 4 very **6** highly **7** notably **9** extremely **10** remarkably, strikingly **11** exceedingly **12** surpassingly **13** exceptionally

emir 5 chief, ruler, sheik, title **6** sheikh **9** chieftain, commander

emissary see **envoy**

emission 4 flow **7** venting **9** discharge, effluvium, emanation, radiation

emit 4 beam, glow, ooze, pour, shed, spew, vent, void **5** eject, expel, exude, issue, loose, utter **6** exhale, let out **7** emanate, excrete, extrude, give off, give out, radiate, release, secrete, send out **8** evacuate, throw off **9** circulate, discharge

emmer 5 grain, spelt, wheat

emmet 3 ant **7** pismire

emollient 4 aloe, balm **5** salve **7** lenient, unguent **8** aloe vera, lenitive, liniment, ointment, sedative, soothing **9** analgesic, softening **10** mollifying

emolument 3 fee, pay **4** wage **5** wages **6** income, reward, salary **7** guerdon, stipend **8** earnings **10** recompense **11** pay envelope **12** compensation

emotion 3 ire, joy **4** fear, glee, hate, love **5** agony, ardor, grief, shame **6** affect, hatred, relief, sorrow, warmth **7** ardency, despair, disgust, ecstasy, feeling, passion, sadness **8** jealousy, surprise **9** affection, agitation, happiness, sentiment

emotional 4 warm **6** ardent, fervid, heated, moving **7** feeling, fervent, intense, soulful, zealous **8** effusive, stirring, touching, vehement **9** affecting, affective, excitable, heartfelt, impetuous, rhapsodic, sensitive **10** hysterical, passionate **11** impassioned, overwrought, rhapsodical, softhearted, susceptible, sympathetic

emotionless 3 icy **4** cold, cool **5** chill, staid, stoic, stony **6** frigid, remote, torpid **7** callous, deadpan, distant, glacial **8** detached, reserved **9** apathetic, immovable, impassive, unfeeling **10** impersonal **11** cold-blooded, indifferent **12** matter-of-fact **13** dispassionate, unimpassioned

empathy 4 pity **6** lenity, warmth **7** rapport **8** affinity, sympathy **9** communion **10** compassion **12** congeniality **13** compatibility, comprehension, fellow feeling, understanding

emperor 4 czar, shah, tsar, tzar **5** ruler **6** caesar, kaiser **7** monarch **8** autocrat, dictator **9** potentate, sovereign *French:* **8** Napoleon (Bonaparte) **9** Bonaparte (Napoleon) **11**

Charlemagne *Indian:* **5** Babur *Japanese:* **6** mikado **7** Akihito **8** Hirohito *Mexican:* **8** Iturbide (Agustín de) **10** Maximilian *Roman:* **4** Nero, Otho **5** Galba, Nerva, Titus **6** Decius, Julian, Trajan **7** Gratian, Hadrian, Severus **8** Augustus, Aurelian, Caligula, Claudius, Commodus, Domitian, Honorius, Tiberius, Valerian **9** Antoninus, Caracalla, Justinian, Vespasian, Vitellius **10** Diocletian, Elagabalus **11** Constantine

emphasis 5 focus, force **6** accent, stress, weight **9** attention, intensity **10** insistence, prominence **12** accentuation

emphasize 6 accent, play up, stress **7** feature **8** pinpoint **9** highlight, italicize, spotlight, underline **10** accentuate, underscore

emphatic 4 firm **6** marked **7** decided, earnest, pointed **8** accented, decisive, forceful, positive, stressed, vigorous **9** assertive, energetic, insistent **10** resounding, underlined **11** accentuated

empire 5 realm **6** domain **7** demesne, kingdom **8** dominion *ancient:* (see **ancient empire**)

Empire State 7 New York

empirical 7 factual **9** fact-based, pragmatic **12** experiential, experimental **13** observational

emplacement 7 battery **8** position

employ 3 job, use **4** busy, hire, work **5** apply, avail **6** devote, engage, occupy, retain, secure, take on **7** exploit, utilize **8** exercise, practice **9** make use of **10** occupation

employee 4 hand, help **5** agent **6** worker **7** servant **8** factotum **9** underling *bank:* **5** clerk, guard **6** teller *hotel:* **7** bellboy, bellhop, doorman **9** concierge, desk clerk **11** chambermaid

employer 4 boss **6** master **10** supervisor

employment 3 job, use **4** line, post, task, toil, work **5** trade, usage **6** hiring, métier, office **7** calling, mission, purpose, pursuit **8** business, exercise, function, position, vocation **9** appliance, operation, situation **10** engagement, occupation **11** application, recruitment, utilization **12** exploitation

emporium 4 mall, mart, shop **5** store **6** bazaar, market **8** exchange **11** marketplace

empower 5 endow **6** charge, enable, invest **7** entitle, entrust, license **8** accredit, delegate, deputize, sanction **9** authorize, privilege **10** commission

empress 5 queen *Byzantine:* **3** Zoe *French:* **7** Eugénie **9** Josephine *Japanese:* **5** Suiko *of India:* **8** Victoria *Mexican:* **7** Carlota *Roman:* **6** Fausta *Russian:* **4** Anna **7** czarina, tsarina, tzarina **9** Alexandra, Catherine, Elizabeth

empressement 6 fervor, warmth **10** cordiality
emprise 4 feat, gest **5** geste **7** exploit, venture **9** adventure **11** undertaking
emptiness 4 void **5** blank **6** hunger, vacuum **7** inanity, vacancy, vacuity
emptor 5 buyer **6** vendee **8** consumer, customer **9** purchaser
____ **emptor 6** caveat
empty 3 rid **4** bare, dump, pour, vain, void **5** blank, clear, drain **6** barren, devoid, hollow, unload, vacant, vacate **7** deplete, drained, exhaust, vacated, vacuous **8** depleted, deserted, evacuate, forsaken **9** abandoned, destitute **10** unoccupied, untenanted *Scottish:* **4** toom
empty-headed 6 simple, vacant **7** vacuous, witless **8** ignorant, untaught **9** benighted, brainless, frivolous **10** illiterate, uneducated, unlettered, unschooled **11** know-nothing **12** uninstructed **13** rattlebrained
empyreal 4 airy, holy **6** aerial, divine **7** sublime **8** beatific, ethereal, heavenly **9** celestial, spiritual, unearthly **12** transcendent
empyrean 3 sky **4** Zion **5** bliss, ether **6** heaven, welkin **7** Elysium, heavens, nirvana **8** paradise **9** firmament
EMT's skill 3 CPR
emu 4 bird, rhea **6** ratite **9** cassowary
emulate 3 ape **4** copy **5** equal, mimic, rival **6** follow, mirror **7** compete, imitate **9** challenge
emulation 7 rivalry **8** striving, tug-of-war **9** imitation **10** contention **11** competition
emulous 5 vying **8** aspiring, striving, vaulting **9** ambitious **11** competitive
emulsifier 4 soap **5** algin
enable 3 fit, let **5** allow, ready **6** permit **7** empower, entitle, license, prepare, qualify **8** accredit, sanction **9** authorize, condition **10** commission, facilitate **12** make possible
enact 4 pass, play **6** decree, depict, effect, ordain, ratify **7** execute, perform, portray **8** proclaim **9** authorize, discourse, establish, institute, legislate, represent **10** accomplish, bring about, constitute, effectuate **11** impersonate
enactment 3 law **6** action, decree **7** statute **9** depiction, ordinance, portrayal **11** legislation, performance **12** ratification
enamel 5 glaze, gloss, japan, paint **7** lacquer
enamored 4 fond **6** loving **7** devoted, smitten **8** besotted **9** bewitched, enchanted, entranced, infatuate **10** captivated, infatuated
encamp 4 tent **6** settle **7** bivouac
encampment 6 billet, laager **7** bivouac, hutment

encase 3 box **4** pack **7** confine, enclose, envelop, sheathe
enceinte 6 gravid **8** pregnant **9** expectant, expecting **10** parturient
enchain 4 bind **6** fetter **7** manacle, shackle
enchant 3 hex **4** lure, wile **5** charm, spell, witch **6** allure, enamor, seduce, thrill, voodoo **7** attract, beguile, bewitch, delight **8** ensorcel, enthrall **9** captivate, enrapture, ensorcell, fascinate, hypnotize, magnetize, mesmerize, spellbind
enchanter 4 mage **5** magus **6** wizard **7** charmer, warlock **8** conjurer, conjuror, magician, sorcerer **11** necromancer, spellbinder
enchanting 5 siren **9** glamorous, seductive **10** attractive, delectable, delightful, intriguing
enchantment 3 hex **5** charm, magic, spell **6** allure **7** glamour, sorcery **8** witchery, wizardry **9** conjuring, seduction **10** necromancy, witchcraft **11** incantation
enchantress 3 hex **5** bruja, Circe, lamia, Medea, siren, witch **9** sorceress
enchiridion 4 text **5** guide **6** manual **8** Baedeker, handbook **9** guidebook, vade mecum
encipher 4 code
encircle 3 hem **4** band, gird, halo, hoop, ring **5** girth **6** begird, engird, enlace, girdle **7** compass, embrace, enclose, environ, wreathe **8** surround **9** encompass **12** circumscribe
enclave 6 colony, ghetto, sector **7** quarter **8** district, homeland
enclose 3 box, hem, mew, pen, rim **4** cage, coop, mure, wall, wrap **5** bound, fence, hedge, limit **6** circle, closet, corral, hold in, immure, shroud, shut in, wall in **7** compass, confine, contain, embosom, include **8** fence off, imprison, surround **9** capsulize **12** circumscribe
enclosed 6 obtect
enclosure 3 box, mew, pen, sty **4** boma, cage, camp, cell, coop, cote, fold, jail, pale, quad, SASE, tank, trap, wall, weir, yard **5** court, fence, kraal, pound, stall **6** aviary, corral, cowpen, kennel, paling, prison **7** chamber, enclave, paddock **8** cloister, stockade **9** courtyard **10** quadrangle
encomiast 7 praiser **8** eulogist **10** panegyrist
encomiastic 9 adulatory, laudative, laudatory **10** eulogistic **11** panegyrical
encomium 4 laud **5** kudos, paean **6** eulogy, homage, praise **7** acclaim, plaudit, tribute **8** accolade, citation, plaudits **9** laudation, panegyric **10** compliment, salutation **11** acclamation **12** commendation
encompass 3 hem **4** belt, gird, ring **5** bound

6 begird, circle, girdle, take in **7** contain, embrace, enclose, include, subsume **8** encircle, surround **10** accomplish, bring about, comprehend

encore 6 recall, repeat, return **10** repetition

encounter 4 face, find, fray, meet **5** brush, clash, fight, run-in, scrap, set-to **6** battle, engage, take on **7** collide, contest, meeting, quarrel, run into **8** argument, bump into, come upon, conflict, confront, meet with, skirmish, struggle **10** contention, experience

encourage 3 egg **4** abet, back, buoy, push, spur, stir, urge **5** boost, cheer, egg on, rally, rouse, serve, steel **6** assist, assure, buck up, excite, foster, incite, induce, praise, spur on **7** advance, animate, approve, bolster, cheer up, endorse, fortify, further, hearten, improve, inspire, promote, provoke, quicken, support, sustain **8** advocate, embolden, energize, inspirit, reassure, sanction **9** enhearten, galvanize, instigate, patronize, reinforce, stimulate, subsidize **10** invigorate, strengthen

encouragement 4 lift, push **5** boost **7** backing, support **8** approval **11** inspiration

encouraging 4 rosy **6** bright, likely **7** hopeful **9** favorable, promising **10** auspicious, propitious

encroach 5 poach **6** invade, meddle, trench **7** impinge, intrude **8** entrench, infringe, overstep, trespass

encrypt 4 code **6** cipher, encode **7** convert **8** disguise, encipher

encumber 4 lade, load **6** burden, charge, fetter, hamper, hinder, impede, saddle, weight **7** freight, oppress **8** handicap, obstruct, overload **9** weigh down **10** overburden

encumbrance 4 lien, load, onus **5** claim **6** burden **7** baggage **8** easement, handicap, mortgage **9** albatross, millstone **10** impediment

encyclical 6 letter **7** general **8** circular

encyclopedic 5 broad **7** general **8** complete, thorough **9** extensive, inclusive, universal **11** compendious, wide-ranging **12** all-embracing, all-inclusive **13** comprehensive

encyclopedist 7 Diderot (Denis)

end 3 aim, tip **4** coda, doom, goal, halt, quit, stop, tail, term **5** cease, close, death, finis, lapse, limit **6** demise, expire, finale, finish, object, period, result, scotch, windup, wrap up **7** abolish, closing, closure, extreme, lineman, outcome, purpose **8** complete, conclude, curtains, surcease, terminal, terminus **9** cessation, extremity, objective, terminate **10** completion, conclusion, denouement, expiration **11** culmination, discontinue, termination **12** consummation

endanger 4 risk **5** peril **6** expose **7** imperil **8** threaten **10** compromise, jeopardize

endearment *term:* **3** hon, pet **4** baby, dear, duck, lamb **5** bubby, bunny, honey, romeo, sugar **6** kitten, poopsy, poppet, sparky **7** darling, dearest, gumdrop, ladybug, lambkin, pumpkin, sweetie **8** cutie pie, doll-face, gorgeous, honey-bun, lady-love, lover-boy, precious, princess, pussycat, snookums, snuggles, sunshine, sweet pea, sweetums **9** angel-face, babycakes, buttercup, sugar-lips **10** heartthrob, honey bunch, honeychild, love-muffin, sweetheart, sweetie pie, tootsie pie

endeavor 3 aim, try **4** push, seek, toil, work **5** assay, essay, labor, trial **6** effort, intend, strain, strive **7** attempt, purpose, travail, venture **8** exertion, striving, struggle **9** determine, undertake **10** enterprise **11** undertaking

ended 4 done, over, past **7** through **8** complete

endemic 5 local **6** innate, native **8** homebred, inherent, primeval **9** homegrown, prevalent **10** aboriginal, indigenous, native-born

ending 4 stop **5** close **6** finale, finish, period, windup **7** closing, closure **8** terminus **9** cessation **10** completion, conclusion, denouement **11** termination

endive 7 lettuce, witloof **8** escarole

endless 7 eternal, undying **8** constant, enduring, immortal, infinite, unending **9** ceaseless, continual, incessant, limitless, perpetual, unbounded, unceasing, unlimited **10** continuous, indefinite, unmeasured **11** everlasting, illimitable, measureless **12** immeasurable, interminable

endmost 4 last **5** final **8** farthest, furthest, ultimate **10** concluding

endocrine gland 3 gonad, ovary **6** pineal, testis, thymus **7** adrenal, thyroid **8** pancreas **9** pituitary **11** parathyroid **12** hypothalamus

endomorphic 5 beefy, heavy, husky, plump, pudgy, stout **6** chubby, portly, pyknic, rotund

endorse 2 OK **4** back, okay, sign **5** bless, vouch **6** attest, ratify, second, uphold **7** approve, certify, command, confirm, stand by, support, witness **8** accredit, advocate, champion, inscribe, make over, notarize, sanction **9** autograph, recommend **10** underwrite **12** authenticate

endorsement 2 OK **4** okay **7** backing, support **8** approval, sanction, thumbs-up **9** signature **10** green light **12** confirmation, ratification **13** authorization

endow 4 back, fund **5** found **6** bestow, confer, enrich, supply **7** empower, enhance, finance, furnish, promote, provide, sponsor, support **8** bequeath **9** subsidize

endowment 4 fund, gift **5** award, dower, dowry, grant, power, skill **6** legacy, talent **7** ability, bequest **8** appanage, aptitude, bestowal, capacity, donation **11** benefaction

end product 5 fruit, issue **6** effect, payoff, result, upshot **7** outcome **11** consequence

endue 3 don **4** vest **5** dower, equip, imbue, put on **6** clothe, invest, outfit **7** furnish, provide **8** accouter **9** crown with, transfuse

endurance 4 grit, guts, wind **5** moxie, pluck **6** mettle **7** stamina **8** patience, strength, tenacity **9** fortitude **10** permanence, resolution **11** persistence **12** perseverance

endure 4 bear, bide, go on, last **5** abide, brook, stand **6** accept, hold on, linger, pocket, remain, suffer **7** carry on, persist, ride out, stomach, survive, sustain, swallow, undergo, weather **8** continue, submit to, tolerate, tough out **9** withstand

enduring 3 old **4** fast, firm, sure **6** steady **7** abiding, durable, eternal, lasting, staunch **8** constant, lifelong **9** long-lived, perennial, permanent, steadfast **10** continuing, inveterate, persistent **11** long-lasting, unfaltering **12** never-failing

Endymion *father:* **8** Aethlius *lover:* **5** Diana **6** Selene *author:* **5** Keats (John)

enemy 3 foe **5** rival **8** attacker, opponent **9** adversary, assailant **10** antagonist, competitor

energetic 4 spry **5** brisk, fresh, hardy, lusty, peppy, zippy **6** active, lively **7** driving, dynamic, vibrant **8** spirited, tireless, vigorous **9** sprightly, strenuous, vivacious **13** indefatigable

energize 3 pep **4** fuel, stir **5** liven, pep up, rouse, spark **6** enable, excite, stir up, turn on **7** empower, enliven, fortify, inspire, juice up **8** activate, inspirit, vitalize **9** electrify, galvanize, stimulate **10** invigorate, strengthen

energy 2 qi **3** chi, pep, vim, zip **4** dash, life, tuck **5** drive, force, juice, moxie, pluck, power, steam, verve, vigor **6** effort, muscle, spirit **7** current, potency, stamina, voltage **8** activity, dynamism, exertion, strength, vitality **9** animation, puissance **10** enterprise, get-up-and-go, initiative *unit:* **3** erg **4** dyne, volt **5** joule **7** quantum **10** horsepower

enervate 3 sap **4** jade, tire **5** weary **6** soften, weaken **7** disable, exhaust, fatigue, unnerve **8** enfeeble, unstring **10** debilitate, devitalize

enfant terrible 3 imp **5** scamp **6** bad boy, urchin **7** skeezix **9** skeezicks

enfeeble 3 sap **6** soften, weaken **7** deplete,

disable, exhaust, fatigue **8** enervate **9** attenuate, undermine **10** debilitate, devitalize

enfold 3 hug **4** wrap **5** clasp, cover, press **6** shroud, swathe **7** contain, embrace, squeeze **8** surround

enforce 5 exact, impel **6** compel, effect, impose, invoke, oblige **7** execute, fulfill **8** carry out **9** constrain, discharge, implement, prosecute **10** accomplish, administer, strengthen

enfranchise 4 free **6** rescue **7** deliver, manumit, release, set free **8** liberate **10** emancipate

engage 4 bind, grip, hire, mesh **5** fight, tie up, troth **6** absorb, attack, battle, commit, employ, enlist, pledge, take on **7** assault, betroth, engross, immerse, involve, promise **8** affiance, interact **9** captivate, encounter, interlace, interlock, intermesh, interplay, preoccupy, undertake

engaged 4 busy, rapt **6** intent **7** working **8** absorbed, employed, immersed, intended, occupied, plighted **9** affianced, betrothed, committed, engrossed, wrapped up **10** contracted **11** preoccupied *person:* **6** fiancé **7** fiancée

engage in 4 wage **5** enter **6** pursue, tackle, take up **7** conduct **8** embark on, practice **9** prosecute, undertake

engagement 3 gig **4** date, fray, word **5** fight, troth, tryst **6** action, battle, combat, hiring, pledge, plight **7** booking, meeting, promise **8** espousal, skirmish **9** betrothal, encounter **10** commitment, employment, rendezvous **11** appointment, assignation

engaging 7 likable, winning, winsome **8** charming, pleasant, pleasing **9** appealing **10** attractive **13** prepossessing

engender 4 sire, stir **5** beget, breed, cause, hatch, rouse, spawn **6** arouse, create, excite, father, induce, lead to, work up **7** develop, produce, provoke **8** generate **9** originate, procreate, stimulate

engine 5 motor, turbo **7** turbine **10** locomotive *fluid:* **7** coolant **10** antifreeze *kind:* **3** gas, jet **5** steam **6** diesel **7** turbine **8** gasoline **9** hydraulic *jet:* **8** turbofan, turbojet *part:* **3** cam, rod **4** gear, plug, pump **5** choke **6** filter, piston, tappet **8** cylinder, manifold, throttle **9** condenser, crankcase **10** carburetor **12** transmission *siege:* **3** ram **6** onager **8** ballista, catapult **9** trebuchet **12** battering ram *sound:* **4** chug, roar **6** rattle

engineer 4 plan, plot **5** set up, swing **6** devise, driver, manage, scheme, wangle **7** arrange, finagle **8** contrive, intrigue, maneuver, motorman **9** machinate, negoti-

ate **10** manipulate, mastermind **11** orchestrate *kind:* **5** civil **6** mining **8** chemical, sanitary **10** electrical, mechanical **12** aeronautical *military:* **6** sapper
engineers' group 4 ASME, IEEE
England 6 Albion **7** Britain **9** Britannia **12** Great Britain see also **United Kingdom**
English 7 British *cathedral city:* **3** Ely **4** York **5** Wells **6** Durham, Exeter **7** Lincoln, Norwich **8** Coventry, Hereford **9** Salisbury, Worcester **10** Canterbury, Winchester *coin:* **5** crown, groat, pence **6** florin, guinea **8** farthing, shilling, sixpence, twopence **9** fourpence, half crown, halfpenny, sovereign **10** threepence *combining form:* **5** Anglo *farm:* **5** croft *forest:* **5** Arden **8** Sherwood *letter:* **3** zed *measure:* **3** rod, tun **4** gill, hand, peck, span **5** chain **6** barrel, bushel, fathom, firkin **7** furlong **8** hogshead **10** barleycorn *military college:* **9** Sandhurst *patron saint:* **6** George *person:* **4** chap, mate **5** bloke **6** Briton *pirate:* **4** Kidd (Capt. William) **5** Avery (Henry), Teach (Edward) **6** Morgan (Henry) **7** Dampier (William) **10** Blackbeard *prince:* **5** Harry **6** Andrew, Edward, Philip **7** Charles, William *princess:* **4** Anne **5** Diana **8** Margaret *professor:* **3** don *royal family:* **5** Tudor **6** Stuart **7** Hanover, Windsor **11** Plantagenet *saint:* **7** Dunstan **8** Cuthbert *school:* **4** Eton **6** Harrow *spa:* **4** Bath *sport:* **5** darts, rugby **7** cricket *tavern:* **3** pub *university:* **5** Leeds **6** Oxford **9** Cambridge *weight:* **5** stone **6** firkin **7** quintal **8** quartern
English Channel *French:* **6** Manche (La) *swimmer:* **6** Ederle (Gertrude)
engrave 3 cut, fix **4** etch **5** carve, chase **6** incise, scrive **7** instill **8** inscribe
engraver 6 chaser, etcher *German:* **5** Dürer (Albrecht) **10** Schongauer (Martin) *Italian:* **8** Raimondi (Marcantonio)
engraving 7 etching, linecut, woodcut **8** drypoint, intaglio **9** xylograph
engross 4 bury, busy, copy, grip **5** apply, write **6** absorb, engage, indite, occupy, scribe **7** consume, immerse, involve **8** enthrall, inscribe **9** captivate, preoccupy **10** transcribe
engrossed 4 rapt **6** intent **7** engaged, riveted **8** absorbed, immersed **9** attentive **10** enraptured **11** preoccupied **12** concentrated
engrosser 6 scribe **7** copyist **9** scrivener **12** calligrapher **13** calligraphist
engulf 4 bury **5** drown, flood, swamp, whelm **6** deluge, devour **7** immerse, overrun, swallow **8** flow over, inundate, overflow, submerge **9** overwhelm, swallow up
enhance 4 lift **5** add to, adorn, exalt, raise **6**

deepen **7** amplify, augment, build up, elevate, enlarge, flatter, improve, magnify **8** beautify, heighten, increase **9** aggravate, embellish, embroider, intensify, reinforce **10** exaggerate, strengthen
enigma 4 crux, knot **5** poser, rebus **6** puzzle, riddle, sphinx, teaser **7** mystery, problem, puzzler **9** conundrum **10** closed book, perplexity, puzzlement **12** question mark **13** Chinese puzzle, mystification
enigmatic 6 mystic **7** cryptic, Delphic, obscure **8** Delphian, oracular, puzzling **9** ambiguous **10** mysterious, mystifying, perplexing **11** inscrutable
enisle 6 cut off **7** isolate **8** insulate, separate **9** segregate, sequester
enjoin 3 ban, bid **4** deny, rule, tell, urge, warn **5** order, taboo **6** adjure, charge, decree, direct, forbid, impose, outlaw **7** caution, command, counsel, dictate, inhibit **8** admonish, disallow, forewarn, instruct, prohibit **9** interdict, prescribe, proscribe
enjoy 4 like, love **5** eat up, fancy, savor **6** relish **9** delight in **10** appreciate
enjoyable 3 fun **8** pleasant, pleasing **9** agreeable **10** delightful, satisfying **11** pleasurable **12** entertaining
enjoyment 4 zest **5** gusto, savor **6** relish **7** benefit, delight **8** felicity, fruition, pleasure **9** diversion **10** indulgence, recreation, relaxation **11** delectation **12** satisfaction **13** gratification
Enki *consort:* **5** Nintu *son:* **6** Ninsar
enkindle 4 fire **5** flame, light **6** ignite **7** inflame **8** touch off **9** set fire to
enlarge 3 wax **4** grow, rise **5** add to, boost, build, mount, widen **6** beef up, dilate, expand, extend **7** amplify, augment, broaden, develop, greaten, inflate, magnify, stretch **8** heighten, increase, multiply **9** elaborate, embroider **10** exaggerate
enlargement 4 node **5** tumor **6** blowup, growth, nodule **7** buildup **8** addition, increase, swelling **9** accretion, expansion, extension **12** augmentation **13** amplification
enlighten 5 edify, guide, teach **6** advise, illume, inform, uplift **7** educate, improve **9** illumine, instruct **10** illuminate
enlist 4 join **5** draft, enter **6** employ, enroll, join up, muster, sign on, sign up **7** attract, recruit **8** register **9** volunteer **11** participate
enliven 3 pep **4** buoy, fire, warm **5** amuse, cheer, pep up, renew, rouse **6** excite, jazz up, perk up, vivify, wake up **7** animate, cheer up, inspire, quicken, refresh, restore, spice up **8** energize, recreate **9** entertain,

galvanize, stimulate **10** exhilarate, invigorate, rejuvenate

en masse 5 as one **6** bodily **8** together **12** collectively

enmesh 4 hook, mire, trap **5** catch, snare **6** draw in, tangle **7** embroil, ensnarl, involve, trammel **8** drag into, entangle **9** embrangle, implicate

enmity 4 hate **6** animus, hatred, rancor, spleen **7** ill will **8** aversion, bad blood, loathing **9** animosity, antipathy, hostility **10** abhorrence, antagonism **11** detestation

ennoble 5 exalt, honor, raise **6** uplift, uprear **7** dignify, elevate, glorify, magnify, sublime **10** aggrandize **11** distinguish

ennui 6 apathy, tedium **7** boredom, fatigue, languor **8** doldrums, dullness, lethargy **9** jadedness, lassitude, tiredness, weariness **11** languidness **12** listlessness

Enoch *father:* **4** Cain *son:* **10** Methuselah

Enoch Arden author 8 Tennyson (Alfred)

enormity 6 infamy **7** outrage **8** atrocity, hugeness, rankness, savagery, vastness **9** barbarity, depravity, flagrancy, graveness, greatness, grossness, immensity, magnitude **11** abomination, heinousness, massiveness, monstrosity, seriousness, weightiness

enormous 4 huge, vast **5** great **7** immense, mammoth, massive, titanic **8** colossal, gigantic **9** humongous, monstrous **10** astronomic, gargantuan, prodigious, stupendous, tremendous **12** astronomical

Enos *father:* **4** Seth *grandfather:* **4** Adam *grandmother:* **3** Eve *uncle:* **4** Abel, Cain

enough 5 ample **6** fairly, plenty **8** adequate, decently, passably **9** competent, tolerably **10** acceptably, adequately, sufficient **11** comfortable, sufficiency **12** satisfactory, sufficiently *poetic:* **4** enow

enounce 3 say **5** state, utter **6** intone **8** proclaim, set forth **10** articulate

enrage 3 ire **4** rile **5** anger **6** madden **7** incense, inflame, steam up **9** infuriate

enrapture 5 charm, elate **6** ravish, trance **7** delight, enchant, rejoice **8** enthrall, entrance **9** captivate, transport

enraptured 6 elated **7** charmed **8** ecstatic, thrilled **9** bewitched, delighted, enchanted, entranced **10** captivated, enthralled, mesmerized, spellbound **11** transported

enrich 5 adorn, endow **6** fatten **7** enhance, improve **8** beautify, ornament **9** embellish, fertilize **10** supplement

enroll 4 book, file, join, list **5** draft, enter **6** enlist, induct, join up, muster, record, sign on, sign up, wrap up **7** catalog, engross, recruit **8** inscribe, register **9** conscript, subscribe **10** transcribe **11** matriculate

ensconce 4 bury, hide **5** cache, cover, place, plant, stash **6** hole up, locate, settle **7** conceal, install, secrete, shelter **9** establish

ensemble 3 duo **4** band, crew, suit, trio **5** choir, combo, decor, group, octet, suite, troop, whole **6** chorus, outfit, septet, sextet, troupe **7** chorale, company, costume, en masse, quartet, quintet **8** together **9** aggregate, orchestra

enshrine 6 hallow, revere **7** cherish **8** dedicate, preserve, sanctify, treasure **10** consecrate **11** memorialize

enshroud 4 hide, veil, wrap **5** cloak **6** clothe, enfold, enwrap, invest **7** blanket, conceal, envelop, obscure

ensign 4 flag, jack, sign **5** badge, crest **6** banner, colors, emblem, pennon **7** officer, pennant **8** gonfalon, insignia, standard, streamer **9** oriflamme

enslave 4 yoke **5** chain **6** fetter, thrall **7** enchain, oppress, shackle, subject **8** dominate, enthrall **9** indenture, subjugate **12** disfranchise

enslavement 4 yoke **6** thrall **7** bondage, helotry, peonage, serfdom, slavery **9** servitude, thralldom

ensnare 3 bag, net **4** hook, lure, mesh, snag, trap **5** benet, catch, decoy **6** enmesh, entrap, tangle **7** capture **8** entangle, inveigle

ensnarl 4 mire **6** enmesh, tangle **7** embroil, perplex, trammel **8** entangle **9** embrangle

ensorcell 3 hex **5** charm, spell, witch **6** allure, voodoo **7** beguile, bewitch, enchant **8** enthrall **9** captivate, enrapture, hypnotize, magnetize, mesmerize, spellbind

ensorcellment 5 magic **7** sorcery **8** witchery, wizardry **9** conjuring **10** necromancy, witchcraft **11** bewitchment, enchantment

ensphere 4 ball **8** conglobe **10** conglobate

ensue 4 stem **5** issue **6** attend, derive, follow, result **7** emanate, proceed, succeed **9** supervene

ensuing 4 next **5** later **9** resultant **10** consequent, subsequent, succeeding

ensure 5 cinch **6** clinch, secure **7** certify, confirm, warrant **9** establish, guarantee

enswathe 4 roll, wrap **5** cloak, drape **6** bundle, enwrap, shroud, wrap up **7** envelop, swaddle

entail 5 imply **6** assign, confer, demand, impose, lead to **7** call for, involve, require **8** occasion, restrict, result in, transmit **11** necessitate

entangle 4 mesh, mire, trap **5** catch, ravel, snare, snarl, tie up, twist **6** enmesh, entrap **7**

capture, catch up, embroil, ensnare, ensnarl, involve, perplex, trammel **10** complicate, intertwine, interweave

entanglement 3 web **4** knot, mesh, mess, toil
5 skein, snare **6** affair, cobweb, muddle **8**
intrigue **9** confusion, imbroglio **11** embroilment, involvement **12** complication

entente 4 pact **6** league, treaty **7** compact **8**
alliance, covenant **9** agreement, coalition,
concordat **13** understanding

enter 4 go in, join, list, open **5** admit, begin,
key in, start **6** come in, enlist, enroll, go
into, insert, join up, muster, record, sign on,
sign up **7** intrude **8** come into, embark on,
inscribe, register **9** introduce, penetrate **10**
embark upon

enterprise 4 deed, feat, firm, push, task **5**
cause, drive, pluck, vigor **6** action, daring,
effort, energy, hustle, outfit, scheme **7** attempt, company, concern, courage, exploit,
project, pursuit, venture **8** activity, ambition, audacity, boldness, business, campaign, endeavor, gumption, industry **9**
adventure, eagerness **10** enthusiasm, get-
up-and-go, initiative **11** corporation, undertaking **12** organization, self-reliance **13**
establishment

enterprising 4 bold **5** eager **6** daring, hungry
7 driving, go-ahead **8** aspiring, hustling **9**
ambitious, audacious, energetic **10** aggressive **11** adventurous, hardworking, industrious, up-and-coming, venturesome

entertain 4 host **5** amuse **6** divert, regale **7**
delight, receive **8** consider

entertainer 4 mime **5** actor, clown, comic **6**
busker, dancer, jester, singer **7** actress, artiste, diseuse, trouper **8** comedian, minstrel
10 comedienne

entertaining 6 lively **7** amusing **8** engaging **9**
diverting, enjoyable

entertainment 4 fete, play, show, skit **5** revue,
sport **6** circus **7** banquet, concert, pastime,
ridotto **8** pleasure **9** amusement, diversion,
enjoyment **10** recreation **11** distraction, performance

enthrall 4 grip **5** charm **6** absorb, subdue **7**
beguile, bewitch, enchant, engross, enslave
9 fascinate, hypnotize, mesmerize, spellbind, subjugate

enthralling 8 exciting, gripping, riveting **9**
absorbing, arresting **10** enchanting, engrossing, entrancing **11** captivating, charismatic, provocative **12** spellbinding

enthuse 4 gush, rave **6** excite, thrill **7** animate, delight, inspire **8** energize **10** rhapsodize

enthusiasm 4 élan, fire, zeal, zest **5** ardor,
craze, fever, mania, verve **6** fervor, spirit **7**
ardency, passion, rapture **9** eagerness, intensity **10** ebullience, excitement, fanaticism

enthusiast 3 bug, fan, nut **4** buff **5** fiend,
freak, lover, maven **6** addict, junkie, maniac, votary, zealot **7** booster, devotee, fanatic, groupie, habitué **8** believer, partisan **9**
extremist **10** aficionado

enthusiastic 4 avid, gaga, keen **5** eager, rabid
6 ardent, fervid, gung ho, hearty, hipped,
rah-rah, raring **7** devoted, excited, fervent,
intense, zealous **8** hopped-up, obsessed,
spirited, vascular **9** fanatical **10** passionate

entice 4 bait, coax, draw, lure, toll, wile **5**
charm, decoy, tempt **6** allure, cajole, entrap,
invite, lead on, seduce **7** attract, wheedle **8**
inveigle, persuade

enticement 4 bait, lure, trap **5** decoy, snare **6**
allure, come-on **9** seduction **10** allurement,
attraction, seducement, temptation **12** blandishment, inveiglement

enticer 4 bait, vamp **5** Circe, decoy, siren **7**
Lorelei **9** attractor, temptress **10** attraction,
seductress **11** enchantress, femme fatale

enticing 5 siren **8** fetching, witching **9** seductive **10** attractive, bewitching, intriguing **11**
captivating, fascinating

entire 3 all **4** full **5** gross, total, whole **6** intact
7 perfect, plenary, unified **8** complete, integral, outright **10** integrated **12** consolidated
combining form: **3** hol, pan **4** holo

entirely 5 fully, quite **6** wholly **7** utterly **9**
perfectly **10** altogether, completely, thoroughly **11** exclusively

entirety 3 sum **5** total, whole **8** sum total, totality **9** aggregate, wholeness **10** everything
12 completeness, universality

entitle 3 dub, let **4** call, name, term **5** allow **6**
enable, permit **7** baptize, empower, license,
qualify **8** christen **9** authorize, designate **10**
denominate

entity 3 sum **4** body, item, unit **5** being, thing,
whole **6** object **7** article, integer **8** quiddity,
totality **9** existence, something, substance
10 individual

entomb 4 bury **5** inter, inurn **6** immure, inhume, shrine **7** mummify **8** enshrine **9** sepulcher, sepulchre

entombment 6 burial **7** funeral, obsequy **9**
obsequies, sepulture **10** inhumation

entourage 5 staff, suite, train **6** escort, milieu
7 cortege, coterie, retinue **8** henchmen **9**
courtiers, followers, following, hangers-on,
retainers **10** associates, attendants **12** surroundings

entr'acte 8 interval **9** interlude **12** intermission

entrails 4 guts **5** pluck, tripe **6** bowels, tripes, umbles, vitals **7** giblets, innards, insides, viscera **8** stuffing **10** intestines

entrance 4 adit, door, gate, port **5** charm, foyer, inlet, lobby, mouth **6** access, portal, ravish **7** arrival, attract, bewitch, delight, doorway, enchant, gateway, ingress, opening **8** aperture, enthrall, open door **9** admission, captivate, enrapture, fascinate, hypnotize, mesmerize, spellbind, threshold, transport, vestibule **10** admittance, ingression **11** penetration

entrant 7 starter **10** competitor, contestant **11** participant

entrap 3 bag, net **4** bait, lure, toll **5** catch, decoy, snare, tempt **6** allure, ambush, entice, entoil, lead on, seduce, tangle **7** beguile, catch up, ensnare **8** entangle, inveigle

entre _____ 4 nous

entreat 3 ask, beg, bid **4** pray, urge **5** crave, plead, press **6** adjure, appeal **7** beseech, implore, wheedle **8** blandish **9** importune **10** supplicate

entreaty 4 plea, suit **6** appeal, orison, prayer **7** request **8** petition **11** application, importunity **12** supplication

entrechat 4 leap

entrée 6 access **7** ingress **8** main dish **9** admission **10** admittance, main course

entrench 3 fix **4** root **5** embed, lodge **6** define, furrow, ground, hole up, invade, settle **7** confirm, impinge, implant, intrude **8** encroach, ensconce, infringe, trespass **9** establish **10** strengthen

entrenched 3 set **4** firm **5** rigid, sworn **8** accepted, deep-dyed **9** hard-shell **10** deep-rooted, deep-seated, inveterate **13** bred-in-the-bone, dyed-in-the-wool

entrepôt 3 hub **4** mart **5** depot **6** bazaar, market **8** emporium, exchange **9** concourse, warehouse **10** depository, storehouse **11** marketplace

entrepreneur 10 capitalist, contractor, impresario

entresol 9 mezzanine

entropy 5 chaos, decay **7** decline **8** disorder **10** randomness **11** degradation

entrust 4 give **5** allot, leave **6** assign, charge, commit, confer, impose **7** commend, confide, consign, deliver, deposit **8** allocate, delegate, hand over, relegate, turn over

entry 3 way **4** adit, door, gate, item, port **5** debit, foyer, inlet, lobby **6** access, credit, portal, record **7** doorway, ingress, opening **8** headword **9** admission, threshold, vesti-

bule **10** admittance, enlistment, enrollment, ingression

entryway 4 door, gate **5** foyer, lobby **6** portal **7** ingress, narthex, portico **9** vestibule

entwine 4 coil, wind **5** braid, plait, twist **6** enmesh **7** wreathe **8** entangle **9** interlace **10** interweave

enumerate 3 sum, tot **4** cite, list, tell, tote **5** add up, count, tally, total, tot up **6** detail, number, recite, reckon, tote up **7** compute, itemize, recount, specify, tick off **8** identify **9** calculate, inventory **13** particularize

enunciate 3 say **5** speak, state, utter, voice **6** affirm, intone **7** declare, express, lay down **8** announce, proclaim, propound, vocalize **9** formulate, postulate, pronounce, verbalize **10** articulate

envelop 3 hem **4** hide, roll, veil, wrap **5** cloak, cover, drape **6** cocoon, enfold, engulf, enwrap, invest, sheath, shield, shroud, swathe, wrap up **7** blanket, embrace, enclose, swaddle **8** encircle, enshroud, enswathe, surround **10** circumfuse

envelope abbreviation 4 ADSR, ATTN

envenom 6 poison **8** embitter **10** exacerbate

envious 7 jealous **8** coveting, covetous, grudging **9** green-eyed, invidious, resentful **10** begrudging

environment 6 medium, milieu **7** ambient, climate, context, habitat, setting, terrain **8** ambiance, ambience, backdrop **9** situation **10** atmosphere, background **11** mise-en-scène **12** surroundings *science:* **7** ecology

environmentalist 4 Gore (Al), Muir (John) **6** Brower (David), Carson (Rachel), Nelson (Gaylord), Wilson (Edward O.) **7** Ehrlich (Paul), Thoreau (Henry David) **8** Commoner (Barry), Cousteau (Jacques-Yves) **9** Burroughs (John), ecologist, Roosevelt (Theodore)

environs 4 nabe **6** bounds, limits **7** compass, fringes, suburbs **8** boundary, confines, locality, purlieus, vicinity **9** districts, outskirts, precincts **12** neighborhood, surroundings

envisage 4 view **5** dream, fancy, grasp, image, think **6** ideate, regard, vision **7** dream up, feature, foresee, imagine, picture, realize **8** conceive, look upon, summon up **9** conjure up, objectify, visualize

envoy 5 agent **6** bearer, consul, deputy, legate, nuncio **7** attaché, carrier, courier **8** diplomat, emissary, minister **9** messenger **10** ambassador **11** internuncio **12** intermediary

envy 5 covet **6** grudge **8** begrudge, grudging, jealousy **10** resentment **12** covetousness **13** invidiousness

enwrap 4 roll, veil **5** clasp, drape **6** enfold, invest, shroud, swathe **7** enclose, engross, envelop, sheathe, swaddle **8** enshroud, enswathe

enzyme 3 ase **5** ficin, lyase, renin, urase **6** kinase, ligase, lipase, mutase, papain, pepsin, rennin, urease, zymase **7** amidase, amylase, cyclase, enolase, guanase, hydrase, inulase, isozyme, lactase, maltase, oxidase, pectase, pepsine, plasmin, ptyalin, rennase, sucrase, trypsin, zymogen **8** aldolase, diastase, elastase, esterase, fumarase, lyzozyme, nuclease, protease, steapsin, thrombin, zymogene **9** cellulase, invertase

eon see **aeon**

Eos see **Aurora**

épée 5 blade, sword **6** rapier

epergne 5 stand **11** centerpiece

ephemeral 5 brief, short **7** passing **8** episodic, fleeting, fugitive, volatile **9** fugacious, momentary, temporary, transient **10** evanescent, short-lived, transitory **11** impermanent

Ephialtes 5 giant *brother:* **4** Otus *father:* **6** Aloeus **8** Poseidon *mother:* **9** Iphimedia *slayer:* **6** Apollo

Ephraim *brother:* **8** Manasseh *father:* **6** Joseph *grandfather:* **5** Jacob *mother:* **7** Asenath

epic 4 Edda, poem, saga **5** grand, Iliad **6** Aeneid, heroic **7** Beowulf, Odyssey **8** imposing, sweeping **9** Gilgamesh, narrative **12** Heimskringla

epicene 10 effeminate **11** intersexual **13** hermaphrodite

epicure 7 gourmet **8** aesthete, hedonist, sybarite **9** bon vivant **10** gastronome **11** connoisseur **12** gastronomist

epicurean 7 gourmet, sensual **8** aesthete, hedonist, sensuous, sybarite **9** bon vivant, luxurious **10** gastronome, voluptuous **11** connoisseur **12** gastronomist, sensualistic

epidemic 3 flu **4** rash, wave **6** plague **7** rampant, scourge **8** catching, outbreak **9** contagion, prevalent **10** contagious, pestilence

epidermis 4 skin **7** cuticle **10** integument

epigram 3 saw **4** poem **5** adage, axiom, maxim **6** bon mot, dictum, saying, truism **7** proverb **8** aphorism, apothegm

epigrammatic 5 meaty, pithy, terse, witty **6** cogent **7** compact, concise, marrowy, piquant, pointed

epigraph 5 motto **9** quotation **11** inscription

epilogue 4 coda **5** close **6** ending, finale, windup **7** closing **8** postlude **9** afterword **10** conclusion, postscript

Epimetheus *brother:* **10** Prometheus *father:* **7** Iapetus *wife:* **7** Pandora

epiphany 6 aperçu, vision **7** insight **9** discovery, intuition **10** appearance, disclosure, revelation **11** inspiration, realization **13** manifestation

episode 5 event, phase **7** passage **8** incident, occasion **9** happening, interlude **10** occurrence **12** circumstance

episodic 5 brief **7** passing **8** fleeting, sporadic **9** ephemeral, irregular, temporary, transient **10** evanescent, occasional, short-lived **12** intermittent

epistaxis 9 nosebleed

epistle 4 note **6** letter **7** lection, missive **13** communication

epitaph 3 R.I.P. **5** elegy **6** eulogy **8** hic jacet **11** inscription

epithet 4 name **5** label, title **7** agnomen, moniker **8** cognomen, nickname **9** sobriquet **11** appellation

epitome 3 sum **4** acme, type **5** brief, short **6** digest, précis, résumé **7** essence, example, outline, summary **8** abstract, breviary, exemplar, synopsis, ultimate **9** archetype, summation, summing-up **10** abridgment, apotheosis, conspectus, embodiment **11** abridgement **12** condensation, quintessence

epitomize 5 sum up **6** digest, embody, mirror, typify **7** abridge, outline, summate **8** abstract, boil down, condense, manifest, tabulate **9** capsulize, exemplify, incarnate, inventory, objectify, personify, represent, summarize, symbolize, synopsize **10** abbreviate, illustrate **11** concentrate, emblematize, incorporate, personalize

epoch 3 age, eon, era **4** aeon, term, time **6** period **8** interval, time span

equable 4 calm, even, just **6** serene, stable, steady **7** orderly, regular, stabile, uniform **8** composed, constant **9** immutable, temperate, unvarying **10** consistent, invariable, unchanging **12** unchangeable

equal 3 tie **4** even, fair, like, mate, peer, same, twin **5** agree, alike, match **7** uniform **8** alter ego, amount to, parallel **9** duplicate, identical, impartial, objective **10** fifty-fifty **11** counterpart, symmetrical **12** commensurate, correspond to, proportional **13** commensurable, proportionate *combining form:* **3** iso **4** equi, pari *French:* **4** égal

equality 3 par **6** equity, parity **7** balance, égalité **8** evenness, fairness, sameness **10** uniformity

Equality State 7 Wyoming

equalize 4 even **5** level **6** square **7** balance **9** harmonize

equalizer 3 gun **6** pistol **8** handicap **10** tying score

equally 10 fifty-fifty **11** impartially

equanimity 4 calm, cool **5** poise **6** aplomb, phlegm **7** balance **8** calmness, coolness, evenness, serenity **9** assurance, composure, equipoise, placidity, sangfroid **10** detachment, steadiness **11** tranquility **12** tranquillity

equate 4 even **5** liken, match, treat **6** adjust, regard, relate, square **7** compare **8** consider, equalize, parallel **10** assimilate

Equatorial Guinea *capital:* **6** Malabo *island, island group:* **5** Bioko **6** Elobey, Pagulu **7** Corisco *language:* **5** Bantu **6** French **7** Spanish *mainland:* **5** Mbini **7** Río Muni *monetary unit:* **5** franc *neighbor:* **5** Gabon **8** Cameroon

equestrian 5 rider **6** horsey **8** horseman, knightly **10** horsewoman

equidistant 3 mid **6** medial, median, middle, midway **7** central, halfway, midmost

equilibrium 5 poise **6** aplomb, stasis **7** balance **8** evenness, symmetry **9** composure, stability **10** steadiness **12** counterpoise **13** stabilization

equine 4 colt, mare **5** filly, horse, steed **6** horsey **8** stallion **9** horselike

equip 3 arm, fit, rig **5** array, dress, endow, rig up **6** attire, fit out, outfit, rig out, supply **7** appoint, furnish, prepare, provide **8** accouter, accoutre **9** provision

equipment 3 rig **4** gear **5** traps **6** attire, outfit, tackle, things **7** baggage, panoply **8** fittings, material, matériel, ordnance, supplies, tackling **9** apparatus, endowment, machinery, trappings **10** provisions **11** accessories, attachments, habiliments, impedimenta **12** accouterment, accoutrement, provisioning **13** accouterments, accoutrements, appurtenances, paraphernalia

equitable 4 even, fair, just **5** level **6** proper, square **7** condign **8** balanced, deserved, unbiased **9** identical, impartial, objective, uncolored **10** evenhanded, impersonal **12** unprejudiced **13** dispassionate

equity 3 law, par **7** justice **8** equality, interest, justness

equivalence 3 par **6** parity, simile **7** analogy **8** equality, identity, likeness, sameness **10** conformity **11** correlation

equivalent 4 akin, copy, like, peer, same, twin **5** alike, match **6** agnate **7** identic, similar **8** parallel **9** analogous, duplicate, identical **10** comparable, homologous, substitute, tantamount **11** convertible, correlative, counterpart **12** commensurate **13** corresponding, proportionate

equivocal 4 hazy **5** fishy, vague **6** unsure **7** clouded, dubious, obscure, suspect, unclear **8** doubtful **9** ambiguous, debatable, enigmatic, uncertain, undecided **10** ambivalent, indecisive, indistinct, irresolute, unresolved **11** problematic **12** disreputable, inconclusive, questionable **13** indeterminate

equivocate 3 fib, lie **5** cavil, dodge, evade, fudge, hedge **6** palter, waffle, weasel **7** shuffle **8** sidestep **9** pussyfoot **11** prevaricate **12** tergiversate

equivocation 3 fib **7** evasion, fibbing, hedging, sophism **8** waffling **9** ambiguity, casuistry, duplicity, sophistry **12** speciousness

equivoque 3 pun **8** wordplay

era 3 age, day, eon **4** aeon, date, term, time **5** epoch, stage **6** period

eradicate 4 dele, raze **5** abate, erase, purge **6** delete, efface, remove, uproot **7** abolish, blot out, destroy, expunge, root out, weed out, wipe out **8** demolish, stamp out **9** eliminate, extirpate, liquidate **10** annihilate, do away with, extinguish, obliterate **11** exterminate

erase 4 dele, void, x out **6** cancel, delete, efface, excise, remove, rub out **7** abolish, blot out, expunge, nullify, scratch, take out, wipe out **8** black out, blank out, cross off, cross out **9** eliminate, extirpate, sponge out, strike out **10** extinguish, obliterate

Erato see **Muse**

Erbin *father:* **9** Custennin *nephew:* **6** Arthur *son:* **7** Geraint

erbium symbol 2 Er

ere 6 before

Erebus *daughter:* **3** Day **6** Hemera *father:* **5** Chaos *home:* **5** Hades *sister, wife:* **3** Nox, Nyx *son:* **6** Aether, Charon

Erec et ____ 5 Enide

Erechteus *daughter:* **8** Chthonia *father:* **6** Vulcan **10** Hephaestus *mother:* **4** Gaea *slayer:* **4** Zeus **7** Jupiter

erect 4 form **5** build, put up, raise, set up **6** create, raised **7** build up, stand-up, upright **8** assemble, elevated, standing, straight, vertical **9** construct, establish **10** upstanding **13** perpendicular

eremite 6 hermit **7** ascetic, recluse, stylite **9** anchoress, anchorite

Erewhon 6 utopia **7** nowhere *author:* **6** Butler (Samuel)

ergo 4 then, thus **5** hence **9** therefore **11** accordingly **12** consequently

Erichthonius *father:* **8** Dardanus *son:* **4** Tros

Eridanus star 8 Achernar

Erin see **Ireland**

Erinyes 6 Alecto, Furies **7** Megaera **9** Eumenides, Tisiphone

Eris *brother:* 4 Ares, Mars *daughter:* 3 Ate *fruit:* 5 apple *goddess of:* 6 strife 7 discord *mother:* 3 Nox, Nyx

Eritrea *archipelago:* 6 Dahlak *capital:* 6 Asmara *island:* 5 Zuqar *language:* 8 Tigrinya *monetary unit:* 5 nakfa *neighbor:* 5 Sudan 8 Djibouti, Ethiopia *river:* 6 Baraka *sea:* 3 Red

ermine 3 fur 5 stoat 6 weasel

erode 3 eat, mar, rot, rub 4 rust, wear 5 decay, scour 6 abrade, rub off 7 consume, corrade, crumble, eat away, oxidize, rub away 8 wear away 9 scrape off 10 scrape away 11 deteriorate 12 disintegrate

Eroica composer 9 Beethoven (Ludwig van)

Eros see **Cupid**

erose 6 craggy, jagged, uneven 9 irregular

erotic 4 lewd, racy, sexy 5 bawdy, spicy 6 carnal, earthy, ribald, risqué 7 fleshly, obscene, profane, sensual 8 off-color, prurient, sensuous 9 salacious 10 voluptuous 11 aphrodisiac, titillating

err 3 sin 4 goof, slip, trip 5 lapse, stray 6 bollix, bungle, foul up, fumble, mess up, slip up 7 balls-up, blunder, deviate, screw up, stumble 8 trespass 10 transgress

errand 3 job 4 task 5 chore 7 mission 10 assignment

errand boy 4 page 5 gofer 7 bellboy, bellhop, courier 9 go-between

errant 5 stray 6 fickle, roving 7 aimless, deviant, erratic, naughty, ranging, roaming, wayward, willful 8 drifting, fallible, rambling, shifting, straying 9 deviating, itinerant, traveling, wandering 10 meandering, unreliable 11 mischievous

erratic 5 flaky 6 fitful, spotty 7 wayward 8 freakish, shifting, unstable, variable, volatile 9 arbitrary, desultory, eccentric, fluctuant, irregular, mercurial, spasmodic, uncertain, wandering, whimsical 10 capricious, changeable, inconstant, meandering 12 inconsistent 13 idiosyncratic, unpredictable

erring see **errant**

erroneous 3 off 4 awry 5 amiss, askew, false, wrong 6 untrue 7 unsound 8 mistaken, specious, spurious 9 defective, incorrect, misguided 10 fallacious, inaccurate, misleading

error 4 flub, goof, muff, slip, trip 5 boner, botch, fault, fluff, gaffe, lapse, snafu 6 booboo, bungle, fumble, howler, miscue, slipup 7 blooper, blunder, fallacy, falsity, faux pas, misdeed, misstep, mistake, screwup, stumble, untruth 8 delusion, illusion, screamer 9 falsehood, indecorum, oversight 10 inaccuracy, misreading 11 impropriety, misjudg-

ment *printing:* 4 typo 6 errata (plural) 7 erratum

ersatz 4 copy, fake, sham 5 bogus, dummy, faked, false, phony, pseud 6 phoney, pseudo 8 spurious 9 imitation, simulated, synthetic 10 artificial, factitious, simulacrum, substitute 11 counterfeit

Erse 5 Irish 6 Celtic, Gaelic

erstwhile 3 old 4 late, once, past 5 prior 6 before, bygone, former, whilom 7 already, earlier, onetime, quondam 8 formerly, previous 10 heretofore, previously

eruct 4 burp, emit, gush, spew 5 belch, eject, expel 7 explode 8 detonate, disgorge

erudite 7 bookish, learned 8 lettered, literate, studious, well-read 9 scholarly 10 scholastic

erudition 7 culture 8 learning, literacy 9 knowledge 11 bookishness, cultivation, learnedness, scholarship 12 studiousness 13 scholarliness

erupt 3 jet 4 spew 5 belch, burst, eject, expel, go off, spout, spurt 7 explode 8 break out, burst out, detonate 9 discharge 10 break forth, burst forth

eruption 4 gust, rush 5 blast, burst, flare, sally 6 access 7 flare-up 8 outbreak, outburst 9 commotion, explosion *skin:* 3 zit 4 rash 6 pimple

Esau *brother:* 5 Jacob *country:* 4 Edom *descendant:* 7 Edomite *father:* 5 Isaac *father-in-law:* 4 Elon *grandson:* 6 Amalek *mother:* 7 Rebecca, Rebekah *new name:* 4 Edom *son:* 5 Korha, Reuel 7 Eliphaz *wife:* 4 Adah 10 Aholibamah

escalade 5 climb, mount, scale 6 ascend 7 scaling

escalate 4 grow, rise, soar 5 boost, climb, mount, widen 6 expand, extend, spread, step up 7 amplify, augment, broaden, enlarge, inflate 8 heighten, increase, multiply 9 intensify 11 proliferate

escapade 4 lark, romp 5 antic, caper, fling, folly, prank, spree, stunt 6 frolic, vagary 7 roguery, rollick 8 mischief 9 adventure

escape 3 fly, lam 4 bolt, duck, flee, shun, skip, slip 5 avoid, break, dodge, elude, evade, shake 6 bypass, depart, eschew, flight, hegira, outlet 7 abscond, duck out, evasion, get away, make off, release, run away, skip out 8 breakout 9 avoidance, desertion, disappear, steal away 10 circumvent, liberation 11 deliverance, evasiveness *artist:* 7 Houdini (Harry) *narrow:* 9 close call 10 close shave

escargot 5 snail

escarole 6 endive

escarpment 5 bluff, cliff, slope

eschar 4 scab **5** crust **6** lesion

eschew 4 shun **5** avoid, elude, evade, forgo, spurn **6** abjure, forego, pass up, refuse, reject **7** decline **8** turn down

eschewal 7 elusion, evasion, refusal **8** shunning, spurning **9** avoidance, rejection

escort 4 beau, date, lead, show **5** guard, guide, pilot, steer, usher **6** attend, convoy, direct, gigolo, squire **7** company, conduct, consort, retinue **8** cavalier, chaperon, henchman, shepherd **9** accompany, bodyguard, chaperone, companion, entourage, safeguard **13** accompaniment

escritoire 4 desk **9** secretary **11** writing desk

escrow 4 bond, deed, fund **7** deposit

esculent 6 edible **7** eatable **10** comestible, digestible

escutcheon 6 flange, shield

Eshcol *ally:* **7** Abraham *brother:* **4** Aner **5** Mamre

esker 2 os **4** kame **5** mound, ridge

Eskimo 4 Inuk **5** Aleut, Inuit *boat:* **5** kayak, umiak *boot:* **6** mukluk *dog:* **5** husky **8** malamute, malemute *dwelling:* **5** igloo *outer garment:* **5** parka **6** anorak *sledge:* **7** komatik

esophagus 6 gullet

esoteric 5 inner **6** arcane, mystic, occult, orphic, secret **7** cryptic, private **8** abstruse, hermetic, profound **9** recondite **10** cabalistic, mysterious **12** confidential

ESP 9 telepathy **10** sixth sense **12** clairvoyance, precognition

espadrille 4 shoe **6** sandal

espalier 7 lattice, railing, trellis

esparto 5 grass

especial 4 main **5** close **7** express, notable, unusual **8** dominant, intimate, peculiar, singular, specific, uncommon **9** paramount **10** individual, particular **11** exceptional

especially 7 notably **8** markedly **9** expressly, primarily, unusually **10** peculiarly, remarkably, singularly **11** principally **12** particularly, specifically **13** distinctively, exceptionally

espial 6 notice **9** detection, discovery **11** observation

espionage 6 spying **9** sleuthing **12** surveillance

espousal 5 troth, union **6** mating **7** embrace, support, wedding **8** adoption, advocacy, approval, ceremony, marriage **9** betrothal, embracing, matrimony, promotion **10** acceptance

espouse 3 wed **4** back **5** adopt, marry **6** accept, take on, take up **7** approve, embrace, support **8** advocate

esprit 3 vim, wit **4** brio, dash, élan, zest, zing **5** oomph, verve, vigor **6** fervor, gaiety, mettle, morale, spirit **7** courage, loyalty, panache, passion, sparkle **8** devotion, vibrancy, vitality **9** animation **10** brightness, enthusiasm, fellowship **11** camaraderie

esprit de corps see **morale**

espy 3 see **4** mark, spot **5** sight **6** descry, detect, notice **7** discern, make out **9** recognize

____ es Salaam 3 Dar

essay 3 try **4** seek, test **5** labor, paper, piece, study, theme, tract, trial **6** effort, strive, thesis **7** article, attempt, venture **8** endeavor, treatise **9** undertake **10** discussion, exposition **11** composition, undertaking **12** dissertation

essayist *American:* **4** Agee (James), Will (George) **5** Baker (Russell), Cooke (Alistair), Gould (Stephen Jay), White (E. B.) **6** Brooks (Cleanth), Fisher (M. F. K.), Holmes (Oliver Wendell), Lowell (James Russell), Sontag (Susan), Thomas (Lewis) **7** Buckley (William F.), Cousins (Norman), Emerson (Ralph Waldo), Mencken (Henry Louis), Thoreau (Henry David) **8** Benchley (Robert), Lippmann (Walter), Repplier (Agnes) **10** Crèvecoeur (Jean de) *English:* **4** Elia, Lamb (Charles) **5** Bacon (Francis), Cecil (Lord David), Pater (Walter), Smith (Sydney) **6** Arnold (Matthew), Cowley (Abraham), Morris (Jan), Ruskin (John), Steele (Richard) **7** Addison (Joseph), Hazlitt (William) **8** Beerbohm (Max) **9** De Quincey (Thomas) **12** Chesterfield (Lord) *French:* **9** Montaigne (Michel de) *Scottish:* **7** Carlyle (Thomas)

essence 3 nub **4** base, core, crux, gist, odor, pith, root, soul **5** attar, basis, being, fiber, fibre, point, stuff **6** center, entity, kernel, marrow, nature, spirit **7** extract, perfume, quality **9** substance **10** distillate **12** distillation, significance

essential 4 main, must, need **5** basal, basic, chief, prime, vital **6** inborn, inbred, innate, primal **7** connate, crucial, element, primary **8** cardinal, foremost, inherent, required, rudiment **9** condition, elemental, intrinsic, necessary, necessity, principal, requisite, substance **10** congenital, deep-seated, elementary, idiopathic, imperative, sine qua non, underlying **11** fundamental, requirement **12** precondition, prerequisite **13** indispensable, part and parcel

essentially 6 almost, au fond, really **7** largely **8** actually, as good as, as much as, wellnigh **9** basically, virtually **11** practically **13** fundamentally, substantially

essonite 6 garnet 13 cinnamon stone

establish 3 fix, lay, put, set 4 base, form, root, show 5 build, enact, endow, erect, found, place, prove, set up, start 6 attest, create, decree, effect, ground, impose, secure, settle, verify 7 build up, certify, clarify, confirm, find out, implant, install, instill, provide, set down 8 document, ensconce, organize 9 authorize, construct, determine, formulate, institute, legislate, originate, prescribe 10 bring about, constitute, inaugurate 11 corroborate, demonstrate 12 authenticate, substantiate

establishment 4 firm 6 outfit 7 company, concern 8 business, old guard 9 institute, workplace 10 enterprise, foundation 11 institution, ruling class

estate 4 farm, land 5 manor, ranch, villa 6 domain, legacy, quinta 7 demesne 8 dominion, hacienda, property 10 plantation *agent:* 7 Realtor *feudal:* 4 fief 7 fiefdom *first:* 6 clergy *fourth:* 5 press *manager:* 7 steward 8 executor, guardian *second:* 6 nobles 8 nobility *third:* 7 commons

esteem 4 deem 5 favor, honor, prize, think, value 6 admire, liking, regard, revere 7 account, believe, cherish, idolize, respect, worship 8 approval, consider, treasure, venerate 9 valuation 10 admiration, appreciate 12 appreciation 13 consideration

ester 6 oleate 7 acetate 8 compound 9 phosphate

Esther *cousin:* 8 Mordecai *enemy:* 5 Haman *father:* 7 Abihail *festival:* 5 Purim *Hebrew name:* 8 Hadassah *husband:* 6 Xerxes 9 Ahasuerus

estimable 5 noble 6 august, valued, worthy 7 admired 8 laudable, sterling 9 admirable, deserving, honorable, reputable, respected, venerable 10 creditable 11 commendable, meritorious, respectable 12 praiseworthy

estimate 3 put 4 call, rank, rate 5 assay, gauge, guess, infer, judge, price, set at, value 6 assess, deduce, figure, rating, reckon, survey 7 imagine, opinion, project, suppose, surmise 8 appraise, conclude, discover, evaluate, forecast, judgment, round off 9 appraisal, calculate, determine, reckoning, valuation 10 assessment, conjecture, evaluation, impression, projection 11 approximate, calculation, measurement

estimation 4 fame 5 favor, honor, stock 6 esteem, regard 7 account, opinion, respect 8 figuring, judgment 9 appraisal, reckoning, valuation 10 admiration, assessment, evaluation, impression 11 calculation 13 consideration

Estonia *capital:* 7 Tallinn *city:* 5 Tartu *gulf:* 4 Riga 7 Finland *inhabitant:* 4 Balt *island:* 4 Muhu 6 Vormsi 7 Hiiumaa 8 Saaremaa *lake:* 5 Pskov 6 Peipus 9 Vorts-Jarv *monetary unit:* 5 kroon *neighbor:* 6 Latvia, Russia *river:* 5 Narva, Pärnu 6 Kasari *sea:* 6 Baltic

estop 3 bar 6 enjoin, forbid 7 prevent 8 disallow, preclude, prohibit, restrain

estrange 4 part 5 split 7 break up, divorce 8 alienate, disunite, separate 9 disaffect

estrangement 4 rift 5 split 6 breach, schism 7 breakup, cooling, divorce, rupture 8 disunity, division 10 alienation, falling-out, withdrawal 12 disaffection

estuary 5 firth, frith, mouth 10 tidal river

esurient 4 avid 6 greedy, hungry 8 covetous, grasping, ravening, ravenous 9 rapacious, voracious 10 avaricious, gluttonous 11 acquisitive

étagère 7 cabinet, whatnot

Etats-____ 4 Unis

etch 3 cut 5 carve, stamp 6 depict, incise 7 engrave, impress, imprint, portray 8 inscribe 9 delineate, represent

etcher *American:* 7 Pennell (Joseph) 8 Whistler (James McNeil) *Dutch:* 9 Rembrandt (van Rijn) *French:* 5 Redon (Odilon) 6 Villon (Jacques) *Italian:* 8 Piranesi (Giambattista) *Spanish:* 6 Ribera (José) *Swiss:* 4 Zorn (Anders)

Eteocles *brother:* 9 Polynices 10 Polyneices *father:* 7 Oedipus *mother:* 7 Jocasta *slayer:* 9 Polynices 10 Polyneices

eternal 7 abiding, ageless, endless, lasting, undying 8 constant, enduring, immortal, infinite, timeless, unending 9 ceaseless, continual, deathless, immutable, incessant, permanent, perpetual, unceasing 10 immemorial, unchanging 11 amaranthine, everlasting, illimitable, inalterable, never-ending, unalterable, unremitting 12 imperishable, interminable

Eternal City 4 Rome

eternally 3 e'er 4 ever 6 always 7 forever 8 evermore, for keeps 11 forevermore, in perpetuum 12 in perpetuity

eternity 3 age, eon 4 aeon 7 dog's age 8 blue moon, coon's age, infinity 9 afterlife 10 infinitude, perpetuity 11 endlessness, immortality 12 infiniteness, timelessness

Etesian 4 wind 6 annual

Ethan ____ 5 Allen, Brand, Frome

Ethbaal's daughter 7 Jezebel

ether 3 air, gas, sky 6 heaven 7 heavens 8 airwaves, empyrean 10 anesthetic, atmosphere

ethereal 4 aery, airy 5 filmy, light 6 aerial 7

fragile 8 delicate, empyreal, empyrean, gossamer, heavenly, rarefied, vaporous **9** celestial, spiritual, unearthly, unworldly **10** immaterial, intangible **13** unsubstantial

ethical 4 good **5** moral, noble **6** decent **7** upright, virtual **8** elevated, virtuous **9** righteous **10** principled, upstanding **11** right-minded **13** conscientious

ethics 5 mores **6** morals, values **8** morality **9** moral code, standards **10** principles

Ethiopia battle site: 5 Adowa **biblical name: 4** Cush **capital: 10** Addis Ababa **city: 6** Gonder **8** Dire Dawa **desert: 4** Haud **7** Danakil **emperor: 7** Menelik, Menilek **8** Selassie **9** Ras Tafari **13** Haile Selassie **former name: 9** Abyssinia **language: 5** Oromo **7** Amharic **monetary unit: 4** birr **mountain: 9** Ras Dashen **neighbor: 5** Kenya, Sudan **7** Eritrea, Somalia **8** Djibouti **region: 5** Tigre **6** Ogaden, Tigray **7** Danakil **river: 4** Abay **5** Awash **6** Tekeze **8** Blue Nile

ethnic 6 racial, tribal **8** minority

etiolate 4 fade, pale **6** bleach, weaken **7** lighten, wash out **8** enfeeble

etiquette 4 code, form **5** mores **7** conduct, customs, decency, decorum, manners **8** behavior, protocol **9** amenities, propriety **10** civilities, convention, deportment, seemliness **11** conventions, formalities, proprieties

Etruscan city, town: 4 Roma, Veii **5** Caere, Vulci **6** Arezzo **7** Clusium, Felsina, Perugia **8** Volsinii **9** Florentia, Tarquinia, Vetulonia **deity: 3** Tin, Tiv, Uni **4** Turm, Usil **5** Tinia, Turan, Turms **6** Menfra, Menrva, Nethun, Trithn **7** Velchan **8** Sethlans, Voltumna **king: 7** Porsena, Tarquin **10** Tarquinius **11** Lars Porsena **kingdom: 7** Etruria

étude 5 study **8** exercise **11** composition

etui 4 case

etymology 11 word history

etymon 4 root **5** radix **6** source **8** morpheme

eucalyptus eater 5 koala

Eucharist container: 3 pyx **plate: 5** paten **service: 4** Mass **9** Communion **vessel: 8** ciborium **wafer: 4** host **8** viaticum

Euclid subject: 8 geometry **work: 8** Elements

____ Eulenspiegel 4 Till, Tyll

eulogistic 9 adulatory, laudative, laudatory **11** encomiastic, panegyrical **12** commendatory **13** complimentary

eulogize 4 hymn, laud **5** cry up, exalt, extol **6** praise **7** acclaim, applaud, commend, glorify, magnify **9** celebrate **10** panegyrize

eulogy 5 paean **6** praise **7** oration, tribute **8** accolade, citation, encomium **9** laudation, panegyric **10** salutation **12** commendation **13** glorification

Eumenides see **Erinyes**

eunuch 7 gelding **8** castrate, castrato

euphony 7 harmony **8** lyricism **9** sweetness **10** consonance

euphoria 3 joy **4** glee **5** bliss **7** ecstasy, elation, rapture **9** transport **10** exaltation, jubilation **11** high spirits **12** exhilaration, intoxication

Euphrosyne see **Graces**

euphuistic 5 fancy, tumid **6** florid, ornate, prolix, purple, turgid **7** elegant, flowery, fustian, orotund, verbose **8** colorful, elevated, inflated, sonorous **9** bombastic, elaborate, high-flown, overblown **10** figurative, flamboyant, rhetorical **11** highfalutin, overwrought **12** magniloquent **13** grandiloquent

eureka 3 aha

Euridice's husband 7 Orpheus

Euripides play 3 Ion **5** Helen, Medea **6** Hecuba **7** Bacchae (The), Cyclops, Electra, Orestes **8** Alcestis **10** Andromache, Hippolytus, Suppliants (The) **11** Trojan Women (The)

Europa brother: 6 Cadmus **father: 6** Agenor **7** Phoenix **husband: 8** Asterius **son: 5** Minos **8** Sarpedon

Europe 9 continent **country: 4** Eire **5** Italy, Malta, Spain **6** Cyprus, France, Greece, Latvia, Monaco, Norway, Poland, Russia, Serbia, Sweden, Turkey **7** Albania, Andorra, Armenia, Austria, Belarus, Belgium, Croatia, Denmark, Estonia, Finland, Georgia, Germany, Hungary, Iceland, Ireland, Moldova, Romania, Rumania, Ukraine **8** Bulgaria, Portugal, Slovakia, Slovenia **9** Lithuania, Macedonia, San Marino **10** Azerbaijan, Luxembourg, Montenegro **11** Netherlands, Switzerland, Vatican City **13** Czech Republic, Liechtenstein, United Kingdom **ethnic group: 4** Celt, Finn, Lapp, Lett, Pole, Serb, Sorb, Turk, Wend **5** Croat, Czech, Dutch, Greek, Gypsy, Irish, Latin, Swede, Swiss, Welsh **6** Basque, Celtic, French, German, Magyar, Polish, Scotch, Slovak **7** Bosnian, Catalan, English, Finnish, Fleming, Italian, Lettish, Maltese, Russian, Slovene, Spanish, Swedish, Walloon **8** Albanian, Andorran, Armenian, Croatian, Romanian **9** Belarusan, Bulgarian, Hungarian, Ukrainian **10** Belarusian, Macedonian, Monegasque, Phoenician **11** Belarussian **12** Byelorussian, Scandinavian **language: 4** Lapp **5** Czech, Dutch, Greek, Irish, Latin, Welsh **6** Basque, Breton, Danish, French, Gaelic, German, Magyar, Polish, Slovak **7** Catalan, English, Finnish, Flemish, Italian, Maltese, Romansh, Russian, Serbian, Slovene, Spanish, Swedish, Turkish, Wendish **8** Albanian, Croatian, Lusatian, Romanian, Rumanian **9** Bulgarian, Hungarian, Icelandic, Norwegian **10** Macedonian, Portuguese **13** Serbo-Croatian *mountain range:* **4** Alps **8** Pyrenees **11** Carpathians

European Union member 5 Italy, Malta, Spain **6** Cyprus, France, Greece, Latvia, Poland, Sweden **7** Austria, Belgium, Denmark, Estonia, Finland, Germany, Hungary, Ireland, Romania, Rumania **8** Bulgaria, Portugal, Slovakia, Slovenia **9** Lithuania **10** Luxembourg **11** Netherlands **13** Czech Republic, United Kingdom

europium symbol 2 Eu

Euryale see **Gorgon**

Eurytus *daughter:* **4** Iole *slayer:* **8** Hercules

Euterpe see **Muse**

evacuate 4 exit, void **5** clear, empty, expel, leave **6** decamp, depart, remove, vacate **7** abandon, excrete, exhaust, pull out, retreat **8** clear out, pull back, withdraw **9** eliminate

evacuee 2 DP **6** émigré **7** refugee **8** fugitive

evade 4 duck, flee, foil **5** avoid, dodge, elude, hedge, parry, shirk, skirt **6** baffle, bypass, escape, eschew, outwit, thwart, weasel **7** shuffle **8** sidestep, slip away **9** pussyfoot, turn aside **10** circumvent, equivocate **11** prevaricate **12** tergiversate

evaluate 4 rank, rate **5** assay, class, gauge, grade, set at, weigh **6** assess, figure, reckon, size up, survey **7** eyeball **8** appraise, classify, estimate **9** calculate, criticize

evaluation 6 rating **7** judging, opinion **8** estimate, judgment **9** appraisal **10** assessment **12** appreciation

Evander *father:* **6** Hermes **7** Mercury *mother:* **8** Carmenta **9** Carmentis *son:* **6** Pallas

evanesce 4 fade **5** clear **6** vanish **7** scatter **8** disperse, dissolve, melt away **9** disappear, dissipate, evaporate **13** dematerialize

evanescent 7 fading **7** elusive, melting, passing **8** fleeting, fugitive, volatile **9** ephemeral, fugacious, momentary, transient, vanishing **10** dissolving, short-lived, transitory **12** disappearing

evangelical 6 ardent, fervid **7** fanatic, fervent, zealous **8** militant **9** crusading **10** missionary **13** proselytizing

Evangeline *author:* **10** Longfellow (Henry Wadsworth) *beloved:* **7** Gabriel *home:* **6** Acadia

evangelist 4 John, Luke, Mark **5** Moody (Dwight) **6** Bakker (Jim, Tammy Faye), Dobson (James), Graham (Billy, Franklin), Sunday (Billy), Warren (Rick), Wesley (John) **7** apostle, Edwards (Jonathan), Fal-

well (Jerry), Matthew, Roberts (Oral) **8** Schuller (Robert), Swaggart (Jimmy) **9** McPherson (Aimee Semple), missioner, Robertson (Pat) **10** colporteur, missionary, revivalist, Whitefield (George)

evangelistic 9 crusading, reforming **10** missionary, revivalist **13** proselytizing

evangelize 6 preach **7** convert **9** sermonize

evaporate 4 fade, melt **5** clear **6** vanish **8** diminish, disperse, dissolve, evanesce, melt away, vaporize **9** disappear, dissipate

evasion 5 dodge, fudge **6** escape, excuse **7** dodging, elusion, fudging **8** escaping **9** avoidance **13** circumvention

evasive 3 sly **5** cagey, dodgy, vague **6** shifty **7** elusive **8** slippery **9** ambiguous, equivocal

Eve *home:* **4** Eden *husband:* **4** Adam *son:* **4** Abel, Cain, Seth *temptation:* **5** apple, fruit

even 3 tie **4** fair, flat, just, same, tied **5** align, equal, exact, flush, grade, level, plane, still, truly **6** as well, equate, smooth, square, stable, steady **7** balance, equable, flatten, uniform **8** balanced, constant, equalize, smoothen, straight **9** equitable, expressly, identical, precisely, unvarying **10** absolutely, comparable, consistent, continuous, fifty-fifty, unchanging **13** fair and square, proportionate

evening 4 dusk **6** soiree, sunset, vesper **7** sundown **8** gloaming, twilight **9** nightfall *French:* **4** soir *Italian:* **4** sera *service:* **7** vespers *star:* **5** Venus **6** Vesper **8** Hesperus

evenness 6 equity, parity **7** balance **8** equality **9** stability **10** equanimity, uniformity **11** consistency, equilibrium

event 3 act **4** case, deed, fact, feat, meet **5** issue, match **6** action, affair, chance, effect, result, upshot **7** contest, episode, outcome, product **8** accident, function, incident, occasion **9** aftermath, happening **10** occurrence, phenomenon **11** achievement, competition, consequence, eventuality **12** circumstance, happenstance

eventful 4 busy **6** lively **9** important, momentous

eventual 4 last **5** final **6** ending **7** closing, endmost, ensuing **8** terminal, ultimate **9** resulting **10** concluding, consequent, inevitable, succeeding

eventuality 4 case **6** effect, result **7** outcome **11** consequence, contingency, possibility

eventually 6 at last, in time, one day **7** finally, someday **8** sometime **9** hereafter **10** ultimately **13** sooner or later

eventuate 5 ensue, occur **6** befall, follow, happen, result **9** come about, take place

ever 4 once **5** at all **6** always **7** forever **9** at

any time, eternally, regularly **10** constantly, invariably **11** perpetually **12** consistently, continuously *poetic:* **3** e'er
evergreen 3 fir, ivy, yew **4** ilex, pine, tree **5** cedar, holly, savin **6** laurel, myrtle, spruce **7** conifer, cypress, hemlock, juniper, lasting, redwood, sequoia, undying **8** magnolia, mangrove, timeless, unfading **9** mistletoe, perennial **10** arborvitae **12** rhododendron
Evergreen State 10 Washington
everlasting 7 abiding, endless, eternal, forever, lasting, undying **8** constant, immortal, infinite, termless, timeless, unending **9** boundless, ceaseless, continual, deathless, limitless, permanent, perpetual, unceasing **10** continuous, perdurable **11** amaranthine, never-ending, unremitting **12** imperishable
evermore 6 always **7** for good **8** for keeps **9** eternally **12** in perpetuity
every 3 all **4** each *prefix:* **3** pan
everybody 3 all **4** each
everyday 5 banal, plain, usual **6** common, normal **7** mundane, prosaic, routine **8** familiar, habitual, ordinary **9** customary, quotidian **11** commonplace **12** conventional, run-of-the-mill, unremarkable
everything 3 all *French:* **4** tout *German:* **5** alles *Spanish:* **4** todo
everywhere 7 all over, overall **8** all round, wherever **9** all around **10** far and near, far and wide, high and low, throughout
evict 3 out **4** boot, oust **5** eject, expel **6** bounce, put out **7** boot out, dismiss, extrude, kick out **8** dislodge, force out, throw out **10** dispossess
evidence 4 clue, mark, show, sign **5** goods, proof, prove **6** attest, evince, expose, reveal **7** confirm, display, exhibit, symptom, testify, witness **8** indicate **9** testament, testimony **10** indication, smoking gun **11** attestation, demonstrate, testimonial **12** confirmation **13** documentation
evident 5 clear, overt, plain **6** marked, patent **7** obvious, visible **8** apparent, distinct, manifest, palpable, tangible **9** prominent **10** noticeable, pronounced **11** conspicuous, perceptible, unambiguous
evidently 9 outwardly, seemingly **10** officially, ostensibly
evil 3 bad, sin **4** foul, vice, vile **5** black **6** infamy, malice, sinful, wicked **7** badness, baleful, baneful, devilry, hateful, heinous, malefic, satanic, vicious **8** damnable, iniquity, satanism, villainy **9** atrocious, diablerie, diabolism, execrable, loathsome, malicious, malignant, nefarious **10** flagitious, iniquitous, maleficent, malevolent,

pernicious, sinfulness, wickedness **11** maleficence *combining form:* **3** mal
evildoer 6 sinner **7** villain **8** criminal **9** miscreant **10** malefactor
evil spirit 3 imp **5** demon, devil, fiend, Satan **6** daemon
evince 4 mark, show **5** educe, evoke, prove **6** attest, betray, elicit, expose, reveal **7** bespeak, betoken, confirm, display, exhibit, signify **8** evidence, indicate, manifest, proclaim **10** illustrate **11** demonstrate
eviscerate 3 gut **4** draw **5** bowel **7** embowel **8** protrude **10** disembowel, exenterate
evocative 6 moving **8** redolent, stirring **9** affecting, emotional, nostalgic **10** expressive, meaningful, suggestive **11** stimulating
evoke 4 cite, stir **5** educe, raise, waken **6** arouse, awaken, call up, elicit, evince, excite, induce, recall **7** conjure **8** recreate, summon up **9** call forth, conjure up, stimulate **11** summon forth
evolution 6 change, growth **8** progress, upgrowth **9** flowering, phylogeny, unfolding **10** biogenesis, maturation **11** development, progression
evolve 4 grow **5** educe, ripen **6** change, derive, emerge, mature, open up, unfold **7** advance, develop, work out **8** progress **9** elaborate
ewe 5 sheep
ewer 3 jug **4** olpe, vase **7** pitcher
ex 4 from, past **5** out of, prior **6** former **7** earlier, without **9** erstwhile
exacerbate 6 worsen **7** envenom, inflame, provoke **8** embitter, heighten **9** aggravate, intensify
exact 4 levy, true **5** claim, force, gouge, pinch, screw, wrest, wring **6** coerce, compel, dead-on, demand, extort, spot-on, strict **7** correct, extract, literal, precise, require, solicit, squeeze **8** accurate, rigorous, selfsame **9** identical, postulate, shake down **10** meticulous, scrupulous **11** painstaking, punctilious, requisition
exacting 5 fussy, rigid, stern, tough **6** severe, strict, taxing, trying **7** exigent, finicky, onerous **8** critical, rigorous **9** demanding, stringent **10** fastidious, nitpicking, particular, scrupulous **11** persnickety **13** hypercritical
exactitude 5 rigor **8** accuracy **9** precision **10** definitude **11** correctness, preciseness **12** definiteness
exactly 4 bang, just **5** quite, right, sharp, spang **6** bang on, square, to a tee, wholly **7** totally, utterly **8** entirely, on the dot, smackdab, squarely **9** on the nose, precisely **10** absolutely, accurately, altogether, completely, positively **12** specifically

exaggerate 6 overdo 7 amplify, enlarge, inflate, magnify, overact, romance 8 overdraw, overrate 9 embellish, embroider, overstate 11 hyperbolize 13 overemphasize

exaggeration 8 travesty 9 hyperbole 10 caricature, stretching 11 enlargement, overdrawing 12 embroidering 13 embellishment, overstatement

exalt 4 fete, laud, lift 5 boost, elate, extol, honor, raise 6 praise, uplift 7 acclaim, adulate, build up, dignify, elevate, enhance, ennoble, glorify, inspire, magnify, promote 8 eulogize, heighten, inspirit 9 intensify 10 aggrandize 11 apotheosize

exaltation 3 joy 5 bliss, glory 6 homage, praise 7 delight, ecstasy, elation, rapture, tribute 8 euphoria, rhapsody 9 panegyric, transport, uplifting 10 apotheosis, jubilation 11 deification 12 exhilaration, intoxication 13 glorification

exalted 4 high 5 grand, lofty, noble 6 august 7 eminent, highest, sublime 9 venerable 11 high-ranking, illustrious, outstanding, prestigious

examination 4 oral, quiz, scan, test 5 assay, final, probe, trial 6 review, survey 7 canvass, checkup, hearing, inquest, inquiry, perusal, sifting, testing 8 analysis, scrutiny 9 breakdown, check-over, diagnosis 10 dissection, inspection 11 inquisition 13 catechization, investigation, perlustration *kind:* 3 bar 4 oral 5 final 7 medical, midterm 8 physical *of accounts:* 5 audit *of a corpse:* 7 autopsy 10 postmortem

examine 3 con, vet 4 pump, quiz, scan, sift, test 5 audit, check, grill, probe, query, study 6 go over, look at, peruse, survey 7 canvass, check up, inquire, inspect, observe 8 check out, look into, look over, question 9 catechize, check over 10 scrutinize 11 interrogate, investigate

examiner 6 censor 7 auditor, coroner 9 inspector 10 inquisitor, prosecutor 12 investigator

example 4 case 5 ideal, model 7 paragon, pattern 8 instance, paradigm, specimen, standard 9 archetype, precedent, prototype 11 case history 12 illustration

exanimate 4 dead 5 inert 8 lifeless, listless, sluggish, stagnant 9 lethargic 10 spiritless

exasperate 3 irk, vex 4 gall, rile, roil 5 anger, annoy, peeve, pique, upset 6 enrage, madden, nettle, rankle 7 agitate, incense, inflame, provoke 8 irritate 9 aggravate, infuriate

exasperation 8 vexation 9 annoyance 10 irritation 11 aggravation

ex cathedra 8 official 9 ex officio 13 authoritative

excavate 3 dig 4 grub 5 scoop, spade 6 dig out, dredge, expose, hollow, quarry, shovel 7 unearth 8 gouge out, scoop out 9 hollow out, scrape out

excavation 3 dig, pit 4 hole, mine 5 ditch, stope 6 dugout, hollow, quarry, trench, trough

exceed 3 cap, top 4 beat, best, pass 5 break, excel, outdo 6 better, outrun, overdo 7 eclipse, outpace, overrun, surpass 8 go beyond, outreach, outshine, outstrip, outweigh, overstep, overtake 9 overreach, transcend

exceedingly 4 very 6 hugely, vastly 7 awfully, notably, vitally 9 extremely 10 remarkably, strikingly 12 surpassingly 13 exceptionally *prefix:* 5 ultra

excel 3 cap, top 4 beat, best, pass 5 outdo, shine 6 better, exceed, outrun, overdo 7 eclipse, outpace, overrun, surpass 8 go beyond, outclass, outreach, outshine, outstrip, outweigh, overstep, overtake 9 overreach, transcend

excellence 5 class, merit, value, worth 6 virtue 7 quality 8 fineness 9 greatness 10 perfection 11 distinction, superiority

excellent 3 top 4 A-one, boss, fine 5 bully, model, neato, prime 6 bang-up, banner, famous, Grade A, superb, tip-top, worthy 7 capital, premium, supreme 8 champion, five-star, splendid, stunning, superior, terrific, top-notch 9 classical, exemplary, first-rate, high-class, high-grade, marvelous, number one, top-drawer, wonderful 10 blue-ribbon, first-class 11 exceptional, magnificent, meritorious, sensational, superlative, unsurpassed 12 incomparable

except 3 bar, but, yet 4 omit, only, save 6 beside, exempt, object, reject, unless 7 barring, besides, exclude, however, outside, rule out, suspend 8 pass over 9 apart from, aside from, eliminate, excluding, outside of 11 exclusive of

exception 5 demur 7 anomaly, dissent 8 question 9 allowance, deviation, exclusion, objection 10 aberration

exceptionable 8 unwanted 9 unwelcome 10 unsuitable 11 regrettable, undesirable 12 unacceptable 13 objectionable

exceptional 4 rare 6 scarce, unique 7 notable, special, unusual 8 abnormal, atypical, distinct, singular, superior, uncommon, unwonted 9 anomalous, excellent, marvelous, wonderful 10 infrequent, noteworthy, phenomenal, remarkable 11 outstanding, uncustomary 13 extraordinary

exceptionally 4 very **6** hugely **7** notably **9** extremely **10** especially, remarkably, strikingly **11** exceedingly **12** particularly, stupendously

excerpt 4 cite, clip, cull, pick **5** glean, quote **6** choose, sample, select **7** extract, passage, pick out, portion, snippet **8** fragment **9** quotation

excess 3 fat **4** glut, rest **5** extra, flood, spare, waste **7** nimiety, overage, surfeit, surplus **8** leavings, leftover, overflow, overkill, overmuch **9** indulgent, overstock, redundant, remainder **10** oversupply, surplusage **11** dissipation, prodigality, superfluity, superfluous, unessential **12** extravagance, immoderation, intemperance **13** overabundance, supernumerary

excessive 4 over **5** dizzy, steep, super, undue **6** dc trop, too-too **7** extreme, sky-high **8** overmuch, prodigal **10** exorbitant, immoderate, inordinate, profligate **11** extravagant, intemperate, overweening, superfluous **12** supernatural, unrestrained

excessively 3 too **6** overly, unduly **8** overmuch *prefix:* **5** hyper

exchange 4 swap, swop **5** bandy, trade, truck **6** barter, market, switch **7** bargain, commute, convert, pay back, replace, traffic **8** displace **9** transpose **10** conversion, substitute **11** reciprocate

exchangerate premium 4 agio

exchequer 5 funds **8** treasury

excise 3 fee, tax **4** toll **5** elide, slash **6** cut out, delete, remove, resect **9** expurgate, extirpate, strike out, surcharge

excision 3 cut **7** removal, surgery **8** deletion **9** resection **11** extirpation

excitable 4 rash **8** volatile **9** impetuous **10** high-strung

excite 4 fire, goad, move, spur, stir **5** elate, evoke, key up, pique, prime, rouse, waken **6** appeal, arouse, elicit, fire up, induce, kindle, stir up, thrill, turn on **7** agitate, animate, commove, inflame, inspire, provoke, quicken **8** activate, charge up, energize, motivate **9** galvanize, impassion, innervate, stimulate **10** exhilarate

excited 3 hot **4** avid **5** eager **6** aflame **7** fevered **8** aflutter, worked up **10** passionate **12** enthusiastic

excitement 3 ado **4** buzz, stir, to-do **5** fever, furor **6** flurry, frenzy, furore, hubbub, thrill **7** turmoil **8** delirium, hysteria **9** agitation, commotion **10** enthusiasm, hullabaloo **11** disturbance, pandemonium **12** exhilaration

exclaim 4 blat, bolt **5** blurt **6** cry out **8** blurt out, burst out **9** ejaculate

exclamation 2 ha, hi, ho, lo **3** aah, aha, bah, boo, cry, eek, feh, fie, gee, hah, hey, huh, oho, ooh, pah, tsk, tut, ugh, wow **4** ahem, alas, amen, damn, dang, darn, drat, egad, gosh, heck, hell, oops, ouch, phew, pish, posh, rats, whew, yell **5** alack, bravo, faugh, golly, humph, pshaw, shout **6** clamor, hurrah, indeed, outcry, phooey, shucks **7** doggone, gee whiz, hosanna, jeepers, whoopee **9** expletive **10** hallelujah **12** interjection *of disappointment:* **4** damn, darn, rats *of disapproval:* **3** tsk **6** tsk-tsk *of discovery:* **3** aha **6** eureka *of disgust:* **3** bah, boo, feh, fie, ugh **4** yech, yuck **5** faugh, yecch **6** phooey *of dismay:* **4** oh no, uh-oh **5** yikes *of enthusiasm:* **4** whee **5** wahoo **7** whoopie *of fear:* **3** eek *of pain:* **2** ow **4** ouch *of relief:* **4** phew *of sorrow:* **3** woe **4** alas **5** alack *of surprise:* **2** ah, oh **3** wow **4** gosh **5** golly *of triumph:* **3** aha, hah **5** yahoo **6** eureka (see also **interjection)**

exclude 3 ban, bar **4** oust **5** block, debar **6** banish, disbar, reject **7** keep out, lock out, obviate, prevent, rule out, shut out, suspend **8** count out, preclude, prohibit **9** blackball, blacklist, eliminate, ostracize

excluding 3 bar, but **4** less, save **6** except **7** barring, besides **9** apart from, aside from, other than, outside of

exclusion 3 bar **6** ouster **7** barring, lockout, removal **8** ejection, eviction, omission **9** blackball, expulsion, ostracism **10** banishment **12** blackballing, nonadmission

exclusive 4 lone, only, sole **5** elect, elite, prime, scoop, smart, swank, swish **6** choice, chosen, picked, select, single **7** cliquey, high-hat, stylish **8** clannish, cliquish, selected, snobbish **9** preferred, undivided **10** privileged **11** fashionable, prohibitive, restrictive **12** aristocratic, concentrated, preferential

exclusively 4 only **5** alone **6** wholly **8** entirely **10** completely **12** particularly

excogitate 6 derive, devise, invent **7** develop, think up **8** contrive, think out

excommunicate 7 cast out **8** unchurch

excoriate 4 flay, lash, skin **5** roast, slash **6** abrade, scathe, scorch **7** blister, censure, scarify, scourge **8** chastise, lambaste, lash into **9** castigate

excrement 6 ordure *of animals:* **4** dung, muck **6** manure *of sea birds:* **5** guano

excrescence 4 blot, lump, mole, wart **5** tumor **6** growth, nodule, pimple **7** blemish, process **9** by-product, outgrowth

excrete 4 emit, spew **5** eject, expel, exude **9** discharge

excruciate 4 rack 6 martyr 7 afflict, crucify, torment, torture 9 martyrize

excruciating 5 acute, sharp 6 severe 7 extreme, intense 8 piercing, shooting, stabbing 9 agonizing, harrowing, torturous 10 unbearable 11 unendurable

exculpate 4 free 5 clear, remit 6 acquit, excuse, let off, pardon 7 absolve, amnesty, condone, forgive, justify 9 exonerate, vindicate 11 rationalize

excursion 4 ride, tour, trek, trip, walk 5 aside, drive, jaunt, paseo, sally, tramp 6 cruise, junket, outing, ramble, safari 7 day trip, journey 9 round trip 10 digression, divagation, expedition 11 parenthesis 12 pleasure trip

excusable 6 venial

excuse 3 out 4 plea 5 alibi, clear, remit 6 acquit, cop-out, defend, exempt, let off, pardon, reason, wink at 7 absolve, apology, condone, defense, forgive, justify, pretext, regrets, relieve 8 mitigate, overlook, palliate, pass over, shrug off, tolerate 9 discharge, exculpate, exonerate, extenuate, gloss over, makeshift, vindicate, whitewash 10 substitute 11 explanation, rationalize 13 justification

execrable 4 base, foul, vile 7 heinous 8 accursed, damnable, horrific, infernal, wretched 9 abhorrent, atrocious, loathsome, monstrous, repulsive, revolting 10 abominable, deplorable, despicable, detestable, horrifying

execrate 4 damn, hate 5 abhor, curse 6 detest, loathe, revile, vilify 7 censure, condemn, despise 8 denounce 9 abominate, imprecate 12 anathematize

execute 2 do 3 act 4 do in, kill, play, slay 5 cause, lynch 6 effect, finish, murder, render 7 achieve, bump off, conduct, enforce, fulfill, perform, realize 8 carry out, complete, dispatch, knock off, transact 9 discharge, eliminate, implement, liquidate 10 accomplish, administer, bring about, put through, put to death 11 assassinate 12 administrate

execution 6 murder 7 killing 11 performance

executioner 7 hangman, headman 8 headsman

executive 4 dean, suit 6 leader 7 manager 8 director, governor 9 president 10 supervisor 13 administrator *ineffective:* 9 empty suit

exegesis 5 gloss 8 analysis 9 construal 10 commentary, exposition 11 elucidation, explanation, explication 12 construction

exemplar 4 copy 5 ideal, model 7 epitome, paragon, pattern 8 instance, paradigm, specimen, standard 9 archetype, criterion, prototype 12 illustration

exemplary 4 pure 5 ideal, model 7 classic, typical 8 laudable, monitory, virtuous 9 admirable, blameless, classical, estimable, faultless, honorable, righteous 10 impeccable, inculpable, prototypal 11 commendable, meritorious 12 illustrative, paradigmatic, praiseworthy, prototypical

exemplify 4 copy 6 embody, mirror, typify 7 clarify 9 enlighten, epitomize, personify, represent, symbolize 10 concretize, illuminate, illustrate

exempt 4 free 5 spare 6 except, excuse, let off, spared 7 absolve, excused, relieve 8 dispense 9 discharge

exemption 7 freedom, release 8 immunity, impunity 9 discharge, exception

exenterate 3 gut 4 draw 7 embowel 10 disembowel, eviscerate

exercise 3 use, vex 4 fret, gall, hone 5 alarm, annoy, apply, drill, étude, exert, sit-up, train, upset, wield 6 chin-up, crunch, employ, pull-up, push-up 7 agitate, develop, exploit, improve, prepare, problem, provoke, utilize, work out 8 activity, maneuver, practice, rehearse 9 athletics, condition, cultivate, discharge, operation 10 employment 11 application 12 calisthenics

exert 3 use 5 apply, wield 6 employ, expend, put out, strain 8 exercise, put forth

exertion 4 toil, work 5 labor, pains 6 effort, strain 7 trouble 8 activity, exercise, striving 11 application, elbow grease

exfoliate 4 peel, shed 5 scale 7 cast off, leaf out 8 flake off 10 desquamate

exhalation 6 breath 8 emission 9 breathing, effluvium, emanation

exhale 4 blow, emit 6 expire, let out 7 breathe, respire 10 breathe out *audibly:* 4 sigh

exhaust 3 fag, sap 4 do in, tire 5 drain, eat up, empty, spend, use up, waste, weary 6 expend, finish, tucker, wash up, weaken 7 burn out, consume, deplete, fatigue, frazzle, tire out, wear out 8 draw down, enervate, squander, wear down 9 discharge, dissipate, prostrate, tucker out 10 debilitate, overextend, run through

exhausted 4 beat, limp, weak 5 all in, spent, tired 6 bushed 7 run-down, worn out 8 dog-tired

exhaustion 7 burnout, fatigue 8 collapse 9 lassitude, tiredness, weariness 11 prostration

exhaustive 8 complete, sweeping, thorough 9 full-blown, full-scale, intensive 10 scrupulous 11 painstaking 13 comprehensive, thoroughgoing

exhibit 4 fair, show 6 evince, expose, flaunt, parade, reveal 7 display, feature, show off 8 evidence, manifest, proclaim, showcase **10** exposition **11** demonstrate

exhibition 4 expo, fair, show **5** rodeo **7** display, pageant, showing **9** trade show **12** presentation **13** demonstration, manifestation

exhibitionist 3 fop **4** toff **6** hot dog **7** peacock, show-off **8** showboat **12** grandstander

exhilarate 4 buoy, lift **5** boost, cheer, elate, exalt, pep up **6** buck up, excite, thrill, uplift **7** animate, cheer up, commove, delight, enliven, gladden, inspire, refresh **8** inspirit, vitalize **9** stimulate **10** invigorate

exhilaration 3 joy **4** glee **7** ecstasy, elation **8** euphoria, gladness **10** exaltation, excitement **11** inspiration **12** vitalization, vivification **13** galvanization

exhort 4 goad, prod, spur, urge, warn **5** egg on, plead, press, prick **6** adjure, call on, incite, prompt, propel **7** beseech, entreat **8** admonish, call upon **9** stimulate

exhortation 4 plea **6** advice, urging / caution, warning **8** entreaty, jeremiad **10** admonition, incitement, injunction **11** inspiration **13** encouragement

exhume 5 dig up **6** redeem **7** reclaim, recover, unearth **8** disinter **9** resurrect

exigency 3 fix, jam **4** need, pass **5** pinch, rigor **6** crisis, demand, pickle, plight, strait **7** urgency **8** juncture, pressure, zero hour **9** extremity, necessity **10** compulsion, constraint, crossroads, difficulty, insistence **11** predicament, requirement

exigent 5 acute, vital **6** crying, taxing **7** burning, clamant, instant, onerous **8** exacting, grievous, pressing **9** clamorous, demanding, insistent, necessary **10** burdensome, imperative **11** importunate

exiguous 4 poor, puny, thin, tiny **5** scant, spare, token **6** meager, meagre, measly, paltry, scanty, shabby, skimpy, slight, sparse **7** minimal, scrimpy **9** miserable **10** inadequate, straitened

exile 4 oust **5** eject, expel **6** banish, deport, emigré **7** cast out, outcast, refugee **8** diaspora, displace, drive out, evacuate, expellee **9** exclusion, expulsion, extradite, migration, ostracism, ostracize **10** banishment, dispossess, expatriate, scattering **11** deportation, extradition **12** displacement, expatriation *place of:* **4** Elba **7** Siberia **8** St. Helena

exist 2 am, be, is **3** are, lie **4** live **5** occur

existence 4 esse, life **5** being **7** reality **8** duration **9** actuality

existent 4 live, real **5** being, thing **6** actual, entity, extant, living **7** current, instant, present **10** present-day **12** contemporary

existentialist writer 5 Buber (Martin), Camus (Albert) **6** Marcel (Gabriel), Sartre (Jean-Paul) **7** Jaspers (Karl) **8** Beauvoir (Simone de) **9** Heidegger (Martin), Nietzsche (Friedrich) **11** Kierkegaard (Søren)

existing 5 alive, being, ontic **6** extant, living *from birth:* **6** innate **10** congenital *Latin:* **6** in esse

exit 2 go **3** die **4** door, gate, quit **5** death, going, leave, scram, split **6** depart, egress, escape, outlet, portal, retire **7** doorway, get away, off-ramp **8** withdraw **9** departure, egression **10** withdrawal

_____ **ex machina 4** deus

exodus 6 flight **9** migration **10** emigration

Exodus author 4 Uris (Leon)

exonerate 4 free **5** clear, remit **6** acquit, excuse, exempt, let off, pardon **7** absolve **8** reprieve **9** exculpate, vindicate

exorbitant 5 undue **7** extreme **9** excessive **10** immoderate, inordinate, outrageous **11** extravagant, unwarranted **12** preposterous

exordium 5 intro, proem **6** lead-in **7** opening, preface, prelude **8** foreword, overture, preamble, prologue **12** introduction, prolegomenon

exotic 4 rare **5** alien **7** bizarre, foreign, strange, unusual **8** alluring, enticing, imported, romantic **9** different, glamorous, nonnative **10** introduced, mysterious **11** fascinating

expand 3 wax **4** grow, open, rise **5** boost, mount, swell, widen **6** beef up, bulk up, dilate, pad out, spread, unfold **7** amplify, augment, bolster, develop, distend, enlarge, inflate, magnify, prolong, stretch **8** escalate, increase, lengthen, multiply, mushroom, protract **9** discourse, elaborate, expatiate, spread out

expanse 4 area, room **5** field, ocean, range, reach, scope, space, sweep, tract **6** domain, extent, sphere, spread **7** breadth, stretch **8** distance **9** territory

expansion 6 growth, spread **8** increase **9** unfolding **11** enlargement **12** augmentation

expansive 3 big **4** wide **5** ample, broad, large, roomy **6** lavish **7** buoyant, elastic, liberal, sizable **8** effusive, extended, generous, outgoing, spacious **9** capacious, garrulous, talkative **10** gregarious, openhanded, unreserved **11** extroverted **13** demonstrative

expatiate 6 ramble, wander **7** dissert, enlarge **8** dilate on, perorate **9** discourse, elaborate, sermonize **10** dilate upon, dissertate

expatriate 5 exile, expel **6** banish, deport, émigré **8** displace, expellee, relegate

expect 4 feel, hope, take **5** await, sense, think, trust **6** assume, divine, gather, look to **7** believe, count on, foresee, imagine, look for, predict, presume, suppose, surmise **8** forecast, foreknow **9** apprehend, count upon **10** anticipate, presuppose

expectant 5 alert **6** gravid **7** anxious, hopeful **8** enceinte, pregnant, vigilant, watchful **10** breathless, parturient **12** anticipatory, apprehensive

expectation 4 hope **5** hunch **8** prospect **9** assurance, intuition **10** assumption, likelihood **11** presumption, probability **12** anticipation, presentiment

expectorate 4 spit

expediency 5 means **6** resort, tactic **7** aptness, fitness, measure, stopgap **8** meetness, recourse, resource, strategy **9** makeshift, propriety, rightness **11** opportunism, suitability **12** appositeness, practicality, suitableness

expedient 3 fit **5** ad hoc, means, shift **6** resort, timely, useful **7** fitting, politic, prudent, stopgap **8** feasible, recourse, resource, suitable, tactical **9** advisable, judicious, makeshift, opportune, practical, pragmatic, well-timed **10** convenient **11** appropriate, practicable, utilitarian **12** advantageous

expedite 4 send **5** hurry, issue, speed **6** hasten **7** quicken, speed up **8** dispatch **10** accelerate, facilitate

expedition 4 trek, trip **5** hurry, speed **6** voyage **7** journey **8** campaign, dispatch **9** excursion, swiftness **10** efficiency, speediness **11** punctuality

expeditious 4 fast **5** brisk, quick, rapid, swift **6** prompt, speedy **9** efficient **11** efficacious

expeditiousness 5 hurry, speed **6** hustle **8** dispatch

expel 4 boot, oust, spew **5** egest, eject, evict, exile **6** banish, bounce, deport, disbar **7** cast out, dismiss, drum out, kick out, turn out **8** disgorge, displace, throw out **9** discharge, eliminate **10** expatriate

expellee 5 exile **6** émigré **7** outcast **8** deportee, emigrant

expend 3 pay, sap **4** blow **5** drain, spend, use up, waste **6** lay out, outlay, pay out **7** consume, deplete, dig into, dole out, exhaust, fork out, utilize **8** disburse, dispense, shell out, squander **9** dissipate **10** run through

expendable 10 disposable **11** dispensable, inessential, replaceable **12** nonessential

expenditure 4 cost **5** outgo **6** outlay, payoff, payout **12** disbursement

expense 4 cost, loss, toll **5** debit, price **6** burden, charge, outlay **7** forfeit, payment **8** overhead **9** decrement, sacrifice **10** forfeiture **12** disbursement

expensive 4 dear, high, posh **5** fancy, pricy,

ritzy, steep, stiff **6** costly, deluxe, lavish, pricey **7** upscale **8** precious, valuable, wasteful **9** big-ticket, luxurious **10** exorbitant, high-priced, overpriced **11** extravagant **12** uneconomical

experience 4 know, live **5** event, savor, skill, trial **6** ordeal, suffer, wisdom **7** episode, know-how, sustain, undergo **8** incident, practice **9** encounter, go through **10** background **11** familiarity, savoir faire *anew:* **6** relive

experienced 4 wise **6** mature, versed **7** old-line, veteran, worldly **8** broken in, seasoned **9** practiced, qualified **12** accomplished

experiential see **empirical**

experiment 3 try **4** test **5** assay, probe, trial **6** try out **7** test out **8** research, trial run **13** trial and error

experimental 9 empirical, tentative **10** innovative **11** exploratory, preliminary, preparatory, provisional **13** developmental, trial-and-error

experimentation 4 test **5** trial **7** testing **8** research, trial run **13** trial and error

expert 3 ace, pro, wiz **4** deft, whiz **5** adept, crack, doyen, maven **6** adroit, master, wizard **7** skilled **8** masterly, skillful, virtuoso **9** authority, dexterous, masterful, virtuosic **10** past master, proficient, specialist **11** crackerjack **12** passed master, professional

expertise 5 craft, skill **7** ability, command, know-how, mastery **8** facility **10** adroitness, competence **11** proficiency **12** skillfulness

expiate 6 offset, pay for, redeem **7** redress **8** atone for

expiation 9 atonement, indemnity **10** recompense, reparation **11** restitution **12** satisfaction

expiatory 7 atoning, lustral **9** purgative **11** penitential, purgatorial **12** propitiatory

expiration 3 end **5** death **10** exhalation **11** termination

expire 3 die, end **4** pass **5** lapse **6** elapse, exhale, pass on, perish, run out **7** decease **8** pass away **9** terminate **10** breathe out

explain 5 gloss, solve **7** analyze, clarify, clear up, condone, expound, justify, resolve, unravel **8** construe, decipher, spell out, unriddle, untangle **9** break down, elucidate, interpret **10** account for, illuminate, illustrate, unscramble **11** disentangle, rationalize

explain away 6 excuse **7** justify **8** minimize **9** extenuate **10** account for **11** rationalize

explanation 3 key **5** gloss **6** excuse, motive, reason **7** account, example, grounds, meaning **8** exegesis **9** construal, rationale **11** elucidation **12** significance **13** clarification

explanatory 10 discursive, exegetical **12** enlightening, illuminating, illustrative, interpretive

expletive 4 cuss, oath **5** curse, swear **8** cussword **9** swearword **12** interjection (see also **exclamation**)

explicate 7 amplify, develop, explain, expound **8** construe, spell out **9** elucidate, interpret

explication 5 gloss **8** exegesis **9** construal **10** commentary **11** development

explicative 10 discursive, exegetical, scholastic **12** interpretive **13** hermeneutical

explicit 4 open, sure **5** clear, exact, frank, lucid, overt, plain **7** certain, correct, express, obvious, precise **8** clear-cut, definite, distinct, specific **10** definitive **11** categorical, perspicuous, unambiguous, unequivocal

explode 3 pop **4** fire **5** blast, burst, erupt, go off **6** blow up, debunk, negate, refute **7** burgeon, deflate **8** break out, burst out, detonate, disprove, dynamite, mushroom, puncture **9** discharge, discredit **10** burst forth **11** proliferate

exploit 3 act, use **4** coup, deed, feat, gest, play **5** abuse, geste, stunt **6** bestow, effort, employ, parlay, play on **7** emprise, utilize, venture **8** escapade, exercise **9** adventure, cultivate **10** enterprise, manipulate **11** achievement, performance, tour de force

explore 5 probe, scout **6** burrow, go into, search **7** dig into, examine **8** look into, prospect, traverse **9** delve into **11** inquire into, investigate

explorer *African:* **3** Cam, Cão (Diogo) **4** Park (Mungo) **5** Grant (James), Laird (Macgregor), Speke (John Hanning) **6** Akeley (Carl, Mary), Burton (Richard), Lander (John, Richard) **7** Covilhâ (Pero da), Stanley (Henry) **8** Covilhâo (Pero da) **10** Clapperton (Hugh) **11** Livingstone (David) *American:* **4** Byrd (Richard), Hall (Charles Francis), Kane (Elisha Kent), Pike (Zebulon) **5** Beebe (Charles William), Clark (William), Lewis (Meriwether), Peary (Robert) **6** Henson (Matthew), Powell (John Wesley), Wilkes (Charles) **7** Ballard (Robert), Frémont (John Charles) *Antarctic:* **4** Byrd (Richard), Cook (Frederick), Ross (James Clark) **5** Fuchs (Vivian), Ronne (Finn), Scott (Robert Falcon) **6** Palmer (Nathaniel), Rymill (John Riddoch), Wilkes (Charles) **7** Weddell (James), Wilkins (George) **8** Amundsen (Roald), d'Urville (Dumont) **9** Ellsworth (Lincoln) **10** Shackleton (Ernest) *Arctic:* **3** Rae (John) **4** Byrd (Richard), Cook (Frederick) **5** Davis

(John), Peary (Robert) **6** Baffin (William), Bering (Vitus), Henson (Matthew), Hudson (Henry), Nansen (Fridtjof), Nobile (Umberto) **7** Barents (Willem), Bennett (Floyd), Wilkins (George), Wrangel (Ferdinand von) **8** Amundsen (Roald) **9** Mackenzie (Alexander), MacMillan (Donald) **10** Stefansson (Vilhjalmur) *Australian:* **7** Wilkins (George) *Austrian:* **9** Weyprecht (Carl) *Canadian:* **9** Mackenzie (Alexander) **10** Stefansson (Vilhjalmur) *Danish:* **9** Rasmussen (Knud) *Dutch:* **6** Tasman (Abel Janszoon) *English:* **4** Cook (James) **5** Cabot (John, Sebastian), Drake (Francis), Scott (Robert Falcon), Smith (John) **6** Baffin (William), Burton (Richard), Hudson (Henry) **7** Raleigh (Walter), Stanley (Henry) **9** Vancouver (George) **10** Shackleton (Ernest) **12** Younghusband (Francis) *French:* **7** Cartier (Jacques), La Salle (Sieur de), Nicolet (Jean) **8** Cousteau (Jacques-Yves) **9** Champlain (Samuel de), La Peroùse (Comte de), Marquette (Jacques) *French Canadian:* **6** Joliet (Louis) **7** Jolliet (Louis) **9** Iberville (Sieur d') *German:* **6** Peters (Carl) **8** Humboldt (Alexander von) *Italian:* **5** Cabot (John) **6** Nobile (Umberto) **8** Vespucci (Amerigo) *New Zealand:* **7** Hillary (Edmund) *Norwegian:* **6** Nansen (Fridtjof) **8** Amundsen (Roald), Sverdrup (Otto) **9** Heyerdahl (Thor) *Portuguese:* **4** Gama (Vasco da) **5** Cunha (Tristão da) **6** Cabral (Pedro) **8** Cabrilho (João Rodrigues), Magellan (Ferdinand) *Scottish:* **3** Rae (John) **4** Park (Mungo), Ross (James Clark) **7** Thomson (Joseph) **11** Livingstone (David) *Spanish:* **6** Balboa (Vasco Núñez de), Cortés (Hernán, Hernando), de Soto (Hernando), Pinzón (Martín Alonso, Vicente Yáñez) **7** Mendoza (Pedro de), Pizarro (Francisco) **8** Bastidas (Rodrigo de), Coronado (Francisco de) **11** Ponce de León (Juan)

explosion 3 pop, pow **4** bang, boom, clap **5** blast, burst, crack, crash, sally, salvo, storm **6** report, volley **7** barrage, blowout, torrent **8** eruption, outburst, paroxysm **9** discharge **10** detonation *cosmic:* **7** big bang

explosive 3 TNT **5** nitro, tense **6** charge, napalm, petard, powder **7** cordite, violent **8** dynamite **9** gunpowder **13** nitroglycerin *device:* **3** cap **4** bomb, mine **5** shell **6** petard **7** grenade **8** firework *inventor:* **5** Maxim (Hudson), Nobel (Alfred) *sound:* **3** pop, pow **4** bang, blam, boom **5** crack

exponent 6 backer **7** booster **8** advocate, champion, defender, partisan, promoter, upholder **9** supporter **12** practitioner

expose 3 air 4 bare, open, show 5 dig up, flash 6 debunk, flaunt, parade, reveal, show up, unmask, unveil 7 abandon, display, exhibit, lay open, publish, show off, subject, uncover, undress 8 brandish, disclose, discover, endanger, unclothe

exposé 10 disclosure, revelation, uncovering

exposed 4 bare, open 5 naked 6 liable 7 evident, subject, visible 8 manifest, stripped, unhidden 9 uncovered 11 susceptible, unconcealed, unprotected

exposition 4 fair, show 6 bazaar 7 display, exhibit 9 trade show

expostulate 5 argue 6 debate, reason 7 discuss, dispute

exposure 4 risk 5 peril 6 airing, baring, danger 8 betrayal, jeopardy, openness 9 liability, publicity 10 revelation 12 helplessness 13 vulnerability

expound 5 state 6 defend 7 clarify, comment, explain, present 8 construe, set forth, spell out 9 discourse, explicate, interpret

expounder 7 teacher 8 advocate, champion, defender, promoter 9 proponent, supporter

express 3 air, say 4 mean, tell, vent 5 couch, crush, frame, state, utter, voice 6 broach, convey, denote, impart, intend, voiced 7 connote, declare, signify, special, uttered 8 announce, clear-cut, definite, disclose, explicit, intended, proclaim, specific 9 enunciate, formulate, high-speed, pronounce, symbolize, ventilate 10 definitive, particular 11 categorical, communicate, intentional, unambiguous *gratitude:* 5 thank *regret:* 9 apologize

expression 4 cast, face, form, look, mien, sign, vent, word 5 idiom, issue, motto, token, voice 6 symbol, visage 7 diction, gesture 8 locution 9 eloquence, statement, utterance, verbalism, vividness 10 embodiment, indication 11 countenance, enunciation, observation 13 demonstration, manifestation *facial:* 4 grin, phiz, pout 5 frown, scowl, smile, smirk, sneer, wince 7 grimace *of assent:* 3 aye, nod, yea, yes 4 okay *of sorrow:* 4 alas, tear *trite:* 6 cliché 7 bromide 8 banality *witty:* 4 quip 5 sally 6 bon mot

expressionless 5 blank 6 stolid, vacant, wooden 7 deadpan 9 impassive 10 poker-faced 11 inscrutable

expressive 5 vivid 7 graphic 8 eloquent 9 revealing 10 meaningful, passionate

expressly 9 precisely, purposely 10 explicitly 12 particularly, specifically 13 intentionally

expressway 4 road 7 freeway, highway, parkway 8 turnpike 12 thoroughfare

expropriate 4 take 5 annex, seize 7 impound, preempt 8 arrogate 9 sequester 10 commandeer, confiscate, dispossess

expulsion 5 exile, purge 6 ouster 7 ousting, removal 8 ejection, eviction 9 ostracism 10 banishment, relegation 11 deportation 12 displacement

expunge 4 dele, x out 5 annul, erase 6 cancel, delete, efface 7 blot out, destroy, exclude, wipe out 8 black out 9 eliminate, eradicate, strike out 10 annihilate, obliterate

expurgate 4 blip 5 bleep, purge 6 censor, purify, screen 7 cleanse 8 sanitize 10 bowdlerize

expurgation 8 ablution 9 catharsis, cleansing 10 lustration 12 purification

exquisite 3 fop 4 fine, keen, rare 5 acute, dandy 6 choice, dainty, select, superb 7 coxcomb, elegant, extreme, intense, refined 8 delicate, finished, flawless, macaroni 9 recherché 10 fastidious, immaculate, impeccable

exsiccate 3 dry 4 sear 5 parch 6 wither 7 shrivel 9 dehydrate

extant 4 live 5 alive 6 actual, living 7 current, present 9 surviving 10 present-day 12 contemporary

extemporaneous 5 ad-lib 6 casual 7 offhand 8 ad-libbed, informal 9 impromptu, impulsive, makeshift, unplanned 10 improvised, unprepared, unscripted 11 spontaneous, unrehearsed 12 unthought-out

extempore see **extemporaneous**

extemporize 5 ad-lib 6 wing it 7 dash off, toss off 8 knock off 9 improvise

extend 4 draw, span, vary 5 award, offer, range, reach 6 bestow, spread, unbend, unfold 7 advance, augment, broaden, drag out, draw out, enlarge, further, hold out, proceed, proffer, project, prolong, spin out, stretch 8 continue, elongate, increase, lengthen, protract 10 outstretch, stretch out

extension 3 arm, ell 4 wing 5 add-on, annex, delay, range, reach, scope, sweep 6 radius, spread 7 adjunct, compass, purview 8 addition, increase 9 appendage, magnitude 10 broadening, elongation 11 enlargement, lengthening, protraction 12 augmentation, continuation, postponement, prolongation

extensity 5 ambit, orbit, range, reach, scope, sweep 6 radius 7 compass, purview

extensive 3 big 4 long, vast, wide 5 broad, large, major 7 general, immense, lengthy, sizable 8 far-flung, sizeable, spacious, sweeping, thorough 9 wholesale 10 large-scale, widespread 11 far-reaching, wide-ranging 12 considerable

extent 4 size 5 ambit, limit, orbit, range, reach, scope, sweep, width 6 amount, degree, domain, radius 7 breadth, compass, measure, purview 8 vicinity 9 magnitude 10 dimensions, proportion

extenuate 6 dilute, excuse, lessen, soften, temper, weaken 7 explain, justify, qualify, varnish 8 diminish, enervate, mitigate, moderate, palliate 9 gloss over 11 rationalize

exterior 4 skin 5 outer, shell 6 facade 7 outmost, outside, outward, surface 8 apparent 9 outermost 11 superficial

exterminate 4 kill 6 rub out 7 destroy, wipe out 8 massacre 9 eliminate, eradicate, finish off, liquidate, slaughter 10 annihilate, extinguish, obliterate

external 3 out 4 over 5 outer 7 foreign, outside, outward, surface 9 outermost 10 peripheral 11 superficial

externalize 4 show 6 embody, evince, excuse, expose, reveal 7 exhibit, justify 8 manifest 9 extenuate, incarnate, objectify, personify 11 rationalize 12 substantiate

extinct 4 cold, dead, gone, late 5 passé 6 bygone 7 archaic, defunct 8 deceased, departed, obsolete, perished, vanished 10 superseded

extinction 3 end 4 doom 5 death 6 demise 11 destruction, eradication, liquidation 12 annihilation, obliteration 13 disappearance, extermination

extinguish 3 end 5 crush, douse, erase, quash, quell, snuff 6 put out, quench, squash, stifle 7 abolish, blot out, blow out, destroy, eclipse, expunge, nullify, put down, wipe out 8 snuff out, stamp out, suppress 9 eliminate, eradicate, extirpate 10 annihilate, obliterate

extirpate 5 erase 6 cut out, efface, excise, resect, uproot 7 abolish, blot out, destroy, expunge, kill off, root out, wipe out 8 demolish 9 eliminate, eradicate 10 annihilate, deracinate, extinguish

extol 4 hymn, laud 5 cry up, exalt 6 praise 7 acclaim, applaud, commend, glorify, magnify 8 eulogize 9 celebrate 10 panegyrize

extort 5 wrest, wring 7 extract

extortion 8 exaction 9 blackmail

extra 3 odd 4 more, over, perk, plus 5 added, add-on, bonus, spare 6 de trop, rarely 7 reserve, surplus 8 leftover 9 lagniappe, redundant, unusually 10 additional, especially, perquisite 11 superfluous 12 particularly, supplemental 13 supernumerary, supplementary

extract 4 pull, yank 5 evoke, glean, quote, wring 6 derive, eke out, elicit, remove 7 abridge, distill, essence, excerpt, passage, pull out, squeeze, take out 8 citation, condense, infusion 9 quotation, selection 11 concentrate

extraction 5 birth, blood, stock 6 origin 7 descent, essence, lineage 8 ancestry, pedigree 9 parentage 10 derivation 12 distillation

extraneous 5 alien, outer 6 exotic 7 foreign, outside 8 external 9 unrelated 10 immaterial, inapposite, incidental, irrelevant, peripheral 11 impertinent, inessential, superfluous, unessential 12 adventitious, inapplicable, nonessential

extraordinary 3 odd 4 rare 6 unique 7 amazing, notable, special, unusual 8 abnormal, atypical, singular, terrific, uncommon, unwonted 9 wonderful 10 noteworthy, phenomenal, remarkable, stupendous, tremendous 11 exceptional, outstanding

extravagance 5 frill, waste 6 excess, luxury 9 hyperbole, profusion 10 indulgence, lavishness 11 ostentation, prodigality, superfluity 12 immoderation, wastefulness

extravagant 4 wild 5 outré, undue 6 lavish 7 bizarre, extreme, profuse 8 overdone, prodigal, reckless, wasteful 9 elaborate, excessive, fantastic, grandiose, overblown 10 exorbitant, hyperbolic, immoderate, inordinate, profligate 11 exaggerated, implausible, intemperate, nonsensical 12 ostentatious, preposterous, unrestrained

extreme 3 max, top 4 apex, dire, last, peak, wild 5 crown, final, limit, ultra, undue 6 climax, excess, height, summit, utmost, zenith 7 drastic, fanatic, intense, maximal, maximum, outmost, radical, violent 8 farthest, furthest, pinnacle, remotest, ultimate 9 desperate, excessive, outermost, uttermost 10 immoderate, inordinate, outlandish, outrageous 11 furthermost, unwarranted 12 unmeasurable, unreasonable 13 revolutionary
    degree: 3 nth

extremely 4 mega, most, unco, very 5 ultra 6 highly, hugely, mighty, overly, plenty, wildly 7 acutely, awfully, greatly, utterly 8 severely, terribly 9 immensely, seriously, unusually 10 remarkably, strikingly 11 exceedingly 12 terrifically

extremist 5 rabid, ultra 6 zealot 7 die-hard, fanatic, radical 8 militant, ultraist 9 fanatical 10 monomaniac, ultraistic 11 reactionary 13 revolutionary

extremity 3 arm, end, leg, tip 4 acme, apex, foot, hand, tail 5 limit, verge 6 apogee, vertex, zenith 8 terminal, terminus

extricate 4 free 5 loose 6 detach, redeem, rescue **7** bail out, deliver, resolve, set free, untwine **8** liberate, untangle **9** disengage **11** disencumber, disentangle, distinguish, individuate **12** discriminate, disembarrass **13** differentiate

extrinsic 5 alien, outer **6** exotic **7** foreign, outside, outward **8** exterior, external, imported **10** incidental, extraneous

extrude 4 spew **5** eject **7** push out **8** press out **10** squeeze out

exuberance 4 glee, life, zest **5** ardor **6** gaiety, spirit **7** abandon **8** buoyancy, hilarity, vivacity **9** profusion **10** ebullience, enthusiasm, friskiness, liveliness **11** flamboyance, high spirits, zestfulness **12** exhilaration **13** effervescence, sprightliness

exuberant 3 gay **4** lush, rank **5** happy **6** bouncy, elated, fecund, lavish, lively **7** buoyant, profuse, rampant, riotous, zestful **8** fruitful, prodigal, prolific, spirited **9** ebullient, luxuriant, sprightly, vivacious **10** flamboyant **11** exhilarated **12** effervescent, enthusiastic, high-spirited

exude 4 emit, leak, ooze, seep, shed **5** issue **7** diffuse, display, emanate, excrete, exhibit, give off, ooze out, radiate, secrete **9** discharge

exult 4 crow **5** cheer, gloat, glory, revel **7** delight, rejoice **8** jubilate **9** celebrate

exultant 6 elated, joyful, joyous **7** gleeful **8** ecstatic, euphoric, jubilant **9** cock-a-hoop, overjoyed, rejoicing, triumphal **10** triumphant

exultation 3 joy **4** glee **7** delight, ecstasy, elation, rapture, triumph **8** euphoria, gloating **9** jubilance, rejoicing **10** jubilation

eye 3 orb **4** lamp, ogle, scan, view **5** sight, watch **6** behold, goggle, look at, ocular, oculus, peeper, regard, size up, vision **7** inspect, observe **8** check out, consider, gaze

upon, scrutiny **9** headlight **10** scrutinize *combining form:* **4** ocul **5** oculo **8** ophthalm **9** ophthalmo *defect:* **6** myopia **9** hyperopia **10** emmetropia, presbyopia **11** astigmatism *disease:* **8** cataract, glaucoma, trachoma *doctor:* **7** oculist **11** optometrist *opening:* **5** pupil *part:* **4** iris, lens, uvea **5** pupil **6** cornea, retina, sclera *relating to:* **5** optic **7** optical *socket:* **5** orbit *Spanish:* **3** ojo *test:* **10** Amsler Grid **12** Snellen Chart

eyeball 4 scan **5** check, study **6** go over, look at, peruse, survey **7** examine, inspect, observe **8** appraise, check out, evaluate, pore over **10** scrutinize

eye-catching 4 bold **5** gaudy, showy **6** flashy **7** salient **8** striking **9** arresting, prominent **10** noticeable, remarkable **11** conspicuous

eyeful 6 looker **7** stunner **8** knockout

eyeglass 7 monocle

eyeglasses 5 specs **6** lenses **7** lorgnon **8** bifocals, pince-nez **9** lorgnette **10** spectacles

eyelash 6 cilium **11** hairbreadth

eyelet 4 hole **7** grommet **8** loophole, peephole

eyelid growth 3 sty **4** cyst, stye **5** nevus **9** chalazion, hordeolum

eyepiece 4 lens **6** ocular

eye-popping 7 amazing **8** exciting, stirring **9** thrilling **10** astounding **11** astonishing, mind-blowing, spectacular **12** breathtaking

eyesore 4 blot, dump, mess **6** blight **7** blemish **8** atrocity **11** monstrosity

eyespot 6 blight, fungus **7** ocellus

eyetooth 6 canine

eyewash 3 rot **4** bunk **5** bilge, hooey, tripe **6** bunkum **7** baloney, garbage, hogwash, rubbish, twaddle **8** malarkey, nonsense **9** poppycock **10** balderdash **13** horsefeathers

eyewitness 8 observer, onlooker **9** bystander, spectator

eyrie see **aerie**

F

Fabergé product 3 egg **9** Easter egg

Fabian 4 Shaw (George Bernard), Webb (Beatrice, Sidney) **7** politic **8** cautious, dilatory **9** socialist **11** circumspect, calculating

fable 4 myth, tale, yarn **5** story **6** legend **7** fantasy, fiction, figment, parable **8** allegory, tall tale *animal:* **8** bestiary

fabled 5 famed **6** famous, unreal **7** storied **8** fanciful, mythical, renowned **9** fictional, imaginary, legendary, pretended **10** fictitious **11** make-believe **12** mythological

fabric 3 aba, rep, web **4** lamé, repp **5** cloth, fiber, grain **7** texture **8** building, material, shirting **9** structure *coarse:* **4** tapa **5** crash, gunny **6** burlap, linsey, ratiné **7** cheviot, hopsack **8** homespun *colorer:* **4** dyer *corded:* **3** rep **4** repp **5** piqué **6** calico, moreen, poplin **7** pinwale **8** corduroy, padu-asoy **9** bengaline *cotton:* **4** jean, leno **5** baize, chino, denim, domet, drill, lisle, scrim, wigan **6** chintz, dimity, faille, madras, muslin, sateen **7** etamine, gingham, nankeen, percale, ticking **8** chambray, dungaree, nainsook, tarlatan **9** crinoline **10** seersucker *cotton and linen:* **4** huck **7** fustian **9** huckaback *crepe:* **8** marocain *dealer:* **6** draper, mercer *durable:* **4** huck, jean **5** chino, denim, drill, scrim **6** frieze, moreen **7** lasting, ticking **8** cretonne, dungaree *embroidered:* **9** baldachin **10** baldachino *finishing process:* **8** lustring **9** mercerize *flag material:* **7** bunting *glazed:* **4** ciré **6** chintz **7** cambric, holland *knitted:* **6** tricot **10** balbriggan *linen:* **7** cambric, lockram *looped:* **6** bouclé *lustrous:* **4** silk **5** moiré, satin, surah **6** sateen **7** taffeta **12** brilliantine *metallic:* **4** lamé *net:* **5** tulle **8** bobbinet, illusion *openwork:* **4** lace **8** filigree *ornamental:* **4** lace **5** braid **6** ribbon **7** bunting *pebbly-surface:* **8** barathea *pile-surface:* **5** panne, plush, terry **6** velour, velvet **7** duvetyn, velours **8** chenille, moleskin **9** velveteen *plaid:* **6** tartan *pleated:* **5** ruche *printed:* **5** batik, toile **6** calico, chintz, damask **7** allover, challis **8** cretonne, jacquard **11** toile de Jouy *puckered:* **6** plissé **10** seersucker *raised pattern:* **4** lamé **7** brocade **10** brocatelle *satin weave:* **5** panne *sheer:* **4** lawn, mull **5** gauze, ninon, voile **6** dimity **7** batiste, chiffon, organdy, organza, tiffany **8** tarlatan *silk:* **6** faille, pongee, samite **7** foulard, grogram **8** paduasoy, sarcenet, sarsenet, shantung **9** bombazine *striped:* **3** aba **7** ticking **8** bayadere *synthetic:* **5** Arnel, ninon, nylon, Orlon, rayon **6** Dacron *trim:* **5** ruche *twill:* **4** jean **5** chino, drill, serge **7** foulard, nankeen, ticking **8** dungaree, shalloon **9** bombazine **10** broadcloth *unfinished:* **6** greige *waterproof:* **7** oilskin *wool:* **5** baize, loden, tweed **6** alpaca, caddis, camlet, duffel, duffle, melton, merino, wadmal, wadmel, wadmol, woolen **7** woollen **8** mackinaw, prunella **9** cassimere *wool, poor quality:* **5** mungo **6** shoddy *wool mixture:* **6** saxony **7** drugget, ratteen **8** moquette, shalloon, zibeline **9** zibelline *woven:* **4** weft **7** textile

fabricate 4 form, make **5** build, erect, frame, set up, shape **6** cook up, create, devise, invent, make up **7** concoct, dream up, fashion, produce, think up **8** assemble, contrive

9 construct, structure **11** manufacture, put together

fabrication 3 fib, lie **4** bull, jive **6** canard, deceit **7** fiction, figment, hogwash, product, untruth **8** assembly, building, creation **9** deception, fairy tale, falsehood, invention **10** concoction, production **11** manufacture **12** construction

fabulist 4 liar *French:* **10** La Fontaine (Jean de) *Greek:* **5** Aesop *Roman:* **8** Phaedrus *Russian:* **6** Krylov (Ivan)

fabulous 5 super **7** amazing **8** mythical, terrific, wondrous **9** fantastic, legendary, marvelous, wonderful **10** astounding, fictitious, incredible, outrageous, phenomenal, prodigious, remarkable, stupendous **11** astonishing, extravagant, spectacular **12** mythological *animal:* **6** dragon **7** centaur, unicorn *bird:* **3** roc *serpent:* **8** basilisk **10** cockatrice

facade 4 face, mask **5** color, front, guise, put-on **6** veneer **8** disguise, exterior, frontage, pretense **10** appearance, camouflage, false front

face 3 mug, pan **4** dare, defy, dial, meet, phiz, puss, show, side **5** abide, brave, front, guise, honor, image, nerve **6** endure, facade, kisser, makeup, mazard, oppose, resist, suffer, take on, visage **7** compete, contend, dignity, surface **8** confront, cope with, deal with, disguise, features, prestige, war paint **9** assurance, encounter, lineament, semblance, withstand **10** appearance, confidence, experience, expression, maquillage, reputation **11** countenance, self-respect

face-off 5 clash, set-to **13** confrontation

facet 4 edge, item, part, side **5** angle, bezel, front, phase, plane, point, trait **6** aspect, detail **7** element, feature, surface **9** attribute, component **10** appearance, particular

facetious 4 flip **5** comic, droll, jokey, smart, witty **6** blithe, breezy, joking **7** amusing, comical, jesting, jocular, joshing, kidding, risible, waggish **8** flippant, humorous **9** ludicrous, unserious, whimsical **10** irreverent, ridiculous **12** wisecracking **13** tongue-in-cheek

face-to-face 6 direct **7** contact, present, vis-à-vis **8** directly, in person, personal **10** personally

facile 4 deft, easy, glib, snap **5** light, quick, ready **6** adroit, expert, fluent, poised, simple, smooth **7** assured, cursory, offhand, shallow, voluble **8** skillful, untaxing **9** dexterous **10** effortless, simplistic **13** uncomplicated

facilitate 3 aid **4** abet, ease, help **6** assist, enable, smooth **7** advance, forward, further, promote **8** expedite, make easy, simplify

facility 3 aid, wit **4** bent, ease **5** knack, privy, skill **6** talent, toilet **7** ability, amenity, comfort, fluency, leaning **8** aptitude, bathroom, building, capacity, lavatory, washroom **9** advantage, dexterity **10** adroitness, competence, smoothness **11** convenience, institution, proficiency **12** installation **13** accommodation, establishment

facing 5 front, panel **6** contra, lining, toward, veneer **7** surface, vis-à-vis **8** covering, opposite, paneling **11** over against *down:* **5** prone *up:* **6** supine

facsimile 4 copy, dupe, fake, twin **5** clone, ditto, match, mimeo, repro, Xerox **6** carbon, double **7** replica **8** knockoff, likeness **9** duplicate, imitation, photocopy **10** carbon copy, dead ringer, similitude **11** counterpart, duplication, replication **12** reproduction

fact 4 dope **5** datum, event, truth **6** detail, gospel, truism, verity **7** episode, reality **8** evidence, incident **9** actuality **10** occurrence, particular, phenomenon **11** information **12** circumstance, intelligence

faction 4 band, bloc, camp, part, ring, sect, side, wing **5** cabal, group, party **6** caucus, circle, clique, sector, strife **7** combine, coterie, discord, section **8** alliance, disunity, splinter **10** contingent

factious 7 warring **8** contrary, divisive, partisan **9** dissident, insurgent, sectarian, seditious, turbulent **10** contending, malcontent **11** contentious, disaffected, dissentious, quarrelsome **12** disputatious **13** troublemaking

factitious 4 sham **5** bogus, false, phony **6** ersatz, forced, made-up, unreal **7** assumed, created, feigned, man-made, shammed **8** affected, invented, spurious **9** concocted, contrived, fashioned, pretended, simulated, synthetic, unnatural **10** artificial, fabricated **11** constructed, counterfeit **12** manufactured **13** counterfeited

_____ **facto 4** ipso **6** ex post

factor 4 gene, item **5** agent, cause, proxy **6** broker, lender, number, symbol **7** divisor, element, exclude, include, resolve **8** attorney, emissary, quantity **9** component, majordomo, substance **10** antecedent, ingredient, multiplier **11** determinant **12** intermediary

factory 4 mill, shop **5** plant, works **8** workshop **9** sweatshop **11** machine shop

factotum 4 grub **5** gofer **6** drudge **7** servant **9** assistant, gal Friday, man Friday, operative **11** functionary

factual 4 real, true **5** exact, valid **6** actual **7**

certain, genuine, literal **8** absolute, positive **9** authentic, undoubted **10** undisputed **12** indisputable

faculty 4 bent, body, gift **5** flair, knack, power **6** talent **7** ability, college **8** aptitude, capacity, facility, function, instinct **9** educators, lecturers **10** department, professors **11** instructors

fad 4 chic, kick, mode, rage, whim **5** craze, furor, mania, style, trend **6** furore, latest, whimsy **7** caprice, fashion **9** bandwagon **10** dernier cri

faddish 3 hot **4** chic **5** today **6** modish, redhot, trendy, with-it **7** stylish, voguish **8** contempo **9** au courant **11** cutting-edge, fashionable

fade 3 die, dim, ebb **4** fail, pale, wane, wilt **6** lessen, vanish, weaken, wither **7** decline, lighten, wash out **8** decrease, discolor, diminish **9** disappear, evaporate

faded 3 dim, wan **4** drab, dull, pale **6** pallid **8** bleached, vanished, withered **9** etiolated, washed-out

Faerie Queene, The *author:* **7** Spenser (Edmund) *character:* **3** Ate, Una **4** Alma **5** Guyon, Talus **6** Abessa, Amavia, Amoret, Arthur, Cambel, Duessa, Palmer **7** Artegal, Corceca, Fidessa, Maleger, Sansloy **8** Calidore, Florimel, Fradubio, Gloriana, Lucifera, Orgoglio, Satyrane **9** Archimago, Britomart **11** Britomartis

Faeroes whirlwind 2 oe

Fafnir 6 dragon *brother:* **5** Regin **6** Fasolt, Reginn *father:* **8** Hreidmar *slayer:* **6** Sigurd **9** Siegfried *victim:* **6** Fasolt **8** Hreidmar

fag 4 do in, moil, tire, toil **5** serve, smoke, stick, weary **6** drudge, overdo, tucker **7** exhaust, fatigue, servant, wear out **8** drudgery, knock out **9** cigarette

fag end 4 butt, edge, fray **7** remnant

faience 7 pottery **11** earthenware

fail 3 die, end **4** bomb, fade, lack, lose, miss, sink, slip, stop, wane **5** break, flunk **6** fizzle, forget, ignore, lessen, weaken **7** decline, default, founder, give out, go under, neglect **8** fall flat, languish, miscarry **9** break down, fall short **10** disappoint, go bankrupt **11** deteriorate

failing 4 flaw, vice **5** fault **6** defect **8** weakness **9** weak point **10** deficiency **11** shortcoming **12** imperfection

failure 3 bum, dud **4** bomb, bust, flop, miss **5** decay, loser **6** fiasco, fizzle, no-good, outage **7** default, washout **8** collapse, fracture, omission **9** breakdown, cessation, oversight, unconcern **10** bankruptcy, deficiency, insolvency, negligence **11** defalcation, dysfunction, miscarriage **12** interruption **13** deterioration

fain 3 apt **5** eager, prone, ready **6** gladly, minded **7** willing **8** amenable, inclined **9** agreeable

fainéant 3 bum **4** idle, lazy **5** idler, sloth **6** loafer, torpid **7** goof-off, slacker **8** deadbeat, inactive, indolent, layabout, slothful, sluggard, sluggish **9** do-nothing, lazybones, shiftless **11** couch potato, ineffectual **13** lackadaisical

faint 3 dim, low, wan **4** hazy, pale, soft, weak, wilt **5** dizzy, light, plotz, swoon, vague, woozy **6** feeble, subtle **7** conk out, obscure, pass out, shadowy, syncope, unclear **8** black out, collapse, keel over **9** undefined **10** ill-defined, indistinct

fair 2 OK **3** due **4** even, expo, fine, join, just, mild, okay, open, so-so **5** blond, bonny, clear, equal, fresh, light, sunny **6** bazaar, blonde, comely, decent, honest, kermis, lovely, market, pretty, square **7** cricket **8** adequate, all right, balanced, carnival, festival, mediocre, middling, pleasant, pleasing, rational, sunshiny, unbiased **9** beautiful, cloudless, equitable, favorable, fortunate, impartial, objective, tolerable, trade show, unclouded **10** acceptable, attractive, evenhanded, exhibition, exposition, openminded, reasonable **11** indifferent, nonpartisan, respectable **12** satisfactory, unprejudiced **13** disinterested, dispassionate, sportsmanlike

fair food 10 candy apple, candy floss, fried dough, funnel cake **11** cotton candy, elephant ear

fair-haired 3 pet **5** blond **6** blonde **7** beloved, darling, favored **8** favorite **9** fortunate

fairly 5 quite **6** nearly, rather **7** plainly **8** passably, properly, somewhat **9** tolerably **10** acceptably, deservedly, distinctly, moderately, reasonably **11** practically

fairness 6 candor, equity **7** honesty **8** justness **9** good faith **12** impartiality

fairy 3 elf, imp, nix **4** peri, puck **5** elfin, nixie, nymph, pixie, sylph **6** goblin, kobold, sprite **7** brownie, gremlin **10** leprechaun *king:* **6** Oberon *queen:* **3** Mab **7** Titania **8** Gloriana *shoemaker:* **10** leprechaun

fairy tale *author:* **4** Lang (Andrew) **5** Grimm (Jacob, Wilhelm), Wilde (Oscar) **7** Kipling (Rudyard) **8** Andersen (Hans Christian), Perrault (Charles) *character:* **4** Jack, Puck **6** Gretel, Hansel **8** Rapunzel, Tom Thumb **9** Snow White **10** Cinderella, Goldilocks, Thumbelina

faith 4 cult, sect **5** credo, creed, stock, troth,

trust **6** belief, church, credit **8** credence, reliance, religion **9** certainty, certitude, communion, credulity **10** confidence, persuasion **12** denomination *article of:* **5** tenet

faithful 4 fast, just, true **5** liege, loyal, pious, tried **6** steady, trusty **7** devoted, dutiful, staunch **8** constant, follower, reliable, resolute, true-blue **9** religious, steadfast **10** dependable, scrupulous, unwavering **11** truehearted, trustworthy

faithfulness 5 piety, troth **6** fealty **7** loyalty **8** devotion, fidelity **9** adherence, constancy **10** allegiance, attachment

faithless 5 false, Punic **6** fickle, untrue **8** disloyal, recreant **10** perfidious, traitorous **11** treacherous **13** untrustworthy

faithlessness 7 perfidy, treason **8** betrayal **9** falseness, treachery **10** disloyalty, infidelity

fake 3 act, gyp **4** hoax, mock, sham **5** bluff, bogus, false, feign, fraud, phony, pseud, put on, spoof **6** affect, doctor, ersatz, forged, framed, humbug, pseudo **7** falsify, pretend **8** impostor, invented, simulate, spurious **9** brummagem, charlatan, concocted, fabricate, imitation, imposture, pinchbeck, pretended, simulated **10** artificial, fabricated, fictitious, fraudulent, simulation **11** counterfeit *combining form:* **5** pseud **6** pseudo

faker 4 sham **5** fraud, phony, quack **6** con man, hoaxer **8** deceiver, impostor **9** charlatan, con artist, pretender **10** mountebank **11** four-flusher **12** double-dealer **13** confidence man

fakir 7 ascetic, dervish **9** mendicant

falafel holder 4 pita, wrap **5** pitta

falcon 4 hawk **5** hobby, saker **6** lanner, merlin **7** kestrel **9** peregrine *eye cover:* **4** seel *male:* **4** jack **6** tercel **7** tiercel **8** lanneret *mature:* **7** haggard *young:* **4** eyas

falcon-headed god see at **Egyptian**

falconry 7 hawking *equipment:* **4** bell, hood, jess, lure *procedure:* **3** imp **4** cope, seel

Falkland Islands *capital:* **7** Stanley *claimant:* **9** Argentina *colony of:* **7** Britain

fall 3 dip, ebb, sag **4** dive, drip, drop, dump, hang, plop, sink, slip, trip, wane **5** abate, crash, lapse, slide, slump, spill **6** autumn, drowse, give up, go down, header, plunge, sprawl, tumble **7** cascade, decline, descend, descent, devolve, go under, plummet, scatter, stumble, subside **8** collapse, decrease, diminish, keel over, nose-dive **9** hairpiece **10** depreciate **11** precipitate

fallacious 6 untrue **7** invalid **8** delusive, delusory **9** deceitful, deceptive, erroneous, sophistic **10** fraudulent

fallacy 5 error **6** canard **7** falsity, sophism, untruth **8** delusion **9** falsehood **11** non sequitur **13** misconception

fall apart 6 lose it **7** crumble **9** break down, decompose **10** go to pieces **11** come unglued, deteriorate **12** disintegrate

fall back 6 recede, recoil, retire **7** retract, retreat **8** withdraw **9** disengage, retrocede **10** retrograde

fall behind 3 lag **4** drag **5** delay, tarry, trail **6** dawdle, linger, loiter

fall flat 4 bomb, fail, flop, miss **6** fizzle

fall guy 4 dupe, fool, goat, gull **5** chump, front, patsy **6** stooge, sucker **8** front man **9** scapegoat **11** whipping boy

fallible 4 iffy, weak **5** dicey, frail, human **6** errant, erring, faulty **9** imperfect **10** unreliable

falling-out 3 row **4** beef, feud, fuss, spat, tiff **5** break, run-in, words **6** bicker, fracas, hassle **7** dispute, quarrel, rhubarb, wrangle **8** argument, conflict, squabble **9** brannigan **11** altercation, controversy **12** disagreement, estrangement

falloff 3 sag **4** drop, slip **5** slump **7** decline **8** downturn **9** downslide, downswing, downtrend **13** deterioration

fall out 5 argue, break, leave, occur **6** bicker **7** brabble, quarrel, wrangle **8** disagree, squabble

fallow 4 idle **5** inert **6** unsown **7** dormant, resting **8** inactive, unseeded, untilled **9** neglected, quiescent, unplanted **12** uncultivated

false 4 fake, mock, sham **5** bogus, dummy, hokey, lying, phony, wrong **6** ersatz, forged, hollow, pseudo, untrue **7** crooked, devious, feigned, seeming, unloyal **8** apostate, apparent, deluding, delusive, delusory, disloyal, recreant, specious, spurious **9** brummagem, deceitful, deceiving, deceptive, dishonest, distorted, erroneous, faithless, illogical, imitation, incorrect, pinchbeck, simulated **10** artificial, fictitious, fraudulent, inaccurate, misleading, perfidious, traitorous, unfaithful, untruthful **11** counterfeit, treacherous *combining form:* **5** pseud **6** pseudo

falsehood 3 fib, lie **5** fable **6** canard **7** fallacy, fiction, untruth, whopper **8** roorback **9** mendacity **11** fabrication **12** misstatement **13** prevarication

falseness 7 fallacy, perfidy **8** apostasy **9** treachery **10** disloyalty, infidelity **11** insincerity

false teeth 8 dentures

falsify 3 fib, lie **4** cook, deny **5** belie, fudge, slant **6** doctor, refute **7** deceive, distort, mis-

lead **8** disprove, misstate **10** contradict **11** prevaricate **12** misrepresent

falsity 3 fib, lie **4** tale, yarn **5** fable **6** canard **7** untruth, whopper **9** falsehood, mendacity **11** fabrication **13** prevarication

Falstaff *companion:* **3** Nym **4** Peto **6** Pistol **8** Bardolph *composer:* **5** Verdi (Giuseppe) *creator:* **11** Shakespeare (William) *drink:* **4** sack *play:* **7** Henry IV *prince:* **3** Hal *tavern:* **9** Boar's Head

Falstaffian 3 fat **6** jovial **7** roguish **8** boastful **9** convivial, dissolute

falter 4 halt, limp, reel, sway, trip **5** quail, waver **6** flinch, teeter, totter, wobble **7** give way, stagger, stammer, stumble **8** hesitate **9** vacillate **12** shilly-shally

fame 4 note **5** éclat, glory, honor, kudos **6** esteem, regard, renown, repute **7** acclaim, stardom **8** standing **9** celebrity, notoriety **10** popularity, prominence, reputation **11** acclamation, immortality, recognition

famed 5 noted **6** marked **7** eminent, notable **8** renowned **9** notorious, prominent, well-known **10** celebrated **11** illustrious **13** distinguished

familiar 4 cozy **6** common, folksy **8** domestic, everyday, frequent, informal, intimate, standard **10** accustomed **11** comfortable, commonplace **12** conventional, recognizable **13** garden-variety

familiarity 4 ease **8** intimacy **9** closeness, knowledge **11** informality **12** acquaintance

family 3 kin **4** clan, folk, home, line, race **5** brood, folks, house, issue, stirp, stock, tribe **6** ménage, strain **7** dynasty, kindred, lineage, progeny **8** pedigree **9** bloodline, household, offspring *branch:* **5** stirp *lineage:* **4** tree **6** stemma **8** pedigree **9** genealogy

famine 4 want **6** dearth, hunger **10** starvation

famished 6 hungry **7** starved **8** ravenous, starving

famous 5 famed, noble, noted **6** fabled **7** eminent, notable, popular **8** historic, renowned **9** legendary, notorious, prominent, well-known **10** celebrated **11** illustrious, prestigious, redoubtable

fan 3 bug, nut **4** blow, buff, open, wind **5** freak, lover, maven, rouse **6** addict, arouse, expand, extend, kindle, rooter, ruffle, spread, stir up, unfold, votary, whip up, winnow **7** admirer, devotee, habitué **8** adherent, enkindle, follower, railbird **9** stimulate **10** aficionado, enthusiast *dance:* **11** balletomane *horseracing:* **7** turfman *India:* **6** punkah *movie:* **7** cineast **8** cineaste **9** cinephile

fanatic 3 bug, nut **4** buff **5** fiend, freak, rabid **6** addict, maniac, votary, zealot **7** devotee, die-hard, habitué **10** aficionado, enthusiast

fanatical 5 fiery, rabid **6** ardent, fervid **7** extreme, fervent, zealous **8** frenetic, frenzied, maniacal, obsessed **9** perfervid **10** passionate **11** impassioned

fanaticism 4 zeal **5** mania **6** frenzy **8** zealotry **9** extremism, monomania, obsession

fancier 6 grower **7** amateur, admirer, breeder, devotee

fanciful 6 absurd, unreal **7** bizarre, fictive **8** fabulous, illusory, imagined, mythical, notional, romantic **9** fantastic, fictional, grotesque, imaginary **10** chimerical, fictitious **11** fantastical **12** preposterous

fancy 3 bee, fad **4** idea, like, posh, whim **5** dream, ritzy, shine, smart, taste **6** dressy, liking, megrim, notion, relish, snazzy, swanky, vision, whimsy **7** caprice, chimera, conceit, concept, dream up, elegant, fantasy, feature, imagine, picture **8** conceive, daydream, envision, fondness, judgment, velleity **9** capriccio, elaborate, intricate, inventive, visualize, whimsical **10** decorative, ornamental, partiality, propensity **11** extravagant, highfalutin, imagination, inclination

fandango 5 dance **9** malaguena

fanfare 4 pomp, show, ta-da **5** array, ta-dah **6** hoopla **7** display, hooplah, panoply **8** ballyhoo, flourish *trumpet:* **6** tucket **7** tantara

fanlike 7 plicate

fanny 3 bum, can **4** buns, butt, duff, moon, rear, rump, seat, tail, tush **5** booty, nates **6** behind, bottom, breech, heinie **7** caboose, hind end, keister, rear end, tail end **8** backside, buttocks, derriere **9** fundament, posterior

fantasia 6 vision **8** daydream, illusion, rhapsody **9** fairyland **10** apparition

fantasize 4 moon **5** dream, fancy **7** imagine **8** daydream **10** woolgather

fantastic 3 odd **4** wild **6** absurd, unreal **7** bizarre, surreal **8** fanciful, singular **9** eccentric, grotesque, imaginary, marvelous, monstrous, unearthly, whimsical **10** chimerical, far-fetched, improbable, incredible, outlandish, outrageous, prodigious, stupendous, tremendous **11** implausible, nonsensical, sensational, superlative **12** preposterous, unbelievable

fantasy 4 moon, whim **5** dream, fancy, freak **6** vagary, vision, whimsy **7** caprice, chimera, fiction, reverie **8** daydream, delusion, phantasm **9** imagining, invention, pipe dream **10** bizarrerie **11** imagination **12** grotesquerie

far 4 long **6** remote **7** distant **8** outlying *combining form:* **3** tel **4** tele, telo

far and wide 7 all over **10** everyplace, everywhere, throughout

faraway 4 lost **5** moony **6** absent, dreamy, remote **7** distant, removed **8** outlying **9** oblivious, unheeding **10** abstracted, distracted **11** preoccupied, inattentive **12** absentminded

farce 5 stuff **6** comedy, satire **7** mockery **8** travesty **9** burlesque, slapstick **10** caricature

farceur 5 clown, cutup, joker **7** buffoon

farcical 5 comic **6** absurd **7** comical, foolish, risible **9** laughable, ludicrous **10** ridiculous **12** preposterous

fare 4 diet, dine, food, pass, rate, toll **5** get on, price, track **6** manage, travel **7** come off, journey, make out, proceed, succeed **8** get along, progress, victuals **9** passenger, surcharge **10** provisions **11** comestibles

farewell 3 ave, bye **4** ciao, ta-ta, vale **5** adieu, adios, aloha, congé **6** bye-bye, pip-pip, shalom, so long **7** aloha oe, cheerio, good-bye, toodles **8** swan song, toodle-oo **9** bon voyage, departure **11** arrivederci, leave-taking, valediction, valedictory

far-fetched 5 fishy **6** absurd **7** dubious **8** doubtful, strained, unlikely **10** improbable, incredible **11** implausible, unrealistic **12** preposterous, unbelievable

far-flung 6 remote **7** distant, removed **8** outlying **10** widespread

farinaceous 5 mealy **6** floury **7** starchy *food:* **4** meal **5** flour, grits **6** cereal, hominy **7** polenta, pudding, tapioca

farm 4 till **5** croft, ranch **6** grange, rancho **7** hennery **8** estancia, hacienda, hatchery **9** cultivate, farmstead **10** plantation *building:* **4** barn, shed, silo *Dutch:* **6** bowery *Israeli collective:* **7** kibbutz *Russian:* **7** kolkhoz, sovkhoz

farmer 6 grower, tiller, yeoman **7** granger, planter, rancher **8** ranchero, ranchman **13** agriculturist *Russian:* **5** kulak *South African:* **4** Boer *tenant:* **6** cottar, cotter **7** crofter **12** sharecropper

farming 7 tillage **8** agronomy **9** husbandry **11** agriculture, cultivation

faro 5 monte *bet:* **7** sleeper *card:* **4** case, hock, soda

Faroes whirlwind 2 oe

far-off 6 remote **7** distant, removed **8** outlying

far-out 3 rad **4** cool **5** outré, weird **6** groovy **7** bizarre, offbeat, radical **9** eccentric **10** avant-garde, off-the-wall, outlandish

farrago 4 hash, mess, olio **5** gumbo **6** jumble, medley, muddle **7** goulash, mélange, mixture **8** mishmash, shambles **9** potpourri **10** hodgepodge, miscellany

far-reaching 5 broad **8** sweeping **9** extensive, momentous, pervasive **10** portentous, widespread **11** significant, wide-ranging **13** comprehensive, consequential

farrier 5 smith **10** blacksmith, horseshoer

farsighted 4 sage, wise **9** hyperopic, prescient, sagacious **10** discerning

farthest 6 utmost **7** apogean, extreme, outmost **8** remotest, ultimate **9** outermost, uttermost

Fasching 8 carnival

fascinate 4 draw, wile **5** charm **6** allure, enamor, entice, please **7** attract, beguile, bewitch, enchant **8** enthrall, intrigue, transfix **9** captivate, enrapture, magnetize, mesmerize, spellbind

fascination 5 charm **6** allure, appeal **7** glamour **8** charisma **9** magnetism **10** attraction, witchcraft **11** enchantment **12** enthrallment

Fascist 4 Nazi **6** despot, Hitler (Adolf), tyrant **8** autocrat **9** Falangist, Mussolini (Benito) **10** Blackshirt

fashion 3 fad, fit, ton, way **4** chic, form, mode, mold, suit, tone, vein, wear **5** craze, shape, style, trend, usage, vogue **6** create, custom, design, devise, manner, method, sculpt, tailor **7** compose, costume, pattern **8** contrive **9** bandwagon, construct, fabricate **10** dernier cri **12** haute couture *magazine:* **3** WWD **4** Elle **5** Vogue **6** Hilary **7** Glamour, InStyle

fashionable 3 hip **4** chic, cool, posh, tony **5** fresh, ritzy, sharp, smart, swank, swish **6** chichi, du jour, modish, trendy, with-it **7** à la mode, current, dashing, faddish, popular, stylish, voguish **8** up-to-date **9** au courant, exclusive, happening **12** silk-stocking

fashionably nostalgic 5 retro

fashion designer *American:* **3** Sui (Anna) **4** Cole (Kenneth), Ford (Tom), Head (Edith), Kors (Michael), Wang (Vera) **5** Beene (Geoffrey), Blass (Bill), Daché (Lilly), Ellis (Perry), Karan (Donna), Klein (Anne, Calvin) **6** Jacobs (Marc), Lauren (Ralph), Mackie (Bob) **7** Galanos (James), Halston, Mizrahi (Isaac) **8** Galliano (John), Hilfiger (Tommy) **9** Claiborne (Liz), de la Renta (Oscar), Gernreich (Rudi) *Anglo-French:* **5** Worth (Charles Frederick) *Dominican:* **9** de la Renta (Oscar) *English:* **5** Quant (Mary) **6** Bailey (Christopher) **7** McQueen (Alexander) **8** Westwood (Vivienne) **9** McCartney (Stella) *French:* **4** Dior (Christian) **5** Bohan (Marc) **6** Cardin (Pierre), Chanel (Coco), Poiret (Paul) **6** Ungaro (Emanuel) **7** Bal-

main (Pierre), Lacroix (Christian), Montana (Claude) **8** Gaultier (Jean-Paul), Givenchy (Hubert de) **9** Courrèges (André), Lagerfeld (Karl) **12** Saint-Laurent (Yves), Schiaparelli (Elsa) *German:* **9** Lagerfeld (Karl) *Israeli:* **7** Mizrahi (Isaac) *Italian:* **5** Ferrè (Gianfranco), Prada (Miuccia), Pucci (Emilio), Ricci (Nina), Zegna (Ermenegildo) **6** Armani (Giorgio) **7** Cassini (Oleg), Versace (Gianni) **9** Valentino **12** Schiaparelli (Elsa) *Japanese:* **6** Miyake (Issey) *Spanish:* **10** Balenciaga (Cristóbal)

fast 3 set **4** ASAP, diet, easy, firm, Lent, soon, sure, true, wild **5** apace, fixed, fleet, hasty, hitch, loose, loyal, quick, rapid, swift **6** firmly, presto, prompt, snappy, speedy, stable **7** abstain, hastily, hurried, lasting, quickly, rapidly, staunch, swiftly **8** chop-chop, constant, faithful, full tilt, immobile, promptly, resolute, speedily **9** breakneck, dissolute, immovable, libertine **10** abstinence, profligate, recklessly, stationary **11** expeditious, promiscuous **12** lickety-split **13** expeditiously

fasten 3 fix, peg, pin, set, sew, tie, zip **4** bind, bolt, clip, hook, join, lace, lash, link, lock, moor, nail, seal, shut, weld **5** affix, cable, catch, chain, cinch, clamp, clasp, close, cramp, dowel, girth, hitch, latch, rivet, screw, stake, stick, strap, tie up, truss **6** anchor, attach, batten, buckle, button, couple, secure, skewer, solder, staple, tether **7** connect, mortise **8** buckle up

fastener 3 nut, peg, pin, tie **4** bolt, brad, clip, cord, frog, hasp, link, lock, nail, rope, snap, stud, tack, tape **5** catch, clamp, clasp, dowel, girth, hinge, hitch, latch, rivet, screw, spike, stake, strap **6** buckle, button, cotter, skewer, staple, tether, toggle, Velcro, zipper **7** grommet, padlock, netsuke, shackle **8** coupling, cuff link, handcuff, seat belt, shoelace **9** connector, cotter pin, safety pin, thumbtack **10** clothespin

fastidious 5 fussy, picky **6** choosy, dainty, queasy **7** choosey, finical, finicky, refined **8** exacting **9** demanding, squeamish **10** meticulous, particular, pernickety **11** persnickety

fastness 4 fort, hold, keep **6** bunker, castle, refuge **7** alcazar, bastion, citadel, crannog, redoubt, sanctum **8** casemate, fortress, presidio **10** stronghold, tower house **11** strongpoint

fast-talking 4 glib **5** slick **6** facile **8** slippery **13** silver-tongued

fat 3 big, oil **4** flab, lard, suet, wide **5** beefy, broad, bulky, burly, cream, dumpy, gross, heavy, husky, large, lipid, obese, plump, pudgy, round, stout, thick, tubby **6** chunky, excess, fleshy, grease, portly, rotund, stocky, stubby, tallow **7** adipose, blubber, paunchy, pinguid, porcine, surfeit, surplus, weighty **8** heavyset, oversize, thickset **9** corpulent **10** full-bodied, overweight, pot-bellied **11** superfluity

fatal 6 deadly, lethal, mortal **7** deathly, ruinous **8** terminal **9** incurable, pestilent **10** pernicious **12** pestilential

fatality 4 doom **5** death **8** casualty **10** deadliness

fata morgana 6 mirage **8** illusion

fat cat 5 mogul, nabob **6** big gun, bigwig, tycoon **7** big shot, magnate, pooh-bah **8** big wheel **9** moneybags, plutocrat **11** mucketymuck **13** high-muck-a-muck

fate 3 end, lot **4** doom, luck, ruin **5** death, karma **6** chance, kismet, upshot **7** destiny, fortune, outcome, portion **13** inevitability

fateful 6 deadly **7** ominous, ruinous **8** decisive **9** momentous, prophetic **10** portentous

Fates see at **Greek; Norse; Roman**

fathead 3 ass, oaf **4** boob, clod, dodo, dope, dolt, gawk, goof, goon, jerk, lump, mutt, yo-yo **5** cluck, clunk, dummy, dunce, idiot, moron, stock, stupe, yahoo **6** cretin, dimwit, donkey, doofus, dum-dum, nitwit, noodle, schlub, turkey **7** buffoon, dullard, jackass, schnook **8** dumbbell, imbecile, numskull **9** birdbrain, ignoramus, lamebrain, numbskull, simpleton

fatheaded 4 dull, dumb **5** dense, dopey, thick **6** obtuse, simple, stupid **7** doltish, idiotic **8** gormless **9** brainless, dim-witted, imbecilic **10** numskulled **11** numbskulled, thick-witted

father 2 pa **3** dad, pop **4** dada, papa, père, sire **5** beget, breed, daddy, hatch, padre, pappy, pater, poppa, spawn **6** author, create, old man, parent, priest **7** builder, creator, founder, produce **8** ancestor, engender, generate, inventor, producer **9** architect, initiator, originate, patriarch, procreate **10** originator, prime mover *combining form:* **4** patr **5** patri, patro *French:* **4** père *German:* **5** Vater *Italian:* **5** padre *Portuguese:* **3** pai *Spanish:* **5** padre

Father Brown creator 10 Chesterton (Gilbert Keith)

fatherland 4 home, soil **7** country

Father Time's implement 6 scythe

fathom 4 know **5** probe, sound **7** discern, explore, measure **9** apprehend, figure out, penetrate **10** comprehend, understand **11** investigate

fathomless 7 abysmal, abyssal **8** profound **12** immeasurable

fatidic 5 vatic **6** mantic **7** Delphic, sibylic **8** Delphian, oracular, sibyllic **9** prophetic, prescient, sibylline, vaticinal **10** divinatory, predictive

fatigue 3 fag **4** poop, tire, wear **5** drain, weary **6** tucker **7** deplete, burn out, exhaust, frazzle, wear out **8** drudgery, wear down **9** tiredness, weariness **10** enervation, exhaustion *combat:* **7** frazzle **10** shell shock

Fatima father: **8** Mohammed, Muhammad *husband:* **9** Bluebeard *son:* **5** Hasan **6** Husayn *stepbrother:* **3** Ali

fatness 7 obesity **9** adiposity **10** corpulence, overweight

fatty 4 oily, rich **6** greasy **7** adipose **8** unctuous **10** oleaginous *combining form:* **4** lipo **5** adipo

fatuous 4 dumb, fond **5** inane, sappy, silly **6** jejune, simple **7** asinine, foolish, puerile, witless

faucet 3 tap **4** bung, cock, gate **5** valve **6** spigot **7** hydrant, petcock **8** stopcock

Faulkner, William *character:* **3** Ike (Snopes), Joe (Christmas) **4** Eula (Varner Snopes), Flem (Snopes), Mink (Snopes) **5** Benjy (Compson), Caddy (Compson), Gavin (Stevens), Henry (Sutpen), Jason (Compson), Lucas (Beauchamp) **6** Dilsey, Temple (Drake) **7** Candace (Compson), Quentin (Compson) **8** Benjamin (Compson) *county:* **13** Yoknapatawpha *family:* **6** Benbow, Snopes, Sutpen **7** Compson **8** McCaslin, Sartoris **9** Beauchamp *novel:* **4** Town (The) **6** Hamlet (The) **7** Mansion (The), Reivers (The) **8** Sartoris **9** Sanctuary, Wild Palms (The) **11** As I Lay Dying **13** Light in August **14** Absalom Absalom **15** Sound and the Fury (The) **17** Intruder in the Dust

fault 3 err, nag, sin **4** flaw, rift, slip, spot, vice, want **5** blame, break, knock, error, scold **6** accuse, defect, foible, miscue **7** censure, demerit, failing, fissure, frailty, mistake, upbraid **8** fracture, weakness **9** criticize, infirmity **10** San Andreas **11** culpability, dereliction, shortcoming **12** imperfection *line:* **4** rift **5** split **6** breach **7** fissure **8** crevasse

faultfinder 4 crab **5** grump **6** critic, griper, grouch, nagger, whiner **7** grouser **8** grumbler **10** bellyacher, complainer, criticizer, crosspatch

faultfinding 7 carping **8** captious, critical, nitpicky **9** criticism **10** censorious, nit-picking, pernickety **11** persnickety **12** overcritical **13** hypercritical

faultless 4 pure **7** perfect **8** innocent, unerring **9** guiltless **10** immaculate, impeccable, inculpable

faulty 4 awry **5** amiss, wrong **6** flawed, marred **7** botched, damaged, defaced, inexact, unsound **8** fallible, specious **9** blemished, defective, deficient, erroneous, imperfect, incorrect **10** fallacious, inaccurate *prefix:* **3** dys

faun 5 satyr

fauna 7 animals

Faunus *grandfather:* **6** Saturn *son:* **4** Acis **7** Latinus

Faust *author:* **6** Goethe (Johann Wolfgang von) *beloved:* **8** Gretchen *composer:* **6** Gounod (Charles)

faux 4 fake, mock, sham **5** bogus, false, phony **6** ersatz **9** imitation, pretended, simulated, synthetic **10** substitute

faux pas 4 flub, goof, slip **5** boner, error, gaffe **6** boo-boo, howler, miscue, slipup **7** blooper, blunder, misstep, mistake, stumble **8** pratfall, solecism **9** gaucherie **11** impropriety

favor 4 baby, back, bias, boon, gift, okay **5** bless, bribe, grace, mercy, token, value **6** accept, behalf, choose, oblige, pamper, prefer, regard **7** indulge, present, support, sustain **8** courtesy, goodwill, interest, keepsake, kindness, resemble, sanction, sympathy **9** attention, patronage, privilege, take after **10** admiration, facilitate, indulgence, partiality **11** approbation, benevolence, countenance

favorable 4 fair **5** lucky **6** benign, biased, golden, timely, toward, useful **7** helpful, partial **8** pleasant, pleasing, positive **9** agreeable, benignant, fortunate, promising **10** auspicious, benevolent, propitious, prosperous **11** affirmative **12** advantageous **13** complimentary

favoring 4 rosy **6** timely, toward, useful **7** helpful **9** opportune **10** auspicious, beneficial, propitious **12** advantageous *prefix:* **3** pro

favorite 3 pet **7** dearest, popular, special **8** precious **9** preferred, well-liked **10** fair-haired, preference **11** front-runner, teacher's pet, white-haired

favoritism 4 bias **8** cronyism, nepotism **10** partiality **12** one-sidedness

fawn 3 kid, tan **4** deer, ecru **5** beige, toady **6** bister, grovel, kowtow **7** flatter, truckle, wheedle **8** blandish, bootlick **9** sweet-talk **11** apple-polish

fawning 6 smarmy **8** unctuous **9** parasitic **10** obsequious **11** sycophantic

fay 3 elf, nix **4** puck **5** elfin, fairy, nixie, pixie **6** elfish, goblin, sprite **7** brownie **10** leprechaun

faze 3 cow **5** abash, daunt, throw **6** dismay, rattle **7** confuse, disturb, nonplus, perturb **8** befuddle, bewilder, confound, unsettle **9** discomfit, dumbfound, embarrass **10** disconcert **11** flabbergast

FBI director 5 Freeh (Louis) **6** Hoover (J. Edgar) **7** Mueller (Robert)

fealty 5 faith, troth **7** loyalty **8** devotion, fidelity **9** adherence, constancy, vassalage **10** allegiance, attachment **11** devotedness **12** faithfulness

fear 3 awe **5** alarm, angst, dread, panic, qualm, scare, worry **6** dismay, fright, horror, phobia, terror **7** anxiety, jitters **8** cold feet, disquiet, timidity **9** agitation, cowardice, misgiving **10** foreboding **11** disquietude, trepidation **12** apprehension, cowardliness, perturbation, presentiment, timorousness *of animals:* **9** zoophobia *of being buried alive:* **11** taphephobia *of cats:* **12** ailurophobia *of crowds:* **11** ochlophobia *of darkness:* **11** nyctophobia *of dirt:* **10** mysophobia *of fire:* **10** pyrophobia *of heights:* **10** acrophobia *of men:* **11** androphobia *of new things:* **9** neophobia *of open areas:* **11** agoraphobia *of pain:* **10** algophobia *of strangers:* **10** xenophobia *of thunder:* **12** brontophobia *of water:* **11** hydrophobia *of women:* **10** gynophobia

fearful 5 timid **6** afraid, aghast, scared, trepid **7** alarmed, anxious, jittery, panicky **8** alarmist, paranoid, timorous **9** terrified, tremulous **12** apprehensive

fearless 4 bold **5** brave **6** daring **7** gallant, valiant **8** intrepid, unafraid **9** dauntless **10** courageous **11** lionhearted **12** greathearted, stouthearted

fearmonger 8 alarmist

Fear of Flying *author* **4** Jong (Erica)

fearsome 3 shy **5** scary, timid **6** afraid **7** extreme, intense **8** daunting, timorous **9** frightful **10** terrifying **11** frightening **12** intimidating

feasible 6 doable, likely, viable **8** possible, suitable, workable **10** reasonable **11** practicable **12** tried-and-true

feast 3 eat **4** dine, meal **5** gorge **6** dinner, regale, repast, spread **7** banquet, indulge **8** potlatch *Hawaiian:* **4** luau *Scottish:* **3** foy

Feast of Lights 8 Chanukah, Hanukkah

Feast of Lots 5 Purim

Feast of Tabernacles 6 Sukkot **7** Sukkoth

feat 3 act **4** coup, deed, gest **5** stunt, trick **6** action **7** exploit **11** achievement, performance, tour de force

feather 3 ilk **4** down, kind, sort, type **5** breed, order, pinna, plume, quill **6** fledge, fletch, pinion **7** species, variety *kind:* **4** down **6** covert **7** contour, plumule, rectrix **8** scapular *part:* **3** web **4** barb, vane **5** shaft **7** barbule, calamus **8** barbicel

featherbrained 5 dizzy, giddy, silly **7** flighty, foolish **8** heedless **9** frivolous **11** light-headed, thoughtless

feathered 7 plumose

feathers 4 down **7** plumage

feature 4 item, mark, part **5** add-on, trait **6** aspect, detail, factor **7** article, element, fixture, gimmick, quality **8** hallmark, property **9** attribute, component, lineament **10** attraction, ingredient **11** drawing card, peculiarity

febrile 3 hot **5** fiery **7** fevered, pyretic **8** feverish

feckless 4 weak **7** useless **8** carefree, impotent **11** incompetent, ineffective, ineffectual **12** undependable **13** irresponsible

fecund 4 rich **7** fertile **8** fruitful, prolific **9** inventive **10** productive

fecundity 9 abundance, fertility **11** prodigality **12** fruitfulness, productivity

Federalist writer 3 Jay (John) **7** Madison (James) **8** Hamilton (Alexander)

federation 5 union **6** league, nation **7** council **8** alliance **10** government **11** confederacy

fed up 4 sick **9** disgusted **11** exasperated

fee 3 cut, pay, tax **4** bill, cost, dues, hire, rate, toll, wage **5** price **6** charge **7** expense, payment, rake-off, stipend, tuition **8** retainer **9** emolument **10** commission, recompense *minting:* **10** seignorage **11** seigniorage *wharf:* **7** quayage

feeble 4 lame, puny, weak **5** anile, frail **6** infirm, senile, sickly, weakly **7** doddery **8** decrepit **9** doddering, unhealthy **10** inadequate

feebleminded 4 daft, dull, slow **5** dense, thick **6** stupid **7** doltish, foolish, idiotic, moronic, witless **8** imbecile, retarded **9** brainless, dim-witted, imbecilic **10** half-witted, slow-witted **11** harebrained, thickheaded

feebleness 7 frailty **8** debility **9** fragility, infirmity **10** enervation, inadequacy **11** decrepitude

feed 3 eat **4** grub, hand, meal **5** feast, gorge, graze, stuff **6** browse, devour, fatten, fodder, ingest, regale, repast, supply, viands **7** banquet, consume, deliver, dish out, edibles, furnish, nourish, nurture, provide, sustain **8** bonemeal, dispense, hand over, victuals **9** partake of, provender, provision, refection **10** provisions

feedback 5 input **8** critique, reaction, response **9** criticism **10** evaluation

feed the kitty 4 ante

feel 5 grope, sense, touch **6** caress, fondle, handle, stroke **7** palpate

feeler 4 palp **5** probe **6** palpus **7** antenna **8** proposal, tentacle **12** trial balloon

feeling 3 air **4** aura, mood, vibe **5** hunch, sense, touch **6** notion, temper **7** emotion, inkling, opinion, outlook, passion, sensate **8** attitude, instinct, sentient **9** affection, emotional, intuition, sensation, sentiment, suspicion **10** atmosphere, impression, persuasion **11** sensibility, sensitivity

feign 3 act **4** fake, play, sham **5** bluff, put on **6** affect, assume **7** pretend **8** simulate **9** dissemble **11** counterfeit, make believe

feigned 4 fake, sham **5** false, phony, put-on **7** assumed **8** imagined **9** imitation, insincere, pretended, simulated **10** fabricated, fictitious **11** counterfeit

feint 4 fake, hoax, play, ploy, ruse, sham, wile **5** trick **6** gambit **8** maneuver **9** stratagem *hockey:* **4** deke

feisty 6 frisky, plucky, spunky, touchy **7** bristly, fidgety **8** petulant, snappish, spirited **9** fractious, irascible **10** aggressive **11** quarrelsome

feldspar 6 albite **8** andesine **9** anorthite, moonstone **10** microcline, orthoclase **11** plagioclase *clay:* **6** kaolin

felicitate 6 salute **7** commend **10** compliment **12** congratulate

felicitous 3 apt, fit **4** meet **5** happy **6** proper, timely **7** apropos, fitting **8** apposite, pleasant, suitable **9** agreeable **10** delightful **11** appropriate

feline 3 cat, sly, tom **4** lion, lynx, pard, puma, puss **5** catty, felid, pussy, sleek, tiger **6** bobcat, cougar, jaguar, margay, ocelot, serval, slinky, sneaky, tomcat **7** caracal, catlike, cheetah, furtive, leonine, leopard, lioness, panther, tigress, wildcat **8** pussycat, stealthy *hybrid:* **5** liger, tigon **6** tiglon

fell 3 cut, hew, mow **4** down, drop, kill, raze **5** floor **6** poleax **7** cut down, flatten **8** knock off **9** bring down, knock down

Fellini film 8 Amarcord, Casanova, La Strada **9** Satyricon **10** I Vitelloni **11** La Dolce Vita **15** Nights of Cabiria **18** Juliet of the Spirits

fellow 3 bub, guy, joe, lad, man **4** buck, chap, dude, gent, mate, peer, twin **5** bloke, match **6** codger, cohort, hombre, person **7** comrade, consort, partner **8** confrere **9** associate, companion, copartner, gentleman **10** coordinate, reciprocal

fellow feeling 5 agape **7** concern, empathy,

rapport 8 affinity, kindness, sympathy **9** affection **10** compassion, kindliness **11** consolation **13** understanding

fellowship 4 club **5** guild **6** league **7** coterie, society, stipend **8** sodality **9** communion, community **10** fraternity **11** association, brotherhood

felon 3 con **7** convict, whitlow **8** criminal **10** malefactor

felt 6 groped, sensed

felt hat 3 fez **5** derby, terai **6** fedora, trilby **7** homburg, stetson **8** snap-brim **9** wideawake

female 4 girl **5** woman **7** girlish, womanly **8** feminine **suffix: 3** ess **4** ette, trix

Feminine Mystique author 7 Friedan (Betty)

feminist 10 suffragist **11** suffragette

femme fatale 5 Circe, siren **6** Carmen, Salome **7** Delilah, Lorelei **8** Mata Hari **9** temptress **10** seductress **11** enchantress

femur 9 thighbone

fen 3 bog **4** mire, quag, wash **5** marsh, swale, swamp **6** morass, muskeg, slough **9** marshland

fence 3 bar, pen **4** cage, rail, palc, wcir **5** hedge, parry **6** corral, paling, picket **7** barrier, enclose, railing **8** backstop, boundary, hoarding, palisade, receiver, sidestep, stockade **9** barricade, stone wall **sunk: 4** ha-ha

fencer 7 duelist, épéeist **8** foilsman **9** swordsman

fencing 9 swordplay **attack: 5** lunge **6** thrust **7** reprise, riposte **cry: 6** touché **7** en garde **defense: 5** parry **movement: 4** volt **term: 4** jury **5** forte, lunge **6** flèche, foible, touché **touch: 3** cut, hit **weapon: 4** épée, foil **5** blade, guard, saber, sabre **6** pommel

fender 4 skid **5** guard **6** buffer, bumper, shield **7** cushion, railing **8** mudguard

fennec 3 fox

Fenrir chain: 8 Gleipnir **father: 4** Loki **form: 4** wolf **mother: 9** Angerboda **10** Angerbotha **slayer: 5** Vidar **6** Vithar **victim: 4** Odin **5** Woden

Fenway Park fence: 12 Green Monster **site: 6** Boston **team: 6** Red Sox

feral 4 wild **5** brute **6** brutal, savage **7** beastly, bestial, brutish, inhuman, untamed

Ferber novel 5 Giant, So Big **8** Cimarron, Show Boat **9** Ice Palace **13** Saratoga Trunk

Ferdinand beloved: 7 Miranda **father: 6** Alonso

Ferdinand, King conquest: 7 Granada **daughter: 6** Joanna **wife: 7** Isabela **8** Germaine, Isabella

fermata 4 hold **5** pause

ferment 4 boil, brew, stir **5** rouse, sweat **6** clamor, enzyme, excite, incite, leaven, seethe, simmer, unrest, work up **7** smolder, turmoil **9** agitation, commotion **12** restlessness

fermentation 7 zymosis **13** bioconversion

fern 4 tree **5** brake, holly, royal **6** Boston **7** bracken **8** polypody **10** maidenhair, spleenwort **leaf: 5** frond

ferocious 4 fell, grim, wild **5** brute, cruel **6** brutal, fierce, savage **7** bestial, extreme, inhuman, intense, vicious, violent **8** barbaric, inhumane, ruthless **9** barbarous, rapacious, truculent

ferret out 4 find **5** dig up, flush **6** elicit **7** unearth **8** discover **9** ascertain

ferrule 3 cap, tip **4** band, ring, virl **6** collet

ferry 5 carry **6** convey **7** shuttle **9** transport

ferryman 6 Charon **9** gondolier

fertile 4 lush, rich **6** fecund **8** abundant, creative, fruitful, pregnant, prolific **9** bountiful, ingenious, inventive, luxuriant, plenteous **10** productive **12** reproductive

fertilize 5 beget, breed **6** enrich **8** generate **9** fecundate, pollinate **10** impregnate, inseminate

fertilizer 4 dung **5** guano, mulch **6** manure **7** compost **8** bonemeal **9** plant food

ferule 3 rod **5** stick

fervent 3 hot **4** avid, keen **5** eager, fiery **6** ardent, devout, gung-ho **7** blazing, burning, earnest, glowing, intense, zealous **8** vehement **9** heartfelt **10** hot-blooded, passionate **11** impassioned, warm-blooded **12** enthusiastic, wholehearted

fervor 4 fire, heat, zeal **5** ardor **6** warmth **7** passion **8** devotion, violence **9** vehemence **10** devoutness, enthusiasm

fescennine 7 obscene **10** scurrilous

fess up 3 own **5** admit **9** come clean

fester 3 rot **6** rankle **7** inflame, putrefy **8** ulcerate **9** suppurate

festina _____ 5 lente

festival 4 fair, fete, gala **5** feast **6** fiesta **7** jubilee **8** carnival, jamboree **11** celebration, merrymaking

festive 3 gay **4** gala **5** jolly, merry **6** joyful, joyous **7** gleeful **8** mirthful **11** celebratory

festivity 4 bash, fair, fete, gala **5** feast, party, revel **6** affair, frolic, gaiety **7** blowout, revelry, whoopee **8** carnival, jamboree **9** rejoicing, merriment **11** celebration, merrymaking

festoon 4 deck, hang **5** adorn **6** bedeck **7** garland **8** decorate, ornament **9** embellish

fetch 3 get **4** draw, earn **5** bring, yield **6** take in **7** attract, bring in, realize **8** retrieve

fetching 4 fair **6** comely, lovely, pretty **7** winsome 8 alluring, charming, enticing, engaging, handsome, pleasing 9 appealing 10 attractive

fete 4 ball, bash, fair, gala 5 feast, honor, party 6 affair, fiesta, soiree 7 banquet, jubilee, shindig 8 carnival, festival, jamboree, wingding 9 celebrate, entertain 11 celebration, commemorate 13 entertainment

fetid 4 foul, high, rank 5 funky 6 putrid, rancid, smelly, strong 8 mephitic, stinking 10 malodorous

fetish 4 idol, juju, luck 5 charm 6 amulet 7 periapt 8 fixation, gris-gris, talisman 10 phylactery

fetor 4 odor, reek 5 stink 6 stench

fetter 3 tie 4 bind, bond, gyve 5 chain, check, irons 6 hobble, hog-tie, impede 7 enchain, manacle, shackle, trammel 8 handcuff, restrain 9 restraint

fettle 5 shape 6 health 7 fitness 9 condition 12 constitution

feud 6 enmity, strife 7 dispute, quarrel 8 argument, vendetta 9 hostility 11 controversy

feudal *estate:* 3 fee 4 feud, fief 6 domain *jurisdiction:* 4 soke *laborer:* 4 serf *lord:* 5 laird, liege, thane 8 suzerain *status:* 9 vassalage *tax:* 7 tallage *tenant:* 6 vassal 7 homager, socager, vavasor 8 vavasour *tenure of land:* 6 socage *tribute:* 6 heriot *warrior:* 5 bushi, ronin 7 samurai

feuilleton 5 essay

fever 4 ague, fire, heat 5 craze, flush, Lassa, mania 6 dengue, frenzy 7 ferment, passion, pyrexia 8 delirium 9 calenture *recurrent:* 7 malaria, quartan, tertian *type:* 3 hay 6 dengue, hectic 7 scarlet

fevered 6 crazed, heated 7 burning, febrile, flushed 8 agitated, frenetic, restless 9 delirious 10 distracted, overheated 11 overwrought

feverish 3 hot 5 fiery 6 hectic 7 burning, febrile, flushed, pyretic 8 frenetic, frenzied 10 passionate 11 overwrought

fever tree 6 acacia 7 blue gum

few 4 rare 5 scant 6 meager, meagre, scanty, scarce, sparse 7 handful, limited 8 sporadic 9 scattered 10 infrequent, occasional, scattering, smattering, spattering, sprinkling *combining form:* 4 olig 5 oligo

fey 4 daft 5 campy, crazy, vatic 7 touched 8 oracular, precious 9 pixilated, prophetic, sibylline, visionary 11 clairvoyant 12 otherworldly

fiasco 3 dud 4 bomb, flop 5 farce, flask 6 bottle, defeat 7 blunder, debacle, failure, washout 8 abortion, disaster 11 miscarriage 13 embarrassment

fiat 5 edict, order 6 decree 7 command, dictate, mandate, warrant 8 sanction 11 endorsement 12 proclamation 13 authorization

fib 3 lie 4 tale 5 story 7 falsify, falsity, untruth 8 white lie 9 falsehood, mendacity 10 taradiddle 11 fabrication, prevaricate

fiber 3 web 4 noil, pita 5 grain, istle 6 fabric, strand, thread 7 texture *basketry:* 5 istle *brain:* 4 pons *coarse:* 4 jute 8 piassava *coconut husk:* 4 coir *rope:* 4 bast, hemp 5 sisal 8 henequen *silky:* 5 kapok *small:* 6 fibril *substructure:* 7 micelle, spongin *synthetic:* 5 nylon, Orlon, rayon, saran, vinal 6 Dacron 7 spandex *woody:* 4 bast *woollike:* 7 lanital

fibrous 4 ropy, wiry 5 tough, woody 6 sinewy 7 stringy

fibula 4 bone 5 clasp

fichu 5 scarf 8 kerchief

fickle 7 flighty 8 unstable, variable, volatile 9 mercurial 10 capricious, changeable, inconstant, unfaithful, unreliable 12 undependable 13 temperamental, unpredictable

fiction 4 tale, yarn 5 fable, story 7 fantasy, figment 8 pretense 9 falsehood, fish story, invention, narrative 10 concoction 11 fabrication

fictional 6 made-up, unreal 8 notional 9 imaginary 11 make-believe 12 suppositious

fictitious 4 fake, mock, sham 5 bogus, faked, false, phony 6 ersatz, made-up, unreal, untrue 7 assumed, created 8 cooked-up, fanciful, illusory, imagined, invented, mythical, spurious 9 concocted, fantastic, imaginary, simulated, trumped-up 10 apocryphal, artificial, chimerical, fabricated 11 make-believe 12 suppositious

fiddle 3 toy 4 fool, play, rack 5 alter, cheat 6 dawdle, diddle, doodle, finger, meddle, monkey, potter, putter, tamper, tinker, trifle, violin 7 swindle 9 interfere 10 fool around, manipulate, mess around

fiddle-faddle 3 rot 4 bosh, bull, bunk, nuts 5 fudge, drool, hokum, hooey, pshaw 6 bunkum, drivel, hoodoo, humbug, piffle 7 baloney, blarney, hogwash, rubbish, twaddle 8 nonsense, pishposh, tommyrot 9 poppycock 10 applesauce, balderdash, flapdoodle 13 horsefeathers

____ **Fideles** 6 Adeste

Fidelio *composer:* 9 Beethoven (Ludwig van) *hero:* 9 Florestan *heroine:* 7 Leonora

fidelity 5 ardor, piety, troth 6 fealty 7 loyalty 8 devotion 9 adherence, constancy 10 allegiance, attachment 11 staunchness 12 faithfulness 13 dependability, steadfastness

Fidel's comrade 3 Che

fidget 6 fantod, fiddle, jitter, squirm, twitch **7** wriggle

fidgety 5 antsy, jumpy **6** uneasy **7** jittery, nervous, restive, squirmy, twitchy **8** restless

fiduciary 7 trustee

field 3 lea **4** area, mead, turf **5** green, major, milpa, orbit, range **6** domain, meadow, métier, region, sphere **7** demesne, pasture, purview, terrain **8** dominion, gridiron, precinct, vocation **9** bailiwick, champaign, specialty, territory **10** department, discipline, occupation

field crop 3 hay **4** corn, oats **5** grain, wheat **6** cotton **7** alfalfa **8** soybeans

field deity 3 Pan **4** Faun **5** Fauna **6** Faunus

field glasses 6 binocs **10** binoculars

field hand 4 hoer **5** sower **6** picker **7** laborer, planter

Fielding novel 6 Amelia **8** Tom Jones **13** Joseph Andrews

field marshal *Austrian:* 8 Radetzky (Joseph) ***British:* 6** Napier (Robert), Raglan (Baron), Wavell (Archibald), Wilson (Henry) **7** Roberts (Frederick) **8** Wolseley (Garnet) **9** Kitchener (Horatio) **10** Montgomery (Bernard) ***French:* 3** Ney (Michel) **4** Foch (Ferdinand) **6** Joffre (Joseph-Jacques-Césaire), Pétain (Philippe) ***German:* 6** Keitel (Wilhelm), Paulus (Friedrich), Rommel (Erwin), Rupert (Prince) **9** Mackensen (August von), Rundstedt (Karl von), Waldersee (Alfred von) **10** Kesselring (Albert) ***Japanese:* 8** Sugiyama (Hajime) ***Prussian:* 6** Moltke (Helmuth von) ***Russian:* 7** Kutuzov (Mikhail), Suvorov (Aleksandr) **8** Potemkin (Grigory)

field mouse 4 vole

field officer 5 major **7** colonel

fieldwork 5 redan

fiend 3 bug, imp, nut **5** demon, devil, freak, Satan **6** addict, Belial, diablo, maniac, zealot **7** devotee, fanatic, habitué, Lucifer, monster, Old Nick, serpent **8** Apollyon, succubus **9** Beelzebub **10** enthusiast, Old Scratch **13** Old Gooseberry

fiendish 3 bad **4** evil **5** cruel **6** malign, savage, wicked **7** baleful, demonic, hellish, inhuman, malefic, satanic, vicious **8** demoniac, devilish, diabolic, infernal, sinister **9** barbarous, difficult, ferocious, malicious, malignant **10** diabolical

fierce 4 fell, grim, wild **5** cruel **6** brutal, savage, wicked **7** brutish, hostile, inhuman, intense, vicious, violent, wolfish **8** inhumane, pitiless, ruthless, terrible, vehement **9** barbarous, bellicose, ferocious, merciless, truculent **10** aggressive, determined

fiery 3 hot, red **5** afire **6** ablaze, aflame, ardent, fervid, fierce, heated, red-hot, torrid **7** burning, febrile, fervent, flaming, flaring, igneous, intense, peppery **8** broiling, feverish, spirited, vehement, white-hot **9** flammable, hotheaded, irritable, perfervid **10** mettlesome, passionate **11** combustible, inflammable, impassioned

fiesta 4 fete **5** party **6** frolic **8** carnival, festival, jamboree **9** merriment

fife 4 pipe **5** flute

fifth *combining form:* 5 quint

fifth columnist 3 spy

fig *genus:* 5 Ficus *sacred:* **5** pipal *variety:* **5** elemi **6** Smyrna

fight 3 row, war **4** bout, buck, duel, feud, fray, spat, tiff **5** brawl, broil, clash, joust, match, melee, repel, scrap, set-to **6** affray, attack, battle, combat, fracas, oppose, oppugn, resist, rumble, scrape, tussle **7** contend, contest, dispute, quarrel, scuffle, wrangle, wrestle **8** conflict, skirmish, slugfest, squabble, struggle, traverse **10** aggression, donnybrook, free-for-all **11** altercation

fighter 2 GI **3** pug **4** swad **5** boxer **7** brawler, soldier, warrior **8** champion, pugilist, scrapper **9** combatant, gladiator, man-at-arms, mercenary **11** interceptor

fighter plane 3 MiG, Roc **4** Zero **5** Sabre **6** bomber, Fokker, Hawker, Mirage, Voodoo **7** Corsair, Harrier **8** Spitfire **11** interceptor

fighting fish 5 betta

figment 5 dream, fable, fancy **7** chimera, fiction **8** daydream, illusion, phantasm **9** invention, unreality **11** contrivance, fabrication

figure 3 add, sum, tot **4** cast, form, mold, rule, tote **5** count, digit, frame, image, model, motif, shape, total **6** cipher, decide, design, device, effigy, motive, number, reckon, settle, symbol **7** compute, integer, numeral, outline, pattern, resolve **8** conclude, estimate, physique **9** calculate, character, determine, enumerate *geometric:* **4** cone, cube **5** rhomb **6** circle, isogon, square **7** decagon, ellipse, hexagon, nonagon, octagon, polygon, rhombus **8** pentacle, pentagon, rhomboid, tetragon, triangle **9** rectangle **10** hexahedron, octahedron **11** icosahedron **12** dodecahedron, rhombohedron *human:* **4** nude **5** atlas **7** telamon **8** caryatid *ornamental:* **6** statue **8** gargoyle

figurehead 4 pawn, tool **5** front **6** minion, puppet **7** cat's-paw **8** creature **10** instrument, mouthpiece

figure of speech 5 trope **6** aporia, simile **7** litotes **8** metaphor, metonymy **10** synecdoche

figure out 5 crack, learn, solve **6** decide, decode, fathom **7** resolve, unravel **8** decipher, discover, unriddle **9** ascertain, determine

figure skater see **ice skater**

figure skating *jump:* **4** axel, loop, lutz **5** split **6** rocker **7** bracket, counter, salchow **11** spreadeagle *spin:* **5** camel

figurine 9 statuette

Fiji *capital:* **4** Suva *explorer:* **4** Cook (Capt. James) **6** Tasman (Abel) *island:* **3** Gau **4** Koro **6** Ovalau **8** Viti Levu **9** Vanua Levu *island group:* **3** Lau **6** Yasawa *language:* **6** Fijian *neighbor:* **5** Samoa **7** Vanuatu

filch 3 cop, nip **4** crib, lift, take **5** boost, pinch, steal, swipe **6** pilfer, snitch **7** purloin

file 3 row, rub **4** line, rank, rasp, tier **5** lodge, march, place, queue **6** smooth **7** archive, arrange, corrupt, dossier **10** emery board

filial 5 sonly **7** duteous, dutiful

filibuster 5 delay, stall **10** adventurer

filigree 4 lace **6** design **7** pattern **8** fretwork, openwork, ornament **10** decoration **13** embellishment, ornamentation

fill 3 jam **4** clog, cloy, cram, glut, heap, lade, load, pack, pile, plug, sate, stop **5** block, choke, close, gorge, stock, stuff **6** charge, stodge **7** congest, engorge, inflate, occlude, pervade, satiate, satisfy, stopper, surfeit **8** permeate *interstices:* **4** calk **5** caulk, chink, putty

filled 5 awash, flush, sated **6** packed **7** replete **9** saturated

filler 5 squib **7** packing, padding, tobacco, wadding **8** stuffing

fillet 4 band **5** slice, snood, strip **6** ribbon, stripe **7** bandeau, banding **8** headband *anatomical:* **9** lemniscus *architectural:* **6** listel, reglet, taenia *meat:* **10** tenderloin

fill in 3 sub **4** clew, clue, post **6** advise, detail, insert, notify **7** apprise **8** acquaint, complete **10** substitute

fill-in 3 sub **4** temp **6** backup **7** stopgap **9** alternate, expedient, makeshift, surrogate, temporary **10** substitute **11** locum tenens, pinch hitter, replacement, succedaneum

filling 5 kapok

fillip 3 tap **4** goad, kick, spur **5** boost, tonic **6** buffet, strike **7** impetus, wrinkle **8** catalyst, stimulus **9** incentive, stimulant, stimulate **10** inducement, motivation **13** embellishment

film 4 coat, scum, skim, skin **5** glaze, layer, Mylar **6** lamina, patina **7** tarnish **8** membrane, pellicle (see also **movie**)

film director see **movie director**

film producer see **movie producer**

filmy 4 hazy **5** gauzy, misty, sheer, wispy **6**

dainty **8** delicate, gossamer **10** diaphanous **11** transparent

fils 3 son

filter 4 sift **5** clean, leach, sieve **6** purify, refine, screen, strain **7** clarify, cleanse **9** percolate

filth 4 crud, dirt, dung, muck, slop, smut **5** dreck, grime, slime, trash **6** ordure, refuse, sludge **7** squalor **9** obscenity

filthy 4 base, foul, vile **5** black, dirty, grimy, gross, gunky, mucky, muddy, nasty **6** coarse, cruddy, grubby, ribald, scuzzy, skanky, smutty, sordid **7** obscene, raunchy, squalid, unclean **8** indecent **9** loathsome, offensive, repulsive, revolting **12** scatological

filthy lucre 4 cash, loot, pelf **5** bread, bucks, dough, money, moola **6** boodle, riches, moolah, wampum **7** cabbage, scratch **8** currency

fin 3 arm **4** bill **5** fiver, pinna **7** airfoil, flipper *type:* **6** caudal, dorsal **7** ventral **8** pectoral

finagle 5 cheat, trick **6** wangle **7** snaffle, swindle, wheedle **8** fast-talk, maneuver, scrounge **9** bamboozle, machinate

final 3 end **4** last **6** ending, latest **7** closing **8** hindmost, terminal, ultimate **10** concluding, conclusive, definitive **11** examination

finale 3 end **4** coda **5** close, finis **6** capper, climax, ending, payoff, windup, wrap-up **7** closing **10** conclusion, denouement **11** culmination, termination

finalize 3 end **5** close, sew up, tie up **6** decide, finish, wind up, wrap up **7** approve **8** complete, conclude, solidify **9** terminate **10** consummate

finally 6 at last, lastly **7** someday **8** at length **9** belatedly **10** at long last, eventually, ultimately **12** subsequently

finance 4 back, bank, fund **5** endow, funds, money, stake **6** credit **7** banking, promote, revenue, sponsor, support **8** bankroll **9** grubstake, patronize, subsidize **10** capitalize, investment, underwrite

financial 6 fiscal, pocket **8** business, economic, monetary **9** pecuniary **10** commercial *plan:* **6** budget *statement:* **12** balance sheet

financier *American:* **4** Hill (James Jerome), Ryan (Thomas Fortune), Sage (Russell) **5** Astor (John Jacob), Baker (George Fisher), Eaton (Cyrus), Field (Cyrus West), Gould (Jay), Grace (William Russell), Green (Hetty), Soros (George) **6** Biddle (Nicholas), Boesky (Ivan), Girard (Stephen), Mellon (Andrew), Morgan (John Pierpont, Junius Spencer), Morris (Robert), Rogers

(Henry Huttleston), Yerkes (Charles Tyson) **7** Buffett (Warren), Peabody (George) **10** Vanderbilt (Cornelius, William) *British:* **6** Baring (Alexander), Rhodes (Cecil) **7** Gresham (Thomas) *French:* **6** Necker (Jacques) **7** Colbert (Jean-Baptiste) *German:* **7** Schacht (Hjalmar) **10** Rothschild (Amschel, Jakob, Karl, Mayer, Nathan, Salomon)

finch 4 pape **5** junco, serin, zebra **6** canary, linnet, siskin, towhee **7** bunting, chewink, redpoll, sparrow **8** cardinal, grosbeak, longspur **9** crossbill, seedeater

find 3 gem **4** gain, meet, spot **5** catch, dig up, hit on, reach, sight **6** attain, detect, locate, supply, turn up **7** discern, furnish, scare up, uncover, unearth **8** bump into, come upon, discover, meet with, perceive, treasure **9** determine, discovery, encounter **10** experience **13** treasure trove

find out 4 hear **5** catch, learn **6** detect **7** catch on **8** discover, perceive **9** ascertain, determine

fine 3 A-OK, end, top **4** fair, keen, levy, pure, thin **5** bonny, close, clear, dandy, mulct, sheer **6** amerce, choice, minute, ornate, punish, purify, subtle **7** clarion, damages, elegant, forfeit, penalty **8** all right, delicate, penalize, pleasant, splendid, superior **9** beautiful, enjoyable, excellent, first-rate **10** punishment, reparation

finery 5 array **6** attire **7** apparel, regalia **8** clothing, frippery, glad rags, ornament **9** caparison, full dress, trappings, trimmings **10** decoration, Sunday best

finesse 5 dodge, evade, skill, skirt **6** jockey **7** beguile, cunning, exploit **8** maneuver, subtlety **9** dexterity **10** adroitness, artfulness, manipulate

fine-tune 4 true **5** tweak **6** adjust

Fingal's Cave *composer:* **11** Mendelssohn (Felix) *island:* **6** Staffa

finger 5 blame, digit, index, pinky, strum, touch **6** accuse, pinkie **7** palpate **8** identify, pinpoint *bone:* **7** phalanx *combining form:* **6** dactyl

finicky 5 fussy, picky **6** choosy, dainty, prissy **7** choosey **8** exacting **9** squeamish **10** fastidious, meticulous, particular, pernickety **11** persnickety

finis 3 end **5** close **6** finale **10** completion, conclusion

finish 3 end **4** do in, kill, slay, stop **5** cease, close, glaze, use up **6** cut off, ending, finale, murder, patina, polish, windup, wrap up **7** closing, consume, destroy, execute, exhaust, surface **8** complete, conclude, dispatch, finalize, terminus **9** cessation, liquidate, terminate **10** completion, conclusion, denouement, run through **11** termination *dull:* **3** mat **4** matt **5** matte *second:* **5** place *third:* **4** show

finished 4 done, over, ripe **5** ideal **7** done for, perfect, refined, through **8** achieved, complete, over with, polished, washed-up **9** perfected **10** consummate

finite 5 bound, fixed **7** bounded, limited, precise **9** definable **10** restricted **12** determinable

fink 3 rat **5** Judas **6** betray, snitch, squeal **7** traitor **8** betrayer, informer, quisling, snitcher **11** backstabber, stool pigeon **13** strikebreaker

Finland 5 Suomi *Arctic region:* **7** Lapland *capital:* **8** Helsinki *city:* **5** Espoo, Turku **6** Vantaa **7** Tampere *ethnic group:* **4** Lapp, Sami *gulf:* **7** Bothnia *invader:* **9** Alexander *island:* **5** Karlö **6** Kimito **9** Vallgrund *island group:* **5** Åland *lake:* **5** Inari **6** Saimaa **7** Keitele **8** Pielinen *language:* **7** Finnish, Swedish *monetary unit:* **4** euro *monetary unit, former:* **6** markka *neighbor:* **6** Norway, Russia, Sweden

Finlandia composer 8 Sibelius (Jean)

Finnigans Wake *author:* **5** Joyce (James) *first word:* **8** riverrun *last word:* **3** the

Finnish bath: **5** sauna *epic:* **8** Kalevala *god:* **6** Jumala

fir 4 pine **6** balsam, Fraser **7** conifer, Douglas **9** evergreen *genus:* **5** Abies

fire 2 ax **3** axe, can, pep, vim, zip **4** bake, brio, burn, cast, dash, hurl, sack, stir, toss, zeal, zest, zing **5** ardor, blaze, drive, flame, flare, fling, glare, ingle, light, pitch, rouse, salvo, shoot, spark, throw, torch, verve, vigor **6** arouse, energy, excite, fervor, flames, ignite, kindle, lay off, spirit **7** animate, boot out, dismiss, enthuse, inferno, inflame, inspire, kick out, passion, provoke **8** enkindle **9** calenture, discharge, holocaust, terminate **10** combustion, enthusiasm, liveliness **13** conflagration *combining form:* **3** pyr **4** igni, pyro *god:* **4** Agni, Loki **6** Vulcan **10** Hephaestus

firearm see **gun**

firebrand 8 agitator **10** incendiary, instigator

firebug 5 torch **8** arsonist **10** incendiary, pyromaniac

firecracker 5 squib **6** banger **9** explosive **10** cherry bomb, noisemaker

firedog 7 andiron

firedrake 6 dragon

firefly 12 lightning bug

fire opal 7 girasol

fireplace 5 grate, ingle **equipment: 6** fender, screen **7** andiron **part: 3** hob **6** hearth, mantel

fireplug 7 hydrant

fire up 5 anger, annoy, rouse, spark **6** excite, ignite, incite, kindle **7** enliven, inflame, inspire, provoke **8** enkindle, irritate

firework 6 petard, rocket **8** pinwheel, sparkler **11** pyrotechnic, Roman candle **cluster: 9** girandole

firkin 3 keg, tun, vat **4** butt, cask, pipe **6** barrel, vessel **8** hogshead

firm 3 set **4** fast, hard, sure **5** fixed, rigid, solid, sound, stiff, tight, tough **6** harden, outfit, secure, settle, stable, steady, strong, sturdy **7** abiding, adamant, certain, company, concern, improve, settled, staunch, unmoved **8** business, constant, definite, enduring, faithful, resolute, specific, vigorous **9** steadfast, tenacious **10** determined, enterprise, inflexible, stipulated, strengthen, unwavering, unyielding **11** established, partnership, substantial, unfaltering, well-founded **13** establishment

firmament 3 sky **5** vault **6** sphere, welkin **7** expanse, heavens **8** empyrean

firmness 7 resolve **8** decision, security, solidity, strength, tenacity **9** constancy, stability **10** durability, resolution **13** determination

first 4 arch, head **5** alpha, chief, prime **6** maiden, primal **7** highest, initial, leading, lead-off, opening, pioneer, premier, primary, supreme **8** champion, dominant, earliest, foremost, headmost, original **9** inaugural, initially, paramount, principal, sovereign **10** aboriginal, preeminent, primordial **prefix: 4** prot **5** proto

firstborn 4 heir **6** eldest, oldest

first-class 3 top **4** A-one, best, fine **5** prime, primo **6** tip-top **7** capital, supreme **8** five-star, superior, top-notch **9** excellent, top-drawer

firsthand 6 direct **7** primary **9** immediate

first man in space 7 Gagarin (Yury)

first showing 5 debut **7** opening **8** premiere

First State 8 Delaware

firth 3 arm, bay **4** cove, gulf **5** inlet **6** harbor, slough **7** estuary

fiscal 8 monetary **9** budgetary, financial

fish 3 aku, bob, cod, dab, eel, gar, koi, net, ray **4** barb, bass, carp, cast, cero, char, chub, chum, coho, cusk, dace, dory, drum, gata, gill, goby, hake, hint, jack, ling, mero, opah, parr, pike, rudd, scup, shad, sild, sisi, sole, spet, tuna, ulua **5** angle, betta, bream, brill, charr, cisco, cobia, danio, fluke, grunt, guppy, jurel, loach, moray, perch, platy, porgy, roach, scrod, seine, shark, skate, smelt, smolt, snook, sprat, tench, tetra, trawl, troll, trout, tunny, wahoo **6** blenny, bonito, burbot, caribe, conger, dorado, grilse, kipper, marlin, minnow, mullet, permit, plaice, pompon, puffer, remora, salmon, sauger, sebago, shiner, sucker, tarpon, tautog, tomcod, turbot, warsaw, wrasse **7** alewife, anchovy, buffalo, capelin, catfish, cavalla, chimera, chinook, cichlid, corbina, cowfish, crappie, dolphin, escolar, gillnet, gourami, grouper, grunion, haddock, hagfish, halibut, herring, hogfish, jewfish, lamprey, mudfish, oarfish, pigfish, pinfish, piranha, pollack, pollock, pompano, pupfish, rainbow, rasbora, sardine, sawfish, sculpin, sea carp, snapper, sniggle, sockeye, sunfish, tilapia, torpedo, whiting **8** albacore, blowfish, bluefish, bluegill, bocaccio, bonefish, brisling, bullhead, chimaera, crevalle, filefish, flounder, gambusia, goldfish, grayling, halfbeak, hornpout, kingfish, ladyfish, lionfish, lookdown, lumpfish, lungfish, mackerel, menhaden, moonfish, pickerel, pilchard, pipefish, porkfish, rock bass, rockfish, rosefish, sailfish, seahorse, sea trout, skipjack, stingray, sturgeon, tilefish, warmouth, weakfish, wolffish **9** amberjack, angelfish, barracuda, brandling, cutthroat, goosefish, greenling, pilotfish, spadefish, stargazer, swordfish, topminnow, trunkfish, whitebait, whitefish **10** butterfish, flying fish, needlefish, parrotfish, sheepshead, silverside, squeteague, tripletail, victorfish, yellowtail **11** Dolly Varden, hatchetfish, jacksmelt, killifish, lanternfish, mummichog, muskellunge, pumpkinseed, stickleback, triggerfish **basket: 5** creel **character: 4** Nemo **5** Wanda **combining form: 6** ichthy **dish: 7** ceviche, seviche **8** cioppino, matelote **13** bouillabaisse **eggs: 3** roe **5** spawn **genus: 4** Amia, Lota **relating to: 7** piscine **spear: 3** gig **7** harpoon, trident **trap: 4** weir **young: 3** fry **4** parr **5** larva, smolt **6** alevin, grilse

fisherman 6 angler

fish hawk 6 osprey

fishhook adjunct: 5 snell **part: 4** barb **5** shank

fishing line 4 trot **7** setline **8** longline, trotline **float: 3** bob **5** quill **leader: 5** snell

fishing lure 3 fly **4** bait **5** spoon **7** spinner

fishing net 5 seine, trawl

fishlike mammal 4 orca **5** whale **6** dugong, sea cow **7** dolphin, grampus, manatee, narwhal **8** cetacean, porpoise

fish story 3 fib, lie **4** bunk, yarn **11** fabrication **12** exaggeration **13** overstatement
fishwife 5 harpy, scold, shrew, vixen **6** virago **9** termagant, Xanthippe
fishy 7 dubious, suspect **8** doubtful, unlikely **9** ambiguous, dubitable, equivocal, uncertain **10** suspicious **11** problematic **12** questionable
fission element 7 uranium **9** plutonium
fissure 3 gap **4** gash, hole, part, rent, rift **5** break, chasm, chink, cleft, crack, split **6** breach, cleave, divide, schism **7** crevice, discord, opening, rupture **8** crevasse, fracture **10** disharmony, separation
fist 4 duke, grip, hand **5** clamp, grasp **6** clench, clinch, clutch
fit 3 apt, set **4** able, buff, hale, jibe, just, sane, suit, turn **5** adapt, agree, frame, ready, sound, spasm, spell, tally, throe, toned **6** access, accord, adjust, attack, become, belong, decent, go with, proper, seemly, square, tailor, useful **7** capable, conform, healthy, prepare, qualify, seizure, tantrum **8** assemble, decorous, dovetail, èligible, paroxysm, suitable **9** agree with, congruous, consonant, harmonize, reconcile **10** applicable, convenient, correspond, felicitous, go together **11** accommodate, appropriate
fitful 6 random, spotty **7** erratic **8** periodic, sporadic, variable **9** haphazard, hit-or-miss, irregular, spasmodic, uncertain **10** changeable, convulsive, herky-jerky, inconstant **12** intermittent
fitness 4 trim **5** order, shape **6** fettle, health, kilter, repair **7** account, decorum, service, utility **8** capacity **9** condition, propriety, relevance **11** eligibility, suitability **13** applicability
fit out 3 arm, rig **5** equip **6** outfit **7** appoint, furnish **8** accouter, accoutre
fitting 3 apt, due **4** able, just, meet, part, true **5** happy, right **6** proper, seemly **7** apropos, germane **8** apposite, relevant, suitable **9** accessory, befitting, pertinent, qualified **10** applicable, attachment, felicitous, harmonious **11** appropriate
fit together 4 hook, join, mesh **6** hook up **7** connect **8** dovetail **9** integrate
Fitzgerald novel 10 Last Tycoon (The) **11** Great Gatsby (The) **16** Tender Is the Night **17** Tales of the Jazz Age **18** This Side of Paradise **17** All the Sad Young Men **21** Beautiful and the Damned (The)
five combining form: 4 pent **5** penta **6** quinqu **7** quinque group of: **6** pentad **7** quintet
five-dollar bill 3 fin
fivefold 9 quintuple

Five Nations 8 Iroquois **member: 7** Cayugas, Mohawks, Oneidas, Senecas **9** Onondagas
five-sided figure 8 pentagon
five-star 6 deluxe, superb **8** superior, top-notch **9** excellent, first-rate **10** first-class **11** outstanding
five-year period 6 luster, lustre **7** lustrum
fix 3 jam, rig, set **4** cook, cure, geld, mend, mess, moor, root, spay, spot, work **5** affix, alter, catch, patch, ready, renew, rivet, solve, state, stick **6** adjust, anchor, assign, attach, change, decide, doctor, fasten, neuter, pickle, plight, repair, revamp, scrape, secure, settle, square, steady **7** appoint, arrange, correct, dilemma, impress, ingrain, resolve, restore, specify, work out **8** castrate, discover, overhaul, position, renovate, solution **9** condition, establish, stabilize, sterilize **11** predicament
fixation 5 craze, mania **6** fetish **9** obsession **11** fascination, infatuation
_____ **fixe 4** idée, prix
fixed 3 pat, set **4** fast, firm, sure **6** frozen, secure, stable, stated, steady **7** abiding, certain, limited, precise, settled **8** constant, definite, enduring, immobile, resolute **9** exclusive, immovable, immutable, permanent, steadfast, tenacious **10** inflexible, invariable, restricted, stationary, stipulated, unswerving, unwavering **11** determinate, unalterable **12** concentrated, unchangeable **13** circumscribed
fixture 9 appliance **10** attachment
fizz 4 buzz, foam, hiss **5** froth **6** bubble, spirit **7** bubbles, sparkle, sputter **10** effervesce, liveliness **13** effervescence
fizzle 4 bomb, fail, flop **6** fiasco **7** failure, misfire **8** miscarry, peter out **10** effervesce **11** fall through
fjord Baffin Island: 9 Admiralty **Denmark: 3** Ise, Lim **5** Lamme **Iceland: 4** Axar, Eyja **5** Horna, Skaga, Vopna **Norway: 3** Tys **4** Bokn, Nord, Salt, Stor, Tana, Vest **5** Lakse, Ranen, Sogne **9** Stavanger, Trondheim **Spitsbergen: 3** Ice **Svalbard: 4** Stor
flab 3 fat **4** bulk, lard **5** flesh **7** blubber, fatness **9** cellulite **10** corpulence **11** love handles
flabbergast 3 awe **4** stun **5** amaze, shock, throw **7** astound, nonplus **8** astonish, bowl over, dumfound, surprise **9** dumbfound, overwhelm
flabby see **flaccid**
flaccid 4 limp, soft, weak **6** feeble, flabby, floppy **8** flexible
flag 3 ebb, lag, sag, tag **4** fade, fail, hail, iris, jack, sign, swag, tail, tire, waft, wane,

wave, wilt **5** abate, color, droop, stone **6** banner, burgee, colors, ensign, falter, guidon, pennon, signal, weaken **7** bunting, decline, pendant, pennant **8** bannerol, gonfalon, languish, Old Glory, penalize, registry, standard, streamer, tricolor, vexillum **9** banderole, blue peter, oriflamme, Union Jack **10** Jolly Roger **11** deteriorate **12** Stars and Bars

flagellate 4 beat, flog, hide, lash, whip **5** whale **6** larrup, lather, stripe, switch, thrash **7** scourge **9** horsewhip

flagitious 4 evil **6** sinful, wicked **7** corrupt, vicious **8** criminal, depraved, infamous, perverse, shameful **9** miscreant, nefarious, perverted **10** degenerate, outrageous, scandalous, villainous **11** disgraceful

flagon 3 jug **4** ewer **5** stein, stoup **6** vessel **7** tankard

flagpole 4 mast **5** staff *rope:* **7** halyard

flag-raising site 7 Iwo Jima

flagrant 4 bold, rank **5** gross **6** wanton **7** blatant, glaring, heinous, obvious **8** striking **9** atrocious, egregious, monstrous **10** outrageous **11** conspicuous

flagstone 5 shale, slate

flag-waver 7 patriot **8** jingoist, loyalist **10** chauvinist **11** nationalist **12** superpatriot

flail 4 club, beat, flog, whip **6** strike, thrash, thresh **7** scourge **8** flounder, thresher

flair 4 bent, chic, élan, gift **5** knack, style **6** genius, talent **7** ability, aptness, faculty **8** aptitude, tendency **10** proclivity **11** inclination

flak 4 fire **5** abuse **6** shells **7** censure, vitriol **9** brickbats, criticism, hostility **10** opposition **11** disapproval **12** condemnation, fault-finding

flake 3 bit **4** chip, kook, peel **5** scale **6** lamina **7** oddball **8** crackpot, fragment **9** eccentric

flake off 4 chip, peel **5** scale **9** exfoliate **10** desquamate

flaky 3 odd **5** ditsy, ditzy, goofy, nutty, wacky, weird **6** fickle, screwy **7** bizarre, erratic, offbeat **9** eccentric

flambé 6 ablaze, aflame, alight **7** blazing, flaming

flamboyant 4 loud **5** gaudy, showy **6** flashy, florid, ornate, rococo **7** baroque, splashy **8** colorful, luscious **10** over-the-top **12** ostentatious

flame 4 beau, dear, fire, glow, love **5** ardor, blaze, flare, flash, honey, light, lover **7** beloved, darling, passion, sweetie **8** ladylove, truelove **9** boyfriend, inamorata, inamorato **10** brilliance, brightness, girlfriend, heartthrob, sweetheart

flamen 6 priest

flaming 5 afire, fiery **6** ablaze, alight, ardent, red-hot **7** blazing, burning, fervent, flaring, ignited, intense **10** hot-blooded, passionate **11** conflagrant, impassioned

flammable 8 burnable **9** ignitable **10** incendiary **11** combustible *liquid:* **3** gas, oil **7** acetone, alcohol, ethanol **8** gasoline, kerosene **9** petroleum **10** turpentine

Flanders *capital:* **5** Lille *language:* **7** Flemish

flaneur 5 idler **12** boulevardier, man-about-town

flank 4 abut, side **6** adjoin, border

flap 3 tab, tap **4** beat, flog, fold, slap, stew, wave, wing **5** fling, panel **6** crisis, dither, lather, pother, tumult, uproar **7** aileron, flutter, turmoil **9** agitation, commotion, confusion

flapdoodle 3 rot **4** bosh, bull, nuts **5** drool, fudge, hokum, hooey **6** bunkum, drivel **7** baloney, blarney, hogwash, rubbish **8** malarkey, nonsense, tommyrot **9** poppycock **10** applesauce, balderdash **12** blatherskite, fiddle-faddle, fiddlesticks

flapjack 7 hotcake, pancake **11** griddle cake

flare 4 burn **5** blaze, burst, flame, flash **6** signal **7** flicker **8** outburst *type:* **5** Hyder **9** air-assist **11** steam-assist

flare-up 5 blaze, burst, flame, flash, surge **8** eruption, outburst **9** explosion

flaring 5 afire, fiery **6** ablaze, aflame, alight **7** blazing, burning **11** conflagrant

flash 3 ray **4** beam, rush, snap, show **5** blaze, bling, blink, crack, flame, flare, glare, gleam, glint, jiffy, shake, shine, showy, spark, speed **6** dazzle, expose, flaunt, glance, minute, moment, second **7** display, disport, exhibit, flicker, glamour, glimmer, glisten, glitter, instant, pizzazz, shimmer, show off, spangle, sparkle, twinkle **8** brandish **9** coruscate **11** coruscation, scintillate, split second **13** scintillation

flashy 4 loud **5** gaudy, jazzy, showy **6** brazen, florid, garish, glitzy, ornate, snazzy, sporty, tawdry, tinsel **7** blatant, chintzy, glaring, insipid **9** sparkling **10** flamboyant, glittering **12** meretricious, ostentatious

flask 4 olpe, vial **6** bottle, fiasco, flacon **7** ampulla, canteen, costrel, thermos

flat 3 dim, mat **4** dead, drab, dull, even **5** banal, bland, exact, fixed, flush, level, muted, plane, prone, rooms, stale, vapid **7** insipid, prosaic **8** lodgings, tenement, unsavory **9** apartment, colorless, innocuous **10** flavorless, lackluster, monotonous

flatfish see at **fish**

flatland 4 mesa 5 plain 6 steppe, tundra 7 plateau 9 tableland

flat-out 8 absolute 9 downright 10 absolutely

flatten 4 deck, down, dull, even, fell, raze 5 crush, floor, level 6 smooth, squash 9 knock down, prostrate

flattened at the poles 6 oblate

flatter 4 coax, suit 5 toady 6 become, cajole, praise, stroke 7 adulate, blarney, gratify, wheedle 8 blandish, bootlick, butter up, soft-soap 9 sweet-talk

flattery 5 smarm 6 butter, praise 7 blarney 8 cajolery, soft soap, toadyism 9 adulation, sweet talk 10 sycophancy 11 compliments 12 blandishment, ingratiation, unctuousness

Flaubert, Gustave *birthplace:* 5 Rouen *heroine:* 4 Emma (Bovary) *novel:* 8 Salammbô 12 Madame Bovary

flaunt 4 show, wave 5 flash, flout, vaunt 6 expose, parade 7 display, disport, exhibit, show off 8 brandish, flourish

flavor 4 race, tang, zest, zing 5 sapor, savor, smack, spice, taste, tinge 6 relish, season 7 variety, version

flavorless 4 flat 5 bland, stale 7 insipid 8 unsavory 11 unpalatable

flavorsome 5 sapid, tasty, yummy 6 savory 9 delicious, palatable 10 appetizing, delectable 11 good-tasting

flaw 3 gap, rip, sin 4 blot, chip, tear, vice 5 crack, fault 6 defect 7 blemish 8 weakness 9 deformity 12 imperfection

flawed 5 amiss 6 faulty, marred 7 damaged, spoiled 8 impaired 9 defective, imperfect

flawless 4 pure 5 ideal, model 6 intact 7 perfect 8 seamless, unmarred 9 exquisite 10 immaculate, impeccable 11 unblemished

flax linen *fiber:* 3 tow *prepare:* 3 ret 4 card 5 dress 6 hackle, scutch

flaxen 4 fair 5 blond, straw 6 blonde, golden, yellow 7 towhead

flay 4 beat, lash, peel, skin 7 blister, censure, lambast, upbraid 8 lambaste 9 castigate, criticize, excoriate

flea 6 chigoe, jigger 7 chigger *water:* 7 daphnid

Fleance's father 6 Banquo

flèche 5 spire

fleck 3 dot 4 mark, mote, spot 5 flake, speck 6 dapple, mottle, streak, stripe 7 spatter, speckle, stipple 8 particle 9 bespeckle

Fledermaus, Die 3 bat *character:* 5 Adele, Falke, Frank 6 Alfred 9 Rosalinde 10 Eisenstein *composer:* 7 Strauss (Johann)

fledge 4 rear 7 feather

fledgling 4 colt, tyro 6 novice, rookie 8 beginner, freshman, neophyte, newcomer 10 apprentice

flee 3 fly, lam, run 4 bolt, scat, skip 5 elude, scoot, scram, skirr, steal 6 decamp, escape 7 abscond, make off, run away, scamper, vamoose 8 stampede, turn tail 9 skedaddle 10 make tracks

fleece 3 rob 4 bilk, clip, gaff, milk, rook, skin, soak, wool 5 bleed, cheat, cozen, mulct, shear, stick, sweat 6 extort, hustle, rip off 7 defraud, swindle 8 flimflam 10 overcharge

fleecy 5 downy 6 fluffy, pilose, woolly 7 hirsute 9 whiskered 10 flocculent

fleer 4 gibe, gird, jeer, jest, mock, quip 5 flout, laugh, scoff, scout, sneer, taunt

fleet 4 fast, navy, spry 5 agile, brisk, group, hasty, quick, rapid, swift 6 argosy, armada, nimble, speedy 8 flotilla 9 breakneck 10 harefooted

fleeting 5 brief 7 passing 8 fugitive, volatile 9 ephemeral, fugacious, momentary, temporary, transient 10 evanescent, short-lived, transitory

Fleming, Ian see **James Bond**

flesh 4 beef, meat, skin 5 stock 7 kindred 9 offspring, relatives, substance

fleshly 5 obese 6 animal, bodily, carnal 7 lustful, profane, secular, sensual 8 corporal, physical, sensuous, temporal 9 corporeal, epicurean, luxurious, sybaritic 10 voluptuous

fleshy 3 fat 5 ample, beefy, burly, gross, heavy, hefty, husky, meaty, obese, plump, pudgy, stout, tubby 6 chubby, chunky, portly, rotund 7 porcine, weighty 9 corpulent 10 overweight, well-padded *fruit:* 4 plum, pome 5 berry, drupe, grape, mango, peach 6 cherry 8 cucumber

Fletcher's partner 8 Beaumont (Francis)

fleur-de-lis 4 iris

flex 4 bend 5 tense

flexible 5 lithe, loose 6 docile, floppy, limber, pliant, supple 7 elastic, pliable, springy, willowy 8 amenable, bendable, stretchy, yielding 9 adaptable, compliant, malleable, tractable

flexion 3 bow 4 bend, fold, turn 5 angle

flexuous 5 fluid, lithe, snaky 7 sinuous, winding 8 tortuous 10 circuitous, convoluted, meandering, serpentine 11 anfractuous

flick 4 film, show 5 movie 13 motion picture, moving picture

flicker 4 bird, film, flit, hint 5 flash, gleam, glint, movie, waver 6 quiver 7 twinkle 10 woodpecker **13** motion picture, moving picture

flickering 7 lambent **8** unsteady

flier 3 ace **5** pilot **6** airman **7** aviator, birdman, handout **8** aviatrix, brochure, circular **9** throwaway

flight 3 hop, lam **4** rout, soar, slip, wing **5** flock, floor, flush, flyby, story **6** escape, flying, series **7** getaway **8** breakout *formation:* **7** echelon *overnight:* **6** redeye

flighty 5 dizzy, giddy, silly, swift **7** foolish **8** freakish, skittish, unstable, volatile **9** frivolous, mercurial, transient **10** capricious, changeable, inconstant **11** empty-headed, harebrained **13** irresponsible

flimflam 3 con, gyp **4** bilk, dupe, fake, fool, gull, hoax, jazz, sham **5** cheat, cozen, fraud, hokum, trick **6** chouse, deceit, diddle, humbug **7** chicane, deceive, defraud, swindle **8** hoodwink, trickery **9** bamboozle, deception, moonshine **10** balderdash, double-talk **11** hornswoggle

flimflammer 3 gyp **5** cheat **6** con man **7** diddler, sharper **8** swindler **9** defrauder **11** fourflusher **12** double-dealer

flimsy 4 limp, weak **5** cheap, filmy, frail, gauzy, sheer **6** feeble, flabby, sleazy, slight **7** flaccid, fragile, rickety, spindly, tenuous, unsound **8** decrepit, delicate, gossamer **10** diaphanous, improbable **11** implausible, transparent **12** unconvincing **13** insubstantial

flinch 5 quail, start, wince **6** blench, cringe, recoil, shrink

fling 3 peg **4** cast, emit, fire, flap, hurl, plop, rush, shot, slap, stab, tear, toss **5** binge, chuck, heave, pitch, shoot, spree, throw **6** affair, charge, hurtle, launch **7** splurge **8** catapult

Flintstones, The *character:* **4** Dino, Fred **5** Betty (Rubble), Wilma **6** Barney (Rubble) **8** Bamm-Bamm *creator:* **5** Hanna (Bill) **7** Barbera (Joe) *setting:* **7** Bedrock *voice:* **5** Blanc (Mel)

flip 4 glib, leaf, pert, riff, toss, wise **6** breezy, invert, riffle, ruffle **8** turn over **10** somersault **11** impertinent, smart-alecky

flip-flop 5 U-turn, waver **6** sandal, switch, waffle **7** reverse **8** reversal **9** about-face, turnabout, vacillate, volte-face **10** turnaround **11** vacillation

flippancy 5 cheek **6** levity **8** archness, pertness **9** cockiness, freshness, frivolity **10** cheekiness, impishness **11** roguishness

flippant 4 glib, pert **5** sassy, saucy **6** breezy, cheeky **11** impertinent, smart-alecky **13** disrespectful

flirt 3 toy **4** flit, fool, minx, ogle, vamp **5** dally, tease **6** coquet, trifle, wanton **8** coquette **10** experiment, mess around

flit 3 fly, zip **4** dart, pass, rush, sail, scud, whiz, wing **5** flash, hurry, scoot, speed **7** flicker, flutter, twinkle

flitter 4 dart, flap, wing **5** hover, waver **6** quiver **7** skitter **9** fluctuate

flivver 6 jalopy **9** tin lizzie

float 3 bob, fly **4** buoy, cork, hang, raft, ride, sail, scud, swim, waft **5** drift, hover **6** wander **7** pontoon, propose **8** levitate **9** negotiate

floater 3 bum, vag **4** hobo, raft **5** tramp **7** drifter, vagrant **8** derelict, vagabond **10** roustabout

floating 5 fluid, loose **6** adrift, natant **7** buoyant, movable **8** moveable, shifting, variable **10** adjustable **11** fluctuating

flocculent 5 flaky **6** fleecy, fluffy, woolly

flock 3 mob **4** army, bevy, herd, host, mass, pack, rout, wisp **5** brood, bunch, cloud, covey, crowd, drove, group **6** flight, gaggle, gather, legion, scores, throng **8** assemble, assembly, converge **9** multitude **11** aggregation **12** congregation

floe 3 ice **4** berg **7** glacier, iceberg **8** ice field

flog 3 tan **4** beat, cane, flap, hide, lash, slog, whip **5** birch, drive, flail, whale **6** larrup, lather, stripe, switch, thrash **7** cowhide, leather, scourge **10** flagellate

flood 4 fill, flow, flux, glut, pour, rush, tide **5** burst, drown, float, spate, swamp **6** deluge, engulf, stream **7** current, freshet, immerse, Niagara, torrent **8** alluvion, cataract, inundate, overflow, submerge **9** avalanche, cataclysm, overwhelm **10** inundation, outpouring

floor 3 awe **4** base, down, drop, fell, stun, tier **5** amaze, level, shock, story **6** ground **7** astound, flatten **8** astonish, audience, bowl down, bowl over, surprise **9** dumbfound, knock down **11** flabbergast

flop 3 dud **4** bomb, bust, fail, fall **5** lemon, loser **6** bummer, fizzle, turkey **7** clinker, failure

floppy 4 disk, limp **6** flimsy **7** flaccid **8** diskette, flexible

flora 6 plants **10** vegetation

flora and fauna 5 biota

Florence *bridge:* **12** Ponte Vecchio *cathedral:* **5** Duomo *family:* **6** Medici *museum:* **6** Uffizi **8** Bargello *palace:* **5** Pitti *river:* **4** Arno

florid 3 red **5** flush, gaudy, ruddy, showy **6** ornate, rococo **7** baroque, flowery, flushed, glowing **8** rubicund, sanguine, sonorous **9**

bombastic, elaborate, overblown **10** euphuistic, flamboyant, rhetorical **11** declamatory **12** magniloquent **13** grandiloquent

Florida *capital:* **11** Tallahassee *city:* **5** Miami, Tampa **6** Naples, Venice **7** Hialeah, Key West, Orlando **8** Sarasota **9** Palm Beach **11** St. Augustine **12** Jacksonville, St. Petersburg *college, university:* **7** Rollins, Stetson *county:* **3** Lee **4** Dade **6** Orange **7** Broward, Volusia **8** Pinellas, Sarasota *key:* **4** Long, Vaca, West **5** Largo **7** Big Pine **9** Matecumbe, Sugarloaf *lake:* **9** Kissimmee **10** Okeechobee *nickname:* **8** Sunshine (State) *park:* **10** Everglades *race site:* **7** Daytona *river:* **6** Indian **7** St. Johns **8** Suwannee **12** Apalachicola *state bird:* **11** mockingbird *state flower:* **13** orange blossom *state tree:* **9** sabal palm

florilegium 5 album **6** reader **7** garland, omnibus **8** analects **9** anthology **10** collection, miscellany

Florimel's husband 7 Marinel

floss 4 down, fuzz, lint **5** fluff **6** thread

flotilla 5 fleet **6** argosy, armada

Flotow opera 5 Indra **6** L'Ombre, Martha

flotsam 6 debris, jetsam **7** remains **8** wreckage **9** driftwood

flounce 5 frill, mince, strut, waltz **6** bounce, prance, ruffle, sashay

flounder 3 dab **5** slosh **6** fumble, muddle, splash, thrash, wallow **7** blunder, flounce **8** flatfish, struggle

flour 4 meal **6** pinole, powder *beetle:* **6** weevil *merchant:* **6** miller

flourish 3 wax **4** grow, wave **5** adorn, bloom **6** flower, stroke, thrive **7** blossom, burgeon, develop, fanfare, prosper, succeed **8** brandish, curlicue, ornament **13** embellishment, ornamentation

flout 4 defy, mock **5** scorn, spurn **6** deride, insult **7** scoff at

flow 4 emit, flux, gush, ooze, pour, rill, rise, rush, stem, tide, well **5** arise, drift, flood, issue, spate, spill, surge, swarm **6** course, deluge, onrush, sluice, spring, stream **7** cascade, current, emanate, give off, outflow, proceed **8** inundate, sequence **9** discharge, originate **10** continuity, inundation, succession **11** progression **12** continuation

flower 4 best, blow, pick, posy **5** bloom, cream, elite, pride, prime, prize **6** choice, thrive **7** blossom, burgeon, develop **10** effloresce **13** inflorescence *buttonhole:* **11** boutonniere *cluster:* **4** cyme **5** spike, umbel **6** corymb, floret, raceme, spadix **7** panicle **8** spikelet **9** capitulum, dichasium, glomerule **11** monochasium **13** inflorescence *cup:* **5**

calyx *garden:* **4** iris, lily, pink, rose **5** aster, canna, daisy, oxlip, pansy, peony, phlox, poppy, tulip **6** azalia, cosmos, crocus, dahlia, orchid, violet **7** jonquil, petunia **8** camellia, daffodil, gardenia, geranium, gloxinia, hyacinth, larkspur, marigold, primrose **9** carnation, gladiolus, narcissus **10** delphinium, heliotrope **13** chrysanthemum *necklace:* **3** lei *opening:* **8** anthesis *part:* **5** bract, calyx, ovary, ovule, petal, sepal, style **6** anther, pistil, spathe, stamen, stigma **7** corolla, nectary, pedicel, petiole **8** calyptra, filament, peduncle, perianth *spike:* **5** ament **6** catkin, spadix *stalk:* **7** pedicel **8** peduncle *type:* **3** ray **4** disk **6** annual, simple **9** composite, perennial *wild:* **4** flag **5** bluet, daisy, vetch **6** lupine **7** anemone, arbutus, cowslip, gentian, vervain **8** bluebell, hepatica, trillium **9** buttercup, columbine, dandelion, saxifrage **10** cinquefoil **12** lady's slipper

flower arranging 7 ikebana

flowering 6 growth **8** progress **9** evolution **11** development, florescence, progression

flowerless plant 4 fern, moss **6** lichen **9** liverwort

flowery 5 wordy **6** florid, ornate, prolix **7** aureate, diffuse, verbose **8** sonorous **9** overblown **10** euphuistic, rhetorical **11** declamatory **12** magniloquent **13** grandiloquent

Flowery Kingdom 5 China

flowing 4 easy **5** fluid **6** fluent, liquid, smooth **7** cursive, running **10** effortless *back:* **6** reflux **8** refluent *in:* **6** influx **8** influent *together:* **7** conflux **9** confluent

flow regulator 4 cock, gate **5** valve **8** throttle

flu 6 grippe

flub 4 goof, mess, muff, slip **5** boner, botch, error, fluff, gaffe, lapse, snarl **6** bobble, bollix, bungle, foul up, goof up, mess up **7** blunder, faux pas, louse up

fluctuate 4 sway, yo-yo **5** swing, waver **6** seesaw **8** undulate **9** alternate, oscillate, vacillate

flue 4 duct, pipe, tube, vent **6** funnel, uptake **7** channel, chimney, outtake

fluent 4 easy, glib **5** fluid **6** facile, liquid, smooth, supple **7** cursive, flowing, voluble **8** eloquent, polished **10** articulate, effortless

fluff 4 down, flub, fuzz, goof, lint, mess, muff, slip, trip **5** boner, botch, error, floss, gaffe, lapse, whisk **6** bobble, bollix, bungle, goof up, mess up **7** blooper, blunder, faux pas, louse up, mistake

fluffy 5 downy **6** flossy **7** cursory, shallow **8**

puffed up **10** flocculent **11** superficial **13** unsubstantial

fluid 4 free, sera (plural) **5** lymph, serum, water **6** liquid, mobile, molten, serous, watery **7** mutable, protean **8** flexible, shifting, unstable, unsteady, variable **9** adaptable, changeful, unsettled **10** changeable *excessive:* **5** edema

fluke 3 hap **4** lobe, worm **5** quirk **6** chance **8** flatfish, fortuity **9** trematode

fluky 3 odd **6** casual, chance, chancy, random **9** arbitrary **10** accidental, fortuitous

flume 5 chute **6** sluice, stream **7** channel **8** aqueduct **11** watercourse

flummox 5 abash, addle **6** baffle, rattle, stymie **7** confuse, fluster, perplex **8** befuddle, bewilder, confound **9** discomfit, embarrass **10** disconcert

flunk 4 fail

flunky 4 peon **5** gofer, toady **6** drudge, lackey, stooge, yes-man **7** footman, servant, steward **8** factotum, follower

flurry 3 ado, fit **4** fuss, gust, spit, stir, to-do **5** haste, whirl **6** bother, bustle, furore, pother, tumult **7** barrage, flutter, turmoil **8** snowfall **9** agitation, commotion, confusion, whirlpool, whirlwind **10** excitement, turbulence

flush 4 even, flat, glow, pink, rich, rose, wash **5** bloom, color, level, plane, raise, rinse, rouge **6** florid, filled, mantle, redden, sluice **7** cleanse, crimson, glowing, inflame, opulent, suffuse, wealthy **8** abundant, abutting, irrigate, rubicund, sanguine, squarely **9** turn color

fluster 5 addle, dizzy, shake, upset **6** ball up, bother, fuddle, muddle, rattle, ruffle **7** agitate, confuse, disturb, nonplus, perturb, unhinge **8** befuddle, bewilder, confound, disquiet, distract **10** discompose

flustered 5 upset **7** abashed, anxious, rattled **8** agitated, confused, troubled **9** chagrined, disturbed, flummoxed, perplexed, perturbed **10** bewildered, disquieted, distracted, distraught, distressed, nonplussed **11** discomposed, embarrassed **12** disconcerted

flute 4 fife, roll **5** pleat **6** goffer, groove **7** chamfer, channel, piccolo **8** recorder **9** wineglass *Japanese:* **10** shakuhachi *oval:* **7** ocarina *player:* **5** piper **7** flutist **8** flautist

flutist *American:* **5** Baker (Julius), Baron (Samuel) **7** Robison (Paula) **8** Zukerman (Eugenia) *French:* **6** Rampal (Jean-Pierre) *Irish:* **6** Galway (James)

flutter 4 beat, flap, flit **5** hover, quake, shake **6** flurry, quaver, quiver, wobble **7** flicker, flitter, pulsate, tremble, vibrate **9** agitation,

commotion, confusion, palpitate, vibration **11** fluctuation

flu type 4 bird **5** Asian, avian, swine

flux 3 run **4** flow, fuse, melt, rush, thaw, tide **5** drift, flood, spate **6** change, stream **7** current, flowing, outflow **8** dissolve

fly 3 zip **4** bolt, dart, dash, flee, flit, lure, scud, skip, soar, whiz, wing **5** fleet, float, glide, hover, hurry, pilot, scoot, shoot, skirr, sweep, whish, whisk **6** aviate, escape, hasten, hustle **7** abscond, flutter *insect:* **3** ked **4** gnat **5** midge **6** botfly, gadfly, mayfly, tsetse **7** deerfly, sandfly **8** blackfly, dipteron, horsefly, housefly, tachinid **10** bluebottle *larva:* **6** maggot

fly-by-night 5 shady **7** passing **9** transient **10** transitory, unreliable **12** disreputable, undependable **13** untrustworthy

flycatcher 5 pewee **6** phoebe, tyrant **8** bellbird, kingbird **9** passerine

flying 5 aloft **6** volant **8** airborne

Flying Dutchman, The *composer:* **6** Wagner (Richard) *heroine:* **5** Senta

flying fish 7 gurnard

flying fox 3 bat **8** fruit bat

flying horse 7 Pegasus **10** hippogriff

flying island 7 Laputa

flying lemur 6 colugo

flying mammal 3 bat

flying saucer 3 UFO

fly in the ointment 5 catch **8** drawback

foam 4 head, scud, scum, suds, surf **5** churn, froth, spume **6** bubble, lather, seethe **7** bubbles **10** effervesce

fob 4 seal **5** chain **6** pocket, ribbon **8** ornament

fob off 5 foist **6** put off **7** palm off, pass off

focus 3 fix, hub **4** node, zoom **5** heart, rivet **6** adjust, center, fixate, home in **8** converge, emphasis, meditate, polestar **9** concenter, epicenter **10** hypocenter **11** concentrate, nerve center

fodder 4 feed, food **6** forage, silage, stover **9** provender *crop:* **3** hay, oat, rye **4** corn **5** maize, vetch, wheat **6** barley, clover, millet **7** alfalfa, sorghum *storage structure:* **4** silo *store:* **6** ensile

foe 5 enemy, rival **8** opponent **9** adversary **10** antagonist

fog 4 blur, daze, foam, haze, mist, murk, soup **5** brume, cloud, vapor **6** miasma, muddle **7** pea soup, pogonip

foggy 4 hazy **5** dirty, grimy, misty, murky, soupy, vague **7** brumous, muddled, obscure, tenuous **8** confused, pea soupy, vaporous

fogy 6 dotard, fossil, square **7** diehard **8** mossback **10** fuddy-duddy **12** antediluvian, conservative **11** standpatter **13** stick-in-the-mud

fogyish 7 old-line **8** outmoded, standpat **9** hidebound, out-of-date **10** antiquated, fuddy-duddy, mossbacked **11** reactionary **12** conservative, old-fashioned

foible 4 vice **5** fault **6** defect **7** failing, frailty **8** weakness **11** shortcoming **12** imperfection

foil 4 balk, beat, curb, dash, faze **5** check, sword **6** baffle, defeat, rattle, thwart **7** buffalo **8** contrast, restrain **9** discomfit, embarrass, frustrate **10** circumvent, disappoint, disconcert **11** straight man

foist 6 fob off **7** palm off, pass off

fold 3 pen, ply **4** bend, fail, tuck **5** drape, flock, pleat, plica, ridge **6** crease, double, furrow, pucker **7** flexure, plicate **9** plication **11** corrugation *skin:* **4** ruga **5** plica, rugae (plural) **6** dewlap, plicae (plural)

folder 4 file **6** binder **9** portfolio

foliage 6 growth, leaves **7** verdure **8** greenery, lushness **10** vegetation

folk 4 race **6** people **9** community

folklore 4 myth, tale **5** fable **6** belief, custom, legend, mythos, wisdom **9** mythology, tradition **12** superstition

folks 6 family **7** parents **9** relatives

folksinger 4 Baez (Joan), Ives (Burl) **5** Dylan (Bob), Niles (John Jacob), White (Josh) **6** Odetta, Seeger (Pete) **7** Collins (Judy), Guthrie (Arlo, Woody), Robeson (Paul) **9** Belafonte (Harry), Ledbetter (Huddie)

folksy 5 homey **6** casual, earthy, mellow, rustic, simple **7** natural **8** down-home, familiar, informal, laid-back, sociable **9** easygoing, ingenuous **10** unaffected, unpolished **13** unpretentious

folktale 4 myth **5** fable **6** legend **7** märchen

follow 3 dog, spy, tag **4** hunt, keep, obey, seek, tail, walk **5** catch, chase, ensue, grasp, hound, trace, track, trail **6** accept, comply, convoy, pursue, search, shadow, travel **7** conform, imitate, proceed, replace, succeed **8** practice, supplant **9** supersede *closely:* **5** draft **10** slipstream

follower 3 fan **5** toady **6** addict, cohort, minion, sequel, votary **7** acolyte, apostle, devotee, groupie, habitué, sectary, trailer, wannabe **8** adherent, advocate, disciple, faithful, hanger-on, henchman, myrmidon, parasite, partisan, tagalong **9** dependent, satellite, supporter, sycophant **10** aficionado

following 4 next **5** after, below, later, since **6** behind, public **7** ensuing, retinue **8** audience **9** adherents, afterward, believers, disciples, entourage, partisans **10** afterwards, sequential, supporters, subsequent, suc-

ceeding, successive **12** subsequently, subsequent to

follow-up 6 sequel

folly 4 whim **6** lunacy, vanity **7** fatuity, foolery, inanity, madness **8** insanity, nonsense **9** absurdity, craziness, dottiness, silliness, stupidity **10** indulgence **11** foolishness **12** extravagance

foment 3 sow **4** brew, goad, spur **5** rouse, set on **6** arouse, excite, foster, incite, stir up, whip up **7** agitate, nurture, provoke **9** cultivate, encourage, instigate

fond 4 dear, warm **5** silly **6** doting, loving, tender **7** devoted, fatuous, foolish, partial **8** desirous, enamored, romantic **9** indulgent **10** infatuated **11** sentimental **12** affectionate

fondle 3 paw, pet **5** grope, touch **6** caress, cosset, dandle, stroke **7** embrace **8** canoodle

fondness 4 love **5** fancy, taste **6** liking, relish **8** appetite, devotion, penchant, soft spot, weakness **9** affection, tendresse **10** attachment, partiality, preference, propensity **11** inclination **12** predilection

font 4 root, type **6** origin, source **8** fountain **10** receptacle

food 3 pap **4** chow, diet, eats, fare, grub, meal, meat **5** bread, manna **6** fodder, viands **7** aliment, cuisine, edibles, nurture, pabulum, vittles **8** delicacy, victuals **9** nutriment, provender **10** provisions, sustenance **11** comestibles, nourishment *disorder:* **7** bulimia **8** anorexia *divine:* **8** ambrosia *element:* **5** fiber, fibre, sugar **6** starch **7** mineral, protein, vitamin **12** carbohydrate *from heaven:* **5** manna *lover:* **7** epicure, gourmet **8** gourmand *provision:* **4** mess **6** ration **7** serving *scarcity:* **6** famine *waste:* **7** garbage

foofaraw 3 ado **4** fuss, stir, to-do **5** hoo-ha, stink **6** bother, finery, frills, furore, hoohah, hurrah, pother, ruckus, rumpus **8** brouhaha **9** commotion **11** disturbance

fool 3 ass, kid, oaf, rag, rib, sap, toy **4** boob, butt, clod, dolt, dope, dupe, fish, gull, hoax, jerk, jest, joke, josh, mook, zany **5** chump, clown, comic, dally, dummy, dunce, goose, idiot, loser, moron, ninny, patsy, schmo, trick **6** banter, cretin, dawdle, delude, diddle, dimwit, doodle, galoot, gammon, jester, lead on, meddle, monkey, motley, nitwit, pigeon, schmoe, stooge, sucker, tamper, trifle, victim **7** beguile, buffoon, chicane, deceive, fake out, fall guy, fritter, half-wit, jackass, mislead, pinhead, saphead, schmuck **8** bonehead, comedian, dumbbell, flimflam, hoodwink, imbecile, lunkhead, numskull, pushover **9** bamboozle, birdbrain, blockhead, interfere, simpleton **10** nincompoop **11** hornswoggle, merry-andrew, string along **13** laughing-stock *around:* **4** futz, idle, laze, loaf, loll **5** flirt **6** dawdle, diddle, lounge **8** lollygag, womanize **9** philander

foolhardy 4 bold, rash **6** daring, madcap **8** headlong, reckless **9** audacious, daredevil, impetuous **11** precipitate, temerarious

foolish 3 mad **4** daft, gaga, rash, zany **5** balmy, batty, crazy, dippy, dizzy, dorky, dotty, goofy, inane, inept, kooky, loony, loopy, nutty, sappy, silly, wacky **6** absurd, insane, simple, stupid, unwise **7** asinine, doltish, fatuous, idiotic, lunatic, meshuga, moronic, witless **8** clueless, meshugge, reckless, trifling **9** cockamamy, half-baked, brainless, fantastic, frivolous, half-baked, imbecilic, insensate, laughable, ludicrous, senseless **10** cockamamie, half-cocked, half-witted, irrational, ridiculous **11** hare-brained, nonsensical

foolishness 4 bull, bunk **5** folly, fudge **6** bêtise, bunkum, lunacy **7** fatuity, inanity, rubbish **8** claptrap, drollery, insanity, nonsense, tommyrot **9** absurdity, craziness, silliness, stupidity **10** imbecility, imprudence **12** fiddle-faddle **13** horsefeathers

fool's gold 6 pyrite

foot 3 paw, pay **4** hoof *ailment:* **4** corn **6** bunion, callus *animal:* **3** pad, paw **4** hoof *bones of:* **5** talus, tarsi (plural) **6** cuboid, tarsal, tarsus **7** phalanx **9** calcaneus, cuneiform, navicular, phalanges (plural) **10** metatarsal *combining form:* **3** ped, pod **4** podo *doctor:* **10** podiatrist **11** chiropodist *metric:* **4** iamb **5** arsis, paeon **6** dactyl, thesis **7** anapest, pyrrhic, spondee, trochee *part:* **3** toe **4** arch, ball, claw, nail **5** ankle, digit, talon **6** hallux, instep

football 4 nerf **5** rugby **6** rugger, soccer **7** pigskin *field:* **8** gridiron *foul:* **7** holding, offside **8** clipping **12** interference *official:* **6** umpire **7** referee **8** linesman **9** back judge, line judge **10** field judge *play:* **4** dive, trap **5** sneak, sweep **6** option, screen **7** audible, counter, handoff, rollout, runback **8** dropback **9** crossbuck, off-tackle **10** buttonhook *player position:* **3** end **4** back, half, wing **5** guard **6** center, kicker, safety, tackle **7** flanker, lineman, wideout **8** defender, fullback, halfback, linesman, receiver, scatback, slotback, split end, tailback, tight end, wingback **9** noseguard **10** cornerback, linebacker, nose tackle **11** placekicker, quarterback, running back, snapper-back **12** defensive end, strong safety, wide receiver *scoring:* **6** safety **9** field goal, touchdown **10** conversion *starting play:* **7** kickoff *team:* **6** eleven *term:* **4** down, kick, pass, punt, rush, snap **5** blitz, block, squad **6** fumble, huddle, kicker, onside, option, player, safety, spiral **7** end zone, handoff, kickoff, offside, pigskin, quarter, spinner, tweener, yardage **8** clipping, crossbar, goal line, goalpost, gridiron, halftime **9** backfield, defensive, field goal, intercept, offensive, placekick, scrimmage, touchback, touchdown **11** ballcarrier, broken field **12** interception, triple threat (see also **National Football League**)

footballer 4 Kemp (Jack), Long (Howie), Lott (Ronnie), Levy (Marv), Monk (Art), Moon (Warren), Reed (Andre), Rice (Jerry) **5** Allen (Marcus), Baugh (Sammy), Berry (Raymond), Brady (Tom), Brown (Bob, Jim), Clark (Gary), Ditka (Mike), Elway (John), Eller (Carl), Favre (Brett), Gibbs (Joe), Groza (Lou), Jones (Bert, Deacon), Kelly (Jim), Kosar (Bernie), Leahy (Pat), Lomax (Neil), Muñoz (Anthony), Shula (Don), Simms (Phil), Smith (Emmitt), Starr (Bart), Stram (Hank), Swann (Lynn), Young (Steve) **6** Aikman (Troy), Blanda (George), Butkus (Dick), Carter (Chris, Ki-Jana), Csonka (Larry), Dawson (Len), Ellard (Henry), Graham (Otto), Grange (Red), Greene (Joe), Harris (Franco), Jaeger (Jeff), Joiner (Charlie), Lofton (James), Lowery (Nick), Marino (Dan), Murray (Eddie), Namath (Joe), Payton (Walter), Rypien (Mark), Sayers (Gale), Slater (Jackie), Taylor (Lawrence), Thorpe (Jim), Tittle (Y. A.), Turner (Jim), Unitas (Johnny), Walker (Herschel) **7** Bledsoe (Drew), Dorsett (Tony), Esiason (Boomer), Gifford (Frank), Hornung (Paul), Johnson (Norm), Largent (Steve), Luckman (Sid), Manning (Eli, Peyton), Montana (Joe), Newsome (Ozzie), Riggins (John), Rozelle (Pete), Sanders (Barry, Deion), Simpson (O. J.), Stabler (Ken), Thurman (Thomas) **8** Andersen (Morten), Anderson (Gary, Ottis), Bradshaw (Terry), Lombardi (Vince), Nagurski (Bronko), Plunkett (Jim), Staubach (Roger) **9** Dickerson (Eric), Jurgensen (Sonny), Hostetler (Jeff), Tarkenton (Fran) **10** Stallworth (John), Singletary (Mike), Stephenson (Dwight), Youngblood (Jack)

Foote play 15 Trip to Bountiful (The) **19** Young Man from Atlanta (The)

footfall 4 step **5** tread

footing 4 base, rank, seat, term **5** basis, place, state **6** bottom, ground, status **7** bedrock, seating, station, warrant **8** basement, capacity, pedestal, position, standing **9** character, situation **10** foundation, groundwork, substratum **12** underpinning

footless 4 dull, dumb **5** crass, dense, inept, unfit **6** apodal, stupid **7** foolish

foot lever 5 pedal **7** treadle

footman 7 servant **10** pedestrian **11** infantryman

footnote abbreviation 4 Ibid., Idem **5** op. cit. **6** loc. cit.

footpad 5 thief **6** mugger, robber **8** criminal **10** highwayman, pickpocket

footprint 3 pug **4** sign, step **5** spoor, trace, track, tract **7** pugmark, vestige

footslog 4 plod, slop, toil **5** tramp, tromp **6** trudge

footstone 6 ledger, marker **8** monument **11** grave marker

footstool 7 cricket, hassock, ottoman

fop 3 jay **4** beau **5** blade, blood, dandy, spark, swell **7** coxcomb, gallant **8** cavalier, macaroni, popinjay **9** exquisite, ladies' man, pretty boy **11** Beau Brummel, petit-maître **12** fashion plate, lounge lizard

foppish 6 chichi **8** dandyish, peacocky **10** peacockish

for 3 pro **7** in favor

forage 4 beat, comb, grub, prog, raid, rake, sack **5** scour **6** browse, fodder, ravage, rustle, search **7** plunder, ransack, rummage **8** finecomb, scrounge **9** pasturage *crop:* **5** grass **6** clover, kochia **7** alfalfa, sorghum (see also **fodder**)

foray 4 raid **6** inroad, sortie **8** invasion **9** incursion, irruption

forbear 4 shun **5** avoid, forgo, spare **6** endure, eschew, resist, suffer **7** abstain, decline; refrain **8** hold back, restrain, tolerate

forbearance 5 grace, mercy **6** lenity **7** charity **8** clemency, lenience, leniency, mildness, patience **9** restraint, tolerance **10** abstinence, toleration **13** consideration

forbearing 4 easy, kind, mild **6** gentle **7** clement, lenient, patient **8** merciful, tolerant **9** indulgent **10** charitable, thoughtful **11** considerate, magnanimous

Forbes hero 8 Tremaine (Johnny)

forbid 3 ban, bar, nix **4** curb, deny, halt, stop, veto **5** block, check, debar **6** enjoin, hinder, impede, outlaw, refuse **7** inhibit, prevent, rule out, shut out **8** disallow, obstruct, preclude, prohibit, restrain **9** interdict, proscribe

forbidden 5 taboo **6** banned, barred **7** illegal, illicit **8** verboten **10** prohibited

Forbidden City 5 Lhasa **6** Gu Gong **7** Beijing

forbidding 4 grim **5** drear, harsh **6** dreary, severe **8** daunting, menacing, sinister **9** repellent **10** formidable **11** threatening

force 2 od **3** jam **4** cram, dint, push **5** drive, foist, impel, might, power, press, vigor, wreak, wreck, wrest **6** coerce, compel, demand, duress, effort, energy, extort, impose, legion, muscle, oblige **7** command, impetus, inflict, potency, require, sandbag **8** coercion, manpower, momentum, obligate, pressure, shoehorn, strength, violence **9** constrain, intensity, puissance, strong-arm **10** compulsion, constraint *apart:* **5** wedge *unit:* **4** dyne

forced 8 strained **9** contrived, unnatural **10** artificial, compulsory **11** involuntary

forceful 5 stiff, stout **6** mighty, potent, punchy, strong, virile **7** dynamic **8** emphatic, powerful, puissant, vigorous **9** assertive **10** compelling

forceless 4 lame, weak **5** wimpy **6** feeble **8** impotent, nugatory **9** powerless **10** inadequate **11** ineffective, ineffectual

force out see **expel**

forcible 8 coercive **9** compelled **10** compulsory, obligatory, peremptory

ford 5 cross

Ford's folly 5 Edsel

for each 3 per **6** apiece

forearm bone 4 ulna **5** radii (plural), ulnae (plural) **6** radius

forebear 8 ancestor **9** precursor **10** antecedent, progenitor **11** predecessor **12** primogenitor

forebode 5 augur **7** betoken, portend, predict, presage **8** foretell, prophesy, soothsay **13** prognosticate

foreboding 4 omen, sign **5** dread **6** augury **7** anxiety, portent, presage, warning **10** prediction, prognostic **11** premonition **12** apprehension, presentiment

forecast 5 augur **6** divine **7** foresee, portend, predict, presage **8** estimate, foretell, indicate, prophecy, prophesy **9** adumbrate, calculate, prevision, prognosis **10** prediction **13** prognosticate

forecaster 4 seer **5** augur **6** oracle **7** diviner, prophet **8** haruspex **9** predictor **10** prophesier, soothsayer, weatherman **11** Nostradamus **12** meteorologist, weatherperson

foreclose 3 bar **5** debar **6** cut off, hinder **7** prevent, shut out **8** preclude

forefather see **forebear**

forefeel 6 divine **9** apprehend, prevision

forefinger 5 index

forefront 3 van **4** lead **8** vanguard **10** avant-garde, firing line **11** cutting edge

foregoer 6 herald **8** ancestor, forebear **9** harbinger, precursor, prototype **10** antecedent, antecessor, forerunner, progenitor **11** predecessor **12** primogenitor

foregoing 5 prior **6** former **7** earlier **8** anterior, previous **9** precedent, preceding **10** antecedent

forehanded 6 frugal **7** prudent, thrifty **8** sensible, well-to-do **9** provident **10** prosperous

forehead 4 brow **5** frons, front **8** sinciput **9** sincipita (plural)

foreign 5 alien **6** exotic **7** strange **8** external, offshore, overseas **9** extrinsic, nonnative **10** accidental, extraneous, immaterial, irrelevant **11** incongruous **12** adventitious, inapplicable, incompatible, inconsistent **13** inappropriate *prefix:* **4** xeno

foreigner 5 alien **8** outsider, stranger **9** outlander **10** tramontane

foreknow 6 divine **9** apprehend, prevision **10** anticipate

foreland 4 beak, cape, head, ness **5** point **10** promontory

forelock 5 bangs, quiff **7** cowlick

foreman 4 bos'n, boss **5** bosun, chief **6** gaffer, ganger, honcho, leader **7** captain, manager, steward **8** overseer **9** boatswain **10** supervisor

foremost 4 arch, head, high, main **5** chief, first, front, grand **7** leading, premier, supreme **9** number one, paramount, principal **10** preeminent **11** cutting-edge, outstanding

forenoon 4 morn **7** morning **12** ante meridiem

forensic 0 judicial **0** debatable **10** rhetorical **13** argumentative

foreordain 4 doom, fate **9** determine **10** predestine **12** predetermine

forerunner 4 omen, sign **5** envoy **6** augury, herald **7** pioneer, portent, presage, symptom, warning **8** ancestor, exemplar, outrider **9** announcer, harbinger, initiator, messenger **10** antecedent, originator, prognostic **11** anticipator, predecessor

foresee 6 divine **7** predict, presage **8** perceive, prophesy **9** apprehend, prefigure, prevision **10** anticipate **13** prognosticate

foreseer 5 augur **6** auspex, oracle **7** diviner, prophet **8** haruspex **9** predictor **10** soothsayer **11** Nostradamus

foreshadow 4 bode, hint **5** augur **6** herald **7** betoken, portend, predict, presage, promise, suggest **8** forecast, intimate **9** adumbrate, prefigure **13** prognosticate

foresight 6 vision **7** caution **8** prudence, sagacity **10** discretion, perception, precaution, prescience, providence

forest 4 bosk, wood **5** copse, grove, weald, woods **6** bosque **7** coppice, thicket, woodlot **8** wildwood, woodland **10** timberland, wilderness *deity:* **5** dryad **6** sylvan **8** Sylvanus *English:* **4** Dean **5** Arden **8** Sherwood *German:* **5** Black **11** Schwarzwald *opening:* **5** glade *relating to:* **6** sylvan *subarctic:* **5** taiga *tropical:* **5** selva **6** jungle

forestall 5 avert, block, deter **6** hinder **7** obviate, preempt, prevent, rule out, ward off **8** preclude, stave off **10** anticipate

Forester, C. S. *hero:* **10** Hornblower (Horatio) *novel:* **12** African Queen (The)

foretell 4 bode, warn **5** augur **6** divine **7** portend, predict, presage, promise **8** proclaim, prophesy, soothsay **9** adumbrate, apprehend, prefigure **10** anticipate, vaticinate **13** prognosticate

forethought 8 judgment, planning, prudence **10** discretion, precaution **12** deliberation **13** premeditation

foretoken 4 bode, hint, omen, sign, warn **5** augur **6** augury, herald **7** portend, portent, presage, promise, symptom, warning **8** forecast **9** harbinger, precursor **10** intimation

forever 3 aye **6** always **7** endless **8** eternity, evermore **9** endlessly, eternally **10** in aeternum **11** ad infinitum, ceaselessly, continually, everlasting, incessantly, permanently, perpetually, unceasingly **12** in perpetuity **13** everlastingly

forewarning 6 caveat, tip-off **7** caution **8** monition **11** premonition

foreword 5 intro, proem **7** preface, prelude **8** exordium, overture, preamble, prologue **12** introduction, prolegomenon

for example 3 say **6** such as

for fear that 4 lest

forfeit 4 fine, lose **5** mulct **6** give up **7** penalty **9** sacrifice **10** amercement

forfend 4 ward **5** avert, deter **6** secure **7** obviate, prevent, protect, rule out, ward off **8** preclude, preserve, stave off

forge 4 copy, fake, form, make **5** pound, shape **6** smithy **7** advance, fashion, imitate, produce, turn out **8** continue **9** construct, fabricate **11** counterfeit, manufacture

forget 4 fail, omit **6** ignore, slight **7** neglect **8** discount, overlook, pass over **9** disregard

forgetful 3 lax **5** slack **6** absent, remiss **7** amnesic **8** amnesiac, careless, heedless **9** negligent, oblivious, unwitting **10** abstracted, neglectful **11** inattentive, thoughtless **12** absentminded

forgetfulness 5 lethe **7** amnesia **8** oblivion **10** negligence **11** inattention

forgivable 6 venial **10** remissible

forgive 5 remit **6** excuse, pardon **7** absolve, condone **8** overlook

forgiveness 6 pardon **7** amnesty **9** remission **10** absolution

forgo 3 bag **5** leave, waive, yield **6** eschew, give up, resign **7** abandon **8** abnegate, jettison, renounce **9** sacrifice, surrender **10** relinquish

fork 6 bisect, branch, crotch **7** diverge, utensil **9** branch off *prong:* **4** tine

fork out 3 pay **5** spend **10** contribute

forlorn 5 alone **6** bereft, futile, lonely **8** desolate, forsaken, hopeless, lonesome, solitary, wretched **9** abandoned, depressed, destitute, miserable **10** despairing, despondent **12** disconsolate

form 3 way **4** body, cast, make, mode, mold **5** build, forge, found, frame, image, model, shape, style **6** create, design, devise, figure, make up, manner **7** compose, contour, develop, fashion, outline, process, produce, profile **8** comprise, organize, practice **9** construct, establish, fabricate, framework, procedure, structure, take shape **10** constitute, convention, regulation **11** materialize **13** configuration *combining form:* **5** morph *set:* **10** stereotype

formal 3 set **4** prim **5** exact, legal, rigid, stiff **6** dressy, lawful, proper, seemly, solemn **7** distant, orderly, regular, stately, starchy, stilted **8** abstract, black-tie, decorous, elevated, official, reserved **10** ceremonial, methodical, systematic **11** ceremonious, syntactical **12** conventional

formality 4 form, rite **6** ritual **7** liturgy, service **8** ceremony, insignia **10** ceremonial, convention, observance

formalize 6 codify **9** establish, normalize **10** regularize **11** standardize

format 4 plan, size **5** shape, style **6** makeup, method **11** arrangement **12** organization

formation 4 rank **6** design, makeup **9** structure **11** arrangement, composition, development **12** architecture, construction

former 3 old **4** late, once, past **5** prior **6** bygone, whilom **7** earlier, onetime, quondam **8** anterior, previous, sometime **9** erstwhile, precedent, preceding **10** antecedent

formerly 3 née **4** erst, once **6** before, whilom **7** already, earlier **9** erstwhile **10** heretofore, previously

formidable 8 daunting **9** difficult **10** impressive **11** redoubtable

formless 5 vague **7** chaotic, obscure, unclear **8** inchoate, nebulous, unshaped **9** amorphous, undefined, unordered **10** immaterial, indefinite, indistinct **11** unorganized

Formosa 6 Taiwan *capital:* **6** Taipei

formula 4 rite, rule **5** canon, maxim, tenet **6** method, recipe, ritual **7** precept, theorem **8** equation **9** algorithm, blueprint, principle, yardstick **10** touchstone **12** prescription

formulate 5 couch, draft, frame, hatch **6** codify, devise, invent, make up, phrase **7** concoct, dream up, express, prepare, work out **8** contrive

forsake 4 quit **5** avoid, leave, spurn **6** defect, depart, desert, give up, reject, resign **7** abandon **8** abdicate, renounce **9** throw over **10** relinquish

forsaken 4 lorn **6** bereft **7** forlorn **8** derelict, deserted, desolate, solitary **9** abandoned

Forseti *father:* **6** Balder, Baldur *palace:* **7** Glitnir

Forster *work:* **7** Maurice **10** Howards End **13** Room with a View (A) **14** Passage to India (A)

forswear 4 deny **5** unsay **6** abjure, recall, recant, reject **7** perjure, retract **8** renounce, take back, withdraw

fort 4 base **6** castle **7** bastion, bulwark, citadel, redoubt **8** fastness, fortress, garrison, martello, stockade **10** stronghold *Baltimore:* **7** McHenry *California:* **3** Ord *Kentucky:* **4** Knox *New Jersey:* **3** Dix *New York:* **7** Niagara, Stanwix **8** Schuyler **11** Ticonderoga *Ontario:* **9** Frontenac *San Antonio:* **5** Alamo *South Carolina:* **6** Sumter *Spanish:* **7** alcazar **8** presidio

forte 3 bag **4** loud **5** thing **6** métier **8** long suit, strength **9** specialty **10** strong suit **11** strong point

forth 6 onward **7** forward

forthcoming 7 pending **8** imminent **9** impending, proximate **10** responsive **11** approaching

for the most part 9 generally, typically **10** on the whole

for the time being 3 now **6** pro tem **9** at present, currently, presently **10** pro tempore

forthright 4 open **5** blunt, frank, plain **6** candid, direct **7** up-front **8** straight **10** aboveboard, foursquare **11** openhearted, straight-out, undisguised, unvarnished

forthwith 3 now **6** at once **8** directly **9** instantly, right away, thereupon **11** immediately, straightway **12** straightaway

fortification 4 moat, wall **6** abatis, buffer, glacis **7** barrier, bastion, bulwark, citadel, parapet, rampart, redoubt **8** barbican, enceinte, fastness, garrison, palisade, presidio, stockade **9** barricade, earthwork **10** breastwork, stronghold *part:* **7** salient

fortify 3 arm **4** gird, stir **5** brace, rally, ready, renew, rouse, steel **6** enrich, secure **7** hearten, prepare, protect, refresh, restore **8** embolden, energize **9** encourage, reinforce **10** invigorate, strengthen

fortitude 4 grit, guts, pith **5** fiber, heart, nerve, pluck, spunk, valor **6** mettle, phlegm, spirit **7** bravery, courage, stamina **8** backbone, boldness, strength, tenacity **9** constancy, endurance, tolerance **10** resolution **11** intrepidity **12** fearlessness, perseverance, resoluteness, staying power **13** dauntlessness, determination

fortress see **fort**

fortuitous 5 fluky, happy, lucky **6** casual, chance **10** accidental, auspicious **12** providential

fortuity 3 hap **4** luck **5** fluke **6** chance **8** accident **9** happening **10** occurrence

Fortuna 5 Tyche *symbol:* **5** wheel **6** rudder

fortunate 5 happy, lucky **9** favorable **10** auspicious, propitious **12** providential

Fortunate Islands 8 Canaries

fortune 3 lot, pot, wad **4** doom, fate, luck, mint, pile, ship **5** worth **6** boodle, bundle, chance, happen, hazard, packet, riches, wealth **7** destiny, success, weather **8** property **9** resources

Fortune founder 4 Luce (Henry)

fortune-teller 4 seer **5** augur, sibyl **7** diviner, palmist **9** wisewoman **10** soothsayer (see also **foreseer**)

fortune-telling see **divination**

forty winks 3 nap **6** catnap, siesta, snooze **7** shut-eye

forum 5 court, panel **6** medium **8** congress, tribunal **9** symposium **10** colloquium, conference, roundtable **11** convocation, marketplace

forward 3 aid **4** abet, bold, send, ship **5** ahead, brash, eager, pushy, ready, relay, remit, sassy, saucy **6** cheeky, foster, onward, uphold **7** address, advance, consign, further, promote, support **8** advanced, champion, dispatch, impudent, transmit **9** encourage, in advance **11** smart-alecky **12** presumptuous **13** self-assertive *prefix:* **4** ante

For Whom the Bell Tolls *author:* **9** Hemingway (Ernest) *character:* **5** Maria, Pablo, Pilar **6** Jordan

Forza del Destino composer 5 Verdi (Giuseppe)

fossa 3 pit **5** fovea **6** cavity, groove **10** depression

fosse 4 dike, moat **5** canal, ditch **6** trench **7** acequia, channel

fossil 4 fogy **5** amber, fogey, relic **6** dotard **7** antique **8** calamite, conodont, mossback **10**

antiquated, fuddy-duddy **12** antediluvian **13** stick-in-the-mud *fuel:* **3** gas, oil **4** coal, peat **9** petroleum **10** natural gas

foster 4 back, help, rear, tend **5** nurse **6** assist, harbor, parent **7** advance, bring up, nourish, nurture, promote, support, sustain **8** champion **9** cultivate, encourage

fou 5 crazy, drunk

foul 4 base, rank, soil, vile **5** botch, dirty, fetid, funky, muddy, nasty, yucky **6** coarse, defile, filthy, grubby, horrid, impure, odious, putrid, rotten, scuzzy, smutty, stormy, turbid, vulgar, wicked **7** abusive, noisome, obscene, pollute, profane, raunchy, squalid, tarnish, unclean **8** indecent, obstruct, polluted, stinking, wretched **9** collision, loathsome, obnoxious, offensive, repellent, repugnant, repulsive, revolting **10** abominable, detestable, disgusting, malodorous **11** contaminate, treacherous **12** dishonorable, scatological

foul play 3 hit **5** blood **6** murder **7** killing, outrage **8** homicide, violence **12** manslaughter

found 4 base, cast, rear **5** begin, erect, raise, set up, start **6** bottom, create, invent **7** fashion, support **8** commence, initiate, organize **9** establish, institute, originate, predicate

foundation 3 bed **4** base, rock **5** basis **6** bottom, corset, makeup **7** bedding, footing, support **8** pedestal **9** endowment **10** groundwork, substratum **11** institution **12** organization, substructure, underpinning

foundational 5 basic **6** bottom **7** primary **10** supportive, underlying **11** fundamental

founder 4 fail, sink **5** wreck **6** author, father, go down **7** creator **8** collapse, inventor, submerge, submerse **9** architect, generator, patriarch, shipwreck **10** originator

foundling 6 infant, orphan

fountain 3 jet **4** head, root **5** spout **6** geyser, origin, source, spring **7** bubbler **8** wellhead **9** inception, reservoir **10** wellspring *nymph:* **6** Egeria

four 6 tetrad **7** quartet **10** quaternion *bagger:* **5** homer **7** home run *combining form:* **4** tetr **5** quadr, tetra **6** quadri, quadru, quater, tessar **7** tessara, tessera *gills:* **4** pint *hundred:* **5** elite **10** upper crust *inches:* **4** hand *pecks:* **6** bushel *quarts:* **6** gallon

four-flush 4 dupe **5** bluff **6** betray, delude, humbug, take in **7** beguile, deceive **11** doublecross

four-footed animal 8 tetrapod **9** quadruped

Four Horsemen 3 War **5** Death **6** Famine **8** Conquest **10** Pestilence

four-in-hand 3 tie **5** coach **7** necktie

fourpence 5 groat
four-poster 3 bed
fourscore 6 eighty
four-sided figure 5 rhomb **6** square **7** rhombus **9** rectangle **13** quadrilateral, parallelogram
foursquare 8 straight **10** forthright **13** quadrilateral
fourteen pounds 5 stone
fourth 7 quarter **8** quadrant, quartern *combining form:* **5** quadr, quart **6** quadri, quadru
fowl 3 hen **4** bird, cock, duck **5** chick, goose, poult **6** bantam, pullet, turkey **7** chicken, rooster (see also **chicken; poultry**)
Fowles novel 5 Magus (The) **9** Collector (The) **22** French Lieutenant's Woman (The)
fox 4 fool **5** trick **6** baffle, outwit **7** confuse, reynard **8** bewilder *African:* **4** asse *female:* **5** vixen *kind:* **3** kit, red **5** swift **6** arctic, fennec, silver **8** bat-eared *Scottish:* **3** tod *young:* **3** cub
foxglove 9 digitalis
fox grape 9 muscadine **11** scuppernong
foxiness 4 wile **5** craft, guile **7** cunning, slyness **8** wiliness **10** artfulness, craftiness, cleverness
foxlike 7 vulpine
foxy 3 sly **4** wily **5** canny, slick **6** artful, astute, clever, crafty, shrewd, tricky **7** cunning, vulpine **8** guileful **9** insidious
foyer 5 lobby **8** anteroom, entrance **9** vestibule
fracas 3 row **4** feud, fray, spat, to-do **5** brawl, broil, fight, melee, run-in, set-to **6** affray, hassle, shindy, uproar **7** dispute, quarrel, ruction **8** squabble **9** bickering **10** donnybrook, free-for-all **11** altercation
fraction 3 bit, cut **4** part **5** piece, scrap **6** divide, little **7** portion, section **8** fragment
fractious 4 wild **6** unruly **7** peevish, pettish, willful **8** contrary **9** bellicose, irritable **10** headstrong, pugnacious, refractory **11** belligerent, contentious, intractable, quarrelsome **12** recalcitrant, ungovernable, unmanageable
fracture 4 rent, rift, tear **5** break, cleft, crack, split **6** breach, schism **7** rupture
Fra Diavolo composer 5 Auber (Esprit)
fragile 4 weak **5** frail **6** feeble, flimsy, infirm **7** brittle, friable, tenuous, unsound **8** decrepit, delicate **9** breakable, frangible
fragment 3 bit **4** chip, iota, part, rive **5** burst, crumb, flake, grain, piece, scrap, shard, sherd, shred, smash **6** morsel, shiver, sliver **7** break up, flinder, shatter **8** fraction, particle, splinter **9** fall apart **12** disintegrate

fragmentary 6 broken **7** partial **10** fractional, incomplete, unfinished
fragrance 4 musk, nose, odor **5** aroma, attar, scent, smell, spice **7** bouquet, cologne, incense, perfume **9** redolence **11** eau de parfum, toilet water **13** eau de toilette
fragrant 7 odorous, scented **8** aromatic, perfumed, redolent **11** odoriferous
frail 4 puny, slim, thin, weak **5** petty, reedy, wispy **6** feeble, flimsy, infirm, sickly, slight **7** brittle, fragile, slender, spindly, tenuous, unsound **8** decrepit, delicate **9** breakable, frangible
frailty 4 vice **5** fault **6** foible **7** failing **8** delicacy, weakness **9** infirmity **10** feebleness
frame 4 body, form, mold, plan, sash **5** build, draft, erect, forge, mount, shape, shell **6** border, casing, cook up, devise, draw up, figure, invent, make up, sketch, system **7** arrange, chassis, concoct, fashion, imagine, prepare **8** assemble, casement, conceive, contrive, regulate, skeleton **9** cartouche, construct, fabricate, formulate, structure *part:* **4** sill, stud **5** joist, plate
framework 4 rack **5** shell, truss **7** trestle **8** cribbing, cribwork, scaffold, skeleton, studding, studwork, trussing **9** bare bones, structure *of crossed strips:* **7** lattice, trellis
France *bay:* **6** Biscay *capital:* **5** Paris *channel:* **6** Manche (La) **7** English *city:* **4** Caen, Lyon, Metz, Nice **5** Brest, Lyons **6** Amiens, Calais, Nantes, Rennes **8** Bordeaux, Grenoble, Toulouse **9** Marseille **10** Marseilles, Strasbourg, Versailles **11** Montpellier *conqueror:* **6** Caesar (Julius) *department:* **3** Var **4** Aude, Gard, Jura, Orne **5** Marne, Rhône, Somme **6** Savoie, Vosges **7** Bas-Rhin **8** Ardennes, Calvados *emperor:* **5** Pepin (III, the Short) **8** Napoleon (Bonaparte) **11** Charlemagne *enclave:* **6** Monaco *former name:* **4** Gaul **6** Gallia *hero:* **6** Clovis *heroine:* **9** Joan of Arc *historic province:* **4** Foix **5** Anjou, Aunis, Bearn, Berry, Maine **6** Alsace, Artois, Marche, Poitou, Vendée **7** Gascony, Guyenne, Picardy **8** Auvergne, Bretagne, Brittany, Burgundy, Dauphine, Flanders, Gascogne, Limousin, Lorraine, Lyonnais, Normandy, Picardie, Provence, Touraine **9** Angoumois, Bourgogne, Champagne, Languedoc, Nivernois, Orléanais, Saintonge, Venaissin **10** Roussillon **11** Bourbonnais, Île-de-France **12** Franche-Comté *island:* **3** Yeu **6** Hyères, Oléron, Ushant **7** Corsica **8** Belle-Île **11** Noirmoutier *monarch:* **5** Henri, Henry, Louis **6** Philip **7** Charles **8** Philippe *monetary unit:* **4** euro *monetary unit, former:* **3** sou **5** franc *moun-*

tain, range: 4 Alps, Jura 6 Vosges 8 Auvergne, Pyrenees 9 Mont Blanc *neighbor:* 5 Italy, Spain 7 Andorra, Belgium, Germany 10 Luxembourg 11 Switzerland *president:* 6 Chirac (Jacques) 8 de Gaulle (Charles) 10 Mitterrand (François) *region:* 4 Midi 5 Corse 6 Alsace, Centre 7 Corsica, Picardy 8 Auvergne, Bretagne, Brittany, Burgundy, Limousin, Normandy, Picardie 9 Aquitaine, Bourgogne, Champagne, Languedoc, Normandie 10 Rhône-Alpes 11 Île-de-France 12 Franche-Comté, Midi-Pyrénées *river:* 4 Aire, Aude, Oise 5 Adour, Isère, Loire, Marne, Rhone, Saône, Seine, Somme, Yonne 7 Garonne *sea:* 13 Mediterranean *spa city:* 5 Evian *strait:* 5 Dover *symbol:* 8 Marianne

Francesca's lover 5 Paolo

franchise 4 vote 6 ballot 7 freedom, license 8 suffrage 9 privilege

frangible 7 brittle, fragile, friable 8 delicate 9 breakable

frank 3 dog 4 fair, free, open 5 blunt, plain 6 candid, direct, honest, hot dog, weenie, wiener, wienie 7 upright 8 man-to-man, out-front, straight 9 barefaced, outspoken 10 forthright, scrupulous, unreserved 11 openhearted, plainspoken, transparent, unconcealed, undisguised, uninhibited, unvarnished, wienerwurst 12 heart-to-heart, unmistakable

Frankenstein *author:* 7 Shelley (Mary) *helper:* 4 Igor

frankfurter 3 dog 6 hot dog, weenie, wiener, wienie 11 wienerwurst

Frankie's lover 6 Johnny

Frankish hero 6 Roland

Franklin, Benjamin *birthplace:* 6 Boston *invention:* 5 stove 8 bifocals *pen name:* 11 Poor Richard

frankness 6 candor 7 honesty

frantic 3 mad 4 wild 5 upset, wired 7 fraught, shook up, unglued 8 feverish, frenetic, frenzied, maniacal, worked up 10 distraught 11 overwrought

Franzen novel 11 Corrections (The)

frappe 7 chilled, liqueur 9 milk shake

fraternal 6 clubby 8 sociable 9 brotherly, comradely, dizygotic 10 like-minded

fraternal society 3 FOE, KOC, SAR 4 BPOE, Elks 5 Lions, Moose 6 Eagles, Masons, Rotary 7 Kiwanis, Woodmen 8 Shriners 10 Freemasons, Hibernians, Odd Fellows

fraternity 4 club 5 guild, order, union 6 league 7 company 8 sodality 10 fellowship 11 association, brotherhood 13 brotherliness

fraud 3 con, gyp 4 fake, gaff, hoax, scam, sham 5 cheat, faker, phony, quack, trick 6 deceit, dupery, humbug, hustle, phoney 7 chicane, con game, swindle 8 cozenage, flimflam, impostor, operator, trickery 9 charlatan, chicanery, deception, imposture, pretender, shell game, trickster 10 dishonesty, mountebank, subterfuge 11 counterfeit 12 double-dealer 13 double-dealing, sharp practice

fraudulence 6 deceit 8 quackery, trickery 9 chicanery, deception, phoniness 10 dishonesty

fraudulent 4 fake 5 false, phony 7 crooked 8 cheating, guileful 9 deceitful, deceptive, dishonest 10 fallacious 11 duplicitous

fraught 4 full 5 laden, tense 6 filled, uneasy 7 charged, replete, stuffed 8 pregnant 9 stressful

fräulein 4 maid, Miss 6 maiden 9 governess 12 mademoiselle

fray 3 row 4 fret 5 brawl, broil, brush, clash, fight, melee, ravel, shred 6 combat, fracas, strain, strife 7 dispute, frazzle, ruction, scuffle 8 irritate, skirmish, struggle 9 commotion, scrimmage 10 donnybrook 11 disturbance

frayed 4 worn 6 tatty 6 ragged, shabby 8 tattered 9 moth-eaten 10 threadbare

frazzle 4 do in, fray, poop, tire, wear 5 upset 6 tucker 7 exhaust, fatigue, wear out

frazzled 4 beat 5 upset 6 bushed, sapped 7 drained, rattled 8 agitated, confused, fatigued, tired out 9 exhausted, fagged out, unsettled 10 distressed 11 overwrought 12 disconcerted

freak 3 bug, nut 4 buff, geek, whim 5 go ape, fancy, fiend, maven 6 addict, hippie, maniac, megrim, oddity, vagary, weirdo, whimsy, zealot 7 anomaly, caprice, chimera, conceit, deviate, fanatic, monster 8 crotchet, flimflam 9 androgyne, curiosity 10 aberration, enthusiast 11 abnormality, monstrosity 12 lusus naturae, malformation

freakish 3 odd 5 kooky, outré, weird 6 far-out, quirky 7 bizarre, erratic, oddball, strange 8 aberrant, abnormal 9 arbitrary, eccentric, grotesque, whimsical 10 capricious, outlandish

freckle 3 dot 4 mole, spot 5 fleck 7 speckle, stipple

free 3 rid 4 comp, open 5 frank, loose, untie 6 acquit, exempt, gratis, loosen, unbind, untied 7 absolve, at large, donated, liberal, manumit, movable, pro bono, release, unbound, unchain, unleash, unloose 8 detached, generous, liberate, separate, unfasten, unloosen **9** at liberty, discharge, exculpate, exonerate, extricate, sovereign, unchained, unchecked, unimpeded, un-shackle, unsparing, voluntary **10** autonomous, democratic, emancipate, gratuitous, unconfined, unfettered, unshackled **11** disentangle, emancipated, independent, spontaneous, untrammeled **12** unrestrained, unrestricted **13** complimentary, self-governing, unconstrained

freebie 4 comp, gift, pass **7** present **8** giveaway

freebooter 5 rover **6** bandit, pirate, raider **7** brigand, corsair **8** marauder, picaroon, pillager, rapparee, sea rover **9** buccaneer, pickaroon, plunderer, ransacker

freedom 5 right **7** liberty, license, release **8** autonomy, immunity, latitude **9** exemption, franchise, privilege **11** prerogative **12** emancipation, independence **13** outspokenness *Swahili:* **5** uhuru

free-for-all 4 fray **5** brawl, broil, melee **6** affray, fracas, rumble **7** ruction **10** donnybrook

freehanded 7 liberal **8** generous **9** bounteous, bountiful **10** munificent

freeloader 3 bum **5** leech **6** cadger, sponge **7** moocher **8** barnacle, hanger-on, parasite **11** bloodsucker

Free State 8 Maryland

free ticket 4 pass **11** Annie Oakley

freeze 4 halt, stop **5** chill, stall **6** benumb **7** congeal **8** glaciate, solidify, stoppage **10** immobilize

freezing 3 icy **4** cold **5** chill, gelid, nippy, polar **6** arctic, bitter, chilly, frigid, frosty, wintry **7** glacial, shivery *combining form:* **4** cryo, kryo

freight 4 haul, lade, load **5** cargo **6** burden, charge, lading **7** payload **9** transport

freighter 4 scow, ship **7** carrier, shipper **9** cargo ship **11** bulk carrier

Freischütz composer 5 Weber (Carl Maria von)

French *article:* **2** la, le, un **3** les, une *attendant:* **9** concierge *back:* **3** dos *bed:* **3** lit **6** couche *black:* **4** noir *born:* **3** née *boy:* **4** garçon *brother:* **5** frère *cap:* **5** beret *cardinal:* **7** Mazarin (Jules) **9** Richelieu (Duc de) *castle:* **7** château *cathedral city:* **4** Albi **5** Paris, Reims, Rouen **6** Amiens, Nantes, Rheims **8** Chartres *clergyman:* **4** abbé, curé, père *coin:* **3** ecu *cold:* **5** froid *combining form:* **5** Gallo **6** Franco *conjunction:* **2** et, ou **4** mais *daughter:* **5** fille *day:* **5** jeudi, lundi, mardi **6** samedi **8** dimanche, mercredi, vendredi *dear:* **4** cher *department*

head: **7** prefect *direction:* **3** est, sud **4** nord **5** ouest *down with:* **4** à bas *dream:* **4** rêve *drink:* **5** boire *dynasty:* **5** Capet **6** Valois **7** Bourbon *egg:* **4** oeuf *emblem:* **10** fleur-de-lis *empress:* **7** Eugénie **9** Joséphine *evening:* **4** soir *exclamation:* **3** zut **4** eheu, hein **9** sacrebleu *eye:* **4** oeil *farewell:* **5** adieu **8** au revoir *farmhouse:* **5** ferme *father:* **4** père *forest:* **7** Argonne, Belleau *friend:* **3** ami **4** amie *game:* **3** jeu **4** jeux (plural) *God:* **4** dieu *good:* **3** bon **5** bonne *gray:* **4** gris *hat:* **7** chapeau *head:* **4** tête *here:* **3** ici *income:* **5** rente *island:* **3** île *king:* **3** roi *language:* **9** Provençal *leather:* **4** cuir *length:* **4** aune *mask:* **4** loup *milk:* **4** lait *month:* **3** mai **4** août, juin, mars, mois **5** avril **7** février, janvier, juillet *mother:* **4** mère *nail:* **4** clou *national anthem:* **12** Marseillaise (La) *nose:* **3** nez *nothing:* **4** rien *number:* **3** dix, six **4** cinq, deux, huit, neuf, onze, sept **5** douze, trois **6** quatre *opera:* **5** Faust, Lakmé, Manon, Thaïs **6** Carmen, Mignon **7** Werther *pancake:* **5** crêpe *pastry:* **6** éclair **8** napoleon *poem:* **3** dit *policeman:* **4** flic **8** gendarme *porcelain:* **6** Sèvres **7** Limoges *preposition:* **2** de **3** par, sur **4** avec, dans, pour, sans, sous *pretty:* **4** joli **5** jolie *prison:* **8** Bastille *pronoun:* **2** il, je, te, tu, un **3** eux, ils, mes, moi, toi, une **4** elle, nous, vous *Protestant:* **6** Calvin (John) **8** Huguenot *pupil:* **5** élève *queen:* **5** reine *quick:* **4** vite *rabbit:* **5** lapin *railroad station:* **4** gare *resort:* **3** Pau **4** Nice **5** Vichy **6** Cannes, Menton **7** Antibes **8** Biarritz *resort area:* **7** Riviera *restaurant:* **6** bistro *revolutionist:* **5** Marat (Jean-Paul) **6** Danton (Georges) **11** Robespierre (Maximilien) *Revolution party:* **7** Gironde, Jacobin **8** Mountain *Revolution song:* **5** Ça Ira *roasted:* **4** rôti *room:* **5** salle *saint:* **4** Joan (of Arc) **5** Denis **6** Martin (of Tours) **7** Thérèse (of Lisieux) *school:* **5** école, lycée *sea:* **3** mer *season:* **3** été **5** hiver **7** automne **9** printemps *servant:* **5** valet *sherry:* **5** xérès *shooting match:* **3** tir *shop:* **8** boutique *shrine:* **7** Lourdes *singer:* **4** Piaf (Edith) **8** chanteuse **9** chanteuse *sister:* **5** soeur *small:* **5** petit **6** petite *soldier:* **5** poilu **6** soldat, Zouave **8** chasseur *son:* **4** fils *song:* **3** dit **7** chanson *soup:* **6** potage *star:* **6** étoile *state:* **4** état *stock exchange:* **6** bourse *street:* **3** rue *subway:* **5** metro *summer:* **3** été *there!:* **5** voilà *too much:* **4** trop *very:* **4** très *wartime capital:* **5** Vichy *water:* **3** eau *well:* **4** bien *wine:* **3** vin *wineshop:* **6** bistro *wood:* **4** bois *yes:* **3** oui *yesterday:* **4** hier

French Guiana *capital:* **7** Cayenne *ethnic*

group: 6 Creole **island:** 6 Devil's **mountain range:** 10 Tumac-Humac **neighbor:** 6 Brazil 8 Suriname **river:** 4 Mana 6 Maroni 7 Oyapock

French Polynesia archipelag: 7 Tuamotu **capital:** 7 Papeete **island, island group:** 6 Tahiti 7 Austral, Gambier, Society 9 Marquesas

frenetic 3 mad 4 loco, wild 5 crazy, wired 6 crazed, hectic 7 berserk, frantic 8 agitated, feverish, frenzied, maniacal 9 delirious, orgiastic 10 corybantic

frenzied see frenetic

frenzy 4 amok, fury, rage 5 amuck, craze, furor, mania 6 madden 7 derange, madness, unhinge 8 delirium, distract, hysteria, insanity, paroxysm 9 unbalance 11 derangement

frequency unit 5 hertz 7 fresnel 9 gigahertz

frequent 5 haunt, often, usual, visit 6 common, hourly 7 regular 8 everyday, familiar, habitual 9 customary

frequenter 7 denizen, habitué, haunter

frequently 4 a lot 5 often 8 commonly 9 routinely 10 oftentimes, repeatedly 11 customarily, recurrently

fresh 3 new, raw 4 rude 5 green, lippy, naive, novel, sassy, saucy, smart 6 callow, cheeky, recent, unused, vernal, virgin 8 brand-new, impudent, insolent, original 9 unspoiled 11 impertinent, smart-alecky 12 invigorating 13 inexperienced

freshet 5 flood, spate 6 influx

freshman 4 pleb, tyro 5 frosh, plebe 6 novice, rookie 8 beginner, neophyte, newcomer 10 apprentice, tenderfoot

fret 4 fume, fuss, stew 5 brood, chafe, worry 6 dither, pother

fretful 5 angry, cross 6 crabby, cranky 7 carping, chafing, peevish, pettish, whining 8 captious, caviling, critical, perverse, petulant, restless, snappish 9 fractious, impatient, irascible, irritable, querulous

Freudian term 2 id 3 ego 5 drive 6 denial, libido 7 complex, Oedipal 8 analysis, cathexis, fixation, neurosis, superego 9 analysand, disavowal, dreamwork, fetishism, psychosis 10 parapraxis, projection, regression, repression 11 association, sublimation, unconscious 12 condensation, displacement, preconscious, transference

Frey father: 5 Njörd 6 Njörth **god of:** 3 sun 4 rain 5 peace 6 fertility **sister:** 5 Freya **wife:** 4 Gerd 5 Gerda, Gerth

Freya brother: 4 Frey **domain:** 9 Folkvangr **father:** 5 Njörd 6 Njörth

friable 5 mealy 7 brittle, crumbly, fragile 9 frangible

friar 7 brother 8 cenobite 9 mendicant

fribble 3 toy 5 dally, flirt 6 coquet, trifle 7 trifler 8 trifling 9 dalliance, frivolity 10 dillydally, fool around

friction 4 drag 7 discord, rubbing 8 abrasion 9 animosity, attrition 10 disharmony, dissension, resistance 12 disagreement

friction match 5 vesta 7 lucifer 8 vesuvian

Friday's rescuer 6 Crusoe (Robinson)

friend 3 pal 4 ally, chum, mate, pard 5 buddy, crony, matey, serve 6 cohort 7 comrade, partner 8 alter ego, compadre, confrere, familiar, intimate, playmate, sidekick 9 colleague, companion, confidant 10 confidante **French:** 3 ami 4 amie **Maori:** 4 ehoa **Spanish:** 5 amiga, amigo

Friend 6 Quaker **founder:** 3 Fox (George)

friendly 5 happy 6 amical, chummy, folksy, genial 7 affable, amiable, cordial 8 amicable, cheerful, familiar, sociable 9 congenial, favorable 10 buddy-buddy, compatible, hospitable, neighborly 12 affectionate, well-disposed 13 accommodating

Friendly Islands 5 Tonga

Friends series character: 4 Joey, Ross 6 Monica, Phoebe, Rachel 8 Chandler **setting:** 9 Manhattan **star:** 3 Cox (Courteney) 5 Perry (Matthew) 6 Kudrow (Lisa) 7 Aniston (Jennifer), LeBlanc (Matt) 9 Schwimmer (David)

friends and neighbors 4 kith

friendship 5 amity 6 accord, comity 7 concord, empathy, harmony 8 affinity, alliance, goodwill

frigate bird 3 ioa, iwa 8 alcatras 11 man-o'-war bird **genus:** 7 Fregata

Frigga, Frigg husband: 4 Odin 5 Woden **son:** 6 Balder, Baldur

fright 4 fear 5 alarm, dread, panic, scare, shock 6 dismay, horror, terror 11 trepidation

frighten 3 cow 5 alarm, bully, daunt, scare, shock, spook 6 appall, dismay 7 horrify, perturb, scarify, startle, terrify, unnerve 9 terrorize 10 intimidate

frightful 4 ugly 5 awful, scary 6 horrid 7 fearful, ghastly, hideous 8 alarming, dreadful, fearsome, horrible, horrific, shocking, terrible, terrific 9 appalling, startling 10 formidable, horrendous, terrifying

frigid 3 icy 4 cold 5 chill 6 arctic, chilly, frosty 7 glacial 8 freezing 11 emotionless, indifferent, passionless, unemotional 12 unresponsive

frijoles 5 beans

frill 4 ruff 5 jabot, ruche 6 doodad, luxury,

ruffle **7** flounce, ruching **8** furbelow **11** affectation, superfluity **12** extravagance

fringe 3 hem, rim **4** brim, ruff **5** bound, brink, skirt, thrum, verge **6** border, edging, margin **7** fimbria **8** penumbra, trimming **9** perimeter, periphery **10** borderland

frippery 6 finery, frills, tawdry **7** regalia **8** foofaraw, trumpery **9** trappings **11** ostentation

frisée 6 endive **7** lettuce

frisk 4 leap, play, romp, skip **5** caper, dance **6** cavort, frolic, gambol, search **7** disport, pat down, rollick

frisky 3 gay **5** antic **6** feisty, lively **7** coltish, playful **8** animated, gamesome, sportive **9** sprightly, vivacious **10** frolicsome

fritter away 4 blow **5** spend, waste **7** consume **8** squander **9** dissipate

frivolity 3 fun **4** play **6** gaiety, levity, whimsy **8** nonsense **12** childishness

frivolous 3 gay **4** idle **5** ditsy, ditzy, dizzy, giddy, light, silly **6** breezy, frothy, yeasty **7** flighty, playful, shallow, trivial **8** carefree, careless, heedless, trifling **11** light-headed, superficial

frizzy 5 kinky **6** coiled, curled **7** twisted

frock 4 gown **5** dress, habit **6** jersey, mantle

Frodo's pal 3 Sam

frog 4 toad **5** ranid **6** anuran **7** croaker **9** amphibian **10** batrachian *family:* **7** Ranidae *genus:* **4** Rana *kind:* **4** hyla **5** coqui **6** peeper **7** leopard **8** bullfrog, tree toad *larva:* **7** tadpole

frolic 3 fun **4** lark, play, romp **5** antic, caper, dance, frisk, party, prank, revel, sport, spree **6** cavort, didoes, gaiety, gambol, prance **7** disport, skylark **8** escapade, hilarity **9** festivity, merriment **10** shenanigan, tomfoolery

frolicsome 3 gay **5** antic **6** frisky, impish **7** coltish, jocular, playful, roguish **8** sportful, sportive **9** sprightly **10** rollicking **11** mischievous

from German: 3 von *Scottish:* **4** frae

From Here to Eternity author 5 Jones (James)

frondeur 5 rebel **8** mutineer, renegade **9** anarchist, dissident, insurgent **10** malcontent

front 3 bow, van **4** face, fore, lend, look, mask, prow **5** beard **6** facade, facing **7** forward **8** anterior, disguise **9** challenge, encounter **10** appearance, figurehead **11** countenance

frontier 5 bound, field, march **6** border **8** backland, backwash, boundary **9** upcountry **10** borderland, hinterland **11** backcountry

frontiersman 5 Boone (Daniel), Clark (George Rogers, William) **6** Carson (Kit) **7**

Frémont (J. C.), pioneer, settler **8** Crockett (Davy) **10** bushranger

fronton game 7 jai alai

frontward 8 anterior

frost 4 hoar, rime **6** freeze

frostfish 5 smelt **6** tomcod

frost heave 5 pingo

frosting 5 icing **7** topping **8** trimming

Frost poem 7 Birches **10** Fire and Ice **11** Mending Wall **12** Road Not Taken (The) **18** Death of the Hired Man (The) **30** Stopping By Woods on a Snowy Evening

frosty 3 icy **4** cold, rimy **5** chill, frore, hoary, nippy **6** chilly, frigid **7** glacial **8** freezing **10** unfriendly

Frosty's eyes 4 coal

froth 4 foam, head, suds **5** cream, spume, yeast **6** lather **8** airiness **9** frivolity, lightness

froufrou 6 frills **8** rustling

froward 5 balky **6** mulish, ornery **7** peevish, restive **8** contrary, perverse, petulant, stubborn **9** obstinate **10** headstrong, refractory **11** disobedient

frown 4 pout, sulk **5** glare, lower, scowl **6** glower

frowsy 5 dowdy, funky, fusty, messy, musty, stale **6** shabby, smelly, sordid, untidy **7** squalid, unkempt **8** slattern, slovenly **10** disheveled, disordered, slatternly **13** draggletailed

frozen 4 cold, hard **5** fixed, frore, rigid, stiff **6** frigid, iced up, numbed **7** chilled **8** benumbed, immobile **9** congealed, petrified

frugal 4 mean **5** canny, scant, spare **6** Scotch, stingy **7** careful, prudent, scrimpy, sparing, thrifty **8** discreet, stinting **9** niggardly, penurious, provident **10** economical, unwasteful **12** cheeseparing, parsimonious **13** penny-pinching

frugality 6 thrift **7** economy **8** prudence **9** husbandry **10** providence **11** thriftiness

fruit 3 fig, nut **4** ansu, date, lime, pear, pepo, plum, pome, seed, sloe **5** apple, berry, drupe, gourd, grape, guava, issue, lemon, mango, melon, olive, papaw, peach, prune, young **6** achene, banana, casaba, cherry, citron, durian, legume, loment, loquat, orange, papaya, pawpaw, pomelo, quince, result, samara **7** acerola, apricot, avocado, capsule, coconut, currant, kumquat, outcome, progeny, silique, syconia (plural), tangelo, utricle **8** bergamot, dewberry, mandarin, rambutan, shaddock, syconium, tamarind **9** blueberry, cherimoya, cranberry, muskmelon, nectarine, offspring, persimmon, pineapple, raspberry, tangerine **10** blackberry, calamondin, gooseberry, grapefruit, loganberry, mangosteen, strawberry **11** boysenberry, hesperidium, huckleberry, pomegranate *dried:* **5** prune **6** raisin *drink:* **3** ade **5** juice, punch *residue:* **4** marc **6** pomace *seed:* **3** pip *study of:* **8** pomology **9** carpology *sugar:* **7** glucose **8** fructose, levulose *undeveloped:* **6** nubbin

fruitful 6 fecund **7** copious, fertile **8** abundant, prolific **9** bountiful, fructuous, plenteous, plentiful **10** productive **11** proliferant

fruition 7 delight **8** pleasure **9** enjoyment **10** attainment, conclusion **11** achievement, delectation, fulfillment, realization

fruitless 4 vain **6** barren, futile **7** sterile, useless **8** abortive **10** unavailing **11** ineffective, ineffectual **12** unproductive, unsuccessful

frumpy 4 drab, dull **5** dated, dowdy, tacky **6** stodgy **8** outmoded **9** out-of-date, unstylish **12** old-fashioned

frustrate 4 balk, bilk, dash, foil, halt **5** block, check, stump **6** arrest, baffle, defeat, hinder, impede, stymie, thwart **7** inhibit, prevent **8** confound, obstruct, preclude, prohibit **9** discomfit, forestall, interrupt **10** disappoint

frustration 6 defeat, dismay **7** chagrin, letdown **8** vexation **9** annoyance, hindrance **10** impediment, irritation **11** displeasure, obstruction

fry 4 burn, sear **5** frizz, grill, sauté **6** fishes, picnic **7** frizzle **11** electrocute

frying pan 6 spider **7** griddle, skillet

fuddle 4 befog, booze **6** ball up, jumble, tipple **7** confuse, fluster, stupefy **8** bewilder **10** intoxicate

fuddy-duddy 4 fogy **5** fogey **6** fossil, square, stodgy **8** mossback, outdated, outmoded **12** antediluvian, Colonel Blimp, old-fashioned, stuffed shirt **13** stick-in-the-mud

fudge 3 pad **4** blur, bosh, fake **5** candy, cheat, color, dodge, hedge, hooey, welsh **6** bunkum **7** distort, falsify, hogwash, penuche **8** contrive, divinity, nonsense **9** embellish, embroider, overstate, poppycock **10** equivocate, flapdoodle **11** foolishness

fuel 3 gas, oil **4** coal, coke, fire, peat, wood **5** stoke **6** biogas, diesel, petrol, Sterno **7** ethanol, gasohol, inflame, propane **8** charcoal, gasoline, kerosene **9** biodiesel, petroleum, stimulate **10** natural gas **13** reinforcement *jelled:* **6** napalm

Fuentes novel 4 Aura **9** Old Gringo (The)

fugacious 7 brittle, passing **8** fleeting, fugitive, volatile **9** ephemeral, momentary, transient **10** evanescent, short-lived, transitory

fugitive 5 exile **6** outlaw **7** escapee, lamster, nomadic, passing, refugee, runaway **8** deserter, fleeting, runagate, vagabond **9**

ephemeral, fugacious, momentary, transient, wandering **10** evanescent, short-lived, transitory

fugue master 4 Bach (Johann Sebastian)

Führer, der 6 Hitler (Adolf)

fulcrum 3 hub **4** axis, prop **5** hinge, nexus, pivot **7** support

fulfill 4 meet **5** honor **6** effect, finish, redeem **7** achieve, execute, perform, satisfy **8** complete **9** discharge, implement **10** accomplish

fulgent 6 bright **7** beaming, glowing, radiant, shining **8** luminous, lustrous **9** brilliant

fuliginous 4 dark **5** dingy, dusky, grimy, murky, sooty **7** obscure

full 5 sated, total, whole **6** entire, gorged, jammed, loaded, packed, utmost **7** crammed, crowded, glutted, maximum, plenary, replete, stuffed **8** brimming, complete, satiated **9** jam-packed, plentiful, surfeited **11** chockablock

full-blooded 4 rich **5** flush, ruddy **6** ardent, florid **7** flushed, genuine, glowing **8** forceful, purebred, rubicund, sanguine **9** pedigreed, pureblood **10** compelling **12** thoroughbred

full-blown 4 lush, ripe **5** adult, total **6** all-out, mature **7** grown-up

full-bodied 4 rich **5** husky, lusty, stout **6** potent, robust, strong **9** corpulent **10** meaningful **11** significant, substantial

full dress 6 finery **7** regalia **8** frippery, glad rags **10** Sunday best

full-figured 5 ample, buxom, plump **6** zaftig **10** curvaceous, Rubenesque, statuesque, voluptuous

full-fledged 4 ripe **5** adult, grown, total **6** mature **7** genuine, grown-up **8** complete **9** full-blown

full-grown 4 ripe **5** adult **6** mature

fullness 6 plenty **7** satiety **9** abundance, amplitude, repletion **10** perfection **12** completeness

full-scale 5 total **6** all-out **8** complete, life-size **9** unlimited

full tilt 7 flat-out, rapidly, swiftly **8** pell-mell, speedily **9** posthaste **12** lickety-split

fulminate 4 boil, burn, foam, fume, rage, rail, rave **5** curse, flare **7** bluster, explode, inveigh

fulsome 4 oily **5** plump, slick, soapy, suave **6** lavish, smarmy, smooth **7** buttery, cloying, copious, profuse **8** abundant, effusive, generous, overdone, unctuous **9** excessive **10** flattering, oleaginous **11** extravagant, pharisaical **12** ingratiating, Pecksniffian

Fulton's steamboat 8 Clermont

fumarole 4 vent

fumble 3 bob, err, paw **4** feel, flub, mess, muff **5** botch, grope **6** bobble, bollix, bungle, muddle **7** blunder, misplay **8** flounder

fume 3 gas **4** boil, burn, odor, rage, rant, rave, reek, snit, stew **5** smoke, vapor **6** seethe, swivet **7** sputter

fun 4 play **5** sport **6** frolic, gaiety **7** amusing, jollity, pastime, whoopee **8** hilarity, pleasant, ridicule **9** amusement, diversion, diverting, enjoyment, frivolity, horseplay, jocundity, joviality, merriment **10** pleasantry **12** entertaining **13** entertainment

function 3 act, job, run, use **4** duty, goal, mark, role, task, work **5** party, power, react, serve **6** affair, behave, object, office, target **7** concern, faculty, operate, perform, purpose, service **8** activity, behavior, business, capacity, ceremony, occasion, province **9** objective, officiate, operation, reception *trigonometric:* **4** sine **6** cosine, secant **7** tangent **8** cosecant **9** cotangent

functional 5 handy, utile **6** useful **7** working **9** practical **11** practicable, serviceable, utilitarian **12** occupational

functioning 6 active **7** dynamic **9** operative

fund 4 back, bank, pool **5** endow, stake, stock, store **6** coffer, supply **7** capital, finance, reserve, support **8** bankroll, treasury **9** inventory, subsidize **10** accumulate, capitalize

fundament 3 bum **4** butt, rear, rump, seat **5** basis, fanny **6** behind, bottom **8** backside, buttocks, derriere **9** posterior, principle **10** foundation, groundwork

fundamental 3 key **5** axiom, basal, basic, prime, vital **6** bottom, factor, primal, simple **7** bedrock, organic, primary, radical, theorem **8** absolute, cardinal, dominant, ultimate **9** component, essential, important, necessary, paramount, primitive, principal, principle, requisite **10** deep-rooted, elementary, grassroots, primordial, rock-bottom, underlying **11** constituent, irreducible, nitty-gritty **12** constitutive, foundational

fund-raiser 8 telethon

funeral 6 burial **7** obsequy **9** obsequies *car:* **6** hearse *director:* **9** mortician **10** undertaker *oration:* **6** eulogy **8** encomium **9** panegyric *procession:* **7** cortege *service:* **7** requiem **9** obsequies *song:* **5** dirge, elegy **8** threnody

funereal 3 sad **4** dark **5** black, bleak, grave **6** dismal, dreary, gloomy, solemn, somber, sombre **7** elegiac **8** mournful **9** deathlike, sorrowful **10** depressing, depressive, lugubrious, oppressive, sepulchral

fungus 4 conk, mold, rust, smut **5** ergot, yeast **6** agaric, dry rot, mildew **7** candida,

truffle **8** mushroom, puffball **9** earthstar, stinkhorn, toadstool *combining form:* **4** myco **5** myces, mycet **6** mycete, myceto *part:* **3** cap **4** gill **5** ascus, hypha, stipe, volva **7** annulus **8** basidium, conidium, mycelium *rust:* **5** Uredo

fungus disease 3 rot **4** mold, rust, scab, smut **5** ergot, tinea **6** blight, mildew, thrush **7** mycosis **8** lumpy jaw, ringworm **12** athlete's foot

funk 4 odor, reek **5** blues, dolor, dumps, ennui, gloom, smell, stink, slump **6** recoil, stench **7** sadness **9** dejection **10** depression, melancholy

funky 3 hip, odd **4** foul, rank **5** fetid, reeky **6** earthy, frowsy, grungy, quaint, quirky, smelly, stinky **7** natural, noisome, oddball, offbeat **8** down-home **10** malodorous

funnel 4 flue, pipe **5** stack **6** hopper **7** channel, conduct, tornado, tundish, twister **8** transmit **10** smokestack

funny 3 odd **4** joke, zany **5** antic, comic, droll, fishy, queer **7** amusing, bizarre, comical, jocular, risible, strange **8** farcical, humorous, peculiar **9** facetious, fantastic, hilarious, laughable, ludicrous **10** ridiculous

Funny Girl 5 Brice (Fanny) *composer:* **5** Styne (Jule) *star:* **9** Streisand (Barbra)

funnyman 3 wag, wit **5** clown, comic, cutup, droll, joker **6** gagman, jester **8** comedian, humorist, jokester, quipster **10** comedienne

fur 4 down, hide, pelt, pile **5** floss, fluff, stole **6** pelage, peltry *kind:* **3** fox **4** mink, seal **5** coypu, fitch, otter, sable **6** ermine, fisher, marten, nutria, rabbit, tanuki **7** raccoon **10** chinchilla *lamb:* **7** caracul, karakul **9** broadtail *medieval:* **4** vair **7** miniver

furbelow 5 frill **7** flounce

furbish 4 buff **5** fix up, renew, shine **6** polish, revive **7** burnish, refresh, restore **8** renovate

Furies 6 Alecto **7** Erinyes, Megaera **9** Eumenides, Tisiphone

furious 3 mad **4** wild **5** angry, livid, irate, rabid, upset **6** crazed, fierce, insane, raging, stormy **7** enraged, excited, extreme, frantic, intense, violent **8** feverish, frenetic, frenzied, incensed, maddened, vehement, wrathful **9** impetuous, turbulent **10** boisterous, corybantic

furl 4 curl, fold, roll, wrap **6** take in

furlough 4 pass **5** leave **6** lay off **7** liberty **10** shore leave **13** authorization

furnace 4 kiln, oven **5** forge, stove **6** heater **7** smelter **8** tryworks **11** incinerator *part:* **4** port, vent **6** tuyere *tender:* **6** stoker

furnish 3 arm, rig **4** give, hand, lend **5** endow, endue, equip **6** fit out, outfit, supply **7** apparel, appoint, deliver, provide, turn out **8** accouter, accoutre, dispense, hand over, transfer **9** provision **10** contribute

furnishings 4 gear **5** decor **9** equipment, trappings **10** housewares **11** appointment **13** accouterments, accoutrements, paraphernalia

furniture designer *American:* **5** Eames (Charles, Ray), Phyfe (Duncan) **7** Goddard (John, Stephen, Thomas), Haldane (William) **8** Stickley (Gustav) *British:* **6** Morris (William) **7** Gibbons (Grinling), Shearer (Thomas) **8** Sheraton (Thomas) **11** Chippendale (Thomas), Hepplewhite (George) *French:* **5** Marot (Daniel) **6** Boulle (André-Charles) *German:* **6** Breuer (Marcel) *Scottish:* **4** Adam (James, Robert)

furniture style 4 Adam **6** Empire, Shaker **7** Bauhaus, Federal, Mission **8** Colonial, Georgian, Jacobean, Sheraton, Stickley **9** Queen Anne **11** chinoiserie, Chippendale, Duncan Phyfe, Hepplewhite **13** Arts and Crafts

furor 3 ado, cry, fad, wax **4** chic, mode, rage, stir, to-do **5** anger, craze, mania, style, vogue **6** flurry, frenzy, pother, ruckus, rumpus, uproar **7** fashion, madness **8** foofaraw **9** commotion **10** dernier cri, excitement **11** controversy

furrow 3 rut **4** ruck **5** plica, ridge, sulci (plural) **6** course, crease, groove, sulcus, trench **7** channel, crinkle, wrinkle **8** entrench **9** corrugate **11** corrugation

furrowed 5 lined **6** rugose **7** grooved, sulcate **8** wrinkled **10** corrugated

further 4 abet, also, help **5** again, fresh **6** beyond **7** advance, besides, forward, promote **8** engender, moreover **9** encourage, propagate **10** additional, in addition **12** additionally

furthermore 3 and, too **4** also **6** as well, withal **7** besides **8** likewise, moreover **9** what's more **12** additionally

furthermost 4 last **7** extreme **8** farthest, remotest, ultimate

furtive 3 sly **4** foxy, wary, wily **6** artful, covert, crafty, feline, masked, secret, shifty, sneaky, stolen, tricky **7** catlike, cunning, evasive, sub-rosa **8** guileful, hush-hush, scheming, stealthy **9** disguised, insidious **11** circumspect, clandestine **12** hugger-mugger **13** surreptitious, under-the-table *look:* **4** peek, peep

fur trader 8 voyageur

furuncle 4 boil **7** abscess

fury 3 ire **4** burn, rage **5** anger, furor, wrath **6** frenzy **7** madness, passion **8** violence **9** vehemence **10** fierceness

furze 4 whin **5** gorse *genus:* **4** Ulex **7** Genista

fuse 3 mix **4** flux, meld, melt, weld **5** blend, merge, smelt, unify, unite **6** anneal, solder **7** liquefy **8** coalesce, conflate, dissolve, intermix **9** commingle, integrate **10** amalgamate **11** consolidate, incorporate

fusillade 4 hail **5** burst, salvo **6** shower, volley **7** barrage **8** drumfire, outburst **9** broadside, cannonade **11** bombardment

fusion 5 alloy, blend, union **6** merger **7** amalgam, mixture **8** compound **9** coalition, immixture, synthesis

fuss 3 ado, nag, row **4** beef, crab, flap, fret, miff, stew, stir, to-do **5** gripe, stink, upset, whine, worry **6** bother, bustle, hassle, hurrah, pother, ruckus, rumpus, squawk **7** protest **8** complain, foofaraw, squabble **9** commotion, complaint, kerfuffle, objection **11** controversy

fussbudget 3 hen **6** granny **8** stickler **10** fuddy-duddy **13** perfectionist

fusspot 8 stickler **9** nitpicker, worrywart

fussy 5 picky **6** cranky, dainty, ornate **7** careful, finicky, fretful **9** crotchety, irritable, querulous **10** fastidious, meticulous, particular, pernickety, scrupulous **11** painstaking, persnickety, punctilious **13** conscientious

fustian 4 rant **7** bombast, pompous **8** affected, inflated **9** high-flown **11** exaggerated, highfalutin, pretentious **13** grandiloquent

fusty 4 rank **5** close, dated, fetid, moldy, passé, stale **6** bygone, old-hat, smelly **7** archaic **8** outdated **10** antiquated, malodorous **11** reactionary **12** old-fashioned

futhark letter 4 rune

futile 4 idle, vain **5** empty **6** hollow, otiose **7** useless **8** abortive, bootless, hopeless, nugatory **9** fruitless, worthless **10** unavailing **11** ineffective, ineffectual **12** unproductive, unsuccessful

future 5 later **6** mañana, offing, to come **7** by-and-by **8** oncoming, tomorrow **9** hereafter

Futurism *founder:* **9** Marinetti (Filippo Tommaso) *painter:* **5** Balla (Giacomo), Carra (Carlo) **7** Russolo (Luigi) **8** Boccioni (Umberto), Severini (Gino) *sculptor:* **8** Boccioni (Umberto)

fuzz 3 cop **4** down, lint **6** police

fuzzy 3 dim **5** faint, gauzy, linty, vague, woozy **6** bleary, blurry **7** blurred, muddled, obscure, shadowy, unclear **8** confused **9** distorted, undefined **10** ill-defined, incoherent, indefinite, indistinct

fylfot 8 swastika

G

gab 3 jaw, rap, yak **4** blab, chat, talk **5** clack, drool, prate, speak **6** babble, drivel, gibber, gossip, jabber, natter, yammer **7** blabber, blather, chatter, palaver, prattle, twaddle **8** chitchat, converse, idle talk **9** gibberish, small talk

gabber 5 yenta **6** gossip, magpie **7** blabber **9** chatterer **10** chatterbox **12** blabbermouth, gossipmonger

gabby 4 glib **5** talky, windy **6** chatty **7** voluble **8** effusive **9** garrulous, talkative **10** long-winded, loquacious **11** loose-lipped **12** loose-tongued

gaberdine 4 coat, suit **5** cloak, cloth **6** capote, fabric **7** garment, manteau **8** material

gable 4 wall **8** pediment *ornament:* **6** finial

Gabon *capital:* **10** Libreville *city:* **10** Port-Gentil *ethnic group:* **4** Fang **5** Bantu *language:* **6** French *monetary unit:* **5** franc *neighbor:* **5** Congo **8** Cameroon *river:* **6** Ogooué

gad 3 bat **4** flit, roam, rove **5** amble, drift, mooch, range, stray, tramp **6** chisel, ramble, wander **7** maunder, meander, traipse **9** gallivant

Gad *brother:* **5** Asher *father:* **5** Jacob *mother:* **6** Zilpah *son:* **3** Eri **5** Ezbon, Haggi

Gaddis *novel* **12** Recognitions (The) **14** Frolic of His Own (A) **16** Carpenter's Gothic

gadfly 3 nag **4** pest, pill **6** bother, critic, insect, nudnik **8** nuisance

gadget 4 tool **5** gizmo, thing **6** device, dingus, doodad, hickey, jigger, widget **7** concern, gimmick, utensil **9** apparatus, appliance, doohickey, implement, mechanism, thingummy **10** instrument **11** contraption, thingamabob, thingamajig, thingumajig

gadwall 4 bird, duck, fowl **9** waterfowl

gadzooks 4 drat, egad **6** crikey, zounds

Gaea *husband:* **6** Uranus *offspring:* **6** Furies, Giants, Titans, Typhon, Uranus **7** Erinyes **8** Cyclopes **9** Eumenides *parent:* **5** Chaos

Gaelic 4 Erse **5** Irish **6** Celtic **8** Scottish *god:* **3** Ler **5** Dagda *hero:* **5** Oisin **6** Cormac, Ossian **8** Diarmaid **11** Finn MacCool *king:* **9** Conchobar, Conchobor *language:* **4** Manx *poet:* **4** bard **6** Ossian *queen:* **4** Medb *soldier:* **4** kern **6** Fenian *spirit:* **7** banshee

gaff 3 fix, rig **4** hoax, hook, spar, spur **5** abuse, fraud, spear, trick **6** fleece, ordeal **7** deceive, gimmick **8** raillery **12** climbing iron

gaffe 4 flub, goof, muff **5** boner, error, fault, fluff, lapse **6** bollix, boo-boo, bungle, foul-up, howler, slipup **7** blooper, blunder, clinker, faux pas, misstep, mistake **8** solecism **9** gaucherie **11** impropriety, misjudgment **12** indiscretion

gag 4 balk, gasp, hoax, jape, jest, joke, quip **5** choke, crack, heave, prank, retch, trick **6** muffle, muzzle, shtick, stifle, strain **7** repress, silence, squelch **8** throttle **9** restraint, wisecrack, witticism

gaga 4 agog, wild **5** crazy, giddy, nutty, wacky **6** doting, fervid, gung ho **7** foolish, gushing, excited, smitten **8** animated, enamored, obsessed, thrilled **9** ebullient, exuberant **10** captivated, infatuated **12** enthusiastic

gage 3 vow **4** bond **5** token **6** pledge, surety **8** gauntlet, security (see also **gauge**)

gaggle 4 crew, gang, pack **5** array, bunch, flock, group **6** clutch, number **7** cluster **10** assemblage, collection **11** aggregation

Gaheris *brother:* **6** Gareth, Gawain *father:* **3** Lot *mother:* **8** Margawse, Morgause *uncle:* **6** Arthur *victim:* **8** Margawse, Morgause

gaiety 3 fun, joy **4** glee **5** mirth, revel **6** finery, frolic, hoopla **7** elation, jollity, revelry, whoopee **8** elegance, hilarity, reveling, vivacity **9** animation, festivity, happiness, joviality, merriment **10** ebullience, exuberance, hullabaloo, joyousness, jubilation, liveliness **11** high spirits, merrymaking **12** conviviality

gain 3 get, net, win **4** earn, land, make, reap **5** clear, cover, reach, score **6** attain, expand, obtain, pick up, profit, rack up, secure **7** achieve, acquire, advance, attract, augment, benefit, bring in, enlarge, procure **8** earnings, increase, persuade, proceeds, windfall **10** accomplish

gainful 6 paying **8** fruitful, generous **9** lucrative, rewarding **10** beneficial, productive, profitable, well-paying, worthwhile **12** advantageous, remunerative

gainsay 4 buck, defy, deny **6** impugn, negate, oppose, refute, resist **7** dispute **8** disclaim, disprove, negative, traverse **9** disaffirm, repudiate, withstand **10** contradict, contravene, controvert

Gainsborough painting 7 Blue Boy

gait 3 air, run **4** clip, dash, lope, pace, rate, step, trot, walk **5** amble, speed, strut, train, tread **6** canter, gallop, stride **7** bearing **8** demeanor

gaiter 4 boot, shoe, spat **7** legging **8** overshoe

gal 4 babe, doll **5** chick

gala 4 ball, bash, fete, prom **5** merry, party **6** lively **7** festive, jubilee, pageant, shindig **8** festival, jamboree, wingding **9** festivity, spectacle **11** celebration **13** entertainment

Galactica commander 5 Adama (Adm. William)

galago 5 lemur **8** bush baby

Galahad *father:* **8** Lancelot **9** Launcelot *mother:* **6** Elaine *quest:* **5** Grail **9** Holy Grail

Galatea *father:* **6** Nereus *husband:* **9** Pygmalion *lover:* **4** Acis *mother:* **5** Doris

galaxy 6 nebula **8** Milky Way, universe

Galba *predecessor:* **4** Nero *successor:* **4** Otho

gale 4 blow, gust, wind **5** blast, storm **6** squall **7** cyclone, tempest, typhoon **8** outburst **9** hurricane

galena 3 ore **4** lead

Galen's forte 7 healing **8** medicine

galilee 5 porch **6** chapel

Galilee town 4 Cana **7** Gergesa **8** Nazareth, Tiberias **9** Bethsaida, Capernaum

Galileo's birthplace 4 Pisa **5** Italy **7** Tuscany

gall 3 irk, nag, rub, vex **4** bile, fray, fret, rile, roil, sore, wear **5** annoy, brass, chafe, cheek, erode, grate, graze, nerve **6** abrade, bother, burn up, harass, pester, plague, rancor, ruffle, scrape **7** conceit, disturb, frazzle, inflame, provoke, scratch, torment **8** audacity, boldness, chutzpah, irritate, temerity **9** aggravate, arrogance, brashness, impudence, insolence **10** bitterness, effrontery *bladder:* **9** cholecyst

gallant 3 fop **4** beau, bold, buck, dude, hero **5** blade, blood, brave, civil, dandy, lover, manly, Romeo, showy, suave, swain, wooer **6** daring, heroic, suitor, urbane **7** courtly, coxcomb, dashing, Don Juan, stately, valiant **8** Casanova, gracious, lothario, paramour, spirited, valorous **9** attentive, courteous, dauntless, ladies' man **10** chivalrous, courageous

gallantry 5 honor, poise, valor **6** daring, mettle, spirit **7** amenity, bravery, courage, heroism, prowess, suavity **8** boldness, chivalry, courtesy, urbanity, valiance, valiancy **9** attention, manliness **10** resolution **11** courtliness **12** fearlessness

galleon 7 warship **12** square-rigger

gallery 5 patio, porch, salon **6** arcade, loggia, museum, piazza **7** balcony, passage, portico, veranda **8** audience, corridor, showroom **9** colonnade, onlookers, promenade *ancient Greek:* **4** stoa

galley 3 gig **4** boat, mess, ship, tray **5** cuddy, proof **6** bireme **7** canteen, kitchen, trireme, warship **8** scullery **9** cookhouse

Gallic 6 French

gallimaufry 3 mix **4** hash, mess, olio, stew **5** chaos **6** jumble, medley **7** clutter, goulash, mélange, mixture, variety **8** mishmash, pastiche **9** patchwork, potpourri **10** assortment, hodgepodge, hotchpotch, miscellany, salmagundi

gallinaceous bird 3 hen **5** quail **6** grouse, turkey **7** chicken, hoatzin, peacock **8** curassow, pheasant **9** partridge **10** guinea fowl

galling 6 bitter, vexing **8** rankling **9** upsetting, vexatious **10** afflictive, irritating, nettlesome **11** aggravating, distressing, troublesome **12** exasperating

gallivant 3 bat, bum, gad **4** flit, roam, rove **5** amble, drift, jaunt, mooch, range, stray **6** cruise, ramble, travel, wander **7** meander, traipse **8** vagabond **10** knock about

gallop 4 dash, race **6** sprint

gallows 6 gibbet *bird:* **7** villain **8** criminal

galoot 3 ape, guy, oaf **4** dupe, goon, lout, slob **5** chump **6** fellow, lummox **7** palooka

galore 4 full, lush, rich **5** ample, great **6** lavish **7** aplenty, copious, endless, profuse **8** abundant, generous **9** bountiful, expansive, plentiful **11** overflowing

galosh 4 boot, shoe **6** rubber **8** overshoe

Galsworthy work 7 Justice **11** Forsyte Saga (The)

galumph 4 plod **5** barge, clomp, clump, stomp, stump, tramp **6** lumber, trudge

galvanize 3 jar, zap **4** coat, fire, jolt, stir, spur, stun **5** pep up, pique, prime, react, rouse, shock **6** arouse, excite, perk up, thrill **7** animate, enliven, immerse, inspire, provoke, quicken **8** activate, astonish, energize, motivate, vitalize **9** electrify, innervate, magnetize, stimulate **10** invigorate

gam 3 leg, pin, pod, rap **4** chat, flap, limb,

talk **5** visit **6** confab **9** drumstick **12** conversation

Gambia *capital:* **6** Banjul *city:* **9** Serekunda *monetary unit:* **6** dalasi *neighbor:* **7** Senegal

gambit 3 con, jig **4** move, play, ploy, ruse, wile **5** dodge, topic, trick **6** design, device, remark, tactic **7** gimmick **8** artifice, maneuver, trickery **9** expedient, stratagem **10** subterfuge

gamble 3 bet, lay, set **4** dare, game, play, punt, risk **5** put on, stake, wager **6** chance, hazard, plunge, raffle **7** imperil, lottery, venture **8** cast lots, long shot **9** crapshoot, speculate **10** jeopardize

gambler 5 dicer, shark, sharp **7** sharper **9** cardsharp **10** cardplayer **11** cardsharper

gambling place 3 den **4** club, dive, Reno **5** joint, Vegas **6** casino **8** Las Vegas, pool hall **9** roadhouse **10** Monte Carlo **12** Atlantic City, betting house

gambol 3 hop **4** jump, lark, leap, romp, skip **5** bound, caper, frisk, revel, sport **6** cavort, frolic, prance, spring **7** carry on, roister, rollick

Gambrinus' invention 3 ale **4** beer **5** lager

game 3 bet, fun, lay, RPG **4** bold, jest, joke, lark, play, prey, romp **5** brave, chase, eager, hardy, sport, stake, trick, wager **6** gamble, quarry, spunky **7** contest, pastime, valiant, willing **8** fearless, intrepid, resolute, unafraid, valorous **9** amusement, dauntless, diversion, undaunted **10** courageous, recreation *arcade:* **7** Gremlin **8** Carnival, Skee-Ball *ball:* **4** golf, polo, pool **5** fives, rogue, rugby **6** hockey, pelota, soccer, squash, tennis **7** cricket, croquet, jai alai **8** baseball, football, handball, hardball, lacrosse, racquets, rounders, softball **9** bagatelle, billiards **10** basketball, volleyball **11** racquetball *Basque:* **6** pelota **7** jai alai *bird:* **4** duck **5** quail **6** chukar, turkey **7** bustard **8** bobwhite, pheasant **9** partridge *board:* **4** Clue, Risk, wari **5** chess, chuba, oware, shogi **7** mancala, pachisi **8** checkers, Monopoly, Scrabble **9** crokinole, Parcheesi **10** backgammon *child's:* **3** tag **5** jacks **7** marbles, ringtaw **8** leapfrog, peekaboo **9** hopscotch, tic-tac-toe *confidence:* **4** scam **5** bunco, bunko, sting *court:* **5** roque **6** pelota, squash, tennis **7** jai alai **8** handball, racquets **9** badminton **10** basketball, volleyball **11** racquetball *electric:* **7** pinball *English:* **5** rugby **7** cricket **8** draughts *Irish:* **7** hurling *of chance:* **4** faro, keno **5** beano, bingo, boule, craps, lotto, rondo **6** fan-tan, hazard, policy, raffle **7** lottery, rondeau **8** roulette *parlor:* **8** Carnelli, charades *piece:* **3** die **4**

tile **5** token **6** domino, marble, top hat **7** checker *racket:* **6** squash, tennis **8** lacrosse, ping-pong, racquets **9** badminton **11** racquetball, table tennis *roulette-like:* **5** boule *rule maker:* **5** Hoyle (Edmond) *string:* **10** cat's cradle *table:* **4** pool **5** craps **7** mah-jong, snooker **8** dominoes, mah-jongg, ping-pong, roulette **9** bagatelle, billiards **11** table tennis *word:* **5** rebus **6** crambo **7** anagram, hangman **8** acrostic, charades, Scrabble **9** crossword, logograph (see also *card game*)

game plan 6 scheme, tactic **8** scenario, strategy **9** blueprint **10** big picture

gamete 3 egg **4** ovum **5** sperm **8** germ cell

gamin 3 elf, imp, tad **4** brat, tyke, waif **5** scamp **6** monkey, rascal, urchin **11** guttersnipe **12** street urchin

gamine 3 elf, imp **4** brat, waif **5** scamp **6** hoyden, rascal, tomboy, urchin **11** guttersnipe **12** street urchin

gaming cubes 4 dice **5** bones

gammon 3 ham **4** dupe, fool, rook **5** bacon, feign **6** delude, fleece, humbug **7** deceive, pretend, swindle **8** flimflam, hoodwink **9** bamboozle **11** hornswoggle

gamut 4 A to Z **5** range, scale, scope, sweep **6** extent, series, spread **7** compass **8** diapason, spectrum

gamy 3 off **4** foul, racy, rank, vile **5** brave, fetid, funky **6** plucky, putrid, rancid, rotten, smelly, sordid, stinky, strong **7** corrupt, decayed, noisome, noxious, reeking **10** decomposed, malodorous, scandalous **12** disagreeable, disreputable

gander 4 look, peek **5** goose **6** glance **7** glimpse **9** simpleton, waterfowl

_____ **Gandhi 5** Rajiv **6** Indira **7** Mahatma **8** Mohandas

gandy dancer 10 railroader, tracklayer

ganef 5 thief **6** rascal **9** scoundrel

Ganesa, Ganesh *father:* **4** Siva **5** Shiva *head:* **8** elephant *mother:* **7** Parvati

gang 3 lot, mob, set **4** band, clan, club, crew, pack, ring, team **5** bunch, crowd, group, horde **6** circle, clique, outfit **7** arrange, cluster, collect, combine, company, coterie **8** assemble **10** accumulate, assemblage **11** combination

gangling 4 bony, lean, slim **5** gaunt, lanky, rangy **6** meager, meagre, skinny **7** angular, scrawny, slender, spindly, stringy **8** rawboned **9** spindling

ganglion 5 tumor **7** nucleus

gangrene 3 rot **5** decay **7** mortify, putrefy **8** necrosis **9** decompose

gangster 4 goon, hood, thug **5** cholo, rough, thief, tough **6** bandit, gunman **7** hoodlum, mafioso, mobster, ruffian **8** criminal **9** cutthroat, racketeer *girlfriend:* **4** moll

gangway 4 hall, path **5** aisle **7** passage, walkway **8** corridor **10** passageway

ganja 3 kef, kif, pot, tea **4** hemp, herb, weed **5** grass, smoke **7** hashish **8** cannabis, Mary Jane **9** marijuana

gannet 4 bird **5** booby **7** seabird

ganoid fish 3 gar **6** beluga, bowfin **7** dogfish, garfish, teleost **8** billfish, sturgeon **10** paddlefish

Ganymede *abductor:* **4** Zeus **7** Jupiter *brother:* **4** Ilus *father:* **4** Tros *function:* **9** cupbearer

gaol 3 jug, pen **4** jail **5** clink, joint, pokey **6** cooler, lockup, prison **7** slammer **8** bastille **9** calaboose, jailhouse **12** penitentiary

gap 3 cut, pit **4** gash, gulf, hole, lull, pass, rent, rift, skip, slit, slot, tear, vent, void, yawn **5** abyss, blank, break, chasm, chink, cleft, clove, crack, gorge, gulch, gully, pause, space, split **6** arroyo, breach, canyon, cavity, cranny, divide, hiatus, hollow, lacuna, ravine, recess, schism, vacuum **7** caesura, crevice, fissure, interim, lacunae (plural), opening, orifice, rupture, vacancy, vacuity **8** aperture, cleavage, division, fracture, interval **9** disparity, interlude **10** deficiency, difference, interstice, separation **12** intermission, interruption **13** discontinuity

gape 3 eye, yaw **4** bore, gawk, gawp, gaze, glom, leer, look, ogle, open, part, peer, yawn **5** crack, glare, gloat, space, split, stare **6** glance, goggle **7** eyeball **10** rubberneck

gaping 4 huge, open, vast, wide **5** broad, great **7** chasmal **9** cavernous

gar 4 fish, pike **8** billfish **10** needlefish

garage 4 shop **7** cabinet, car park, carport, shelter

Garand 5 rifle

garb 4 clad, duds **5** array, cover, dress, getup, style **6** attire, clothe, livery, outfit **7** apparel, clothes, garment, raiment, threads **9** trappings **10** appearance

garbage 4 junk, muck, slop **5** dreck, dregs, filth, offal, trash, waste **6** debris, litter, refuse, sewage **7** rubbish **8** detritus, riffraff *heap:* **6** midden

garble 4 sift, warp **5** alter, belie, color, twist **6** jumble, mangle, muddle **7** becloud, confuse, contort, distort, falsify, obscure, pervert **8** miscolor, misstate, mutilate **9** obfuscate **10** impurities **12** misrepresent

garçon 3 boy **6** waiter **7** servant

garden 4 Eden, park **7** nursery *shelter:* **5** arbor **6** arbour

gardener 6 grower **7** yardman **9** topiarist

garden house 6 alcove, gazebo **9** belvedere

Garden State 9 New Jersey

garden tool 3 hoe **4** claw, fork, rake **5** edger, mower, spade **6** dibble, pruner, scythe, shears, shovel, sickle, trowel, weeder **8** clippers

Gardner character 10 Perry Mason **11** Della Street

Gareth *brother:* **6** Gawain **7** Gaheris *father:* **3** Lot *mother:* **8** Margawse, Morgause *slayer:* **8** Lancelot **9** Launcelot *uncle:* **6** Arthur *wife:* **6** Liones

Garfield *creator:* **5** Davis (Jim) *dog:* **4** Odie

Gargamelle's son 9 Gargantua

Gargantua *abbey:* **7** Thélème *author:* **8** Rabelais (François) *father:* **12** Grandgousier *first word:* **5** drink *mother:* **10** Gargamelle *son:* **10** Pantagruel

gargantuan see **gigantic**

Garibaldi follower 8 redshirt

garish 4 loud **5** gaudy, showy, vivid **6** brassy, brazen, flashy, tawdry, tinsel, vulgar **7** blatant, chintzy, glaring, raffish **12** meretricious

garland 3 ana, lei **5** album, crown **6** anadem, digest, laurel, wreath **7** chaplet, coronal, coronet, laurels, omnibus **8** analects **9** anthology, selection **10** collection, compendium, miscellany **11** florilegium

garlic 4 moly, ramp **5** aglio, clove **6** allium *mayonnaise:* **5** aioli

garment 4 garb, gear **5** array, habit **6** attire **7** apparel, raiment **8** clothing, vestment **10** habiliment *African:* **6** kaross **7** dashiki *Arab:* **3** aba **4** haik *British:* **10** mackintosh *clergy's:* **3** alb **4** cope **7** cassock, soutane **8** vestment *close-fitting:* **6** girdle, tights **7** leotard *for sleeping:* **6** pajama **7** nightie **9** nightgown *Greek:* **5** tunic **6** chiton, peplos **7** chlamys **8** himation *Hindu:* **4** sari **6** patola *hooded:* **8** djellaba *Japanese:* **6** kimono *lace:* **10** chemisette *Malay:* **6** sarong *Mexican:* **6** sarape, serape *outer:* **4** cape, coat, robe, wrap **5** apron, cloak, parka, shawl, smock, stole **6** capote, jacket, kimono, poncho, sarong, ulster, wammus **7** overall, pelisse, surtout, sweater, topcoat **8** overcoat, pinafore, pullover, scapular **9** coveralls, gaberdine, polonaise *Polynesian:* **5** pareo, pareu *rain:* **6** poncho **7** oilskin, slicker *Roman:* **4** toga **5** tunic *Scottish:* **4** jupe, kilt **7** sporran *sleeveless:* **3** aba **4** cape **6** mantle, tabard *Turkish:* **6** dolman *women's:* **4** gown **5** dress, skirt, teddy **6** blouse, vestee **7** blouson, chemise, nightie, partlet **8** camisole, negligee, peignoir, pelerine

garner 4 cull, earn, hive, reap **5** amass, glean, hoard, lay up, store **6** gather, pick up, roll up **7** collect, extract, harvest, store up **8** cumulate, ingather **9** stockpile **10** accumulate

garnet 5 jewel, stone **6** pyrope **8** essonite **9** hessonite *black:* **8** melanite *red:* **9** almandine, almandite

garnish 4 deck, trim **5** adorn **6** bedeck **7** dress up, enhance **8** beautify, decorate, ornament **9** embellish

garret 4 loft, room **5** attic **8** cockloft

garrison 4 camp, fort, post **6** assign, billet, occupy, troops **7** station **8** fortress **10** stronghold

garrote 5 choke **8** strangle, throttle **11** strangulate

garrulous see **gabby**

garter 4 band, belt **5** strap **7** support **9** supporter

garth 4 yard **5** close **9** enclosure

gas 4 fuel, fume **5** fumes, steam, vapor **6** petrol **8** gasoline **9** petroleum *atmospheric:* **4** neon **5** argon, oxide, ozone, xenon **6** helium, oxygen **7** krypton, methane **8** hydrogen, nitrogen *flammable:* **6** butane, ethane, ethyne **7** methane, propane, propene **8** ethylene *inert:* **4** neon **5** argon, radon, xenon **6** helium **7** krypton *mine:* **8** firedamp **9** black damp *oxygen:* **5** ozone *toxic:* **5** sarin, soman, tabun **6** arsine, ketene **7** mustard **8** phosgene **9** phosphine

gasconade 4 brag **7** bravado **8** boasting, bragging **11** braggadocio

gash 4 cut, rip **4** rend, slit, tear **5** carve, cleft, gouge, slash, slice, split **6** incise **8** lacerate **10** depression, laceration

gasket 4 ring, seal **5** O-ring **6** sealer

gasoline 4 fuel **6** petrol *rating:* **6** octane

gasp 4 blow, huff, pant, puff **5** heave **6** wheeze **11** exclamation

Gaspar *companion:* **8** Melchior **9** Balthazar *gift:* **12** frankincense

gassy 5 windy **7** verbose **8** inflated, vaporous **9** flatulent

gastronome 7 epicure, gourmet **8** gourmand **9** bon vivant **11** connoisseur

gastropod 4 slug **5** conch, murex, snail, whelk **6** cowrie, limpet, volute **7** abalone, mollusc, mollusk, sea slug **8** pteropod, univalve **10** periwinkle

gat 3 gun, rod **6** pistol, roscoe **7** channel, firearm, handgun, passage **8** revolver

gate 3 tap **4** cock, door, exit, port **5** entry, hatch, toril, valve **6** faucet, portal, spigot, switch, wicket **7** hydrant, opening, petcock **8** entrance, entryway, stopcock **9** turnstile **10** attendance

gâteau 4 cake

gatefold 6 insert **7** foldout

Gates of Hercules 9 Gibraltar **12** promontories

gateway 4 arch, door, exit **5** pylon, toril **6** portal **7** archway, doorway, opening **8** entrance

gather 4 brew, cull, gain, grow, heap, herd, loom, mass, meet, pick, pile, pool, reap **5** amass, bunch, flock, glean, group, horde, infer, judge, pluck, shirr, swarm **6** assume, deduce, derive, expect, garner, muster, pick up, pucker, summon, take in **7** cluster, collect, convene, extract, harvest, marshal, round up, suppose, surmise, suspect **8** assemble, conclude, converge, increase **9** aggregate, intensify **10** accumulate, congregate, understand **11** concentrate

gathering 4 bevy, crew, gang, herd, mass, ruck **5** bunch, crowd, crush, drove, flock, group, horde, party, press, rally, swarm **6** caucus, klatch, muster, throng **7** company, harvest, klatsch, meeting, reunion, turnout **8** assembly, congress, junction **9** concourse, congeries **10** assemblage, collection, conference, confluence **11** aggregation, gettogether **12** congregation

Gath's giant 7 Goliath **10** Philistine

gauche 5 crude, gawky, inept **6** clumsy **7** awkward, halting, loutish, uncouth **8** bumbling, tactless **9** graceless, ham-handed, inelegant, maladroit **10** blundering

gaucho 6 cowboy **8** herdsman *weapon:* **4** bola **5** bolas **7** machete

gaudeamus ____ 6 igitur

gaudy 4 loud **5** showy **6** brassy, brazen, coarse, flashy, garish, tawdry, tinsel, vulgar **7** blatant, chintzy, glaring **9** brummagem, tasteless **10** outlandish **12** meretricious, ostentatious

Gaugamela *loser:* **6** Darius, Persia *victor:* **9** Alexander (the Great)

gauge 4 bore, rule, size **5** check, judge, meter, scale, weigh, width **6** assess, degree **7** compute, measure **8** diameter, estimate, evaluate, quantify, standard **9** benchmark, criterion, dimension, thickness, yardstick **10** instrument, touchstone **11** measurement

Gauguin's island 6 Tahiti

Gaul 4 Celt **6** France **9** Frenchman *ancient inhabitants:* **4** Remi **6** Belgae

Gaulish 6 French *god:* **4** Esus **7** Taranis *goddess:* **8** Belisama *priest:* **5** druid

gaunt 4 bare, bony, grim, lank, lean, thin **5** harsh, lanky, spare **6** barren, gangly, skinny, wasted **7** angular, scraggy, scrawny **8** gan-

gling, rawboned, skeletal 9 emaciated 10 cadaverous
gauntlet 4 dare, test 5 glove, trial 6 attack, ordeal 9 challenge, onslaught
Gautama 6 Buddha 10 Siddhartha *mother:* 4 Maya 8 Mahamaya *son:* 6 Rahula *wife:* 9 Yasodhara
gauze 4 film, haze, leno, mesh, mist 5 cloth, crepe, tulle 6 fabric, tissue 7 bandage, chiffon, tiffany 8 compress, dressing 11 cheesecloth
gauzy 4 thin 5 filmy, fuzzy, sheer, vague 6 flimsy 8 delicate, pellucid 9 gossamery 10 diaphanous 11 transparent
gavel 6 hammer, mallet
gavial 7 gharial, reptile 9 crocodile
gavotte 4 tune 5 dance
Gawain *brother:* 6 Gareth 7 Gaheris *father:* 3 Lot *mother:* 8 Margawse, Morgause *slayer:* 8 Lancelot 9 Launcelot *uncle:* 6 Arthur *victim:* 6 Uwayne 7 Lamerok 9 Pellinore
gawk 3 oaf 4 bore, gape, gaze, hick, look, lout, lump, peer, rube 5 churl, glare, gloat, klutz, looby, stare, yokel 6 goggle, lubber
gawky 5 inept, splay 6 clumsy, coarse, gauche, oafish 7 awkward, loutish, lumpish, uncouth 8 bumbling, bungling, lubberly, ungainly 9 graceless, ham-handed, lumbering, maladroit
gay 4 glad 5 happy, jolly, merry, queer, showy, sunny, vivid 6 blithe, bouncy, bright, cheery, festal, frisky, jocund, jovial, joyful, lively 7 excited, festive, gleeful, lesbian, playful, raffish 8 animated, cheerful, colorful, mirthful, spirited, sportive 9 exuberant, sparkling, vivacious 10 frolicsome, homosexual, insouciant, nonchalant 12 light-hearted
____ **Gay** 4 John 5 Enola
Gaza victor 7 Allenby (Edmund)
gaze 3 eye 4 bore, gape, gawk, leer, look, ogle, peer, pore, scan, view 5 glare, gloat, stare, watch 6 goggle 7 eyeball, observe 8 consider 10 rubberneck 11 contemplate
gazebo 6 alcove 8 pavilion 9 belvedere 11 garden house, summerhouse
gazelle 3 goa 4 cora, kudu, mohr, oryx 5 eland, nyala 6 koodoo 7 gemsbok 8 antelope
gazette 5 paper 6 record 7 journal, publish 9 newspaper 10 periodical 11 publication 12 announcement
gazetteer 5 atlas, guide, index
Ge see **Gaea**
gear 3 cam, cog, rig 5 dress, goods, shift, stuff, wheel 6 adjust, tackle, things 7 apparel, harness, rigging 8 clothing, cog-

wheel, garments, materiel, property, sprocket, tackling, trapping 9 apparatus, equipment, machinery 10 belongings 11 accessories, habiliments, possessions 13 accouterments, accoutrements, paraphernalia
Geats *king:* 7 Hygelac *prince:* 7 Beowulf
Geb *daughter:* 4 Isis 8 Nephthys *father:* 3 Shu *mother:* 6 Tefnut *sister:* 3 Nut *son:* 3 Set 6 Osiris *wife:* 3 Nut
gecko 6 lizard 7 reptile
Gedaliah *father:* 6 Ahikam 7 Pashhur 8 Jeduthun *slayer:* 7 Ishmael
gee 3 wow 4 gosh, turn 5 golly, right 8 goodness, gracious 9 turn right
geek 4 buff, guru, nerd, whiz 5 carny, fiend, freak 6 carney, carnie, expert, pundit, weirdo 7 devotee, egghead, fanatic, oddball 9 authority, eccentric 10 enthusiast 12 intellectual
geezer 4 coot, fogy 5 bloke, crank, fogey 6 codger, dotard, fossil
Gehenna 3 pit 4 hell 5 abyss, hades, Sheol 6 Tophet 7 inferno 8 Tartarus 9 perdition 10 underworld 11 netherworld
Geisel pseudonym 7 Dr. Seuss
geisha wear 3 obi 6 kimono
gel 3 dry, set 4 agar, clot 6 harden, mousse 7 colloid, congeal, thicken 8 solidify 9 coagulate
gelatin 3 jam 4 agar 5 jelly 7 sericin
geld 3 cut, fix, tax 5 alter, desex, unsex 6 change, neuter 7 deprive 8 castrate, mutilate 9 sterilize 10 emasculate 11 desexualize
gelid 3 icy 4 cold 5 chill, nippy, polar 6 arctic, chilly, frigid, frosty, frozen, steely 7 glacial 8 freezing
gelt 5 money
gem 3 jet 4 jade, onyx, opal, rock, ruby, sard 5 agate, amber, beryl, bijou, coral, jewel, lapis, pearl, stone, topaz 6 amulet, garnet, jasper, scarab, sphene, spinel, zircon 7 bejewel, cat's-eye, citrine, diamond, emerald, enjewel, olivine, peridot 8 amethyst, corundum, diopside, fluorite, intaglio, lazurite, obsidian, sapphire, sardonyx, sparkler, tigereye 9 brilliant, carnelian, jadestone, moonstone, phenakite, scapolite, spodumene, tiger's-eye, turquoise 10 aquamarine, cordierite, tourmaline 11 alexandrite, chrysoberyl, chrysoprase, lapis lazuli, masterpiece *blue:* 6 zircon 8 sapphire 9 turquoise 10 aquamarine 11 lapis lazuli *carved:* 5 cameo 8 intaglio *changeable:* 9 chatoyant *cut:* 7 marquis 8 baguette, cabochon, marquise 9 brilliant *face:* 5 culet, facet *green:* 4 jade 7 emerald, peridot, smaragd 10 chrysolite 11 chrysoprase *red:* 4

ruby, sard **6** garnet, pyrope, spinel **9** carnelian *support:* **7** setting *weight:* **5** carat *yellow:* **5** amber, topaz **6** sphene **7** citrine
Gemini star 6 Castor, Pollux
gemmule 3 bud
gemsbok 4 oryx **8** antelope
Gem State 5 Idaho
gemütlich see **genial**
gendarme 3 cop **5** bobby **7** officer, soldier **8** flatfoot **9** constable, patrolman, policeman
gender 3 sex **4** kind, male, sort, type **5** class **6** female, neuter **8** feminine **9** masculine
genealogy 5 roots, stirp, stock **6** origin, stemma **7** descent, history, lineage **8** ancestry, heredity, pedigree **9** bloodline **10** family tree
general 4 wide **5** broad, usual, vague **6** common, global, normal, public **7** blanket, generic, overall, regular, routine, typical **8** catholic, everyday, sweeping **9** all-around, prevalent, universal **10** collective, prevailing, unspecific, widespread **11** commonplace **13** comprehensive *American:* **3** Lee (Robert E.) **4** Haig (Alexander), Pike (Zebulon), Wood (Leonard) **5** Clark (Mark, Wesley, William), Grant (Ulysses S.), Meade (George), Scott (Charles, Hugh, Winfield), Smith (Andrew Jackson, Giles, Holland, Morgan, Samuel, Walter, Bedell), Stark (John), Worth (William) **6** Abrams (Creighton), Custer (George Armstrong), Franks (Tommy), Hooker (Joseph), Kearny (Philip, Stephen), Patton (George S.), Porter (Fitz-John), Powell (Colin), Slocum (Henry), Spaatz (Carl), Taylor (Maxwell, Richard, Zachary) **7** Bradley (Omar), Frémont (John Charles), Houston (Samuel), Jackson (Andrew, Thomas "Stonewall"), Lejeune (John), Ridgway (Matthew B.), Sherman (William Tecumseh), Twining (Nathaniel), Wallace (Lewis), Wheeler (Joseph) **8** Burnside (Ambrose), Goethals (George Washington), Marshall (George), Mitchell (Billy), Pershing (John J.), Sheridan (Philip), Stilwell (Joseph) **9** MacArthur (Arthur, Douglas), McClellan (George), Rosecrans (William), Schofield (John), Wilkinson (James) **10** Beauregard (P. G. T.), Eisenhower (Dwight D.), Vandegrift (Alexander), Wainwright (Jonathan) **11** Schwarzkopf (Norman) **12** Westmoreland (William) *American Revolutionary:* **4** Knox (Henry), Ward (Artemas) **5** Gates (Horatio), Wayne ("Mad Anthony") **6** de Kalb (Baron), Greene (Nathanael), Morgan (Daniel), Putnam (Israel, Rufus) **8** Moultrie (William), Sullivan (John) **10** Washington (George)

Austrian: **11** Wallenstein (Albrecht von) *British:* **4** Gage (Thomas), Howe (William) **5** Clive (Robert), Monck (George), Wolfe (James) **6** Rupert (Prince) **7** Amherst (Jeffery), Wingate (Orde Charles, Reginald) **8** Burgoyne (John), Cromwell (Oliver) **10** Abercromby (Ralph, Robert), Cornwallis (Charles), Wellington (Duke of) *Carthaginian:* **8** Hamilcar, Hannibal **9** Hasdrubal *Chinese:* **3** Tso, Yan (Xishan), Yen (Hsi-shan) **4** Feng (Guozhang, Kuo-chang, Yü-hsiang, Yuxiang) **5** Chang (Tso-lin), Zhang (Zuolin) *Confederate:* **3** Lee (Robert E.) **4** Hill (Ambrose), Hood (John Bell) **5** Bragg (Braxton), Ewell (Richard Stoddart), Price (Sterling), Smith (Edmund Kirby) **6** Morgan (John Hunt), Stuart (Jeb) **7** Forrest (Nathan Bedford), Hampton (Wade), Jackson (Thomas "Stonewall"), Pickett (George) **8** Johnston (Albert Sidney, Joseph Eggleston) **9** Pemberton (John) **10** Beauregard (Pierre G. T.), Longstreet (James) *French:* **3** Ney (Michel) **4** Foch (Ferdinand) **6** Moreau (Victor), Pétain (Philippe) **7** Weygand (Maxime) **8** de Gaulle (Charles), Lefebvre (Pierre), Montcalm (Marquis de), Saint-Cyr (Laurent de Gouvion-) **9** Frontenac (Comte de) **10** Rochambeau (Comte de) *German:* **4** Jodl (Alfred) **6** Kleist (Paul Ludwig von), Rommel (Erwin) **9** Rundstedt (Gerd von) **10** Kesselring (Albert), Ludendorff (Erich) *Greek:* **6** Nicias **9** Miltiades **10** Alcibiades **12** Themistocles *Japanese:* **4** Tojo (Hideki) **5** Koiso (Kuniaki) **6** Yasuda (Yoshisada) **8** Yamagata (Aritomo) **9** Yamashita (Tomoyuki) *Mexican:* **9** Santa Anna (Antonio López de) *Prussian:* **11** Scharnhorst (Gerhard von) *Roman:* **5** Sulla (Lucius Cornelius) **6** Caesar (Julius), Fabius (Quintus), Marius (Gaius), Pompey (the Great), Scipio (Gnaeus Cornelius, Publius Cornelius) **7** Regulus (Marcus Atilius), Ricimer (Flavius) **8** Agricola (Gnaeus Julius), Lucullus (Lucius Licinius), Stilicho (Flavius) **9** Marcellus (Marcus Claudius), Sertorius (Quintus) **10** Theodosius (the Great) **11** Cincinnatus (Lucius Quinctius) *Russian:* **6** Zhukov (Georgy) **7** Kutuzov (Mikhail), Trotsky (Leon), Wrangel (Pyotr), Zhdanov (Andrey) **9** Yeremenko (Andrey) *Spanish:* **4** Alba (Duke of), Alva (Duke of) **6** Franco (Francisco) *Swedish:* **7** Wrangel (Karl Gustav)
general assembly 4 diet **6** plenum **8** congress **10** parliament **11** legislature
generalize 5 infer, widen **6** derive, extend, in-

duce, spread **7** broaden **8** conclude **12** universalize

generally 6 mainly, mostly, widely **7** all told, as a rule, broadly, chiefly, en masse, largely, overall, usually **8** all in all, commonly, normally **9** on average, primarily, typically **10** altogether, by and large, frequently, on the whole, ordinarily **11** customarily, principally

generate 4 bear, make, sire **5** beget, breed, cause, hatch, spawn, yield **6** create, effect, father, induce, work up **7** achieve, develop, produce, provoke **8** engender, initiate, multiply **9** originate, procreate, propagate, reproduce **10** bring about, bring forth

generic 5 broad **6** common, global **7** blanket **9** inclusive, unbranded, universal **10** indistinct **12** nonexclusive

_____ **generis 3** sui

generosity 7 charity **8** altruism, kindness, largesse **9** abundance **10** liberality **11** beneficence, benevolence, magnanimity, munificence **12** philanthropy **13** unselfishness

generous 4 free, kind **5** ample **6** lavish **7** copious, helpful, liberal, profuse, willing **8** abundant **9** bounteous, bountiful, plenteous, plentiful, unselfish, unsparing **10** altruistic, benevolent, bighearted, charitable, munificent, openhanded, ungrudging, unstinting **11** considerate, kindhearted, magnanimous, overflowing **12** greathearted

genesis 4 dawn, root **5** alpha, birth, start **6** origin, outset, source **7** dawning, opening **8** creation **9** beginning, formation, inception **10** provenance **12** commencement

Genet play 5 Maids (The) **6** Blacks (The) **7** Balcony (The)

genetic 10 congenital, hereditary _material:_ **3** DNA, RNA **7** cistron **9** chromatid **10** chromosome _term:_ **8** synapsis **9** backcross

genial 4 kind, warm **5** jolly, merry **6** benign, blithe, hearty, jocund, jovial, kindly, mellow, social **7** affable, amiable, cordial **8** amicable, friendly, gracious, pleasant, sociable **9** agreeable, congenial, convivial, easygoing **10** neighborly **11** good-humored, good-natured, warmhearted

genie 3 imp **4** jann, jinn, puck **5** afrit **6** afreet, spirit, sprite

geniture 4 dawn **5** birth, start **6** origin **8** nativity **9** beginning, inception

genius 3 wiz **4** bent, gift, head, turn, whiz **5** flair, jinni, knack **6** acumen, brains, master, spirit, talent, wizard **7** aptness, faculty, prodigy **8** aptitude, brainiac, capacity, penchant **9** ingenuity, intellect **10** brilliance, creativity, mastermind, propensity **12** intelligence **13** inventiveness

Genoa's liberator 5 Doria (Andrea)

genre 3 ilk **4** kind, sort, type **5** class, style **6** family, stripe **7** species, variety **8** category, division

gens 3 kin **4** clan **5** group **6** family, people **7** kinfolk **9** relations, relatives

Genseric's subjects 7 Vandals

genteel 4 nice, prim **5** civil **6** formal, polite, prissy, strict, stuffy, urbane **7** courtly, elegant, prudish, refined, stilted, stylish **8** affected, cultured, graceful, gracious, ladylike, mannerly, polished, priggish, well-bred **9** courteous **10** cultivated **11** gentlemanly, pretentious, straitlaced, well-behaved

gentile 3 goy **5** pagan **7** heathen **9** Christian, non-Jewish

gentility 5 elite **6** gentry **7** decorum, manners, quality, society **8** breeding, courtesy, nobility **9** blue blood **10** aristocrat, refinement, upper class, upper crust **11** aristocracy

gentle 4 calm, easy, kind, meek, mild, soft, tame **5** balmy, quiet, tamed **6** benign, docile, genial, kindly, mellow, placid, serene, smooth, tender **7** amiable, lenient **8** delicate, peaceful, pleasant, soothing, tranquil **9** agreeable **11** softhearted, sympathetic, warmhearted **13** compassionate _creature:_ **4** lamb

gentleman 3 sir **6** aristo, fellow, mister **8** cavalier **9** blue blood, chevalier, patrician **10** aristocrat _English:_ **6** milord _French:_ **8** monsieur _Hindu:_ **4** babu _Spanish:_ **3** don **5** señor

gentleman friend 4 beau **5** lover, swain **6** fiancé, squire, suitor **7** gallant

gentlemanly 5 civil, noble, suave **6** polite, urbane **7** elegant, gallant, genteel, refined **8** mannerly, well-bred **9** courteous, honorable **10** chivalrous, cultivated **11** considerate

Gentlemen Prefer Blondes author 4 Loos (Anita)

gentry 5 elite, folks **7** quality, society **8** nobility **9** gentility, patrician **10** gentlefolk, patriciate, upper class, upper crust **11** aristocracy, high society, ruling class

genuflect 3 bow **4** fawn **5** kneel **6** kowtow

genuine 4 echt, pure, real, true **5** plain, pucka, pukka, valid **6** actual, dinkum, honest, tested **7** factual, natural, sincere **8** absolute, bona fide, positive, trueborn **9** authentic, certified, unalloyed, undoubted, unfeigned, veritable **10** sure-enough, unaffected

genus 3 ilk **4** kind, mode, sort, type **5** class, group, order **6** family **7** species, variety **8** category _amphibian:_ **4** Hyla, Rana _antelope:_ **4** Oryx _bee:_ **4** Apis _bird:_ **4** Alca,

Anas, Chen, Olor, Pavo, Pica, Rhea, Sula, Uria, Xema **5** Sitta *fish:* **4** Amia, Lota *herb:* **4** Arum, Geum *insect:* **4** Nepa *lily:* **4** Aloe *orchid:* **4** Disa *owl:* **4** Bubo, Otus *palm:* **4** Nipa *sheep:* **4** Ovis *shrub:* **4** Ilex, Itea, Ulex *snake:* **4** Eryx *tree:* **4** Acer, Cola, Maba, Olea *turtle:* **4** Emys

geode 4 rock **5** stone **6** cavity, nodule

geoduck 4 clam

geographer *American:* **10** Huntington (Ellsworth) *Flemish:* **8** Mercator (Gerardus) *German:* **6** Ratzel (Friedrich) *Greek:* **6** Strabo **7** Ptolemy *Italian:* **8** Vespucci (Amerigo)

geologic period 5 azoic **6** Eocene, Hadean **7** Archean, Miocene, Permian **8** Cambrian, Cenozoic, Devonian, Holocene, Jurassic, Mesozoic, Pliocene, Silurian, Triassic **9** Oligocene, Paleocene, Paleozoic **10** Cretaceous, Ordovician **11** Phanerozoic, Pleistocene, Precambrian, Proterozoic **13** Mississippian, Pennsylvanian

geometer 6 Euclid **13** mathematician

geometric *coordinate:* **8** abscissa, ordinate *curve:* **3** arc **6** spiral **7** ellipse, evolute **8** parabola *figure:* **5** rhomb **6** circle, oblong, square **7** ellipse, hexagon, octagon, polygon, rhombus **8** heptagon, pentagon, rhomboid, triangle **9** rectangle *solid:* **4** cone, cube **5** prism **6** sphere **7** pyramid **8** cylinder, spheroid, spherule *surface:* **5** nappe, torus **6** toroid

geometry letters 3 QED

geophagy 4 pica

Georgia *capital:* **7** Atlanta *city:* **5** Macon **6** Albany, Athens **7** Augusta **8** Columbus, Marietta, Savannah *college, university:* **5** Clark, Emory **6** Mercer **7** Spelman **8** Valdosta **9** Morehouse *founder:* **10** Oglethorpe (James) *nickname:* **5** Peach (State) *river:* **8** Ocmulgee **13** Chattahoochee *state bird:* **13** brown thrasher *state flower:* **12** Cherokee rose *state tree:* **7** live oak *swamp:* **10** Okefenokee

Georgia, Republic of *ancient kingdom:* **6** Iberia **7** Colchis *capital:* **6** Tiflis **7** Tbilisi *city:* **7** Kutaisi, Rustavi *includes:* **6** Ajaria **8** Abkhazia, Adzharia **12** South Ossetia *monarch:* **6** Tamara (Queen) *monetary unit:* **4** lari *mountain range:* **8** Caucasus *neighbor:* **6** Russia, Turkey **7** Armenia **10** Azerbaijan *river:* **4** Kura **5** Rioni *sea:* **5** Black

Georgics author 6 Vergil, Virgil

Geraint's wife 4 Enid

Gerda's husband 4 Frey

geriatric 3 old **4** aged **5** aging **6** senior **7** elderly **8** outmoded **12** old-fashioned **13** superannuated

germ 3 bud, bug **4** seed **5** spark, spore, virus **6** embryo, origin, source **7** microbe, nucleus **8** pathogen **9** bacterium *cell:* **3** egg **4** ovum **5** sperm

German 3 Hun **4** Goth **6** Teuton *after:* **4** nach *airport:* **9** Flughafen *always:* **5** immer *article:* **3** das, der, des, die, ein **4** eine *attention:* **7** Achtung *bad:* **8** schlecht *battle:* **4** Kampf **8** Schlacht *bomber:* **5** Gotha, Stuka *beneath:* **5** unter *border:* **6** Grenze *breakfast:* **9** Frühstück *cabbage:* **5** Kraut *child:* **4** Kind *city:* **5** Stadt *coin:* **4** Mark **5** Taler **6** Thaler **7** Pfennig *count:* **4** Graf *day:* **3** Tag *doctor:* **4** Arzt *dog:* **4** Hund *empire:* **5** Reich *entire, whole:* **4** ganz *fairy tale:* **7** Märchen *fast:* **7** schnell *forbidden:* **8** verboten *fruit:* **4** Obst *good:* **3** gut **4** gute *hardly, scarcely:* **4** kaum *head:* **4** Kopf *hero:* **4** Held *highway:* **8** Autobahn *history, story:* **10** Geschichte *honor:* **4** Ehre *hope:* **8** Hoffnung *horse:* **5** Pferd *I:* **3** ich *labor:* **6** Arbeit *leader:* **6** Führer, Kaiser *lightning:* **5** Blitz *liquor:* **8** Schnapps *little:* **5** klein **6** kleine *love:* **5** Liebe *measles:* **7** rubella *Miss:* **8** Fräulein *money:* **4** Geld *moon:* **4** Mond *mountain:* **4** Berg *musical:* **9** Singspiel *no:* **4** nein *Mr.:* **4** Herr *Mrs.:* **4** Frau **4** nein *nobleman:* **6** Junker *nothing:* **6** nichts *numbers:* **3** elf **4** acht, drei, eins, fünf, neun, vier, zehn, zwei **5** sechs, zwölf **6** sieben *over:* **4** über *picture:* **4** Bild *please:* **5** bitte *portion:* **4** Teil *prince:* **5** Fürst *pronoun:* **2** du, er, es **3** ich, sie, wir **4** dich, mich, sich *proud:* **5** stolz *railroad:* **9** Eisenbahn *rifle:* **6** Gewehr, Mauser *rule:* **5** Regel *silence:* **4** Ruhe **6** Stille *song:* **4** Lied **6** Lieder (plural) *space:* **4** Raum *spirit:* **5** Geist *strength, power:* **5** Kraft, Macht *submarine:* **5** U-boat, U-boot *success:* **6** Erfolg *tank:* **6** Panzer *television:* **9** Fernseher *thank you:* **5** danke *today:* **5** heute *tomorrow:* **6** morgen *train:* **3** Zug *train station:* **7** Bahnhof *tree:* **4** Baum *truth:* **8** Wahrheit *valley:* **3** Tal *value:* **4** Wert *victory:* **4** Sieg *war:* **5** Krieg *weight:* **3** Lot **5** Pfund, Stein **8** Vierling *with:* **3** mit *work:* **6** Arbeit *world:* **4** Welt *woman:* **4** Frau **8** Fräulein *youth:* **6** Jugend

germane 3 apt **5** ad rem **7** apropos, fitting, related **8** material, relevant **9** pertinent **10** applicable **11** appropriate

Germany 11 Deutschland *capital:* **6** Berlin *city:* **3** Ulm **4** Bonn, Jena, Kiel **5** Essen, Mainz **6** Bremen, Erfurt, Lübeck, Munich **7** Cologne, Dresden, Hamburg, Hanover, Leipzig, München, Potsdam **8** Augsburg,

Dortmund, Duisburg, Freiburg, Hannover, Schwerin **9** Frankfurt, Nuremberg, Stuttgart, Wiesbaden **10** Baden Baden, Düsseldorf *leader:* **4** Kohl (Helmut) **6** Brandt (Willy), Hitler (Adolf), Merkel (Angela) **7** Schmidt (Helmut), Wilhelm (Kaişer) **8** Bismarck (Otto) *monetary unit:* **4** euro *monetary unit, former:* **4** mark **5** taler **6** thaler **12** deutsche mark *mountain, range:* **4** Harz **7** Brocken *neighbor:* **6** France, Poland **7** Austria, Belgium, Denmark **10** Luxembourg **11** Netherlands, Switzerland **13** Czech Republic *region:* **4** Ruhr **6** Saxony **11** Black Forest *river:* **4** Eder, Elbe, Isar, Main, Oder, Ruhr, Saar **5** Fulda, Mosel, Rhein, Rhine, Weser **6** Danube **7** Moselle *sea:* **5** North **6** Baltic *state:* **5** Hesse **6** Saxony **7** Bavaria **8** Saarland **9** Thuringia **11** Brandenburg

germinate 3 bud **6** evolve, spring, sprout **7** blossom, develop **9** originate, pullulate

Gershom, Gershon *father:* **4** Levi *son:* **5** Libni **6** Shimei

Gershwin 3 Ira **6** George *opera:* **12** Porgy and Bess *piece:* **14** Rhapsody in Blue **15** American in Paris (An) *show:* **5** Oh Kay **9** Funny Face, Girl Crazy **10** Lady Be Good **11** Of Thee I Sing **15** Strike Up the Band *song:* **10** I Got Rhythm, Summertime

Gertrude *husband:* **8** Claudius *son:* **6** Hamlet

Gervaise's daughter 4 Nana

Geryon *dog:* **6** Orthus *father:* **8** Chrysaor *mother:* **10** Callirrhoë *slayer:* **8** Hercules

gestalt 4 form **5** shape **6** figure **7** pattern **9** structure **13** configuration

Gestapo chief 7 Himmler (Heinrich)

geste 4 deed, feat **7** emprise, exploit, romance, venture **9** adventure **10** enterprise **11** undertaking

gesticulate 3 nod **4** move, wave **6** beckon, motion, signal

gesticulation 4 wave **6** motion **7** gesture **8** high sign **9** pantomime **12** body language, sign language

gesture 3 nod **4** sign, wave **5** shrug, token **6** motion, salute, signal **8** reminder **9** signalize **10** expression, indication *graceful:* **9** beau geste

get 3 bag **4** draw, earn, gain, land **5** catch, cause, seize **6** access, attain, become, elicit, extort, obtain, pick up, secure **7** achieve, acquire, bring in, capture, chalk up, deliver, extract, procure, receive **8** contract **10** understand **12** come down with

get around 4 roam, rove, tour, trek, walk **5** avoid, dodge, elude, evade, skirt **6** cruise, detour, escape, ramble, travel, wander **8** ambulate, outflank, sidestep **10** circumvent

get away see **get out**

getaway 3 lam **4** exit, slip **6** escape, flight **7** retreat **8** breakout, vacation

get back 6 go home, recoup, regain, return, revert **7** recover, reclaim, revenge, revisit **8** retrieve **9** repossess, retaliate

get by 4 cope, fare, pass **5** slide **6** eke out, endure, manage **7** carry on, survive **8** maintain

get off 4 walk **5** leave **6** alight, depart, go free, launch **7** pull out **8** dismount **9** disembark **10** beat the rap

get out 2 go **4** exit, kite, leak **5** break, issue, leave, scram, split **6** alight, beat it, begone, decamp, depart, egress, escape **7** buzz off, publish, skiddoo, take off, vamoose **8** dispatch, hightail **9** circulate, skedaddle **10** make tracks

Gettysburg general 3 Lee (Robert E.) **5** Meade (George)

get up 4 gain **5** arise, breed, cause, dress, hatch, mount, raise, stand **6** create, induce, summon **7** acquire, prepare, produce **8** engender, generate **12** rise and shine

getup 3 rig **4** duds, garb, togs **5** array, dress, guise **6** outfit **7** costume, threads

get-up-and-go 3 pep, vim, zip **4** bang, push, snap, zeal, zest **5** drive, moxie, oomph, punch, spunk, steam, verve, vigor **6** energy, spirit, starch **8** ambition **10** enterprise, initiative

gewgaw 3 toy **4** dido **5** bijou, curio **6** bangle, bauble, doodad, trifle **7** bibelot, novelty, trinket, whatnot **8** gimcrack, kickshaw **9** bagatelle, objet d'art **10** knickknack

geyser 3 jet **5** fount, spout, spurt **6** gusher, spring **8** fountain **10** wellspring **11** Old Faithful

Ghana *capital:* **5** Accra *city:* **4** Tema **6** Kumasi, Tamale *ethnic group:* **4** Akan **5** Mossi *former name:* **9** Gold Coast *gulf:* **6** Guinea *lake:* **5** Volta *monetary unit:* **4** cedi *neighbor:* **4** Togo **10** Ivory Coast **11** Burkina Faso *river:* **5** Volta

ghastly 4 grim, pale **5** awful, lurid **6** grisly, horrid, pallid **7** ghostly, hideous, macabre **8** dreadful, ghoulish, gruesome, horrible, shocking, spectral, terrible **9** appalling, deathlike, frightful, ghostlike, repulsive, sickening **10** cadaverous, corpselike, disgustful, disgusting, horrifying, nauseating, terrifying **11** frightening

ghee 3 fat **6** butter

gherkin 4 vine **6** pickle **8** cucumber

ghetto 4 slum

ghost 4 soul **5** demon, haunt, shade, spook,

trace 6 kelpie, shadow, spirit, wraith, zombie 7 eidolon, phantom, specter 8 phantasm 10 apparition 11 poltergeist *cartoon:* 6 Casper

ghostly 5 eerie, scary 6 spooky 7 shadowy 8 ethereal, spectral 9 deathlike, spiritual, unearthly, unworldly 10 cadaverous, corpselike, phantasmal 12 supernatural

Ghosts author 5 Ibsen (Henrik)

ghoul 4 ogre 5 fiend 7 monster 11 grave robber

GI 5 grunt 7 dogface, fighter, soldier, warrior 8 doughboy 9 man-at-arms 10 serviceman

Gianni Schicchi composer 7 Puccini (Giacomo)

giant 4 huge, hulk, ogre, Otus, vast 5 gross, Gyges, Hymir, jumbo, titan, whale 6 Cottus, Typhon 7 Aloadae (plural), Antaeus, Cyclops, Goliath, immense, monster, titanic, whopper 8 behemoth, Briareus, colossal, colossus, enormous, gigantic, Orgoglio 9 cyclopean, Enceladus, Ephialtes, Gargantua, humongous, leviathan, monstrous 10 gargantuan, prodigious 11 elephantine *biblical:* 4 Anak 7 Goliath *cactus:* 7 saguaro *hundred-armed:* 9 Enceladus *hundred-eyed:* 5 Argus *killer:* 4 Jack 5 David *movie monster:* 6 Mothra 8 Godzilla, King Kong *one-eyed:* 5 Arges 7 Cyclops 10 Polyphemus *rime-cold:* 4 Ymer, Ymir *sea god:* 5 Aegir

Giant author 6 Ferber (Edna)

giaour 7 infidel 10 unbeliever 11 nonbeliever

gib 3 tom 6 tomcat

gibber 3 gab, yak 4 blab 5 prate 6 babble, drivel, gabble, jabber, yammer 7 blabber, blather, chatter, palaver, prattle, twaddle

gibberish 3 gab 5 Greek, hokum 6 babble, bunkum, burble, drivel, gabble, jabber, yammer 7 blabber, blather, chatter, palaver, prattle, twaddle 8 claptrap, flimflam, nonsense 10 balderdash, double-talk, hocus-pocus, mumbo jumbo 11 abracadabra, jabberwocky 12 gobbledygook

gibbet 4 hang 5 lynch, noose, scrag 7 execute, gallows 8 string up

gibbon 3 ape, lar 7 primate, siamang 10 anthropoid

gibbous 6 arched, convex, humped 7 bulging, rounded, swollen 10 humpbacked 11 protuberant

gibe 4 gird, jape, jeer, jest, mock, quip, rail 5 fleer, flout, scoff, scorn, scout, sneer, taunt, tease 6 deride, insult 8 ridicule

Gibraltar *colony of:* 7 Britain, England *conqueror:* 5 Tarik, Tariq *neighbor:* 5 Spain *opposite:* 5 Ceuta

Gibran work 7 Prophet (The)

giddy 4 gaga 5 dizzy, inane, light, silly, woozy 6 elated, yeasty 7 flighty, foolish, vacuous 8 euphoric 9 frivolous, slaphappy 10 hoity-toity 11 empty-headed, harebrained, light-headed, vertiginous

____ **Gide** 5 André

Gideon *father:* 5 Joash *servant:* 5 Purah *son:* 9 Abimelech

gift 3 set, tip 4 alms, bent, boon, head, turn 5 award, bonus, endow, favor, flair, forte, grant, knack 6 genius, legacy, reward, talent 7 ability, aptness, cumshaw, faculty, freebie, handout, present, subsidy 8 aptitude, bestowal, capacity, donation, gratuity, largesse, oblation, offering 9 endowment, lagniappe 11 benefaction, benevolence 12 contribution, presentation

gifted 4 able 5 smart 6 expert 7 hotshot, skilled 8 masterly, skillful, talented 9 ingenious, masterful

gig 3 jab, job, top 4 boat, fool, goad, prod, spur 5 annoy, freak, rotor, spear 6 chaise, harass 7 booking, demerit, provoke, rowboat 8 carriage 10 engagement

gigantic 4 huge, vast 5 giant, jumbo 7 hulking, immense, mammoth, massive, titanic 8 behemoth, colossal, enormous, king-size, whopping 9 cyclopean, humongous, king-sized, monstrous, walloping 10 gargantuan, prodigious, stupendous 11 elephantine

giggle 5 laugh 6 guffaw, hee-haw, titter 7 chortle, chuckle, snicker, snigger, twitter

Gigi author 7 Colette

Gilbert and Sullivan opera 6 Mikado (The) 8 Iolanthe, Patience, Sorcerer (The) 9 Grand Duke (The), Ruddigore 10 Gondoliers (The) 11 H.M.S. Pinafore, Princess Ida, Trial by Jury

Gil Blas author 6 Lesage (Alain-René)

gild 4 coat, deck 5 adorn, cover, tinge 6 bedeck, tinsel 7 enhance, overlay 8 brighten, ornament 9 embellish, embroider

Gilda's father 9 Rigoletto

Gilead *father:* 6 Machir *grandfather:* 8 Manasseh *son:* 7 Jephtha 8 Jephthah

Gilgamesh 4 epic *companion:* 6 Eabani, Enkidu *goddess:* 5 Aruru 6 Ishtar, Siduri *home:* 4 Uruk 5 Erech *mother:* 6 Ninsun *victim:* 6 Huwawa 7 Humbaba

gill 4 race 5 brook, creek 6 runnel, stream, wattle 7 rivulet *relating to:* 9 branchial

gillyflower 4 pink 9 carnation, clove pink

Gilroy play 15 Subject Was Roses (The)

gilt 3 hog, pig, sow 4 bond, gold 5 swine 6 gilded, golden 10 brilliance

gimcrack 5 cheap 6 bauble, gewgaw, shoddy,

trifle 7 bibelot, chintzy, trinket **8** kickshaw **10** knickknack

gimlet 4 tool **5** drill, drink **8** cocktail *ingredient:* **3** gin **5** vodka **9** lime juice

gimmick 3 con **4** ploy, ruse, wile **5** angle, catch, dodge, feint, gizmo, trick **6** device, gadget, gambit, jigger, scheme, widget **8** artifice, maneuver **9** stratagem **10** subterfuge

gimp 3 vim **4** cord, halt **5** braid, hitch **6** dodder, falter, hobble, spirit **7** cripple **8** lameness

gimpy 4 game, halt, lame **7** hobbled, limping **8** crippled

gin 3 net **4** sloe, trap **5** catch, rummy, snare **6** device, liquor **7** springe **8** beverage, generate, separate

ginger 3 fig, pep, vim, zip **4** herb, stir, zing **5** liven, spice, verve, vigor **6** energy, mettle, revive, spirit **7** sparkle *cookie:* **4** snap

gingerly 4 safe, wary **5** canny, chary **7** careful, guarded **8** cautious, delicate, discreet

gingery 4 tart **5** fiery, peppy, sharp, spicy, tangy, zesty **6** snappy, spunky **7** peppery, piquant, pungent **8** spirited **10** mettlesome **12** high-spirited

gingham 5 cloth **6** fabric **7** textile **8** material

gingiva 3 gum

gin mill 3 bar, pub **4** dive **5** joint **6** saloon, tavern **7** barroom, taproom **8** alehouse **9** roadhouse **11** public house **12** watering hole

Ginsberg poem 4 Howl **7** Kaddish

ginseng 4 herb, root

Gioconda, La 8 Mona Lisa *composer:* **10** Ponchielli (Amilcare) *painter:* **7** da Vinci (Leonardo) **8** Leonardo (da Vinci)

giraffe 8 ruminant **9** quadruped **10** camelopard

girandole 7 earring **10** candelabra **11** candelabrum, candlestick, composition

girasol 3 gem **4** opal **5** jewel, stone **7** mineral **8** fire opal **9** artichoke

gird 3 hem **4** band, belt, bind, ring, wrap **5** brace, equip, hem in, ready, round, steel **6** circle **7** bolster, enclose, fortify, prepare, provide, shore up, wreathe **8** buttress, cincture, encircle, surround **9** encompass, reinforce **10** strengthen

girder 4 beam **5** brace, I-beam **7** support **8** crossbar **9** crossbeam **10** crosspiece, transverse

girdle 4 band, belt, ring, sash **6** cestus, circle **8** ceinture, cincture, encircle, surround **9** encompass, waistband *of Aphrodite:* **6** cestus

girl 4 babe, bird, coed, doll, lass, maid, miss **5** chick, filly, missy, wench **6** damsel, lassie, maiden **8** daughter **10** sweetheart

girth 4 band, belt, bind, size **5** brace, cinch, strap **6** circle, fasten, girdle **7** measure **8** cincture, encircle, surround **9** thickness **10** dimensions **13** circumference

Giselle composer 4 Adam (Adolphe)

gist 3 nub, sum **4** core, meat, pith **5** sense **6** burden, ground, kernel, marrow, matter, thrust, upshot **7** essence **9** main point, substance

give 3 pay **4** deal, hand **5** allot, allow, award, grant, issue, offer, remit **6** accord, afford, assign, bestow, commit, confer, convey, devote, direct, donate, extend, market, pony up, render, supply, tender **7** deliver, dish out, display, dole out, fall out, fork out, furnish, hand out, mete out, present, produce, proffer, provide **8** allocate, bequeath, disburse, dispense, give away, hand over, shell out, turn over **9** apportion, sacrifice **10** administer, contribute, distribute

give-and-take 6 banter **8** exchange, repartee, trade-off **10** compromise **11** cooperation, reciprocity

give away 4 blab, leak **5** award, grant, spill **6** bestow, betray, confer, devote, donate, expose, reveal, tattle **7** deliver, divulge, hand out, let slip, present **8** bequeath, disclose

giveaway 4 deal, gift, leak **5** steal, value **6** tip-off **7** bargain, freebee, freebie, premium, present, sellout **8** betrayal, exposure **10** disclosure, revelation

give back 6 refund, retire, return **7** replace, restore, retreat **8** withdraw **9** reinstate

give in 4 cave, fold, quit, stop **5** yield **6** assent, comply, desist, relent, submit **7** concede, deliver, indulge, succumb **8** back down, cry uncle **9** surrender **10** relinquish

given 5 prone **6** donnée **7** assumed, granted **8** inclined **9** presented, specified **10** particular **11** considering, susceptible

give off 4 beam, emit, flow, vent **5** exude, issue **6** effuse **7** emanate, radiate, release **9** discharge

give out 4 deal, dole, emit, fail, mete, vent **5** issue **6** cave in **7** declare, release, succumb **8** collapse, throw off **9** break down **10** distribute

giver 5 donor **7** donator, grantor

give up 4 cede, quit **5** allow, cease, forgo, waive, yield **6** abjure, devote, resign, vacate **7** abandon, despair **8** abdicate, hand over, renounce, withdraw **9** sacrifice, surrender **10** relinquish

give way 5 yield **6** buckle, cave in **7** retreat, succumb **8** collapse **9** surrender

gizmo see **gadget**

glabrous 4 bald, bare **6** shaven, smooth **8** hairless **9** beardless **10** bald-headed **12** smooth-shaven

glacial 3 icy, raw **5** chill, gelid, nippy, polar **6** arctic, biting, chilly, frigid, frosty, frozen, wintry **8** freezing **11** Pleistocene

glacier 3 ice **6** ice cap **8** ice field, ice sheet *Alaska:* **4** Muir, Taku **6** Bering **10** Mendenhall *Antarctica:* **9** Beardmore *deposit:* **4** kame **5** esker **6** placer **7** moraine *fissure:* **8** crevasse *fragment:* **4** berg **7** iceberg *Greenland:* **8** Humboldt *hill:* **7** drumlin *Karakoram:* **5** Biafo **7** Baltoro *New Zealand:* **6** Tasman *pinnacle:* **5** serac *surface:* **4** névé

glacis 5 grade, slope **7** incline **10** buffer zone **11** buffer state

glad 3 gay **4** fain **5** happy, jolly, merry **6** blithe, bright, cheery, genial, jocund, jovial, joyful, joyous **7** beaming, gleeful, pleased, radiant, tickled, willing **8** cheerful, mirthful, pleasant, rejoiced **9** delighted, gratified

gladden 4 buoy **5** cheer, elate **6** buck up, perk up, please, uplift **7** cheer up, delight, gratify, hearten

glade 6 meadow **8** clearing **9** open space

gladiator 7 fighter **9** combatant, Spartacus

gladly 4 fain, lief **6** freely **7** happily, readily **8** heartily **9** willingly **10** cheerfully, with relish **12** with pleasure

gladness 3 joy **4** glee **5** bliss, cheer, mirth **6** gaiety **7** delight, jollity **9** happiness, merriment

gladstone 3 bag **8** suitcase

glamorous 7 elegant **8** alluring, charming, dazzling, enticing, magnetic **9** seductive **10** attractive, bewitching, enchanting **11** captivating, fascinating **13** sophisticated

glamour 5 charm, magic, spell **6** allure, appeal **7** romance **8** charisma, witchery **9** magnetism, sex appeal **10** attraction, witchcraft **11** fascination **12** razzle-dazzle

glance 4 peek, peep, skim, skip **5** brush, carom, flash, glaze, graze, shine **6** bounce, careen **7** glimpse **8** ricochet *lascivious:* **4** leer

gland 5 gonad, liver, organ **6** pineal, thymus **7** adrenal, mammary, parotid, thyroid **8** exocrine, pancreas, prostate, salivary **9** endocrine, pituitary **11** parathyroid *secretion:* **7** hormone *swelling:* **4** bubo

glare 4 gaze, glow, peer **5** blaze, flame, flash, frown, gleam, light, lower, scowl, shine, stare **6** dazzle, glower **7** obtrude **8** stand out **10** garishness

glaring 4 loud, rank **5** gaudy, plain, vivid **6** brazen, flashy, garish, tawdry, tinsel **7** blatant, obvious **8** blinding, flagrant **9** audacious, egregious, obtrusive **10** noticeable **11** conspicuous, outstanding **12** ostentatious

glass 4 lens, pane **5** image, lense, prism **6** mirror **7** reflect **9** barometer, telescope *combining form:* **5** vitro *container:* **3** jar **6** beaker, bottle *decorative:* **7** schmelz **8** schmelze *drinking:* **4** pony **5** flute **6** goblet, jigger, rummer, seidel **7** snifter, tumbler **8** schooner, stemware *gem:* **5** paste **6** strass *magnifying:* **5** loupe *milky:* **7** opaline *volcanic:* **7** perlite **8** obsidian

glasses 5 specs **6** shades **7** goggles **8** bifocals, pince-nez, tumblers **9** lorgnette, trifocals **10** spectacles

glass-like 5 clear **6** glazed, limpid, smooth **8** pellucid, vitreous **9** vitrified **11** translucent, transparent

glassmaker 6 Blenko (William) **7** Lalique (René), Tiffany (Louis Comfort) **9** Waterford

glassmaking tool 5 punty **6** pontil **8** blowpipe

Glass Menagerie author 8 Williams (Tennessee)

glassy 5 blank, dazed, shiny **6** glazed, smooth, vacant **7** hyaloid **8** polished, vitreous **9** burnished

glaucous 4 waxy **7** frosted, powdery

Glaucus *beloved:* 6 Scylla *father:* **5** Minos **8** Sisyphus *mother:* **6** Merope **8** Pasiphaë *son:* **11** Bellerophon

glaze 3 rub **4** buff, coat, film **5** cover, glint, gloss, sheen, shine **6** enamel, finish, luster, patina, polish **7** burnish, coating, furbish, lacquer, overlay, varnish

glazed 5 blank **6** glassy

gleam 3 ray **4** beam, burn, glow **5** flare, flash, glint, sheen, shine **6** glance **7** glimmer, glisten, glitter, radiate, shimmer, sparkle, twinkle **8** radiance **11** coruscation, scintillate **13** scintillation

gleaming 5 aglow, shiny **6** glossy, sheeny **7** beaming, burning, glowing, lambent, radiant, shining **8** flashing, luminous, lustrous, polished **9** brilliant, burnished, refulgent, sparkling, twinkling **10** glimmering, glistening, glittering, shimmering **13** scintillating

glean 4 cull, reap, sift **5** amass, learn **6** garner, gather, pick up **7** extract, find out, harvest

glebe 4 land **5** field, tract **7** acreage **8** cropland, farmland

glee 3 joy **5** mirth **6** gaiety, levity **7** delight, elation, jollity **8** gladness, hilarity, partsong **9** enjoyment, festivity, good cheer, happiness, jocundity, joviality, merriment **10** exuberance, joyfulness, jubilation **12** exhilaration

gleeful 3 gay **5** jolly, merry **6** blithe, elated, jocund, jovial, joyous **8** cheerful, exultant, jubilant, mirthful **9** exuberant **12** lighthearted

glen 4 dale, vale **5** swale **6** dingle, valley *deep:* **5** gorge **6** ravine

glengarry 3 cap **6** bonnet

glib 4 easy **5** slick **6** facile, fluent, smooth **7** offhand, shallow, voluble **8** eloquent, flippant **10** articulate, nonchalant **11** superficial

glide 3 fly **4** flow, sail, skim, slip, soar, waft **5** coast, creep, drift, float, skate, skirr, skulk, slide, slink, sneak, steal **7** descend, slither **8** glissade, volplane **10** portamento

glimmer 4 glow, hint **5** blink, flash, gleam, glint, shine, spark, trace **6** glance **7** flicker, glisten, glitter, inkling, shimmer, sparkle, twinkle **9** coruscate **10** suggestion **11** coruscation, scintillate **13** scintillation

glimpse 4 espy, peek, peep **5** flash, glint, stime **6** glance

glint 3 ray **5** flash, glaze, gleam, sheen, shine, trace **6** glance, luster **7** glimmer, glisten, glitter, shimmer, sparkle, twinkle **9** coruscate **11** coruscation, scintillate **13** scintillation

glissade 4 skim, slip **5** glide, slide

glissando 3 run **5** slide **7** gliding, sliding

glisten 4 glow **5** flash, gleam, glint, shine **6** glance **7** flicker, glimmer, glitter, shimmer, spangle, sparkle, twinkle **9** coruscate **11** coruscation, scintillate **13** scintillation

glitch 3 bug **4** flaw, snag **5** fault, snafu **6** defect **7** failing, failure, gremlin, problem **8** obstacle **10** difficulty **11** malfunction

glitter 5 flash, gleam, glint, shine **7** glimmer, glisten, shimmer, spangle, sparkle, twinkle **9** coruscate **11** coruscation, scintillate **13** scintillation

glittering 5 gaudy, shiny, showy **6** flashy **7** fulgent **9** brilliant, clinquant, coruscant, effulgent **11** spectacular

gloaming 3 eve **4** dusk **5** gloom **7** evening **8** eventide, twilight **9** nightfall

gloat 4 crow **5** exult, revel, vaunt **6** relish **7** triumph **9** celebrate

glob 4 clot, lump **6** dollop

global 5 grand **6** cosmic **7** blanket, general, overall **8** all-round, catholic **9** inclusive, planetary, spherical, universal, worldwide **12** encyclopedic **13** comprehensive

globe 3 orb **4** ball **5** earth, round, world **6** planet, sphere **7** rondure *half:* **10** hemisphere

globule 4 ball, bead, drip, drop **6** gobbet, pellet **7** driblet, droplet **8** spherule

glom 4 grab, take **5** catch, latch, seize, steal

gloom 3 dim **4** dusk, funk, loom, murk **5** bedim, blues, cloud, dumps, frown, lower, mopes, scowl **6** darken, glower, shadow **7** becloud, despair, dimness, obscure, sadness **8** darkness, overcast, twilight **9** adumbrate, bleakness, dejection **10** blue devils, depression, melancholy, overshadow **11** despondency, unhappiness **12** mournfulness

gloomy 3 dim, dun, sad **4** cold, dark, dour, down, drab, dull, glum **5** black, bleak, drear, dusky, mopey, murky, muzzy, sulky, surly **6** dismal, dreary, morose, solemn, somber, sullen **7** forlorn, joyless, obscure, stygian, unhappy **8** dejected, desolate, downcast, funereal, mournful **9** cheerless, depressed, mirthless, oppressed, saturnine, tenebrous, woebegone **10** caliginous, chapfallen, depressing, depressive, dispirited, despondent, forbidding, lugubrious, melancholy, oppressive, tenebrific **11** dispiriting, pessimistic **12** disconsolate, discouraging

glorify 4 hymn, laud **5** bless, cry up, erect, exalt, extol, honor **6** admire, praise, revere **7** acclaim, dignify, elevate, ennoble, light up, lionize, magnify, sublime, worship **8** eulogize, venerate **9** celebrate **10** aggrandize

glorious 5 grand, great, noble, proud **6** august, divine, superb **7** eminent, exalted, radiant, sublime **8** esteemed, gorgeous, lustrous, majestic, renowned, splendid, stunning **9** beautiful, brilliant, effulgent, excellent, marvelous, ravishing, wonderful **11** illustrious, magnificent, resplendent, splendorous

glory 4 crow, fame, halo, pomp **5** exalt, exult, gloat, honor, revel **6** heaven, praise, relish, renown **7** acclaim, aureole, delight, majesty, rejoice, triumph **8** eminence, eternity, grandeur, jubilate, radiance, splendor **9** greatness, hereafter **10** effulgence, exaltation, exultation **11** distinction **12** magnificence, resplendence

gloss 4 buff **5** glaze, glint, sheen, shine **6** define, enamel, facade, finish, luster, patina, polish, veneer **7** burnish, comment, explain, furbish, varnish **8** annotate **9** interpret, sleekness, slickness, translate **10** annotation, appearance, brilliance, commentary, definition **11** elucidation, explanation, translation

glossary 7 lexicon **8** wordbook **9** word-hoard **10** dictionary, vocabulary

gloss over 4 mask **5** slant **6** veneer **7** conceal, cover up, distort, falsify, varnish **8** disguise, palliate **9** dissemble, extenuate, sugarcoat, whitewash **10** camouflage

glossy 5 glacé, shiny, sleek, slick **7** shining **8** gleaming, lustrous, polished **9** burnished **10** glistening *fabric:* **4** silk **5** satin *paint:* **6** enamel

glove 4 gage, mitt **5** catch, cover **6** mitten, sheath **8** covering, gauntlet

glow 4 burn, pink, rose **5** bloom, blush, flush, gleam, rouge, shine **6** mantle, redden **7** blossom, crimson, fox fire, glisten, glitter, radiate **8** brighten, radiance **10** brilliance, luminosity **13** incandescence

glower 5 frown, scowl, stare **11** look daggers

glowing 3 hot, red **4** avid **5** flush, ruddy, shiny **6** ardent, fervid, florid, heated, red-hot **7** beaming, burning, fervent, flushed, lambent, radiant, vibrant **8** blushing, dazzling, gleaming, luminous, lustrous, rubicund, sanguine, suffused **9** brilliant **10** candescent, hot-blooded, passionate **11** impassioned **12** enthusiastic, incandescent

Gluck opera 5 Orfeo **6** Armide **7** Alceste

glucose 5 sugar, syrup

glue 3 fix, gum **4** bind, join **5** epoxy, paste, stick **6** adhere, attach, cement, fasten **7** plaster, stickum **8** adhesive, mucilage

gluey 5 gummy, tacky **6** sticky, viscid **7** viscous **8** adhesive **12** mucilaginous

glum 3 sad **4** blue, dour, down **5** moody, sulky, surly **6** dismal, dreary, gloomy, morose, sullen, woeful **7** crabbed **8** brooding, dejected, downcast, taciturn **9** depressed, oppressed, saturnine, sorrowful, woebegone **10** despondent, dispirited, melancholy **11** downhearted, melancholic

glut 4 clog, cloy, cram, fill, pack, pall, sate **5** feast, flood, gorge, stuff **6** deluge, excess, stodge **7** satiate, surfeit, surplus, swallow **8** saturate **10** oversupply **13** overabundance

glutinous 4 ropy **5** gluey, gooey, gummy, pasty, tacky, thick **6** sticky, viscid **7** viscous **10** gelatinous **12** mucilaginous

glutton 3 hog, pig **8** gourmand **9** chowhound, wolverine **11** gormandizer

gluttonous 7 hoggish, piggish **8** edacious, ravening, ravenous **9** dissolute, indulgent, rapacious, voracious **10** insatiable **11** intemperate

gluttony 6 excess **7** edacity **8** gulosity, rapacity, voracity **11** piggishness

glyph 6 figure, groove, symbol **7** graphic **9** character

G-man 3 fed **4** narc, Ness (Eliot) **5** agent **6** Hoover (J. Edgar) **10** gangbuster

gnarl 4 bend, knot, warp **5** growl, snarl, twist **6** deform **7** contort, distort

gnash 4 bite **5** grind

gnat 3 bug, fly **4** pest **5** midge **6** insect, punkie **7** no-see-um

gnaw 3 eat, nag, vex **4** bite, chaw, chew **5** annoy, chomp, erode, munch, scour, tease, worry **6** bother, crunch, nibble, pester,

plague, rankle **7** bedevil, corrode, eat away **8** irritate, wear away **9** masticate

gnome 3 elf, saw **4** rule **5** adage, axiom, dwarf, maxim, moral, troll, truth **6** dictum, goblin, saying, truism **7** proverb **8** aphorism, apothegm **10** shibboleth

gnostic 6 occult, secret **8** abstruse **10** mysterious

gnu 10 wildebeest

go *against:* **4** defy **5** fight **6** oppose, resist **7** counter, protest **10** contradict *ahead:* **4** lead **7** precede, proceed **8** continue, progress *along:* **5** agree, yield **6** accede, comply, concur **7** consent **9** acquiesce *around:* **5** avoid, skirt **6** bypass, detour **7** compass **8** outflank, sidestep **10** circumvent *ashore:* **6** debark **9** disembark *at:* **6** assail, attack, tackle **7** assault *away:* **3** git **4** exit, scat, shoo **5** leave, scram, split **6** beat it, begone, cut out, depart, move on, retire **7** buzz off, get lost, pull out, take off **8** clear out, run along, shove off, withdraw **9** skedaddle *back:* **6** recede, return, revert **7** regress, retreat *back on:* **6** betray, renege **7** abandon **8** abrogate *back over:* **6** rehash, review, rework **7** recheck, retrace *before:* **4** lead **7** precede, predate **8** antedate *beyond:* **4** pass **5** excel, outdo **6** exceed, outrun **7** eclipse, surpass **8** outshine, outstrip, overtake **9** transcend *forward:* **6** move on, push on **7** advance, press on, proceed **8** continue, progress *in:* **5** enter **9** penetrate *out:* **4** exit **5** leave **6** expire *Scottish:* **3** gae *through:* **4** bear **5** audit, brave, check, spend **6** endure, suffer **7** consume, deplete, examine, exhaust, ride out, survive, sustain, undergo **8** squander **9** penetrate, withstand **10** experience *together:* **3** fit **4** date, jibe, suit **5** agree, match, tally **6** accord, square **7** conform **8** dovetail **9** accompany, harmonize **10** correspond *with:* **4** suit **5** befit, match **9** accompany

goad 3 egg, rod, sic **4** prod, push, spur, urge **5** drive, egg on, impel, prick, thorn **6** coerce, exhort, incite, motive, needle, prompt, propel **7** impetus, impulse **8** catalyst, motivate, stimulus **9** encourage, impulsion, incentive, stimulant, stimulate **10** inducement

go-ahead 4 okay **7** consent **8** spirited **9** ambitious, authority, clearance, energetic **10** green light, permission **11** progressive, up-and-coming **12** enterprising **13** authorization

goal 3 aim, end, use **4** duty, hope, mark **5** score **6** design, intent, object, target **7** mission, purpose **8** ambition, function **9** intention, objective

goat 3 kid, ram **4** lech **5** billy, letch, nanny **6**

alpaca, angora, lecher, Saanen **8** cashmere **10** Toggenburg *female:* **3** doe **5** nanny *genus:* **5** Capra *Himalayan:* **4** tahr, thar *male:* **4** buck **5** billy *neutered:* **6** wether *relating to:* **7** caprine *wild:* **4** ibex *wool:* **6** mohair **8** cashmere, pashmina

goat antelope 5 serow **7** chamois

goatee 5 beard **7** Vandyke **8** imperial, whiskers

goatfish 6 mullet

goatish 3 hot **4** lewd **6** carnal **7** caprine, lustful, satyric **8** prurient **9** indulgent, lecherous, lickerish **10** lascivious, libidinous, passionate **12** concupiscent

goat-man deity 3 Pan **5** satyr **7** silenus

goat nut 6 jojoba, pignut

gob 3 wad **4** blob, clod, glob, hunk, lump, mass **5** chunk, mouth **6** nugget, sailor **7** extract

gobbet 4 drib, drip, drop, hunk, lump, mass **5** chunk, piece **7** driblet, droplet, globule, portion **8** fragment

gobble 3 eat **4** bolt, cram, grab, glut, gulp, slop, wolf **5** gorge **6** devour, guzzle **7** swallow **11** ingurgitate

gobbledygook see **gibberish**

go-between 5 agent, envoy, proxy **6** broker, deputy, factor **7** courier, liaison **8** emissary, mediator, procurer **9** middleman **10** arbitrator, interagent, interceder, matchmaker, negotiator, procurator **11** intercessor **12** intermediary, intermediate

goblet 3 cup **5** glass, grail **6** vessel **7** chalice

goblin 3 elf, fay, hob, imp **4** puck **5** bogey, bogle, fairy, ghost, gnome **6** sprite **7** brownie, bugbear **8** bogeyman

____ go bragh 4 Erin

gobs 4 lots, tons, wads **5** heaps, loads, lumps, piles, rafts, reams, scads **6** oodles **8** slathers **10** quantities

god 4 idol **5** deity **7** creator **8** Almighty, divinity, immortal *combining form:* **4** theo *false:* **4** baal *French:* **4** dieu *Hebrew:* **6** Elohim, Yahweh *Latin:* **4** deus *Spanish:* **4** dios see specific entries— **Greek, Roman,** etc.— for names of specific gods and goddesses

god-awful 4 foul **6** horrid, rotten **7** beastly **8** dreadful, horrible, shameful, shocking, terrible, wretched **9** appalling, atrocious, miserable **10** abominable, deplorable, despicable, detestable, disgusting, outrageous

God Bless America composer 6 Berlin (Irving)

goddess 4 idol **5** deity **8** divinity, immortal *Italian:* **4** diva *Latin:* **3** dea (see note at **god**)

godfather 3 don **4** boss, capo **6** leader **7** sponsor

Godfather, The 8 Corleone (Don) *actor:* **6** Brando (Marlon), De Niro (Robert), Pacino (Al) *author:* **4** Puzo (Mario) *director:* **7** Coppola (Francis Ford)

God-fearing 5 pious **6** devout **8** faithful, reverent **9** pietistic, religious, righteous

godforsaken 4 bare **5** bleak **6** barren, dismal, gloomy, remote **7** pitiful **8** deserted, desolate, pitiable, wretched **9** miserable, neglected **11** unfortunate

Godiva's husband 7 Leofric

godless 5 pagan **6** unholy, wicked **7** atheist, heathen, impious, infidel, profane **8** agnostic **9** atheistic **11** irreligious, unreligious

godlike 4 holy **6** divine **7** blessed, supreme **8** almighty, immortal **10** omniscient **11** all-powerful

godliness 5 piety **6** purity **8** devotion, divinity, holiness, sanctity **9** beatitude, reverence **10** devoutness, sacredness **11** religiosity, saintliness **12** spirituality, virtuousness

godly 4 holy **5** pious **6** devout, divine **7** angelic, blessed, saintly, supreme **8** almighty, hallowed, immortal, virtuous **9** pietistic, prayerful, religious **10** omniscient **11** all-powerful

go down 3 dip, set **4** drop, fall, fold, lose, sink **5** ensue, lower, occur, pitch, slide, slump **6** cave in, happen, plunge, settle, topple, tumble **7** crumple, decline, descend, founder, succumb **8** collapse, keel over, submerge, submerse **9** surrender, take place

God's acre 8 boneyard, catacomb, cemetery **9** graveyard **10** churchyard, necropolis **12** burial ground, memorial park, potter's field

godsend 4 boon, gift, good **5** manna **7** benefit **8** blessing, windfall **9** advantage **11** benevolence, serendipity

Goethe work 5 Faust **6** Egmont, Stella **7** Clavigo **10** Prometheus

gofer 4 aide, peon **5** toady **6** drudge, flunky, helper, lackey, menial **7** courier, servant **8** factotum **9** assistant, attendant

goffer 5 crimp, flute, pinch, plait, pleat

go-getter 6 dynamo **7** hustler, rustler **8** live wire **10** ball of fire, powerhouse **11** self-starter

goggle 3 eye **4** bore, gape, gawk, gaze, look, ogle, peer **5** glare, gloat, stare **10** rubberneck

goggles 5 specs **7** glasses **10** eyeglasses, spectacles

go-go 5 hyper **6** hectic **7** frantic **8** frenetic, frenzied

Gogol novel *novel:* **9** Dead Souls *story:* **8** Overcoat (The) **10** Taras Bulba **14** Diary of a Madman

goiter 6 struma **8** swelling

Golconda see **gold mine**

gold 4 gilt **5** money **6** riches, wealth, yellow **7** bullion **8** treasure *bar:* **5** ingot *combining form:* **4** auri, auro **5** chrys **6** chryso *fool's:* **6** pyrite *heraldic:* **2** or *imitation:* **6** ormolu *measure:* **5** carat, karat *Spanish:* **3** oro *symbol:* **2** Au

goldbrick 3 bum **4** idle, laze, lazy, loaf, loll **5** cheat, dally, dog it, idler, shirk, slack **6** dawdle, loafer, loiter, lounge **7** lounger, shirker, slacker, swindle **8** lollygag, malinger, sluggard **9** lazybones **10** dillydally, malingerer

Gold Bug author 3 Poe (Edgar Allan)

gold cloth 4 lamé

gold-covered 4 gilt **6** gilded

golden 4 gilt, rich **5** auric, blond, shiny, straw **6** blonde, flaxen, gilded, mellow, superb, yellow **7** aureate, honeyed, shining **8** glorious, lustrous, resonant **9** favorable **10** auspicious, prosperous **11** flourishing

golden-ager 5 elder **6** senior **7** ancient, oldster, retiree **8** old-timer **13** senior citizen

golden-apples guardian 5 Ithun **6** Ithunn

golden bough 9 mistletoe

Golden Bough author 6 Frazer (James George)

Golden Boy playwright 5 Odets (Clifford)

golden-crowned accentor 7 warbler **8** ovenbird

goldeneye 3 bug **4** duck, fowl **6** insect **8** lacewing

Golden Fleece seeker 5 Jason **8** Argonaut

Golden Hind captain 5 Drake (Francis)

Golden Horde 6 Tatars **7** Mongols *leader:* **4** Batu

golden horse 7 Trigger **8** palomino

golden shiner 4 dace, fish

Golden State 10 California

goldfinch 4 bird **8** songbird **12** yellowhammer

Golding novel 14 Lord of the Flies

gold mine 7 bonanza, pay dirt **8** El Dorado, Golconda, treasure, treasury **13** treasure trove

golem 3 oaf **4** clod, dolt, dope **5** dunce, idiot, robot **6** nitwit **7** halfwit, machine **8** imbecile **9** automaton, blockhead **10** nincompoop **11** blunderhead

golf *assistant:* 5 caddy **6** caddie *ball material:* **6** balata **11** gutta-percha *club:* **4** iron, wood **5** billy, spoon, wedge **6** driver, mashie, putter **7** niblick, pitcher **9** metal wood, sand wedge *club part:* **3** toe **4** face, grip, head, heel, neck, sole **5** hosel, shaft *course:* **5** links *cup:* **5** Ryder **6** Curtis, Walker *hazard:* **4** trap **6** bunker **8** sand trap *score:* **3** ace, par **5** bogey, eagle **6** birdie *stroke:* **4** baff, chip, draw, fade, hook, putt **5** drive, pitch, shank, slice **6** sclaff *target:* **3** cup, par, pin **4** flag **5** green **7** fairway *term:* **3** lie, tee **4** club, fore, hole, loft **5** divot, rough, swing **6** dormie, hazard, marker, stance, stroke **8** foursome, handicap **9** backswing, downswing, flagstick

golfer 8 linksman *man:* **3** Els (Ernie) **4** Aoki (Isao), Daly (John), Ford (Doug), Haas (Jay), Kite (Tom), Lyle (Sandy), Mize (Larry), Tway (Bob) **5** Boros (Julius), Faldo (Nick), Floyd (Ray), Grady (Wayne), Green (Hubert), Hagen (Walter), Hogan (Ben), Jones (Bobby), Irwin (Hale), North (Andy), Pavin (Corey), Peete (Calvin), Price (Nick), Shute (Denny), Singh (Vijay), Snead (Sam), Woods (Tiger) **6** Casper (Billy), Graham (David), Janzen (Lee), Langer (Bernhard), Miller (Johnny), Nelson (Byron, Larry), Norman (Greg), Ouimet (Francis), Palmer (Arnold), Player (Gary), Sluman (Jeff), Sutton (Hal), Vardon (Harry), Watson (Tom) **7** Azinger (Paul), Couples (Fred), Guldahl (Ralph), Mayfair (Billy), Sarazen (Gene), Simpson (Scott), Stewart (Payne), Strange (Curtis), Trevino (Lee), Woosnam (Ian), Zoeller (Fuzzy) **8** Crenshaw (Ben), Nicklaus (Jack), Olazabal (José), Weiskopf (Tom) **9** Mickelson (Phil), Rodriguez (Chi Chi), Elkington (Steve) **10** Middlecoff (Cary) **11** Ballesteros (Seve) *woman:* **3** Pak (Se Ri) **4** Berg (Patty), King (Betsy) **5** Baker (Kathy), Lopez (Nancy), Rawls (Betsy), Stacy (Hollis), Suggs (Louise) **6** Alcott (Amy), Carner (Joanne), Daniel (Beth), Davies (Laura), Geddes (Jane), Mallon (Meg), Merten (Lauri), Wright (Mickey) **7** Bradley (Pat), Inkster (Juli), Mochrie (Dottie), Sheehan (Patty) **8** Zaharias (Babe) **9** Didrikson (Babe), Sorenstam (Annika), Whitworth (Kathy) **10** Stephenson (Jan)

Golgotha 7 Calvary

Goliath 5 giant **10** Philistine *deathplace:* **4** Elah *home:* **4** Gath *slayer:* **5** David

Gollum creator 7 Tolkien (J. R. R.)

gonad 5 gland, ovary **6** testis **8** testicle

gondola 3 car **4** boat **7** ski lift **11** railroad car

gone 4 away, dead, left, lost, past **5** flown **6** absent **7** defunct, extinct, lacking, missing **8** departed, vanished

gonef see **ganef**

goner 8 dead duck **9** lost cause

Goneril *father:* 4 Lear (King) *husband:* **6** Albany *sister:* **5** Regan **8** Cordelia *victim:* **5** Regan

Gone with the Wind *author:* 8 Mitchell (Margaret) *character:* 5 Rhett (Butler) 6 Ashley (Wilkes) 7 Melanie (Wilkes) 8 Scarlett (O'Hara) *plantation:* 4 Tara

gonfalon 4 flag, jack 6 banner, ensign 7 pendant, pennant 8 banderol, standard 9 banderole

gong 6 cymbal, tam-tam

gonzo 6 far-out 7 bizarre, offbeat 9 wigged-out 10 outrageous

goo 4 crud, glop, guck, gunk, muck 5 slime

goober 6 peanut

good 4 pure 5 right, sound, whole 6 decent, humane, kindly, worthy 7 benefit, upright, welfare 8 innocent, virtuous 9 admirable, blameless, exemplary, favorable, honorable, righteous, well-being, wholesome 10 altruistic, beneficent, beneficial, benevolent, charitable, worthwhile 11 respectable, well-behaved *French:* 3 bon 5 bonne *German:* 3 gut 4 gute *Spanish:* 5 buena, bueno

good-bye 4 ciao, ta-ta 5 adieu, congé, later 6 so long 7 cheerio, parting, send-off, toodles 8 farewell, toodle-oo 9 departing, departure 11 leave-taking, valediction, valedictory *French:* 5 adieu 8 au revoir 9 bon voyage *German:* 8 lebe wohl *Italian:* 11 arrivederci *Japanese:* 8 sayonara *Spanish:* 5 adios 10 hasta luego 12 hasta la vista

Good Earth *author:* 4 Buck (Pearl S.) *heroine:* 4 O-lan

good-for-nothing 3 bum 6 rascal, waster 7 inutile, rounder, useless, wastrel 8 fainéant, feckless, rascally, unworthy 9 dissolute, scoundrel, valueless, worthless 10 ne'er-do-well, profligate, scapegrace 11 purposeless

good-looking 4 cute, fair, foxy 5 bonny, dishy, hunky 6 comely, lovely, pretty 8 alluring, drop-dead, fetching, handsome, stunning 9 beauteous, beautiful, bodacious, ravishing 10 attractive

goodly 4 fair, tidy 5 ample, hefty, large 7 sizable 8 generous 9 bountiful, plentiful 11 significant, substantial 12 considerable

good-natured 4 easy, kind, mild, warm 6 genial, jovial, mellow 7 affable, amiable, cordial, lenient 8 cheerful, friendly, laid-back, obliging, pleasant, pleasing, sanguine 9 agreeable, congenial, easygoing, gemütlich 10 altruistic, benevolent, charitable 11 complaisant

goodness 5 honor, merit, worth 6 purity, virtue 7 decency, honesty, probity, quality 8 morality 9 integrity, rectitude 11 benevolence

goods 4 gear 5 cargo, stock, stuff, wares 7 effects 8 chattels, movables, property 9 vendibles 10 belongings 11 commodities, merchandise, possessions 13 paraphernalia *smuggled:* 10 contraband *stolen:* 4 loot, swag 5 booty 6 boodle, spoils 7 plunder *thrown overboard:* 5 lagan 6 jetsam

good-tasting 5 sapid, yummy 6 delish, savory, toothy 8 luscious 9 delicious, palatable, relishing, toothsome 10 appetizing, delectable, flavorsome 11 scrumptious 13 mouthwatering

goodwill 5 amity, favor 6 comity 7 charity, rapport 8 altruism, kindness, sympathy 9 tolerance 10 compassion, friendship, generosity, kindliness 11 benevolence, helpfulness 12 friendliness

goody 5 candy, treat 6 bonbon, dainty, morsel, tidbit 8 delicacy, kickshaw

goody-goody 4 prig 5 prude 6 Grundy 7 prudish, puritan, uptight 8 bluenose, Comstock, priggish 9 Mrs. Grundy, nice-nelly 11 puritanical

gooey 5 gluey, gummy, mushy, sappy, soupy 6 cloggy, drippy, slushy, sticky, viscid 7 maudlin, viscous 8 adhesive 9 glutinous 11 sentimental 12 mucilaginous

goof 3 err, kid 4 boob, dolt, flub, fool, mess, muff, slip 5 boner, booby, botch, chump, dunce, error, fluff, gaffe, gum up, idiot, put on 6 bobble, boggle, bollix, boo-boo, bumble, bungle, fumble, mess up, slip-up 7 blooper, blunder, fathead, louse up, mistake 8 dolthead, lunkhead 9 blockhead

go off 4 blow 5 blast, burst, erupt, leave, sound 6 blow up, depart 7 explode 8 detonate

goofy 5 balmy, batty, crazy, daffy, dippy, loony, nutty, potty, silly 6 simple, stupid 7 foolish, idiotic 9 ludicrous 10 ridiculous 11 harebrained

gook 4 crud, glop, gunk, muck 5 gumbo, slime 6 debris, sludge

go on 4 last, stay 5 occur 6 endure, happen, keep up 7 persist, proceed 8 continue 9 persevere

goon 3 oaf, sap 4 boob, dodo, dolt, dope, fool, hood, thug 5 dummy, idiot 6 dimwit, hit man, nitwit 7 hoodlum 8 dumbbell, enforcer 10 triggerman

gooney 7 seabird 9 albatross

goop 4 crud, gunk, muck 5 gumbo, tripe

Goops author 7 Burgess (Gelett)

goose 4 poke, spur 9 stimulate *cry:* 4 honk 5 clang *formation:* 3 vee 5 skein, wedge 6 gaggle *genus:* 5 Anser *Hawaiian:* 4 nene *male:* 6 gander *wild:* 5 brant 7 greylag 8 barnacle *young:* 7 gosling

gooseberry 7 currant

Goosebumps author 5 Stine (R. L.)

goose egg 3 nil, nix, zip 4 nada, zero 5 aught, zilch 6 bubkes, bupkes, bupkus, cipher, naught, nought 7 no score, nothing
gooseflesh 5 bumps 7 pimples
go over 4 scan, skim 5 study 6 peruse, review 7 examine, inspect
gopher 6 rodent 8 tortoise
Gopher State 9 Minnesota
Gordian knot cutter 9 Alexander
Gordius' son 5 Midas
gore 3 jab 4 stab 5 blood, slime, wound 6 gusset, pierce 7 carnage 12 gruesomeness
gorge 3 gap 4 cloy, fill, glut, jade, pall, sate 5 abyss, chasm, cleft, clove, flume, gulch, stuff 6 arroyo, canyon, clough, defile, pig out, ravine 7 couloir, overeat, satiate, surfeit 11 overindulge *Arizona:* 11 Grand Canyon *Colorado:* 5 Royal
gorgeous 5 grand, plush 6 comely, lavish, lovely, pretty, superb 7 opulent, sublime 8 alluring, dazzling, glorious, splendid 9 beautiful, brilliant, exquisite, luxurious, sumptuous 10 attractive, glittering 11 magnificent, resplendent, splendorous
gorgon 3 hag 5 crone, harpy, witch 6 Medusa, ogress, virago 8 battle-ax, fishwife, harridan, slattern 9 battle-axe, termagant *father:* 7 Phorcus, Phorcys *mother:* 4 Ceto
gorilla 3 ape 4 goon, hood, thug 5 tough 6 simian 7 primate 8 gangster 10 anthropoid
Gorky drama 11 Lower Depths (The)
gormless 4 dumb, slow 6 stupid
gorse 4 whin 5 furze, shrub 6 legume
gory 5 lurid 6 bloody, grisly 8 gruesome, sanguine 10 sanguinary 11 ensanguined, sanguineous, sensational 12 bloodstained 13 bloodcurdling
gosh 3 gee, wow 4 dang, darn, drat, egad, geez, heck 5 golly 6 crikey, cripes, shucks 7 doggone 8 goodness, gracious
gospel 5 truth 6 truism 7 message 8 doctrine 9 scripture 11 evangelical
gossamer 4 airy, film, fine, webs 5 filmy, gauzy, sheer 6 flimsy 7 cobwebs, tenuous 8 delicate 10 diaphanous 11 transparent
gossip 4 blab, buzz, chat, dirt, dish, talk 5 clack, prate, rumor, yenta 6 babble, rumble, tattle 7 babbler, chatter, hearsay, prattle, tattler 8 bigmouth, busybody, informer, prattler, quidnunc, telltale 10 talebearer 11 rumormonger, scandalizer, scuttlebutt 12 blatherskite
gossipy 5 gabby, talky 6 chatty 8 babbling, blabbing 9 garrulous, talkative
Gotham 7 New York (City)
Gothic 4 dark, wild 5 crude 6 brutal, coarse, savage 7 uncouth 8 barbaric, Germanic, medieval, Teutonic 9 barbarian, barbarous, sans serif 11 black letter, uncivilized
Götterdämmerung composer 6 Wagner (Richard)
Gouda 6 cheese
gouge 3 dig 4 milk, ream, tool 5 cheat, exact, pinch, screw, wrest, wring 6 chisel, coerce, extort, groove, wrench 7 squeeze 8 scoop out 9 blackmail, extortion, shake down 10 overcharge
goulash 4 olio, stew 6 jumble, medley 7 mélange 8 mishmash 9 potpourri 10 bridge hand, hodgepodge, hotchpotch, salmagundi 11 gallimaufry
go under 4 fall, flop, fold, lose, sink 5 drown 6 plunge, submit 7 founder, immerse, succumb 8 collapse, submerge, submerse 9 surrender 10 capitulate
Gounod work 5 Faust 8 Ave Maria
gourd 4 pepo 5 fruit, melon 6 bottle, squash, vessel 7 chayote, gherkin, pumpkin 8 calabash, cucumber, cucurbit *instrument:* 6 maraca
gourmand see **glutton; gourmet**
gourmet 7 epicure 9 bon vivant, epicurean 10 gastronome 11 connoisseur 12 gastronomist
gout 4 blob, clot, gush 5 spurt 6 splash 7 disease, podagra 8 eruption, swelling
govern 4 head, lead, rule 5 guide, order, reign, steer 6 direct, manage, master 7 command, conduct, control, execute, oversee 8 dominate, hold sway, regulate 9 supervise 10 administer 11 superintend
governess 5 nanny, nurse 6 duenna 8 mistress 9 nursemaid 10 babysitter 11 Mary Poppins
government 4 rule 5 power 6 polity, regime 7 regency, regimen 8 monarchy, republic, Uncle Sam 9 authority, autocracy, democracy, hierarchy, oligarchy 10 Big Brother 11 aristocracy, sovereignty *autocratic:* 7 czarism, fascism, tyranny 9 despotism 10 absolutism 12 dictatorship *by a few:* 9 oligarchy *by one:* 8 monarchy *by three:* 8 triarchy 11 triumvirate *by women:* 8 gynarchy *official:* 10 bureaucrat 11 functionary *without:* 7 anarchy
government agency 3 ATF, BIA, BLM, CDC, CIA, DEA, EPA, FAA, FBI, FCC, FDA, FEC, FHA, GAO, GPO, HUD, ICC, INS, IRS, NBS, NEA, NIH, NRC, TVA 4 FDIC, FEMA, FEPC, NASA, NOAA, NTSB, OSHA
governor 3 bey, dey 4 head 5 chief, nabob, ruler 6 leader, regent 7 manager, viceroy 8 director 9 executive, regulator 10 commandant, magistrate *Chinese:* 6 tuchun *of a*

fort: 7 alcaide, alcayde 9 castellan, chatelain **Persian:** 6 satrap

gown 4 robe, toga 5 dress, frock, habit, tunic 6 camise, kimono, kirtle, mantua 7 cassock, chemise 8 peignoir **dressing:** 8 bathrobe **hospital:** 6 johnny

goy 6 non-Jew 7 gentile

grab 3 nab 4 glom, grip, snag, take 5 catch, clasp, grasp, pluck, seize 6 clutch, collar, snatch, tackle 7 capture, grapple, seizure

grabby 6 greedy 8 covetous, desirous, grasping 9 rapacious 10 avaricious, prehensile 11 acquisitive

grace 4 ease 5 adorn, charm, favor, mercy, poise 6 allure, lenity, pardon, polish, prayer, thanks, virtue 7 charity, dignify, dignity, enhance 8 approval, blessing, clemency, easiness, elegance, goodness, kindness, leniency, petition, reprieve 9 embellish, privilege 10 indulgence, invocation, refinement 11 benediction, forbearance 12 thanksgiving

graceful 4 airy, deft, easy 5 lithe 6 nimble, poised, smooth 7 elegant, flowing 8 debonair, polished

graceless 4 rude 5 crude, gawky, inept 6 clumsy, coarse, gauche, klutzy, vulgar 7 awkward, boorish, uncouth 8 barbaric, ungainly 9 barbarian, barbarous 10 outlandish, unmannered 12 infelicitous

Graces 6 Charis 8 Charites (plural) **brilliance:** 6 Aglaia **bloom:** 6 Thalia **joy:** 10 Euphrosyne **mother:** 5 Aegle

gracious 4 kind 5 suave 6 benign, genial, kindly, urbane 7 affable, amiable, cordial, courtly, gallant, stately, tactful 8 charming, generous, mannered, merciful, obliging, sociable 9 congenial, courteous 11 complaisant, good-natured 13 compassionate

grackle 4 myna 5 mynah 7 jackdaw 8 starling 9 blackbird

gradation 4 rank, step 5 order, range, scale, shade, stage 6 ablaut, change, degree, nuance, series 8 ordering, position, spectrum 9 continuum, variation 10 difference, succession

grade 3 peg 4 cant, form, kind, lean, mark, rank, rate, rung, sort, step, tier, tilt 5 blend, class, group, level, notch, order, pitch, place, slant, slope, stage 6 assess, assort, degree, league, rating 7 arrange, caliber, echelon, incline, leaning, quality 8 appraise, category, classify, division, evaluate, grouping, position, standard 10 categorize 11 inclination

Grade A 3 ace, top 4 best, boss, fine, tops 5 grand, great, prime, primo, super 6 choice, tip-top 7 capital, supreme 8 five-star, superior, top-notch 9 excellent, first-rate, nonpareil, number one, top-drawer 10 first-class 11 outstanding 13 par excellence

gradient 4 lean, ramp, rise, tilt 5 angle, pitch, slant, slope 7 incline, leaning 9 acclivity, declivity 11 inclination

gradual 4 even, slow 6 Psalms, steady 7 ongoing 8 bit-by-bit, creeping 9 piecemeal, prolonged 10 continuous, developing, protracted, step-by-step 11 progressive

gradually 6 slowly 7 by steps 8 bit by bit 9 by degrees, piecemeal 10 step by step 12 deliberately 13 imperceptibly, incrementally

graduate 4 alum **acquisition:** 6 degree 7 diploma **female:** 6 alumna 7 alumnae (plural) **male:** 6 alumni (plural) 7 alumnus

Graeae, Graiae 4 Enyo 5 Deino 8 Pephredo **father:** 7 Phorcus, Phorcys **mother:** 4 Ceto **sisters:** 7 Gorgons

graffiti artist 6 tagger **signature:** 3 tag

graft 3 imp 4 join, mend, scam, skim 5 affix, crime, fraud, scion, unite 6 attach, boodle, fasten, payola, splice 7 implant, swindle, topwork 8 kickback 10 corruption

Grafton character 8 Millhone (Kinsey)

Grahame, Kenneth character: 3 Rat 4 Toad, Mole 6 Badger **novel:** 16 Wind in the Willows (The)

grail 3 cup, end 4 goal 6 goblet, object, target 7 chalice 9 objective **seeker:** 7 Galahad

grain 3 bit, jot, rye 4 corn, flax, iota, meal, mite, oats, rice 5 crumb, fiber, kamut, maize, speck, spelt, trace, wheat 6 barley, cereal, millet, quinoa, tittle 7 granule, smidgen, sorghum, texture 8 amaranth, molecule, particle 9 buckwheat, triticale **beard:** 3 awn **bundle:** 4 bale 5 sheaf **chute:** 6 hopper **ear:** 5 spike **elevator:** 4 silo **mixture:** 6 fodder **row:** 5 swath 7 windrow

grainy 5 rough 6 coarse 8 granular 10 unfinished, unpolished

grammarian 7 Donatus (Aelius)

grammatical case 6 dative 7 oblique 8 ablative, genitive, locative, vocative 9 objective 10 accusative, nominative, possessive, subjective

grampus 3 orc 5 whale 7 dolphin 8 cetacean, porpoise, scorpion 9 blackfish 12 whip scorpion

Granada building: 8 Alhambra **citadel:** 8 Alcazaba **last Moorish king:** 7 Boabdil

granary 3 bin 4 silo 10 repository, storehouse

grand 3 fab 4 epic, fine, huge, vast 5 gaudy, lofty, noble, regal, royal, showy, super 6 august, garish, lavish, lordly, mighty, ornate, superb 7 exalted, opulent, pompous, stately, sublime **8** baronial, elevated, gorgeous, imposing, majestic, princely, splendid **9** first-rate, inclusive, luxurious, sumptuous, wonderful **10** first-class, impressive, monumental, prodigious, stupendous, tremendous **11** magnificent **12** ostentatious

Grand Canyon *explorer:* **6** Powell (John Wesley) *state:* **7** Arizona

grande dame 5 queen **6** matron **7** dowager, doyenne **9** matriarch

grandee 4 duke, earl, king, lord, peer **5** baron, noble, pasha **6** bashaw, prince **8** mandarin, marquess, viscount **10** panjandrum **11** muckety-muck

grandeur 4 pomp **5** glory **7** dignity, majesty **8** nobility, opulence, splendor, vastness **9** greatness, immensity, largeness, loftiness, nobleness, sublimity **10** augustness **11** stateliness **12** magnificence

grandiloquent 5 lofty **7** aureate, bloated, fustian, orotund, pompous **8** inflated **9** bombastic, flatulent, high-flown, overblown **10** histrionic, portentous **11** declamatory, highfalutin, pretentious **12** magniloquent

grand inquisitor 10 Torquemada (Tomás de)

grandiose 4 epic, vast **5** lofty, noble, regal, royal, showy **6** august, cosmic, lavish, lordly **7** pompous, stately, sublime, utopian **8** affected, imposing, majestic, princely, splendid **9** ambitious, high-flown **11** extravagant, highfalutin, magnificent, pretentious **12** ostentatious

grand mal 7 seizure **8** epilepsy

grandmother 4 nana *Russian:* **8** babushka

grange 4 farm **9** farmhouse, farmstead

granite 3 ore **4** rock **5** stone **6** aplite **7** mineral **11** igneous rock

Granite State 12 New Hampshire

grant 3 aid **4** alms, avow, cede, dole, gift, give **5** admit, allow, award, endow, yield **6** accord, assert, assign, assume, bestow, confer, convey, donate, permit **7** charity, concede, consent, entitle, handout, present, subsidy, suppose **8** bequeath, donation, property, transfer **9** endowment, vouchsafe **10** assistance, concession, relinquish, subvention **11** acknowledge, benefaction **12** contribution **13** appropriation

granular 5 rough, sandy **6** coarse, grainy **7** powdery **8** powdered **10** unfinished, unpolished

granule 3 bit, jot **4** iota, pill, spot **5** grain **6** pellet **8** fragment, particle

grape 3 fox, uva **4** Bual **5** Gamay, Pinot, Syrah **6** Arinto, Burger, Gentil, merlot, muscat, Shiraz **7** Albillo, Aligote, Barbera, Catawba, Concord, Furmint, Niagara, sultana **8** Aleatico, Cabernet, Charbono, Delaware, Friularo, Grenache, Isabella, malvasia, muscadel, Muscadet, Nebbiolo, Riesling, Semillon, Sylvaner, Thompson, Traminer, vinifera, Viognier **9** Carmenère, Chasselas, Lambrusco, Malvoisie, muscadine, Pinot Gris, pinot noir, Sauvignon, Trebbiano, zinfandel **10** chardonnay, Grignolino, muscadelle, pinot blanc, Sangiovese, Verdicchio **11** Chenin Blanc, Petite Sirah, pinot grigio, scuppernong *disease:* **4** esca *dried:* **6** raisin *drink:* **4** wine *pulp:* **4** rape **6** pomace *residue:* **4** marc

grapefruit 6 pomelo

Grapes of Wrath, The *author:* **9** Steinbeck (John) *family:* **4** Joad *people:* **5** Okies

grapevine 4 buzz **5** rumor **6** gossip **7** hearsay **9** rumor mill **11** scuttlebutt

graph 3 map **4** plot **5** chart **6** sketch **7** diagram, outline **8** nomogram, pie chart

graphic 3 map **5** clear, lucid, photo, vivid **6** cogent, visual **7** picture, precise, telling, written **8** clear-cut, definite, detailed, explicit, incisive, striking **9** pictorial, realistic **10** compelling, photograph **11** descriptive, picturesque

graphite 4 lead **6** carbon **8** plumbago

grapnel 4 hook **6** anchor

grappa 6 brandy

grapple 3 nab **4** bind, cope, grab, grip, hold **5** catch, clamp, clasp, fight, grasp, seize **6** battle, bucket, clench, clinch, clutch, fasten, tackle, tussle **7** contest, scuffle, wrestle **8** struggle

grasp 3 dig, ken, see **4** glom, grip, hold, know, take **5** catch, clamp, clasp, cling, seize **6** accept, clench, clinch, clutch, fathom, follow, handle, take in, tenure **7** cognize, compass, control, embrace, grapple, realize **8** envisage, perceive **9** apprehend, awareness **10** appreciate, comprehend, take hold of, understand **12** apprehension **13** comprehension, understanding

graspable 5 clear, lucid **6** lucent **8** coherent, knowable, palpable **10** fathomable **11** perspicuous **12** intelligible **13** apprehensible

grasping 4 avid **6** grabby, greedy **8** covetous, desirous **9** rapacious **10** avaricious, prehensile **11** acquisitive

grass 3 Poa, pot, sod, tea, Zea **4** lawn, reed, turf, weed **6** redtop **7** herbage, panicum, pasture **8** cannabis, Mary Jane **9** cocksfoot, marijuana *African:* **6** imphee *annual:* **6** darnel **8** teosinte *Asian:* **7** vetiver, whangee *Australian:* **8** spinifex *beach:* **6** marram *cereal:* **3** oat, rye, Zea **4** milo, teff **5** kafir, maize, proso, sorgo, wheat **6** millet **7** sorghum **8** triticum *clump:* **4** tuft **7** tussock *cover:* **3** dew *dried:* **3** hay **5** straw *European:* **7** Bermuda, timothy *fiber:* **4** flax *fragrant:* **10** citronella *meadow:* **3** Poa *pasture:* **5** Bahia, grama *perennial:* **6** fescue, quitch, zoysia **7** esparto, galleta *prairie:* **8** bluestem *second growth:* **5** rowen *tropical:* **5** cogon **6** bamboo

grasshopper 6 locust **7** katydid **8** cocktail

grassland 3 lea **5** field **6** meadow **7** pasture, prairie *African:* **4** veld **5** veldt *flat:* **7** savanna **8** savannah *South American:* **5** pampa **6** pampas

Grass novel 7 Tin Drum (The) **8** Dog Years, Flounder (The) **11** Cat and Mouse

grate 3 irk, jar, rub, vex **4** file, fray, fret, gall, rasp, rile **5** annoy, chafe, gnash, grill, grind, peeve, pique **6** abrade, grille, nettle, rankle, scrape **7** provoke, scratch **8** irritate **9** aggravate, fireplace

grateful 7 obliged, pleased, restful, welcome **8** beholden, indebted, pleasant, pleasing, thankful **9** agreeable, congenial, favorable **10** refreshing **11** restorative **12** appreciative

Gratiano *brother:* **9** Brabantio *friend:* **7** Antonio **8** Bassanio *niece:* **9** Desdemona *wife:* **7** Nerissa

gratify 4 baby, sate **5** favor, humor, spoil **6** coddle, oblige, pamper, pander, please **7** appease, cater to, content, delight, gladden, indulge, satisfy

gratin 5 crust

grating 3 dry **4** grid, rasp **5** grill, harsh, rough **6** grille, hoarse **7** irksome, jarring, lattice, rasping, raucous **8** gridiron, strident **9** vexatious **10** stridulous

gratis 4 comp, free **6** comped **8** costless **10** chargeless **13** complimentary

gratitude 6 thanks **12** appreciation, gratefulness, thankfulness

gratuitous 6 wanton **8** baseless **9** unfounded, voluntary **10** groundless, reasonless, ungrounded **11** uncalled-for, unnecessary, unwarranted **12** indefensible

gratuity 3 tip **4** gift, perk **5** bonus **6** reward **7** cumshaw, douceur **8** donation, largesse, offering **9** baksheesh, lagniappe, pourboire **10** perquisite **11** benefaction **12** contribution

grave 3 pit, sad **4** dire, dour, fell, grim, tomb **5** acute, awful, crypt, fatal, heavy, major, sober, staid, vault **6** burial, deadly, gloomy, sedate, severe, solemn, somber, sombre, urgent **7** austere, ghastly, ominous, ossuary, serious, subdued, weighty **8** catacomb, critical, dreadful, perilous, pressing, terrible **9** dangerous, mausoleum, momentous, ponderous, saturnine, sepulcher, sepulchre,

sepulture, unsmiling *marker:* **5** stela, stele **8** memorial, monument **9** footstone, headstone, tombstone **11** sarcophagus *mound:* **6** barrow **7** tumulus *robber:* **5** ghoul

gravel 4 dirt, grit, sand *ridge:* **5** esker

gravelly 5 raspy, rough **6** gritty, hoarse **7** rasping, grating **8** abrasive, granular, guttural, scratchy

graven image 4 icon, idol

graver 4 tool **5** burin **8** sculptor

graveyard 8 boot hill, catacomb, cemetery, God's acre **10** necropolis **12** burial ground, memorial park, potter's field

gravid 5 heavy **8** enceinte, pregnant **9** expectant, expecting, with child **10** parturient **12** childbearing

gravity 5 force **6** weight **7** dignity, urgency **8** sobriety **9** heaviness, solemnity **10** importance, somberness **11** consequence, seriousness **12** significance

gravlax 3 lox **6** salmon

gravy 4 perk **5** bonus, bribe, graft, juice, sauce **6** payola **8** dressing, windfall *French:* **3** jus

gray 3 ash, old **4** aged, ashy, blah, drab, dull **5** ashen, bleak, color, hoary, slate, slaty **6** dismal, gloomy, leaden **7** elderly, grizzly, neutral **8** grizzled, gunmetal, overcast **9** cinereous, colorless *brownish:* **3** dun **5** taupe **7** fuscous

gray duck 7 gadwall, pintail

grayfish 5 shark **7** dogfish

gray matter 3 wit **4** head, mind **5** brain **6** brains, noddle, noggin, noodle **8** cerebrum **9** intellect **10** encephalon **12** intelligence, neural tissue

graze 3 eat, rub **4** feed, gall, kiss, skim, skip, wear **5** brush, chafe, erode, shave, touch **6** abrade, browse, bruise, forage, glance, scrape **7** contuse, corrade, pasture **8** abrasion, ricochet

grazier 7 rancher

grease 3 fat, oil **4** lard **5** smear **6** smooth **7** lanolin **9** lubricant, lubricate *combining form:* **4** sebi, sebo

greasy 4 oily **5** fatty, slick **8** slippery, unctuous **10** lubricious, oleaginous

greasy spoon 4 café **5** diner, grill **6** eatery **7** beanery, hashery **9** chophouse, hash house, lunchroom **10** coffee shop **12** luncheonette

great 3 big, fat **4** huge, vast **5** boffo, grand, jumbo, large, noble, socko **6** famous, heroic **7** awesome, eminent, exalted, immense, mammoth, notable, sublime, supreme, titanic **8** colossal, enormous, gigantic, glorious, renowned, terrific, towering **9** excellent, fantastic, humongous, paramount, prominent, wonderful **10** celebrated, impressive, noteworthy, prodigious, remarkable, stupendous, tremendous **11** illustrious, magnificent, outstanding, superlative **13** distinguished *combining form:* **4** mega **6** megalo

Great Bear 9 Big Dipper, Ursa Major **13** constellation

Great Britain see **England, United Kingdom**

Great Commoner, the 4 Pitt (William) **5** Bryan (William Jennings) **7** Lincoln (Abraham)

Great Emancipator, the 7 Lincoln (Abraham)

greater 4 more **5** metro **6** better, bigger, higher, larger **8** superior **9** exceeding **10** surpassing **12** metropolitan

greatest 4 best, most **6** utmost **7** maximum, supreme **8** foremost

Great Expectations *author:* **7** Dickens (Charles) *character:* **3** Joe (Gargery), Pip **5** Biddy **7** Estella, Jaggers **8** Havisham (Miss), Magwitch (Abel)

greathearted 4 bold, kind **5** brave, lofty, noble **6** heroic **7** gallant **8** fearless, generous, princely **10** benevolent, chivalrous, courageous, high-minded **11** considerate, magnanimous

Great Lake 4 Erie **5** Huron **7** Ontario **8** Michigan, Superior *acronym:* **5** HOMES

Great Lake State 8 Michigan

greave 7 legging

grebe 4 bird, fowl **8** dabchick **10** diving bird

Greece 6 Hellas *ancient city-state:* **5** Argos **6** Athens, Sparta, Thebes **7** Corinth *ancient town:* **6** Delphi *capital:* **6** Athens *city:* **6** Patras **7** Larissa, Piraeus **8** Salonika **12** Thessaloníki *conqueror:* **6** Philip (of Macedonia) **9** Alexander (the Great) *island, island group:* **5** Crete **6** Aegean, Euboea, Ionian **8** Cyclades, Sporades *monetary unit:* **4** euro *monetary unit, former:* **6** lepton **7** drachma *mountain, range:* **3** Ida **4** Ossa **5** Athos **6** Pelion, Pindus **7** Olympus **9** Parnassus *neighbor:* **6** Turkey **7** Albania **8** Bulgaria **9** Macedonia *part of:* **7** Balkans *peninsula:* **6** Balkan **10** Chalcidice **11** Peloponnese *region:* **6** Attica, Epirus, Thrace **8** Thessaly *sea:* **6** Aegean, Ionian **13** Mediterranean *vale:* **5** Tempe

greed 4 lust **6** excess, hunger **7** avarice, avidity, craving **7** edacity, longing **8** cupidity, gluttony, rapacity, voracity **12** covetousness, ravenousness

greedy 4 avid **5** itchy **6** grabby **7** hoggish, miserly, selfish **8** covetous, desirous, edacious, esurient, grasping **10** avaricious, gluttonous **11** acquisitive

Greek 6 Argive, babble, drivel, jabber **7** Achaean, Hellene **8** Hellenic, nonsense **9** gibberish *assembly:* **5** agora, boule *cheese:* **4** feta *coin:* **4** obol **6** lepton, stater *column:* **5** Doric, Ionic **10** Corinthian *contest:* **4** agon *counselor:* **6** Nestor *dictator:* **7** Metaxas (Ioannis) *dragon:* **9** Eurythion *drink:* **4** ouzo *epic:* **5** Iliad **7** Odyssey *Fates:* **6** Clotho, Moirae **7** Atropos **8** Lachesis *gift:* **11** Trojan Horse
god:
  chief: **4** Zeus *messenger:* **6** Hermes *of agriculture:* **6** Cronus *of death:* **8** Thanatos *of dreams:* **8** Morpheus *of fire:* **10** Hephaestus *of healing:* **9** Asclepius **11** Aesculapius *of love:* **4** Eros *of marriage:* **5** Hymen *of the sun:* **6** Apollo *of physicians:* **6** Hermes *of sleep:* **6** Hypnos *of the sea:* **6** Nereus, Triton **7** Oceanus **8** Poseidon *of the sun:* **6** Helios *of the underworld:* **5** Pluto *of the winds:* **5** Eurus, Notus **6** Aeolus, Boreas **8** Zephyrus *of war:* **4** Ares *of wine:* **8** Dionysus *of woods:* **3** Pan
goddess:
  of agriculture: **7** Demeter *of beauty:* **9** Aphrodite *of dawn:* **3** Eos *of discord:* **4** Eris *of fertility:* **6** Cybele *of flowers:* **6** Chloris *of fortune:* **5** Tyche *of harvests:* **4** Rhea *of hunting:* **7** Artemis *of justice:* **7** Astraea *of love:* **9** Aphrodite *of marriage:* **4** Hera *of night:* **3** Nyx *of peace:* **5** Irene *of retribution:* **7** Nemesis *of ruin:* **3** Ate *of the earth:* **4** Gaea, Gaia *of the hearth:* **6** Hestia *of magic:* **6** Hecate, Hekate *of the moon:* **6** Hecate, Hekate, Selena, Selene **7** Artemis, Astarte *of the rainbow:* **4** Iris *of the seasons:* **5** Horae *of the underworld:* **6** Hecate, Hekate **10** Persephone *of vengeance:* **7** Nemesis *of victory:* **4** Nike *of wisdom:* **6** Athena *of witchcraft:* **6** Hecate, Hekate *of womanhood:* **4** Hera *of youth:* **4** Hebe *hero:* **4** Aias, Ajax **5** Jason **7** Theseus **8** Achilles, Argonaut, Heracles, Hercules, Odysseus **9** Achilleus *historian:* **8** Xenophon **9** Herodotus **10** Thucydides *lawgiver:* **5** Draco, Solon *leader:* **9** Agamemnon *letter:* **2** mu, nu, pi, xi **3** chi, eta, phi, psi, rho, tau **4** beta, iota, zeta **5** alpha, delta, gamma, kappa, omega, sigma, theta **6** lambda **7** epsilon, omicron, upsilon *magistrate:* **6** archon *marketplace:* **5** agora *physician:* **5** Galen *porch:* **4** stoa *sandwich:* **4** gyro *soldier:* **7** hoplite *theater:* **5** odeon, odeum *underworld:* **5** Hades *war cry:* **5** alala *warrior:* **4** Ajax **7** Ulysses **8** Achilles, Diomedes, Odysseus

9 Agamemnon, Palamedes *weeper:* **5** Niobe *wine:* **7** retsina

green 3 raw **4** jade, lime, moss **5** alive, fresh, kelly, leafy, naive, virid, young **6** callow, forest, unripe **7** avocado, celadon, emerald, envious, untried, verdant **8** immature, juvenile, unversed, youthful **9** unfledged **10** unseasoned **11** unpracticed **13** inexperienced *bluish:* **8** glaucous *combining form:* **4** verd **6** chloro *grayish:* **5** olive *heraldry:* **4** vert *yellowish:* **7** luteous **10** chartreuse

greenbacks 4 cash, jack, loot **5** bread, bucks, dough, lucre, money, moola **6** moolah, wampum **7** dollars, scratch **8** currency, smackers **11** legal tender

green beryl 7 emerald

greenery 7 foliage, leafage **8** verdancy

green-eyed 7 envious, jealous **9** invidious *monster:* **8** jealousy

greenfly 5 aphid

greengage 4 plum

greenhead 3 fly **8** horsefly

greenheart 6 laurel **9** evergreen

greenhorn 4 babe, hick, jake, naïf, rube, tiro, tyro **5** newbie, novice, rookie **7** ingenue **8** beginner, neophyte, newcomer **10** provincial

greenhouse 7 nursery **12** conservatory

Greenland *capital:* **4** Nuuk **7** Godthåb *city:* **5** Thule *ethnic group:* **5** Inuit **6** Eskimo *explorer:* **4** Eric (the Red), Erik (the Red), Leif (Eriksson) **9** Rasmussen (Knud) *language:* **6** Danish *monetary unit:* **5** krone *possession of:* **7** Denmark

green light 2 OK **3** nod **4** okay **5** leave **6** assent **7** consent, go-ahead, mandate **8** approval, blessing, sanction, thumbs-up **9** authority, clearance **10** permission **11** endorsement **13** authorization

Green Mansions *author:* **6** Hudson (W. H.) *character:* **4** Rima

green monkey 6 guenon, simian, vervet

Green Mountain State 7 Vermont

greenness 5 youth **6** spring **7** puberty **8** verdancy, viridity **9** youthhood **10** immaturity, juvenility, pubescence, springtide, springtime **11** adolescence **12** inexperience

green osier 6 willow **7** dogwood

green plover 7 lapwing **9** shorebird

greenroom 6 lounge

greenstone 4 jade **7** diabase **8** nephrite **9** tremolite **10** actinolite

greet 3 bow **4** hail, meet **6** accost, call to, salaam, salute **7** address, react to, receive, welcome

greeting 3 ave, bow, nod **4** ahoy, ciao, g'day, hail **5** aloha, hello, howdy **6** salaam, salute

7 address, welcome **9** handshake, reception **10** salutation

gregarious 6 clubby, genial, social **7** affable **8** outgoing, sociable **9** clubbable, congenial, convivial **11** extroverted **13** companionable

gremlin 3 bug, elf, imp **5** dwarf, gnome **6** defect, glitch **7** brownie

Grenada *capital:* **9** St. George's *discoverer:* **8** Columbus (Christopher) *former name:* **10** Concepción *location:* **10** West Indies *nickname:* **11** Isle of Spice

grenade 4 bomb **5** shell **7** missile **9** explosive, pineapple

grenadier 7 rattail, soldier

grenadine 4 pink, yarn **5** syrup **6** fabric **9** carnation

Grendel's *slayer* **7** Beowulf

Gretchen's *lover* **5** Faust

greylag 5 goose

grid 3 net **5** grate, grill **6** grille **7** grating, lattice, network, trellis

griddle 3 pan **5** grill

griddle cake 7 hotcake, pancake **8** flapjack

gridiron 3 net **5** field, grate, grill **7** grating, network

grief 3 rue, woe **4** care **5** agony, dolor, gloom, tears **6** mishap, regret, sorrow **7** anguish, chagrin, sadness, trouble **8** disaster, distress, hardship **9** adversity, heartache, suffering **10** affliction, heartbreak, misfortune **11** despondency

Grieg *work* **8** Peer Gynt

grievance 4 beef **5** cross, gripe, trial, wrong **6** burden, grouse, injury, squawk **8** hardship, jeremiad **9** complaint, injustice **10** affliction, allegation, unfairness **11** tribulation

grieve 3 cry **4** ache, keen, moan, wail, weep **5** mourn **6** burden, lament, sadden, sorrow, suffer **7** afflict, agonize **8** distress

grievous 3 sad **4** dire, fell, sore **5** cruel, grave, great, major **6** bitter, severe, taxing, tragic, woeful **7** galling, heinous, onerous, painful, serious, weighty **9** egregious **10** abominable, burdensome, calamitous, deplorable, lamentable, oppressive **11** distressing, regrettable, troublesome, unfortunate **12** heartrending

grift 3 con, gyp **4** bilk, rook **7** defraud, swindle **8** flimflam

grifter 3 gyp **5** cheat, crook, thief **6** con man, gouger **7** cheater, scammer, sharper, slicker **8** swindler **9** defrauder, trickster **13** confidence man

grill 3 fry, vex **4** cook, grid, pump, quiz **5** broil, grate, sauté, toast **6** eatery **7** afflict, debrief, grating, griddle, torment **8** gridiron, question **10** restaurant **11** interrogate **12** cross-examine

grilse 6 salmon

grim 3 set **4** cold, dour, fell, firm, hard **5** bleak, cruel, fixed, grave, harsh, rigid, stern **6** dismal, dogged, dreary, fierce, grisly, intent, savage, severe, somber **7** adamant, austere, inhuman, joyless, ominous **8** gruesome, inhumane, obdurate, resolute, ruthless, stubborn **9** merciless, offensive, truculent **10** determined, forbidding, implacable, inevitable, inexorable, inflexible, melancholy, relentless, unyielding, vindictive **11** unforgiving, unrelenting

grimace 3 mow, mug **4** face, moue, pout **5** frown, lower, mouth, scowl, sneer

grimalkin 3 cat **5** tabby **6** feline **9** female cat

grime 4 crud, dirt, gunk, muck, smut, soot **5** filth

grim reaper 5 death

grimy 5 dingy, dirty **6** filthy, grubby, grungy, soiled, scuzzy, smutty **10** besmirched

grin 4 beam **5** smile, smirk

grind 3 rut, vex **4** chew, grub, mill, moil, pace, plod, plug, rote, slog, toil, whet **5** crank, crush, gnash, grate, labor, slave, sweat **6** abrade, crunch, drudge, groove, harass, kibble, powder, rotate **7** oppress, routine, travail **8** drudgery, monotony, wear down **9** pulverize, treadmill **10** donkeywork

grinder 3 sub **4** gyro, hero **5** molar, tooth **6** hoagie **8** sandwich **9** submarine

grinding 5 harsh **6** severe **7** arduous, grating, wearing **9** fatiguing, strenuous **stone: 4** mano **6** mortar, muller, pestle

griot 11 storyteller

grip 4 glom, hold, take **5** clamp, clasp, grasp, seize **6** clench, clinch, clutch, handle, tenure, valise **7** grapple **8** enthrall, suitcase **9** fascinate, mesmerize, restraint, spellbind, stagehand **10** constraint

gripe 3 bug, vex **4** beef, carp, crab, fuss, yawp **5** annoy, bitch, bleat, cavil, croak, groan, whine **6** bother, grouch, grouse, kvetch, murmur, mutter, object, squawk, yammer **7** afflict, grumble **8** complain, distress, irritate **9** bellyache, complaint, grievance, objection

griper see **grumbler**

grippe 3 flu **9** influenza

gripper 4 clip, hand, vise **5** clamp, clasp, tongs **6** pliers

gris-gris 4 juju **5** charm, spell **6** amulet, fetish **8** talisman **11** incantation

Grisham novel 4 Firm (The) **6** Broker (The), Client (The) **7** Chamber (The), Partner

(The) **8** Brethren (The) **12** Pelican Brief (The)

grisly 4 gory, grim **5** awful, lurid **6** horrid **7** ghastly, hideous, macabre **8** fearsome, godawful, gruesome, horrible, terrible **9** frightful, repellent, repulsive, sickening **10** disgusting, horrifying, terrifying

grist 3 lot **5** grain, input, stint **6** amount, output **7** product **8** quantity

gristle 9 cartilage

grit 4 guts, sand **5** grate, grind, heart, moxie, nerve, pluck, spunk **6** gravel, mettle, powder, smooth, spirit **7** bravery, courage, granule **8** backbone, tenacity **9** fortitude **10** doggedness **13** determination

gritty 4 game **5** dirty, gutsy, rough, sandy **6** dogged, plucky, spunky **8** abrasive, gravelly, resolute, spirited **9** steadfast, tenacious **10** courageous, determined

groan 4 beef, carp, moan **5** cavil, creak, gripe **6** bemoan, grouse, lament, object, repine **7** grumble **8** complain **9** bellyache

grocery 5 store **11** supermarket **Spanish: 6** bodega

grog 3 rum **5** booze, drink, hooch, juice, sauce **6** liquor, tipple **7** alcohol, spirits **9** firewater

groggy 4 dull, hazy, logy, weak **5** dazed, dopey, foggy, muzzy, tired, woozy **6** dulled, sleepy **7** muddled **8** befogged, confused, sluggish **9** befuddled, slaphappy, stupefied **10** punch-drunk

groin 4 fold **6** crotch

grok 6 intuit

grommet 6 eyelet **7** cringle

groom 4 comb, tend, tidy **5** brush, clean, curry, primp, ready, shave **6** neaten, ostler, polish **7** hostler, prepare, servant **8** benedict **9** attendant **Indian: 4** syce

groove 3 rut **4** dado, pace, rote, slot **5** canal, flute, glyph, gouge, grind, niche, score, stria **6** furrow, gutter, hollow, rabbet, rhythm **7** chamfer, channel, routine, top form **8** monotony **10** depression

groovy 3 hip **4** cool, neat **5** ducky, great, nifty, sharp, slick, super, swell **6** choice, gnarly, peachy **7** right-on **8** smashing **9** copacetic, excellent, hunky-dory, marvelous, wonderful **10** delightful, marvellous, peachy keen

grope 4 feel, grub, poke, root **6** fondle, fumble, search **7** grabble **8** scrabble

grosbeak 5 finch **8** hawfinch, songbird

gross 3 fat, raw, sum **4** earn, foul, mass, rude **5** brute, bulky, crude, obese, rough, utter, whole **6** carnal, coarse, entire, vulgar **7** blatant, boorish, capital, extreme, glaring, hulking, obscene, overall, porcine, uncouth **8** absolute, complete, flagrant, ignorant, improper, indecent, outright, sum total, tangible, totality **9** aggregate, before tax, corporeal, corpulent, downright, egregious, excessive, loathsome, offensive, out-and-out, repulsive, revolting, unrefined **10** disgusting, exorbitant, immoderate **11** twelve dozen

grotesque 6 absurd, rococo, unreal **7** baroque, bizarre, extreme **8** aberrant, abnormal, deformed, fanciful, freakish **9** distorted, fantastic, ludicrous, misshapen, monstrous **11** incongruous

grotto 4 cave, hole **5** crypt, vault **6** cavern *Capri:* **4** Blue

grouch 4 beef, carp, crab, kick, sulk, yawp **5** crank, croak, growl, grump, pique **6** carper, griper, grouse, grudge, kicker, kvetch, murmur, mutter, repine, squawk, whiner, yawper **7** crabber, grouser, growler, grumble **8** complain, grumbler, kvetcher, sorehead, sourpuss, squawker **9** bellyache, complaint **10** bellyacher, complainer, crosspatch, malcontent

ground 3 bed, sod **4** base, dirt, land, root, seat, soil, turf **5** basis, cause, earth, floor, proof **6** bottom, reason **7** bedrock, dry land, footing, support, sustain, terrain **8** argument, buttress, evidence **9** establish, testimony **10** foundation, terra firma

groundbreaking 10 innovative, innovatory, pioneering **11** cutting-edge, leading-edge

grounded 6 stable **7** beached **8** marooned, sensible, stranded **9** realistic **13** unpretentious

groundhog 6 marmot **9** woodchuck

grounding 8 practice, training, tutelage **11** instruction, preparation

groundless 4 idle **5** empty, false **6** hollow **8** baseless **9** causeless, unfounded **10** gratuitous **11** uncalled-for, unjustified, unwarranted

groundwork 3 bed **4** base, foot, root **5** basis **6** bottom **7** bedrock, footing, support **8** basement **10** foundation, substratum **11** cornerstone, preparation **12** substruction, substructure, underpinning

ground zero 5 focus, get-go **6** center, outset, target **8** bull's-eye **9** epicenter, square one

group 3 lot, set **4** band, bevy, body, club, crew, gang, pack, ruck, sect, team, tier **5** array, batch, bunch, class, clump, combo, covey, crowd, horde, panel, squad, taxon, troop **6** assort, bundle, cartel, circle, clique, clutch, huddle, klatch, league, passel **7** battery, brigade, cluster, combine, company,

coterie, council, echelon, klatsch, platoon **8** assemble, assembly, category, classify, ensemble, organize **9** congeries, gathering, syndicate **10** assemblage, categorize, collection *of angels:* **4** host *of ants:* **6** colony *of bees:* **4** hive **5** swarm *of birds:* **6** flight *of cats:* **7** clowder, clutter *of cattle:* **5** drove *of chicks:* **5** brood **6** clutch *of clams:* **3** bed *of crows:* **6** murder *of ducks:* **5** brace *of eight:* **5** octad, octet *of elephants:* **4** herd *of elks:* **4** gang *of fish:* **5** shoal **6** school *of five:* **5** quint **6** pentad **7** quintet *of four:* **6** tetrad **7** quartet *of foxes:* **5** leash, skulk *of geese:* **5** flock, skein **6** gaggle *of gnats:* **5** cloud, horde *of goats:* **5** tribe *of gorillas:* **4** band *of greyhounds:* **5** leash *of grouse:* **5** covey *of hares:* **4** down, husk *of hawks:* **4** cast *of hounds:* **3** cry **4** mute, pack *of kangaroos:* **3** mob **5** troop *of kittens:* **6** litter *of larks:* **10** exaltation *of lions:* **5** pride *of locusts:* **6** plague *of monkeys:* **5** troop *of mules:* **4** span *of nine:* **5** nonet **6** ennead *of oysters:* **3** bed *of partridges:* **5** covey *of peacocks:* **6** muster *of pheasants:* **4** nest *of plovers:* **4** wing **12** congregation *of quail:* **4** bevy **5** covey *of seals:* **3** pod **5** patch *of seven:* **6** pleiad, septet *of sheep:* **5** drove, flock *of six:* **6** sextet *of swans:* **4** bevy *of teals:* **6** spring *of ten:* **6** decade *of three:* **4** trio **5** triad **7** ternary, trinity, triplet *of vipers:* **4** nest *of whales:* **3** gam, pod *of wolves:* **4** pack

grouper 8 rockfish

grouse 4 beef, carp, crab **5** croak, gripe, quail, scold **6** mutter, yammer **7** grumble **8** complain, pheasant **9** bellyache, blackcock, ptarmigan **12** capercaillie *extinct:* **8** heath hen *red:* **8** moorfowl *strut:* **3** lek

grout 4 lees, lute **5** dregs **6** cement, filler, mortar **7** grounds, plaster **8** concrete

grove 4 holt, wood **5** copse **7** boscage, coppice, orchard, thicket

grovel 4 fawn **5** abase, cower, crawl, creep, toady **6** cajole, cringe, kowtow, snivel, wallow **7** eat dirt, truckle **8** blandish, bootlick **9** brownnose **10** curry favor, ingratiate **11** apple-polish

grow 3 age, wax **4** flow, gain, rise, tend **5** amass, breed, nurse, raise, ripen, swell **6** abound, become, expand, foster, mature, sprout, thrive **7** burgeon, care for, develop, enlarge, gestate, nurture, produce **8** escalate, flourish, increase, multiply, mushroom, spring up **9** cultivate, propagate

growl 4 beef, carp, crab, fuss, gnar, roar **5** bitch, gripe, gnarr, groan, snarl **6** grouse, kvetch, mutter, repine, rumble, yammer **7** grumble **8** complain **9** bellyache

growler 3 can **4** crab, floe **5** crank, grump **6** grouch, vessel **7** ice floe, iceberg, pitcher **8** sorehead, sourpuss **9** container **10** crosspatch, malcontent **11** faultfinder

grown-up 5 adult **6** mature **8** seasoned **9** developed **11** full-fledged

grow old 3 age **4** wane **5** ripen, wizen **6** mature, mellow

growth 4 gain, rise **5** surge, swell, tumor **7** buildup **8** increase, progress, swelling **9** accretion, evolution, expansion, flowering, unfolding **11** development, enlargement, progression *malignant:* **6** cancer *skin:* **3** tag, wen **4** corn, cyst, mole, wart **5** nevus **6** bunion, callus, keloid **7** verruca

grow up 3 age **5** ripen **6** evolve, mature, mellow **7** advance, develop **8** maturate **9** come of age

grub 3 dig **4** chow, comb, eats, feed, food, hack, moil, plod, poke, rake, root, slog, toil **5** grind, larva, scour, slave, spade, stump **6** burrow, drudge, forage, menial, shovel, slavey, uproot, viands **7** edibles, ransack, rummage, unearth, vittles **8** excavate, hireling, victuals **9** provender **11** comestibles

grubby 4 foul **5** dirty, grimy, messy, seedy **6** filthy, frowsy, frowzy, grungy, scuzzy, shabby, sloppy, soiled **7** scruffy, squalid, unclean, unkempt **8** slovenly, unwashed

grubstake 3 aid **4** back, fund, help, loan **5** funds **6** assist **7** backing, capital, finance, support **8** bankroll **9** financing **10** assistance, capitalize, underwrite

grudge 4 deny, envy **5** spite **6** refuse, spleen **7** ill will **9** grievance **10** resentment **12** hard feelings, spitefulness

gruel 4 mush **5** atole, kasha **6** burgoo, congee, sowens **8** flummery, loblolly, porridge **9** stirabout

gruesome see **grisly**

gruff 4 curt, dour **5** bluff, blunt, cross, harsh, husky, stern, surly **6** abrupt, crabby, crusty, hoarse, morose, sullen **7** bearish, brusque, crabbed, grating, grouchy **8** churlish, croaking, snappish, snippety **9** saturnine **10** illnatured **11** bad-tempered

grumble 4 beef, carp, crab, fuss, moan, yawp **5** bitch, croak, gripe, groan, growl, snarl, whine **6** bemoan, grouch, grouse, murmur, mutter, repine, squawk **8** complain **9** bellyache

grumbler 4 crab **5** crank, grump **6** grouch **8** sorehead **10** crosspatch, malcontent

grump 3 pet **4** beef, carp, crab, pout, sulk **5** crank, gripe, growl **6** griper, grouch **7**

growler, grumble 8 complain, sorehead, sourpuss **9** bellyache **10** bellyacher, malcontent

grumpy 4 dour, sour **5** cross, moody, sulky, surly, testy **6** crabby, cranky, sullen **7** crabbed, peevish **8** petulant, vinegary **9** crotchety, irascible **11** bad-tempered, illtempered **12** cantankerous

grunion 10 silverside

grunt 5 groan, growl, snort **7** dogface, draftee, soldier

G sharp 5 A flat

guacharo 7 oilbird

Guadeloupe *capital:* **10** Basse-Terre *department of:* **6** France *dependency:* **8** Désirade, St. Martin **12** Marie-Galante, St. Barthélemy *discoverer:* **8** Columbus (Christopher) *island:* **10** Basse-Terre **11** Grande-Terre *location:* **10** West Indies *volcano:* **9** Soufrière

Guam *capital:* **5** Agana *ethnic group:* **8** Chamorro *island group:* **7** Mariana

guanaco 5 llama **6** alpaca *kin:* **5** camel

guano 6 manure **9** excrement

guarantee 3 vow **4** bail, bond, oath, seal, word **5** token, vouch **6** assert, assure, ensure, insure, pledge, surety **7** certify, earnest, promise, warrant **8** security, warranty **9** agreement, assurance, insurance, undertake **11** stand behind, undertaking

guarantor 5 angel **6** backer, patron, surety **7** ensurer, insurer, sponsor **8** bondsman **11** underwriter

guard 4 fend, mind, tend, ward **5** aegis, alert, armor, cover, watch **6** convoy, defend, escort, jailer, keeper, minder, patrol, picket, police, screen, secure, sentry, shield, warden, warder **7** bulwark, defense, lookout, oversee, protect, turnkey **8** chaperon, overseer, preserve, security, sentinel, shepherd, watchdog, watchman **9** chaperone, custodian, look after, patrolman, protector, watch over **10** protection

guarded 4 safe, wary **5** cagey, chary, leery **7** careful, politic, prudent **8** cautious, discreet, gingerly, reserved **11** circumspect, considerate

guardhouse 4 brig, jail, keep **5** clink **6** lockup, prison **8** stockade

guardian 6 escort, keeper, patron, warden, warder **7** curator, trustee **8** Cerberus, defender, overseer, watchdog **9** custodian, protector **10** genius loci **11** conservator

guardianship 4 care, keep, ward **5** aegis, trust **6** charge **7** custody, keeping **8** auspices **10** protection **11** safekeeping

Guare play 17 House of Blue Leaves (The) **22** Six Degrees of Separation

Guatemala *capital:* **9** Guatemala (City) *ethnic group:* **4** Maya **5** Mayan *lake:* **6** Izabal **7** Atitlán **9** Petén Itzá *language:* **7** Spanish *monetary unit:* **7** quetzal *mountain, range:* **6** Tacaná **9** Tajumulco **10** Acatenango, Santa María **11** Sierra Madre *neighbor:* **6** Belize, Mexico **8** Honduras **10** El Salvador *peninsula:* **7** Yucatán *river:* **7** Motagua **8** Polochic, Sarstoon **10** Usumacinta

guck 3 bog, goo, mud **4** clay, crud, dirt, glop, goop, mire, ooze, smut **5** filth, slime **7** stickum

gudgeon 3 pin **4** fish **5** pivot **6** socket **7** journal

Gudrun *brother:* **6** Gunnar **7** Gunther *father:* **5** Hetel *husband:* **4** Atli **5** Etzel **6** Sigurd **9** Siegfried

guerrilla 8 partisan **9** irregular *Greek:* **6** klepht

guess 4 call, shot, stab **5** fancy, hunch, infer **7** believe, predict, presume, suppose, surmise **8** estimate **9** speculate **10** conjecture, prediction **11** presumption, supposition, speculation

guest 6 caller, lodger, roomer **7** boarder, company, visitor **9** sojourner

guff 3 jaw, lip **4** bosh, sass **5** bilge, cheek, hokum, hooey, mouth, sauce, trash **6** bunkum, drivel, hot air, humbug **7** baloney, hogwash, palaver, twaddle **8** back talk, claptrap, malarkey, nonsense, tommyrot **9** poppycock **10** balderdash **13** horsefeathers

guffaw 6 cackle, hee-haw **7** chortle

guidance 6 advice **7** control, counsel **8** handling **9** direction, oversight **10** leadership, management **11** instruction, supervision

guide 4 dean, guru, help, lead, show **5** doyen, pilot, route, steer, usher **6** beacon, convoy, direct, docent, escort, handle, leader, manage, manual, mentor **7** adviser, conduct, control, marshal, oversee **8** Baedeker, chaperon, director, handbook, instruct, maneuver, navigate, shepherd, signpost **9** accompany, chaperone, conductor, vade mecum, Sacagawea **10** bellwether, compendium, instructor, pathfinder **11** enchiridion

guidebook 6 Fodor's, manual **8** Baedeker, Frommer's, handbook, Michelin **9** itinerary, vade mecum **10** compendium **11** enchiridion

guided missile 3 ABM **4** Hawk, ICBM, IRBM, Nike, Scud, Thor, Zuni **5** Atlas, drone, Snark, Titan **6** Bomarc, cruise, Exocet, Falcon, Navaho, rocket **7** Bullpup, Matador, Polaris, Regulus, Terrier **8** Redstone, Tomahawk **9** Minuteman **10** projectile, Sidewinder

Guiderius *brother:* **9** Arviragus *father:* **9** Cymbeline

guidon 4 flag **6** banner, burgee, ensign, pennon

guild 4 club **5** lodge, order, union **6** cartel, league **7** society **8** sodality **10** fellowship, fraternity **11** association, brotherhood *medieval:* **5** Hansa, Hanse

guile 4 wile **5** craft, fraud **6** deceit **7** cunning **8** artifice, trickery, wiliness **9** deception, duplicity, stratagem **10** cleverness **13** dissimulation

guileful 3 sly **4** foxy, wily **5** cagey, canny, slick **6** artful, astute, crafty, shifty, shrewd, sneaky, tricky **7** cunning, devious **8** indirect, slippery, sneaking **9** designing, insidious, underhand **11** calculating, duplicitous, underhanded

guileless 4 open **5** frank, naive **6** candid, direct, honest **7** genuine, natural, sincere, upfront **8** innocent, truthful **9** ingenuous **10** aboveboard, forthright

guillemot 3 auk **5** murre **7** seabird

guillotine 6 behead **9** decollate **10** decapitate

guilt 4 onus **5** blame, fault, shame **6** regret, stigma **7** offense, remorse **10** contrition **11** culpability **12** self-reproach

guiltless 4 pure **5** clean **6** chaste **8** innocent, virtuous **9** blameless, exemplary, faultless, righteous, stainless **10** immaculate, inculpable

guilty 6 liable, rueful, sinful **7** ashamed, at fault **8** blamable, contrite, culpable, indicted, penitent **9** impeached, regretful **10** answerable, remorseful **11** accountable, blameworthy, responsible

guimpe 6 blouse

Guinea *capital:* **7** Conakry *city:* **4** Labé **6** Kankan, Kindia *ethnic group:* **6** Fulani **7** Malinke *island, island group:* **3** Los **5** Tombo *language:* **6** French *monetary unit:* **5** franc *mountain:* **5** Nimba *neighbor:* **4** Mali **7** Liberia, Senegal **10** Ivory Coast **11** Sierra Leone **12** Guinea-Bissau *river:* **5** Niger **6** Gambia **7** Senegal

Guinea-Bissau *archipelago:* **7** Bijagós *capital:* **6** Bissau *ethnic group:* **6** Fulani **7** Malinke **8** Mandyako *language:* **10** Portuguese *monetary unit:* **5** franc *neighbor:* **6** Guinea **7** Senegal *river:* **4** Gêba

guinea fowl *genus:* **6** Numida *young:* **4** keet

guinea pig 4 cavy **6** rodent *genus:* **5** Cavia

Guinevere *court:* **7** Camelot *husband:* **6** Arthur *lover:* **8** Lancelot **9** Launcelot

guise 4 mask **5** cloak, cover, dress, getup **6** aspect, facade, outfit, veneer **7** costume, pretext **8** coloring, pretense **9** posturing, semblance **10** appearance, false front

guitar *accessory:* **4** capo *Mexican:* **5** tiple **6**

cuatro **8** charango *part:* **3** nut, peg **4** fret, neck **5** brace **6** bridge, string **7** peghead *small:* **3** uke **7** ukulele *tool:* **4** pick **8** plectrum

guitarist *American:* **3** Guy (Buddy) **4** Byrd (Charlie), King (Albert, B. B., Freddie), Page (Jimmy), Pass (Joe), Paul (Les) **5** Berry (Chuck), Ellis (Herb), Isbin (Sharon) **6** Allman (Duane), Atkins (Chet), Cooder (Ry), Garcia (Jerry), Kessel (Barney), Kottke (Leo), Watson (Doc) **7** Burrell (Kenny), Hendrix (Jimi), Johnson (Robert), Metheny (Pat), Santana (Carlos), Vaughan (Stevie Ray) **8** Van Halen (Eddie) **9** Christian (Charlie), Parkening (Christopher) **10** Montgomery (Wes), Pizzarelli (Bucky, John) *Australian:* **8** Williams (John) *British:* **4** Beck (Jeff) **5** Bream (Julian) **7** Clapton (Eric) **8** Richards (Keith) **9** Townshend (Pete) *French:* **9** Reinhardt (Django) *Italian:* **7** Ghiglia (Oscar) *Spanish:* **5** Yepes (Narciso) **6** Romero (Celedonio) **7** Segovia (Andrés)

guitarlike instrument **3** uke **4** lute, vina **5** banjo, sitar **7** bandore, pandora, samisen, ukulele **8** mandolin, shamisen

gulch **3** gap **4** glen **5** gorge, gully **6** arroyo, canyon, coulee, hollow, ravine, valley **7** couloir

gules **3** red

gulf **3** bay, pit **4** cove **5** abysm, abyss, bayou, bight, chasm, firth, gorge, gulch, inlet **6** cavity, harbor, hollow, ravine, slough **8** crevasse *Adriatic Sea:* **6** Venice *Aegean Sea:* **7** Saronic **8** Salonika *Africa:* **6** Guinea *Arabian Sea:* **4** Oman **7** Persian *Australia:* **9** Van Diemen **11** Carpentaria *Baltic Sea:* **4** Riga **6** Danzig, Gdansk **7** Bothnia, Finland *Bering Sea:* **6** Anadyr *Canada:* **13** Saint Lawrence *Central America:* **7** Fonseca *Djibouti:* **6** Tajura **8** Tadjoura *Europe:* **7** Bothnia, Gascony **8** Gascogne *Greece:* **7** Corinth, Lepanto *Indian Ocean:* **4** Aden *Ionian Sea:* **4** Arta **7** Taranto *Iran:* **7** Arabian *Italy:* **5** Genoa *Mediterranean Sea:* **5** Sidra, Tunis **8** Valencia **10** Khalij Surt **11** Syrtis Major *Middle East:* **7** Persian *New Guinea:* **5** Papua **7** McCluer *New Zealand:* **7** Hauraki *North America:* **6** Mexico *Northwest Territories:* **7** Boothia **8** Amundsen **9** Queen Maud *Philippines:* **4** Asid **5** Davao, Leyte, Panay, Ragay *Red Sea:* **4** Suez **5** Aqaba **11** Aelaniticus *Russia:* **8** Sakhalin *Solomon Sea:* **4** Huon, Kula **5** Vella *South China Sea:* **4** Siam **6** Tonkin **8** Lingayen *Tyrrhenian Sea:* **7** Paestum *Yellow Sea:* **6** Chihli

Gulf State **5** Texas **7** Alabama, Florida **9** Louisiana **11** Mississippi

gull **3** con, mew, sap **4** bird, dupe, fool, hoax, scam, Xema **5** chump, cozen **6** fleece, pigeon, stooge, sucker, take in **7** chicane, fall guy **8** flimflam, hoodwink **9** bamboozle **11** hornswoggle

gullet **3** maw **4** crop, tube **6** dewlap, throat **7** channel **9** esophagus

gullible **4** easy **5** green, naive **8** innocent, trusting **9** believing, credulous **11** susceptible **12** unsuspecting

Gulliver's Travels *author:* **5** Swift (Jonathan) *horses:* **10** Houyhnhnms *land:* **6** Laputa **8** Lilliput **11** Brobdingnag *people:* **6** Yahoos

gully **3** gap **4** glen, wadi, wash **5** gorge, gulch **6** arroyo, coulee, hollow, nullah, ravine, valley **7** couloir

gulp **4** bolt, chug, cram, glut, slop, swig, wolf **5** gorge, quaff, scarf, scoff, stuff, swill **6** devour, gobble, guzzle **7** swallow **8** mouthful **11** ingurgitate

gum **4** chew **5** botch **6** bobble, bollix, bungle, chicle, gluten, goof up, tupelo **7** exudate, gingiva, louse up **8** adhesive, mucilage **9** sapodilla **10** eucalyptus *kind:* **6** acacia, Arabic, balata, bubble **7** chewing, dextrin *resin:* **5** myrrh **7** gamboge **8** ammoniac, galbanum, scammony **9** asafetida **10** asafoetida **12** frankincense

gumbo **3** mud **4** okra, olio, soil, soup, stew **6** creole **7** mélange, mixture *ingredient:* **4** crab, duck, filé, okra **5** quail, tasso **6** shrimp **8** crawfish

gummy **5** gooey, pasty **6** cloggy, sticky, viscid **7** viscous **8** adhesive **9** glutinous **10** gelatinous **12** mucilaginous

gumption **5** drive, moxie, nerve, savvy **6** energy **8** industry **10** enterprise, get-up-and-go, initiative

gumshoe **3** cop, tec **4** bull, dick, fuzz, G-man, heat, narc **6** copper, peeler, shamus, sleuth **7** officer **8** flatfoot, hawkshaw, Sherlock **9** detective, policeman **10** bloodhound, private eye **12** investigator

gun **3** gat, rev, rod **4** Colt **5** rev up, rifle **6** cannon, Garand, heater, mortar, musket, pistol, weapon **7** bazooka, carbine, firearm **8** Browning, howitzer, revolver **9** derringer, Remington **10** Winchester **11** Springfield *antiaircraft:* **6** ack-ack, Bofors *Austrian:* **5** Glock *British:* **4** Sten *French:* **8** arquebus **9** harquebus *German:* **5** Luger *Israeli:* **3** Uzi *Italian:* **7** Beretta *mount:* **6** turret *part:* **3** pin **4** bolt, bore, butt, lock **5** sight, stock **6** barrel, breech, hammer, muzzle, safety **7**

chamber, trigger **8** cylinder, magazine **9** buttstock *stun:* **5** Taser

gunfire 4 shot **5** blast, salvo **6** volley **7** barrage **9** broadside, discharge, fusillade

gung ho 4 avid, keen **6** ardent, fervid, raring **7** fervent, zealous **9** exuberant **11** impassioned **12** enthusiastic

Guni's father 8 Naphtali

gunk 3 goo **4** crud, glop, gook, goop, muck **5** slime

gunman 5 bravo **6** hit man, killer **7** shooter, torpedo **8** assassin, enforcer

Gunnar *brother-in-law:* **6** Sigurd *father:* **5** Hetel *sister:* **6** Gudrun *wife:* **8** Brunhild, Brynhild

gunner 6 sniper **7** shooter **8** marksman, rifleman **9** musketeer **11** infantryman **12** artilleryman

Gunther *sister:* **7** Gutrune **9** Kriemhild *slayer:* **5** Hagen *uncle:* **5** Hagen *wife:* **8** Brunhild **9** Brynhilde

gurgle 3 lap **4** flow, purl, wash **5** plash, slosh, swash **6** babble, bubble, burble, ripple

Gurkha knife 5 kukri

gurney 3 cot **9** stretcher

guru 4 sage **5** guide, swami, tutor **6** expert, leader, master, mentor **7** teacher **9** maharishi

gush 3 jet **4** emit, flow, pour, rave, roll, rush, spew, teem, well **5** burst, flood, flush, issue, spout, spurt, surge **6** babble, effuse, sluice, spring, stream **7** cascade, emanate **10** effervesce, outpouring

gushy 5 gooey, mushy, sappy, soppy **6** sloppy, slushy, sticky **7** cloying, maudlin, mawkish, tearful **8** bathetic, effusive **9** schmaltzy, sickening **10** nauseating, saccharine **11** sentimental

gusset 4 fold, gore, tuck **5** armor, plate, pleat **6** insert **7** bracket

gussy up 5 adorn **6** bedeck **7** furbish **8** decorate, renovate

gust 3 fit **4** blow, gale, rush, wind **5** blast, burst, draft, sally, surge, whiff **6** breeze, flurry, squall **7** bluster, delight, flare-up **8** eruption, outburst, paroxysm

gusto 3 vim **4** brio, élan, zeal, zest **5** ardor, heart, oomph, taste, verve **6** fervor, palate, relish, spirit **7** delight, passion **9** enjoyment **10** enthusiasm

gusty 5 blowy, windy **6** breezy **8** blustery

gut 4 draw, loot, silk **5** belly, bowel, dress, empty, tummy **6** bowels, paunch **7** abdomen, ransack, stomach **8** clean out, entrails, visceral **9** intestine **10** disembowel, eviscerate, exenterate, intestines **11** instinctive

Gutenberg, Johannes *city:* **5** Mainz *inven-*

tion: **11** movable type *partner:* **4** Fust (Johann)

gutless 5 sissy, wimpy, wussy **6** coward, craven, yellow **7** chicken, unmanly **8** cowardly, timorous **9** spineless, spunkless, weak-kneed **11** lily-livered, poltroonish **12** fainthearted **13** pusillanimous

guts 4 grit, sand **5** bowel, heart, moxie, nerve, pluck, spunk, tripe **6** bowels, mettle, spirit **7** bravery, courage, innards, insides, stamina, viscera **8** backbone, entrails, stuffing **9** fortitude, intestine **10** intestines, resolution

gutsy 4 bold **5** brave **6** plucky, spunky **7** valiant **8** intrepid, resolute **10** courageous, determined, mettlesome

gutter 5 chase, ditch, flume, gully **6** furrow, groove, trench, trough **7** channel, conduit

guttersnipe 3 bum **4** hobo, scum, waif **5** gamin **6** beggar, gamine, urchin **7** outcast, vagrant, wastrel **8** derelict, riffraff, vagabond **10** ragamuffin

guttural 4 deep **5** gruff, harsh, husky, rough, velar **6** croaky, hoarse **7** grating, palatal, rasping, throaty **8** gravelly *warning:* **5** growl

guy 3 cat, joe, lad, man **4** buck, chap, dude, male, rope, stud, wire **5** bloke, brace, chain, guide **6** effigy, fellow, steady **7** support

Guyana *capital:* **10** Georgetown *mountain range:* **9** Pacaraima *neighbor:* **6** Brazil **8** Suriname **9** Venezuela *river:* **9** Essequibo

Guys and Dolls *author:* **6** Runyon (Damon) *character:* **3** Sky (Masterson) **6** Nathan (Detroit) **8** Adelaide (Miss) *composer:* **7** Loesser (Frank)

guzzle 4 belt, chug, gulp, slop, soak, swig, toss, tope **5** booze, drink, quaff, slosh, swill **6** imbibe, tank up, tipple **7** consume, swizzle

Gwendolen's husband 7 Locrine

gymnast 7 acrobat, athlete, tumbler *American:* **4** Hamm (Paul) **5** Rigby (Cathy) **6** Conner (Bart), Miller (Shannon), Retton (Mary Lou), Thomas (Kurt) *Romanian:* **8** Comaneci (Nadia) *Russian:* **3** Kim (Nelly) **6** Korbut (Olga) *Ukrainian:* **5** Baiul (Oksana)

gymnastics 5 sport **8** exercise, tumbling **9** athletics **10** acrobatics **12** calisthenics *apparatus:* **3** bar **4** bars, beam, buck, ring, rope **5** horse **11** balance beam *feat:* **3** kip **4** flip **5** vault **6** tumble **9** handstand, headstand **10** handspring, headspring, somersault

gyp 3 con **4** bilk, dupe, fake, hoax, rook, scam, sham **5** bunco, cheat, cozen, cross, fraud, spoof, trick **6** chisel, chouse, con

man, diddle, fleece, humbug, rip-off, rip off
7 cheater, deceive, defraud, diddler, finagle,
sharper, swindle **8** chiseler, hoodwink,
swindler **9** bamboozle, defrauder, imposture, trickster **10** mountebank **11** double-
cross, flimflammer **12** double-dealer
gypsum 7 drywall, mineral **8** selenite **9** ala-
baster, wallboard
gypsy 3 Rom **5** caird, nomad, rover **6** roamer,
Romany, tinker **7** drifter, tzigane **8** Bohemian, vagabond, wanderer *Spanish:* **6** gitano
gyrate 4 coil, purl, roll, spin, turn, wind **5** orbit, twirl, whirl **6** circle, rotate **7** revolve **9**
oscillate, pirouette
gyration 4 coil, turn **5** cycle, orbit, twirl,
wheel, whirl **6** circle **7** circuit, turning **8** rotation **10** revolution
gyre 4 coil, gird, ring, spin, wind **5** cycle, orbit, twirl, whirl **6** circle, girdle, rotate, spiral, vortex **7** circuit, revolve **8** rotation **10**
revolution
gyro 8 sandwich
gyve 4 bond, iron **5** chain **6** fetter **7** shackle **8**
restrain **9** restraint

Habakkuk 7 prophet
habeas corpus 4 writ **5** right **7** mandate
habiliments 4 gear **5** dress **6** attire, outfit **7**
apparel, clothes **8** clothing **9** apparatus,
equipment, trappings
habilitate 5 dress **6** clothe **7** qualify
habit 3 rut **4** bent, form, garb, mode, rote,
wont **5** dress, quirk, style, usage **6** attire,
clothe, custom, groove, manner, outfit **7**
costume, fashion, pattern, routine **8** behavior, clothing, practice, tendency **9** addiction,
mannerism **10** consuetude, convention, proclivity **11** disposition, inclination *riding:* **8**
jodhpurs *wearer:* **3** nun **5** rider
habitable 7 livable
habitant 5 liver **7** denizen, dweller, resider **8**
occupant, resident
habitat 4 home, site, turf **5** abode, haunt,
range **6** locale, milieu **7** terrain **8** domicile **9**
territory **11** environment **12** surroundings
habitation 3 pad **4** digs, flat, home, nest, seat
5 abode, haunt, haven, house, place, roost **7**
housing, lodging, tenancy **8** domicile,
dwelling, lodgment, quarters **9** homestead,
residence, residency **10** settlement
habitual 3 set **5** fixed, usual **6** addict, inborn,
native, normal, steady, wonted **7** chronic,
regular, routine, settled **8** accepted, addicted,
constant, familiar, frequent, inherent **9** automatic, confirmed, continual, customary, ingrained **10** accustomed, inveterate, persistent
11 established, instinctive, involuntary
habitually 8 commonly, normally, wontedly **9**
generally, regularly, routinely **10** ordinarily
11 customarily **12** consistently

habituate 4 bear **5** inure, train **6** addict, adjust, endure, harden, school, season, take
to **7** break in, prepare, support **8** accustom,
tolerate **9** acclimate, condition **11** familiarize
habitué 3 fan **4** buff, user **5** hound, lover **6**
addict, patron **7** denizen, devotee, haunter **8**
adherent, customer **10** enthusiast, frequenter
hacienda 4 farm **5** ranch, villa **6** estate,
quinta **8** estancia **10** plantation
hack 3 cab, cut, hew, try, vex **4** blow, chip,
chop, dull, gash, grub, jade, loaf, mean,
ride, taxi **5** annoy, cabby, cough, grind,
horse, petty, sever, usual **6** cabbie, cliché,
drudge, lackey, mangle, stroke, writer **7** clichéd, machine, plodder, taxicab, trivial **8**
inferior, low-grade, mediocre, tolerate **9**
cabdriver, mercenary, potboiler **10** second-
rate, uninspired
hacker 4 geek, nerd **6** duffer
hackney 3 cab **4** taxi **5** horse **6** jitney **7** taxicab **8** carriage
hackneyed 4 dull, worn **5** banal, corny, stale,
stock, tired, trite **6** cliché, common, old hat,
old saw **7** archaic, clichéd, worn-out **8** everyday, obsolete, outdated, overused, outmoded, timeworn **9** out-of-date **10**
antiquated, overworked, pedestrian
Hadad *father:* **5** Bedad **7** Ishmael *victim:* **6**
Midian
Hades 4 Hell **5** Pluto, Sheol **6** blazes, Tophet
7 Gehenna, inferno **8** Tartarus **9** perdition
10 underworld **11** netherworld *Babylonian:*
5 Aralu *god:* **3** Dis **5** Orcus, Pluto *goddess:*

10 Persephone *guard:* **8** Cerberus *lake:* **7** Avernus *river:* **4** Styx **5** Lethe **7** Acheron, Cocytus **10** Phlegethon

haft 4 grip, hilt, knob **5** helve **6** handle

hag 3 hex **5** biddy, crone, harpy, shrew, vixen, witch **6** beldam, gorgon, virago **8** battle-ax, fishwife, harridan, slattern **9** hobgoblin

Hagar 9 concubine *lover:* **7** Abraham *rival:* **5** Sarah, Sarai *son:* **7** Ishmael

Hagen *father:* **8** Alberich *nephew:* **7** Gunther *slayer:* **9** Kriemhild *victim:* **9** Siegfried

haggard 3 wan **4** hawk, lank, pale, thin, weak, wild, worn **5** ashen, drawn, faded, gaunt, tired **6** fagged, pallid, skinny, wasted **7** angular, pinched, scraggy, scrawny, starved, wearied **8** careworn, fatigued, shrunken, worn-down **9** emaciated, exhausted

Haggard, H. Rider *novel:* **3** She **17** King Solomon's Mines

Haggith *husband:* **5** David *son:* **8** Adonijah

haggle 4 deal **5** argue, cavil, trade **6** barter, bicker, dicker **7** bargain, chaffer, dispute, quibble, stickle, wrangle **8** squabble **10** horse-trade

hagiography subject 5 saint

hail 3 ave **4** ahoy, call **5** greet, salvo, shout, storm **6** accost, call to, holler, praise, salute, shower, volley **7** acclaim, address, applaud, barrage, call out, commend **8** greeting **9** broadside, cannonade, fusillade, originate, recommend **10** salutation **11** acclamation, bombardment

Haile Selassie 9 Ras Tafari *follower:* **11** Rastafarian *nation:* **8** Ethiopia

hair 3 bit, jot **4** hint, mite, wool **5** cilia (plural), pilus, trace **6** cilium, trifle **7** eyelash, whisker **8** fraction, particle *animal:* **3** fur **4** mane, pelt, wool **8** vibrissa **9** vibrissae (plural) *braid:* **5** plait, queue **7** pigtail *clip:* **8** barrette *coarse:* **7** bristle *combining form:* **3** pil **4** pili, pilo **5** trich **6** tricho *covering of:* **3** wig *dressing:* **3** gel **6** mousse **6** pomade **7** pomatum **8** macassar **12** brilliantine *facial:* **5** beard, patch **6** goatee **7** Vandyke **8** mustache, whiskers **9** burnsides, handlebar, moustache, sideburns, soul patch **11** muttonchops *fine:* **6** lanugo *fringe:* **5** bangs *head of:* **9** chevelure *knot:* **3** bun *lock of:* **4** curl **5** tress **7** cowlick *loose roll:* **4** pouf *matted:* **6** dreads **10** dreadlocks *net:* **5** snood *ornament:* **7** topknot *preparation:* **3** gel **6** mousse, pomade **12** brilliantine *root:* **6** fibril *set:* **4** perm *stiff:* **4** seta **5** setae (plural) *tangled:* **7** elflock *tuft of:* **5** quiff **7** cowlick, fetlock *unruly:* **3** mop *without:* **4** bald

haircutter 6 barber **7** stylist **8** coiffeur **9** coiffeuse

hairdo 2 DA **3** bob, bun **4** afro, flip, perm, pomp, shag, trim, updo **5** bangs, braid, butch, taper, wedge **6** Caesar, Mohawk, mullet **7** beehive, bowl cut, buzz cut, chignon, crew cut, flattop, pageboy, tonsure **8** brush cut, coiffure, cornrows, ducktail, pigtails, ponytail, razor cut **9** permanent, pompadour **10** dreadlocks

hairdresser see **haircutter**

hair-raising 5 eerie, scary **6** spooky **7** amazing, awesome **8** exciting **9** thrilling **10** terrifying **11** astonishing, fright ening

hairsplitting 7 finicky **8** exacting **9** quibbling **10** nit-picking **12** overcritical **13** hypercritical

hairstyle see **hairdo**

hairy 5 bushy, downy, furry, fuzzy, nappy, risky, rough **6** chancy, fleecy, fluffy, shaggy, tufted, woolly **7** bristly, hirsute, scraggy, unshorn, villous **8** perilous, strigose **9** dangerous, difficult, hazardous, tomentose, whiskered **11** treacherous

Haiti *capital:* **12** Port-au-Prince *island:* **7** Tortuga **10** Hispaniola *language:* **6** Creole, French *leader:* **8** Aristide (Jean-Bertrand), Duvalier (François, Jean-Claude) *location:* **10** West Indies *monetary unit:* **6** gourde *passage:* **8** Windward *peninsula:* **7** Tiburon *river:* **10** Artibonite

hajj 10 Umrah **10** pilgrimage *site:* **4** Mina **5** Mecca **6** Arafat **10** Muzdalifah

hake 4 fish, ling **7** codling, whiting *relative:* **3** cod

halcyon 4 calm **5** happy, lucky, quiet, still **6** golden, hushed, placid, serene **8** affluent, peaceful, tranquil **9** favorable **10** auspicious, felicitous, kingfisher, prosperous, untroubled

Halcyone *father:* **6** Aeolus *husband:* **4** Ceyx

hale 3 fit **4** sane, well **5** sound, stout **6** hearty, robust **7** healthy **8** vigorous **9** strapping, wholesome

Hale character 5 Nolan (Philip)

Haley epic 5 Roots

half 6 moiety *prefix:* **4** demi, hemi, semi

half-baked 8 slapdash, slipshod **9** imbecilic, senseless, underdone **11** harebrained, impractical, nonsensical, unrealistic **12** illconceived, shortsighted **13** irresponsible

half-cocked 4 rash **5** brash **8** reckless **9** foolhardy, imprudent, impulsive, misguided, premature **10** incautious, unprepared **11** precipitate

halfhearted 4 weak **5** tepid **6** feeble **8** lukewarm **12** uninterested

half-moon 4 arch **5** curve **6** lunule **8** crescent

halfway 3 mid **6** center, medial, median, middle **7** midmost **10** centermost **11** equidistant **12** intermediate

half-wit 4 dolt, dope, fool **5** dunce, idiot, moron **6** cretin **8** imbecile **9** blockhead, simpleton

half-witted 4 dull, slow **7** moronic **8** backward, imbecile **9** imbecilic **12** feebleminded, simpleminded

hall 4 dorm **5** foyer, lobby **6** lyceum **7** passage **8** corridor **9** dormitory **10** auditorium, passageway *exhibition:* **5** salon *Salvation Army:* **7** citadel

Halley's _____ 5 comet

hallmark 4 logo, seal, sign **5** badge, stamp, trait **6** device, emblem, symbol, virtue **7** feature, imprint, quality **8** logotype **9** attribute **11** distinction

hallow 5 bless, honor **6** anoint, devote, revere **8** dedicate, make holy, sanctify, venerate **10** consecrate

hallowed 4 holy **6** sacred

hallucination 4 trip **5** ghost **6** mirage, vision, wraith **7** fantasy, phantom, specter, spectre **8** delusion, illusion, phantasm **10** apparition **11** fata morgana, ignis fatuus

hallucinogen 3 LSD **9** mescaline **10** psilocybin **11** scopolamine

halo 4 aura, nimb **5** nimbi (plural) **6** corona, nimbus **7** aureole

halogen 6 iodine **7** bromine, element **8** astatine, chlorine, fluorine

halt 3 bar, end **4** lame, limp, quit, stay, stop **5** avast, cease, check, close, hitch, lapse, stall, waver **6** arrest, desist, dither, falter, finish, pull up **7** adjourn, bring up, stagger, suspend **8** conclude, cut short, hesitate, knock off, leave off **9** determine, interrupt, terminate, vacillate **10** standstill **11** discontinue

halter 3 bit **4** hang, rope **5** noose **6** blouse, bridle, hamper **8** restrain, trammels **9** hackamore, headstall, restraint

halvah base 6 sesame

ham 4 hock **5** bacon, emote, thigh **7** buttock, overact **8** overplay, strutter **10** scene-eater **13** exhibitionist

Ham *brother:* **4** Shem **7** Japheth *father:* **4** Noah *son:* **4** Cush, Phut **6** Canaan **7** Mizraim

Haman's adversary 6 Esther

ham-handed 5 inept **6** clumsy, gauche **8** bumbling **9** all thumbs, graceless, inelegant, maladroit **10** blundering, unskillful

Hamilcar *conquest:* **5** Spain *home:* **8** Carthage *son:* **8** Hannibal *surname:* **5** Barca

hamlet 4 dorp **7** village *Irish, Scottish:* **7** clachan

Hamlet *author:* **11** Shakespeare (William) *beloved:* **7** Ophelia *castle:* **8** Elsinore *country:* **7** Denmark *friend:* **7** Horatio *mother:* **8** Gertrude *slayer:* **7** Laertes *uncle:* **8** Claudius *victim:* **7** Laertes **8** Claudius, Polonius

Hamlet, The *author:* **8** Faulkner (William) *family:* **6** Snopes

hammer 4 drub, maul, peen **5** forge, gavel, pound **6** batter, mallet, pummel, sledge **7** malleus **8** lambaste *end:* **4** peen *type:* **3** air **4** claw, maul **6** sledge **8** ball-peen **9** pneumatic

hammerhead 4 dolt, dope, fool **5** dunce, idiot, shark **8** clodpoll, numskull **9** numbskull **10** thickskull

hamper 3 bin, tie **4** balk, curb, snag **5** block, check, cramp, crimp, leash, limit **6** baffle, basket, fetter, hinder, hobble, hold up, impede, retard, stymie, thwart **7** inhibit, manacle, pannier, prevent, trammel **8** encumber, handicap, obstacle, obstruct, restrain, restrict, slow down **9** frustrate

hamstring 4 lame **6** muscle, tendon **7** cripple, disable **10** immobilize **12** incapacitate

Hamutal *father:* **8** Jeremiah *husband:* **6** Josiah *son:* **8** Jehoahaz, Zedekiah

hand 3 aid, paw **4** fist, mitt, pass **5** manus **6** script, worker **7** deliver, dish out, laborer, workman **8** employee, transfer **10** assistance, penmanship **11** calligraphy, chirography *clenched:* **4** fist *combining form:* **4** chir **5** chiro *counting zero:* **8** baccarat *covering:* **5** glove **6** mitten *down:* **8** bequeath *gesture:* **5** mudra *on hip:* **6** akimbo *part:* **4** palm **5** thumb **6** finger *poker:* **5** flush **8** straight **9** full house *protector:* **5** glove **7** gantlet **8** gauntlet

handbag 4 grip **5** purse **6** clutch **8** reticule, suitcase **10** pocketbook

handbill 5 flier, flyer **6** poster **7** affiche, leaflet, placard **8** circular

handbook 5 guide **6** manual **8** Baedeker **9** vade mecum **10** compendium **11** enchiridion *religious:* **9** catechism

handcuff 6 fetter **7** manacle, shackle *British:* **7** darbies (plural)

hand down 4 will **6** bestow, pass on **7** deliver **8** bequeath, transmit

Handel, George Frideric *aria:* **5** Largo *birthplace:* **5** Halle **7** Germany *opera:* **4** Nero **5** Serse **6** Admeto, Alcina, Almira, Ottone, Xerxes **7** Arminio, Orlando, Rinaldo, Rodrigo **8** Berenice **9** Agrippina, Ariodante **12** Giulio Cesare, Julius Caesar *oratorio:* **4** Saul **6** Esther, Joshua, Samson, Semele **7** Athalia, Deborah, Jephtha, Messiah, Solomon **8** Theodora

handicap 4 edge, load, odds **6** burden, hamper, hinder, impede **8** drawback, encumber, restrict **9** advantage, allowance, detriment, head start, hindrance **10** disability, limitation **11** encumbrance **12** disadvantage

handicraft 5 skill **8** artefact, artifact

hand in 6 submit, tender **7** deliver, present

handkerchief 5 hanky **6** hankie **7** bandana **8** bandanna, mouchoir **9** accessory

handle 3 paw, use **4** ansa, feel, grip, haft, hilt, knob, name, test **5** crank, see to, touch, trade, treat, wield **6** manage **7** control, moniker, operate **8** deal with, doorknob, exercise, maneuver, nickname **10** manipulate *scythe:* **5** snath **6** snathe

handling 4 care **6** charge **9** packaging, treatment *partner:* **8** shipping

hand out 4 give, mete **6** bestow, donate **7** deliver, present, provide **8** disburse, dispense, give away **10** administer, distribute

hand over 4 cede, feed, give **5** leave, yield **6** commit, donate, fork up, give up, supply **7** commend, confide, consign, deliver, entrust, present **8** dispense, give back, relegate, transfer **9** deliver up, surrender **10** relinquish

handrail 8 banister

handsome 4 buff, cute, fair **5** hunky, noble **6** comely **7** dashing **10** attractive **11** good-looking

handspring 6 tumble *lateral:* **9** cartwheel

handwriting 6 script **8** longhand **10** autography, manuscript, penmanship **11** calligraphy, chirography, copperplate *bad:* **10** cacography *study of:* **10** graphology

handy 4 able, deft, near, yare **5** adept, close, utile **6** adroit, clever, nearby, nimble, useful **7** close-by, skilled **8** adjacent, skillful **9** adaptable, available, dexterous **10** accessible, convenient, proficient **11** practicable, within reach

handyman 6 helper **7** go-to guy **8** factotum

hang 3 jut, sag **4** hook, idle, loll **5** cling, drape, droop, float, hoist, knack, lynch, sling, swing **6** dangle, depend **7** suspend *back:* **3** lag **4** drag, poke **5** trail **6** dawdle, schlep **7** schlepp **8** straggle *loosely:* **3** sag **6** dangle

hang around 4 stay, wait **5** abide, dally, tarry **6** dawdle, linger, loiter **7** goof off **8** frequent

hangdog 3 sad **4** blue, glum **5** cowed **6** guilty **7** abashed, ashamed, pitiful, unhappy **8** dejected, sheepish **9** chagrined, depressed **11** embarrassed

hanger-on 5 leech **6** sponge, sucker **7** sponger **8** barnacle, follower, parasite **9** sycophant **10** freeloader **11** bloodsucker

hanging 5 arras, slope **7** curtain, drapery, pendant, pendent **8** covering, tapestry **9** declivity, execution, pendulous, suspended

Hanging Gardens site 7 Babylon

hang on 4 grip **5** grasp **6** clutch, endure, remain **7** persist, survive **8** continue, hold fast **9** persevere

hang out 4 idle, loaf **5** chill, dally, relax **6** loiter, lounge **7** goof off

hangout 4 haunt, joint **6** resort **7** purlieu, retreat **10** rendezvous **12** watering hole

hang up 4 mire, snag **5** delay **6** detain, impede, retard **7** bog down, set back, suspend **8** slow down

hang-up 5 block **7** dilemma, problem **9** obsession **10** difficulty, inhibition

hank 4 clip, coil, loop, ring **6** bundle

hanker 3 yen **4** ache, itch, long, lust, want, wish **5** covet, crave, yearn **6** desire, hunger, thirst

hankering 3 yen **4** ache, itch, lust, urge **5** ardor **6** desire, hunger, pining, thirst **7** craving, longing, passion **8** appetite, yearning

hanky-panky 5 fraud, trick **7** chicane **8** mischief, trickery **9** chicanery, dalliance, deception **13** double-dealing, sharp practice

Hannibal *defeat:* **4** Zama *father:* **8** Hamilcar *home:* **8** Carthage *surname:* **5** Barca *vanquisher:* **6** Scipio *victory:* **6** Cannae

Hansa 5 guild **6** league

Hans Brinker author 5 Dodge (Mary Mapes)

Hanseatic League city 6 Bremen, Lübeck, Wismar **7** Cologne, Hamburg, Rostock

Hänsel und Gretel composer 11 Humperdinck (Engelbert)

Hansen's disease 7 leprosy

hansom 3 cab **5** coach **8** carriage

haole 5 white **9** Caucasian

haphazard 6 casual, chance, random **7** aimless **8** at random, careless, slipshod **9** desultory, hit-or-miss, irregular, unplanned **10** accidental, willy-nilly **11** unorganized **12** unsystematic **13** helter-skelter

hapless 4 poor **6** woeful **7** unhappy, unlucky **8** ill-fated, wretched **9** miserable **10** ill-starred **11** star-crossed, unfortunate

happen 4 pass **5** occur **6** befall, betide **7** develop, fall out, turn out **8** bechance **9** transpire *again:* **5** recur *together:* **6** concur **8** coincide

happening 3 new **5** event, scene, thing **7** episode **8** incident, occasion **9** adventure **10** experience, occurrence, phenomenon **11** fashionable **12** circumstance

happen on 4 find **8** bump into, discover

happenstance 5 event **6** chance **8** incident,

occasion 9 condition, situation 11 coincidence

happiness 3 joy 4 glee 5 bliss, cheer, mirth 6 gaiety 7 aptness, content, delight, elation, jollity 8 felicity, gladness, pleasure 9 enjoyment, well-being 11 contentment 12 satisfaction

happy 4 glad 5 jolly, lucky, merry 6 joyful, joyous, upbeat 7 blessed, content, pleased 8 friendly, jubilant 9 contented, favorable, satisfied 12 enthusiastic, lighthearted

Happy Days *character:* 5 Chuck 6 Chachi, Fonzie, Howard, Joanie, Marion, Potsie, Richie *family:* 10 Cunningham *site:* 9 Milwaukee *star:* 4 Baio (Scott), Ross (Marion) 5 Moran (Erin) 6 Bosley (Tom), Howard (Ron) 7 Winkler (Henry) 8 O'Herlihy (Gavan), Williams (Anson)

happy-go-lucky 4 easy 6 blithe, breezy, casual 8 carefree, careless, cheerful, heedless, laid-back, reckless 9 easygoing, unworried 10 insouciant, nonchalant 11 unconcerned 12 devil-may-care, light-hearted

hara-kiri 7 seppuku, suicide 8 felo-de-se

Haran *brother:* 7 Abraham *daughter:* 5 Iscah 6 Milcah *father:* 5 Terah 6 Shimei *son:* 3 Lot

harangue 4 rant, rave 5 orate, spiel 6 exhort, hassle, tirade 7 declaim, lecture, oration 8 bloviate, diatribe, jeremiad 9 discourse, philippic 11 declamation, exhortation

harass 3 irk, vex 4 bait, raid, ride 5 annoy, beset, bully, chivy, harry, hound, tease, worry 6 badger, chivvy, hassle, heckle, hector, pester, plague, stress 7 bedevil, exhaust, fatigue, torment, trouble 8 bullyrag, distress 9 beleaguer, persecute

harbinger 4 omen, sign 5 augur 6 augury, herald 7 apostle, portent 9 messenger, precursor 10 forerunner, indication

harbor 3 bay 4 cove, port 5 haven, inlet, lodge, put up 6 billet, refuge, shield, take in 7 nurture, protect, seaport, shelter 9 anchorage, safeguard, sanctuary *Hawaii:* 5 Pearl

hard 4 firm, iron 5 cruel, harsh, solid, tough 6 brutal, knotty, packed, rugged, tiring, trying 7 arduous, callous, onerous 8 absolute, concrete, exacting, granitic, grinding, indurate, pitiless, rigorous 9 demanding, difficult, fatiguing, intensely, intensive, laborious, unfeeling 10 adamantine, exhausting, spirituous, thoroughly, vigorously 11 complicated, intensively, intractable, troublesome, unrelenting, unremitting 12 backbreaking *cover:* 5 crust *to please:* 7 finicky

hard-boiled 4 grim 5 rough, stoic, tough 6 coarse 7 callous 8 seasoned 9 impassive,

pragmatic, unfeeling 11 insensitive, unemotional 12 stonyhearted, thick-skinned 13 unsympathetic

harden 3 dry, set 5 enure, inure, steel 6 anneal, freeze, ossify, season, temper 7 calcify, compact, congeal, densify, lithify, petrify, stiffen, toughen 8 solidify 9 acclimate, fossilize, habituate 10 strengthen

hardfisted 4 mean 5 close, tight 6 stingy, strict 11 penny-pinching

hardheaded 5 sober, tough 6 mulish, shrewd 7 willful 8 obdurate, perverse, stubborn 9 obstinate, practical, pragmatic, realistic 10 determined 11 down-to-earth, intractable

hardhearted 4 cold 5 stony 8 pitiless, uncaring 9 merciless, unfeeling

hard-hitting 6 strong 8 emphatic, forceful, powerful 9 effective

hardihood 3 pep 4 gall, grit, guts 5 cheek, moxie, nerve, pluck, vigor 6 daring 7 courage 8 audacity, boldness, temerity 9 assurance, brashness, cockiness, fortitude, impudence, insolence 10 brazenness, robustness

hard-line 4 firm 5 fixed, rigid, tough 8 obdurate 9 obstinate, unbending 10 inflexible, unyielding 11 stiff-necked 12 intransigent

hardness 5 rigor 7 density 8 rigidity, severity 10 difficulty, resistance

hardscrabble 6 barren 8 marginal 9 infertile, unbearing, unfertile 12 impoverished, unproductive

hardship 4 need, toil 5 rigor, trial 6 burden 7 travail 8 asperity, distress, drudgery 9 adversity, privation, suffering 10 affliction, difficulty, discomfort, misfortune 11 tribulation

Hard Times *author* 7 Dickens (Charles)

hard up 4 poor 5 broke, needy 6 bad off 8 beggared, bankrupt, deprived, indigent, strapped 9 desperate, destitute, penniless 10 down-and-out 11 necessitous 12 impoverished

hardy 4 bold, hale 5 brave, tough 6 daring, robust, rugged, strong 7 healthy 8 intrepid, resolute 9 audacious

Hardy, Thomas *character:* 3 Sue (Bridehead) 4 Alec (D'Urberville), Clym (Yeobright), Jude (Fawley), Tess (Durbeyfield) 5 Angel (Clare) 7 Gabriel (Oak) 8 Arabella (Donn), Eustacia (Vye), Henchard (Michael) 9 Bathsheba (Everdene) *novel:* 11 Woodlanders (The) 14 Jude the Obscure 17 Return of the Native (The) 19 Mayor of Casterbridge (The) 21 Tess of the D'Urbervilles 22 Far from the Madding Crowd *setting:* 6 Wessex

Hardy Boys *author:* 5 Dixon (Franklin W.) 9

McFarlane (Leslie) *character:* 3 Joe 4 Biff (Hooper), Chet (Morton), Iole 5 Frank, Laura 6 Callie, Fenton 12 Aunt Gertrude *city:* 7 Bayport *jalopy:* 5 Queen *motorboat:* 6 Napoli, Sleuth

hare 5 lapin 6 rabbit *female:* 3 doe *genus:* 5 Lepus *male:* 4 buck *tail:* 4 scut *young:* 7 leveret

harebrained 5 crazy, loony, silly, wacky 6 absurd, insane, stupid 7 asinine, foolish 9 frivolous 10 ridiculous 12 preposterous

harem 5 serai 6 zenana 8 seraglio *attendant:* 6 eunuch *concubine:* 9 odalisque

haricot 3 pod 4 bean 10 kidney bean

hark 4 hear, heed, mind, note 6 attend, listen, notice

harlequin 5 clown, joker 6 jester, mottle 7 buffoon 9 prankster

Harlequin *beloved:* 9 Columbine *rival:* 7 Pierrot

harm 3 mar 4 hurt, maim, ruin 5 abuse, spoil, wound, wrong 6 damage, ill-use, impair, injure, injury, misuse, molest 7 tarnish 8 illtreat, maltreat, mischief, mistreat 9 undermine 10 disservice, misfortune

harmful 3 bad 4 evil 5 risky, toxic 6 malign, unsafe 7 noisome, noxious 8 damaging 9 dangerous, hazardous, injurious, malignant, unhealthy 10 pernicious 11 deleterious, detrimental, unhealthful

harmless 4 safe 6 benign 8 innocent, nontoxic 9 innocuous 11 inoffensive

Harmonia *daughter:* 3 Ino 5 Agave 6 Semele 7 Autonoë *father:* 4 Ares, Mars *husband:* 6 Cadmus *mother:* 5 Venus 9 Aphrodite *son:* 9 Polydorus

harmonious 5 sweet 7 chiming, chordal, musical, pacific 8 blending, friendly, in accord, peaceful, pleasing 9 agreeable, congenial, congruous, consonant, symphonic 10 compatible, concordant 11 cooperative, symmetrical, sympathetic

harmonize 3 fit 4 jibe, sing 5 agree, blend, match 6 accord, attune 7 arrange, concert, conform 8 coincide, dovetail 9 integrate 10 coordinate, correspond, synthesize 11 orchestrate

harmony 4 sync 5 grace, peace, unity 6 accord 7 balance, concert, concord, oneness, rapport 8 affinity, sonority, symmetry 9 agreement, congruity, polyphony 10 accordance, concinnity, conformity, consonance, proportion 11 concordance, consistency, cooperation *lack of:* 7 discord 10 dissonance *of movement:* 8 eurythmy

harness 4 curb, gear, yoke 5 hitch, leash 6 bridle, tackle 7 utilize 11 domesticate *part:* 3 bit 4 rein 5 girth, trace 6 collar 7 blinder, crupper 9 bellyband, breeching, checkrein 12 breast collar *ring:* 6 terret

harp 4 lyre 9 harmonica *Greek:* 7 cithara, kithara *Japanese:* 4 koto

harpsichord 7 cembalo 8 clavecin

harpsichordist *American:* 6 Fuller (Albert, David), Kipnis (Igor), Newman (Anthony) 7 Marlowe (Sylvia), Pinkham (Daniel), Valenti (Fernando) 11 Kirkpatrick (Ralph) *Dutch:* 9 Leonhardt (Gustav) *English:* 7 Malcolm (George), Pinnock (Trevor) *German:* 7 Richter (Karl) *Italian:* 7 Sgrizzi (Luciano) *Polish:* 9 Landowska (Wanda)

harpy 3 nag 5 leech, scold, shrew, vixen 6 virago 8 fishwife, harridan 9 termagant

Harpy 5 Aello 7 Celaeno, Ocypete *father:* 7 Thaumas *mother:* 7 Electra *sister:* 4 Iris

harridan 3 hag 4 fury 5 biddy, harpy, shrew, vixen, witch 6 dragon, gorgon, ogress, virago 7 hellcat 8 battle-ax, fishwife 9 battle-axe, termagant

harrier 3 dog 4 hawk 6 hector, runner 10 persecutor

Harris, Joel Chandler *character:* 7 Brer Fox 8 Brer Bear 10 Brer Rabbit *narrator:* 10 Uncle Remus

harrow 3 try, vex 4 bait, rack 5 devil, tease 6 badger, heckle, hector, needle, pester, suffer 7 afflict, bedevil, torment, torture, trouble 8 distress, irritate 9 cultivate 10 excruciate

harry 3 dog, irk, vex 4 gnaw, raid, ride, sack 5 annoy, tease, upset, worry 6 attack, badger, harass, hassle, maraud, pester, plague, ravage 7 assault, bedevil, despoil, perturb, pillage, plunder, torment 8 desolate, maltreat 9 beleaguer, depredate

harsh 5 cruel, gruff, rough, stern 6 biting, brutal, coarse, severe, uneven, unkind 7 austere, caustic, grating, jarring, painful, pungent, raucous, stubbly 8 exacting, grinding, jangling, scraping, scratchy, strident, unsmooth 9 dissonant, inclement 10 discordant, irritating, unpleasant

harshness 8 asperity 9 roughness

hart 4 deer, stag 7 red deer *mate:* 4 hind

hartebeest 4 tora 8 antelope *family:* 7 Bovidae

Harte *story* 17 Luck of Roaring Camp (The) 19 Outcasts of Poker Flat (The)

Hartford *college:* 7 Trinity *specialty:* 9 insurance

Hart, Moss *autobiography:* 6 Act One *collaborator:* 7 Kaufman (George S.) *musical:* 13 Lady in the Dark *play:* 15 Once in a Lifetime 18 Man Who Came to Dinner (The) 20 You Can't Take It with You

haruspex 4 seer 5 augur 7 diviner, prophet 8

foreseer 9 predictor **10** forecaster, foreteller, soothsayer

harvest 4 crop, pick, reap **5** amass, cache, glean, hoard, stash, yield **6** garner, gather **7** collect, reaping, store up, vintage **8** ingather, squirrel, stow away **9** garnering, gathering *bug:* **4** mite **7** chigger *fly:* **6** cicada *festival:* **6** Lammas **7** Cerelia **10** Michaelmas **12** Thanksgiving *god, goddess:* **3** Ops **5** Ceres **6** Consus **7** Demeter

harvester 7 gleaner *grain:* **6** binder, header *of grapes:* **8** vintager

Harvey 5 pooka **6** rabbit *author:* **5** Chase (Mary) *character:* **6** Elwood (P. Dowd)

hash 4 chop, mess, stew **5** botch, mince, mix-up **6** jumble, medley, muddle, review **7** clutter, confuse, mélange, mixture **8** consider, shambles **9** patchwork **10** assortment, hodgepodge, miscellany

hash house 4 café **5** diner **6** bistro, eatery **7** beanery, pit stop **10** coffee shop **11** greasy spoon **12** luncheonette

hashish 5 bhang, ganja **6** charas **8** cannabis, narcotic *plant:* **4** hemp

hash out 6 review **7** discuss **8** talk over **9** talk about

hasp 5 catch **6** fasten **8** fastener **9** fastening

hassle 3 row **4** beef, to-do **5** annoy, argue, brawl, fight, run-in **6** bicker, clamor, harass, hubbub, tumult, uproar **7** dispute, problem, quarrel, rhubarb, turmoil, wrangle **8** argument, squabble, struggle **9** commotion **11** altercation, controversy

hassock 4 pouf **7** cushion, kneeler, ottoman **9** footstool

haste 3 hie, run **4** dash, rush **5** hurry, speed **6** barrel, bustle, flurry, hustle **7** beeline, hotfoot **8** celerity, dispatch, rapidity, velocity **9** fleetness, quickness, swiftness **10** speediness **11** hurriedness, impetuosity

hasten 3 fly, hie, run **4** rush, urge **5** hurry, press, speed **6** barrel, hustle, step up, urge on **7** hurry up, quicken, speed up **8** expedite **10** accelerate

hasty 4 fast, rash **5** brisk, eager, fleet, quick, rapid, swift **6** abrupt, rushed, speedy, sudden **7** cursory, hurried, rushing **8** careless, fleeting, headlong, heedless, reckless, slapdash **9** hotheaded, impatient, impetuous, irritable, quickened **10** ill-advised, incautious **11** expeditious, perfunctory, precipitate, precipitous, superficial, thoughtless

hat 5 derby, toque, tuque **6** boater, cloche, fedora, panama, topper **7** bicorne, chapeau, homburg, porkpie, Stetson, tricorn **8** sombrero, tricorne **9** headpiece **11** deerstalker *ancient Greek:* **7** petasos, petasus *brimless:*

7 pillbox *close-fitting:* **4** kufi **5** toque, tuque **6** cloche, turban *felt:* **5** busby, derby **6** bowler, trilby *fur:* **5** busby **6** castor *helmet-like:* **4** topi **5** topee *maker:* **7** modiste **8** milliner *Middle Eastern:* **3** fez *military:* **4** kepi **5** busby, shako **8** bearskin *Muslim:* **3** fez **6** turban **8** tarboosh *Scottish:* **3** tam **9** glengarry **11** tam-o'-shanter *sheepskin:* **6** calpac **7** calpack *soft:* **5** toque, tuque *straw:* **6** boater, panama, sailor **7** bangkok, leghorn, skimmer **8** sombrero *sun:* **5** terai *tall:* **9** stovepipe *waterproof:* **9** sou'wester *woman's:* **4** coif **5** toque, tuque **6** bonnet **7** pillbox

hatch 4 door, plan, plot **5** breed, brood, cover, inlay, spawn **6** cook up, create, design, devise, emerge, invent, make up, work up **7** concoct, dream up, opening, produce, think up **8** contrive, engender, generate, incubate, occasion **9** floodgate, formulate, give birth, give forth, originate, procreate **11** compartment

hatchet 3 axe **8** tomahawk

hatchet man 5 bravo **6** killer **7** torpedo **8** assassin, enforcer, murderer **9** attack dog, cutthroat **10** eliminator

hate 5 abhor, scorn **6** animus, detest, enmity, loathe, malice, rancor **7** despise **8** aversion, execrate, loathing **9** abominate, animosity, antipathy **10** abhorrence, repugnance

hateful 4 evil, foul, mean, vile **5** nasty **6** horrid, malign, odious, scurvy **7** vicious **8** accursed, damnable, infamous **9** abhorrent, execrable, malicious, obnoxious, repellent, repulsive **10** abominable, despicable, detestable, malevolent **11** blasphemous, opprobrious, unspeakable **13** reprehensible

Hatfields vs. _____ 6 McCoys

hatred 5 odium, spite **6** animus, enmity, rancor **7** dislike **8** aversion, loathing **9** animosity, antipathy, hostility, repulsion, revulsion **10** abhorrence, repugnance **11** abomination, detestation, malevolence *of change:* **9** misoneism *of humankind:* **11** misanthropy *of marriage:* **8** misogamy *of men:* **8** misandry *of women:* **8** misogyny

hats 9 millinery

hauberk 5 armor **9** chain mail, habergeon

haughtiness 4 airs **5** pride, scorn **7** conceit, disdain, hauteur **9** arrogance, insolence, pomposity **12** snobbishness

haughty 5 aloof, proud **6** lordly, sniffy **7** distant **8** arrogant, cavalier, scornful, snobbish, superior **9** egotistic **10** disdainful **11** overbearing **12** contemptuous, supercilious

haul 3 lug, tow, tug **4** cart, drag, draw, hump, lift, load, loot, pull, swag, take, tote **5** boost, booty, cargo, hoist, raise, truck **6**

burden, lading, schlep, spoils **7** freight, payload, schlepp *with a tackle:* **5** bowse

haul up 5 hoise, hoist *with a rope:* **5** trice

haunch 3 hip **11** hindquarter

haunches 4 butt, rump **7** hind end, rear end **8** backside, buttocks **9** posterior **12** hindquarters

haunt 4 site **5** spook **6** obsess, prey on **7** habitat, hang out, inhabit, torment, trouble **8** frequent **9** preoccupy **10** hang around, rendezvous, stay around, visit often

haunter 5 ghost **7** denizen, habitué

hautbois 4 oboe

hauteur see **haughtiness**

haut monde 5 elite **6** jet set **7** society, who's who **10** glitterati, upper crust **11** aristocracy, high society **13** carriage trade

have 3 own **4** hold **7** contain, include, possess

haven 4 port, roof **5** house, oases (plural), oasis **6** asylum, harbor, refuge **7** retreat, shelter **9** anchorage, sanctuary

haversack 3 bag **4** pack **8** backpack

havoc 4 loss, ruin, sack **5** chaos, waste **6** mayhem **8** calamity, disorder, ravaging **9** confusion, ruination **11** catastrophe, destruction, devastation, pandemonium

haw 4 left, tree **5** berry, fruit, shrub **8** turn left **10** equivocate

Hawaii *author:* **8** Michener (James A.) *beach:* **7** Waikiki *capital:* **8** Honolulu *city:* **4** Hilo *coast:* **4** Kona *discoverer:* **4** Cook (Capt. James) *island:* **4** Maui, Oahu **5** Kauai, Lanai **6** Niihau **7** Molokai *mountain:* **7** Kilauea **8** Mauna Kea, Mauna Loa *nickname:* **5** Aloha (State) *park:* **9** Haleakala *state bird:* **4** nene *state flower:* **8** hibiscus *state tree:* **5** kukui **9** candlenut

Hawaiian *dance:* **4** hula *feast:* **4** luau *food:* **3** poi *god:* **4** Kane, Lono **5** Wakea **7** Kanaloa *goddess:* **4** Pele *goose:* **4** nene *gooseberry:* **4** poha *grass:* **4** hilo *instrument:* **3** uke **7** ukulele *lava:* **2** aa *neckwear:* **3** lei *nonnative:* **5** haole **8** malihini *resident:* **8** kamaaina *shaman:* **6** kahuna *soup:* **6** saimin *thrush:* **4** omao *tree:* **3** koa

hawk 4 kite, sell, vend **5** buteo **6** falcon, monger, osprey, peddle **7** Cooper's, goshawk, haggard, harrier **8** caracara, huckster, roughleg **9** accipiter, red-tailed, warmonger **10** militarist **11** ferruginous, rough-legged *Hawaiian:* **2** io *male:* **6** tercel **7** tiercel *young:* **4** eyas

hawker 6 coster, monger, seller, vendor **7** packman, peddler **8** pitchman **12** costermonger

hawkeyed 11 keen-sighted **12** sharp-sighted

Hawkeye State 4 Iowa

hawkish 7 martial, warlike **9** combative **10** aggressive **11** belligerent **12** militaristic

_____ **Hawley Tariff 5** Smoot

Hawthorne, Nathaniel *birthplace:* **5** Salem *character:* **6** Hester (Prynne) **8** Clifford (Pyncheon), Hepzibah (Pyncheon), Pyncheon (Judge) **10** Dimmesdale (Rev. Arthur) **13** Chillingworth (Roger) *novel:* **10** Marble Faun (The) **13** Scarlet Letter (The) **21** House of the Seven Gables (The)

hay 3 bed **4** feed **5** grass **6** fodder, reward **7** herbage *crops:* **6** clover **7** alfalfa, timothy

Haydn oratorio 7 Seasons (The) **8** Creation (The)

hay fever 7 allergy **10** pollenosis, pollinosis *cause:* **6** pollen **7** ragweed

haying machine 5 baler

haymaker 3 box **4** blow, sock **5** clout, punch **6** wallop

hayseed see **hick**

haywire 4 amok, awry **5** amuck, crazy, upset **6** faulty **8** confused **10** out of order **12** out of control

hazard 3 bet, try **4** dare, game, luck, risk **5** peril, shoal, wager **6** chance, danger, gamble, menace **7** fortune, imperil, venture **8** accident, endanger, jeopardy, obstacle

hazardous 5 hairy, risky **6** chancy, unsafe **7** unsound **8** perilous **9** dangerous, unhealthy **10** precarious

haze 3 fog **4** film, mist, murk, smog **5** brume, cloud, drive, smoke, vapor **6** harass **7** dimness, obscure **8** dullness, initiate, overcast **9** mistiness, murkiness, vagueness **10** cloudiness

hazel 4 wood **5** birch, shrub **7** filbert

hazy 3 dim **5** faint, filmy, foggy, fuzzy, misty, murky, smoky, vague **6** cloudy, unsure **7** blurred, clouded, obscure, unclear **8** nebulous, vaporous **9** uncertain **10** indefinite, indistinct

head 3 nob, nut, top **4** bean, boss, capo, foam, john, main, mind, pate, poll **5** brain, caput, chief, first, gourd, poise, prime, privy, scalp, skull **6** honcho, leader, master, noggin, noodle, talent, toilet **7** cranium, faculty, latrine, premier, supreme **8** director, foremost, lavatory **9** chieftain, principal **10** promontory *area:* **5** crown **6** temple *back part:* **7** occiput *bone:* **5** skull **7** cranium **8** parietal *combining form:* **6** cranio **7** cephalo *covering:* **3** cap, hat **6** bonnet **8** kerchief *monastery:* **4** dean **5** abbot **8** superior *nunnery:* **6** abbess **8** superior *of hair:* **4** mane **6** fleece **9** chevelure *relating to:* **8** cephalic *shaving of:* **7** tonsure *skin:* **5** scalp *top:* **4** pate **5** crown

headache 4 pain 5 worry 6 bother, megrim 7 problem 8 migraine, nuisance, vexation 9 annoyance 10 irritation

headband 7 bandeau, circlet, coronal *ancient Greek:* 6 taenia 7 taeniae (plural)

headdress 7 topknot *American Indian:* 9 warbonnet *Arab:* 8 kaffiyeh, keffiyeh *bishop's:* 5 miter, mitre *medieval:* 4 barb *Eastern:* 6 turban *nobleman's:* 7 coronet *royal:* 5 crown, tiara 6 diadem *Spanish women's:* 8 mantilla *women's:* 6 bonnet (see also **hat**)

headland 4 cape 5 point 10 promontory

headline 6 banner 7 feature, promote 8 screamer 9 emphasize, publicize, spotlight 10 noteworthy

headlong 4 rash 5 brash, hasty 6 abrupt, daring, rashly, sudden 7 hurried, rushing 8 heedless, reckless 9 foolhardy, impetuous, impulsive 10 heedlessly, recklessly 11 precipitate, precipitous

headmaster 6 leader 9 principal

head off 4 stop 5 avert, block 6 thwart 7 deflect, obviate, prevent, ward off 8 stave off, turn back 9 forestall, intercept

headquarters 3 hub 4 base, seat 6 center

head start 4 edge, jump, lead, odds 5 boost 7 advance, vantage 8 handicap 9 advantage, allowance

headstone 6 marker 8 memorial, monument 11 grave marker

headstrong 6 dogged, mulish, unruly 7 willful 8 contrary, perverse, stubborn 9 obstinate 10 bullheaded, refractory, self-willed 11 intractable, stiff-necked

heads-up 5 alarm, alert 6 signal, tip-off 7 warning 8 high sign 11 resourceful

headway 4 gain 6 growth 7 advance 8 anabasis, progress 11 advancement, improvement

heady 4 rash, rich 5 giddy 6 elated, potent 7 willful 8 exciting 9 impetuous 11 exhilarated, intoxicated 12 intoxicating

heal 3 fix 4 cure, mend 5 sew up, treat 6 cement, remedy, repair 7 patch up, restore 8 make well

healer 6 doctor, shaman

healing 8 curative, remedial, salutary, sanative 9 vulnerary, wholesome 10 salubrious 11 restorative, therapeutic 12 convalescent *goddess of:* 3 Eir

health 7 fitness, welfare 8 haleness, vitality, wellness 9 soundness, well-being, wholeness *club:* 3 gym, spa

healthful 8 curative, hygienic, remedial, salutary 9 favorable, wholesome 10 beneficial, corrective, profitable, salubrious 11 restorative

healthy 3 fit 4 hale, spry, well 5 sound, tonic 6 benign, robust, strong, sturdy 7 chipper 8 blooming, hygienic, positive, salutary, thriving, vigorous 9 wholesome 10 able-bodied, beneficial, prosperous, salubrious 11 flourishing

Heaney work 5 North 9 Field Work 12 Wintering Out *translation:* 7 Beowulf

heap 3 lot 4 cock, fill, gobs, hill, load, lump, mass, much, pack, pile, rick, scad 5 amass, bunch, clump, crate, loads, mound, shock, stack, wreck 6 barrel, charge, gather, jalopy, junker, lumber, oodles 7 clunker, collect, deposit, jillion 8 assemble, mountain, slathers 9 abundance, profusion, stockpile

hear 4 heed, oyez 5 catch, learn 8 listen to, perceive 9 apprehend

hearing 4 oyer, test 5 trial 6 tryout 7 earshot, inquiry 8 audience, audition 9 interview 10 conference, discussion *distance:* 7 earshot

hearken 4 heed, mind, note 6 attend, listen, notice 7 observe

hearsay 4 buzz, news, talk 5 rumor 6 gossip, report 7 account, chatter 9 grapevine 11 scuttlebutt

heart 3 cor, hub 4 core, crux, gist, guts, love, pith, root, seat, soul, zest 5 ardor, bosom, focus, gusto, moxie, pluck, spunk 6 breast, center, kernel, mettle, relish, spirit, ticker 7 courage, resolve 8 feelings, sympathy 9 character, fortitude 10 compassion *chart:* 3 ECG, EKG *combining form:* 6 cardio *contraction:* 7 systole *dilation:* 8 diastole *part:* 5 valve 6 atrium, septum 9 ventricle

heartache 3 rue, woe 4 care, pain, pang 5 grief 6 regret, sorrow 7 anguish, sadness 8 distress 10 affliction

heartbeat 5 flash, jiffy, pulse, throb, trice 6 moment, second 9 pulsation *irregular:* 10 arrhythmia

heartbreak 3 rue, woe 5 agony, grief 6 misery, regret, sorrow 7 anguish, despair, torment, torture 9 suffering 10 desolation 12 wretchedness

heartbreaking 6 bitter, tragic 8 grievous 9 agonizing 10 calamitous, deplorable, lamentable 11 devastating, distressing

heartbroken 7 crushed, grieved 8 mournful, overcome, wretched 9 sorrowful 10 despairing, despondent 12 disconsolate

heartburn 7 pyrosis

hearten 4 buoy, stir 5 cheer, rally, rouse 6 arouse, buck up, buoy up, perk up 7 animate, cheer up, enliven, inspire 8 embolden, energize, inspirit 9 encourage

heartfelt 4 deep, true 6 honest 7 earnest, fervent, genuine, sincere 8 profound 9 unfeigned

hearth 4 home 5 abode 8 domicile, dwelling, fireside 9 fireplace, residence

heartily 6 wholly 9 sincerely, with gusto, zestfully 10 completely, thoroughly

heartless 4 cold, hard 5 cruel 6 unkind 7 callous 8 uncaring 9 unfeeling 10 hard-boiled 11 insensitive, unemotional 13 unsympathetic

Heart of Dixie 7 Alabama

heartsease 5 pansy, viola 6 violet 11 peace of mind, tranquility 12 johnny-jump-up, tranquillity

heart-shaped 7 cordate

heartsick 4 blue, down 8 dejected, desolate, dismayed, downcast 9 depressed 10 despondent, dispirited 11 demoralized 12 disconsolate

heartthrob 4 idol, love 5 flame, honey, sweet 7 beloved, darling, passion 9 dreamboat 10 sweetheart

heart-to-heart 4 open, talk 5 frank 6 candid, honest 7 sincere 8 truthful 12 conversation

hearty 4 hale, warm 5 ample 6 jovial, robust, sailor, strong 7 cordial, healthy, profuse, sincere 8 abundant, vehement, vigorous 9 approving, energetic, exuberant, flavorful, unfeigned 12 enthusiastic, unrestrained

heat 4 cook, rage, warm, zeal 5 ardor, fever 6 fervor, simmer, warmth 7 caloric, inflame, passion, swelter 8 pyrolyze *combining form:* 4 pyro 6 calori, thermo 7 thermia *measuring device:* 11 calorimeter, thermometer *quantity:* 3 BTU

heated 3 hot, mad 5 angry, fiery, irate 6 ardent, fervid, fierce, ireful, raging, steamy 7 boiling, burning, fevered, furious 8 broiling, feverish, scalding, sizzling, vehement, wrathful 9 indignant, scorching 10 passionate 11 acrimonious

heater 3 gun, rod 4 etna 5 stove 6 boiler, pistol 7 furnace, handgun 8 fastball, radiator

heath 4 ling, moor 5 broom, Erica, shrub 7 Calluna 9 crowberry, wasteland

heathen 5 pagan 7 infidel 8 barbaric 11 irreligious, uncivilized

heat-producing 9 calorific

heave 3 lob 4 cast, draw, fire, gasp, haul, heft, huff, hurl, lift, pant, puff, pull, push, toss 5 fling, hoist, labor, pitch, raise, retch, sling, surge, throw, vomit 6 launch

heave-ho 4 boot 6 ouster 8 bum's rush 9 dismissal

heaven 4 Eden, Zion 5 bliss, glory 6 utopia 7 arcadia, ecstasy, elysium, nirvana, rapture 8 empyrean, eternity, paradise 9 firmament, Shangri-la 10 wonderland 11 immortality, kingdom come 12 promised land

heavenly 4 lush 6 divine, sacred 7 blessed 8 beatific, empyreal, empyrean, ethereal 9 ambrosial, celestial, delicious 10 delectable, delightful, enchanting

heavy 3 big, fat 5 beefy, bulky, gross, hefty, obese, stout, thick 6 bad guy, chunky, fleshy, leaden, portly 7 labored, porcine, villain, weighty 8 cumbrous, sluggish, unwieldy 9 corpulent, laborious, lumbering, ponderous, strenuous 10 burdensome, cumbersome, oppressive, overweight

heavy-handed 5 crude, harsh, inept 6 clumsy, gauche, klutzy 7 awkward 8 bumbling, despotic 9 maladroit 10 oppressive 11 domineering, overbearing

heavyhearted 3 sad 4 glum 5 sorry 7 unhappy 8 dejected, downcast, mournful, saddened 9 depressed, miserable, sorrowful 10 despondent, dispirited, melancholy

heavyset 5 beefy, husky, stout, thick 6 chunky, portly, stocky 11 thick-bodied

heavyweight 3 VIP 4 lion 5 boxer, chief 6 big gun, bigwig, honcho, leader 7 big shot, notable 8 big-timer

Hebe *father:* 4 Zeus 7 Jupiter *husband:* 8 Hercules *mother:* 4 Hera, Juno *successor:* 8 Ganymede

hebetude 6 stupor, torpor 7 languor 8 dullness, lethargy 9 lassitude, torpidity 10 drowsiness

hebetudinous 4 dull, logy 5 dopey 6 drowsy, stupid, torpid 8 listless, sluggish 9 lethargic

Hebrew 3 Jew 6 Jewish *coin:* 6 lepton, shekel *festival:* 5 Purim 6 Pesach, Sukkot 7 Hanukah, Sukkoth 8 Chanukah, Lag b'Omer, Passover, Shabuoth 9 Tishah-b'Ab, Yom Kippur 12 Rosh Hashanah, Simchas Torah *God:* 6 Adonai, Elohim, Yahweh 7 Jehovah *judge:* 6 Gideon *lawgiver:* 5 Moses *leader:* 4 Saul 5 Moses 6 Joshua 7 Solomon *letter:* (see at **alphabet**) *lyre:* 6 kinnor *measure:* 4 beka, omer 5 bekah, cubit, ephah *month:* 2 Ab 4 Abib, Adar, Elul, Iyar 5 Nisan, Sivan, Tebet 6 Kislev, Shebat, Tammuz, Tishri 6 Veadar (in leap year) 7 Heshvan *patriarch:* 3 Dan, Gad, Gad 4 Cain, Levi, Seth 5 Asher, David, Isaac, Jacob, Judah 6 Joseph, Lamech, Reuben, Simeon 7 Abraham, Zebulun 8 Benjamin, Issachar, Naphtali *sacred city:* 5 Safad, Safed 6 Hebron 8 Tiberias 9 Jerusalem *tribe:* 3 Dan, Gad 4 Levi 5 Asher, Judah 6 Reuben, Simeon 7 Ephraim, Zebulon 8 Benjamin, Issachar, Manasseh, Naphtali (see also **Jewish**)

Hebrides island 4 Eigg, Rhum, Skye, Uist 5 Lewis 6 Harris

Hecate *father:* **6** Perses *goddess of:* **5** night **10** underworld, witchcraft *mother:* **7** Asteria

hecatomb **7** killing, slaying **8** butchery **9** bloodbath, sacrifice, slaughter

heck **4** darn, drat, geez, gosh, hell, jeez **5** golly **6** shucks

heckle **3** nag **4** bait, faze, gibe, ride **5** annoy, chivy, hound, tease, worry **6** badger, bother, harass, hassle, hector, molest, needle, pester, plague, rattle **7** disrupt, disturb, torment **9** interrupt **10** disconcert

hectic **3** red **6** fervid **7** burning, excited, fevered, flushed **8** confused, exciting, feverish, frenetic, restless **9** turbulent **10** persistent

hector **3** cow, nag **4** bait, ride **5** bully, chivy, hound **6** badger, harass, lean on **7** bedevil, swagger **8** browbeat, bullyrag, domineer **10** intimidate

Hector *brother:* **5** Paris **7** Helenus, Troilus **9** Deiphobus, Polydorus *father:* **5** Priam *mother:* **6** Hecuba *sister:* **6** Creusa **8** Polyxena **9** Cassandra *slayer:* **8** Achilles *victim:* **9** Patroclus *wife:* **10** Andromache

Hecuba *daughter:* **6** Creusa **8** Polyxena **9** Cassandra *father:* **5** Dymas *husband:* **5** Priam *son:* **5** Paris **6** Hector **7** Helenus, Troilus **9** Deiphobus, Polydorus *victim:* **11** Polymnestor

hedge **4** trim **5** avoid, evade, fence, guard, hem in, limit **6** hinder **7** barrier, defense, enclose, evasion, protect **8** boundary, encircle, restrict **9** shrubbery **10** protection

hedgehog **9** porcupine **10** stronghold

hedonist **4** rake **7** epicure, gourmet **8** gourmand, sybarite **9** bon vivant, epicurean, libertine **10** sensualist, voluptuary

heebie-jeebies **5** jumps **6** creeps, nerves, shakes **7** jitters, shivers, willies **11** nervousness

heed **4** care, hark, mark, mind, note, obey **5** watch **6** attend, harken, listen, notice, regard, remark **7** be aware, concern, hearing, hearken, observe, respect **8** consider, interest, listen to **9** attention **10** observance

heedful **5** alert, aware **7** on guard **8** vigilant **9** attentive, observant, observing **10** interested, meticulous, scrupulous **13** conscientious

heedless **9** negligent, oblivious, unmindful **10** unthinking **11** inadvertent, inattentive, unobservant **12** unreflective **13** inconsiderate

heedlessness **7** neglect **9** disregard, unconcern **11** disinterest, inattention, insouciance **12** indifference

hee-haw **4** bray **5** laugh **6** guffaw **10** horse laugh

heel **3** bum, cad, tip **4** cant, hock, lean, list, tilt **5** creep, knave, louse, rogue, skunk, slope **6** rascal, rotter **7** bounder, incline, lowlife, villain **9** scoundrel *bone:* **8** calcanea (plural), calcanei (plural) **9** calcaneum, calcaneus

heft **4** bulk, lift, load **5** hoist, raise, weigh **6** weight **7** heave up **9** heaviness, influence **10** importance

hefty **3** big **5** beefy, burly, bulky, heavy, husky, large, major **6** brawny, mighty, rugged, strong **7** massive, sizable **8** imposing, powerful **9** extensive, good-sized, plentiful, ponderous, strapping **11** substantial

hegira **6** escape, exodus, flight **7** journey **10** emigration, evacuation **11** deliverance

Heidi *author:* **5** Spyri (Johanna) *goatherd:* **5** Peter *setting:* **4** Alps

heifer **4** calf

_____ **Heifetz** **6** Jascha

height **3** top **4** acme, apex, cusp, peak, rise **6** apogee, climax, heyday, summit, vertex, zenith **7** stature **8** altitude, pinnacle **9** elevation, loftiness **10** prominence *combining form:* **4** acro

heighten **3** wax **5** boost, mount, raise **6** beef up, expand, extend **7** amplify, augment, build up, elevate, enhance, enlarge, improve, magnify **8** increase **9** highlight, intensify **10** aggrandize

heinie **3** bum **4** butt, rear, rump, tush **5** fanny **6** bottom **7** hind end, rear end **8** backside

heinous **4** evil **6** odious **7** hateful **8** infamous, shocking **9** abhorrent, atrocious, execrable, monstrous **10** abominable, detestable, outrageous

heinousness **4** evil **6** horror, infamy **8** atrocity, enormity **13** monstrousness

heir **5** scion **7** grantee, heritor, legatee **9** inheritor, successor **11** beneficiary *joint:* **8** parcener **10** coparcener

heist **3** cop, rob **4** lift, loot **5** boost, caper, filch, pinch, steal, swipe, theft **6** holdup, rip off **7** larceny, purloin, robbery **8** burglary **9** strong-arm

Helen of Troy *abductor:* **5** Paris *husband:* **8** Menelaus

Helenus *brother:* **5** Paris **6** Hector **7** Troilus **9** Deiphobus, Polydorus *father:* **5** Priam *mother:* **6** Hecuba *sister:* **6** Creusa **8** Polyxena **9** Cassandra *wife:* **10** Andromache

Hel, Hela *father:* **4** Loki *hall:* **7** Niflhel **8** Niflheim *mother:* **9** Angerboda

helical **6** spiral

helicopter **7** chopper **9** eggbeater **10** whirlybird *armed:* **7** gunship **9** Black Hawk

blade: 5 rotor **manufacturer: 8** Sikorsky (Igor)

Helios 6 Apollo **daughter: 5** Circe **8** Pasiphaë **father: 8** Hyperion **mother: 5** Theia **sister: 3** Eos **6** Aurora, Selene **son: 8** Phaethon

heliotrope 4 herb **5** shrub **6** borage **10** bloodstone

helium symbol 2 He

hell 5 hades, Sheol **6** blazes, Tophet **7** Gehenna, inferno **9** perdition, tarnation **10** blue blazes

hell-bent 6 driven, intent **8** obsessed, resolved **10** determined

Hellen father: 9 Deucalion **mother: 6** Pyrrha **son: 5** Dorus **6** Aeolus, Xuthus

hellhole 3 pit **8** dystopia, snake pit **9** mare's nest

hellion 3 elf, imp **4** puck, punk **5** demon, rogue, scamp **6** rascal **7** gremlin

hellish 6 horrid **7** ghastly, hideous, satanic, stygian **8** damnable, diabolic, dreadful, gruesome, horrible, infernal, terrible **9** appalling, frightful, monstrous, plutonian **10** diabolical

Hellman play 11 Little Foxes (The) **13** Children's Hour (The) **15** Watch on the Rhine

hello 3 hey **4** ciao, hail **5** aloha, howdy **7** hi there, welcome **8** greeting **9** greetings

helm 4 head **5** wheel **7** cockpit **8** controls

helmet 6 casque, sallet, tin hat **7** morrion **8** burgonet, headgear **medieval: 6** sallet **7** basinet **part: 5** nasal **7** ventail **8** aventail **sun: 4** topi **5** topee

helmsman 5 pilot

Heloïse husband: 7 Abelard (Peter) **son: 9** Astrolabe

helot 4 peon, serf **5** slave **6** vassal **7** laborer, peasant, servant

helotry 4 yoke **6** thrall **7** bondage, peonage, serfdom, slavery **9** servitude, thralldom **11** enslavement

help 3 aid **4** abet, back, mend **5** avail, boost, guide, serve **6** assist, relief, remedy, succor **7** advance, benefit, bolster, further, promote, relieve, secours, service, support **8** mitigate, palliate **9** alleviate, meliorate **10** ameliorate, assistance, facilitate **11** cooperation **forward: 7** further **hired: 5** labor

helper 4 aide, ass't **6** deputy, server **7** ancilla, servant **8** employee **9** assistant, associate, attendant, auxiliary **10** apprentice **11** subordinate

helpful 5 of use **6** usable, useful **8** salutary, valuable **9** effective, favorable, practical **10** beneficial, profitable, propitious **11** encouraging **12** advantageous, constructive

helping 4 dose **5** share **7** portion, serving **9** auxiliary

helpless 4 weak **6** feeble, futile, unable **7** forlorn **8** desolate **9** abandoned, dependent **11** unprotected

helter-skelter 6 anyhow **7** anywise, flighty, hastily, turmoil **8** at random, disorder, pellmell, randomly **9** confusion, haphazard, hitor-miss **11** any which way, haphazardly, in confusion, precipitate

helve 4 haft **6** handle

Helvetian 5 Swiss

hem 3 pen, rim **4** brim, edge, gird, ring, seam, shut **5** bound, brink, fence, hedge, skirt, verge **6** border, circle, corral, edging, fringe, immure, margin, stitch **7** close in, enclose, selvage, shorten **8** encircle, surround **9** encompass, perimeter, periphery **turned-back: 4** cuff

he-man 4 hunk, stud **5** macho

Heman father: 4 Joel **grandfather: 6** Samuel

hematite 3 ore **7** mineral **12** black diamond

Hemingway, Ernest work: 9 In Our Time **12** Sun Also Rises (The) **13** Moveable Feast (A) **14** Farewell to Arms (A) **15** Old Man and the Sea (The) **16** To Have and Have Not **18** Islands in the Stream, Snows of Kilimanjaro (The) **19** For Whom the Bell Tolls **sobriquet: 4** Papa

hemipterous insect 3 bug

hemlock 4 drug, herb, tree, wood **6** poison

hemophiliac 7 bleeder

hemp 3 kef, kif **7** hashish **8** cannabis **9** marijuana **fiber: 5** oakum **kind: 4** aloe

hen 5 biddy, layer **broody: 6** sitter **spayed: 8** poularde **young: 6** pullet

hence 4 away, ergo, thus **5** since **6** hereat **9** as a result, from now on, therefore, thereupon **11** accordingly **12** consequently

henceforth 9 from now on, hereafter

henchman 6 cohort, lackey, minion, stooge **7** abettor **8** adherent, disciple, follower, partisan, retainer **9** attendant, supporter **10** accomplice

Henley poem 8 Invictus

henpeck 3 nag **4** carp, fuss **5** annoy **6** badger, carp at, harass, hector **8** domineer **9** find fault

Henry II adversary: 6 Becket (Thomas à) **son: 4** John (Lackland) **7** Richard (Lionheart) **surname: 5** Anjou **11** Plantagenet **wife: 7** Eleanor

Henry IV 11 Bolingbroke **surname: 9** Lancaster **victim: 10** Richard III

Henry VIII archbishop: 7 Cranmer (Thomas) **10** Thomas More **daughter: 9** Elizabeth **son: 6** Edward **surname: 5** Tudor **victim: 4**

Anne (Boleyn) **9** Catherine (Howard) **10** Thomas More *wife:* **4** Anne (Boleyn, of Cleves), Jane (Seymour) **9** Catherine (Howard, of Aragon, Parr)

hepatic 9 liverwort

Hephaestus 6 Vulcan *father:* **4** Zeus **7** Jupiter *mother:* **4** Hera, Juno *wife:* **5** Venus **6** Charis **9** Aphrodite

Hephzibah *husband:* **8** Hezekiah *son:* **8** Manasseh

hepped up 5 eager **7** charged, excited, fervent **8** enthused **12** enthusiastic

Hera 4 Juno *father:* **6** Cronus, Saturn *husband:* **4** Zeus **7** Jupiter *messenger:* **4** Iris *mother:* **4** Rhea

Heracles *beloved:* **4** Iole *brother:* **8** Iphicles *charioteer:* **6** Iolaus *father:* **4** Zeus **7** Jupiter *mother:* **7** Alcmene *son:* **6** Hyllus *victim:* **5** Hydra, Ladon **6** Geryon, Megara, Orthus **10** Nemean lion *wife:* **4** Hebe **6** Megara **8** Deianira

herald 4 hail, tout **5** crier, greet **6** signal **7** courier, declare, portend, precede, presage, trumpet **8** announce, ballyhoo, exponent, outrider, proclaim **9** advertise, harbinger, messenger, precursor, publicize, spokesman **10** forerunner, foreshadow

heraldic *border:* **7** bordure *cross:* **6** fleury, formée, moline, pommée **8** fourchée *term:* **4** aile, bend, fess, orle, pale, semé, vair, vert **5** crest, flank, gules **6** argent, blazon, canton, charge, device, dexter, emblem, impale, manche, sejant, voided, volant **7** chevron, nombril, passant, purpure, rampant, saltire, statant, urinant **8** guardant, sinister, tincture **9** regardant **10** escutcheon

heraldry 6 armory **9** pageantry

herb 3 Iva, oca, pia, udo **4** arum, dill, flax, forb, geum, hemp, leek, mint, nard, sage, wort **5** basil, canna, chive, cumin, tansy, thyme **6** allium, arnica, borage, catnip, endive, eryngo, fat hen, fennel, garlic, hyssop, lovage, orpine, squill, yarrow **7** boneset, caraway, catmint, chervil, chicory, comfrey, episcia, ginseng, milfoil, mullein, oregano, parsley, pinesap, pussley, salsify, sanicle **8** angelica, camomile, capsicum, cardamom, centaury, cilantro, costmary, feverfew, freewort, hepatica, lungwort, mandrake, marjoram, origanum, pokeweed, purslane, rapeseed, selfheal, tarragon, turmeric, euphrasy, valerian, woodruff, wormwood **9** birthwort, bush basil, chamomile, goosefoot, patchouli, spikenard **10** basil thyme, cuckoo pint **12** balm of Gilead *beverage:* **6** tisane *genus:* **4** Arum, Geum *mythical:* **4** moly *poisonous:* **4** atis **7** aconite, dogbane,

hemlock, henbane **8** veratrum **9** hellebore, monkshood

herbicide 6 dioxin, diquat, diuron **7** monuron **8** picloram, simazine **11** Agent Orange

Herculean 4 huge, vast **5** giant **7** arduous, immense, mammoth, titanic **8** colossal, enormous, gigantic, powerful **10** formidable, superhuman

Hercules see **Heracles**

herd 3 mob **4** bevy, lead **5** covey, crowd, drive, drove, flock, swarm **6** gather, throng **9** associate, multitude

herdsman 6 Boötes, cowboy **7** breeder **8** shepherd

here and there 6 passim **7** at times **9** sometimes **11** irregularly

hereditary 6 inborn, inbred, innate, lineal **7** genetic **9** ancestral, inherited **10** congenital **11** traditional, transmitted

heredity 7 lineage **8** ancestry **9** tradition **11** inheritance *unit:* **4** gene

heresy 6 schism **7** dissent, fallacy, impiety **9** defection, deviation, misbelief **10** dissidence, heterodoxy, infidelity, radicalism **11** revisionism, unorthodoxy **13** nonconformism, nonconformity

heretic 7 infidel **8** apostate, defector, recusant, renegade **9** dissenter, dissident **10** iconoclast, schismatic, separatist, unbeliever **11** misbeliever, nonbeliever, revisionist **13** nonconformist

heretical 7 infidel **8** apostate **9** dissident, heterodox, miscreant, sectarian **10** dissenting, schismatic, unorthodox **11** revisionist **12** misbelieving **13** nonconformist

heretofore 6 ere now **7** up to now

heritage 6 legacy **7** bequest **9** patrimony, tradition **10** birthright

Hermes 7 Mercury *attribute:* **7** petasos, petasus **8** caduceus *father:* **4** Zeus **7** Jupiter *mother:* **4** Maia

hermetic 6 arcane, closed, occult, sealed, secret **7** recluse **8** abstruse, airtight, profound, secluded, solitary **9** recondite **10** cloistered, impervious **11** sequestered

Hermia *beloved:* **8** Lysander *father:* **5** Egeus

Hermione *father:* **8** Menelaus *husband:* **7** Orestes, Pyrrhus **11** Neoptolemus *mother:* **5** Helen

hermit 5 loner **6** cookie **7** eremite, recluse **8** solitary **9** anchorite

hermitage 7 retreat **8** cloister, hideaway **9** monastery

hernia 6 breach **7** rupture **10** protrusion *support:* **5** truss *type:* **6** cystic, hiatal **7** femoral **9** umbilical **10** incisional

hero 4 idol, lion **6** knight **7** demigod, paladin

8 champion **11** protagonist *American:* **6** Bunyan (Paul) **8** Superman *Armenian:* **10** Skanderbeg *Babylonian:* **9** Gilgamesh *Celtic-French:* **7** Tristan **8** Tristram *Crusades:* **7** Tancred **8** Tancredi *English:* **6** Arthur **7** Beowulf **9** Robin Hood *French:* **6** Roland **11** Charlemagne *German:* **5** Etzel **8** Arminius **9** Siegfried *Greek:* **4** Ajax **5** Jason **7** Perseus, Ulysses **8** Achilles, Heracles, Hercules, Leonidas, Odysseus **11** Bellerophon *Hebrew:* **5** David **6** Daniel, Samson *Hungarian:* **5** Arpad **7** Hunyadi (János) *Irish:* **9** Cuchulain, Cuchulinn, Cuchullin *Italian:* **7** Orlando *Roman:* **7** Romulus **8** Horatius *Scandinavian:* **6** Sigurd **9** Siegfried *Scottish:* **5** Bruce (Robert) **6** Rob Roy *Spanish:* **3** Cid **5** El Cid *Spartan:* **8** Leonidas *Trojan:* **6** Aeneas, Hector

Herod *daughter:* **6** Salome *father:* **7** Antipas **9** Antipater *kingdom:* **5** Judea **6** Judaea *mother:* **6** Cyprus *son:* **5** Herod (Antipas) **6** Joseph **7** Pheroas **9** Phasaelus

Herodias *daughter:* **6** Salome *father:* **11** Aristobulus *husband:* **5** Herod (Antipas)

heroic 4 bold, epic **5** brave, noble **6** daring **7** drastic, extreme, radical, valiant **8** fearless, intrepid, unafraid, valorous **9** dauntless, Herculean, undaunted **10** courageous

heroin 4 gear, skag, snow **5** horse, smack **8** narcotic **11** diamorphine

heroism 5 valor **6** daring, spirit **7** bravery, courage, prowess **8** boldness, chivalry, nobility, valiance **9** gallantry **11** intrepidity

heron relative 5 egret **7** bittern

Hero's lover 7 Leander

herring 7 sardine **8** brisling, pilchard *measure:* **4** cran *smoked:* **7** bloater

Herse *father:* **7** Cecrops *sister:* **8** Aglauros *son:* **8** Cephalus

Hersey *novel:* **4** Wall (The) **12** Bell for Adano (A) *town:* **5** Adano

Hesione *brother:* **5** Priam *father:* **8** Laomedon *husband:* **7** Telamon *rescuer:* **8** Heracles, Hercules *son:* **6** Teucer

hesitant 4 slow **5** chary, loath, timid **6** afraid, averse, unsure **7** halting, uneager **9** faltering, reluctant, tentative, uncertain, unwilling **10** irresolute **11** disinclined, vacillating

hesitate 4 balk **5** delay, demur, hedge, pause, stall, stick, waver **6** dawdle, dither, falter, waffle **7** stammer, stutter **8** hang back, hold back **9** temporize, vacillate **12** shilly-shally

Hesperides 6 nymphs

Hesperus 5 Venus **11** evening star *father:* **8** Astraeus *mother:* **3** Eos

Hesse novel **6** Demian **10** Siddhartha **11** Steppenwolf **12** Magister Ludi

Hestia 5 Vesta *father:* **6** Cronus, Saturn *mother:* **4** Rhea

heterodox 9 dissident, heretical, sectarian **10** schismatic, unorthodox **13** nonconformist

heterodoxy 6 heresy, schism **7** dissent **9** misbelief **10** dissidence **13** nonconformism, nonconformity

heterogeneous 5 mixed **6** motley, sundry, varied **7** diverse, various **8** assorted **9** disparate **12** conglomerate

het up 5 irate, upset **7** excited **8** agitated

hew 3 axe, cut **4** chop, fell, form **5** shape, stick **6** adhere **7** conform, cut down

hex 4 jinx **5** charm, curse, spell, witch **6** voodoo, whammy **7** bad luck, bewitch, enchant **9** sorceress **11** enchantment, enchantress

hey 4 psst

heyday 4 acme, peak **5** prime **6** height, zenith **9** high point

Hezekiah *father:* **4** Ahaz **7** Neariah *mother:* **3** Abi *son:* **8** Manasseh *wife:* **9** Hephzibah

hiatus 3 gap **5** break, space **6** breach, lacuna **7** interim **8** aperture, downtime, interval **10** suspension **12** interruption **13** discontinuity

Hiawatha *author:* **10** Longfellow (Henry Wadsworth) *craft:* **5** canoe *grandmother:* **7** Nokomis *mother:* **7** Wenonah *tribe:* **6** Ojibwa, Ojibwe **8** Onondaga **7** Ojibway *wife:* **9** Minnehaha

hibernal 6 wintry **8** winterly

Hibernia 4 Eire, Erin **7** Ireland

hick 4 rube **5** yokel **6** rustic **7** bumpkin, hayseed **8** cornball **10** clodhopper, provincial

hidden 5 privy **6** buried, covert, occult, secret, veiled **7** obscure **8** obscured, shrouded, ulterior **9** concealed **11** undisclosed *combining form:* **6** crypto, krypto

hide 3 fur **4** bury, lurk, mask, pelt, skin, veil **5** cache, cloak, cover, inter, shade, stash **6** harbor, lie low, screen, shroud **7** conceal, cover up, leather, obscure, seclude, secrete, shelter **8** ensconce

hideaway see **hideout**

hidebound 8 obdurate **9** parochial **10** inflexible, provincial **11** reactionary, straitlaced **12** conservative, narrow-minded **13** straightlaced

hideous 4 ugly **5** awful, gross, lurid, nasty **6** grisly, horrid **7** ghastly, hateful **8** gruesome, horrible, shocking, terrible **9** appalling, dismaying, frightful, loathsome, monstrous, offensive, repellent, repugnant, repulsive, revolting, sickening **10** disgusting, horrifying

hideout 3 den **4** lair **5** cache, haven **6** covert, refuge **7** retreat, shelter **9** hermitage, safe house, sanctuary

hie 3 run 4 dash, push, trot 5 hurry, scoot 6 hasten, hustle

hierarch 4 boss, head 5 chief 6 honcho, leader, master 7 headman 9 chieftain 10 high priest

hierarchy 5 group, order, ranks 6 ladder, system 7 pyramid 9 food chain, structure 11 bureaucracy 12 pecking order

hieratic 6 formal 8 priestly, stylized 10 priest-like, sacerdotal

high 4 tall 5 drunk, giddy, grand, lofty, noble, tipsy 6 elated, raised, stoned, treble, zonked 7 drugged, keyed up, soaring, supreme 8 abstruse, elevated, eloquent, euphoric, hopped-up, piercing, towering 9 climactic, delirious, prominent, spaced-out 11 extravagant, intoxicated *combining form:* 4 alti

high ____ 3 hat, tea 4 card, five, noon, road, sign, tech, tide, time 5 chair, heels, hopes, jinks 6 priest, roller, school

high-and-mighty 5 bossy, proud 6 lordly 7 haughty 8 arrogant, cavalier, insolent, superior 9 imperious 10 disdainful 11 domineering, overbearing 12 supercilious

highball 3 fly, run 4 dash, rush, whiz 5 hurry, speed 6 barrel, hustle, signal 7 hotfoot 8 cocktail

highboy 5 chest 6 bureau 7 dresser 9 furniture

highbrow 4 snob 7 egghead 8 cerebral, cultured, educated 9 intellect 12 intellectual

high-class 7 elegant 8 five-star, superior 9 exclusive, exquisite, first-rate, patrician 11 fashionable 12 aristocratic 13 sophisticated

highest 3 top 5 chief 6 apical, upmost 7 exalted, supreme, topmost 9 top-drawer, uppermost 10 top-ranking *point:* 4 acme, apex 5 crest 6 summit, zenith 8 pinnacle

highfalutin 5 fancy, windy 6 florid 7 aureate, flowery, fustian, orotund, pompous 8 affected 9 bombastic, grandiose, overblown, rhapsodic 10 oratorical, rhetorical 11 declamatory, pretentious

high-flown 5 showy, tumid, windy 6 turgid 7 aureate, flowery, fustian, orotund, pompous, swollen 8 elevated, inflated, sonorous 9 bombastic, grandiose, overblown 10 flamboyant 11 declamatory, pretentious 12 magniloquent, ostentatious 13 grandiloquent

high-handed 5 bossy 8 arrogant, dogmatic, imperial 9 arbitrary, imperious 10 autocratic, disdainful, imperative, peremptory 11 dictatorial, domineering, magisterial, overbearing

high-hat 4 snub 6 slight, snobby, snooty 7 disdain, haughty 8 arrogant, snobbish 9 conceited, disregard 11 pretentious 12 supercilious

high jinks 3 fun 6 antics 7 fooling, revelry 9 horseplay, rowdiness, whoop-de-do

Highlander 4 Gael, Scot

highlight 4 mark 5 focus 6 accent, stress 7 feature 8 point out 9 emphasize, underline 10 accentuate, focal point

high-minded 5 lofty, moral, noble 7 ethical, upright 8 elevated 10 principled

high-muck-a-muck 3 VIP 5 nabob 6 bigwig 7 big shot, notable

high-pitched 6 shrill 7 excited 8 agitated, feverish, frenetic, piercing

high point 3 top 4 acme, peak 6 apogee, summit, zenith 8 best part, pinnacle

high-powered 6 driven, strong 7 dynamic 8 animated, forceful, vigorous 9 energetic, strenuous 10 aggressive, compelling 12 enterprising

high-pressure 7 intense 8 forceful 9 insistent, stressful 10 aggressive

high roller 7 gambler, spender, wastrel 8 prodigal 10 big spender, profligate, squanderer 11 spendthrift

high sign 3 nod, tip 4 wink 5 alarm 6 signal, tipoff 7 gesture, warning 8 thumbs-up

Highsmith novel 11 Ripley's Game 16 Talented Mr. Ripley (The)

high-sounding 7 fustian, pompous 8 affected, imposing, inflated, puffed-up 9 grandiose, overblown 11 pretentious

high-spirited 4 bold 5 brash, fiery, jolly, merry 6 bubbly, daring, joyful, lively, plucky, spunky 7 excited, gleeful 9 ebullient, energetic, exuberant, vivacious 12 effervescent, lighthearted

high-strung 4 edgy, taut 5 hyper, jumpy, nervy, tense, tight, wired 6 touchy 7 fidgety, jittery, keyed up, nervous, uptight 8 restless 9 excitable, sensitive

hightail it 3 run 4 bolt, dash, flee 5 scoot, scram 6 get out, run off 7 take off 8 clear out 9 skedaddle

highway 4 pike, road 5 track 6 artery 8 corridor, turnpike 10 interstate 12 thoroughfare *German:* 8 autobahn *Italian:* 10 autostrada

highwayman 5 thief 6 bandit, robber 7 brigand

hijack 5 seize, steal 6 abduct, kidnap 8 take over 10 commandeer 11 appropriate

hike 2 up 4 jump, rove, snap, trek, walk 5 boost, raise, tramp, tromp 6 jack up, rise up, travel 7 journey, traipse, upgrade 8 backpack, increase

hilarious 5 funny, merry 7 comical 8 humorous, mirthful 9 laughable, priceless 10 rollicking

hilarity 4 glee **5** cheer, mirth **6** gaiety **7** delight **8** jocosity, laughter **9** merriment **12** cheerfulness

hill 4 bank, brae, bump, cock, dune, heap, knob, pile, rick, rise **5** bluff, butte, knoll, mound, ridge, shock, slope, stack **6** cuesta, height **7** hummock, incline **8** mountain **9** elevation, monadnock *African veld:* **5** kopje **6** koppie *Boston:* **6** Bunker *craggy:* **3** tor *Cuba:* **7** San Juan *D.C.:* **7** Capitol *elongate:* **7** drumlin *level-topped:* **4** mesa **5** butte *of stratified drift:* **4** kame *rounded:* **5** swell *sand:* **4** dune *small:* **5** knoll, kopje, mound **6** koppie *surrounded by ice:* **7** nunatak

hillbilly 4 rube **5** yokel **6** rustic **7** bumpkin, hayseed **10** clodhopper **12** backwoodsman

hillock 4 rise **5** knoll, mound

hillside 5 slope *Scottish:* **4** brae

hilt 4 grip, haft **6** handle **8** handgrip

Himalayan *country:* **5** Nepal **6** Bhutan *creature:* **4** yeti *peak:* **6** Makalu **7** Everest **9** Annapurna **10** Dhaulagiri **11** Nanga Parbat **13** Kangchenjunga

hind 3 doe **4** back, deer, rear **5** after **7** grouper **9** posterior *mate:* **4** hart

hinder 4 balk, curb, mire **5** block, check, delay, deter **6** baffle, burden, fetter, hamper, hold up, impede, retard, thwart **7** inhibit, prevent, shackle, trammel **8** handicap, hold back, obstruct, restrain **9** frustrate, hamstring, interfere, interrupt

hindmost 3 end **4** back, last, rear **5** after, final **6** latter **7** closing **8** farthest, terminal, ultimate **9** posterior **10** concluding

hindquarters 8 haunches

hindrance 3 bar **4** snag **6** hurdle **7** barrier **8** obstacle **9** impedance **10** impediment **11** obstruction

Hindu *age:* **4** yuga *ascetic:* **4** yogi **5** fakir, swami *camel:* **4** oont *caste (varna):* **5** Sudra **6** Vaisya **7** Brahman **9** Kshatriya *class:* **5** caste, varna *community:* **6** ashram *demon:* **4** Rahu **6** Ravana *essence:* **5** atman *force:* **5** karma *garment:* **4** sari *gentleman:* **4** babu *god:* **4** deva, Rama, Siva **5** Shiva **6** Brahma, Vishnu *goddess:* **4** devi *goddess of beauty:* **7** Lakshmi *goddess of destruction:* **4** Kali *goddess of speech:* **4** Vach *god of destruction:* **4** Siva **5** Shiva *god of fire:* **4** Agni *god of love:* **4** Kama *god of the heavens:* **7** Krishna *god of the wind:* **4** Vayu *god of war:* **6** Skanda **10** Karttikeya *god of wisdom:* **6** Ganesa, Ganesh *hell:* **6** Naraka *holy man:* **5** sadhu *honorific:* **3** Sri **5** Swami **6** Pandit *hundred thousand:* **4** lakh *instrument:* **5** sitar, tabla *leader:* **6** Gandhi (Mahatma) *lowest caste:* **5** Sudra *nobleman:* **4**

raja **5** rajah *philosophy:* **7** Vedanta *precept:* **5** sutra *prince:* **4** raja **5** rajah **8** maharaja **9** maharajah *queen:* **4** rani **5** ranee **8** maharani **9** maharanee *salvation:* **7** nirvana *scripture:* **4** Veda **6** Purana **12** Bhagavad Gita *social group:* **5** caste, varna *teacher:* **4** guru **5** swami **9** maharishi *term of respect:* **5** sahib *treatise:* **9** Upanishad *twice-born:* **6** Vaisya **7** Brahman **9** Kshatriya *weaver:* **5** tanti

hinge 4 pawl **5** joint, mount **12** turning point *kind:* **4** butt **5** piano **10** hook-and-eye

hint 3 cue, tip **4** clue, dash, sign, wisp **5** imply, taste, tinge, touch, trace **6** allude, notion, shadow, tipoff **7** inkling, soupçon, suggest **8** allusion, indicate, innuendo, intimate **9** insinuate, scintilla, suspicion **10** indication, intimation, suggestion **11** implication, insinuation

hinterland 4 bush **6** sticks **8** frontier, interior **9** backwater, backwoods, boondocks, upcountry **10** wilderness **11** backcountry

hip 3 hot **4** chic, coxa **5** aware, savvy **6** haunch, trendy, with-it **7** tuned in **11** fashionable *bone:* **5** ilium, pubis **6** pelvis **7** ischium *cattle:* **5** thurl *disorder:* **8** sciatica

hip-hop *star:* **3** DMC, DMX, Nas **4** Dash (Damon), Jay-Z, West (Kanye), Zola **5** Combs (Sean "Diddy"), Dr. Dre, Kelis **6** Eminem, Franti (Michael), Ja Rule, Lil' Kim **7** Ice Cube, LL Cool J, OutKast, Simmons (Russell) **8** Jadakiss, Ludacris **9** Biz Markie, Fifty Cent, Foxy Brown, Snoop Dogg **11** Busta Rhymes, Tupac Shakur *term:* **3** dap, def, dip, dis **4** bima, simp, wack **5** busta, chill, crunk, floss, freak, homey, peeps, props, sherm, stilo, whodi **6** gaffle, hottie, nucker, step to **7** all that, be geese, down low, homeboy, hooptie, puff lye, shizzle, wangsta **9** dukey rope, freestyle, throw bows **10** bling bling, ghetto bird, scrap a lick **12** South Central

hippie 8 bohemian, longhair **11** flower child **13** nonconformist

Hippocratic _____ 4 oath

Hippodamia *father:* **8** Oenomaus *husband:* **6** Pelops **9** Pirithous **10** Peirithous *son:* **6** Atreus **8** Thyestes

Hippolytus *father:* **7** Theseus *mother:* **7** Antiope **9** Hippolyte *stepmother:* **7** Phaedra

hire 3 fee, let, pay **4** rent, wage **5** lease, wages **6** employ, engage, retain, sign on, take on **7** charter, payment, recruit **8** contract **10** employment **11** contract for

hireling 4 hack **6** worker **7** servant **8** employee **9** mercenary

Hirschfeld's daughter 4 Nina

hirsute 5 hairy **6** shaggy, woolly **9** whiskered
Hispania 6 Iberia **9** peninsula *part:* **5** Spain **8** Portugal
Hispaniola country 5 Haiti
hiss 3 boo **4** hoot, jeer **5** decry **6** deride, revile, sizzle, wheeze **7** catcall, whisper, whistle **8** sibilate
historian 8 annalist **10** chronicler *American:* **4** Webb (Charles Richard) **5** Adams (Brooks, Charles Kendall, Hannah, Henry, Herbert Baxter), Beard (Charles, Mary), Foote (Shelby) **6** Brooks (Van Wyck), Catton (Bruce), DeVoto (Bernard), Durant (Ariel, Will), Malone (Dumas), Miller (Perry), Muzzey (David), Nevins (Allen), Sarton (George Alfred), Shirer (William), Sparks (Jared), Turner (Frederick Jackson) **7** Ambrose (Stephen), Morison (Samuel Eliot), Parkman (Francis), Ridpath (John Clark), Tuchman (Barbara), Woodson (Carter G.) **8** Bancroft (George), Boorstin (Daniel), Channing (Edward), Commager (Henry Steele), Prescott (William H.), Robinson (James Harvey), Woodward (C. Vann) **10** McCullough (David) **11** Schlesinger (Arthur) *Arab:* **10** Ibn Khaldun *Danish:* **4** Saxo (Grammaticus) *Dutch:* **8** Huizinga (Johan) *English:* **4** Bede (Venerable), Stow (John), Ward (Adolphus) **5** Acton (Lord), Grote (George), Wells (Herbert George) **6** Camden (William), Gibbon (Edward), Keegan (John), Namier (Lewis Bernstein), Stubbs (William), Taylor (A. J. P.) **7** Hakluyt (Richard), Raleigh (Walter), Toynbee (Arnold), Whewell (William) **8** Geoffrey (of Monmouth), Macaulay (Thomas Babington) **9** Holinshed (Raphael), Trevelyan (George) *French:* **5** Bloch (Marc), Renan (Ernest), Taine (Hippolyte) **6** Guizot (François), Thiers (Louis-Adolphe), Volney (Comte de) **7** Braudel (Ferdinand) **8** Hanotaux (Gabriel), Michelet (Jules) *German:* **5** Ranke (Leopold von) **7** Mommsen (Theodor), Niebuhr (Barthold Georg) **8** Spengler (Oswald) *Greek:* **8** Plutarch, Polybius, Xenophon **9** Dionysius, Herodotus **10** Thucydides *Italian:* **4** Vico (Giovanni) **5** Croce (Benedetto) **9** Salvemini (Gaetano) *Jewish:* **8** Josephus (Flavius) *Roman:* **4** Livy **7** Sallust, Tacitus (Cornelius) **9** Suetonius *Scottish:* **7** Carlyle (Thomas) **9** Robertson (William) *Swiss:* **6** Müller (Johannes von) *Welsh:* **7** Nennius
historical period 3 age, era **5** epoch
history 4 past, saga **5** diary **6** annals, memoir, record **7** account, done for, journal **9** chronicle, narrative, treatment **10** chronology

histrionic 5 showy, stagy **6** staged **8** affected, dramatic **10** artificial, theatrical
hit 3 bop, jab, rap **4** bang, bash, bean, biff, blow, bump, bunt, butt, conk, cuff, ding, lick, slap, slug, sock, swat **5** clout, knock, paste, pound, punch, smack, smash, smite, swipe, whack **6** batter, buffet, chance, larrup, strike, stroke, thwack, wallop **7** clobber, sellout, success **8** bludgeon, lambaste **9** collision, sensation *baseball:* **5** homer, liner **6** double, single, triple **7** home run **9** line drive *topposite:* **4** bomb, flop, miss *golf ball:* **5** shank
hitch 4 jerk, join, halt, hook, knot, lift, limp, snag, yoke **5** delay, thumb, unite **6** attach, couple, fasten, hobble, tether **7** connect, harness **8** make fast, stoppage **10** connection, difficulty, impediment **11** obstruction **12** entanglement
Hitchcock, Alfred film: **4** Rope **5** Birds (The), Topaz **6** Frenzy, Marnie, Psycho **7** Rebecca, Vertigo **8** Lifeboat, Sabotage **9** Notorious, Suspicion **10** Rear Window, Spellbound **12** Lady Vanishes (The) **13** To Catch a Thief **14** Shadow of a Doubt **16** North by Northwest *forte:* **8** suspense
hitchhike 5 thumb
hither 4 here **6** nearer **11** to this place
hitherto 5 as yet, so far **7** earlier, thus far, till now **8** formerly, until now **10** previously
Hitler, Adolf follower: **4** Nazi *title:* **6** Führer **7** Fuehrer *wife:* **5** Braun (Eva)
hit man 5 bravo **6** killer **7** torpedo **8** assassin, enforcer, hired gun, murderer **9** cutthroat
hit-or-miss 6 casual, chance, random **7** aimless, erratic **8** careless **9** desultory, haphazard, irregular, unplanned
hive 6 apiary, colony **7** cluster **9** stockpile
HMS Pinafore composer: **8** Sullivan (Arthur) *librettist:* **7** Gilbert (W. S.)
hoagie 3 sub **4** hero **5** po'boy **7** grinder, torpedo **8** sandwich **9** submarine
hoar 4 rime **5** frost
hoard 4 save **5** amass, cache, lay by, lay up, stash, stock, store, trove **6** supply **7** collect, lay away, nest egg, reserve **8** squirrel, treasure **9** stockpile **10** accumulate, collection, cumulation **11** aggregation **12** accumulation
hoarder 5 miser **7** scrooge
hoarse 5 gruff, husky, raspy, rough, thick **6** croaky **7** grating, rasping, raucous, throaty **8** croaking, gravelly, guttural
hoary 3 old **4** aged **5** stale **6** age-old **7** ancient, antique, graying **8** grizzled, timeworn **9** venerable
hoax 3 con **4** dupe, fake, fool, gull, sham **5** fraud, phony, trick **6** befool, delude, hum-

bug, take in **7** deceive, mislead **8** flimflam, hoodwink, trickery **9** bamboozle, deception, imposture

Hobbit creator 7 Tolkien (J. R. R.)

hobble 4 lame, limp **6** fetter, hamper, hinder, hog-tie, impede **7** cripple, trammel **8** handicap

hobby 6 falcon **7** pastime, pursuit **8** activity, sideline **9** avocation, diversion

hobgoblin *4* Puck **5** bogey **6** sprite **7** bugaboo

hobnob 3 mix **6** mingle **7** consort **9** associate, rub elbows, socialize **10** fraternize **11** get together

hobo 3 bum **5** gypsy, tramp **7** drifter, floater, swagman, vagrant **8** derelict, vagabond

hock 4 debt, pawn **5** ankle **6** prison

hockey 6 shinny *arena:* **4** rink *cup:* **7** Stanley *implement:* **4** puck **5** stick *official:* **7** referee **8** linesman *player:* **3** Orr (Bobby), Roy (Patrick) **4** Bure (Pavel), Fuhr (Grant), Hall (Glenn), Howe (Gordie), Hull (Bobby, Brett), Jagr (Jaromir), wing **5** Bossy (Mike), Bucyk (John), Hasek (Dominik), Kurri (Jari), Maruk (Dennis), Sakic (Joe), Shore (Eddie), Shutt (Steve) **6** center, Clarke (Bobby), Coffey (Paul), Dionne (Marcel), Dryden (Ken), goalie, Harvey (Doug), Juneau (Joe), Kariya (Paul), Leetch (Brian), Mikita (Stan), Morenz (Howie), Parent (Bernie), Plante (Jacques), Potvin (Denis), Recchi (Mark), Savard (Denis), Sundin (Mats) **7** Belfour (Ed), Bourque (Ray), Brodeur (Martin), Chelios (Chris), Fedorov (Sergei), forward, Francis (Ron), Gretzky (Wayne), Lafleur (Guy), Lemieux (Claude, Mario), Lindros (Eric), Messier (Mark), Mogilny (Alexander), Richard (Maurice), Richter (Mike), Sawchuk (Terry), Selanne (Teemu), Stastny (Peter), Yzerman (Steve) **8** Beliveau (Jean), Esposito (Phil, Tony), Forsberg (Peter), Nicholls (Bernie), pointman, Shanahan (Brendan), Trottier (Bryan), Ysebaert (Paul) **9** Hawerchuk (Dale) **10** Carbonneau (Guy), defenseman, goalkeeper *term:* **3** box **4** cage, deke, goal, puck, rink **5** bandy, bench, check, icing, stick **6** charge, crease, shinny **7** face-off, offside **8** blue line **9** back-check, body-check **10** center line, penalty box *variation of:* **9** broomball (see also **National Hockey League**)

hocus-pocus 4 sham **8** artifice, nonsense, trickery **9** conjuring, deception, imposture **10** mumbo jumbo **11** abracadabra, incantation, legerdemain **13** sleight of hand

hod 4 tray **6** trough **7** scuttle **11** coal scuttle

Hoder, Hoth *brother:* **6** Balder, Baldur *slayer:* **4** Vali *victim:* **6** Balder, Baldur

hodgepodge 4 hash, olio **6** jumble, medley **7** mélange, mixture **8** mishmash, mixed bag **9** patchwork, potpourri **10** assortment, miscellany, salmagundi **11** gallimaufry

hoe 4 till, weed **6** tiller, weeder **9** cultivate

hoedown 9 barn dance **11** contra dance, square dance

hog 3 pig, sow **4** boar, suid **5** swine *family:* **6** Suidae *female:* **3** sow **4** gilt *genus:* **3** Sus *red:* **5** duroc *young:* **5** shoat

hogback 5 crest, ridge

hogshead 3 keg, tun **4** butt, cask **6** barrel **9** container

hog-tie 4 bind **6** fetter **7** shackle, trammel

Hogwarts lesson 6 charms, spells **7** Muggles, potions

hogwash 3 rot **4** bosh, bunk, slop **5** bilge, hokum, hooey, swill **6** piffle **7** baloney, garbage, rubbish **8** nonsense, tommyrot **9** moonshine, poppycock **10** applesauce, balderdash, flapdoodle, taradiddle **12** gobbledygook

hog wild 5 crazy **6** crazed, madcap **7** berserk

ho-hum 4 dull **5** bored **6** boring **7** tedious **8** tiresome **10** unexciting **11** indifferent

hoi polloi 3 mob **5** horde **6** masses **8** populace **9** multitude **10** lower class **11** proletariat

hoist 4 lift **5** drink, raise, winch **6** lift up, pick up, take up **7** derrick, elevate **8** windlass

hoity-toity 4 smug **5** dizzy, giddy, silly **7** flighty, pompous **9** conceited, frivolous **11** highfalutin

hokey 4 fake, mock, sham **5** banal, bogus, corny, hammy, phony, stale, stagy, trite **6** ersatz, pseudo **7** clichéd **8** cornball, outdated **9** contrived, hackneyed **12** melodramatic

hokum 4 bosh **5** hooey **7** baloney, hogwash **8** malarkey, nonsense **9** moonshine, poppycock **10** applesauce, balderdash, flapdoodle, taradiddle **11** foolishness **12** gobbledygook

hold 3 own **4** bear, deem, grab, grip, keep **5** carry, clamp, clasp, cling, grasp, gripe, judge, sense, think, value **6** arrest, clench, clinch, clutch, detain, harbor, regard, retain **7** contain, convene, convoke, fermata, grapple, keep out, possess, reserve, support, sustain **8** keep back, maintain, preserve, restrict *close:* **6** cuddle *dear:* **7** cherish *in check:* **7** repress *in common:* **5** share *out:* **4** last **6** endure *together:* **4** bond **5** clamp **6** fasten *wrestling:* **6** nelson **8** headlock, scissors **10** full nelson, half nelson

hold back 4 curb, keep, stop **5** check, delay **6** bridle, detain, impede, retain **7** inhibit, keep out, prevent, refrain, reserve **8** restrain, suppress, withhold **9** constrain

holder 3 cup, pot **4** bowl, cone, vase **5** owner **6** tenant **7** pitcher

hold forth 4 rant **5** orate, speak, spout **7** declaim, expound, lecture **8** harangue, proclaim **9** expatiate **10** dilate upon

hold off 4 stay, wait **5** defer, delay, pause, repel **6** rebuff, resist **7** abstain, adjourn, repulse, suspend **8** hesitate, postpone, prorogue **9** withstand **11** discontinue

holdup 5 heist, theft **7** mugging, robbery

hold up 3 rob **4** halt, lift, stay **5** check, defer, delay, raise **6** hinder, impede, put off, retard **7** support, suspend **8** postpone, prorogue, slow down

hole 3 den, gap, jam, pit **4** cave, flaw, lair, rent, spot, void **5** fault, niche **6** breach, burrow, cavity, cranny, defect, eyelet, lacuna, outlet **7** dilemma, opening, orifice **8** aperture, weakness **9** perforate **10** excavation, interstice **11** perforation, predicament

hole in one 3 ace

holiday 4 Xmas **5** leave **6** May Day **7** Flag Day **8** Labor Day, New Year's, vacation **9** Christmas, Hallowmas, Halloween **10** Father's Day, Mother's Day **11** Memorial Day, Veterans Day **12** All Saints' Day, Groundhog Day, Thanksgiving **13** Presidents' Day, St. Patrick's Day, Valentine's Day *British:* **9** Boxing Day *Canadian:* **11** Dominion Day, Victoria Day *Jewish:* **8** Passover *Vietnamese:* **3** Tet

holiness 5 piety **6** purity **8** devotion, divinity, sanctity **9** beatitude **11** religiosity **12** consecration, spirituality

Holland see **Netherlands**

holler 3 cry **4** call, yell **5** shout **6** bellow, clamor, cry out, outcry **7** call out **8** complain **9** complaint

hollow 3 dip, sag **4** void **5** basin, empty, false **6** cavity, ravine, sunken, vacant **7** concave, echoing, sinkage **8** sinkhole, thorough **9** cavernous, concavity **10** depression, sepulchral *out:* **3** dig, gut **4** mine **5** gouge **8** excavate

holly 4 tree **5** shrub *genus:* **4** Ilex

Hollywood 10 Tinseltown *street:* **4** Vine

holocaust 4 fire **7** inferno **8** genocide **9** sacrifice **10** mass murder **11** destruction **13** conflagration

Holofernes' slayer 6 Judith

holy 6 adored, divine, sacred **7** angelic, blessed, revered, sainted, saintly, sublime **8** hallowed **9** glorified, religious, spiritual, venerated, worshiped **10** reverenced, sacrosanct, sanctified **11** consecrated *combining*

form: **5** hagio, hiero *communion:* **9** Eucharist *oil:* **6** chrism *person:* **5** saint **6** zaddik **7** tzaddik *Spirit:* **9** Paraclete *vessel:* **5** grail **7** chalice **8** ciborium

holy place 6 church, shrine, temple **7** sanctum **9** sanctuary

Holy Roman Emperor 4 Karl, Otto **5** Adolf, Franz, Henry, Louis **6** Albert, Arnulf, Conrad, Joseph, Lothar, Ludwig, Philip, Rudolf, Rupert, Wenzel **7** Charles, Francis, Leopold, Lothair **8** Heinrich **9** Ferdinand, Frederick, Friedrich, Sigismund **10** Maximilian **11** Charlemagne

Holy Thursday 6 Maundy (Thursday) **9** Ascension (Day)

holy war 5 jihad **7** crusade

holy writ 5 Bible **9** Scripture

homage 5 honor **6** praise **7** respect, tribute **9** deference, obeisance, reverence

hombre 3 cat, guy, lad, man **4** buck, chap, dude, gent, stud **6** fellow, honcho **7** comrade

home 3 den **4** digs, lair, land, site **5** abode, haunt, house, range **6** family, hearth **7** country, habitat, housing **8** domicile, dwelling, locality **9** household, residence **10** fatherland, habitation, motherland **12** headquarters *country:* **5** cabin **7** cottage **8** bungalow

homeless 5 stray **6** exiled **7** outcast, vagrant **8** derelict **9** abandoned, displaced, wandering **12** dispossessed

homely 4 cozy **5** plain **6** direct, modest, simple **7** natural **8** familiar, ordinary **11** comfortable, commonplace **12** unattractive **13** unpretentious

Homer epic 5 Iliad **7** Odyssey

homesickness 7 longing **9** nostalgia

homespun 5 plain **6** fabric, folksy, russet, simple **8** ordinary **9** practical **13** unpretentious

Home, Sweet Home *music:* **6** Bishop (Henry) *words:* **5** Payne (John Howard)

homicidal 6 bloody **8** sanguine **9** murdering, murderous **10** sanguinary **11** sanguineous **12** bloodthirsty

homicide 5 blood **6** killer, murder, slayer **7** killing **8** foul play, murderer **9** manslayer **12** manslaughter

homily 6 sermon **7** lecture **9** discourse

homogeneous 7 uniform **10** consistent

Homo sapiens 3 man **7** mankind **8** humanity **9** humankind, human race

homunculus 5 dwarf, pygmy **6** midget, peewee **7** manikin **8** Tom Thumb

honcho 4 boss, head **5** chief, Mr. Big **6** bigwig, leader, master, top gun **7** big shot, foreman, headman **8** hierarch, overseer **9** chieftain, Mister Big

Honduras *capital:* **11** Tegucigalpa *city:* **7** La Ceiba **9** Choluteca **10** El Progreso **12** San Pedro Sula *coast:* **8** Mosquito *discoverer:* **8** Columbus (Christopher) *Indian people:* **4** Maya **5** Mayan *language:* **7** Spanish *monetary unit:* **7** lempira *neighbor:* **9** Guatemala, Nicaragua **10** El Salvador *river:* **4** Coco, Ulúa **5** Aguán **6** Patuca *sea:* **9** Caribbean

hone 4 edge, whet **6** finish, polish, refine, smooth **7** perfect, sharpen **9** whetstone

honest 4 fair, just, open, real, true **5** frank, plain **6** candid **7** genuine, sincere, upright **8** innocent, reliable, truthful **9** objective, reputable, unfeigned, veracious **10** creditable, forthright, legitimate, scrupulous **13** conscientious, unimpeachable

honesty 4 herb **5** honor **6** candor, virtue **7** probity **8** fairness, goodness, justness, veracity **9** integrity, rectitude, sincerity **11** uprightness **12** truthfulness

honey *combining form:* **3** mel **4** meli, mell **5** melli *drink:* **4** mead

honeybee *genus* **4** Apis

honeycomb 3 pit **4** fill, fret **5** cells **6** impair, infest, riddle, weaken **7** subvert **9** perforate

honeydew 5 melon

honeyed 5 sweet **6** golden, liquid, mellow **9** sweetened **10** flattering **11** mellifluous

Honeymooners, The *bus company:* **6** Gotham *character:* **5** Alice (Kramden) **6** Trixie (Norton) **8** Ed Norton **12** Ralph Kramden *lodge:* **7** Raccoon *setting:* **8** Brooklyn **11** Bensonhurst *star:* **6** Carney (Art) **7** Gleason (Jackie), Meadows (Audrey) **8** Randolph (Joyce)

honeysuckle 6 azalea **9** columbine **13** pinxter flower

honk 4 blow, toot **5** blare, blast **7** trumpet

honky-tonk 4 dive **5** joint **7** hangout **9** juke joint, roadhouse **11** barrelhouse

honor 4 fete, laud **5** adorn, asset, award, badge, exalt, glory, kudos, medal **6** credit, esteem, homage, praise, purity, regard, trophy **7** commend, dignify, ennoble, fulfill, glorify, laurels, respect **8** accolade, approval, carry out, chastity, decorate, devotion, good name **9** adulation, deference, integrity, privilege, recognize, reverence **10** admiration, decoration, reputation, veneration **11** distinction, distinguish, recognition **12** commendation

honorable 4 just, true **5** moral, right **6** honest, worthy **7** ethical, upright **8** laudable **9** dignified **10** creditable, scrupulous **11** illustrious **13** conscientious

honorarium 7 payment **8** gratuity **10** recompense **12** compensation **13** consideration

hooch 6 liquor, rotgut **7** bootleg **8** dwelling, home brew **9** firewater, moonshine **10** bathtub gin

hood 4 cowl, thug **5** tough **6** bonnet, helmet **7** capuche **8** covering, gangster, hooligan **10** delinquent

hoodlum 4 punk, thug **5** bully **7** mobster, ruffian **8** criminal, gangster, hooligan **10** delinquent

hoodoo 3 hex **4** jinx, juju, rock **5** curse, haunt, hokum, magic, spell, spook **6** harass, whammy **7** bewitch, evil eye, sorcery, terrify, torment **8** nonsense **9** conjuring **10** black magic, hocus-pocus, mumbo jumbo, witchcraft

hoodwink 3 con **4** bilk, dupe, fool, gull, hoax, rook **5** trick **6** befool **7** deceive, mislead **8** flimflam **9** bamboozle

hooey 3 rot **4** bunk **5** bilge **6** bunkum **7** baloney, eyewash, hogwash **8** claptrap, malarkey, nonsense, tommyrot **10** balderdash

hoof 4 foot, walk **5** troop **6** ungula **7** traipse **8** ambulate *cloven:* **5** cloot *sound:* **4** clop **8** clip-clop

hoofer 6 dancer **7** danseur **8** coryphée, danseuse, showgirl **9** ballerina, tap dancer

hooflike 6 ungual

hook 3 nab, nip **4** gore, hasp **5** catch, curve, hitch, pinch, steal **6** anchor, fasten, pilfer **7** hamulus **8** crotchet *a fish:* **4** gaff, snag *for keys:* **10** chatelaine

hooklike 7 falcate **8** unciform, uncinate *part:* **5** uncus **7** hamulus

hookup 7 circuit, linkage **8** alliance **10** assemblage, connection **11** affiliation, association, combination, conjunction, partnership

hooky 6 truant **7** truancy **8** truantry

hooligan see **hoodlum**

hoop 4 band, ring **6** circle **7** circlet

hoopla 4 bash, fuss, stir, to-do **6** bustle, frolic **7** revelry, shindig, whoopee **8** ballyhoo, wingding **9** commotion, festivity, merriment, promotion

hoops 5 b-ball **10** basketball

hooray 3 rah, yay **5** cheer, huzza **6** huzzah, yippee **7** acclaim, whoopee **10** hallelujah

hoosegow 3 jug, pen **4** brig, cage, coop, jail, keep, stir **5** clink, pokey **6** cooler, lockup, prison **7** slammer **8** bastille, big house **9** calaboose, jailhouse **12** penitentiary

Hoosier State 7 Indiana

hoot 3 bit, boo, jot **4** hiss, iota, jeer, whit **5**

laugh, scrap, shout, whoop **6** assail, deride, heckle **7** catcall, modicum **8** particle

hooter 3 owl **5** owlet

Hoover Dam lake 4 Mead

hop 4 jump, leap, trip, vine **5** bound, dance **6** bounce, spring, wait on **7** rebound **8** jump over

hope 4 goal, wish **5** await, dream, faith, trust **6** aspire, desire, expect **7** count on, longing, promise **8** ambition, optimism, prospect **9** count upon **10** anticipate, aspiration, confidence *loss of:* **7** despair

hopeful 4 rosy **5** eager, sunny **6** bright, cheery, golden, seeker, upbeat **7** assured **8** aspirant, aspiring **9** candidate, confident, expectant, promising **10** auspicious, contestant, optimistic, propitious **11** encouraging **12** advantageous

hopeless 4 glum, lost, vain **6** futile, gloomy, morose **7** forlorn **8** downcast **9** desperate, incurable, insoluble **10** despairing, despondent, impossible **11** ineffectual, irreparable, pessimistic **12** incorrigible, irredeemable, irremediable

hoper 7 truster **8** optimist **9** expectant, Pollyanna

hopped-up 4 high **5** giddy **6** stoned, zonked **7** drugged, excited **9** delirious **12** enthusiastic

hopper 3 box, mix **4** frog, hare, tank, toad **5** bunny, chute **6** rabbit **7** cricket **10** freight car, receptacle

____ **Hopper 5** Grace (Murray), Hedda **6** Edward

hopping 4 busy **5** irate, livid **6** lively **7** furious **9** extremely, violently **10** infuriated

Horae 4 Dike **6** Eirene **7** Eunomia, seasons

Horam *kingdom:* **5** Gezer *slayer:* **6** Joshua

horde 3 mob **4** army **5** crowd, crush, drove, press, swarm **6** throng **9** multitude

horizon 4 goal **5** limit, range, reach, scope, vista **6** extent **7** purview, skyline **8** prospect **11** perspective

horizontal 4 flat **5** level **8** parallel

hormone 4 ACTH **5** kinin **6** estrin **7** estriol, estrone, gastrin, insulin, relaxin **8** autacoid, estrogen, glucagon, kallidin, secretin *female:* **8** estrogen *insect:* **8** ecdysone *pituitary:* **8** oxytocin

horn 4 toot **5** cornu **6** antler, klaxon, shofar **7** trumpet **10** cornucopia, projection *ancient Greek:* **5** rhyta (plural) **6** rhyton *animal:* **6** antler

Hornblower, Horatio *creator:* **8** Forester (C. S.) *ship:* **6** Le Reve **7** Atropos, Hotspur **10** Sutherland

horn in 6 meddle **7** intrude, obtrude **9** insinuate, interfere, interlope, interrupt

hornlike 8 corneous **10** keratinous

hornswoggle 3 con **4** dupe, fool, gull, hoax, hose **5** trick **7** deceive **8** flimflam, hoodwink **9** bamboozle

horrendous 5 awful **7** fearful, ghastly, heinous, hideous **8** alarming, dreadful, gruesome, horrible, horrific, shocking, terrible **9** abhorrent, appalling, execrable, frightful, repugnant, revolting **11** distressing, unspeakable

horrible 4 grim **5** awful, lurid **6** grisly **7** fearful, ghastly, hateful, hellish, hideous **8** dreadful, gruesome, shocking **9** abhorrent, appalling, frightful, loathsome, repellent, repugnant, repulsive, revolting **10** abominable, disgusting, terrifying

horrid 5 nasty **7** noisome **8** shocking **9** loathsome, offensive, repulsive, sickening **10** detestable, disgusting

horrific 5 awful **7** fearful **8** dreadful, shocking, terrible **9** appalling, dismaying, frightful, harrowing

horrified 6 aghast **8** appalled

horrify 5 daunt, shock **6** appall, dismay

horrifying 4 grim **5** awful, lurid **6** grisly **7** ghastly, hideous **8** gruesome, terrible **9** appalling, atrocious

horror 4 fear, hate, pain **5** alarm, dread, panic, shock **6** dismay, fright, hatred, terror **7** disgust **8** aversion, loathing **9** repulsion, revulsion **10** abhorrence, repugnance **11** abomination, detestation, trepidation

hors d'oeuvre 4 whet **5** snack **6** canape, tidbit **7** crudité **9** antipasto, appetizer

horse 3 nag **4** buck **5** bronc, mount, pacer, steed **6** bronco, brumby, equine **7** cavalry, palfrey, sawbuck, trestle, trotter **8** footrope, jackstay, stallion, traveler *Australian-bred:* **5** waler *battle:* **7** charger *breed:* **4** Arab **5** pinto **6** Morgan **7** Arabian, Belgian, Iceland **8** Palomino, Shetland **9** Appaloosa, Percheron **10** Lippizaner **12** standardbred, Thoroughbred *champion:* **7** Barbaro, Man o' War **8** Affirmed, Citation **10** Seabiscuit **11** Seattle Slew, Secretariat, Smarty Jones *collar part:* **4** hame *color:* **3** bay, dun **4** roan **6** grullo, sorrel **8** buckskin, chestnut, palomino *combining form:* **4** hipp **5** hippo *covering:* **8** trapping *draft:* **5** shire **10** Clydesdale *extinct:* **8** eohippus *farm:* **6** dobbin *female:* **4** mare **5** filly *foot part:* **7** pastern *gait:* **4** trot **6** canter, gallop *gear:* **3** bit **4** rein **6** saddle **7** harness **9** checkrein *leg joint:* **7** fetlock *leg part:* **6** gaskin **7** gambrel *male:* **4** colt **8** stallion *mark:* **5** blaze *of the movies:* **4** Fury **6** Flicka, Silver **7** Trigger **8** Champion **11** Black Beauty *race:* **5** Ascot, derby **7** Belmont **9** Preakness *rump:* **7** crupper *small:* **4** pony **6** garron, jennet *spotted:* **5** pinto **7** piebald *talking:* **4** Mr. Ed *tan:* **8** palomino *thoroughbred:* **8** hotblood *tooth:* **4** tush *war:* **8** destrier *wild:* **7** mustang

horsefeathers 3 rot **4** bull, bunk **5** bilge, hokum, hooey, trash **6** bunkum, drivel, piffle **7** baloney, garbage, hogwash, rubbish, twaddle **8** claptrap, flimflam, nonsense, tommyrot **9** poppycock **10** applesauce, balderdash

horseman 5 rider **6** cowboy **7** vaquero **8** cavalier **9** caballero, chevalier **10** equestrian

horsemanship 6 manège **10** equitation

horse opera 5 oater **7** western

horseplay 7 fooling **8** clowning, rowdyism **9** high jinks, rowdiness **10** buffoonery, roughhouse **11** shenanigans **12** roughhousing

horse-racing term 3 bug, cup **4** bolt, calk, gait, oaks, pill, prop, show, tack **5** float, place, purse, silks, washy **6** bobble, closer, exacta, impost, mudder, router, stayer **7** also-ran, blowout, clocker, paddock, spit box **8** breakage, claiming, climbing, dead heat, handicap, hand ride, off track, perfecta, post time, quiniela **9** hot walker **10** allowances, in the money, parimutuel, shadow roll **11** backstretch, daily double, morning line, triple crown **12** morning glory

horseshoer 6 smithy **10** blacksmith

hortative 8 advisory **9** exhorting, homiletic

horticulturist 6 Carver (George Washington) **7** Burbank (Luther)

Horus *brother:* **6** Anubis *father:* **6** Osiris *mother:* **4** Isis *victim:* **3** Set **4** Seth

hose 4 sock, tube, wash **5** cheat, spray, trick, water **6** tights **8** stocking

hoser 6 barfly, boozer **7** redneck

hospice see **hostel**

hospitable 4 kind, open **6** social **7** cordial **8** friendly, generous, gracious **9** convivial, receptive, welcoming **10** gregarious

hospital 6 clinic **7** lazaret **9** infirmary, lazaretto *attendant:* **7** orderly *ship's:* **7** sickbay

Hospitallers' island 5 Malta **6** Rhodes

host 2 MC **4** army **5** array, cloud, crowd, emcee, flock, horde **6** angels, legion, myriad, scores, server **7** compere, present, receive **8** assemble **9** innkeeper, introduce, moderator, multitude, presenter

hostage 4 pawn **5** token **6** pledge, surety **7** captive, earnest **8** guaranty, prisoner, security **9** guarantee

hostel 3 inn **4** stay **5** lodge **6** tavern, travel **7** auberge, lodging **11** caravansary, public house

hostile 4 anti, mean **5** enemy **6** bitter, fierce **7** adverse, opposed, warlike **8** contrary, inimi-

cal, opposite **9** bellicose, combative, resistant, resisting **10** malevolent, pugnacious, unfriendly **11** belligerent, contentious **12** antagonistic **13** argumentative

hostility 3 war **6** animus, enmity, hatred, rancor **7** ill will **8** conflict **9** antipathy **10** aggression, antagonism, opposition, resistance **12** belligerence

hot 3 new **4** fast, heat, sexy **5** angry, close, eager, fiery, lucky, spicy **6** ardent, baking, banned, heated, hectic, on fire, raging, stolen, sultry, torrid, urgent **7** boiling, burning, excited, fevered, illicit, lustful, peppery, popular, pungent, zealous **8** broiling, feverish, in demand, scalding, sizzling, tropical, vehement **9** energized, lecherous, scorching **10** blistering, contraband, passionate, sweltering **11** radioactive

hot air 4 bosh **6** bunkum **7** blather, prattle, twaddle **8** malarkey, nonsense **9** empty talk, poppycock **10** double-talk

hotbed 3 hub **4** core, seat **5** heart **6** center **7** nucleus **10** focal point **11** nerve center

hot-blooded 5 fiery **6** ardent **7** burning, fervent, flaming **9** excitable, impetuous, impulsive **10** passionate **11** impassioned **12** high-spirited

hotchpotch see **hodgepodge**

hot dog 5 frank **6** weenie, wiener, wienie **7** sausage, show-off **11** frankfurter, wienerwurst

hotel 3 inn **5** lodge **6** tavern **7** auberge, hospice, pension **8** motor inn **11** public house **12** lodging house, rooming house **13** boardinghouse *chain:* **5** Hyatt **6** Hilton, Ramada, Westin **7** Days Inn **8** Marriott, Radisson, Sheraton, Stouffer **10** Holiday Inn **11** Best Western, Four Seasons *inferior:* **7** fleabag **9** flophouse

hothead 5 rebel **7** fanatic, inciter, radical **8** agitator **9** demagogue, firebrand **10** incendiary **12** rabble-rouser, troublemaker **13** revolutionary

hotheaded 4 rash **5** brash, fiery, hasty **6** madcap **8** reckless **9** excitable, impetuous, imprudent, impulsive, irritable

hotshot 3 ace **4** star, whiz **5** comer **6** expert, master, wizard **8** virtuoso **10** powerhouse **11** heavyweight

hot-tempered see **quick-tempered**

hot water 3 box, fix, jam **4** bind, hole **6** corner, pickle **7** dilemma, trouble **9** tight spot **11** predicament *in:* **10** up the creek

____ Houdini 5 Harry

hound 3 dog, fan **4** bait, buff, ride **5** chivy **6** badger, basset, beagle, bowwow, canine, harass, hassle, heckle, hector, pester, pursue, Talbot **7** devotee **8** bullyrag **9** dachs-hund, persecute **10** aficionado *Russian:* **6** borzoi

hourglass 5 timer

house 3 cot, hut, ken **4** home, shed **5** abode, board, cabin, dwell, hovel, lodge, put up, shack **6** billet, chalet, harbor, shanty **7** contain, cottage, enclose, mansion, quarter, saltbox, shelter, theater **8** audience, bungalow, domicile, dwelling, quarters **9** residence *clergyman's:* **5** manse **7** rectory **9** parsonage *country:* **5** manor **7** cottage **8** bungalow *dog:* **6** kennel *earth:* **5** adobe *Eskimo:* **5** igloo *mean:* **5** hovel, shack *of prostitution:* **4** crib **6** bagnio **7** brothel **8** bordello *religious:* **5** abbey **6** priory **7** convent, nunnery **9** monastery *rooming:* **5** lodge *Russian:* **5** dacha *small:* **4** camp **5** cabin, shack **6** shanty **7** cottage **8** bungalow *Spanish:* **4** casa

housebreaker 4 yegg **5** thief **7** burglar, prowler **8** picklock

household 4 home **5** folks **6** family, ménage **8** domestic, familiar *gods (Roman):* **5** lares **7** penates

house of worship 6 bethel, chapel, church, mosque, pagoda, shrine, temple **7** chantry, minster, oratory **8** basilica **9** cathedral, sanctuary, synagogue **10** tabernacle **11** conventicle

housing 4 case, room **7** shelter **8** barracks, quarters **9** enclosure

hovel 3 hut, sty **4** dump, shed **5** hutch, shack **6** burrow, pigpen, pigsty, shanty **7** shelter

hover 4 flit, hang, loom **5** dance, drift, float, poise, waver **7** flitter, flutter, suspend **9** fluctuate, hang about

howbeit 3 yet **4** when **5** still, while **6** even if, much as, though **7** whereas **8** after all, although **11** nonetheless **12** nevertheless

however 3 but, yet **4** only **5** still **6** except, though **8** after all **11** nonetheless

howl 3 bay, cry **4** bark, keen, wail, yell, yelp **6** cry out **9** caterwaul

howler 4 flub, gaff, goof **5** boner, fluff, gaffe **6** boo-boo **7** blooper, blunder

huarache 6 sandal

hub 4 axis, core **5** focus, heart, pivot **6** center **8** polestar **10** focal point **11** nerve center *opposite:* **3** rim

hubbub 3 din **4** fuss, stir, to-do **5** babel, furor, hoo-ha, noise **6** clamor, furore, hassle, jangle, pother, racket, rumpus, tumult, uproar **7** turmoil **8** brouhaha, foofaraw **9** commotion, confusion **10** hullabaloo, hurly-burly **11** disturbance, pandemonium

hubris 3 ego **4** gall **5** brass, cheek, nerve,

pride **7** conceit, hauteur, swagger **8** audacity, chutzpah **9** arrogance, cockiness, vainglory **11** braggadocio

hubristic 4 vain **5** cocky, proud **7** haughty **8** arrogant, insolent, superior **11** overbearing, overweening **13** overconfident

Huckleberry Finn *author:* **5** Twain (Mark) **7** Clemens (Samuel) *character:* **3** Jim, Tom (Sawyer) **4** Duke, King *river:* **11** Mississippi

huckster 4 hawk, plug, tout, vend **5** pitch **6** dicker, haggle, hawker, peddle, vendor **7** bargain, chaffer, haggler, packman, peddler, promote **8** pitchman

huddle 4 lump, mass **5** bunch, crowd, group, hunch **6** confab, confer, crouch, curl up, gather, parley, powwow **7** cluster, consult, meeting **8** assemble **10** conference, discussion

Hudson's ship 8 Half Moon

hue 4 cast, tint, tone **5** color, shade, shape, tinge, value **6** aspect, manner **8** coloring, tincture **10** coloration, complexion

huff 3 pet **4** blow, gasp, pant, rile, roil, snap, snit, tiff **5** annoy, grate, heave, peeve, pique, storm **6** nettle, put out **7** bluster, inflate **8** irritate

huffy 5 angry, proud, testy **6** piqued, touchy **7** annoyed, fretful, haughty, peevish, prickly, waspish **8** arrogant, petulant, snappish **9** irritable, irritated, querulous

hug 4 hold **5** clasp, press, prize, value **6** clinch, clutch, cuddle, enfold **7** cherish, embrace, envelop, squeeze **8** hold fast, hold onto **12** congratulate

huge 4 epic, vast, wide **5** bulky, giant, grand, great, jumbo, mondo **6** heroic, mighty, untold **7** immense, mammoth, massive, titanic **8** colossal, enormous, gigantic, whopping **9** extensive, monstrous **10** monumental, prodigious, stupendous, tremendous **11** magnificent, mountainous

hugeness 8 enormity **9** immensity, magnitude

hugger-mugger 4 hash **6** jumble, muddle, secret, tangle **7** clutter, furtive, jumbled, secrecy **8** confused, covertly, disorder, secretly **9** by stealth, confusion, furtively **10** disordered, disorderly, stealthily, undercover **11** clandestine **13** clandestinely

Hugo, Victor *character:* **6** Javert (Inspector) **7** Cosette, Fantine, Valjean (Jean) **9** Esmeralda, Quasimodo *novel:* **13** Les Misérables **20** Hunchback of Notre Dame (The)

Huguenot 10 Protestant *leader:* **5** Condé (Prince de), Rohan (Henri) **6** Mornay (Philippe) **7** Coligny (Gaspard II de)

Huguenots composer 9 Meyerbeer (Giacomo)

hulk 4 body, loom, ship **5** shell, wreck **8** skeleton **9** shipwreck

hulking 4 huge **5** beefy, bulky, burly, husky **7** immense, mammoth, massive **8** colossal, enormous, gigantic, oversize **9** humongous, lumbering, monstrous, ponderous, strapping **11** heavyweight

hull 3 pod **4** bark, body, case, husk, peel, rind, skin **5** chaff, frame, shell, shuck **6** casing **8** covering **11** decorticate

hullabaloo 3 ado, din **4** roar, to-do **5** hoo-ha, noise **6** clamor, hoo-hah, hubbub, jangle, pother, racket, tumult, uproar **8** ballyhoo, foofaraw **9** commotion, hue and cry **11** pandemonium

hum 4 buzz, purr, sing, zing **5** drone **6** murmur **7** vibrate

human 5 being, party **6** mortal, person **7** hominid **8** hominoid **10** individual *race:* **7** mankind

Human Comedy author 6 Balzac (Honoré de) **7** Saroyan (William)

humane 4 kind **6** gentle, kindly, tender **8** merciful **10** altruistic, benevolent, charitable **11** considerate, kindhearted, softhearted, sympathetic, warmhearted **13** compassionate, philanthropic

humanitarian 5 giver **8** generous **10** altruistic, benefactor, beneficent, benevolent, charitable **13** compassionate, philanthropic

humanity 6 people **7** mankind **8** kindness, sympathy **10** compassion, generosity **11** benevolence, Homo sapiens

humble 3 low **4** meek **5** abase, abash, crush, lowly, quiet **6** demean, modest, simple **7** chagrin, deflate, degrade, subdued **8** cast down, disgrace, ordinary **9** compliant, diffident, discomfit, embarrass, humiliate **10** submissive, unassuming **11** acquiescent, deferential **13** insignificant, unpretentious

humbug 3 con, rot **4** fake, fool, hoax, sham **5** faker, fraud, hokum, phony, spoof, trick **6** bunkum, delude, drivel, take in **7** beguile, deceive, mislead **8** flimflam, impostor, malarkey, nonsense, pretense, quackery **9** deception, hypocrite, imposture, pretender, trickster **10** balderdash

humdinger 3 ace, gem, pip **4** lulu **5** beaut, dandy, dilly, doozy, jewel, peach, prize **6** doozie **8** jim-dandy, knockout **11** crackerjack

humdrum 4 blah, dull, flat **6** boring, dreary, stodgy **7** prosaic, tedious **8** monotone, monotony, plodding, unvaried, workaday **10** monotonous, uneventful **13** uninteresting

humid 3 wet **4** damp, dank **5** close, moist, muggy, soggy **6** clammy, sodden, steamy, sticky, stuffy **10** oppressive

humidify 6 dampen **7** moisten

humiliate 5 abase, crush, lower, shame **6** bemean, debase, demean, humble **7** chagrin, degrade, mortify **8** belittle, cast down, disgrace **9** embarrass

humiliation 5 shame **7** chagrin, put-down **8** disgrace, ignominy, reproach **9** abasement, disrepute, indignity **11** degradation **13** embarrassment, mortification

humility 7 modesty, shyness **8** meekness **9** abasement, lowliness **10** diffidence, submission **12** subservience **13** self-abasement

humming 4 busy **5** brisk **6** active, lively **8** bustling, hustling **9** energetic

hummock 4 hump **5** couch, knoll, mound **7** hillock

humongous 4 huge, vast **5** giant, jumbo **7** immense, mammoth, massive, titanic **8** colossal, enormous, gigantic **9** monstrous **10** gargantuan, prodigious, tremendous

humor 3 wit **4** baby, bent, mind, mood, tone, vein, whim **5** fancy, fluid, spoil, yield **6** banter, coddle, comedy, cosset, esprit, joking, levity, nature, pamper, temper **7** caprice, cater to, conceit, gratify, indulge, jesting, kidding **8** crotchet, drollery, jocosity, repartee **9** character, drollness, flippancy, funniness, witticism, wittiness **10** complexion, jocularity, pleasantry **11** disposition, temperament

humorist 3 Ade (George), wag, wit **4** card, Nash (Ogden), Shaw (Henry Wheeler), Ward (Artemus, Edward) **5** Adams (Franklin Pierce), Allen (Fred), Barry (Dave), clown, comic, cutup, droll, Dunne (Finley Peter), joker, Twain (Mark), White (E. B.) **6** Blount (Roy), Browne (Charles Farrar), Diller (Phyllis), gagman, jester, kidder, Martin (Steve), Parker (Dorothy), Rogers (Will), Rourke (P. J.), Runyon (Damon), Thorpe (Thomas Bangs) **7** buffoon, Bombeck (Erma), Burgess (Gelett), Clemens (Samuel Langhorne), gagster, Hubbard (Kin), Keillor (Garrison), Marquis (Don), punster, Sedaris (David), Thurber (James), Trillin (Calvin) **8** Aleichem (Shalom), Benchley (Robert), comedian, funnyman, jokester, Perelman (S. J.), quipster **9** jokesmith, prankster, Wodehouse (P. G.) *Canadian:* **7** Leacock (Stephen)

humorous 5 comic, droll, funny, jokey, merry, witty **6** jocose **7** amusing, comical, jocular, risible, waggish **8** mirthful **9** facetious, laughable, whimsical

hump 3 lug **4** bump, race, tote **5** bulge, carry, hunch, mound, range **6** hustle, schlep **7** hummock, schlepp **8** mountain, obstacle, swelling **9** transport **10** protrusion

humpback 5 whale **8** kyphosis **10** pink salmon

humpbacked 6 convex, curved **7** gibbous

Humperdinck opera 15 Hansel and Gretel

humus 3 mor **4** mull, soil **7** compost **8** material

hunch 4 arch, clod, idea, lump, hump, push **5** chunk, clump, crook, squat, stoop **6** crouch, curl up, huddle, jostle, notion, nugget **7** feeling, inkling **9** intuition

Hunchback of Notre Dame *author:* **4** Hugo (Victor) *character:* **9** Esmeralda, Quasimodo

hundred *combining form:* **5** centi, hecto *dollar bill* **5** C-note

Hungary *capital:* **8** Budapest *city:* **4** Pécs **6** Szeged **7** Miskolc **8** Debrecen *ethnic group:* **6** Magyar *lake:* **7** Balaton *monetary unit:* **6** forint *mountain range:* **10** Carpathian *national hero:* **5** Árpád *neighbor:* **6** Serbia **7** Austria, Croatia, Romania, Ukraine **8** Slovakia, Slovenia *plain:* **11** Great Alföld *river:* **4** Eger **5** Tisza **6** Danube

hunger 3 yen **4** ache, itch, long, lust, need, pine, want **5** crave, greed, yearn **6** desire, hanker, thirst **7** craving, longing

hungry 4 avid, keen, poor **5** eager **6** barren **7** craving, starved, thirsty **8** desirous, famished, ravenous, starving, underfed, yearning **9** hankering, motivated

hunk 3 gob, wad **4** clod, lump, stud **5** chunk, clump, himbo, piece, wedge **6** nugget **7** portion

hunker down 5 dig in, squat **6** crouch **8** settle in

hunky 4 buff **5** burly **6** buffed **8** athletic, muscular **9** strapping, well-built

hunky-dory 4 fine, okay **5** dandy, ducky, nifty, swell **6** peachy **10** peachy keen **12** satisfactory

Hunnish 4 rude, wild **6** savage **7** fearful, uncivil **9** barbarian, barbarous, ferocious **11** uncivilized

hunt 3 dog, run **4** hawk, seek **5** chase, hound, prowl, quest, shoot, snare, stalk, track, trail **6** battue, course, dig out, prey on, pursue, safari, search **7** explore, pursuit, rummage **9** ferret out, search for, search out *birds:* **4** fowl *illegally:* **5** poach

hunter 6 jaeger, nimrod **8** predator *biblical:* **6** Nimrod *cap:* **7** montero *constellation:* **5** Orion *mythological:* **6** Orion **7** Actaeon

hunting 5 chase **6** venery **7** gunning, hawking **8** coursing, falconry **9** predatory **10** preda-

cious *bird:* **6** falcon *call:* **7** recheat *cry:* **6** yoicks **7** tallyho **10** view halloo *dog:* **5** hound **6** basset, beagle, borzoi, saluki, setter, vizsla, vizsla **7** harrier, pointer, spaniel **9** ridgeback, wolfhound **10** bloodhound *expedition:* **6** safari *garb:* **4** camo **10** camouflage *horn:* **5** bugle

huntress 5 Diana **7** Artemis **8** Atalanta

hurdle 3 bar **4** leap, snag **5** bound, clear, vault **6** hamper, spring **7** barrier **8** leap over, obstacle, overcome, overleap, surmount, traverse **9** negotiate **10** difficulty, impediment **11** obstruction

hurl 4 cast, fire **5** chuck, fling, heave, pitch, sling, throw, vomit **6** launch, thrust **8** catapult

hurly-burly 3 din **4** riot, to-do **5** melee **6** clamor, furore, hassle, hubbub, racket, rumpus, tumult, uproar **7** turmoil **8** confused **9** commotion, confusion

hurrah 3 olé, yay **4** fuss, to-do, zeal **5** cheer **6** fervor, rumpus **7** fanfare, ovation **8** approval **9** commotion **10** enthusiasm **11** acclamation

hurricane 7 typhoon

hurried 4 fast, sped **5** hasty, quick, swift **6** abrupt, rushed, sudden **7** cursory, rushing **8** headlong **9** impetuous **11** precipitant, precipitate

hurry 3 fly, hie, jog, run, zip **4** post, prod, push, rush **5** fleet, haste, scoot, speed, whirl, whish, whisk **6** barrel, breeze, bullet, bustle, hasten, hustle, rocket, rustle, step up, tumult **7** beeline, hotfoot, quicken, shake up, skelter, speed up, swiften **8** celerity, dispatch, expedite, highball, make time **9** commotion, make haste, swiftness **10** accelerate, speediness

hurt 3 mar **4** ache, blow, harm, pain **5** smart, wound, wrong **6** damage, grieve, hamper, harmed, impair, injure, injury, in pain, misuse, offend, pained, suffer **7** afflict, anguish, blemish, damaged, wounded **8** aggrieve, distress, mischief, mistreat **9** constrain, detriment, prejudice, resentful, suffering **10** resentment

hurtful 4 mean, sore **6** aching, unkind **7** harmful, painful **8** damaging, wounding **9** injurious **11** deleterious, destructive, detrimental, distressing, prejudicial

hurtle 3 fly **4** race, rush, tear **5** fling, shoot, speed, throw **6** charge, plunge, rocket

husband 3 man **4** mate, save **6** manage, mister, spouse **7** consort, partner **8** conserve, helpmate, helpmeet **9** economize, other half **10** bridegroom

husbandry 6 thrift **7** control, economy, farming **8** prudence **9** frugality **10** management **11** agriculture, thriftiness **12** conservation, preservation

hush 4 calm **5** quell, quiet **6** shut up, stifle **7** cover up, mollify, secrecy, silence **8** choke off, suppress **9** cessation, quietness, stillness

hush-hush 6 covert, secret **7** private, subrosa **9** top secret **11** clandestine **12** confidential **13** surreptitious, under-the-table

husk 3 pod **4** case, hull, peel, rind, skin **5** shell, shuck, strip **6** casing

husky 3 big, dog **5** beefy, burly, great, hefty, large, rough, stout **6** brawny, croaky, hoarse, mighty, robust, strong, sturdy **7** throaty **8** muscular, oversize, stalwart, thickset **9** strapping

hustings 5 stump

hustle 3 fly, rob, run **4** earn, move, push, rush, sell, urge, work **5** cheat, elbow, fraud, haste, hurry, press, shove, speed **6** hasten **7** hotfoot, promote, solicit, swindle **8** bulldoze, dispatch **9** deception, swiftness

hustler 4 doer **6** dynamo, vendor **8** go-getter, live wire **10** powerhouse

hustling 4 busy **5** eager **6** active, lively, speedy **7** hopping, humming **9** energetic **10** aggressive

hut 3 cot **4** camp, crib, shed **5** cabin, dacha, hooch, hovel, hutch, jacal, lodge, roost, shack **6** cabana, chalet, lean-to, shanty **7** cottage **8** bungalow *American Indian:* **6** wigwam **7** wickiup *Scottish:* **5** bothy, shiel **8** shieling

hutch 3 bin, pen **4** cage, coop **5** chest, shack **6** locker, shanty **8** cupboard **9** enclosure

Huxley novel 8 Antic Hay **11** Crome Yellow **13** Brave New World, Eyeless in Gaza

Hyacinthus *father:* **7** Amyclas *slayer:* **6** Apollo

hybrid 5 blend, cross, mixed, Prius, spork **7** amalgam, mixture **8** combined, compound **9** composite, crossbred **10** crossbreed **11** combination *animal:* **4** mule **5** hinny, liger, tigon *fruit:* **4** Ugli **7** tangelo

hybridize 4 join **5** blend, cross **7** combine **10** crossbreed, interbreed, intercross

Hydra 5 polyp **6** plague **7** monster, serpent **13** constellation *father:* **6** Typhon *mother:* **7** Echidna *slayer:* **8** Heracles, Hercules

hydrant 3 tap **4** pipe **5** valve **6** faucet, spigot **7** petcock **8** fireplug

hydraulic device 3 ram **4** jack, lift, pump **5** brake, press **8** elevator

hydrocarbon 5 xylol **6** dioxin, ethane, xylene **7** benzene, methane, styrene, toluene **8** biphenyl, butylene, ethylene, paraffin *liquid:* **6** octane **7** retinol, styrene **8** menthene

hydroid 5 polyp **6** medusa, obelia **9** jellyfish

hydrometer scale 4 Brix **5** Baumé

hydrophobia 5 lyssa **6** rabies

hyena 5 dingo **6** jackal **9** scavenger

Hygeia 5 Salus *father:* **9** Asclepius **11** Aesculapius *goddess of:* **6** health

hygiene 6 health **10** sanitation **11** cleanliness

hygienic 5 clean **7** aseptic, healthy, sterile **8** sanitary **9** healthful **10** antiseptic, unpolluted

Hyllus' father 8 Heracles, Hercules

hymeneal 6 bridal, wedded **7** marital, married, nuptial, spousal **8** conjugal **9** connubial **11** matrimonial

hymn 4 laud, song **5** bless, carol, chant, extol, paean, psalm **6** anthem, choral, praise, Te Deum **7** chorale, glorify **8** canticle, doxology, eulogize

hype 4 plug, tout **5** boost, thump **7** acclaim, enliven, glorify, promote, puffery, trumpet **8** ballyhoo, increase **9** advertise, excellent, publicity, publicize, stimulate **11** advertising

hyper 4 edgy **5** antsy, jumpy, wired **6** on edge **7** anxious, frantic **8** agitated, frenetic, hopped-up **9** excitable **10** high-strung, overactive **11** overwrought

hyperbole 6 excess **12** embroidering, exaggeration **13** embellishment, overstatement

hypercritical 6 severe **7** carping **8** captious, exacting **10** censorious, nit-picking **12** faultfinding

Hyperion *daughter:* **3** Eos **6** Aurora, Selene *father:* **6** Uranus *mother:* **4** Gaea *son:* **6** Helios *wife:* **5** Theia

hypnotic 6 opiate, sleepy **8** mesmeric, narcotic, sedative **9** somnolent, soporific **11** mesmerizing, somniferous **12** somnifacient, spellbinding

hypnotize 4 drug **5** charm **6** dazzle, trance **8** enthrall, entrance, overcome **9** captivate, fascinate, mesmerize, overpower, spellbind

hypocorism 7 pet name **8** nickname **9** sobriquet

hypocrisy 4 cant, sham **6** deceit, humbug **7** falsity, pietism **8** quackery **9** deception, duplicity, phoniness **10** sanctimony **11** insincerity, religiosity

hypocrite 4 fake, sham **5** actor, faker, fraud, phony, poser **6** humbug, poseur **7** bluffer, pietist **8** deceiver, impostor, pharisee **9** charlatan, pretender **10** dissembler **11** masquerader **12** dissimulator

hypocritical 5 false **7** canting **8** affected, specious, two-faced **9** deceitful, insincere, pietistic **10** Janus-faced **11** dissembling, double-faced, duplicitous **12** mealy-mouthed, pecksniffian **13** sanctimonious

hypothesis 6 belief, theory 7 premise 8 position, supposal 9 condition, inference 10 antecedent, assumption, conjecture 11 explanation, speculation, supposition
hypothetical 7 assumed 8 abstract, academic, supposed 10 assumptive 11 conditional, conjectural, suppositous, theoretical 12 suppositious 13 suppositional

hyrax 4 cony 5 coney 6 dassie, mammal 8 ungulate
hysteria 4 fear 5 craze, furor, mania, panic 6 excess, frenzy 7 madness 8 delirium
hysterical 5 rabid 6 crazed, raving 7 berserk, frantic 8 agitated, frenzied, neurotic 9 delirious, hilarious 10 convulsive, distraught, uproarious 11 overexcited, overwrought 13 side-splitting

I

Iago general: 7 Othello victim: 6 Cassio, Emilia 7 Othello 9 Desdemona wife: 6 Emilia
Iapetus father: 6 Uranus mother: 4 Gaea son: 5 Atlas 9 Menoetius 10 Epimetheus, Prometheus wife: 7 Clymene
Iasion brother: 8 Dardanus father: 4 Zeus 7 Jupiter lover: 5 Ceres 7 Demeter mother: 7 Electra son: 6 Plutus
ibex 4 tahr 8 wild goat family: 7 Bovidae genus: 5 Capra
Ibhar's father 5 David
ibis-headed god 5 Thoth
ibis relative 5 heron, stork
Ibsen, Henrik character: 3 Ase 4 Nora (Helmer) 5 Brack (Judge), Brand, Hedda (Gabler), Helen (Alving), Werle (Gergers) 6 Ejlert (Lovberg), Hedvig (Ekdal), Jorgen (Tesman), Oswald (Alving) 7 Solness (Halvard), Solveig, Torvald (Helmer) 8 Peer Gynt 9 Stockmann (Thomas) country: 6 Norway play: 6 Ghosts 8 Peer Gynt, Wild Duck (The) 10 Doll's House (A) 11 Hedda Gabler, Little Eyolf, Rosmersholm 13 Master Builder (The) 16 Enemy of the People (An)
Icarus' father 8 Daedalus
ICBM part 4 MIRV 7 booster, warhead
ice area: 4 rink dessert: 6 sorbet 7 sherbet floating: 6 berg, floe hanging: 6 icicle pinnacle: 5 serac sheet: 7 glacier
icebox 6 cooler, fridge 12 refrigerator
ice cream 6 gelato 7 spumoni, tortoni brand: 4 Edy's 7 Breyers 8 Klondike 9 Good Humor dish: 6 sundae 11 baked Alaska drink: 4 soda 6 frappe headache: 11 brain freeze holder: 4 cone
iced 5 glacé 6 glazed 7 chilled
ice field 4 floe 7 glacier

ice game 6 hockey 7 curling
ice house 5 igloo
Iceland capital: 9 Reykjavik monetary unit: 5 krona possession: 9 Greenalnd sea: 9 Norwegian snowfield: 11 Vatnajökull strait: 7 Denmark volcano: 5 Hekla
Icelandic epic: 4 Edda, saga hero: 5 Njáll 6 Gunnar 7 Grettir
ice skater figure skater: 4 Witt (Katarina) 5 Baiul (Oksana), Henie (Sonja), Kulik (Ilia) 6 Hughes (Sarah), Umanov (Alexei) 7 Arakawa (Shizuka), Cousins (Robin), Fleming (Peggy), Yagudin (Alexei) 8 Hamilton (Scott), Lipinski (Tara) 9 Plushenko (Evgeny) speed skater: 4 Koss (Johann Olav), Ohno (Apolo Anton), Yang (Yang) 5 Blair (Bonnie), Davis (Shani) 6 Heiden (Eric), Timmer (Marianne) 7 Hedrick (Chad), Klassen (Cindy), Zhurova (Svetlana) 9 Pechstein (Claudia)
ice smoother 7 Zamboni
Ichabod Crane's beloved 7 Katrina
icing 7 topping 8 frosting
icky 4 vile 5 awful, gross, nasty 9 loathsome, offensive, repellent, repulsive, revolting, sickening 10 disgusting 11 distasteful
icon 4 idol, sign 5 image 6 emblem, symbol
iconoclastic 9 dissident, heretical 10 rebellious, unorthodox 13 nonconformist
icy 4 cold 5 gelid, polar 6 arctic, chilly, frigid, frosty, frozen, steely 7 glacial 8 freezing 11 emotionless, unemotional
Idaho capital: 5 Boise city: 6 Moscow 9 Pocatello, Twin Falls 10 Idaho Falls 11 Coeur d'Alene mountain: 5 Borah (Peak) nickname: 3 Gem (State) river: 5 Snake 6 Salmon state bird: 8 bluebird state flower: 7 syringa state tree: 9 white pine

Idas *brother:* **7** Lynceus *father:* **8** Aphareus *slayer:* **4** Zeus *victim:* **6** Castor *wife:* **8** Marpessa

idea 4 whim **5** fancy, guess, motif **6** belief, notion, theory, thesis, vagary **7** caprice, conceit, concept, inkling, meaning, opinion, subject, surmise, thought **8** estimate **9** sentiment, suspicion **10** assumption, brainchild, brainstorm, conception, conclusion, conjecture, conviction, estimation, hypothesis, impression, perception, reflection **11** abstraction, formulation, supposition

ideal 4 best, goal **5** model **7** chimera, classic, epitome, paragon, perfect, utopian **8** absolute, ensample, exemplar, flawless, nonesuch, paradigm, standard, ultimate **9** archetype, classical, exemplary, nonpareil **10** archetypal, conceptual, consummate **11** theoretical

idealist 7 dreamer, quixote, utopian **9** ideologue, visionary

idealistic 6 dreamy **7** utopian **8** poetical, quixotic, romantic **9** visionary **10** starry-eyed **11** impractical, unrealistic

idealize 5 deify, exalt, extol **7** elevate, ennoble, glorify, worship **8** venerate

ideate 5 think **7** imagine **8** conceive, envisage, envision

idée fixe 5 mania **6** fetish, phobia **7** complex **8** fixation **9** obsession **13** preoccupation

identical 3 one **4** like, same, very **5** alike, equal, exact **8** selfsame **9** duplicate **10** equivalent, synonymous

identification mark 4 logo **5** badge, brand, label **6** emblem

identify 3 peg, tag **4** mark, name, spot **5** brand, place **6** finger, select **7** make out, pick out **8** pinpoint **9** determine, recognize **11** distinguish

identity 4 name, self **7** oneness **8** sameness, selfhood **9** character **10** congruence, uniformity, uniqueness **11** personality, singularity **13** individuality, particularity

ideological 8 notional **10** conceptual, ideational **11** speculative **13** philosophical

ideologue 8 believer, idealist, partisan, theorist

ideology 3 ism **5** credo, creed **7** beliefs **8** doctrine **10** philosophy, principles

idiocy 7 fatuity **9** cretinism, stupidity **10** imbecility **11** foolishness

idiomatic 7 demotic **8** peculiar **9** dialectal **10** colloquial, vernacular

idiosyncrasy 3 tic **5** quirk **6** oddity **7** anomaly **11** peculiarity, singularity **12** eccentricity

idiosyncratic 3 odd **5** kooky, queer, weird **6** quirky **7** erratic, oddball, offbeat, unusual **8** peculiar, singular **9** eccentric **11** distinctive

idiot 3 ass **4** dolt, fool, jerk, simp **5** dummy, dunce, moron, ninny **6** cretin, doofus, nitwit, stupid **7** airhead, dullard, half-wit, jackass, natural, tomfool **8** dumbbell, imbecile, numskull **9** ignoramus, numbskull, simpleton **10** nincompoop

idiotic 5 dopey **6** stupid **7** foolish, moronic **8** ignorant **9** brainless, imbecilic, senseless

idle 3 bum **4** laze, lazy, loaf, loll, rest, vain **5** dally, drone, empty, inert, slack, tarry **6** asleep, dawdle, diddle, fallow, futile, linger, loiter, lounge, otiose, unused, vacant **7** aimless, dormant, passive **8** inactive, indolent, slothful **9** shiftless **10** unoccupied

idleness 4 ease **5** sloth **6** vanity **7** leisure, loafing **8** lethargy **9** indolence **10** inactivity

idler 3 bum **4** slug **5** drone **6** loafer, slouch **7** dawdler **8** deadbeat, fainéant, loiterer, slugabed, sluggard **9** do-nothing, lazybones **11** couch potato

Idmon *daughter:* **7** Arachne *father:* **6** Apollo *mother:* **6** Cyrene

idol 3 god **4** hero, icon, star **5** deity, image, totem **6** fetish, minion, symbol **8** likeness *Chinese:* **4** joss

idolatry 7 worship **8** devotion **9** adoration **10** exaltation, veneration **11** deification **13** glorification

idolize 5 adore, deify, exalt **6** revere **7** glorify, worship **8** venerate

Idomeneo *composer* **6** Mozart (Wolfgang Amadeus)

idyllic 5 ideal **6** rustic **7** bucolic, halcyon, perfect, utopian **8** arcadian, heavenly, pastoral, peaceful, romantic **9** idealized, unspoiled **11** picturesque, sentimental

Idylls of the King *author:* **8** Tennyson (Alfred) *character:* **4** Enid **6** Arthur, Elaine, Gareth, Merlin, Vivien **7** Geraint, Lynette **8** Lancelot

iffy 5 dicey, risky **6** chancy, unsure **7** dubious, erratic **8** doubtful **9** uncertain **10** unreliable **12** inconsistent **13** unpredictable

igneous rock 4 lava **5** magma **6** basalt, gabbro **7** diabase, granite **8** porphyry

ignis fatuus 6 mirage **7** chimera **8** delusion, illusion, phantasm **9** pipe dream **12** will-o'-the-wisp **13** hallucination

ignitable 8 burnable **9** excitable, flammable **10** incendiary **11** combustible, inflammable

ignite 4 fire **5** light, spark **6** excite, kindle **7** inflame **8** enkindle, touch off

ignited 3 lit **5** afire, fiery **6** ablaze, aflame, alight **7** blazing, burning, flaming, flaring **11** conflagrant

ignoble 3 low **4** base, mean, poor, vile **5** lowly **6** abject, coarse, common, scurvy, s'ordid, vulgar **7** lowborn, servile **8** base-born, indecent, inferior, plebeian, shameful, unwashed, wretched **10** despicable, inglorious **11** disgraceful **12** contemptible, dishonorable

ignominious 6 odious **8** infamous, shameful **9** degrading **10** despicable, inglorious **11** disgraceful, humiliating, opprobrious **12** contemptible, dishonorable, disreputable **13** discreditable, unrespectable

ignominy 5 odium, shame **6** infamy **7** obloquy, scandal **8** disgrace, dishonor **9** discredit, disesteem, disrepute **10** opprobrium **11** humiliation **13** mortification

ignoramus 4 dolt **5** dummy, dunce, idiot, moron **6** dimwit, nitwit, stupid **7** airhead, dullard, half-wit **8** dumbbell, imbecile, numskull **9** numbskull, simpleton

ignorance 7 naiveté **9** innocence, nescience, stupidity **10** illiteracy, simpleness, simplicity **11** unawareness **12** incognizance

ignorant 5 naive **6** simple **7** unaware **8** clueless, nescient, untaught **9** benighted, ingenuous, oblivious, unknowing, unlearned, untutored, unwitting **10** illiterate, uncultured, uneducated, uninformed, unlettered, unschooled **11** incognizant, know-nothing **12** uninstructed **13** unenlightened

ignore 4 omit, snub **5** avoid **6** forget, reject, slight **7** neglect **8** overlook **9** disregard

Igraine *husband:* **5** Uther **7** Gorlois *son:* **6** Arthur

iguana 5 anole **6** lizard **8** basilisk **10** chuckwalla

ilex 4 maté **5** holly **6** yaupon **7** holm oak **8** inkberry

Iliad 4 epic *author:* **5** Homer *character:* **4** Ajax **5** Helen, Paris, Priam **6** Aeneas, Hector **8** Achilles, Diomedes, Odysseus **9** Agamemnon, Patroclus *city:* **4** Troy

Ilium 4 Troy

ilk 4 kind, sort, type **5** breed, class, genre **6** family, kidney, nature, stripe **7** variety

ill 4 sick **6** ailing, infirm, laid up, malady, peaked, queasy, unwell **7** ailment, disease, trouble, unlucky **8** diseased, disorder, distress, feverish, nauseous, scarcely, sickness, syndrome **9** afflicted, infirmity, nauseated, unhealthy **10** misfortune

ill-adapted 8 unfitted, unsuited **10** unsuitable

ill-advised 4 rash **5** brash, hasty **6** madcap, unwise **7** foolish **8** careless, heedless, reckless **9** foolhardy, impolitic, imprudent **10** incautious, indiscreet, unthinking **11** inexpedient, injudicious, thoughtless

ill at ease 3 shy **4** edgy **6** on edge **7** anxious, awkward, fidgety, nervous **8** insecure, restless **9** unsettled **11** discomfited **12** apprehensive **13** self-conscious, uncomfortable

ill-boding 4 dire **7** baleful, doomful, fateful, ominous, unlucky **8** sinister **10** portentous **11** apocalyptic **12** inauspicious, unpropitious

ill-bred 4 rude **5** crude **7** boorish, loutish, uncivil, uncouth **8** impolite **9** unrefined **10** uncultured, ungracious, unmannered, unmannerly, unpolished **11** uncivilized **12** discourteous

ill-defined 5 faint, fuzzy, vague **7** shadowy **10** indistinct

illegal 3 hot **6** banned **7** bootleg, illicit, lawless **8** criminal, outlawed, unlawful, wrongful **9** felonious, forbidden **10** actionable, prohibited, proscribed, unlicensed **12** illegitimate *act:* **5** crime **6** felony *payment:* **5** bribe **6** payola *scheme:* **4** scam

illegible 8 scrawled **10** unreadable **11** inscrutable

illegitimacy 8 bastardy **11** bar sinister **12** unlawfulness

illegitimate 7 bastard, bootleg, erratic, invalid, lawless, natural **8** criminal, improper, spurious, unlawful **11** misbegotten **12** unauthorized

ill-fated 6 cursed, doomed **7** unhappy, unlucky **8** accursed, luckless, untoward **10** disastrous **11** star-crossed, unfortunate

ill-favored 4 ugly **5** plain **6** homely **12** unattractive

ill-humored 4 dour, sour **5** cross, surly, testy **6** crabby, cranky, crusty, grumpy, morose, ornery, sullen, tetchy, touchy **7** crabbed, grouchy, peevish, prickly **8** choleric, churlish, snappish **9** dyspeptic, irascible, irritable, saturnine, splenetic **12** cantankerous, disagreeable, misanthropic

illiberal 6 biased, narrow **7** bigoted, insular **9** hidebound, parochial, penurious **10** intolerant, prejudiced, provincial **11** reactionary, small-minded **12** conservative, narrow-minded, uncharitable

illicit 7 bootleg, crooked, lawless **8** criminal, unlawful **9** forbidden **10** contraband, prohibited **11** black-market, clandestine **12** unauthorized

illimitable 7 endless **8** infinite, unending **9** boundless **11** measureless

Illinois *capital:* **11** Springfield *city:* **6** Aurora, Cicero, Joliet, Peoria **7** Chicago **8** Rockford *college, university:* **4** Knox **6** DePaul **7** Wheaton **12** Northwestern *nickname:* **7** Prairie (State) *river:* **6** Wabash *state bird:* **8** cardinal *state flower:* **6** violet *state tree:* **8** white oak

illiterate 6 unread **8** untaught **9** untutored **10** uneducated, unlettered, unschooled

ill-mannered 4 rude **6** coarse **7** boorish, loutish, uncivil, uncouth **8** churlish, impolite **10** ungracious **12** discourteous

ill-natured 4 sour **5** cross, huffy, surly, testy **6** bitchy, crabby, grumpy, ornery, tetchy **7** grouchy, peevish, waspish **8** choleric, churlish, snappish, spiteful **9** dyspeptic, fractious, irascible, irritable **10** malevolent **11** belligerent, contentious, quarrelsome **12** cantankerous, disagreeable

illness 6 malady **7** ailment, disease, malaise **8** cachexia, disorder, sickness **9** infirmity **10** affliction **13** indisposition

illogical 6 absurd **7** invalid, unsound **8** specious **9** plausible, senseless, sophistic **10** fallacious, irrational, unreasoned **11** nonrational **12** preposterous, unreasonable

ill-starred 6 cursed, doomed, malign **7** fateful, ominous, unhappy, unlucky **8** luckless, untoward **10** disastrous, foreboding, portentous **11** unfavorable, unfortunate, unpromising **12** inauspicious, unpropitious

ill-tempered 4 sour **5** cross, huffy, surly **6** crabby, bitchy, grumpy, ornery, snippy **7** grouchy, peevish, waspish **8** choleric, churlish, petulant, shrewish, snappish, spiteful **9** dyspeptic, fractious, irascible, irritable **11** belligerent, contentious, quarrelsome **12** cantankerous, disagreeable

ill-timed 11 inopportune **12** unseasonable

ill-treat 4 harm, hurt **5** abuse **6** injure, misuse, molest **7** torment **8** aggrieve **10** traumatize

illuminate 5 clear, edify, exalt, gloss, light **6** uplift **7** clarify, clear up, explain, lighten **8** brighten, decorate **9** elucidate, embellish, enlighten, highlight, irradiate, spotlight

illuminati 5 elite **7** clerisy, scholar **8** academic **11** academician **13** intellectuals

illumination 5 light **8** lighting *unit of:* **3** lux **4** phot **5** lumen **6** candle **7** candela **10** footcandle

illusion 4 myth **5** dream, fancy, ghost **6** facade, mirage **7** chimera, fantasy **8** phantasm, phantasy **9** invention, pipe dream, semblance **11** ignis fatuus **12** will-o'-the-wisp **13** hallucination

illusionist 8 conjurer, magician **9** trickster

illusive see **illusory**

illusory 4 sham **6** unreal **7** seeming **8** apparent, fanciful **9** deceptive, fictional, imaginary, visionary **10** chimerical, fallacious, fictitious, misleading, ostensible

illustrate 4 mark, show **6** depict, evince, expose, reveal **7** clarify, display, exhibit, explain, picture, portray **8** decorate, describe, evidence, instance, manifest **9** elucidate, epitomize, exemplify **11** demonstrate

illustration 4 case **6** sample **7** diagram, drawing, example, picture, problem **8** instance

illustrative 7 graphic **9** pictorial **10** clarifying **11** descriptive **12** iconographic

illustrator *American:* **4** Kent (Rockwell), Pyle (Howard) **5** Abbey (Edwin Austin), Flagg (James Montgomery), Smith (Jessie Willcox), Wyeth (Newell Convers) **6** Gibson (Charles Dana) **7** Burgess (Gelett), Parrish (Maxwell) **8** Rockwell (Norman) **9** Remington (Frederic) *English:* **5** Crane (Walter) **6** Morris (William), Potter (Beatrix) **7** Nielsen (Kay), Rackham (Arthur), Tenniel (John) **9** Beardsley (Aubrey), Caldecott (Randolph), du Maurier (George), Greenaway (Kate) *French:* **4** Doré (Gustave) **5** Dulac (Edmund) *German:* **5** Dürer (Albrecht)

illustrious 5 famed, great, lofty, noted **6** famous **7** eminent, exalted, notable, sublime **8** glorious, renowned, splendid **9** acclaimed, prominent **10** celebrated, preeminent **11** outstanding, prestigious **13** distinguished

illustriousness 4 fame **5** glory **6** renown **8** eminence, prestige **9** celebrity **10** prominence **11** distinction, preeminence

ill will 5 spite, venom **6** animus, enmity, malice, rancor, spleen **7** despite, dislike **8** acrimony, aversion, bad blood **9** animosity, antipathy, hostility, malignity **10** resentment **11** malevolence **12** spitefulness **13** maliciousness

Ilus *father:* **4** Tros *grandson:* **5** Priam *mother:* **10** Callirrhoë *son:* **8** Laomedon

image 4 copy, form, icon, idea, idol, ikon **5** equal, match **6** double, effigy, figure, mirror, notion, ringer, vision **7** concept, fantasm, feature, picture **8** likeness, phantasm, portrait **9** facsimile, semblance **10** conception, equivalent, impression, reflection, simulacrum **12** illustration *Polynesian:* **4** tiki *Semitic:* **6** teraph **8** teraphim (plural)

imaginary 5 ideal **6** made-up, unreal **7** fancied, fictive **8** abstract, fabulous, fanciful, illusive, illusory, notional, quixotic **9** dreamlike, fantastic, fictional, legendary, visionary **10** apocryphal, chimerical, fictitious, phantasmal **11** make-believe **12** hypothetical, supposititious

imagination 5 fancy **7** fantasy **8** phantasy **9** invention **10** creativity **11** inspiration **13** inventiveness

imaginative 5 false **7** blue-sky, fictive **8** artistic, creative, fanciful, original, poetical **9**

ingenious, inventive, visionary, whimsical 11 resourceful 12 enterprising

imagine 5 dream, fancy 6 assume, invent, make up 7 dream up, feature, picture, suspect 8 conceive, envisage, envision 9 fabricate, visualize 10 conjecture

imbecile 4 dodo, dolt, dull, fool, jerk 5 dunce, idiot, moron, ninny 6 cretin, dimwit, nitwit 7 half-wit, jackass, moronic, pinhead, tomfool 8 numskull 9 birdbrain, blockhead, numbskull 10 dunderhead, nincompoop

imbibe 3 sip, sup 4 chug, soak, swig, tope, toss 5 booze, drink, quaff, swill 6 absorb, guzzle, tipple 7 consume, swallow, swizzle 10 assimilate

imbricate 3 lap 7 overlap, shingle 11 overlapping

imbroglio 3 row 4 maze, mess, spat, to-do 5 brawl, broil, mix-up 6 fracas, muddle, tangle 7 dispute, quarrel, rhubarb, scandal, wrangle 8 argument, disorder, squabble 9 confusion, intricacy 10 falling-out 11 altercation, predicament 12 complication, entanglement

imbrue 4 soil 5 stain 8 discolor

imbue 3 dye 4 soak 5 bathe, endow, steep, tinge 6 infuse, invest, leaven 7 ingrain, instill, pervade, suffuse 8 permeate, saturate 9 influence, inoculate

imitate 3 ape 4 copy, echo, mime, mock 5 forge, mimic, spoof 6 parody 7 emulate, take off 8 resemble, simulate, travesty 9 burlesque, duplicate, replicate, reproduce 11 counterfeit, impersonate

imitation 4 copy, fake, mock, sham 5 clone, ditto, dummy, false, match, phony 6 ersatz, parody, ringer 7 forgery, replica 8 likeness, parallel, spurious, travesty 9 duplicate, semblance, simulated 10 artificial, simulacrum, simulation, substitute 11 counterfeit, counterpart 12 reproduction, substitution

imitative 4 mock 5 apish 6 echoic 7 copycat, mimetic, parodic, slavish 11 counterfeit 12 onomatopoeic 13 onomatopoetic

imitator 4 aper, mime 5 mimic 6 parrot 7 copycat

immaculate 4 pure 5 clean 6 chaste, virgin 7 cleanly, perfect, sinless 8 flawless, spotless, unsoiled, virtuous 9 stainless, undefiled, unsullied 11 spic-and-span, unblemished 12 spick-and-span

immaterial 7 trivial 8 bodiless, ethereal 10 extraneous, inapposite, intangible, irrelevant 11 disembodied, incorporeal, nonphysical, unimportant 12 inapplicable 13 insignificant, insubstantial, unsubstantial

immature 3 raw 5 crude, green, young 6 callow, infant, unripe 7 puerile 8 childish, juvenile, youthful 9 infantile, primitive, unfledged 10 unfinished 11 undeveloped

immaturity 6 nonage 7 infancy 8 minority 9 childhood, salad days 11 adolescence 12 juvenescence

immeasurable 4 vast 6 untold 7 endless 8 infinite 9 boundless, extensive, limitless, unbounded, unlimited 11 illimitable, inestimable, uncountable 12 incalculable, unfathomable

immediate 4 next, nigh 5 close 6 at hand, direct, nearby, urgent 7 current, instant, ongoing, primary 9 firsthand, proximate 10 unmediated 12 straightaway 13 instantaneous

immediately 3 now, PDQ 4 anon, ASAP, stat 6 at once, presto, pronto 8 directly, promptly 9 forthwith, instanter, instantly, right away 11 straightway 12 straightaway

immense 4 huge, mega, vast 5 great, large, mondo 6 mighty 7 mammoth, massive, titanic 8 colossal, enormous, gigantic 9 humongous, monstrous 10 gargantuan, monumental, prodigious, tremendous 11 elephantine

immensely 4 a lot 8 terribly 9 extremely 11 exceedingly 12 inordinately

immensity 8 enormity, hugeness, vastness 9 greatness 12 enormousness

immerse 3 dip 4 duck, dunk, sink, soak 5 bathe, douse 6 drench, engage, plunge 7 baptize, engross, involve 8 saturate, submerge

immigrant 5 alien 7 settler 8 newcomer 10 transplant *Japanese:* 5 issei

imminent 4 near 6 at hand 6 coming 7 brewing, nearing, ominous, pending 8 upcoming 9 gathering, proximate 11 approaching, overhanging

immobile 3 set 5 fixed, inert, still 6 frozen, stable, static 9 unmovable 10 motionless, stationary

immobilize 5 still 7 cripple, disable 8 paralyze 9 hamstring 12 incapacitate

immoderate 5 undue 7 extreme 9 excessive 10 exorbitant, inordinate, untempered 11 extravagant, intemperate 12 unreasonable, unrestrained 13 extraordinary, overindulgent

immoderation 6 excess 11 exorbitance, prodigality 12 extravagance, intemperance

immodest 4 lewd, vain 7 stuck-up 8 arrogant, boastful, indecent, puffed-up, unchaste 9 conceited, egotistic 11 pretentious

immolate 4 burn, kill 7 destroy 9 sacrifice

immoral 4 evil, vile **5** dirty, wrong **6** sinful, wanton, wicked **7** corrupt, unclean, vicious **8** depraved, indecent, unchaste **9** dissolute, reprobate, uncleanly **10** degenerate, iniquitous, licentious

immorality 3 sin **4** vice **8** iniquity **9** depravity **10** corruption, unchastity, wickedness

immortal 7 endless, eternal, godlike, undying **8** timeless, unending **9** ceaseless, deathless, perpetual **11** amaranthine, everlasting, sempiternal

immotile 5 fixed, inert **6** rooted, static **9** paralyzed **10** stationary

immovable 3 pat, set **4** fast, firm **5** fixed, rigid **6** rooted, stable **7** adamant **8** constant, obdurate, stubborn **9** steadfast **10** inflexible, invariable, stationary, unyielding

immune 4 free, safe **6** exempt, secure **9** protected **10** impervious **12** invulnerable, unassailable

immunity 7 defense, freedom **9** exemption, privilege **10** protection

immure 3 pen **4** cage, coop, jail, wall **6** entomb, intern, shut in **7** confine, enclose **8** imprison **11** incarcerate

immutable 4 firm **5** fixed **8** constant **9** permanent, steadfast **10** changeless, inflexible, invariable, unchanging **11** inalterable, unalterable **12** unchangeable

Imogen *father:* **9** Cymbeline *husband:* **9** Posthumus

imp 3 elf **4** brat, puck **5** demon, devil, fiend, gamin, gnome, pixie, scamp **6** goblin, kobold, rascal, sprite, urchin **7** gremlin **9** hobgoblin

impact 3 hit, jar, rap **4** blow, bump, jolt, rock, slam, slap **5** brunt, embed, pound, punch, shock, smash, smite **6** affect, buffet; effect, strike, wallop **9** collision, influence **10** concussion, percussion

impair 3 mar, sap **4** harm, hurt **5** spoil **6** damage, injure, lessen, weaken, worsen **7** cripple, tarnish, vitiate **8** enfeeble **9** prejudice, undermine **10** debilitate

impala 8 antelope

impale 4 gore, spit, stab **5** lance, prick, spear, spike, stick **6** pierce, skewer **8** puncture, transfix **11** transpierce

impalpable 4 fine **7** powdery **8** ethereal **10** intangible **11** disembodied, incorporeal **12** imponderable **13** imperceptible, indiscernible

impart 4 cede, give, lend, tell **5** grant, share, yield **6** afford, bestow, confer, convey, pass on, relate, render **8** disclose, transmit **11** communicate *knowledge:* **5** teach **6** inform **7** educate **8** instruct

impartial 4 even, fair, just **5** equal **7** neutral **8** detached, unbiased **9** equitable, objective, uncolored **10** evenhanded **12** unprejudiced **13** disinterested, dispassionate

impassable 6 closed **7** blocked **10** obstructed **12** impenetrable

impasse 3 box, fix, jam **6** aporia, corner, logjam, pickle, pocket **7** dead end, dilemma **8** cul-de-sac, deadlock, standoff **9** stalemate **10** blind alley, bottleneck

impassioned 3 hot **5** fiery **6** ardent, fervid, fierce, heated, red-hot, torrid **7** burning, fervent, intense, zealous **8** feverish, romantic, vehement, white-hot **9** emotional, perfervid **10** hot-blooded, overheated **11** dithyrambic **12** melodramatic

impassive 4 calm, cold, cool **5** stoic **6** serene, stolid, vacant **7** deadpan **8** composed, hardened, reserved, reticent, taciturn **9** heartless **10** insensible, insentient, phlegmatic, poker-faced **11** cold-blooded, emotionless, insensitive, unconcerned, unemotional, unexcitable, unflappable **12** inexpressive, unexpressive, unresponsive **13** dispassionate, self-possessed

impassivity 6 apathy, phlegm **8** stoicism **9** sangfroid, stolidity **12** indifference **13** insensibility

impatient 4 edgy **5** antsy, eager, hasty **7** anxious, fretful, restive **8** restless

impeach 5 blame, doubt **6** accuse, charge, indict **7** censure **9** inculpate, reprehend **11** incriminate

impeccable 4 pure **5** exact **7** perfect, precise **8** absolute, accurate, flawless, unerring **9** blameless, errorless, faultless, guiltless **10** infallible **11** unblemished

impecunious 4 poor **5** broke, needy **7** pinched **8** bankrupt, beggarly, indigent **9** destitute, insolvent, penniless, penurious **10** down-and-out **11** necessitous

impecuniousness 4 need, want **6** penury **7** poverty **9** indigence, neediness, pauperism, privation **11** destitution

impedance 3 bar **4** clog **5** block **8** blockage, obstacle **9** hindrance **10** opposition **11** obstruction

impede 3 bar, dam **4** clog, slow **5** block, check, debar, delay, deter, stall **6** hinder, hang up, hold up, stymie, thwart **7** bog down **8** encumber, obstruct **9** embarrass, interfere, stonewall

impediment 3 bar **4** clog, snag **5** block, hitch **6** hurdle **7** barrier **8** obstacle **9** barricade, hindrance, roadblock **10** difficulty **11** encumbrance, obstruction

impel 4 goad, prod, push, spur, urge **5** drive,

force, rouse **6** excite, incite, prompt **7** actuate, inspire **8** mobilize, motivate **9** instigate, stimulate

impend 4 loom, near **6** menace **8** approach, overhang, threaten

impenetrable 5 dense **6** arcane **7** obscure **9** enigmatic, recondite **10** impervious, invincible, mysterious, unknowable **11** impermeable, bulletproof, inscrutable, ungraspable **12** unfathomable

imperative 4 duty, need, rule, writ **5** acute, vital **6** crying, urgent **7** burning, clamant, command, crucial, exigent **8** critical, pressing, required **9** clamorous, essential, insistent, mandatory, necessary, necessity, requisite **10** compulsory, obligation, obligatory **11** fundamental, necessitous **12** prerequisite

imperceptible 3 dim **5** faint, vague **6** slight, subtle **7** gradual **9** invisible **10** impalpable, indistinct, insensible, intangible, unapparent **12** undetectable, unnoticeable, unobservable **13** inappreciable, inconspicuous, indiscernible

imperceptive 4 dull **7** shallow, unaware **11** inattentive, insensitive

imperfect 6 faulty, flawed **9** defective, deficient, irregular **10** defeasible, inadequate

imperfection 3 sin **4** flaw, wart **5** fault **6** defect, foible **7** blemish, demerit, failing, frailty **8** weakness **10** deficiency **11** shortcoming

imperial 5 regal, royal **6** kingly, lordly **7** haughty **8** absolute, majestic **9** masterful, sovereign **10** high-handed, peremptory **11** domineering, magisterial, monarchical

imperil 4 risk **6** hazard, menace **7** venture **8** endanger, threaten **10** jeopardize

imperious 5 bossy **6** urgent **7** haughty **8** absolute, arrogant, despotic, dominant **9** arbitrary, masterful **10** autocratic, commanding, high-handed, oppressive, peremptory, tyrannical **11** dictatorial, domineering, heavy-handed, magisterial, overbearing

impermanent 7 passing **8** fleeting, fugitive **9** ephemeral, fugacious, momentary, temporary, transient **10** evanescent, short-lived, transitory

impersonal 4 cold **5** aloof **8** abstract, detached **11** cold-blooded, emotionless **13** dispassionate, unimpassioned

impersonate 3 ape **4** play **5** mimic **6** act out **7** imitate, playact, portray **9** represent **11** counterfeit

impersonator 3 ape **4** aper, mime **5** actor, mimic **6** mummer, player, ringer **7** actress, copycat **8** thespian *female:* **9** drag queen

impertinence 3 lip **4** gall, guff, sass **5** brass, cheek **8** audacity, boldness, chutzpah, rudeness, temerity **9** brashness, impudence, insolence **10** brazenness, effrontery, incivility **11** discourtesy, irrelevance

impertinent 4 bold, busy, rude **5** brash, fresh, sassy, saucy **6** brazen, cheeky **7** uncivil **8** insolent, meddling **9** audacious, intrusive, obtrusive, officious **10** inapposite, irrelative, irrelevant, meddlesome **11** ill-mannered **12** discourteous, inapplicable, presumptuous

imperturbability 5 poise **6** aplomb, phlegm **8** calmness, coolness, serenity, stoicism **9** composure, placidity, sangfroid **10** dispassion, equanimity **11** equilibrium, nonchalance, tranquility **12** tranquillity

imperturbable 4 calm, cool **5** stoic **6** placid, poised, serene, smooth, steady, stolid **7** unmoved **8** composed, tranquil **9** collected, unruffled **10** nonchalant, phlegmatic, unaffected **11** unflappable

impervious 4 safe **6** immune **8** hardened **10** inviolable **12** inaccessible, invulnerable

impetuous 3 hot **4** rash, wild **5** fiery, hasty **6** ardent, fervid, madcap, sudden **8** headlong, vehement, volatile **9** hotheaded, mercurial **10** irrational, passionate **11** precipitant, precipitate, precipitous, spontaneous **13** temperamental

impetus 4 goad, push, spur **5** force **6** motive **8** catalyst, momentum, stimulus **9** incentive, stimulant **10** incitement, motivation **13** encouragement

impinge 5 press **6** border **7** intrude, obtrude **8** encroach

impious 6 sinful, unholy, wicked **7** godless, infidel, profane, secular, ungodly **8** agnostic, apostate **9** atheistic **10** irreverent, unfaithful, unhallowed **11** blasphemous, irreligious, unrighteous **12** iconoclastic, sacrilegious **13** unconsecrated

impish 4 arch **5** elfin **6** elvish **7** playful, puckish, roguish, waggish **11** mischievous

impishness 7 devilry, roguery, waggery **8** deviltry, mischief **9** devilment **11** roguishness, waggishness

implacable 4 grim **8** ruthless **9** merciless **10** inexorable, unyielding **11** intractable **12** unappeasable

implant 3 fix **4** root **5** embed, graft, infix **6** enroot, infuse, insert **7** ingrain, inspire, instill **9** establish, inculcate, inoculate, introduce **10** inseminate **12** augmentation

implausible 5 fishy **6** flimsy **7** dubious, suspect **8** doubtful, fanciful, unlikely **10** farfetched, incredible **12** questionable, unbelievable, unconvincing

implement 4 tool **6** device, effect, enable, gadget **7** enforce, execute, fulfill, perform, realize, utensil **8** carry out, complete, make good **9** actualize, apparatus, appliance **10** accomplish, instrument, supplement **11** contraption, contrivance *carpentry:* **3** adz, die, saw **4** adze, file **5** brace, clamp, drill, punch, tongs **6** chisel, hammer, pliers, reamer, sander, wrench **7** hacksaw, scraper **9** blowtorch **11** screwdriver *cleaning:* **3** mop **5** broom, brush, whisk **6** duster, vacuum **7** sweeper **10** whiskbroom *cutting:* **5** knife, mower, razor **6** scythe, shears, sickle **8** scissors *digging:* **5** spade **6** dibber, dibble, shovel *drawing:* **3** pen **6** eraser, pencil **7** compass **8** template *eating:* **4** fork **5** knife, spoon **9** chopstick *engraving:* **5** burin **6** graver *farm:* **4** plow **6** binder, harrow, plough, scythe, seeder, sickle **8** gangplow, reaphook, spreader, thresher **9** pitchfork **10** cultivator *fireplace:* **5** poker, tongs **7** andiron *fishing:* **3** rod **4** hook, lure, reel **6** sinker **7** harpoon, trident *garden:* **3** hoe **4** rake **5** edger, spade **6** dibber, dibble, digger, tiller, trowel **7** mattock *grooming:* **4** comb, file **5** brush, razor **7** clipper **8** clippers, nail file, tweezers **10** toothbrush *kitchen:* **3** pan, pot **4** mold **5** mixer, whisk **6** grater, kettle, mortar, pestle **7** blender, skillet, spatula **8** colander, saucepan, stockpot *logging:* **5** peavy **6** peavey **8** cant hook *measuring:* **3** cup **4** gage, rule **5** gauge, ruler, scale **7** caliper, divider, trammel, T-square **10** micrometer, protractor *stone:* **5** burin **7** neolith **9** paleolith

implicate 4 link, mire **5** blame **6** tangle **7** concern, embroil, entwine, include, involve **8** entangle, intimate **11** incriminate

implication 4 hint **8** allusion, overtone **9** inference, undertone **10** connection, intimation, suggestion **11** association, connotation **12** significance

implicit 5 tacit **6** unsaid **8** inherent, unspoken **9** doubtless, potential, unuttered **10** undeclared, understood **11** unexpressed

implied 5 tacit **6** unsaid **8** inherent, unspoken **9** suggested **10** undeclared, understood **11** unexpressed

implore 3 ask, beg **4** coax, pray **5** crave, plead **6** adjure, appeal **7** beseech, entreat, solicit **10** supplicate

imply 4 hint, mean **5** get at **7** connote, include, involve, signify, suggest **8** indicate, intimate **9** insinuate

impolite 4 rude **5** crude **7** ill-bred, uncivil, uncouth **10** ungracious, unladylike, unmannered, unmannerly **11** ill-mannered **12** discourteous **13** ungentlemanly

impolitic 5 brash **6** unwise **8** tactless **9** imprudent, maladroit, untactful **10** ill-advised, indiscreet **11** inadvisable, inexpedient, injudicious **12** shortsighted, undiplomatic

import 4 bear, gist, mean, pith **5** sense, value, worth **6** convey, denote, intend, intent, matter, moment, stress, thrust, weight **7** concern, connote, express, meaning, message, purpose, signify **8** emphasis, indicate, transfer **9** magnitude, substance **10** intendment **11** acceptation, consequence **12** significance **13** signification

importance 4 mark, note, pith **5** value, worth **6** moment, weight **7** account, gravity **8** eminence, priority, salience, standing **9** greatness, magnitude, substance **10** prominence, worthiness **11** consequence, distinction, seriousness, weightiness **12** significance

important 3 big **5** chief, grave, great, heavy, major, noted, vital **6** famous, marked, potent, urgent, worthy **7** big-time, capital, crucial, eminent, fateful, notable, salient, serious, telling, weighty **8** critical, eventful, foremost, material, powerful, pressing, valuable **9** essential, estimable, imperious, memorable, momentous, prominent **10** meaningful, noteworthy, preeminent, worthwhile **11** outstanding, significant, substantial **12** considerable **13** consequential, distinguished, indispensable

importune 3 beg **4** pray, urge **5** annoy, plead, worry **6** appeal, invoke, plague **7** beseech, besiege, entreat, solicit, trouble **8** petition

impose 3 fob **4** lade, levy **5** abuse, enact, exact, foist, force, order, place, put on, visit, wreak **6** assess, burden, charge, compel, decree, demand, enjoin, fob off, ordain, saddle **7** command, dictate, exploit, inflict, intrude, lay down, obtrude, palm off, pass off, require **8** encroach, encumber, infringe, trespass **9** authorize, constrain, establish

imposing 4 huge **5** grand, noble, regal, royal **6** august **7** awesome, massive, pompous, stately **8** baronial, majestic, towering **9** dignified **10** commanding, monumental **11** magnificent, outstanding **12** high-sounding **13** distinguished

imposition 3 tax **4** duty, fine, levy **6** burden, demand **7** penalty **9** deception **13** inconvenience

impossible 6 absurd **8** hopeless **10** infeasible, unfeasible, unworkable **11** unthinkable **12** preposterous, unacceptable, unattainable, unbelievable, unimaginable, unrealizable, unreasonable **13** inconceivable

impost 3 fee, tax **4** duty, levy, toll **6** charge, tariff **7** tribute **9** surcharge **10** assessment

impostor 4 fake, sham 5 actor, cheat, faker, fraud, mimic, phony, poser, quack 6 humbug, poseur 8 deceiver 9 charlatan, con artist, hypocrite, pretender 10 dissembler, mountebank 11 masquerader 12 impersonator

imposture 4 fake, hoax, sell, sham, wile 5 cheat, fraud 6 deceit, humbug 8 flimflam 9 deception, mare's nest, stratagem 11 counterfeit

impotence 8 weakness 9 sterility 10 inadequacy 12 helplessness 13 powerlessness

impotent 4 lame, weak 6 effete, feeble 7 sterile 8 helpless 9 forceless, incapable, powerless 11 ineffective, ineffectual 12 invertebrate

impound 5 seize 6 immure, lock up 7 confine, enclose, put away 8 imprison 10 confiscate

impoverish 4 bust, ruin 5 break 6 beggar 8 bankrupt 9 pauperize

impoverished 4 poor 5 broke, needy 8 bankrupt, indigent 9 destitute, penniless, penurious

impoverishment 4 need, want 6 penury 9 indigence, neediness, privation 11 destitution

impracticable 8 unusable 10 infeasible, unfeasible, unworkable 11 insuperable, unrealistic 12 inaccessible, unattainable

impractical 7 utopian 8 quixotic, romantic, unusable 9 visionary 10 idealistic, infeasible, ivory-tower, starry-eyed, unfeasible, unworkable 11 theoretical, unrealistic

imprecation 3 hex 4 cuss 5 curse 7 malison 8 anathema 11 malediction

imprecise 5 rough, vague 7 inexact 9 estimated 10 indefinite 11 approximate, unspecified

impregnable 4 safe 6 immune, secure 9 protected 10 invincible, inviolable, unbeatable 11 indomitable, insuperable 12 unassailable 13 unconquerable

impregnate 3 sop 4 fill, soak 5 imbue, souse, steep 6 drench, infuse 7 pervade 8 conceive, permeate, saturate 9 fecundate, fertilize, penetrate, transfuse 10 inseminate

impresario 4 Bing (Rudolf) 5 Carte (Richard D'Oyly), Hurok (Sol) 6 Pastor (Tony) 7 manager 8 director, Kirstein (Lincoln), producer, promoter 9 Diaghilev (Sergei) 10 D'Oyly Carte (Richard)

impress 3 fix, set 4 dent, etch, mark, move, seal, sway 5 brand, carry, drive, exert, force, grave, infix, print, stamp, touch 6 affect, effect, excite, strike 7 engrave, ingrain, inspire 8 inscribe, transfer, transmit 9 establish, influence, stimulate

impressible 8 gullible, immature, moldable 9 malleable, receptive, sensitive 10 affectable, susceptive, vulnerable 11 persuadable, suggestible, susceptible

impression 4 dent, idea, mark, sign 5 image, print, stamp, trace, track 6 effect, hollow, notion 7 concept, edition, feeling, reissue, thought, vestige 8 printing, reaction 9 influence

impressionable 8 sensible, sentient 9 malleable, receptive, sensitive 10 responsive 11 suggestible, susceptible

impressionist *composer:* 5 Ravel (Maurice) 7 Debussy (Claude) *mimic:* 6 Carvey (Dana), Little (Rich) *painter:* 5 Degas (Edgar), Manet (Edouard), Monet (Claude) 6 Renoir (Auguste), Sisley (Alfred) 7 Cassatt (Mary), Morisot (Berthe) 8 Pissarro (Camille) (see also **postimpressionist**)

impressive 5 grand, noble 6 moving, superb 7 amazing, awesome, notable, stately, sublime 8 dazzling, dramatic, gorgeous, majestic, powerful, splendid, stirring, striking, touching 9 admirable, affecting, arresting, inspiring 11 magnificent

imprimatur 6 permit 7 license 8 approval, sanction 10 permission 13 authorization

imprint 3 fix 4 dent, etch, mark 5 grave, press, stamp 6 dimple, effect 7 engrave 8 inscribe 9 engraving, influence 10 depression 11 indentation, inscription

imprison 3 jug 4 cage, jail 6 coop up, detain, immure, intern, send up 7 confine, enclose 8 restrain, restrict, stockade 9 constrain 11 incarcerate

improbable 5 fishy 7 dubious 8 doubtful, fanciful, unlikely 10 far-fetched 11 implausible

impromptu 5 ad-lib 7 offhand 9 extempore, makeshift, unplanned, unstudied 10 off-the-cuff, unprepared, unscripted 11 extemporary, spontaneous, unrehearsed

improper 5 inapt, inept, outré, undue, wrong 6 gauche, risqué 7 illicit, naughty 8 ill-timed, indecent, tactless, unseemly, untimely, untoward 9 incorrect, unethical, unfitting 10 inaccurate, inapposite, indecorous, indelicate, malapropos, unbecoming, undecorous, unsuitable 11 impertinent, unbefitting 12 illegitimate, inadmissible, inapplicable, infelicitous, unseasonable 13 inappropriate

impropriety 5 gaffe 7 blooper, blunder, faux pas 8 solecism 9 barbarism, gaucherie, indecorum, vulgarism 12 unseemliness 13 incorrectness

improve 4 edit, help, mend 5 amend, boost, edify, emend, raise 6 better, enrich, look up, perk up, refine, reform, remedy, revise, revive, update, uplift **7** advance, amplify, augment, build up, correct, develop, enhance, enlarge, further, perfect, recover, rectify, upgrade **8** increase, progress **9** cultivate, intensify, meliorate **10** ameliorate, recuperate, strengthen

improvident 4 rash **6** lavish **8** careless, feckless, heedless, prodigal, reckless, wasteful **9** impetuous, negligent, unthrifty **10** profligate **11** extravagant, spendthrift **12** shortsighted

improvise 4 scat **5** ad-lib **6** cook up, invent, make up, wing it **7** concoct **8** contrive **9** fabricate **11** extemporize

improvised 7 offhand **9** extempore, unstudied **10** off-the-cuff, unprepared, unscripted **11** extemporary, unrehearsed

imprudent 4 rash **6** unwise **7** foolish **8** reckless **9** foolhardy **10** ill-advised, incautious, indiscreet **11** inadvisable, inexpedient, injudicious **12** shortsighted

impudence 4 gall **5** brass, cheek, nerve **8** audacity, boldness, chutzpah, temerity **9** brashness, cockiness, hardihood, insolence, nerviness **10** disrespect, effrontery **11** presumption

impudent 4 bold, flip, pert, rude, wise **5** brash, cocky, fresh, lippy, nervy, sassy, saucy, smart **6** brassy, brazen, cheeky **7** blatant, forward **8** flippant, insolent, overbold **9** audacious, barefaced, bold-faced **11** brazen-faced, smart-alecky **12** contumelious **13** disrespectful

impugn 5 cross **6** assail, attack, defame, malign, oppose, vilify **7** asperse, gainsay, impeach **8** chastise, reproach, traverse **9** castigate, denigrate, deprecate, disparage, reprehend **9** criticize, denigrate

impugnable 5 fishy, shady **6** guilty **7** suspect **8** doubtful **9** equivocal, uncertain **10** assailable, suspicious **11** problematic **12** disreputable

impulse 4 goad, push, spur, urge, whim **5** drive, force **6** motive, thrust, whimsy **7** caprice, passion **8** catalyst, excitant, stimulus **9** actuation, incentive, stimulant **10** incitation, incitement, motivation **11** inspiration, instigation *conductor:* **4** axon

impulsive 4 rash **5** brash, hasty **6** abrupt, fickle, sudden **7** erratic, flighty, offhand **8** headlong, volatile **9** extempore, mercurial, unplanned, whimsical **10** capricious **11** instinctive, precipitate, spontaneous

impunity 7 freedom, liberty, license **8** immunity **9** exception, exemption, indemnity, privilege **10** absolution, protection

impure 3 raw **5** mixed **6** soiled, sordid, unholy **7** alloyed, defiled, profane, sullied, unclean **8** indecent, polluted, unchaste **9** uncleanly, unrefined **10** desecrated, unhallowed **11** adulterated

impute 3 lay **4** cite **5** blame, refer **6** accuse, adduce, assign, charge, credit, indict **7** ascribe **8** accredit **9** attribute, implicate

inaccessible 5 aloof **6** arcane, closed, far-off, remote **7** cryptic, distant, faraway, obscure **8** abstruse, esoteric, hermetic **9** recondite **11** unavailable, unreachable **12** unattainable, unobtainable

inaccurate 5 false, wrong **6** all wet, faulty, untrue **7** unsound **8** specious **9** distorted, erroneous **10** fictitious

inaction 6 repose **7** latency **8** dormancy, idleness, lethargy **9** indolence, passivity, slackness, torpidity **10** quiescence

inactive 4 idle, lazy **5** inert, quiet, slack, still **6** asleep, latent, sleepy, static, torpid **7** abeyant, dormant, passive, resting **8** slothful, sluggish **9** do-nothing, lethargic, quiescent, sedentary

in addition 4 also **6** as well, to boot, withal **7** besides, further **8** moreover **11** furthermore

inadequacy 4 lack, want **6** dearth **7** deficit, failure, paucity **8** shortage, weakness **9** impotence **10** deficiency, scantiness **11** shortcoming

inadequate 3 shy **5** scant, short **6** meager, scanty, scarce, skimpy **7** lacking, scrimpy, wanting **8** impotent **9** defective, deficient

inadmissible 5 unapt, unfit **8** unusable, unworthy **9** unwelcome **10** unsuitable **11** unqualified **12** unacceptable

inadvertent 8 careless, heedless **9** negligent, unmindful, unplanned, unwitting **10** accidental, unintended, unthinking **13** unintentional

inadvisable 4 rash **6** unwise **7** foolish **8** careless, reckless **9** foolhardy, impolitic, imprudent, pointless **10** ill-advised **11** harebrained

inalterable 5 fixed **6** stable **8** constant **9** immovable, immutable, steadfast, unmovable, unvarying **12** unchangeable

inamorata, inamorato 4 beau, dear **5** flame, honey, lover **6** steady **7** beloved, darling, squeeze, sweetie **8** ladylove, mistress, paramour, truelove **9** boyfriend **10** girlfriend, heartthrob, sweetheart

inane 4 idle, vain **5** blank, dotty, empty, silly, vapid **6** absurd, jejune, vacant **7** asinine, fatuous, foolish, idiotic, insipid, trivial, vacuous, witless **8** mindless **9** frivolous, laughable, pointless, senseless

inanimate 4 dead, dull **5** inert **5** still **6** asleep, torpid **7** dormant **8** immotile, lifeless **9** quiescent **10** motionless **11** unconscious

inanity 5 folly **6** idiocy, lunacy **7** fatuity, vacuity **8** vapidity **9** absurdity, dottiness, emptiness, silliness **10** hollowness **11** foolishness, vacuousness, witlessness **13** senselessness

inappreciable 6 meager, scanty, skimpy, slight **10** impalpable, unapparent **13** imperceptible

inappropriate 5 amiss, undue, unfit **6** unmeet **8** improper, unseemly, untimely, untoward **9** ill-suited **10** malapropos, unsuitable **11** impertinent

inapt 5 unfit **6** clumsy, gauche, jejune, unmeet **7** awkward, unhandy **8** improper, unfitted, unsuited, untimely **9** maladroit, unfitting, unskilled **10** amateurish, irrelevant, malapropos, unskillful, unsuitable

inarticulate 4 dumb, mute **5** tacit **6** silent **7** halting, unvocal **8** mumbling, unspoken, wordless **9** voiceless **10** maundering, speechless, tongue-tied, undeclared **11** unexpressed

inasmuch as 5 since **7** because, whereas **11** considering

inattentive 6 absent, remiss **8** distrait, heedless **9** forgetful, negligent, unheeding, unmindful **10** abstracted, distracted, unthinking **12** absentminded

inaugural 5 first **6** maiden, speech **7** address, initial, leading, opening, premier **8** foremost **9** beginning

inaugurate 5 begin, set up, start **6** launch **7** kick off **8** commence, dedicate, initiate **9** establish, institute, originate **10** consecrate

inauspicious 4 dire **7** adverse, baleful, direful, fateful, ominous, unlucky **8** sinister **9** ill-boding **11** threatening, unfavorable, unpromising **12** unpropitious

inborn 6 innate, native **7** connate, natural **8** inherent **9** intrinsic **10** congenital, connatural, hereditary, unacquired

inbred 7 connate, genetic, natural **8** inherent **9** intrinsic **10** congenital, connatural, deepseated, hereditary

Inca capital: 5 Cuzco **conqueror: 7** Pizarro (Francisco) **god: 4** Inti **9** Viracocha **10** Pachacamac **language: 7** Quechua **record: 5** quipu **ruin: 11** Machu Picchu **ruler: 9** Atahualpa, Pachacuti **10** Atahuallpa

incalculable 4 huge, iffy, vast **6** untold **8** enormous **9** boundless, countless, limitless, uncertain **10** tremendous, unnumbered **11** illimitable, measureless, uncountable **12** immeasurable, unmeasurable **13** unpredictable

in camera 7 privily, sub rosa **8** covertly, secretly **9** furtively, privately **10** stealthily **13** clandestinely

incandescent 3 hot **5** lucid **6** ardent, bright, lucent **7** beaming, fulgent, glowing, intense, lambent, radiant **8** dazzling, luminous **9** brilliant, effulgent, refulgent **11** resplendent

incantation 3 hex **4** rune **5** chant, charm, magic, spell **10** hocus-pocus, mumbojumbo, necromancy **11** abracadabra, conjuration, enchantment **Buddhist, Hindu: 6** mantra

incapable 5 unfit **6** unable **8** impotent, unexpert, unfitted **9** powerless, unskilled **10** unequipped, unskillful **11** unqualified **12** disqualified

incapacitate 6 disarm **7** cripple, disable **8** paralyze **10** debilitate, devitalize, disqualify, immobilize

incapacity 9 impotence, unfitness **10** impairment **11** disablement **12** fecklessness

incarcerate 3 jug **4** jail **6** coop up, immure, intern, send up **7** confine, enclose, impound **8** imprison

incarnadine 3 red **4** rosy **5** ruddy **6** redden **7** pinkish **8** bloodred

incarnate 5 human, reify **6** embody **7** realize **8** embodied, manifest **9** actualize, corporeal, personify **11** materialize, personalize **12** substantiate

incarnation 6 avatar **10** embodiment **11** reification **of Christ: 7** kenosis **of Vishnu: 4** Rama

incautious 4 rash **5** brash, hasty **6** daring, madcap, unwary **8** careless, heedless, reckless **9** daredevil, foolhardy, impetuous, imprudent, negligent, unmindful **10** ill-advised, neglectful, regardless **11** precipitate, thoughtless

incendiary 5 fiery, torch **7** firebug **8** agitator, arsonist, arsonous **9** explosive, firebrand, ignitable **10** pyromaniac **12** pyromaniacal

incense 3 ire, mad, oil **4** balm, burn, rile **5** anger, aroma, scent, spice **6** arouse, enrage, homage, incite, madden **7** inflame, provoke **8** irritate **9** infuriate **vessel: 6** censer **8** thurible

incentive 4 goad, spur **5** spark **6** motive **7** impetus, impulse **8** catalyst, stimulus **9** stimulant **10** inducement, motivation **11** provocation **13** encouragement

inception 4 root **5** birth, start **6** origin, outset, source **7** genesis, kickoff, opening **9** beginning **10** derivation, provenance **11** provenience **12** commencement

inceptive 7 initial, leadoff, nascent **9** beginning **10** initiatory

incertitude 5 doubt **7** dubiety **8** mistrust **9** suspicion **10** skepticism **11** dubiousness, uncertainty, vacillation **12** irresolution

incessant 6 steady **7** endless, eternal, nonstop **8** constant **9** ceaseless, continual, perpetual, unceasing **10** continuous **11** everlasting, unremitting **12** interminable **13** uninterrupted

inch 3 bit **5** crawl, creep **7** modicum

inchoate 8 formless, immature, unformed, unshaped **9** amorphous, embryonic, incipient, potential, shapeless **10** disjointed, incoherent **11** rudimentary, unorganized **12** disconnected

incident 5 event **7** episode **8** occasion **9** happening **10** affiliated, collateral, occurrence **11** concomitant

incidental 5 fluky, minor **6** casual, chance **9** accessory **10** contingent, fortuitous **11** subordinate **12** nonessential

incidentally 7 by the by **8** by the bye, by the way, casually **12** fortuitously

incinerate 4 burn **7** cremate

incipient 7 nascent **9** beginning, embryonic **10** commencing

incipit 5 start **7** opening **9** beginning

incise 3 cut **4** etch, gash, kerf, slit **5** carve **6** chisel **7** engrave

incision 3 cut **4** gash, slit **5** blaze, notch **10** laceration

incisive 4 keen **5** acute, crisp, sharp, terse **6** direct **7** cutting, mordant **8** clear-cut, piercing, slashing, succinct **9** trenchant **11** penetrating **13** perspicacious

incite 3 egg **4** abet, goad, prod, spur, urge **5** egg on, raise, rouse, set on **6** arouse, exhort, foment, kindle, set off, spur on, stir up, whip up **7** actuate, agitate, provoke, trigger **8** motivate **9** instigate, stimulate

incitement see **incentive**

inclement 3 raw **5** harsh, rough **6** bitter, brutal, severe, stormy **8** rigorous

inclination 3 bow, nod **4** bent, bias, lean, tilt, will **5** fancy, grade, pitch, slant, slope, taste, trend **6** ascent, liking **7** descent, incline, leaning **8** affinity, appetite, fondness, gradient, penchant, soft spot, tendency, velleity, weakness **9** affection **10** attachment, partiality, proclivity, propensity **11** disposition **12** predilection

incline 3 tip **4** bend, bias, cant, cast, heel, lean, list, sway, tend, tilt, turn **5** grade, impel, slant, slide, slope **6** affect, induce **7** dispose, leaning **8** gradient, persuade **9** influence, prejudice

inclined 3 apt **5** atilt, given, leant, prone, raked, ready **6** liable, likely, minded **7** dip-

ping, leaning, oblique, sloping, tilting, willing **8** diagonal, pitching **11** predisposed

***way:* 4** ramp

include 5 admit, bound, cover **6** enfold, number, take in **7** confine, contain, embrace, enclose, receive, subsume **8** comprise, encircle **9** encompass **10** comprehend **11** accommodate

inclusive 5 all up, broad **6** global **7** general, overall **8** complete, sweeping **9** all-around, embracive **11** compendious **12** encompassing, encyclopedic **13** comprehensive

incognito 6 veiled **7** cloaked **9** anonymous, disguised **11** camouflaged

incognizant 7 unaware **8** ignorant **9** oblivious, unknowing, unmindful, unwitting **10** unfamiliar, uninformed **11** unconscious **12** unacquainted

incoherent 5 loose **6** broken, raving **7** muddled, unclear **8** confused **9** illogical **10** disjointed, disordered, irrational, maundering, tongue-tied **11** unconnected, unorganized **12** disconnected, disorganized **13** discontinuous

incombustible 9 fireproof **10** unburnable **12** nonflammable

income 4 gain, take **5** wages **6** profit **7** revenue **8** entrance, proceeds, receipts **9** emolument

incommode 3 irk, vex **5** annoy, upset **6** bother, burden, hinder, plague, put out **7** disturb, perturb, trouble **8** disquiet, distress, irritate **9** disoblige **10** disconcert

incommodious 7 awkward, cramped, crowded **8** confined **9** congested

incommunicable 8 reserved, taciturn **9** ineffable, withdrawn **11** unspeakable, unutterable **13** undescribable, unexpressible

incomparable 6 unique **7** supreme **8** peerless, singular, ultimate **9** matchless, nonpareil, paramount, unequaled, unmatched, unrivaled **10** preeminent, surpassing, unequalled, unrivalled **11** outstanding, superlative, unequalable, unmatchable **12** transcendent, unparalleled **13** unsurpassable

incompatible 7 adverse, counter **8** contrary, opposite **9** dissonant, unmixable **10** discordant, discrepant **11** conflicting, disagreeing, uncongenial, unfavorable **12** antagonistic, antithetical **13** contradictory, unsympathetic

incompetence 9 unfitness **10** disability, ineptitude **12** fecklessness

incompetent 5 inept, unfit **6** clumsy **8** helpless, inexpert, unfitted **9** incapable, maladroit, unskilled **10** unequipped **11** inefficient, unqualified

incomplete 4 part **5** short **6** broken, undone **7**

partial, sketchy **8** abridged, immature **9** truncated **10** unfinished **11** fragmentary

incompliant 5 rigid, stiff **6** mulish **7** defiant **8** perverse, stubborn **9** obstinate, pigheaded, resistant, unbending **10** bullheaded, headstrong, inflexible, self-willed, unyielding **11** intractable **12** pertinacious, recalcitrant

incomprehensible 7 cryptic, obscure, unclear **8** abstruse, baffling, esoteric **9** fantastic **10** fathomless, mysterious, mystifying, unknowable **11** ungraspable **12** impenetrable, unfathomable, unimaginable

inconceivable 10 improbable, unknowable **11** implausible, unthinkable **12** unbelievable, unconvincing, unimaginable

in conclusion 6 lastly **7** finally

inconclusive 4 open **9** equivocal, uncertain, undecided, unsettled **10** unfinished

incongruous 5 alien **6** absurd **7** foreign, variant **9** anomalous, dissonant **10** discordant, discrepant, unsuitable **11** conflicting, disagreeing **12** disconsonant

inconsequential 5 petty, small **6** measly, paltry **7** trivial **8** picayune, trifling **9** illogical, smalltime **10** immaterial, irrelevant, negligible **11** impertinent, superficial, unimportant

inconsiderable 4 puny **5** minor, petty **6** meager, meagre, paltry, scanty, skimpy, slight **7** scrimpy, trivial **8** picayune, trifling **9** frivolous, small-beer **10** negligible **11** unimportant

inconsiderate 4 rash **5** brash, hasty **6** unkind **8** careless, heedless, impolite, reckless **9** hotheaded, impulsive **10** ill-advised, ungracious **11** precipitate, thoughtless **12** discourteous, uncharitable

inconsistent 6 fickle **8** contrary **9** dissonant, illogical, mercurial **10** capricious, changeable, discordant, discrepant **11** conflicting **13** contradictory

inconsolable 7 forlorn **8** desolate **9** heartsick **11** comfortless, heartbroken

inconspicuous 6 hidden, subtle **7** obscure **9** concealed **11** unobtrusive **12** unnoticeable

inconstant 6 fickle, untrue **7** erratic, mutable, protean, vagrant **8** unstable, unsteady, variable, volatile, wavering **9** changeful, faithless, fluctuant, irregular, mercurial, uncertain, unsettled **10** capricious, changeable, irresolute, perfidious, unfaithful **11** chameleonic, vacillating **13** temperamental

incontestable 4 sure **7** certain **8** absolute, clear-cut, ironclad, positive **9** apodictic, undoubted **10** conclusive, inarguable, undeniable **11** irrefutable, unequivocal **12** unassailable, undisputable **13** unimpeachable

incontinent 5 loose **6** wanton **9** dissolute **10** licentious, profligate **12** unrestrained

incontrovertible 4 sure **7** certain **8** absolute, clear-cut, definite, positive **10** conclusive, undeniable **11** irrefutable, unequivocal **12** undisputable

inconvenience 3 irk, vex **5** annoy **6** bother, meddle, put out **7** disrupt, disturb, trouble **8** handicap, vexation **9** annoyance **10** discomfort, discommode, disruption, exasperate **11** aggravation

inconvenient 7 awkward, unhandy **8** annoying **10** bothersome, unsuitable **11** pestiferous, troublesome

incorporate 3 mix **4** form, fuse, join **5** blend, merge, unite **6** absorb, embody, imbibe, mingle **7** combine **8** organize **9** establish **10** amalgamate, assimilate

incorporeal 8 bodiless, formless **9** spiritual **10** discarnate, immaterial, unphysical **11** disembodied, nonmaterial, nonphysical **12** metaphysical **13** unsubstantial

incorrect 5 false, wrong **6** faulty, untrue **7** unsound **8** improper, specious **9** erroneous, imprecise **10** fallacious, inaccurate, unbecoming

incorrigible 6 unruly **8** depraved **9** incurable **10** delinquent, inveterate **11** unalterable **12** irredeemable

increase 2 up **3** add, wax **4** gain, grow, hike, jump, plus, rise, soar, teem **5** add to, boost, build, mount, raise, run up, surge, swarm, swell **6** accrue, amount, beef up, dilate, expand, extend, growth, jack up, markup, step up **7** accrual, advance, amplify, augment, burgeon, enhance, enlarge, inflate, magnify, prolong, upsurge **8** addition, compound, escalate, flourish, heighten, lengthen, manifold, multiply, protract, snowball **9** accession, accretion, expansion, extension, increment, inflation, intensify, reinforce **10** accelerate, accumulate, aggrandize, appreciate **11** enlargement **12** augmentation **13** amplification

incredible 7 amazing, awesome **8** unlikely **9** cockamamy, fantastic **10** astounding, cockamamie, far-fetched, impossible, improbable, outlandish, phenomenal, remarkable **11** astonishing, implausible **12** preposterous, unbelievable, unconvincing, unimaginable **13** extraordinary

incredulity 7 unfaith **8** distrust, mistrust, unbelief **9** disbelief, nonbelief, suspicion **10** skepticism

incredulous 6 show-me **7** dubious **8** doubting **9** quizzical, sceptical, skeptical **10** suspicious **11** distrustful, mistrustful, questioning, unbelieving, unconvinced **12** disbelieving

increment 4 gain, hike, rise, step 5 raise 6 degree, growth 7 quantum 8 addition 9 accession, accretion 11 enlargement 12 augmentation

incriminate 6 accuse, charge 7 arraign, impeach 9 implicate

incrustation 4 film, rime, scab 5 scale 6 tartar 7 coating

incubate 5 hatch

incubus 5 demon, fiend 9 nightmare

inculcate 5 teach, train 6 impart 7 educate, implant, impress, instill

inculpable 4 pure 5 clean 8 innocent, spotless, virtuous 9 blameless, guiltless, righteous 10 impeccable

incumbent 7 leaning, resting 8 occupant, required 9 overlying 10 obligatory 12 officeholder

incur 7 acquire, bring on 8 contract

incurable 5 fatal 6 deadly, lethal 8 hopeless, terminal 9 immutable 11 immedicable, irreparable 12 irremediable, unchangeable 13 uncorrectable

incursion 4 raid 5 blitz, foray, sally 6 attack, sortie 7 assault 9 irruption

incus 4 bone 5 anvil

indebted 5 bound 7 obliged 8 beholden 9 obligated

indebtedness 3 due, IOU 7 arrears 9 arrearage, gratitude, liability 10 obligation 11 delinquency 12 thankfulness

indecent 4 blue, lewd, racy 5 bawdy, dirty, gross 6 coarse, filthy, impure, risqué, smutty, vulgar 7 obscene, profane, raunchy 8 immodest, improper, off-color, unseemly, untoward 9 offensive 10 scurrilous 13 objectionable

indecision 5 doubt 8 wavering 9 hesitancy 11 ambivalence, uncertainty, vacillation 12 equivocation, irresolution, shilly-shally

indecisive 5 vague 6 unsure 7 dubious, unclear 8 wavering 9 equivocal, tentative, uncertain, undecided, unsettled 10 irresolute 11 problematic, vacillating

indecorous 4 rude 5 gross, rough 6 coarse, vulgar 7 uncivil 8 impolite, improper, unseemly, untoward 9 graceless, irregular, offensive, tasteless, unrefined 10 unbecoming 11 ill-mannered, undignified 12 discourteous

indecorum 5 gaffe 6 breach 7 blooper, blunder, faux pas, offense 8 solecism 11 impropriety

indeed 4 amen 5 truly 6 really, surely, verily 8 forsooth, honestly 9 assuredly, certainly 10 positively, undeniably 11 doubtlessly, undoubtedly 13 unequivocally

indefatigable 6 dogged 8 tireless, untiring,

vigorous 9 energetic, tenacious 10 persistent, relentless, unflagging, unwearying 11 unrelenting

indefensible 9 unguarded, untenable 10 assailable, vulnerable 11 unprotected 12 unforgivable, unpardonable 13 unjustifiable

indefinable 5 vague 7 elusive 9 uncertain 11 unspeakable, unutterable 13 undescribable

indefinite 4 wide 5 broad, loose, vague 7 endless, general, inexact, obscure, unclear, unfixed 8 infinite 9 ambiguous, boundless, imprecise, limitless, unbounded, uncertain, undefined, unlimited 10 indistinct, inexplicit, unmeasured, unspecific 12 inconclusive 13 indeterminate *article:* 2 an *pronoun:* 3 all, any, few 4 each, many, most, none, some 6 anyone, nobody 7 anybody, several, someone 8 everyone, somebody 9 everybody

indehiscent fruit 3 key, nut 4 pepo 5 berry, grain, grape, melon 6 achene, loment, samara, squash 7 pumpkin 8 cucumber 9 caryopsis 10 schizocarp

indelible 4 fast 5 fixed 7 lasting 8 enduring 9 memorable, permanent 13 unforgettable

indelicate 3 raw 4 lewd, rude 5 crude, gross, rough 6 coarse, vulgar 7 uncouth 8 impolite, immodest, improper, tactless, unseemly, untoward 9 unrefined 10 unbecoming

indemnify 5 repay 6 secure 7 redress, requite 9 reimburse 10 compensate, recompense, remunerate

indemnity 6 amends 7 redress 8 requital, security 9 exemption, quittance, reprisals 10 protection, recompense, reparation 11 restitution 12 compensation, remuneration 13 fee-for-service

indentation 4 dent, nick, pock 5 notch 6 dimple, recess 10 depression

indenture 4 nick 5 notch 8 contract 9 agreement 11 certificate

indentured 5 bound 10 controlled 11 apprenticed

independent 4 free 8 absolute, autarkic, separate 9 autarchic, sovereign 10 autonomous 11 self-reliant 13 self-contained

indescribable 11 unspeakable, unutterable 13 unexplainable

indestructible 7 lasting 8 enduring, immortal 9 permanent 12 imperishable, irrefragable, unperishable

indeterminate 5 vague 9 imprecise, uncertain, unlimited

index 4 list, mark, sign 5 ratio, table 7 catalog, symptom 8 classify, evidence, regulate 9 catalogue 11 systematize

India *bay:* 6 Bengal *capital:* 8 New Delhi *city:* 5 Delhi 6 Bombay, Kanpur, Madras, Mumbai, Nagpur 7 Benares, Chennai, Kolkata, Lucknow 8 Calcutta 9 Ahmadabad, Bangalore, Hyderabad *coast:* 7 Malabar 10 Coromandel *European discoverer:* 4 Gama (Vasco da) *language:* 5 Hindi *leader:* 3 Rao (P. V. N.) 5 Nehru (Jawaharlal) 6 Gandhi (Indira, Mohandas, Rajiv) *monetary unit:* 5 rupee *mountain range:* 7 Vindhya 9 Himalayas *neighbor:* 5 Burma, China, Nepal 6 Bhutan 7 Myanmar 8 Pakistan 10 Bangladesh *pass:* 5 Bolan, Gumal 6 Khyber *plateau:* 6 Deccan *river:* 5 Indus 6 Ganges, Yamuna 7 Krishna 11 Brahmaputra *sea:* 7 Arabian

Indian *bread:* 3 nan 4 naan 7 chapati *butter:* 3 ghi 4 ghee *caste:* 4 Bahr 5 Sudra 6 Vaisya 7 Brahman 9 Kshatriya *cattle:* 4 dhan *cavalry commander:* 8 risaldar *crop-related:* 4 rabi 6 kharif *female dancer:* 8 bayadere *groom:* 4 syce *harem:* 6 zenana *instrument:* 4 vina 5 sarod, sitar, tabla 7 tambura *lady:* 4 bibi 5 begum 8 memsahib *musical term:* 4 raga, tala *musician:* 7 Shankar (Ravi) *nurse:* 4 amah, ayah *outcast:* 6 pariah *peasant:* 4 ryot *prince:* 4 raja, rana 5 rajah 8 maharaja 9 maharajah *princess:* 5 begum *queen:* 4 rani 5 ranee *scholar:* 6 pandit, pundit *screen:* 6 purdah *seal, stamp:* 4 chop *soldier:* 4 peon 5 sepoy *steps:* 4 ghat *teacher:* 4 guru *title:* 5 sahib *viceroy:* 5 nabob, nawab *weight unit:* 3 ser 4 cash, dhan, pank, pice, powe, rati, tank, tola 5 adpao, fanam, hubba, masha, maund, pally, pouah, ratti 6 dhurra, pagoda, pollam 7 chinnam, chittak

Indian, American *baby:* 7 papoose *ball game:* 8 lacrosse *carrier:* 7 travois *Central and South American:* 3 Mam, Ona 4 Cuna, Inca, Maya 5 Arara, Aztec, Carib, Huave, Olmec, Taino, Yagua 6 Arawak, Aymara, Jivaro, Omagua, Toltec, Yahgan 7 Chibcha, Quechua, Zapotec 8 Tarascan, Yanomamo 10 Araucanian 11 Tupi-Guaraní *food:* 4 samp 5 maize 8 pemmican *home:* 5 hogan, lodge, tepee 6 pueblo, teepee, wigwam 7 wickiup *leader:* 4 Popé 6 Wovoka 7 Cochise, Osceola, Pontiac, Sequoia, Sequoya 8 Geronimo, Hiawatha, Powhatan, Sequoyah, Tecumseh 9 Black Hawk, Massasoit 10 Crazy Horse 11 Cornplanter, Sitting Bull *money:* 6 wampum *North American:* 3 Aht, Fox, Hoh, Kaw, Oto, Sac, Sia, Ute, Wea 4 Coos, Cora, Cree, Crow, Erie, Hopi, Hupa, Iowa, Otoe, Pima, Pomo, Sauk, Taos, Yuma, Zuni 5 Aleut, Caddo, Creek, Haida, Huron, Kansa, Kiowa, Maidu, Miami, Modoc, Omaha, Osage, Sioux, Uinta 6 Apache, Cayuga, Dakota, Lenape, Mandan, Micmac, Mohawk, Munsee, Navaho, Navajo, Nootka, Oglala, Ojibwa, Oneida, Paiute, Pawnee, Pueblo, Quapaw, Salish, Santee, Seneca, Siwash 7 Anasazi, Arapaho, Arikara, Bannock, Chilkat, Chinook, Choctaw, Dakotah, Esselen, Klamath, Kutenai, Mohican, Naskapi, Natchez, Ojibway, Pontiac, Shawnee, Tlingit 8 Cherokee, Cheyenne, Chippewa, Comanche, Delaware, Illinois, Iroquois, Kickapoo, Kwakiutl, Nez Percé, Onondaga, Powhatan, Seminole, Shoshoni 9 Blackfoot, Chickasaw, Menominee, Tsimshian, Tuscarora, Wampanoag, Winnebago 10 Assiniboin, Chiricahua, Gros Ventre, Potawatomi 11 Massachuset, Narraganset *pipe:* 7 calumet *spirit:* 5 totem 6 manitu 7 kachina, manitou

Indiana *capital:* 12 Indianapolis *city:* 4 Gary 6 Muncie 9 Fort Wayne, South Bend 10 Evansville, Terre Haute 11 Bloomington *college, university:* 6 DePauw, Purdue 9 Ball State, Notre Dame *nickname:* 7 Hoosier (State) *river:* 5 White 6 Wabash *state bird:* 8 cardinal *state flower:* 5 peony *state tree:* 5 tulip

Indian paintbrush 8 hawkweed 10 painted cup

indicate 4 bode, hint, mark, mean, show 5 augur, imply, point, prove 6 attest, convey, denote, evince, import, reveal 7 bespeak, betoken, connote, display, exhibit, express, presage, signify, suggest 8 disclose, evidence, foretell, manifest, register 9 designate 10 foreshadow, illustrate 11 demonstrate

indication 3 cue 4 clue, hint, mark, sign 5 proof, token, trace 6 augury, signal 7 gesture, inkling, portent, symptom 8 evidence, reminder, telltale 9 testimony 10 expression, suggestion 13 foreshadowing, manifestation

indicative 10 expressive, suggestive 11 evidentiary, symptomatic 12 illustrative 13 demonstrative

indicia 5 marks, signs 8 imprints, markings

indict 5 blame 6 accuse, charge 7 arraign, censure, impeach 9 criticize

indifference 6 apathy 9 aloofness, unconcern 10 detachment, dispassion 11 disinterest 12 carelessness, impartiality

indifferent 4 cold, cool, numb, so-so 5 aloof, blasé, stoic 6 casual, remote 7 average, neutral 8 careless, detached, mediocre, middling, moderate, ordinary, passable, unbiased, uncaring **9** apathetic, impartial, impassive, objective **10** nonchalant, unaffected **11** unconcerned, unemotional **12** uninterested, unprejudiced **13** disinterested, dispassionate

indigence 4 need, want **6** penury **7** poverty **9** neediness, pauperism, privation **11** deprivation, destitution

indigene 6 native **9** aborigine **10** aboriginal

indigenous 6 native **7** endemic, natural **10** aboriginal, congenital, connatural, unacquired **13** autochthonous

indigent 4 poor **5** broke, needy **9** destitute, penniless **11** impecunious, necessitous **12** impoverished

indigestion 9 dyspepsia, heartburn

indignant 3 mad **5** irate, riled, upset, vexed **6** galled, heated **7** annoyed **8** offended, outraged, provoked **9** affronted, irritated, resentful

indignation 5 pique **7** dudgeon **10** irritation, resentment

indignity 3 cut **4** slap **6** injury, insult, slight **7** affront, outrage **9** contumely, grievance **10** disrespect **11** humiliation **13** disparagement, embarrassment

indigo 4 anil, blue **8** deep blue

indigo bird 5 finch **7** bunting

Indira's father 5 Nehru (Jawaharlal)

indirect 7 devious, oblique, vagrant, winding **8** circular, sidelong, tortuous **9** deceitful, underhand, wandering **10** backhanded, circuitous, collateral, meandering, roundabout **11** duplicitous, underhanded

indiscreet 5 gabby **6** unwise **7** foolish, gossipy **8** tactless **9** impolitic, imprudent, untactful **10** ill-advised **11** loose-lipped

indiscretion 4 slip **5** folly, gaffe, lapse **7** blunder, faux pas, mistake, misstep **8** solecism **10** imprudence **11** impropriety

indiscriminate 5 mixed **6** hybrid, motley, random, varied **7** aimless, jumbled, vagrant **8** assorted, careless **9** arbitrary, desultory, haphazard, hit-or-miss, unplanned, wholesale **10** uncritical **11** promiscuous **12** conglomerate, multifarious, unrestrained **13** heterogeneous, miscellaneous

indispensable 5 basic, vital **6** needed **7** crucial, needful, pivotal **8** cardinal, critical **9** essential, necessary, requisite **10** imperative, obligatory **11** fundamental

indisposed 3 ill **4** down, sick **5** loath **6** ailing, averse, poorly, sickly, unwell **7** uneager **8** hesitant **9** reluctant, resistant, unwilling **11** disinclined

indisposition 6 malady **7** ailment, dislike, illness, malaise **8** aversion, disfavor, distaste, sickness, unhealth **10** affliction, reluctance

indisputable 4 sure, true **7** certain, evident, obvious **8** absolute, ironclad, positive **9** apodictic **10** undeniable **11** irrefutable, unequivocal **12** irrefragable, unassailable

indistinct 3 dim **4** hazy **5** faint, foggy, misty, murky, vague **6** bleary, blurry, cloudy **7** blurred, obscure, shadowy, unclear **8** confused **9** uncertain, undefined **12** undetermined

indistinguishable 4 same **5** alike, equal, vague **7** unclear **9** duplicate, identical **10** equivalent

indite 3 pen **5** write **6** record, scribe **7** compose, engross **10** transcribe

individual 3 one **4** body, lone, self, sole, soul, unit **5** being, human, party, thing **6** entity, mortal, person, proper, single **7** special **8** creature, discrete, distinct, peculiar, personal, separate, singular, solitary, specific **10** particular, respective **11** distinctive **13** idiosyncratic *combining form:* **4** idio

individualist 5 loner **6** hermit **8** lone wolf, maverick **13** nonconformist

individuality 4 self **7** essence, oneness **8** identity, selfhood **9** character **10** uniqueness **11** personality, singularity **12** idiosyncrasy, separateness

individualize 4 mark **7** specify **9** customize **10** specialize **11** distinguish, personalize, singularize **12** characterize **13** differentiate, particularize

Indochinese country 4 Laos **5** Burma **7** Myanmar, Vietnam **8** Cambodia, Thailand **9** Kampuchea

indoctrinate 5 teach, tutor **7** educate, program **8** convince, persuade **9** brainwash, inculcate

indolence 4 laze **5** sloth **7** inertia, languor **8** idleness, laziness, lethargy **9** torpidity **12** slothfulness, sluggishness **13** shiftlessness *fruit of:* **5** lotus

indolent 4 idle, lazy **6** torpid **8** fainéant, slothful, sluggish **9** lethargic, shiftless

indomitable 7 staunch **9** steadfast **10** invincible, unbeatable **11** impregnable **13** unconquerable

Indonesia *archipelago:* **5** Malay *capital:* **7** Jakarta **8** Djakarta *city:* **5** Medan **7** Bandung, Cilacap **8** Semarang, Surabaja, Surabaya **9** Palembang *island group:* **5** Sunda **8** Moluccas *language:* **6** Bahasa *leader:* **7** Suharto, Sukarno *monetary unit:* **6** rupiah *regions:* **4** Bali, Java **5** Ceram, Timor **6** Bangka, Borneo, Flores, Lombok, Madura

7 Celebes, Sumatra 8 Sulawesi 9 Irian Jaya
volcano: 8 Krakatau, Krakatoa
indubitable 4 sure 6 patent 7 certain, evident, obvious 8 definite, ironclad, positive 9 apodictic, veritable 10 undeniable 11 irrefutable, self-evident, unequivocal 12 irrefragable
induce 5 cause 6 effect, elicit, prompt 7 actuate, procure 8 convince, engender, generate, motivate, occasion, persuade 9 encourage
inducement 4 bait, lure 6 come-on, motive 10 attraction, motivation 13 consideration
induct 4 lead 5 admit 6 enlist, enroll 7 appoint, install
inductance unit 5 henry
induction 8 entrance 9 accession, reasoning 10 enlistment 11 appointment 13 ratiocination
inductive 7 logical 9 prefatory, prelusive 11 a posteriori
indulge 3 pet 4 baby, bask 5 allow, favor, humor, spoil 6 cocker, coddle, cosset, oblige, pamper, permit, please, wallow 7 cater to, delight, gratify, satisfy 9 luxuriate 11 mollycoddle
indulgence 5 favor, mercy, treat 6 luxury 7 charity 8 clemency, courtesy, kindness, lenience, leniency 9 allowance, remission, tolerance 10 compassion, kindliness, permission, toleration 11 forbearance, forgiveness 12 dispensation, mercifulness 13 gratification
indulgence seller 5 Tezel (Johann) 6 Tetzel (Johann)
indulgent 4 easy, kind 7 clement, lenient 8 generous, merciful, tolerant 9 forgiving 10 charitable, permissive
indurate 6 harden 7 callous, confirm, congeal 8 hardened, solidify, stubborn 9 unfeeling 11 hard-hearted
industrialist 6 tycoon 7 magnate 12 manufacturer
industrious 4 busy 8 diligent, sedulous 9 assiduous, laborious
industry 4 work 5 labor 8 business, commerce 9 assiduity, diligence 10 enterprise
Indy 500 winner 4 Foyt (A. J.) 5 Mears (Rick), Unser (Al, Bobby) 8 Andretti (Mario)
inebriant see **intoxicant**
inebriate 3 sot 4 lush, soak 5 drunk, souse, tight, tipsy, toper 6 bibber, boozer 7 stupefy, tippler, tosspot 8 drunkard 10 intoxicate
inebriated 3 lit 5 drunk, lit up, oiled, stiff, tight, tipsy 6 blotto, juiced, loaded, plowed, potted, soused, stewed, tanked, wasted 7

crocked, pickled, pie-eyed, sloshed, smashed 8 polluted 9 plastered
inedible 9 poisonous 12 unappetizing
ineffable 5 taboo 9 forbidden 11 unspeakable, unutterable 13 undescribable
ineffaceable 7 lasting 8 enduring 9 indelible, permanent
ineffective 4 vain, weak 6 futile 7 useless 8 abortive, bootless, feckless, impotent 9 fruitless, powerless 10 emasculate, unavailing 12 unproductive, unsuccessful
ineffectiveness 8 futility 9 impotence
ineffectual see **ineffective**
inefficient 5 slack 6 clumsy 8 careless, slipshod, wasteful 9 negligent
inelastic 5 rigid, stiff 7 brittle 9 unbending 10 unyielding
inelegant 5 crass, crude, gross, rough 6 coarse, gauche, vulgar 7 awkward, uncouth 9 graceless, unrefined 10 uncultured, ungraceful 12 uncultivated
ineligible 5 unfit 8 unfitted, unworthy 10 unequipped, unsuitable 11 unqualified 12 disqualified
ineluctable 4 sure 5 bound, fated 6 doomed 7 certain 8 destined 9 necessary 10 inevitable, unevadable 11 unavoidable, unescapable 13 unpreventable
inept 5 unfit 6 clumsy, gauche, klutzy 7 artless, awkward, foolish, halting, unhandy 8 bumbling, bungling 9 all thumbs, hamhanded, maladroit, unskilled 10 malapropos, unskillful, unsuitable 11 heavy-handed, undexterous, unfortunate
inequality 8 imparity 9 disparity 10 unevenness 12 irregularity, variableness 13 disproportion, heterogeneity
inequitable 6 biased, unfair, unjust 7 partial 10 prejudiced 11 unjustified, unrighteous
inequity 4 bias 6 wrong 9 prejudice 10 unfairness, unjustness
ineradicable 6 innate 7 chronic 8 constant, inherent, stubborn 9 ingrained 10 deep-rooted, deep-seated, entrenched, inveterate 11 established, ever-present, never-ending
inert 4 calm, dead, idle 5 quiet, still 6 asleep, sleepy 7 dormant, passive 8 immobile, lifeless, sluggish 9 apathetic, lethargic 10 motionless
inert gas 4 neon 5 argon, radon, xenon 6 helium 7 krypton
inertia 5 sloth 6 apathy, stupor, torpor 7 languor 8 idleness, laziness, lethargy 9 indolence, inertness, lassitude, passivity, torpidity 10 immobility, inactivity 11 disinterest 12 listlessness, sluggishness
inescapable see **inevitable**

inessential see **unessential**

inestimable 9 priceless 11 measureless 12 immeasurable, unmeasurable, unfathomable

inevitable 4 sure 5 bound, fated 6 doomed 7 certain 8 destined 9 necessary 11 unavoidable, unescapable 12 foreordained 13 unpreventable

inevitably 8 perforce 10 willy-nilly 11 like it or not, unavoidably

inexcusable 6 guilty 8 blamable, culpable 9 untenable 10 censurable 11 blameworthy, condemnable 12 criticizable, unforgivable, unpardonable 13 reprehensible, unjustifiable

inexhaustible 8 tireless, untiring 9 unfailing, weariless 10 bottomless, unflagging 13 indefatigable

inexorable 5 rigid 6 strict 7 adamant 8 immobile, obdurate, stubborn 9 immovable, unbending 10 relentless, unyielding 11 unrelenting

inexpensive 3 low 5 cheap 7 cut-rate 8 moderate 10 reasonable

inexperience 7 naïveté, rawness 8 verdancy 9 freshness, greenness 10 callowness

inexperienced 3 raw 5 fresh, green, naive, young 6 callow 7 untried 8 unversed 9 unskilled, untrained, unworldly 10 amateurish, unseasoned

inexpert 9 maladroit, unskilled, untrained 10 amateurish

inexplicable 6 arcane, obtuse, opaque 7 cryptic 9 enigmatic 10 mysterious, mystifying, unsolvable 12 impenetrable, unfathomable 13 unaccountable, unexplainable

inexpressible 8 nameless 11 unspeakable, unutterable 13 undescribable, unexplainable

inexpressive 5 blank, stoic 6 stolid, vacant, wooden 7 deadpan 9 impassive 10 poker-faced 13 straight-faced

inextricable 9 insoluble 10 unsolvable

infallible 4 sure 5 exact 6 trusty 7 certain, correct, perfect 8 absolute, accurate, flawless, surefire, unerring 9 errorless, unfailing 10 dependable, impeccable 11 trustworthy 12 tried-and-true 13 unimpeachable

infamous 4 evil, vile 6 odious 7 hateful, heinous 8 flagrant, shameful 9 abhorrent, miscreant, nefarious, notorious 10 abominable, despicable, detestable, flagitious, scandalous, villainous 11 disgraceful, ignominious, opprobrious 12 contemptible, disreputable

infamy 5 odium, shame 7 obloquy 8 disgrace, dishonor, ignominy 9 disrepute, notoriety 10 opprobrium

infancy 6 nonage 8 babyhood 9 childhood

infant 4 babe, baby 5 bairn, child, green 7 bambino, neonate, newborn, papoose, toddler 8 bantling, immature, nursling 9 unfledged *bed:* 4 crib 6 cradle 8 bassinet *condition:* 5 colic *food:* 3 pap 4 milk 7 pabulum *room:* 7 nursery

infanta 8 princess

infantile 7 babyish, puerile 8 childish, immature

infantryman 7 dogface 8 doughboy 11 foot soldier *Algerian:* 6 Zouave

infatuated 4 gaga 5 dotty, silly 7 foolish 8 besotted, enamored, obsessed 9 bewitched, rapturous 10 captivated, passionate

infatuation 4 rage 5 ardor, craze, crush, folly 7 passion, rapture 8 devotion 9 obsession, puppy love 11 fascination

infect 5 taint 6 defile, poison 7 corrupt, pollute 11 contaminate

infection 3 bug 6 sepses (plural), sepsis *carrier:* 6 vector *fungous:* 8 mycetoma

infectious 8 catching, epidemic, virulent 9 pestilent 10 contagious, corrupting 12 communicable 13 contaminating, transmittable

infelicitous 5 unapt, unfit 6 unmeet 7 awkward, unhappy 8 improper 9 imperfect 10 malapropos, unsuitable 11 regrettable, unfortunate

infer 5 judge 6 deduce, deduct, derive, gather, reason 7 collect, make out, suppose, surmise 8 conclude, construe 10 conjecture 11 extrapolate, hypothesize

inference 7 surmise 8 illation, sequitur 9 deduction 10 assumption, conclusion, conjecture, derivation 11 presumption, supposition

inferior 3 low 4 base, fair, hack, mean, poor, puny 5 cheap, lousy, lower, minor, petty, scrub, sorry, under, worse 6 common, deputy, feeble, impure, junior, lesser, nether, no-good, paltry, satrap, shoddy, sleazy, tawdry, tinpot, vassal 7 average, subject, unequal 8 declassé, low-grade, mediocre, middling, ordinary, unworthy, wretched 9 attendant, auxiliary, no-account, satellite, secondary, subaltern, subjacent, underling, worthless 10 inadequate, second-rate 11 substandard *prefix:* 3 sub 4 demi 5 infra

infernal 6 Hadean 7 demonic, hellish, satanic 8 chthonic, damnable, demoniac, devilish, diabolic, plutonic 9 chthonian, plutonian, Tartarean 10 diabolical, sulphurous

inferno 3 pit 4 fire, hell 5 Hades, Sheol 6 blazes, Tophet 7 Gehenna 9 holocaust, perdition 10 underworld 11 netherworld 13 conflagration

Inferno *division:* **5** canto *poet:* **5** Dante
(Alighieri) *verse form:* **9** terza rima

infertile 6 barren, effete **7** sterile **8** impotent
10 unfruitful **12** hardscrabble, unproductive

infest 4 teem **5** beset, swarm **6** plague **7** overrun **10** parasitize

infidel 5 pagan **7** atheist, heathen, heretic,
skeptic **8** agnostic **10** unbeliever

infidelity 7 perfidy, treason **8** adultery, betrayal, cheating **9** disbelief, treachery **10**
disloyalty **13** faithlessness

infinite 4 vast **7** endless, eternal, immense **8**
unending **9** boundless, countless, limitless,
perpetual, unlimited **11** everlasting, illimitable, measureless, sempiternal **12** immeasurable

infinity 8 eternity **10** perpetuity **11** endlessness **12** sempiternity **13** boundlessness, lim-
itlessness

infirm 4 lame, sick, weak **5** frail **6** ailing, feeble, sickly **7** failing, fragile, unsound **8** decrepit, unstable **9** doddering **11** debilitated

infirmity 3 ill **4** flaw **5** decay **6** malady **7** ailment, disease, frailty, illness, malaise **8** debility, disorder, sickness, syndrome,
weakness **9** complaint, condition **10** affliction, feebleness, sickliness **11** decrepitude
12 debilitation, enfeeblement

infix 4 root **5** embed, lodge **6** fasten, pierce **7**
engrave, implant, impress

inflame 4 fire, gall, goad, rile, roil **5** anger,
light, rouse **6** arouse, enrage, excite, foment, ignite, kindle, madden, redden, stir
up **7** provoke **8** enkindle, irritate **9** aggravate **10** exacerbate, exasperate

inflammable 5 fiery **6** ardent **8** burnable, volatile **9** excitable, ignitable, irascible **11**
combustible

inflammation 4 gout, sore **6** otitis, quinsy **7**
catarrh, colitis **8** adenitis, bursitis, cystitis,
neuritis, pleurisy, rachitis, swelling **9** arthritis, chilblain, gastritis, nephritis, phlebitis
10 bronchitis, cellulitis, combustion, dermatitis, gingivitis, laryngitis, tendinitis **12**
encephalitis **13** poliomyelitis *eye:* **6** iritis **7**
pinkeye **9** keratitis *horse:* **7** fistula, quittor
intestines: **7** ileitis **9** enteritis *suffix:* **4** itis

inflammatory 8 exciting **9** explosive, seditious **11** provocative **13** rabble-rousing, revolutionary

inflate 4 fill **5** bloat, elate, swell **6** expand **7**
amplify, distend **9** supersize **10** aggrandize

inflated 5 tumid, windy **6** turgid **7** bloated,
swollen, verbose **9** bombastic, distended,
dropsical, flatulent, overblown **10** heightened **11** exaggerated, pretentious

inflection 4 bend, tone **5** curve, pitch **6** accent, change, stress, timbre **8** emphasis, tonality **9** accidence **10** modulation

inflexible 3 set **4** grim, hard, iron **5** fixed,
rigid, stiff **6** strict **7** adamant, die-hard **8**
granitic, hard-line, ironclad, obdurate, stubborn **9** immovable, immutable, obstinate,
steadfast, unbending **10** adamantine, brassbound, implacable, rock-ribbed, unbendable, unyielding **11** unalterable, unrelenting
12 unchangeable

inflict 5 visit, wreak **7** mete out, subject **8** dispense **10** administer

inflow 4 rush **7** arrival

influence 4 move, pull, sway **5** alter, bribe,
clout, force, impel, lobby, touch **6** affect,
compel, impact, modify, moment, strike,
weight **7** command, control, impress, mastery **8** dominate, militate, persuade, prestige
9 authority, dominance

influenceable 8 gullible **9** malleable, receptive, tractable **11** persuadable, persuasible,
suggestible

influential 6 potent **8** forceful, powerful **9** effective **10** persuasive **13** authoritative

influx 7 arrival **8** entrance, invasion **9** accession

inform 3 rat, tip **4** blab, clue, leak, post, tell,
warn **5** brief, edify, endow, endue, imbue,
teach **6** advise, betray, fill in, impart,
leaven, notify, reveal, snitch, squeal, tattle,
turn in, update **7** animate, apprise, caution,
educate **8** acquaint, disclose, forewarn **9** advertise, enlighten **11** familiarize

informal 6 casual, dégagé, folksy **7** natural,
offhand, relaxed **8** down-home, familiar,
laid-back **9** easygoing **10** colloquial, unofficial **13** unceremonious

information 3 tip **4** data, fact, lore, news,
poop, word **5** scoop **6** advice, notice,
skinny, wisdom **7** lowdown, tidings **9**
knowledge **12** intelligence *manager:* **9** cy-
brarian *secondhand:* **7** hearsay

information bureau *abbreviation:* **4** USIA,
USIS

informative 8 edifying, exegetic **10** exegetical
11 educational, elucidative, explanatory **12**
enlightening, illuminating

informed 4 wise **5** aware **6** au fait, versed **7**
abreast, knowing **8** apprised, educated **9** au
courant, cognizant **10** acquainted, conversant **11** enlightened **13** knowledgeable

informer 3 rat, spy **4** fink, mole, narc **5** stool
6 canary, gossip, snitch **7** rat fink, stoolie,
tattler, tipster **8** squealer, telltale **10** deep
throat, talebearer, tattletale **11** stool pigeon
13 whistle-blower

infra 5 after, below, later, under **7** beneath

infract 3 sin **6** breach, offend **7** violate **8** trespass **10** contravene, transgress

infraction 3 sin **4** foul **5** crime, error **6** breach **7** faux pas, misdeed, offense **8** trespass **9** violation **12** encroachment **13** contravention, transgression

infrastructure 4 base **5** basis **9** framework **10** foundation, groundwork, substratum **12** underpinning

infrequent 3 odd **4** rare **6** scarce, seldom **7** unusual **8** isolated, sporadic, uncommon, unwonted **10** occasional **11** exceptional

infringe 6 breach, impose, meddle, offend **7** disturb, obtrude, violate **8** encroach, entrench, trespass **10** transgress

infuriate 3 ire, mad **4** rile **5** anger, pique **6** enrage, madden, rankle **7** incense, inflame, outrage, provoke, steam up

infuse 4 fill, soak **5** imbue, steep **6** leaven **7** animate, implant, pervade, suffuse **8** permeate, saturate **10** impregnate

ingenious 5 acute, canny, sharp, smart, witty **6** adroit, clever, crafty **7** cunning, fertile **8** creative, original **11** imaginative, resourceful

ingenuity 5 knack, savvy, skill **6** acumen, smarts, talent **7** know-how, mastery **8** deftness, keenness **9** adeptness, handiness **10** adroitness, capability, cleverness, perception, shrewdness **11** proficiency **12** intelligence, skillfulness **13** inventiveness

ingenuous 4 open **5** naive **6** simple **7** artless, natural **8** innocent **9** childlike, guileless, unstudied **10** unaffected

ingest 3 eat **4** feed **6** devour **7** consume, partake, swallow

Inge work 6 Picnic **7** Bus Stop **18** Splendor in the Grass **19** Come Back Little Sheba

inglorious 8 shameful **11** disgraceful, ignominious, opprobrious **12** dishonorable, disreputable **13** discreditable, unrespectable

ingot 3 bar, pig, rod **4** mold **6** billet

ingrain 4 etch **5** imbue

ingrained 6 innate **8** inherent **9** essential **10** congenital, deep-rooted, deep-seated

ingratiating 5 silky **6** silken, smarmy **7** fawning **8** pleasing, unctuous **9** adulatory **10** flattering **11** sycophantic

ingredient 4 part **5** piece **6** factor **7** element **9** component **11** constituent

ingress 4 door **5** entry **6** access, entrée, portal **7** doorway, passage **8** entrance, entryway **9** admission, vestibule **10** admittance **11** entranceway

ingurgitate 4 bolt, cram, gulp, slop, wolf **5** gorge, scarf, stuff, swill **6** devour, gobble, guzzle **7** swallow

inhabit 4 live **5** dwell, haunt **6** occupy, people, settle, tenant **8** populate

inhabitant 5 liver **6** inmate, native **7** citizen, denizen, dweller, resider **8** indigene, resident **9** aborigine **10** autochthon *foreign:* **5** alien *indigenous:* **6** native **9** aborigine

inhale 7 breathe, consume, respire, swallow

inharmonious 6 atonal **7** jarring **9** dissonant, unmusical **10** discordant **11** cacophonous, conflicting, conflictive, disagreeing, quarrelsome, uncongenial **12** antagonistic

inhere 3 lie **5** dwell **6** belong, reside

inherent 4 born **5** basic, per se **6** inborn, native **7** built-in, connate, natural **8** immanent **9** elemental, essential, intrinsic **10** congenital, deep-seated **11** fundamental

inherit 7 acquire, receive, succeed

inheritance 3 DNA **4** gene, gift **6** devise, estate, legacy **7** bequest **8** heirloom, heritage **9** patrimony, tradition **10** birthright **13** primogeniture

inherited 6 native **7** connate, genetic, natural **10** bequeathed, congenital, connatural, handed-down, hand-me-down

inheritor 4 heir **7** heiress, legatee **11** beneficiary

inhibit 4 curb, slow **5** check **6** arrest, bridle, enjoin, fetter, hamper, hinder, hobble, impede **7** prevent, repress, trammel **8** hold back, obstruct, restrain, suppress, withhold **9** constrain **10** discourage

inhibition 4 curb **5** taboo **6** hang-up **7** barrier **9** hindrance, restraint, stricture **10** impediment, repression **11** suppression

inhuman 5 cruel, feral **6** brutal, savage **7** beastly, bestial, brutish **8** fiendish **9** barbarous, monstrous **10** diabolical

inhumane 4 fell, grim **5** cruel **6** brutal, fierce, malign, savage **8** ruthless, sadistic **9** barbarous, ferocious, heartless, merciless, truculent

inhumation 6 burial **9** interment, sepulture **10** entombment

inhume 4 bury **5** plant **6** entomb **7** put away **9** lay to rest

inimical 7 adverse, harmful, hostile **10** malevolent, unfriendly **11** belligerent, contentious **12** antagonistic, antipathetic

iniquitous 3 bad **4** base, evil, vile **5** wrong **6** sinful, unjust, wicked **7** immoral, vicious **9** nefarious

iniquity 3 sin **4** evil **5** crime, wrong **7** offense **9** turpitude **8** trespass **10** immorality, wickedness, wrongdoing **13** transgression

initial 5 first, prime **6** anlage, letter, maiden **7** approve, engrave, leading, opening, primary **8** earliest, foremost, monogram, original **9** beginning

initiate 4 open **5** begin, enter, set up, start **6** enroll, get off, induct, invest, launch, take up **7** install, kick off, usher in **8** commence **9** originate **10** inaugurate

initiation 5 debut **7** baptism **9** admission, beginning, induction **10** admittance **11** investiture, origination **12** commencement, introduction

initiative 4 push **5** drive, spunk **6** energy **8** ambition, aptitude, gumption **9** beginning **10** enterprise, get-up-and-go

inject 3 add **6** insert **7** implant, instill **9** inoculate, introduce, vaccinate

injection 3 fix **4** hypo, shot **5** serum **7** booster, vaccine **10** hypodermic **11** inoculation, vaccination

injudicious 4 rash **5** hasty **6** unwise **8** heedless, reckless **9** ill-judged, impolitic, imprudent **10** ill-advised, indiscreet **11** inexpedient **12** shortsighted

injunction 3 ban, bar **4** writ **5** order **6** behest, charge **7** bidding, command, dictate, mandate **9** direction **11** prohibition

injure 3 mar **4** foul, harm, hurt, maim **5** spoil, wound, wrong **6** blight, bruise, damage, deface, deform, impair, mangle **7** contort, cripple, disable, torture **8** maltreat, mutilate **9** disfigure **12** incapacitate

injurious 6 nocent **7** abusive, adverse, harmful, hurtful **8** damaging **9** offensive **10** defamatory **11** detrimental

injury 3 ill **4** harm, hurt **5** wound, wrong **6** bruise, damage, trauma **8** distress **9** detriment

injustice 4 tort **5** crime, wrong **6** breach, damage **7** outrage **8** inequity, trespass **9** grievance, violation **10** favoritism, wrongdoing

ink 3 dye, pen **4** sign **8** inscribe **9** autograph, signature, subscribe **roller: 6** brayer

inkling 3 cue, tip **4** clue, hint, idea, lead, wind **5** hunch **6** notion, tip-off **8** telltale **9** suspicion **10** indication, intimation, suggestion

inky 3 jet **4** ebon **5** black, ebony, jetty, raven, sable **9** Cimmerian, pitch-dark **10** pitch-black

inlaid 5 piqué **6** boolle **7** hatched **8** enchased, nielloed **9** damascene, incrusted

Inland Empire 8 Illinois

inlet 3 arm, bay, ria **4** cove, gulf, loch **5** bayou, bight, creek, fiord, firth, fjord, sound **6** harbor, slough, strait **7** estuary *Admiralties:* **4** Kali *Adriatic Sea:* **5** Vlorë *Aegean Sea:* **7** Saronic *Alaska:* **4** Cook **5** Cross, Taiya **8** Chilkoot *Aleutians:* **5** Holtz, Nazan *Angola:* **5** Bengo, Tiger **6** Tigres *Antarctica:*
7 McMurdo **8** Amundsen **10** Shackleton *Arabian Sea:* **4** Qamr **5** Kamar *Australia:* **4** King **7** Repulse **10** Broad Sound *Baffin Island:* **9** Admiralty *Baltic Sea:* **6** Gdansk *Barents Sea:* **4** Kola **7** Pechóra *Bismarck Sea:* **5** Kimbe *Canada:* **9** Howe Sound *Cape Breton Island:* **4** Mira *Chile:* **5** Otway *Crete:* **4** Suda **5** Canea *Denmark:* **3** Ise *Djibouti:* **6** Tajura **8** Tadjoura *Ecuador:* **5** Manta *Florida:* **10** Saint Lucie *Georgia:* **8** Altamaha *Gulf of Alaska:* **3** Icy **5** Woman *Gulf of Mexico:* **8** Suwannee **9** Matagorda **10** Terrebonne *Hawaii:* **11** Pearl Harbor *Honshu:* **3** Ise **5** Owari **6** Atsuta *Iceland:* **4** Axar, Eyja, Huna **5** Horna, Skaga, Vopna **8** Hunafloi *Indonesia:* **4** Bima **5** Saleh *Ionian Sea:* **7** Taranto *Java:* **4** Lada **5** Peper *Kara Sea:* **6** Enisei **7** Yenisei *Labrador:* **8** Hamilton *Lake Erie:* **8** Put-in-Bay, Sandusky *Long Island:* **8** Rockaway *Madagascar:* **8** Antongil *Massachusetts:* **9** Annisquam *Massachusetts Bay:* **10** Lynn Harbor *Mediterranean Sea:* **8** Valencia **9** Famagusta **10** Khalij Surt **11** Syrtis Major *Mozambique:* **5** Memba, Pemba *Nantucket Sound:* **5** Lewis *New Guinea:* **3** Oro **5** Berau, Hansa **11** McCluer Gulf *New Jersey:* **9** Little Egg *New Zealand:* **5** Hawke **6** Tasman *North Carolina:* **9** Albemarle *Northern Ireland:* **12** Belfast Lough *North Sea:* **4** Lyse **9** Hardanger *Northwest Territories:* **5** Wager **8** Bathurst, Franklin **9** Frobisher **12** Prince Albert *Norway:* **3** Tys **4** Bokn, Tana **5** Lakse, Sogne *Norwegian Sea:* **4** Nord, Salt, Stor, Vest **5** Ranen **8** Scoresby **9** Trondheim *Ontario:* **4** Owen *Potomac:* **10** Tidal Basin *Philippines:* **5** Baler, Pilar, Sogod **6** Butuan **9** Davao Gulf, Leyte Gulf, Panay Gulf *Puget Sound:* **4** Carr, Case *Quebec:* **6** Ungava *Red Sea:* **4** Foul Bay **5** Chaun **8** Sakhalin *Santa Cruz Islands:* **8** Basilisk *Solomon Islands:* **4** Deep **8** Huon Gulf *South Africa:* **5** Table *South Carolina:* **4** Bull *South China Sea:* **4** Bias, Datu, Siam, Taya **5** Dasol **6** Brunei, Paluan **8** Lingayen *Spitsbergen:* **3** Ice **4** Bell **5** Kings *Sumatra:* **5** Bajur **10** Koninginne *Wales:* **5** Burry *Washington:* **11** Grays Harbor (see also **bay**)

inmate 7 convict **8** occupant, prisoner, resident **10** inhabitant

inmost part 4 core, pith **5** heart **6** center, depths, kernel, marrow **7** nucleus

inn 5 hotel, lodge, motel, serai **6** hostel, tavern **7** auberge, hospice, pension **8** hostelry **9** roadhouse **11** caravansary, public house **12** caravansarai **13** boardinghouse *French:* **7** auberge *German:* **7** Gasthof **8** Gasthaus

Spanish: 5 fonda 6 posada 7 parador *Turkish:* 6 imaret

innards 4 guts 5 belly 6 bowels, tripes 7 viscera 8 entrails, stuffing 10 intestines

innate see **inherent**

inner 3 gut 5 focal 6 hidden, middle, secret 7 central, nuclear, private 8 familiar, interior, internal, personal, visceral 9 concealed, essential *prefix:* 3 ent 4 ento

innervate 4 jolt, move 5 pique, rouse 6 excite 7 animate, provoke, quicken 8 motivate, vitalize 9 electrify, galvanize, stimulate

Innisfail 4 Eire, Erin 7 Ireland

innkeeper 4 host 8 boniface, hosteler, hotelier, landlord, publican

innocence 6 purity 7 naiveté 8 chastity 10 simplicity 11 artlessness, sinlessness

innocent 4 good, lamb, naïf, pure, void 5 clean, legal, licit, naive 6 chaste, devoid, lawful 7 artless, natural, unaware 8 harmless, ignorant, virtuous 9 blameless, childlike, exemplary, faultless, guileless, guiltless, ingenuous, innocuous, righteous, stainless, unstained, unsullied, untainted 10 inculpable, legitimate 12 unsuspecting

innocuous 5 banal, bland 6 pallid 7 insipid 8 harmless 11 inoffensive, unoffending 13 insignificant

innovation 6 change 7 novelty

innovative 3 new 5 novel 6 creative, original 9 inventive 10 newfangled 11 cutting-edge, leading-edge 12 trailblazing

innovator 9 architect, developer 10 originator 11 trailblazer 13 revolutionary

innuendo 4 clue, hint, slur 7 calumny 8 allusion 9 aspersion 10 backbiting, intimation 11 implication, insinuation

innumerable 4 many 6 legion, myriad, untold 7 umpteen 9 countless, uncounted 10 numberless 13 multitudinous

Ino *brother:* 9 Polydorus *father:* 6 Cadmus *grandfather:* 6 Agenor *husband:* 7 Athamas *mother:* 8 Harmonia *sister:* 5 Agave 6 Semele 7 Autonoë *son:* 8 Learchus, Palaemon 10 Melicertes

inobtrusive 4 meek 5 muted, quiet 6 modest 7 subdued 8 discreet, tasteful 10 restrained

inoculate 5 imbue, shoot, steep 6 infuse 7 implant, suffuse 9 vaccinate

inoffensive 5 bland 7 neutral 8 harmless 9 innocuous, peaceable

inopportune 8 ill-timed, mistimed, untimely 12 unseasonable

inordinate 5 undue 6 wanton 7 extreme 8 overmuch 9 excessive 10 exorbitant, gratuitous, immoderate, irrational 11 extrava-

gant, intemperate, superfluous, uncalled-for 12 unreasonable 13 extraordinary

inorganic 7 mineral 10 artificial

in passing 5 aside 6 obiter 7 by the by 8 by the bye, by the way 12 incidentally

in perpetuum 4 ever 6 always 7 forever, for good 8 evermore, for keeps 9 eternally 10 enduringly 11 forevermore

input 4 data 6 advice, energy 7 comment, counsel, opinion 8 feedback, guidance, material, stimulus 11 information

inquest 5 probe 7 hearing, inquiry 11 examination 13 investigation

inquietude 5 angst 6 unease, unrest 7 anxiety, ferment, turmoil 8 distress 10 uneasiness 11 restiveness 12 restlessness 13 Sturm und Drang

inquire 3 ask, pry 4 seek 5 probe, query 7 examine 8 question 9 catechize 11 interrogate, investigate

inquiry 5 audit, probe, query 7 hearing 8 grilling, question, research, scrutiny 11 examination, questioning 13 investigation

inquisition 4 hunt 5 probe, quest, trial 6 search 7 inquiry 8 grilling, research 11 examination 13 interrogation, investigation

inquisitive 4 nosy 5 nosey 6 prying, snoopy 7 curious 8 meddling, snooping 9 intrusive 10 meddlesome 11 questioning

inquisitor 10 Torquemada (Tomás de)

in re 4 as to 5 about, as for 7 apropos 9 as regards, regarding 10 as respects, concerning, respecting 12 with regard to 13 with respect to

in respect to see **in re**

inroad 4 raid 5 foray 7 advance 8 invasion 9 incursion 12 encroachment

ins and outs 5 ropes 6 quirks 7 details 8 minutiae, oddities 11 incidentals, particulars 12 lay of the land

insane 3 mad, off 4 daft, nuts 5 batty, crazy, daffy, dotty, loony, manic, nutsy, nutty, rabid, silly, wacky 6 absurd, crazed, cuckoo, maniac, raving, schizo, screwy, teched 7 berserk, bonkers, cracked, haywire, lunatic, tetched, touched, unsound 8 demented, deranged, unhinged 9 eccentric, psychotic 10 disordered, irrational, moonstruck, unbalanced 11 harebrained 12 crackbrained, preposterous, unreasonable

insane asylum 6 bedlam 8 loony bin, madhouse, nuthouse, snake pit 10 sanatorium, sanitarium

insanity 5 folly, mania 6 frenzy, lunacy 7 madness 8 delirium, delusion, dementia, hysteria, illusion 9 craziness, dottiness, psychosis 11 derangement, psychopathy

insatiable 6 crying, greedy, urgent 7 exigent 8 pressing, ravenous 9 clamorous, demanding, voracious 10 quenchless 11 importunate 12 unappeasable, unquenchable

inscribe 4 etch, list 5 carve, enter, print, write 6 enroll, record 7 engrave, engross, impress, imprint 8 dedicate, enscroll, register

inscription 5 title 6 legend 7 epigram, epitaph, heading 8 epigraph 10 dedication *Calvary:* 4 INRI

inscrutable 6 arcane 7 deadpan 10 mysterious, poker-faced, sphinxlike, unknowable, unreadable 12 impenetrable, unfathomable

insect 3 bee, bug, fly 6 beetle *adult:* 5 imago *antenna:* 4 palp 6 feeler, palpus *combining form:* 5 entom 6 entomo *covering:* 6 chitin *genus:* 4 Nepa *immature:* 4 grub, pupa 5 larva, nymph 6 larvae (plural), maggot 8 wriggler 9 chrysalis 11 caterpillar *kind:* 3 ant, bee 4 flea, moth, wasp 5 aphid, scale 6 bedbug, beefly, beetle, cicada, earwig, hornet, mantid, mantis, mayfly 7 ant lion, cricket, firefly, June bug, katydid, ladybug, termite 8 honeybee, horsefly, housefly, lacewing, mosquito, stinkbug 9 bumblebee, butterfly, damselfly, dragonfly 10 silverfish, springtail 11 grasshopper 12 walkingstick *luminous:* 7 firefly 8 glowworm *molt:* 7 ecdysis *moth:* 4 luna 5 gypsy 6 miller, sphinx 7 noctuid, pyralid, tortrix, tussock 8 cecropia, cinnabar, forester, sphingid 9 clearwing, geometrid, saturniid, tortricid 10 Polyphemus *multi-legged:* 8 diplopod 9 centipede, millipede *noisy:* 6 cicada *part:* 4 palp 5 cerci (plural) 6 arista, cercus, labium, labrum, ocelli (plural), palpus, thorax 7 antenna, maxilla, ocellus 8 antennae (plural), mandible, maxillae (plural) 9 proboscis, spiracles 10 ovipositor 11 exoskeleton *pest:* 4 flea, lice (plural), mite 5 louse, midge, scale 7 blowfly, termite 8 horsefly, housefly, mealybug 9 cockroach, gypsy moth 10 boll weevil, Hessian fly, silverfish *science:* 10 entomology *stage:* 6 instar *sucking:* 5 aphid *winged:* 5 alate *wingless:* 4 flea, lice (plural) 5 louse 8 firebrat 10 silverfish, springtail 11 bristletail

insecticide 3 DDT 5 mirex, naled 6 aldrin, endrin 7 lindane, phorate 8 carbaryl, dieldrin, rotenone 9 chlordane, malathion, parathion 10 permethrin

insecure 5 shaky 6 unsafe, unsure, wobbly 7 anxious 8 unstable 9 uncertain 10 precarious 11 unconfident 12 apprehensive

inseminate 7 implant, instill 9 fertilize, pollinate 10 impregnate

insensate 4 dull, hard, numb 5 stony 6 brutal, numbed 7 callous 8 comatose 9 bloodless, heartless, impassive, unfeeling

insensibility 4 coma 6 apathy, torpor 8 lethargy, stoicism 12 indifference

insensible 4 cold, dead, dull, hard, numb, rapt 5 stoic 6 asleep, intent, numbed, obtuse, stolid 7 callous 8 absorbed, comatose, deadened, hardened, obdurate 9 apathetic, bloodless, engrossed, impassive, unfeeling 11 unconscious 12 anesthetized

insensitive 4 dull, hard, numb, rude 5 crass 6 numbed, obtuse, unkind 7 callous 8 benumbed, deadened, hardened, tactless, uncaring 9 bloodless, heartless, unfeeling 10 anesthetic, impossible 11 indifferent, unconcerned 12 anesthetized, unresponsive

insert 5 enter 7 implant, obtrude 9 interpose 10 interleave 11 intercalate, interpolate

insertion 8 addendum, addition 13 interpolation *symbol:* 5 caret

in short 7 briefly, tersely 9 concisely 10 succinctly

inside 6 closet, secret, within 7 private 8 hush-hush, interior 12 confidential *combining form:* 4 endo

insidious 3 sly 4 foxy, wily 6 artful, crafty, subtle, tricky 7 cunning, gradual 8 creeping, guileful 9 deceitful 13 surreptitious

insight 6 acumen, aperçu, wisdom 8 sagacity, sapience 9 intuition 11 discernment, penetration 13 understanding

insightful 4 keen, sage, wise 7 gnostic, knowing 9 intuitive, sagacious 10 discerning, perceptive 11 penetrating

insignia 4 mark, sign 5 badge 6 emblem 8 brassard 10 decoration

insignificant 4 mere, puny 5 dinky, minor, petty, small 6 casual, little, minute, paltry 7 minimal, trivial 8 nugatory, trifling 9 secondary, small-time 10 negligible 11 Mickey Mouse, minor-league, unimportant

insincere 5 false, lying, phony 6 double, forced, hollow, phoney, shifty, tricky 7 feigned 8 mala fide, slippery, spurious 9 deceitful, deceptive, dishonest, pretended, simulated 10 left-handed, mendacious, untruthful 11 dissembling, double-faced 12 hypocritical

insinuate 4 hint 5 imply 6 inject, insert, work in, worm in 7 implant, instill, suggest 9 introduce

insipid 4 drab, dull, mild, pale, thin, weak 5 banal, bland, vapid 6 jejune, watery 7 mundane, prosaic, tedious 8 bromidic, lifeless, ordinary 9 innocuous, tasteless 10 flavorless, monotonous, namby-pamby, wishy-washy 11 commonplace

insist 4 hold 5 argue, claim, swear 6 affirm, assert, demand, stress 7 certify, contend, declare, require, testify 8 maintain

insistent 6 crying, dogged, urgent 7 adamant, burning, clamant, exigent 8 emphatic, forceful, pressing, resolute 9 assertive, clamorous, obtrusive 10 determined, imperative, relentless 11 persevering

insolence 4 gall, guff, sass 5 brass, cheek, nerve 8 audacity, boldness, chutzpah, contempt, rudeness 9 arrogance, impudence 10 brazenness, disrespect, effrontery 11 haughtiness, presumption 12 impertinence

insolent 4 bold, flip, pert, rude 5 cocky, lofty, sassy, saucy 6 brazen, cheeky 7 haughty, uncivil 8 arrogant, cavalier, flippant, impolite, impudent, superior 9 audacious, barefaced, bold-faced 10 disdainful, peremptory 11 impertinent 12 contumelious, discourteous

insouciance 6 aplomb 9 disregard, unconcern 10 breeziness 11 disinterest, nonchalance 12 carelessness, heedlessness, indifference

insouciant 4 airy, flip 6 blithe, breezy, casual, jaunty 8 carefree, flippant, heedless 9 easygoing 10 nonchalant, untroubled 11 indifferent, thoughtless, unconcerned 12 devil-may-care, happy-go-lucky, light-hearted

inspect 3 con, vet 4 scan, view 5 audit, check, probe, study 6 review, size up, survey 7 canvass, examine, observe 8 appraise, check out, look over, question 9 check over 10 scrutinize 11 investigate

inspiration 4 idea, muse 6 animus, genius, vision 7 insight 8 afflatus 9 brainwave, influence 10 brainchild, brainstorm, creativity 13 enlightenment

inspire 4 fire, stir 5 elate, exalt, imbue, rouse 6 arouse, excite, foment, incite, prompt, strike 7 animate, enliven, impress, instill, quicken 8 motivate 9 encourage, galvanize, influence, stimulate 10 exhilarate

inspiring 6 moving 7 awesome, rousing 8 exalting, stirring 9 animating, uplifting 10 vitalizing

inspirit 4 fire, lift, spur, stir 5 cheer, elate, exalt, liven, rally, rouse, spark, steel 6 arouse, excite, incite, kindle, revive, uplift, vivify 7 animate, comfort, console, delight, enliven, gladden, hearten, nourish, quicken, refresh, restore 8 activate, embolden, energize, revivify, vitalize 9 encourage, stimulate 10 invigorate, strengthen

instability 8 fluidity 9 shakiness 10 insecurity, volatility 11 inconstancy 12 unsteadiness

install 4 seat, vest 5 put in, set up 6 induct, invest 8 ensconce, enthrone, entrench 9 establish

instance 4 case, cite, item 6 detail, ground, reason, sample 7 example 8 specimen 10 particular 12 illustration

instant 3 sec 4 wink 5 flash, jiffy, point, shake, trice 6 moment, second, urgent 7 current, exigent, present 8 existent, occasion, pressing 9 heartbeat, immediate, insistent, twinkling 10 imperative, present-day

instantaneous 4 fast 5 quick, rapid 9 immediate, ligntning, momentary 11 hair-trigger, split-second

instantly 3 now, PDQ 4 ASAP, stat 6 at once, pronto 8 directly 9 forthwith, right away 11 immediately

instead 4 else 6 in lieu, rather 11 alternately 13 alternatively

instigate 4 abet, fire, goad, plan, plot, prod, spur, urge 5 egg on, impel, raise 6 excite, foment, incite, stir up, whip up 7 provoke, suggest 8 motivate 9 stimulate 10 bring about

instill 5 imbue 6 impart, infuse, inject 7 implant, suffuse 8 engender 9 inculcate, introduce

instinct 4 nose 5 hunch, sense 7 feeling, impulse 8 aptitude, behavior 9 intuition 10 proclivity, sixth sense 11 gut reaction

instinctive 3 gut 6 inborn, innate, normal 7 natural 8 habitual, inherent, visceral 9 automatic, ingrained, intrinsic, intuitive, reflexive, unlearned 10 congenital, unprompted 11 involuntary, spontaneous, unmeditated

instinctual 6 reflex 7 natural, routine 8 habitual, knee-jerk, untaught 9 automatic, impulsive, intuitive, reflexive 10 mechanical, unthinking 11 involuntary, spontaneous, unconscious

institute 5 begin, found, set up, start 6 decree, launch, ordain 7 academy, pioneer, usher in 8 initiate, organize 9 establish, introduce, originate 10 inaugurate 12 organization

institution 4 firm, rite 5 habit 6 custom 9 enactment 10 foundation 13 establishment *kind:* 6 asylum, school 7 academy, college 8 hospital 10 sanatorium, sanitarium, sanitorium, university

instruct 4 show 5 coach, drill, guide, order, steer, teach, train, tutor 6 direct, enjoin, inform, school 7 apprise, command, counsel, educate, lecture 9 enlighten, prescribe

instruction 5 drill 6 advice, lesson 7 precept 8 coaching, guidance, teaching, training, tutelage 9 catechism, education, schooling

10 directions *place of:* **6** school **7** academe, academy, college **10** university

instructive 8 didactic, edifying, pedantic **9** pedagogic **11** educational, explanatory, explicative, informative **12** enlightening

instructor 3 don **4** guru **5** coach, guide, swami, tutor **6** mentor **7** teacher, trainer **8** educator, lecturer **9** pedagogue, preceptor

instrument 4 deed, gear, mean, tool **5** agent, means, organ **6** agency, device, gadget, medium **7** utensil, vehicle **9** apparatus, appliance, machinery, mechanism **11** contraption, contrivance **13** paraphernalia *aircraft:* **5** radar, radio **7** compass **9** altimeter, gyroscope **10** altazimuth, tachometer **11** transponder *calculating:* **6** abacus **8** computer **9** slide rule *graphic:* **6** camera **8** otoscope **9** telescope **10** binoculars, microscope **11** fluoroscope, stethoscope, stroboscope **12** bronchoscope, oscilloscope, spectrograph, spectroscope *measuring:* **4** gage **5** clock, gauge, radar, scale, sonar **7** alidade, ammeter, balance, caliper, sextant, transit **8** quadrant **9** altimeter, astrolabe, barometer, bolometer, manometer, pedometer, sonometer, voltmeter **10** anemometer, Fathometer, hydrometer, hygrometer, micrometer, radiometer, radiosonde, spirometer, tachometer, theodolite **11** chronometer, lie detector, range finder, seismograph, speedometer, thermometer **12** electroscope, galvanometer, oscillograph, oscilloscope **13** Geiger counter, potentiometer *medical:* **6** lancet, trocar **7** curette, forceps, specula (plural) **8** tenacula (plural) **9** tenaculum *radiation-producing:* **5** laser, maser (see also **implement; musical instrument; tool**)

instrumental 5 vital **6** useful **7** crucial, helpful **9** conducive, essential, necessary, requisite **10** imperative **13** indispensable

instrumentality 5 agent, force, means, organ **6** agency, energy, medium **7** channel, vehicle **8** ministry **9** mechanism

insubordinate 6 unruly **8** factious, mutinous **9** fractious, seditious **10** headstrong, rebellious, refractory **11** disobedient, intractable, uncompliant **12** contumacious, recalcitrant, ungovernable

insubstantial 4 airy, weak **5** frail **6** feeble, flimsy, jejune **7** fragile, tenuous **8** bodiless, ethereal **9** unfleshly **10** intangible **11** disembodied **12** apparitional

insufferable 10 unbearable **11** intolerable, unendurable **13** insupportable

insufficiency 4 lack **6** dearth **7** paucity, poverty **8** scarcity, shortage **10** deficiency, inadequacy, scantiness, scarceness **11** defalcation

insufficient 5 scant **6** scanty, scarce, skimpy **7** lacking, wanting **10** inadequate, incomplete

insular 5 local **6** narrow **7** bigoted, limited **8** confined, isolated, secluded **9** illiberal, parochial, sectarian, small-town **10** prejudiced, provincial, restricted

insulate 6 cut off, enisle **7** isolate **8** close off **9** segregate, sequester

insult 4 gibe, jeer, mock, slap, slur **5** abuse, fleer, scoff, scorn, shame, sneer, taunt **6** debase, deride, offend, revile **7** affront, disdain, obloquy, offense, outrage **8** derision, disgrace, ignominy, ridicule **9** contumely, humiliate **10** opprobrium **12** vituperation

insurance 8 guaranty, warranty **10** protection *agency:* **7** actuary **8** adjuster **11** underwriter *term:* **6** policy **7** annuity **8** coverage **9** bordereau **11** beneficiary *type:* **4** crop, fire **5** crime, flood, title **6** dental **7** no-fault **8** accident, casualty **9** liability **10** disability, homeowner's **11** workers' comp

insure 5 cinch, guard **6** shield **7** confirm, protect **9** guarantee, safeguard **10** underwrite

insurgent 5 rebel **6** anarch **8** factious, frondeur, mutineer, mutinous, revolter **9** anarchist, seditious **10** incendiary, rebellious **12** contumacious **13** insubordinate, revolutionary

insurrection 4 coup **6** mutiny, putsch, revolt, rising **8** uprising **9** rebellion

insurrectionist 5 rebel **6** anarch **8** frondeur, mutineer, revolter **10** malcontent

insusceptible 6 exempt, immune **9** resistant **10** impervious **11** unreceptive

intact 5 sound, whole **6** entire, unhurt, virgin **7** perfect **8** complete, unbroken, unmarred, virginal **9** undamaged, uninjured, untouched **10** unimpaired

intangible 4 airy **5** vague **7** elusive, ghostly **8** ethereal **10** evanescent, immaterial, impalpable **11** incorporeal

integer 4 unit **5** digit **6** entity, figure, number **7** numeral **11** whole number

integral 4 full **5** whole **6** entire **7** perfect **8** complete, inherent **9** composite, elemental, essential, necessary, requisite **11** constituent **13** indispensable

integrate 3 mix **4** fuse, join, link **5** blend, merge, unify, unite **6** embody, mingle **7** combine, conjoin **8** coalesce **9** harmonize, reconcile **10** amalgamate, assimilate, coordinate, synthesize **11** consolidate, desegregate

integrity 5 honor **6** virtue **7** honesty, probity **8**

cohesion 9 coherence, constancy, rectitude, soundness, wholeness 12 completeness

integument 4 coat 5 testa 7 coating, cuticle 8 covering, envelope

intellect 3 wit 4 mind 5 brain 6 acumen, brains, genius, reason, smarts 9 intuition, mentality 12 intelligence 13 comprehension, understanding

intellectual 5 brain 6 brainy, mental, pundit 7 bookish, egghead, erudite, psychic, thinker 8 academic, cerebral, highbrow, longhair 9 scholarly

intelligence 3 wit 4 dope, info, mind, news, word 5 brain, savvy, sense 6 acuity, acumen, brains, notice, reason, smarts, wisdom 7 hearsay, tidings 8 aptitude, judgment, learning, sagacity 9 knowledge, mentality, mother wit 10 brainpower, shrewdness

intelligent 4 keen, wise 5 acute, alert, aware, quick, sharp, smart, sound 6 adroit, astute, brainy, bright, clever, shrewd 7 cunning, knowing, logical 8 rational, sensible 9 brilliant, ingenious, sagacious 10 reasonable 11 quick-witted, ready-witted 13 perspicacious

intelligentsia 7 clerisy 8 literati, vanguard 10 avant-garde, illuminati

intelligible 5 clear, lucid, plain

intemperance 6 excess 7 license 9 depravity 10 debauchery, profligacy 11 dissipation, drunkenness 12 immoderation, incontinence

intemperate 5 harsh 6 bitter, brutal, severe 7 drunken, extreme, violent 8 bibulous 9 crapulous, dissolute, excessive 10 dissipated, exorbitant, gluttonous, immoderate, inordinate, profligate 12 unrestrained 13 overindulgent

intend 3 aim, try 4 mean, plan 5 essay, spell 6 assign, denote, design, scheme, strive 7 attempt, connote, propose, purpose, signify 8 endeavor 9 designate

intended 6 fiancé 7 engaged, fiancée 8 destined, plighted, promised, proposed 9 affianced, betrothed 10 calculated, deliberate

intense 4 keen 5 acute, vivid 6 ardent, fervid, fierce, severe, strong 7 extreme, fervent, furious, violent, zealous 8 powerful, vehement 9 assiduous, excessive, exquisite 10 heightened 12 concentrated

intensify 4 rise 5 mount, rouse 6 accent, heat up, stress 7 enhance, sharpen 8 escalate, heighten, increase, redouble 9 aggravate, emphasize 10 accentuate, aggrandize, exacerbate 11 concentrate

intensity 6 energy, fervor 7 passion 8 emphasis, ferocity, fervency, loudness 9 vehemence

intensive 6 all-out 7 zealous 8 sweeping, thorough 10 exhaustive 12 concentrated

pronoun: 6 itself, myself 7 herself, himself 8 yourself 9 ourselves 10 themselves, yourselves

intent 3 aim, set 4 bent, goal, plan, rapt, will 5 eager, fixed 6 design, import, object 7 decided, earnest, engaged, meaning, purport, purpose, riveted, wrapped 8 absorbed, conation, decisive, diligent, immersed, resolute, resolved, sedulous, volition 9 engrossed, objective, wrapped up 10 determined

intention 3 aim, end 4 goal, hope, plan, wish 6 design, desire, object 7 meaning, purpose 8 ambition 9 objective 10 aspiration

intentional 5 meant 7 advised, studied, willful, willing, witting 8 designed, proposed 9 voluntary 10 considered, deliberate 12 premeditated

intentionally 9 on purpose, purposely

inter 4 bury 5 plant 6 entomb, inhume 9 lay to rest

interact 9 cooperate 11 collaborate

interbreed 5 cross 9 hybridize 10 mongrelize

intercede 6 step in 7 mediate 9 arbitrate

intercept 4 grab 5 catch, seize, steal 6 cut off, hijack

intercessor 5 agent 6 broker 8 advocate, mediator 9 go-between, middleman

interconnect 4 join, link, mesh 5 unite 6 couple, hook up, link up

intercourse 3 sex 5 trade, truck 7 contact, dealing, traffic 8 business, commerce, dealings 9 communion 10 connection, networking 11 give-and-take 12 conversation 13 communication

intercross 9 hybridize 10 mongrelize

interdict 3 ban, bar 4 veto 5 block, taboo 6 cut off, enjoin, forbid, outlaw 7 censure, condemn, embargo 8 disallow, prohibit, sanction 9 proscribe 11 prohibition

interest 4 gain, grab, hook, lure, pull 5 pique, stake, tempt 6 appeal, arouse, behalf, engage, profit, regard 7 attract, concern, engross, involve, welfare 8 appeal to, intrigue 9 attention, curiosity, fascinate, tantalize, well-being 10 prosperity

interested 4 rapt 5 drawn 7 curious, partial 8 invested, partisan 9 attentive

interface 3 GUI 6 border 8 boundary 9 cooperate 11 communicate

interfere 6 butt in, horn in, meddle, step in 7 barge in, intrude

interim 3 gap 5 break, pause 6 acting, breach, hiatus, lacuna, pro tem 7 stopgap, time-out 8 downtime, meantime 9 makeshift, temporary 10 pro tempore 11 provisional

interior 3 gut **4** pith **5** belly, bosom, heart, inner **6** center, inland, inside, inward, marrow **8** visceral **9** heartland **10** hinterland
interject 3 add **6** fill in, insert **7** throw in
interjection *agreement:* **4** amen **5** roger **6** righto **7** right on *attention-getter:* **3** hey **4** ahem, ahoy, psst **6** yoo-hoo *cheer:* **3** rah, yay **5** wahoo **6** hooray, hurrah, hurray *contempt:* **4** pooh **5** pshaw *disappointment:* **4** rats **5** shoot **6** shucks *disapproval:* **3** boo, fie *disbelief:* **2** aw **3** huh *disgust:* **3** bah, boo, pah, ugh **4** rats, yuck **5** faugh, yecch **6** phooey *dismay:* **2** oy **4** oh no, uh-oh *dismissal:* **3** git **4** shoo *in golf:* **4** fore *in hunting:* **6** yoicks *in marching:* **3** hup, hut *joy:* **4** whee **6** hooray, hurrah, hurray, yippee **7** hosanna, whoopee **8** alleluia **10** hallelujah *mild apology:* **4** oops **6** whoops *mild oath:* **3** gad **4** darn, drat, egad, geez, gosh, heck, jeez **5** egads, golly, zooks **6** jiminy, zounds **7** begorra, gee whiz, jeepers **8** gadzooks **13** gee whillikers *O.K.:* **5** roger, wilco *pain:* **2** ow **4** ouch *regret:* **3** woe **4** alas **5** alack **8** lackaday *relief:* **4** phew *silence:* **2** sh **3** shh *sneeze:* **5** achoo **6** atchoo **7** kerchoo *sorrow:* **4** alas **5** alack **8** lackaday *stop:* **4** whoa **5** avast *surprise:* **2** ah, ho, lo, oh **3** aha, huh, oho, wow **4** gosh, oops **5** blimy, yikes, yipes, zowie **6** blimey *triumph:* **3** aha, hah **6** eureka (see also **exclamation**)
interlace 3 mix **5** braid, plait, twine, weave **7** entwine **9** alternate
interlard 3 mix **6** mingle
interlock 4 mesh **5** unite **6** enmesh
interlocuter 4 host **5** emcee
interlope 6 butt in, horn in, meddle **7** intrude **8** encroach, infringe **9** interfere
interlude 4 halt, lull, rest **5** break, idyll, letup, pause, spell **6** hiatus, recess **7** episode, respite **8** breather, entr'acte, meantime, stoppage **9** meanwhile **10** suspension
intermediary 3 mid **4** mean **5** agent, envoy, organ **6** agency, broker, center, medium, middle, midway **7** central, channel, vehicle **8** delegate, emissary, mediator, ministry **9** go-between, middleman
intermediate 3 mid **4** fair, mean, so-so **5** mesne **6** broker, center, middle, midway, step in **7** arbiter, average, between, central, halfway **8** middling **9** arbitrate, go-between, middleman
intermediator 6 broker **7** arbiter, liaison, referee **9** go-between, middleman
interment 6 burial **9** sepulture **10** inhumation
intermesh 4 lock **6** engage **8** dovetail
interminable 7 endless, eternal, lasting **8** constant, infinite, unending **9** boundless, cease-

less, continual, limitless, permanent, perpetual, unceasing **10** protracted **11** everlasting, never-ending
intermission 4 lull, rest, stop **5** break, pause, spell **6** hiatus, recess **7** latency, respite, time-out **8** abeyance, dormancy, interval **10** quiescence, suspension **11** parenthesis
intermit 4 halt, stay **5** break, defer, delay **6** arrest, hold up, put off **7** suspend **8** postpone, prorogue **9** interrupt **11** discontinue
intermittent 6 broken, cyclic, fitful, serial **8** cyclical, metrical, periodic, seasonal, sporadic **9** irregular, recurrent, recurring, spasmodic, stop-and-go **10** occasional
intermix 4 meld **5** blend **6** mingle **8** comingle, compound **9** commingle, integrate **10** amalgamate
intermixture 4 brew **5** blend **7** amalgam **8** compound **9** composite, synthesis **12** amalgamation **13** miscegenation
intern 4 jail **6** immure **7** confine, impound, put away, trainee **8** imprison **11** incarcerate
internal 6 native **7** private **8** visceral **10** subjective *concretion:* **9** gallstone *prefix:* **5** intra
internal organs 4 guts **6** bowels, vitals **7** innards, viscera **8** entrails **10** intestines, penetralia
international organization 2 UN **3** FAO, IAM, ICJ, IFC, ILO, ITO, ITU, OAS, WHO, WMO, WTO **4** IAAF, IABA, IAEA, IARU, IATA, ICAO, IFIP, IMCO, NATO **5** ICFTU, SEATO **6** UNESCO, UNICEF
Internet forum 9 newsgroup
internuncio 5 envoy **6** bearer, legate **7** carrier, courier **8** delegate, emissary **9** go-between, messenger, middleman
interpolate 3 add **5** admit, annex, enter **6** append, fill in, inject, insert **7** throw in **9** introduce
interpose 6 butt in, fill in, insert, meddle, step in **7** intrude, mediate, obtrude, throw in **8** moderate **9** arbitrate, insinuate, introduce, negotiate **11** come between
interpret 5 gloss **6** decode **7** explain, expound **8** annotate, construe **9** elucidate, explicate **10** paraphrase
interpretation 5 gloss **7** meaning, reading, version **8** exegesis **9** construal, rendering **11** explanation, translation
interpretive 8 exegetic **10** diagnostic, exegetical, expository **11** explanatory, explicatory
interregnum 5 break, lapse, pause **6** hiatus **7** time-out
interrogate 3 ask **4** pump, quiz **5** grill, query **7** examine **8** question **9** catechize **12** cross-examine

interrupt 4 halt, stay, stop **5** abort, break, cut in **7** break in, chime in, suspend **8** cut short

interruption 3 gap **4** halt **5** break, pause, split **6** breach, cutoff, hiatus, lacuna, recess **7** caesura **8** stoppage

intersect 4 meet **5** cross **9** decussate **10** criss-cross

intersection 3 hub **4** node **8** crossing, junction, juncture **10** crossroads

intersperse 7 diffuse, scatter **8** sprinkle

interstice 3 gap **4** slit, slot, vent **5** chink, cleft, crack, space **6** breach, cavity, cranny **7** crevice, fissure, opening, orifice **8** aperture

intertwine 4 mesh **5** braid, plait, twist, weave **6** enlace **7** network **9** convolute **10** criss-cross

interval 3 gap **4** lull, wait **5** break, comma, delay, letup, pause, space **6** breach, hiatus, lacuna **7** caesura, interim, respite, time-out **8** downtime **9** pausation **11** parenthesis *music:* **4** rest

intervene 6 butt in, meddle, step in **7** intrude, mediate, obtrude

interweave 3 mix **4** fuse, join, knit, link, mesh **5** blend, plait, twine **6** enmesh **7** entwine, wreathe

intestinal 5 ileal **7** colonic, jejunal **8** duodenal

intestinal fortitude 4 grit, guts **5** nerve, pluck, spunk **6** mettle, spirit **7** courage **8** backbone **10** resolution

intestine 3 gut **4** tube **5** bowel, canal **7** viscera (plural) *combining form:* **4** coli, colo **6** entero *part:* **5** cecum, colon, ileum **7** jejunum **8** duodenum

in the same place 6 ibidem

intimacy 9 closeness **11** familiarity **12** acquaintance

intimate 3 gut **4** cozy, dear, fond, hint **5** amigo, close, crony, imply, inner, privy **6** attest, friend, impart, loving, secret **7** comrade, connote, devoted, nearest, suggest **8** familiar, inherent **9** close-knit, companion, confidant, ingrained, insinuate, intrinsic **12** confidential

intimation 3 cue **4** clue, hint **5** shade, tinge, trace **6** breath **7** inkling **8** telltale **10** suggestion

intimidate 3 awe, cow **4** bait **5** bully, chivy, daunt, scare **6** badger, coerce, hector **7** buffalo, overawe **8** browbeat, bulldoze, bullyrag **9** strong-arm, terrorize

intolerable 10 unbearable **11** unendurable **12** insufferable **13** insupportable

intolerant 6 biased, narrow **7** bigoted **8** dogmatic **9** hidebound, illiberal **10** inflexible, prejudiced **11** small-minded **12** narrowminded

intonation 5 chant, pitch **6** accent, timbre **7** cadence **8** chanting **10** inflection, modulation, recitation

intone 5 chant, croon, drone **10** cantillate

in toto 3 all **6** wholly **7** all told, en masse **10** altogether

intoxicant 5 booze, drink, hooch, sauce **6** hootch, liquor, rotgut **7** alcohol, spirits **9** aqua vitae, firewater, moonshine

intoxicated 3 lit, wet **4** high **5** blind, drunk, fried, giddy, lit up, oiled, stiff, tight, tipsy **6** blotto, bombed, canned, elated, juiced, loaded, looped, potted, sodden, soused, stewed, stoned, tanked, tiddly, zonked **7** blitzed, crocked, drunken, excited, maudlin, muddled, pickled, pie-eyed, sloshed, smashed, sozzled **8** cockeyed, polluted, squiffed **9** crapulous, plastered **11** exhilarated

intoxication 3 joy **5** bliss **6** frenzy **7** ecstasy, elation, rapture **8** delirium, euphoria **9** transport **10** exaltation **11** drunkenness, inebriation

intractable 4 wild **5** balky **6** mulish, ornery, unruly **7** froward, willful **8** mutinous, obdurate, perverse, stubborn **9** fractious, obstinate, pigheaded, unbending **10** bullheaded, headstrong, inflexible, rebellious, refractory, unyielding **12** pertinacious, recalcitrant, ungovernable **13** undisciplined

intransigent 5 rigid, tough **7** willful **8** obdurate, perverse, resolute, stubborn **9** obstinate, unbending, unpliable **10** refractory, self-willed, unyielding **12** contumacious, pertinacious

intrepid 4 bold, game **5** brave, gutsy, hardy **6** daring, heroic **7** doughty, gallant, valiant **8** fearless, resolute, stalwart, unafraid, valorous **9** audacious, dauntless, undaunted **10** courageous **11** adventurous, temerarious

intricate 4 mazy **6** daedal, knotty **7** complex, gordian, tangled **8** abstruse, involved, tortuous **9** Byzantine, elaborate **10** circuitous, convoluted **11** complicated **12** labyrinthine **13** sophisticated

intrigue 4 plot, wile **5** amour, cabal, cheat, pique, trick **6** affair, appeal, excite, scheme **7** attract, beguile, collude, connive, liaison, romance **8** cogitate, conspire, contrive, interest **9** machinate **10** conspiracy **11** machination

intriguing 8 enticing **9** absorbing, beguiling **10** engrossing, entrancing **11** captivating, fascinating, stimulating

intrinsic see **inherent**

intrinsically 5 per se **6** as such **7** at heart **10** inherently

introduce 5 begin, enter, found, set up 6 broach, fill in, insert, launch, unveil, work in 7 bring up, implant, install, instill, precede, preface, present, propose, throw in, usher in 8 initiate, innovate 9 insinuate, institute, interject, interpose, originate 10 inseminate

introduction 5 debut, proem 6 lead-in 7 introit, opening, preface, prelude 8 entrance, exordium, foreword, overture, preamble, prologue, protases (plural), protasis 12 prolegomenon

introductory 5 basic 7 initial, nascent, opening 8 proemial 9 beginning, prefatory 10 elementary 11 preliminary, preparatory

intrude 5 cut in 6 butt in, horn in, impose, invade, meddle 7 barge in, burst in, presume 8 encroach, infringe, trespass 9 interfere, interlope, interrupt

intrusive 4 busy, nosy 5 nosey 6 prying, snoopy 7 curious 8 meddling, snooping 9 officious 10 meddlesome 11 impertinent

in truth 6 indeed, really, verily 8 actually, candidly 9 veritably

intuit 5 infer, sense 6 deduce, divine 7 surmise

intuition 5 hunch 7 feeling, inkling, insight 8 instinct 10 sixth sense 11 second sight 12 presentiment

intuitive 6 innate 7 natural 8 unwilled, visceral 10 unthinking 11 instinctive, instinctual, involuntary, spontaneous, unconscious

Inuit 6 Eskimo

inundate 4 glut 5 drown, flood, swamp, whelm 6 deluge, engulf 7 overrun 8 overflow, submerge 9 overwhelm

inundation 5 flood, spate 6 deluge 7 Niagara, torrent 8 cataract, flooding, overflow 9 avalanche, cataclysm, landslide 10 cloudburst

inure 5 steel, train 6 harden, season 7 prepare, toughen 8 accustom 9 acclimate, habituate 10 discipline 11 familiarize

inutile 6 no-good 7 useless 8 unusable 9 valueless, worthless

invade 4 loot, raid 6 breach, occupy, ravage 7 overrun, pillage, plunder 8 encroach, infringe, trespass 9 penetrate

invader 8 intruder 10 encroacher, interloper, trespasser 11 infiltrator

invalid 3 bad 4 null, sick, void 5 false 6 ailing, infirm, shut-in, sickly 7 expired, unsound 8 baseless, disabled 9 bedridden, illogical, sophistic 10 fallacious, irrational 11 null and void 12 convalescent

invalidate 4 undo, void 5 annul, quash 6 cancel, offset, vacate 7 abolish, nullify 9 discredit, repudiate 10 counteract, disqualify, neutralize

invaluable 7 crucial 8 precious 9 essential, priceless 11 beyond price, inestimable 13 irreplaceable

invariable 4 same 5 fixed 6 static, steady 7 uniform 8 constant 9 continual, immovable, immutable, unfailing, unvarying 10 changeless, consistent, unchanging 11 inalterable, unalterable 12 unchangeable

invariably 4 ever 6 always 7 forever

invasion 4 raid 5 foray 6 attack, inroad 7 assault, offense 8 trespass 9 incursion, intrusion, offensive, onslaught 12 encroachment

invective 5 abuse 6 tirade 7 abusive, obloquy 8 diatribe, jeremiad 9 contumely, philippic, truculent 10 opprobrium, scurrility, scurrilous 11 opprobrious 12 billingsgate, contumelious, vituperation, vituperative

inveigh 4 kick, rail, rant 6 object 7 protest 8 complain 9 fulminate 11 expostulate, remonstrate

inveigle 4 coax, lure 5 decoy, snare, tempt 6 allure, cajole, entice, entrap, lead on, rope in, seduce, wangle 7 blarney, win over 8 blandish, butter up, maneuver, persuade

invent 4 coin, mint 6 cook up, create, design, devise, make up, patent, vamp up 7 concoct, dream up, fashion, hatch up, pioneer, think up 8 conceive, contrive, discover, engineer, envision 9 fabricate, formulate, originate

invention 7 coinage, fiction 8 creation 10 brainchild, innovation 11 contrivance

inventive 7 fertile, teeming 8 creative, fruitful, original 9 demiurgic, ingenious 10 innovative, innovatory 11 imaginative

inventor 5 maker 6 author, father, mother 7 creator, founder 8 engineer 9 architect, generator, innovator 10 discoverer, introducer, originator *air brake:* 12 Westinghouse (George) *air conditioning:* 7 Carrier (Willis) *automobile:* 7 Daimler (Gottlieb) *ballpoint pen:* 4 Loud (John) *barbed wire:* 7 Glidden (Joseph Farwell) *barometer:* 10 Torricelli (Evangelista) *bifocal lens:* 8 Franklin (Benjamin) *camera:* 7 Eastman (George) *cash register:* 5 Ritty (James) *cotton gin:* 7 Whitney (Eli) *cylinder lock:* 4 Yale (Linus) *dirigible:* 8 Zeppelin (Ferdinand von) *dynamite:* 5 Nobel (Alfred) *electric battery:* 5 Volta (Alessandro) *electric fan:* 7 Wheeler (George) *electric organ:* 7 Hammond (Laurens) *electric razor:* 6 Schick (Jacob) *electric stove:* 7 Hadaway (W. S.) *elevator:* 4 Otis (Elisha) *fountain pen:* 8 Waterman (Lewis) *friction match:* 6

Walker (John) *gyrocompass:* 6 Sperry (Elmer) *helicopter:* 8 Sikorsky (Igor) *hot-air balloon:* 11 Montgolfier (Jacques, Joseph) *incandescent lamp:* 6 Edison (Thomas Alva) *induction motor:* 5 Tesla (Nikola) *lawn mower:* 5 Hills (Amariah) *Linotype:* 12 Mergenthaler (Ottmar) *logarithm:* 6 Napier (John) *machine gun:* 7 Gatling (Richard) *microphone:* 8 Berliner (Emile) *microwave oven:* 7 Spencer (Percy) *movable type:* 9 Gutenberg (Johannes) *parachute:* 9 Blanchard (Jean-Pierre) *pendulum clock:* 7 Huygens (Christiaan) *phonograph:* 6 Edison (Thomas Alva) *photography:* 6 Niepce (Nicéphore), Talbot (W. H. Fox) 8 Daguerre (Louis) *piano:* 10 Cristofori (Bartolomeo) *radio:* 7 Marconi (Guglielmo) *reaper:* 9 McCormick (Cyrus) *revolver:* 4 Colt (Samuel) *rocket engine:* 7 Goddard (Robert) *safety pin:* 4 Hunt (Walter) *safety razor:* 8 Gillette (King) *sewing machine:* 4 Howe (Elias) *sleeping car:* 7 Pullman (George) *spinning jenny:* 10 Hargreaves (James) *steamboat:* 5 Fitch (John) 6 Fulton (Robert), Miller (Patrick), Rumsey (James) 8 Jouffroy (Claude de) *steam engine:* 4 Watt (James) *steam locomotive:* 10 Stephenson (George) *stethoscope:* 7 Laënnec (René) *submarine:* 7 Holland (John Philip) *synthesizer:* 4 Moog (Robert) *tank:* 7 Swinton (Ernest) *telegraph:* 5 Morse (Samuel F. B.) *telephone:* 4 Bell (Alexander Graham) *telescope:* 10 Lippershey (Hans) *television:* 5 Baird (John) 6 Nipkow (Paul) 8 Zworykin (Vladimir) 10 Farnsworth (Philo) *thermometer:* 7 Galileo (Galilei) *torpedo:* 9 Whitehead (Robert) *tractor:* 5 Deere (John) *transistor:* 7 Bardeen (John) 8 Brattain (Walter), Shockley (William) *vulcanized rubber:* 8 Goodyear (Charles) *writing for the blind:* 7 Braille (Louis) *zipper:* 6 Judson (Whitcomb)
inventory 3 sum 4 fund, list 5 hoard, stock, store, tally 6 assets, digest, record, supply, survey 7 account, backlog, catalog, itemize, reserve, specify, summary 8 register, tabulate 9 catalogue, checklist, enumerate, reservoir, stockpile, summarize, synopsize
inverse 8 contrary, opposite
inversion 7 reverse 8 flipping, reversal, upending 9 about-face, turnabout, volte-face
invert 4 flip 5 upend 7 reverse 8 overturn, turn over 9 transpose
invertebrate 4 weak 5 timid 7 chicken, doormat, milksop 8 boneless, impotent, weakling 9 jellyfish, spineless 10 namby-pamby 11 ineffectual, milquetoast *kind:* 4 worm 6

insect, sponge 7 mollusc, mollusk 8 arachnid 9 arthropod 12 coelenterate
invest 4 gird, veil, wrap 5 adorn, array, dress, endow, imbue 6 clothe, confer, enfold, induct, infuse, ordain 7 empower, enclose, envelop, ingrain, install, suffuse
investigate 3 pry 4 sift 5 audit, probe, study 6 go into, search 7 dig into, examine, explore, inquire, inspect 8 check out, look into, muckrake, prospect, research 9 delve into 10 scrutinize 11 inquire into
investigation 5 audit, probe 6 survey 7 inquest, inquiry 8 research, scrutiny 11 factfinding, inquisition
investigator 3 spy, tec 4 dick 5 hound 6 shamus, sleuth 7 gumshoe 8 hawkshaw, sherlock 9 detective 10 private eye
investiture 9 inaugural, induction 10 initiation, ordination 12 inauguration, installation, ratification
inveterate 3 old, set 5 fixed, sworn 6 rooted 7 abiding, chronic, settled 8 deep-dyed, enduring, habitual, hard-core, hardened, lifelong 9 confirmed, ingrained, perennial 10 continuing, deep-rooted, deep-seated, entrenched, habituated, persistent, persisting 11 established 12 incorrigible 13 dyed-in-the-wool
Invictus author 6 Henley (William Ernest)
invidious 7 envious, envying, jealous 9 green-eyed, obnoxious, resentful
invigorate 4 stir 5 brace, liven, pep up, rally, renew, rouse 6 perk up, vivify 7 animate, brace up, enliven, fortify, juice up, refresh, restore 8 energize, vitalize 9 reinforce, stimulate 10 rejuvenate, revitalize, strengthen
invincible 10 inviolable, unbeatable 11 impregnable, indomitable, insuperable 12 invulnerable, unassailable, undefeatable 13 unconquerable
in vino ____ 7 veritas
inviolable 4 safe 6 secure 10 impervious, sacrosanct 11 consecrated, impregnable 12 unassailable 13 incorruptible
invisible 6 hidden 9 concealed 10 intangible 12 unnoticeable 13 imperceptible
Invisible Man author: 5 Wells (H. G.) 7 Ellison (Ralph) *character:* 7 Griffin (Herbert)
invitation 4 call, lure 6 come-on 7 bidding, proffer 8 entreaty, proposal 10 enticement 11 proposition 12 solicitation
invite 3 ask, bid 4 call, lure 5 tempt 6 allure, call in, entice, summon 7 propose, request, solicit
inviting 8 engaging, enticing, tempting 9 ap-

pealing, beguiling, seductive **10** attractive, intriguing

invocation 6 appeal, prayer **8** entreaty, petition **11** conjuration, incantation **12** supplication

invoice 3 tab **4** bill, list **5** score **7** account **8** manifest **9** reckoning, statement **11** consignment

invoke 3 beg **4** pray **5** crave, plead **6** appeal, call on, effect **7** beseech, conjure, enforce, entreat, implore, solicit **8** call upon, petition **9** call forth, conjure up, implement, importune **10** supplicate

involuntary 6 forced, reflex **8** knee-jerk **9** automatic, impulsive, reflexive, unwitting **10** compulsory, unintended, unprompted **11** instinctive, spontaneous, unconscious, unmeditated **13** unintentional

involve 4 mire **6** affect, embody, engage, entail, take in **7** call for, concern, contain, embrace, embroil, include, require, subsume **8** comprise, entangle **9** encompass, implicate **10** complicate, comprehend **11** necessitate

involved 6 daedal, knotty **7** complex, gordian **8** confused **9** Byzantine, elaborate, intricate **10** convoluted **11** complicated **12** labyrinthine

invulnerable 6 immune, secure **10** impervious, invincible, unbeatable **11** impregnable, indomitable **12** unassailable

Io *father:* **7** Inachus *guard:* **5** Argus *son:* **7** Epaphus

iodine *source* **4** kelp

Iolanthe *composer:* **8** Sullivan (Arthur) *librettist:* **7** Gilbert (W. S.)

Iolcus *king* **5** Aeson **6** Pelias

Iole *captor:* **8** Heracles, Hercules *father:* **7** Eurytus *husband:* **6** Hyllus

ion 6 ligand *kind:* **5** anion **6** cation **8** thermion

Ion *father:* **6** Apollo *mother:* **6** Creusa *stepfather:* **6** Xuthus

Ionesco, Eugène *play:* **6** Chairs (The), Lesson (The) **10** Rhinoceros **11** Bald Soprano (The)

iota 3 bit, jot, ray **4** atom, hint, mite, whit **5** crumb, grain, ounce, scrap, shred, speck, trace **6** smidge, tittle **7** smidgen, smidgin **8** molecule, particle, smidgeon **9** scintilla

IOU 4 chit, debt *part:* **3** owe, you

Iowa *capital:* **9** Des Moines *city:* **4** Ames **7** Dubuque **8** Waterloo **9** Davenport, Sioux City **11** Cedar Rapids **13** Council Bluffs *college, university:* **5** Drake **8** Grinnell *nickname:* **7** Hawkeye (State) *river:* **9** Des Moines *state bird:* **9** goldfinch *state flower:* **15** wild prairie rose *state tree:* **3** oak

Iphicles *brother:* **8** Heracles, Hercules *mother:* **7** Alcmene *son:* **6** Iolaus

Iphigenia *avenger:* **12** Clytemnestra *brother:* **7** Orestes *father:* **9** Agamemnon *mother:* **12** Clytemnestra *sister:* **7** Electra

Iran *ancient civilization:* **4** Elam **5** Medes, Media **6** Persia *capital:* **6** Tehran **7** Teheran *city:* **3** Qom, Qum **6** Shiraz, Tabriz **7** Esfahan, Isfahan, Mashhad *conqueror:* **9** Alexander (the Great) *gulf:* **4** Oman **7** Persian *island:* **5** Qeshm *language:* **3** Tat **5** Farsi **7** Persian *leader:* **7** Pahlavi (Mohammad Reza, Reza Shah) **8** Khomeini (Ayatollah Ruholla) *monetary unit:* **4** rial *mountain, range:* **6** Elburz, Zagros **8** Damavand **9** Hindu Kush *neighbor:* **4** Iraq **6** Turkey **7** Armenia **8** Pakistan **10** Azerbaijan **11** Afghanistan **12** Turkmenistan *river:* **5** Atrek, Karun, Safid **7** Karkheh *sea:* **7** Caspian *strait:* **6** Hormuz

Iranian 7 Persian *parliament:* **6** Majlis *religious movement:* **5** Baha'i *sect:* **4** Shia *sect member:* **6** Shiite

Iraq *ancient civilization:* **5** Akkad, Sumer **8** Akkadian, Sumerian **9** Babylonia **10** Babylonian *ancient name:* **11** Mesopotamia *capital:* **7** Baghdad *city:* **5** Basra, Mosul, Najaf **6** Kirkuk **7** Falluja, Karbala **8** Fallujah *conqueror:* **9** Alexander (the Great) *desert:* **6** Syrian *gulf:* **7** Persian *leader:* **6** Faisal **7** Hussein (Saddam) *monetary unit:* **5** dinar *neighbor:* **4** Iran **5** Syria **6** Jordan, Kuwait, Turkey **11** Saudi Arabia *port:* **5** Basra **7** Umm Qasr *river:* **6** Tigris **9** Euphrates

irascible 4 tart **5** huffy, surly, testy **6** crabby, cranky, feisty, tetchy, touchy **7** bristly, grouchy, peevish, peppery, prickly **8** choleric, petulant, snappish **9** crotchety, fractious, irritable, querulous, splenetic **11** hot-tempered **12** cantankerous **13** quick-tempered

irate 3 mad **5** angry, livid, riled, vexed, wroth **6** fuming **7** enraged, furious, steamed **8** choleric, incensed, provoked, wrathful **9** indignant **10** infuriated

ire 4 fury, rage, rile **5** anger, wrath **6** choler, enrage, madden, temper **7** incense, steam up, umbrage **9** infuriate **10** exasperate **11** indignation **12** exasperation

Ireland 4 Eire, Erin **8** Hibernia *capital:* **6** Dublin *city:* **4** Cork **5** Kerry, Louth, Meath, Sligo **6** Galway **7** Donegal, Kildare, Wexford, Wicklow **8** Kilkenny, Limerick **9** Waterford **12** Dun Laoghaire *county:* **4** Cork, Mayo **5** Clare, Kerry, Louth, Meath, Sligo **6** Galway **7** Donegal, Kildare, Wexford **8** Limerick *flag color:* **5** green, white **6** orange *flower:* **8** shamrock *island group:* **4** Aran **8** Hibernia *lake:* **3** Ree (Lough) **4**

Derg (Lough) **5** Neagh (Lough) **6** Corrib (Lough) *language:* **4** Erse **5** Irish **6** Gaelic **7** English *legislature:* **4** Dail *monetary unit:* **4** euro *nickname:* **11** Emerald Isle *province:* **7** Munster **8** Connacht, Leinster *river:* **4** Erne, Nore **5** Boyne **6** Barrow, Liffey **7** Shannon *symbol:* **4** harp

Irene 3 Pax *father:* **4** Zeus **7** Jupiter *mother:* **6** Themis

irenic 4 calm **7** pacific **8** pacifist **9** peaceable, placative, placatory **10** nonviolent **12** conciliatory, propitiatory

iridescent 8 gleaming, lustrous **10** opalescent *gem:* **4** opal **5** pearl **7** apatite **8** ammolite **9** fire agate, moonstone *shell:* **7** abalone

iridium symbol 2 Ir

Iris father: **7** Thaumas *mother:* **7** Electra

Irish 4 Erse **6** Celtic, Gaelic *accent:* **6** brogue *airline:* **9** Aer Lingus *cattle:* **5** Kerry *chief heir oloct:* **6** tanist *clan:* **4** sept *combining form:* **7** Hiberno *coronation stone:* **7** Lia Fail *cudgel:* **9** shillalah **10** shillelagh *death spirit:* **7** banshee *design:* **8** claddagh *dog:* **6** setter **7** terrier *elf:* **10** leprechaun *fortification:* **4** liss *girl:* **4** lass **6** lassie **7** colleen *god:* **3** Ler **5** Dagda **6** Aengus *goddess:* **4** Badb, Bodb **6** Brigit **8** Morrigan *hero:* **9** Cuchulain **10** Cú Chulainn *heroine:* **7** Deirdre *king:* **9** Brian Boru *lake:* **5** lough *language:* **4** Erse *militant force:* **3** IRA *nationalist:* **4** Tone (Wolfe) **6** Pearse (Padraig) **7** Collins (Michael), Parnell (Charles) **8** De Valera (Eamon), O'Connell (Daniel) **9** Sarsfield (Patrick) *nationalist society:* **8** Sinn Fein *patron saint:* **7** Patrick *police officer:* **5** garda *singer:* **4** Enya **5** Makem (Tommy), Margo **6** Clancy (Bobby, Liam, Paddy, Patrick, Tom) **8** O'Donnell (Daniel) *symbol:* **4** harp *theater:* **5** Abbey *writing system:* **4** ogam **5** ogham (see also **Gaelic; Celtic**)

Irish moss 7 seaweed **9** carrageen

irk 3 try, vex **4** fret, gall, miff, pain, rile **5** annoy, peeve, pique, upset **6** abrade, bother, harass, nettle, ruffle, strain, stress **7** provoke, trouble **8** exercise, irritate **10** exasperate

irksome 6 vexing **7** tedious **8** annoying, rankling **9** provoking, upsetting, vexatious **10** bothersome, irritating, nettlesome, unpleasant **11** aggravating, troublesome, unpalatable

iron 4 firm, gyve, hard **5** press, rigid **6** fetter, strong **7** adamant, manacle, shackle **8** handcuff, obdurate **9** unbending **10** inexorable, inflexible *combining form:* **5** ferro **6** sidero *German:* **5** Eisen *relating to:* **6** ferric **7** ferrous **11** ferruginous *symbol:* **2** Fe

ironbound 5 harsh, rocky, rough, stern **6** craggy, jagged, rugged, severe, strict, uneven **7** scraggy **8** asperous, exacting, rigorous, scabrous **9** stringent **10** inflexible

Iron City 10 Pittsburgh

ironclad 5 fixed **7** binding **8** constant **9** immovable, immutable **10** inflexible, invariable **11** inalterable, irrefutable, unalterable **12** indisputable, irrefragable, unchangeable **13** unimpeachable

ironfisted 4 grim, hard, mean **5** harsh **6** brutal, severe, stingy **7** callous, miserly **8** pitiless, ruthless **9** penurious **10** implacable, unmerciful **11** hard-hearted, intractable, remorseless **12** unappeasable

ironhanded 5 harsh, rigid **6** severe, strict **8** despotic, rigorous **9** draconian, stringent **10** tyrannical **12** unpermissive

ironhearted 5 stony **7** callous **8** hardened, obdurate, ruthless **9** merciless, unfeeling **10** hard-boiled **11** cold-blooded **13** unsympathetic

iron horse 10 locomotive

ironic 3 wry **6** biting **7** caustic, cutting, cynical, mordant, satiric **8** sardonic **9** sarcastic, trenchant

iron ore 8 goethite, hematite, limonite, siderite, taconite **9** magnetite

Iron Pants 6 Patton (George)

irons 5 bonds, gyves **6** chains **7** bilboes, darbies, fetters **8** manacles, shackles

Iroquois tribe 6 Cayuga, Mohawk, Oneida, Seneca **8** Onondaga **9** Tuscarora

irradiate 4 beam, glow **5** edify, light, shine **6** uplift **7** light up **8** illumine **9** enlighten **10** illuminate

irrational 3 mad **5** crazy **6** absurd, insane **7** invalid **8** demented **9** cockamamy, illogical, senseless, sophistic **10** cockamamie, fallacious, ridiculous **12** preposterous, unreasonable *number:* **4** surd

irrefutable 4 sure **6** proven **7** certain **8** airtight, ironclad, positive **9** apodictic, veracious **10** conclusive, inarguable **11** indubitable **12** indisputable **13** incontestable

irregular 3 odd **5** erose, queer **6** fitful, patchy, random, spotty, uneven **7** aimless, erratic, unequal **8** aberrant, abnormal, atypical, informal, lopsided, peculiar, singular, sporadic, unstable, unsteady, variable **9** anomalous, desultory, divergent, eccentric, guerrilla, haphazard, hit-or-miss, spasmodic, unregular, unsettled **10** asymmetric, capricious, changeable, inconstant, off-balance, unbalanced, unofficial **11** exceptional, fluctuating **12** intermittent, unsystematic

irregularity 5 freak, quirk **6** oddity, vagary **7**

anomaly **8** deviance **9** deviation, roughness **10** aberration, inequality, unevenness **11** abnormality

irrelevant 5 inapt **9** unrelated **10** extraneous, immaterial, inapposite, peripheral **11** inessential, unessential, unimportant **12** inapplicable **13** insignificant

irreligious 6 unholy **7** godless, impious, profane, ungodly **11** blasphemous

irreparable 8 cureless, hopeless **9** incurable **11** immedicable **12** irredeemable, irremediable **13** irretrievable, unrecoverable

irreproachable 4 pure **8** flawless, innocent, spotless, virtuous **9** blameless, errorless, exemplary, faultless, guiltless, righteous **10** immaculate, impeccable, inculpable, unblamable

irresolute 5 shaky **6** fickle, unsure, wobbly **7** halting **8** doubtful, hesitant, unstable, waffling, wavering **9** equivocal, faltering, tentative, uncertain, undecided **10** ambivalent, changeable, inconstant, wishy-washy **11** fluctuating, half-hearted, vacillating

irresponsible 4 rash, wild **8** carefree, careless, feckless, reckless **10** incautious, unreliable **12** undependable **13** unaccountable, untrustworthy

irreverent 4 flip **7** impious, profane, ungodly **8** flippant **9** satirical **11** blasphemous **12** sacrilegious

irrevocable 4 firm **5** final **9** immutable **11** unalterable **12** irreversible, unchangeable **13** nonreversible

irrigate 3 wet **4** soak **5** flush, water

irrigation ditch 5 flume **6** sluice **7** acequia

irritability 5 pique **6** choler **8** edginess **9** petulance **10** crabbiness, impatience **11** fretfulness, peevishness *abnormal:* **8** eretism

irritable 4 edgy, sour **5** cross, huffy, ratty, testy, waspy, whiny **6** crabby, cranky, crusty, grumpy, ornery, snappy, tetchy, touchy **7** fretful, grouchy, peevish, pettish, prickly, waspish **8** captious, choleric, petulant, snappish **9** crotchety, fractious, impatient, irascible, querulous, splenetic **12** cantankerous, disagreeable

irritant 4 itch, pest **5** nudge, peeve **6** bother, gadfly, noodge, nudnik, pester, plague **7** nudnick **8** headache, nuisance, vexation **9** annoyance **11** botheration

irritate 3 bug, irk, rub, vex **4** fret, gall, goad, rile, roil **5** anger, annoy, chafe, grate, peeve, pique, spite **6** abrade, badger, bother, burn up, harass, hector, madden, needle, nettle, offend, ruffle **7** inflame, provoke **9** aggravate, stimulate **10** exacerbate, exasperate

irritated 5 irate, testy **7** fretful, peevish **8** choleric **9** impatient, irascible

irritation 4 itch, pest, rash, sore **6** bother, plague **7** chagrin **8** nuisance, vexation **9** annoyance

irrupt 5 belch, eruct, surge **6** invade **7** intrude

irruption 4 raid **5** foray **6** inroad **7** upsurge **8** invasion **9** incursion, intrusion

I.R.S. employee 7 auditor **10** accountant

Irving novel 15 Cider House Rules (The) **17** Hotel New Hampshire (The) **20** World According to Garp (The)

Isaac *father:* **7** Abraham *mother:* **5** Sarah *son:* **4** Esau **5** Jacob *wife:* **7** Rebekah

Isabella I *country:* **5** Spain *home:* **7** Castile *husband:* **9** Ferdinand

Isaiah 7 prophet *father:* **4** Amoz

Iscah *brother:* **3** Lot *father:* **5** Haran *sister:* **6** Milcah

Iseult, Isolde *beloved:* **7** Tristan **8** Tristram *husband:* **4** Mark

Ishbak *father:* **7** Abraham *mother:* **7** Keturah

Ishbosheth's father 4 Saul

Ishmael 6 pariah **7** outcast **8** castaway, outsider **11** untouchable *captain:* **4** Ahab *father:* **7** Abraham *mother:* **5** Hagar *ship:* **6** Pequod

Ishtar *brother:* **7** Shamash *father:* **3** Anu, Sin *lover:* **6** Tammuz

Ishui's father 4 Saul **5** Asher

Isis *brother:* **6** Osiris *father:* **3** Geb *husband:* **6** Osiris *mother:* **3** Nut *son:* **4** Sept **5** Horus

Islam *adherent:* **6** Moslem, Muslim *founder:* **8** Mohammed, Muhammad *god:* **5** Allah *holy city:* **5** Mecca *holy month:* **7** Ramadan *law:* **6** Sharia *place of worship:* **6** mosque *priest:* **4** imam *scriptures:* **5** Koran, Quran *sect:* **4** Shia, Sufi **5** Sunni **6** Salafi, Shiite, Sufism **7** Ismaili, Wahhabi **8** Salafism (see also **Muslim**)

island 3 ait, cay, key **4** holm **5** atoll, oasis **6** skerry **7** crannog *Adriatic Sea:* **3** Vis **4** Brac, Cres, Hvar **5** Brach, Ciovo, Mljet, Solta **6** Lesina, Pharus *Aegean Sea:* **4** Scio **5** Chios, Khios, Samos, Thira **6** Ikaria, Lemnos, Lesbos, Limnos **7** Nikaria **8** Mitilini, Mytilene, Santorin **10** Sakis-Adasi, Susam-Adasi *Alaska:* **4** Adak, Atka, Attu, Kuiu **8** Wrangell *American Samoa:* **3** Ofu, Tau **4** Rose **6** Swains *Andaman Sea:* **4** Mali **5** Tavoy *Antarctica:* **5** Scott, Young *Arafura Sea:* **5** Dolak *Arctic Archipelago:* **6** Baffin **8** Victoria *Arctic Ocean:* **5** Senja *Australian:* **5** Cocos **8** Tasmania *Azores:* **4** Pico **5** Corvo, Faial *Bahamas:* **3** Cat, Rum **4** Long **5** Abaco, Exuma **6** Andros, Inagua **7** Acklins, Crooked **8** Watlings **9** Eleuthera, Maya-

guana 11 San Salvador *Bahrain:* 5 Sitra 8
Muharraq *Baltic Sea:* 4 Moon, Muhu 5
Faron, Mukhu, Rugen, Worms 6 Vormsi 7
Gotland 8 Bornholm, Gothland, Gottland
Barents Sea: 4 Bear *Bay of Naples:* 5 Capri
Bay of Panama: 4 Naos *Bering Sea:* 5
Medny 7 Nunivak 10 Big Diomede 13 Little
Diomede *Bismarck Archipelago:* 5 Lihir 10
New Britain *Bristol Channel:* 5 Lundy *Buz-
zards Bay:* 9 Cuttyhunk *Canadian:* 5
Banks, Devon 6 Baffin 8 Bathurst, Mel-
ville, Somerset, Victoria 9 Anticosti, Elles-
mere 10 Cape Breton 11 Axel Heiberg,
Southampton 12 Newfoundland, Prince Ed-
ward *Canaries:* 6 Gomera 7 La Palma 8
Tenerife 9 Lanzarote *Cape Verde:* 4 Fogo,
Maio, Mayo 5 Brava, Rombo *Caribbean
Sea:* 4 Cuba 5 Aruba, Utila, Vache 6 To-
bago 7 Antigua, Curaçao, Jamaica 8 Barba-
dos, Dominica, Trinidad 10 Guadeloupe,
Martinique, Puerto Rico (see also **Virgin
group**) *Carolines:* 3 Uap, Yap 4 Truk 5
Chuuk, Nomoi, Sorol 6 Ponape 7 Hogoleu,
Pohnpei 9 Ascension *Chagos Archipelago:*
11 Diego Garcia *Chesapeake Bay:* 4 Deal,
Kent 5 Smith, Watts *Chukchi Sea:* 6 Herald
Comoro group: 7 Mayotte *Congo River:* 4
Bamu *Croatia:* 3 Krk, Pag, Rab 5 Susak,
Unije *Cyclades:* 3 Ios, Kea, Nio 4 Ceos,
Keos, Milo 5 Delos, Melos, Milos, Naxos,
Paros, Siros, Syros 6 Andros, Dhilos 7
Amorgos, Cythnos, Kithnos, Kythnos,
Mykonos *Denmark:* 3 Als, Fyn, Mon 4
Aero, Fano, Moen, Mors 5 Alsen, Funen,
Moers, Samso 8 Bornholm 9 Greenland 13
Fanum Fortunae *East River:* 5 Ward's 7
Welfare 9 Roosevelt *England's:* 7 Britain 9
Britannia 12 Great Britain *English Chan-
nel:* 5 Wight *Fiji:* 4 Koro 5 Mango, Vatoa
French: 7 Corsica 12 New Caledonia
French Polynesia: 4 Rapa, Reao, Ua Pu 5
Ua Pau *Futunas:* 5 Alofi *Galápagos:* 5 Pinta
7 Chatham, Isabela 8 Abingdon 10 Alber-
marle *Georgia:* 5 Tybee *Germany:* 4 Fohr 7
Fehmarn 9 Helgoland 10 Heligoland
Greater Antilles: 4 Cuba 7 Jamaica 10 His-
paniola, Puerto Rico *Greece:* 4 Milo, Rodi
5 Creta, Crete, Hydra, Idhra, Kriti, Rodos,
Tenos, Tinos 6 Euboea, Evvoia, Hydrea,
Lesbos, Rhodes, Rhodus 9 Negropont 10
Negroponte *Grenadines:* 5 Union *Gulf of
Alaska:* 6 Kodiak *Gulf of Bothnia:* 5 Karlö
Gulf of Carpentaria: 5 Maria 6 Groote 7
Eylandt *Gulf of Guinea:* 7 Sao Tomé 8
Príncipe, Sao Thomé 11 Saint Thomas *Gulf
of Mexico:* 3 Cat 5 Lobos *Gulf of Panama:*
3 Rey *Gulf of St. Lawrence:* 5 Brion *Gulf of*

Thailand: 3 Kut 5 Samui *Haiti:* 6 Gonâve
Hawaii: 4 Maui, Oahu 5 Kauai, Lanai 6 Nii-
hau 7 Molokai 9 Kahoolawe *Hudson Bay:* 5
Coats *Indian Ocean:* 4 Mahé, Nias 5 Heard,
Pemba 7 La Dique, Praslin, Réunion 8 Sri
Lanka, Zanzibar 9 Mauritius 10 Madagas-
car *Indonesia:* 4 Bali, Biak, Java, Maja,
Muna, Nias, Rhio, Riau, Roma, Roti, Savu,
Sawu 5 Batam, Boano, Buton, Djawa,
Japen, Lakor, Moena, Riouw, Rotti, Rupat,
Sawoe, Solor, Sumba, Wetar, Wokam 6 Bu-
tung, Flores, Jappen, Lombok, Madura, Pa-
dang, Roepat, Romang, Soemba 7 Celebes,
Madoera, Sumatra, Sumbawa 8 Boetoeng,
Soembawa, Sulawesi 10 Bandanaira, Banda
Neira, Sandalwood *Iran:* 5 Shahi *Ireland:* 4
Aran *Irish Sea:* 3 Man *Italy:* 4 Elba 6 Sicily
8 Sardinia *Japan:* 3 Iki, Uku 4 Naru, Yezo 5
Awaji, Fukae, Fukue, Hondo, Shodo 6
Honshu, Kyushu 7 Shikoku 8 Hokkaido 10
Shodoshima *Java Sea:* 4 Laut *Kiribati:* 6
Tarawa *Lake Champlain:* 5 Grand *Lake
Erie:* 9 North Bass, South Bass 10 Middle
Bass *Lake Huron:* 8 Drummond 10 Mani-
toulin *Lake Michigan:* 3 Hog 4 High 6 Bea-
ver *Lake Ontario:* 5 Wolfe *Lake Superior:* 4
Sand 6 Royale 7 Manitou *Lake Winnipeg:* 5
Hecla *largest:* 9 Greenland *Leeward group:*
5 Nevis 7 Antigua, Barbuda, Redonda 8
Anguilla, Sombrero 10 Montserrat, Saint
Kitts 13 St. Christopher *legendary:* 7
Cipango *Lesser Sundas:* 4 Alor 5 Ombai
Long Island Sound: 4 City, Hart 5 Goose,
Harts *Malay Archipelago:* 5 Kisar, Larat,
Timor 6 Borneo 9 New Guinea *Malaysia:* 6
Penang, Pinang 13 Prince of Wales *Malta:* 4
Gozo *Massachusetts:* 9 Nantucket *Mediter-
ranean Sea:* 4 Elba 5 Corfu, Crete, Malta 6
Cyprus, Euboea, Rhodes, Sicily 7 Corsica 8
Sardinia *Moluccas:* 4 Buru 5 Ambon, Ce-
ram, Seram 6 Boeroe *Mozambique chan-
nel:* 10 Juan de Nova *Myanmar:* 5 Daung,
Kadan, Lanbi *Narragansett Bay:* 5 Rhode 8
Prudence 9 Aquidneck, Conanicut *Nether-
lands:* 5 Texel 7 Ameland 8 Vlieland *Neth-
erlands Antilles:* 7 Curaçao *New York:* 4
Fire, Long 5 Ellis 6 Staten 7 Liberty 9 Gar-
diners, Governors, Manhattan, Roosevelt
New York Bay: 5 Ellis 6 Staten 7 Liberty 9
Governors, Manhattan *New Zealand:* 5
South, White 7 Chatham, Stewart 8
D'Urville *Niagara River:* 4 Goat *Nile River:*
4 Argo, Roda, Ruda 5 Rhoda 6 Rawdah 11
Elephantine *North Channel:* 3 Mew 8
Manihiki 9 Tongareva *North Pacific:* 4
Wake *Northwest Territories:* 5 Banks, Bylot,
Devon 8 Bathurst, Melville 9 Ellesmere 10

Cornwallis, Resolution **13** Prince of Wales *Norwegian:* **8** Jan Mayen *Norwegian Sea:* **5** Donna, Smola, Vikna *Nova Scotia:* **5** Sable **10** Cape Breton *off Alaska:* **4** Dall **5** Kayak *off Albania:* **5** Sazan **6** Saseno *off Australia:* **4** Dunk *off Belize:* **9** Ambergris *off Brazil:* **4** Apeu **5** Rocas *off British Columbia:* **4** King, Pitt **9** Vancouver *off Cape Cod:* **8** Muskeget **9** Nantucket *off Chile:* **5** Guafo, Mocha *off China:* **4** Amoy **5** Ma-tsu **6** Hainan, Quemoy, Taiwan *off Crete:* **3** Dia *off Ecuador:* **4** Puna *off England:* **3** Man **4** Sark **5** Wight **6** Jersey, Walney **8** Alderney, Guernsey *off Florida:* **3** Dog **4** Pine **6** Amelia **7** Pelican, Sanibel **9** Anastasia *off French Guiana:* **6** Devil's *off Georgia:* **10** Cumberland **11** Saint Simons *off Germany:* **4** Sylt *off Greenland:* **5** Disko *off Guinea:* **5** Tombo *off Hispaniola:* **5** Beata *off Honduras:* **5** Tigre *off Iceland:* **7** Surtsey *off India:* **5** Sagar *off Ireland:* **4** Tory **5** Clare, Clear *off Kenya:* **4** Lamu *off Long Island:* **7** Fishers *off Louisiana:* **5** Marsh *off Maine:* **4** Deer, Orrs **5** Swans **8** Monhegan **11** Mount Desert *off Malay Peninsula:* **6** Phuket **9** Singapore *off Maryland:* **10** Assateague *off Massachusetts:* **4** Plum **7** Naushon *off Mexico:* **7** Cozumel *off Mississippi:* **4** Horn, Ship *off Mozambique:* **3** Ibo *off New Brunswick:* **10** Campobello *off Newfoundland:* **4** Bell *off Nigeria:* **5** Lagos *off North Carolina:* **5** Bodie *off Norway:* **5** Bomlo, Froya, Hitra, Sotra, Stord, Vardo **8** Hitteren *off Panama:* **4** Naos **5** Coiba **6** Parida *off Poland:* **5** Wolin **6** Wollin *off Puerto Rico:* **4** Crab **7** Culebra, Vieques *off Rhode Island:* **5** Block *off Scotland:* **4** Bute, Iona, Jura **5** Arran, Islay *off South Carolina:* **5** North **6** Parris **10** Hilton Head *off Sri Lanka:* **5** Delft *off Staten Island:* **7** Hoffman *off Sumatra:* **3** Weh *off Sweden:* **5** Graso, Oland, Vaddo *off Syria:* **5** Arvad, Arwad, Rouad **6** Aradus *off Tanzania:* **5** Mafia, Pemba *off Tasmania:* **5** Bruni, Bruny *off Tunisia:* **5** Jerba **6** Djerba, Meninx *off Venezuela:* **5** Aruba **7** Bonaire **8** Buen Aire *off Virginia:* **5** Wreck *off Wales:* **5** Caldy **6** Caldey *Orkneys:* **3** Hoy *Outer Hebrides:* **5** Barra, Scarp *Palmer Archipelago:* **6** Anvers **7** Antwerp, Brabant *Pearl Harbor:* **4** Ford *Persian Gulf:* **4** Qeys **5** Kharg, Khark *Philippines:* **4** Buad, Cebu, Fuga, Ilin, Poro, Sulu **5** Balut, Batan, Bohol, Coron, Daram, Leyte, Luzon, Panay, Samal, Samar, Sugbu, Talim, Ticao, Verde **6** Negros **7** Masbate, Mindoro, Palawan, Samar **9** Limasawa, Mindanao **10** Corregidor *Puerto Rico:* **4** Mona *Quebec:* **4** Alma *Red Sea:* **5** Tiran,

Zugur, Zuqar *Russia:* **7** Wrangel *St. Lawrence River:* **4** Hare **5** Jesus **8** Montreal *San Francisco Bay:* **5** Angel *Santa Cruz:* **5** Anuda, Ndeni **6** Cherry *Sea of Japan:* **4** Sado **5** Rebun *Sea of Marmara:* **4** Avsa *second largest:* **9** New Guinea *Senegal:* **5** Gorée *Seychelles:* **4** Mahé **7** La Digue, Praslin *Shetland archipelago:* **4** Unst, Yell **5** Foula *Sierra Leone:* **5** Tasso *South Atlantic:* **5** Gough **6** Gough's **11** Saint Helena *South Korea:* **5** Cheju *South of Tokyo:* **3** Iwo **7** Iwo Jima, Naka Iwo *South Orkneys:* **10** Coronation *South Pacific:* **3** Hiu **4** Niue **5** Raoul **6** Savage, Sunday **7** Norfolk **8** Pitcairn *Spitsbergen archipelago:* **4** Edge *Strait of Hormuz:* **5** Qeshm, Qishm *Sulu Archipelago:* **4** Jolo **5** Lapac *Svalbard:* **4** Hope *Sverdrup:* **11** Axel Heiberg **12** Amund Ringnes *Swedish:* **3** Ven **4** Hven **5** Hveen, Orust *Tanzania:* **8** Zanzibar *Texas:* **5** Padre *Thames River:* **7** Sheppey *third largest:* **6** Borneo *Tierra del Fuego:* **5** Hoste *Tonga:* **3** Eua, Foa **4** Uiha **5** Haano *Tuamotu Archipelago:* **4** Anaa **5** Chain *Turkish:* **5** Imroz **6** Imbros *Tuvalu:* **7** Nanumea **9** Nukufetau *Tyrrhenian Sea:* **6** Ischia **11** Montecristo *Vanuatu:* **3** Api, Epi, Oba **4** Aoba, Gaua, Tana, Vate **5** Efate, Maewo, Tanna *Venezuelan:* **5** Patos **9** La Tortuga *volcanic:* **5** Tofua **7** Iwo Jima *Wales:* **8** Anglesea, Anglesey, Holyhead *Weddell Sea:* **4** Ross **6** Hearst *Western Samoa:* **5** Upolu **6** Savaii *West Indies:* **4** Mona, Saba, Salt **5** Nevis, Peter, Saona **6** Tobago, Tortue **7** Grenada, Tortuga **8** Trinidad **9** Santa Cruz **10** Concepción, Hispaniola, Montserrat, Saint Croix (see also **Bahamas; Greater Antilles; Leeward group; Virgin group; Windward group**) *West of England:* **7** Ireland *West Pacific:* **5** Dyaul, Fauro, Ocean **6** Banaba, Marcus **7** Iwo Jima, Kita Iwo **9** Minami Iwo *with former penitentiary:* **8** Alcatraz **island group** *Admiralty:* **5** Manus *Alaska:* **3** Rat **8** Aleutian, Pribilof **9** Andreanof, Catherine *Aleutians:* **4** Near *Aleutian:* **3** Rat **4** Adak, Akun, Attu **5** Amlia, Kiska, Umnak **6** Kanaga, Tanaga, Unimak **8** Amchitka, Unalaska *American Samoa:* **5** Manua *Apostle:* **3** Oak **4** Long, Sand **5** Outer **8** Madeline, Michigan, Stockton *Arabian Sea:* **9** Laccadive *Arctic Archipelago:* **8** Sverdrup *Arctic Ocean:* **8** Svalbard **12** Novaya Zemlya *Bahamas:* **5** Berry, Exuma **6** Bimini *Balearic:* **5** Ibiza **7** Majorca, Menorca, Minorca **8** Mallorca *Banda Sea:* **5** Damar *Bangladesh:* **5** Hatia, Hatya *Bay of Bengal:* **7** Andaman, Nicobar *between England and*

France: 7 Channel *Bismarck Archipelago:* 4 Feni 5 Tabar, Tanga *Bismarck Sea:* 4 Vitu *British:* 7 Bermuda *Caribbean Sea:* 4 Swan 5 Pearl 6 Cayman, Perlas, Pigeon 8 Pichones 10 Grenadines, West Indies *Central Pacific Ocean:* 4 Line 5 Samoa, Union 6 Danger, Midway 7 Phoenix, Tokelau 8 Manihiki 9 Polynesia 12 Northern Cook *Channel:* 4 Herm, Sark 5 Lihou, Sercq 6 Jersey 8 Guernsey *Cook:* 4 Atiu 5 Mauke *Coral Sea:* 4 Huon *Cuba:* 8 Camagüey *Denmark:* 6 Faroes 7 Faeroes *D'Entrecasteaux:* 8 Kaluwawa 9 Fergusson *Dodecanese:* 3 Coo, Cos, Kos 4 Caso, Lero, Simi, Syme 5 Kasos, Leros, Lipso, Lisso, Patmo, Telos 6 Calino, Lipsos, Nisiro, Patmos 7 Calimno, Nisiros, Nisyros 8 Kalymnos *east of Philippines:* 10 Micronesia *East Siberian Sea:* 4 Bear 8 Medvezhi *Ecuador:* 3 Colón 9 Galápagos *England:* 5 Farne *Faeroes, Faroes:* 4 Vago 5 Bordo, Sando *Fiji:* 3 Lau 7 Eastern *Florida Keys:* 4 Long, Vaca, West 5 Largo 7 Big Pine 9 Matecumbe, Sugarloaf *Formosa Strait:* 4 Hoko 6 Peng hu 10 Pescadores *Fox:* 5 Umnak 6 Akutan, Unimak 8 Unalaska *France:* 5 Salut 6 Safety 9 Kerguelen *French Polynesia:* 3 Low 6 Tubuai 7 Austral, Paumotu, Société, Society, Tuamotu 9 Marquesas, Touamotou *Frisian:* 3 Rom 4 Föhr, Sylt 5 Amrum, Juist, Mando, Texel 6 Borkum 7 Ameland 8 Langeoog, Pellworm, Vlieland 9 Helgoland, Norderney *Germany:* 8 Halligen *Greece:* 6 Aegean, Ionian 8 Cyclades 10 Dodecanese 11 Dodecanesus *Hudson Bay:* 7 Belcher *Indian Ocean:* 7 Aldabra *Indonesia:* 4 Asia, Batu, Pagi, Sula 5 Babar, Batoe, Pagai, Pageh, Penju, Spice, Wakde 6 Maluku *Inner Hebrides:* 4 Coll, Eigg, Iona, Jura, Muck, Mull, Skye 5 Canna, Gigha, Islay, Tiree, Tyree *Ionian:* 5 Corfu, Paxos, Zante 6 Cerigo, Ithaca, Leukas, Levkas 10 Santa Maura *Ireland:* 4 Aran *Italy:* 6 Lipari *Japan:* 5 Osumi *Kuril:* 4 Urup 5 Ketoi, Matua 6 Iturup 7 Etorofu, Matsuwa 8 Kunashir 9 Kunashiri *largest:* 5 Malay 8 Malaysia *Lesser Antilles:* 8 Windward *Leti:* 3 Moa 5 Lakor *Line:* 5 Flint 6 Malden, Vostok 7 Fanning, Palmyra 8 Starbuck 9 Christmas *Loyalty:* 3 Uea 6 Lifu, Maré, Uvea 5 Lifou *Malay Archipelago:* 5 Sunda 6 Soenda *Marianas:* 4 Maug, Rota 5 Pagan 6 Saipan *Marquesas:* 4 Eiào, Ua Pu 6 Hatutu, Hiva Oa, Ua Huka 7 Tahuata 8 Fatu Hiva, Nuku Hiva *Marshall:* 5 Wotho, Wotje 8 Eniwetok 9 Kwajalein *Mediterranean Sea:* 8 Baleares, Balearic *Midway:* 4 Sand 7 Eastern *Moluccas:* 3 Kai, Kei, Obi 4 Buru, Leti 5 Ambon, Banda, Letti, Seram 6 Boeroe 8 Tanimbar 9 Timorlaut *New Caledonia:* 7 Loyalty 9 Loyalties *Northern Cook:* 7 Penrhyn *north of Australia:* 9 Melanesia *north of British Isles:* 5 Faroe 7 Faeroes *north off Fiji:* 5 Hoorn 6 Futuna *north of Madagascar:* 7 Aldabra 8 Farquhar *north of New Caledonia:* 5 Belep *north of New Guinea:* 8 Bismarck 9 Admiralty 11 Admiralties *Northwest Territories:* 5 Parry *off Alaska:* 3 Fox *off Alaska Peninsula:* 8 Shumagin *off Cape Cod:* 9 Elizabeth *off eastern Asia:* 5 Kuril 6 Kurile *off England:* 6 Scilly *off Florida:* 11 Dry Tortugas *off Guinea:* 3 Los 4 Loos *off Honduras:* 5 Bahia *off Morocco:* 7 Madeira *off New Guinea:* 3 Aru 4 Aroe *off Nicaragua:* 4 Corn *off northern Africa:* 6 Canary 8 Canaries *off northern Australia:* 6 Wessel 7 Dampier *off Sicily:* 5 Egadi 8 Aegadian *Okinawa:* 4 Kume *Outer Hebrides:* 4 Uist *Papua New Guinea:* 5 Green *Persian Gulf:* 4 Tunb *Philippines:* 4 Cuyo 5 Tapul 6 Lubang 7 Basilan, Bisayas, Visayan *Phoenix:* 4 Hull, Mary 6 Birnie, Canton 9 Enderbury *Portuguese:* 6 Azores *Quebec:* 8 Magdalen 9 Madeleine *Queen Charlotte:* 7 Moresby *Ryukyus:* 5 Amami 7 Okinawa *St. Lawrence River:* 8 Thousand *Sea of Japan:* 3 Oki *Sea of Marmara:* 5 Kizil 7 Princes 11 Kizil Adalar *Shumagin:* 4 Unga *Society:* 5 Eimeo, Tahaa, Tahao, Taiti 6 Moorea, Tahiti 8 Otaheite *Solomon:* 4 Buka, Gizo, Savo 7 Malaita 11 Guadalcanal 12 Bougainville *South Atlantic Ocean:* 8 Falkland, Malvinas *South China Sea:* 6 Hirata 7 Paracel, Spratly *south of New Zealand:* 8 Auckland *South Pacific:* 11 Austronesia *Sulu Sea:* 7 Cagayan 9 Cagayanes *Tonga:* 5 Vavau *Treasury:* 4 Mono *Truk:* 3 Tol 4 Haru, Moen, Udot, Uman 5 Fefan *Tyrrhenian Sea:* 5 Ponza *Venezuelan:* 4 Aves, Bird 9 Los Roques *Virgin, American:* 9 Saint John 10 Saint Croix 11 Saint Thomas *Virgin, British:* 5 Peter 6 Norman 7 Anegada, Tortola 11 Jost Van Dyke *West Europe:* 12 British Isles *West Indies:* 6 Virgin 10 Guadeloupe *west of French Polynesia:* 4 Cook *west of Scotland:* 7 Western 8 Hebrides *west Pacific Ocean:* 4 Duff 5 Belau, Bonin, Mapia, Palau, Pelew 7 Ladrone, Mariana, Solomon, Vanuatu 8 Marshall, Treasury 9 Ogasawara 10 Saint David *Windward:* 10 Martinique

island nation *Atlantic Ocean:* 9 Cape Verde *Indian Ocean:* 8 Malagasy, Malgache, Sri Lanka 9 Mauritius 10 Madagascar, Seychelles *Mediterranean Sea:* 6 Cyprus Mo-

zambique Channel: **6** Comoro **7** Comores ***off southern China:*** **6** Taiwan ***south of Greenland:*** **7** Iceland ***West Indies:*** **4** Cuba **7** Jamaica **8** Barbados **10** Saint Lucia ***West Pacific Ocean:*** **4** Fiji **5** Belau, Nauru, Palau, Samoa **6** Tuvalu **7** Vanuatu ***Windward group:*** **8** Dominica

island province 12 Prince Edward

island state 6 Hawaii

isle see **island**

Ismene ***brother:*** **9** Polynices **10** Polyneices ***father:*** **7** Oedipus ***mother:*** **7** Jocasta ***sister:*** **8** Antigone ***uncle:*** **5** Creon

isochronous 7 regular **8** cyclical, periodic, rhythmic **9** recurrent, recurring **10** periodical **12** intermittent

isolate 6 cut off, detach, enisle **7** seclude **8** close off, insulate, pinpoint, separate, set apart **9** segregate, sequester **10** quarantine

isolated 5 alone **6** random, remote, unique **7** unusual **8** solitary, sporadic **9** separated, withdrawn **11** exceptional, quarantined

Isolde see **Iseult**

Israel ***airline:*** **4** El Al ***ancient name:*** **4** Zion **5** Judea **6** Canaan, Judaea **9** Palestine ***capital:*** **9** Jerusalem ***city:*** **4** Acre **5** Haifa, Jaffa **7** Tel Aviv **9** Beersheba ***desert:*** **5** Negeb, Negev ***gulf:*** **5** Aqaba ***lake:*** **8** Tiberias **12** Sea of Galilee ***language:*** **6** Arabic, Hebrew ***monetary unit:*** **6** shekel ***neighbor:*** **5** Egypt, Syria **6** Jordan **7** Lebanon ***plain:*** **9** Esdraelon ***river:*** **6** Jordan ***sea:*** **4** Dead **13** Mediterranean

Israeli 5 sabra ***dance:*** **4** hora **5** horah ***gun:*** **3** Uzi

Israelite see **Hebrew; Jewish**

Issachar ***father:*** **5** Jacob ***mother:*** **4** Leah

issue 4 emit, flow, gush, pour, rise, seed, stem, vent **5** arise, birth, brood, child, empty, fruit, scion, topic **6** affair, appear, effect, emerge, get out, matter, put out, result, scions, sequel, source, spring, upshot **7** concern, debouch, descent, edition, emanate, give off, give out, outcome, problem, proceed, progeny, publish, release, subject **8** bulletin, children, question, throw off **9** come forth, offspring, originate, posterity **10** derive from, distribute, end product, promulgate **11** consequence, descendants, progeniture, publication

Istanbul ***ancient name:*** **9** Byzantium ***business section:*** **6** Galata ***country:*** **6** Turkey ***foreign quarter:*** **4** Pera **7** Beyoglu ***park:*** **8** Seraglio ***residential section:*** **7** Uskudar

isthmus ***Africa-Asia:*** **4** Suez ***America:*** **6** Panama ***Greece:*** **7** Corinth ***Malay Peninsula:*** **3** Kra

Italian ***after:*** **4** dopo ***against:*** **6** contro ***ahead:*** **6** avanti ***apple:*** **4** mela ***article:*** **2** il, la ***aunt:*** **3** zia ***automobile:*** **4** Fiat **6** Lancia **7** Ferrari **8** Maserati **9** Alfa Romeo **11** Lamborghini ***be:*** **6** essere ***book:*** **5** libro ***brandy:*** **6** grappa ***brother:*** **8** fratello ***cake:*** **5** torta ***cat:*** **5** gatto ***cathedral:*** **5** duomo ***cheers:*** **6** cin cin ***chicken:*****5** pollo ***child:*** **7** bambino ***coffee:*** **5** caffè ***come:*** **6** venire ***day:*** **6** giorno ***deer:*** **5** cervo ***dialect:*** **6** Tuscan **8** Sicilian ***dictator:*** **9** Mussolini (Benito) ***die:*** **6** morire ***dinner:*** **6** pranzo ***do, make:*** **4** fare ***dog:*** **4** cane ***enough:*** **5** basta ***evening:*** **4** sera ***everyone:*** **5** tutti ***family:*** **4** Este **5** Cenci, Savoy **6** Borgia, Medici, Orsini, Pepoli, Savoia, Sforza **7** Colonna, Gonzaga, Spinola **8** Visconti ***fascist:*** **10** Blackshirt ***game:*** **5** bocce, bocci **6** boccie ***gentleman:*** **6** signor **7** signore ***give:*** **4** dare ***go:*** **6** andare ***goat:*** **5** capra ***good-bye:*** **4** ciao ***grape:*** **3** uva ***hear:*** **7** sentire ***hello:*** **4** ciao ***highway:*** **10** autostrada ***honey:*** **5** miele ***how much:*** **6** quanto ***ice cream:*** **6** gelato ***lady:*** **5** donna **7** signora **9** signorina ***leave:*** **7** partire ***magistrate:*** **7** podestà ***maybe:*** **5** forse ***meat:*** **5** carne **6** salami **8** pancetta **9** pepperoni, salsiccia **10** mortadella, prosciutto ***man:*** **4** uomo ***milk:*** **5** latte ***mountain soldier:*** **6** Alpino ***much:*** **5** molto ***mushroom:*** **5** fungo ***night:*** **5** notte ***nothing:*** **6** niente ***numbers:*** **3** due, sei, tre, uno **4** nove, otto **5** dieci, sette **6** cinque **7** quattro ***often:*** **6** spesso ***oil:*** **4** olio ***open:*** **6** aprire ***opera house:*** **7** La Scala ***over:*** **5** sopra ***patriot:*** **6** Cavour (Conte di), Rienzo (Cola di) **7** Mazzini (Giuseppe) **9** Garibaldi (Giuseppe) ***peach:*** **5** pesca ***pencil:*** **6** matita ***please:*** **9** per favore ***red:*** **5** rosso ***religious reformer:*** **10** Savonarola (Girolamo) ***resort:*** **4** Lido **5** Abano, Capri **8** Sorrento, Taormina ***road:*** **6** strada ***sandwich:*** **6** panino ***sell:*** **7** vendere ***shrimp:*** **6** scampi ***sing:*** **7** cantare ***sister:*** **7** sorella ***soldier:*** **7** soldato ***soup:*** **5** zuppa **10** minestrone ***speak:*** **7** parlare ***square:*** **6** piazza ***squid:*** **8** calamari ***star:*** **6** stella ***street:*** **3** via **5** corso ***summer:*** **6** estate ***sun:*** **4** sole ***tell, say:*** **4** dire ***thanks:*** **6** grazie ***think:*** **7** pensare ***toward:*** **5** verso ***uncle:*** **3** zio ***under:*** **5** sotto ***voice:*** **4** voce ***weight:*** **5** libra, oncia ***white:*** **6** bianco ***wine:*** **4** vino ***with:*** **3** con ***without:*** **5** senza ***write:*** **8** scrivere

Italy ***bay:*** **6** Naples ***capital:*** **4** Roma, Rome ***city:*** **4** Asti, Bari, Pisa **5** Aosta, Genoa, Milan, Padua, Parma, Siena, Turin **6** Genova, Mantua, Milano, Modena, Naples, Napoli, Padova, Torino, Venice, Verona **7** Bergamo, Bologna, Bolzano, Catania, Cremona, Firenze, Leghorn, Livorno, Mantova, Palermo, Perugia, Ravenna, Salerno, Taranto,

Trieste, Venezia **8** Florence, Siracusa, Syracuse *enclave:* **9** San Marino **11** Vatican City *gulf:* **5** Gaeta **7** Salerno, Taranto **11** Sant' Eufemia *island, island group:* **4** Elba, Lido **5** Capri **6** Ischia, Lipari, Sicily **7** Aeolian, Capraia **8** Sardinia *lake:* **4** Como **5** Garda **7** Bolsena **8** Maggiore **9** Bracciano *leader:* **9** Mussolini (Benito) *monetary unit:* **4** euro *monetary unit, former:* **4** lira **5** scudi (plural), scudo, soldi (plural), soldo *mountain, range:* **4** Alps, Etna **9** Apennines, Mont Blanc, Monte Rosa **10** Monte Corno *neighbor:* **6** France **7** Austria **8** Slovenia **11** Switzerland *peninsula:* **9** Salentina *river:* **4** Arno, Liri **5** Adige, Piave, Tiber **6** Isonzo, Tevere **8** Volturno *sea:* **6** Ionian **8** Adriatic, Ligurian **10** Tyrrhenian **13** Mediterranean *strait:* **7** Messina, Otranto *volcano:* **4** Etna **8** Vesuvius *wine region:* **4** Asti

itch 3 yen **4** ache, long, lust, pine, urge **5** crave, yearn **6** desire, hanker, hunger, thirst **7** craving, longing **8** appetite, pruritus, yearning **9** hankering

itchy 4 avid, edgy, keen **5** antsy, eager, jumpy **7** fidgety, restive **8** prurient, pruritic, restless **9** impatient

item 3 bit **5** entry, point, scrap, story, thing, topic **6** detail, matter **7** account, article, element, feature, product **8** clipping **9** commodity **10** particular

itemize 4 list **5** count, tally **6** number **7** catalog, run down, specify, tick off **8** document, spell out **9** catalogue, enumerate, inventory

iterate 5 drill, recap, renew **6** rehash, repeat, replay, retell **7** reprise, restate **12** recapitulate

Ithaca king 8 Odysseus

Ithamar's father 5 Aaron

itinerant 5 gypsy, nomad **6** roving **7** migrant, nomadic, roaming, vagrant **8** drifting, rambling, traveler, vagabond, wanderer **9** migratory, transient, unsettled, wandering, wayfaring **11** peripatetic

itty-bitty 3 wee **4** tiny **5** teeny, weeny **6** teensy **10** teeny-weeny **12** teensy-weensy

Ivanhoe author: 5 Scott (Walter) *character:* **5** Isaac **6** Cedric, Rowena, Ulrica **7** Rebecca, Wilfred **9** Robin Hood

Ivory Coast 11 Côte d'Ivoire *capital:* **7** Abidjan **12** Yamoussoukro *city:* **6** Bouaké *language:* **6** French *monetary unit:* **5** franc *mountain:* **5** Nimba *neighbor:* **4** Mali **5** Ghana **6** Guinea **7** Liberia **11** Burkina Faso *river:* **7** Bandama **9** Sassandra

ivory-tower 8 academic **11** conjectural, impractical, theoretical, unrealistic

Ivy League 4 Penn, Yale **5** Brown **7** Cornell, Harvard **8** Columbia **9** Dartmouth, Princeton **12** Pennsylvania

J

jab 3 hit **4** barb, blow, poke, prod, sock, stab **5** nudge, prick, punch **6** pierce, strike, thrust **8** puncture

jabber 3 gab, jaw, yak **6** babble, drivel, gabble **7** blather, chatter, prattle **8** nonsense **9** gibberish

jabberer 6 gabber, magpie **7** babbler, blabber, gabbler **8** prattler **9** chatterer **10** chatterbox

Jabberwocky author 7 Carroll (Lewis), Dodgson (Charles)

jabot 4 fall **5** frill **6** ruffle

____ **jacet 3** hic

jack 3 tar **4** bird, card, fish, flag, hike, lift, move, salt **5** boost, brace, bread, dough, knave, knife, money, put up, raise **6** brandy, cheese, device, donkey, rabbit, sailor, seaman **7** laborer, mariner, servant **8** increase,

standard **9** criticize, mechanism **10** take to task

jackal 4 dupe, pawn **5** agent, canid, patsy **6** canine, flunky, lackey, minion, stooge **7** cat's-paw **9** accessory, auxiliary **10** accomplice **11** stool pigeon *god:* **4** Anpu **6** Anubis

jackanapes 3 ape, imp **4** brat, fool **6** monkey

jackass 4 dolt, dope, fool, jerk **5** burro, dunce, idiot, schmo **6** donkey, nitwit **7** nebbish **8** bonehead, imbecile, numskull **9** blockhead, numbskull **10** nincompoop *deer:* **3** kob **8** antelope

jackdaw 7 grackle **9** blackbird

jacket 3 tux **4** Eton **5** parka, tunic **6** anorak, blazer, bolero, jerkin, reefer, sacque, tuxedo **7** doublet, Norfolk, peacoat, spencer **8** camisole **10** roundabout *armored:* **7** hauberk **9**

habergeon *sleeveless:* 4 vest 6 bolero, jerkin 9 waistcoat

jackhammer 5 drill 9 rock drill

jack-in-the-pulpit 4 arum

jackknife 4 dive 6 barlow *game:* 11 mumblety-peg

jackleg 6 make-do, novice 7 amateur, shyster, stopgap 9 dishonest, greenhorn, makeshift, temporary, unskilled 10 substitute 11 pettifogger 12 unscrupulous

jack-of-all-trades 6 tinker 7 go-to guy 8 factotum, handyman

jack-o'-lantern 6 fungus 7 pumpkin

jackpot 3 sum 4 pool 5 award, kitty, prize 6 reward, stakes 7 bonanza, success 8 windfall

jackrabbit 4 hare

jackstay 3 bar, rod 4 rope 7 rigging, support

Jacob *brother:* 4 Esau *daughter:* 5 Dinah *father:* 5 Isaac *father-in-law:* 5 Laban *mother:* 7 Rebekah *new name:* 6 Israel *son:* 3 Dan, Gad 4 Levi 5 Asher, Judah 6 Joseph, Reuben, Simeon 7 Zebulun 8 Benjamin, Issachar, Naphtali *variant:* 5 James *wife:* 4 Leah 6 Rachel

Jacobin 7 radical 9 Dominican, extremist

Jacob's ladder 4 herb 5 phlox 9 perennial

jade 3 gem, nag 4 bore, cloy, dull, minx, pall, tire, wear 5 color, drain, flirt, green, hussy, jewel, stone, tramp, weary, wench 6 wanton 7 fatigue, jezebel, mineral, trollop, wear out 8 gemstone, nephrite, strumpet, wear down

jaded 4 worn 5 blasé, bored, sated, tired, weary 6 dulled 7 cynical, wearied, worn-out 8 fatigued, satiated, worn down 9 apathetic, exhausted, surfeited 10 overworked

jaeger 4 skua 6 hunter 8 huntsman

Jael *husband:* 5 Heber *victim:* 6 Sisera

jag 3 cut 4 barb, jerk, load, pink, tear 5 binge, notch, prick, spell, spree 6 bender, indent, thrill, thrust 7 serrate

jagged 5 erose, harsh, rough, sharp 6 broken, craggy, rugged, spiked, uneven 7 scraggy 8 serrated, unsmooth 9 irregular

Jaguar model 3 XKE

jai alai 6 pelota *basket:* 5 cesta *court:* 6 cancha 7 fronton

jail 3 can, jug, pen 4 coop, gaol, poky 5 clink, pokey 6 cooler, lockup, prison 7 confine, freezer, slammer 8 hoosegow, imprison, stockade 9 constrain 11 confinement, incarcerate

jailbird 3 con 5 felon, loser 7 convict 8 criminal, prisoner, repeater 10 recidivist

jailer 5 guard, screw 6 keeper, warden 7 turnkey 8 overseer

jakes 3 loo 5 privy 7 latrine 8 outhouse 9 backhouse

jalopy 3 car 4 auto, heap 5 crate, wreck 6 beater, junker 7 clunker, vehicle 10 automobile, rattletrap

jalousie 5 blind 6 window 7 shutter

jam 3 box, fix 4 bind, clog, cram, dunk, pack, push 5 block, crowd, crush, force, jelly, press, stuff, wedge 6 bruise, impede, plight, scrape, squash, squish 7 dilemma, squeeze 8 compress, conserve, obstacle, preserve 9 confiture, preserves 10 difficulty 11 predicament

Jamaica *capital:* 8 Kingston *cay:* 5 Pedro 6 Morant *city:* 10 Montego Bay 11 Spanish Town *discoverer:* 8 Columbus (Christopher) *location:* 10 West Indies *mountain range:* 4 Blue 10 Dry Harbour *sea:* 9 Caribbean

Jamaican *export:* 3 rum 5 sugar *hair style:* 6 dreads 10 dreadlocks *music:* 3 dub, ska 6 reggae *musician:* 5 Cliff (Jimmy) 6 Marley (Bob, Ziggy) 7 Wailers *nationalist:* 6 Garvey (Marcus)

jambalaya 4 olio 5 gumbo 6 medley 7 mélange, mixture 8 mishmash 10 hodgepodge, hotchpotch, salmagundi

jamboree 4 gala 5 revel 6 fiesta, frolic 7 carouse, shindig 8 carnival, festival, wingding 9 merriment 11 celebration 13 entertainment

James *brother:* 4 John 5 Jesus, Joses *cousin:* 5 Jesus *father:* 7 Zebedee 8 Alphaeus *mother:* 4 Mary 6 Salome

James *novel* 8 American (The) 9 Europeans (The) 10 Bostonians (The), Confidence, Golden Bowl (The), Tragic Muse (The) 11 Ambassadors (The), Daisy Miller 14 Turn of the Screw (The), Wings of the Dove (The) 15 Portrait of a Lady (The) 16 Washington Square

James, P. D. *detective:* 9 Dalgliesh (Adam) *novel:* 11 Original Sin

James Bond *actor:* 5 Craig (Daniel), Moore (Roger) 6 Dalton (Timothy) 7 Brosnan (Pierce), Connery (Sean), Lazenby (George) *author:* 7 Fleming (Ian) *cocktail:* 12 vodka martini *film:* 4 Dr. No 9 GoldenEye, Moonraker, Octopussy 10 Goldfinger 11 Thunderball, View to a Kill (A) 12 Casino Royale 13 Die Another Day, License to Kill, Live and Let Die, Spy Who Loved Me (The) 15 For Your Eyes Only, Living Daylights (The), Quantum of Solace 16 World Is Not Enough (The), You Only Live Twice 17 Tomorrow Never Dies 18 Diamonds Are Forever, From Russia with Love

19 Man with the Golden Gun (The) **26** On Her Majesty's Secret Service *gun:* **7** Beretta, Walther **8** Lilliput *novel:* **4** Dr. No **9** Moonraker **10** Goldfinger **11** Thunderball **12** Casino Royale **13** Live and Let Die, Spy Who Loved Me (The) **15** For Your Eyes Only **16** You Only Live Twice **18** Diamonds Are Forever, From Russia with Love **19** Man with the Golden Gun (The) **26** On Her Majesty's Secret Service *secretary:* **10** Moneypenny (Miss) *villain:* **4** Drax (Sir Hugo), Dr. No, Khan (Kamal), King (Elektra) **5** Klebb (Rosa), Largo (Emilio), Mr. Big, Zorin **6** Carver (Elliot), Graves (Gustav), Renard **7** Blofeld (Ernst Stavro), Mr. White, Sanchez (Franz) **8** Gen. Orlov, Whitaker (Brad) **9** Dr. Kananga, Gen. Koskov, Kristados (Aristotle), Le Chiffre, Stromberg (Karl), Trevelyan (Alec) **10** Goldfinger (Auric), Scaramanga (Francisco)

Jammu and _____ **7** Kashmir

Jane Eyre *author:* **6** Brontë (Charlotte) *lover:* **9** Rochester

jangle 3 jar **4** ring **5** babel, clash **6** clamor, excite, hubbub **7** discord, quarrel **8** conflict **11** discordance, discordancy **12** disharmonize

jangling 5 harsh, noisy, tense **7** grating **9** dissonant **10** discordant, quarreling

janitor 5 super **6** porter **7** cleaner **9** caretaker, concierge, custodian **10** doorkeeper

japan 4 coat **7** coating, varnish **11** lacquerware

Japan 5 Nihon **6** Nippon *capital:* **3** Edo **5** Tokyo *city:* **4** Kobe **5** Kyoto, Osaka, Otaru **6** Nagoya **7** Fukuoka, Okinawa, Sapporo **8** Kawasaki, Nagasaki, Yokohama **9** Hiroshima *island:* **6** Honshu, Kyushu **7** Shikoku **8** Hokkaido *lake:* **4** Biwa **8** Chuzenji *monetary unit:* **3** yen *mountain:* **4** Fuji **8** Fujiyama

Japanese *aborigine:* **4** Ainu *art:* **6** bonsai, ukiyo-e **7** origami *baron:* **6** daimyo *battle cry:* **6** banzai *Buddha:* **5** Amida, Amita *business alliance:* **8** keiretsu *cartoons:* **5** anime *coin:* **2** bu *comics:* **5** manga *dancing girl:* **6** geisha *dish:* **4** miso, soba **5** gyoza, katsu, kombu, sushi **7** sashimi, tempura **8** sukiyaki, teriyaki *drama:* **3** Noh **6** Bugaku, Kabuki **7** Bunraku *drink:* **4** sake, saki *emperor:* **6** Mikado **7** Akihito **8** Hirohito *fencing:* **5** kendo *festival:* **3** Bon *fish:* **4** fugu *flower arrangement:* **7** ikebana *garment:* **6** kimono *gateway:* **5** torii *god:* **5** Ebisu, Hotei **7** Daikoku, Jurojin **8** Bishamon *goddess:* **6** Benten **9** Amaterasu *governor:* **6**

shogun *grill:* **7** hibachi *honorific:* **3** san *immigrant:* **5** issei *instrument:* **4** biwa, koto **7** samisen **8** shamisen **10** shakuhachi *language:* **4** Ainu *martial art:* **4** judo **5** kendo **6** aikido, karate **7** jujitsu *martial artist:* **5** ninja *mat:* **6** tatami *measure:* **2** bu, ri *money:* **3** sen, yen *plum:* **6** loquat *poem:* **5** haiku, tanka *porcelain:* **5** imari *pottery:* **4** raku **7** satsuma *race:* **4** Ainu *radish:* **6** daikon *religion:* **6** Shinto **8** Buddhism **9** Shintoism *rice wine:* **4** sake, saki *robe:* **6** kimono *samurai clan:* **5** Taira **8** Minamoto *sash:* **3** obi *song:* **3** uta *suicide:* **7** seppuku **8** hara-kiri, hari-kari, kamikaze *theater:* **2** No **3** Noh **6** Bugaku, Kabuki **7** Bunraku *tidal wave:* **7** tsunami *vehicle:* **8** rickshaw *warrior:* **7** samurai *warrior code:* **7** bushido *weight:* **2** mo *wrestling:* **4** sumo *writing:* **4** kana **5** kanji **8** hiragana, katakana *zither:* **4** koto

Japanese-American 5 Issei, Nisei *second-generation:* **6** Sansei

jape 3 gag, kid, rib **4** gibe, jest, jibe, joke, mock, quip **5** crack, laugh, prank, tease **7** waggery **8** drollery **9** wisecrack, witticism

Japheth *brother:* **3** Ham **4** Shem *father:* **4** Noah *son:* **5** Gomer, Javan, Madai, Magog, Tiras, Tubal **7** Meshech

jar 4 bump, jolt, olla **5** cruse, quake, shake, shock, upset **6** jangle, jounce **7** tremble, vibrate **8** mismatch **9** container *ancient:* **6** krater **7** amphora, canopic

jardiniere 5 stand **6** holder **7** garnish

jargon 4 cant **5** argot, idiom, lingo, slang **6** patois, pidgin **7** dialect, lexicon, palaver **8** language **9** gibberish **10** mumbo-jumbo, vernacular, vocabulary **11** terminology *lawyer's:* **8** legalese *tinkers':* **5** shelta

jarl 4 earl **5** noble **8** nobleman **12** Scandinavian

jarring 5 harsh, rough **6** hoarse, jangly **7** grating, rasping, raucous **8** strident **9** dissonant **10** discordant, unsettling

jasmine 3 tea **4** vine **5** shrub **6** flower, yellow **7** perfume

Jason *father:* **5** Aeson *helper:* **5** Medea *lover:* **6** Creusa, Glauce, Glauke *quest:* **6** Fleece **12** Golden Fleece *ship:* **4** Argo *shipmate:* **8** Argonaut *teacher:* **6** Chiron **7** Cheiron *uncle:* **6** Pelias *wife:* **5** Medea

jasper 6 morlop, quartz **9** stoneware **10** chalcedony

jaundice 4 bias **7** disease, icterus **9** prejudice

jaundiced 6 biased, warped, yellow **7** colored, cynical, envious, hostile, jealous **9** distorted **10** suspicious

jaunt 4 ride, trip **5** drive, sally **6** junket, outing, ramble **7** journey **9** excursion

jaunty 4 airy, pert **5** fresh, light, peppy, perky **6** breezy, lively **7** buoyant **8** debonair **9** sprightly **10** nonchalant

java 6 coffee

Java *almond:* **7** talisay *cotton:* **5** kapok *jute:* **5** kenaf *lake:* **4** Ijen **5** Dieng, Kelut *plum:* **5** jaman **6** jambul **7** jambool *strait:* **4** Bali **5** Sunda *volcano:* **4** Gede, Kawi, Lawu **5** Bromo, Kelut, Raung **7** Ciremai

Javanese *civet:* **5** rasse *orchestra:* **7** gamelan *tree:* **4** upas

Javan squirrel 8 jelerang

javelin 5 lance, shaft, spear **7** assagai, assegai, harpoon

Javert's prey 7 Valjean (Jean)

jaw 3 gab, yak **4** chat, rail, talk **5** chops, clack, prate **6** babble, gabble **7** chatter, prattle **9** yakety-yak

jawbone 7 maxilla **8** arm-twist, mandible, persuade, talk into

jawbreaker 9 hard candy

jay 4 bird, blue, hick, rube **5** dandy **6** rustic **7** bumpkin, hayseed **9** chatterer, greenhorn

Jayhawker 9 guerrilla *State:* **6** Kansas **8** Missouri

jazz 3 bop **4** guff, jive **5** bebop, swing **6** boogie **7** ragtime **8** malarkey, nonsense *group:* **5** combo *term:* **3** axe **4** blow, riff, scat, tune, vamp **5** bebop, chart, chops **6** bridge, groove, improv **7** changes **8** stop time **9** front line **10** broken time *up:* **5** rouse **6** vivify **7** animate, enliven **9** stimulate

jazz musician 3 Ory (Kid) **4** Cole (Nat "King"), Getz (Stan), Hirt (Al), Mann (Herbie), Monk (Thelonious), O'Day (Anita), Rich (Buddy), Shaw (Artie) **5** Baker (Chet), Basie (Count), Brown (Clifford), Corea (Chick), Davis (Miles), Evans (Bill, Gil), Hines (Earl "Fatha"), James (Harry), Jones (Hank), Krall (Diana), Krupa (Gene), McRae (Carmen), Roach (Max), Smith (Jimmy), Sun Ra, Tatum (Art), Terry (Clark), Tormé (Mel), Young (Lester) **6** Bechet (Sidney), Blakey (Art), Burton (Gary), Carter (Benny, Betty), Dorsey (Jimmy, Tommy), Farmer (Art), Garner (Erroll), Gordon (Dexter), Herman (Woody), Hodges (Johnny), Jordan (Louis), Kenton (Stan), Miller (Glenn), Mingus (Charles), Morton (Jelly Roll), Oliver (King), Parker (Charlie "Bird"), Pepper (Art), Powell (Bud), Puente (Tito), Silver (Horace), Waller (Fats), Wilson (Teddy) **7** Brubeck (Dave), Coleman (Ornette), Connick (Harry), Goodman (Benny), Hampton (Lionel), Hancock (Herbie), Hawkins (Coleman), Holiday (Billie), Jarrett (Keith), Mehldau (Brad), Metheny (Pat), Rollins (Sonny), Rushing (Jimmy), Russell (Pee Wee), Shorter (Wayne), Vaughan (Sarah), Webster (Ben) **8** Adderley (Cannonball), Calloway (Cab), Coltrane (John), Eldridge (Roy), Marsalis (Wynton), Mulligan (Gerry), Peterson (Oscar), Williams (Mary Lou) **9** Armstrong (Louis), Blanchard (Terence), Christian (Charlie), Ellington (Duke), Gillespie (Dizzy), Grappelli (Stéphane), Henderson (Fletcher), Lunceford (Jimmie), Reinhardt (Django), Teagarden (Jack) **10** Fitzgerald (Ella), Montgomery (Wes), Washington (Dinah) **11** Beiderbecke (Bix)

jazzy 5 gaudy **6** brassy, flashy, glitzy, lively, rakish, sporty **7** raffish, splashy **8** animated, colorful, exciting, spirited **9** vivacious **10** flamboyant

jealous 5 green **7** envious **9** green-eyed, invidious, resentful **10** possessive

jeans brand 3 Lee **5** Levi's **8** Wrangler

jeer 4 gibe, jibe, mock **5** fleer, flout, scoff, scorn, sneer, taunt **6** deride, heckle, hector, insult **7** contemn, laugh at, mockery **8** derision, ridicule

Jeeves *creator:* **9** Wodehouse (P. G.) *employer:* **7** Wooster (Bertie) *position:* **5** valet **6** butler

jeez 4 gosh, heck **5** golly, shoot **6** shucks **7** jeepers

jefe 4 boss, head, lord **5** chief, ruler **6** honcho, leader **9** chieftain, commander

Jefferson, Thomas *home:* **10** Monticello *lover:* **5** Sally (Hemings) *state:* **8** Virginia

Jehoram *brother:* **7** Ahaziah *father:* **4** Ahab **11** Jehoshaphat *kingdom:* **5** Judah *slayer:* **4** Jehu *wife:* **8** Athaliah

Jehoshaphat *father:* **3** Asa **6** Ahilud, Nimshi, Paruah *father-in-law:* **4** Ahab *son:* **4** Jehu **7** Jehoram *wife:* **8** Athaliah

Jehovah 3 God **6** Adonai, Elohim, Yahweh

Jehu 6 driver *father:* **6** Hanani **11** Jehoshaphat *grandfather:* **6** Nimshi *son:* **8** Jehoahaz *victim:* **5** Joram **7** Jehoram

jejune 4 dull, flat **5** banal, bland, empty, inane, silly, trite, vapid **7** insipid, puerile **8** lifeless **9** colorless **13** uninteresting

Jekyll's alter ego 4 Hyde (Mr.)

jell 3 set **4** form **6** cohere, gelate **7** congeal, thicken **8** coalesce **9** coagulate, take shape

jelly 3 set **4** mass **5** aspic **6** spread **7** congeal, thicken **9** coagulate

jellyfish 6 coward, medusa **7** doormat, medusan **8** medusoid, pushover, weakling **10**

ctenophore **12** coelenterate, invertebrate, siphonophore

jennet 3 ass **5** hinny, horse **6** donkey

jenny 4 bird **6** donkey, female

jeopardize 4 risk **5** peril **6** chance, expose, hazard **7** imperil **8** endanger

jeopardy 4 risk **5** peril **6** danger, hazard, menace **8** exposure **9** liability **12** endangerment

jeremiad 6 lament, screed, tirade **7** lecture **8** diatribe, harangue **9** complaint, philippic **11** declamation, lamentation

Jeremiah's scribe 6 Baruch

Jericho's conqueror 6 Joshua

jerk 3 ass, lug, tic, tug **4** dolt, dope, fool, jolt, pull, push, snap, twit, yank **5** brute, creep, idiot, lurch, ninny, spasm, twist, wrest **6** bounce, nitwit, thrust, twitch, wrench **7** jackass **8** preserve **10** nincompoop

jerkin 6 jacket

jerky 4 meat **5** inane **6** abrupt, stupid, sudden **7** foolish, idiotic, jolting **8** saccadic **9** senseless

Jerome's Bible 7 Vulgate

jersey 3 cow **4** fabric **7** sweater **8** pullover

Jerusalem 4 Sion, Zion **5** Salem **8** Holy City *hill:* **4** Sion, Zion **6** Moriah *mosque:* **4** Omar **6** Al-Aqsa **13** Dome of the Rock *pool:* **6** Siloam **8** Bethesda

Jerusalem artichoke 5 tuber **8** girasole **9** sunflower

Jerusalem thorn 9 horsebean

jess 5 strap

Jesse *daughter:* **7** Abigail, Zeruiah *father:* **4** Obed *grandfather:* **4** Boaz *son:* **4** Ozem **5** David, Eliab, Elihu **6** Raddai **7** Shammah **8** Abinadab, Nethanel *youngest son:* **5** David

Jessica *father:* **7** Shylock *husband:* **7** Lorenzo

jest 3 fun, gag, kid, rag, rib **4** butt, game, gibe, jape, jeer, joke, josh, mock, quip, razz **5** crack, fleer, flout, humor, prank, scoff, sneer, spoof, sport, tease **6** banter, gaiety **7** mockery, waggery **8** derision, drollery, ridicule **9** merriment, wisecrack, witticism

jester 3 wag, wit **4** fool **5** actor, clown, comic, joker **7** buffoon **8** comedian, funnyman, humorist, jokester, quipster **9** prankster **11** entertainer

Jesuit *founder:* **6** Loyola (Ignatius) *leader:* **6** Xavier (St. Francis)

jet 4 coal, ebon, emit, gush, inky, Lear, rush, spew **5** black, ebony, plane, spout, spurt **6** engine, nozzle, squirt, stream, travel **7** current, jewelry **8** airplane **9** pitch-dark **10** pitch-black

Jethro *daughter:* **8** Zipporah *son-in-law:* **5** Moses

jetsam 7 flotsam **8** wreckage **9** driftwood

jet set 5 A-list, elite **9** beau monde, haut monde **10** glitterati

jettison 4 drop, dump, junk, omit **5** eject, forgo, scrap **6** reject, remove **7** deep-six, discard **8** disposal, get rid of, throw out **9** sacrifice, throw away

jetty 4 dock, ebon, inky, pier, quay **5** black, ebony, groin, wharf **7** project, seawall **9** pitch-dark **10** breakwater, pitch-black

Jew 6 Essene, Hebrew, Semite **7** Israeli, Judaist **9** Israelite

jewel 3 gem **4** rock **5** adorn, bijou, ideal, prize, stone **7** bearing **8** gemstone, ornament, treasure **9** embellish

jeweler 8 lapidary *famous:* **7** Cartier (Jacques, Louis, Pierre), Fabergé (Carl), Lalique (René), Tiffany (Charles Lewis)

jewelry 5 bling **10** bijouterie, bling-bling *artificial:* **5** glass, paste **6** strass **7** costume *piece:* **3** pin **4** ring **6** brooch **7** earring **8** bracelet, cufflink, necklace, tieclasp **9** lavaliere *set:* **6** parure

Jewish *bread:* **5** matzo **6** matzoh *ceremony:* **4** bris **8** havdalah **10** bar mitzvah, bas mitzvah, bat mitzvah *combining form:* **5** Judeo **6** Judaeo *credo:* **6** shema *doctrine:* **6** Mishna **7** Mishnah *New Year:* **12** Rosh Hashanah *organization:* **8** Hadassah **9** B'nai B'rith *prayer:* **7** kaddish, kiddush *prayer book:* **6** siddur *sabbath:* **8** Saturday *scripture:* **5** Torah **6** Talmud *synagogue:* **4** shul *teacher:* **5** rabbi, rebbe **6** Hillel *village:* **6** shtetl (see also **Hebrew**)

Jezebel 4 slut **5** hussy, tramp, trull, wench **6** wanton **7** trollop **8** slattern, strumpet *father:* **7** Ethbaal *home:* **5** Sidon *husband:* **4** Ahab *slayer:* **4** Jehu *victim:* **6** Naboth

jib 3 arm, shy **4** balk, boom, sail, stop **5** demur **6** refuse **9** stop short

jibe 5 agree, fit in, match, shift, tally **6** accord, concur, square **7** conform **8** dovetail **9** harmonize **10** correspond, go together **12** change course

jiffy 3 sec **4** snap, tick, wink **5** flash, hurry, shake, trice **6** minute, moment, second **7** instant **11** split second

jig 4 fish, game, hoax, hook, jerk, play, ploy, ruse, sham, wile **5** catch, dance, feint, trick **6** device, gambit **7** gimmick **9** deception

jigger 4 jerk, mold, sail **5** alter, gismo, gizmo **6** device, dingus, doodad, gadget, widget **7** gimmick, machine, measure **9** doohickey, rearrange, shot glass, thingummy **10** manipulate

jiggle 4 jerk **5** shake **7** agitate **9** oscillate

jigsaw 3 cut **4** tool **6** puzzle **7** arrange, machine

jihad 3 war **6** strife **7** crusade, holy war **8** campaign, struggle

jilt 4 drop **5** ditch, leave **6** desert, reject **7** abandon, cast off, discard

jim-dandy 3 ace, gem, pip **4** A-one, lulu **5** doozy, great, ideal, nifty, peach, super, swell **6** doozie **7** perfect **8** knockout **9** excellent, first-rate, humdinger **11** outstanding

jimmy 3 bar, pry **4** open **5** crack, force, lever **7** crowbar **9** break open, force open

jimsonweed 6 datura **10** thorn apple

jingle 4 call, ring, song **5** clink, rhyme, sound, verse **6** tinkle

jingoistic 7 hawkish **11** belligerent **12** chauvinistic, militaristic **13** nationalistic

jinn 5 afrit, genie **6** afreet, spirit

jinx 3 hex **5** charm, curse, spell **6** plague, whammy **7** bad luck, evil eye **8** foredoom **10** affliction, misfortune

jitters 5 jumps, panic **6** nerves, shakes **7** anxiety, shivers, willies **9** whim-whams **11** nervousness, stage fright **13** heebie-jeebies

jittery 4 edgy **5** jumpy, nervy **6** goosey, spooky **7** anxious, fearful, fidgety, nervous, panicky **10** high-strung

jive 3 kid **4** fool, jazz, talk **5** dance, music, swing, tease **6** cajole, hot air, jargon

Joab *brother:* **6** Asahel **7** Abishai *father:* **7** Seraiah, Zeruiah *slayer:* **7** Benaiah *uncle:* **5** David *victim:* **5** Abner, Amasa

Joan of Arc *birthplace:* **7** Domremy *epithet:* **7** Pucelle (La) **13** Maid of Orléans *king:* **7** Charles (VII) *victory:* **7** Orléans

Joan's husband 5 Darby

Joash *father:* **4** Ahab **7** Ahaziah **8** Jehoahaz *son:* **6** Gideon **7** Amaziah **8** Jeroboam *victim:* **9** Zechariah

job 3 gig **4** duty, hire, item, post, role, spot, task, work **5** chore, stint, trade **6** effort, office **7** calling, posting, pursuit, robbery **8** business, function, position, vocation **9** situation **10** assignment, employment, engagement, livelihood, occupation, profession **11** undertaking

Job *daughter:* **6** Keziah **7** Jemimah *father:* **8** Issachar *friend:* **6** Bildad, Zophar **7** Eliphaz

jobber 6 broker, dealer, seller, trader **8** merchant **10** contractor, wholesaler

job-safety agency 4 OSHA

job-training program 4 JTPA

Jocasta *daughter:* **6** Ismene **8** Antigone *husband:* **5** Laius **7** Oedipus *son:* **7** Oedipus **8** Eteocles **9** Polynices **10** Polyneices

jock 5 pilot **7** athlete

jockey 4 play **5** rider, trick **7** beguile, exploit, finesse **8** maneuver **10** manipulate *famous:* **5** Baeza (Braulio), Krone (Julie) **6** Arcaro (Eddie), Bailey (Jerry), Murphy (Isaac), Pincay (Laffit) **7** Cauthen (Steve), Cordero (Angel), Hartack (Bill), Longden (Johnny), Stevens (Gary) **8** McCarron (Chris), McHargue (Darrel), Turcotte (Ron) **9** Shoemaker (Willie)

jocular 5 comic, funny, jolly, merry, witty **6** jocose, jocund, jovial, lively **7** amusing, comical, jesting, playful **8** cheerful, humorous **9** facetious

jocularity 3 fun, wit **4** glee **5** humor, mirth **6** gaiety **7** jollity **8** hilarity **9** joviality, merriment **11** high spirits, playfulness

jocund 3 gay **5** happy, jolly, merry **6** elated, jovial, lively **7** festive, gleeful, playful **8** mirthful **12** lighthearted

joe 3 guy **4** dude, java **6** coffee, fellow

jog 3 dig, jab, run **4** lope, move, pace, poke, prod, push, ride, stir, trot **5** nudge, punch, rouse, shake **6** bounce, change, jounce, prompt, remind

joggle 4 join, trot **5** dowel, joint, notch, shake, tooth **6** jostle

john 2 WC **3** lav, loo **4** head **5** jacks, privy **6** toilet **7** latrine **8** bathroom, lavatory **11** water closet

John Hancock 9 autograph, signature

Johnson, Samuel *biographer:* **7** Boswell (James) *work:* **8** Rasselas **10** dictionary

John the Baptist *father:* **9** Zacharias *mother:* **9** Elisabeth

John the Evangelist *brother:* **5** James *father:* **7** Zebedee *mother:* **6** Salome

joie de vivre 4 elan, zest **5** gusto **6** esprit **10** love of life

join 3 tie, wed **4** abut, ally, bind, bond, fuse, line, link, mate, yoke **5** affix, align, blend, marry, merge, piece, touch, unify, union, unite **6** attach, border, couple, engage, enlist, enroll, sign on, sign up, splice **7** combine, connect **8** compound, federate, side with **9** affiliate, associate, integrate **12** come together

joint 3 bar, ell, hip, tie **4** butt, crux, dive, knee, link, node, seam **5** ankle, elbow, hinge, nexus, union, wrist **6** common, mutual, public, shared, suture, united **7** hangout, knuckle, shiplap **8** abutment, combined, communal, conjunct, coupling, junction, juncture, shoulder **9** concerted, honky-tonk **10** collective, connection **11** cooperative **12** articulation *combining form:* **5** arthr **6** arthro, condyl **7** condylo *disease:* **9** arthritis **10** rheumatism

joist 4 beam **6** rafter, timber **7** support

joke 3 gag, kid, pun, rag, rib, yak 4 fool, jape, jest, josh, quip, razz 5 crack, humor, prank, sally 6 banter, corker, parody 7 mockery, sarcasm, waggery 8 drollery, one-liner 9 burlesque, wisecrack, witticism 11 monkeyshine *hilarious:* 12 sidesplitter *stale:* 8 chestnut

joker 3 guy, wag, wit 4 card, fool 5 catch, clown, comic, cutup 6 fellow, jester, kicker 7 proviso 8 comedian, humorist 9 condition 10 limitation 11 stipulation

jollity 3 fun 4 glee 5 cheer, mirth 6 gaiety, revels 7 revelry, whoopee 8 hilarity 9 festivity, jocundity, joviality, merriment 10 ebullience, jocularity 11 high spirits, merrymaking 12 cheerfulness, conviviality

jolly 3 fun, gay, kid 4 glad, jest, josh, very 5 humor, merry 6 banter, jocund, jovial, joyful, joyous 7 festive, gleeful, jocular, playful, roguish, waggish 8 cheerful, mirthful 9 convivial 10 frolicsome 12 lighthearted

Jolly Roger 4 flag 6 ensign *user:* 6 pirate

jolt 3 hit, jar 4 blow, bump, jerk, shot, slug, stun 5 check, clash, crash, knock, lurch, shake, shock, upset 6 impact, jounce, rattle 7 disturb, shake up, startle 8 astonish, surprise 9 collision

Jonah 7 prophet *swallower:* 4 fish 5 whale

Jonathan *brother:* 7 Johanan *father:* 4 Saul *friend:* 5 David

Jones, John Paul *ship:* 15 Bonhomme Richard *victim:* 7 Serapis

Jones novel 11 Thin Red Line (The) 15 Some Came Running 18 From Here to Eternity

jongleur 4 bard 6 singer 7 juggler 8 minstrel 10 troubadour 11 entertainer

jonquil 8 daffodil 9 narcissus, perennial

Jonson play 7 Volpone 9 Alchemist (The) 15 Bartholomew Fair

Joplin creation 3 rag 7 ragtime 11 Entertainer (The) 12 Maple Leaf Rag

Joram *brother:* 7 Ahaziah *father:* 3 Toi 4 Ahab 11 Jehoshaphat *slayer:* 4 Jehu *son:* 7 Ahaziah

Jordan *capital:* 5 Amman *city:* 5 Irbid, Zarqa *gulf:* 5 Aqaba *language:* 6 Arabic *monarch:* 7 Hussein 8 Abdullah *monetary unit:* 5 dinar *mountain:* 4 Ramm *neighbor:* 4 Iraq 5 Syria 6 Israel 11 Saudi Arabia *sea:* 4 Dead

jorum 3 cup, jug 6 vessel

Joseph *brother:* (see **Jacob** son) *buyer:* 8 Potiphar *father:* 5 Asaph, Jacob 9 Zacharias 10 Mattathias *mother:* 6 Rachel *son:* 5 Jesus 7 Ephraim 8 Manasseh *wife:* 4 Mary 7 Asenath

josh 3 kid, rag, rib 4 jest, joke, razz 5 chaff, jolly, tease 6 banter

Joshua's victory 7 Jericho

Joshua tree 5 yucca

joss 4 idol 5 image

Jo's sister 3 Amy, Meg 4 Beth

jostle 3 jar, jog 4 bump, push 5 crowd, elbow, nudge, press, shove 7 agitate, collide, compete, contend, vie with 8 shoulder

jot 3 bit 4 atom, iota, note, whit 5 grain, minim, speck, write 6 tittle 7 smidgen 8 particle

joule component 3 erg

jounce 3 bob, jar, jog 4 bump, jolt 5 shake, shock, thump 6 impact

journal 3 log 4 blog 5 diary, organ 6 ledger, record 7 account, gazette, minutes 8 magazine, register 9 chronicle, newspaper 10 periodical

journalist 3 Bly (Nellie) 4 Dowd (Maureen), Drew (Elizabeth), King (Larry), Pyle (Ernie), Reed (John), Rose (Charlie), Will (George F.), Zahn (Paula) 5 Baker (Russell), Brown (George), Cooke (Alistair), Dunne (Finley Peter), Evans (Rowland), Hersh (Seymour), Novak (Robert), Rowan (Carl), Royko (Mike), Safer (Morley), Smith (Hedrick), Stahl (Lesley), Stone (I. F.), Szulc (Tad), White (William Allen), Wolfe (Tom) 6 Arnett (Peter), Bierce (Ambrose), Broder (David), Brokaw (Tom), Couric (Katie), Ephron (Nora), Koppel (Ted), Gibson (Charles), Kuralt (Charles), Lehrer (Jim), Moyers (Bill), Murrow (Edward R.), Osgood (Charles), Rather (Dan), Reston (James), Reuter (Paul Julius), Rivera (Geraldo), Runyon (Damon), Safire (William), Shirer (William L.), Thomas (Helen, Lowell), Zenger (John Peter) 7 Blitzer (Wolf), Bradlee (Benjamin), Breslin (Jimmy), Cousins (Norman), Greeley (Horace), Gunther (John), Huntley (Chet), Kempton (Murray), McGrory (Mary), Mencken (H. L.), Pearson (Drew), Royster (Vermont), Russert (Tim), Tarbell (Ida), Trillin (Calvin), Wallace (Chris, Mike), Walters (Barbara) 8 Amanpour (Christiane), Anderson (Jack, Terry), Atkinson (Brooks), Brinkley (David), Cronkite (Walter), Garrison (William Lloyd), Jennings (Peter), Lippmann (Walter), Pulitzer (Joseph), Salinger (Pierre), Sevareid (Eric), Steffens (Lincoln), Thompson (Dorothy, Hunter), Williams (Brian), Winchell (Walter), Woodward (Bob) 9 Bernstein (Carl), Donaldson (Sam), Frederick (Pauline), Salisbury (Harrison), Schieffer (Bob)

journey 3 hie **4** hike, roam, tour, trek, trip **5** jaunt, quest **6** cruise, junket, safari, travel, voyage **7** caravan, odyssey, proceed, travels **8** progress **9** excursion **10** expedition, pilgrimage *route:* **9** itinerary *stage:* **3** leg

joust 4 duel, feud, spar, tilt **5** clash, fight **6** combat **7** contest **8** conflict **10** tournament *arena:* **5** lists **8** tiltyard

Jove see **Jupiter**

jovial 5 happy, jolly, merry **6** cheery **7** amiable **8** cheerful **9** convivial **11** good-humored, good-natured

jowl 3 jaw **5** cheek **6** dewlap, wattle **8** mandible

joy 4 glee **5** bliss, mirth **6** gaiety **7** delight, elation **8** felicity, fruition, gladness, pleasure **9** enjoyment, happiness, merriment **11** delectation

Joyce, James *birthplace:* **6** Dublin *character:* **5** Bloom (Leopold), Bloom (Molly) **7** Dedalus (Stephen) *work:* **6** Exiles **7** Ulysses **9** Dubliners **13** Finnegans Wake

joyful 3 gay **4** glad **5** happy, jolly, merry **6** elated, jocund **7** buoyant, gleeful, pleased **8** ecstatic, jubilant, mirthful **9** delighted, rapturous **12** lighthearted

jubilant 5 happy **6** elated, joyful, joyous **8** euphoric, exultant, exulting **9** cock-a-hoop, delighted, overjoyed, triumphal **10** triumphant

jubilate 5 exult, glory **7** delight, rejoice **9** celebrate

jubilation 3 joy **4** glee **7** ecstasy, rapture **8** euphoria, rhapsody **9** rejoicing, transport **10** exaltation, exultation, joyfulness, joyousness **11** celebration **12** exhilaration

jubilee 6 flambé **8** festival **9** festivity **10** indulgence **11** anniversary, celebration **13** commemoration

Judah *brother:* (see **Jacob** son) *father:* **5** Jacob *king:* **3** Asa **4** Ahaz, Amon **5** Joash **6** Abijam, Josiah, Jotham, Uzziah **7** Ahaziah, Amaziah, Jehoram **8** Hezekiah, Jehoahaz, Manasseh, Rehoboam, Zedekiah **9** Jehoiakim **10** Jehoiachin **11** Jehoshaphat *mother:* **4** Leah *son:* **4** Onan **6** Shelah

Judas 7 traitor **8** informer, turncoat *father:* **5** Simon **7** Chalphi **10** Mattathias *replacement:* **8** Matthias *suicide place:* **8** Aceldama, Akeldama

judge 3 ref, try, ump **4** call, deem, rate, rule, test **5** infer **6** critic, decide, deduce, jurist, reckon, settle, umpire **7** arbiter, justice, mediate, referee **8** assessor, critique, estimate, mediator **9** arbitrate, criticize, determine, moderator **10** adjudicate, arbitrator, chancellor, magistrate, negotiator **11** conciliator

12 intermediary *bench:* **4** banc *chamber:* **6** camera *in Hades:* **5** Minos **6** Aeacus **12** Rhadamanthus *mallet:* **5** gavel *Muslim:* **4** cadi, qadi **5** mufti

judgment 5 award, dicta (plural), sense **6** acumen, decree, dictum, ruling, result, wisdom **7** finding, insight, opinion, verdict **8** decision, sagacity, sentence **9** appraisal, deduction, good sense, inference **10** assessment, conclusion, discretion, estimation, evaluation, horse sense, punishment **11** common sense, discernment **13** determination

judgmental 7 carping **8** captious, critical **10** belittling, censorious, derogatory **11** disparaging, reproachful **12** disapproving, faultfinding **13** hypercritical

Judgment Day 8 doomsday

_____ **judicata 3** res

judicial *assembly:* **5** court *document:* **4** writ *order:* **10** injunction

judicious 3 apt **4** fair, just, sage, sane, wise **5** right, sound **6** astute **7** careful, prudent, sapient **8** accurate, discreet, rational, sensible **9** equitable, objective, sagacious **10** discerning, reasonable

Judith *father:* **5** Beeri *home:* **8** Bethulia *husband:* **4** Esau *victim:* **10** Holofernes

judo 10 martial art *school:* **4** dojo *teacher:* **6** sensei

Judy's husband 5 Punch

jug 3 jar, pen **4** coop, ewer, gaol, jail, olla, olpe, stew, stir, toby **5** clink, pokey **6** cooler, flagon, immure, intern, noggin, prison, vessel **7** confine, pitcher, slammer **8** demijohn, imprison **9** constrain, container **11** incarcerate

jug-band instrument 5 kazoo **6** bottle **7** washtub **9** stovepipe, washboard

juggernaut 11 steamroller

juggle 3 fix **4** fool, toss **5** bluff, trick **6** change, delude, doctor, handle, humbug, take in **7** balance, beguile, deceive, mislead, shuffle **9** rearrange **10** manipulate

juice 3 sap **4** fuel, must **5** fluid **7** current, essence **8** vitality **10** succulence **11** electricity *fermented:* **4** wine **5** cider, perry

juicy 4 racy **5** lusty **7** piquant **8** dripping **9** succulent **10** profitable **11** sensational

juju 4 luck **5** charm, magic **6** amulet, fetish, grigri, mascot **8** gris-gris, talisman **10** lucky charm

jujube 4 tree **5** fruit **7** gumdrop, lozenge

julep 5 drink

Juliet *betrothed:* **5** Paris *father:* **7** Capulet *lover:* **5** Romeo

July 14 11 Bastille Day

jumble 3 mix **4** cake, hash, mess, olio **5**

chaos, mix up, shake **6** cookie, medley, mess up, muddle, muss up **7** clutter, confuse, disturb, mélange, rummage, shuffle **8** disarray, disorder, mishmash, pastiche, scramble **9** confusion, patchwork, potpourri **10** assortment, hodgepodge, hotchpotch, miscellany

jumbo 4 huge, vast **5** giant **6** mighty **7** immense, mammoth, massive **8** colossal, enormous, gigantic, oversize **9** humongous, oversized **10** prodigious **11** elephantine

jump 3 hop **4** bolt, hike, leap, move, trip **5** avoid, begin, boost, bound, clear, flush, hurry, leave, put up, raise, shift, start, vault **6** attack, bounce, bustle, change, hurdle, hustle, jack up, pounce, spring **7** bail out, elevate, startle **8** increase, leap over

jumper 4 sled **5** dress, horse, smock **6** blouse, jacket

jumping-frog county 9 Calaveras

jumpy 4 edgy **6** on edge **7** anxious, jittery, nervous **9** excitable **10** high-strung

junction 4 seam **5** joint, union **7** joining, meeting **8** coupling **9** interface **10** confluence, connection, crossroads **12** intersection

juncture 4 seam **5** joint, point, union **6** crisis, moment **7** instant, joining **8** coupling **10** connection, crossroads **11** concurrence, convergence **12** turning point

jungle 3 web, zoo **4** hash, mash, maze **5** selva, snarl **6** jumble, morass, muddle, tangle **7** clutter, thicket **8** mishmash **9** labyrinth

Jungle Books, The *author:* **7** Kipling (Rudyard) *bear:* **5** Baloo *boy:* **6** Mowgli *panther:* **8** Bagheera *python:* **3** Kaa *tiger:* **9** Shere Khan *wolf:* **5** Akela

Jungle, The *author:* **8** Sinclair (Upton) *locale:* **7** Chicago **10** stockyards

junior 3 son **5** lower, minor, sonny, youth **6** lesser **7** student, younger **8** inferior, young man, youthful **9** secondary, youngster **11** subordinate

juniper 4 cade, cone **5** cedar, fruit, savin, shrub **7** conifer **9** evergreen

junk 4 boat, dope, drug, ship **5** scrap, trash, waste **6** debris, heroin, litter, refuse, reject **7** cashier, clutter, discard, rubbish, rummage **8** get rid of, jettison, throw out **9** narcotics, throw away *e-mail:* **4** spam

junker 4 heap **5** crate, wreck **6** beater, jalopy **10** rattletrap, rust bucket

junket 4 trip **5** feast, jaunt, spree **6** outing, picnic **7** banquet, dessert, journey **9** excursion

junk mail 4 spam

Juno *bird:* **7** peacock *epithet:* **6** Moneta *Greek equivalent:* **4** Hera *husband:* **7** Jupiter (see also **Hera**)

Junoesque 7 stately **10** curvaceous, statuesque

junta 5 cabal, group **7** council, faction **9** committee

Jupiter 4 Jove, Zeus *angel:* **7** Zadkiel *cupbearer:* **8** Ganymede *daughter:* **5** Venus **7** Minerva *epithet:* **6** Fidius, Fulgur, Stator, Tonans **7** Pluvius *father:* **6** Saturn *lover:* **6** Europa **8** Callisto *mother:* **3** Ops *satellite:* **6** Europa **8** Callisto, Ganymede *son:* **5** Arcas **6** Castor, Pollux *temple:* **7** Capitol *wife:* **4** Juno

juridical 5 legal **6** lawful **8** juristic **10** legalistic

jurisdiction 3 law, see **4** sway, zone **5** might, orbit, power, range, reach, scope, venue **6** county, domain, parish, sphere **7** circuit, command, compass, control, diocese, mastery, purview **8** dominion, hegemony, province **9** authority, bailiwick, territory **10** domination **11** supervision

jurisprudence 3 law

jurist 5 judge

jury 5 panel *decision:* **7** verdict

jury-rigged 6 make-do **7** stopgap **9** makeshift, temporary **10** improvised

just 3 apt, due, fit **4** even, fair, good, meet, only, true **5** equal, legal, right **6** barely, hardly, honest, lawful, proper, simply, square **7** correct, ethical, exactly, fitting, merited, precise, upright **8** accurate, deserved, rightful, suitable, unbiased **9** equitable, honorable, impartial, objective, requisite, righteous **10** legitimate, reasonable, scrupulous **11** appropriate, well-founded **12** unprejudiced

justice 3 law **5** court, judge, right **6** equity **7** honesty **8** evenness, fairness, fair play **10** lawfulness, magistrate **11** correctness **12** impartiality

justification 6 excuse, reason **7** account, apology, defense, grounds **8** apologia **9** rationale **10** validation **11** explanation, vindication

justify 5 argue, claim, prove **6** assert, defend, uphold, verify **7** account, bear out, confirm, contend, explain, support, warrant **8** maintain, make even, validate **9** vindicate **10** legitimate, legitimize **11** corroborate, rationalize **12** authenticate, legitimatize, substantiate

jut 4 hang, poke **5** bulge, pouch **6** beetle, thrust **7** project **8** extend up, overhang, protrude, stand out, stick out **9** extend out, extension **10** projection, protrusion **12** protuberance

jute 5 gunny **6** burlap **7** hessian, sacking

Juvenal 4 poet **5** Roman *forte:* **6** satire
juvenile 3 kid **5** actor, child, green, young, youth **6** callow, jejune, junior, moppet **7** preteen, puerile **8** childish, immature, youthful **9** childlike, fledgling, unfledged, youngling, youngster **11** undeveloped
juvenility 5 youth **9** childhood, greenness **10** immaturity, springtide, springtime **12** youthfulness
juxtaposed 4 next **8** abutting, adjacent, neighbor, proximal, touching **9** adjoining, bordering **10** appositive, contiguous, side-by-side **11** coterminous, neighboring **12** conterminous

K

kabob see **kebab**
kachina 4 doll **6** spirit **12** impersonator
kaddish 6 prayer
Kafka, Franz *character:* **4** Olga **6** Gregor (Samsa), Joseph (K.) *novel:* **5** Trial (The) **6** Castle (The) **7** Amerika *story:* **8** Judgment (The) **12** Hunger Artist (A) **13** Metamorphosis (The)
kaiser 5 ruler **7** emperor, monarch **8** autocrat **9** sovereign
kaka 6 parrot
kale 4 cash, cole **5** bucks, lucre, money, moola **6** moolah **7** cabbage **8** Brassica, colewort
kaleidoscopic 8 changing, colorful **10** variegated
Kali *aspect:* **5** Durga **7** Parvati *husband:* **4** Siva **5** Shiva
Kama *god of:* **4** love *mount:* **6** parrot **7** sparrow *wife:* **4** Rati
Kama ____ **5** Sutra
kamikaze 7 suicide **8** suicidal
kampong 6 hamlet **7** village
Kampuchea see **Cambodia**
kangaroo 6 hopper, leaper **7** wallaby **8** wallaroo **9** marsupial *herd:* **3** mob *young:* **4** joey
Kansas *capital:* **6** Topeka *city:* **4** Iola **6** Olathe, Salina **7** Abilene, Emporia, Shawnee, Wichita **8** Lawrence *nickname:* **9** Jayhawker (State), Sunflower (State) *prison:* **11** Leavenworth *river:* **8** Arkansas *state bird:* **10** meadowlark *state flower:* **9** sunflower *state tree:* **10** cottonwood
kaolin 4 clay
kaput 5 spent **6** ruined **7** done for, useless **8** defeated, finished, outmoded **9** destroyed
karakul 5 sheep **9** broadtail
karate *level:* **4** belt *school:* **4** dojo *teacher:* **6** sensei

karma 4 fate **7** destiny **9** emanation
kaross 3 rug **7** garment
kasha 5 grain **8** porridge **9** buckwheat
Katharina *father:* **8** Baptista *suitor:* **9** Petruchio
Katrina's suitor 9 Brom Bones **12** Ichabod Crane
katydid 3 bug **6** insect **11** grasshopper
katzenjammer 3 din **5** hoo-ha, noise **6** clamor, hoo-hah, hubbub, racket, rumpus **8** brouhaha, distress, foofaraw, hangover, headache **9** commotion
kava 5 shrub **6** pepper **8** beverage
kayo 5 defeat, finish **8** knockout **9** finish off **11** coup de grace
Kazakhstan *capital:* **6** Akmola, Astana *city:* **5** Semey **8** Pavlodar, Shymkent *lake:* **6** Tengiz **8** Balkhash *language:* **6** Kazakh **7** Russian *monetary unit:* **5** tenge *mountain:* **10** Khan-Tengri *neighbor:* **5** China **6** Russia **10** Kyrgyzstan, Uzbekistan **12** Turkmenistan *river:* **4** Ural **6** Irtysh **8** Syr Dar'ya *sea:* **4** Aral **7** Caspian
Kazantzakis hero 5 Zorba (Alexis)
kea 6 parrot
Keats poem 5 Lamia **8** Endymion, Hyperion, Isabella, To Autumn **11** Ode to Psyche **12** Eve of St. Agnes (The) **16** Ode on a Grecian Urn **17** Ode to a Nightingale
kebab 8 shashlik
kedge 6 anchor
keel 4 boat, lean, ship **5** barge, pitch, ridge, slump **6** carina **7** capsize **8** overturn **11** centerboard
keen 4 avid, fine, wail, yowl **5** acute, alert, eager, honed, mourn, neato, nifty, sharp, smart, super **6** ardent, astute, bewail, bright, clever, gung ho, intent, lament, peachy, shrewd **7** anxious, fervent, intense, whetted, zealous **8** animated, spirited **9** fine-edged,

impatient, sensitive, wonderful **10** perceptive, razor-sharp **11** lamentation, penetrating, quick-witted, sharp-witted **12**
enthusiastic, sharp-sighted
keenness 3 wit **4** edge, zeal **6** acuity, acumen
10 enthusiasm **11** discernment, penetration
12 incisiveness, perspicacity
keep 3 own **4** hold, jail, mind, obey, save,
stay, stet, tend **5** lodge, stock **6** castle, comply, detain, living, lockup, manage, prison,
retain **7** abstain, conduct, confine, forbear,
fulfill, possess, refrain, reserve **8** conserve,
fortress, maintain, preserve, withhold **9**
constrain **10** livelihood, sustenance **11**
maintenance, subsistence
keep back 3 bar, dam **4** curb, hold, save, stay
6 detain, retain, retard, stifle **7** contain, inhibit, repress, reserve **8** restrain, restrict,
suppress, withhold
keeper 5 guard **6** warden **7** big fish, curator **8**
Cerberus, guardian, watchdog **9** custodian,
protector
keeping 4 care, ward **5** aegis, trust **6** charge **7**
custody, support **8** wardship **9** provision **10**
caretaking, conformity, observance **11**
maintenance **12** conservation, guardianship
keep on 4 last **5** abide **6** endure **7** persist **8**
continue **9** hang tough, persevere
keep out 3 ban, bar **4** hold, stop **5** block,
check, debar **6** forbid **7** embargo, exclude **8**
prohibit, turn back **9** blackball
keepsake 5 token **6** trophy **7** memento **8** memorial, reminder, souvenir **11** remembrance
keep up 7 persist, prolong, sustain **8** continue, maintain, preserve **9** persevere
kef 3 pot **4** hash, hemp **5** grass **7** hashish **9**
marijuana **10** dreaminess **12** tranquillity
keg 3 tun **4** butt, cask, pipe **6** barrel, firkin,
vessel **8** hogshead **9** container
kegler 6 bowler
keister 3 bum, end **4** buns, butt, duff, rear,
rump, seat, tail, tush **5** fanny **6** behind, bottom, heinie **8** backside, buttocks, derriere **9**
posterior
keloid 4 scar
kelp 4 alga **7** seaweed
kelpie 3 dog **5** naiad, nixie **6** sprite
Kemo Sabe 10 Lone Ranger
ken 4 view **5** grasp, range, reach, scope, sight
7 horizon, purview **9** knowledge **10** perception **13** comprehension, understanding
kenaf 5 fiber **8** hibiscus
Kenilworth author 5 Scott (Walter)
Kennedy novel 8 Ironweed
kennel 4 pack **5** board **6** gutter **7** shelter **9** enclosure
keno 4 game *similar to:* **5** beano, bingo, lotto

Kentucky *capital:* **9** Frankfort *city:* **9** Lexington **10** Louisville **12** Bowling Green *nickname:* **9** Bluegrass (State) *park:* **11**
Mammoth Cave *racecourse:* **14** Churchill
Downs *river:* **4** Ohio *state bird:* **8** cardinal
state flower: **9** goldenrod *state tree:* **11** tulip
poplar
Kentucky bluegrass 3 Poa
Kenya *capital:* **7** Nairobi *city:* **6** Kisumu, Nakuru **7** Mombasa *lake:* **7** Turkana **8** Victoria
monetary unit: **8** shilling *mountain:* **5** Elgon, Kenya *neighbor:* **5** Sudan **6** Uganda **7**
Somalia **8** Ethiopia, Tanzania *river:* **4** Tana
kepi 3 cap
kerchief 6 hankie **7** bandana **8** babushka, bandanna, kaffiyeh *Scottish:* **5** curch
kerf 3 cut **4** nick, slit **5** cleft, notch **6** groove
kerfuffle 3 ado, row **4** flap, fuss, stir, to-do **5**
hoo-ha **6** dust-up, hoo-hah, ruckus, rumpus
7 turmoil **8** foofaraw **9** commotion **11** disturbance
kermis 4 fair **8** carnival, festival
kernel 3 nub, nut **4** core, crux, gist, meat,
pith, seed **5** grain **6** nubbin, upshot **7** essence, nucleus **9** substance
Kerouac novel 6 Big Sur **9** On the Road **10**
Dharma Bums (The) **13** Subterraneans
(The)
Kesey novel 21 Sometimes a Great Notion
25 One Flew over the Cuckoo's Nest
kestrel 4 bird, hawk **6** falcon **9** windhover
ketch 4 boat **6** vessel **8** sailboat **10** watercraft
ketone 7 acetone, camphor
kettle 3 pot **6** hollow, vessel **7** caldron, marmite, pothole **8** cauldron *handle:* **4** bail
kettledrum 5 naker **7** timpani (plural), tim-
pano *Moorish:* **6** atabal
key 4 clue, isle, reef **5** basic, islet, vital **6** cotter, island, legend, master, opener, samara,
spline, ticket, tip-off **7** central, crucial, digital, pivotal **8** critical, password, solution,
tonality **9** essential, important **10** open sesame **11** fundamental *combining form:* **5**
clavi, clavo *notch:* **4** ward *type:* **8** skeleton
keyboard 6 manual **7** clavier
key fruit 6 samara
Key Largo *director:* **6** Huston (John) *star:* **6**
Bacall (Lauren), Bogart (Humphrey)
key man 5 chief **7** kingpin **9** locksmith
keynote 4 core, crux, gist, pith, tone **5** theme,
tonic
keynoter 6 orator **7** speaker
Keystone Kops director 7 Sennett (Max)
Keystone State 12 Pennsylvania
khaki 3 tan **5** brown, cloth, color **7** garment,
uniform
khamsin 4 wind

khan 5 chief, ruler **9** chieftain, sovereign **11** caravansary

khedive 5 ruler **7** viceroy

Khomeini 4 imam **9** ayatollah

Ki *mother:* **5** Nammu *son:* **5** Enlil

kiang 3 ass

kibble 4 meal **5** grain, grind **9** pulverize

kibbutz 4 co-op, farm **7** commune **10** collective, settlement **11** cooperative

kibe 4 heel, sore **8** swelling **9** chilblain

kibitz 4 chat **6** banter, butt in, meddle **7** comment, intrude, obtrude **9** interfere

kibitzer 7 meddler **8** busybody, observer **9** buttinsky, spectator **10** rubberneck

kibosh 3 hex **4** jinx, stop **5** check, curse

kick 4 bang, boot, punt **6** recoil, thrill, wallop

kicker 5 catch **6** clause, punter **9** condition, fine print

kick in 3 die, pay **4** give **5** begin, put up, start **6** donate, pony up **7** cough up, fork out **8** fork over, hand over **10** contribute

kick off 3 die **4** open **5** begin, croak, start **6** launch **8** commence, drop dead, embark on, initiate **10** inaugurate

kick out 2 ax **3** axe, can **4** fire, oust, sack **5** eject, evict, expel **6** bounce **7** cashier, dismiss **9** discharge

kickshaw 5 curio, goody, treat **6** bauble, dainty, gewgaw, morsel, tidbit, trifle **7** bibelot, trinket **8** delicacy **9** bagatelle

kid 3 guy, rag, rib **4** dupe, fool, gull, hoax, jest, joke, josh, razz **5** bairn, child, jolly, trick, youth **6** banter, befool, moppet, nipper **7** deceive, younger **8** flimflam, hoodwink, juvenile **9** bamboozle, youngling, youngster

kidnap 6 abduct, snatch **8** shanghai

kidney 3 ilk **4** kind, sort, type **5** gland, organ *combining form:* **4** reni, reno **5** nephr **6** nephro

kidney-shaped 8 reniform *delicacy:* **6** cashew

kielbasa 7 sausage

kilderkin 3 keg **4** cask **6** barrel

kilim 3 mat, rug **6** carpet

kill 2 ax **3** axe, end, ice, nix, off, zap **4** do in, prey, slay, stop, veto **5** creek, croak, erase, quash, scrag, snuff, waste **6** defeat, delete, finish, murder, quarry, stifle **7** bump off, butcher, channel, destroy, execute **8** blow away, carry off, dispatch, knock off, massacre **9** sacrifice, slaughter **10** annihilate **11** assassinate, exterminate

killer 5 bravo **6** gunman, hit man **7** butcher, torpedo **8** assassin, homicide *combining form:* **4** cide

Killer Angels author 6 Shaara (Michael)

killer whale 4 orca **8** cetacean

killing 5 blood, fatal **6** deadly, lethal, mortal, murder **7** carnage **8** butchery, foul play, homicide **9** bloodbath, bloodshed, slaughter **12** manslaughter *of a race:* **8** genocide *of bacteria:* **11** bactericide *of a brother:* **10** fratricide *of a father:* **9** patricide *of a king:* **8** regicide *of a mother:* **9** matricide *of a relative:* **9** parricide *of a sister:* **10** sororicide *of oneself:* **7** suicide *of plants:* **9** herbicide

killjoy 5 downer, grinch, grouch **7** spoiler **8** doomster, sourpuss **9** Cassandra, defeatist, doomsayer, gloomy Gus, pessimist, worrywart **10** spoilsport, wet blanket

Kilmer poem 5 Trees

kiln 4 oast, oven **7** furnace

kilt 5 skirt *accessory:* **7** sporran *fabric:* **5** plaid **6** tartan

kilter 4 trim **5** order, shape **6** fettle, repair **7** fitness **9** condition

kimono 4 gown, robe *sash:* **3** obi

kin 3 sib **4** clan, folk, sept **5** blood, flesh, house, stock, tribe **6** family **7** lineage, related **8** relation, relative

kind 3 ilk **4** good, like, sort, type, warm **5** breed, class, genre **6** benign, gentle, humane, loving, nature, stripe, tender **7** affable, amiable, clement, essence, feather, lenient, quality, species, variety **8** category, merciful, tolerant **9** character **10** altruistic, benevolent, charitable, forbearing, responsive **11** considerate, good-hearted, good-humored, good-natured, openhearted, softhearted, sympathetic, warmhearted

kindle 4 bear, fire, stir, wake, whet **5** light, rally, rouse, spark, start, waken **6** arouse, awaken, bestir, excite, foment, ignite, incite **7** inflame, provoke **8** activate **9** galvanize, instigate, stimulate **10** illuminate

kindliness 8 goodwill, sympathy **9** affection **10** solicitude **11** benevolence

kindly 6 benign, gentle **7** benefic **8** friendly, generous, gracious, pleasant **9** agreeable, benignant **10** beneficent, beneficial **11** considerate, good-hearted, sympathetic

kindness 5 favor, mercy **7** service **8** clemency, courtesy, goodwill, sympathy **10** compassion, generosity, indulgence **11** benevolence **13** consideration

kind of 5 quite **6** fairly, pretty, rather **8** passably, somewhat **9** tolerably **10** more or less, reasonably, relatively

kindred 3 sib **4** clan, folk, like, sept **5** alike, blood, flesh, house, stock, tribe **6** agnate, allied, family **7** cognate, connate, lineage, related, similar **9** relatives **10** affiliated, connatural **11** consanguine

king 3 rex **4** czar, tsar, tzar **5** mogul, ruler **6** tycoon **7** magnate, monarch **9** sovereign *Albanian:* **3** Zog **7** William *Assyrian:* **6** Sargon **11** Sennacherib, Shalmaneser *Babylonian:* **6** Sargon **9** Hammurabi **10** Belshazzar *Belgian:* **6** Albert **7** Leopold **8** Baudouin *Bohemian:* **9** Wenceslas **10** Wenceslaus *Bulgarian:* **5** Boris **6** Simeon *Damascus:* **8** Benhadad *Danish:* **4** Abel, Eric, Gorm, Hans, John, Olaf **5** Sweyn **6** Canute, Harold, Magnus **8** Nicholas, Waldemar **9** Christian, Frederick **11** Christopher *Dutch:* **7** William *Egyptian:* **3** Tut **4** Pepi, Seti **5** Khufu, Menes, Necho **6** Cheops, Ramses **7** Harmhab, Osorkon, Psamtik, Ptolemy **8** Ikhnaton, Thothmes, Thutmose **9** Amenhotep, Sesostris **11** Tutankhamen *English:* **4** John **5** Henry, James **6** Alfred, Canute, Edmund, Edward, Egbert, George, Harold **7** Charles, Richard, Stephen, William **8** Ethelred **9** Athelstan, Ethelbald, Ethelbert *French:* **3** Odo, roi **4** Jean, John **5** Henri, Henry, Louis, Pepin, Raoul **6** Philip, Robert, Rudolf **7** Charles, Francis, Lothair **8** François **9** Hugh Capet **11** Charlemagne *German:* **4** Carl, Karl **5** König, Louis **6** Lothar, Ludwig **7** Charles, Lothair *Greek (modern):* **4** Paul **6** George **9** Alexander **11** Constantine *Hawaiian:* **10** Kamehameha *Hungarian:* **6** Attila *Indian:* **4** raja **5** rajah *Irish:* **9** Brian Boru *Italian:* **7** Humbert, Umberto *Jordanian:* **5** Talal **7** Hussein **8** Abdullah *Judah:* (see at **Judah**) *Judean:* **5** Herod *legendary:* **3** Lud **4** Atli, Cole *Lydian:* **5** Gyges **7** Croesus **8** Alyattes *Norwegian:* **4** Eric, Erik, Inge, Olaf **5** Sweyn **6** Haakon, Harald, Harold, Magnus, Sigurd, Sverre *Ostrogothic:* **9** Theodoric *Persian:* **5** Cyrus **6** Darius, Xerxes *Portuguese:* **4** John **5** Henry, Louis, Peter **6** Carlos, Edward, Manuel, Sancho **7** Alfonso **9** Ferdinand, Sebastian *Prussian:* **7** Wilhelm, William **9** Frederick, Friedrich *relating to:* **5** regal, royal *Saudi Arabian:* **4** Saud **6** Faisal **9** Abdul-Aziz *Scottish:* **4** John **5** David, Edgar, James **6** Duncan **7** Macbeth, Malcolm, William **9** Alexander, Donalbane **10** David Bruce **11** Robert Bruce *Spanish:* **3** rey **5** Louis **6** Philip **7** Alfonso, Amadeus, Charles **9** Ferdinand **10** Juan Carlos *Spartan:* **8** Leonidas *Swedish:* **4** Eric, John **5** Oscar **6** Birger, Gustav, Haakon, Magnus **7** Charles **8** Gustavus, Waldemar **9** Frederick, Sigismund, Sten Sture *Visigothic:* **6** Alaric **King Arthur** *birthplace:* **8** Tintagel *chronicler:* **8** Geoffrey (of Monmouth) *court site:* **7** Camelot **8** Caerleon *deathplace:* **6** Camlan *father:* **5** Uther *father-in-law:* **9** Laodogant, Leodegran **11** Leodegrance *foster father:* **5** Ector *jester:* **7** Dagonet *knight:* **3** Kay **4** Bors **5** Balan, Balin **6** Gareth, Gawain, Modred **7** Galahad, Geraint, Lamerok, Mordred, Tristan **8** Bedivere, Lancelot, Parsifal, Percival, Tristram **9** Launcelot *lance:* **3** Ron *last abode:* **6** Avalon *last name:* **9** Pendragon *magician:* **6** Merlin *mother:* **6** Ygerne **7** Igraine *nephew:* **6** Gareth, Modred **7** Mordred *queen:* **9** Guinevere *shield:* **7** Pridwin *sister:* **7** Morgain **11** Morgan le Fay *slayer:* **6** Modred **7** Mordred *son:* **6** Modred **7** Mordred *steward:* **3** Kay *sword:* **9** Excalibur *victim:* **6** Modred **7** Mordred *wife:* **9** Guinevere

king crab 7 limulus

kingdom 5 realm **6** domain, empire **7** demesne **8** monarchy

kingdom come 4 Zion **6** heaven **8** paradise **9** hereafter **10** afterworld

kingfish 4 boss **6** bigwig, honcho, master **7** big shot, croaker **8** mackerel

kingfisher 7 halcyon **10** kookaburra

King Kong *character:* **4** Dwan **6** Darrow (Ann), Denham (Carl), Wilson (Fred) **8** Driscoll (Jack), Prescott (Jack) *director:* **6** Cooper (Merian C.) **7** Jackson (Peter) **10** Guillermin (John) *home:* **11** Skull Island *star:* **4** Wray (Fay) **5** Black (Jack), Brody (Adrien), Cabot (Bruce), Lange (Jessica), Watts (Naomi) **6** Grodin (Charles) **7** Bridges (Jeff) **9** Armstrong (Robert)

King Lear *actor:* **3** Cox (Brian) **4** Holm (Ian) **5** Booth (Edwin), Jones (James Earl), Magec (Patrick) **7** Burbage (Richard), Garrick (David), Gielgud (John), Olivier (Laurence) **8** Scofield (Paul) *author:* **11** Shakespeare (William) *daughter:* **5** Regan **7** Goneril **8** Cordelia *servant:* **6** Oswald *son:* **5** Edgar **6** Edmund

kingly 5 regal, royal **6** august, lordly, regnal **7** exalted **8** imperial, majestic **9** imperious, masterful, monarchal, sovereign **10** monarchial **11** monarchical

King novel 6 Carrie **7** Shining (The) **8** Dead Zone (The) **9** Dark Tower (The), Green Mile (The), Salem's Lot **11** Firestarter, Pet Sematary

King Philip 9 Metacomet

kingpin 4 boss, guru, head **5** chief, mogul **6** bigwig, top dog **7** magnate **9** top banana **10** mastermind

Kings Peak *range* **5** Uinta

Kingu *consort:* **6** Tiamat *slayer:* **6** Marduk

kink 4 bend, curl, knot, whim **5** cramp, crick,

quirk, snarl, spasm, twist **6** tangle **11** peculiarity **12** eccentricity, imperfection
kinky 3 odd **4** bent **5** curly, outré, ultra, weird
6 curled, far-out, frizzy, quirky **7** bizarre,
deviant, knotted, strange, twisted **9** eccentric **10** outlandish
kiosk 5 booth, stand **8** pavilion **9** newsstand
11 summerhouse
kip 3 bed, nap **4** hide, pelt, skin **5** sleep
Kipling work 3 Kim **6** L'Envoi **8** Gunga Din,
Mandalay **10** Fuzzy Wuzzy **11** Jungle
Books (The), Recessional **13** Just So Stories, Soldiers Three **15** Light That Failed
(The), Puck of Pook's Hill **18** Captains
Courageous
Kiribati *capital:* **6** Tarawa *island, island
group:* **4** Line **6** Banaba **7** Gilbert, Phoenix
location: **7** Oceania
kirk 6 church
kirsch 6 brandy, liquor
kirtle 4 coat, gown **5** dress, tunic **7** garment
Kish *father:* **3** Ner **4** Abdi **5** Abiel, Jeiel **6** Jehiel *son:* **4** Saul
kismet 3 lot **4** doom, fate, luck **5** weird **6**
Moirai **7** destiny, fortune
kiss 4 buss, neck, peck **5** graze, smack,
spoon **6** cookie, glance, smooch **7** lip-lock
8 osculate, pucker up **10** osculation
kisser 3 mug **4** face, lips **5** mouth
Kiss sculptor 5 Rodin (Auguste)
kit 3 set **4** gear, pelt **5** group **6** outfit, tackle,
violin **7** package **8** caboodle **9** container **10**
collection
kitchen 4 mess **6** galley **7** cuisine **8** scullery
appliance: (see at **appliance**) *boss:* **4** chef
(see also **cooking**)
kite 4 hawk, sail, soar **5** check, glede, hurry,
mosey **7** saunter, take off **8** clear out, hightail, predator **9** spinnaker
kith 3 kin, sib **4** clan, folk **6** family **7** friends,
kindred, kinfolk **9** neighbors, relatives
kitsch 4 camp, junk **9** vulgarity
kittenish 3 coy **6** elvish, frisky, impish **7** coltish, playful **10** frolicsome **11** mischievous
kitty 3 cat, pot **4** ante, fund, pool, puss **5**
pussy **6** feline, stakes **7** jackpot
kiwi 4 bird **5** fruit **7** Apteryx **12** New Zea-
lander
klatch 5 bunch, group **7** meeting **9** gathering
11 get-together
kleptomaniac 5 thief **7** booster **10** shoplifter
klutz 3 oaf **4** boob, clod, gawk, lout, lump **5**
looby **6** lubber, lummox **7** bungler, palooka
8 shlemiel **9** schlemiel **10** stumblebum
klutzy 5 inept **6** clumsy **7** awkward **9** all
thumbs, maladroit **10** blundering
knack 4 bent, gift, head **5** flair, forte, skill,

trick **6** genius, talent **7** ability, aptness,
command, faculty, know-how, mastery **8**
aptitude, capacity, facility **9** dexterity, expertise, stratagem
knapsack 4 pack **8** backpack
knave 3 cad **4** heel, jack **5** fraud, rogue,
scamp **6** rascal, varlet **7** bounder, lowlife,
villain **8** scalawag, swindler **9** scoundrel **10**
blackguard **11** rapscallion
knavery 5 fraud **6** deceit **8** mischief, trickery,
villainy **9** chicanery, deception, rascality **10**
dishonesty
knavish 5 lying **6** shifty, tricky **7** devious,
roguish **8** rascally **9** deceitful, deceptive,
dishonest **10** mendacious **12** unscrupulous
knead 4 form, mold, work **5** press, shape **7**
massage **10** manipulate
knee 5 joint *bend:* **9** genuflect **12** genuflection *bone:* **7** patella
kneeler 5 stool **7** cushion **8** prie-dieu **9** footstool
knell 4 bong, peal, ring, toll **5** chime **6** summon **7** warning **8** announce, proclaim
knickknack 3 toy **4** dido **5** curio **6** bauble,
gadget, gewgaw, trifle **7** bibelot, novelty,
trinket, whatnot, whatsit **8** gimcrack, ornament, souvenir **9** bagatelle, bric-a-brac, objet d'art
knife 3 ulu **4** bolo, kris, shiv, snee **5** blade,
bowie, panga, shank, sword **6** barong, cutter, dagger, lancet, parang, sickle **7** cleaver,
machete, scalpel **8** stiletto, yataghan **11**
switchblade *case:* **6** sheath *handle:* **4** haft,
hilt *maker:* **6** cutler **7** grinder
knifelike 4 keen **5** acute, sharp **7** cutting **8**
piercing, stabbing **11** penetrating
knight 3 dub, sir **5** eques **8** cavalier, chess-
man, horseman **9** caballero, chevalier *code:*
8 chivalry *competition:* **7** listing, tilting **8**
jousting **10** tournament *German:* **6** Ritter
servant: **4** page **5** valet **6** squire *title:* **3** sir
wife: **4** lady
knighthood 8 chivalry
knightly 4 bold **5** brave, noble **6** heroic **7** gallant, valiant **10** chivalrous
Knight of the Round Table see **King Arthur**
Knight of the Rueful Countenance 10 Don
Quixote
knit 4 bind, heal, join, link, mend, purl **5**
plait, unite, weave **6** fabric, stitch **7** conjoin,
crochet **8** contract **9** interlace **10** intertwine
knitting *material:* **4** yarn *stitch:* **3** rib **4** purl **6**
garter *tool:* **6** needle
knob 3 bun, bur, nub **4** bump, burl, burr, dial,
hill, hump, lump, node, umbo **5** bulge,
gnarl, knoll, mound **6** button, finial, handle,
nubble, pommel **7** hillock **12** protuberance

knobkerrie 3 bat **4** club, mace **5** billy **6** cudgel, weapon **7** war club **8** bludgeon **9** billy club, shillalah, truncheon **10** shillelagh

knock 3 bob, hit, rap, tap **4** bash, blow, bump, cuff, lick, swat **5** blame, clout, fault, pound, swipe, thump **6** strike **7** censure, condemn, setback **8** denounce, reversal **9** criticize **10** denunciate

knockabout 5 rough, rowdy, sloop, tough **7** roaming, vagrant **10** boisterous

knock down 4 drop, earn, fell, gain, raze **5** floor, level, lower **6** lay low, reduce **7** acquire, bring in, flatten **9** dismantle **11** disassemble

knocker 6 carper, critic **7** caviler **8** quibbler **10** complainer, criticizer **11** fault-finder

knock off 3 rob **4** copy, do in, halt, kill, quit, slay, stop **5** cease **6** deduct, defeat, desist, finish, murder **7** execute, imitate, take out, take ten **8** discount, overcome, subtract, take five **9** liquidate **11** assassinate, call it quits, counterfeit

knockout 2 KO **4** kayo, lulu **5** dandy, doozy, final **6** beauty, doozie, eyeful, looker, lovely **7** stunner **8** decisive, jim-dandy, striking, stunning **9** deathblow, finishing, humdinger **10** attractive **11** coup de grace, crackerjack

knock over 3 rob **4** down, drop, fell **5** amaze, floor, steal, upset **6** boggle, hijack, hold up, lay low, topple **7** flatten, stick up **9** bring down, eliminate, overpower, overthrow, overwhelm, prostrate

knoll 4 hill, knob, rise **5** mound **7** hillock

knot 3 bow, tie **4** bond, burr, link, loop, lump, node **5** bunch, gnarl, hitch, nexus **6** jungle, tangle **8** ligament, ligature, vinculum *hair:* **/** chignon *in fiber:* **3** nep *kind:* **4** bend, loop, slip **5** hitch **6** granny, splice, square **7** bowline **9** sheet bend **10** clove hitch, sheepshank

knotty 4 hard **6** sticky **7** complex, gnarled, Gordian **8** involved **9** byzantine, difficult, elaborate, intricate **10** formidable **11** complicated, problematic

knout 4 flog, lash, whip **7** scourge

know 3 wot **5** grasp **6** fathom, intuit **7** discern, realize **9** apprehend, recognize **10** comprehend, understand *Scottish:* **3** ken

knowable 9 graspable **11** cognizable, fathomable **12** intelligible **13** apprehensible

know-how 5 craft, knack, skill **6** talent **7** ability, cunning, faculty, mastery **8** aptitude **9** dexterity, expertise **10** adroitness, expertness **11** proficiency

knowing 3 hep, hip **4** sage, wise **5** aware, blasé, canny, savvy, smart **6** bright, clever **7** witting, worldly **8** sentient **9** cognizant, conscious, sagacious **10** conversant, discerning, insightful, perceptive **11** worldly-wise **13** sophisticated

know-it-all 6 smarty **7** wise guy **8** wiseacre **10** smart aleck **11** smarty-pants, wisenheimer

knowledge 3 ken **4** data, info, lore, news **5** facts **6** wisdom **7** science **8** learning **9** cognition, education, erudition **10** cognizance **11** information, scholarship **12** intelligence *lack of:* **9** ignorance *mystical:* **6** gnosis

knowledgeable 5 savvy **8** educated, informed

know-nothing 4 dolt, dope, fool **5** dummy, dunce, idiot, yahoo **6** dimwit **7** pinhead **8** agnostic, ignorant, numskull **9** benighted, blockhead, brainless, ignoramus, lamebrain, numbskull **10** illiterate, uneducated **11** empty-headed

knuckle 5 joint *combining form:* **6** condyl **7** condylo

knucklehead 4 dolt, dope, fool **5** dummy, dunce, idiot, yahoo **6** dimwit **8** clodpole, numskull **9** ignoramus, lamebrain, numbskull

knuckle under 3 bow **4** cave **5** yield **6** cave in, give in, submit **7** succumb **8** say uncle **9** surrender **10** capitulate

knurl 3 nub **4** bead, knob **5** ridge **12** protuberance

KO 8 knockout

koan 7 paradox

kobold 3 nis **5** dwarf, gnome **6** goblin, spirit, sprite

Kohinoor 3 gem **7** diamond

kohlrabi 7 cabbage **8** Brassica

kola 3 nut **4** tree

komatik 4 sled **6** sledge

kook 3 nut **5** crank, loony, wacko **6** cuckoo, weirdo **7** dingbat, lunatic, oddball **8** crackpot **9** ding-a-ling, fruitcake, screwball **10** crackbrain

kooky 4 bats, daft, nuts **5** batty, crazy, daffy, ditsy, ditzy, dotty, flaky, loony, nutty, silly, wacky, weird **6** freaky, fruity, insane, screwy **7** bizarre, idiotic, lunatic, offbeat, touched **8** demented **9** eccentric, fantastic **10** flipped out, freaked-out, off-the-wall, outlandish

kopeck 4 coin *one hundred:* **5** ruble

Koran *chapter:* **4** sura *revealer of:* **7** Gabriel *scholar:* **5** ulama, ulema

Korea, North *capital:* **9** P'yongyang *city:* **7** Hamhung **8** Ch'ongjin *leader:* **9** Kim Il-sung, Kim Jong II **10** Kim Chong-II *monetary unit:* **3** won *mountain:* **6** Paektu *neighbor:* **5** China **6** Russia **10** South Korea *sea:* **6** Yellow

Korea, South *captial:* **5** Seoul *city:* **5** Pusan,

Taegu **6** Inch'on, Taejon **7** Kwangju *island:* **5** Cheju *monetary unit:* **3** won *neighbor:* **10** North Korea *river:* **3** Han **7** Naktong *sea:* **5** Japan **6** Yellow

Korean *dynasty:* **5** Silla **7** Koguryo *national dish:* **6** kimchi

kosher 3 fit **4** pure **5** clean **6** proper **10** acceptable, legitimate, sanctioned **12** satisfactory *not:* **4** tref **7** terefah

Kosinski *novel* **5** Steps **10** Being There **11** Painted Bird (The)

Kosovo *capital:* **8** Priština *city:* **7** Prizren *lake:* **6** Badovc **8** Gazivoda *monetary unit:* **4** euro **5** dinar *neighbor:* **6** Serbia **7** Albania **9** Macedonia **10** Montenegro *river:* **3** Lab **4** Ibar **6** Erenik **7** Sitnica **9** White Drin

kowtow 3 bow **4** fawn **5** cower, defer, kneel, toady **6** cringe, grovel **7** honey up, truckle **8** bootlick **11** apple-polish

kraal 3 pen **6** corral **7** village **9** enclosure

kraken 5 squid **9** leviathan **10** giant squid, sea monster

krater 3 jar **4** vase **6** vessel

Kriemhild *brother:* **7** Gunther *husband:* **5** Etzel **6** Attila **9** Siegfried *slayer:* **10** Hildebrand *victim:* **5** Hagen

kris 6 dagger

Krishna *avatar of:* **6** Vishnu *brother:* **8** Balarama *father:* **8** Vasudeva *mother:* **6** Devaki *uncle:* **5** Kansa *victim:* **5** Kansa

Krupp works site 5 Essen

krypton symbol 2 Kr

Kubla Khan *author:* **9** Coleridge (Samuel Taylor) *intruder's home:* **7** Porlock *palace:* **6** Xanadu *river:* **4** Alph

kudos 4 bays, fame **5** award, glory, honor **6** honors, praise, renown **7** acclaim, bouquet, laurels **8** accolade, bouquets **10** compliment **11** distinction, recognition

kudu 8 antelope

kukri 5 sword

Kumin *work* **9** Up Country **12** Long Marriage (The)

kumquat 5 fruit *kin:* **6** orange

Kushner *play* **15** Angels in America

Kuwait *gulf:* **7** Persian *island:* **7** Bubiyan **8** Faylakah *language:* **6** Arabic **7** Persian *monetary unit:* **5** dinar *neighbor:* **4** Iraq **11** Saudi Arabia *oasis:* **8** Al-Jahrah

kvass 4 beer

kvetch 4 beef, crab, fret, fuss **5** gripe, whine **6** grouch, grouse **7** grumble **8** complain **9** bellyache

kyphosis 8 humpback **9** curvature, hunchback

Kyrgyzstan *capital:* **7** Bishkek *city:* **3** Osh *conqueror:* **9** Jöchi Khan *lake:* **8** Issyk-Kul *language:* **6** Kyrgyz **7** Russian *monetary unit:* **3** som *mountain, range:* **4** Alai **6** Pobedy **7** Victory **8** Tian Shan **10** Khan-Tengri **11** Kok Shaal-Tau *neighbor:* **5** China **10** Kazakhstan, Tajikistan, Uzbekistan *river:* **5** Naryn

L

Laadah *father:* **6** Shelah *grandfather:* **5** Judah

laager 4 camp **6** encamp **7** bivouac

lab see **laboratory**

Laban *daughter:* **4** Leah **6** Rachel *father:* **7** Bethuel *grandfather:* **5** Nahor *sister:* **7** Rebekah

label 3 tag **4** band, mark **6** marker, ticket **7** epithet, sticker **8** classify, hallmark, identify, insignia

labium 3 lip

La Bohème *composer:* **7** Puccini (Giacomo) *librettist:* **6** Illica (Luigi) **7** Giacosa (Giuseppe) *role:* **4** Mimi **6** Benoit **7** Colline, Musetta, Rodolfo **8** Marcello **9** Alcin-doro, Schaunard *setting:* **5** Paris *source author:* **6** Murger (Henri)

labor 4 moil, task, toil, work **5** chore, grind, sweat **6** drudge, effort, strain, strive **7** slavery, travail **8** drudgery, endeavor, exertion, struggle **10** birth pangs, childbirth, donkeywork **12** childbearing *camp:* **5** gulag *group:* **3** AFL, CIO **5** ILGWU, union **6** AFL-CIO *leader:* **5** Hoffa (James, Jimmy), Lewis (John L.), Meany (George) **6** Chavez (Cesar) **7** Gompers (Samuel), Reuther (Walter), Sweeney (John J.) **8** Kirkland (Lane), Randolph (A. Philip)

laboratory *device:* **5** flask **6** beaker, mortar, pestle, retort **7** burette, pipette **8** crucible, test tube 9 petri dish 12 Bunsen burner 13 proving ground

labored 4 hard 6 forced, taxing, tiring 7 arduous 8 strained 9 difficult, effortful, fatiguing, strenuous

laborer 4 esne, hack, hand, peon 5 grind, navvy, prole 6 coolie, menial 7 workman 10 roustabout, workingman *Mexican:* 7 bracero

laborious 4 hard 6 tiring, uphill 7 arduous, onerous, operose 8 diligent, grueling, sedulous, toilsome 9 assiduous, difficult, effortful, strenuous 10 burdensome, unflagging 11 hardworking, industrious, persevering 12 backbreaking

La Brea 4 pits 7 tar pits *fossil:* 7 mammoth 8 mastodon 10 saber-tooth

labyrinth 3 web 4 coil, knot, maze, mesh 5 skein, snarl 6 jungle, morass, tangle *builder:* 8 Daedalus *hero:* 7 Theseus *monster:* 8 Minotaur

labyrinthine 4 mazy 6 daedal, knotty 7 complex, gordian 8 involved, mazelike, tortuous 9 Byzantine, elaborate, intricate 10 convoluted, perplexing 11 bewildering, complicated

lace 3 net, tat, tie 4 cord, trim 5 adorn, braid, frill, plait, twine 6 fasten, string 7 entwine, netting, tatting 8 filigree, openwork 9 embroider 10 embroidery, intertwine 11 needlepoint *edge:* 5 picot *fall:* 5 jabot *ground:* 6 reseau *into:* 5 abuse 6 attack 7 condemn *kind:* 6 bobbin 7 Alençon, guipure, macramé, Maltese, Mechlin, torchon 8 Brussels, Venetian 9 Chantilly 11 needlepoint 12 Valenciennes *make:* 3 tat *pattern:* 5 toilé

Lacedaemon 6 Sparta

lacerate 3 cut, rip 4 gash, rend, tear 5 slash, wound 6 mangle, pierce 7 afflict, mangled, torment 8 distress

lacework 7 tatting

lachrymose 3 sad 5 teary, weepy 7 doleful, tearful, weeping 8 dolorous, mournful 11 tear-jerking

lack 4 need, want 6 dearth, defect 7 absence, default, deficit, failure, paucity, poverty, require 8 scarcity, shortage 9 privation 10 deficiency, inadequacy, scantiness 13 insufficiency

lackadaisical 4 idle, lazy, limp, slow 5 moony 6 dreamy 7 languid, passive 8 fainéant, indolent, listless, slothful 9 apathetic, enervated 10 languorous, spiritless 11 halfhearted

lackey 5 toady 6 fawner, flunky, minion, vassal 7 footman, servant 8 truckler 9 attendant, sycophant

lacking 3 shy 4 sans 5 minus, short 6 absent, flawed, needed 7 missing, needing, omitted, wanting, without 8 devoid of, impaired 9 defective, deficient 10 deprived of, inadequate, incomplete 11 halfhearted 12 insufficient

lackluster 3 dim 4 arid, blah, drab, dull, flat 5 blind, ho-hum, matte, muted, prosy, rusty, vapid 6 boring, leaden 7 prosaic 8 lifeless, mediocre 9 colorless, tarnished 10 uninspired 13 unimaginative

Laconian 7 Spartan *king:* 5 Lelex, Myles 8 Menelaus

laconic 4 curt 5 bluff, blunt, brief, pithy, short, terse 7 brusque, concise 8 succinct

lacquer 5 glaze, gloss 6 enamel, finish 7 shellac, varnish

lacrosse *related game:* 7 jai alai *term:* 5 clamp 6 crease, crosse, pocket 7 face-off *team:* 3 ten

lactate 4 salt 5 ester, nurse 6 suckle 7 secrete 8 wet-nurse 10 breast-feed

lacteal 5 milky 6 cloudy, pearly

lacuna 3 gap, pit 4 void 5 blank, break, space 6 breach, cavity, hiatus 7 caesura 10 deficiency 12 interruption

lacy 4 fine 5 meshy 6 dainty 7 netlike 8 delicate, gossamer 9 filigreed

lad 3 boy, son, tad 4 tike, tyke 5 youth 6 shaver 9 shaveling, stripling *Irish:* 4 boyo 5 bucko *Scottish:* 5 chiel 7 callant

ladder 3 run 5 ranks, scale 6 series 7 ranking 9 hierarchy *piece:* 4 rung 6 rundle

ladderlike 6 scalar, scaled 7 stepped 11 scalariform

lade 3 dip, tax 4 bail, load, pack, ship, stow 5 ladle, scoop 6 burden, saddle, weight 8 encumber

la-di-dah 6 chichi, too-too 7 elegant, genteel, stuck-up 8 affected, snobbish 9 conceited, grandiose, high-flown 10 hoity-toity 11 pretentious

ladies' man 4 stud, wolf 5 Romeo 7 amorist, Don Juan, gallant 8 lothario 9 womanizer

lading 4 haul, load 5 cargo, goods 6 burden 7 bailing, dipping, freight, loading, payload 8 shipment 11 consignment

ladle 3 dip 4 bail 5 scoop, spoon 6 dipper

Ladon 6 dragon *father:* 7 Phorcus, Phorcys *mother:* 4 Ceto *slayer:* 8 Heracles, Hercules

lady 4 dame 5 madam, woman 6 female, matron *French:* 4 dame *German:* 4 Frau *Italian:* 5 donna 7 signora *Muslim:* 5 begum *Spanish:* 4 doña 6 señora

lady ____ 4 luck 5 apple 6 beetle, chapel

ladybug 6 beetle *Australian:* 7 vedalia

Lady Chatterley's Lover *author:* 8 Lawrence

(David Herbert) *character:* 6 Connie 7 Mellors (Oliver) 9 Constance

lady-killer 4 dude, hunk, roué, stud 7 playboy, seducer 8 Casanova, lothario 12 heartbreaker

Lady of the Lake, The 5 Ellen (Douglas), Nimue 6 Vivien *author:* 5 Scott (Walter)

Lady Windermere's Fan author 5 Wilde (Oscar)

Laertes *father:* 8 Acrisius, Polonius *sister:* 7 Ophelia *son:* 7 Ulysses 8 Odysseus *victim:* 6 Hamlet *wife:* 8 Anticlea

La Fontaine's forte 5 fable

lag 4 drag, flag, last, poke, slow, tire 5 dally, delay, tarry, trail 6 dawdle, linger, loiter 7 slacken 8 hang back, hindmost, interval 10 dillydally 13 procrastinate

lager 4 beer, brew, malt, suds 7 brewski

laggard 3 lax 4 slow 5 tardy 6 loafer 7 dawdler 8 dallying, dawdling, delaying, dilatory, flagging, lingerer, loiterer, slowpoke, sluggish, tarrying 9 apathetic, lazybones, lethargic, loitering, straggler 10 behindhand

La Gioconda 8 Mona Lisa *composer:* 10 Ponchielli (Amilcare) *painter:* 7 da Vinci (Leonardo) 8 Leonardo (da Vinci)

lagniappe 3 tip 4 gift, perk 5 bonus, extra 7 cumshaw, largess 8 dividend, gratuity 9 baksheesh, pourboire 10 perquisite

lagomorph 4 hare, pika 6 rabbit

lagoon 4 pond, pool 5 bayou, sound 6 strait 7 channel, narrows *rim:* 5 atoll

_____ **La Guardia** 8 Fiorello

Lahmi *brother:* 7 Goliath *slayer:* 7 Elhanan

laid-back 4 cool 6 breezy, casual 7 relaxed 8 carefree, informal 9 easygoing, hang-loose 10 nonchalant

lair 3 den 4 cave 5 haunt, lodge 6 burrow, refuge 7 hideout, retreat 8 hideaway 9 sanctuary

Laius *father:* 8 Labdacus *slayer, son:* 7 Oedipus *wife:* 7 Jocasta

lake 4 loch, mere, pond, pool, tarn 5 lough 6 lagoon *Adriatic:* 6 Varano *Alberta:* 6 Louise *Algeria:* 5 Hodna *Alps:* 6 Annecy *Arizona-Nevada:* 4 Mead *Armenia:* 5 Sevan 6 Gokcha, Sevang 9 Lychnitis *Aswan's:* 6 Nasser *Australia:* 4 Eyre 5 Carey, Cowan, Frome, Wells 6 Barlee 7 Amadeus, Everard, Torrens 8 Gairdner *Austria:* 5 Atter, Traun 6 Kammer 8 Attersee 9 Kammersee *Bolivia:* 5 Poopó *Botswana:* 5 Ngami *British Columbia:* 4 Pitt 5 Atlin *California:* 4 Mono, Tule 5 Clear, Eagle, Honey *Cambodia:* 8 Tonle Sap *Canada:* 4 Dyke 8 Manitoba *central Africa:* 4 Kivu 5 Mweru 6 Albert *Central America:* 5 Guija *central Europe:* 5 Leman 6 Geneva, Lugano 7 Ceresio 8

Bodensee 9 Constance *central North America:* 5 Rainy *Chile:* 4 Laja 5 Ranco *China:* 6 Poyang 8 Dongting *Colorado:* 5 Grand *Denmark:* 5 Esrum *east Africa:* 6 Rudolf 7 Turkana *east Asia:* 6 Khanka 7 Xingkai 8 Hsingkai *east central Africa:* 8 Victoria 10 Tanganyika *east China:* 3 Tai 5 Dalai, Hulun *Ethiopia:* 4 Tana, Zwai 5 Abaya, Shala, Shamo, Tsana 8 Stefanie 9 Chew Bahir *Finland:* 5 Inari *Florida:* 5 Worth 10 Okeechobee *Germany:* 5 Ammer, Chiem 8 Ammersee, Chiemsee *Ghana:* 5 Volta *Great:* 4 Erie 5 Huron 7 Ontario 8 Michigan, Superior *Greece:* 5 Bolbe, Volvi *Guatemala:* 7 Atitlán *Honduras:* 5 Yojoa *Honshu:* 3 Omi 4 Biwa, Suwa, Yodo *Hungary:* 7 Balaton 10 Plattensee *Idaho:* 4 Waha 5 Grays 6 Priest 11 Coeur d'Alene, Pend Oreille *India:* 3 Dal 5 Wular 6 Chilka *Indonesia:* 4 Poso, Toba 5 Ranau *Iowa:* 5 Storm *Iran:* 5 Niriz, Shahi, Urmia 8 Matianus, Urumiyeh 9 Bakhtigan *Ireland:* 3 Gur, Ree 4 Conn, Derg, Mask 5 Allen, Arrow, Leane *Israel:* 12 Bahr Tabariya, Sea of Galilee *Israel-Jordan:* 7 Dead Sea *Italy:* 4 Como, Iseo, Nemi 5 Garda 6 Albano 7 Bolsena, Perugia 8 Maggiore 9 Trasimene *Japan:* 4 Imba 8 Imbanuma *Kazakhstan:* 7 Balqash 8 Balkhash *Louisiana:* 4 Soda 9 Catahoula 13 Pontchartrain *Maine:* 6 Sebago 9 Moosehead *Mali:* 4 Debo *Manitoba:* 4 Gods 5 Cedar, Moose 8 Winnipeg *Mexico:* 7 Chapala *Michigan:* 4 Burt *Minnesota:* 3 Red 4 Cass, Gull, Swan 5 Leech 6 Itasca 9 Mille Lacs 10 Minnetonka, of the Woods 11 Lac qui Parle *Minnesota-Wisconsin:* 5 Pepin *Mongolian:* 3 Har 5 Har Us, Khara 8 Khara Usu *Montana:* 8 Medicine *mountain:* 4 tarn *Myanmar:* 4 Inle *Nevada:* 4 Ruby 7 Pyramid *New Hampshire:* 5 Squam 13 Winnipesaukee *New Jersey:* 5 Union *New York:* 4 Long 5 Chazy, Keuka 6 Cayuga, George, Oneida, Otsego, Owasco, Placid, Seneca 7 Crooked, Saranac 8 Onondaga, Saratoga 9 Champlain 10 Chautauqua 11 Canandaigua, Skaneateles *New Zealand:* 4 Ohau 5 Hawea, Taupo 6 Pukaki, Wanaka 8 Wakatipu *Nicaragua:* 7 Managua *North Africa:* 4 Chad *Northern Ireland:* 5 Neagh *Northwest Territories:* 4 Gras 5 Baker, Garry, Pelly 9 Great Bear 10 Great Slave *Norway:* 5 Mjosa *Nova Scotia:* 7 Bras d'Or *Ontario:* 4 Rice, Seul 5 Trout *Oregon:* 5 Abert 6 Crater 7 Malheur, Wallowa *Paraguay:* 4 Ypoá *Peru:* 5 Junín 13 Chinchaycocha *Philippines:* 4 Bato, Taal 5 Lanao 6 Bombon *Poland:* 5 Mamry, Mauer *Quebec:*

5 Minto, Payne *Russia:* **3** Seg **5** Chany, Ilmen, Lacha, Onega **6** Baikal, Ladoga **7** Rybinsk **10** Eltonskoye **11** Ladozhskoye *Saskatchewan:* **4** Cree **5** Ronge *Scotland:* **3** Ard, Awe **4** Doon, Earn, Ness, Oich, Shin, Sloy **5** Leven, Lochy, Maree, Morar, Shiel **6** Lomond *Siberia:* **6** Baikal, Baykal *South Africa:* **4** Kosi *South America:* **5** Merin, Mirim **8** Titicaca *South Carolina:* **7** Wateree *South Dakota:* **5** Andes *southeast Africa:* **5** Nyasa **6** Nyassa *southwest Europe:* **5** Ohrid **7** Okhrida *Sweden:* **5** Asnen, Roxen **6** Siljan, Vänern, Vetter **7** Malaren, Vattern *Switzerland:* **3** Zug **4** Biel, Joux **5** Zuger **6** Bieler, Bienne, Brienz, Sarnen, Sarner, Zurich **7** Lucerne, Lungern **8** Brienzer, Züricher **9** Neuchâtel, Zürichsee *Tajikistan:* **7** Karakul *Tanzania:* **5** Rukwa *Texas-Louisiana:* **4** Caddo *Tibet:* **4** Na-mu **6** Nam Tso, Tengri *Turkey:* **3** Tuz, Van **4** Bafa, Nice **5** Iznik, Sugla **6** Nicaea *Uganda:* **5** Kyoga *Utah:* **6** Powell, Sevier **9** Great Salt *Vermont:* **9** Champlain *Wales:* **4** Bala *Washington:* **4** Omak **5** Moses **6** Chelan **9** Wenatchee *western China:* **4** Ai-pi **6** Ebinur *western United States:* **4** Bear **5** Tahoe *Wisconsin:* **5** Green **9** Winnebago *Yellowstone National Park:* **5** Heart, Lewis **8** Shoshone *Zaire:* **5** Tumba *Zambia:* **9** Bangweolo, Bangweulu

lake group *central North America:* **5** Great *Egypt:* **5** Balah *Maine:* **8** Rangeley *New York:* **6** Finger *Saskatchewan:* **5** Quill *Twin:* **8** Washinee **9** Washining

lake herring 5 cisco

Lake poet 7 Southey (Robert) **9** Coleridge (Samuel Taylor) **10** Wordsworth (William)

Lake Wobegon Days author 7 Keillor (Garrison)

Lakmé *aria:* **8** Bell Song *composer:* **7** Delibes (Léo)

Lakshmi *husband:* **6** Vishnu *son:* **4** Kama

L. A. Law *actor:* **3** Dey (Susan) **5** Drake (Larry), Smits (Jimmy) **6** Dysart (Richard), Greene (Michele), Hamlin (Harry), Ruttan (Susan), Tucker (Michael) **7** Bernsen (Corbin), Rachins (Alan) **10** Eikenberry (Jill) *character:* **5** Kuzak (Michael) **6** Becker (Arnie), Kelsey (Ann), Melman (Roxanne) **7** Van Owen (Grace), Perkins (Abby) **8** Brackman (Douglas), McKenzie (Leland) **9** Markowitz (Stuart), Sifuentes (Victor) *creator:* **6** Bochco (Steven)

lam 3 hit **4** beat, blow, bolt, drub, flay, flee, flog, pelt, skip, whip **5** baste, paste, pound, scram, smack, split, whale **6** batter, beat it, buffet, cut out, decamp, escape, flight, hammer, pummel, strike, thrash, wallop **7** getaway, take off, vamoose **8** breakout, escaping **9** skedaddle

La Mancha's knight 10 Don Quixote

lamb 4 cade **5** sheep **6** cosset **8** yearling *leg of:* **5** gigot *parent:* **3** ewe, ram

lambaste 3 pan **4** beat, drub, flay, flog, lash, lick, pelt, slam, slap, trim, whip **5** paste, pound, roast, scold, score, slash, smear **6** assail, attack, berate, cudgel, hammer, pummel, scathe, scorch, thrash, wallop **7** assault, blister, censure, clobber, reprove, scourge, shellac, upbraid **8** bludgeon, denounce, harangue, lash into **9** castigate, excoriate **10** tongue-lash

lambent 5 aglow **6** ardent, bright, lucent **7** beaming, glowing, radiant, shining **8** gleaming, luminous, lustrous **9** brilliant, effulgent, refulgent, twinkling **10** flickering, glittering, shimmering **12** incandescent

lamblike 4 meek **6** docile

lamb of God 5 Jesus **6** Christ **8** Agnus Dei

Lamb's pseudonym 4 Elia

lame 4 gimp, halt, limp **5** gimpy, stiff **6** feeble, flimsy **7** cripple, disable, halting, limping **8** crippled, disabled, hobbling, inferior **10** inadequate **11** ineffectual **12** contemptible, unconvincing

lamebrain 3 oaf **4** dolt, dope, goof, mutt, simp, yo-yo **5** chump, dummy, dunce, idiot, moron, ninny, noddy, stupe **6** dimwit, donkey, dum-dum, nitwit, noodle **7** airhead, dullard, pinhead, schnook **8** bonehead, clodpoll, dumbbell, dumbhead, imbecile, lunkhead, meathead, numskull **9** blockhead, ignoramus, numbskull, simpleton, thickhead **10** dunderhead, hammerhead, nincompoop **11** chowderhead, chucklehead, knucklehead

Lamech *daughter:* **6** Naamah *father:* **10** Methuselah *son:* **4** Noah **5** Jabal, Jubal **9** Tubalcain *wife:* **4** Adah **6** Zillah

lament 3 cry, rue **4** keen, moan, pine, wail, weep **5** dirge, elegy, mourn **6** bemoan, bewail, grieve, plaint, regret, repent, sorrow **7** deplore, elegize, wailing **8** jeremiad, threnody **9** complaint, ululation

lamentable 6 rueful, woeful **7** doleful, pitiful **8** dolorous, grievous, mournful **9** plaintive, sorrowful **10** afflictive, deplorable, lugubrious, melancholy **11** distressing, regrettable, unfortunate **13** heartbreaking

lamentation 5 elegy, grief **7** anguish, remorse, wailing **8** grieving, mourning, threnody **9** sorrowing, ululation

Lamerok *father:* **9** Pellinore *lover:* **8** Margawse *slayer:* **6** Gawain

lamia 3 hex **5** witch **7** hellcat, vampire **8** succubus **9** sorceress **11** enchantress

Lamia *country:* **5** Libya *form:* **7** serpent *lover:* **4** Zeus

lamina 5 blade, flake, layer, plate, scale

lamp 3 arc **4** bulb, davy **5** klieg, light, torch **7** lantern **10** candelabra **11** candelabrum *floor:* **8** torchère **9** torchiere *hanging:* **10** chandelier

lampblack 4 soot **6** carbon

Lampetia *father:* **6** Apollo, Helios *husband:* **9** Asclepius *mother:* **6** Neaera *sister:* **9** Phaethusa

lampoon 4 mock **5** roast, spoof, squib **6** parody, satire, send-up **7** take off **8** ridicule, satirize **9** burlesque **10** caricature, pasquinade

lamprey 3 eel **8** nine-eyes

lanai 5 patio, porch **6** piazza **7** terrace, veranda

lance 4 gash, hurl, open **5** slash, spear **6** impale, pierce, skewer **7** javelin **8** transfix

Lancelot, Launcelot *father:* **3** Ban *lover:* **6** Elaine **9** Guinevere *son:* **7** Galahad *victim:* **6** Gawain

lancer 10 cavalryman *Prussian:* **5** uhlan

lancet 4 arch **5** blade, knife **6** cutter, window **7** scalpel

land 4 dirt, dock, gain, soil **5** acres, berth, earth, light, manor, shore, terra, tract **6** alight, estate, ground, obtain, pick up, secure **7** acquire, acreage, country, expanse, grounds, procure, set down, terrain, terrene **9** touch down **10** terra firma *alluvial:* **5** delta *barren:* **5** waste **6** desert *cultivated:* **4** farm **5** glebe, tilth **7** tillage *for grazing:* **3** lea, ley **5** range **6** meadow **7** pasture *high:* **4** hill, mesa **7** plateau **8** mountain *level:* **4** mesa **5** plain **7** plateau *low:* **4** vale **6** valley **9** intervale *measure:* **3** rod **4** acre *open:* **3** lea **5** field, green, plain **6** meadow **7** pasture *piece:* **3** lot **4** plot **5** tract **6** estate, parcel *reclaimed:* **6** polder *sloping:* **6** cuesta *strip:* **7** isthmus *wet:* **3** bog, fen **5** marsh, swamp **6** marish

land east of Eden 3 Nod

landed 4 alit

landlord 6 lessor, squire **9** innkeeper **10** freeholder

landmark 5 cairn, guide **9** benchmark, milestone, watershed **11** achievement **12** breakthrough, turning point

Land of Enchantment 9 New Mexico

Land of Lakes 8 Michigan

Land of Opportunity 3 USA **8** Arkansas **12** United States

Land of the Midnight Sun 6 Norway

landowner 6 squire, yeoman *Anglo-Saxon:* **5** thane, thegn *Dutch:* **7** patroon *Scottish:* **5** laird

landscape 5 scene, vista **7** scenery, setting, terrain **8** backdrop, prospect

lane 3 way **4** path, road **5** aisle, alley, byway, track **6** street **7** pathway, roadway **8** footpath **10** passageway

Langland work 12 Piers Plowman

lang syne 4 past, yore **10** yesteryear

language 4 cant **5** argot, idiom, lingo, prose, slang **6** jargon, patois, speech, tongue **7** dialect, lexicon, palaver **10** vernacular, vocabulary **11** terminology *ambiguous:* **8** newspeak **10** double-talk *ancient:* **5** Greek, Latin **6** Hebrew **8** Etruscan, Sanskrit *artificial:* **3** Ido **7** Volapük **9** Esperanto *Bantu:* **3** Ila *classical:* **5** Greek, Latin *combining form:* **5** gloss, glott **6** glosso, glotto *expert:* **8** linguist, polyglot *informal:* **4** jive **5** lingo, slang *meaningless:* **6** babble, jabber **7** blather **9** gibberish **10** mumbo-jumbo *mixed:* **6** creole, pidgin *pretentious:* **7** bombast, fustian **8** claptrap *regional:* **7** dialect *relating to:* **10** linguistic *Romance:* **6** French **7** Catalan, Italian, Spanish **8** Romanian, Rumanian **10** Portuguese *Scotch-Irish:* **4** Erse **6** Gaelic *secret:* **4** cant, code **5** argot *Siamese:* **3** Lao, Tai *structure:* **6** syntax **7** grammar *suffix:* **3** ese *written:* **5** prose

languid 4 lazy, limp **5** inert **6** draggy, supine, torpid **8** drooping, flagging, inactive, listless, slothful, sluggish **9** apathetic, enervated, impassive, lethargic **10** languorous, phlegmatic, spiritless **13** lackadaisical

languish 4 fade, fail, pine, tire, wilt **5** brood, droop **6** weaken **7** decline **9** waste away

languishing 4 limp, weak **6** feeble, pining **7** languid **8** fainéant, indolent, listless, weakened **9** depressed, enervated, enfeebled **10** dispirited, spiritless **11** debilitated, devitalized **13** lackadaisical

languor 3 kef, kif **5** ennui **6** stupor, tedium, torpor **7** fatigue **8** doldrums, dullness, hebetude, lethargy **9** heaviness, inertness, lassitude, torpidity, weariness **10** exhaustion

languorous 4 lazy, limp **5** inert **6** draggy, supine, torpid **7** laggard, languid, passive, relaxed **8** dilatory, drooping, fainéant, flagging, inactive, indolent, indulged, listless, pampered, slothful, sluggard **9** apathetic, enervated, impassive, lethargic **10** phlegmatic, spiritless **13** lackadaisical

lank 4 bony, lean, thin **5** rangy, spare **6** gangly **7** angular, scraggy, slender **8** gangling

lanky 4 bony, lean, thin **5** gaunt, spare **6** gangly **7** scraggy, scrawny **8** gangling, rawboned

lanyard 4 cord, line, rope 7 cordage
Laocoön *city:* 4 Troy *killer:* 8 serpents
Laodamia *father:* 7 Acastus *husband:* 11
Protesilaus
Laomedon *daughter:* 7 Hesione *father:* 4
Ilus *kingdom:* 4 Troy *mother:* 8 Eurydice
slayer: 8 Heracles, Hercules *son:* 5 Priam 8
Tithonus
Laos *capital:* 9 Vientiane *city:* 11 Savannakhet *ethnic group:* 5 Hmong *monetary
unit:* 3 kip *neighbor:* 5 Burma, China 7
Myanmar, Vietnam 8 Cambodia, Thailand 9
Kampuchea *river:* 6 Mekong
lap 3 sip 4 fold, join, wind 5 drink 6 cuddle,
splash, swathe 7 circuit, control, custody,
shingle 9 imbricate
lapidary 6 cutter 7 elegant, jeweler 8 engraver, polisher
lapillus 4 lava 6 cinder
lapin 6 rabbit
Lapiths *foes:* 8 centaurs *king:* 5 Ixion
lappet 4 flap, fold 5 lapel
lapse 3 err, gap, sin 4 fall, flub, goof, sink,
slip, vice 5 boner, cease, error, fluff, gaffe,
slide 6 breach, bungle, expire, foible, miscue 7 blooper, blunder, decline, failing,
failure, faux pas, forfeit, frailty, mistake,
screwup, subside 8 abeyance, apostasy, interval, trespass 9 backslide, deviation, oversight, violation 10 apostatize 11
backsliding, impropriety 12 indiscretion,
interruption
lapsed 4 sunk 5 ended 6 ceased 7 expired 8
obsolete 9 forfeited
Laputan 6 absurd 9 visionary
Lar 3 god 6 spirit 12 household god
larboard 4 left, port 8 leftward
larcenist 5 thief 6 bandit, robber 7 burglar,
filcher, stealer 8 pilferer 9 embezzler, plunderer, purloiner 10 pickpocket, shoplifter
larcenous 7 robbing 8 thieving 9 pilfering 10
plunderous 13 light-fingered
larceny 5 theft 7 looting, robbery 8 burglary,
stealing, thievery, thieving *kind:* 5 grand,
petty
lard 3 fat 6 fatten, grease 10 shortening
larder 6 pantry
large 3 big, fat 4 bull, huge, vast 5 ample,
bulky, giant, grand, great, gross, hefty,
jumbo, major 6 goodly 7 copious, immense, mammoth, massive, outsize, sizable
8 colossal, enormous, gigantic, king-size,
oversize, spacious, whopping 9 capacious,
excessive, extensive, humongous, monstrous 10 exorbitant, large-scale, monumental, prodigious, stupendous, tremendous,
voluminous 11 extravagant, substantial

combining form: 4 macr, mega 5 macro 6
megalo
largesse 4 alms, gift 6 bounty 7 bequest,
charity, cumshaw, gifting, present 8 donation, gratuity 9 endowment, pourboire 10
almsgiving, generosity, liberality 11 benefaction, beneficence, benevolence, magnanimity, munificence 12 philanthropy
largo 4 slow 5 broad, tempo
lariat 4 bola, bolo, rope 5 lasso, noose, reata,
riata *user:* 6 cowboy, drover 10 cowpuncher
lark 4 bird, dido, romp 5 antic, caper, prank,
shine, stunt, trick 6 frolic 7 rollick 8 escapade, songbird 9 diversion 10 tomfoolery 11
distraction, shenanigans 12 monkeyshines
larrup 3 tan 4 beat, cane, drub, dust, flay,
flog, hide, lash, lick, whip, whup 5 pound,
spank, whale 6 cudgel, lather, paddle,
thrash, wallop 7 clobber, scourge, shellac,
trounce 8 lambaste 10 flagellate
larva 3 bot 4 grub, worm 6 dobson, maggot 8
cercaria, hornworm, mealworm 10 casebearer 11 caterpillar 12 hellgrammite *amphibian:* 7 tadpole *crustacean:* 4 zoea
flatworm: 5 redia *free-swimming:* 7 planula
mollusk: 7 veliger *moth:* 8 leafworm *tape-
worm:* 6 measle
larynx 7 trachea 8 voice box
lasagna 5 pasta 7 noodles
lascivious 4 lewd 5 bawdy, loose, randy 6
carnal, coarse, rakish, wanton 7 fleshly,
goatish, immoral, lustful, satyric 8 depraved,
prurient 9 lecherous, libertine, lickerish, salacious 10 libidinous, licentious, lubricious,
profligate 12 concupiscent
lash 4 beat, bind, dash, flay, flog, hide, whip
5 baste, birch, fling, pound, scold, slash,
whale 6 assail, berate, buffet, pummel,
scathe, strike, stripe, switch, thrash 7 blister, scarify, scourge, upbraid 8 lambaste 9
castigate, excoriate, horsewhip 10 flagellate
lass 3 gal 4 girl, maid 5 wench 6 damsel,
maiden 7 colleen
lassitude 5 ennui, sloth 6 apathy, stupor, tedium, torpor 7 fatigue, languor 8 debility,
doldrums, dullness, hebetude, laziness,
lethargy 9 indolence, tiredness, torpidity,
weariness 10 exhaustion 11 insouciance 12
heedlessness, indifference, listlessness,
sluggishness
lasso see lariat
last 3 end, lag, nth 5 abide, final 6 endure,
latest, latter, utmost 7 closing, extreme, perdure, persist 8 continue, crowning, eventual, farthest, furthest, hindmost, rearmost,
remotest, terminal, ultimate 9 umpteenth,
uttermost 10 concluding, conclusive 11 ter-

minating *French:* **7** dernier *next to:* **6** penult **11** penultimate

last-ditch 5 final **7** defiant **8** ultimate **9** desperate **10** concluding

lasting 6 stable **7** abiding, durable, undying **8** enduring, lifelong, long-term, longtime **9** continual, indelible, perennial, permanent, unceasing **10** continuing, continuous, perdurable, persisting **12** indissoluble, longstanding

Last of the Mohicans, The 5 Uncas *author:* **6** Cooper (James Fenimore) *character:* **4** Cora **5** Alice, Magua, Uncas **11** Natty Bumppo **12** Chingachgook

Last Supper, The *painter:* **7** da Vinci (Leonardo) **8** Leonardo (da Vinci) *location:* **5** Milan

latch 4 bolt, glom, hasp, hook **5** catch **6** fasten, secure **8** fastener *British:* **5** sneck

latchet 4 band, cord, lace **5** strap, thong **8** shoelace

late 4 dead, past, slow **5** tardy **6** former, recent, whilom **7** defunct, delayed, onetime, overdue, quondam **8** deceased, departed, sometime **9** preceding

latent 4 idle **5** inert **6** covert, fallow, hidden, innate, unripe **7** abeyant, dormant, lurking **8** immature, inactive, inherent **9** concealed, intrinsic, potential, quiescent

later 4 anon, soon **5** after, infra **6** behind **7** by and by, ensuing **9** afterward, following, posterior **10** subsequent, succeeding **12** subsequently

lateral 4 pass, side **6** branch **8** crabwise, flanking, sidelong, sideward, sideways, sidewise

laterally 8 crabwise, sideward, sideways, sidewise

latest 6 newest, red-hot **7** current **8** contempo **9** au courant **10** dernier cri **13** up-to-the-minute

latex 6 balata **8** emulsion *product:* **5** paint **6** chicle, rubber **11** gutta-percha

lath 4 slat **5** board, frame, stave, stick, strip

lather 4 flap, flog, foam, hide, lash, soap, stew, suds, whip **5** froth, spume, tizzy, yeast **6** dither, hoopla, pother, thrash, welter **7** scourge, turmoil **8** soapsuds

Latin 5 Roman **7** Italian **8** Hispanic *after:* **4** post *always:* **6** semper *and:* **2** et *as directed:* **6** ut dict *be, being:* **4** esse *before:* **4** ante, prae *behold:* **4** ecce *believe:* **5** credo *book:* **5** liber *boy:* **4** puer *brother:* **6** frater *but:* **3** sed *day:* **4** dies *dog:* **5** canis *earth:* **5** terra *egg:* **3** ova *father:* **5** pater *foot:* **3** pes *friend:* **6** amicus *girl:* **6** puella *god:* **4** deus *goddess:* **3** dea *good-bye:* **4** vale **5** salve

grammarian: **7** Donatus (Aelius) *greeting:* **3** ave *hail and farewell:* **12** ave atque vale *hand:* **5** manus *hello:* **3** ave *horse:* **5** equus *house:* **5** domus *is:* **3** est *law:* **3** ius, jus, lex *let it stand:* **4** stet *life:* **4** vita *light:* **3** lux *love:* **3** amo **4** amas, amat, amor *man:* **4** homo *mother:* **5** mater *moon:* **4** luna *night:* **3** nox *nothing:* **5** nihil *now:* **4** nunc *peace:* **3** pax *pronoun:* **2** tu **3** ego, nos, vos *road:* **3** via *same:* **4** idem *sea:* **4** mare *see:* **4** vide *sister:* **5** soror *step:* **6** gradus *sun:* **3** sol *that is:* **5** id est *thing:* **3** res *this:* **3** hic, hoc **4** haec *thus:* **3** sic *truth:* **7** veritas *war:* **6** bellum *welcome:* **5** salve *wife:* **4** uxor *woman:* **6** femina *year:* **4** anno **5** annus

Latin American *country:* **4** Cuba, Peru **5** Chile **6** Belize, Brazil, Guyana, Mexico, Panama **7** Bolivia, Ecuador, Uruguay **8** Colombia, Honduras, Paraguay, Suriname **9** Argentina, Costa Rica, Guatemala, Nicaragua, Venezuela **10** El Salvador *dance:* **4** juba **5** conga, mambo, rumba, samba **6** maxixe, rhumba **7** carioca, lambada **8** capoeira, habanera, merengue **9** bossa nova *revolutionary:* **6** Castro (Fidel) **7** Bolívar (Simón), Guevara (Ché), Hidalgo (Father Miguel) **8** O'Higgins (Bernardo) **9** San Martín (José de)

Latinus *daughter:* **7** Lavinia *father:* **6** Faunus **8** Odysseus *son-in-law:* **6** Aeneas *wife:* **5** Amata

latitude 4 play, room **5** range, scope, space, width **6** leeway, margin **7** breadth, compass, freedom, liberty, license **9** elbowroom **10** discretion **12** independence

latke 7 pancake **13** potato pancake

Latona 4 Leto *daughter:* **5** Diana **7** Artemis *father:* **5** Coeus *mother:* **6** Phoebe *son:* **6** Apollo

Latter-day Saint 6 Mormon

lattice 4 grid, mesh **5** grate, grill **7** grating, network, trellis **12** reticulation

Latvia *capital:* **4** Riga *city:* **7** Liepaja **10** Daugavpils *gulf:* **4** Riga *language:* **7** Lettish *monetary unit:* **3** lat *native:* **4** Lett *neighbor:* **6** Russia **7** Belarus, Estonia **9** Lithuania *river:* **7** Daugava **12** Western Dvina *sea:* **6** Baltic

Latvian 4 Balt, Lett **7** Lettish

laud 5 adore, bless, cry up, extol, glory, honor **6** admire, praise, revere **7** acclaim, flatter, glorify, magnify, worship **8** eulogize, venerate **9** celebrate, reverence

laudable 6 worthy **9** admirable, deserving, estimable **11** commendable, meritorious, thankworthy **12** praiseworthy

laudatory 7 glowing **9** adulatory, approving

10 eulogistic, flattering **11** approbative, encomiastic, panegyrical **12** commendatory **13** complimentary

laugh 3 yuk **4** ha-ha, roar, yuck **5** tehee, whoop **6** cackle, giggle, guffaw, hee-haw, titter **7** chortle, chuckle, snicker **10** cachinnate

laughable 4 rich **5** comic, droll, funny, goofy, witty **6** absurd, jocose **7** amusing, comical, jocular, mocking, risible **8** derisive, derisory, farcical, humorous **9** ludicrous **10** ridiculous

Laugh-In *cast:* **4** Sues (Alan), Hawn (Goldie) **5** Buzzi (Ruth), Carne (Judy), Owens (Gary) **6** Dawson (Richard), Gibson (Henry), Tomlin (Lily) **7** Johnson (Arte) *catch phrase:* **10** sock it to me **12** go to your room *guest:* **6** Wilson (Flip) **7** Tiny Tim **8** Youngman (Henny) *host:* **5** Rowan (Dan) **6** Martin (Dick)

laughing 5 merry, riant **6** blithe **8** mirthful **9** sparkling

laughingstock 4 butt, dupe, fool, jest, joke, mark, mock **5** sport **6** target **7** mockery **8** derision

launch 4 boat, cast, fire, hurl **5** begin, debut, fling, heave, pitch, sling, start, throw **6** get off **7** jump off, kick off, lift off, release, take off, usher in **8** blast off, catapult, commence, embark on, initiate **9** inception, institute, introduce, motorboat, set afloat **10** inaugurate, initiation **12** inauguration

launder 4 wash **5** clean **6** trough **7** cleanse **8** sanitize, transfer

Laura's lover 8 Petrarch

laurels 4 bays, fame **5** award, honor, kudos, prize **6** awards, badges, honors, prizes, renown **7** acclaim **8** accolade, citation **9** accolades, citations **10** decoration, reputation **11** decorations, distinction **12** achievements, distinctions

laurel-tree nymph 6 Daphne

lava 2 aa **4** slag **5** magma **6** scoria **8** andesite, trachyte *fragment:* **8** lapillus *stream:* **4** flow **6** coulee

lavalava 5 cloth, skirt **6** sarong

lavaliere 7 pendant **8** necklace

lavatory 2 WC **3** loo **4** head, john **5** basin, jakes, potty, privy **6** johnny, toilet **7** latrine **8** bathroom, restroom, washroom **11** water closet

lave 4 pour, wash **5** bathe

Lavinia *father:* **7** Latinus *husband:* **6** Aeneas *mother:* **5** Amata

Lavinium's founder 6 Aeneas

lavish 4 lush, posh, pour **5** plush, spend, waste **6** swanky **7** liberal, opulent, profuse **8** effusive, prodigal, splendid, squander **9**

bountiful, excessive, exuberant, luxuriant, luxurious, sumptuous **10** immoderate, inordinate, munificent **11** extravagant

law 3 act, lex **4** bill, code, rule **5** axiom, canon, edict, Torah **6** assize, decree, equity **7** dictate, justice, mandate, precept, statute, theorem **8** exigency **9** enactment, ordinance, principle **10** principium, regulation **11** commandment, fundamental **12** prescription *body of:* **4** code **7** pandect **12** constitution *degree:* **2** JD **3** LLB, LLD *expert:* **5** judge **6** jurist **7** justice *practitioner:* **6** lawyer **7** counsel **8** attorney **9** barrister, solicitor *relating to:* **5** jural, legal **7** canonic **8** forensic, juristic **9** judiciary *violation of:* **4** tort **5** crime **6** felony **11** misdemeanor

law-abiding 6 decent **7** duteous, dutiful, orderly, upright **8** obedient, obliging, straight **9** compliant, peaceable **10** forthright, respectful **11** respectable, well-behaved

Law & Order *actor:* **4** Röhm (Elisabeth) **6** Govich (Milena), Martin (Jesse), Orbach (Jerry) **7** Hendrix (Leslie) **8** Thompson (Fred) **9** Merkerson (S. Epatha), Waterston (Sam) *character:* **5** Green (Ed), McCoy (Jack) **6** Branch (Arthur) **7** Briscoe (Lennie), Cassady (Nina), Rodgers (Elizabeth) **8** Van Buren (Anita) **10** Southerlyn (Serena) *creator:* **4** Wolf (Dick)

lawbreaker 3 con **4** hood, thug **5** crook, felon **6** outlaw, sinner **7** convict, hoodlum, mobster **8** criminal, gangster, hooligan, jailbird, offender, scofflaw, violator **9** desperado, wrongdoer **10** malefactor, trespasser **12** transgressor

lawful 3 due **4** just **5** legal, legit, licit, valid **6** kosher **7** condign **8** bona fide, innocent, mandated, ordained **9** allowable, canonical, juridical, legalized **10** authorized, legitimate **11** permissible

lawgiver 5 Draco, Moses, solon **7** senator **8** alderman **10** councilman, legislator **11** congressman, thesmothete

lawlessness 5 chaos **6** strife **7** anarchy, discord, misrule, turmoil **8** conflict, disorder **9** mobocracy **10** illegality, misconduct, ochlocracy, unruliness, wrongdoing **11** criminality, pandemonium

lawman 7 marshal, officer, sheriff **9** policeman

Lawrence novel 7 Rainbow (The) **8** Kangaroo, Lost Girl (The) **9** Aaron's Rod **11** Women in Love **13** Plumed Serpent (The), Sons and Lovers

lawrencium symbol 2 Lr

lawsuit 4 case **5** cause, claim **6** action **8** replevin **9** assumpsit **10** litigation, proceeding **11** presentment, prosecution

lawyer 6 jurist, legist **7** counsel, pleader **8** advocate, attorney **9** barrister, counselor, solicitor *dishonest:* **7** shyster **11** pettifogger *fictional:* **5** Finch (Atticus) **7** Matlock (Ben), Rumpole (Horace) **10** Perry Mason *French:* **6** avocat *title:* **3** Esq. **7** Esquire

lax 5 loose, slack **6** casual, remiss, sloppy **7** lenient **8** careless, derelict, lacrosse **9** deficient, forgetful, negligent **10** neglectful, permissive **11** inattentive

lay 3 bet, put, set **5** apply, hatch, place, wager **6** assert, assign, ballad, charge, credit, devise, impute, settle, spread **7** amateur, arrange, ascribe, concoct, deposit, prepare, present **11** nonclerical

lay by 4 keep, save **5** amass, hoard, store **7** deposit, discard, store up **8** preserve, salt away, set aside **10** accumulate

lay down 3 set **4** rule **5** order, store, yield **6** assert, decree, define, give up, impose, ordain, record, resign **7** abandon, command, dictate, specify **8** hand over, preserve, proclaim **9** establish, prescribe, surrender **10** relinquish

layer 3 hen, ply **4** coat, film, seam, tier **5** paver, sheet **6** folium, lamina, strata (plural), veneer **7** coating, stratum **8** covering, laminate, membrane, sandwich, stratify *inner:* **6** lining *of skin:* **6** dermis **9** epidermis *outer:* **4** skin **6** veneer

lay for 6 ambush **8** surprise

lay in see **lay by**

layman 6 novice, oblate **7** amateur, secular **11** parishioner

lay off 4 fire, halt, quit, stop **5** avoid, cease, let go, lie by **6** desist **7** abstain, dismiss, measure, release **9** discharge, terminate **10** inactivity **11** discontinue

lay out 3 pay **4** give, plan **5** chart, dummy, place, spend **6** design, expend **7** arrange, display, exhibit, prepare **8** disburse

lay waste 4 ruin **5** wreck **6** ravage **7** destroy **8** desolate **9** devastate

lazar 5 leper

Lazarus' sister 4 Mary **6** Martha

laze 3 bum, lag **4** bask, hang, idle, loaf, loll **5** chill **6** dawdle, loiter, lounge, slouch **7** goof off, hang out **8** chill out **9** goldbrick **10** hang around

laziness 5 sloth **6** torpor **7** inertia, languor, laxness, loafing **8** idleness, lethargy, otiosity **9** indolence, lassitude, loitering, slackness **10** inactivity **11** languidness **12** listlessness

lazy 3 lax **4** idle **5** inert, slack **6** droopy, remiss, supine, torpid **7** languid, loafing, passive **8** fainéant, inactive, indolent, listless, slothful, sluggish **9** lethargic, negligent, shiftless, slowgoing **10** languorous

lazy Susan 4 tray **9** turntable

leach 4 drip, leak, ooze, perk, seep, suck, weep **5** bleed, drain, exude, issue **7** draw out, dribble, trickle **8** filtrate, perspire **9** discharge, lixiviate, percolate

lead 3 tip **4** head, hint, show, star **5** guide, metal, plumb, route, steer, trace, usher **6** bullet, ceruse, direct, escort, leader **7** captain, conduct, precede, preface **8** graphite, persuade, shepherd **9** spearhead **10** bellwether *combining form:* **5** plumb **6** plumbo *ore:* **6** galena **9** anglesite *oxide:* **6** sinter *sounding:* **5** plumb **7** plummet *symbol:* **2** Pb

lead astray 6 seduce **7** corrupt

leaden 4 drab, dull, flat, gray **5** heavy, inert **6** gloomy, somber **7** languid, weighty **8** dragging, lifeless, sluggish **9** ponderous

leader 4 boss, dean, duce, guru, head, jefe, lord **5** chief, guide, pilot **6** despot, honcho, rector **7** captain, foreman, general, headman, manager, warlord **8** chairman, director, hierarch, superior **9** chieftain, commander, conductor, demagogue, harbinger, precursor, president, principal, straw boss **10** bellwether, forerunner, pacesetter *authoritarian:* **10** Big Brother *Cossack:* **6** ataman, hetman *German:* **6** führer **7** fuehrer *Japanese:* **6** shogun *military:* **7** admiral, general, warlord **9** commander **12** field marshal *Muslim:* **3** aga **4** agha, amir, emir, imam **5** ameer **6** caliph, mullah *national:* **7** premier **9** president **12** chief of state

leading 4 arch, head, main **5** ahead, chief, first, major **6** famous, master **7** premier, primary **8** champion, foremost, headmost, peerless **9** paramount, principal, prominent, well-known **10** preeminent

lead on 3 con **4** bait, dupe, fool, gull, hoax, lure, scam, tole, toll, wile **5** cozen, flirt, tempt **6** allure, betray, cajole, coquet, delude, entice, entrap, humbug, seduce, suck in, take in, trifle **7** beguile, deceive, toy with **8** coquette, hoodwink, inveigle **9** bamboozle **11** string along

leaf 4 flip, foil, page, riff, scan, skim **5** blade, bract, folio, frond, petal, scale, sepal, thumb **6** browse, glance, riffle, spathe *angle:* **4** axil *aperture:* **5** stoma *axis:* **6** rachis *combining form:* **5** phyll **6** phyllo **7** phyllum *edge:* **9** crenation *lily:* **3** pad *part:* **4** lobe, vein **5** blade, costa, stoma **7** petiole, stipule, tendril *pine:* **6** needle *vein:* **5** costa

leafage 7 foliage, umbrage, verdure

leaflet 5 flier, flyer, pinna, sheet, tract **6** folder **7** handout **8** brochure, circular, handbill, pamphlet

leafy 4 lush **5** green, shady **6** shaded, wooded **7** foliate, verdant **8** foliated, laminate **9** verdurous

league 4 band, bond, club, crew **5** class, grade, group, guild, order, union, unite **6** circle **7** circuit, combine, society **8** alliance, category, division, grouping, sodality **9** coalition **10** conference, consortium, federation, fellowship, fraternity **11** association, brotherhood, confederacy **13** confederation

Leah *daughter:* **5** Dinah *father:* **5** Laban *husband:* **5** Jacob *sister:* **6** Rachel *son:* **4** Levi **5** Judah **6** Reuben, Simeon **7** Zebulun **8** Issachar

leak 4 drip, ooze, seep **5** break, crack, spill **6** escape, get out, reveal, source **7** come out, divulge, seepage **8** disclose **9** discharge **10** make public

leaky 6 broken, faulty, porous **7** cracked, damaged

lea, ley 4 veld **5** field, veldt **6** fallow, meadow **7** pasture **9** grassland, pasturage

lean 3 sag, tip **4** bend, bony, cant, heel, lank, list, slim, thin, tilt **5** gaunt, lanky, shift, slant, slope, spare **6** meager, meagre, skinny, slight, wasted **7** angular, deviate, haggard, incline, pinched, scraggy, scrawny, slender, stringy, wizened **8** gradient, rawboned **9** deficient **11** inclination

Leander's beloved 4 Hero

Leaning Tower site 4 Pisa

lean-to 3 hut **4** shed **5** shack **6** shanty **7** bivouac, shelter

leap 3 hop **4** buck, jump, loup, lutz, rise, soar **5** bound, caper, clear, mount, vault **6** ascend, gambol, hurdle, spring **7** saltate **8** capriole, surmount *ballet:* **4** jeté **9** entrechat *by a horse:* **7** gambado

Lear, King *daughter:* **5** Regan **7** Goneril **8** Cordelia *son:* **5** Edgar **6** Edmund

learn 3 con **4** hear **5** grasp, study **6** attain, detect, master, pick up **7** acquire, catch on, discern, find out, realize, uncover, unearth **8** discover, memorize **9** apprehend, ascertain, determine **10** comprehend, understand **11** stumble onto

learned 4 sage, wise **6** expert, versed **7** bookish, erudite, sapient, studied **8** abstruse, academic, cultured, educated, esoteric, highbrow, lettered, pedantic, well-read **9** recondite, scholarly **10** cultivated, scholastic **12** intellectual

learner 4 tiro, tyro **5** pupil **6** novice, rookie **7** student, trainee **8** beginner, disciple, initiate, neophyte **9** greenhorn, postulant **10** apprentice, catechumen **11** abecedarian

learning 4 lore **6** wisdom **7** science, tuition **8** booklore, pedantry **9** education, erudition, knowledge **11** scholarship *person of:* **7** egghead, scholar **9** professor **12** intellectual

lease 3 let **4** hire, rent **6** sublet **7** charter, compact **8** contract, covenant, document **11** continuance

leash 3 tie **4** bind, cord, curb, rein, rope **5** strap **6** bridle, fetter, hamper, tether **7** shackle, trammel **8** restrain **9** entrammel

least 6 fewest **7** minimal, minimum **8** smallest

leather 3 tan **4** hide, skin, whip **6** thrash *kind:* **3** kid, kip, oak **4** bock, buff, calf, roan **5** crown, grain, mocha, strap, suede, whang **6** castor, latigo, oxhide, patent, roller, saddle, skiver **7** buffalo, chamois, morocco, ostrich, peccary **8** capeskin, cordovan, cowhide, shagreen *maker:* **5** tawer **6** tanner **7** tannery *piece:* **4** welt **5** strap, thong *prepare:* **3** tan, taw **5** curry *soft:* **5** mocha, suede **8** cabretta

leatherneck 6 marine

Leatherstocking Tales, The *author:* **6** Cooper (James Fenimore) *hero:* **5** Natty (Bumppo) *title:* **7** Prairie (The) **8** Pioneers (The) **10** Deerslayer (The), Pathfinder (The) **17** Last of the Mohicans (The)

leave 2 go **3** fly, let **4** blow, cede, exit, flee, move, part, quit, will **5** allow, scram, split **6** assent, assign, beat it, begone, commit, cut out, decamp, depart, desert, devise, escape, get off, legate, permit, resign, retire, set out, vacate **7** abandon, abscond, absence, consent, consign, entrust, forsake, get away, liberty, pull out, take off, vamoose **8** bequeath, clear out, farewell, furlough, hand down, transmit, vacation, withdraw **9** departure, disappear, surrender, terminate **10** permission, relinquish, sabbatical **13** authorization

leaved 5 green **7** foliate, verdant **8** foliated

leaven 5 imbue, steep, yeast **6** infuse, invest, modify, temper, vivify **7** enliven, ingrain, lighten, suffuse **8** moderate **9** alleviate, inoculate, sourdough **12** baking powder

leavening 5 yeast **9** sourdough **10** baking soda **12** baking powder

leave of absence 8 furlough

leave off 3 end **4** halt, quit, stop **5** cease **6** desist, give up **7** abstain **8** give over, surcease **9** terminate **11** discontinue

leave out 4 omit, skip **5** elide **7** exclude

Leaves of Grass author 7 Whitman (Walt)

leavings 4 lees, orts, rest **5** dregs, scrap **6** debris, grouts **7** balance, remains, remnant, residue, rubbish **8** discards, oddments, remnants, residual, residuum **9** fragments, leftovers, remainder

Lebanon *capital:* **6** Beirut *city:* **4** Tyre **5** Sidon **6** Zahlah **7** Tripoli *language:* **6** Arabic, French *monetary unit:* **5** pound *mountain:* **6** Hermon *neighbor:* **5** Syria **6** Israel *river:* **6** Litani **7** Orontes *sea:* **13** Mediterranean *valley:* **5** Bekaa

Le Carré, John *character:* **6** Smiley (George) *novel:* **11** Russia House (The) **17** Little Drummer Girl (The) **22** Tinker Tailor Soldier Spy **23** Spy Who Came in from the Cold (The)

lecher 4 rake, roué, wolf **7** Don Juan, seducer **8** Casanova, lothario **9** debauchee, reprobate, libertine, womanizer **10** degenerate, profligate, voluptuary **11** philanderer

lecherous 4 lewd **5** bawdy, loose, randy **6** carnal, coarse, rakish, wanton **7** fleshly, goatish, immoral, lustful, satyric **8** depraved, prurient, scabrous **9** debauched, libertine, lickerish, salacious **10** lascivious, libidinous, licentious, lubricious, profligate **11** promiscuous **12** concupiscent

lectern 4 desk **5** podia (plural), stand **6** podium

lecture 4 talk **5** chide, scold, speak **6** berate, preach, rebuke, sermon, speech **7** address, declaim, expound, oration, reproof, reprove, upbraid **8** admonish, briefing, harangue, scolding **9** chalk talk, criticism, criticize, discourse, hold forth, reprimand, talking-to **10** allocution **12** disquisition, dressing-down

lecturer 3 don **6** docent, fellow, master, orator, reader **7** scholar, speaker, teacher, trainer **9** pedagogue, preceptor, professor **10** instructor **11** academician

Leda *daughter:* **5** Helen **12** Clytemnestra *father:* **8** Thestius *husband:* **9** Tyndareus *lover:* **4** swan, Zeus *son:* **6** Castor, Pollux

ledge 3 bar, rim **4** berm, lode, reef, sill, vein **5** bench, ridge, shelf **6** mantle **7** bedrock, molding **10** projection

ledger 4 book **5** tally **6** record **7** account, balance **8** notebook, register **9** reckoning

lee 5 haven **7** shelter **9** protected, sheltered

leech 4 milk, worm **5** bleed, drain **6** sponge, sucker **7** exhaust, sponger **8** barnacle, hanger-on, parasite **10** freeloader **11** bloodsucker **12** lounge lizard

leer 3 eye **4** ogle **5** fleer, gloat, smirk, sneer, stare **6** glance, goggle, squint **7** grimace

leery 4 wary **5** chary **6** unsure **7** dubious, guarded **8** cautious, doubtful, doubting **10**

suspicious **11** circumspect, distrustful, mistrustful

lees 5 dregs **6** grouts, refuse **7** deposit, grounds, residue **8** leavings, residual, residuum, sediment **9** settlings **11** precipitate

leeward 8 downwind *opposite:* **8** windward

leeway 4 play, room **5** scope, space **6** margin **7** breadth, compass, freedom, liberty **8** latitude **9** elbowroom, tolerance

left 4 port **7** liberal, radical **8** departed, deserted, larboard, residual, sinister **9** abandoned, discarded, remaining, sinistral

left-handed 5 inept **6** clumsy, gauche **7** awkward, dubious **8** fumbling, southpaw **9** ambiguous, equivocal, insincere, maladroit **10** morganatic

left-hand page 5 verso

leftover 5 extra, spare **6** excess, unused **7** remnant, reserve, residue, surplus, uneaten, vestige **8** residual, unneeded **9** redundant, remainder, remaining **10** unconsumed **11** superfluous

leftovers see **leavings**

leftward 4 levo **5** aport *go:* **3** haw

leg 3 bow, gam **4** limb **5** shank, stage **6** branch **7** support, upright **8** cabriole **9** appendage, drumstick *bone:* **4** shin **5** femur, tibia **6** fibula **7** patella *part:* **4** calf, crus, foot, knee, shin **5** ankle, thigh

legacy 4 gift **5** trust **6** devise, estate **7** bequest **8** heirloom, heritage **9** endowment, patrimony, tradition **10** birthright **11** benefaction, inheritance

legal 5 legit, licit **6** lawful **7** allowed **8** innocent **9** juridical, statutory **10** legitimate, sanctioned *matter:* **3** res **4** case, suit *order:* **4** writ **7** summons **8** subpoena *organization:* **3** ABA *party:* **6** suitor **8** litigant **9** defendant, plaintiff *restraint:* **8** estoppel

legal tender 3 wad **4** cash **5** bread, dough, money, moola, notes **6** moolah, specie **7** coinage **8** banknote, currency **9** long green

legate 4 will **5** endow, envoy, grant, leave **6** bestow, commit, devise, deputy, devise, pass on **7** entrust, leave to **8** bequeath, delegate, emissary, hand down, transmit **10** ambassador

legatee 4 heir **7** devisee **9** inheritor

legato 5 fluid **6** smooth **7** flowing

legend 3 key **4** lore, myth, saga, tale, yarn **5** fable, motto, story **6** mythos **7** caption, fiction **8** epigraph, folklore, folktale, tall tale **9** mythology, tradition **11** inscription

legendary 5 famed **6** fabled, famous, mythic **7** fabular, fancied, fictive, storied **8** fabulous, mythical, renowned, supposed **9** well-known **10** apocryphal, celebrated **11** illustrious, traditional **12** mythological

legerdemain 5 magic **8** prestige, trickery **9** chicanery, conjuring, deception **13** sleight of hand

leggings 5 chaps **7** puttees **9** gambadoes

leghorn 3 hat **4** fowl **5** straw **7** chicken

legible 5 clear **8** distinct, readable **12** decipherable, intelligible

legion 4 army, host, many, mass, rout **5** cloud, crowd, drove, flock, horde **6** myriad, scores, sundry, throng **7** phalanx, various **8** numerous, populous **9** countless, multitude **10** numberless

legislate 5 enact, order **6** codify, decree, ordain, permit, ratify **7** empower, mandate **8** legalize, regulate, sanction **9** establish

legislation 3 act, law **4** acts, bill, code, laws **5** bills, codes, rules **6** edicts **7** statute **8** charters, dictates, statutes **9** enactment, lawmaking **10** enactments, ordinances, regulation **11** regulations **12** codification

legislator 5 solon **7** senator **8** alderman, lawgiver, lawmaker **10** councilman **11** assemblyman, congressman, thesmothete

legislature 4 diet **5** house, junta **6** senate **7** council **8** assembly, congress **10** parliament *Communist:* **6** soviet **9** politburo, presidium *Danish:* **9** Folketing *Finnish:* **9** Eduskunta *German:* **9** Bundesrat, Bundestag *Iceland:* **7** Althing *Ireland:* **4** Dáil *Israel:* **7** Knesset *Norway:* **8** Storting *one-house:* **10** unicameral *Poland:* **4** Sejm *Russian:* **4** duma *Spain:* **6** Cortes *Sweden:* **7** Riksdag *two-house:* **9** bicameral *Ukraine:* **4** Rada

legitimate 4 fair, just, true **5** legal, licit, sound, usual, valid **6** kosher, lawful, normal, proper **7** genuine, regular, typical **8** accepted, innocent, orthodox, rightful **9** allowable, authentic, canonical, customary **10** admissable, authorized, reasonable, recognized **11** justifiable, well-founded

Le Guin, Ursula K. *novel:* **7** Telling (The) **8** Solitude (The) **12** Dispossessed (The) **18** Left Hand of Darkness (The) *series:* **8** Earthsea

legume 3 dal, pea, pod **4** bean, dhal, guar, seed **5** pulse **6** clover, lentil **7** soybean

leg up 3 aid **4** edge, lift **5** boost **6** assist **9** advantage, head start

lei 6 wreath **7** garland **8** necklace

Leibniz's invention 8 calculus

Leif Eriksson *discovery:* **7** Vinland *father:* **4** Eric, Erik (the Red)

leisure 4 ease, rest, time **6** casual, chance, repose **7** freedom, liberty **8** downtime **10** relaxation **11** opportunity

leisurely 4 easy, slow **6** lazily, slowly **7** relaxed, restful **8** laid-back **9** unhurried

leitmotiv 4 idea **5** theme, topic **6** burden, motive, thesis **7** subject **8** idée fixe

lemma 5 bract, theme **7** heading, premise, theorem **8** argument **11** proposition

lemon 3 dud **4** bomb, bust, flop **5** fruit, loser, scent **6** flavor, yellow **7** failure

lemur 4 lori **5** indri, loris, potto **6** aye-aye, colugo, galago **7** tarsier **8** bush baby

lend 4 give, loan **5** allow, grant **6** afford, oblige, supply **7** advance, furnish, provide **11** accommodate

L'Engle novel 10 Many Waters **13** Wind in the Door (A), Wrinkle in Time (A)

length 4 span **5** ambit, range, reach, realm, scope **6** extent, radius **7** compass, expanse, measure, purview, section, stretch, yardage **8** distance, duration

lengthen 6 expand, extend, let out **7** draw out, prolong, spin out, stretch **8** elongate, increase, protract **9** string out *Scottish:* **3** eke

lengthy 4 long **8** dragging, drawn-out, extended, overlong **9** elongated, prolonged **10** long-winded, protracted, voluminous **12** interminable

leniency 5 mercy **7** quarter **8** clemency **9** tolerance **10** indulgence, toleration **11** forbearance

lenient 4 easy, kind, mild, soft **6** benign, gentle, kindly **7** amiable, clement **8** merciful, obliging, tolerant **9** benignant, forgiving, indulgent **10** forbearing, permissive

lenity 5 mercy **7** quarter **8** clemency **9** tolerance **10** humaneness, indulgence **11** forbearance

lens 5 glass **6** lentil **8** meniscus *kind:* **5** toric **6** convex **7** bifocal, concave **8** trifocal

lento 4 slow **5** tempo

Leofric's wife 6 Godiva

Leoncavallo opera 9 Pagliacci (I) **10** Chatterton

leonine 8 lionlike

Leonora 7 heroine *alias:* **7** Fidelio *husband:* **9** Florestan

leopard 3 cat **4** pard **5** ounce **7** panther

leper 6 pariah **7** Ishmael, outcast **8** castaway, derelict **9** incurable **10** Ishmaelite **11** untouchable *hospital:* **9** lazaretto *island:* **7** Molokai *priest:* **6** Damien (Father)

Leper Priest 6 Damien (Father)

lepers' hospital 9 lazaretto

lepers' island 7 Molokai

lepidoptera 5 moths **8** skippers **11** butterflies **12** caterpillars

Leporello's master 11 Don Giovanni

leprechaun 3 elf 5 dwarf, fairy 6 sprite 7 brownie *trade:* 8 cobbling

lepton 4 coin, muon 8 electron, neutrino

Lesage hero 7 Gil Blas

Lesbos poet 6 Sappho 7 Alcaeus

____ LeShan 3 Eda

lesion 3 cut 4 boil, flaw, harm, sore 5 ulcer, wound 6 injury 7 blister

Lesotho *capital:* 6 Maseru *ethnic group:* 5 Sotho *former name:* 10 Basutoland *language:* 5 Sotho *monetary unit:* 4 loti *mountain:* 9 Ntlenyana *neighbor:* 11 South Africa *river:* 6 Orange 7 Caledon

less 5 lower, minus 7 reduced, without

lessen 3 cut 4 clip, crop, ease, thin, wane 5 abate, erode, lower, taper 6 dilute, impair, minify, recede, reduce, shrink, weaken 7 abridge, assuage, curtail, degrade, dwindle, lighten, relieve, subside 8 decrease, diminish, minimize, mitigate, taper off 9 attenuate

lessening 4 drop, fall 5 letup 8 decrease, slowdown 9 abatement, reduction 10 curtailing, diminution 11 degradation

lesser 5 lower, minor 7 smaller 8 inferior 9 secondary, small-time, subjacent 11 minor-league, subordinate 13 insignificant

lesson 4 text 5 chide, moral, study 6 rebuke 7 example, lecture, reading, reprove, warning 8 admonish, exercise, homework, reproach 9 reprimand 10 admonition, assignment 11 instruction

lessor 8 landlady, landlord 9 landowner 10 freeholder

let 4 make, rent 5 allow, grant, lease, leave 6 assign, permit, suffer 9 authorize 11 obstruction

letdown 5 slump 6 defeat 7 decline, descent, failure, reverse, setback 10 anticlimax, depression, misfortune 11 frustration

let go 3 can 4 boot, fire, free, sack 5 remit 6 unhand 7 dismiss, neglect, release, set free 8 liberate 9 discharge, terminate

lethal 4 fell 5 fatal 6 deadly, mortal, poison 7 baleful, deathly 8 poisoned, virulent 9 murderous, poisonous 11 destructive, devastating

lethargic 4 dull, idle, slow 5 dopey, heavy, inert 6 draggy, supine, torpid 7 dormant, laggard, languid, passive 8 comatose, dilatory, inactive, listless, slothful, sluggish 9 apathetic, impassive 10 languorous, phlegmatic, spiritless 11 indifferent 12 hebetudinous 13 lackadaisical

lethargy 5 sloth 6 apathy, phlegm, stupor, torpor 7 inertia, languor, slumber 8 dullness, hebetude, idleness, laziness 9 disregard, inanition, indolence, inertness, lassitude, torpidity 10 inactivity, supineness 11 impassivity, passiveness 12 listlessness

lethe 7 amnesia 8 oblivion 13 forgetfulness

Leto see Latona

let off 5 spare 6 excuse, exempt 7 absolve, relieve 8 dispense 9 discharge

let on 3 own 5 admit, allow, grant, own up, spill 6 betray, fess up, reveal 7 concede, confess, confirm, divulge, pretend 8 disclose, give away

let out 5 blurt, loose 6 exhale 7 release, set free, unloose 8 lengthen, liberate, set loose 9 discharge, turn loose

letter 2 ar, ef, el, em, en, ex 3 bee, cee, cue, dee, eff, ell, ess, gee, jay, kay, pee, tee, vee, wye, zed, zee 4 line, mail, memo, note, rune 5 aitch, print, vowel 6 report, screed, symbol 7 epistle, message, missive 8 dispatch, inscribe 9 consonant *airmail:* 8 aerogram *Anglo-Saxon:* (see Anglo-Saxon) *Arabic:* (see alphabet) *Greek:* (see alphabet) *Hebrew:* (see alphabet) *kind:* 4 open 5 chain, roman 6 italic, uncial 8 Dear John *large:* 7 capital 9 majuscule, uppercase *papal:* 4 bull 10 encyclical *small:* 9 lowercase, minuscule *start:* 4 Dear

lettuce 3 cos 4 Bibb, head 6 Boston 7 iceberg, romaine, Simpson 10 butterweed

let up 3 ebb 4 fall, stop, wane 5 abate, cease 6 lessen, relent 7 die away, die down, ease off, slacken, subside 8 decrease, diminish, moderate, taper off

letup 4 lull 5 break, pause 7 respite 9 abatement, cessation, lessening, reduction 10 slackening

levee 4 dike, dock, pier, quay 5 jetty, ridge, wharf 7 seawall 8 assembly, function 9 reception 10 breakwater, embankment, riverfront

level 3 aim, lay, par 4 calm, even, flat, raze, same, tier, true 5 equal, floor, flush, grade, plane 6 direct, ground, smooth, status, steady 7 aligned, flatten, mow down 8 balanced, bulldoze, demolish, equalize, parallel, smoothen, standing 9 bring down, intensity, knock down, magnitude 10 equivalent, horizontal, reasonable 11 equilibrium

lever 3 bar, pry 4 jack, tool 5 jimmy, peavy, prize 6 peavey, tappet 7 crowbar

leverage 5 clout, power 7 exploit 9 advantage, dominance, influence 11 superiority 13 effectiveness

leveret 4 hare

Levi *father:* 5 Jacob *mother:* 4 Leah *son:* 6 Kohath, Merari 7 Gershon

leviathan 4 huge 5 giant, jumbo, large, titan,

whale **7** Goliath, immense, mammoth, massive, monster, titanic **8** behemoth, colossal, colossus, enormous, gigantic **9** cyclopean, monstrous **10** formidable, gargantuan **11** elephantine, monstrosity

Leviathan *author* **6** Hobbes (Thomas)

levitate 4 lift, rise **5** float, raise **7** elevate, suspend

levity 5 folly, humor **8** buoyancy **9** absurdity, flippancy, frivolity, giddiness, lightness, silliness **10** jocularity, volatility

levy 3 tax **4** duty, toll, wage **5** exact, lay on **6** assess, charge, custom, enlist, impose, impost, tariff **7** carry on, collect **9** conscript **10** assessment, enlistment **12** conscription

lewd 5 bawdy, gross **6** coarse, ribald, smutty, vulgar **7** fleshly, goatish, lustful, obscene, satyric **8** depraved, improper, indecent, prurient, unchaste **9** debauched, lecherous, libertine, lickerish, salacious **10** indelicate, lascivious, libidinous, licentious, lubricious

Lewis and Clark *interpreter* **9** Sacagawea, Sacajawea

Lewis *work* **7** Babbitt **9** Dodsworth **10** Arrowsmith, Main Street **11** Elmer Gantry **16** Screwtape Letters (The) **18** Chronicles of Narnia (The)

lexicographer 8 compiler *American:* **6** Porter (Noah) **7** Webster (Noah) **9** Worcester (Joseph) *English:* **4** Wyld (Henry) **6** Fowler (Francis, Henry), Murray (James), Onions (Charles) **7** Craigie (William), Johnson (Samuel) **9** Partridge (Eric) *French:* **6** Littré (Paul-Emile) **8** Larousse (Pierre) *German:* **5** Grimm (Jakob, Wilhelm)

lexicon 4 cant **6** jargon **8** glossary, language, wordbook **9** inventory, word-hoard **10** dictionary, repertoire, vocabulary **11** terminology

liable 3 apt **4** open **5** given, prone **6** likely **7** exposed, subject **8** inclined **9** sensitive **10** answerable, assailable, vulnerable **11** accountable, responsible, susceptible

liaison 4 bond, link **5** amour, fixer **6** affair, broker, hookup **7** contact, romance **8** intrigue **9** go-between **10** connection **12** entanglement, intermediary, relationship **13** communication

liana 4 vine

liar 6 fibber **7** Ananias **8** fabulist, perjurer **9** falsifier **12** prevaricator *female:* **8** Sapphira

libation 5 drink **6** liquid, liquor **7** potable **8** beverage, oblation, offering, potation

libel 4 slur **5** smear **6** defame, malign, vilify **7** asperse, calumny, obloquy, slander, traduce **8** bad-mouth, tear down **9** aspersion, denigrate **10** calumniate, defamation, scandalize **11** denigration

libelous 6 untrue **9** injurious, invidious, maligning, traducing, vilifying **10** backbiting, calumnious, defamatory, derogative, derogatory, detracting, detractive, malevolent, pejorative, scandalous, slanderous

liberal 4 full, open **5** ample, broad, loose **6** lavish **7** copious, profuse, radical **8** abundant, generous, prodigal, tolerant **9** bounteous, bountiful, indulgent, plentiful, unsparing **10** benevolent, bighearted, charitable, freehanded, munificent, openhanded, permissive, unorthodox **11** broad-minded

liberal arts *quadrivium:* **5** music **8** geometry **9** astronomy **10** arithmetic *trivium:* **5** logic **7** grammar **8** rhetoric

liberate 4 free **5** loose **7** manumit, release, unchain **9** discharge, unshackle **10** commandeer, emancipate **11** appropriate, expropriate

liberator 6 savior **7** messiah **9** deliverer *of Argentina:* **9** San Martín (José de) *of Chile:* **8** O'Higgins (Bernardo) *of Ecuador:* **5** Sucre (Antonio José de) *of Scotland:* **5** Bruce (Robert the) *of South America:* **7** Bolívar (Simón)

Liberia *capital:* **8** Monrovia *coast:* **3** Kru **5** Grain *neighbor:* **6** Guinea **10** Ivory Coast **11** Côte d'Ivoire, Sierra Leone

Liberian *language:* **3** Kwa *native:* **3** Kru, Vai **4** Gola, Toma **5** Bassa, Grebo **6** Kruman

libertine 4 lewd, rake, roué **5** bawdy, loose, randy **6** carnal, rakish, wanton **7** Don Juan, lustful, raffish, satyric **8** Casanova **9** debauched, debauchee, dissolute, lecherous, salacious **10** degenerate, dissipated, lascivious, libidinous, licentious, profligate **11** promiscuous

liberty 4 risk **5** leave **6** chance **7** freedom, license **8** autonomy **9** franchise, privilege **10** permission **11** familiarity **12** emancipation, independence

libidinous 4 lewd **5** bawdy, loose, randy **6** carnal, rakish, wanton **7** fleshly, goatish, lustful, satyric **8** depraved, prurient **9** debauched, lecherous, libertine, lickerish, salacious **10** lascivious, licentious, lubricious, profligate **11** promiscuous **12** concupiscent

librarian 5 Dewey (Melvil)

library 7 archive **8** atheneum **9** athenaeum **11** bibliotheca *desk:* **6** carrel

Libya *capital:* **7** Tripoli *city:* **8** Benghazi *desert:* **6** Sahara *gulf:* **5** Sidra *language:* **6** Arabic **7** Hamitic *leader:* **7** Gadhafi, Qaddafi (Mu'ammar) *monetary unit:* **5** dinar *neigh-*

bor: 4 Chad 5 Egypt, Niger, Sudan 7 Algeria, Tunisia *sea:* 13 Mediterranean

lice 7 cooties

license 3 let, tag 5 allow, grant, leave 6 enable, laxity, permit, suffer, ticket 7 certify, empower, freedom, go-ahead, liberty 8 accredit, document, sanction, variance 9 authority, authorize, slackness 10 permission, profligacy 11 certificate, impropriety 12 carte blanche 13 authorization

licentious 4 lewd 5 bawdy, loose, randy 6 amoral, carnal, rakish, wanton 7 fleshly, goatish, immoral, lustful, satyric 8 depraved, prurient, scabrous 9 abandoned, debauched, dissolute, lecherous, libertine, salacious 10 lascivious, libidinous, lubricious, profligate 11 promiscuous 12 concupiscent

lichen 4 moss 6 archil, litmus 7 oakmoss *genus:* 5 Usnea

licit 4 okay 5 legal 6 lawful 7 allowed 8 approved, innocent, licensed 9 allowable, permitted 10 admissible, authorized, legitimate, sanctioned 11 permissible

lick 3 bit, dab, dig, hit, lap, rap, tan 4 beat, dash, deck, down, drub, hint, swat, whip, wipe 5 cream, pinch, pound, smack, smear, spank, taste, touch, trace, whiff 6 defeat, master, punish, thrash, tongue, wallop 7 clobber, conquer, shellac, trounce 8 lambaste, outstrip, overcome, surmount 9 overwhelm

lickerish see **libidinous**

lickety-split 4 fast 5 apace 6 presto, pronto 7 flat out, hastily, quickly, rapidly, swiftly 8 chop-chop, full tilt, headlong, pell-mell, speedily 9 posthaste 13 expeditiously, precipitately

licorice 4 root 5 candy *pill:* 6 cachou

lid 3 cap, top 5 cover 8 covering *moss:* 9 operculum

lie 3 fib 4 rest, tale 5 exist, fable, libel 6 belong, canard, covert, delude, extend, inhere, remain, repose, reside 7 consist, falsify, falsity, perjure, recline, untruth, whopper 8 misspeak, misstate, tall tale 9 dissemble, falsehood, fish story, mendacity 10 inaccuracy, taradiddle 11 prevaricate 12 misstatement

Liechtenstein *capital:* 5 Vaduz *language:* 6 German *monetary unit:* 4 euro *mountain range:* 4 Alps *neighbor:* 7 Austria 11 Switzerland *river:* 5 Rhein, Rhine

lied 4 song 7 art song

lief 4 fain, soon 6 freely, gladly 7 happily, readily 9 willingly 11 contentedly

liege 4 lord, true 5 loyal 6 ardent, master, vassal 7 abiding, staunch 8 constant, endur-

ing, faithful, reliable, resolute, stalwart 9 dedicated, steadfast 10 dependable

lien 5 claim 6 charge, demand 8 interest, mortgage 10 imposition

lieu 5 place, stead

lieutenant 4 aide 5 looey, looie 6 backup, deputy 7 officer 9 assistant, coadjutor 10 aide-de-camp, coadjutant 11 subordinate

life 3 vim 4 brio, dash, élan, soul 5 verve 6 energy, esprit, spirit 8 vitality 9 animation, existence *animal:* 5 fauna *animal and plant:* 5 biota *combining form:* 3 bio *plant:* 5 flora *relating to:* 5 vital 8 biologic 10 biological *science:* 7 biology

life jacket 7 Mae West

lifeless 4 dead, drab, dull 5 inert 6 asleep, barren, torpid, wasted 7 defunct, extinct 8 comatose, deceased, departed 9 inanimate, inorganic, insensate 10 lackluster

lifelike 5 exact 7 natural, precise 8 accurate, faithful, veristic 9 realistic

life of ____ 5 Riley 8 the party

lift 4 heft, hike, jack, load, rear, rise 5 boost, exalt, filch, heave, hoist, pinch, raise, steal, swipe, theft 6 assist, pick up, pilfer, repeal, revoke, snitch, take up 7 elevate, purloin, rescind, reverse, support 8 levitate, stealing, thievery 10 plagiarize

lift-off 6 ascent, launch 7 takeoff 9 launching

ligament 3 tie 4 band, bond, link, yoke 5 nexus 8 ligature, vinculum 10 connection

ligature see **ligament**

Ligeia *author* 3 Poe (Edgar Allan)

light 4 airy, dawn, deft, easy, fair, fire, lamp, land, luck, neon 5 blond, flash, minor, perch, roost, sunny, torch 6 beacon, blithe, bright, candle, casual, facile, flimsy, fluffy, ignite, kindle, settle, simple, slight, strobe 7 lantern, sunrise, trivial 8 cheerful, daybreak, enkindle, illumine, luminous, trifling 9 frivolous, touch down 10 chandelier, effortless, illuminate *and shade interplay:* 11 chiaroscuro *combining form:* 4 luci, phot 5 lumin, photo 6 lumini, lumino *indicator:* 3 LED *measure:* 3 lux 4 phot 5 lumen 6 candle 7 candela *refractor:* 5 prism *relating to:* 6 photic *ring:* 4 halo 6 corona 7 aureola, aureole *science:* 6 optics *source:* 3 sun 4 lamp

light-emitting 6 lasing, lucent 7 beaming, fulgent, glowing, lambent, shining 8 luminous 9 effulgent, refulgent

lighten 4 dawn, ease, fade 5 allay, cheer 6 bleach, lessen, reduce 7 assuage, gladden, hearten, mollify, relieve 8 decrease, mitigate, unburden 9 alleviate, attenuate, extenuate 11 disencumber

light-headed 5 dizzy, faint, giddy, silly **6** swimmy **7** flighty **9** frivolous, slaphappy **10** unbalanced **11** disoriented, vertiginous

lighthearted 3 gay **4** glad **5** happy, jolly, merry, sunny **6** blithe, jocund, jovial, joyful, joyous, lively, upbeat **7** buoyant, festive, gleeful, playful **8** carefree, cheerful, mirthful, volatile **9** easygoing, expansive, sprightly, vivacious **10** blithesome, insouciant **12** effervescent, happy-go-lucky, highspirited

lighthouse 6 beacon **7** warning

lighting crew member 6 gaffer

lightless 4 dark **5** unlit **7** aphotic, stygian **9** tenebrous, pitch-dark **10** caliginous, pitch-black **11** unillumined

lightness 6 bounce, gaiety, levity **8** buoyancy, vivacity **9** animation, frivolity **10** cheeriness, liveliness, resiliency, volatility **12** cheerfulness **13** effervescence

lightning bug 7 firefly

lignite 4 coal **9** brown coal

likable 4 nice **6** genial **7** affable, amiable, popular, winning, winsome **8** charming, engaging, friendly, pleasant, pleasing **9** agreeable, appealing, congenial **10** attractive, personable **11** good-natured

like 3 à la, dig **4** akin, same, such **5** close, enjoy, equal, match **6** admire, agnate, akin to, allied, prefer, relish **7** approve, cognate, kindred, related, similar, uniform **8** parallel, selfsame **9** analogous, consonant, identical **10** appreciate, comparable, comprehend, equivalent, resembling

likelihood 6 chance **8** prospect **11** eventuality, possibility, presumption, probability

likely 3 apt **5** given, prone **6** liable, odds-on **7** assumed **8** credible, inclined, possible, presumed, probable, probably, reliable, suitable **9** doubtless, plausible, promising **10** achievable, attractive, believable, presumably

liken 5 match **6** equate **7** compare **8** parallel **10** assimilate

likeness 4 copy, twin **5** clone, image **6** double, effigy **7** analogy, picture, replica **8** affinity, portrait, sameness **9** depiction, facsimile, look-alike, semblance **10** appearance, photograph, similarity, similitude, uniformity **11** resemblance

likewise 3 and, too **4** also **5** ditto **6** as well, withal **7** besides **8** moreover **9** similarly **10** in addition **11** furthermore

liking 4 bent **5** fancy, taste **6** desire **8** affinity, appetite, fondness, penchant, pleasure, soft spot, weakness **9** affection **10** attraction,

partiality **11** inclination **12** appreciation, predilection

Lilith *husband:* **4** Adam *successor:* **3** Eve

lilliputian 3 wee **4** runt, tiny **5** dwarf, petty, pygmy, small **6** bantam, little, midget, peanut, peewee, shrimp **7** manikin **8** mannikin, pint-size, Tom Thumb **9** miniature, pint-sized, undersize **10** diminutive, homunculus

lilt 3 air **4** flow, purl, sing, song, tune **5** carol, pulse, swing, tempo **6** melody, rhythm **7** cadence **8** buoyancy

lily 3 pad **4** aloe, sego **5** calla, tiger, yucca **6** flower **7** leopard **8** mariposa *genus:* **4** Aloe

lily-livered 5 sissy, wimpy **6** craven, yellow **7** caitiff, chicken, fearful, gutless **8** cowardly, cowering, poltroon, recreant, timorous **9** spineless, spunkless, weak-kneed **12** fainthearted, poor-spirited **13** pusillanimous

lily-white 4 pure **6** chaste **7** upright **8** innocent, virtuous **9** blameless, estimable, exclusive, exemplary, guiltless, righteous, untainted **10** inculpable **11** uncorrupted

limb 3 arm, fin, gam, leg **4** lobe, twig, wing **5** bough, shoot, spray, sprig **6** branch, member, pinion **7** flipper **8** offshoot **9** appendage, dismember, extremity

limber 4 spry **5** agile, lithe, loose **6** nimble, pliant, supple **7** elastic, lissome, pliable, springy **8** flexible **9** lithesome, resilient

limbo 5 dance **7** neglect **8** oblivion **9** detention, purgatory **11** confinement, uncertainty

lime 4 tree **5** color, fruit, green **6** citrus, linden **7** calcium

limen 8 doorsill, doorstep **9** threshold

limerick 4 poem **5** verse *writer:* **4** Lear (Edward)

limestone 4 tufa, tuff **5** chalk **6** marble, oolite **7** coquina **10** travertine

lime tree 6 linden

limit 3 bar, cap, end, fix, max, set **4** curb **5** check, quota **6** border, bounds, curfew, define, extent, hinder, lessen **7** confine, curtail, enclose, extreme, mark out, measure **8** boundary, deadline, restrain, restrict **9** constrict, demarcate, determine, extremity, prescribe **12** circumscribe

limitless 4 vast **7** endless **8** infinite, wide-open **9** boundless, unbounded **10** indefinite **11** illimitable, innumerable, measureless **12** immeasurable, incalculable **13** inexhaustible

limn 4 draw **5** image, paint **6** depict, render, sketch **7** outline, picture, portray **8** describe **9** delineate, interpret, represent

Limoges product 5 china **9** porcelain

limp 3 lax **4** bent, halt, lame, wilt **5** hitch, loose, slack, spent, weary **6** dodder, droopy, falter, hobble **7** flaccid, languid, shamble, shuffle, slumped **8** drooping **9** enervated, exhausted **10** spiritless

limpid 4 pure **5** clear, lucid **6** glassy, serene **8** pellucid **10** see-through, untroubled **11** crystalline, translucent, transparent **12** crystal clear

limping 4 halt, lame **5** gimpy **7** halting **8** hobbling, lameness **9** faltering **12** claudication

linchpin 8 backbone, mainstay

Lincoln *assassin:* **5** Booth (John Wilkes) *biographer:* **8** Sandburg (Carl) *debater:* **7** Douglas (Stephen) *law partner:* **7** Herndon (William) *mother:* **5** Nancy (Hanks) *nickname:* **9** Honest Abe **12** Railsplitter *photographer:* **5** Brady (Mathew) *secretary of state:* **6** Seward (William) *secretary of war:* **7** Stanton (Edwin) *wife:* **8** Mary Todd

Lindsay poem 5 Congo (The)

line 3 row **4** file, rank, rope **5** array, goods, queue, route **6** border, column, cordon, series, strain, string **7** contour, descent **8** business, pedigree, sequence **10** employment, occupation, succession *curved:* **3** arc *mathematical:* **6** vector *metrical:* **5** verse **6** verset **8** versicle *of rulers:* **7** dynasty *weather map:* **6** isobar

lineage 3 kin **4** clan, folk, race **5** birth, blood, breed, house, stirp, stock, tribe **6** family, origin, strain **7** descent, kindred **8** ancestry, breeding, pedigree **9** forebears, genealogy **10** derivation, extraction, succession **11** forefathers, progenitors

lineal 6 direct **8** familial **9** ancestral, inherited **10** bequeathed, hereditary

lineament 4 form **6** figure, relief **7** contour, feature, outline, profile **10** figuration, silhouette

lined 5 drawn, ruled **7** aligned, striate, striped **8** streaked, wrinkled

linen 4 lawn **5** cloth, toile **6** byssus, damask, fabric, napery, sheets **7** batiste, bedding, cambric, taffeta **8** cretonne, lingerie *fiber:* **3** tow *source:* **4** flax

lineup 6 roster

linger 3 lag **4** bide, drag, loll, mope, poke, stay, wait **5** abide, dally, delay, mosey, tarry **6** dawdle, loiter, put off, remain **7** saunter **10** dillydally **11** stick around **13** procrastinate

lingerie 8 negligee

lingo 4 cant **5** argot, idiom, slang **6** jargon, patois, patter, speech, tongue **7** dialect **10** vernacular, vocabulary

linguist 8 polyglot **11** philologist

linguistics 9 philology

liniment 3 oil **4** aloe, balm **5** salve **6** lotion **7**

anodyne, unction, unguent **8** aloe vera, lenitive, ointment **9** demulcent **11** embrocation

lining 6 facing, insert **8** wainscot

link 3 tie **4** bind, bond, join, knot, ring, yoke **5** hitch, nexus, unite **6** attach, copula, couple, hookup, relate, splice **7** bracket, combine, conjoin, connect, contact, joining **8** catenate, division, vinculum **9** associate, conjugate **10** attachment, connection **11** association **12** relationship

linksman 6 golfer

linnet 5 finch

lint 3 fur, nap **4** down, fuzz, pile **5** floss, fluff **9** ravelings

lion 3 cat **4** puma **6** cougar **7** notable **8** eminence, luminary **9** carnivore, personage *group:* **5** pride *young:* **3** cub

lionhearted 4 bold **5** brave **6** heroic **7** valiant **8** fearless, intrepid, stalwart, unafraid, valorous **9** dauntless **10** courageous

lionize 4 fete **5** exalt, extol, honor **7** glorify **8** venerate **9** celebrate

Lion King, The *character:* **4** Nala, Scar, Zazu **5** Simba, Timon **6** Banzai, Mufasa, Pumbaa, Rafiki, Sarabi, Shenzi **8** Sarafina *composer:* **4** John (Elton) *film score:* **6** Zimmer (Hans) *lyricist:* **4** Rice (Tim) *setting:* **10** Pride Lands *voice:* **5** Irons (Jeremy), Jones (James Earl), Marin (Cheech) **8** Atkinson (Rowan), Goldberg (Whoopi) **9** Broderick (Matthew)

lion monkey 7 tamarin **8** marmoset

Lion of Judah 8 Selassie (Haile)

lip 3 rim **4** brim, edge, guff, kiss, sass **6** labium, labrum, margin **8** back talk *relating to:* **6** labial

lipid 3 fat, wax

lipped 7 labiate **9** bilabiate

liquefy 4 run **4** flux, melt, thaw **5** smelt **6** render **8** dissolve **10** deliquesce

liqueur 4 arak, ouzo, raki **5** crème **6** arrack, brandy, Kahlua, kirsch, kummel, pastis, Pernod **7** Campari, Cinzano, cordial, curaçao, ratafia, sambuca, sloe gin **8** absinthe, amaretto, anisette, Drambuie, Galliano, Tía Maria **10** Chartreuse, pousse-café

liquid 5 drink, fluid, sauce, water **6** watery **7** flowing **8** beverage, emulsion **11** mellifluous *container:* **3** cup, jug, keg, mug **4** vial **5** glass **6** bottle, goblet **7** pitcher, tumbler *flammable:* **3** gas, oil **5** ether, furan **6** butane, toluol **7** alcohol, toluene **8** gasoline, pyridine *measure:* **2** cc, ml, oz, pt, qt **3** cup, gal **4** pint **5** liter, litre, ounce, quart **6** gallon *thick:* **5** syrup **8** molasses

liquidate 3 pay **4** do in, kill **5** pay up, purge **6** murder, remove, rub out, settle, square **7**

bump off, convert, satisfy **8** amortize, dispatch, dissolve, knock off **9** eliminate, terminate **10** annihilate **11** assassinate

liquor 5 booze, drink, hooch **7** alcohol, potable, spirits **8** potation **9** firewater, inebriant **10** intoxicant *add:* **4** lace **5** spike *Asian:* **4** arak **6** arrack *homemade:* **5** hooch **9** moonshine **10** bathtub gin *inferior:* **5** hooch **6** redeye, rotgut *Japanese:* **4** sake, saki *kind:* **3** gin, rum, rye **5** vodka **6** brandy, geneva, scotch, whisky **7** aquavit, bourbon, schnaps, whiskey **8** schnapps, vermouth **9** aqua vitae **10** barley-bree *malt:* **3** ale **4** beer **5** nappy, stout **6** porter *measure:* **4** dram, shot **6** jigger **7** shooter *Mexican:* **5** sotol **6** mescal **7** tequila

lissome 5 agile, lithe **6** limber, nimble, supple, svelte **7** slender **8** flexible, graceful

list 3 tip **4** book, cant, file, heel, lean, menu, note, post, roll, tilt **5** arena, count, index, slant, slate, slope, tally **6** agenda, census, docket, lineup, record, roster **7** catalog, incline, itemize, specify **8** calendar, glossary, manifest, register, roll call, schedule, tabulate **9** chronicle, enumerate, inventory **13** particularize *type:* **3** hit **4** life, to-do, wish **5** punch, short **6** linked **7** laundry, mailing, waiting **8** shopping **10** best-seller

listen 4 hark, hear, heed, hist, note **5** audit **6** attend, harken **7** hearken, monitor **8** overhear **9** eavesdrop

listeners 8 audience

listless 4 dull, limp, weak **5** inert, slack **6** torpid, vacant **7** languid **8** indolent, sluggish **9** apathetic, enervated, lethargic, lymphatic **10** languorous, phlegmatic, spiritless **11** indifferent, languishing **13** lackadaisical

listlessness 6 apathy, stupor, torpor **7** fatigue, inertia, languor **8** doldrums, lethargy **9** indolence, lassitude, torpidity **10** enervation

litany 4 list **5** chant **6** prayer **7** account, listing, recital, refrain **8** petition, rogation **9** catalogue **10** invocation, recitation **11** enumeration **12** supplication

literal 4 bald, bare **5** blunt, exact, stark **6** actual, simple, strict **7** precise **8** accurate, bona fide, faithful, verbatim **9** authentic **11** unvarnished, word-for-word **13** unembellished

literally 5 truly **6** direct, indeed, openly, simply **7** plainly, totally, utterly **8** candidly, directly, verbatim **9** genuinely, virtually **11** word for word

literary 7 bookish, erudite, learned **8** lettered, well-read **9** authorial, scholarly **12** belletristic

literary work 4 book, opus, play, poem **5** drama, essay, novel **10** short story

literature 5 prose **6** poetry **7** fiction **13** belleslettres

lithe 4 lean, slim **5** agile, spare **6** limber, supple, svelte **7** lissome, pliable, slender **8** flexible, graceful

lithium symbol 2 Li

lithographer 4 Ives (James Merritt) **7** Currier (Nathaniel)

Lithuania *capital:* 7 Vilnius *city:* **6** Kaunas **8** Klaipeda *monetary unit:* **5** litas *neighbor:* **6** Latvia, Poland, Russia **7** Belarus *river:* **5** Neman, Venta **7** Lielupe *sea:* **6** Baltic

litigant 4 suer **6** suitor **9** defendant, disputant, plaintiff

litigate 3 sue **6** indict **7** arraign, contest, dispute **9** prosecute

litigation 4 case, suit **7** lawsuit **11** prosecution, proceedings

litter 3 bed **4** cubs, junk **5** brood, couch, issue, strew, trash, waste, young **6** clutch, debris, refuse **7** bedding, clutter, garbage, kittens, piglets, progeny, puppies, rubbish, scatter **8** detritus **9** offspring, stretcher **10** scattering

little 3 bit, dab, toy, wee **4** dash, hint, mean, puny, tiny **5** brief, dinky, minor, petty, pinch, runty, short, small, taste, trace, young **6** bantam, meager, meagre, minute, narrow, paltry, petite, skimpy **7** limited, trivial **8** dwarfish, slightly, smallish, trifling **9** miniature, small-beer **10** diminutive, short-lived, undersized **11** microscopic, unimportant

Little Bighorn *state:* 7 Montana *victim:* **6** Custer (George Armstrong) *victor:* **11** Sitting Bull

little by little 6 slowly **8** inchmeal, steadily **9** gradually, piecemeal

Little Dipper *constellation:* 9 Ursa Minor *star:* **5** North **7** Polaris

Little Women *author:* 6 Alcott (Louisa May) *character:* **3** Amy, Meg **4** Beth **6** Laurie, Marmee *surname:* **5** March

littoral 5 beach, coast, shore **6** strand **7** coastal, seaside **8** seaboard, sea front, seashore **9** shoreline **10** oceanfront

liturgy 4 rite **6** ritual **7** service **8** ceremony **9** sacrament **10** ceremonial, observance, repertoire

livable 6 viable **8** adequate, bearable, passable **9** endurable, habitable, tolerable **11** inhabitable, supportable

live 4 fare, stay **5** abide, dwell, exist, on air, vital, vivid **6** actual, reside, thrive **7** breathe, current, subsist, survive

livelihood 3 job 4 game, keep, work 5 craft, trade 7 support 8 business, vocation 10 employment, handicraft, occupation, profession, sustenance 11 subsistence

liveliness 3 pep, zip 4 brio, élan, zing 5 verve, vigor 6 energy, hustle, spirit 8 dispatch, vibrance, vibrancy, vitality, vivacity 9 animation

lively 3 gay 4 busy, keen, pert, spry, yare 5 agile, alert, brisk, fresh, jazzy, jolly, merry, peppy, zippy 6 active, bouncy, bright, chirpy, frisky, jocund, nimble 7 animate, buoyant, chipper, intense, rousing 8 animated, bustling, hustling, spirited, vigorous, volatile 9 energetic, resilient, sparkling, sprightly, vivacious 11 stimulating

liven 3 pep up 6 jazz up, vivify 7 animate, freshen, quicken 8 energize, inspirit, vitalize 10 invigorate

liver 7 denizen 8 habitant, occupant, resident 10 inhabitant *combining form:* 5 hepat 6 hepato *disease:* 9 cirrhosis, hepatitis *French:* 4 foie *lobster's:* 8 tomalley

liverwort 8 hepatica 9 bryophyte

livestock 4 cows, hogs, pigs 5 bulls, goats, sheep 6 beasts, calves, cattle 7 animals *feed:* 6 silage 8 ensilage

live wire 6 dynamo 7 hustler, rustler 8 go-getter, promoter 9 energizer, generator 11 self-starter

livid 3 hot, mad, wan 4 ashy, pale 5 ashen, lurid, waxen 6 fuming, leaden, pallid, sultry 7 boiling, bruised, enraged, furious, reddish 8 blanched, contused, incensed 9 colorless 10 discolored, infuriated 12 black-and-blue 13 beside oneself

living 5 means, vital 6 extant, income 8 animated, existent 10 livelihood, sustenance *combining form:* 3 bio

living room 6 parlor 10 lebensraum

lizard 3 eft, Uta 4 gila, newt, uran 5 agama, anole, gecko, skink, teiid 6 dragon, goanna, iguana 7 monitor, reptile, saurian 8 basilisk, mosasaur, slowworm, squamate, whiptail 9 alligator, blindworm, chameleon, crocodile 10 chuckwalla, salamander *combining form:* 4 saur 5 saura, sauro

llama 7 camelid *country:* 4 Peru 7 Bolivia, Ecuador *habitat:* 5 Andes *relative:* 6 alpaca, vicuña 7 guanaco

Lloyd's business 9 insurance

lo 4 ecce, hark, heed, look, mark, mind 6 attend, behold 7 observe

load 3 tax 4 bias, copy, fill, haul, heap, lade, onus, pack, pile, stow, task 5 cargo, laden, swamp, weigh 6 burden, debase, doctor, dope up, eyeful, lading, saddle, weight 7

freight 8 encumber, shipment, transfer 9 liability, millstone, transport 11 consignment, encumbrance

loaded 4 full, high, rich 5 awash, doped 6 aboard, biased, filled, packed, stoned 7 boarded, brimful, crowded, wealthy 8 affluent, brimming, chockful, tripping, turned on 9 chock-full

loaf 3 bum, bun 4 idle, laze, lazy, loll 5 bread, dough 6 dawdle, lounge 7 goof off 8 lollygag 9 bum around, goldbrick 10 fool around

loafer 3 bum 4 shoe, slug 5 idler 6 slouch 7 goof-off, lounger 8 deadbeat, dolittle, fainéant, slugabed, sluggard 9 do-nothing, goldbrick, lazybones 11 beachcomber, lollygagger

loam 4 clay, dirt, sand, silt, soil 7 topsoil *deposit:* 5 loess

loan 3 pay 4 lend 6 credit 7 advance, imprest 9 grubstake *figure:* 3 APR

loan shark 6 lender, usurer 7 Shylock 10 pawnbroker 11 moneylender

loath 6 afraid, averse 8 hesitant 9 reluctant, unwilling 10 indisposed 11 disinclined 12 antipathetic

loathe 4 hate 5 abhor, scorn, spurn 6 detest, refuse, reject 7 despise 8 execrate 9 abominate

loathsome 4 foul, ugly, vile 5 gross, nasty 6 odious 7 beastly, hateful, hideous 8 horrible 9 abhorrent, execrable, obnoxious, offensive, repellent, repugnant, repulsive, revolting 10 abominable, deplorable, detestable, disgusting, nauseating

lob 4 loft, toss 5 chuck, fling, heave, pitch, sling, throw 6 propel

lobby 4 hall 5 foyer 7 promote 8 anteroom, corridor 9 influence, vestibule 10 passageway 11 waiting room

lobe 4 flap 7 pendant

lobo 4 wolf 8 gray wolf 10 timber wolf

lobster 8 crawfish 10 crustacean *claw:* 5 chela 6 pincer *female:* 3 hen *male:* 4 cock *trap:* 3 pot 5 creel

local 6 native 7 endemic, insular, topical 9 parochial 10 provincial

locale 4 area, belt, site, turf, ward 5 place, scene, venue 6 milieu, parish, region, sector 7 commune, quarter, setting 8 district, precinct, vicinage, vicinity 9 community, territory 11 mise-en-scène 12 neighborhood

locality 4 area, belt, city, site, turf, zone 5 block, field, haunt, place, tract 6 county, domain, hamlet, region, sector, sphere, square 7 habitat, section 8 district, environs, precinct, province, purlieus, township, vicinage, vicinity **9** bailiwick, situation, territory **12** neighborhood

localize 4 mass **5** amass, focus **7** cluster, collect **8** coalesce, pinpoint **10** accumulate **11** concentrate, consolidate **12** conglomerate

locate 3 fix, spy **4** espy, find, site, spot **5** dwell, place, trace **6** detect, reside, settle **7** nose out, situate, station, uncover **8** come upon, discover, pinpoint, position **9** establish, ferret out, search out **10** come across

location 4 area, site, post, spot **5** locus, place, point, scene, venue, where **7** bearing, habitat, setting **8** position **9** situation **11** mise-en-scène, whereabouts

loch 3 bay **4** lake

lock 4 bolt, curl, hank, hold, tuft **5** latch, tress **6** fasten, secure **7** ringlet **8** fastener **9** enclosure, fastening

lockjaw 7 tetanus, trismus

lock up 3 ice **4** seal **5** sew up **6** assure, clinch, ensure, ratify, secure, settle **7** confirm **8** complete, conclude, finalize, validate **9** guarantee

lockup 3 jug, pen **4** brig, cell, coop, gaol, jail, stir, tank **5** clink, pokey, pound **6** cooler, prison **7** slammer **8** bastille, hoosegow

loco 3 ape, mad **4** bats, nuts **5** balmy, batty, crazy, kooky, loony, nutty **6** crazed, insane, screwy **7** bananas, berserk, bonkers, cracked, flipped, lunatic **8** demented, deranged, frenzied, unhinged **10** flipped out

locomotive 5 cheer, dolly, train **6** engine *small:* **5** dinky **6** dinkey *type:* **5** steam **6** diesel **8** electric

locum tenens 3 sub **5** proxy **6** backup, fill-in, supply **7** stand-in **9** alternate, auxiliary, surrogate **10** substitute **11** pinch hitter, replacement, succedaneum

locus 3 hub **4** seat, site **5** focus, heart, stage **6** center **7** setting **8** cynosure, location, polestar **10** focal point **11** nerve center **12** headquarters

locust 4 tree, wood **5** carob **6** cicada, insect **11** grasshopper

locution 4 word **5** argot, idiom, lingo **6** jargon, patois, phrase **7** dialect **8** parlance, phrasing **9** utterance **10** expression **11** phraseology

lode 4 seam, vein **5** store **6** source, supply **7** deposit *mother:* **7** bonanza

lodestar 4 guru **5** gauge, guide, ideal, model **6** beacon, leader, mentor **7** epitome **8** exemplar, paradigm **9** archetype, guidepost **11** inspiration

lodestone 6 magnet **9** magnetite

lodge 3 den, fix, inn **4** bunk, camp, club, file, lair, nest, root, stay **5** abide, abode, board, cabin, couch, dwell, embed, guild, hotel, house, motel, order, put up **6** billet, burrow, hostel, league, remain, shanty, tavern, wigwam **7** auberge, contain, cottage, deposit, hospice, quarter, receive, shelter **8** domicile, hostelry, sodality **9** gatehouse **10** fellowship **11** accommodate, brotherhood, caravansary, public house

lodger 5 guest **6** renter, roomer, tenant **7** boarder, resider

lodging 3 inn, pad **4** dorm, room **5** abode, hotel, motel, place **7** shelter **8** chambers, diggings, domicile, dwelling, quarters **9** apartment, residence **10** pied-à-terre **13** accommodation

loess 4 clay, loam, marl **7** deposit

loft 4 rise **5** attic, raise **6** dormer, garret, propel **7** gallery

loftiness 5 pride **6** height **7** disdain, hauteur, stature **8** altitude, eminence **9** aloofness, arrogance, elevation, pomposity, sublimity **11** haughtiness, superiority **13** condescension

lofty 4 airy, epic, high, tall **5** grand, noble, proud **6** aerial, august, raised, remote, superb **7** exalted, haughty, soaring, stately, sublime, utopian **8** arrogant, cavalier, elevated, eloquent, imposing, insolent, majestic, superior, towering **9** ambitious, grandiose, visionary **10** disdainful **11** overbearing, pretentious, skyscraping **12** supercilious

log 5 diary, tally **6** record, timber **7** journal **8** register *cutter:* **8** chain saw *mover:* **5** peavy **6** peavey **7** cant dog

loge 3 box **5** booth, stall **7** balcony **9** mezzanine

logger 9 lumberman **10** lumberjack, woodcutter *legendary:* **10** Paul Bunyan

loggerhead 6 shrike, turtle

loggia 6 arcade **7** balcony, gallery, veranda

logic 6 reason **9** reasoning **10** syntactics *specious:* **7** sophism **9** sophistry

logical 5 sound, valid **6** cogent **8** analytic, sensible **9** deducible, deductive, plausible **10** analytical, compelling, convincing, diagnostic, reasonable, scientific, systematic

logjam 5 crowd **7** impasse **8** blockage, deadlock, stoppage **11** obstruction

logo 5 badge, brand, motto **6** cipher, device, emblem, symbol **8** colophon, hallmark, monogram **9** trademark

logograph 6 puzzle **7** anagram

logroll 4 birl

logy 4 dull, slow **5** dopey, heavy **6** drowsy, groggy, torpid **9** listless, sluggish

Lohengrin *composer:* **6** Wagner (Richard) *father:* **8** Parsifal, Parzival *wife:* **4** Elsa

loincloth 5 dhoti **11** breechcloth, breechclout
Loire city 5 Blois, Tours **6** Nantes **7** Orléans
loiter 3 bum, lag **4** drag, idle, laze, lazy, loaf, loll, poke **5** dally, delay, tarry, trail **6** dawdle, diddle, linger, lounge, put off, putter **8** lollygag **10** dillydally, fool around, hang around **11** screw around **13** procrastinate
Loki *father:* **8** Farbauti *mother:* **3** Nal **6** Laufey *offspring:* **3** Hel **4** Hela **6** Fenris **7** Midgard *slayer:* **8** Heimdall *victim:* **6** Balder, Baldur *wife:* **5** Sigyn **9** Angurboda
Lolita *author:* **7** Nabokov (Vladimir) *suitor:* **7** Humbert (Humbert)
loll 3 bum, lag **4** drag, idle, laze, lazy, loaf, poke **5** chill, dally, delay, droop, slump, tarry, trail **6** dawdle, diddle, linger, lounge, putter, slouch **8** chill out **10** dillydally, fool around, hang around **13** procrastinate
lollapalooza 4 lulu **5** beaut, doozy **6** doozie **8** knockout **9** humdinger
Lollards' leader 8 Wycliffe (John)
lollygag 4 idle, loaf, loll, poke, drag **5** chill **6** dawdle, diddle, loiter, piddle, putter **10** dilly-dally, fool around
Lombard 6 banker **11** moneylender *king:* **5** Cleph **6** Alboin, Audoin **7** Aistulf, Aripert, Authari **9** Liudprand
London *attraction:* **3** Eye **5** Tower *borough:* **5** Brent **6** Barnet, Bexley, Ealing, Harrow, Sutton **7** Barking, Bromley, Chelsea, Croydon, Enfield, Hackney, Lambeth **8** Haringey, Havering, Hounslow, Lewisham **9** Greenwich, Islington, Redbridge **10** Kensington **11** Westminster *cathedral:* **2** St. Paul's *clock:* **6** Big Ben *district:* **4** Soho **5** Acton **7** Chelsea, Mayfair **9** Belgravia, Southwark *gallery:* **4** Tate *gardens:* **3** Kew *policeman:* **5** bobby *prison:* **7** Newgate *river:* **6** Thames *square:* **9** Leicester, Trafalgar *street:* **4** Bond **5** Fleet **6** Strand **7** Downing **9** Whitehall **10** Piccadilly *subway:* **4** tube
London novel 7 Sea Wolf (The) **8** Iron Heel (The) **9** White Fang **10** Martin Eden **13** Call of the Wild (The)
lone 4 only, sole, solo **5** alone **6** single, unique **8** deserted, forsaken, isolated, secluded, separate, singular, solitary **13** unaccompanied
lonely 4 left, lorn **5** alone **7** forlorn **8** deserted, forsaken, homesick, lonesome, rejected, solitary **9** abandoned
loneness 8 solitude **9** isolation **10** detachment **12** separateness, solitariness
loner 6 hermit **7** isolate, outcast, recluse **8** outsider, solitary **13** individualist
Lone Ranger, The *creator:* **7** Striker (Fran) *companion:* **5** Tonto *epithet:* **8** Kemo Sabe

horse: **6** Silver *trademark:* **4** mask **12** silver bullet
Lone Star State 5 Texas
long 3 far, yen **4** ache, itch, pine, tall **5** wordy, yearn **6** hanker, hunger, prolix, thirst **7** endless, lengthy **8** dragging, drawn-out, extended, unending **9** extensive **10** full-length, protracted
long ago 4 yore
long-drawn-out 7 endless, lengthy **8** dragging, unending **10** protracted **12** interminable
Longfellow poem 8 Christus, Hiawatha, Hyperion, Kavanagh **10** Evangeline **11** My Lost Youth, Psalm of Life (A)
long for 4 want **5** covet, crave, mourn **6** desire, repine **8** aspire to
longing 3 yen **4** itch, lust, urge, wish **5** greed **6** desire, hunger, thirst **7** avidity, craving, passion **8** appetite
longshoreman 9 stevedore **10** roustabout
long-suffering 7 patient, stoical **8** enduring, resigned **9** compliant **10** forbearing, submissive **13** accommodating, uncomplaining
long suit 3 bag **4** gift **5** forte **6** métier, talent **8** strength **9** specialty
long-winded 5 wordy **6** prolix **7** diffuse, lengthy, verbose **8** rambling **9** garrulous, redundant **10** loquacious
loo 2 WC **3** lav **4** head, john **5** jakes, privy **6** toilet **7** latrine **8** bathroom, outhouse
look 3 air, eye **4** gape, gawk, gaze, leer, mien, ogle, peek, peep, peer, seem, view **5** glare, stare, watch **6** admire, appear, aspect, behold, expect, eyeful, glance, glower, goggle, regard, squint, survey, visage **7** bearing, examine, eyeball, glimpse, observe **8** demeanor, once-over **10** appearance, rubberneck
look after 4 mind, tend **5** nurse, serve, watch **6** attend, wait on **7** care for, husband **8** wait upon **9** watch over **10** provide for
look-alike 4 twin **5** clone **6** double **7** similar **8** matching **9** duplicate
look at 3 eye, see **4** face, ogle, scan, view **5** check **6** behold, ponder, regard **7** examine, inspect **8** confront, consider **11** investigate
look back 6 recall, review **7** reflect **8** remember **9** reminisce
look down on 5 abhor, scorn, scout, spurn **7** contemn, despise, disdain **8** dominate **9** tower over **10** tower above
looker 6 beauty, eyeful, lovely, vision **7** stunner, witness **8** knockout, ornament **9** bystander, sightseer, spectator **10** eyewitness
looker-on 5 gaper **6** viewer **7** watcher, witness **8** beholder, observer **9** bystander, spectator **10** eyewitness **12** rubbernecker

look for 4 seek **5** await **6** expect, plan on **9** search out **10** anticipate

looking glass 6 mirror **9** reflector

look into 5 check, probe, study **6** pursue, survey **7** examine, explore, inspect **8** check out, question, research **10** scrutinize **11** investigate

look out 4 mind **6** beware

lookout 4 aery, view **5** aerie, guard, scout, tower, vista, watch **6** cupola, picket, sentry **7** spotter **8** panorama, prospect, sentinel, watchman **9** belvedere, crow's nest, firetower **10** watchtower, widow's walk **11** observatory, perspective

look over 3 vet **4** read **5** check **6** review, size up **7** examine, inspect **8** appraise, evaluate

loom 4 brew, bulk, near, rear **5** hover, mount, tower **6** appear, come on, emerge, gather, impend **7** portend **8** approach, overhang, stand out, threaten **9** take shape *part:* **6** heddle **7** harness, shuttle, treadle, trundle

loon 3 nut, oaf **4** bird, clod, dodo, dolt, goof, lout, yo-yo **5** chump, dummy, dunce, ninny, noddy, stupe, yokel **6** dimwit, dum-dum, nitwit **7** airhead, buffoon, dullard, pinhead **8** bonehead, dumbbell, crackpot, imbecile, lunkhead, meathead, numskull **9** birdbrain, blockhead, ignoramus, lamebrain, numbskull, simpleton **10** dunderhead, nincompoop **11** chowderhead, chucklehead

loony 3 nut **4** bats, loco **5** balmy, batty, crazy, daffy, dippy, goofy, nutty, silly, wacky **6** absurd, insane, madman, screwy **7** fatuous, foolish, idiotic **8** demented **9** bedlamite, half-baked, ludicrous, senseless **10** ridiculous **11** harebrained **12** preposterous

loony bin 6 asylum, bedlam **8** bughouse, madhouse, nuthouse **9** funny farm **10** booby hatch, crazy house

loop 3 arc, eye **4** ansa, ring **5** curve, noose, picot **6** circle, eyelet, league, staple **7** circlet, circuit **8** doubling

looped 4 high **5** bowed, drunk, stiff **6** blotto, bombed, curved, juiced, loaded, potted, stewed, tanked, zonked **7** crocked, pickled, pie-eyed, sloshed, smashed **9** plastered **10** inebriated **11** curvilinear, intoxicated

loophole 3 out **6** escape, outlet **7** opening

loopy 4 bats, daft, nuts, wavy **5** arced, batty, bowed, crazy, daffy, dotty, flaky, nutty, silly, snaky, wacky **6** arched, curved, freaky, fruity, screwy, swirly **7** bizarre, idiotic, lunatic, offbeat, sinuous, touched **8** demented **9** eccentric **10** flipped out, off-the-wall, outlandish

loose 3 lax **4** easy, fast, free, lewd, limp **5** baggy, slack, untie, vague **6** flabby, wanton

7 flaccid, relaxed **8** flexible **9** debauched, desultory, dissolute, imprecise **10** disjointed, dissipated, ill-defined, licentious, unattached, unconfined **12** disconnected, unrestrained

loose end 6 detail **8** fragment

loose-lipped see **loquacious**

loosen 4 ease, free, undo **5** relax, slack, untie **6** unbind **7** ease off, manumit, release, slacken, unchain **8** liberate, unbuckle, unfasten **10** emancipate

loosen up 5 relax **6** unbend, unwind **7** ease off, stretch

loot 3 rob **4** haul, lift, pelf, raid, sack, swag **5** boost, booty, dough, lucre, money, moola, reave, rifle, spoil **6** boodle, moolah, ravish, spoils **7** despoil, pillage, plunder, ransack, stick up **9** knock over

looter 5 thief **7** brigand **8** marauder

lop 3 cut **4** chop, clip, crop, snip, trim **5** prune, sever **6** excise **8** amputate, truncate **9** dismember **10** guillotine

lope 3 jog, run **4** gait, romp, trot **5** amble **6** canter

lopsided 4 awry **5** askew **6** aslant, uneven **7** crooked, leaning, tilting **8** top-heavy **10** asymmetric, off-balance, unbalanced **12** asymmetrical **13** unsymmetrical

loquacious 5 gabby, talky, wordy **6** chatty, mouthy, prolix **7** verbose, voluble, yakking **8** babbling **9** garrulous, jabbering, talkative **10** blathering, chattering, long-winded **11** loose-lipped **12** motormouthed

Lorca play 5 Yerma **12** Blood Wedding

lord 3 sir **4** boss, duke, earl, peer **5** noble, ruler **6** master **7** marquis **8** governor, marquess, nobleman, viscount **9** sovereign, tyrannize *feudal:* **5** liege **8** seigneur, suzerain *Muslim:* **6** sayyid

Lord High Executioner 4 Koko

Lord Jim author 6 Conrad (Joseph)

lordly 5 grand, lofty, noble, proud **6** august, uppity **7** exalted, haughty, pompous, stately, swollen **8** affected, arrogant, cavalier, gracious, imposing, insolent, majestic, princely, snobbish, superior **9** dignified, egotistic, grandiose **10** disdainful, highhanded **11** dictatorial, magisterial, magnificent, overbearing, patronizing **12** aristocratic, supercilious **13** authoritarian, high-and-mighty

Lord of the Flies *author:* **7** Golding (William) *character:* **4** Jack **5** Piggy, Ralph

Lord of the Rings *author:* **7** Tolkien (J. R. R.) *book:* **9** Two Towers (The) **15** Return of the King (The) **19** Fellowship of the Ring (The) *character:* **3** Sam **5** Arwen, Frodo, Gimli **6**

Elrond, Gollum, Sauron 7 Aragorn, Baggins (Bilbo, Frodo), Boromir, Gandalf, Legolas, Saruman, Théoden 9 Galadriel, Treebeard *film director:* 7 Jackson (Peter) *illustrator:* 3 Lee (Alan) 4 Howe (John) *race:* 4 ents, orcs 5 wargs 6 huorns 7 hobbits 11 ringwraiths *realm:* 5 Arnor, Moria, Rohan 6 Gondor, Mordor 10 Lothlórien 11 Middle-earth 12 Undying Lands *site:* 5 Shire (The) 8 Isengard 9 Mount Doom, Rivendell *star:* 3 Lee (Christopher) 4 Hill (Bernard), Holm (Ian), Wood (Elijah) 5 Astin (Sean), Baker (Sala), Bloom (Orlando), Tyler (Liv) 6 Serkis (Andy) 7 Weaving (Hugo) 8 McKellen (Ian), Monaghan (Dominic) 9 Blanchett (Cate), Mortensen (Viggo) *sword:* 5 Sting 6 Narsil 7 Andúril 9 Glamdring

Lord's Prayer 9 Our Father 11 Paternoster

lore 6 mythos, wisdom 7 history 8 folkways, learning 9 knowledge, mythology, tradition 11 information 12 superstition

Lorelei 5 siren 9 temptress 10 seductress 11 femme fatale *poet:* 5 Heine (Heinrich) *river:* 5 Rhein, Rhine *victim:* 6 sailor 7 mariner

lorgnette 10 eyeglasses, spectacles 12 opera glasses

Lorna Doone *author:* 9 Blackmore (Richard) *hero:* 4 Ridd (John)

____ **Lorraine** 6 Alsace

lorry 3 rig, van 4 semi 5 truck

lose 4 miss, shed 5 evade, shake, waste, yield 6 escape, give up, mislay 7 destroy, forfeit, succumb 8 misplace, shake off, throw off 9 sacrifice, surrender

lose it 5 go ape 7 crack up, flip out, go crazy, run amok 8 freak out, run amuck

loser 3 dud 4 bomb, bust, flop 5 lemon 6 bummer, fiasco, misfit, turkey 7 also-ran, debacle, failure, washout 8 deadbeat 11 incompetent

loss 4 bath, harm, ruin 5 waste 6 damage, defeat, injury 7 deficit, failure, forfeit 8 casualty, decrease, fatality 9 depletion, privation, sacrifice, shrinkage 10 divestment, forfeiture, misfortune, misplacing 11 bereavement, deprivation, destruction

lost 4 asea, dead, gone, rapt 6 absent, astray, bygone, damned, doomed, futile, hidden, wasted 7 defunct, faraway, lacking, mislaid, missing 8 absorbed, departed, distrait, helpless, hopeless, vanished 9 condemned, desperate, destroyed 10 abstracted, insensible, overlooked 11 irrevocable, preoccupied 12 irredeemable, unregenerate

Lost Horizon *author:* 6 Hilton (James) *character:* 6 Conway (Hugh) *land:* 9 Shangri-La

lot 3 cut, ilk 4 doom, fate, heap, kind, mass, plat, yard 5 batch, block, bunch, field, moira, patch, quota, share, slice, tract, weird 6 assign, barrel, bundle, parcel, stripe 7 acreage, cluster, destiny, fortune, mete out, portion, species 8 allocate, clearing, frontage 9 aggregate, allowance, apportion

Lot *father:* 5 Haran *sister:* 5 Iscah 6 Milcah *son:* 4 Moab 5 Ammon *uncle:* 7 Abraham

lothario 4 lech, stud, wolf 5 letch, Romeo 6 lecher, tomcat 7 amorist, Don Juan, gallant, seducer 8 Casanova, paramour 9 debaucher, ladies' man, womanizer 10 lady-killer 11 philanderer

lotion 3 oil 4 balm 5 cream, salve 6 cerate 7 unguent 8 ablution, cosmetic, lenitive, liniment, ointment 9 demulcent 11 embrocation

lottery 6 raffle 7 drawing 11 sweepstakes

lotus-eater 7 dreamer 8 escapist, romantic 10 daydreamer 13 castle-builder

loud 5 forte, gaudy, noisy, showy 6 brassy, brazen, flashy, garish, glitzy, tawdry, vulgar 7 blaring, blatant, booming, chintzy, glaring, pealing, raucous, roaring 8 piercing, resonant, sonorous, strident 9 clamorous, deafening, obnoxious, obtrusive, offensive, tasteless 10 bigmouthed, boisterous, flamboyant, fortissimo, resounding, stentorian, thunderous, vociferous 12 earsplitting

loudmouth 6 ranter 7 stentor 8 blowhard, braggart 9 blusterer

loudspeaker 3 amp 6 Tannoy, woofer 7 tweeter 9 amplifier

Louisiana *capital:* 10 Baton Rouge *city:* 10 New Orleans, Shreveport *college, university:* 6 Tulane *county:* 6 parish *lake:* 13 Pontchartrain *nickname:* 7 Pelican (State) *river:* 11 Mississippi *state bird:* 12 brown pelican *state flower:* 8 magnolia *state tree:* 11 bald cypress

lounge 3 bar, bum, lie, pub, tap 4 idle, laze, loaf, loll, sofa 5 couch, dally, drift, lobby, relax 6 dawdle, loiter, parlor, repose, saloon 7 barroom, goof off, lie down, recline, taproom 8 restroom, kill time 10 living room

lounge lizard 3 fop 4 rake, toff 5 blade, dandy, leech 6 gigolo, sponge 9 ladies' man

Lourdes saint 10 Bernadette

louse 3 cad, cur, dog, rat 4 toad 5 aphid, creep, skunk, snake 6 cootie, psylla, rotter, slater, wretch 7 bounder, stinker *egg:* 3 nit

louse up 4 blow, flub, muff, ruin 5 botch, spoil, wreck 6 bobble, bollix, bumble, bungle, fumble

lousy 3 ill 4 poor, rife 5 awful 6 crummy, shoddy, rotten 7 replete, teeming 8 crawling, horrible, inferior, infested, terrible **9** miserable, repulsive **10** despicable **12** contemptible

lout 3 oaf **4** boob, boor, dolt, gawk, hick, rube **5** brute, chuff, churl, klutz, looby, scorn, yahoo, yokel **6** galoot, lubber, lummox, rustic **7** bumpkin, hayseed, palooka **9** simpleton **10** clodhopper

Louvre masterpiece 8 Mona Lisa **11** Venus de Milo

lovable 4 dear **5** sweet **6** cuddly **7** winning, winsome **8** adorable **9** appealing, endearing **11** embraceable

love 4 zeal **5** adore, ardor, crush, Cupid, prize, value **6** desire, dote on, fervor, revere **7** adulate, cherish, idolize, passion, romance, worship **8** devotion, fondness, idolatry, treasure, venerate, yearning **9** adoration, adulation, delight in **10** attachment **11** amorousness, infatuation *combining form:* **4** phil **5** philo, phily **6** philia *French:* **5** amour *Italian:* **5** amore *tennis:* **3** nil **4** zero **7** nothing

love apple 6 tomato

lovebird 6 budgie, parrot **10** budgerigar

love-bite 3 nip **6** hickey

love feast 5 agape

love god 4 Amor, Eros, Kama **5** Bhaga, Cupid

love goddess 5 Athor, Freya, Venus **6** Hathor, Inanna, Ishtar **7** Astarte **9** Aphrodite, Ashtoreth

love letter 8 mash note **9** valentine **10** billet-doux

lovely 4 fair **5** sweet, swell **6** comely, dainty, pretty **7** elegant **8** adorable, alluring, charming, delicate, engaging, graceful, knockout **9** beauteous, beautiful, exquisite **10** attractive, delightful, enchanting, entrancing **11** captivating, good-looking

love potion 7 philter, philtre **11** aphrodisiac

lover 3 fan **4** beau, buff **5** flame, leman, Romeo, swain **6** addict, steady, suitor, votary **7** amorist, darling, devotee, Don Juan, gallant, habitué, squeeze **8** fancy man, lothario, mistress, paramour **9** boyfriend, inamorata, inamorato **10** aficionado, girlfriend, sweetheart

lovey-dovey 5 mushy **6** doting **7** amorous **12** affectionate

loving 4 dear, fond **6** ardent, erotic, tender **7** amatory, amorous, cordial, devoted, fervent **8** attached, enamored, faithful **10** benevolent, infatuated, passionate, solicitous **11** impassioned **12** affectionate

low 3 moo **4** base, blue, dead, deep, flat, mean, neap **5** cheap **6** abject, ailing, humble, hushed, lesser, nether, poorly, sickly,

sordid, unwell **7** cut-rate, reduced, scrubby **8** cast down, dejected, depleted, downcast, inferior, mediocre, wretched **9** declining, depressed, miserable, subnormal, woebegone **10** inadequate, indisposed **11** crestfallen, downhearted, unfavorable

lowbred 4 base, rude **6** coarse, oafish, vulgar **7** boorish, brutish, loutish, uncouth **8** churlish, cloddish, lubberly **11** uncivilized

low-cost 5 cheap **6** budget, cheapo **7** bargain, cut-rate **10** affordable, reasonable **11** inexpensive

low-down 4 base, mean, ugly, vile **6** grubby, odious, scurvy, sleazy, sordid **7** ignoble, squalid **8** shameful, wretched **9** abhorrent, worthless **10** despicable, disgusting **11** ignominious **12** contemptible

lowdown 4 dope, info **5** facts, goods, scoop, specs **6** skinny **8** briefing **11** information

lower 3 cut **4** clip, drop, fall, sink **5** frown, gloom, scowl, shave, slash, under **6** debase, demean, demote, humble, lesser, menace, nether, reduce **7** cut down, deflate, degrade, demerit, depress, descend, devalue, let down **8** inferior, mark down, overcast, submerge, threaten **9** devaluate, downgrade *prefix:* **5** infra

Lower Depths author 5 Gorki, Gorky (Maksim, Maxim)

lowest point 5 nadir *in the U.S.:* **11** Death Valley *on earth's crust:* **13** Mariana Trench *on earth's surface:* **7** Dead Sea

low-grade 4 hack **5** junky, lousy **6** cheesy, cruddy, shabby, shoddy, sleazy, tawdry **8** below par, déclassé, inferior, mediocre **9** deficient **10** second-rate **11** second-class, substandard **12** second-drawer

low-key 4 soft **5** muted, quiet **7** relaxed, subdued **8** laid-back, softened, tasteful **9** easygoing, minimized, temperate, toned down **10** played down, restrained **11** understated

lowland 4 flat, sump, vale **5** basin **6** bottom, slough, valley **7** bottoms *Scottish:* **6** lallan **7** lalland

lowlife 4 fink, heel **5** knave, rogue **6** no-good, outlaw, rascal, wretch **7** hoodlum, ruffian, villain **9** miscreant, reprobate, scoundrel **10** blackguard, black sheep, sleazeball **11** rapscallion, slimebucket **12** bottom-feeder

lowly 4 base, mean, meek **6** abject, humble, menial, modest **7** ignoble, mundane, obscure, prosaic, servile **8** baseborn, plebeian, unwashed

low-pressure 4 calm **6** casual, dégagé, folksy, mellow **7** relaxed **8** flexible, informal, laidback **9** easygoing **10** nonchalant

low-spirited 3 sad **4** blue, down, glum **6** abject, droopy, gloomy, morose **7** doleful **8** cast down, dejected, downcast, saddened **9** bummed out, cheerless, depressed, woebegone **10** dispirited, melancholy **11** discouraged, downhearted **12** disheartened, heavyhearted

low tide 3 ebb **4** neap

loyal 4 firm, true **5** liege **6** ardent, trusty **7** devoted, dutiful, staunch **8** constant, faithful, resolute, true-blue **9** allegiant, steadfast, unfailing **10** dependable **11** trustworthy

loyalist 4 Tory **7** patriot **8** partisan **10** countryman **11** nationalist

loyalty 6 fealty **8** adhesion, devotion, fidelity **9** adherence, constancy **10** allegiance, attachment, dedication **11** staunchness **12** faithfulness **13** dependability, steadfastness

lozenge 4 pill **6** troche **7** diamond, rhombus **8** pastille

LSD 4 acid *user:* **8** acidhead

lubricate 3 oil **6** grease, smooth **7** moisten

lubricious 4 lewd, oily **5** slick **6** carnal, greasy, slippy, wanton **8** prurient, slippery, slithery, ticklish **9** lecherous, salacious **10** lascivious, libidinous **12** concupiscent

lucent 5 clear **6** bright, limpid **7** beaming, crystal, glowing, lambent, radiant, shining **8** clear-cut, luminous, pellucid **9** brilliant, effulgent, refulgent **11** unambiguous

Lucia di Lammermoor *character:* **7** Edgardo *composer:* **9** Donizetti (Gaetano) *novelist:* **5** Scott (Walter)

lucid 4 sane **5** clear **6** bright, limpid **7** crystal, lambent, radiant **8** clear-cut, knowable, luminous **9** brilliant, effulgent, graspable, refulgent, unblurred **10** articulate, fathomable **11** translucent, transparent, unambiguous **12** compos mentis, incandescent, intelligible, transpicuous

lucidity 6 acumen, sanity **7** clarity **8** sagacity, saneness **9** clearness, plainness, soundness **10** cognizance, perception **12** clairvoyance

Lucifer 5 devil, fiend, Satan, Venus **7** Old Nick **8** Apollyon **9** archfiend, Beelzebub **10** Old Scratch **13** Old Gooseberry

Lucinde *beloved:* **7** Leandre **9** Clitandre *father:* **7** Geronte **10** Sganarelle

luck 3 hap, hit **4** juju, meet **5** fluke, light **6** chance, happen, hazard, kismet **7** fortune, godsend, stumble **8** fortuity, occasion, windfall **9** advantage **11** opportunity *token:* **5** charm **6** amulet, clover, fetish, mascot **8** talisman **9** horseshoe **11** rabbit's foot

luckless 7 adverse, hapless, unhappy **8** illfated, untoward, wretched **9** miserable **10** ill-starred **11** star-crossed, unfavorable, unfortunate **12** misfortunate, unpropitious

lucky 6 golden, timely **7** favored **9** favorable, fortunate **10** auspicious, beneficial, felicitous, fortuitous, propitious **12** advantageous, providential **13** serendipitous *Scottish:* **5** canny

Lucky Jim author 4 Amis (Kingsley)

lucrative 6 paying **7** gainful **8** fruitful **10** high-income, productive, profitable, well-paying, worthwhile **11** moneymaking **12** advantageous, remunerative

lucre 3 pay **4** cash, gain, jack, loot, pelf, swag **5** booty, dough, green, money, moola **6** boodle, dinero, do-re-mi, moolah, profit, wampum **7** cabbage, revenue **9** long green **10** greenbacks

Lucrezia _____ 6 Borgia

Lucy's husband 4 Desi **5** Arnaz (Desi)

ludicrous 4 zany **5** antic, comic, droll, funny, goofy, nutty, silly **6** absurd **7** amusing, bizarre, comical, foolish, risible **8** farcical **9** fantastic, grotesque, laughable **10** off-the-wall, outlandish, ridiculous **11** incongruous **12** preposterous

Ludlum novel 14 Bourne Identity (The) **15** Bourne Supremacy (The) **16** Holcroft Covenant (The)

lug 3 nut, oaf, tow, tug **4** bear, buck, drag, draw, haul, hump, jerk, pull, tote **5** carry, ferry, shlep **6** convey, schlep **7** bruiser, schlepp **9** transport

luggage 4 bags, gear **7** baggage

lugubrious 3 sad **4** blue, dour, down, glum **5** bleak **6** dismal, dreary, gloomy, morose, rueful, somber, sullen, woeful **7** doleful, joyless **8** cast down, dejected, dolesome, downcast, mournful **9** cheerless, depressed, plaintive, saturnine, sorrowful, woebegone **10** depressing, despondent, lamentable, melancholy, oppressive **11** discouraged, dispiriting, downhearted **12** disconsolate

lukewarm 5 blasé, tepid **7** dubious, offhand **8** hesitant **9** uncertain, undecided **10** wishy-washy **11** halfhearted, indifferent

lull 3 ebb **4** balm, calm, hush, wane **5** letup, pause, quiet, still **6** becalm, pacify, soothe, temper **7** compose, decline, ease off, slacken **8** abeyance, interval **9** stillness **10** quiescence **11** tranquilize

lullaby 8 berceuse **10** cradlesong

lulu 3 ace, gem, pip **5** beaut, dandy, dilly, doozy, dream, honey **6** doozie, wonder **7** delight **8** jim-dandy, knockout **9** humdinger, sensation

lumber 3 tax **4** clog, lade, load, logs, plod, slog, wood **5** barge, clump, stump, weigh **6** burden, charge, rumble, saddle, timber, trudge **8** encumber

lumberjack see **logger**
luminance 10 brightness
luminary 3 sun, VIP 4 lion, name, star 5 celeb, light, nabob 6 leader, worthy 7 big name, notable 8 big-timer, eminence, somebody 9 celebrity, dignitary, superstar 10 notability 12 leading light
luminous 5 clear, lucid 6 bright, lucent 7 beaming, crystal, fulgent, lambent, radiant, shining 8 clear-cut, lustrous, pellucid 9 brilliant, effulgent, refulgent 11 illustrious, translucent, transparent 12 enlightening, incandescent
lummox 3 oaf 4 boor, clod, gawk, goon, hulk, lout 5 klutz, looby 6 lubber 7 palooka
lump 3 gob, lot, oaf, wad 4 blob, bulk, chip, clod, gawk, glob, heap, hunk, lout, mass, pile, welt 5 abide, batch, block, brook, bulge, bunch, chunk, hunch, klutz, knurl, looby, piece, scrap, stand, tumor 6 digest, endure, entire, lubber, morsel, nugget 7 handful, palooka, portion, stomach, swallow 8 swelling, totality 9 aggregate 10 protrusion, tumescence 12 protuberance
lumpy 5 crude, gawky, rough 6 choppy, clumsy, coarse, oafish 8 clumpish, unformed 9 roughhewn
lunacy 5 folly, mania 6 idiocy 7 fatuity, foolery, inanity, madness 8 delirium, dementia, insanity 9 absurdity, craziness, silliness, stupidity 10 imbecility 11 derangement, foolishness 13 senselessness
lunar *dark area:* 4 mare 5 maria (plural) *valley:* 4 rill 5 rille
lunatic 3 mad, nut 4 bats, daft, kook, loco, yo-yo, zany 5 balmy, batty, crank, crazy, nutty, raver, wacko, wacky 6 absurd, crazed, cuckoo, insane, madman, maniac, nitwit, psycho, screwy 7 bonkers, cracked, foolish 8 crackpot, demented, demoniac, deranged, frenzied, maniacal, paranoid, schizoid, unhinged 9 bedlamite, ding-a-ling, fruitcake, harebrain, screwball 10 crackbrain 11 nonsensical
lunch 3 eat 4 meal, nosh 5 snack
luncheonette 4 café 5 diner 6 bistro, eatery 7 beanery, canteen, tearoom 8 snack bar 9 cafeteria 10 coffee shop, restaurant 11 greasy spoon
lune 3 bow 5 curve 6 sickle 8 crescent, meniscus
lung *combining form:* 5 pneum, pulmo 6 pneumo, pulmon *disease:* 9 emphysema, pneumonia 10 byssinosis 12 tuberculosis
lunge 3 jab 4 dash, dive, stab 5 bound, drive, pitch, surge 6 charge, plunge, pounce, thrust
lunkhead 3 oaf 4 boob, clod, dodo, dolt,

goof, yo-yo 5 booby, chump, dummy, dunce, idiot, moron, ninny, noddy, stupe 6 dimwit, dum-dum, nitwit 7 dullard 8 dumbbell, imbecile, numskull 9 birdbrain, ignoramus, lamebrain, numbskull, simpleton 10 nincompoop
lupine 5 feral 6 brutal, fierce 7 wolfish 8 ravening 9 predatory, rapacious 10 bluebonnet, sanguinary
lurch 3 bob, yaw 4 jerk, lean, list, reel, rock, roll, sway, tilt, toss 5 heave, pitch, slide, swing 6 bumble, careen, falter, plunge, seesaw, swerve, teeter, totter 7 blunder, stagger, stumble 8 flounder
lure 3 bag 4 bait, call, draw, fake, hook, pull, rope, toll, trap, wile 5 blind, catch, charm, decoy, snare, tempt, trick 6 appeal, cajole, come-on, draw in, draw on, entice, entrap, invite, lead on, seduce 7 attract, beguile, bewitch, capture, con game, enchant, ensnare, gimmick, wheedle 8 blandish, delusion, illusion, inveigle 9 captivate, fascinate, incentive, seduction, siren song 10 attraction, camouflage, enticement, inducement, seducement, temptation *fishing:* 3 fly 4 worm 5 spoon 6 minnow 8 bucktail
lurid 4 ashy, gory, gray, grim, pale 5 ashen, fiery, gross, livid, waxen 6 grisly, malign, sultry 7 baleful, ghastly, graphic, hideous, macabre, malefic, tabloid 8 blanched, gruesome, horrible, shocking, sinister, terrible 9 colorless 10 horrifying, maleficent, terrifying 11 sensational 12 melodramatic
Lurie *novel* 14 Foreign Affairs 18 War Between the Tates (The)
lurk 4 hide, slip 5 creep, prowl, skulk, slide, slink, sneak, snoop, steal 9 pussyfoot
luscious 4 rich, sexy 5 sapid, sweet, tasty, yummy 6 delish, divine, ornate, savory 7 opulent, piquant, sensual 8 sensuous 9 ambrosial, epicurean, exquisite, flavorful, luxurious, seductive, sumptuous, toothsome 10 delectable, delightful, flamboyant, flavorsome, voluptuous 11 scrumptious 13 mouth-watering
lush 3 sot 4 rank, rich, wino 5 dense, drink, drunk, yummy 6 bibber, boozer, deluxe, lavish, savory 7 fertile, opulent, profuse, sensual, teeming, tippler 8 abundant, drunkard, palatial, prodigal, sensuous, thriving 9 ambrosial, epicurean, exuberant, inebriate, luxuriant, luxurious, plentiful, sumptuous, toothsome 10 boozehound, delectable, delightful, profitable, prosperous, voluptuous 11 extravagant, flourishing
Lusitania 8 Portugal
lust 3 rut, yen 4 ache, itch, pine, urge, wish,

zeal, zest **5** ardor, crave, drive, greed, letch, yearn **6** desire, fervor, hanker, hunger, libido **7** avidity, craving, lechery, longing, passion **8** appetite, coveting, cupidity, lewdness, priapism, salacity, satyrism, yearning **9** carnality, eagerness, eroticism, lubricity, prurience, pruriency **10** enthusiasm, excitement, satyriasis, wantonness **11** nymphomania **13** concupiscence, lecherousness, salaciousness

luster 4 glow **5** glaze, gleam, glint, gloss, sheen, shine **6** polish **7** burnish, shimmer **8** lambency, radiance **9** afterglow **10** brightness, brilliance, brilliancy, effulgence, luminosity, refulgence **11** candescence, iridescence

lusterless 3 dim, wan **4** blah, drab, dull, flat, gray, matt **5** brown, dingy, dusky, faded, matte, muddy, muted, vapid **6** boring **10** uninspired

lustful 3 hot **4** lewd **5** bawdy, horny **6** carnal, erotic, wanton **7** burning, goatish, itching, ruttish, satyric **8** prurient **9** debauched, lecherous, libertine, lickerish, salacious **10** hot-blooded, lascivious, libidinous, licentious, lubricious, passionate **12** concupiscent

lustrate 5 purge **6** purify **7** cleanse

lustration 6 ritual **8** ablution **9** catharsis, cleansing, purgation **10** sprinkling **12** purification

lustrous 4 naïf **5** nitid, shiny **6** bright, gleamy, glossy, pearly, sheeny **7** fulgent, glowing, lambent, radiant, shining **8** gleaming, luminous, polished, splendid **9** brilliant, burnished, effulgent, refulgent **10** glimmering, glistening **11** resplendent **12** incandescent

lusty 4 hale **5** hardy, vital **6** brawny, hearty, mighty, potent, robust, strong, virile **7** dynamic, healthy, rousing **8** vigorous **9** energetic, strapping, strenuous **10** prodigious, red-blooded **12** enthusiastic

lute 4 clay, seal **5** grout **6** cement **7** bandora **8** mandolin **10** chitarrone, instrument *Arabic:* **3** oud *Indian:* **5** sitar *Japanese:* **4** biwa **7** samisen **8** shamisen *Oriental:* **3** tar *two-necked:* **7** theorbo

lutenist 5 Bream (Julian) **7** Dowland (John) **8** Gaultier (Denis)

Lutetia 5 Paris

Luxembourg *capital:* **10** Luxembourg *monetary unit:* **4** euro *monetary unit, former:* **5** franc *mountain range:* **8** Ardennes *neighbor:* **6** France **7** Belgium, Germany *river:* **4** Sûre **7** Alzette

luxuriant 4 lush, rank, rich **5** dense **6** fecund, lavish **7** copious, fertile, opulent, profuse, rampant, riotous, teeming **8** abundant, fruitful, luscious, prodigal, prolific **9** excessive, exuberant, sumptuous

luxuriate 4 bask **5** bloom, enjoy, feast, revel **6** abound, relish, thrive, wallow **7** delight, indulge **8** flourish

luxurious 4 lush, posh, rich **5** fancy, grand, plush, ritzy, showy **6** costly, deluxe, lavish, plushy **7** opulent, sensual, stately **8** imposing, majestic, palatial, splendid **9** elaborate, epicurean, expensive, grandiose, sumptuous **10** impressive **11** extravagant, magnificent *situation:* **7** fat city **10** bed of roses, easy street

luxury 5 frill, treat **6** dainty **7** amenity, comfort **8** delicacy, opulence **9** abundance, affluence **10** indulgence **11** superfluity **12** extravagance

lycée 6 school **10** high school

lyceum 4 hall **6** school **7** academy, chamber **9** institute

Lycidas *author* **6** Milton (John)

Lycomedes *daughter:* **8** Deidamia *victim:* **7** Theseus

Lycus *brother:* **7** Nycteus *father:* **7** Pandion *slayer:* **6** Zethus **7** Amphion *wife:* **5** Dirce

Lydian *king:* **5** Gyges **7** Croesus **8** Alyattes *queen:* **7** Omphale

lye 7 caustic **9** hydroxide

lynch 4 hang **5** scrag **6** gibbet, murder **7** execute **8** string up

Lynette see **Line**

lynx 4 puma **6** bobcat, cougar **7** caracal, wildcat **9** catamount

Lyra *star* **4** Vega

lyre 4 harp

lyric 3 ode **4** odic, poem **5** melic, verse **6** poetic **7** melodic, musical **8** operatic **9** exuberant, rhapsodic

lyrical 7 lilting, melodic, musical, songful, tuneful **8** operatic **9** melodious

lyricist 4 poet **10** librettist see **songwriter**

Lysander's *beloved* **6** Hermia

M

Maacah *father:* 5 Nahor 6 Talmai 7 Absalom
  husband: 5 David 6 Jehiel, Machir 8 Rehoboam *son:* 5 Hanan 6 Abijam, Achish 7 Absalom 10 Shephatiah
macabre 4 grim 5 lurid 6 grisly, horrid, morbid 7 deathly, ghastly, hideous 8 ghoulish,
  gruesome, horrible 9 deathlike 10 horrifying
macadam 3 tar 7 asphalt, roadway 8 pavement
macaque 6 monkey, rhesus
macaroni 3 fop 4 beau, buck, dude, toff 5
  dandy, pasta, swell 7 coxcomb, gallant
macaw 3 Ara 6 parrot
Macbeth *character:* 4 Ross 5 Angus 6
  Hecate, Lennox 7 Fleance *slayer:* 7
  Macduff *successor:* 7 Malcolm *title:* 5
  thane *victim:* 6 Banquo, Duncan
mace 4 club 5 baton, staff 6 cudgel, nutmeg 8
  bludgeon
Macedonia *capital:* 6 Skopje *city:* 6 Tetovo
  monetary unit: 5 denar *neighbor:* 6 Greece,
  Serbia 7 Albania 8 Bulgaria *part of:* 7 Balkans *peninsula:* 6 Balkan
macerate 3 ret 4 soak 5 steep 6 drench,
  soften 7 immerse, suffuse 8 saturate
machete 4 bolo 5 knife 6 scythe
Machiavellian 4 wily 6 shrewd 7 cunning, devious 8 guileful, scheming 9 conniving, deceitful, insidious 10 conspiring 11
  duplicitous, treacherous 12 unscrupulous
Machiavelli *work* 6 Prince (The) 8 Mandrake
  (The) 10 Mandragola (La)
machinate 4 plot 6 scheme 7 connive, finagle
  8 conspire, intrigue, maneuver
machination 4 plot, ploy, ruse 5 cabal, dodge
  6 gambit, scheme 8 artifice, intrigue, maneuver, scheming, trickery 9 chicanery, collusion, deception, dirty work, expedient,
  stratagem 10 hanky-panky, subterfuge 11
  contrivance, skulduggery 12 gamesman-
  ship, skullduggery
machine 6 device, engine, gadget 9 apparatus, appliance, automaton 11 contraption
  part: 3 cam 4 gear 5 lever, shaft, valve 6
  caster, flange, router, switch 7 bearing
machine-gun 4 rake 6 strafe 8 enfilade 9
  rapid-fire

machine-gun *inventor* 7 Gatling (Richard)
machinery 5 works 9 apparatus, equipment,
  mechanism
machismo 7 swagger 8 virility 9 manliness
  11 masculinity
macho 4 stud 5 he-man, manly 6 virile 9
  masculine
Machu Picchu *resident* 4 Inca
mackinaw 4 coat 5 cover, trout 7 blanket
mackintosh 7 slicker 8 raincoat
macrocosm 5 world 6 cosmos 8 creation,
  universe
mad 4 daft, nuts, rash, sore, wild 5 angry,
  crazy, irate, irked, kooky, livid, loony,
  loopy, nutty, rabid, upset, wacky 6 absurd,
  crazed, cuckoo, heated, insane, ireful,
  screwy 7 berserk, bonkers, cracked, enraged, foolish, frantic, furious, lunatic 8
  choleric, demented, deranged, frenetic,
  frenzied, incensed, offended, outraged,
  seething, unhinged, worked up, wrathful 9
  delirious, fanatical, fantastic, hilarious, illogical, senseless 10 distracted, infuriated,
  irrational, unbalanced
Madagascar *capital:* 10 Tananarive 12 Antananarivo *channel:* 10 Mozambique *city:* 9
  Mahajanga, Toamasina *language:* 6 French
  8 Malagasy *monetary unit:* 6 ariary *mountain range:* 9 Ankaratra
madame 4 Mrs. 4 wife 6 milady, missus *German:* 4 Frau *Spanish:* 3 Sra. 6 Señora
Madame Bovary *author:* 8 Flaubert
  (Gustave) *character:* 4 Emma (Bovary) 7
  Charles (Bovary) 8 Rodolphe
Madame Butterfly *character:* 9 Cho-Cho-
  San, Cio-Cio-San, Pinkerton, Sharpless
  composer: 7 Puccini (Giacomo)
madcap 4 rash, wild, zany 5 antic 7 foolish 8
  reckless 9 frivolous, hotheaded 10 capricious, incautious
Mad Cavalier 6 Rupert (Prince)
madden 3 ire, vex 4 goad 5 anger, craze 6 enrage 7 derange, incense, inflame, outrage,
  possess, steam up, unhinge 9 infuriate, unbalance
Madeira Islands *capital:* 7 Funchal *export:* 4
  wine *part of:* 8 Portugal

mademoiselle 4 girl, Miss **6** maiden **9** governess **10** yellowtail **11** silver perch

made-to-order 6 custom **7** bespoke **10** customized **11** custom-built

made-up 5 bogus, faked, false, phony **6** phoney **7** painted **8** invented, mythical, specious **9** fictional, imaginary, pretended, trumped-up **10** apocryphal, fabricated, fictitious **11** make-believe **12** cosmeticized

madhouse 6 asylum, bedlam **8** loony bin **9** funny farm **10** booby hatch

madman 3 nut **4** kook, loon **5** loony, raver **6** cuckoo, maniac, psycho **7** lunatic, nutcase **9** bedlamite, psychotic, fruitcake

madness 4 rage **5** folly **6** lunacy **8** insanity **9** psychosis **11** derangement

Madonna initials 3 BVM

Madras 9 Tamil Nadu *founder:* **3** Day (Francis)

Madrid museum 5 Prado

madrigal 4 glee, poem, song **8** part-song

madrigalist *English:* 4 Byrd (William) **6** Morley (Thomas), Wilbye (John) **7** Tomkins (Thomas), Weelkes (Thomas) *Flemish:* **8** Willaert (Adriaan) *Italian:* **5** Lasso (Orlando di) **6** Lassus (Orlandus) **8** Marenzio (Luca) **10** Monteverdi (Claudio)

maelstrom 4 eddy **5** whirl, whorl **6** vortex **7** turmoil **9** whirlpool

maenad 9 bacchante, priestess *cry:* **4** evoe

maestro see **conductor**

Mafia 3 mob **4** ring **6** clique **7** rackets **8** gangland **9** Black Hand, syndicate **10** Cosa Nostra, underworld *code:* **6** omertà

mafioso 4 capo, goon **6** hit man **7** goombah, made man, mobster **8** gangster **9** racketeer

magazine 4 dump **5** cache, depot, organ, store **6** armory, digest, review, weekly **7** arsenal, gazette, journal, monthly **8** biweekly **9** bimonthly, quarterly, warehouse **10** depository, periodical, repository, storehouse **11** publication *type:* **3** box, pan **4** drum, news, tube **5** humor, trade **6** glossy, little, rotary **7** popular **8** literary

mage 6 priest **8** magician, sorcerer

maggot 3 bee **4** grub, whim **5** fancy, larva **6** megrim, vagary **7** caprice, conceit

Magi 6 Caspar, Gaspar **8** Melchior **9** Balthasar, Balthazar *gift:* **4** gold **5** myrrh **7** incense **12** frankincense

magic 4 juju **5** obeah, wicca **6** hoodoo, voodoo **7** alchemy, devilry, sorcery **8** satanism, witchery, witching, wizardry **9** conjuring, diablerie, diabolism, occultism, sortilege **10** hocus-pocus, mumbo jumbo, necromancy, witchcraft **11** abracadabra, bewitchment, enchantment, legerdemain, thaumaturgy

magical 5 runic **6** occult **8** wizardly **10** bewitching, entrancing **11** necromantic **12** thaumaturgic *expression:* **6** presto, shazam **8** alakazam **11** abracadabra

Magic Flute composer 6 Mozart (Wolfgang Amadeus)

magician 5 brujo, witch **6** shaman, wizard **7** Houdini, warlock **8** conjurer, satanist, sorcerer **9** diabolist, enchanter, trickster, voodooist **11** medicine man, necromancer, thaumaturge *Arthurian:* **6** Merlin *Shakespearean:* **8** Prospero *stage:* **5** Randi (James) **11** Copperfield (David), illusionist *Tolkien's:* **7** Gandalf

Magic Mountain, The *author:* 4 Mann (Thomas) *character:* **7** Castorp (Hans)

magisterial 6 lordly **7** pompous **8** dogmatic **9** imperious, masterful **10** high-handed **11** doctrinaire, domineering, overbearing **13** authoritative, self-important

Magister Ludi author 5 Hesse (Hermann)

magistrate 5 court, judge **7** bencher, justice **8** official *ancient Greek:* **5** ephor **6** archon *ancient Roman:* **6** aedile **7** duumvir, praetor, questor **8** quaestor *Italian:* **4** doge **7** podesta *Scottish:* **6** bailie

Magna Carta *king:* 4 John *place signed:* **9** Runnymede

magnanimous 5 noble **7** liberal **8** generous, princely **9** forgiving, unselfish **10** benevolent, bighearted, charitable, chivalrous, high-minded, munificent

magnate 5 baron, mogul, nabob **6** fat cat, prince, tycoon **9** personage, plutocrat

magnesium symbol 2 Mg

magnet 9 lodestone **10** attraction

magnetic 8 alluring **9** appealing, seductive **10** attractive **11** captivating, charismatic, fascinating **12** irresistible *substance:* **4** iron **7** ferrite

magnetism 4 draw, lure, pull **5** charm **6** allure, appeal **7** glamour **8** charisma **10** attraction **11** fascination

magnetize 4 draw, lure, wile **5** charm **6** seduce **7** attract, bewitch, enchant **9** captivate, fascinate

magnification unit 8 diameter

magnificence 4 pomp **7** majesty **8** grandeur, splendor **9** pageantry **13** sumptuousness

magnificent 5 grand, noble, regal, royal **6** august, lavish, lordly, superb **7** exalted, opulent, stately, sublime **8** glorious, imposing, majestic, palatial, princely, splendid **9** brilliant, grandiose, luxurious, sumptuous **11** extravagant, resplendent, splendorous **13** splendiferous

magnifier 4 lens 9 telescope *jeweler's:* 5 loupe

magnify 4 hymn, laud 5 add to, boost, cry up, exalt, extol, swell 6 expand, extend, praise 7 amplify, augment, enhance, enlarge, ennoble, glorify, inflate 8 heighten, increase, maximize, multiply, overplay 9 aggravate, celebrate, embellish, embroider, intensify, overstate 10 aggrandize, exaggerate 13 overemphasize

magniloquent 5 tumid, windy 6 florid, turgid 7 aureate, flowery, fustian, orotund, pompous, swollen 8 sonorous 9 bombastic, highflown, overblown, rhapsodic 10 euphuistic, rhetorical 11 declamatory

magnitude 4 size 5 order, range 6 extent, import, number, volume 7 bigness, caliber, measure, quality 8 enormity, hugeness, quantity, vastness 9 greatness, immensity, largeness 10 dimensions, importance, proportion 11 consequence

Magnolia State 11 Mississippi

magnum opus 7 classic 10 masterwork 11 chef d'oeuvre, masterpiece, tour de force

Magog's king 3 Gog

magpie 3 jay 4 bird 6 gabber, prater 7 blabber, hoarder 8 jabberer, prattler 9 chatterer, collector 10 chatterbox 12 blabbermouth

maguey 5 agave, fiber 7 cantala *relative:* 4 aloe

magus 6 wizard 7 diviner, warlock 8 conjurer, magician, sorcerer 9 enchanter 10 astrologer 11 necromancer

Magyar 9 Hungarian *leader:* 6 Attila

Mahalath *father:* 7 Ishmael 8 Jerimoth *husband:* 4 Esau 8 Rehoboam

Mahfouz work 12 Cairo Trilogy

mah-jongg piece 4 tile

Mahlon *father:* 9 Elimelech *mother:* 5 Naomi *wife:* 4 Ruth

Maia *father:* 5 Atlas *mother:* 7 Pleione *sisters:* 8 Pleiades *son:* 6 Hermes 7 Mercury

maid 4 girl, lass, miss 5 biddy, bonne, wench 6 au pair, damsel, lassie, live-in, virgin 7 servant 8 domestic 9 charwoman, hired girl 10 au pair girl *Indian:* 4 ayah *lady's:* 7 abigail *stage:* 9 soubrette

maiden 3 gal 4 girl, lass, miss 5 first, fresh, missy, prime, wench 6 damsel, lassie, unused, virgin 7 initial, pioneer, primary 8 earliest, original, spinster, virginal 10 spinsterly *Norse mythological:* 8 valkyrie

maidenhair tree 6 ginkgo

maidenhead 5 hymen 6 purity 9 virginity

maidenhood 9 virginity

Maid of Astolat 6 Elaine

Maid of Orleans, The 7 Pucelle (La) 9 Joan of Arc *author:* 8 Schiller (Friedrich von)

mail 4 post 5 armor 7 hauberk, letters 8 messages

_____ mail 3 air 5 chain, snail

maim 4 maul 6 mangle 7 cripple, disable 8 mutilate, paralyze 9 disfigure

main 3 sea 5 chief, great, major, ocean, prime, trunk 7 central, high sea, leading, premier, primary 8 cardinal, foremost, high seas 9 paramount, principal 10 preeminent, prevailing 11 fundamental, outstanding, predominant

Maine *capital:* 7 Augusta *city:* 6 Bangor 8 Lewiston, Portland *college, university:* 5 Bates, Colby 7 Bowdoin *lake:* 6 Sebago *motto:* 6 Dirigo *mountain:* 8 Cadillac, Katahdin *nickname:* 8 Pine Tree (State) *park:* 6 Acadia *river:* 8 Kennebec 9 Penobscot *state bird:* 9 chickadee *state flower:* 22 white pine cone and tassel *state tree:* 9 white pine

mainly 6 mostly 7 chiefly, largely 8 above all 9 primarily 10 especially 11 principally 13 predominantly

mainstay 4 prop 5 brace 6 pillar 7 bulwark, standby, support 8 backbone, buttress 9 supporter, sustainer

Main Street author 5 Lewis (Sinclair)

maintain 4 aver, avow 5 argue, claim 6 affirm, allege, assert, back up, defend, insist, keep up, manage, stress, uphold 7 care for, carry on, contend, declare, justify, persist, profess, support, sustain, warrant 8 continue, preserve 9 cultivate, emphasize, look after 10 provide for

maintenance 4 care, keep 6 living, upkeep 7 alimony, support 10 livelihood 11 subsistence 12 alimentation *worker:* 7 janitor 9 custodian

maize 4 corn, milo 10 Indian corn

majestic 5 grand, noble, regal, royal 6 august, kingly, lordly, superb 7 exalted, stately 8 elevated, imperial, imposing, princely, splendid 9 dignified, grandiose 11 ceremonious, magnificent

majesty 4 pomp 5 glory 8 eminence, grandeur, splendor 9 greatness, loftiness 11 stateliness 12 magnificence

major 3 big 4 main, star 5 chief, grave, large 6 higher, larger 7 capital, greater, notable, primary, serious, sizable 8 sizeable, superior 9 principal, prominent 10 large-scale, preeminent 11 outstanding, predominant, significant 12 considerable

Major Barbara author 4 Shaw (George Bernard)

majority 4 bulk, edge **6** margin **13** preponderance

make 3 net **4** earn, form, mold **5** build, cause, erect, forge, frame, hatch, shape, spawn **6** create, effect, output **7** achieve, bring in, compose, fashion, prepare, produce **8** comprise, conclude, generate **9** construct, establish, fabricate, originate **10** constitute **11** manufacture, put together *amends:* **5** atone *believe:* **7** pretend *certain:* **6** assure **8** convince *fast:* **3** fix **4** gird **6** secure *good:* **7** succeed **9** indemnify *known:* **3** air **6** expose, reveal, spread **7** declare, divulge, uncover **8** announce, disclose, proclaim *use of:* **6** employ

make-believe 4 mock, sham **7** charade, fantasy, feigned, fiction **8** disguise, pretense **9** fictional, imaginary, insincere, pretended, simulated **10** fictitious

make do 4 cope **5** get by, get on, shift **6** endure, fake it, manage, wing it **7** survive **8** get along **9** improvise **11** extemporize **13** muddle through

make off 3 fly, run **4** flee, skip **5** leave, scoot, scram **6** decamp, depart, escape **7** abscond, run away **9** skedaddle

make out 3 pet, see **4** fare, neck **5** grasp, infer, spoon **6** accept, cuddle, deduce, derive, follow, gather, manage, take in, thrive **7** discern, prosper, succeed **8** conclude, flourish, get along, perceive **9** apprehend, determine, establish, interpret **10** comprehend, understand

make over 4 cede, deed **6** assign, convey, reform **7** remodel, reshape **8** renovate, transfer

maker 7 builder, creator **8** borrower, designer, inventor, producer **10** originator **11** constructor **12** manufacturer

makeshift 6 resort **7** stopgap **8** recourse, resource **9** expedient, temporary **10** expediency, jerry-built, jury-rigged, substitute **11** provisional **13** quick-and-dirty, rough-and-ready

make up 4 form **5** atone **6** devise, invent **7** arrange, compile, compose, concoct, fashion, prepare **8** comprise, contrive **9** apologize, construct, fabricate, formulate, improvise, reconcile **10** compensate

makeup 4 cast, form, kohl, mold **5** blush, fiber, gloss, grain, paint, rouge, shape, stamp, style **6** design, nature, powder, stripe, temper **7** blusher, mascara **8** eyeliner, lip gloss, war paint **9** character, eye shadow, formation **10** complexion, maquillage **11** arrangement, composition, disposition, greasepaint, personality, temperament **12**

architecture, constitution, construction, organization

maladroit 5 inept **6** clumsy, gauche, klutzy **7** awkward, unhandy **8** bumbling, bungling, tactless **9** ham-handed, impolitic **10** blundering, ungraceful **11** heavy-handed **12** undiplomatic

malady 3 ill **7** ailment, disease, illness **8** disorder, sickness, syndrome **9** complaint, condition, infirmity **10** affliction

malaise 4 funk **5** dumps, ennui **8** debility, doldrums **10** enervation

Malamud, Bernard *novel:* **5** Fixer (The) **7** Natural (The) **9** Assistant (The) *story:* **11** Magic Barrel (The)

malapert 4 rude **5** brash, fresh, nervy, sassy, saucy, smart **6** brassy, brazen, cheeky **7** forward **8** impudent, insolent **12** presumptuous

Malaprop creator 8 Sheridan (Richard Brinsley)

malapropos 5 inapt, undue **8** improper, unseemly, untimely **10** unsuitable **11** inopportune **13** inappropriate, inopportunely

malaria 4 ague **6** miasma *medicine:* **7** quinine **8** Atabrine, cinchona **10** quinacrine *mosquito:* **9** anopheles

malarkey 4 bosh, bunk, guff **5** bilge, hokum, hooey, tripe **6** bunkum, drivel **7** baloney, eyewash, hogwash, rubbish, twaddle **8** nonsense, tommyrot **9** poppycock **10** balderdash **12** blatherskite

Malawi *capital:* **8** Lilongwe *city:* **8** Blantyre *explorer:* **11** Livingstone (David) *former name:* **9** Nyasaland *lake:* **5** Nyasa **6** Malawi *language:* **8** Chichewa *monetary unit:* **6** kwacha *neighbor:* **6** Zambia **8** Tanzania **10** Mozambique *river:* **5** Shire

Malaysia *capital:* **11** Kuala Lumpur *city:* **4** Ipoh **6** Penang **11** Johor Baharu *island:* **6** Borneo *monetary unit:* **7** ringgit *neighbor:* **8** Thailand **9** Indonesia *peninsula:* **5** Malay *sea:* **10** South China *strait:* **7** Malacca

malcontent 5 rebel **6** griper, grouch, unruly **8** agitator, factious, frondeur, grumbler, mutinous, restless **9** alienated **10** bellyacher, complainer, rebellious **11** disaffected, disgruntled **12** contumacious, dissatisfied

mal de mer 6 nausea **8** vomiting **10** queasiness **11** seasickness

Maldives *capital:* **4** Male *language:* **6** Divehi *monetary unit:* **7** rufiyaa

male 3 guy, tom **4** gent **5** macho, manly **6** manful, virile **7** manlike **9** masculine, staminate

malediction 4 jinx, oath **5** curse **7** malison **8** anathema **10** execration **11** imprecation

malefactor 5 felon, knave, rogue **6** sinner **8**

criminal, evildoer, offender **9** miscreant,
reprobate, scoundrel, wrongdoer **10** blackguard, lawbreaker
maleficent 4 evil, vile **5** toxic **6** malign, sinful, wicked **7** baleful, baneful, beastly,
harmful, noxious, vicious **8** damnable, sinister, virulent **9** execrable, injurious, nefarious, repugnant **10** pernicious, villainous **11**
destructive
malevolence 4 evil **5** spite **6** grudge, malice,
spleen **7** ill will **9** hostility, malignity **12**
spitefulness **13** maliciousness
malevolent 4 evil **6** malign, wicked **7** baleful,
hateful, hurtful, vicious **8** sinister, spiteful,
venomous **9** injurious, malicious, malignant, poisonous
malfunction 6 glitch **7** misfire
Mali *capital:* **6** Bamako *city:* **5** Mopti, Ségou
7 Sikasso **8** Timbuktu **10** Tombouctou *des-*
ert: **6** Sahara *former name:* **11** French Sudan *language:* **6** French *monetary unit:* **5**
franc *neighbor:* **5** Niger **6** Guinea **7** Algeria, Senegal **10** Ivory Coast, Mauritania **11**
Burkina Faso, Côte d'Ivoire *river:* **5** Niger
malice 4 bile, hate **5** spite, venom **6** animus,
enmity, grudge, hatred, poison, spleen **7** ill
will **8** meanness **9** animosity, antipathy **10**
bitterness, resentment **11** hatefulness, malevolence **12** spitefulness **13** invidiousness
malicious 4 evil, mean **5** nasty, petty **6**
wicked **7** baneful, hateful, heinous, jealous
8 spiteful, vengeful, venomous, virulent **9**
poisonous, poison-pen, rancorous **10** malevolent
maliciousness see **malevolence**
malign 4 evil, soil **5** abuse, decry, libel,
smear, stain, sully, taint **6** befoul, defame,
defile, revile, smirch, vilify, wicked **7**
asperse, baleful, baneful, blacken, detract,
hateful, hostile, noxious, slander, tarnish,
traduce, vicious **8** besmirch, derogate, inimical, sinister, spiteful, tear down, virulent
9 denigrate, disparage, injurious, rancorous
10 calumniate, depreciate, maleficent, malevolent, pernicious, scandalize, vituperate
11 deleterious, opprobriate **12** antagonistic,
antipathetic
malignant 4 evil **5** fatal **6** deadly, lethal,
wicked **7** baleful, hateful, vicious **8** devilish, fiendish, spiteful **9** injurious, rancorous
10 diabolical, malevolent
malison 5 curse **8** anathema **11** commination,
imprecation, malediction
mall 4 lane **5** alley, plaza, strip **7** passage **9**
concourse, esplanade, promenade **10** passageway **11** median strip

malleable 6 pliant, supple **7** ductile, plastic,
pliable **8** flexible **9** adaptable
mallet 6 hammer
malodorous 4 foul, gamy, rank **5** fetid,
fuggy, funky, fusty, musty, stale **6** frowsy,
putrid, rancid, rotten, smelly, stinky **7** noisome, noxious, reeking, spoiled **8** mephitic,
stinking **9** offensive **10** nauseating **11** ill-
smelling **12** pestilential
Malraux novel 8 Man's Fate
Malta *capital:* **8** Valletta *city:* **5** Qormi **10**
Birkirkara *island:* **4** Gozo **6** Comino *lan-*
guage: **6** French **7** Maltese *monetary unit:*
4 lira *sea:* **13** Mediterranean
Maltese Falcon, The *actor:* **5** Astor (Mary),
Lorre (Peter) **6** Bogart (Humphrey) **11**
Greenstreet (Sydney) *author:* **7** Hammett
(Dashiell) *detective:* **5** Spade (Sam) *direc-*
tor: **6** Huston (John)
maltreat 5 abuse **6** ill-use, misuse, molest
Mamet, David *film:* **5** Heist **7** Verdict (The) **9**
Wag the Dog **12** House of Games, Un-
touchables (The) *play:* **7** Oleanna, Romance
14 Boston Marriage **15** American Buffalo
17 Glengarry Glen Ross
mammal 2 ox **3** ass, bat, cat, cow, dog, elk,
fox, pig, rat **4** bear, deer, goat, Homo, lion,
mink, mole, oxen (plural), pika, seal, tahr,
unau, urva, wolf **5** camel, civet, coati, fossa,
genet, hippo, hyena, hyrax, koala, lemur,
llama, moose, okapi, otter, panda, ratel, sable, sheep, shrew, sloth, takin, tapir, tiger,
tigon, zebra **6** alpaca, badger, beaver,
colugo, dassie, grison, jackal, marten, ocelot, rabbit, racoon, rodent, sifaka, tenrec, tiglon, vicuña, wombat **7** caracal, giraffe,
guanaco, hyraces (plural), leopard, lioness,
opossum, linsang, peccary, polecat, primate, raccoon, tigress **8** aardvark, aardwolf,
edentate, elephant, hedgehog, kangaroo,
kinkajou, mongoose, pangolin, pinniped,
ruminant, squirrel, starnose, ungulate **9** armadillo, bandicoot **10** cacomistle **12** hippopotamus *aquatic:* **4** orca, seal **6** dugong, sea
cow, walrus **7** cowfish, dolphin, grampus,
manatee, narwhal, platypi (plural) **8** cetacean, platypus, porpoise, sirenian *extinct:* **6**
quagga **8** mastodon, stegodon
mammon 4 pelf **5** lucre **6** riches, wealth **8**
treasure **9** abundance, affluence **10** prosperity **11** possessions
mammoth 4 huge, vast **5** giant, jumbo **6**
mighty **7** immense, massive, monster, titanic **8** colossal, enormous, gigantic **9** leviathan, monstrous **10** gargantuan, mastodonic,
monumental **9** humongous **11** elephantine
man 2 Mr. **3** guy **4** buck, chap, cuss, dude,

gent, male **5** being, bloke **6** fellow, mister, mortal, person **7** husband **8** creature, paramour **9** boyfriend, mortality, personage **10** individual **11** Homo sapiens *castrated:* **6** eunuch *combining form:* **4** andr **5** andro, homin **6** homini *common:* **7** Joe Blow, John Doe **11** John Q. Public *French:* **5** homme *Italian:* **4** uomo *Latin:* **3** vir **4** homo *old:* **6** codger, geezer *Spanish:* **6** hombre *Yiddish:* **6** mensch

manage 3 run **4** cope, fare, head, keep, mind, tend **5** get by, get on, shift **6** afford, direct, effect, govern, handle **7** achieve, carry on, conduct, control, execute, finagle, operate, oversee, succeed **8** carry out, contrive, cope with, deal with, dominate, engineer, get along, maintain **9** cultivate, supervise **10** accomplish, administer, bring about **11** orchestrate, superintend

manageable 6 docile, pliant **8** amenable, bearable, biddable, passable **9** agreeable, compliant, endurable, tractable **10** responsive **11** cooperative, supportable, sustainable **13** accommodating

management 4 care **5** brass **6** charge **7** conduct, control, running **8** guidance, handling **9** direction, oversight **10** conducting **11** front office, supervising, supervision

manager 4 boss, exec **6** gerent **7** handler, officer **8** director, official, overseer, producer **9** conductor, executive **10** impresario, supervisor **13** administrator *museum:* **7** curator

mañana 7 someday **8** sometime, tomorrow

Man and Superman author 4 Shaw (George Bernard)

Manassas battle 7 Bull Run

Manasseh, Manasses *brother:* **7** Ephraim *father:* **6** Hashum, Joseph **8** Hezekiah **10** Pahathmoab *grandfather:* **5** Jacob *grandson:* **6** Gilead *mother:* **7** Asenath *son:* **6** Machir

man-at-arms 2 GI **7** fighter, soldier, warrior **10** serviceman

Mandalay author 7 Kipling (Rudyard)

mandarin 5 elder **6** orange **8** official **9** tangerine **10** bureaucrat, panjandrum

mandate 4 fiat, word **5** edict, order, ukase **6** behest, charge, decree **7** bidding, command, dictate **9** authority, directive **10** imperative, injunction **13** authorization

mandatory 6 forced **7** binding **8** required **9** de rigueur, necessary, requisite **10** compulsory, imperative, obligatory **11** involuntary

mandible 3 jaw **8** lower jaw

man-eater 4 lion, ogre **5** shark, tiger **8** cannibal **13** mackerel shark

Manette's daughter 5 Lucie

maneuver 3 ply **4** move, plan, plot, ploy, step **5** feint, trick, wield **6** design, device, gambit, handle, jockey, scheme, tactic, wangle **7** exploit, finagle, finesse **8** artifice, démarche, engineer, exercise, intrigue, movement, navigate **9** machinate, procedure, stratagem **10** manipulate, proceeding, subterfuge **11** contrivance, machination **12** manipulation

maneuvering room 8 latitude

Man for All Seasons, A *author:* **4** Bolt (Robert) *subject:* **4** More (Thomas)

manganese *ore:* **10** pyrolusite *symbol:* **2** Mn

manger 4 rack **6** cratch, feeder, trough

mangle 3 mar **4** iron, maim, maul **5** press **6** damage, deface, deform, impair, injure **7** butcher, contort, distort **8** lacerate, mutilate **9** disfigure

mangy 5 seedy **6** ragtag, shabby **7** scruffy, squalid **8** decrepit, tattered **9** moth-eaten **10** down-at-heel, threadbare

manhandle 5 abuse **6** batter **7** rough up **8** maltreat, mistreat **10** push around, slap around

Manhattan *building:* **8** Chrysler **11** Empire State *district:* **4** Soho **6** Harlem **7** Chelsea, Tribeca *entertainment district:* **11** Times Square *financial district:* **10** Wall Street *museum:* **3** Met **4** MOMA **7** Whitney **10** Guggenheim **12** Metropolitan *opera house:* **3** Met **12** Metropolitan *purchaser:* **6** Minuit (Peter) *river:* **4** East **6** Hudson *school:* **3** NYU **6** Hunter **8** Columbia **9** Juilliard

mania 4 rage, zeal **5** craze, fancy **6** frenzy, lunacy **7** madness, passion **8** fixation, idée fixe, insanity **9** cacoëthes, obsession **10** compulsion, enthusiasm **11** infatuation

maniac 3 bug, nut **4** loon **5** fiend, freak **6** madman, psycho, zealot **7** fanatic, lunatic, nutcase **8** crackpot **9** bedlamite **10** enthusiast

manifest 4 show **5** clear, overt, plain, shown, utter, voice **6** appear, embody, evince, expose, patent, reveal **7** display, evident, evinced, exhibit, express, invoice, obvious, visible **8** apparent, distinct, evidence, palpable, proclaim, revealed **9** evidenced, incarnate, objectify, prominent **10** illustrate, noticeable, observable **11** demonstrate, exteriorize, externalize, perceptible, unambiguous

manifestation 4 show, sign **5** proof **7** display, symptom **8** epiphany **10** appearance, revelation

manifesto 4 fiat, rule, writ **5** credo, creed, edict, ukase **6** decree, dictum, gospel, notice, policy, ruling **7** mandate **8** doctrine, document, platform **9** directive, statement, testament, testimony, ultimatum **10** deposi-

tion, injunction, resolution 11 declaration
12 announcement, notification, proclamation 13 pronouncement

manifold 7 diverse, various 8 compound,
multiple, multiply, numerous 9 multiform,
multiplex 10 multiphase 12 multifarious

manikin 4 runt 5 dummy, dwarf, gnome,
model, pygmy 6 midget, peewee 8 Tom
Thumb 10 homunculus

Manila *founder:* 7 Legazpi (Miguel López
de) *site:* 5 Luzon 11 Philippines *victor:* 5
Dewey (George)

manioc 4 yuca 5 yucca 6 casava 7 cassava,
tapioca

manipulate 3 ply, rig 4 play 5 steer, swing,
tweak, wield 6 adjust, direct, doctor, handle, jockey, juggle, manage 7 beguile, conduct, control, exploit, finagle, finesse,
massage 8 engineer, maneuver 9 machinate
10 tamper with

Man, Isle of *capital:* 7 Douglas *cat:* 4 Manx
possession of: 7 Britain *sea:* 5 Irish

Manitoba *capital:* 8 Winnipeg *lake:* 8 Winnipeg 12 Winnipegosis *mountain:* 5 Baldy
provincial flower: 13 prairie crocus *river:* 6
Nelson 9 Churchill

mankind 6 humans, people 8 humanity 11
Homo sapiens

manlike 4 male 6 virile 8 hominoid, humanoid 9 masculine 10 anthropoid

manly 4 male 5 macho 6 virile 9 masculine

man-made 9 synthetic 10 artificial, factitious
object: 8 artefact, artifact

Mann character 6 Joseph 9 Leverkühn
(Adrian) 10 Aschenbach (Gustav von), Felix Krull 11 Hans Castorp, Tonio Kröger

manner 3 air, way 4 form, kind, mien, mode,
sort, vein, wont 5 habit, modus, style, usage
6 aspect, custom, method 7 bearing, conduct, fashion 8 behavior, demeanor, habitude, practice, presence 9 demeanour,
etiquette, technique 10 consuetude, deportment 11 affectation, comportment 12 idiosyncrasy

mannered 7 stilted 8 affected, precious 10 artificial 13 self-conscious

mannerism 3 tic 4 pose 5 quirk 10 preciosity
11 affectation, peculiarity, singularity 12 eccentricity, idiosyncrasy 13 artificiality

mannerless 4 rude 6 coarse 7 boorish, ill-
bred, uncivil, uncouth 8 impolite 12 discourteous

mannerly 5 civil 6 polite 7 genteel, refined 8
decorous, gracious, well-bred 9 civilized,
courteous 10 respectful

Manon composer 8 Massenet (Jules)

Manon Lescaut *author:* 7 Prévost (Abbé)

composer: 7 Puccini (Giacomo) 8 Massenet (Jules) *lover:* 9 des Grieux

manor 5 villa 6 estate, quinta 7 château, demesne 12 landed estate

manservant 5 valet 6 butler

mansion 4 hall 5 villa 6 palace 7 château

manslayer 6 killer 8 homicide, murderer

manta 3 ray 5 cloak, cloth, shawl 7 blanket

manteau 4 coat, robe, wrap 5 cloak 6 capote,
domino, mantle, tabard

mantic 5 vatic 6 orphic 7 Delphic, fatidic 8
Delphian, oracular 9 prophetic, sibylline,
vaticinal 10 divinatory

mantilla 4 cape, wrap 5 cloak, fichu, scarf,
shawl 8 kerchief

mantle 4 cope, glow, pink, robe, rose 5 blush,
cloak, color, cover, flush, rouge 6 capote,
casing, pinken, redden 7 crimson

man-to-man 4 open 5 frank, plain 6 candid,
direct, honest 10 forthright, unreserved 11
openhearted

mantra 2 om 5 chant, motto 6 prayer, slogan
9 watchword 10 invocation 11 incantation

manual 4 text 5 guide 6 primer 8 Baedeker,
handbook, hornbook, textbook 9 guidebook, vade mecum 10 compendium 11
abecedarium, enchiridion *religious:* 9 catechism *worker:* 6 menial 7 laborer

manufacture 4 form, make 6 create 7 fashion,
produce 8 assemble 9 construct, fabricate
11 put together

manumit 4 free 6 unbind 7 release, set free,
unchain 8 liberate 9 unshackle 10 emancipate

manure 4 dung 6 ordure 7 excreta 9 excrement 10 fertilizer

manuscript 4 hand 6 scrawl 8 longhand 9 autograph 10 penmanship 11 calligraphy,
handwriting *ancient:* 5 codex 6 scroll 7 co-
dices (plural) *red part:* 6 rubric *style:* 6 uncial *symbol:* 6 obelus

many 5 scads 6 divers, legion, myriad, sundry 7 copious, diverse, umpteen, various 8
abundant, manifold, multiple, numerous 9
abounding, bounteous, bountiful, countless,
multitude, plentiful 12 multifarious 13 multitudinous *combining form:* 4 poly 5 multi,
pluri

many-sided 7 diverse 8 all-round, talented 9
all-around, versatile 10 variegated 11 diversified 12 multifaceted, multifarious 13 comprehensive

Mao's successor 3 Hua (Guofeng, Kuo-feng)
4 Deng (Xiaoping), Teng (Hsiao-p'ing)

map 4 plan, plat 5 chart, draft, globe, graph 6
design, lay out, set out, sketch, survey 7 arrange, diagram, drawing, outline, tracing 9

delineate **collection:** 5 atlas **line:** 6 isobar 7 contour, isogram, isohyet 8 isogloss, isogonic, isopleth, isotherm **maker:** 12 cartographer **making:** 11 cartography

maple genus: 4 Acer **product:** 5 syrup **type:** 3 red 5 sugar 8 box elder

map projection 5 conic 8 Mercator 9 polyconic 10 sinusoidal 12 orthographic 13 stereographic

maquillage 6 makeup

mar 4 ding, harm, hurt, scar, warp 5 spoil, stain 6 bruise, damage, deface, deform, impair, injure 7 blemish, scratch, tarnish, vitiate 9 disfigure

marabou 5 stork

Marat/Sade author 5 Weiss (Peter)

Marat, Jean-Paul colleague: 6 Danton (Georges) 11 Robespierre (Maximilien) **slayer:** 6 Corday (Charlotte)

maraud 4 loot, raid, sack 5 foray, harry 6 harass, ravage, ravish 7 despoil, pillage, plunder, ransack

marauder 6 bandit, pirate 7 brigand, spoiler, wrecker 9 buccaneer, desperado 10 freebooter

marble 3 mib, mig, taw 4 immy, migg 5 agate, aggie, alley, rance 6 blotch, miggle, mottle, streak 7 cipolin, glassie, steelie 9 limestone

marbled 6 veined 7 dappled, flecked, mottled 8 speckled, streaked

Marble Faun, The author: 9 Hawthorne (Nathaniel) **character:** 5 Hilda 6 Kenyon, Miriam 9 Donatello **setting:** 4 Rome

marcel 4 wave

march 3 hem, rim 4 abut, file, line 5 skirt 6 adjoin, border, parade 7 advance, headway, proceed 8 anabasis, boundary, frontier, outlands, progress, traverse 9 periphery 10 borderland

March date: 4 ides **mother:** 6 Marmee **sisters:** 3 Amy, Meg 4 Beth

March King 5 Sousa (John Philip)

Mardi Gras 8 carnival 10 Fat Tuesday **city:** 10 New Orleans

Marduk city: 7 Babylon **consort:** 8 Zarbanit, Zarpanit **victim:** 5 Kingu 6 Tiamat

mare 3 sea 5 horse 6 equine

mare's nest 3 con, din 4 hoax, scam 5 babel, cheat, fraud, put-on, spoof 6 bedlam, clamor, hubbub, humbug, racket, ruckus, tumult, uproar 7 swindle, turmoil 8 brouhaha, flimflam, illusion 9 confusion, imposture 10 hullabaloo 11 pandemonium

margarine 4 oleo

margin 3 hem, rim 4 brim, edge, join, line, play, room, side 5 bound, brink, frame, scope, shore, skirt, verge 6 border, fringe, leeway 7 minimum, outline, selvage 8 boundary, latitude, selvedge, surround, trimming 9 elbowroom, perimeter, periphery 13 circumference **tiny:** 4 hair

marginal 5 minor 7 limited, minimal 9 bordering 10 borderline, negligible, peripheral, subsidiary 13 insignificant

Marguerite's lover 5 Faust

Maria ____ 5 Elena 7 Stuarda

Marianas discoverer: 8 Magellan (Ferdinand) **island:** 4 Guam, Rota 5 Pagan 6 Guguan, Saipan, Tinian 7 Agrihan, Aguijan

marijuana 3 kef, kif, pot 4 hash, hemp, weed 5 bhang, grass 6 reefer 7 hashish 8 cannabis

marina 4 dock, pier, quay 5 basin, berth, wharf 8 boatyard

marinate 4 soak 5 steep 6 drench, pickle 7 immerse 8 macerate

marine 5 naval 7 abyssal, aquatic, deep-sea, oceanic, pelagic 8 nautical, seagoing, seascape 9 seafaring, thalassic 10 oceangoing 12 hydrographic 13 oceanographic **crustacean:** 6 shrimp 7 lobster 8 barnacle **deposit:** 5 coral **plant:** 4 kelp, nori 5 dulse 6 wakame 7 seaweed

mariner 3 gob, tar 4 jack, salt, swab 5 limey 6 hearty, rating, sailor, sea dog, seaman 7 jack-tar, old salt, swabbie 8 seafarer 9 sailorman, shellback, tarpaulin 10 bluejacket

marital 6 wedded 7 married, nuptial, spousal 8 conjugal, hymeneal 9 connubial

maritime 7 oceanic, pelagic 8 nautical 9 thalassic 12 navigational

mark 3 aim, jot, sap, tee 4 butt, dupe, fool, goal, gull, heed, look, nick, note, pick, show, sign, view 5 blaze, bound, brand, chart, chump, elect, grade, label, notch, stamp, token, trait 6 behold, choose, denote, evince, lay off, notice, object, opt for, rating, record, select, sucker, target, victim, virtue 7 betoken, delimit, discern, exhibit, fall guy, feature, gudgeon, indicia, initial, measure, observe, qualify, scratch, signify, symptom 8 function, indicate, perceive, register 9 attribute, character, designate, objective, single out 10 indication 11 differentia, distinction, distinguish 12 characterize **distinctive:** 7 indicia 8 indicium **identifying:** 4 logo, seal 6 emblem, signet, symbol 8 colophon, logotype **of insertion:** 5 caret **of omission:** 4 dele 8 ellipsis 10 apostrophe **of retention:** 4 stet **over a vowel:** 5 breve, haček 6 accent, macron, umlaut 8 dieresis 9 diaeresis 10 circumflex **over n:** 5 tilde **punctuation:** 4 dash 5 brace, colon, comma, slant, slash 6 hyphen, period 7 bracket, solidus **9** backslash, guillemet, semicolon **10** apostrophe *under a letter:* **7** cedilla

Mark 6 Gospel *cousin:* **8** Barnabas *mother:* **4** Mary

mark down 3 cut **4** pare **5** shave, slash **6** reduce **7** devalue **8** discount **9** devaluate **10** depreciate, undervalue

marked 5 noted **6** patent, signal **7** evident, notable, obvious, pointed, salient **8** distinct, manifest, striking **9** arresting, prominent **10** noticeable, remarkable **11** conspicuous, outstanding **12** considerable **13** distinguished *man:* **4** Cain

marker 3 IOU, run **5** score **7** felt-tip

market 3 suq **4** fair, mall, sell, shop, souk, vend **5** store **6** bazaar, outlet, retail, rialto **8** emporium, exchange, showroom **9** advertise, traffic in, wholesale **11** merchandise *kind:* **4** flea **5** money, stock

marketable 5 sound **7** salable **8** vendible **10** commercial

marketplace 3 suq **4** mall, souk **5** agora **6** bazaar, rialto **8** emporium

marksman 4 shot **6** sniper **7** deadeye, shooter **12** sharpshooter

marl 4 clay, silt

marlin 8 billfish **9** spearfish

Marlowe play 8 Edward II **9** Dr. Faustus **10** Jew of Malta (The) **11** Tamburlaine **13** Doctor Faustus

marmot 6 rodent **9** woodchuck **10** prairie dog

maroon 3 red **6** claret, desert, strand **7** abandon, crimson, forsake, isolate, outcast **8** burgundy, castaway

Marquand character 4 Gray (Charles), Moto (Mr.) **5** Apley (George), Wayde (Willis) **6** Pulham (H.M.) **7** Goodwin (Melville)

Marquis, Don *cat:* **9** Mehitabel *cockroach:* **5** Archy

marriage 5 match, union **6** bridal **7** nuptial, spousal, wedding, wedlock **8** coupling, espousal, monogamy, nuptials, polygamy **9** matrimony **11** conjugality **12** connubiality *combining form:* **4** gamy **6** gamous *notice:* **5** banns *outside a group:* **7** exogamy *within a group:* **8** endogamy

marriageable 6 nubile **8** eligible

marriage broker 5 yenta **9** go-between **10** matchmaker

Marriage of Figaro composer 6 Mozart (Wolfgang Amadeus)

marrow 4 core, meat, pith, soul **5** heart, stuff **6** kernel **7** essence **12** quintessence

marry 3 tie, wed **4** join, link, mate, wive, yoke **5** hitch, merge, unite **6** couple, splice,

spouse **7** combine, conjoin, espouse **9** conjugate

Mars 4 Ares **6** planet *combining term:* **4** areo *feature:* **4** face **5** basin **6** canyon, crater **7** volcano **8** polar cap *lover:* **5** Venus *mission:* **6** Viking **7** Mariner **10** Pathfinder *moon:* **6** Deimos, Phobos *relating to:* **7** martian (see also **Ares**)

Marseillaise composer 13 Rouget de Lisle (Claude-Joseph)

marsh 3 bog, fen **4** mire, ooze, quag **5** bayou, glade, swale, swamp **6** morass, muskeg, slough **7** wetland **8** quagmire **9** swampland

marshal 5 align, array, guide, order, rally, usher **6** deploy, direct, escort, muster **7** arrange, officer, round up **8** assemble, mobilize, organize, shepherd **9** methodize, systemize (see also **field marshal**)

Marshall Islands *atoll:* **6** Bikini **8** Enewetak **9** Kwajalein *capital:* **6** Majuro *ethnic group:* **11** Micronesian *island chain:* **5** Ralik, Ratak **6** Sunset **7** Sunrise **11** Marshallese

marshy 4 miry **5** boggy, mucky **6** quaggy, swampy **7** sloughy

marsupial 3 roo **4** euro **5** koala **6** possum, wombat **7** opossum, wallaby **8** kangaroo, wallaroo **9** bandicoot

marten 6 fisher, weasel

Martha *brother:* **7** Lazarus *sister:* **4** Mary

martial 7 warlike **8** militant, military, spirited **9** bellicose, combative, soldierly **11** belligerent **12** militaristic

martial art 4 judo **5** kendo **6** aikido, karate, kung fu, neijia, tai chi **7** shaolin **8** capoeira, jiujitsu **9** tae kwon do **11** tai chi chuan *expert:* **5** ninja *school:* **4** dojo *teacher:* **6** sensei

Martial's forte 7 epigram

Martin Chuzzlewit author 7 Dickens (Charles)

Martinique *capital:* **12** Fort-de-France *department of:* **6** France *discoverer:* **8** Columbus (Christopher) *island group:* **8** Windward *location:* **10** West Indies *neighbor:* **8** Dominica **10** Saint Lucia *volcano:* **5** Pelée

martyr 4 Paul, rack **5** Agnes, Alban, James, Peter, saint, wring **6** George, harrow, Justin **7** afflict, agonize, Clement, crucify, Cyprian, Stephen, torment, torture **8** Ignatius, Lawrence, Polycarp, sufferer **9** Joan of Arc, Sebastian **10** excruciate, Thomas More *Protestant:* **6** Ridley (Nicholas) **7** Cranmer (Thomas), Latimer (Hugh)

marvel 4 gape **6** wonder **7** miracle, portent, prodigy, stunner **9** curiosity, sensation **10** phenomenon **12** astonishment

marvelous 5 super, swell **6** divine **7** amazing, awesome, ripping **8** glorious, striking, stunning, superior, terrific, wondrous **9** excellent, wonderful **10** astounding, incredible, miraculous, phenomenal, prodigious, remarkable, staggering, stupendous, surprising **11** astonishing, exceptional, sensational, spectacular **12** awe-inspiring, supernatural **13** extraordinary

Marx brother 5 Chico, Gummo, Harpo, Zeppo **7** Groucho

Marxist 9 socialist **9** communist

Marx, Karl *book:* **7** Kapital (Das) *collaborator:* **6** Engels (Friedrich)

Mary *husband:* **6** Clopas, Joseph **8** Alphaeus *kinswoman:* **9** Elisabeth *son:* **4** Mark **5** James, Jesus

Maryland *bay:* **10** Chesapeake *capital:* **9** Annapolis *city:* **9** Baltimore, Frederick *college, university:* **6** Towson **7** Goucher **9** Annapolis **12** Johns Hopkins **12** Naval Academy (U.S.) *fort:* **7** McHenry *nickname:* **7** Old Line (State) *river:* **7** Potomac **8** Patuxent *state bird:* **15** Baltimore oriole *state flower:* **14** black-eyed Susan *state tree:* **8** white oak

mascot 4 juju **5** charm **6** amulet, fetish, symbol **8** gris-gris, talisman

masculine 4 male **5** macho, manly **6** manful, virile **7** manlike

masculinity 8 machismo, virility **9** manliness

Masefield *work:* **7** Cargoes **8** Sea Fever

mash 4 pulp **5** crush, smash **6** squash, squish **7** squoosh **8** macerate **9** pulverize

masher 4 wolf **5** flirt **6** chaser **7** Don Juan, seducer **8** Casanova, lothario **9** ladies' man, womanizer **10** lady-killer **11** philanderer, skirt chaser

mash note 10 billet-doux, love letter

mask 4 hide, pose, sham, veil **5** cover, front, guard, guise, visor **6** facade, screen, vizard **7** dress up, frisket, pretext **8** coloring, disguise, pretense **9** dissemble, semblance **10** appearance, camouflage, false front, simulation **11** dissimulate

masonry 9 brickwork, stonework *in a frame:* **7** nogging

masquerade 4 pose **6** facade **7** costume, posture **8** carnival, disguise **10** camouflage, masked ball **11** costume ball

mass 3 lot, sum, wad **4** bank, body, bulk, clot, core, glob, heap, hill, lump, pack, peck, pile **5** clump, mound **6** corpus, volume **7** expanse, globule, wadding **8** assemble, quantity **9** aggregate, stockpile, substance **11** aggregation **12** conglomerate *compacted:* **4** cake *for the dead:* **7** requiem

of individuals: **3** mob **4** host **5** crowd, crush, flock, horde, swarm **6** throng **12** congregation **13** agglomeration *part:* **5** Kyrie **6** proper **8** Agnus Dei, ordinary

Massachusetts *cape:* **3** Ann, Cod *capital:* **6** Boston *city:* **6** Lowell, Quincy **9** Cambridge, Worcester **10** New Bedford **11** Springfield *college, university:* **3** MIT **5** Clark, Smith, Tufts **7** Amherst, Berklee, Harvard, Wheaton **8** Brandeis, Williams **9** Hampshire, Holy Cross, Radcliffe, Wellesley **12** Mount Holyoke, Northeastern *island:* **9** Nantucket **15** Martha's Vineyard *mountain, range:* **8** Greylock **9** Berkshire *nickname:* **3** Bay (State) **9** Old Colony (State) *river:* **11** Connecticut *state bird:* **9** chickadee *state flower:* **9** mayflower *state tree:* **3** elm (American) *symbol:* **3** cod

massacre 4 kill **6** mangle, murder, pogrom **7** butcher, carnage **8** butchery, decimate, genocide, mangling, mutilate **9** bloodbath, bloodshed, slaughter **10** annihilate, blood purge, decimation, mutilation **11** exterminate **12** annihilation

massage 3 rub **5** knead **7** flatter, rubdown, shiatsu **8** blandish **10** manipulate

Massenet *opera* **5** Le Cid, Manon, Sapho, Thaïs **7** Werther

massive 4 huge, mega, vast **5** bulky, giant, jumbo, mondo, solid **6** mighty **7** hulking, immense, mammoth, weighty **8** colossal, cumbrous, enormous, gigantic, towering **9** humongous, monstrous **10** gargantuan, monumental, prodigious, stupendous, tremendous **11** elephantine, mountainous

master 4 best, boss, guru, head, lick, rule, tame **5** adept, bwana, chief, crack, learn, ruler, sahib, tutor **6** artist, expert, genius, honcho, leader, subdue, victor **7** captain, conquer, headman, maestro, padrone, prevail, skilled, triumph **8** dominant, dominate, employer, governor, overcome, overlord, overseer, regulate, skeleton, skillful, superior, surmount, virtuoso **9** authority, chieftain, conqueror, dominator, paramount, principal, sovereign **10** proficient **11** predominant *of ceremonies:* **4** host **5** emcee **7** compere

masterful 4 deft **5** adept **6** adroit, expert **7** skilled **8** skillful **10** high-handed, proficient **11** magisterial **13** authoritative

masterly 5 adept, crack **6** adroit, expert **7** skilled **8** skillful **9** dexterous **10** proficient **11** crackerjack **12** accomplished

Master of Ballantrae, The 6 Durrie *author:* **9** Stevenson (Robert Louis)

masterpiece 7 classic **10** magnum opus **11** chef d'oeuvre, tour de force

mastery 5 knack, skill **7** ability, command, control, know-how, prowess **8** dominion **9** authority, expertise **10** ascendancy, domination, expertness, virtuosity **11** proficiency, superiority

masticate 4 chaw, chew, pulp **5** champ, chomp, crush, munch **6** crunch **7** scrunch **8** macerate, ruminate **9** break down

mat 3 rug **4** felt **6** border, carpet, tatami

matador 6 torero **8** toreador **11** bullfighter *adjunct:* **6** muleta *move:* **4** pase **5** faena **8** veronica

Mata Hari 3 spy **10** seductress **11** femme fatale

match 3 pit **4** bout, game, meet, peer, suit, twin **5** array, equal, rival, touch, union **6** double, equate, oppose **7** compare, contest, counter, paragon, play off **8** alliance, analogue, marriage, opponent, parallel **9** adversary, correlate, duplicate, encounter, measure up, smackdown **10** antagonist, complement, coordinate, engagement, equivalent, reciprocal, supplement, tournament **11** counterpart **12** correspond to *a bet:* **3** see *friction:* **7** lucifer

matchless 6 unique **7** supreme **8** peerless, singular **9** nonpareil, unequaled, unrivaled **10** inimitable **12** incomparable, unparalleled

matchmaker see **marriage broker**

mate 3 bud, pal, tie, wed **4** chum, pair, twin **5** amigo, breed, buddy, crony, equal, hitch, marry **6** cohort, couple, double, fellow, friend, helper, splice, spouse **7** compeer, comrade, consort, partner **8** confrere, sidekick **9** associate, companion, copartner, duplicate, procreate **10** complement, equivalent, reciprocal **11** concomitant

maté 3 tea **5** holly **8** beverage

mater 3 mom, mum **6** mother **9** matriarch
_____ **mater 4** alma

material 4 real, true **5** cloth, stuff **6** actual, fabric, matter, object **7** element, germane, worldly **8** palpable, physical, relevant, sensible, tangible **9** component, corporeal, essential, important, objective, pertinent, substance **10** applicable, ingredient, meaningful, phenomenal **11** appreciable, constituent, fundamental, perceptible, significant, substantial *building:* **5** adobe, brick **6** stucco **7** lagging, plaster, plywood, shingle **8** concrete

materialistic 7 secular, worldly **11** acquisitive

materialize 4 loom, rise **5** arise, issue **6** appear, embody, emerge, evolve, show up **7** develop, surface **8** manifest **9** come about, incarnate, take shape **12** substantiate

matériel 4 gear **5** stock **8** supplies **9** apparatus, equipment, machinery **10** provisions **13** accouterments, accoutrements, paraphernalia

maternal 8 motherly

matey 5 pally, tight **6** clubby **7** affable **8** amicable, familiar, friendly, intimate, sociable **9** congenial

mathematician *American:* **5** Wiles (Andrew) **6** Peirce (Charles S.), Veblen (Oswald), Wiener (Norbert) *Austrian:* **5** Gödel (Kurt) *British:* **6** Stokes (George) *Dutch:* **7** Huygens (Christiaan) *English:* **6** Newton (Isaac), Taylor (Brook), Turing (Alan), Wallis (John) **7** Pearson (Karl), Russell (Bertrand) **8** Hamilton (James Rowan) **9** Sylvester (James Joseph), Whitehead (Alfred North, Henry) *French:* **4** Weil (André) **5** Borel (Emile), Comte (Auguste), Viète (François) **6** Galois (Evariste), Pascal (Blaise), Picard (Charles-Emile) **7** Fourier (Jean-Baptiste), Laplace (Marquis de), Vernier (Pierre) **8** Painlevé (Paul), Poincaré (Jules-Henri) **9** Descartes (René) *German:* **5** Gauss (Carl Friedrich), Wolff (Freiherr von) **6** Staudt (Karl von) **7** Leibniz (Gottfried Wilhelm), Riemann (Georg) **11** Weierstrass (Karl) *Greek:* **6** Euclid **10** Archimedes, Pythagoras *Hungarian:* **5** Erdos (Paul) *Italian:* **8** Volterra (Vito) **10** Torricelli (Evangelista) *Norwegian:* **7** Stormer (Fredrik) *Russian:* **11** Lobachevsky (Nikolay) *Scottish:* **4** Tait (Peter) **6** Napier (John) **8** Stirling (James) *Swiss:* **5** Euler (Leonhard), Sturm (Jacques) **7** Steiner (Jakob)

mathematics *branch:* **4** trig **7** algebra **8** calculus, geometry, topology **10** arithmetic, statistics **12** trigonometry *proven statement in:* **7** theorem
_____ **Mather 6** Cotton **7** Richard **8** Increase

mating arena 3 lek

matriarch 4 dame **6** mother **7** dowager **10** grande dame

matriculate 4 join **5** enter **6** enroll, sign on **8** register

matrimonial 6 bridal, wedded **7** marital, married, nuptial, spousal **8** conjugal, hymeneal **9** connubial **11** epithalamic

matrimony 7 wedlock **8** marriage **11** conjugality **12** connubiality

matrix 3 die, net, web **4** grid, mesh **5** array **6** cradle, gangue **7** complex, network **10** groundmass, truth table

matron 4 dame **7** dowager **8** chaperon **9** chaperone **10** grande dame

Mattathias *father:* **5** Simon **6** Ananos **7** Absalom, Boethus **10** Theophilus *son:* **8** Josephus

matter 4 body, core, gist, meat, pith, text **5** being, cause, order, point, sense, stuff, theme, thing, topic, value, weigh **6** affair, amount, burden, entity, import, object **7** concern, signify, subject **8** argument, material **9** grievance, magnitude, substance **11** constituent **12** circumstance

matter-of-fact 3 dry **5** plain, prose, sober, stoic **6** stolid **7** prosaic **9** impassive, objective, practical, pragmatic, realistic **10** hardboiled, hardheaded, impersonal, phlegmatic **11** down-to-earth **13** unimpassioned, unsentimental

mattress 3 pad **4** sack *case:* **4** tick *fabric:* **7** ticking *straw:* **6** pallet

mature 3 age, due **4** grow, ripe **5** adult, grown, owing, ready, ripen **6** flower, grow up, mellow, season, unpaid **7** advance, blossom, decline, develop, grown-up, overdue, payable, ripened **8** progress **9** developed, full-blown, full-grown **11** full-fledged

maudlin 5 gushy, mushy, silly, sappy, soppy **6** slushy, sticky **7** cloying, gushing, mawkish **8** bathetic **11** sentimental, tear-jerking

Maugham character 4 Kear, Liza **5** Carey, Rosie, Sadie **7** Mildred **8** Ashenden, Craddock **10** Strickland

maul 4 bang, bash, beat, club, drub, flog, whip **5** abuse, flail, pound **6** batter, bruise, buffet, cudgel, hammer, injure, mangle, molest, pummel, sledge, thrash **7** clobber, rough up **8** bludgeon, lambaste **9** manhandle

Mauna ____ **3** Kea, Loa

maunder 3 bat, gad **4** rove **5** drift, mooch, range **6** mumble, mutter, ramble, wander **7** blather, digress, traipse **8** divagate

Mauritania *capital:* 10 Nouakchott *desert:* **6** Sahara *language:* **5** Wolof **6** Arabic, Fulani **7** Soninke *monetary unit:* **7** ouguiya *neighbor:* **4** Mali **6** Guinea **7** Senegal **7** Algeria **13** Western Sahara *river:* **7** Senegal

Mauritius *capital:* 9 Port Louis *island group:* **9** Mascarene *language:* **6** Creole *monetary unit:* **5** rupee

mauve 5 lilac **6** purple, violet

maven 3 ace **4** buff, whiz **5** adept, freak, shark **6** addict, expert, master, savant **7** devotee, fanatic, hotshot **8** virtuoso **9** authority **10** enthusiast **11** connoisseur

maverick 5 rogue, stray **7** heretic **8** unmarked **9** dissident, unbranded **10** iconoclast **11** independent, loose cannon **13** nonconformist

maw 4 crop **5** chasm, mouth **6** cavity, gullet **7** stomach

mawkish 5 gushy, mushy, sappy, soppy **6** sloppy, slushy, sticky, syrupy **7** cloying, gushing, insipid, maudlin **8** bathetic, roman-

tic **9** schmaltzy, sickening **10** lovey-dovey, nauseating **11** sentimental, tear-jerking

maxilla 3 jaw **4** bone

maxim 3 law, saw **4** rule **5** adage, axiom, gnome, moral, motto, tenet, truth **6** byword, dictum, saying, truism **7** precept, proverb, theorem **8** aphorism, apothegm **9** platitude, prescript, principle **11** commonplace

maximal 3 nth, top **6** utmost **7** highest, largest, supreme, topmost **8** complete, greatest, ultimate **9** paramount

maximum 3 nth, top **6** utmost **7** highest, largest, supreme, topmost **8** extremum, greatest, ultimate **9** paramount

may 5 might, shrub **6** spirea **8** hawthorn

maybe 7 perhaps **8** possibly **9** perchance **11** conceivably, uncertainty

Mayberry resident 4 Andy (Taylor), Opie (Taylor) **5** Gomer (Pyle) **6** Barney (Fife) **7** Aunt Bee

Mayflower *document:* 7 Compact *passengers:* **8** Pilgrims

mayhem 4 maim, riot **5** chaos, havoc **7** cripple, dislimb **8** mutilate **9** dismember **10** mutilation

mayor 11 burgomaster *Boston:* **6** Curley (James Michael) *Chicago:* **5** Daley (Richard) *New York:* **4** Koch (Edward) **6** Walker (Jimmy) **7** Lindsay (John) **8** Giuliani (Rudolph) **9** Bloomberg (Michael), La Guardia (Fiorello) *Spanish:* **7** alcalde

Mayor of Casterbridge, The *author:* 5 Hardy (Thomas) *character:* **8** Henchard (Michael)

maze 3 web **4** knot, mesh **5** skein, snarl **6** jungle, morass, tangle **7** confuse, network, perplex **8** bewilder, mishmash **9** labyrinth

Mazel ____! **3** tov

McCarthy novel 4 Road (The) **8** Crossing (The) **13** Blood Meridian **16** Cities of the Plain **18** All the Pretty Horses, No Country for Old Men

McCourt memoir 3 'Tis **10** Teacher Man **12** Angela's Ashes

McCullers, Carson *novel:* 18 Ballad of the Sad Cafe (The) **18** Member of the Wedding (The) **20** Heart Is a Lonely Hunter (The) **23** Reflections in a Golden Eye

McCullough novel 10 Thorn Birds (The)

McEwan novel 8 Saturday **9** Amsterdam, Atonement, Black Dogs **12** Enduring Love

McMurtry novel 12 Buffalo Girls, Lonesome Dove **14** Horseman Pass By **15** Last Picture Show (The) **17** Terms of Endearment

McTeague author 6 Norris (Frank)

MD 3 doc **6** doctor, medico **8** sawbones **9** physician

mea culpa 5 error, fault **7** apology **9** admission **10** concession, confession

meadow 3 lea, ley **4** vega **5** field, green **7** pasture **9** grassland *historic:* **9** Runnymede *low-lying:* **5** haugh

meadow mushroom 6 agaric

meager 4 bare, bony, lean, mere, thin **5** gaunt, lanky, scant, short, spare **6** paltry, scanty, shabby, skimpy, skinny, slight, sparse **7** angular, minimum, scraggy, scrawny, scrimpy **8** exiguous, rawboned **9** deficient, miserable **10** inadequate **12** insufficient

meal 4 chow, fare, feed, grub **5** board, feast, lunch, snack **6** brunch, dinner, farina, picnic, repast, spread, supper **7** high tea, nooning **8** luncheon, victuals **9** breakfast, collation, elevenses, refection *army:* **3** MRE **4** mess

mealy 6 spotty, uneven **11** farinaceous

mean 3 low, mid, par **4** base, fair, hint, norm, poor, want, wish **5** cheap, cruel, imply, lousy, lowly, mingy, petty, rough, small, snide, spell, tight, weigh **6** attest, center, common, denote, design, humble, intend, matter, medial, medium, middle, paltry, scummy, scurvy, shabby, shoddy, sleazy, stingy, unwell **7** average, betoken, connote, express, lowborn, miserly, pitiful, portend, propose, purport, signify, suggest, vicious **8** déclassé, indicate, inferior, mediocre, middling, midpoint, moderate, ordinary, pitiable, plebeian, stand for **9** designate, penurious, represent, symbolize **10** despicable, second-rate **11** closefisted, tightfisted **12** contemptible, intermediary, intermediate

meander 4 roam, rove, turn, wind **5** amble, drift, range, snake, stray, twist **6** ramble, wander **7** traipse, winding **8** vagabond **9** gallivant, labyrinth

meandering 5 snaky **7** sinuous **8** flexuous, tortuous **10** convoluted, serpentine **11** anfractuous

meaning 3 aim **4** gist, pith **5** drift, force, point, sense **6** effect, import, intent **7** essence, message, purport **9** intention, substance **10** definition, denotation, intimation **11** connotation, implication **12** significance **13** signification

meaningful 5 valid **7** pointed, serious, weighty **8** eloquent, material **9** important, momentous **10** expressive **11** sententious, significant, substantial **13** consequential

meaningless 5 empty, inane **6** absurd, futile, hollow, jejune **7** trivial **8** nugatory **11** nonsensical **13** insignificant

meanings *diverse:* **8** polysemy *study of:* **9** semantics

means 5 funds, money **6** assets, avenue, income **7** backing, capital **8** finances, holdings, property, reserves **9** equipment, resources, substance **11** wherewithal

meantime 7 interim **8** interval

measly 4 poor, puny **5** petty, scant **6** meager, meagre, paltry, scanty, skimpy **7** pitiful, trivial **8** niggling, pathetic, picayune, piddling, trifling **9** miserable **10** picayunish **13** insignificant

measure 3 bar, ken **4** bill, size, step, test **5** bound, gauge, index, quota, scale, share, weigh **6** amount, bounds, effort, extent, figure, ration, reckon, resort, size up, survey **7** caliper, compute, delimit, mark out, portion **8** calliper, estimate, regulate, resource, standard **9** allotment, benchmark, calculate, calibrate, criterion, demarcate, determine, expedient, magnitude, yardstick **10** dimensions, indication, proportion, touchstone *area:* **3** are, cho, mou, tan **4** acre **7** hectare *capacity:* **3** cab, cor, pin, zak **4** fass, gill, peck, pint **5** liter, minim, quart, stere **6** bushel, gallon **8** fluidram **9** fluid dram **10** fluid ounce, milliliter *cloth:* **3** ell *combining form:* **6** metric **8** metrical *depth:* **5** plumb, sound *dry:* **4** peck **6** bushel *electrical:* **3** amp, mho, ohm **4** volt, watt **6** ampere **7** coulomb *energy:* **3** erg *force:* **4** dyne *horse height:* **4** hand *interstellar space:* **6** parsec *length:* **3** mil, pik, rod **4** alen, aune, foot, hiro, inch, link, mile, tsun, vara, yard **5** chain, cubit, meter **6** league **7** braccio, furlong **9** kilometer **10** centimeter, hectometer *liquid:* **3** hin, tun **4** gill, pint **5** minim, quart **6** gallon *mixed drinks:* **6** jigger *of comparison:* **8** standard *paper:* **4** ream *printer's:* **2** em, en **4** pica **5** point *radioactive decay:* **8** halflife *rotation:* **5** angle *strength of solution:* **7** titrate *surface:* **3** are *thermodynamic:* **7** entropy **8** enthalpy *yarn:* **3** lea (see also **weight**)

measured 7 regular, stately **8** metrical **9** regulated, temperate, unhurried **10** calculated, controlled, deliberate, restrained **13** proportionate

Measure for Measure *character:* **6** Angelo, Juliet **7** Claudio, Mariana **8** Isabella **9** Vincentio *setting:* **6** Vienna

measurement 4 area **6** degree **8** capacity, quantity **9** dimension, magnitude **11** calibration, mensuration

measure up to 3 tie **4** meet **5** equal, match, rival, touch **7** emulate **10** qualify for

measuring device 4 gage, tape **5** buret, gauge, ruler, scale, timer **7** burette, caliper, sextant, venturi **8** calipers **8** dipstick **9** altimeter, barometer, dosimeter, pedometer, yardstick **11** tensiometer, velocimeter

meat 4 core, food, gist, pith, pork, veal **5** flesh, jerky, steak **6** thrust, upshot **7** edibles **8** victuals **9** foodstuff, provender, substance **10** provisions **11** comestibles *broth:* **8** bouillon *cake:* **6** burger **9** hamburger *cured:* **7** biltong *cut:* **3** rib **4** loin, rump **5** chuck, flank, plate, round, shank **7** brisket, sirloin **8** rib roast **9** club steak, rump roast, short loin, short ribs **10** blade roast, flank steak, round steak, T-bone steak **12** sirloin steak *dealer:* **7** butcher *deer:* **7** venison *dried:* **5** jerky *fastening pin:* **6** skewer *holding rod:* **4** spit **10** rotisserie *juices:* **5** gravy *packer:* **5** Swift **6** Armour *raw:* **6** gobbet *roasted:* **8** barbecue *roasting shop:* **10** rotisserie *seasoned:* **7** sausage **8** pastrami, scrapple *sheep:* **6** mutton *side:* **8** sowbelly *skewered:* **5** kebab, kebob *slice:* **6** cutlet, rasher *small portion:* **6** collop *tough part:* **7** gristle

meat-eating 11 carnivorous

meathead 3 lug, oaf **4** clod, dodo, dolt, gawk, goon, lout **5** chump, klutz, looby **6** dimwit, lubber **7** bungler, palooka **8** dumbbell, numskull **9** birdbrain, ignoramus, lamebrain, numbskull **10** nincompoop

Mebd *husband:* **6** Ailill *victim:* **10** Cuchulainn

Mecca 4 goal *country:* **11** Saudi Arabia *pilgrim:* **5** hadji, hajji *pilgrimage:* **4** hadj, hajj *port:* **5** Jedda, Jidda **6** Jeddah, Jiddah *shrine:* **5** Kaaba

mechanic 7 artisan **9** machinist

mechanical 4 cold **7** cursory, pasteup, robotic **8** lifeless **9** automated, automatic, unfeeling **10** impersonal **11** emotionless, instinctive, involuntary, perfunctory, unemotional

mechanism 4 gear **5** gizmo, means, works **6** agency, doodad, jigger, medium, widget **7** whatsit **8** dohickey **9** apparatus, appliance, procedure, technique, thingummy **10** instrument **11** contraption, contrivance, thingamabob, thingamajig, thingumajig

medal 5 badge, honor, prize **6** reward **7** laurels **8** accolade **10** decoration **13** commemoration

meddle 3 pry **4** fool, nose **5** snoop **6** butt in, dabble, horn in, kibitz, monkey, putter, tamper, tinker **7** intrude, obtrude **8** trespass **9** interfere, interlope, intervene **10** mess around

meddler 5 snoop, yenta **7** snooper **8** busybody, intruder, kibitzer **9** buttinsky **12** troublemaker

meddlesome 4 busy, nosy **5** nosey **6** prying **9** intrusive, obtrusive, officious **11** impertinent, interfering

Medea 5 witch **9** sorceress **11** enchantress *aunt:* **5** Circe *brother:* **8** Absyrtus *father:* **6** Aeëtes *husband:* **5** Jason **6** Aegeus *sister:* **5** Circe *son:* **6** Medeus *victim:* **6** Creusa, Glauce, Glauke

medial 3 mid **4** mean **6** center, middle **7** average, central, halfway, midmost **8** middling, moderate **10** centermost, middlemost **11** equidistant **12** intermediary, intermediate

median see **medial**

mediate 5 judge **6** broker, convey, liaise, settle, step in, umpire **7** adjudge, referee, resolve **8** moderate, transmit **9** arbitrate, intercede, interfere, interpose, intervene, negotiate **10** conciliate

mediator 3 ref, ump **5** judge **6** broker, umpire **7** arbiter, liaison, referee **9** go-between, middleman **10** interceder, negotiator, peacemaker **11** intercessor

medical instrument 6 needle **7** forceps, scalpel, scanner, syringe **8** otoscope, speculum **9** endoscope **11** cardiograph, stethoscope

medical practitioner 2 PA, RN **3** doc, LPN **5** nurse **6** doctor, intern **7** interne, surgeon **9** physician

medicament 4 cure, pill **6** elixir, physic, remedy **7** nostrum **8** antidote, curative **10** palliative *inert:* **7** placebo

medicate 4 cure, dose, drug, heal **5** treat

medicinal 8 curative, remedial, salutary, sanative **9** healthful **12** health-giving, pharmaceutic

medicine 4 cure, pill **5** bromo **6** physic, remedy **7** anodyne, nostrum **8** busulfan, poultice **11** antipyretic *African:* **4** muti *bottle:* **4** vial *branch:* **7** surgery **8** oncology **9** neurology, pathology **10** bariatrics, cardiology, geriatrics, gynecology, nephrology, obstetrics, pediatrics, psychiatry *cathartic:* **8** evacuant **9** purgative *combining form:* **5** iatro **8** pharmaco *quantity of:* **4** dose **6** dosage *shell:* **7** capsule *soothing:* **7** anodyne **8** lenitive, narcotic, sedative **9** calmative, soporific

medicine man 6 doctor, kahuna, shaman **9** curandero

medieval study 5 logic **7** grammar, trivium **8** rhetoric **10** quadrivium

mediocre 4 dull, fair, hack, so-so **6** common **7** average, fairish **8** inferior, middling, moderate, ordinary, passable **9** tolerable **10** pedestrian, uninspired **11** commonplace, indifferent **12** run-of-the-mill **13** unexceptional

meditate 4 mull, muse **5** weigh **6** intend, ponder **7** purpose, reflect, revolve **8** cogitate, consider, mull over, ruminate, turn over **9** reflect on **10** deliberate **11** contemplate

meditative 6 broody **7** pensive **8** brooding **10** reflective, ruminative, thoughtful

meditator 4 yogi

Mediterranean 11 Mare Nostrum **12** Mare Internum *coastal region:* **7** Riviera *eastern shores:* **6** Levant *island:* (see at **island**) *wind:* **7** mistral, sirocco **8** scirocco

medium 3 par **4** fair, mean, so-so **5** agent, organ **6** agency, métier, milieu, normal **7** ambient, average, channel, climate, culture, neutral, vehicle **8** ambience, middling, moderate, passable, standard **9** tolerable **10** atmosphere **11** clairvoyant, environment **12** run-of-the-mill *of exchange:* **5** money **8** currency **11** legal tender

medley 4 brew, olio, stew **5** combo, gumbo **6** jumble, ragout **7** farrago, mélange, mixture **8** mishmash, pastiche **9** pasticcio, patchwork, potpourri **10** assortment, hodgepodge, hotchpotch, miscellany, salmagundi **11** gallimaufry

Medusa 6 Gorgon *father:* **7** Phorcus, Phorcys *hair:* **6** snakes *mother:* **4** Ceto *offspring:* **7** Pegasus **8** Chrysaor *sister:* **6** Stheno **7** Euryale *slayer:* **7** Perseus

medusa 9 jellyfish

meed 3 due **4** part **5** quota, share **6** amount, desert, ration, return, reward **7** guerdon, measure, portion **8** dividend **9** allotment, allowance **10** recompense

meek 3 shy **4** mild, tame **5** lowly, timid **6** docile, gentle, humble, modest **7** patient **8** tolerant **10** submissive, unassuming **11** deferential **13** long-suffering

meerschaum 4 pipe **9** sepiolite

meet 3 apt, fit **4** face, fair, fill, find, join, just, open, spot **5** cross, event, hit on, match, right, touch, unite **6** answer, chance, engage, oppose, proper, settle, take on **7** contest, convene, fitting, fulfill, hit upon, satisfy, stumble **8** approach, assemble, come upon, concours, conflict, confront, converge, suitable **9** encounter, measure up **10** congregate **11** competition *a bet:* **3** see *a need:* **7** suffice *athletic:* **8** gymkhana **10** tournament *by appointment:* **10** rendezvous

meeting 4 moot, talk **5** tryst **6** huddle, parley, powwow **7** session **8** assembly, conclave, concours, congress, junction **9** concourse, encounter, gathering, rencontre **10** conference, confluence, convention, rendezvous **11** competition, convocation, get-together **12** intersection *Anglo-Saxon:* **5** gemot **6** gemote *place:* **5** forum *spiritual:* **6** séance

Mefistofele composer 5 Boito (Arrigo)

Megaera see **Erinyes**

megaphone 8 bullhorn **10** mouthpiece

Megara father: **5** Creon *husband:* **8** Heracles, Hercules *king:* **5** Nisus

megillah 5 story **7** account

megrim 3 bee **4** urge, whim **5** fancy, freak, humor **6** notion, vagary, whimsy **7** caprice, conceit, impulse, vertigo **8** crotchet, migraine **9** dizziness

Mehitabel 3 cat *creator:* **7** Marquis (Don) *friend:* **5** Archy

Mein Kampf author 6 Hitler (Adolf)

meiosis 7 litotes **12** cell division

Meissen 5 china **8** ceramics **9** porcelain

Meistersinger 5 Sachs (Hans) **9** Frauenlob

Meistersinger, Die beloved: **3** Eva *composer:* **6** Wagner (Richard) *hero:* **6** Walter *mentor:* **5** Sachs (Hans)

melancholia 5 gloom **6** sorrow **7** despair, sadness **9** dejection, morbidity **10** depression, desolation, gloominess **11** despondency, dolefulness

melancholic 3 low, sad **4** blue, glum **6** gloomy, morose, triste **7** joyless **8** dejected, downcast, mournful **9** depressed, saddening **10** depressing, despondent, dispirited

melancholy 3 low, sad **4** blue, funk, glum **5** blues, dumps, ennui, gloom **6** dismal, dreary, gloomy, misery, morose, rueful, somber, tedium, triste, woeful **7** boredom, despair, doleful, joyless, sadness, unhappy **8** dejected, dolorous, downcast, funereal, mournful, saddened **9** black bile, dejection, depressed, plaintive, saddening, sorrowful **10** depressing, depression, despondent, dispirited, lachrymose, lugubrious **11** despondency, unhappiness **12** heavyhearted, wretchedness

mélange see **medley**

Melanippus father: **7** Theseus *slayer:* **10** Amphiaraus *victim:* **6** Tydeus

Melchior companion: **6** Caspar, Gaspar **9** Balthasar, Balthazar *gift:* **4** gold

Melchizedek's kingdom 5 Salem

meld 3 mix **4** fuse **5** blend, merge **6** mingle **7** combine, mixture **8** compound **9** commingle, interfuse **10** amalgamate **11** intermingle

Meleager beloved: **8** Atalanta *father:* **6** Oeneus *mother:* **7** Althaea *victim:* **4** boar

melee 3 row **4** fray, riot **5** brawl, broil, clash, fight, set-to **6** affray, fracas, ruckus, rumpus **7** scuffle **8** skirmish **9** scrimmage **10** donnybrook, free-for-all

meliorate 4 help **5** amend **6** better, soften **7** improve **8** mitigate, palliate

Mélisande's lover 7 Pelléas

melisma 7 cadenza, descant
mellifluous 5 sweet **6** dulcet, fluent, golden, liquid, smooth **7** flowing, honeyed, silvery **8** euphonic, soothing **10** euphonious **13** silver-tongued
mellow 3 age **4** aged, ripe **5** ripen **6** genial, golden, grow up, mature, season, smooth **7** honeyed, matured, ripened **8** laid-back, pleasant, seasoned **9** agreeable
melodic 5 sweet **6** dulcet **7** musical, songful, tuneful **8** canorous, euphonic **10** euphonious
melodious 5 lyric, sweet **6** dulcet **7** musical, songful, tuneful **8** euphonic **9** cantabile **10** euphonious
melody 3 air, lay **4** aria, lilt, song, tune **5** canto, music, theme **6** chorus, strain, warble **7** descant, refrain **11** tunefulness
melon 4 pepo **5** gourd **6** casaba, profit **8** crenshaw, honeydew, windfall **10** cantaloupe
Melpomene see **Muse**
melt 3 run **4** flux, fuse, thaw **6** relent, soften **7** liquefy **8** dissolve, liquesce, unfreeze **9** disappear **10** deliquesce **down: 6** render **together: 4** fuse
Melville, Herman character: 3 Pip **4** Ahab, Toby **5** Bembo, Chase **6** Cereno (Benito), Jermin, Pierre **7** Fayaway, Ishmael **8** Bartleby, Queequeg, Starbuck **work: 4** Omoo **5** Mardi, Typee **6** Pierre **7** Redburn **8** Moby Dick **11** White-Jacket **12** Benito Cereno **13** Confidence-Man (The)
member 3 cut **4** part **5** piece **6** clause, parcel **7** portion, section, segment **8** division **9** appendage, component **10** ingredient **Parliament: 2** MP **political party: 4** Tory, Whig **7** Liberal **8** Democrat, Laborite **9** Labourite **10** Republican **12** Conservative **service club: 3** Elk **4** Lion **8** Kiwanian, Rotarian
membrane 4 film, tela **5** velum **6** pleura **7** pleurae (plural) **bodily: 6** serosa **brain: 3** pia **diffusion through: 7** osmosis **dividing: 5** septa (plural) **6** septum **ear: 8** tympanum **enclosing: 5** tunic **8** indusium **thin: 6** lamina **7** lamella, laminae (plural) **8** lamellae (plural) **wing: 8** patagium
memento 5 relic, token, trace **6** trophy **7** vestige **8** keepsake, reminder, souvenir **11** remembrance
Memnon father: 8 Tithonus **mother: 3** Eos **6** Aurora **slayer: 8** Achilles
memoir 3 bio **4** life **5** diary **6** record, report, thesis **7** account, journal **8** anecdote **9** biography **11** confessions **12** recollection, reminiscence **13** autobiography
memoirist 7 Boswell, diarist **10** biographer
memorable 7 lasting, notable **8** historic **9**

deathless, indelible, momentous, red-letter **10** noteworthy **11** significant **13** distinguished
memorandum 4 chit, note **6** minute, notice, record **7** tickler **8** notation, reminder **12** announcement
memorial 4 note **5** relic, token, trace **6** record, trophy **7** relique **8** keepsake, monument, reminder, souvenir **10** dedicatory **11** celebrative, remembrance **12** consecrative, remembrancer **13** commemoration, commemorative **mound: 5** cairn
memorial park see **cemetery**
memorize 3 con, get **6** retain **8** remember
memory 6 recall **8** mind's eye, souvenir **9** anamnesis, awareness, flashback, retention **10** reflection **11** remembrance **12** recollection, reminiscence **13** retentiveness, retrospection **assisting: 8** mnemonic **loss: 7** amnesia **trace: 6** engram **unit: 3** meg
menace 4 risk **5** alarm, peril, scare **6** danger, hazard, threat **7** imperil, jeopard, torment **8** endanger, frighten, jeopardy, threaten **9** terrorize **10** intimidate, jeopardize
ménage 4 clan **5** house **6** family **8** quarters **9** household **12** housekeeping
menagerie 3 zoo **7** mixture
mend 3 fix, sew **4** cure, darn, heal, knit **5** patch, renew **6** cobble, doctor, look up, perk up, reform, remedy, repair, revamp **7** correct, improve, patch up, rebuild, rectify, redress, restore **8** overhaul, renovate **9** condition, refurbish **10** ameliorate, convalesce, recuperate **11** recondition, reconstruct
mendacious 5 false, lying **6** shifty **7** fibbing **9** deceitful, deceptive, dishonest, paltering **10** untruthful **11** dissembling **13** prevaricating
mendacity 3 lie **6** deceit **9** deception, duplicity, falsehood **10** dishonesty **12** equivocation **13** truthlessness
mendelevium symbol 2 Md
mendicancy 7 beggary, begging, bumming, cadging **8** mooching, sponging **11** panhandling
mendicant 5 friar **6** beggar **7** begging
Mending Wall author 5 Frost (Robert)
Menelaus brother: 9 Agamemnon **father: 6** Atreus **kingdom: 6** Sparta **mother: 6** Aerope **wife: 5** Helen
menial 4 dull **5** lowly **6** humble **7** servant, servile, slavish **8** obeisant, retainer **9** unskilled **10** obsequious **11** subservient, undignified
meniscus 4 lens **9** cartilage
Menlo Park inventor 6 Edison (Thomas Alva)
menopause 11 climacteric **12** change of life

menorah 10 candelabra
Menotti, Gian Carlo *character:* **5** Amahl *opera:* **6** Consul (The), Medium (The) **9** Telephone (The)
men's store 12 haberdashery
mental 5 inner **7** psychic **8** cerebral, rational, thinking **9** reasoning, spiritual **10** immaterial, telepathic **11** intelligent **12** intellective, intellectual **13** psychological *faculty:* **6** memory
mentalist 6 Geller (Uri) **7** Kreskin **8** Banachek
mentality 3 wit **5** sense **6** brains **7** mindset, outlook **9** intellect, mother wit **10** brainpower **12** intelligence
mention 4 cite, name, note **7** refer to, specify **8** advert to, allude to, citation, instance **9** reference
mentor 4 guru **5** coach, guide, tutor **7** teacher **9** counselor **10** counsellor
Mentor's pupil 10 Telemachus
menu 4 card, diet **5** carte **10** bill of fare **11** carte du jour *item:* **4** soup **5** salad **6** entrée **7** dessert **9** appetizer
Mephibosheth *father:* **4** Saul **8** Jonathan *mother:* **6** Rizpah
Mephistophelian 7 satanic **8** devilish, diabolic **10** diabolical
mephitic 4 rank **5** fetid, funky, musty **6** putrid, smelly **7** noisome, noxious, reeking **8** stinking **9** poisonous **10** malodorous
Merab *father:* **4** Saul *husband:* **6** Adriel
mercenary 4 hack **5** ninja, ronin, venal **6** greedy **7** corrupt, soldier **8** hireling **10** gun for hire
merchandise 4 line, sell **5** cargo, goods, stock, trade, wares **6** deal in, job lot, market, retail **7** effects, promote, staples, traffic **8** products **9** publicize, vendibles **11** commodities
merchandiser 6 dealer, trader, vendor **8** retailer **9** tradesman **10** wholesaler **11** businessman **13** businesswoman
merchant 5 buyer **6** dealer, jobber, seller, trader, vendor **7** peddler **8** purveyor, retailer **9** tradesman **10** trafficker, wholesaler **11** businessman, storekeeper *guild:* **5** Hansa, Hanse *League:* **9** Hanseatic *ship:* **5** oiler **6** argosy, coaler, galiot, packet, tanker, trader **7** collier, galliot, steamer **8** Indiaman **9** freighter *wine:* **7** vintner
Merchant of Venice, The 7 Antonio *character:* **6** Portia **7** Jessica, Lorenzo, Nerissa, Shylock **8** Bassanio
merciful 4 kind **6** benign, humane, kindly **7** clement, lenient **8** tolerant **9** forgiving, indulgent **10** charitable, forbearing **11** softhearted **13** compassionate
merciless 4 grim **5** cruel, harsh **6** brutal, savage, wanton **9** cutthroat, ferocious, unfeeling **10** gratuitous, implacable, ironfisted, unyielding **11** hardhearted, unrelenting **12** unappeasable
mercurial 5 flaky **6** fickle, mobile **7** erratic **8** unstable, variable, volatile **9** impulsive **10** capricious, changeable, inconstant **13** temperamental, unpredictable
mercury 5 azoth **11** quicksilver *ore:* **8** cinnabar *symbol:* **2** Hg
Mercury 6 planet (see also **Hermes**)
Mercutio *friend:* **5** Romeo *slayer:* **6** Tybalt
mercy 4 pity, ruth **5** grace **6** lenity **7** caritas, charity **8** clemency, goodwill, kindness, leniency **9** benignity, tolerance **10** compassion, generosity, kindliness **11** benevolence, forbearance **13** commiseration *petition for:* **5** kyrie **8** miserere
mere 4 bare, lake, pool, pure **6** meager, meagre, paltry **7** trivial **8** boundary, landmark, piddling **9** undiluted
merely 4 just, only **6** simply, solely, wholly
meretricious 4 loud, sham **5** gaudy, phony, showy **6** flashy, garish, glitzy, sleazy, tawdry, tinsel, trashy **7** chintzy **8** delusive, delusory, illusory **9** contrived, deceptive **10** misleading **11** counterfeit, pretentious
merganser 4 duck, smew
merge 3 mix **4** fuse, join **5** blend, unify, unite **6** mingle **7** combine **8** coalesce, compound **9** commingle, interfuse **10** amalgamate, assimilate **11** consolidate, intermingle
merger 5 union **6** fusion **7** melding **8** alliance, takeover **9** coalition **10** absorption **11** combination, unification **12** amalgamation **13** consolidation
meridian 4 acme, apex, peak **6** apogee, climax, summit, zenith **8** pinnacle
merit 3 due **4** earn, rate **5** arete, value, worth **6** virtue **7** caliber, deserts, deserve, entitle, justify, quality, stature, warrant **10** excellence, perfection, recompense **11** achievement
merited 3 due **4** fair, just **5** right **7** condign, fitting **8** deserved, rightful, suitable **9** justified, requisite **11** appropriate
meritorious 6 worthy **8** laudable **9** admirable, deserving, estimable, honorable **10** creditable **11** commendable, thankworthy **12** praiseworthy
Merlin 4 seer **5** augur, magus **6** shaman, wizard **7** prophet **8** magician **10** soothsayer **11** necromancer, thaumaturge
merlin 6 falcon **10** pigeon hawk

mermaid 3 nix **5** Ariel, nixie **7** manatee **8** sirenian **10** water nymph **11** water sprite
Merope *father:* **5** Atlas **8** Oenopion *husband:* **7** Polybus **8** Sisyphus **11** Cresphontes *lover:* **5** Orion *mother:* **7** Pleione *sisters:* **8** Pleiades *son:* **7** Aepytus, Glaucus
merriment 4 glee **5** mirth, revel **6** gaiety **7** jollity, revelry, whoopee **8** hilarity, reveling **9** festivity, jocundity, joviality **10** jocularity, jubilation **13** entertainment
merry 3 gay **4** glad **5** happy, jolly **6** blithe, jocund, jovial, joyful, joyous, lively **7** festive, gleeful **8** animated, cheerful, mirthful **9** hilarious, sprightly, vivacious **12** high-spirited, lighthearted
merry-andrew 4 fool, zany **5** clown, joker **6** jester, madcap **7** buffoon **9** harlequin **10** mountebank
merrymaker 7 partyer, reveler **8** carouser
merrymaking 5 party, revel **6** frolic, gaiety **7** jollity, revelry, whoopee **8** hilarity **9** festivity **12** conviviality
Merry Widow composer 5 Lehár (Franz)
Merry Wives of Windsor character 3 Nym **4** Ford, Page **5** Caius **6** Fenton, Pistol **7** Slender **8** Falstaff
mesa 5 bench, butte **7** plateau **9** tableland
mescal 5 agave **6** cactus, liquor, maguey, peyote
mesh 3 net, web **4** jibe, maze **5** skein, snare, snarl **6** engage, morass, tangle **7** entwine, netting, network **8** dovetail, entangle **9** harmonize, interlock, labyrinth **10** coordinate **12** reticulation
meshuga 3 mad **4** nuts **5** crazy, goofy, kooky, loony, nutty, wacky **6** insane, screwy **7** foolish
mesmeric 8 alluring, hypnotic **9** glamorous, seductive **10** bewitching, enchanting **11** captivating, fascinating
mesmerize 4 vamp **6** dazzle, seduce **7** bewitch **8** ensorcel, enthrall, entrance **9** captivate, ensorcell, fascinate, hypnotize, spellbind
Mesopotamia 4 Iraq *civilization:* **4** Elam **5** Akkad, Sumer **7** Assyria, Elamite **8** Akkadian, Assyrian, Sumerian **9** Babylonia **10** Babylonian *river:* **6** Tigris **9** Euphrates
mess 4 hash **5** botch, snafu **6** fright, jumble, muddle **7** eyesore **8** botchery, disarray, disorder, shambles, wreckage **9** confusion **10** hodgepodge, hotchpotch, miscellany *around:* **4** hang, idle **5** chill, dally **6** dawdle, doodle, fiddle, potter, putter **7** goof off, hang out **8** chill out, lollygag **10** dilly-dally *up:* **3** err **4** blow, flub, muff, ruin **5** botch,

fluff, fudge, spoil, touse **6** bungle, fumble, tousle **7** butcher
message 4 note, post **5** sense, theme **6** letter, report **7** epistle, meaning, mission, missive, purport **8** bulletin, dispatch, telegram **9** directive, telegraph **10** communiqué **12** significance **13** communication, signification
Messalina's husband 8 Claudius
mess around 4 fool, idle **5** flirt **6** dabble, dawdle, fiddle, meddle, monkey, potter, putter, tamper, tinker **8** womanize **9** associate, interfere, interlope, philander
messenger 4 post **5** envoy **6** herald, runner **7** apostle, courier **8** emissary **9** go-between, harbinger **10** ambassador **11** internuncio **12** intermediary *God's:* **5** angel *of the gods:* **4** Iris **6** Hermes **7** Mercury *Turkish:* **6** chiaus
messiah 6 savior **7** saviour **8** defender **9** deliverer, liberator
Messiah composer 6 Handel (George Frideric)
messy 6 frowsy, frowzy, sloppy, unneat, untidy **7** chaotic, rumpled, unkempt **8** careless, confused, ill-kempt, slapdash, slipshod, slovenly **10** disheveled, disorderly **11** dishevelled *abode:* **3** sty **6** pigpen, pigsty
mestizo 5 métis **6** ladino **10** mixed-blood
Mestor *father:* **7** Perseus *mother:* **9** Andromeda
metal 4 gold, iron **5** steel **6** bronze *alloy:* (see alloy) *casting mold:* **5** ingot *corrosion:* **4** rust *fuse:* **6** solder *in mass:* **7** bullion *layer:* **7** plating *lump:* **6** nugget *magnetic:* **4** iron *refuse:* **4** slag **6** scoria *sheath:* **5** armor *source:* **3** ore *thin:* **4** foil, leaf **5** plate *worker:* **5** smith **10** blacksmith
metallic element 3 tin **4** gold, iron, lead, zinc **6** barium, cobalt, copper, nickel, radium, silver, sodium **7** arsenic, bismuth, cadmium, calcium, lithium, mercury, uranium **8** aluminum, chromium, platinum, titanium, tungsten, vanadium **9** magnesium, manganese, potassium, strontium **10** molybdenum
metamere 6 somite **7** segment
metamorphic rock 5 slate **6** gneiss, marble, schist **9** quartzite, soapstone
metamorphose 6 change, mutate **7** convert, develop **9** transform, translate, transmute **11** transfigure **12** transmogrify
metamorphosis 6 change **8** changing, mutation **9** evolution, sea change **10** changeover **13** transmutation
Metamorphosis author 5 Kafka (Franz)
_____ me tangere 4 noli
metaphor 5 trope **6** simile, symbol **7** analogy **8** allegory **10** comparison, similitude
metaphorical compound 7 kenning

metaphysical 8 bodiless, numinous **9** unearthly, unfleshly **10** immaterial, suprahuman **12** supermundane, supramundane, supranatural, transcendent **13** preternatural *poet:* **5** Donne (John) **6** Cowley (Abraham) **7** Crashaw (Richard), Herbert (George), Marvell (Andrew), Vaughan (Henry) **9** Cleveland (John)

mete 4 deal, dole, give **5** allot, bound **6** border, parcel, ration **7** portion **8** allocate, boundary, disburse, dispense **9** apportion **10** distribute

meteor 8 fireball **12** shooting star *exploding:* **6** bolide *shower:* **5** Lyrid **6** Leonid, Taurid **7** Aquarid, Geminid, Orionid, Perseid **10** Quadrantid

meteorite 8 aerolite **10** siderolite

meter 4 beat, scan **6** rhythm **7** cadence, measure, pattern

motor maid 4 Rita

metheglin 4 mead **8** beverage *ingredient:* **5** honey

method 3 way **4** mode, modi (plural), plan **5** means, modus, order, style **6** course, design, manner, schema, scheme, system **7** fashion, formula, pattern, process, routine, wrinkle **8** practice **9** procedure, technique **11** orderliness **13** modus operandi *careful:* **8** strategy *of employing troops:* **6** tactic **7** tactics *of procedure:* **4** game

methodical 5 exact **7** careful, logical, orderly, precise, regular **9** efficient, organized **10** deliberate, scrupulous, systematic, systemized **12** systematized

Methuselah *father:* **5** Enoch *grandson:* **4** Noah *son:* **6** Lamech

meticulous 5 exact, fussy, picky **6** strict **7** careful, finicky, precise **8** detailed, thorough **10** fastidious, nitpicking, pernickety, scrupulous **11** microscopic, painstaking, persnickety, punctilious **13** conscientious

métier 4 work **5** craft, field, forte, trade **7** calling, pursuit **8** business, strength, vocation **9** specialty **10** employment, occupation, profession

metrical foot 4 iamb **5** ionic, paeon **6** cretic, dactyl, iambic, iambus **7** anapest, pyrrhic, pyrrhus, spondee, triseme, trochee **8** bacchius, choriamb, dactylic, spondaic, tribrach, trochaic **9** anapestic **10** tribrachic

metric unit *area:* **3** are **7** hectare *capacity:* **5** liter, litre **9** decaliter, deciliter, kiloliter **10** centiliter, hectoliter, milliliter *length:* **5** meter **9** decameter, decimeter, dekameter, kilometer **10** centimeter, hectometer, millimeter *mass and weight:* **4** gram **7** quintal **8** decagram, decigram, dekagram, kilogram **9** centigram, hectogram, metric ton, milligram *volume:* **5** liter, litre

metro 4 tube **6** subway **11** underground

metropolis 4 city **7** capital

metropolitan 5 urban **6** urbane **7** primate **9** municipal **10** archbishop

mettle 4 fire, grit, guts **5** heart, moxie, nerve, pluck, spunk, steel, valor, vigor **6** daring, spirit, starch, temper **7** cojones, courage, resolve, stamina **8** backbone, boldness, tenacity, vitality **9** fortitude **10** resolution

mettlesome 4 bold, game **5** brave, fiery, gutsy **6** plucky, spunky **7** staunch, valiant **8** intrepid, resolute, spirited, vigorous **9** tenacious **10** courageous, determined

mew 3 hem, pen **4** cage, coop, gull **5** alley, fence **6** corral, immure, shut in, stable **7** enclose **8** hideaway

mewl 4 moan, pule **5** whine **6** snivel **7** whimper

Mexican *crop:* **5** sisal **8** henequen *estate:* **8** hacienda *food:* **4** masa, taco **5** chili, salsa **6** fajita, tamale **7** burrito, panocha, penuche, tostada **8** frijoles, tortilla **9** enchilada, guacamole **10** quesadilla **11** chimichanga *hut:* **5** jacal *liquor:* **6** mescal, mezcal **7** tequila

Mexico *ancient city:* **12** Tenochtitlán *ancient culture:* **4** Maya **5** Aztec, Mayan, Olmec **6** Toltec *bay:* **8** Campeche *capital:* **10** Mexico City *city:* **4** León **6** Juárez, Mérida, Oaxaca, Puebla **7** Nogales, Tijuana **8** Acapulco, Mexicali, Saltillo **9** Chihuahua, Matamoros, Monterrey **10** Cuernavaca **11** Guadalajara **12** Ciudad Juárez *conqueror:* **6** Cortés (Hernán, Hernando) *discoverer:* **7** Córdoba (Fernández de) *emperor:* **10** Maximilian *gulf:* **10** California *island:* **7** Cozumel *island group:* **13** Revillagigedo *lake:* **7** Chapala, Cuitzeo, Texcoco **9** Pátzcuaro *language:* **7** Spanish *leader:* **4** Díaz (Porfirio) **6** Juárez (Benito) **8** Carranza (Venustiano) *monetary unit:* **4** peso *mountain, range:* **8** Malinche **11** Sierra Madre *neighbor:* **6** Belize **9** Guatemala *peninsula:* **4** Baja **7** Yucatán *port:* **7** Tampico **8** Ensenada, Mazatlán, Veracruz *resort:* **6** Cancún **8** Acapulco *revolutionist:* **5** Villa (Pancho) **6** Zapata (Emiliano) **7** Hidalgo (Padre Miguel) *river:* **4** Mayo **5** Bravo, Yaquí **6** Balsas, Grande, Pánuco **7** Conchos **8** Grijalva, Río Bravo, Santiago **9** Rio Grande **10** Usumacinta *ruined city:* **5** Tulum, Uxmal **7** Mayapán **8** Palenque **11** Chichén Itzá *state:* **6** Oaxaca, Puebla, Sonora **7** Chiapas, Durango, Hidalgo, Tabasco, Yucatán **8** Veracruz *sea:* **9** Caribbean *volcano:* **6** Colima **9** Paricutín **11**

Ixtacihuatl **12** Citlaltépetl, Ixtaccihuatl, Popocatépetl

mezzanine 4 loge **5** story **7** balcony **8** entresol

mezzo 4 half **6** singer **7** soprano

mezzo-soprano *American:* **5** Elias (Rosalind), Horne (Marilyn), Jones (Sissieretta) **6** Bumbry (Grace), Graves (Denyce) **7** Stevens (Risë), Verrett (Shirley) **8** Troyanos (Tatiana), von Stade (Frederica) *Austrian:* **6** Ludwig (Christa) *English:* **5** Baker (Janet) *Italian:* **7** Bartoli (Cecilia) **8** Cossotto (Fiorenza)

Miami *bowl:* **6** Orange *chief:* **12** Little Turtle *county:* **4** Dade *stadium:* **9** Joe Robbie *team:* **4** Heat **7** Marlins **8** Dolphins, Panthers

miasma 3 fog **4** haze, mist, murk, smog **5** brume, vapor **9** effluvium

mica 7 biotite **8** silicate **9** isinglass, muscovite

Michelangelo Buonarotti *painting:* **10** Holy Family (The) **12** Last Judgment (The) *statue:* **5** David, Moses, Pietà **7** Bacchus

Michener novel 5 Space, Texas **6** Hawaii, Poland, Source (The) **8** Caravans, Covenant (The), Drifters (The), Sayonara **10** Centennial, Chesapeake **13** Fires of Spring (The) **15** Bridges at Toko-Ri (The)

Michigan *capital:* **7** Lansing *city:* **5** Flint **7** Detroit, Pontiac **8** Ann Arbor, Dearborn **9** Kalamazoo **11** Grand Rapids **13** Sault Ste. Marie *college, university:* **6** Calvin **9** Kalamazoo **10** Wayne State *lake:* **4** Erie **5** Huron **8** Michigan, Superior *nickname:* **9** Wolverine (State) **10** Great Lakes (State) *state bird:* **5** robin *state flower:* **12** apple blossom *state tree:* **9** white pine

mickey 5 flask, split

Mickey Mouse 5 dinky, petty **7** trivial **8** trifling **9** pointless, small-time, worthless **10** irrelevant

microbe 3 bug **4** germ **5** virus **8** bacillus, pathogen **9** bacterium **13** microorganism see **microorganism**

microfilm sheet 5 fiche

Micronesia *capital:* **7** Palikir *island, island group:* **3** Yap **5** Chuuk **6** Kosrae **7** Pohnpei **8** Caroline

microorganism 3 bug **4** germ **5** ameba, virus **6** aerobe, amoeba **7** bacilli (plural), microbe, protist **8** bacillus, bacteria (plural), pathogen, protozoa (plural) **9** bacterium, protozoan, protozoon

microphone 3 bug **4** mike *shield:* **4** gobo

microscope 9 magnifier *inventor:* **11** Leeu-

wenhoek (Antoni van) *part:* **5** stage **6** mirror **8** eyepiece **9** objective

microscopic 4 tiny **5** small **6** minute **13** infinitesimal

Microsoft founder 5 Gates (Bill)

microwave 3 zap **4** nuke

Mid-Atlantic state 7 New York **8** Delaware, Maryland, Virginia **9** New Jersey **12** Pennsylvania, West Virginia

midday 4 noon, sext **8** high noon, noontide, noontime

middle 4 core, mean **5** mesne, waist **6** center, medial, median **7** average, central, halfway **8** interior **10** centermost **11** equidistant, intervening **12** intermediary, intermediate *combining form:* **3** mes **4** meso

Middle American country 4 Cuba **5** Haiti **6** Belize, Mexico, Panama **7** Bahamas, Grenada, Jamaica **8** Barbados, Dominica, Honduras **9** Costa Rica, Guatemala, Nicaragua **10** El Salvador

middlebrow 7 Babbitt

middle class 11 bourgeoisie

middle-class 9 bourgeois

middle ear *bone:* **5** incus **6** stapes **7** malleus *membrane:* **7** eardrum **8** tympanum

Middle Eastern country 4 Iran, Iraq, Oman **5** Egypt, Qatar, Sudan, Syria, Yemen **6** Cyprus, Israel, Jordan, Kuwait, Turkey **7** Bahrain, Lebanon **11** Saudi Arabia

Middle Kingdom 5 China

middleman 5 agent **6** broker **8** mediator **9** go-between **11** distributor, intercessor **12** intermediary, intermediate

Middlemarch author 5 Eliot (George), Evans (Mary Ann)

middle-of-the-road 7 neutral **8** moderate **9** impartial **11** nonpartisan

middling 4 fair, okay, so-so **6** decent, fairly, medium, rather **7** average, fairish, typical **8** adequate, mediocre, moderate, ordinary, passable **9** tolerable **10** moderately, secondrate **11** indifferent **12** intermediate, run-of-the-mill

midge 3 fly **4** gnat **6** punkie **7** no-see-um **8** dipteran **10** chironomid *larva:* **9** bloodworm

midget 4 runt **5** dwarf, pygmy **6** bantam, peewee **7** manikin **8** Tom Thumb **10** homunculus **11** hop-o'-my-thumb, Lilliputian

Midian *father:* **7** Abraham *mother:* **7** Keturah *son:* **5** Abida, Ephah, Epher **6** Eldaah, Hanoch

midpoint 3 par **4** mean, norm **6** center, median, middle **7** average, centrum, halfway **8** bull's-eye, standard

midwife 4 dhai **5** doula **6** granny, Lucina **10** accoucheur

mien 3 air, set **4** look **6** aspect, manner **7** address, bearing **8** carriage, demeanor, presence **9** mannerism **10** appearance, deportment, expression **11** comportment

miff 3 fit, irk, vex **4** beef, flap, spat **5** annoy, pique, run-in, upset **6** bother, fracas, nettle, offend, put out **7** dispute, provoke, quarrel, rhubarb **8** irritate, squabble **10** conniption, falling-out **11** altercation

might 3 may **4** sway **5** brawn, clout, force, means, power **6** energy, muscle **7** ability, command, control, mastery, potency **8** capacity, strength **9** authority, resources **12** forcefulness

mighty 4 huge, very **5** grand, great **6** heroic, potent, strong **7** eminent, immense, massive, titanic **8** enormous, forceful, gigantic, imposing, powerful, puissant **10** impressive, monumental, prodigious, stupendous, tremendous

Mignon composer 6 Thomas (Ambroise)

mignonette 4 herb **5** sauce **6** annual **6** reseda

migrant 5 exile, mover, nomad **7** drifter, nomadic, refugee **8** traveler, wanderer **9** itinerant, transient **10** expatriate

migrate 4 move, trek **5** drift, range, shift **6** wander **8** transfer

migration 6 exodus **8** diaspora *of professionals:* **10** brain drain

migratory 5 nomad **6** errant, mobile, moving, roving **7** nomadic, ranging **9** wandering

Mikado, The *character:* 4 Ko-Ko **6** Yum-Yum **7** Pooh-Bah **8** Nanki-Poo **9** Pitti-Sing *composer:* **8** Sullivan (Arthur) *librettist:* **7** Gilbert (W. S.)

milady 6 madame **10** noblewoman **11** gentlewoman

Milan *family:* 6 Sforza **8** Visconti *opera house:* **7** La Scala

Milcah *brother:* 3 Lot *father:* **5** Haran **10** Zelophehad *husband:* **5** Nahor *son:* **7** Bethuel

mild 4 calm, easy, meek, soft, tame **5** balmy, bland, faint, tepid **6** benign, docile, gentle, placid, serene, smooth, tender **7** amiable, clement, equable, insipid, lenient, patient, subdued **8** moderate, obliging **9** benignant, temperate **10** forbearing, submissive

mildew 4 mold, rust **6** fungus, growth

___ **mile 7** country, statute **8** nautical

mileage recorder 8 odometer

milestone 5 event **6** marker **8** landmark, occasion

milieu 5 scene **6** medium, sphere **7** ambient, climate, setting **8** ambiance, ambience **10** atmosphere, background **11** environment, mise-en-scène **12** surroundings

militant 7 fighter, martial, warlike, warrior **8** activist, fighting **9** assertive, bellicose, combatant, combative, truculent **10** aggressive, pugnacious **11** belligerent, contentious, quarrelsome **12** gladiatorial

military 5 troop **6** forces, troops **7** martial, warlike **8** soldiery **9** soldierly **10** servicemen **11** armed forces, soldierlike *alert protocol:* **6** DEFCON *alliance:* **4** NATO *base:* **4** camp, fort, post **5** depot, field **6** billet **8** barracks, garrison, quarters **10** encampment *officer:* **5** major **7** captain, colonel, general **9** brigadier **10** lieutenant *prisoner:* **3** POW *school:* **3** OCS, OTS **4** ROTC, USMA **9** Annapolis, West Point *sector:* **10** combat zone, front lines **11** battlefront *store:* **2** BX, PX **10** commissary *storehouse:* **5** depot **6** armory **7** arsenal *supplies:* **8** matériel, ordnance *unit:* **5** corps, squad, troop **7** company, platoon **8** division, regiment **9** battalion **11** battle group *vehicle:* **4** jeep, tank **6** Abrams, Humvee **7** Bradley **9** Black Hawk, half-track

militate 4 tell **5** count, weigh **6** matter **11** carry weight

militia 7 reserve

milk 4 pump, rook, suck **5** drain, educe, empty, evoke, exact, mulct, nurse, wring **6** elicit, extort, fleece **7** exhaust, exploit, extract *coagulated:* **4** curd *combining form:* **4** lact **5** lacti, lacto *curdled:* **7** clabber *fermented:* **5** kefir **6** kumiss, yogurt **7** koumiss, yoghurt *liquid part:* **4** whey *store:* **5** dairy *sugar:* **7** lactose

milkfish 3 awa

milk shake 6 frappe **7** frosted

milky 4 fair, meek, mild, pale, tame **5** white **6** chalky, cloudy, gentle **7** lacteal, whitish **8** timorous *lymph:* **5** chyle

mill 5 grind, plant, shape, works **7** factory, machine **9** circulate, pulverize **11** manufactory

millenary 8 thousand

Miller, Arthur *film:* 7 Misfits (The) *play:* **5** Price (The) **9** All My Sons **8** Crucible (The) **12** After the Fall **16** Death of a Salesman **17** View from the Bridge (A) *salesman:* **5** Loman (Willy)

milliner 6 hatter

million *combining form:* 3 meg **4** mega

millionth *combining form:* 4 micr **5** micro

Mill on the Floss author 5 Eliot (George), Evans (Mary Ann)

millstone 4 duty, load, onus **6** burden, charge, weight **9** albatross **10** affliction, deadweight

Milne character 3 Roo **4** Pooh (Winnie the) **5** Kanga **6** Eeyore, Piglet, Tigger

milord 8 nobleman 9 gentleman, patrician 10 aristocrat 12 silk stocking

milquetoast see **milksop**

Miltiades' victory 8 Marathon

Milton work 5 Comus 7 Lycidas 8 L'Allegro 12 Areopagitica, Paradise Lost

mime 3 act 5 actor 6 act out 7 Marceau (Marcel) 9 performer, represent 11 impersonate 12 impersonator

mimic 3 act, ape, tui 4 aper, copy, mock, play 5 actor, enact 6 mummer, parody, parrot, player 7 copycat, imitate 8 resemble, simulate, travesty 9 burlesque, pantomime 11 impersonate 12 impersonator

mimicry 4 echo 6 parody 8 travesty 9 imitation, parroting 10 caricature 13 impersonation

minatory 4 dire, grim 7 baleful, baneful, direful, hostile, malefic, ominous 8 menacing, sinister 9 ill-boding 10 forbidding, foreboding, maleficent 11 frightening, threatening 12 intimidating

mince 4 chop, dice, hash 5 cut up, strut 6 prance, sashay, soften 8 moderate, restrain, tone down 9 euphemize

mincing 5 fussy 6 dainty, la-di-da, too-too 7 finical, finicky, stilted 8 affected, delicate 10 fastidious, pernickety 11 persnickety

mind 3 wit 4 mood, obey, soul, tend, will, wits 5 brain, fancy, watch, weigh 6 attend, belief, beware, brains, follow, memory, notice, psyche, reason, senses, spirit 7 care for, discern, dislike, feeling, observe, oversee, purpose 8 consider 9 intellect, intention, mentality, supervise 10 brainpower, gray matter 11 disposition, temperament 12 intelligence 13 consciousness *combining form:* 5 psych 6 psycho

mindful 5 alert, awake, aware 7 knowing 8 sensible, vigilant 9 attentive, cognizant, conscious, observant 10 conversant 13 conscientious

mindless 4 rash 5 ditsy, ditzy, inane, silly 6 jejune, simple, stupid 7 asinine, foolish, unaware, vacuous 9 nitwitted, oblivious 10 irrational, unthinking 13 unintelligent

mine 3 dig, pit, sap 4 fund, lode, vein, well 5 delve, drill, hoard, stock, store, trove 6 burrow, quarry, spring 7 bonanza, deposit, extract 8 eldorado, excavate, Golconda 10 excavation, wellspring 13 treasure trove *coal:* 8 colliery *entrance:* 4 adit

miner 6 pitman 7 collier

mineral 5 beryl, topaz, trona 6 augite, barite, garnet, iolite, pinite, rutile, sphene, spinel, sulfur, zircon 7 apatite, axinite, azurite, bornite, calcite, citrine, coesite, cyanite, jade-ite, kernite, kunzite, olivine, zeolite 8 boracite, cinnabar, dolomite, epsomite, fayalite, feldspar, fluorite, hematite, lazulite, lazurite, siderite, sodalite, stibnite, triplite, wellsite 9 aragonite, celestite, cerussite, danburite, fosterite, kaolinite, lawsonite, magnetite, malachite, muscovite, phenakite, scapolite, tridymite, turquoise, wulfenite 10 chalcedony, orthoclase, pyrrhotite, tourmaline 11 alexandrite, chrysoberyl, melanterite 12 brazilianite, chalcopyrite, tincalconite 13 rhodochrosite *flaky:* 4 mica *greasy:* 4 talc 10 serpentine *hard:* 6 spinel 7 diamond 8 corundum *iridescent:* 4 opal *nonmetallic:* 5 boron 6 gypsum, halite 8 asbestos, graphite *shiny:* 4 gold 6 galena, pyrite, silver *soft:* 4 talc 6 gypsum 8 graphite *transparent:* 6 quartz

mineral water 7 seltzer 8 club soda

Minerva see **Athena**

mingle 3 mix 4 meld 5 blend, merge 6 commix 7 combine 8 intermix 9 associate, socialize

mingy 4 mean 5 cheap, tight 7 chintzy, miserly, scrimpy 8 grudging, ungiving 9 niggardly, penurious 10 pinchpenny 11 closefisted, tightfisted

miniature 3 wee 4 tiny 5 small, teeny, weeny 6 little, minute, petite, teensy 9 itsy-bitsy, itty-bitty 10 diminutive, small-scale, teeny-weeny 11 Lilliputian 12 illumination

minify 4 trim 6 lessen, shrink 7 abridge, curtail 8 decrease, diminish 10 abbreviate

minim 3 bit, jot 4 atom, iota 5 grain, speck 7 modicum, smidgen 8 particle *music:* 8 half note

minimal 5 basic, least, token 6 lowest 7 nominal 8 littlest, smallest 9 slightest

minimize 5 decry 6 reduce 7 run down 8 belittle, derogate, discount, downplay, play down 9 disparage, soft-pedal, underrate 10 depreciate 13 underestimate

minimum 3 dab, jot 4 iota, whit 5 least, speck 6 lowest, margin 7 smidgen 8 particle, pittance, smallest

minion 4 idol 5 toady 6 flunky, lackey, vassal, yes-man 7 devotee, flunkey, flunkie, spaniel 8 favorite, follower, parasite, truckler 9 sycophant, toadeater, underling 10 bootlicker 11 lickspittle, subordinate

minister 4 tend 5 agent, clerk, serve 6 cleric, curate, divine, parson 8 clerical, preacher, reverend 9 churchman, clergyman 10 ambassador 12 ecclesiastic *of state:* 10 chancellor *plenipotentiary:* 5 envoy 6 consul 8 diplomat, emissary

ministry 5 agent, organ 6 agency, clergy, medium **7** cabinet **10** department, instrument **11** bureaucracy

mink kin 5 otter, skunk, stoat **6** ermine, ferret, fisher, weasel

Minnehaha's husband 8 Hiawatha

Minnesota *capital:* 6 St. Paul ***city:* 5** Edina **6** Duluth **9** Rochester **11** Minneapolis ***college, university:* 8** Carleton **9** Saint Olaf **10** Macalester ***nickname:* 6** Gopher (State) **9** North Star (State) ***park:* 9** Voyageurs ***river:* 7** St. Croix **9** Minnesota **11** Mississippi ***state bird:* 4** loon (common) ***state flower:* 12** lady's slipper ***state tree:* 7** red pine

minor 5 lower, petty, small, youth **6** casual, lesser, little, paltry, slight **7** trivial **8** inferior, mediocre, piddling, small-fry, trifling, underage **9** dependent, secondary, smallbeer, small-time **10** bush-league, secondrate, shoestring **11** indifferent, unimportant **13** insignificant

minority 5 youth **6** nonage **7** infancy **9** childhood **10** immaturity

minor-league 5 small **6** lesser **9** secondary, small-time **11** unimportant

Minos *daughter:* 7 Ariadne, Phaedra ***father:* 4** Zeus **7** Jupiter ***kingdom:* 5** Crete ***monster:* 8** Minotaur ***mother:* 6** Europa ***son:* 9** Androgeos ***wife:* 8** Pasiphaë

Minotaur *father:* 4 bull ***home:* 9** labyrinth ***mother:* 8** Pasiphaë ***slayer:* 7** Theseus

minstrel 4 bard, wait **6** harper, singer **7** gleeman **8** jongleur **9** balladist **10** troubadour ***end man:* 5** Bones (Mr.), Tambo (Mr.) ***instrument:* 4** lute, lyre **5** naker, rebec, shawm, tabor **8** crumhorn, psaltery **9** krummhorn **10** tambourine

mint 3 pot **4** cast, coin, heap, pile, sage **5** basil, bugle, forge, issue, stamp, trove **6** boodle, bundle, create, intact, packet, savory, strike, unused **7** fortune, like-new, menthol, perfect, produce **8** brand-new, lavender, marjoram, original **9** blue curls, bugleweed, undamaged **10** pennyroyal

Minuit's purchase 9 Manhattan

minus 4 flaw, lack, less, sans **6** absent, defect **7** lacking, missing, wanting, without **8** drawback, negative, subtract **10** deficiency

minuscule 4 tiny **5** small **6** letter, little, minute **7** trivial **9** lowercase, miniature **10** negligible, small-scale **11** meaningless, microscopic **13** imperceptible, inappreciable, insignificant

minute 3 wee **4** jiff, memo, note, tiny **5** draft, flash, jiffy, small, teeny, weeny **6** little, moment, record, teensy **7** careful, instant, precise, trivial **8** detailed, itemized, thorough, trifling **9** itsy-bitsy, itty-bitty, miniature, mi-

nuscule **10** diminutive, memorandum, meticulous, scrupulous, teeny-weeny **11** Lilliputian, punctilious **13** infinitesimal

minutes 3 log **6** annals, record **7** summary **10** transcript **11** proceedings

minutiae 6 trivia **7** details **10** fine points, triviality **11** particulars

minx 4 bawd, moll, slut, tart **5** bimbo, tramp, wench, whore **6** floozy, harlot, hooker **7** hustler, trollop **8** strumpet **10** prostitute

miracle 4 boon, feat **6** marvel, wonder **7** godsend, portent, prodigy, stunner **8** windfall **9** sensation **10** phenomenon

miraculous 7 amazing **8** wondrous **9** marvelous, unearthly, wonderful **10** astounding, prodigious, superhuman **11** astonishing, spectacular **12** inexplicable, supernatural **13** preternatural

mirage 6 vision, wraith **8** delusion, illusion, phantasm **11** fata morgana, ignis fatuus **13** hallucination

Miranda *father:* 8 Prospero ***lover:* 9** Ferdinand

mire 3 bog, fen, mud **4** muck, ooze, sink, trap **5** delay, marsh, slush, swamp **6** detain, enmesh, entrap, hang up, morass, slough, tangle **7** bog down, embroil, ensnare, involve, set back **8** entangle **9** imbroglio, implicate, quicksand

Miriam's brother 5 Aaron, Moses

mirror 5 glass **6** embody, typify **7** reflect **8** speculum **9** exemplify, personify, reflector **10** illustrate **11** cheval glass **12** looking glass ***signaling:* 10** heliograph

mirth 3 fun, joy **4** glee **5** cheer **6** gaiety, levity **7** jollity, revelry **8** gladness, hilarity **9** festivity, frivolity, happiness, jocundity, joviality, merriment **10** jocularity **11** merrymaking **12** cheerfulness

mirthful 3 gay **5** jolly, merry, riant **6** jocund, jovial **7** festive **9** exuberant, hilarious **12** lighthearted

miry 4 oozy **5** boggy, mucky, muddy **6** marshy, slushy, swampy

misadventure 4 slip **5** boner, error, lapse **6** howler, mishap **7** blunder, faux pas **8** accident, calamity, casualty, disaster **9** cataclysm **10** misfortune **11** catastrophe

misanthrope 5 cynic, grump, loner **6** grinch **7** killjoy, recluse, scoffer **10** curmudgeon

misanthropic 7 cynical **10** antisocial

misappropriate 5 filch, steal **6** pilfer **7** purloin **8** embezzle, peculate **9** defalcate

misbegotten 7 bastard, illicit, natural **8** baseborn, deformed, spurious **10** fatherless, unfathered **12** contemptible, disreputable, ill-conceived, illegitimate

misbehave 5 act up, cut up, lapse, rebel, stray **6** act out, offend **7** carry on, disobey **8** trespass **10** roughhouse, transgress

misbehavior 7 misdeed **8** rudeness **9** high jinks **10** misconduct, wrongdoing **11** delinquency, dereliction, naughtiness **13** transgression

miscalculate 3 err **8** miscount, misgauge

miscarry 4 fail, flop **5** abort **6** fizzle **7** go wrong

miscellaneous 3 odd **5** mixed **6** motley, sundry, varied **7** diverse **8** assorted **9** different, disparate, scrambled **13** heterogeneous

miscellany 3 ana **4** hash, olio, stew **5** salad **6** jumble, medley, motley, muddle **7** farrago, mélange, mixture, omnibus **8** mixed bag, pastiche **9** anthology, congeries, pasticcio, patchwork, potpourri **10** assortment, hodgepodge, hotchpotch, salmagundi **11** aggregation, gallimaufry, odds and ends, olla podrida, smorgasbord

mischance 6 mishap **7** bad luck, tragedy **8** accident, casualty **9** adversity **10** misfortune **11** contretemps

mischief 3 ill **4** evil, harm **5** prank **6** damage, strife **7** devilry, roguery, trouble, waggery **8** deviltry, sabotage **9** devilment, diablerie, vandalism **10** wrongdoing **11** naughtiness, shenanigans **12** monkeyshines

mischief-maker 3 imp **4** puck **5** devil, knave, rogue, scamp **6** rascal **7** villain **8** agitator, scalawag **9** prankster, trickster **11** rapscallion **12** rabble-rouser

mischievous 3 sly **4** arch, foxy **5** antic, saucy **6** artful, bratty, impish, tricky, vexing **7** harmful, irksome, larkish, naughty, playful, puckish, roguish, tricksy, waggish **8** annoying, damaging, perverse, prankish, rascally, sportive **9** injurious, malicious **10** bothersome, frolicsome, ill-behaved

misconception 5 error **7** fallacy, mistake **8** delusion, illusion

misconduct 8 adultery **10** wrongdoing **11** dereliction, impropriety, malfeasance, malpractice, misbehavior **12** malversation **13** transgression

miscreant 4 heel **5** felon, knave, rogue **6** outlaw, rascal, sinner, wretch **7** corrupt, culprit, heretic, hoodlum, infidel, lowlife, vicious, villain **8** apostate, criminal, depraved, infamous, perverse **9** heretical, nefarious, scoundrel, unhealthy, wrongdoer **10** blackguard, degenerate, delinquent, unbeliever, villainous

miscue 4 goof, miss, slip, trip **5** error, fluff, lapse **6** slipup **7** blooper, blunder, mistake

misdeed 3 sin **5** crime, wrong **6** breach **7** offense **9** violation **10** infraction **13** transgression

misdoubt 4 fear **5** dread **7** suspect

mise-en-scène 3 set **4** site **6** locale, medium, milieu **7** ambient, climate, context, scenery, setting **8** ambiance, ambience, stage set **10** atmosphere, background **11** environment **12** stage setting, surroundings

miser 5 piker **7** hoarder, niggard, scrooge **8** tightwad **9** skinflint **10** cheapskate, pinchpenny

miserable 6 gloomy, meager, meagre, paltry, rueful, sordid, woeful **7** doleful, forlorn, piteous, pitiful, squalid **8** desolate, dolorous, downcast, hopeless, shameful, tortured, wretched **9** afflicted, destitute, sorrowful, worthless **10** despairing, despondent, melancholy

Miserables, Les *author:* **4** Hugo (Victor) *character:* **6** Javert (Inspector) **7** Cosette, Fantine, Valjean (Jean)

miserly 4 mean **5** close, tight **6** greedy, stingy **7** scrimpy **8** covetous, grasping **9** niggardly, penurious, scrimping **10** avaricious **11** closefisted, tightfisted **12** cheeseparing, parsimonious **13** penny-pinching

misery 3 woe **5** agony, dolor, grief **6** sorrow **7** anguish, squalor **8** calamity, distress **9** adversity, dejection, suffering **10** affliction, depression, desolation **11** despondency **12** wretchedness

misfit 6 oddity, weirdo **7** oddball **8** maverick **9** eccentric, screwball

misfortune 3 ill, woe **4** blow, harm, loss **5** cross, trial **7** reverse, setback, tragedy, trouble **8** accident, calamity, casualty, disaster, hardship **9** adversity, cataclysm **10** affliction, visitation **11** catastrophe, contretemps, tribulation

misgiving 4 fear **5** doubt, dread, qualm **6** unease **7** anxiety, scruple **8** distrust **9** suspicion **10** foreboding **11** premonition, trepidation **12** apprehension, presentiment

misguided 5 wrong **9** erroneous **10** ill-advised **11** injudicious **12** short-sighted

mishandle 4 flub **5** abuse, botch **6** bungle, fumble, mess up **7** rough up **8** maltreat **10** knock about, slap around

mishap 7 bad luck, tragedy **8** accident, casualty **9** adversity **11** contretemps

mishmash 4 olio, stew **6** jumble, litter, medley, motley, muddle **7** clutter, farrago, mélange, mixture, rummage **8** pastiche, scramble **9** pasticcio, patchwork, potpourri **10** hodgepodge, hotchpotch, salmagundi **11** gallimaufry

misidentify 5 mix up **7** confuse **8** confound

misinterpret 7 confuse, misread
mislay 4 lose
mislead 4 dupe, fool, gull, lure **5** bluff, cheat **6** betray, delude, entice, seduce, take in **7** beguile, deceive **8** hoodwink, inveigle **11** double-cross
misleading 5 false, wrong **8** delusive, delusory, specious **9** deceitful, deceptive **10** fallacious, inaccurate **11** casuistical, sophistical
mismatch 3 jar **5** clash **6** jangle **7** discord **8** conflict
misplace 4 lose
misprint 4 typo
misprision 5 scorn **7** despite, disdain, neglect **8** contempt, sedition **9** contumely, disregard **10** misconduct, negligence **11** concealment, dereliction, impropriety, malpractice
misrepresent 4 warp **5** twist **6** garble **7** distort, falsify, varnish **8** disguise **9** embellish, embroider **10** camouflage **11** counterfeit
misrepresentation 3 fib, lie **4** tale **5** story **6** canard **7** falsity, untruth **9** falsehood **10** distortion
miss 3 err, gal **4** fail, girl, lass, maid, omit, skip **5** avoid **6** damsel, escape, forget, ignore, lassie, maiden **7** failure, misfire, neglect **8** discount, leave out, overlook **9** disregard *French:* **4** Mlle. **12** Mademoiselle *German:* **8** Fräulein *Spanish:* **4** Srta. **8** Señorita
Missa Solemnis composer 9 Beethoven (Ludwig van)
misshape 4 warp **6** deform **7** contort, distort, torture **9** disfigure
missile 4 bolt, dart **5** arrow, shell, spear **6** bullet, rocket **10** cannonball, projectile *shelter:* **4** silo *underwater:* **7** torpedo (see also **guided missile**)
missing 4 AWOL, lost **6** absent
mission 3 aim, job **4** duty, goal, task **5** quest, recon **6** charge, errand, object, sortie **7** calling, embassy, purpose **8** legation, lifework, ministry, vocation **9** objective **10** assignment
missionary 7 apostle **8** emissary **10** evangelist, revivalist **12** propagandist, proselytizer
Mississippi *capital:* **7** Jackson *city:* **6** Biloxi **8** Gulfport **10** Greenville *college, university:* **12** Jackson State **8** Millsaps *nickname:* **8** Magnolia (State) *river:* **5** Pearl **11** Mississippi *state bird:* **11** mockingbird *state flower:* **8** magnolia *state tree:* **8** magnolia
missive 4 memo, note **6** letter, report **7** epistle, message **8** dispatch
Miss Julie author 10 Strindberg (August)
Miss Lonelyhearts author 4 West (Nathanael)

Missouri *capital:* **13** Jefferson City *city:* **7** St. Louis **10** Kansas City **11** Springfield **12** Independence *college, university:* **10** Washington *lake:* **15** Lake of the Ozarks *nickname:* **6** Show Me (State) *river:* **8** Missouri **11** Mississippi *state bird:* **8** bluebird *state flower:* **8** hawthorn *state tree:* **7** dogwood
misstate 4 warp **5** color, twist **6** garble **7** distort, falsify
misstatement 3 fib, lie **4** tale **7** falsity, untruth **9** falsehood **13** prevarication
misstep 4 flub, goof, slip **5** boner, error, fluff, gaffe, lapse **6** slipup **7** blooper, blunder, faux pas
mist 3 dim, fog **4** blur, film, haze, murk **5** befog, brume, cloud **7** becloud, obscure
mistake 4 flub, slip **5** boner, error, fluff, folly, gaffe, lapse, snafu **6** boo-boo, bungle, howler, slipup **7** blooper, blunder, confuse, faux pas, take for **8** confound **10** inaccuracy
mistaken 5 false, wrong **6** all wet, faulty, flawed, untrue **7** invalid **8** specious **9** defective, erroneous, incorrect, misguided, unfounded **10** fallacious, fraudulent, inaccurate **11** misinformed
mister 3 sir **7** husband *French:* **8** Monsieur *German:* **4** Herr *Italian:* **6** Signor *Spanish:* **5** Señor
mistreat 5 abuse **6** ill-use, molest **7** rough up **9** brutalize, manhandle
mistress 4 doxy, moll **5** lover, woman **7** hetaira **8** dulcinea, ladylove, paramour **9** concubine, courtesan, inamorata, kept woman **10** chatelaine, girlfriend *of Charles II:* **4** Gwyn (Nell) **8** Villiers (Barbara) *of Edward III:* **7** Perrers (Alice) *of Henry II (England):* **8** Clifford (Rosamund) *of Henry II (France):* **10** de Poitiers (Diane) *of Louis XV:* **9** Pompadour (Madame de) *of Ludwig I:* **6** Montez (Lola)
mistrust 5 doubt **7** concern, dispute, dubiety, surmise, suspect **8** wariness **9** apprehend, misgiving, suspicion **10** foreboding, skepticism **11** incertitude, uncertainty **12** apprehension
mistrustful 4 wary **5** leery **6** uneasy **7** dubious, jealous **8** doubting **9** skeptical **10** suspicious
misty 3 dim **4** hazy **5** foggy, vague **6** cloudy, vapory **7** blurred, obscure, tearful, unclear **8** confused, nebulous, vaporous **10** indistinct
misunderstanding 4 rift, spat, tiff **5** mix-up **6** breach **7** dispute, quarrel, rupture **8** squabble **10** falling-out **12** disagreement
misuse 5 waste *of a word:* **8** malaprop **11** malapropism

Mitchell novel 15 Gone with the Wind
mite 3 bit, jot **4** atom, iota **5** grain, minim, ounce, speck **6** acarid, tittle **7** chigger, modicum, smidgen **8** molecule, particle *family:* **8** oribatid
miter 5 crown, joint **9** headdress
mitigate 4 ease **5** abate, allay, relax, slake **6** lessen, soften, subdue, temper **7** assuage, lighten, mollify, relieve **8** palliate, moderate, tone down **9** alleviate, extenuate, meliorate
mitigation 4 ease **6** relief **8** easement
mitosis 12 cell division, karyokinesis *stage:* **8** anaphase, prophase **9** metaphase, telophase
mix 4 fuse, link, lump, meld, stir **5** blend, merge, unite **6** fusion, jumble, mingle, tangle, work in **7** amalgam, combine, concoct, confuse, conjoin **8** coalesce, compound, confound **9** associate, commingle, interfuse **10** amalgamate, crossbreed **11** intermingle **12** amalgamation
mixed 6 hybrid, impure, motley, sundry, varied **7** diluted, diverse, mongrel **8** assorted, compound **9** composite, crossbred, interbred, irregular **12** multifarious **13** heterogeneous, miscellaneous
mixed bag 4 hash, olio **5** gumbo, salad **6** jumble, medley **7** mélange **8** mishmash, pastiche **9** potpourri **10** assortment, hodgepodge, hotchpotch, miscellany, salmagundi **11** gallimaufry
mixed-up 5 fazed **6** addled **7** jumbled **8** confused **9** flustered, nonplused, perplexed **10** bewildered, disjointed, distracted, incoherent, nonplussed **12** disconcerted
mixologist 6 barman **7** tapster **9** barkeeper, bartender
mixture 4 brew, hash, olio, stew **5** alloy, blend, gumbo, hybrid, jumble, medley **7** amalgam, farrago, mélange **8** compound, mishmash, solution **9** composite, potpourri **10** concoction, confection, miscellany, salmagundi **11** combination **12** amalgamation
mix up 5 addle **6** fuddle, jumble, muddle **7** confuse, fluster, mistake **8** befuddle, bewilder, confound **10** disarrange, discompose **11** disorganize, misidentify
mix-up 4 hash, mess, muss **5** botch, chaos, error, melee **6** muddle, tangle **7** mistake **8** shambles **9** commotion, confusion
MKS unit 3 lux, ohm **4** mole, volt, watt **5** farad, henry, hertz, joule, lumen, meter, metre, tesla, weber **6** ampere, kelvin, newton, pascal, second **7** candela, coulomb, siemens **8** kilogram

Mnemosyne 6 Memory *daughters:* **5** Muses *father:* **6** Uranus *lover:* **4** Zeus *mother:* **4** Gaea
Moabite *city:* **3** Kir *god:* **7** Chemosh *king:* **5** Eglon, Mesha
Moab's father 3 Lot
moan 4 wail, weep **5** gripe, groan, whine **6** bewail, grieve, grouse, lament **7** deplore **8** complain
mob 3 jam **4** clan, gang, herd, pack, push, ring, riot **5** crowd, crush, horde, mafia, press, swarm **6** jostle, masses, rabble, throng **8** canaille, riffraff **9** hoi polloi, multitude **11** proletariat
mobile 5 fluid **6** moving **7** migrant, movable **8** cellular, moveable, variable **9** itinerant, migratory, unsettled, versatile **10** ambulatory **11** peripatetic
mobile home 4 tent **6** camper **7** trailer **9** Airstream
mobile-phone area 4 cell
mobilize 5 drive, impel, rally, ready, rouse **6** arouse, call up, muster, prompt, propel **7** actuate, animate, marshal **8** activate, assemble, organize **9** circulate
mobster 4 capo, goon, thug **6** hit man **7** goombah, made man, mafioso **8** criminal, gangster **9** godfather, racketeer
Moby Dick 5 whale **10** white whale *author:* **8** Melville (Herman) *character:* **3** Pip **6** Daggoo, Parsee **7** Ishmael **8** Queequeg, Starbuck, Tashtego *pursuer:* **4** Ahab *ship:* **6** Pequod
moccasin 6 loafer **7** slipper **8** larrigan
mock 3 ape **4** defy, fake, gibe, jape, jeer, razz, twit **5** bogus, chaff, dummy, false, feign, mimic, phony, quasi, sneer, taunt, tease **6** deride, ersatz, parody, pseudo, send up **7** deceive, feigned, imitate, lampoon, mislead **8** ridicule, satirize, so-called, spurious **9** imitation, simulated **10** artificial **11** counterfeit
mockery 4 sham **5** farce, scorn, sport **6** japery, parody, satire **7** take-off **8** contempt, derision, raillery, ridicule, travesty **9** burlesque, imitation **10** caricature **13** laughingstock
mocking 8 derisive, sardonic, scornful **9** sarcastic
mode 3 fad, way **4** chic, rage **5** state, style, vogue **6** custom, manner, method, status, system **7** fashion **9** condition, procedure, situation, technique **10** convention, dernier cri
model 4 copy, type **5** dummy, ideal, shape **6** design, effigy, mirror, mockup, symbol **7** classic, epitome, example, imitate, mani-

kin, paragon, pattern, perfect, replica, typical **8** ensample, exemplar, flawless, mannikin, maquette, nonesuch, paradigm, standard **9** archetype, beau ideal, blueprint, classical, criterion, exemplary, miniature, nonpareil **10** apotheosis, embodiment, prototypal, touchstone **12** paradigmatic, prototypical, reproduction *famous:* **4** Iman, Moss (Kate) **5** Banks (Tyra), Tiegs (Cheryl) **6** Hutton (Lauren), Parker (Suzy), Twiggy **8** Brinkley (Christie), Bündchen (Gisele), Campbell (Naomi), Crawford (Cindy), Schiffer (Claudia) **9** Shrimpton (Jean) **10** MacPherson (Elle), Turlington (Christy)

moderate 3 ebb **4** bate, curb, even, fair, mild, so-so, wane **5** abate, sober **6** lessen, medium, reduce, relent, soften, steady, subdue, temper **7** average, control, ease off, equable, lighten, limited, neutral, relieve, subside, trivial **8** centrist, constant, discreet, middling, mitigate, restrain **9** alleviate, constrain, temperate **10** abstemious, controlled, reasonable, restrained **11** indifferent **12** conservative

moderation 7 control, measure **9** restraint **10** abstinence, constraint, limitation, temperance **13** temperateness

moderator 5 judge **7** arbiter **8** chairman, examiner, governor, mediator **10** peacemaker **11** chairperson

modern 3 new **5** fresh, novel **6** recent **7** current **8** neoteric, up-to-date **10** newfangled, present-day **12** contemporary

modernize 4 redo **5** renew **6** update **7** remodel **8** renovate **9** refurbish **10** rejuvenate

modest 3 coy, shy **4** meek, prim **5** plain, timid **6** decent, demure, humble, proper, seemly, simple **7** bashful, prudish **8** decorous, discreet, moderate, reserved, reticent, retiring **9** diffident **10** unassuming **11** straitlaced, unassertive **12** self-effacing **13** unpretentious

Modest Proposal author 5 Swift (Jonathan)

modesty 7 decency, reserve **8** chastity, humility, timidity **9** propriety, reticence **10** diffidence

modicum 3 bit, jot, tad **4** atom, iota, mite, whit **5** grain, minim, ounce, pinch, scrap, speck, trace **7** smidgen, soupçon **8** particle

modify 4 vary **5** adapt, alter, amend, limit, tweak **6** adjust, change, mutate, revise, rework, temper **7** qualify **8** mitigate, moderate, restrain **9** refashion

modish 4 chic **5** smart, swank **6** chichi, trendy, with-it **7** dashing, stylish **11** fashionable

Modred *father:* **6** Arthur *mother:* **8** Margawse *slayer, victim:* **6** Arthur

module 4 item, unit **7** element **9** component **11** constituent

modulate 4 vary **5** tweak **6** adjust, attune, temper **8** fine-tune, regulate, restrain

modus operandi 5 style **6** custom, manner, method, system **7** process, program, routine **8** approach, practice, strategy **9** procedure, technique

modus vivendi 9 way of life

mogul 4 czar, king, lord **5** baron, nabob, ruler **6** bigwig, honcho, prince, sachem, top gun, tycoon **7** kingpin, magnate **9** plutocrat, potentate

Mohammed see **Muhammad**

Mohawk chief 5 Brant (Joseph) **8** Hiawatha

Mohican chief 5 Uncas

moiety 3 cut **4** half, part **5** piece **7** element, portion, section, segment **8** division **9** component

moil 3 tug, wet **4** grub, to-do, work **5** churn, dirty, drive, grind, labor, swirl **6** bustle, clamor, drudge, hubbub, lather, seethe, strain, strive, uproar **7** ferment, travail, trouble, wrangle **8** drudgery **9** agitation, commotion, confusion **10** hurly-burly, turbulence

moist 3 wet **4** damp, dank, dewy **5** humid **6** clammy, steamy, sticky **7** dampish, maudlin, tearful, wettish

moisten 3 wet **6** dampen **8** humidify, saturate

moisture 4 damp **5** vapor **7** wetness **8** humidity **13** precipitation

mojo 3 hex **4** jinx **5** charm, magic, power, spell **6** hoodoo, whammy

molar 5 tooth **7** grinder *neighbor:* **6** canine

molasses 7 treacle **10** blackstrap

mold 3 die **4** cast, form, sort, type **5** forge, ingot, knead, shape, stamp **6** design, fungus **7** fashion, pattern **8** template **9** construct

moldable 6 pliant, supple **7** ductile, plastic, pliable **9** adaptable, malleable

molder 3 rot **5** decay, waste **7** crumble **9** break down, decompose **11** deteriorate **12** disintegrate

molding 4 bead, gula, ogee **5** congé, ogive, talon, torus **6** reglet **7** annulet, beading, cavetto, cornice, reeding **8** cincture **9** baseboard *compound:* **4** beak, cyma, ogie **10** serpentine *edge:* **5** arris *flat:* **5** splay **6** fascia, fillet, listel, regula **7** chamfer *simple curve:* **4** roll **5** flute, ovolo, torus **6** scotia **8** astragal

Moldova *capital:* **8** Chisinau, Kishinev *former name:* **8** Moldavia *language:* **8** Romanian *monetary unit:* 3 leu *neighbor:* 7 Romania, Ukraine *river:* 8 Dniester

moldy 5 dated, fusty, musty, passé 6 bygone, old hat 7 ancient, antique, archaic, outworn 8 mildewed, outdated 9 crumbling, moth-eaten 10 antiquated 12 old-fashioned

mole 3 spy 4 pier, quay 5 jetty, nevus 6 burrow, tunnel 9 birthmark 10 breakwater

molecule 3 bit, jot 4 iota 5 minim, speck 7 modicum 8 particle

molest 3 vex 4 bait 5 abuse, annoy, harry, tease 6 badger, bother, harass, heckle, hector, pester, plague 7 disturb, torment, trouble 9 persecute

Moll Flanders author 5 Defoe (Daniel)

mollify 4 calm, ease 5 allay 6 pacify, soften, soothe, temper 7 appease, assuage, lighten, placate, relieve, sweeten 8 mitigate 9 alleviate 10 ameliorate, conciliate, propitiate

mollusk 6 chiton *bivalve:* 4 clam 6 cockle, mussel, oyster, teredo 7 geoduck, scallop 8 shipworm *cephalopod:* 5 squid 7 octopus 8 argonaut, nautilus 10 cuttlefish *part:* 6 mantle, radula, siphon *tooth shell:* 9 dentalium *univalve:* 4 slug 5 conch, cowry, murex, snail, whelk 6 cowrie, limpet, triton 7 abalone 10 nudibranch, periwinkle

Molly ____ 7 Maguire, Pitcher

mollycoddle 3 pet 4 baby 5 humor, spoil 6 cocker, cosset, dandle, pamper 7 cater to, indulge, milksop 8 mama's boy 11 milquetoast

Moloch's pit 6 Tophet

molt 4 cast, shed, slip 6 change, slough 7 cast off, discard, ecdysis 9 slough off

molted skins 7 exuviae

molten 6 melted 7 glowing 9 liquefied

molten rock 4 lava 5 magma

molybdenum symbol 2 Mo

moment 3 sec 4 jiff 5 flash, jiffy, point, shake, trice 6 import, minute, second 7 instant 8 juncture, occasion 9 magnitude 10 importance 11 consequence, split second 12 significance

momentary 5 brief, quick 8 fleeting, fugitive 9 ephemeral, fugacious, transient 10 evanescent, short-lived, transitory

momentous 5 grave 7 epochal, fateful, serious, weighty 9 important 10 meaningful 11 significant, substantial 12 considerable 13 consequential

momentousness 6 import, weight 9 magnitude 10 importance 11 consequence, weightiness 12 significance

momentum 5 drive 6 energy, thrust 7 impetus, impulse 10 propulsion

Momo author 4 Ende (Michael)

momus 6 carper, critic, mocker 7 caviler 8 caviller 9 detractor 11 faultfinder

Monaco *commune:* 10 Monte Carlo *language:* 6 French *monetary unit:* 4 euro *monetary unit, former:* 5 franc *neighbor:* 6 France *prince:* 6 Albert 7 Rainier *princess:* 5 Grace 8 Caroline

monad 3 one 4 atom, unit 8 zoospore 9 protozoan

Mona Lisa 10 La Gioconda *painter:* 7 da Vinci (Leonardo) 8 Leonardo (da Vinci)

monarch 4 czar, king, raja, tsar, tzar 5 queen, rajah, ruler 6 kaiser, prince 7 emperor, empress, majesty 9 butterfly, potentate, sovereign *daughter:* 7 infanta 8 princess *heir:* 7 dauphin 11 crown prince *son:* 6 prince 7 infante

monarchical 5 regal, royal 6 kingly 8 imperial, kinglike, majestic 9 sovereign

monarchy 4 rule 5 realm, reign 7 kingdom 8 kingship 9 autocracy, monocracy 11 sovereignty

monastery 5 abbey 6 friary, priory 7 convent, nunnery 8 cloister *Buddhist:* 8 lamasery *Eastern Orthodox:* 5 laura *head:* 5 abbot, prior

monastic 4 abbé, monk 7 ascetic, brother 8 isolated, secluded 9 reclusive 10 cloistered 11 sequestered

____ **Mondrian** 4 Piet

monetary 6 fiscal 9 financial, pecuniary 10 numismatic

monetary rate 7 millage

monetary unit see at individual countries

money 4 cash, coin, gelt, jack, kale, loot, pelf, swag 5 bread, chips, dough, funds, lolly, lucre, moola, rhino, scrip 6 boodle, change, dinero, do-re-mi, mammon, moolah, riches, specie, wampum, wealth 7 cabbage, capital, coinage, lettuce, needful, scratch, stipend 8 bankroll, currency, finances, treasure 9 resources 10 greenbacks 11 filthy lucre, legal tender

moneyed 4 rich 5 flush 6 loaded 7 opulent, wealthy, well-off 8 affluent, well-to-do 10 prosperous, well-heeled

money-grubber 5 miser 7 hoarder, niggard, scrooge 8 tightwad 9 skinflint 10 cheapskate 12 penny-pincher

moneymaking 6 paying 7 gainful 9 lucrative 10 profitable, well-paying, worthwhile 12 advantageous, remunerative

monger 4 hawk, sell, vend 6 broker, dealer, hawker, peddle, trader, vendor 7 higgler, packman, peddler 8 huckster

Mongol *conqueror:* 9 Tamerlane 10 Kublai Khan 11 Genghis Khan, Tamburlaine *peo-*

ples: **4** Daur, Olöt, Urat **5** Ordos **6** Bargut, Buryat, Buzawa, Chahar, Dorbet, Torgut **7** Karchin, Khalkha, Monguor

Mongolia *capital:* **9** Ulan Bator **11** Ulaanbaatar *conqueror:* **6** Ögödei **11** Genghis Khan *desert:* **4** Gobi *lake:* **6** Baikal *monetary unit:* **6** tugrik *mountain range:* **5** Altai, Altay **6** Kentai **7** Hentiyn **9** Altai Shan, Altay Shan *neighbor:* **5** China **6** Russia *river:* **4** Yalu **5** Orhun **7** Selenga

mongoose 4 urva

mongrel 3 cur **4** mule, mutt **5** cross **6** hybrid **7** bastard, mixture **8** half-bred **9** crossbred, half blood, half-breed **10** crossbreed

moniker 3 tag **4** name **6** handle **8** cognomen, nickname **9** sobriquet **11** appellation, designation

monish 4 warn

monition 6 caveat **7** caution, portent, warning **11** forewarning

monitor 4 test **5** check, watch **6** screen **7** adviser, observe, oversee **8** watchdog **11** keep track of

Monitor *designer:* **8** Ericsson (John) *opponent:* **8** Virginia **9** Merrimack

monitory 7 warning **8** advisory **10** cautionary

monk 4 abbé **5** friar **7** brother **8** cenobite, monastic **9** anchorite *Buddhist:* **4** lama **5** bonze *Hindu:* **4** sannyasi *Roman Catholic:* **8** Capuchin, Salesian, Trappist **9** Carmelite, Dominican **10** Carthusian, Cistercian, Franciscan **11** Augustinian *room:* **4** cell *shaven crown:* **7** tonsure *title:* **3** Dom, Fra **5** Padre

monkey 3 imp **4** mess **5** gamin **6** meddle, simian, tamper, urchin **8** busybody **9** interfere, interlope *Ceylon:* **4** maha *Cochin China:* **4** douc *New World:* **4** mico, saki, titi **6** howler, spider, uakari, woolly **7** sapajou, tamarin **8** capuchin, marmoset, squirrel **11** douroucouli *Old World:* **4** mona **5** Diana, drill **6** guenon, langur, rhesus, vervet **7** colobus, hanuman, macaque **8** mandrill, mangabey **9** proboscis **10** Barbary ape

monkeyshine 3 gag **4** dido, jape, lark **5** antic, caper, prank, stunt, trick **6** frolic **10** shenanigan, tomfoolery

monocratic 8 absolute, despotic **9** arbitrary, autarchic, tyrannous **10** autocratic, tyrannical

monogram 8 initials

monograph 5 study **6** thesis **8** tractate, treatise **9** discourse **12** disquisition, dissertation

monopolize 3 hog **5** sew up **6** absorb, corner **7** control, engross **8** dominate, take over

monopoly 5 trust **6** cartel, corner **7** control **9** ownership, syndicate **10** consortium, domination **11** exclusivity

monotone 5 drone, thrum **8** sameness

monotonous 4 blah, dull **6** boring, dreary **7** droning, humdrum, one-note, uniform **8** singsong, unvaried **9** unvarying **10** pedestrian, repetitive **11** repetitious

monotony 6 tedium **7** humdrum **8** flatness, sameness **10** uniformity

monsoon 6 deluge **8** downpour **9** rainstorm **10** cloudburst

monster 3 orc **4** ogre **5** beast, freak, giant, whale **6** mutant, ogress **8** behemoth, bogeyman, colossus, giantess **9** hellhound, leviathan, manticore *biblical:* **5** Rehab **6** Behemoth **9** Leviathan *female:* **6** Gorgon, Medusa, Scylla *fire-breathing:* **6** dragon, Typhon **7** Chimera **8** Chimaera *fowl-dragon:* **10** cockatrice *French:* **8** Tarasque *Hebrew:* **5** golem *horse-fish:* **11** hippocampus *hundred-armed:* **9** Enceladus *hundred-eyed:* **5** Argus *hundred-handed:* **8** Briareus *lion-eagle:* **7** griffin *nine-headed:* **5** Hydra *serpent-headed:* **6** gorgon *study of:* **10** teratology *three-bodied:* **6** Geryon *three-headed dog:* **8** Cerberus *two-headed dog:* **6** Orthos *water:* **6** kraken *woman-bird:* **5** Harpy *woman-lion:* **6** Sphinx *woman-serpent:* **7** Echidna (see also **dragon, giant**)

monstrosity 5 freak **6** horror **7** eyesore, outrage, prodigy **8** atrocity, enormity **11** abomination **12** malformation

monstrous 4 huge, vast **5** awful, giant, large **7** glaring, heinous, hellish, hideous, immense, inhuman, mammoth, massive, titanic **8** aberrant, abnormal, colossal, deformed, dreadful, enormous, fiendish, freakish, gigantic, god-awful, gruesome, horrible, infamous, shocking, towering **9** atrocious, egregious, fantastic, frightful, grotesque, humongous, loathsome, malformed, unnatural **10** diabolical, flagitious, gargantuan, horrendous, impressive, monumental, outrageous, prodigious, scandalous, stupendous, tremendous

montage 4 olio **6** jumble, medley **7** mélange, mixture **9** composite, patchwork, potpourri **10** assortment, miscellany **12** conglomerate

Montagues' enemies 8 Capulets

Montaigne's forte 5 essay

Montana *capital:* **6** Helena *city:* **5** Butte **7** Bozeman **8** Billings, Missoula **10** Great Falls *lake:* **8** Flathead *motto:* **9** Oro y plata *mountain:* **7** Granite (Peak) *nickname:* **8** Treasure (State) *park:* **7** Glacier *river:* **8** Missouri **11** Yellowstone *state bird:* **10** meadowlark *state flower:* **10** bitterroot *state tree:* **13** ponderosa pine

Montenegro *capital:* **7** Cetinje **9** Podgorica *language:* **7** Serbian *monetary unit:* **4** euro *park:* 8 Durmitor *river:* 3 Lim 4 Piva, Tara, Zita 6 Morača *sea:* 8 Adriatic

Monteverdi opera 5 Orfeo 7 Arianna

Montezuma *capital:* 12 Tenochtitlán *conqueror:* 6 Cortés, Cortéz (Hernán, Hernando) *people:* 6 Aztecs *revenge:* 8 diarrhea

month *Hindu:* 3 Pus 4 Asin, Jeth, Magh 5 Aghan, Chait, Sawan 6 Asargh, Bhadon, Kartik, Phagun 7 Baisakh *Jewish:* 2 Ab 4 Adar, Elul, Iyar 5 Nisan, Sivan, Tebet 6 Kislev, Shebat, Tammuz, Tishri 7 Heshvan *Muslim:* 4 Rabi 5 Rajab, Safar 6 Jumada, Sha'ban 7 Ramadan, Shawwal 8 Muharram 9 Dhu'l-Hijja, Dhu'l-Qa'dah

Montmartre church 10 Sacré Coeur

Montserrat *capital:* 8 Plymouth *discoverer:* 8 Columbus (Christopher) *location:* 10 West Indies *territory of:* 7 Britain *volcano:* 9 Soufrière

monument 5 cairn, stela, stupa 7 memento, tribute 8 archives, cenotaph, document, memorial 9 footstone, headstone, tombstone 10 gravestone 11 grave marker, testimonial *prehistoric:* 6 dolmen, menhir 8 cromlech, megalith

monumental 4 epic, huge, vast 6 mighty, mortal 7 awesome, immense, mammoth, massive 8 enormous, gigantic, historic, majestic, towering 9 monstrous 10 prodigious, stupendous, tremendous 11 mountainous, outstanding 12 overwhelming

mooch 3 bat, beg, bum 4 grub, roam, rove 5 amble, cadge, drift, range, slink, sneak, steal, stray 6 ramble, sponge, wander 7 maunder, meander, saunter 8 freeload, scrounge 9 panhandle

mooching 7 beggary 9 mendicity 10 mendicancy

mood 3 air 4 aura, feel, tone, whim 5 fancy, humor 6 spirit, temper, vagary 7 caprice, emotion, feeling, mind-set 8 ambiance, ambience 9 character, semblance 10 atmosphere 11 disposition, personality, temperament

moody 4 glum 5 mopey 6 fickle, gloomy 7 pensive 8 unstable 9 mercurial, whimsical 10 capricious, changeable, depressive, inconstant, melancholy 13 temperamental

moola 4 cash, coin, pelf, swag 5 bread, dough, money 6 dinero, specie, wampum 7 cabbage, scratch 9 long green

moon 4 gape, mope 5 dream 6 dawdle 8 languish 9 satellite *dark area:* 4 mare 5 maria (plural) 7 farside *god:* 3 Sin 5 Nanna 6 Meztli *goddess:* 4 Luna 5 Diana, Tanit 6 Hecate, Hekate, Selena, Selene, Tanith 7 Artemis, Astarte *period:* 5 phase *valley:* 4 rill *vehicle:* 3 LEM (see also **satellite**)

Moon and Sixpence *author:* 7 Maugham (W. Somerset)

mooncalf 4 dolt, fool 5 dunce, ninny 7 jackass, tomfool 9 simpleton

moonfish 4 opah 5 platy

Moon River composer 7 Mancini (Henry)

moonshine 4 bosh, jake 5 hokum 6 bunkum, humbug 7 bootleg, eyewash, hogwash 8 homebrew, malarkey, nonsense, tommyrot 9 poppycock 10 balderdash, bathtub gin, contraband, flapdoodle 11 mountain dew 12 blatherskite

Moonstone, The *author:* 7 Collins (Wilkie) *detective:* 4 Cuff

moonstruck 4 daft, nuts 5 batty, corny, flaky, kooky, mushy, nutty, sappy, wacko, wacky 6 crazed, cuckoo, fruity, insane, screwy 7 berserk, bonkers, lunatic, maudlin, touched 8 romantic 9 nostalgic, schmaltzy 10 lovey-dovey, saccharine, unbalanced 11 sentimental

moor 3 bog, fen 4 dock, fell 5 berth, catch, tie up 6 anchor, Berber, fasten, Muslim, secure, tether 7 peat bog 8 make fast, Moroccan *fictional:* 7 Othello

moose 6 cervid *female:* 3 cow *male:* 4 bull *relative:* 3 elk 4 deer 6 wapiti 7 caribou 8 reindeer

moot 5 argue, plead 6 broach, debate 7 agitate, bring up, canvass, discuss, dispute, dubious, suggest, suspect 8 abstract, academic, arguable, disputed, doubtful 9 debatable, introduce, thrash out, uncertain, unsettled, ventilate 10 disputable, unresolved 11 problematic 12 questionable 13 controversial

mop 4 swab, wipe

mope 4 fret, idle, moon, pine, pout, sigh, stew, sulk 5 brood, drift, mosey 6 dawdle, linger 7 maunder, meander, saunter 8 languish

mopes 4 funk 5 blues, dumps, ennui, slump 7 dismals, malaise, sadness 8 dolefuls 10 depression, melancholy 11 unhappiness

mopey 3 low 4 blue, down, glum 6 broody, droopy, morose 7 doleful 8 cast down, dejected, downcast 9 depressed 10 dispirited, melancholy, spiritless

moppet 3 kid, tot 4 tike, tyke 5 chick, child 7 toddler 8 juvenile 9 youngster

mop up 4 beat, drub, dust, lick, whip 6 absorb, garner, gather 7 shellac, trounce 8 complete, lambaste 9 overwhelm

moral 3 saw 4 good, just, pure, rule 5 adage, axiom, gnome, maxim, noble, right 6 chaste, decent, dictum, honest, lesson, proper, saying, truism **7** epigram, ethical, preachy, precept, proverb, upright, virtual **8** aphorism, apothegm, didactic, elevated, sermonic, virtuous **9** honorable, righteous **10** high-minded, principled, scrupulous, upstanding **11** right-minded **13** conscientious

morale 4 mood **5** heart **6** esprit, mettle, spirit, temper **7** resolve **10** confidence **13** esprit de corps

moralistic 5 noble, pious **7** canting, ethical **8** didactic, virtuous **9** righteous **10** principled **11** pharisaical, right-minded **13** sanctimonious

morality 5 ethic, honor, mores **6** purity, virtue **7** decency, probity **8** goodness **9** integrity, rectitude, rightness **11** saintliness, uprightness **13** righteousness

moralize 6 preach **7** lecture **9** preachify, sermonize **11** pontificate

morals 5 mores **6** ethics, ideals **8** scruples **9** integrity, standards **10** principles

morass 3 bog, fen, web **4** knot, maze, mesh, mire, quag, trap **5** marsh, skein, snarl, swamp **6** jungle, muddle, tangle **8** quagmire **9** imbroglio

moratorium 3 ban **5** delay **8** interval **10** suspension

moray 3 eel

morbid 4 dark, sick **5** moody **6** gloomy, grisly, morose, sickly, sullen **7** unsound **8** diseased, gruesome **9** saturnine, unhealthy **11** melancholic, unwholesome **12** pathological

mordancy 7 acidity **8** acerbity, acridity, acrimony, asperity, pungency **9** harshness, sharpness **10** causticity, trenchancy **11** astringency

mordant 4 acid, keen **5** acerb, acrid, salty, sharp **6** biting **7** acerbic, burning, caustic, cutting, pungent **8** incisive, sardonic, scathing **9** sarcastic, trenchant

Mordecai *cousin:* **6** Esther *father:* **4** Jair *mother:* **6** Esther

more 3 new, too **4** also, else, plus **5** added, again, along, extra, fresh, older, other, spare **6** as well, better, nearer, withal **7** another, besides, farther, further, greater **8** likewise, moreover **9** increased **10** additional

More book 6 Utopia

more or less 5 about, circa **7** roughly **13** approximately

moreover 3 and, too **4** also **6** as well, withal **7** besides, further **8** likewise **10** in addition **11** furthermore **12** additionally

mores 6 ethics, habits, values **7** beliefs, customs, manners **8** folkways **9** amenities, etiquette **10** civilities **11** proprieties

Morgan le Fay 9 sorceress *brother:* **6** Arthur (King)

moribund 5 dying **6** ebbing, fading **7** dormant, outworn **8** decaying, expiring, inactive **9** declining **11** obsolescent **13** deteriorating

Mormon Church *administrative unit:* **4** ward **5** stake *founder:* **5** Smith (Joseph) *leader:* **5** Young (Brigham) *priest:* **5** elder

Mormon State 4 Utah

morning 4 dawn **5** sunup **6** aurora **7** dawning, sunrise **8** cockcrow, daybreak, daylight, forenoon *moisture:* **3** dew **8** dewdrops *song:* **6** aubade

Morocco *capital:* **5** Rabat *city:* **3** Fès **6** Agadir, Meknès **7** Tangier **9** Marrakech, Marrakesh **10** Casablanca *coast:* **7** Barbary *language:* **6** Arabic, Berber *monetary unit:* **6** dirham *mountain, range:***3** Rif **5** Atlas **7** Toubkal *neighbor:* **5** Spain **7** Algeria **13** Western Sahara *sea:* **13** Mediterranean

moron 4 dodo, dolt, dope, fool **5** dummy, dunce, idiot **6** cretin, dimwit, stupid **7** dullard, half-wit **8** dumbbell, imbecile, numskull **9** ignoramus, lamebrain, numbskull, simpleton

moronic 4 dull, dumb **6** simple, stupid **8** backward, retarded **9** brainless, dim-witted, imbecilic **10** half-witted, slow-witted **12** feebleminded, simpleminded

morose 4 dour, glum, sour **5** moody, sulky **6** cranky, crusty, gloomy, morbid, sullen **7** crabbed, unhappy **9** depressed, saturnine **10** depressive, ill-humored, melancholy

morph 6 change, mutate **7** convert **9** transform, transmute **12** metamorphose, transmogrify

Morpheus *father:* **6** Hypnos *god of:* **5** sleep

Morrison *novel* **4** Jazz, Love, Sula **7** Beloved **9** Bluest Eye (The) **13** Song of Solomon

Morse code *dash:* **3** dah *dot:* **3** dit

morsel 3 bit, ort **4** bite **5** crumb, goody, piece, scrap, snack, taste, treat **6** dainty, nibble, tidbit **7** soupçon **8** delicacy, fragment, kickshaw, mouthful

mortal 3 man **5** awful, being, fatal, frail, human, party **6** deadly, lethal, person **7** deathly, earthly, extreme, fleshly, tedious, worldly **8** creature, ruthless, temporal **9** merciless, personage **10** implacable, individual, perishable **11** conceivable

mortality 5 flesh **7** mankind **8** fatality, humanity **9** death rate, humankind, lethality **10** deadliness

mortar 5 grout **6** binder, cannon, cement, vessel **7** plaster, sealant **8** howitzer, ordnance

Morte d'Arthur author 6 Malory (Thomas)

mortgage 4 hock, lien, pawn **6** pledge **10** obligation

mortician 8 embalmer **10** undertaker

mortified 6 shamed **7** ascetic, ashamed, austere **8** red-faced **9** chagrined **10** humiliated, shamefaced **11** embarrassed

mortify 5 abash, shame **6** deaden, dismay **7** chagrin, perturb **8** disgrace **9** discomfit, embarrass, humiliate

mortuary 8 funereal **10** sepulchral **11** funeral home

mosaic 5 inlay **7** chimera **8** terrazzo **9** composite, patchwork **12** tessellation *piece:* **6** smalto **7** tessera **8** tesserae (plural)

Moscow *cathedral:* **8** St. Basil's **11** Saint Basil's *citadel:* **7** Kremlin *resident:* **9** Muscovite

Moses *brother:* **5** Aaron *brother-in-law:* **5** Hobab *deathplace:* **4** Nebo *father-in-law:* **6** Jethro *sister:* **6** Miriam *son:* **7** Eliezer, Gershom *spy:* **5** Caleb *successor:* **6** Joshua *wife:* **8** Zipporah

mosey 4 mope **5** amble, drift **6** dawdle, linger, ramble, stroll, wander **7** maunder, meander, saunter

mosh 4 slam **9** slam-dance

Moslem see **Muslim**

mosque 6 masjid *niche:* **6** mihrab *prayer caller:* **7** muezzin *turret:* **7** minaret

mosquito 5 culex **7** skeeter *eater:* **3** bat **4** bird, frog **9** dragonfly *genus:* **5** Aëdes, Culex **9** Anopheles

moss 9 bryophyte *kind:* **4** peat **8** sphagnum *part:* **4** seta **7** capsule, rhizoid *study of:* **8** bryology

mossback 4 fogy **6** fossil **10** fuddy-duddy **11** reactionary **12** antediluvian, conservative **13** stick-in-the-mud

mostly 6 mainly **7** chiefly, largely, overall, usually **9** generally, primarily **11** principally **13** predominantly

mote 3 bit, dot, jot **4** iota, whit **5** grain, point, speck, trace **8** flyspeck, particle

moth *immature:* **5** larva **6** larvae (plural) **11** caterpillar *kind:* **4** luna **7** codling, tussock **8** Cecropia, silkworm **9** browntail *order:* **11** Lepidoptera

moth-eaten 4 worn **5** dated, dingy, faded, mangy, moldy, musty, passé, ratty, seedy **6** bygone, old hat, patchy, shabby **7** antique, archaic, raggedy, run-down, unkempt **8** decrepit, outdated, outmoded, tattered, timeworn **10** antiquated, down-at-heel, threadbare **11** dilapidated

mother 2 ma **3** dam, mom **4** mama, root **5** fount, mammy, mater, momma, mommy, mummy, nurse **6** matrix, origin, source **7** care for, nurture **9** prototype, rootstock **10** provenance, wellspring *combining form:* **4** matr **5** matri, matro *French:* **4** mère German: **6** Mutter *Italian:* **5** madre *Portuguese:* **3** mãe *Spanish:* **5** madre

mother country 8 homeland **10** fatherland

Mother Courage author: **6** Brecht (Bertolt)

motherly 8 maternal **9** nurturing **10** protective

mother-of-pearl 5 nacre

Mother of Presidents 8 Virginia

Mother of the Gods 3 Ops **4** Rhea **6** Cybele

motif 4 idea, text **5** point, theme, topic **6** design, device, figure, matter **7** pattern, subject **8** idée fixe **13** subject matter

motion 4 stir, sway **6** signal **7** gesture **8** movement, proposal, stirring **9** agitation

motionless 5 fixed, inert, still **6** frozen, static **7** stalled **8** becalmed, immobile, stagnant, unmoving **9** immovable, steadfast **10** stationary, stock-still

motion picture see **movie**

motivate 4 fire, goad, move, spur **5** impel, pique, rouse **6** arouse, excite, incite, induce, prompt **7** actuate, inspire, provoke, quicken, trigger **8** inspirit, persuade **9** galvanize, influence, stimulate

motivation 4 spur **5** drive **7** impetus, impulse **8** ambition, catalyst, stimulus **9** impulsion, incentive, stimulant **10** incitation, incitement **11** inspiration, instigation, provocation

motive 3 aim, end **4** spur **5** cause, point, theme, topic **6** design, device, figure, intent, matter, object, reason, spring **7** impulse, pattern, purpose, subject **8** stimulus **9** incentive, intention, rationale **10** incitement, inducement **11** inspiration

motley 4 olio, stew **5** mixed, salad **6** jumble, medley, varied **7** dappled, diverse, piebald **8** assorted, pastiche **9** disparate, multihued **10** assortment, hodgepodge, hotchpotch, miscellany, multicolor, salmagundi, variegated **11** gallimaufry, varicolored **12** conglomerate, multicolored, multifarious, parti-colored **13** heterogeneous, miscellaneous, polychromatic

motor 3 car **4** auto, ride **5** buggy, drive **6** cruise, engine **7** machine **10** automobile

motorboat 6 launch **7** cruiser, inboard **8** outboard, runabout **12** cabin cruiser

motorcycle 7 chopper **8** minibike **9** trail bike *adjunct:* **7** sidecar

Motown 7 Detroit *founder:* **5** Gordy (Berry) *group:* **8** Four Tops, Miracles, Supremes **9** Vandellas **11** Temptations

mottle 4 spot **5** fleck **6** blotch, dapple, marble **7** spatter, speckle, stipple, splotch

mottled 5 tabby 7 blotchy, dappled, flecked, spotted 8 blotched, brindled, speckled 9 checkered 10 variegated

motto 3 cry 5 adage, axiom, maxim 6 byword, saying, slogan, war cry 7 precept, proverb 8 aphorism 9 battle cry, catchword, watchword 10 shibboleth 11 catchphrase

moue 3 mow, mug 4 face, pout 7 grimace

mound 4 bank, berm, cock, heap, hill, hump, mass, pile 5 cairn, drift, knoll, shock, stack 6 barrow, tumuli (plural) 7 bulwark, hillock, rampart, tumulus 9 elevation 10 embankment *Buddhist:* 5 stupa *burial, Eastern Europe:* 6 kurgan *of detritus:* 4 kame *of sand:* 4 dune *of stones:* 5 cairn

mount 3 alp, wax 4 lift, peak, rise, show, soar 5 arise, build, climb, frame, horse, put on, raise, rouse, scale, set up, stage, steed, swell 6 ascend, aspire, deepen, expand, launch, uprear 7 advance, augment, display, enhance, enlarge, install, magnify, produce, support, upsurge 8 bestride, escalade, escalate, heighten, increase, multiply, redouble 9 aggravate, intensify 10 promontory

mountain 3 alp, lot 4 bank, crag, dome, heap, hill, hulk, lump, mass, mesa, much, peak, pile, slew 5 bluff, butte, drift, mound, shock, stack 6 height, massif *Adirondack:* 9 Whiteface *Africa's highest:* 4 Kibo *Alaska:* 4 Bona 6 Denali 7 Foraker, Sanford 8 McKinley, Wrangell *Alaska-Canada:* 10 Saint Elias *Alberta:* 6 Castle 10 Eisenhower *Alps:* 4 Rosa (Monte) 8 Blanc, Eiger 8 Jungfrau 10 Matterhorn *Andes:* 4 Ruiz 5 Torrá *Angola:* 4 Moco *Antarctica:* 4 Mohl 6 Vinson (Massif) 7 Gardner 9 Elizabeth *Apennines:* 5 Amaro *Appalachians:* 8 Mitchell 10 Kittatinny 10 Washington 13 Clingmans Dome *Argentina:* 4 Azul 5 Negra, Payún 9 Aconcagua *Asia Minor:* 3 Ida *Australia:* 4 Ziel 5 Bruce 6 Cradle 9 Kosciusko *Bavaria:* 5 Arber *Berkshires:* 8 Greylock *biblical:* 5 Horeb, Sinai, Tabor 6 Ararat, Carmel, Gilboa, Gilead, Hermon, Moriah, Olivet, Pisgah 7 Lebanon 8 Har Tavor *Black Hills:* 6 Harney (Peak) 8 Rushmore *Bolivia:* 5 Cuzco, Tahua, Ubina 6 Sajama, Sorata 8 Illimani *Borneo:* 4 Raja 8 Kinabalu, Kinabulu *California:* 5 Guyot 6 Shasta, Sonora 7 Palomar, Whitney 8 Half Dome, Tuolumne 9 Excelsior 10 Buena Vista, Stanislaus *Canada:* 5 Keele, Logan *Canaries:* 5 Telde 8 Tenerife *Carpathian:* 4 Rysy *Cascades:* 7 Rainier *Catskill:* 6 Pisgah *Caucasus:* 5 Ushba 6 Elbrus *Chile:* 4 Mayo, Pili 5 Paine, Pular *China:* 4 Emei, Song *Colombia:* 4 Tama 6 Neiva *Colorado:*

3 Ute 5 Eolus, Pikes (Peak) 9 Purgatory (Peak) *Costa Rica:* 6 Blanco 14 Chirripó Grande *Cuba:* 8 Turquino *Cyprus:* 7 Olympus, Troodos *depression:* 3 col *Dominican Republic:* 6 Duarte 8 Trujillo *Ecuador:* 10 Chimborazo *Egypt:* 4 Musa 5 Sinai *England:* 11 Scafell Pike *Ethiopia:* 4 Guna 5 Holla *Fiji:* 8 Victoria 9 Tomaniivi *foot:* 8 piedmont *France:* 5 Blanc (Mont), Pilat *French Guiana:* 5 Amana *Gabon:* 8 Iboundji *Georgia:* 8 Springer 10 Oglethorpe *Germany:* 7 Zollern 9 Zugspitze 11 Fichtelberg *Glacier National Park:* 8 Kootenal *Greece:* 3 Ida 4 Ossa 5 Athos, Levka 6 Pelion 7 Helicon, Olympus 9 Parnassus, Psiloriti 10 Pendelikon, Pentelicus *Greenland:* 9 Gunnbjorn *Himalayas:* 3 Api 6 Khamet, Lhotse 7 Everest 9 Annapurna 10 Gasherbrum *Honshu:* 4 Yari 10 Yarigatake *Idaho:* 11 Pend Oreille *India:* 5 Japvo *Indonesia:* 4 Lawu 5 Kwoka, Lawoe, Raung 6 Raoeng, Semeru 7 Kerinci *Iran:* 8 Damavand *Israel:* 5 Meron 6 Carmel *Italy:* 4 Etna 8 Vesuvius *Ivory Coast:* 5 Nimba *Japan:* 4 Fuji, Sobo 5 Iwate, Oyama 7 Fujisan, Sobozan 8 Fujiyama *Java:* 5 Liman 6 Slamet *Jordan:* 3 Hor 5 Hārūn 6 Gilead *Karakoram Range:* 7 Dapsang 10 Masherbrum 12 Godwin Austen *Maine:* 8 Katahdin 10 Saddleback *Malaysia:* 5 Ophir, Tahan 6 Ledang *Mediterranean entrance:* 5 Calpe 9 Gibraltar *Mexico:* 7 Orizaba (Pico de) *Montana:* 8 Gallatin *Nevada:* 3 Ely *Newfoundland:* 9 Gros Morne *New Hampshire:* 9 Monadnock *New York:* 4 Bear 5 Marcy *New Zealand:* 3 Una 4 Cook 7 Aorangi 8 Aspiring *North America's highest:* 6 Denali 8 McKinley *North Carolina:* 8 Mitchell *Oahu:* 5 Kaala *Oman:* 4 Sham *Oregon:* 4 Hood *Pakistan:* 9 Tirich Mir *Papua New Guinea:* 7 Wilhelm 8 Victoria *peak:* 3 top 4 acme, apex, roof 5 crest, crown 6 summit, vertex, zenith 8 pinnacle *Pennine Alps:* 4 Rosa (Monte) 10 Matterhorn, Mont Cervin *Philippines:* 3 Apo, Iba 4 High, Labo 5 Silay *Pyrenees:* 11 de Vignemale *ridge:* 4 spur 5 arête, crest 7 sawbuck *Romania:* 11 Moldoveanul *Russia's highest:* 6 Elbrus *Scotland:* 8 Ben Nevis *Sicily:* 4 Etna *South America:* 7 Roraima 9 Aconcagua *South Dakota:* 6 Custer (Peak) *Spain:* 5 Yelmo 8 Mulhacén 11 Pico de Aneto *Switzerland:* 3 Dom 4 Dôle, Rosa (Monte), Tödi 5 Eiger, Mönch 6 La Dôle, Rusein 7 Pilatus 8 Jungfrau 10 Matterhorn *Syria:* 4 Druz 5 Duruz *Tanzania:* 11 Kilimanjaro *Tasmania:* 4 Ossa *Tennessee:* 13 Clingmans Dome *Togo:* 4

Agou *Turkey:* 3 Ida *Utah:* 5 Kings *Vermont:* 8 Ascutney, Haystack, Stratton 9 Mansfield *Vietnam:* 8 Ngoo Linh *Virginia:* 6 Rogers *Washington:* 7 Olympus, Rainier 11 Saint Helens *Western Hemisphere's highest:* 9 Aconcagua *White Mts.:* 10 Washington *world's highest:* 7 Everest *Wyoming:* 3 Elk 5 Cloud 7 Gannett (Peak) 10 Grand Teton *Yukon:* 4 King 5 Logan

mountain climbing *equipment:* 2 ax 3 axe, nut 5 piton 7 crampon 9 carabiner *maneuver:* 6 rappel 10 rappelling

mountain dew see **moonshine**

mountain formation 7 orogeny 10 orogenesis

mountainous 4 huge, vast 6 alpine, mighty 7 immense, mammoth, massive 8 enormous, gigantic, towering 10 monumental, prodigious

mountain pass 3 col, gap *Afghanistan-Pakistan:* 6 Khyber *Alps:* 5 Gries *California:* 4 Muir 6 Sonora *China-Myanmar:* 5 Namni *Colorado:* 3 Ute 5 Mosca, Muddy, Music, Raton *Europe:* 8 Moravian *Greece:* 5 Rupel *Hindu Kush Mts.:* 5 Dorah, Durah *Pakistan:* 5 Bolan, Gomal, Gumal *Sierra Nevada:* 4 Mono *Switzerland:* 5 Furka, Gemmi 7 Grimsel 8 Lötschen *Tunisia:* 4 Faïd *Ukrainian:* 5 Uzhok *Wyoming:* 5 Union

mountain range *Asia:* 5 Altai, Altay 8 Himalaya, Tien Shan 9 Altai Shan, Altay Shan, Himalayan, Himalayas, Hindu Kush *Australia:* 8 Flinders *Europe:* 4 Alps 10 Carpathian *Germany:* 4 Harz 5 Hartz *Greece:* 4 Oeta *India:* 5 Ghats *Iran:* 6 Zagros *Italy:* 9 Apennines, Dolomites *Mexico:* 11 Sierra Madre *North Africa:* 5 Atlas *North America:* 5 Rocky 7 Rockies 11 Appalachian *Russia:* 4 Ural *Scotland:* 9 Grampians *Sinai:* 9 Gebel Musa *Slovakia:* 5 Tatra, Tatry 9 High Tatra *South America:* 5 Andes *Spain:* 8 Pyrenees *Turkey:* 3 Ida 6 Taurus 7 Kazdagi *United States:* 5 Rocky, White 6 Brooks 7 Cascade, Olympic, Rockies, Sawatch, Wasatch 8 Absaroka, Aleutian, Catskill, Wrangell 9 Blue Ridge, Wind River 10 Adirondack, Bitterroot, Black Hills, Clearwater, Grand Teton *Zimbabwe:* 6 Matopo (Hills) 7 Matoppo (Hills)

Mountain State 7 Montana 12 West Virginia

mountebank 5 quack 6 con man 8 swindler 9 charlatan 11 flimflammer, quacksalver 13 confidence man

Mount St. Helens 7 volcano

mourn 3 rue 6 bemoan, bewail, grieve, lament, sorrow 7 deplore, protest

mournful 3 sad 6 dismal, gloomy, rueful, triste, woeful 7 doleful, forlorn, unhappy 8 dejected, desolate, dolorous, funereal, grievous, wretched 9 dirgelike, plaintive 10 depressing, despondent, dispirited, lugubrious, melancholy 11 melancholic 12 heavyhearted

mournfulness 5 blues, dumps, gloom 7 dismals, sadness 9 dejection 10 blue devils, depression, melancholy

mourning 5 grief 7 keening, remorse, wailing, weeping 8 grieving 9 lamenting, morbidity, sorrowing, ululation 10 heartbreak 11 bereavement, lamentation

Mourning Becomes Electra author 6 O'Neill (Eugene)

mourning period, Jewish 5 shiva 6 shivah

mourning symbol 7 armband

mouse 6 rodent, shiner 8 black eye *meadow:* 4 vole

mousy 3 shy 4 drab, dull 5 plain, quiet, timid 7 bashful 8 retiring, timorous 9 colorless, diffident, shrinking 11 unassertive 12 self-effacing

mouth 3 gob, maw 4 trap 5 chops 6 kisser 8 entrance 10 embouchure

mouthlike opening 5 stoma 7 stomata (plural)

mouthpiece 5 organ 6 puppet 7 speaker 8 front man 9 spokesman 10 figurehead 11 spokeswoman 12 spokesperson

mouthwatering 5 sapid, tasty, yummy 6 savory, toothy 9 delicious, palatable, succulent, toothsome 10 appetizing, delectable 11 good-tasting

mouthy 4 glib 5 gabby, talky, windy 7 verbose, voluble 8 effusive 9 bombastic, garrulous, talkative

movable 5 loose 6 mobile, motile, roving 8 portable 10 changeable

movables 5 goods 7 effects 8 chattels 10 belongings 11 furnishings

move 4 relo 5 budge, leave, march, shift, start, touch 6 affect, depart, incite, induce 7 advance, conduct, inspire, migrate, proceed, propose, request 8 dislodge, displace, motivate, persuade, progress, relocate, resettle, transfer, withdraw 9 influence, instigate, stimulate, transport 10 relocation

movement 4 flow, stir 5 tempo, trend 6 action, motion 7 crusade 8 activity, campaign, dynamism, maneuver, progress, stirring, tendency, velocity 9 migration *music:* 4 moto *reflex:* 5 taxis *stimulated:* 7 kinesis

movie 4 cine, film, show 5 flick 6 cinema, talkie 7 picture 9 photoplay 11 picture show 13 motion picture 7 western *genre:* 3 war 4 cult, epic 5 adult, anime, crime, oater 6 action, comedy, cowboy, family, horror, silent

7 cartoon, fantasy, Western **9** adventure, animation **11** documentary, martial arts **12** mockumentary *short:* **4** clip **8** newsreel **movie director** *American:* **3** Lee (Spike), Ray (Nicholas) **4** Coen (Joel), Ford (John), Hill (George Roy), Mann (Anthony), Penn (Arthur), Ritt (Martin), Ross (Herbert), Sirk (Douglas), Wise (Robert) **5** Allen (Woody), Ashby (Hal), Brown (Clarence), Capra (Frank), Cukor (George), Demme (Jonathan), Donen (Stanley), Fosse (Bob), Hawks (Howard), Ivory (James), Jonze (Spike), Kazan (Elia), LeRoy (Mervyn), Logan (Joshua), Lucas (George), Lumet (Sidney), Lynch (David), Moore (Michael), Roach (Hal), Stone (Oliver), Vidor (King), Walsh (Raoul), Whale (James), Wyler (William), Zwick (Ed) **6** Altman (Robert), Beatty (Warren), Benton (Robert), Brooks (Richard), Burton (Tim), Cimino (Michael), Corman (Roger), Curtiz (Michael), Fuller (Samuel), Gibson (Mel), Hanson (Curtis), Howard (Ron), Huston (John), Kramer (Stanley), Malick (Terrence), Pakula (Alan), Parker (Alan), Seaton (George), Waters (John), Welles (Orson), Wilder (Billy) **7** Borzage (Frank), Cameron (James), Chaplin (Charlie), Coppola (Francis Ford, Sofia), Costner (Kevin), De Mille (Cecil B.), De Palma (Brian), Fleming (Victor), Gilliam (Terry), Jewison (Norman), Kubrick (Stanley), McCarey (Leo), Nichols (Mike), Pollack (Sydney), Redford (Robert), Siodmak (Robert), Stevens (George), Sturges (Preston), Van Sant (Gus), Wellman (William) **8** Avildsen (John), Eastwood (Clint), Flaherty (Robert), Friedkin (William), Griffith (David Wark), Grosbard (Ulu), Jarmusch (Jim), Levinson (Barry), Lubitsch (Ernst), Marshall (Penny), Minnelli (Vincente), Mulligan (Robert), Scorsese (Martin), Zemeckis (Robert) **9** Carpenter (John), Hitchcock (Alfred), Milestone (Lewis), Peckinpah (Sam), Preminger (Otto), Spielberg (Steven), Sternberg (Josef von), Streisand (Barbra), Tarantino (Quentin), Zinnemann (Fred) **10** Cassavetes (John), Heckerling (Amy), Mankiewicz (Joseph), Soderbergh (Steven) **11** Bogdanovich (Peter) **13** Frankenheimer (John) *Australian:* **4** Weir (Peter) **6** Noonan (Chris) **9** Armstrong (Gillian), Beresford (Bruce) *Austrian:* **4** Lang (Fritz) **8** Stroheim (Erich von) **9** Sternberg (Josef von) *British:* **4** Lean (David), Reed (Carol) **5** Leigh (Mike), Loach (Ken), Losey (Joseph), Reisz (Karel), Scott (Ridley) **6** Fig-

gis (Mike), Frears (Stephen), Jordan (Neil), Newell (Mike), Parker (Alan), Powell (Michael) **7** Boorman (John), Branagh (Kenneth), Forsyth (Bill) **8** Anderson (Lindsay) **9** Hitchcock (Alfred) **10** Richardson (Tony) **11** Schlesinger (John) *Chinese:* **3** Lee (Ang) **4** Chen (Kaige) **5** Zhang (Yimou) *French:* **4** Demy (Jacques), Tati (Jacques), Vigo (Jean) **5** Malle (Louis) **6** Godard (Jean-Luc), Ophüls (Marcel), Renoir (Jean), Rohmer (Eric) **7** Bresson (Robert), Chabrol (Claude), Cocteau (Jean), Resnais (Alain), Rivette (Jacques) **8** Truffaut (François) *German:* **6** Herzog (Werner), Ophüls (Max) **7** Wenders (Wim) **8** Petersen (Wolfgang) **10** Fassbinder (Rainer Werner) **11** Riefenstahl (Leni), Schlöndorff (Volker) *Italian:* **5** Leone (Sergio) **6** De Sica (Vittorio) **7** Fellini (Federico) **8** Pasolini (Pier Paolo), Visconti (Luchino) **9** Antonioni (Michelangelo) **10** Bertolucci (Bernardo), Rossellini (Roberto), Wertmüller (Lina), Zeffirelli (Franco) *Japanese:* **3** Ozu (Yasujiro) **5** Itami (Juzo) **8** Kurosawa (Akira), Miyazaki (Hayao) **9** Mizoguchi (Kenji) *Mexican:* **6** Cuarón (Alfonso) *New Zealand:* **7** Campion (Jane) *Polish:* **5** Wajda (Ardrzej) **7** Holland (Agnieszka) **8** Polanski (Roman) *Russian:* **9** Tarkovsky (Andrei) **10** Eisenstein (Sergei) *Spanish:* **6** Buñuel (Luis) **9** Almodóvar (Pedro) *Swedish:* **7** Bergman (Ingmar) **10** Zetterling (Mai) **movie producer** *American:* **3** Fox (William) **4** Cohn (Jack) **5** Lasky (Jesse), Mayer (Louis B.), Zukor (Adolph) **6** Warner (Jack L.), Zanuck (Darryl, Richard) **7** Goldwyn (Samuel), Laemmle (Carl) **8** Selznick (David O.) **9** Weinstein (Bob, Harvey) *Austrian:* **9** Reinhardt (Max)

moving 5 astir **6** mobile **7** emotive, rousing **8** arousing, exciting, gripping, pathetic, poignant, stirring, touching **9** affecting, emotional, inspiring, transient **11** stimulating

moving stairs 9 escalator

mow 3 cut **4** clip, crop, fell, heap, moue, pile, raze, rick **5** level, shave, shear, stack **7** grimace **9** knock down

moxie 3 pep, vim, zip **4** grit, guts **5** brass, heart, nerve, oomph, pluck, savvy, spunk, vigor **6** energy, mettle, spirit, starch **7** cojones, courage, know-how **8** backbone **9** fortitude **10** get-up-and-go, resolution **13** determination

Mozambique *capital:* **6** Maputo *language:* **5** Bantu **7** Swahili **10** Portuguese *monetary unit:* **7** metical *neighbor:* **6** Malawi, Zambia **8** Tanzania, Zimbabwe **9** Swaziland **11**

South Africa *river:* 6 Ruvuma 7 Limpopo, Zambezi

Mozart, Wolfgang Amadeus *birthplace:* 8 Salzburg *cataloger:* 6 Köchel (Ludwig) *deathplace:* 6 Vienna *opera:* 8 Idomeneo 10 Magic Flute (The) 11 Don Giovanni, Il Rè Pastore 12 Così Fan Tutte 16 Marriage of Figaro (The)

MP's prey 4 AWOL 8 deserter

Mr. *French:* 8 Monsieur *German:* 4 Herr *Italian:* 6 Signor *Spanish:* 5 Señor

Mr. Moto star 5 Lorre (Peter)

Mrs. *French:* 3 Mme. 6 Madame *German:* 4 Frau *Italian:* 3 Sra. 7 Signora *Spanish:* 3 Sra. 6 Señora

Mrs. Grundy 4 prig 5 prude 7 puritan 8 bluenose

much 3 oft 4 long, many, most 5 often 6 highly, hugely, plenty 7 greatly, notably 8 abundant 9 eminently, extremely *combining form:* 4 poly 5 multi

Much Ado About Nothing character 4 Hero 7 Claudio, Don John 8 Beatrice, Benedick, Dogberry

muck 3 goo, mud 4 crap, crud, dirt, dung, glop, gook, goop, grub, gunk, junk, mess, mire, murk, plod, slog, slop, soil, toil 5 dirty, dreck, filth, grime, gumbo, slave, slime, swill, trash, waste 6 drudge, litter, manure, meddle, putter, sleaze, sludge, smirch, tinker 7 garbage, rubbish 8 nonsense 9 interfere

muckety-muck 3 VIP 5 nabob 6 bigwig, fat cat, honcho 7 big shot, kingpin, notable 8 kingfish, somebody 9 dignitary

mucky 4 foul 5 dirty, grimy, muddy, muggy, murky, nasty, soggy 6 cruddy, filthy, grubby, grungy 7 squalid, unclean

mucous 5 slimy 6 viscid

mud 4 dirt, mire, muck, ooze 5 dregs, slime 6 depths, sludge

muddle 3 mix 4 hash, mess, muck, rile, roil 5 addle, botch, mix up, snarl 6 ataxia, bungle, drivel, foul up, fumble, jumble, jungle, litter, mess up, tangle, tumble 7 clutter, confuse, fluster, perplex, rummage, shuffle, snarl up, stumble, stupefy 8 befuddle, bewilder, confound, disarray, disorder, distract, entangle, mishmash, scramble, shambles, throw off, unsettle 9 confusion, throw away 10 complicate, disarrange, discompose 11 disorganize

muddled 5 drunk, tight, tipsy, vague 7 mixed-up 8 inchoate 10 disjointed, disordered, incoherent, inebriated 11 intoxicated, unorganized

muddle through 4 cope, fare 5 get by, get on 6 manage 7 carry on, make out 8 get along

muddy 3 dim, fog 4 base, blur, drab, dull, fade, foul, hazy, oozy, roil, soil 5 befog, cloud, dingy, dirty, grime, grimy, murky 6 cloudy, gloomy, grubby, sordid, turbid 7 becloud, begrime, confuse, obscure, squalid, tarnish, unclean, unclear 8 confused

muff 4 blow, flub 5 botch, fluff 6 bobble, bollix, bungle, fumble, goof up, mess up 7 louse up, misplay, screw up 9 mishandle

muffle 3 gag 4 dull, mute, veil 5 shush 6 dampen, deaden, lessen, shroud, soften, stifle, subdue, wrap up 7 envelop, repress, silence, smother, squelch 8 bundle up, suppress, tone down

muffled 5 muted 6 dulled 7 stifled, subdued 8 deadened, obscured, silenced 9 distorted, enveloped 10 indistinct, suppressed

muffler 4 mask, veil 5 cloak, scarf

mug 3 cup, ham, mop, mow, rob 4 boob, dolt, dope, face, fool, moue, phiz, punk, puss, thug 5 dunce, idiot, mouth, rowdy, stein, tough 6 ambush, dimwit, kisser 7 assault, grimace, tankard 8 bullyboy, dumbbell, features, numskull 9 blockhead, bushwhack, ignoramus, roughneck

mugger 4 thug 6 robber 9 assailant, crocodile

muggy 4 damp 5 humid, moist 6 sticky, sultry 7 dampish

Muhammad *adopted son:* 3 Ali *birthplace:* 5 Mecca *camel:* 5 Kaswa *daughter:* 6 Fatima *deathplace:* 6 Medina *deity:* 5 Allah *father:* 8 Abdallah, Abdullah *father-in-law:* 7 Abu Bakr *flight:* 6 hegira, hejira *follower:* 6 Moslem, Muslim *horse:* 5 Buraq 7 Alborak *religion:* 5 Islam *scripture:* 5 Koran *son:* 7 Ibrahim *son-in-law:* 3 Ali *successor:* 6 caliph 7 Abu Bakr *tribe:* 7 Koreish, Quraysh *uncle:* 8 Abu Talib *wife:* 5 Aisha 6 Ayesha 7 Khadija

mulatto 5 métis, mixed 7 mestizo 9 half-breed, half-caste 10 crossbreed

mulberry 3 fig 10 breadfruit *type:* 6 banyan 11 India rubber, osage orange

mulct 4 fine, milk, rook 5 bleed, cheat, gouge 6 extort, fleece 7 deceive, defraud, forfeit, penalty, swindle 8 penalize 9 blackmail

mule 5 cross, scuff 6 bagman, hybrid 7 bastard, courier, mongrel 8 smuggler 9 crossbred, half blood, half-breed 10 crossbreed

mulish 8 contrary, perverse, stubborn 9 obstinate, pigheaded 10 bullheaded, headstrong, inflexible, refractory, unyielding 11 stiffnecked

mull 4 hash, muse 5 brood, think, weigh 6 ponder 7 reflect 8 cogitate, consider, meditate, ruminate, turn over 9 pulverize 10 deliberate 11 contemplate

multicolored 4 pied 6 motley 7 dappled 9 prismatic 10 variegated 13 polychromatic

multifarious 5 mixed 6 motley, sundry, varied 7 diverse, various 8 assorted, manifold 13 heterogeneous, miscellaneous

multiform 6 sundry, varied 7 diverse, various 8 assorted, manifold 9 disparate 12 multifarious

multilateral 9 many-sided

multiple 4 many 6 shared, sundry 7 diverse, several, various 8 assorted, manifold, numerous 9 composite

multiplicity 3 lot 4 heap, load, mass, peck 5 flood, hoard, horde 6 barrel 7 variety 8 mountain, plethora 9 diversity, great deal, profusion

multiply 3 wax 4 rise 5 boost, breed, build, mount 6 expand, extend, spread 7 amplify, augment, enlarge, magnify 8 generate, heighten, increase 9 procreate, propagate, reproduce 10 aggrandize 11 proliferate

multitude 3 mob 4 army, herd, host, mass, slew 5 crowd, crush, drove, flock, horde, swarm 6 legion, myriad, public, throng 8 populace

multitudinous 4 many 6 legion, myriad, sundry 7 copious, various 8 abundant, manifold, numerous, populous 9 countless 10 numberless, voluminous 11 innumerable

mum 4 dumb, mute 5 quiet 6 silent 8 wordless 10 speechless, tongue-tied

mumble 6 murmur, mutter 7 maunder

mumbo jumbo 4 juju 6 fetish 9 gibberish 10 hocus-pocus 11 abracadabra 12 gobbledygook, superstition

mummer 4 mime 5 actor, mimic 12 impersonator

mummify 5 dry up, wizen 6 embalm, wither 7 shrivel 9 desiccate

munch 3 eat 4 chaw, chew 5 champ, chomp, snack 6 crunch 9 masticate

mundane 4 lowly 6 earthy, normal 7 earthly, humdrum, prosaic, routine, terrene, worldly 8 banausic, day-to-day, everyday, familiar, ordinary, telluric, workaday 9 practical, sublunary, tellurian 11 commonplace, terrestrial, uncelestial 13 materialistic

municipal 5 civic, local, urban 12 metropolitan

munificent 6 lavish 7 liberal 8 generous, handsome 9 bounteous, bountiful 10 benevolent, freehanded, openhanded 11 magnanimous 13 philanthropic

munitions maker 5 Krupp

muralist 4 Sert (José María) 6 Benton

(Thomas Hart), Giotto, Orozco (José Clemente), Rivera (Diego) 7 La Farge (John) 9 Siqueiros (David Alfaro) 12 Michelangelo (Buonarotti)

murder 3 hit, off 4 do in, kill, slay 5 blood, lynch, scrag, snuff, waste 6 rub out 7 bump off, execute, garrote, killing, smother, take out 8 foul play, homicide, knock off, strangle 9 eradicate, liquidate, slaughter 10 annihilate, asphyxiate, decapitate, extinguish 11 assassinate, electrocute, exterminate 12 manslaughter *brother:* 10 fratricide *father:* 9 patricide *king:* 8 regicide *mother:* 9 matricide *parent:* 9 parricide *sister:* 10 sororicide

murderer 6 hit man, killer, slayer 7 butcher 8 assassin, homicide 9 cutthroat, manslayer 11 slaughterer

Murder in the Cathedral *author:* 5 Eliot (Thomas Stearns) *character:* 5 Henry (II) 6 Becket (Thomas à)

murderous 6 deadly, lethal 10 sanguinary 12 bloodthirsty

murk 3 fog 4 haze, mist 5 brume, gloom 6 miasma 8 darkness 9 obscurity

murky 3 dim 4 dark, dull, foul, gray 5 dirty, dusky, foggy, misty, muddy, roily, vague 6 cloudy, gloomy, opaque, somber, turbid 7 obscure 8 nebulous 9 ambiguous, equivocal, tenebrous 10 caliginous

murmur 3 hum 4 buzz, purr 5 drone, rumor 6 grouch, grouse, mumble, mutter, rumble 7 grumble, whisper 8 complain 9 grumbling, undertone 11 scuttlebutt, susurration

Muscat sultanate 4 Oman

muscle 4 beef, thew 5 brawn, force, might, power, sinew 6 energy 7 potency 8 strength 9 strong arm *abdomen:* 3 abs 7 abdomen *arm:* 3 bis 4 tris 6 biceps 7 triceps *back:* 4 lats 5 traps 9 trapezius *buttock:* 6 glutes *calf:* 6 soleus *chest:* 4 pecs 10 pectoralis *jaw:* 8 masseter *kind:* 6 flexor, tensor 7 dilator, evertor, levator, rotator 8 abductor, adductor, extensor *leg:* 4 hams *loin:* 5 psoas *neck:* 5 traps 8 platysma 9 trapezius *shoulder:* 5 delts 7 deltoid 10 deltoideus *side:* 4 lats *stomach:* 3 abs *straight:* 6 rectus *study of:* 7 myology *thigh:* 5 quads 8 gracilis 9 sartorius

muscle-bound 5 rigid, stiff 6 wooden

muscular 4 ropy 5 beefy, burly, husky 6 brawny, mighty, robust, sinewy, strong, sturdy 8 athletic, forceful, powerful, resolute, stalwart, vigorous 9 Herculean, strapping, well-built

muse 5 angel, brood, guide, think 6 genius, ponder, trance 7 reflect, reverie 8 cogitate, meditate, mull over, ruminate, turn over **10** deliberate **11** contemplate

Muse *father:* **4** Zeus **7** Jupiter *home:* **7** Helicon *leader:* **6** Apollo *mother:* **9** Mnemosyne *of astronomy:* **6** Urania *of choral song:* **11** Terpsichore *of comedy:* **6** Thalia *of dancing:* **11** Terpsichore *of epic poetry:* **8** Calliope *of history:* **4** Clio *of love poetry:* **5** Erato *of lyric poetry:* **5** Erato *of music:* **7** Euterpe *of pastoral poetry:* **6** Thalia *of sacred poetry:* **8** Polymnia **10** Polyhymnia *of tragedy:* **9** Melpomene

museum 5 salon **7** archive, exhibit, gallery **8** atheneum **10** collection, repository *famous:* **3** Met **4** Fogg, MoMA, Tate **5** Field, Frick, Getty, Orsay, Prado **6** Louvre **7** Peabody, Walters, Whitney **9** Henry Ford, Hermitage, Hirshhorn **10** Guggenheim **11** Norton Simon, Smithsonian

mush 4 slop **5** grits, gruel, hokum **6** bathos, drivel, hominy **8** porridge, schmaltz

mushroom 4 grow **6** expand, spread **7** burgeon, explode, inflate **8** snowball **11** proliferate *combining form:* **3** myc **4** myco **5** mycet **6** myceto *edible:* **5** enoki, morel **6** bolete **7** cremini, crimini, porcini **8** shiitake **9** mousseron **10** champignon, portabella, portabello, portobello **11** chanterelle *kind:* **6** agaric, bolete **7** inky cap, russula *part:* **3** cap **4** gill, ring **5** stipe, volva **6** pileus **7** annulus **8** mycelium *poisonous:* **7** amanita **8** death cap **9** fly agaric, toadstool

mushy 4 soft **5** pulpy, soppy, vague **6** quaggy, spongy **7** amorous, maudlin, mawkish, squashy, squishy **8** bathetic, effusive, romantic, squooshy **9** schmaltzy **10** lovey-dovey, saccharine **11** sentimental

music *abbreviation:* **3** fff, ppp, sfz **5** cresc *bass staff lines:* **5** GBDFA *bass staff spaces:* **4** ACEG *characteristic phrase:* **9** leitmotif, leitmotiv *chord:* **5** major, minor, tonic **7** harmony **8** dominant **9** augmented **10** diminished *closing:* **4** coda *embellishment:* **3** run **4** turn **5** trill **7** cadenza, mordent, roulade **8** arpeggio, flourish **9** grace note *for eight:* **5** octet *for five:* **7** quintet *for four:* **7** quartet *for nine:* **5** nonet *for one:* **4** solo *for seven:* **6** septet *for six:* **6** sextet *for three:* **4** trio *for two:* **5** duo **4** a due, duet *god:* **6** Apollo *hall:* **5** odeum **7** cabaret, theater *instrumental form:* **3** jig, rag **4** jazz, reel **5** étude, fugue, gigue, march, polka, rondo, suite, waltz **6** minuet, pavane, sonata **7** bourrée, gavotte, mazurka, prelude, toccata **8** chaconne, concerto, courante, fantasia, galliard, nocturne, overture, rhapsody, ricercar, saraband, serenade, symphony,

tone poem **9** allemande, polonaise *morning:* **6** aubade *Muse:* **7** Euterpe *night:* **8** nocturne, serenade *note:* **4** half **5** breve, minim, neume, whole **6** eighth, quaver **7** quarter **8** crotchet **9** sixteenth **10** semiquaver *patron saint:* **7** Cecilia *period:* **6** Modern, Rococo **7** Baroque **8** Medieval, Romantic **9** Classical *symbol:* **3** bar, key **4** clef, flat, note, rest, slur, turn **5** G clef, neume, sharp, staff **7** fermata, mordent **8** bass clef **9** alla breve **10** accidental, treble clef *treble staff lines:* **5** EGBDF *treble staff spaces:* **4** FACE *vocal form:* **3** air **4** aria, hymn, lied, mass, song **5** chant, motet, opera, round **6** anthem, ballad **7** cantata, chanson, chorale **8** cavatina, madrigal, operetta, oratorio, serenade **9** cabaletta

musical 4 show **5** revue **6** choral **7** lyrical, melodic, songful, tuneful **8** harmonic, operetta, zarzuela **9** melodious, symphonic **10** euphonious, harmonious *famous:* **4** Cats, Hair, Mame, Rent **5** Annie, Evita, Gypsy **6** Grease, Kismet, Les Miz, Oliver **7** Cabaret, Camelot, Candide, Chicago, Company, Follies **8** Carousel, Fiorello, Godspell, King and I (The), Lion King (The), Music Man (The), Oklahoma, Show Boat **9** Brigadoon, Funny Girl, Girl Crazy, On the Town, Over There, State Fair **10** Chorus Line (A), Dreamgirls, Hello Dolly, Kiss Me Kate, Miss Saigon, My Fair Lady, Pajama Game (The), She Loves Me **11** Damn Yankees, Of Thee I Sing, Sweeney Todd **12** Anything Goes, Bye Bye Birdie, Guys and Dolls, Into the Woods, Sound of Music (The), South Pacific, Sweet Charity **13** Les Misérables, Man of La Mancha, Silk Stockings, West Side Story, Wonderful Town **14** Finian's Rainbow, Flower Drum Song, Paint Your Wagon **15** Annie Get Your Gun **16** Fiddler on the Roof **17** Phantom of the Opera (The) **20** Jesus Christ Superstar

musical composition 4 aria, coda, hymn, lied, opus, song, trio **5** chant, canon, carol, dirge, étude, fugue, march, motet, opera, rondo, suite **6** anthem, ballad, sextet, sonata **7** cantata, chanson, chorale, prelude, quartet, quintet, requiem, scherzo, toccata **8** concerto, fantasia, madrigal, nocturne, operetta, oratorio, overture, postlude, serenade, sonatina, symphony **9** bagatelle, barcarole, cabaletta, interlude **10** intermezzo, recitative

musical direction *accented:* **7** marcato **8** sforzato **9** sforzando *all:* **5** tutti *bowed:* **4** arco *brisk:* **4** brio, vivo **6** vivace **7** allegro, animato *connected:* **6** legato *detached:* **8**

spiccato, staccato *dignified:* 8 maestoso *disconnected:* 8 staccato *emotional:* 12 appassionato *emphatic:* 7 marcato *excited:* 7 agitato *fast:* 4 vite, vivo 6 presto, veloce, vivace 7 allegro *faster:* 7 stretto 11 accelerando *fluctuating tempo:* 6 rubato *forcefully:* 7 furioso *freely:* 9 ad libitum *from the beginning:* 6 da capo *gay:* 7 giocoso *gentle:* 5 dolce 7 amabile, amoroso 10 affettuoso *graceful:* 8 grazioso *half:* 5 mezzo *heavy:* 7 pesante *held firmly:* 6 tenuto *less:* 4 meno *little:* 4 poco *little by little:* 9 poco a poco *lively:* 4 vite, vivo 6 vivace 7 allegro, animato, giocoso *loud:* 5 forte *louder:* 9 crescendo *majestic:* 8 maestoso *moderate:* 7 andante 8 moderato *moderately loud:* 10 mezzo forte *moderately soft:* 10 mezzo piano *playful:* 10 scherzando *plucked:* 9 pizzicato *quick:* 4 vite, vivo 6 presto, veloce, vivace 7 allegro *quickening:* 11 affrettando *repeat:* 3 bis 8 da capo *run:* 8 arpeggio 9 glissando *sad:* 7 dolente 8 doloroso *separate:* 6 divisi *silent:* 5 tacet *singing:* 9 cantabile *sliding:* 9 glissando *slow:* 5 grave, largo, lento 6 adagio 7 andante 9 larghetto *slowing:* 3 rit 6 ritard 10 ritardando 11 rallentando *smooth:* 6 legato *soft:* 5 dolce, piano *softening:* 10 diminuendo 11 decrescendo *solemn:* 5 grave *spirited:* 4 vivo 6 vivace 7 animato 9 spiritoso *stately:* 7 pomposo 8 maestoso *sustained:* 6 tenuto 9 sostenuto *sweet:* 5 dolce *tender:* 7 amabile, amoroso 10 affettuoso *together:* 4 a due 5 tutti *very:* 5 assai *very fast:* 11 prestissimo *very loud:* 10 fortissimo *very soft:* 10 pianissimo

musical drama 5 opera 8 operetta, zarzuela 9 singspiel

musical group 4 band, trio 5 choir, combo 6 chorus, sextet 7 quartet, quintet 8 ensemble, glee club 9 orchestra

musical instrument *African:* 5 mbira, rebab 7 kalimba *ancient:* 4 lyre, rote 5 crwth 6 syrinx 7 cithara, kithara, sistrum, timbrel 8 psaltery *Arabic:* 3 oud *bagpipe:* 7 musette, pibroch 8 psaltery *brass:* 4 horn, tuba 5 bugle 6 cornet 7 althorn, clarion, helicon, saxhorn, trumpet 8 trombone 10 flugelhorn, French horn, sousaphone *Indian:* 4 vina 5 sarod, sitar, tabla *Japanese:* 4 biwa, koto 7 samisen 8 shamisen 10 shakuhachi *keyboard:* 5 organ, piano 6 spinet 7 celesta, cembalo, clavier 8 calliope, melodeon, virginal 9 accordion 10 clavichord, concertina, pianoforte 11 harpsichord *medieval:* 4 lute 5 naker, rebab, rebec, shawm, tabor 7 gittern, mandola 8 cornetto, gemshorn, horn-

pipe, oliphant 9 monochord 10 hurdy-gurdy *percussion:* 4 bell, drum 5 anvil, güiro, piano 6 cymbal, maraca 7 maracas, marimba, timpani, tympani 8 bass drum, castanet, triangle 9 castanets, snare drum, xylophone 10 kettledrum, tambourine, vibraphone *Persian:* 6 santir *reed:* 4 oboe 7 bassoon 8 clarinet 9 harmonica, saxophone 11 English horn *Renaissance:* 4 viol 5 regal, shawm 6 curtal, spinet 7 bagpipe, bandora, cittern, rackett, sackbut, serpent, theorbo, vihuela, violone 8 crumhorn, recorder, virginal 9 krummhorn 10 chitarrone, colascione 11 harpsichord *Russian:* 9 balalaika *stringed:* 3 uke 4 harp, lute, lyre, viol 5 banjo, cello, piano, rebab, viola 6 fiddle, guitar, violin, zither 7 bandora, cittern, gittern, kantele, pandura, ukulele 8 autoharp, dulcimer, mandolin 10 contrabass, double bass 11 harpsichord, violoncello *toy:* 5 kazoo 7 ocarina *woodwind:* 4 oboe 5 flute 7 bassoon, piccolo 8 clarinet 9 saxophone 11 English horn

musical interval 5 fifth, major, minor, sixth, third 6 fourth, octave, second 7 perfect, seventh, tritone

musical syllable 2 do, fa, la, mi, re, si, ti, ut 3 sol

musician 4 bard 5 piper 6 player 7 jazzman, maestro 8 minstrel, virtuoso 9 performer 10 troubadour

muskeg 3 bog, fen 4 mire, quag 5 marsh, swamp 6 morass, slough 8 quagmire

musket 5 fusil 9 flintlock, matchlock 12 muzzleloader

Musketeer 5 Athos 6 Aramis 7 Porthos *author:* 5 Dumas (Alexandre) *friend:* 9 d'Artagnan

muskmelon 10 cantaloupe

Muslim *ascetic:* 4 Sufi 5 fakir 7 dervish 8 marabout *body of scholars:* 5 ulama, ulema *branch:* 4 Shia 5 Sunni 6 Shiite *caller to prayer:* 7 muezzin *decree:* 5 fatwa, irade *devil:* 5 Iblis *garment:* 5 burka, burqa 6 chador *god:* 5 Allah *heavenly virgin:* 5 houri *holy city:* 5 Mecca 6 Medina *holy war:* 5 jihad *judge:* 4 qadi 5 mufti *lady:* 5 begum *law:* 6 Sharia *leader:* 3 aga 4 agha, amir, emir, imam 5 ameer 6 caliph, sayyid, sultan 9 ayatollah *lord:* 5 omrah *mendicant:* 5 fakir *messiah:* 5 Mahdi *month:* (see at **month**) *month of fasting:* 7 Ramadan *mosque:* 6 masjid *mystic:* 4 Sufi *official:* 3 dey 6 mullah, vizier *pilgrim:* 5 hajji *pilgrimage:* 4 hadj, hajj 5 omrah *prayer:* 5 salat *priest:* 4 imam *prophet:* 8 Mohammed, Muhammad *religion:* 5 Islam *scripture:* 5

Koran, Quran *school:* 7 madrasa 8 madrasah, madrassa 9 madrassah *shrine:* 5 Kaaba *spirit:* 4 jinn 5 djinn, jinni 6 djinni *temple:* 6 masjid, mosque *theological student:* 5 softa *title:* 3 aga 4 emir 6 caliph *tradition:* 5 sunna *veil:* 7 yashmak (see also **mosque; Muhammad**)

muss 3 row 4 mess 5 botch, chaos, mix-up, upset 6 jumble, mess-up, muddle, rumple, tousle 7 disrupt, rummage 8 disarray, dishevel, disorder, shambles 9 confusion 10 disarrange 11 disorganize

mussel 5 naiad *genus:* 4 Unio 7 Mytilus 8 Anodonta *larva:* 9 blackhead

Mussolini, Benito 4 Duce (Il) *son-in-law:* 5 Ciano (Galeazzo)

mussy 6 sloppy, untidy 7 tousled, unkempt 8 slovenly 9 cluttered 10 disheveled

must 4 duty, mold, need, want 5 gotta, juice, ought 6 devoir, should 9 condition, essential, necessity, requisite 10 obligation, sine qua non 11 requirement 12 precondition, prerequisite

muster 4 call, roll 5 crowd, group, raise, rally, rouse 6 enlist, enroll, gather, induce, invoke, join up, roster, sample, sign on, sign up, summon, work up 7 collect, convene, develop, include, marshal, produce 8 assemble, assembly, comprise, congress, generate, mobilize, organize, roll call, specimen 9 gathering, inventory, nose count 10 accumulate, assemblage, collection, congregate, rendezvous 12 accumulation, congregation

muster out 5 demob, let go 9 discharge 10 demobilize

musty 4 dank 5 funky, moldy, stale, tired, trite 6 frowsy, frowzy, old hat, smelly 7 airless, antique, mildewy, squalid 8 shopworn, timeworn 10 antiquated, malodorous, threadbare

Mut *husband:* 4 Amen, Amon *son:* 5 Chons 6 Chonsu, Khonsu

mutable 5 fluid 6 fickle, mobile, shifty 7 erratic, protean 8 slippery, unstable, unsteady, variable, volatile, wavering 9 changeful, mercurial, unsettled 10 capricious, changeable, inconstant 11 fluctuating, vacillating 12 inconsistent

mutate 4 vary 5 alter, morph 6 change, modify 9 refashion, transform, transmute 11 transfigure 12 metamorphose, transmogrify

mutation 5 sport 6 change 7 novelty 9 deviation, variation 10 alteration 11 vicissitude 12 modification 13 metamorphosis

mute 3 mum 4 dumb 5 quiet 6 dampen, deaden, muffle, muzzle, reduce, silent, soften, stifle, subdue 7 silence 8 silencer, wordless 9 voiceless 10 speechless, tongue-tied

muted 3 dim, mat 4 dull 6 low-key, silent 10 speechless

mutilate 3 mar 4 maim 6 damage, deface, injure, mangle 7 cripple 9 disfigure, dismember

mutineer 5 rebel

mutinous 6 unruly 8 factious 9 insurgent, seditious, turbulent 10 rebellious 12 contumacious 13 insubordinate

mutiny 5 rebel 6 revolt, rise up 8 uprising 9 rebellion 12 insurrection

mutt 3 cur, dog 4 mule 5 cross 6 hybrid 7 mixture, mongrel 9 half blood, half-breed 10 crossbreed

Mutt and ____ 4 Jeff

mutter 5 growl 6 grouch, grouse, mumble, murmur 7 grumble 9 undertone

muttonchops 9 burnsides, sideburns 10 sideboards 11 dundrearies 12 side-whiskers

mutual 5 joint 6 common, public, shared, united 7 related 8 communal, conjoint, conjunct 9 bilateral, connected 10 associated, reciprocal, respective *prefix:* 5 inter

muumuu 6 caftan

muzzle 3 gag 4 hush, mute, nose, phiz 5 snout 7 silence, squelch

muzzy 3 dim 4 dull, hazy 5 faint, vague 6 blurry, gloomy 7 blurred, muddled, unclear 8 confused, nebulous 9 imprecise

myalgia 4 ache, pain 5 cramp 6 strain 8 soreness

Myanmar 5 Burma *bay:* 6 Bengal *capital:* 6 Yangon 7 Rangoon *monetary unit:* 4 kyat *neighbor:* 4 Laos 5 China, India 8 Thailand 10 Bangladesh *peninsula:* 9 Indochina *river:* 7 Salween 9 Irrawaddy *sea:* 7 Andaman

My Antonia author 6 Cather (Willa)

My Last Duchess author 8 Browning (Robert)

My Lost Youth author 10 Longfellow (Henry Wadsworth)

Myra Breckenridge author 5 Vidal (Gore)

myriad 3 lot 4 heap, host, raft, slew 5 flood, horde, swarm 6 throng 9 countless, multitude 10 infinitude, numberless 11 innumerable 12 incalculable 13 multitudinous

myrmecology subject 3 ant 4 ants

myrmidon 6 minion 8 follower, retainer 9 attendant, underling 11 subordinate

Myron's statue 10 Discobolos, Discobolus 13 Discus Thrower (The)

Myrrha's son 6 Adonis

mysterious 6 arcane, mystic, occult, secret 7

cryptic, obscure, strange **8** abstruse, esoteric, numinous **9** ambiguous, enigmatic, equivocal, recondite **10** cabalistic, unknowable **11** inscrutable **12** impenetrable, inexplicable, unfathomable **13** unaccountable

mystery 5 poser **6** enigma, puzzle, riddle, secret **7** arcanum, problem, stumper **8** whodunit **9** conundrum **10** closed book, perplexity, puzzlement **13** Chinese puzzle *writer:* **3** Poe (Edgar Allan), Tey (Josephine) **5** Blake (Nicholas), Cross (Amanda), Doyle (Arthur Conan), Innes (Michael), James (P. D.), Lynds (Dennis), Marsh (Ngaio), Oates (Joyce Carol), Queen (Ellery), Stout (Rex), Waugh (Hillary) **6** Dexter (Colin), Parker (Robert B.), Peters (Ellis), Sayers (Dorothy) **7** Barnard (Robert), Collins (Michael, Wilkie), Gardner (Erle Stanley), Grafton (Sue), Hammett (Dashiell), MacLeod (Charlotte), Rendell (Ruth), Upfield (Arthur) **8** Chandler (Raymond), Christie (Agatha), Paretsky (Sara), Spillane (Mickey) **9** MacDonald (John D.), Macdonald (Ross) **10** Chesterton (G. K.)

mystic 4 seer **6** arcane, medium, occult, oracle, secret **7** obscure **8** anagogic, esoteric, hermetic, numinous **9** enigmatic, visionary **10** cabalistic, unknowable **11** inscrutable,

necromantic **12** impenetrable, thaumaturgic **13** unaccountable

mystical 4 holy **6** arcane, covert, divine, occult, orphic, sacred, secret **7** cryptic, subrosa **8** anagogic, esoteric, hermetic, oracular, profound **9** recondite, spiritual **10** miraculous, symbolical **11** clandestine **12** supernatural, supranatural

mysticism 7 Orphism **8** cabalism, quietism **11** hermeticism

mystify 6 baffle, puzzle **7** confuse, obscure, perplex **8** befuddle, bewilder, confound **9** obfuscate

mystifying 7 cryptic, delphic **8** Delphian **9** enigmatic

mystique 4 aura **5** charm, magic **6** glamor **7** glamour **8** charisma **9** magnetism

myth 4 lore, saga, tale **5** fable, story **6** legend **7** fiction, figment, parable **8** allegory, folklore **9** tradition **11** fabrication

mythical 6 fabled, made-up, unreal **7** created, fictive **8** fabulous, fanciful, invented **9** fantastic, fictional, imaginary, legendary **10** apocryphal, fictitious

mythologist 4 Jung (Carl Gustav), Ovid **5** Tylor (Edward Burnett) **6** Eliade (Mircea), Frazer (James George), Müller (Friedrich Max) **8** Campbell (Joseph) **9** Euhemerus **10** Malinowski (Bronislaw)

N

Naamah *brother:* **9** Tubalcain *father:* **6** Lamech *husband:* **7** Solomon *mother:* **6** Zillah *son:* **8** Rehoboam

nab 4 grab **5** catch, pinch, run in, seize **6** arrest, clutch, collar, pick up, pull in, snatch **7** capture **9** apprehend

nabob 3 VIP **5** mogul, noble **6** bigwig, fat cat, tycoon **7** big shot, magnate, notable **8** big chief, eminence, governor **9** big cheese, dignitary, personage **10** notability

Nabokov novel 3 Ada **4** Gift (The), Pnin **6** Lolita **7** Defense (The), Despair **8** Pale Fire **14** King Queen Knave

nacre 13 mother-of-pearl

nada 3 nil, nix, zip **4** zero **5** zilch **6** naught **7** nothing, nullity **11** nothingness

nadir 4 base, foot **5** depth **6** bottom **8** low point *opposite:* **6** zenith

nag 3 irk, vex **4** bait, carp, goad, ride **5** annoy, chivy, harry, horse, hound, shrew, worry **6** badger, bother, carp at, harass, heckle, hector, needle, peck at, pester, plague **7** henpeck, torment **8** complain, harangue, irritate

naiad 5 nymph

naïf 7 ingenue

nail 3 bag, get, nab **4** brad, grab, spad, stud, tack, trap **5** catch, clone, spike, sprig **6** arrest, collar, secure **7** capture **9** apprehend

naive 6 simple **7** artless, natural **8** gullible, innocent, wide-eyed **9** childlike, credulous, guileless, ingenuous, unstudied **10** selftaught, unaffected, unschooled **11** susceptible

naked 3 raw **4** bald, bare, mere, nude, pure **5** clear, sheer **6** peeled, scanty, simple, unclad

7 denuded, evident, exposed, obvious **8** revealed, starkers, stripped **9** au naturel, disclosed, unclothed, uncovered, undressed *combining form:* **4** gymn **5** gymno

Naked and the Dead author 6 Mailer (Norman)

namby-pamby 4 weak **5** banal, bland, inane, sissy, vapid **6** effete, jejune **7** insipid, milksop, nebbish **8** nebbishy, weakling **9** spineless **10** effeminate, indecisive, pantywaist, wishy-washy **11** milquetoast **12** milk-and-water **13** characterless

name 3 dub, nom, tab, tag, tap **4** cite, term **5** alias, label, nomen, title **6** finger, repute, rubric **7** appoint, baptize, epithet, moniker, specify **8** christen, identify, nominate **9** designate, incognito, sobriquet **10** denominate, reputation **11** appellation, appellative, designation *ancient Rome:* **7** agnomen **8** prenomen *assumed:* **5** alias **9** sobriquet *family:* **8** cognomen *fictitious:* **9** pseudonym *giver:* **6** eponym

nameless 6 unsung **7** obscure, unknown **9** anonymous **11** indefinable, unutterable **12** uncelebrated, unidentified

namely 3 viz. **5** id est, to wit **6** that is **8** scilicet **9** expressly, specially, videlicet **10** especially **12** particularly, specifically

Name of the Rose author 3 Eco (Umberto)

Namibia *capital:* **8** Windhoek *city:* **8** Oshakati, Rehoboth *desert:* **5** Namib **8** Kalahari *language:* **5** Bantu **6** German **9** Afrikaans *neighbor:* **6** Angola **8** Botswana **11** South Africa *river:* **6** Cunene, Orange **8** Okavango

nana 7 grandma **11** grandmother

Nana *author:* **4** Zola (Emile) *mother:* **8** Gervaise

Nancy Drew *aunt:* **6** Eloise *author:* **5** Keene (Carolyn) *boyfriend:* **3** Ned *creator:* **11** Stratemeyer (Edward) *dog:* **4** Togo *father:* **6** Carson *friend:* **4** Bess **5** Helen **6** George *housekeeper:* **6** Hannah

Nanna *brother:* **6** Nergal, Ninazu *father:* **5** Enlil *husband:* **6** Balder, Baldur *mother:* **6** Ninlil *son:* **3** Utu *wife:* **6** Ningal

nanny 5 nurse **9** caregiver, governess, nursemaid

Naomi 4 Mara *daughter-in-law:* **4** Ruth **5** Orpah *husband:* **9** Elimelech *son:* **6** Mahlon **7** Chilion

nap 4 doze, pile, rest, shag, wale, warp, weft, woof **5** sleep, weave **6** drowse, nod off, siesta, snooze **7** drop off, surface **10** forty winks

nape 6 scruff

Naphtali *brother:* **3** Dan *father:* **5** Jacob

mother: **6** Bilhah *son:* **4** Guni **5** Jezer **7** Jahzeel, Jahziel, Shallum

naphtha 7 solvent **9** petroleum

napkin 5 cloth, doily, towel **9** serviette

napoleon 4 boot **6** pastry **8** card game **9** solitaire *bid:* **7** blucher **10** wellington

Napoleon *adversary:* **6** Nelson (Horatio) **7** Kutuzov (Mikhail) **10** Wellington (Duke of) *birthplace:* **7** Ajaccio, Corsica *brother:* **5** Louis **6** Jérome, Joseph, Lucien *brother-in-law:* **5** Murat (Joachim) *deathplace:* **8** St. Helena *defeat:* **7** Leipzig **8** Waterloo **9** Trafalgar *doctor:* **11** Antommarchi (Francesco) *father:* **5** Carlo *island of exile:* **4** Elba **8** St. Helena *marshal:* **3** Ney (Michel) **5** Murat (Joachim), Soult (Nicolas-Jean) **6** Suchet (Louis-Gabriel) *sister:* **5** Maria **8** Carlotta, Carolina *victory:* **3** Ulm **4** Jena, Lodi **5** Ligny **6** Abukir, Abu Qir, Arcole, Wagram **7** Bautzen, Dresden, Marengo **8** Borodino **10** Austerlitz *wife:* **9** Josephine **11** Marie Louise

narcissism 6 egoism, vanity **7** conceit, egotism **8** self-love, vainness **9** vainglory **11** egocentrism, self-conceit **13** conceitedness

narcissistic 4 vain **7** stuck-up **9** conceited, egotistic **10** self-loving **11** egotistical **12** self-absorbed, self-admiring, self-centered, vainglorious

Narcissus *admirer:* **4** Echo *father:* **9** Cephissus *mother:* **7** Liriope

narcotic 3 hop **4** dope, drug, junk **5** opium **6** heroin, opiate **7** anodyne, cocaine, hashish **8** hypnotic, morphine, nepenthe **9** somnolent, soporific **10** somnorific **11** somniferous *peddler:* **6** dealer, pusher

narrate 4 tell **5** state **6** detail, recite, relate, report **7** express, outline, recount **8** describe **9** chronicle

narrative 4 epic, myth, saga, tale, yarn **5** fable, story **6** legend, report **7** account, history, recital, version **8** anecdote **9** chronicle *medieval French:* **5** roman **7** romance *prose:* **5** novel **7** novella

narrator 6 teller **7** reciter **8** reporter **9** describer, performer **10** chronicler

narrow 5 close, small, taper **6** lessen, strait **7** bigoted, limited, precise, slender **8** contract, decrease, straiten **9** confining, constrict, hidebound, illiberal **10** brassbound, inflexible, intolerant, prejudiced, restricted

narrowly 6 barely **7** closely **8** scarcely, strictly

narrow-minded 5 petty **7** bigoted, insular **9** hidebound, illiberal **10** brassbound, intolerant, prejudiced, provincial

nasal 6 rhinal, twangy **9** nosepiece *combining form:* **4** rhin **5** rhino *sprayer:* **9** nebulizer

NASCAR champion 5 Busch (Kurt), Petty (Lee, Richard) **6** Gordon (Jeff), Martin (Mark), Newman (Ryan) **7** Jarrett (Dale), Johnson (Jimmie), Kenseth (Matt), Labonte (Bobby, Terry), Stewart (Tony) **9** Earnhardt (Dale)

nascency 5 birth **6** origin **7** genesis **8** birthing, creation, nativity **9** inception **11** parturition

nascent 7 budding, growing, newborn **8** emergent **9** beginning, embryonic, fledgling, incipient, sprouting **10** blossoming, burgeoning, initiative, initiatory

Naseby victor 7 Fairfax (Thomas) **8** Cromwell (Oliver)

_____ **Nastase 4** Ilie

nasty 4 evil, foul, icky, mean, vile **5** awful, dirty, gross, snide **6** filthy, grubby, horrid, malign, odious, wicked **7** beastly, harmful, hateful, ill-bred, painful, raunchy, squalid, vicious **8** god-awful, indecent, spiteful **9** loathsome, malicious, malignant, obnoxious, offensive, repugnant, repulsive **10** disgusting, malevolent **11** distasteful **12** disagreeable

natant 8 floating, swimming

Nathan *father:* **4** Bani **5** Attai, David *son:* **5** Zabad

nation 4 race **5** realm, state, tribe **6** domain, people, polity **7** country, kingdom, society **8** dominion, populace, republic **11** sovereignty **12** commonwealth, principality *Africa:* **4** Chad, Mali, Togo **5** Benin, Congo, Egypt, Gabon, Ghana, Kenya, Libya, Niger, Sudan **6** Angola, Gambia, Guinea, Malawi, Rwanda, Uganda, Zambia **7** Algeria, Burundi, Comoros, Eritrea, Lesotho, Liberia, Morocco, Namibia, Nigeria, Senegal, Somalia, Tunisia **8** Botswana, Cameroon, Djibouti, Ethiopia, Tanzania, Zimbabwe **9** Cape Verde, Mauritius, Swaziland **10** Ivory Coast, Madagascar, Mauritania, Mozambique, Seychelles **11** Burkina Faso, Côte d'Ivoire, Sierra Leone, South Africa **12** Guinea-Bissau **16** Equatorial Guinea **18** São Tomé and Principe **22** Central African Republic *Americas:* **4** Peru **5** Chile **6** Belize, Brazil, Canada, Guyana, Mexico, Panama **7** Bolivia, Ecuador, Uruguay **8** Colombia, Honduras, Paraguay, Suriname **9** Argentina, Costa Rica, Guatemala, Nicaragua, Venezuela **10** El Salvador **12** United States *Asia:* **4** Laos **5** Burma, China, India, Japan, Korea, Nepal **6** Bhutan, Brunei, Ceylon, Taiwan **7** Armenia, Georgia, Myanmar, Vietnam **8** Cambodia, Malaysia, Maldives, Mongolia, Pakistan, Sri Lanka, Thailand **9** East Timor,

Indonesia, Singapore **10** Azerbaijan, Bangladesh, Kazakhstan, Kyrgyzstan, North Korea, South Korea, Tajikistan, Timor-Leste **11** Afghanistan, Philippines **12** Turkmenistan *Caribbean:* **4** Cuba **5** Haiti **7** Bahamas, Grenada, Jamaica **8** Barbados, Dominica **10** Saint Lucia **15** St. Kitts and Nevis **17** Antigua and Barbuda, Dominican Republic, Trinidad and Tobago **18** Saint Kitts and Nevis **25** St. Vincent and the Grenadines **28** Saint Vincent and the Grenadines *Europe:* **5** Italy, Malta, Spain **6** Bosnia, Cyprus, France, Greece, Latvia, Monaco, Norway, Poland, Russia, Serbia, Sweden, Turkey **7** Albania, Andorra, Austria, Belarus, Belgium, Croatia, Denmark, Estonia, Finland, Germany, Hungary, Iceland, Ireland, Moldova, Romania, Ukraine **8** Bulgaria, Portugal, Slovakia, Slovenia **9** Lithuania, Macedonia, San Marino **10** Luxembourg, Montenegro, Yugoslavia **11** Netherlands, Switzerland **13** Czech Republic, Liechtenstein, United Kingdom *Middle East:* **3** UAE **4** Iraq, Iran, Oman **5** Qatar, Syria, Yemen **6** Israel, Jordan, Kuwait **7** Bahrain, Lebanon **11** Saudi Arabia **18** United Arab Emirates *Oceania:* **4** Fiji **5** Samoa, Tonga **7** Vanuatu **8** Kiribati **9** Australia **10** Micronesia, New Zealand **14** Papua New Guinea, Solomon Islands **15** Marshall Islands

national 6 native **7** citizen, federal, subject **8** resident **10** countryman **11** countrywide

National Basketball Association *Atlanta:* **5** Hawks *Boston:* **7** Celtics *Charlotte:* **7** Bobcats *Chicago:* **5** Bulls *Cleveland:* **9** Cavaliers *Dallas:* **9** Mavericks *Denver:* **7** Nuggets *Detroit:* **7** Pistons *Golden State:* **8** Warriors *Houston:* **7** Rockets *Indiana:* **6** Pacers *Los Angeles:* **6** Lakers **8** Clippers *Memphis:* **9** Grizzlies *Miami:* **4** Heat *Milwaukee:* **5** Bucks *Minnesota:* **12** Timberwolves *New Jersey:* **4** Nets *New Orleans:* **7** Hornets *New York:* **6** Knicks *Oklahoma City:* **7** Thunder *Orlando:* **5** Magic *Philadelphia:* **13** Seventy-sixers *Phoenix:* **4** Suns *Portland:* **12** Trail Blazers *Sacramento:* **5** Kings *San Antonio:* **5** Spurs *Toronto:* **7** Raptors *Utah:* **4** Jazz *Washington:* **7** Wizards

National Football League *Arizona:* **9** Cardinals *Atlanta:* **7** Falcons *Baltimore:* **6** Ravens *Buffalo:* **5** Bills *Carolina:* **8** Panthers *Chicago:* **5** Bears *Cincinnati:* **7** Bengals *Cleveland:* **6** Browns *Dallas:* **7** Cowboys *Denver:* **7** Broncos *Detroit:* **5** Lions *Green Bay:* **7** Packers *Houston:* **6** Texans *Indianapolis:* **5** Colts *Jacksonville:* **7** Jaguars *Kansas City:*

6 Chiefs *Miami:* 8 Dolphins *Minnesota:* 7 Vikings *New England:* 8 Patriots *New Orleans:* 6 Saints *New York:* 4 Jets 6 Giants *Oakland:* 7 Raiders *Philadelphia:* 6 Eagles *Pittsburgh:* 8 Steelers *St. Louis:* 4 Rams *San Diego:* 8 Chargers *San Francisco:* 11 Forty-niners *Seattle:* 8 Seahawks *Tampa Bay:* 4 Bucs 10 Buccaneers *Tennessee:* 6 Titans *Washington:* 8 Redskins

National Hockey League *Anaheim:* 5 Ducks *Atlanta:* 9 Thrashers *Boston:* 6 Bruins *Buffalo:* 6 Sabres *Calgary:* 6 Flames *Carolina:* 10 Hurricanes *Chicago:* 10 Blackhawks *Colorado:* 9 Avalanche *Columbus:* 11 Blue Jackets *Dallas:* 5 Stars *Detroit:* 8 Red Wings *Edmonton:* 6 Oilers *Florida:* 8 Panthers *Los Angeles:* 5 Kings *Minnesota:* 4 Wild *Montreal:* 9 Canadiens *Nashville:* 9 Predators *New Jersey:* 6 Devils *New York:* 7 Rangers 9 Islanders *Ottawa:* 8 Senators *Philadelphia:* 6 Flyers *Phoenix:* 7 Coyotes *Pittsburgh:* 8 Penguins *St. Louis:* 5 Blues *San Jose:* 6 Sharks *Tampa Bay:* 9 Lightning *Toronto:* 10 Maple Leafs *Vancouver:* 7 Canucks *Washington:* 8 Capitals

nationalism 8 jingoism 10 chauvinism, patriotism

National League *Arizona:* 12 Diamondbacks *Atlanta:* 6 Braves *Chicago:* 4 Cubs *Cincinnati:* 4 Reds *Colorado:* 7 Rockies *Florida:* 7 Marlins *Houston:* 6 Astros *Los Angeles:* 7 Dodgers *Milwaukee:* 7 Brewers *New York:* 4 Mets *Philadelphia:* 8 Phillies *Pittsburgh:* 7 Pirates *St. Louis:* 9 Cardinals *San Diego:* 6 Padres *San Francisco:* 6 Giants *Washington:* 9 Nationals

national military park *Alabama:* 13 Horseshoe Bend *Arkansas:* 8 Pea Ridge *Mississippi:* 9 Vicksburg *Pennsylvania:* 10 Gettysburg *South Carolina:* 13 Kings Mountain *Tennessee:* 6 Shiloh

national monument *Alabama:* 11 Russell Cave *Alaska:* 9 Aniakchak *Arizona:* 5 Tonto 6 Navajo 7 Saguaro, Wupatki 8 Tuzigoot 10 Chiricahua, Pipe Spring, Tumacacori 11 Hohokam Pima 12 Sunset Crater, Walnut Canyon *California:* 8 Cabrillo, Lava Beds 9 Muir Woods, Pinnacles 10 Joshua Tree 11 Death Valley *Colorado:* 10 Yucca House *Colorado-Utah:* 8 Dinosaur 9 Hovenweep *Florida:* 12 Fort Matanzas 13 Fort Jefferson *Georgia:* 8 Ocmulgee 11 Fort Pulaski 13 Fort Frederica *Iowa:* 12 Effigy Mounds *Louisiana:* 12 Poverty Point *Maryland:* 11 Fort McHenry *Minnesota:* 9 Pipestone 12 Grand Portage *Nebraska:* 10 Homestead 11 Scotts Bluff *New Mexico:* 5 Pecos 7 El

Morro 9 Bandelier, El Malpais, Fort Union 10 Aztec Ruins, White Sands *New York:* 11 Fort Stanwix 13 Castle Clinton *South Carolina:* 10 Fort Sumter 13 Congaree Swamp *South Dakota:* 9 Jewel Cave *Utah:* 11 Cedar Breaks 13 Rainbow Bridge *Wyoming:* 11 Devils Tower, Fossil Butte

national park *Alaska:* 6 Denali, Katmai 9 Lake Clark 10 Glacier Bay 11 Kenai Fjords, Kobuk Valley *Angola:* 4 Iona, Mupa *Arizona:* 11 Grand Canyon *Arkansas:* 10 Hot Springs *Botswana:* 5 Chobe *California:* 7 Redwood, Sequoia 8 Yosemite 11 King's Canyon *Chad:* 5 Manda *Colombia:* 5 Uraba *Colorado:* 9 Mesa Verde 13 Rocky Mountain *eastern Africa:* 10 Mount Kenya *Florida:* 8 Biscayne 10 Everglades *Hawaii:* 9 Haleakala *India:* 5 Kanha *Japan:* 5 Nikko *Kentucky:* 11 Mammoth Cave *Kenya:* 4 Meru 5 Tsavo 10 Royal Tsavo *Lake Superior:* 10 Isle Royale *Maine:* 6 Acadia *Malaysia:* 8 Kinabalu *Minnesota:* 9 Voyageurs *Montana:* 7 Glacier *Nevada:* 10 Great Basin *Oregon:* 10 Crater Lake *Poland:* 5 Ojcow, Tatra *South Africa:* 6 Kruger *South Dakota:* 8 Badlands, Wind Cave *Sri Lanka:* 4 Yala *Sweden:* 5 Sarek *Tanzania:* 5 Ruaha 9 Serengeti *Texas:* 7 Big Bend *Utah:* 4 Zion 6 Arches 11 Bryce Canyon, Canyonlands, Capitol Reef *Virginia:* 10 Shenandoah *Washington:* 7 Olympic 12 Mount Rainier 13 North Cascades *Wyoming:* 10 Grand Teton *Wyoming-Idaho-Montana:* 11 Yellowstone *Zambia:* 5 Kafue *Zimbabwe:* 13 Rhodes Inyanga, Victoria Falls

native 3 raw 4 wild 5 local 6 inborn, innate 7 connate, endemic, natural 8 domestic, indigene, inherent, internal, national 9 inherited 10 aboriginal, congenital, connatural, indigenous, unacquired *Acadian Louisiana:* 5 Cajun *China:* 3 Han 9 Celestial *India:* 5 sepoy *Japan:* 9 Nipponese *London:* 7 Cockney *Mindanao:* 3 Ata *New England:* 4 Yank 6 Yankee *New York:* 13 Knickerbocker

Native American see **Indian, American**

Native Son author 6 Wright (Richard)

Nativity 4 Noel, Xmas, yule 8 yuletide 9 Christmas *scene:* 6 crèche

nativity 5 birth, start 6 origin, outset 7 genesis 8 delivery 9 beginning, horoscope, inception 11 parturition

natter 3 gab, jaw, yak, yap 4 blab, buzz, chat, go on 5 prate, run on 6 babble, gabble, gossip, tattle 7 chatter, prattle, twaddle 8 chitchat, converse

natty 4 neat, tidy, trim 5 doggy, nobby, sassy, smart, swank 6 classy, dapper, jaunty, snazzy, spiffy, spruce, sprucy, swanky **7** bandbox, doggish, stylish **9** turned out **11** well-groomed

natural 4 pure, wild **5** naive, usual **6** candid, inborn, innate, native, normal, simple **7** artless, connate, organic **8** homespun, inherent, innocent **9** childlike, ingenuous, ingrained, primitive **10** congenital, indigenous, legitimate, unaffected **11** commonplace, instinctive, spontaneous

naturalist *American:* **4** Muir (John) **5** Gould (Stephen Jay), Hyatt (Alpheus) **6** Carson (Rachel) **7** Agassiz (Louis), Audubon (John James), Thoreau (H. D.), Verrill (Addison, Alpheus) **9** Burroughs (John) *English:* **3** Ray (John) **5** White (Gilbert) **6** Darwin (Charles) **7** Wallace (Alfred Russel) **10** Williamson (William) *French:* **5** Fabre (Jean-Henri) **7** Lamarck (Chevalier de), Réaumur (René Antoine) *German:* **8** Humboldt (Alexander von) *Scottish:* **6** Wilson (Alexander) **10** Richardson (John)

nature 3 ilk, way **4** kind, sort, type **6** makeup, manner, stripe, temper **7** essence, scenery **8** creation, tendency, universe **9** character, landscape **10** complexion **11** description, disposition, personality, temperament **12** constitution

naught 3 nil, nix, zip **4** love, nada, zero **5** zilch **6** cipher **7** nothing, nullity **8** goose egg **11** nothingness

naughty 3 bad **4** lewd **5** bawdy **6** unruly, ribald, risqué, smutty, vulgar **7** froward, obscene, raunchy, wayward, willful **8** contrary, improper, perverse, rascally **10** ill-behaved **11** disobedient, mischievous **12** obstreperous, recalcitrant

Nauru *capital:* **5** Yaren *former name:* **8** Pleasant (Island)

nauseate 5 repel **6** offend, sicken **7** disgust, repulse

nauseated 6 queasy **7** carsick **8** qualmish **9** disgusted, squeamish **10** grossed out

nauseating 6 putrid **7** noisome **9** loathsome, offensive, repellant, repugnant, repulsive, revolting, sickening **10** disgusting

Nausicaa *father:* **8** Alcinous *mother:* **5** Arete

nautical 5 naval **6** marine **7** oceanic **8** maritime **12** navigational *instrument:* **3** aba **7** compass, pelorus, sextant

Navajo *dwelling* **5** hogan

naval hero 5 Drake (Francis), Jones (John Paul), Perry (Matthew, Oliver Hazard) **6** Nelson (Horatio) **8** Farragut (David, George), Lawrence (James)

navel 6 middle **7** nombril **9** umbilicus **11**

belly button *combining form:* **6** omphal **7** omphalo *type:* **5** innie, outie

navigate 4 helm, plot, sail **5** guide, pilot, steer **6** cruise **8** maneuver, traverse

navigation 8 piloting **10** seamanship **12** helmsmanship

navigational system 5 loran

navigator 5 flyer, pilot **6** airman **7** copilot *Danish:* **6** Bering (Vitus) *Dutch:* **6** Tasman (Abel) **7** Barents (Willem) *English:* **4** Cook (Captain James) **5** Cabot (John, Sebastian), Drake (Francis) **6** Hudson (Henry) **7** Gilbert (Humphrey), Raleigh (Walter) **9** Vancouver (George) *French:* **7** Cartier (Jacques) **9** La Perouse (Comte de) *Italian:* **6** Caboto (Giovanni) **8** Columbus (Christopher), Vespucci (Amerigo) **9** Verrazano (Giovanni) **10** Verrazzano (Giovanni) *Norwegian:* **4** Eric (the Red), Erik (the Red) **8** Ericsson (Leif), Eriksson (Leif) **12** Leif Ericsson, Leif Eriksson *Portuguese:* **4** Dias (Bartolomeu, Dinis) **6** Cabral (Pedro Alvares), da Gama (Vasco) **8** Magellan (Ferdinand) *Spanish:* **9** Fernández (Juan)

navy 4 blue **5** fleet **6** argosy, armada **8** flotilla *officer:* **3** ADM, CWO, ENS **4** CAPT, LCDR, LTJG, RADM, VADM **6** ensign **7** admiral, captain **9** commander **10** lieutenant

Nazi 9 Hitlerite **10** brownshirt *admiral:* **6** Dönitz (Karl), Raeder (Erich) **7** Doenitz (Karl) *air force:* **9** Luftwaffe *armed forces:* **9** Wehrmacht *cheer:* **8** Siegheil *collaborator:* **5** Laval (Pierre) **8** Quisling (Vidkun) *concentration camp:* **6** Belsen, Dachau **8** Auschwitz, Treblinka **10** Buchenwald, Nordhausen *field marshal:* **5** Model (Walter) **6** Keitel (Wilhelm), Paulus (Friedrich), Rommel (Erwin) **9** Rundstedt (Karl von) **10** Kesselring (Albert) *greeting:* **4** heil **10** heil Hitler *leader:* **3** Ley (Robert) **4** Hess (Rudolf), Röhm (Ernst) **5** Roehm (Ernst) **6** Führer, Göring (Hermann), Hitler (Adolf) **7** Fuehrer, Goering (Hermann), Himmler (Heinrich) **8** Goebbels (Joseph), Heydrich (Reinhard) **9** Rosenberg (Alfred) *police:* **7** Gestapo *propagandist:* **8** Goebbels (Joseph) *submarine:* **5** U-boat *surrender signer:* **4** Jodl (Alfred) **6** Keitel (Wilhelm) *symbol:* **6** fylfot **8** swastika *tactic:* **10** blitzkrieg *tank:* **6** Panzer

NCO 3 cpl, sgt **8** corporal, sergeant

neap 3 low **4** tide

near 4 nigh **5** about, circa, close, round **6** almost, around **7** close by, close on **8** adjacent, approach **9** immediate, proximate **11** approximate

nearby 4 nigh **5** about, aside, close, handy **6**

around, beside **8** adjacent **9** adjoining, proximate **10** contiguous, convenient **11** neighboring

nearest 4 next **7** closest **8** adjacent, proximal **9** proximate **10** contiguous

nearsighted 6 myopic

neat 4 deft, nice, prim, snug, tidy, trig, trim **5** clean, clear, kempt **6** bovine, cattle, clever, smooth, spruce **7** orderly, precise, unmixed **8** straight, well-kept **9** shipshape, undiluted **10** methodical, systematic **11** spic-and-span, uncluttered, well-groomed **12** spick-and-span **13** unadulterated

neb 3 tip **4** beak, bill, nose, prow **5** snoot, snout **9** proboscis

Nebraska *capital:* **7** Lincoln *city:* **5** Omaha *college, university:* **9** Creighton *nickname:* **10** Cornhusker (State) *river:* **6** Platte **8** Missouri *state bird:* **10** meadowlark *state flower:* **9** goldenrod *state tree:* **10** cottonwood

nebula 6 galaxy

nebulous 4 hazy **5** vague **6** cloudy, turbid **7** clouded, obscure, unclear **9** ambiguous, amorphous, uncertain **10** indefinite, indistinct **13** indeterminate

necessary 5 basic, vital **6** needed **7** crucial, needful **8** cardinal, integral, required **9** de rigueur, essential, mandatory, requisite **10** compulsory, imperative, inevitable, obligatory, undeniable **11** fundamental, ineluctable, inescapable, unavoidable **12** all-important, prerequisite **13** indispensable

necessitate 5 cause, exact, force **6** compel, demand, entail **7** call for, involve, require **8** occasion

necessity 4 must, need **6** crisis, duress **7** poverty **8** exigency **9** essential, privation, requisite **10** compulsion, imperative, obligation, sine qua non **11** dire straits, needfulness, requirement **12** precondition, prerequisite

neck 3 pet **4** kiss **5** spoon **6** fondle, smooch *back of:* **4** nape **5** nucha, nuque **6** scruff *ornament:* **6** gorget, torque

necklace 5 chain **6** choker **7** rivière **8** carcanet *floral:* **3** lei

necktie 4 bolo **5** ascot **6** cravat **10** four-in-hand

necrology 4 obit **8** obituary

necromancy 4 juju, mojo **5** magic, vodun **6** hoodoo, voodoo **7** devilry, sorcery **8** witchery, wizardry **9** conjuring, diabolism, magicking **10** black magic, witchcraft **11** bewitchment, conjuration, enchantment, incantation, thaumaturgy

necropolis 8 boneyard, boot hill, cemetery, God's acre **9** graveyard **10** churchyard **12** memorial park, potter's field

necropsy 7 anatomy, autopsy **10** dissection, postmortem

née 4 born **10** originally

need 3 use **4** call, duty, lack, must, want **5** crave **6** demand, devoir, hunger, penury, thirst **7** poverty, require **8** distress, exigency, occasion, shortage **9** indigence, necessity, privation, requisite **10** compulsion, deficiency, obligation **11** deprivation, destitution, requirement

neediness 4 want **6** penury **7** poverty **9** essential, indigence, privation **11** deprivation, destitution **13** insufficiency

needle 3 rib **5** annoy, tease **6** harass, pester, plague **7** bedevil, hagride, obelisk, pricker, syringe **10** hypodermic *case:* **4** etui *hole:* **3** eye

needlefish 3 gar **8** pipefish

needlelike 7 styloid **8** belonoid *part:* **7** acicula

needlepoint 4 lace **7** alençon, crochet, tatting **8** bargello **10** embroidery **11** cross-stitch

needlework 4 lace **6** sewing **7** alençon, crochet, sampler, tatting **8** bargello, knitting **9** stitching **10** crocheting, embroidery **11** cross-stitch

needy 4 poor **5** broke **6** hard up **8** beggared, dirt-poor, indigent, strapped **9** destitute, penniless, penurious **10** down-and-out **11** impecunious, necessitous **12** impoverished

ne'er-do-well 3 bum, dud **5** loser **6** loafer, no-good **7** failure, wastrel **8** derelict, fainéant **9** shiftless **10** profligate, scapegrace

nefarious 4 evil, vile **6** savage, wicked **7** heinous, impious, noxious **8** depraved, dreadful, flagrant, infamous, perverse **9** execrable, miscreant, monstrous, offensive **10** abominable, degenerate, detestable, iniquitous, outrageous, villainous **11** opprobrious **13** reprehensible

negate 4 deny, undo, void **5** annul, belie, quash, rebut **6** cancel, impugn, refute, vacate **7** abolish, gainsay, nullify, redress, vitiate **8** abrogate, disallow, disprove, overturn, traverse **9** cancel out, disaffirm, repudiate **10** contradict, contravene, counteract, invalidate, neutralize

negative 2 no **3** nay, nix **4** deny, kill, veto **5** annul, cross, minus **6** impugn **7** adverse, gainsay, nullify, redress, refusal **8** abrogate, disprove, traverse **9** cancel out, frustrate **10** contradict, contravene, counteract, invalidate, neutralize **11** detrimental, unfavorable *battery terminal:* **5** anode *ion:* **5** anion *Scottish:* **3** nae *sign:* **5** minus

neglect 4 fail, omit **5** let go, shirk **6** forget, ignore, laxity, slight **7** failure, laxness **8** omission, overlook, overpass, pass over **9**

avoidance, disregard, oversight, pretermit **10** negligence **11** dereliction, inattention **12** carelessness

neglectful see **negligent**

negligee 4 gown **5** teddy **7** chemise, nightie **8** camisole, peignoir **9** nightgown

negligent 3 lax **5** slack **6** remiss **8** careless, derelict, heedless **9** forgetful, imprudent **10** delinquent, neglectful, nonchalant, regardless, unthinking **11** inattentive, pococurante, unconcerned **13** irresponsible, lackadaisical

negligible 4 puny, slim **5** minor, petty, small **6** meager, meagre, minute, remote, paltry, skimpy, slight **7** minimal, slender, trivial **8** nugatory, picayune, trifling **9** minuscule **11** meaningless, unimportant **13** imperceptible, insignificant

negotiable 8 passable **11** convertible **12** transferable

negotiate 4 cash **6** confer, dicker, hurdle, manage, parley, settle **7** arrange, bargain, develop, mediate, work out, wrangle **8** contract, covenant, moderate, surmount, transact, transfer **9** arbitrate **10** horse-trade

neigh 6 nicker, whinny

neighbor 4 abut **5** flank, frame, skirt, touch **6** adjoin, border **7** abutter **8** border on

neighborhood 4 area, nabe, turf, ward **5** block, range **6** parish **8** district, environs, locality, precinct, purlieus, vicinage, vicinity **9** community, proximity

neighborly 6 genial **7** amiable, cordial, helpful **8** amicable, friendly, obliging, sociable **9** congenial **10** gregarious, hospitable **11** considerate, cooperative, good-natured **13** accommodating

nematode 4 worm **7** eelworm **9** roundworm

Nemean predator **4** lion

nemesis 4 bane, doom **5** curse, enemy, rival **8** opponent **9** bête noire **11** retribution

neologism 7 coinage, new word

neon symbol **2** Ne

neophyte see **newcomer**

Neoptolemus 7 Pyrrhus *father:* **8** Achilles *slayer:* **7** Orestes *victim:* **5** Priam *wife:* **8** Hermione

neoteric 6 modern, recent

Nepal *capital:* **8** Katmandu **9** Kathmandu *city:* **7** Pokhara **8** Lalitpur *monetary unit:* **5** rupee *mountain, range:* **7** Everest **8** Himalaya **9** Himalayan, Himalayas **10** Dhaulagiri **11** Gauri Sankar **12** Kanchenjunga *neighbor:* **5** China, India *river:* **6** Ganges

nepenthe 6 opiate, potion **7** anodyne **8** lenitive, narcotic **9** analgesic **10** anesthetic, painkiller **11** anaesthetic

Nephthys *brother, husband:* **3** Set **4** Seth

nepotism 10 favoritism, partiality

Neptune 6 planet *satellite:* **6** Nereid, Triton (see also **Poseidon**)

nerd 4 drip, geek **5** dweeb **6** misfit, weenie **7** egghead, nebbish, oddball **10** pointy-head

Nereid 6 Thetis **7** Galatea **10** Amphitrite *father:* **6** Nereus *mother:* **5** Doris

Nereus *daughters:* **8** Nereides *emblem:* **7** trident *father:* **6** Pontus *mother:* **4** Gaea *wife:* **5** Doris

Nergal *brother:* **5** Nanna **6** Ninazu *father:* **5** Enlil *mother:* **6** Ninlil

Nero *birthplace:* **4** Rome *mother:* **9** Agrippina *successor:* **5** Galba *tutor:* **6** Seneca *victim:* **5** Lucan **6** Seneca **7** Octavia, Poppaea **9** Agrippina *wife:* **7** Octavia, Poppaea

Nero Wolfe creator **5** Stout (Rex)

nerve 4 face, gall, grit, guts **5** brass, cheek, crust, heart, moxie, spunk **6** daring **7** sciatic **8** audacity, backbone, boldness, chutzpah, temerity **9** assurance, brashness, fortitude, hardihood, hardiness **10** confidence, effrontery **11** presumption *cell:* **6** neuron *cell group:* **7** ganglia (plural) **8** ganglion *cell part:* **4** axon **8** dendrite, receptor *combining form:* **4** neur **5** neura, neuro *cranial:* **4** vagi (plural) **5** optic, vagus **8** abducens *lesion:* **8** neuritis

nerve center 3 hub **4** core, seat **5** focus, heart, locus **7** capital **8** cynosure, polestar **10** crossroads, focal point **12** headquarters

nerve gas 5 sarin, soman, tabun

nervous 4 edgy **5** antsy, jerky, jumpy, tense, timid **6** fitful, goosey, on edge, spooky, uneasy **7** erratic, fidgety, fretful, jittery, restive, twitchy, uptight **8** aflutter, agitated, skittery, skittish, spirited, twittery, unsteady, vigorous, volatile **9** excitable, irritable **10** high-strung **12** apprehensive

nervy 4 bold, edgy, flip, pert **5** brash, cocky, fresh, jerky, jumpy, sassy, tense **6** brassy, cheeky, goosey, plucky, uneasy **7** fidgety, forward, jittery, restive, twitchy, uptight **8** flippant, impudent, intrepid, twittery **9** excitable **10** high-strung **11** smart-alecky

ness 4 cape **8** foreland, headland **9** peninsula **10** promontory

Nessus' *victim:* **8** Heracles, Hercules

nest 4 den **5** aery, home, lair, nidi (plural) **6** aerie, eyrie, nidus **7** hangout, shelter **11** aggregation *eagle's:* **4** aery **5** aerie, eyrie *pheasant's:* **4** nide *wasp's:* **8** vespiary

nest egg 5 cache, funds, hoard, kitty, stash **6** assets **7** reserve

nestle 4 snug **6** bundle, burrow, cuddle, huddle, nuzzle **7** snuggle

Nestor *father:* **6** Neleus *kingdom:* **5** Pylos

net 4 gain, gist, mesh **5** basic, catch, clear, seine, tulle, yield **6** maline **7** clean up, essence, malines *conical:* **5** trawl *fishing:* **5** seine *hair:* **5** snood

Nethanel *brother:* **5** David *father:* **5** Jesse **7** Pashhur **8** Obededom *son:* **8** Shemaiah

nether 3 low **4** down **5** below, lower, under **6** lesser **8** chthonic, inferior **9** subjacent **10** underworld **11** underground **12** subterranean

Netherlands 7 Holland *capital:* **9** Amsterdam *city:* **5** Hague (The) **7** Utrecht **8** The Hague **9** Rotterdam *former inlet:* **9** Zuider Zee *island group:* **11** West Frisian *lake:* **10** IJsselmeer *language:* **5** Dutch *monetary unit:* **4** euro *monetary unit, former:* **6** gulden, stiver **7** guilder *neighbor:* **7** Belgium, Germany *river:* **4** Maas **5** Meuse, Rhein, Rhine **7** Scheldt *sea:* **5** North

Netherlands Antilles *capital:* **10** Willemstad *discoverer:* **8** Columbus (Christopher) *former name:* **7** Curaçao *island:* **4** Saba **7** Bonaire **7** Curaçao *location:* **10** West Indies

netherworld 3 pit **4** hell **5** abyss, hades, Sheol **6** blazes, Tophet **7** Gehenna, inferno **8** hellfire **9** perdition **10** no-man's-land, underworld **11** underground

netlike 9 reticular **10** reticulate

nettle 3 irk, nag, vex **4** gall, huff, rile, roil **5** annoy, chafe, peeve, pique, upset **6** abrade, badger, harass, incite, put out, pester, ruffle, stir up **7** agitate, disturb, perturb, provoke **8** irritate **10** exasperate

nettle rash 5 hives **9** urticaria

nettlesome 5 pesky **6** vexing **7** galling, irksome, prickly **8** annoying, rankling **9** irritable, upsetting, vexatious **10** irritating

network 3 ABC, CBS, CNN, CTV, Fox, HBO, NBC, PBS, QVC, TBS, TNT, web **4** ESPN, grid, INHD, mesh, NESN, rete **8** gridiron, Internet **9** reticulum *anatomical:* **4** rete **5** retia (plural)

neurotic 6 phobic, touchy **7** anxious **8** abnormal, unstable **9** disturbed, obsessive **10** compulsive, disordered

neuter 3 fix **4** geld, spay **5** alter, unsex **7** sexless **8** castrate, mutilate **9** sterilize **11** desexualize **12** intransitive

neutral 7 hueless **8** detached, middling, unbiased **9** colorless, impartial, unaligned **10** achromatic, disengaged, even-handed, impersonal, nonaligned, pokerfaced **11** indifferent, nonpartisan **13** disinterested, dispassionate

neutralize 4 undo **5** annul **6** negate, offset **7** balance, nullify, redress, reverse **9** cancel

out **10** counteract, invalidate **11** countervail **12** countercheck, counterpoise

Nevada *capital:* **10** Carson City *city:* **4** Elko, Reno **8** Las Vegas *dam:* **6** Hoover **7** Boulder *lake:* **4** Mead **5** Tahoe *mountain:* **8** Boundary (Peak) *nickname:* **6** Silver (State) *river:* **8** Humboldt *state bird:* **8** bluebird (mountain) *state flower:* **9** sagebrush *state tree:* **5** piñon **6** pinyon **15** bristlecone pine

névé 4 firn, snow

never-ending 7 eternal **8** immortal **9** ceaseless **11** everlasting

Never-Ending Story *author* **4** Ende (Michael)

nevertheless 3 but, yet **5** still **6** anyhow, anyway, though, withal **7** howbeit, however **8** after all **10** regardless **11** nonetheless, still and all

nevus 4 mole **9** birthmark

new 5 fresh, novel **6** modern, recent **7** another, revived **8** neoteric, pristine **9** fledgling **10** additional, unfamiliar **11** modernistic **12** contemporary *combining form:* **3** neo, nov **4** novo *word:* **7** coinage **9** neologism

New Age *belief:* **5** karma **6** cabala, holism, kabala **7** kabbala **8** kabbalah **9** occultism, pantheism, shamanism, theosophy, wholeness **10** numerology, soul travel **12** spiritualism **13** reincarnation, synchronicity *community:* **6** Esalen, Sedona, Totnes **7** Dornach **8** Byron Bay, Damanhur, Findhorn **9** Arcosanti, Auroville *healing technique:* **5** auras **8** Ayurveda, crystals **9** iridology **10** homeopathy **11** acupressure, acupuncture, biofeedback **12** aromatherapy *practice:* **4** yoga **5** reiki **7** fasting **10** channeling, meditation, syncretism *teacher:* **3** Orr (Leonard) **4** Dass (Ram), Long (Barry), Myss (Caroline) **5** Cohen (Andrew) **6** Chopra (Deepak), Walsch (Neale Donald), Wilber (Ken) **7** Kabbani (Hisham), Quanjer (Johan) **8** Cottrell (Douglas James), Rajneesh (Bhagwan Shree), Spangler (David) **9** Castaneda (Carlos), Helminski (Kabir) **10** Williamson (Marianne)

New Brunswick *capital:* **11** Fredericton *city:* **6** St. John **7** Moncton *mountain:* **8** Carleton *provincial flower:* **12** purple violet *river:* **9** Miramichi, Saint John **10** Nepisiguit **11** Restigouche

New Caledonia *capital:* **6** Nouméa *department of:* **6** France *discoverer:* **4** Cook (Capt. James) *island:* **7** Loyalty, Walpole **11** Isle of Pines

newcomer 4 colt, tiro, tyro **6** novice, rookie **7** trainee **8** beginner, freshman, initiate, neophyte **9** greenhorn, immigrant, novitiate **10** apprentice, tenderfoot

New Deal agency 3 CCC, NRA, REA, RFC, SEC, TVA, WPA **4** FDIC, NLRB

Newfoundland and Labrador *capital:* **7** St. John's *mountain:* **8** Caubvick *provincial flower:* **12** pitcher plant *river:* **6** Gander **8** Exploits **9** Churchill

New Hampshire *capital:* **7** Concord *city:* **6** Nashua **10** Manchester, Portsmouth *college, university:* **9** Dartmouth *motto:* **13** Live Free or Die *mountain, range:* **5** White **10** Washington *nickname:* **7** Granite (State) *river:* **9** Merrimack **11** Connecticut *state bird:* **11** purple finch *state flower:* **11** purple lilac *state tree:* **10** white birch

New Jersey *capital:* **7** Trenton *city:* **6** Camden, Newark **7** Cape May **8** Paterson **9** Elizabeth **10** Jersey City *college, university:* **4** Drew **7** Rutgers **9** Princeton, Seton Hall *nickname:* **6** Garden (State) *river:* **6** Hudson **7** Raritan **8** Delaware *state bird:* **9** goldfinch *state flower:* **6** violet *state tree:* **6** red oak

New Mexico *capital:* **7** Santa Fe *caverns:* **8** Carlsbad *city:* **4** Taos **7** Roswell **9** Las Cruces, Los Alamos **10** Farmington **11** Albuquerque *mountain, range:* **7** Wheeler (Peak) **14** Sangre de Cristo *nickname:* **17** Land of Enchantment *river:* **5** Pecos **9** Rio Grande *state bird:* **10** roadrunner *state flower:* **5** yucca *state tree:* **5** piñon **6** pinyon

news 4 dope, poop, word **5** rumor **6** advice, gossip, report, tattle **7** lowdown, tidings **9** knowledge, speerings **11** information, scuttlebutt **12** announcement, intelligence *agency:* **2** AP **3** AFP, UPI **4** TASS **7** Reuters **8** ITAR-TASS

newspaper 3 rag **5** daily, organ **6** review **7** gazette, journal, tabloid **8** magazine **10** periodical *goof:* **4** typo *publisher:* **6** Hearst (William Randolph) **7** Murdoch (Rupert) **11** Beaverbrook (Lord) *section:* **4** arts, op-ed **6** comics, sports **8** business **10** classified

newt 3 eft **6** triton *green:* **5** ebbet

New Testament see at **Bible**

New York *capital:* **6** Albany *city:* **4** Rome, Troy **5** Utica **6** Elmira, Ithaca **7** Buffalo, Yonkers **8** Saratoga, Syracuse **9** Rochester *college, university:* **3** RPI **4** Pace, CUNY, SUNY **5** Pratt, Siena **6** CW Post, Hunter, Vassar **7** Adelphi, Barnard, Colgate, Cornell, Fordham, Hofstra, St. Johns, Yeshiva **8** Columbia, Skidmore, Syracuse **9** Juilliard, West Point **13** Sarah Lawrence *county:* **5** Tioga **6** Albany, Oneida, Queens **7** Clinton, Niagara **8** Dutchess, Onandaga *island:* **4** Long, Fire *lake, lake group:* **4** Erie **6** Cayuga, Finger, Oneida **7** Saranac. **9** Champlain *motto:* **9** Excelsior *mountain, range:* **5** Marcy **8** Catskill **10** Adirondack *nickname:* **6** Empire (State) *prison:* **6** Attica *river:* **6** Hudson **7** Niagara **10** St. Lawrence *state bird:* **8** bluebird *state flower:* **4** rose *state tree:* **10** sugar maple

New York City 6 Gotham **8** Big Apple *borough:* **5** Bronx **6** Queens **8** Brooklyn, Richmond **9** Manhattan **12** Staten Island *neighborhood:* **4** Soho **6** Harlem **7** Tribeca

New Zealand *capital:* **10** Wellington *city:* **8** Auckland **12** Christchurch *ethnic group:* **5** Maori *evergreen:* **4** tawa *explorer:* **4** Cook (Capt. James) **6** Tasman (Abel) *island:* **7** Chatham, Stewart *island group:* **4** Cook **8** Manihiki **12** Northern Cook *lake:* **5** Taupo *language:* **5** Maori *mountain, range:* **4** Cook **6** Egmont **12** Southern Alps *native:* **4** Kiwi *parrot:* **4** kaka *shrub:* **4** tutu *strait:* **4** Cook *volcano:* **7** Ruapehu **9** Ngauruhoe

next 4 then **5** after, later **6** behind, beside, second **7** closest, ensuing, nearest **8** abutting, adjacent, touching **9** adjoining, afterward, alongside, following, proximate **10** contiguous, subsequent, succeeding **11** neighboring

next to 4 near **6** almost, beside **7** abreast, close by **8** abutting, adjacent, opposite, touching **9** adjoining, alongside, bordering **11** neighboring

nexus 3 tie **4** bond, knot, link, yoke **5** focus **6** center **8** ligament, ligature, vinculum **10** connection

Nez Percé chief 6 Joseph

Niagara 5 flood, spate **6** deluge **7** torrent **8** alluvion, cataract, flooding, overflow **9** cataclysm, waterfall **10** inundation

nib 3 tip **4** beak, bill, nose, prow **5** prong, snoot, snout, tooth **8** pen point **9** proboscis

nibble 3 eat, nip **4** bite, chew, crop, gnaw, nosh, peck, pick **5** graze, munch, snack, taste **6** morsel, tidbit

Nicaragua *capital:* **7** Managua *city:* **4** León **6** Masaya **7** Grenada *coast:* **8** Mosquito *ethnic group:* **4** Maya **5** Mayan *discoverer:* **8** Columbus (Christopher) *language:* **7** Spanish *monetary unit:* **7** córdoba *neighbor:* **8** Honduras **9** Costa Rica *sea:* **9** Caribbean

nice 4 fine, good, kind, mild, neat **5** right **6** benign, decent, polite, proper, seemly **7** affable, cordial, correct, fitting, refined **8** becoming, charming, decorous, obliging, pleasant, pleasing, suitable, virtuous, wellbred **9** admirable, agreeable, courteous,

congenial, enjoyable, favorable 10 attractive, personable 11 appropriate, respectable
niche 4 nook 6 alcove, corner, cranny, recess 7 calling 8 vocation 9 cubbyhole 11 compartment
Nicholas Nickleby author 7 Dickens (Charles)
nick 3 cut 4 chip, gash 5 cheat, notch, score 6 groove, record 10 overcharge 11 indentation
nickel symbol 2 Ni
nickname 3 tag 5 label 6 byword, handle 7 agnomen, epithet, moniker 8 cognomen 9 sobriquet 10 diminutive, hypocorism
Nicomede conquest: 10 Cappodocia dramatist: 9 Corneille (Pierre) half-brother: 6 Attale stepmother: 7 Arsinoë
nictitate 3 bat 4 wink 5 blink 7 flutter, twinkle
nifty 4 cool, keen, neat 5 dandy, ducky, super, swell 6 clever, groovy, peachy 7 stylish 8 jim-dandy, splendid, terrific 9 ingenious
Niger capital: 6 Niamey city: 6 Maradi, Zinder desert: 5 Sahel 6 Sahara ethnic group: 5 Hausa language: 5 Hausa 6 Arabic, French monetary unit: 5 franc neighbor: 4 Chad, Mali 5 Benin, Libya 7 Algeria, Nigeria 11 Burkina Faso river: 5 Niger
Nigeria capital: 5 Abuja, Lagos city: 4 Kano 6 Ibadan, Ilorin 7 Oshogbo 9 Ogbomosho ethnic group: 4 Igbo 5 Hausa 6 Fulani, Yoruba gulf: 6 Guinea lake: 4 Chad language: 5 Hausa monetary unit: 5 naira neighbor: 4 Chad 5 Benin, Niger 8 Cameroon river: 5 Benue, Niger 6 Kaduna
niggard 5 churl, miser, piker, screw 7 hoarder, scrooge 8 tightwad 9 skinflint 10 cheapskate, curmudgeon 12 money-grubber, penny-pincher
niggardly 5 tight 6 scanty, stingy 7 chintzy, miserly 9 penurious 10 begrudging 11 closefisted, tightfisted 12 cheeseparing, parsimonious 13 penny-pinching
niggling 5 minor, petty 6 measly, paltry, two-bit 7 trivial 8 picayune, piddling, tiresome, trifling 9 small-time 10 bothersome, picayunish 11 Mickey Mouse, small-minded
nigh 4 near 5 about, close, round 6 all but, almost, around, beside, nearby, nearly 7 close to 8 approach 9 immediate, just about, proximate, virtually 10 near at hand 11 practically
night blindness 10 nyctalopia
nightclub 5 disco 6 bistro, casino 7 cabaret 9 honky-tonk, speakeasy 11 discotheque
nightfall 3 eve 4 dusk, even 6 sunset 7 evening, sundown 8 eventide, gloaming, twilight

nighthawk 6 petrel 7 bullbat 10 goatsucker
nightjar 9 nighthawk 10 goatsucker 12 whip-poor-will
nightly 9 nocturnal
nightmare 5 dream, fancy, worry 6 fright, horror, ordeal, vision 7 bugbear, fantasy, incubus, torment 8 phantasm, phantasy, succubus 12 apprehension 13 hallucination
nightshade 6 tomato 7 henbane 8 eggplant 10 belladonna 11 bittersweet
nightstick 3 bat 4 club, mace 5 baton, billy, staff 6 cudgel 8 bludgeon 9 billy club, blackjack, shillalah, truncheon 10 shillelagh
Nike father: 6 Pallas goddess of: 7 victory mother: 4 Styx
nil 3 nix, zip 4 love, nada, wind, zero 5 zilch 6 naught 7 nothing
Nile 6 Al-Bahr dam: 5 Aswan 6 Makwar 10 Gebel Aulia enclave: 4 Lado explorer: 5 Baker (Sir Samuel), Bruce (James), Grant (James Augustus), Speke (John Hanning) queen: 4 Cleo 9 Cleopatra section: 4 Abay 5 Abbai source lake: 4 Tana
nilgai 8 antelope
nimble 4 deft, spry, yare 5 agile, alert, fleet, handy, light, quick, zippy 6 adroit, limber, lively 7 lissome 8 dexterous, sprightly 10 responsive 11 quick-witted
nimbus 4 aura, halo 5 glory 6 corona 7 aureole
Nimrod 6 hunter father: 4 Cush
Nin, Anaïs father: 7 Joaquin friend: 6 Miller (Henry)
Ninazu brother: 5 Nanna 6 Nergal father: 5 Enlil mother: 6 Ninlil
nincompoop 3 oaf 4 boob, clod, dodo, fool, goof, mutt, simp, yo-yo 5 chump, dummy, dunce, idiot, moron, ninny, noddy, stupe 6 dimwit, donkey, dum-dum, nitwit 7 airhead, dullard, pinhead, schnook, tomfool 8 bonehead, clodpoll, dumbbell, dumbhead, imbecile, lunkhead, meathead, numskull 9 birdbrain, blockhead, ignoramus, lamebrain, numbskull, simpleton, thickhead 10 dunderhead, hammerhead 11 chowderhead, chucklehead, knucklehead, ninnyhammer
nine 12 baseball team combining form: 3 non 4 nona 5 ennea goddesses: 5 Muses group: 6 ennead inches: 4 span instruments: 5 nonet
nine-eyes 7 lamprey
Nine Worlds 3 Hel 6 Asgard 7 Alfheim, Midgard 8 Niflheim, Vanaheim 10 Jotunnheim 12 Muspellsheim 13 Svartalfaheim
ninny see nincompoop
Ninsum's son 9 Gilgamesh
Nintu consort: 4 Enki son: 6 Ninsar

Ninurta *father:* 5 Enlil *victim:* 3 Kur

Ninus *father:* 5 Belus *wife:* 9 Semiramis

Niobe *brother:* 6 Pelops *father:* 8 Tantalus *husband:* 7 Amphion *sister-in-law:* 5 Aedon

nip 3 bit, nab, sip 4 bite, dart, dash, dram, drop, jolt, peck, shot, slug, swig 5 chill, clamp, hurry, pinch, sever, snort, steal 6 imbibe, snatch, thwart, tipple 7 cabbage, snifter, swallow 9 frustrate

nipper 3 kid 4 tike, tyke 5 child 6 moppet, shaver 7 pincers 9 youngling, youngster

nipple 3 pap 4 teat 7 mammila

Nippon 5 Japan

nippy 3 icy, raw 4 cold, cool 5 algid, chill, crisp, sharp 6 arctic, biting, bitter, chilly, frosty, wintry 7 caustic, glacial, numbing, shivery 8 chilling, freezing

nirvana 5 bliss, dream 6 heaven 7 Elysium, rapture 8 empyrean, euphoria, oblivion, paradise 9 Shangri-la

Nisus *betrayer, daughter:* 6 Scylla *father:* 7 Pandion

nitid 6 bright, glossy, lucent 7 fulgent, glowing, shining 8 gleaming, glinting, luminous, lustrous, polished 9 burnished

nitpick 4 carp 5 cavil 7 quibble 10 split hairs

nitrogen 5 azote *combining form:* 3 azo

nitty-gritty 4 core, gist, meat, pith 5 heart, stuff 6 burden, kernel 7 essence 9 substance 10 bottom line, brass tacks

nitwit 3 oaf 4 boob, clod, dodo, dolt, dope, goof, mutt, simp 5 chump, cluck, dummy, dunce, idiot, moron, ninny, noddy, stupe 6 donkey, dum-dum 7 airhead, dullard, pinhead, schnook 8 bonehead, clodpoll, dumbbell, imbecile, lunkhead, meathead, numskull 9 birdbrain, blockhead, ignoramus, lamebrain, numbskull, simpleton, thickhead 10 dunderhead, hammerhead, nincompoop 11 chowderhead, chucklehead, knucklehead

nix 2 no 3 nay, nil, zap 4 kill, nada, nope, veto, zero 5 quash 6 cancel, naught, reject, scotch, sprite 7 call off, nothing, nullify

Njord, Njorth *daughter:* 5 Freya *son:* 4 Frey *wife:* 6 Skadhi, Skathi

no 3 nay, nix 4 uh-uh 6 denial 7 refusal 8 negative 10 thumbs-down *German:* 4 nein *Scottish:* 3 nae

no-account see **no-good**

Noachian 3 old 4 aged 5 fusty, hoary 6 ageold 7 ancient, antique, archaic 8 timeworn 9 venerable 10 antiquated, oldfangled 12 antediluvian, old-fashioned 13 superannuated

Noah *father:* 6 Lamech 10 Zelophehad *grandson:* 4 Aram 6 Canaan *great-grand-*

son: 3 Hul *landing place:* 6 Ararat *son:* 3 Ham 4 Shem 6 Canaan 7 Japheth

Nobel Prize winner

chemistry:
1901: 8 van't Hoff (Jacobus) **1902:** 7 Fischer (Emil) **1903:** 9 Arrhenius (Svante) **1904:** 6 Ramsay (William) **1905:** 9 von Baeyer (Adolf) **1906:** 7 Moissan (Henri) **1907:** 7 Buchner (Eduard) **1908:** 10 Rutherford (Ernest) **1909:** 7 Ostwald (Wilhelm) **1910:** 7 Wallach (Otto) **1911:** 5 Curie (Marie) **1912:** 8 Grignard (François), Sabatier (Paul) **1913:** 6 Werner (Alfred) **1914:** 8 Richards (Theodore) **1915:** 11 Willstatter (Richard) **1918:** 5 Haber (Fritz) **1920:** 6 Nernst (Walther) **1921:** 5 Soddy (Frederick) **1922:** 5 Aston (Francis) **1923:** 5 Pregl (Fritz) **1925:** 9 Zsigmondy (Richard) **1926:** 8 Svedberg (Theodor) **1927:** 7 Wieland (Heinrich) **1928:** 7 Windaus (Adolf) **1929:** 6 Harden (Athur) 12 Euler-Chelpin (Hans von) **1930:** 7 Fischer (Hans) **1931:** 5 Bosch (Karl) 7 Bergius (Friedrich) **1932:** 8 Langmuir (Irving) **1934:** 4 Urey (Harold) **1935:** 11 Joliot-Curie (Frédéric, Irene) **1936:** 5 Debye (Peter) **1937:** 6 Karrer (Paul) 7 Haworth (Walter) **1938:** 4 Kuhn (Richard) **1939:** 7 Ruzicka (Leopold) 9 Butenandt (Adolf) **1943:** 6 Hevesy (Georg de) **1944:** 4 Hahn (Otto) **1945:** 8 Virtanen (Artturi) **1946:** 6 Sumner (James) 7 Stanley (Wendell) 8 Northrop (John Howard) **1947:** 8 Robinson (Robert) **1948:** 8 Tiselius (Arne) **1949:** 7 Glauque (William) **1950:** 5 Alder (Kurt), Diels (Otto) **1951:** 7 Seaborg (Glenn) 8 McMillan (Edwin) **1952:** 5 Synge (Richard) 6 Martin (Archer) **1953:** 10 Staudinger (Hermann) **1954:** 7 Pauling (Linus) **1955:** 10 du Vigneaud (Vincent) **1956:** 7 Semenov (Nikolay) 11 Hinshelwood (Cyril) **1957:** 4 Todd (Alexander) **1958:** 6 Sanger (Frederick) **1959:** 9 Heyrovsky (Jaroslav) **1960:** 5 Libby (Willard) **1961:** 6 Calvin (Melvin) **1962:** 6 Perutz (Max) 7 Kendrew (John) **1963:** 5 Natta (Giulio) 7 Ziegler (Karl) **1964:** 7 Hodgkin (Dorothy) 8 Woodward (Robert) **1966:** 8 Mulliken (Robert) **1967:** 5 Eigen (Manfred) 6 Porter (George) 7 Norrish (Ronald) **1968:** 7 Onsager (Lars) **1969:** 6 Barton (Derek), Hassel (Odd) **1970:** 6 Leloir (Luis) **1971:** 8 Herzberg (Gerhard) **1972:** 5 Moore (Stanford), Stein (William) 8 Anfinsen (Christian) **1973:** 7 Fischer (Ernst) 9 Wilkinson (Geoffrey) **1974:** 5 Flory (Paul) **1975:** 6

Prelog (Vladimir) 9 Cornforth (John) 1976: 8 Lipscomb (William) 1977: 9 Prigogine (Ilya) 1978: 8 Mitchell (Peter) 1979: 5 Brown (Herbert) 6 Wittig (Georg) 1980: 4 Berg (Paul) 6 Sanger (Frederick) 7 Gilbert (Walter) 1981: 5 Fukui (Kenichi) 8 Hoffmann (Roald) 1982: 4 Klug (Aaron) 1983: 5 Taube (Henry) 1984: 10 Merrifield (R. Bruce) 1985: 5 Karle (Jerome) 8 Hauptman (Herbert) 1986: 3 Lee (Yuan) 7 Polanyi (John) 10 Herschbach (Dudley) 1987: 4 Cram (Donald), Lehn (Jean-Marie) 8 Pedersen (Charles) 1988: 5 Huber (Robert) 6 Michel (Hartmut) 11 Deisenhofer (Johann) 1989: 4 Cech (Thomas) 6 Altman (Sidney) 1990: 5 Corey (Elias) 1991: 5 Ernst (Richard) 1992: 6 Marcus (Rudolph) 1993: 5 Smith (Michael) 6 Mullis (Kary) 1994: 4 Olah (George) 1995: 6 Molina (Mario) 7 Crutzen (Paul), Rowland (F. Sherwood) 1996: 4 Curl (Robert) 5 Kroto (Harold) 7 Smalley (Richard) 1997 4 Skou (Jens) 5 Boyer (Paul) 6 Walker (John) 1998: 4 Kohn (Walter) 5 Pople (John) 1999: 6 Zewail (Ahmed) 2000: 6 Heeger (Alan) 9 Shirakawa (Hideki) 10 MacDiarmid (Alan) 2001: 6 Noyori (Ryoji) 7 Knowles (William) 9 Sharpless (K. Barry) 2002: 4 Fenn (John) 6 Tanaka (Koichi) 8 Wüthrich (Kurt) 2003: 4 Agre (Peter) 9 MacKinnon (Roderick) 2004: 4 Rose (Irwin) 7 Hershko (Avram) 11 Ciechanover (Aaron) 2005: 6 Grubbs (Robert) 7 Chauvin (Yves), Schrock (Richard) 2006: 8 Kornberg (Roger) 2007: 4 Ertl (Gerhard) 2008: 5 Tsien (Roger) 7 Chalfie (Martin) 9 Shimomura (Osamu) 2009: 6 Steitz (Thomas), Yonath (Ada) 12 Ramakrishnan (Venkatraman) 2010: 4 Heck (Richard) 6 Suzuki (Akira) 7 Negishi (Ei-Ichi)

economics:
1969: 6 Frisch (Ragnar) 9 Tinbergen (Jan) 1970: 9 Samuelson (Paul) 1971: 7 Kuznets (Simon) 1972: 5 Arrow (Kenneth), Hicks (John) 1973: 8 Leontief (Wassily) 1974: 5 Hayek (Friedrich von) 6 Myrdal (Gunnar) 1975: 8 Koopmans (Tjalling) 11 Kantorovich (Leonid) 1976: 8 Friedman (Milton) 1977: 5 Meade (James), Ohlin (Bertil) 1978: 5 Simon (Herbert) 1979: 5 Lewis (Arthur) 7 Schultz (Theodore) 1980: 5 Klein (Lawrence) 1981: 5 Tobin (James) 1982: 7 Stigler (George) 1983: 6 Debreu (Gerard) 1984: 5 Stone (Richard) 1985: 10 Modigliani (Franco) 1986: 8 Buchanan (James) 1987: 5 Solow (Robert)

1988: 6 Allais (Maurice) 1989: 8 Haavelmo (Trygve) 1990: 6 Miller (Merton), Sharpe (William) 9 Markowitz (Harry) 1991: 5 Coase (Ronald) 1992: 6 Becker (Gary) 1993: 5 Fogel (Robert), North (Douglass) 1994: 4 Nash (John) 6 Selten (Reinhard) 8 Harsanyi (John) 1995: 5 Lucas (Robert) 1996: 7 Vickrey (William) 8 Mirrlees (James) 1998: 3 Sen (Amartya) 1999: 7 Mundell (Robert) 2000: 7 Heckman (James) 8 McFadden (Daniel) 2001: 6 Spence (Michael) 7 Akerlof (George) 8 Stiglitz (Joseph) 2002: 5 Smith (Vernon) 8 Kahneman (Daniel) 2003: 5 Engle (Robert) 7 Granger (Clive) 2004: 7 Kydland (Finn) 8 Prescott (Edward) 2005: 6 Aumann (Robert) 9 Schelling (Thomas) 2006: 6 Phelps (Edmund) 2007: 6 Maskin (Eric) 7 Hurwicz (Leonid), Myerson (Roger) 2008: 7 Krugman (Paul) 2009: 6 Ostrom (Elinor) 10 Williamson (Oliver) 2010: 7 Diamond (Peter) 9 Mortensen (Dale) 10 Pissarides (Christopher)

literature:
1901: 9 Prudhomme (Sully) 1902: 7 Mommsen (Theodor) 1903: 8 Bjornson (Bjornstjerne) 1904: 7 Mistral (Frédéric) 9 Echegaray (José) 1905: 11 Sienkiewicz (Henryk) 1906: 8 Carducci (Giosue) 1907: 7 Kipling (Rudyard) 1908: 6 Eucken (Rudolf) 1909: 8 Lagerlof (Selma) 1910: 5 Heyse (Paul) 1911: 11 Maeterlinck (Maurice) 1912: 9 Hauptmann (Gerhart) 1913: 6 Tagore (Rabindranath) 1915: 7 Rolland (Romain) 1916: 10 Heidenstam (Verner von) 1917: 9 Gjellerup (Karl) 11 Pontoppidan (Henrik) 1919: 9 Spitteler (Carl) 1920: 6 Hamsun (Knut) 1921: 6 France (Anatole) 1922: 9 Benavente (Jacinto) 1923: 5 Yeats (William Butler) 1924: 7 Reymont (Wladyslaw) 1925: 4 Shaw (George Bernard) 1926: 7 Deledda (Grazia) 1927: 7 Bergson (Henri) 1928: 6 Undset (Sigrid) 1929: 4 Mann (Thomas) 1930: 5 Lewis (Sinclair) 1931: 9 Karlfeldt (Erik Axel) 1932: 10 Galsworthy (John) 1933: 5 Bunin (Ivan) 1934: 10 Pirandello (Luigi) 1936: 6 O'Neill (Eugene) 1937: 12 Martin du Gard (Roger) 1938: 4 Buck (Pearl) 1939: 9 Sillanpää (Frans Eemil) 1944: 6 Jensen (Johannes) 1945: 7 Mistral (Gabriela) 1946: 5 Hesse (Hermann) 1947: 4 Gide (André) 1948: 5 Eliot (Thomas Stearns) 1949: 6 Faulkner (William) 1950: 7 Russell (Bertrand) 1951: 10 Lagerkvist (Pär) 1952: 7 Mauriac (Fran-

çois) **1953: 9** Churchill (Winston) **1954: 9** Hemingway (Ernest) **1955: 7** Laxness (Halldór) **1956: 7** Jiménez (Juan Ramón) **1957: 5** Camus (Albert) **1958: 9** Pasternak (Boris) **1959: 9** Quasimodo (Salvatore) **1960: 5** Perse (Saint-John) **1961: 6** Andric (Ivo) **1962: 9** Steinbeck (John) **1963: 7** Seferis (George) **1964: 6** Sartre (Jean-Paul) **1965: 9** Sholokhov (Mikhail) **1966: 5** Agnon (Shmuel Yosef), Sachs (Nelly) **1967: 8** Asturias (Miguel Angel) **1968: 8** Kawabata (Yasunari) **1969: 7** Beckett (Samuel) **1970: 12** Solzhenitsyn (Alexander) **1971: 6** Neruda (Pablo) **1972: 4** Böll (Heinrich) **1973: 5** White (Patrick) **1974: 7** Johnson (Eyvind) **9** Martinson (Edmund) **1975: 7** Montale (Eugenio) **1976: 6** Bellow (Saul) **1977: 10** Aleixandre (Vicente) **1978: 6** Singer (Isaac Bashevis) **1979: 6** Elytis (Odysseus) **1980: 6** Milosz (Czeslaw) **1981: 7** Canetti (Elias) **1982: 13** García Márquez (Gabriel) **1983: 7** Golding (William) **1984: 7** Seifert (Jaroslav) **1985: 5** Simon (Claude) **1986: 7** Soyinka (Wole) **1987: 7** Brodsky (Joseph) **1988: 7** Mahfouz (Naguib) **1989: 4** Cela (Camilo José) **1990: 3** Paz (Octavio) **1991: 8** Gordimer (Nadine) **1992: 7** Walcott (Derek) **1993: 8** Morrison (Toni) **1994: 2** Oe (Kenzaburo) **1995: 6** Heaney (Seamus) **1996: 10** Szymborska (Wislawa) **1997: 2** Fo (Dario) **1998: 8** Saramago (José) **1999: 5** Grass (Günter) **2000: 3** Gao (Xingjian) **2001: 7** Naipaul (V. S.) **2002: 7** Kertész (Imre) **2003: 7** Coetzee (J. M.) **2004: 7** Jelinek (Elfriede) **2005: 6** Pinter (Harold) **2006: 5** Pamuk (Orhan) **2007: 7** Lessing (Doris) **2008: 8** Le Clézio (J.-M. Gustave) **2009: 6** Müller (Herta) **2010: 11** Vargas Llosa (Mario)
peace:
1901: 5 Passy (Frédéric) **6** Dunant (Jean-Henri) **1902: 5** Gobat (Charles Albert) **8** Ducommun (Elie) **1903: 6** Cremer (William) **1905: 7** Suttner (Bertha von) **1906: 9** Roosevelt (Theodore) **1907: 6** Moneta (Ernesto) **7** Renault (Louis) **1908: 5** Bajer (Fredrik) **9** Arnoldson (Klas Pontus) **1909: 9** Beernaert (Auguste) **13** d'Estournelles (Paul) **1911: 5** Asser (Tobias), Fried (Alfred) **1912: 4** Root (Elihu) **1913: 10** La Fontaine (Henri) **1919: 6** Wilson (Woodrow) **1920: 9** Bourgeois (Léon) **1921: 5** Lange (Christian Louis) **8** Branting (Karl Hjalmar) **1922: 6** Nansen (Fridtjof) **1925: 5** Dawes (Charles) **11** Chamberlain (Austen) **1926: 6** Briand

(Aristide) **10** Stresemann (Gustav) **1927: 6** Quidde (Ludwig) **7** Buisson (Ferdinand) **1929: 7** Kellogg (Frank) **1930: 9** Soderblom (Nathan) **1931: 6** Addams (Jane), Butler (Nicholas Murray) **1933: 6** Angell (Norman) **1934: 9** Henderson (Arthur) **1935: 9** Ossietzky (Carl von) **1936: 13** Saavedra Lamas (Carlos de) **1937: 5** Cecil (Robert) **1945: 4** Hull (Cordell) **1946: 4** Mott (John) **5** Balch (Emily Greene) **1949: 3** Orr (John Boyd) **1950: 6** Bunche (Ralph) **1951: 7** Jouhaux (Léon) **1952: 10** Schweitzer (Albert) **1953: 8** Marshall (George) **1957: 7** Pearson (Lester) **1958: 4** Pire (Dominique Georges) **1959: 9** Noel-Baker (Philip) **1960: 7** Luthuli (Albert John) **1961: 12** Hammarskjöld (Dag) **1962: 7** Pauling (Linus) **1964: 4** King (Martin Luther) **1968: 6** Cassin (René) **1970: 7** Borlaug (Norman) **1971: 6** Brandt (Willy) **1973: 8** Le Duc Tho **9** Kissinger (Henry) **1974: 4** Sato (Eisaku) **8** MacBride (Sean) **1975: 8** Sakharov (Andrey) **1976: 8** Corrigan (Mairead), Williams (Betty) **1978: 5** Begin (Menachem), Sadat (Anwar el-) **1979: 12** Mother Teresa **1980: 8** Esquivel (Adolfo Pérez) **1982: 6** Myrdal (Alva) **12** García Robles (Alfonso) **1983: 6** Walesa (Lech) **1984: 4** Tutu (Desmond) **1986: 6** Wiesel (Elie) **1987: 12** Arias Sánchez (Oscar) **1989: 9** Dalai Lama **1990: 9** Gorbachev (Mikhail) **1991: 13** Aung San Suu Kyi **1992: 6** Menchú (Rigoberta) **1993: 7** de Klerk (F. W.), Mandela (Nelson) **1994: 5** Peres (Shimon), Rabin (Yitzhak) **6** Arafat (Yasir) **1995: 7** Rotblat (Joseph) **1996: 10** Ramos-Horta (José) **11** Ximenes Belo (Carlos Felipe) **1997: 8** Williams (Jody) **1998: 4** Hume (John) **7** Trimble (David) **2000: 3** Kim (Dae-jung) **2001: 5** Annan (Kofi) **2002: 6** Carter (Jimmy) **2003: 5** Ebadi (Shirin) **2004: 7** Maathai (Wangari) **2005: 9** ElBaradei (Mohamed) **2006: 5** Yunus (Muhammad) **2007: 4** Gore (Al) **2008: 9** Ahtisaari (Martti) **2009: 5** Obama (Barack) **2010: 3** Liu (Xiaobo)
physics:
1901: 8 Roentgen (Wilhelm) **1902: 6** Zeeman (Pieter) **7** Lorentz (Hendrik Antoon) **1903: 5** Curie (Marie, Pierre) **9** Becquerel (Antoine-Henri) **1904: 6** Strutt (John) **8** Rayleigh (Lord) **1905: 6** Lenard (Philipp von) **1906: 7** Thomson (Joseph) **1907: 9** Michelson (Albert) **1908: 8** Lippmann (Gabriel) **1909: 5** Braun (Karl) **7** Marconi (Guglielmo) **1910: 11** van der Waals (Jo-

hannes) **1911: 4** Wien (Wilhelm) **1912: 5**
Dalen (Nils) **1914: 4** Laue (Max von) **1915:
5** Bragg (William) **1917: 6** Barkla
(Charles) **1918: 6** Planck (Max) **1919: 5**
Stark (Johannes) **1920: 9** Guillaume
(Charles) **1921: 8** Einstein (Albert) **1922: 4**
Bohr (Niels) **1923: 8** Millikan (Robert)
1924: 8 Siegbahn (Karl) **1925: 5** Hertz
(Gustav) **6** Franck (James) **1926: 6** Perrin
(Jean-Baptiste) **1927: 6** Wilson (Charles) **7**
Compton (Arthur) **1928: 10** Richardson
(Owen) **1929: 7** Broglie (Louis-Victor de)
1930: 5 Raman (Chandrasekhara) **1932: 10**
Heisenberg (Werner) **1933: 5** Dirac (Paul)
11 Schrödinger (Erwin) **1935: 8** Chadwick
(James) **1936: 4** Hess (Victor) **8** Anderson
(Carl) **1937: 7** Thomson (George) **8** Davis-
son (Clinton) **1938: 5** Fermi (Enrico) **1939:
8** Lawrence (Ernest) **1943: 5** Stern (Otto)
1944: 4 Rabi (Isidor Isaac) **1945: 5** Pauli
(Wolfgang) **1946: 8** Bridgman (Percy)
1947: 8 Appleton (Edward) **1948: 8** Black-
ett (Patrick) **1949: 6** Yukawa (Hideki)
1950: 6 Powell (Cecil) **1951: 6** Walton (Ernest) **9** Cockcroft (John) **1952: 5** Bloch
(Felix) **7** Purcell (Edward) **1953: 7** Zernike
(Frits) **1954: 4** Born (Max) **5** Bothe
(Walther) **1955: 4** Lamb (Willis) **5** Kusch
(Polykarp) **1956: 7** Bardeen (John) **8** Brattain (Walter), Shockley (William) **1957: 3**
Lee (Tsung Dao) **4** Yang (Chen Ning)
1958: 4 Tamm (Igor) **5** Frank (Ilya) **9**
Cherenkov (Pavel) **1959: 5** Segrè (Emilio)
11 Chamberlain (Owen) **1960: 6** Glaser
(Donald) **1961: 9** Mossbauer (Rudolf) **10**
Hofstadter (Robert) **1962: 6** Landau (Lev)
1963: 5 Mayer (Maria) **6** Jensen (J. Hans),
Wigner (Eugene) **1964: 5** Basov (Nikolay)
6 Townes (Charles) **9** Prochorov (Alexander) **1965: 7** Feynman (Richard) **8** Tomo-
naga (Shinichiro) **9** Schwinger (Julian)
1966: 7 Kastler (Alfred) **1967: 5** Bethe
(Hans) **1968: 7** Alvarez (Luis) **1969: 8**
Gell-Mann (Murray) **1970: 4** Néel (Louis)
6 Alfven (Hannes) **1971: 5** Gabor (Dennis)
1972: 6 Cooper (Leon) **7** Bardeen (John)
10 Schrieffer (John) **1973: 5** Esaki (Leo) **7**
Giaever (Ivar) **9** Josephson (Brian) **1974: 4**
Ryle (Martin) **6** Hewish (Antony) **1975: 4**
Bohr (Aage) **9** Mottelson (Ben), Rainwater
(L. James) **1976: 4** Ting (Samuel) **7** Rich-
ter (Burton) **1977: 4** Mott (Nevill) **8** Ander-
son (Philip), Van Vleck (John) **1978: 6**
Wilson (Robert) **9** Kapitsa (Pyotr), Penzias
(Arno) **1979: 5** Salam (Abdus) **7** Glashow
(Sheldon) **8** Weinberg (Steven) **1980: 5**
Fitch (Val) **6** Cronin (James) **1981: 8**

Schawlow (Arthur), Siegbahn (Kai) **11**
Bloembergen (Nicholaas) **1982: 6** Wilson
(Kenneth) **1983: 6** Fowler (William) **13**
Chandrasekhar (Subrahmanyan) **1984: 6**
Rubbia (Carlo) **11** van der Meere (Simon)
1985: 8 Klitzing (Klaus von) **1986: 5**
Ruska (Ernst) **6** Binnig (Gerd), Rohrer
(Heinrich) **1987: 6** Müller (K. Alex) **7** Bed-
norz (J. Georg) **1988: 8** Lederman (Leon),
Schwartz (Melvin) **11** Steinberger (Jack)
1989: 4 Paul (Wolfgang) **6** Ramsey (Nor-
man) **7** Dehmelt (Hans) **1990: 6** Taylor
(Richard) **7** Kendall (Henry) **8** Friedman
(Jerome) **1991: 8** De Gennes (Pierre-
Gilles) **1992: 7** Charpak (Georges) **1993: 5**
Hulse (Russell) **6** Taylor (Joseph) **1994: 5**
Shull (Clifford) **10** Brockhouse (Bertram)
1995: 4 Perl (Martin) **6** Reines (Frederick)
1996: 3 Lee (David) **8** Osheroff (Douglas)
10 Richardson (Robert) **3** Chu (Steven) **8**
Phillips (William) **14** Cohen-Tannoudji
(Claude) **1998: 4** Tsui (Daniel) **7** Störmer
(Horst) **8** Laughlin (Robert) **1999: 6** 't
Hooft (Gerardus) **7** Veltman (Martinus)
2000: 5 Kilby (Jack) **7** Alferev (Zhores),
Kroemer (Herbert) **2001: 6** Wieman (Carl)
7 Cornell (Eric) **8** Ketterle (Wolfgang)
2002: 5 Davis (Raymond) **7** Koshiba
(Masatoshi) **8** Giacconi (Riccardo) **2003: 7**
Leggett (Anthony) **8** Ginzburg (Vitaly) **9**
Abrikosov (Alexei) **2004: 5** Gross (David)
7 Wilczek (Frank) **8** Politzer (David) **2005:
4** Hall (John) **6** Hänsch (Theodor) **7** Glau-
ber (Roy) **2006: 5** Smoot (George) **6**
Mather (John) **2007: 4** Fert (Albert) **8**
Grünberg (Peter) **2008; 5** Nambu (Yo-
ichiro) **7** Maskawa (Toshihide) **9** Ko-
bayashi (Makoto) **2009: 3** Kao (Charles
K.) **5** Boyle (Willard), Smith (George)
2010: 4 Geim (Andre) **9** Novoselov (Konstantin)

physiology or medicine:
1901: 7 Behring (Emil von) **1902: 4** Ross
(Ronald) **1903: 6** Finsen (Niels Ryberg)
1904: 6 Pavlov (Ivan) **1905: 4** Koch (Robert) **1906: 5** Golgi (Camillo) **11** Ramón y
Cajal (Santiago) **1907: 7** Laveran (Alphonse) **1908: 7** Ehrlich (Paul) **11** Metchnikoff (Elie) **1909: 6** Kocher (Emil) **1910:
6** Kossel (Albrecht) **1911: 10** Gullstrand
(Allvar) **1912: 6** Carrel (Alexis) **1913: 6**
Richet (Charles) **1914: 6** Barany (Robert)
1919: 6 Bordet (Jules) **1920: 5** Krogh
(August) **1922: 4** Hill (Archibald) **8** Mey-
erhof (Otto) **1923: 7** Banting (Frederick),
Macleod (John) **1924: 9** Einthoven (Willem) **1926: 7** Fibiger (Johannes) **1927: 13**

Wagner-Jauregg (Julius) **1928: 7** Nicolle (Charles) **1929: 7** Eijkman (Christiaan), Hopkins (Frederick) **1930: 11** Landsteiner (Karl) **1931: 7** Warburg (Otto) **1932: 6** Adrian (Edgar) **11** Sherrington (Charles) **1933: 6** Morgan (Thomas) **1934: 5** Minot (George) **6** Murphy (William) **7** Whipple (George) **1935: 7** Spemann (Hans) **1936: 4** Dale (Henry) **5** Loewi (Otto) **1937: 12** Szent-Györgyi (Albert) **1938: 7** Heymans (Corneille) **1939: 6** Domagk (Gerhard) **1943: 3** Dam (Henrik) **5** Doisy (Edward) **1944: 6** Gasser (Herbert) **8** Erlanger (Joseph) **1945: 5** Chain (Ernst) **6** Florey (Howard) **7** Fleming (Alexander) **1946: 6** Muller (Hermann) **1947: 4** Cori (Carl, Gerty) **7** Houssay (Bernardo) **1948: 7** Mueller (Paul) **1949: 4** Hess (Walter) **5** Moniz (Antonio) **1950: 5** Hench (Philip) **7** Kendall (Edward) **10** Reichstein (Tadeus) **1951: 7** Theiler (Max) **1952: 7** Waksman (Selman) **1953: 5** Krebs (Hans) **7** Lipmann (Fritz) **1954: 6** Enders (John), Weller (Thomas) **7** Robbins (Frederick) **1955: 8** Theorell (Hugo) **1956: 8** Cournand (André), Richards (Dickinson) **9** Forssmann (Werner) **1957: 5** Bovet (Daniel) **1958: 5** Tatum (Edward) **6** Beadle (George) **9** Lederberg (Joshua) **1959: 5** Ochoa (Severo) **8** Kornberg (Arthur) **1960: 6** Burnet (Macfarlane) **7** Medawar (Peter) **1961: 6** Bekesy (Georg von) **1962: 5** Crick (Francis) **6** Watson (James) **7** Wilkins (Maurice) **1963: 6** Eccles (John), Huxley (Andrew) **7** Hodgkin (Alan) **1964: 5** Bloch (Konrad), Lynen (Feodor) **1965: 5** Jacob (Francois), Monod (Jacques) **5** Lwoff (André) **1966: 4** Rous (Francis) **7** Huggins (Charles) **1967: 4** Wald (George) **6** Granit (Ragnar) **8** Hartline (H. Keffer) **1968: 6** Holley (Robert) **7** Khorana (H. Gobind) **9** Nirenberg (Marshall) **1969: 5** Luria (Salvador) **7** Hershey (Alfred) **8** Delbruck (Max) **1970: 4** Katz (Bernard) **5** Euler (Ulf von) **7** Axelrod (Julius) **1971: 10** Sutherland (Earl) **1972: 6** Porter (Rodney) **7** Edelman (Gerald) **1973: 6** Frisch (Karl von), Lorenz (Konrad) **9** Tinbergen (Nikolaas) **1974: 4** Duve (Christian) **6** Claude (Albert), Palade (George) **1975: 5** Temin (Howard) **8** Dulbecco (Renato) **9** Baltimore (David) **1976: 8** Blumberg (Baruch), Gajdusek (D. Carleton) **1977: 5** Yalow (Rosalyn) **7** Schally (Andrew) **9** Guillemin (Roger) **1978: 5** Arber (Werner), Smith (Hamilton) **7** Nathans (Daniel) **1979: 7** Cormack (Allan) **10**

Hounsfield (Godfrey) **1980: 5** Snell (George) **7** Dausset (Jean) **10** Benacerraf (Baruj) **1981: 5** Hubel (David) **6** Sperry (Roger), Wiesel (Torsten) **1982: 4** Vane (John) **9** Bergstrom (Sune) **10** Samuelsson (Bengt) **1983: 10** McClintock (Barbara) **1984: 5** Jerne (Niels) **7** Koehler (Georges) **8** Milstein (Cesar) **1985: 5** Brown (Michael) **9** Goldstein (Joseph) **1986: 5** Cohen (Stanley) **14** Levi-Montalcini (Rita) **1987: 8** Tonegawa (Susumu) **1988: 5** Black (James), Elion (Gertrude) **9** Hitchings (George) **1989: 6** Bishop (J. Michael), Varmus (Harold) **1990: 6** Murray (Joseph), Thomas (E. Donnall) **1991: 5** Neher (Erwin) **7** Sakmann (Bert) **1992: 5** Krebs (Edwin) **7** Fischer (Edmond) **1993: 5** Sharp (Phillip) **7** Roberts (Richard) **1994: 6** Gilman (Alfred) **7** Rodbell (Martin) **1995: 5** Lewis (Edward) **9** Wieschaus (Eric) **15** Nüsslein-Volhard (Christiane) **1996: 7** Doherty (Peter) **11** Zinkernagel (Rolf) **1997: 8** Prusiner (Stanley) **1998: 5** Murad (Ferid) **7** Ignarro (Louis) **9** Furchgott (Robert) **1999: 6** Blobel (Günter) **2000: 6** Kandel (Eric) **8** Carlsson (Arvid) **9** Greengard (Paul) **2001: 4** Hunt (Tim) **5** Nurse (Paul) **8** Hartwell (Leland) **2002: 7** Brenner (Sydney), Horvitz (Robert), Sulston (John) **2003: 9** Lauterbur (Paul), Mansfield (Peter) **2004: 4** Axel (Richard), Buck (Linda) **2005: 6** Warren (J. Robin) **8** Marshall (Barry) **2006: 4** Fire (Andrew) **5** Mello (Craig) **2007: 5** Evans (Martin) **8** Capecchi (Mario), Smithies (Oliver) **2008: 9** zur Hausen (Harald) **10** Montagnier (Luc) **13** Barré-Sinoussi (Françoise) **2009: 7** Greider (Carol), Szostak (Jack) **9** Blackburn (Elizabeth) **2010: 7** Edwards (Robert)

Nobel's invention 8 dynamite

nobility 6 virtue **7** dignity, peerage, royalty **8** eminence, noblesse **9** loftiness **10** exaltation, excellence, worthiness **11** aristocracy, superiority, uprightness

noble 4 lord, peer **5** grand, lofty, moral **6** august, lordly, titled, worthy **7** courtly, eminent, exalted, notable, stately, sublime, upright **8** baronial, elevated, generous, gracious, highborn, highbred, imposing, magnific, majestic, princely, sterling, virtuous, wellborn **9** dignified, estimable, excellent, grandiose, honorable, righteous **10** highminded, impressive, principled **11** illustrious, magnanimous, magnificent, outstanding, right-minded **12** aristocratic

nobleman 4 duke, earl, lord, peer **5** baron,

count **6** aristo, prince **7** baronet, marquis **8** marquess, viscount **10** aristocrat *French:* **5** comte **7** vicomte *German:* **4** Graf **8** margrave **9** landgrave *Indian:* **6** sardar, sirdar **8** maharaja **9** maharajah *Islamic:* **4** amir, emir **5** ameer *Italian:* **8** marchese *Japanese (former):* **6** daimyo *Scandinavian:* **4** jarl *Spanish:* **7** hidalgo

noblewoman 4 lady **7** duchess, peeress **8** baroness, countess, princess **11** marchioness, viscountess *French:* **7** baronne **8** marquise *Italian:* **8** marchesa

nobody 4 zero **6** cipher **7** nothing, nullity, upstart **9** nonentity **11** lightweight, small potato

nocturnal 7 nightly **9** nighttime

nocuous 3 bad **6** nocent **7** harmful, hurtful **8** damaging **9** injurious **11** deleterious, destructive, detrimental, mischievous

nod 3 bob, err **4** doze, okay **5** agree, droop, slump **6** assent, invite, signal **7** approve **8** approval **10** acceptance

nodding 6 casual, slight **7** passing **8** drooping **9** pendulous **11** superficial

noddle 3 nob, nut **4** bean, head, pate, poll **6** noggin

noddy 3 oaf **4** boob, clod, dodo, dolt, dope, fool, goof, mutt, simp, yo-yo **5** chump, dummy, dunce, moron, ninny, stupe **6** dimwit, donkey, dum-dum **7** airhead, dullard, pinhead, schnook **8** bonehead, clodpoll, dumbbell, dumbhead, imbecile, lunkhead, meathead, numskull **9** birdbrain, blockhead, ignoramus, lamebrain, numbskull, simpleton, thickhead **10** dunderhead, hammerhead, nincompoop **11** chowderhead, chucklehead, knucklehead

node 4 bump, burl, knob, knot, lump, mass **5** bulge, point **6** growth, vertex **8** swelling **11** enlargement, predicament **12** entanglement, protuberance

Noel 4 Xmas **5** carol **9** Christmas

nog 3 ale **4** beer, brew, malt, suds **5** lager, stout

noggin 3 cup, mug, nip, nob, nut **4** bean, gill, head, pate, poll **6** noddle, noodle

no-good 3 bum, dud **4** base, vile, worm **5** loser **6** scurvy, wretch **7** dirtbag, inutile, lowlife, rounder, wastrel **8** deadbeat, fainéant, shameful, unworthy, wretched **9** no-account, valueless, worthless **10** ne'er-do-well, profligate, scapegrace **11** ignominious **12** contemptible, disreputable **13** reprehensible

noise 3 din **4** blab, talk **5** babel, rumor, sound **6** clamor, gossip, hubbub, racket, ruckus, rumpus, tattle, uproar **7** ruction, sonance, stridor **8** resonant **11** pandemonium

noiseless 4 hush, mute **5** muted, quiet, still, whist **6** hushed, silent, stilly

noisemaker 4 horn **6** rattle **7** clapper, whistle

noisome 4 foul, rank, vile **5** fetid, funky, fusty, musty, nasty **6** filthy, horrid, putrid, rancid, smelly **7** harmful, noxious, squalid **8** stinking **9** obnoxious, offensive, repulsive, revolting, sickening **10** disgusting, malodorous, nauseating

noisy 4 loud **5** rowdy **7** blatant, booming, clamant, rackety, raucous, squeaky **8** clattery, strident **9** clamorous, deafening, turbulent **10** boisterous, chattering, clangorous, tumultuous, uproarious, vociferous **11** conspicuous **12** earsplitting, obstreperous

nomad 4 bedu, hobo **5** gipsy, gypsy, rover **6** beduin, Tuareg **7** bedouin, migrant, rambler, Touareg **8** vagabond, wanderer, wayfarer

nomadic 5 gipsy, gypsy **6** roving **7** roaming, vagrant **8** drifting, vagabond **9** itinerant, migratory, wandering, wayfaring **11** peripatetic **13** perambulatory

nom de plume see **pen name**

nomen 4 name **7** moniker **11** appellation, designation

nomenclature 4 list, name **7** catalog **8** glossary, taxonomy **11** appellation, designation, phraseology, terminology **12** codification

nominal 3 low **5** given, named, rated, small **6** formal, puppet **7** alleged, minimal, seeming, titular **8** apparent, so-called, trifling **9** pretended, professed **10** ostensible **11** approximate, inexpensive **12** satisfactory **13** insignificant

nominate 3 tap **4** call, name **5** offer, put up **7** appoint, propose, suggest **9** designate, recommend

nominee 6 choice **8** aspirant **9** candidate, contender **10** contestant

nonage 5 youth **7** infancy **8** minority **9** childhood **10** immaturity, juvenility

nonchalant 4 cool, easy **5** blasé **6** casual, mellow, serene **7** offhand **8** carefree, careless, cheerful, laid-back **9** easygoing **10** effortless, insouciant, untroubled **11** unconcerned, unflappable, unperturbed **12** lighthearted **13** lackadaisical

noncommittal 7 neutral **8** reserved **9** impassive **10** disengaged

nonconformist 5 loner, rebel **7** beatnik, heretic, oddball, offbeat, radical **8** bohemian, maverick **9** dissenter, dissident, eccentric, heretical, heterodox, protester, sectarian **10** schismatic, separatist, unorthodox **11** misbeliever, schismatist

nonconformity 6 heresy, schism **7** dissent **9** misbelief, recusancy **10** dissidence, heterodoxy, opposition **11** unorthodoxy **13** individualism

nonentity 4 zero **5** aught, zilch **6** cipher, nobody **7** nothing, nullity, whiffet **8** unperson **10** figurehead, mouthpiece

nonesuch 5 ideal **7** epitome, paragon, pattern **8** exemplar, paradigm, standard **9** archetype, beau ideal, matchless, nonpareil, unequaled, unrivaled **10** apotheosis

nonetheless 3 yet **5** still **6** anyway, though, withal **7** howbeit, however **8** although, after all **10** regardless **11** still and all

nonexistence 4 nada, void **7** nullity, vacuity **11** nothingness

nonflammable 9 fireproof **10** unburnable **13** incombustible

non-Hawaiian 5 haole

non-Jewish 3 goy **6** goyish **7** gentile

non-Muslim 6 giaour

no-nonsense 5 grave, sober **6** solemn **7** earnest, serious **8** resolute **9** pragmatic, realistic **10** hardheaded, sobersided **11** plainspoken **12** businesslike **13** unsentimental

nonpareil see **nonesuch**

nonpartisan 7 neutral **8** unbiased **9** equitable, impartial, objective, uncolored **10** nonaligned **11** independent **12** unprejudiced

nonplus 4 faze **5** stump **6** baffle, boggle, muddle, puzzle, rattle, stymie **7** buffalo, confuse, dilemma, flummox, fluster, mystify, perplex, stagger **8** bewilder, confound, distract, overcome, paralyze, quandary **9** discomfit, dumbfound, frustrate **10** disconcert

nonresistant 6 docile, pliant **7** passive, pliable **8** resigned, yielding **9** complying, malleable, tractable **10** conforming, submissive **11** acquiescent, conformable **13** accommodating

nonsense 3 rot **4** blah, bosh, bull, bunk, crap, gook, guff, jazz, punk, tosh **5** bilge, crock, drool, folly, fudge, Greek, hokum, hooey, trash, tripe **6** babble, blague, bunkum, drivel, hot air, humbug, jabber, piffle **7** baloney, blather, eyewash, flubdub, foolery, fooling, hogwash, inanity, rubbish, trifles, twaddle **8** buncombe, claptrap, falderal, folderol, flimflam, malarkey, pishposh, slipslop, tommyrot, trumpery **9** gibberish, moonshine, poppycock **10** applesauce, balderdash, double-talk, flapdoodle, tomfoolery **11** jabberwocky **12** blatherskite, fiddle-faddle, fiddlesticks **13** horsefeathers *British:* **10** codswallop

nonsensical 5 crazy, daffy, flaky, goofy, inane, kooky, loony, nutty, silly, wacky **6** absurd, screwy **7** foolish, idiotic, risible **9** illogical, laughable, ludicrous, senseless **10** irrational **12** preposterous, unreasonable

nonviolent 6 irenic **7** pacific **8** pacifist **9** peaceable **10** pacifistic

noodle 3 oaf **4** bean, boob, clod, dodo, dope, goof, head, mutt, poll, simp, yo-yo **5** chump, dummy, dunce, idiot, moron, ninny, noddy, stupe **6** dimwit, donkey, dum-dum, nitwit, noggin **7** airhead, dullard, pinhead, schnook **8** bonehead, clodpoll, dumbbell, dumbhead, imbecile, lunkhead, meathead, numskull **9** birdbrain, blockhead, ignoramus, lamebrain, numbskull, simpleton **10** dunderhead, hammerhead, nincompoop **11** chowderhead, chucklehead, knucklehead *dish:* **5** pasta **7** lasagna, lasagne **8** linguine, linguini **10** fettuccine, fettuccini **11** pappardelle

nook 3 bay **4** cove **5** hutch, niche **6** alcove, cavity, corner, cranny, recess **9** cubbyhole **11** compartment

noose 3 tie **4** bait, bind, hang, loop, lure, trap **5** lasso, snare **6** entrap, secure

norm 3 par **4** mean, rule, type **5** gauge, maxim, model **6** median **7** average, measure, pattern **8** paradigm, standard **9** benchmark, criterion **10** touchstone

Norma *composer:* **7** Bellini (Vincenzo) *librettist:* **6** Romani (Felice)

normal 4 sane **5** usual **6** common **7** average, general, natural, regular, typical **8** ordinary, standard **9** customary, prevalent **11** commonplace, traditional **12** conventional **13** perpendicular

Normandy's capital 5 Rouen

Norns 5 fates, Skuld, Urdur **9** Verthandi

Norris novel 3 Pit (The) **4** Blix **7** Octopus (The) **8** McTeague

Norse *abode of the dead:* **8** Niflheim *alphabet:* **5** Runic *archer:* **4** Egil *bard:* **5** scald, skald *chieftain:* **4** jarl, Rolf **5** Rollo *demon:* **4** Mara, Surt **5** Surtr *dragon:* **6** Fafnir **8** Nithhogg *epic:* **4** Edda *explorer:* **4** Eric, Erik, Leif **8** Ericsson (Leif), Eriksson (Leif) *first man:* **3** Ask **4** Askr *first woman:* **5** Embla *giant:* **4** Egil, Wade, Wate, Ymer, Ymir **5** Aegir, Egill, Hymir, Jotun, Mimir **6** Fafnir, Jotunn *giantess:* **4** Egia, Norn, Nott *god:* **3** Asa, Ass **4** Surt, Vali, Vili **5** Aesir (plural), Surtr, Vanir (plural) **6** Hoenir, Vithar **7** Vitharr *blind:* **4** Hoth **5** Hoder, Hodur, Hothr *chief:* **4** Oden, Odin **5** Othin, Wodan, Woden, Wotan *guardian:* **7** Heimdal **8** Heimdall **9** Heimdallr *messenger:* **6** Hermod **7** Hermodr *of beauty:* **5** Baldr **6** Balder, Baldur *of evil:* **4** Loke, Loki *of fertility:* **4** Frey **5** Freyr *of fire:* **4** Loke, Loki *of justice:* **7** Forsete, Forseti *of light:* **3** Dag *of peace:* **5** Baldr **6**

Balder, Baldur **of poetry: 5** Brage, Bragi **of the hunt: 3** Ull **4** Ullr **of the seas: 5** Njord **6** Njoerd, Njorth **4** Hler **5** Aegir, Gymir **of the sky: 4** Odin **5** Othin, Wodan, Woden, Wotan **of thunder: 4** Thor **5** Donar **of war: 3** Tiu, Tiw, Tyr, Zio, Ziu **wolf: 6** Fenrir

goddess: 3 dis **4** Saga **5** disir (plural) **7** Asynjur **of fate: 3** Urd **4** Norn, Urth, Wyrd **5** Skuld **9** Verthandi **of healing: 3** Eir **of love: 5** Freya **of marriage: 5** Frigg **6** Frigga **of night: 4** Natt, Nott **of storms: 3** Ran **of the earth: 4** Erda **5** Joerd, Jorth **of the moon: 5** Nanna **of the sea: 3** Ran **of the sky: 5** Frigg **6** Frigga **of the underworld: 3** Hel **4** Hela **of youth: 4** Idun **5** Ithun **6** Ithunn **gods' abode: 6** Asgard **hall of heroes: 8** Valhalla **king: 4** Atli, Olaf **nobleman: 4** jarl **patron saint: 4** Olaf **poem: 4** rune **poet: 5** scald, skald **rainbow bridge: 7** Bifrost **sea serpent: 4** Wade, Wate **6** kraken **7** Midgard **smith: 6** Völund **tale: 4** saga **toast: 5** skoal **watchdog: 4** Garm **5** Garmr **world's destruction: 8** Ragnarok **world tree: 8** Ygdrasil **10** Yggdrasill

north combining form: 4 arct **5** arcto
North African country: 5 Egypt, Libya **7** Algeria, Morocco, Tunisia **fruit: 3** fig **4** date **garment: 4** haik **7** burnous **8** burnoose **grass: 4** alfa **7** esparto **jackal: 4** dieb **language: 6** Arabic, Berber **Muslim sect: 6** Sanusi **7** Senussi **people: 4** bedu **6** beduin, Berber, Hamite **7** bedouin **seaport: 4** Oran, Sfax **6** Annaba **7** Tangier **10** Casablanca
North America country: 6 Belize, Canada, Mexico, Panama **8** Honduras **9** Costa Rica, Guatemala, Nicaragua **10** El Salvador **12** United States
North Carolina capital: 7 Raleigh **city: 6** Durham **9** Asheville, Charlotte **10** Greensboro **12** Winston-Salem **college, university: 4** Duke, Elon **10** Chapel Hill, Wake Forest **mountain, range: 8** Mitchell **9** Blue Ridge **10** Great Smoky **nickname: 7** Tar Heel (State) **state bird: 8** cardinal **state flower: 7** dogwood **state tree: 4** pine
North Dakota capital: 8 Bismarck **city: 5** Fargo, Minot **10** Grand Forks **nickname: 5** Sioux (State) **11** Flickertail (State) **river: 3** Red **8** Missouri **state bird: 10** meadowlark **state flower: 11** prairie rose **state tree: 3** elm (American)
North Korea see **Korea, North**
northern 4 pike **6** boreal **11** hyperborean
Northern Ireland capital: 7 Belfast **city: 5** Derry, Newry **6** Armagh **7** Lisburn **conflict:**

8 Troubles (The) **county: 4** Down **6** Antrim, Armagh, Tyrone **9** Fermanagh **11** Londonderry **lake: 10** Lough Neagh **language: 3** BSL, ISL **5** Irish **11** Ulster Scots **monetary unit: 5** pound **mountains: 6** Mourne **7** Sperrin **prison, former: 4** Maze **province: 6** Ulster **university: 6** Queens
Northern Mariana Islands commonwealth of: 12 United States **discoverer: 8** Magellan (Ferdinand) **island: 4** Rota **6** Saipan, Tinian
North Star State 9 Minnesota
Northwest Territories capital: 11 Yellowknife **gulf: 8** Amundsen **island: 5** Banks **8** Victoria **lake: 9** Great Bear **10** Great Slave **river: 9** Mackenzie **sea: 8** Beaufort
north wind see at **wind**
Norway Arctic region: 7 Lapland **cape: 7** Nordkyn **capital: 4** Oslo **city: 5** Hamar **6** Bergen **9** Stavanger, Trondheim **inlet: 9** Skagerrak **island: 5** Senja **6** Sørøya **8** Magerøya, Steinsøy **10** Nord-Kvaløy, Ringvassøy **island group: 7** Lofoten **10** Vesterålen **king: 4** Eric, Olaf, Olav **5** Oscar **6** Haakon, Harald, Magnus **7** Charles **9** Christian, Frederick **11** Christopher **lake: 5** Mjøsa **monetary unit: 5** krone **mountain range: 6** Kjølen **11** Jotunheimen **neighbor: 6** Russia, Sweden **7** Finland **part of: 11** Scandinavia **patron saint: 4** Olaf, Olav **port: 5** Vardø **6** Tromsø **8** Kirkenes **10** Hammerfest **river: 4** Tana **5** Glåma, Lågen **9** Dramselva **sea: 5** North
Norwegian goblin: 5 nisse **language: 5** Norse **6** Bokmal **7** Bokmaal, Nynorsk, Riksmal **8** Landsmal, Riksmaal **9** Landsmaal
nose 3 pry **4** beak, bent, bump, head, poke **5** aroma, flair, knack, scent, smell, sniff, snift, snoop, snoot, snout, snuff **6** muzzle, nuzzle, schnoz, talent **7** aptness, faculty, schnozz, smeller, sneezer **8** smell out **9** olfaction, proboscis, schnozzle **combining form: 4** naso, rhin **5** rhino **French: 3** nez **kind: 3** pug **5** Roman **8** aquiline **lengthener: 3** lie **opening: 5** nares (plural) **7** nostril
nosebleed 9 epistaxis
nosedive 4 drop, fall **6** header, plunge **7** plummet
nosegay 4 posy **6** flower **7** bouquet, corsage **11** boutonniere
nosh 4 bite **5** graze, munch, snack **6** nibble
Nostradamus 4 seer **7** prophet **birthplace: 6** St. Remy
Nostromo author 6 Conrad (Joseph)
nostrum 4 cure **6** elixir, remedy **7** cure-all, panacea **8** antidote, medicine **10** catholicon, corrective **11** restorative
nosy 6 prying, snoopy **7** curious, peeping **8**

snooping 9 intrusive 11 inquisitive, inquisitory

not 4 nary

notable 3 VIP 4 lion, star 5 celeb, chief, famed, mogul, nabob, power 6 big boy, biggie, big gun, bigwig, famous, fat cat, honcho, leader, prince, worthy 7 big name, big shot, eminent, magnate, pooh-bah 8 big chief, big-timer, big wheel, eminence, luminary, renowned, somebody, striking 9 big cheese, celebrity, character, chieftain, dignitary, distingué, personage, prominent, superstar 10 celebrated, celebrious, noteworthy, remarkable 11 conspicuous, heavyweight, illustrious, muckety-muck, personality 13 distinguished, high-muck-a-muck

notarize 7 certify, endorse 8 validate 12 authenticate

not at all 5 nohow, noway 6 noways, nowise

notch 3 cut, gap, jag 4 gash, kerf, mark, nick, nock, rung, slit, step 5 cleft, grade, score, stage 6 degree, groove, indent, rabbet, record 7 achieve, scratch 8 incision, undercut 11 indentation

notched 5 erose

note 3 jot 4 bond, chit, heed, mark, memo, show, sign, tone 5 catch, sound, token 6 letter, notice, record, regard 7 comment, discern, jotting, missive, observe, promise, set down 8 eminence, indicate, perceive, reminder 9 attention, knowledge 10 cognizance, memorandum, reputation 11 distinction, distinguish, observation

notebook 3 log 5 diary 7 journal

noted 5 famed 6 famous 7 eminent, leading, popular 8 esteemed, renowned, striking 9 acclaimed, prominent, well-known 10 celebrated, recognized, remarkable 11 illustrious 13 distinguished

noteworthy 7 salient 8 singular, striking 9 arresting, bodacious, memorable, prominent, red-letter 10 impressive, meaningful, remarkable 11 conspicuous, exceptional, high-profile, major-league, outstanding, significant 12 considerable 13 extraordinary

nothing 3 nil, nix, zip 4 nada, zero 5 aught, nihil, zilch 6 cipher, naught, nobody, nought, trifle 7 nullity, whiffet 8 goose egg, whipster 9 no-account, nonentity *French:* 4 rien *German:* 6 nichts *Latin:* 5 nihil *Spanish:* 4 nada

nothingness 4 nada, void 5 death 6 vacuum 7 nullity, vacuity 9 emptiness 12 nonexistence

notice 2 ad 3 eye, see 4 espy, heed, mark, memo 5 catch, sight 6 descry, regard, review 7 discern, observe, respect 8 handbill, perceive 9 attention, directive, recognize 10 cognizance, evaluation 11 declaration, information, observation 12 announcement, proclamation

noticeable 6 marked, patent, signal 7 evident, obvious, pointed, salient 8 apparent, manifest, striking 9 arresting, prominent 10 noteworthy, observable, remarkable 11 appreciable, conspicuous, eye-catching, outstanding, perceptible, significant 12 unmistakable

notify 3 cue 4 tell, warn 5 alert, brief 6 advise, clue in, fill in, inform 7 apprise 8 acquaint 9 enlighten

notion 4 clue, hint, idea, whim 5 fancy 6 belief, maggot, theory, vagary 7 caprice, conceit, concept, inkling, thought 8 crotchet 10 conception, impression, intimation, perception 11 inclination

notional 5 ideal 6 unreal 7 fancied, fictive 8 fanciful, illusory, imagined 9 imaginary, visionary, whimsical 10 capricious, conceptual 11 speculative, theoretical 12 hypothetical

notoriety 4 fame 6 infamy, renown 7 obloquy 9 disrepute 10 opprobrium, prominence 11 recognition

notorious 5 noted 6 famous 8 ill-famed, infamous 9 prominent, well-known 10 outrageous, scandalous 12 disreputable

Notus 6 Auster *brother:* 5 Eurus 6 Boreas 8 Zephyrus *father:* 6 Aeolus 8 Astraeus *mother:* 3 Eos

noun 4 name 7 nominal 11 substantive *inflectional form:* 4 case *verbal:* 6 gerund

nourish 4 feed, rear 5 nurse, raise 6 foster 7 bring up, build up, nurture, promote, support 8 maintain 9 cultivate, encourage 10 provide for, strengthen

nourishment 3 pap 4 diet, eats, feed, food, grub 6 viands 7 aliment, pabulum, vittles 8 victuals 9 nutriment, provender 10 sustenance

_____ **nous** 5 entre

nouveau riche 7 climber, parvenu, upstart 9 arriviste

Nova Scotia *capital:* 7 Halifax *city:* 9 Dartmouth *island:* 10 Cape Breton *lake:* 7 Bras D'Or *provincial flower:* 9 mayflower

novel 3 new, odd 4 book 5 fresh 6 unique 7 fiction, offbeat, unusual 8 atypical, original, peculiar, singular, uncommon 9 different, narrative 10 avant-garde, innovative, newfangled

novelist see **author**

Novello, _____ 4 Ivor

novelty 5 curio 6 bauble, gewgaw, oddity, trifle 7 bibelot, gimmick, newness, trinket, whatnot **8** gimcrack, souvenir **9** bagatelle, curiosity, objet d'art **10** innovation, knick-knack

novice 3 cub **4** colt, punk, tyro **5** plebe **6** newbie, rookie **7** amateur, learner, recruit, student, trainee **8** aspirant, beginner, freshman, neophyte, newcomer, prentice **9** fledgling, greenhorn, novitiate, postulant **10** apprentice, tenderfoot **11** probationer

Novum Organum author 5 Bacon (Francis)

now 3 PDQ **4** ASAP, soon, stat **5** today **6** at once, pronto **7** anymore, present **8** directly, first off, promptly **9** forthwith, instanter, instantly, presently, right away, sometimes **11** immediately, straightway **12** straightaway

now and then 7 at times, betimes **9** sometimes **12** infrequently, occasionally, periodically, sporadically

Nox _brother:_ 6 Erebus **_daughter:_ 3** Day **4** Eris **5** Light **_father:_ 5** Chaos **_husband:_ 6** Erebus **_son:_ 6** Charon, Hypnos **8** Thanatos

noxious 4 foul **5** fetid, toxic **6** deadly, putrid **7** baneful, harmful, noisome **8** stinking **9** dangerous, pestilent, poisonous, unhealthy **10** corrupting, pernicious **11** deleterious, destructive, detrimental, pestiferous **12** disagreeable, pestilential

nozzle 4 nose, vent **5** spout **7** channel

nth 4 last **6** utmost **7** extreme, highest, maximal, maximum, supreme **8** greatest, ultimate

nuance 4 hint **5** shade, tinge, touch, trace **6** nicety **7** shading, soupçon **8** overtone, subtlety **9** gradation, suspicion **10** refinement, suggestion **11** distinction

nub 4 bump, core, crux, gist, knob, knot, lump, meat, node, pith **5** bulge, point, short **6** kernel, upshot **8** swelling **9** substance **10** projection **12** protuberance

Nubian 5 Mahas **6** Birked, Kenuzi, Midobi **7** Dongola **8** Cushitic **9** Chari-Nile

nubile 4 ripe **10** attractive **12** marriageable

nuchal 4 nape

nuclear agency 3 AEC, NRC

nuclear particle 5 meson **6** proton **7** neutron

nucleus 3 bud **4** core, germ, head, kern, ring, seed **5** focus, spark **6** embryo **_material:_ 8** karyotin

nude 3 raw **4** bald, bare **5** naked, stark **6** barren, peeled, unclad **8** disrobed, starkers, stripped **9** au naturel, buck naked, unattired, unclothed, uncovered, undressed **10** stark naked

nudge 3 dig, jab, jog **4** near, poke, prod, push **5** elbow, shove **8** approach

nudnik 4 bore, drip, pest, pill, twit **8** nuisance

nugatory 4 idle, vain **5** empty, inane, vapid **6** futile, hollow, otiose **7** invalid, vacuous **8** trifling **9** fruitless, worthless **11** inoperative, meaningless

nugget 4 hunk, lump, plum **5** chunk **6** tidbit

nuisance 4 pain, pest, pill **6** bother, nudnik **7** nudnick **8** headache, irritant, pesterer, vexation **11** botheration

nuke 3 zap **4** bomb **5** crush, smash **6** attack **7** destroy **8** demolish **9** eradicate, microwave **10** annihilate **11** exterminate

null 4 void, zero **5** annul, empty **6** futile **7** invalid, useless **8** nugatory **9** worthless **10** invalidate, obliterate, unavailing **11** ineffective, ineffectual, inoperative

nullify 3 zap **4** undo, veto, void **5** abate, annul, limit, quash, scrub, trash **6** cancel, efface, negate, offset, repeal, revoke, squash **7** abolish, rescind, scratch, take out, wipe out **8** abrogate **10** annihilate, compensate, counteract, invalidate, neutralize **11** countervail

nullity 4 nada, zero **5** zilch **6** cipher, nobody **7** nothing, vacuity, whiffet **9** annulment, nonentity **11** nothingness **12** nonexistence

numb 5 chill, dazed **6** deaden, freeze **7** callous **8** deadened **9** insensate, paralyzed, stupefied, unfeeling **10** insensible, insentient **11** desensitize **12** anesthetized, desensitized

number 5 add up, count, digit, run to, sum to, tally, total **6** amount, cipher, figure **7** chiffer, include, integer, numeral, ordinal, several **8** cardinal, paginate **9** aggregate, enumerate **_added to another:_ 6** augend **_great:_ 4** army, host **5** horde **6** googol, legion **9** multitude **10** googolplex **_irrational:_ 4** surd **_resulting from division:_ 8** quotient **_resulting from multiplication:_ 7** product **_resulting from subtraction:_ 10** difference **_science:_ 11** mathematics

number one 3 top **4** best, main **5** chief, first, major **6** finest, Grade A, tip-top, top dog **7** capital, highest, leading, primary, stellar **8** dominant, five-star, foremost, superior **9** excellent, first-rate, front-rank, numero uno, principal, top-drawer **10** blue-ribbon, first-class, preeminent **11** first-string, outstanding, predominant

numbness 5 shock **6** stupor **10** anesthesia **11** anaesthesia **12** stupefaction **_combining form:_ 4** narc **5** narco

numeral 5 digit **6** cipher, figure, number **7** integer **11** whole number

numerate 4 list **5** count, tally **6** number **7** compute, itemize, tick off **8** tabulate **9** calculate

numerous 4 many **6** legion **7** profuse, umpteen **8** abundant, populous **9** plentiful **10** voluminous **13** multitudinous

Numitor _brother:_ 7 Amulius **_daughter:_ 9** Rea

Silvia **10** Rhea Silvia *grandson:* **5** Remus **7** Romulus

numskull 3 oaf **4** boob, clod, dodo, dolt, dope, goof, mutt, simp **5** chump, dummy, dunce, idiot, moron, ninny, noddy, stupe **6** dimwit, donkey, dum-dum, nitwit **7** airhead, dullard, pinhead, schnook **8** bonehead, clodpate, clodpoll, dumbbell, dumbhead, imbecile, lunkhead, meathead **9** birdbrain, blockhead, ignoramus, lamebrain, simpleton, thickhead **10** dunderhead, hammerhead, nincompoop **11** chowderhead, chucklehead, knucklehead

nun 4 buoy **6** sister *headcloth:* **6** wimple

Nunavut *capital:* **7** Iqaluit *island:* **5** Devon **6** Baffin **9** Ellesmere **11** Southampton *mountain:* **7** Barbeau (Peak) *peninsula:* **7** Boothia **8** Melville *provincial flower:* **11** Arctic poppy

nunnery 7 convent **8** cloister **10** sisterhood *head:* **8** superior

nuptial 6 bridal, wedded **7** marital, married, spousal, wedding **8** conjugal, espousal, hymeneal, marriage **9** connubial **11** matrimonial

nurse 3 LPN, LVN **4** feed, nana, rear, suck **5** nanny, serve **6** attend, foster, pamper, suckle **7** care for, cherish, nourish, nurture **9** cultivate **10** minister to *children's:* **5** nanny *English:* **11** Nightingale (Florence) *Indian:* **4** ayah *Chinese:* **4** amah

nursemaid 4 nana **5** nanny **6** minder, sitter **9** governess **10** babysitter *Indian:* **4** ayah *Chinese:* **4** amah

nursery 6 crèche **7** brooder **8** hothouse **9** fosterage **10** greenhouse **12** conservatory

nurture 4 care, feed, rear, tend **5** nurse, raise, train **6** cradle, foster, parent, suckle **7** bring up, care for, develop, educate, nourish, rearing **8** breeding, instruct, training, tutelage **9** cultivate **10** upbringing

nut 3 bug **4** cola, kola, kook, loon, pili **5** acorn, betel, crank, fiend, freak, hazel, loony, pecan, piñon **6** almond, cashew, cuckoo, madman, maniac, walnut, zealot **7** buckeye, fanatic, filbert, hickory, lunatic **8** crackpot **9** bedlamite, ding-a-ling, macadamia, pistachio, screwball **10** enthusiast, Tom o' Bedlam *of a violin bow:* **4** frog, heel

Nut *consort:* **3** Geb, Keb *daughter:* **4** Isis **8** Nephthys *son:* **6** Osiris

nuthouse 6 asylum, bedlam **8** loony bin **9** funny farm **10** booby hatch **11** institution **12** insane asylum

Nutmeg State 11 Connecticut

nutria 5 coypu

nutriment 4 diet, fare, food, grub, keep **6** viands **7** aliment, pabulum **8** victuals **9** provender **10** provisions, sustenance **11** comestibles, nourishment, subsistence

nutrition 4 diet **7** vittles **8** victuals **10** sustenance **11** nourishment

nutritious 9 healthful, wholesome **10** alimentary, nourishing

nuts 3 mad **4** daft, keen, wild, zany **5** batty, crazy, dotty, kooky, loony, rabid, wacky **6** absurd, cuckoo, insane, screwy **7** bonkers, cracked, excited, foolish, idiotic **8** animated, demented, deranged **9** exuberant, fanatical, screwball **10** passionate, unbalanced **12** enthusiastic *on forest floor:* **4** mast

nutty see **nuts**

nuzzle 3 rub **4** root, snug **5** nudge **6** burrow, cuddle, nestle **7** snuggle

Nycteus *brother:* **5** Lycus *daughter:* **7** Antiope

nymph 3 nix **5** dryad, larva, naiad, nixie, oread, sylph **6** kelpie, maiden, sprite **7** mermaid *changed into a bear:* **8** Callisto *changed into a laurel:* **6** Daphne *changed into a rock:* **4** Echo *mountain:* **5** oread *sea:* **6** Nereid **7** Calypso *water:* **5** naiad **6** undine *wood:* **5** dryad

Nyx see **Nox mythology** see **myth**

oaf 3 ape, dub, lug **4** boob, boor, bull, clod, dodo, dolt, goof, goon, hulk, lout, lump, slob **5** booby, chump, clown, dummy, dunce, klutz **6** dum-dum, galoot, lubber, lummox **7** fathead, palooka **8** bonehead, lunkhead, meathead **9** blockhead, blunderer, lamebrain, simpleton

oafish 5 dense **6** clumsy, klutzy, rustic **7** boorish, doltish, loutish **8** bungling, churlish, clownish, lubberly

oak *African:* 7 turtosa *fruit:* 5 acorn *genus:* 7 Quercus *kind:* 3 bur, pin, red 4 bear, cork, holm, ilex, live 5 black, holly, roble, white 6 barren, cerris, encina 7 durmast, English, moss-cup, valonia 9 blackjack *Mexican:* 8 chaparro *young:* 8 flittern

oar 3 row 4 pole, pull 5 rower, scull 6 paddle 7 paddler *part:* 4 loom, palm 5 blade, shaft 6 button, collar *pin:* 5 thole

oarsman 3 bow 5 rower 6 stroke 7 sculler *captain:* 3 cox 8 coxswain

oasis 3 spa 4 wadi 6 refuge, relief *ancient:* 4 Merv *Egypt:* 4 Siwa 5 Gafsa 6 Dakhla 7 Farafra 8 Ammonium *Libya:* 5 Mizda, Sebha 6 Sabhah 7 Gadames 8 Ghudamis *Niger:* 5 Bilma *Saudi Arabia:* 5 Hofuf, Taima 7 Al-Hufuf

oast 4 kiln, oven

oat 5 grain, grass 6 cereal *genus:* 5 Avena *Scottish:* 3 ait

oater 7 western 10 horse opera

oath 3 vow 4 cuss 5 curse, swear 6 pledge 7 promise 8 cussword 9 expletive, profanity, swearword *mild:* 4 darn, drat, egad 6 jiminy, zounds

oatmeal 5 gruel 6 burgoo 8 porridge *Scottish:* 8 drammock

obdurate 3 set 4 firm, hard 5 harsh, rigid, stony 6 dogged, mulish 7 adamant, callous 8 stubborn 9 heartless, immovable, unbending, unfeeling 10 hard-boiled, inflexible, unshakable, unyielding 11 coldhearted, hardhearted, insensitive 12 intransigent, stonyhearted 13 unsympathetic

obeah 5 charm, magic *relative:* 5 vodun 6 vodoun, voodoo 8 Santeria 9 Candomblé

Obed *father:* 4 Boaz 6 Ephlal 8 Shemaiah *mother:* 4 Ruth *son:* 5 Jesse 7 Azariah

obedient 5 loyal 6 docile 7 devoted, duteous, dutiful, willing 8 amenable, biddable, obliging, yielding 9 compliant, tractable 10 law-abiding, manageable, respectful, submissive 11 acquiescent, cooperative, deferential, subservient

obeisance 3 bow 5 honor 6 curtsy, esteem, fealty, homage, kowtow, salaam 7 gesture, loyalty, respect 9 deference, reverence 10 allegiance, submission

obelisk 6 dagger, pillar, symbol

Oberon 9 fairy king *messenger:* 4 Puck *wife:* 7 Titania

obese 3 fat 5 bulky, gross, heavy, tubby 6 fleshy, portly 7 adipose, outsize, porcine 9 corpulent 10 overweight

obey 3 bow 4 heed, keep, mind 5 agree, defer, serve, yield 6 accede, accept, assent, comply, follow, regard, submit 7 abide by, conform, execute, fulfill, observe, satisfy 9 acquiesce

obfuscate 4 blur 5 cloud, muddy 6 darken 7 becloud, conceal, confuse, cover up, obscure 9 adumbrate

obi 4 sash

obiter dictum 4 note 6 remark 7 comment, opinion 10 commentary, incidental 11 observation

obituary 9 necrology 11 death notice

object 3 aim, end, use 4 goal, item, kick, view, wish 5 demur, focus, frown, point, thing 6 design, entity, except, intent, matter, motive, oppose, target 7 article, dissent, protest, purpose 8 complain, disagree, material 9 criticize, intention, something 10 disapprove

objection 5 demur 7 protest 8 argument, demurral, demurrer, question 9 challenge, complaint, exception 10 difficulty, opposition 11 disapproval 12 disagreement, remonstrance 13 remonstration

objectionable 5 unfit 8 unwanted 9 invidious, obnoxious, offensive, unwelcome 10 unpleasant 11 displeasing, distasteful, undesirable 12 disagreeable

objective 3 aim, end 4 fair, goal, just, lens, mark 6 actual, design, intent, target 7 mission, purpose 8 ambition, function, material, physical, sensible, unbiased 9 corporeal, equitable, impartial, intention 10 impersonal 11 independent, substantial 12 unprejudiced 13 dispassionate

objet d'art 5 curio, virtu (plural) 7 bibelot, novelty 8 kickshaw 10 knickknack

objurgate 5 chide, decry, scold 6 rebuke 7 censure, reprove, upbraid 8 admonish, reproach 9 castigate, reprimand

oblate 7 lay monk 9 flattened, religious

oblation 4 gift 6 corban 8 holy gift, offering 9 sacrifice 12 presentation

obligate 4 bind 7 require 8 encumber, restrict 9 constrain

obligated 5 bound, owing 6 liable 8 beholden, indebted 11 accountable, responsible

obligation 3 IOU, vow 4 bond, call, debt, dues, duty, need, oath 5 cause 6 burden, charge, pledge 7 promise 8 business, contract 9 committal, liability, necessity, restraint 10 commitment, compulsion, constraint 11 requirement 12 indebtedness

obligatory 7 binding 8 required 9 essential, mandatory, necessary, requisite 10 compulsory, imperative 11 unavoidable

oblige 3 aid 4 bind, help, make 5 avail, favor, force 6 assist, coerce, compel, please, profit

7 benefit, command, gratify, require **9** constrain **10** contribute **11** accommodate, necessitate

obliged 4 made **5** bound **6** forced **8** beholden, grateful, indebted, thankful **11** constrained **12** appreciative

obliging 4 kind **5** civil **7** amiable, helpful, willing **8** friendly, pleasant **11** complaisant, considerate, cooperative, good-humored, good-natured **12** good-tempered

oblique 6 sloped, tilted **7** devious, leaning, obscure, slanted, sloping, tilting **8** diagonal, inclined, indirect **9** inclining **10** roundabout

obliterate 4 raze, x out **5** erase **6** cancel, delete, efface, remove, rub out **7** blot out, destroy, expunge, wipe out **8** black out, cross out **9** extirpate, liquidate **10** annihilate

oblivion 5 lethe, limbo **7** amnesia, nirvana, nowhere **9** emptiness **11** nothingness **13** forgetfulness

oblivious 4 lost **5** blind **7** unaware **8** absorbed, heedless, ignorant **9** unknowing, unmindful, unwitting **10** unfamiliar, uninformed **11** incognizant, unconscious

oblong 4 oval **5** ovate **7** ellipse **8** elongate **9** elongated, rectangle **11** rectangular

obloquy 4 slam, slur **5** abuse, odium, shame **6** infamy, rebuke **7** calumny, censure **8** disgrace, dishonor, ignominy **9** aspersion, contumely, discredit, disrepute, invective, stricture **10** defamation, opprobrium, scurrility **11** disapproval **12** billingsgate, condemnation, vituperation

obnoxious 4 vile **5** awful **6** odious, rotten **7** hateful **9** abhorrent, invidious, loathsome, offensive, repellant, repellent, repugnant, revulsive, sickening **10** abominable, detestable, disgusting

oboe 4 reed **7** hautboy **8** hautbois, woodwind **10** double reed *early:* **5** shawm *relative:* **7** bassoon **10** cor anglais **11** English horn

O'Brian character 6 Aubrey (Jack) **7** Maturin (Stephen)

obscene 4 foul, lewd, rank, vile **5** bawdy, crude, dirty, gross, lurid, taboo **6** coarse, filthy, ribald, risqué, smutty, vulgar **7** immoral, noisome, profane, raunchy **8** indecent, scabrous **9** abhorrent, appalling, offensive, repellent, repugnant, repulsive, salacious **10** disgusting, lascivious, scurrilous **11** foulmouthed, unprintable **12** pornographic, scatological

obscure 3 dim **4** blur, hide, mask, veil **5** blind, cloak, cloud, cover, dusky, faint, minor, murky, shade, shady, vague **6** cloudy, darken, hidden, opaque, remote, screen, secret, shadow, shroud, veiled **7** clouded, conceal, cryptic, eclipse, removed, shadowy, unclear, unknown, unnoted **8** disguise, nameless, overcast, puzzling, secluded, shrouded **9** ambiguous, enigmatic, tenebrous, uncertain, undefined **10** camouflage, ill-defined, indefinite, indistinct, mysterious, overshadow **11** out-of-the-way, unimportant **12** inaccessible **13** inconspicuous

obscurity 3 fog **4** haze, mist, murk **5** gloom **6** enigma, miasma, puzzle **7** dimness, mystery, shadows **8** darkness **9** ambiguity

obsequies 4 rite **5** rites **6** burial **7** funeral **10** burial rite

obsequious 4 oily **6** abject, smarmy **7** fawning, fulsome, servile, slavish **8** obedient, obeisant, toadying, unctuous **9** parasitic **10** flattering, submissive **11** deferential, subservient, sycophantic

observance 4 rite, rule **6** custom, notice, regard, ritual **7** liturgy, service **8** ceremony, practice **9** adherence, attention, formality **10** ceremonial

observant 4 keen **5** alert, awake, aware, sharp **7** heedful, mindful **8** watchful **9** advertent, attentive **10** perceptive

observation 4 note **6** notice, record, remark **7** comment, finding, opinion **8** judgment, notation **9** attention, inference **10** commentary **12** obiter dictum

observatory 5 tower **7** lookout, outlook **8** overlook *famous:* **4** Lick **6** Wilson, Yerkes **7** Palomar *instrument:* **9** telescope

observe 3 eye, see **4** espy, keep, look, mark, mind, note, obey, twig, view **5** honor, opine, sight, state, study, watch **6** behold, comply, follow, look at, notice, remark **7** abide by, comment, conform, discern, respect **8** perceive **9** celebrate, solemnize **10** comply with **11** commemorate

obsess 5 beset, haunt, hound, rivet **6** absorb, plague **7** consume, possess **9** captivate, preoccupy

obsessed 6 dogged, driven, hipped, hooked **7** gripped, haunted, plagued **8** overcome, troubled **9** dominated, possessed **11** preoccupied **12** prepossessed

obsession 5 craze, mania **6** fetish, hang-up **8** fixation, idée fixe **11** infatuation **13** preoccupation

obsessive 5 rabid **8** frenetic, maniacal, neurotic **9** fanatical, possessed **10** passionate **11** preoccupied

obsolete 3 old **5** dated, passé, stale **6** old hat **7** disused, worn-out **8** outmoded, time-worn **9** out-of-date **10** antiquated, superseded **12** antediluvian, old-fashioned

obstacle 3 bar **4** bump, clog, snag **5** block,

catch, check, crimp, hitch **6** hurdle **7** barrier **8** handicap, hardship **9** hindrance, imped-ance, roadblock **10** difficulty, impediment **11** encumbrance, vicissitude **12** interference

obstinate 4 deaf, firm **5** balky, fixed **6** dogged, mulish, ornery **7** staunch, willful **8** obdurate, perverse, resolute, stubborn **9** pigheaded, resistant, unbudging, immov-able **10** hardheaded, headstrong, inflexible, persistent, refractory, unyielding **11** intrac-table, stiff-necked, wrongheaded **12** intran-sigent, pertinacious, recalcitrant

obstreperous 4 loud **5** noisy, rowdy **6** unruly **7** blatant, raucous **8** strident **9** clamorous, insistent **10** boisterous, disorderly, vocifer-ant, vociferous **11** disobedient, loud-mouthed **12** rambunctious

obstruct 3 bar, dam **4** clog, hide, plug, stop **5** block, check, choke, close **6** cut off, ham-per, hinder, impede, stymie, thwart **7** con-gest, occlude, prevent, shut off, shut out, trammel **9** interfere

obstruction 3 bar **4** snag **5** hitch **6** hamper, hurdle **7** barrier **8** blockage, obstacle, stop-page **9** hindrance, impedance **10** impedi-ment

obtain 3 buy, get, win **4** earn, gain, have, reap **5** annex, reach **6** pick up, secure **7** achieve, acquire, chalk up, procure **8** purchase

obtrude 5 cut in **6** butt in, horn in, impose, meddle **7** presume, push out **8** chisel in, in-fringe **9** interfere, thrust out

obtrusive 4 nosy **5** pushy **6** prying **7** forward **8** meddling **9** bumptious, officious **10** med-dlesome, protruding **11** impertinent, inter-fering

obtuse 4 dull, dumb, slow **5** blunt, dense, thick **6** stupid **7** rounded, unclear **11** insen-sitive

obverse 4 face, side **5** front **8** opposite **9** other side **10** complement **11** counterpart

obviate 4 ward **5** avert, deter, block **7** for-fend, prevent, rule out **8** preclude, stave off **9** forestall, interfere, interpose, intervene **10** anticipate

obvious 5 clear, overt, plain **6** patent, simple **7** blatant, evident, glaring **8** apparent, clear-cut, distinct, manifest, palpable **10** undeni-able **11** conspicuous, self-evident, transparent, unambiguous, unequivocal

oca 5 tuber **6** sorrel

O'Casey, Sean 9 dramatist **10** playwright *plays:* **17** Juno and the Paycock, Plough and the Stars (The)

occasion 3 call, need, shot, show, time **5** ba-sis, break, cause, event **6** chance, demand, effect, excuse, ground, lead to, moment,

reason **7** episode, instant, opening, produce **8** ceremony, incident, instance **9** condition, happening, necessity **10** bring about, foun-dation, occurrence **11** celebration, opportu-nity **12** circumstance **13** justification

occasional 3 few, odd **4** rare **6** casual, fitful, random, scarce, seldom **7** special, unusual **8** specific, sporadic, uncommon **9** irregular **10** incidental, infrequent

occasionally 7 at times

Occidental 7 Western **8** European **9** West-erner

occlude 4 clog, fill, hide, plug, stop **5** block, choke, close, cover **6** screen, stop up **7** close up, conceal, congest **8** block off, ob-struct

occult 5 eerie, magic **6** arcane, orphic, secret **8** abstruse, esoteric, hermetic, mystical **9** recondite, unearthly **10** cabalistic, mysteri-ous **12** supernatural

occupant 5 liver **6** inmate, tenant **7** denizen, dweller, resider **8** habitant, resident **10** in-habitant

occupation 3 job, use **4** line, work **5** trade **6** career, métier, office **7** calling, control, pur-suit, seizure **8** activity, business, position, vocation **9** occupancy, residence **10** em-ployment, habitation, possession, settle-ment

occupy 3 use **4** busy, fill, hold, take **5** seize, tie up **6** absorb, employ, engage, live in, people, take up, tenant **7** control, engross, immerse, inhabit, involve, possess **8** popu-late, reside in, take over

occur 3 hap **4** pass **5** arise, ensue, pop up **6** appear, befall, betide, chance, dawn on, happen, result, strike **7** come off, develop **9** take place, transpire

occurrence 3 hap **4** pass **5** event, state **7** epi-sode **8** exigency, incident, juncture, occa-sion **9** adventure, condition, emergency, happening, situation

ocean 3 sea **4** blue, deep, main **5** brine, drink **6** Arctic, Indian **7** Pacific **8** Atlantic **9** Ant-arctic *movement:* **4** tide, wave

Oceania *country:* **4** Fiji **5** Belau, Nauru, Palau, Samoa, Tonga **6** Tuvalu **7** Vanuatu **8** Kiribati **9** Australia **10** New Zealand *terri-tory:* **7** Tokelau **12** New Caledonia **13** American Samoa *ethnic group:* **6** Fijian, Papuan, Samoan **10** Melanesian, Polynesian **11** Micronesian *language:* **5** Maori **6** Fijian, Papuan, Pidgin, Samoan **10** Melanesian

oceanic 4 huge, vast **5** great **6** marine **7** im-mense, pelagic **8** enormous, maritime **9** saltwater, thalassic

Ocean State 11 Rhode Island

Oceanus *daughter:* 5 Doris 7 Oceanid 8 Eurynome *father:* 6 Uranus *mother:* 4 Gaea *sister:* 6 Tethys *son:* 6 Peneus 7 Alpheus *wife:* 6 Tethys

ocellus 3 eye 7 eyespot

ocelot 3 cat 7 wildcat

O'Connor novel 9 Wise Blood

octave 5 eight, scale 6 eighth, stanza 8 interval

Octavia *brother:* 8 Augustus *grandson:* 8 Caligula *husband:* 4 Nero 6 Antony

octopus 7 mollusc, mollusk 9 devilfish 10 cephalopod *arm:* 8 tentacle *genus:* 7 Polypus *kin:* 5 squid 10 cuttlefish

ocular 4 seen 5 optic 6 visual 7 eyelike, optical, visible 8 eyepiece, viewable 9 perceived

Odalisque painter 6 Ingres (Jean-Auguste-Dominique) 7 Matisse (Henri)

odd 4 lone, rare 5 extra, fluky, queer, rummy, weird 6 casual, chance, single, uneven 7 curious, erratic, strange, unusual 8 peculiar, singular 9 eccentric, unmatched 13 idiosyncratic

oddball 4 kook 5 kooky, weird 6 weirdo 7 bizarre, curious, offbeat, strange, unusual 8 original, peculiar 9 character, eccentric 10 outlandish 13 idiosyncratic

Odd Couple, The *author:* 5 Simon (Neil) *character:* 5 Felix, Oscar *director:* 4 Saks (Gene) 7 Nichols (Mike) *star:* 6 Carney (Art), Lemmon (Jack) 7 Klugman (Jack), Matthau (Walter), Randall (Tony)

oddity 5 freak, quirk 6 weirdo 7 anomaly 9 character, curiosity, departure, deviation, eccentric, weirdness 10 aberration, difference 11 abnormality, peculiarity, strangeness 12 eccentricity, idiosyncrasy, irregularity

odds 4 edge 5 favor, ratio 7 benefit, chances 8 handicap, variance 9 advantage, allowance, disparity 10 difference, likelihood, partiality 11 probability 12 disagreement

odds and ends 4 bits, olio 6 jumble, medley, motley, scraps 7 mélange, mixture 8 remnants, sundries 9 etceteras, leftovers, potpourri 10 assortment, hodgepodge, hotchpotch, miscellany 13 paraphernalia

ode 4 hymn, poem 5 lyric, psalm, verse *part:* 5 epode 7 strophe 11 antistrophe

Odets play 9 Golden Boy 11 Country Girl (The) 12 Awake and Sing 15 Waiting for Lefty

odeum 4 hall 7 theater 11 concert hall

Odin *brother:* 4 Vili *daughter-in-law:* 5 Nanna *father:* 3 Bor *hall:* 8 Valhalla *horse:* 8 Sleipnir *maiden:* 8 Valkyrie *mansion:* 9 Gladsheim *mother:* 6 Bestla *raven:* 5 Hugin, Munin *ring:* 8 Draupnir *son:* 3 Tyr 4 Thor, Vali 6 Balder, Baldur *spear:* 7 Gungnir *sword:* 4 Gram *wife:* 4 Fria, Rind 5 Frigg 6 Frigga *wolf:* 4 Geri 5 Freki

odious 4 foul, vile 6 horrid 7 hateful, heinous, noxious 8 horrible 9 abhorrent, execrable, invidious, loathsome, malicious, repellent, repugnant 10 abominable, despicable, detestable, disgusting

odium 4 hate, onus 5 shame 6 hatred, infamy, stigma 7 censure, obloquy 8 contempt, disgrace, dishonor, ignominy, loathing 9 disrepute 10 abhorrence, opprobrium 11 detestation 12 condemnation

odor 4 funk 5 aroma, scent, smell, stink, whiff 6 stench 7 bouquet, perfume 9 fragrance, redolence

odorous 5 heady, sweet 6 smelly, strong 7 pungent, scented 8 aromatic, fragrant, perfumed, redolent, unsavory 9 offensive

Odysseus 7 Ulysses *dog:* 5 Argos *enchantress:* 5 Circe *father:* 7 Laertes *friend:* 6 Mentor *harasser:* 8 Poseidon *herb:* 4 moly *kingdom:* 6 Ithaca *mother:* 8 Anticlea *rescuer:* 3 Ino 8 Nausicaa *son:* 9 Telegonus 10 Telemachus *swineherd:* 7 Eumaeus *voyage:* 7 odyssey *wife:* 8 Penelope

odyssey 4 trek 5 quest 6 voyage 7 journey 9 wandering 13 peregrination

Odyssey author 5 Homer

Oedipus *brother-in-law:* 5 Creon *daughter:* 6 Ismene 8 Antigone *father:* 5 Laius *foster father:* 7 Polybus *foster mother:* 8 Periboea *kingdom:* 6 Thebes *mother:* 7 Jocasta *son:* 8 Eteocles 9 Polynices 10 Polyneices *victim:* 5 Laius *wife:* 7 Jocasta

Oeneus *kingdom:* 7 Calydon *son:* 8 Meleager *wife:* 7 Althaea

Oenomaus *charioteer:* 8 Myrtilus *daughter:* 10 Hippodamia *kingdom:* 4 Pisa *slayer:* 6 Pelops

Oenone *husband:* 5 Paris *rival:* 5 Helen

oeuvre 4 work 6 corpus, output 8 lifework 10 collection 11 compilation

of *German:* 3 aus, von *Italian:* 5 degli, della, delle

off 4 away, kill, slay 5 aside 6 depart, murder, remote, slight 7 seaward, spoiled 8 dispatch 9 eccentric, incorrect

offal 4 guts 4 junk 5 gurry, trash, waste 6 debris, litter, refuse, spilth 7 carrion, garbage, innards, rubbish, viscera 8 entrails 9 sweepings 10 intestines

offbeat 3 odd 5 fresh, outré, weird 6 way out 7 bizarre, oddball, strange, unusual 8 bohemian, peculiar, singular, uncommon 9 different, eccentric, whimsical **10** outlandish, unorthodox **11** distinctive **13** idiosyncratic

off-color 3 ill, low **4** blue, racy **5** bawdy, broad, salty, shady **6** ailing, peaked, poorly, risqué, sickly, unwell **7** dubious, naughty **8** improper, indecent **10** indisposed, suggestive

offend 3 sin, vex **4** gall, hurt, miff, pain **5** anger, annoy, pique, repel, shock, upset **6** appall, breach, insult, nettle **7** affront, disturb, provoke, violate **8** aggrieve, distress, irritate **9** displease **10** antagonize, transgress

offender 5 felon **6** sinner **7** culprit **8** criminal, violator **9** wrongdoer **10** lawbreaker, malefactor **12** transgressor

offense 3 sin **4** huff, hurt, miff, tort, vice **5** crime, fault, pique, wrong **6** attack, breach, felony, injury, insult **7** affront, assault, dudgeon, misdeed, mistake, outrage, umbrage **9** indignity, onslaught, violation **10** aggression, infraction, resentment **11** misdemeanor

offensive 3 bad **4** foul, rank, vile **5** drive, onset **6** attack, odious **7** assault, fulsome, noisome, obscene, painful **8** nauseous, unsavory **9** loathsome, obnoxious, onslaught, repellent, repugnant, repulsive, sickening **10** aggression, aggressive, disgusting, nauseating, unpleasant **12** disagreeable, unappetizing **13** objectionable

offer 3 bid, try **4** seek, show **5** assay, essay, pitch, put up **6** afford, extend, submit, tender **7** advance, attempt, display, exhibit, hold out, present, propose, provide, suggest **8** endeavor, proposal, threaten **9** sacrifice **10** submission **11** proposition

offering 3 IPO **4** alms, gift **5** grant **6** course, corban **7** charity, present **8** donation, oblation **9** sacrifice **11** benefaction, beneficence **12** contribution

offhand 5 ad-lib **6** blithe, breezy, casual **8** informal **9** extempore, impromptu, unstudied **10** improvised, nonchalant, unprepared **11** extemporary, spontaneous, unrehearsed

office 3 job **4** duty **5** berth, suite **6** agency, billet, bureau **7** station **8** business, cube farm, function, province **9** situation, workplace **10** department *head:* **4** boss **7** manager *holder:* **9** incumbent **11** functionary *machine:* **3** fax **6** copier **7** printer **8** computer **10** calculator, fax machine **11** photocopier *seeker:* **9** candidate **10** politician *without work:* **8** sinecure *worker:* **5** clerk **6** typist **9** file clerk, secretary **10** bookkeeper

officer 3 cop **4** exec **6** noncom, police **7** John Law, manager **8** official **9** executive *abbreviation:* **2** Lt. **3** Adm., Col., Ens., Gen., Maj.

4 Capt., Cmdr. **5** Comdr., Lieut. *army:* **5** looey, looie, major **7** captain, colonel, general **10** lieutenant *British:* **9** brigadier *court:* **7** bailiff *king's:* **11** chamberlain *law-enforcement:* **3** cop **6** deputy, police **7** marshal, sheriff **9** constable, patrolman, policeman *naval:* **4** mate **6** ensign **7** admiral, captain **9** commander, commodore **10** lieutenant *noncommissioned:* **5** sarge **8** corporal, sergeant *petty:* **4** bos'n **5** bosun **6** yeoman **9** boatswain *prison:* **5** guard **6** warden

official 4 exec **7** cleared, manager **8** approved, bona fide, endorsed **9** authentic, canonical, cathedral, certified, executive **10** accredited, authorized, ex cathedra, magistrate, sanctioned **13** administrator, authoritative *city or town:* **5** mayor **8** alderman **9** councilor, selectman **10** councillor *diplomatic:* **5** envoy **6** consul **7** attaché **10** ambassador *governmental:* **6** syndic *parish:* **6** beadle *sports:* **3** ref, ump **6** umpire **7** referee **8** linesman *university:* **4** dean **6** bursar **7** provost **9** registrar **10** chancellor

officiate 5 chair, serve **6** direct, umpire **7** conduct, oversee, preside, referee **9** supervise **11** superintend

officious 4 busy, nosy **5** nosey, pushy **7** forward **8** meddling **9** assertive, intrusive, obtrusive **10** meddlesome **11** impertinent **13** self-important

offing 4 future **7** by-and-by **9** aftertime, hereafter **10** near future

off-key 3 odd **4** sour **7** jarring **9** anomalous, dissonant, unnatural **10** discordant **12** inharmonious

off-putting 8 daunting **9** dismaying, offensive, repellent **10** forbidding **11** distasteful **12** disagreeable, discouraging **13** disconcerting, disheartening, objectionable

offscouring 5 leper, trash **6** pariah, refuse, reject **7** outcast **8** castaway, derelict **11** untouchable

offset 6 square **7** balance **8** equalize **10** balance out, compensate, neutralize **11** counterpose, countervail **12** counterpoise, displacement

offshoot 4 twig **5** scion **6** branch **7** product, spin-off **9** affiliate, by-product, outgrowth **10** derivative, descendant

offspring 3 cub, kid **4** kids, seed **5** brood, child, hatch, issue, scion, spawn, swarm, young **7** produce, product, progeny **8** children **9** posterity **10** descendant **11** progeniture

off-the-wall 3 odd **5** kooky, weird **6** far-out, way-out **7** bizarre, oddball, unusual **8** freak-

ish **9** eccentric, fantastic, grotesque **10** outlandish
off-white 4 bone **5** cream, ivory **6** oyster, vellum **9** parchment
Of Human Bondage author: 7 Maugham (W. Somerset)
Of Mice and Men *author:* **9** Steinbeck (John) *character:* **6** George (Milton), Lennie (Small)
often 9 generally **10** frequently, habitually, repeatedly **11** recurrently
ogee 3 ess **4** arch **5** curve **7** molding
Ogier the ____ 4 Dane
ogive 3 rib **4** arch **5** graph
ogle 3 eye **4** gape, gaze, leer, look **5** stare **6** goggle **7** stare at **10** rubberneck
ogre 3 orc **5** bogey, giant, Shrek **6** Grinch **7** bugbear, monster **8** bogeyman **9** boogeyman *Algonquian:* **7** wendigo, windigo
ogress 5 harpy, scold, shrew, vixen **6** amazon, virago **8** fishwife **9** termagant, Xanthippe
O'Hara novel 7 Pal Joey **16** Butterfield Eight **17** Ten North Frederick
Ohio *capital:* **8** Columbus *city:* **5** Akron, Xenia **6** Canton, Dayton, Toledo **9** Cleveland **10** Cincinnati *college, university:* **5** Miami **6** Kenyon **7** Antioch, Denison, Oberlin **9** Kent State **12** Bowling Green *nickname:* **7** Buckeye (State) *river:* **4** Ohio **6** Maumee **8** Sandusky *state bird:* **8** cardinal *state flower:* **16** scarlet carnation *state tree:* **7** buckeye
Oholibamah *father:* **4** Anah *husband:* **4** Esau
oil 3 fat, gas **4** balm, fuel, lube, oleo **5** oleum, slick **6** anoint, grease, pomade **7** blarney, incense, lanolin **8** flattery, soft soap **9** adulation, lubricant, lubricate, petroleum *combining form:* **3** ole **4** olei, oleo *company:* **3** Sun **4** Arco, Esso, Gulf, Hess, Hunt, Pure **5** ADNOC, Amoco, Citgo, Exxon, Getty, Mobil, Pemex, Shell, Sohio, Union, YUKOS **6** Aramco, Conoco, Lukoil, Sunoco, Texaco, Valero **7** Ashland, Chevron **8** Marathon, Pennzoil, Phillips, Sinclair, Standard **9** Petrobras **10** ExxonMobil, Occidental, PetroChina *consecrated:* **6** chrism *fragrant:* **5** attar **6** neroli *fuel:* **3** gas **6** butane, petrol **7** benzene, propane **8** gasoline, kerosene *relating to:* **5** oleic *ship:* **6** tanker *source:* **4** rape **5** olive, shale **6** canola **7** linseed **8** flaxseed, rapeseed **9** sunflower *well:* **6** gusher
oilbird 8 guacharo
oily 5 fatty, slick, soapy, suave **6** greasy, smarmy, smooth **7** fulsome **8** slippery, unctuous **10** lubricious, obsequious, oleaginous

ointment 4 balm, nard **5** cream, salve **6** lotion **7** unction, unguent **8** calamine, liniment **9** emollient, spikenard **11** embrocation
OK, okay 3 aye, yea, yes **4** fine, good, safe, well, yeah **5** agree, allow, favor, licit **6** agreed, assent, decent, permit **7** approve, certify, endorse, support **8** accredit, adequate, all right, approval, blessing, high sign, passable, sanction, thumbs-up **9** authorize, hunky-dory **10** acceptable, permission **11** endorsement, permissible **12** satisfactory
Okinawa capital 4 Naha
Oklahoma *capital:* **12** Oklahoma City *city:* **3** Ada **4** Enid **5** Tulsa **6** Norman *college, university:* **11** Oral Roberts *mountain:* **9** Black Mesa *nickname:* **6** Sooner (State) *river:* **3** Red **8** Arkansas, Canadian *state bird:* **10** flycatcher *state flower:* **9** mistletoe *state tree:* **6** redbud
okra 4 soup **5** gumbo **6** mallow
old 4 aged, gray, late, past **5** dated, hoary, passé, stale **6** bygone, démodé, former, mature, senior, whilom **7** ancient, antique, archaic, elderly, lasting, onetime, overage, quondam, veteran **8** enduring, lifelong, Noachian, outmoded, timeworn **9** erstwhile, geriatric, long-lived, perennial, perpetual, primitive, venerable **10** antiquated, inveterate **13** superannuated *Scottish:* **4** auld
old age 3 eld **6** dotage **8** caducity **10** senescence **11** decreptitude, elderliness, senectitude
Old Bailey 5 court
Old Colony State 13 Massachusetts
Old Curiosity Shop *author:* **7** Dickens (Charles) *character:* **4** Nell **10** Little Nell
Old Dominion State 8 Virginia
Old Faithful 6 geyser
old-fashioned 4 aged **5** dated, dowdy, fusty, moldy, passé, stale, tired **6** bygone, démodé, quaint, stodgy **7** ancient, antique, archaic, outworn, vintage **8** obsolete, outdated, outmoded **9** out-of-date, unstylish **10** antiquated
old hand 3 pro, vet **6** expert, master **7** veteran **9** authority **10** past master, specialist
old hat 5 dated, passé, stale, tired, trite **6** démodé **7** antique, clichéd, vintage **8** outmoded, timeworn, well-worn **9** hackneyed, out-of-date **10** antiquated
Old Ironsides 12 Constitution (U.S.S.) *poet:* **6** Holmes (Oliver Wendell)
Old Line State 8 Maryland
old maid 6 fusser **7** fusspot **8** spinster **10** fussbudget
Old North State 13 North Carolina

Old Rough and Ready 6 Taylor (Zachary)

Olds' car 3 Reo

old-time 5 dated **6** bygone **7** antique, vintage **10** antiquated **12** long-standing

old-timer 3 vet **5** elder **6** senior **7** ancient, antique, veteran

Old World 6 Europe

oleaginous see **oily**

oleaster 5 shrub **12** Russian olive

olecranon 9 funny bone

oleo 9 margarine

oleoresin 10 turpentine

oleum 3 oil

olfaction 5 sense, smell **8** smelling

olid 4 rank **5** fetid **6** putrid, rancid, rotten **7** stenchy **8** stinking **9** offensive **10** malodorous

olio 3 mix **4** hash, stew **5** gumbo, umble **6** medley **7** grab bag, mélange, mixture **8** mishmash, mixed bag **9** potpourri **10** assortment, collection, hodgepodge, hotchpotch, miscellany, salmagundi **11** gallimaufry

Oliver Twist *author:* **7** Dickens (Charles) *character:* **5** Fagin, Nancy, Sikes (Bill) **6** Bumble (Mr.) **12** Artful Dodger

Ollie's partner 4 Stan

Olympian 3 god **5** lofty, noble **6** lordly **7** athlete, exalted, godlike **8** majestic, superior **10** competitor

Olympics site *1972:* **6** Munich **7** Sapporo *1976:* **8** Montreal **9** Innsbruck *1980:* **6** Moscow **10** Lake Placid *1984:* **10** Los Angeles **8** Sarajevo *1988:* **5** Seoul **7** Calgary *1992:* **9** Barcelona **11** Albertville *1994:* **11** Lillehammer *1996:* **7** Atlanta *1998:* **6** Nagano *2000:* **6** Sydney *2002:* **12** Salt Lake City *2004:* **6** Athens *2006:* **5** Turin **6** Torino *2008:* **7** Beijing *2010:* **9** Vancouver *2012:* **6** London *2016:* **3** Rio **12** Rio de Janeiro

Oman *capital:* **6** Masqat, Muscat *language:* **6** Arabic **7** Baluchi *monetary unit:* **4** rial *mountain range:* **7** Al-Hajar *neighbor:* **5** Yemen **11** Saudi Arabia *peninsula:* **7** Arabian *sea:* **7** Arabian

Omar 4 poet **7** Khayyám *country:* **6** Persia *father:* **7** Eliphaz *poem:* **8** Rubaiyat

omega 3 end **6** ending, finale, letter *kin:* **3** zed, zee

omen 3 sign **5** augur, token **6** augury, boding **7** auspice, portent, presage, warning **8** bodement, prophecy **9** foretoken **10** foreboding, prediction, prognostic

ominous 4 dark, dire, grim **6** dismal **7** baleful, direful, doomful, fateful **8** alarming, lowering, menacing, sinister **9** ill-boding, prophetic **10** forbidding, foreboding, portentous **11** frightening, threatening **12** inauspicious, unpropitious

omission 3 cut, gap **4** lack, skip, slip **5** blank, break, chasm, error, lapse **6** hiatus, lacuna **7** elision, failure **8** eclipsis, ellipsis, overlook **9** exclusion *mark:* **5** caret **8** ellipsis **10** apostrophe

omit 4 drop, fail, skip **5** elide **6** except, forget, ignore, slight **7** exclude, neglect **8** leave out, overlook, pass over

omnibus 3 ana **4** posy **5** album **7** garland **8** analects, treasury **9** anthology **10** miscellany **11** florilegium

omnipotent 6 divine **7** godlike, supreme **8** almighty **9** unlimited **11** all-powerful

omnipresent 7 allover, endless **8** infinite, unending **9** boundless, limitless, universal **10** ubiquitous

omniscient 4 wise **7** learned **9** know-it-all **10** all-knowing

omnium-gatherum see **olio**

Omphale *domain:* **5** Lydia *slave:* **8** Heracles, Hercules

omphalos 3 hub **5** focus, navel **9** umbilicus **10** focal point **11** belly button

on 4 atop, over **5** above, along, going **7** working **9** operating **11** functioning

onager 3 ass **5** kiang **8** catapult

Onan's father 5 Judah

once 4 ever, late, past **5** at all **6** before, bygone, former, whilom **7** already, earlier, long ago, onetime, quondam **8** formerly, sometime

once-over 4 look **5** check **6** gander, glance, survey **10** inspection **11** examination

one 4 lone, only, sole, unit **5** monad **6** single, unique **7** numeral **8** separate, singular, solitary **9** undivided **10** individual, particular *combining form:* **4** mono *French:* **2** un **3** une *German:* **3** ein **4** eine *prefix:* **3** uni *Scottish:* **2** ae **3** ane, yin *Spanish:* **2** un **3** una, uno

one and a half *combining form:* **6** sesqui

one-eyed giant 7 Cyclops **10** Polyphemus

one-handed god 3 Tiu, Tyr

one-horse town 4 burg **5** thorp **6** hamlet, Podunk **7** village **11** whistle-stop

one hundred 6 centum *years:* **7** century

O'Neill, Eugene *daughter:* **4** Oona *heroine:* **4** Anna, Nina *play:* **3** Ile **4** Gold **8** Hairy Ape (The) **12** Ah Wilderness, Anna Christie, Emperor Jones, Iceman Cometh (The) **13** Great God Brown (The), Marco Millions **16** Strange Interlude **18** Desire Under the Elms **22** Mourning Becomes Electra **24** Long Day's Journey into Night

oneiric 6 dreamy **8** anagogic **9** dreamlike

oneness 3 all **5** union, unity, whole **7** harmony **8** entirety, identity, sameness, totality **9** integrity, unanimity **10** singleness, uniformity **11** singularity, unification **13** individuality

onerous 4 hard **5** heavy, tough **6** taxing, trying **7** arduous, exigent, wearing, weighty **8** exacting, grievous, imposing, pressing, toilsome **9** demanding, difficult, laborious **10** burdensome, cumbersome, oppressive **11** troublesome

one-sided 6 biased, uneven **7** colored, partial, unequal **8** inclined, partisan, weighted **10** prejudiced, unbalanced, unilateral

onetime 3 old **4** once, past **6** bygone, former, whilom **7** quondam **8** previous **9** erstwhile

ongoing 7 current, growing **8** evolving **9** advancing, in process **10** continuing, continuous, developing, in progress, unfinished **11** progressing

on hand 4 here **5** ready **6** nearby **7** pending, present **9** available

onion 4 bulb **7** shallot *bulb:* **3** set *genus:* **6** Allium *kin:* **4** leek **6** garlic *kind:* **7** Bermuda, Danvers, Spanish *roll:* **5** bialy *young:* **8** scallion

online 5 wired **9** connected *business:* **5** e-tail *guffaw:* **3** LOL *pages:* **7** Web site *system:* **3** Web **8** Internet

onlooker 6 viewer **7** watcher, witness **8** beholder, kibitzer, observer **9** bystander, kibbitzer, spectator **10** eyewitness **12** rubbernecker

only 3 but, few, one, yet **4** just, lone, mere, save, sole, solo **5** alone **6** and yet, at most, except, merely, simply, single, solely, unique **7** however, utterly **8** entirely, singular, solitary **11** exclusively

onomasticon 7 lexicon **8** wordbook

onomatopoeic 5 mimic **6** echoic **7** mimetic **9** emulative, imitative **10** simulative

onset 4 dawn, rush **5** birth, get-go, start **6** attack, coming, origin **7** arrival, assault, dawning, offense, opening **8** invasion **9** beginning, inception, offensive **10** aggression **12** commencement

onslaught 5 blitz **6** attack, charge, deluge **7** assault, barrage, offense, torrent **8** invasion **9** offensive **10** aggression

on-target 3 apt, fit **5** exact, right **7** correct, perfect, precise **8** accurate **11** appropriate

Ontario *bay:* **8** Georgian *capital:* **7** Toronto *city:* **4** York **6** London, Ottawa **7** Markham, Windsor **8** Hamilton **9** Etobicoke, Kitchener, North York **10** Thunder Bay **11** Mississauga, Scarborough **13** Sault Ste. Marie *lake:* **4** Erie **5** Huron **7** Nipigon, Ontario **8**

Superior *provincial flower:* **13** white trillium *river:* **5** Moose **6** Albany, Severn, Winisk

on the go 4 busy **6** active

on the house 4 free **6** comped, gratis **13** complimentary

on the nose 5 bingo **6** dead-on, spot-on **7** exactly **8** accurate **9** precisely **10** accurately

on the other hand 3 but **7** however **11** nonetheless **12** nevertheless

on the rocks 4 iced **7** with ice, wrecked

on the whole 6 mainly, mostly **7** usually **8** all in all **9** generally, in general, typically **10** altogether, by and large

onus 3 tax **4** duty, load, task **5** blame, brand, fault, guilt, odium, stain **6** burden, charge, stigma, weight **8** black eye **9** liability **10** obligation, oppression

onward 5 ahead, along, forth **7** forward **9** advancing

onyx 5 agate **10** chalcedony

oodles 4 gobs, lots, tons, wads **5** heaps, loads, piles, rafts, reams, scads **6** plenty

oolong 3 tea

oomph 3 pep, vim, zip **4** brio, dash, élan, push, zest, zing **5** drive, punch, verve, vigor **6** esprit, pizazz, spirit **7** pizzazz **8** strength, vitality **9** sex appeal

ooze 3 goo, mud **4** emit, goop, leak, seep, weep **5** bleed, exude, issue, marsh, slime, sweat **7** secrete, seepage **8** transude

opacity 9 murkiness, obscurity **10** obtuseness

opal 3 gem **5** jewel, stone **6** silica **7** girasol, hyalite **8** gemstone

opaque 3 dim **4** dull, hazy **5** dense, filmy, murky, vague **6** cloudy **7** clouded, obscure, unclear **8** abstruse

OPEC nation 3 UAE **4** Iran, Iraq **5** Libya, Qatar **6** Kuwait **7** Algeria, Nigeria **9** Indonesia, Venezuela **11** Saudi Arabia

open 4 ajar, bare, free, wide **5** frank, lance, overt, unzip **6** broach, candid, expand, expose, public, reveal, spread, unfold, unlock, unseal, unveil **7** convene, outdoor, uncover, unlatch **8** disclose, outdoors, unlocked, unsealed **9** available, uncovered, undecided **10** unfastened **11** susceptible, unconcealed, undisguised **12** unrestricted

open-air 7 outdoor, outside **8** alfresco, outdoors **9** out-of-door **10** out-of-doors

open-and-shut 4 easy **5** clear, plain **6** patent, simple **7** evident, obvious

openhanded 6 giving, lavish **7** liberal **8** generous **9** bounteous, bountiful, unselfish, unsparing **10** beneficent, bighearted, charitable, munificent **11** magnanimous

openhearted 4 kind, warm **5** frank, plain **6**

candid, honest **8** generous **10** responsive **11** sympathetic

opening 2 os **3** gap **4** dawn, door, gate, hole, pass, pore, slit, slot, vent **5** break, chasm, chink, cleft, crack, debut, intro, mouth, onset, start, stoma **6** breach, chance, lacuna, outlet, outset **7** crevice, dawning, fissure, orifice, pinhole **8** aperture, overture **9** beginning **11** opportunity *ship's:* **5** hatch **8** hatchway, porthole

open-minded 7 liberal **8** tolerant, unbiased **9** receptive **12** freethinking, unprejudiced

openmouthed 4 agog, awed, rapt **5** agape **6** amazed, gaping **7** stunned **9** astounded, surprised **10** astonished, speechless

open sesame 3 key **5** charm **6** ticket **8** passport, password

open up 4 fire, talk **5** shoot **6** reveal **7** cut into, divulge **8** disclose **9** make plain, spread out **11** communicate

opera *comic:* **5** buffa **6** bouffe *glasses:* **9** lorgnette *house:* **3** Met **7** La Scala **12** Covent Garden, Metropolitan *kind:* **4** soap **5** comic, grand, horse, space *part:* **3** act **4** aria **5** scena *solo:* **4** aria *star:* **4** diva **10** prima donna *text:* **8** libretto (see also individual titles and composers)

opera (famous) 4 Aida **5** Faust, Manon, Norma, Tosca **6** Carmen, Otello, Salome **7** Elektra, Fidelio, Macbeth, Nabucco, Walküre (Die), Wozzeck **8** Don Carlo, Falstaff, Idomeneo, La Bohème, Turandot **9** Don Carlos, Lohengrin, Rheingold (Das), Rigoletto, Siegfried **10** I Pagliacci, La Gioconda, La Traviata, Magic Flute (The), Prince Igor, Tannhäuser **11** Don Giovanni, William Tell **12** Così Fan Tutte, Manon Lescaut, Pearl Fishers (The) **14** Flying Dutchman (The) **15** Barber of Seville (The), Götterdämmerung, Madama Butterfly **16** Marriage of Figaro (The), Tristan und Isolde

operant 8 behavior **9** effective **10** measurable, observable, productive **12** conditioning

operate 3 act, run, use **4** work **5** drive, exert, steer **6** behave, direct, effect, handle, manage **7** carry on, conduct, control, perform, produce **8** function, maneuver **9** influence **10** manipulate

operation 3 use **4** step **6** action **7** concern, mission, process, surgery **8** activity, business, exercise, exertion, function, maneuver **9** procedure **10** employment, engagement, enterprise **11** performance, transaction

operative 3 key **5** agent, alive **6** active, moving, usable **7** dynamic, in force, running,

working **8** relevant **9** effective **10** functional **11** efficacious, secret agent

operator 4 user **5** agent, fixer, pilot **6** doctor, driver **7** schemer, surgeon **9** conductor

operculum 3 lid **4** flap **8** covering

operetta composer 5 Friml (Rudolf), Lehár (Franz), Suppé (Franz von) **6** Straus (Oscar) **7** Herbert (Victor), Romberg (Sigmund), Strauss (Johann) **8** Sullivan (Arthur) **9** Offenbach (Jacques)

operose 4 dull **6** boring, tiring **7** tedious **8** tiresome, toilsome, weariful **9** difficult, laborious, wearisome

Ophelia *beloved:* **6** Hamlet *brother:* **7** Laertes *father:* **8** Polonius

ophidian 5 snake **9** snakelike

opiate 4 dope, drug **7** anodyne **8** hypnotic, narcotic, nepenthe, sedative **9** analgesic, soporific **10** anesthetic, painkiller **11** somniferous **12** somnifacient, tranquilizer *type:* **7** codeine **8** morphine

opine 4 aver, deem, hold, view **5** claim, judge, state, think **6** advise, assert **7** believe, express, suppose **8** point out **9** recommend

opinion 4 idea, view **5** tenet **6** belief, notion, theory **7** feeling, thought **8** attitude, estimate, judgment, reaction **9** sentiment **10** assumption, conclusion, conjecture, conviction, estimation, hypothesis, persuasion **11** speculation, supposition *express an:* **4** vote **5** judge **9** criticize

opium 4 dope, drug **8** narcotic *derivative:* **6** heroin **7** codeine **8** laudanum, morphine **9** paregoric *source:* **5** poppy

opossum 9 marsupial *kin:* **8** kangaroo

opponent 3 con, foe **4** anti **5** enemy, rival **6** muscle **7** nemesis **9** adversary, assailant, combatant **10** antagonist, challenger, competitor **12** counteragent

opportune 3 apt, fit **6** timely **8** suitable **9** favorable, well-timed **10** auspicious, convenient, felicitous, propitious **11** appropriate

opportunity 4 turn **5** break, space, spell **6** chance **7** opening **8** juncture, occasion, prospect **12** circumstance

oppose 4 buck, defy, deny, duel **5** cross, fight, repel **6** attack, combat, debate, differ, object, refute, resist **7** assault, contest, counter, dispute, prevent, protest **8** confront, contrast, disagree, obstruct **9** withstand **10** contradict, contravene, controvert, disapprove

opposed 3 con **4** agin, anti **6** contra **7** adverse, against **11** adversarial **12** antagonistic, antipathetic

opposite 4 foil **5** polar **6** contra, facing **7** antonym, counter, inverse, obverse, opposed,

reverse 8 antipode, antipole, contrary, contrast, converse **9** antipodal, diametric **10** antipodean, antithesis **11** contrasting, counterpole **12** antithetical, counterpoint **13** contradictory **prefix: 3** dis **5** retro **6** contra **7** counter

opposition 3 con, foe **5** enemy **7** rivalry **8** conflict, defiance **9** adversary, animosity, hostility **10** antagonism, antithesis, resistance **11** contrariety, disapproval

oppress 5 abuse, crush, wrong **6** burden, injure, sadden, subdue **7** afflict, torment, torture, trouble **8** aggrieve, distress, overload **9** persecute, subjugate, weigh down

oppressive 5 harsh, heavy **6** brutal, dismal, gloomy, severe, somber, sombre, taxing **7** exigent, onerous, weighty **8** crushing, exacting, grievous, stifling **9** demanding **10** burdensome, depressing, tyrannical **11** dispiriting, overbearing, suffocating **12** discouraging, overwhelming **force: 4** onus, yoke **6** burden, weight

oppressor 5 bully **6** despot, tyrant **8** autocrat, dictator **9** strongman

opprobrious 4 evil, vile **6** odious, vulgar **7** abusive, hateful **8** infamous **9** notorious, truculent **10** despicable, scurrilous **11** disgraceful, ignominious **12** contemptible, contumelious, vituperative

opprobrium 5 abuse, blame, odium, scorn, shame **6** infamy **7** obloquy **8** contempt, disgrace, dishonor, ignominy, reproach **9** contumely, discredit, disesteem, disrepute **10** scurrility **12** vituperation

oppugn 5 argue, fight **6** battle, combat **7** contend, contest, dispute **8** question

Ops 4 Rhea **consort: 6** Cronus, Saturn **daughter: 5** Ceres **7** Demeter

opt 3 tap **4** pick **5** elect, favor **6** choose, decide, prefer, select

optical 6 ocular, visual **8** visional **debris: 7** floater **instrument: 4** lens **5** scope **7** transit **9** magnifier, periscope, telescope **10** microscope

optimal 4 best **5** ideal **6** choice, finest **7** perfect, supreme **8** choicest

optimist 4 bull **5** hoper **7** dreamer **8** idealist, Micawber **9** Pollyanna **10** positivist

optimistic 4 rosy **5** happy, merry, sunny **6** bright, hoping, upbeat **7** assured, buoyant, hopeful, roseate **8** cheerful, positive, sanguine, trusting **9** confident, promising **11** rose-colored **12** Pollyannaish

option 4 pick **5** claim, extra, grant, right **6** choice **7** license **8** contract, election **9** accessory, privilege, selection **10** preference **11** alternative, prerogative

optional 4 free **5** extra **8** elective **9** voluntary **11** alternative **13** discretionary **item: 5** add-on, extra

opulence 4 luxe **6** bounty, luxury, plenty, riches, wealth **7** fortune **9** abundance, affluence, plenitude, profusion **10** luxuriance **12** extravagance

opulent 4 lush, rich **5** plush, showy, swank **6** deluxe, lavish **7** moneyed, profuse, wealthy **8** affluent, palatial **9** luxuriant, luxurious, plentiful, sumptuous **11** extravagant **12** ostentatious

opuntia 6 cactus

opus 4 work **5** piece **6** oeuvre **7** product **8** creation **11** composition

or 4 else, gold **6** golden, yellow **9** otherwise

oracle 4 sage, seer **5** augur, sibyl **6** augury, medium, Pythia, vision **7** prophet **8** haruspex, prophecy **10** apocalypse, revelation, soothsayer **site: 6** Claros, Delphi, Didyma, Dodona **7** Olympia **9** Epidaurus

oracular 5 vatic **6** mantic, orphic **7** cryptic, Delphic, fatidic, obscure **8** Delphian, dogmatic **9** ambiguous, arbitrary, prophetic, sibylline, vaticinal

oral 4 exam **5** vocal **6** spoken, verbal, voiced **8** narrated, viva voce **9** unwritten **11** examination

orange 6 citrus **brownish: 6** Titian **deep: 11** bittersweet **gem: 7** jacinth **genus: 6** Citrus **kin: 4** lime **5** lemon **7** kumquat, satsuma **8** mandarin **9** tangerine **10** grapefruit **kind: 4** sour **5** blood, chino, navel, Osage, sweet **7** Seville **8** bergamot, mandarin, Valencia **oil: 6** neroli **seed: 3** pip **skin: 4** rind

orangutan 3 ape **6** pongid **7** primate **10** anthropoid

Oranjestad island 5 Aruba

orate 4 rant **5** mouth, speak, spiel **6** preach **7** address, declaim, lecture **8** bloviate, harangue, perorate **9** discourse, sermonize, speechify **11** pontificate

oration 6 homily, sermon, speech **7** address, lecture **9** discourse **funeral: 6** eulogy

orator 7 speaker **American: 4** Clay (Henry) **5** Bryan (William Jennings), Henry (Patrick) **7** Calhoun (John C.), Douglas (Stephen), Webster (Daniel) **British: 5** Burke (Edmund) **8** Disraeli (Benjamin) **9** Churchill (Winston), Gladstone (William) **French: 8** Mirabeau (Comte de) **Greek: 5** Corax **8** Pericles **11** Demosthenes **Roman: 6** Cicero

oratory 6 chapel, speech **7** bombast **8** rhetoric **9** discourse, elocution, eloquence **10** expression **11** exhortation, speechcraft

orb 3 eye **4** ball **5** globe, round **6** circle, sphere

orbit 4 path 5 ambit, range, reach, scope, sweep, track 6 extent, radius 7 ellipse *farthest point:* 4 apse 5 apsis 6 apogee 8 aphelion *nearest point:* 4 apse 5 apsis 7 perigee 10 perihelion

orchard 5 trees 10 plantation

orchestra 4 band 7 gamelan 8 ensemble, symphony 12 philharmonic *instrument:* 4 harp, oboe, tuba 5 cello, flute, viola 6 chimes, violin 7 bassoon, cymbals, piccolo, timpani, trumpet 8 bass drum, clarinet, triangle, trombone 9 castanets, snare drum, xylophone 10 double bass, French horn, tambourine 11 English horn, violoncello 12 glockenspiel *leader:* 9 conductor *section:* 5 brass 6 string 7 brasses, strings 8 woodwind 9 woodwinds 10 percussion

orchestrate 5 blend, score, unify 6 manage 7 arrange, compose 8 organize 9 harmonize, integrate 10 coordinate

orchid *genus:* 4 Disa *kind:* 7 calypso, pogonia 8 cattleya, oncidium 9 cymbidium 11 cypripedium *petal:* 3 lip 8 labellum *product:* 5 salep *tuber:* 5 salep

ordain 4 will 5 enact, order 6 decree, direct, impose, invest 7 appoint, command, conduct, destine, dictate, install, lay down 9 establish, prescribe, pronounce 10 predestine

ordeal 4 test 5 agony, cross, trial 7 calvary, torment, trouble 8 crucible 9 suffering 10 affliction, difficulty, visitation 11 tribulation

order 4 book, fiat, rank 5 array, caste, class, genre, range 6 decree, lineup, method, scheme, series, system 7 command, harmony, mandate, marshal, pattern, reserve 8 classify, neatness, position, shipment, tidiness 9 directive, hierarchy, procedure, structure 10 injunction, regularity 11 progression *lack of:* 5 chaos 6 ataxia 7 anarchy, clutter 9 confusion 11 pandemonium *of business:* 6 agenda, docket *of preference:* 8 priority

orderly 4 aide, calm, neat, tidy, trim 6 batman 7 correct, precise, regular, soldier, uniform 8 methodic, peaceful 9 attendant, organized, peaceable, regulated, shipshape 10 methodical, systematic 11 uncluttered, well-behaved 12 businesslike

ordinance 3 law 4 code, rule 5 edict 6 decree 7 precept, statute 9 direction, prescript 10 regulation

ordinary 4 so-so 5 banal, cheap, judge, plain, trite, usual 6 common, normal 7 average, humdrum, mundane, natural, popular, prelate, prosaic, regular, routine, typical 8 everyday, familiar, inferior, mediocre, workaday 9 clergyman, customary, quotid-

ian 10 uneventful, unoriginal 11 commonplace

ordnance 4 arms, guns 6 cannon 7 weapons 8 armament, supplies, weaponry 9 artillery, munitions 10 ammunition

ore 4 gold, rock 5 metal 6 copper, silver 7 mineral 8 platinum *analysis:* 5 assay *deposit:* 4 lode, vein *excavation:* 5 stope *iron:* 5 ocher, ochre 8 goethite, hematite, limonite *lead:* 6 galena *process:* 8 leaching, smelting *refuse:* 4 slag 5 dross, matte 6 scoria *smelted:* 7 regulus

oread 5 nymph

Oregon *capital:* 5 Salem *city:* 4 Bend 6 Eugene 7 Coos Bay, Medford 8 Portland *college, university:* 4 Reed *lake:* 6 Crater *mountain, range:* 4 Hood 7 Cascade *nickname:* 6 Beaver (State) *river:* 5 Snake 8 Columbia *state bird:* 10 meadowlark *state flower:* 11 Oregon grape *state tree:* 10 Douglas fir

Orestes *father:* 9 Agamemnon *friend:* 7 Pylades *mother:* 12 Clytemnestra *sister:* 7 Electra 9 Iphigenia *victim:* 9 Aegisthus 12 Clytemnestra *wife:* 8 Hermione

organ 5 agent, means 6 agency, medium, review 7 channel, journal, vehicle 8 magazine, ministry 9 newspaper 10 instrument, periodical *ancient:* 9 hydraulus *barrel:* 10 hurdy-gurdy *bodily:* 3 ear, eye 4 lung, nose, skin 5 gland, heart, liver 6 kidney, larynx, spleen, tongue, tonsil, viscus 9 intestine *displacement:* 8 prolapse *mouth:* 8 harmonica *part:* 4 pipe, reed, stop 5 pedal, valve 6 blower 7 console, tremolo 8 keyboard 9 wind chest *reed:* 8 melodeon 9 harmonium *stop:* 4 oboe, sext 5 gamba, quint, viola 6 dulcet 7 bassoon, celesta, melodia, subbass, tertian 8 carillon, diapason, dulciana, gemshorn *tactile:* 6 feeler 8 tentacle

organ cactus 7 saguaro

organic 5 basic 6 innate 7 natural, primary 8 inherent, integral 9 essential 10 structural 11 fundamental

organism 5 being, plant 6 animal *disease-producing:* 4 germ 5 virus 8 pathogen 9 bacterium *single-celled:* 5 monad 6 amoeba 9 protozoan

organist *American:* 3 Fox (Virgil) 5 Biggs (E. Power) 6 Newman (Anthony) *Dutch:* 9 Sweelinck (Jan) *English:* 6 Wesley (Samuel) 7 Gibbons (Christopher, Edward, Ellis, Orlando) *French:* 5 Alain (Marie-Claire), Widor (Charles) 6 Franck (César) 8 Messiaen (Olivier) 10 Schweitzer (Albert) *German:* 4 Bach (Johann Sebastian) 6 Handel (George Frideric), Walcha (Helmut) 7

Richter (Anton, Ernst, Ferdinand, Johann, Karl) *Swiss:* 4 Rogg (Lionel)

organization 4 body, club, unit 5 group, guild, setup 6 agency, system 7 pattern 9 framework, structure 11 arrangement, association, corporation, institution 13 establishment *college:* 4 frat 8 sorority 10 fraternity *criminal:* 3 Mob 4 gang 5 Mafia *fraternal:* (see **fraternal society**) *government:* (see **government agency**) *lack of:* 5 chaos *political:* 4 bloc 5 party 7 apparat, machine *service:* 3 USO, VFW

organize 4 form 5 array, group, order, rally, set up, start 6 create, line up 7 arrange 8 classify, unionize 9 construct, establish, institute, integrate 10 constitute, coordinate 11 put together

orgulous 5 proud

orgy 4 rite 5 binge, revel, spree 7 blowout, carouse, debauch, rampage, revelry, splurge 8 carousal 9 bacchanal 10 indulgence, saturnalia 11 bacchanalia

oriel 3 bay 6 window

orient 3 set 4 face 5 adapt, align, pearl, sheen 6 adjust, direct, inform, locate, luster 7 arrange 8 acquaint, lustrous 9 sparkling 11 accommodate, familiarize

Orient 4 Asia, East 7 Far East

Oriental 3 rug 5 Asian 6 carpet 7 Eastern 10 Far Eastern

orientation 7 bearing 8 location, position 9 alignment, direction 10 adjustment 11 arrangement

orifice see **opening**

oriflamme 4 flag 5 ideal 6 banner, pennon, symbol 7 pendant, pennant 8 standard, streamer

origami 12 paper folding *bird:* 5 crane

origin 4 root, seed, well 5 birth, blood, start 6 source 7 descent, genesis, lineage 8 ancestry, fountain, pedigree 9 beginning, inception, maternity, parentage, paternity 10 derivation, extraction, provenance, wellspring

original 3 new 5 first, model, novel, prime 6 native, unique 7 initial, pattern, pioneer, primary 8 creative, earliest 9 archetype, ingenious, innovator, inventive, precursor, primitive, prototype 10 archetypal, forerunner, innovative, primordial

originally 5 first 7 at first 8 formerly 9 initially, primarily

originate 4 coin, flow, hail, make, rise, stem 5 arise, begin, found, hatch, issue, set up, start 6 create, derive, invent, launch, spring 7 emanate, proceed, produce, think up 8 commence, generate, initiate, innovate 9 institute, introduce

originator 5 maker 6 author 7 creator, founder, planner 8 inventor, producer 9 initiator, innovator 10 institutor, introducer

oriole 4 bird 8 troupial *European:* 6 loriot *genus:* 7 Icterus *golden:* 6 loriot *kind:* 6 golden 7 orchard 8 Bullock's 9 Baltimore

Orion 6 hunter 13 constellation *beloved:* 3 Eos *belt:* 7 Ellwand *father:* 7 Hyrieus 8 Poseidon *slayer:* 5 Diana 7 Artemis *star:* 5 Rigel 9 Bellatrix 10 Betelgeuse

orison 6 prayer 8 entreaty, petition 12 supplication

Orithyia *lover:* 6 Boreas *son:* 5 Zetes 6 Calais

Orlando author 5 Woolf (Virginia)

Orlando Furioso author 7 Ariosto (Ludovico)

Orléans heroine 9 Joan of Arc

orlop 4 deck

ormolu 5 brass 6 bronze

ornament 3 gem 4 bead, deck, trim 5 adorn, jewel 6 bedeck, finial, tassel 7 dress up, garnish, jewelry, pendant, whatnot 8 beautify, decorate, filigree 9 embellish, embroider, lavaliere *Christmas tree:* 4 bulb 5 angel 6 tinsel *lip:* 6 labret *shoulder:* 7 epaulet

ornamental case 4 etui

ornate 4 lush, rich 5 fancy, gaudy, showy 6 florid, frilly, gilded, glitzy, rococo 7 baroque, flowery, opulent 8 overdone 9 elaborate, luxuriant, sumptuous 10 flamboyant

ornery 5 balky, cross, testy 6 crabby, cranky, crusty, grumpy 7 bearish, froward, grouchy 8 contrary, perverse, stubborn, vinegary 9 crotchety, difficult, irascible, irritable 10 inflexible, vinegarish 12 cantankerous

ornithic 5 avian 8 birdlike

ornithologist *American:* 4 Bond (James) 7 Audubon (John James), Bartram (William) 8 Peterson (Roger Tory) *English:* 5 Gould (John) *Scottish:* 6 Wilson (Alexander)

orotund 4 full, loud 5 round 7 flowery, fustian, pompous, ringing 8 resonant, sonorous 9 bombastic, high-flown, overblown 10 euphuistic, oratorical, resounding, rhetorical, stentorian 11 declamatory 12 magniloquent 13 grandiloquent

Orpah *husband:* 7 Chilion *sister-in-law:* 4 Ruth

orphan 4 waif 5 Annie, gamin, stray 6 bereft, gamine, urchin 7 cast-off, ignored 8 forsaken, homeless 9 abandoned, foundling, neglected 10 motherless, parentless

Orpheus *father:* 6 Apollo 7 Oeagrus *home:* 6 Thrace *instrument:* 4 lyre *mother:* 8 Calliope *wife:* 8 Euridice

orphic 6 arcane, mystic, occult 7 cryptic,

Delphic, obscure 8 abstruse, Delphian, esoteric, hermetic, mystical, oracular, profound
9 enigmatic, recondite
ort 3 bit 4 bite 5 crumb, piece, scrap 6 morsel
7 remnant 8 leftover
orthodox 6 proper 8 accepted, approved, official, received, standard 9 canonical, customary 10 conformist, recognized,
sanctioned 11 established, traditional 12 acknowledged, conservative, conventional 13
authoritative
orthography 7 writing 8 spelling
ortolan 7 bunting
Orwell novel 10 Animal Farm 18 Nineteen
Eighty-four
oryx 7 gemsbok 8 antelope
os 3 ora (plural) 4 bone, ossa (plural) 5
mouth 7 orifice
Osborne play 6 Luther 11 Entertainer (The)
15 Look Back in Anger
oscillate 3 wag 4 sway, vary 5 swing, waver
6 change, seesaw 7 vibrate 9 alternate, fluctuate
oscillation 4 sway 5 swing 9 variation, vibration 10 undulation 11 fluctuation, periodic-
ity
osculate 3 lip 4 buss, kiss, peck 5 smack 6
smooch
osculation 4 buss, kiss, peck 6 smooch 7 lip-
lock
osier 3 rod 6 willow 7 dogwood
Osiris brother: 3 Set 4 Seth father: 3 Geb,
Keb, Seb mother: 3 Nut scribe: 5 Thoth
sister: 4 Isis slayer: 3 Set 4 Seth son: 5
Horus 6 Anubis wife: 4 Isis
osmium symbol 2 Os
osmosis 4 flow 8 transfer 9 diffusion 10 absorption 12 assimilation 13 incorporation
osprey 4 hawk 8 fish hawk
osseous 4 bony 8 bonelike
ossicle 4 bone 5 incus 6 stapes 7 malleus
ossify 3 set 6 harden 7 stiffen 8 solidify 9
fossilize
osso ____ 4 buco
ossuary 4 tomb 5 vault 8 boneyard, cemetery
9 sepulcher, sepulchre
ostensible 6 stated 7 alleged, seeming 8 apparent, asserted, illusive, illusory, so-called,
supposed 9 pretended, professed, purported, semblable 11 superficial
ostentation 4 pomp, show 5 flash, swank 7
display 9 pomposity, showiness, vainglory
10 flashiness, pretension 11 flamboyance
ostentatious 4 loud 5 gaudy, showy, swank 6
flashy, garish, swanky 7 pompous, splashy
8 overdone, peacocky 10 flamboyant, peacockish 11 pretentious 12 vainglorious

ostiole 4 pore 7 orifice 8 aperture
ostracism 5 exile 7 removal 9 exclusion 10
banishment, relegation 11 deportation
ostracize 3 bar, cut 4 shun, snub 5 exile 6
banish, deport 7 exclude, keep out, shut out
8 throw out 9 blackball 10 expatriate 12
cold-shoulder
ostrich 4 rhea 6 ratite
Ostrogoth king 9 Theodoric
Oswego tea 7 bee balm
otalgia 7 earache
Otello composer 5 Verdi (Giuseppe) 7
Rossini (Gioacchino)
O tempora! O ____! 5 mores
Othello ancient / ensign: 4 Iago author: 11
Shakespeare (William) lieutenant: 6 Cassio
maid: 6 Emilia victim, wife: 9 Desdemona
others 4 rest 9 remainder and: 4 et al 6 et
alia, et alii 7 et aliae
other than 3 but 4 save 6 except 7 besides 9
apart from, aside from, except for, excepting, excluding
otherwise 3 not 4 else 5 if not 6 or else 7
changed 9 different 11 differently 12 anything else 13 alternatively
otic 5 aural 8 auditory 9 auricular
otiose 4 idle, vain 5 empty 6 futile, hollow 7
surplus, useless 8 nugatory 9 fruitless,
pointless, worthless 11 ineffective, purposeless, superfluous 12 functionless 13 supernumerary
Ottawa chief 7 Pontiac
ottoman 4 seat 5 couch 6 fabric 9 footstool
Ottoman 4 Turk 7 Turkish council: 5 divan
governor: 3 bey official: 3 aga, dey 6 vizier
ruler: 3 bey 5 Osman, Selim 8 Suleiman,
Süleyman
Otus 5 giant brother: 9 Ephialtes father: 6
Aloeus 8 Poseidon mother: 9 Iphimedia
slayer: 6 Apollo
ouch 5 bezel, jewel 6 brooch, buckle 7 setting 8 ornament 11 exclamation
ounce 3 bit, cat 4 dram 5 pinch, scrap, shred
6 amount, splash, weight 7 measure, modicum, smidgen 8 fraction, particle 11 snow
leopard
our French: 5 notre Italian: 6 nostra Spanish:
7 nuestro
Our Town author 6 Wilder (Thornton)
oust 4 fire, sack 5 eject, evict, expel 6 banish,
deport, remove, topple, unseat 7 boot out,
cast out, deprive, dismiss, kick out 8 displace, drive out, force out, relegate, supplant, take away, throw out 10 dispossess
ouster 7 removal 8 ejection, eviction 9 discharge, dismissal, expulsion 10 banishment
out 4 away, exit 5 forth, loose 6 absent, ex-

cuse *of control:* 4 amok, wild 5 amuck 7 chaotic *of gas:* 5 tired 7 drained 9 exhausted *of line:* 4 awry, rude 5 askew, fresh *of place:* 13 inappropriate *of sorts:* 5 cross 7 grouchy, peevish 9 irritable *of the ordinary:* 3 odd 7 bizarre, strange, unusual

outage 4 loss 5 break 7 failure 8 blackout 12 interruption

out-and-out 5 gross, sheer, total, utter 7 perfect 8 absolute, complete, positive 9 downright 10 consummate 11 unmitigated, unqualified 13 thoroughgoing

outback 4 bush 6 sticks 7 boonies 9 boondocks 10 hinterland, wilderness

Outback call 5 cooee

outboard 4 boat 5 motor 6 engine

outbreak 4 rash, rise, rush 5 burst, flare, spike, surge 6 attack, blowup, plague, revolt 7 flare-up 8 epidemic, eruption, increase, uprising 9 rebellion 12 insurrection

outbuilding 4 barn, shed

outburst 3 fit 4 gush, gust 5 flare, sally, scene, spasm, storm, surge 6 frenzy, tirade 7 flare-up, tantrum, torrent 8 eruption, paroxysm, upheaval 9 explosion

outcast 4 hobo 5 exile, leper, tramp 6 pariah 7 Ishmael, vagrant 8 castaway, derelict, vagabond 9 reprobate 10 expatriate, Ishmaelite 11 offscouring, untouchable

outclass 3 top 4 best 5 excel 6 exceed 7 surpass

outcome 3 end 5 event, fruit, issue 6 effect, result, sequel, upshot 9 aftermath 10 conclusion 11 aftereffect, consequence, development

outcrop 4 rock 5 ledge 6 appear 7 project 8 protrude 10 projection, protrusion 12 protuberance

outcry 3 hue 4 yell 5 noise, shout 6 clamor, tumult, uproar 7 auction, ferment, protest 8 upheaval 9 commotion, objection 11 exclamation

outdated 3 old 5 passé 6 bygone, démodé, old hat 7 antique, archaic, vintage 10 antiquated, old-fangled 12 old-fashioned

outdistance 3 top 4 beat, best, pass 5 excel, trump 6 better, exceed 7 eclipse, surpass

outdo 3 top 4 beat, best, pass 5 excel, trump 6 better, defeat, exceed 7 eclipse, surpass, triumph 8 overcome 9 transcend

outdoor 7 open-air 8 alfresco

outer 6 remote 7 surface 8 exoteric, exterior, external 9 extrinsic 10 extraneous 11 superficial

outermost 4 last 5 final 6 far-off 7 distant, extreme 8 farthest, furthest, remotest

outfit 3 kit, rig, set 4 band, firm, gear, suit, team, togs, unit 5 corps, dress, equip, getup, group, squad, troop 6 clothe, supply, tackle, troupe 7 appoint, company, concern, costume, furnish 8 accouter, accoutre, business, clothing, ensemble, matériel, tackling 9 equipment, provision 10 enterprise 12 organization 13 accouterments, accoutrements, establishment

outflank 5 evade 6 bypass 9 get around 10 circumvent

outflow 6 efflux 8 drainage, effluent 9 effluence

out-front 4 open 5 frank 6 candid, honest 10 forthright

outgoing 4 open 7 affable 8 friendly, sociable 9 departing, expansive 10 gregarious, responsive 11 extroverted

outgrowth 6 effect, result 7 product, spin-off 8 offshoot 9 by-product, offspring 10 derivative 11 aftereffect, consequence

outhouse 5 jakes, privy 7 latrine

outing 4 spin, trip 5 drive, jaunt, sally 6 junket, picnic 9 excursion 10 appearance, disclosure

outlandish 3 odd 4 wild 5 alien, outré, ultra, weird 6 exotic 7 bizarre, curious, extreme, foreign, offbeat, strange, uncouth, unusual 8 peculiar, singular 9 eccentric, fantastic, tasteless 10 ridiculous, unorthodox 11 extravagant

outlast 6 endure 7 survive, weather 9 withstand

outlaw 3 ban, con 4 wild 5 crook 6 bandit, banned, enjoin, forbid 7 exclude, illegal 8 criminal, disallow, fugitive, prohibit, renegade, restrict 9 desperado, interdict, proscribe 10 illegalize, rebellious

outlay 3 pay, tab 4 cost, give 5 spend 6 amount, expend 7 expense, payment 8 disburse 11 expenditure 12 disbursement

outlet 4 exit, hole, mart, shop, vent 5 issue, store 6 avenue, egress, escape, market 7 channel, opening, passage, release 8 aperture 10 discounter, receptacle

outline 4 edge, form, limn, plan 5 brief, draft, shape, trace 6 bounds, border, précis, schema, sketch 7 contour, profile, summary 8 abstract, boundary, skeleton, syllabus, synopsis 9 delineate, summarize 10 figuration, silhouette 11 skeletonize

outlive 7 survive, weather

outlook 4 side, view 5 angle, scope, sight, slant, vista 6 aspect, future 7 promise 8 attitude, forecast, position, prospect 9 direction, viewpoint 10 standpoint 11 expectation, observatory, perspective, point of view

outlying 3 far 6 far-off, remote 7 distant, far-away, removed 8 far-flung

outmoded 4 dead 5 dated, passé, tired 6 old hat 7 antique, archaic 8 obsolete 9 moth-eaten, unstylish 10 oldfangled 11 obsolescent 12 old-fashioned

Out of Africa author 7 Dinesen (Isak)

out-of-date 3 old 4 past 5 passé, stale 6 démodé, old hat, square 7 antique, archaic, old-time, vintage 8 obsolete 9 unstylish 10 antiquated, oldfangled 12 old-fashioned

out of it 4 lost 5 dazed, spacy 6 addled, spacey 7 muddled 8 confused, demented 10 bewildered

out-of-the-way 4 rare 6 remote 7 distant, obscure, removed, unusual 8 secluded, uncommon

outpost 4 base 6 branch, colony 7 station 8 foothold 10 detachment, settlement

outpouring 4 flow, gush, rush 5 burst, flood, spate, spurt 6 deluge, stream 7 torrent 8 effusion

output 4 crop, gain, take 5 power, yield 6 amount, profit 7 harvest, produce, product 10 production 11 achievement, information

outrage 4 fury, rape 5 abuse, shock, wrong 6 injury, insult, offend 7 affront, incense, violate 8 aggrieve, atrocity, ill-treat, mischief, violence 9 brutality, infuriate 10 resentment, scandalize

outrageous 5 awful, gross 6 horrid, insane, odious, unholy, wicked 7 beastly, ghastly, heinous, ignoble, obscene 8 dreadful, flagrant, horrible, indecent, shocking, terrible 9 atrocious, egregious, excessive, fantastic 10 abominable, inordinate, scandalous 11 intolerable

outré 3 odd 5 ultra 6 far-out 7 bizarre, extreme, offbeat, strange 8 peculiar 9 eccentric 10 off-the-wall

outrigger 4 boat, beam, prau, proa, spar

outright 4 pure 5 total, utter, whole 6 entire 7 perfect 8 absolute, complete, entirely, positive 9 on the spot 10 completely, consummate 11 unequivocal, unmitigated, unqualified 13 thoroughgoing

outrun 3 top 4 beat, pass 6 exceed 7 surpass

outset 4 dawn 5 birth, get-go, start 7 opening 9 beginning, inception 12 commencement

outshine 3 top 4 beat, best 5 excel 6 better, exceed 7 eclipse, surpass

outside 5 alien 7 foreign, open-air 8 alfresco, exterior, external *combining form:* 3 ect, exo 5 extra

outsider 5 alien 7 inconnu 8 newcomer, stranger 9 foreigner

outsmart see **outwit**

outspoken 4 free, open 5 blunt, frank, plain, vocal 6 candid, direct, honest 7 up front 8 explicit 10 forthright, point-blank, unreserved 11 unequivocal

outstanding 3 due 4 A-one, star 5 boffo, noted, owing, socko 6 signal, superb, tiptop, unpaid 7 capital, eminent, notable, salient, stellar 8 dominant, striking, superior, top-notch 9 arresting, excellent, first-rate, prominent, unsettled 10 noticeable, preeminent, remarkable, unresolved 11 conspicuous, distinctive, exceptional, magnificent, superlative, uncollected 13 extraordinary

outstrip 3 top 4 beat, best, pass 5 excel 6 better, exceed 7 surpass 8 distance, go beyond, overtake 9 transcend 11 leave behind

outward 5 overt 7 evident, visible 8 apparent, exterior, external 10 noticeable, ostensible 11 superficial

outweigh 6 exceed 8 overbear 10 overshadow 11 overbalance 12 preponderate

outworn see **outmoded**

ouzel 6 dipper, thrush 9 blackbird

oval 5 track 6 oblong 7 ellipse 8 elliptic 9 egg-shaped, racetrack 10 elliptical 11 ellipsoidal

ovation 5 kudos 6 homage, praise 7 acclaim, tribute 8 applause, approval, cheering, clapping, plaudits 11 acclamation

oven 4 kiln, oast 5 range, stove

over 4 anew, atop, done, past, upon 5 above, again, aloft, ended 6 across, beyond 8 done with, finished, once more *French:* 3 sur *German:* 4 über *prefix:* 3 epi, sur 5 extra, hyper, super, supra *Spanish:* 5 sobre

overabundance 4 glut 6 excess 7 surfeit, surplus 8 plethora 10 surplusage 11 superfluity

overact 3 ham, mug 4 rant 5 emote 10 exaggerate

overage 6 excess 7 surplus

overall 5 smock, total 6 global, mainly, mostly 7 chiefly, general, largely 8 as a whole, sweeping 9 generally, inclusive, in general, primarily 10 far and wide 11 principally 13 comprehensive, predominantly

overalls 5 pants 8 trousers

over and above 4 also 6 as well, beyond 7 besides 8 as well as 10 in addition

over and over 3 oft 5 often 8 ofttimes 10 frequently, oftentimes, repeatedly 11 continually, recurrently

overbearing 5 bossy 6 lordly 7 haughty, pompous 8 absolute, arrogant, despotic, dominant, imperial, insolent, scornful, superior 9 imperious, tyrannous 10 autocratic, disdainful, dominating, high-handed, oppressive, peremptory, tyrannical 11 dictatorial, domineering, magisterial **12** supercilious **13** high-and-mighty

overblown 6 turgid **7** flowery, hyped up, orotund, pompous **8** inflated **9** bombastic, excessive, high-flown **10** euphuistic, oratorical, rhetorical **11** declamatory, exaggerated, pretentious **12** magniloquent **13** grandiloquent

overcast 3 sew **4** dull, gray, hazy **5** cloud, cover **6** cloudy, darken, shadow **7** becloud, blanket, clouded, obscure **8** covering, lowering **9** adumbrate

overcharge 3 pad **4** bilk, clip, rook, skin, soak **5** cheat, stick **6** fleece **7** inflate

overcoat 5 paint **6** capote, raglan, ulster **7** surtout **9** balmacaan, outerwear **12** chesterfield

overcome 4 beat, best, lick **5** drown, throw **6** defeat, hurdle, master **7** conquer, prevail, triumph **8** surmount **9** prostrate

overconfident 4 rash **5** brash, cocky, pushy **8** arrogant, cocksure, reckless **9** hubristic, presuming **12** presumptuous

overdo 7 exhaust, fatigue, wear out **9** embellish **10** exaggerate

overdue 4 late **5** owing, tardy **6** behind, unpaid **7** belated, delayed, payable **8** dilatory **9** unsettled **10** behindhand, delinquent, unpunctual **11** outstanding

overemphasize 7 magnify **8** heighten **9** dramatize, embellish **10** exaggerate

overflow 4 pour **5** cover, drown, flood, slosh, spate, spill, swamp **6** deluge, engulf, excess, outlet **7** surfeit, surplus, torrent **8** flooding, inundate, spillage, submerge **10** inundation, surplusage **11** superfluity

overgrown 4 lush **5** dense, thick **6** brushy **7** hulking **8** ungainly **9** excessive, ponderous **10** junglelike

overhang 3 jut **4** loom **5** bulge **6** beetle, extend, impend **7** project **8** protrude, stick out, threaten **10** projection

overhaul 3 fix **4** mend, redo **5** patch, renew **6** doctor, remake, repair, revamp, revise **7** rebuild, restore **8** renovate **11** recondition, reconstruct

overhead 4 atop **5** above, aloft, smash **7** ceiling, expense **8** expenses

overheated 5 fiery **7** fervent **8** inflated **9** perfervid **11** impassioned

overindulgence 6 excess **7** surfeit **8** gluttony **11** dissipation **12** immoderation, intemperance

overjoyed 6 elated **7** gleeful **8** blissful, ecstatic, euphoric, exultant, jubilant, thrilled **9** rapturous **11** transported

overkill 4 glut **6** excess **7** surfeit, surplus, too much **8** plethora **10** obliterate, redundancy, surplusage **11** superfluity

overlap 7 shingle **9** imbricate

overlay 3 cap **4** coat **5** cover, glaze **6** finish, veneer **7** blanket, coating, lacquer, varnish **8** covering **11** superimpose **12** transparency

overload 4 glut **5** stuff **6** burden, excess, pile on, strain **7** surfeit

overlook 4 fail, miss, omit, skip **5** check, let go **6** excuse, forget, ignore, pass by, slight, slip up, survey, wink at **7** blink at, condone, forgive, inspect, let pass, neglect **8** discount, dominate, surmount **9** disregard, supervise **11** superintend

overlord 4 czar, tsar, tzar **5** chief, mogul, ruler **6** tycoon **7** magnate **8** suzerain **9** potentate, sovereign

overly 3 too **6** too-too, unduly **11** exceedingly, excessively **12** immoderately, inordinately

overpass 5 cross **6** bridge **8** crossing, traverse **9** traversal **11** interchange

overplay 4 hype **6** expand **7** enlarge, inflate, magnify, point up, stretch **8** maximize **9** dramatize **10** exaggerate **11** hyperbolize

overpower 4 rout **5** crush, swamp, whelm **6** defeat, master, subdue **7** conquer **8** vanquish **9** prostrate, subjugate **11** steamroller

overreach 3 con **4** beat, bilk **5** cheat, outdo **6** defeat, outfox, outwit **7** defraud **8** flimflam, outsmart **10** exaggerate **11** outmaneuver

override 4 veto **5** annul **6** cancel **7** nullify **10** counteract, neutralize

overriding 3 key **4** main **5** chief, major, prime, vital **7** central, crucial, pivotal, primary, supreme **8** cardinal, dominant, foremost **9** paramount, principal

overrule 4 undo, veto **5** upset **6** negate, revoke **7** reverse **8** set aside **11** countermand

overrun 4 beat, raid, teem, whip **5** swamp, swarm **6** defeat, excess, infest, invade, occupy, ravage, spread, thrash **7** clobber, conquer

overseas 6 abroad **11** transmarine, ultramarine **12** transoceanic, transpacific **13** transatlantic

oversee 3 run **4** boss, tend **5** watch **6** direct, manage, survey **7** command, examine, inspect **9** supervise **11** superintend

overseer 4 boss, exec, head **5** chief **7** foreman, manager **8** director **9** executive **10** supervisor **13** administrator

overshadow 4 veil **5** cloud, dwarf, shade **6** darken, exceed **7** becloud, eclipse, obscure, surpass **8** dominate, outshine, outweigh **9** adumbrate

overshoe 4 boot 6 arctic, galosh, patten, rubber

oversight 4 care, slip 5 aegis, check, error, lapse 6 charge, slip-up 7 control, failure, mistake, neglect 8 omission 10 intendance, management 11 supervision

overspread 3 cap 5 beset, cover, flood, swarm 6 infest, invade 7 blanket, obscure, pervade 8 permeate

overstate 3 pad 7 amplify, enlarge, magnify 9 embellish, embroider 10 exaggerate

overstep 6 exceed, offend 7 surpass, violate 8 infringe, trespass 10 transgress

overstock 4 glut 5 extra 6 excess 7 surplus 9 remainder 10 surplusage

overstress 7 magnify 8 maximize 10 exaggerate

overt 4 open 5 clear 6 patent 7 evident, obvious, outward, visible 8 apparent, manifest 10 observable

overtake 4 pass 5 catch 6 pass by 7 outpace, surpass 8 come upon, outstrip 11 outdistance

Over the Rainbow *composer:* 5 Arlen (Harold) *lyricist:* 7 Harburg (E. Y.) *movie:* 10 Wizard of Oz (The) *singer:* 7 Garland (Judy)

over there 3 yon 6 yonder

over-the-top 5 outré 7 extreme 8 reckless 9 egregious, excessive 10 exorbitant, flamboyant, outrageous 11 extravagant

overthrow 4 fell, oust, rout 5 evert, purge, upset 6 defeat, depose, remove, topple, unseat 7 conquer 8 dethrone, downfall 9 bring down

overtone 4 hint 5 sense 8 coloring, harmonic 9 inference 10 suggestion 11 association, connotation, implication 12 undercurrent

overture 3 bid 5 proem 7 advance, preface, prelude, present 8 approach, foreword, preamble, prologue, proposal 9 prelusion 10 initiative 11 proposition 12 introduction, presentation

overturn 3 tip 4 flip, void 5 upend, upset 6 topple, tumble 7 capsize, nullify, reverse 8 set aside 10 invalidate

overused 5 banal, musty, stale, tired, trite 7 clichéd, worn-out 9 hackneyed 10 threadbare

overview 6 aperçu, précis, survey 7 epitome, summary 10 conspectus

overweening 5 brash, pushy 6 lordly, uppish, uppity 7 forward 8 arrogant 9 conceited, presuming 10 immoderate 11 exaggerated 12 presumptuous

overweight 3 fat 5 beefy, burly, dumpy, gross, heavy, husky, obese, plump, pudgy, stout 6 chubby, chunky, flabby, fleshy, portly, rotund 7 outsize 8 heavyset, thickset 9 corpulent

overwhelm 4 beat, bury, rout, ruin, sink, whip 5 crush, drown, flood, swamp, upset, wreck 6 boggle, defeat, deluge, engulf, thrash 7 conquer, destroy, oppress, shatter, shellac, smother 8 inundate, submerge 9 devastate, prostrate 10 demoralize 11 steamroller, subordinate

overwhelmed 6 aghast 7 shocked, stunned, touched 8 defeated, helpless 10 distressed 13 thunderstruck

overwhelming 4 huge 5 great 7 extreme 8 numerous

overwrought 5 hyper, upset 7 anxious, frantic, wound up 8 agitated, frenetic, stressed, troubled 9 disturbed, emotional 10 distracted, freaked out, high-strung, hysterical 11 discomposed

Ovid work 5 Fasti 6 Amores 7 Tristia 8 Heroides 13 Metamorphoses

ovine 5 sheep 9 sheeplike

ovoid 9 egg-shaped

ovule 3 egg *fertilized:* 4 seed

ovum 3 egg 6 gamete 7 egg cell 11 macrogamete

owing 3 due 6 in debt, mature, unpaid 7 overdue, payable 9 unsettled 11 outstanding

owing to 4 over 7 through 9 because of 10 by reason of 11 on account of

owl *cry:* 4 hoot *genus:* 4 Bubo, Otus *kind:* 3 elf 4 barn, gray, lulu 5 eagle, gnome, madge, pygmy, snowy 6 barred, horned 7 saw-whet, screech 9 long-eared 10 short-eared 11 great horned

Owl and the Pussycat author 4 Lear (Edward)

own 4 avow, have, hold 5 admit, allow, enjoy, grant, let on 6 accept, fess up, retain 7 concede, confess, possess 8 disclose 9 recognize 11 acknowledge

owner 6 holder 8 landlady, landlord 9 possessor, purchaser 10 proprietor

ownership 4 hand 5 title 8 dominion, property 10 possession 11 proprietary *perpetual:* 8 mortmain

ox 3 yak 4 anoa, gaur, musk, zebu 5 bison, steer 6 bovine 7 banteng, buffalo *Asian:* 4 zebu *attachment:* 4 yoke *extinct:* 4 urus 7 aurochs *family:* 7 Bovidae *relating to:* 6 bovine *wild:* 4 anoa, gaur 7 banteng

oxeye 5 daisy 6 flower

oxford 4 shoe 5 cloth, sheep 6 cotton, fabric

oxide *calcium:* 4 lime 9 quicklime *ferric:* 4 rust *sodium:* 4 soda

oxidize 4 rust

oxygen 3 air, gas 5 ozone 7 element *discov-*

erer: 9 Lavoisier (Antoine) *form:* 5 ozone *liquid:* 3 lox

oyster 7 bivalve, mollusc, mollusk *bed:* 4 park 6 claire, cultch *eggs:* 5 spawn *genus:* 6 Ostrea *lining:* 5 nacre *Long Island:* 9 bluepoint *product:* 5 pearl *shell:* 4 test 5 shuck *young:* 4 spat

oyster plant 7 salsify

Oz 9 Australia, Down Under *creator:* 4 Baum (L. Frank) *inhabitant:* 8 Munchkin *princess:* 4 Ozma

Ozark State 8 Missouri

Ozem *brother:* 5 David *father:* 5 Jesse 9 Jerahmeel

Ozymandias author 7 Shelley (Percy Bysshe)

P

pabulum 3 pap 4 food 7 aliment 8 nutrient 9 blandness, nutriment 10 insipidity, sustenance 11 nourishment

paca 4 cavy

pace 3 set 4 beat, clip, gait, lead, rate, step, time, walk 5 speed, tempo, tread, troop 6 motion, stride, timing 7 example, fluency, measure, precede, proceed, routine, step off 8 ambulate, antecede, movement, progress, regulate

pachyderm 8 elephant

pacific 4 calm, mild 6 gentle, irenic, placid, serene 8 dovelike, peaceful, soothing, tranquil 9 peaceable, temperate 12 conciliatory

Pacific *island:* 3 Yap 4 Wake 6 Easter, Jarvis, Saipan, Tahiti, Tarawa 7 Iwo Jima, Tokelau 8 Pitcairn, St. Helena 11 Guadalcanal *nation:* 4 Fiji 5 Belau, Japan, Nauru, Palau, Tonga 6 Tuvalu 7 Vanuatu 8 Kiribati

Pacificator, Great 4 Clay (Henry)

Pacific Ocean discoverer 6 Balboa (Vasco Núñez de)

pacifist 4 dove 6 irenic 8 appeaser, peaceful, peacenik 9 peaceable 10 nonviolent 11 peacemonger

pacify 4 calm, cool, ease, lull 5 allay, quell, quiet, still 6 disarm, settle, soften, soothe, subdue, temper 7 appease, assuage, mollify, placate 9 subjugate 10 conciliate, propitiate

pack 3 jam, kit, lot, lug, ram, set, wad 4 band, bear, cram, deck, fill, gang, heap, load, lump, mass, pile, stow, tamp, tote, unit 5 bunch, carry, cover, crowd, ferry, group, store, stuff, troop 6 bundle, charge, clique, convey, depart, gather 7 possess 8 assemble, compress, knapsack 9 container, equipment, influence, transport 10 collection, congregate

package 3 box 4 bale, deal, unit, wrap 5 array, combo, whole 6 bundle, parcel 7 enclose, present, wrapper 8 shipment 9 container 10 collection 11 combination

pack animal 3 ass 4 mule 5 burro, camel, horse, llama 6 donkey 7 jackass 13 beast of burden

packed 4 full 5 awash, dense, flush 6 filled, jammed 7 brimful, crowded, stuffed 8 brimming 9 chock-full 10 compressed

packet 3 wad 4 boat, mass, pile 5 group 6 bundle, parcel 7 cluster

pact 4 bond, deal 6 accord, treaty 7 bargain, concord 8 alliance, contract, covenant 9 agreement

pad 3 bed, mat, wad 4 foot, mute 5 fudge, guard, paper, stuff 6 buffer, expand, muffle, shield, tablet 7 augment, bolster, cushion, stretch 8 dressing, increase 9 embellish, embroider, overstate 10 exaggerate, overcharge

paddle 3 oar, row 4 beat, stir 5 spank 6 propel, thrash

paddock 5 field 7 pasture 9 enclosure

paddy wagon 10 Black Maria

padre 3 Fra 6 father, priest 8 chaplain, minister 9 clergyman, confessor

paean 4 hymn, song 6 anthem, eulogy, praise 7 tribute 8 accolade, encomium 9 panegyric

page 4 book, call, leaf 5 folio, sheet 6 locate, summon 7 bellhop, equerry *left-hand:* 5 verso *right-hand:* 5 recto

pageant 4 sham, show 7 charade, display, tableau 8 pretense 9 spectacle 10 exhibition

pageantry 4 pomp, show 7 display, panoply 8 flourish, splendor 9 spectacle 10 exhibition 11 flamboyance, ostentation 12 magnificence

Pagliacci, I *character:* 5 Canio, Nedda, Tonio

6 Silvio *composer:* **11** Leoncavallo (Ruggero)

pagoda 2 ta **6** temple

pail 3 hod **6** bucket, piggin, vessel **7** scuttle

pain 3 irk **4** ache, care, hurt, pang **5** agony, cramp, grief, throe, upset **6** grieve, harass, stitch, twinge **7** afflict, anguish, torture, travail, trouble **8** aggrieve, distress **9** suffering **10** affliction, discomfort *back:* **7** lumbago *muscular:* **7** myalgia

painful 3 raw **4** hard, sore **5** acute, sharp **6** aching, trying **7** arduous, irksome **8** annoying, piercing, stinging **9** agonizing, difficult, laborious, torturous, upsetting, vexatious **10** afflictive, tormenting

painkiller 4 drug **6** opiate **7** anodyne, codeine **8** morphine, narcotic **9** analgesic **10** anesthetic

painstaking 5 exact **7** careful, heedful **8** diligent, exacting, thorough **9** assiduous, diligence, laborious **10** meticulous, scrupulous **11** punctilious

paint 4 coat, daub, limn, swab, tint **5** adorn, brush, color, cover, horse, pinto, rouge, stain **6** depict, makeup **7** coating, pigment, portray, produce, touch up **8** cosmetic, decorate **9** delineate, represent **10** maquillage

painter 6 artist *American:* **4** Cole (Thomas), Haas (Richard), West (Benjamin), Wood (Grant) **5** Abbey (Edwin Austin), Davis (Stuart), Gorky (Arshile), Grosz (George), Henri (Robert), Hicks (Edward), Homer (Winslow), Johns (Jasper), Kline (Franz), Kroll (Leon), Marin (John), Marsh (Reginald), Moses (Grandma), Peale (Anna, Charles Willson, James, Raphaelle, Rembrandt, Sarah, Titian), Ryder (Albert Pinkham), Shahn (Ben), Sloan (Eric, John), Weber (Max), Wyeth (Andrew, Jamie, Newell Convers) **6** Albers (Josef), Benton (Thomas Hart), Catlin (George), Church (Frederick Edwin), Coburn (Alvin Langdon), Copley (John Singleton), Durand (Asher), Eakins (Thomas), Hassam (Childe), Hopper (Edward), Inness (George), Leutze (Emanuel), Martin (Agnes, Homer), Newman (Barnett), Rivers (Larry), Rothko (Mark), Stella (Frank), Stuart (Gilbert), Tanguy (Yves), Thorpe (Thomas), Warhol (Andy) **7** Allston (Washington), Bearden (Romare), Bellows (George), Bingham (George Caleb), Cassatt (Mary), Duchamp (Marcel), Harnett (William), Hartley (Marsden), Kinkade (Thomas), La Farge (John), O'Keeffe (Georgia), Parrish (Maxfield), Pollock (Jackson), Sargent (John Singer), Sheeler

(Charles), Tiffany (Louis Comfort), Tworkov (Jack), Wiggins (Carleton) **8** Basquiat (Jean-Michel), Melchers (Gari), Rockwell (Norman), Sullivan (Patrick), Trumbull (John), Whistler (James McNeill) **9** Bierstadt (Albert), de Kooning (Willem), Feininger (Lyonel), Reinhardt (Ad), Remington (Frederic), Twachtman (John Henry), Vanderlyn (John), Walkowitz (Abraham) **10** Motherwell (Robert), Whittredge (Thomas) **12** Lichtenstein (Roy), Rauschenberg (Robert) *Austrian:* **5** Klimt (Gustav) **9** Kokoschka (Oskar) *Belgian:* **5** Ensor (James) **6** Campin (Robert) **8** Magritte (René) *Canadian:* **4** Kane (Paul) **6** Harris (Lawren), Watson (Homer) **7** Jackson (Alexander Young), Thomson (Tom) **9** MacDonald (James Edward Hervey) *Chinese:* **4** Wu Li **6** Ma Yüan **7** Wang Wei **8** Yen Li-pen *Dutch:* **3** Dou (Gerrit) **4** Hals (Frans), Lely (Peter), Maas (Nicolas) **5** Bosch (Hieronymus), Hooch (Pieter de), Steen (Jan) **6** Potter (Paul) **7** de Hooch (Pieter), de Witte (Emanuel), Hobbema (Meindert), van Gogh (Vincent), Vermeer (Jan) **8** Mondrian (Piet), Ruisdael (Jacob van, Salomon), Ruysdael (Salomon), Terborch (Gerard) **9** de Kooning (Willem), Rembrandt (van Rijn), Wouwerman (Philips) **11** Terbrugghen (Hendrik) *English:* **4** Hunt (William Holman), John (Augustus), Lear (Edward) **5** Bacon (Francis), Blake (William), Brown (Ford Madox), Lewis (Wyndham), Watts (George Frederick) **6** Fuseli (Henry), Romney (George), Stubbs (George), Turner (Joseph Mallord William), Wilson (Richard), Wright (Joseph) **7** Hockney (David), Hogarth (William), Kneller (Godfrey), Millais (John), van Dyke (Anthony) **8** Landseer (Edwin), Lawrence (Thomas), Reynolds (Joshua), Rossetti (Dante Gabriel) **9** Constable (John), Nicholson (Ben, William) **10** Alma-Tadema (Lawrence), Burne-Jones (Edward) **12** Gainsborough (Thomas) *Finnish:* **9** Järnefelt (Edvard) *Flemish:* **4** Eyck (Hubert van, Jan van), Goes (Hugo van der) **6** Rubens (Peter Paul), Weyden (Rogier van der) **7** Memling (Hams), Teniers (David), Van Dyck (Anthony), van Eyck (Hubert, Jan) **8** Breughel, Brueghel (Abraham, Ambrose, Jan, Pieter) *French:* **3** Arp (Hans) **4** Doré (Gustave), Dufy (Raoul), Erté, Gros (Antoine-Jean) **5** Corot (Camille), David (Jacques-Louis), Degas (Edgar), Léger (Fernand), Manet (Edouard), Monet (Claude), Redon (Odilon), Vouet (Simon) **6**

Braque (Georges), Breton (André), Claude (of Lorrain), Clouet (François, Jean), Gérôme (Jean-Léon), Greuze (Jean-Baptiste), Ingres (Jean-Auguste-Dominique), Le Brun (Charles), Le Nain (Antoine, Louis, Mathieu), Millet (Jean-François), Renoir (Pierre-Auguste), Seurat (Georges), Sisley (Alfred), Tanguy (Yves), Vernet (Carle, Horace, Joseph) **7** Balthus, Bonheur (Rosa), Bonnard (Pierre), Boucher (François), Cézanne (Paul), Chagall (Marc), Chardin (Jean-Baptiste), Courbet (Gustave), Daumier (Honoré), Duchamp (Gaston, Marcel), Gauguin (Paul), Matisse (Henri), Morisot (Berthe), Poussin (Nicolas), Rouault (Georges), Utrillo (Maurice), Watteau (Antoine) **8** Dubuffet (Jean), Magritte (René), Pissarro (Camille), Rousseau (Henri, Théodore), Vlaminck (Maurice de), Vuillard (Edouard) **9** Delacroix (Eugène), Fragonard (Jean-Honoré), Géricault (Théodore), Laurencin (Marie) **10** Bouguereau (William), Meissonier (Jean-Louis) **11** Caillebotte (Gustave) **13** Claude Lorrain *German:* **5** Dürer (Albrecht), Ernst (Max), Grosz (George), Nolde (Emil) **6** Albers (Josef), Müller (Friedrich "Maler") **7** Cranach (Lucas), Holbein (Hans), Lochner (Stefan), Richter (Gerhard), Schwind (Moritz von), Zoffany (Johann) **8** Kirchner (Ernst), Kollwitz (Käthe) **9** Grünewald (Matthias), Kandinsky (Wassily) **10** Schongauer (Martin), Wohlgemuth (Michael) *Greek:* **6** Zeuxis **7** Apelles **10** Polygnotus *Irish:* **5** Yeats (Jack, John Butler) *Italian:* **4** Reni (Guido), Rosa (Salvator), Tura (Cosme) **5** Campi (Antonio, Bernardino, Giulio, Vincenzo), Lippi (Fra Filippo, Filippino, Lorenzo), Piero (della Francesca, di Cosimo), Sarto (Andrea del) **6** Andrea (del Sarto), Cosimo (Agnolo di, Piero di), Giotto, Romano (Giulio), Sodoma (Il), Titian, Vasari (Giorgio) **7** Bellini (Gentile, Giovanni, Jacopo), Chirico (Giorgio De), Cimabue, da Vinci (Leonardo), Fiesole (Giovanni da), Martini (Simone), Orcagna, Peruzzi (Baldassare), Raphael, Tiepolo (Giovanni), Uccello (Paolo), Zuccari (Taddeo) **8** del Sarto (Andrea), Fabriano (Gentile da), Giordano (Luca), Leonardo (da Vinci), Mantegna (Andrea), Masaccio, Montagna (Bartolommeo), Perugino, Pontorno (Jacopo da), Severini (Gino), Veronese (Paolo), Vivarini (Alvise, Antonio, Bartolomeo) **9** Carpaccio (Vittore), Correggio, Francesca (Piero della) **10** Caravaggio, Modigliani (Amedeo), Signorelli (Luca),

Tintoretto, Verrocchio (Andrea del), Zuccarelli (Francesco) **11** Ghirlandaio (Domenico), Ghirlandajo (Domenico) **12** Michelangelo (Buonarotti), Parmigianino *Japanese:* **5** Korin **6** Sesshu *Lithuanian:* **7** Soutine (Chaim) *Mexican:* **6** Orozco (José Clemente), Rivera (Diego), Tamayo (Rufino) **9** Siqueiros (David Alfaro) *Norwegian:* **5** Munch (Edvard) *Russian:* **7** Chagall (Marc), Roerich (Nikolay) **9** Kandinsky (Wassily) *Scottish:* **6** Ramsay (Allan) **7** Nasmyth (Alexander), Raeburn (Henry) *Spanish:* **4** Dalí (Salvador), Goya (Francisco), Gris (Juan), Miró (Joan), Sert (José Maria) **6** Ribera (José), Rincón (Antonio del), Tapiés (Antonio) **7** El Greco, Herrera (Francisco de), Murillo (Bartolomé Esteban), Picasso (Pablo), Zuloaga (Ignacio) **8** Zurbarán (Francisco de) **9** Velázquez (Diego) *Swedish:* **4** Zorn (Anders) **6** Roslin (Alexander) *Swiss:* **4** Klee (Paul), Witz (Konrad) **6** Fuseli (Henry)

painting 3 oil **7** acrylic, picture **10** watercolor *circular:* **5** tondo *one-color:* **8** monotint **10** monochrome *plaster:* **5** secco **6** fresco *style:* **4** Dada **5** fauve **6** cubism, cubist, Gothic, pop art, rococo **7** baroque, Bauhaus, dadaism, fauvism, fauvist, realism, realist **8** Barbizon, futurism, futurist, romantic **9** Byzantine, geometric, mannerism, mannerist **10** classicism, classicist, surrealism, surrealist **11** romanticism **13** expressionism, expressionist, impressionism, impressionist *technique:* **3** oil **6** fresco, pastel **7** gouache, polymer, tempera **9** encaustic **10** watercolor *tool:* **5** brush, easel, knife, paint **6** canvas **7** palette *wall:* **5** mural

pair 3 duo, two **4** dyad, item, join, mate, span, team, twin, yoke **5** brace, match, twins, unite **6** couple **7** doublet, twosome **8** geminate

Pakistan *capital:* **9** Islamabad *city:* **6** Lahore, Multan **7** Karachi **9** Hyderabad **10** Faisalabad, Rawalpindi *language:* **4** Urdu *leader:* **6** Bhutto (Benazir) **9** Musharraf (Pervez) *monetary unit:* **5** rupee *mountain, range:* **8** Himalaya **9** Himalayan, Himalayas **11** Nanga Parbat *neighbor:* **4** Iran **5** China, India **11** Afghanistan *sea:* **7** Arabian

pal 3 bud **4** chum, mate, pard **5** amigo, buddy, crony **6** comate, friend **7** comrade, partner **9** companion

palace 5 court, manor, manse **6** castle **7** alcazar, château, mansion **8** seraglio

paladin 6 leader **8** advocate, champion, defender, official

Palamedes *brother:* **6** Sforza **8** Achilles *fa-*

ther: 8 Nauplius *slayer:* 7 Corinda, Ulysses 8 Odysseus

palatable 5 sapid, tasty 6 savory 8 pleasing, savorous, tasteful 9 agreeable, appealing, delicious, toothsome 10 acceptable, appetizing 12 satisfactory

palate 5 taste 6 liking 6 relish

palatial 4 rich 5 grand, large, noble, plush, regal 6 deluxe, ornate 7 opulent, stately 8 imposing, majestic, splendid 9 grandiose, luxuriant, luxurious, sumptuous 10 impressive 11 magnificent

Palau *capital:* 5 Koror *former name:* 5 Pelew *island:* 5 Koror 6 Angaur 7 Eli Malk 10 Babelthuap, Urukthapel *language:* 7 Palauan

palaver 3 gas, yak 4 blab, cant, chat, guff, talk 6 babble, cajole, hot air, jargon, parley, powwow, speech 7 chatter, prattle 8 colloquy, converse, dialogue 10 conference, discussion, rap session 12 conversation

pale 3 dim, wan 4 area, ashy, dull, fade, sick, weak 5 ashen, faded, faint, fence, field, light, livid, pasty, stake, waxen 6 anemic, blanch, chalky, doughy, feeble, pallid, picket, sallow, sickly, weaken, whiten 7 enclose, ghastly, insipid 8 blanched, district, encircle 9 bloodless, colorless, enclosure

palindrome 3 aha, bib, dad, dud, DVD, eke, ere, eve, ewe, eye, gag, gig, huh, mem, mom, mum, nun, pap, PCP, pep, pip, pop, pup, sis, SOS, tat, TNT, tot, tut, wow 4 deed, kook, ma'am, noon, peep, poop, toot 5 alula, civic, imami, kayak, Kazak, level, madam, minim, put-up, radar, refer, rotor, stats, Tebet, tenet, we few 6 pull-up, terret 7 deified, race car, reviver, top spot 9 Malayalam, never even 11 borrow or rob, drawn inward, Kinnikinnik, Madam I'm Adam

palinode 10 retraction 11 recantation

pall 4 bore, cloy, damp, jade, sate, tire 5 cloak, cloth, cloud, drape, ennui, gloom, weary 6 coffin, damper, mantle, shadow 7 dwindle, satiate, surfeit 8 covering

palladium 9 safeguard *symbol:* 2 Pd

Pallas 6 Athena *brother:* 6 Aegeus *father:* 7 Pandion *slayer:* 7 Theseus *wife:* 4 Styx (see also **Athena**)

palliate 4 ease, help 5 cover, salve 6 excuse, lessen, reduce, soften, soothe, temper 7 assuage, cover up, lighten 8 mitigate, moderate 9 alleviate, sugarcoat, whitewash 10 ameliorate

pallid 3 wan 4 ashy, dull, pale, weak 5 ashen, pasty, waxen 6 anemic, doughy, sickly 8 blanched, lifeless 9 bloodless, colorless

pallor 8 lividity, paleness 9 pastiness, whiteness 10 etiolation 12 glaucousness

pally 4 cozy 5 close, matey 6 chummy 7 devoted 8 familiar, friendly, intimate

palm 5 prize, steal, swipe 6 trophy 7 conceal, triumph, victory *beverage:* 4 nipa *fiber:* 4 bass, bast, coir 8 piassava *fruit:* 4 date 7 coconut 11 coquilla nut *kind:* 3 fan, wax 4 atap, coco, date, doom, hemp, nipa, sago 5 areca, betel, ivory, royal, sabal 6 miriti, raffia, rattan 7 cabbage, feather, palmyra 8 carnauba, palmetto, piassava 12 Washingtonia *leaf:* 4 olla 5 frond *lily:* 2 ti *starch:* 4 sago *vine:* 6 rattan

palmer 7 pilgrim

Palmetto State 13 South Carolina

palmistry 6 augury 8 prophecy 10 divination 11 soothsaying

palm off 5 foist 7 deceive, pretend 8 disguise

palmy 6 golden 7 booming, halcyon, opulent 8 affluent, thriving 10 prospering, prosperous 11 flourishing

Palmyra's queen 7 Zenobia

palooka 3 oaf 4 boob, dolt, goon, lout, lump 5 boxer, klutz 6 baboon, galoot, lummox 7 bruiser

palpable 4 real, sure 5 clear, plain 6 patent 7 certain, evident, obvious, tactile 8 apparent, concrete, definite, distinct, manifest, material, positive, tangible 10 noticeable 11 discernible, perceptible, unequivocal

palpate 4 feel 5 touch 6 finger 7 examine

palpitate 4 beat 5 pulse, throb 6 quiver 7 flutter, pulsate 12 pitter-patter

palsy-walsy 4 cozy 5 close, thick, tight 6 chummy 8 intimate 10 buddy-buddy

palter 3 fib, lie 5 evade 6 dicker, haggle 7 bargain, chaffer, deceive, falsify, wrangle 10 equivocate 11 prevaricate 12 misrepresent

paltry 3 low 4 base, mean, poor, puny, vile 5 cheap, petty, tatty 6 meager, measly, narrow, shabby, shoddy, sleazy, trashy 7 lowdown, pitiful, trivial 8 beggarly, inferior, picayune, piddling, rubbishy, trifling 9 worthless 10 despicable, picayunish 11 unimportant 12 contemptible 13 insignificant

paludal place 3 fen 5 marsh

Pamela author 10 Richardson (Samuel)

pampa 5 plain 7 prairie 9 grassland

pamper 3 pet 4 baby 5 humor, spoil 6 caress, cocker, coddle, cosset, cuddle, dandle, fondle 7 cater to, cherish, gratify, indulge 9 spoon-feed 11 mollycoddle

pamphlet 5 flier, flyer, tract 6 folder 7 leaflet 8 brochure, circular 9 throwaway 10 broadsheet

pan 3 pot, rap 4 slam, wash 5 basin, knock, roast, trash 6 attack, vessel 7 censure, condemn, skillet 8 denounce, ridicule 9 betel leaf, container, criticism, criticize 10 receptacle

Pan 5 Inuus 6 Faunus *father:* 6 Hermes *invention:* 6 syrinx *lower part:* 4 goat *mother:* 8 Penelope *pipe:* 6 syrinx *seat of worship:* 7 Arcadia *son:* 7 Silenus

panacea 4 cure 6 elixir, remedy 7 cure-all, nostrum 10 catholicon

Panacea's father 9 Asclepius 11 Aesculapius

panache 4 brio, dash, élan, tuft, zest 5 ardor, crest, flair, style, verve, vigor 6 esprit, polish, spirit 8 aigrette, flourish, vivacity 11 flamboyance

panama 3 hat

Panama *discoverer:* 6 Balboa (Vasco Núñez de) 8 Columbus (Christopher) *gulf:* 7 San Blas 8 Mosquito *language:* 7 Spanish *leader:* 7 Noriega (Manuel) *monetary unit:* 6 balboa *neighbor:* 8 Colombia 9 Costa Rica *peninsula:* 6 Azuero *sea:* 9 Caribbean *volcano:* 8 Chiriquí

pancake 8 flapjack, slapjack *chain:* 4 IHOP *French:* 5 crepe *Jewish:* 5 latke 6 blintz 7 blintze *Russian:* 4 blin 5 blini

Pandarus 6 archer 8 procuror *father:* 6 Lycaon *slayer:* 8 Diomedes

pandect 4 code, laws 8 treatise 10 compendium 11 compilation

pandemic 4 rife 7 general, rampant 9 contagion, extensive, prevalent 10 contagious, widespread 11 wide-ranging

pandemonium 3 din 5 babel, chaos, furor 6 bedlam, clamor, hubbub, tumult, uproar 7 anarchy, discord, inferno, misrule, turmoil 8 disorder 9 confusion 10 hullabaloo

pander 4 pimp 5 cater 9 exploiter, go-between

Pandion *daughter:* 6 Procne 9 Philomela *son:* 6 Pallas

Pandora *creator:* 10 Hephaestus *husband:* 10 Epimetheus

pane 4 side 5 sheet 7 section

panegyric 6 eulogy, praise 7 tribute 8 citation, encomium 9 laudation 10 compliment 12 commendation

panegyrical 8 praising 9 laudative, laudatory 10 eulogistic 11 encomiastic 12 commendatory 13 complimentary

panel 4 jury 5 board, frame 6 hurdle 7 console, section 9 dashboard

panfry 5 sauté

pang 4 ache, pain, stab 5 agony, prick, spasm, throe 6 stitch, twinge 7 anguish, torment 8 distress

Pangloss's pupil 7 Candide

panhandle 3 beg, bum, tap 5 cadge, hit up, touch 6 hustle 7 solicit

panhandler 6 beggar

panic 4 fear, riot, rush 5 alarm, scare 6 dismay, frenzy, fright, horror, terror 7 anxiety, terrify 8 frighten, hysteria, stampede

pannier 4 hoop, pack 6 basket, hamper 9 overskirt

panoply 4 pomp, show 5 armor, array 6 attire 7 display, fanfare 9 trappings

panorama 4 view 5 range, reach, scene, scope, sweep, vista 7 display, expanse, picture, purview 12 presentation

panoramic 8 sweeping, synoptic 12 all-inclusive, unobstructed 13 comprehensive

pan out 4 work 5 click, prove, score 7 come off, succeed

pant 4 blow, gasp, gulp, huff, puff 5 chuff, heave 6 wheeze

Pantagruel 5 giant *companion:* 7 Panurge *father:* 9 Gargantua *mother:* 7 Badebec

pantaloon 7 buffoon, trouser

Pantaloon's daughter 9 Columbine

pantheon 4 gods 5 Aesir 6 temple 9 hierarchy 10 hall of fame

panther 4 pard, puma 6 cougar, jaguar 7 leopard 12 mountain lion

pantomime 5 drama, mimic 6 act out, ballet, dancer 7 charade 12 harlequinade *clown:* 7 Pierrot

pantry 6 closet, larder 7 buttery 9 storeroom

pants 5 jeans 6 slacks 7 drawers, garment 8 breeches, britches, knickers, trousers

Panurge's companion 10 Pantagruel

Paolo's lover 9 Francesca

pap 4 food, mash, mush 7 aliment, pabulum 8 soft food 9 blandness, nutriment 10 sustenance 11 nourishment

papal 8 pontific 9 apostolic 10 pontifical *court:* 5 Curia *decree:* 8 decretal *envoy:* 6 nuncio *letter:* 4 bull 10 encyclical

paper 5 essay, sheet, theme 6 letter, report 7 article 8 document 9 monograph, newsprint 10 memorandum 11 composition, publication 12 dissertation *measure:* 4 ream 5 quire *roll:* 6 scroll *scrap:* 4 chad *size:* 3 cap 5 atlas, crown, folio, legal, royal, sexto, sixmo 6 octavo, quarto 7 emperor 8 elephant, foolscap, imperial *stiff:* 7 bristol 9 cardboard 12 bristol board *strong:* 5 kraft 6 manila *thin:* 6 tissue 9 onionskin *transparent:* 8 glassine *writing:* 3 rag 6 vellum 9 parchment

paper folding 7 origami

paperwork 7 red tape

papillon 7 spaniel 9 butterfly

Papua New Guinea *archipelago:* 8 Bismarck

capital: 11 Port Moresby **city:** 3 Lae **island:** 12 Bougainville **language:** 4 Motu 8 Tok Pisin **monetary unit:** 4 kina **neighbor:** 9 Indonesia, Irian Jaya

par 4 mean, norm 5 equal, score, usual 6 median, normal 7 average, typical 8 equality, standard

parable 4 myth, tale 5 fable, moral, story 7 example 8 allegory

parachute 7 bailout, skydive **part:** 5 riser 6 canopy 7 harness, ripcord

Paraclete 9 Holy Ghost 10 Holy Spirit

parade 4 brag, pomp 5 array, boast, flash, march, shine, strut 6 expose, flaunt, review 7 display, exhibit, fanfare, marshal, panoply, show off 8 brandish, ceremony, proclaim 9 advertise, cavalcade, pageantry, promenade 10 masquerade, procession

paradigm 5 ideal, model 6 mirror 7 example, pattern 8 exemplar, standard 9 archetype, beau ideal, framework, prototype

paradise 4 Eden, Zion 5 bliss 6 heaven, utopia 7 arcadia, elysium, nirvana 8 empyrean 9 Shangri-la 10 wonderland 12 New Jerusalem, promised land

Paradise Lost author 6 Milton (John)

paragon 3 gem 4 tops 5 champ, cream, ideal, jewel, match, model, peach, saint 6 beauty 7 compare, epitome 8 champion, exemplar, last word, nonesuch, parallel, ultimate 9 archetype, beau ideal, nonpareil 10 apotheosis

Paraguay capital: 8 Asunción **lake:** 4 Ypoá **language:** 7 Guarani, Spanish **monetary unit:** 7 guarani **neighbor:** 6 Brazil 7 Bolivia 9 Argentina **river:** 9 Pilcomayo

parallel 4 akin, copy, even, like 5 agree, align, alike, along, equal, liken, match 6 double, equate, line up 7 aligned, compare, similar 8 analogue 9 alongside, analogous, companion, consonant, corollary, correlate, duplicate 10 comparable, comparison, correspond, equivalent, similarity 11 coextensive, counterpart, duplication, resemblance 13 correspondent, corresponding

parallelogram 5 rhomb 6 oblong, square 7 rhombus 8 rhomboid 9 rectangle 13 quadrilateral

paralysis 5 palsy 7 inertia 9 impotence

paralyze 3 awe 4 daze, numb, stun 6 benumb, deaden, dismay 7 cripple, disable, nonplus, petrify, stupefy 8 shut down 10 immobilize 12 incapacitate

paramount 5 chief, ruler 6 master 7 capital, leading, primary, regnant, supreme 8 cardinal, crowning, dominant, foremost, headmost, superior 9 principal, sovereign,

uppermost 10 commanding, preeminent 11 predominant

paramour 5 lover, Romeo 7 Don Juan, gallant 8 Casanova, lothario, mistress 9 courtesan, inamorata, inamorato

parapet 4 wall 7 bastion, bulwark, rampart 10 battlement, breastwork **part:** 6 merlon 12 crenellation

paraphernalia 4 gear 5 items 6 outfit, tackle 7 effects 8 property 9 equipment, trappings 10 belongings 11 accessories, furnishings 13 accouterments, accoutrements, appurtenances

paraphrase 6 reword 7 restate, version 9 interpret, rendering, translate 11 restatement, translation

parasite 5 leech, toady 6 sponge, sucker 7 sponger 8 barnacle, deadbeat, hanger-on 9 dependent, exploiter, sycophant 10 freeloader, self-seeker 11 bloodsucker

parasitic 8 sponging, toadying 9 leechlike 11 freeloading, sycophantic 12 bloodsucking **flatworm:** 5 fluke 9 trematode

parasol 8 umbrella

_____ **paratus** 6 semper

Parcae 5 Fates, Norns 6 Moirai **name:** 4 Nona 5 Morta 6 Decuma

parcel 3 box, cut, lot 4 deal, dole, land, mete, pack, part, plot, wrap 5 allot, array, batch, bunch, group, share, tract 6 assign, bundle, divide, packet, ration 7 package, partial, portion, prorate, section, segment 8 allocate, disburse, disperse, division 9 apportion, partition 10 distribute

parch 3 dry 4 burn, sear 5 dry up, roast, toast 6 dry out, scorch 7 shrivel 9 dehydrate, desiccate

parched 3 dry 4 arid, sere 5 dusty 7 bone-dry, thirsty 8 scorched, withered 9 shriveled, waterless 10 dehydrated

parchment 4 skin 5 paper 6 vellum 7 diploma 8 document

pardon 4 free 5 remit, spare 6 excuse, let off 7 absolve, amnesty, condone, forgive, release 8 liberate, reprieve, tolerate 9 acquittal, exculpate, indemnity, remission 10 absolution, indulgence 11 exculpation, exoneration, forgiveness

pardonable 6 venial 9 allowable, excusable 11 permissible

pare 3 cut 4 clip, crop, peel, trim 5 lower, prune, shave 6 reduce, remove 7 curtail, cut back, cut down, trim off, whittle 8 diminish

parent 4 make, rear 5 beget, cause, hatch, raise, spawn 6 author, create, father, mother, origin 7 bring up, care for, produce

8 begetter, generate **9** originate, procreate **10** progenitor

parenthetically 7 by the by **8** by the bye, by the way **9** in passing **12** incidentally

parentless 6 orphan **8** orphaned

par excellence 3 top **5** prime **6** superb **7** premier, supreme **8** foremost, peerless, superior **9** matchless, number one, unmatched **10** first-class, preeminent **11** outstanding

pariah 5 leper **7** Ishmael, outcast **8** castaway **10** Ishmaelite **11** offscouring, untouchable

Japanese: 3 eta

Paris *airport:* **4** Orly *ancient name:* **7** Lutetia *avenue:* **13** Champs-Elysées *basilica:* **10** Sacré Coeur *cathedral:* **9** Notre Dame *city hall:* **12** Hôtel de Ville *college:* **8** Sorbonne *garden:* **9** Tuileries **10** Luxembourg *island:* **11** Île de la Cité *museum:* **5** Cluny **6** Louvre *palace:* **6** Louvre **7** Bourbon *patron saint:* **9** Geneviève *racecourse:* **7** Auteuil *river:* **5** Seine *section:* **8** Left Bank **9** Right Bank **10** Montmartre, Rive Gauche **12** Latin Quarter *stock exchange:* **6** Bourse *subway:* **5** Métro *tower:* **6** Eiffel

Paris *beloved:* **5** Helen *betrothed:* **6** Juliet *father:* **5** Priam *mother:* **6** Hecuba *slayer:* **11** Philoctetes *wife:* **6** Oenone

parish 6 county **8** district **9** community **12** congregation, neighborhood

Parisina *author:* **5** Byron (Lord) *husband:* **3** Azo *lover:* **4** Hugo *slayer:* **3** Azo

parity 8 equality, sameness, symmetry **10** similarity, similitude **11** equivalence, equivalency, parallelism

park 4 stop **5** green, plaza **7** deposit, funfair, reserve **8** carnival, preserve **9** esplanade **11** reservation

parka 6 anorak, jacket **7** garment **8** pullover **9** outerwear

park designer 4 Vaux (Calvert) **6** Paxton (Joseph) **7** Alphand (Jean), Le Nôtre (André), Olmsted (Frederick Law)

parlance 4 cant, talk **5** argot, idiom, lingo, style, usage **6** jargon, patois, phrase, speech **7** wording **8** language, locution, phrasing **9** verbalism **11** phraseology

parlay 3 bet **4** risk **5** bid up, boost, stake, wager **6** expand, extend, hazard **7** build up, enhance, enlarge, exploit, venture **8** increase, leverage **9** transform

parley 4 talk **5** speak **6** confab, confer, huddle, powwow **7** discuss, meeting **8** colloquy, converse, dialogue **9** discourse, negotiate **10** conference, discussion **11** confabulate **12** conversation **13** confabulation

parliament see **legislature**

parlor 4 room **5** salon **11** drawing room **13** reception room

parlous 5 dicey, hairy, risky **6** chancy, touchy, tricky, unsafe **8** critical, ticklish **9** dangerous, hazardous **10** precarious

Parnassian 4 poet **6** poetic

parochial 5 local **6** narrow **7** insular, limited **9** sectarian, small-town **10** provincial, restricted

parody 3 rib **4** mock **5** mimic, spoof **6** satire **7** imitate, lampoon, mockery, takeoff **8** ridicule, travesty **9** burlesque, imitation **10** caricature

parole 4 free, word **6** let out, pledge **7** promise, release **9** discharge, probation, watchword **11** performance

paronomasia 3 pun **11** play on words

paroxysm 3 fit **4** bout **5** spasm, throe **6** attack, frenzy **7** flare-up, seizure **8** eruption, outbreak, outburst **9** explosion **10** conniption, convulsion

parrot 3 ape **4** aper, copy, echo **5** mimic **6** repeat **7** chatter, copycat, imitate *kind:* **3** ara, kea **4** jako, kaka, lory **5** macaw **6** Amazon, budgie, kakapo **8** cockatoo, lorikeet, lovebird, parakeet **9** cockatiel **10** budgerigar **11** African gray

parrot fever 11 psittacosis

parry 4 duck, fend **5** avert, avoid, block, dodge, elude, evade **7** counter, deflect, evasion, fend off, prevent, respond, ward off **8** sidestep, stave off **9** turn aside **10** circumvent

parse 4 scan **7** analyze, dissect, examine, resolve **8** construe **9** anatomize, explicate, interpret

Parsi 11 Zoroastrian

Parsifal *composer:* **6** Wagner (Richard) *magician:* **8** Klingsor *quest:* **5** Grail *son:* **9** Lohengrin *temptress:* **6** Kundry

parsimonious 4 mean **5** cheap, close, tight **6** frugal, stingy **7** chintzy, miserly, sparing, thrifty **9** penurious **10** restrained **11** closefisted, tightfisted **12** cheese-paring **13** penny-pinching

parsley 4 herb **7** garnish *family:* **6** carrot *piece:* **5** sprig

parson 6 cleric, pastor, rector **8** clerical, minister, preacher, reverend **9** clergyman **12** ecclesiastic

parsonage 5 manse **7** rectory

part 3 bit, cut **4** chip, role, unit **5** chunk, piece, quota, scrap, sever, share, slice **6** detail, divide, member, moiety, ration, sector **7** element, measure, portion, quantum, quarter, section, segment **8** division, fraction, fragment, function, separate **9** component

partake of 3 eat **5** savor, share **6** accept, sample **7** acquire, consume, receive **9** enter into **11** participate

Parthenon *sculptor:* **7** Phidias **8** Pheidias *sculpture:* **6** frieze *site:* **9** Acropolis

partial 6 biased, unfair, warped **7** colored, half-way **8** inclined, one-sided **9** jaundiced **10** fractional, incomplete, prejudiced **11** fragmentary, predisposed

partiality 4 bent, bias **5** favor, taste **6** liking **7** leaning **8** affinity, fondness, tendency **10** favoritism, preference **11** inclination **12** onesidedness, predilection

participant 5 party **6** fellow, member, player, sharer **7** partner, sharing **11** contributor, shareholder

participate 4 join, play **5** share **6** engage, join in **7** partake **8** take part

particle 3 ace, bit, dab, dot, jot, ort, tad **4** atom, doit, dram, drop, hint, hoot, iota, mite, mote, spot, whit **5** atomy, crumb, fleck, grain, minim, ounce, scrap, shred, speck **6** morsel, tittle **7** granule, modicum, smidgen, smidgin, soupçon **8** fragment, smidgeon **9** scintilla *atomic:* **3** ion **5** anion **6** baryon, cation *elementary:* **3** psi, tau **4** kaon, muon, pion **5** boson, meson **6** baryon, hadron, lambda, lepton, photon, proton **7** fermion, hyperon, neutron, nucleon, upsilon **8** electron, mesotron, neutrino, positron *hypothetical:* **5** gluon, quark **6** parton **8** graviton *virus:* **6** virion *with negative charge:* **8** electron *with positive charge:* **6** proton **8** positron

particular 4 fact, full, item **5** exact, fussy, picky, point **6** detail, minute, single, unique **7** careful, correct, element, feature, finicky, precise, special, unusual **8** accurate, detailed, distinct, especial, exacting, itemized, separate, solitary, specific **10** fastidious, individual, meticulous, pernickety, scrupulous **11** distinctive, exceptional, persnickety, punctilious **12** circumstance

particularize 4 list **6** detail **7** catalog, itemize, specify **8** spell out **9** enumerate, inventory **13** individualize

parting 4 last **5** adieu, break, congé, final **6** good-by **7** good-bye **8** division, farewell **10** divergence, separation **11** leave-taking, valedictory

partisan 6 backer, biased, warped **7** devotee, die-hard, fanatic, patriot, sectary **8** adherent, advocate, disciple, follower, guerilla, one-sided, stalwart, upholder **9** factional,

guerrilla, irregular, satellite, sectarian, supporter

partition 4 wall **6** divide, screen **7** divider, section, wall off **8** disunion, division, fence off, separate **10** separation

partner 4 ally, chum, mate **5** buddy, crony **6** cohort, fellow **7** comrade **8** confrere, sidekick **9** assistant, associate, colleague, companion **10** accomplice **11** confederate

partnership 4 axis, firm **5** union **7** cahoots, company, sharing **8** alliance, business, marriage, relation **11** affiliation, association, combination **12** consociation, togetherness **13** participation

parturient 6 gravid, parous **8** enceinte, pregnant **9** expecting

parturition 5 birth **8** delivery **10** childbirth **12** childbearing

party 4 ball, band, bash, bevy, bloc, crew, fete, gala, luau, orgy, rave, side **5** actor, corps, covey, feast, group, revel, troop **6** fiesta, frolic, kegger, mortal, person, social, soiree, troupe **7** blowout, carouse, faction, roister, shindig **8** carousal, litigant, wingding **9** bacchanal, gathering, make merry, raise hell **10** detachment, individual, saturnalia **11** bacchanalia, celebration, participant

parvenu 7 upstart **9** arriviste **12** nouveau riche

Pascal essay 6 Pensée

pasha 3 dey

Pasiphaë *daughter:* **7** Ariadne, Phaedra *husband:* **5** Minos *son:* **8** Minotaur

pass 3 bye, die, end **4** fare, hand **5** cease, enact, get by, lapse, occur, relay, spend, while **6** crisis, depart, elapse, exceed, expire, hand on, happen, permit, push on, slight, slip by, strait **7** come off, develop, journey, proceed, succumb **8** bequeath, fork over, hand down, juncture, outshine, outstrip, transmit **9** while away *Afghanistan:* **5** Murgh *Afghanistan-Pakistan:* **6** Khyber *Alaska:* **5** White *Alps:* **5** Cenis, Loibl **7** Brenner, Ljubelj, Simplon **9** St. Bernard *California:* **5** Cajon *China-India:* **9** Karakoram *Colorado:* **3** Ute *mountain:* 3 col, gap **4** ghat **5** notch *Pakistan:* **5** Kilik *Russian:* **12** Caspian Gates *Tennessee:* **10** Cumberland *Turkey:* **13** Cilician Gates

passable 4 okay, open, so-so **6** decent **8** adequate, all right **9** tolerable, unblocked **10** accessible, good enough **12** satisfactory

passably 6 enough **8** all right, somewhat **10** moderately

passage 3 way **4** exit, fare, hall, iter, path, text **5** route, shift **6** access, arcade, avenue, course, egress, strait, travel, tunnel, voyage **7** channel, excerpt, hallway, journey, transit **8** corridor, transfer, traverse **9** enactment, quotation **10** transition **11** transmittal **12** transference, transmission *air:* **7** windway *arched:* **6** arcade *Atlantic-Pacific:* **9** Northwest *narrow:* **3** gut *roofed:* **6** arcade **9** breezeway

Passage to India author 7 Forster (E. M.)

pass away 3 die, end **6** demise, depart, elapse, expire, perish **7** decease, succumb **9** disappear

pass by 4 miss, omit **6** forget, ignore **7** neglect **8** overlook **9** disregard

passé 4 dead **5** dated, stale **6** démodé, old hat **7** demoded, disused, extinct, outworn **8** obsolete, outdated, outmoded **9** out-of-date **10** antiquated, oldfangled, superseded **12** old-fashioned

passel 3 lot **4** heap, pack **5** bunch **6** bundle **9** multitude

passenger 4 fare

passing 5 brief, death, quick **6** demise, highly **7** cursory, decease **8** fleeting **9** ephemeral, fugacious, extremely, momentary, transient **10** evanescent, short-lived, transitory **11** exceedingly, superficial

passion 4 fire, heat, itch, love, lust, zeal **5** agony, amour, ardor, craze, crush, drive **6** desire, fervor, hunger **7** avidity, craving, ecstasy, emotion, rapture **8** appetite, devotion, yearning **9** eagerness, suffering, transport **10** enthusiasm, excitement **11** amorousness, infatuation

passionate 3 hot **5** angry, fiery **6** ardent, fervid, heated **7** amorous, aroused, blazing, burning, excited, fervent, furious, intense **8** incensed, vehement **9** impetuous, steamed up **10** hot-blooded, stimulated **11** hot-tempered **12** enthusiastic **13** quick-tempered

passive 4 idle **5** inert **6** docile, latent **8** enduring, immobile, inactive, listless, resigned, yielding **9** apathetic, compliant, lethargic, quiescent **10** motionless, nonviolent, phlegmatic, submissive **11** acquiescent, complaisant, indifferent, unresistant

pass out 3 die **5** faint, swoon **7** divvy up **8** disburse, keel over **10** distribute

pass over 4 miss, omit, skip **6** forget, ignore **7** dismiss, neglect **8** discount, leave out **9** disregard

Passover 5 Pasch **6** Pesach *bread:* **5** matzo **6** matzoh *meal:* **5** seder

pass up 5 forgo **6** refuse, reject **7** decline

past 3 ago, old **4** gone, late, once, yore **5** above, after, prior **6** beyond, bygone, former, whilom **7** onetime, quondam **8** ante-

rior, foretime, lang syne, previous, sometime **9** antiquity, erstwhile, foregoing, precedent, preceding, yesterday **10** antecedent, yesteryear

pasta 5 dough *kind:* **4** orzo, ziti **5** penne, ruote **6** rotini **7** fusilli, gemelli, gnocchi, lasagna, lasagne, mafalda, noodles, ravioli **8** farfalle, linguine, linguini, macaroni, rigatoni **9** cannelloni, capellini, cavatappi, fettucine, fettucini, manicotti, radiatore, spaghetti, tubettini **10** cannelloni, conchiglie, fettuccine, fettuccini, tortellini, vermicelli **11** cappelletti, orecchiette, pappardelle

paste 3 fix, hit **4** beat, clay, drub, food, glue, sock **5** affix, dough, pound, stick, stuff **6** adhere, attach, cement, defeat, fasten, thrash, wallop **7** trounce **8** adhesive, material

Pasternak character 4 Lara **7** Zhivago (Dr.)

pastiche 4 olio **6** jumble, medley **7** farrago, mélange, mixture **8** mishmash **9** potpourri **10** assortment, hodgepodge, hotchpotch, miscellany, salmagundi **11** gallimaufry

pastime 4 game **5** hobby, sport **9** amusement, diversion **10** recreation **13** entertainment

past master 3 ace, pro, wiz **4** whiz **5** adept, maven **6** expert, wizard **8** virtuoso **9** authority

pastor 5 padre **6** cleric, parson **8** minister, preacher, reverend, sky pilot **9** clergyman

pastoral 4 idyl **5** idyll, rural **6** rustic **7** bucolic, country, crosier, idyllic **8** agrarian, clerical, innocent, peaceful **10** campestral

pastor's assistant 6 curate

pastry 3 bun, pie **4** baba, cake, flan, tart **5** torte **6** cornet, Danish, éclair, gâteau **7** baklava, beignet, bouchée, dariole, gâteaux (plural), palmier, savarin, strudel, tartlet **8** napoleon, papillon, piroshki, pirozhki, turnover **9** barquette, cream puff, madeleine, petit four, vol-au-vent **10** cheesecake **11** profiterole **12** millefeuille *kind:* **4** filo, puff **5** flaky **6** phyllo *shell:* **7** timbale **8** meringue

pasture 3 lea, ley **4** feed, land **5** field, grass, graze **6** browse, meadow **9** grassland

pasty 3 wan **4** pale **6** doughy, pallid, sickly **7** meat pie **8** turnover **9** unhealthy

pat 3 apt, dab, set **4** firm **5** fixed, slice, stiff, trite **6** dead-on **7** apropos, fitting **8** apposite, standard, suitable **9** contrived, pertinent, rehearsed

patch 3 bit, fix **4** area, fill, mend, plot **5** cover, piece, scrap, spell **6** doctor, emblem, fill up, repair, shield **7** connect, plaster **8** material **10** connection

patchwork 4 olio **5** quilt **6** jumble **7** mixture **8**

covering, mishmash, mixed bag **10** assortment, hodgepodge, hotchpotch, miscellany, salmagundi

patchy 6 fitful, random, spotty, uneven **7** erratic **8** sporadic **9** haphazard, hit-or-miss, irregular **12** intermittent

pate 4 bean, dome, head, poll **5** brain, crown **6** noddle, noggin, noodle

patella 7 kneecap, kneepan

patent 4 open **5** clear, plain, right **6** secure **7** evident, license, obvious, visible **8** apparent, distinct, manifest **9** exclusive, privilege, prominent, protected **11** proprietary

paternal 8 fatherly *relative:* **6** agnate

paternity 7 lineage **8** ancestry **10** fatherhood, provenance **11** progenitors

Pater Noster 9 Our Father **11** Lord's Prayer

path 3 way **4** lane, line, road, tack, walk **5** byway, orbit, route, track, trail **6** avenue, bridle, course **7** passage, walkway **9** direction **10** trajectory

pathetic 3 sad **4** poor **5** sorry **6** absurd, moving, paltry **7** piteous, pitiful, risible, useless **8** inferior, pitiable, poignant, touching **9** affecting, laughable, miserable **10** lamentable, ridiculous

Pathfinder, The *author:* **6** Cooper (James Fenimore) *hero:* **6** Bumppo (Natty)

pathogen 4 germ **5** E. coli, virus **9** bacterium

pathological 7 deviant **8** aberrant, abnormal, diseased, maniacal, schizoid **9** psychotic

pathos 4 pity **7** emotion **8** sympathy **9** poignance, poignancy

pathway 4 line, walk **5** route, track, trail **6** course **7** channel, conduit, network, passage

patience 4 cool **8** calmness, stoicism **9** composure, endurance **10** equanimity, sufferance **11** forbearance, resignation, self-control

Patience *composer:* **8** Sullivan (Arthur) *librettist:* **7** Gilbert (W. S.)

patient 4 case, meek **8** enduring **9** easygoing **10** persistent **11** susceptible **13** long-suffering *man:* **3** Job

patina 4 aura, coat, film **6** finish, polish **7** coating **8** covering **10** appearance, coloration

patio 5 atria (plural), court **6** atrium **7** terrace **9** courtyard

patois 4 cant **5** argot, lingo, slang **6** jargon **7** dialect **10** colloquial, vernacular

patriarch 4 sire **6** father, nestor **7** creator, founder **9** architect, graybeard *biblical:* **5** David, Isaac, Jacob **7** Abraham

patrician 5 noble **6** aristo **9** blue blood, gentleman **10** aristocrat, upper-class

patriciate 5 elite **6** gentry **9** blue blood, gentility **10** upper crust **11** aristocracy

patrimony 6 estate, legacy **8** heritage **9** endowment **10** birthright **11** inheritance

patriot 5 jingo **8** jingoist, loyalist **9** flag-waver **10** chauvinist **11** nationalist

patriotism 8 jingoism **10** chauvinism **11** nationalism

Patroclus *friend:* **8** Achilles *slayer:* **6** Hector

patrol 5 guard, round, scout, troop, watch **7** protect **8** sentinel **9** keep watch

patrolman 3 cop **5** guard **6** police **7** officer

patrol wagon see **paddy wagon**

patron 5 angel **6** backer, client **7** sponsor **8** customer, guardian **9** protector, supporter **10** benefactor

patronage 4 help **5** aegis, trade **6** custom **7** backing, subsidy, support, traffic **8** activity, advocacy, auspices, business, cronyism **9** clientage, clientele, influence **10** pork barrel, protection **11** benefaction, sponsorship **12** guardianship

patronize 3 aid, use **4** back **5** deign, favor **6** assist, shop at **7** protect, support **8** frequent **10** condescend

patron saint *of beggars, cripples:* **5** Giles *of children:* **8** Nicholas *of England:* **6** George *of fishermen:* **5** Peter *of France:* **5** Denis *of Ireland:* **7** Patrick *of lawyers:* **4** Ives *of musicians:* **7** Cecilia *of Norway:* **4** Olaf *of physicians:* **4** Luke *of sailors:* **4** Elmo **8** Nicholas *of Scotland:* **6** Andrew *of shoemakers:* **7** Crispin *of Spain:* **5** James **8** Santiago *of travelers:* **11** Christopher *of Wales:* **5** David *of winegrowers:* **7** Vincent *of workers:* **6** Joseph

patsy 3 sap **4** dupe, fool, mark **5** chump **6** pigeon, sucker, victim **8** easy mark, pushover

patter 4 cant **5** argot, lingo, slang, spiel **6** babble, jargon, patois **7** chatter, prattle

pattern 4 copy, form, plan **5** guide, ideal, model, motif, order, plaid, shape **6** argyle, design, figure, floral, follow, method, mirror, system **7** diagram, emulate, example, imitate, paisley **8** exemplar, grouping, paradigm, standard, template **9** archetype, incidence, prototype **10** flight path, stereotype **11** arrangement, orderliness **12** distribution **13** configuration

paucity 4 lack, want **6** dearth **7** poverty **8** scarcity, shortage **9** scantness, smallness **10** deficiency, meagerness, meagreness **13** insufficiency

Paul the Apostle *birthplace:* **6** Tarsus *companion:* **5** Silas, Titus **7** Artemas, Timothy **8** Barnabas *original name:* **4** Saul *place of conversion:* **8** Damascus *prosecutor:* **9**

Tertullus *teacher:* 8 Gamaliel *tribe:* 8 Benjamin

paunch 3 gut, pot 5 belly, tummy 7 abdomen, stomach 8 potbelly 9 bay window, beer belly 11 breadbasket, corporation

paunchy 3 fat 5 beefy, plump, tubby 6 chunky, portly, rotund 8 thickset 10 overweight, potbellied

pauper 6 beggar 7 have-not 8 bankrupt, indigent 9 mendicant

pauperism 4 need, ruin, want 6 penury 7 beggary, poverty 9 indigence, neediness, privation 11 destitution

pause 3 gap 4 halt, hush, lull, rest, stop, wait 5 break, comma, delay, lapse, letup 6 hiatus, linger, recess 7 caesura, respite, take ten, time out 8 breather, hesitate, inaction, interval, take five 9 cessation, interlude 10 hesitation, suspension 12 intermission, interruption

pave 3 lay, tar 5 cover 7 asphalt, surface 8 blacktop, concrete

pavement 6 tarmac 7 asphalt, macadam, surface 8 concrete, sidewalk

pavilion 4 tent 5 kiosk 6 canopy, gazebo 9 belvedere 11 summerhouse

paw 4 feel, foot, grab, hand, mitt 5 grope, touch 6 fondle, handle, molest, scrape

pawn 4 hock, tool 6 pledge, puppet, stooge, victim 7 deposit, hostage, warrant 8 guaranty, security 9 guarantee 10 chess piece, instrument

pax 5 peace 6 tablet

Pax _____ 3 Dei 6 Romana 10 Britannica

pay 3 fee 4 ante, wage 5 remit, serve, spend 6 answer, ante up, defray, expend, kick in, lay out, pony up, profit, render, salary, settle, tender, reward 7 benefit, bring in, cough up, forfeit, fork out, satisfy, stipend 8 disburse, earnings, shell out 9 discharge, emolument, indemnify, reimburse 10 compensate, recompense, remunerate 12 compensation, remuneration

payable 3 due 4 owed 5 owing 6 mature, unpaid 7 overdue 9 unsettled 10 obligatory 11 outstanding, uncollected

paycheck 5 wages 6 salary

payload 4 haul 5 cargo, goods 6 burden, lading, weight 7 freight, tonnage 8 shipment

payment 3 fee 4 dues 5 award, money 6 amends, outlay, return, reward 7 penance 8 defrayal, requital 11 restitution 12 compensation, remuneration, satisfaction

payoff 3 fix 5 bribe 6 climax, profit, result, reward, upshot 7 outcome 8 clincher, decisive 10 conclusion, conclusive, denouement 11 retribution

payola 5 bribe

PDQ 4 ASAP, stat 6 at once, pronto 8 directly, right now, right off 9 forthwith, instanter, instantly, right away 11 immediately, straightway 12 straightaway

peace 3 pax 4 calm, ease, pact 5 amity, order, quiet 6 accord, repose 7 concord, harmony, silence 8 serenity 11 tranquility 12 tranquillity

peaceable 6 dovish, irenic 7 amiable, pacific 8 amicable, friendly, pacifist, tranquil 10 nonviolent 11 complaisant 12 conciliatory

peaceful 4 calm 5 still, quiet 6 irenic, placid, serene 7 equable, halcyon, pacific 8 composed, tranquil 9 unruffled 10 harmonious, nonviolent, untroubled

peacemaker 7 arbiter 8 mediator, pacifier, placater 10 arbitrator, negotiator 11 conciliator, pacificator

peace officer 3 cop 6 police 9 policeman 11 policewoman

peach 3 ace, pip, rat 4 blab, lulu, tree 5 fruit, honey 6 betray, inform, reveal, snitch, squeal 7 Elberta 8 knockout 9 freestone, humdinger, nectarine 10 clingstone 11 crackerjack *family:* 4 rose

Peach State 7 Georgia

peachy 4 fine, good, neat, nice 5 dandy, neato, nifty, super, swell 8 pleasant, pleasing 9 excellent, hunky-dory, marvelous, wonderful

peacockish 5 showy, swank 6 chichi, flashy, swanky 7 splashy 8 show-offy 10 flamboyant 11 pretentious 12 ostentatious

peak 3 top 4 acme, apex, roof 5 crest, crown 6 summit, vertex, zenith 8 pinnacle *Arizona:* 9 Humphreys *Bighorn Mtns.:* 5 Cloud *Black Hills:* 6 Harney *California:* 6 Lassen 9 Telescope *Cascade Range:* 6 Lassen *Colorado:* 5 Grays, Longs, Pikes 6 Blanca 7 La Plata 11 Uncompahgre *Idaho:* 5 Borah *Kyrgyzstan:* 5 Lenin 6 Pobeda *Montana:* 7 Granite 8 Electric *Nevada:* 7 Wheeler 8 Boundary 10 Charleston *New Mexico:* 7 Truchas, Wheeler 12 Sierra Blanca *South Dakota:* 6 Harney *Sri Lanka:* 5 Adam's 8 Samanala *Tajikistan:* 5 Lenin 9 Communism *Utah:* 5 Kings *White Mtns.:* 8 Boundary *Wyoming:* 5 Cloud 6 Franks 7 Gannett (see also **mountain**)

peaked 3 ill, wan 4 ashy, pale, sick 5 acute, ashen, drawn, sharp 6 ailing, pallid, sickly 7 pointed 9 emaciated

peal 4 bell, bong, ring, toll 5 chime, knell, sound 7 ring out, ringing 8 ding-dong

peanut 4 mani 6 goober, legume, peewee, shrimp 9 pipsqueak

Peanuts *character:* 4 Lucy (van Pelt) 5 Linus, Patty (Peppermint), Rerun, Sally (Brown), Spike 6 Frieda, Marcie, Pig-Pen, Snoopy 8 Franklin 9 Schroeder, Woodstock 12 Charlie Brown *creator:* 6 Schulz (Charles M.) *expression:* 4 rats *forerunner:* 8 Li'l Folks

pear 4 Bosc, pome 5 Anjou, Hardy 6 Comice, Garber, Seckel 7 Kieffer, LeConte 8 Bartlett *cider:* 5 perry

pearl 3 gem 4 dear 5 jewel 7 paragon 8 treasure

Pearl Mosque site 4 Agra

pearly 8 lustrous, nacreous, precious 10 iridescent, opalescent

pear-shaped 8 pyriform

peasant 4 carl, kern, peon, serf 5 churl 6 rustic 7 bumpkin, hayseed, villein *Arab:* 6 fellah *Indian:* 4 ryot *Latin-American:* 9 campesino *Philippine:* 3 tao *Russian:* 5 mujik 6 moujik, muzhik

peccary 8 javelina *genus:* 7 Tayassu

peck 3 lot, nag 4 buss, carp, fuss, heap, kiss, load, mess, pile, poke 6 carp at, nibble, pick at, pick up, pierce, strike 8 quantity

pecking order 6 ladder 7 pyramid 9 food chain, hierarchy

peculate 5 steal 8 embezzle 9 defalcate 11 appropriate

peculiar 3 odd 4 rare 5 queer, weird 6 unique 7 bizarre, curious, oddball, offbeat, special, strange, unusual 8 abnormal, singular, specific, uncommon 9 eccentric 10 individual, particular 11 distinctive

peculiarity 3 tic 4 mark 5 quirk, trait 6 oddity 7 feature, quality 8 property 9 attribute, character, mannerism 12 eccentricity, idiosyncrasy

pecuniary 6 fiscal 8 economic, monetary 9 financial

pedagogue 5 tutor 6 pedant 7 teacher 8 educator 12 schoolmaster

pedagogy 8 teaching 9 education

pedal 5 lever 7 bicycle, treadle *digit:* 3 toe

pedant 7 teacher 9 formalist 10 schoolmarm 12 precisionist

pedantic 3 dry 4 arid, dull 6 stodgy 7 bookish, donnish, erudite, learned, tedious 8 academic, didactic, priggish 9 ponderous 10 pedestrian, scholastic 11 pedagogical 13 unimaginative

peddle 4 hawk, push, sell, vend 5 pitch 6 monger 8 huckster

peddler 6 coster, dealer, hawker, monger, vendor 8 huckster, merchant, promoter 9 tradesman 12 costermonger

pedestal 4 base, foot 5 stand 7 footing, support 10 foundation 12 underpinning *part:* 4 dado 6 plinth 7 subbase

pedestrian 4 blah, dull 5 banal 6 dreary, stodgy, walker 7 humdrum, mundane, prosaic 8 everyday, ordinary 11 commonplace 13 unimaginative *crossing:* 5 zebra 10 footbridge

pedigree 6 origin, purity 7 descent, history, lineage 8 ancestry, purebred 9 bloodline, genealogy 10 background, extraction, family tree

peduncle 4 stem 5 stalk 7 pedicel

peek 3 spy 4 look 6 glance 7 glimpse

peel 4 bark, pare, rind, skin 5 flake, scale, strip 7 take off 8 flake off 9 break away, exfoliate

peeled 4 bare, open 5 naked 7 denuded, exposed 8 stripped 9 uncovered

peep 3 see, spy 4 look 5 chirp, tweet, watch 6 glance, squeak 7 glimpse, twitter 9 sandpiper

Peeping Tom 5 snoop 6 voyeur 7 prowler, snooper

peer 3 pry 4 gaze, lord 5 equal, glare, noble, stare 6 goggle, squint 9 associate *British:* 4 duke, earl 5 baron 7 marquis 8 marquess, viscount

Peer Gynt *author:* 5 Ibsen (Henrik) *beloved:* 7 Solveig *character:* 6 Anitra *composer:* 5 Grieg (Edvard) *mother:* 3 Ase 4 Aase

peerless 4 best 6 unique 7 perfect, supreme 8 superior 9 matchless, nonpareil, paramount, unequaled, unmatched, unrivaled 12 incomparable, unparalleled

peeve 3 bug, irk, vex 4 miff, rile 5 anger, annoy, pique 6 bother, nettle, put out 7 disturb, provoke 8 irritate, nuisance, vexation 9 aggravate, annoyance, grievance 10 exasperate 11 aggravation

peevish 4 sour 5 cross, testy 6 cranky, grumpy, ornery 7 fretful, whining 8 petulant 9 fractious, irritable, obstinate, querulous 11 ill-tempered

peewee 4 runt, tike, tyke 5 dwarf, pigmy, pygmy, small 6 midget, shaver, shrimp, squirt 9 miniature 10 diminutive, flycatcher 11 lilliputian

peg 3 fix, pin, tee 4 mark, plug, step 5 dowel, prong, stake, throw 6 attach, fasten, marker 7 pin down, pretext, support 8 identify

Pegasus 5 horse, steed *rider:* 11 Bellerophon

pejorative 7 adverse 8 critical, debasing 9 slighting 10 belittling, derogatory, detractive 11 denigrating, deprecatory, disparaging, opprobrious, unfavorable 12 depreciatory

pelagic 6 marine 7 oceanic 8 maritime

Peleus *brother:* 7 Telamon *father:* 6 Aeacus *half brother:* 6 Phocus *son:* 8 Achilles *victim:* 8 Eurytion *wife:* 6 Thetis

pelf 4 loot, swag 5 booty, lucre, money, moola 6 boodle, moolah, riches, spoils 7 plunder

Pelias *country:* 6 Iolcus *father:* 8 Poseidon *half brother:* 5 Aeson *son:* 7 Acastus

Pelican State 9 Louisiana

Pelléas *beloved:* 9 Mélisande *brother, slayer:* 6 Golaud

Pelles *daughter:* 6 Elaine *grandson:* 7 Galahad

pellet 3 wad 4 ball, shot 6 sphere 10 projectile

Pellinore *slayer:* 6 Gawain *son:* 5 Torre 6 Dornar 7 Lamerok 8 Percival 9 Agglovale

pell-mell 5 chaos, snarl 6 muddle, rashly 7 chaotic, clutter, hastily 8 confused, disarray, disorder, headlong, reckless 9 confusion, haphazard, hurriedly 10 carelessly, heedlessly 11 hurry-scurry 13 helter-skelter

pellucid 5 clear, plain, sheer 6 limpid 7 crystal, evident, obvious 8 clear-cut, luminous 9 unblurred 10 see-through 11 crystalline, transparent

Pelops *father:* 8 Tantalus *son:* 6 Atreus 8 Pittheus, Thyestes *wife:* 10 Hippodamia

pelota 4 ball 7 jai alai

pelt 3 fur, run 4 beat, blow, dash, drub, hide, hurl, rush, skin, whop 5 hurry, pound, scoot, speed, strip, throw, whack 6 assail, batter, pepper, pummel, strike, wallop 7 hombard, hotfoot

pen 3 sty 4 cage, coop, jail, swan 5 pound, quill, write 6 cooler, corral, indite, prison, shut in, stylus, writer 7 close in, confine, enclose, fence in 9 ballpoint, enclosure

penal 8 punitive 12 correctional, disciplinary

penalize 4 dock, fine 5 mulct 6 punish 7 deprive 8 handicap 10 discipline 12 disadvantage

penalty 4 fine, loss 5 mulct 7 damages, forfeit 8 hardship 10 amercement, forfeiture, punishment 12 disadvantage

penance 4 rite 7 penalty 8 hardship 9 atonement 10 punishment

penchant 4 bent 5 taste 6 liking 7 leaning 8 affinity, fondness, tendency 9 inclining 10 partiality, proclivity, propensity 11 inclination 12 predilection

pendant 4 flag, jack, rope 7 fixture 8 lavalier, ornament 10 supplement

pendent 7 hanging 9 suspended, undecided, unsettled 11 overhanging 12 undetermined

pending 6 during 8 awaiting, imminent 9 undecided, unsettled 12 undetermined

_____ **Pendragon** 5 Uther

pendulous 7 hanging 8 dangling, drooping, wavering 9 faltering, suspended, tentative, uncertain 10 hesitating, indecisive 11 vacillating

Penelope *father:* 7 Icarius *father-in-law:* 7 Laertes *husband:* 7 Ulysses 8 Odysseus *mother:* 8 Periboea *son:* 10 Telemachus *suitor:* 7 Agelaus

penetrable 6 porous 8 pervious 9 permeable

penetrate 3 jab 4 bore, go in, stab 5 break, drive, enter, probe, touch 6 affect, charge, invade, pierce 7 pervade 8 discover, encroach, perceive, permeate, puncture, saturate 9 percolate, perforate 10 understand

penetrating 4 keen 5 acute, sharp 6 astute, shrewd 8 incisive, piercing 9 trenchant 10 discerning, insightful, perceptive 11 quick-witted, sharp-witted 12 sharp-sighted

Peneus *daughter:* 6 Daphne *father:* 7 Oceanus *mother:* 6 Tethys

penguin type 6 Adélie

_____ **Penh** 5 Phnom

peninsula 4 neck 10 chersonese *Alaska:* 5 Kenai 6 Seward *Australia:* 6 Tasman *Barents Sea:* 5 Kanin *British colony:* 9 Gibraltar *Canada:* 5 Bruce, Gaspé 6 Ungava 8 Labrador *Chile:* 5 Swett *China:* 8 Shandong *Costa Rica:* 3 Osa *Croatia:* 6 Istria *Denmark:* 7 Jutland *eastern United States:* 8 Delmarva *Estonia:* 5 Sorve *Florida:* 8 Pinellas 9 Canaveral *France:* 5 Giens *Greece:* 5 Acte 10 Chalcidice 11 Peloponnese 12 Peloponnesus *Guam:* 5 Orote *Hong Kong:* 7 Kowloon *Honshu:* 3 Izu 5 Miura *Massachusetts:* 7 Cape Ann, Cape Cod *Mexico:* 4 Baja 7 Yucatan 14 Baja California *Michigan:* 8 Keweenaw *Middle East:* 5 Sinai *New Guinea:* 4 Huon *New Jersey:* 9 Sandy Hook *New Zealand:* 5 Banks, Mahia *Nunavut:* 7 Boothia 8 Melville *Ontario:* 5 Bruce *Persian Gulf:* 9 Ras Tanura *Quebec:* 5 Gaspé *Russia:* 4 Kola 5 Taman, Yamal 6 Kolski, Taimyr 9 Kamchatka *Scotland:* 7 Kintyre *South Australia:* 4 Eyre 5 Yorke *Southeast Asia:* 5 Malay 9 Indochina *southeastern Europe:* 6 Balkan *southwestern Asia:* 6 Arabia 7 Arabian *southwestern Europe:* 7 Iberian *Texas:* 9 Matagorda *Tierra del Fuego:* 5 Mitre *Turkey:* 8 Anatolia 9 Asia Minor *Ukraine:* 5 Kerch 6 Crimea 7 Crimean *Wales:* 5 Gower, Lleyn *Washington:* 7 Olympic *Wisconsin:* 4 Door

Peninsular State 7 Florida

penitence 3 rue 4 ruth 6 regret, sorrow 7 anguish, remorse 8 distress, humbling 10 con-

trition, repentance **11** compunction, self-reproof **12** self-reproach
penitent 5 sorry **6** rueful **8** contrite **9** regretful, repentant **10** apologetic, remorseful
penitentiary see **prison**
penman 5 clerk **6** author, scribe, writer **7** copyist **9** scrivener **12** calligrapher
penmanship 4 hand **5** style **6** script **7** writing **11** calligraphy, chirography, handwriting
pen name 6 anonym **9** pseudonym **10** nom de plume *Addison, Joseph:* **4** Clio *Arouet, François-Marie:* **8** Voltaire *Beyle, Marie-Henri:* **8** Stendhal *Blair, Eric:* **12** George Orwell *Blixen, Karen:* **11** Isak Dinesen *Brontë, Anne:* **9** Acton Bell *Brontë, Charlotte:* **10** Currer Bell *Brontë, Emily:* **9** Ellis Bell *Clemens, Samuel:* **9** Mark Twain *Dickens, Charles:* **3** Boz *Dodgson, Charles Lutwidge:* **12** Lewis Carroll *Dupin, Amandine-Aurore:* **10** George Sand *Evans, Mary Ann:* **11** George Eliot *Faust, Frederick:* **8** Max Brand *Franklin, Benjamin:* **11** Poor Richard *Geisel, Theodore:* **7** Dr. Seuss *Glidden, Frederick:* **9** Luke Short *Lamb, Charles:* **4** Elia *Lederer, Esther:* **10** Ann Landers *Munro, Hector Hugh:* **4** Saki *Poquelin, Jean-Baptiste:* **7** Molière *Porter, William Sidney:* **6** O. Henry *Ramé, Maria Louise:* **5** Ouida *Thibault, J.-A.-F.:* **13** Anatole France *Viaud, L.-M.-J.:* **10** Pierre Loti *Wofford, Chloe Anthony:* **12** Toni Morrison
pennant 4 flag, jack **5** color **6** banner, ensign **8** standard, streamer **9** banderole **12** championship
penniless 4 poor **5** broke, needy **8** bankrupt, indigent **9** destitute, insolvent **11** impecunious
pennon 4 flag, jack, wing **5** color **6** banner, ensign **8** bannerol, gonfalon, streamer **9** banderole, oriflamme
Pennsylvania *capital:* **10** Harrisburg *city:* **4** Erie **7** Reading **8** Scranton **9** Allentown **10** Pittsburgh **12** Philadelphia *college, university:* **6** Drexel, Lehigh, Temple **7** LaSalle **8** Bryn Mawr, Bucknell **9** Dickinson, Haverford, Lafayette, Penn State, Villanova **10** Swarthmore **14** Carnegie Mellon *mountain range:* **6** Pocono *nickname:* **8** Keystone (State) *river:* **9** Allegheny **10** Schuylkill **11** Monongahela, Susquehanna *state bird:* **12** ruffed grouse *state flower:* **14** mountain laurel *state tree:* **7** hemlock
penny-pincher 5 miser **7** niggard, scrooge **8** tightwad **9** skinflint **10** cheapskate
penny-pinching 4 mean **6** frugal, stingy, thrift **7** miserly, thrifty **9** frugality, nig-

gardly, parsimony, penurious **11** tightfisted **12** cheeseparing, parsimonious
penny-wise 5 canny, tight **6** frugal, stingy **7** prudent, sparing, thrifty **9** provident **10** economical **12** parsimonious
pen point 3 neb, nib
pension 3 inn **5** hotel, lodge **6** hostel, reward **7** annuity, auberge, payment, stipend **8** gratuity **9** allowance **12** room and board, roominghouse **13** boardinghouse
pensioner 7 retiree
pensive 3 sad **6** dreamy, musing **7** wistful **10** meditative, melancholy, reflective, ruminative, thoughtful **11** preoccupied **13** contemplative
Pentateuch 5 Torah *books:* **6** Exodus **7** Genesis, Numbers **9** Leviticus **11** Deuteronomy
Penthesilea *queen of:* **7** Amazons *slayer:* **8** Achilles
Pentheus *grandfather:* **6** Cadmus *king of:* **6** Thebes *mother:* **5** Agave
penumbra 4 veil **5** cover, shade **6** fringe, screen, shadow, shroud **7** curtain
penurious 4 mean, poor **5** needy, tight **6** frugal, stingy **7** miserly **8** indigent, stinting **9** destitute, niggardly **11** impecunious, tightfisted **12** impoverished, parsimonious **13** penny-pinching
penury 4 need, want **7** beggary, poverty **8** distress **9** indigence, privation, pauperism **11** destitution, needfulness
peon 4 serf **5** prole, slave **6** drudge, toiler, worker **7** laborer, peasant **11** galley slave *Anglo-Saxon:* **4** esne
peonage 4 yoke **6** thrall **7** bondage, helotry, serfdom, slavery **9** servitude, thralldom, villenage **11** enslavement
people 3 kin **4** folk **5** folks, peeps, plebs **6** public **7** society **8** populace **9** commoners, community, plebeians **10** commonalty **11** inhabitants, rank and file, third estate *combining form:* **5** ethno
pep 3 vim, zip **4** brio, dash **5** gusto, moxie, punch, verve, vigor **6** energy, spirit **7** sparkle **8** vitality, vivacity **10** get-up-and-go, liveliness **11** high spirits
pepo 5 gourd, melon **6** squash **7** pumpkin **8** cucumber
pepper 4 kava, pelt **5** chili **6** season, shower **7** cayenne, paprika, pimento, tabasco **8** capsicum, cascabel, chipotle, habanero, jalapeño, pimiento, sprinkle **9** condiment, seasoning **12** Scotch bonnet
peppery 3 hot **5** cross, fiery, sharp, spicy, testy, zesty **6** biting, lively, snappy, touchy **7** piquant, pungent **8** choleric, poignant,

seasoned, stinging **9** irascible, irritable **11** hot-tempered **13** quick-tempered

peppy 4 spry **5** alert, perky **6** active, bright, lively **7** vibrant **8** animated, spirited, vigorous **9** energetic, sprightly, vivacious

Pequod *cabin boy:* **3** Pip *captain:* **4** Ahab *harpooner:* **6** Daggoo **8** Queequeg, Tashtego *mate:* **8** Starbuck *seaman:* **7** Ishmael

per 3 via **4** a pop, each, with **6** apiece **7** by way of, for each, through **9** by means of **12** individually

perambulate 4 walk **6** ramble, stroll **8** traverse **9** promenade

per capita 4 each **6** apiece, by each **7** equally, for each

perceive 3 see **4** espy, feel, know, mark, note **5** grasp, seize, sense **6** detect, notice, remark **7** discern, observe, realize **8** identify **9** apprehend, recognize **10** comprehend, understand

percentage 3 cut **4** part **5** piece, share, slice **6** profit **7** portion **9** advantage **10** commission, proportion **11** probability

perceptible 5 clear **6** marked **7** visible **8** apparent, definite, distinct, palpable, sensible, tangible **10** detectable, noticeable, observable **11** appreciable, discernible **12** recognizable

perception 3 ken **4** idea **5** grasp, image **6** acumen, notion **7** concept, feeling, insight, thought **9** awareness, cognition **10** impression **11** discernment, observation

perceptive 4 keen, sage, wise **5** acute, alert, aware, sharp **7** knowing **9** intuitive, observant, sagacious, sensitive **10** discerning, insightful, responsive **13** understanding

perch 3 bar, peg, set **4** fish, land, rest, seat **5** light, roost, sit on **6** alight, settle **7** set down, sit atop, sit down

perchance 5 maybe **6** mayhap **7** perhaps **8** possibly **11** conceivably

percipience 6 acumen **8** keenness **9** cognition, intuition **10** astuteness **11** discernment **12** appreciation, perspicacity **13** comprehension

percolate 4 drip, ooze, seep **5** exude, leach **6** charge, filter, simmer, spread **7** pervade, trickle **9** penetrate

percussion 3 jar **4** bump, jolt **5** clash, crash, shock **6** impact **9** collision **10** concussion *instrument:* (see at **musical instrument**)

Perdita *father:* **7** Leontes *mother:* **8** Hermione

perdition 4 hell **5** hades **7** inferno **9** damnation **10** underworld **11** netherworld

Père Goriot author 6 Balzac (Honoré de)

peregrination 4 trek, trip, walk **7** journey, travels **9** traversal **10** expedition

peremptory 5 bossy, final **7** haughty **8** absolute, arrogant, decisive, dogmatic, imperial **9** imperious, masterful **10** autocratic, commanding, disdainful, high-handed, imperative **11** dictatorial, domineering, magisterial, overbearing

perennial 7 durable **8** constant, enduring, lifelong **9** continual, long-lived, permanent, perpetual, recurrent, unceasing **10** continuing, persistent, persisting, unchanging **11** long-lasting

Perez *brother:* **5** Zerah *father:* **5** Judah *mother:* **5** Tamar

perfect 4 full, pure **5** exact, ideal, model, right, sound, total, utter, whole **6** entire, expert, intact, polish, proper, refine **7** correct, improve, precise **8** absolute, accurate, complete, finished, flawless, peerless, spotless, unbroken, unflawed **9** downright, excellent, faultless, matchless, stainless, unalloyed, undiluted **10** consummate, impeccable, proficient **11** unequivocal, unmitigated, unqualified

perfection 4 acme **5** ideal **6** purity, virtue **7** paragon **9** integrity, wholeness **10** excellence, excellency **12** flawlessness

perfectly 5 fully, quite **6** wholly **7** to a turn, utterly **8** entirely **10** altogether, completely, thoroughly

perfidious 5 false **6** untrue **8** disloyal **9** deceitful, dishonest, faithless **10** treasonous, traitorous, unfaithful, unreliable **11** treacherous

perfidy 6 deceit **7** falsity, sellout, treason **8** betrayal **9** falseness, treachery **10** disloyalty, infidelity **13** faithlessness

perforate 3 pit **4** bore **5** drill, prick, punch **6** pierce **8** puncture **9** penetrate

perform 2 do **3** act **4** play, work **5** enact **6** behave, comply, effect **7** achieve, execute, fulfill, operate, playact, present, satisfy **8** bring off, carry out, complete, function **9** discharge, entertain, implement **10** accomplish

performance 3 act **4** deed, feat, show, work **6** acting, action **7** conduct, display **8** behavior, efficacy, exercise **9** discharge, execution, operation **10** efficiency, exhibition **11** achievement, fulfillment **12** presentation

performer 4 doer, mime **5** actor, mimic **6** mummer, player **7** actress, artiste, trouper **8** thespian **9** playactor **12** impersonator

perfume 4 balm **5** aroma, cense, scent, smell, spice **6** sachet **7** bouquet, incense, odorize **9** aromatize, fragrance, redolence *source:* **4** musk **5** attar, myrrh, orris **8** bergamot

perfumer 4 Dior (Christian), Nose (The) 5 Estée 6 Chanel (Coco), Lanvin, Lauder 8 Guerlain (Aimé, Jacques), Guichard (Aurelien, Jean)

perfunctory 7 cursory, routine 8 careless 9 automatic 10 impersonal, mechanical 11 superficial

pergola 5 arbor, bower 7 trellis

perhaps 5 maybe 8 feasibly, possibly 9 perchance 11 conceivably

periapt see amulet

Pericles *father:* 10 Xanthippus *mistress:* 7 Aspasia *mother:* 8 Agariste

peril 4 risk 6 danger, hazard, menace 8 exposure, jeopardy 9 liability 12 endangerment

perilous 5 hairy, risky 6 chancy, unsafe 7 unsound 9 dangerous, desperate, hazardous, uncertain 11 treacherous

_____ **Perilous** 5 Siege

perimeter 4 edge 5 limit, verge 6 border, bounds, margin 8 boundary

period 3 age, end, era 4 span, stop, term, time 5 cycle, phase, point, spell, stage 6 extent 8 division, duration, interval, sentence

periodic 6 cyclic, fitful 7 regular 8 cyclical, repeated, sporadic 9 recurrent, recurring 10 occasional 11 fluctuating 12 intermittent

periodical 3 mag 5 organ 6 cyclic, review 7 journal 8 cyclical, magazine 9 alternate, newspaper, recurrent, recurring 10 isochronal 11 isochronous, publication 12 intermittent

peripatetic 6 moving, roving 7 nomadic, walking 8 ambulant, vagabond 9 itinerant, traveling, wayfaring 10 ambulatory, pedestrian, travelling 13 perambulatory

peripheral 6 remote 7 lateral, surface 8 farflung, marginal, outlying 9 auxiliary, secondary 10 borderline, tangential 11 out-of-the-way 13 supplementary

perish 3 die, end 4 pass 5 cease 6 be lost, demise, depart, expire, vanish 7 decease, decline, go under, succumb 8 collapse, pass away 9 disappear

perjure 3 lie 6 delude 7 deceive, distort, falsify, mislead 8 forswear 9 misinform 10 equivocate 11 prevaricate

perk 4 gain, mend, plus 5 bonus, cheer, extra 7 benefit, freshen, improve, refresh, smarten 8 brighten

perky 5 alert, cocky, happy 6 bouncy, bubbly, cheery, chirpy, frisky, jaunty, lively, upbeat 7 buoyant, chipper 8 animated, cheerful, spirited, sportive 9 energetic, sparkling, sprightly, vivacious 12 effervescent, high-spirited

permanent 5 fixed 6 stable 7 abiding, durable, lasting 8 constant, enduring, hair wave 9 continual, perennial 10 changeless, invariable, unchanging 11 established, everlasting 12 imperishable

permeable 6 porous, spongy 8 pervious 9 absorbent, diffusive 10 penetrable

permeate 5 imbue 6 drench, infuse, spread 7 diffuse, pervade, suffuse 8 saturate 9 penetrate, percolate 10 impregnate, infiltrate 11 pass through

permissible 4 okay 5 legal 7 allowed 8 approved 9 allowable, tolerable, tolerated 10 acceptable, authorized, sanctioned

permission 5 leave 6 assent, permit 7 consent, license 8 approval, sanction 9 agreement, allowance 11 approbation, endorsement 12 acquiescence 13 authorization

permissive 3 lax 4 open 7 lenient, liberal 8 tolerant 9 easygoing, forgiving, indulgent 10 forbearing 11 acquiescent, complaisant

permit 3 let 4 okay, pass 5 agree, allow, grant, leave 6 accede, enable, say yes, suffer 7 consent, license, warrant 8 sanction, tolerate 9 allowance, authorize, give leave 10 permission 13 authorization

permutation 6 change 7 variety, version 9 variation 10 alteration, innovation 11 arrangement, vicissitude 12 modification

pernicious 4 evil 5 fatal, toxic 6 deadly, lethal, malign, wicked 7 baleful, baneful, harmful, hurtful, killing, malefic, noxious, ruinous 8 damaging, sinister, virulent 9 injurious, malignant, offensive, poisonous 10 maleficent 11 deleterious, destructive, detrimental, devastating

Pernod flavor 5 anise 8 licorice

perorate 5 speak 7 declaim, lecture 8 bloviate, harangue, proclaim 9 hold forth, speechify

perpend 5 study, weigh 6 ponder 7 examine, reflect 8 consider, think out 9 reflect on, think over 10 excogitate, think about 11 contemplate

perpendicular 5 plumb, sheer, steep 7 upright 8 straight, vertical 11 precipitate, precipitous

perpetrate 6 commit, effect 7 inflict, execute, perform 8 carry out 10 bring about

perpetual 7 endless, eternal, undying 8 constant, unending 9 ceaseless, continual, incessant, perennial, recurrent, unceasing 10 continuous 11 everlasting, unremitting

perpetuate 7 sustain 8 conserve, continue, eternize, maintain, preserve 9 keep alive 10 eternalize 11 immortalize

perplex 5 befog, mix up, stump 6 baffle, bemuse, muddle, puzzle **7** buffalo, confuse, mystify, nonplus, perturb **8** befuddle, bewilder, confound, distract, entangle **9** dumbfound **10** discompose

perplexed 7 at a loss, mixed up, puzzled **8** confused

Perry Mason *author:* **7** Gardner (Erle Stanley) *character:* **5** Drake (Paul), Drumm (Lt. Steve), Mason (Perry), Tragg (Lt. Arthur) **6** Burger (Hamilton), Street (Della) **8** Anderson (Lt. Andy) *TV star:* **4** Burr (Raymond), Hale (Barbara)

perquisite 3 tip **4** gain **5** right **6** profit **7** benefit, payment **8** gratuity **9** privilege

per se 6 as such, solely **8** in itself **11** essentially **13** intrinsically

persecute 4 bait, ride **5** annoy, harry, hound, worry, wrong **6** badger, harass, hector, injure, molest, pester, pick on, plague, punish, pursue **7** afflict, oppress, torment, torture **8** aggrieve

Persephone 4 Kore **10** Proserpina *father:* **4** Zeus **7** Jupiter *husband:* **5** Hades, Pluto *mother:* **5** Ceres **7** Demeter

Perseus *father:* **4** Zeus **7** Jupiter *grandfather:* **8** Acrisius *mother:* **5** Danaë *victim:* **6** Medusa **8** Acrisius *wife:* **9** Andromeda

perseverance 8 tenacity **9** diligence, endurance **10** dedication **11** persistence **13** steadfastness

persevere see **persist**

Persia 4 Iran

Persian *ancient:* **4** Mede *fairy:* **4** peri *governor:* **6** satrap *language:* **5** Farsi, Parsi *mystic:* **4** sufi *New Year's:* **6** Nowruz *poet:* **4** Omar **5** Hafez, Hafiz **7** Firdusi **8** Ferdowsi, Firdausi, Firdawsi, Firdousi **11** Omar Khayyám *prophet:* **9** Zoroaster *robe:* **6** caftan *sacred books:* **6** Avesta *sun-god:* **7** Mithras *title:* **4** shah *writing:* **9** cuneiform

persiflage 6 banter, joking **7** jesting, kidding, ribbing **8** badinage, raillery, repartee

persist 4 go on, last **5** abide **6** endure, hang on, keep on, linger **7** carry on, prevail **8** continue **9** persevere

persistence 8 duration **9** endurance **10** continuity **11** continuance **12** continuation

persistent 6 dogged **7** lasting **8** enduring, obdurate, stubborn **9** continual, steadfast, tenacious **10** continuing, determined, relentless, unshakable **11** persevering, unremitting

persnickety 5 fussy, picky **6** choosy **7** finicky **8** exacting **10** fastidious, particular

person 3 guy **4** self, soul **5** being, human **6** entity, mensch, mortal **8** creature, specimen **10** individual

personable 4 nice **6** genial **7** affable, amiable **8** charming, friendly, pleasant, pleasing **9** appealing, congenial **10** attractive

personage 3 VIP **5** human, mogul **6** bigwig, figure, honcho **7** big shot, magnate, notable **8** creature, luminary, somebody **9** celebrity, character, dignitary **10** individual

personal 3 own **5** privy **7** private, special **8** peculiar **10** individual, particular

personal effects 5 stuff **10** belongings **11** possessions

personality 3 ego, VIP **4** self **6** makeup, nature, temper **7** notable **8** identity, selfhood **9** celebrity, character **10** complexion **11** disposition, singularity, temperament **13** individuality

personate 3 act **4** play **5** enact **6** embody, typify **7** perform **9** epitomize, exemplify, represent **10** illustrate

personify 6 embody, typify **8** stand for **9** actualize, epitomize, exemplify, incarnate, represent, symbolize **11** emblematize

perspective 4 view **5** angle, scene, slant, vista **7** outlook **8** position, prospect **9** viewpoint **10** standpoint **11** point of view

perspicacious 4 keen **5** acute, quick, savvy, sharp **6** astute, clever, shrewd **9** observant, sagacious **10** discerning, insightful, perceptive **11** penetrating

perspicacity 6 acumen **7** insight **8** keenness **10** astuteness, shrewdness **11** discernment, penetration, percipience

perspicuous 5 clear, lucid, plain **6** lucent, simple **7** crystal, precise **8** clear-cut, pellucid **11** unambiguous

perspiration 5 sweat

perspire see **sweat**

persuadable 4 open **7** willing **9** receptive **11** suggestible, susceptible

persuade 3 win **4** coax, lead, sell, sway, urge **5** argue **6** entice, induce, prompt **7** convert, impress, win over **8** convince **9** influence, prevail on **11** bring around

persuasion 4 kind, mind, sort, type, view **5** group **6** belief, school **7** faction, opinion **8** argument **9** character, prejudice, sentiment **10** connection, conviction **11** affiliation, description

Persuasion *author* **6** Austen (Jane)

persuasive 6 cogent **7** telling, winning **8** credible **10** compelling, convincing **11** influential

pert 4 bold, chic, flip, trim **5** alert, cocky, fresh, lippy, sassy, saucy, smart **6** brazen, bright, cheeky, jaunty, lively **7** forward **8** animated, flippant, spirited **9** audacious, sprightly, vivacious

pertain 5 apply, refer **6** affect, bear on, belong, regard, relate **7** concern **8** bear upon **9** touch upon

pertinacious 4 firm **5** fixed **6** dogged, mulish **7** willful **8** resolute, stubborn **9** obstinate, tenacious **10** inflexible, persistent, unshakable, unyielding

pertinent 3 apt, fit **5** ad rem **7** apropos, fitting, germane **8** apposite, material, relevant **10** applicable **11** appropriate

perturb 5 upset, worry **6** bother **7** agitate, disturb, fluster, trouble **8** disorder, disquiet, unsettle **10** discompose, disconcert

Peru *ancient civilization:* **4** Inca *capital:* **4** Lima *city:* **5** Cusco, Cuzco **6** Callao **8** Arequipa, Trujillo *conqueror:* **7** Pizarro (Francisco) *ethnic group:* **7** Quechua *lake:* **8** Titicaca *language:* **6** Aymara **7** Quechua, Spanish *leader:* **8** Fujimori (Alberto) *monetary unit:* **3** sol *mountain, range:* **5** Andes **9** Huascarán *neighbor:* **5** Chile **6** Brazil **7** Bolivia, Ecuador **8** Colombia *river:* **6** Amazon **7** Marañón *volcano:* **5** Misti **7** El Misti **8** Yucamani

peruse 4 read, scan **5** study **6** survey **7** examine **8** consider, look over, pore over

Peruvian singer 5 Sumac (Yma)

pervade 5 imbue **6** spread **7** diffuse **8** permeate, saturate **9** penetrate, percolate, transfuse **10** impregnate

perverse 5 balky **6** cranky, mulish, ornery **7** corrupt, deviant, froward, peevish, wayward, willful **8** contrary, depraved, improper, stubborn **9** incorrect, irritable, obstinate **10** degenerate, headstrong, refractory **11** stiff-necked, wrongheaded **12** crossgrained, unreasonable

pervert 4 ruin, skew, warp **5** abuse, twist **6** debase, divert, garble, misuse **7** corrupt, debauch, deprave, distort, deviant, falsify, vitiate **8** misstate, mistreat **9** misdirect

pervious 4 open **6** porous **9** permeable **10** accessible, penetrable

pesky 6 vexing **7** irksome **8** annoying **9** vexatious **10** bothersome **11** troublesome

pessimist 5 cynic **9** Cassandra, defeatist, doomsayer, worrywart **11** misanthrope

pessimistic 6 gloomy, morose **7** cynical **10** despairing **11** distrustful **12** misanthropic

pest 4 bane **5** trial, worry **6** bother, nudnik, plague, vermin **7** nudnick, trouble **8** irritant, nuisance, vexation **9** annoyance, tormentor

pester 3 bug, irk, nag **4** ride **5** annoy, harry, tease, worry **6** badger, bother, harass, hassle, plague **7** bedevil, disturb, torment **8** irritate

pestiferous 7 baneful, noxious **8** annoying, infected **9** infective, pestilent **10** pernicious **11** troublesome

pestilence 5 curse **6** plague **7** scourge

pestilential 5 fatal **6** deadly, lethal, vexing **7** baneful, deathly, noxious, ruinous **8** annoying **10** pernicious

pestle 4 mano **6** muller *vessel:* **6** mortar

pet 3 cat, dog, hug **4** dear, kiss, love, neck, pout, sulk **5** loved, spoon **6** caress, cosset, dandle, fondle, pamper, stroke **7** beloved, cherish, darling, indulge **8** favorite, treasure **9** cherished

petcock 3 tap **5** valve **6** faucet, spigot

Peter Grimes composer 7 Britten (Benjamin)

peter out 4 fade, wane **5** abate, cease **6** lessen, recede, run dry **7** dwindle **8** decrease, diminish, taper off **9** drain away

Peter Pan *author:* **6** Barrie (James) *character:* **5** Wendy **7** Michael **9** Tiger Lily **10** Tinker Bell *dog:* **4** Nana *family:* **7** Darling *pirate:* **4** Hook, Smee

Peter the Apostle *brother:* **6** Andrew *father:* **5** Jonah *original name:* **5** Simon

Peter the Great *father:* **6** Alexis *mother:* **8** Nataliya *wife:* **7** Eudoxia **9** Catherine

petite 5 small **6** little **8** smallish **10** diminutive

petition 3 ask **4** plea **5** plead **6** appeal **7** beseech, entreat, implore, request, solicit **8** entreaty **10** supplicate **11** application **12** supplication

Petrarch's beloved 5 Laura

Petrified Forest author 8 Sherwood (Robert)

petrify 4 daze, numb, stun **5** chill, scare **6** benumb, deaden, harden **7** startle **8** confound, frighten, paralyze

Petruchio's wife 9 Katharina, Katharine

pettifogger 7 shyster **8** quibbler **9** nitpicker

petty 4 mean **5** minor, small **6** measly, narrow, paltry **7** trivial **8** niggling, picayune, piddling, trifling **9** frivolous, secondary **10** irrelevant, negligible **11** small-minded, subordinate, unimportant **13** insignificant

petty officer 6 noncom

petulant 5 huffy, moody, sulky, testy, whiny **6** touchy **7** grouchy, peevish **8** snappish **9** irascible, irritable, querulous **10** ill-humored

pew 3 row **4** seat **5** bench

peyote 6 cactus, mescal *drug:* **9** mescaline

Phaedra *father:* **5** Minos *husband:* **7** Theseus *mother:* **8** Pasiphaë *sister:* **7** Ariadne *stepson:* **10** Hippolytus

Phaëthon's father 6 Helios **7** Phoebus

phalanx 4 army, host, mass **5** horde **6** myriad, throng **6** troops

phantasm 5 dream, fancy, ghost 6 spirit, vision 7 fantasy, fiction, figment, specter, spectre 8 daydream, delusion, illusion 9 invention 10 apparition 11 fabrication 13 hallucination

phantom 5 dummy, ghost, shade, spook 6 goblin, shadow, spirit, vision 7 bugbear, chimera, eidolon, specter, spectre 8 illusory, spectral 9 imaginary 10 apparition, fictitious 12 will-o'-the-wisp

pharaoh 3 Tut 4 Seti 5 Menes, ruler 6 Ahmose, Ramses, tyrant 7 Harmhab 8 Ikhnaton, Thutmose 9 Amenhotep, Merneptah 11 Tutankhamen, Tutankhaten

pharisee 9 hypocrite

pharmacist 8 druggist 10 apothecary *British:* 7 chemist

pharos 6 beacon 10 lighthouse

Pharsalus, battle of *vanquished:* 6 Pompey *victor:* 6 Caesar (Julius)

phase 4 part, side, view 5 point, stage, state 6 adjust, aspect 7 conduct 8 carry out, position 9 condition, situation, viewpoint 10 appearance

PhD exam 5 orals

Phèdre author 6 Racine (Jean)

phenomenal 6 actual 7 unusual 8 material, physical, sensible, singular, tangible, uncommon 9 corporeal, fantastic, objective 10 astounding, remarkable 11 astonishing, exceptional, outstanding, perceivable, perceptible, substantial 13 extraordinary

phenomenon 4 fact 5 event 6 marvel, object, rarity, wonder 7 miracle, reality 9 actuality, sensation 10 experience, uniqueness 11 peculiarity, singularity

philander 8 womanize

philanthropic 6 giving, humane 8 generous 10 altruistic, benevolent, bighearted, charitable 11 magnanimous 12 eleemosynary, humanitarian

philanthropist *American:* 5 Gates (Bill) 6 Cooper (Peter), Girard (Stephen), Mellon (Andrew) 7 Buffett (Warren), Cornell (Ezra), Eastman (George), Packard (David), Whitney (Gertrude Vanderbilt) 8 Carnegie (Andrew), Stanford (Leland) 9 Rosenwald (Julius) 10 Vanderbilt (Cornelius) 11 Rockefeller (J. D.) *English:* 11 Wilberforce (William) *Swedish:* 5 Nobel (Alfred)

Philemon's wife 6 Baucis

philharmonic 8 symphony 9 orchestra, symphonic

Philip of Macedonia *father:* 7 Amyntas *son:* 9 Alexander

philippic 4 rant 6 tirade 8 diatribe, harangue, jeremiad 12 condemnation

Philippics author 6 Cicero

Philippines *capital:* 6 Manila *city:* 4 Cebu 5 Davao 10 Quezon City *discoverer:* 8 Magellan (Ferdinand) *guerrilla:* 3 Huk 10 Hukbalahap *island:* 4 Cebu 5 Leyte, Luzon, Panay, Samar 6 Negros 7 Masbate, Mindoro, Palawan 8 Mindanao *language:* 7 Ilocano, Tagalog 8 Filipino, Pilipino *leader:* 6 Aquino (Corazon), Marcos (Ferdinand) *liberator:* 9 MacArthur (Douglas) *patriot:* 5 Rizal (José) *monetary unit:* 4 peso *people:* 3 Ati 4 Moro *sea:* 4 Sulu 5 Samar 7 Celebes, Sibuyan, Visayan 8 Mindanao 10 Philippine, South China *volcano:* 4 Taal 5 Mayon

Philippi victor 6 Antony (Marc, Mark) 8 Octavian

Philip the Tetrarch *father:* 5 Herod *mother:* 9 Cleopatra

philistine 4 boob 7 Babbitt 9 bourgeois, vulgarian 10 capitalist 11 materialist

Philistine *champion:* 7 Goliath *city:* 4 Gath, Gaza 5 Ekron 6 Ashdod 8 Ashkelon *foe:* 5 David 6 Samson *god:* 5 Dagon

Philoctetes *father:* 5 Poeas *victim:* 5 Paris

Philomela 11 nightingale *father:* 7 Pandion *ravisher:* 6 Tereus *sister:* 6 Procne

philosopher *American:* 5 Adler (Mortimer), Dewey (John), James (William), Quine (Willard), Rorty (Richard), Royce (Josiah) 6 Langer (Susanne), Peirce (C. S.) 7 Marcuse (Herbert), Mumford (Lewis), Strauss (Leo) 9 Santayana (George) *Arab:* 8 Averroës, Avicenna *Austrian:* 6 Popper (Karl) 12 Wittgenstein (Ludwig) *Chinese:* 5 Laoxi 6 Lao-tsu 7 Dai Zhen, Mencius, Tai Chen 9 Confucius *Danish:* 11 Kierkegaard (Soren) *Dutch:* 7 Erasmus (Desiderius), Spinoza (Baruch de) *English:* 4 Ayer (A. J.), Joad (C. E. M.), Mill (John Stuart), More (Henry, Thomas), Watt (James) 5 Bacon (Francis), Burke (Edmund), Locke (John), Moore (G. E.), Occam (William of), Paine (Thomas) 6 Berlin (Isaiah), Hobbes (Thomas), Huxley (Thomas), Ockham (William), Popper (Karl) 7 Bentham (Jeremy), Russell (Bertrand), Spencer (Herbert), Whewell (William) 9 Whitehead (Alfred North) 12 Wittgenstein (Ludwig) *Finnish:* 11 Westermarck (Edward) *French:* 4 Weil (Simone) 5 Comte (Auguste), Taine (Hippolyte) 6 Pascal (Blaise), Sartre (Jean-Paul), Valéry (Paul) 7 Abelard (Peter), Bergson (Henri), Derrida (Jacques), Diderot (Denis), Fourier (Charles) 8 Foucault

(Michel), Maritain (Jacques), Rousseau (Jean-Jacques), Voltaire **9** Descartes (René), Montaigne (Michel de) **10** Saint-Simon (Comte de) **11** Montesquieu (Baron de) **12** Merleau-Ponty (Maurice) *German:* **4** Kant (Immanuel), Marx (Karl) **5** Frege (Gottlob), Hegel (Georg Wilhelm Friedrich), Wolff (Christian von) **6** Carnap (Rudolf), Fichte (Immanuel, Johann), Herder (Johann von) **7** Husserl (Edmund), Jaspers (Karl), Leibniz (Gottfried) **8** Spengler (Oswald) **9** Heidegger (Martin), Nietzsche (Friedrich), Schelling (Friedrich von) **12** Schopenhauer (Arthur) **14** Albertus Magnus *Greek:* **4** Zeno **5** Plato, Timon **6** Thales **7** Gorgias, Proclus **8** Diogenes, Epicurus, Longinus, Socrates **9** Aristotle, Epictetus **10** Anaxagoras, Democritus, Empedocles, Heraclitus, Parmenides, Protagoras, Pythagoras, Xenocrates, Xenophanes **11** Anaximander **12** Theophrastus *Irish:* **8** Berkeley (George) *Italian:* **5** Croce (Benedetto) **6** Ficino (Marsilio) **11** Machiavelli (Niccolo) *Jewish:* **5** Buber (Martin), Philo **10** Maimonides (Moses) **12** Philo Judaeus *Roman:* **6** Seneca (Lucias Annaeus) **8** Boethius (Anicius), Plotinus **9** Lucretius *Scottish:* **4** Hume (David), Mill (James), Reid (Thomas) **7** Stewart (Dugald) *Spanish:* **6** Suárez (Francisco) **7** Unamuno (Miguel de) **13** Ortega y Gasset (José) *Swedish:* **10** Swedenborg (Emanuel)
philosopher's stone 3 key **6** elixir
philosophical 4 calm **7** stoical **8** composed, rational, resigned **9** unruffled **10** thoughtful
philosophy 6 system, theory, values **7** beliefs, inquiry **8** attitude, calmness **10** discipline *component:* **5** logic **6** ethics **10** aesthetics **11** metaphysics **12** epistemology
philter 4 drug **5** charm, tonic **6** potion **9** stimulant **10** love potion **11** aphrodisiac, restorative
Phineas *beloved:* **9** Andromeda *tormentors:* **7** Harpies *wife:* **9** Cleopatra
phlegm 5 humor, mucus **6** apathy **8** calmness, coolness, dullness **9** composure, sangfroid **10** equanimity **11** impassivity, nonchalance **12** indifference
phlegmatic 4 calm, cool, dull **5** aloof, stoic **6** stolid **8** detached **9** apathetic, impassive, lethargic **11** indifferent, unconcerned
Phlegyas *daughter:* **7** Coronis *father:* **4** Ares, Mars *son:* **5** Ixion
phobia see **fear**
Phobos 4 moon **9** satellite *brother:* **6** Deimos *father:* **4** Ares, Mars
Phocus *father:* **6** Aeacus **8** Ornytion *half brother:* **6** Peleus **7** Telamon *mother:* **8** Psa-

mathe *slayer:* **6** Peleus **7** Telamon *wife:* **7** Antiope
Phoebe 5 Diana **7** Artemis *daughter:* **4** Leto *father:* **9** Leucippus *mother:* **4** Gaea
Phoebus see **Apollo**
Phoenician *city:* **4** Acre, Tyre **5** Sidon *colony:* **8** Carthage *god:* **4** Baal **6** Eshmun *goddess:* **6** Baltis **7** Astarte
Phoenix *pupil:* **8** Achilles *sister:* **6** Europa *team:* **4** Suns **7** Coyotes **9** Cardinals **12** Diamondbacks
phony 4 fake, sham **5** bogus, cheat, faker, false, fraud **6** ersatz, humbug, pseudo **8** impostor, specious, spurious **9** charlatan, dishonest, pretender **10** ficticious, suspicious **11** counterfeit **12** hypocritical
photograph 3 pic **4** film, snap **5** shoot **6** glossy **7** picture, tintype **8** snapshot *color:* **5** sepia *three-dimensional:* **8** hologram
photographer 8 photoist **9** cameraman **10** shutterbug *famous:* **3** Ray (Man) **4** Capa (Cornell, Robert), Haas (Ernst), Hine (Lewis), Penn (Irving), Riis (Jacob) **5** Adams (Ansel), Arbus (Diane), Atget (Eugène), Brady (Mathew), Evans (Frederick, Walker), Frank (Robert), Horst (Horst Peter), Karsh (Yousuf), Lange (Dorothea), Model (Lisette), Nadar, Parks (Gordon), Ritts (Herb), Smith (W. Eugene), Weber (Bruce), White (Clarence, Minor) **6** Abbott (Berenice), Avedon (Richard), Beaton (Cecil), Brandt (Bill), Coburn (Alvin), Curtis (Edward S.), Newton (Helmut), Porter (Eliot), Rowell (Galen), Siegel (Eliot), Strand (Paul), Talbot (William Henry Fox), Weegee, Wegman (William), Weston (Brett, Edward) **7** Brassaï, Cameron (Julia Margaret), Emerson (Peter), Halsman (Philippe), Jackson (William Henry), Kertész (André), Salomon (Erich), Siskind (Aaron), Snowdon (Earl of), Thomson (John), Watkins (Carleton) **8** Callahan (Harry), Cosindas (Marie), Daguerre (Louis-Jacques-Mandé), Kasebier (Gertrude), Scavullo (Francesco), Steichen (Edward), Steinert (Otto) **9** Caponigro (Paul), Feininger (Andreas), Leibovitz (Annie), Meyrowitz (Joel), Muybridge (Eadweard), O'Sullivan (Timothy), Rejlander (Oscar), Rothstein (Arthur), Stieglitz (Alfred), Winogrand (Garry) **10** Cunningham (Imogen), Heartfield (John), Moholy-Nagy (Laszlo) **11** Bourke-White (Margaret), Eisenstaedt (Alfred) **12** Mapplethorpe (Robert)
photographic 5 exact, vivid **7** graphic **8** accurate, detailed **9** pictorial **11** picturesque

solution: **4** hypo **5** fixer, toner **7** reducer **9** developer

phrase 5 couch, frame, idiom **6** slogan **7** diction, express, styling, wording **8** locution, verbiage **9** catchword, formulate, verbalism, watchword **10** expression

Phrygian *god:* **4** Atys **5** Attis *goddess:* **6** Cybele *king:* **5** Midas **7** Gordius

phthisis 2 TB **11** consumption **12** tuberculosis

phylactery 5 charm **6** amulet **7** periapt **8** talisman

physic 4 cure, heal **5** purge **6** remedy **8** medicine **9** cathartic, purgative **10** medication

physical 4 real **5** lusty, rough **6** actual, bodily, carnal, sexual **7** fleshly, natural, somatic **8** concrete, corporal, material, sensible, tangible **9** corporeal, objective **10** phenomenal **11** perceivable, perceptible, substantial

physician 2 MD **3** doc **5** medic **6** doctor, medico **7** surgeon **8** sawbones *American:* **4** Koop (C. Everett), Rush (Benjamin), Salk (Jonas) **5** Minot (George), Spock (Benjamin), Still (Andrew) **6** Jarvik (Robert), Murphy (John), Weller (Thomas) **7** Huggins (Charles), Robbins (Frederick), Theiler (Max) **8** Richards (Dickinson) **9** Sternberg (George Miller) *Arab:* **8** Avicenna *Canadian:* **5** Osler (William) *English:* **4** Ross (Ronald) **6** Harvey (William), Jenner (Edward, William), Willis (Thomas) **8** Sydenham (Thomas) *French:* **5** Widal (Fernand) **7** Laveran (Charles) **10** Schweitzer (Albert) *German:* **7** Sylvius (Franciscus) *Greek:* **5** Galen **11** Hippocrates *Italian:* **7** Galvani (Luigi) *organization:* **3** AMA *South African:* **7** Barnard (Christiaan) *Swiss:* **10** Paracelsus (see also **Nobel Prize winner** *physiology or medicine; surgeon*)

physicist *American:* **4** Rabi (I. I.), Ting (Samuel) **5** Fermi (Enrico), Gibbs (J. Willard), Kusch (Polykarp), Mayer (Maria-Goeppert), Pauli (Wolfgang), Pupin (Michael), Segré (Emilio), Smyth (Henry DeWolf), Stern (Otto) **6** Teller (Edward), Townes (Charles), Wigner (Eugene) **7** Alvarez (Luis), Feynman (Richard), Goddard (Robert), Purcell (Edward) **8** Einstein (Albert), Gell-Mann (Murray), McMillan (Edwin), Millikan (Clark, Robert), Mulliken (Robert), Shockley (William), Van Allen (James) **9** Michelson (Albert), Schwinger (Julian) **11** Oppenheimer (J. Robert) *Austrian:* **4** Mach (Ernst) **7** Doppler (Christian) **11** Schrödinger (Erwin) *British:* **4** Snow (C. P.) **5** Dirac (B. A. M.), Jeans (James), Joule (James) **6** Dalton (John), Kelvin (Baron), Newton (Isaac), Powell (Cecil), Stokes (George) **7** Faraday (Michael), Hodgkin (Dorothy), Thomson (George, Joseph, William) **7** Tyndall (John) **8** Rayleigh (Lord), Robinson (Robert), Thompson (Benjamin, Silvanus) **9** Wollaston (William) **10** Richardson (Owen), Rutherford (Ernest), Wheatstone (Charles) *Chinese:* **4** Yang (Chen-Ning) *Danish:* **4** Bohr (Aage, Niels) *Dutch:* **6** Zeeman (Pieter) **7** Huygens (Christian), Lorentz (Hendrik), Zernike (Frits) **11** Van der Waals (Johannes) *French:* **4** Néel (Louis) **5** Arago (François) **6** Ampère (André-Marie), Perrin (Jean-Baptiste) **7** Coulomb (Charles-Augustin de), Kastler (Alfred), Réaumur (René-Antoine de) **8** Lippmann (Gabriel) *German:* **3** Ohm (Georg) **4** Laue (Max von), Wien (Wilhelm) **5** Hertz (Gustav, Heinrich), Stark (Johannes), Weber (Wilhelm) **6** Jensen (Hans), Lenard (Philipp), Nernst (Walther), Planck (Max) **7** Meitner (Lise) **8** Roentgen (Wilhelm) **9** Helmholtz (Hermann von), Kirchhoff (Gustav), Mossbauer (Rudolf) **10** Fahrenheit (Daniel), Hofstadter (Robert) *Indian:* **5** Raman (Chandrasekhara) *Irish:* **6** Walton (Ernest) *Italian:* **5** Rossi (Bruno), Volta (Alessandro) **7** Galileo (Galilei), Galvani (Luigi) **10** Torricelli (Evangelista) *Japanese:* **6** Yukawa (Hideki) **8** Tomonaga (Shinichiro) *Mexican:* **8** Vallarta (Manuel) *Russian:* **4** Tamm (Igor) **6** Landau (Lev) **9** Prokhorov (Aleksandr) *Scottish:* **4** Tait (Peter) **6** Wilson (Charles) **7** Maxwell (James Clerk) *Swedish:* **7** Rydberg (Johannes) **8** Angstrom (Anders), Siegbahn (Kai, Karl) *Swiss:* **6** Zwicky (Fritz) **7** Piccard (Auguste) (see also **Nobel Prize winner** *physics*)

physiognomy 3 mug **4** face **5** front **6** aspect, visage **7** profile **8** features **9** character **10** lineaments **11** countenance, temperament

physiologist *English:* **8** Starling (Ernest) *German:* **5** Weber (Ernst), Wundt (Wilhelm) **7** Schwann (Theodor) **9** Helmholtz (Hermann von) *Italian:* **11** Spallanzani (Lazzaro) (see also **Nobel Prize winner** *physiology or medicine*)

physique 3 bod **4** body, form **5** build, shape **6** figure, makeup **7** anatomy **9** structure **12** constitution

pianist *American:* **4** Nero (Peter), Tesh (John), Wild (Earl) **5** Janis (Byron), Watts (André) **6** Duchin (Peter), Joplin (Scott), Serkin (Peter, Rudolf) **7** Cliburn (Van), Istomin (Eugene), Ohlsson (Garrick), Perahia (Murray), Winston (George) **8** Graffman

(Gary), Horowitz (Vladimir), Pennario (Leonard) **9** Fleischer (Leon) **10** Johannesen (Grant), Rubinstein (Arthur) *Argentinian:* **8** Argerich (Martha) **9** Barenboim (Daniel) *Austrian:* **6** Czerny (Karl) **7** Brendel (Alfred) **8** Schnabel (Artur) *Bulgarian:* **11** Weissenberg (Alexis) *Canadian:* **5** Gould (Glenn) *Chilean:* **5** Arrau (Claudio) *Cuban:* **5** Bolet (Jorge) *English:* **4** Hess (Myra) **5** Ogdon (John) **6** Curzon (Clifford) *French:* **6** Cortot (Alfred) **7** Cziffra (Gyorgy) **9** Casadesus (Robert), Entremont (Philippe) **10** Saint-Saëns (Camille) *German:* **6** Kempff (Wilhelm) **8** Schumann (Clara) **9** Gieseking (Walter) *Hungarian:* **5** Liszt (Franz) **7** Cziffra (Gyorgy) *Italian:* **6** Busoni (Ferruccio) **7** Pollini (Maurizio) **8** Clementi (Muzio) *Japanese:* **6** Uchida (Mitsuko) *Polish:* **6** Chopin (Frédéric) **7** Hofmann (Josef) **10** Paderewski (Ignacy), Rubinstein (Arthur) *Romanian:* **4** Lupu (Radu) **7** Lipatti (Dinu) *Russian:* **6** Berman (Lazar), Gilels (Emil), Kissin (Evgeny) **7** Richter (Sviatoslav) **8** Horowitz (Vladimir), Pachmann (Vladimir von) **9** Ashkenazy (Vladimir) **10** Rubinstein (Anton) **12** Rachmaninoff (Sergey) *Spanish:* **6** Iturbi (José) **8** Granados (Enrique) **10** de Larrocha (Alicia) *Swiss:* **4** Anda (Geza) (see also **jazz musician**)

piano 5 grand **6** softly, spinet **7** quietly, upright **9** baby grand *builder:* **5** Knabe (William), Stein (Johann), Zumpe (Johann) **7** Baldwin (Dwight) **8** Steinway (Henry) **9** Bechstein (Friedrich) **10** Chickering (Jonas), Silbermann (Johann) *inventor:* **10** Cristofori (Bartolomeo) *keys:* **7** ivories *pedal:* **6** damper **9** sostenuto

piazza 5 patio, plaza, porch **6** square **7** balcony, gallery, portico, terrace, veranda **9** courtyard

picaro 5 rogue, rover, thief **6** pirate **7** brigand, corsair **8** bohemian, sea rover **9** buccaneer **10** freebooter

picayune 5 petty **6** measly, paltry, trifle **7** trivial **8** piddling **11** small-minded **13** insignificant

pick 3 rob, tap **4** best, carp, cull, open, pull, take, tool **5** elect, pluck, probe, prize **6** choice, choose, chosen, option, pierce, pilfer, remove, select, unlock **7** harvest, provoke **8** selected **9** exclusive, single out

picket 4 pale, post **5** fence, guard, stake, watch **6** sentry, tether **7** enclose, lookout, protest **8** palisade, sentinel, watchman **11** demonstrate

pickle 3 fix, jam **4** dill, spot **5** brine, treat **6** plight, scrape **7** dilemma, gherkin, trouble **8** marinate, preserve **10** difficulty **11** predicament

pick on 5 bully, harry, taunt, tease **6** hector, pester **9** criticize, single out

pick out 4 espy, name, spot **6** choose, descry, detect, select, take in **7** discern **8** identify, perceive **9** apprehend, ascertain, recognize **11** distinguish

pickpocket 3 dip **5** thief **6** dipper **8** cutpurse

pick up 3 buy, get **4** cull, gain, earn, land, lift, tidy **5** catch, glean, hoist, learn, raise, run in **6** arrest, detain, gather, notice, obtain, pull in, resume, revive **7** acquire, clean up, collect, restart **8** perceive **9** apprehend **10** appreciate, understand

pickup 3 ute **5** truck **9** detention **10** hitchhiker **11** improvement **12** acceleration

picky 5 fussy **6** choosy **7** finicky **10** fastidious, particular, pernickety **11** persnickety

picnic 4 snap **5** cinch **6** breeze, outing **7** cookout **8** cakewalk **11** piece of cake

picture 4 limn, show **5** image, photo, pinup **7** drawing, tableau **8** describe, painting, portrait **9** depiction, portrayal **10** simulacrum **11** delineation, description **13** spitting image *stand:* **5** easel

picturesque 5 vivid **6** quaint, scenic **8** artistic, charming

piddling 4 puny **5** petty **6** meager, meagre, measly, paltry **7** trivial **8** picayune, trifling **11** Mickey Mouse, unimportant **13** insignificant

pie 4 flan, tart **5** pasty **6** pastry **7** cobbler, dessert **8** turnover

piebald 5 mixed **6** motley **7** mottled **10** multicolor, variegated

piece 4 part **5** patch, slice **6** member, parcel **7** firearm, portion, section, segment **8** division, fraction, fragment **9** allotment **10** allocation

pièce de résistance 8 main dish **9** showpiece **11** centerpiece, chef d'oeuvre, masterpiece

piecemeal 5 apart **6** slowly **7** gradual **8** bit by bit **9** by degrees, gradually **11** fragmentary

piece of cake 4 snap **5** cinch **6** breeze, picnic, shoo-in **8** duck soup, kid stuff, pushover

pied 6 motley **7** blotchy, brindle, dappled, mottled **8** brindled, speckled **9** multihued **10** variegated **11** varicolored **12** parti-colored

pier 4 anta, dock, quay, slip **5** berth, jetty, levee, wharf **6** column, pillar **8** pilaster *architectural:* **4** anta

pierce 3 cut **4** stab **5** probe, spear **6** impale, incise, skewer **8** puncture **9** penetrate, perforate **10** run through

piercing 4 high, keen **5** acute, sharp **6** piping, shrill **8** shooting, stabbing, strident **9** knifelike **12** earsplitting *tool:* **3** awl

piety 6 fealty **7** loyalty **8** devotion, fidelity, sanctity **9** reverence **10** allegiance, dedication, devoutness **12** faithfulness

piffle 4 bosh, bunk **5** bilge, hokum, hooey **6** bunkum, drivel **7** baloney, eyewash, hogwash, rubbish, twaddle **8** malarkey, nonsense, tommyrot **9** poppycock **10** balderdash, codswallop

pig 3 hog **4** Babe, slob **5** Porky, shoat, swine **6** farrow, piglet, porker **7** casting, glutton *breed:* **5** Duroc **8** Tamworth **9** Berkshire, Hampshire, Yorkshire *female:* **3** sow **4** gilt *feral:* **9** razorback *litter:* **6** farrow *male:* **4** boar **6** barrow *meat:* **3** ham **4** pork **5** bacon **7** sausage **8** chitlins **12** chitterlings *sound:* **3** wee *wild:* **4** boar **7** peccary, warthog **8** babirusa

pigeon 3 Nun, sap **4** dupe, fool, gull, mark **5** chump, decoy, patsy **6** culver, stooge, sucker **7** fall guy, stoolie **8** rock dove *genus:* **7** Columba *house:* **4** cote, loft *kind:* **4** barb, rock **5** homer **6** homing, pouter, roller **7** carrier, crowned, fantail, tumbler *relative:* **4** dove *young:* **5** squab

pigeon hawk 6 merlin

pigeonhole 4 slot, sort **5** class, cubby, grade, group, niche **6** recess, shelve **7** catalog **8** category, classify, grouping **10** categorize **11** compartment

piggish 6 greedy **7** selfish, swinish **10** gluttonous

pigheaded 5 rigid **6** dogged, mulish **7** willful **8** contrary, perverse, stubborn **9** obstinate **10** inflexible, unyielding

piglet 5 shoat

pigment 3 dye **4** tint **5** color, paint, stain **8** colorant, dyestuff, tincture *black:* **9** lampblack *blue:* **4** cyan **5** azure, smalt **6** indigo **7** cyanine **8** cerulean **9** verdigris **11** ultramarine *brown:* **5** sepia *umber:* **6** bister, sienna *combining form:* **5** chrom **6** chromo *dark:* **7** melanin *green:* **7** celadon **8** viridian **10** biliverdin *orange:* **7** realgar **8** carotene *red:* **4** lake **5** eosin *toxic:* **8** gossypol *yellow:* **5** ocher, ochre **6** flavin, lutein **7** flavine, xanthin

pigpen 3 sty **4** dump, mess **5** hovel

pigskin 6 saddle **8** football

pike 4 dive, Esox, fish **5** spear **7** highway **8** pickerel

piker 5 miser **7** scrooge **8** tightwad **9** skinflint **10** cheapskate **12** penny-pincher

pilaster 4 pier **6** column, pillar

pilchard 7 herring, sardine

pile 3 fur, lot, nap **4** coat, fill, heap, hill, load, mass, much, pack, peck, pyre, rick **5** amass, crowd, drive, mound, stack **6** bundle, column, jumble **7** collect, fortune, reactor **8** quantity **9** great deal **10** assemblage, collection **11** aggregation **12** accumulation

pileup 4 mass **5** crash, smash **8** accident **9** collision **12** accumulation

pilfer 3 rob **4** lift, take **5** filch, pinch, steal, swipe **6** finger, snitch, thieve **7** purloin **11** appropriate

pilgarlic 4 butt **8** baldhead **13** laughingstock

Pilgrim 5 Alden (John) **6** Carver (John) **7** Puritan, Winslow (Edward) **8** Bradford (William), Brewster (William), Standish (Myles) *interpreter:* **7** Squanto *ship:* **9** Mayflower

pilgrim 5 hadji, hajji **6** palmer **8** traveler, wanderer, wayfarer

pilgrimage 4 hadj, hajj, trip **7** journey *destination:* **5** Mecca **6** Assisi, Delphi, Dodona, Fátima, Medina **7** Lourdes **8** Bodh Gaya **10** Canterbury, Kusinagara

Pilgrim's Progress 8 allegory *author:* **6** Bunyan (John) *hero:* **9** Christian

pill 4 ball, bore, pain, pest **5** bolus **6** pellet **7** capsule, lozenge **8** medicine, nuisance **9** annoyance

pillage 4 lift, loot, sack **5** booty, prize, reave, reive, spoil, steal **6** maraud, ravage, thieve **7** despoil, plunder, purloin **8** spoliate **9** depredate, desecrate

pillar 4 pier, post, prop **5** pylon, shaft, stela, stele **6** column, stelae (plural) **7** obelisk, support, upright **8** backbone, mainstay, pedestal, pilaster

pillory 6 stocks

pillow 3 pad **4** rest **7** bolster, cushion, support

pillowcase 4 sham

pilot 3 ace **4** lead, show, tool **5** drive, flier, guide, steer **6** airman, direct, leader **7** aviator, conduct, guiding, tracing **8** aviatrix, helmsman, shepherd *seat:* **7** cockpit

pimple 3 dot, zit **4** acne, boil, spot, stud **6** papule **7** blemish, blister, pustule, speckle **8** sprinkle, swelling

pin 3 leg, peg **4** clip, hold, join **5** affix, blame, rivet, stake **6** attach, broach, brooch, cotter, emblem, fasten, secure, trifle **8** fastener, hold down, ornament, restrain

pinafore 5 apron, dress, frock

pinch 3 bit, nab, nip **4** dash, lift, pain, take **5** filch, press, prune, run in, skimp, steal, swipe, taper, theft, tweak **6** arrest, crisis, narrow, pilfer, snatch, stress **7** confine, deficit, larceny, squeeze, straits **8** compress, exigency, hardship, juncture, pressure, stealing, straiten **9** apprehend, constrict, emergency, privation, tight spot **10** substitute

pinchbeck 4 fake, sham **5** alloy, bogus, false, phony **6** pseudo **8** spurious **9** brummagem **11** counterfeit

pinch hitter 3 sub **6** backup, fill-in, relief **7** stand-in **9** alternate, surrogate **10** substitute **11** alternative, replacement

pinchpenny 4 mean **5** cheap, close, mingy, tight **6** stingy **7** chintzy, costive, miserly, scrimpy **9** niggardly, penurious **11** closefisted, tightfisted **12** parsimonious

Pindar *home:* **6** Thebes *poem:* **3** ode

pine 4 ache, long, mope, sigh, tree, wish, wood **5** brood, crave, dream, yearn **6** desire, grieve, hanker, hunger, lament, thirst **7** conifer **8** languish **9** evergreen *textile screw:* **3** ara **4** hala **7** lauhala

Pine Tree State 5 Maine

pinhead 4 dolt, dope, fool **5** dunce **6** dimwit, doofus, nitwit **7** dullard **8** dumbbell **9** birdbrain

pinion 3 cog **4** bind, gear, wing **5** quill, tie up, truss **6** fetter, tether **7** disable, feather, shackle **8** cogwheel, restrain **9** hamstring

pink 3 cut **4** best, peak, stab **5** blush **6** flower, height, pierce **7** excited, paragon **9** perforate

pinna 3 ear, fin **4** wing **7** feather, leaflet

pinnacle 3 top, tor **4** acme, apex, peak **5** crest, crown, serac, spire **6** apogee, climax, height, summit, zenith **7** steeple **8** capsheaf, meridian **11** culmination

pinniped 4 seal **6** walrus

Pinocchio author 7 Collodi (Carlo) **9** Lorenzini (Carlo)

pinochle *card:* **3** ace, ten **4** jack, king, nine **5** queen *term:* **4** meld **5** widow **7** auction *two-handed:* **7** goulash

pinpoint 3 aim, fix **4** spot, tiny **5** exact, place **6** locate **7** precise **8** identify, stand out **9** determine, highlight, recognize **11** distinguish

Pinter play 8 Betrayal **9** Caretaker (The) **10** Homecoming (The)

pinto 4 pied, pony **5** horse, paint **7** mottled, piebald **8** skewbald

pint-size 3 wee **5** dwarf, small **6** midget, pocket **9** miniature **10** diminutive

pioneer 5 first, prime **6** maiden **7** explore, founder, initial, primary, settler **8** colonist, earliest, explorer, original **9** innovator **10** avant-garde, pathfinder **11** trailblazer **12** frontiersman *famous:* **5** Boone (Daniel), Bowie (Jim), Clark (William), Lewis (Meriwether) **6** Carson (Kit), Colter (John) **7** Bridger (Jim), Chapman (John), Frémont

(John C.), Whitman (Marcus) **8** Crockett (Davy)

pious 4 holy **5** godly **6** devout, worthy **7** devoted, dutiful **8** reverent, virtuous **9** hypocrite, pietistic, prayerful, religious **10** devotional **12** hypocritical

pip 3 dot **4** blip, peep, seed, spot **5** speck **9** break open

pipe 3 keg, tun **4** butt, cask, duct, flue, hose, tube **5** briar **6** barrel, convey, funnel, siphon **7** channel, conduct, conduit **8** aqueduct, hogshead **10** meerschaum *ceremonial:* **7** calumet *part:* **4** bowl, stem

pipe down 4 hush **5** dry up, quiet **6** shut up **7** be quiet

pipe dream 4 wish **7** chimera, fantasy **8** illusion

pipeline 5 works **6** system **7** channel, conduit, process **8** activity, supplier **10** connection

pipsqueak 6 shaver, squirt **7** tadpole **8** half-pint, small fry

piquancy 4 zest **5** gusto **6** relish

piquant 4 racy, tart **5** sharp, spicy, tangy, zesty **6** biting, lively, savory, snappy **7** peppery, pungent **8** poignant, spirited **9** flavorful, sparkling **10** appetizing **11** provocative, stimulating

pique 3 irk, vex **4** huff, miff, move **5** anger, annoy, peeve, pride, rouse **6** arouse, excite, nettle, offend, put out **7** dudgeon, offense, provoke, quicken **8** irritate, motivate, vexation **9** aggravate, annoyance, challenge, stimulate **10** exasperate, irritation, resentment

piracy 5 theft **7** lifting, looting, pillage, plunder, robbery **8** stealing, thievery **10** plagiarism

piranha 6 caribe

pirate 5 rover **6** looter, picaro, raider, robber, sea dog **7** brigand, corsair, sea wolf **8** marauder, picaroon, pillager, sea rover **9** buccaneer, plunderer, privateer, sea robber **10** freebooter *address:* **5** matey *English:* **4** Read (Mary) **5** Bonny (Anne), Teach (Edward) **6** Morgan (Henry) **7** Dampier (William) **10** Blackbeard *flag:* **10** Jolly Roger *French:* **7** Laffite (Jean), Lafitte (Jean) *Scottish:* **4** Kidd (William)

Pirates of Penzance, The *composer:* **8** Sullivan (Arthur) *librettist:* **7** Gilbert (W. S.)

pirogue 5 canoe **6** dugout

pirouette 4 spin, turn **5** twirl, wheel, whirl

piscator 6 angler **9** fisherman

pismire 3 ant

pistol 3 gat, rod **4** Colt **5** Glock, Luger **6** Magnum, Mauser, roscoe **7** bulldog, handgun **8** revolver, small arm **9** derringer, pepperbox *case:* **7** holster

pit 3 vie **4** dent, hell, hole, scar **5** arena, hades, match, shaft, stone **6** cavity, hollow, oppose **7** counter, play off **8** pockmark **11** indentation

Pit and the Pendulum author 3 Poe (Edgar Allan)

pitch 3 dip, set **4** buck, dive, drop, fall, hurl, line, play, plug, tilt, tone, toss **5** erect, fling, heave, lurch, put up, resin, slant, sling, slope, spiel, throw **6** encamp, go down, plunge **7** discard, incline, present, promote, sidearm **8** distance **9** advertise, declivity **13** advertisement *uneven:* **3** rub

pitch-dark 3 jet **4** ebon, inky **5** black, ebony, jetty

pitcher 4 ewer, olla, olpe, toby **5** cruse **6** beaker, flagon **7** creamer *area:* **5** mound *handle:* **3** ear **4** ansa see also **baseballer**

pitch in 3 aid **4** help **5** begin, set to, start **6** fall to **8** commence, get going, start off **9** subscribe, volunteer **10** contribute

piteous 3 sad **4** poor **8** pathetic **9** affecting **10** lamentable **11** distressing

pitfall 4 risk, snag, trap **5** catch, peril, snare **6** danger, hazard **9** booby trap **10** difficulty **12** entanglement

pith 3 nub **4** core, kill, meat, pulp **5** focus, heart **6** center, import, kernel **7** essence, nucleus **9** substance **10** importance **12** significance

pith helmet 4 topi **5** topee

pithy 5 brief, crisp, meaty, short, terse **6** cogent **7** compact, concise, pointed **8** succinct **12** epigrammatic **13** short and sweet

pitiable 4 poor **5** cheap, sorry **8** shameful **10** deplorable, lamentable **12** contemptible

pitiful 3 sad **4** mean, poor **5** cheap, sorry **6** meager, meagre, paltry, shabby **7** forlorn **8** beggarly, pathetic, wretched **9** miserable **10** despicable, inadequate **12** contemptible **13** heartbreaking

pitiless 4 cold, hard **5** cruel, harsh, stony **6** brutal **8** inhumane, uncaring **9** barbarous, unfeeling **10** unmerciful **11** coldhearted, hardhearted

pittance 4 wage **5** scrap, trace **6** trifle **7** modicum, peanuts **9** allowance

pity 3 rue **4** ache, ruth **5** mercy **6** regret, sorrow **7** empathy, feel for, sadness **8** distress, sympathy **10** compassion, condolence, sympathize **11** commiserate **13** commiseration

pivot 3 pin **4** slew, slue, turn **5** hinge, shaft, swing, wheel **6** center, swivel

pivotal 3 key **5** chief, vital **7** central, crucial **8** critical, decisive **9** essential, important

pixie 3 elf, fay, imp **5** antic, fairy, scamp **6** elvish, impish, rascal, sprite **7** brownie, coltish, playful, puckish **8** prankish **11** mischievous

pixilated 3 fey **7** bemused, erratic, flighty, muddled, touched **9** eccentric, whimsical **10** capricious

Pizarro, Francisco *brother:* **7** Gonzalo *city founded:* **4** Lima *conquest:* **4** Peru *victims:* **5** Incas **9** Atahualpa **10** Atahuallpa

pizzazz 3 pep, vim, zip **4** bang, brio, dash, élan, snap, zest, zing **5** éclat, flair, flash, gusto, moxie, oomph, punch, verve **6** dazzle, energy, hoopla, sizzle, spirit **7** glamour, panache **8** vitality **10** excitement

placard 4 bill, post **6** notice, plaque, poster **7** affiche **8** handbill

placate 4 calm, ease **6** pacify, soothe **7** appease, assuage, comfort, mollify, satisfy, sweeten, win over **10** conciliate, propitiate

place 3 lay, put, set **4** area, lieu, loci (plural), post, rank, site, spot, zone **5** locus, point, stead, tract **6** region, status **7** situate, station **8** district, identify, locality, location, pinpoint, position, standing **9** establish, recognize *combining form:* **3** top **4** loco, topo, topy

placid 4 calm, easy, mild **5** quiet, still **6** gentle, serene **7** halcyon **8** composed, peaceful, tranquil, waveless, windless **9** unruffled **10** complacent, unagitated, untroubled **11** undisturbed **13** imperturbable

plagiarize 4 copy, crib **5** steal **6** pirate **11** appropriate

plague 3 vex **4** bane, evil, pest **5** annoy, beset, curse, harry, hound, smite, trial, worry **6** blight, bother, infest, harass, hassle, hector, pester **7** afflict, bedevil, disease, disturb, scourge, torment, trouble **8** calamity, distress, epidemic, invasion, irritant, irritate, nuisance, outbreak, pandemic **9** annoyance, beleaguer **10** affliction, black death, pestilence **11** infestation

plaid 6 tartan

plain 3 lea **4** bald, bare, open, pure, veld **5** blunt, clear, field, frank, llano, pampa, usual, veldt **6** candid, common, homely, modest, pampas, patent, severe, simple, steppe, tundra **7** expanse, evident, obvious, prairie, savanna **8** apparent, distinct, everyday, homespun, manifest, ordinary, savannah, straight **9** outspoken, unadorned **10** absolutely, forthright, unaffected **11** undecorated, unvarnished **13** uncomplicated

plainclothesman 3 tec **4** dick **6** shamus,

sleuth **7** gumshoe **8** hawkshaw **9** detective **12** investigator

plainness 6 candor, purity **7** clarity, honesty **8** lucidity **10** simplicity

plainsong 5 chant **12** cantus firmus

plainspoken 4 open **5** frank **6** candid, direct, honest **8** straight, truthful **10** forthright **11** undisguised, unvarnished

plaintive 3 sad **4** glum **6** woeful **7** doleful, piteous, pitiful **8** dolorous, downcast, mournful **9** sorrowful **10** dispirited, lamentable, lugubrious, melancholy

plait 4 fold **5** braid, pleat, weave **7** pigtail **10** intertwine, interweave

plan 3 aim, map, way **4** cast, goal, idea, mean, plot **5** chart, frame **6** design, devise, intend, intent, lay out, map out, method, scheme, set out **7** arrange, diagram, drawing, outline, pattern, program, project, propose, purpose, work out **8** contrive, engineer, organize, strategy, think out **9** blueprint, formulate, intention, procedure **11** arrangement, formulation

plane 3 fly **4** even, flat, tool, tree **5** flush, level **6** smooth (see also **airplane**)

planet 4 Mars **5** Earth, Venus **6** Saturn, Uranus **7** Jupiter, Mercury, Neptune **dwarf:** 4 Eris **6** Ceres, Pluto **path:** 5 orbit **satellite:** 4 moon **shadow:** 5 umbra **small:** 8 asteroid

planetary 4 vast **6** global **7** erratic, immense **8** colossal, enormous **9** universal, wandering, worldwide **11** terrestrial

plangent 7 orotund, ringing, vibrant **8** resonant, sonorous **9** consonant, plaintive **10** expressive, resounding **11** reverberant

plank 4 item, wood **5** board, floor **6** lumber, timber **7** article, support

plant 3 fix, pot, set, sow **4** bury, grow, hide, mill, park, root, seed, tomb **5** cache, cover, imbed, inter, place, plunk, put in, stash, works **6** entomb, inhume, occult, screen **7** conceal, factory, install, lay away, put away, secrete **8** colonize, populate **9** cultivate **angiosperm:** 5 dicot **7** monocot **aquatic:** 4 reed **5** lotus, sedge **7** awlwort, cattail, fanwort, papyrus **8** duckweed, eelgrass, hornwort, pondweed **9** water lily **10** watercress **11** bladderwort **12** pickerelweed **aromatic:** 4 nard **6** lovage **9** spikenard **Australian:** 6 mallee **7** banksia **8** blackboy **10** eucalyptus **body:** 4 stem **7** thallus **bulbous:** 4 Ixia, lily **5** camas, onion, tulip **7** jonquil **8** hyacinth **9** narcissus **carnivorous:** 6 sundew **10** butterwort **12** pitcher plant, Venus flytrap **cell layer:** 7 phellem **climbing:** 3 ivy **4** vine **5** betel, liana, vetch **6** bryony, derris, smilax **7** creeper, jasmine **8** bignonia, fumitory,

moonseed, scammony, wisteria **12** morning glory **coloring agent:** 8 carotene **11** chlorophyll, xanthophyll **combining form:** 4 phyt **5** phyto **cone-bearing:** 3 fir, yew **4** pine **5** cedar, cycad **6** ginkgo, spruce **7** conifer, cypress, redwood **10** arborvitae, gymnosperm **desert:** 4 aloe **5** agave **6** cactus, cholla **8** mesquite, ocotillo **9** paloverde **11** brittlebush **disease:** 3 rot **4** gall, mold, rust, scab, smut, wilt **5** ergot **6** blight, mildew, mosaic **7** blister **8** clubroot **9** black spot **10** black heart **extinct:** 8 calamite **flowerless:** 4 alga, fern, kelp, moss **5** algae (plural), fungi (plural) **6** fungus, lichen **7** seaweed **8** clubmoss **9** bryophyte, equisetum, horsetail, liverwort **fluid:** 3 gum, sap **4** milk **5** latex, resin **gland:** 7 nectary **hallucinogenic:** 4 hemp **5** poppy **6** mescal **8** cannabis **9** marijuana **hard-to-grow:** 5 miffy **largest:** 7 sequoia **life:** 5 flora **marine:** 4 kelp, nori **5** dulse, fucus **6** wakame **7** seaweed **8** gulfweed **10** sea lettuce **marsh:** 4 reed **5** carex, sedge **7** bogbean, bulrush, calamus, cattail **8** red maple, sphagnum **10** rose mallow **11** loosestrife **medicinal:** 4 aloe, sage **5** poppy, senna, tansy **6** catnip, fennel, garlic, hyssop, ipecac, nettle **7** aconite, boneset, burdock, camphor, comfrey, ginseng, hemlock, henbane, juniper, lobelia, mullein, mustard, parsley **8** camomile, capsicum, cinchona, feverfew, licorice, pilewort, plantain, wormwood **9** asafetida, chamomile, dandelion, echinacea, fenugreek, monkshood **10** asafoetida, goldenseal, peppermint **microscopic:** 4 mold **6** diatom **7** euglena **8** bacteria (plural) **9** bacterium **oldest:** 11 bristlecone **onion-like:** 4 leek **5** chive **7** shallot **8** scallion **opening:** 5 stoma **7** stomata (plural) **parasitic:** 6 dodder, fungus **7** pinesap **8** gerardia **9** broomrape, mistletoe, rafflesia, witchweed **10** beechdrops **part:** 3 bud, nut, sap **4** bark, bulb, cell, cone, corm, leaf, pome, root, seed, stem, wood **5** bract, drupe, fruit, grain, spore, stool, thorn, tuber, xylem **6** catkin, flower, nectar, phloem, raceme, spadix **7** rhizome **8** lenticel **9** cellulose, cotyledon **11** chlorophyll, chloroplast **13** inflorescence **pepper:** 3 ava **4** kava **pest:** 5 aphid, scale **6** chafer, thrips, weevil **7** cutworm **8** fruit fly, wireworm **9** gypsy moth **10** cankerworm, leafhopper, phylloxera **11** codling moth **poisonous:** 4 poke, upas **5** sumac **6** castor, croton, datura **7** amanita, cassava, cowbane, henbane, lobelia, tobacco **8** foxglove, larkspur, locoweed, mayapple, oleander, pokeweed **9** baneberry, monkshood **10** belladonna, jimsonweed, manchineel, nightshade *saprophytic:* 5 fungi (plural) 6 fungus 7 pinesap 9 pinedrops, snow plant 10 beechdrops, Indian pipe *succulent:* 4 aloe 5 agave 6 cactus 10 bitterroot *thorny:* 4 rose 5 briar 6 cactus, nettle, teasel 7 caltrop, thistle 9 cocklebur *tissue:* 5 xylem 6 phloem 7 cambium, medulla 8 meristem *young:* 5 scion, shoot 6 sprout 7 cutting 8 seedling

plantain 5 fruit 6 banana

plantation 5 manor 6 colony, estate, quinta 7 acreage, demesne 8 hacienda 10 encampment, habitation, settlement

plant louse 5 aphid

plaque 4 film 5 badge, patch 6 brooch, lesion, tablet 7 tribute 8 bacteria, memorial 13 commemoration

plaster 3 dab 4 coat 5 affix, cover, gesso 6 stucco 7 coating, conceal, overlay 8 dressing *of paris:* 5 gesso 6 gypsum

plastered 3 lit 4 high 5 drunk, lit up, oiled 6 bashed, blotto, bombed, juiced, potted, soaked, soused, stewed, stoned, tanked, wasted, zonked 7 crocked, drunken, pickled, pie-eyed, sloshed, smashed, sottish 10 inebriated, liquored up 11 intoxicated

plastic 4 soft 5 vinyl 6 pliant, supple 7 ductile, pliable 8 creative, flexible, moldable, workable 9 adaptable, formative, malleable, synthetic 10 artificial, credit card, sculptural

plat 3 lot, map 4 plan 5 chart, tract 6 parcel 7 quadrat

plate 4 base, coat, disc, dish, disk, gild, tile 5 layer, paten, scute, slice 6 enamel, fascia, lamina, plaque 7 anodize, lamella, overlay

plateau 4 mesa 5 table 6 upland 9 altiplano, tableland *arid:* 4 puna *barren:* 5 field 6 paramo *dry:* 5 karoo 6 karroo

platform 3 map 4 bank, base, dais, deck, plan 5 bimah, forum, ledge, riser, shelf, stage, stump 6 design, pallet, perron, podium, pulpit, scheme 7 balcony, pattern, rostrum 8 hustings, scaffold 9 banquette, manifesto 11 declaration *temporary:* 7 staging 8 scaffold *wooden:* 9 boardwalk

Plath, Sylvia *novel:* 7 Bell Jar (The) *poem:* 5 Ariel, Daddy

platinum symbol 2 Pt

platitude 6 cliché, truism 7 bromide 8 banality, prosaism 10 shibboleth

Plato *father:* 7 Ariston *literary form:* 6 dialog 8 dialogue *original name:* 10 Aristocles *school:* 7 Academy *work:* 3 Ion 4 Meno 5 Crito, Lysis 6 Laches, Phaedo 7 Apology, Gorgias 8 Phaedrus, Republic (The) 9 Charmides, Symposium

platter 5 plate 6 record 8 trencher

platypus 8 duckbill

plaudits 5 kudos 6 cheers, praise 7 acclaim, ovation 8 applause, approval, encomium 9 accolades 11 acclamation

plausible 8 credible, specious 10 believable, convincing, creditable, persuasive, reasonable

play 3 act, fun 4 game, jest, joke, romp 5 drama, feint, serve, sport, treat, trick, wager 6 cavort, comedy, fiddle, frolic, gambit, gambol, leeway, margin 7 delight, disport, perform 8 latitude, pleasure 9 amusement, diversion, enjoyment, stratagem 10 manipulate, recreation *an instrument:* 3 bow 4 beat, blow, pick 5 pluck, sound, strum 6 strike 7 squeeze *kind:* 5 farce 6 comedy 7 musical, tragedy 8 one-acter 9 melodrama, pantomime *part:* 3 act 5 scene 8 epilogue, prologue *passionate:* 9 melodrama *site:* 8 stage set

playact 5 put on 7 perform, posture, pretend 9 personate 11 impersonate, make believe

playboy 4 rake, roué 7 swinger 8 hedonist, lothario 9 bon vivant, libertine

play down 8 minimize 9 deprecate, softpedal, underrate 11 de-emphasize

player 5 actor 6 mummer 7 actress, athlete, trouper 8 musician, thespian 9 contender, performer 10 competitor, contestant 11 participant *reserve:* 11 benchwarmer

player piano 7 Pianola 10 Disklavier

play for time 5 stall

playful 5 antic, jolly, ludic, merry, pixie 6 elvish, frisky, impish, jocund, joking, jovial, lively 7 coltish, jocular, puckish, waggish 8 humorous, sportive 9 kittenish, sprightly 10 frolicsome

play off 3 pit, vie 5 match 6 oppose 7 counter 8 contrast

plaything 3 toy

play up 6 stress 7 feature 9 dramatize, emphasize, highlight, overstate, underline 10 accentuate, exaggerate, underscore

playwright 9 dramatist 10 dramaturge (see also **dramatist**)

plaza 6 circus, common, square, zocalo 9 carrefour 11 marketplace

plea 4 suit 5 alibi 6 appeal, excuse, orison, prayer 7 apology, defense, pretext, request 8 entreaty, overture, petition 11 application, imploration 12 supplication *defendant's:* 4 nolo 6 guilty 8 innocent 9 not guilty

plead 3 beg 4 pray 5 argue 6 allege, answer, appeal 7 beseech, entreat, implore 8 advocate, maintain 9 importune 10 supplicate

pleasant 4 fair, fine, good, nice 5 clear, sunny, sweet 6 cheery, genial, pretty 7 amiable, clarion, likable, welcome **8** amicable, charming, cheerful, engaging, gracious, grateful, likeable, pleasing, sunshine, sunshiny **9** agreeable, appealing, cloudless, congenial, convivial, enjoyable, favorable, unclouded **10** delightful, gratifying

pleasantry 3 fun **4** jest, joke **6** banter, levity **8** badinage, repartee **9** wittiness **10** jocularity

please 4 like, suit, wish **5** agree, amuse, enjoy, serve **6** choose **7** content, delight, gladden, gratify, indulge, satisfy *French:* **12** s'il vous plait *German:* **5** bitte *Spanish:* **8** por favor

pleasing 4 good, nice **6** pretty **7** welcome **8** suitable **9** agreeable, congenial, favorable, palatable **10** attractive, delightful, gratifying **12** satisfactory

pleasure 3 fun, joy **4** will **5** bliss, fancy **6** desire, liking, relish **7** delight, gladden, gratify **8** felicity, gladness, hedonism **9** amusement, diversion, enjoyment, happiness, merriment **11** inclination

pleat 4 fold **5** crimp **6** crease

plebe 5 frosh **8** freshman

plebeian 3 low **4** base **5** crude, lowly **6** coarse, common, humble, menial **8** commoner, everyday, ordinary **10** lower-class

plebiscite 4 vote

plectrum 4 pick

pledge 3 vow **4** bail, bind, bond, gage, hock, oath, pawn, seal, sign, word **5** drink, swear, toast, token **6** parole, plight, surety **7** chattel, earnest, promise, warrant **8** bailment, contract, covenant, guaranty, security, warranty **9** agreement, assurance, certainty, guarantee, undertake **11** hypothecate

pledget 3 pad **8** compress

Pleiades 4 Maia **6** Merope **7** Alcyone, Celaeno, Electra, Sterope, Taygeta **8** Asterope *brightest star:* **7** Alcyone

plenary 4 full **5** whole **6** entire **7** general **8** absolute, complete **9** inclusive **11** unqualified **12** unrestricted

plenitude 4 glut **6** excess **7** satiety, surfeit **8** fullness **9** abundance, profusion, repletion **11** copiousness, sufficiency, superfluity **12** completeness

plenteous 7 fertile **8** abundant, fruitful, prolific **9** abounding **10** productive

plentiful 4 full, rich, rife **5** ample, flush **7** copious, profuse **8** abundant, affluent, generous **9** abounding, bounteous, unstinted **10** sufficient

plenty 3 lot **4** heap, lots, pack, peck, pile **6** stacks, wealth **8** adequacy, fullness, mountain **9** abundance, affluence, great deal **10** cornucopia

pleonasm 8 verbiage **9** prolixity, tautology, verbosity, wordiness **10** redundancy **11** periphrasis, superfluity

plethora 4 glut **5** flood **6** excess **7** overrun, surfeit, surplus **8** fullness, overflow **9** abundance, profusion, repletion **11** superfluity **13** overabundance

plexus 4 rete **7** network

pliable 6 supple **7** plastic **9** adaptable **10** adjustable **11** complaisant, manipulable

pliant 5 lithe, supple **6** limber, supple **7** ductile, plastic, springy **8** flexible, moldable, workable, yielding **9** adaptable, malleable, tractable **10** manageable

plica 4 fold **6** crease, groove

plight 3 fix, jam, vow **4** hole, spot, word **5** swear **6** engage, pickle, pledge, scrape **7** betroth, dilemma, promise **8** quandary **9** betrothal **10** difficulty, engagement **11** predicament

plod 4 slog, toil **5** grind, slave, tramp, tread, tromp **6** drudge, lumber, trudge **8** plug away

plot 3 map **4** area, land, mark, note, plan, ruse **5** cabal, chart, story, tract **6** design, devise, invent, lay out, locate, parcel, scheme **7** collude, compact, connive, diagram, outline **8** conspire, contrive, intrigue, scenario **9** collusion, conniving, machinate **10** complicity, connivance, conspiracy **11** machination

plover 5 pewit, stilt **6** peewit **7** lapwing **8** dotterel, killdeer *relative:* **9** sandpiper, turnstone

plow 3 dig **4** till, turn **5** break **6** furrow, harrow, trench **8** turn over **9** cultivate *part:* **4** beam, frog **5** share **7** coulter **8** landside **9** moldboard

ploy 4 ruse, scam, wile **5** feint, trick **6** device, frolic, gambit, tactic **7** gimmick **8** artifice, escapade, maneuver **9** stratagem **11** contrivance

pluck 3 rob, tug **4** grit, guts, pick, pull, yank **5** cheek, grasp, heart, moxie, nerve, spunk **6** daring, fleece, mettle, remove, snatch, spirit, tweeze **7** bravery, courage, pull out

plucky 4 bold, game **5** brave **6** feisty, spunky **7** doughty **8** fearless, spirited, unafraid **9** dauntless **10** courageous

plug 3 tap **4** bung, clog, core, cork, fill, hype, pack, push, stop, tout **5** block, blurb, boost, choke, close, cry up, shoot, spile **6** device, remedy **7** congest, fitting, hydrant, promote, stopper **8** obstruct **9** advertise, publicity, publicize **10** connection

plug-ugly 4 goon, thug **5** bully, rowdy, tough

7 goombah, hoodlum, ruffian **8** enforcer **9** roughneck

plum 5 prize **6** purple, reward **7** guerdon, premium **8** dividend *dried:* **5** prune *kind:* **6** damson **7** bullace **9** greengage *spiny:* **4** sloe **10** blackthorn

plumage 8 feathers *early:* **4** down

plumb 5 delve, probe, sound **6** fathom, weight **7** examine, explore, install, measure **8** vertical **10** vertically **13** perpendicular

plume 4 tail **5** array, preen, pride, prize **6** column **7** feather **8** aigrette

plummet 4 dive, drop, fall **5** crash **6** plunge, tumble **8** collapse, nose-dive **11** precipitate

plump 3 fat **4** drop, fall, full **5** ample, buxom, favor, pudgy, round, stout, tubby **6** chubby, portly, rotund, zaftig **7** rounded, support **8** roly-poly **9** pneumatic **10** Rubenesque

plumply 7 frankly, plainly **8** candidly **12** forthrightly

plunder 3 rob **4** loot, sack, swag, take **5** booty, prize, seize, spoil, steal, strip **6** boodle, rapine, spoils **7** despoil, pillage, ransack, relieve, stick up **9** pillaging

plunge 3 bet, ram, run **4** dive, drop, fall, jump, rush, sink, stab, swim **5** drive, lunge, pitch, stick **6** charge, gamble, hasten, hurtle, thrust, topple, tumble **7** descend, immerse, plummet **8** nose-dive, submerge **9** penetrate

plus 3 and **4** also, more, perk **5** added, asset, bonus, boost, extra **6** excess **7** benefit **8** addition, increase, positive

plush 4 full, rich **6** deluxe, fabric, lavish, velvet **7** opulent **8** luscious, palatial **9** expensive, luxuriant, luxurious, sumptuous

Pluto 3 Dis **5** Hades *brother:* **4** Zeus **7** Jupiter, Neptune **8** Poseidon *father:* **6** Cronus, Saturn *mother:* **3** Ops **4** Rhea *wife:* **10** Persephone, Proserpina

plutocrat 5 mogul **6** fat cat, tycoon **7** magnate **9** financier, moneybags **10** capitalist

plutonian 8 infernal **10** underworld

plutonium symbol 2 Pu

Plutus *father:* 6 Iasion *god of:* **6** riches, wealth *mother:* **5** Ceres **7** Demeter

ply 3 use **4** bias, sail **5** apply, exert, layer, wield **6** employ, handle, strand, supply, travel, voyage **7** furnish, perform **8** maneuver, practice **11** inclination

pneuma 4 soul **5** anima **6** psyche, spirit

pneumatic 4 airy **5** ample, buxom, plump **6** aerial, zaftig **9** spiritual **10** curvaceous **11** atmospheric

poach 4 cook **5** steal **6** coddle, simmer **7** intrude **8** encroach, trespass **9** interlope **11** appropriate

Pocahontas *father:* 8 Powhatan *husband:* **5** Rolfe (John)

pock 3 pit **4** hole, spot **7** pustule

pocket 3 bag **4** lift, sack **5** filch, pinch, pouch, purse, steal, swipe **6** cavity **7** capsule, dead end, impasse **8** cul-de-sac **9** condensed **10** blind alley *billiards:* **4** pool

pocketbook 3 bag **4** poke **5** purse **6** clutch, income, wallet **7** handbag **8** billfold **9** clutch bag

pocket bread 4 pita **5** pitta

pocket money 6 change **9** petty cash **11** small change

pocket-size 4 tiny **5** small **9** miniature **10** diminutive

pod 3 bag, gam, sac **4** boll, case, hull, husk, skin **5** shell, shuck **6** cocoon **7** capsule, silique **8** seedcase *plant:* **3** pea **4** bean, okra **5** chili, gumbo **6** cassia, cowpea, legume, lentil, peanut, pepper **8** capsicum, mesquite, milkweed **9** lespedeza

pod-bearing tree 5 carob **6** locust **7** catalpa

podiatry 9 chiropody

podium 4 dais **6** pulpit **7** lectern, rostrum **8** platform

____ podrida 4 olla

Poe, Edgar Allan *detective:* 5 Dupin (C. Auguste) *poem:* **5** Bells (The), Raven (The) **6** Lenore **7** Israfel, To Helen, Ulalume **8** Eldorado, For Annie **10** Annabel Lee *tale:* **6** Ligeia, Shadow **7** Gold-Bug (The), Morella, Silence **8** Black Cat (The) **13** Tell-tale Heart (The) **15** Purloined Letter (The) **17** Cask of Amontillado (The), Pit and the Pendulum (The) **19** Masque of the Red Death (The) **21** Fall of the House of Usher (The)

poem 3 ode **4** epic, epos, idyl, rime, rune, song **5** ditty, elegy, epode, idyll, lyric, rhyme, verse **6** ballad, epopee, jingle, rondel, sonnet **7** eclogue, rondeau **8** limerick, madrigal *closing:* **5** envoi, envoy *division:* **4** foot, line **5** canto, epode, stich, verse **6** stanza **7** refrain **8** epilogue, prologue *Japanese:* **5** haiku, tanka *of eight lines:* **6** octave **7** triolet *of four lines:* **8** quatrain *of fourteen lines:* **6** sonnet *of three lines:* **7** triplet *pastoral:* **7** eclogue, georgic *short:* **5** ditty **7** epigram

poet 4 bard, muse, scop **5** skald **6** lyrist **7** elegist **8** idyllist, lyricist **9** balladist, sonneteer **10** Parnassian *American:* **3** Poe (Edgar Allan) **4** Dove (Rita), Hass (Robert), Nash (Ogden), Read (Thomas), Rich (Adrienne), Ryan (Kay), Tabb (John Banister), Tate (Allen) **5** Auden (Wystan Hugh), Benét (Stephen Vincent), Crane (Hart), Field (Eugene), Frost (Robert), Guest (Edgar), Moore (Marianne), Plath (Sylvia), Pound (Ezra), Riley (James Whitcomb), Wylie (Elinor) 6 Barlow (Joel), Bishop (Elizabeth), Brooks (Gwendolyn), Bryant (William Cullen), Ciardi (John), Dickey (James), Dunbar (Paul Laurence), Hughes (Langston), Kilmer (Joyce), Lanier (Sidney), Lowell (Amy, James Russell, Robert), McKuen (Rod), Millay (Edna St. Vincent), Pinsky (Robert), Ransom (John Crowe), Seeger (Alan), Strand (Mark), Taylor (Edward), Warren (Robert Penn), Wilbur (Richard) 7 Angelou (Maya), Ashbery (John), Collins (Billy), Emerson (Ralph Waldo), Freneau (Philip), Halleck (Fitz-Greene), Jeffers (Robinson), Lindsay (Vachel), Markham (Edwin), Merrill (James), Nemerov (Howard), Roethke (Theodore), Shapiro (Karl), Stevens (Wallace), Whitman (Walt) 8 Berryman (John), Cummings (E. E.), Ginsberg (Allen), MacLeish (Archibald), Robinson (Edwin Arlington), Sandburg (Carl), Teasdale (Sara), Wheatley (Phillis), Whittier (John Greenleaf), Williams (C. K., William Carlos) 9 Dickinson (Emily), Santayana (George) 10 Bradstreet (Anne), Longfellow (Henry Wadsworth) 12 Wigglesworth (Michael) *Anglo-Saxon:* 7 Caedmon, Cynwulf 8 Cynewulf, Kynewulf *Arab:* 5 Jarir 6 Hariri 8 al-Hariri *Australian:* 8 Paterson (Andrew Barton) *Belgian:* 11 Maeterlinck (Maurice) *Canadian:* 5 Pratt (Edwin John) 6 Hébert (Anne) 7 Roberts (Charles G. D.), Service (Robert) 8 Drummond (William Henry) 9 Fréchette (Louis-Honoré) *Chilean:* 6 Neruda (Pablo) 7 Mistral (Gabriela) *Chinese:* 4 Li Po, Tu Fu 7 Wang Wei *Danish:* 4 Rode (Helge) 5 Ewald (Johannes) *English:* 3 Gay (John) 4 Gray (Thomas), Owen (Wilfred), Pope (Alexander), Rowe (Nicholas), Tate (Nahum), Wyat (Thomas) 5 Blake (William), Byron (Lord), Carew (Thomas), Clare (John), Donne (John), Eliot (Thomas Stearns), Gower (John), Hardy (Thomas), Keats (John), Noyes (Alfred), Wilde (Oscar), Wyatt (Thomas), Young (Edward) 6 Arnold (Matthew), Austin (Alfred), Belloc (Hilaire), Brooke (Rupert), Butler (Samuel), Clough (Arthur Hugh), Cowper (William), Dryden (John), Graves (Robert), Larkin (Philip), Milton (John), Savage (Richard), Sidney (Philip), Surrey (Earl of), Symons (Arthur), Waller (Edmund), Warton (Thomas), Watson (William), Wotton (Henry) 7 Bridges (Robert), Campion (Thomas), Chaucer (Geoffrey), Gilbert (W. S.), Herbert (George), Herrick (Robert), Hopkins (Gerard Manley), Housman (A. E.), Kipling (Rudyard), Layamon, Marvell (Andrew), Patmore (Coventry), Quarles (Francis), Shelley (Percy Bysshe), Skelton (John), Southey (Robert), Spender (Stephen), Spenser (Edmund) 8 Betjeman (John), Browning (Elizabeth Barrett, Robert), de la Mare (Walter), Langland (William), Lovelace (Richard), Meredith (George), Rossetti (Christina, Dante Gabriel), Suckling (John), Tennyson (Alfred Lord), Thompson (Francis) 9 Coleridge (Samuel Taylor), Masefield (John), Swinburne (Algernon Charles) 10 Chatterton (Thomas), FitzGerald (Edward), Wordsworth (William) 11 Shakespeare (William) *Finnish:* 8 Runeberg (Johan Ludvig) *French:* 5 Marot (Clément) 6 Musset (Alfred de), Valéry (Paul), Villon (François) 7 Bourget (Paul), Chénier (André de, Marie-Joseph), Gautier (Théophile), Rimbaud (Arthur), Ronsard (Pierre de) 8 Malherbe (François de), Mallarmé (Stéphane), Verlaine (Paul) 9 Lamartine (Alphonse de) 10 Baudelaire (Charles) 11 Apollinaire (Guillaume) *German:* 5 Heine (Heinrich), Rilke (Rainer Maria), Sachs (Hans), Storm (Theodor) 6 Brecht (Bertolt), Goethe (Johann Wolfgang von), Uhland (Ludwig) 7 Walther (von der Vogelweide), Wolfram (von Eschenbach) 8 Schiller (Friedrich von) 9 Klopstock (Friedrich Gottlieb) 10 Tannhäuser *Greek:* 5 Arion, Homer 6 Elytis (Odysseus), Erinna, Hesiod, Pindar, Ritsos (Yannis), Sappho 7 Agathon, Alcaeus, Orpheus, Seferis (George), Thespis 8 Anacreon 9 Simonides 10 Apollonius, Theocritus *Hindu:* 5 Naidu (Sarojini) 6 Tagore (Rabindranath) 8 Kalidasa, Tulsidas *Hungarian:* 6 Petofi (Sandor), Zrinyi (Miklos) *Irish:* 5 Moore (Thomas), Wolfe (Charles), Yeats (William Butler) 6 Heaney (Seamus) 7 Dunsany (Lord), Muldoon (Paul) 8 Drummond (William Henry), MacNeice (Louis) *Italian:* 4 Rosa (Salvator), Vida (Marco) 5 Dante (Alighieri), Tasso (Torquato) 7 Ariosto (Ludovico), Manzoni (Alessandro), Montale (Eugenio) 8 Carducci (Giosuè), Leopardi (Giacomo), Petrarch 9 Boccaccio (Giovanni), D'Annunzio (Gabriele), Marinetti (Filippo Tommaso), Quasimodo (Salvatore), Ungaretti (Giuseppe) *Japanese:* 5 Basho 6 Matsuo *medieval:* 8 minstrel, trouvère 10 troubadour *Mexican:* 3 Paz (Octavio) *nonsense:* 4

Lear (Edward) **7** Dr. Seuss *Norwegian:* **8** Bjornson (Bjornstjerne), Welhaven (Johan) **9** Wergeland (Henrik) *Persian:* **4** Sadi **5** Attar, Hafez, Hafiz **11** Omar Khayyám *Roman:* **4** Ovid **6** Horace, Vergil, Virgil **7** Juvenal, Martial, Statius **8** Catullus, Tibullus **9** Lucretius *Russian:* **4** Blok (Aleksandr) **7** Brodsky (Joseph), Pushkin (Aleksandr), Yesenin (Sergey) **9** Akhmatova (Anna), Kheraskov (Mikhail), Pasternak (Boris), Tsvetaeva (Marina) **10** Mandelstam (Osip), Mayakovsky (Vladimir) **11** Yevtushenko (Yevgeny) *Saint Lucian:* **7** Walcott (Derek) *Scottish:* **4** Hogg (James), Muir (Edwin) **5** Burns (Robert), Scott (Alexander, Walter) **6** Dunbar (William), Ramsay (Allan) **7** Thomson (James) **10** MacDiarmid (Hugh) *Spanish:* **5** Lorca (Federico García) **7** Jiménez (Juan Ramón) **8** Figueroa (Francisco) **10** Aleixandre (Vicente) **11** García Lorca (Federico) *Swedish:* **5** Sachs (Nelly) **6** Tegner (Esaias) **8** Snoilsky (Carl Johan) **9** Karlfeldt (Erik Axel) *Swiss:* **5** Amiel (Henri Frédéric) **9** Spitteler (Carl) *Welsh:* **6** Thomas (Dylan) **7** Aneurin, Watkins (Vernon)

poetic 5 lyric **6** dreamy **8** romantic **9** aesthetic, beautiful *word:* **3** ere, e'er, thy **4** dost, doth, hast, hath, kine, ne'er, thee, thou, wert, wilt **5** thine **8** forsooth **9** beauteous

poet laureate *British:* **3** Pye (Henry) **4** Rowe (Nicholas), Tate (Nahum) **6** Austin (Alfred), Cibber (Colley), Dryden (John), Hughes (Ted), Jonson (Ben), Motion (Andrew) **7** Bridges (Robert), Southey (Robert) **8** Betjeman (John), Davenant (William), Day-Lewis (Cecil), Shadwell (Thomas), Tennyson (Alfred) **9** Masefield (John), Whitehead (William) **10** Wordsworth (William) *American:* **4** Dove (Rita), Hall (Donald), Hass (Robert) **5** Glück (Louise) **6** Kooser (Ted), Kunitz (Stanley), Merwin (W. S.), Pinsky (Robert), Strand (Mark), Warren (Robert Penn), Wilbur (Richard) **7** Brodsky (Joseph), Collins (Billy), Nemerov (Howard), Van Duyn (Mona)

poetry 5 verse

poetry term 4 iamb, mora, scan **5** arsis, canto, envoi, ictus, ionic, paeon, rhyme, stave, stich **6** dactyl, septet, sestet, stanza, thesis **7** anapest, cadence, elision, euphony, quintet, refrain, spondee, strophe, trochee **8** chiasmus, choriamb, cinquain, end rhyme, eye rhyme, quatrain, rhopalic **9** decameter, dithyramb, hexameter, near rhyme, octameter, terza rima **10** enjambment, fourteener, heptameter, ottava rima, rhyme royal **11** Al-

exandrine, antistrophe, heroic verse, rhyme scheme, shaped verse **12** sprung rhythm

Pogo creator 5 Kelly (Walt)

poi 4 taro

poignancy 6 pathos **7** emotion, sadness **9** sentiment

poignant 3 sad **4** keen **5** acute, sharp **6** biting, moving **7** painful, piquant, pointed, pungent **8** incisive, piercing, stirring, touching **9** affecting

point 3 aim, dot, end, jag, nib, tip **4** apex, crux, item, mark, show, site, spot, step, tine, turn, unit **5** motif, place, stage, theme, topic, trace, verge **6** detail, direct, intent, moment, motive, object, period, reason **7** decimal, essence, instant, meaning, purpose, subject **8** headland, juncture, locality, location, particle, position **9** direction **10** promontory **12** significance

pointed 5 acute, sharp **6** barbed, marked, signal **7** salient **8** incisive, striking **9** arresting, pertinent, prominent **11** conspicuous, penetrating

pointer 3 dog, tip **4** clue, hint **5** arrow, guide **6** gundog **9** indicator **10** suggestion

pointillist 6 Seurat (Georges), Signac (Paul) **8** Pissarro (Camille)

pointless 4 idle, vain **5** inane, silly **6** futile **7** useless **8** bootless **9** fruitless, senseless, worthless **10** immaterial, irrelevant, unavailing, unfruitful **11** meaningless **12** unprofitable

point of view 5 angle, slant **7** outlook **8** position, prospect **11** perspective

poise 4 ease, hang, tact **5** brace, grace, hover, skill **6** aplomb, steady **7** address, balance, bearing, dignity, support, suspend **8** carriage, elegance, serenity **9** assurance, composure, diplomacy, sangfroid **10** confidence, equanimity **11** delicatesse, equilibrium, savoir faire, tactfulness

poised 4 calm **6** at ease, serene, steady **7** assured, equable **8** composed, tranquil **9** collected, confident **13** self-possessed

poison 4 bane, upas **5** toxin, venom **6** toxoid **7** arsenic, botulin, cyanide, envenom **8** toxicant **9** botulinum, contagion **10** strychnine **13** contamination *arrow:* **4** inée, upas **6** curare **7** ouabain *combining form:* **3** tox **4** toxi, toxo **6** toxico

poisoning *food:* **8** botulism *lead:* **8** plumbism

poisonous 5 toxic **7** baneful, miasmal, nocuous, noxious **8** mephitic, venomous, virulent **9** pestilent **10** pernicious

poke 3 dig, hit, jab, jut, lag, pry **4** cuff, nose, prod, push, sock, stab, stir, urge **5** bulge, dally, delay, elbow, nudge, punch, snoop, tarry **6** dawdle, meddle, pierce, putter, thrust **7** intrude, project, rummage **8** stick out **9** interfere, interject, interpose

poker *bet total:* **3** pot *bullet:* **3** ace *form:* **4** stud *hand:* **4** pair **5** flush **8** straight **9** full house **10** royal flush **13** straight flush *ploy:* **5** bluff *stake:* **4** ante *term:* **3** see **4** call, draw, open **5** raise *token:* **4** chip

poker-faced 5 blank, staid **7** deadpan, neutral **9** impassive **11** inscrutable, noncommittal **12** inexpressive

pokey 3 can, jug, pen **4** brig, coop, jail, stir **5** clink **6** cooler, prison **7** slammer **9** calaboose

poky 4 slow **5** dingy, seedy **6** dreary, shabby **7** cramped, laggard, run-down **8** dilatory, plodding, sluggish

Poland *capital:* **6** Warsaw *city:* **4** Lódz **6** Gdansk, Kraków, Poznan **7** Wroclaw **8** Katowice, Szczecin *leader:* **6** Walesa (Lech) *monetary unit:* **5** zloty *mountain range:* **10** Carpathian *national hero:* **10** Kosciuszko (Thaddeus) *neighbor:* **6** Russia **7** Belarus, Germany, Ukraine **8** Slovakia **9** Lithuania **13** Czech Republic *river:* **4** Oder **7** Vistula *sea:* **6** Baltic

polar 6 arctic **7** pivotal **8** opposite **9** diametric

pole 3 rod **4** punt, spar **5** anode, shaft, staff, stick, stilt **7** cathode *Indian:* **5** totem *Scottish:* **5** caber

polecat 5 fitch, skunk **6** ferret **7** fitchet

polemic 6 attack, debate, screed, tirade **7** defense, dispute **8** argument, diatribe, harangue, jeremiad **9** assertion, philippic **10** contention, refutation **11** controversy, disputation **12** denunciation, remonstrance

polemical 11 contentious, opinionated **12** disputatious **13** argumentative, controversial

polestar 3 hub **5** focus, guide **10** focal point

police 3 law, man **4** fuzz, heat **6** govern, patrol **7** control, monitor **8** regulate *officer:* **3** cop **4** flic, fuzz, heat **5** bobby **6** copper, lawman, peeler **7** John Law, sheriff, trooper **8** bluecoat, Dogberry, flatfoot, gendarme **9** constable, patrolman **11** carabiniere

policy 4 plan **6** course, method, number **7** lottery, program **8** contract, practice **9** procedure **10** management

polio vaccine developer 4 Salk (Jonas) **5** Sabin (Albert)

polish 3 rub, wax **4** buff **5** glaze, glint, gloss, sheen, shine **6** luster, refine, smooth, soften **7** burnish, culture, enhance, improve, perfect, touch up **8** brighten **10** refinement

Polish *dumpling:* **6** pirogi **7** pierogi *leader:* **6** Walesa (Lech) *patriot:* **9** Kosciusko (Thad-

deus) *pope:* **8** John Paul *sausage:* **8** kielbasa, kielbasy *soldier:* **7** Pulaski (Casimir)

polish off 5 eat up **6** devour **7** consume, put away **8** dispatch **9** dispose of

polite 5 civil **7** courtly, genteel, refined **8** cultured, mannerly, polished, well-bred **9** attentive, courteous **10** thoughtful **11** considerate **12** well-mannered

politeness 7 manners **8** civility, courtesy **10** refinement

politic 4 wise **5** suave **6** adroit, shrewd, smooth **7** prudent, tactful **8** tactical **9** advisable, expedient, judicious, sagacious **10** diplomatic

political *meeting:* **6** caucus *party:* **3** GOP **10** Democratic, Republican *system:* **7** fascism **9** communism, democracy, socialism

poll 4 cast, clip, crop, head, nape, pate **5** count, shear, tally, votes **6** noggin, record, sample, survey **7** canvass, pollard **8** question **9** interview **10** canvassing *type:* **4** exit **5** straw

pollack 4 fish **6** saithe **8** bluefish *family:* **3** cod

pollard 3 top **4** crop, tree **7** cut back

pollen-producing organ 6 stamen

pollex 5 thumb

_____ **polloi 3** hoi

pollster 5 Zogby (John) **6** Gallup (George), Harris (Lou)

pollute 4 foul, soil **5** dirty, spoil, stain, sully, taint **6** befoul, damage, debase, defile **7** corrupt, profane **10** adulterate **11** contaminate

pollution 4 smog **5** abuse **8** impurity **10** defilement

Pollux 10 Polydeuces *brother:* **6** Castor *father:* **4** Zeus *mother:* **4** Leda *sister:* **5** Helen **12** Clytemnestra

Pollyanna 8 optimist *author:* **6** Porter (Eleanor)

Pollyannaish 6 blithe, cheery, upbeat **8** cheerful, positive **10** optimistic **11** rose-colored

pollywog 7 tadpole

Polonius *daughter:* **7** Ophelia *hiding place:* **5** arras *slayer:* **6** Hamlet *son:* **7** Laertes

poltergeist 5 ghost **6** spirit

poltroon 6 coward, craven, yellow **7** chicken, dastard, gutless **8** cowardly **9** dastardly **11** lily-livered

Polydorus *father:* **5** Priam **6** Cadmus *mother:* **6** Hecuba **8** Harmonia *slayer:* **8** Achilles **10** Polymestor **11** Polymnestor

polygon *eight-sided:* **7** octagon *five-sided:* **8** pentagon *four-sided:* **8** tetragon *nine-sided:* **7** nonagon *seven-sided:* **8** heptagon *six-sided:* **7** hexagon *ten-sided:* **7** decagon

three-sided: 8 triangle ***twelve-sided:*** 9 dodecagon

Polyhymnia 4 Muse ***invention:*** 4 lyre

polymer 5 amber, nylon 6 rubber, Teflon 7 shellac 8 Bakelite, silicone

Polynesian 5 Maori 6 Samoan, Tongan 8 Hawaiian, Tahitian 9 Marquesan

Polynices ***brother:*** 8 Eteocles ***father:*** 7 Oedipus ***mother:*** 7 Jocasta ***wife:*** 5 Argia 6 Argeia

polyp 5 tumor, zooid 6 growth 7 hydroid ***freshwater:*** 5 hydra

Polyphemus 7 Cyclops ***beloved:*** 7 Galatea ***father:*** 8 Poseidon ***victim:*** 4 Acis

pome 4 pear 5 apple, fruit

pommel 4 knob 6 handle

pomp 4 show 5 array 6 parade, ritual 7 display, fanfare, panoply 8 ceremony, grandeur, splendor 9 pageantry, vainglory 11 ostentation

pompano 4 fish 8 carangid 10 butterfish

Pompeii's volcano 8 Vesuvius

pompous 4 vain 5 proud, showy 6 lordly, ornate, stuffy 7 stuck-up 8 arrogant, boastful, inflated 9 bombastic, conceited, important, overblown 10 egocentric, flamboyant, pontifical 11 magisterial, pretentious 12 ostentatious, vainglorious

pond 4 mere, pool, tarn 5 stank 6 lagoon ***growth:*** 4 scum 5 algae

ponder 4 mull, muse 5 study, think, weigh 6 reason 7 examine, perpend, reflect 8 appraise, cogitate, consider, evaluate, meditate, mull over, ruminate 9 reflect on, speculate 10 deliberate, think about 11 contemplate

ponderous 4 dull 5 heavy 6 clumsy, dreary, stodgy, wooden 7 labored, massive, weighty 8 cumbrous, lifeless, plodding, unwieldy 9 lumbering 10 burdensome, cumbersome, oppressive

poniard 6 dagger

Ponte Vecchio ***city:*** 8 Florence ***river:*** 4 Arno

Pontiac 5 chief ***tribe:*** 6 Ottawa

pontiff 4 pope

pontifical 7 pompous 8 dogmatic 9 episcopal 11 magisterial

pony 4 crib, trot 5 horse 6 bronco, cayuse 7 mustang ***breed:*** 6 Exmoor 8 Shetland

pony up 3 pay 6 lay out, pay out 7 dish out, dole out, fork out 8 hand over, shell out, turn over 10 compensate, remunerate

pooch 3 dog, pup 4 tyke 5 hound, puppy 6 bowwow, canine

Pooh ***creator:*** 5 Milne (A. A.) ***friend:*** 5 Kanga 6 Eeyore, Piglet, Tigger ***illustrator:*** 7 Shepard (Ernest)

pooh-bah 3 VIP 4 czar, king, star, tsar, tzar 5 baron, heavy, mogul 6 big gun, bigwig, honcho, kahuna, prince, worthy 7 big name, big shot, kingpin, magnate, notable 8 big wheel, eminence, luminary 9 big cheese, personage, superstar 11 heavyweight

pooh-pooh 5 scorn 6 deride 7 disdain, dismiss, sneer at 8 minimize, play down

pool 3 pot 4 mere, pond, tarn 5 chain, group, kitty, merge, trust 6 cartel, lagoon, laguna, puddle 7 combine, jackpot 9 syndicate ***player:*** 7 Mosconi (Willie) 13 Minnesota Fats (see also **billiards**)

poop 4 dirt, info, tire 7 fatigue

poor 4 base, mean 5 broke, needy, scant, skimp, spare 6 humble, meager, meagre, paltry, scanty, skimpy, sparse 8 bankrupt, beggarly, indigent, strapped 9 destitute, insolvent, penniless, penurious 10 down-and-out, pauperized, stone-broke 11 impecunious, necessitous

poorly 3 ill, low 4 sick 5 badly 6 ailing, sickly, unwell 10 indisposed 11 imperfectly

pop 3 dad, dot, gun, hit, try 4 dada, dart, ding, shot, slap, slog, sock, soda 5 catch, crack, daddy, drink, fling, shoot, whack, whirl 6 attack, bug out, effort, father, strike 7 assault, attempt, explode 8 backfire

pop artist 5 Blake (Peter), Johns (Jasper) 6 Warhol (Andy) 7 Hockney (David), Indiana (Robert) 9 Oldenburg (Claes), Wesselman (Tom) 10 Rosenquist (James) 12 Lichtenstein (Roy) (see also **pop singer**)

pope 3 Leo 4 John, Mark, Paul, Pius 5 Caius, Conon, Donus, Felix, Gaius, Lando, Linus, Peter, Soter, Urban 6 Adrian, Agatho, Fabian, Julius, Lucius, Martin, Sixtus, Victor 7 Anterus, Clement, Damasus, Gregory, Hadrian, Hyginus, Marinus, Paschal, Pontian, Romanus, Sergius, Stephen, Zosimus 8 Agapetus, Anicetus, Benedict, Boniface, Calixtus, Eugenius, Eusebius, Formosis, Gelasius, Hilarius, Honorius, Innocent, John Paul, Liberius, Nicholas, Pelagius, Siricius, Theodore, Vigilius, Vitalian 9 Adeodatus, Alexander, Anacletus, Callistus, Celestine, Cornelius, Densdedit, Dionysius, Eutychian, Evaristus, Hormisdas, Marcellus, Miltiades, Severinus, Silverius, Silvester, Sisinnius, Sylvester, Symmachus, Valentine, Zacharias 10 Anastasius, Melchiades, Sabinianus, Simplicius, Zephyrinus 11 Christopher, Constantine, Eleutherius, Eutychianus, Marcellinus, Telesphorus

Pope poem 7 Dunciad (The) **10** Essay on Man (An) **13** Rape of the Lock (The)

Popeye accessory: 4 pipe *baby:* **7** Swee'Pea **8** Sweet Pea *creator:* **5** Segar (E. C.) *energizer:* **7** spinach *friend:* **5** Wimpy **8** Olive Oyl *occupation:* **6** sailor *rival:* **5** Bluto

pop in 4 call **5** visit **6** drop by, look up, stop by **8** come over

popinjay 3 fop **4** toff **5** dandy, swell **7** peacock **8** macaroni

poplar 5 abele, alamo, aspen **6** balsam **9** tulip tree **10** cottonwood **12** balm of Gilead

Poppaea's husband 4 Nero

poppycock 3 rot **4** bosh, bunk, guff **5** bilge, hokum, hooey **6** bunkum **7** baloney **8** malarkey, nonsense, tommyrot **10** balderdash

pop singer 3 Lee (Brenda), Ray (Johnnie), Vee (Bobby) **4** Cher, Como (Perry), Enya, Gore (Lesley), Joel (Billy), Page (Patti), Ross (Diana) **5** Abdul (Paula), Aiken (Clay), Arden (Toni), Cline (Patsy), Lopez (Trini), Simon (Carly, Paul), Valli (Frankie) **6** Avalon (Frankie), Brewer (Teresa), Crosby (Bing), Fisher (Eddie), Martin (Dean, Tony), Mathis (Johnny), Midler (Bette), Murray (Billy), Pitney (Gene), Spears (Britney), Summer (Donna), Vallee (Rudy), Vinton (Bobby) **7** Bennett (Tony), Buffett (Jimmy), Diamond (Neil), Estefan (Gloria), Francis (Connie), Houston (Whitney), Jackson (Michael), Loggins (Kenny), Madonna, Rodgers (Jimmie), Simpson (Jessica), Sinatra (Frank), Warwick (Dionne) **8** Aguilera (Christina), Williams (Andy) **9** Streisand (Barbra)

populace 5 plebs **6** masses, people, public **9** citizenry, commonage, commoners, plebeians **10** commonalty **11** commonality, rank and file, third estate

popular 5 cheap, noted **6** common, famous **7** admired, current, favored, general, leading **8** accepted, approved, favorite, ordinary **9** preferred, prevalent, prominent, well-known, well-liked **10** democratic, prevailing, widespread **11** inexpensive

populate 6 occupy, people, settle **7** inhabit

populous 6 packed **7** crowded, teeming **8** numerous **9** congested **13** multitudinous

porcelain Chinese: 9 Lowestoft *English:* **3** Bow **5** Derby, Spode **6** Minton **7** Aynsley, Belleek, Bristol, Chelsea **8** Caughley, Wedgwood *French:* **6** Sèvres **7** Limoges *German:* **7** Dresden, Meissen *ingredient:* **6** kaolin *Italian:* **6** Doccia *Japanese:* **5** Imari

porch 4 deck **5** lanai **6** piazza **7** gallery, veranda **8** verandah

porcupine 8 hedgehog

pore 6 outlet **7** opening, orifice, reflect **8** meditate **10** interstice

pore over 4 read, scan **5** study **6** peruse **10** scrutinize

porgy 3 tai **4** fish, scup **6** sparid **8** menhaden

Porgy and Bess composer: 8 Gershwin (George) *librettist:* **7** Heyward (DuBose) **8** Gershwin (Ira)

Po River city 5 Milan, Padua, Turin **6** Milano, Padova, Torino, Verona **7** Brescia

pork 3 ham, pig **5** bacon, swine **8** sowbelly *cut:* **3** ham **4** jowl, loin, side **7** fatback **8** forefoot, hind foot, spare rib **9** picnic ham **10** Boston butt

pork-barreling 9 patronage

pornographic 7 obscene

porous 5 leaky **6** spongy **8** pervious **9** permeable **10** penetrable

porpoise 5 whale **7** dolphin

porridge 4 mush **5** gruel, kasha **6** burgoo, cereal, congee, pablum, sowens **7** oatmeal, pabulum **8** flummery, loblolly **9** stirabout

port 4 hole, jack, left, wine **5** cover, haven **6** harbor, refuge **7** bearing, opening, retreat, shelter **8** larboard, left side **9** anchorage, harborage, roadstead, sanctuary **11** comportment *opposite:* **9** starboard

portable 5 handy **6** mobile, wieldy

portal 4 door, gate **5** entry **7** doorway, gateway **8** approach, entrance, entryway

portcullis 4 gate **5** orgue **7** grating, lattice

portend 4 bode **5** augur **6** signal **7** betoken, predict, presage, promise, signify **8** forebode, forecast, foretell, indicate, prophesy **9** adumbrate, foretoken **10** foreshadow, vaticinate

portent 4 omen, sign **6** augury, boding **7** presage, prodigy **9** foretoken, sensation **10** foreboding, indication **11** premonition

portentous 5 grave **6** solemn **7** ominous, pompous, serious, weighty **8** inflated **9** marvelous, momentous, ponderous **10** prodigious

porter 5 hamal, stout **6** bearer, redcap, skycap **7** bellboy, bellhop, carrier **9** transport **10** doorkeeper

Porter novel 11 Ship of Fools

Portia 6 lawyer *husband:* **6** Brutus **8** Bassanio *maid:* **7** Nerissa

portico 4 stoa **9** colonnade

portion 3 cut, lot **4** bite, part **5** dower, moira, piece, quota, share, slice **6** moiety, parcel **7** measure, quantum, segment **8** division *largest:* **10** lion's share *unused:* **8** leftover

portly 3 fat **5** bulky, heavy, large, stout **6** fleshy **7** rotound, stately, weighty **8** imposing **9** corpulent **10** overweight

portmanteau 7 holdall **8** carryall, suitcase

portrait 4 bust **5** image **6** figure, statue **7** picture **8** painting **9** depiction

portray 4 draw, limn, play **5** enact, paint **6** depict, render **7** picture **8** describe **9** delineate, interpret, represent

portrayal 5 image **7** account, picture **8** likeness, painting **9** depiction **11** delineation, description, performance **12** illustration

Portugal *capital:* **6** Lisbon *city:* **5** Porto **6** Oporto **7** Amadora *former colony:* **3** Goa **5** Macao **6** Angola, Brazil *former name:* **9** Lusitania *island group:* **6** Azores **7** Madeira *leader:* **4** Luís **7** Salazar (Antonio de) *monetary unit:* **4** euro *monetary unit, former:* **6** escudo *neighbor:* **5** Spain *peninsula:* **6** Iberia **7** Iberian *river:* **5** Tagus

pose 3 act, air, ask, set, sit **4** airs, fake, role, sham **5** feign, front, offer, place, stand, state, strut **6** affect, assume, pass as, stance **7** pass for, pass off, present, pretend, show off, suggest **8** attitude, pretense, set forth **9** mannerism **10** pretension **11** affectation

Poseidon 7 Neptune *brother:* **4** Zeus **5** Hades, Pluto **7** Jupiter *consort:* **4** Tyro **6** Medusa **7** Demeter *father:* **6** Cronus *mother:* **4** Rhea *offspring:* **7** Pegasus *son:* **5** Orion **6** Neleus, Pelias, Triton **7** Antaeus **10** Polyphemus *weapon:* **7** trident *wife:* **10** Amphitrite

poser 6 puzzle, riddle **7** problem **9** conundrum **11** brainteaser

poseur 4 fake **5** bluff, decoy, fraud, phony, pseud, quack **6** phoney **7** bluffer **8** deceiver, imposter **9** charlatan, hypocrite, pretender **10** mountebank **11** masquerader **12** impersonator

posh 4 chic, rich, tony **5** fancy, grand, smart, swank **7** elegant, stylish **9** exclusive, expensive, luxurious **11** fashionable, highfalutin, pretentious

posit 3 fix **5** offer **6** affirm, assert, assume **7** premise, present, presume, propose, suggest **9** postulate

position 3 job **4** rank, site, spot **5** locus, place, point, situs, stand, state **6** belief, locate, stance **7** emplace, footing, stature **8** attitude, capacity, location, prestige, standing **10** standpoint *without work:* **8** sinecure

positive 4 firm, real, sure **6** actual, useful **7** assured, certain, decided, factual, genuine, reality **8** absolute, complete, definite, forceful, outright **9** confident, doubtless, effective, favorable **10** beneficial, inarguable, optimistic, undeniable **11** categorical, irrefutable, unequivocal, unqualified **12** indisputable, unmistakable **13** incontestable

possess 3 own **4** have, hold, keep **5** carry **6** retain **7** acquire, control

possessed 3 mad **6** crazed, hooked **8** frenzied **9** bewitched

possession 7 control **8** property **9** occupancy, ownership **10** occupation

possessive 7 jealous **8** watchful **10** protective **11** proprietary

possibility 2 if **4** odds **6** chance **8** instance **9** potential **10** likelihood **11** contingency, feasibility

possible 6 doable, likely, viable **7** earthly **8** feasible **9** expedient, potential **10** imaginable, realizable **11** practicable

possibly 5 maybe **7** perhaps **8** by chance **9** perchance **11** conceivably

post 3 set **4** camp, mail, pole, ride, send, spot, stem, task **5** affix, after, hurry, newel, place, put up, score, stage, stake **6** advise, column, fill in, inform, notify, office, pillar **7** apprise, express, placard, publish, station **8** announce, denounce, position **9** advertise **10** assignment

poster 4 bill, sign **6** notice **7** affiche, placard **9** broadside, signboard **12** announcement **13** advertisement

posterior 4 back, butt, hind, rear, rump, seat, tail **5** after, fanny, later **6** behind, caudal, dorsal, heinie, hinder **7** ensuing, rear end, tail end **8** backside, buttocks, derriere, hindmost, rearward **9** following **10** subsequent

posterity 6 future **7** progeny **8** children **9** offspring **11** descendants

posthaste 4 fast **6** at once, pronto **7** fleetly, quickly, rapidly, swiftly **8** promptly, speedily **11** immediately

Postimpressionist painter 6 Seurat (Georges) **7** Cezanne (Paul), Gauguin (Paul), Van Gogh (Vincent) **8** Pissarro (Camille), Rousseau (Henri)

postmortem 7 autopsy **8** necropsy

postpone 5 defer, delay, table **6** hold up, put off, shelve **7** hold off, lay over, suspend **8** hold over, prorogue

postulate 5 axiom, claim **6** assert, assume, demand, thesis **7** premise, suppose **10** assumption, hypothesis, presuppose **11** hypothesize, presumption, supposition

posture 4 mode, pose **5** state **6** affect, assume, manner, stance, status **7** bearing, outlook **8** attitude, carriage, position **9** condition, situation **12** attitudinize

posy 5 bloom **6** flower **7** blossom, bouquet, corsage, nosegay **9** sentiment

pot 3 bet, pan, wad **4** ante, hemp, olla, weed **5** grass, kitty, stake, wager **6** boodle, bundle, pipkin **7** marmite **8** cannabis **9** marijuana

potable 5 clean, drink, fresh **6** liquid, liquor **8** beverage **9** drinkable

potassium ore 7 sylvite

potato 3 yam **4** spud **5** tater *bud:* **3** eye

pot-au-____ 3 feu **5** creme

potbelly 3 gut **5** stove **6** paunch **9** bay window, spare tire **11** corporation

Potemkin mutiny site 6 Odessa

potency 3 pep **5** force, might, power, vigor **6** energy, muscle **8** strength **9** influence, puissance **10** capability **13** effectiveness

potent 4 rich **6** mighty, robust, strong, virile **7** dynamic **8** forceful, forcible, powerful **9** effective **10** persuasive **11** influential

potential 6 latent, likely **7** ability, promise **8** capacity, possible **9** plausible, promising **10** imaginable **11** conceivable, possibility

pother 3 ado **4** flap, fret, fuss, stir, to-do **5** furor, whirl, worry **6** bustle, flurry, furore, hassle, hubbub, tumult, uproar **7** fluster, turmoil **9** agitation, annoyance, commotion, confusion

potion 6 liquid **7** mixture, philter, philtre **8** medicine **10** concoction

Potiphar's slave 6 Joseph

Potiphera *daughter:* **7** Asenath *son-in-law:* **6** Joseph

Potok novel 6 Chosen (The) **16** My Name Is Asher Lev

potpourri 4 olio **5** blend **6** medley, sachet **7** grab bag, mélange, variety **8** mishmash, pastiche **10** assortment, collection, hodgepodge, hotchpotch, miscellany, salmagundi **11** gallimaufry

potshot 3 cut, dig **4** barb, gibe, jibe **5** crack, shoot, swipe **6** attack, insult **9** criticism

potter see **putter**

Potter character 5 Mopsy, Mr. Tod **6** Flopsy, Jemima (Puddleduck) **10** Cotton-tail, Hunca Munca **11** Peter Rabbit **12** Jeremy Fisher

potter's field 8 cemetery, God's acre **9** graveyard

pottery 4 raku **5** delft, Imari **7** redware **8** ceramics, clayware, slipware **10** lusterware, terra-cotta, yellowware **11** earthenware

pouch 3 bag, sac **4** sack **5** bulge, bursa, burse **6** pocket **7** saccule **8** sacculus

pouf 5 quilt **7** ottoman **9** comforter

poultry 4 fowl *type:* **4** duck, swan **5** goose, quail **6** grouse, pigeon, turkey **7** chicken, ostrich, peacock **8** pheasant **9** partridge

pounce 5 seize, swoop, talon **6** attack, powder **7** assault, stencil

pound 4 bang, bash, beat, slam, slug, sock **5** drive, money, smite, stamp, throb, thump, tramp **6** batter, buffet, hammer, pummel, strike, thrash, wallop **7** belabor, impress, pulsate **9** enclosure

Pound work 6 Cantos (The)

poupée 4 doll

pour 4 flow, gush, rain, rill, rush, teem **5** flood, issue, skink, spate, surge, swarm **6** decant, deluge, drench, sluice, spring, stream **7** cascade, torrent **8** inundate, overflow

pourboire 3 tip **7** cumshaw **8** gratuity **9** baksheesh

pout 3 pet **4** fish, moue, sulk **5** grump **8** protrude **10** expression, protrusion

poverty 4 need, want **6** dearth, penury **7** beggary, paucity **8** hardship, poorness, scarcity, shortage **9** indigence, neediness, pauperism, privation **10** mendicancy, scarceness **11** destitution **13** pennilessness

POW camp 6 stalag

powder 4 bray, dust, talc **5** crush **6** talcum **8** sprinkle **9** comminute, pulverize, triturate **10** besprinkle

power 3 vis **4** sway **5** force, might, sinew, steam, vigor, vires (plural) **6** energy, muscle **7** command, ability, control, potency, voltage **8** dominion, dynamism, imperium, strength **9** authority, influence, privilege, puissance, strong arm **10** ascendancy, domination **11** prerogative, sovereignty, superiority **12** jurisdiction, potentiality *combining form:* **5** dynam **6** dynamo *unit:* **4** watt

powerful 5 great **6** mighty, potent, strong **7** dynamic **8** dominant, puissant, vigorous **9** energetic, strenuous **10** convincing, impressive, invincible, persuasive

powerless 4 weak **5** inert **6** feeble, unable **7** passive **8** impotent **9** incapable **11** incompetent, ineffective

powwow 4 chat, talk **6** confab, confer, huddle, parley **7** discuss, meeting **8** ceremony **9** gathering **10** discussion **11** confabulate, gettogether

practicable 5 utile **6** doable, likely, usable, useful **8** feasible, possible **9** operative **10** functional

practical 5 handy, utile **6** active, useful, versed **7** applied, skilled, trained, virtual **8** sensible **9** pragmatic, realistic **10** functional **11** down-to-earth, experienced **12** businesslike

practically 5 about **6** all but, almost, near to, nearly **7** close to **8** in effect **9** in essence, just about

practice 3 ply, use, way **4** form, mode, wont **5** drill, habit, usage **6** custom, manner, method, repeat, system, tryout, warm up **7** perform, process, workout **8** drilling, engage in, exercise, habitude, rehearse **9** procedure, rehearsal **10** convention

pragmatic 7 factual, logical **8** rational **9** practical, realistic **11** down-to-earth

prairie 4 veld **5** pampa, plain, veldt **6** pampas **7** plateau **9** grassland

prairie chicken 6 grouse

prairie wolf 6 coyote

praise 4 hail, hymn, laud, puff **5** bravo, cry up, exalt, extol, honor, kudos **6** belaud, kudize **7** acclaim, adulate, applaud, commend, flatter, glorify, hosanna, magnify, ovation, plaudit, puffery **8** accolade, applause, approval, citation, encomium, eulogize, flattery **9** celebrate, laudation, panegyric, recommend **10** aggrandize, compliment, panegyrize **11** acclamation **12** commendation

praiseworthy 8 laudable **9** admirable, deserving, estimable **11** commendable, meritorious

prance 4 step **5** mince, strut **6** sashay, spring **8** cakewalk

prank 3 gag **4** deck, dido, lark, whim **5** adorn, antic, caper, fancy, spiff, sport, trick **6** doll up, frolic, gambol, levity, shavie, vagary, whimsy **7** caprice, deck out, doll out, dress up, garnish, rollick, spiff up **8** beautify, decorate, escapade, ornament, spruce up **9** embellish, frivolity, horseplay, smarten up **10** shenanigan, tomfoolery **11** monkeyshine

prankster 3 wag **5** cutup, joker

prate 3 gab, jaw, yak **4** blab, chat, go on **5** run on **6** babble, gabble, jabber **7** blabber, blather, chatter **9** yakety-yak

prater 5 yenta **6** gossip, magpie **10** chatterbox **12** blabbermouth

pratfall 6 mishap, tumble **7** blunder, stumble **11** humiliation

prattle 3 gab **4** blab **5** prate **6** babble, gabble, jabber, natter **7** blabber, chatter

prawn 6 shrimp **11** langoustine *French:* **8** crevette

praxis 5 habit **6** action, custom, manner **7** conduct **8** exercise, habitude, practice

Praxiteles statue 5 Satyr **6** Hermes **9** Aphrodite

pray 3 ask, beg **5** plead **6** appeal **7** beseech, entreat, implore, request **8** petition **10** supplicate

prayer 4 plea, suit **6** appeal, litany, orison **7** angelus, begging, worship **8** blessing, devotion, entreaty, petition, pleading, rogation **9** adoration **11** application, imploration, imprecation **12** supplication *beads:* **6** rosary

ending: **4** amen *for the dead:* **7** requiem *Jewish:* **7** kaddish, kiddush *period:* **6** novena **7** triduum *shawl:* **7** tallith

prayer book 6 missal, siddur **8** breviary

prayerful 4 holy **5** godly, pious **6** devout **7** earnest, sincere

preach 4 urge **6** exhort **7** address, deliver, lecture **8** admonish, advocate, moralize **9** sermonize **10** evangelize

preacher 5 padre **6** cleric, divine, parson, pastor **8** chaplain, clerical, minister, reverend **9** churchman, clergyman **10** evangelist, sermonizer **12** ecclesiastic

preaching friar 9 Dominican

preachy 4 smug **7** donnish **8** didactic, pedantic, sermonic, unctuous **9** homiletic, hortative, pedagogic, pietistic **10** moralizing **11** exhortative, sermonizing **13** sanctimonious, self-righteous

preamble 5 intro, proem **8** exordium, foreword, overture, prologue **12** introduction

precarious 4 iffy **5** dicey, risky, shaky **6** chancy, touchy, tricky, unsafe **7** dubious **8** delicate, doubtful, insecure, ticklish, unstable **9** dangerous, hazardous, sensitive, uncertain **10** unreliable

precaution 4 care **8** prudence **9** foresight, insurance, provision, safeguard **11** forethought

precede 4 lead, rank **5** usher **6** herald **7** forerun, outrank, surpass **8** announce, antedate, go before **9** introduce

precedence 5 order **8** priority **9** seniority

precedent 4 past, rule **5** model, prior **6** former **7** earlier, example **8** anterior **9** foregoing **10** convention

preceding 4 past **5** prior **6** before, former **7** ahead of, prior to **8** anterior, hitherto **9** erstwhile **10** heretofore **11** in advance of *prefix:* **4** ante

precept 3 law **4** rule **5** axiom, edict, order, tenet **6** behest, decree **7** bidding, command **8** doctrine **9** principle **10** injunction, regulation **11** fundamental

preceptive 8 didactic

preceptor 4 head **5** tutor **7** teacher **9** principal **10** headmaster

precinct 4 area **6** domain, region, sector, sphere **7** quarter, section **8** district, division, township **9** bailiwick, enclosure

precious 3 pet **4** dear, nice, rare, rich, very **5** fussy, great, loved, showy **6** adored, choice, costly, la-di-da, prized **7** beloved, darling **8** affected, esteemed, favorite, valuable **9** cherished, exquisite, extremely, priceless **10** invaluable

precipice 5 brink, cliff **8** overhang

precipitancy 4 rush 5 haste, hurry 9 hastiness 10 abruptness, suddenness 11 hurriedness

precipitate 4 fall, hurl 5 hasty, sheer, steep, throw 6 abrupt, madcap, sudden, upshot 7 bring on, deposit, grounds, hurried, outcome, product 8 condense, headlong, sediment, separate 9 breakneck, impatient 10 unexpected, unforeseen 11 consequence

precipitation 4 hail, mist, rain, snow 5 sleet 7 deposit 8 sediment

precipitous 4 rash 5 hasty, sheer, steep 6 abrupt, sudden 7 hurried, rushing 8 headlong, heedless, plunging 9 breakneck 13 perpendicular

précis 6 digest, survey 7 summary 8 abstract, overview, syllabus 10 abridgment, compendium 11 abridgement 12 condensation

precise 4 nice 5 exact, fixed, right 6 narrow, strict 7 correct, limited 8 accurate, clearcut, definite, rigorous, specific 9 clocklike, stringent 10 particular

precisely 4 just 5 right 7 exactly 8 strictly

precision 4 care 5 rigor 6 nicety 8 accuracy 9 exactness 10 exactitude, refinement 11 correctness

preclude 5 avert, deter 7 forfend, obviate, prevent, rule out 8 prohibit, stave off 9 forestall

precocious 5 smart 6 brainy, bright, mature 7 forward 8 advanced

precondition 4 must, need 7 proviso 9 essential, necessity, provision, requisite 10 sine qua non 11 requirement, stipulation

precursor 6 herald 8 ancestor, forebear 9 harbinger, indicator, prototype 10 antecedent, forerunner

predator 6 hunter, preyer, raptor 7 stalker 8 devourer 9 destroyer 10 bird of prey

predatory 6 greedy 8 ravening, ravenous 9 pillaging, rapacious 10 plundering 12 exploitative

predecessor 8 ancestor, forebear 9 precursor, prototype 10 antecedent, forerunner

predicament 3 fix, jam 4 bind, hole, spot 5 pinch, state 6 corner, muddle, pickle, plight, puzzle, scrape, strait 7 dilemma, impasse, trouble 8 hardship, nuisance, quagmire 9 condition, situation 10 difficulty

predicate 4 aver, avow, base, rest 5 found, imply 6 affirm, assert, avouch 7 declare, profess 9 establish

predict 5 augur, guess, infer 6 expect 7 forbode, foresee, portend, surmise 8 announce, conclude, forebode, forecast, foretell, indicate, prophesy, soothsay 10 conjecture, vaticinate 13 prognosticate

prediction 6 augury 8 forecast, prophecy 9 prognosis 10 expectancy 11 expectation

predilection 4 bent, bias 5 fancy, taste 6 liking 7 leaning 8 fondness, penchant, tendency 9 inclining 10 partiality, proclivity, propensity 11 inclination

predispose 4 bend, bias, tend, sway 5 prime 6 affect 7 incline 9 influence

predisposed 5 prone, ready 6 biased 7 partial, willing 8 inclined 11 susceptible

predisposition 4 bent, bias 7 leaning 8 penchant, tendency 9 inclining 10 partiality, proclivity, propensity 11 inclination

predominant 3 top 4 main 5 chief, major 6 master, ruling 7 capital, general, leading, primary, supreme 8 reigning, superior 9 number one, paramount, principal, sovereign 10 prevailing 11 outstanding

predominate 4 rule 5 reign 6 govern, master 7 command, control, prevail 8 outweigh

preeminence 6 renown 7 primacy 8 dominion, prestige 9 supremacy 10 ascendancy, domination, excellence, importance 11 distinction, superiority

preeminent 3 top 4 main 5 chief, first 7 capital, stellar, supreme 8 dominant, foremost, peerless, towering, ultimate 9 matchless, number-one, paramount, principal, unrivaled 10 surpassing, unrivalled 11 outstanding, unmatchable 12 incomparable, transcendent *prefix:* 4 arch

preempt 4 bump, take 5 annex, seize, usurp 6 assume 7 acquire, replace 8 arrogate 9 forestall 10 confiscate, substitute 11 appropriate, expropriate

preen 5 gloat, groom, pride, primp, swell 6 smooth

preface 4 lead, open 5 begin, intro, proem, usher 6 herald 8 exordium, foreword, overture, preamble, prologue 9 introduce 11 preliminary 12 introduction

prefatory 7 opening 8 proemial 12 introductory

prefect 7 head boy, monitor 8 head girl 10 magistrate

prefer 5 elect, favor 6 choose, opt for, select 7 advance, elevate, promote, upgrade

preferable 5 finer 6 better 8 superior, worthier

preference 4 pick 6 choice, option 8 election, priority 9 advantage, elevation, promotion, selection, upgrading 10 favoritism, partiality

prefigure 4 hint 7 foresee 8 indicate 9 adumbrate 10 foreshadow

pregnancy 9 gestation, gravidity

pregnant 4 full, rich 5 heavy 6 gravid, parous

7 teeming, weighty **8** eloquent, enceinte, profound **9** expectant, expecting, gestating, inventive, momentous, with child **10** expressive, meaningful, parturient **11** significant

prehensile 8 grasping

prejudice 3 mar **4** bias, harm, hurt, sway **5** color, favor **6** damage, injure, injury, racism, sexism **7** bigotry, leaning **8** aversion **9** antipathy, hostility, influence **10** partiality **11** intolerance **12** one-sidedness

prejudicial 6 biased **7** bigoted **8** damaging **9** injurious **11** deleterious, detrimental

prelate 6 bishop **7** primate **8** cardinal, diocesan **9** patriarch **10** archbishop **12** ecclesiastic

preliminary 4 heat **5** basic, match, trial **7** initial, opening **8** proemial **9** beginning **10** qualifying **11** fundamental **12** introductory

prelude 5 intro, proem **7** opening **8** exordium, foreword, overture, prologue **12** introduction, prolegomenon

premature 5 early **8** untimely **10** beforehand

premeditated 5 set up **7** planned, studied, willful **8** designed, intended **9** conscious **10** calculated, considered, deliberate, thought-out **11** intentional

premier 4 head, main **5** chief, first **7** leading, primary **8** earliest, foremost, original **9** principal **13** prime minister

premiere 5 debut **7** opening **8** earliest, original **9** beginning **10** first night

premise 4 base **5** posit **6** assume, thesis **8** building, property, set forth **9** postulate **10** assumption **11** postulation, proposition, supposition

premium 4 agio **5** bonus, extra, prize **6** reward **8** dividend, superior **9** excellent **10** recompense **11** exceptional

premonition 4 omen **9** misgiving, suspicion **10** foreboding **11** forewarning **12** apprehension, presentiment

preoccupied 4 deep, lost, rapt **6** absent, intent **7** engaged, faraway, worried **8** absorbed, immersed **9** concerned, engrossed, wrapped up **10** abstracted, distracted **11** inattentive **12** absentminded

prep 5 basic, coach, drill, equip, groom, prime, ready, train, trial **8** get ready **11** preliminary **12** introductory

preparation 4 base, plan **5** study **7** fitness, measure **8** compound, medicine, training **9** alertness, foresight, readiness **10** background, concoction

preparatory 5 basic **11** preliminary, rudimentary **12** introductory

prepare 3 fit, fix, set **4** gird **5** draft, groom,

prime, ready, train **6** draw up, make up, outfit **7** fortify, furnish **9** formulate

prepared 3 set **4** up on **5** fixed, ready **6** primed **7** treated **9** processed

preponderance 4 bulk **8** dominion, majority, main part **9** ascendant, dominance, supremacy **10** ascendancy, domination **11** superiority

preponderant 7 supreme **8** dominant, superior **9** paramount **10** prevailing

preponderate 4 rule **5** reign **6** exceed **7** command, dictate, outrank, prevail **8** dominate, outweigh

preposition 2 at, by, in, of, on, to, up **3** for, off **4** down, from, into, like, near, onto, over, past, upon, with **5** about, above, after, along, among, below, since, under, until **6** across, around, before, behind, beside, during, except, inside, toward, within **7** against, beneath, between, outside, through, without

prepossess 4 bias, sway **5** favor **6** absorb, engage, occupy **7** engross, immerse, involve **9** influence

prepossessing 7 likable **9** appealing **10** attractive

preposterous 4 wild **5** crazy, wacky **6** absurd, insane **7** asinine, foolish, idiotic **9** fantastic, laughable, senseless **10** irrational, ridiculous **11** harebrained **12** unreasonable

prerequisite 4 must, need **5** vital **8** required **9** condition, essential, mandatory, necessary, necessity **10** imperative, sine qua non **11** requirement **13** indispensable

prerogative 5 power, right **8** appanage, immunity **9** authority, exemption, privilege **10** birthright, perquisite

presage 4 bode, omen, warn **5** augur, sense **6** augury, boding, herald, intuit **7** portend, portent, predict, promise, warning **8** announce, forebode, forecast, foretell, forewarn, indicate, prophesy, soothsay **9** foretoken, harbinger, intuition, misgiving **10** foreboding, foreshadow, prediction, prognostic, vaticinate

presbyter 5 elder **6** priest

prescience 9 foresight **12** anticipation, clairvoyance **13** foreknowledge

prescribe 3 fix, set **4** rule **5** guide, order **6** assign, choose, decide, decree, define, direct, impose, ordain, select **7** dictate, lay down, pick out, require, specify **9** designate, determine, stipulate

prescript 3 law **4** rule **5** edict, order **6** decree **10** regulation

prescription 3 med **4** drug, rule **5** claim,

presence right, title **6** custom, remedy **8** medicine **9** direction **10** medication

presence 3 air **4** look, mien **5** poise **6** aspect, spirit **7** address, bearing **8** carriage, demeanor **9** composure

present 3 act, aim, now **4** boon, gift, give, here, pose, show **5** award, bring, favor, offer, point, stage, tense, today **6** at hand, bestow, confer, convey, direct, donate, extend, in view, modern, render, submit, tender **7** hand out, largess, perform, proffer **8** existing, nominate **9** introduce **12** contemporary

presentable 3 fit **6** decent, proper **8** becoming **9** befitting **10** acceptable **11** appropriate **12** satisfactory

present-day 6 living, recent **7** current, ongoing, popular, topical **8** contempo, existent, existing, pressing, up-to-date **9** prevalent, surviving **10** prevailing **12** contemporary

presently 3 now **4** anon, soon **5** today **6** in time, one day **7** by and by **9** forthwith, these days **10** before long

preservation 4 care **6** saving, shield **7** defense, keeping **8** pickling **10** husbanding, protection **11** conservancy, maintenance, safekeeping

preserve 3 can, jam **4** save **5** jelly, put up **6** embalm, ensile, keep up, pickle **7** protect, shelter, sustain **8** keep safe, maintain **9** confiture

preside 3 run **4** head, lead **5** chair **6** direct, handle, manage **7** conduct, control, operate, oversee **8** moderate **9** officiate

president, U. S. 3 Abe, DDE, FDR, HST, Ike, JFK, LBJ, RMN **4** Bush (George, George W.), Ford (Gerald R.), Polk (James K.), Taft (William H.) **5** Adams (John, John Quincy), Grant (Ulysses S.), Hayes (Rutherford B.), Nixon (Richard M.), Obama (Barack), Tyler (John) **6** Arthur (Chester A.), Carter (Jimmy), Hoover (Herbert), Monroe (James), Pierce (Franklin), Reagan (Ronald), Taylor (Zachary), Truman (Harry S.), Wilson (Woodrow) **7** Clinton (Bill), Harding (Warren), Jackson (Andrew), Johnson (Andrew, Lyndon), Kennedy (John F.), Lincoln (Abraham), Madison (James) **8** Buchanan (James), Coolidge (Calvin), Fillmore (Millard), Garfield (James), Harrison (Benjamin, William Henry), McKinley (William), Van Buren (Martin) **9** Cleveland (Grover), Jefferson (Thomas), Roosevelt (Franklin D., Theodore) **10** Eisenhower (Dwight D.), Washington (George)

presidential nominee 4 Dole (Robert J.), Gore (Albert) **5** Dewey (Thomas), Kerry (John) **6** McCain (John) **7** Dukakis (Michael), Mondale (Walter) **8** Humphrey (Hubert), McGovern (George) **9** Goldwater (Barry), Stevenson (Adlai)

presidio 4 fort **7** bastion, citadel **8** fastness, fortress, garrison **10** stronghold **13** fortification

Presley, Elvis 4 King (The) **6** Pelvis (The) *daughter:* **9** Lisa Marie *manager:* **6** Parker (Col. Tom) *middle name:* **4** Aron **5** Aaron *property:* **9** Graceland *wife:* **9** Priscilla

press 3 hug, jam, ram **4** cram, iron, mass, pack, pile, push, rush, urge **5** clasp, crowd, crush, drive, force, horde, hurry, media, shove **6** demand, hustle, insist, jostle, propel, squash, stress, throng, thrust **7** beseech, entreat, imprint, printer, squeeze **9** constrain, influence, multitude

pressing 5 acute, vital **6** urgent **7** crucial, earnest, exigent, serious **8** critical **9** immediate, important, insistent **10** compelling, imperative

pressure 4 push, rush **5** drive, impel **6** burden, coerce, strain, stress **7** tension **10** constraint *combining form:* **5** piezo *instrument:* **9** barometer *unit:* **3** bar **6** pascal

prestige 4 fame, rank, sway **5** power **6** cachet, credit, esteem, regard, renown, repute, status, weight **7** dignity, stature **8** eminence, position, standing **9** authority, influence **10** importance, prominence **11** consequence, distinction

prestigious 5 famed, great **6** famous **7** eminent, honored, notable **8** esteemed, renowned **9** prominent, respected **10** celebrated **11** influential **13** distinguished

presto 4 fast **7** hastily, quickly, rapidly **8** suddenly **9** posthaste **11** immediately

presumably 6 likely, surely **8** probably **9** doubtless

presume 4 dare **5** guess, imply, infer, think, trust **6** expect, gather, impose, reason **7** believe, intrude, suppose, surmise, venture **8** infringe **9** postulate **10** conjecture

presumption 4 gall **5** brass, cheek, nerve **6** belief, daring, ground, reason, thesis **7** conceit **8** audacity, chutzpah, evidence **9** brashness, inference, postulate **10** confidence, effrontery

presumptuous 4 bold, smug **5** brash, fresh, pushy **6** cheeky, uppity **7** forward **8** arrogant **9** audacious, confident **11** overweening, self-assured

presuppose 5 posit **6** assume, expect **7** imagine, require, surmise **9** postulate

pretend 3 act **4** fake, pose, sham **5** bluff, claim, false, feign, guess, put on **6** affect, assume, delude, invent **7** deceive, imitate, mislead, playact, profess, purport, suppose, surmise **8** simulate **9** imaginary **11** counterfeit, make-believe

pretender 4 fake, sham **5** actor, faker, fraud, phony **6** humbug **8** claimant, impostor **9** hypocrite

pretense 3 act, air **4** face, fake, mask, pose, sham **5** claim, cloak, cover, front, guise **6** deceit, facade, humbug **7** charade, fiction **8** disguise **9** deception, false show, imposture **10** masquerade, simulation **11** affectation, make-believe, ostentation

pretension 5 claim, right **6** vanity **8** ambition **10** allegation, aspiration **11** affectation

pretentious 4 arty **5** lofty, put-on, showy **6** chichi, la-de-da, la-di-da, too-too **7** pompous, stilted **8** affected, inflated, lah-de-dah, lah-di-dah, puffed up, snobbish, specious **9** bombastic, conceited, grandiose, lah-dee-dah, overblown **10** euphuistic, rhetorical **11** highfalutin **12** high-sounding, magniloquent, vainglorious

preternatural 7 psychic, unusual **8** abnormal, atypical **9** anomalous, unearthly, untypical **10** mysterious **12** inexplicable, supernatural **13** extraordinary

pretext 4 mask, ploy **5** alibi, cloak, cover, front, guise **6** device, excuse **7** apology **10** subterfuge

pretty 4 cute, fair **5** bonny, quite **6** comely, fairly, lovely, rather, sort of **7** cunning **8** graceful, pleasant, pleasing, somewhat **9** appealing, beautiful **10** attractive, more or less **11** good-looking **12** considerable

prevail 4 beat, rule **5** reign **6** master **7** conquer, impress, persist, triumph **8** convince, dominate, domineer, overcome, override, persuade **9** influence

prevalent 4 rife **6** ruling **7** favored, popular, regnant **8** accepted, dominant, superior **9** ascendant, customary, paramount, sovereign **10** accustomed, widespread

prevaricate 3 fib, lie **5** avoid, evade **6** palter **7** confuse, deceive, distort, falsify, quibble **12** misrepresent

prevarication 3 fib, lie **4** tale **5** lying, story **6** canard, deceit **7** falsity **9** deception, falsehood

prevent 3 bar, dam **4** balk, foil, ward **5** avert, avoid, block, check, debar, deter, estop **6** arrest, baffle, forbid, hinder, impede, thwart **7** forfend, head off, inhibit, obviate **8** obstruct, preclude, prohibit, stave off **9** forestall, frustrate, interdict **10** anticipate

previous 4 fore, past **5** early, prior **6** before, former **7** earlier, onetime **8** anterior **9** erst-

while, foregoing, in advance **10** antecedent, beforehand

previously 4 once **5** afore, ahead **6** before **7** already, earlier **8** formerly **9** erstwhile **10** heretofore

prewar 10 antebellum

prey 4 feed, game, mark **5** chase **6** quarry, target, victim **8** casualty, distress

Priam *daughter:* **6** Creusa **8** Polyxena **9** Cassandra *father:* **8** Laomedon *grandfather:* **4** Ilus *kingdom:* **4** Troy **5** Ilium *slayer:* **7** Pyrrhus **11** Neoptolemus *son:* **5** Paris **6** Hector, Lycaon **7** Helenus, Troilus **9** Deiphobus, Polydorus *wife:* **6** Arisbe, Hecuba

Priapus *father:* **7** Bacchus **8** Dionysus *mother:* **5** Venus **9** Aphrodite

price 3 fee, fix, tab **4** cost, fare, rate, toll **6** amount, assess, charge, figure, outlay, reward, tariff **7** expense, payment **8** appraise

priceless 4 rare, rich **5** droll, funny, witty **6** absurd, costly, prized, valued **7** amusing **8** precious, valuable **9** cherished, treasured **10** invaluable

pricey 4 dear **5** steep **6** costly **9** expensive

prick 3 jab **4** goad, mark, prod, spur, urge **5** egg on, point, sting, thorn **6** affect, excite, exhort, pierce, prompt **7** pinhole **8** puncture **9** perforate

prickly 5 burry, sharp, spiny **6** briary, thorny, tetchy, tingly, touchy, trying **7** brambly, waspish **8** annoying, nettling, snappish, stinging **9** difficult, fractious, irritable, vexatious **10** bothersome, irritating, nettlesome **11** troublesome

pride 3 ego, top **4** best, brag, pack, pick **5** boast, cream, elite, exult, group, preen, prime, prize, vaunt **6** choice, egoism, hubris, vanity **7** conceit, delight, elation, dignity, disdain, egotism **8** smugness, treasure **9** arrogance, cockiness, vainglory **10** self-esteem, self-regard **11** self-respect **12** congratulate

Pride and Prejudice author 6 Austen (Jane)

prideful 6 elated **7** haughty **8** exultant **10** disdainful

prier 5 snoop **7** meddler **8** busybody, quidnunc **9** buttinsky

priest 5 padre **6** cleric, divine, father, rector **8** chaplain **9** clergyman, presbyter *ancient Roman:* **6** flamen **8** pontifex *Biblical:* **3** Eli *Buddhist:* **4** lama *Celtic:* **5** druid *French:* **4** abbé, curé *Muslim:* **4** imam *prop:* **4** bell, book **6** candle *tribal:* **6** shaman

priestly 8 clerical, hieratic **10** sacerdotal

prig 5 prude, thief **6** pedant **8** bluenose **9** Mrs. Grundy **10** goody-goody

priggish 5 fussy **6** stuffy **7** genteel, pompous,

prudish **8** affected, pedantic **11** puritanical, straitlaced

prim 4 neat, nice, snug, tidy, trig **5** stiff **6** formal, proper, strict, stuffy, wooden **7** correct, genteel, orderly, precise, prudish **8** decorous, priggish **11** straitlaced

prima donna 4 diva, snob, star **7** artiste **9** chanteuse **10** narcissist **11** leading lady

prima facie 4 true **5** valid **8** apparent **11** self-evident

primal 5 basic **6** age-old **7** ancient, premier **8** cardinal, original **9** atavistic, paramount, primitive **10** preeminent **11** prehistoric

primary 4 main **5** basal, basic, chief, first **6** direct **7** initial, pioneer, radical **8** cardinal, earliest, original **9** elemental, essential, firsthand, immediate, number-one, paramount, principal **10** aboriginal, underlying **11** fundamental, rudimentary **12** foundational, introductory **combining form: 4** prot **5** proto **prefix: 4** arch **5** archi

primate 3 ape, man **5** human, lemur, loris **6** aye-aye, bishop, bonobo, monkey **7** gorilla **10** anthropoid, archbishop, chimpanzee, human being **11** Homo sapiens **nocturnal: 5** loris **7** tarsier **small: 6** galago

prime 3 top **4** best, dawn, fill, load, morn, peak, pick, rate **5** coach, cream, elite, first, paint, sunup, tonic, youth **6** choice, excite, height, spring, symbol **7** capital, highest, initial, morning, prepare, provoke, quicken **8** earliest, motivate, original, superior **9** excellent, first-rate, principal, stimulate **10** first-class

primer 4 book **5** guide **6** manual, reader **8** hornbook

primeval 7 ancient **8** earliest, original **10** aboriginal

primitive 3 raw **4** rude **5** basic, crude, early **6** savage **7** archaic, Spartan **8** barbaric, original, primeval **9** atavistic, barbarian, barbarous, elemental, essential, unevolved **10** elementary, primordial, underlying **11** fundamental, preliterate, uncivilized, undeveloped **12** uncultivated **combining form: 5** palae, paleo **6** archae, archeo, palaeo **7** archaeo **prefix: 4** arch **5** archi

primogenitor 4 sire **8** ancestor, forebear **9** precursor **10** forefather

primordial 5 basic, early, first **7** ancient **8** earliest, original

primp 4 fuss **5** adorn, dress, fix up, preen **7** dress up

prince Anglo-Saxon: 8 atheling **Arab: 4** amir, emir **5** ameer **Austrian: 8** archduke **Ethiopian: 3** ras **Indian: 4** raja, rana **5** rajah **of demons: 9** Beelzebub **of Monaco: 6** Albert

7 Rainier **of the church: 8** cardinal **of Wales: 7** Charles

Prince and the Pauper author 5 Twain (Mark) **7** Clemens (Samuel)

Prince Edward Island capital: 13 Charlottetown **provincial flower: 12** lady's slipper

Prince Igor composer 7 Borodin (Aleksandr)

princely 5 grand, noble, royal **8** generous, imposing, majestic **9** dignified **11** magnificent

princess 7 infanta **fictional: 3** Ida, Mia **4** Aura, Leia, Miyu, Ozma, Xena **5** Ariel, Belle, Fiona, She-Ra, Storm, Vespa, Zelda **6** Anelle, Aurora, Kadiya **7** Camilla, Jasmine **8** Angelica, Starfire **9** Belphoebe, Blackfire, Britomart, Buttercup, Gwenevere, Snow White **10** Bradamante, Cinderella, Pocahontas **11** Casamassima **mythical: 3** Ino **5** Medea **of Monaco: 5** Grace

Prince Valiant artist: 6 Foster (Hal) **son: 3** Arn **wife: 5** Aleta

principal 4 arch, dean, head, main, star **5** chief, first, major, prime **6** assets **7** capital, leading, premier, primary, stellar **8** cardinal, champion, dominant, foremost **9** paramount **10** headmaster, preeminent **11** outstanding, predominant **combining form: 4** prot **5** proto **prefix: 4** arch **5** archi

principium 3 law **5** axiom, basis **7** element, theorem **10** foundation **11** fundamental

principle 3 law **4** code, form, rule **5** axiom, basis, canon, ethic, tenet **6** ground, origin, source **7** conduct, faculty, precept **8** doctrine, polestar, rudiment **10** assumption, convention, foundation **11** fundamental

principled 5 moral, noble **6** honest **7** ethical, upright **8** virtuous **9** righteous **10** moralistic

print 4 type **5** issue, litho, stamp, write **7** engrave, impress, publish, typeset **10** impression **style: 4** bold **5** roman **6** italic **7** cursive **8** boldface

printer English: 6 Caxton (William) **German: 9** Gutenberg (Johann, Johannes) **Italian: 6** Bodoni (Giambattista) **8** Manutius (Aldus)

printing 7 edition, reissue **10** impression **measure: 4** pica **5** agate **plate: 10** stereotype **process: 4** roto **7** gravure **11** lithography **tool: 6** brayer

priority 4 lead **5** order **8** ordering **9** supremacy **10** importance, precedence, preference

prison 3 can, pen **4** brig, coop, jail, keep **5** clink **6** cooler, lockup **7** dungeon, slammer **8** bastille, big house, stockade **9** calaboose **11** reformatory **12** penitentiary **British: 4** gaol **California: 8** Alcatraz **10** San Quentin **New York: 6** Attica **8** Sing Sing **12** Rikers

Island **Northern Ireland:** 4 Maze **resident:** 6 inmate 7 convict 8 jailbird **Russian:** 5 gulag

prisoner 7 captive, convict, hostage 8 criminal, detainee, jailbird

prissy 5 picky 7 finicky, precise, prudish 8 exacting 10 fastidious, particular 11 strait-laced

pristine 4 pure 5 clean, fresh 8 earliest, original 9 unspoiled

privacy 6 secret 7 retreat, secrecy 9 seclusion 11 concealment

private 5 inner 6 secret 7 soldier 8 eyes-only, hush-hush, intimate, personal 9 concealed 10 closed-door, restricted, unofficial 11 independent, sequestered 12 confidential

privateer 4 ship 6 pirate 7 gunship 9 mercenary

private eye 3 spy, tec 4 tail 6 sleuth, shamus 7 gumshoe 8 sherlock 9 detective 12 investigator

privately 7 sub rosa 8 covertly, in camera, in secret, secretly

privation 4 lack, loss, need, want 6 dearth, penury 7 absence, poverty 8 distress 9 indigence, neediness, suffering

privilege 4 boon 5 favor, grant, right 7 license 8 appanage 9 allowance, exemption 10 birthright, concession, perquisite 11 entitlement, opportunity, prerogative **pope-granted:** 6 indult

privy 2 WC 3 can, loo 4 head, john 5 jakes 6 secret, toilet 7 latrine 8 bathroom, informed, lavatory, outhouse, personal 9 concealed, withdrawn 11 water closet

prize 3 pry, top 4 best, loot, pick, plum, rate, swag 5 award, booty, cream, elite, force, lever, purse, spoil, value 6 choice, esteem, reward, spoils, trophy 7 capture, cherish, jackpot, plunder, premium 8 treasure 10 appreciate 11 outstanding

prizefighting 6 boxing 8 pugilism

pro 3 for 6 expert, master 8 skillful 9 authority, in favor of 11 affirmative **opposite:** 3 con 4 anti

probable 6 likely 7 seeming 8 apparent, credible, expected, feasible, rational, reliable 10 reasonable

probe 4 poke, quiz, test 5 query, sonde, study 6 search 7 dig into, examine, explore, feel out, inquest, inquire, inquiry 8 check out, look into, research, sound out 9 delve into, penetrate 11 exploration, investigate, reconnoiter 13 investigation

probity 5 honor 6 virtue 7 honesty 8 fairness, goodness 9 integrity, rectitude 11 uprightness

problem 4 mess, snag 5 hitch, issue, poser 6 enigma, hassle, puzzle, riddle 7 dilemma, example, mystery, puzzler, trouble 8 hardship, headache, question 10 difficulty

problematic 4 iffy, moot, open 7 dubious 8 arguable, doubtful 9 debatable, uncertain, unsettled 10 precarious 12 questionable

proboscis 4 beak, nose 5 snoot, snout, trunk

procedure 4 plan, step 6 course, custom, method, policy, system 7 formula, measure, routine 8 protocol 9 operation 11 instruction

proceed 2 go 4 flow, move, rise, stem, wend 5 arise, get on, issue, segue 6 emerge, push on, spring, travel 7 advance, carry on, emanate, journey 8 continue 9 originate

proceedings 8 goings-on **recorded:** 4 acta 6 annals 7 minutes

proceeds 4 gain, take 5 yield 6 profit, result, return 8 earnings

process 3 way 4 mode, wise 5 modus, treat 6 handle, manner, method, refine, system 7 fashion, prepare, recycle, routine 8 workings 9 evolution, operation, outgrowth, procedure, technique 11 development **nerve cell:** 4 axon

procession 5 march, order, train 6 parade, series, string 7 caravan, cortege 8 sequence 9 cavalcade, march-past, motorcade 11 consecution

proclaim 5 extol 6 assert, insist 7 declare, exhibit, glorify, publish 8 announce, evidence, manifest 9 advertise, broadcast, make known 10 annunciate, bruit about

proclivity 4 bent 5 taste 6 liking 7 leaning 8 affinity, fondness, penchant, tendency 9 proneness 11 inclination 12 predilection

Procne father: 7 Pandion **husband:** 6 Tereus **sister:** 9 Philomela **son:** 4 Itys

procrastinate 5 dally, delay 6 dawdle

procreate 5 beget, breed 7 produce 8 conceive, generate, multiply 9 reproduce

Procris' husband 8 Cephalus

Procrustean ____ 3 bed

proctor 7 monitor, oversee 9 supervise 10 supervisor

procure 3 buy, get 4 gain 6 obtain, pick up 7 achieve, acquire 8 purchase 10 bring about

prod 3 dig, jab, jog 4 goad, poke, push, spur, stir, urge 5 egg on, elbow, nudge, point, prick, rouse 6 excite, exhort, incite, thrust 8 motivate 9 stimulate 10 incitement

prodigal 4 lush 6 lavish 7 opulent, profuse, riotous, spender, wastrel 8 reckless, wasteful 9 exuberant, luxuriant 10 profligate, squanderer 11 extravagant, spendthrift

prodigious 4 huge, vast 6 mighty, unreal 7 amazing, immense, mammoth, massive, strange, unusual 8 colossal, enormous, gi-

produce

gantic **9** fantastic, marvelous, wonderful **10** astounding, impressive, monumental, phenomenal, remarkable, staggering, stupendous, surprising **11** astonishing **13** extraordinary

produce 4 bear, form, grow, make, show, sire **5** beget, breed, build, cause, erect, frame, hatch, mount, put on, raise, spawn, stage, yield **6** create, effect, father, output, parent, secure, work up **7** deliver, fashion, turn out **8** engender, generate, multiply **9** construct, fabricate, originate, procreate, propagate **10** bring about **11** manufacture, put together

product 5 fruit, issue, yield **6** effect, legacy, output, result, upshot **7** harvest, outcome, turnout **8** artifact, creation, multiple, offshoot **9** handiwork, outgrowth **11** consequence, manufacture *combining form:* **3** gen

production 5 fruit, yield **6** output **7** staging, turnout **8** artifact, assembly, creation **9** execution, handiwork, rendering **11** achievement, manufacture, realization

productive 4 rich **6** fecund, useful **7** fertile **8** abundant, fruitful, prolific **9** rewarding **10** beneficial

proem 5 intro **7** preface, prelude **8** exordium, foreword, overture, prologue **11** preliminary **12** introduction

profane 3 lay **4** damn, foul **5** abuse, dirty, pagan **6** coarse, debase, defile, filthy, impure, unholy, vulgar **7** impious, obscene, secular **8** indecent, temporal, unsacred **9** desecrate **10** irreverent, unhallowed **11** blasphemous, irreligious **12** sacrilegious, unsanctified

profanity 4 oath **5** abuse, curse **7** cursing, cussing **8** swearing **9** blasphemy, sacrilege **10** execration **11** imprecation, irreverence

profess 4 aver, avow **5** claim, teach **6** affirm, allege, assert, avouch **7** declare, pretend, protest, purport **8** maintain, practice

profession 3 art, job, vow **5** craft, trade **6** avowal, career, métier **7** calling **8** business, vocation **9** assertion, specialty, statement, testimony **10** handicraft, occupation, walk of life **11** affirmation

professional 4 paid **6** expert, master **7** learned, skilled **9** authority **10** proficient, specialist **11** experienced **12** businesslike

professor 3 don **6** expert **7** teacher **8** academic, educator

proffer 4 give, pose **6** extend, submit, tender **7** hold out, present, suggest **10** invitation, suggestion

proficiency 5 savvy, skill **7** ability, advance, mastery, prowess **8** facility, progress **9** adeptness, dexterity, expertise, knowledge **10** competence

proficient 4 able **5** adept **6** expert **7** capable, skilled **8** advanced, masterly, skillful **9** authority, competent, effective, masterful, qualified **11** crackerjack, experienced **12** accomplished

profile 3 bio **5** chart **6** sketch, survey **7** contour, diagram, outline **8** exposure, portrait, side view **9** biography **10** silhouette **11** description

profit 3 net **4** gain, take **5** serve, yield **6** excess, income, payoff, return **7** benefit, receipt **8** earnings, proceeds **10** percentage **12** compensation *sudden:* **7** killing

profitable 6 paying, useful **7** gainful **8** fruitful **9** lucrative, rewarding **10** beneficial, well-paying, worthwhile **11** moneymaking **12** advantageous, remunerative

profligate 4 wild **6** waster **7** immoral, spender, wastrel **8** prodigal, reckless, wasteful **9** abandoned, dissolute, indulgent, reprobate **10** dissipated, immoderate, licentious, squanderer **11** extravagant, promiscuous, spendthrift **13** self-indulgent

profound 4 deep, wise **5** heavy, total, utter **7** abysmal, intense **8** absolute, abstruse, complete, esoteric, thorough **9** intensive **10** deep-seated, insightful

profundity 5 depth **6** wisdom **7** insight **8** deepness **12** abstruseness

profuse 4 lush **6** lavish **7** copious, fulsome, liberal, opulent **8** abundant, generous, prodigal **9** abounding, bounteous, bountiful, excessive, exuberant, luxuriant, plentiful **10** munificent **11** extravagant

profusion 4 glut, riot **5** flood, spate, surge **6** bounty, deluge, excess, wealth **7** nimiety, satiety, surfeit, surplus, torrent **8** overflow, overload, plethora **9** abundance, plenitude **10** lavishness, luxuriance, oversupply, plentitude, redundancy **11** copiousness, prodigality, sufficiency, superfluity **12** extravagance **13** overabundance

progenitor 4 sire **6** author, father, mother **8** ancestor, forebear **9** initiator, precursor **10** antecessor, forefather, forerunner, originator **11** predecessor

progeny 4 line **5** issue **6** litter, result, scions **7** outcome, product **8** children **9** offspring, posterity **11** descendants

prognosis 8 estimate, forecast, prophecy **9** prevision **10** estimation, prediction **11** expectation **12** anticipation

prognostic 4 omen, sign **6** augury **7** portent, presage **10** foreboding, indication

prognosticate 6 divine **7** foresee, predict, presage **8** forecast, foretell, prophesy

program 4 bill, book, plan, show **5** plans, slate **6** agenda, course, docket, lineup, policy **7** listing **8** calendar, playbill, schedule, syllabus **9** broadcast, procedure, timetable **10** bill of fare, curriculum

programming language 3 SQL **4** DASL, JADE, Java, LISP, Perl, Thue **5** Algol, BASIC, COBOL, CORAL **6** Euclid, Groovy, Inform, Pascal, Prolog, Python, Scheme, Simula **7** FORTRAN, Haskell, Miranda **10** JavaScript, PostScript **11** Visual Basic

progress 4 fare, gain, grow **5** get on, march **6** course, growth **7** advance, headway, passage, proceed **8** anabasis, get along, momentum **9** evolution, flowering, unfolding **11** advancement, development, improvement *planned:* **7** telesis

progressing 5 afoot **7** en route **8** under way

progression 4 path **5** chain **6** course, growth, series **7** advance **8** sequence **9** evolution, unfolding **10** trajectory **11** development

progressive 6 modern **7** growing, liberal, radical **8** advanced, tolerant **9** advancing **10** developing, increasing

prohibit 3 ban, bar **4** stop **5** block, debar **6** enjoin, forbid, outlaw **7** prevent **8** preclude **9** interdict

prohibited 4 tabu **5** taboo **6** banned, barred **7** illegal, illicit **8** verboten **9** forbidden

prohibition 3 ban, bar **5** taboo **7** embargo **8** sanction **9** interdict **10** constraint, forbidding, injunction **12** disallowance, interdiction, proscription

prohibitive 5 steep **6** costly **7** sky-high **9** excessive **10** exorbitant, forbidding **11** restrictive

project 3 jut **4** cast, feat, plan **5** bulge **6** affair, design, devise, extend, intend, scheme, vision **7** arrange, concern, emprise, exploit, feature, imagine, propose, purpose, venture **8** business, conceive, envisage, envision, game plan, overhang, protrude, stand out, stick out, strategy **9** blueprint, visualize **10** enterprise **11** proposition, undertaking

projection 3 jut **4** bump, knob, view **5** bulge **7** display **8** estimate, forecast, overhang, scheming, swelling **9** extension **10** jutting out, perception **11** expectation *vaulted:* **4** apse

prolapse 3 sag

proletariat 6 masses **7** workers **8** laborers **9** commoners, hoi polloi **12** working class

prolific 4 rich **6** fecund, gifted, lavish **7** fertile **8** abundant, creative, fruitful **9** abounding,

bountiful, inventive **10** generating, generative **11** reproducing **12** reproductive

prolix 4 long **5** windy, wordy **7** diffuse, lengthy, tedious, verbose **8** drawn out, rambling, tiresome **9** redundant, wearisome **10** long-winded

prologue 7 opening, preface, prelude **8** exordium, foreword, overture, preamble **9** beginning **12** introduction

prolong 6 extend **7** drag out, draw out, spin out, stretch **8** continue, elongate, lengthen

prolonged 7 lasting, lengthy **8** drawn-out **9** lingering **10** continuing, persistent, persisting

prom 4 ball, fete, gala **5** dance **6** formal

promenade 4 deck, walk **6** parade, stroll **9** boardwalk

Prometheus *brother:* **5** Atlas **9** Menoetius **10** Epimetheus *creation:* **3** man **7** mankind *father:* **7** Iapetus *gift:* **4** fire *mother:* **7** Clymene *muralist:* **6** Orozco *rescuer:* **8** Heracles, Hercules *tormentor:* **5** eagle

prominence 4 crag, fame, rise, spur **5** bulge **6** height, renown, status **8** eminence, headland, prestige, salience, standing **9** celebrity, elevation **10** importance, projection **11** distinction

prominent 5 famed, great, noted **6** famous, marked, signal **7** eminent, jutting, leading, notable, popular, salient **8** renowned, striking **9** arresting, notorious, well-known **10** celebrated, noticeable, pronounced, remarkable **11** conspicuous, eye-catching, illustrious, outstanding **13** distinguished *person:* **3** VIP **4** BMOC, lion **5** mogul, nabob **6** bigwig, honcho **7** big shot, grandee **8** luminary, mandarin, somebody **9** dignitary **13** high-muck-a-muck

promiscuous 5 mixed **6** casual, random, varied **7** immoral **8** careless **9** haphazard, hitor-miss, irregular **10** licentious **11** unselective **12** unrestrained

promise 3 vow **4** bode, bond, oath, word **5** agree, augur, swear, vouch **6** assure, engage, ensure, expect, insure, parole, pledge, plight **7** betroth, compact, consent, declare, outlook, portend, presage, suggest **8** contract, covenant, indicate **9** assurance, betrothal, potential, undertake **11** declaration, expectation

promised land 4 Zion **6** Canaan, heaven **8** paradise **11** kingdom come

promising 6 likely **7** hopeful **9** favorable **10** auspicious **11** encouraging

promissory note 3 IOU

promontory 4 beak, bill, cape, head, ness **5** bulge, point **8** foreland, headland

promote 3 aid **4** help, hype, plug, puff, push, sell, tout **5** boost, favor, raise **6** foster, launch, prefer **7** advance, build up, elevate, endorse, forward, further, nurture, present, support **8** advocate, champion **9** advertise, encourage, publicize, recommend

promotion 6 step up **7** advance, buildup, puffery **9** elevation, publicity, upgrading **10** preference, preferment **11** advancement, advertising, improvement **13** advertisement

prompt 3 apt, cue, jog **4** fast, goad, help, hint, move, spur, urge **5** alert, quick, rapid, ready **6** assist, incite, induce, on time, remind, speedy, stir up, timely **7** suggest **8** convince, persuade, punctual, reminder **10** responsive

promulgate 5 issue **6** decree **7** declare, publish **8** announce, proclaim **9** advertise, broadcast **10** annunciate **11** disseminate

prone 3 apt **4** flat, open **5** given, level **6** liable, likely, supine **7** subject, tending, willing **8** disposed, facedown, inclined **9** lying down, reclining, prostrate, recumbent **10** horizontal **11** predisposed, susceptible

prong 4 barb, fang, fork, spur, stab, tine **5** point, thorn **6** pierce

pronghorn 8 antelope

____ **pro nobis 3** ora

pronoun *archaic:* **2** ye **3** thy **4** thou **5** thine *demonstrative:* **4** that, this **5** these, those *indefinite:* **3** all, any, few, one **4** both, each, none, some **5** no one, other **6** anyone, either, nobody **7** another, anybody, neither, nothing, someone **8** anything, somebody **9** everybody, something **10** everything *personal:* **2** he, it, my, we **3** her, him, she, you **4** them, they *possessive:* **2** my **3** her, his, its, our **4** hers, mine, ours, your **5** their, yours **6** theirs *reflexive:* **6** itself, myself **7** herself, himself, oneself, ourself **8** yourself **9** ourselves **10** themselves, yourselves *relative:* **3** who **4** that, what, whom **5** which, whose, whoso **6** whomso **7** whoever **8** whatever, whomever **9** whichever, whosoever **10** whatsoever, whomsoever **11** whichsoever

pronounce 3 say **5** judge, sound, speak, state, utter **6** affirm, assert, decree, recite **7** declare **9** enunciate **10** articulate

pronounced 5 clear **6** marked, strong **7** assured, decided, evident, obvious **8** clear-cut, definite, distinct **12** unmistakable

pronouncement 5 edict **6** decree **9** manifesto, statement **11** declaration, publication **12** notification

pronto 3 now, PDQ **4** ASAP, fast, stat **6** at once **7** quickly **8** directly **9** forthwith, instanter, instantly, posthaste, right away **11** immediately

pronunciation *distinctive:* **4** burr, lilt **5** drawl, twang **6** accent, brogue *study:* **8** orthoepy **9** phonetics

proof 4 test **5** facts, goods, repro **6** galley **8** argument, evidence **9** testament, testimony **10** impression **11** attestation **12** confirmation

proofreaders' mark 4 dele, stet **5** caret

prop 4 stay **5** brace, shore **6** buoy up, hold up **7** bolster, shore up, support, sustain **8** buttress **10** strengthen **12** underpinning

propaganda 4 hype **8** agitprop, lobbying

propagandize 4 tout **5** boost, extol **7** advance, promote, trumpet **9** brainwash, catechize, inculcate **10** promulgate **11** proselytize **12** indoctrinate

propagate 5 beget, breed, raise, strew **6** extend, spread **7** diffuse, publish, radiate **8** disperse, generate, increase, multiply, transmit **9** circulate, cultivate, publicize, reproduce **10** distribute **11** disseminate

propel 4 goad, move, push, spur, urge **5** drive, egg on, power, shoot, shove **6** exhort, launch, thrust **7** actuate **8** activate

propellant 3 gas **4** fuel, spur **7** impetus, impulse **8** catalyst, stimulus **9** explosive, incentive, stimulant **10** motivation

propensity 7 leaning **8** penchant **10** preference **11** inclination

proper 3 apt, due, fit **4** good, just, meet, nice, prim, true **5** exact, right **6** au fait, decent, prissy, seemly, useful **7** correct, desired, fitting, genteel **8** becoming, decorous, priggish, rightful, rigorous, suitable **9** befitting **10** felicitous **11** appropriate, comme il faut, distinctive *combining form:* **4** orth **5** ortho

property 4 land, mark **5** acres, trait, worth **6** assets, estate, realty, riches, virtue, wealth **7** acreage, chattel, effects, feature, fortune, quality **8** chattels, dominion, hallmark, holdings, premises **9** attribute, ownership, resources, substance **10** belongings, possession, real estate *conveyor:* **7** alienor *recipient:* **7** alienee *seller:* **7** Realtor *transfer:* **8** alienate

prophecy 6 vision **8** forecast **10** divination, prediction **11** foretelling

prophesy 5 augur **6** divine, preach **7** foresee, portend, predict, presage **8** forecast, foretell, instruct, soothsay **9** adumbrate, prefigure **10** vaticinate **13** prognosticate

prophet 4 seer **5** augur, sibyl **6** auspex, oracle **7** diviner, seeress **8** foreseer, haruspex **9** predictor **10** forecaster, foreteller, prophesier, soothsayer **11** Nostradamus **13** fortune-teller *Arthurian:* 6 Merlin *Major:* 6 Daniel, Isaiah 7 Ezekiel 8 Jeremiah *Minor:* 4 Amos, Joel, Osee 5 Hosea, Jonah, Micah, Nahum 6 Haggai 7 Malachi, Obadiah 8 Habakkuk 9 Zechariah, Zephaniah

Prophet author 6 Gibran (Khalil)

prophetess 5 sibyl 6 Pythia 7 Deborah 9 Cassandra

prophetic 5 vatic 6 orphic 7 Delphic 8 Delphian, oracular 9 presaging, prescient, sibylline, vaticinal 10 predictive, revelatory 11 apocalyptic, foretelling

propinquity 7 kinship 8 nearness 9 closeness, proximity 10 contiguity

propitiate 5 adapt, atone 6 adjust, pacify, soothe 7 appease, assuage, gratify, mollify, placate, satisfy 9 intercede, reconcile 10 conciliate

propitious 4 good, rosy 5 lucky 6 benign, bright 7 benefic, helpful 8 favoring 9 favorable, fortunate, opportune, promising 10 auspicious, beneficent, beneficial, benevolent 12 advantageous

proponent 6 backer 8 advocate, champion, defender 9 expounder, supporter 10 enthusiast

proportion 4 rate, size 5 allot, ratio, quota, share 6 adjust, divide 7 balance, conform, harmony 8 symmetry 9 dimension 10 percentage 12 relationship

proportional 5 scale 7 in scale, pro rata 8 relative 9 equalized 10 contingent, equivalent, reciprocal 11 correlative, symmetrical 12 commensurate 13 commensurable, corresponding

proposal 3 bid 4 idea, plan 6 motion, scheme 7 outline, proffer, project 8 scenario 10 invitation, suggestion 11 proposition *final:* 9 ultimatum

propose 3 aim, ask, put 4 name, plan, pose 5 offer 6 design, intend, submit, tender 7 advance, move for, present, request, solicit, suggest 8 nominate, put forth, set forth, theorize 9 recommend 10 put forward

proposition 4 plan 5 offer 6 scheme, thesis 7 premise, suggest, theorem 8 proposal 10 invitation, suggestion

propound 3 put 4 pose 5 offer 7 present, suggest 8 put forth

proprietor 5 owner 8 landlord 9 possessor

propriety 7 aptness, decency, decorum, manners 8 behavior, civility, good form 9 etiquette, rightness 10 seemliness 11 correctness, fittingness, suitability 12 decorousness

·**propulsion** 4 fuel, push 5 drive, force, power 6 energy, thrust

prorate 5 allot, divvy, quota, share, split 6 assess, divide, parcel, ration 7 divvy up, portion 9 apportion, partition 10 distribute

prorogue 3 end 4 rise, stay 5 defer, delay 6 hold up, put off, recess, shelve 7 adjourn, hold off, suspend 8 dissolve, hold over, postpone 9 terminate

prosaic 4 dull, flat 5 banal, prose, prosy, trite, vapid 6 boring, common 7 factual, literal, mundane, tedious 8 everyday, lifeless, ordinary, workaday 9 colorless 10 lackluster, uneventful 11 commonplace 13 unimaginative

proscenium 5 frame, stage 9 forestage 10 foreground

proscribe 3 ban 4 damn 6 enjoin, forbid, outlaw 7 condemn 8 prohibit, sentence 9 interdict

proscription 3 ban 4 tabu 5 taboo 8 sanction 11 prohibition 12 condemnation, interdiction

prosecute 3 sue 4 wage 5 press 6 charge, indict, pursue 7 carry on, perform 8 continue 9 bring suit, persevere

prosecutor 2 DA

proselyte 7 convert, recruit 8 neophyte

proselytize 5 draft 6 enlist, enroll, sign up 7 convert, recruit, win over 8 convince 9 brainwash, catechize 11 prevail upon 12 indoctrinate

_____ **prosequi** 5 nolle

prospect 4 mine, view 5 scene, vista 6 chance, survey, vision 7 dig into, explore, lookout, outlook 8 customer, exposure 9 candidate 10 expectancy 11 expectation, possibility 12 anticipation

prospective 6 coming, future, likely 7 awaited, ensuing, nearing, pending, planned, would-be 8 destined, eventual, expected, hoped-for, intended, proposed, soon-to-be 9 impending, looked-for, potential, scheduled 10 consequent, succeeding 11 anticipated, approaching, predestined, forthcoming

prospectus 4 list, plan 6 design, layout, précis 7 epitome, outline, program, summary 8 bulletin, synopsis 9 catalogue, timetable 10 projection 11 description 12 announcement

prosper 5 score, yield 6 arrive, do well, thrive 7 make out, produce, succeed, turn out 8 flourish, grow rich

prosperity 4 ease 6 riches, wealth 7 success 8 thriving 9 abundance, advantage, affluence, well-being

Prospero *daughter:* 7 Miranda *servant:* 5 Ariel *slave:* 7 Caliban

prosperous 4 rich, well 5 happy, lucky 6 robust, strong **7** booming, halcyon, opulent, wealthy, well-off **8** affluent, thriving, well-to-do **9** desirable, favorable, fortunate, promising, well-fixed **10** auspicious, successful, well-heeled **11** comfortable, flourishing

prostitute 4 bawd, doxy, drab, moll **5** abuse, B-girl, madam, quean, whore **6** callet, debase, floozy, harlot, hooker, misuse, wanton **7** chippie, cocotte, corrupt, cyprian, floozie, hustler, Paphian **8** call girl, meretrix, strumpet **9** courtesan, party girl **11** fille de joie, nightwalker **12** camp follower, streetwalker *reformed:* **8** magdalen **9** magdalene

prostitution 8 harlotry, whoredom **13** streetwalking *house of:* **4** crib, stew **6** bagnio **7** brothel, lupanar **8** bordello, cathouse **10** bawdy house **13** sporting house

prostrate 4 fell, flat **5** abase, level, prone **6** humble, lay low, submit, supine **7** exhaust, wear out **8** helpless, overcome **9** decumbent, exhausted, overpower, overwhelm, powerless, recumbent **10** procumbent, submissive

protagonist 4 hero, lead, star **5** actor **6** leader **7** heroine, sponsor **8** advocate, champion **9** principal

protean 6 mobile, varied **7** diverse, mutable **8** variable **9** adaptable, versatile **10** changeable

protect 4 save **5** cover, guard **6** defend, screen, secure, shield **7** shelter **8** preserve, restrict **9** safeguard

protection 4 care **5** aegis, armor, bribe, graft, guard **6** safety, shield **7** bulwark, defense, shelter, support **8** armament, coverage, immunity, security **9** extortion, insurance, safeguard **11** supervision

protector 5 armor, guard **6** patron, regent, shield **8** guardian **9** caretaker

protégé 4 ward **5** pupil **7** student, trainee **8** disciple

protein 4 zein **5** actin, opsin **6** avidin, enzyme, fibrin, globin **7** albumin, elastin, fibroin, histone, keratin, legumin, sericin **8ʹ** creatine, globulin, glutelin, prolamin, protamin, proteose, vitellin *complex:* **6** mucoid *derivative:* **7** peptide, peptone *poisonous:* **5** abrin, ricin

pro tem 6 acting **7** interim **9** ad interim, temporary

protest 4 aver, avow, beef **5** sit-in **6** affirm, assert, avouch, except, object, oppose, picket, resist **7** declare, dissent, profess **8** maintain **9** challenge, complaint, objection **10** disapprove **11** demonstrate, disapproval **13** demonstration

Protestant 5 Amish **6** Mormon, Quaker, Shaker **7** Baptist, Lollard, Pilgrim, Puritan **8** Anglican, Lutheran, Moravian **9** Adventist, Mennonite, Methodist, Unitarian **11** Pentecostal **12** Episcopalian, Presbyterian *Bohemian:* **7** Hussite *French:* **8** Huguenot

protocol 4 code, form, rule **6** custom, ritual **7** compact, conduct, decorum, manners **8** courtesy **9** concordat, etiquette, politesse, propriety **11** conventions, formalities

prototype 4 norm **5** model, pilot **6** design **7** example, pattern **8** original, paradigm, standard

prototypical 5 ideal, model **7** classic **9** classical, exemplary **10** archetypal

protozoan 4 cell **5** ameba **6** amoeba **7** ciliate, stentor **10** flagellate, paramecium

protract 6 drag on, extend **7** drag out, draw out, prolong, stretch **8** continue

protrude 3 jut **4** poke, pout **5** bulge **6** jut out **7** project **8** overhang, stand out, stick out

protrusion 3 jut, nub **4** bump **5** bulge **8** swelling **10** projection

protuberant 5 bulgy **7** bulging **9** prominent **11** conspicuous

proud 4 vain **5** huffy, lofty, noble **6** lordly, stuffy, superb **7** haughty, pleased, pompous, stuck-up, stately **8** arrogant, exultant, glorious, scornful, snobbish, spirited, splendid, superior, vigorous **9** conceited, delighted, imperious **10** disdainful, high-handed **11** magnificent, pretentious, resplendent **12** ostentatious, supercilious

Proulx novel 9 Postcards **12** Shipping News (The)

Proust character 5 Swann (Charles) **6** Marcel, Odette (Swann) **7** Charlus (Baron de) **8** Gilberte (Swann) **9** Albertine

prove 3 try **4** show, test **5** argue, check **6** attest, pan out, verify **7** bear out, certify, confirm, examine, explain, turn out **8** document, indicate, validate **9** determine, establish **11** corroborate, demonstrate **12** substantiate

provenance 4 root, well **6** origin, source **7** history **9** inception **10** derivation

provender 4 feed, food **8** victuals **10** provisions

proverb 3 saw **5** adage, axiom, maxim **6** byword, saying **7** epigram **8** aphorism

provide 4 give, hand **5** endow, endue, equip, serve, state **6** afford, outfit, render, supply **7** deliver, furnish, prepare, specify, support **8** dispense, hand over, maintain **9** stipulate

provided 5 given **6** if only **8** equipped, supplied

providence 4 care **6** thrift **7** caution, economy 8 prudence 9 foresight, frugality 11 forethought, thriftiness

provident 5 canny, chary 6 frugal, saving 7 careful, prudent, sparing, thrifty 8 prepared 10 economical, unwasteful 11 foresighted

providential 5 happy, lucky 9 benignant, fortunate 10 auspicious, fortuitous

province 4 area, duty, role, work 5 field, shire 6 canton, county, domain, office, region, sphere 7 demesne, pursuit, terrain 8 district, dominion, function 9 bailiwick, champaign, territory 10 department 12 jurisdiction

provincial 5 local, rural 6 narrow, rustic, simple 7 country, insular, limited 8 pastoral 9 parochial, sectarian, small-town 11 countrified

proving ground 10 laboratory, White Sands

provision 5 stock, store 6 supply 9 condition 11 preparation, requirement, reservation, stipulation

provisional 5 stamp 6 acting, pro tem 9 temporary 10 contingent 11 conditional

provisions 4 feed, food, grub 5 stock 6 viands 7 aliment, edibles, nurture, vittles 8 supplies, victuals 9 provender 10 sustenance 11 comestibles *dealer:* 8 chandler

proviso 6 clause 7 article 9 condition 11 stipulation

provocation 5 cause, wrong 7 offense 8 stimulus, vexation 9 annoyance, incentive 10 incitement 11 instigation

provocative 4 edgy 5 heady 8 alluring, annoying, arousing, exciting 9 offensive 10 intriguing 11 challenging, stimulating

provoke 3 bug, irk, vex 4 abet, rile, stir, wake 5 anger, annoy, cause, evoke, pique, rouse, upset, waken 6 arouse, awaken, bother, excite, foment, harass, incite, induce, kindle, nettle, stir up, whip up 7 incense, inflame, inspire, outrage, quicken 8 generate, irritate, motivate, occasion 9 challenge, galvanize, instigate, stimulate

provost 4 head 6 keeper 7 marshal 8 director 10 magistrate 13 administrator

prow 3 bow 4 stem 5 front 10 projection

prowess 5 skill, valor 7 bravery, command, courage, heroism, mastery 9 expertise, gallantry 10 excellence

prowl 4 hunt, roam 5 skulk, slink, sneak, steal 6 search, wander

proximate 4 near, next 5 close 6 nearby 8 adjacent, imminent 9 following, immediate, preceding 10 near-at-hand 11 forthcoming

proximity 8 nearness, vicinity 9 adjacency, closeness, immediacy 10 contiguity 11 propinquity

proxy 5 agent 6 deputy 7 stand-in 8 attorney 9 surrogate 10 substitute

pro ____ 3 tem 4 bono, rata 5 forma, tanto 7 tempore

prude 4 prig 7 old maid, Puritan 8 bluenose 9 Mrs. Grundy

prudence 4 care 5 skill 6 acumen, reason, thrift, wisdom 7 caution, economy 8 sagacity 9 foresight, frugality 10 astuteness, discretion, expediency, precaution, providence, shrewdness 11 calculation, forethought, thriftiness

prudent 4 sage, sane, wary, wise 5 canny, chary 6 frugal 7 careful, politic 8 cautious, discreet, sensible 9 expedient, judicious 11 circumspect

prudish 4 prim 5 stern 6 narrow, prissy, proper, severe, strict, stuffy 7 austere, genteel 8 affected, decorous, priggish 11 puritanical, straitlaced

prune 3 cut, lop 4 clip, crop, pare, plum, thin, trim 5 shear 6 cut off, reduce, remove 7 cut away, cut back, shorten 8 pare down, truncate

prurience 4 lust 6 desire, libido 7 lechery, passion 8 cupidity 9 carnality, eroticism 11 lustfulness 13 concupiscence

prurient 4 lewd 5 bawdy 6 erotic 7 goatish, lustful, satyric, sensual 9 lickerish 10 lascivious, libidinous, passionate 12 concupiscent

pruritic 5 itchy

Prussian *aristocrat:* 6 Junker 12 Hohenzollern *prime minister:* 8 Bismarck (Otto von) *ruler:* 7 Wilhelm 9 Frederick (the Great)

pry 4 nose, open, poke 5 jimmy, lever, snoop 6 meddle 7 inquire 9 interfere

prying 4 nosy 6 snoopy 7 curious 8 meddling, snooping 9 intrusive, obtrusive, officious 10 meddlesome 11 impertinent, inquisitive

psalm 3 ode 4 hymn, poem, song 5 paean *book:* 7 psalter *selection:* 6 Hallel *word:* 5 selah

psalmist 4 poet 5 Asaph, David 6 cantor

pseudo 4 fake, mock, sham 5 bogus, false, phony 7 pretend 8 spurious 9 imitation 10 artificial 11 counterfeit

pseudonym 5 alias 7 pen name 9 false name, stage name 10 nom de plume 11 nom de guerre

psyche 4 mind, soul 5 anima 6 animus, pneuma, spirit *part:* 2 id 3 ego 8 superego

Psyche's beloved 4 Eros 5 Cupid

psychiatrist 6 shrink 8 alienist 11 neurologist *American:* 3 May (Rollo) 5 Reich (Wilhelm) 6 Kramer (Peter), Rogers (Carl) 7

Erikson (Erik) **8** Sullivan (Harry Stack) **9** Menninger (Karl) *Austrian:* **5** Adler (Alfred), Freud (Anna, Sigmund), Reich (Wilhelm) *British:* **5** Laing (R. D.) *French:* **5** Lacan (Jacques) *German:* **5** Fromm (Erich) **6** Horney (Karen) *Swiss:* **4** Jung (Carl) **9** Rorschach (Hermann)

psychic 4 seer **6** medium, mental, occult **8** cerebral **9** mentalist, prophetic, spiritual **10** mind reader, telepathic **11** clairvoyant, telekinetic **12** intellectual, supersensory *American:* **5** Cayce (Edgar), Dixon (Jeane) **10** Montgomery (Ruth) *power:* **3** ESP

psycho 3 nut **5** crazy, sicko, wacko **6** madman, maniac, mental, schizo, weirdo **7** berserk, haywire, lunatic, nutcase **8** crackpot, demented, deranged, head case **9** fruitcake, screwball, sociopath

psychoanalyst 4 Jung (Carl Gustav), Rank (Otto) **5** Adler (Alfred), Freud (Sigmund), Fromm (Erich), Klein (Melanie), Kohut (Heinz), Lacan (Jacques) **6** Horney (Karen) **7** Erikson (Erik) **8** Ferenczi (Sandor)

psychologist 6 shrink **9** therapist *American:* **5** James (William) **6** Terman (Lewis), Watson (John), Yerkes (Robert) **7** Skinner (B. F.) **9** Thorndike (Edward L.) *English:* **4** Ward (James) **8** Spearman (Charles), Tichener (Edward) *German:* **5** Wundt (Wilhelm) **6** Müller (Georg), Stumpf (Carl) **10** Wertheimer (Max)

psychotic 3 mad **5** crazy **6** insane **8** demented, deranged, schizoid **13** schizophrenic

ptarmigan 6 grouse

ptomaine 6 poison

pub 3 bar, inn **4** dive **5** joint **6** tavern **7** barroom, gin mill, taproom **8** grogshop **9** roadhouse **11** rathskeller

puberty 11 adolescence

public 4 open **5** civic, civil, state **6** common, mutual, people, shared, social **7** general, popular, society **8** communal, national, populace **9** community, municipal, universal **10** accessible, government

publican 7 barkeep **8** landlord, licensee, taverner **9** bartender, collector, innkeeper **12** tax collector

publication 4 book **7** article, journal **8** magazine, pamphlet **9** broadside, newspaper **10** periodical *list:* **12** bibliography

public house 3 bar, inn **6** hostel, saloon, tavern **7** auberge, hospice **8** hostelry

publicity 3 ink **4** hype, plug **5** blurb, press, promo **6** hoopla, notice **7** billing, fanfare, write-up **8** ballyhoo **9** attention, promotion

11 advertising **12** announcement **13** advertisement

publicize 3 air **4** bill, hype, plug, puff, push, tout **5** boost **7** promote, trumpet **8** announce **9** advertise, broadcast **10** press-agent, promulgate

publish 3 air **5** issue, print **6** get out, inform, put out, report **7** release **8** announce, bring out, proclaim **9** advertise, broadcast, make known **10** distribute, promulgate **11** disseminate

Puccini opera 5 Tosca **7** Le Villi **8** La Bohème, Turandot **12** Manon Lescaut **15** Madame Butterfly

puck 3 elf, imp **4** disk **5** fairy **6** spirit, sprite **9** hobgoblin, prankster

pucker 4 fold **5** purse **6** cockle, crease **7** wrinkle **8** compress, contract **9** constrict

puckish 5 antic, elfin, larky, pixie **6** elvish, impish **7** playful **8** prankish **9** whimsical **11** mischievous

Puck's master 6 Oberon

pudding 4 duff **6** burgoo **7** custard, tapioca *baked:* **5** kugel **10** brown Betty

pudgy 3 fat **5** plump, round, stout, tubby **6** chubby, chunky, flabby, rotund **8** plumpish, roly-poly

pueblo 4 town **7** village **8** dwelling *ceremonial room:* **4** kiva

Pueblo tribe 3 Zia **4** Hopi, Taos, Zuñi **5** Acoma, Jemez, Keres, Tigua **6** Laguna **7** Cochiti

puerile 5 inane, silly **6** jejune **7** foolish **8** childish, immature, juvenile

Puerto Rico *capital:* **7** San Juan *city:* **5** Ponce **7** Bayamon **8** Mayagüez *discoverer:* **8** Columbus (Christopher) *language:* **7** Spanish *location:* **10** West Indies

puff 3 pad **4** blow, brag, crow, drag, emit, huff, pant, plug, pouf, push, tout, waft **5** blurb, boast, boost, elate, expel, quilt, swell, vaunt, whiff **6** exhale, pastry, praise **7** flatter, inflate **8** swelling **9** advertise, comforter, publicize **10** exaggerate

puffer 8 blowfish **9** globefish, swellfish

puffery 4 buzz, hype, plug **7** fanfare **8** ballyhoo **9** promotion, publicity **11** advertising **12** exaggeration, press-agentry

puffin 4 bird **7** seabird **9** sea parrot **10** shearwater *cousin:* **3** auk

puffy 7 swollen **8** inflated

pug 3 bun, dog **4** nose **5** boxer, track **9** footprint

Puget Sound port 6 Tacoma **7** Seattle

pugilism 6 boxing **13** prizefighting

pugilist 5 boxer **7** fighter **12** prizefighter

pugnacious 7 defiant, scrappy **8** brawling,

fighting, militant **9** bellicose, combative, truculent **10** aggressive, rebellious **11** belligerent, contentious, quarrelsome **13** argumentative

pugnacity 9 hostility **10** aggression, truculence, truculency **12** belligerence **13** combativeness

puisne 6 junior **8** inferior

puissance 5 force, might, power **6** energy **7** potency **8** strength

puissant 6 mighty, potent, strong **8** forceful, powerful

pukka 4 real, tops **7** genuine **8** bona fide **9** authentic **10** first-class

pule 3 cry **4** mewl **5** whine **7** whimper

Pulitzer Prize fiction winner *1918:* **5** Poole (Ernest) *1919:* **10** Tarkington (Booth) *1921:* **7** Wharton (Edith) *1922:* **10** Tarkington (Booth) *1923:* **6** Cather (Willa) *1924:* **6** Wilson (Margaret) *1925:* **6** Ferber (Edna) *1926:* **5** Lewis (Sinclair) *1927:* **9** Bromfield (Louis) *1928:* **6** Wilder (Thornton) *1929:* **8** Peterkin (Julia) *1930:* **7** La Farge (Oliver) *1931:* **6** Barnes (Margaret) *1932:* **4** Buck (Pearl) *1933:* **9** Stribling (T. S.) *1934:* **6** Miller (Caroline) *1935:* **7** Johnson (Josephine) *1936:* **5** Davis (Harold) *1937:* **8** Mitchell (Margaret) *1938:* **8** Marquand (John) *1939:* **8** Rawlings (Marjorie Kinnan) *1940:* **9** Steinbeck (John) *1942:* **7** Glasgow (Ellen) *1943:* **8** Sinclair (Upton) *1944:* **6** Flavin (Martin) *1945:* **6** Hersey (John) *1947:* **6** Warren (Robert Penn) *1948:* **8** Michener (James) *1949:* **7** Cozzens (James Gould) *1950:* **7** Guthrie (A. B.) *1951:* **7** Richter (Conrad) *1952:* **4** Wouk (Herman) *1953:* **9** Hemingway (Ernest) *1955:* **8** Faulkner (William) *1956:* **6** Kantor (MacKinlay) *1958:* **4** Agee (James) *1959:* **6** Taylor (Robert Lewis) *1960:* **5** Drury (Allen) *1961:* **3** Lee (Harper) *1962:* **7** O'Connor (Edwin) *1963:* **8** Faulkner (William) *1965:* **4** Grau (Shirley Ann) *1966:* **6** Porter (Katherine Anne) *1967:* **7** Malamud (Bernard) *1968:* **6** Styron (William) *1969:* **7** Momaday (N. Scott) *1970:* **8** Stafford (Jean) *1972:* **7** Stegner (Wallace) *1973:* **5** Welty (Eudora) *1975:* **6** Shaara (Michael) *1976:* **6** Bellow (Saul) *1978:* **9** McPherson (James Alan) *1979:* **7** Cheever (John) *1980:* **6** Mailer (Norman) *1981:* **5** Toole (John Kennedy) *1982:* **6** Updike (John) *1983:* **6** Walker (Alice) *1984:* **7** Kennedy (William) *1985:* **5** Lurie (Alison) *1986:* **8** McMurtry (Larry) *1987:* **6** Taylor (Peter) *1988:* **8** Morrison (Toni) *1989:* **5** Tyler (Anne) *1990:* **8** Hijuelos (Oscar) *1991:* **6** Updike (John)

1992: **6** Smiley (Jane) *1993:* **6** Butler (Robert Olen) *1994:* **6** Proulx (E. Annie) *1995:* **7** Shields (Carol) *1996:* **4** Ford (Richard) *1997:* **10** Millhauser (Steven) *1998:* **4** Roth (Philip) *1999:* **10** Cunningham (Michael) *2000:* **6** Lahiri (Jhumpa) *2001:* **6** Chabon (Michael) *2002:* **5** Russo (Richard) *2003:* **9** Eugenides (Jeffrey) *2004:* **5** Jones (Edward P.) *2005:* **8** Robinson (Marilynne) *2006:* **6** Brooks (Geraldine) *2007:* **8** McCarthy (Cormac) *2008:* **4** Diaz (Junot) *2009:* **6** Strout (Elizabeth) *2010:* **7** Harding (Paul)

pull 3 oar, row, tow, tug **4** drag, draw, haul, lure, root, yank **5** clout, draft, drive, force, pluck, put on, wrest **6** appeal, assume, entice **7** attract, draw out, extract, stretch **9** advantage, influence **10** attraction

pull back 6 rein in **7** retreat **8** withdraw

pull down 4 draw, earn, raze, ruin **5** lower, wreck **6** reduce **7** depress, destroy **8** demolish, overcome **9** dismantle

pullet 3 hen **5** chick **7** chicken

pulley 5 wheel **6** sheave *watch's:* **5** fusee

pull in 3 nab **4** stop **5** check, pinch **6** arrest, arrive, collar, detain, pick up **7** inhibit **8** hold back, restrain **9** apprehend

pulling 6 towage **7** draught, haulage **8** traction *cable:* **7** towline

Pullman 3 car **7** sleeper **8** suitcase **11** railroad car

pull off 6 attain, manage **7** achieve, succeed **8** carry out **10** accomplish

pull out 4 exit, quit **5** leave **6** depart **7** abandon, retreat, take off **8** shove off, withdraw

pull through 5 rally **7** get over, recover, ride out, survive, weather **9** get better

pullulate 4 teem **5** breed, crawl, swarm **6** abound, sprout **7** produce **9** germinate

pull up 4 halt, stop **5** check **6** rebuke **8** draw even **9** reprimand

pulp 4 mash, pith **5** crush **6** bruise, squash **7** tabloid **8** soft part

pulpit 4 ambo, dais **6** podium **7** lectern, rostrum **8** ministry, platform

pulpy 4 soft **5** cheap, juicy, lurid, mushy **6** spongy **11** sensational

pulsate 4 beat, pump **5** pound, throb **7** vibrate **9** oscillate, palpitate

pulse 4 beat **5** throb **6** rhythm

pulverize 4 beat, ruin **5** crush, grind, smash, wreck **6** crunch, powder **7** atomize, destroy **8** demolish **9** micronize **10** annihilate

puma 3 cat **6** cougar **7** panther **12** mountain lion

pummel 3 hit **4** beat, drub **5** pound, punch **6** batter, buffet, hammer, thrash, wallop **7** belabor

pump 4 draw, shoe, quiz **5** exert, grill, heart, raise **6** device, elicit **7** operate **8** energize, question

pumpernickel 3 rye **5** bread

pumpkin 4 pepo **6** orange, squash **12** jack-o'-lantern *family:* **5** gourd

pump up 4 fill **6** excite, expand **7** enthuse, inflate **8** energize, increase, motivate **9** stimulate

pun 4 joke **11** paronomasia, play on words **13** double meaning

punch 3 box, cut, die, dig, hit, jab, jog, pep **4** bang, blow, cuff, poke, prod, push, snap, sock **5** clout, drive, notch, smack, vigor **6** buffet, emboss, energy, impact, pummel, strike, thrust **8** uppercut, vitality **9** emphasize, perforate

punch bowl 8 monteith

punch-drunk 5 dazed, dizzy, woozy **6** addled, groggy **8** unsteady **9** befuddled, slaphappy **10** staggering **11** disoriented

puncheon 3 log **4** cask, slab, tool **6** timber

puncher 5 boxer **6** cowboy

Punch's wife 4 Judy

punchy 5 dazed, dizzy, vivid **6** addled, lively **7** dynamic, vibrant **8** forceful, spirited, vigorous **9** befuddled, energetic, slaphappy **11** light-headed

punctilious 5 exact, fussy **7** careful, precise **9** attentive, observant **10** meticulous, particular, scrupulous **11** painstaking

punctual 5 ready **6** on time, prompt, timely

punctuate 4 mark **5** point **6** accent, divide, stress **8** separate **9** emphasize, interrupt **10** accentuate

punctuation mark 4 dash **5** brace, colon, comma, slant, slash **6** hyphen, parens, period **7** bracket, solidus, virgule **8** diagonal, ellipsis **9** backslash, guillemet, semicolon **10** apostrophe **11** parenthesis

puncture 3 jab **4** bore, flat, hole, stab **5** burst, drill, prick, punch **6** blow up, debunk, pierce, riddle **7** deflate, explode **8** disprove **9** discredit, perforate **11** perforation

pundit 4 guru, sage **5** maven, swami **6** critic, expert **7** teacher, wise man **9** authority, columnist **11** talking head

pungency 4 bite **5** sting **8** piquancy **9** intensity, sharpness

pungent 5 acrid, acute, harsh, sharp, spicy, tangy, zesty **6** barbed, biting **7** caustic, cutting, intense, mordant, painful, peppery, piquant, pointed **8** exciting, incisive, poignant, stinging **9** trenchant **10** irritating **11** provocative, stimulating

punish 4 fine, hurt **5** mulct, spank **6** amerce, avenge **7** chasten, correct, put down, re-prove, revenge, scourge, torture **8** chastise, penalize **9** castigate, criticize **10** discipline

punishment 3 rod **4** fine **5** lumps, mulct **7** penalty, reproof **10** amercement, chastening, correction, discipline **11** castigation, comeuppance, just deserts **12** chastisement *instrument:* **7** scourge

punitive 5 penal **11** castigating, vindicative **12** correctional, disciplinary

punk 4 hood, thug **5** cholo, rowdy, tough **6** novice, rookie, tinder **7** hoodlum, ruffian, toughie **8** beginner, gangster, inferior **9** roughneck **10** delinquent *rock group:* **7** Ramones **10** Sex Pistols

punkah 3 fan

punt 4 boat, boot, kick, play **6** gamble, propel

Punta del _____ 4 Este

puny 4 weak **5** dinky, petty, small **6** feeble, little, measly, paltry, slight **7** trivial **8** inferior, niggling, picayune, piddling, trifling

pupa 9 chrysalid, chrysalis

pupil 5 cadet, tutee **7** learner, scholar, student **8** disciple **9** schoolboy **10** apprentice, schoolgirl *French:* **5** élève

puppet 4 doll, dupe, pawn, tool **6** figure, stooge **10** figurehead, marionette

puppy 3 dog **5** whelp

Purcell opera 13 Dido and Aeneas

purchase 3 buy **4** hold **6** obtain, pay for **7** acquire, procure **9** advantage **11** acquisition

pure 5 clean, fresh, plain, sheer, total, utter **6** chaste, decent **7** a priori, genuine, perfect, unmixed **8** absolute, abstract, innocent, spotless, virtuous **9** authentic, continent, exemplary, inviolate, stainless, unalloyed, undiluted, untainted **10** immaculate **11** theoretical, unblemished, unmitigated, unqualified **13** unadulterated

purebred 8 pedigree **9** full-blood, pedigreed **10** registered **11** full-blooded

puree 4 soup **5** paste

purely 4 just **5** quite **6** merely, simply, wholly **7** exactly, totally, utterly **8** entirely **10** altogether, completely **11** exclusively

purfle 4 trim **6** border **8** decorate, ornament

purgation 9 catharsis, cleansing **10** lustration

purgative 5 jalap **7** lustral **9** cathartic

purge 3 rid **4** oust **5** clear, expel **6** purify, remove **7** cleanse, wipe out **8** get rid of, lustrate **9** eliminate, liquidate

purification 8 ablution **9** catharsis, cleansing, expiation, purgation **10** absolution, lustration **11** expurgation **12** regeneration *sacrament:* **7** baptism

purify 5 clean, purge **6** filter, refine **7** clarify, cleanse

Purim 11 Feast of Lots *queen:* **6** Esther

puritan 4 prig **5** prude **8** bluenose **9** Mrs. Grundy

puritanical 4 prim **5** rigid **6** severe, strict **7** ascetic, austere, prudish **8** priggish **9** bluenosed **11** straitlaced

purity 8 chastity **9** innocence

purl 4 eddy, edge, knit **5** swirl, whirl **6** border, murmur, stitch **9** embroider

purlieu 5 haunt **7** hangout

purlieus 6 bounds, limits **7** suburbs **8** boundary, confines, environs **9** outskirts, precincts **12** neighborhood

purloin 3 nip **4** lift, take **5** filch, pinch, steal, swipe **6** pilfer, remove, rip off, snitch **11** appropriate

purloiner 5 crook, thief **8** larcener **9** larcenist

purple 4 plum, robe **5** cloth, grape, lilac, mauve, regal **6** florid, maroon, orchid, ornate, turgid, violet **7** flowery, pigment, pompous **8** imperial, lavender **9** bombastic, high-flown, overblown **10** rhetorical

Purple Heart 5 award, medal **10** decoration

purport 4 gist, mean **5** claim, drift, sense, tenor **6** allege, intend, thrust **7** meaning, message, profess, purpose **8** maintain **9** substance **11** connotation, implication **12** significance, significancy

purported 7 alleged, reputed, seeming **8** apparent, so-called, supposed **9** professed **10** ostensible

purpose 3 aim, end, use **4** goal, plan **5** point **6** action, design, intent, object **7** meaning, mission, resolve, subject **8** ambition, function, proposal **9** direction, intention, objective **10** aspiration, resolution **13** determination

purposeful 5 telic **6** driven, intent **7** earnest, planned, studied, willful **8** resolute **9** conscious, dedicated **10** calculated, considered, deliberate, determined **11** intentional **12** premeditated

purposeless 6 random **9** desultory, haphazard, hit-or-miss, irregular, unplanned

purposely 9 expressly **10** explicitly **12** deliberately **13** intentionally

purr 3 hum **6** murmur

purse 3 bag, sum **4** knit **5** money, pouch, prize **6** pucker, wallet **7** handbag **8** reticule **9** clutch bag **10** pocketbook, prize money *Scottish:* **7** sporran

pursue 3 woo **4** hunt, seek **5** chase, haunt, hound, stalk, track, trail **6** badger, follow **7** afflict, go after, proceed **8** continue, engage in **9** persecute, persevere

pursuit 3 job **4** hunt, work **5** chase, quest, trade **6** search **8** activity, business, vocation **9** avocation, following **10** employment, occupation, profession

purvey 6 obtain, peddle, supply **7** furnish, provide **9** provision

purview 3 ken **5** ambit, limit, orbit, range, reach, scope, sweep **6** extent **8** boundary

push 3 pep **4** goad, plug, prod, sell, spur, urge **5** boost, drive, elbow, exert, force, impel, press, punch, shove, vigor **6** attack, effort, energy, expand, peddle, propel, throng, thrust **7** advance, assault, impetus, promote **8** ambition, pressure, vitality **9** incentive, influence, offensive **10** enterprise, get-up-and-go, initiative

Pushkin, Alexander *novel:* **12** Eugene Onegin *play:* **10** Stone Guest (The) **12** Boris Godunov *story:* **13** Queen of Spades (The)

push off 4 exit **5** leave, start **6** depart, set out

push on 6 travel **7** advance, journey, proceed **8** continue, progress

pushover 4 snap **5** chump, cinch, softy **6** breeze, picnic, stooge, sucker **9** soft touch

pushy 4 bold **5** brash, nervy **7** forward **8** forceful **9** assertive, obnoxious **10** aggressive **12** presumptuous

pusillanimous 5 timid **6** coward, craven **7** chicken, gutless **8** cowardly, poltroon, timorous **9** spineless **11** lily-livered

puss 3 cat, mug **4** face **6** kisser, kitten

pussycat 5 sissy, softy **6** softie **8** pushover, weakling **9** soft touch **10** namby-pamby **13** bleeding heart

pussyfoot 5 creep, dodge, evade, glide, skulk, slink, sneak, steal **6** tiptoe **10** equivocate

pustule 4 boil **6** pimple **7** abscess, blister **8** furuncle **9** carbuncle

put 3 lay, set **4** park **5** place **8** position

putative 7 assumed, reputed **8** accepted, believed, presumed, supposed **11** conjectural **12** hypothetical

put away 3 eat **4** stow **5** eat up, swill **6** commit, devour, lock up **7** confine, consume **9** polish off **11** incarcerate

put by 4 save **5** lay in, store **7** lay away **8** lay aside, salt away

put down 5 crush, quash, quell **6** demean, demote, depose, squash, subdue **7** squelch **8** belittle, suppress **9** criticize, disparage, downgrade, humiliate

put forth 5 issue **6** assert **7** present, propose

put off 5 defer, delay **7** suspend **8** hold over, postpone

put on 3 act, don, kid **4** fake **5** apply, bluff, feign, mount, stage **6** affect, assume **7** mislead, perform, pretend, produce

put-on 3 act **4** fake, sham, show **5** faked, phony, spoof **6** parody **7** assumed, feigned

. **8** affected, disguise **9** pretended **10** artificial, false front

put out 3 vex **4** gall **5** annoy, douse, evict, issue, upset **6** bother, quench **7** disturb, produce, publish, trouble **8** irritate **9** aggravate, displease, embarrass **10** disconcert, exasperate, extinguish **13** inconvenience

putrefy 3 rot **5** decay, spoil, taint **6** molder **7** corrupt **9** break down, decompose

putrid 4 foul **5** fetid **6** rancid, rotten **7** corrupt, decayed, noisome, spoiled

putsch 4 coup **6** revolt **8** takeover, uprising **9** coup d'état, overthrow, rebellion **10** usurpation

putter 4 club, idle **6** fiddle, golfer, tinker **8** golf club

putting area 5 green

putto 5 cupid **6** cherub **8** amoretto

put together 4 form, join, make **5** build, unite **7** combine, connect, fashion, produce **8** assemble **9** construct, fabricate

putty 3 mud **4** clay **6** cement

put up 4 bunk **5** board, build, erect, house, lodge, raise **6** billet, harbor **7** quarter **8** domicile **9** construct

put up with 4 bear **5** stand **6** endure **8** tolerate

Puzo novel 6 Omerta **7** Last Don (The) **8** Fools Die, Sicilian (The) **9** Godfather (The)

puzzle 3 why **4** foil, koan **5** poser, rebus **6** baffle, enigma, fuddle, muddle, riddle **7** anagram, confuse, mystery, mystify, nonplus, paradox, perplex, problem, tangram **8** acrostic, befuddle, bewilder, confound **9** conundrum, crossword, dumbfound, frustrate **10** disconcert **11** brainteaser *number:* **6** Sudoku

puzzle out 5 solve **6** answer, decode **7** clarify,

clear up, explain, unravel **8** decipher, unriddle

puzzling 6 knotty **7** cryptic **8** baffling **9** confusing, difficult, enigmatic **10** mystifying, perplexing **11** bewildering, paradoxical **12** inexplicable

Pygmalion *beloved:* **7** Galatea *character:* **5** Eliza (Doolittle) **7** Higgins (Henry) *father:* **5** Belus *musical:* **10** My Fair Lady *playwright:* **4** Shaw (George Bernard) *sister:* **4** Dido *victim:* **8** Sichaeus

pygmy 4 tiny **5** dwarf **6** bantam, little, midget **8** dwarfish **10** diminutive, homunculus **11** lilliputian

Pylades *companion:* **7** Orestes *father:* **9** Strophius *wife:* **7** Electra

pylon 4 post **5** tower **6** marker **7** gateway

Pym's creator 3 Poe (Edgar Allan)

Pynchon novel 13 Mason and Dixon **15** Gravity's Rainbow

pyramid builder 5 Khufu **6** Cheops

Pyramus' beloved 6 Thisbe

pyre 4 heap, pile

pyretic 3 hot **7** burning, febrile, fevered **8** feverish

pyromaniac 5 torch **8** arsonist **10** incendiary

pyrosis 9 heartburn

pyrotechnics 7 display **9** fireworks, spectacle

Pyrrha's husband 9 Deucalion

Pyrrhonist 7 doubter, skeptic **10** unbeliever

Pyrrhus *kingdom:* **6** Epirus *victory:* **7** Asculum

Pythias' friend 5 Damon

python 3 boa **5** snake *slayer:* **6** Apollo

pyx 3 box **4** case **6** vessel **9** container **10** receptacle

Qatar *capital:* **4** Bida, Doha *gulf:* **7** Persian *language:* **6** Arabic *monetary unit:* **4** rial **5** riyal *neighbor:* **11** Saudi Arabia *peninsula:* **7** Arabian

QED word 4 erat, quod **13** demonstrandum

q.t., on the 7 sub rosa **8** covertly, secretly **13** under the table

quack 3 cry **4** honk, sham **6** con man, humbug **7** shammer **9** charlatan **10** mountebank **12** saltimbanque

quackery 4 hoax, scam **5** fraud, hokum **6** de-

ceit **8** flimflam, pretense **9** deception, duplicity, imposture **11** dissembling

quad see **quadrangle**

quadrangle 4 yard **5** close, court, patio **6** square **7** polygon **9** courtyard, curtilage, enclosure

quadrant 3 arc **6** fourth **9** one-fourth **10** instrument

quadratic 4 boxy **6** square **7** boxlike **10** foursquare

quadriga 7 chariot

quadrille 5 dance, ombre **8** card game **11** square dance

quadrivium subject 5 music **8** geometry **9** astronomy **10** arithmetic

quaestor 6 bursar **8** official **9** paymaster, treasurer

quaff 3 sip **4** swig, toss **5** drink, sup up **6** guzzle, imbibe, sup off **7** carouse, swallow

quagga 3 ass

quaggy 4 soft **5** boggy, mushy, pulpy **6** flabby, marshy, spongy **7** flaccid, squashy, squishy **8** squooshy, yielding

quagmire 3 bog, fen, fix, jam **4** mire **5** marsh, pinch, swamp **6** morass, pickle, plight, scrape, slough **7** dilemma **8** quandary **9** imbroglio, marshland, swampland **11** predicament

quahog 4 clam **7** mollusc, mollusk **9** shellfish **11** cherrystone

quail 5 cower, wince **6** blanch, blench, cringe, flinch, recoil, shrink **7** shudder, squinch, tremble **8** bobwhite *flock of:* **4** bevy

quaint 3 odd **5** funny, queer **7** antique, archaic, curious, oddball, strange, unusual **8** peculiar, singular **9** different, eccentric, whimsical **10** antiquated, unfamiliar **12** old-fashioned

quake 5 shake, waver **6** dither, quaver, quiver, shiver, tremor **7** shudder, temblor, tremble, twitter, vibrate **8** trembler

Quaker 6 Friend *city:* **12** Philadelphia *colonizer:* **4** Penn (William) *color:* **4** gray *founder:* **3** Fox (George) *poet:* **6** Barton (Bernard) **8** Whittier (John Greenleaf) *pronoun:* **3** thy **4** thee, thou **5** thine *State:* **12** Pennsylvania

qualification 6 caveat **7** ability, fitness **8** adequacy, aptitude, capacity, standard **9** condition, criterion **10** capability, competence **11** requirement, restriction, stipulation

qualified 3 fit **4** able **6** au fait, proper, proved, proven, tested **7** capable, limited, partial, skilled, trained **8** eligible, modified, reserved **9** competent **10** restricted **11** conditional **12** accomplished

qualify 3 fit **5** limit **6** lessen, modify, reduce, soften, temper **7** certify, entitle, license, mollify, prepare **8** describe, mitigate, moderate **9** authorize **12** characterize

quality 4 rank **5** class, elite, grade, merit, prime, savor, state, trait, value, worth **6** factor, flower, gentry, status, virtue **7** caliber, element, feature, stature **8** position, property, standing **9** attribute, blue blood, character, gentility, parameter **10** excellence, patriciate, perfection

qualm 4 fear **5** demur, doubt **6** nausea, unease **7** illness, scruple **8** mistrust **9** faintness, misgiving, objection **10** conscience, foreboding, reluctance, uneasiness **11** compunction, nervousness, uncertainty **12** apprehension, remonstrance **13** unwillingness

qualmish 3 ill **4** sick **5** queasy, uneasy, unwell **8** hesitant, nauseous **9** nauseated, reluctant, squeamish, uncertain **10** scrupulous **12** apprehensive

quandary 3 fix, jam **4** bind, hole, spot **5** pinch **6** pickle, plight, scrape **7** dilemma **8** quagmire **10** difficulty **11** predicament

quantity 4 body, bulk, dose **5** total **6** amount, degree, volume **9** abundance, aggregate, magnitude *fixed:* **8** constant *small:* **3** bit **7** modicum, smidgen

quantum 5 quota, share, total **6** amount, budget, ration **7** measure, portion **9** aggregate, allotment, allowance, increment **13** apportionment *of gravity:* **8** graviton *of radiant energy:* **6** photon *of vibrational energy:* **6** phonon *theory originator:* **6** Planck (Max)

quarantine 6 detain **7** confine, isolate **8** restrain **9** isolation, restraint **10** detainment **11** confinement

quarrel 3 row **4** beef, bolt, dust, fray, fuss, miff, spar, spat, tiff **5** argue, arrow, brawl, broil, clash, fight, melee, run-in, scrap, set-to **6** affray, battle, bicker, differ, dustup, fracas, ruckus, squall, strife **7** brabble, discord, dispute, dissent, fall out, rhubarb, ruction, scuffle, wrangle **8** argument, catfight, conflict, disagree, skirmish, squabble **9** altercate, bickering, brannigan, lock horns, imbroglio, scrimmage **10** contention, difference, dissension, falling-out **11** altercation, embroilment **12** disagreement

quarrelsome 6 brawly **7** adverse, counter, hostile, scrappy, warlike **8** brawling, choleric, inimical, militant **9** bellicose, combative, irascible, irritable, rancorous, truculent **10** pugnacious **11** bad-tempered, belligerent, contentious **12** cantankerous, disputatious **13** argumentative

quarry 3 dig, pit **4** game, mine, pane, prey **5** chase, delve **6** source, victim **8** excavate **10** excavation

quarter 4 area, bunk, part **5** board, house, lodge, mercy, put up **6** barrio, billet, canton, fourth, ghetto, harbor, sector **7** barrack, section, shelter **8** clemency, district, division, locality, precinct, quadrant *circle:* **8** quadrant *note:* **8** crotchet *pint:* **4** gill *ship's:* **6** fo'c'sle **10** forecastle

quarterback 4 boss, head, lead **6** direct, leader, player **7** athlete, oversee **8** director, overseer **9** supervise **10** footballer, supervisor

quartet 4 four **5** group **6** tetrad **8** ensemble, foursome **10** quadruplet, quaternion **11** composition

quart, metric 5 liter, litre

quartz 4 onyx, sard **5** agate **6** jasper **7** citrine, mineral **8** amethyst, sardonyx **9** cairngorm, carnelian **10** chalcedony

quash 2 ax **3** axe, nix **4** undo, veto, void **5** annul, crush, quell **6** defeat, negate, quench, stifle, subdue **7** abolish, nullify, put down, repress, smother, squelch **8** abrogate, dissolve, suppress **10** extinguish, invalidate

quasi 6 almost **7** nominal, seeming, virtual **8** apparent

Quasimodo 9 hunchback *creator:* **4** Hugo (Victor) *occupation:* **10** bell ringer *residence:* **5** Paris **9** Notre Dame

quaver 4 note **5** quake, shake, trill, waver **6** dither, shiver, tremor **7** shudder, tremble, twitter **10** eighth note

quay 4 dock, pier, slip **5** berth, jetty, levee, wharf **6** marina **7** moorage

quean 4 bawd, slut, tart **5** tramp, wench, whore **6** harlot, hooker **7** chippie, hustler **8** strumpet **9** courtesan **10** prostitute **12** streetwalker

queasy 3 ill **4** sick **6** qualmy, uneasy, unwell **7** dubious **8** delicate, doubtful, hesitant, nauseous, qualmish, troubled **9** hazardous, nauseated, reluctant, squeamish

Quebec *province capital:* **6** Quebec *city:* **5** Laval **8** Montreal **9** Longueuil *island:* **9** Anticosti *mountain:* **9** Tremblant **10** D'Iberville *peninsula:* **5** Gaspé *provincial flower:* **10** fleur-de-lys **11** madonna lily *river:* **10** St. Lawrence

Queeg's ship 5 Caine

queen *Austria-Hungary:* **12** Maria Theresa *Belgian:* **6** Astrid *Danish:* **8** Margaret, Margrete *Egyptian:* **9** Cleopatra **10** Hatshepsut *English:* **4** Anne, Mary **8** Victoria **9** Elizabeth *French and English:* **7** Eleanor *Netherlands:* **7** Beatrix, Juliana **10** Wilhelmina *of Carthage:* **4** Dido *of heaven:* **4** Mary, moon **7** Astarte *of Isles:* **6** Albion *of Ithaca:* **8** Penelope *of Navarre:* **8** Margaret *of Scots:* **4** Mary *of Sheba:* **6** Balkis *of the Adriatic:* **6** Venice *of the Antilles:* **4** Cuba *of the East:* **7** Zenobia *of the fairies:* **3** Mab **7** Titania *of the gods:* **4** Hera, Juno, Sati *of the Nile:* **9** Cleopatra *of the North:* **9** Edinburgh *of the underworld:* **3** Hel **4** Hela **10** Persephone, Proserpina *Spanish:* **7** Isabela **8** Isabella *Spartan:* **4** Leda *Swedish:* **9** Christina

Queen Anne's lace 6 carrot **10** wild carrot

Queen of Spades *author:* **7** Pushkin (Alexander) *composer:* **11** Tchaikovsky (Peter Ilyich)

Queensland *capital:* **8** Brisbane *explorer:* **4** Cook (Captain James)

queer 3 odd **5** bogus, weird **7** bizarre, curious, deviant, dubious, oddball, strange, touched, unusual **8** doubtful, peculiar, singular **9** eccentric, worthless **10** homosexual, outlandish, suspicious **11** counterfeit

quell 4 calm, stop **5** allay, check, crush, quash, quiet **6** pacify, quench, squash, subdue **7** conquer, put down, squelch **8** overcome, suppress, vanquish **9** overwhelm, subjugate **10** extinguish

Quemoy's neighbor 4 Amoy **5** Matsu

quench 4 sate **5** allay, douse, quash, quell, slake **6** lessen, put out, reduce **7** appease, assuage, gratify, lighten, put down, relieve, satiate, satisfy **8** mitigate, suppress **9** alleviate, eliminate **10** extinguish

quenelle 8 dumpling, meatball **9** forcemeat

quern 4 mill

querulous 5 whiny **7** fretful, peevish, pettish, whining **8** petulant **9** lamenting **10** whimpering **11** complaining

query 3 ask **4** quiz **5** doubt, grill **7** dubiety, inquire, inquiry **8** question **9** catechize **11** interrogate **13** interrogation

quest 4 hunt **5** probe **6** pursue, search **7** delving, inquire, inquiry, probing, pursuit, seeking **8** research **9** pursuance **11** inquisition **13** investigation *object:* **5** grail

question 3 ask, pry **4** poll, pump, quiz **5** doubt, grill, issue, probe, query **6** chance, matter **7** debrief, dispute, examine, inquire, inquiry, problem, suspect **8** distrust, mistrust **9** catechize, challenge, objection **10** difficulty, puzzle over **11** interrogate, possibility **13** interrogation, interrogatory

questionable 4 iffy, moot **5** shady, vague **6** unsure **7** dubious, obscure, suspect **8** arguable, doubtful, unproven **9** debatable, equivocal, refutable, uncertain **10** disputable, fly-by-night, improbable, unreliable **11** problematic **12** undependable

questioning 5 probe, query **6** show-me **7** delving, dubious, inquiry, probing **8** doubtful, grilling **9** inquiring, quizzical, skeptical, uncertain **11** incredulous, inquisitive, unbelieving **12** disbelieving **13** interrogation, interrogatory, investigative

quetzal 4 bird, coin **6** trogon

queue 3 row **4** file, line, rank, wait **5** braid **6** column **8** sequence

quibble 4 carp **5** argue, cavil **6** argufy, bicker, niggle, object **7** dispute, evasion, nitpick, wrangle **8** squabble **9** criticism, criticize, objection **10** split hairs

quick 4 core, deft, fast, keen, pith, root **5** acute, adept, agile, brisk, fleet, hasty, rapid, sharp, smart, swift **6** abrupt, bright, clever, nimble, prompt, speedy, sudden **7** hurried **9** breakneck, impetuous **10** harefooted **11** expeditious **12** lickety-split *combining form:* **5** tachy

quick bread 6 muffin **7** biscuit

quicken 4 goad, grow, move, spur, stir, wake **5** hurry, liven, pique, rouse, speed **6** arouse, awaken, excite, hasten, incite, induce, kindle, revive, step up, vivify **7** actuate, animate, enliven, provoke, shake up, sharpen, speed up **8** activate, energize, motivate, vitalize **9** galvanize, stimulate **10** accelerate, exhilarate, invigorate

quickly 5 apace **6** at once, pronto **9** forthwith, posthaste **12** straightaway

quickness 5 haste, speed **8** alacrity, celerity, dispatch, legerity, rapidity, velocity **9** fleetness, rapidness, swiftness **10** promptness

quicksand 3 bog **4** mire **6** morass

quicksilver 7 mercury **9** mercurial **10** inconstant

quick-tempered 5 cross, fiery, ratty, testy **6** cranky, touchy **7** peppery **8** choleric, petulant **9** irascible, irritable, splenetic **10** passionate

quick-witted 3 apt **4** keen **5** acute, agile, alert, canny, ready, sharp, smart **6** astute, brainy, bright, clever, prompt **9** brilliant **10** perceptive **11** intelligent, penetrating

quid 3 cut, wad **4** chew, coin **5** money, pound **9** sovereign

quiddity 3 nub **4** gist, meat, pith **6** trifle **7** essence, quibble **8** crotchet **12** eccentricity, quintessence

quidnunc see **rumormonger**

quiescent 4 calm **5** quiet, still **6** benign, hushed, latent, placid, serene, stilly **7** abeyant, dormant, halcyon, lurking **8** inactive, tranquil **10** untroubled

quiet 4 calm, hush, idle, lull, mute, stop **5** abate, allay, inert, muted, shush, still, whist **6** asleep, becalm, gentle, hushed, lessen, placid, serene, settle, silent, soothe, subdue **7** compose, halcyon, pacific, passive, restful, silence, subdued **8** decrease, inactive, peaceful, reserved, secluded, taciturn, tranquil **9** noiseless, soundless, stillness, unruffled **11** tranquility, tranquilize, unobtrusive **12** tranquillity

quietus 3 end **5** death, sleep **6** damper, demise, finish **7** decease, passing, silence **8**

curtains **10** inactivity, settlement **11** termination

quill 3 pen **5** float, shaft, spine, spool **6** bobbin **7** feather, spindle

quilt 4 pouf, puff **5** duvet **8** coverlet **9** comforter, eiderdown **11** counterpane *design:* **8** trapunto

quince 3 bel

quintessence 4 gist, meat, pith, soul **5** ideal, model, stuff **6** marrow **7** epitome **8** exemplar, last word, quiddity, ultimate **9** substance **10** apotheosis **12** essentiality

quintessential 5 ideal, model **7** classic, typical **8** ultimate **9** classical, exemplary **10** archetypal, consummate, prototypal **12** prototypical

quintillionth combining form 4 atto

quintuple 8 fivefold

quip 3 dig, gag, kid **4** gibe, gird, jape, jeer, jest, jibe, joke **5** crack, fleer, sally, scoff, sneer, tease **6** banter, oddity, retort, zinger **7** quibble **8** drollery, repartee **9** wisecrack, witticism **12** equivocation

quipster 3 wag, wit **4** card **5** clown, comic, droll, joker **6** jester **8** comedian, funnyman, humorist, jokester **11** wisecracker

quirk 3 tic **4** bend, kink, quip, whim **5** crook, curve, twist **6** groove, oddity, vagary **7** caprice **8** accident, crotchet **9** mannerism **11** peculiarity **12** idiosyncrasy

quirky 3 odd **7** erratic, offbeat **8** peculiar **9** eccentric, irregular, whimsical **10** capricious **13** idiosyncratic

quirt 4 lash, whip

quisling 5 Judas, rebel **7** traitor **8** apostate, betrayer, defector, turncoat **10** copperhead **11** backstabber **12** collaborator

quit 3 end, pay **4** drop, free, halt, stop **5** cease, chuck, leave **6** depart, desert, desist, give up, resign, retire, settle **7** abandon, drop out, forsake, release, relieve, satisfy **8** knock off, leave off, released, renounce, withdraw **9** discharge, liquidate, surrender, terminate **10** relinquish **11** discontinue

quite 3 all **4** just, very, well **5** fully, in all **6** in toto, purely, rather, wholly **7** exactly, totally, utterly **8** entirely **9** perfectly **10** absolutely, altogether, completely, positively, thoroughly **12** considerably

quittance 6 amends **7** redress **8** reprisal, requital **9** atonement, discharge, expiation, repayment **10** recompense, reparation **11** restitution **12** compensation

quitter 4 funk **6** coward, craven **7** chicken, dastard **8** poltroon, recreant **9** defeatist **11** yellowbelly

quiver 4 beat, case **5** pulse, quake, shake,

throb, waver **6** arrows, dither, jitter, quaver, shiver, tremor **7** pulsate, shudder, tremble, twitter, vibrate **9** palpitate, vibration
qui vive 5 alert **7** lookout
Quixote see **Don Quixote**
quixotic 7 foolish **8** fanciful, illusory, romantic **9** fantastic, imaginary, visionary **10** capricious, chimerical, idealistic **11** impractical
quiz 3 ask **4** exam, test **5** grill, query **7** examine, inquire **8** question **9** catechize **11** interrogate **12** cross-examine
quizzical 3 odd **5** queer **6** quaint, show-me **7** curious, dubious, mocking, probing, puzzled, teasing **8** doubtful, doubting, sardonic **9** inquiring, skeptical **11** incredulous, inquisitive, questioning, unbelieving **12** disbelieving
quodlibet 5 issue, point **6** debate, medley **7** mélange **8** fantasia, question **11** disputation
quoin 5 angle, block, wedge **6** corner **8** keystone, voussoir
quoit 4 hoop, ring **6** circle
quoits peg 3 hob
quondam 4 late, once, past **6** bygone, former,

whilom **7** defunct, onetime **8** sometime **9** erstwhile **10** occasional
quorum 4 body **5** group **7** council **8** majority
quota 3 cut, lot **4** bite, meed, part **5** share, slice, whack **6** amount, parcel, ration **7** measure, portion, quantum **9** allotment, allowance **10** allocation, percentage, proportion
quotation 3 bid **5** offer, price **7** excerpt, extract, passage **8** citation
quotation mark, French 9 guillemet
quote 3 bid **4** cite, list **5** blurb, offer, price, refer **6** adduce, borrow, repeat **7** excerpt, extract, passage **8** citation
quotidian 5 daily, plain, usual **6** common **7** average, diurnal, prosaic, regular, routine, vanilla **8** day-to-day, everyday, ordinary, workaday **9** circadian **11** commonplace **12** unremarkable
quotient 5 ratio, share **7** caliber, portion **9** allotment, magnitude **10** percentage, proportion
Quo Vadis *author:* **11** Sienkiewicz (Henryk) *character:* **4** Nero **5** Lygia, Peter **8** Vinicius **9** Petronius

R

Ra *son:* **6** Khonsu *wife:* **3** Mut
Raamah *father:* **4** Cush *son:* **5** Dedan, Sheba
Rabbi Ben Ezra author 8 Browning (Robert)
rabbit 4 cony, hare **5** bunny, coney *female:* **3** doe *fictional:* **5** Fiver, Hazel, Mopsy, Peter **6** Flopsy, Harvey **7** Thumper **8** Crusader, Ricochet **9** Bugs Bunny **10** Cotton-tail **11** Easter Bunny *food:* **5** salad **6** carrot **7** lettuce *neutered:* **5** lapin *tail:* **4** scut
rabble 3 mob **4** mass, rout **5** crush, horde **6** masses **8** canaille, populace, riffraff, unwashed **10** lower class **11** proletariat, rank and file
rabble-rouser 7 inciter **8** agitator, fomenter **9** demagogue **10** incendiary **12** troublemaker
Rabelais character 7 Panurge **9** Gargantua **10** Pantagruel
rabid 3 mad **4** wild **5** crazy, ultra **6** crazed, insane **7** extreme, fanatic, frantic, furious, radical, zealous **8** demented, deranged, frenetic, frenzied, obsessed, ultraist **9** delirious, extremist **10** corybantic **11** hydrophobic

rabies 11 hydrophobia
raccoon 8 ringtail *dog:* **6** tanuki *relative:* **5** civet, coati, panda **8** civet cat, kinkajou **10** cacomistle, coatimundi
race 3 rev **4** bolt, dart, dash, gill, lash, meet, rush, tear, type **5** brook, chase, creek, fling, hurry, match, rally, relay, shoot, speed, spurt **6** charge, course, gallop, runnel, scurry, sprint, stream **7** channel, contest, rivalry, rivulet, scamper **8** marathon **9** grand prix **11** competition, watercourse *zigzag:* **6** slalom
race car 4 Elva, Lola, Ralt **5** Lotus, March, Swift **6** Abarth, Cooper, Merlyn, Royale, Turner **7** Avenger, Brabham, Chevron, Crosslé, Ferrari, Mallock, McLaren, Reynard, TransAm, Triumph **8** Corvette **9** Van Diemen **12** Austin Healey
racecourse 4 oval, turf **5** track **8** speedway
racehorse 5 Alsab, Kelso **6** Forego **7** Assault, Barbaro, Man O' War **8** Affirmed, Citation **9** Riva Ridge, War Emblem **10** War Admiral

11 Forward Pass, Seattle Slew, Secretariat, Smarty Jones **12** Native Dancer

Rachel *father:* **5** Laban *husband:* **5** Jacob *servant:* **6** Bilhah *sister:* **4** Leah *son:* **6** Joseph **8** Benjamin

rachis 4 back **5** chine, spine **8** backbone **12** spinal column

rachitic 5 shaky **6** wobbly **7** rackety, rickety, tenuous **9** tremulous **10** ramshackle, rattletrap

____ **Rachmaninoff 6** Sergei, Sergey

racing enthusiast 8 railbird

racism 7 bigotry, jim crow **9** apartheid, prejudice **11** segregation

racist 4 nazi **5** bigot **7** bigoted **10** intolerant, prejudiced **11** supremacist

rack 3 bed **4** buck, bunk, pace, pain, sack, scud **5** frame, wring **6** harass, harrow, martyr, strain, wrench **7** afflict, agonize, antlers, crucify, ratchet, sawbuck, stretch, torment, torture **8** distress, sawhorse **9** framework, persecute **10** excruciate

racket 3 con, din **4** game **5** babel, fraud, hooha, noise **6** clamor, hubbub, rattle, scheme, tumult, uproar **7** pursuit, swindle **8** ballyhoo, brouhaha, foofaraw **10** hullabaloo **11** pandemonium

racketeer 7 goombah, mafioso, mobster **8** extorter, gangster **9** godfather *law:* **4** RICO (Act)

rack up 3 win **4** gain **5** reach, score **6** attain **7** achieve, realize **10** accomplish

raconteur 11 storyteller

racy 4 blue, gamy **5** bawdy, broad, juicy, salty, spicy, vampy, zesty **6** purple, risqué, smutty, snappy, vulgar, wicked **7** piquant, pungent **8** indecent, off-color, vigorous **10** suggestive

Radames' beloved 4 Aïda

radar image 3 pip **4** blip, spot **5** trace

Raddai *brother:* **5** David *father:* **5** Jesse

radiance 3 ray **4** glow **5** glory, shine **6** luster **7** aureola, aureole **8** splendor **10** brightness, brilliance

radiant 4 glad **5** aglow, beamy, shiny **6** bright, cheery, lucent **7** beaming, fulgent, glowing, lambent **8** cheerful, luminous, lustrous **9** brilliant, effulgent **10** effulgence **12** incandescent

radiate 4 beam, glow **5** gleam, shine, strew **6** spread **7** diverge **8** illumine **10** illuminate

radiation unit 3 rad, rem, rep **7** langley, sievert **8** roentgen

radiator 6 cooler, heater **9** convector **11** transmitter **13** heat exchanger

radical 4 acyl, root **5** basal, basic, rebel, ultra **7** extreme, fanatic, primary **8** agitator, car-

dinal, inherent, militant, ultraist **9** anarchist, essential, extremist, intrinsic **10** subversive, underlying **11** fundamental **12** foundational, iconoclastic **13** revolutionary *mathematical:* **4** surd

radicle 4 root **5** radix **9** hypocotyl

radio 4 AM-FM **8** wireless *frequency range:* **8** waveband *shortwave:* **3** ham **7** amateur

radioactive 3 hot **7** nuclear

radium *discoverer:* **5** Curie (Marie, Pierre) *symbol:* **2** Ra

radius 5 ambit, orbit, range, reach, sweep **6** extent **7** compass, purview **9** extension

radix 4 base, root **6** source

radon symbol 2 Rn

raffish 6 coarse, jaunty, rakish, sporty, vulgar **9** dissolute **12** devil-may-care

raffle 7 drawing, lottery

raft 3 lot, ton **4** heap, mess, pile, scad, slew **5** balsa, float **6** bundle *Maori:* **4** moki

rafter 4 balk, beam, viga

rag 3 jaw, kid, rib **4** bait, jive, josh, rail, razz, rock **5** baste, cloth, scold, tease **6** berate, harass, hector, needle, pester **7** tabloid, torment **9** newspaper

ragamuffin 3 bum **4** hobo, waif **5** gamin, tramp **6** beggar, gamine, orphan, urchin **7** wastrel **8** vagabond **9** scarecrow **11** guttersnipe

rage 3 cry, fad, ire, mad, wax **4** chic, fume, fury, mode, rant **5** anger, craze, fancy, furor, go ape, mania, storm, style, vogue, wrath **6** blow up, frenzy, furore, lose it, seethe **7** fashion, madness, passion **8** boil over, hysteria, violence **10** dernier cri **11** indignation

ragged 4 rent, torn **5** seedy **6** frayed, jagged, shabby, uneven **7** unkempt, worn-out **8** frazzled, straggly, tattered **10** threadbare

raging 4 wild **6** stormy **7** furious, extreme, intense, violent **8** blustery **9** ferocious, turbulent **10** blustering **11** tempestuous

ragout 4 stew **5** salmi **6** burgoo, jumble, medley **7** farrago, goulash, mélange, mixture **8** mishmash **9** potpourri **10** hodgepodge, salmagundi **11** gallimaufry

rags 4 duds, garb **5** dress **6** attire, shreds **7** apparel, clothes, raiment, threads **8** clothing **10** attirement **11** habiliments

ragtag see **rabble**

ragwort 7 senecio **9** cineraria, groundsel **10** butterweed

raid 4 bust, loot, sack **5** foray, harry **6** attack, forage, harass, inroad, invade, maraud, ravage, sortie **7** assault, despoil, overrun, plunder **8** invasion, spoliate **9** incursion, onslaught

raider 6 pirate **10** freebooter

rail 3 bar, jaw **5** fence, scold, track **6** berate, revile **7** barrier, inveigh, upbraid **8** banister **10** tongue-lash, vituperate

rail bird 4 coot, sora **5** crake **7** clapper **8** marsh hen, water hen *extinct:* **4** moho

railing 8 banister **10** balustrade *part:* **8** baluster

raillery 5 scorn **6** banter **7** mockery, teasing **8** badinage, derision, ridicule, taunting **10** lampoonery, persiflage

railroad *branch:* **6** siding *car:* **5** coach, diner, stock **6** hopper **7** caboose, gondola, Pullman *engine:* **10** locomotive *locomotive:* **9** iron horse *station:* **5** depot *underground:* **4** tube **5** metro **6** subway *worker:* **6** porter **7** fireman **8** brakeman, engineer **9** conductor **11** gandy dancer

raiment 4 duds, garb, gear, togs **5** array, dress **6** attire **7** apparel, clothes, threads, vesture **8** clothing, garments, glad rags, vestiary **9** caparison, vestments **10** attirement **11** habiliments

rain 4 spit **6** deluge, mizzle, shower **7** drizzle **8** downpour, sprinkle **10** cloudburst **13** precipitation

rainbow 3 arc **4** irid, iris **5** array, gamut **7** fantasy **8** illusion, spectrum **9** pipe dream *bridge:* **7** Bifrost *chaser:* **9** visionary *goddess:* **4** Iris

rainbow fish 5 guppy, trout **6** wrasse

raincoat 3 mac **4** mack **6** poncho, trench **7** oilskin, slicker **10** mackintosh

rain leader 9 downspout

rain tree 9 monkeypod

raise 2 up **4** ante, grow, hike, jack, jump, lift, pump, rear **5** boost, breed, erect, exalt, hoist, put up **6** foment, incite, jack up, leaven, muster, uplift **7** augment, bring up, collect, elevate, enhance, inflate, produce **8** heighten, increase **9** construct, cultivate, increment, propagate

raisin 5 grape **7** currant, sultana **10** dried grape

Raisin in the Sun author 9 Hansberry (Lorraine)

raison d' ____ **4** état, être

raja 4 king **5** chief, ruler **6** prince **9** dignitary

rake 3 rip **4** comb, roué, scan **5** angle, blood, pitch, rifle, scamp, scour, slope **6** forage, glance, lecher, rascal, scrape, search, strafe **7** incline, playboy, ransack, rummage, scratch **8** enfilade, lothario **9** debauchee, libertine **10** profligate

rakehell 4 fast, wild **5** blood, rogue, scamp **6** rascal, sporty **7** playboy, raffish **8** lothario, rascally **9** debauchee, dissolute, lecherous, libertine **10** licentious, profligate

rake-off 3 cut **4** bite, take **5** chunk, share **7** portion **9** baksheesh, lagniappe **10** commission, percentage

rake's look 4 leer, ogle

Rake's Progress artist 7 Hogarth (William)

rakish see **rakehell**

rally 4 race, stir, wake **5** harry, renew, rouse, waken **6** arouse, awaken, bestir, kindle, muster, perk up, pick up, repair, volley **7** convene, enliven, marshal, rebound, recover **8** assemble, clambake, comeback, mobilize, recovery **9** challenge, re-collect **10** invigorate, reorganize

rallying cry 5 motto **6** byword, slogan **9** watchword **10** shibboleth **11** catchphrase

ram 5 Aries, crash, crowd, drive, pound, sheep, stuff **6** batter, plunge, strike, thrust **7** warship

Rama's wife 4 Sita

ramble 3 gad **4** roam, rove **5** drift, range, run on, stray, troll **6** stroll, wander **7** blather, digress, diverge, maunder, meander, saunter, traipse **8** divagate, straggle **9** gallivant

rambler 4 rose **5** gypsy, hiker, nomad, rover **6** roamer, walker **7** drifter, vagrant **8** stroller, vagabond, wanderer **9** itinerant **10** ranch house

rambunctious 5 rowdy **6** unruly **7** raucous, willful **10** boisterous, headstrong **11** intractable **12** recalcitrant, ungovernable

ramification 5 shoot **6** branch, offset **8** offshoot **9** outgrowth, offspring **11** consequence

ramify 6 branch, divide, extend **7** develop, radiate **9** branch out, propagate **11** proliferate

Ramona author 7 Jackson (Helen Hunt)

ramose 8 branched

ramp 5 apron **7** incline

rampage 4 rage, riot, tear **5** binge, fling, spree, storm

rampageous 4 wild **6** unruly **7** riotous

rampant 4 rank, rife, wild **7** rearing, regnant **9** prevalent, unbridled **10** widespread **12** uncontrolled, unrestrained

rampart 4 wall **5** ridge **7** bulwark, parapet **9** barricade **10** breastwork

ramshackle 6 flimsy **7** rickety, run-down **8** decrepit **10** tumbledown **11** dilapidated

ram's mate 3 ewe

ranch 5 finca **6** quinta, spread **8** estancia, hacienda *worker:* **6** cowboy, gaucho **7** cowgirl, cowhand, cowpoke **10** cowpuncher

rancher 6 cowboy **7** breeder **9** cattleman

rancid 4 high, rank, sour **5** fetid **6** putrid, skunky, smelly **7** noisome, spoiled **8** stinking **9** offensive **10** malodorous

rancor 4 gall **6** animus, enmity, hatred **7** ill

will **9** animosity, antipathy, hostility **10** antagonism, bitterness

rancorous 6 bitter **7** hateful, hostile **8** spiteful, venomous **9** malicious, malignant, vitriolic **10** malevolent **11** acrimonious **12** antagonistic

Rand, Ayn *novel:* **6** Anthem **12** Fountainhead (The) **13** Atlas Shrugged

random 6 casual **7** aimless **8** slapdash **9** arbitrary, desultory, haphazard, hit-or-miss, unplanned **10** accidental, contingent, hit-and-miss, incidental **11** purposeless

randy 4 lewd **5** bawdy, lusty **7** lustful, satyric **9** lecherous, libertine, lickerish, salacious **10** lascivious, libidinous, licentious

range 3 row, run **4** area, band, roam, rove, shot, site, sort, span, vary **5** align, ambit, carry, drift, field, gamut, orbit, order, reach, realm, ridge, scale, scope, space, stove, stray, sweep, width **6** assort, domain, extent, length, limits, ramble, sierra, sphere, spread, wander **7** compass, earshot, expanse, eyeshot, habitat, meander, purview, stretch **8** confines, distance, latitude, locality, panorama, province, stovetop, traverse, vicinity **9** amplitude, extension, gallivant, magnitude, territory **12** distribution

range finder 9 telemeter

ranger 3 spy **5** scout **6** lawman, patrol, warden **8** overseer **9** caretaker, protector

rangy 4 lean **5** lanky **6** gangly **7** spindly **8** gangling

rani's mate 4 raja **5** rajah

rank 3 row **4** file, foul, lush, rate, seed, sort, tier **5** class, fetid, funky, grade, gross, humid, order, place, queue **6** assort, cachet, coarse, filthy, lavish, putrid, rancid, rating, smelly, status **7** arrange, dignity, echelon, footing, noisome, profuse, rampant, reeking, station, stature **8** classify, evaluate, flagrant, outright, position, standing, stinking **9** downright, egregious, loathsome, luxuriant, overgrown, repulsive **10** consummate, malodorous **11** conspicuous, unmitigated

rank and file 5 plebs **6** people, plebes **8** populace **9** commonage, commoners, plebeians **10** commonalty **11** enlisted men

rankle 3 irk, vex **4** rile **5** annoy **6** bother, fester, nettle, seethe **8** embitter, irritate **9** aggravate **10** exasperate

ransack 3 rob **4** comb, grub, loot, rake **5** rifle, scour **6** forage, ravage **7** plunder, rummage

Ran's husband 5 Aegir

ransom 3 buy **4** free **6** redeem, regain, rescue **7** deliver, recover **8** liberate **13** consideration

rant 3 jaw, rag **4** huff, rage, rail, rate, rave **5**

mouth, scold **6** screed, tirade **7** bluster, bombast, declaim, fustian **8** bloviate, harangue, perorate **10** vituperate **11** rodomontade

ranula 4 cyst

rap 3 hit, tap **4** blow, chat, swat, talk, wipe **5** blame, chide, knock, swipe **6** charge, patter, rebuke **7** censure, condemn, reproof **8** causerie, denounce, reproach, sentence **9** criticize, criticism, reprehend, reprimand, reprobate **10** discussion **12** conversation

rapacious 6 greedy **8** covetous, grasping, ravening, ravenous **9** predatory, raptorial, voracious **10** gluttonous, predaceous

rapacity 5 greed **7** avarice, avidity **8** cupidity, voracity **10** greediness **12** covetousness, ravenousness

rape 4 ruin **5** colza, force, spoil **6** canola, defile, ravage, ravish **7** assault, debauch, despoil, outrage, plunder, violate **9** violation **10** ravishment, spoliation

Rape of the Lock, The *author:* **4** Pope (Alexander) *heroine:* **7** Belinda

Raphael *birthplace:* **6** Urbino *subject:* **7** Madonna *teacher:* **8** Perugino

rapid 4 fast **5** brisk, chute, fleet, hasty, quick, swift **6** speedy **7** hurried **9** breakneck **11** expeditious

rapidity 5 haste, hurry, speed **8** celerity, velocity

rapids 5 chute **8** cataract **10** white water

rapier 4 épée **5** blade, sword

rapine 4 loot, pelf, swag **5** booty, prize, spoil **6** boodle, spoils **7** pillage, plunder **10** spoliation

Rappaccini's Daughter 8 Beatrice *author:* **9** Hawthorne (Nathaniel)

rapper 3 DMX, Eve, GZA, Jin **4** Ice T, Jay-Z **5** Cee-Lo, Rakim **6** Eminem, Heavy D, KRS-ONE, Mac Dre, Mos Def, Run DMC, Twista **7** Caushun, LL Cool J, OutKast **8** Ludacris, Melle Mel, Paul Wall **9** Kanye West, Method Man, Snoop Dogg **10** Kool Moe Dee, Lupe Fiasco, Spoonie Gee, Vanilla Ice **11** Busta Rhymes, Public Enemy

rapport 5 unity **6** accord **7** concord, harmony **8** affinity **9** communion **13** communication

rapscallion see **rascal**

rap session 6 confab, parley **7** palaver **8** colloquy **10** discussion

rapt 7 intent **7** engaged **8** absorbed, immersed **9** engrossed **10** enthralled **11** carried away, preoccupied, transported

raptor 3 owl **4** hawk **5** eagle **6** condor, falcon, merlin, osprey **7** kestrel, vulture **9** gyrfalcon **10** bird of prey **11** deinonychus

rapture 5 swoon **6** heaven **7** delight, ecstasy,

nirvana **9** transport **10** exaltation **13** seventh heaven

rara _____ **4** avis

rare 3 few, red **4** pink, thin **6** choice, dainty, exotic, scarce, seldom, select **7** elegant, unusual **8** delicate, singular, sporadic, superior, uncommon, unwonted **9** exquisite, recherché, underdone **10** infrequent, occasional **11** distinctive, exceptional **13** extraordinary

rarefied 4 fine, thin **7** tenuous **8** esoteric **10** attenuated

rarefy 4 thin **6** refine **9** attenuate

rarely 6 little, seldom **9** extremely, unusually **12** infrequently

raring 4 avid, keen **5** eager **6** gung-ho **12** enthusiastic

rarity 5 curio **6** oddity **7** curiosa **8** scarcity **9** curiosity **10** aberration **11** collectible

rascal 3 imp **4** rake **5** devil, knave, rogue, scamp **7** lowlife, villain, wastrel **8** scalawag **9** miscreant, reprobate, scoundrel, skeezicks **10** blackguard **11** rapscallion *Irish:* **8** spalpeen

rash 5 hasty, heady **6** abrupt, brazen, daring, madcap, plague, sudden, unwary, unwise **7** foolish **8** careless, epidemic, eruption, headlong, heedless, outbreak, reckless **9** audacious, daredevil, foolhardy, hotheaded, impetuous, imprudent, impulsive **10** ill-advised, incautious, indiscreet, unthinking **11** injudicious, precipitate, temerarious, thoughtless

rasp 4 file, fret **5** annoy, chafe, grate **6** abrade, scrape **7** scratch **8** irritate

raspberry 7 catcall **8** blackcap **10** Bronx cheer

raspy 3 dry **5** harsh, rough **6** hoarse **7** grating, jarring, raucous **8** scrabbly, scratchy

rat 4 blab, fink, heel, scab, sing **5** louse **6** defect, desert, inform, rodent, snitch, squeak, squeal, tattle **7** stoolie **8** apostate, defector, informer, recreant, renegade, squealer, turncoat **9** bandicoot, repudiate, turnabout **11** stool pigeon **12** tergiversate *female:* **3** doe

ratchet 4 pawl **6** detent

rate 3 fee, set, tab **4** cost, earn, rank **5** assay, class, grade, merit, price, scale, set at, value **6** amount, assess, charge, degree, esteem, regard, survey, tariff **7** apprize, deserve, valuate **8** appraise, classify, consider, estimate, evaluate, price tag **9** valuation **10** proportion

rather 4 a bit **5** quite **6** fairly, in lieu, kind of, pretty, sort of **7** instead **8** somewhat **10** more or less, preferably **11** alternately **13** alternatively

rathskeller 3 bar, inn, pub **4** dive **6** saloon, tavern **7** barroom, taproom **8** alehouse, basement

ratify 4 seal **5** enact **7** approve, certify, confirm, endorse, license **8** accredit, sanction, validate

rating 4 mark, rank **5** class, grade **6** number **8** estimate, standing

ratio 5 scale **7** percent **8** fraction, quotient **10** percentage, proportion

ratiocination 8 judgment, sequitur **9** inference, reasoning **10** conclusion

ration 4 dole, food, meal, mete **5** allot, divvy, quota, share **6** divide, parcel **7** measure, mete out, prorate **8** allocate **9** allotment, allowance **10** provisions **13** apportionment

rational 4 calm, cool, sane **5** lucid, sober, sound **6** stable **7** logical, prudent **8** sensible, thinking **9** judicious **10** consequent, reasonable **11** circumspect, intelligent, levelheaded **12** intellectual

rationale 5 basis, logic **6** reason **7** grounds **9** reasoning **11** explanation **13** justification

rationalize 7 explain, justify **10** account for **11** externalize

ratite 3 emu, moa **4** kiwi, rhea **7** ostrich

rattail 3 cod **9** grenadier

rattan 4 cane, palm **6** switch **7** malacca

Rattigan play 10 Winslow Boy (The) **14** Separate Tables

rattle 3 gab, jaw, yak **4** chat, faze, rale **5** abash, addle, clack, noise, rouse, run on, upset **6** babble, gabble, jangle, racket **7** chatter, clatter, confuse, disturb, flummox, perplex, unnerve **8** bewilder, confound, distract **9** discomfit, embarrass **10** disconcert, noisemaker

rattlebrained 5 dizzy, giddy, silly **7** flighty **8** skittish **9** frivolous

rattling 4 very **5** brisk, quick **6** damned, lively, mighty **8** whacking, whopping **9** energetic, extremely **11** exceedingly

ratty 4 mean **5** dowdy, dumpy, seedy, tacky **6** cheesy, scurvy, shabby **7** unkempt **8** slovenly **9** irritable **10** despicable **11** treacherous **12** contemptible

raucous 4 loud **5** harsh, noisy, rough, rowdy **6** hoarse, unruly **7** grating, jarring, squawky **8** rowdyish, strident **9** termagant, turbulent **10** boisterous, disorderly, stridulent, stridulous, tumultuous **11** cacophonous **12** rambunctious

raunchy 4 foul **5** dirty, nasty **6** coarse, filthy, sloppy, smutty, vulgar **7** obscene **8** indecent **9** salacious

ravage 4 loot, raze, ruin, sack **5** foray, harry, spoil, strip, waste, wreck **6** forage, invade,

ravish 7 despoil, overrun, pillage, plunder, ransack, scourge 8 desolate, spoliate 9 depredate, desecrate, devastate

rave 4 gush, rant 5 storm 6 babble, jabber 7 enthuse 10 rhapsodize

ravel 3 run 4 fray 5 snarl 6 muddle, tangle 7 perplex, untwine 8 entangle 9 extricate 10 complicate 11 disentangle

ravelings 4 lint 7 threads

Ravel work 6 Boléro 7 La Valse 14 Daphnis et Chloé 17 Rapsodie espagnole

raven 3 jet 4 ebon, inky, prey 5 black, ebony, jetty, sable 7 despoil, plunder 9 pitch-dark 10 pitch-black *relative:* 3 jay 4 crow 6 magpie 7 blue jay

Raven, The *author:* 3 Poe (Edgar Allan) *lost love:* 6 Lenore *refrain:* 9 Nevermore

ravenous 6 greedy, hungry 7 starved 8 edacious, famished, starving 9 rapacious, voracious 10 gluttonous

ravine 3 cut, gap 4 gulf, pass, wadi 5 abyss, chasm, cleft, clove, flume, gorge, gulch, gully, notch 6 arroyo, canyon, clough, coulee, defile, gutter, nullah 7 crevice, fissure 8 barranca, crevasse *Mt. Washington's:* 9 Tuckerman

raving 3 mad 5 manic, rabid, upset 6 crazed 7 frantic, lunatic, unglued 8 demented, deranged, frenetic, frenzied, maniacal, obsessed, unhinged, worked up 9 ravishing 10 distraught, flipped out, hysterical, irrational 11 overwrought

ravish 4 rape 5 force, spoil 6 defile 7 assault, despoil, outrage, pillage, plunder, violate 8 deflower, entrance, overcome 9 enrapture, transport

raw 4 cold, nude, rude 5 bleak, chill, crass, crude, fresh, green, naked, rough, young 6 callow, coarse, impure, native, unclad, unripe, vulgar 7 uncouth 8 immature, uncooked, unformed 9 au naturel, inelegant, irritated, run-of-mine, unbridled, unclothed, undressed, unrefined 10 unfinished, unpolished 13 inexperienced

rawboned 4 bony, lank, lean 5 gaunt, gawky, lanky, spare 6 skinny 7 angular, scraggy, scrawny

ray 4 beam 5 gleam, manta, shaft, skate, trace 6 radius, streak, stream 7 radiate, sawfish, sunbeam, torpedo 8 moonbeam 9 devilfish, thornback 10 guitarfish

raze 4 ruin 5 level 7 destroy 8 demolish, pull down, tear down

razor 4 Atra 6 shaver

razz 3 rag, rib 4 bait, josh, mock, twit 5 scout, taunt 6 badger, banter, deride, heckle, hector 8 ridicule (see also **raspberry**)

RBI 11 run batted in 12 runs batted in

re 4 as to 5 about, as for 7 apropos 9 apropos of, as regards, regarding 10 as respects, concerning, relating to, respecting 12 with regard to 13 with respect to

reach 4 beat, gain, pass, span, tack 5 carry, get at, get to, grasp, level, range, scope, sweep, touch 6 arrive, attain, extend, extent, rack up, thrust 7 achieve, contact, horizon, project, stretch 9 encompass, influence 10 accomplish, get through

_____ reaction 4 dark 5 alarm, chain, light 7 nuclear 8 chemical

reactivate 5 renew 6 revive 8 rekindle, revivify 9 resurrect 10 revitalize 11 resuscitate

read 4 scan, skim 6 peruse 8 pore over *inability to:* 8 dyslexia

readable 7 legible

reader 6 lector, primer 7 proofer, scanner 8 bookworm 9 anthology

readily 4 well 6 easily, freely 7 lightly 9 willingly 12 effortlessly

readiness 4 ease 5 skill 6 DEFCON 7 aptness 8 alacrity, dispatch, facility 9 dexterity, quickness 10 promptness 11 inclination, promptitude 12 preparedness

reading 6 lesson 7 lection, version, vulgate 9 rendition 10 recitation

ready 3 set 4 prep, ripe, yare 5 equip 6 active, gear up, make up, primed, prompt 7 prepare 8 inclined, prepared 9 available

real 4 true, very 5 pukka, sound, valid 6 actual, honest 7 certain, genuine, sincere 8 bona fide, concrete, existent, tangible 9 authentic, undoubted, veridical 10 sure enough, undeniable 11 substantive 12 indisputable

real-estate abbreviation 3 ARM, apt, flr, gar, gdn, kit, lux, mbr, MLS, TLC, vic 4 bsmt, bdrm, frpl, FSBO, furn, HVAC, PITI, util, wbfp 5 RESPA

realism 6 verism 7 verismo 10 naturalism, pragmatism 11 objectivism, objectivity

realistic 4 sane 5 sober, sound 7 genuine, natural 8 lifelike, rational, sensible, veristic 9 practical, pragmatic 10 bottom-line, hardboiled, hardheaded, reasonable, unromantic 11 down-to-earth 12 matter-of-fact 13 unsentimental

reality 4 fact, true 5 being, sooth, truth 9 actuality, existence, substance 13 flesh and blood

realize 4 gain, reap 5 grasp, reach, score 6 attain, rack up 7 achieve, feature, imagine, reflect 8 conceive, envisage, envision 9 actualize, recognize 10 accomplish, comprehend

really 4 very **5** truly **6** indeed, verily **7** awfully, clearly **8** actually, honestly **9** assuredly, certainly, decidedly, genuinely **10** definitely, positively **11** exceedingly, indubitably, undoubtedly **12** unmistakably

realm 5 orbit, range, scope, sweep **6** domain, empire, estate, extent, radius, sphere **7** compass, demesne, kingdom, purview **8** dominion

ream 4 load, scad **5** widen **7** enlarge **11** countersink

reanimation 7 rebirth, revival **10** renascence, resurgence **11** reawakening, renaissance **12** risorgimento

reap 3 cut **4** earn, gain **5** glean, shear **6** garner, gather, obtain, sickle, thresh **7** harvest

rear 3 aft **4** back, butt, hind, lift, ramp, rump, seat, tail **5** after, breed, build, erect, fanny, hoist, nurse, put up, raise, set up, stern **6** behind, bottom, fledge, foster, heinie, uphold **7** bring up, caboose, elevate, nurture **8** backside, buttocks, hindmost **9** construct, posterior

rear end 3 bum, bun, can **4** butt, duff, moon, rump, seat, tail, tush **5** booty, fanny, stern **6** behind, bottom, heinie **7** caboose, keister **8** backside, buttocks, derriere **9** posterior

rearmost 3 end **4** last **5** final **8** terminal, ultimate

rearrange see **readjust**

rearward 3 aft **4** back **6** behind **8** backward **9** posterior **10** retrograde

Rea Silvia *father:* **7** Numitor *son:* **5** Remus **7** Romulus

reason 3 why, wit **4** mind, nous **5** basis, cause, infer, proof, think **6** excuse, ground, motive, sanity, senses **7** account, reflect **8** argument, cogitate, conceive, persuade **9** inference, intellect, rationale, soundness, speculate, wherefore **10** deliberate **11** explanation **12** intelligence **13** consideration, justification, ratiocination, understanding

reasonable 4 fair, just **5** cheap, level, sound **6** modest **7** logical, low-cost, tenable **8** credible, feasible, moderate, rational, sensible **9** equitable, plausible **10** acceptable, affordable, restrained **11** inexpensive, intelligent

reasoning 4 case **5** logic **8** argument **9** deduction

reasonless 7 invalid **8** baseless **9** illogical, senseless, unfounded **10** fallacious, groundless, irrational **11** meaningless, purposeless

reawaken 5 renew **6** revive **7** refresh **8** revivify **9** reanimate **10** regenerate **12** reinvigorate

rebate 6 lessen, refund, return **8** decrease, diminish, give back **9** deduction, reduction

Rebecca *beloved:* **7** Ivanhoe *father:* **5** Isaac

Rebekah *brother:* **5** Laban *father:* **7** Bethuel *husband:* **5** Isaac *nurse:* **7** Deborah *son:* **4** Esau **5** Jacob

rebel 6 anarch, mutiny, resist, revolt **7** disobey **8** frondeur, mutineer **9** insurgent **10** malcontent **13** revolutionary, revolutionist

rebellion 6 émeute, mutiny, revolt, rising **8** defiance, intifada, sedition, uprising **10** insurgence, insurgency, resistance, revolution **12** insurrection

rebellious 6 unruly **8** mutinous, stubborn **9** insurgent **10** refractory **11** disaffected, disobedient **12** contumacious, unmanageable **13** insubordinate

rebirth 7 revival **9** awakening **10** conversion, renascence, resurgence **11** reanimation, reawakening, renaissance **12** resurrection, risorgimento

rebound 5 rally **6** bounce, reecho, recoil, repeat **7** recover **8** comeback, recovery, ricochet, snap back **10** convalesce

rebozo 5 scarf, shawl

rebuff 4 slap, snub **5** repel **6** reject **7** fend off, repulse, ward off **8** turn away

rebuild 6 repair, revamp **7** remodel, restore **8** overhaul, renovate, retrofit **9** modernize, refurbish **11** recondition, reconstruct **12** rehabilitate

rebuke 3 rap **4** snub **5** chide, scold, scorn **6** berate, earful, lesson, rebuff **7** bawl out, lecture, reproof, reprove **8** admonish, call down, reproach, scolding **9** reprimand, talking-to **10** tongue-lash **11** comeuppance, objurgation **12** admonishment, dressing-down **13** tongue-lashing

rebut 5 repel **6** refute, reject **7** confute, fend off, repulse, ward off **8** confound, disprove, stave off **10** controvert, disconfirm

rebuttal 5 reply **6** answer, retort **7** defense, riposte **8** argument, comeback, response **9** rejoinder **10** refutation **11** repudiation

recalcitrant 6 unruly **7** froward, willful **8** contrary, perverse, stubborn, untoward **9** fractious, obstinate, resistant **10** headstrong **11** intractable **12** ungovernable, unmanageable

recall 4 stir **5** evoke, renew, rouse, waken **6** arouse, awaken, cancel, memory, remind, repeal, revive, revoke **7** bethink, rescind, restore, retract, reverse **8** callback, remember, resemble, take back, withdraw **9** anamnesis, recollect, reinstate, reminisce, represent, reproduce **10** revocation **11** bring to mind, countermand, remembrance **12** recollection, reminiscence

recant 5 unsay **6** abjure, revoke **7** retract **8**

forswear, renounce, take back, withdraw 9 backtrack, repudiate

recap 5 sum up 6 précis, résumé, review 7 reprise, retread, summary 8 overview 9 summarize 10 retrograde

recapitulate 5 sum up 6 resume, review 9 summarize 10 retrograde

recapitulation 5 sum-up 6 précis, résumé, review 7 epitome, reprise, summary 9 summing-up

recede 3 ebb 4 back 5 abate, taper 6 lessen, reduce, retire 7 dwindle, regress, retract, retreat 8 decrease, diminish, fall back, withdraw 10 retrograde, retrogress

receipts 4 gate, take 5 sales 6 income 7 revenue, takings 8 earnings, proceeds

receive 4 host 5 admit, catch, greet 6 accept, endure, suffer, take in 7 acquire, sustain, welcome 10 experience

received 5 plain, sound 6 common 7 popular 8 accepted, familiar, ordinary, orthodox 12 acknowledged, conventional

receiver 4 dish 5 donee, fence, pager 6 aerial 7 antenna, catcher, scanner 9 recipient, treasurer

recent 3 new 4 late 5 fresh, novel 6 latest, modern 8 neoteric

receptacle 6 hamper, holder, hopper, trough, vessel 9 container 10 repository

receptive 4 open 7 passive 8 amenable 9 sensitive 10 accessible, hospitable, open-minded, responsive 11 persuadable, persuasible, suggestible, susceptible

recess 4 cove, nook 5 break, cleft, niche 6 alcove, grotto, hiatus 7 adjourn 8 prorogue 9 prorogate, terminate 11 indentation

Recessional author 7 Kipling (Rudyard)

recessive 3 shy 8 retiring 9 reclusive, withdrawn 10 unsociable

recherché 4 rare 5 novel 6 choice, dainty, exotic, select 7 elegant, unusual 8 affected, delicate, original, superior, uncommon 9 exquisite 11 pretentious

recipe 7 formula 9 procedure 12 prescription

recipient 5 donee 7 grantee 8 receiver 11 beneficiary

reciprocal 4 mate, twin 5 match 6 double, fellow, mutual 8 requited 9 bilateral, companion, duplicate 10 coordinate 11 interactive **prefix:** 5 inter

reciprocate 5 repay 6 retort, return 7 requite 8 exchange 9 retaliate 10 compensate, recompense 11 interchange

recital 5 story 6 soiree 7 concert, reading 9 discourse, narration 10 recounting 11 enumeration, performance

recite 4 tell 5 chant, count, state 6 detail, number, relate, repeat, report, set out 7 declaim, narrate, recount, reel off 8 describe, rehearse 9 pronounce

reckless 4 rash, wild 5 brash, hasty 6 daring, madcap 8 carefree, heedless 9 audacious, daredevil, foolhardy, hotheaded 10 ill-advised, incautious 11 harebrained, temerarious, thoughtless 12 devil-may-care 13 irresponsible

reckon 3 sum 5 count, gauge, guess, judge, opine, tally, total 6 cipher, figure, number, regard 7 account, compute, suppose, surmise 8 consider, estimate 9 calculate, enumerate 10 conjecture 11 approximate

reckoning 3 tab 4 bill 5 tally, score 7 account, invoice 9 statement 10 arithmetic, estimation 11 calculation, computation

reclaim 4 save, tame 6 redeem, reform, rescue 7 deliver, recover, restore 9 restitute 11 recondition, reconstruct 12 rehabilitate

recline 3 lie 4 rest, tilt 5 couch, slant, slope 6 lounge, repose 7 lie down 10 stretch out

reclining 4 flat 5 prone 6 supine 9 decumbent, prostrate, recumbent

recluse 5 loner 6 hermit, shut-in 7 eremite 8 cenobite, solitary 9 anchorite **female:** 7 ancress 9 anchoress

reclusive 8 eremitic, hermetic, reserved, solitary 9 withdrawn 10 antisocial, eremitical, unsociable 12 misanthropic

recognition 6 credit, esteem, notice 9 attention, awareness, gratitude 10 cognizance, perception 11 realization 12 appreciation

recognize 4 note, spot 5 admit 6 notice 7 observe, realize 8 accredit, diagnose, identify 9 apprehend 10 appreciate 11 acknowledge, determinate, distinguish

recoil 4 balk, kick 5 cower, dodge, quail, start, wince 6 blench, cringe, flinch, shrink 7 rebound, retract, squinch 8 reaction

recollect 5 evoke 6 recall, remind, revive 7 bethink 8 remember 9 reminisce

recollection 6 memory, recall 9 anamnesis, flashback 11 remembrance 12 reminiscence

recommence 5 renew 6 pick up, reopen, resume, take up 7 restart 8 continue

recommend 4 tout 6 advise, praise, prefer 7 acclaim, commend, counsel, endorse, entrust, propose, suggest 8 advocate

recommendation 4 plug 5 pitch 6 advice 7 counsel 11 endorsement, testimonial

recompense 3 pay 4 wage 5 repay 6 amends, reward 7 guerdon, premium, redress, requite 8 gratuity, requital 9 indemnify, indemnity, quittance, reimburse, repayment 10 compensate, remunerate, reparation 11 reciprocate, restitution, retribution 12 compensation, remuneration **13** consideration, gratification

reconcile 4 suit, tune **5** adapt **6** accept, accord, adjust, attune, make up, resign, settle, square, submit, tailor **7** conform, get over, resolve **9** harmonize, integrate **10** conciliate, coordinate **11** accommodate

recondite 4 deep **6** arcane, hidden, mystic, occult, orphic, secret **7** cryptic, erudite, learned, obscure **8** abstruse, academic, esoteric, hermetic, profound **9** concealed, difficult, enigmatic, scholarly

recondition 3 fix **4** mend **6** doctor, repair, revamp **7** rebuild, restore **8** make over, overhaul, retrofit **9** restitute **10** rejuvenate **12** rehabilitate

reconnoiter 5 scout **6** survey

reconsider 6 review, revise **7** rethink, reweigh **8** reassess **9** reexamine **10** reevaluate **13** think better of

reconstruct 6 recast, re-form, remake, revamp **7** rebuild, reclaim, remodel, restore **8** make over, overhaul, readjust, renovate **9** refashion, restitute **10** reassemble, reorganize

record 4 disc, disk, tape **5** album **6** annals, enroll **7** archive, journal, platter **8** archives, document, register **9** chronicle **10** transcript *of a meeting:* **7** minutes *of proceedings:* **4** acta *ship's:* **3** log **7** logbook

recorder 4 TiVo **5** flute **9** registrar *flight:* **8** black box

record player 4 hi-fi **5** phono **8** Victrola **9** turntable **10** gramophone, phonograph

recount 4 tell **5** state **6** recite, relate, report, retail **7** narrate **8** describe, rehearse **9** enumerate

recoup 6 regain **7** get back, reclaim, recover **8** retrieve **9** repossess

recourse 6 backup, refuge, resort **7** standby, stopgap, support **8** resource **9** expedient, makeshift

recover 4 heal, mend **5** evict, rally, renew **6** recoup, redeem, regain, revive **7** get back, get over, improve, rebound, reclaim, recycle, restore **8** retrieve, snap back **9** come round, reacquire, recapture, re-collect, repossess, restitute **10** bounce back, convalesce, recuperate

recreant 3 rat **5** false **6** coward, craven, untrue **7** chicken, dastard, unloyal **8** apostate, cowardly, defector, deserter, disloyal, poltroon, renegade, turncoat **9** dastardly, faithless, turnabout **10** perfidious, traitorous, unfaithful **13** pusillanimous

recreate 4 play **5** evoke, renew **7** freshen, refresh, restore **11** reconstruct

recreation 4 play **5** hobby, sport **7** leisure, pastime **8** activity **9** avocation, diversion **10** relaxation **13** entertainment

recrudesce 5 recur **6** return, revert, revive **7** reoccur **8** break out

recruit 4 boot, hire **5** raise **6** engage, enlist, enroll, muster, novice, rookie **7** draftee **8** beginner, enlistee, freshman, headhunt, neophyte, newcomer **9** conscript, fledgling, reinforce, replenish **10** apprentice, tenderfoot

rectifier 4 tube **5** diode **8** detector, ignitron

rectify 3 fix **4** mend **5** amend, emend **6** adjust, remedy, repair **7** correct

rectitude 6 virtue **7** honesty, probity **8** morality **9** rightness **11** uprightness **13** righteousness

rector 6 parson, pastor, priest **9** clergyman **10** headmaster

rectory 5 manse **8** benefice **9** parsonage

recumbent 4 flat **5** prone **6** supine **7** leaning, resting **8** reposing **9** lying down, prostrate, reclining

recuperate 4 heal, mend **5** rally **6** regain, revive **7** rebound, recover **8** snap back **10** convalesce

recur 5 cycle, haunt **6** repeat, resort, return **7** iterate, revolve **8** turn back

recurring 7 chronic **8** periodic **10** continuous, isochronal, periodical, persistent **11** isochronous **12** intermittent

red 4 puce, ruby **5** coral, gules, rouge, ruddy **6** cerise, claret, florid, maroon **7** carmine, crimson, flushed, glowing, magenta, oxblood, scarlet, vermeil **8** burgundy, sanguine **9** vermilion *combining form:* **4** rhod **5** rhodo

Red 6 Bolshy, commie **7** Bolshie, comrade **9** Bolshevik, Communist

redact 4 edit **6** censor, revise

Red and the Black author 8 Stendhal

red ape 9 orangutan

red arsenic 7 realgar

red-backed sandpiper 6 dunlin

Red Badge of Courage, The *author:* **5** Crane (Stephen) *hero:* **7** Fleming (Henry)

red-bellied snipe 9 dowitcher

redbird 7 tanager **8** cardinal **13** summer tanager

red blood cell 11 erythrocyte

red-blooded 5 juicy, lusty, manly **6** hearty, robust, virile **8** vigorous **9** energetic

redbreast 4 knot **5** robin **7** sunfish

red-breasted snipe 9 dowitcher

Redburn author 8 Melville (Herman)

red carp 8 goldfish

red cobalt 9 erythrite

red copper ore 7 cuprite
Red Cross *founder:* 6 Barton (Clara), Dunant (Henri) *Knight:* 6 George
redden 5 blush, color, flush, rouge 6 mantle, ruddle 11 incarnadine
red dog 5 blitz
redecorate 4 redo 5 fix up 9 refurbish
redeem 4 free, save 5 atone, loose, renew 6 offset, pay off, ransom, reform, rescue 7 expiate, reclaim, recover, restore 9 exonerate
redeemer 5 Jesus 6 Christ, savior 7 messiah, saviour
redemption 6 ransom 7 release 9 atonement, expiation, salvation 11 deliverance
red-eye 5 hooch 6 flight, rotgut 7 whiskey 8 home brew, rock bass 9 moonshine
red-faced 5 ruddy 6 florid, shamed 7 abashed, flushed, glowing 8 blushing, rubicund, sanguine, sheepish 9 mortified 11 embarrassed
red felt hat 3 fez
redfish 4 bass, drum 5 perch 6 salmon 10 ocean perch 11 channel bass
red hickory 6 pignut
red-hot 5 fiery 6 ardent, fervid 7 blazing, boiling, burning, fervent, flaming, glowing 8 brand-new, scalding, sizzling 9 scorching 10 blistering, passionate, sweltering 11 impassioned
red Indian paint 9 bloodroot 11 sanguinaria
red ink 7 arrears, deficit 8 shortage
red inkberry 8 pokeweed
red ironbark 8 eucalypt 10 eucalyptus
red iron ore 5 ocher, ochre 8 hematite
red lauan 8 mahogany
red-legged crow 6 chough
red-legged sandpiper 9 turnstone
red-letter 7 notable 8 historic 9 important, memorable 10 noteworthy, observable, remarkable 11 significant
red-light district 5 stews 10 tenderloin
red mite 7 chigger
redneck 4 clod, hick, rube 5 Bubba, yahoo, yokel 6 rustic 7 bumpkin, hayseed 9 hillbilly 10 clodhopper, good old boy, good ole boy
redo 5 renew 6 repeat, revamp 7 remodel, restyle 8 make over, overhaul, refinish, renovate 9 refurbish 10 redecorate
red ocher 8 hematite
redolence 4 balm, odor 5 aroma, attar, scent, spice 7 bouquet, incense, perfume 9 fragrance
redolent 5 balmy, spicy, sweet 7 odorous, scented 8 aromatic, fragrant, perfumed 9 ambrosial, evocative 10 suggestive 11 reminiscent

redouble 4 dupe 7 dualize, enhance, magnify 8 heighten 9 duplicate, intensify, reinforce 10 strengthen
redoubt 4 fort 7 bastion, citadel 8 fastness, fortress 10 stronghold
redoubtable 5 famed, great 6 famous, mighty 7 awesome, eminent 8 imposing, puissant, renowned 9 prominent 10 celebrated, formidable, impressive 11 illustrious 12 intimidating, overwhelming 13 distinguished
redound 6 accrue, recoil 7 conduce, reflect 10 contribute
red pigment 4 lake 5 eosin, ocher, ochre 6 ruddle
Red Planet 4 Mars
redpoll 5 finch 6 linnet
redraft 6 revamp, revise, rework 7 restyle, rewrite 8 make over, overhaul, rescript, revision, work over 9 recension
redress 4 heal 6 amends, avenge, negate, offset, relief, remedy 7 correct 8 reprisal, requital 9 cancel out, indemnity, quittance, vindicate 10 compensate, counteract, correction, neutralize, recompense, reparation 11 restitution, retribution 12 compensation
red roe 5 coral 6 caviar
redroot 7 alkanet, pigweed 9 bloodroot 12 New Jersey tea
red sable 8 kolinsky
red silver ore 9 proustite
red squirrel 9 chickaree
reduce 2 ax 3 axe, cut 4 cull, diet, melt, pare 5 abate, force, lower, shade, shave, slash, smelt 6 humble, lessen, recede, weaken 7 abridge, curtail, cut back, cut down, dwindle, liquefy, squeeze 8 boil down, compress, contract, decrease, diminish, discount, mark down, minimize, simplify, taper off 10 depreciate, slenderize 11 consolidate
reductio ad ____ 8 absurdum
reduction 6 digest, précis, rebate 7 cutback, cutdown, epitome, summary 8 abstract, discount, markdown, synopsis 9 abatement 10 shortening 11 curtailment 12 condensation
redundancy 6 excess 7 nimiety, surfeit 8 pleonasm 9 abundance, profusion, prolixity, tautology 10 repetition 11 periphrasis, reiteration, superfluity 13 supernumerary
redundant 5 extra, spare, windy, wordy 6 de trop, prolix 7 surplus, verbose 9 duplicate, excessive, iterative 11 duplicative, reiterative, repetitious, superfluous, tautologous 13 supernumerary
redux 7 revived 8 restored
redwing 6 thrush 9 blackbird
redwood 7 amboyna, sequoia 8 mahogany

reed 4 di mo, pipe 5 arrow, grass

reed instrument 3 sax 4 dizi, oboe 5 shawm 6 curtal 7 bagpipe, bassoon, dulcian 8 bagpipes, clarinet, crumhorn, melodeon 9 accordion, harmonica, krummhorn, saxophone 10 concertina 11 English horn

reedy 4 thin 6 skinny, stalky, twiggy 7 spindly

reef 3 bar, cay, key 4 lode, vein 5 atoll, ledge 6 reduce, skerry 7 sandbar

reek 4 funk 5 fetor, smell, stink 6 stench 9 effluvium

reeking 4 rank 5 fetid, funky, fusty 6 putrid, rancid, smelly, stinky 7 noisome, stenchy 10 malodorous

reel 4 spin, sway, turn 5 lurch, spool, weave, whirl 6 bobbin, careen, teeter, totter, waggle, wobble 7 stagger, stumble 8 fall back

reestablish 5 renew 6 revive 7 restore 9 reinstate 10 reinscribe 11 reintroduce

reevaluate 6 review 7 rethink, reweigh 8 reassess 9 reexamine 10 reconsider

reeve 4 ruff 6 thread 9 sandpiper 10 magistrate

reexamine see **reevaluate**

refashion 5 alter 6 change, modify, recast, remake, revamp 7 remodel 8 make over, overhaul 9 transmute

refection 4 feed, meal 6 repast 11 nourishment, refreshment

refectory 7 commons 10 dining hall

refer 6 advert, allude, assign, relate, submit 7 ascribe 9 attribute

referee 3 ump 5 judge 6 umpire 7 adjudge, arbiter, mediate 8 mediator 9 arbitrate, officiate 10 adjudicate, arbitrator

reference 6 credit, source 7 meaning, mention 8 allusion, citation, innuendo, relation, resource 11 testimonial *guide:* 5 index 12 bibliography *work:* 5 atlas, bible, guide 6 manual 7 almanac 8 handbook 9 directory, guidebook, thesaurus 10 dictionary 11 enchiridion 12 encyclopedia

referendum 4 poll, vote 10 plebiscite

refine 5 prune, smelt 6 polish, purify, smooth 7 elevate, improve, perfect, process 8 civilize 9 cultivate

refined 4 pure 6 subtle, urbane 7 elegant, genteel, raffiné 8 cultured, elevated, ladylike, raffinée, well-bred 9 civilized 10 cultivated, fastidious 13 sophisticated

refinement 5 couth, grace, taste 6 finish, polish 7 culture, finesse, suavity 8 breeding, civility, courtesy, elegance, subtlety, urbanity 9 politesse 10 politeness 11 cultivation 12 civilization, distillation, purification 13 clarification

reflect 4 echo, pore, show 5 weigh 6 bounce, mirror, ponder, reason, return 7 redound 8 chew over, cogitate, consider, ruminate 9 cerebrate 10 deliberate, retrospect 11 contemplate, demonstrate

reflection 4 slur 5 image 6 musing 7 replica, thought 8 reproach 9 aspersion 10 cogitation, meditation, rumination, simulacrum 11 cerebration 12 deliberation, reproduction 13 animadversion, consideration, contemplation

reflective 7 pensive 9 reflexive 10 cogitative, indicative, meditative, ruminative, thoughtful 12 deliberative 13 contemplative

reflux 3 ebb 4 GERD 8 backflow

reform 5 amend, emend 6 redeem, revise 7 correct, improve, reclaim, shape up 8 make over 10 correction, houseclean, regenerate

Reformation leader 4 Knox (John) 6 Calvin (John), Luther (Martin) 7 Zwingli (Huldrych)

reformatory 3 pen 6 prison 7 borstal 8 big house, remedial 10 corrective 12 penitentiary

refractory 6 mulish, unruly 7 froward, restive 8 contrary, perverse, stubborn 9 obstinate 10 bullheaded, headstrong, rebellious, unyielding 11 intractable, stiff-necked 12 unmanageable

refrain 4 fa-la, keep, la-la, stop 5 eieio, tra-la 6 burden, chorus, fa-la-la, shrink 7 abstain, forbear, tra-la-la 8 hold back

refresh 5 renew 6 revive 7 animate, enliven, quicken, restore 8 irrigate, recreate, renovate 9 replenish, stimulate 10 rejuvenate

refresher 5 drink, tonic 6 bracer 8 reminder 9 stimulant 11 restorative

refreshing 5 brisk, tonic 7 bracing 8 reviving 9 analeptic, animating 10 delightful, energizing 11 restorative, stimulating 12 invigorating, rejuvenating

refrigerant 3 ice 5 freon 7 coolant, cryogen 12 fluorocarbon 13 sulfur dioxide

refrigerator 6 cooler, fridge, icebox, walk-in 9 condenser 10 Frigidaire

refuge 3 den 4 lair, port 5 cover, haven 6 asylum, covert, harbor, resort 7 hideout, protect, retreat, shelter 8 hideaway, recourse, resource 9 expedient, harborage, sanctuary, safe house

refugee 2 DP 5 exile 6 émigré 7 evacuee 8 emigrant, fugitive 10 boat person, expatriate

refulgent 6 bright 7 glowing, radiant 8 luminous 9 brilliant

refund 5 repay 6 rebate 8 give back 9 reimburse, repayment, restitute 11 restitution

refurbish 4 redo 5 fix up, renew 6 revamp 7

restore 8 make over, overhaul, renovate, retrofit 10 redecorate, rejuvenate 11 recondition

refusal 4 veto 6 denial 7 regrets 8 negative, negation 9 disavowal 10 abnegation, thumbs-down 11 declination, repudiation

refuse 3 jib, nix 4 chum, deny, junk, scum 5 dreck, dross, offal, spurn, swill, trash, waste 6 debris, litter, reject, scraps, spilth 7 decline, garbage, residue, rubbish 8 disallow, leavings, remnants, turn down, withhold 9 reprobate, repudiate, sweepings 10 disapprove

refutation 8 disproof, elenchus, rebuttal

refute 4 deny 5 rebut 7 confute 8 confound, disprove 10 controvert, disconfirm

regain 6 recoup 7 get back, recover 8 reoccupy, retrieve 9 recapture, repossess *possession:* 7 replevy 8 replevin

regal 5 grand 6 august, kingly, purple 7 queenly, stately, sublime 8 glorious, imperial, imposing, kinglike, majestic, princely, splendid 9 monarchal, sovereign 10 monarchial 11 magnificent, monarchical, resplendent

regale 4 feed 5 amuse, feast 6 dinner, divert, spread 7 banquet 9 entertain

regalia 5 array 6 finery 8 frippery, insignia 9 caparison, full dress, trappings 10 decoration 11 habiliments

Regan *father:* 4 Lear *husband:* 8 Cornwall *sister:* 7 Goneril 8 Cordelia

regard 4 deem, heed, mark, note, rate, view 5 assay, favor, honor, judge, value 6 admire, assess, esteem, homage, liking, look at, notice, reckon, repute 7 account, concern, respect 8 approval, consider, devotion, estimate, fondness 9 attention 10 admiration, cognizance, estimation, observance, solicitude 11 approbation, contemplate, observation 12 appreciation, satisfaction 13 consideration

regardful 7 heedful 8 watchful 9 advertent, attentive, observant 10 perceptive, respectful

regarding 4 as to, in re 5 about, anent, as for 7 apropos 8 touching 9 apropos of 10 as respects, concerning, relative to, respecting 11 in respect to 13 with respect to

regatta 4 race *site:* 6 Henley 10 Argenteuil

regenerate 5 renew 6 reform, revive 7 rebirth, restore 8 recreate 9 reproduce

regent 5 ruler 6 warden 8 governor 9 protector

regicide's victim 4 king 7 monarch

regime 4 rule, term 5 reign 6 empire, tenure 7 dynasty 10 government, leadership

regimen 4 diet, plan, rule 6 course 10 government

region 4 area, belt, part, zone 5 field, tract 6 domain, locale, sector, sphere 7 demesne, terrain 8 locality, province, vicinity 9 bailiwick, territory 12 neighborhood

regional 5 local 9 localized, sectional 10 provincial 11 territorial

register 4 file, list, note, roll, till 5 enter, range, tally 6 annals, docket, enroll, ledger, record, roster 7 catalog, check in, express 8 indicate 9 catalogue

regnant 4 rife 6 ruling 7 current, popular 8 dominant, reigning 9 paramount, prevalent, sovereign 10 prevailing, widespread

regress 6 revert 9 backslide 10 retrograde

regret 3 rue, woe 4 care 5 grief, mourn 6 bemoan, bewail, excuse, grieve, lament, repent, sorrow 7 anguish, apology, deplore, remorse 9 heartache, penitence 10 contrition, heartbreak 11 compunction

regretful 5 sorry 6 rueful 8 contrite, mournful, penitent 9 repentant, sorrowful 10 apologetic, remorseful 11 penitential

regrettable 3 sad 6 too bad, woeful 8 grievous 10 lamentable 11 distressing, unfortunate 13 heartbreaking

regular 3 due, set 4 even 5 fixed, usual 6 common, normal, steady 7 average, equable, general, natural, orderly, typical, uniform 8 complete, constant, everyday, methodic, ordinary, standard 9 clocklike, customary, prevalent 10 methodical, systematic 11 commonplace 12 run-of-the-mill

regulate 5 order, scale 6 adjust, direct, govern, police, square, temper 7 arrange, control 8 organize 9 methodize, systemize 11 systematize

regulation 3 law 4 rule 5 canon, edict, order 6 decree 7 precept, statute 9 ordinance, prescript 11 restriction 12 codification

regulator 8 governor

rehabilitate 4 cure, heal 7 reclaim, recover, restore 8 renovate 9 reeducate, restitute 11 recondition

rehash 5 reuse 6 repeat, review, rework 7 restate, version 8 chew over, rehearse, talk over 9 rendering, rendition, rewording 11 restatement 12 recapitulate

rehearsal 5 trial 6 dry run, tryout 7 recital 8 dummy run, practice 10 run-through, simulation 11 reiteration 12 woodshedding

rehearse 5 drill, train 6 repeat 7 run over 8 exercise, practice 10 run through

Rehoboam *father:* 7 Solomon *kingdom:* 5 Judah 6 Israel *mother:* 6 Naamah

reign 4 rule, sway 6 govern 7 prevail 8 dominate, dominion 11 predominate, sovereignty

reimburse 3 pay 5 repay 6 recoup, refund 7

pay back, requite **9** indemnify **10** compensate, remunerate

rein 4 curb, stem **5** check **6** bridle **7** compose, control, repress **8** hold back, restrain, suppress

reinforce 4 prop **5** brace **7** augment, bolster, enlarge, fortify, recruit, sustain **8** buttress, increase, redouble **10** invigorate, strengthen

reinstate 6 recall **7** restore **11** reestablish, reintroduce **12** rehabilitate

reintroduce 6 recall, revive **7** restore **9** reinstate **11** reestablish

reinvestment 4 DRIP **8** plowback

reiterate 5 renew, resay **6** repeat, resume, retell **7** reprise

reject 3 nix **4** jilt, junk, shed **5** debar, scorn, scrap, spurn **6** abjure, pariah, pass up, rebuff, refuse **7** cashier, castoff, decline, discard, dismiss, exclude, outcast, repulse, shut out **8** castaway, jettison, throw out, turn away, turn down **9** eliminate, repudiate, shoot down, throw away **10** disapprove

rejoice 5 cheer, exult, glory **7** delight, gladden **8** jubilate

rejoinder 5 reply **6** answer, retort **8** comeback, rebuttal, repartee, response

rejuvenate 5 green, renew **7** refresh **8** renovate **9** modernize **10** revitalize

rekindle 5 renew **6** revive **7** restart **8** reawaken, reignite, revivify **10** reactivate, revitalize

relate 4 link, tell **5** apply, refer **6** assign, detail, recite, report **7** connect, express, narrate, pertain, recount **8** describe, disclose, interact, rehearse **9** appertain, chronicle

related 4 akin **5** alike, enate **6** agnate, allied **7** cognate, connate, germane, kindred **8** incident **9** analogous, connected, identical, pertinent **10** associated, connatural, homologous **11** consanguine

relation 3 kin **6** agnate **7** hinship, kinsman **8** affinity **9** kinswoman, reference **11** propinquity

relationship 3 tie **4** bond, link **5** ratio, tie-in, union **6** affair **7** analogy, contact, liaison **8** affinity, alliance **10** connection **11** affiliation, association **13** confederation, consanguinity

relative 2 ma, pa **3** mom, pop, sib, sis, son **4** aunt, mama, papa **5** blood, madre, mamma, momma, niece, pappy, pater, poppa, uncle **6** agnate, cousin, father, mother, nephew, parent, sister **7** apropos, brother, cognate, germane, kinsman, sibling **8** ancestor, daughter, grandson, relation, relevant **9** ascendant, dependent, kinswoman, pertinent **10** applicable, collateral, descendant, grand-

child **11** comparative, conditional, grandfather, grandmother, grandparent **13** granddaughter

relatives 3 kin **4** kith **5** folks **7** kindred, kinfolk **8** kinfolks **9** relations

relax 4 bask, ease, laze, loaf, loll, rest **5** chill, let go, loose, remit **6** loosen, lounge, modify, unbend, unkink, unwind **7** slacken **8** chill out, kick back, loosen up, unbuckle, wind down **9** untighten **10** decompress

relaxation 3 fun **4** ease, rest **5** hobby **6** repose **7** leisure, pastime **9** amusement, diversion, enjoyment **10** recreation

relaxed 5 loose, slack **6** casual, dégagé, mellow **8** informal **9** easygoing **11** low-pressure

release 4 emit, free, vent **5** issue, let go, loose, untie, yield **6** acquit, let out, loosen, pardon, ransom, unbind, uncage **7** give off, give out, manumit, set free, unchain, unleash **8** liberate, unfetter **9** acquittal, discharge, exculpate, exonerate, surrender **10** emancipate **11** manumission **12** emancipation *conditional:* **6** parole

relegate 5 exile, expel **6** assign, banish, charge, commit, demote, resign **7** commend, confide, consign, entrust **8** delegate, hand over, transfer, turn over

relent 3 ebb **4** cave, ease, wane **5** abate, let up, yield **6** give in, submit **7** die away, die down, ease off, slacken, subside **8** moderate **9** acquiesce **10** capitulate

relentless 5 cruel, rigid, stern **6** dogged **7** adamant, nonstop **8** constant, obdurate, rigorous, unabated **9** ferocious, incessant, stringent **10** implacable, inexorable, inflexible, unyielding **11** remorseless, unfaltering

relevant 3 apt, fit **5** ad rem **6** cogent **7** apropos, germane **8** apposite, material, relative **9** pertinent **10** admissible, applicable **11** applicative, appropriate **12** proportional

reliable 4 safe, sure **5** solid, sound, tried, valid **6** proven, secure, trusty **7** bedrock, certain **8** constant, verified **9** foolproof, validated **10** dependable **11** trustworthy **12** tried-and-true

reliance 4 hope **5** faith, stock, trust **10** dependence

relic 5 token **6** corpse **7** antique, memento, remains, remnant, vestige **8** artifact, fragment, keepsake, memorial, reminder, souvenir **11** remembrance

relict 5 widow **8** survivor

relief 3 aid **4** ease, fret, hand, help, lift **5** break, cameo **6** assist, raised, remedy, succor **7** comfort, redress, respite, support, welfare **8** breather, fretwork, repoussé **9** abatement, diversion **10** assistance, mitigation **11** alleviation, deliverance *pitcher:* **6** closer **7** fireman, stopper

relieve 3 rid **4** calm, ease, free, help, quit, vent **5** allay, relax, spell **6** assist, exempt, lessen, loosen, reduce, remedy, soften, solace, soothe, succor, supply **7** absolve, assuage, comfort, deprive, lighten, mollify, release **8** diminish, dispense, mitigate, moderate, palliate, unburden **9** alleviate

religion 4 cult, Jain, sect, Sikh **5** Baha'i, cause, creed, dogma, faith, Hindu, Islam **6** belief, church, Jewish, Mormon, Muslim, Shinto **7** Friends, Jainism, Judaism, Quakers, Sikhism **8** Buddhism, Buddhist, devotion, doctrine, Hinduism **9** Christian, Mormonism, Shintoism **11** Zoroastrian **12** Christianity

religious 3 nun **4** holy, monk **5** friar, godly, pious **6** devout, priest, sacred, votary **7** staunch, upright **8** cenobite, faithful, monastic, priestly, reverent **9** pietistic, prayerful, spiritual, steadfast **10** scriptural, scrupulous, worshipful

relinquish 4 cede, quit, shed **5** forgo, leave, waive, yield **6** desert, give up, resign **7** abandon, discard, lay down, release **8** abdicate, hand over, renounce **9** quitclaim, sacrifice, surrender

relish 4 like, tang, zest **5** enjoy, fancy, flair, gusto, savor, taste **6** flavor, liking, palate **7** chutney, delight **8** chowchow, fondness, penchant, pleasure, sapidity **9** appetizer, condiment, enjoyment **10** appreciate, piccalilli **11** delectation, hors d'oeuvre

relucent 6 bright **7** glaring, radiant, shining **10** reflecting

reluctant 3 shy **4** wary **5** chary, loath **6** afraid, averse **8** cautious, grudging, hesitant **9** unwilling **10** indisposed **11** disinclined *prophet:* **5** Jonah

rely 3 bet **4** bank, plan **5** count **6** depend, gamble, reckon

rely on 5 trust **6** expect **10** anticipate

remain 4 bide, last, live, stay, wait **5** abide, stand, tarry **6** endure, linger, loiter **7** persist, survive **8** continue **10** hang around **11** stick around

remainder 4 rest **5** dregs, trace **6** excess **7** balance, residue, remnant, surplus, vestige **8** leavings, leftover, residual, residuum

remains 4 body **5** ashes, bones, ruins **6** corpse, debris, relics **7** balance, cadaver, -carcass, flotsam **8** leavings, remnants **9** reliquiae

remand 8 send back

remark 4 gibe, note **5** aside, crack **7** comment, mention **9** utterance, wisecrack, witticism **10** annotation **11** observation **12** obiter dictum

remarkable 4 rare **5** great **6** signal, unique **7** salient, strange, unusual **8** singular, striking, uncommon **9** arresting, bodacious, momentous, prominent **10** impressive, noteworthy, noticeable **11** conspicuous, exceptional, outstanding, significant **13** extraordinary

remarkably 4 unco

remedial 8 curative, salutary, sanative **9** medicinal **10** corrective **11** restorative, therapeutic **12** recuperative

remedy 3 fix **4** cure, drug, heal **5** salve, solve **6** elixir, relief, repair **7** correct, cure-all, nostrum, panacea, rectify, redress, relieve **8** antidote, medicine, specific **9** alleviate, treatment **10** corrective, medicament, medication

remember 5 educe, evoke **6** recall, record, relive, retain, reward **7** bethink **9** flash back, recollect, reminisce **10** bear in mind **11** commemorate, memorialize

remembrance 4 gift **5** favor, relic, token **6** déjà vu, memory, recall, trophy **7** memento, present, thought **8** keepsake, memorial, reminder, souvenir **9** anamnesis, flashback **12** recollection, reminiscence

remind 6 advise, prompt **7** bethink **8** admonish

reminder 4 hint, memo **5** relic, token **6** prompt, trophy **7** memento **8** keepsake, memorial, monument, souvenir **9** refresher **10** admonition, memorandum **11** remembrance

reminisce see **remember**

reminiscence 6 memory, recall **8** anecdote **9** anamnesis, flashback **11** remembrance **12** recollection

remise 4 cede, deed **5** alien, grant **6** assign, convey **8** make over, transfer **9** quitclaim

remiss 3 lax **4** lazy **5** slack **8** careless, derelict, heedless, indolent, slothful **9** negligent **10** delinquent, neglectful, slatternly **11** inattentive

remit 4 send, ship, stay, stop **5** abate, defer, delay, relax **6** desist, hold up, pardon, put off, remand, shelve **7** condone, consign, forgive, forward, hold off **8** dispatch, moderate, postpone

remnant 3 end **4** heel, husk, part, rest, rump **5** relic, trace, wrack **6** fag end, relict **7** balance, oddment, residue **8** leavings, leftover, residuum **9** remainder

remodel 4 redo **6** recast, revamp **8** make over, overhaul, redesign **9** refashion **11** reconstruct

remonstrance 5 demur 7 protest 8 demurral, demurrer, scolding 9 challenge, objection

remonstrate 5 argue, demur, plead, scold 6 combat, object, oppose, reason 7 protest 9 challenge

remora 4 clog, drag 6 sucker 9 hindrance 10 impediment 11 encumbrance, shark sucker

remorse 3 rue 4 ruth 5 guilt, smart 6 regret, sorrow 9 penitence 10 contrition, repentance 11 compunction 12 self-reproach

remorseful see **regretful**

remote 3 far, off 4 slim 5 aloof 6 far-off, slight 7 distant, faraway, obscure, outside, slender 8 detached, far-flung, frontier, isolated, lonesome, off-lying, outlying, secluded 9 backwoods, withdrawn 10 negligible 11 godforsaken, out-of-the-way *combining form:* 3 tel 4 tele

remotest 6 utmost 7 extreme, outmost 8 farthest 9 outermost, uttermost 11 furthermost

remove 4 doff, skim 5 purge 6 delete, unseat 7 extract, take off, take out 8 dislodge, evacuate, take away, withdraw 9 clear away, eliminate *from office:* 6 depose *hair:* 8 depilate *surgically:* 6 resect

removed 5 aloof, apart 6 far-off, remote 7 devious, distant, faraway, obscure 8 detached, far-flung, isolated, outlying, separate 10 distracted 11 unconnected

remunerate 3 pay 5 repay 7 requite 9 indemnify, reimburse 10 compensate, recompense

remunerative 6 paying 7 gainful, payable 9 lucrative 10 productive, profitable 11 moneymaking

Remus *brother:* 7 Romulus *father:* 4 Mars *mother:* 9 Rea Silvia 10 Rhea Silvia *slayer:* 7 Romulus

renaissance see **rebirth**

renal 7 nephric 9 nephritic

rend 3 rip 4 rive, tear 5 split 6 cleave, divide

render 3 pay 4 cede, limn 5 yield 6 depict, give up, impart, return, submit 7 deliver, execute, pay back, picture, portray, present, proffer, provide, restore 8 carry out, describe, hand over, turn over 9 delineate, interpret, represent, translate, transpose 10 administer, relinquish 12 administrate

rendering 4 copy 7 version 9 depiction 10 paraphrase 11 description, performance, restatement, translation 12 reproduction

rendezvous 4 date 5 haunt, tryst 6 gather, muster 7 collect, hangout, meeting 8 assemble 10 congregate, engagement 11 appointment, assignation, get-together

rendition 7 reading, version 10 adaptation 11 performance, translation

renegade 3 rat 5 rebel 6 outlaw 7 heretic 8 apostate, defector, deserter, maverick, recreant, turncoat 9 turnabout 10 schismatic

renege 4 deny 5 welch, welsh 6 cry off, recall, recant, revoke 7 back off, back out, retract 8 renounce, withdraw 9 backpedal

renew 6 redeem, reform, revamp, revive 7 freshen, refresh, remodel 8 make over, overhaul, recharge, recreate, rekindle, renovate, revivify 9 refurbish, resurrect 10 reactivate, recommence, regenerate, rejuvenate, revitalize

rennet 8 abomasum

renounce 4 deny, quit 5 demit 6 abjure, defect, desert, give up, recant, renege, resign 7 abandon, decline, forsake, put away, retract 8 abdicate, abnegate, disclaim, forswear, swear off 9 repudiate, sacrifice 10 apostatize

renovate 4 redo 5 renew 6 remake, repair, revamp, revive 7 furbish, refresh, restore 8 overhaul, revivify 9 modernize, refurbish, resurrect 10 rejuvenate, revitalize 12 rehabilitate

renown 4 fame 5 éclat, glory, kudos 6 repute 7 acclaim 8 eminence, prestige 9 celebrity, notoriety 10 prominence, reputation 11 distinction

renowned 5 famed, great, noted 6 fabled, famous 7 eminent, notable 8 extolled 9 acclaimed, legendary, notorious, prominent, well-known 10 celebrated 11 illustrious, outstanding 13 distinguished

rent 3 let, rip 4 hire, rift, tear, torn 5 lease, split 6 breach, sublet 7 charter, fissure, rupture 8 fracture

rental 4 hire 7 tenancy

renter 6 lessee, tenant 11 leaseholder

renunciation 6 denial 7 refusal 8 apostasy, eschewal, forgoing 9 disavowal, sacrifice, surrender 10 abdication, abnegation, disclaimer, self-denial 11 abandonment, forswearing, repudiation, resignation

reorder 5 shift 7 permute 9 rearrange, reshuffle

reorganization 7 shake-up 8 turnover

repair 3 fix 4 mend 5 patch 6 cobble, doctor 7 fitness, service 8 overhaul 9 condition 11 recondition

reparations 6 amends 7 redress 9 indemnity, quittance 10 recompense, settlement 11 restitution 12 satisfaction

repartee 4 quip 6 banter, retort 7 riposte 8 backchat, badinage, comeback 9 cross talk, rejoinder 10 persiflage

repast 3 eat 4 feed, meal 5 feast 9 refection

repay 6 offset, return, reward 7 requite 9 indemnify, reimburse **10** compensate, recompense, remunerate **11** get even with

repeal 4 lift, null, void **5** annul **6** recall, revoke **7** abandon, abolish, nullify, rescind, reverse **8** abrogate, renounce

repeat 4 copy, echo **5** recap, recur, rerun, resay **6** go over, parrot, reecho, recite, rehash, relate, retell **7** imitate, iterate, reprise, restate **9** duplicate, reiterate, replicate **11** reduplicate **12** recapitulate

repeater 7 firearm **10** recidivist

repeating 7 iterant **9** perennial, recurrent **11** reiterative, repetitious

repel 5 rebut **6** rebuff, reject, revolt, sicken **7** disgust, fend off, hold off, repulse, ward off **8** nauseate, stave off

repellent 4 foul, vile **5** nasty **7** noisome **8** aversive **9** abhorrent, loathsome, obnoxious, offensive, repulsive, revolting **10** forbidding, disgusting, off-putting **11** rebarbative

repent 3 rue **6** regret

repentance 3 rue **4** ruth **6** sorrow **7** remorse **10** contrition **11** compunction

repentant see **regretful**

repetition 4 copy, echo **5** rerun **7** recital, reprise **11** duplication

rephrase 6 recast, reword **7** restate

repine 4 beef, fuss, kick, long, moan, wail **5** gripe, yearn **6** grouse, hanker, murmur **7** grumble **8** complain

replace 7 put back, restore **8** exchange, supplant **9** supersede **10** substitute

replacement 3 sub **6** fill-in, loaner, makeup **7** stand-in **9** alternate, surrogate, temporary **10** substitute **11** locum tenens, pinch hitter, succedaneum

replenish 4 fill **5** renew, stock **6** refill **7** refresh, restock, restore

replete 4 full, rife **5** awash, lousy **6** packed **7** brimful, crammed, stuffed **8** brimming **9** chock-full **11** overflowing

replica 4 copy, dupe, fake **5** clone, ditto **6** carbon **9** duplicate, facsimile, imitation **10** carbon copy, simulacrum **12** reproduction

replicate 4 copy **5** clone **6** repeat **9** reproduce

reply 4 echo, RSVP **6** answer, rejoin, retort **7** respond **8** comeback, repartee, response **9** rejoinder

report 4 bang, boom, news, tell **5** crack, relay, rumor, study **6** record, relate, return, review, show up **7** account, article, check in, hearsay, narrate, recount, rundown **8** advisory, bulletin, describe, dispatch **9** broadcast, chronicle, narrative, statement **11** compte rendu

reporter 7 newsman **8** pressman **9** newshound, newswoman **10** journalist *inexperienced:* **3** cub

repose 3 lie **4** calm, rest **5** peace, poise, quiet, sleep **7** lie down, recline **8** quietude **9** composure, stillness **10** inactivity, quiescence, relaxation **11** restfulness, tranquility **12** tranquillity

repository 3 ark **5** depot, store **7** archive, arsenal **8** magazine, treasury **10** storehouse

repossess see **regain**

reprehend 3 rap **4** rate, skin **5** blame, chide, fault, knock, scold **6** berate, rebuke **7** censure, condemn, upbraid **8** admonish, denounce **9** criticize **10** denunciate

reprehensible 4 base, evil **6** guilty, sinful, unholy, wicked **8** blamable, criminal, culpable **10** censurable **11** blameworthy, disgraceful

represent 3 act **6** denote, depict, embody, mirror, recall, relate, render, sketch, typify **7** display, exhibit, express, hold out, imitate, make out, narrate, outline, picture, portray, present, protest, realize, signify, suggest **8** describe, stand for **9** delineate, epitomize, exemplify, interpret, personify, symbolize **10** constitute, illustrate, substitute **11** emblematize, impersonate

representation 5 draft, image **6** effigy, symbol **7** picture **8** likeness **9** portrayal, statement **10** caricature, delegation

representative 5 agent, envoy, model, proxy **6** deputy, sample **7** burgess, example, typical **8** delegate, emissary, sampling, specimen **9** exemplary, spokesman **10** ambassador, legislator, prototypal, substitute **11** congressman **12** illustrative, prototypical **13** congresswoman

repress 4 curb **5** check, sit on **6** bridle, muffle, stifle, subdue **7** smother, squelch, swallow **8** keep down, restrain, suppress

repression 4 curb **7** amnesia, control **8** stifling **9** clampdown, crackdown, restraint **10** constraint

reprieve 4 stay **5** grace **7** respite, suspend

reprimand 3 rap **4** rate, ream, task **5** chide, scold **6** rebuke **7** bawl out, censure, chew out, reproof, reprove **8** admonish, call down, reproach, scolding **9** reprimand, talking-to **10** admonition **12** admonishment, dressing-down **13** tongue-lashing

reprisal 7 redress, revenge **8** revanche **9** vengeance **11** counterblow, retaliation, retribution

reprise 5 recap **6** repeat **9** reiterate **10** recurrence, repetition

reproach 3 rap **4** rail **5** blame, chide, scold **6** berate, rebuke **7** bawl out, censure, chew out, remorse, reprove, upbraid **8** admonish, call down **9** reprimand **10** admonition, opprobrium **12** admonishment

reprobate 3 rap **4** skin **5** blame, scamp, spurn **6** refuse, reject, sinner **7** censure, condemn, lowlife, villain **8** denounce, scalawag **9** miscreant, scoundrel **10** blackguard, degenerate

reproduce 4 bear, copy, sire **5** beget, breed, spore **7** imitate **8** multiply **9** duplicate, procreate, propagate, replicate **10** regenerate **11** reduplicate

reproduction see **replica**

reproductive cell 3 egg **4** ovum **5** sperm, spore **6** gamete **12** spermatozoid, spermatozoon

reproof 3 rap **6** rebuke **7** censure, lecture **8** scolding **9** criticism, reprimand **10** admonition **11** castigation **12** admonishment, reprehension **13** remonstration

reprove 5 chide, scold **6** rebuke **7** censure, chasten **8** admonish, call down, lambaste, reproach **9** criticize, dress down, reprimand

reptile 4 croc **5** gator, skink, snake **6** caiman, cayman, gavial, iguana, lizard, turtle **7** tuatara **8** tortoise **9** alligator, crocodile, sphenodon *combining form:* **6** herpet **7** herpeto *extinct:* **8** dinosaur

republic 5 state **6** nation **9** democracy

Republican Party 3 GOP *symbol:* **8** elephant

Republic author 5 Plato

repudiate 4 deny **5** spurn **6** abjure, disown, recant, refuse, reject **7** decline, disavow, dismiss **8** disclaim, renounce **9** disaffirm **10** apostatize, disapprove

repugnance 6 horror **7** disgust **8** aversion, loathing **9** repulsion, revulsion **10** abhorrence, antagonism, odiousness **11** abomination, detestation

repugnant 4 foul, vile **5** nasty, yucky **6** creepy, horrid, skanky **7** noisome **8** aversive, gruesome **9** abhorrent, loathsome, obnoxious, offensive, repulsive, revolting **10** disgusting

repulse 5 rebut, repel, spurn **6** rebuff, reject, revolt, sicken **7** disgust, fend off, hold off, ward off **8** nauseate, stave off

repulsion see **repugnance**

repulsive see **repugnant**

reputable 7 eminent, upright **8** esteemed **9** estimable, honorable **10** creditable, legitimate, recognized, sanctioned **11** respectable, trustworthy **13** well-thought-of

reputation 4 fame, name, note **5** éclat, honor **6** esteem, renown, report **8** position, prestige, standing **9** celebrity, character, notoriety

reputed 6 honest **7** alleged **8** putative, supposed **9** estimable, purported **10** creditable, ostensible **11** respectable **12** hypothetical

request 3 ask, dun, sue **4** pray, seek, wish **5** plead, press **6** appeal, ask for, demand, invite **7** entreat, solicit **8** entreaty, petition **10** invitation

Requiem for a Nun author 8 Faulkner (William)

require 3 ask, beg **4** lack, need, want **5** claim, crave **6** demand, desire **7** call for, dictate, mandate, solicit **8** insist on **11** necessitate

required 3 due **5** vital **7** crucial **9** essential, mandatory, necessary, requisite **10** compulsory, obligatory **11** fundamental

requirement 4 must, need, want **5** claim **6** charge, demand **9** condition, essential, necessity, requisite **10** imperative, sine qua non **11** stipulation

requisite 3 due **4** must **5** vital **7** crucial, needful **8** cardinal **9** condition, essential, necessity **10** imperative, sine qua non **11** fundamental **12** precondition **13** indispensable

requisition 4 call **5** claim, exact **6** demand **7** solicit **11** application

requite 3 pay **5** repay **6** return **7** revenge, satisfy **9** indemnify, reimburse **10** compensate, recompense, remunerate **11** reciprocate

reredos 6 screen **9** partition

rescind 4 lift **5** annul **6** cancel, recall, repeal, revoke **7** retract, reverse **8** roll back, take back

rescue 4 free, save **6** ransom, redeem **7** bailout, deliver, reclaim, recover, release, salvage **8** liberate, preserve **9** extricate **11** deliverance

rescuer 6 savior **7** saviour

research 5 probe, study **7** inquest, inquiry **8** look into **9** delve into **10** experiment **11** examination, inquisition, investigate **13** investigation

resect 6 cut out, excise **8** amputate **9** extirpate

resemblance 7 analogy **8** likeness **9** alikeness **10** comparison, similarity, similitude **11** parallelism

resemble 5 favor **6** recall **8** look like, simulate **9** take after **11** approximate

resembling 3 à la **4** like **6** akin to

resentful 4 sore **6** bitter, piqued, sullen **7** envious

resentment 5 pique **6** animus, grudge, malice, rancor **7** dudgeon, offense, umbrage **9** animosity **11** indignation

reservation 5 doubt **7** booking, enclave, proviso **8** homeland, preserve **9** condition, misgiving, sanctuary **10** limitation

reserve 4 book, fund, hold, keep **5** hoard, put by, stash, stock, store, tract **6** retain, supply

7 nest egg, savings, standby **8** contract, distance, fallback, hold back, postpone, set aside, squirrel, withhold **9** inventory, restraint, reticence, stockpile **10** constraint, discretion, diffidence **13** qualification

reserved 4 cool **5** aloof, stiff **6** demure, formal, remote **7** distant **8** reticent, retiring, taciturn **9** diffident, reclusive, secretive, withdrawn **10** unsociable **11** tight-lipped **12** closemouthed **13** self-contained

reservoir 5 hoard, stock, store **6** supply **7** nest egg **9** inventory, stockpile

reside 3 lie **4** hive, live, stay **5** dwell, exist **6** inhere **7** consist

residence 4 home, stay **5** abode, house **7** address **8** domicile, dwelling **9** occupancy **10** habitation

resident 5 liver **6** inmate, lodger, native, tenant **7** citizen, denizen, dweller, present **8** inherent, occupant **10** inhabitant **11** householder

residential area 9 community **12** neighborhood

residual 7 balance, payment, remnant **8** leavings, leftover **9** remainder

residue 3 ash **4** heel, lees, marc, rest, silt, slag **5** ashes, dregs, grout **6** debris, excess, scraps **7** balance, grounds, remains, remnant, surplus **8** leavings, remnants, residuum **9** leftovers, remainder, scourings

resign 4 cede, quit **5** demit, leave, yield **6** give up, retire, submit **7** abandon, consign **8** abdicate, hand over, relegate, renounce, step down **9** reconcile, surrender **10** relinquish

resignation 8 meekness **9** demission, surrender **10** abdication, compliance, submission **12** acquiescence, renunciation

resigned 9 compliant **10** submissive **11** acquiescent, complaisant

resile 6 recede, recoil, spring **7** rebound, retract, retreat **8** draw back, snap back

resilient 6 bouncy, supple, whippy **7** buoyant, elastic, springy **8** flexible, stretchy **9** adaptable

resin 4 balm **5** copal, damar, roset **6** dammar **7** acrylic, copaiba *aromatic:* **6** balsam, mastic **8** sandarac *fragrant:* **5** elemi **6** storax, styrax **7** ladanum **8** labdanum *gum:* **5** myrrh **7** benzoin *medicinal:* **6** guaiac **8** guaiacum *of an insect:* **3** lac *synthetic:* **8** phenolic *used by bees:* **8** propolis

resist 4 buck, defy, kick **5** rebel **6** baffle, combat, oppose, revolt **7** contest, counter, gainsay **8** traverse **10** contradict, contravene

resistance 7 dissent **8** defiance, variance **10**

dissension, dissidence, opposition **11** contrariety, obstruction

resistance unit 3 ohm

resistor 8 rheostat, varistor **10** thermistor

resolute 3 set **4** bent, bold, fast, firm, true **6** intent, steady, sturdy **7** decided, staunch **8** constant, decisive, faithful, intrepid, stubborn **9** obstinate, steadfast, tenacious, undaunted **10** determined, persistent **12** pertinacious, single-minded

resolution 4 guts **5** heart, nerve, pluck, spunk **6** mettle, spirit **7** courage, outcome **8** decision, firmness, tenacity **10** conclusion **12** perseverance **13** determination, steadfastness

resolve 5 clear, crack **6** decide, settle **7** clear up, iron out, unravel, work out **8** boldness, conclude, decipher, firmness **9** breakdown, determine, intention, reconcile **10** unscramble **13** determination, steadfastness

resonant 4 deep, full, rich **6** silver **7** booming, echoing, orotund, vibrant **8** powerful, sonorous **11** reverberant

resonate 4 echo, peal, ring **7** resound, vibrate **11** reverberate

resort 3 spa **4** lido **5** haven, hotel, lodge, shift **6** harbor, refuge **7** retreat, riviera, stopgap **8** recourse **9** expedient, makeshift **10** substitute *last:* **8** pis aller

resound 4 boom, echo, peal, ring **11** reverberate

resounding 7 booming, echoing, orotund, vibrant **8** emphatic, sonorous **10** clangorous, resonating, thunderous **11** unequivocal

resource 3 aid **5** asset, means, shift **6** supply **7** standby

resourceful 5 adept **6** adroit, artful, clever, shrewd **7** capable, cunning **8** creative, skillful **9** ingenious, inventive **10** innovative **11** imaginative **12** enterprising

resources 5 funds, means, money, purse **6** assets, riches, wealth **7** capital, fortune, reserve **8** bankroll, finances, property, reserves **9** substance **11** wherewithal

respect 3 awe **5** favor, honor, props **6** admire, detail, devoir, esteem, homage, regard, revere **7** account, concern **8** venerate **9** deference **10** admiration, estimation, particular, veneration

respectable 4 fair **5** ample **6** decent, proper, worthy **8** adequate **9** admirable, estimable, honorable **10** sufficient **11** appropriate, presentable **12** satisfactory **13** well-thought-of

respectful 5 civil **6** polite **8** obeisant, reverent **9** courteous **11** deferential, reverential

respecting 3 per **4** as to, in re **5** about **7** apropos **9** as regards, regarding **10** as concerns, concerning, relating to **11** considering

respire 7 breathe

respite 4 lull, rest **5** break, delay, pause, spell, truce **6** hiatus, recess, relief **8** breather, reprieve, surcease **12** intermission

resplendent 5 regal **7** glowing, shining **8** glorious, gorgeous **9** brilliant, refulgent **11** magnificent

respond 5 react, reply **6** answer, rejoin, retort **8** come back

response 5 reply **6** answer, retort, return **7** riposte **8** antiphon, comeback, reaction **9** rejoinder *involuntary:* **6** reflex **7** tropism

responsibility 4 buck, duty, onus **5** blame, brief, fault **6** burden, charge, devoir **10** obligation **11** reliability

responsible 6 liable **8** amenable, reliable **10** answerable, chargeable, dependable **11** accountable, trustworthy

responsive 4 open **8** sentient **9** sensitive **11** susceptible, sympathetic

rest 3 nap, sit **4** calm, ease, laze, loaf, loll, lull, stay **5** let up, pause, peace, quiet, relax, spell **6** catnap, depend, excess, lounge, repose **7** balance, leisure, lie down, recline, remains, remnant, surplus **8** breather, leavings, vacation **9** interlude, predicate, remainder

restate 4 echo **6** reword **8** rephrase **9** translate **10** paraphrase **12** recapitulate

restatement 10 paraphrase **11** translation

restaurant 4 café **5** diner **6** eatery **7** beanery **9** brasserie, cafeteria **10** coffee shop **11** coffeehouse, greasy spoon *price:* **8** à la carte, prix fixe **10** table d'hôte *worker:* **4** chef, cook **6** busboy, server, waiter **7** maître d', waitron **8** waitress **10** dishwasher, headwaiter, waitperson **12** maître d'hôtel

restful 4 calm **5** quiet **6** placid **8** peaceful, tranquil

restitute 6 refund, return **7** reclaim, recover, restore **8** give back **11** recondition, reconstruct **12** rehabilitate

restitution 6 amends, refund, return **7** redress **8** reprisal **9** indemnity, quittance **10** recompense, reparation **11** restoration **12** remuneration, satisfaction

restive 4 edgy **5** balky, nervy, tense **6** ornery, uneasy **7** fidgety, froward, uptight, wayward **8** contrary, perverse, skittish

restiveness 7 anxiety, ferment, turmoil **8** disquiet **9** balkiness **10** inquietude, perversity **11** contrariety, disquietude, waywardness **12** contrariness

restless 5 antsy, itchy, jumpy **6** fitful, uneasy **7** anxious, fidgety, fretful, jittery, nervous,

unquiet **8** agitated, troubled **9** disturbed, perturbed, unsettled **12** discontented, dissatisfied

restorative 4 balm **5** tonic **7** healing **8** curative, remedial, sanative **12** recuperative

restore 4 cure, heal, mend, stet **5** amend, remit, renew, right **6** recall, recoup, reform, remedy, render, repair, return, revive **7** get back, improve, reclaim, recover, rectify, refresh, replace **8** give back, recreate, renovate, revivify **9** refurbish, reinstate, replenish, restitute **10** regenerate, rejuvenate **11** recondition, reestablish **12** rehabilitate

restrain 3 bit, gag **4** bate, curb, rein **5** check, leash **6** arrest, bridle, halter, hamper, hinder, hold in, impede, muzzle, temper **7** collect, control, harness, inhibit, repress **8** hold back, hold down, moderate, suppress

restrained 4 cool **6** low-key **5** canny, quiet **6** modest **7** subdued **8** discreet, reserved, reticent, retiring, tasteful **9** contained, inhibited, temperate **10** controlled, reasonable

restraint 5 stint **6** bridle **7** durance, embargo, reserve **8** estoppel, pullback **9** hindrance **10** deterrence, inhibition, limitation, moderation **11** confinement, forbearance **12** straitjacket

restrict 3 bar, tie **4** bind, curb **5** hem in, limit **6** hamper, hobble, impede, narrow, shrink **7** confine, curtail, delimit, inhibit, trammel **8** hold back, prelimit **10** delimitate **12** circumscribe *a will:* **6** entail

restriction 4 curb **5** check, limit, stint **7** control **9** restraint **10** constraint, limitation, regulation **11** confinement, prohibition **12** proscription **13** qualification

restyle 4 redo **6** revamp, revise, rework **8** make over

result 3 end **4** flow, stem **5** close, ensue, fruit, issue **6** effect, emerge, finish, follow, payoff, sequel, upshot **7** outcome, product **8** sequence, solution **9** aftermath, come about, eventuate **10** conclusion, denouement, production **11** aftereffect, consequence, eventuality *incidental:* **7** spinoff

resume 4 go on **5** renew **6** pick up, reopen **7** carry on, proceed, restart **8** continue **10** recommence

résumé 2 CV **4** vita **5** sum-up **6** précis **7** summary **9** summation, summing-up

resurgence 5 rally **7** rebirth, revival **8** comeback, recovery **10** renascence **11** renaissance **12** risorgimento

resurrect 5 raise, renew **6** come to, revive **8** retrieve, revivify **10** reactivate

resurrection 7 rebirth, revival **10** renascence **11** renaissance **12** risorgimento

resuscitate see **resurrect**

retail 4 sell, tell, vend **6** market **7** narrate **11** merchandise

retailer 6 dealer, seller, trader, vendor **8** merchant **9** tradesman **10** shopkeeper **11** storekeeper **12** merchandiser

retain 3 own **4** hire, hold, keep **6** detain **7** reserve **8** hold over, preserve, remember, withhold

retainer 3 fee **6** lackey, menial, minion, yeoman **7** deposit, servant **8** employee, follower **9** bite plate, dependent, pensioner

retaliate 7 get back, get even **10** strike back

retaliation see **reprisal**

retaliatory 8 punitive, vengeful **10** vindictive

retard 4 clog, mire, slow **5** delay, stunt **6** detain, fetter, hamper, hang up, hinder, impede, slow up **7** set back, slacken **8** decrease, hold back, restrain **10** decelerate

retarded 3 dim **4** dull, dumb, slow **6** opaque, simple, stupid **8** backward **9** dim-witted **10** half-witted, slow-witted **11** exceptional

retch 3 gag **4** barf, hurl, puke, spew **5** heave, vomit **6** spit up **7** bring up, throw up, upchuck **8** disgorge

retention 6 memory **7** storage

reticent see **reserved**

reticulate 4 vein **5** veiny **6** meshed, netted **7** netlike **10** crisscross

retinue 4 band, tail **5** suite, train **6** livery **7** company, cortege **9** entourage, following

retire 4 exit, quit **5** leave, yield **6** bow out, depart, recede, resign, turn in **7** dismiss, pension **8** step down, withdraw **9** discharge, strike out, terminate **10** relinquish

retired person 7 emerita **8** emeritus **9** pensioner

retiree 6 senior **9** pensioner **10** golden-ager **13** senior citizen

retirement allowance 3 SEP **7** pension

retiring 3 shy **5** mousy, timid **6** demure, modest **7** bashful **8** reserved **9** diffident, withdrawn **11** unassertive

retool 7 reequip **10** reengineer

retort 5 reply, sally **6** answer, rejoin **7** counter, respond, riposte **8** comeback, repartee, response **9** rejoinder, retaliate, wisecrack

retouch 5 alter, emend, renew **6** repair **7** correct, enhance, improve, restore

retract 4 deny **5** unsay **6** abjure, recall, recant, recede, renege, resile, revoke **7** disavow, rescind, retreat, swallow **8** forswear, renounce, take back, withdraw

retreat 3 den, ebb **4** flee, quit **5** cover, haven, leave **6** ashram, asylum, bow out, covert, decamp, depart, escape, recede, recoil, refuge, shrink, vacate **7** abandon, back off,

back out, pull out, shelter **8** back down, draw back, evacuate, fall back, hideaway, withdraw **9** backtrack, climb down, sanctuary **10** give ground, withdrawal

retrench 3 cut **4** pare **5** slash **6** excise, lessen, reduce **7** abridge, curtail **9** economize

retribution 6 return, reward **7** deserts, revenge **8** avenging, reprisal, requital, revanche **9** vengeance **10** punishment, recompense **11** counterblow, retaliation *goddess of:* **3** Ate **4** Fury **7** Nemesis

retrieve 5 fetch **6** recall, recoup, redeem, rescue **7** get back, recover, restore, salvage **9** resurrect

retro 5 campy **7** antique, revival, vintage **9** nostalgic **12** old-fashioned

retrograde 4 back **7** inverse, reverse **8** backward, inverted, rearward

retrogress see **revert**

retrospect 9 hindsight **12** recollection **13** reexamination

retrospective 6 review **8** backward **10** exhibition, reflective, ruminative

return 5 recur, repay, reply, yield **6** answer, rebate, regain, rejoin, render, repeat, retort, revert **7** bring in, get back, rebound, recover, reprise, requite, respond, reverse, riposte **8** comeback, dividend, earnings, give back, proceeds, reappear, response **9** rejoinder, repayment, reversion **10** recompense, recurrence **11** reciprocate, restitution

Return of the Native *author:* **5** Hardy (Thomas) *character:* **4** Clym (Yeobright) **8** Eustacia (Vye)

Reuben *brother:* **6** Joseph *father:* **5** Jacob *mother:* **4** Leah *son:* **5** Carmi **6** Hanoch, Hezron, Phallu

Réunion *capital:* **7** St.-Denis *city:* **6** St.-Paul **7** St.-Louis **8** St.-Pierre *department of:* **6** France *ethnic group:* **6** Creole *former name:* **7** Bourbon **9** Bonaparte *island group:* **9** Mascarene

revamp 4 redo **5** renew **6** remake, repair, revise, rework **7** remodel, restyle, rewrite **8** make over, overhaul, redesign, renovate **9** refurbish **11** recondition

reveal 4 bare, blab, jamb, leak, open, show, tell **5** admit, let on, peach, spill **6** betray, evince, expose, impart, unmask, unveil **7** confess, declare, display, divulge, exhibit, publish, uncover, undress **8** announce, decipher, disclose, discover, give away, unclothe **9** broadcast, made known **11** acknowledge, communicate **12** bring to light

revel 4 bask, orgy, riot **5** binge, feast, party, spree **6** boogie, frolic, gaiety, hoopla, wallow **7** carouse, delight, indulge, jollity, rois-

ter, rollick, wassail, whoopla **8** carnival, carousal, festival **9** bacchanal, celebrate, festivity, luxuriate, merriment, whoop-de-do **11** bacchanalia, celebration, merrymaking

revelation 6 kicker **8** epiphany, giveaway, prophecy, surprise **9** discovery **10** apocalypse, disclosure **13** manifestation

reveler 7 orgiast **8** bacchant, carouser **9** bacchante, wassailer **10** merrymaker

revelry 4 orgy, riot **6** gaiety **7** carouse, jollity, wassail, whoopee, whoopla **8** carousal, partying **9** festivity, high jinks, merriment, whoop-de-do **10** whoop-de-doo **11** merrymaking

revenant 5 ghost, haunt, shade, spook **6** shadow, spirit, undead, wraith, zombie **7** phantom, specter, spectre **8** phantasm, prodigal, visitant **10** apparition

revenge 5 right **6** defend **7** get back, get even, redress, requite **8** reprisal, requital, revanche **9** retaliate, vindicate **11** retaliation, retribution

revenue 4 rent **5** gains, issue, yield **6** income, profit, return **7** comings **8** earnings, interest, proceeds, receipts, taxation

reverberant 6 hollow **7** booming, echoing **8** resonant **10** resounding

reverberate 4 echo, gong, ring **6** reecho **7** resound

revere 4 laud **5** adore, exalt, extol, honor, prize, value **6** admire, esteem, regard **7** cherish, magnify, respect, worship **8** treasure, venerate **10** appreciate

revered 6 sacred **9** estimable, venerable

reverence 3 awe **5** adore, dread, honor, piety **6** esteem, fealty, homage **7** loyalty, respect, worship **8** devotion, venerate **9** deference, obeisance, solemnity **10** veneration *gesture of:* **3** bow **6** kowtow **8** kneeling **12** genuflection

reverend 4 abbé, holy **5** clerk, vicar **6** clergy, cleric, deacon, divine, parson, rector **8** chaplain, clerical, minister, preacher **9** churchman, clergyman **11** clergywoman **12** ecclesiastic

reverent 5 godly, pious **6** devout **7** dutiful **9** prayerful **10** God-fearing, respectful, worshipful

reverie 4 muse **5** dream **6** trance, vision **7** fantasy **8** daydream **10** absorption, brown study, meditation **11** abstraction **13** woolgathering

reversal 4 turn **5** U-turn **6** double, switch **7** setback, undoing **8** backfire, flip-flop **9** about-face, inversion, turnabout, volte-face **10** switcheroo **12** solarization **13** change of heart

reverse 4 lift, undo **6** change, contra, defeat, invert, recall, repeal, revoke **7** capsize, counter, rescind, setback **8** antipode, backward, contrary, disaster, exchange, opposite, overrule, overturn **9** about-face, backwards, diametric, overthrow, transpose, turnabout, volte-face **10** antithesis, misfortune

reversion 4 turn **5** lapse **6** return **7** atavism, escheat **9** about-face, throwback, turnabout, volte-face **10** regression, succession

revert 4 turn **6** return **7** decline, devolve, escheat, inverse, regress **8** turn back **9** backslide **10** degenerate, retrograde, retrogress

revetment 4 berm **6** bunker, riprap **9** barricade, earthwork **10** embankment

review 4 scan **5** audit, recap, study **6** assess, go over, parade, report, revise, survey **7** analyze, journal, rethink **8** analysis, critique, magazine, revision, scrutiny, talk over **9** criticism, reexamine, refresher **10** evaluation, inspection, periodical, reconsider, reevaluate **11** examination **13** reexamination, retrospective

revile 4 rail, rate **5** abuse, scold **6** attack, berate, defame, malign, vilify **7** asperse, bawl out, chew out, upbraid **8** belittle, disgrace, execrate **9** blaspheme **10** tongue-lash, vituperate

revise 4 edit **5** alter, amend, emend, proof, renew **6** change, polish, redraw, reform, retool, revamp, rework **7** correct, improve, redraft, restore, restyle, rewrite **8** overhaul, redesign, work over **9** red-pencil **10** bluepencil

revision 6 change, revamp, update **7** redraft **8** facelift, overhaul, updating **10** alteration, correction, emendation **11** overhauling **12** modification

revitalize see **revive**

revival 7 rebirth, renewal **8** comeback **10** renascence, resurgence **11** reanimation, renaissance, restoration **12** regeneration, rejuvenation, resurrection, risorgimento **13** recrudescence, resuscitation

revive 4 wake **5** rally, renew, rouse **6** arouse, awaken, come to, recall **7** bring to, enliven, freshen, quicken, refresh, restore **8** reawaken, rekindle, renovate, retrieve **9** reanimate, resurrect **10** reactivate, recuperate, regenerate, rejuvenate **11** bring around, reintroduce, resuscitate **12** reinvigorate

revoke 4 lift, void **5** annul, erase **6** abjure, cancel, recall, recant, renege, repeal **7** abolish, nullify, rescind, retract, reverse **8** abrogate, call back **10** invalidate **11** countermand

revolt 4 riot **5** rebel, repel, shock **6** mutiny, resist, sicken **7** disgust, repulse **8** nauseate, outbreak, uprising **9** jacquerie, rebellion **10** insurgence, insurgency **12** insurrection

revolter 5 rebel **6** anarch **8** frondeur, mutineer **9** anarchist, insurgent **10** malcontent

revolting 4 foul, ugly, vile **5** nasty **6** horrid **7** hideous, noisome, obscene **8** shocking **9** atrocious, loathsome, repellent, repugnant, repulsive **10** disgusting, nauseating

revolution 4 gyre, reel, riot, roll, spin, turn **5** cycle, orbit, twirl, wheel, whirl **6** mutiny **7** circuit **8** gyration, rotation, uprising **9** pirouette, rebellion **10** barrel roll, changeover, somersault **12** insurrection

revolutionary 5 rebel, ultra **7** extreme, radical **8** mutineer, rotating, ultraist **9** extremist, insurgent *American:* **4** Hale (Nathan), Reed (John) **5** Adams (Samuel), Allen (Ethan), Henry (Patrick), Shays (Daniel) **6** Revere (Paul) *English:* **5** Paine (Thomas) *French:* **5** Marat (Jean-Paul) **6** Danton (Georges) **8** Mirabeau (Comte de) **9** Saint-Just (Louis) **11** Robespierre (Maximilien) *Irish:* **4** Tone (Wolfe) **6** Pearse (Padraig, Patrick) **7** Collins (Michael), Parnell (Charles Stewart) **8** Casement (Roger), de Valera (Eamon), Griffith (Arthur), O'Connell (Daniel) *Mexican:* **5** Villa (Pancho) **6** Zapata (Emiliano) **7** Hidalgo (Padre Miguel) *Russian:* **5** Kirov (Sergey), Lenin (Vladimir Ilyich) **7** Trotsky (Leon) **8** Kerensky (Aleksandr) **9** Kropotkin (Pyotr)

revolutionize 9 transform **11** transfigure

revolve 4 spin, turn **5** twirl, wheel, whirl **6** circle, gyrate, rotate

revolver 3 gat, gun, rod **4** Colt **5** Glock, Luger, Ruger **6** Magnum, pistol, six-gun **7** firearm, handgun, shooter, sidearm **10** six-shooter

revue 4 show **9** burlesque **10** production, vaudeville **13** entertainment

revulsion 4 hate **6** hatred, horror **7** disgust **8** aversion, loathing **10** abhorrence, repugnance **11** abomination, detestation

reward 5 bonus, booty, crown, medal, price, prize **6** bounty, carrot, payoff, trophy **7** guerdon, jackpot, premium **8** dividend **10** compensate, honorarium, recompense, remunerate **12** compensation, remuneration

rewarding 7 gainful **8** edifying, fruitful, valuable **9** lucrative **10** beneficial, fulfilling, gratifying, productive, profitable, satisfying, worthwhile **12** advantageous, remunerative

reword see **restate**

rework 6 revamp, revise **7** restyle, rewrite

Reynard 3 fox

rhadamanthine 3 due **4** just **5** right **6** strict **7** condign, fitting, merited **8** deserved, rigorous, rightful, suitable **9** requisite, stringent **11** appropriate

Rhadamanthus 5 judge *brother:* **5** Minos *father:* **4** Zeus **7** Jupiter *mother:* **6** Europa

rhapsodic 5 lyric **8** ecstatic, effusive **9** emotional, exuberant

rhapsodize 4 gush, rave **5** drool **6** effuse **7** enthuse

Rhea 3 Ops *daughter:* **4** Hera, Juno **5** Ceres, Vesta **6** Hestia **7** Demeter *father:* **6** Uranus *husband:* **6** Cronus, Saturn *mother:* **4** Gaea *son:* **4** Zeus **5** Hades, Pluto **7** Jupiter, Neptune **8** Poseidon

Rheingold, Das *character:* **4** Loge, Loki **5** Freya, Wotan **6** Fafner, Fafnir, Fasolt **8** Alberich *composer:* **6** Wagner (Richard)

rheostat 8 resistor

rhesus 6 monkey **7** macaque

rhetoric 4 rant **6** speech **7** bombast, fustian, oratory **8** rhapsody **9** elocution, eloquence, verbosity **11** rodomontade, speechcraft *term:* **6** aporia, simile **7** litotes **8** metaphor **10** apostrophe, digression **12** alliteration, onomatopoeia

rhetorical 4 glib **5** gassy, grand, tumid, windy **6** florid, fluent, ornate, purple, turgid **7** aureate, flowery, orotund, pompous, stilted **8** eloquent, forensic, inflated, overdone, sonorous **9** bombastic, grandiose, high-flown, overblown, tumescent **10** euphuistic, flamboyant, oratorical **11** declamatory, highfalutin, overwrought, pretentious **12** high sounding, magniloquent **13** grandiloquent

rhetorician 6 orator, writer **7** speaker *Roman:* **10** Quintilian

Rhine River *city:* **4** Bonn, Köln **5** Basel, Mainz **7** Coblenz, Cologne, Koblenz **8** Duisburg, Mannheim **9** Rotterdam, Wiesbaden **10** Düsseldorf *nymph:* **7** Lorelei *tributary:* **3** Aar, Ill, Lek **4** Aare, Lahn, Main, Ruhr, Waal

rhizome 4 root **5** tuber

Rhode Island *bay:* **12** Narragansett *capital:* **10** Providence *city:* **7** Newport, Warwick **9** Pawtucket *college, university:* **4** RISD **5** Brown *island:* **5** Block *nickname:* **5** Ocean (State) **11** Little Rhody *river:* **8** Pawtuxet *state bird:* **14** Rhode Island red *state flower:* **6** violet *state tree:* **8** red maple

Rhodesia 8 Zimbabwe

rhombus 7 diamond, lozenge **13** parallelogram

rhonchus 5 snore

Rhône River *city:* 4 Lyon 5 Arles, Lyons 6 Geneva 7 Avignon *lake:* 6 Geneva *mountain range:* 4 Jura *tributary:* 5 Isère, Saône

rhubarb 3 row 4 flap 5 run-in 6 ruckus, tangle 7 dispute, quarrel, wrangle 8 argument, pieplant 11 altercation, controversy

rhyme 4 poem, song 5 agree, ditty, verse 6 accord, jingle, poetry 7 conform 8 dovetail 9 harmonize 10 coordinate, correspond *scheme:* 4 ABAB

rhymer 4 bard, poet 5 odist 7 metrist 8 lyricist 9 poetaster, rhymester, sonneteer, versifier

rhythm 4 beat, flow, lilt, time 5 meter, pulse, swing 6 accent, groove 7 cadence, measure, pattern 8 sequence

rhythmic 7 pulsing, regular 8 measured, metrical

rialto 6 market 8 district, exchange 11 marketplace

riant 3 gay 5 jolly, merry 6 blithe, bright, jocund, jovial 7 buoyant, gleeful 8 cheerful, mirthful 10 blithesome

riata 4 rope 5 lasso 6 lariat

rib 3 fun, kid, rag 4 band, bone, dike, fool, jape, jest, joke, josh, purl, razz, stay, wale 5 chaff, costa, ridge, tease 6 banter, costae (plural), lierne, needle

ribald 3 raw 4 blue, racy, rude, sexy 5 bawdy, crude, dirty, salty, spicy 6 coarse, earthy, filthy, purple, risqué, smutty, vulgar 7 naughty, obscene, profane, raunchy 8 indecent, off-color 9 offensive, reprobate, salacious 10 suggestive

ribbon 3 bow 4 band, tape 5 braid, shred, strip 6 cordon, fillet, stripe, tatter 7 bandeau

rice 7 arborio, basmati, risotto *dish:* 5 pilaf 6 congee 7 risotto 9 jambalaya *drink:* 4 sake, saki 5 mirin 6 arrack *field:* 5 paddy *husk:* 5 lemma

rich 4 dear, lush, oily, posh 5 ample, fatty, flush, grand, heavy, plush, swank, vivid 6 costly, creamy, deluxe, fecund, gilded, lavish, loaded, monied, ornate, potent, rococo 7 baroque, copious, elegant, fertile, filling, moneyed, opulent, orotund, profuse, wealthy, well-off 8 abundant, affluent, eloquent, fruitful, palatial, well-to-do 9 abounding, bountiful, elaborate, luxuriant, luxurious, plentiful, sumptuous, well-fixed 10 productive, prosperous, well-heeled 11 extravagant *person:* 4 have 5 Midas, mogul, nabob 6 fat cat 7 Croesus, magnate 9 moneybags, plutocrat

Richardson work 6 Pamela 8 Clarissa

Richelieu's successor 7 Mazarin

riches 4 gold, pelf 5 booty, lucre, worth 6 mammon, wealth 7 fortune 8 opulence, property, treasure 9 resources *demon of:* 6 Mammon

rick 4 cock, heap, pile 5 shock, stack

rickety 4 weak 5 shaky 6 flimsy, wobbly 7 unsound 8 decrepit, insecure, rachitic, unstable, unsteady 10 ramshackle, rattletrap

ricochet 4 ping, skim, skip 5 carom 6 bounce, glance 7 rebound 9 boomerang

rid 6 divest 7 relieve 8 unburden 11 disencumber

riddle 5 rebus 6 enigma, puzzle 7 mystery, perplex, problem 9 conundrum, perforate 10 closed book, puzzlement 11 brainteaser

ride 4 spin, tour, trip 5 drive, jaunt, mount 6 travel 7 journey 8 carousel 9 excursion

ride out 6 endure 7 outlast, survive, weather 9 withstand

rider 6 clause, cowboy, jockey 7 codicil 8 addendum, addition, appendix, horseman, reinsman 9 amendment 10 equestrian, horsewoman, supplement

ridge 3 rib, top 4 bank, berm, brow, fold, keel, reef, roll, ruck, seam, wave 5 arête, arris, chine, crest, esker, knurl, plica, spine 6 crease, divide, furrow, rimple, saddle, summit 7 annulet, breaker, crinkle, hogback, wrinkle 8 shoulder 9 razorback 11 corrugation *gravelly:* 5 esker *on the skin:* 4 wale, weal, welt *sharp:* 7 hogback

ridicule 3 pan, rib 4 gibe, haze, jape, jeer, mock, razz, ride, twit 5 chaff, flout, mimic, roast, scoff, scout, sneer, squib, taunt 6 deride, satire 7 lampoon, mockery, pillory, sarcasm 8 derision, raillery, satirize, travesty 9 burlesque 10 caricature *god of:* 5 Momus *object of:* 4 butt 13 laughingstock

ridiculous 5 comic, daffy, dotty, goofy, silly, wacky 6 absurd, insane 7 bizarre, comical, foolish, risible 8 derisory, farcical 9 cockamamy, fantastic, grotesque, laughable, ludicrous, monstrous, senseless 10 cockamamie, outrageous 11 for the birds, harebrained 12 preposterous, unbelievable

riding *academy:* 6 manège *costume:* 5 habit *pants:* 8 jodhpurs *whip:* 3 bat 4 crop 5 quirt

Rienzi composer 6 Wagner (Richard)

rife 4 full 5 flush 6 common 7 replete, teeming 8 abundant, swarming 9 abounding, plentiful, prevalent 10 widespread 11 overflowing

riff 4 flip, leaf, scan, skim 5 theme, thumb 6 browse 8 ostinato

riffle 4 flip, leaf, fret, scan, skim, wave 5 shoal, thumb 6 browse, sluice 7 shallow, shuffle 10 interstice

riffraff 3 mob 5 trash, waste 6 debris, kelter,

litter, masses, rabble, refuse **7** garbage, rubbish **8** canaille, unwashed **9** hoi polloi, multitude **11** proletariat

rifle 3 arm, gun, rob **4** loot, sack **5** steal **6** burgle, groove, weapon **7** carbine, despoil, firearm, pillage, plunder, ransack, rummage **9** chassepot *accessory:* **6** ramrod *attachment:* **5** scope **8** silencer *kind:* **6** Garand, Mauser **7** Enfield **8** Browning **9** Remington **10** Winchester **11** Springfield

rift 3 gap **4** rent **5** break, chasm, chink, cleft, crack, fault, space, split **6** breach, cleave, divide, hiatus, schism **7** fissure, opening, rupture **8** crevasse, division, fracture, interval **9** fault line **10** separation **12** estrangement

rig 3 arm, fit, fix **4** fake, gear, semi **5** dress, equip, getup, trick **6** adjust, clothe, doctor, outfit, tackle **7** apparel, arrange, costume, derrick, furnish, turn out **8** accouter, accoutre, clothing, equipage **9** apparatus, construct, equipment **10** manipulate

rigging 3 net **4** duds, gear, togs **5** dress, lines, ropes **6** attire, chains, tackle, things **7** apparel, clothes, raiment **8** clothing **9** apparatus, equipment

right 3 apt, due, fit **4** fair, just, sane, true, well **5** amend, amply, claim, droit, emend, exact, sound, title **6** at once, common, decent, dexter, direct, equity, honest, lawful, proper, square, strict **7** condign, correct, exactly, fitting, freedom, genuine, healthy, liberty, license, merited, old-line, rectify, redress **8** accurate, bona fide, orthodox, smack-dab, suitable **9** authentic, befitting, equitable, privilege, veracious, veritable **10** perquisite **11** appropriate, correctness, prerogative *combining form:* **4** orth, rect **5** dextr, ortho, recti **6** dextro *feudal:* **4** soke *legal:* **5** droit **8** usufruct *royal:* **7** regalia (plural)

right away 3 now **6** at once, pronto **8** directly, promptly **9** forthwith, instanter, instantly **11** immediately, straight off, straightway **12** then and there

righteous 4 good, holy, just, pure **5** godly, moral, noble, pious **6** devout, worthy **7** ethical, genuine, sinless, upright **8** innocent, virtuous **9** blameless, guiltless **10** inculpable, principled

righteousness 5 honor **6** equity, virtue **7** honesty, justice, probity **8** holiness, morality **9** integrity, rectitude

rightful 3 apt, due, fit **4** fair, just, true **5** legal **6** honest, lawful, proper **7** condign, fitting **8** deserved, suitable **9** befitting, equitable, impartial **10** applicable, legitimate **11** appropriate

right-handed 6 dexter **7** dextral **9** clockwise

right-hand page 5 recto

rightist 4 tory **11** reactionary **12** conservative

right-minded 5 moral, noble **6** decent, honest **7** ethical **8** virtuous **10** upstanding

Rights of Man author 5 Paine (Thomas)

rigid 3 set **4** firm, hard, taut **5** fixed, stiff, tense **6** severe, strict **7** austere, precise, hard-set **8** cast-iron, ironclad, obdurate, rigorous **9** draconian, immovable, inelastic, rockbound, stringent, unbending **10** adamantine, brassbound, inflexible, relentless, unyielding **11** unbudgeable **13** rhadamanthine

rigidity 6 turgor **7** buckram **8** hardness **9** stiffness *muscular:* **8** myotonia

rigmarole 6 bunkum, drivel, ramble **7** blather **8** nonsense **9** gibberish, procedure **10** balderdash, mumbo jumbo **12** gobbledygook

Rigoletto composer: **5** Verdi (Giuseppe) *daughter:* **5** Gilda *setting:* **6** Mantua

rigor 7 cruelty **8** asperity, hardness, hardship, severity **9** austerity, exactness, harshness, roughness, sharpness, sternness **10** affliction, difficulty, exactitude, strictness **11** tribulation **13** inflexibility

rigorous 5 exact, harsh, rigid, rough, stern, stiff **6** bitter, brutal, proper, rugged, severe, strict **7** ascetic, drastic, onerous, precise **8** accurate, exacting **9** draconian, ironbound, stringent **10** burdensome, inflexible, ironhanded, oppressive **11** punctilious **13** rhadamanthine

rile 3 bug, rub, vex **4** roil **5** anger, annoy, grate, muddy, peeve, pique, upset **6** muddle, nettle, put out, rankle **7** agitate, disturb, fluster, inflame, perturb, provoke **8** disorder, disquiet, irritate **9** aggravate **10** discompose, exasperate

rill 3 run **4** burn, purl **5** bourn, brook, creek **6** runnel, stream, valley **7** freshet, rivulet **8** brooklet **9** streamlet **11** watercourse

rim 3 hem, lip **4** bank, boss, brim, edge, ring **5** bezel, bezil, bound, brink, skirt, verge **6** border, flange, fringe, margin, shield **7** annulus, horizon, outline **8** boundary, surround **9** perimeter, periphery *of a basket:* **4** hoop *of a cask:* **5** chime *of an insect's wing:* **6** termen *of a spoked wheel:* **5** felly **6** felloe

Rimbaud work 12 Season in Hell (A) **13** Illuminations (Les)

rime 3 ice **4** hoar **5** crust, frost **7** coating, encrust **9** hoarfrost, Jack Frost **12** incrustation

Rinaldo beloved: **8** Angelica *cousin:* **7** Orlando *father:* **5** Aymon *horse:* **6** Bayard *mother:* 3 Aya *sister:* 10 Bradamante *uncle:* 11 Charlemagne

rind 4 bark, husk, peel, skin 5 crust 9 crackling

ring 3 eye, hem, rim 4 band, bloc, bong, echo, gird, gyre, hoop, loop, peal, toll 5 arena, bezel, cabal, chime, clang, cycle, group, knell, knoll, round, sound 6 circle, clique, collar, girdle, staple 7 annulus, clangor, combine, compass, resound, vibrate 8 bracelet, cincture, encircle, surround 9 coalition, encompass 11 combination, reverberate *around sun or moon:* 6 corona *curtain:* 3 eye *for a compass:* 6 gimbal *harness:* 3 dee 6 button, terret *heraldic:* 7 annulet *in a hinge:* 7 gudgeon *of chain:* 4 link *of color:* 8 stocking *of leaves or flowers:* 6 wreath 7 garland *of light:* 4 halo 5 glory 6 corona, nimbus 7 aureole 8 halation *of rope or metal:* 4 hank 6 becket 7 garland, grommet, thimble *of two hoops:* 6 gimmal *relating to:* 7 annular *used as a valve or diaphragm:* 5 wafer *wedding:* 4 band

Ring and the Book author 8 Browning (Robert)

ringed 8 annulate, bordered 9 encircled 10 surrounded

ringer 4 fake, spit 5 clone, image 6 double 7 clapper, picture 8 impostor, portrait 10 simulacrum 13 spitting image

ringing 7 orotund, vibrant 8 decisive, emphatic, plangent, resonant, sonorous 10 clangorous, resounding 11 reverberant, unequivocal

ringleader 4 boss 5 chief 6 honcho, top dog 7 kingpin 9 godfather, top banana 10 head honcho, instigator, mastermind

ringlet 4 curl, lock 5 crimp, tress 7 circlet, earlock, tendril

Ring of the Nibelung composer 6 Wagner (Richard)

ringworm 5 tinea

rinse 4 dunk, lave, wash 5 bathe, douse, swill 6 shower, sluice 7 cleanse *the mouth:* 6 gargle

riot 5 brawl, broil, melee, revel, spree 6 bedlam, émeute, jumble, revolt, tumult, uproar 7 carouse, debauch, rampage, revelry, roister, wassail 8 carousal, disorder, uprising 9 commotion 10 debauchery, donnybrook, revolution 11 disturbance

riotous 4 lush, wild 6 stormy, unruly, wanton 7 bacchic, profuse, untamed 8 abundant 9 abounding, clamorous, exuberant, luxuriant, plentiful, turbulent, unchecked 10 boisterous 11 saturnalian, tempestuous 12 unrestrained

rip 4 gash, hole, rend, rent, rive, spit, tear 5 shred, slash, split 6 attack, cleave 7 current, sputter 8 lacerate, undertow 9 criticize, disparage 12 undercurrent *into:* 5 go for 6 assail, attack 8 lambaste *off:* 3 con, rob 4 copy 5 cheat, steal, theft 7 defraud, imitate, swindle 9 imitation

ripe 4 aged, full, late 5 adult, grown, ready, ruddy, plump 6 mature, mellow, smelly, timely 7 grown-up 8 prepared, suitable 9 developed, full-blown, full-grown, offensive, opportune 10 seasonable 11 appropriate, full-fledged

ripen 3 age 4 cure, grow 6 better, grow up, mature, mellow, season 7 develop, enhance, improve, perfect 8 heighten, maturate

rip off 3 con, rob 4 copy 5 cheat, steal 7 defraud, imitate, swindle

rip-off 4 copy, scam 5 fraud, theft 7 swindle 8 stealing 9 deception, imitation 12 exploitation

riposte 5 parry, reply 6 retort, return, thrust 8 back talk, comeback, repartee 13 counterattack

ripping 4 fine 5 grand, nifty, super, swell 6 divine, peachy 7 capital 8 glorious, splendid, terrific 9 admirable, delicious, excellent, fantastic, marvelous, wonderful 10 delightful, delectable, remarkable 11 scrumptious, sensational

ripple 3 lap 4 curl, fret, riff, wave 6 cockle, dimple, lipper, popple, ruffle, spread, wimple 7 crinkle, wavelet, wrinkle 8 undulate

rip-roaring 5 noisy 6 lively 8 exciting 9 hilarious 10 boisterous, rollicking, uproarious

ripsnorter 3 ace, pip 4 lulu 5 dandy, doozy 6 doozie, hummer 8 jim-dandy, knockout 9 humdinger 11 crackerjack

riptide 7 current 8 undertow 12 undercurrent

Rip Van Winkle author: 6 Irving (Washington) *dog:* 4 Wolf

rise 3 wax 4 grow, hill, lift, rear, soar 5 awake, get up, issue, mount, stand, surge, swell 6 ascend, ascent, awaken, emerge, expand, growth, origin, spring, uprear 7 advance, augment, develop, emanate, enhance, enlarge, hilltop, stand up, succeed, surface, upsurge 8 eminence, heighten, increase 9 ascension, beginning, increment, intensify, originate, terminate *above:* 8 surmount *again:* 7 resurge 9 resurrect *against:* 5 rebel 6 mutiny, revolt *and fall:* 4 tide 5 heave 6 welter *and shine:* 5 get up *gradually:* 4 loom

Rise of Silas Lapham author 7 Howells (William Dean)

riser 4 dais, step 8 platform

risible 4 rich **5** comic, droll, funny, jokey **6** absurd **7** comical **8** farcical **9** laughable, ludicrous **10** ridiculous

risk 4 ante, dare, defy **5** peril, stake, throw, wager **6** chance, danger, gamble, hazard, menace, stakes **7** imperil, jeopard, venture **8** endanger, exposure, jeopardy **9** adventure, encounter, liability **10** jeopardize

risky 4 bold **5** dicey, hairy **6** chancy, daring, touchy, tricky **7** parlous, unsound **8** delicate, perilous, ticklish **9** dangerous, hazardous, unhealthy **10** jeopardous, precarious **11** adventurous, speculative, treacherous

risqué 4 blue, lewd, racy, sexy **5** broad, crude, dirty, salty, spicy, vampy **6** coarse, daring, earthy, purple, ribald, vulgar **7** naughty, obscene, raunchy **8** indecent, off-color, scabrous **9** salacious **10** indecorous, indelicate, suggestive

rite 6 office **7** liturgy, mystery, service **8** ceremony **9** formality, ordinance, sacrament, solemnity **10** ceremonial, initiation, observance **11** celebration, sacramental *funeral:* **6** exequy **7** obsequy **8** exequies **9** obsequies *Jewish:* **4** bris *of initiation or purification:* **7** baptism *of knighthood:* **8** accolade (see also **sacrament**)

ritual see **rite**

ritzy 4 posh **5** fancy, swank **6** chichi, classy, modish, snazzy, swanky **7** elegant, high-hat, stylish **9** au courant, exclusive, expensive, luxurious **11** fashionable **12** ostentatious

rival 3 tie, try, vie **4** even, peer, side **5** equal, match **6** strive **7** attempt, compete, contend, contest, emulate **8** approach, opponent **9** adversary, competing, contender, measure up **10** antagonist, competitor, contending, contestant **11** comparative, competition

rivalry 6 strife **7** contest, warfare **8** conflict, jealousy, tug-of-war **9** emulation **10** contention, opposition **11** competition

rive 3 rip **4** rend, tear **5** break, burst, crack, sever, smash, split **6** cleave, divide, shiver, sunder **7** fissure, shatter **8** fracture, fragment, lacerate, separate, splinter

river *Afghanistan:* **5** Kabul *Africa:* **4** Bomu, Juba, Nile, Uele **5** Chari, Congo, Shari, Tsavo, Zaire **6** Atbara, Mbomou, Songwe, Ubangi **7** Aruwimi, Limpopo, Zambesi, Zambezi **9** Astaboras, Crocodile *Alabama:* **5** Coosa **6** Mobile **7** Conecuh, Perdido **9** Tombigbee **10** Tallapoosa *Alaska:* **5** Kobuk **6** Copper, Noatak, Tanana **7** Koyukuk, Susitna **9** Kuskokwim *Albania:* **4** Drin **5** Drini *Argentina:* **5** Negro **6** Paraná **7** Matanza *arm:* **6** branch **9** tributary *Asia:* **3** Ili **4** Amur,

Lena, Oxus **5** Indus **6** Jayhun, Sutlej **7** Oedanes **8** Amu Darya **9** Dyardanes **11** Brahmaputra *Australia:* **4** Daly **5** Roper, Yarra **6** Barwon, Culgoa, Dawson, DeGrey, Murray **7** Darling, Fitzroy, Lachlan **8** Victoria **10** Yarra Yarra *Austria:* **4** Enns *bank:* **5** levee *Belgium:* **4** Leie, Yser **5** Rupel, Senne, Weser **6** Dender, Dindar, Ourthe **8** Visurgis *Bolivia:* **4** Beni **5** Abuná **6** Mamoré *Borneo:* **5** Kajan *bottom:* **3** bed *Brazil:* **3** Ica **4** Pará, Paru **5** Negro, Xingu **6** Paraná **7** Madeira, Tapajos, Tapajoz *British Columbia:* **6** Skeena **10** Bella Coola *Burma:* **4** Pegu **7** Irawadi **8** Chindwin **9** Irrawaddy *California:* **3** Eel, Pit **4** Kern, Yuba **6** Merced **7** Feather, Salinas, Trinity **8** Tuolumne *Cambodia:* **8** Tonle Sap *Canada:* **3** Bow **4** Back **5** Moose, Peace, Slave **6** Beaver, Fraser, Nelson **8** Gatineau, Saguenay **9** Athabasca, Great Fish, Mackenzie, Richelieu **11** Assiniboine *Carolinas:* **7** Catawba *central United States:* **3** Fox **5** Grand **6** Neosho, Platte, Wabash **8** Keya Paha, Missouri, Niobrara **9** Tennessee, Verdigris **10** Republican, Saint Croix **11** Mississippi *channel:* **6** alveus *Chile:* **3** Loa **5** Itata, Maule **6** Bío-Bío **8** Valdivia *China:* **3** Bei, Han, Hun, Nen, Wei **4** Amur, Dong **5** Baihe, Chang, Huang, Tarim **6** Yellow **7** Kashgar, Yangtze *China-North Korea:* **4** Yalu *Colombia:* **4** Meta, Tomo **6** Atrato **9** Magdalena *Colorado:* **5** Yampa **8** Gunnison *Connecticut:* **6** Thames **7** Niantic, Shepaug **9** Naugatuck **10** Farmington, Housatonic, Quinnipiac **11** Willimantic *Crimea:* **4** Alma *crossing:* **4** ford *current:* **4** eddy **6** rapids *Czech Republic:* **4** Iser **6** Jizera, Moldau, Vltava *dam:* **4** weir *Denmark:* **4** Stor *dried bed:* **4** wadi *East Asia:* **4** Yalu **5** Amnok **7** Oryokko *Ecuador:* **4** Napo **10** Esmeraldas *England:* **3** Esk, Exe, Nen, Ure **4** Aire, Avon, Eden, Nene, Ouse, Tees, Tyne, Wear, Yare **5** Swale, Trent **6** Mersey, Ribble, Thames *Ethiopia:* **3** Omo **4** Baro, Dawa *Europe:* **4** Eger, Elbe, Labe, Oder, Ohre, Saar **5** Albis, Meuse, Saale **6** Danube, Ticino *Florida:* **6** Indian **9** Kissimmee **10** Saint Johns **12** Apalachicola *Foster's:* **6** Swanee *France:* **3** Ain, Lot, Lys, Var **4** Aire, Aude, Cher, Eure, Gers, Loir, Oise, Orne, Saar, Tarn, Yser **5** Adour, Aisne, Drôme, Indre, Isère, Loire, Marne, Rhône, Saare, Sâone, Seine, Somme, Yonne **6** Allier, Ariège, Scarpe, Vienne **7** Durance, Garonne, La Riège, Moselle **8** Charente, Dordogne *Georgia:* **6** Etowah, Oconee **8** Altamaha, Ocmulgee **13** Chattahoochee *Germany:* **3** Ems, Rur **4** Eder, Eger, Elbe,

Isar, Main, Rems, Ruhr, Saar **5** Hunte, Lippe, Mosel, Rhine, Spree, Werra, Weser **6** Neckar **Germany-Poland: 4** Oder **Ghana: 5** Volta **god: 7** Alpheus, Inachus **8** Achelous **Greece: 3** Iri **4** Arta **5** Lerna, Lerne **7** Alpheus, Eurotas **8** Achelous **9** Arakhthos **Honduras: 4** Ulúa **5** Aguán **6** Patuca **Iberian: 5** Douro, Duero **Idaho: 5** Lemhi **Illinois: 8** Mackinaw **India: 4** Sind **5** Sindh, Tapti **6** Chenab, Ganges, Jhelum, Kaveri, Kistna **7** Cauvery, Krishna **8** Acesines, Godavari **inlet: 5** bayou **6** slough **Iran: 3** Kor **4** Mand, Mund **5** Karun **8** Safid Rud, Sefid Rud **Ireland: 3** Lee **4** Deel, Erne, Suir **5** Boyne, Clare, Foyle **6** Barrow, Liffey **7** Shannon **Italy: 4** Adda, Arno, Liri, Nera **5** Adige, Arnus, Etsch, Liris, Oglio, Padus, Piave, Tiber **6** Ollius, Rapido, Tevere, Trebia **7** Athesis, Rubicon, Secchia, Tiberis, Trebbia **8** Rubicone, Volturno **Kansas: 6** Pawnee **Kazakhstan-Russia: 4** Emba, Ural **5** Tobol **6** Irtysh **Kenya: 4** Athi, Tana **Kubla Khan's: 4** Alph **land: 4** holm **5** flats **7** bottoms **Latvia: 5** Gauja **Latvia-Lithuania: 7** Lielupe **Lebanon: 6** Litani **Little Rock's: 8** Arkansas **living on the bank of: 8** riparian **longest: 4** Nile **Louisiana: 11** Atchafalaya **Maine: 8** Kennebec **9** Aroostook, Penobscot **Malaysia: 9** Trengganu **Maryland: 8** Monocacy, Patapsco, Patuxent **9** Nanticoke **Massachusetts: 7** Charles, Taunton **9** Merrimack, Westfield **10** Housatonic **Mexico: 6** Pánuco, Sonora **7** Tabasco **8** Grijalva **Michigan: 4** Cass **5** Huron **7** Saginaw **8** Manistee, Muskegon **9** Cheboygan, Kalamazoo **10** Michigamme, Shiawassee **Mississippi: 5** Pearl, Yazoo **10** Pascagoula **Moldova-Ukraine: 8** Dneister **Missouri: 5** Osage **mouth: 5** delta **Myanmar: 4** Pegu **7** Irawadi **8** Chindwin **9** Irrawaddy **Nebraska: 4** Loup **6** Nemaha, Platte **7** Elkhorn **Netherlands: 4** Maas, Waal **5** Issel, Yssel **6** Amstel, IJssel **7** Vahalis **New England: 4** Saco **6** Nashua **9** Merrimack **10** Blackstone **11** Connecticut **12** Androscoggin **New Jersey: 6** Rahway **7** Passaic, Raritan **8** Tuckahoe **New York: 5** Tioga **6** Hudson, Mohawk, Oneida, Oswego, Seneca **7** Chemung, Niagara **8** Chenango **New Zealand: 7** Waikato **Nicaragua: 4** Coco **5** Segovia **Nigeria: 5** Benin **North Carolina: 3** Haw, Tar **5** Neuse **6** Chowan **8** Alamance **northeast United States: 4** Ohio **6** Hoosic **7** Genesee, Hocking **8** Delaware, Mahoning **9** Allegheny **11** Monongahela, Susquehanna **Northern Ireland: 4** Bann **6** Mourne **North Korea: 4** Yalu **5** Daido **7** Taedong **northwest United**

States: 5 Snake **7** Klamath **8** Columbia **11** Pend Oreille **Norway: 4** Otra, Tana, Teno **nymph: 5** naiad **of fire: 10** Phlegethon **of forgetfulness: 5** Lethe **of ice: 7** glacier **of woe: 7** Acheron **Ohio: 5** Miami **8** Cuyahoga, Sandusky **9** Muskingum **10** Tuscarawas **Oklahoma: 8** Cimarron **Oregon: 5** Rogue **6** Owyhee **7** Malheur **8** McKenzie **9** Clackamas, Deschutes **10** Willamette **Nevada: 7** Truckee **Pakistan: 4** Ravi **Panama: 5** Tuira **7** Chagres **Papua New Guinea: 3** Fly **5** Sepik **Paraguay: 3** Apa **9** Pilcomayo **Pennsylvania: 6** Lehigh **10** Schuylkill **Peru: 5** Rímac, Santa **7** Marañón **8** Apurímac, Huallaga, Urubamba **Philippines: 4** Abra, Agno **5** Pasig **7** Cagayan **8** Cotabato, Mindanao, Pampanga **Poland: 3** San **7** Vistula **Portugal: 4** Sado **7** Mondego **relating to: 7** fluvial **Rhode Island: 7** Seekonk **8** Sakonnet **10** Providence **Romania: 5** Arges **Russia: 3** Don, Oka, Ufa, Usa **4** Kama, Kara, Lena, Msta, Neva, Sura, Svir **5** Onega, Terek, Volga **6** Anadyr, Angara, Belaya, Kolima, Kolyma, Ussuri, Vyatka **7** Dnieper, Pechora, Yenisey **8** Barguzin, Kostroma, Voronezh, Vychegda **Russia-Ukraine: 6** Donets **sacred: 6** Ganges **Scotland: 3** Dee, Don, Esk, Tay **4** Doon, Nith, Spey, Tyne **5** Afton, Annan, Clyde, Forth, Tweed **6** Teviot **7** Deveron **8** Findhorn **Shanghai's: 7** Huangpu, Hwang Pu **Sicily: 5** Salso **6** Simeto **siren: 7** Lorelei **Slovakia: 3** Vag, Vah **4** Gran, Hron, Waag **5** Garam, Nitra **6** Neutra, Nyitra **South Africa: 4** Vaal **6** Orange **South America: 3** Apa **6** Amazon **8** Amazonas, Orellana **9** Pilcomayo **South Carolina: 6** Saluda, Santee **7** Wateree **8** Congaree **South Dakota: 3** Bad **Southeast Asia: 6** Dza-chu, Mekong **7** Salween **8** Lan-ts'ang **southeast United States: 6** Pee Dee **7** Noxubee, Washita **8** Escambia, Ouachita, Suwannee **10** Okanoxubee **southern United States: 6** Sabine **South Korea: 3** Kum **southwest United States: 3** Red **4** Gila, Zuni **5** Pecos **8** Canadian, Colorado **Spain: 4** Ebro **5** Tagus **6** Aragon **12** Guadalquivir **Sweden: 4** Göta **5** Kalix **Switzerland: 3** Aar **4** Aare **5** Reuss **7** Obringa **Syria: 6** Khabur **7** Orontes **Tasmania: 4** Huon **Tbilisi's: 4** Kura **Texas: 5** Llano **6** Brazos, Nueces **7** San Saba, Trinity **9** Guadalupe **Texas-Mexico: 8** Rio Bravo **9** Rio Grande **tidal: 7** estuary **Tokyo's: 6** Sumida **Turkey: 4** Aras **5** Araks **6** Seihun, Seyhan **Ukrainian: 3** Bug **4** Alma, Styr **underworld: 4** Styx **5** Lethe **7** Acheron, Cocytus **10** Phlegethon **Uruguay: 5** Negro **Utah: 5** Provo, Uinta, Weber **6** Jordan,

Sevier *valley:* 6 strath *Venezuela:* 5 Apure, Caura 6 Caroní 7 Orinoco *Vermont:* 3 Mad 5 Onion, White 8 Winooski *Virginia:* 3 Dan 5 James 7 Rapidan 9 Nansemond 10 Appomattox, Shenandoah 12 Chickahominy, Rappahannock *wailing:* 7 Cocytus *Wales:* 4 Dyfi 5 Clwyd, Dovey, Teifi *Washington:* 6 Skagit, Yakima 9 Klickitat, Snohomish, Wenatchee *West Africa:* 5 Niger 6 Gambia 7 Senegal *western United States:* 7 Laramie 8 Columbia, Flathead 11 Yellowstone *West Virginia:* 7 Kanawha *Wisconsin:* 8 Kickapoo 9 Menominee *Wyoming:* 8 Shoshone 10 Gros Ventre 11 Medicine Bow

Rivera's wife 5 Kahlo (Frida)

river duck 4 teal 6 wigeon 7 dabbler, mallard, widgeon 8 shoveler 9 greenwing

river horse 5 hippo 12 hippopotamus

riverine 8 riparian

river island 3 ait 4 eyot

rivet 3 fix, pin 4 bolt, brad, stud 5 affix 6 absorb, attach, clinch, fasten 7 engross 8 fastener

Riviera city 4 Nice 6 Cannes, Monaco 7 Antibes, San Remo 8 St. Tropez 10 Monte Carlo

rivulet 3 run 4 beck, burn, gill, race, rill 5 bourn, brook, creek 6 runlet, runnel, stream 9 streamlet

Rizpah *father:* 4 Aiah *lover:* 4 Saul *son:* 6 Armoni 12 Mephibosheth

roach 3 hog 6 shiner 7 sunfish

road 3 way 4 fare, lane, line, path 5 drive, going, route, track 6 artery, avenue, career, causey, course, street 7 highway, journey, passage 8 causeway, chaussée, crossway, highroad, pavement, speedway, turnpike 9 boulevard 12 thoroughfare *along a cliff:* 8 corniche *around a city:* 6 bypass 7 beltway *bend:* 7 hairpin *edge:* 4 berm 8 shoulder *French:* 6 chemin *Irish:* 6 boreen *machine:* 5 paver 6 grader 9 bulldozer *Roman:* 3 via 4 iter *shoulder:* 4 berm *side:* 6 branch 8 shunpike *Spanish:* 6 camino *surface:* 3 tar 6 gravel 7 asphalt, macadam 8 pavement

roadblock 7 barrier 8 blockade 9 barricade 11 obstruction

road book 3 map 5 atlas 9 gazetteer, itinerary

roadhouse 3 bar, inn 4 dive 5 hotel, lodge 6 tavern 9 nightclub

roadrunner 6 cuckoo 13 chaparral cock

road rut 6 kettle 7 pothole 9 chuckhole

roam 3 bat, bum, gad, run 4 rove, walk 5 drift, prowl, range, stray 6 ramble, stroll, travel, wander 7 meander, traipse 8 straggle, vagabond 9 gallivant

roamer 3 bum 5 gipsy, gypsy, nomad, rover 6 ranger, walker 7 drifter, prowler, rambler,

vagrant 8 marauder, stroller, traveler, vagabond, wanderer 11 nightwalker

roar 3 din 4 bawl, bell, boom, bray, howl, yell 5 shout 6 bellow, clamor, outcry 7 bluster 10 vociferate *bullring:* 3 olé

roast 4 bake, mock, rack, sear 5 broil, grill, joint, parch 6 scathe, scorch 7 banquet, blister, mockery, swelter 8 barbecue, ridicule 9 criticize

rob 3 cop, mug 4 lift, loot, nick, raid, roll, sack 5 boost, filch, heist, pinch, pluck, reave, steal 6 burgle, fleece, hijack, hold up, pilfer, rip off, snitch, thieve 7 defraud, deprive, despoil, pillage, plunder, purloin, ransack, stick up, swindle 8 knock off 9 knock over 10 burglarize

robber 4 yegg 5 crook, thief 6 bandit, looter, mugger, pirate, reiver 7 brigand, burglar, footpad, rustler 8 hijacker, swindler 9 holdup man 10 cat burglar, highwayman, sandbagger, stickup man 12 housebreaker *grave:* 5 ghoul

robbery 5 heist, theft 6 holdup, piracy 7 larceny, mugging, stickup 8 banditry

robe 3 aba 4 cape, gown, wrap 5 cloak, habit 6 caftan, mantle 7 garment, manteau 8 covering, dalmatic, vestment *baptismal:* 7 chrisom *bishop's:* 7 chimere *of Roman emperors:* 6 purple *Turkish:* 6 dolman

Robin Goodfellow 4 Puck 6 sprite

Robinson Crusoe *author:* 5 Defoe (Daniel) *character:* 6 Friday

robot 5 droid, golem 7 android 8 automata (plural) 9 automaton

Rob Roy author 5 Scott (Walter)

robust 4 hale, rude 5 hardy, husky, lusty, rough, sound, stout 6 hearty, potent, rugged, sinewy, strong, sturdy 7 healthy 8 athletic, muscular, vigorous 9 energetic, strapping 10 boisterous, red-blooded, full-bodied, prosperous

robustious 4 rude 5 lusty, rough, rowdy, wooly 6 rugged 7 boorish, ill-bred, loutish 8 churlish, clownish 9 unrefined 10 boisterous, unpolished

rock 4 crag, reel, roll, sway, toss 5 geode, pitch, quake, shake, swing 6 totter 7 boulder, breccia 8 astonish, convulse, undulate 9 oscillate *basaltic:* 5 wacke *cavity:* 3 vug *combining form:* 4 lite, lith, lyte, petr 5 clast, petri, petro *decomposed:* 6 gossan *fissile:* 5 shale *formation:* 4 sill 5 butte, nappe 6 pluton 7 rimrock, terrane 8 isocline, syncline *fragment:* 8 xenolith *igneous:* 4 lava, sial, sima 5 magma 6 basalt, gabbro, pumice 7 diabase, diorite, granite 8 eruptive, felstone, obsidian, porphyry, traprock **10** travertine *layer:* **10** mantlerock *mass:* **5** scree **9** batholith *metamorphic:* **5** slate **6** gneiss, marble, schist **9** quartzite, soapstone *molten:* **4** lava *sedimentary:* **4** clay, coal **5** chalk, chert, coral, flint, shale **8** mudstone **9** limestone, sandstone, siltstone *volcanic:* **4** tuff **6** basalt

rock band 3 REM, Who (The) **4** Cure (The) **5** Byrds (The), Clash (The), Cream, Doors (The), Kinks (The), Queen **6** Eagles (The), Pixies (The), Police (The) **7** Animals (The), Beatles (The), Bee Gees (The), Blondie, Bon Jovi, Chicago, Nirvana, Ramones (The), Rascals (The), Santana **8** Coldplay, Drifters (The), Green Day, Megadeth, Pearl Jam, Platters (The), Supremes (The), Van Halen **9** Aerosmith, Alice Cooper, Beach Boys (The), Metallica, Pink Floyd, Radiohead, Steely Dan, Yardbirds (The) **10** Deep Purple, Duran Duran, Jethro Tull, Moody Blues, Sex Pistols (The), Spice Girls **11** Four Seasons (The), King Crimson, Led Zeppelin **12** Black Sabbath, Fleetwood Mac, Grateful Dead (The), Talking Heads (The) **13** Nine Inch Nails, Rolling Stones (The)

rock bass 7 sunfish

rock-bottom 4 root **6** lowest **8** cheapest **9** lowermost **11** fundamental

rocket 3 fly, zip **4** soar, whiz, zoom **5** mount **6** ascend, bullet **7** missile, shoot up **8** firework, starship **10** projectile *European:* **6** Ariane *landing:* **7** reentry **10** splashdown *launcher:* **7** bazooka *launching:* **7** liftoff **8** blastoff *scientist:* **5** Braun (Wernher von) **7** Goddard (Robert) *section:* **5** stage

rockfish 4 cony, hind **5** coney **7** grouper, jewfish, sea bass **8** bocaccio **10** scorpaenid **11** striped bass

Rockies resort 4 Vail **5** Aspen **8** Snowmass **9** Telluride

____ **Rockne 5** Knute

rock rabbit 4 cony, pika **5** coney, hyrax **6** dassie

rock-ribbed 5 rigid **8** dogmatic, obdurate **9** unbending **10** inflexible, unyielding

rock star 3 J. Lo, Pop (Iggy) **4** Bono, Cher, Crow (Sheryl), Dion (Celine), Flea, Gaga (Lady), Joel (Billy), John (Elton), King (Carole), Love (Courtney), Moon (Keith), Rose (Axl), Roth (David Lee) **5** Abdul (Paula), Berry (Chuck), Bowie (David), Haley (Bill), Harry (Debbie), Holly (Buddy), Lewis (Jerry Lee), Lopez (Jennifer), Paige (Jimmy), Plant (Robert), Seger (Bob), Smith (Patti), Starr (Ringo), Tyler (Stephen), Wyman (Bill), Young (Neil) **6** Burdon (Eric), Cobain (Kurt), Cooper (Alice), Domino (Fats), Eminem, Garcia (Jerry), Jagger (Mick), Joplin (Janis), Lennon (John), Manson (Marilyn), Prince, Spears (Britney), Vaughn (Stevie Ray), Vedder (Eddie) **7** Bon Jovi (Jon), Clapton (Eric), Cochran (Eddie), Daltrey (Roger), Diddley (Bo), Fogerty (John), Hendrix (Jimi), Lavigne (Avril), Madonna, Mercury (Freddie), Michael (George), Perkins (Carl), Presley (Elvis), Shannon (Del), Stefani (Gwen), Stewart (Rod), Vincent (Gene), Winwood (Steve) **8** Costello (Elvis), Harrison (George), Morrison (Jim, Van), Osbourne (Ozzy), Richards (Keith), Van Halen (Eddie) **9** Boy George, McCartney (Paul), Townshend (Pete) **10** Mellencamp (John) **11** Springsteen (Bruce) **13** Little Richard

rockweed 5 algae, fucus **7** seaweed **12** bladder wrack

rocky hill 3 tor **5** kopje

rococo 4 busy **5** showy **6** florid, frilly, ornate **7** baroque, elegant, opulent **9** elaborate, intricate **10** decorative, flamboyant **11** overwrought

rod 3 bar, gat **4** cane, pole, wand **5** baton, dowel, spoke, staff, stave, stick **6** pistol **7** scepter **8** revolver **10** correction, discipline, punishment **11** castigation **12** chastisement *bundle of:* **6** fasces

rodent 3 rat **4** cavy, cony, mole, paca, pika, vole **5** cavie, coney, coypu, mouse, shrew **6** agouti, beaver, gerbil, gopher, jerboa, marmot, murine, nutria, rabbit **7** hamster, lemming, leveret, muskrat **8** capybara, chipmunk, dormouse, squirrel, tuco tuco, viscacha, vizcacha, water rat **9** guinea pig, porcupine **10** chinchilla, field mouse, prairie dog **11** kangaroo rat, meadow mouse, pocket mouse **12** pocket gopher *aquatic:* **5** coypu **6** beaver, nutria **7** muskrat **8** musquash *burrowing:* **4** mole, paca **6** gerbil, gopher **7** hamster **8** viscacha, vizcacha *family:* **5** murid **6** murine **7** sciurid *genus:* **3** Mus **5** Lepus *tropical:* **6** agouti

rodeo 7 contest, roundup **9** enclosure **10** exhibition **11** competition *animal:* **5** horse, steer **10** Brahma bull *event:* **10** calf roping **11** bulldogging **12** bronco riding *performer:* **5** clown **6** cowboy

____ **Rodin 7** Auguste

rodomontade 4 blow, brag, rant **5** boast, swash, vaunt **7** bluster, swagger **9** gasconade **11** braggadocio

Rodomonte *beloved:* **8** Doralice *slayer:* **8** Ruggiero

Rodrigo Díaz de Bivar 5 El Cid
rod-shaped 7 virgate **8** bacillar **9** bacillary
roe 4 deer, eggs **6** beluga, caviar, osetra **7** sevruga
Roentgen's discovery 4 X-ray
Roethke work 6 Waking (The) **8** Far Field (The)
rogation 6 litany, prayer **8** entreaty, petition **10** beseeching **12** supplication
____ **Rogers 3** Roy **4** Carl, Fred, Will **6** Ginger, Robert
rogue 5 cheat, gypsy, knave, scamp **6** rascal **7** lowlife, sharper, villain **8** picaroon, scalawag, swindler **9** defrauder, miscreant, reprobate, scoundrel, skeezicks, trickster **10** blackguard, mountebank **11** rapscallion *relating to:* **10** picaresque
roguery 5 fraud **7** devilry, knavery, waggery **8** deviltry, mischief, trickery **9** devilment, diablerie **11** waggishness **12** sportiveness
roguish 3 sly **4** arch **6** impish, wicked **7** knavish, devilish, espiègle, scampish **10** picaresque **11** mischievous
roil 3 mud, vex **4** foul, rile, romp **5** annoy, dirty, grate, muddy, peeve, upset **6** befoul, muddle, nettle, stir up **7** agitate, disturb **8** disorder, irritate **9** aggravate **10** exasperate
roily 5 muddy, riley **6** turbid **9** turbulent
roister 4 riot **5** revel **6** frolic **7** carouse, reveler, wassail **9** wassailer
Roland 7 Orlando *battle site:* **9** Roncevaux **12** Roncesvalles *beloved:* **4** Aude *betrayer:* **4** Gano **7** Ganelon *friend:* **6** Oliver **7** Olivier *horn:* **7** Olivant *sword:* **8** Durandal, Durendal *uncle:* **11** Charlemagne
role 3 bit **4** duty, lead, part, pose **5** cameo, cloak, guise, niche **6** aspect, office **7** quality **8** capacity, function, position **9** character **13** impersonation
roll 3 bun, rob **4** bolt, coil, flow, furl, gyre, list, pour, rock, toss, turn, wind, wrap **5** heave, pitch, surge **6** bundle, roster, rotate, stream, swathe, wallow, wrap up **7** biscuit, brioche, envelop, revolve, swaddle, trundle **8** involute, register, schedule, turn over *ring-shaped:* **5** bagel
roll about 6 wallow, welter
roll back 5 lower **6** reduce, repeal **7** curtail, rescind
roller 3 rod **4** bowl, drum, wave **6** canary, caster, platen **7** breaker, carrier, tumbler **8** cylinder
Roller Derby round 3 jam
rollick 4 lark, play, romp **5** caper, frisk, party, revel, sport **6** cavort, frolic, gambol **7** disport, skylark **8** escapade **9** merriment
rollicking 4 wild **5** antic, merry **6** frisky,

lively **8** sportive **10** boisterous, frolicsome **12** high-spirited
rolling stock 4 cars **7** coaches, engines **8** cabooses, Pullmans, sleepers, trailers **11** locomotives
rolling stone 4 hobo **5** gipsy, gypsy, nomad, rover, tramp **6** roamer **7** drifter, rambler, vagrant **8** vagabond, wanderer
Rolling Stones 4 Wood (Ron) **5** Jones (Brian), Watts (Charlie), Wyman (Bill) **6** Jagger (Mick), Taylor (Dick, Mick) **7** Stewart (Ian) **8** Richards (Keith)
roly-poly see **rotund**
Roman 5 Latin **7** Italian *amphitheater:* **9** Colosseum *assembly:* **5** forum **6** senate **7** comitia *building:* **5** Forum **6** Circus **8** basilica, Pantheon *clan:* **4** gens *comedy writer:* **7** Plautus (Titus), Terence *conspirator:* **6** Brutus (Marcus Junius) **7** Cassius (Gaius) **8** Catiline *date:* **4** Ides **7** calends, kalends *Doric:* **6** Tuscan *emperor:* **4** Nero, Otho **5** Galba (Servius Sulpicius), Nerva (Marcus Cocceius), Titus, Verus (Lucius Aurelius) **6** Julian, Trajan **7** Hadrian, Maximus (Magnus Clemens, Marcus Clodius, Petronius), Severus (Lucius Septimius) **8** Augustus, Caligula, Claudius, Commodus (Lucius Aelius), Domitian, Tiberius, Valerian **9** Caracalla, Vespasian **10** Diocletian, Theodosius **11** Constantine, Valentinian *entrance hall:* **5** atria (plural) **6** atrium *epic:* **6** Aeneid *epigrammatist:* **7** Martial *family:* **7** Gracchi *Fates:* **4** Nona **5** Morta **6** Decuma, Parcae *festival:* **10** Saturnalia *founder:* **5** Remus **7** Romulus *fountain:* **5** Trevi **6** Triton *garment:* **4** toga **5** tunic *general:* **5** Sulla (Lucius Cornelius), Titus **6** Antony (Marc), Marius (Gaius), Scipio (Publius Cornelius) **8** Agricola (Gnaeus Julius)
god: **3** Lar **4** deus **6** Plutus *chief:* **4** Jove **7** Jupiter *messenger:* **7** Mercury *of agriculture:* **6** Saturn *of animals:* **6** Faunus *of death:* **4** Mors *of dreams:* **8** Morpheus *of fire:* **6** Vulcan *of gates and doors:* **5** Janus *of healing:* **9** Asclepius **11** Aesculapius *of heaven:* **6** Uranus *of households:* **3** Lar **5** Lares **7** Penates *of love:* **4** Amor **5** Cupid *of medicine:* **9** Asclepius **11** Aesculapius *of mirth:* **5** Comus *of regeneration:* **7** Priapus *of sleep:* **6** Somnus *of the sea:* **6** Pontus **7** Neptune, Proteus *of the sun:* **3** Sol **6** Apollo *of the underworld:* **3** Dis **5** Orcus, Pluto **8** Dispater *of the wind:* **5** Eurus, Notus **6** Aeolus, Aquilo, Auster, Boreas **8** Favonius, Zephyrus *of war:* **4** Mars **8** Quirinus *of*

wealth: 6 Plutus of wine: 7 Bacchus of woods: 6 Faunus two-faced: 5 Janus *goddess:* 3 dea of agriculture: 5 Ceres of beauty: 5 Venus of dawn: 6 Aurora *of death:* 5 Morta of flowers: 5 Flora of handicrafts: 7 Minerva of harvests: 3 Ops of health: 7 Minerva of hope: 4 Spes of hunting: 5 Diana of justice: 7 Astraea of love: 5 Venus of marriage: 4 Juno of night: 3 Nox of peace: 3 Pax of springs: 7 Juturna of strife: 9 Discordia of the earth: 5 Terra 6 Tellus of the hearth: 5 Vesta of the moon: 4 Luna of the sea: 10 Amphitrite of the underworld: 10 Proserpina of victory: 6 Vacuna of war: 7 Bellona of wisdom: 7 Minerva of womanhood: 4 Juno *greeting:* 3 ave *hero:* 6 Caesar (Julius) 11 Cincinnatus (Lucius Quinctius) *hill:* 7 Caelian, Viminal 8 Aventine, Palatine, Quirinal 9 Esquiline 10 Capitoline *historian:* 4 Livy 5 Nepos 7 Sallust, Tacitus 9 Suetonius *king:* 7 Romulus, Servius, Tullius 12 Ancus Martius 13 Numa Pompilius *marketplace:* 5 agora *military formation:* 3 ala 6 alares (plural) 7 phalanx *miltary unit:* 6 cohort, legion 7 maniple *officer:* 9 centurion *official:* 5 augur, edile 6 aedile, censor, consul, lictor 7 praetor, prefect, tribune 8 quaestor 9 proconsul *people:* 5 Laeti, plebs 6 populi (plural) 7 populus, Sabines 9 plebeians *philosopher:* 4 Cato 6 Seneca 8 Apuleius 9 Epictetus, Lucretius *physician:* 9 Asclepius 11 Aesculapius *port:* 5 Ostia *procurator:* 6 Pilate (Pontius) *province:* 4 Asia 5 Lycia, Syria 6 Achaea, Africa, Arabia, Cyprus, Raetia 7 Baetica, Belgica, Galatia, Numidia, Sicilia, Thracia 8 Aegyptus, Dalmatia 9 Aquitania, Britannia, Lusitania 10 Cappadocia, Mauretania *racecourse:* 6 circus *road:* 4 iter *slave:* 9 Spartacus *statesman:* 4 Cato 5 Pliny 6 Caesar, Cicero, Pompey, Seneca 7 Agrippa 8 Augustus, Gracchus, Maecenas 9 Flaminius *symbol of authority:* 6 fasces
roman à _____ 4 clef
romance 3 woo 4 gest, love 5 amour, court, fling, geste, novel 6 affair 7 fantasy, fiction 8 stardust 10 love affair 12 bodice ripper
Romance language 6 French 7 Catalan, Italian, Spanish 8 Romanian, Rumanian 9 Sardinian 10 Portuguese
romance writer 4 Holt (Victoria), Robb (J. D.) 5 Brown (Sandra), Chase (Loretta), Clark (Mary Higgins), Heyer (Georgette), Steel (Danielle) 6 Dailey (Janet), Graham (Heather), Howard (Linda), Krantz (Ju-

dith), Krentz (Jayne Ann), Putney (Mary Jo), Stuart (Anne) 7 Baldwin (Faith), Collins (Jackie), Cookson (Catherine), Coulter (Catherine), Estrada (Rita Clay), Garwood (Julie), Hatcher (Robin Lee), Maxwell (Anne), Osborne (Maggie), Roberts (Nora), Spencer (LaVyrle), Stewart (Mary), Whitney (Phyllis) 8 Bradford (Barbara Taylor), Cartland (Barbara), Deveraux (Jude), Gabaldon (Diana), McNaught (Judith), Phillips (Susan Elizabeth) 9 Alsobrook (Rosalyn), Evanovich (Janet), Woodiwiss (Kathleen)
Romania *capital:* 9 Bucharest *city:* 4 Iasi 6 Brasov, Galati 7 Craiova 9 Constanta, Timisoara *monetary unit:* 3 leu 4 bani *mountain range:* 10 Carpathian *neighbor:* 6 Serbia 7 Hungary, Moldova, Ukraine 8 Bulgaria *part of:* 7 Balkans *peninsula:* 6 Balkan *river:* 5 Siret, Tisza 6 Danube *sea:* 5 Black
romantic 5 gauzy, ideal, idyll, mushy 6 ardent, dreamy, exotic, gothic, poetic, unreal 7 amorous, maudlin, mawkish 8 fanciful, quixotic 9 fantastic, imaginary, visionary 10 idealistic, lovey-dovey 11 sentimental
Romany 5 Gipsy, Gypsy
Romeo 5 lover, swain 7 amorist, Don Juan, gallant 8 Casanova, lothario, paramour *beloved:* 6 Juliet *enemy:* 6 Tybalt *father:* 8 Montague *friend:* 8 Mercutio
Rommel, Erwin 9 Desert Fox
romp 4 lark, play 5 caper, frisk, sport 6 cavort, frolic, gambol, hoyden 7 rollick, runaway, skylark 8 escapade
Romulus *brother:* 5 Remus *father:* 4 Mars *mother:* 9 Rea Silvia 10 Rhea Silvia *victim:* 5 Remus
rondure 3 arc, orb 4 arch, ball, ring 5 curve, globe, round 6 circle, sphere 9 curvature
rood 5 cross 8 crucifix
roof 3 hip, top 4 apex, peak 5 cover, crest, crown 6 summit 7 ceiling 8 covering, housetop *material:* 3 tar, tin 4 tile 5 slate, straw, terne 6 copper, thatch 7 shingle *of a cavern:* 4 dome *of the mouth:* 6 palate *part:* 3 hip 4 eave 5 eaves 6 soffit 8 overhang 9 ridgepole *structure:* 9 penthouse *type:* 5 gable 6 hipped 7 gambrel, lamella, mansard 9 butterfly *vaulted:* 4 dome
roofer 5 tiler
rook 4 bilk, colt, crow, scam, tyro 5 cheat, mulct, raven, stick 6 castle, fleece, novice 7 amateur, defraud, recruit, swindle, trainee 8 beginner, flimflam, freshman, neophyte, newcomer 10 apprentice, tenderfoot
rookery 5 roost 6 colony

rookie 4 colt, tyro **5** plebe **6** novice **7** amateur, recruit, trainee **8** beginner, freshman, neophyte, newcomer **10** apprentice, tenderfoot

room 3 den **4** cell, hall, play, rein **5** divan, house, lodge, put up, salon, scope, space **6** alcove, billet, leeway, margin, reside, studio **7** chamber, cubicle, expanse, gallery, lodging **9** clearance *ancient Roman:* **5** atria (plural) **6** atrium *eating:* **4** nook **6** alcove **7** commons, kitchen **8** mess hall **9** refectory *food storage:* **6** larder, pantry *for paintings:* **7** gallery *in a harem:* **3** oda *in a monastery:* **4** cell **9** refectory **11** calefactory *in a prison:* **4** cell *on a ship:* **5** cabin **6** galley *round:* **7** rotunda

roomer 5 guest **6** lodger, renter, tenant **7** boarder

roomy 4 wide **5** ample, broad, large **8** spacious **9** capacious **10** commodious

Roosevelt, Franklin D. *birthplace:* **8** Hyde Park *dog:* **4** Fala *message:* **12** fireside chat *mother:* **4** Sara *predecessor:* **6** Hoover (Herbert) *program:* **7** New Deal *successor:* **6** Truman (Harry) *vacation home:* **10** Campobello *wife:* **7** Eleanor

roost 3 sit **4** land, nest, rest **5** perch **6** alight, settle **7** rookery **8** dovecote

rooster 4 cock **5** capon **8** cockerel, gamecock **10** cockalorum **11** chanticleer

root 3 dig, fix **4** base, bulb, core, grub, pith, stem, well **5** basis, cheer, embed, grout, lodge, plant, radix, tuber **6** bottom, etymon, ground, marrow, origin, settle, source **7** applaud, bedrock, essence, footing, radical **8** radicate **9** beginning, establish, inception **10** foundation *aromatic:* **7** ginseng *edible:* **3** oca, yam **4** beet, taro, yuca **5** yucca **6** carrot, daikon, ginger, jicama, manioc, potato, radish, turnip **7** burdock, cassava, parsnip, salsify **8** celeriac, kohlrabi, rutabaga, tuckahoe **11** horseradish *fragrant:* **6** orris **7** vetiver *main:* **7** taproot *medicinal:* **5** jalap **7** ginseng *relating to:* **7** radical *starch:* **4** arum **7** tapioca *word:* **6** etymon

rootlet 7 radicle, rhizoid

root out 4 grub **9** eradicate, extirpate **10** deracinate

Roots *author:* **5** Haley (Alex) *character:* **3** Lea (George, Tom) **4** Toby **5** Haley (Alex, Simon Alexander) **6** Bertha, Waller (Bell, John, Kizzy, Dr. William) **7** Cynthia, Matilda **8** Kintango **9** Missy Anne **10** Kunta Kinte

rope 3 guy, tie **4** bind, cord, line, stay **5** belay, bight, brace, cable, chord, lasso, riata, sheet **6** binder, fasten, halter, hawser, lariat, marlin, shroud, strand, string, tether **7** halyard, lashing, marline, painter, towline **8** buntline, lifeline *fiber:* **4** coir, hemp, jute **5** abaca, sisal **6** Manila **8** henequen *loop:* **7** cringle *mooring:* **6** hawser *ship's:* **4** vang **5** sheet **6** marlin, parral, parrel, shroud **7** lanyard, marline, ratline **9** mainsheet

ropedancer 11 funambulist

rope off 6 cordon

ropes 10 ins and outs, procedures, techniques

ropy 4 wiry **6** sinewy **7** stringy, viscous **8** muscular

roque 7 croquet

rorqual 5 whale **7** finback **8** fin whale **11** baleen whale

Rosalind's beloved 7 Orlando

rosary 5 beads **7** chaplet **8** beadroll, devotion **11** prayer beads

rose 4 glow, pink **5** blush, color, flush, rouge **6** mantle, pinken, redden **7** crimson **10** erysipelas *Chinese:* **8** Cherokee *cotton:* **7** cudweed *feature:* **5** thorn *kind:* **4** moss **5** Peace, Vogue **6** Circus, damask **7** Fashion, Granada, Iceberg, New Dawn, Pascali, Tiffany **8** Rubaiyat **9** Floradora, Montezuma, polyantha, Tropicana **10** Floribunda **11** grandiflora, Mount Shasta **12** Crimson Glory

roseate see **rosy**

rose-colored see **rosy**

Rosenkavalier composer 7 Strauss (Richard)

rose of ____ 6 Sharon

rose oil 5 attar

Rose Tattoo author 8 Williams (Tennessee)

rosette 7 cockade **8** ornament

Rosinante's master 7 Quixote (Don)

Rosmersholm author 5 Ibsen (Henrik)

____ Rossetti 5 Dante (Gabriel) **9** Christina *work:* **8** Sing-Song **11** Annus Domini, House of Life (The), Seek and Find, Sister Helen **12** Beata Beatrix, Goblin Market

Rossini opera 6 Otello **8** Tancredi **11** Cenerentola (La), William Tell **14** Siege of Corinth (The) **15** Barber of Seville (The)

Rostand hero 6 Cyrano (de Bergerac)

roster 4 list, roll, rota **5** slate **6** muster, scroll **8** register, roll call, schedule **9** honor roll **10** muster roll **11** waiting list

rostrum 4 dais **5** bimah **6** pulpit **7** lectern, tribune **8** platform

rosy 3 red **4** pink **5** sunny **6** bright, upbeat **7** beamish **8** cheerful, sanguine **10** optimistic

rot 4 bosh, bull, mold **5** decay, hooey, spoil, taint, trash **6** fester, molder **7** corrupt, crapola, crumble, eyewash, garbage, hogwash, putrefy, rubbish **8** gangrene, nonsense **9** break down, decompose, poppycock **10** balderdash, degenerate **11** deteriorate, putrescence **12** disintegrate, putrefaction **13** decomposition

rotary 6 circle **8** gyratory, spinning, whirling **10** roundabout **11** vertiginous **13** traffic circle

rotate 4 gyre, roll, spin, turn **5** pivot, twirl, wheel, whirl **6** gyrate, swivel **7** revolve, trundle **9** alternate, pirouette *a log:* **4** birl

rotation 4 gyre, loop, turn **5** cycle, orbit, pivot, round, wheel, whirl **7** circuit, turning **8** gyration **10** revolution, succession

rote 5 crowd, grind **6** custom, groove, memory **7** routine **8** practice **9** automatic, treadmill **10** mechanical, repetition **12** memorization

Roth novel 11 Call It Sleep **15** Goodbye Columbus **16** American Pastoral **17** Portnoy's Complaint

rotten 4 foul **5** fetid, lousy **6** crummy, putrid **7** corrupt, decayed, spoiled, tainted **9** nefarious, offensive, putrified **10** decomposed, degenerate, putrescent

rotter 3 cad, cur **4** heel, lout **5** creep, louse **7** bounder **9** scoundrel **10** blackguard

rotund 4 fat **5** obese, plump, podgy, pudgy, round, stout, thick, tubby **6** chubby, chunky, portly, stocky **7** rounded **8** heavyset, roly-poly, thickset **9** corpulent **10** potbellied

roué 4 lech, rake, wolf **6** lecher **7** amorist, Don Juan, gallant, seducer, swinger **8** Casanova, lothario, sybarite **9** bon vivant, debauchee, libertine, womanizer **10** sensualist, voluptuary **11** philanderer

rouge 3 red **4** glow, pink, rose **5** blush, color, flush **6** mantle, pinken, redden **7** crimson

rough 3 raw **4** rude, wild **5** brute, bumpy, crass, crude, hairy, harsh, raspy, rowdy, yahoo **6** choppy, coarse, craggy, crusty, hoarse, jagged, rugged, stormy, uneven **7** cragged, grating, jarring, rasping, raucous, ruffian, scraggy, uncivil, uncouth **8** bullyboy, churlish, impolite, scabrous, unformed **9** difficult, imperfect, strenuous, turbulent, unrefined **10** boisterous, tumultuous, unfinished, unpolished **11** approximate, tempestuous

rough-and-ready 5 crude **6** make-do **7** stopgap **8** slapdash **9** expedient, impromptu, makeshift **10** improvised **11** provisional **13** quick-and-dirty

rough-hewn 4 rude **5** crude, plain **10** unfinished, unpolished **12** uncultivated

roughly 5 about, circa **9** virtually **10** more or less **13** approximately

roughneck see **ruffian**

rough out 5 block, chalk, draft **6** sketch **7** outline **9** adumbrate **11** skeletonize

rough up 4 beat, maul **6** batter, pummel **8** maltreat **9** brutalize, manhandle **10** slap around

roulette *bet:* **4** noir, trio **5** rouge, split **7** sixline **10** straight up *term:* **5** passe, tiers **6** impair, manque, mucker **7** orphans **8** croupier **9** house edge

round 4 gyre, tour, turn **5** bowed, cycle, globe, wheel **6** circle, curved, rotund **7** annular, circuit **8** circular, globular, roly-poly, rotation, sequence **9** orbicular, spherical **10** conglobate

roundabout 6 circle, detour, rotary **7** circuit, compass, curving, devious, oblique, winding **8** circular, indirect **10** circuitous, meandering **13** traffic circle

rounded 5 bowed, plump **6** arched, convex, curved, rotund, zaftig **7** concave **9** developed **10** curvaceous, Rubenesque **13** well-developed

rounder 4 rake, roué, waif **6** no-good, waster **7** wastrel **8** prodigal, vagabond **9** libertine **10** ne'er-do-well, profligate

roundly 4 well **5** fully, quite **6** widely, wholly **7** bluntly, sharply, smartly, utterly **8** candidly, entirely **9** brusquely **10** altogether, completely, rigorously, scathingly, thoroughly, vigorously

round off 3 cap, top **5** crown **6** climax, finish **8** conclude **9** culminate

round-robin 6 appeal, letter, series **7** protest **8** petition, sequence **9** statement **10** tournament

round trip 4 tour **7** circuit **9** excursion

round up 4 herd **5** drive, group **6** gather **7** cluster, collect **8** assemble

rouse 3 jog **4** call, goad, rock, stir, wake, whet **5** alarm, awake, pique, rally, roust, waken **6** awaken, bestir, excite, foment, incite, kindle, muster, rattle, recall, revive, vivify, work up **7** agitate, animate, commove, disturb, enliven, provoke, quicken **8** motivate **9** aggravate, challenge, galvanize, instigate, stimulate

rousing 5 brisk, peppy **6** lively **8** animated, exciting, spirited, stirring **9** inspiring **11** stimulating **12** exhilarating, intoxicating

Rousseau work 5 Émile

roustabout 4 hand **6** worker **7** laborer, workman **8** deckhand **10** workingman **12** longshoreman, troublemaker

route 3 way **4** path, road, send, ship **5** guide, pilot, steer, track, trail **6** avenue, bypass, course, detour, direct, divert, escort, flyway, seaway, skyway **7** channel, circuit, conduct, consign, forward, highway, journey, passage, portage, sea-lane **8** corridor, dispatch, transmit, traverse **9** direction, itinerary

routine 3 act, bit, rut **4** dull, pace, rote **5** chore, drill, grind, habit, ho-hum, plain, round, trial, usual **6** course, groove, improv, shtick, wonted **7** chronic, formula, program, regimen, regular, utility **8** accepted, everyday, habitual, ordinary, standard, workaday **9** customary, monologue, procedure, quotidian, treadmill **10** accustomed, donkeywork, mechanical **11** commonplace, cut-and-dried, perfunctory **12** housekeeping, unremarkable

rove 3 gad **4** roam **5** drift, range, stray **6** ramble, wander **7** meander, traipse **8** straggle, vagabond **9** gallivant

rover 5 gipsy, gypsy, nomad, stray **6** picaro, pirate, roamer, viking **7** corsair, drifter, floater, rambler, vagrant **8** picaroon, runabout, traveler, vagabond, wanderer **9** buccaneer, meanderer **10** freebooter **12** rolling stone

roving 6 errant, mobile **7** movable, nomadic, vagrant **8** straying, vagabond **9** itinerant, migratory, wayfaring **11** peripatetic

row 3 oar, way **4** bank, crew, file, fray, fuss, line, muss, rank, spat, tier, tiff **5** align, brawl, broil, chain, fight, melee, order, queue, range, run-in, scrap, scull, strip, swath **6** bicker, clamor, column, dustup, fracas, kickup, paddle, propel, ruckus, series, string, stroke **7** brabble, dispute, quarrel, rhubarb, wrangle **8** argument, diagonal, sequence, squabble **9** commotion **10** falling-out, single file, succession **11** altercation, disturbance, progression

rowdy 4 punk, rude **5** bully, crude, rough, yahoo **6** unruly **7** hoodlum, rackety, raffish, raucous, ruffian **8** bullyboy, hooligan **9** roughneck **10** boisterous, disorderly, robustious **11** rumbustious **12** rambunctious

Rowena *father:* **7** Hengist *guardian:* **6** Cedric *husband:* **7** Ivanhoe **9** Vortigern

Rowling character 3 Ron (Weasley) **5** Harry (Potter), Snape (Severus) **6** Malfoy (Draco), Sirius (Black) **8** Hermione (Granger) **9** Voldemort (Lord) **10** Dumbledore (Albus)

Roxana *husband:* **9** Alexander *rival:* **7** Statira

royal 5 grand, noble, regal **6** kingly, lordly **7** stately **8** glorious, imperial, imposing, majestic, princely, splendid **9** grandiose, monarchal, sovereign **10** monarchial **11** magnificent, monarchical

rub 4 buff **5** chafe, grate, shine **6** abrade, polish, smooth, stroke **7** burnish, massage

Rubaiyat author 4 Omar (Khayyám)

rubber 4 buna **5** crepe **6** caucho, eraser **10**

caoutchouc *basis:* **5** latex *hard:* **7** ebonite *synthetic:* **8** neoprene *tree:* **3** Ule **4** Para

Rubber City 5 Akron

rubberneck 3 eye **4** gape, gawk, gaze **5** snoop, stare **6** goggle **8** sightsee

rubber-stamp 2 OK **4** okay **7** approve, certify, endorse **9** authorize

rubbish 3 rot **4** bosh, crap, crud, junk, muck, slop, tosh **5** bilge, dreck, hooey, offal, trash, truck, waste **6** debris, litter, refuse, raffle, rubble, spilth **7** crapola, garbage, hogwash **8** nonsense, riffraff, tommyrot **9** poppycock, sweepings **11** foolishness

rubbishy 5 cheap, tatty **6** paltry, shoddy, sleazy, trashy **9** worthless

rubble 5 ruins, scree **6** debris, litter **8** detritus, wreckage

rube 4 boor, hick, naïf **5** churl, cluck, swain, yahoo, yokel **6** rustic **7** bumpkin, hayseed, redneck **9** greenhorn, hillbilly **10** clodhopper **12** apple-knocker, backwoodsman

rubicund 3 red **5** flush, ruddy **6** florid **7** glowing, reddish **8** sanguine **11** full-blooded, incarnadine

rubidium symbol 2 Rb

____ **Rubik 4** Erno

rub out 3 ice, off, zap **4** do in, kill, slay **5** erase, smoke, waste, whack **6** finish, murder **7** bump off, destroy, put away **8** dispatch, knock off **9** liquidate, terminate **10** extinguish, obliterate **11** assassinate

rubric 4 name, rule **5** canon, class, gloss, style, title **6** custom **7** concept, heading **8** category, headline **9** tradition **11** appellation, designation **13** interpolation

ruck 3 mob **4** fold, heap, mass, pile **5** crimp, crowd, group, purse, ridge **6** cockle, crease, furrow, gather, jumble, pucker, rumple **7** crinkle, crumple, scrunch, wrinkle **10** generality **11** corrugation

rucksack 4 pack **6** kit bag **7** musette **8** backpack

ruckus 3 ado, row **4** fuss, to-do **5** brawl, melee, scrap **6** fracas, furore, hassle, pother, rumpus, shindy, uproar **7** dispute, quarrel, rhubarb, shindig, wrangle **8** squabble **9** commotion **10** falling-out **11** altercation, controversy, disturbance

ruddle see **redden**

ruddy 3 red **4** ripe, rosy **5** flush **6** blowsy, florid **7** flushed, glowing **8** rubicund, sanguine **11** full-blooded, incarnadine

rude 3 raw **4** curt **5** crass, gross, gruff, harsh, rough, rowdy, surly **6** abrupt, callow, clumsy, coarse, crusty, robust, rugged, rustic, sturdy, unhewn, vulgar **7** boorish, brusque, ill-bred, loutish, lowbred, uncivil, uncouth **8** arrogant, churlish, clownish, impolite, tactless **9** barbarian, barbarous, elemental, inelegant, primitive, rough-hewn, unrefined **10** ungracious, unmannered, unmannerly, unpolished **11** ill-mannered, impertinent, uncivilized **12** discourteous, uncultivated **13** disrespectful

rudimentary 5 basal, basic **6** simple **7** initial, primary **8** simplest **9** beginning, elemental, vestigial **10** elementary **11** fundamental, undeveloped **12** introductory

rudiments 4 ABCs **6** basics **10** essentials **12** fundamentals

rue 3 woe **4** pity, ruth **5** dolor, grief, mourn, prick **6** grieve, lament, regret, repent, sorrow **7** anguish, deplore, remorse **8** sympathy **9** heartache, penitence **10** affliction, compassion, contrition, heartbreak, repentance **11** compunction

rueful 5 sorry **6** woeful **8** contrite, penitent **9** regretful, sorrowful **10** remorseful

ruff 5 frill, perch, trump **6** collar, fringe **9** sandpiper **11** pumpkinseed *female:* **5** reeve

ruffian 4 goon, hood, punk, thug **5** beast, brute, bully, rowdy, tough, yahoo **6** Apache, hector **7** gorilla, hoodlum **8** bullyboy, hooligan **9** muscleman, roughneck, swaggerer

ruffle 3 bug, irk, rub, vex **4** fret, gall, wear **5** annoy, brawl, chafe, frill, graze, jabot, pleat, ruche **6** abrade, bother, nettle, ripple **7** agitate, bristle, disturb, flounce, provoke, trouble, wrinkle **8** drumbeat, furbelow, irritate, skirmish **9** commotion

rug 3 mat **6** carpet, runner, toupee **7** laprobe *kind:* **3** rag, rya **6** hooked **7** braided, dhurrie, drugget, flokati, Persian **8** Aubusson, bearskin, Oriental **10** Savonnerie

rugby *formation:* 5 scrum **9** scrummage *goal:* **7** dropped, penalty *period:* **4** half *player:* **6** center, hooker, winger **8** standoff **9** scrum half *scoring:* **3** try **4** goal **10** conversion *team:* **7** fifteen *term:* **4** heel **5** match **7** convert, dribble, hand off, knock on **9** fair catch *time-out:* **8** stoppage *version:* **5** union **6** league

rugged 5 burly, hardy, harsh, heavy, husky, rough, tough **6** brawny, coarse, craggy, jagged, robust, severe, stable, stormy, strong, sturdy, uneven **7** arduous, austere, scraggy **8** leathery, muscular, rigorous, scabrous, stalwart, vigorous **9** difficult, inclement, strenuous, unrefined, weathered **10** formidable, unpolished **11** tempestuous

Ruggiero *guardian:* 7 Atlante *sister:* **7** Marfisa *slayer:* **11** Tisaphernes *wife:* **10** Bradamante

rug rat 3 tot **4** tyke **6** moppet **7** toddler

Ruhr city 5 Essen **8** Dortmund

ruin 4 bane, bust, dash, do in, doom, fall, loss, rape, raze, sack, undo **5** decay, havoc, smash, spoil, trash, use up, waste, wrack, wreck **6** beggar, finish, pauper, perish, ravage **7** corrupt, deplete, despoil, destroy, exhaust, failure, nemesis, pillage, shatter, undoing, wipe out **8** bankrupt, collapse, decimate, demolish, downfall, spoliate **9** depredate, devastate, disrepair, overthrow, pauperize, shipwreck **10** desolation, impoverish **11** destruction, devastation, dissolution **12** degeneration **13** deterioration

ruination 4 bane, loss, rack **5** havoc **7** undoing **8** calamity, disaster, downfall **10** decimation **11** destruction, devastation

ruinous 5 fatal **7** baneful **10** calamitous, disastrous, pernicious **11** cataclysmic, destructive **12** catastrophic

rule 3 law, Raj **4** lead, sway **5** axiom, bylaw, canon, edict, habit, judge, maxim, moral, order, reign **6** assize, custom, decree, deduce, dictum, direct, govern, regime, truism **7** brocard, command, control, precept, prevail, regency, regimen, resolve, statute **8** decretum, doctrine, dominate, domineer, dominion **9** authority, determine, etiquette, ordinance, principle, procedure **10** regulation *absolute:* **7** autarky **8** autarchy *by a god:* **8** theonomy

Rule Britannia composer 4 Arne (Thomas)

rule out 3 bar **5** block, debar **6** forbid, refuse, reject **7** dismiss, exclude, forfend, head off, obviate, prevent **8** preclude, prohibit, stave off **9** eliminate

ruler 4 king, lord **5** queen **6** archon, dynast, ferule, gerent, prince, regent, satrap, sultan **7** emperor, monarch, viceroy **8** governor, hierarch, oligarch, pentarch, princess, theocrat **9** dominator, imperator, matriarch, patriarch, potentate, sovereign **12** straightedge *absolute:* **6** despot, tyrant **8** autocrat, dictator, overlord *Arab:* **4** amir, emir **5** ameer, sheik **6** sharif, sheikh, sultan *Asian:* **4** khan *Byzantine Empire:* **6** exarch *Egyptian:* **7** pharaoh *family:* **7** dynasty *Iranian:* **4** shah *one of four:* **8** tetrarch *one of seven:* **8** heptarch *one of three:* **7** triarch **8** triumvir *Persian:* **6** satrap *Russian:* **4** czar, tsar, tzar *Turkish:* **3** bey, dey **6** sultan

ruling 3 law **4** call **5** chief, edict, order, ukase **6** decree **7** current, finding, popular, regnant, verdict **8** decision, judgment **9** directive, judgement, prevalent, statement **10** prevailing, widespread **11** predominant **12** adjudication

Rumania see **Romania**

rumble 4 buzz, roar, roll **5** brawl, drone, fight, growl, rumor **6** murmur, report **7** hearsay, quarrel, resound, thunder **8** feedback **9** complaint **11** altercation, disturbance, reverberate, scuttlebutt

ruminant 3 Bos, cow, yak **4** deer, goat, tahr **5** bison, camel, llama, okapi, serow, sheep, takin **6** alpaca, cattle, musk ox, vicuña **7** buffalo, chamois, chewing, giraffe, guanaco **8** antelope **9** pronghorn *stomach:* **5** rumen **6** omasum **8** abomasum **9** reticulum

ruminate 4 chew, mull, muse **5** champ, chomp, weigh **6** ponder **7** reflect **8** cogitate, consider, meditate **9** masticate **10** deliberate **11** contemplate

ruminative 7 pensive **8** thinking **9** pondering **10** cogitative, meditative, reflective, thoughtful **11** speculative **13** contemplative, introspective

rummage 4 comb, fish, grub, hash, hunt, poke, rake, rout, seek **5** delve, scour **6** ferret, forage, jumble, litter, search **7** clutter, ransack **8** mishmash **9** potpourri **10** hodgepodge, hotchpotch, miscellany

rummy 3 gin, odd, sot **4** lush, soak, wino **5** drunk, souse, toper **6** boozer **7** bizarre, canasta, curious, guzzler, strange, swiller, tippler, tosspot **8** drunkard, peculiar **9** eccentric, inebriate **10** boozehound

rumor 4 blab, buzz, talk **5** bruit, noise, story **6** canard, gossip, murmur, mutter, report, rumble, tattle **7** hearsay, tidings, whisper **9** grapevine **11** scuttlebutt, susurration *personified:* **4** Fama

rumormonger 5 yenta **6** gossip **8** gossiper, informer, quidnunc, telltale **9** whisperer **10** talebearer, tattletale

rump 3 can **4** beam, butt, duff, hind, rear, tush **5** fanny **6** behind, bottom, breech, heinie **7** keester, keister, rear end **8** backside, buttocks, derriere, haunches **9** posterior

rumple 4 fold, muss, ruck **5** crimp, screw, touse **6** pucker, tousle **7** crimple, crinkle, scrunch, wrinkle **8** dishevel, disorder

rumpus see **ruckus**

run 3 fly, hie, jog **4** bolt, dart, dash, flee, flow, race, rush, scud, tear **5** chase, haste, hurry, scoot, skirr, speed **6** career, gallop, hasten, scurry, sprint, streak, stream **7** scamper, scuttle, smuggle **9** skedaddle

run across 4 meet **8** bump into, discover **9** encounter, stumble on

runagate 4 hobo **5** gipsy, gypsy, nomad, tramp **6** outlaw **7** drifter, floater, lamster, vagrant, wastrel **8** bohemian, fugitive, rapparee, vagabond, wanderer **11** guttersnipe

run along 2 go **5** leave, scram **6** beat it, begone, cut out, depart **7** buzz off, get lost, skiddoo, take off, vamoose **8** shove off **9** skedaddle **10** make tracks

runaround 4 duck, slip **5** dodge **7** elusion, evasion

run away 4 bolt, flee, skip **5** elope, leave, scram, skirr, split, steal **6** depart, desert, escape **7** abscond, make off **8** clear out, light out, stampede **9** skedaddle **10** make tracks

runaway 4 romp, wild **5** loose **6** outlaw **7** escapee, lamster **8** deserter, fugitive **10** delinquent **12** uncontrolled

run down 3 hit, ram, tag **5** catch, knock, trace **6** pursue **7** decline, belittle, derogate, diminish **9** apprehend, disparage **10** depreciate **11** catch up with

run-down 5 dingy, seedy, tacky, tired **6** beatup, bushed, shabby **7** rickety, ruinous, worn-out **8** decrepit, tattered, untended **9** burned-out, exhausted, neglected **10** bedraggled, down-at-heel, ramshackle, uncared-for **11** dilapidated

rundown 4 dope, poop **5** recap, scoop **6** report, review, skinny, update **7** outline, summary **8** briefing, synopsis

runes 4 ogam **5** ogham **7** futhark

rung 3 bar **4** step **5** grade, notch, round, spoke, staff, stage, stair, tread **6** degree, rundle **10** crosspiece

run-in 3 row **4** tiff **5** brush, fight, set-to **6** hassle, scrape, tangle **7** dispute, quarrel, rhubarb, wrangle **8** skirmish, squabble **9** encounter **10** falling-out **11** altercation

run into 3 hit, ram **4** meet **9** encounter, stumble on **11** collide with

runner 3 rug **5** gofer, miler, racer **6** carpet, stolon **7** carrier, courier, tendril **8** smuggler, sprinter **9** go-between, messenger **10** marathoner **11** ballcarrier see **track star**

running 6 active, fluent **7** cursive, dynamic, flowing, working **9** operative **10** continuous **11** functioning

run-of-the-mill 4 dull, so-so **5** usual **6** common, normal **7** average, humdrum, regular, typical **8** everyday, familiar, mediocre, middling, moderate, ordinary **9** prevalent **10** monotonous **11** commonplace, indifferent **12** intermediate **13** unexceptional

run on 3 gab, yak **4** blab **5** clack **6** babble, cackle, gabble, jabber, ramble, rattle **7** chatter, prattle **8** continue

run out of 5 use up **6** finish **7** exhaust

run over 5 spill **6** exceed, repeat **7** examine **8** overfill, overflow, rehearse

runt 5 dwarf, pygmy **6** midget, peanut, peewee, shrimp, squirt **7** manikin **8** mannikin,

Tom Thumb **10** homunculus **11** hop-o'-my-thumb, lilliputian

run through 3 jab **4** blow, gore, read, scan, stab **5** spend, use up, waste **6** expend, finish, impale, pierce **7** consume, examine, exhaust **8** rehearse, squander, transfix

runty 3 wee **4** puny **6** peewee **7** stunted **8** dwarfish **10** diminutive, undersized

run up 5 build, erect, mount **6** expand **7** augment, enlarge **8** increase, multiply **9** construct **10** accumulate

runway 4 duct, path **5** strip, track, trail **6** sluice, tarmac **7** channel, conduit **8** airstrip, platform

rupture 4 rend, rent, rift, rive **5** break, burst, cleft, sever, split **6** breach, cleave, hernia, schism, sunder **7** blowout, break up, disrupt, divorce, fissure, parting, split-up **8** division, fracture, separate **9** partition **10** separation **11** dissolution **12** estrangement

R.U.R. *author:* **5** Capek (Karel) *character:* **5** robot

rural 6 rustic **7** bucolic, country, idyllic **8** agrarian, arcadian, down-home, pastoral **10** campestral **11** countrified

ruse 3 con, jig **4** hoax, ploy, wile **5** dodge, feint, fraud, stall, trick **6** deceit, gambit **7** gimmick, swindle **8** artifice, maneuver, trickery **9** deception, stratagem **10** subterfuge **13** double-dealing

rush 3 fly, rip, run **4** boil, bolt, dart, dash, flit, flow, hurl, lash, race, roar, scud, tear, tide, whiz **5** blitz, break, carry, chase, court, daily, flash, haste, hurry, lunge, onset, sally, scoot, sedge, shoot, spate, speed, storm, surge **6** attack, barrel, beat it, bustle, career, charge, course, hasten, hurtle, hustle, irrupt, plunge, streak, stream, thrill, whoosh **7** assault, cattail, current, rampage, torrent **8** stampede **9** whirlwind, wire grass **13** precipitation

Rushdie novel 5 Shame **13** Satanic Verses (The) **17** Midnight's Children

rushing 5 hasty **6** abrupt, sudden **7** hurried **8** headlong **9** impetuous **11** precipitate, precipitous

rusk 7 biscuit **8** biscotto

Russia *capital:* **6** Moscow *city:* **3** Ufa **4** Omsk, Orel, Perm' **5** Kazan', Kursk **6** Grozny, Samara **7** Groznyy, Izhevsk, Ivanovo **8** Murmansk **9** Leningrad, Volgograd **10** Stalingrad **11** Chelyabinsk, Novosibirsk, Vladivostok **12** St. Petersburg **13** Yekaterinburg *czar:* **4** Ivan **5** Basil, Boris (Godunov), Peter (the Great) **6** Alexis, Dmitry, Feodor, Vasily **7** Dimitri, Godunov (Boris), Michael (Romanov), Romanov

(Michael) **8** Nicholas, Romanoff, Theodore **9** Alexander *empress:* **4** Anna (Ivanovna) **9** Catherine (the Great), Elizabeth (Petrovna) *ethnic group:* **7** Cossack *island:* **8** Sakhalin *island group:* **5** Kuril **6** Kurile *lake:* **5** Il'men', Onega **6** Baikal, Ladoga *leader:* **5** Lenin (Vladimir), Putin (Vladimir) **6** Stalin (Joseph) **7** Trotsky (Leon) **8** Brezhnev (Leonid) **10** Khrushchev (Nikita) *legislature:* **4** Duma *monetary unit:* **5** kopek, ruble **6** kopeck *mountain, range:* **4** Ural **5** Altai, Altay, Sayan **6** Elbrus, Kolyma, Koryak **8** Caucasus, Stanovoy *neighbor:* **5** China **6** Latvia, Norway **7** Belarus, Estonia, Finland, Georgia, Ukraine **8** Mongolia **9** Kazakstan **10** Azerbaijan, Kazakhstan, North Korea *peninsula:* **4** Kola **5** Gydan, Kanin, Yamal **6** Taymyr **7** Chukchi **9** Kamchatka *region:* **7** Siberia **9** Circassia **11** Golden Horde *revolution:* **9** Bolshevik *river:* **3** Don **4** Amur, Lena, Neva, Ural **5** Desna, Dvina, Vitim, Volga **6** Belaya, Kolyma, Vilyui, Vilyuy **7** Pechora, Yenisey **9** Indigirka *sea:* **4** Azov, Kara **5** Black, White **6** Laptev **7** Barents, Caspian, Chukchi, Okhotsk *secret police:* **3** KGB, MVD **4** NKVD *strait:* **6** Bering

Russian *aristocrat:* **5** boyar *caviar:* **6** beluga *comrade:* **8** tovarich, tovarish *country house:* **5** dacha *dog:* **6** borzoi **7** Samoyed *drink:* **5** kvass, vodka *family:* **7** Romanov **9** Stroganov *farmer:* **5** kulak *forest:* **5** taiga *grandmother:* **8** babushka *instrument:* **9** balalaika *monk:* **8** Rasputin *no:* **4** nyet *pancakes:* **5** blini *peasant:* **5** kulak, mujik **6** moujik, muzhik *republic:* **6** oblast *saint:* **15** Alexander Nevsky *urn:* **7** samovar *vehicle:* **6** troika *villa:* **5** dacha

rustic 4 hick, rube, rude **5** churl, clown, plain, rough, rural, swain, yokel **6** farmer **7** bucolic, bumpkin, country, granger, hayseed, peasant, plowboy, plowman, redneck, uncouth **8** agrarian, pastoral **9** chawbacon, hillbilly **10** campestral, clodhopper, countryman, husbandman **11** countrified **12** apple-knocker, backwoodsman

rustle 5 haste, hurry, speed, steal, swish **6** forage, swoosh **7** crackle, crinkle **8** susurrus

rustler 5 thief **6** duffer, robber **7** forager **8** marauder

Rustum's son 6 Sohrab

rusty 4 slow **6** bygone, creaky **7** outworn **8** outdated, outmoded **10** antiquated, discolored **12** old-fashioned

rut 5 gouge, grind, track **6** furrow, groove **7** channel, routine **9** treadmill

rutabaga 5 swede **6** turnip

ruth 3 rue, woe **4** pity **5** grief, mercy **6** regret, sorrow **7** anguish, remorse, sadness **8** distress, sympathy **9** attrition, penitence **10** compassion, contrition, repentance **11** compunction **13** commiseration
Ruth *husband:* **4** Boaz **6** Mahlon *mother-in-law:* **5** Naomi *son:* **4** Obed
ruthful 6 woeful **7** doleful **8** dolorous, wretched **9** miserable, sorrowful
ruthless 4 hard **5** cruel, harsh **6** brutal, savage **7** inhuman **8** pitiless **9** barbarous, cutthroat, dog-eat-dog, ferocious, heartless, merciless, unsparing **10** implacable, ironfisted **11** cold-blooded
ruttish 4 lewd **5** lusty, randy **6** wanton **7** goatish, lustful, satyric **9** lecherous, lickerish, salacious **10** lascivious, libidinous **12** concupiscent
Rwanda *capital:* **6** Kigali *ethnic group:* **4** Hutu **5** Tutsi *language:* **6** French, Rwanda *monetary unit:* **5** franc *neighbor:* **5** Congo **6** Uganda **7** Burundi **8** Tanzania

S

____ Saarinen 4 Eero **5** Eliel
Sabatini novel 11 Scaramouche **12** Captain Blood
sabbatical 4 rest **5** leave **7** time off **8** vacation
saber 5 sword **7** cutlass **8** scimitar
sabertooth 3 cat **5** tiger
sable 3 fur **4** dark, inky **5** black, ebony, raven **6** gloomy, somber, sombre, weasel **8** mourning
sabot 4 clog, shoe **10** wooden shoe
sabotage 5 wreck **6** damage, hamper, hinder **7** cripple, disable, subvert, torpedo **8** obstruct, wreckage, wrecking **9** frustrate, undermine, vandalize **10** subversion **11** undermining
Sabra *father:* **7** Ptolemy *rescuer:* **8** St. George *son:* **3** Guy **5** David **9** Alexander
sac 4 caul, cyst **5** pouch **7** vesicle
saccharine 5 mushy, sweet **6** sugary, syrupy **7** candied, cloying, honeyed, maudlin, mawkish, sugared **9** oversweet, schmaltzy **11** sentimental, sugar-coated **12** ingratiating
sacerdotal 8 hieratic, pastoral, priestly **10** priestlike **11** ministerial
sachem 4 boss **5** chief **6** leader
sachet 3 bag **6** powder **7** perfume **9** potpourri
sack 2 ax **3** axe, bag, bed, can **4** bunk, drop, fire, loot, raid, wine **5** expel, pouch, strip, waste **6** pocket, ravage, tackle **7** boot out, cashier, despoil, dismiss, hammock, kick out, pillage, plunder **8** desolate, spoliate **9** container, depredate, desecrate, devastate, white wine
sackbut 8 trombone
sacque 6 jacket
sacrament 4 rite **6** ritual **7** baptism, penance **8** ceremony, marriage **9** Communion, Eucharist, matrimony **10** holy orders **12** confirmation
sacrarium 6 chapel, shrine **7** oratory, piscina **8** sacristy **9** sanctuary
sacred 4 holy **5** godly **6** divine, immune **7** angelic, blessed, saintly **8** hallowed, numinous **9** inviolate, spiritual **10** inviolable, sacrosanct, sanctified **11** consecrated, sacramental *combining form:* **4** hagi, hier, sacr **5** hagio, hiero, sacro *monkey:* **6** baboon, rhesus **7** hanuman *place:* **7** sanctum *song:* **4** hymn *weed:* **7** vervain
sacrifice 4 bunt, cede, lamb, lose, loss **5** forgo, yield **6** devote, donate, eschew, give up, martyr, victim **7** forfeit, offer up **8** dedicate, hecatomb, immolate, oblation, offering **12** renunciation
sacrilege 6 heresy **7** impiety, offense **9** blasphemy, violation **11** desecration, irreverence, profanation
sacrilegious 7 impious, profane, ungodly **10** irreverent **11** blasphemous
sacristan 6 sexton
sacristy 6 vestry
sacrosanct 9 inviolate **10** inviolable
sad 4 blue, down, glum **5** sorry **6** dismal, dreary, gloomy, morose, triste, woeful **7** doleful, joyless, piteous, pitiful, unhappy **8** dejected, desolate, dolorous, downbeat, downcast, grieving, mournful, pathetic, pitiable **9** depressed, sorrowful, woebegone **10** depressing, dispirited, lamentable, melancholy **11** melancholic **12** heavyhearted
sadden 7 depress, oppress, trouble **8** aggrieve, dispirit **9** weigh down **10** discourage

saddle 3 tax 4 lade, load, task 5 weigh 6 burden, charge, hamper, impede, impose, weight 7 aparejo, inflict 8 encumber, restrict *adjunct:* 7 stirrup *part:* 6 cantle, pommel *strap:* 5 cinch, girth 6 latigo 7 harness

sadness 3 woe 4 funk 5 blues, dolor, dumps, gloom, grief, mopes 6 misery, sorrow 7 dismals, megrims 8 doldrums, glumness, mourning 9 dejection, dysphoria, heartache 10 blue devils, depression, desolation, melancholy 11 despondency, melancholia, unhappiness

safari 4 hunt, trek, trip 7 caravan, journey 10 expedition

safe 4 snug, wary 5 chary 6 secure, unhurt 7 careful, guarded 8 cautious, defended, shielded, unharmed 9 innocuous, protected, sheltered, strongbox, uninjured, unscathed 10 inviolable, sheltering 11 impregnable 12 invulnerable, unassailable

safecracker 4 yegg 8 picklock 9 cracksman

safeguard 4 ward 6 convoy, defend, escort, shield, surety 7 bulwark, defense, protect 8 armament, preserve 10 precaution, protection

safety 6 asylum, refuge 7 defense, shelter 8 immunity, security 9 assurance, sanctuary 10 protection 13 inviolability

sag 3 dip 4 bend, drop, flag, flap, flop, hang, sink, slip, wilt 5 droop, slide, slump 6 dangle, hollow, slouch 7 decline, drop off, falloff, sinkage, sinking 8 downturn, prolapse, settling, sinkhole 9 concavity, downswing 10 depression

saga 4 Edda, epic, myth, tale 5 story 6 legend 9 chronicle, narrative 12 Heimskringla

sagacious 4 keen, wise 5 acute, smart 6 astute, clever, shrewd 7 knowing, prudent, sapient 8 critical 9 far-seeing, judicious 10 discerning, insightful, perceptive 11 intelligent 13 perspicacious

sagacity 5 grasp 6 acuity, acumen, wisdom 7 insight 8 judgment, keenness, prudence, sapience 10 perception, shrewdness 11 discernment, penetration, percipience, perspicuity 12 perspicacity 13 comprehension, judiciousness, understanding

sagamore 5 chief 6 sachem

Sagan work 6 Cosmos 16 Bonjour tristesse

sage 4 Bias, guru, mint, wise 5 Solon, Vyasa 6 Buddha (Gautama), Chilon, expert, Gandhi (Mohandas), Lao Tzu, master, Narada, Nestor, nestor, pundit, savant, shrewd, Thales 7 gnostic, knowing, learned, prudent, sapient, scholar, Solomon, Valmiki, wise man 8 polymath, profound, sensible 9 Confucius, judicious 10 discerning, insight-

ful, perceptive 11 penetrating, philosophic *Hindu:* 6 pandit, pundit 7 mahatma

Sage *of Chelsea:* 7 Carlyle (Thomas) *of Concord:* 7 Emerson (Ralph Waldo) *of Emporia:* 5 White (William Allen) *of Ferney:* 8 Voltaire *of Monticello:* 9 Jefferson (Thomas) *of Pylos:* 6 Nestor

Sagebrush State 6 Nevada

Sagittarius 6 archer 7 centaur 13 constellation

sago 4 palm 6 starch

saguaro 6 cactus

sahib 3 sir 6 master 9 gentleman

sail 3 fly 4 dart, flit, scud, skim, wing 5 fleet, float, shoot, skirr, sweep 6 cruise, mizzen 7 spencer 9 spinnaker *into wind:* 4 luff *support:* 4 mast *triangular:* 3 jib 5 genoa

sailing term 3 aft, bow, lee, yaw 4 alee, beam, boom, port, tack, trim 5 abaft, abeam, aloft, belay, brale, stern 6 astern, adrift, fouled, pay out 7 cast off, heading, rigging, sea room 8 downhaul, overhaul, sounding, underway 9 starboard 10 batten down, Cunningham, lubber line, scandalize 11 self-tacking

sailing vessel 4 bark, brig, moth, yawl 5 xebec, yacht 6 barque, cutter 7 clipper, frigate, galleon 8 schooner, skipjack 10 barkentine, brigantine 11 barquentine

sailor 3 gob, tar 4 jack, mate, salt, swab 6 hearty, sea dog, seaman 7 jack-tar, mariner, matelot, old salt, swabbie 8 flatfoot, seafarer, shipmate, water dog 9 shellback, tarpaulin, yachtsman 10 bluejacket *British:* 5 limey *East Indian:* 6 lascar *fictional:* 6 Sinbad *patron saint:* 4 Elmo *song:* 6 chanty 7 chantey 9 barcarole

saint 7 paragon *biography:* 11 hagiography *list:* 9 hagiology *Muslim:* 3 pir (see also **patron saint**)

Saint, The 12 Simon Templar *creator:* 9 Charteris (Leslie)

Saint Anthony's cross 3 tau

Saint Elmo's Fire 9 corposant

Saint Helena capital: 9 Jamestown *colony of:* 7 Britain *island:* 9 Ascension

Saint Joan author 4 Shaw (George Bernard)

Saint John's bread 5 carob

Saint Kitts and Nevis capital: 10 Basseterre *island group:* 7 Leeward *location:* 10 West Indies

Saint Louis attraction 11 Gateway Arch

Saint Lucia capital: 8 Castries *island group:* 8 Windward *location:* 10 West Indies *volcano:* 8 Quilabou

saintly 4 holy, pure 5 godly, pious 6 devout,

worthy 7 angelic, blessed, upright 8 be-
atific, seraphic, virtuous 9 righteous
Saint Paul's architect 4 Wren (Christopher)
Saint Peter's Basilica *architect:* 7 Bernini
(Gian Lorenzo) 12 Michelangelo (Buona-
rotti) *sculpture:* 5 Pietà
Saint-Pierre and Miquelon *capital:* 8 St.-
Pierre *department of:* 6 France
Saint Teresa birthplace 5 Avila
Saint Vincent and the Grenadines *capital:* 9
Kingstown *island group:* 8 Windward *location:* 10 West Indies *volcano:* 9 Soufrière
Saint Vitus' dance 6 chorea
sake 3 end 4 good 5 drink 7 benefit, purpose,
welfare
Saki 5 Munro (H. H.)
salaam 3 bow 6 kowtow 8 greeting 9 obeisance
salacious 4 blue, fast, lewd, racy 5 bawdy 6
erotic, ribald, risqué, smutty 7 lustful, obscene, satyric 8 indecent, off-color, prurient
9 lecherous, libertine 10 lascivious, libidinous, licentious
salad *item:* 3 egg, udo 4 bean, cuke, herb 5
cress, olive, onion, pasta 6 carrot, celery,
cheese, endive, pepper, potato, radish, tomato 7 anchovy, arugula, cabbage, crouton,
lettuce, mesclun, niçoise, parsley, spinach 8
chickpea, cucumber, garbanzo, mushroom,
scallion 9 radicchio 10 watercress *dressing:*
5 ranch 6 French 7 Italian, Russian 10 blue
cheese, buttermilk, gorgonzola 11 vinaigrette *type:* 4 Cobb 5 chef's 6 Caesar 7
Waldorf 8 coleslaw
salamander 3 eft, olm 4 newt 7 urodele 8
mud puppy, water dog 10 hellbender *Mexican:* 7 axolotl
salary 3 pay 4 take, wage 6 income 7 stipend
8 earnings 9 emolument 10 recompense 12
compensation, remuneration
sale 6 bazaar, demand 7 auction 8 closeout,
disposal, transfer 9 clearance 11 transaction
salesperson 3 rep
salient 6 marked, signal 7 obvious, weighty 8
striking 9 arresting, important, obtrusive,
pertinent, prominent 10 impressive, noticeable, projecting, pronounced, remarkable
11 conspicuous, outstanding, significant
saline 5 briny, salty 8 brackish
Salinger, J. D. *character:* 4 Esmé 6 Holden
(Caulfield) *novel:* 14 Franny and Zooey 15
Catcher in the Rye
saliva 4 spit 6 slaver, sputum 7 spittle
salivate 5 drool 6 drivel, slaver 7 slobber
_____ **Salk** 5 Jonas
sallow 3 wan 4 pale, waxy 5 pasty 6 pallid,
sickly, willow, yellow 7 bilious 9 jaundiced

sally 3 gag 4 gust, jape, jest, joke, quip 5
blast, burst, crack, jaunt 6 depart, junket,
outing, set out, sortie, volley, zinger 7 barrage, flare-up 8 drollery, eruption, outbreak,
outburst, paroxysm 9 discharge, excursion,
explosion, wisecrack, witticism
salmagundi see **hodgepodge**
salmon 3 dog 4 chum, coho, kelt, parr, pink 5
smolt 6 grilse, Sebago 7 chinook, sockeye 9
brandling *cured:* 4 nova 7 gravlax 8 grav-
laks *male:* 6 kipper *smoked:* 3 lox
Salome *composer:* 7 Strauss (Richard) *father:* 5 Herod *husband:* 6 Philip 7 Zebedee
11 Aristobulus *mother:* 8 Herodias *son:* 4
John 5 James *victim:* 4 John (the Baptist)
salon 4 hall, shop 5 suite 6 parlor 7 gallery 9
apartment, reception 10 exhibition
saloon 3 bar, pub 6 tavern 7 barroom, cantina, gin mill, taproom 9 beer joint 12 watering hole
salt 3 gob, tar 4 jack, keep, NaCl, swab 5
brine, limey 6 sailor, saline, sea dog, seaman 7 jack-tar, mariner 8 salinize, seafarer
9 sailorman
salt away 4 bank, save 5 hoard, lay by, lay
up, put by, stash, store 7 deposit 8 lay aside,
squirrel
saltpeter 5 niter, nitre
salty 4 blue, racy 5 briny, crude, spicy, tangy
6 earthy, purple, risqué, saline 7 caustic,
mordant, pungent 8 brackish, off-color,
scathing 9 trenchant
salubrious 5 tonic 7 bracing, healthy 8 hygienic, salutary 9 healthful, wholesome 10
beneficial 11 restorative 12 invigorating
Salus see **Hygeia**
salutary 5 tonic 6 benign 7 bracing, healing 8
curative, remedial, sanative 9 analeptic,
healthful, vulnerary, wholesome 10 beneficial, salubrious 11 restorative, therapeutic
12 advantageous, health-giving
salutation 2 hi 4 hail 5 hello, howdy 7 welcome 8 greeting *Arab:* 6 salaam *French:* 5
salut *Hawaiian:* 5 aloha *Italian:* 4 ciao *Latin:*
3 ave *Spanish:* 4 hola
salute 4 hail 5 greet, honor 6 praise 7 address, commend 8 greeting 12 congratulate
salvage 4 save 6 ransom, recoup, redeem, regain, rescue 7 deliver, reclaim, recover 8 retrieve
salvation 6 saving 7 keeping 10 redemption
11 deliverance 12 conservation, preservation
Salvation Army founder 5 Booth (General
William)
salve 4 balm 5 cream, quiet 6 cerate, chrism,

lotion, remedy **7** assuage, unction, unguent **8** ointment **9** emollient

salver 4 tray

salvo 4 hail **5** burst, spray, storm **6** attack, shower, volley **7** barrage, proviso **9** broadside, cannonade, discharge, fusillade **11** bombardment

Samaritan 6 helper **10** benefactor

same 4 idem, like, very **5** equal, exact **7** coequal, similar **8** constant **9** duplicate, identical, unvarying **10** consistent, equivalent, invariable, unchanging *combining form:* **3** hom **4** homo

Samoa *capital:* **4** Apia *island:* **5** Upolu **6** Savai'i *monetary unit:* **4** tala

samovar 3 urn

samp 6 cereal, hominy

sampan 4 boat **5** skiff

sample 3 try **4** case, part, test, unit **5** piece, taste **7** dip into, element, example, excerpt, portion, segment **8** fragment, instance, specimen **10** indication **11** case history, constituent **12** illustration

Samson *betrayer:* **7** Delilah *birthplace:* **5** Zorah *deathplace:* **4** Gaza *father:* **6** Manoah *tribe:* **3** Dan

Samson Agonistes *author* **6** Milton (John)

Samuel *father:* **7** Elkanah *grandson:* **5** Heman *mentor:* **3** Eli *mother:* **6** Hannah

samurai code 7 Bushido

San Antonio *team:* **5** Spurs *landmark:* **5** Alamo

sanatorium 3 spa **8** hospital, rest home

sanctify 5 bless **6** hallow, ordain, purify **8** dedicate **10** consecrate

sanctimonious 5 pious **7** canting, preachy **8** unctuous **9** pharisaic **11** pharisaical **12** hypocritical, Pecksniffian **13** self-righteous

sanction 2 OK **4** fiat, okay **5** bless, leave **6** assent, decree, permit, ratify **7** approve, backing, boycott, certify, consent, embargo, endorse, license, penalty, support **8** accredit, approval **9** allowance, authorize **10** commission, permission, sufferance **11** approbation, endorsement **12** confirmation, ratification **13** authorization, encouragement

sanctity 8 holiness **9** godliness **11** saintliness, uprightness **13** inviolability, righteousness

sanctuary 5 haven, oasis **6** asylum, covert, harbor, refuge, shrine, temple **7** reserve, retreat, shelter **8** preserve **9** holy place

sanctum 4 lair **6** shrine **7** retreat, shelter **9** holy place, sanctuary

sand 3 tan **4** buff, ecru, fawn, grit **5** beach, beige, camel, grind, khaki, scour, shore **6** gravel, polish, smooth **7** burnish **8** granules

sandal 4 clog, zori **5** sabot, thong **6** patten **8** flip-flop, huarache **10** espadrille

sandbag 3 hit **4** stun **6** ambush, waylay **7** deceive

sandbar 4 reef, spit **7** tombolo

Sandburg, Carl *biographical subject:* **7** Lincoln (Abraham) *work:* **9** People Yes (The) **12** Chicago Poems, Harvest Poems **13** Smoke and Steel **16** Rootabaga Stories

Sand County Almanac *author* **7** Leopold (Aldo)

sandpiper 4 knot, ruff **5** reeve **6** dunlin **9** shorebird

sandstone deposit 6 flysch

sandwich 3 BLT, sub **4** club, gyro, hero, roti **5** butty, Cuban, po'boy **6** Denver, hoagie, Reuben **7** grinder, Western **9** submarine **10** muffuletta *shop:* **4** deli

sandy 4 fair **5** blond **6** blonde, grainy, gritty

sane 3 fit **4** good, hale, sage, well, wise **5** lucid, right, sober, sound **6** cogent, normal **7** healthy, logical, prudent, sapient **8** all there, balanced, oriented, rational, sensible **9** judicious, wholesome **10** reasonable **11** levelheaded **12** compos mentis

San Francisco *hill:* **3** Nob **7** Russian *tower:* **4** Coit

sangfroid 4 calm **5** poise **6** aplomb, phlegm **8** serenity **9** composure **10** equanimity **11** self-control

sanguinary 4 gory **6** bloody **9** homicidal, murdering, murderous **12** bloodstained, bloodthirsty

sanguine 4 gory **5** flush, ruddy **6** bloody, florid, secure, upbeat **7** assured, buoyant, flushed, glowing, hopeful **8** bloodred, cheerful, rubicund **9** confident, homicidal, murdering, murderous **10** optimistic **11** self-assured **12** blood-stained, bloodthirsty, Pollyannaish **13** self-confident

sanitary 5 clean **7** sterile **8** hygienic **9** healthful **10** antiseptic, salubrious

sanitize 5 clean, purge **6** bleach, censor, purify **7** cleanse, launder **8** black out **9** disinfect, expurgate, sterilize **10** bowdlerize

sanity 6 health, reason **7** balance **8** lucidity, prudence **9** normality, soundness, stability

San Marino *capital:* **9** San Marino *monetary unit:* **4** euro *monetary unit, former:* **4** lira *neighbor:* **5** Italy

sans 7 lacking, missing, wanting, without

Sanskrit *dialect:* **4** Pali *epic:* **8** Ramayana *Scripture:* **4** Veda **6** Purana

Santa Lucia *composer* **5** Denza (Luigi)

São Tomé and Príncipe *capital:* **7** São Tomé *language:* **10** Portuguese *location:* **12** Gulf of Guinea *monetary unit:* **5** dobra

sap 4 dupe, fool, gull, mark **5** chump, drain, ninny **6** pigeon, sucker, weaken **7** cripple, deplete, disable, exhaust, fall guy **8** enervate, enfeeble **9** attenuate, schlemiel, undermine **10** debilitate *pine:* **5** resin, rosin

sapid 5 tasty **6** savory **9** delicious, flavorful, palatable, toothsome **10** appetizing **11** scrumptious

sapience see **sagacity**

sapient see **sagacious**

sapling 4 tree **5** child, youth **9** youngster

Sapphira's husband 7 Ananias

Sappho *forte:* **6** poetry *island:* **6** Lesbos *student:* **6** Erinna

sappy 5 ditzy, flaky, mushy, silly, soupy **6** drippy, slushy, sticky, syrupy **7** cloying, foolish, maudlin, mawkish **8** bathetic **11** sentimental

Saracen hero 9 Rodomonte

Sarah *husband:* **7** Abraham *maid:* **5** Hagar *son:* **5** Isaac

sarcasm 3 wit **4** gibe **5** irony, scorn **6** satire **7** mockery **8** acerbity, mordancy, ridicule, sneering **10** causticity

sarcastic 4 acid, tart **5** acerb, sharp **6** biting, ironic **7** acerbic, caustic, cutting, cynical, jeering, mocking, mordant, satiric **8** sardonic, scathing, scornful, stinging **9** corrosive

sarcophagus 4 tomb **6** coffin

sardine 4 sild **7** anchovy, herring **8** pilchard

Sardinia *capital:* **8** Cagliari *neighbor:* **7** Corsica

sardonic 3 wry **6** ironic **7** caustic, cynical, jeering, mocking, satiric **8** derisive, scornful, sneering **9** corrosive, sarcastic **10** disdainful **12** contemptuous

sarong 5 skirt **7** garment

Sarpedon *brother:* **5** Minos **12** Rhadamanthus *father:* **4** Zeus **7** Jupiter *mother:* **6** Europa **8** Laodamia

Sartor ____ **8** Resartus

Sartre work 4 Wall (The) **5** Flies (The) **6** Nausea, No Exit **8** Huis Clos **10** Saint Genet

sash 3 obi **4** belt **6** girdle **8** ceinture, cincture **9** waistband **10** cummerbund

sashay 5 mince, strut **6** prance **7** flounce, saunter, swagger

Saskatchewan *capital:* **6** Regina *city:* **8** Moose Jaw **9** Saskatoon **12** Prince Albert *mountain range:* **12** Cypress Hills *provincial flower:* **7** red lily **11** prairie lily *river:* **9** Churchill **11** Assiniboine

sass 3 lip **4** guff **5** brass, cheek, mouth, sauce **8** back talk **9** impudence, insolence **12** impertinence

sassy 4 bold, flip, pert, wise **5** fresh, lippy, nervy, smart **6** brazen, cheeky **7** forward **8** flippant, impudent, insolent, malapert **9** audacious, unabashed **11** smart-alecky

Satan 5 demon, devil, fiend **6** diablo **7** Lucifer, Old Nick, serpent, villain **9** archfiend, Beelzebub **10** Old Scratch

satanic 4 evil **6** wicked **7** demonic, hellish **8** demoniac, devilish, diabolic, fiendish, infernal

satanism 9 diabolism

satchel 3 bag **4** case, tote **5** pouch **6** valise **7** handbag **9** briefcase

sate 4 cloy, fill, glut, jade, pall **5** gorge, stuff **6** stodge **7** appease, overeat, placate, surfeit **8** overfill **9** overstuff **10** conciliate

sated 4 full **6** filled, gorged **7** glutted, overfed, replete, stuffed **8** appeased, chockful **9** chock-full, surfeited

satellite 4 moon **5** toady **6** cohort, minion **7** Sputnik **8** adherent, disciple, follower, henchman, partisan **9** attendant, supporter, sycophant, tributary *of Jupiter:* **6** Europa **8** Callisto, Ganymede *of Mars:* **6** Deimos, Phobos *of Neptune:* **6** Nereid, Triton *of Saturn:* **4** Rhea **5** Dione, Janus, Mimas, Titan **6** Phoebe, Tethys **7** Iapetus **8** Hyperion **9** Enceladus *of Uranus:* **5** Ariel **6** Oberon **7** Miranda, Titania, Umbriel

satiate see **sate**

satire 3 wit **5** irony, spoof, squib **6** parody **7** lampoon, mockery, takeoff **8** raillery, ridicule, spoofery, travesty **9** burlesque **10** caricature, lampoonery, pasquinade, persiflage

satiric 6 ironic **7** mocking **8** farcical, ironical

satirist *American:* **5** Twain (Mark) **6** Bierce (Ambrose) *English:* **4** Pope (Alexander) **5** Swift (Jonathan), Waugh (Evelyn) **7** Marston (John) *French:* **7** Molière **8** Rabelais (François), Voltaire *Greek:* **8** Menippus **12** Aristophanes *Italian:* **7** Aretino (Pietro) *Roman:* **6** Horace **7** Juvenal, Martial, Persius **8** Apuleius **9** Petronius

satirize 4 mock **5** spoof **6** parody, send up **7** lampoon **8** ridicule **10** caricature

satisfaction 6 amends **7** redress **8** pleasure, serenity **9** atonement **10** reparation **11** contentment, fulfillment, restitution, vindication **12** propitiation **13** gratification

satisfactory 4 fair, good, okay **5** sound **6** decent **7** alright **8** adequate, all right, passable **9** agreeable, competent, tolerable **10** acceptable, sufficient **13** unexceptional

satisfy 3 pay **4** fill, meet, sate, suit **5** clear, humor, pay up, serve **6** answer, assure, dispel, pacify, please, settle, square **7** appease, content, fulfill, gladden, gratify, indulge, placate, satiate, suffice, win over **8** convince, persuade **9** conform to, discharge, indemnify **10** comply with

satori 12 illumination **13** enlightenment

satrap 5 ruler **6** cohort **7** viceroy **8** governor, henchman, sidekick **11** subordinate

saturate 3 sop, wet **4** fill, soak **5** bathe, douse, imbue, souse, steep **6** charge, drench, infuse **7** pervade, suffuse **8** permeate, waterlog **9** transfuse

Saturday Night Live *cast member:***3** Fey (Tina) **4** Sanz (Horatio) **5** Chase (Chevy), Myers (Mike), Short (Martin), Vance (Danitra) **6** Carvey (Dana), Curtin (Jane), Dratch (Rachel), Farley (Chris), Kattan (Chris), Morgan (Tracy), Murphy (Eddie), Murray (Bill), Nealon (Kevin), Newman (Laraine), Radner (Gilda), Rocket (Charles) **7** Aykroyd (Dan), Belushi (John), Crystal (Billy), Ferrell (Will), Franken (Al), Hammond (Darrell), Hartman (Phil), Meadows (Tim), Parnell (Chris), Rudolph (Maya), Sandler (Adam), Shearer (Harry) **9** MacDonald (Norm), O'Donoghue (Michael) *creator:* **8** Michaels (Lorne)

Saturn *moon:* **4** Rhea **5** Dione, Janus, Mimas, Titan **6** Phoebe, Tethys **7** Iapetus **8** Hyperion **9** Enceladus see also **Cronus**

saturnalia 4 orgy **5** party, revel **6** excess **7** debauch **9** bacchanal **11** bacchanalia, dissipation

saturnine 4 dour, glum, grim **5** sulky, surly **6** gloomy, moping, morose, somber, sombre, sullen **7** crabbed **8** funereal, sardonic

satyr 4 faun, goat, lech, rake, wolf **5** letch **6** lecher **8** Casanova, lothario **9** butterfly

satyric 4 lewd **5** randy **6** wanton **7** goatish, lustful **8** prurient **9** lecherous, libertine, lickerish, salacious **10** lascivious, libidinous, licentious, lubricious **11** promiscuous **12** concupiscent

sauce 3 lip **4** guff, sass **5** mouth **6** relish **7** topping **8** back talk **9** condiment, impudence *kind:* **3** soy **4** hard, mole, roux **5** aioli, chili, curry, gravy, melba, pesto, ponzu, salsa **6** Mornay, panada, tamari, tartar **7** chutney, marengo, Newburg, piquant, soubise, tartare, velouté **8** béchamel, duxelles, marinara, matelote, noisette, normande **9** béarnaise, lyonnaise, rémoulade **10** bordelaise, Provençale **11** hollandaise, vinaigrette

saucy see **sassy**

Saudi Arabia *capital:* **6** Riyadh *city:* **5** Jedda, Jidda, Mecca **6** Jeddah, Jiddah, Medina *desert:* **7** Arabian **10** Rub Al-Khali **12** Empty Quarter *gulf:* **7** Persian *monetary*

unit: **4** rial **5** riyal *neighbor:* **3** UAE **4** Iraq, Oman **5** Qatar, Yemen **6** Jordan *peninsula:* **7** Arabian *sea:* **3** Red

Saul *concubine:* **6** Rizpah *cousin:* **5** Abner *daughter:* **5** Merab **6** Michal *father:* **4** Kish *general:* **5** Abner *son:* **8** Jonathan *successor:* **5** David *uncle:* **3** Ner *wife:* **7** Ahinoam

saunter 4 mope, roam, rove **5** amble, drift, mosey **6** loiter, ramble, sashay, stroll, wander **7** meander, traipse

sausage 5 wurst **6** banger, kishke, salami, Vienna, wiener **7** baloney, bologna, boloney, chorizo, saveloy **8** cervelat, kielbasa, kielbasy **9** andouille, bratwurst, frankfurt, pepperoni, Thuringer **10** knackwurst, knockwurst, liverwurst, mortadella **11** frankfurter

sauté 3 fry **4** sear **5** brown, grill **6** sizzle **7** frizzle

savage 4 grim, wild **5** brute, cruel, feral **6** bloody, brutal, fierce, Gothic, rugged **7** bestial, brutish, inhuman, untamed, vicious, wolfish **8** barbaric, inhumane, primeval, ravenous, unbroken **9** barbarian, barbarous, ferocious, heartless, murderous, primitive, rapacious, truculent, voracious **10** implacable, relentless **11** uncivilized **12** bloodthirsty, uncontrolled, uncultivated, unsocialized

savagery 7 cruelty **8** atrocity **9** barbarity, brutality, depravity **10** bestiality, inhumanity **11** abomination, monstrosity, viciousness **12** ruthlessness

savanna 4 veld **5** plain, veldt **9** grassland

savant 4 sage **7** scholar, thinker, wise man

save 3 bar, but, yet **4** bank, keep, only, stow **5** amass, avoid, cache, guard, hoard, lay by, lay in, lay up, put by, set by, skimp, spare, store **6** defend, except, gather, keep up, manage, ransom, redeem, rescue, scrimp, shield, unless **7** barring, besides, collect, deliver, deposit, however, husband, lay away, protect, reclaim, reserve, salvage, set free, store up **8** conserve, lay aside, liberate, maintain, preserve, salt away, set aside, squirrel **9** aside from, economize, excluding, safeguard, stash away, stockpile **10** accumulate

savior 7 messiah, paladin, rescuer **8** defender **9** deliverer, liberator, preserver, protector, salvation **11** white knight

savoir faire 4 tact **5** grace, poise **6** aplomb **7** address, dignity, finesse, manners **8** urbanity **10** confidence, refinement **13** self-assurance

savor 4 odor, tang **5** enjoy, scent, smack,

smell, spice, taste, tinge **6** flavor, relish, season **8** sapidity

savory 5 sapid, spicy, tangy, tasty **7** piquant **9** flavorful, palatable, toothsome **10** appetizing

savvy 4 deft **5** adept, craft, handy, knack, skill **6** clever, talent **7** ability, know-how, skilled **8** deftness **9** adeptness, expertise, handiness, ingenuity **10** capability, cleverness, competence

saw 3 cut, hew **5** adage, axiom, maxim **6** byword, cliché, cutter, saying **7** precept, proverb **8** aphorism, apothegm

_____ **saw 3** bow, jig, pit, rip **4** band, buck, buzz, fret, hack, whip **5** chain, crown, saber **6** coping, scroll **7** compass, keyhole **8** circular, crosscut

sawbones 3 doc **6** doctor **7** surgeon **9** physician

sawbuck 6 tenner **7** trestle

sawhorse see **sawbuck**

saw-toothed 7 serrate, serried **8** serrated **11** denticulate

Saxon _assembly:_ **4** moot **5** gemot **6** gemote _nobleman:_ **8** atheling _serf:_ **4** esne **6** thrall _warrior:_ **5** thane

say 4 talk, tell **5** mouth, speak, state, utter, voice **6** affirm, assert, assume, recite, remark **7** comment, declare, express **8** announce, proclaim **9** enunciate, pronounce **10** articulate

Sayers character 6 Wimsey (Lord Peter)

saying 3 mot, saw **5** adage, axiom, maxim, motto **6** byword, dictum, truism **7** precept, proverb **8** aphorism, apothegm

scab 5 crust **6** eschar **8** blackleg **13** strikebreaker

scabbard 6 sheath

scabrous 4 lewd **5** bawdy, harsh, rough, salty, scaly **6** craggy, crusty, grubby, jagged, knobby, knotty, ribald, rugged, scurfy, sordid, uneven **7** bristly, prickly, scraggy, squalid **8** indecent, prurient **9** salacious **10** scandalous

scads 4 gobs, lots, tons, wads **5** heaps, loads, piles, rafts, reams **6** oodles, plenty **8** slathers **10** quantities

scaffold 5 stage, truss **7** staging **8** platform **9** framework

Scala, La _city:_ **5** Milan **6** Milano _production:_ **5** opera

scalawag see **scamp**

scald 4 boil, burn **6** scorch

scale 4 peel, rate, skin **5** climb, flake, gamut, gauge, mount, ratio, scute, strip **6** ascend, degree, extent, ladder, lamina, scutum, squama **7** measure, ranking **8** escalade,

flake off, spall off **9** exfoliate, hierarchy **10** desquamate, proportion **11** decorticate _auxiliary:_ **7** vernier _earthquake:_ **7** Richter _musical:_ **2** do, fa, la, mi, re, ti, ut **3** sol _temperature:_ **6** Kelvin **7** Celsius, Réaumur **10** centigrade, Fahrenheit _wind:_ **8** Beaufort

scallion 4 leek **5** onion **7** shallot **10** green onion

scalp 4 flay, skin **5** cheat **6** resell, trophy

scam 3 con, gyp **4** bilk, dupe, fool, hoax **5** cheat, fraud, stick, trick **6** delude, diddle, take in **7** beguile, deceive, defraud, swindle **8** flimflam, hoodwink, phishing **11** double-cross

scamp 3 imp **4** brat, rake, tyke **5** devil, joker, knave, rogue **6** rascal, urchin **7** hellion **8** scalawag, slyboots **9** prankster, scoundrel, skeezicks **11** rapscallion

scamper 3 run **4** dash, skip **5** scoot **6** scurry **7** scuttle

scan 3 eye, MRI **4** skim, view **5** audit, check **6** browse, review, survey **7** examine, eyeball, inspect **8** glance at **10** run through, scrutinize

scandal 5 rumor **6** gossip, infamy **7** calumny, obloquy, offense, slander **8** disgrace, dishonor, reproach **9** aspersion, discredit, disrepute **10** backbiting, defamation, detraction, opprobrium

scandalize 5 libel, shock, smear **6** defame, malign **7** asperse, slander **9** denigrate **10** calumniate

scandalmonger 6 gossip **8** busybody, gossiper, quidnunc, telltale **9** backbiter, muckraker **10** talebearer

scandalous 7 heinous **8** infamous, libelous, shameful, shocking **9** notorious, offensive **10** defamatory, outrageous, scurrilous **11** disgraceful

Scandinavian see **Norse**

Scandinavian country 6 Norway, Sweden **7** Denmark, Finland, Iceland

scant 5 short, skimp, spare, stint, tight **6** meager, meagre, paltry, scarce, scrimp, skimpy, slight, sparse **7** scrimpy, wanting **8** exiguous **10** inadequate **12** insufficient

scantiness 4 lack **6** dearth **7** deficit, paucity **8** scarcity, shortage, sparsity **10** deficiency, inadequacy, scarceness, sparseness **13** insufficiency

scanty see **scant**

scapegoat 6 target, victim **7** fall guy **9** sacrifice **11** whipping boy

scapegrace 5 knave, rogue, scamp **6** bad egg, rascal, sinner **7** ruffian, varmint, villain **8** hooligan, recreant, scalawag **9** miscreant, reprobate, scoundrel **10** blackguard, black sheep, delinquent **11** rapscallion

Scapin 5 rogue, valet **6** rascal *author:* **7** Molière *employer:* **7** Léandre

scar 3 mar **4** flaw **5** score **6** deface, defect, keloid **7** blemish, scratch **8** cicatrix, pockmark **9** cicatrize, disfigure *on a seed:* **5** hilum

scarab 6 beetle

scaramouch see **scamp**

scarce 3 few **4** rare **5** scant **6** barely, hardly, scanty, sparse **7** limited, wanting **8** sporadic, uncommon **9** deficient **10** inadequate, infrequent, occasional **12** insufficient

scarcity see **scantiness**

scare 5 alarm, panic, spook **6** fright **7** horrify, petrify, shake up, startle, terrify **8** frighten, paralyze **9** terrorize

scaredy-cat 4 wimp, wuss **5** mouse, sissy **6** coward **7** chicken, dastard **8** alarmist, poltroon **11** milquetoast, yellowbelly

scare up 4 find, snag **5** rally **6** corral, gather, locate, obtain, secure **7** acquire, collect, procure, unearth **8** smoke out **9** ferret out, track down

scarf 3 boa **4** gulp, wolf **5** ascot, fichu, plaid, shawl, stole **6** cravat, devour, gobble, inhale **8** babushka, liripipe, mantilla, puggaree **10** lambrequin *Mexican:* **6** rebozo

Scarlet Letter, The *author:* **9** Hawthorne (Nathaniel) *character:* **5** Pearl **6** Hester (Prynne) **10** Dimmesdale (Arthur) **13** Chillingworth (Roger)

Scarlet Pimpernel author **5** Orczy (Baroness Emmuska)

Scarlett's home 4 Tara

scary 6 creepy, spooky **8** chilling **9** frightful *cry:* **3** boo

scathe 4 burn, flay, flog, harm, lash, sear **5** roast, slash **6** assail, berate, scorch, thrash **7** blister, scarify, scourge, upbraid **8** lambaste **9** castigate, excoriate

scathing 6 biting, brutal **7** caustic, mordant **8** stinging **9** trenchant

scatter 3 sow, ted **4** cast, part, shed **5** strew **6** divide, spread **7** bestrew, break up, diffuse, disband, diverge **8** disperse, sprinkle **9** broadcast, dissipate **10** besprinkle, distribute **11** disseminate

scatterbrained 5 dizzy, giddy, silly **7** flighty, foolish **8** heedless **9** frivolous

scattering 8 diaspora **10** dispersion

scavenger 5 hyena **6** jackal **7** vulture

scenario 4 plot **6** script **7** outline **8** libretto, synopsis **10** screenplay

scene 3 row, set **4** fuss, site, spot, view **5** arena, field, place, sight, vista **6** locale, milieu, sphere **7** episode, outlook, setting, tableau, tantrum **8** backdrop, locality, location, stage set **9** commotion, landscape, situation **10** background **11** environment **12** stage setting

scenery 3 set **5** decor, props **7** setting **8** stage set **10** properties **11** furnishings **12** stage setting

scent 4 nose, odor **5** aroma, smell, sniff, snuff, whiff **7** bouquet, essence, incense, odorize, perfume **9** aromatize, fragrance, redolence

scepter 4 mace **5** baton, staff **11** sovereignty

schedule 4 list, roll **5** chart, slate, table **6** agenda, docket, record, roster **7** catalog, program, reserve **8** calendar, register, roll call **9** catalogue, timetable

scheme 4 plan, plot, ploy, ruse **5** bunco, bunko, cabal, order **6** design, device, devise **7** collude, connive, diagram, program, project **8** cogitate, conspire, contrive, game plan, intrigue, proposal, strategy **9** blueprint, expedient, machinate **10** conspiracy, strategize **11** arrangement, contrivance, machination *type:* **5** Ponzi **7** pyramid

schism 4 rent, rift **5** break, chasm, cleft, split **6** breach, divide, heresy **7** discord, dissent, fissure, rupture **8** cleavage, division, fracture **10** disharmony, dissidence, divergence, falling-out, heterodoxy, separation **11** unorthodoxy **12** estrangement

schlemiel 4 fool **5** chump, klutz **7** bungler

schlep 3 lug, tow **4** drag, haul, hump, plod, pull, slog, tote **5** carry, truck **6** trudge **7** shamble, shuffle **8** straggle

schlock 4 junk, mean **5** cheap, dreck, gaudy, junky, tacky, tatty **6** cheesy, common, kitsch, shoddy, sleazy, tawdry, trashy **8** inferior, low-grade **11** second-class, substandard

schmaltzy 5 mushy, soppy **6** drippy **7** maudlin, mawkish **11** sentimental, tear-jerking

schmo 4 dolt, dope, dork, fool, goof, jerk, mutt, simp, twit, yo-yo **5** brute, chump, idiot, moron, ninny, noddy, scamp **6** dimwit, donkey, dumdum, nitwit, noodle, nudnik, rascal **7** dullard, halfwit, jackass, schmuck, schnook **8** bonehead, clodpoll, imbecile, lunkhead, meathead, numskull **9** birdbrain, blockhead, ignoramus, lamebrain, numbskull, thickhead **10** dunderhead, hammerhead, nincompoop **11** chowderhead, chucklehead, knucklehead

schmooze 3 gab, yak **4** chat **6** chat up **8** converse

schnoz 4 beak, nose **5** snout **6** honker

scholar 4 sage, wonk **5** pupil **6** savant **7**

bookman, egghead, student, wise man **8** bookworm, polymath **12** intellectual *Hindu:* **6** pandit, pundit *Muslim:* **5** ulama, ulema

scholarly 7 bookish, erudite, learned **8** academic, educated, studious **10** scholastic **12** intellectual

scholarship 5 award, grant **7** stipend **8** learning **9** education, erudition, knowledge **11** learnedness

scholastic 7 bookish, erudite, learned **8** academic, lettered, literary, pedantic **9** scholarly *life:* **8** academia

school 3 gam, pod **5** shoal, teach, train, tutor **7** academy, college, educate **8** instruct **9** alma mater, institute **10** discipline, university *English:* **4** Eton **6** Harrow *French:* **5** école, lycée *grounds:* **6** campus *Jewish:* **5** heder **7** yeshiva *judo:* **4** dojo *organization:* **3** PTA, PTO *religious:* **8** seminary *term:* **7** quarter **8** semester **9** trimester *type:* **4** coed

schoolbook 4 text **6** primer, reader **7** speller

School for Scandal author 8 Sheridan (Richard Brinsley)

schooner 4 ship **5** stoup **6** goblet, seidel **7** tumbler **8** sailboat

Schubert forte 4 lied, song

science *of agriculture:* **8** agronomy *of animals:* **7** zoology *of criminal punishment:* **8** penology *of environment:* **7** ecology *of fermentation:* **8** zymology *of health:* **7** hygiene **9** hygienics *of heredity:* **8** genetics *of human behavior:* **10** psychology *of measuring time:* **8** horology **11** chronometry *of motion:* **8** kinetics *of mountains:* **7** orology *of plants:* **6** botany *of projectiles:* **10** ballistics *of the earth:* **7** geology

scientific classification 8 taxonomy

sci-fi writer 3 Lem (Stanislaw) **4** Card (Orson Scott), Dick (Philip K.), Pohl (Frederik) **5** Disch (Thomas M.), Lewis (C. S.), Niven (Larry), Verne (Jules), Wells (H. G.) **6** Aldiss (Brian), Asimov (Isaac), Bester (Alfred), Bishop (Michael), Butler (Octavia), Clarke (Arthur C.), Delany (Samuel), Farmer (Philip José), Gibson (William), Le Guin (Ursula), Leiber (Fritz), Miller (Walter), Norton (Andre) **7** Ballard (J. G.), Clement (Hal), Ellison (Harlan), Herbert (Frank), Hubbard (L. Ron), Van Vogt (A. E.), Zelazny (Roger) **8** Anderson (Poul), Bradbury (Ray), Heinlein (Robert A.), Sterling (Bruce), Sturgeon (Theodore), Vonnegut (Kurt) **9** Gernsback (Hugo), Kornbluth (C. M.) **10** Silverberg (Robert)

scimitar 5 saber, sabre, sword **7** cutlass

scintilla 3 bit, jot **4** atom, iota, whit **5** grain, spark, speck, trace **7** smidgen **8** particle

scintillate 5 flash, gleam, glint, spark **6** glance **7** glimmer, glisten, glitter, shimmer, sparkle, twinkle **9** coruscate

scion 4 heir **5** child, graft, issue **7** progeny **8** offshoot **9** inheritor, offspring, successor **10** descendant

scoff at 4 mock, twit **5** fleer, scorn **6** deride **7** contemn, disdain **8** belittle, pooh-pooh, ridicule

scold 3 rag **4** chew, lash, rail, rant **5** baste, blame, chide, grill, harpy, hound, shrew, vixen **6** berate, grouch, grouse, harass, murmur, mutter, rebuke, revile, virago **7** bawl out, blister, censure, chasten, chew out, grumble, lecture, reprove, tell off, upbraid **8** admonish, execrate, fishwife, lambaste, reproach, Xantippe **9** criticize, dress down, excoriate, objurgate, reprehend, reprimand, termagant, Xanthippe **10** tongue-lash, vituperate

scoop 3 dig, dip **4** bail, beat, lift **5** gouge, ladle, spade **6** dig out, pick up, shovel **8** excavate **9** exclusive

scoot 3 fly, run, zip **4** dash, flee, race, rush, skip **5** hurry, scram, skirr, slide **6** hustle, scurry, sprint **7** scamper **9** skedaddle

scope 3 ken **4** area, room **5** ambit, gamut, orbit, range, reach, sweep **6** extent, leeway, margin, radius **7** breadth, compass, purview **8** capacity, fullness, latitude **9** amplitude, extension

Scopes trial lawyer 5 Bryan (William Jennings) **6** Darrow (Clarence)

scorch 4 bake, burn, char, flay, sear **5** broil, roast, singe **6** scathe **7** blacken, blister, scarify, scourge, swelter **8** lambaste **9** castigate, excoriate

score 3 cut, tab, win **4** bill, gain, goal, line, mark, nick, slit **5** cleft, count, notch, reach, tally, total **6** attain, furrow, groove, grudge, rack up, record, thrive, twenty **7** account, achieve, invoice, prosper, scratch, succeed **8** flourish **9** reckoning **10** accomplish

scorn 4 gibe, jeer, mock **5** abhor, flout, scoff, spurn, taunt **6** deride **7** contemn, despise, despite, disdain, jeering, mockery **8** contempt, derision, ridicule, scoffing, taunting **9** contumely

Scorpius star 7 Antares

Scot 4 Celt, Gael

Scotch cocktail 6 Rob Roy **9** Rusty Nail

scoter 7 sea coot, sea duck

Scotland *capital:* **9** Edinburgh *church:* **11** the Auld Kirk *city:* **6** Dundee **7** Glasgow **8** Aberdeen **9** Inverness **11** Dunfermline *emblem:* **7** thistle *firth:* **5** Clyde, Forth, Moray **6** Solway *former capital:* **5** Perth *island, is-*

land group: 4 Iona, Jura, Mull, Skye, Uist 5 Arran, Islay 7 Orkneys 9 Shetlands 8 Hebrides *lake:* 8 Loch Ness 10 Loch Lomond *mountain, range:* 8 Ben Nevis 9 Grampians *patron saint:* 6 Andrew *river:* 3 Dee, Esk 5 Clyde

Scott, Sir Walter *novel:* 5 Abbot (The) 6 Rob Roy 7 Ivanhoe 8 Talisman (The), Waverley 9 Woodstock 10 Kenilworth 11 Redgauntlet 12 Old Mortality 14 Quentin Durward *poem:* 7 Marmion 13 Lady of the Lake (The)

_____ **Scott case** 4 Dred

Scottish 4 Erse 6 Gaelic *cap:* 3 tam 9 glengarry 11 tam-o'-shanter *child:* 5 bairn *coin:* 6 bawbee *dance:* 4 reel 5 fling 10 strathspey *Gaelic:* 4 Erse *guide:* 6 gillie *hero:* 5 Bruce (Robert) 7 Wallace (William) *hill:* 4 brae *lake:* 4 loch *landowner:* 5 laird *language:* 4 Erse 6 Gaelic *no:* 3 nae *outlaw:* 6 Rob Roy *plaid:* 6 tartan *pudding:* 6 haggis *skirt:* 4 kilt *spirit:* 6 kelpie 7 banshee *sword:* 8 claymore *trousers:* 5 trews

scoundrel 3 cad 4 heel 5 knave, rogue, scamp 6 bad guy, rascal 7 lowlife, villain 9 miscreant, reprobate 10 blackguard

scour 4 comb, rake 5 erode, purge, range, scrub 6 forage, search 7 corrode, eat away, ransack, rummage 8 wear away 9 ferret out

scourge 4 bane, flay, flog, hide, lash, whip, whop 5 curse, flail, slash, whale 6 plague, ravage, scathe, stripe, thrash 7 afflict, blister, despoil, pillage, scarify 8 chastise, lambaste 9 castigate, depredate, desecrate, devastate, excoriate 10 affliction, flagellate, pestilence

Scourge of God 6 Attila

scout 3 spy 6 ranger, survey 7 explore, lookout 8 searcher, watchman 11 investigate, reconnoiter

scouting group 3 BSA, GSA

scow 3 hoy 5 barge 6 garvey 7 lighter

scowl 5 frown, glare, lower 6 glower

scrabble 5 grope 6 scrawl 7 clamber 8 flounder

scraggly 6 ragged, shaggy, uneven 7 unkempt 9 irregular

scraggy 4 bony, lank, lean 5 gaunt, harsh, lanky, rocky, rough 6 jagged, rugged, skinny, uneven 7 angular, scrawny, spindly, unlevel 8 gangling, rawboned, scabrous

scram 3 git 4 scat, shoo 5 scoot, split 6 beat it, begone, get out 7 buzz off, get lost, skiddoo, take off, vamoose 8 clear out 9 skedaddle

scramble 4 hash 6 jumble, jungle, muddle, scurry, tumble 7 clamber, clutter, rummage,

scuttle, shuffle 8 mishmash, scrabble, straggle 9 confusion

scrambled 7 chaotic, jumbled, mixed-up 8 confused 9 corrupted 10 disordered, disorderly

scrap 3 bit, jot, ort, row 4 chip, dump, fray, iota, junk, spat, tiff, whit 5 abort, brawl, chuck, crumb, fight, melee, piece, set-to, shred, speck 6 bicker, fracas, reject, sliver, tittle 7 brabble, cutting, discard, fall out, quarrel, scuffle, smidgen, wrangle 8 fragment, jettison, leftover, particle, squabble, throw out 9 throw away

scrape 3 fix, jam, rub 4 mess, rasp, spot 5 chafe, fight, grate, graze, pinch, scour, scuff, shave, skimp, spare, stint 6 abrade, pickle, plight, scrimp 7 dilemma, scratch, trouble 8 abrasion, struggle 11 predicament

scrappy 6 feisty 8 brawling 9 combative, truculent 10 pugnacious 11 belligerent, contentious, quarrelsome

scratch 4 claw, rake, rasp 5 grate, money, score, scrup 6 scotch, scrape, scrawl 7 call off 8 scrabble, scribble

scratchy 5 rough 6 gritty 7 itching, prickly, rasping 8 abrasive, granular, tingling 10 irritating

scrawl 6 doodle 7 scratch 8 scrabble, scribble

scrawny 4 bony, lank, lean 5 gaunt, lanky 6 skinny 7 scraggy 8 rawboned

scream 3 cry 4 riot, yell, yowl 5 shout 6 screak, shriek, shrill, squeal 7 screech

screech 6 screak, scream, shriek, shrill, squeal

screed 4 rant 5 level, spiel 6 letter, tirade 8 diatribe, harangue, jeremiad 9 discourse, philippic 11 disputation 12 disquisition

screen 4 cull, hide, sift, veil 5 blind, sieve 6 facade, filter, movies, shroud, winnow 7 conceal, obscure, pick out 9 partition 10 camouflage *Japanese:* 5 shoji

screw 9 propeller

screwball 3 nut, wag 4 kook, zany 5 clown, crazy, cutup, flake, flaky, freak, gonzo, joker, kooky, loony, loopy, nutty, silly, wacko, wacky 6 madcap, weirdo 7 buffoon, dingbat, farceur 8 crackpot, jokester 9 ding-a-ling, eccentric, fruitcake, whimsical

Screwtape Letters author 5 Lewis (C. S.)

screwy 3 mad 4 daft, nuts 5 batty, crazy, goofy, loony, nutty, wacky 6 absurd, insane 7 bizarre, cracked, lunatic 9 eccentric 10 unbalanced

scribble 5 write 6 scrawl 7 scratch 8 squiggle

scribe 5 clerk, write 6 author, penman, writer 7 copyist 9 scrivener, secretary 10 amanuensis

scrimmage 4 fray **5** brawl, broil, clash, fight, melee, scrap, scrum, set-to **6** battle, fracas, ruckus, rumpus **7** scuffle **8** skirmish **10** donnybrook, free-for-all

scrimp 4 save **5** stint **6** save up, scrape **8** conserve **9** economize

script 4 hand, text **5** write **8** longhand, scenario **10** penmanship, screenplay **11** calligraphy, chirography, handwriting, orchestrate

scrivener 5 clerk **6** notary, scribe, writer **7** copyist **10** amanuensis

scrooge 5 miser **7** niggard **8** tightwad **9** skinflint **10** cheapskate **12** moneygrubber

scrounge 3 beg, bum, tap **4** grub, hunt, loot **5** cadge, filch, mooch, pinch, steal, swipe, touch **6** forage, hustle, pilfer, snitch, sponge, thieve **7** finagle, solicit, wheedle **8** freeload **9** panhandle

scroungy 5 dirty, seedy **6** grubby, grungy, scurvy, scuzzy, shabby, sleazy, sordid **7** scruffy, squalid, unkempt **8** slovenly **10** slatternly

scrub 3 rub **4** buff, drop, wash **5** abort, brush, scour **6** cancel, mallee, maquis, polish **7** abandon, call off, cleanse, scratch **9** chaparral, eliminate

scrubby 4 drab, mean **5** dingy, dowdy, runty **6** paltry, ragged, shabby, shoddy **7** rundown, runtish, stunted **8** inferior **9** neglected **10** bedraggled, broken-down

scruff 4 nape, neck

scruffy 5 mangy, seedy, tacky **6** frowsy, frowzy, shabby, shaggy **7** run-down, scrubby, unkempt **8** slovenly, tattered **10** down-at-heel, threadbare

scrumptious 5 tasty, yummy **8** heavenly, luscious **9** ambrosial, delicious, succulent, toothsome **10** delectable, delightful **13** mouthwatering

scruple 3 bit, jot **4** balk, iota **5** demur, doubt, grain, qualm, scrap, shred, worry **7** concern, modicum **8** particle, question **9** hesitancy **11** compunction

scrupulous 5 exact, fussy **6** honest, minute, strict **7** careful, heedful, upright **8** critical, punctual, rigorous **9** honorable **10** fairminded, fastidious, meticulous, principled, upstanding **11** painstaking, punctilious **12** conscionable **13** conscientious

scrutinize 4 comb, scan **5** audit, probe, study **6** peruse **7** analyze, canvass, dig into, dissect, examine, eyeball, inspect **8** look over, pore over **9** check over **11** contemplate, investigate

scrutiny 4 scan **5** audit **6** review, survey **7** perusal **8** analysis **10** inspection **11** examination **12** surveillance

scuba diver 7 frogman **8** aquanaut

scud 3 fly **4** race, rain, rush, sail, skim **5** brume, froth, scoot, speed, spray, spume **6** clouds, scurry, shower

scuff 6 scrape **7** scratch, shamble, shuffle

scuffle 3 row **4** fray **5** brawl, broil, fight, scrap, set-to **6** affray, fracas, hubbub, tussle **7** bobbery, grapple, shamble, shuffle, wrestle **10** roughhouse

scull 3 oar, row **4** boat **5** shell **6** propel

sculpt 3 hew **5** carve, shape **6** chisel

sculptor *American:* **3** Lin (Maya) **4** Gabo (Naum), Judd (Donald), Taft (Lorado) **5** Andre (Carl), Koons (Jeff), Pratt (Bela), Segal (George), Serra (Richard), Smith (David), Story (William) **6** Aitkin (Robert), Calder (Alexander), Fraser (James Earle), French (Daniel Chester), Powers (Hiram), Zorach (William) **7** Borglum (Gutzon), Cornell (Joseph), Noguchi (Isamu) **8** Lachaise (Gaston), Lipchitz (Jacques), Nadelman (Elie), Nevelson (Louise) **9** Bourgeois (Louise), Mestrovic (Ivan), Oldenburg (Claes), Remington (Frederic) **12** Saint-Gaudens (Augustus) *Czech:* **6** Stursa (Jan) *Danish:* **11** Thorvaldsen (Bertel), Thorwaldsen (Bertel) *Dutch:* **6** Sluter (Claus) *English:* **5** Moore (Henry), Watts (George) **7** Epstein (Jacob), Flaxman (John) **8** Hepworth (Barbara) *French:* **3** Arp (Hans, Jean) **4** Bloc (André) **5** Rodin (Auguste) **6** Dubois (Paul), Houdon (Jean-Antoine) **7** Maillol (Aristide), Pevsner (Antoine) **9** Bartholdi (Frédéric-Auguste), Roubillac (Louis-François) *German:* **5** Hesse (Eva) *Greek:* **5** Myron **7** Phidias **8** Pheidias **10** Polyclitus, Praxiteles **11** Polycleitus *Italian:* **5** Leoni (Leone), Salvi (Niccolò, Nicola) **6** Canova (Antonio), Pisano (Andrea, Nino), Robbia (Andrea, Giovanni, Girolamo, Luca della) **7** Bernini (Gian Lorenzo), Cellini (Benvenuto), da Vinci (Leonardo), Orcagna, Quercia (Jacopo della) **8** Ghiberti (Lorenzo), Leonardo (da Vinci), Vittoria (Alessandro) **9** Donatello, Sansovino (Jacopo) **10** Giocometti (Alberto), Verrocchio (Andrea del) **12** Michelangelo (Buonarroti) *Rhodian:* **9** Polydorus *Romanian:* **8** Brancusi (Constantin) *Russian:* **7** Zadkine (Ossip) *Swedish:* **6** Milles (Carl) **9** Oldenburg (Claes) *Swiss:* **10** Giacometti (Alberto)

scum 5 algae, dregs, dross **6** refuse, vermin **8** riffraff

scummy 3 low **4** base, mean, vile **5** dirty,

mucky, slimy **6** grubby, odious, sleazy, sordid **7** squalid **10** despicable **12** contemptible

scurrilous 4 foul **5** dirty, gross, nasty **6** coarse, filthy, vulgar **7** abusive, obscene, profane **8** indecent **9** insulting, offensive **10** outrageous **11** opprobrious **12** contumelious, vituperative

scurry 3 run **4** dart, dash **5** scoot, shoot **6** bustle **7** scamper, scuffle, scuttle

scurvy see **scummy**

scut 4 tail

scuttle 3 run **4** hole, pail, sink **5** abort, scrap, wreck **6** basket, scurry **7** destroy, opening

scuttlebutt 4 buzz, talk **5** rumor **6** gossip, report **7** chatter, hearsay **9** grapevine

Scylla 4 rock *counterpart:* **9** Charybdis *father:* **5** Nisus *lover:* **5** Minos

scythe handle 5 snath **6** snathe

sea 4 blue, deep, main **5** brine, drink, ocean *Antarctica:* **4** Ross **5** Davis **7** Weddell **8** Amundsen *Arctic:* **4** Kara **7** Chukchi **8** Beaufort, Karskoye **9** Chuckchee, Norwegian **11** Chukotskoye **12** East Siberian *Asia-Europe:* **5** Black *Asia Minor:* **7** Icarian *Atlantic:* **5** North **7** Weddell **9** Caribbean *Australia-Indonesia:* **7** Arafura *Balkan Peninsula-Italy:* **8** Adriatic *Bay of Bengal:* **7** Andaman *China-Korea:* **5** Huang, Hwang **6** Yellow *combining form:* **3** mer **4** mari **5** pelag **6** pelago **7** thalass **8** thalasso *Corsica-Italy:* **10** Tyrrhenian *Denmark-Norway:* **9** Skagerrak *Denmark-Sweden:* **8** Kattegat *England-Ireland:* **5** Irish *Fiji:* **4** Koro *France-Italy:* **8** Ligurian *Greece:* **5** Crete *Greece-Italy:* **6** Ionian *Greece-Turkey:* **6** Aegean **8** Thracian *Honshu:* **6** Sagami *Indian Ocean:* **5** Timor **7** Arabian *Indonesia:* **4** Bali **6** Flores *inland:* **3** Red **4** Aral **7** Caspian *Japan:* **3** Suo **6** Inland *Kazakhstan:* **4** Aral *Malay Archipelago:* **5** Banda *Mexico:* **6** Cortés *Netherlands:* **6** Wadden *North Atlantic:* **8** Sargasso *Northern Europe:* **6** Baltic, Ostsee **8** Suevicum *North Pacific:* **6** Bering *off Scotland:* **8** Hebrides *off Sweden:* **5** Aland *Pacific:* **4** Java **5** China, Coral **6** Maluku **7** Celebes, Eastern, Molucca, Solomon **9** East China **10** South China *Philippine:* **4** Sulu *Russia:* **5** White **7** Okhotsk *Russia-Ukraine:* **4** Azov *South Pacific:* **4** Ross **6** Tasman **8** Amundsen *Turkey:* **7** Marmara **9** Propontis *Uzbekistan:* **4** Aral *West Pacific:* **5** Ceram, Japan **8** Bismarck **10** Philippine

sea anemone 5 polyp

seabird see **bird** *aquatic*

seacoast 5 beach, coast, shore **6** strand **8** littoral **9** shoreline

sea cucumber 7 trepang **11** holothurian

sea dog see **sailor**

sea duck 5 eider, scaup **6** scoter **9** merganser

sea eagle 4 erne **6** osprey **8** fish hawk

seafarer 3 tar **4** salt **6** sailor **7** jack-tar, mariner

seafood dish 4 clam, crab **5** clams, squid **6** cockle, mussel, oyster, scampi, shrimp **7** ceviche, lobster, mussels, oysters, scallop, seviche **8** calamari, scallops

seagoing 8 maritime, nautical

seal 5 sigil, stamp **6** cachet, signet **7** sticker *female:* **3** cow *herd:* **3** pod **5** patch *joint:* **6** gasket *young:* **3** pup

sealant 4 lute **5** caulk, grout **6** luting, mastic **8** caulking

sea lily 7 crinoid

seam 4 bond **5** joint, union **8** coupling, juncture **10** connection

seaman see **sailor**

sea monster 3 Orc **6** kraken **9** leviathan

seamount 5 guyot

seamy 5 dirty, rough, seedy **6** sordid **7** squalid **12** disreputable

séance 7 meeting, session, sitting *holder:* **6** medium

seaport *Alaska:* **6** Juneau **9** Anchorage *Albania:* **5** Vlorë **6** Durres, Valona *Algeria:* **4** Bône, Oran **6** Annaba *Angola:* **6** Lobito, Luanda **7** Cabinda **8** Benguela *Argentina:* **11** Buenos Aires, Mar del Plata *Australia:* **4** Eden **5** Bowen, Perth **6** Darwin, Hobart, Sydney **8** Brisbane **9** Melbourne **10** Wollongong *Azores:* **5** Horta *Balearic:* **5** Ibiza *Belgium:* **6** Ostend **7** Antwerp *Benin:* **7** Cotonou **9** Porto-Novo *Black Sea:* **5** Varna **6** Burgas, Odessa **9** Constanta *Brazil:* **3** Rio **4** Pará **5** Bahia, Belém, Natal **6** Recife, Santos **7** Vitoria **8** Salvador **9** Fortaleza **10** Pernambuco **11** Pôrto Alegre, São Salvador **12** Rio de Janeiro *Bulgaria:* **5** Varna **6** Burgas *Cameroon:* **6** Douala *Canaries:* **8** Arrecife **9** Las Palmas *Chile:* **5** Arica **8** Coquimbo **10** Valparaíso *China:* **4** Amoy **6** Dalian, Fuzhou, Lüshun, Xiamen **7** Foochow, Hsiamen, Qingdao, Tianjin **8** Shanghai, Shenzhen, Tientsin, Tsingtao **9** Guangzhou, Zhenjiang **10** Chen-chiang, Port Arthur *Colombia:* **6** Lorica **9** Cartagena **12** Barranquilla *Corsica:* **5** Calvi **7** Ajaccio *Costa Rica:* **5** Limón **10** Puntarenas *Crimean:* **5** Kerch, Yalta **10** Sebastopol, Sevastopol *Croatia:* **5** Rieka, Split **6** Rijeka **9** Dubrovnik *Cuba:* **6** Havana **8** La Habana, Matanzas, Santiago *Cyprus:* **9** Famagusta *Denmark:* **5** Arhus **6** Aarhus, Alborg **7** Aalborg **8** Elsinore **10** Copenhagen *Ecuador:* **9** Guayaquil *Egypt:* **4** Said **10** Alexandria

England: 4 Hull 5 Dover 9 Liverpool 10 Portsmouth 11 Southampton *Equatorial Guinea:* 4 Bata *Eritrea:* 4 Aseb *Estonia:* 5 Pärnu 7 Tallinn *Finland:* 3 Abo 4 Kemi, Oulu, Pori, Vasa 5 Hango, Kotka, Rauma, Turku, Vaasa 6 Vyborg *Florida:* 5 Miami, Tampa 9 Pensacola 12 Apalachicola, Jacksonville *France:* 4 Nice 5 Brest, Havre 6 Calais, Cannes, Toulon 7 Dunkirk, Le Havre 8 Bordeaux, Boulogne 9 Cherbourg, Dunkerque, Marseille 10 Marseilles *French Polynesia:* 7 Papeete *Georgia:* 8 Savannah 9 Brunswick *Georgia, Republic of:* 4 Pot'i *Germany:* 4 Kiel 5 Emden 6 Bremen, Lübeck, Wismar 7 Hamburg, Rostock 8 Cuxhaven 11 Bremerhaven *Ghana:* 4 Tema 5 Accra *Greece:* 5 Pylos, Syros, Volos 7 Piraeus *Guatemala:* 7 San José 10 Livingston *Haiti:* 5 Cayes 10 Cap Haitien *Honduras:* 7 La Ceiba 8 Trujillo *India:* 3 Goa 4 Puri 5 Marud 6 Bombay, Madras, Mumbai, Old Goa 7 Calicut, Chennai 8 Calcutta 9 Jagannath 10 Trivandrum *Iran:* 4 Jask 7 Bushehr *Iraq:* 5 Basra *Ireland:* 4 Cork 5 Sligo 6 Dingle, Dublin, Galway, Tralee 8 Drogheda, Limerick 9 Waterford 10 Balbriggan *Israel:* 4 Acre, Akko, Elat, Yafo 5 Accho, Eilat, Haifa, Jaffa, Joppa 6 Ashdod 8 Ashqelon *Italy:* 4 Bari 5 Anzio, Gaeta, Genoa 6 Genova, Naples, Napoli, Pesaro, Rimini, Venice 7 Leghorn, Livorno, Marsala, Messina, Rapallo, Salerno, Taranto, Trieste, Venezia 8 Brindisi, Siracusa, Sorrento, Syracuse *Ivory Coast:* 5 Tabou 7 Abidjan *Jamaica:* 7 Kingston 10 Montego Bay *Japan:* 4 Kobe, Oita 5 Kochi, Osaka, Rumoi, Ujina, Uraga 6 Sasebo 7 Fukuoka 8 Nagasaki, Yokohama 9 Hiroshima *Java:* 5 Tegal, Tuban 7 Cilacap, Jakarta 8 Semarang, Surabaya *Jordan:* 5 Aqaba, Elath 6 Aelana *Latvia:* 4 Riga *Lebanon:* 4 Tyre 5 Saida, Sidon 6 Beirut 7 Tripoli *Libya:* 6 Tobruk 7 Tripoli 8 Benghazi *Lithuania:* 5 Memel 8 Klaipeda *Madagascar:* 8 Tamatave *Maine:* 7 Belfast 8 Portland *Malaysia:* 4 Miri, Weld 5 Pekan 6 Melaka, Pinang 7 Malacca 10 George Town *Massachusetts:* 6 Boston 9 Fall River 10 New Bedford *Mauritius:* 9 Port Louis *Mediterranean:* 4 Gaza, Oran 5 Genoa, Haifa, Jaffa 6 Beirut, Naples, Venice 7 Algiers, Bizerte, Catania, Palermo, Piraeus, Tripoli 8 Benghazi, Port Said 9 Barcelona, Marseille 10 Alexandria, Marseilles *Mexico:* 7 Tampico 8 Acapulco, Mazatlán, Veracruz *Minorca:* 5 Mahón *Moluccas:* 5 Ambon *Montenegro:* 5 Kotor *Morocco:* 4 Safi, Salé 5 Ceuta 6 Agadir 7 Tangier, Tétouan 10

Casablanca *Mozambique:* 5 Beira, Pemba 6 Amelia, Maputo, Xai Xai 11 Porto Amelia *New Hampshire:* 10 Portsmouth *New Zealand:* 8 Auckland 10 Wellington *Nicaragua:* 5 Brito *Nigeria:* 5 Lagos 8 Harcourt *Niger mouth:* 5 Bonny *North Korea:* 4 Yuki 5 Nampo, Unggi 6 Wonsan *Norway:* 4 Bodo, Moss 5 Vadso 6 Bergen, Tromso 9 Stavanger, Trondheim 11 Fredrikstad *Oman:* 6 Masqat, Muscat 7 Salalah *Pakistan:* 5 Pasni 6 Gwadar 7 Karachi *Papua New Guinea:* 3 Lea *Peru:* 3 Ilo 4 Eten 5 Paita, Pisco 6 Callao *Philippines:* 4 Cebu 5 Davao, Laoag 6 Aparri, Cavite, Iloilo, Manila 7 Legaspi 8 Tacloban 9 Zamboanga *Poland:* 6 Danzig, Gdansk, Gdynia 7 Stettin 8 Szczecin *Portugal:* 4 Faro 5 Porto 6 Oporto 7 Funchal, Setúbal *Puerto Rico:* 5 Ponce 7 Arecibo, San Juan 8 Mayagüez *Russia:* 6 Vyborg 8 Murmansk 11 Kaliningrad, Vladivostok *Ryukyu:* 4 Naha, Nawa *Sakhalin Island:* 8 Korsakov *Saudi Arabia:* 5 Jedda, Jidda, Yanbu, Yenbo 6 Jeddah, Jiddah, Jubail *Scotland:* 3 Ayr 5 Leith, Leven 6 Dundee 7 Glasgow 8 Aberdeen *Sicily:* 7 Catania, Marsala, Messina, Palermo 8 Syracuse *Slovenia:* 5 Kopar, Koper, Piran *Somalia:* 7 Berbera 9 Mogadishu *South Africa:* 5 Natal 6 Durban 8 Cape Town *South Carolina:* 8 Savannah 10 Charleston *South Korea:* 5 Masan, Mokpo, Pusan 6 Inchon 7 Incheon, Masampo *Spain:* 4 Vigo 5 Cádiz, Gijón 6 Abdera, Málaga 8 Alicante 9 Algeciras, Barcelona, Cartagena, Las Palmas *Sri Lanka:* 7 Colombo 10 Batticaloa *Sumatra:* 5 Medan 6 Padang 9 Banda Aceh *Sweden:* 4 Umea 5 Gavle, Lulea, Malmö, Pitea, Ystad 8 Göteborg 9 Stockholm 10 Gothenburg 11 Helsingborg *Tanzania:* 5 Lindi, Tanga 8 Zanzibar 11 Dar es Salaam *Thailand:* 4 Trat 8 Bang Phra *Tunisia:* 4 Sfax 5 Gabès 6 Sousse 7 Bizerta, Bizerte *Turkey:* 4 Rize 5 Izmir, Sinop 6 Samsun, Smyrna 7 Antalya 8 Istanbul *Ukraine:* 5 Kerch, Yalta 6 Odessa 7 Kherson *Vanuatu:* 4 Vila 8 Port-Vila *Vietnam:* 3 Hue 6 Da Nang 7 Tourane 8 Haiphong, Nha Trang *Virginia:* 7 Norfolk 10 Portsmouth *Yemen:* 4 Aden 5 Mocha

seaport capital 4 Aden, Apia, Dili, Lomé, Suva 5 Accra, Adana, Dakar, Lagos 6 Banjul, Belize, Bissau, Dublin, Havana, Kuwait, Lisbon, Maputo, Masqat, Muscat, Roseau 7 Algiers, Batavia, Colombo, Jakarta, Moresby, San Juan 8 Castries, Djakarta, Freetown, Hamilton, Helsinki, Honolulu, Kingston, Monrovia, Valletta 9

Mogadishu, Nuku'alofa, Porto-Novo, Reykjavík, Singapore **10** Bridgetown, Daressalem, Libreville, Mogadiscio, Paramaribo **11** Dar es Salaam, Port of Spain **12** Port-au-Prince

sear 3 dry **5** brand, parch, singe **6** burn up, scorch, sizzle **7** shrivel **9** cauterize, dehydrate, desiccate

search 4 beat, comb, grub, hunt, scan, seek **5** chase, check, delve, frisk, grope, quest, rifle, scour **6** ferret, forage, google **7** fossick, hunting, manhunt, pursuit, ransack, rummage, run down **8** finecomb, scavenge, scout out **9** cast about, ferret out **10** scrutinize

searing 3 hot **5** harsh **6** severe **7** blazing, burning, intense **8** scathing **9** agonizing, scorching **10** blistering **12** excruciating

sea robber 5 rover **6** pirate **7** corsair **8** picaroon **9** buccaneer **10** freebooter

seasickness 6 nausea **8** mal de mer

season 3 fit **4** fall, term, time, Yule **5** spice, train, treat **6** autumn, flavor, harden, pepper, period, school, spring, summer, winter **7** prepare, toughen **8** marinade, marinate **9** acclimate, Christmas **10** case-harden, discipline **11** acclimatize

seasonable 3 apt **6** timely **7** welcome **9** favorable, opportune, pertinent, well-timed **10** auspicious, convenient, propitious **11** appropriate

seasoned 6 inured, mature, tested, versed **7** adapted, matured, veteran **8** flavored, hardened **9** flavorful, practiced **10** acclimated, habituated **11** experienced **12** acclimatized, accomplished

seasoning 3 bay **4** dill, herb, mace, sage, salt **5** anise, basil, chili, clove, cumin, spice, thyme **6** cloves, fennel, garlic, ginger, nutmeg, pepper, savory **7** cayenne, chervil, mustard, oregano, paprika, parsley, saffron **8** allspice, cardamom, cinnamon, rosemary, tarragon, turmeric **9** condiment, coriander

seat 3 hub **4** base, beam, duff, rear, rest, rump **5** basis, chair, place, usher **6** behind, bottom, center, settee **7** fulcrum **8** backside, buttocks, derriere **9** fundament, posterior **10** foundation *church:* **3** pew *on a camel or elephant:* **6** howdah *upholstered:* **9** banquette

sea urchin 7 echinus **8** echinoid

seaweed 4 agar, alga, kelp, limu, nori, tang, ulva **5** dulse, fucus, kombu **6** fucoid, wakame **8** sargasso **9** carrageen, Irish moss **12** bladder wrack

Sea Wolf, The *author:* **6** London (Jack) *captain:* **10** Wolf Larsen *ship:* **5** Ghost

Sebastian *brother:* **6** Alonso *sister:* **5** Viola

secco 3 dry **8** painting, staccato

secede 4 quit **5** leave **8** separate, withdraw

seclude 4 hide **6** closet, immure, retire, screen **7** confine, enclose, isolate, shut off **8** cloister, separate, withdraw **9** sequester

secluded 6 hidden, remote **7** private, recluse, shut off **8** hermetic, isolated, screened, solitary **9** concealed, reclusive, withdrawn **10** cloistered, tucked away **11** out-of-the-way, quarantined, sequestered

seclusion 7 privacy **8** solitude **9** isolation **10** separation, withdrawal

second 4 wink **5** flash, jiffy, place, trice **6** moment **7** endorse, instant, support **9** twinkling

secondary 3 sub **6** lesser **7** derived **8** borrowed, inferior **9** resultant, tributary **10** collateral, derivative, subsequent **11** subordinate, subservient

second-class 6 common **8** déclassé, inferior, low-grade, mediocre

secondhand 4 used, worn **7** derived **8** borrowed **10** derivative

second-string 3 sub **6** backup **9** alternate **10** substitute

secrecy 7 silence, stealth **10** covertness, subterfuge **11** concealment, furtiveness

secret 5 sneak **6** arcane, closet, covert, hidden, occult **7** cryptic, furtive, obscure, subrosa **8** abstruse, backdoor, discreet, hermetic, hush-hush, stealthy **9** concealed, recondite **10** classified, restricted, undercover **11** clandestine, out-of-the-way, underhanded **12** confidential, hugger-mugger **13** surreptitious, under-the-table *combining form:* **5** crypt, krypt **6** crypto, krypto

secret agent 3 spy **8** emissary

secretary 4 aide, desk **5** clerk **6** scribe **9** assistant **10** amanuensis, escritoire *king's:* **10** chancellor

Secretary-General 3 Ban (Ki-moon), Lie (Trygve) **4** Jebb (Gladwyn) **5** Annan (Kofi), Thant (U) **8** Waldheim (Kurt) **12** Boutros-Ghali (Boutros), Hammarskjöld (Dag)

secrete 4 bury, emit, hide **5** cache, exude, plant, stash **6** screen **7** conceal, deposit, emanate

secretion 3 pus **5** mucus

secretive 7 furtive **8** reticent, taciturn **10** backstairs, buttoned-up **11** tight-lipped **12** close-mouthed **13** unforthcoming

secretly 7 sub rosa **9** furtively **10** stealthily

secret police *East Germany:* **5** Stasi *Soviet Union:* **3** KGB, MGB, MVD **4** NKVD, OGPU **5** Cheka

secret society 3 KKK **4** tong **5** cabal, Mafia, Triad **6** Mau Mau, Yakuza **7** camorra **9** camarilla, Carbonari **10** Cosa Nostra, Freemasons, Ku Klux Klan

sect 4 cult **5** creed, party **7** faction **8** division, religion **12** denomination

sectarian 5 local **8** splinter **9** dissident, heretical, heterodox, parochial **10** provincial, schismatic, unorthodox **13** nonconformist

sectary 5 rebel **7** heretic **8** adherent, disciple, follower, partisan **9** dissenter, dissident **10** schismatic, separatist **13** nonconformist, revolutionary

section 3 cut **4** area, belt, part, unit, zone **5** chunk, piece, slice, tract **6** member, moiety, parcel, region, sector, sphere **7** portion, quarter, segment **8** district, division, locality, precinct **11** subdivision

sector 4 area, zone **7** quarter, section **8** district, precinct **11** subdivision

secular 3 lay **4** laic **7** earthly, profane, worldly **8** temporal, unsacred **11** nonclerical, terrestrial **12** nonreligious

secure 3 fix, ice, tie **4** bind, fast, firm, gain, land, lock, moor, nail, safe, seal **5** catch, cinch, clamp, cover, fixed, guard, solid, sound, tried **6** anchor, assure, cement, clinch, defend, effect, ensure, fasten, insure, obtain, shield, stable **7** acquire, assured, capture, procure, protect, tie down **8** reliable, sanguine **9** confident, safeguard **10** batten down, bring about **11** established, impregnable

security 4 bail, bond, pawn **5** guard, T-note, token **6** pledge, safety, shield, surety **7** defense, earnest, warrant **8** guaranty, immunity, warranty **9** assurance, guarantee, safeguard, soundness, stability **10** collateral, protection, steadiness **13** certification

sedate 4 calm **5** grave, sober, staid **6** placid, proper, seemly, serene, steady **7** earnest, serious **8** composed, decorous, tranquil **9** collected, dignified, unruffled **10** sobersided **13** dispassionate, imperturbable

sedative 4 balm **6** downer, Valium **7** calmant, Librium, Miltown, Seconal **8** barbital, hyoscine, Nembutal **9** calmative, soporific **10** depressant **11** barbiturate **12** sleeping pill, tranquilizer **13** tranquillizer

sedentary 4 lazy **6** seated **7** alluvia, settled, sitting **8** inactive **10** stationary

sediment 4 lees, silt **5** dregs, dross **7** bottoms, deposit, grounds, heeltap, residue **8** residuum **9** settlings **11** precipitate *layer:* **5** varve

sedition 4 coup **6** mutiny, putsch, revolt, strike **7** protest, treason **8** intrigue, uprising **9** coup d'état, rebellion **10** revolution **12** insurrection

seditious 8 disloyal, factious, mutinous **9**
dissident, insurgent **10** rebellious, traitorous **11** treacherous

seduce 4 bait, coax, lure **5** decoy, tempt **6** allure, betray, delude, entice, entrap, lead on, ravish **7** corrupt, debauch, deceive **8** entrance, inveigle

seducer 4 rake, roué, vamp **7** Don Juan, playboy **8** Casanova, lothario **9** libertine, womanizer **11** philanderer

seduction 4 lure **8** conquest **9** siren song **10** allurement, attraction, ravishment, temptation

seductive 5 siren **8** alluring, magnetic, tempting **9** beguiling **10** attractive, bewitching, enchanting **11** captivating

seductress 5 siren **7** Lorelei **9** temptress **11** femme fatale

sedulous 8 diligent, tireless **9** assiduous, laborious **10** persistent **11** industrious, persevering, unremitting

see 4 call, espy, gaze, look, mark, peer, scan, view **5** sight, watch **6** behold, descry, divine, notice, take in **7** discern, find out, glimpse, make out, observe, realize **8** consider, envisage, envision, perceive **9** apprehend, ascertain, recognize, visualize

seed 3 pip, sow **4** core, germ **5** brood, grain, issue, ovule, plant, spark, spawn, spore **6** embryo, kernel, notion **7** concept, nucleus, progeny **8** children **9** offspring **11** descendants *aromatic:* **5** anise **6** fennel *coating:* **5** testa **6** testae (plural) *covering:* **4** aril *of a bean:* **7** haricot *of a vine:* **6** peanut *poisonous:* **10** castor bean *poppy:* **3** maw *scar:* **5** hilum *small:* **3** pip *vessel:* **3** pod **5** fruit, pyxis **7** silicle, silique

seedcase 3 pod **4** aril

seedy 5 dingy, faded, mangy, ratty, tired **6** droopy, frowsy, frowzy, shabby, used up, wilted **7** run-down, scruffy, squalid, unkempt, wilting **8** decaying, decrepit, drooping, flagging, inferior, slovenly, tattered **9** neglected, overgrown **10** bedraggled, down-at-heel, threadbare **12** disreputable

seek 3 try **4** fish, hunt, root **5** assay, delve, essay, offer, quest, sniff **6** pursue, strive **7** attempt, inquire, look for, request **8** endeavor, smell out **9** search for, search out, undertake

seem 3 act **4** look **5** imply **6** appear, behave **7** suggest **8** resemble

seemly 3 fit **6** decent, proper, suited **7** apropos, correct, fitting **8** becoming, decorous, suitable **9** befitting, congenial, congruous **10** compatible, conforming **11** appropriate, comme il faut

seep 4 drip, leak, ooze, weep **5** bleed, exude,

leech, sweat **6** filter, strain **7** diffuse, dribble, trickle **8** transude **9** percolate

seer 5 augur, sibyl **6** oracle **7** diviner, prophet **8** foreseer, haruspex **9** predictor **10** forecaster, foreteller, soothsayer **11** clairvoyant, Nostradamus, vaticinator **13** fortune-teller

seesaw 3 yaw **4** rock, veer **5** lurch, pitch, swing **6** teeter **7** bascule **8** flip-flop **9** alternate, fluctuate, oscillate **11** teeterboard **12** teeter-totter

seethe 3 sop **4** boil, burn, foam, fret, fume, rage, soak, stew **5** churn, erupt, froth, souse, steam, steep **6** bubble, drench, simmer, sizzle **7** bristle, ferment, parboil, smolder **8** saturate, smoulder, waterlog

see-through 5 clear **6** limpid **8** pellucid **11** translucent, transparent

segment 3 bit, cut, lap, leg **4** clip, part **5** phase, piece **6** divide, member, moiety **7** portion, section **8** division, fragment, separate **10** categorize

sego 4 lily

segregate 6 enisle, select **7** isolate **8** separate **9** sequester **10** disconnect

segregation 9 apartheid, isolation **10** jim crowism, separatism **13** ghettoization

segue 7 proceed **8** continue **10** transition **11** progression

seidel 5 stoup **8** schooner

seine 3 net **5** trawl

Seine tributary 4 Oise **5** Marne, Yonne

seismologist 7 Richter (Charles)

seize 3 bag, nab **4** glom, grab, take **5** annex, catch, clasp, grasp, usurp **6** abduct, arrest, clinch, clutch, kidnap, occupy, secure, snatch **7** capture, grapple, impound **8** arrogate, carry off **9** apprehend, sequester **10** commandeer, confiscate **11** appropriate, expropriate

seizure 3 fit **4** turn **5** spasm, spell, throe **6** access, attack, taking **7** capture **8** paroxysm, takeover **9** breakdown **10** annexation, convulsion, usurpation **12** confiscation

seldom 6 hardly, rarely **8** scarcely **10** hardly ever **12** infrequently, occasionally, sporadically

select 4 best, cull, fine, pick, rare **5** A-list, cream, elite, prime **6** choice, choose, chosen, culled, opt for, picked **7** favored, pick out **8** screened, superior **9** exclusive, exquisite, preferred, recherché, single out

selection 6 choice **7** culling, excerpt, picking **8** choosing **10** assortment, preference

selective 5 fussy, picky **6** choosy **7** choosey, finicky **8** specific **10** discerning, particular, scrupulous **11** persnickety

Selene 4 Luna **6** Hecate **7** Artemis *beloved:* **8** Endymion *brother:* **6** Helios *father:* **8** Hyperion *mother:* **4** Thea *sister:* **3** Eos

selenium symbol 2 Se

self 3 ego *combining form:* **3** aut **4** auto

self-absorbed 4 smug **8** egoistic **9** conceited, egotistic **10** complacent, egocentric **11** egotistical, introverted **12** narcissistic **13** inner-directed

self-acting 9 automatic

self-assertive 4 bold **5** brash, pushy **6** cheeky **7** forward **8** cocksure, militant **9** audacious, obtrusive, officious **10** aggressive **11** impertinent, overweening **12** presumptuous

self-assurance 5 poise **6** aplomb **8** coolness **9** composure, sangfroid **10** confidence, equanimity **13** collectedness

self-assured 4 smug **6** poised **8** sanguine **9** confident

self-centered 9 conceited, egotistic **10** egocentric **11** egotistical **12** narcissistic

self-composed 4 calm **6** poised, serene **7** assured **9** collected, confident, possessed **10** controlled

self-confidence 5 poise **6** aplomb **9** assurance

self-confident 5 cocky **6** jaunty, poised **7** assured **8** sanguine

self-conscious 4 prim **5** stiff **6** formal, uneasy **7** awkward, stilted, studied **8** affected, mannered **9** contrived, ill at ease **10** artificial

self-contained 6 closed, formal **7** built-in **8** composed, enclosed, reserved, reticent **9** exclusive **10** restrained **11** independent

self-control 7 balance, dignity, reserve **9** restraint, stability, willpower **10** abstinence, constraint, discipline, temperance **11** forbearance

self-defense art 4 judo **6** aikido, karate, kung fu **7** jujitsu **9** tai kwan do

self-destruction 7 seppuku, suicide **8** felo-de-se, hara-kiri, hari-kari

self-discipline 4 will **8** stoicism **9** willpower **10** abstinence

self-educated 12 autodidactic

self-effacing 3 shy **5** timid **6** modest **7** bashful **8** retiring, sheepish **9** diffident, unassured **11** unassertive

self-esteem 5 pride **6** vanity **7** conceit, dignity, egotism **10** narcissism **11** amour propre

self-evident 5 clear, plain **6** patent **7** obvious **8** manifest, palpable **10** prima facie, undeniable **12** demonstrable, unmistakable *truth:* **5** axiom

self-explanatory 5 clear, plain **7** evident, obvious **8** manifest **11** perspicuous, transparent

self-governing 7 popular **9** sovereign **10** autonomous, democratic

self-importance 3 ego **5** pride **6** egoism, hubris **7** conceit, egotism **9** arrogance, pomposity, vainglory

self-important 4 smug, vain **6** lordly **7** bloated, haughty, pompous **8** arrogant **9** conceited, egotistic **10** pontifical **11** magisterial, pretentious

self-indulgent 9 libertine, sybaritic **10** hedonistic

self-interest 6 egoism

selfish 6 stingy **8** egoistic **9** egotistic **10** egocentric, ungenerous **11** egomaniacal **12** selfcentered **13** self-indulgent

selfless 8 generous **10** altruistic, benevolent, charitable

self-love 6 egoism, vanity **7** conceit, egotism **8** vainness **9** vainglory **10** narcissism **11** amour propre **13** conceitedness

self-possessed 4 calm **6** poised, serene **7** equable **8** composed, sanguine **9** collected, unruffled **11** unflappable **13** imperturbable

self-proclaimed 8 so-called **9** soi-disant **10** self-styled

Self-Reliance author 7 Emerson (Ralph Waldo)

self-respect 5 pride **7** dignity **11** amour propre

self-restraint 8 chastity, sobriety **9** willpower **10** abnegation, abstention, abstinence, continence, discipline **11** forbearance

self-righteous 5 pious **7** canting, preachy **8** unctuous **9** pharisaic **10** complacent, goodygoody **11** pharisaical **12** hypocritical, pecksniffian **13** sanctimonious

self-sacrificing 8 generous, selfless **9** unselfish

self-satisfied 4 smug **8** priggish **10** complacent

self-seeking 6 greedy **7** selfish **8** egoistic **9** egotistic **10** egocentric **11** egotistical

self-serving see **self-seeking**

self-starter 7 hustler **8** go-getter

self-styled 7 nominal, would-be **8** so-called **9** soi-disant

self-taught 12 autodidactic

sell 4 hawk, vend **5** trade **6** barter, deal in, hustle, market, peddle, retail, unload **7** auction **8** exchange

sell out 4 dump, move **6** betray, turn in, unload **7** deceive **8** inform on **11** double-cross

selvage, selvedge 3 hem **4** edge **6** border

semblance 3 air **4** face, look, mask, pose, show, veil **5** front, guise, image **6** aspect, facade, simile, veneer **7** analogy, feeling, modicum **8** affinity, disguise, likeness, pretense **10** apparition, appearance, comparison, false front, masquerade, similarity, similitude, simulacrum **11** countenance

Semele *father:* **6** Cadmus *mother:* **8** Harmonia *sister:* **3** Ino **5** Agave **7** Autonoë *son:* **7** Bacchus **8** Dionysus

semi 3 rig **4** demi, half, hemi **5** truck **6** partly

seminar 5 forum **8** colloquy **10** colloquium, conference, roundtable

Seminole chief 7 Osceola

Semiramis *husband:* **5** Ninus *kingdom:* **7** Babylon

Semite 3 Jew **4** Arab **6** Hebrew **7** Moabite **8** Akkadian, Assyrian **9** Canaanite **10** Babylonian, Phoenician

Senapo *daughter:* **8** Clorinda *kingdom:* **8** Ethiopia

senate 7 chamber, council **8** assembly **11** legislature

senator 5 solon **8** lawmaker **10** legislator

send 4 mail, post, ship **5** relay, remit, route **6** commit, export, launch **7** address, advance, airmail, consign, forward, traject **8** dispatch, transmit *back:* **6** remand

Sendak book 17 In the Night Kitchen **21** Where the Wild Things Are

send in 6 submit

send-up 5 roast, spoof **6** parody, satire **7** lampoon, takeoff **9** burlesque **10** caricature, pasquinade

Senegal *capital:* **5** Dakar *enclave:* **6** Gambia *ethnic group:* **5** Wolof **6** Fulani **7** Malinke *language:* **6** French *monetary unit:* **5** franc *neighbor:* **4** Mali **6** Guinea **10** Mauritania **12** Guinea-Bissau *river:* **6** Gambia

senescence 6 old age **8** caducity **11** elderliness, senectitude

senility 6 dotage

senior 5 doyen, elder, older, prior **7** ancient, doyenne, oldster **8** higher-up, old-timer, superior **10** golden-ager

Sennacherib *domain:* **7** Assyria *father:* **6** Sargon *kingdom:* **7** Assyria *slayer, son:* **8** Sharezer **11** Adrammelech

sensation 4 bomb **5** éclat **6** marvel, tingle, wonder **7** feeling, miracle, prodigy, stunner **8** response **9** bombshell **10** impression, perception, phenomenon **13** consciousness

sensational 3 hot **5** boffo, juicy, lurid **6** purple, vulgar **7** tabloid **8** dramatic, exciting, fabulous, glorious, slambang, smashing, stunning **9** hunky-dory, marvelous, thrilling **10** astounding, impressive, incredible, remarkable, scandalous **11** astonishing, extravagant, outstanding, spectacular **12** electrifying

sense 3 wit **4** feel **5** sight, smell, taste, touch **6** divine, intuit, pick up **7** believe, discern, feeling, hearing, meaning, message, realize **8** consider, judgment, perceive, prudence **9** awareness, foresight, intuition **10** anticipate, cognizance, discretion, perception **12** intelligence, significance **13** comprehension, consciousness, understanding *sixth:* **3** ESP

Sense and Sensibility author 6 Austen (Jane)

senseless 4 cold, numb **5** silly **6** absurd, numbed, simple, stupid **7** fatuous, foolish, idiotic, moronic, trivial, witless **8** benumbed, comatose, deadened, mindless **9** brainless, pointless **10** irrational **11** meaningless, purposeless, unconscious

senselessness 5 folly **7** inanity **8** insanity **9** absurdity, stupidity **12** illogicality

sense organ 3 ear, eye **4** nose, skin **6** tongue **8** receptor

sensibility 5 taste **7** emotion, feeling, insight **8** judgment, keenness **9** affection, awareness, sensation **11** discernment, penetration **12** appreciation

sensible 4 sage, sane, wise **5** solid, sound **6** astute, shrewd **7** logical, prudent, sapient **8** rational **9** judicious, objective, sagacious **10** reasonable

sensitive 4 keen, sore **5** aware, prone **6** liable, tender, touchy, tricky **7** feeling, nervous **8** delicate, sensible, sentient, ticklish **9** emotional **10** high-strung, perceptive, precarious, responsive **11** susceptible **13** understanding

sensitive plant 6 mimosa *family:* **3** pea

sensual 4 lush **6** animal, carnal, earthy **7** fleshly, mundane, worldly **8** temporal **9** epicurean, luxurious, sybaritic **10** hedonistic, voluptuous **11** irreligious, unspiritual

sensuality 4 lust **6** desire, luxury **7** lechery, license **8** hedonism, lewdness, pleasure **9** carnality, depravity, eroticism, prurience **10** debauchery, degeneracy, immorality, indulgence, perversion, profligacy, sybaritism **11** dissipation **13** dissoluteness, gratification, salaciousness

sensuous 4 lush **6** carnal **7** fleshly **8** luscious **9** epicurean, luxurious, sybaritic **10** hedonistic, voluptuous **13** self-indulgent

sentence 3 rap **4** damn, doom **5** blame, judge **6** dictum, ordain, punish **7** adjudge, condemn, convict, verdict **8** decision, denounce, judgment, penalize **10** adjudicate, punishment

sententious 5 crisp, pithy, terse **7** concise, piquant, pointed **8** eloquent, pregnant, succinct **10** aphoristic, expressive, meaningful, moralistic, moralizing

sentient 5 alert, aware, savvy **7** knowing **8** sensible **9** attentive, cognizant, conscious, receptive, sensitive **10** conversant, discerning, perceptive, percipient, responsive **12** appreciative

sentiment 4 view **5** ethos **6** belief **7** emotion, feeling, leaning, opinion, passion, posture **8** penchant, position, tendency **9** affection, inclining, sensation **10** conception, conviction, partiality, persuasion, propensity **11** disposition, inclination, sensibility

sentimental 4 soft **5** corny, gooey, gushy, mushy, sappy, soupy, sweet **6** dreamy, drippy, slushy, sticky, sugary, syrupy, tender **7** cloying, gushing, insipid, maudlin, mawkish **8** bathetic, effusive, romantic **9** misty-eyed, nostalgic, schmaltzy **10** idealistic, lovey-dovey, moonstruck, namby-pamby, saccharine, soft-boiled **11** tear-jerking **12** affectionate

sentimentality 4 mush **8** schmaltz

sentinel see **sentry**

sentry 5 guard, watch **6** picket **7** lookout **8** sentinel, watchman

separate 4 comb, only, part, sift, sole, sort **5** apart, sever, split **6** cut off, detach, divide, single, unique **7** asunder, diverse, divided, divorce, isolate, several, split up, unravel, various **8** alienate, detached, discrete, disjoint, distinct, insulate, isolated, solitary, splinter, uncouple **9** different, divergent, extricate, segregate **11** compartment, distinctive, distinguish, independent, unconnected **12** disconnected, discriminate **13** differentiate

separation 3 gap **4** rift **5** break, split **6** schism **7** breakup, divorce, parting, rupture, split-up **8** disunion, disunity, division **9** apartheid, dichotomy, partition **11** disjunction, dissolution, segregation **12** dissociation, estrangement **13** disconnection, sequestration

separatism 9 apartheid **11** segregation

separatist 10 schismatic **12** secessionist

sepia 3 ink **5** brown, umber **6** sienna

sepulchral 4 grim **5** bleak, grave **6** dismal, gloomy, solemn, somber **7** doleful, macabre **8** funereal, ghoulish, mortuary **9** tenebrous

sepulchre 4 tomb **5** grave, vault **9** mausoleum

sequel 3 end **5** close **6** effect, ending, finish, result, upshot **7** closing, outcome **8** epilogue **9** aftermath **10** succession **11** aftereffect, consequence, development, eventuality, progression, termination **12** continuation

sequence 3 row, run, set **4** flow **5** chain, order, train **6** course, series, string **8** disposal, ordering **9** placement **10** procession, succession **11** arrangement, disposition, progression **12** distribution

sequential 6 serial **9** succedent **10** continuous, succeeding, successive **11** consecutive **12** successional **13** chronological

sequester 4 hide, take **5** annex, seize **6** attach, cut off, enisle **7** impound, isolate, preempt, seclude, secrete **8** accroach, arrogate, cloister, close off, insulate, separate, set apart, withdraw **9** segregate **10** commandeer, confiscate, dispossess **11** appropriate, expropriate

sequoia 7 big tree, redwood **12** coast redwood

seraglio 5 harem

serape 5 shawl

seraph 5 angel **8** guardian **9** messenger

seraphic 4 pure **7** angelic, sublime **8** beatific, cherubic, ethereal

Serbia capital: 8 Belgrade **city: 3** Bar, Niš **7** Novi Sad, Pancevo **10** Kragujevac **former leader: 9** Milošević (Slobodan) **monetary unit: 4** euro **5** dinar **neighbor: 6** Bosnia, Kosovo **7** Albania, Croatia, Hungary, Romania **8** Bulgaria **9** Macedonia **10** Montenegro **part of: 7** Balkans **peninsula: 6** Balkan **province: 9** Vojvodina **province, former: 6** Kosovo **river: 4** Sava **6** Danube **sea: 8** Adriatic

sere 3 dry **4** arid **5** dried **7** parched, thirsty **8** withered **9** shriveled, unwatered

serenade 7 lullaby **8** shivaree **9** charivari

serene 4 calm **5** quiet, still **6** limpid, placid, poised, sedate **7** halcyon **8** composed, tranquil **9** unruffled **10** untroubled

serenity 4 calm **5** peace **8** calmness, quietude **9** composure, placidity, stillness **10** equanimity **11** contentment, tranquility **12** peacefulness, tranquillity

serf 4 esne, peon **5** churl, helot, slave **6** thrall **7** bondman, villein **freeborn: 7** colonus

sergeant 3 NCO **6** noncom

serial 4 soap **10** sequential, successive **11** consecutive, installment

series 3 row, run, set **4** list, tier **5** chain, range, scale, train **6** catena, column, parade, sequel, string **8** sequence **9** cavalcade, gradation **10** procession, succession **11** progression **12** continuation

serious 4 grim, hard **5** grave, heavy, major, sober, staid, stern, tough **6** intent, sedate, severe, solemn, somber, sombre, steady **7** austere, earnest, intense, pensive, sincere, unfunny, weighty **8** funereal, menacing, resolute, sobering **9** difficult, humorless, important, laborious, strenuous, unamusing **10** determined, formidable, meditative, nononsense, poker-faced, purposeful, reflective, sobersided, thoughtful, unhumorous **11** significant, threatening **12** businesslike **13** contemplative

sermon 6 homily, speech, tirade **7** address, lecture, oration **8** harangue **9** preaching **10** preachment **11** exhortation

sermonize 5 orate **6** dilate, exhort, preach **7** dissert, lecture **8** moralize **9** discourse, expatiate, preachify **10** dissertate, evangelize **11** pontificate

serpent 5 fiend, Satan, snake **fabled: 8** basilisk **mythical: 10** cockatrice **sound: 4** hiss

serpentine 4 rock, wily **5** snaky **6** snakey **7** cunning, devious, mineral, sinuous, winding **8** flexuous, tempting, tortuous **9** snakelike **10** circuitous, convoluted, meandering

serrated 7 notched, toothed **8** saw-edged, sawtooth **10** saw-toothed **11** denticulate

servant 4 maid, peon **5** slave, valet **6** butler, flunky, helper, lackey, menial **7** famulus, footman **8** domestic, handmaid, hireling, houseboy **9** attendant **11** chamberlain, chambermaid **India: 4** syce **kitchen: 8** scullion **Wodehouse: 6** Jeeves

serve 3 act, fit, use **4** help, make, play, suit, work **5** avail, nurse, spend, treat **6** foster, handle, wait on **7** advance, benefit, care for, present, promote, provide, satisfy, suffice, work for **8** deal with, function **9** encourage, officiate **10** minister to

service 3 use **4** duty, help, rite **5** favor **6** employ, repair, ritual **7** account, benefit, fitness, liturgy **8** ceremony, courtesy, disposal, maintain **10** active duty, assistance, ceremonial, observance, usefulness **11** maintenance **12** dispensation

serviceable 5 handy, utile **6** decent, usable, useful **7** durable, helpful **8** adequate, suitable **9** efficient, practical **10** acceptable, beneficial, convenient, dependable, functional **11** utilitarian **12** satisfactory

servile 6 abject, craven, humble, menial **7** fawning, slavish **8** obedient, obeisant **9** groveling **10** obsequious, submissive **11** subservient

servility 7 bondage, helotry, peonage, serfdom, slavery **9** thralldom **11** enslavement

serving 6 dollop **7** helping, portion

servitude 5 labor **6** corvée, thrall **7** bondage, helotry, peonage, serfdom, slavery **9** captivity, indenture, thralldom, villenage **10** subjection **11** enslavement **12** enthrallment

sesame 3 til **4** teel *grass:* **4** gama *seed paste:* **6** tahini

Sesame Street *human character:* **3** Bob, Tom **4** Alan, Gabi, Luis **5** David, Linda, Maria, Miles, Susan **6** Gordon, Savion **8** Mr. Hooper (Harold) *Muppet:* **3** Zoe **4** Abby, Bert, Biff, Elmo **5** Count (The), Ernie, Oscar, Sully, Telly **6** Fluffy, Grover, Kermit, Rosita, Slimey, Snuffy **7** Barkley, Big Bird **9** Guy Smiley, Miss Piggy **13** Cookie Monster, Count von Count *puppeteer:* **6** Henson (Jim)

sessile 5 fixed **6** rooted **7** settled **8** attached **11** established

session 6 assize, séance **7** meeting, sitting

set 3 aim, dry, fix, gel, lay, lot, put **4** firm, jell **5** array, batch, bunch, fixed, group, place, put on, ready, rigid, scene **6** belong, harden, impose, placed, rooted, secure, stated **7** arrange, certain, cluster, congeal, decided, deposit, dictate, jellify, lay down, located, prepare, scenery, situate, specify, station **8** prepared, resolute, resolved, situated, solidify, specific **9** confirmed, designate, establish, prescribe, specified, stipulate, tenacious **10** assortment, determined, gelatinize, inflexible, positioned, prescribed, stipulated **11** established, mise-en-scène *a gem:* **6** collet *right:* **7** redress

set aside 4 void **5** annul **7** discard, dismiss, reserve **8** overrule

set back 4 mire **5** delay **6** detain, hang up, hinder, retard, slow up

setback 4 snag **5** check, hitch **6** defeat, glitch, holdup, rebuff **7** reverse **8** obstacle, reversal **9** hindrance **10** impediment, regression

set down 4 land **5** light, perch, roost **6** alight, record **9** establish, touch down

set fire to 4 burn **5** light, spark **6** ignite, kindle **7** emblaze, inflame **8** enkindle, touch off

set forth 4 cite **5** state **6** adduce, affirm, allege, avouch, depart, embark, launch, submit **7** advance, declare, express, present, proffer, propose, take off **8** proclaim, spell out **9** introduce **10** account for

set free 5 loose **6** redeem, rescue, unbind **7** deliver, manumit, unchain, unloose **8** liberate, unloosen **9** unshackle **10** emancipate

Seth *brother:* **4** Abel, Cain *father:* **4** Adam *mother:* **3** Eve *son:* **4** Enos

set out 5 start **6** embark, intend **7** take off **9** undertake

Set *brother:* **6** Osiris *mother:* **3** Nut *opponent:* **5** Horus *victim:* **6** Osiris

settee 4 seat, sofa **5** bench, divan **6** lounge

setting 5 scene **7** context, scenery **8** ambience **10** background **11** mise-en-scène *for a stone:* **4** ouch

settle 3 fix, lay, pay, put **4** calm, sink **5** allay, judge, light, pay up, perch, place, quiet, roost, still **6** alight, clinch, decide, soothe, square, verify, wind up **7** arrange, clarify, compose, confirm, dispose, install, mediate, resolve, satisfy, work out **8** colonize, conclude, ensconce, nail down **9** determine, discharge, establish, negotiate, reconcile, touch down

settlement 4 deal, mise **6** colony, hamlet **7** outpost, quietus, village **8** decision **9** agreement **10** conclusion, encampment, habitation, resolution **11** arrangement **13** determination *Israeli:* **6** moshav

settler 7 pioneer **8** colonist, squatter **9** colonizer

set-to 3 row **4** fray, spat **5** brawl, broil, brush, fight, run-in, scrap **6** affray, blowup, fracas, tussle **7** dispute, quarrel, rhubarb, scuffle **8** argument, skirmish **9** encounter **10** falling-out **11** altercation

set up 4 open **5** erect, found, raise, start **6** create, launch **7** arrange, install **8** assemble, generate, initiate, organize **9** construct, establish, institute, originate

setup 4 plan, trap **5** array, trick **6** layout, scheme, shoo-in **7** pattern, project, setting **8** assembly, carriage, position, slam dunk **9** alignment, apparatus, structure, sure thing **11** arrangement, preparation **12** constitution

Seuss, Dr. 6 Geisel (Theodore) *character:* **6** Grinch, Horton, Sam-I-Am, Yertle *work:* **11** Cat in the Hat (The) **15** Green Eggs and Ham, Horton Hears a Who, Yertle the Turtle

seven *combining form:* **4** hept, sept **5** hepta, septi *group of:* **6** heptad **8** hebdomad

seventeenth century 8 seicento

sever 3 cut, lop **4** part, rend **5** slice, split **6** cleave, cut off, detach, divide, lop off, sunder **7** break up, divorce **8** amputate, disjoint, separate

several 4 a few, many, some **6** divers, plural, sundry, varied **7** certain, diverse, various **8** assorted, discrete, distinct, manifold, numerous, separate, specific **9** different **10** respective

severe 4 dour, grim, hard **5** acute, grave, harsh, heavy, rigid, sober, stern, tough **6** bitter, brutal, rugged, strict **7** arduous, ascetic, austere, extreme, intense, onerous, serious, weighty **8** exacting, pitiless, rigorous **9** demanding, difficult, laborious, strenuous, stringent, unbending **10** forbidding, implacable, inflexible, iron-willed, oppressive, unyielding **11** disciplined, heavy-handed

severity 5 rigor **7** gravity, urgency **8** exigency, grimness, obduracy, rigidity **9** austerity, harshness, intensity, plainness, privation, restraint, spareness, starkness, sternness **10** strictness, stringency **11** seriousness

sew 4 darn, mend, seam **5** baste **6** needle, stitch, suture

Seward's Folly 6 Alaska

sewer 4 duct **5** ditch, drain **6** tailor **7** cesspit, conduit **8** cesspool, stitcher

sewing *aid:* **7** thimble *case:* **4** etui *kit:* **9** housewife

sewing-machine inventor 4 Howe (Elias)

sew up 3 ice **4** darn, mend, seal **5** patch **6** clinch, decide, ensure, secure, settle, stitch, tailor **7** confirm **8** complete, conclude, finalize, nail down **9** determine

sexless 6 neuter **7** epicene **8** neutered

sex manual 9 Kama-sutra

sexton 6 deacon **9** custodian, sacristan

sexual 4 blue, lewd, racy **6** carnal, erotic, ribald, risqué, smutty **7** obscene **8** venereal **9** salacious **12** pornographic

sexual desire 4 eros, lust **6** libido

sexy 4 blue, racy **5** bawdy, spicy **6** erotic, purple, ribald, risqué, steamy, sultry **7** naughty **8** alluring, off-color, sensuous **9** appealing, salacious, seductive **10** attractive, suggestive

Seychelles *capital:* **8** Victoria *island:* **4** Mahé **7** La Digue, Praslin *language:* **6** Creole, French *monetary unit:* **5** rupee

Sganarelle *brother:* **6** Ariste *daughter:* **7** Lucinde *ward:* **7** Leonore **8** Isabelle *wife:* **7** Martine

shabby 5 dingy, dowdy, faded, mangy, ratty, seedy, sorry, tacky, tatty, tired **6** frayed, scurvy, shoddy, sleazy, sordid **7** outworn, rickety, run-down, scrubby, scruffy, squalid, worn-out **8** beggarly, decaying, decrepit, dog-eared, tattered **9** miserable, moth-eaten, neglected, worm-eaten **10** bedraggled, down-at-heel, ramshackle, threadbare **11** dilapidated **12** deteriorated, disreputable **13** deteriorating, unrespectable

shack 3 cot, hut **4** camp, shed **5** cabin, hovel, lodge **6** shanty **7** cottage

shackle 4 gyve **5** bilbo, chain, leash, strap **6** fetter, hobble, hog-tie, impede, pinion, secure **7** enchain, leg-iron, manacle, trammel **8** handcuff **9** entrammel

shad 7 clupeid, herring

shade 3 bit, hue, tad **4** cast, tint, tone, veil **5** ghost, tinge, trace, umbra **6** awning, darken, nuance, screen **7** dimness, eclipse, phantom, shelter, specter, spectre, umbrage **8** darkness, penumbra, phantasm, tincture **9** gradation, intensity, obscurity **10** apparition **11** distinction

shadow 3 dim, dog, tag **4** haze, hint, tail **5** cloud, shade, tinge, touch, trace, trail, umbra **6** screen, spirit, wraith **7** eidolon, obscure, phantom, specter, umbrage, vestige **8** overcast, penumbra, phantasm, revenant, tincture **9** inumbrate, overcloud, suspicion **10** apparition, intimation, suggestion **11** adumbration

shadowy 3 dim **4** dark **5** dusky, faint, murky, vague **6** gloomy, shaded **7** ghostly, obscure **9** tenebrous **10** indistinct

shady 4 dark **5** bosky, dusky, fishy **6** purple, shabby, shoddy **7** clouded, dubious, suspect **8** doubtful, screened **9** equivocal, sheltered, uncertain **10** suggestive, suspicious, umbrageous, unreliable **12** disreputable

Shaffer play 5 Equus **7** Amadeus

shaft 3 jab, ray, rod **4** axle, barb, beam, dart, pole, stem **5** arrow, lance, shoot, spear, stalk, thill **6** thrust **7** chimney, spindle **8** short end

shag 3 nap, rug **4** pile **5** chase, fetch **7** thicket, tobacco **9** cormorant

shaggy 5 bushy **7** unkempt **8** uncombed

shake 3 jar, jog, rid **4** deal, jerk, jolt, lose, rock, roil, sway **5** avoid, churn, daunt, elude, jiffy, quake, shock, waver, worry **6** escape, frappe, jiggle, joggle, quaver, quiver, shimmy, shiver, tremor **7** agitate, shingle, shudder, temblor, tremble, unnerve, vibrate **8** brandish, convulse, unsettle **9** palpitate **10** earthquake

shake down 5 frisk, gouge, screw, wrest, wring **6** coerce, extort, fleece, search **7** squeeze **9** blackmail

shakedown 3 bed **4** test **5** dance, trial **6** pallet, search, tryout **7** pursuit, testing **8** exaction **9** blackmail, extortion **10** inspection

Shaker leader 3 Lee (Ann) **9** Mother Ann

Shakespearean actor 4 Kean (Edmund) **5** Booth (Edwin), Dench (Judi), Evans (Maurice), Terry (Ellen) **6** Irving (Henry), Jacobi (Derek) **7** Branagh (Kenneth), Burbage (Richard), Garrick (David), Gielgud (John), Olivier (Laurence), Siddons (Sarah) **8** Ashcroft (Peggy), Macready (William), McKellen (Ian), Redgrave (Michael), Scofield

(Paul) **9** Barrymore (Ethel, John, Lionel, Maurice) **10** Richardson (Ralph)
Shakespeare, William 4 bard *character:* **3** Hal **4** Doll (Tearsheet), Hero, Iago, Kent, Lear, Puck **5** Ariel, Edgar, Feste, Harry, Percy (Henry), Poins (Ned), Regan, Romeo, Timon, Titus (Andronicus), Viola **6** Antony, Banquo, Bottom, Brutus, Caesar, Cassio, Duncan, Edmund, Emilia, Fabian, Hamlet, Hecate, Hermia, Jaques, Juliet, Oberon, Olivia, Orsino, Pistol, Portia **7** Antonio, Caliban, Cassius, Claudio, Fleance, Goneril, Horatio, Hotspur, Jessica, Laertes, Lavinia, Macbeth, Macduff, Malcolm, Miranda, Ophelia, Orlando, Othello, Perdita, Shylock, Sir Toby (Belch), Theseus, Titania, Troilus **8** Bassanio, Beatrice, Benedick, Claudius, Cordelia, Cressida, Dogberry, Falstaff (Sir John), Gertrude, Hermione, Lysander, Malvolio, Mercutio, Mortimer, Pericles, Polonius, Prospero, Rosalind **9** Cleopatra, Cymbeline, Demetrius, Desdemona, Hippolyta, Katherine, Petruchio, Sir Andrew (Aguecheek), Vincentio **10** Fortinbras, Holofernes **11** Bolingbroke, John of Gaunt, Lady Macbeth, Lady Macduff, Peter Quince **13** Queen Gertrude, Queen Margaret *contemporary:* **6** Jonson (Ben) **7** Marlowe (Christopher) *forest:* **5** Arden *mother:* **9** Mary Arden *play:* **6** Hamlet, Henry V **7** Henry IV, Henry VI, Macbeth, Othello, Tempest (The) **8** King John, King Lear, Pericles **9** Cymbeline, Henry VIII, Richard II **10** Coriolanus, Richard III **11** As You Like It, Winter's Tale (The) **12** Julius Caesar, Twelfth Night **13** Timon of Athens **14** Comedy of Errors (The), Romeo and Juliet **16** Love's Labour's Lost, Merchant of Venice (The), Taming of the Shrew (The) **17** Measure for Measure **18** Antony and Cleopatra **19** Much Ado About Nothing **20** All's Well That Ends Well, Midsummer Night's Dream (A) *theater:* **5** Globe *wife:* **12** Anne Hathaway
shaky 4 weak **6** infirm, unsure, wobbly **7** aquiver, dubious, jittery, quaking, rackety, rickety, suspect, trembly, unsound **8** doubtful, insecure, rachitic, unstable, unsteady, wavering **9** quivering, tottering, trembling, tremulous, uncertain, unsettled **10** indecisive, precarious, rattletrap, unreliable **11** problematic, vacillating
shale 4 rock **5** slate
shallot 4 herb **5** onion **10** green onion
shallow 4 idle, vain **5** petty, shoal **7** cursory, sketchy, trivial **8** trifling **9** depthless, frivolous **11** perfunctory, superficial

shallows 6 lagoon, shoals
Shallum *father:* **5** Shaul, Zadok **6** Jabesh, Josiah, Sismai, Tikvah **8** Colhozeh, Naphtali **9** Hallohesh *mother:* **6** Bilhah *nephew:* **8** Jeremiah *slayer:* **7** Menahem *son:* **6** Mibsam **7** Hilkiah **8** Maaseiah *victim:* **9** Zechariah
shalom 5 peace
sham 3 act, ape **4** fake, hoax, mock **5** bluff, bogus, bunco, cheat, dummy, false, farce, feign, fraud, phony, pseud, put on, spoof **6** deceit, ersatz, facade, fakery, forged, invent, pseudo **7** assumed, feigned, forgery, imitate, mislead, mockery, pretend **8** affected, flimflam, simulate, spurious, travesty **9** brummagem, burlesque, deception, hypocrisy, imitation, imposture, pinchbeck, simulated **10** artificial, caricature, false front, fictitious, fraudulent, sanctimony, substitute **11** counterfeit, make-believe **12** pecksniffery *combining form:* **5** pseud **6** pseudo
shaman 6 healer, priest, wizard **7** diviner **8** conjurer, conjuror, magician, sorcerer **9** enchanter, priestess **10** high priest, soothsayer **11** faith healer, necromancer, thaumaturge, witch doctor
Shamash 6 sun-god *father:* **3** Sin *sister:* **6** Ishtar *wife:* **3** Aya
shamble see **shuffle**
shambles 4 mess **5** chaos **6** jumble, muddle **8** disarray, disorder, wreckage **9** confusion
shame 4 pity **5** abash, guilt, odium **6** infamy, stigma **7** chagrin, mortify, obloquy, remorse, scandal **8** disgrace, dishonor, ignominy **9** disrepute, embarrass, humiliate, ill repute **10** opprobrium **11** humiliation **12** self-reproach **13** embarrassment, mortification
shamefaced 7 abashed **8** blushing, sheepish **9** mortified **10** humiliated **11** crestfallen, embarrassed
shameless 6 arrant, brazen, wanton **7** blatant, immoral **8** depraved, flagrant, immodest, impudent **9** abandoned, bald-faced, barefaced, dissolute, unabashed **10** outrageous, profligate, unblushing **11** brazenfaced, disgraceful **12** presumptuous
Shammah *brother:* **5** David *father:* **4** Agee **5** Jesse, Reuel *grandfather:* **4** Esau **7** Ishmael *son:* **7** Jonadab **8** Jonathan
Shammua *father:* **5** David, Galal **6** Bilgah, Zaccur *mother:* **9** Bathsheba *son:* **4** Abda
shamus 3 cop **4** dick, tail **6** copper, shadow, sleuth **7** gumshoe **8** flatfoot, sherlock **9** constable, detective, operative, policeman **10** private eye **12** investigator **13** police officer

shanghai 6 abduct, hijack, kidnap

Shangri-la 5 Tibet **6** utopia **7** arcadia **8** paradise **9** Cockaigne, fairyland **10** wonderland

shank 3 leg **4** shin, stem **5** stalk, tibia

shanty 3 cot, hut **4** camp, shed **5** cabin, hovel, lodge, shack **7** cottage

shape 3 fit **4** case, cast, form, mold, plan, trim **5** forge, frame, state, whack **6** aspect, devise, fettle, figure, kilter, repair, sculpt, tailor, work up **7** contour, fitness, outline, pattern, profile **8** assemble **9** condition, construct, fabricate, semblance **10** appearance, silhouette **12** conformation **13** configuration *combining form:* **5** morph **6** morpho *dark:* **6** shadow **10** silhouette

shapeable 6 pliant, supple **7** ductile, plastic, pliable **8** flexible **9** tractable

shapeless 8 inchoate, unformed **9** amorphous

shapely 4 trim **5** buxom **9** Junoesque **10** curvaceous, statuesque, well-turned **11** clean-limbed

shard 4 chip **5** chunk, scale, scrap, shell **6** sliver **7** elytron **8** carapace, fragment

share 3 cut, lot **4** part **5** chunk, claim, quota, slice, stake **6** divide, parcel, ration **7** dole out, give out, helping, partake, portion, prorate, quantum **8** dispense, fraction, interest, quotient **9** allotment, allowance, apportion **10** experience, percentage, proportion **11** participate

shared 5 joint **6** common, mutual, public **8** communal, conjoint, conjunct **9** concerted **10** collective **11** cooperative

Sharezer *father, victim:* 11 Sennacherib

shark 5 cheat **8** swindler *kind:* **4** gata, mako, sand, tope **5** nurse, tiger **7** basking, dogfish, leopard **8** mackerel, man-eater, thresher **9** porbeagle **10** great white, hammerhead *skin:* **8** shagreen

sharp 3 sly **4** acid, keen, tony, trig **5** acerb, acrid, acute, alert, canny, crisp, honed, quick, slick, smart, swank **6** astute, biting, brainy, bright, clever, jagged, nimble, peaked, shrewd, shrill, snappy, snazzy **7** caustic, dashing, intense, pointed, prickly, stylish, whetted **8** clean-cut, clear-cut, incisive **9** brilliant, ingenious, knifelike, vitriolic **10** astringent, perceptive **11** intelligent, penetrating, quick-witted, resourceful

sharpen 4 edge, file, hone, whet **5** grind, strop

sharper 6 con man **7** diddler **8** chiseler, swindler **9** defrauder, trickster **10** mountebank **12** double-dealer

sharp-eyed 4 keen **5** alert **8** vigilant, watchful

9 attentive, observant **10** discerning, perceptive

sharpie see **sharper**

sharpness 4 edge **6** acuity, acumen **9** precision

sharpshooter 6 sniper **7** deadeye **8** marksman

sharp-sighted 8 hawk-eyed, lynx-eyed **9** eagle-eyed

sharp-witted 4 keen **5** acute, canny, quick, smart **6** astute, clever, shrewd **11** intelligent

shatter 4 dash **5** break, burst, crush, smash **6** shiver **8** demolish, fragment, splinter **9** pulverize **10** annihilate **11** fragmentize **12** disintegrate

shatterable 7 brittle, fragile **9** breakable, frangible

shave 3 cut **4** clip, crop, pare, peel, skim, trim **5** lower, plane, prune, shear, skive **6** barber, cut off, deduct, reduce, scrape, sliver **7** cut back, whittle **8** mark down

shaver 3 boy, kid, lad, tad **4** tike, tyke **5** child, razor **6** barber, laddie, squirt **9** stripling, youngster

shawl 4 wrap **5** fichu, manta **6** afghan, chador, serape **7** tallith **8** mantilla

shawm's descendant 4 oboe

Shawnee chief 8 Tecumseh, Tecumtha **9** Cornstalk

Shaw play 6 Geneva **7** Candida **9** Pygmalion, Saint Joan **11** Misalliance **12** Major Barbara **13** Arms and the Man

shay 6 chaise **8** carriage

shear 3 cut, mow **4** clip, crop, pare, snip, trim **5** prune, shave, skive **6** barber

shears 8 scissors

shearwater 4 bird **6** petrel **7** skimmer

sheath 4 case, skin **5** cover **7** holster **8** scabbard

sheathe 4 case, clad, face, side, skin, wrap **5** cover, panel **6** encase, jacket

Sheba *father:* 6 Bichri *queen:* **6** Balkis

shebang 4 mess **6** affair **7** schmear **8** business, caboodle **9** ball of wax, enchilada

shed 3 hut **4** cast, doff, drop, emit, molt **5** exude, hovel, hutch, scrap, shack, stall **6** divest, lean-to, reject, slough **7** cast off, diffuse, discard, radiate, take off **8** jettison, throw out **9** throw away

sheen 5 glaze, gleam, glint, gloss, shine **6** finish, luster, lustre, polish **7** burnish, glitter, shimmer **8** radiance **9** shininess **10** brightness

sheeny see **shiny**

sheep 5 ovine *breed:* **5** Tunis **6** Dorper, Dorset, Exmoor, Merino, Navajo, No-Tail, Oxford, Panama, Romney **7** Cheviot, Colbred,

Karakul, Lincoln, Ryeland, Suffolk **8** Columbia, Cotswold, Polwarth **9** Hampshire, Leicester, Montadale, Southdown **10** Corriedale, Debouillet **11** Rambouillet *coat:* **4** wool **6** fleece *disease:* **3** gid, orf *female:* **3** ewe *genus:* **4** Ovis *male:* **3** ram **6** wether *meat:* **6** mutton *relating to:* **5** ovine *Scottish:* **9** blackface *sound:* **5** bleat *tender:* **8** shepherd *wild:* **3** sha **5** urial **6** aoudad, argali, bharal **7** bighorn, mouflon *young:* **4** lamb

sheepish 4 meek **5** timid **7** abashed, ashamed, bashful **8** timorous **9** diffident **10** shamefaced **11** embarrassed

sheepskin 4 roan **6** mouton **7** diploma **9** parchment *prepare:* **3** taw

sheer 4 pure, skew, thin, turn, veer **5** filmy, gauzy, steep, utter **6** abrupt, arrant, flimsy, simple, swerve **7** chiffon, deflect, deviate, perfect, unmixed **8** absolute, complete, gossamer, outright **9** out-and-out, unalloyed, undiluted **10** diaphanous, see-through **11** precipitate, precipitous, transparent, unmitigated

sheet 3 ply **4** film, leaf, page, sail, slab **5** cover, linen, paper **6** lamina, veneer **8** membrane **9** newspaper

sheet _____ **3** ice **4** film **5** glass, metal, music **6** anchor

shelf 3 hob **4** bank, edge, reef, sill **5** ledge, shoal **6** mantel **7** counter **8** sandbank

shell 3 pod **4** boat, bomb, case, hull, husk, rake, skin **5** blitz, conch, shuck **6** pepper **7** bombard, capsule, grenade, mollusc, mollusk **8** carapace **9** cannonade, cartridge *defective:* **3** dud *explosive:* **4** bomb *layer:* **5** nacre *ornamental:* **6** cowrie *study:* **10** conchology

shellac 4 beat, drub, flay, lick, rout, trim, whap, whip, whop, whup **5** resin, smear, whomp **6** defeat, thrash **7** clobber, smother, trounce **8** lambaste, vanquish

Shelley, Percy Bysshe *friend:* **5** Byron (Lord), Keats (John) *poem:* **5** Cloud (The) **7** Adonais, Alastor **8** Queen Mab **10** Ozymandias, To a Skylark **16** Ode to the West Wind *wife:* **4** Mary

shellfish 4 clam, crab **5** conch, cowry, prawn, snail, whelk **6** cockle, limpet, mussel, oyster, quahog, triton **7** abalone, crawdad, geoduck, lobster, mollusc, mollusk, scallop **8** barnacle, crayfish, escargot **10** crustacean, periwinkle

shell out 3 pay **4** give **5** spend **8** fork over, hand over

shell-shaped 6 spiral **9** cochleate

shelter 3 den, hut, lee **4** cote, fold, hide, port, roof, shed, tent **5** bower, cloak, cover, haven, house, shack **6** asylum, burrow, covert, defend, harbor, refuge, shield **7** defense, foxhole, hideout, hospice, housing, lodging, pillbox, protect, retreat **8** hideaway, hidy-hole, security **9** dwellings, hermitage, hidey-hole, sanctuary *for aircraft:* **6** hangar *for cows:* **4** barn, byre *toward:* **4** alee

shelve 4 dish, drop, stay, tilt **5** defer, delay, slope, stock, waive **6** freeze, give up, hold up, put off **7** hold off, suspend **8** hold over, mothball, postpone, prorogue, set aside

Shem *brother:* **3** Ham **7** Japheth *father:* **4** Noah

Shema's father 4 Joel **6** Hebron

Shemida's father 6 Gilead

shenanigan 4 dido, lark **5** antic, caper, prank, stunt, trick **6** frolic **8** escapade, mischief **10** tomfoolery **11** monkeyshine

Sheol see **hades**

shepherd 4 lead, show, tend **5** guide, pilot, route, steer, watch **6** direct, escort, leader **7** conduct **8** guardian *dog:* **6** collie **12** border collie *stick:* **5** crook, staff

Sheridan, Richard Brinsley *character:* **8** Bob Acres, Malaprop (Mrs.) **10** Lady Teazle **13** Lady Sneerwell, Lydia Languish *play:* **6** Critic (The), Rivals (The) **7** Pizarro **16** School for Scandal (The)

sheriff 5 reeve **6** lawman **7** marshal, officer *aide:* **6** deputy

sherlock 4 dick, tail **5** snoop **6** shadow, shamus, sleuth **7** gumshoe **8** hawkshaw **9** detective **10** private eye **12** investigator

Sherlock Holmes *address:* **11** Baker Street *creator:* **5** Doyle (Arthur Conan) *sidekick:* **6** Watson (Dr.)

sherry 4 fino, wine **7** oloroso **10** manzanilla **11** amontillado

shibboleth 3 saw, tag **5** axiom, maxim **6** byword, cliché, phrase, saying, slogan, truism **7** bromide **8** banality, chestnut, password, prosaism **9** catchword, platitude, watchword **11** catchphrase, commonplace

shield 4 fend, roof, ward **5** aegis, armor, cover, guard, haven, house, pavis **6** buffer, defend, harbor, screen, secure **7** buckler, bulwark, defense, protect, shelter **8** defilade **9** safeguard **10** escutcheon *band:* **4** fess *bullfighter's:* **9** burladero *light:* **5** targe *part:* **4** boss, umbo **7** bordure *Roman:* **7** testudo

shield-like 7 peltate

shift 3 yaw **4** bend, bout, move, stir, tack, time, tour, turn, vary, veer **5** alter, budge, get by, spell, stint, trick **6** change, make do, manage, remove, resort, swerve **7** deviate, replace, shuffle, stopgap **8** get along, relocate, resource, transfer **9** deviation, expedient, fluctuate **10** alteration, changeover, conversion, transition **11** fluctuation

shiftless 4 idle, lazy **5** inept **8** feckless, indolent, slothful **11** inefficient

shifty 3 sly **4** foxy, wily **5** cagey, lying, shady, slick **6** crafty, sneaky, tricky **7** cunning, devious, elusive, evasive, furtive **8** guileful, slippery, sneaking **9** conniving, deceitful, deceptive, dishonest, insidious, underhand **10** inconstant, untruthful **11** duplicitous, underhanded **12** equivocating

shill 5 blind, decoy, pitch **6** capper **8** promoter **10** accomplice, sales pitch

shillelagh 3 bat **4** club, cosh, mace **5** baton, billy, stick **6** cudgel **8** bludgeon **9** bastinado, billy club, blackjack, truncheon **10** nightstick

shilling 3 bob

shilly-shally 5 fudge, hedge, stall, waver **6** dawdle, dither, waffle **7** whiffle **8** hesitate **9** temporize, vacillate **11** prevaricate **12** tergiversate

Shimea brother: **5** David **father:** **5** David, Jesse **son:** **7** Jonadab **8** Jonathan

shimmer 5 flash, gleam, glint, sheen **6** luster, lustre **7** glimmer, glisten, glitter, spangle, sparkle, twinkle **9** coruscate **11** coruscation, scintillate **13** scintillation

shimmy 5 dance, shake **6** quiver, shiver, tremor **7** chemise, shudder, tremble, vibrate **9** vibration

shin 3 run **4** dash **5** scoot, tibia **6** scurry, sprint **7** scamper

shindig 4 ball, bash, fête, gala **5** binge, dance, party, revel **6** affair, frolic **7** blowout **8** wingding

shine 3 ray, rub **4** beam, buff, burn, glow **5** blaze, flare, flash, glare, glaze, gleam, glint, gloss, sheen **6** luster, lustre, polish **7** burnish, glimmer, glisten, glitter, radiate, shimmer, sparkle, twinkle **9** luminesce **10** incandesce

shiner 4 fish **8** black eye, cyprinid

shingle 5 beach, coast, shore **7** haircut, overlap, overlay **8** detritus **9** signboard

shiny 6 agleam, bright, glossy **7** fulgent, radiant **8** dazzling, gleaming, lustrous, polished **9** burnished, effulgent **10** glistening

ship 4 boat, send **5** remit, route **6** export **7** consign, forward, freight **8** dispatch, transfer, transmit **ancient:** **6** bireme, galley **7** galleon, trireme **attendant:** **7** steward **beam:** **7** keelson **berth:** **4** dock, slip **boat:** **6** dinghy **7** lighter **body:** **4** hull **cabin:** **9** stateroom **commercial:** **5** liner, oiler **6** argosy, tanker, trader **9** freighter **crew member:** **4** hand,

mate **6** sailor **deck:** **4** boat, main, poop **5** orlop **6** bridge **10** forecastle **fishing:** **6** lugger **7** trawler **fleet:** **6** armada **floor:** **4** deck **front:** **3** bow **4** prow, stem **8** cutwater **hoister:** **4** boom **5** davit **7** capstan **kitchen:** **6** galley **left side:** **4** port **8** larboard **military:** **6** cutter, PT boat **7** carrier, cruiser **9** destroyer, submarine **officer:** **4** mate **5** bosun **6** purser **7** captain, steward **9** boatswain **part:** **3** bow **4** beam, deck, helm, hold, hull, keel, mast, skeg, stem **5** bilge, hatch, stern **6** bridge, rudder **7** scupper **partition:** **7** bulwark **8** bulkhead **personnel:** **4** crew **platform:** **9** crow's nest, gangboard, gangplank **poetic:** **4** bark **post:** **4** bitt, mast **7** bollard **prison:** **4** brig **projection:** **7** sponson **rear:** **5** stern **record:** **3** log **right side:** **9** starboard **room:** **4** brig **5** cabin **6** galley **rope:** **4** line **5** sheet **7** halyard **sailing:** **3** hoy **4** brig, dhow, prau, proa, yawl **5** ketch, sloop, xebec, yacht **6** lugger **7** caravel, galleon **8** schooner **steerer:** **4** helm **6** tiller **storage area:** **4** hold **to the rear of:** **3** aft **5** abaft **6** astern **valve:** **7** seacock **window:** **4** port **8** porthole

shipment 5 cargo **6** lading **7** freight, payload **8** delivery **11** consignment

Ship of Fools author 6 Porter (Katherine Anne)

Shipping News author 6 Proulx (Annie)

ships, group of 4 navy **5** fleet, flota **6** armada **8** flotilla

shipshape 4 neat, snug, tidy, trig, trim **7** orderly **11** spic-and-span, uncluttered **12** spick-and-span

shipworm 6 teredo

shire 5 horse **6** county **8** district **10** draft horse

shirk 4 duck, lurk, shun **5** avoid, creep, dodge, elude, evade, skulk, slink, sneak, steal **8** sidestep

shirker see **slacker**

shirt 3 tee **4** polo, sark **5** dress, kurta, sport **6** blouse, jersey **9** guayabera

shirty 3 mad **5** angry, cross, irate **6** heated, ireful **7** annoyed **8** choleric, incensed, offended **9** indignant, irritated

shiv 5 blade, knife, shank **6** dagger **8** stiletto

Shiva consort: **3** Uma **4** Devi, Kali **5** Durga, Gauri **6** Ambika, Chandi **7** Parvati **9** Haimavati **son:** **6** Ganesa, Ganesh, Skanda **7** Ganesha **10** Karttikeya

shiver 5 burst, quake, shake, smash **6** quaver, quiver, tremor **7** shatter, shudder, tremble, twitter **8** fragment, splinter, splitter

shlep see **schlep**

shoal 3 bar **4** bank, hook, reef, spit **6** school

7 barrier, sandbar, shallow, tombolo **8** sandbank, sand reef

shoat 3 hog, pig **4** gilt **5** swine **6** piglet, porker

Shobab father: 5 Caleb, David **mother: 6** Azubah **9** Bathsheba

shock 3 jar **4** blow, bump, daze, jolt, pile, rick, stun **5** amaze, clash, crash, mound, quake, shake, sheaf **6** appall, dismay, impact, insult, offend, trauma, tremor **7** astound, disgust, horrify, outrage, stagger, startle, stupefy, temblor **8** astonish, surprise **9** collision, electrify **10** concussion, earthquake, percussion, scandalize, traumatize **11** flabbergast **12** stupefaction

shock absorber 6 spring **7** dashpot, snubber

shocker 4 blow **7** stunner **8** surprise, thriller **9** bombshell, eye-opener, sensation **11** showstopper

shocking 5 awful, lurid **6** horrid **7** glaring, heinous **8** dreadful, horrible, horrific, shameful, terrible **9** appalling, atrocious, frightful, monstrous, revolting, traumatic **10** outrageous, scandalous **11** disgraceful, distressing, unspeakable

shoddy 4 base, mean, poor **5** cheap, dingy, gaudy, junky, seedy, tacky, tatty **6** cheesy, common, flimsy, paltry, shabby, sleazy, tawdry, trashy **7** run-down, scruffy **8** inferior, rubbishy, shameful **9** makeshift **10** broken-down, down-at-heel, jerry-built, jury-rigged **11** dilapidated, disgraceful, ignominious, pretentious **12** dishonorable, disreputable **13** discreditable

shoe 3 pac **4** boot, clog, geta, mule, pump **5** sabot, wedge **6** brogan, brogue, buskin, gaiter, galosh, gillie, loafer, oxford, patten, sandal, slip-on **7** chopine, ghillie, slipper, sneaker **8** balmoral, moccasin, platform, plimsoll **10** clodhopper, espadrille **armored: 8** solleret **athlete's: 7** sneaker **form: 4** last, tree **kind: 8** elevator, open-toed **10** high-heeled **part: 3** tip, toe **4** arch, heel, lace, lift, sole, vamp **5** cleat, shank, upper **6** box toe, collar, foxing, insole, lining, throat, tongue **7** counter, outsole **8** backstay **protective: 6** galosh, rubber **shiner: 6** polish **9** bootblack **wooden: 5** sabot **7** chopine

shoelace tip 5 aglet

shoeless 6 unshod **8** barefoot **9** discalced

shoemaker 7 cobbler **patron saint: 7** Crispin **Scottish: 6** souter

Shogun author 7 Clavell (James)

Sholem Aleichem character 5 Golde, Tevye, Yente

shoo 4 scat **5** drive, leave, scare, scram, split **6** beat it, begone, bug off, skidoo **7** buzz

off, get lost, skiddoo, vamoose **8** clear out **9** skedaddle, take a hike **10** hit the road

shoo-in 6 winner **7** sure bet **8** slam dunk **9** sure thing

shoot 3 bud, fly, gun, ray **4** beam, bolt, dart, dash, fire, lash, race, rush, sail, scud, skim, spew, tear **5** blast, chase, fling, photo, plink, shaft, skirr, snipe, spurt **6** branch **7** project **9** discharge **10** photograph

shoot down 3 pan, rap **4** bash, kill, slam **5** blast, decry, knock, scorn, trash **6** assail, deride, dump on, reject, squash **7** deflate, squelch, torpedo **8** bad-mouth, belittle, derogate, discount, disprove, puncture, ridicule **9** discredit

shooting 4 keen **5** acute, sharp **7** gunplay **8** piercing, stabbing

shooting star 6 meteor **8** fireball

shoot up 4 soar **6** inject, rocket **7** burgeon **8** mushroom **9** skyrocket

shop 4 hunt **5** store **6** browse, market, outlet, search **8** boutique, emporium, showroom

shoplift 3 bag, cop **4** lift, palm **5** boost, filch, pinch, steal, swipe **6** pilfer, rip off, snitch

shop owner 8 merchant, retailer **9** tradesman **10** proprietor

shopworn 5 banal, faded, stale, tired, trite **6** cliché, soiled **7** clichéd **8** overused **9** hackneyed **10** threadbare

shore 4 bank, prop, stay **5** beach, brace, brink, coast **6** bear up, strand, uphold **7** bolster, shingle, support, sustain **8** buttress, littoral, seacoast **9** coastland, coastline, riverbank, riverside, waterside **10** embankment, waterfront

shorebird see at **bird**

short 3 shy **4** curt **5** blunt, brief, crisp, scant, skimp, spare, squat, stint, terse **6** abrupt, meager, meagre, scanty, scarce, skimpy, stubby **7** brusque, compact, concise, lacking, laconic, stunted, wanting **8** abridged, succinct **9** deficient **10** inadequate **11** abbreviated **12** insufficient

shortage 4 lack **5** pinch **6** dearth, ullage **7** deficit, paucity **8** scarcity **10** deficiency, inadequacy, scantiness

shortcoming 3 bug, sin **4** flaw, lack **5** fault, lapse **6** defect **7** demerit, failing **8** weakness **9** weak point **10** deficiency **12** imperfection

shortcut 5 macro **6** bypass, cutoff

shorten 3 bob, cut **4** clip, dock **5** elide, slash **6** lessen, reduce, shrink **7** abridge, curtail, cut back, cut down, excerpt **8** boil down, compress, condense, contract, decrease, diminish, minimize, truncate **10** abbreviate

shorthand 11 stenography **method: 5** Gregg **6** Pitman

shorthanded 7 wanting **11** undermanned **12** understaffed

short-lived 5 brief **7** passing **8** fleeting **9** ephemeral, fugacious, momentary, temporary **10** evanescent, transitory

shortly 4 anon, soon **6** pronto **7** briefly, by and by, in brief, quickly, tersely **8** directly **9** concisely, presently **10** succinctly **11** laconically

shortness 7 brevity **9** concision

shortsighted 6 myopic **8** heedless, reckless **10** astigmatic

short-spoken 4 curt **5** bluff, blunt, brief, gruff, terse **6** abrupt, crusty, snippy **7** brusque **8** snippety

short-tempered 5 testy **6** touchy **7** prickly **8** snappish **9** irascible, irritable

Shoshone chief 8 Washakie **9** Pocatello

shot 3 nip, pop, try **4** dose, dram, drop, jolt, stab **5** blast, break, carom, crack, fling, guess, ounce, photo, range, reach, snort, swipe, whack, whirl **6** chance, effort, stroke **7** attempt, snifter **8** marksman, occasion **9** discharge **11** opportunity

shoulder 4 bear, edge, push, side **5** elbow, press, shove **6** assume, hustle, jostle, take on **8** bulldoze *bone:* **7** scapula **8** clavicle *covering:* **6** tippet **8** scapular *muscle:* **7** deltoid *relating to:* **7** humeral **8** scapular

shoulder blade 7 scapula

shout 3 cry **4** bark, bawl, bray, call, roar, yell **5** blare, whoop **6** bellow, clamor, holler, scream **7** exclaim **10** vociferate

shove 3 dig, jab, jam **4** cram, prod, push **5** crowd, drive, elbow, press **6** jostle, propel, thrust **8** bulldoze, shoulder

shovel 3 dig **4** grub **5** delve, scoop, spade **6** dig out, dredge, trowel **8** excavate

shoveler 4 duck **9** broadbill

shove off 2 go **3** git **4** blow, exit **5** leave, scoot, scram, split **6** beat it, cut out, decamp, depart, move on **7** move out, pull out, vamoose **8** clear out, run along

show 4 fair, film, lead, pomp, sham **5** array, flick, front, guide, mount, movie, offer, prove, revue, sport, stage **6** appear, arrive, direct, effect, evince, expose, flaunt, lay out, parade, reveal, set out, submit, unveil **7** conduct, display, divulge, exhibit, explain, fanfare, panoply, picture, present, produce, project, trot out **8** brandish, disclose, evidence, illusion, indicate, instruct, manifest, proclaim **9** determine, establish, pageantry, represent, semblance, spectacle **10** appearance, exhibition, exposition, illustrate, production **11** demonstrate, materialize,

performance **13** demonstration, manifestation

Show Boat *author:* **6** Ferber (Edna) *composer:* **4** Kern (Jerome) *lyricist:* **11** Hammerstein (Oscar)

showcase 6 flaunt, parade **7** cabinet, exhibit, feature, vitrine

shower 4 hail, rain, wash **5** bathe, burst, party, salvo, spray, storm **6** deluge, lavish, volley **7** barrage, cascade, shatter, spatter **8** cataract, downpour, fountain, rainfall **9** broadside, cannonade, fusillade **10** cloudburst **11** bombardment

showman 8 producer, promoter **10** impresario *famous:* **4** Cody (William F.) **6** Barnum (Phineas T.)

Show Me State 8 Missouri

show off 4 brag **5** boast, flash, model, strut, vaunt **6** expose, flaunt, hotdog, parade **7** display, exhibit, swagger, trot out **8** brandish **10** grandstand

show-off 3 ham **6** hotdog **7** boaster, hotshot, peacock **8** blowhard, braggart **9** swaggerer **13** exhibitionist

showpiece 3 gem **5** jewel, prize **10** magnum opus, masterwork **11** chef d'oeuvre, masterpiece

show up 4 come **6** appear, arrive, debunk, expose, reveal, unmask **8** discover **9** discredit, embarrass **10** invalidate **11** materialize

showy 4 loud **5** gaudy, jazzy **6** flashy, garish, ornate, sporty, tawdry **7** opulent, splashy **8** gorgeous, overdone, striking **9** luxurious, sumptuous **10** flamboyant **11** overwrought, pretentious, resplendent, sensational **12** meretricious, orchidaceous, ostentatious

shred 3 bit, dag, jot, rag **4** chip, iota, whit **5** crumb, grain, grate, ounce, scrap, shave, speck, trace **6** sliver, tatter **7** modicum, smidgen, snippet **8** demolish, fragment, particle **9** scintilla

shrew 3 erd, nag **4** mole **5** harpy, scold, vixen, witch **6** dragon, gorgon, ogress, rodent, virago **7** hellcat **8** battle-ax, fishwife, harridan, she-devil, spitfire, Xantippe **9** battle-axe, termagant, Xanthippe

shrewd 3 sly **4** cagy, foxy, keen, wily, wise **5** acute, cagey, canny, savvy, sharp, slick, smart **6** artful, astute, clever, crafty, smooth **7** knowing, prudent **8** sensible **9** ingenious, judicious, sagacious **10** discerning **11** intelligent, penetrating, quick-witted **13** perspicacious

shrewish 5 cross, testy **6** cranky, snappy **7** nagging, peevish, peppery **8** choleric, petulant **9** crotchety, fractious, irascible, splenetic **10** ill-natured **11** contentious,

intractable, quarrelsome 12 disputatious 13 quick-tempered, short-tempered
shriek 3 cry 4 yell 6 screak, scream, shrill, squawk, squeal 7 screech
shrill 4 keen 5 acute, sharp 6 piping 8 piercing, strident 9 deafening 12 earsplitting
shrimp 4 runt 5 prawn 6 peanut, peewee, scampi, shorty 9 pipsqueak 10 crustacean
shrine 5 altar 6 temple 7 sanctum 9 reliquary, sacrarium, sanctuary *Buddhist:* 4 tope 5 stupa 7 chorten
shrink 3 shy 4 wane 5 cower, quail, slink, start, wince 6 blench, boggle, cringe, flinch, huddle, recede, recoil, wither 7 analyst, dwindle, refrain 8 compress, condense, contract, draw back, withdraw 9 constrict, shrivel up, therapist, waste away 12 psychiatrist, psychologist
shrinking 3 shy 5 mousy, timid 7 bashful 8 retiring, skittish 9 withdrawn
shrive 5 purge 6 pardon, purify 7 absolve, confess, expiate 8 lustrate
shrivel 4 wilt 5 dry up, parch, wizen 6 shrink, wither 7 dwindle, wrinkle 9 dehydrate, desiccate
Shropshire Lad author 7 Housman (A. E.)
shroud 4 hide, rope, veil, wrap 5 cloak, cover, shade 6 enfold, enwrap, screen 7 conceal, enclose, envelop, obscure 8 cerement, obstruct 9 cerecloth 12 winding-sheet
shrouded 5 privy 6 covert, hidden, secret 7 obscure 10 mysterious
shrub 4 bush 5 elder, erica, hazel 6 muskit, privet 7 arboret, dyeweed, guayule 8 barberry, bluewood, boxthorn, inkberry, ironweed, rosebush 9 bearberry 10 bladdernut *Asian:* 4 bago 6 kerria 8 caragana, japonica *desert:* 4 jhow 7 ephedra 8 tamarisk *dwarf:* 6 bonsai *East Indian:* 3 aal 4 sunn *European:* 4 cade 8 woodbine *evergreen:* 3 box, kat, yew 4 ilex, khat, titi 5 furze, heath, holly, pyxie, savin, taxus 6 kalmia, laurel, myrtle, nandin, protea, sabine, savine 7 boxwood, heather, jasmine, juniper, rosebay 8 lambkill, oleander, rosemary, tamarisk *flowering:* 5 ribes, tiara, wahoo 6 daphne, laurel, myrtle, spirea 7 chamise, chamiso, mahonia, maybush, rhodora, spiraea, weigela 8 magnolia, mezereon, nineback, oleander, oleaster, snowball, snowbush, tornillo, viburnum, wisteria *genus:* 3 Iva 4 Ilex, Inga, Itea, Rhus, Rosa, Ulex 7 Solanum 8 Euonymus *hardwood:* 4 pelu 6 cornel, kowhai *Mexican:* 8 ocotillo *New Zealand:* 4 tutu *ornamental:* 6 privet 7 syringa 9 bluebeard *pasture:* 8 cowberry *prickly:* 4 Ulex 5 briar,

chico, furze, gorse 7 bramble 8 hawthorn, mesquite 9 buckthorn *thicket:* 6 maquis 7 macchia 9 chaparral *tropical:* 4 kava, Sida 5 henna 7 lantana 8 buddleia 10 frangipani *West Indian:* 4 anil 7 acerola
shrug off 8 belittle, downplay, minimize
shtick 3 act, bag, bit 5 spiel 6 number 7 routine 9 specialty 11 performance
Shuah *father:* 7 Abraham *mother:* 7 Keturah
shuck 3 pod 4 case, cast, hull, husk, junk, peel, shed, skin 5 ditch, scrap, shell, strip 6 reject, remove, slough 7 discard, peel off, take off 8 jettison 11 decorticate
shudder 5 quake, shake 6 quaver, quiver, shimmy, shiver, tremor 7 frisson, tremble, twitter, vibrate
shuffle 3 mix 4 hash 5 dodge, evade, hedge, scuff, shift 6 jumble, mess up, muddle, weasel 7 clutter, reorder, rummage, shamble 8 disarray, disorder, intermix, mishmash 9 rearrange 10 disarrange, equivocate 11 disorganize
shun 3 cut 4 duck, snub 5 avoid, dodge, elude, evade, scorn 6 escape, eschew, refuse, reject 7 decline, disdain
shunt 4 turn 5 avert, shift 6 change, divert, switch 7 deflect, shuttle 8 transfer 9 sidetrack
shush 4 hush 5 quiet, still 6 muffle, muzzle, shut up, stifle 7 repress, silence, squelch 8 suppress
shut 3 bar 4 lock, seal, slam 5 close 6 fasten 9 close down 10 batten down
Shute novel 10 On the Beach
shut in 3 hem, mew, pen 4 cage, coop, wall 5 fence 6 coop up, immure 7 confine, enclose 8 imprison
shut-in 7 invalid 8 confined 9 withdrawn 12 convalescent
shut out 3 bar 6 screen 7 exclude 9 ostracize
shutter 5 blind 6 screen
shuttle 5 ferry, shunt 6 bobbin 7 commute, spindle 9 alternate
shuttlecock 4 bird 5 bandy
shut up 3 gag, mew, pen 4 cage, hush, jail, mute 5 burke, choke, quiet, shush, still 6 muzzle, stifle 7 confine, enclose, impound, silence, squelch 8 choke off, imprison, pipe down, suppress 9 quiet down 11 incarcerate
shy 3 coy 4 balk, duck, meek, shun, wary 5 avoid, chary, elude, evade, mousy, quail, scant, short, timid 6 averse, blench, demure, modest, recoil, scanty, scarce, shrink 7 bashful, fearful, lacking, wanting 8 hesitant, reserved, reticent, retiring, sheepish, timorous 9 diffident, withdrawn 11 intro-

verted, unassertive **12** apprehensive, insufficient, self-effacing **13** self-conscious

Shylock 6 usurer **9** loan shark *daughter:* **7** Jessica

shyster 11 pettifogger

Siam see **Thailand**

sib 3 bro, kin, sis **4** akin **6** sister **7** brother, kindred, kinsman, related **8** relation, relative **9** relatives

Sibelius composition 9 Finlandia **11** Valse Triste

Siberian *dog:* 5 husky **7** Samoyed *native:* **5** Tatar, Yakut **6** Tartar, Tungus **7** Chukchi **9** Mongolian *plain:* **6** steppe *tent:* **4** yurt

sibilate 4 buzz, fizz, hiss, whiz **6** fizzle, sizzle **7** whisper

sibling 3 bro, sis **6** sister **7** brother

sibyl 4 seer **6** oracle **7** prophet **10** prophetess, soothsayer **13** fortune-teller

sic 3 set **4** thus **5** chase **6** attack

Sicilian secret organization 5 Mafia **10** Cosa Nostra

Sicily *capital:* 7 Palermo *city:* **4** Enna **7** Catania, Messina **8** Siracusa, Syracuse, Taormina *volcano:* **4** Etna

sick 3 ill **5** fed up, tired, weary **6** ailing, laid up, morbid, peaked, rotten, unwell, wobbly **7** fevered, invalid **8** confined, diseased **9** bedridden, defective, disgusted, unhealthy **10** indisposed **11** debilitated

sicken 5 upset **7** afflict, disgust, fall ill **8** nauseate

sickle 5 blade, mower **6** scythe **8** crescent

sickle-shaped 7 falcate

sickly 3 ill, low, wan **4** puny, weak **5** frail **6** ailing, anemic, feeble, infirm, morbid, peaked, poorly, unwell **8** delicate, diseased **9** unhealthy **10** indisposed **11** unhealthful, unwholesome **12** insalubrious

sickness 3 bug **6** malady **7** ailment, disease, illness **8** disorder, syndrome **9** complaint, condition, infirmity **10** affliction **13** indisposition

sick-out 7 blue flu

sic transit gloria ____ 5 mundi

side 4 clad, team **5** angle, facet, flank **6** aspect **9** direction **10** standpoint *combining form:* **5** later **6** lateri, latero *exposed:* **8** windward *of a coin:* **7** obverse, reverse *sheltered:* **3** lee

sideboard 5 table **6** buffet **8** credence, credenza *for wine:* **8** cellaret **10** cellarette

sideburns 9 burnsides **10** sideboards **11** dundrearies, muttonchops

sidekick 3 pal **4** chum **5** buddy, crony **7** partner **9** assistant, companion **10** accomplice

sideline 5 eject, hobby **6** injure **7** disable,

pastime, take out **9** avocation, diversion **10** recreation **11** distraction **12** incapacitate

sidereal 6 astral, starry **7** stellar

side road 5 byway **8** bystreet, shunpike

sideshow 9 diversion **11** distraction

sidestep 4 duck **5** avoid, burke, dodge, evade, hedge, skirt **6** bypass, swerve, weasel **10** circumvent, equivocate **12** tergiversate

sideswipe 5 brush, carom, graze, shave **6** glance, scrape

sidetrack 5 shunt **6** divert, switch **7** deflect

sidewhiskers see **sideburns**

side with 4 back **5** favor **6** second, uphold **7** endorse, support **8** backstop, champion

sidle 4 edge, inch, slip

siege 4 bout **5** spell **6** attack **7** assault, seizure **8** blockade **9** onslaught

Siegfried *composer:* 6 Wagner (Richard) *lover:* **8** Brunhild *mother:* **9** Sieglinde *slayer:* **5** Hagen *sword:* **7** Balmung *vulnerable spot:* **4** back **8** shoulder *wife:* **9** Kriemhild

Sienkiewicz novel 8 Quo Vadis

sierra 3 saw **4** fish **5** range **8** mackerel **13** mountain range

Sierra ____ 4 Club **5** Ancha, Leone, Madre **6** Blanca, Nevada

Sierra Leone *capital:* 8 Freetown *ethnic group:* **5** Mende, Temne *language:* **4** Krio **7** English *monetary unit:* **5** leone *neighbor:* **6** Guinea **7** Liberia

Sierra Nevada lake 5 Tahoe

siesta 3 nap **4** doze **5** sleep **6** catnap, snooze **10** forty winks

sieve 4 sift **6** filter, screen, winnow **8** colander, filtrate, strainer

Sif's husband 4 Thor

sift 3 pan **4** comb, cull, sort **5** glean, sieve **6** filter, screen, strain, winnow **8** filtrate, separate

sigh 3 sob **4** gasp, long, moan, pine **5** groan, sough, whine, yearn **6** exhale, grieve, hanker, murmur **7** breathe, respire, suspire

sight 3 aim, eye, spy **4** espy, view **5** scene, vista **6** notice, vision **7** make out, outlook *relating to:* **5** optic **6** ocular, visual **7** optical

sightseer 7 tourist **10** rubberneck **12** rubbernecker

sign 3 cue, ink **4** flag, hint, mark, omen **5** index, proof, token, trace **6** motion, signal, symbol **7** endorse, gesture, indicia, initial, symptom, vestige, warning **8** evidence, exponent, reminder **9** autograph, indicator **10** expression, indication, suggestion *box office:* **3** SRO *magic:* **4** rune *directional:* **5** arrow *of the zodiac:* (see zodiac sign)

signal 3 cue, nod **4** flag **5** alarm, alert **6** beckon, wigwag **7** gesture **8** high sign **9** indicator, semaphore *distress:* **3** SOS **6** Mayday

signature 4 name **9** autograph **11** John Hancock *flourish:* **6** paraph

signet 4 ring, seal **5** stamp **6** device **8** hallmark, intaglio

significance 4 pith **5** merit, point, sense **6** credit, import, moment, weight **7** gravity, meaning **9** authority, magnitude **10** importance **11** consequence, weightiness

significant 5 major, sound, valid **7** notable, telling, weighty **8** material, powerful **9** important, momentous **10** compelling, convincing, meaningful, noteworthy **11** substantial **12** considerable **13** consequential

signification 4 gist **5** point, sense **6** import **7** essence, meaning, message, purport **9** substance **10** intendment **11** implication **12** notification **13** understanding

signify 4 mean, show **5** count, imply, spell, weigh **6** convey, denote, intend, matter **7** add up to, bespeak, connote, express, purport, suggest **8** indicate

sign on 4 book, hire, join **5** draft **6** engage, enlist, enroll, induct, join up, retain, secure **7** recruit **9** conscript

sign over 4 cede, deed **5** alien, grant **6** assign, convey, remise **7** consign **8** alienate, transfer

sign up 4 join **5** enrol, enter **6** enlist, enroll, muster

Sigurd *horse:* **5** Grani *slayer:* **5** Hogni *victim:* **6** Fafner, Fafnir *wife:* **6** Gudrun

Sigyn's husband 4 Loki

Sikhism *deity:* **4** Akal *founder:* **5** Nanak **9** Guru Nanak *leader:* **5** Arjan **9** Guru Arjan **11** Gobind Singh *scripture:* **9** Adi Granth *shrine:* **12** Golden Temple

silage 6 fodder

silence 3 gag **4** calm, hush, lull, mute **5** quash, quell, quiet, shush, still **6** dampen, deaden, muffle, muzzle, shut up, squash, stifle **7** secrecy, squelch **8** choke off, muteness, quietude, suppress **9** quietness, reticence, stillness

silent 3 mum **4** dumb, mute **5** muted, quiet, still, tacit, whist **6** hushed, stilly **8** reticent, taciturn, unspoken, wordless **9** noiseless, soundless, voiceless **10** speechless **11** close-lipped, tight-lipped **12** closemouthed, tight-mouthed

Silent Night writer 4 Mohr (Joseph) **6** Gruber (Franz)

silhouette 6 shadow **7** contour, outline, pro-file **9** lineament, lineation **10** figuration **11** delineation

silicon symbol 2 Si

Silicon Valley city 7 San Jose **8** Palo Alto

silk 5 fiber **7** foulard **8** sarcenet, sarsenet *fabric:* **4** gros **5** caffa, ninon, Pekin, satin, surah, tulle **6** mantua, pongee, samite, sendal, tussah **7** taffeta *factory:* **8** filature *hat:* **6** topper *maker:* **4** worm *raw:* **6** greige *source:* **6** cocoon *waste:* **4** noil **5** floss *wild:* **6** tussah

sill 5 bench, ledge, shelf **9** threshold

silliness 5 folly **6** idiocy **7** inanity **9** absurdity, stupidity

silly 4 daft **5** balmy, crazy, daffy, dippy, dizzy, funny, giddy, inane, loony, sappy, wacky **6** absurd, simple **7** asinine, fatuous, flighty, foolish, idiotic, vacuous, witless **9** brainless, frivolous, ludicrous, nitwitted, senseless **10** irrational, ridiculous, weakminded **11** empty-headed, harebrained, light-headed **12** preposterous, simple-minded **13** rattlebrained

silt 4 marl **5** dregs **7** deposit, residue **8** alluvium, sediment

silver 4 coin **5** money, shiny **6** argent, dulcet **7** bullion, element **8** flatware, lustrous, sterling **9** argentine, tableware *relating to:* **9** argentine *symbol:* **2** Ag

silverfish 6 insect, tarpon

silversmith 6 Revere (Paul) **11** metalworker

silver-tongued 4 glib **6** fluent **7** voluble **8** eloquent

silvery 6 argent **7** shining **9** argentine, brilliant **10** glittering, shimmering

Silvia's beloved 9 Valentine

____. Simbel 3 Abu

Simenon character 7 Maigret (Inspector)

Simeon *father:* **5** Jacob *mother:* **4** Leah *son:* **4** Ohad **6** Nemuel

simian 3 ape **5** chimp, lemur, loris **6** baboon, bonobo, galago, monkey **7** apelike, gorilla, primate, tarsier **9** orangutan **10** anthropoid, chimpanzee, monkeylike

similar 4 akin, like **5** alike **6** agnate **7** uniform **8** parallel, suchlike **9** analogous, consonant **10** comparable, reciprocal **11** correlative **13** complementary, corresponding

similarity 6 parity **7** analogy, harmony, kinship **8** affinity, likeness, parallel, sameness **9** alikeness, closeness, congruity, semblance **10** conformity, congruence **11** coincidence, correlation, homogeneity, parallelism, resemblance

similarly 8 likewise

simile 7 analogy **8** affinity, likeness, metaphor **9** alikeness, semblance **10** comparison

11 correlation, resemblance *word:* **2** as **4** like

similitude 4 copy **5** image **6** double **7** analogy, kinship, replica **8** affinity, likeness, metaphor, relation, sameness **9** alikeness, congruity, semblance **10** comparison, similarity **11** correlation, counterpart, equivalence, resemblance

simmer 4 boil, fret, fume, stew, stir **5** churn **6** bubble, seethe **7** ferment, smolder

simmer down 5 relax

Simon *brother:* **5** Jesus **6** Andrew *father:* **5** Jonah *new name:* **5** Peter *son:* **5** Judas, Rufus **9** Alexander

Simon ___ **5** Magus **6** Legree **8** of Cyrene **9** the Zealot

Simon Maccabaeus *father:* **10** Mattathias *nickname:* **6** Thassi *slayer:* **7** Ptolemy

Simon *play* **9** Odd Couple (The) **10** Chapter Two, Plaza Suite **11** Biloxi Blues **12** Sunshine Boys (The) **13** Lost in Yonkers **16** Come Blow Your Horn **17** Barefoot in the Park **20** Brighton Beach Memoirs **21** Last of the Red Hot Lovers **22** Prisoner of Second Avenue (The)

simp 4 dope **5** dunce, idiot, moron **6** dimwit, nitwit **7** pinhead **8** bonehead, imbecile, lunkhead, numskull **9** blockhead, lamebrain, numbskull **10** nincompoop

simple 4 easy, mere, pure **5** basic, lucid, naive, plain, sheer **6** modest **7** artless, natural, unmixed **8** absolute, trusting **9** childlike, credulous, ingenuous, unadorned **10** effortless, elementary, unaffected **11** fundamental, undecorated, unelaborate **13** unpretentious *combining form:* **4** hapl **5** haplo

simpleminded 4 dull, slow **5** naive **6** stupid **7** foolish, idiotic, moronic **8** gullible, retarded **9** dim-witted, imbecilic **10** half-witted, slow-witted

simpleton 4 dolt, dope, fool **5** dummy, dunce, idiot, moron **6** cretin, dimwit, nitwit **7** dullard, half-wit, pinhead **8** bonehead, dumbbell, imbecile, lunkhead **9** blockhead, ignoramus, lamebrain **10** nincompoop

simplify 4 ease **7** clarify, clear up **8** boil down **10** facilitate, streamline, unscramble **11** disentangle **13** straighten out

simply 4 just, only **6** merely

Simpsons, The *catchphrase:* **3** d'oh **12** don't have a cow *character:* **3** Abe, Apu, Moe **4** Bart, Lisa **5** Homer, Marge, Patty, Selma, Snake **6** Barney, Krusty, Maggie, Martin, Willie **7** Bouvier, Mr. Burns, Skinner (Principal Seymour) **8** Chalmers (Supt.), Milhouse, Smithers **9** Dr. Hibbert, Joe Quimby (Mayor) **11** Chief Wiggum (Clancy), Ned Flanders, Nelson Muntz, Sideshow Bob, Sideshow Mel, Troy McClure **12** Kent Brockman, Mrs. Krabappel *creator:* **8** Groening (Matt) *Lisa's instrument:* **3** sax **9** saxophone *setting:* **11** Springfield *voice:* **5** Smith (Yeardley) **6** Azaria (Hank), Kavner (Julie) **10** Cartwright (Nancy) **12** Castellaneta (Dan)

simulacrum 4 copy **5** clone, ditto, guise, image, trace **6** double, ersatz, mirror, ringer **7** picture, replica **8** likeness, portrait **9** facsimile, imitation, semblance **10** appearance **12** reproduction **13** impersonation, spitting image

simulate 3 ape **4** fake, sham **5** feign, mimic **6** embody, mirror, parody, parrot **7** imitate **8** resemble **9** incarnate **11** counterfeit

simulated 4 fake, mock, sham **5** bogus, dummy, false, phony **6** ersatz **8** spurious **9** imitation, insincere, pretended **10** artificial, fictitious, substitute **11** counterfeit

simultaneous 6 coeval **10** coexistent, coexisting, coincident, coinciding, concurrent, synchronic **11** synchronous **12** contemporary

simultaneously 6 at once **7** jointly **8** together **9** meanwhile

sin 3 err **4** debt, evil, no-no, tort, vice **5** crime, fault, guilt, lapse, misdo, stray, wrong **6** offend **7** demerit, misdeed, offense **8** hamartia, iniquity, trespass **10** deficiency, peccadillo, transgress, wickedness, wrongdoing **11** shortcoming **12** imperfection *deadly:* **4** envy, lust **5** anger, greed, pride, sloth **8** gluttony **12** covetousness

Sin 7 moon-god *daughter:* **6** Ishtar *son:* **7** Shamash *wife:* **6** Ningal

since 3 ago **5** after **6** behind **7** because, whereas **8** as long as **9** following **10** inasmuch as **11** considering *Scottish:* **4** syne

sincere 4 real, true **5** frank, plain **6** actual, candid, devout, honest **7** artless, earnest, genuine, serious **8** bona fide, truthful **9** authentic, heartfelt, ingenuous, unfeigned **10** aboveboard, forthright **12** wholehearted **13** unpretentious

sincerity 6 candor **7** honesty **8** goodwill, openness **9** frankness, good faith **11** artlessness, earnestness

Sinclair *novel* **6** Jungle (The)

sine qua non 4 must **9** condition, essential, necessity, requisite **11** requirement **12** precondition, prerequisite

sinew 6 tendon

sinewy 4 ropy, wiry **5** tough **6** brawny **7** fibrous, stringy **8** muscular

sinful 3 bad **4** base, evil, vile **5** wrong **6** guilty, unholy, wicked **7** immoral, peccant, vicious **8** blamable, culpable, damnable, depraved, shameful **9** reprobate **10** iniquitous **11** blameworthy, disgraceful **13** reprehensible

sing 3 rat **4** fink, hymn **5** carol, chant, chirp, croon, troll, yodel **6** inform, intone, snitch, squeal, warble **7** confess, descant, lullaby **8** serenade, vocalize **10** cantillate

singe 4 burn, char, sear **6** scorch

singer 4 alto, bass **5** mezzo, tenor **6** canary **7** crooner, soloist, soprano **8** baritone, choirboy, songbird, songster, vocalist **9** balladeer, chorister, contralto **10** troubadour **12** mezzo-soprano *cabaret:* **11** chansonnier *female:* **9** chanteuse *opera:* **4** diva **10** cantatrice, prima donna *religious:* **6** cantor (see also **alto, baritone, bass, folksinger, mezzo-soprano, pop singer, rock star, soprano**)

singing *exercise:* **7** solfège *group:* **5** choir **6** chorus **7** chorale **8** glee club

single 3 hit, odd, one **4** free, lone, only, sole **5** unwed **6** maiden, unique **7** base hit, unitary **8** distinct, isolated, separate, solitary, specific **9** exclusive, unmarried **10** individual, particular, unattached *combining form:* **3** mon **4** hapl, mono **5** haplo *prefix:* **3** uni

single-minded 5 rigid **6** dogged, driven, intent **7** adamant, devoted, diehard **8** hellbent, obdurate, resolute, resolved, stubborn **9** dedicated, steadfast, unbending **10** brassbound, determined, inexorable, inflexible, purposeful, relentless, unyielding

single out 4 cull, mark, pick **5** elect, favor **6** choose, opt for, select **9** designate **11** distinguish

singsong 4 cant

singular 3 odd **4** lone, only, rare, sole, solo **5** weird **6** unique **7** bizarre, oddball, strange, unusual **8** peculiar, solitary, uncommon **9** exclusive **10** individual, outlandish, particular, unexampled **11** exceptional **13** extraordinary

singularity 5 quirk, unity **6** oddity **7** anomaly, oneness **8** identity **9** exception **11** peculiarity, personality **12** idiosyncrasy **13** individuality, particularity

singularize 4 mark **11** distinguish, individuate **12** characterize **13** differentiate, individualize

sinister 4 dark, dire, evil, left **6** creepy, malign **7** baleful, fateful, malefic, ominous **8** lowering, menacing **9** ill-omened, malicious **10** foreboding, maleficent, portentous **11** apocalyptic, threatening **12** inauspicious, unpropitious

sink 3 dip, pit, sag **4** bore, bury, dive, drop, fall, sump, wane **5** basin, drill, droop, lower, sewer, slope, slump, stoop, swamp **6** hollow, invest, plunge, settle, thrust, worsen **7** capsize, cesspit, decline, depress, descend, founder, go under, immerse, let down, scuttle, subside, torpedo **8** cesspool, hellhole, submerge, submerse **9** concavity, disappear **10** depression

sinker 3 bob **5** plumb **6** weight **8** doughnut, fastball, plumb bob

sinkhole 3 dip, sag **4** bowl **5** basin **6** hollow **8** cesspool **9** concavity **10** depression

sinless 4 pure **6** chaste **8** innocent **9** righteous **10** impeccable

sinner 5 rogue, scamp **6** bad egg, outlaw, rascal, wretch **7** lowlife, villain **8** criminal, evildoer, offender **9** libertine, miscreant, reprobate, scoundrel, wrongdoer **10** black sheep, delinquent, profligate, malefactor **11** rapscallion

Sinn ____ **4** Fein

sinuous 4 wavy **5** lithe, snaky **7** winding **8** flexuous, tortuous **10** convoluted, meandering, serpentine **11** anfractuous, snake-shaped

sinus 6 cavity, hollow, recess

Sioux 6 Dakota *chief:* **8** Red Cloud **10** Crazy Horse **11** Sitting Bull *language:* **6** Dakota, Lakota *people:* **3** Ofo **4** Crow **6** Biloxi, Tutelo **7** Catawba, Hidatsa **9** Winnebago

sip 5 drink, savor, taste **6** imbibe

siphon 3 tap **4** draw, pipe, pump **5** draft, drain **6** convoy, divert, funnel **7** channel, conduct, draw off **8** transmit

sir 4 lord **5** title **6** knight, mister **9** gentleman

sire 4 lord **5** beget, breed, hatch, spawn **6** father, parent **7** founder **8** engender **9** patriarch, procreate, propagate, reproduce **10** forefather

siren 4 vamp **5** alarm **7** Lorelei **9** temptress **10** seductress **11** femme fatale *film:* **4** Bara (Theda)

Siren 5 Ligea **8** Leucosia **10** Parthenope *German:* **7** Lorelei

sirenian 6 dugong, sea cow **7** manatee

siren song 4 lure **5** decoy, snare **6** come-on **10** allurement, enticement, temptation

Sirius 7 Dog Star

sister 3 nun **7** sibling *French:* **5** soeur *Latin:* **5** soror *Spanish:* **7** hermana

Sister Carrie *author* **7** Dreiser (Theodore)

sisterly 7 sororal

Sisyphus *brother:* **7** Athamas **9** Salmoneus *father:* **6** Aeolus *mother:* **7** Enarete *son:* **7** Glaucus

sit 4 pose **5** perch, roost

Sita *abductor:* 6 Ravana *husband, rescuer:* 4 Rama

sitarist 7 Shankar (Ravi)

sitcom 3 ALF 4 MASH, Mr. Ed, Soap 5 Ellen, Maude 6 Cheers 7 Frasier, Friends, Jetsons (The), Newhart 8 Get Smart, Love Boat (The), Mister Ed, Munsters (The), Roseanne, Seinfeld, Simpsons (The) 9 Bewitched, Cosby Show (The), Full House, Happy Days, I Love Lucy, Odd Couple (The) 10 Brady Bunch (The), Green Acres, Jeffersons (The), Night Court 11 Flintstones (The), Golden Girls (The), Murphy Brown, My Three Sons, Wonder Years (The) 12 Addams Family (The), Barney Miller, Fawlty Towers, Hogan's Heroes, Honeymooners (The), King of Queens (The), Mork and Mindy, Will and Grace 13 One Day at a Time, Our Miss Brooks, Sanford and Son, Three's Company 14 All in the Family 15 Diff'rent Strokes, Father Knows Best, Gilligan's Island, Home Improvement, I Dream of Jeannie, Leave It to Beaver, Ozzie and Harriet 17 Are You Being Served, Laverne and Shirley, My Favorite Martian, Petticoat Junction 18 Beverly Hillbillies (The) 19 Married with Children 20 Keeping Up Appearances 21 Everybody Loves Raymond

site 3 dig 4 home, spot 5 haunt, locus, place, point, scene, venue 6 locale 7 station 8 locality, location, position

sit-in 7 protest

sitting 6 séance 7 session *prolonged:* 8 sederunt

Sitting Bull's tribe 5 Sioux 6 Dakota

sitting duck 4 butt, mark 6 target

situate 3 put, set 5 place 6 locate 7 install 8 position

situation 3 job 4 post, rank 5 point, state 6 plight, status 7 footing, setting, station 8 location, position, standing 9 condition 13 circumstances

situs 5 place, venue 6 locale

Siva see **Shiva**

six *combining form:* 3 hex, sex 4 hexa, sexi 5 sexti *group of:* 6 sestet, sextet 9 sextuplet *relating to:* 6 senary

sixfold 8 sextuple

six-pack 3 abs

six-shooter 3 gun 6 pistol 8 revolver

sixth sense 3 ESP 5 hunch 7 insight 9 intuition, telepathy 12 clairvoyance

sizable 3 big 5 ample, hefty, large, major, roomy 8 spacious 9 capacious, extensive 10 commodious, large-scale 11 substantial 12 considerable

size 2 sm, xl 3 lge, med 4 area, bulk, mass 5 range, scope, width 6 extent, height, length, spread, volume 7 bigness, breadth, caliber, expanse, measure, stature 9 amplitude, dimension, extension, greatness, largeness, magnitude 10 dimensions, proportion 11 measurement, proportions

size up 3 peg 4 rate, read 5 assay, gauge, judge, value 6 assess, review, survey 7 adjudge, dope out 8 appraise, estimate, evaluate 9 figure out

sizzle 3 fry 4 buzz, fizz, hiss, whiz 5 grill 6 hoopla, seethe 7 pizzazz 8 sibilate 10 excitement

sizzling 3 hot 6 red-hot, torrid 7 burning 8 scalding, white-hot 9 scorching

skald 4 bard, poet

Skanda 6 war-god *brother:* 6 Ganesa, Ganesh 7 Ganesha *father:* 4 Siva 5 Shiva

skate 3 nag, ray 4 skid, skim 5 glide, skirr, slide 8 glissade *blade:* 6 runner *kind:* 6 figure, hockey, in-line 11 Rollerblade

skateboard maneuver 3 air 4 bail, hang 5 carve, grind, ollie, pivot 8 kickflip

skater see **ice skater**

skating *area:* 10 kiss and cry *game:* 8 ringette 9 broomball, ice hockey 12 in-line hockey, roller hockey *site:* 3 ice 4 rink *term:* 3 COP 4 axel, lobe, lutz, quad 5 T-stop 6 Mohawk, rocker, spiral 7 bracket, choctaw, gliding, salchow, sit spin, swizzle, toe loop, twizzle 8 heel stop, star lift, striding, stroking, toe picks 9 camel spin, crossover, free dance, free skate, waltz jump, Zayak Rule 11 death spiral, falling leaf, hydrant lift *type:* 3 ice 5 trail 6 in-line, roller

skedaddle 3 run 4 bolt, flee, skip 5 scoot, scram, split 6 beat it, begone, bug off, cut out, decamp, get out 7 make off, run away, scamper, skiddoo, take off, vamoose 8 clear out 10 make tracks

skein 4 coil, hank 5 flock, snarl, twist 6 tangle 12 entanglement

skeletal 4 bony 5 gaunt 6 wasted 7 angular, scraggy, starved 8 rawboned 9 emaciated 10 cadaverous

skeleton 5 bones, draft, frame 6 sketch 7 diagram, outline 9 bare bones, framework *marine:* 5 coral, shell

skeptic 5 cynic 7 doubter, scoffer 8 agnostic 10 Pyrrhonist, questioner, unbeliever 11 disbeliever

skeptical 4 wary 5 leery 6 show-me 7 cynical, dubious 8 doubtful, doubting 9 quizzical 10 dissenting, suspicious 11 mistrustful, questioning, unbelieving 12 disbelieving, freethinking

skepticism 5 doubt **7** dubiety **8** distrust, mistrust, wariness **9** dubiosity, misgiving, suspicion **11** incertitude, uncertainty

skerry 4 isle, reef **6** island

sketch 4 draw, plot **5** draft, rough, trace **6** depict, design, doodle, lay out, map out, précis **7** develop, diagram, outline, portray **8** block out, chalk out, rough out **9** blueprint, delineate **12** characterize

sketchy 4 iffy **5** crude, rough, vague **6** skimpy, slight **7** cursory, shallow **8** skeletal **10** incomplete **11** preliminary, superficial **12** questionable

skew 4 bias, veer **5** angle, fudge, slant, slide **6** swerve **7** distort

skewer 3 rod **4** spit **5** lance, spear, spike **6** impale, pierce **8** puncture, ridicule, transfix **9** brochette, criticize

ski 5 glide, slide *lift:* **4** J-bar, T-bar **5** chair **7** gondola

skid 5 glide, skate, slide **6** pallet, runner **7** spinout **8** sideslip

skiddoo 4 scat **5** leave, scram, split **6** beat it, begone, bug off, decamp, depart, vacate **7** buzz off, take off, vamoose **8** clear out, shove off **9** skedaddle, take a hike **10** hit the road, make tracks

skid row 6 bowery

skier *American:* **3** Moe (Tommy) **4** Kidd (Billy) **5** Mahre (Phil, Steve) **6** Miller (Bode) **7** Johnson (Bill) *Austrian:* **5** Maier (Hermann) **6** Proell (Annemarie), Sailer (Toni) **7** Klammer (Franz), Schranz (Karl) **10** Girardelli (Marc) **11** Moser-Proell (Annemarie) *French:* **5** Killy (Jean-Claude) *Italian:* **5** Tomba (Alberto) **6** Thoeni (Gustavo) *Luxembourg:* **10** Girardelli (Marc) *Swedish:* **8** Stenmark (Ingemar) *Swiss:* **10** Zurbriggen (Pirmin)

skiff 4 boat **7** rowboat

skiing *area:* **3** run **5** slope *cross-country:* **7** touring *event:* **6** schuss, slalom **8** downhill **11** giant slalom *horse-drawn:* **9** skijoring *kind:* **6** Alpine, Nordic *position:* **7** vorlage *technique:* **6** wedeln **8** snowplow, traverse *turn:* **7** christy **8** christie

skill 3 art **5** craft, knack **7** ability, address, command, cunning, finesse, know-how, mastery, prowess, sleight **8** deftness, facility **9** dexterity, expertise, ingenuity, readiness, technique **10** adroitness, competence **11** proficiency

skilled 3 apt **4** able **5** adept **6** expert **7** capable, trained **8** masterly, talented **9** competent, masterful, practiced **10** proficient **12** accomplished

skillet 3 pan **6** spider **9** frying pan

skillful 4 able, deft **5** adept, crack, handy **6** adroit, clever, daedal, expert **7** skilled **8** masterly **9** competent, dexterous, masterful, practiced, workmanly **10** proficient **11** crackerjack, workmanlike **12** accomplished

skim 4 sail, scan, scud, skip **5** brush, carom, glide, graze, skirr **6** browse **8** embezzle, ricochet

skimp 4 save **5** pinch, scant, spare, stint **6** meager, scanty, scrape, sparse **7** slender **8** begrudge, conserve, retrench, withhold **9** economize

skimpy 5 scant, spare **6** meager, meagre, paltry, scanty, scarce, sparse **7** limited, wanting **8** exiguous **9** deficient **10** inadequate **12** insufficient

skim through 4 scan **6** browse

skin 3 fur, gyp, pod, rap **4** clad, clip, flay, husk, hide, pare, peel, pelt, rind, soak **5** blame, cheat, cover, scale, shell, stiff, strip **6** fleece, sheath, slough **7** censure, condemn, sheathe **8** denounce **9** epidermis, sheathing **10** integument, overcharge **11** decorticate *animal:* **4** coat, hide, pelt **6** hackle, peltry *beaver:* **4** plew *combining form:* **3** cut **4** cuti, derm **5** derma, dermo, dermy **6** dermat, dermia, dermis **7** cutaneo, dermata (plural), dermato, epiderm **8** epidermo *depression:* **6** dimple *disease:* **4** acne **5** hives, mange **6** eczema, herpes, tetter **8** ringworm **10** dermatitis *dry:* **5** scurf *fold:* **5** plica *layer:* **5** derma **6** corium, dermis **7** cuticle **9** epidermis *opening:* **4** pore *protuberance:* **3** tag, wen **4** mole, wart **6** pimple *rabbit:* **5** coney *relating to:* **6** dermal **9** cuticular, epidermal *spot:* **7** freckle

skin-deep 7 shallow, trivial **11** superficial

skinflint 5 miser **7** niggard, scrooge **8** tightwad **10** cheapskate, pinchpenny

skin game 3 con **4** scam **5** bunco, bunko, cheat, fraud, sting, trick **6** hustle, racket **7** swindle **8** flimflam

skink 4 adda **6** lizard

skinny 4 bony, dope, info, lank, lean, thin **5** gaunt, lanky, scoop, spare, weedy **6** twiggy **7** angular, lowdown, scraggy, scrawny **8** rawboned, skeletal **9** emaciated

Skin of Our Teeth author 6 Wilder (Thornton)

skip 3 hop, run **4** flee, jump, leap, omit, trip **5** bound, caper, carom, frisk, leave, scoot, skirr **6** cavort, gambol, ignore, pass up, spring **7** abscond, misfire, scamper, skitter **8** leave out, overlook, pass over, ricochet **9** skedaddle

skipjack 4 boat, fish, tuna **8** bluefish, ladyfish, sailboat

skipper 5 pilot **6** leader **7** captain **9** butterfly, commander

ski resort *Austrian:* **9** Kitzbühel *Canadian:* **5** Banff **8** Big White, Sun Peaks, Whistler **9** Tremblant (Mont) **10** Lake Louise *French:* **8** Chamonix *Italian:* **7** Cortina *Swiss:* **5** Davos **6** Gstaad **7** Verbier, Zermatt **8** St. Moritz **9** Engelberg, Sugarloaf *U. S.:* **4** Alta, Taos, Vail **5** Aspen, Stowe **6** Big Sky **8** Snowbird, Snowmass **9** Camelback, Lake Tahoe, Snowbasin, Sun Valley, Telluride **10** Killington **11** Jackson Hole, Squaw Valley **12** Breckenridge

skirmish 3 row **4** fray **5** broil, brush, clash, melee, run-in, scrap, set-to **6** affray, battle, fracas **7** assault, dispute **8** conflict, struggle **9** encounter, scrimmage

skirr 3 run **4** bolt, flee, sail, scud, skim, skip **5** float, scoot, shoot **7** make off, scamper **9** skedaddle

skirt 3 hem, rim **4** brim, duck, edge **5** avoid, bound, brink, burke, dodge, elude, evade, hedge, verge **6** border, bypass, define, detour, escape, fringe, ignore, margin **8** sidestep, surround **9** perimeter, periphery **10** circumvent *ballet:* **4** tutu *feature:* **3** hem **4** slit *long:* **4** maxi *Polynesian:* **5** pareo, pareu *Scottish:* **4** kilt *short:* **4** mini *style:* **5** A-line **6** sheath **9** crinoline *support:* **11** farthingale

skit 6 shtick, sketch **9** burlesque *show:* **5** revue

skitter 3 hop **4** flit, skip, trip **6** scurry, spring **7** scamper

skittery see **skittish**

skittish 3 coy, shy **4** edgy, wary **5** chary, dizzy, jumpy, leery **6** fickle **7** bashful, fidgety, flighty, nervous, rabbity, restive **8** unstable, volatile **9** excitable, frivolous, impulsive, mercurial, whimsical **10** capricious, unreliable

skive 4 pare **5** carve, shave, slice

skivvies 9 underwear

skoal 5 toast **6** health

skua 4 bird **6** jaeger **7** seabird

skulduggery 5 fraud **8** foul play, trickery **9** chicanery, duplicity **10** hanky-panky

skulk 4 lurk, slip **5** creep, prowl, shirk, slink, sneak, steal

skull 4 head, mind **5** brain **7** cranium **8** brainpan **9** braincase *back of:* **7** occiput *bone:* **5** vomer **6** zygoma **7** ethmoid, frontal **8** parietal, sphenoid, temporal *jawless:* **9** calvarium *joint:* **6** suture *part:* **3** jaw **5** inion

skullcap 6 beanie, pileus **7** calotte **8** yarmulke **9** calvarium, zucchetto

skunk 4 beat, drub, lick, scum, whip, whup **6** thrash, wallop **7** clobber, polecat, shellac,

stinker, trounce **8** civet cat, lambaste **9** overwhelm, slaughter *genus:* **8** Mephitis

sky 5 azure **6** heaven, welkin **7** heavens **8** empyrean **9** firmament

sky-blue 5 azure **8** cerulean

skylarking 5 revel **7** revelry, whoopee **9** high jinks, horseplay, rowdiness, whoop-de-do **10** roughhouse **12** roughhousing

skylight 6 window

skyline 7 horizon, outline

sky pilot 5 padre **6** cleric, parson, pastor **8** chaplain, minister, preacher **9** churchman, clergyman

skyrocket 4 rise, soar **7** shoot up **8** catapult

sky sighting 3 UFO

slab 5 block, chunk, slice, strip **8** pavement

slack 3 lax **4** lazy, slow, soft **5** inert, loose, relax **6** remiss **7** ease off, laggard, passive, relaxed **8** careless, derelict, dilatory, inactive, indolent, slothful, sluggish, stagnant **9** leisurely, lethargic, negligent **10** neglectful

slacken 3 ebb, lax **4** ease, slow, wane **5** abate, let up, loose, relax **6** detain, ease up, lessen, loosen, relent, retard, slow up **7** die down, dwindle, ease off, subside **8** diminish, moderate, slow down **9** untighten **10** decelerate

slacker 3 bum **4** slug **5** idler, sloth **6** loafer **7** goof-off, shirker, wastrel **8** deadbeat, layabout, slugabed, sluggard **9** goldbrick, lazybones **10** delinquent **11** couch potato

slag 4 lava **5** dross **6** cinder, debris, scoria

slake 5 allay **6** deaden, quench **7** crumble, hydrate, relieve, satisfy **9** alleviate

slam 3 bat, hit, jab, pan, rap **4** bang, bash, beat, belt, blow, boom, dash, drub, flay, slug, slur, swat, wham **5** blast, crack, crash, fling, knock, pound, slash, smack, smash, swipe, whack **6** batter, cudgel, hammer, scathe, strike, thwack, wallop **7** clobber, potshot **8** lambaste **9** castigate

slam-dance 4 mosh

slam dunk 5 cinch, setup **6** shoo-in **7** safe bet **9** certainty, sure thing

slammer 3 can, jug, pen **4** brig, coop, jail, stir **5** clink, pokey **6** cooler, lockup, prison **9** calaboose **12** penitentiary

slander 4 slur, tale **5** libel, slime, smear, sully **6** defame, malign, smirch, vilify **7** asperse, calumny, scandal, tarnish, traduce **8** besmirch **9** denigrate **10** backbiting, calumniate, defamation, detraction, scandalize **11** mud-slinging **12** back-stabbing

slang 4 cant, jive **5** argot, lingo **6** jargon, patois, patter **7** dialect **10** vernacular

slant 3 tip **4** bank, bias, cant, heel, lean, list, skew, tilt, veer, warp **5** angle, aside, bevel, grade, slope, splay **7** distort, incline, leaning, outlook **8** gradient **9** prejudice, viewpoint **10** standpoint **11** inclination **12** predilection **combining form:** **4** clin **5** clino

slap 3 hit, pop **4** bash, blow, cuff, shot, slam, swat **5** clout, smack, spank, whack **6** buffet, insult, rebuff, strike **7** affront, putdown **8** brickbat, lambaste, penalize **9** castigate

slapdash 5 hasty, messy **6** random, sloppy **7** cursory **8** careless, slipshod **9** half-baked, haphazard, hit-or-miss, makeshift

slap down 5 quell **6** kibosh **7** squelch **8** prohibit, suppress

slaphappy 5 dazed, dizzy, woozy **6** punchy **10** punch-drunk

slash 3 cut **4** clip, gash, hack, pare, slit **5** lower, shave, slice **6** reduce, scathe, scorch **7** abridge, blister, curtail, cut back, cut down, scarify, scourge, shorten **8** lacerate, lambaste, mark down **9** castigate, excoriate **10** abbreviate

slat 4 lath **5** board, stave, strip **6** louver, louvre **7** airfoil

slate 4 gray, list, rock, tile **6** lineup, record, tablet, ticket **7** shingle **8** schedule **9** designate

slather 5 smear **6** spread **8** squander

slattern 4 bawd, moll, slut, tart **5** hussy, tramp, wench **6** floozy, harlot **7** chippie, jezebel, trollop **8** strumpet **10** prostitute **11** painted lady **12** scarlet woman, streetwalker

slaughter 4 kill, slay **6** murder **7** butcher, carnage, killing, wipe out **8** butchery, decimate, demolish, hecatomb, massacre **9** bloodbath, bloodshed, liquidate **10** annihilate, butchering **11** destruction, exterminate, liquidation **12** annihilation

slaughterhouse 8 abattoir, shambles

Slav 4 Pole, Serb, Sorb, Wend **5** Croat, Czech **6** Bulgar, Slovak **7** Russian, Serbian, Slovene **8** Bohemian, Croatian, Moravian **9** Bulgarian, Ruthenian, Ukrainian

slave 4 grub, help, peon, plod, serf, slog, toil **5** grind, helot, swink **6** drudge, menial, thrall, toiler, vassal **7** bondman, chattel, servant **feudal: 4** serf **harem: 9** odalisque **liberated: 8** freedman **Muslim: 6** Mamluk **8** Mameluke **Spartan: 5** helot

slave driver 6 tyrant **7** foreman **8** martinet, overseer **10** taskmaster **11** Simon Legree

slaver 4 spit **5** drool, froth **6** drivel, saliva **7** dribble, slobber, spittle **8** salivate

slavery 6 thrall **7** bondage, helotry, peonage, serfdom **9** indenture, servitude, thralldom **11** subjugation

Slavic apostle 5 Cyril **9** Methodius

slavish 6 abject, menial **7** servile **8** obeisant,

wretched **9** groveling, imitative, laborious **10** obsequious, unoriginal **11** subservient

slay 4 do in, kill **6** murder **7** bump off, butcher, execute, put away **8** dispatch, knock off **9** liquidate, slaughter **11** assassinate

slayer 7 butcher **11** executioner

sleazy 3 low **5** cheap, dingy, seedy, tacky, tatty **6** cheesy, flimsy, shabby, shoddy, trashy **7** run-down, squalid **8** gimcrack **10** down-at-heel **11** dilapidated **12** disreputable

sled 4 luge, pung **6** sleigh **7** coaster, travois **8** toboggan **Russian: 6** troika

sled dog 5 husky **8** malamute

sledge 4 maul **6** hammer, sleigh **Eskimo: 7** komatik **Lapp: 5** pulka

sleek 4 oily **6** glassy, glossy, smooth **7** elegant, stylish **8** lustrous, polished **10** glistening

sleep 3 nap **4** doss, doze, rest **6** catnap, repose, siesta, snooze **7** shut-eye, slumber **11** slumberland **bringer: 7** sandman **combining form: 4** hypn, narc **5** hypno, narco, somni **god: 6** Hypnos, Somnus **noise: 5** snore

sleeper 3 tie **4** beam, mole **7** Pullman **8** long shot **11** double agent, stringpiece

sleeping 7 dormant **8** comatose **.disease: 10** narcolepsy

sleepless 7 wakeful **8** vigilant **9** insomniac

sleeplessness 8 insomnia

sleepwalker 12 somnambulist

sleepy 4 dozy **6** drowsy **7** nodding **9** somnolent **10** slumberous

sleigh 4 pung **6** sledge

sleight 4 ploy, ruse, wile **5** skill, trick **7** gimmick, prowess **8** artifice, deftness, maneuver **9** dexterity, stratagem **10** adroitness

sleight of hand 11 legerdemain

slender 4 lean, slim, thin, trim **5** lithe, reedy, spare **6** skinny, slight, svelte, twiggy **7** spindly, willowy

sleuth 4 dick, Drew (Nancy) **5** Brown (Encyclopedia, Father), Hardy (Frank, Joe), Kojak (Theo), Lupin (Arsène), McGee (Travis), Morse, Queen (Ellery), Saint (The), snoop, Spade (Sam), Tracy (Dick), Vance (Philo), Wolfe (Nero) **6** Alleyn (Roderick), Archer (Lew), Belden (Trixie), Hammer (Mike), Holmes (Sherlock), Marple (Miss), Poirot (Hercule), shamus, Wimsey (Peter) **7** Cadfael (Brother), Columbo, Fansler (Kate), gumshoe, Maigret, Marlowe (Philip), Rawlins (Easy), Templar (Simon "The Saint") **8** Drummond (Bulldog), hawkshaw, Millhone (Kinsey), Rockford (Jim), sherlock **9** Dalgliesh (Adam), detective, Scarpetta (Kay), Wallander (Kurt) **10** private eye, Warshawski (V. I.) **12** investigator

slew 3 lot, mob, ton **4** army, heap, host, load, mess, pile, raft, skid, turn, veer **5** batch, bunch, crowd, flock, pivot, twist **6** myriad, passel, swerve, throng **9** abundance, multitude

slice 3 cut **4** gash, slit **5** allot, carve, divvy, quota, sever, share, slash, split, wedge **6** cleave, divide, incise, sample **7** dissect, portion, segment **8** allocate **9** allotment, allowance

slick 4 film, glib, oily, slip, wily **5** sharp, sleek, soapy **6** crafty, glossy, greasy, shrewd, smarmy, smooth, tricky **7** cunning **8** slippery, slithery, unctuous **10** lubricious, oleaginous

slicker 4 dude **5** dandy, shark **6** con man **7** cheater, diddler, grifter, oilskin, sharper **8** raincoat, swindler **9** trickster **11** flimflammer

slide 3 dip, sag **4** flow, ramp, skid, slip **5** chute, coast, chute, drift, glide, skate, slump, spill **6** scooch, stream **7** decline, slither **8** downturn **9** downswing, downtrend **12** transparency

slight 4 omit, skip, slim, snub, thin **5** frail, reedy, scorn, small **6** flimsy, ignore, meager, meagre, modest, offend, paltry, remote, skinny **7** contemn, neglect, outside, putdown, slender, tenuous, trivial **8** brush-off, delicate, discount, overlook, smallish, trifling **9** disregard, pint-sized **10** disrespect, negligible

slightly 4 a bit, a tad **6** a touch **7** a little

slim 4 thin **5** lithe, reedy, small, spare **6** meager, meagre, minute, narrow, paltry, remote, skinny, slight, svelte, twiggy **7** lissome, outside, slender, tenuous **9** lithesome **10** negligible

slim down 4 diet, fast **6** reduce **10** slenderize

slime 3 goo, mud **4** glop, gook, guck, gunk, muck, ooze, scum **5** filth **6** sleaze, sludge **7** slander

slimy 4 oozy **6** mucous **7** viscous

sling 3 lob **4** cast, fire, hang, hurl, sock, toss **5** chuck, heave, march, pitch, throw **6** dangle, launch **7** suspend **8** catapult

slink 4 lurk **5** creep, prowl, skulk, slide, sneak, steal **7** gumshoe

slinky 4 sexy **5** lithe, sleek **6** svelte **7** furtive, lissome, sinuous, slender, willowy **8** graceful, sensuous, stealthy

slip 3 sag **4** dock, drop, fall, flow, flub, goof, lurk, shed, sink, skid **5** berth, boner, creep, error, fluff, gaffe, glide, lapse, slide, slink,

slump, sneak, steal **6** escape **7** blooper, blunder, decline, drop off, fall off, faux pas, mistake, slither **8** downturn, throw off **9** downswing, downtrend

slipper 4 mule, shoe **5** scuff **6** bootee, bootie, sandal **8** flip-flop, pantofle

slippery 3 icy **4** eely, oily **5** slick **6** greasy, shifty, smooth **7** devious, evasive **8** illusive, slithery **10** lubricious

slipshod 6 blowsy, blowzy, flimsy, frowsy, frowzy, shabby, shoddy, sloppy, untidy **7** rumpled, scrubby, scruffy, unkempt **8** careless, ill-kempt, slapdash, slovenly, tattered **9** haphazard, makeshift, negligent **10** bedraggled, disheveled, down-at-heel

slipup 4 goof **5** boner, error, fluff, lapse **6** bungle, glitch, miscue, mishap **7** blooper, blunder, faux pas, misstep, mistake, setback, stumble **8** accident **9** mischance, oversight **10** misfortune **11** misjudgment

slit 3 cut, gap **4** gash, rent **5** chink, crack, slash, slice **6** cranny, incise **7** crevice, fissure, opening

slither 4 slip **5** creep, glide, sidle, slide, slink, snake, sneak, steal **7** wriggle **8** undulate

slithery see **slippery**

sliver 5 scrap, shard, shave, shred, slice **6** paring **7** shaving, snippet **8** splinter

slob 3 oaf **4** boor, clod, goon, lout **6** galoot, sloven

slobber 4 gush **5** drool, froth **6** drivel, effuse, slaver **7** dribble, enthuse **8** salivate

sloe 4 plum **10** blackthorn

slog 4 grub, moil, plod, plug, toil **5** chore, grind, labor, shlep, slave, sweat **6** drudge, schlep, trudge **7** schlepp

slogan 5 maxim, motto **6** byword **9** battle cry, catchword, watchword **10** shibboleth **11** catchphrase

sloop 4 boat **5** yacht **8** sailboat

slop 3 mud, pap **4** gush, muck **5** douse, dreck, dregs, offal, slosh, slush, spill, swill **6** guzzle, pablum, refuse, splash, sludge **7** garbage, pabulum, rubbish **8** splatter

slope 3 tip **4** bend, brae, cant, heel, lean, list, rise, skew, swag, sway, tilt **5** grade, pitch, scarp, slant **6** ascent, glacis **7** descent, incline, leaning, recline **8** gradient **9** acclivity, declivity, obliquity **11** inclination ***combining form:*** **5** cline **6** clinal

sloppy 5 dowdy, gushy, messy **6** slushy, untidy **7** gushing, unkempt **8** careless, effusive, ill-kempt, slapdash, slipshod, slovenly **10** bedraggled, disheveled **11** dishevelled

slosh 4 gush, slop, wash **5** churn, swash **6** gurgle, splash **8** flounder, splatter

slot 4 vent **5** niche, notch **6** groove, keyway **7**

keyhole, opening, passage 8 aperture 10 pigeonhole

sloth 4 laze, unau 5 idler 6 acedia, apathy, idling, lazing, loafer, slouch, torpor 7 goof-off, languor, loafing, slacker 8 idleness, laziness, lethargy 9 heaviness, indolence, lassitude, lazybones, torpidity 11 couch potato 12 listlessness, sluggishness 13 shiftlessness *three-toed:* 2 ai

slothful 4 idle, lazy 8 fainéant, indolent 9 shiftless

slouch 3 bum, oaf, sag 4 laze, loaf, loll, lout, mope, slug 5 droop, idler, sloth, slump, stoop 6 loafer, loiter, lounge 7 saunter, shamble, shuffle 8 fainéant, slugabed, sluggard 9 do-nothing, lazybones

slough 3 bog, fen 4 cast, mire, molt, quag, shed, sump 5 inlet, marsh, scrap, swamp 6 morass, reject 7 discard 8 jettison, quagmire, throw out 9 backwater, marshland, swampland, throw away

Slovakia *capital:* 10 Bratislava *city:* 6 Kosice *monetary unit:* 6 koruna *mountain range:* 10 Carpathian *neighbor:* 6 Poland 7 Austria, Hungary, Ukraine 13 Czech Republic *river:* 3 Váh 4 Hron 6 Danube, Morava

Slovenia *capital:* 9 Ljubljana *city:* 7 Maribor *monetary unit:* 4 euro *monetary unit, former:* 5 tolar *neighbor:* 5 Italy 7 Austria, Croatia, Hungary *part of:* 7 Balkans *peninsula:* 6 Balkan

slovenly 5 dingy, messy, mussy, seedy, slack 6 frowsy, frowzy, grubby, grungy, scuzzy, shabby, skanky, sleazy, sloppy, untidy 7 squalid, unkempt 8 careless, slapdash, slipshod 10 bedraggled, slatternly

slow 4 late, poky 5 brake, check, lento, pokey, tardy 6 adagio, hinder, impede, leaden, retard, torpid 7 halting, lagging, slacken 8 dilatory, dragging, plodding, sluggish, stagnant 9 leisurely, snaillike, unhurried 10 decelerate, snail-paced, straggling

slowpoke 5 snail 6 lagger 7 dawdler, laggard 8 lingerer, loiterer 9 straggler

sludge 3 mud 4 crud, gook, guck, gunk, mire, muck, ooze, slop 5 slime 6 sewage 8 sediment

slug 3 bum, hit, nip, tot 4 bash, belt, dram, drop, jolt, shot, slam, swat 5 blast, clout, idler, larva, pound, punch, smack, smash, snail, snort, thump 6 buffet, bullet, loafer, slouch, thwack, wallop 7 clobber, goof-off, slacker 8 fainéant, toothful 9 do-nothing, lazybones 11 couch potato *genus:* 5 Limax

slugfest 4 bout 5 brawl, set-to 6 rumble 8 dogfight 10 donnybrook, prizefight

sluggard 3 bum 5 idler 6 loafer, slouch 7 dawdler, goof-off, laggard, shirker, slacker 8 deadbeat, fainéant, slowpoke 9 do-nothing, goldbrick, lazybones

slugger 5 boxer 6 batter, hitter 7 palooka

sluggish 4 lazy, logy, slow 5 inert, slack 6 draggy, leaden, stupid, torpid 7 lumpish 8 dragging, indolent, listless, slothful 9 apathetic, lethargic

sluice 4 duct, flow, gush, pour, race, wash 5 flush, surge 6 trough 7 channel 8 spillway 9 floodgate

slum 6 ghetto 7 skid row

slumber 3 nap 4 doze 5 sleep 6 catnap, drowse, snooze, stupor, torpor 8 dormancy, hebetude, lethargy 9 lassitude, torpidity

slumberous see **sleepy**

slumgullion 4 stew 6 burgoo, ragout 7 goulash

slump 3 dip, sag 4 drop, fall, flag, funk, loll, sink, slip 5 droop, hunch, slide 6 slouch, trough 7 decline, drop off, falloff 8 collapse, downturn 9 downslide, downswing, downtrend, recession 10 depression, stagnation

slur 4 blot, blur, lisp, onus, slam, spot 5 brand, knock, libel, odium, smear, stain 6 befoul, defame, insult, malign, stigma, vilify 7 blacken, calumny, obloquy, obscure, slander, spatter, traduce 8 black eye, brickbat, innuendo, tear down 9 aspersion, bespatter, denigrate, discredit, disparage 10 accusation, calumniate

slurp 3 lap 4 gulp, suck 5 lap up, swill 6 guzzle

slush 3 mud 4 mire, muck, slop 6 drivel 8 schmaltz

sly 4 arch, foxy, wily 5 cagey, saucy, shady, slick 6 artful, clever, crafty, shifty, shrewd, smooth, sneaky, subtle, tricky 7 cunning, devious, furtive, roguish, vulpine 8 guileful, scheming, slippery, stealthy 9 designing, insidious, underhand 11 mischievous, underhanded

slyboots see **scamp**

slyness 4 wile 5 guile 7 cunning 8 caginess, foxiness, wiliness 9 canniness 10 craftiness

smack 3 bat, bop, box 4 bang, bash, belt, biff, blow, buss, chop, clip, cuff, dash, hint, kiss, peck, reek, slam, slap, sock, tang, whop 5 clout, crack, plumb, punch, right, savor, smell, spang, spank, stink, taste, tinge, trace, whack 6 buffet, heroin, relish, smooch, square, strike, thwack 7 clobber, soupçon

smack-dab 4 bang, just 5 plumb, right, spang

6 square **7** exactly **8** squarely **9** perfectly, precisely

small 3 wee **4** mean, mini, puny, tiny **5** bitty, dinky, dwarf, micro, minor, petty, runty, short, teeny **6** bantam, little, meager, meagre, minute, monkey, narrow, paltry, petite, slight, teensy **7** cramped, stunted, trivial **8** picayune, piddling, pint-size, trifling **9** miniature, minuscule, pint-sized **10** diminutive, negligible, undersized **11** ineffectual, unimportant *combining form:* **4** micr, mini **5** micro

small fry 4 kids, tots **8** children **10** youngsters

small-minded 4 mean **5** petty **6** narrow **7** bigoted **9** hidebound, illiberal, parochial **10** brassbound, intolerant, provincial

smallpox 7 variola

small talk 4 chat **6** banter **7** chatter, palaver, prattle **8** badinage, chitchat, raillery, repartee **10** persiflage

small-time 5 minor, petty **6** paltry, two-bit **7** trivial **8** picayune, piddling, trifling **10** bush-league, negligible, shoestring **11** minor-league, unimportant **13** insignificant

smalt 4 blue

smarmy 4 glib, oily **5** slick **6** sleazy **7** buttery, fawning, fulsome **8** unctuous **10** obsequious, oleaginous **12** ingratiating

smart 3 apt **4** ache, chic, keen **5** acute, alert, canny, fresh, natty, nobby, quick, sassy, saucy, savvy, sharp, slick, sting, swank, throb **6** brainy, bright, cheeky, clever, dapper, shrewd, spiffy, spruce, suffer **7** dashing, stylish **8** impudent **11** fashionable, intelligent, quick-witted, ready-witted, sharp-witted

smart aleck 7 show-off, wise guy **8** wiseacre **9** know-it-all **11** wisecracker, wisenheimer

smart-alecky 4 wise **5** fresh, sassy, saucy **6** cheeky **8** impudent, insolent **9** bold-faced **11** impertinent

smart set 5 elect, elite **6** bon ton, gentry **7** in crowd, quality, society, who's who **9** beau monde, haut monde **10** blue bloods, upper crust **11** aristocracy, Four Hundred, high society

smarty-pants 7 wise guy **9** know-it-all, swellhead **11** wisenheimer

smash 3 hit, jar **4** bang, bash, belt, blow, boom, clap, jolt, raze, ruin, slam, slug, sock, wham, whop **5** blast, boffo, burst, clash, crack, crash, crush, shock, whack, wreck **6** batter, impact, pileup, shiver, wallop **7** clobber, crack-up, debacle, destroy, shatter, success **8** collapse, decimate, demolish, knockout, overhand, splinter **9**

breakdown, collision, pulverize, sensation, succès fou **10** annihilate **12** disintegrate

smashup 5 crash, wreck **6** fiasco, pileup **7** crack-up, debacle **8** accident, collapse, disaster **9** breakdown, collision

smattering 3 few **7** handful **10** sprinkling

smear 3 dab, tar **4** beat, coat, daub, drub, lick, slur, soil, whip **5** cover, libel, stain, sully, taint **6** befoul, defame, defile, malign, smirch, smudge, spread, thrash, vilify **7** asperse, blacken, calumny, plaster, shellac, slander, tarnish, traduce **8** besmirch **9** bespatter, denigrate **10** calumniate

smell 4 funk, nose, odor, reek **5** aroma, scent, sense, smack, sniff, snuff, stink, trace, whiff **6** detect, stench **7** bouquet, perfume **9** fragrance, redolence *rotten egg:* **6** sulfur

smell, sense of 9 olfaction

smelly 4 rank **5** fetid, funky, reeky **6** foetid, putrid, rancid, stinky **7** noisome, reeking, stenchy **8** mephitic, stinking **10** malodorous

smelt 4 flux, fuse, slag **6** reduce, refine, tomcod **8** sparling **9** sand lance, whitebait

smidgen 3 bit, dab, jot **4** atom, iota, mite **5** crumb, speck, touch **6** morsel

smile 4 beam, grin **5** smirk **6** simper

smirch see **smudge**

smirk 4 grin, leer **5** fleer, sneer **6** simper **7** grimace

smite 3 hit **4** belt, kill, sock **5** clout, whack **6** assail, attack, strike **7** afflict, assault, clobber, torment

smithereens 4 bits **6** pieces **9** fragments, particles

smitten 4 gaga **5** taken **6** hooked **8** besotted, enamored **9** enamoured, enchanted, entranced **10** captivated, enraptured, infatuated **11** intoxicated

smock 5 apron, dress, frock **8** pinafore

smoke 4 cure, fume **5** fumes, vapor **8** fastball, fumigate **9** cigarette

smoky 4 fumy, gray, hazy **5** murky, sooty **6** turbid **7** reeking **10** caliginous, smoldering

smolder 4 fume, glow, stew **5** churn **6** bubble, seethe, simmer **7** ferment **9** fulminate

smooch 4 buss, kiss, neck, peck **5** smack **8** osculate

smooth 4 easy, even, flat, oily **5** fluid, flush, level, plane, sleek, slick, suave **6** facile, fluent, glassy, glossy, polish, urbane **7** cursive, flatten, flowing, running **8** glabrous, hairless, soothing, unbroken **10** effortless, unwrinkled

smooth-spoken 4 glib **6** fluent **8** eloquent **10** articulate **13** silver-tongued

smorgasbord 4 hash, olio **6** buffet, jumble, medley **7** farrago, grab bag, mélange **8**

mishmash, mixed bag, pastiche **9** potpourri **10** hodgepodge, hotchpotch, miscellany, salmagundi **11** gallimaufry

smother 5 choke, douse, quell **6** hush up, muffle, quench, stifle **7** blanket, repress, squelch **8** inundate, restrain, suppress **9** overwhelm, suffocate **10** asphyxiate

smudge 3 dab **4** blot, blur, daub, foul, soil **5** dirty, smear, stain, sully, taint **6** bedaub, blotch, defile, smirch **7** begrime, besmear, blacken, blemish, splotch, tarnish **8** besmirch

smug 8 priggish **9** conceited **10** complacent **13** self-satisfied

smuggle 3 run **7** bootleg

smut 4 porn **5** filth **9** obscenity **11** pornography

smutty 4 blue, foul, lewd, racy **5** bawdy, dirty, nasty, sooty **6** coarse, filthy, risqué, vulgar **7** obscene, raunchy **8** indecent, off-color, prurient **9** salacious **12** pornographic, scatological

Smyrna 5 Izmir

snack 3 tea **4** bite, nosh, tapa **6** morsel, nibble **11** refreshment

snaffle 3 bit, cop **4** lift **5** filch, pinch, swipe **6** pilfer, pocket **7** purloin

snafu 5 botch, error, mix-up, snarl **6** bungle, foul up, mess up, muddle **7** chaotic, screwup **9** confusion

snag 3 nab **4** curb, grab, hook, nail, tear **5** catch, hitch **6** glitch, holdup, hurdle, obtain, secure **7** capture **8** drawback, obstacle **9** apprehend **10** impediment **11** obstruction

snail 5 whelk **6** limpet **7** mollusc, mollusk **8** escargot, ramshorn, slowpoke **9** gastropod **10** periwinkle

snake 3 boa **4** fink **5** crawl, creep, racer, slide **6** python, writhe **7** hognose, serpent, slither **8** anaconda, ophidian, undulate *genus:* **4** Eryx *poisonous:* **3** asp **5** adder, cobra, coral, krait, mamba, viper **6** elapid, taipan **7** rattler **8** pit viper **10** bushmaster, copperhead, fer-de-lance **11** cottonmouth **13** water moccasin

snakebird 6 darter **7** anhinga

snake-eater 8 mongoose **13** secretary bird

snakelike 7 sinuous **8** ophidian **10** serpentine

snakeroot 7 bugbane **10** wild ginger **11** blazing star

snakeweed 7 bistort **13** poison hemlock

snaky 7 sinuous, winding **8** flexuous, tortuous **10** convoluted, meandering, serpentine **11** anfractuous

snap 4 bang, bark **5** break, cinch, crack **6** breeze, lose it, picnic **7** crackle **8** duck soup, kid stuff, pushover **10** child's play

snap back 6 revive **7** rebound, recover **10** convalesce, recuperate

snappy 4 edgy, fast, tart **5** brisk, hasty, huffy, natty, quick, rapid, sharp, smart, swank, swift, testy **6** lively, prompt, speedy, touchy **7** dashing, stylish, waspish **8** animated, petulant, vigorous **9** breakneck, fractious, irritable, vivacious

snapshot 4 view **5** image, photo **6** précis, sketch, visual **7** picture **8** overview, synopsis **10** shadow copy

snare 3 bag, get, net **4** bait, hook, lure, trap **5** catch, decoy, noose, tempt **6** come-on, enmesh, entice, entrap, seduce, tangle **7** capture, catch up, chicane, embroil, ensnare, ensnarl, involve, mantrap, pitfail, trammel **8** entangle, inveigle **9** chicanery, deception **10** enticement, temptation

snarl 3 jam, web **4** bark, gnar, knot, maze, mesh **5** chaos, growl, ravel, skein **6** jungle, morass, muddle, tangle **7** perplex **8** disarray, disorder, entangle, gridlock, mishmash **9** confusion, labyrinth **10** complexity, complicate **12** complication, entanglement

snatch 3 bit, nab **4** grab, jerk, take, yank **5** catch, pluck, seize, swipe **6** abduct, clutch, kidnap, wrench **8** fragment

snazzy 4 chic **5** fancy, gaudy, jazzy, nobby, ritzy, sassy, sharp, smart, showy, swank **6** chichi, classy, flashy, garish, glitzy, jaunty, spiffy, swanky **7** elegant

sneak 3 cur, pad **4** lurk, slip, worm **5** crawl, creep, glide, mooch, prowl, shirk, skulk, skunk, slide, slink, steal **6** covert, secret, tiptoe, weasel **7** furtive, gumshoe, slither, smuggle **8** hush-hush, slyboots, stealthy **9** pussyfoot, scoundrel **10** undercover **11** clandestine

sneaky 4 foxy **6** shifty, tricky **7** devious, furtive **8** guileful, indirect, slippery, stealthy **9** underhand **11** duplicitous, underhanded

sneer 4 gibe, jeer **5** fleer, scoff, smirk **7** grimace, snigger

sneeze 5 achew, achoo **6** ahchoo *cause:* **5** snuff **6** dander, pollen **7** allergy **8** dust mite *French:* **7** atchoum *German:* **7** hatschi *Spanish:* **6** atchís

snicker 5 laugh **6** giggle, titter **7** chortle, chuckle

snide 4 mean **5** nasty **8** spiteful **9** malicious **11** insinuating

sniff 4 jeer, nose **5** scent, scoff, smell, snoop **6** inhale

sniffy 4 smug **5** aloof, lofty **6** lordly, snooty, uppity **7** haughty, pompous, stuck-up **8** scornful, superior **10** disdainful, hoity-toity **12** contemptuous, supercilious

snifter 3 nip, sip, tot **4** dram, drop, jolt, shot, slug **5** glass, snort **6** finger, goblet

snip 3 bit, cut **4** clip, crop, trim **5** notch, scrap **8** fragment

snipe 4 carp **9** sandpiper

sniper 6 gunman, killer **7** shooter **8** marksman, rifleman **12** sharpshooter

snippety see **snippy**

snippy 4 curt, tart **5** bluff, blunt, brief, gruff, short, terse **6** abrupt, crusty **7** brusque **8** snappish

snit 3 fit **4** flap, fume, huff, stew **5** panic, pique, sweat, tizzy **6** dither, frenzy, lather, pother, swivet **10** conniption

snitch 3 cop, nip, rat **4** beak, blab, fink, hook, lift, palm, sing, tell **5** filch, peach, pinch, spill, steal, swipe **6** inform, pilfer, pocket, squeal, tattle **7** purloin, rat fink, stoolie, tattler, tipster **8** betrayer, informer, squealer **11** stool pigeon

snivel 3 sob **4** weep **5** cower, whine **6** cringe, whinge **7** blubber, snuffle, whimper

snob 5 snoot **6** poseur **7** parvenu

snobbish 6 la-de-da, la-di-da, snooty, uppity **7** elitist, haughty, high-hat, stuck-up **8** lah-de-dah, lah-di-dah **9** lah-dee-dah **10** hoity-toity **11** patronizing, pretentious **12** supercilious **13** condescending

snook 5 cobia **6** robalo **12** sergeant fish

snooker 3 con **4** dupe, fool, hoax, pool **5** trick **6** delude **7** beguile, deceive, defraud **8** flimflam, hoodwink **9** bamboozle **11** hornswoggle

snoop 3 pry, spy **4** nose, peek, peep, peer, poke **5** prier, pryer **6** ferret, meddle, sleuth **7** gumshoe, intrude, meddler **8** busybody, quidnunc **9** detective, inspector, interfere **10** rubberneck

snooper 3 spy **9** detective, inspector **12** investigator

snoopy 4 nosy **6** prying **7** curious **8** meddling **9** intrusive **10** meddlesome **11** inquisitive

snoot see **snout**

snooty see **snobbish**

snooze 3 kip, nap **4** doze **5** sleep **6** catnap, drowse, nod off, siesta **7** drop off, slumber **10** forty winks

snore 8 rhonchus

snort 3 nip, tot **4** dram, drop, jolt, shot, slug **5** scoff, snarl **6** exhale, inhale **7** snifter

snout 3 neb **4** beak, nose **6** muzzle, schnoz **7** schnozz **9** proboscis

snow *glacial:* **4** firn, névé *melted:* **5** slush *pellet:* **7** graupel *ridge:* **8** sastruga

snow apple 8 mushroom

snowball 5 mount, run up **6** expand **7** augment, burgeon, explode, inflate **8** increase, multiply, mushroom, viburnum **10** accumulate **11** proliferate

snowbird 5 finch, junco **6** thrush **7** bunting **9** fieldfare, ivory gull

Snow-Bound author 8 Whittier (John Greenleaf)

snow finch 9 brambling

snow grouse 9 ptarmigan

snow leopard 5 ounce

Snow Leopard author 11 Matthiessen (Peter)

snowstorm 8 blizzard

snub 3 cut **4** shun **5** blunt, scorn, spite, spurn **6** rebuff, rebuke, slight, stubby **7** put down **9** ostracize, repudiate **12** cold-shoulder

snuff 3 ice, off **4** kill, nose **5** pinch, scent, smell **6** murder, rappee **7** execute **10** extinguish **11** exterminate

snug 4 cozy, neat, taut, tidy, trim **5** comfy, cushy, tight **6** burrow, cuddle, nestle, nuzzle, secure **7** orderly **9** sheltered, shipshape **11** comfortable

snuggle 5 spoon **6** burrow, cuddle, curl up, huddle, nestle, nuzzle

so 3 sae **4** ergo, then, thus, true **5** hence **6** indeed **9** similarly, therefore **11** accordingly **12** consequently

soak 3 ret, sop, sot, wet **4** bilk, clip, lush, skin, swig, wino **5** douse, drink, gouge, imbue, souse, steep **6** boozer, drench, fleece, infuse, rip off, seethe **7** drinker, guzzler, immerse **8** drunkard, permeate, saturate, submerge **9** alcoholic, penetrate **10** boozehound, impregnate, overcharge *flax:* **3** ret

soap 4 suds **6** stroke **7** flatter, wheedle **8** blandish, butter up, inveigle **9** sweet-talk *hard:* **7** castile *ingredient:* **3** lye, oil **5** scent **9** fragrance

soapbox 4 dais **6** podium **7** rostrum **8** hustings, platform, scaffold

soap plant 5 amole

soapstone 4 talc **8** steatite

soapwort 7 cowherd **11** bouncing bet

soar 3 fly **4** lift, rise **5** arise, climb, glide, hover, mount, shoot **6** ascend, rocket **7** shoot up **8** increase **9** skyrocket

sob 3 cry **4** bawl, blub, wail, weep **7** blubber, whimper

sober 4 calm, cool **5** grave, staid **6** low-key, proper, sedate, solemn **7** austere, earnest, serious, subdued **8** composed, low-keyed, moderate, rational, reserved **9** abstinent, collected, practical, pragmatic, realistic, temperate **10** abstaining, abstemious, controlled, hardheaded, no-nonsense, reasonable, restrained **11** disciplined, down-to-earth **12** matter-of-fact **13** imperturbable, self-possessed

sobriety 7 gravity 10 abstinence, continence, sedateness, temperance 11 seriousness

sobriquet 3 tag 5 alias 6 byname 7 epithet, moniker 8 cognomen, nickname 10 hypocorism

so-called 6 formal 7 alleged, nominal, titular 8 supposed 9 pretended, professed, purported 10 ostensible, self-styled

soccer *cup:* 5 World *official:* 7 referee 8 linesman *player:* 6 booter, goalie, kicker, winger 7 forward, link man, striker, sweeper 8 defender, fullback, halfback 10 goalkeeper *star:* 4 Hamm (Mia), Pelé 5 Akers (Michelle), Henry (Thierry), Klose (Miroslav) 6 Zidane (Zinedine) 7 Beckham (David), Ronaldo 8 Chastain (Brandi), Maradona (Diego) 10 Ronaldinho 11 Beckenbauer (Franz) *term:* 3 net 4 boot, chip, kick, trap 6 corner, header, tackle, volley 7 dribble, kickoff, throw-in 8 back-heel, free kick, goal kick, goal line 9 touchline 10 center spot, corner flag, corner kick 11 dropped ball, halfway line, penalty kick, penalty spot

sociable 5 close 6 genial 7 affable, amiable, cordial 8 familiar, gracious 9 clubbable, congenial, convivial 10 gregarious, hospitable 11 good-natured

social 5 civic, civil 8 communal 9 clubbable, convivial 10 collective, gregarious, hospitable 11 extroverted 13 companionable *class:* 5 caste

Social Contract author 8 Rousseau (Jean-Jacques)

socialist *American:* 4 Debs (Eugene) 6 Ripley (George), Thomas (Norman) *British:* 4 Owen (Robert, Robert Dale), Webb (Beatrice, Sidney) 6 Morris (William) *French:* 7 Fourier (Charles), Viviani (René) 10 Saint-Simon (Henri de) *German:* 4 Marx (Karl) 6 Engels (Friedrich) 9 Luxemburg (Rosa) 10 Liebknecht (Wilhelm)

socialize 3 mix 5 party, visit 6 hobnob, mingle 7 consort 9 associate 10 fraternize

social worker 4 Riis (Jacob), Wald (Lillian D.) 6 Addams (Jane) 7 Alinsky (Saul), Lathrop (Julia C.)

society 4 club 5 elite, guild 6 gentry, league, people, public 7 company, quality, who's who 8 populace, sodality 9 beau monde, community, haut monde 10 fellowship, fraternity, upper class, upper crust 11 aristocracy, association, brotherhood 13 companionship *branch:* 7 chapter

sociologist *American:* 4 Bell (Daniel), Ward (Lester Frank) 5 Balch (Emily Green), Whyte (William H.) 6 Du Bois (W. E. B.),

Glazer (Nathan), Sumner (William Graham) 7 Johnson (Charles Spurgeon), Riesman (David) *English:* 7 Spencer (Herbert) *French:* 8 Durkheim (Emile) *German:* 5 Weber (Max) *Italian:* 6 Pareto (Vilfredo) *Swedish:* 6 Myrdal (Alva, Gunnar)

sock 3 bop, box, hit 4 bash, belt, blow, chop, cuff, ding, slap, slog 5 clout, punch, smack, smash, whack 6 argyle, buffet, strike, thwack, wallop 7 clobber 8 stocking

sock away 4 bank, save, stow 5 cache, hoard, lay by, put by, stash 8 lay aside

socks 4 hose 7 hosiery

Socrates *birthplace:* 6 Athens *poison:* 7 hemlock *pupil:* 5 Plato *wife:* 8 Xantippe 9 Xanthippe

Socratic 8 maieutic

sod 4 land, peat, turf 5 earth, grass 6 ground

soda 3 pop 4 cola 5 tonic 7 seltzer

sodality 4 club 5 guild, lodge, order, union 6 league 7 society 9 community 10 fellowship, fraternity 11 association, brotherhood

sodden 3 wet 5 soggy, soppy 6 soaked, soused 7 soaking, sopping 8 drenched, dripping 9 saturated 11 waterlogged, wringing-wet

sodium symbol 2 Na

Sodom and ____ 8 Gomorrah *visitor:* 3 Lot

sofa 5 couch, divan 7 ottoman 9 banquette, davenport

so far 3 yet 5 as yet, still 6 to date 7 till now 8 hitherto, until now 10 heretofore

Sofia native 6 Bulgar 9 Bulgarian

soft 4 cozy, easy, mild, snug 5 balmy, comfy, cushy, downy, faint, mushy, silky 6 doughy, flabby, gentle, low-key, pliant, satiny, silken, simple, smooth, spongy, tender 7 cottony, lenient, pillowy, pliable, squashy, squishy, subdued, velvety 8 cushiony, workable, yielding 9 malleable 11 comfortable

softcover 9 paperback

soften 4 ease, tame 5 abate, allay, relax 6 dampen, lessen, mellow, soothe, subdue, temper, weaken 7 assuage, lighten, mollify 8 diminish, mitigate, moderate, palliate, tone down 9 alleviate

soft hail 7 graupel

softhearted 4 kind, warm 6 humane, kindly, tender 7 lenient 10 responsive 11 sympathetic 13 compassionate

soft palate 5 velum

soft-pedal 4 mute 6 dampen, hush up, muffle, subdue 8 minimize, play down, suppress, tone down 9 underplay 11 de-emphasize

soft-soap 3 con 4 coax 6 cajole, soothe, wangle 7 blarney, flatter, wheedle 8 blandish, butter up, inveigle 9 sweet-talk

soggy 3 wet 6 doughy, soaked, sodden 7 soaking, sopping 8 drenched, dripping 9 saturated 10 bedraggled 11 waterlogged

Sohrab and Rustum author 6 Arnold (Matthew)

soi-disant 7 alleged 8 putative, so-called, supposed 9 pretended, professed, purported 10 ostensible, self-styled

soil 3 mud, tar 4 daub, dirt, foul, land, loam, mess, muck, murk 5 dirty, earth, grime, muddy, smear, stain, sully, taint 6 defile, ground, smirch, smudge 7 begrime, blacken, country, pollute, tarnish 8 besmirch, discolor, homeland 10 fatherland, motherland, terra firma 11 contaminate **aggregate:** 3 ped **clay:** 5 gault **combining form:** 3 geo 4 agro **dark:** 9 chernozem **deposit:** 5 loess 7 eluvium **infertile:** 6 podzol **layer:** 4 gley, sola (plural) 5 solum **rich:** 6 hotbed **tropical:** 7 latosol

soiree 4 fete, gala 5 party 6 affair, social 7 evening, shindig 8 function 9 festivity, reception 11 celebration 13 entertainment

sojourn 4 bide, stay, stop 5 abide, lodge, tarry, visit 6 linger 7 layover 8 stopover

Sol 3 sun 7 daystar, phoebus **horse:** 4 Eous 5 Ethon 9 Erythreos (see also **Helios**)

solace 5 allay, amuse, cheer 6 buck up 7 comfort, console, hearten 8 inspirit 10 condolence

solar disk 4 Aten, Aton

solarium 7 sunroom

solar-system model 6 orrery

solder 4 fuse, weld 5 braze

soldier 2 GI 5 grunt, sepoy 7 dogface, draftee, fighter, private, recruit, trooper, veteran, warrior 8 bluecoat, doughboy, fusilier, rifleman 9 free lance, guerrilla, man-at-arms, mercenary 10 carabineer, carabinier, serviceman 11 condottiere, infantryman **ancient Greece:** 7 hoplite **British:** 5 Tommy 7 redcoat **cavalry:** 6 hussar 8 chasseur **Confederate:** 3 reb **French:** 5 poilu 6 Zouave **German:** 5 jerry **irregular:** 8 guerilla 9 guerrilla **Prussian:** 5 uhlan **Turkish:** 9 janissary

sole 3 one 4 lone, only 5 alone 6 bottom, single, unique 8 flatfish, singular 9 exclusive

solecism 4 goof, slip 5 boner, error, gaffe, lapse 6 misuse 7 blooper, blunder, faux pas, mistake 9 barbarism, indecorum, vulgarism 11 impropriety

solemn 5 grand, grave, sober, staid, stern 6 august, formal, ritual, sedate, somber, sombre 7 earnest, plenary, serious, stately,

weighty 8 funereal, imposing, majestic 9 dignified 10 ceremonial, impressive, nononsense, sobersided 11 ceremonious, magnificent

solemnize 4 keep 5 bless, honor 6 hallow 7 dignify, observe 8 venerate 9 celebrate, ritualize 10 consecrate 11 commemorate

solicit 3 ask, beg 4 lure, tout, urge 5 apply 6 demand, drum up, entice 7 beseech, bespeak, canvass, entreat, implore, request 8 petition 9 importune 11 proposition, requisition

solicitor 6 jurist, lawyer, suitor 7 pleader 8 advocate, attorney 9 counselor

solicitous 4 avid, keen 5 eager, fussy 6 ardent, tender 7 anxious, careful, devoted, fearful, finicky, worried 8 rigorous 9 assiduous, attentive, concerned, impatient 10 fastidious, meticulous, scrupulous 11 considerate, punctilious, sympathetic 12 apprehensive 13 conscientious

solicitude 4 care, heed 5 qualm, worry 6 unease 7 anxiety, concern, scruple 9 attention, vigilance 10 uneasiness 11 compunction 12 watchfulness 13 consideration

solid 4 firm, hard 5 dense, sound, valid 6 cogent, secure, stable, sturdy, united 7 compact 8 reliable, unbroken 9 steadfast, unanimous, undivided 10 convincing 11 substantial

solidarity 5 union, unity 6 cement, esprit 7 concord, oneness 8 cohesion 9 integrity 10 singleness 12 cohesiveness, togetherness 13 esprit de corps

solidify 3 dry, fix, gel, set 4 cake, jell 6 freeze, harden, secure 7 compact, congeal 8 compress, contract, indurate 11 consolidate

solitary 4 lone, lorn, only, solo 5 alone 6 hermit, lonely, single, unique 7 recluse 8 derelict, deserted, desolate, eremitic, forsaken, isolated, lonesome, separate, singular 9 abandoned, reclusive, withdrawn 10 antisocial, particular, unsociable 11 standoffish 12 misanthropic 13 unaccompanied

solitude 7 privacy 8 loneness 9 aloneness, isolation, seclusion 10 detachment, loneliness, quarantine, retirement, withdrawal 11 confinement 12 separateness

solo 4 aria, lone 5 alone 6 single 7 unaided 8 solitary 13 independently, unaccompanied

Solomon brother: 8 Adonijah **daughter:** 7 Taphath 8 Basemath **father:** 5 David **kingdom:** 6 Israel **mother:** 9 Bathsheba **son,** **successor:** 8 Rehoboam **victim:** 4 Joab 8 Adonijah

Solomon Islands capital: 7 Honiara **ethnic group:** 10 Melanesian **island:** 7 Florida,

Malaita, Rennell **8** Choiseul **11** Guadalcanal, Santa Isabel **12** San Cristóbal
solon 8 lawgiver **10** legislator
so long 4 by-by, ciao, ta-ta **5** adieu, adios **6** bye-bye, good-by **7** cheerio, good-bye, toodles **8** farewell, Godspeed, toodle-oo
solution 6 answer, result *salt:* **6** saline
solve 3 fix **5** break, crack **6** decode, reveal, settle **7** clarify, clear up, dope out, explain, unravel, work out **8** construe, decipher, unriddle, untangle **9** elucidate, figure out, interpret, puzzle out **11** disentangle
Somalia *capital:* **9** Mogadishu *gulf:* **4** Aden *language:* **6** Arabic, Somali *location:* **12** Horn of Africa *monetary unit:* **8** shilling *neighbor:* **5** Kenya **8** Djibouti, Ethiopia
somatic 6 bodily, carnal **7** fleshly **8** corporal, parietal, physical **9** corporeal
somber 3 dim **4** dark, drab, dull, grim **5** bleak, dusky, grave, heavy, murky, staid **6** dismal, dreary, gloomy, sedate, solemn **7** doleful, joyless, obscure, serious, weighty **8** funereal, mournful **9** tenebrous **10** caliginous, depressing, depressive, lugubrious, melancholy, sepulchral, sobersided, tenebrific **11** dispiriting
somersault 4 flip
somewhat 4 a bit, a tad **5** quite **6** fairly, kind of, rather, sort of **7** a little **8** slightly **9** partially, tolerably **10** moderately
sommelier's *offering* **4** wine
_____ **Sommer 4** Elke
somniferous see **sleepy**
somnolent see **sleepy**
Somnus *brother:* **4** Mors *god of:* **5** sleep *mother:* **3** Nox
son *French:* **4** fils *Italian:* **6** figlio *Spanish:* **4** hijo
song 3 air, lay **4** aria, glee, hymn, lied, tune **5** carol, chant, ditty, lyric, paean **6** ballad, melody, number **7** chanson **8** madrigal *biblical:* **8** canticle *boat:* **9** barcarole **10** barcarolle *French:* **7** chanson *German:* **4** lied **6** lieder (plural) *lamentation:* **5** dirge **8** threnode, threnody *medieval:* **8** sirvente **9** sirventes *morning:* **6** aubade *of joy:* **5** paean *operatic:* **4** aria **7** arietta **8** cavatina **9** cabaletta *Portuguese:* **4** fado *sacred:* **5** psalm *sailor's:* **6** chanty, shanty **7** chantey *short:* **8** canzonet *wedding:* **8** hymeneal
song and dance 5 pitch, spiel
songbird see at **bird**
Song of Myself *author* **7** Whitman (Walt)
Song of Solomon 9 Canticles
songwriter 8 composer, lyricist *famous:* **3** Ebb (Fred) **4** Anka (Paul), Bock (Jerry), Cahn (Sammy), Duke (Vernon), Hart

(Lorenz), Kern (Jerome), King (Carole), Nyro (Laura), Webb (Jimmy), Wolf (Hugo) **5** Arlen (Harold), Berry (Chuck), Byrne (David), Cohan (George M.), Cohen (Leonard), Cooke (Sam), David (Hal), Dietz (Howard), Dylan (Bob), Evans (Ray), Green (Adolph), Holly (Buddy), Loewe (Frederick), Simon (Carly, Paul), Styne (Jule), Waits (Tom), Weill (Kurt) **6** Berlin (Irving), Comden (Betty), Coward (Noel), Denver (John), Dozier (Lamont), Fields (Dorothy), Foster (Stephen), Goffin (Gerry), Herman (Jerry), Kander (John), Leiber (Jerry), Lennon (John), Lerner (Alan Jay), Lovett (Lyle), McHugh (Jimmy), Mercer (Johnny), Nelson (Willie), Newman (Randy), Parton (Dolly), Porter (Cole), Sedaka (Neil), Seeger (Pete), Taupin (Bernie), Taylor (James), Travis (Merle), Warren (Harry), Wonder (Stevie) **7** Diamond (Neil), Guthrie (Woody), Harburg (E. Y.), Harnick (Sheldon), Holland (Brian, Eddie), Loesser (Frank), Mancini (Henry), Manilow (Barry), Novello (Ivor), Orbison (Roy), Rodgers (Richard), Romberg (Sigmund), Spector (Phil), Stoller (Mike), Youmans (Vincent) **8** Costello (Elvis), Gershwin (George, Ira), Hamlisch (Marvin), Mayfield (Curtis), Mitchell (Joni), Morrison (Van), Robinson (Smokey), Schubert (Franz), Schwartz (Arthur), Sondheim (Stephen) **9** Bacharach (Burt), Donaldson (Walter), McCartney (Paul), Strayhorn (Billy), Von Tilzer (Albert, Harry), Van Heusen (Jimmy) **10** Carmichael (Hoagy) **11** Hammerstein (Oscar), Springsteen (Bruce)
Sonja _____ **5** Henie
Sonnambula *composer* **7** Bellini (Vincenzo)
sonnet *developer:* **8** Petrarch *part:* **5** octet **6** octave, sestet
sonorous 7 ringing, vibrant **8** resonant **10** oratorical, resounding, rhetorical **11** declamatory **12** magniloquent **13** grandiloquent
Sons and Lovers *hero* **5** Morel (Paul)
Sontag *novel* **9** In America **12** Volcano Lover (The)
soon 4 anon **6** any day, pronto **7** betimes, by and by, quickly, rapidly, shortly **8** directly, promptly, speedily **9** forthwith, presently, right away **10** before long
Sooner State 8 Oklahoma
soothe 4 balm, calm, ease, hush, lull **5** allay, quiet, salve, still **6** becalm, pacify, settle, solace, subdue **7** appease, assuage, comfort, compose, console, massage, mollify, placate, relieve **8** calm down, reassure **9** alleviate **10** conciliate, propitiate **11** tranquilize

soothsay 5 augur 8 prophesy 9 adumbrate 10 vaticinate 13 prognosticate

soothsayer 4 seer 5 sibyl 6 oracle 7 diviner, prophet 8 foreseer 9 predictor 10 forecaster, foreteller *ancient Roman:* 5 augur 6 auspex 8 haruspex *blind:* 8 Tiresias (see also **prophet**)

sop 3 wet 4 gift, soak 5 bribe, douse, goody, souse, steep 6 deluge, drench, reward, seethe 7 douceur 8 gratuity, saturate, waterlog 9 incentive, lagniappe, sweetener 10 enticement

sophism see **sophistry**

sophistic 5 false, phony 7 invalid, seeming, unsound 8 delusive, illusory, spurious 9 beguiling, casuistic, deceptive, plausible 10 fallacious, fraudulent, misleading, ostensible

sophisticated 5 blasé, jaded, suave 6 smooth, svelte, urbane 7 complex, knowing, refined, worldly 8 cultured, involved, schooled, seasoned 9 Byzantine, elaborate, intricate, practiced 10 world-weary 11 complicated, experienced, worldly-wise 12 cosmopolitan

sophistry 9 casuistry 12 equivocation 13 dissimulation, prevarication

Sophocles play 4 Ajax 7 Electra 8 Antigone 10 Oedipus Rex

Sophonisba *brother:* 8 Hannibal *father:* 9 Hasdrubal *husband:* 6 Syphax

soporific 4 dozy 6 drowsy, opiate, sleepy 7 anodyne, calming, numbing 8 hypnotic, narcotic, sedative 9 calmative, deadening, somnolent 10 anesthetic, slumberous 11 somniferous 12 somnifacient 13 tranquilizing

soprano *American:* 4 Pons (Lily) 5 Costa (Mary), Gluck (Alma), Moffo (Anna), Moore (Grace), Price (Leontyne), Sills (Beverly) 6 Arroyo (Martina), Battle (Kathleen), Callas (Maria), Curtin (Phyllis), Donath (Helen), Farrar (Geraldine), Garden (Mary), Munsel (Patrice), Norman (Jessye), Peters (Roberta), Piazza (Marguerite), Resnik (Regina), Upshaw (Dawn) 7 Farrell (Eileen), Fleming (Renée), Kirsten (Dorothy), Stevens (Risë), Traubel (Helen) 8 Ponselle (Rosa) *Australian:* 5 Melba (Nellie) 10 Sutherland (Joan) *Austrian:* 4 Popp (Lucia) 7 Rysanek (Leonie) 8 Sembrich (Marcella) *Canadian:* 7 Stratas (Teresa) *French:* 7 Crespin (Régine) *German:* 6 Leider (Frida) 7 Lehmann (Lilli, Lotte) 11 Schwarzkopf (Elisabeth) *Italian:* 5 Freni (Mirella), Grisi (Giuditta, Giulia), Patti (Adelina) 6 Scotto (Renata) 7 Bartoli (Cecilia), Tebaldi (Renata) 10 Tetrazzini (Lu-

isa) 11 Ricciarelli (Katia) *Korean:* 6 Sumi Jo *Mexican:* 8 Cruz-Romo (Gilda) *New Zealand:* 8 Te Kanawa (Kiri) *Norwegian:* 8 Flagstad (Kirsten) *Romanian:* 8 Cotrubas (Ileana) *Russian:* 8 Netrebko (Anna) *Spanish:* 7 Caballé (Montserrat) 8 Berganza (Teresa) 12 de los Angeles (Victoria) *Swedish:* 4 Lind (Jenny) 7 Nilsson (Birgit) (see also **mezzo-soprano**)

sorcerer 4 mage 5 magus 6 wizard 7 warlock 8 conjurer, conjuror, magician 9 enchanter 11 necromancer, thaumaturge 13 thaumaturgist

sorceress 3 hag, hex 5 Circe, witch

sorcery 5 magic 8 diablery, wizardry 9 conjuring 10 necromancy, witchcraft 11 bewitchment, enchantment, thaumaturgy *West Indian:* 5 obeah

sordid 3 low 4 base, foul, mean, vile 5 dirty, nasty, seamy, shady, venal 6 blowsy, blowzy, filthy, frowsy, frowzy, grubby, scurvy, shabby, sleazy 7 ignoble, lowdown, squalid, unclean 8 degraded, shameful, wretched 9 loathsome, mercenary 10 despicable, scandalous, slatternly 11 disgraceful 12 contemptible, disreputable 13 reprehensible

sore 3 raw 4 achy, boil 5 angry, irked, ulcer, upset, vexed 6 aching, bitter, canker, peeved, tender 7 abscess, chancre, hurting, painful 8 inflamed, smarting 9 chilblain, irritated, rancorous, resentful, sensitive 10 affliction

sorehead 4 crab 5 grump 6 griper, grouch 7 grouser 8 grumbler, sourpuss 10 bellyacher, complainer, crosspatch, malcontent

sorrel 3 oca 4 dock 8 chestnut, sourwood

sorrow 3 rue, sob, woe 4 moan, ruth 5 dolor, grief, mourn 6 grieve, lament, misery, regret 7 anguish, remorse, sadness 8 distress, grieving, mourning 9 dejection, heartache, suffering 10 affliction, heartbreak, melancholy 11 lamentation, unhappiness 12 mournfulness

sorrowful 3 sad 6 rueful, triste, woeful 7 doleful, forlorn, piteous, ruthful, unhappy 8 dolorous, downcast, grieving, mournful, tristful, wretched 9 afflicted, miserable, plaintive, woebegone 10 lamentable, lugubrious, melancholy 11 heartbroken 12 disconsolate

sorry 3 bad, sad 4 mean, poor 5 cheap 6 cheesy, paltry, scummy, scurvy, shabby, shoddy 7 scruffy, unhappy 8 beggarly, contrite, mournful, penitent, pitiable, saddened, trifling, wretched 9 miserable, regretful, repentant 10 apologetic, despicable, inadequate, melancholy, remorseful **11** disgraceful, penitential **12** contemptible, heavyhearted

sort 3 ilk, lot, set **4** comb, cull, kind, pick, sift, type **5** class, order **6** choose, screen, select, stripe, winnow **7** arrange, catalog, species, variety **8** classify, separate **9** catalogue, character **10** categorize, pigeonhole

sortie 4 dash, raid **5** foray, sally **7** assault, mission **9** excursion **10** expedition

sortilege 6 augury **7** sorcery **8** divining, witchery **10** divination, necromancy, witchcraft **11** thaumaturgy

so-so 4 fair, okay **6** decent, enough, fairly, medium, rather **7** average, fairish **8** adequate, mediocre, middling, moderate, passable, passably **9** tolerably **10** moderately **11** indifferent **12** run-of-the-mill

sot 4 lush, wino **5** drunk, souse **6** bibber, boozer **7** guzzler, tippler, tosspot **8** drunkard **9** alcoholic, inebriate **10** boozehound

sotto voce 3 low **5** aside **6** softly **7** faintly, mutedly, quietly **9** privately

souchong 3 tea

sough 4 sigh **7** suspire, whisper

soul 4 pith **5** anima, being, heart, stuff **6** animus, breast, marrow, pneuma, psyche, spirit **7** essence **8** élan vital, substance **10** conscience, vital force **12** quintessence *combining form:* **5** psych **6** psycho

soulful 6 moving, tender **7** emotive, fervent **8** poignant, stirring, touching **9** affecting, emotional **11** impassioned, sentimental

soul singer 4 Gaye (Marvin) **5** Bland (Bobby), Brown (James), Cooke (Sam), Flack (Roberta), Green (Al), Hayes (Isaac) **6** Butler (Jerry), Knight (Gladys), Sledge (Percy) **7** Charles (Ray), Pickett (Wilson), Redding (Otis) **8** Franklin (Aretha), Mayfield (Curtis)

sound 3 fit **4** firm, hale, kyle, safe, sane **5** audio, legit, noise, plumb, probe, right, sober, solid, valid, whole **6** cogent, fathom, intact, secure, stable, sturdy, unhurt **7** correct, earshot, healthy, logical, prudent **8** rational, reliable, sensible, unharmed **9** judicious, resonance, undamaged, vibration, wholesome **10** convincing, reasonable **11** wellfounded **12** satisfactory, well-grounded **13** reverberation *combining form:* **3** son **4** phon, soni, sono **5** audio, audit, phone, phono, phony **6** audito, phonia *gentle:* **6** rustle *high-pitched:* **4** ping, ting *pleasant:* **7** euphony *quality:* **6** timbre *repeating:* **7** rat-a-tat **8** rataplan **10** rat-a-tat-tat *science:* **6** sonics **7** phonics **9** acoustics

Sound *Alaska:* **5** Cross *Antarctica:* **7** McMurdo *Australia:* **4** King **5** Broad *Bahamas:* **5** Exuma *Canada:* **4** Howe **6** Nansen *Connecticut-New York:* **10** Long Island *English Channel:* **8** Plymouth *Georgia:* **8** Altamaha *Greenland:* **5** Smith *Gulf of Mexico:* **8** Suwannee **11** Mississippi *Massachusetts:* **8** Vineyard **9** Nantucket *New England:* **11** Block Island *North Carolina:* **4** Core **5** Bogue **7** Pamlico, Roanoke **9** Albemarle, Currituck *Northwest Territories:* **4** Peel **8** Melville **9** Lancaster **12** Prince Albert *Norwegian Sea:* **8** Scoresby *Ontario:* **4** Owen *Scotland:* **3** Hoy **4** Jura, Mull **5** Inner *Spitsbergen:* **4** Bell *Washington:* **5** Puget

Sound and the Fury, The *author:* **8** Faulkner (William) *character:* **5** Benjy (Compson), Caddy (Compson), Jason (Compson) **6** Dilsey **7** Quentin (Compson)

soundness 6 health, sanity **7** balance **8** lucidity, prudence, security, solidity, strength **9** integrity, stability **11** reliability **12** practicality

sound off 7 speak up **8** speak out

soup *beet:* **6** borsch **7** borscht *bowl:* **6** tureen *clear:* **5** broth **8** bouillon, consommé, julienne *cold:* **8** gazpacho **11** vichyssoise *curry:* **12** mulligatawny *okra:* **5** gumbo *seafood:* **7** chowder *soy:* **4** miso *thick:* **6** gumbo, puree **6** bisque, burgoo, potage *vegetable:* **10** minestrone

soupçon see **particle**

soupy 5 foggy, gooey, gushy, murky, mushy **6** drippy, slushy, smoggy **7** cloying, maudlin, mawkish **8** cornball **9** schmaltzy **10** saccharine **11** sentimental, tear-jerking

sour 4 acid, dour, tart **5** acerb, acrid, tangy, testy **6** acidic, bitter, crabby, cranky, curdle, grumpy, morose, rancid, rotten, sullen, turned **7** acerbic, grouchy, peevish, prickly, spoiled, unhappy **8** embitter, vinegary **9** acidulous, fermented **12** disagreeable

source 4 font, root, well **5** basis, cause, fount, model, onset, start **6** mother, origin, spring **7** dawning, genesis **8** begetter, fountain, wellhead **9** beginning, inception, informant, precursor, prototype, reference, rootstock **10** antecedent, authorship, birthplace, derivation, originator, progenitor, provenance, wellspring **11** origination, provenience **12** fountainhead

sourness 7 acidity **8** acerbity, asperity

sourpuss 4 crab **5** crank, grump **6** griper, grouch **7** grouser, killjoy **8** grumbler, sorehead **10** bellyacher, complainer, crosspatch, curmudgeon **11** misanthrope

souse 3 dip, sop, sot **4** lush, soak, wino **5**

binge, drown, steep **6** boozer, drench, pickle, plunge, seethe **7** immerse **8** drunkard, inundate, marinate, preserve, saturate, submerge, submerse **9** alcoholic, immersion, inebriate **10** boozehound, intoxicate **11** dipsomaniac

soused 3 lit **4** high **5** drunk, lit up, oiled **6** bashed, blotto, bombed, juiced, potted, soaked, soused, stewed, stoned, tanked, wasted, zonked **7** crocked, drunken, pickled, pie-eyed, sloshed, smashed, sottish **8** polluted **9** plastered **10** inebriated, liquored up **11** intoxicated

south *combining form:* **5** austr **6** austro *French:* **3** sud *Spanish:* **3** sur

South Africa *capital:* **8** Cape Town, Pretoria **12** Bloemfontein *city:* **6** Durban **12** Johannesburg *desert:* **8** Kalahari *enclave:* **7** Lesotho *grassland:* **4** veld **5** veldt *language:* **5** Bantu **7** English **9** Afrikaans *monetary unit:* **4** rand *mountain range:* **11** Drakensberg *native:* **3** San **4** Khoi, Zulu **5** Pondo, Sotho, Swazi, Venda, Xhosa **6** Tswana **7** Bushmen, Khoisan **9** Hottentot *neighbor:* **7** Namibia **8** Botswana **9** Swaziland **10** Mozambique, Zimbabwe *plateau:* **5** Karoo **6** Karroo *province:* **7** Gauteng **8** Northern **9** Free State **10** Mpumalanga *river:* **6** Molopo, Orange *settlers:* **5** Boers

South America *country:* **4** Peru **5** Chile **6** Brazil, Guyana **7** Bolivia, Ecuador, Uruguay **8** Colombia, Paraguay, Suriname **9** Argentina, Venezuela *ethnic group:* **6** Aymara, Creole, Indian **7** mestizo, mulatto, Quechua, Spanish **10** Amerindian, Portuguese *language:* **6** Aymara **7** Guaraní, Quechua, Spanish **10** Portuguese

South Carolina *capital:* **8** Columbia *city:* **10** Charleston, Greenville *college, university:* **7** Citadel, Clemson *fort:* **6** Sumter *island, island group:* **3** Sea **6** Edisto, Parris **10** Hilton Head *nickname:* **6** Palmetto (State) *river:* **6** Edisto, Pee Dee, Santee **7** Tugaloo **8** Savannah *state bird:* **12** Carolina wren *state flower:* **13** yellow jasmine *state tree:* **8** palmetto

South Dakota *capital:* **6** Pierre *city:* **9** Rapid City **10** Sioux Falls *mountain:* **6** Harney (Peak) **8** Rushmore **10** Black Hills *nickname:* **6** Coyote (State) **10** Mt. Rushmore (State) *park:* **8** Badlands, Wind Cave *river:* **8** Missouri **11** Belle Forche *state bird:* **18** ring-necked pheasant *state flower:* **12** pasqueflower *state tree:* **6** spruce

southerly 7 austral

South Korea see **Korea, South**

southpaw 5 lefty

South-West Africa 7 Namibia

south wind see at **wind**

souvenir 5 relic, token **6** trophy **7** memento **8** keepsake, memorial, reminder **11** remembrance

sovereign 4 coin, czar, free, king, tsar **5** queen, regal, royal, ruler **6** kingly, ruling **7** emperor, empress, highest, monarch, regnant, supreme **8** absolute, autarkic, autocrat, dominant, imperial, kinglike, majestic **9** ascendant, autarchic, monarchal, number one, paramount, potentate **10** autonomous, monarchial **11** independent, monarchical, predominant **12** self-governed

soviet 7 council **9** committee

Soviet Union 4 CCCP, USSR

sow 4 seed, toss **5** drill, fling, plant, strew **7** bestrew, scatter **9** broadcast **11** disseminate

soybean paste 4 miso

spa 5 baths, hydro, wells **6** hot tub, resort, spring, waters **7** springs **13** watering place *Czech:* **6** Bilina **8** Karlsbad *English:* **4** Bath **6** Buxton **9** Harrogate *French:* **3** Dax **5** Evian *German:* **3** Ems **5** Baden **6** Bad Ems **9** Kissingen

space 3 gap **4** area, room **5** blank, ether, plena (plural), scope **6** cavity, extent, plenum, spread, volume **7** breadth, expanse, stretch **8** capacity, distance, interval, universe **9** amplitude, expansion

spaced-out 4 high **5** doped **6** stoned, zonked **7** drugged **8** hopped-up, turned on

space station 3 Mir **6** Salyut, Skylab

spacious 3 big **4** vast, wide **5** ample, large, roomy **7** immense **8** enormous, extended **9** boundless, capacious, cavernous, expansive, extensive **10** commodious, voluminous

spade 3 dig, loy **4** grub **5** dig up, scoop **6** dig out, shovel **8** excavate

Spade, Sam 4 dick **6** shamus, sleuth **7** gumshoe **9** detective **10** private eye *creator:* **7** Hammett (Dashiell) *novel:* **13** Maltese Falcon (The)

Spain *ancient name:* **8** Hispania *capital:* **6** Madrid *city:* **6** Málaga **7** Seville **8** Pamplona, Valencia, Zaragoza **9** Barcelona, Saragossa *island group:* **6** Canary **8** Balearic *king:* **10** Juan Carlos *leader:* **6** Franco (Francisco) *monetary unit:* **4** euro *monetary unit, former:* **4** real **6** peseta *mountain:* **8** Mulhacén **11** Pico de Aneto *mountain range:* **8** Pyrenees *neighbor:* **6** France **8** Portugal *peninsula:* **7** Iberian *region:* **6** Aragon, Murcia **7** Galicia **8** Valencia **9** Andalusia, Catalonia *river:* **4** Ebro **12**

Guadalquivir *sea:* **13** Mediterranean *strait:* **9** Gibraltar

spall 4 chip **5** flake **7** shaving **8** fragment **9** exfoliate

span 4 arch, term, time **5** cross, reach **6** extent, length, period, spread **7** compass, measure, stretch **8** duration, interval, lifetime, straddle, traverse

spangle 4 trim **5** flash, gleam **6** sequin **7** glitter, shimmer, sparkle, twinkle **9** coruscate **11** scintillate

Spaniard 9 Castilian

Spanish *aunt:* **3** tia *bay:* **5** bahia *bed:* **4** cama **5** lecho *bird:* **6** pájaro *boss:* **7** cacique *bread:* **3** pan *bridge:* **6** puente *bull:* **4** toro **6** el toro *chaperone:* **6** duenna *church:* **7** iglesia *combining form:* **7** hispano *crossword puzzle:* **10** crucigrama *dance:* **4** jota **5** baile, salsa **6** bailar **8** fandango, flamenco **9** zapateado *devil:* **6** diablo *dictator:* **8** caudillo *door:* **6** puerta *dress:* **7** vestido *folksong:* **6** tonada *fortress:* **7** alcazar *game:* **5** juego *garrison:* **8** presidio *gift:* **6** regalo *gold:* **3** oro *good-bye:* **5** adiós *hello:* **4** hola *hors d'oeuvre:* **4** tapa *house:* **4** casa *husband:* **6** esposo, marido *ice cream:* **6** helado *inn:* **6** posada *journey:* **5** viaje *library:* **10** biblioteca *light:* **3** luz *mayor:* **7** alcalde *milk:* **5** leche *money:* **5** plata **6** dinero *movie:* **8** pelicula *movies:* **4** cine *number:* **3** dos, uno **4** diez, doce, ocho, once, seis, tres **5** cinco, nueve, siete **6** cuatro *national hero:* **3** Cid (El) **5** El Cid *nobleman:* **7** grandee *operetta:* **8** zarzuela *penal settlement:* **8** presidio *plain:* **4** vega **5** llano, pampa *plantation:* **8** hacienda *please:* **8** por favor *princess:* **7** infanta *ranch:* **5** finca **8** estancia *river:* **3** rio *room:* **4** sala **6** cuarto *saint:* **7** Dominic **8** Ignatius *sale:* **5** venta *scarf:* **7** pañuelo **8** mantilla *school:* **7** colegio, escuela *shawl:* **6** rebozo, serape *shirt:* **6** camisa *shoe:* **6** zapato **7** calzado *singer:* **8** cantante *skirt:* **5** falda *soccer:* **6** fútbol *street:* **5** calle *thank you:* **7** gracias *title:* **3** don, Sra. **4** doña, Srta. **5** señor **6** señora **8** señorita *tree:* **5** árbol *trousers:* **10** pantalones *uncle:* **3** tío *wife:* **6** esposa *wine:* **4** sack **6** sherry

Spanish fly 9 cantharis

spank 4 cane, flog, lash, slap **5** smack **6** larrup, paddle, punish, thrash **7** scourge **8** chastise

spar 3 box, vic **4** pole **5** joust, sprit, stall **7** dispute, wrangle **8** longeron *ship's:* **4** boom, gaff, mast, yard **7** yardarm **8** bowsprit

spare 4 lank, lean, pity, save, slim **5** avoid, extra, gaunt, lanky **6** backup, excess, excuse, exempt, let off, meager, meagre, par-

don, scanty, scrape, scrimp, skimpy, skinny, slight, unused **7** absolve, relieve, reserve, scrawny, scrimpy, surplus **8** leftover **10** additional **11** superfluous

sparing 4 bare, wary **5** canny, chary, tight **6** frugal, meager, meagre, saving, stingy **7** prudent, thrifty **9** provident **10** economical, restrained, unwasteful **11** tightfisted **12** parsimonious

spark 3 woo **5** court, ember, glint **6** foment, incite, kindle, set off **7** provoke, trigger **8** activate, touch off **9** instigate, scintilla

sparkle 4 zing **5** flash, gleam, glint, verve **7** glimmer, glisten, glitter, shimmer, twinkle **8** vivacity **9** animation, coruscate **10** effervesce, liveliness **11** coruscation, scintillate **13** scintillation

sparkling 6 bubbly, lively **8** animated, bubbling **9** brilliant **12** effervescent

Spark novel 11 Memento Mori **21** Prime of Miss Jean Brodie (The)

sparse 4 rare, thin **5** scant **6** meager, meagre, scanty, scarce, skimpy **7** limited, scrimpy **8** exiguous, sporadic, uncommon **9** dispersed, scattered **10** inadequate, infrequent, occasional **12** insufficient

Sparta 10 Lacedaemon *country:* **7** Laconia *king:* **8** Leonidas, Menelaos *opponent:* **6** Athens *queen:* **4** Leda

Spartacus *author:* **4** Fast (Howard) *slayer:* **7** Crassus

spasm 3 fit, tic **4** pang **5** burst, crick, throe **6** twitch **8** paroxysm **10** convulsion *muscular:* **6** clonus

spasmodic 5 jerky **6** fitful, spotty **7** erratic **8** sporadic **9** desultory, excitable **10** convulsive **12** intermittent

spat 3 row **4** flap, miff, tiff **5** fight, scene, scrap **6** bicker, gaiter, hassle, oyster **7** brabble, dispute, fall out, quarrel, rhubarb, wrangle **8** argument, outburst, squabble **10** falling-out **11** altercation

spate 4 flow, flux, gush, pour, rain, rush, tide **5** flood, river, spurt, surge **6** deluge, series, shower, stream **7** current, freshet, torrent **8** cataract, outburst, overflow **10** inundation, outpouring

spatter 4 slop, slur, spit **5** douse, fleck, plash, slosh, smear, spray, spurt, swash **6** befoul, defame, malign, splash, splosh, vilify **7** asperse, blacken, handful, slander, speckle, splurge, stipple, traduce **8** besmirch, sprinkle **9** denigrate, disparage

spawn 4 eggs, sire **5** beget, breed, brood, hatch, issue **6** create, father, parent **7** produce, product, progeny, provoke **8** engender, generate **9** offspring, originate, procreate, propagate, reproduce, stimulate

speak 3 gab, jaw, say, yak **4** blab, chat, chin, talk **5** blurt, drawl, mouth, orate, spiel, spout, utter, voice **6** assert, convey, intone, mumble, murmur, mutter, parley **7** address, declaim, declare, lecture, phonate, whisper **8** converse, dilate on, perorate, vocalize **9** discourse, enunciate, expatiate, hold forth, verbalize *combining form:* **4** phon *confusedly:* **7** stammer, stutter **8** splutter *for:* **7** testify

speaker 5 voice **6** orator **9** spokesman **10** mouthpiece **12** spokesperson

spear 3 gig **4** pike, spit **5** gouge, lance, spike **6** impale, pierce, skewer **7** assagai, assegai, harpoon, leister, trident **8** puncture, transfix **9** penetrate

spearhead 4 lead **5** front **6** direct

spear-thrower 6 atlatl **7** woomera

special 4 rare **6** unique **7** express, notable, unusual **8** peculiar, uncommon **10** designated, individual, noteworthy, particular **11** distinctive, exceptional, outstanding

species 4 kind, sort, type **5** breed, class, order

specific 3 set **5** exact **6** strict, unique **7** express, limited, precise, special **8** clean-cut, clear-cut, definite, distinct, especial, explicit **10** individual, particular **11** categorical, unambiguous

specify 3 fix, set **4** cite, list, name **6** detail **7** itemize, mention, pin down, tick off **8** instance, spell out **9** determine, enumerate, establish, inventory, stipulate **13** particularize

specimen 4 case, sort, type **6** sample **7** example, neotype, variety **8** exemplar, holotype, instance, sampling **12** illustration

specious 5 empty, false **6** hollow **8** spurious **9** casuistic, plausible, sophistic **10** misleading, ostensible **11** sophistical

speciousness 7 sophism **9** casuistry, sophistry

speck 3 bit, dot, jot **4** atom, iota, mite, mote, spot, tick, whit **5** crumb, fleck, grain, point, shred, trace **7** freckle, smidgen **8** molecule, particle, pinpoint

speckle 3 dot **4** spot **5** flake, fleck **6** dapple, pepper **7** stipple **8** sprinkle

spectacle 4 pomp, show **5** drama, sight **6** parade **7** display, pageant, panoply, tableau **10** exhibition, exposition **12** extravaganza

spectacular 5 stagy **7** amazing, pageant **8** dazzling, dramatic, striking, wondrous **9** marvelous, thrilling, wonderful **10** astounding, eye-popping, histrionic, miraculous,

phenomenal, prodigious, staggering, stupefying, stupendous, theatrical **11** astonishing, sensational **12** extravaganza

spectator 5 gazer **6** viewer **7** watcher, witness **8** beholder, observer, onlooker **9** bystander **10** eyewitness

Spectator author 6 Steele (Richard) **7** Addison (Joseph)

specter 5 ghost, shade **6** shadow, spirit, wraith **7** eidolon, phantom **8** phantasm, revenant, visitant **10** apparition

spectral 6 spooky **7** ghastly, ghostly, phantom **9** ghostlike, unearthly **10** shadowlike **11** disembodied, phantomlike

spectrum 5 ambit, gamut, range, scale, sweep **7** compass **8** diapason **9** continuum *producer:* **5** prism

speculate 4 muse **5** study, think, weigh **6** ponder, reason, review, wonder **7** reflect **8** cogitate, consider, meditate, ruminate, theorize **9** cerebrate **10** conjecture, deliberate **11** contemplate

speculation 5 guess, hunch **6** gamble, review, theory **7** surmise **9** brainwork **10** conjecture

speculative 5 risky **7** curious, pensive **8** academic **10** thoughtful **11** conjectural, theoretical **12** hypothetical

speech 4 talk **5** idiom, spiel, voice **6** debate, homily, parley, sermon, tirade, tongue **7** address, dialect, diction, lecture, monolog, oration, palaver **8** dialogue, diatribe, harangue, language, parlance, rhetoric **9** discourse, monologue, utterance **10** allocution, expression, vernacular **11** declamation **12** articulation, disquisition, vocalization **13** verbalization *defect:* **4** lisp **7** stutter

speechcraft 7 oratory **8** rhetoric **9** elocution

speechless 3 mum **4** dumb, mute **6** silent **7** aphonic **10** dumbstruck, tongue-tied

speed 3 fly, hie, run, zip **4** clip, gait, pace, race, rush, tear, whiz **5** chase, haste, hurry, tempo **6** barrel, burn up, career, hasten, hustle, whoosh **7** quicken **8** alacrity, celerity, dispatch, expedite, highball, legerity, momentum, rapidity, velocity **9** fleetness, quickness, swiftness **10** accelerate, cannonball, facilitate, promptness

speed skater see **ice skater**

speedway 5 track **8** turnpike **9** racetrack **10** racecourse

speedy 4 fast **5** brisk, fleet, hasty, quick, rapid, swift **6** nimble, prompt **8** headlong **9** breakneck **11** expeditious

spell 3 hex **4** bout, jinx, mojo, rune, time, tour, turn **5** charm, hitch, shift, stint, throe, while **6** attack, period, streak, voodoo **7** relieve, stretch **11** conjuration, incantation

spellbind 3 hex **4** grip, vamp **5** charm **7** bewitch, catch up, enchant **8** enthrall, entrance **9** enrapture, fascinate, hypnotize, mesmerize

spelling 11 orthography *bad:* **10** cacography

spell out 7 clarify, explain, expound **8** construe, set forth **9** elucidate, explicate, interpret

spelunker 5 caver

spend 3 pay **4** blow, drop, pass **5** use up, waste **6** lavish, lay out, outlay **7** consume, exhaust, fork out, hand out, splurge **8** disburse, shell out, squander **9** dissipate, go through, throw away, while away **10** contribute, run through

spender 7 wastrel **8** prodigal **10** high roller, profligate, squanderer **11** scattergood

spendthrift see **spender**

Spenser poem 11 Faerie Queen (The)

spent 4 shot **5** all in **6** effete, pooped, used-up, wasted **7** drained, worn-out **8** burnt out, consumed, depleted, washed-up **9** exhausted, washed-out

spew 4 gush, ooze **5** belch, eject, eruct, erupt, expel, exude, flood, heave, shoot, spray, vomit **6** irrupt, spit up, squirt **7** throw up, upchuck **8** disgorge

sphagnum 4 moss

sphere 3 orb **4** area, ball, star, turf, zone **5** arena, field, globe, range, realm, round, scope **6** circle, domain, planet **7** demesne, rondure, terrain **8** dominion, province **9** bailiwick, territory **12** jurisdiction

spherical 5 round **6** global **7** globose **8** globular **9** orbicular

Sphinx *builder:* **6** Khafre *father:* **6** Typhon *mother:* **7** Echidna *query:* **6** riddle *site:* **4** Giza **6** Thebes

spice 3 pep, zip **4** kick, mace, tang, zest **5** anise, aroma, clove, cumin, poppy, savor, scent, smack, smell, taste **6** cloves, fennel, ginger, nutmeg, pepper, relish, sesame **7** bouquet, caraway, perfume **8** cardamom, cinnamon, piquancy **9** fragrance, redolence, seasoning

Spice Islands 8 Moluccas

spick-and-span 3 new **4** mint, neat, snug, tidy, trig, trim **5** clean, fresh **6** spruce **7** orderly **8** brand-new, spotless **9** shipshape **10** immaculate **11** well-groomed

spicy 3 hot **4** racy **5** bawdy, fiery, salty, tangy, zesty **6** lively, purple, ribald, risqué, savory, snappy, wicked **7** gingery, peppery, piquant, pungent, scented, zestful **8** aromatic, fragrant, off-color, perfumed, redolent, seasoned, spirited **9** flavorful, salacious **10** scandalous, suggestive **11** titillating

spider 6 Aranea, frypan **7** skillet **8** arachnid **9** frying pan **10** black widow

spiel 4 jive, line **5** pitch **6** patter **12** song and dance

Spielberg film 4 Hook, Jaws **6** Always, Munich **7** Amistad **8** Terminal (The) **9** Lost World (The) **11** Color Purple (The) **12** Jurassic Park, Twilight Zone (The) **14** Empire of the Sun, Minority Report, Schindler's List, War of the Worlds **15** Catch Me if You Can **16** Sugarland Express (The) **17** Saving Private Ryan **19** Raiders of the Lost Ark

spieler 4 tout **6** barker, hawker, talker **8** huckster

spigot 3 tap **4** cock, gate **5** valve **6** faucet **7** hydrant, petcock, shutoff **8** stopcock

spike 3 pin **4** brob, heel, lace, nail **5** lance, piton, spear **6** antler, impale, needle, skewer **7** spindle **8** increase, mackerel, puncture, transfix

spile 4 bung **5** spout

spill 4 blab, drip, drop, fall, flow, slop, tell **5** spray **6** betray, inform, reveal, splash, squeal, tattle **7** divulge, dribble, run over, spatter **8** disclose, overflow

Spillane detective 10 Mike Hammer

spilth 5 dregs, dross, swill, trash, waste **6** debris, refuse, scraps **7** garbage, rubbish **8** leavings

spin 4 gyre, reel, ride, swim, turn **5** dizzy, swirl, twirl, wheel, whirl **6** gyrate, rotate **7** revolve **8** rotation **9** pirouette, whirligig **10** revolution *a log:* **4** birl *out:* **4** draw **6** extend **7** prolong, stretch **8** elongate, lengthen, protract **10** prolongate

spinal column 5 chine **6** rachis *curvature:* **8** lordosis *part:* **8** vertebra (see also **spine**)

spindle 3 pin, rod **5** newel, shaft, spike **6** impale, rachis

spindly 5 frail, lanky, rangy, shaky, weedy **6** flimsy, gangly, skinny, twiggy, wobbly **7** fragile, rickety, tottery **8** gangling, skeletal, unsteady **9** emaciated **10** jerry-built

spine 4 back **6** rachis **7** spicule **8** backbone **9** vertebrae

spineless 5 timid **8** cowardly, timorous **9** weak-kneed **10** weak-willed **12** invertebrate

spin-off 8 offshoot **9** by-product, outgrowth **10** derivative, descendant

____ **Spinoza 6** Baruch

spinster 7 old maid **10** maiden lady

spiny 6 barbed, thorny **7** prickly **8** echinate **10** nettlesome

spiral 4 coil, curl, wind **5** helix, twine, twist **6** volute **7** helical, helices (plural) **8** gyroidal, volution **9** cochleate, corkscrew *combining form:* **3** gyr **4** gyro **5** helic **6** helico

spire 4 coil 5 twist, whorl 7 steeple 8 pinnacle

spirit 3 pep, vim, zip 4 brio, dash, élan, gimp, grit, guts, life, mood, snap, soul, zeal, zest, zing 5 anima, ardor, drive, force, heart, moxie, oomph, pluck, shade, spunk, tenor, verve, vigor 6 animus, daimon, energy, esprit, fervor, ginger, mettle, morale, pneuma, psyche, starch, temper, wraith 7 courage, passion, phantom, specter, spectre 8 phantasm, revenant, vitality 9 animation, élan vital, substance 10 apparition, enthusiasm, get-up-and-go, liveliness *away:* 6 abduct, kidnap, snatch *bottled:* 5 genie *evil:* 3 ker 4 aitu 5 afrit, demon 6 afreet 7 erlking, shaitan *female:* 5 nymph 7 banshee *Hopi:* 7 kachina *of a place:* 10 genius loci *Persian:* 4 peri

spirited 4 bold, game, keen 5 eager, fiery, peppy 6 ardent, gritty, lively, plucky, spunky 7 chipper, fervent, gingery, peppery, valiant, zealous 8 animated, cheerful, intrepid, resolute 9 audacious, dauntless, energetic, sprightly, vivacious 10 courageous, mettlesome, passionate 12 enthusiastic

spirits 5 booze, drink 6 liquor, tipple 9 aqua vitae, firewater *low:* 5 blues, dumps, ennui 8 doldrums 10 blue devils, depression, melancholy

spiritual 6 sacred 7 saintly 8 churchly, mystical, numinous, platonic 9 religious 10 high-minded, immaterial, unphysical 11 disembodied, incorporeal, nonmaterial, nonphysical 12 metaphysical, supernatural, transcendent

spiritualist 6 medium, mystic 7 psychic

spit 5 spear 6 impale, saliva, skewer, slaver, sputum 7 spatter, sputter 8 splutter 9 brochette 11 expectorate

spite 5 venom 6 grudge, malice, rancor, spleen 7 ill will, revenge 9 pettiness, vengeance 11 malevolence 13 maliciousness

spiteful 4 mean 5 catty, nasty, snide 6 malign, wicked 7 vicious, waspish 8 venomous 9 malicious, malignant, rancorous 10 malevolent, vindictive

spitfire 4 fury 5 harpy, shrew, vixen 6 dragon, virago 7 hellcat, tigress 8 fishwife, harridan 9 termagant

spitting image 4 twin 5 clone 6 double, ringer 9 duplicate 10 carbon copy, dead ringer, simulacrum

spittoon 8 cuspidor

splash 3 sop, wet 4 slop, soak 5 douse, slosh, spray, swash 6 drench 7 spatter 8 sprinkle

splashy 5 gaudy, jazzy, showy 6 flashy, garish, glitzy, tawdry 7 blatant, dashing 8 colorful, dazzling, striking 10 flamboyant, theatrical 11 sensational 12 meretricious, ostentatious

splatter 4 slop 5 douse, plash, slosh, spray, swash 6 splash 8 sprinkle

splay 4 cant, tilt 5 angle, bevel, gawky, slant, slope 6 clumsy, extend, spread 7 awkward, incline 8 ungainly 9 expansion 11 inclination

spleen see **spite**

splendid 4 fine 5 grand, showy 6 superb 7 elegant, shining 8 glorious, gorgeous 9 brilliant, excellent, marvelous, wonderful 10 first-class, impressive 11 illustrious, magnificent, outstanding 12 transcendent

splendor 4 pomp 5 glory 6 dazzle 7 panoply 8 grandeur, richness 9 pageantry, spectacle 10 brilliance, brilliancy 12 magnificence

splenetic 5 cross, surly 6 fuming 8 incensed, spiteful 9 malicious 10 ill-natured, malevolent 11 ill-tempered

splice 3 tie 4 join, mate, mesh 5 braid, graft, plait, unite

splint 5 brace, strip 7 support 10 immobilize

splinter 4 rive 5 burst, smash 6 shiver, sliver 7 faction, shatter 8 fragment 12 disintegrate

split 3 rip 4 part, rend, rent, rift, rima, rime, rive, tear 5 break, carve, chasm, chink, cleft, crack, sever, slice 6 breach, cleave, cloven, divide, schism, sunder 7 break up, disjoin, dissect, diverge, divorce, divvy up, fission, fissure, rupture 8 cleavage, dissever, fracture, separate 11 dichotomize *combining form:* 5 schiz 6 schizo 7 schisto

splotch 4 blob, blot, spot 5 fleck, stain 6 smudge

splurge 4 orgy 5 binge, fling, spree 7 blowout, rampage 10 indulgence 12 extravagance

splutter 4 spit 6 babble, jabber 7 stammer

spoil 3 mar, rob, rot 4 baby, harm, prey, ruin, sack 5 decay, humor, taint, waste, wreck 6 coddle, cosset, curdle, damage, defile, impair, molder, pamper, ravish 7 blemish, cater to, destroy, indulge, pillage, putrefy, tarnish, vitiate 8 demolish 9 break down, decompose 11 mollycoddle

spoiled 4 rank, sour 6 putrid, rancid, rotten, ruined 7 coddled, decayed, gone bad 8 impaired, indulged, pampered 9 indulgent

spoils 4 haul, loot, swag 5 booty 7 pillage, plunder

spoilsport 7 killjoy

spoken 4 oral, said, told 6 verbal, voiced 7 uttered 8 phonetic, viva voce 9 delivered, unwritten 11 articulated

sponge 4 grub 5 cadge, leech, mooch 6 absorb, loofah **7** moocher **8** freeload, parasite, scrounge **10** freeloader *material:* **8** mesoglea *opening:* **6** oscula (plural) **7** osculum, ostiole

sponger 5 leech **7** moocher **8** parasite **10** freeloader

spongy 4 soft **5** mushy, pulpy **6** porous, quaggy **7** squashy, squishy **9** absorbent

sponsor 4 back, fund **5** angel, stake **6** backer, patron, surety **7** endorse, finance **8** advocate, bankroll, champion, Maecenas, mainstay, promoter, vouch for **9** grubstake, guarantee, guarantor, patronize, subsidize, supporter **10** benefactor, underwrite **11** underwriter

sponsorship 5 aegis **7** backing, support **8** advocacy, auspices **9** patronage

spontaneous 5 ad-lib **7** natural, offhand **8** ad-libbed, unforced **9** automatic, extempore, impromptu, impulsive, unstudied **10** improvised, off-the-cuff, unprompted **11** instinctive, unmeditated **13** unconstrained

spontoon 4 pike **5** lance, spear

spoof 4 sham **5** farce, put-on **6** parody, satire, send-up **7** lampoon, takeoff **8** travesty

spook 3 spy **5** agent, alarm, ghost, haunt, scare **7** specter, spectre, startle, terrify **8** frighten

spooky 5 eerie, weird **6** creepy **7** ghostly, ominous, uncanny **8** eldritch **9** unearthly

spool 4 reel, wind **6** bobbin

spoon 3 pet, woo **4** neck **5** court, ladle, scoop **6** cuddle

spoonbill 4 ibis **8** shoveler **9** ruddy duck **10** paddlefish

Spoon River poet 7 Masters (Edgar Lee)

spoony 5 mushy, silly **6** simple, slushy, syrupy **7** fatuous, foolish, mawkish, smitten, witless **9** schmaltzy **10** saccharine **11** sentimental

spoor 5 scent, trace, track, tract, trail **7** vestige **8** footstep **9** droppings, footprint

sporadic 4 rare **6** catchy, fitful, random, scarce, sparse, spotty **7** erratic **8** episodic, isolated, uncommon **9** desultory, irregular, scattered, spasmodic **10** infrequent, occasional

sport 3 fun **4** game, jest, joke, mock, play **6** frolic, racing, trifle **7** mockery, show off **9** diversion, high jinks, horseplay **10** recreation *indoor:* **6** boxing, hockey, squash **7** bowling **8** handball **9** wrestling **10** acrobatics, basketball, gymnastics **11** racquetball, table tennis *Olympic:* **4** judo **6** boxing, diving, hockey, rowing **7** archery, cycling, fencing, shot put **8** canoeing, football, high jump, long jump, marathon, shooting,

swimming, yachting **9** decathlon, pole vault, water polo, wrestling **10** basketball, gymnastics, pentathlon, triple jump, volleyball **11** discus throw, hammer throw **12** javelin throw, steeplechase **13** weightlifting *water:* **6** diving, rowing **7** sailing, surfing **8** canoeing, swimming, yachting *winter:* **4** luge **6** hockey, skiing **7** curling, lugeing, skating **8** biathlon, sledding **10** ski jumping **11** bobsledding, tobogganing

sporting house 6 bagnio **7** brothel **8** bordello

sportive 5 antic **6** frisky, impish **7** playful, roguish, waggish **10** frolicsome **11** mischievous

sportiveness 7 devilry, roguery, waggery **8** deviltry, mischief **9** devilment, rascality

sporty 4 fast **5** peppy **6** breezy, casual, jaunty, lively **7** dashing, relaxed **8** debonair, informal **10** insouciant **11** streamlined

spot 3 fix, jam, nip, pip, see **4** espy, post, site **5** fleck, hit on, locus, place, point, speck **6** blotch, detect, pickle, plight, scrape **7** dilemma, smidgen, spatter, speckle **8** diagnose, flyspeck, identify, location, pinpoint, position **9** recognize, situation **11** predicament

spotless 4 pure **5** clean **6** chaste **8** hygienic, sanitary, unsoiled **9** undefiled, unstained, unsullied **10** immaculate **11** unblemished

spotlight 5 focus **6** notice **7** feature, point up **8** interest, point out **9** attention, emphasize, public eye, publicity **10** illuminate **12** illumination

spotted 4 seen **6** calico, motley **7** brindle, dappled, flecked, piebald **8** brindled, speckled, stippled

spouse 4 mate, wife **5** bride, groom, hubby **7** consort, husband

spout 3 jet **4** gush **5** chute, eject, spray, spurt **6** nozzle, squirt

sprain 4 pull, tear, turn **5** twist **6** wrench **7** stretch

sprawl 4 flop, loll **5** drape, slump **6** extend, lounge, slouch, spread **7** stretch **11** spread-eagle

spray 3 fog **4** hose, mist **6** shower, spritz **7** aerosol, atomize, diffuse, spatter **8** atomizer, droplets, fumigate, nebulize **9** spindrift

spread 3 jam, lay, set, sow, ted **4** deal, oleo, open, pâté, push **5** apply, feast, jelly, space, splay, strew, sweep **6** butter, expand, extend, fan out, pass on, retail **7** banquet, breadth, diffuse, expanse, overrun, pervade, radiate, scatter, slather, stretch, suffuse **8** bedcover, coverlet, dispense, disperse, mushroom, permeate **9** amplitude, broadcast, circulate, diffusion, dissipate, expansion, extension, profusion, propagate, radiation **10** dispersion, distribute, outstretch **11** counterpane, disseminate **12** transmission **13** proliferation

spree 3 jag **4** bash, bust, lark, orgy, riot, tear **5** binge, drunk, fling, revel **6** bender, frolic **7** blowout, carouse, rampage, splurge **8** carousal, wingding **10** indulgence **11** bacchanalia

sprig 4 brad, heir, twig **5** scion, shoot **7** pintail **9** ruddy duck

sprightly 3 gay **4** keen, spry, yare **5** agile, alert, antic, brisk, peppy, perky, zesty, zingy, zippy **6** active, breezy, chirpy, frisky, jaunty, lively, nimble **7** animate, chipper, coltish, piquant, playful, pungent **8** animated, cheerful, spirited, sportive **9** energetic, vivacious **10** frolicsome, rollicking

spring 3 hop **4** flow, free, jump, leap, lope, rise, root, skip, stem, trip, well **5** arise, begin, bound, cause, fount, issue, start **6** appear, bounce, emerge, hurdle, pounce, reason, source, uncoil, vernal **7** come out, emanate, proceed, rebound, startle **8** commence, fountain, stimulus, wellhead **9** originate **10** incitement, resilience **12** fountainhead *back:* **6** resile *mineral:* **3** spa

springe 4 trap **5** noose, snare **7** pitfall **9** booby trap

springlike 6 vernal

springy 6 supple **7** elastic **8** flexible, stretchy **9** recoiling, resilient

sprinkle 3 dot **4** rain, spot **5** shake, speck, spray, strew **6** pepper, powder, spritz **7** asperse, drizzle, freckle, scatter, speckle, stipple **9** bespeckle

sprint 3 run **4** dart, dash, race, shin, tear **5** scoot **6** gallop, hurtle, scurry **7** scamper

sprite 3 elf, fay, nix **4** puck **5** dryad, fairy, naiad, nixie, nymph, oread, pixie, sylph **6** kelpie **7** brownie **9** hamadryad, hobgoblin

spritz 3 jet **5** spray, spurt **6** shower, squirt

sprout 3 bud **4** grow **5** scion, shoot **6** ratoon, sucker **7** burgeon **8** offshoot **9** germinate

spruce 4 trim **5** natty, sassy, spiff **6** dapper, spiffy **11** well-groomed

spry 4 yare **5** agile, brisk, sound, zesty, zippy **6** active, lively, nimble, robust **7** healthy **8** animated, spirited, vigorous **9** energetic, vivacious

spud 5 tater **6** potato

____ **Spumante 4** Asti

spume 4 fizz, foam, head, scum, suds **5** froth, spray, yeast **6** lather

spunk 4 grit, guts **5** heart, moxie, nerve, pluck **6** mettle, spirit, tinder **7** cojones,

courage **8** backbone, gumption **9** fortitude, toughness **10** liveliness, resolution

spunky 4 bold **5** brave, fiery **6** daring **7** doughty, gingery, peppery **8** fearless, spirited **9** dauntless **10** courageous, mettlesome **12** high-spirited

spur 4 goad, prod, stir, urge **5** egg on, impel, prick, rally, rouse, spine **6** arouse, branch, exhort, motive, prompt, propel **7** impetus, impulse **8** buttress, catalyst, excitant, stimulus **9** actuation, incentive, instigate, stimulant, stimulate **10** incitement, inducement, motivation, projection *part:* **5** rowel

spurious 4 fake, mock, sham **5** bogus, dummy, false, phony, put-on **6** ersatz, pseudo **7** assumed, feigned, pretend **8** affected **9** brummagem, imitation, pinchbeck, pretended, simulated **10** apocryphal, artificial, substitute **11** counterfeit, make-believe **12** illegitimate *combining form:* **5** pseud **6** pseudo

spurn 4 snub **5** flout, scoff, scorn, scout, sneer **6** rebuff, refuse, reject **7** contemn, decline, despise, disdain, dismiss, repulse **8** turn down **9** disregard, reprobate, repudiate **10** disapprove **12** cold-shoulder

spurt 3 jet **4** gush, jump **5** burst, expel, spout, surge **6** shower, spritz, squirt **7** upsurge **8** eruption, increase **9** discharge

sputter 4 fizz, fume, rage, rant, rave, spew, spit **6** gibber, jabber **7** bluster, stammer

spy 5 agent, scout, snoop, spook **6** beagle, sleuth **7** gumshoe **8** informer, saboteur **9** detective **12** investigator **13** undercover man *name:* **4** Ames (Aldrich), Boyd (Belle) **5** André (John), Blunt (Anthony), Fuchs (Klaus) **6** Philby (Kim), Smiley (George) **7** Burgess (Guy), Hanssen (Robert), Maclean (Donald), Pollard (Jonathan) **8** Mata Hari

spyglass 9 telescope

spying 9 espionage

Spyri's heroine 5 Heidi

squab 5 couch **6** pigeon **7** cushion

squabble 3 row **4** miff, spat, tiff **5** argue **6** bicker, dustup **7** brabble, dispute, quarrel, wrangle

squad 4 crew, side, team, unit **5** cadre **6** detail, lineup, patrol

squalid 3 low **4** base, foul, mean, vile **5** dingy, dirty, nasty, seedy **6** filthy, frowsy, frowzy, grubby, scurvy, shabby, shoddy, sleazy, slummy, sordid **7** ignoble, lowdown, run-down, scrubby, unclean, unkempt **8** slovenly, wretched **10** despicable, disheveled **11** dilapidated **12** disreputable

squall 3 caw, row, yap, yip **4** bark, bawl, beef, feud, fuss, gust, howl, roar, tiff, wail, yawp, yell, yelp, yowl **5** brawl, fight, hoo-ha, shout **6** bellow, clamor, flurry, fracas, hubbub, ruckus, rumpus, scream, shriek, squeal, yammer **7** dispute, flare-up, quarrel, rhubarb, screech **8** brouhaha, squabble **9** bickering, caterwaul, commotion **10** falling-out, hullabaloo **11** altercation

squalor 5 filth **6** misery **7** neglect, poverty **8** baseness, iniquity **9** depravity, dirtiness **10** sordidness **11** degradation **12** wretchedness

squander 4 blow **5** spend, waste **7** consume, exhaust, fritter, scatter **9** dissipate, throw away **10** trifle away **11** fritter away

squanderer see **spender**

square 3 fit, fix **4** bang, boxy, even, fair, jibe, just, tied **5** adapt, agree, align, clear, equal, exact, match, pay up, plaza, sharp, spang, tally **6** accord, adjust, settle **7** balance, conform, satisfy, settled **8** check out, dovetail, orthodox, quadrate, smack-dab, straight, unbiased **9** equitable, liquidate, objective, quadratic, reconcile, rectangle

squash 3 jam **4** cram, mash, pepo, pulp **5** crush, gourd, press, quell **7** flatten, put down, squeeze, squelch **8** suppress *variety:* **5** acorn **6** cushaw, Sibley, turban **7** Hubbard, scallop **8** pattypan, zucchini **9** butternut, crookneck **10** Marblehead

squat 3 low **5** dumpy, hunch, stoop, stout, thick **6** chunky, crouch, hunker, stocky, stubby **8** heavyset, thickset **10** hunker down **11** thick-bodied

squawfish 4 chub **8** cyprinid **10** pikeminnow

squawk 3 caw, yap, yip **4** beef, crab, fuss, yawp **5** bleat, gripe **6** yammer **7** protest, screech **8** complain **9** bellyache, complaint

squeak 3 rat **4** blab, fink, peep, pipe, sing **5** cheep, creak **6** escape, inform, snitch, tattle **10** tattletale

squeal 3 rat, yip **4** blab, howl, sing, yell, yelp, yowl **5** bleat, creak, grate, gripe, peach **6** inform, screak, scream, shriek, shrill, snitch, squawk, tattle **7** protest, screech **8** complain **10** tattletale

squealer 3 rat **4** fink **6** canary, snitch, weasel **7** ratfink, stoolie, tattler, tipster **8** betrayer, informer **10** talebearer, tattletale **11** stool pigeon

squeamish 5 fussy, upset **6** queasy **7** finical, finicky **8** nauseous **9** nauseated **10** fastidious, particular, pernickety **11** persnickety

squeeze 3 hug, jam **4** bind, cram, grip, milk, pack, push **5** clasp, crowd, crush, exact, gouge, juice, pinch, press, screw, wring **6** clutch, coerce, compel, crunch, eke out, enfold, extort, jostle, squash, squish **7** dilemma, embrace, extract **8** compress,

contract, pressure, quandary **9** shake down **11** compression, predicament

squelch 5 quell, shush, sit on **6** muffle, muzzle, squash, squish, stifle, subdue **7** repress, silence, smother **8** strangle, suppress **10** extinguish

squib 4 fire **6** filler **7** lampoon **8** shoot off **9** detonator **11** firecracker

squid 7 mollusc, mollusk **8** calamari, calamary **10** cephalopod *kin:* **7** octopus **10** cuttlefish

squiggle 4 worm **6** doodle, scrawl, squirm, writhe **7** scratch **8** curlicue, scrabble, scribble

squinch 5 quail, start, wince **6** blench, crouch, recoil, shrink

squint 4 peek, peep, peer **10** hagioscope, strabismus

squire 6 attend, escort, lawyer **7** consort, gallant **8** cavalier, chaperon **9** accompany, landowner

squirm 4 worm **6** fidget, wiggle, writhe **7** wriggle

squirrel 4 stow **5** cache, hoard, stash **7** secrete *red:* **9** chickaree

squirt 3 jet, kid, pup, tot **4** brat, tyke **5** sprat, spray, spurt, twerp **6** shaver, shrimp, splurt, spritz **7** spatter

squish 3 jam **4** cram, mash, mush, pack, push **5** crush, press, quash, smash **7** flatten, scrunch, squeeze, squelch, trample

squishy 4 soft **6** flabby, quaggy, slushy, spongy

Sri Lanka *aborigine:* **5** Vedda *bay:* **6** Bengal *capital:* **7** Colombo *city:* **5** Kandy **8** Moratuwa *ethnic group:* **9** Sinhalese *former name:* **6** Ceylon *language:* **5** Tamil **9** Sinhalese *monetary unit:* **5** rupee *shoals:* **11** Adam's Bridge *strait:* **4** Palk

SRO 7 sellout

SS chief 7 Himmler (Heinrich)

S-shaped 7 sigmoid *arch, molding:* **4** ogee

stab 3 dig, pop, try **4** pang, poke, shot **5** crack, drive, fling, guess, prick, spear, stick, whack, whirl **6** effort, pierce, thrust, twinge **7** attempt **8** puncture **9** penetrate

Stabat ____ 5 Mater

stabile 6 steady **9** sculpture **10** stationary

stabilize 3 fix, set **4** prop **5** brace, poise **6** cement, firm up, fixate, prop up, secure, settle, steady **7** balance, ballast, support, sustain **8** solidify **9** reinforce

stable 3 set **4** barn, fast, firm, mews, safe, sure **5** fixed, solid, sound **6** secure, steady, sturdy **7** abiding, durable, lasting, staunch **8** balanced, constant, enduring, resolute **9** immutable, permanent, steadfast, unvarying

10 perdurable, stationary, unchanging, unshakable

stack 4 cock, heap, hill, load, mass, pile, pipe, rick **5** mound, sheaf **7** chimney, pyramid

stack up 3 add **5** equal, total **6** equate, gather **7** compare, measure

stadium 4 bowl, dome, rink, ring **5** arena **6** garden **8** coliseum **10** hippodrome **12** amphitheater *level:* **4** tier

staff 3 rod **4** cane, club, prop, rung, team, wand **5** baton, billy **6** cudgel **7** faculty, support **9** personnel *bishop's:* **7** crosier, crozier *medical:* **8** caduceus *of office:* **4** mace

stag 4 male, solo **5** alone

stage 3 lot **4** dais, play, rung, show, step **5** grade, level, mount, notch, phase, put on **6** degree, period, status **7** execute, perform, present, produce **8** platform *direction:* **4** exit **5** enter **6** exeunt *scenery:* **3** set **8** backdrop *show:* **4** play **5** drama, revue **7** musical **9** burlesque **10** vaudeville *signal:* **3** cue *whisper:* **5** aside

stage set 5 decor, scene **7** scenery **8** backdrop **11** mise-en-scène

stagger 4 daze, reel, stun, sway **5** amaze, floor, lurch, pitch, stump, waver, weave **6** boggle, careen, dither, falter, teeter, topple, totter, wobble, zigzag **7** astound, nonplus, perplex, shatter, stumble, stupefy **8** astonish, bowl over **9** dumbfound, overwhelm, vacillate **11** flabbergast

stagnant 5 musty, stale **6** static **8** immobile, unmoving **10** motionless, stationary

stagnate 4 idle **5** stall **6** fester **8** languish, stultify, vegetate

stagy 10 artificial, histrionic, theatrical **11** pretentious **12** melodramatic

staid 5 grave, sober **6** formal, sedate, solemn, somber, sombre, stuffy **7** earnest, serious, starchy **8** composed, decorous, priggish **9** dignified

stain 3 dye, tar **4** blot, daub, onus, slur, soil, spot **5** brand, color, odium, shame, smear, sully, taint, tinge **6** blotch, defile, embrue, imbrue, smirch, smudge, stigma **7** blemish, pigment, tarnish **8** besmirch, colorant, discolor, dishonor, dyestuff, tincture

staircase *handrail:* **8** banister **9** bannister *outdoor:* **6** perron *post:* **5** newel **8** baluster

stake 3 bet, lay, pot, set **4** ante, back, game, pale, play, post, risk **5** claim, put on, share, wager **6** gamble, paling, picket, pledge, tether **7** finance **8** bankroll, interest **10** capitalize, investment

stalag 7 POW camp **10** prison camp

stale 5 banal, dusty, faded, fusty, moldy, musty, passé, tired, trite **7** clichéd, tedious, worn-out **8** overused, shopworn, stagnant, timeworn **9** hackneyed, tasteless **11** commonplace, stereotyped

stalemate 3 tie **4** draw **7** impasse **8** deadlock, gridlock, standoff

stalk 4 hunt, prey **5** chase, track **6** ambush, follow, pursue, stride **8** flush out *flower:* **8** peduncle *leaf:* **7** petiole *short:* **5** stipe

stall 3 bay, pew **4** halt **5** booth, brake, check, delay, hedge, kiosk, stand **6** arrest, put off **7** conk out, counter, hold off **8** obstruct **9** stonewall **10** filibuster **11** compartment, prevaricate

stalwart 4 bold **5** brave, gutsy, hardy, husky, stout, tough **6** brawny, robust, sinewy, strong, sturdy **7** valiant **8** fearless, intrepid, unafraid, valorous, vigorous **9** dauntless, tenacious, undaunted **10** courageous

stamen part 6 anther **8** filament

stamina 8 tenacity **9** endurance, fortitude, tolerance **11** persistence **12** staying power

stammer 6 gibber, jabber **7** sputter, stutter **8** hesitate, splutter

stamp 3 ilk, lot **4** etch, kind, mark, mint, mold, seal, sort, type **5** clomp, clump, pound, print, tromp **6** hammer, stripe **7** impress, imprint, trample **8** hallmark, inscribe **9** character **10** impression **12** characterize

stampede 4 bolt, dash, rout, rush, tear **5** crush, panic, rodeo **6** charge

stamps 7 postage

stance 4 pose **7** bearing, posture **8** attitude, carriage, position **10** deportment

stanch 4 stem, stop **5** check **6** stop up **8** hold back

stanchion 4 post, prop **5** brace **7** support

stand 4 bear **5** abide, booth, brook, kiosk, stall, treat **6** endure, handle, suffer **7** counter, stomach, swallow, weather **8** attitude, platform, position, tolerate *artist's:* **5** easel *three-legged:* **6** tripod, trivet *ornamental:* **7** étagère

standard 3 law, par **4** flag, jack, mean, norm, rule **5** color, gauge, ideal, model, stock, usual **6** banner, common, ensign, median, normal, pennon **7** average, classic, example, general, labarum, measure, pattern, pennant, regular, typical, uniform **8** accepted, everyday, exemplar, familiar, ordinary, orthodox, paradigm **9** archetype, benchmark, criterion, customary, principle, yardstick **10** recognized, regulation, touchstone **11** established, fundamental

standardize 6 adjust **7** conform **8** regulate **9** reconcile

stand for 4 bear, mean **5** allow **6** denote, permit **7** signify **8** indicate, tolerate **9** put up with, represent, symbolize

stand-in 3 sub **5** proxy **6** backup, second **9** alternate, surrogate **10** substitute, understudy **11** pinch hitter, replacement **12** impersonator

standing 4 rank, term **5** erect, fixed, place **6** cachet, credit, repute, status **7** dignity, footing, station, stature, upright **8** capacity, duration, eminence, position, prestige, stagnant **9** character, permanent, situation **10** estimation, reputation **11** consequence, established

standoff see **stalemate**

standoffish 5 aloof **6** chilly **7** distant, haughty **8** detached, reserved **9** reclusive, withdrawn **10** unfriendly, unsociable **12** misanthropic

stand out 3 jut **4** bulk, loom **5** bulge **7** project **8** protrude

standpatter 4 fogy, tory **5** fogey **7** diehard **8** mossback **11** bitter-ender **12** conservative

standpoint 4 side **5** angle, slant **7** outlook **9** direction **11** perspective

standstill 4 halt, stop **5** check, pause **7** impasse **8** deadlock, dead stop **9** cessation, stalemate

Stanford site 8 Palo Alto

Stanley Kowalski's wife 6 Stella

Stanleys' car 7 steamer

Stan's partner 5 Ollie

stanza 7 strophe *combining form:* **5** stich *final:* **5** envoi *of eight lines:* **6** octave *of four lines:* **6** ballad **8** quatrain *of six lines:* **6** sestet *of three lines:* **6** tercet **7** triplet *Persian:* **8** rubaiyat

star 4 icon, idol, lead, main, nova **5** actor, chief, major **6** étoile **7** actress, capital **8** asterisk, dominant, luminary **9** celebrity, headliner, principal **10** preeminent **11** outstanding *bright:* **4** Vega **5** Algol, Deneb, Rigel, Spica **6** Altair, Castor, Pollux, Sirius **7** Antares, Canopus, Capella, Polaris, Procyon, Regulus **8** Arcturus **9** Aldebaran, Archernar, Fomalhaut **10** Beta Crucis, Betelgeuse **11** Alpha Crucis **12** Beta Centauri **13** Alpha Centauri *combining form:* **4** astr **5** aster, astro **6** astero, sidero *envelope:* **6** corona *exploding:* **4** nova *five-pointed:* **8** pentacle, stellate **9** pentagram *giant:* **10** Betelgeuse *North:* **7** Polaris *six-pointed:* **8** hexagram

starch 3 pep **4** push, snap **5** drive, moxie, punch, spunk, vigor **7** stiffen **8** gumption, vitality **9** formality *combining form:* **4** amyl **5** amylo

starchy 4 prim **5** aloof, stiff **6** doughy, formal, wooden **7** stilted

star-crossed 6 doomed **7** hapless, unlucky **8** ill-fated, luckless **10** ill-starred **11** unfortunate **12** misfortunate

Stardust composer 10 Carmichael (Hoagy)

stare 3 eye **4** gape, gawk, gaze, ogle, peer **6** goggle **10** rubberneck

stark 3 raw **4** bare, nude, pure **5** bleak, blunt, clear, harsh, naked, quite, rigid, sheer, utter **6** barren, strict, unclad, vacant, wholly **8** absolute, complete, desolate, stripped **9** au naturel, out-and-out **10** absolutely

starry 6 astral **7** stellar **8** sidereal

starry-eyed 6 dreamy, unreal **7** utopian **8** ecstatic **9** rapturous, visionary **11** impractical, unrealistic **13** impracticable

Star-Spangled Banner writer 3 Key (Francis Scott)

start 4 bolt, dawn, draw **5** arise, begin, crank, found, get-go, issue, onset, quail, react, set up, wince **6** blench, create, embark, flinch, launch, outset, recoil, shrink, spring, take up **7** actuate, genesis, infancy, kickoff, opening, trigger **8** activate, commence, embark on, initiate, organize, reaction **9** beginning, establish, institute, originate **10** inaugurate **12** commencement

startle 4 jolt, jump **5** alarm, scare, shock, spook **8** astonish, frighten, surprise

Star Trek *captain:* **4** Kirk (James T.) **5** Sisko (Benjamin) **6** Archer (Jonathan), Picard (Jean-Luc) **7** Janeway (Kathryn) *character:* **3** Dax (Jadzia), Kim (Harry), Nog, Odo, Rom, Yar (Natasha) **4** Data, Kurn, Lore, Sulu, Troi (Deanna, Lwaxana), Worf **5** Adami (Kai Winn), Dukat, Duras (Lursa, B'Etor), McCoy ("Bones"), Nerys (Kira), Paris (Tom), Quark, Riker (Will), Sarek, Scott, Spock, Tuvok, Uhura **6** Bashir (Julian), Chekov, Doctor (The), Guinan, Gowron, O'Brien (Keiko, Miles), Torres (B'Elanna), Weyoun **7** Crusher (Dr. Beverly, Wesley), La Forge (Geordi) **8** Chakotay **9** Borg Queen **11** Seven of Nine *creator:* **11** Roddenberry (Gene) *fan:* **7** Trekker, Trekkie *race:* **4** Borg, Gorn, Voth **5** Breen, Human, Trill, Vorta **6** Lurian, Pakled, Terran, Vulcan **7** Bajoran, Ferengi, Iconian, Klingon, Romulan, Tribble **8** Andorian, Betazoid, El-Aurian, Jem'Hadar **9** Nausicaan, Tellarite **10** Cardassian, Changeling *actor:* **5** Nimoy (Leonard), Takei (George) **6** Kelley (DeForest) **7** Mulgrew (Kate), Shatner (William), Stewart (Patrick) **8** Fletcher (Louise), Goldberg (Whoopi) **11** Auberjonois (René) *starship:* **10** Enterprise

starved 6 hungry **8** famished, ravenous, underfed

Star Wars 3 SDI *actor:* **3** Lee (Christopher) **4** Ford (Harrison) **5** Jones (James Earl) **6** Fisher (Carrie), Hamill (Mark), Neeson (Liam) **7** Jackson (Samuel L.), Portman (Natalie) **8** Guinness (Alec), McGregor (Ewan), Williams (Billy Dee) **9** McDiarmid (Ian) *character:* **4** Fett (Boba, Jango), Jinn (Qui-Gon), Leia (Princess), Maul (Darth), Solo (Han), Yoda (Master) **5** Binks (Jar Jar), Dooku (Count), Vader (Darth) **8** Grievous (General) **9** Chewbacca, Palpatine (Senator, Chancellor, Emperor), Skywalker (Anakin, Luke) **10** Calrissian (Lando) **12** Jabba the Hutt *composer:* **8** Williams (John) *creator:* **5** Lucas (George) *film:* **7** New Hope (A) **13** Phantom Menace (The) **15** Return of the Jedi **16** Revenge of the Sith **17** Attack of the Clones, Empire Strikes Back (The) *group:* **4** Jedi, Sith **5** Ewoks **6** Clones, Droids **8** Wookiees **13** Rebel Alliance *parody:* **6** Troops **10** Spaceballs **12** Hardware Wars *planet:* **4** Hoth **5** Naboo **7** Dagobah **8** Alderaan, Tatooine **9** Coruscant *threat:* **9** Death Star

stash 4 bury, hide, pile **5** cache, hoard, plant, store **7** conceal, lay away, nest egg, secrete **8** lay aside, sock away, squirrel **9** stockpile

stasis 7 balance, inertia **9** equipoise **10** immobility, stagnation **11** equilibrium

stat 3 now, PDQ **4** ASAP **6** at once, pronto

state 3 air, put, say **4** aver, mode, rank, tell, vent **5** utter **6** affirm, assert, recite, relate, report **7** declare, dignity, explain, expound, express, posture, recount **8** attitude, capacity, describe, position, set forth, standing **9** condition, enunciate, situation, ventilate *subdivison:* **6** county

state *easternmost:* **5** Maine *largest:* **6** Alaska *smallest:* **11** Rhode Island *southernmost:* **6** Hawaii

state abbreviation *Alabama:* **3** Ala. *Alaska:* **4** Alas. *Arizona:* **4** Ariz. *Arkansas:* **3** Ark. *California:* **3** Cal. **5** Calif. *Colorado:* **3** Col. **4** Colo. *Connecticut:* **4** Conn. *Delaware:* **3** Del. *Florida:* **3** Fla. *Idaho:* **3** Ida. *Illinois:* **3** Ill. *Indiana:* **3** Ind. *Kansas:* **3** Kan. **4** Kans. *Kentucky:* **3** Ken. *Massachusetts:* **4** Mass. *Michigan:* **4** Mich. *Minnesota:* **4** Minn. *Mississippi:* **4** Miss. *Montana:* **4** Mont. *Nebraska:* **3** Neb. **4** Nebr. *Nevada:* **3** Nev. *New Mexico:* **4** N. Mex. *North Carolina:* **4** N. Car. *North Dakota:* **4** N. Dak. *Oklahoma:* **4** Okla. *Oregon:* **3** Ore. **4** Oreg. *Pennsylvania:* **4** Penn. **5** Penna. *South Carolina:* **4** S. Car. *South Dakota:* **4** S. Dak. *Tennessee:* **4** Tenn. *Texas:* **3** Tex. *Vermont:* **4** Verm. *Virginia:* **4** Virg. *Washington:* **4** Wash. *West*

Virginia: **3** W. Va. *Wisconsin:* **3** Wis. **4** Wisc. *Wyoming:* **3** Wyo.

stately 5 grand, lofty, noble, regal, royal **6** august, formal, kingly, lordly, solemn **7** courtly, elegant, gallant, haughty **8** gracious, imperial, imposing, majestic, palatial, princely **9** dignified **10** ceremonial, impressive, monumental **11** ceremonious, magnificent

statement 3 tab **4** bill **5** score **6** avowal, charge, dictum, remark, report **7** account, comment, invoice, recital **8** averment **9** affidavit, assertion, manifesto, narrative, reckoning, testimony, utterance **10** deposition, expression **11** description *introductory:* **7** preface **8** foreword, prologue

stateroom 5 cabin

statesman 10 politician *American:* **3** Hay (John Milton) **4** Clay (Henry), Hull (Cordell), Otis (James), Root (Elihu) **5** Adams (Samuel), Henry (Patrick), Lodge (Henry Cabot), Vance (Cyrus) **6** Bunche (Ralph), Bunker (Ellsworth), Dulles (John Foster), Kennan (George F.), Morris (Gouverneur), Powell (Colin), Sumner (Charles) **7** Acheson (Dean), Hancock (John), Kellogg (Frank B.), Lansing (Robert), Sherman (John, Roger), Stimson (Henry L.), Webster (Daniel) **8** Franklin (Benjamin), Hamilton (Alexander), Harriman (Averell), Pinckney (Charles, Thomas), Randolph (Edmund Jennings, John, Payton), Rutledge (John), Trumbull (Jonathan, Joseph) **9** Kissinger (Henry), Stevenson (Adlai) **10** Stettinius (Edward Reilly) *Australian:* **9** Wentworth (William Charles) *Austrian:* **6** Renner (Karl) **7** Kaunitz (Wenzel von) **8** Dollfuss (Engelbert) **10** Metternich (Klemens von) **13** Schwarzenberg (Felix zu) *Canadian:* **4** King (W. L. Mackenzie) **7** Laurier (Wilfrid) **8** Thompson (John Sparrow) **9** Macdonald (John Alexander, John Sandfield), Mackenzie (Alexander, William Lyon) *Chinese:* **3** Yen (Hsishan) **4** Deng (Xiaoping), Kung (Hsiang-hsi), Teng (Hsiao-p'ing), Wang (Anshih, Chingwei), Yuan (Shih-kai) **9** Sun Yat-Sen *Dutch:* **6** de Witt (Johan de) **7** Grotius (Hugo), Stikker (Dirk) *East German:* **8** Ulbricht (Walter) *English:* **3** Fox (Charles, Henry) **4** Eden (Anthony, George, William), More (Thomas), Peel (Arthur, Robert, William), Pitt (William), Vane (Henry) **5** Cecil (Robert, William), North (Francis, Frederick, Roger) **6** Morley (John), Sidney (Algernon, Henry, Philip, Robert), Temple (Henry, William), Wolsey (Thomas) **7** Halifax (Earl of), Reading (Marquis of), Russell

(John, William), Stanley (Edward George, Edward Henry), Stewart (Robert), Warwick (Earl of) **8** Cromwell (Oliver, Thomas), Disraeli (Benjamin), Robinson (George Frederick Samuel), Villiers (George) **9** Cavendish (Spencer, William), Churchill (Randolph, Winston), Gladstone (William), Salisbury (Earl, Marquis of), Strafford (Earl of), Wellesley (Arthur, Richard Colley) **10** Palmerston (Lord), Rockingham (Marquis of), Sunderland (Earl of), Walsingham (Francis), Wellington (Duke of) **11** Chamberlain (Austen, Joseph, Neville), Shaftesbury (Earl of) **12** Chesterfield (Earl of) *Finnish:* **9** Stahlberg (Kaarlo Juho) *French:* **5** Sully (Duc de) **6** Guizot (François-Pierre-Guillaume), Thiers (Louis-Adolphe), Turgot (Anne-Robert-Jacques) **7** Herriot (Edouard), Mazarin (Jules), Schuman (Robert), Viviani (René) **8** Hanotaux (Gabriel) **9** Lafayette (Marquis de), Millerand (Alexandre), Richelieu (Duc de) **10** Clemenceau (Georges) **11** Tocqueville (Alexis de) *German:* **5** Wirth (Joseph) **10** Stresemann (Gustav) *German-Danish:* **9** Struensee (Johann Friedrich) *Greek:* **6** Zaimis (Alexandros) **8** Pericles **9** Aristides **11** Cleisthenes, Demosthenes **12** Themistocles *Israeli:* **4** Eban (Abba) **5** Begin (Menachem), Dayan (Moshe), Peres (Shimon), Rabin (Yitzhak) **7** Sharett (Moshe) **9** Ben-Gurion (David) *Italian:* **6** Cavour (Conte di), Crispi (Francesco) **7** Orlando (Vittorio Emanuele) **11** Machiavelli (Niccolo) *Japanese:* **3** Ito (Hirobumi) **5** genro, Kanoe **6** Kanoye *Norwegian:* **6** Nansen (Fridtjof) *Polish:* **7** Zaleski (August) **9** Pilsudski (Jozef) **10** Paderewski (Ignacy) *Prussian:* **5** Stein (Karl) *Roman:* **4** Cato (Marcus Porcius) **6** Cicero (Marcus Tullius), Pompey, Seneca (Lucius Annaeus) **7** Agrippa (Marcus Vipsanius) **8** Gracchus (Gaius, Tiberius), Maecenas (Gaius) **9** Symmachus (Quintus Aurelius) *Russian:* **5** Witte (Sergey) **7** Molotov (Vyacheslav) **8** Potemkin (Grigory) **9** Vyshinsky (Andrey) *Scottish:* **4** Knox (John) *South American:* **7** Bolívar (Simón) **9** San Martín (José de) *Swiss:* **4** Ador (Gustave) **5** Welti (Emil)

static 5 fixed, inert **6** stable, steady **7** stabile, stalled, stopped **8** constant, immobile, inactive, stagnant, unmoving **9** immovable, unvarying **10** changeless, unchanging

station 4 post, rank, site, spot **5** depot, locus, place, point **6** assign **7** footing **8** capacity, standing **9** character **10** white noise

stationary 5 fixed **6** static **8** immobile, stag-

nant, unmoving **9** immovable **10** motionless, stock-still

statue *base:* **6** plinth **8** pedestal *gigantic:* **8** Colossus *Greek:* **5** atlas **7** telamon **8** caryatid *religious:* **5** Pietà *small:* **8** figurine

stature see **status**

status 4 rank **5** merit, place, worth **6** cachet, rating, renown **7** caliber, dignity, footing, posture, quality **8** capacity, eminence, position, prestige, standing **9** character, condition, situation **10** prominence **11** consequence, distinction

statute 3 act, law **4** bill **5** canon, edict **9** enactment, ordinance

staunch 4 fast, firm, sure, true **5** liege, loyal, solid, sound **6** secure, stable, strong, trusty **8** constant, faithful, reliable, resolute, stalwart **9** steadfast **10** dependable **11** substantial, trustworthy

stave off 4 foil **5** avert, block, deter, dodge, elude, parry, rebut, repel **6** rebuff, thwart **7** forfend, obviate, prevent, repulse **8** preclude **9** forestall **10** circumvent

stay 3 guy, lag **4** bide, halt, prop, rest, stop, wait **5** abide, brace, check, defer, delay, dwell, lodge, tarry, visit **6** linger, put off, remain **7** sojourn, support, suspend **8** hold over, postpone, stop over **9** interrupt **10** suspension **11** stick around

stead 4 lieu **5** place **9** advantage

steadfast 4 firm, sure, true **5** fixed, liege, loyal **7** abiding, adamant, patient, staunch **8** constant, enduring, faithful, immobile, reliable, resolute, stubborn **9** immovable, unbending, unmovable **10** dependable, unwavering, unyielding **11** unfaltering, unflinching **12** never-failing, single-minded, wholehearted **13** unquestioning

steady 3 set **4** beau, even, fast, firm, sure **5** fixed, liege, loyal, sober **6** stable, static **7** abiding, ballast, certain, durable, equable, nonstop, regular, stabile, staunch, uniform **8** constant, enduring, faithful, habitual, reliable, resolute, unbroken, unshaken **9** ceaseless, incessant, stabilize, unvarying **10** changeless, consistent, continuous, dependable, persistent, sweetheart, unchanging, unswerving, unwavering **11** unfaltering **12** unchangeable, wholehearted

steak 4 club, cube, loin **5** chuck, flank, round, T-bone **6** rib eye **7** brisket, sirloin **9** Delmonico, hamburger, Salisbury **10** tenderloin **11** filet mignon, London broil, porterhouse **13** chateaubriand

steal 3 bag, cop, nab, nip, rob **4** glom, grab, hook, kite, lift, loot, lurk, slip, take **5** boost, creep, filch, glide, heist, pinch, poach, prowl, seize, shirk, sidle, skulk, slide, slink, sneak, swipe **6** burgle, fleece, hijack, pilfer, pocket, snatch, snitch, thieve, tiptoe **7** bargain, pillage, plunder, purloin **8** embezzle, shanghai, shoplift **9** pussyfoot **10** burglarize, plagiarize **11** appropriate *a vehicle:* **6** hijack **8** highjack

stealing 5 theft **6** piracy **7** larceny, robbery **8** burglary

stealthy 3 sly **4** wily **6** covert, crafty, feline, secret, shifty, silent, slinky, sneaky **7** catlike, cunning, furtive, sub-rosa **8** hush-hush, skulking, slinking, sneaking **9** noiseless **10** undercover **11** clandestine **13** surreptitious

steam 3 gas, pep, zip **4** foam, fume, mist, rage **5** anger, force, might, power, vapor **6** energy, seethe **8** momentum

steam bath 5 sauna

steamboat structure 5 texas

steamer 4 boat, clam, ship

steam organ 8 calliope

steamy 3 hot **5** humid, muggy **6** erotic, sticky, sultry, torrid **8** stifling

steed 5 horse, mount **7** charger

steel 4 gird **5** brace, nerve, rally **6** buck up, harden **7** fortify, hearten, stiffen **8** embolden, inspirit **9** reinforce **10** strengthen

steep 3 sop **4** high, soak **5** bathe, dizzy, imbue, sheer **6** abrupt, drench, infuse **7** arduous, extreme, immerse, suffuse **8** elevated, marinate, saturate **9** excessive **10** exorbitant, immoderate, impregnate, inordinate **11** precipitate, precipitous

steeple 5 spire, tower **6** flèche

steer 4 helm, lead **5** guide, pilot, point, route **6** direct, escort, tip-off **7** channel, conduct, skipper **8** shepherd *a ship:* **4** conn, helm, luff

steersman 3 cox **7** captain **8** coxswain

Stegner novel 13 Angle of Repose, Spectator Bird (The) **20** Big Rock Candy Mountain (The)

stein 3 mug **5** stoup **6** goblet **7** tankard

Steinbeck novel 5 Pearl (The) **10** Cannery Row, East of Eden **12** Of Mice and Men, Tortilla Flat **13** Grapes of Wrath (The)

Stein's companion 6 Toklas (Alice B.)

Steinway product 5 piano

stellar 6 astral, starry **7** leading, shining **8** sidereal, standout, starlike **10** preeminent **11** outstanding, predominant, superlative

stem 4 flow, head, rise, stop **5** abate, arise, check, issue **6** arrest, derive, spring, stanch **7** control, develop, emanate, proceed **8** peduncle **9** originate *plant:* **4** axis **5** haulm *underground:* **5** tuber **7** rhizome

stench 4 funk, reek **5** smell, stink

stentorian 4 loud **7** blaring, booming, orotund, raucous, roaring **8** sonorous, strident **9** clamorous, deafening **10** thundering **12** earsplitting

step 4 hoof, pace, rung, walk **5** grade, level, notch, stage, stair, stile, track, tread **6** degree **7** measure, traipse **8** footfall **9** gradation *dance:* **3** pas

step-by-step 7 gradual **9** piecemeal

steppe 5 plain **6** tundra

Steppenwolf author 5 Hesse (Hermann)

stereotype 4 mold **5** plate **7** pattern **10** categorize, pigeonhole **11** standardize

stereotypical 4 hack **5** banal, stale, trite **7** clichéd **8** shopworn, timeworn **9** hackneyed **11** commonplace

sterile 4 arid, bare, vain **6** barren, fallow **7** aseptic, worn-out **8** desolate, hygienic, impotent, lifeless, sanitary **9** fruitless, infertile **10** antiseptic, unfruitful, uninspired **11** disinfected **12** unproductive

sterilize 3 fix **4** geld, spay **5** alter **6** neuter, purify **7** cleanse **8** sanitize **9** disinfect **10** emasculate

sterilized 7 aseptic

sterling 4 pure, true **5** noble **6** worthy **8** virtuous **9** estimable, exemplary, honorable

stern 4 grim **5** harsh, rigid, sober, stony **6** gloomy, severe, strict **7** ascetic, austere **8** obdurate **10** forbidding, implacable, inexorable, inflexible **11** unrelenting

Sterne novel 14 Tristram Shandy

sternutation 8 sneezing

sternward 3 aft **5** abaft

Sterope *father:* 5 Atlas *mother:* **7** Pleione *sisters:* **8** Pleiades

Stevenson, Robert Louis *character:* 3 Jim (Hawkins) **4** Hyde (Mr.) **5** David (Balfour) **6** Jekyll (Dr.), Silver (Long John) *novel:* **9** Kidnapped **14** Treasure Island

stew 4 boil, brew, flap, fret, fume, fuss, hash, olio, olla, snit **5** daube, gumbo, salmi, sweat, tizzy, worry **6** burgoo, dither, jumble, lather, medley, menudo, pother, ragout, seethe, simmer, swivet, tumult **7** brothel, goulash, mélange, mixture, parboil, swelter, turmoil **8** bordello, mishmash, mulligan, pot-au-feu **9** Brunswick, cassoulet, commotion, confusion, pasticcio, potpourri **10** hodgepodge, hotchpotch, miscellany, turbulence **11** gallimaufry, olla podrida, ratatouille, slumgullion **13** bouillabaisse

steward 6 manage **7** manager **8** overseer **10** supervisor

stewed 3 lit **4** high **5** drunk, lit up, oiled **6** bashed, blotto, bombed, cooked, juiced, potted, soaked, soused, stewed, stoned, tanked, wasted, zonked **7** crocked, drunken, pickled, pie-eyed, sloshed, smashed, sottish **8** simmered **9** plastered **10** inebriated, liquored up **11** intoxicated

Stheno see **Gorgon**

stick 3 put, rod **4** glue, pole, stab **5** affix, baton, cling **6** adhere, attach, cleave, cohere, fasten **7** scruple **10** overcharge

stick around 4 bide, stay, wait **5** abide, dally, tarry **6** linger, remain

sticker 3 pin **4** barb, seal, shiv, spur **5** decal, point, prong, shank, spike, spine, stamp **6** dagger **8** stiletto

stick-in-the-mud 4 fogy **5** fogey **6** fossil **8** mossback **10** fuddy-duddy

stick out 3 jut **5** bulge **6** beetle **7** project **8** overhang, protrude

stick up 3 mug, rob **6** waylay **7** project **8** protrude

sticky 5 gluey, gooey, gummy, humid, muggy, mushy, soggy, tacky **6** clammy, knotty, slushy, sultry, thorny, viscid **7** awkward, cloying, maudlin, mawkish, viscous **8** adhesive, bathetic, clinging, romantic **9** difficult **11** problematic, sentimental, tearjerking

stiff 3 lit, set **4** body, firm, hard, lush **5** cheat, drunk, harsh, oiled, rigid, stark, steep, stick, tense, tight, tipsy **6** buzzed, corpse, frozen, jelled, juiced, person, plowed, potent, potted, severe, soused, stewed, wooden **7** cadaver, carcass, sloshed, starchy, stilted **8** hardened, reserved, stubborn **9** cardboard, inelastic, petrified, plastered, unbending **10** inflexible, mechanical, unyielding **11** intoxicated, intractable

stiffen 5 tense **6** harden **7** thicken **8** rigidify, solidify **9** stabilize **10** immobilize

stifle 3 gag **4** hush, mute **5** burke, choke, deter **6** dampen, deaden, hush up, muffle, muzzle **7** repress, silence, smother, squelch **8** stultify, suppress **9** suffocate **10** asphyxiate, discourage

stigma 4 blot, onus, spot **5** brand, odium, shame, stain, taint **6** smudge, smutch **8** black eye, disgrace, dishonor, petechia, tainting

stigmatize 5 brand, label, stamp

still 3 but, yet **4** calm, even, hush, lull **5** allay, inert, quiet, shush, whist **6** even so, hushed, placid, serene, settle, silent, though, withal **7** alembic, halcyon, silence **8** peaceful, stagnant, tranquil **9** noiseless, quietness, soundless **10** motionless, stationary **11** furthermore, nonetheless, tranquility **12** nevertheless

stilt 4 bird, pile, pole **8** longlegs **9** shorebird

stilted 4 prim **5** stiff **6** formal, wooden **7** pompous, starchy **8** affected **9** cardboard

stilt-like bird 6 avocet

Stimpy's pal 3 Ren

stimulant 4 goad, spur **5** tonic **7** impetus, impulse **8** caffeine, catalyst, excitant **9** analeptic, energizer, incentive **10** incitement, motivation

stimulate 4 fire, goad, move, prod, spur, urge, whet **5** impel, pique, rouse, set up, spark **6** arouse, excite, fire up, foment, incite, prompt, vivify, work up **7** agitate, enliven, inspire, provoke, quicken, trigger **8** activate, energize, motivate, vitalize **9** galvanize **10** exhilarate

stimulus 4 goad, kick, push, spur **5** boost, cause **6** charge, motive **7** impetus, impulse **8** catalyst **9** incentive **10** incitement, inducement, motivation **11** instigation, provocation **13** encouragement

sting 3 con **4** scam, trap **5** cheat, prick, smart, snare **6** hustle, tingle **7** con game **8** skin game

stinging 8 aculeate

stingy 4 mean **5** close, tight **6** frugal, narrow, paltry, skimpy **7** chintzy, costive, miserly, niggard, scrimpy, sparing, thrifty **8** grudging **9** niggardly, penny-wise, penurious **10** economical, ironfisted, pinchpenny, ungenerous **11** tightfisted **12** cheeseparing, parsimonious **13** penny-pinching

stink 4 flap, funk, fuss, reek **5** smell **6** stench **7** malodor

stinker 3 dog, dud **4** bomb, bust, flop **5** lemon, loser, skunk **6** petrel, turkey **7** washout

stinking see **smelly**

stinky see **smelly**

stint 3 job **4** bout, task, time, tour, turn **5** chore, cramp, pinch, scant, share, shift, skimp, spare, spell **6** amount, scrape, scrimp **8** quantity, restrict **9** allotment, stricture **10** assignment, limitation **11** restriction

stipend 3 fee, pay **4** hire, wage **5** award **6** salary **7** payment **9** allowance, emolument **13** consideration

stipple 3 dot **5** fleck, speck **6** pepper **7** freckle, speckle **8** sprinkle

stipulate 5 state **6** detail **7** specify **8** contract, spell out **13** particularize

stipulation 5 limit, terms **7** proviso, strings **9** condition, provision **11** requirement

stir 3 ado, din, mix **4** fuss, rout, to-do, wake, whet **5** blend, budge, churn, impel, rally, rouse, roust, spark, waken **6** arouse, bustle, excite, flurry, foment, hubbub, incite, kindle, pother, seethe, simmer, tumult, whip up **7** agitate, disturb, ferment, inspire, provoke, quicken **8** activity **9** agitation, commotion, galvanize, stimulate **11** disturbance

stirrup 6 stapes **8** footrest

stithy 5 anvil

stoat 6 ermine, weasel

stock 4 butt, fund, hope, race **5** brace, carry, faith, goods, hoard, store, talon, trunk, trust **6** family, supply **7** furnish, lineage **8** pedigree, reliance **9** inventory, selection **10** confidence, dependence **11** merchandise

stockade 4 jail **5** fence **6** paling, prison **8** palisade **9** enclosure, guardroom

stock exchange 4 AMEX, FTSE, NYSE **6** bourse, NASDAQ

stockings 4 hose **5** socks **7** hosiery

stockpile 4 bank, heap, mass **5** amass, cache, hoard, lay up, store **6** garner, supply **7** backlog, collect, nest egg, reserve, store up **9** inventory, reservoir **10** accumulate, repository

stocky 3 fat **5** beefy, burly, dumpy, husky, plump, pudgy, squat, stout, thick **6** chunky, stubby, stumpy **8** heavyset, thickset **9** corpulent

stodge 4 fill, sate **5** gorge, stuff **7** overeat, surfeit

stodgy 5 fusty **6** stuffy **9** hidebound, out-of-date **12** old-fashioned

stogie 4 shoe **5** cigar **6** brogan

stoic 4 Zeno **6** stolid **7** Spartan **9** apathetic, impassive **10** phlegmatic **11** indifferent, unconcerned

stoicism 9 stolidity **11** impassivity *founder:* **4** Zeno

stoke 3 fan **4** feed, fuel, poke, stir, tend **6** supply

Stoker novel 7 Dracula

stolid 3 dry **4** dull, flat **5** stoic **6** wooden **8** rocklike **9** apathetic, impassive, unruffled **10** phlegmatic **11** unemotional

stomach 3 gut, maw **4** bear, craw **5** abide, belly, brook, stand, taste, tummy **6** digest, endure, paunch, venter **7** abdomen, swallow **8** appetite, tolerate *combining form:* **5** gastr **6** gastro, ventri, ventro *enzyme:* **6** pepsin, rennin *muscle:* **7** pylorus *ruminant:* **6** omasum **8** abomasum **9** reticulum *Scottish:* **4** kyte

stomachache 5 colic, gripe **12** collywobbles

stomp 5 clomp, clump, pound, tramp, tromp **7** trample

stone 3 gem **4** rock **5** lapis **6** pebble **7** boulder *base:* **6** plinth *block of:* **8** monolith *carving:* **7** epitaph *chip:* **5** spall *combining form:* **4** lite, lith, lyte *cosmic:* **6** meteor **9** chondrite, meteorite *facing:* **6** ashlar *for grinding grains:* **6** metate *fruit:* **5** drupe *me-*

morial: **5** cairn, stela **7** obelisk *monument:* **6** dolmen **8** megalith *of a fruit:* **3** pit *paving:* **3** set **4** sett

____ **Stone 7** Blarney, Rosetta

Stone novel 11 Lust for Life **18** Agony and the Ecstasy (The)

stonecrop 5 sedum

stoned 3 lit **4** high **5** boozy, doped, drunk, fried, oiled, tight, tipsy **6** buzzed, canned, juiced, loaded, plowed, potted, soused, stewed, tanked, wasted, zonked **7** crocked, drugged, muddled, pickled, pie-eyed, sloshed, smashed **8** hopped-up, turned on, wiped out **9** pixilated, plastered, spaced-out, strung out **10** inebriated, tripped out **11** intoxicated

stonewall 5 delay, stall **6** hamper, hinder, impede, stymie **8** obstruct

stooge 3 act, sap **4** dupe, foil, gull, mark, pawn, tool **5** chump, dummy, patsy, proxy **6** puppet, sucker, victim **7** fall guy **8** sidekick **9** represent **11** stool pigeon, straight man **12** second banana

Stooge 3 Moe (Howard) **5** Curly (Howard), Larry (Fine)

stool pigeon 3 rat **4** fink, nark **5** decoy **6** canary, snitch **7** ratfink, tipster **8** informer

stoop 3 dip **4** bend, duck, sink **5** deign, hunch, porch, slump **6** resort, slouch **7** descend, portico, veranda **8** stairway **10** condescend

stop 3 bar, can, dam, end **4** clog, fill, halt, plug, quit, stay, stem **5** block, brake, cease, check, close, stall, tarry **6** arrest, desist, ending, kibosh, stanch **7** disrupt, occlude, prevent, sojourn, suspend **8** knock off, obstruct **9** cessation, interrupt, terminate **10** conclusion, standstill **11** discontinue, termination *up:* **4** cork, plug **7** occlude

stopgap 5 shift **6** resort **8** recourse, resource **9** expedient, makeshift **10** expediency, substitute

stopover 4 stay **5** visit **7** sojourn

stoppage 4 halt **6** cutoff, strike **7** walkout **8** shutdown **10** standstill **11** obstruction

Stoppard play 7 Jumpers **9** Real Thing (The) **10** Travesties **13** Coast of Utopia (The)

stopper 4 bung, cork, fill, plug **5** close

store 3 bin **4** fund, mart, pack, shop, stow, tank **5** amass, cache, depot, hoard, lay up, stash **6** ensile, garner, market, outlet, shoppe, supply **7** arsenal, backlog, bootery, deposit, reserve **8** boutique, cumulate, emporium, mothball, showroom, squirrel **9** abundance, chandlery, inventory, reservoir, stockpile, warehouse **10** accumulate, depository, five-and-ten, repository **11** five-and-dime 12 accumulation *display:* 6 endcap 8 showcase

storehouse 5 depot 7 arsenal, granary 8 magazine 9 stockpile 10 depository, repository

storekeeper 8 merchant, retailer 9 tradesman

storeroom 6 larder, pantry 7 buttery

storm 3 row 4 fury, gale, hail, rage, rant, rave, roar, rush, to-do 5 beset, blast, blitz, burst, furor, onset, salvo 6 assail, attack, charge, clamor, fall on, flurry, furore, hubbub, outcry, pother, racket, shower, squall, tumult 7 assault, bluster, cyclone, monsoon, ruction, tempest, thunder, tornado, turmoil; twister, typhoon 8 blizzard, downpour, fall upon, outbreak, outburst, paroxysm, upheaval 9 broadside, commotion, discharge, hurricane, nor'easter, onslaught 10 cloudburst, hurly-burly 11 northeaster, northwester

storm trooper 10 brownshirt

stormy 4 foul 5 rainy, rough 6 raging 7 furious 8 blustery 9 turbulent 10 tumultuous 11 tempestuous, threatening

story 3 fib, lie 4 epic, saga, tale, yarn 5 conte, fable 6 canard, legend, report 7 account, fiction, märchen, parable, version 8 allegory, anecdote, folktale, megillah, tall tale 9 chronicle, fairy tale, narration, narrative 11 description, fabrication

storyteller 4 liar 6 fibber 8 fabulist 9 raconteur

stoup 4 font 5 basin 6 flagon, goblet 7 chalice, tankard

stout 3 ale, fat 4 brew 5 beefy, bulky, burly, heavy, husky, obese, plump, thick 6 fleshy, porter, portly, strong, sturdy 9 corpulent 10 overweight

Stout detective 5 Wolfe (Nero)

stouthearted 4 bold, game 5 brave, gutsy 7 doughty, gallant, valiant 8 fearless, intrepid, resolute, stalwart, stubborn, unafraid 9 audacious, dauntless, undaunted 10 courageous

stove 4 kiln, oven 5 range 8 Franklin, potbelly

stow 3 bin 4 lade, load, pack 5 stash, store 7 arrange, deposit

stower 9 stevedore

Stowe work 4 Dred

strabismus 6 squint

straddle 4 span 6 sprawl 8 bestride 11 spread-eagle

strafe 4 rake 6 attack 8 enfilade 10 machine-gun

straggle 3 lag 4 poke, roam, rove 5 drift, range, stray 6 dawdle, loiter, ramble, wander 7 maunder, meander 8 trail off 9 string out

straight 4 even, fair, neat, pure, true 5 erect, plain, plumb, right 6 at once, candid, direct, honest, linear, square 7 unmixed, upright 8 orthodox 9 bourgeois, forthwith, undiluted 10 aboveboard, button-down, forthright 12 conventional 13 unadulterated *combining form:* 4 orth, rect 5 ortho, recti

straightaway 3 now 6 at once 7 stretch 8 directly, first off, promptly 9 forthwith, instanter 11 immediately

straighten 4 even, tidy 5 align 6 neaten, unbend, uncurl 7 rectify

straightforward 5 frank, lucid 6 candid, direct, honest 7 genuine, precise, sincere 8 clear-cut 9 outspoken 10 forthright 11 undeviating

strain 3 air, tax, try 4 hint, kind, pull, sort, toil, tune, vein 5 exert, stock, sweat, tinge, touch, trace, twist 6 filter, melody, screen, streak, stress, strive, wrench 7 lineage, overtax, tension, trouble 8 ancestry, exertion, overwork, pedigree, pressure, struggle 9 overexert

strait 4 bind, kyle, pass 5 pinch 6 crisis, plight 7 channel, dilemma, narrows, squeeze 8 exigency, hardship, juncture 9 crossroad, emergency 10 difficulty 11 contingency *Adriatic Sea-Ionian Sea:* 7 Otranto *Alaska:* 3 Icy *Alaska-Russia:* 6 Bering *Albania-Greece:* 5 Corfu *Asia-Europe:* 11 Dardanelles *Atlantic-Baffin Island:* 5 Davis *Atlantic-Mediterranean:* 9 Gibraltar *Atlantic-Nantucket Sound:* 8 Muskeget *Atlantic-North Sea:* 7 English *Atlantic-Pacific:* 5 Drake 8 Magellan *Atlantic-Saint Lawrence:* 5 Cabot *Baffin Island-Quebec:* 6 Hudson *Bering Sea-Sea of Okhotsk:* 5 Kuril 6 Kurile *Bismarck Sea-Solomon Sea:* 6 Vitiaz *Canada:* 3 Rae 5 Dease *East China Sea:* 5 Korea 8 Tsushima *East China-South China:* 6 Taiwan 7 Formosa *England-France:* 5 Dover *Flores Sea-Indian Ocean:* 4 Sape *Flores Sea-Savu Sea:* 4 Alor *Indian Ocean-Java Sea:* 5 Sunda *Indian Ocean-Sri Lanka:* 4 Palk *Indonesia:* 4 Alas, Alor, Bali 5 Tioro 6 Lombok 7 Dampier 8 Macassar, Makassar, Surabaya *Inner Hebrides:* 5 Tiree *Iran-Oman:* 6 Hormuz *Italy:* 7 Messina *Japan:* 4 Yura 5 Bungo, Kitan 7 Hayasui *Japan-Sakhalin Island:* 4 Soya *Lake Huron:* 10 Mississagi *Lake Huron-Lake Michigan:* 8 Mackinac *Malay Archipelago:* 5 Wetar *Malaysia-Singapore:* 6 Johore *Malay-Sumatra:* 7 Malacca *New Jersey-Staten Island:* 7 van Kull *New South Wales-Tasmania:* 4 Bass

New Zealand: 4 Cook *Northwest Territories:* 6 Barrow 8 Franklin, Victoria 13 Prince of Wales *Nova Scotia:* 5 Canso *Pacific-San Francisco Bay:* 10 Golden Gate *Pacific-South China Sea:* 5 Luzon *Philippines:* 5 Bohol, Tanon 6 Iloilo 7 Basilan *Russia:* 4 Kara *Suvu Sea-Timor Sea:* 4 Roti *Sea of Azov-Black Sea:* 5 Kerch 7 Enikale *Sea of Japan:* 5 Tatar *Solomon Islands:* 12 Bougainville *South China Sea:* 7 Mindoro 9 Singapore *Turkey:* 8 Bosporus 9 Bosphorus, Karadeniz *Vancouver-Washington:* 10 Juan de Fuca *Wales:* 5 Menai *Washington Sound:* 4 Haro

straitened 7 lacking, pinched, wanting 8 deprived, strapped 9 deficient, destitute 10 distressed, inadequate 12 impoverished

straitlaced 4 prim 5 staid, stiff 6 formal, narrow, prissy, strict, stuffy 7 genteel, prudish, starchy, stilted 8 priggish 9 hidebound, Victorian 11 puritanical

strand 4 bank 5 beach, coast, fiber, leave, shore, wreck 6 desert, maroon, thread 7 abandon, shingle 8 cast away, filament, littoral, seacoast, seashore 9 shipwreck 10 run aground, waterfront

strange 3 odd 5 alien, crazy, eerie, fishy, funny, kinky, kooky, nutty, outré, queer, weird 6 exotic, far-out, freaky 7 bizarre, curious, oddball, offbeat, uncanny, unknown, unusual 8 aberrant, abnormal, atypical, peculiar, singular 9 eccentric, fantastic, grotesque 10 mysterious, off-the-wall, outlandish, unfamiliar 11 exceptional 12 unaccustomed

Strange Interlude author 6 O'Neill (Eugene)

stranger 5 alien, guest 7 visitor 8 newcomer, outsider, wanderer 9 auslander, foreigner, immigrant, transient

strangle 5 burke, choke, shush 6 muffle, quelch, stifle 7 garotte, garrote 8 suppress, throttle 10 asphyxiate

strap 4 band, beat, belt, bind, rein 5 leash 6 attach, punish, secure, suffer 7 binding, leather 8 distress 9 constrict

strapping 5 beefy, burly, hardy, husky 6 brawny, robust, rugged, sturdy 8 muscular, vigorous 10 able-bodied

stratagem 4 play, plot, ploy, ruse, wile 5 feint, trick 6 device, gambit, scheme, tactic 8 artifice, intrigue, maneuver 10 conspiracy, subterfuge 11 machination

strategy 4 plan 6 design, method, scheme 7 project, tactics 8 game plan 9 blueprint

stratum 3 bed 4 rank 5 class, grade, layer, level

Strauss, Richard *opera:* 6 Salome 7 Elektra 13 Rosenkavalier (Der) 15 Ariadne auf Naxos 16 Frau ohne Schatten (Die) *tone poem:* 7 Don Juan 10 Don Quixote 11 Heldenleben (Ein) 20 Thus Spake Zarathustra 23 Death and Transfiguration

straw 3 hay 5 blond 6 flaxen, golden, thatch *braided:* 6 sennit *mat:* 6 tatami *plaited:* 7 leghorn

straw man 4 dupe, foil, sham

stray 3 err, gad 4 lost, roam, rove, waif 5 drift, range 6 depart, errant, ramble, random, wander 7 deviate, digress, diverge, erratic, meander, runaway, traipse, vagrant 8 divagate, homeless, sporadic 9 gallivant

streak 4 hint, vein 5 fleck, tinge, trace 6 dapple, marble, mottle, strain, stripe 7 striate 8 tincture 9 suspicion, variegate 10 intimation, suggestion

streaked 5 upset 7 brindle, marbled, striped 8 brindled, grizzled 9 disturbed

stream 3 run 4 beck, burn, flow, flux, gill, gush, pour, race, rill, rush, sike, tide 5 bourn, brook, creek, spate, surge 6 bourne, branch, rindle, runnel, sluice 7 current, freshet, rivulet, torrent 8 affluent

streambed 4 wadi, wash 5 gully

streamer 4 flag, jack 6 banner, burgee, ensign, pennon 7 pennant 8 banderol, bannerol, standard 9 banderole

streamline 7 contour 8 organize, simplify 9 modernize

street 3 way 4 drag, road, wynd 5 alley, drive 6 artery, avenue 7 roadway 9 boulevard 12 thoroughfare *border:* 4 curb 7 curbing *material:* 6 cobble 7 asphalt, macadam 11 cobblestone *name:* 3 Elm 4 Main, Park 5 Maple, State

streetcar 4 tram 7 trolley

Streetcar Named Desire, A *author:* 8 Williams (Tennessee) *character:* 6 Stella (Kowalski) 7 Blanche (DuBois), Stanley (Kowalski)

Street Scene author 4 Rice (Elmer)

strength 5 brawn, force, forte, might, power, sinew, vigor 6 energy, muscle 7 potency 8 firmness, security 9 fortitude, intensity, soundness, stability, toughness 10 steadiness, sturdiness

strengthen 4 gird 5 brace, steel 6 anneal, beef up, harden, prop up 7 bolster, enhance, fortify, support, toughen 8 buttress, embolden, energize 9 intensify, reinforce, undergird 10 invigorate, rejuvenate

strenuous 4 hard 5 tough 6 taxing, uphill 7 arduous, operose 9 demanding, difficult, effortful, Herculean, laborious 12 backbreaking

Strephon 8 shepherd *beloved:* 5 Chloe 6 Urania

stress 6 accent, burden, import, play up, strain, weight 7 anxiety, feature, tension, trouble, urgency 8 emphasis, pressure 9 emphasize, italicize, underline 10 accentuate, underscore 12 accentuation *in poetry:* 5 ictus

stretch 4 area, draw, time 5 crane, range, reach, scope, space, spell, sweep, tract, while 6 extend, extent, length, limber, region, spread 7 breadth, compass, draw out, expanse, magnify, prolong, purview, spin out, tighten 8 distance, elongate, lengthen, protract 9 embellish, embroider, expansion, overstate 10 exaggerate *on a frame:* 6 tenter *out:* 6 sprawl 7 lie down, recline

stretchable 7 ductile, elastic, tensile

stretched 4 taut

stretcher 4 yarn 6 gurney, litter 8 tall tale

strew 3 sow 4 dust 5 cover 6 pepper, spread 7 scatter 8 disperse, sprinkle 9 broadcast, circulate, propagate 10 distribute 11 disseminate

stricken 3 hit, ill 4 hurt, sick 6 bereft 7 injured, wounded 9 afflicted 11 overwhelmed

strict 4 firm 5 exact, harsh, rigid, stern, tough 6 narrow, severe 7 precise 8 exacting, faithful, rigorous 9 draconian, stringent, unsparing 10 inflexible, ironhanded, meticulous, scrupulous 11 punctilious

stricture 5 cramp, stint 7 censure, reproof 8 reproach 9 aspersion, criticism, reprimand 10 constraint, limitation 11 restriction 13 animadversion

stride 4 gait, pace, step 5 march, stalk 7 advance 8 straddle

strident 4 loud 5 harsh 6 shrill 7 grating, jarring, rasping, raucous, squawky 8 piercing 9 clamorous, insistent, obtrusive 10 boisterous, discordant, stentorian, vociferous 11 loudmouthed 12 earsplitting, obstreperous

strife 4 fray 5 broil, fight 6 battle, combat 7 discord, dispute, dissent, quarrel, rivalry, warfare, wrangle 8 argument, conflict, disunity, friction, struggle, tug-of-war 10 contention, difference, dissension, dissidence 11 altercation, competition, controversy

strike 3 hit, pop, rap 4 bash, beat, find, poke, slam, slap, slug, sock, swat, whap, whop 5 clout, knock, punch, smack, smite, swipe, thump, whack 6 affect, assail, attack, cudgel, delete, hammer, pummel, thrash 7 assault, impress, inflict, inspire, wildcat 8 discover, stoppage

strike out 4 dele 5 elide 6 delete, efface 7 expunge

striking 5 showy, vivid 6 cogent, marked, signal 7 salient, telling 8 forceful 9 arresting, prominent 10 compelling, noticeable, remarkable 11 conspicuous, outstanding

Strindberg play 6 Easter, Father (The) 8 Comrades 9 Creditors (The), Dream Play (A), Miss Julie 10 Master Olaf 11 Ghost Sonata (The) 12 Dance of Death (The), Gustavus Vasa

string 3 row 4 file, line, rank, tier 5 chain, order, queue, train, twine 6 sequel, series 7 echelon 8 recourse, resource, sequence 10 succession *together:* 4 bead *up:* 4 hang 5 noose, scrag 6 gibbet

stringent see **strict**

stringy 4 lean, ropy, wiry 6 sinewy 7 fibrous 8 muscular

strip 4 band, bare, doff, flay, husk, peel, sack, skin 5 scale 6 billet, denude, divest, expose, fillet, ravage, ribbon 7 bandeau, deprive, disrobe, pillage, uncover, undress 8 unclothe *leather:* 5 thong *of wood:* 4 lath, slat *skin, blubber:* 5 scarf 6 flense

stripe 3 ilk 4 band, kind, lash, sort, type 5 order 6 strake, streak 7 banding, chevron, lineate, striate, variety

stripling 3 boy, lad 5 youth 9 youngster 10 adolescent

stripper 6 peeler, teaser 9 ecdysiast

stripteaser see **stripper**

strive 4 try, vie 5 seek 5 labor 6 strain 7 attempt, contend 8 endeavor, struggle 9 undertake

stroke 3 fit, hit, pet, rub 4 blow, hone, whet 5 swing 6 attack, caress, fondle, soothe 7 flatter 8 apoplexy, ischemia 9 heartbeat

stroll 4 rove, turn, walk 5 amble, drift, mosey, paseo 6 cruise, linger, ramble, wander 7 saunter, traipse 9 promenade

stroller 4 pram 6 go-cart 8 carriage 12 baby carriage, perambulator

strong 4 fast, firm, hard 5 burly, hardy, lusty, solid, sound, stout, tough 6 brawny, hearty, heroic, mighty, potent, robust, rugged, secure, sinewy, stable, sturdy 7 durable, intense, staunch 8 forceful, muscular, powerful, stalwart, vigorous 9 resilient, strapping, tenacious 10 able-bodied, full-bodied, spirituous 12 concentrated

strong-arm 5 bully 6 bounce, coerce, hector, lean on 7 assault, dragoon 8 browbeat, bulldoze, bullyrag 9 terrorize 10 intimidate

strongbox 4 arca, safe 5 chest 6 coffer 9 reliquary 13 treasure chest

stronghold 4 fort 7 bastion, bulwark, citadel, redoubt 8 fastness, fortress

strongman 4 Amin (Idi), Tito 5 Assad

(Hafez), Perón (Juan) **6** Castro (Fidel), Chávez (Hugo), despot, Marcos (Ferdinand), Mobutu (Sese Seko), Samson, Taylor (Charles), tyrant **7** Batista (Fulgencio), Hussein (Saddam), Noriega (Manuel), Suharto **8** caudillo, Pinochet (Augusto) **9** Milošević (Slobodan), Mussolini (Benito)

strong point 5 forte **6** métier

strong suit see **strong point**

strontium symbol 2 Sr

strophe 5 verse **6** stanza

struck 3 hit **5** smote

structure 4 form **5** frame **6** format, makeup, system **7** anatomy, complex, edifice, network **8** building, erection, skeleton **9** framework **10** morphology **11** arrangement, composition

struggle 3 try, vie **4** agon **5** trial **6** battle, effort, hassle, strain, strife, strive, tussle **7** attempt, compete, contend, contest, grapple, scuffle **8** endeavor, exertion, flounder, skirmish, striving **9** undertake **11** undertaking

strumpet 4 bawd, jade, slut, tart **5** hussy, tramp, trull, wench **6** floozy, harlot, hooker, wanton **7** jezebel,.trollop **8** slattern

strut 6 flaunt, parade, prance, sashay **7** flounce, peacock, show off, swagger

stub 3 end **4** butt, tail **5** stump **6** put out, strike **7** remnant **10** extinguish

stubborn 5 balky, rigid **6** cussed, dogged, mulish, ornery **7** adamant, lasting, willful **8** obdurate, perverse **9** obstinate, pigheaded, steadfast, unbending **10** bullheaded, determined, headstrong, inexorable, inflexible, persistent, rebellious, refractory, relentless, unyielding **11** intractable **12** contumacious, pertinacious, single-minded

stubby 5 dumpy, short, squat, stout **0** stocky, stumpy **8** heavyset, thickset

stuck 5 clung, glued **6** jammed, wedged **7** adhered, baffled, blocked, saddled, stabbed, stopped, stumped **8** attached, held fast **11** overcharged

stuck-up 4 vain **6** sniffy, snippy, snooty **7** haughty **8** snobbish **9** conceited **12** narcissistic, supercilious

stud 3 guy **4** dude, hunk, male, nail, post **5** cleat, he-man, himbo, macho **6** button, pillar **7** earring, speckle, upright **8** sprinkle, stallion

student 4 tiro, tyro **5** pupil, tutee **6** novice **7** protégé, scholar **8** disciple, neophyte **10** apprentice *college:* **9** undergrad **13** undergraduate *female:* **4** coed *first-year:* **5** frosh **8** freshman *fourth-year:* **6** senior *French:* **5** élève **8** étudiant *military:* **5** cadet, middy **10** midshipman *second-year:* **4** soph **9** sopho-

more *third-year:* **6** junior *wandering:* **7** goliard

studio 4 shop **7** atelier **8** workroom, workshop

studious 7 bookish, learned **9** scholarly

Studs Lonigan creator 7 Farrell (James T.)

study 3 con, den, vet **4** case, cram, muse **5** étude **6** ponder, survey **7** analyze, examine, inspect, reverie **8** consider **9** attention, think over **10** excogitate, scrutinize

stuff 3 jam, ram **4** cram, fill, glut, junk, pack, sate, tamp **5** crowd, gorge, shove **6** matter, things **7** essence, jam-pack, squeeze, surfeit **8** material, overfill **9** substance **11** possessions

stuffy 4 dull, prim **5** close, fuggy, heavy, humid, stale, thick **6** narrow, stodgy **7** airless, bloated, genteel, humdrum, pompous, prudish, stilted **8** priggish, stagnant, stifling **9** hidebound, Victorian **10** oppressive, pontifical **11** puritanical, suffocating **12** narrow-minded **13** self-important, self-righteous

stultify 4 dull **6** deaden, impair, stifle, weaken **7** inhibit, nullify, repress, smother, trammel **8** restrain, stagnate, suppress **9** suffocate **10** discourage, invalidate

stumble 3 err **4** reel, slip, trip **5** error, fluff, gaffe, lapse, lurch **6** falter, muddle, slipup, totter **7** blunder, faux pas, mistake, stagger, stammer **8** flounder

stump 3 end **4** beat, butt, dare, defy, plod, stub **5** barge, clomp, clump, stick **6** baffle, outwit, puzzle, stymie, trudge **7** buffalo, flummox, galumph, mystify, nonplus, perplex **8** bewilder, campaign, confound, hustings, politick **9** barnstorm, challenge **11** electioneer

stun 4 daze **5** amaze, floor, shock **6** dazzle **7** astound, nonplus, stagger, stupefy **8** astonish, bewilder, bowl over, knock out, paralyze **9** dumbfound **11** flabbergast

stunning 6 superb **7** amazing, awesome **8** gorgeous, striking **9** excellent, wonderful **10** astounding, impressive, remarkable, staggering, surprising **11** astonishing

stunt 4 curb, feat **5** antic, caper, check, dwarf, prank, trick **6** hinder, impair, retard **8** escapade, hold back, suppress

stupefy 4 daze, dull, faze, stun **5** addle, amaze **6** muddle, rattle **7** astound, nonplus, petrify, stagger **8** astonish, bewilder, paralyze **9** disorient, dumbfound **11** flabbergast

stupendous 4 huge **6** amazing, awesome, massive, titanic **8** colossal, enormous, gigantic, stunning, towering, wondrous **9** fantastic, humongous, marvelous, monstrous, wonderful **10** astounding, miraculous, mon-

umental, phenomenal, prodigious, staggering, tremendous **11** astonishing, spectacular
12 breathtaking, mind-boggling, overwhelming

stupid 3 dim **4** dull, dumb, slow **5** dense,
dopey, inane, silly, thick **6** oafish, obtuse,
simple, torpid **7** asinine, brutish, doltish,
fatuous, foolish, idiotic, moronic, witless **8**
backward, ignorant, mindless, retarded **9**
brainless, fatheaded, imbecilic, laughable,
ludicrous, pinheaded, senseless, vexatious
10 half-witted, slow-witted **11** blockheaded,
thickheaded, thick-witted **12** exasperating
13 chuckleheaded

stupor 6 torpor, trance **7** languor **8** dullness,
hebetude, lethargy, narcosis **9** lassitude, torpidity **10** anesthesia, somnolence **13** insensibility *combining form:* **4** narc **5** narco

sturdy 5 hardy, solid, sound, stout, tough **6**
robust, rugged, secure, strong **7** durable,
healthy, staunch **8** stalwart, vigorous **9**
strapping

sturgeon 6 beluga *roe:* **6** caviar

Sturm und Drang 5 angst **6** unease, unrest **7**
anxiety, ferment, turmoil **8** disquiet **9** agitation **10** inquietude, turbulence **11** disquietude, restiveness **12** restlessness

St. Vitus' _____ 5 dance

sty 3 pen **4** coop, cyst **6** pigpen **7** piggery

stygian 4 dark **6** gloomy **7** hellish, sunless **8**
infernal, plutonic **9** Cimmerian, plutonian

style 3 fad, way **4** chic, élan, mode, rage,
vein **5** craze, decor, flair, trend, vogue **6**
manner **7** fashion, panache **10** dernier cri **11**
savoir-faire *hair:* **4** coif **8** coiffure

stylish 3 mod **4** chic, posh, tony, trig **5**
doggy, natty, ritzy, sassy, sharp, showy,
sleek, slick, smart, swank, swell **6** chichi,
dapper, dressy, modern, modish, snappy,
snazzy, spiffy, trendy, with-it **7** à la mode,
dashing, doggish **8** spiffing, up-to-date **10**
newfangled **11** fashionable

stymie 4 stop **5** block **6** hamper, hinder, impede, thwart **7** flummox, prevent **8** confound, obstruct **9** frustrate, hamstring

Stymphalides' slayer 8 Heracles, Hercules

Styron novel 13 Sophie's Choice **22** Confessions of Nat Turner (The)

Styx *father:* 7 Oceanus *ferryman:* **6** Charon
location: **5** Hades *mother:* **6** Tethys

Styx's counterpart 5 Lethe **7** Acheron, Cocytus **10** Phlegethon

suave 4 oily **5** slick **6** smarmy, smooth, urbane **7** cordial, courtly, gallant, politic, refined, tactful, worldly **8** debonair, gracious,
polished, unctuous, well-bred **9** courteous

10 cultivated, diplomatic **12** ingratiating **13**
sophisticated

sub 5 below, proxy, under **6** backup, fill-in **7**
stand-by, stand-in **8** pinch-hit **9** alternate,
secondary, surrogate **10** understudy **11**
locum tenens, pinch hitter, replacement

subaltern 8 inferior **9** secondary, underling

subdue 4 curb, tame **5** crush, quash, quell **6**
defeat, master, quench **7** conquer, control,
put down, repress, squelch **8** beat down,
overcome, suppress, tone down, vanquish **9**
overpower, overthrow, subjugate

subdued 4 soft, tame **5** muted, quiet, sober **6**
low-key, mellow, subtle **7** neutral, serious **8**
low-keyed, softened, tasteful, tempered **9**
moderated, toned down **10** controlled, restrained, submissive **11** unobtrusive

subjacent 3 low **5** lower, under **6** lesser,
nether **8** inferior

subject 3 apt **4** core, open **5** liege, motif,
point, prone, theme, topic **6** expose, liable,
likely, matter, motive, vassal **7** citizen, exposed, lay open, problem **8** argument, inferior, material, question **9** dependent,
leitmotif, secondary, sensitive, subjugate,
substance, tributary **11** subordinate, subservient, susceptible

subjective 6 biased **10** prejudiced

subjugate see **subdue**

sublime 4 holy **5** ideal, lofty, noble, proud **6**
august, divine, sacred, superb **7** blessed, exalted **8** elevated, glorious, heavenly, majestic, splendid **9** celestial, spiritual **11**
magnificent, resplendent **12** transcendent

submarine 4 hero **5** po'boy, U-boat **6** hoagie
7 grinder *detector:* **5** sonar

submerge 3 dip **4** duck, dunk, sink **5** drown,
flood, swamp **6** deluge, engulf, plunge **7**
founder, go under, immerse **8** inundate,
overflow

submerse see **submerge**

submissive 4 meek, tame **6** abject, docile,
pliant **7** servile, slavish, subdued **8** amenable, obedient, obeisant, yielding **9** compliant, tractable **10** obsequious **11** acquiescent,
deferential, subservient, unresisting **12** nonresisting

submit 3 bow **4** cave, fold, obey **5** defer, offer, yield **6** accede, comply, give in, hand
in, relent, send in, tender **7** concede, deliver, go under, present, proffer, provide,
subject, succumb, suggest **9** acquiesce, surrender **10** capitulate **11** buckle under **12**
knuckle under

subordinate 5 minor, scrub, under **6** junior **7**
adjunct, subject **8** inferior **9** accessory, ancillary, auxiliary, dependent, secondary,

subaltern, tributary, underling **10** collateral, submissive, subsidiary **11** subservient

sub rosa 6 covert, secret **7** furtive, private **8** covertly, in camera, secretly, stealthy **9** by stealth, furtively, privately, secretive, underhand **10** stealthily **11** clandestine, underhanded **13** clandestinely, surreptitious

subscribe 3 ink **4** sign **5** agree **6** accede, adhere, assent, attest, pledge **7** approve, consent, endorse, support **8** sanction **9** acquiesce

subsequent 4 next **5** after, later **6** serial **7** ensuing **9** following, resultant, resulting **10** sequential, succeeding, successive **11** consecutive *prefix:* **4** post

subsequently 4 next, then **5** after, later, since **9** afterward **10** afterwards, thereafter

subservient 6 abject, docile **7** fawning, ignoble, servile, slavish **8** adjuvant, obeisant **9** accessory, ancillary, auxiliary, compliant, truckling **10** collateral, obsequious, submissive **11** acquiescent, deferential, subordinate, sycophantic

subside 3 die, ebb **4** ease, fall, lull, sink, wane **5** abate, let up, taper **6** ease up, recede, settle **7** decline, descend, die away, die down, dwindle, ease off, slacken **8** decrease, diminish, moderate

subsidiary 5 minor **6** backup, branch **7** subject **8** adjuvant **9** accessory, ancillary, auxiliary, secondary, tributary **10** collateral **11** subordinate **12** supplemental **13** supplementary

subsidize 4 back, fund **5** endow, stake **7** finance, promote, sponsor, support **8** bankroll **9** grubstake **10** underwrite

subsidy 4 gift **5** grant **6** reward **10** subvention **13** appropriation

subsistence 4 keep, salt **5** bread, means **6** income, living **7** support **9** resources **10** livelihood, sustenance **11** maintenance, wherewithal **12** alimentation

substance 3 nub **4** bulk, core, crux, gist, mass, meat, pith, soul **5** being, drift, focus, heart, point, sense, stuff, tenor **6** amount, burden, entity, import, kernel, marrow, matter, nubbin, object, thrust, upshot, wealth **7** essence, meaning, nucleus, purport **8** material, property, sum total **9** resources **12** essentiality, quintessence

substantial 3 big **4** full **5** ample, hefty, large, meaty, solid **6** strong, sturdy **7** massive, sizable, weighty **8** abundant, concrete, material, physical, sensible, tangible **9** corporeal, important, objective **10** meaningful, phenomenal **11** significant **12** considerable

substantiate 5 prove **6** embody, evince, verify **7** bear out, confirm, justify **8** evidence, manifest, validate **9** establish, incarnate, objectify, vindicate **11** corroborate, demonstrate **12** authenticate

substantive 4 firm, noun, real **5** solid **8** definite **9** essential

substitute 4 mock, sham, swap **5** dummy, locum, proxy, trade **6** acting, backup, deputy, double, ersatz, fill-in, refuge, resort, second, switch **7** replace, reserve, standby, stand-in, stopgap **8** exchange, recourse, resource, spurious **9** alternate, expedient, imitation, makeshift, simulated, surrogate, temporary **10** artificial, expediency, understudy **11** alternative, locum tenens, pinch hitter, replacement, succedaneum

substratum 4 base **5** basis **6** bottom, ground **7** bedrock, footing **10** foundation, groundwork **12** underpinning

substructure 4 base, seat **5** basis **6** bottom **7** footing **10** foundation, groundwork **12** underpinning

subsume 6 embody, take in **7** contain, embrace, include, involve **8** comprise **9** encompass **10** comprehend

subterfuge 4 ploy, ruse, scam, sham **5** cheat, feint, fraud **6** deceit, dupery **7** chicane **8** trickery **9** chicanery, deception **10** dishonesty

subterranean 11 underground

subtle 4 fine **5** faint **6** artful, astute **7** cunning, refined **8** delicate, finespun, guileful, skillful **9** insidious **10** indistinct **13** inconspicuous

subtract 6 deduct, remove **7** take off **8** discount, knock off, take away, withdraw, withhold

subtraction 6 rebate **8** discount **9** abatement, deduction **10** diminution, withdrawal *term:* **7** minuend **9** remainder **10** subtrahend

suburb 5 slurb **8** edge city

suburbs 7 fringes **8** environs, purlieus **9** outskirts

subversion 8 sabotage **11** undermining **12** undercutting

subvert 5 upset **6** debase **7** corrupt, deprave, vitiate **8** overturn, sabotage **9** overthrow, undermine

subway *British:* **4** tube **11** underground *French:* **5** métro

succeed 3 win **4** boom **5** click, ensue, go far, score **6** arrive, follow, go over, make it, pan out, thrive, win out **7** catch on, come off, make out, prevail, prosper, replace, triumph **8** displace, flourish, get ahead, make good, supplant **9** supervene succes ____ 3 fou 7 d'estime

success 3 hit 4 fame 5 smash, éclat 6 wealth 7 arrival, fortune, killing, triumph, victory 8 fruition 10 attainment, prosperity 11 achievement, fulfillment

successful 5 boffo, smash, socko 7 booming 8 fruitful, thriving 9 effective, lucrative 10 prosperous, triumphant, victorious 11 flourishing

succession 3 row 5 chain, cycle, march, order, round, suite, train 6 course, sequel, series, string 8 sequence 11 progression

successive 4 next 7 ensuing 9 following 10 subsequent

successor 4 heir 8 claimant, follower 9 inheritor 11 beneficiary

succinct 4 curt 5 blunt, brief, pithy, short, terse 7 brusque, compact, concise, laconic, summary 11 compendious

succor 3 aid 4 help, lift 6 assist, relief 7 comfort, relieve, support 10 assistance, sustenance

succulent 5 juicy 8 luscious *plant:* 4 aloe, hoya 5 agave, ficus, yucca 6 cactus, cereus, hoodia, viscum 7 begonia

succumb 3 bow, die 4 cave, fold, wilt 5 defer, yield 6 accede, buckle, cave in, expire, give in, perish, relent, resign, submit 7 give out, go under, knuckle 8 collapse 9 break down, surrender 10 capitulate 11 buckle under 12 knuckle under

sucker 3 con, gyp, sap 4 bilk, dupe, fool, gull, mark, rook 5 cheat, chump, patsy, shoot 6 diddle, pigeon 7 defraud, fall guy, swindle 8 hoodwink, pushover 9 bamboozle

suckle 5 nurse 7 nourish, nurture 10 breastfeed

Sudan *capital:* 8 Khartoum *desert:* 6 Libyan *language:* 6 Arabic *monetary unit:* 5 dinar *neighbor:* 4 Chad 5 Congo, Egypt, Kenya, Libya 6 Uganda 7 Eritrea 8 Ethiopia *river:* 4 Nile *sea:* 3 Red

sudden 4 rash 5 hasty, swift 6 abrupt, prompt 7 hurried 8 headlong 9 impetuous, impromptu, impulsive 10 unexpected, unforeseen 11 precipitant, precipitate, precipitous

suddenly 5 aback 7 hastily, shortly, unaware 8 abruptly, promptly, unawares 9 all at once 10 by surprise 12 unexpectedly

suds 4 beer, fizz, foam, head, soap 5 froth, spume 6 lather

sue 8 litigate

suer 8 litigant

suet 3 fat 4 lard 6 tallow

Suez Canal *builder:* 7 Lesseps (Ferdinand de) *city:* 8 Ismailia, Port Said

suffer 4 ache, bear, lump 5 abide, admit, allow, brook, leave, stand, yield 6 accept, endure, permit, submit 7 agonize, anguish, stomach, sustain, swallow, undergo 8 tolerate 10 experience 11 countenance

sufferer 6 victim

suffering 4 ache 5 agony, dolor 6 misery, ordeal 7 anguish, passion, torment, torture 8 distress 10 affliction, misfortune

suffice 5 avail, serve

sufficient 3 due 5 ample 6 common, decent, enough, plenty 8 adequate, all right 9 competent, tolerable 10 acceptable 11 comfortable 12 commensurate, satisfactory 13 commensurable, proportionate *poetic:* 4 enow

suffocate 5 burke, choke 6 stifle 7 smother 8 snuff out, strangle 10 asphyxiate

suffrage 4 vote 5 voice 6 ballot 9 franchise

suffragist 4 Catt (Carrie Chapman), Howe (Julia Ward), Mott (Lucretia), Paul (Alice) 5 Stone (Lucy) 7 Anthony (Susan B.), Bloomer (Amelia), Stanton (Elizabeth Cady) 8 Woodhull (Victoria Claflin) 9 Pankhurst (Emmeline)

suffuse 4 fill 5 bathe, flush, imbue, steep 7 pervade 8 permeate, saturate 10 impregnate

sugar 6 aldose, fucose, ribose, xylose 7 glucose, lactose, maltose, mannose, pentose, sorbose, sucrose, sweeten 8 fructose, furanose, levulose 10 saccharose *burnt:* 7 caramel *combining form:* 4 gluc, glyc, sucr 5 gluco, glyco, sucro 7 sacchar 8 sacchari, saccharo *from palm sap:* 7 jaggery *Mexican:* 7 panocha, penuche *source:* 4 beet, cane, corn 5 maple

sugarcane refuse 7 bagasse

sugarcoat 5 candy 6 veneer 7 sweeten, varnish 8 palliate 9 extenuate, gloss over, gloze over, whitewash

sugary 6 syrupy 7 cloying, honeyed, mawkish 10 saccharine 11 sentimental

suggest 4 hint 5 evoke, imply 6 submit 7 connote, propose, signify 8 indicate, intimate 9 adumbrate, insinuate

suggestion 3 cue 4 clue, hint 5 shade, smack, tinge, trace 6 advice 7 inkling 8 allusion, innuendo, overtone, proposal, reminder 9 suspicion, undertone 10 indication, intimation 11 implication, insinuation

suggestive 4 racy 5 salty, spicy 6 ribald, risqué 8 off-color 9 evocative 10 indicative 11 reminiscent

suicidal pilot 8 kamikaze

suicide 8 felo-de-se 10 self-murder 13 self-slaughter *Japanese:* 7 seppuku 8 hara-kiri, hari-kari

suit 3 fit **4** case, jibe, plea **5** adapt, agree, befit, cause, check, serve, tally **6** accord, action, adjust, appeal, become, go with, please, prayer, square, tailor **7** conform, enhance, flatter, lawsuit, request, satisfy **8** entreaty, petition **9** agree with, reconcile **10** go together **11** accommodate, application, imploration, imprecation **12** solicitation, supplication *card:* **5** clubs **6** hearts, spades **8** diamonds *type:* **4** zoot **6** monkey, vested **9** paternity **10** pin-striped **11** class-action

suitable 3 apt, due, fit **4** just, meet **5** right **6** proper, seemly, useful **7** condign, fitting **8** apposite, becoming, deserved, eligible **9** pertinent, qualified, requisite **10** acceptable, felicitous **11** appropriate

suitcase 3 bag **4** grip **6** valise **7** carry-on, holdall **8** carryall

suite 3 lot, row, set **4** flat **5** array, group, rooms, staff, train **6** sequel, series, string **7** lodging, retinue **8** chambers, sequence **9** apartment, entourage, following

suitor 4 beau **5** lover, spark, swain, wooer **7** admirer, gallant, sparker **8** cavalier, paramour **9** boyfriend **10** petitioner

sulfur 9 brimstone

sulk 4 mope, pout **5** brood, gloom

sulky 4 cart, dour, glum **5** moody **6** gloomy, morose, sullen **7** crabbed **9** saturnine

sullen 4 dour, glum, mean, sour **5** moody, pouty, surly **6** crabby, dismal, gloomy, grumpy, morose, somber, sombre **7** crabbed, pouting **8** lowering, scowling **9** glowering, saturnine **10** ill-humored **11** pessimistic

Sullivan's partner 7 Gilbert (William Schwenk)

sully 3 tar **4** soil **5** dirty, shame, smear, stain, taint **6** defame, defile, malign, vilify **7** asperse, blacken, pollute, slander, tarnish, traduce **8** besmirch, disgrace, dishonor **9** denigrate

Sultan of Swat 8 Babe Ruth

sultry 3 hot **4** sexy **5** close, humid, muggy **6** steamy, sticky, stuffy, torrid **7** airless **8** stifling **9** seductive **10** passionate, sweltering, voluptuous

sum 3 add, all, tot **4** mass, tote **5** gross, total, whole **6** amount, digest, entity, figure, resumé **7** epitome **8** entirety, integral, nutshell, totality **9** aggregate, epitomize

Sumatra *country:* **9** Indonesia *highest peak:* **7** Kerinci **8** Kerintji *largest city:* **5** Medan *shrew:* **4** tana

Sumerian *city:* **4** Kish, Umma **5** Erech **6** Lagash, Nippur *dragon:* **3** Kur *god:* **3** Abu, Kur, Utu **4** Enki **5** Enlil, Lahar, Nanna, Nintu **6** Dumuzi, Nergal, Ninazu **7** Enkimdu *goddess:* **6** Ningal, Ninlil

summarize 5 recap **6** digest **7** abridge, outline **8** boil down, condense **9** epitomize, synopsize **11** encapsulate **12** recapitulate

summary 5 recap **6** aperçu, digest, précis, résumé, review, wrap-up **7** compend, epitome, outline, roundup, rundown **8** abstract, overview, scenario, synopsis **9** inventory **10** abridgment, compendium, conspectus **11** abridgement **12** condensation

summer *French:* **3** été *Spanish:* **6** verano

summerhouse 6 alcove, gazebo, pagoda **9** belvedere

summery 7 estival

summit 3 top **4** acme, apex, peak, roof **5** crest, crown **6** apogee, climax, height, vertex, zenith **8** capstone, meridian, pinnacle **11** culmination

summon 3 bid **4** call, cite **5** evoke, order **6** beckon, call in, invite, muster **7** arraign, command, conjure, convene, convoke, send for **8** assemble, subpoena

sump 4 sink **8** cesspool

sumptuous 4 lush, rich **5** grand **6** costly, deluxe, lavish, superb **7** opulent **8** gorgeous, luscious, palatial, splendid **9** grandiose, luxurious **11** extravagant, resplendent **12** awe-inspiring

sun 3 orb, Sol **4** bask, star **7** daystar, phoebus **8** daylight, luminary, radiance **9** radiation *combining form:* **4** heli **5** helio *disk:* **4** Aten *god:* **3** Lug, Sol, Tem, Utu **4** Amen, Atmu, Atum, Inti, Lleu, Llew, Lugh, Utug **5** Horus, Sunna, Surya **6** Apollo, Babbar, Helios, Marduk **7** Khepera, Ninurta, Phoebus, Shamash **8** Hyperion, Merodach

Sun Also Rises, The *author:* **9** Hemingway (Ernest) *character:* **6** Ashley (Brett), Barnes (Jake)

sunder 3 cut **4** rend, rive **5** break, sever, slice, split **6** cleave, divide **8** dissever, disunite, separate

sundial part 6 gnomon

sundown 4 dusk **7** evening **8** eventide, gloaming, twilight

sundries 7 notions **8** oddments **9** etceteras **11** odds and ends

sundry 4 many, some **6** varied **7** diverse, several, various **8** assorted, manifold, numerous **9** different, disparate **12** multifarious **13** miscellaneous, multitudinous

sunfish 4 opah **7** pompano **8** bluegill **11** pumpkinseed

Sunflower State 6 Kansas

sun-god see at **sun**

Sun King 8 Louis XIV

sunny 4 fair, fine, warm **5** clear, happy **6** blithe, bright, cheery, chirpy, golden **7** beaming, clarion, radiant **8** cheerful, pleasant, rainless **9** brilliant, cloudless, unclouded **10** optimistic

sunrise 4 dawn, morn **6** aurora **7** dawning, morning **8** cockcrow, daybreak, daylight *goddess:* **3** Eos **6** Aurora

sunroom 8 solarium

sunset 3 eve **4** dusk **7** evening **8** gloaming, twilight

Sunset State 6 Oregon

Sunshine State 7 Florida

sunup see **sunrise**

sup 3 eat **4** dine **5** feast

super 4 very **5** great **8** powerful, splendid, terrific **9** excellent, extremely, fantastic, first-rate, wonderful **11** outstanding

superannuated 4 aged **5** hoary, passé **6** bygone **7** ancient, archaic, elderly, outworn **8** obsolete, outdated, outmoded **9** out-of-date **10** antiquated **11** obsolescent **12** old-fashioned

superb 4 A-one, rich **5** grand, lofty, noble, prime, primo, super **7** elegant, exalted, optimal, optimum, opulent, stately, sublime, supreme **8** glorious, gorgeous, imposing, majestic, peerless, splendid, standout **9** excellent, marvelous, matchless, wonderful **11** magnificent, outstanding, resplendent, sensational, splendorous **13** splendiferous

supercilious 5 lofty **6** lordly, sniffy, snippy **7** haughty, stuck-up **8** cavalier, snobbish, superior **10** disdainful **11** patronizing **13** condescending, high-and-mighty

superficial 5 hasty **6** breezy, casual, slight **7** cursory, shallow, sketchy, surface, trivial **8** external, skin-deep **9** depthless, frivolous **11** perfunctory

superfluity 4 glut **5** frill **6** excess **7** nimiety, overrun, surfeit, surplus **8** overflow, overkill, overload, overmuch, overplus, plethora **10** oversupply, redundancy, surplusage **11** prodigality **12** extravagance **13** overabundance

superfluous 5 extra, spare **6** de trop, excess, otiose **7** surplus **8** needless **9** excessive, redundant **10** gratuitous **11** uncalled-for, unnecessary

superintend 4 boss **6** direct, manage **7** control, oversee **10** administer

superintendence 4 care **6** charge **7** conduct, running **8** handling **9** authority, direction, oversight **10** management

superior 4 rare **5** above, lofty, major, prime, proud, upper **6** better, choice, higher, lordly, select, sniffy, snippy, snooty **7** capital,

greater, haughty, premium, stuck-up **8** arrogant, brass hat, cavalier, dominant, higher-up, insolent **9** excellent, first-rate, marvelous **10** disdainful, first-class, preeminent, preferable, remarkable **11** exceptional, overbearing, patronizing, predominant **13** condescending, high-and-mighty

superiority 9 advantage, dominance, seniority, supremacy, upper hand **10** ascendancy

superjacent 4 over **6** higher **7** greater **9** overlying

superlative 3 ace **4** A-one, best **8** peerless, standout **9** matchless **10** consummate **11** magnificent, outstanding

Superman 9 Clark Kent *actor:* **4** Alyn (Kirk), Cain (Dean) **5** Reeve (Christopher), Routh (Brandon) **6** Reeves (George) **7** Collyer (Bud) *bane:* **10** kryptonite *birthplace:* **7** Krypton *creator:* **7** Shuster (Joe) *employer:* **11** Daily Planet (The) *father:* **5** Jor-El *foe:* **3** Zod (General) **6** Luthor (Lex) **7** Bizarro **8** Brainiac, Darkseid, Doomsday, Mxyzptlk (Mr.) *friend:* **5** Olsen (Jimmy) *girlfriend:* **8** Lois Lane *mother:* **4** Lara *original name:* **5** Kal-El

supernatural 5 magic **6** divine, mystic **7** magical, psychic, uncanny **8** heavenly **9** celestial, unearthly **10** miraculous, paranormal, phenomenal **12** metaphysical, transcendent **13** extraordinary

supernatural being 3 elf, fay, god, hob, imp, nix **4** jinn, ogre, peri, puck **5** afrit, angel, bogle, deity, demon, fairy, gnome, jinni, lamia, naiad, nixie, nymph, pixie, satyr, sylph, Titan, troll **6** afreet, goblin, kelpie, seraph, spirit, sprite **7** banshee, brownie, bugbear, goddess, incubus, silenus, vampire, wendigo, windigo **8** bogeyman, demiurge, succubus **9** boogeyman, hobgoblin **10** leprechaun

supernumerary 5 extra, spare **6** de trop, excess, walk-on **7** reserve, surplus **8** leftover **9** redundant

supersede 5 usurp **7** replace, succeed **8** displace, supplant

supervene 5 ensue, occur **6** befall, follow, result **7** succeed **9** eventuate, transpire

supervise 3 run **4** boss **5** steer **6** direct, govern, manage **7** conduct, control, monitor, oversee, proctor, referee **8** chaperon, overlook **10** administer

supervision 4 care **6** charge **7** control, running **8** auspices, handling **9** direction, oversight **10** intendance, management **11** stewardship

supervisor 7 foreman, manager **8** director, overseer **13** administrator

supine 5 inert, prone, slack 7 passive 8 inactive, indolent 9 prostrate, recumbent 10 horizontal 12 outstretched

supper club 6 nitery 7 cabaret 9 night spot

supplant 4 oust 5 usurp 6 cut out, unseat 7 replace, succeed 8 crowd out, displace, force out 9 overthrow, supersede

supple 5 agile, lithe, withy 6 limber, nimble, pliant, whippy 7 ductile, elastic, lissome, plastic, pliable, springy, willowy 8 flexible, graceful, moldable 9 adaptable, malleable, resilient

supplement 3 add, pad 4 coda 5 rider 6 append, beef up, enrich, extend, sequel 7 adjunct, augment, codicil, enhance, fill out, fortify 8 addendum, addition, appendix, buttress, increase 9 accessory, reinforce 10 postscript, strengthen

suppliant 5 asker 6 beggar, suitor 9 solicitor 10 petitioner

supplicant see **suppliant**

supplicate 3 ask, beg, sue 4 pray 5 crave, plead 6 appeal, invoke 7 beseech, entreat, implore, solicit 8 petition 9 importune

supplication 4 plea, suit 6 appeal, orison, prayer 8 entreaty, petition 11 application

supplies 6 stores 8 matériel 9 equipment, materials 10 provisions

supply 3 man 4 feed, fund, hand, help 5 cache, equip, hoard, stock, store 6 afford, outfit, purvey 7 deliver, fulfill, furnish, provide, reserve, satisfy, surplus 8 dispense, hand over, transfer, turn over 9 inventory, provision, reservoir, stockpile 10 contribute 12 accumulation

support 3 aid 4 back, base, bear, hand, help, lift, prop, root, side, stay 5 abide, adopt, boost, brace, bread, brook, carry, favor, shore, strut, truss 6 anchor, assist, bear up, buoy up, column, crutch, defend, endure, girder, pillar, prop up, second, suffer, uphold, verify 7 alimony, applaud, approve, backing, bolster, comfort, confirm, embrace, endorse, espouse, fortify, fulcrum, nourish, nurture, pull for, shore up, stiffen, sustain, trestle 8 abutment, advocate, backstop, buttress, champion, mainstay, maintain, sanction, side with, tide over, underpin 9 encourage, reinforce, underprop 10 assistance, foundation, livelihood, provide for, strengthen, sustenance 11 corroborate, hand-holding, maintenance, subsistence 12 underpinning

supporter 3 fan 4 ally 6 patron 7 booster, sectary 8 adherent, advocate, champion, disciple, exponent, follower, henchman, partisan 9 proponent

suppose 4 deem 5 allow, guess, infer, opine, posit, think 6 assume, expect, gather, reckon 7 believe, imagine, presume, pretend, surmise, suspect 8 consider 9 postulate, speculate 10 conjecture 11 hypothesize

supposed 7 alleged, seeming 8 apparent, putative 10 ostensible

supposition 2 if 5 guess, hunch, posit 6 notion, theory, thesis 7 premise, surmise 9 postulate 10 assumption, conjecture, hypothesis 11 postulation, presumption, speculation

supposititious 6 unreal 7 dubious, fictive, reputed 8 doubtful, fanciful, illusory, putative, spurious 9 fantastic, fictional, imaginary, pretended, simulated 10 chimerical, fictitious, fraudulent 11 conjectural 12 hypothetical, illegitimate, questionable

suppress 4 curb, stop 5 burke, check, choke, crush, drown, quash, quell, shush, spike, stunt 6 arrest, censor, cut off, hush up, muffle, muzzle, quench, retard, squash, stifle, subdue 7 abolish, collect, conceal, control, prevent, put down, silence, smother, squelch, swallow 8 prohibit, restrain, snuff out, withhold 9 overthrow 10 extinguish

suppurate 6 fester

supra 5 above

supremacy 7 control, mastery 8 dominion 9 authority, dominance 10 ascendancy, domination, mastership, prepotency 11 preeminence, sovereignty 12 predominance 13 preponderance

supreme 4 best 5 chief, final, prime 6 superb, utmost 7 highest, leading, maximum, perfect 8 absolute, cardinal, crowning, foremost, greatest, peerless, towering, ultimate 9 matchless, paramount, principal, sovereign, unequaled, unmatched, unrivaled 10 preeminent, surpassing 11 culminating, predominant, superlative, unmatchable, unsurpassed 12 incomparable, transcendent, unparalleled 13 unsurpassable

Supreme Being 3 God 5 Allah 7 creator, Jehovah 8 Almighty *belief in:* 5 deism

Supreme Court justice 3 Jay (John) 4 Taft (William Howard) 5 Alito (Samuel), Black (Hugo), Chase (Salmon P.), Kagan (Elena), Stone (Harlan Fiske), Story (Joseph), Taney (Roger B.) 6 Breyer (Stephen G.), Burger (Warren), Holmes (Oliver Wendell), Hughes (Charles Evans), Scalia (Antonin), Souter (David), Thomas (Clarence), Vinson (Fred), Warren (Earl) 7 Brennan (William), Cardozo (Benjamin), Douglas (William O.), O'Connor (Sandra Day), Roberts (John G.), Stevens (John Paul), Kennedy (Anthony M.) **8** Blackmun (Harry), Brandeis (Louis), Ginsburg (Ruth Bader), Marshall (John, Thurgood) **9** Rehnquist (William), Sotomayor (Sonia) **11** Frankfurter (Felix)

surcease 3 end **4** halt, quit, rest, stay, stop **6** desist **7** refrain, respite, suspend **8** knock off, leave off, postpone, stoppage **9** cessation, remission **10** suspension **11** discontinue **12** postponement

sure 3 set **4** fast, firm, safe **5** fixed **6** indeed, secure, stable, steady, strong **7** certain, staunch **8** absolute, definite, enduring, positive, reliable, unerring **9** confident, convinced, steadfast **10** convincing, dependable, inevitable, infallible, undeniable, unshakable, unwavering **11** indubitable, trustworthy, unequivocal, unfaltering **12** indisputable **13** incontestable, unquestioning

surefire 7 assured, certain **8** reliable **10** dependable, guaranteed

sure thing 6 shoo-in, winner **9** certainty

surety 4 bail, bond **5** angel **6** backer, patron, pledge **7** sponsor **8** guaranty, security, warranty **9** certainty, certitude, guarantee, guarantor **10** confidence, conviction

surf 4 scan, skim **6** browse **9** bodyboard, kneeboard

surfing term 4 deck, tube **5** leash **6** A-frame, barrel, drop in, hollow, turtle **7** bail out, carving, cutback, grommet, hang ten, snaking, wipeout **8** backdoor, blown out **9** goofy foot **10** impact zone **12** kneeboarding

surface 3 top **4** face, pave, rise, skin **5** cover **6** appear, come up, emerge, facade, facing, finish, patina, show up, veneer **7** outside **8** covering, exterior **11** superficial

surfeit 4 cloy, fill, glut, jade, pall, sate **5** gorge, stuff **6** excess **7** replete, satiate, surplus **8** overfill, overflow, overkill, overmuch, overplus, plethora **10** surplusage **11** overindulge, superfluity **13** overabundance

surge 4 flow, gush, pour, rise, roll, rush, soar, tide, wave **5** flood, swell **6** billow, deluge, sluice, stream **7** torrent

surgeon 8 sawbones *American:* **4** Mayo (Charles, William), Reed (Walter) **6** Thorek (Max) **7** Cushing (Harvey), DeBakey (Michael) **8** McDowell (Ephraim) *English:* **5** Paget (James) **6** Lister (Joseph) *French:* **4** Paré (Ambroise) **5** Broca (Paul) *South African:* **7** Barnard (Christiaan)

surgery 9 operation *instrument:* **5** clamp, curet, laser **6** gorget, lancet, splint, stylet, trocar **7** forceps, scalpel

surgical removal 8 ablation *combining form:* **6** ectomy

Suriname *capital:* **10** Paramaribo *former name:* **11** Dutch Guiana **6** Sranan *monetary unit:* **7** guilder *mountain range:* **10** Tumac-Humac *neighbor:* **6** Brazil, Guyana **12** French Guiana *river:* **6** Maroni **8** Suriname **10** Courantyne

surly 4 dour, glum **5** cross, gruff, sulky **6** crusty, grumpy, morose, sullen **7** bearish, crabbed, grouchy **8** churlish, menacing, snappish **9** irritable, saturnine **10** ungracious **11** ill-mannered, threatening **12** discourteous

surmise see **suppose**

surmount 3 cap, top **4** best, down, leap, lick **5** clear, climb, crest, crown, excel, outdo, vault **6** better, hurdle, master **7** conquer, surpass **8** outstrip, overcome, vanquish **9** negotiate, transcend

surpass 3 cap, top **4** beat, best **5** excel, outdo, trump **6** better, exceed, outrun **7** eclipse, outpace **8** go beyond, outclass, outshine, outstrip, outweigh, overstep **9** transcend **10** overshadow

surplice 5 cotta, ephod **8** vestment

surplus 5 extra, spare **6** excess **7** overage, overrun, reserve, surfeit **8** leftover, overflow, overkill, overmuch, plethora **9** overstock, remainder **10** oversupply **11** superfluity, superfluous

surprise 4 faze, stun **5** amaze, floor **6** ambush, dismay, rattle, waylay, wonder **7** astound, capture, nonplus, stagger, startle, stupefy **8** astonish, bewilder, bowl over **9** amazement, dumbfound, overpower, take aback **11** flabbergast **12** astonishment, stupefaction

surreal 5 weird **7** bizarre **9** dreamlike, fantastic **10** outlandish **12** unbelievable

surrealist 3 Arp (Jean), Ray (Man) **4** Dalí (Salvador), Népo **5** Ernst (Max) **6** Breton (André), Tanguy (Yves) **8** Magritte (René) **9** de Chirico (Giorgio)

surrender 4 cave, cede, fold **5** waive, yield **6** cave in, give in, give up, resign, submit **7** abandon, concede, succumb **8** cry uncle, hand over **10** abdication, capitulate, relinquish, submission **12** capitulation *sign:* **7** hands up **9** white flag

surreptitious see **stealthy**

surrogate 3 sub **5** proxy **6** acting, deputy, fill-in **7** stand-in, stopgap **9** makeshift **10** substitute **11** locum tenens, pinch hitter, replacement

surround 3 hem, rim **4** edge, gird, loop, ring **5** beset, bound, hem in, limit, round, skirt, verge **6** border, circle, fringe, girdle, margin **7** besiege, compass, confine, enclose, envelop, outline **8** encircle **9** encompass **12** circumscribe

surrounding 5 about **7** ambient **12** circumjacent *prefix:* **4** peri **6** circum

surroundings 6 milieu **7** ambient **8** ambience **11** environment

surveillance 3 eye, tab **4** tail **5** vigil, watch **7** lookout **8** scrutiny, stakeout **9** vigilance **11** supervision

survey 3 con, vet **4** case, poll, scan, view **5** assay, audit **6** assess, précis, review, size up **7** canvass, examine, inspect, pandect, perusal, preview **8** analysis, appraise, estimate, evaluate, look over, overlook, overview, scrutiny, syllabus **9** check over **10** scrutinize **11** reconnoiter

survive 4 keep, last **6** endure **7** carry on, hold out, outlast, outlive, outwear, persist, recover, ride out, weather **8** continue, live down **9** withstand **11** come through, live through, pull through

Surya 6 sun-god *son:* **4** Manu, Yama **5** Karna **6** Asvins *temple site:* **7** Konarak

susceptible 4 open **5** naive, prone **6** liable **7** exposed, pliable, subject **8** disposed, inclined, sensible **9** malleable, receptive, sensitive **10** responsive, vulnerable **11** impressible, persuadable

suspect 5 doubt, fishy, guess **6** assume, unsure **7** believe, dubious, imagine, suppose, surmise **8** distrust, doubtful, mistrust **9** doubtable, uncertain **10** disbelieve **11** problematic

suspend 3 bar **4** bate, halt, hang, stay, stop **5** debar, defer, delay, hover, sling **6** dangle, depend, hold up, put off, shelve **7** adjourn, hold off **8** intermit, postpone, prorogue **9** eliminate **11** discontinue

suspended 6 frozen **7** hanging, pendant, pendent, stopped **8** dangling, swinging **9** pendulous

suspenders 6 braces **8** galluses

suspense 7 anxiety, mystery, tension **10** expectancy **11** expectation, uncertainty **12** apprehension

suspension 4 halt, stay, stop **5** delay, letup, pause **6** cutoff, freeze **7** latency, respite, time-out **8** abeyance, dormancy, stoppage **9** remission **10** moratorium, quiescence **11** cold storage, withholding **12** intermission, interruption, postponement

suspicion 4 hint **5** doubt, dread, guess, hunch, qualm, shade, smell, tinge, touch, trace, whiff **7** concern, dubiety, surmise **8** distrust, mistrust, wariness **9** chariness, misgiving **10** foreboding, intimation, skep-

ticism, suggestion **11** incertitude, premonition, supposition, uncertainty

suspicious 4 wary **5** chary, fishy, leery **7** dubious, jealous, suspect **8** doubtful, watchful **9** doubtable, skeptical **11** distrustful, mistrustful, problematic **12** apprehensive, questionable

suspire 4 sigh **5** sough

sustain 4 bear, feed, prop, save **5** brace, carry, stand **6** bear up, buoy up, endure, foster, hold up, keep up, succor, suffer, uphold **7** bolster, confirm, nourish, nurture, prolong, relieve, shore up, support, undergo **8** buttress, preserve

sustenance 3 pap **4** food, keep, meat **5** bread, means **6** living, viands **7** aliment, alimony, pabulum, support **8** victuals **9** nutriment, provender **10** livelihood, provisions **11** maintenance, nourishment, subsistence, wherewithal

susurration 4 purr **6** mumble, murmur, mutter, rustle **7** whisper **9** undertone

suture 3 sew **4** seam **6** stitch

suzerain 5 ruler **8** overlord **9** sovereign

svelte 4 slim **5** lithe, sleek, suave **6** smooth, urbane **7** elegant, slender **8** graceful

swab 3 mop **4** Q-Tip **5** clean **6** sponge

swaddle 4 roll, wrap **5** drape **6** enfold, swathe, wrap up **7** blanket **8** enshroud, enswathe

swag 3 sag, yaw **4** loot, sway, tilt **5** booty, droop, lurch, money, prize **6** boodle, spoils **7** festoon, garland, pillage, plunder **10** contraband

swagger 4 brag **5** boast, bully, strut, swank, swash, swell **6** sashay **7** bluster, bravado, peacock, saunter **9** arrogance, cockiness, gasconade **11** braggadocio, swashbuckle

swagman 4 hobo **5** rover, tramp **7** drifter, vagrant **8** vagabond, wanderer

swain 4 beau **5** lover, spark, wooer **6** rustic, suitor **7** admirer **8** shepherd **9** boyfriend

swallow 3 buy, sip **4** bear, belt, bolt, down, gulp, swig, take, toss, wolf **5** abide, brook, drink, quaff, slurp, stand, swill **6** absorb, accept, digest, endure, guzzle, imbibe, ingest, inhale **7** believe, consume, fall for, repress, retract, stomach **8** chugalug, take back, tolerate **11** ingurgitate

swamp 3 bog, fen **4** holm, mire, moss, muck, quag **5** drown, flood, glade, marsh, whelm **6** deluge, engulf, morass, muskeg, slough **7** bottoms **8** inundate, overcome, overflow, quagmire, submerge **9** everglade, marshland, overwhelm *Everglades:* **10** Big Cypress *Georgia:* **10** Okefenokee *North Carolina-Virginia:* **6** Dismal swamped **716**

swamped 5 awash **7** brimful, flooded, overrun **8** engulfed **9** inundated, submerged **11** overflowing, overwhelmed
Swamp Fox 6 Marion (Francis)
swan *female:* **3** pen *genus:* **4** Olor **6** Cygnus *male:* **3** cob **4** cobb *young:* **6** cygnet
swank 4 posh, tony, trig **5** boast, fancy, ritzy, sharp, showy, smart, swell, swish **6** chichi, classy, dapper, deluxe, lavish, plushy, snappy, trendy **7** elegant, peacock, show off, splashy, stylish, swagger **8** peacocky **9** glamorous, luxurious **10** flamboyant, peacockish
Swan Lake *character:* **5** Odile **6** Odette **9** Siegfried (Prince) **11** Von Rothbart *composer:* **11** Tchaikovsky (Pyotr Ilyich)
swap 5 trade, truck **6** barter, change, switch **7** bargain, traffic **8** exchange **10** substitute
swarm 3 jam, mob **4** army, bevy, herd, host, mass, pack, push, shin, teem **5** crawl, crowd, crush, drove, flock, group, horde, mount, press **6** abound, gather, myriad, throng **7** climb up, cluster, overrun **9** multitude, pullulate **10** congregate
swarthy 4 dark **5** dusky, sooty **6** brunet **8** bistered
swash 3 lap **4** brag, dash, gush, rush, slop **5** boast, churn, douse, froth, plash, slosh **6** bubble, burble, gurgle, seethe, splash **7** bluster, channel, saunter, spatter, splurge, swagger
swat 3 bat, box, hit, rap **4** bash, belt, blow, cuff, lick, slap, slog, slug, sock **5** blast, clout, homer, knock, smack, smash, smite, swipe, whack **6** buffet, larrup, strike, wallop **7** clobber
swath 4 belt, path **5** strip, sweep **6** stroke
swathe see **swaddle**
sway 4 bend, bias, rock, rule **5** lurch, range, reach, scope, sweep, swing, waver, weave **6** affect, careen, direct, govern, totter, wobble **7** command, control, dispose, impress, incline, mastery, stagger, win over **8** dominate, dominion, overrule, persuade, undulate **9** authority, dominance, fluctuate, influence, oscillate, vacillate **10** domination, predispose
Swaziland *capital:* **7** Lobamba, Mbabane *language:* **5** Swazi *monetary unit:* **9** lilangeni *neighbor:* **10** Mozambique **11** South Africa *river:* **5** Usutu **6** Komati **8** Umbeluzi
swear 3 vow **4** avow, bind, cuss, damn, oath, rail, rant **5** abuse, curse, vouch **6** adjure, affirm, assert, attest, depone, depose, pledge, plight **7** declare, promise, testify, warrant **8** covenant, maintain **9** blaspheme, imprecate **10** asseverate

swearword 4 cuss, oath **5** curse **9** expletive, obscenity
sweat 4 emit, glow, moil, ooze, seep, toil, weep **5** exude, grind, labor **6** strain, swivet **7** excrete **8** perspire, transude **12** perspiration
sweater 8 cardigan, pullover, slipover **10** turtleneck
sweaty 6 clammy, sticky **7** glowing **10** perspiring
Sweden *Arctic region:* **7** Lapland *capital:* **9** Stockholm *city:* **5** Malmö **8** Göteborg *gulf:* **7** Bothnia **8** Kattegat *island:* **5** Öland **7** Gotland *lake:* **6** Vänern **7** Mälaren, Vättern **9** Hjälmaren *monetary unit:* **5** krona *mountain range:* **5** Kölen *neighbor:* **6** Norway **7** Finland *part of:* **11** Scandinavia *river:* **3** Dal *sea:* **6** Baltic
Swedish Nightingale 4 Lind (Jenny)
Swedish pop group 4 ABBA
sweep 3 arc, fly, mop, win **4** flit, sail, scud, skim, wing **5** ambit, broom, brush, clean, clear, curve, drive, orbit, range, reach, scope, surge, whisk **6** extent, radius, search **7** compass, purview, victory **9** extension
sweeping 5 broad **6** all-out **7** blanket, general, overall, radical **8** thorough, whole-hog **9** extensive, inclusive, out-and-out, universal, wholesale **11** far-reaching **12** all-embracing
sweepings 4 dust **5** trash, waste **6** debris, litter, refuse **7** garbage, residue, rubbish **8** detritus
sweet 5 candy, honey **6** bonbon, dulcet, lovely, sugary, syrupy **7** angelic, cloying, dessert, melodic, scented, sugared, winning, winsome **8** aromatic, fragrant, heavenly, luscious, perfumed **9** ambrosial, delicious **10** delectable, saccharine *combining form:* **4** glyc **5** glyco
Sweet ____ 7 Adeline, Charity **8** Caroline **12** Georgia Brown
sweeten 5 candy, honey, sugar **6** soften **7** appease, assuage, enhance, mollify, placate **9** sugarcoat, sugar over **10** conciliate, propitiate
sweetheart 3 gra **4** dear, love **5** flame, honey **7** beloved, darling, tootsie **10** heartthrob, honeybunch
sweetmeat 5 candy **6** comfit **8** delicacy, preserve **10** confection
sweet potato 3 yam **7** boniato
sweet-talk 4 coax **5** charm **6** banter, cajole, wangle **7** blarney, flatter, wheedle **8** blandish, butter up, inveigle, soft-soap
swell 4 fine, grow, keen, neat, pout, puff **5** bloat, bulge, dandy, neato, nifty, pouch, su-

per, surge, swank **6** abound, billow, blow up, dilate, expand, groovy, peachy **7** amplify, augment, balloon, distend, enlarge, inflate, peacock, swagger, upsurge **8** increase, jim-dandy, terrific **9** crescendo, marvelous, wonderful *British:* **3** nob **4** toff

swelled head 5 pride **6** egoism, vanity **7** conceit, egotism **8** smugness **9** arrogance, vainglory **10** narcissism **11** amour propre, self-conceit

swelling 3 sty **4** boil, bubo, bump, corn, gall, node **5** bulge, edema, tumid, tumor **6** bunion, growth, nodule **7** gibbous **8** tubercle **9** carbuncle, chilblain, expansion, tumescent **10** tumescence **11** excrescence **12** inflammation, protuberance

sweltering 3 hot **5** fiery **6** baking, sultry, torrid **7** burning **8** broiling, roasting, sizzling **9** scorching

swerve 3 yaw **4** skew, turn, veer **5** sheer, shift, stray, waver **6** depart, wander **7** deflect, deviate

swift 4 fast **5** fleet, hasty, quick, rapid, ready **6** prompt, snappy, speedy, sudden **8** full-tilt, headlong **9** breakneck

___ **Swift 3** Tom **8** Jonathan *character:* **8** Gulliver

swiftness 4 gait, pace **5** haste, hurry, speed **6** hustle **8** celerity, dispatch, legerity, rapidity, velocity

swig 4 belt, down, drag, gulp, pull, slug **5** booze, draft, drain, drink, quaff, swill **6** guzzle, imbibe, tipple **7** swallow, swizzle

swill 4 bolt, gulp, slop, swig, tope, wolf **5** booze, draft, drink, gorge, scarf, scoff, slops **6** debris, gobble, guzzle, inhale, spilth, tank up, tipple **7** consume, garbage, hogwash, rubbish, swizzle

swim 3 dip **4** reel, spin, turn **5** bathe, crawl, float, swoon, whirl **9** dizziness, dog-paddle

swimmingly 6 easily **8** smoothly **10** splendidly

swimming stroke 5 crawl **7** dolphin, trudgen **9** butterfly, dog paddle

swindle 3 con, gyp **4** bilk, clip, dupe, fake, hoax, rook, scam, sell, sham, skin, soak **5** bunco, bunko, cheat, cozen, fraud, gouge, phony, rogue, shaft, skunk, sting **6** chouse, diddle, fleece, humbug, hustle, take in **7** con game, defraud **8** flimflam, hoodwink **9** bamboozle, imposture, victimize **11** hornswoggle

swindler 5 cheat, crook, ganef, gonif, shark **6** con man, goniff **7** sharper, shyster **8** deceiver **9** charlatan, defrauder **10** mountebank

swine see **hog**

swing 4 jive, slew, slue, sway, veer **5** flail, lurch, pivot, twirl, waver, weave, whirl, wield **6** dangle, divert, rhythm, rotate, seesaw, stroke, swerve, switch **7** revolve, suspend **8** brandish **9** alternate, fluctuate, oscillate, vacillate

swinish 5 feral **6** coarse **7** beastly, bestial, porcine

swipe 3 cop, hit, nab, rap **4** blow, clip, conk, grab, hook, lick, lift, nick, sock, swat, wipe **5** clout, filch, heist, knock, pinch, smack, steal **6** pilfer, snatch, snitch, strike, wallop

swirl 4 eddy, purl, roil **5** curve, twist, whirl, whorl **6** swoosh, vortex **9** whirlpool **11** convolution

swish 4 buzz, chic, fizz, hiss, posh, tony, whiz **5** ritzy, smart, swank, whisk **6** classy, dressy, sizzle, trendy, whoosh **7** elegant, stylish **8** sibilate

Swiss Family Robinson author 4 Wyss (Johann David)

switch 3 rod, wag **4** beat, flay, flog, lash, swap, veer, wand, whip **5** shift, shunt, trade, whisk **6** change, strike, waggle **7** scourge **8** exchange, flip-flop, reversal **9** about-face, sidetrack **10** substitute **12** substitution

Switzerland *canton:* **3** Uri, Zug **4** Jura, Vaud **5** Berne **6** Geneva, Ticino, Valais *capital:* **4** Bern **5** Berne *city:* **5** Basel **6** Geneva, Zürich **8** Lausanne *lake:* **6** Geneva, Lausanne **7** Lucerne **9** Constance, Neuchâtel, Thunersee, Zürichsee *language:* **6** French, German **7** Italian *monetary unit:* **5** franc *mountain, range:* **4** Alps, Jura **9** Monte Rosa *neighbor:* **5** Italy **6** France **7** Austria, Germany **13** Liechtenstein *resort:* **5** Davos, Vevey **7** Zermatt **8** Montreux, St. Moritz **10** Interlaken *river:* **3** Aar **4** Aare **5** Rhine, Rhône *state:* **6** canton

swivel 4 spin, turn **5** pivot, swing, twirl, whirl **6** rotate **7** revolve **9** pirouette

swivet see **snit**

swizzle 3 mix **4** stir **5** swill **6** guzzle, tipple

swollen 5 puffy, tumid **6** turgid **7** bloated, bulbous, bulging, pompous **8** enlarged, inflated, varicose **9** bombastic, distended, tumescent **10** rhetorical

swoon 4 coma, daze, fade **5** droop, faint **6** torpor **7** pass out, rapture, syncope **8** black out

swoosh 4 eddy, gush, purl, rush **5** swirl, whirl, whorl

sword 4 épée, foil **5** saber, sabre **6** barong, bilboa, rapier, Toledo **7** cutlass **8** claymore, falchion, scimitar, yataghan

sword-shaped 6 ensate **8** ensiform

sworn 6 avowed **7** devoted **8** affirmed **9** committed, confirmed **10** deep-rooted, deep-seated, entrenched, inveterate

sybarite 7 epicure **8** hedonist **9** libertine **10** sensualist, voluptuary

sybaritic 6 carnal **7** sensual **8** sensuous **9** epicurean, libertine, luxurious **10** hedonistic, voluptuous

sycophancy 7 fawning **8** flattery, toadying **9** truckling **11** bootlicking

sycophant 5 leech, toady **6** flunky, lackey, minion, yes-man **8** groveler, hanger-on, parasite, truckler **9** easy rider, flatterer, toadeater **10** bootlicker, self-seeker **11** lickspittle **13** apple-polisher

sycophantic 7 fawning, servile, slavish **8** toadying, unctuous **9** groveling, kowtowing, parasitic, truckling **10** obsequious **11** bootlicking

Sycorax's son 7 Caliban

syllable *deletion:* **7** apocope *last:* **6** ultima *lengthening of:* **7** ectasis *musical:* **2** do, fa, la, mi, re, si, ti, ut **3** sol *next to last:* **6** penult *shortening:* **7** elision, systole *stressed:* **5** arsis

syllabus 6 aperçu, digest, précis, sketch, survey **7** epitome, outline, pandect, summary **8** abstract, headnote, synopsis **10** compendium

sylph 5 fairy, nymph **6** sprite

sylvan 5 bosky, woody **6** rustic, wooded *deity:* **3** Pan **4** Faun **5** dryad, satyr **6** Faunus **7** Silenus **8** Arethusa, Silvanus, Sylvanus

symbol 4 icon, logo, mark, sign **5** badge, glyph, motif, stamp, token **6** design, device, emblem, mascot *chemical:* see individual element *musical:* **4** clef, flat, hold, note, rest, turn **5** shake, sharp **7** fermata, mordent, natural

symbolic 5 token **10** emblematic **11** allegorical

symbolist poet 7 Rimbaud (Arthur) **8** Mallarmé (Stéphane), Verlaine (Paul)

symbolize 4 mean **6** embody, mirror, typify **7** signify **8** stand for **9** epitomize, exemplify, personify, represent **10** illustrate **11** emblematize

symmetrical 5 equal **7** regular **8** balanced

symmetry 5 order **6** parity **7** balance, harmony **8** equality, evenness **9** agreement, congruity **10** conformity, proportion, regularity **11** arrangement

sympathetic 4 kind, warm **6** benign, caring, humane, kindly, tender **8** amenable, friendly **9** agreeable, approving, benignant, congenial, congruous, consonant, favorable, receptive **10** compatible, consistent,

responsive **11** considerate, kindhearted, softhearted, warmhearted

sympathize 4 pity **7** condole **11** commiserate

sympathy 4 pity, ruth **5** heart **6** accord, solace, warmth **7** comfort, harmony, rapport **8** affinity, kindness **9** agreement **10** benignancy, compassion, condolence, kindliness, tenderness **11** consolation, sensitivity **13** commiseration

symphonic 10 orchestral

symphony 9 orchestra **12** philharmonic *movement:* **5** rondo **6** minuet

symposium 5 forum **7** meeting, seminar **9** gathering **10** conference, discussion

symptom 4 mark, sign **5** index, token **8** evidence **10** indication

symptoms 7 indicia **8** syndrome

synagogue 4 shul **6** temple *platform:* **5** bimah

sync 4 jibe **5** agree, match **7** harmony **8** coincide **9** harmonize **10** concurrent **12** simultaneous

synchronize 5 agree **6** concur **8** coincide

synchronous 6 coeval **10** coetaneous, coexistent, coexisting, coincident, concurrent **11** concomitant **12** contemporary, simultaneous **13** geostationary

syncope 4 coma **5** faint, swoon **8** blackout

syndicate 3 mob **4** pool **5** chain, group, mafia, trust, union **6** cartel, league **7** combine **11** association, partnership **12** conglomerate, organization

syndrome 3 ill **6** malady **7** ailment, disease **8** disorder, sickness **9** complaint, condition, infirmity

synergic 5 joint **6** shared **8** coacting, coactive, conjoint **9** collusive, concerted **11** cooperating, cooperative, coordinated

synod 4 body, diet **7** council, meeting **8** assembly, conclave, congress **10** conference, convention **11** convocation

synopsis 5 brief, recap **6** aperçu, digest, précis, review **7** capsule, epitome, outline, rundown, summary **8** abstract, breviary, syllabus **10** abridgment, compendium, conspectus **12** condensation

synopsize 5 recap, sum up **6** digest **7** outline, summate **8** abstract, boil down, compress, condense **9** epitomize, inventory, summarize

synthesis 5 blend, union **6** fusion, merger **7** amalgam **8** blending, compound **9** composite **11** combination **12** amalgamation **13** incorporation

synthesize 4 fuse, meld **5** blend, merge, unify **7** combine **8** compound **9** harmonize, integrate **10** amalgamate **11** incorporate

synthetic 6 ersatz **7** man-made, plastic **9** imitation, unnatural **10** artificial, fabricated **11** counterfeit *fiber:* **3** PBI, PLA **5** Modal, Mylar, Nomex, nylon, Orlon, saran, Zylon **6** Kevlar, olefin, sulfar, Twaron, vinyon **7** acetate, acrylic, lyocell, spandex, vectran, vinalon **9** polyester **10** modacrylic

Syria *capital:* **8** Damascus *city:* **4** Homs **6** Aleppo *language:* **6** Arabic, French *monetary unit:* **5** pound *neighbor:* **4** Iraq **6** Israel, Jordan, Turkey **7** Lebanon

syringe 4 hypo **6** needle **10** hypodermic

Syrinx 5 nymph *pursuer:* **3** Pan

syrinx 7 panpipe **8** panpipes

syrup 6 orgeat **9** grenadine

syrupy 5 gooey, mushy, sappy, sweet **6**

dripply, dulcet, slushy, sticky, sugary **7** cloying, maudlin, mawkish **9** schmaltzy **10** saccharine **11** sentimental

system 3 way **4** mode, plan **5** modus, order, setup **6** entity, manner, method, scheme **7** complex, network, pattern, process, regimen, routine **8** strategy **9** procedure, structure, technique

systematic 7 logical, ordered, orderly, regular **8** arranged **9** organized **10** analytical, methodical

systematize 5 array, order **6** codify **7** arrange, catalog, dispose, marshal **8** classify, organize, regiment **9** catalogue, methodize

system of weights 4 troy **11** avoirdupois **12** apothecaries

T

tab 4 bill, cost, flap, list, loop, rate **5** check, count, price, score **6** charge, record **7** account, invoice **8** eagle eye, price tag, scrutiny **9** appendage, designate, extension, reckoning, statement **12** surveillance

tabard 4 cape, coat **5** tunic **10** coat of arms

tabby 3 cat **6** feline, cement **8** brindled

tabernacle 4 tent **5** hovel **6** church, temple

tabes 7 atrophy, wasting **12** degeneration

Tabitha's Greek name 6 Dorcas

table 4 fare, list **5** bench, board, chart, defer, stand **6** buffet, put off, record, shelve, teapoy **7** counter **8** mahogany, postpone **9** sideboard *ornament:* **7** epergne **11** centerpiece *writing:* **4** desk **9** secretary **10** escritoire

table d'___ 4 hôte

tableland 4 mesa **5** butte **6** upland **7** plateau *Alabama-West Virginia:* **10** Cumberland *Arizona:* **5** Kanab **6** Kaibob *England:* **8** Dartmoor *India:* **5** Malwa (see also **plateau**)

tablet 3 bar, pad **4** cake, disk, pill, slab **5** panel, slate **6** pellet, plaque, troche **7** lozenge, notepad **8** steno pad

tableware 4 cups **5** bowls, china, forks **6** dishes, knives, plates, silver, spoons **7** glasses, saucers **8** settings, utensils **9** stainless

tabloid 3 rag **5** lurid, pulpy **6** digest **7** summary **9** condensed, newspaper **11** sensational **12** scandal sheet

taboo 3 ban **4** no-no **6** banned, enjoin, forbid, outlaw **7** inhibit, obscene **9** forbidden, ineffable, interdict, off-limits, restraint **10** inhibition **11** restriction, unspeakable **12** interdiction

tabor 4 drum

tabulate 4 list **5** count, order **6** codify, figure, record **7** arrange **9** enumerate **11** systematize

tabulation 4 list **5** chart, tally **6** record **7** account

tabula ___ 4 rasa

tacit 6 silent, unsaid **7** assumed, implied **8** implicit, inferred, unspoken **9** intimated, suggested **10** subtextual, undeclared, underlying, understood **11** acquiescent, unexpressed **12** inarticulate

taciturn 4 dumb **6** silent **7** laconic **8** reserved, reticent, wordless **9** secretive **11** tightlipped **12** closemouthed

Tacitus work 7 Annales **8** Dialogus, Germania **9** Historiae

tack 3 pin, yaw **4** beat, brad, gear, join, nail, stay, turn **5** baste, reach, shift **6** attach, course, double, stitch, swerve, turn up, zigzag **7** tangent **8** put about **9** come about, deviation **10** alteration, deflection, digression, sea biscuit **11** ship biscuit **12** pilot biscuit

tackle 3 cat, rig **4** gear, sack **6** outfit, take on, take up **7** halyard, lineman, rigging **8** set about **9** apparatus, equipment, machinery, undertake **10** footballer, linebacker, plunge into **13** paraphernalia

tacky 5 cheap, crude, dingy, dowdy, gaudy, messy, seedy, ratty, tatty **6** blowsy, frowsy, frumpy, kitsch, shabby, sleazy, sloppy, sticky, frumpy, tawdry, untidy, vulgar **7** run-down, unkempt **8** adhesive, frumpish, slovenly **9** inelegant, tasteless, unstylish **10** down-at-heel, threadbare

tact 5 poise, touch **6** acumen **7** address, finesse, suavity **8** civility, courtesy, delicacy, urbanity **9** diplomacy, politesse **10** adroitness, politeness, smoothness **11** savoir faire, sensitivity

tactful 5 civil, suave **6** adroit, urbane **7** politic **8** delicate, discreet, polished **9** courteous, sensitive **10** diplomatic, perceptive, thoughtful **11** considerate

tactic 4 hoax, plan, play, ploy, ruse, scam **5** dodge, feint, means, stunt, trick **6** device, gambit, method **7** sleight **8** approach, artifice, maneuver, strategy **9** procedure, stratagem

tactical 7 politic, prudent **9** advisable, expedient, strategic

tactics 4 plan **6** method, scheme **8** maneuver, playbook, strategy **9** stratagem

tactile 8 palpable, tangible **9** touchable

taction 4 feel **5** touch **7** contact **9** palpation

tactless 4 rude **5** blunt, crude, inept **6** candid, clumsy, gauche **7** awkward **8** impolite **9** impolitic, maladroit **10** indiscreet **11** insensitive

tad 3 bit, boy, lad, son **4** lick, mite, snap, spot, whit **5** child, crumb, shade, sonny, speck **6** laddie, nipper, shaver **7** smidgen **8** fraction

tadpole 8 polliwog, pollywog

taffy 5 candy **8** flattery

tag 3 bit, dog, end **4** cost, flag, game, logo, mark, name, tail **5** aglet, brand, label, price, trail **6** append, charge, follow, select, shadow, slogan, tassel, tatter, ticket **7** license, run down **8** graffito, identify, insignia

tagline 5 motto **6** byword, slogan

Tahiti *city:* **7** Papeete *painter:* **7** Gauguin (Paul) *war god:* **3** Oro

tail 3 dog, end, tag **4** butt, rear **5** hound, stalk **6** follow, pursue, shadow **7** hind end, rear end **8** backside, buttocks **9** posterior *bone:* **6** coccyx *relating to:* **6** caudal *short:* **4** scut

tailed 7 caudate

tailor 3 fit, hem, sew **4** suit **5** adapt, alter, style **7** fashion **8** clothier, seamster **11** haberdasher

tailor-made 6 fitted, suited **7** bespoke, fitting **8** suitable **10** well-suited **11** appropriate

taint 3 rot **4** blot, blur, foul, harm, hurt, smut, soil, spot, turn, vice **5** brand, cloud, color, decay, dirty, fault, smear, spoil, stain, sully, touch **6** befoul, darken, defile, poison, smudge, smutch **7** blacken, blemish, corrupt, pollute, putrefy, tarnish **8** besmirch, discolor **9** discredit **10** adulterate, stigmatize **11** contaminate

taipan 5 snake **8** merchant **11** businessman

Taiwan 7 Formosa *capital:* **6** Taipei *channel:* **5** Bashi *city:* **6** T'ai-nan **8** Pan-ch'iao, T'ai-chung **9** Kao-hsiung *language:* **8** Mandarin *leader:* **13** Chiang Kai-shek *mountain:* **6** Yü Shan

Tajikistan *capital:* **8** Dushanbe *monetary unit:* **5** diram **6** somoni *monetary unit, former:* **5** ruble, tanga *mountain, range:* **6** Pamirs **9** Communism (Peak), Trans Alai **10** Revolution (Peak) *neighbor:* **5** China **10** Kyrgyzstan, Uzbekistan **11** Afghanistan *river:* **8** Amu Dar'ya, Syr Dar'ya

Taj Mahal 9 mausoleum *builder:* **9** Shah Jahan *site:* **4** Agra

take 3 cop, get, nab **4** glom, grab **5** annex, catch, seize, steal, swipe **6** endure, gather, obtain, secure **7** capture, receive **8** proceeds, receipts *account of:* **6** notice *advantage of:* **5** abuse **7** exploit *after:* **6** follow **8** resemble *apart:* **7** analyze, dissect **9** dismantle *care:* **6** beware *care of:* **3** fix **4** tend **5** nurse **6** attend *exception:* **6** object *five:* **4** rest **5** break, relax *from:* **7** deprive, detract **8** subtract *it easy:* **5** relax *on the:* **7** corrupt, crooked *part:* **4** join **5** share **11** participate *place:* **5** occur **6** happen *to task:* **5** scold **7** reprove *turns:* **9** alternate *unawares:* **8** surprise

take away 4 grab **5** wrest **6** arrest, commit, deduct, detach, detain, remove, revoke **7** deprive, detract **8** diminish, discount, minimize, subtract, withdraw

take back 5 unsay **6** abjure, recall, recant, return, revoke **7** replace, restore, retract, swallow **8** forswear, withdraw **9** repossess

take down 4 note **5** lower, write **6** humble, record, reduce **7** deflate **8** dismount **9** dismantle **11** disassemble

take in 3 con **4** dupe, fool, furl, jail **5** admit, bluff, board, house, trick **6** absorb, accept, arrest, attend, betray, delude, embody **7** beguile, compass, contain, deceive, embrace, include, involve, mislead, observe, receive, shelter, snooker, subsume **8** flimflam, hoodwink, perceive **9** apprehend, bamboozle, encompass, four-flush **10** assimilate, comprehend, understand **11** double-cross

take off 2 go **4** doff, exit, quit, soar **5** leave,

scram 6 begone, deduct, depart, remove, set out **7** pull out, skiddoo, vamoose **8** clear out, discount, hightail, light out, subtract, withdraw **9** skedaddle

takeoff 5 spoof **6** launch, parody, satire, send-up **7** lampoon **8** travesty **9** burlesque **10** caricature *area:* **3** pad **6** runway

take on 3 don **4** face, hire, meet **5** adopt, annex, fight **6** accept, append, assume, attack, battle, employ, engage, strike, tackle **7** contest, embrace, espouse, venture **8** endeavor, set about **9** encounter, undertake

take out 4 date, dele, kill, omit **5** loose, whack **6** deduct, excise, remove **7** destroy, release, unleash **8** discount, knock off, separate, subtract, withdraw, withhold **9** eliminate **10** annihilate

take over 5 seize, spell, usurp **6** assume **7** capture, relieve

take up 3 use **4** fill, open **5** adopt, begin, enter, raise, renew, set to, start **6** absorb, accept, assume, gather, occupy, resume, shrink, tackle **7** embrace, espouse, kick off, restart, shorten, tighten **8** commence, continue, initiate **10** recommence

talc 6 powder **8** steatite **9** soapstone

tale 3 fib, lie **4** myth, saga, yarn **5** fable, rumor, story **6** canard, legend **7** fiction **8** anecdote **9** narration, narrative

talebearer 3 rat **4** fink **5** yenta **6** canary, gossip, snitch **7** rat fink, tattler **8** busybody, gossiper, informer, quidnunc, squealer, telltale **9** informant **10** newsmonger, tattletale **11** rumormonger, stool pigeon **12** blabbermouth **13** scandalmonger

talent 4 bent, gift, head, nose **5** craft, dowry, flair, forte, knack, skill **6** genius **7** ability, aptness, faculty **8** aptitude **9** endowment, expertise

talented 4 able **6** clever, expert, gifted **8** skillful

Tale of Two Cities, A *author:* **7** Dickens (Charles) *character:* **5** Lucie (Manette) **6** Carton (Sidney), Darnay (Charles) **7** Defarge (Madame), Manette (Alexander)

Tales of a Traveller author 6 Irving (Washington)

Tales of a Wayside Inn author 10 Longfellow (Henry Wadsworth)

Tales of Hoffman composer 9 Offenbach (Jacques)

talisman 4 juju, luck **5** charm **6** amulet, fetish, grigri, mascot, scarab **7** periapt **8** grisgris **10** phylactery

Talisman author 5 Scott (Walter)

talk 3 gab, rap, yak **4** blab, buzz, chat, chin, yarn **5** prate, rumor, run on, speak, utter, voice **6** babble, gabble, gossip, parley, patter, report, speech **7** address, chatter, declaim, hearsay, lecture, prattle **8** colloquy, converse, dialogue, harangue **9** discourse, utterance **10** discussion **12** conversation *about:* **7** discuss *back:* **4** sass *empty:* **3** gas **6** hot air **7** bombast *foolish:* **4** bunk **6** babble **7** chatter, palaver *indistinctly:* **6** mumble, mutter *over:* **7** discuss *shop:* **5** argot *slowly:* **5** drawl *small:* **6** banter **8** chitchat **10** persiflage *wildly:* **4** rant, rave

talkative 4 glib **5** gabby, vocal **6** chatty, fluent **7** gossipy, voluble **9** garrulous **10** loquacious **13** communicative

talk over 6 debate **7** discuss, hash out **8** consider **9** thrash out **10** deliberate

talky 5 gabby, windy, wordy **6** chatty, prolix **7** verbose, voluble

tall 4 high, long **5** lanky, large, lofty, rangy **6** absurd **7** pompous **8** towering **9** high-flown **10** far-fetched **11** skyscraping **12** altitudinous

tallow 3 fat **4** lard, suet **6** grease

tally 3 tab **4** jibe, list, tale **5** agree, count, match, score, total **6** accord, census, number, reckon, square **7** account, balance, catalog, compute, conform, itemize **8** check off, register, tabulate **9** agreement, catalogue, enumerate, harmonize, inventory, reckoning **10** complement, correspond

talon 4 claw, hand **5** stock **6** finger

talus 5 ankle, scree, slope **9** anklebone **10** astragalus

tam 3 cap

Tamar *brother:* **7** Absalom *father:* **5** David **7** Absalom *father-in-law:* **5** Judah *half brother:* **5** Amnon *seducer:* **5** Amnon *son:* **5** Perez, Zerah

tamarisk 9 salt cedar

tambour 3 cup **4** drum **9** embroider **10** embroidery

Tamburlaine the Great author 7 Marlowe (Christopher)

tame 4 bust, dull, meek, mild **5** break, train, vapid **6** bridle, docile, gentle, humble, soften, subdue **7** harness, insipid, reclaim, subdued **8** domestic, familiar, obedient **9** tractable **10** housebreak, submissive **11** domesticate, housebroken **12** domesticated

Taming of the Shrew, The *character:* **6** Bianca **8** Baptista **9** Katharina, Petruchio *locale:* **5** Padua

Tammany boss 5 Tweed (William)

Tammuz's lover 6 Ishtar

tam-o'-shanter 3 cap

tamp 3 ram **4** pack **5** pound, press, stuff

tampion 4 plug **5** cover

tan 3 sun, taw **4** beat, ecru, flog, whip **5**

beige, brown, taupe, tawny, toast **6** bronze, darken, thrash **7** biscuit

Tan novel 11 Joy Luck Club (The) **15** Kitchen God's Wife (The) **19** Bonesetter's Daughter (The)

tanager 7 redbird

Tancred, Tancredi *beloved:* **8** Clorinda *composer:* **7** Rossini (Gioacchino) *father:* **3** Odo *mother:* **4** Emma *victim:* **8** Clorinda

tandem 4 pair **7** bicycle, concert **8** carriage

tang 3 nip **4** bite, fang, odor, ring, zest **5** aroma, clang, prong, sapor, savor, shank, smack, taste, trace **6** flavor, relish **8** piquancy, pungency, sapidity **9** spiciness

tangible 4 real **7** tactile **8** concrete, material, palpable, physical, sensible **9** corporeal, touchable **10** detectable, observable, phenomenal **11** appreciable, discernible, perceptible, substantial

tangle 3 mat, web **4** foul, knot, maze, mesh, shag **5** ravel, skein, snare, snarl **6** entrap, hamper, jumble, jungle, morass, muddle, pileup, raffle **7** dispute, embroil, ensnare, ensnarl, involve, thicket **8** obstruct **9** implicate **10** complicate **11** altercation, predicament **12** complication

Tanglewood Tales author 9 Hawthorne (Nathaniel)

tango 5 dance **8** circuity **11** indirection **13** deceitfulness

tangy 5 sharp **6** lively **7** piquant, pungent, zestful **9** flavorful

tank 3 vat **5** basin **7** cistern **8** aquarium **9** reservoir *American:* **6** Abrams **7** Bradley, Sherman *German:* **6** panzer *part:* **6** turret

tankard 3 mug **5** stein, stoup **6** flagon **9** blackjack

tanked 3 lit **4** high, lost **5** drunk, lit up, oiled **6** bashed, blotto, bombed, failed, gave up, juiced, potted, soaked, soused, stewed, stoned, tanked, wasted, zonked **7** crocked, drunken, pickled, pie-eyed, sloshed, smashed, sottish **9** collapsed, plastered **10** inebriated, liquored up **11** intoxicated

tanker 4 ship **5** oiler

Tannhäuser *character:* **5** Venus **9** Elisabeth *composer:* **6** Wagner (Richard) *locale:* **8** Wartburg **9** Venusberg

tantalize 3 rag **4** bait, lure **5** tease, tempt **6** entice, needle **7** torment **9** frustrate

Tantalus *daughter:* **5** Niobe *father:* **4** Zeus *son:* **6** Pelops

tantamount 4 same **5** alike, equal **8** parallel, selfsame **9** duplicate, identical **10** equivalent **12** commensurate

tantara 5 blare **7** fanfare

tantivy 3 run **6** gallop

tantrum 3 fit **6** blowup **8** outburst, paroxysm **9** hysterics **10** conniption

Tanzania *capital:* **6** Dodoma **11** Dar es Salaam *city:* **6** Arusha *former name:* **10** Tanganyika *island:* **5** Mafia, Pemba **8** Zanzibar *lake:* **5** Rukwa **6** Malawi **8** Victoria **10** Tanganyika *language:* **7** Swahili *monetary unit:* **8** shilling *mountain:* **11** Kilimanjaro *neighbor:* **5** Congo, Kenya **6** Malawi, Rwanda, Uganda, Zambia **7** Burundi **10** Mozambique *plain:* **9** Serengeti *river:* **6** Kagera, Rufiji, Ruvuma **7** Pangani *volcano:* **6** Lengai

Taoism founder 5 Laozi **6** Lao-tzu

tap 3 hit, pat **4** cock, draw, flap, name, plug, tick **5** chuck, draft, drain, nudge, touch, valve **6** faucet, select, siphon, spigot, strike **7** appoint, draw off, hydrant, percuss, petcock **8** drumbeat, half sole, nominate, stopcock **9** designate

tape 4 band, belt, bind **5** strip **6** fillet, ribbon **7** bandage *kind:* **5** inkle **6** ferret **7** masking **8** adhesive *machine:* **4** deck **8** recorder

taper 4 wane, wick **5** abate, close, draft, pinch, spire **6** candle, lessen, narrow, reduce **7** dwindle, glimmer **8** decrease, diminish

tapering 5 conic, spiry **6** spired, terete **7** conical **8** ensiform, fusiform, napiform, subulate **9** acuminate, attenuate **10** lanceolate

tapestry 5 arras, kilim **6** dossal **7** curtain, Gobelin, hanging *pattern:* **7** cartoon *subject:* **4** hunt **7** unicorn

Taphath's father 7 Solomon

tapioca 4 yuca **5** yucca **6** manioc **7** cassava, farinha, pudding

tapir 4 anta

taproom 3 bar, pub **4** café **6** bodega, saloon, tavern **7** cantina **8** dramshop **9** roadhouse

tapster 6 barman **7** barkeep, barmaid, skinker **9** barkeeper, bartender **10** mixologist

tar 3 gob **4** jack, salt, soil, swab **5** pitch, smear, stain, sully, taint **6** defile, hearty, sailor, seaman **7** asphalt, besmear, mariner, shipman **8** besmirch, creosote, deckhand, flatfoot **9** shellback

taradiddle 3 fib, lie **5** hooey, story, trash **6** bunkum, canard **7** baloney, falsity **8** claptrap, nonsense **9** falsehood **10** balderdash **13** prevarication

tarantella 5 dance

tarantula 6 spider **10** wolf spider

Taras Bulba author 5 Gogol (Nikolai)

tarboosh 3 fez, hat

tardy 4 dull, late, lazy, slow **7** belated, delayed, laggard, overdue **8** dilatory, sluggish **10** behindhand, delinquent, unpunctual

tare 4 seed, weed **5** vetch, weigh **6** darnel, weight **11** undesirable **13** counterweight

target 3 aim 4 butt, goal, mark, prey 5 aim at 6 object, quarry, victim 9 objective 11 sitting duck *center:* 8 bull's-eye *shooter's:* 10 clay pigeon

Tar Heel State 13 North Carolina

tariff 3 tax 4 cost, duty, levy, rate 5 price 6 charge, impost 7 tribute 10 assessment

Tarkington character 6 Penrod 10 Alice Adams

tarn 4 lake, pool

tarnish 3 dim, mar 4 dull, foul, harm, hurt, soil 5 dirty, muddy, smear, spoil, stain, sully, taint 6 damage, darken, defile, injure, smirch, smudge, smutch 7 begrime, besmear, blemish, vitiate 8 besmirch, discolor

taro 3 yam 4 eddo 5 aroid 6 yautia 7 dasheen, malanga *product:* 3 poi *root:* 4 eddo

tarpaulin 3 gob 4 jack, salt, swab 5 cover, sheet 6 hearty, sailor, seaman 7 mariner, shipman 9 shellback

tarpon 8 ladyfish 10 silverfish

tarry 3 lag 4 bide, drag, stay, wait 5 abide, dally, delay, visit 6 dawdle, linger, loiter, pitchy, remain 7 sojourn

tarsus 5 ankle

tart 3 pie 4 acid, bawd, moll, slut, sour 5 acerb, quean, sharp, tramp, trull, whore 6 biting, harlot, pastry 7 acerbic, cutting, piquant, pungent, tootsie 8 chess pie, strumpet 10 prostitute

tartar 5 argol 6 plaque 8 calculus

Tartar see **Tatar**

Tartuffe author 7 Molière

Tarzan *chimpanzee:* 7 Cheetah *creator:* 9 Burroughs (Edgar Rice) *mate:* 4 Jane *son:* 3 Boy 4 Jack 5 Korak

task 3 job 4 duty, lade, load, post, slog, toil, work 5 chare, chore, labor, stint 6 assign, burden, charge, detail, devoir 7 mission, project 8 business, encumber, function 9 challenge, dress down, reprimand 10 assignment, commission 11 undertaking 12 dressing-down

Tasmanian 4 wolf 5 devil *capital:* 6 Hobart *pine:* 4 Huon

tassel 3 tag 4 tuft 5 adorn 6 fringe 7 pendant, tzitzit 8 ornament 13 inflorescence

Tasso, Torquato *patron:* 4 Este (Alfonso II d') *work:* 6 Aminta 7 Rinaldo 18 Jerusalem Delivered

taste 3 eat, sip, try 4 tang, zest 5 savor, smack 6 flavor, liking, palate, relish 7 stomach 8 appetite, elegance, fondness, sapidity, soft spot, weakness 10 experience, partiality, preference, refinement 11 inclination *kind:* 4 salt, sour 5 sweet 6 bitter *organ:* 3 bud

tasteful 4 fine 7 elegant, genteel, refined, stylish 8 artistic, becoming 9 aesthetic

tasteless 4 dull, flat 5 bland, crass, gaudy, showy, stale, tacky, vapid 6 vulgar 7 insipid 8 off-color, unsavory 9 inelegant, savorless, unrefined 10 flavorless

tasty 5 sapid, yummy 6 dainty, delish, savory 8 luscious 9 delicious, flavorful, palatable, succulent, toothsome 10 appetizing, delectable, flavorsome 11 scrumptious

Tatar 6 Mongol, Turkic 7 Turkish 9 Mongolian *leader:* 4 Vatu

tattered 4 torn 5 dingy, seedy 6 frayed, ragged, ripped, shabby 7 raggedy, run-down, worn-out 10 bedraggled, threadbare 11 dilapidated

tattle 3 rat, wag, yak 4 blab, buzz, dish, talk, tell 5 clack, prate, rumor 6 gossip, inform, report, snitch, squeal 7 chatter, hearsay, prattle 8 chitchat 9 grapevine 11 scuttlebutt

tattletale see **talebearer**

tatty 5 cheap, dingy, dowdy, dumpy, seedy, tacky 6 beat-up, cheesy, paltry, scuzzy, shabby, shoddy, sleazy, trashy 7 run-down, scrubby 8 rubbishy 10 threadbare 11 dilapidated

taunt 3 jab 4 gibe, jeer, mock, quip, razz, skit, twit 5 scout, tease 6 deride, insult 7 affront, provoke 8 reproach, ridicule 9 challenge

taurine 6 bovine 8 bull-like

Taurus 4 bull *star:* 9 Aldebaran

taut 4 firm, snug, trim 5 rigid, tense, tight 6 corded 10 high-strung

tautology 8 iterance, pleonasm 9 iteration 10 redundancy, repetition

tavern 3 bar, inn, pub 4 café, dive 6 bistro, bodega, saloon 7 barroom, cantina, gin mill, taproom 8 alehouse, pothouse, wineshop 9 roadhouse 11 public house, rathskeller 12 watering hole 13 watering place

taverner 7 barkeep 8 boniface, publican 9 barkeeper, bartender, innkeeper 12 saloonkeeper

taw 3 tan 6 marble 7 partner

tawdry 4 loud 5 cheap, gaudy, tacky 6 brazen, flashy, garish, tinsel 7 chintzy, glaring, ignoble 9 brummagem, dime-store 12 meretricious

tawny 3 tan 4 buff 5 beige, brown, sandy 6 copper, tanned

tax 4 cess, duty, lade, levy, load, onus, scot, toll 5 drain, tithe 6 assess, burden, cumber, impost, saddle, strain, tariff, weight 7 tribute 8 encumber 10 imposition *agency:* 3 IRS *feudal:* 7 scutage, tallage *kind:* 4 geld 5 sales, tithe 6 excise, income 8 property 9 ad valorem, surcharge *on salt:* 7 gabelle *rate:* 10 assessment

taxi 3 cab, car 4 hack 5 cyclo

taxi driver 5 cabby 6 cabbie, hackie 7 hackman

taxing 5 tough 6 trying 7 exigent, onerous, wearing 8 exacting, grievous, grueling 9 demanding, difficult 10 burdensome, oppressive

Taygeta *father:* 5 Atlas *mother:* 7 Pleione *sisters:* 8 Pleiades

tazza 3 cup 4 vase

Tchaikovsky, Pyotr Ilyich *ballet:* 8 Swan Lake 10 Nutcracker (The) 14 Sleeping Beauty *opera:* 12 Eugene Onegin 13 Queen of Spades (The)

tea 5 party 6 repast 8 beverage 9 reception *black:* 5 bohea, pekoe 8 souchong *box:* 5 caddy *cake:* 6 cookie *genus:* 4 Thea *herbal:* 6 ptisan, tisane *kind:* 4 herb, Java 5 Assam, black, bohea, green, hyson, pekoe 6 Ceylon, congou, oolong 7 cambric, rooibos 8 Earl Grey, souchong 9 chamomile, sassafras 10 Darjeeling

teach 5 coach, edify, guide, train, tutor 6 impart, school 7 educate, instill, profess 8 instruct 9 enlighten, inculcate 12 indoctrinate

teacher 4 guru, prof 5 coach, guide, tutor 6 docent, master, mentor, pedant 7 maestro, trainer 8 educator 9 pedagogue, preceptor, professor 10 instructor 12 schoolmaster *Hindu:* 5 swami *Jewish:* 5 rabbi, rebbe *Muslim:* 6 mullah *organization:* 3 NEA *religious:* 9 catechist 10 mystagogue

Tea for Two composer 7 Youmans (Vincent)

team 4 band, club, crew, gang, join, pair, side, yoke 5 group, squad, troop, wagon 6 stable, troupe 8 carriage *baseball:* 4 nine *basketball:* 4 five 7 quintet *football:* 6 eleven *kind:* 2 JV 6 jayvee 7 varsity

teamster 6 driver 7 trucker

tear 3 cry, cut, fly, rip, run 4 bolt, claw, dash, drop, flaw, gash, hole, lash, pull, race, rend, rift, rive, rush, slit, snag, weep 5 chase, hurry, shoot, shred, slash, speed, split, spree 6 career, charge, course, sunder, tatter, wrench 7 droplet, fissure, rupture 8 lacerate 10 laceration

tear down 4 raze, ruin, slur 5 knock, smash, smear, wreck 6 defame, malign, vilify 7 asperse, traduce, destroy, shatter, slander 8 demolish 9 denigrate, disparage, take apart 10 annihilate, calumniate 11 disassemble

tearful 3 sad 5 misty, moist, weepy 6 crying, watery, woeful 7 bawling, sobbing, weeping 8 mournful, pathetic 9 lamenting, sniveling, sorrowful 10 blubbering, lachrymose

tear-jerking 5 mushy 6 drippy, sticky 7 maudlin, mawkish 8 touching 9 schmaltzy 11 sentimental

teary-eyed 5 blear, moist

tease 3 bug, kid, rag, rib, rip 4 bait, coax, comb, gibe, jive, josh, ride, tear, twit 5 annoy, chaff, chivy, harry, shred, taunt, worry 6 cajole, harass, needle, pester, pick on, plague 7 bedevil, torment 8 ridicule 9 tantalize

teaser 4 lure 5 promo 7 preview

teched 3 mad 4 daft 5 batty, crazy 6 insane 7 cracked, lunatic 8 demented

technicality 6 detail 8 loophole

technique 4 mode 5 modus 6 method, system 8 approach 9 procedure 13 modus operandi

ted 5 strew 6 spread 7 scatter

tedious 3 dry 4 dull 5 ho-hum, stale 6 boring, dreary, trying 7 irksome, operose 8 drudging, tiresome 9 dryasdust, wearisome 10 monotonous 11 mind-numbing 13 uninteresting

tedium 4 yawn 5 ennui 7 boredom 8 doldrums, dullness, monotony, sameness

teem 4 flow, pour 5 crawl, empty, swarm 6 abound, bustle 7 produce 9 pullulate

teeming 4 lush, rife 5 alive 6 aswarm 7 replete 8 abundant, swarming, thronged 9 abounding 11 overflowing

teen 5 youth 10 adolescent

tee off 4 open 5 begin, drive, enter, start 8 commence, initiate

teeter 4 rock, sway 5 waver 6 falter, seesaw, wobble 9 vacillate

telamon 5 atlas *counterpart:* 8 caryatid

Telamon *brother:* 6 Peleus *father:* 6 Aeacus *half-brother:* 6 Phocus *son:* 4 Ajax 6 Teucer

Telegonus *father:* 7 Ulysses 8 Odysseus *mother:* 5 Circe

telegraph 4 wire 5 cable 6 signal *code:* 5 Morse *inventor:* 5 Morse (Samuel F. B.)

Telemachus *father:* 7 Ulysses 8 Odysseus *mother:* 8 Penelope

telephone 4 buzz, call, cell, dial, ring 5 mobile, ring up 8 cordless, landline *inventor:* 4 Bell (Alexander Graham)

Telephus *father:* 8 Heracles, Hercules *mother:* 4 Auge

telescope 5 glass 6 finder 7 compact 8 compress, condense, contract, spyglass 9 reflector, refractor

television 2 TV 4 tube 5 video 8 boob tube, idiot box *antenna:* 10 rabbit ears *award:* 4 Emmy *British:* 5 telly *children's:* 6 kidvid *frequency:* 3 UHF, VHF *interference:* 4 snow *network:* 3 ABC, BBC, CBS, Fox, HBO, NBC, NET, PBS, QVC, TNT 4

ESPN, INHD *pioneer:* 5 Baird (John Logie) 8 De Forest (Lee), Goldmark (Peter Carl), Zworykin (Vladimir) 10 Farnsworth (Philo T.) *program:* 4 news 5 pilot, rerun 6 series, sitcom 7 western 8 game show, talk show 9 broadcast, docudrama, soap opera 11 infomercial *tube:* 9 kinescope

tell 3 rat, say 4 blab, clue 5 count, mound, order, spill, state, utter 6 advise, betray, fill in, inform, notify, relate, report, retail, reveal, tattle 7 confess, declare, divulge, narrate, recount 8 disclose, give away 9 come clean

teller 5 clerk 6 banker 7 cashier, counter 8 informer, narrator 12 communicator

telling 5 solid, sound, valid 6 cogent 7 weighty 8 powerful 9 effective 10 convincing, expressive

tell off 4 flay, rate, ream 5 chide, scold 6 berate, rebuke 7 bawl out, chew out, reprove, upbraid 8 admonish, call down 9 dress down, excoriate, reprimand 10 take to task, tongue-lash, vituperate

tell on 6 inform, snitch, tattle

telltale 3 cue 4 clue, fink, lead, sign 5 proof 6 canary, gossip, signal, snitch, tip-off 7 rat fink, tattler 8 evidence, gossiper, informer, quidnunc, signpost, squealer 9 indicator 10 indication, newsmonger 12 blabbermouth, gossipmonger 13 scandalmonger

telluric 6 earthy 7 earthly, mundane, terrene, worldly 9 sublunary 11 terrestrial

tellurium symbol 2 Te

temblor 5 quake, shake, shock 6 tremor 8 upheaval 10 aftershock, earthquake

temerarious 4 rash 6 daring 8 heedless, reckless 9 audacious, daredevil, foolhardy, venturous 11 adventurous, venturesome 13 adventuresome

temerity 4 gall 5 cheek, nerve 6 daring 8 audacity, chutzpah, rashness 9 assurance, brashness, hardihood, hardiness 10 effrontery 12 recklessness 13 foolhardiness

temper 4 heat, mean, mind, mood, tone, vein 5 admix, alloy, anger, blood, grain, humor, trend 6 anneal, attune, dander, dilute, govern, hackle, makeup, medium, season, soften, spirit, strain 7 courage, mollify, passion, quality, toughen 8 hardness, moderate, modulate, restrain 9 character, composure, condition 10 resilience, resiliency 11 disposition, personality

temperament 4 mood 5 humor 6 manner, makeup, mettle, nature 9 character 10 complexion 11 disposition, personality

temperamental 5 moody 6 ornery, touchy 7 erratic 8 contrary, ticklish, unstable, variable, volatile 9 mercurial 10 capricious,

changeable, high-strung, inconstant 13 unpredictable

temperance 8 sobriety 9 austerity, restraint 10 abstinence, continence, moderation, self-denial 11 self-control *advocate of:* 6 Nation (Carry) 7 Willard (Frances)

temperate 4 calm, even, mild, soft 5 balmy, sober 6 modest, steady 7 clement 8 discreet, moderate 9 abstinent, continent 10 abstemious, controlled, reasonable, restrained 11 abstentious

temperature 4 heat, mood 5 fever 6 degree, warmth 7 hotness 8 coldness 9 intensity

tempered 7 diluted, treated 8 adjusted, hardened, softened 9 mitigated, moderated, qualified 12 strengthened

tempest 3 din 4 blow, gale, rage, wind 5 furor, hurly, storm 6 hubbub, squall, tumult, uproar 8 brouhaha, foofaraw 9 commotion, hurricane 10 hullabaloo, hurly-burly

Tempest character 5 Ariel 6 Alonso 7 Caliban, Miranda 8 Prospero 9 Ferdinand

tempestuous 4 wild 5 roily, rough 6 raging, stormy 7 furious, moiling, violent 8 blustery 9 turbulent 10 tumultuous

temple 4 fane 6 church 9 synagogue 10 tabernacle *ancient:* 8 pantheon *Aztec:* 8 teocalli *Buddhist:* 2 ta 3 wat *Eastern:* 6 pagoda *Greek:* 9 Parthenon *sanctuary:* 4 naos 5 cella, Nemea 6 adytum 10 penetralia

tempo 4 pace, rate, time 5 speed 6 rhythm *fast:* 6 presto, vivace 7 allegro *moderate:* 7 andante *slow:* 5 grave, lento 6 adagio

temporal 3 lay 5 civil 6 carnal 7 earthly, mundane, profane, secular, worldly 13 chronological, synchronistic

temporary 6 acting 7 Band-Aid, interim 8 fleeting 9 ad interim, makeshift, transient 10 short-lived, substitute, transitory 11 provisional

temporize 5 delay, stall, yield 6 palter 7 draw out 8 gain time 10 equivocate 11 prevaricate

tempt 3 woo 4 bait, lure, risk, sway 5 court, decoy 6 allure, entice, entrap, invite, lead on, seduce 7 provoke 8 inveigle 9 tantalize

temptation 4 bait, lure, trap 5 decoy, siren, snare 6 allure, come-on 9 seduction 10 attraction, enticement

tempting 8 alluring 9 appealing, delicious, seductive 10 attractive, come-hither

temptress 4 vamp 5 siren 7 Lorelei 10 seductress 11 femme fatale

ten *cents:* 4 dime *combining form:* 3 dec, dek 4 deca, deka 5 decem *dollars:* 7 sawbuck *mills:* 4 cent *thousand:* 6 myriad *years:* 6 decade

tenable 5 sound **8** rational **10** defendable, defensible, reasonable **12** maintainable

tenacious 3 set **4** fast, firm, true **5** fixed, stout **6** dogged, secure, sturdy **8** adhesive, clinging, resolute, stalwart, stubborn **9** obstinate, steadfast **10** persistent **11** persevering

tenacity 4 grit, guts **5** moxie, pluck, spunk **6** mettle, spirit **7** courage **8** firmness **10** resolution **11** persistence **13** determination

tenant 6 holder, lessee, lodger, renter **7** boarder, dweller **8** occupant *feudal:* **6** vassal

tenantable 7 livable **9** habitable **11** inhabitable

Ten Commandments 9 Decalogue *director:* **7** DeMille (Cecil B.)

tend 4 lean, mind, till, work **5** guard, labor, nurse, serve, watch **6** foster **7** babysit, care for, conduce, incline, nurture, oversee **8** minister **9** cultivate, look after, watch over

tendency 4 bent, bias **5** drift, tenor, trend **7** current, leaning **8** penchant **10** partiality, proclivity, propensity **11** disposition, inclination **12** predilection

tendentious 6 biased **7** colored, partial **8** one-sided, partisan **10** prejudiced

tender 3 bid **4** fond, mild, soft, sore, warm **5** green, money, mushy, offer **6** extend, gentle, humane, loving, submit, touchy **7** fragile, lenient, painful, present, proffer, propose **8** delicate, proposal **9** sensitive, succulent **11** considerate, warmhearted **12** affectionate **13** compassionate

tenderfoot 4 colt, punk, tiro, tyro **6** novice, rookie **7** amateur **8** beginner, freshman, neophyte, newcomer **9** cheechako, fledgling, greenhorn, novitiate **10** apprentice

tenderhearted 6 kindly **11** sympathetic **13** compassionate

Tender Is the Night author 10 Fitzgerald (F. Scott)

tendon 4 band, cord **5** nerve, sinew **6** leader **9** hamstring

tendril 4 curl, vine **6** cirrus, spiral **7** ringlet

tenebrific 4 dark, glum, gray, grim **5** black, bleak, sable **6** dismal, dreary, gloomy, somber, sombre **8** desolate, funereal **10** depressing, oppressive **11** dispiriting

tenebrous 3 dim **4** dark, deep, dusk, hazy **5** dusky, foggy, muddy, murky, vague **6** cloudy, gloomy **7** cryptic, obscure, shadowy, unclear **9** ambiguous, lightless **10** caliginous

tenement 4 flat **6** rental, walk-up, warren **7** lodging, rookery **8** building **9** apartment, residence

tenet 3 ism **5** canon, creed, dogma **6** belief **7** paradox **8** doctrine **9** principle **10** empiricism

tenfold 7 decuple

Tennessee *capital:* 9 Nashville *city:* **7** Memphis **9** Knoxville **11** Chattanooga *college, university:* **10** Vanderbilt *mountain, range:* **7** Lookout **10** Great Smoky **13** Clingmans Dome *nickname:* **9** Volunteer (State) *public works:* **3** TVA **9** Norris Dam *river:* **9** Tennessee **11** Mississippi *state bird:* **11** mockingbird *state flower:* **4** iris *state tree:* **11** tulip poplar

tennis *award:* 8 Davis Cup *item:* **3** net **4** ball **6** racket **7** racquet *kind:* **5** table **7** doubles, singles **8** platform *score:* **4** ad-in, love **5** add-in, ad-out, deuce **6** add-out *serve:* **3** ace *shoe:* **7** sneaker *stroke:* **3** cut, lob **4** chop, drop **5** serve, slice **6** volley **8** backhand, forehand *term:* **3** let, set **5** court, fault **7** service **9** advantage, backcourt

tennis champ 4 Ashe (Arthur), Borg (Bjorn), Cash (Pat), Graf (Steffi), King (Billie Jean), Noah (Yannick), Wade (Virginia) **5** Budge (Don), Chang (Michael), Court (Margaret Smith), Evert (Chris), Gómez (Andres), Henin (Justine), Laver (Rod), Lendl (Ivan), Nadal (Rafael), Perry (Fred), Safin (Marat), Seles (Monica), Stich (Michael), Vilas (Guillermo), Wills (Helen) **6** Agassi (André), Austin (Tracy), Becker (Boris), Casals (Rosie), Edberg (Stefan), Fraser (Neale), Gibson (Althea), Hewitt (Lleyton), Hingis (Martina), Kramer (Jack), Muster (Thomas), Pierce (Mary), Stolle (Fred), Tilden (Bill) **7** Connors (Jimmy), Courier (Jim), Emerson (Roy), Federer (Roger), Lacoste (René), McEnroe (John), Nastase (Ilie), Novótna (Jana), Sampras (Pete) **8** Connolly (Maureen), González (Pancho), Martínez (Conchita), Newcombe (John), Rosewall (Ken), Sabatini (Gabriela), Wilander (Mats), Williams (Serena, Venus) **9** Davenport (Lindsay), Goolagong (Evonne) **10** Mandlikova (Hana) **11** Navratilova (Martina)

Tennyson poem 4 Maud **7** Ulysses **8** Princess (The), Tiresias **10** Enoch Arden, In Memoriam **12** Locksley Hall **23** Charge of the Light Brigade (The)

tenor 4 mood, tone **5** drift, voice **6** singer **7** meaning, purport **8** tendency **9** substance *American:* **5** Lanza (Mario) **6** Hadley (Jerry), Peerce (Jan), Tucker (Richard) **9** McCracken (James) *Belgian:* **6** Maison (René) *Canadian:* **7** Vickers (Jon) *Czech:* **6** Slezak (Leo) *Danish:* **8** Melchior (Lauritz) *English:* **5** Pears (Peter) *German:* **10** Wunderlich (Fritz) *Irish* 9 McCormack (John) *Italian:* 5 Gigli (Beniamino) 6 Alagna (Roberto), Caruso (Enrico) 7 Bocelli (Andrea), Corelli (Franco) 8 Bergonzi (Carlo) 9 del Monaco (Mario), di Stefano (Giuseppe), Pavarotti (Luciano) *Spanish:* 5 Kraus (Alfredo) 7 Domingo (Plácido) 8 Carreras (José) *Swedish:* 5 Gedda (Nicolai) 8 Björling (Jussi) 9 Bjoerling (Jussi)

tenpins 7 bowling

tense 4 edgy, taut 5 nervy, rigid, tight, wired 6 uneasy 7 anxious, jittery, nervous, restive, uptight 8 strained, stressed 10 high-strung *grammatical:* 4 past 6 future 7 perfect, present 8 preterit 9 preterite 10 pluperfect 11 progressive

tension 5 state, steam 6 nerves, strain, stress, unease 7 anxiety, balance 8 edginess, pressure, tautness 9 agitation, hostility, stiffness 10 discomfort, opposition, uneasiness 11 nervousness, uptightness

tent 4 camp 6 canopy, encamp, laager 7 bivouac, shelter *kind:* 3 ger, pup 4 yurt 5 Baker, tepee 6 teepee 7 marquee 8 pavilion, umbrella *maker:* 4 Omar *material:* 6 canvas *part:* 3 fly, guy, peg 4 pole 5 stake

tentacle 3 arm 6 barbel, feeler

tentative 4 test 5 chary, loath, probe, trial 6 averse 7 halting 8 hesitant, insecure 9 diffident, makeshift, reluctant, uncertain, undecided, unsettled 10 irresolute 11 conditional, disinclined, problematic, provisional

tenth 5 tithe *combining form:* 4 deci

tenuous 4 slim, thin, weak 5 reedy, shaky 6 feeble, flimsy, slight, stalky 7 fragile, sketchy, slender 8 gossamer 10 precarious 11 implausible 13 insubstantial, unsubstantial

tenure 4 term 6 estate 10 incumbency *feudal:* 7 burgage

tepid 4 mild, warm 7 warmish 8 lukewarm 9 apathetic 11 halfhearted, indifferent

tequila source 5 agave

terbium symbol 2 Tb

Terentia's husband 6 Cicero

Tereus son: 4 Itys *wife:* 6 Procne

tergiversate 3 haw, hem, rat 5 dodge, evade, hedge 6 defect, desert, waffle, weasel 7 abandon, shuffle 8 renounce, sidestep 9 pussyfoot, repudiate 10 apostatize, equivocate

term 3 dub, end 4 call, name, span, tour, word 5 label, spell, stint, title 6 detail, period, tenure 7 quarter, session 8 duration, semester 9 designate 10 conclusion, de-

nominate, expression, limitation, particular 11 appellation, designation

termagant 5 harpy, scold, shrew, vixen 6 ogress, virago 8 fishwife, harridan 9 Xanthippe

terminable 6 finite

terminal 3 end, lag 4 last 5 anode, depot, fatal, final 6 finial, latest, latter, lethal 7 cathode, closing, extreme, station 8 eventual, hindmost, junction, ultimate 9 extremity 10 concluding *negative:* 7 cathode *positive:* 5 anode

terminate 2 ax 3 end 4 boot, drop, fire, halt, kill, quit, sack, stop 5 abort, cease, close, issue, leave 6 cut off, finish, wind up 7 abolish, dead-end, dismiss 8 complete, conclude, dissolve 9 determine, discharge 10 extinguish 11 assassinate, discontinue

terminology 4 cant 5 argot, idiom, lingo 6 jargon, patois 7 lexicon 8 language, shoptalk 10 vernacular, vocabulary 12 nomenclature

termite 5 alate 8 white ant

ternary 5 third 6 triple 9 threefold

Terpsichore see **Muse**

terrace 4 bank, deck, mesa, park, roof, step 5 bench, porch, shelf 6 street 7 balcony, sundeck 8 platform 9 promenade

terra-cotta 4 clay 7 pottery

terra firma 4 dirt, land, soil 5 earth 6 ground

terrain 4 area, land, turf 5 field 6 domain, ground, milieu, sphere 8 province 9 bailiwick, territory 10 topography 11 environment

terrapin 6 turtle

terrestrial 4 land 6 earthy, ground 7 earthly, mundane, worldly 8 everyday, ordinary, telluric, workaday 9 earthlike, planetary, sublunary 10 earthbound

terrible 4 dire 5 awful, dread 6 grisly, horrid 7 dreaded, fearful, ghastly, heinous, hideous, intense, macabre, vicious, violent 8 dreadful, gruesome, horrible, horrific, shocking, vehement 9 abhorrent, appalling, atrocious, frightful, harrowing, loathsome, monstrous 10 disastrous, formidable, horrendous, horrifying

terrier 3 dog *kind:* 3 fox 4 blue, bull, Skye 5 cairn, Irish, Welsh 6 Boston 8 Airedale, Lakeland 9 Yorkshire

terrific 5 boffo, socko, super, swell 6 superb 7 amazing, awesome 8 dreadful, dynamite, glorious 9 appalling, fantastic, frightful, marvelous, upsetting, wonderful 10 formidable, incredible 11 magnificent, sensational 13 extraordinary

terrify 5 alarm, scare **7** scarify, startle **8** affright, frighten **10** intimidate

terrifying 4 grim **5** scary **6** grisly, horrid **7** ghastly, hideous, macabre **8** alarming, dreadful, fearsome, gruesome, horrible, horrific, terrible **9** frightful **10** formidable, horrifying

territory 4 area, belt, land, turf, zone **5** field, route, state, tract **6** domain, region, sphere **7** country, demesne, terrain **8** conquest, district, dominion, province **9** bailiwick **10** borderland **12** jurisdiction

terror 4 fear **5** alarm, dread, panic, worry **6** dismay, fright, horror **7** scourge **9** nightmare **11** fearfulness, trepidation

terrorize 3 cow **5** alarm, bully, scare **6** coerce, fright, menace **7** scarify **8** browbeat, bulldoze, frighten, threaten **9** strong-arm **10** intimidate

terry 4 loop **5** cloth **6** fabric **12** Turkish towel

terse 4 curt **5** brief, crisp, pithy, short **6** abrupt **7** brusque, compact, concise, elegant, laconic, summary **8** polished, succinct **11** compendious, sententious, telegraphic **12** monosyllabic

tertiary 5 third

terza ____ **4** rima

tessera 3 die **4** tile **6** tablet, ticket

test 3 try **4** exam, quiz **5** assay, check, essay, final, proof, prove, taste, touch, trial, try on **6** sample, tryout, verify **7** confirm, examine, midterm **8** evaluate, gut check, sounding, trial run **9** benchmark, criterion **10** evaluation, experiment, touchstone **11** examination

testa 6 cupule **7** coating **8** envelope, seed coat, tegument **10** integument

testament 4 will **5** credo, creed, proof **7** tribute, witness **8** evidence **9** scripture **11** attestation **12** confirmation

tester 4 coin **6** canopy, prover **7** analyst, assayer **8** examiner **12** investigator

testifier 7 witness **8** deponent

testify 5 prove, swear **6** affirm, attest, depone, depose, evince **7** certify, witness **11** certificate

testimonial 5 proof **6** salute **7** tribute, witness **8** evidence, memorial, monument **9** affidavit, character, reference **11** attestation **12** appreciation, commendation, confirmation **13** commemoration

testimony 5 proof **6** avowal **7** witness **8** evidence **9** affidavit, authority **10** deposition, profession **11** affirmation, attestation, declaration **12** confirmation **13** corroboration, documentation

testy 4 edgy **5** cross, fussy, hasty **6** cranky,

ornery, tetchy, touchy **7** fretful, grouchy, peevish **8** choleric **9** crotchety, irascible, irritable **10** ill-humored, out of sorts **12** cantankerous **13** quick-tempered

tetanus 7 lockjaw, trismus

tetchy see **testy**

tête-à-tête 4 chat, talk **5** à deux **7** private, vis-à-vis **8** causerie **10** face-to-face **12** conversation

tether 3 tie **4** bind, rope **5** cable, chain, stake **6** fasten, fetter, lariat, picket **8** restrain **9** restraint

Tethys *daughters:* **9** Oceanides *father:* **6** Uranus *husband:* **7** Oceanus *mother:* **4** Gaea **5** Terra

tetrad 4 four **7** quartet **8** foursome **10** quaternion

Teutonic 6 German **8** Germanic *language:* **5** Dutch **6** Danish, German, Gothic **7** English, Flemish, Frisian, Swedish **9** Afrikaans, Norwegian

Texas *capital:* **6** Austin *city:* **4** Waco **6** Dallas, El Paso **7** Houston **8** Amarillo **9** Arlington, Fort Worth **10** San Antonio *college, university:* **3** SMU **4** Rice **5** Lamar **6** Baylor **9** Texas Tech *island:* **5** Padre *mountain:* **9** Guadalupe (Peak) *nickname:* **8** Lone Star (State) *park:* **7** Big Bend *river:* **3** Red **5** Pecos **6** Brazos **8** Colorado **9** Rio Grande *state bird:* **11** mockingbird *state flower:* **10** bluebonnet *state tree:* **5** pecan

text 6 script

textbook 6 primer

textile 5 cloth **6** fabric *dealer:* **6** mercer *machine:* **8** calender *pattern:* **7** paisley **11** houndstooth *shop:* **7** mercery *starch:* **4** sago *treat:* **9** mercerize

texture 3 web **4** feel, hand, wale, woof **5** weave **6** fabric

Thackeray *novel* **9** Pendennis **10** Vanity Fair **11** Barry Lyndon, Henry Esmond

Thailand *capital:* **7** Bangkok *city:* **9** Chiang Mai *former name:* **4** Siam *island:* **6** Phuket *monetary unit:* **4** baht *neighbor:* **4** Laos **5** Burma **7** Myanmar **8** Cambodia, Malaysia *river:* **10** Chao Phraya *sea:* **7** Andaman

Thaïs 7 hetaera, hetaira **9** courtesan *author:* **6** France (Anatole) *composer:* **8** Massenet (Jules) *husband:* **7** Ptolemy *lover:* **9** Alexander (the Great)

thalassic 6 marine **7** oceanic **8** maritime

Thalia see **Graces; Muse**

thallium symbol 2 Tl

Thanatopsis author 6 Bryant (William Cullen)

Thanatos 5 death *brother:* **6** Hypnos *mother:* **3** Nyx

thankful 4 glad 8 grateful 12 appreciative
thanks 5 grace 8 blessing 9 gratitude 11
  benediction 12 appreciation, gratefulness
Thanksgiving 5 feast 7 holiday *first cele-*
  brant: 6 Indian 7 Pilgrim *food:* 6 turkey
thatch 3 mop 4 hair, roof 5 cover
that is *Latin:* 5 id est
Thaumas *daughter:* 4 Iris 5 Aello, Harpy 7
  Celaeno, Ocypete *daughters:* 7 Harpies *fa-*
  ther: 6 Pontus *mother:* 4 Gaea *wife:* 7 Electra
thaumaturgic 5 magic 6 Magian, mystic,
  witchy 7 magical 8 wizardly 9 marvelous
  10 miraculous 11 necromantic 12 supernatural
thaumaturgy 5 magic 7 sorcery 8 cabbalah,
  kabbalah, witchery, wizardry 10 necromancy
thaw 4 melt 5 deice, relax 6 unbend 7 defrost,
  liquefy 8 dissolve, unfreeze 10 condescend,
  deliquesce
the 7 article *French:* 2 la, le, un 3 les, une
  German: 3 das, der, die, ein 4 eine *Italian:* 2
  il, la 3 una, uno *Spanish:* 2 el, la, un 3 las,
  los, una, uno
Thea *daughter:* 6 Selene *father:* 6 Uranus
  husband: 8 Hyperion *mother:* 4 Gaea
theater 4 nabe 5 drama, stage 6 boards 9
  playhouse 10 footlights *award:* 4 Obie,
  Tony *district:* 6 rialto *drop:* 5 scrim *en-*
  trance: 5 foyer, lobby *Greek:* 5 odeum
  movie: 6 cinema 8 cineplex, megaplex 9
  multiplex *outdoor:* 7 drive-in *part:* 3 box,
  pit 4 loge 5 apron, stage, wings 6 stalls 7
  balcony, parquet 8 parterre 9 greenroom,
  mezzanine, orchestra 10 proscenium 11
  dress circle, grand circle, royal circle, upper circle
theatrical 5 stagy 6 staged 8 dramatic, thespian 10 artificial, flamboyant, histrionic 11
  dramaturgic 12 melodramatic *agent:* 6
  Morris (William) *device:* 4 prop *group:* 6
  troupe
Theban Eagle 6 Pindar
Thebes *founder:* 6 Cadmus *king:* 5 Laius 7
  Oedipus *queen:* 5 Niobe 7 Jocasta
Theda _____ 4 Bara
theft 5 heist, pinch 6 holdup, piracy 7 break-
  in, larceny, robbery 8 burglary, stealing,
  thievery 9 pilferage *combining form:* 5
  klept 6 klepto
theme 4 stem, text, tune 5 essay, lemma, motif, paper, point, topic, topos 6 burden, matter, melody, mythos, thesis 7 article,
  conceit, message, subject 8 argument 11
  composition 12 dissertation
Themis *father:* 6 Uranus *goddess of:* 3 law 7

justice *husband:* 4 Zeus 7 Jupiter *mother:* 4
  Gaea
then 4 also, anon, ergo, next, thus, when 5
  again, hence, later 7 besides, further 8
  moreover 9 therefore, thereupon 10 in addition 11 accordingly, furthermore 12 additionally, consequently
thence 4 away 7 thereof 9 from there, therefrom
Theogony poet 6 Hesiod
theologian *American:* 6 Merton (Thomas) 7
  Edwards (Jonathan), Niebuhr (Reinhold),
  Tillich (Paul), Walther (Carl) *Dutch:* 6
  Jansen (Cornelis) *English:* 4 Bede (Vener-
  able) 5 Pusey (Edward), Watts (Isaac) 6 Al-
  cuin, Wesley (John) 7 Langton (Stephen) 8
  Pelagius, Wycliffe (John) *French:* 6 Calvin
  (John) 7 Abelard (Peter), William (of Au-
  vergne, of Auxerre) 8 Maritain (Jacques),
  Sabatier (Auguste), Teilhard (de Chardin,
  Pierre) *German:* 6 Rahner (Karl) 7 Eckhart
  (Meister) 8 Albertus (Magnus) 9 Niemöller
  (Martin) 10 Bonhoeffer (Dietrich) *Greek:* 9
  Zygomalas (Theodore) *Italian:* 6 Thomas
  (Aquinas) 7 Aquinas (Thomas), Socinus
  (Fausto, Laelius) *Scottish:* 10 Duns Scotus
  (John) *Spanish:* 6 Suárez (Francisco) 7 Vi-
  toria (Francisco de) 8 Servetus (Michael)
  Swedish: 9 Soderblom (Nathan) *Swiss:* 4
  Küng (Hans) 5 Barth (Karl), Vinet (Alexan-
  dre-Rodolphe) 6 Calvin (John), Cauvin
  (Jean)
theological *school:* 8 seminary *virtue:* 4 hope
  5 faith 7 charity
_____ Theologica 5 Summa
theorbo 4 lute
theorem 3 law 4 rule 5 axiom 7 formula, inverse, stencil 8 converse 9 principle 10
  principium 11 fundamental, proposition
theoretical 4 pure 5 ideal 8 abstract, academic, notional, unproved 11 conjectural,
  speculative 12 hypothetical 13 problematical, suppositional
theorize 5 guess 6 submit 7 suggest 9 formulate, postulate, speculate 10 conjecture 11
  hypothesize
theory 7 perhaps, premise, surmise 8 supposal 10 conjecture, hypothesis 11 speculation, supposition *astronomical:* 7 big bang
  suffix: 3 ism
therapeutic 5 tonic 7 healing, helpful 8 curative, remedial, salutary, sanative 9 healthful, medicinal, vulnerary, wholesome 10
  beneficial, corrective 11 restorative 12
  health-giving
therapy 9 treatment

therefore 4 ergo, then, thus **5** hence **6** hereat, thence **11** accordingly **12** consequently
therefrom 4 away **6** thence
thereupon 4 ergo, then, thus **6** at once, at that, thence **8** directly **9** right away, therefore, wherefore **11** accordingly, straightway **12** consequently
thermal unit 3 Btu **6** degree **7** calorie
thermometer 5 gauge **9** indicator *kind:* **7** Celsius, Réaumur **10** centigrade, Fahrenheit
thermos 5 dewar **10** Dewar flask
Theroux work 9 Saint Jack **13** Mosquito Coast (The) **14** Half Moon Street **18** Great Railway Bazaar (The)
Thersites' slayer 8 Achilles
thesaurus editor 5 Roget (Peter Mark)
Theseus *beloved:* 7 Ariadne *father:* **6** Aegeus *mother:* **6** Aethra *slayer:* **9** Lycomedes *son:* **10** Hippolytus *victim:* **6** Sciron **8** Minotaur **10** Procrustes *wife:* **7** Phaedra
thesis 5 essay, point, theme **6** belief **7** premise **8** downbeat, position, tractate, treatise **9** discourse, monograph, postulate, synthesis **10** contention, exposition **11** postulation, proposition, supposition **12** disquisition, dissertation
thespian 5 actor **6** mummer, player **7** actress, trouper **8** dramatic **9** performer **10** histrionic, theatrical **11** dramaturgic **12** impersonator, melodramatic
Thespis' forte 5 drama **7** tragedy
Thessalian hero 5 Jason **8** Achilles
Thetis 6 Nereid *father:* **6** Nereus *husband:* **6** Peleus *mother:* **5** Doris *son:* **8** Achilles
theurgist 5 witch **7** warlock **8** magician, sorcerer **12** wonder-worker
thew 4 beef **5** brawn, might, power, sinew, vigor **6** muscle **8** strength, vitality
thick 3 fat **4** wide **5** broad, bulky, burly, close, dense, dumpy, husky, squat, stout **6** chummy, chunky, packed, stocky **7** compact, crammed, crowded, viscous **8** familiar, heavyset, intimate **11** inspissated
thicken 3 set **4** blur, clot, jell **6** curdle **7** broaden, compact, congeal **8** condense **9** coagulate **10** inspissate **11** concentrate
thicket 4 bosk, bush, shaw, wood **5** clump, copse, grove, hedge **6** bosket, covert, mallee, tangle **7** boscage, bosquet, coppice, spinney **8** hedgerow, quickset **9** brushwood, canebrake, chaparral
thickness 3 ply **4** bulk, loft **5** depth, gauge, layer, sheet **7** density **9** viscosity
thickset 5 bulky, burly, heavy, husky, plump, pudgy, stout, tubby **6** chubby, chunky, portly, stocky, sturdy **7** compact **9** corpulent
thief 3 dip **4** prig, yegg **5** ganef, gonif **6** bandit, goniff, lifter, looter, pirate, rascal, robber **7** booster, burglar, filcher, stealer **8** hijacker, larcener, pilferer, water rat **9** larcenist, purloiner **10** cat burglar, highwayman, pickpocket, shoplifter **12** housebreaker
thieve 3 rob **4** hook, lift, pick, roll **5** boost, filch, pinch, pluck, steal, swipe **6** hijack, hold up, pilfer, rip off, snitch **7** purloin **8** knock off **9** knock over
thievery see theft
thievish 7 corrupt, crooked **9** larcenous **13** light-fingered
thigh 3 ham **5** flank **6** gammon *bone:* **5** femur *relating to:* **6** crural **7** femoral
thimble 3 cup **5** cover
thin 4 fine, lank, lean, slim **5** gaunt, lanky, reedy, scant, sharp, sheer, spare **6** dilute, flimsy, meager, meagre, rarefy, scanty, skimpy, skinny, slight, sparse, stalky, treble, twiggy, watery **7** diluted, scraggy, scrawny, slender, spindly, squinny, subtile, tenuous **8** rarefied, skeletal **9** attenuate, extenuate **10** attenuated **11** watered-down **13** unsubstantial
thing 4 item, unit **5** being, event **6** entity, matter, object **7** article, concern, element **10** occurrence, phenomenon *in law:* **3** res
thingamajig 5 gismo, gizmo **6** dingus, doodad, gadget, hickey, jigger, widget **7** whatsit **9** doohickey
things 4 gear **5** goods, stock, stuff **7** baggage, clothes, effects, luggage **8** chattels, clothing, matériel, movables, property, supplies **10** belongings, provisions **11** impedimenta, merchandise **13** accoutrements, paraphernalia
think 4 mull, muse **5** brood, study, weigh **6** ideate, ponder, reason **7** believe, imagine, reflect, suppose, surmise **8** cogitate, consider, meditate, ruminate **9** cerebrate, speculate **10** conjecture, deliberate, excogitate **11** contemplate
Thinker sculptor 5 Rodin (Auguste)
Thin Man, The *actor:* 3 Loy (Myrna) **6** Powell (William), Skippy **9** O'Sullivan (Maureen) *author:* **7** Hammett (Dashiell) *character:* **4** Nick (Charles), Nora (Charles) **6** Wynant (Clyde, Dorothy) *dog:* **4** Asta
third 4 show **8** tertiary *combining form:* **3** tri *power:* **4** cube
third degree 7 torture **8** grilling **11** inquisition, questioning **13** interrogation
third estate 5 plebs **6** people, plebes **8** populace **9** commonage, commoners, plebeians **10** commonalty **11** rank and file
Third Man author 6 Greene (Graham)
Third of May painter 4 Goya (Francisco)

thirst 3 yen **4** itch, long, lust, pine **5** crave, yearn **6** desire, hanker, hunger **7** craving, dryness, longing **8** appetite

thirsty 3 dry **4** arid, avid **5** eager **6** ardent **7** anxious, bone-dry, parched **8** droughty **9** absorbent, waterless

this and that 8 oddments, sundries **9** etceteras **11** miscellanea, odds and ends

Thisbe's lover 7 Pyramus

This Side of Paradise author 10 Fitzgerald (F. Scott)

thistle 4 weed **7** caltrop *Russian:* **10** tumbleweed

thistlebird 9 goldfinch

thither 3 yon **5** there **6** yonder

thole 3 peg, pin **6** endure

Thomas à _____ 6 Becket, Kempis

Thomas's Greek name 7 Didymus

Thomas opera 6 Mignon

_____ Thompson 4 Emma **5** Sadie **6** Hunter **7** Dorothy, Francis, J. Walter **8** Benjamin

thong 4 band, lace, lash, rein, zori **5** lasso, strap, strip, whang **6** sandal **7** latchet **8** flip-flop

Thor 5 Donar *father:* **4** Odin **5** Wotan *god of:* **7** thunder *hammer:* **8** Mjollnir *mother:* **5** Jordh, Jorth

thorax 5 chest, trunk **6** pereon

Thoreau, Henry David *friend:* **7** Emerson (Ralph Waldo) *pond:* **6** Walden *town:* **7** Concord *work:* **6** Walden

thorium symbol 2 Th

thorn 4 barb **5** briar, spike, spine **7** prickle, spinule **9** annoyance **10** irritation

thorny 5 sharp, spiny **6** briary, touchy, tricky **7** awkward, prickly, spinous **8** ticklish **9** difficult, vexatious **10** nettlesome **11** troublesome

thorough 4 full **6** minute **7** careful, in-depth **8** complete, detailed, diligent, whole-hog **9** downright **10** blow-by-blow, exhaustive, meticulous **11** painstaking **13** conscientious

thoroughbred 5 racer **8** pedigree, purebred **9** pedigreed, pureblood **10** bloodstock **11** full-blooded

thoroughfare 3 way **4** road **5** track **6** artery, avenue, street **7** highway, parkway **8** corridor **9** boulevard

thoroughgoing 5 utter **6** all-out **7** extreme **8** absolute, complete, outright, whole-hog **9** out-and-out **10** consummate, exhaustive **11** straight-out, unmitigated **13** dyed-in-the-wool

thou 3 you **5** grand *French:* **5** mille

though 3 yet **5** still, while **6** albeit **7** however, whereas **8** after all **11** nonetheless **12** nevertheless

thought 4 idea **6** notion, reason **7** concept, opinion **8** ideation **9** brainwork **10** cogitation, conception, meditation, reflection, rumination **11** cerebration, speculation **12** deliberation, intellection **13** contemplation

thoughtful 6 polite **7** gallant, heedful, mindful, pensive, serious **8** gracious, studious, thinking **9** attentive, courteous **10** cogitative, meditative, reflective, ruminative, solicitous **11** considerate **12** deliberative, intellectual **13** contemplative

thoughtless 4 rash, rude **5** brash, hasty **6** madcap **7** selfish **8** careless, feckless, heedless, impolite, reckless, uncaring **9** insensate **10** incautious, ungracious **12** discourteous **13** inconsiderate

thousand *combining form:* **4** kilo *cubed:* **7** billion *dollars:* **5** grand *squared:* **7** million *years:* **10** millennium

thousandth 10 millesimal *combining form:* **5** milli

thrall 4 peon, serf, yoke **5** helot, slave **7** bondage, bondman, helotry, peonage, serfdom, slavery, villein **9** servitude, villenage **10** absorption **11** enslavement

thrash 3 tan **4** beat, belt, drub, flog, hide, lash, lick, maul, pelt, trim, whip **5** baste, flail, pound, smear, swing, thump, whale, whang **6** batter, buffet, larrup, pummel, stripe, wallop **7** scourge, shellac, trounce **8** flounder, lambaste, work over **10** flagellate

thrash out 4 moot **5** argue **6** debate **7** discuss, dispute **10** deliberate, kick around

thread 4 line, vein, yard **5** fiber, trail, weave **6** strand, stream, string **8** filament *ball of:* **4** clew *dental:* **5** floss *holder:* **6** bobbin *kind:* **4** silk, yarn **5** floss, lisle **6** cotton **8** surgical *loose:* **8** raveling **9** ravelling *surgical:* **6** catgut, suture

threadbare 4 hack, worn **5** dingy, faded, seedy, stale, tacky, tatty, tired, trite **6** beat-up, cheesy, cliché, frayed, ragged, shabby, shoddy **7** clichéd, run-down, tedious, worn-out **8** shopworn, slipshod, tattered, timeworn, well-worn **9** destitute, hackneyed **10** down-at-heel **11** commonplace, dilapidated, down-at-heels, stereotyped **13** down-at-the-heel

threadlike 6 filate **11** filamentous

threads 4 duds **7** clothes **8** clothing, garments

threat 6 danger, duress, menace **7** assault, warning **8** big stick, coercion **11** thunderbolt

threaten 3 cow **4** warn **5** augur, lower **6** coerce, menace **7** caution, portend, presage **8** endanger, forebode, forewarn, overhang **10** intimidate

three 4 trey **5** crowd *combining form:* **3** ter, tri

threefold 5 trine **6** thrice, treble, trinal, triple **7** triplex

Three Musicians artist 7 Picasso (Pablo)

Three Musketeers 5 Athos **6** Aramis **7** Porthos *author:* **5** Dumas (Alexandre) *friend:* **9** D'Artagnan

Threepenny Opera, The *author:* **6** Brecht (Bertolt) *composer:* **5** Weill (Kurt)

threescore 5 sixty

Three Sisters, The 4 Olga **5** Irina, Masha *author:* **7** Chekhov (Anton)

threesome 4 trio **5** triad, trine **6** triple, triune, troika **7** trinity **8** triangle **11** triumvirate

three-wheeler 5 cycle, trike **7** pedicab **8** tricycle **10** velocipede

threnody 5 dirge, elegy **6** lament

thresh 3 lam, tan **4** beat, belt, drub, flog, hide, lash, lick, pelt, trim, wave, whip **5** baste, forge, flail, pound, slate, smear, swing, thump, whale, whang **6** batter, buffet, larrup, pummel, strike, stripe, wallop, winnow **7** scourge, shellac, trounce **8** lambaste, work over **10** flagellate

threshold 3 eve **4** door, edge, gate, sill **5** brink, limen, verge **6** outset **8** boundary

thrift 6 saving **7** economy, sea pink **8** prudence **9** frugality, parsimony

thrifty 5 canny **6** frugal, saving **7** sparing **9** provident **10** economical **12** cheeseparing, parsimonious **13** penny-pinching

thrill 3 wow **4** bang, boot, kick, rush, send **5** blast, throb **6** charge, excite, shiver, tingle, wallop **7** frisson, tremble, vibrate **9** electrify **10** excitement **11** titillation

thriller 6 gothic **7** chiller, mystery, shocker **8** whodunit **9** dime novel **10** hair-raiser **13** penny dreadful

thrive 4 boom, grow **7** advance, burgeon, develop, prosper, succeed **8** flourish, get ahead

throat 3 maw **4** tube **5** gorge **6** groove, gullet **7** channel, weasand *infection:* **5** strep **12** epiglottitis *inflammation:* **5** croup **6** angina, quinsy **10** laryngitis **11** pharyngitis *relating to:* **8** guttural *warmer:* **5** scarf

throaty 5 gruff, husky, thick **6** hoarse **8** gravelly, guttural

throb 4 ache, beat, drum **5** pound, pulse **6** thrill **7** pulsate, vibrate **9** palpitate

throe 3 fit **4** pain, pang **5** agony, spasm **6** attack **7** seizure **9** suffering **10** convulsion **11** contraction

thrombus 4 clot **8** blockage, coagulum

throne 4 seat **5** chair, crown, power, reign **8** cathedra, dominion **11** sovereignty

throng 3 jam, mob **4** host, pack, push, rout **5** bunch, crowd, crush, drove, flock, group, horde, press, scrum, shoal, swarm **6** resort **9** multitude **10** assemblage

throttle 3 gun **5** choke **6** throat **7** garrote, trachea **8** strangle, suppress **11** accelerator, strangulate

through 3 per, via **4** done, past **5** due to, ended **6** direct **7** by way of, done for, nonstop, owing to **8** by dint of, complete, finished, washed-up **9** because of, by means of, completed, concluded **10** by virtue of, terminated, throughout **13** dia, per

throughout 3 mid **4** amid **5** midst **6** during **7** all over, overall **10** everywhere, far and near, far and wide, high and low

Through the Looking Glass *author:* **7** Carroll (Lewis) *character:* **5** Alice

throve 9 burgeoned, prospered **10** flourished

throw 3 lob, peg, put **4** cast, fire, hurl, toss **5** chuck, fling, heave, pitch, sling **6** afghan, launch, propel **7** buck off, project *in the towel:* **4** quit **6** give up

throw away 4 blow, cast, junk, shed **5** scrap, waste **7** discard, fritter **8** jettison, squander

throwback 7 atavism **9** reversion **11** anachronism

throw off 4 lose, shed **5** addle, shake **7** confuse, fluster **8** befuddle, bewilder, distract *the track:* **6** derail **7** confuse, mislead

throw out 4 emit, junk, shed **5** chuck, eject, evict, scrap **6** reject **7** discard **8** jettison

throw up 4 barf, cast, hurl, lose, puke, quit, spew, toss **5** heave, retch, vomit **7** upchuck **8** disgorge **11** regurgitate

thrush 4 omao **5** mavis, ouzel, robin, veery **6** mistle **8** bluebird **9** blackbird, fieldfare, mistletoe **11** nightingale

thrust 3 dig, jab, ram **4** barb, butt, core, cram, dash, dive, duck, gist, hurl, kick, pith, poke, prod, push, stab, tilt **5** barge, crowd, cut in, drive, force, lunge, press, punch, sense, shoot, shove, spear, stick, stuff **6** burden, extend, insert, pierce, plunge, propel, upshot **7** assault, obtrude, project, purport, riposte **8** pressure **9** substance

thud 3 jar **4** bump, jolt, plop **5** clunk, throb, thump **6** impact **10** concussion

thug 3 mug **4** goon, hood, punk **5** bully, rough, rowdy, tough **6** Apache, Capone, gunman, hit man **7** hoodlum, mobster, ruffian **8** enforcer, gangster, hooligan, plugugly **9** cutthroat, roughneck

thulium symbol 2 Tm

thumb 4 leaf, turn **5** digit, hitch, ovolo **6** pollex, riffle **8** pollices (plural) **9** hitchhike

thumbs-up 3 AOK, nod **4** okay **7** go-ahead **10** green light

thumb through 4 scan **6** browse, riffle **7** dip into

thump 3 bop, hit **4** bash, beat, belt, blow, drub, jolt, pelt, whip, whup **5** knock, paste, pound, punch, shock, smack, sound, whack **6** batter, buffet, defeat, impact, pummel, strike, thrash, thwack, wallop **7** clobber, endorse, promote, shellac, trounce **8** advocate

thunder 4 bang, boom, clap, peal, roar **6** rumble **7** resound **8** rumbling **9** fulminate

thunderbolt 9 lightning

thunder lizard 11 apatosaurus **12** brontosaurus

thunderstruck 5 agape **6** amazed **7** shocked, stunned **8** dismayed **9** astounded, staggered **10** astonished, bewildered, confounded **11** dumbfounded **13** flabbergasted

Thurber character 5 Mitty (Walter)

thurible 6 censer

thus 3 sic **4** ergo, then **5** hence **9** therefore **11** accordingly **12** consequently *French:* **5** ainsi

Thus Spake Zarathustra author 9 Nietzsche (Friedrich)

thwack 3 bop **4** belt, biff, blow, pelt, sock, whop **5** crack, pound, smack, thump, whack **6** wallop **7** clobber

thwart 4 balk, beat, dash, foil **5** bench, block, deter **6** baffle, hamper, hinder, oppose, scotch, stymie **7** flummox, prevent **8** confound, obstruct **9** checkmate, frustrate **10** circumvent, contravene, disappoint

Thyestes *brother:* 6 Atreus *daughter:* **7** Pelopia *father:* **6** Pelops *mother:* **10** Hippodamia *son:* **9** Aegisthus

Tiamat *husband:* 4 Apsu *slayer:* **6** Marduk

tiara 5 crown **6** diadem **8** headband

Tibetan *animal:* 3 yak **5** takin *capital:* **5** Lhasa *coin:* **5** tanga *dog:* **5** Lhasa **9** Lhasa apso *monk:* **4** lama *people:* **6** Bhotia, Sherpa

tibia 8 shinbone

tic 5 quirk, spasm **6** twitch **9** twitching

tick 5 check **8** arachnid, parasite **9** checkmark **11** bloodsucker

ticker 4 bomb **5** clock, heart, watch

ticket 3 key, tag **4** comp, pass, vote **5** slate **6** ballot **7** receipt **8** passport, password **10** open sesame *seller:* **7** scalper

tickle 4 stir **5** amuse, tease, touch **6** arouse, excite, please, tingle **7** delight, gratify, provoke **9** stimulate, titillate

tickled 5 happy **6** amused **7** pleased **9** delighted

ticklish 5 dicey **6** tender, thorny, touchy,

tricky 8 delicate, unstable **9** sensitive **10** precarious **13** oversensitive

tick off 3 ire, irk **5** anger **6** rankle **7** incense, provoke **9** aggravate

tidal flood 4 bore

tidbit 3 ort **4** bite **5** goody, treat **6** dainty, morsel, nugget

tide 4 flow, flux, rush **5** drift, flood, spate, surge **6** stream **7** current, holiday *type:* **3** ebb, low **4** high, neap **5** flood **6** spring

tidings 4 news, word **6** advice **7** message **11** information **12** intelligence

tidy 4 fair, neat, smug, snug, trim **5** kempt **6** pick up **7** clean up, orderly, precise **9** shipshape **10** acceptable, methodical **11** respectable, spic-and-span, substantial, uncluttered, well-groomed **12** satisfactory, spick-and-span

tie 3 guy, rod **4** band, bind, bolo, bond, cord, draw, gird, join, knit, knot, lash, link, moor, rope, yoke **5** equal, leash, match, truss **6** attach, clip-on, cravat, fasten, fetter, hamper, oxford, ribbon, secure **7** connect, harness, shackle **8** dead heat, deadlock, fastener, ligament, ligature, restrain, shoelace, standoff, vinculum **9** constrain, stalemate **10** attachment, four-in-hand

tied 4 even **5** bound **6** joined, united **8** attached, fastened **9** connected

tier 3 row **4** bank, deck, file, line, rank **5** class, grade, group, story **6** league **7** echelon **8** category, grouping

tie-up 3 jam **4** snag **5** crimp, delay, hitch, snarl **6** glitch **7** problem **8** gridlock, slowdown, stoppage **10** connection, traffic jam **11** association

tiff 3 row **4** fuss, spat **5** run-in, scrap **6** bicker **7** brabble, dispute, quarrel, wrangle **8** argument, squabble **10** falling-out **11** altercation **12** disagreement

tiffany 5 gauze **11** cheesecloth

tiger 3 cat **6** feline **9** carnivore *young:* **3** cub

tight 4 fast, firm, snug, taut, trim **5** cheap, close, drunk, fixed, tipsy **6** firmly, secure, stingy **7** compact, crowded, drunken, miserly **8** intimate **9** difficult, tenacious **10** inebriated **11** closefisted, intoxicated **12** cheeseparing, parsimonious **13** pennypinching

tighten 4 bind **5** choke, close, cramp, pinch, screw **6** clench, fasten, narrow, secure, shrink **8** compress, restrict **9** clamp down, constrict

tightfisted see **stingy**

tight-lipped 6 silent **8** reserved, reticent, taciturn **12** closemouthed

tightwad 5 miser, piker 7 niggard, scrooge 9 skinflint 10 cheapskate 12 penny-pincher

tile 5 plate, slate 6 domino 7 tessera 8 linoleum

till 3 hoe, sow 4 disk, plow, tend, turn, up to, work 6 before, harrow 7 prior to 9 cultivate 11 in advance of 12 cash register

tillable 6 arable 10 cultivable 12 cultivatable

tillage 4 farm, land 5 tilth 7 culture 11 cultivation

tiller 4 helm 5 stalk 6 farmer, sprout 7 planter, steerer 9 sodbuster 10 cultivator

tilt 3 tip 4 bank, bent, bias, cant, cock, heel, lean, list, toss 5 grade, joust, level, lurch, pitch, slant, slope, speed 6 attack, charge, thrust 7 dispute, incline, leaning, recline 8 gradient 11 inclination

timbal 4 drum 10 kettledrum

timber 3 log 4 balk, beam, stud, tree, wood 5 board, joist, plank, trees, woods 6 forest, girder, lumber, rafter 8 woodland *uncut:* 8 stumpage *wolf:* 4 lobo

timbre 4 tone 6 temper 7 quality 9 resonance, tone color

timbrel 4 drum 10 tambourine

time 3 age, era 4 bout, date, hour, pace, span, term 5 clock, epoch, shift, space, spell, stint, tempo, while 6 moment, period, season 7 instant, stretch 8 duration, occasion 11 opportunity *abbreviation:* 3 CDT, CST, EDT, EST, MDT, MST, PDT, PST *combining form:* 5 chron 6 chrono *gone by:* 3 ago 4 past 9 yesterday 10 yesteryear 12 auld lang syne *long:* 3 age, eon, era 4 aeon *of day:* 4 dawn, dusk, noon 5 night 6 sunset 7 evening, morning, sunrise 8 daybreak, twilight 9 afternoon *olden:* 4 yore 10 yesteryear *period:* 3 age, day, eon, era 4 aeon, hour, week, year 5 epoch, month 6 decade, minute, moment, second 7 century, instant 9 fortnight 10 millennium *present:* 3 now *relating to:* 8 temporal *short:* 5 jiffy 6 moment, second 7 instant *to come:* 6 future 8 tomorrow *waste:* 4 loaf 5 dally 6 loiter

time and again 3 oft 5 often 6 hourly 8 commonly, ofttimes 10 constantly, frequently, oftentimes, repeatedly 11 continually, over and over 12 periodically

Time founder 4 Luce (Henry R.) 6 Hadden (Briton)

timeless 7 ageless, eternal, unaging 8 unageing 9 atemporal, perpetual 11 everlasting

timely 5 early 6 prompt, proper 8 punctual, suitable 9 opportune 10 seasonable 11 appropriate

Time Machine author 5 Wells (H. G.)

time-out 4 rest 5 break, pause 6 hiatus, recess 7 respite 8 breather 9 interlude 12 interruption

timepiece 5 clock, watch 7 sundial 8 horologe 9 clepsydra, metronome, stopwatch 10 water clock 11 chronograph, chronometer

timetable 6 agenda, docket 7 program 8 calendar, schedule

timeworn 3 old 4 aged, hack 5 hoary, stale, trite 6 age-old 7 ancient 8 dog-eared, Noachian 9 hackneyed 10 threadbare

time zone 7 Central, Eastern, Pacific 8 Mountain

timid 3 shy 4 wary 5 chary, mousy 6 afraid, yellow 7 bashful, chicken, fearful, halting, nervous, panicky 8 cowardly, retiring, timorous 9 diffident, tentative, trepidant, uncertain 11 unassertive 12 apprehensive, fainthearted

timidity 4 fear 7 modesty, shyness 8 meekness 9 hesitancy, reticence 10 diffidence, hesitation

Timon's servant 7 Flavius

timorous 4 wary 5 timid 6 afraid 7 fearful 8 retiring 9 shrinking, tremulous 12 apprehensive

Timothy's associate 4 Paul 5 Titus

tin 3 box, can 5 metal 7 element 9 container *mining region:* 8 stannary *relating to:* 7 stannic 8 stannous *sheet:* 6 latten *symbol:* 2 Sn

tincture 3 dye 4 cast, hint, tint 5 color, shade, smack, stain, tinge, touch, trace 6 iodine, streak 8 colorant, dyestuff, laudanum 9 paregoric 10 intimation, suggestion

tinder 4 punk 5 spunk 8 kindling

tine 5 point, prong, spike 6 branch

tinge 3 dye, hue 4 cast, hint, tint, tone 5 color, imbue, shade, stain, tinct, touch 8 tincture 10 intimation

tingle 5 sting 6 thrill 7 prickle 9 sensation

tinker 3 fix 4 mend, mess, muck, play 5 gypsy 6 adjust, diddle, fiddle, mender, potter, putter, repair 7 bungler, twiddle 9 repairman

tinkle 4 ring, ting 5 chink, clink, plink 6 jingle

tinny 4 thin 5 cheap, harsh 8 metallic

tinsel 5 gaudy 6 flashy, garish, tawdry 7 chintzy, glaring, trinket 8 ornament, specious 9 clinquant 11 superficial 12 meretricious

tint 3 dye, hue 4 cast, tone, wash 5 color, shade, tinge, touch 8 tincture 10 coloration 12 pigmentation

tiny 3 wee 4 itsy 5 bitsy, bitty, elfin, micro, pygmy, teeny, weeny 6 minute, peewee, pocket, teensy, weensy 8 pint-size 9 itsy-bitsy, itty-bitty, miniature, minuscule **10** diminutive, pocket-size, teeny-weeny **11** lilliputian, microscopic **12** teensy-weensy **13** infinitesimal

tip 3 cap, cue, top **4** apex, cant, clue, cusp, heel, hint, lean, list, peak, perk, tilt **5** point, slant, slope, steer, upset **6** advice, topple **7** cumshaw, incline **8** gratuity, overturn, turn over **9** baksheesh, lagniappe, pourboire **11** information

tip off 4 warn **5** alert

tip-off 4 clue, hint, sign **6** advice **7** pointer, red flag, warning **8** giveaway, jump ball **10** indication

Tippecanoe and ____ too 5 Tyler

tippet 4 cape **5** scarf **8** liripipe

tipple 3 bib, sip **4** swig, tope **5** booze, drink **6** guzzle, imbibe **7** swizzle **8** liquor up

tippler 3 sot **4** lush, soak **5** drunk, toper **6** bibber, boozer **7** tosspot **8** drunkard **9** inebriate

tipstaff 7 bailiff

tipster 4 fink, tout **6** canary, snitch **7** adviser, rat fink, stoolie, tattler **8** informer, squealer **11** stool pigeon

tipsy 3 lit **4** high **5** askew, drunk, lit up, oiled, tight **7** drunken, fuddled, sloshed **8** unsteady **10** inebriated **11** intoxicated

tiptoe 5 creep, skulk, slink, sneak, steal **9** pussyfoot

tirade 4 rant **6** screed **8** diatribe, harangue, jeremiad **9** philippic **12** denunciation, vituperation **13** tongue-lashing

tire 3 sap **4** bore, fail, flag, jade, pall, poop, wear **5** drain, droop, ennui, weary, wheel **6** tucker, weaken **7** exhaust, fatigue, wear out **8** enervate, wear down *airless:* **4** flat **7** blowout *kind:* **4** bias, snow **6** radial **7** retread **9** whitewall

tired 4 worn **5** spent, weary **6** done in **7** drained, run-down, worn out **8** fatigued, flagging **9** enervated, exhausted

tiredness 7 fatigue **8** collapse **9** lassitude **10** enervation, exhaustion **11** prostration

tireless 10 unflagging **13** indefatigable, inexhaustible

Tiresias 4 seer **10** soothsayer

tiresome 4 dull **5** stale **6** boring **7** irksome, lumpish, operose, tedious

Tirol *capital:* 9 Innsbruck *country:* **7** Austria *mountains:* **4** Alps

Tisiphone see **Erinyes**

tissue 3 web **4** film, mesh **5** fiber, gauze, paper **6** fabric *anatomical:* **4** tela **5** fiber **6** diploe **8** ganglion **10** epithelium *connective:* **4** tela **6** stroma, tendon **9** cartilage *kind:* **3** fat **5** nerve **6** muscle **7** nervous **8** muscular **10** connective *layer:* **6** dermis **7**

stratum *plant:* **4** bast, wood **5** xylem **6** phloem

titan 5 giant **8** colossus

Titan *father:* 6 Uranus *female:* **4** Rhea **6** Tethys, Themis *male:* **6** Cronus **7** Iapetus, Oceanus *mother:* **4** Gaea

Titan author 7 Dreiser (Theodore)

Titania's husband 6 Oberon

titanic 4 huge, vast **5** great **6** mighty **7** immense, mammoth, massive **8** colossal, enormous, gigantic **9** cyclopean, Herculean, monstrous **10** gargantuan, tremendous

Titanic *actor:* 4 Zane (Billy) **5** Bates (Kathy) **6** Stuart (Gloria) **7** Winslet (Kate) **8** DiCaprio (Leonardo) *director:* **7** Cameron (James) *last U. S. survivor:* **7** Asplund (Lillian) *line:* **9** White Star *rescuing vessel:* **9** Carpathia *sister ship:* **7** Olympic **9** Britannic

titanium symbol 2 Ti

tithe 3 tax **4** levy **5** tenth **12** contribution

Tithonus *beloved by:* 3 Eos *father:* **8** Laomedon

Titian painting 5 Danaë **8** Ecce Homo **10** Assumption (The), Holy Family (The) **12** Rape of Europa (The) **13** Maltese Knight, Medea and Venus, Venus and Cupid **14** Worship of Venus (The) **17** Bacchus and Ariadne

titillate 6 arouse, excite, stir up, thrill, tickle **9** stimulate

title 3 dub, due **4** call, deed, dibs, name, term **5** claim, merit, nomen **7** baptize, caption, heading **8** cognomen **9** designate **10** denominate **11** appellation, appellative, designation **12** championship, compellation, denomination *academic:* **4** dean, Prof. **7** provost **9** president, professor *Dutch:* **7** mynheer *ecclesiastic:* **3** Rev. **5** abbot **6** bishop **8** cardinal, reverend **10** archbishop *Etruscan:* **3** lar *feminine:* **2** Ms. **3** Mrs. **4** dame, lady, ma'am, miss **5** madam **6** abbess, madame, milady, missus **8** mistress *French:* **6** madame **8** monsieur **12** mademoiselle *German:* **4** Frau, Herr **8** Fräulein *Hindu:* **4** babu, raja, rani **5** baboo, rajah, ranee *holder:* **5** noble **8** champion *Indian:* **3** sri **5** sahib *Islamic:* **4** amir, emir, imam **5** ameer, hadji, hajji **6** sayyid **9** ayatollah *Italian:* **5** donna **6** signor **7** signora **9** signorina *masculine:* **2** Mr. **6** mister *monk's:* **3** fra **7** brother *of nobility:* **3** sir **4** duke, earl, king, lady, lord, sire **5** baron, count, queen **6** prince **7** baronet, duchess, marquis **8** Archduke, baroness, countess, marchesa, marchese, marquise, princess, viscount **11** marchioness, viscountess *Oriental:* **4** khan

Persian: 5 mirza *Portuguese:* 3 dom 4 dona 6 senhor 7 senhora 9 senhorita *Spanish:* 3 don 4 doña *Turkish:* 3 aga, bey

titmouse 4 bird 6 tomtit 7 bushtit 9 chickadee

Tito 4 Broz (Josip)

titter 5 laugh 6 giggle 7 chortle, chuckle, snicker, snigger

tittle 3 bit, jot 4 atom, iota, mite 5 minim, speck 7 smidgen 8 particle 9 diacritic

titular 5 legal 6 titled 7 nominal 8 so-called 11 designative

Tityus *father:* 4 Zeus *slayer:* 6 Apollo

Tiu see **Tyr**

tizzy 4 flap, fume, snit, stew 5 sweat 6 dither, swivet, uproar

T-man 5 agent 8 revenuer

to (Scottish) 3 tae

toad 4 agua 6 anuran, peeper 8 truckler 9 amphibian, brownnose, sycophant 10 batrachian, bootlicker 11 lickspittle *genus:* 4 Bufo, Hyla

toady 4 fawn 5 cower, leech 6 cringe, flunky, grovel, kowtow, lackey, sponge 7 truckle 8 bootlick, parasite, truckler 9 brownnose, sycophant 10 bootlicker 11 apple-polish, lickspittle

toast 5 bread, drink, salud, singe, skoal 6 cheers, health, l'chaim, pledge, prosit, salute 7 wassail 8 mazel tov 9 celebrate *kind:* 5 melba 6 French 8 zwieback

toastmaster 2 MC 5 emcee

To a Waterfowl author 6 Bryant (William Cullen)

tobacco 4 leaf, weed *cask:* 8 hogshead *chewing:* 4 chaw, quid *ingredient:* 3 tar 8 nicotine *juice:* 6 ambeer *kind:* 4 shag 5 flake, snuff 6 burley 7 caporal, latakia, perique, Turkish 8 Virginia 9 broadleaf, mundungus *pipe:* 4 heel 6 dottle *rolled:* 5 cigar 9 cigarette *Turkish:* 7 latakia

Tobacco Road author 8 Caldwell (Erskine)

to be *Latin:* 4 esse

to be sure 6 indeed 7 granted 9 certainly

Tobias *father:* 5 Tobit *son:* 8 Hyrcanus

toby 3 jug, mug 7 pitcher

tocsin 3 SOS 5 alarm, alert 6 signal

today 3 now 9 currently, presently

toddler 3 tot 4 tike, tyke 6 rug rat

to-do 4 fuss, rout, stir 5 hoo-ha, rouse, stink, whirl 6 bother, bustle, clamor, furore, hoohah, hubbub, hurrah, pother, ruckus, rumpus, tumult, uproar 7 turmoil 8 foofaraw 9 agitation, commotion 10 hurly-burly 11 disturbance

toe 5 digit *big:* 6 hallux *combining form:* 6 dactyl

toehold 7 footing

toff 3 fop 4 beau 5 blade, dandy, swell 7 coxcomb, peacock 8 macaroni, popinjay 9 exquisite 12 clotheshorse

toga 4 gown, robe, wrap

together 5 as one 6 at once, joined, united 7 jointly 8 mutually 10 conjointly 11 concertedly 12 coincidently, collectively, concurrently *prefix:* 3 col, com, con, cor, sym, syn

togetherness 5 union 7 cahoots 8 alliance 10 connection, solidarity 11 affiliation, association, combination, conjunction, partnership

toggle 3 pin 6 fasten, switch 9 alternate 10 crosspiece

Togo *capital:* 4 Lomé *language:* 3 Ewe 6 French *monetary unit:* 5 franc *neighbor:* 5 Benin, Ghana 11 Burkina Faso

togs 3 rig 4 duds, suit 5 dress 6 attire, outfit 7 apparel, clothes, raiment, rigging, threads 8 clothing, ensemble, garments

To His Coy Mistress author 7 Marvell (Andrew)

toil 3 fag, net, tug 4 grub, plod, plug, slog, trap, work 5 grind, labor, slave, snare, sweat 6 drudge 7 slavery, travail 8 drudgery

toiler 4 peon 5 slave 6 drudge, slavey 9 workhorse

toilet 3 loo 4 head, john 5 bidet, potty, privy 6 johnny 7 latrine 8 bathroom, lavatory 11 water closet

toilsome 4 hard 5 heavy 6 uphill 7 arduous, labored 9 difficult, effortful, laborious, strenuous

Tokay 4 wine

token 4 buck, chip, gift, mark, note, sign 5 badge, check, favor, index, piece, plume, prize, relic, scrip 6 copper, emblem, pledge, symbol, ticket, trophy 7 earnest, gesture, memento, symptom, warrant 8 evidence, keepsake, memorial, reminder, security, souvenir 9 indicator 10 expression, indication 11 perfunctory, remembrance

To Kill a Mockingbird *author:* 3 Lee (Harper) *character:* 3 Jem (Finch), Tom (Robinson) 4 Dill (Harris) 5 Ewell (Bob), Scout (Finch) 7 Atticus (Finch), Mayella (Ewell) 9 Boo Radley, Calpurnia 10 Cunningham (Walter) *town:* 7 Maycomb

Tokyo *formerly:* 3 Edo *island:* 6 Honshu

tolerable 2 OK 4 fair, okay 6 common, decent 7 livable 8 adequate, all right, bearable, passable 9 endurable 10 acceptable, sufferable 11 respectable 12 satisfactory

tolerably 4 so-so 5 quite 6 fairly, pretty, rather 8 passably 9 averagely 10 moderately

tolerance 6 leeway 8 patience 9 allowance, endurance, deviation, fortitude, variation 10 indulgence, resistance, sufferance **11** forbearance, habituation

tolerant 4 easy **5** broad **7** lenient, liberal **8** placable **9** easygoing, eurytopic, forgiving, indulgent, tractable **10** open-minded, permissive **11** broad-minded, sympathetic **13** understanding

tolerate 4 bear, bide, hack **5** abide, allow, brook, stand **6** accept, endure, pardon, permit, suffer **7** condone, stomach, swallow **8** bear with, live with **9** put up with **11** countenance

Tolkien creature 3 Ent, Orc **4** Warg **5** Ainur, Huorn, Troll **6** Balrog, Hobbit, Nazgul, Shelob **9** Oliphaunt **10** Ringwraith

toll 3 fee, tax **4** bell, bong, cost, levy, peal, ring **5** chime, knell, price, sound **6** charge, summon, tariff **7** expense **8** casualty **10** assessment

tollbooth 11 customhouse

Tolstoy work 8 Cossacks (The) **11** War and Peace **12** Anna Karenina **16** Death of Ivan Ilich (The)

tomato 9 love apple

tomb 5 crypt, grave **6** burial **9** mausoleum, sepulcher, sepulchre, sepulture *ancient Egyptian:* **7** mastaba *empty:* **8** cenotaph

tomboy 6 gamine, hoyden

tombstone 4 slab **8** memorial, monument **11** grave marker *inscription:* **3** RIP **8** hic jacet

tome 4 book **6** volume

tomfool 3 ass **4** dolt, fool, jerk **5** crazy, idiot, loony, ninny, silly, wacky **6** absurd, donkey, stupid **7** doltish, foolish, jackass **8** clodpoll, dummkopf, imbecile **9** blockhead, fantastic, horse's ass, thickhead **10** dunderhead, nincompoop **11** chowderhead, chucklehead, harebrained **12** preposterous

tomfoolery 4 dido, lark **5** antic, caper, prank, shine, trick **6** frolic **8** escapade, fandango **9** high jinks **10** shenanigan **11** monkeyshine

Tom Jones author 8 Fielding (Henry)

tommyrot 4 bosh, bull, bunk **5** bilge, hooey, trash **7** baloney, eyewash, hogwash, rubbish **8** claptrap, nonsense **9** poppycock **10** balderdash **13** horsefeathers

Tom o'Bedlam 3 nut **4** loon **5** loony **6** madman, maniac **7** lunatic

tomorrow 6 future, mañana

Tom Sawyer *author:* **5** Twain (Mark) **7** Clemens (Samuel) *character:* **5** Becky (Thatcher) **8** Huck Finn, Injun Joe **9** Aunt Polly **10** Muff Potter

Tom Thumb 4 runt **5** dwarf, pygmy **6** midget, peanut, peewee **7** manikin **8** half-pint, mannikin **10** homunculus **11** lilliputian

ton 3 lot **4** chic **5** bunch, style, trend, vogue **6** bundle **7** fashion

tone 3 hue **4** cast, mode, mood, note, tint, vein **5** color, pitch, shade, sound, style, tinge **6** accent, manner, spirit, strain, temper, timbre **7** fashion **10** inflection

toned 3 cut, fit **4** buff, firm, trim **6** buffed **7** defined **8** muscular

toned down 4 mute, soft **5** muted, quiet, sober **6** low-key, mellow **7** subdued **8** laidback, low-keyed, softened **10** restrained **11** understated

Tonga *capital:* **9** Nuku'alofa *ethnic group:* **10** Polynesian *explorer:* **4** Cook (Capt. James) **6** Tasman (Abel) *island group:* **5** Vava'u **6** Haapai **9** Tongatapu *monetary unit:* **6** pa'anga

tongue 4 lick, pole, tang **6** glossa, lingua, speech **7** clapper, dialect, languet **8** language **10** vernacular *combining form:* **4** glot **5** gloss, lingu **6** glossa, glosso, lingua, lingui, linguo **7** glossia

tongue-lash 4 lash, rail **5** chide, scold **6** berate, rebuke, revile **7** bawl out, chew out, tell off, reprove, upbraid **8** admonish, call down, reproach **9** castigate, reprimand **10** vituperate

tongue-lashing 6 rebuke, tirade **7** censure, reproof **8** scolding **9** reprimand, talking-to **11** castigation **12** dressing-down

tongue-tied 3 mum, shy **4** mute **6** silent **7** bashful **9** diffident **10** speechless **12** inarticulate

tonic 3 pop **4** cola, soda **5** brisk **7** bracing, soda pop **8** curative, salutary **10** refreshing **11** restorative, stimulating **12** exhilarating, invigorating *extract:* **4** cola **9** berberine

tons 4 gobs, lots **5** heaps, loads, piles, reams, scads **6** oodles

tony 4 chic, posh **5** smart, swank, swish **6** classy, modish, uptown **7** à la mode, elegant, stylish **9** exclusive **11** fashionable

too 4 also, ever, over, very **5** along **6** as well, overly, unduly, withal **7** awfully, besides, further, greatly **8** likewise, moreover, overmuch **9** extremely, immensely **10** in addition, remarkably, strikingly **11** exceedingly, excessively, furthermore **12** additionally, exorbitantly, immoderately, inordinately **13** exceptionally

tool 4 pawn **5** means **6** puppet, rimmer, stooge **7** cat's-paw, hayfork, machine, rounder, utensil **8** picklock **9** appliance, implement, mechanism **10** instrument *axlike:* **3** adz **4** adze *boring:* **5** auger, drill *carving:* **6** veiner *cleaving:* **4** froe *cobbler's:* **3** awl *cooper's:* **3** adz **4** adze *cutting:* **2** ax **3** adz,

axe, saw **4** adze **5** edger, knife **6** shears **8**
billhook *digging:* **4** pick **5** spade **6** shovel **7**
mattock *engraving:* **5** burin *farm:* **6** seeder
filing: **4** rasp **7** riffler *garden:* **3** hoe **4** rake **5**
spade **6** trowel, weeder *grasping:* **6** pincer **7**
tweezer **8** tweezers *mining:* **3** gad **6** trepan
piercing: **3** awl *prehistoric:* **6** eolith *pruning:* **6** shears **9** secateurs *rubbing:* **9** burnisher *scooping:* **6** router *toothed:* **3** saw **7**
ripper *woodworking:* **3** adz, saw **4** adze **5**
bevel, plane **6** chisel, hammer

toot 3 bat, jag **4** bout, bust, honk, tear **5**
binge, blast, drunk, snort, sound, souse,
spree **6** bender **7** carouse

tooth 5 molar **7** incisor **8** bicuspid, premolar
combining form: **4** dent **5** denti, dento *cuspid:* **6** canine **8** dogtooth, eyetooth *cutting:*
10 carnassial *decay:* **6** caries *doctor:* **7** dentist *gear:* **3** cog *horse:* **4** tush *material:* **4**
pulp **6** dentin, enamel **8** cementum *pointed:*
4 fang **6** canine, cuspid *small:* **8** denticle

toothless 7 useless **8** edentate **10** edentulous
11 ineffective, ineffectual

toothsome 5 sapid, tasty **6** delish, savory **8**
luscious, pleasant, pleasing, tasteful **9**
agreeable, delicious, palatable, succulent **10**
appetizing, attractive **11** scrumptious

too-too 6 la-di-da **7** extreme **8** affected, overdone, overmuch, precious **9** excessive **10**
hoity-toity, inordinate **11** exaggerated, overrefined, pretentious

tootsie 3 pet **4** dear **5** honey, sugar **7** beloved,
darling, sweetie **10** sweetheart, sweetie pie

top 3 cap, tip **4** acme, apex, best, cusp, head,
peak, pick, roof **5** cream, crest, crown, elite,
point, prime, prize **6** apical, choice, climax,
height, summit, utmost, vertex **7** capital,
highest, maximal, maximum, surface **8**
five-star, loftiest, pinnacle, superior **9** firstrate, uppermost **10** first-class **11** culmination

tope 3 nip **4** soak **5** booze, drink, shark, stupa
6 guzzle, imbibe, tipple **7** swizzle **8** liquor
up

toper 3 sot **4** lush, soak, wino **5** drunk,
rummy, souse **6** bibber, boozer **7** tippler,
tosspot **8** drunkard **9** inebriate **10** boozehound

Tophet 4 hell **5** hades, Sheol **6** blazes **7** Gehenna, inferno **9** perdition **10** underworld

topic 4 talk, text **5** issue, motif, point, score,
theme **6** burden, matter, motive, thread **7**
content, subject **8** argument **11** proposition

topical 5 local **7** current, nominal **8** regional
9 temporary **11** superficial

topmost 7 highest, leading, supreme **8**

crowning, ultimate **9** paramount, principal
10 consummate, preeminent **11** culminating

top-notch 4 A-one **5** prime, primo **6** choice **7**
capital **8** five-star, superior **9** excellent,
first-rate **10** first-class **11** first-string

top off 3 cap **5** crown **6** climax, finish, refill **8**
complete, conclude, resupply **9** culminate

topography 7 surface, terrain **8** features

topple 3 tip **4** drop, fall **5** crash, lurch, pitch,
slump, upset **6** defeat, falter, plunge, totter,
tumble **8** collapse, keel over, overturn **9**
overthrow

tops 4 A-one, best **5** primo **6** at most **7** highest, supreme **8** peerless, superior **9** at the
most, first-rate, matchless, nonpareil **11** outstanding

topsy-turvy 7 chaotic, jumbled, mixed-up **8**
cockeyed, confused, inverted **10** disjointed,
disordered, upside down

toque 3 cap, hat

tor 4 crag, hill, peak **5** butte, cliff, mound, talus

Torah 10 Pentateuch

torch 4 fire **5** flame, light **6** ignite **7** firebug **8**
arsonist, flambeau, guidance **10** flashlight,
incendiary

toreador 6 torero **7** matador **11** bullfighter

torero see **toreador**

torment 3 rag, try, vex **4** bait, bane, hell, hurt,
pain, pang, rack **5** abuse, agony, curse, grill,
harry, tease, worry, wring **6** harass, harrow,
heckle, misery, molest, needle, plague **7** afflict, agonize, anguish, bedevil, crucify, distort, hagride, torture, travail, trouble **8**
distress **9** persecute, tantalize **10** affliction,
excruciate

torn 4 rent **5** split **6** ragged, ripped, unsure **7**
mangled **8** tattered, wrenched **9** lacerated,
uncertain, undecided

tornado 6 funnel **7** cyclone, twister **9** windstorm, whirlwind

toro 4 bull

torpedo 3 gun, ray **4** mine, thug **5** blast,
bravo, smash, wreck **6** gunman, gunsel, hit
man, killer, weapon **7** destroy, nullify, scuttle **8** assassin, firework **9** explosive, shoot
down **10** hatchet man, projectile, triggerman **11** electric ray

torpid 4 dull, lazy, numb **5** dopey, inert **6** sodden, stupid **7** dormant **8** comatose, inactive,
sluggish **9** apathetic, lethargic **12** hebetudinous

torpor 4 coma, daze **5** swoon **6** apathy, stupor
7 languor **8** dopiness, dullness, hebetude,
lethargy **9** lassitude, passivity, stolidity **10**
stagnation **12** listlessness

torque 5 twist

torrent 4 rush **5** flood, spate **6** deluge, stream **7** cascade, Niagara **8** cataract, flooding **9** cataclysm **10** inundation, outpouring

torrid 3 hot **5** fiery **6** ardent, fervid, heated, red-hot, sultry **7** boiling, burning, flaming, parched **8** broiling, white-hot **9** scorching **10** hot-blooded, passionate, sweltering **11** impassioned

tort 5 crime, wrong **7** offense **10** wrongdoing

tortilla dish 4 taco **6** flauta **7** burrito, chalupa, tostada **9** enchilada **10** quesadilla **11** chimichanga

Tortilla Flat author 9 Steinbeck (John)

tortoise 6 turtle **8** terrapin **9** chelonian *beak:* **3** neb *shell:* **8** carapace

tortuous 5 snaky **6** cranky, tricky **7** crooked, devious, sinuous, winding **8** flexuous, indirect, involute, involved **9** meandrous **10** circuitous, convoluted, meandering, serpentine **11** anfractuous, vermiculate **12** labyrinthine

torture 4 pain, rack, warp **5** agony, wring **6** harrow, martyr **7** afflict, agonize, anguish, crucify, torment **9** martyrdom **10** excruciate **11** third degree

tortured 4 bent **6** racked, warped **7** twisted **8** deformed **9** distorted

tory 5 right **7** old-line **8** loyalist, old guard, orthodox, rightist, royalist **12** conservative

Tosca *character:* 5 Mario (Cavaradossi) **7** Scarpia (Baron) *composer:* **7** Puccini (Giacomo)

tosh 3 rot **4** bosh, bunk **5** bilge, hooey **6** bunkum, drivel, humbug **7** baloney, eyewash, hogwash, twaddle **8** malarkey, nonsense, tommyrot, trumpery

toss 4 cast, flap, flip, hurl, rock, roll **5** chuck, drink, fling, heave, match, pitch, quaff, sling, surge, throw, vomit **6** imbibe, tumble, welter, writhe **7** discard **9** knock back, throw away

tosspot see **tippler**

tot 3 add, kid, nip, sum **4** dram, shot, slug, tike, tyke **5** child, snort **6** figure, infant, nipper, shaver, squirt **7** snifter, toddler

total 3 add, all, sum **4** foot, full **5** add up, equal, gross, run to, smash, sum to, utter, whole, wreck, yield **6** all-out, amount, entire, figure, number **7** crack up, destroy, overall, perfect, quantum **8** absolute, complete, demolish, entirety, outright, quantity **9** aggregate, full-blown, full-scale, inclusive, unlimited **10** consummate, unreserved **11** unmitigated **13** comprehensive, thoroughgoing

totalitarian 8 absolute, despotic **10** autocratic **11** dictatorial **13** authoritarian

totality 3 all, sum **4** lump **5** whole **7** oneness **8** entirety **9** aggregate, wholeness **12** completeness

totalize 3 add, sum **5** sum up **6** figure **7** summate

tote 3 lug **4** cart, haul, load, pack **5** carry, ferry, shlep, sum up **6** burden, convey, figure, schlep, shlepp **7** schlepp, summate **9** transport **10** pari-mutuel

totem 6 emblem, symbol

To the Lighthouse author 5 Woolf (Virginia)

totter 4 reel, sway **5** lurch, shake, waver **6** falter, toddle, topple, wobble **7** stagger

touch 3 dab, tad **4** abut, feel, meet, move, stir **5** brush, graze **6** adjoin, border, caress, finger, stroke **7** contact, palpate, smidgen **9** palpation, tactility

touchable 7 tactile **8** palpable, tangible

touch down 4 land **5** light, perch, roost **6** alight, settle

touched 3 odd, off **5** batty, crazy, moved **7** stirred **8** affected **9** emotional

touching 4 as to, in re **5** about, anent, as for **6** moving, tender **7** against, apropos, emotive, meeting, piteous, pitiful, tangent **8** abutting, adjacent, pathetic, pitiable, poignant, stirring **9** adjoining, affecting, apropos of, as regards, bordering, immediate, impinging, regarding **10** as respects, back-to-back, concerning, contiguous, respecting, tangential **11** coterminous **12** conterminous

touch off 5 erupt, spark, start **6** ignite, incite, kindle **7** explode, inflame, provoke, trigger **8** initiate **9** instigate **11** precipitate

touchstone 4 test **5** check, gauge, proof, trial **7** measure **8** standard **9** barometer, benchmark, criterion, yardstick

touch up 3 fix **5** patch **6** rework **7** improve, perfect

touchy 5 dicey, huffy, risky, testy **6** tender, tricky **7** peppery **8** delicate, ticklish **9** explosive, hazardous, irascible, irritable, sensitive **10** precarious **11** inflammable, quarrelsome, thin-skinned **13** oversensitive, temperamental, unpredictable

tough 3 mug **4** goon, hard, hood, lout, punk, thug **5** bully, hardy, harsh **6** rugged, severe, unruly **7** arduous, hoodlum, onerous, ruffian **8** bullyboy, hooligan, obdurate **9** arbitrary, demanding, difficult, effortful, hard-nosed, hidebound, laborious, resistant, roughneck, strenuous **10** hard-bitten, hardboiled, hardheaded, refractory **11** unbreakable

toughen 5 inure **6** anneal, harden, season, temper **9** acclimate, habituate **10** strengthen **11** acclimatize

toughie 4 goon, hood, lout, punk, thug **5**
poser, rowdy **7** hoodlum, ruffian, stumper **8**
bullyboy, hooligan, plug-ugly **9** roughneck
toupee 3 rug, wig **6** peruke, wiglet **7** periwig
8 postiche **9** hairpiece
tour 4 bout, trip, turn **5** jaunt, round, shift,
spell, stint **6** junket, period, travel, troupe **7**
circuit, journey **8** progress **9** barnstorm, excursion **10** expedition, rubberneck
tour de force 4 deed, feat **7** classic, display,
exploit **10** magnum opus, masterwork **11**
achievement, chef d'oeuvre, masterpiece
Tour de France winner 4 Riis (Bjarne) **5**
Roche (Stephen) **6** Fignon (Laurent), Lan-
dis (Floyd), LeMond (Greg), Sastre (Carlos) **7** Delgado (Pedro), Hinault (Bernard),
Pantani (Marco), Pereiro (Oscar), Ullrich
(Jan) **8** Contador (Alberto), Induráin
(Miguel) **9** Armstrong (Lance)
tour guide 8 cicerone
tourist 7 tripper, visitor **8** traveler **9** sightseer,
traveller **10** day-tripper, rubberneck, vacationer **12** excursionist, globe-trotter
tournament 4 meet, open, tilt **5** pro-am **6**
jousts, series **7** contest, tourney **8** carousel
10 round-robin **11** competition **12** championship
tourney 4 meet **5** event, games, match **7** compete, contest **8** concours **11** competition
tousle 4 mess, muss **6** rumple **8** dishevel, disorder
tout 3 spy, tip **4** brag, hype, laud, plug **5**
watch **6** blow up, peddle, praise, talk up **7**
acclaim, crack up, promote, solicit **8** ballyhoo, persuade, proclaim **9** publicize
tovarich 7 comrade
tow 3 lug, tug **4** drag, draw, haul, pull, rope,
yarn **5** chain, trail **6** hawser *truck:* **7**
wrecker
towel word 3 his **4** hers
tower 4 loom **5** spire **6** turret **8** overlook *biblical:* **4** Edar **5** Babel *on a mosque:* **7** minaret
towering 4 high, tall **5** grand, lofty **6** aerial **7**
soaring **8** imposing, majestic **9** excessive,
grandiose **10** monumental, prodigious **11**
magnificent, skyscraping **12** altitudinous,
overwhelming
towhee 5 finch **7** chewink
to wit 3 viz **6** namely, that is **8** scilicet **9** c'est-
à-dire, videlicet
town 4 burg **6** hamlet, podunk **7** borough, village *medieval:* **5** bourg
town and ____ 4 gown **7** country
townsman 7 burgher, citizen
town square 5 plaza *Italian:* **6** piazza
toxic 6 poison **7** harmful, noxious **8** venomous, virulent **9** poisonous **10** infectious

toxin 5 venom **6** poison
toy 3 top **4** fool, play, yo-yo **5** antic, curio,
dally, flirt, knack, mouse, tease **6** bauble,
caress, coquet, diddle, fiddle, gewgaw, puzzle, rattle, Slinky, trifle **7** bibelot, Frisbee,
foot bag, novelty, pastime, trinket, whatnot
8 gimcrack **9** plaything, pogo stick **10** diminutive, Erector Set, knickknack, Silly
Putty, sock monkey, Spirograph, View-
Master **11** jumping jack **12** kaleidoscope
trace 3 jot, ray, run, tug **4** blip, echo, hint,
iota, mark, path, scan, wisp **5** relic, shade,
spoor, tinge, trail, tread **6** derive, detect, nuance, shadow, strain, streak **7** outline, remains, remnant, run down, soupçon,
symptom, vestige **8** discover, tincture, traverse **9** delineate, footprint, remainder,
scintilla, suspicion **10** intimation, suggestion
trachea 6 larynx, throat, vessel **7** weasand **8**
throttle, windpipe
track 3 way **4** drag, oval, path, rail, road,
sign, slot, step, tail **5** chase, cover, print,
spoor, trace, trail, tread **6** artery, follow,
pursue, shadow, travel **7** footway, imprint,
monitor, pathway, vestige **8** footpath, footstep **9** footprint **10** racecourse *cycle:* **9** velodrome
track-and-field event 4 dash **5** relay **6** discus
7 javelin, hurdles, shot put **8** footrace, high
jump, long jump **9** broad jump, decathlon,
pole vault **10** heptathlon, triple jump **11** discus throw **12** steeplechase
track star 3 Coe (Sebastian) **4** Nool (Erki) **5**
Flo-Jo, Jones (Marion), Lewis (Carl), Mo-
ses (Edwin), Nurmi (Paavo), Ovett (Steve),
Owens (Jesse), Pérec (Marie-José), Viren
(Lasse) **6** Beamon (Bob), Devers (Gail),
Jenner (Bruce), O'Brien (Dan), Oerter (Al),
Sebrie (Roman), Toomey (Bill) **7** Johnson
(Michael, Rafer), Mathias (Bob), Rudolph
(Wilma), Shorter (Frank), Zátopek (Emil) **8**
Thompson (Daley), Zaharias (Babe Didrikson) **9** Bannister (Roger), Didrikson (Babe)
12 Joyner-Kersee (Jackie)
tract 3 lot **4** area, belt, farm, land, plat, plot,
zone **5** block, claim **6** parcel, region **7** leaflet, portion, terrain **8** pamphlet, preserve **9**
territory
tractable 4 tame **6** docile, gentle, pliant **7**
ductile, plastic, pliable **8** amenable, biddable, flexible, obedient, workable **9** adaptable, breakable, malleable **10** manageable
tractate 5 summa **6** memoir, thesis **7** pandect
8 hornbook, monument, treatise **9** discourse, monograph **10** commentary **12** disquisition, dissertation, introduction

traction 4 drag, pull **5** force **7** drawing, tension **8** friction

tractor maker 4 Case **5** Deere (John) **6** Kubota **7** Farmall

trade 4 deal, sell, swap **5** craft, truck **6** barter, change, custom, market, métier, peddle, switch **7** bargain, calling, pursuit, traffic **8** business, commerce, exchange, industry, vocation **10** employment, occupation, profession, substitute **11** merchandise, transaction *illicit:* **11** black market

trademark 3 tag **4** logo **5** brand, label, stamp **6** patent, symbol **8** colophon, logotype **9** brand name

trader 4 ship **6** broker, dealer, vendor **8** merchant

trade route 7 sea-lane

trade show 4 expo **10** exhibition, exposition

tradition 4 lore, myth **5** habit **6** belief, custom, legacy, legend, mythos, rubric **7** folkway **8** folklore, heredity, heritage, practice **9** mythology **10** convention **12** old wives' tale

traditional 4 oral **5** usual **6** common, spoken, verbal **7** classic, old-line, popular **8** habitual, orthodox **9** classical, customary, old-school, unwritten **10** button-down **11** established **12** acknowledged, buttoned-down, conservative, conventional

traditionalist 6 purist **12** conservative

traditionalistic 4 tory **7** die-hard, old-line **8** orthodox, standpat **12** conservative

traduce 4 slur **5** libel, smear, wrong **6** betray, breach, defame, malign, vilify **7** asperse, slander, violate **8** disgrace, tear down **9** denigrate **10** calumniate

Trafalgar commander 6 Nelson (Horatio)

traffic 4 deal **5** cargo, fence, trade, truck **6** barter, custom **7** bootleg, freight **8** commerce, dealings, exchange, movement **9** patronage, transport **11** black-market *circle:* **6** rotary **10** roundabout *cone:* **5** pylon *jam:* **5** tie-up **6** holdup **8** blockage, gridlock **10** bottleneck

trafficker 6 dealer, trader

tragedy 3 woe **6** mishap, plague **8** calamity, disaster **9** cataclysm, mischance **10** misfortune **11** catastrophe **12** misadventure

trail 3 dog, lag, tag **4** drag, flag, path, plod, poke **5** chase, dally, delay, tarry, trace, track **6** dawdle, follow, linger, pursue, shadow **7** draggle, gumshoe, pathway, traipse **8** footpath, footwalk **10** bridle path *emigrant:* **6** Oregon *Florida:* **7** Tamiami *Georgia-Maine:* **11** Appalachian *Indian:* **5** Great

trailer 5 truck **7** preview **9** motor home, transport **10** mobile home

trailer truck 4 semi

train 2 el **3** row **4** file, tame **5** coach, drill, teach, track **6** column, convoy, course, school, sequel, series, thread **7** caravan, cortege, educate, prepare, retinue **8** exercise, instruct, sequence **9** cultivate, entourage, following, habituate **10** succession **11** progression

trainee 4 tiro, tyro **6** novice **7** learner **8** beginner, neophyte **10** apprentice

training 7 tuition **8** teaching, tutelage **9** education, schooling **11** instruction *horse:* **6** manège

traipse 3 gad **4** hoof, pace, roam, rove, step, walk **5** amble, range, trail, tramp, tread **6** ramble, stroll, wander **7** maunder, meander **8** ambulate **9** gallivant

trait 4 mark **5** point, quirk, touch, trace **6** oddity, stroke **7** feature, quality **8** hallmark, property, specific **9** attribute

traitor 3 rat **5** Judas **8** apostate, betrayer, defector, deserter, quisling, renegade, turncoat **9** turnabout

traitorous 5 Punic **8** apostate, disloyal, mutinous, recreant, renegade **9** faithless **10** perfidious, rebellious, unfaithful **11** treacherous

traject 4 beam, pass, pipe, send **5** carry **6** convey, render **7** conduct, forward, impress **8** hand down, transfer, transmit **9** broadcast, transfuse

trajectory 3 arc **4** path **5** curve **11** progression

tram 3 car **7** trolley **9** streetcar

trammel 3 tie **4** bind, curb **5** check, gauge, leash **6** fetter, hamper, hobble **7** compass, confine, ensnare, manacle, pothook, shackle **8** entangle, handcuff **9** restraint

tramontane 8 outsider **9** foreigner, outlander **11** transalpine

tramp 3 bum **4** hike, hobo, jade, plod, slog, thud **5** bimbo, caird, clump, gipsy, gypsy, march, stamp, stiff, stomp, tread **6** ramble, stroll, travel, trudge, wander **7** chippie, drifter, floater, saunter, traipse, vagrant **8** clochard, derelict, footslog, homeless, stroller, vagabond, wanderer **10** prostitute

trample 4 mash **5** crush, pound, stamp, stomp, tread, tromp

trance 4 daze, muse **5** swoon **7** ecstasy, rapture, reverie **8** hypnosis **9** catalepsy, enrapture **10** absorption, brown study **11** abstraction

tranquil 4 calm, easy **5** quiet, still **6** dreamy, placid, poised, serene **7** restful **8** composed, peaceful **10** untroubled **13** self-possessed

tranquilize 4 calm, hush, lull **5** quiet, relax, still **6** becalm, pacify, sedate, settle, soothe, subdue **7** compose, mollify

tranquilizer 6 downer 8 diazepam, pacifier, sedative 10 depressant 11 barbiturate

tranquillity 4 calm 5 peace, quiet 8 calmness, serenity 9 composure, placidity

transaction 4 deal 5 trade 7 bargain, dealing 8 contract, covenant 9 agreement

transcend 3 top 4 beat, best 5 excel, outdo 6 better, exceed 7 surpass 8 outshine, outstrip, overcome, surmount

transcendent 5 ideal 7 perfect, sublime, supreme 8 abstract, immanent 10 consummate, surpassing

Transcendentalist 6 Alcott (Bronson), Fuller (Margaret) 7 Emerson (Ralph Waldo), Thoreau (Henry David)

transcribe 4 copy 5 write 6 record 8 transfer 9 translate, write down 13 transliterate

transfer 4 cede, deed, hand, pass, ship 5 carry, grant, shift 6 assign, convey, remove, supply 7 consign, convert, deliver, devolve, dispose 8 alienate, hand over, make over, relocate, turn over 9 carry over 10 assignment, conveyance 11 disposition

transfix 4 spit 5 lance, spear, spike, stick 6 impale, skewer 7 spindle 8 entrance 9 fascinate, hypnotize, mesmerize

transform 5 alter, morph 6 change, mutate 7 commute, convert 12 metamorphose

transformation 8 reaction 10 changeover, conversion 13 metamorphosis

transfuse 5 endue, imbue 7 pervade, suffuse, traject 8 permeate, saturate 9 penetrate, percolate 10 impregnate

transgress 3 err, sin 6 breach, exceed, offend 7 violate 8 infringe, overpass, overstep, trespass 10 contravene

transgression 3 sin 5 crime, error, wrong 6 breach 7 misdeed, offense 9 violation 12 infringement

transient 4 hobo 5 brief, tramp 7 drifter, migrant, passing 8 fleeting, flitting, fugitive, volatile 9 ephemeral, fugacious, momentary, temporary 10 evanescent, fly-by-night, short-lived 11 impermanent

transit 7 passage 8 traverse 10 conveyance

transition 4 leap 5 segue, shift 6 change 7 passage 10 conversion 13 metamorphosis

transitory see **transient**

translate 6 render 7 convert 9 interpret, reproduce 10 paraphrase

translation 9 rendition 10 conversion, paraphrase

transmarine 7 oversea 8 overseas

transmission 7 gearbox 8 handover 9 broadcast, infection

transmit 3 air 4 beam, hand, pass, pipe, send 6 convey, hand on, impart, pass on, render,

signal 7 channel, conduct, consign, diffuse, forward, traject 8 bequeath, dispatch, hand down 9 broadcast

transmogrify see **transform**

transmute see **transform**

transoceanic message 4 wire 5 cable 9 cablegram

transparent 5 clear, filmy, gauzy, sheer 6 limpid 7 crystal 8 clear-cut, gossamer, pellucid 10 diaphanous, see-through 11 crystalline

transpire 3 hap 4 leak 5 exude, occur, sweat 6 chance, emerge, happen 7 develop 9 come about, take place 11 come to light

transplant 8 relocate, resettle

transport 3 bus, fly, lag, lug, wow, zap, zip 4 haul, hump, lift, pack, pass, send, ship, taxi, tote 5 carry, ferry, motor, truck 6 convey, excite, ravish, remove, thrill 7 delight, ecstasy, freight, rapture, sealift, trundle, vehicle 8 carriage, displace, railroad, rhapsody 9 carry away, chauffeur, troopship 10 conveyance, helicopter

transportation 6 moving 7 freight, hauling, removal, vehicle 8 carriage, carrying 10 conveyance 12 displacement

transpose 6 invert 7 convert, permute, reorder, reverse 9 rearrange 11 interchange

transude 4 ooze, reek, seep, weep 5 bleed, sweat 7 diffuse, give off 8 permeate 9 transfuse

transverse 5 cross 6 across, lintel, thwart 7 transom 8 crossbar, crossing 9 crossbeam, crosswise 10 crosspiece

trap 3 bag, net 4 bait, snag 5 catch, decoy, set up, snare 6 ambush, enmesh, tangle 7 ensnare, pitfall 8 birdlime, deadfall, entangle, quagmire 9 ambuscade

trappings 4 gear 5 dress 6 finery 8 equipage, ornament 9 adornment, caparison, equipment 10 decoration 11 habiliments 13 accouterments, accoutrements, embellishment, paraphernalia

Trappist 4 monk *writer:* 6 Merton (Thomas)

trash 3 rag, rot 4 bosh, bunk, junk, ruin, scum, slop 5 bilge, blast, dreck, dregs, hokum, offal, spoil, tripe, waste, wreck 6 bunkum, debris, insult, litter, refuse, rubble 7 clutter, destroy, garbage, hogwash, put down, rubbish 8 claptrap, malarkey, nonsense, tommyrot 9 disparage, poppycock, throw away, vandalize 10 balderdash 11 guttersnipe, proletariat

trash can 7 dustbin

trashy 5 bawdy, cheap, tatty 6 cruddy, shoddy, sleazy, smutty, vulgar 8 rubbishy 9 third-rate

trauma 4 blow, pain **5** shock, upset, wound **6** crisis, injury, stress **8** collapse **9** suffering

travail 4 grub, moil, task, toil, work **5** grind, labor, pains **6** drudge, effort **7** slavery, torment **8** drudgery, struggle

travel 4 fare, pass, roam, tour, trek, trip, wend **5** jaunt, range, tramp **6** junket, push on, voyage **7** explore, journey, passage, proceed, traffic, transit **8** movement, traverse **9** gallivant **10** hit the road *term:* **3** ETA **4** fare **9** all aboard

traveler 5 gipsy, gypsy, nomad, rover **7** drummer, tourist **8** runabout, runagate, salesman, vagabond **9** itinerant, sightseer **10** journeyman **11** peripatetic **12** rolling stone

traveling library 10 bookmobile

traverse 4 ride, span, walk **5** cover, cross, march, route, trace, track **6** course, thwart, travel, voyage **7** examine, transit **8** crossing, navigate, obstacle, pass over **9** adversity **10** crisscross, pass across **11** perambulate, peregrinate

travesty 3 ape **4** mock, sham **5** farce, mimic, spoof **6** parody **7** imitate, lampoon, mimicry, mockery, take off **8** ridicule **9** burlesque **10** caricature, distortion *satanic:* **9** Black Mass

Traviata, La *character:* **7** Alfredo (Germont), Germont **8** Violetta (Valéry) *composer:* **5** Verdi (Giuseppe)

trawl 3 net **4** fish **7** setline

tray 6 salver, server **7** platter **8** teaboard *revolving:* **9** lazy Susan

treacherous 5 false, Punic, risky **6** chancy, tricky **7** unsound **8** disloyal, perilous, recreant **9** dangerous, deceptive, faithless, hazardous, insidious **10** perfidious, traitorous, unfaithful, unreliable

treachery 7 perfidy, treason **8** bad faith, betrayal **9** duplicity **10** disloyalty, infidelity **11** double-cross **13** dastardliness, double-dealing, faithlessness

treacle 4 mush **5** slush, syrup **6** bathos **8** molasses, schmaltz **11** golden syrup

tread 4 hoof, pace, plod, step, walk **5** dance, march, stamp, stomp, trace, track, tramp, tromp, troop **6** follow, stride **7** footing, traipse, trample **8** footstep

treadle 5 lever, pedal

treadmill 3 rut **4** rote **5** chore, grind **6** groove **7** routine **8** drudgery, turnspit

treason 7 perfidy **8** betrayal, sedition **9** treachery **10** disloyalty, misprision **11** lèse-majesté

treasure 4 haul, save **5** adore, cache, hoard, pearl, prize, trove, value **6** esteem, revere, riches, wealth **7** apprize, cherish, idolize, worship **8** conserve, preserve, venerate **9** reverence **10** appreciate

Treasure Island *author:* **9** Stevenson (Robert Louis) *character:* **7** Ben Gunn **8** Long John (Silver) *narrator:* **10** Jim Hawkins

treasurer 6 bursar, purser **7** curator **8** receiver **11** chamberlain

Treasure State 7 Montana

treasure trove 4 find, mine **7** bonanza, pay dirt **8** El Dorado, Golconda, gold mine

treasury 4 fisc, mine **5** cache, chest, hoard **6** argosy, coffer, museum **7** bonanza, gallery, omnibus **8** archives, El Dorado, Golconda, gold mine, war chest **9** anthology, exchequer **10** depositary, depository, repository, storehouse

treat 5 goody, nurse **6** bonbon, dainty, doctor, goodie, handle, manage, morsel, tidbit **7** care for **8** deal with, delicacy, medicate **10** minister to *animals:* **3** vet *leather:* **3** tan, taw **7** tanning

treatise 6 thesis **8** tractate **9** discourse, monograph **10** exposition **12** disquisition, dissertation

treatment 4 care **7** therapy

treaty 4 pact **6** accord **7** charter, compact, concord **8** alliance, contract, covenant **9** agreement, concordat **10** convention

treble 4 high **6** shrill, triple **7** descant, soprano **9** threefold **11** high-pitched

tree 3 apa, ash, box, dao, dar, elm, eng, fir, koa, kou, lin, oak, sal, ule, yew **4** ague, atle, copa, dhak, kaki, lime, linn, mora, neem, pine, poon, tawa, teak, teil, titi, tung, upas, wych **5** aalii, abele, alamo, alder, athel, beech, birch, carob, cedar, ebony, holly, larch, lemon, maire, maple, osier, pipal, roble, rowan, sauch, saugh, sumac, taxus, yulan **6** arbute, banyan, cherry, cornel, deodar, ginkgo, kamala, linden, loquat, lychee, mallee, medlar, mimosa, myrtle, orange, poplar, redbud, sapota, spruce, tan oak, tupelo **7** arariba, arbutus, camphor, conifer, cypress, deodara, dogwood, hemlock, inkwood, juniper, kumquat, lentisk, madrona, madrone, murmast, redwood, sequoia, seringa, wallaba, zelkova **8** basswood, bergamot, black gum, bluejack, cinchona, corkwood, laburnum, loblolly, longleaf, magnolia, mahogany, sourwood, sweetgum, sycamine, sycamore, tamarisk **9** balsam fir, sassafras **10** candlewood, chinaberry, chinquapin **11** bald cypress **12** balm of Gilead, rhododendron *African:* **4** akee, cola, shea **5** limba, sassy **6** baobab **7** avodire, bubinga **8** sasswood **9** berberine *Australian:* **4** toon, yate **5** wilga **7** blue gum **8** lacewood, quandong **9** casuarina **10** eucalyptus **11** bottle-brush *branch:* **5** bough *combining form:* **3** dry **4** dryo **5** arbor, dendr **6** arbori, dendra (plural), dendro *genus:* **4** Acer, Cola, Maba, Olea, Para **5** Abies **11** Callistemon *palm:* **4** coco, nipa **5** ratan **6** pinang, raffia, rattan **7** coquito **8** carnauba *tropical:* **3** ake, ama **4** akee, copa, dita, ohia, palm, pili, sago, teak, upas, yaya **5** areca, assai, balsa, cacao, ceiba, cycad, lehua, mamey **6** acajou, balata, baobab, bataan, citrus **7** genipap, logwood, majagua, palmyra, quassia, soursop **8** allspice, barbasco, mahogany, mangrove, milkwood, palmetto, rosewood, soapbark, sweetsop, tamarind **9** candlenut, jacaranda, sapodilla **10** breadfruit, calamondin, manchineel **11** candleberry, coconut palm *trunk:* **4** bole *young:* **7** sapling

trefoil 4 leaf **6** clover **8** ornament *part:* **3** arc

trek 4 hike, trip **6** travel, trudge **7** journey **9** migration **10** expedition

trellis 5 arbor **6** screen **7** lattice, pergola **8** espalier **11** latticework

tremble 5 quake, shake **6** dither, quaver, quiver, shiver **7** shudder, twitter, vibrate

tremblor see **temblor**

tremendous 4 huge, vast **6** mighty **7** awesome, immense, massive, titanic **8** colossal, enormous, fearsome, gigantic, terrific, towering **9** fantastic, monstrous **10** formidable, gargantuan, incredible, monumental, prodigious, stupendous **13** extraordinary

tremolo 7 vibrato

tremor 5 quake, shake, shock **6** quaver, quiver, shiver **7** shudder, temblor **10** earthquake *muscular:* **8** dystaxia

tremulous 5 shaky, timid **6** afraid **7** aquiver, fearful, quaking, shivery **8** timorous **9** quivering, shivering

trench 4 sink **5** ditch, fosse, gully, verge **6** border, furrow, trough *Caribbean:* **6** Cayman *Pacific:* **7** Mariana

trenchant 4 acid, keen **5** acerb, crisp, sharp **6** biting **7** acerbic, caustic, cutting, mordant, probing, satiric **8** clear-cut, distinct, incisive, sardonic, scathing **9** sarcastic **11** penetrating

trencher 4 tray **7** platter

trencherman 5 eater **7** glutton **8** gourmand

trend 3 fad, run **4** flow, mode **5** curve, drift, shift, style, swing, tenor, vogue **6** course, temper **7** current, fashion, incline **8** approach, movement, tendency **9** direction

trendy 3 hep, hip, hot **4** cool, tony **5** faddy **6** groovy, modish, with-it **7** à la mode, faddish, stylish **8** downtown, nouvelle, up-to-date **11** fashionable, ultramodern

trepang 10 bêche-de-mer **11** sea cucumber

trepidation 4 fear **5** alarm, dread **6** dismay **7** anxiety **12** apprehension **13** consternation

trespass 3 err, sin **4** debt **5** lapse, poach **6** breach, invade, offend **7** impinge, intrude **8** encroach, entrench, infringe **9** interlope, violation **10** infraction, transgress **12** encroachment, infringement **13** transgression

tress 4 curl, lock **5** braid, plait

trestle 4 buck **5** frame **6** bridge **7** sawbuck, support **8** sawhorse **9** framework

trey 5 three

triad 4 trio **5** chord **6** triple, troika **7** harmony, trinity **9** threesome **11** triumvirate

trial 3 woe **4** care, test **5** cross, essay, rigor, worry **6** dry run, hassle, misery, ordeal, sorrow, tryput **7** anguish, attempt, contest, trouble **8** crucible, distress, endeavor, gauntlet, hardship, struggle, vexation **9** adversity, rehearsal, suffering **10** affliction, coup d'essai, difficulty, experiment, misfortune, proceeding, temptation **11** preliminary, tribulation **12** experimental

trial balloon 6 feeler, tryout

trial run 4 test **5** essay **7** break-in **10** experiment

triangle type 5 acute, right **6** obtuse **7** scalene **9** isosceles **11** equilateral

tribal unit 6 moiety **7** phratry

tribe 4 clan, folk, race **5** house, phyle, stock **6** family **7** kindred, lineage

tribulation 3 woe **5** cross, trial **6** burden, ordeal **9** adversity **10** affliction, oppression, visitation **11** persecution

tribunal 3 bar **4** dais, rota **5** bench, court **8** platform **10** consistory **12** court of honor

tributary 5 bayou, creek **6** branch, feeder, stream **7** subject **8** affluent, influent **9** backwater, confluent, dependent, satellite **12** contributory

tribute 5 paean, toast **6** eulogy, homage **8** citation, encomium **9** panegyric **10** salutation **11** recognition, testimonial **12** appreciation

trice 4 lash, wink **5** blink, flash, jiffy, shake **6** moment, second, secure **7** instant **8** eyeblink **9** twinkling **11** split second

trick 3 jig **4** bilk, dido, dupe, fool, gull, hoax, hose, lark, play, ploy, ruse, scam, sham **5** antic, caper, dodge, feint, fraud, prank, stunt **6** gambit, outwit, scheme **7** chicane, finagle, gimmick, sleight **8** escapade, flimflam, hoodwink **9** bamboozle, deception, stratagem, victimize **10** red herring, shenanigan, tomfoolery **11** hornswoggle, monkeyshine **13** practical joke

trickery 4 scam, wile **5** cheat, fraud **6** deceit **7** chicane, dodgery **8** jugglery **9** chicanery, deception **10** subterfuge **11** double cross **13** double-dealing, jiggery-pokery, sharp practice

trickle 4 drip, seep **5** creep, trill **7** dribble

trickster 5 cheat, shark **6** con man **7** cheater, diddler, grifter, sharper **8** conjurer, deceiver, magician, swindler **9** defrauder **11** flimflammer, illusionist **12** double-dealer

tricksy 5 rough **6** trying **7** arduous **8** prankish

tricky 3 sly **4** foxy, wily **5** dodgy **6** catchy, clever, crafty, shifty, sticky, thorny, touchy, trying **7** cunning, knavish **8** delusive, guileful, slippery, ticklish, tortuous, unstable **9** deceptive, difficult, dishonest, ingenious, intricate **10** misleading, nettlesome, precarious, unreliable **11** complicated, treacherous, troublesome **12** undependable

trident 5 spear

tried 6 proved, proven, secure, tested, trusty **7** staunch **8** approved, faithful, reliable, stalwart, true-blue **9** certified, steadfast **10** dependable **11** trustworthy

tried and true 5 loyal **6** proven, secure, steady, tested, trusty **8** faithful, reliable, stalwart **9** steadfast **10** dependable **11** trustworthy

trifle 3 bob, fig, pin, toy **4** doit, fool, mess, play **5** curio, dally, flirt, sport, waste **6** bauble, coquet, diddle, doodle, fiddle, fidget, footle, frivol, gewgaw, monkey, niggle **7** bibelot, conceit, fribble, fritter, novelty, trinket, twiddle, whatnot **8** folderol, gimcrack, kickshaw, nonsense, squander **9** bagatelle, cream puff, dalliance **10** knickknack, triviality **11** small change

trifling 4 tiny **5** petty **6** measly, paltry, piddly, slight **7** trivial **8** niggling, nugatory, picayune, piddling, piffling **9** frivolous, worthless **10** negligible **11** Mickey Mouse, unimportant **13** insignificant

trifolium 6 clover **8** shamrock

trig 4 chic, neat, prim, snug, tidy, trim **5** sharp, smart, swank, trick **6** classy, modish, snappy **7** chipper, dashing, orderly, precise, stylish **9** shipshape

trigger 4 fire **5** cause, spark, start **6** ignite, kindle, set off **7** actuate, release **8** activate, initiate, touch off

triggerman 3 gun **5** bravo **6** gunsel, killer **7** torpedo **8** assassin **9** cutthroat, pistolero

trigonometric function see at **function**

trill 4 burr, drop, roll **5** chirr, shake, twirl **6** quaver, warble **7** dribble, revolve, trickle, twitter, vibrato

trillion combining form 4 tera, treg **5** trega

trillionth combining form 4 pico

trim 3 cut, fit **4** buff, clip, crop, deck, neat, pare, snug, tidy, trig **5** adorn, order, prune, shape, shave, shear, skive, toned **6** barber, dapper, fettle, kilter, repair, spruce **7** chipper, dress up, garnish, orderly, shapely **8** clean-cut, decorate, manicure **9** shipshape **11** spic-and-span, streamlined, well-groomed **12** spick-and-span **a tree: 5** prune **7** pollard

Trinidad and Tobago capital: 11 Port of Spain **monetary unit: 6** dollar **sea: 9** Caribbean

trinity see **triad**

trinket 3 toy **5** curio, jewel **6** bauble, doodad, gewgaw, trifle **7** bibelot, novelty, whatnot **8** gimcrack, kickshaw **9** bagatelle, plaything, tchotchke **10** knickknack

trinkets 10 bijouterie

trio of goddesses 5 Fates **6** Furies, Graces

trip 3 hop, run **4** fall, ride, skip, slip, step, tour, trek **5** boner, caper, dance, error, lapse **6** bungle, junket, outing, sashay, travel, tumble, voyage **7** blooper, blunder, journey, mistake, misstep, stumble **9** excursion **10** expedition

tripe 4 guts **5** bilge, trash **6** menudo, waffle, viscus **7** innards, viscera (plural) **8** entrails, stuffing **9** internals

triple 4 trio **5** triad, trine **6** treble, triune, troika **7** triform, trilogy, trinity **8** trifecta **9** threefold, threesome **11** three-bagger, triumvirate

Triple Crown winner 1919: 9 Sir Barton **1930: 10** Gallant Fox **1935: 5** Omaha **1937: 10** War Admiral **1941: 9** Whirlaway **1943: 10** Count Fleet **1946: 7** Assault **1948: 8** Citation **1973: 11** Secretariat **1977: 11** Seattle Slew **1978: 8** Affirmed

Triple Crown site 7 Pimlico **11** Belmont Park **14** Churchill Downs

tripped out 4 high **5** doped **6** stoned, zonked **7** drugged **8** hopped-up, turned on, wiped out **9** spaced-out **10** freaked-out

Tristan's beloved 6 Iseult, Isolde

Tristan und Isolde composer 6 Wagner (Richard)

triste 3 sad **5** sorry **7** doleful, pensive, wistful **8** mournful **9** depressed, sorrowful **10** melancholy **11** melancholic

Tristram Shandy author 6 Sterne (Laurence)

trite 3 pat, set **4** dull, flat, hack **5** banal, corny, musty, slick, stale, stock, tired, vapid **6** cliché, jejune, old-hat **7** prosaic, worn-out **8** bathetic, bromidic, flyblown, ordinary, shopworn, timeworn, well-worn **9** hackneyed **10** threadbare **11** commonplace, stereotyped **13** platitudinous, stereotypical

triton 5 conch **7** mollusc, mollusk **9** shellfish

Triton 6 merman *attribute:* 5 conch *father:* 7 Neptune **8** Poseidon *mother:* **10** Amphitrite

triturate 4 bray **5** crush, grind **6** powder **9** comminute, pulverize

triumph 3 joy, win **4** crow, palm **5** exult, glory, vaunt **6** master **7** conquer, prevail, succeed, success, victory **8** conquest, overcome, surmount **10** exultation, jubilation

triumphant 8 exultant, exulting, jubilant **10** conquering, victorious

triumvirate see **triad**

Triumvirate member 6 Antony (Marc), Caesar (Julius), Pompey (the Great) **7** Anthony (Mark), Crassus (Marcus Licinius), Lepidus (Marcus Aemilius) **8** Octavius (Gaius)

trivet 4 rack **5** stand **6** tripod

trivia 8 factoids, minutiae **9** small beer **11** small change **13** small potatoes

trivial 5 dinky, light, minor, petty, small **6** casual, measly, paltry, piddly, slight **8** nugatory, picayune, piddling, piffling, trifling **9** small-beer **10** negligible **11** Mickey Mouse, unimportant **13** insignificant

troche 6 tablet **7** lozenge **8** pastille **9** cough drop

troglodyte 6 hermit **7** caveman, recluse **11** cave dweller

Troilus *beloved:* **8** Cressida, Criseyde *father:* 5 Priam *mother:* **6** Hecuba *slayer:* **8** Achilles

Trojan *horse builder:* **5** Epeus *king:* **5** Priam *priest:* **7** Laocoön *queen:* **6** Hecuba *soothsayer:* **7** Helenus **9** Cassandra *warrior:* **5** Paris **6** Aeneas, Agenor, Hector **7** Glaucus **8** Sarpedon **9** Euphorbus, Polydamas

Trojan Horse builder 5 Epeus **6** Epeius

troll 4 fish, lure, sing, spin **5** angle, dwarf, prowl **6** goblin, search

trolley 3 car **4** cart, tram **8** carriage **9** streetcar

Trollope novel 10 Claverings (The) **11** Ayala's Angel, Phineas Finn **12** Phineas Redux **12** Way We Live Now (The) **15** Eustace Diamonds (The) **16** Barchester Towers

trombone 7 sackbut

tromp 4 beat, drub, hike, pelt, slog, walk, whup **5** pound, stamp, stomp, stump, tread **6** batter, buffet, pummel, thrash, trudge, wallop **7** belabor, clobber, trample **8** lambaste

troop 4 army, band, crew, host, pace, step, walk **5** corps, crowd, flock, tread **6** legion, outfit **7** brigade, company, soldier, traipse **8** assembly **9** associate, battalion, gathering, multitude **10** collection

trooper 3 cop **5** actor, horse **7** soldier **9** policeman **10** cavalryman

trope 6 cliché, simile **8** metaphor, metonymy **10** synecdoche

Trophonius *brother:* **8** Agamedes *temple site:* **6** Delphi

trophy 3 cup **5** award, prize, relic, scalp, token **6** spoils **7** memento **8** hardware, keepsake, memorial, reminder, souvenir **9** loving cup **11** remembrance

tropical 3 hot **4** lush, warm **5** balmy, humid **6** jungly, steamy, sultry, torrid **10** equatorial

tropical storm see **typhoon**

Tropic of Cancer author 6 Miller (Henry)

Tros' son 4 Ilus **8** Ganymede

trot 3 jog **4** gait, lope, pony, rack **5** amble, hurry **7** setline **11** translation

troth 6 commit, engage, pledge **7** loyalty **8** affiance, contract, espousal, fidelity **10** engagement **12** faithfulness

trot out 4 show **6** expose, parade **7** display, disport, exhibit, show off

Trotsky, Leon *associate:* **5** Lenin (Vladimir) *rival:* **6** Stalin (Joseph)

troubadour 4 bard, poet **6** singer **8** jongleur, minstrel, musician **9** balladist **10** folksinger

trouble 3 ado, ail, ill, irk, vex, woe **4** care, pain **5** annoy, beset, Dutch, grief, harry, haunt, pains, trial, upset, worry **6** bother, effort, harass, kiaugh, misery, pester, plague, ruffle, strain, stress, unrest **7** afflict, agitate, ailment, bedevil, concern, disturb, oppress, perturb, torment **8** aggrieve, disquiet, distress, hardship, hot water, irritate, vexation **9** suffering **10** difficulty, disconcert **11** disturbance, predicament

troubled 6 uneasy **7** anxious, worried **9** concerned, disturbed **10** distressed

troublemaker 7 hellion **8** agitator **9** firebrand **10** instigator **11** provocateur **12** rabble-rouser

troublesome 5 pesky **6** thorny, tricky, trying, vexing **7** carking, onerous, prickly **8** annoying **9** difficult, upsetting, vexatious **10** bothersome, burdensome, cumbersome, disturbing **11** disquieting, importunate, pestiferous

troublous 5 pesky **6** rugged, stormy **7** onerous **8** turbulent, vexatious **10** tumultuous **11** tempestuous

trough 3 hod **4** bowl, tank **5** basin, drain **6** vessel **7** channel **10** depression

trounce 4 beat, drub, lick, rout, whip, whup **5** crush, whomp **6** defeat, larrup, punish, thrash, thresh, wallop **7** clobber, shellac **9** overwhelm

troupe 4 band **5** corps, party **6** outfit **7** company

trouper 4 mime **5** actor, mimic **6** mummer,

player **7** actress, artiste **8** thespian **9** performer **11** entertainer

trousers 5 pants **6** slacks **7** drawers **8** breeches, britches *tartan:* **5** trews

trout *kind:* **3** sea **4** char, lake **5** brook, brown, river **7** rainbow **8** speckled **9** steelhead

Trovatore, Il *character:* **7** Azucena, Leonora, Manrico **11** Count di Luna *composer:* **5** Verdi (Giuseppe)

trove 4 find, haul **5** hoard, store **8** treasure **10** collection **11** aggregation **12** accumulation

Troy 5 Ilium *epic of:* **5** Iliad *excavator:* **10** Schliemann (Heinrich) *founder:* **4** Ilus *modern site:* **9** Hissarlik **11** Dardanelles (see also **Trojan**)

truant 4 idle **5** shirk **7** shirker, slacker **8** shirking **10** delinquent

truce 4 lull **5** letup, pause, peace **6** accord **7** respite **9** armistice, cease-fire

truck 3 ute, van **4** semi, swap **5** lorry, trade **6** barter, handle, peddle, retail **7** bargain, traffic **8** commerce, dealings, exchange *military:* **6** camion

Truckee River city 4 Reno

truckle 4 fawn **5** cower, defer, toady **6** cringe, grovel, kowtow **8** bootlick **11** apple-polish

truckler 5 leech, toady **6** lackey, sponge **7** spaniel **8** parasite **9** sycophant **10** bootlicker **11** lickspittle **13** apple-polisher

truculent 4 fell, grim **5** cruel, harsh, rough, sharp **6** brutal, deadly, fierce, savage, severe **7** abusive, warlike **9** barbarous, bellicose, combative, ferocious **10** pernicious, pugnacious **11** belligerent, contentious, destructive, opprobrious, quarrelsome

trudge 4 plod, slog, trek **5** march, tramp, tromp **8** footslog

true 4 real, very **5** valid **6** actual, honest, trusty **7** factual, genuine, staunch, upright **8** accurate, bona fide, constant, faithful, resolute, rightful **9** authentic, honorable, steadfast, undoubted, veracious, veritable **10** ‘ dependable, legitimate, undeniable **11** indubitable, trustworthy **12** indisputable **13** authoritative

true-blue 5 loyal **6** proven, steady, trusty **7** genuine **8** bona fide, constant, faithful, reliable, stalwart **9** steadfast **10** unswerving

truism 3 saw **4** rule **5** adage, axiom, gnome, maxim, moral **6** cliché, dictum, gospel, saying, verity **8** aphorism, apothegm **9** platitude **10** shibboleth **11** commonplace

Truk Island 3 Tol **4** Moen, Udot, Uman **5** Fefan **6** Dublon

truly 4 well **6** easily, indeed, really, surely, verily **7** de facto **8** actually **9** doubtless, genuinely, sincerely, veritably **10** absolutely,

definitely, positively, truthfully, undeniably **11** confidently, doubtlessly, undoubtedly

Truman, Harry S *birthplace:* **5** Lamar **8** Missouri *predecessor:* **3** FDR *successor:* **3** DDE *wife:* **4** Bess

trump 3 cap, top **4** beat, best, pass, ruff **5** excel, outdo **6** better **7** manille, surpass **8** clincher, jew's harp, outstrip, override, spadille *up:* **6** invent **7** concoct **9** fabricate **11** manufacture

trumpery 4 bosh, junk, muck, slop, tosh **5** bilge, cheap, dreck, hokum, trash **6** bunkum, cheesy, common, humbug, paltry, piffle, shoddy, trashy **7** baloney, twaddle **8** claptrap, flimflam, malarkey, nonsense, rubbishy, tommyrot **10** double-talk

trumpet 4 horn, tout **6** herald **7** clarion **8** ballyhoo *call:* **6** sennet *ram's horn:* **6** shofar

trumpeter 4 Hirt (Al), swan **5** André (Maurice), Baker (Chet), Botti (Chris), Brown (Clifford), Davis (Miles), James (Harry) **6** Alpert (Herb), Balsom (Alison), Bolden (Buddy), Farmer (Art), Voisin (Roger) **7** Schwarz (Gerard) **8** advocate, Eldridge (Roy), eulogist, Marsalis (Wynton), Masekela (Hugh), Sandoval (Arturo) **9** Armstrong (Louis), encomiast, Gillespie (Dizzy), spokesman **10** mouthpiece, panegyrist, Severinsen (Doc)

truncate 3 lop, top **4** crop, trim **5** prune, shear **6** cut off **7** abridge, shorten **10** abbreviate

truncheon 3 bat **4** club **5** baton, billy **6** cudgel, warder **8** bludgeon **9** billy club **10** nightstick, shillelagh

trundle 3 bed, tub **4** cart, haul, roll, spin **5** churn, wheel **6** rotate **7** revolve **9** transport

trunk 3 box **4** body, bole, case, stem **5** chest, torso **7** channel, circuit, luggage *elephant:* **9** proboscis *tree:* **4** bole **5** stump

truss 3 tie **4** band, bind **5** brace **7** bandage, bracket, support **9** framework, supporter **10** strengthen

trust 4 hope, pool, rely **5** faith, stock **6** assume, bank on, belief, cartel, charge, commit, credit, rely on **7** build on, combine, confide, consign, count on, custody, keeping, presume **8** bank upon, credence, depend on, reckon on, reliance, rely upon **9** assurance, certainty, certitude, syndicate **10** confidence, conviction, dependence, depend upon **11** safekeeping **12** conglomerate

trustee 8 guardian **9** custodian, protector **10** supervisor

trustworthy 4 sure, true **5** tried, valid **6** honest, proven, secure **8** accurate, credible, faithful, reliable, stalwart, true-blue **9** authentic, realistic, steadfast, veracious **10** dependable 11 responsible 12 tried and true 13 authoritative

trusty 4 true 5 tried 6 proven, secure, stable, steady 7 certain, convict 8 faithful, reliable 9 steadfast, truepenny 10 dependable 11 responsible 12 tried and true

truth 5 axiom, maxim, sooth 6 candor, gospel, verity 7 lowdown, reality, veritas 8 veracity 9 rightness 11 genuineness 12 authenticity *goddess:* 4 Maat *serum:* 11 scopolamine

truthful 5 frank 6 candid, honest 7 factual, sincere 8 accurate 9 realistic, veracious, veridical

truthfulness 6 candor, verity 7 honesty 8 veracity

try 3 aim, tax, vex 4 seek, shot, stab, test 5 annoy, assay, essay, judge, offer, prove, study, whack, whirl, worry 6 aspire, harass, harrow, sample, strain, stress, strive 7 afflict, adjudge, attempt, trouble 8 endeavor, struggle 9 undertake 10 adjudicate, experiment

trying 6 taxing, thorny, tricky, vexing 7 arduous, onerous 8 annoying, exacting, grueling 9 demanding, difficult, strenuous, vexatious 10 irritating

try out 4 test 5 check, prove 6 verify 7 confirm 8 audition

tryst 4 date 7 meeting 10 engagement, rendezvous 11 appointment, assignation

tsar see **czar**

tsunami 9 tidal wave

tub 3 vat 4 boat 9 container *hot:* 3 spa 7 Jacuzzi

tuba 7 helicon 9 bombardon, euphonium 10 sousaphone

tubby 3 fat 5 plump, podgy, porky, pudgy 6 chubby, chunky, rotund 8 roly-poly

tube 2 TV 4 duct, flue, hose, pipe 5 buret 6 siphon, subway, tunnel, vessel 7 burette, channel, conduit, cuvette, pipette, syringe 8 cylinder, pipeline 10 television *anatomical:* 3 vas 4 duct, vasa (plural) 7 salpinx 9 salpinges (plural)

tuber 3 oca, set 4 bulb, corm, root, stem, taro, yamp, yuca 5 salep, yucca 6 manioc, potato 7 cassava, rhizome 10 prominence

tuberculosis 8 phthisis, scrofula 11 consumption

tucker out 4 do in, poop, tire 5 drain, weary 7 exhaust

tuft 5 clump, mound 7 cluster *of feathers:* 7 panache *ornamental:* 6 pom-pom *vascular:* 6 glomus

tufted 7 crested

tug 3 tow 4 drag, draw, haul, moil, pull, toil 5 labor 6 strain, strive

tug-of-war 5 match 6 strife 7 contest, grapple, rivalry 8 conflict, struggle 11 competition

tuition 3 fee 6 charge 8 teaching, training, tutelage 9 education, schooling 11 instruction *collector:* 6 bursar

tumble 4 drop, fall, trip 5 upset 6 plunge, topple 8 collapse, keel over 9 bring down, overthrow

tumbledown 8 decrepit 10 ramshackle 11 dilapidated

tumbler 5 glass 6 roller 7 acrobat, gymnast 11 cartwheeler

tumbrel 4 cart 5 wagon 7 tipcart

tumescent 6 turgid 7 aureate, bloated, bulging, flowery, swollen 8 inflated, swelling 9 bombastic, dropsical, overblown 10 euphuistic, rhetorical

tummy 3 gut 5 belly 6 paunch 7 abdomen, stomach 8 potbelly 9 bay window 11 breadbasket

tumult 3 din 4 flap, riot, to-do 5 babel, broil, hoo-ha, hurly, noise, whirl 6 clamor, dither, hoo-haw, hubbub, lather, outcry, pother, racket, strife, uproar 7 ferment, tempest, turmoil 8 disorder, foofaraw, outburst, paroxysm, upheaval 9 agitation, commotion, confusion, kerfuffle, maelstrom 10 convulsion, hullabaloo, hurly-burly, turbulence

tumultuous 5 rowdy 6 stormy, unruly 7 raucous, riotous 9 clamorous, turbulent 10 boisterous, disorderly 11 rumbustious, tempestuous 12 rambunctious

tumulus 5 grave, knoll, mound 6 barrow 7 hillock

tun 3 keg, vat 4 butt, cask, pipe 6 barrel 8 hogshead, puncheon

tuna 3 ahi 4 pear 6 bigeye, bonito 7 bluefin 8 albacore, skipjack 9 scombroid, yellowfin

tune 3 air 4 dial, lilt, song 5 theme, tweak 6 accord, adjust, amount, attune, extent, jingle, melody, strain, temper 7 descant 8 modulate, regulate

tuneful 5 sweet 6 dulcet 7 melodic 9 melodious

tungsten 7 wolfram 9 scheelite 10 wolframite

tunic 4 jama 5 jupon 6 kirtle 7 hauberk *Greek:* 6 chiton

tunicate 4 salp 8 ascidian, chordate 9 sea squirt 11 urochordate

Tunisia *capital:* 5 Tunis *city:* 4 Sfax 6 Ariana *island:* 5 Jerba *language:* 6 Arabic *monetary unit:* 5 dinar *neighbor:* 5 Libya 7 Algeria *ruins:* 8 Carthage

tunnel 4 tube 6 burrow 7 conduit 8 crawlway *Alps:* 7 Simplon 11 Loetschberg *France:* 4 Rove *Hudson river:* 7 Holland, Lincoln *Nevada:* 5 Sutro *railroad:* 6 Hoosac 7 Cascade

Turandot *character:* 3 Liu 5 Calaf *author:* 5 Gozzi (Carlo) *composer:* 6 Busoni (Ferruccio) 7 Puccini (Giacomo)

turban 7 bandana, pugaree 8 bandanna 9 headdress

turbid 4 dark 5 dense, mucky, muddy, murky, riley, roily, smoky, thick 6 cloudy, opaque, roiled 7 clouded, obscure

turbot 8 flatfish

turbulence 3 din 4 flap, stew 5 babel, fight, hoo-ha 6 dither, fracas, lather, pother, tumult, uproar 7 turmoil 8 foofaraw 9 agitation, commotion

turbulent 4 wild 5 bumpy, roily, rough, rowdy 6 raging, stormy, unruly 7 furious, moiling, raucous, riotous, roaring 8 agitated, blustery, swirling 9 clamorous 10 boisterous, tumultuous

tureen 3 pot 4 bowl 5 crock 6 vessel 9 casserole

turf 3 sod 4 area, peat 5 grass, sward, track 6 domain, region 7 terrain 9 racetrack, territory 11 horse racing 12 neighborhood

turgid see **tumescent**

Turkey *capital:* 6 Ankara *city:* 5 Adana, Bursa, Izmir, Konya 8 Istanbul *enclave:* 8 Naxçivan *lake:* 3 Van *leader:* 7 Atatürk (Kemal) *monetary unit:* 4 lira *mountain, range:* 6 Ararat, Taurus *neighbor:* 4 Iran, Iraq 5 Syria 6 Greece 7 Armenia, Georgia 8 Bulgaria *peninsula:* 6 Balkan 9 Asia Minor *river:* 6 Tigris 8 Menderes 9 Euphrates *sea:* 6 Aegean 7 Marmara 13 Mediterranean

turkey *buzzard:* 7 vulture *disease:* 9 blackhead *head growth:* 5 snood 7 dewbill *male:* 3 tom 7 gobbler *throat pouch:* 6 wattle *young:* 5 poult

Turkish *cavalryman:* 5 spahi *empire:* 7 Ottoman *governor:* 4 vali *inn:* 4 kahn 6 imaret *soldier:* 5 nizam 9 janissary *sultan:* 5 Ahmed, Selim 7 Bajazet, Bayezid, Ilderim *sword:* 8 yataghan *title:* 3 aga, bey 4 agha 5 pasha 6 vizier 7 effendi

Turkmenistan *capital:* 8 Ashgabat 9 Ashkhabad *desert:* 7 Kara-Kum *monetary unit:* 5 manat, tenne *neighbor:* 4 Iran 10 Kazakhstan, Uzbekistan 11 Afghanistan *river:* 6 Murgab 7 Murghab 8 Amu Dar'ya *sea:* 7 Caspian

Turks and Caicos Islands *capital:* 9 Grand Turk *location:* 10 West Indies *passage:* 6 Caicos 8 Mouchoir *territory of:* 7 Britain

turmeric 3 dye 4 herb 5 spice 6 ginger 8 dyestuff

turmoil 4 coil, flap, moil, riot, stew, stir, to-do 5 chaos, whirl 6 clamor, dither, hassle, hubbub, lather, pother, strife, tumult, unease,

unrest, uproar, welter 7 ferment 8 disorder, upheaval 9 agitation, commotion, confusion 10 disruption, hurly-burly, turbulence, uneasiness 11 pandemonium 13 helter-skelter, Sturm und Drang

turn 3 yaw, zag, zig 4 bend, bias, bout, cast, grow, gyre, reel, spin, tack, tour, veer, whip, wind 5 angle, curve, pivot, refer, shunt, spell, stint, swirl, train, twirl, whirl 6 detour, divert, gyrate, mutate, revert, rotate, switch, swivel 7 circuit, convert, deflect, deviate, digress, diverge, reverse, revolve 8 gyration, rotation 9 about-face, deviation, pirouette, volte-face

turnabout 3 rat 6 coward 7 reverse 8 apostate, defector, recreant, reversal 9 about-face, reversion, volte-face 11 retaliation 12 merry-go-round

turn aside 4 veer, shun, sway, veer 5 avert, repel, shunt, stave 6 divert, refuse, reject, swerve 7 deflect, deviate, digress, dismiss, diverge, fend off, reflect, ward off 9 sidetrack

turncoat 3 rat, spy 5 Judas 7 traitor 8 apostate, betrayer, defector, deserter, quisling, recreant, renegade 9 traitress, turnabout 13 tergiversator

turn down 4 jilt, veto 5 spurn 6 rebuff, refuse, reject 7 decline, dismiss 9 repudiate 10 disapprove

turned on 4 high 5 doped 6 stoned, zonked 7 aroused, drugged, excited 8 hopped-up, tripping 9 activated, spaced-out, zonked-out 10 passionate 12 enthusiastic

turn in 5 crash, rat on 6 betray, inform, rat out, retire, submit 7 deliver, produce, sack out 8 hand over 9 hit the hay 10 hit the sack, relinquish

turning point 4 cusp 5 pivot 6 climax, crisis 8 landmark 11 climacteric

turn inside out 5 evert

turnip 5 swede 8 rutabaga *Scottish:* 4 neep

turnip-shaped 8 napiform

turnkey 6 jailer

turn left 3 haw

Turn of the Screw, The *author:* 5 James (Henry) *character:* 5 Flora, Miles 10 Peter Quint *composer:* 7 Britten (Benjamin)

turn on 5 start 6 excite, ignite 7 start up 8 activate, motivate 9 stimulate, titillate

turn over 4 plow, roll 5 upend, upset 6 assign, commit, give up, rotate 7 capsize, consign, deliver, entrust, furnish, provide, revolve 8 delegate, transfer 9 overthrow, surrender 10 relinquish

turnpike 7 highway

turn right 3 gee

turn up 4 find **6** appear, arrive, reveal **7** uncover, unearth **8** discover **9** encounter **11** materialize

Turow work 4 One L **16** Presumed Innocent

turpentine 7 galipot, solvent, thinner *ingredient:* **6** pinene *tree:* **4** pine **9** terebinth

turret 5 tower **6** cupola, louver, louvre **7** mirador **8** bartizan **9** belvedere

turtle 8 terrapin, tortoise **9** chelonian *edible part:* **7** calipee **8** calipash *genus:* **4** Emys *sea:* **6** ridley **8** hawkbill *shell:* **8** carapace *shell part:* **8** plastron

Tuscany city: 4 Pisa **8** Florence *river:* **4** Arno *tower:* **4** Pisa *wine:* **7** chianti

tusk 4 fang **5** ivory, tooth

tusker 6 dugong, walrus **7** mammoth, muntjac, narwhal, warthog **8** elephant, musk deer **11** barking deer

tussle 4 spar **5** scrap, scrum **6** hassle, scrape **7** scuffle, wrangle, wrestle **8** argument, skirmish, struggle **9** scrimmage **11** controversy

tussock 4 tuft **5** clump, mound **7** cluster

tutelage see **tuition**

tutor 3 don **5** coach, teach **6** docent, mentor **7** teacher **9** pedagogue, preceptor **10** instructor

Tut's tomb discoverer 6 Carter (Howard)

tutti 3 all **8** everyone **9** everybody

Tuvalu *capital:* 8 Funafuti *ethnic group:* **10** Polynesian *former name:* **6** Ellice (Islands)

TVA dam 5 Ocoee

twaddle 3 jaw, yak **4** bosh, bull, bunk, chat, guff, muck, talk, tosh **5** clack, drool, hooey, prate, run on **6** babble, bunkum, burble, drivel, gabble, hot air, humbug, jabber, tattle **7** baloney, blabber, blarney, blather, chatter, hogwash, prattle, rubbish **8** claptrap, malarkey, nonsense, tommyrot, trumpery **9** poppycock **10** applesauce, balderdash **12** blatherskite

Twain character 3 Jim **5** Becky (Thatcher) **8** Huck Finn, Injun Joe **9** Aunt Polly, Joe Harper, Tom Sawyer

tweak 4 jerk, mock, pull, zing **5** annoy, pinch, pluck **6** adjust, bother, modify, twitch **8** fine-tune **9** poke fun at

tweet 4 call, note **5** cheep, chirp **7** chirrup, twitter

Twelfth Night character 5 Viola **6** Olivia, Orsino (Duke) **7** Antonio, Cesario **8** Malvolio **9** Sebastian, Toby Belch

twelve *combining form:* 5 dodec **6** dodeca

twenty 5 score *combining form:* **4** icos **5** icosa, icosi

twerp 4 brat, drip, fool, jerk, nerd, twit **6** squirt

twibil 2 ax **3** axe

twice 3 bis **7** twofold *combining form:* **3** bis *prefix:* **3** dis

twice a day 3 b.i.d. **8** bis in die **11** semidiurnal

twice a year 8 biannual **10** semiannual, semiyearly

twig 5 shoot, sprig, withe **6** branch *bundle of:* **5** fagot **6** faggot

twiggy 4 slim, thin **5** reedy **6** skinny, slight, stalky **7** slender **9** sticklike

twilight 3 eve **4** dusk **5** gloam, gloom **6** sunset **7** decline **8** gloaming **9** nightfall **10** crepuscule

Twilight of the Gods 8 Ragnarok *composer:* **6** Wagner (Richard)

twill 5 chino, cloth, serge, toile, tweed, weave **6** fabric **7** cheviot **8** dungaree **9** bombazine, gabardine **11** herringbone

twin 4 dual, like, mate **5** clone, match **6** bifold, binary, double, fellow, paired **7** matched, similar, twofold **8** matching **9** companion, duplicate, identical **10** coordinate, reciprocal

Twin Cities 6 St. Paul **11** Minneapolis

twine 4 coil, cord, curl, wind, wrap **5** twist, weave **6** spiral, string **7** embrace, meander, wreathe **8** entangle **9** interlace **10** interweave

twinge 4 ache, pain, pang, stab **5** pluck, shoot, throe, twang, tweak **6** stitch

twinkle 3 bat **4** flit, wink **5** blink, flash, flirt, gleam, glint, light, shake, shine, trice **7** flicker, flutter, glimmer, glisten, glitter, shimmer, sparkle **9** coruscate, nictitate **11** coruscation, scintillate

twin stars 6 Castor, Pollux

twirl 4 coil, gyre, spin **5** pitch, trill, whirl, whorl **6** gyrate **7** revolve **9** pirouette

twist 3 wry **4** coil, curl, skew, turn, warp, wind **5** belie, gnarl, pivot, twine, twirl, wring **6** garble, spiral, sprain, squirm, torque, wrench, writhe **7** contort, distort, entwine, falsify, pervert, wriggle

twisted 3 wry **4** awry, sick **5** askew, kinky **6** swirly, warped **9** perverted

twister 6 funnel **7** tornado **9** dust devil, whirlwind **10** waterspout

twit 4 dolt, fool, gibe, jeer, jive, josh, mock, quiz, razz **5** chide, rally, scout, taunt, tease, twerp **6** deride **8** bonehead, numskull, ridicule **9** blockhead, numbskull **10** nincompoop

twitch 3 tic **4** jerk, pang, pull, yank **5** pluck, spasm, throe, tweak **6** quiver **10** quack grass

twitter 4 chat, peep **5** cheep, chirp, quake, tweet **6** cackle, giggle, jargon, quiver, shiver, titter, tremor, warble **7** chatter, chirrup, tremble

twittery 6 giggly **8** chattery **9** flustered, tremulous

two 3 duo 4 duet, pair 5 twain 6 couple *combining form:* 3 bis, duo, dyo *divide into:* 4 fork 6 bisect 9 bifurcate *prefix:* 3 twi

two-faced 9 deceitful, dishonest, insincere 11 duplicitous 12 hypocritical 13 double-dealing *god:* 5 Janus

twofold 4 dual, twin 5 binal, duple 6 binary, double, duplex, dyadic, paired 9 dualistic

two-footed 7 bipedal

Two Gentlemen of Verona *author:* 11 Shakespeare (William) *character:* 5 Julia 6 Silvia, Thurio 7 Proteus 9 Valentine

two-sided 9 bilateral

twosome 3 duo 4 dyad, item, pair 5 brace 6 couple 7 doublet

two-time 4 dupe 6 betray, delude, humbug, take in 7 beguile, cheat on, deceive, mislead 9 bamboozle 11 double-cross

two-wheeler 4 bike 5 cycle 7 bicycle, scooter 10 motorcycle

Tybalt *cousin:* 6 Juliet *family:* 7 Capulet *slayer:* 5 Romeo *victim:* 8 Mercutio

tycoon 5 mogul, nabob 7 magnate

tyke 3 dog, kid 5 child, hound, puppy 6 canine, moppet, nipper, shaver 7 mongrel

tympanum 7 eardrum 9 middle ear

Tyndareus *kingdom:* 6 Sparta *wife:* 4 Leda

type 3 cut, ilk, key, lot, way 4 cast, form, kind, mold, sort 5 breed, class, genre, order, print, serif, stamp 6 kidney, nature, stripe 7 feather, species, variety 8 category, keyboard *bar:* 4 slug *font:* 5 Arial, Goudy 6 Bodoni 7 Antigua, Century, Courier 8 Garamond, Palatino, Perpetua 9 Helvetica 10 Times Roman *measure:* 2 em, en 4 pica 5 point *set:* 7 compose *setter:* 10 compositor *size:* 4 pica 5 agate, elite, pearl *stroke:* 5 serif *style:* 4 bold 5 roman, serif 6 Gothic, italic 7 Fraktur 8 boldface 9 lightface, sans serif *tray:* 6 galley

Typee *author:* 8 Melville (Herman) *character:* 4 Toby

typewriter *part:* 3 key 6 platen, spacer *type size:* 4 pica 5 elite

Typhon 3 Set 7 monster 8 Typhoeus *offspring:* 6 Sphinx 7 Chimera 8 Cerberus, Chimaera *wife:* 7 Echidna

typhoon 7 cyclone 9 hurricane 13 tropical storm

typical 5 ideal, model, usual 6 common, normal 7 classic, general, natural, regular 8 symbolic

typify 6 embody, mirror 9 epitomize, exemplify, personify, represent, symbolize 10 illustrate 11 emblematize 12 characterize

typo 5 error 7 erratum 8 misprint 11 corrigendum

typographer 7 printer 10 compositor

Tyr 3 Tiu *brother:* 4 Thor *father:* 4 Odin 5 Woden *god of:* 3 war *mother:* 5 Jordh, Jorth

tyrannical 8 absolute, despotic 9 arbitrary 10 absolutist, autocratic, oppressive 11 dictatorial

tyrannize 7 oppress 8 dominate, domineer, overbear

tyrannous 5 harsh 6 brutal, severe 8 absolute, despotic 9 arbitrary, fascistic 10 autocratic 11 dictatorial

tyranny 7 cruelty, fascism 9 autocracy, despotism, monocracy 10 absolutism, domination, oppression 12 dictatorship

tyrant 4 czar, duce, tsar, tzar 5 ruler 6 despot, führer 7 fuehrer, pharaoh, usurper 8 autocrat, dictator 9 oppressor, strongman 10 absolutist

Tyrian ____ 6 purple

tyro 4 punk 6 novice, rookie 7 amateur, dabbler, student 8 beginner, freshman, neophyte, newcomer 9 novitiate 10 apprentice, dilettante, tenderfoot 11 abecedarian

Tyrol see **Tirol**

tzar see **czar**

tzigane 3 Rom 5 gypsy 6 Romany

U

übermensch 8 superman

ubiquitous 7 allover 9 pervasive, universal 10 everywhere, wall-to-wall, widespread 11 omnipresent

U-boat 3 sub 7 pigboat 9 submarine

Uganda *capital:* 7 Kampala *falls:* 5 Ripon *lake:* 5 Kyoga 6 Albert, Edward, George 8 Victoria *leader:* 4 Amin (Idi) *monetary unit:* 8 shilling *mountain:* 5 Elgon *mountain range:* 9 Ruwenzori *neighbor:* 5

Congo, Kenya, Sudan **6** Rwanda **8** Tanzania *river:* **4** Nile

ugly 4 vile **7** hideous **8** deformed **9** loathsome, misshapen, offensive, repugnant, repulsive, unsightly **10** disfigured **12** unattractive

Ugly Duckling author 8 Andersen (Hans Christian)

ukase 4 fiat **5** edict, order **6** decree, dictum, ruling **7** command, dictate, mandate **9** directive **10** injunction **12** proclamation **13** pronouncement

Ukraine *capital:* 4 Kiev *city:* **4** Lviv, Lvov **5** Yalta **6** Odessa **7** Kharkiv **9** Chernobyl *ethnic group:* **7** Cossack *monetary unit:* **6** hryvny *mountain range:* **10** Carpathian *neighbor:* **6** Poland, Russia **7** Belarus, Hungary, Moldova **8** Slovakia *peninsula:* **5** Kerch **6** Crimea **7** Crimean *river:* **3** Bug **5** Tisza **6** Donets **7** Dnieper **8** Dniester *sea:* **4** Azov **5** Black

Ulalume author 3 Poe (Edgar Allan)

ulcer 4 sore **6** fester **7** corrupt *kind:* **6** peptic **8** duodenal *mouth:* **10** canker sore

ulna 7 forearm

Ulster hero 6 Fergus **7** Deirdre **9** Conchobar, Cuchulain, Cuchullin **10** Cú Chulainn

ulterior 5 privy **6** covert, future, hidden, latent **7** further, obscure, remoter **9** ambiguous, concealed **10** subsequent, succeeding **11** undisclosed

ultimate 3 end, nth **4** acme, last, peak **5** basic, final, utter **6** summit, utmost, zenith **7** closing, epitome, extreme, maximum, primary, supreme, topmost **8** absolute, deciding, decisive, eventual, farthest, furthest, greatest, original, terminal **9** elemental, paramount **10** apotheosis, concluding, conclusive, consummate, preeminent **11** categorical, fundamental, furthermost, indivisible **12** incomparable, quintessence

ultimatum 5 order **6** demand, threat **7** mandate **9** challenge **12** notification

ultra 5 kinky, outré, rabid **6** beyond, far-out, too-too **7** extreme, fanatic, radical **9** excessive, extremist, fanatical **10** outlandish **11** extravagant

ultraconservative 11 reactionary

ultraist 5 rabid **6** zealot **7** extreme, fanatic, radical **9** extremist

ultramarine 7 oversea, sea-blue **8** overseas **11** lapis lazuli

ululate 3 bay **4** howl, wail, yowl

Ulysses *author:* 5 Joyce (James) *character:* **5** Bloom (Leopold), Molly (Bloom) **6** Blazes (Boylan) **7** Dedalus (Stephen) *last word:* **3** yes (see also **Odysseus**)

umber 5 brown, sepia, shade **6** darken, shadow

umbilicus 3 hub **4** core **5** heart, hilum, navel **6** center

umbra 5 shade **6** shadow

umbrage 4 hint, huff **5** anger, pique, shade **6** shadow **7** chagrin, dudgeon, foliage, leafage, offense **9** annoyance, suspicion **10** irritation, resentment **11** displeasure, indignation **12** exasperation

umbrageous 5 shady **6** shaded, touchy **7** shadowy **8** shadowed **9** defensive, sensitive

umbrella 5 cover, guard, shade **6** brolly, pileus, screen **7** parasol, protect, shelter **8** sunshade **10** protection **11** bumbershoot

umph see **oomph**

umpire 3 ref **5** judge **6** decide, settle **7** arbiter, referee **9** arbitrate **10** arbitrator *call:* **3** out **4** balk, ball, safe **6** strike

unabashed 5 blunt, brash, frank, naked, overt **6** arrant, brassy, brazen, candid **7** blatant, forward **8** outright **9** audacious, barefaced, shameless, undaunted **10** unblushing **11** undisguised, unmitigated **12** unapologetic

unabbreviated see **unabridged**

unable 5 inept, unfit **8** helpless, impotent **9** incapable, maladroit, powerless, unskilled **10** unequipped **11** incompetent, unqualified **13** incapacitated

unabridged 5 uncut, whole **6** entire, intact **8** complete **10** full-length **11** uncondensed **13** unabbreviated

unacceptable 8 unwanted **9** unwelcome **10** unsuitable **11** intolerable, undesirable **12** inadmissible **13** exceptionable, inappropriate, insupportable, objectionable

unaccompanied 4 lone, sole, solo, stag **5** alone, apart **6** single **8** detached, solitary **9** a cappella **10** unattended, unescorted

unaccountable 6 arcane, mystic **7** strange **8** baffling, puzzling **9** enigmatic **10** mysterious, mystifying, unknowable, unreliable **12** impenetrable, inexplicable, undependable, unfathomable **13** irresponsible, unexplainable

unaccustomed 3 new **5** alien, novel **6** unused **7** strange, unusual **8** singular, uncommon, unwonted **10** unexpected, unfamiliar

unadorned 4 bald, bare **5** naked, plain, spare, stark **6** rustic, severe, simple **7** artless, austere, natural, spartan **11** undecorated **13** unembellished, unembroidered, unpretentious

unadulterated 4 neat, pure **5** sheer, utter **7** genuine, unmixed **8** absolute, straight **9** unalloyed, undiluted **11** unmitigated, unqualified

unaffected 5 naive **6** candid, simple **7** artless, callous, genuine, natural, sincere, unmoved **9** guileless, impassive, ingenuous, unaltered, unchanged, unstudied, untouched **10** hard-boiled, impervious **13** unpretentious

unalloyed 4 pure **5** sheer, total **7** genuine, unmixed **8** absolute, straight **9** authentic, out-and-out, undiluted **11** unmitigated, unqualified **13** thoroughgoing, unadulterated

unalterable 5 fixed **7** binding, bounden, certain, decided **8** constant, required **9** immutable, mandatory, necessary **10** compulsory, invariable **12** unchangeable **13** predetermined

unambiguous 5 clear, lucid, plain **6** patent **7** evident, express, obvious, precise **8** apparent, clean-cut, clear-cut, decisive, definite, distinct, explicit, manifest, specific, univocal **10** definitive, forthright **11** categorical, translucent, transparent, unequivocal **12** transpicuous

unanimous 5 as one **6** united **8** communal, univocal **9** unopposed **10** collective **11** uncontested **13** consentaneous

unanimously 5 as one **6** wholly **7** en masse **10** altogether

unanticipated 9 unplanned **10** surprising, unexpected, unforeseen **12** out of the blue

unappeasable 4 grim **7** adamant **8** obdurate, resolute **9** insatiate, unbending **10** implacable, insatiable, relentless, unyielding **11** unrelenting **12** unquenchable

unappetizing 4 icky **5** gross, yucky **7** insipid **8** unsavory **9** repugnant **11** unappealing, unpalatable **12** unattractive

unapproachable 5 aloof **6** remote, offish **7** distant **8** reserved **10** unfriendly, unsociable **11** standoffish, unreachable **12** inaccessible, unattainable

unasked 7 willing **8** unbidden, unsought, unwanted **9** uninvited, unwelcome, voluntary **10** gratuitous, unprompted **11** spontaneous, uncalled-for, unrequested, voluntarily

unassailable 6 secure **8** airtight **10** invincible, inviolable, undeniable **11** impregnable, irrefutable **12** indisputable, invulnerable **13** incontestable, unconquerable

unassertive 3 shy **4** meek **5** mousy, timid **6** modest, mousey **7** bashful **8** backward, reticent, retiring, sheepish, timorous **9** diffident, shrinking **10** submissive **12** self-effacing

unassuming 3 shy **6** humble, modest, simple **8** ordinary, retiring **9** diffident **11** unassertive **12** self-effacing **13** unpretentious

unattached 4 free **5** loose **6** single **8** separate

9 unmarried **10** unassigned **11** uncommitted, unconnected **12** disconnected, freestanding, unassociated

unattainable 7 elusive **10** impossible **12** inaccessible

unattractive 4 drab, dull, ugly **5** dowdy, plain **6** homely **8** frumpish **10** unalluring, unsuitable **11** unappealing, undesirable **12** unflattering

unauthentic 4 fake, mock, sham **5** bogus, dummy, faked, false, phony **6** ersatz, forged, pseudo **7** feigned **8** affected, spurious **9** contrived, imitation, pretended, simulated **10** apocryphal, artificial **11** counterfeit, make-believe **12** illegitimate

unavailable 4 busy **6** absent, tied up **7** missing **8** occupied

unavailing 4 idle, vain **5** empty **6** barren, futile **7** useless **8** abortive, bootless **9** fruitless, pointless **11** ineffective, ineffectual **12** unproductive

unavoidable 5 fated **7** certain **8** destined **9** impending, necessary **10** compulsory, inevitable, obligatory **11** ineluctable, inescapable

unavoidably 8 perforce **10** helplessly, inevitably, willy-nilly **11** inescapably, necessarily, whether or no

unaware, unawares 5 aback **7** unready **8** abruptly, heedless, ignorant, off guard, suddenly **9** oblivious, unknowing, unmindful, unwitting **10** by surprise, unfamiliar, uninformed, unprepared **12** unacquainted, unexpectedly

unbalance 11 destabilize

unbalanced 3 mad **4** daft **5** batty, nutty **6** crazed, insane, uneven, wobbly **7** unequal, unsound **8** demented, deranged, lopsided, unhinged, unstable **9** psychotic **10** disordered, moonstruck

unbearable 11 intolerable, unendurable **12** excruciating, insufferable

unbeautiful 4 ugly **5** plain **6** homely **8** uncomely, unlovely **9** unsightly **10** ill-favored, unbecoming, uninviting **12** unattractive

unbecoming 8 improper, unlovely, unseemly, untimely, untoward, unworthy **9** inelegant, tasteless, unfitting **10** indecorous, indelicate, malapropos, unsuitable **11** disgraceful **12** unattractive **13** inappropriate

unbelievable 7 amazing, awesome **8** fabulous **9** fantastic **10** astounding, improbable, incredible, phenomenal, staggering, stupendous **11** astonishing, implausible, spectacular **12** unconvincing, unimaginable **13** extraordinary, inconceivable

unbeliever 5 pagan **6** giaour **7** atheist, doubter, gentile, heathen, heretic, infidel, scoffer, skeptic **8** agnostic **10** Pyrrhonist **11** freethinker

unbelieving 5 leery **6** show-me **8** agnostic, apostate, doubting **9** quizzical, skeptical **10** dissenting, suspicious **11** incredulous, mistrustful, questioning

unbending 4 iron **5** rigid, stern, stiff **6** severe **8** hard-line, obdurate, resolute **9** inelastic **10** brassbound, inexorable, inflexible, unyielding

unbiased 4 fair, just **5** equal **7** neutral **8** detached, tolerant **9** equitable, impartial, objective, unbigoted **10** even-handed, open-minded **11** broad-minded, uncommitted **12** unprejudiced **13** disinterested, dispassionate

unbidden 7 unasked, willing **8** unsought, unwanted **9** impromptu, uninvited, unwelcome, voluntary **10** gratuitous, unprompted **11** spontaneous, unrequested

unbind 4 free, undo **5** loose, untie **6** detach, loosen **7** manumit, release, unchain, unloose **8** dissolve, liberate, unfasten, unloosen **9** discharge, disengage, unshackle **10** emancipate

unblemished 4 pure **7** perfect **8** flawless, spotless, unmarred, virtuous **9** exemplary, faultless, stainless, undefiled, unspotted, unsullied **10** immaculate **11** untarnished

unbosom 4 bare, open, tell **6** betray, expose, reveal, unveil **7** divulge, express, uncover **8** disclose

unbound 4 free **5** freed, loose **6** loosed **10** unattached, unconfined, unfastened

unbounded 4 open **6** untold **7** endless **8** infinite, unending **9** excessive, limitless, unchecked, unlimited **10** immoderate, indefinite, inordinate **11** extravagant, measureless **12** immeasurable, incalculable, uncontrolled, unrestrained

unbreakable 7 durable, lasting **10** unyielding **11** everlasting

unbridled 4 free **5** loose **6** madcap **8** reckless, uncurbed **9** dissolute, unchecked **10** immoderate, licentious, unconfined, unfettered, ungoverned **11** spontaneous, uninhibited, unrepressed **12** uncontrolled, unrestrained, unrestricted **13** unconstrained

unbroken 5 solid, sound, whole **6** entire, intact, single **8** complete, constant, enduring **9** ceaseless, steadfast, unceasing, undamaged, undivided, unsubdued, unvarying **10** continuous, unimpaired **13** uninterrupted

unburden 3 rid **4** dump, ease, lose **5** shake **6** reveal, unload **7** cast off, confess, confide, off-load, relieve **8** shake off, throw off **9** discharge **10** relinquish **11** disencumber

uncalled-for 8 baseless, needless **9** officious, unfounded **10** gratuitous, groundless **11** unessential, unjustified, unnecessary, unwarranted **13** unjustifiable

uncanny 5 eerie, weird **6** creepy, spooky **7** ghostly, strange **9** unearthly, unnatural **10** mysterious, mystifying, superhuman **11** supernormal, supranormal **12** supernatural

uncared-for 5 dingy **6** beat-up, shabby **7** rickety, run-down, worn-out **8** decrepit, derelict, deserted, desolate, forsaken, tattered, untended **9** neglected **10** broken-down, down-at-heel, ramshackle, tumble-down **11** dilapidated

uncaring 4 cold **7** callous **9** heartless, negligent, oblivious, unfeeling, unheeding **11** coldhearted, hard-hearted, indifferent, insensitive, thoughtless, unconcerned **13** inconsiderate, unsympathetic

unceasing 7 abiding, endless, eternal, nonstop, undying **8** constant, enduring, unbroken, unending **9** continual, perennial, perpetual **10** continuous **11** amaranthine, everlasting, unremitting **12** imperishable, interminable **13** uninterrupted

unceremonious 4 curt, rude **5** bluff, blunt, frank, hasty, sharp, short, terse **6** abrupt, breezy, casual, sudden **7** brusque, hurried, offhand **8** familiar, informal **10** ungracious **11** precipitate, precipitous

uncertain 4 hazy, iffy, moot **5** vague **6** chancy, fitful, unsure, wobbly **7** dubious, erratic, halting, unclear **8** arguable, doubtful, insecure, slippery, unstable, unsteady, variable **9** ambiguous, debatable, undecided, unsettled **10** ambivalent, disputable, inconstant, indefinite, precarious **11** problematic, speculative **12** questionable, undependable **13** indeterminate, problematical, unforeseeable, unpredictable, untrustworthy

uncertainty 5 doubt **7** dubiety **8** distrust, mistrust **9** ambiguity, suspicion **10** indecision, perplexity, puzzlement, skepticism, uneasiness **11** ambivalence **12** doubtfulness, irresolution

unchain 4 free **5** loose **6** loosen, unbind **7** manumit, release **8** liberate, unfasten, unfetter **9** discharge, unshackle **10** emancipate **11** disenthrall

unchangeable 3 set **4** firm **5** fixed **7** settled **8** constant **9** immutable, permanent **10** continuing, inflexible, invariable **11** established, inalterable

unchanging 5 fixed **6** stable, static, steady **7** abiding, equable, eternal, settled, stabile, uniform **8** constant, enduring **9** immutable, steadfast, unvarying **10** consistent, continuing, invariable

unchaste 4 easy, lewd **5** bawdy, loose **6** impure, vulgar, wanton **7** immoral, lustful, obscene, scarlet, unclean **8** depraved, prurient **9** debauched, dissolute, lecherous, salacious **10** adulterous, lascivious, libidinous, licentious, profligate **11** promiscuous

unchecked 5 loose **7** rampant **9** spreading, unbounded, unbridled **10** widespread **11** uninhibited **12** unrestrained, unrestricted

uncivil 4 rude **5** crass, crude **6** coarse, savage, vulgar **7** boorish, ill-bred, uncouth **8** barbaric, impolite **9** barbarous **10** indecorous, uncultured, ungracious **11** ill-mannered, uncourteous **12** discourteous **13** disrespectful

uncivilized 4 rude, wild **5** crude **6** brutal, coarse, Gothic, savage **7** boorish, Hunnish, ill-bred, loutish, lowbred, uncouth **8** barbaric, churlish **9** barbarian, barbarous, primitive, unrefined **10** mannerless, uncultured, unmannerly, unpolished **12** uncultivated **13** unenlightened

unclad see **unclothed**

uncle *cry:* **6** give up **9** surrender *Dutch:* **6** critic **7** advisor *French:* **5** oncle *Scottish:* **3** eme *Spanish:* **3** tío *U.S. symbol:* **3** Sam

unclean 4 foul **5** dingy, dirty, grimy **6** filthy, grubby, grungy, impure, soiled, sordid **7** corrupt, defiled, immoral, obscene, squalid, stained, sullied, tainted **8** befouled, indecent, polluted, unchaste **10** besmirched, desecrated **12** contaminated

unclear 3 dim **4** hazy **5** murky, vague **6** bleary, blurry, cloudy, opaque, unsure **7** clouded, cryptic, dubious, obscure, shadowy **8** doubtful, nebulous, overcast, puzzling **9** ambiguous, enigmatic, tenebrous, unsettled **10** ill-defined, indistinct, indefinite, inexplicit **13** indeterminate

Uncle Remus creator 6 Harris (Joel Chandler)

Uncle Tom's Cabin *author:* **5** Stowe (Harriet Beecher) *character:* **5** Eliza, Topsy **6** Legree (Simon) **9** Little Eva

Uncle Vanya author 7 Chekhov (Anton)

unclothe 5 strip **6** denude, divest, expose, unveil **7** display, disrobe, uncloak, uncover, undress

unclothed 4 bare, nude **5** naked **6** peeled, unclad **7** denuded, exposed **8** in the raw, stripped **9** au naturel, buck-naked, undressed **10** stark naked

unclouded 4 fair **5** clear, lucid, sunny **6** bright **7** halcyon **8** rainless, sunshiny

uncluttered 4 neat, tidy, trig, trim **7** orderly **9**

organized, shipshape **11** spic-and-span, well-ordered **12** spick-and-span

uncombed 5 messy, mussy **6** matted, mussed **7** ruffled, snarled, tangled, tousled, unkempt **10** disheveled

uncommon 3 odd **4** rare **5** novel **6** choice, scarce, unique **7** special, unusual **8** esoteric, especial, singular, sporadic, unwonted **10** infrequent, noteworthy, remarkable **11** distinctive, exceptional **12** unaccustomed **13** extraordinary

uncommunicative 3 mum **4** dumb **5** aloof **6** offish, silent **7** distant, guarded, private **8** reserved, reticent, taciturn **9** reclusive, secretive, withdrawn **10** antisocial, pokerfaced, speechless, tongue-tied, unsociable **11** inscrutable, standoffish, tight-lipped **12** closemouthed, tight-mouthed, unresponsive **13** unforthcoming

uncompassionate 4 cold, hard **5** stony **7** callous **8** obdurate, pitiless, uncaring **9** heartless, unfeeling **10** hard-boiled **11** coldhearted, hardhearted, insensitive **12** stonyhearted **13** unsympathetic

uncomplicated 4 easy **5** basic, clear, plain **6** simple **8** clear-cut **10** effortless, elementary, manageable, uninvolved

uncomplimentary 7 adverse **8** critical **9** degrading **10** belittling, derogatory, pejorative **11** deprecatory, disparaging, unfavorable **12** depreciative, depreciatory, unflattering

uncompromising 4 firm **5** rigid **8** hard-line, obdurate, resolute, stubborn **9** hard-nosed, immovable, insistent, unbending **10** brassbound, determined, inexorable, inflexible, unshakable, unyielding **12** intransigent, single-minded

unconcealed 4 bald, bare, open **5** frank, naked, overt, plain **6** candid **7** blatant, evident, exposed, express, obvious, visible **8** apparent, explicit, manifest, palpable **10** forthright **11** openhearted, transparent, undisguised, unvarnished

unconcern 6 apathy **7** neglect **9** aloofness, disregard **10** alienation, detachment, dispassion **11** disinterest, inattention, insouciance, nonchalance **12** carelessness, heedlessness, indifference **13** preoccupation

unconcerned 4 cool **6** remote **7** unmoved **8** careless, detached, heedless **9** alienated, apathetic, oblivious, unmindful, unruffled **10** insouciant, neglectful, untroubled **11** inattentive, indifferent, unperturbed **12** uninterested **13** disinterested, dispassionate

unconditional 5 sheer, total, utter **8** absolute, definite, explicit, outright **9** downright, out-

and-out **10** unreserved **11** unequivocal, unqualified **12** unrestricted **13** thoroughgoing
unconfined 4 free, vast **5** loose **7** at large **9** at
liberty, boundless, limitless, unlimited **12**
unrestrained, unrestricted
uncongenial 6 at odds **8** unfitted **9** repellent,
repugnant, unlikable **10** discordant, unsociable, unsuitable **11** conflicting, displeasing **12** antipathetic, disagreeable,
incompatible, unattractive **13** unsympathetic
unconnected 5 alone, apart **8** discrete, detached, disjoint, disjunct, distinct, inchoate,
rambling, separate **9** unrelated **10** unattached **11** independent **12** unassociated **13**
discontinuous, noncontinuous
unconquerable 10 invincible, inviolable, unbeatable **11** bulletproof, impregnable, indomitable, insuperable **12** invulnerable,
unassailable
unconscionable 5 undue **6** unfair, unholy,
unjust, wanton, wicked **7** immoral, ungodly
8 barbaric, criminal **9** barbarous, unethical
10 exorbitant, inordinate, outrageous **11** inexcusable, uncivilized **12** unprincipled, unscrupulous
unconscious 3 out **6** asleep, chance **7** out
cold, stunned, unaware **8** comatose **9** insensate, passed out, unplanned, unwitting **10**
blacked out, insensible, knocked out **11** inadvertent, instinctual, involuntary **12** uncalculated **13** unintentional
unconsciousness 4 coma **5** faint **6** stupor,
torpor, trance **7** syncope **13** obliviousness
unconsidered 4 rash **5** brash, hasty **6** casual
7 offhand **8** careless, reckless, slapdash **9**
desultory, haphazard, hit-or-miss, hotheaded, impetuous, unplanned **10** ill-advised, incautious, unthinking **11** thoughtless
unconstrained 4 free, open **6** blithe, dégagé,
wanton **7** buoyant, gushing, relaxed **8** animated, carefree, effusive, informal, outgoing **9** easygoing, expansive, liberated **10**
expressive, nonchalant, unreserved
uncontrollable 4 wild **6** unruly **7** wayward,
willful **9** fractious **10** headstrong, refractory, self-willed **11** intractable **12** overwhelming, recalcitrant, ungovernable,
unmanageable **13** irrepressible, undisciplined
uncontrolled 4 free, wild **5** loose **6** wanton **9**
automatic, excessive, unbounded, unlim-
ited, unmanaged **10** autonomous, immoderate, licentious, ungoverned **11** independent,
instinctual, involuntary, unconscious, uninhibited, unregulated **12** disorganized, unrestrained **13** self-governing

unconventional 3 odd **4** beat, boho **5** kinky,
kooky, outré **6** casual, far-out, freaky,
quirky, unique, way-out, weirdo **7** bizarre,
deviant, oddball, offbeat, unusual, wayward
8 aberrant, abnormal, atypical, bohemian,
freakish, original, peculiar **9** anomalous,
eccentric, irregular **10** avant-garde, unexpected, unorthodox **11** uncustomary **13** idiosyncratic
unconvinced 5 leery **6** unsure **7** dubious **8**
doubtful **9** skeptical, undecided **10** suspicious
unconvincing 4 lame **6** feeble, flimsy, forced
7 dubious, suspect **8** doubtful, strained **10**
farfetched, improbable, incredible **11** implausible, unrealistic **12** unbelievable **13** unsubstantial
uncooked 3 raw
uncouple 4 part **6** detach, divide **7** disjoin, divorce, unhitch **8** separate, unfasten **9** disengage **10** disconnect, dissociate **12**
disaffiliate
uncouth 3 odd, raw **4** rude **5** crass, crude,
gross, rough **6** clumsy, coarse, rugged, vulgar **7** awkward, bizarre, boorish, ill-bred,
loutish, strange, uncivil **8** barbaric, clownish, impolite, ungainly **9** eccentric, graceless, inelegant, unrefined **10** outlandish,
uncultured, unpolished **11** ill-mannered, uncivilized **12** discourteous, uncultivated *person:* **3** oaf **4** boor, dolt, lout **5** clown **7**
bumpkin **9** barbarian
uncover 4 bare **5** strip **6** betray, detect, divest,
expose, remove, reveal, unmask, unveil **7**
display, divulge, unearth **8** disclose
uncritical 5 naive **9** credulous **11** perfunctory
unction 3 oil **4** balm **5** cream, salve **6** balsam,
cerate, chrism **7** suavity, unguent **8** liniment, ointment **9** emollient **11** embrocation
unctuous 4 oily **5** fatty, slick, soapy, suave **6**
greasy, smarmy **7** cloying, fawning, ful-
some **8** slippery **9** wheedling **10** flattering,
oleaginous, saccharine **11** sycophantic
uncultivated 4 wild **5** crass, crude, gross **6**
coarse, desert, fallow, savage, vulgar **7**
boorish, lowbrow, uncouth **8** barbaric, un-
plowed, untilled **9** barbarian, barbarous, inelegant, unrefined **10** unpolished **11**
uncivilized
uncultured 3 raw **4** rude **5** crass, crude, gross,
rough **6** coarse, vulgar **7** artless, boorish,
ill-bred, loutish, lowbred, lowbrow, natural,
uncouth **8** barbaric, churlish, cloddish **9**
barbarian, barbarous, benighted, inelegant,
unrefined **10** unpolished **11** uncivilized **13**
unenlightened
uncustomary 4 rare **7** special, strange, un-

usual **8** aberrant, abnormal, atypical, singular, uncommon **9** anomalous **10** surprising, unfamiliar, unorthodox **11** exceptional **13** extraordinary

uncut 5 whole **6** entire, intact **8** complete **9** undiluted **10** full-length, unabridged **11** uncondensed **13** unabbreviated

undamaged 5 sound, whole **6** intact, unhurt **8** unbroken, unmarred **9** uninjured, unscathed **10** unimpaired **11** unblemished

undaunted 4 bold **5** brave **6** daring, heroic **7** doughty, Spartan, valiant **8** fearless, intrepid, resolute, unafraid, valorous **9** audacious **10** courageous **11** lionhearted, unconquered, unflinching **12** stouthearted

____ **und Drang 5** Sturm

undeceive 8 disabuse **11** disillusion

undecided 4 iffy, moot, open **6** unsure **7** dubious, pending **8** doubtful, wavering **9** equivocal, tentative, uncertain, unsettled **10** ambivalent, indefinite, unresolved **12** undetermined

undeclared 5 tacit **6** unsaid **7** assumed, implied **8** accepted, implicit, inferred, presumed, unspoken, unstated **10** understood

undecorated 4 bare **5** plain, stark **6** homely, severe, simple **8** no-frills **9** unadorned **12** unornamented **13** unembellished, unembroidered

undefiled 4 pure **6** chaste, intact, vestal, virgin **8** innocent, spotless, virginal, virtuous **9** stainless, unstained, unsullied, untainted **10** immaculate **11** unblemished, untarnished

undefined 3 dim **4** hazy **5** faint, vague **6** bleary **7** obscure, shadowy, unclear **8** inchoate, nebulous, unformed **9** amorphous, shapeless **10** indistinct **12** undetermined

undemonstrative 4 calm, cold, cool **5** aloof, chill **7** aseptic, distant, laconic **8** reserved, retiring **9** contained, inhibited, shrinking, withdrawn **10** restrained, unsociable **11** emotionless, passionless, standoffish, unemotional **12** matter-of-fact, unresponsive **13** self-contained

undeniable 6 patent **7** certain, evident, genuine, obvious **8** manifest **9** veridical **10** inarguable **11** indubitable, irrefutable, unequivocal **12** indisputable **13** incontestable

undependable 6 fickle, tricky, unsafe **7** erratic **10** capricious, fly-by-night, inconstant, unreliable **12** inconsistent, questionable **13** irresponsible, unpredictable, untrustworthy

under 3 low, sub **4** down, less **5** below, lower, short **7** lesser **8** beneath, covered, subject **8** downward, inferior **9** dependent, receiving,

secondary, subjacent **11** subordinate *prefix:* **3** hyp, sub **4** hypo

undercarriage 5 frame **9** framework **11** landing gear

undercover 6 covert, hidden, secret **7** furtive, stealth, sub-rosa **8** hush-hush, stealthy **11** clandestine **12** confidential **13** surreptitious *person:* **3** spy **4** mole **5** agent, spook **6** sleuth **9** detective, operative **10** counterspy **11** double agent, secret agent **12** counteragent

undercroft 5 crypt, vault **7** chamber **8** catacomb

undercut 7 subvert **8** sabotage

underdeveloped 4 poor **7** dwarfed, stunted **8** backward, immature **9** unevolved **10** third-world

underdog 5 loser **6** victim **7** also-ran, fall guy, wannabe **9** dark horse

underdone 3 raw, red **4** rare

underestimate 6 slight **7** dismiss **8** belittle, discount, disprize, minimize **9** deprecate, disparage, sell short **10** depreciate

undergarment 3 bra **4** BVDs, slip **5** teddy **6** bikini, bodice, briefs, corset, girdle, shorts, undies **7** chemise, drawers, panties, stammel, step-ins **8** lingerie, pretties, Skivvies, woollies **9** brassiere, jockstrap, long johns, petticoat, underwear **10** foundation

undergo 4 bear, face **5** abide, brave, brook **6** endure, suffer **7** sustain, weather **8** submit to, tolerate **9** withstand **10** experience

undergraduate 4 coed, soph **5** frosh **6** junior, senior **8** freshman **9** collegian, sophomore

underground 4 tube **5** metro, train **6** buried, hidden, nether, secret, subway **7** illegal, offbeat, railway **8** hypogeal, hypogean **10** undercover **11** alternative, clandestine **12** subterranean **13** surreptitious

underhanded 3 sly **4** wily **5** shady **6** covert, crafty, secret, shifty, sneaky, tricky **7** cunning, devious, elusive, evasive, furtive, subrosa **8** guileful, sneaking, stealthy **9** deceitful, deceptive **10** circuitous **11** clandestine, duplicitous **13** surreptitious

underlie 4 bear **6** prop up **7** subtend, support **8** buttress

underline 4 mark **6** play up, stress **9** emphasize, italicize **10** accentuate, underscore

underling 4 aide, peon, serf **5** gofer, scrub, slave **6** flunky, gopher, lackey, menial, minion **7** fall guy **8** inferior **9** assistant, attendant, subaltern **11** subordinate

underlying 4 root **5** basal, basic **7** primary **8** implicit **9** elemental, essential **11** fundamental

Under Milk Wood author 6 Thomas (Dylan)

undermine 3 sap **4** foil **5** blunt, erode **6** impair, thwart, weaken **7** cripple, disable, subvert **8** sabotage **9** attenuate, frustrate **10** debilitate, demoralize

undermost 6 bottom, lowest **9** lowermost **10** bottommost, nethermost, rock-bottom

underneath 4 sole **5** below, lower **6** bottom **7** covered

underpin 4 back, base, prop, root **5** brace **6** uphold **7** bolster, justify, shore up, support **8** buttress, validate **10** strengthen **11** corroborate

underpinning 4 base, prop, root, stay **5** basis, brace **7** bedrock, footing, seating, support **8** buttress **10** foundation, groundwork **12** substructure

underprivileged 4 poor **5** needy **7** hapless, unlucky **8** deprived **11** handicapped, unfortunate **13** disadvantaged

underrate 7 devalue **8** discount, mark down, minimize, write off **9** devaluate, write down **10** depreciate

underscore 6 accent, play up, stress **9** emphasize, italicize **10** accentuate

underside 4 sole **6** bottom **7** reverse

undersized 4 toy **4** baby, mini, puny **5** dinky, dwarf, pygmy, runty, short, small **6** bantam, little, pocket, slight **7** scrubby, stunted **9** miniature **10** diminutive **11** Lilliputian

understand 3 con, dig, ken, see **4** grok, know **5** grasp, guess, infer, savvy, sense, think **6** accept, assume, deduce, expect, fathom, figure, follow, gather, reason, reckon, take in, take it **7** believe, discern, imagine, presume, realize, suppose, surmise, suspect, suss out **8** conceive, conclude, consider, perceive **9** apprehend, interpret **10** appreciate, comprehend, conjecture

understandable 5 clear, lucid, plain **8** clearcut, coherent, knowable **9** excusable, graspable, plausible **10** articulate, believable, defensible, fathomable, reasonable **11** justifiable, perceivable, unambiguous **12** intelligible **13** apprehensible

understanding 3 ken, wit **4** deal, pact **5** grasp, sense **6** accord, humane, kindly **7** compact, empathy, entente, insight, mastery **8** sympathy **9** agreement, awareness, knowledge, tolerance **10** acceptance, impression, perception **11** considerate, discernment, explanation, sympathetic **12** apprehension, relationship **13** comprehension

understatement 7 litotes

understood 5 tacit **7** assumed, implied **8** accepted, implicit, inferred, unspoken

understudy 6 double, backup, fill-in **7** standby, stand-in **9** surrogate **10** substitute **11** replacement

undertake 3 try **4** dare **5** assay, begin, essay, start **6** accept, assume, pledge, strive, tackle, take on, take up **7** attempt, certify, execute, perform, promise, warrant **8** commence, contract, covenant, endeavor, set about, set forth, shoulder **9** guarantee

undertaker 8 embalmer **9** mortician

undertaking 3 job **4** task **6** affair, charge, effort **7** calling, emprise, exploit, mission, project, pursuit, venture **8** endeavor **9** adventure, guarantee, operation **10** enterprise **11** proposition, transaction

under-the-table 6 covert, hidden, secret, sneaky **7** furtive, on the q.t., sub-rosa **8** hush-hush, stealthy **9** concealed, underhand **10** undercover **11** clandestine **13** surreptitious

undertone 3 hue, hum **4** buzz, cast, hint, tint **5** drone, shade **6** mumble, murmur, mutter, rumble **7** inkling **10** suggestion **11** association, connotation, implication

undertow 4 eddy **7** current, riptide, sea puss

undervalue see **underrate**

underwater 9 submarine **10** subaquatic, subaqueous *breathing apparatus:* **5** scuba *captain:* **4** Nemo *chamber:* **7** caisson *device:* **8** paravane *missile:* **7** torpedo *sound detector:* **5** sonar

underwear see **undergarment**

underwood 5 brush, copse, hedge, scrub **7** boscage, coppice, thicket **9** shrubbery

underworld 4 hell **5** hades, Sheol **6** Erebus, Tophet **7** Gehenna, inferno **8** gangland **9** antipodes **11** Pandemonium *boatman:* **6** Charon *deity:* **3** Dis **4** Bran **5** Pluto **6** Osiris *goddess:* **6** Hecate **10** Persephone *organization:* **4** tong **5** Mafia, Triad **6** Yakuza **10** Cosa Nostra *relating to:* **8** chthonic *watchdog:* **8** Cerberus

underwrite 4 back, fund, sign **5** endow, stake **6** assure, insure, pay for, secure **7** agree to, endorse, finance, sponsor, support **8** bankroll **9** grubstake, guarantee **11** subscribe to

undesigning 5 frank **6** candid, honest **7** artless, earnest, genuine, sincere **9** guileless, ingenuous, unfeigned **10** aboveboard, forthright

undesirable 8 annoying, unwanted **9** offensive, unwelcome **10** ill-favored, unpleasant, unsuitable **11** displeasing, inadvisable, troublesome **12** disagreeable, unacceptable, unattractive **13** inappropriate, objectionable

undesired 8 needless, unsought, unwanted **9** uninvited, unwelcome **10** gratuitous **11** uncalled-for, unnecessary **12** nonessential

undetermined 5 vague **7** dubious, obscure, pending, unclear **8** doubtful **9** ambiguous, equivocal, uncertain, undecided, undefined, unsettled **10** ill-defined, indefinite, indistinct **12** inconclusive

undeveloped 5 crude, green, rough **6** latent **8** backward, immature, inchoate **9** embryonic, incipient, primitive, unevolved **10** unfinished

undiluted 4 neat, pure **5** sheer, utter **7** genuine, unmixed **8** absolute, straight **9** authentic, unalloyed **11** unmitigated, unqualified **13** unadulterated

undiplomatic 4 rash, rude **5** brash, cocky **6** brazen, cheeky **8** impudent, tactless **9** audacious, hotheaded, impolitic, impulsive, maladroit, untactful **10** ill-advised, indiscreet **11** impertinent, injudicious, insensitive, thoughtless **12** presumptuous

undisciplined 4 wild **6** unruly, wanton **7** froward, restive, wayward, willful **8** contrary, untoward **9** fractious **10** disorderly, rebellious, refractory **11** intractable **12** contumacious, noncompliant, obstreperous, recalcitrant, ungovernable, unmanageable

undisclosed 6 hidden, sealed, secret **7** unknown, unnamed **8** ulterior, withheld **9** anonymous **10** unreported, unrevealed **11** clandestine, unmentioned, unspecified **12** confidential, undesignated, unidentified

undisguised 4 bald, open, pure **5** frank, naked, overt, sheer, stark **6** candid, patent **7** obvious **8** apparent, explicit, manifest, palpable **9** barefaced **11** openhearted, unconcealed, unvarnished

undistinguished 5 cheap, stock **6** common **7** humdrum, obscure, routine **8** déclassé, everyday, inferior, low-grade, mediocre, middling, ordinary, workaday **10** second-rate **11** commonplace, nondescript, second-class **12** run-of-the-mill **13** insignificant

undisturbed 6 in situ

undivided 3 one **4** full **5** fixed, total, whole **6** entire, intact, united **8** complete, unbroken **9** unanimous **10** continuous, unswerving **11** indivisible **12** concentrated, undistracted

undo 4 free, open, ruin, veto **5** annul, loose, untie, upset, wrack, wreck **6** cancel, defeat, loosen, negate, stymie, unbind, unsnap **7** abolish, destroy, nullify, release, reverse, vitiate, wipe out **8** abrogate, disallow, overturn, unfasten, unloosen **9** disengage **10** contravene, invalidate **11** disentangle, outmaneuver

undoing 4 bane, doom, ruin, slip **5** shame **7** misstep **8** downfall, reversal **9** destroyer,

overthrow, ruination **10** misfortune **11** destruction, humiliation

undoubted 4 real, sure, true **7** certain, genuine **8** definite, positive **9** authentic **10** undisputed

undoubtedly 5 truly **6** indeed, really, surely **7** clearly **8** of course **9** assuredly, certainly **10** definitely, positively, presumably, undeniably **11** indubitably

undress see **unclothe**

undressed 4 nude, rude **5** naked **6** unclad **7** exposed **8** in the raw, stripped **9** au naturel, unclothed

undue 5 inapt **7** extreme **8** ill-timed, improper, needless, untimely **9** excessive, unfitting **10** immoderate, indecorous, inordinate, unsuitable **11** extravagant, uncalled-for, unnecessary, unwarranted **12** unreasonable **13** inappropriate, unjustifiable

undulant fever 11 brucellosis

undulate 4 roll, swag, sway, wave **5** heave, snake, swell, swing **6** billow, ripple **7** slither **9** fluctuate, oscillate

unduly 3 too **6** overly **9** extremely, immensely **11** excessively **12** immoderately, inordinately, unreasonably **13** unnecessarily

undying 7 abiding, ageless, endless, eternal **8** enduring, immortal, unending **9** continual, deathless, perennial, perpetual, unceasing **10** continuing **11** amaranthine, everlasting **12** imperishable, unquenchable

unearth 4 find, show **5** dig up, learn **6** exhume, expose, reveal **7** exhibit, find out, root out, uncover **8** come upon, disclose, discover, dredge up, excavate **9** ascertain, determine **10** come across

unearthly 5 eerie, weird **6** absurd, insane, spooky **7** awesome, ghostly, uncanny, ungodly **8** abnormal, ethereal, heavenly, numinous, spectral **9** appalling, fantastic **10** miraculous, mysterious, outlandish, superhuman, suprahuman **12** preposterous, supermundane, supernatural **13** preternatural

unease 4 care, fear **5** agita, angst, worry **6** strain, stress, unrest **7** anxiety, concern, tension **8** disquiet, distress **9** abashment, confusion, misgiving **10** discomfort, discontent, solicitude **11** disquietude, fretfulness, nervousness, uncertainty, uptightness **12** apprehension, discomfiture, discomposure **13** embarrassment

uneasy 4 edgy **5** jumpy, tense **6** afraid **7** anxious, awkward, fearful, fidgety, fretful, nervous, restive, unquiet, uptight, worried **8** agitated, doubtful, insecure, restless, unstable **9** ambiguous, concerned, difficult, disturbed, perturbed, uncertain, unsettled **10**

disquieted, precarious, solicitous **11** embarrassed **12** apprehensive **13** uncomfortable

uneducated 5 crude, rough **8** ignorant, untaught **9** benighted, untutored **10** illiterate, unlettered, unschooled **12** uncultivated, uninstructed

unembellished 4 bald, bare **5** blunt, plain, spare, stark **6** severe **7** austere **9** essential, unadorned **11** undecorated, unelaborate, ungarnished, unvarnished **12** unornamented **13** unembroidered, unpretentious

unemotional 4 cold, cool **5** chill, stoic, stony **6** frigid, sedate, serene **7** deadpan, equable, glacial, stoical **8** composed, obdurate, reserved, reticent **9** apathetic, impassive **10** hard-boiled, phlegmatic **11** insensitive, passionless, unexcitable **12** intellectual, thick-skinned, unresponsive **13** dispassionate

unemployed 4 idle **5** fired **6** otiose, unused **7** jobless, laid off, loafing **8** inactive, leisured, workless **10** unoccupied

unending 7 eternal, undying **8** constant, immortal, infinite, timeless **9** boundless, ceaseless, continual, incessant, limitless, perennial, perpetual, unceasing **10** continuous **11** amaranthine, everlasting, unremitting **12** interminable **13** uninterrupted

unenlightened 5 naive **6** unread **7** heathen, unaware **8** backward, ignorant, nescient **9** benighted, unknowing **10** uneducated, uninformed **11** uninitiated **12** uncultivated

unenthusiastic 4 cool **5** tepid **8** grudging, listless, lukewarm **9** apathetic, unexcited **10** lackluster, lacklustre, spiritless **11** half-hearted, indifferent, perfunctory **12** uninterested

unequal 3 odd **6** uneven, unfair **7** diverse **8** inferior, lopsided, one-sided **9** different, disparate, divergent, irregular **10** asymmetric, dissimilar, inadequate, mismatched, off-balance **12** insufficient

unequaled 6 unique **7** supreme **8** foremost, nonesuch, peerless **9** matchless, paramount, unmatched, unrivaled **10** preeminent, surpassing **12** incomparable, transcendent, unparalleled **13** unprecedented

unequivocal 5 clear **6** direct, patent **7** certain, evident **8** apparent, definite, distinct, explicit, manifest, palpable **10** undeniable **11** categorical, indubitable, unambiguous **12** indisputable, undisputable

unerring 5 exact **6** dead-on **7** certain, correct, perfect, precise **8** accurate, reliable **9** faultless, unfailing **10** dependable, infallible **11** trustworthy

unessential 8 marginal, needless, unneeded **9** redundant **10** expendable, gratuitous, irrel-

evant, peripheral, unrequired **11** dispensable, superfluous, uncalled-for, unimportant, unnecessary

unethical 5 venal, wrong **7** corrupt, crooked, immoral **9** dishonest, reprobate **12** disreputable, unprincipled, unscrupulous

uneven 3 odd **4** wavy **5** bumpy, erose, harsh, jaggy, rough **6** craggy, jagged, patchy, ragged, random, rugged, spotty **7** scraggy, unequal, varying **8** lopsided, scabrous, scraggly, variable **9** haphazard, hit-or-miss, irregular **10** asymmetric, imbalanced, unbalanced

unevenness 4 bump, wave **7** anomaly **8** asperity, imparity **9** disparity, imbalance, roughness, variation **10** inequality **12** irregularity, lopsidedness **13** disproportion

uneventful 5 usual **6** placid **7** humdrum, prosaic, routine **8** ordinary **10** unexciting **11** commonplace **12** unremarkable

unexampled 4 lone, only, sole, solo **5** alone **6** unique **8** singular, solitary **9** matchless, unequaled, unmatched, unrivaled **10** consummate, inimitable, sui generis, unequalled, unrivalled **12** incomparable, unparalleled **13** unprecedented

unexcited 4 calm **5** blasé, stoic **6** placid, sedate, serene **7** relaxed, stoical **8** composed, tranquil **9** apathetic, collected, unruffled **10** nonchalant **11** indifferent **12** uninterested **13** dispassionate

unexciting 4 arid, dull, tame **5** banal, bland, ho-hum **6** boring, stodgy **7** humdrum, insipid, prosaic, tedious **8** lifeless, tiresome **10** monotonous **11** commonplace

unexpected 10 surprising, unforeseen **11** unpredicted **13** unanticipated

unexpectedly 5 aback, short **6** sudden **7** unaware **8** abruptly, suddenly, unawares **9** forthwith **11** unwittingly **12** accidentally **13** inadvertently

unexpended 5 saved **7** reserve, surplus **8** left over, reserved **9** remaining

unexpired 5 valid **9** operative

unexpressed 5 tacit **6** silent, unsaid **7** assumed, implied **8** implicit, presumed, unspoken, wordless **9** unuttered **10** undeclared, understood

unfailing 4 fast, sure **7** certain, devoted **8** constant, faithful, reliable, resolute, sure-fire, unerring **9** steadfast, unvarying **10** consistent, dependable, infallible, invariable, persistent, unchanging, unflagging, unwavering **11** everlasting, persevering, unrelenting **12** tried-and-true **13** inexhaustible

unfair 4 foul **5** wrong **6** biased, shabby, uneven, unjust **7** unequal **8** wrongful **9** arbi-

trary, dishonest, unethical **10** prejudiced **11** inequitable, underhanded, unrighteous
unfaithful 5 false **6** untrue **8** cheating, disloyal, recreant, turncoat **9** faithless, two-timing **10** adulterous, inaccurate, perfidious, traitorous **11** treacherous **13** untrustworthy
unfaltering 3 set **4** firm **6** steady **7** abiding **8** constant, enduring, resolute, tireless **9** steadfast, unfailing **10** continuous, unflagging, unwavering **11** persevering **12** never-failing, wholehearted
unfamiliar 3 new, odd **5** alien, novel, weird **6** exotic **7** foreign, strange, unaware, unknown, unusual **8** abnormal, peculiar **11** incognizant, out-of-the-way **12** unaccustomed, unacquainted
unfashionable 5 dated, dowdy, passé, stale **6** bygone, démodé, old-hat, shabby **7** outworn **8** outdated, outmoded **9** out-of-date, unstylish **10** antiquated, oldfangled
unfasten 4 free, open, undo **5** loose, unbar, unfix, unpin, untie **6** detach, loosen, unbind, unbolt, unlace, unlock, unsnap **7** release, unclasp, unhitch, unlatch, unleash, unloose, unstrap **8** unbuckle, unfetter, unloosen, untether **9** disengage
unfathomable 7 abysmal, obscure **8** profound **9** boundless, enigmatic, unplumbed **10** bottomless, fathomless, unknowable **11** inscrutable **12** immeasurable, impenetrable
unfavorable 3 bad, ill **4** poor **6** averse, unfair, unkind **7** adverse, hostile, opposed **8** contrary, damaging, inimical, negative **9** disliking, troubling **11** detrimental, displeasing **12** antagonistic, disapproving, inauspicious
prefix: **3** dys
unfavorably 4 awry **5** amiss, badly **6** astray, poorly **7** wrongly **10** negatively, unsuitably **13** unfortunately
unfeasible 8 quixotic **9** visionary **10** chimerical, impossible, unworkable **11** impractical, speculative, theoretical, unrealistic **12** unattainable, unrealizable **13** impracticable
unfeeling 4 cold, hard, numb **5** cruel, harsh, stern, stony **6** brutal, leaden, marble, numbed, severe, stolid, unkind **7** callous **8** benumbed, deadened, hardened, obdurate, pitiless, ruthless, uncaring **9** apathetic, heartless, indurated, insensate, senseless **10** hardboiled, insensible, insentient **11** cold-blooded, coldhearted, hardhearted, insensitive, unemotional **12** anesthetized **13** unsympathetic
unfeigned 4 real, true **6** actual, hearty, honest **7** artless, earnest, genuine, natural, sincere **8** innocent **9** guileless, heartfelt, ingenuous **12** wholehearted

unfinished 3 raw **5** crude, rough **7** sketchy **9** imperfect, roughhewn, undressed **10** incomplete, unpolished
Unfinished Symphony composer 8 Schubert (Franz)
unfit 4 sick, weak **5** inapt, inept **6** faulty **7** deprive, disable, unsound, useless **8** disabled, improper, unsuited **9** ill-suited, incapable, maladroit **10** disqualify, ill-adapted, inadequate, ineligible, unsuitable **11** ill-equipped, incompetent, unqualified **12** disqualified, incompatible **13** inappropriate, incapacitated
unfitting 5 inapt **8** improper, unseemly **9** imprudent **10** ill-advised, inapposite, malapropos, unbecoming, unsuitable **11** inadvisable **13** inappropriate
unfix 4 part, undo **5** loose, sever **6** cut off, detach, loosen, sunder, unbind **7** unloose **8** uncouple, unfasten, unloosen **9** disengage **10** disconnect, dissociate
unflagging 6 steady **7** staunch **8** constant, tireless, untiring **9** unceasing, unfailing, unwearied **11** persevering, unfaltering, unrelenting, unremitting **13** indefatigable, inexhaustible
unflappable 4 calm **6** poised, serene **7** assured, equable **8** composed, laid-back **9** collected, unruffled **10** deliberate, nonchalant **11** self-assured **13** imperturbable, self-possessed
unfledged 5 green, young **6** callow, jejune, unripe **7** puerile **8** immature, juvenile **10** unseasoned **11** undeveloped, unfeathered **13** inexperienced
unflinching 4 firm, grim **6** dogged **7** doughty, staunch, valiant **8** fearless, intrepid, resolute **9** dauntless, steadfast **10** courageous, relentless, unwavering, unyielding **11** unfaltering, unrelenting **12** stouthearted
unfold 4 open **6** deduce, evolve, expand, expose, extend, flower, mature, reveal, unwrap **7** blossom, burgeon, clear up, develop, display, dope out, exhibit, explain, resolve **8** decipher, disclose, evidence, manifest **9** elaborate, explicate, figure out, puzzle out, transpire **10** effloresce, outstretch **11** come to light
unforced 4 easy **7** natural, willing, witting **8** elective, optional **9** available, easygoing, voluntary **10** deliberate, volitional **11** intentional **12** unprescribed **13** discretionary, noncompulsory
unforeseeable 9 uncertain, unplanned **10** accidental
unforeseen 6 chance **8** surprise **10** accidental,

surprising, unexpected **11** unlooked-for, un-predicted **13** unanticipated

unforgivable 9 untenable **10** censurable, inex-piable, outrageous **11** blameworthy, inex-cusable, intolerable **12** indefensible, unacceptable, unpardonable **13** insupport-able, reprehensible, unjustifiable

unformed 4 rude **5** crude, rough, vague **6** cal-low **8** immature, inchoate, nebulous, un-shaped **9** amorphous, roughhewn, shapeless **10** indefinite, unfinished, unpolished **11** un-developed, unfashioned **12** unstructured **13** indeterminate

unfortunate 3 bad, sad **4** dire, poor **6** woeful, wretch **7** adverse, awkward, hapless, un-happy, unlucky **8** grievous, ill-fated, luck-less, untoward, wretched **9** desperate, graceless, ill-chosen, miserable **10** afflic-tive, calamitous, deplorable, disastrous, ill-starred, lamentable, unsuitable **11** distressing, regrettable, star-crossed, unfa-vorable **12** disagreeable, inauspicious, infe-licitous, unsuccessful **13** heartbreaking

unfounded 4 idle, vain **5** false **8** baseless, spurious, unproven **9** deceptive, dishonest, untenable **10** fabricated, fallacious, gratu-itous, groundless, mendacious, misleading, untruthful **11** uncalled-for, unsupported, un-warranted

unfriendly 4 cold, cool **5** alien, aloof, chill, gruff, surly **6** chilly, frosty, remote **7** dis-tant, grouchy, hostile, opposed, warlike **8** inimical, unsocial **10** antisocial, censorious, inimicable, unsociable **11** ill-disposed, un-congenial **12** antagonistic, disagreeable, in-hospitable, misanthropic, unneighborly **13** unsympathetic

unfruitful 4 arid, idle **5** empty, waste **6** bar-ren, desert, effete, fallow, futile, wasted **7** parched, sterile, useless **8** abortive, boot-less, depleted, impotent **9** infertile, point-less **10** unavailing **11** ineffective, ineffectual **12** impoverished, unproductive, unprofit-able

unfurl 4 open **6** expose, reveal, spread, un-fold, unroll, unwind **7** develop, display, ex-hibit, uncover **8** disclose **9** elaborate, spread out

unfurnished 4 bare **5** empty **6** vacant

unfussy 5 loose **6** breezy, casual, common, dégagé, folksy, mellow **7** cursory, relaxed **8** familiar, informal, laid-back **9** easygoing **10** unreserved **11** low-pressure, pococurante, unconcerned **12** unparticular **13** unceremo-nious, uncomplicated

ungainly 5 gawky, lanky, splay **6** clumsy, klutzy, oafish **7** awkward, boorish, hulking, loutish, lumpish, uncouth **8** bungling, clownish, lubberly, unwieldy **9** lumbering, maladroit **10** blundering

ungarnished 5 plain **6** modest, simple **9** un-adorned **11** undecorated, unelaborate **12** un-ornamented **13** unembellished, unembroidered

ungenerous 4 mean **5** petty, tight **6** paltry, shabby, skimpy, stingy **7** chintzy, miserly **8** grudging, picayune, ungiving **9** illiberal, niggardly, penurious **10** pinchpenny **11** closefisted, tightfisted **12** parsimonious **13** penny-pinching

ungodly see **unholy**

ungovernable 4 wild **6** unruly **7** froward, lawless, willful **8** mutinous, untoward **9** fractious, turbulent, unbridled **10** disor-derly, headstrong, rebellious, refractory, tu-multuous **11** intractable **12** recalcitrant, uncontrolled, unmanageable **13** irrepress-ible, undisciplined

ungraceful 5 crude, gawky, inept, stiff **6** clumsy, gauche, klutzy, oafish, wooden **7** artless, awkward, halting, labored, stilted **8** bumbling, bungling, ungainly, untoward **9** all thumbs, inelegant, lumbering, maladroit **10** blundering

ungracious 4 rude **5** gruff **6** crusty **7** brusque, uncivil **8** churlish, impolite **9** offensive **10** unmannerly **11** disobliging, ill-mannered, impertinent, thoughtless, uncalled-for **12** disagreeable, discourteous **13** disrespectful, inconsiderate, unceremonious

ungraspable 6 opaque **7** obscure **8** baffling **9** enigmatic **10** unknowable **12** impenetrable, inexplicable, unfathomable

ungrateful 9 thankless

unguarded 5 frank, hasty **6** candid, direct, unwary **7** offhand **8** careless, heedless, reckless **9** impolitic, imprudent, impulsive **10** incautious, indiscreet, unthinking **11** de-fenseless, thoughtless, unprotected

unguent 4 balm **5** cream, salve **6** balsam, cer-ate, chrism, lotion **8** ointment **9** emollient, lubricant **11** embrocation

ungulate 3 hog, pig **4** deer **5** horse, tapir **6** hoofed **8** elephant **10** rhinoceros

unhallowed 4 evil **6** impure, unholy, wicked **7** immoral, impious, profane, ungodly **8** in-fernal **9** nefarious **10** desecrated, iniquitous, irreverent **13** unconsecrated

unhampered 4 free, open **5** frank, loose **6** di-rect **8** uncurbed **9** unbridled, unchecked, unimpeded, unlimited **10** unhindered **11** un-inhibited, untrammeled **12** unrestrained, un-restricted, unobstructed **13** unconstrained

unhand 5 let go **7** release

unhandy 5 bulky, inept **6** clumsy, gauche, klutzy **7** awkward, halting, hulking **8** bumbling, bungling, cumbrous, unwieldy **9** all thumbs, ham-handed, maladroit, ponderous **10** cumbersome, unskillful **12** inconvenient

unhappiness 3 woe **5** blues, dolor, dumps, gloom, grief, worry **6** misery, mishap, sorrow **7** anxiety, sadness **8** distress **9** dejection **10** depression, desolation, discontent, heartbreak, melancholy **11** despondency, dolefulness **12** mournfulness, wretchedness **13** cheerlessness

unhappy 3 sad **4** down, glum, grim **5** sorry **6** dismal, dreary, gloomy **7** joyless **8** dejected, downcast, mournful, saddened, troubled, wretched **9** cheerless, depressed, sorrowful, woebegone **10** despondent, dispirited, melancholy **11** melancholic, unfortunate **12** disconsolate, heavyhearted

unharmed 4 safe **5** sound **6** intact, secure, unhurt **8** unbroken, unmarred **9** protected, undamaged, undefiled, uninjured, unscathed **10** unimpaired **11** unblemished

unhealthiness 7 ailment, disease, illness, malaise **8** debility, sickness **9** infirmity **10** affliction, sickliness **11** decrepitude **13** indisposition

unhealthy 3 ill **4** sick **6** ailing, infirm, sickly, unwell **7** baneful, noisome, noxious, unsound **8** diseased **9** injurious **11** deleterious, unwholesome **12** insalubrious

unheard-of 3 new **6** unique **7** obscure, unknown, unnoted **8** nameless **10** phenomenal, unrenowned **12** uncelebrated **13** extraordinary, unprecedented

unhesitating 7 assured, earnest **8** decisive, positive, resolute **9** confident, immediate, unchecked **10** determined, forthright, purposeful **11** unflinching **12** wholehearted

unhinge 5 addle, craze **6** madden, ruffle **7** derange **9** unbalance

unhinged 3 mad **4** daft, loco, nuts **5** balmy, crazy, loony, wacky **6** insane **7** lunatic, unglued **8** demented, deranged **9** disturbed **10** unbalanced

unholy 4 base, evil, vile **6** impure, sinful, wicked **7** heinous, immoral, impious, profane, ungodly **8** dreadful, fiendish, godawful, shocking **9** atheistic, barbarous **10** iniquitous, irreverent, outrageous, scandalous, unhallowed **11** irreligious, unbelieving **12** sacrilegious, unsanctified **13** reprehensible

unhorse 5 pitch, throw **6** topple, tumble, unseat **7** buck off **8** dislodge, dismount, overturn, unsaddle **9** overthrow

unhurried 4 easy, slow **6** casual **7** laggard, relaxed **8** dilatory, laid-back **9** easygoing, leisurely **10** deliberate **11** low-pressure

unhurt 4 safe **5** sound, whole **6** entire, intact **7** perfect **8** unbroken, unharmed, unmarred **9** undamaged, uninjured, unscathed, untouched **10** unimpaired **11** unblemished

unification 5 union **6** fusion, hookup, merger **7** amalgam, joining, linkage, melding, merging **8** alliance, coupling **9** coalition **10** connection, federation **11** affiliation, coalescence, combination **12** amalgamation **13** confederation, consolidation

uniform 4 even, like, suit **5** alike, dress, equal, level **6** attire, outfit, stable, steady **7** ordered, orderly, regular, similar, stabile **8** constant, unvaried **9** consonant, unvarying **10** comparable, consistent, invariable, unchanging **11** homogeneous **13** unfluctuating
combining form: **3** iso *type:* **3** BDU **5** blues, habit, khaki **6** livery, whites

uniformity 6 parity **7** oneness **8** equality, evenness, identity, monotony, sameness **9** agreement, congruity, constancy **11** consistency **13** invariability

uniformly 6 always, evenly **7** equally **8** smoothly **10** comparably **11** analogously, identically **12** equivalently

unify 3 tie, wed **4** bind, bond, fuse, knit, link, mesh **5** blend, marry, merge, unite **6** cement, couple **7** combine, conjoin **8** coalesce, compound, federate **9** integrate **10** amalgamate, centralize, synthesize **11** concatenate, consolidate

unimaginable 10 incredible, unknowable **11** unthinkable **12** mind-boggling, unbelievable **13** extraordinary, inconceivable, indescribable

unimaginative 4 dull, flat **5** banal, bland, trite, vapid **6** common **7** literal, prosaic, routine, vanilla **8** bromidic **10** derivative, pedestrian, uncreative, uninspired **11** commonplace

unimpaired 4 safe **5** sound **6** intact, unhurt **7** perfect **8** unbroken, unharmed, unmarred **9** undamaged, uninjured, unscathed **11** unblemished

unimpassioned 4 calm, cool **5** sober, stoic **6** placid, remote, stolid **7** deadpan **8** detached, lukewarm, reserved, tranquil **9** impassive, temperate **10** phlegmatic, spiritless **11** coldblooded, emotionless **12** matter-of-fact

unimpeachable 5 valid **7** correct **8** flawless, reliable, virtuous **9** blameless, exemplary, faultless, unspotted, unsullied **10** conclusive, impeccable, undisputed **11** unblemished, untarnished **13** authoritative

unimportant 4 mere **5** minor, petty **6** casual,

minute, paltry **7** trivial **8** piddling **9** small-beer, worthless **10** expendable, immaterial, irrelevant, negligible **11** dispensable, meaningless, superfluous **13** insignificant

uninformed 7 unaware **8** ignorant, nescient **9** oblivious, unknowing, unwitting **10** unfamiliar **11** incognizant, superficial **12** unacquainted, undiscerning

uninhabited 5 empty, waste **6** barren, vacant **7** vacated **8** deserted, desolate, forsaken **9** abandoned, evacuated **10** unoccupied

uninhibited 3 lax **4** free **5** loose **8** uncurbed **9** expansive, fancy-free, liberated, unbridled **10** boisterous, ungoverned, unhampered, unreserved **11** spontaneous, unrepressed, untrammeled **12** unrestrained, unsuppressed **13** unconstrained

uninjured 4 safe **5** sound, whole **6** intact, unhurt **8** unharmed, unmarred **9** undamaged, undefiled, unscathed, untouched **10** unimpaired

uninspired 4 blah, drab, dull **5** banal, stock, trite, vapid **6** boring, leaden, old-hat, stodgy **7** humdrum, insipid, plastic, sterile, vanilla **8** bromidic, lifeless, ordinary **9** colorless **10** lackluster, lacklustre, pedestrian, uncreative, unoriginal **11** commonplace **13** unimaginative

unintelligent 4 dumb **5** dense **6** obtuse, stupid **7** asinine, brutish, doltish, fatuous, foolish, moronic, vacuous, witless **8** mindless **9** brainless, ludicrous **10** half-witted, ill-advised, irrational, ridiculous, weak-minded **11** harebrained, lamebrained **12** feebleminded

unintentional 6 chance, random **9** haphazard, unplanned, unwitting **10** accidental, fortuitous, incidental, unexpected, unforeseen, unthinking **11** inadvertent, unconscious, unlooked-for **12** adventitious, coincidental

uninterested 5 aloof, blasé, bored, jaded **9** apathetic, incurious, unexcited **10** uninvolved **11** indifferent, unconcerned

uninteresting 3 dry **4** arid, blah, drab, dull, flat **5** banal, dusty, ho-hum, stale **6** boring, jejune **7** humdrum, insipid, prosaic, tedious **8** bromidic, plodding, tiresome **9** colorless, dryasdust, wearisome **10** monotonous, pedestrian, uneventful, unexciting

uninterrupted 6 direct **7** endless, nonstop **8** constant, unbroken, unending **9** ceaseless, continual, incessant, perpetual, sustained, unceasing **10** continuous **11** undisturbed, unremitting

uninvited 7 unasked **8** unbidden, unsought **9** intruding **10** gratuitous **11** uncalled-for, unrequested, unsolicited **12** presumptuous

union 4 bloc, bond, club **5** alloy, artel, group, guild, joint **6** fusion, league, merger **7** amalgam, joining, melding, merging, society **8** alliance, congress, coupling, junction, juncture, marriage, sodality **9** coalition **10** connection, federation, fellowship **11** association, brotherhood, coalescence, combination, confederacy, cooperative, unification **13** confederation, consolidation **branch: 5** local **labor: 3** AFL, CIO, UAW, UMW **5** ILGWU

unique 3 odd, one **4** lone, only, sole, solo **5** alone, novel **6** single **8** peculiar, peerless, singular, solitary, uncommon, unwonted **9** anomalous, exclusive, matchless, unequaled, unmatched, unrivaled **10** inimitable, particular, sui generis, unequalled, unexampled, unrivalled **11** distinctive, exceptional **12** incomparable, unparalleled, unrepeatable **13** extraordinary, idiosyncratic, unprecedented

uniqueness 8 identity **10** singleness **11** singularity **13** individuality

____-Unis 5 Etats

unit 3 arm, one **4** area, item, part, wing **5** digit, group, monad, piece, whole **6** entity **7** element, measure **8** molecule **9** component **10** individual **11** constituent **administrative: 6** agency, bureau, sector **8** district **boy scout: 5** troop **educational: 6** course **military:** (see at **military**) **of acceleration: 3** gal **of action: 7** episode **of advertising space: 4** line **6** column **of an element: 4** atom **8** molecule **of angular measure: 6** radian **of area: 3** are **4** acre **6** morgen **7** hectare **9** square rod **10** square mile, square yard **of astronomical distance: 6** parsec **9** light-year **of brightness: 7** lambert **of capacitance: 5** farad **of capacity: 2** cc, ml **3** cup, tun **4** cord, dram, gill, peck, pint **5** liter, litre, minim, ounce, quart **6** barrel, bushel, firkin, gallon **of computer information: 3** bit, gig, meg **4** byte **8** gigabyte, megabyte **of conductance: 3** mho **7** siemens **of distance: 4** mile, yard **5** meter **6** league **7** furlong **of electricity: 3** amp **4** volt, watt **6** ampere **7** coulomb **of energy: 3** erg **5** joule **7** quantum **8** watt-hour **of explosive force: 7** megaton **of fineness: 5** carat, karat **of force: 4** dyne **6** newton **7** poundal **of frequency: 5** hertz **7** fresnel **of grain: 5** sheaf **of heat: 3** BTU **5** therm **7** calorie **of illumination: 3** lux **5** lumen **of inductance: 5** henry **of length: 3** mil, rod **4** foot, hand, inch, mile, rood, yard **5** chain, fermi, meter **6** fathom, micron **7** furlong **9** kilometer **historic: 5** cubit **of loudness: 4** sone **7** decibel **of lumber:**

9 board foot *of magnetic flux:* **5** gamma, gauss, tesla, weber **7** maxwell *of magnetic intensity:* **7** oersted *of magnetomotive force:* **7** gilbert *of pressure:* **3** bar, psi **4** torr **6** pascal **10** atmosphere *of radiation:* **3** rad **8** roentgen *of radioactivity:* **5** curie *of resistance:* **3** ohm *of solar radiation:* **7** langley *of sound absorption:* **5** sabin *of speech:* **4** word **6** toneme **7** phoneme **8** morpheme, syllable *of speed:* **3** CPS, MPH, RPM **4** knot *of temperature:* **6** degree, kelvin *of time:* **3** age, day, eon **4** beat, bell, hour, week, year **5** month **6** minute, season, second **8** svedberg *of viscosity:* **5** poise *of volume:* **5** stere **9** cubic foot, cubic yard **10** cubic meter *of weight:* **3** cwt, ton **4** dram, gram, tael **5** carat, grain, ounce, pound, tonne **6** drachm **7** gigaton, kiloton, quintal, scruple **8** kilogram, millieme **9** metric ton, microgram, milligram *historic:* **3** tod **5** gerah, libra *Indian:* **4** tola *Russian:* **4** pood *of work:* **3** erg **5** ergon, joule *social:* **4** clan **5** tribe **6** family **7** chapter
unitary 5 whole **9** undivided **11** indivisible
unite 3 mix, tie, wed **4** ally, band, bind, bond, fuse, join, knit, link, meld, pool, weld **5** blend, graft, marry, merge, unify **6** cement, couple, gather, league, mingle, splice **7** combine, conjoin, connect **8** assemble, coadjute, coalesce, compound, federate **9** affiliate, aggregate, commingle **10** amalgamate, federalize **11** confederate, incorporate
united 3 one, wed **5** joint **6** allied, linked, merged, wedded **7** made one **8** agreeing, combined, in accord **10** harmonious
United Arab Emirates *capital:* **8** Abu Dhabi *city:* **5** Dubai **6** Dubayy *coast:* **6** Pirate **7** Trucial *emirate:* **5** Dubai **6** Dubayy **8** Abu Dhabi *former name:* **13** Trucial States *gulf:* **4** Oman **7** Persian *monetary unit:* **6** dirham *neighbor:* **4** Oman **11** Saudi Arabia *peninsula:* **7** Arabian *strait:* **6** Hormuz
United Kingdom *capital:* **6** London *city:* **3** Ely **4** Bath **5** Derby, Dover, Leeds **6** Exeter, Oxford **7** Bristol, Cardiff, Glasgow, Paisley **8** Bradford, Brighton, Coventry, Plymouth **9** Cambridge, Edinburgh, Leicester, Liverpool, Newcastle, Sheffield **10** Birmingham, Manchester, Nottingham **11** Bournemouth *colony:* **8** Falkland (Islands) *component:* **5** Wales **7** England **8** Scotland **12** Great Britain *conqueror:* **6** Caesar (Julius) **7** William (the Conqueror) *county:* **4** Kent **5** Devon, Essex **6** Dorset, Surrey, Sussex **7** Norfolk, Suffolk **8** Cornwall, Somerset **9** Berkshire, Wiltshire, Yorkshire *island:* **3** Man **4** Jura,

Skye **5** Islay, Lewis, Wight **6** Jersey **8** Anguilla, Guernsey, Mainland *island group:* **6** Orkney **7** Channel **8** Hebrides, Shetland *language:* **5** Welsh **6** Gaelic *leader:* **8** Cromwell (Oliver) **9** Churchill (Winston) *monarch:* **4** Anne, Mary **5** Henry, James **6** Alfred (the Great), Edward, George **7** Charles, Richard, William **8** Victoria **9** Elizabeth *monetary unit:* **5** pence, penny, pound *monetary unit, former:* **3** bob **5** crown, groat **6** florin, guinea **7** ha'penny **8** farthing, shilling, sixpence **9** halfpenny **10** threepence *mountain, range:* **7** Scafell (Peak), Snowdon **8** Ben Nevis, Cumbrian, Grampian **12** Cheviot Hills *peninsula:* **7** Kintyre *prehistoric site:* **7** Avebury **9** Skara Brae **10** Stonehenge *river:* **3** Dee, Exe, Wye **4** Aire, Avon, Ouse **5** Clyde **6** Mersey, Severn, Thames *sea:* **5** Irish, North **6** Celtic *territory:* **8** Anguilla
United Nations secretary-general 3 Ban (Ki-moon), Lie (Trygve) **5** Annan (Kofi), Thant (U) **8** Waldheim (Kurt) **12** Boutros-Ghali (Boutros), Hammarskjöld (Dag)
United States *desert:* **6** Mojave **7** Sonoran **8** Colorado *highest point:* **6** Denali (Mt.) **8** McKinley (Mt.) *island:* **6** Hawaii, Kodiak, Unimak **7** Nunivak **9** Admiralty, Chichagof **10** St. Lawrence **13** Prince of Wales *island group:* **3** Fox **6** Hawaii **8** Aleutian, Pribilof, Thousand *lowest point:* **11** Death Valley *mountain range:* **5** Coast, Green, Ozark, Rocky, White **7** Cascade, Olympic **8** Catskill **9** Blue Ridge **10** Adirondack, Great Smoky **11** Appalachian **12** Sierra Nevada *national park:* **4** Zion **6** Denali **7** Glacier, Olympic, Redwood, Sequoia **8** Badlands, Carlsbad, Wind Cave, Yosemite **9** Mesa Verde, Mt. Rainier **10** Everglades, Grand Teton, Hot Springs, Isle Royale, Shenandoah **11** Dry Tortugas, Grand Canyon, Kenai Fjords, Mammoth Cave, Yellowstone *possession:* **10** Puerto Rico *state:* **4** Iowa, Ohio, Utah **5** Idaho, Maine, Texas **6** Alaska, Hawaii, Kansas, Nevada, Oregon **7** Alabama, Arizona, Florida, Georgia, Indiana, Montana, New York, Vermont, Wyoming **8** Arkansas, Colorado, Delaware, Illinois, Kentucky, Maryland, Michigan, Missouri, Nebraska, Oklahoma, Virginia **9** Louisiana, Minnesota, New Jersey, New Mexico, Tennessee, Wisconsin **10** California, Washington **11** Connecticut, Mississippi, North Dakota, Rhode Island, South Dakota **12** New Hampshire, Pennsylvania, West Virginia **13** Massachusetts, North Carolina,

South Carolina *territory:* **4** Guam **13** American Samoa, Virgin Islands

unity 5 union **6** accord **7** concord, harmony, oneness **8** identity, soleness **9** agreement, consensus **10** continuity, singleness, solidarity

universal 3 all **5** broad, total, whole **6** common, cosmic, entire, global **7** general, generic **8** catholic **9** extensive, planetary, unlimited, worldwide **10** ecumenical, ubiquitous **11** omnipresent **12** all-embracing, all-inclusive, cosmopolitan **13** comprehensive *combining form:* **4** omni

universe 3 all **5** whole, world **6** cosmos, system **8** creation **9** macrocosm

unjust 5 wrong **6** biased, shabby, unfair **7** partial, unequal **8** one-sided, improper, wrongful **9** inequable **10** prejudiced, undeserved **11** inequitable, unrighteous

unjustifiable 5 undue **7** invalid **8** baseless **9** unfounded, untenable **10** groundless **11** inexcusable, unsupported, unwarranted **12** indefensible

unkempt 5 messy **6** frowsy, frowzy, ragtag, shaggy, sloppy, untidy **7** ruffled, rumpled, scruffy, tousled **8** scraggly, slipshod, slovenly, uncombed **10** bedraggled, disarrayed, disheveled, disordered, unpolished **11** disarranged

unkind 4 mean, vile **5** cruel, harsh, rough, stern **6** severe **7** callous **8** uncaring **9** inclement, malicious **10** ungenerous, ungracious **11** insensitive, thoughtless, unfavorable **12** uncharitable **13** unsympathetic

unknowable 6 arcane, hidden, mystic, occult, secret **7** cryptic **8** mystical, numinous **9** enigmatic, recondite **10** mysterious **11** inscrutable, ungraspable **12** impenetrable, unfathomable

unknowing 6 unwary **7** unaware **8** heedless, ignorant **9** oblivious, unmindful, unwitting **10** insensible, unfamiliar, uninformed **11** incognizant **12** unsuspecting

unknown 6 hidden, nobody, secret **7** obscure, strange **8** nameless **9** anonymous, incognito

unlawful 6 banned **7** bootleg, corrupt, crooked, illegal, illicit, immoral **8** criminal, outlawed, verboten, wrongful **9** forbidden, felonious, nefarious **10** contraband, flagitious, indictable, iniquitous, prohibited, proscribed, unlicensed **11** black-market **12** illegitimate, unauthorized

unlearned 5 naive **6** unread **7** unaware **8** ignorant, nescient, untaught **10** illiterate, uneducated, unlettered, unschooled **11** instinctive **13** unenlightened

unleash 4 free, vent **5** let go, loose, untie, visit, wreak **6** unbind **7** inflict, release **8** carry out, liberate **10** bring about

unless 3 but **4** save **6** except, saving **7** barring, but that, without **9** excepting, excluding

unlettered see **uneducated**

unlikable 9 obnoxious, offensive, repellent **10** unpleasant **11** displeasing, distasteful **12** disagreeable

unlike 5 mixed **6** varied **7** diverse, unequal, various **8** assorted **9** different, disparate, divergent **10** dissimilar **11** contrasting, distinctive, diversified **13** heterogeneous

unlikely 5 faint, unfit **6** remote, slight **7** distant, dubious **8** doubtful **10** farfetched, improbable, unsuitable **11** implausible, unpromising **12** questionable

unlimited 4 full, vast **5** total **6** untold **7** endless, immense **8** absolute, infinite, wide-open **9** boundless, countless, unbounded, universal **10** unconfined, unfettered **11** unqualified, untrammeled **12** immeasurable, interminable, unrestrained, unrestricted **13** comprehensive, unconditional, unconstrained

unlit 4 dark, inky **6** gloomy **7** shadowy **9** lightless, tenebrous

unload 4 drop, dump, junk **5** chuck, ditch, empty **6** debark, remove **7** confess, confide, deep-six, deliver, discard, divulge, lighten, relieve **8** disclose, disgorge, jettison **9** disburden, discharge, disembark, eighty-six, stevedore **11** disencumber

unloose 4 free, undo **5** let go, relax, untie **6** detach, unbind **7** break up, manumit, release, set free, slacken **8** liberate, uncouple, unfasten **9** disengage, extricate, untighten **10** disconnect

unlucky 6 jinxed **7** hapless, ominous **8** ill-fated, untoward **9** ill-boding **10** ill-starred **11** detrimental, inopportune, regrettable, star-crossed, unfavorable, unfortunate **12** inauspicious, unpropitious

unmanageable 4 wild **5** balky, bulky **6** unruly **7** awkward **8** contrary, cumbrous, perverse, stubborn, unwieldy **9** fractious **10** cumbersome, disorderly, headstrong, rebellious, refractory **11** intractable **12** obstreperous, recalcitrant, ungovernable **13** uncooperative, undisciplined

unmannered 4 rude **5** crude, rough **6** coarse, gauche **7** boorish, ill-bred, loutish **8** impolite **10** indecorous, ungracious **12** discourteous **13** disrespectful

unmarred 5 sound, whole **6** intact, unhurt **7** perfect **8** pristine, unflawed, unharmed **9**

undamaged, undefiled, unscathed, unstained 10 unimpaired 11 unblemished, untarnished

unmask 6 debunk, detect, expose, reveal, show up 7 deflate, uncover 8 disclose, discover, disprove 9 demystify

unmatched 3 odd 4 only 5 alone 6 unique 8 peerless, singular 9 unequaled, unrivaled 10 inimitable, unequalled, unrivalled 11 exceptional 12 incomparable, unparalleled

unmerciful 5 cruel, harsh 6 brutal 7 callous, extreme 8 inhumane, pitiless, ruthless, uncaring, vengeful 9 heartless, unfeeling, unsparing 10 relentless

unmindful 7 unaware 8 careless, heedless 9 forgetful, negligent, oblivious, unheeding, unwitting 10 abstracted, distracted, neglectful 11 inattentive

unmistakable 5 clear, frank, plain 6 patent 7 certain, decided, evident, express, obvious 8 apparent, definite, distinct, explicit, manifest, palpable 11 unambiguous, unequivocal

unmitigated 4 pure, rank 5 gross, sheer, utter 6 arrant 7 perfect, unmixed 8 absolute, clearcut, complete, outright 9 downright, out-and-out, unalloyed, undiluted 10 consummate, unmodified, unrelieved 11 straight-out, unqualified 13 thoroughgoing

unmixed 4 mere, neat, pure 5 plain, sheer, utter 6 simple 7 perfect, sincere 8 absolute, straight 9 unalloyed, unblended, undiluted, undivided 11 unmitigated, unqualified 13 unadulterated

unmoved 4 calm, cool, firm 5 aloof, stony 6 in situ, stolid 7 adamant, callous, stoical 8 obdurate 9 impassive, untouched 10 insensible, untroubled 11 unconcerned, unemotional, unimpressed 12 unresponsive

unnamed 5 incog 6 secret 7 obscure, unknown 9 anonymous, incognito 11 unspecified 12 unidentified

unnatural 7 uncanny 8 aberrant, abnormal 9 anomalous, contrived, irregular, synthetic 10 artificial, fabricated, factitious

unnecessary 6 excess 7 surplus 8 needless, optional, prodigal 9 avoidable, redundant 10 expendable, extraneous, gratuitous 11 dispensable, inessential, superfluous, uncalled-for, unessential 12 nonessential

unnerve 5 daunt, shake, throw, upset, worry 6 dismay, rattle 7 agitate, disturb, fluster, perturb, trouble, unhinge 8 bewilder, confound, distress 9 undermine 10 disconcert, discourage, dishearten, intimidate

unobstructed 4 open 5 clear 8 passable 9 unblocked, unimpeded 10 unhampered, unhindered 12 unrestricted

unobtrusive 5 quiet 6 modest 7 subdued 8 reserved, retiring, tasteful 10 restrained 13 inconspicuous

unoccupied 4 free, idle 5 empty 6 vacant 7 jobless, vacated 8 deserted 9 abandoned, available 10 employable, unemployed 11 uninhabited

unofficial 7 pirated, private, wildcat 8 informal 9 irregular 10 unapproved, unorthodox 12 unauthorized, unsanctioned

unorganized 7 aimless, chaotic, muddled 8 confused, inchoate, nebulous, rambling, unformed 9 amorphous, arbitrary, haphazard, shapeless, unplanned 10 disjointed, disordered, incoherent, incohesive 11 spontaneous

unoriginal 5 banal, stock 6 copied, old-hat 7 clichéd, humdrum, prosaic, sterile 8 borrowed, ordinary 9 hackneyed, imitative 10 derivative, uninspired 11 commonplace, plagiarized 12 conventional 13 unimaginative

unornamented 4 bare 5 plain, spare, stark 6 chaste, modest, severe, simple 7 austere 9 unadorned 11 unelaborate, ungarnished 13 unembellished, unembroidered

unorthodox 3 odd 5 kinky, novel, weird 6 far-out 7 offbeat, strange, unusual 8 abnormal, maverick 9 different, dissident, eccentric, heretical, irregular, sectarian 10 schismatic, unexpected 13 nonconformist

unorthodoxy 6 heresy, schism 7 dissent 8 variance 9 ingenuity, recusancy 10 contention, dissidence, innovation 13 nonconformism, nonconformity

unpaid 3 due 5 owing 6 mature 7 donated, overdue, payable, pro-bono 8 freewill, honorary, wageless 9 unsettled, voluntary, volunteer 10 delinquent, gratuitous, receivable 11 contributed, outstanding

unpalatable 8 unsavory 10 flavorless 11 distasteful 12 unappetizing

unparalleled 6 unique 8 peerless, singular 9 matchless, unequaled, unmatched, unrivaled 10 inimitable, unequalled, unrivalled 11 exceptional 12 incomparable

unplanned 5 fluky 6 chance, random 7 aimless 9 desultory, haphazard, hit-or-miss 10 accidental, unexpected, unforeseen, unintended 11 inadvertent 12 adventitious, coincidental, unconsidered 13 unintentional

unpleasant 4 sour 5 seamy 7 painful 8 annoying 9 offensive, troubling 10 disturbing, irritating 11 displeasing, distasteful, distressing 12 disagreeable 13 objectionable

unpolished 4 rude 5 crude, gruff, rough 6 crusty, vulgar 7 brusque, uncivil, uncouth 8 homespun **9** inelegant, roughhewn, unrefined **10** amateurish, uncultured, unfinished, ungracious **11** ill-mannered, uncivilized

unpredictable 4 iffy **5** dicey, fluky **6** chancy, fickle, random, touchy **7** erratic, mutable **8** unstable, variable, volatile **9** arbitrary, mercurial, uncertain, whimsical **10** capricious, changeable **13** unforeseeable

unprejudiced 4 fair, just **5** equal **8** balanced, unbiased **9** equitable, impartial, objective, unbigoted, uncolored **10** even-handed, fairminded, open-minded **11** nonpartisan **12** uninfluenced **13** disinterested, dispassionate

unpressed 7 rumpled, wrinkly **8** crinkled, puckered, wrinkled

unpretentious 5 frank, plain **6** candid, honest, modest, simple **7** genuine **8** ordinary **9** unadorned **10** forthright, unaffected, unassuming **11** plain-spoken

unprincipled 5 venal **7** corrupt, crooked, immoral **9** deceitful, dishonest, dissolute, mercenary, reprobate, unethical **10** inconstant, iniquitous, profligate, unfaithful **11** underhanded **12** unscrupulous

unproductive 4 vain **6** barren, futile **7** sterile, useless **8** bootless, depleted, feckless, impotent **9** fruitless, infertile **10** unavailing **11** ineffectual **12** hardscrabble

unprofitable 4 idle, vain **6** barren, futile **7** useless **8** bootless **9** fruitless **10** unavailing **11** ineffective **12** unproductive, unsuccessful

unprogressive 8 orthodox **9** illiberal **11** tradiional **12** conservative

unpropitious 4 grim **5** bleak **7** ominous, unlucky **9** ill-boding, ill-omened **10** foreboding **11** inopportune, threatening, unfavorable **12** discouraging

unprosperous 4 poor **5** needy **8** strapped **9** penurious **11** impecunious

unprotected 6 unsafe **7** exposed **8** helpless, insecure **9** unguarded **10** endangered, undefended, unshielded, vulnerable **11** defenseless, susceptible, unsheltered

unproved 7 untried **8** untested **10** postulated **11** conjectural, preliminary, provisional, speculative, theoretical **12** experimental, hypothetical

unpunctual 4 late **5** tardy **6** remiss **7** belated, delayed, overdue **10** behindhand, delinquent

unqualified 4 firm, rank **5** sheer, total, unfit, utter **7** express **8** absolute, explicit, unfitted **9** incapable, out-and-out, steadfast, unalloyed, undiluted, unskilled **10** ineligible, unequipped, unreserved, unsuitable **11** ill-equipped, incompetent, unmitigated **12**

wholehearted **13** unadulterated, unconditional

unquenchable 7 exigent **9** demanding, insatiate, insistent **10** insatiable **12** effervescent, unrestrained **13** irrepressible, unconstrained

unquestionable 4 real, sure, true **7** certain, genuine **8** absolute, bona fide **9** authentic, undoubted **10** sure-enough, undeniable **11** established, indubitable, self-evident, wellfounded **12** indisputable, well-grounded **13** authoritative, incontestable, unimpeachable

unquestioning 4 firm, sure **5** fixed **6** steady **7** abiding **8** enduring, gullible, resolute, trusting, unshaken **9** accepting, believing, credulous, steadfast **10** uncritical, unshakable, unwavering **11** unfaltering, unqualified **12** never-failing, unsuspecting

unravel 4 fray **5** break, solve **6** answer, decode, unknit, unwind **7** clear up, dope out, explain, resolve, unsnarl **8** decipher, dissolve, untangle **9** elucidate, extricate, figure out, interpret, puzzle out, translate **11** disentangle

unreadable 7 deadpan **9** illegible **10** pokerfaced **11** inscrutable **12** hieroglyphic **13** cacographical

unreal 4 fake **5** bogus, false **6** fabled **7** fictive **8** chimeric, fanciful, illusory, mythical **9** fantastic, fictional, imaginary, imitation **10** artificial, chimerical, fictitious, improbable, incredible **11** nonexistent **12** unbelievable
combining form: **5** pseud **6** pseudo

unrealistic 7 blue-sky, idyllic, utopian **8** fanciful, quixotic, romantic **9** distorted, idealized, overblown **10** farfetched, ivory-tower, overstated, starry-eyed, unworkable **11** exaggerated, extravagant, impractical, sensational

unreasonable 5 undue **6** absurd **7** invalid **9** arbitrary, excessive, illogical, senseless **10** exorbitant, fallacious, headstrong, immoderate, inordinate, irrational, peremptory, ridiculous **11** extravagant, incongruous, uncalled-for, unwarranted **12** preposterous **13** unjustifiable

unreasoned 7 invalid, unsound **9** deceptive, illogical, sophistic, unfounded **10** fallacious, ill-founded, irrational, misleading, ungrounded **11** nonrational

unrefined 3 raw **4** rude **5** crass, crude, rough, tacky **6** coarse, earthy, impure, vulgar **7** natural, uncouth **9** graceless, inelegant, maladroit, roughhewn **10** uncultured, unpolished **11** ill-mannered, uncivilized, unprocessed **12** uncultivated

unreflective 6 casual **7** offhand **8** careless, feckless, heedless, mindless **9** imprudent, impulsive, oblivious, unheeding **10** indiscreet, nonchalant, unthinking **11** inadvertent, perfunctory, thoughtless **13** ill-considered

unrehearsed 5 ad-lib **7** offhand **8** ad-libbed, informal **9** extempore, impromptu, unstudied **10** improvised, off-the-cuff, unprepared **11** extemporary, spontaneous **12** extemporized

unrelated 8 discrete, separate **9** different, disparate **10** dissimilar, extraneous, irrelevant **11** independent

unrelenting 3 set **4** grim **5** stern **7** adamant, endless **8** constant, resolute, ruthless, tireless **9** ceaseless, continual, hard-nosed, incessant, tenacious, unbending, unsparing **10** continuous, determined, implacable, inexorable, inflexible, persistent, unflagging, unshakable, unwavering, unyielding **12** unappeasable

unreliable 6 fickle, shifty, tricky, unsafe **7** dubious **8** fallible, slippery, two-faced **9** deceitful, deceptive, faithless, trustless, uncertain **10** capricious, fly-by-night, inaccurate, inconstant, perfidious, unfaithful **11** vacillating **12** falsehearted, questionable, unconvincing, undependable **13** irresponsible, unpredictable, untrustworthy

unremarkable 4 so-so **5** plain, usual **6** common, decent, normal **7** average, mundane, prosaic, routine **8** adequate, everyday, familiar, habitual, mediocre, ordinary, workaday **9** customary, quotidian **11** commonplace, nondescript **12** run-of-the-mill **13** unexceptional

unremitting 7 abiding, chronic, endless, lasting, nonstop, ongoing **8** constant, enduring, unending **9** ceaseless, continual, incessant, perennial, perpetual, sustained, unceasing **10** continuous, persistent, persisting, relentless **12** interminable **13** uninterrupted

unrepentant 10 impenitent **11** remorseless **12** unregenerate

unrepresentative 7 deviant, unusual **8** aberrant, abnormal, atypical **9** anomalous, divergent, eccentric, irregular, untypical **11** exceptional, heteroclite **13** nonconforming

unreserved 4 open **5** frank, plain **6** candid **8** effusive, explicit, outgoing, outright **9** expansive, talkative **10** definitive **11** forthcoming, openhearted, unconcealed, undisguised, unqualified **13** demonstrative, unconstrained

unresolved 4 moot **7** pending **8** hesitant, wavering **9** faltering, tentative, uncertain, undecided, unsettled **10** ambivalent,

hesitating, indecisive, irresolute, unanswered **11** vacillating

unrespectable 3 low **5** shady **6** shabby, shoddy **8** shameful, unworthy **10** inglorious **11** disgraceful, ignominious **12** dishonorable, disreputable **13** discreditable

unresponsive 4 cold **5** aloof, stoic **6** frigid, remote, stolid **7** distant, passive **8** detached, reserved **9** inhibited, withdrawn **10** forbidding, insentient **11** insensitive, passionless, unemotional **12** uninterested **13** insusceptible, unsusceptible

unrest 6 strife, tumult **7** anarchy, anxiety, ferment, tension, turmoil **8** disorder, disquiet, distress, edginess, upheaval **9** agitation, commotion, confusion **10** inquietude, turbulence, uneasiness **11** disquietude, disturbance, instability **12** perturbation **13** Sturm und Drang

unrestrained 6 wanton **7** rampant **8** uncurbed **9** audacious, excessive, unbridled **10** immoderate, inordinate, ungoverned, unhampered **11** extravagant, intemperate, spontaneous, uninhibited, untrammeled **12** uncontrolled **13** demonstrative, irrepressible, overindulgent

unrestricted 4 free, full, open **9** boundless, extensive, unlimited **10** accessible, unconfined, unfettered, unhampered **11** far-reaching, unqualified, wide-ranging **12** unobstructed **13** unconditional

unripe 3 raw **5** green, young **6** callow, jejune **7** untried **8** emergent, immature, juvenile, unformed, youthful **9** unfledged, untrained **10** unprepared, unseasoned **11** undeveloped **13** inexperienced

unrivaled 4 only, sole **5** alone **6** unique **7** leading, stellar, supreme **8** champion, foremost, greatest, peerless **9** matchless, paramount, principal, unequaled, unmatched **10** inimitable, preeminent, unequalled **11** outstanding, predominant **12** incomparable, unparalleled

unroll 6 expose, extend, reveal, unfurl, unwind **7** exhibit, open out **8** disclose **9** spread out

unromantic 5 sober **8** sensible **9** practical, pragmatic, realistic **10** hard-boiled, hardheaded **11** down-to-earth, level-headed, utilitarian **12** businesslike, matter-of-fact **13** unsentimental

unruffled 4 calm, cool **6** poised, placid, serene, smooth **7** equable, unmoved **8** composed, tranquil **9** collected, unexcited **10** nonchalant, untroubled **11** unconcerned, undisturbed, unflappable **13** imperturbable, self-possessed

unruly 4 wild **5** rowdy **7** froward, raucous, wayward, willful **8** contrary, perverse, untoward **9** fractious, obstinate, turbulent **10** boisterous, disorderly, headstrong, ill-behaved, rebellious, refractory, tumultuous **11** disobedient, intractable **12** contumacious, incorrigible, obstreperous, rambunctious, recalcitrant, ungovernable, unmanageable **13** undisciplined

unsafe 5 risky, shaky **6** chancy **7** erratic, harmful, parlous, rickety, tottery, unsound **8** insecure, perilous, slippery, unstable **9** dangerous, hazardous, uncertain **10** precarious, ramshackle, unreliable, vulnerable **11** threatening, treacherous **12** undependable

unsaid 5 known, tacit **6** silent **7** assumed, implied **8** accepted, implicit, indirect, inferred, presumed, unspoken, unstated, wordless **9** customary, unuttered **10** insinuated, undeclared, understood **11** traditional, unexpressed

unsatisfactory 3 bum **4** lame **8** mediocre **9** defective, deficient **10** inadequate **11** displeasing, substandard **12** unacceptable **13** disappointing

unsavory 4 rank **5** gross, shady **7** insipid **9** repugnant, repulsive, sickening, tasteless **11** distasteful, ill-flavored **12** disagreeable, unappetizing

unsay 4 lift, void **6** abjure, cancel, disown, recall, recant, revoke **7** nullify, rescind, retract, reverse, suspend **8** abnegate, abrogate, disclaim, forswear, renounce, take back, withdraw **11** countermand

unscathed 4 safe **5** sound, whole **6** intact, unhurt **8** unharmed **9** uninjured, unscarred, untouched **11** unscratched

unscented 8 odor-free, odorless

unschooled 5 naive **7** artless, natural, vacuous **8** ignorant **9** ingenuous, unstudied **10** illiterate, unaffected, uneducated, unlettered **11** empty-headed

unscramble 5 solve, untie **6** decode, unwind **7** clarify, clear up, resolve, restore, sort out, unravel, untwine **8** decipher, untangle **9** extricate, figure out **11** disentangle **12** disembarrass

unscrupulous 5 shady, venal **7** corrupt, crooked, knavish **8** scheming, wrongful **9** deceitful, dishonest, mercenary, shameless, underhand, unethical **11** underhanded **12** exploitative, unprincipled

unseasonable 8 ill-timed, untimely **12** inconvenient

unseasoned 3 raw **4** flat **5** bland, fresh, green, young **6** callow **7** untried **8** immature **9** credulous, tasteless, unfledged, untrained **10** flavorless **11** unpracticed **13** inexperienced

unseat 3 axe, can **4** boot, buck, fire, oust, sack **5** eject, pitch, purge, throw **6** depose, recall, remove **7** buck off, dismiss, unhorse **8** dethrone, dislodge, displace **9** ostracize

unseemliness 8 solecism **9** barbarism, gaucherie, immodesty, impudence, indecency, vulgarity **10** imprudence, incivility, indelicacy **11** impropriety **12** indiscretion

unseemly 8 improper, untoward **9** inelegant, unrefined **10** indecorous, indelicate, malapropos, unbecoming, unsuitable **11** unbefitting **13** inappropriate

unseen 6 hidden **9** concealed, invisible, unnoticed **10** overlooked, unobserved **11** unsuspected

unsentimental see **unromantic**

unserviceable 7 useless **10** inoperable, unfeasible, unworkable **11** impractical, unrealistic **13** impracticable, nonfunctional

unsettle 3 vex **4** faze **5** spook, upset **6** bother, flurry, jumble, rattle, ruffle **7** agitate, disturb, fluster, perturb, trouble, unhinge, unnerve **8** bewilder, confound, disarray, disorder, disquiet **9** discomfit **10** discompose, disconcert

unsettled 4 open **5** fluid, owing, shaky **6** mobile, queasy, shaken, uneasy, unpaid **7** anxious, dubious, mutable, overdue, payable, pending, restive **8** agitated, bothered, doubtful, frontier, restless, troubled, unstable, unsteady, variable **9** disturbed, uncertain, undecided **10** changeable, unbalanced, unresolved **11** outstanding, problematic **12** undetermined

unsex 3 fix **4** geld, spay **5** alter **6** change, neuter **8** castrate **9** sterilize **10** emasculate

unshackle 4 free **5** loose **6** loosen, unbind **7** manumit, release, unchain **8** liberate, unfetter **10** emancipate

unshakable 4 firm, sure **5** fixed **6** stable, steady **7** abiding, adamant, settled, staunch **8** resolute **9** steadfast, tenacious **10** determined, persistent, unwavering, unyielding **11** unfaltering **12** never-failing

unshaped 5 vague **7** nascent **8** formless, inchoate, unformed **9** amorphous, embryonic **10** incoherent **11** preliminary

unshared 4 sole **6** single, unique **7** private **8** singular **9** exclusive, undivided **10** individual **11** distinctive

unshod 8 barefoot, shoeless **9** discalced **10** barefooted

unsightly 4 ugly **5** gross **6** grisly **7** hideous **9** repulsive **10** ill-favored **12** unattractive

unskillful 5 inept **6** clumsy, gauche **7** awkward, unhandy **8** bumbling, bungling, inexpert **9** ham-handed, incapable, maladroit, stumbling, untrained

unsnarl see **untangle**

unsociable 3 shy **4** cool **5** aloof, timid **6** offish, remote, shut-in **7** distant **8** reserved, secluded, solitary **9** diffident, reclusive, withdrawn **10** unfriendly **11** introverted, standoffish **12** inaccessible, unneighborly

unsoiled 5 clean **8** spotless **9** unspotted, unstained, unsullied, untainted **10** immaculate **11** unblemished, untarnished

unsophisticated 5 corny, green, naive **6** callow, folksy, rustic, simple **7** artless, natural, sincere, uncouth **8** gullible, innocent **9** childlike, ingenuous, unrefined, unworldly

unsorted 5 mixed **6** divers, motley, sundry, varied **7** diverse, jumbled, mingled **9** disparate, scrambled, unmatched, unrefined **10** variegated **11** diversified **12** multifarious **13** heterogeneous, miscellaneous

unsought 7 unasked, willing **8** unbidden, unwanted **9** undesired, uninvited, unwelcome, voluntary **10** gratuitous **11** spontaneous, unsolicited

unsound 3 mad **4** weak **5** frail, shaky, wrong **6** faulty, flawed, flimsy, infirm, insane, sickly, untrue **7** damaged, fragile, invalid **8** decrepit, specious **9** defective, erroneous, imperfect, incorrect, unhealthy **13** insubstantial

unsparing 5 ample, harsh, stern, tough **6** lavish, severe, strict **7** copious, liberal, onerous, profuse **8** abundant, exacting, generous, prolific, rigorous, ruthless **9** bounteous, bountiful, demanding, plenteous **10** freehanded, munificent, openhanded, unmerciful **11** magnanimous

unspeakable 4 dire, evil **5** awful **6** grisly **7** beastly, ghastly, hateful, heinous, hideous **8** dreadful, ghoulish, gruesome, horrific, shocking **9** appalling, atrocious, execrable, frightful, loathsome, monstrous, obnoxious, repugnant, repulsive, revolting **10** abominable, detestable, disgusting, horrendous, outrageous, scandalous **11** unutterable **13** inexpressible

unspoiled 5 ideal **6** intact, virgin **7** halcyon, idyllic, perfect, untamed **8** arcadian, pastoral, pristine, virginal **9** idealized, undefiled, untouched **10** unimpaired **11** unblemished, uncorrupted

unspoken 4 mute **5** tacit **6** hinted, silent, unsaid **7** assumed, implied **8** implicit, inferred, presumed, unstated, wordless **9** intimated, suggested, unuttered **10** undeclared, understood **11** unexpressed

unstable 5 fluid, shaky **6** fickle, shifty, tricky, wobbly **7** dubious, rickety, suspect **8** insecure, slippery, unsteady, variable, volatile, wavering **9** ambiguous, changeful, fluctuant, irregular, mercurial, teetering, uncertain, unsettled **10** capricious, inconstant, precarious **11** vacillating **13** temperamental, unpredictable

unstated 5 tacit **6** latent, unsaid **7** assumed, implied **8** implicit **10** understood

unsteady 5 rocky, shaky, tippy **6** uneven, wobbly **7** erratic, mutable, rickety, varying **8** shifting, unstable, variable **9** changeful, irregular, tottering **10** changeable, inconstant *British:* **5** wonky

unstudied 5 naive **6** casual **7** artless, natural, offhand **8** careless, informal, unforced, unversed **9** extempore, guileless, impromptu, ingenuous, makeshift, unplanned **10** improvised, nonchalant, unaffected, unpolished **11** extemporary, spontaneous, unrehearsed **13** improvisatory

unstylish 4 drab, dull **5** dated, dowdy, fusty, passé, ratty, tacky **6** démodé, frumpy, oldhat, shabby, stodgy **7** vintage **8** outdated, outmoded **9** inelegant, moth-eaten, out-of-date **10** antiquated, oldfangled **12** old-fashioned **13** unfashionable

unsubstantial 4 thin **5** frail, shaky **6** feeble, flimsy, infirm **7** fragile, shadowy, tenuous **8** ethereal, illusory **9** dreamlike, imaginary **10** immaterial, impalpable, intangible **11** implausible, incorporeal, nonmaterial, nonphysical

unsuitable 5 inapt, undue, unfit **7** awkward, jarring **8** ill-timed, improper, unfitted, unseemly, untimely **9** ill-suited **10** ill-adapted, inadequate, inapposite, malapropos, mismatched, unbecoming **11** inadvisable, inopportune, unbefitting, unqualified **12** incompatible, infelicitous, unacceptable, unseasonable **13** inappropriate

unsullied 4 pure **5** clean **6** chaste **8** flawless, spotless, unsoiled **9** blameless, exemplary, guiltless, stainless, taintless, undefiled **10** immaculate **11** unblemished, untarnished

unsure 5 dicey, shaky **6** wobbly **7** dubious, unclear **8** doubtful, insecure, unstable, wavering **9** fluctuant, skeptical, uncertain, undecided **10** ambivalent, indecisive, irresolute, unreliable **11** unconvinced, vacillating **12** questionable, undependable **13** untrustworthy

unsurpassable 7 supreme **8** ultimate **9** matchless **10** consummate, preeminent **12** transcendent

unsusceptible 6 immune, inured **8** hardened

9 impassive, resistant **10** impervious **11** insensitive **12** invulnerable, unresponsive

unsuspecting 5 naive **6** unwary **8** gullible, trustful, trusting **9** confiding, credulous, imprudent **10** incautious

unswerving see **unfaltering**

unsympathetic 4 cold, cool **5** chill, stony **6** averse **7** callous, unmoved **8** detached **9** apathetic, unfeeling, unpitying **10** hard-boiled **11** coldhearted, hardhearted, indifferent, insensitive, unconcerned **12** stonyhearted **13** disinterested

untactful 4 flip, rash, rude **5** brash **6** brazen **8** flippant, insolent **9** audacious, impolitic, imprudent, maladroit **10** indiscreet **11** impertinent, thoughtless **12** presumptuous, undiplomatic

untamed 4 wild **5** brute, feral **6** carnal, fierce, savage **7** bestial, brutish **8** barbaric **9** primitive **11** uncivilized

untangle 5 solve **7** clear up, explain, resolve, unravel, unsnarl, untwine, untwist **9** elucidate, extricate, interpret **10** disembroil, disentwine, straighten, unscramble **11** disencumber **12** disembarrass

untaught 5 naive **7** natural **8** ignorant, nescient **9** intuitive, untrained, untutored **10** uneducated, unlettered, unschooled **11** empty-headed, instinctual, spontaneous

untempered 6 wanton **7** extreme **9** excessive **10** gratuitous, immoderate, inordinate **11** extravagant **12** unrestrained

untenable 5 wrong **6** faulty, flimsy **10** inadequate **12** indefensible

untended 5 seedy **7** rickety, run-down **8** decrepit, derelict, deserted, forsaken, tattered **9** neglected **10** ramshackle, tumbledown, uncared-for **11** dilapidated

Unter den ____ 6 Linden

untested 6 intact, unused **7** untried **8** unproved, unproven **11** unpracticed

unthinkable 10 impossible, incredible, outlandish **12** preposterous, unimaginable **13** extraordinary, inconceivable, unprecedented

unthinking 8 careless, feckless, habitual, heedless, knee-jerk **9** automatic, reflexive, unheeding, unmindful **10** distracted, unintended **11** inattentive, inadvertent, instinctive, instinctual, involuntary, perfunctory, spontaneous, thoughtless **12** unreflective

unthrifty 6 lavish, wanton **7** ruinous **8** prodigal, wasteful **9** imprudent **10** profligate **11** extravagant, improvident **12** uneconomical

untidy 5 messy **6** sloppy **7** chaotic, jumbled, unkempt **8** confused, littered, slapdash, slipshod, slovenly **9** cluttered **10** dishev-

eled, disordered, disorderly, topsy-turvy **11** disarranged, dishevelled **12** disorganized

untie 5 let go **6** loosen, unbind, unknot, unlace, unlash **7** release, resolve, set free **8** unstring **9** extricate **11** disencumber, disentangle **12** disembarrass

until 4 up to **6** before **7** prior to **11** in advance of

untimely 5 early, undue **9** premature **10** malapropos **11** ill-seasoned, inopportune **12** unseasonable

untiring 7 devoted, patient **8** diligent, enduring **9** assiduous, ceaseless, dedicated, energetic, unceasing **10** determined, persistent, unflagging, unwavering, unwearying **11** persevering, unfaltering **13** indefatigable, inexhaustible

untold 4 huge, vast **7** immense **8** enormous, gigantic **9** countless **10** prodigious **11** innumerable, uncountable **12** incalculable **13** indescribable

untouchable 5 dalit, leper **6** pariah **7** harijan, outcast **8** outcaste

Untouchables leader 4 Ness (Eliot) **5** Stack (Robert) **7** Costner (Kevin)

untouched 4 pure **5** sound, whole **6** intact, virgin **7** unmoved **8** flawless, pristine, unharmed, unmarred, untapped, virginal **9** undamaged, unspoiled **10** unaffected **11** unblemished, unconcerned, unimpressed

untoward 7 adverse, awkward, froward, unlucky **8** ill-fated, improper, indecent, luckless, unseemly **9** unfitting, vexatious **10** ill-starred, indecorous, indelicate, unbecoming **11** intractable, unfortunate **12** inconvenient, recalcitrant, ungovernable, unmanageable, unpropitious

untrained see **unskilled**

untrammeled 8 uncurbed **9** unimpeded **10** unconfined, unfettered, ungoverned, unhampered **11** uninhibited **12** unobstructed, unrestrained, unrestricted

untried 3 raw **5** fresh, green **6** callow, rookie **8** unproved, untested **10** innovative, pioneering, unseasoned **11** unpracticed **13** inexperienced, unprecedented

untroubled 4 calm **5** still **6** blithe, placid, serene **7** halcyon **8** carefree, composed, peaceful, tranquil **9** easygoing, unruffled **10** insouciant, nonchalant **11** unconcerned, unperturbed **12** lighthearted

untrue 4 fake **5** false, wrong **8** disloyal, specious **9** erroneous, faithless, incorrect **10** fictitious, inaccurate, unfaithful *combining form:* **5** pseud **6** pseudo

untrustworthy 5 shady **6** shifty, unsafe, unsure **7** devious, dubious **8** disloyal, slippery, two-faced 9 deceptive, negligent, two-timing 10 fly-by-night, unreliable 11 duplicitous 12 questionable, undependable 13 double-dealing, irresponsible

untruth 3 fib, lie 4 sham 5 error 6 canard, deceit 7 blarney, fallacy, falsity, fiction, hogwash 9 deception, duplicity, falsehood, falseness, hypocrisy, mendacity 11 fabrication, insincerity 12 misstatement 13 prevarication

untruthful 4 sham 5 bogus, false, lying, phony 7 knavish 8 specious 9 deceitful, dishonest, erroneous, incorrect 10 fictitious, inaccurate, mendacious

untutored see **unschooled**

unusable 7 outworn, useless 8 obsolete 9 worthless 10 inoperable, unavailing, unworkable 11 impractical, unrealistic 12 inapplicable 13 nonfunctional

unused 3 new 4 idle 5 fresh 6 excess 7 dormant, surplus 8 leftover, residual 9 untouched

unusual 3 odd 4 rare 5 outré 6 quaint, unique 7 bizarre, curious, special, strange 8 aberrant, abnormal, peculiar, singular, uncommon, atypical, unwonted 9 anomalous, different, eccentric, irregular 11 exceptional 13 extraordinary

unusually 4 very 5 extra 6 highly, rarely, seldom 8 markedly 9 curiously, extremely, strangely 10 abnormally, especially, peculiarly, remarkably, strikingly, uncommonly 11 exceedingly 12 infrequently, particularly

unutterable 5 taboo 7 awesome 9 ineffable 11 unspeakable 13 indescribable, inexpressible

unvaried 4 like, same 5 alike 7 uniform 9 identical 10 consistent, unchanging 11 undeviating

unvarnished see **undisguised**

unvarying see **unchanging**

unveil see **uncover**

unversed 3 raw 5 green 6 callow 7 untried 8 inexpert 9 unfledged 10 unfamiliar, unseasoned 11 uninitiated, unpracticed 13 inexperienced

unwanted see **unwelcome**

unwarranted 5 undue 8 baseless 9 misguided, unfounded 10 gratuitous, groundless, immoderate, unprovoked 11 extravagant, inexcusable, injudicious, uncalled-for, unjustified 12 unreasonable 13 insupportable, unjustifiable, unsupportable

unwary 5 brash, hasty 8 careless, gullible, heedless, reckless 9 credulous, impetuous, imprudent, unguarded 10 ill-advised, incautious, indiscreet 11 thoughtless 12 unsuspecting

unwavering see **unfaltering**

unwelcome 7 unasked 8 unsought, unwanted 9 undesired, uninvited 11 undesirable 12 unacceptable 13 objectionable

unwell 3 ill 4 sick 5 frail, shaky 6 ailing, feeble, infirm, offish, peaked, queasy, sickly, wobbly 8 diseased, stricken 9 afflicted, enfeebled, unhealthy 10 indisposed 11 debilitated

unwholesome 4 foul 5 toxic 6 sickly 7 adverse, corrupt, harmful, immoral, noisome, noxious, unsound 8 diseased 9 injurious, loathsome, offensive, unhealthy 10 pernicious, subversive 11 deleterious, detrimental, unhealthful 12 insalubrious

unwieldy 5 bulky 7 awkward, massive 8 cumbrous 9 ponderous 10 burdensome, cumbersome 12 unmanageable

unwilling 5 loath 6 averse 8 grudging, hesitant 9 obstinate, reluctant 10 indisposed 11 disinclined

unwind 4 rest, undo 5 let go, relax 6 loosen, unbend, uncoil, unfold, unreel, unroll 7 ease off, slacken, unravel 8 calm down, kick back, loosen up

unwise 4 rash 5 silly 6 stupid 7 asinine, fatuous, foolish, idiotic, witless 8 reckless 9 brainless, foolhardy, ill-judged, imbecilic, impolitic, imprudent, ludicrous, misguided, senseless 10 ill-advised, indiscreet, ridiculous 11 impractical, injudicious, thoughtless, undesirable, unfortunate 13 unintelligent

unwitting 6 chance 7 unaware 8 ignorant, innocent 9 haphazard, oblivious, unknowing, unmindful, unplanned 10 unfamiliar, uninformed, unintended 11 inadvertent 12 unacquainted

unwonted 4 rare 6 signal, unique 7 notable, unusual 8 singular, uncommon 10 remarkable, unexpected 11 exceptional 12 unaccustomed 13 extraordinary

unworkable 7 useless 8 quixotic 9 half-baked 10 impossible, infeasible, inoperable, unfeasible 11 impractical, unrealistic 12 inapplicable 13 impracticable, nonfunctional

unworldly 5 naive 6 astral, dreamy, simple 7 artless, natural 8 ethereal, innocent, trusting 9 celestial, ingenuous, spiritual, unearthly, visionary 11 impractical 13 inexperienced

unworthy 6 no-good 7 ignoble 8 shameful, unseemly 9 no-account, unmerited, worthless 10 unbecoming 11 disgraceful, inexcusable, undeserving

unwrap see **uncover**

unwritten 4 oral 5 blank, tacit 6 latent, spoken, verbal 7 assumed 8 accepted, implicit

10 understood 11 traditional, word-of-mouth 12 conventional

unyielding 4 firm, grim, hard, iron 5 fixed, rigid, stern, stiff, stony, tough 6 dogged, mulish 7 adamant 8 hard-core, obdurate, stubborn 9 hard-nosed, immovable, insistent, obstinate, pigheaded, steadfast, unbending 10 determined, headstrong, implacable, inexorable, inflexible, persistent, relentless, unshakable 11 intractable, unrelenting 12 pertinacious, single-minded, unappeasable

up 4 hike, jump, lift, rise 5 above, ahead, arise, astir, boost, built, mount, raise, risen 6 ascend, arisen, lifted, versed 7 abreast, promote 8 familiar, increase, informed, positive 9 au courant, northward 10 acquainted, conversant *prefix:* 3 ana, sur

up-and-coming 7 go-ahead, hot-shot 8 aspiring 9 promising 11 presumptive, prospective 12 enterprising

upbeat 4 rosy 5 arsis 6 cheery 7 buoyant, hopeful 8 cheerful, positive, sanguine 9 confidant, expectant, promising 10 heartening, optimistic 12 Pollyannaish

upbraid 3 rap 4 lash, rate 5 chide, scold 6 berate, rail at, rebuke, revile, scorch 7 bawl out, censure, chasten, chew out, reprove, scourge, tell off 8 admonish, chastise, reproach 9 castigate, criticize, dress down, reprimand 10 tongue-lash, vituperate

upbringing 7 nurture, rearing 8 training 9 schooling

upchuck 4 barf, hurl, puke, spew, toss 5 heave, retch, vomit 6 spit up 7 bring up, throw up 8 disgorge 11 regurgitate

upcoming 7 looming, nearing, pending 8 expected, foreseen, imminent 9 advancing, impending, onrushing 11 anticipated, approaching, forthcoming, prospective

up-country 4 bush 6 inland, sticks, upland 7 outback 8 backland, frontier, interior, outlying, woodland 9 backwater, backwoods, boondocks 10 hinterland, timberland

update 5 amend, brief, renew 6 inform, revamp, revise, revive 7 apprise, enhance, improve, refresh, restore, rundown, upgrade 8 renovate 9 modernize, refurbish 10 rejuvenate

Updike, John *character:* 6 Rabbit (Angstrom) *novel:* 7 Centaur (The), Couples 9 Rabbit Run 11 Rabbit Redux 12 Rabbit at Rest, Rabbit Is Rich 17 Witches of Eastwick (The)

upend 4 beat, best, drub, flip, lick, skin, trim, whip 5 cream, crush, upset 6 invert, subdue, thrash, topple, unseat, wallop 7 capsize, clobber, conquer, overrun, shellac, trounce 8 dethrone, lambaste, overcome, overturn, vanquish 9 overpower, overwhelm, subjugate

upgrade 4 hike, rise 5 boost, raise 6 prefer 7 advance, elevate, enhance, improve, promote 8 increase 9 promotion 10 betterment 11 advancement, improvement 12 breakthrough

upheaval 6 clamor, outcry, tumult, upturn 7 ferment, turmoil 8 churning, disaster, disorder 9 cataclysm, commotion 10 alteration, convulsion, disruption 11 catastrophe

uphill 4 hard 6 rising, rugged, taxing 7 arduous, labored, operose, tedious 8 climbing, grueling, toilsome 9 ascending, difficult, effortful, gruelling, laborious, punishing, strenuous, wearisome

uphold 3 aid 4 back, help, lift, prop 5 brace, carry, hoist, raise 6 assist, back up, bear up, buoy up, defend, second 7 bolster, elevate, justify, shore up, support, sustain 8 advocate, backstop, buttress, champion, maintain, side with 9 vindicate

upkeep 4 cost 7 expense 8 overhead 11 expenditure, maintenance

upland 4 mesa 5 table 7 plateau

uplift 4 buoy 5 cheer, edify, hoist, raise 6 take up 7 animate, elevate, enliven, gladden, hearten 8 brighten, embolden, inspirit 9 encourage 10 exhilarate, strengthen

upon 4 atop *prefix:* 3 epi

upper class 4 rank 5 elite 6 gentry 7 peerage, quality, society, who's who 8 affluent, nobility, noblesse, well-to-do 9 blue blood, gentility, haut monde 10 patricians, patriciate 11 aristocracy 13 carriage trade, Establishment

upper hand 4 edge, sway 5 leg up 7 control, mastery 8 leverage 9 advantage, dominance 10 ascendancy 11 superiority 12 predominance

uppermost 3 top 6 apical 7 highest 8 loftiest

uppity 4 smug 5 aloof, brash 6 lordly, sniffy, snippy, snooty, snotty 7 forward, haughty, pompous 8 arrogant, cavalier 9 conceited, egotistic, imperious, know-it-all, presuming 10 disdainful, high-handed 11 overweening, pretentious 12 contemptuous, presumptuous, supercilious 13 self-asserting, self-assertive, self-important

upright 4 fair, good, just, pure, true 5 erect, moral, noble, piano 6 honest, raised 7 correct, ethical 8 elevated, goalpost, standing, vertical, virtuous 9 equitable, exemplary, honorable, impartial 10 principled, scrupulous 13 conscientious, perpendicular

uprightness 5 honor **6** repute, virtue **7** honesty, probity **8** morality, nobility **9** character, integrity, rectitude **13** righteousness

uprising 4 riot **6** mutiny, revolt **8** upheaval **9** rebellion **10** insurgence, revolution **12** insurrection

uproar 3 din, row **4** coil, fuss, to-do, riot **5** babel, brawl, broil, chaos, furor, hoo-ha, melee, whirl **6** bedlam, clamor, fracas, furore, hassle, hoo-hah, hubbub, mayhem, pother, racket, ruckus, rumpus, shindy, tumult **7** shindig, turmoil **8** brouhaha, disorder, foofaraw **9** commotion, confusion **10** hullabaloo, hurly-burly, turbulence **11** pandemonium

uproarious 5 noisy, rowdy **7** comical, rackety, raucous, riotous **8** brawling, clattery, mirthful, strident **9** clamorous, hilarious **10** clangorous, hysterical, resounding, rollicking, tumultuous **12** obstreperous **13** side-splitting

uproot 4 grub, move, weed **8** displace, overturn, supplant **9** eradicate, extirpate, overthrow, supersede **10** annihilate, transplant **11** exterminate

upset 3 ail, ill, irk, vex **4** rile, roil **5** annoy, evert, worry **6** bother, defeat, dismay, invert, jumble, muddle, topple, tumble **7** afflict, agitate, capsize, disturb, fluster, invalid, jittery, jumbled, muddled, perturb, rattled, reverse, shook up, tip over, toppled, trouble, unnerve, worried **8** agitated, bewilder, bothered, confound, confused, disarray, dismayed, disorder, distress, overturn, troubled, turn over, unnerved **9** afflicted, confusion, disturbed, flustered, knock over, overthrow, perturbed **10** bewildered, confounded, disconcert, disordered, distracted, distressed, indisposed, invalidate, overthrown, overturned, tipped over **11** overwrought **12** apprehensive, disconcerted

upshot 5 issue **6** burden, climax, effect, ending, finish, result **7** outcome, purport **9** substance **10** conclusion, denouement **11** consequence, culmination, termination **12** significance

upside-down 7 chaotic, haywire, jumbled **8** backward, confused, inverted, pell-mell, reversed **10** disordered, overturned, topsy-turvy **13** helter-skelter

upstanding see **upright**

upstart 5 comer **7** parvenu **8** outsider **9** arriviste, pretender **12** nouveau riche **13** social climber

upsurge 4 gain, jump, rise, rush, tide, wave **5** boost, flood, spurt, swell **6** deluge, growth **7** advance **8** increase

uptight 4 edgy **5** riled, tense **6** uneasy **7** anxious, nervous, restive, worried **8** stressed **10** high-strung

up to 4 till **5** until **6** before **11** in advance of

up-to-date 6 modern, modish, timely, trendy, with-it **7** abreast, à la mode, current, stylish **8** advanced, brand-new, contempo **9** au courant, plugged-in **10** avant-garde **11** cutting-edge, fashionable **12** contemporary **13** state-of-the-art

upturn 4 jump, rise **6** growth **8** increase **11** improvement

Urania see **Muse**

Uranus 6 planet *moon:* **5** Ariel **6** Oberon **7** Titania *mother, wife:* **4** Gaea *offspring:* **6** Titans **8** Cyclopes *overthrower, son:* **6** Cronus

urban 9 municipal **12** metropolitan

urbane 5 suave **6** poised, smooth **7** elegant, genteel, politic, refined **8** cultured, debonair, gracious, polished **9** civilized, distingué **10** cultivated, diplomatic **12** cosmopolitan **13** sophisticated

urbanize 6 citify

urchin 3 imp **4** brat **5** child, gamin, scamp **10** ragamuffin

Urdur see **Norn**

urge 3 egg, sic, yen **4** coax, goad, itch, lust, prod, push, spur, wish **5** drive, egg on, impel, press, prick, set on, tar on **6** adjure, cajole, compel, demand, desire, exhort, incite, induce, needle, prompt, propel **7** beseech, conjure, craving, entreat, implore, impulse, inspire, longing, passion, promote, propose, provoke, solicit, wheedle **8** advocate, appetite, blandish, pressure, yearning **9** encourage, instigate, stimulate **12** high-pressure

urgency 5 haste **6** duress, stress **8** exigence, exigency, pressure **9** necessity **10** compulsion, insistence

urgent 5 vital **6** crying **7** burning, clamant, crucial, driving, exigent, instant, present **8** critical, pressing **9** clamorous, demanding, immediate, impelling, insistent, momentous **10** compelling, imperative **11** importunate

Uriel 9 archangel

Uris novel 3 Haj (The) **5** QB VII **6** Exodus **7** Trinity **9** Battle Cry, Mitla Pass **10** Angry Hills (The), Redemption

urn 4 vase **6** vessel **7** samovar *Greek:* **7** amphora

Ursa Major 9 Great Bear **11** Great Dipper

Ursa Minor 10 Little Bear **12** Little Dipper *star:* **7** Polaris **8** polestar **9** North Star

Uruguay *capital:* **10** Montevideo *language:* **7** Spanish *monetary unit:* **4** peso *neighbor:* **6**

Brazil **9** Argentina *river:* **7** La Plata **8** Río Negro

usable 6 liquid **7** running, working **9** adaptable, available, operative **10** accessible, applicable, employable, expendable, functional, marketable, negotiable **11** exploitable, functioning, operational, serviceable

usage 3 way **4** form, mode, wont **5** habit, sense **6** action, amount, custom, manner, method, praxis **7** process **8** habitude, practice **9** formality, procedure **10** convention

use 3 ply **4** wont, work **5** apply, avail, habit, serve, treat, value, wield, worth **6** custom, demand, employ, handle, liking, manage, manner **7** benefit, exploit, operate, purpose, service, utility, utilize **8** deal with, exercise, exertion, function, impose on, occasion, practice, regulate **9** advantage, habituate, objective, relevance **10** employment, manipulate **11** application

used 8 pre-owned, shopworn **10** secondhand

used up 5 all in, spent **6** bleary, effete, sapped, wasted **7** drained, emptied, fargone, worn-out **8** consumed, depleted **9** exhausted, washed-out

useful 3 fit **4** meet **5** handy, utile **7** helpful **8** fruitful, suitable, valuable **9** favorable, practical **10** beneficial, convenient, functional, productive, profitable, propitious, worthwhile **11** appropriate, practicable, serviceable, utilitarian **12** advantageous

usefulness 5 value, worth **7** fitness, service, utility **8** function **9** advantage, relevance, substance **10** expedience, expediency **12** practicality **13** applicability

useless 4 idle, vain **5** inept **6** futile **7** inutile **8** bootless, hopeless, unusable **9** fruitless, pointless, worthless **10** unavailing, unworkable **11** impractical, ineffective, ineffectual, inoperative **12** unproductive, unprofitable **13** impracticable, nonfunctional

user 5 buyer **6** addict **8** consumer, customer, utilizer

use up 5 drain, spend **6** devour, expend **7** consume, deplete, exhaust **8** draw down **10** run through

usher 4 lead, seat **5** guide **6** escort **7** conduct, precede **9** conductor **10** doorkeeper

usher in 5 begin, greet, start **6** launch **7** kick off, trumpet, welcome **8** announce, commence, initiate, proclaim **9** institute, introduce, originate **10** inaugurate

usual 5 stock, typic **6** common, kosher, normal, wonted **7** average, regular, routine, typical, vanilla **8** accepted, everyday, expected, familiar, habitual, ordinary, orthodox, standard, workaday **9** customary, prevalent, quotidian **10** accustomed, prevailing **11** commonplace, established **12** conventional, unremarkable

usually 6 mainly, mostly **7** as a rule **8** commonly, normally **9** generally, routinely **10** habitually, ordinarily **11** customarily

usurer 7 Shylock **9** loan shark **11** moneylender

usurp 4 take **5** seize, wrest **6** assume **7** preempt **8** arrogate, displace, supplant **10** commandeer **11** appropriate

Utah *capital:* **12** Salt Lake City *city:* **4** Orem **5** Ogden, Provo *college, university:* **12** Brigham Young *lake:* **6** Powell **9** Great Salt *motto:* **8** Industry *mountain:* **5** Kings (Peak) *nickname:* **7** Beehive (State) *park:* **4** Zion **5** Bryce **6** Arches **11** Canyonlands *river:* **5** Green **6** Sevier *state bird:* **14** California gull *state flower:* **8** sego lily *state tree:* **10** blue spruce

utensil 3 pan, pot **4** fork, tool **5** knife, spoon **6** device, vessel **8** saucepan, teaspoon **9** implement **10** instrument

uterus 4 womb

Uther Pendragon *son:* **6** Arthur *wife:* **6** Ygerne **7** Igraine

utile 5 handy **6** useful **7** working **9** available, operative, practical **10** accessible, convenient, dependable, functional **11** practicable, serviceable

utilitarian 6 useful **9** practical, pragmatic **10** functional *philosopher:* **4** Mill (John Stuart) **7** Bentham (Jeremy)

utility 3 use **7** benefit, fitness, service **8** function **9** advantage, relevance **10** efficiency, usefulness **12** practicality **13** applicability

utilize 3 use **5** apply, spend **6** bestow, deploy, employ, handle, occupy **7** exploit **8** exercise **11** appropriate

utmost 3 nth, top **4** acme, apex, best, peak **6** height, zenith **7** extreme, highest, maximal, maximum, supreme **8** farthest, furthest, greatest, pinnacle, remotest, ultimate **9** damnedest, extremity

utopia 4 Eden, Zion **5** bliss **6** heaven **7** Elysium **8** paradise **9** Cockaigne, dreamland, Shangri-la **10** dreamworld **12** promised land **13** Elysian fields

Utopia author 4 More (Thomas)

utopian 3 ideal, lofty **6** edenic **7** dreamer **8** arcadian, fanciful, idealist, quixotic **9** grandiose, ideologue, visionary **10** chimerical, idealistic, impossible, millennial, unfeasible **11** impractical **12** otherworldly **13** castle-builder, impracticable

utter 3 say **4** damn, dang, darn, rank, talk, tell

5 sheer, speak, stark, state, total, voice **6** arrant, dashed, deuced, reveal **7** blasted, blessed, declare, deliver, divulge, express, flat-out **8** absolute, bring out, complete, crashing, disclose, infernal, outright, positive, throw out **9** downright, out-and-out, pronounce, verbalize **10** articulate, confounded, consummate **11** come out with, straight-out, unmitigated, unqualified **13** thoroughgoing

utterance 4 rant, vent, word **5** voice **6** speech **7** oration **8** delivery, speaking **9** assertion, discourse, statement **10** expression, revelation **11** declaration **12** announcement, articulation **13** pronouncement, verbalization

utterly 4 just **5** plumb, quite **6** in toto **7** totally **8** entirely **9** perfectly **10** absolutely, altogether, completely, thoroughly

uttermost 4 last **5** final **7** extreme, outmost **8** farthest, furthest, remotest

Utu see **Shamash**

Uzbekistan *capital:* **8** Tashkent *city:* **7** Bokhara, Bukhara **9** Samarkand, Samarqand *desert:* **8** Kyzyl Kum *enclave:* **10** Karakalpak *monetary unit:* **3** som **5** tiyin *neighbor:* **9** Kazakstan **10** Kazakhstan, Kyrgyzstan, Tajikistan **11** Afghanistan **12** Turkmenistan *river:* **8** Amu Dar'ya, Syr Dar'ya **9** Zeravshan *sea:* **4** Aral

V

vacancy 4 void **6** vacuum **7** opening **8** idleness **9** blankness, emptiness

vacant 4 bare, free, idle, open, void **5** blank, clear, empty, inane, stark **6** unused **7** deadpan, vacuous **8** deserted, unfilled **9** abandoned, impassive **10** tenantless, unoccupied **11** empty-headed **12** inexpressive

vacate 4 quit, void **5** annul, clear, empty, leave **6** bow out, give up, repeal, revoke **7** abandon, rescind, retract, reverse **8** abrogate, check out, dissolve, evacuate **9** discharge **10** relinquish

vacation 4 rest, trip **5** break, leave **6** recess **7** holiday, leisure, respite, time off **8** furlough, interval **10** sabbatical **12** intermission

vacationer 7 tourist, tripper **9** weekender **10** rubberneck **12** holidaymaker

vaccination 4 shot **7** booster **9** injection **11** inoculation

vaccine 4 shot **5** serum **9** antiserum **11** preparation *inventor:* **4** Salk (Jonas), Zhou (Jian) **5** Cohen (Joe), Sabin (Albert) **6** Frazer (Ian), Jenner (Edward), Talwar (Gursaran) **8** Hilleman (Maurice)

vacillate 4 sway, yo-yo **5** waver **6** dither, falter, seesaw, teeter, waffle, waggle **7** swither, whiffle **8** hesitate **9** alternate, fluctuate, oscillate **10** equivocate **12** shilly-shally

vacillating 4 weak **6** fickle, unsure, wobbly **8** hesitant, shifting, unstable, unsteady **9** fluctuant, tentative, uncertain, undecided, unsettled **10** changeable, inconstant, indecisive, irresolute **12** shilly-shally

vacillation 5 doubt **8** to-and-fro, wavering **9** hesitancy **10** fickleness, indecision **12** irresolution, shilly-shally

vacuity 4 hole, void **6** cavity, hollow, vacuum **7** inanity **9** black hole, blankness, ditsiness, ditziness, emptiness, stupidity **10** hollowness **11** nothingness

vacuous 4 idle, void **5** blank, empty, inane, silly **6** stupid, vacant **7** foolish, shallow **11** birdbrained, empty-headed, superficial

vacuum 4 void **5** space **7** suction **9** emptiness **11** nothingness *bottle:* **5** dewar **7** thermos

vacuum tube 5 diode **6** triode **7** tetrode *casing:* **4** bulb

vade mecum 5 guide **6** manual **8** Baedeker, handbook **9** guidebook **11** enchiridion

_____ **Vadis 3** Quo

vagabond 3 bum **4** hobo **5** gipsy, gypsy, idler, nomad, rogue, rover, tramp **6** picaro, roamer **7** drifter, floater, migrant, nomadic, vagrant, wastrel **8** bohemian, clochard, picaroon, runabout, runagate, traveler, wanderer **9** itinerant, transient, wandering **11** peripatetic

vagarious 6 fickle **7** erratic, flighty, mutable, wayward **8** unstable, volatile **9** impulsive, mercurial, whimsical **10** capricious, inconstant **13** unpredictable

vagary 3 bee **4** whim **5** crank, fancy, freak,

humor, quirk **6** megrim, whimsy **7** caprice, fantasy **8** crotchet

vagrancy 6 roving **7** roaming **8** drifting, nomadism, rambling **9** wandering **10** itinerancy

vagrant see **vagabond**

vague 3 dim **4** hazy **5** blear, faint, foggy, fuzzy, gauzy, misty, muddy, woozy **6** bleary, blurry, cloudy, dreamy, slight, vacant **7** inexact, obscure, shadowy, unclear **8** confused, nebulous, vaporous **9** ambiguous, dreamlike, enigmatic, imprecise, uncertain **10** diaphanous, ill-defined, indefinite, indistinct **13** indeterminate, unsubstantial

vain 4 idle **5** empty, proud **6** futile, hollow, otiose **7** foppish, haughty, stuck-up, trivial, useless **8** abortive, arrogant, boastful, bootless, nugatory **9** conceited, fruitless, valueless, worthless **10** egocentric, profitless, sophomoric, unavailing **11** egotistical, ineffective, ineffectual **12** narcissistic, unproductive, unprofitable, unsuccessful **13** self-important

vainglorious 8 arrogant, boastful, bragging, puffed-up, vaunting **9** conceited, egotistic **10** swaggering **11** egotistical **12** supercilious

vainglory 4 pomp **5** pride **6** egoism, vanity **7** conceit, egotism **9** arrogance **10** pretension **11** haughtiness **12** boastfulness

valance 5 drape **6** pelmet **7** curtain, drapery **10** lambrequin

vale 4 dale, dell, glen **5** combe **6** dingle, hollow, valley

valediction 5 adieu **7** good-bye **8** farewell **11** leave-taking

valedictory see **valediction**

valentine 4 card, dear, love **7** beloved, darling, tribute **10** sweetheart

valet 7 servant **9** attendant **10** manservant

valiant 4 bold **5** brave **6** heroic, plucky **7** doughty, gallant, valiant **8** fearless, intrepid **9** dauntless **10** chivalrous, courageous **11** lionhearted **12** greathearted, stouthearted

valid 4 just, true **5** legal, solid, sound **6** cogent, lawful, potent, proven **7** binding, in force, logical, telling **8** attested, bona fide, credible, forceful **9** effective, effectual, operative **10** acceptable, compelling, convincing, legitimate, persuasive **11** justifiable, trustworthy **12** well-grounded

validate 5 prove **6** affirm, ratify, verify **7** approve, bear out, certify, confirm, endorse, justify, probate **8** legalize, sanction **10** legitimate, legitimize **11** corroborate, rubber-stamp **12** authenticate, substantiate

validity 5 force, proof **7** cogency, potency **8** efficacy **9** soundness **10** lawfulness **13** effectiveness

valise 3 bag **4** grip **6** kit bag, suiter **7** handbag, Pullman **8** gripsack, suitcase **9** gladstone, two-suiter **10** weekend bag **11** portmanteau **12** overnight bag, traveling bag **13** traveling case

Valjean's pursuer 6 Javert

Valkyrie 6 maiden **8** Brynhild *mother:* **4** Erda

valley 4 dale, dell, dene, glen, vale, wadi **5** basin, combe, gulch, gully, swale **6** canyon, dingle, hollow, ravine **10** depression *Africa-Asia:* **4** Rift **9** Great Rift *Alps:* **11** Grindelwald *ancient Greece:* **5** Nemea *Asia:* **7** Fergana *California:* **3** Noe **4** Napa **5** Death, Squaw **7** Central **8** Imperial, Yosemite **10** San Joaquin **11** San Fernando *Dead Sea area:* **6** Arabah *Dominican Republic:* **5** Cibao *Egypt:* **6** Kharga *England:* **5** Doone *Germany:* **4** Ruhr *Greece:* **5** Tembi, Tempe *India:* **4** Kulu **7** Kashmir (Vale of) *Ireland:* **5** Avoca, Ovoca *Israel:* **4** Elah *Lebanon:* **4** Biqa **5** Bekaa *moon:* **4** rill **5** rille *New York:* **12** Sleepy Hollow *Pennsylvania:* **7** Nittany *Scotland:* **7** Glen Roy *Switzerland:* **5** Hasli **8** Engadine **11** Grindelwald *Virginia:* **10** Shenandoah *Washington:* **11** Grand Coulee

Valmiki's epic 8 Ramayana

valor 4 guts **6** mettle, spirit, virtue **7** bravery, courage, heroism, prowess, stomach **8** chivalry, valiance, valiancy **9** fortitude, gallantry **10** resolution

valorous see **valiant**

valse 5 waltz

valuable 4 dear **5** utile **6** costly, prized, useful, worthy **8** precious **9** expensive, important, rewarding, treasured **10** satisfying, worthwhile

valuate 4 rate **5** assay, price **6** assess, survey **7** adjudge **8** appraise, estimate

valuation 4 cost, rate **5** price, worth **6** rating **7** opinion **8** estimate, judgment **9** appraisal **10** assessment, estimation **12** appreciation

value 4 cost, rate **5** assay, gauge, judge, price, prize, scale, worth **6** assess, assign, charge, esteem, figure, reckon, regard, return, survey **7** account, apprize, care for, cherish, compute, quality, respect, utility **8** appraise, estimate, evaluate, quantity, treasure **9** appraisal, principle **10** appreciate, assessment, equivalent, importance **11** market price **12** denomination

valve 3 tap **4** cock, flap, gate **6** device, faucet, poppet, spigot **7** hydrant, petcock, shutoff **8** stopcock **9** regulator *cardiac:* **6** mitral **8** bicuspid

vamoose 3 git **4** scat **5** leave, scram, split **6**

beat it, begone, cut out, decamp, depart, get out **7** run away, skiddoo, take off **8** clear out **9** skedaddle

vamp 3 fix **4** fake, lure, mend, wile **5** ad-lib, flirt, intro, patch, siren, tempt **6** cook up, entice, groove, lead-in, make up, repair, seduce **7** beguile, charmer, rebuild **8** inveigle **9** fabricate, formulate, improvise, refurbish, temptress **10** gold digger, seductress **11** enchantress, extemporize, femme fatale **famous: 4** Bara (Theda) **5** Negri (Pola) **6** Golden (Eve), Harlow (Jean), Lamarr (Hedy), Salome **7** Delilah, Jezebel **8** Dietrich (Marlene), Mata Hari **9** Cleopatra

vampire 3 bat **5** lamia **6** Lestat, undead **7** Dracula **9** Nosferatu **11** bloodsucker **novelist: 4** Rice (Anne) **6** Stoker (Bram)

van 3 car **4** head, lead, wing **5** front, truck, wagon **7** minibus **9** forefront **11** cutting edge, leading edge

vandal 3 Hun **5** yahoo **6** looter **8** pillager **9** despoiler, destroyer, plunderer, spoliator

vandalize 5 smash, trash, wreck **6** damage, deface, ravage, tear up **7** destroy **8** demolish, sabotage

Vandal king 8 Gaiseric, Genseric

Vandyke 5 beard **6** border, collar, edging, goatee

vane 3 web **7** feather, wind tee **8** vexillum **10** bellwether **11** weathercock

Van Gogh, Vincent brother: 4 Theo **friend: 7** Gauguin (Paul) **residence: 5** Arles **subject: 10** sunflowers

vanguard 4 lead **5** front **9** forefront **11** cutting edge, leading edge

vanilla 4 tame **5** beige, cream, plain **7** extract **8** ordinary **9** innocuous **10** white-bread **12** conventional **13** garden-variety

vanish 3 die, fly **4** fade, flee, melt **5** clear **8** dissolve, evanesce **9** disappear, dissipate, evaporate **13** dematerialize

vanity 3 ego **5** pride **6** egoism **7** conceit, egotism **8** self-love, smugness **9** vainglory **10** narcissism, pretension **13** dressing table

Vanity Fair author 9 Thackeray (William Makepeace)

vanquish 4 beat, best, drub, lick, rout **5** cream, crush, quell **6** defeat, humble, subdue, thrash **7** clobber, conquer, destroy, smother, trounce **8** surmount **9** overpower, overthrow, subjugate **10** annihilate

vantage 4 edge, odds **8** handicap **9** head start, upper hand **point: 3** POV **5** perch **7** lookout, outlook **8** position **10** watchtower

Vanuatu capital: 8 Port-Vila **ethnic group: 10** Melanesian **explorer: 4** Cook (Capt. James) **former name: 11** New Hebrides **island: 3**

Epi **5** Efate, Maéwo, Tanna **6** Ambrim **8** Aneityum, Malekula **9** Erromango, Pentecost **13** Espíritu Santo **language: 6** French **monetary unit: 4** vatu

vapid 4 dull, flat, weak **5** banal, bland, ditsy, ditzy, inane, silly **6** jejune **7** fatuous, insipid, sapless, vacuous **9** brainless, colorless, innocuous **10** namby-pamby, wishy-washy **13** uninteresting

vapor 3 fog, gas **4** brag, haze, mist, smog **5** brume, cloud, smoke, steam **6** breath, miasma, nimbus **7** bluster **8** phantasm **condensed: 3** dew **frozen: 4** hoar, rime **5** frost **9** hoarfrost

vaporize 5 steam **6** ablate **8** disperse, dissolve, evanesce **9** dissipate, evaporate

vaporous 4 airy, hazy **5** foggy, misty, vague, wispy **6** cloudy, unreal **7** gaseous **8** ethereal, illusory, volatile **10** evanescent **13** unsubstantial

vaquero 5 waddy **6** cowboy, gaucho, herder, waddie **7** cowpoke **8** buckaroo, herdsman, wrangler **10** cowpuncher

varia 6 medley **7** mélange, mixture, omnibus **8** treasury **9** anthology **10** compendium, miscellany **11** compilation

variable 5 fluid **6** fickle, fitful, mobile, symbol **7** mutable, protean **8** unstable, unsteady, volatile **9** irregular, mercurial, uncertain, unsettled, versatile **10** capricious, changeable, inconstant **13** temperamental

variance 3 war **4** odds **6** change, strife **7** discord, dispute, dissent **8** conflict, disunity, division **9** variation **10** contention, difference, dissension, dissidence **11** fluctuation **12** disagreement

variation 4 riff **5** shade, shift **6** change, nuance **7** partita **8** mutation **9** disparity **10** alteration, difference, divergence **11** fluctuation, declination, discrepancy, oscillation **12** modification **13** dissimilarity

varicolored see **variegated**

varicose 7 bulging, dilated, swollen

varied 5 mixed **6** motley, sundry **7** diverse, various **8** assorted **9** different, disparate, divergent **10** dissimilar **12** multifarious **13** heterogeneous, kaleidoscopic, miscellaneous

variegated 4 pied **5** mixed, pinto **6** calico, motley **7** checked, dappled, diverse, mottled, piebald, spotted **8** skewbald, stippled, streaked **9** checkered, multihued **10** multicolor, parti-color, polychrome **12** multicolored, parti-colored **13** kaleidoscopic, polychromatic

variety 3 ilk **4** kind, mode, sort, type **5** array, breed **6** flavor, medley, nature, stripe **8**

mixed bag **9** diversity, variation **10** assortment, collection, miscellany, subspecies **12** multiformity, multiplicity

various 4 some **5** mixed **6** divers, sundry, unlike **7** diverse, several, unalike **8** assorted, separate **9** different, disparate, divergent, unsimilar **10** dissimilar **12** multifarious **13** heterogeneous, miscellaneous

varlet 3 cur **4** page **5** knave, rogue, skunk **6** menial, rascal, wretch **8** coistrel **9** attendant, miscreant, scoundrel **10** blackguard

varmint 4 pest **5** knave, rogue, scamp, skunk, sneak **6** rascal **7** critter **9** scoundrel

varnish 4 coat **5** adorn, cover, glaze, gloss, japan **6** veneer **7** coating, conceal, cover up, shellac **8** covering **9** embellish, gloss over, sugarcoat, whitewash *component:* **5** elemi, resin

vary 5 alter, range **6** change, depart, differ, modify, mutate **7** deviate, digress, diverge **8** modulate **9** diversify

vase 3 urn **5** tazza **6** crater, krater, vessel **7** amphora

Vashni's father 6 Samuel

Vashti's husband 6 Xerxes **9** Ahasuerus

vassal 4 leud, serf **5** helot, liege, slave **6** tenant **7** bondman, homager, peasant, servant, subject **8** bondsman, liege man **9** dependent, underling **11** subordinate **12** feudal tenant *high-ranking:* **7** vavasor **8** vavasour

vast 4 huge, mega **5** giant, great, jumbo **6** untold **7** immense, mammoth, oceanic, titanic **8** colossal, enormous, gigantic, spacious, whopping **9** boundless, expansive, humongous **10** gargantuan, tremendous, widespread **12** astronomical

vastness 5 sweep **8** enormity, hugeness **9** immensity, magnitude **13** expansiveness

vat 3 tub, tun **4** beck, butt, cask, kier, tank **5** keeve, kieve **6** barrel, liquor, vessel **7** cistern **8** cauldron *cheese:* **7** chessel

vatic 6 mantic **7** fatidic **8** oracular **9** fatidical, prophetic, sibylline **10** predictive **11** apocalyptic

Vatican City 10 papal state *army:* **11** Swiss Guards *chapel:* **7** Sistine *church:* **11** Saint Peter's *court:* **4** Rota *ruler:* **4** Pope *site:* **4** Rome

vaticinal see **vatic**

vaticinate 5 augur **6** divine **7** portend, predict, presage **8** forebode, forecast, foretell, prophesy, soothsay **9** adumbrate **13** prognosticate

vaudeville 5 revue **9** burlesque, music hall **11** variety show **12** song and dance

vaudevillian 11 entertainer

vault 3 pit, sky **4** arch, cave, dome, jump,

leap, room, safe, tomb **5** bound, crypt **6** cavern, cellar, cupola, hurdle, spring, welkin **7** archway, dungeon **8** catacomb, overleap **9** firmament **10** undercroft

vaulting 4 arch, dome **7** emulous **8** aspiring **9** ambitious **12** enthusiastic **13** opportunistic

vaunt 4 blow, brag, crow, puff, rant **5** boast, strut **6** flaunt, parade **7** bluster, display, exhibit, show off **8** brandish **9** gasconade **11** rodomontade

veal 4 calf *cutlet:* **9** schnitzel *roasted:* **10** fricandeau *shank:* **8** osso buco

vector 5 agent **7** carrier **9** direction **10** pollinator

Vedic religion *country:* **5** India *god:* **4** Agni, deva, Soma **5** Indra **6** Varuna *language:* **8** Sanskrit *priest:* **7** Brahman *treatise:* **9** Upanishad *writing:* **7** Rig Veda, Samhita

veer 3 yaw **4** cast, chop, slew, sway, turn **5** fetch, sheer, shift, trend **6** depart, swerve **7** deflect, deviate, digress, diverge

vegetable 3 pea, soy, udo, yam **4** bean, beet, corn, kale, leek, okra, soya, spud, taro, wort **5** chard, chive, cress, green, onion, plant **6** carrot, celery, cowpea, endive, garlic, legume, lentil, peanut, pepper, potato, radish, sorrel, squash, tomato, turnip **7** cabbage, chayote, dullard, lettuce, mustard, parsley, parsnip, pumpkin, rhubarb, salsify, shallot, soybean, spinach **8** broccoli, collards, cucumber, eggplant, kohlrabi, lima bean, rutabaga, scallion, snap bean **9** artichoke, asparagus, muskmelon **10** watermelon **11** cauliflower, horseradish, sweet potato *bog:* **6** muskeg *covering:* **4** peel, rind, skin *dish:* **5** salad *mold:* **5** humus *seller:* **6** grocer **7** grocery **12** costermonger *sponge:* **5** luffa **6** loofah *spread:* **4** oleo **9** margarine

vegetarian 9 herbivore **11** herbivorous

vegetate 4 idle, laze, loaf, loll **5** chill, slack **9** loiter, lounge **7** goof off, hang out **8** chill out, languish, lollygag, slack off, stagnate **9** goldbrick, hibernate

vegetation 5 flora **6** growth, plants **7** verdure **8** greenery **9** plant life *floating:* **4** sudd **8** pleuston

vehement 3 hot **4** wild **5** fiery, rabid **6** ardent, bitter, fervid, fierce, heated **7** excited, fervent, vicious, violent, zealous **8** forceful, powerful **9** perfervid **10** passionate **11** impassioned **12** antagonistic

vehicle 3 ATV, bus, cab, car, SUV, van **4** auto, bike, taxi, tool **5** agent, buggy, means, organ, plane, sedan, train, truck, wagon **6** agency, binder, medium, vector **7** bicycle, carrier, channel, machine, solvent, travois **8** airplane, ministry **9** ambulance, implement, motor home, transport **10** automobile, conveyance, instrument, motorcycle *baby's:* **4** pram **8** carriage, stroller **9** baby buggy *child's:* **5** trike **7** scooter **8** tricycle *farm:* **4** wain **7** tractor *horse-drawn:* **4** cart, dray **5** buggy, lorry, sulky, wagon **6** hansom, landau, troika **7** calèche, phaeton **8** carriage **9** buckboard *military:* **4** jeep, tank **6** Humvee *one-wheeled:* **8** unicycle *passenger:* **3** bus, cab, car **4** auto, taxi **7** ricksha **8** cable car, rickshaw *public:* **3** bus **4** tram **5** train **6** subway **7** omnibus, trolley *Roman:* **7** chariot *winter:* **4** sled **6** sleigh **8** snowplow **10** snowmobile

veil 4 caul, hide, mask, wrap **5** cloak, cloth, cloud, cover, velum **6** chador, mantle, screen, shield, shroud **7** conceal, cover up, curtain, obscure, secrete, yashmak **8** covering, disguise, enshroud **10** camouflage, false front *chalice:* **3** aer *Muslim:* **7** yashmak *netting:* **6** maline **7** malines

vein 3 bed, way **4** line, lode, mind, mode, mood, seam, tone, tube **5** style, tenor **6** manner, nature, spirit, strain, streak, vessel **7** channel, fashion, pattern, quality, stratum **8** aptitude **11** blood vessel *combining form:* **3** ven **4** veni, veno *deposit:* **3** ore *fluid:* **5** blood *heart:* **8** vena cava *leaf:* **3** rib *leg:* **7** saphena **9** saphenous *neck:* **7** jugular *small:* **6** venule *varicose:* **5** varix

velar 8 guttural *nasal consonant:* **3** eng **4** agma

veld 7 prairie **9** grassland

velleity 4 bent, wish **5** fancy **6** desire, liking **7** leaning **10** propensity **11** inclination

velocipede 4 bike **5** cycle, trike **6** tandem **7** bicycle, pedicab **8** tricycle

velocity 4 pace **5** haste, speed, tempo **7** headway **8** celerity, rapidity **9** quickness, swiftness **12** acceleration

velum 4 caul, veil **8** membrane **10** soft palate

velvet 4 gain, mild, rich, soft **5** cloth **6** fabric, profit, smooth **8** winnings **10** antler skin

velvety 4 mild, soft **5** plush **6** smooth

venal 4 paid **6** sordid **7** corrupt **8** bribable **9** mercenary, unethical **11** corruptible, purchasable **12** unprincipled, unscrupulous

vend 4 hawk, sell, toot **6** market, monger, peddle, retail **8** huckster **9** advertise, broadcast

vendee 5 buyer **6** client **8** customer **9** purchaser

vendetta 4 feud **7** rivalry **9** blood feud

vendible 7 salable **8** sellable **10** marketable **12** merchantable

vendor 6 dealer, duffer, hawker, seller **7** packman, peddler **8** huckster, merchant, retailer, salesman

vendue 4 sale **7** auction **10** public sale

veneer 3 ply **4** burl, coat, face, mask, show, veil **5** cover, front, gloss, layer, plate **6** facade, facing **7** conceal, overlay **8** disguise

venerable 3 old **4** aged **5** hoary **6** sacred **7** ancient, antique, elderly, honored, revered, stately **8** esteemed **9** admirable, dignified, estimable, honorable, respected

venerate 5 adore, honor, prize **6** admire, esteem, revere **7** cherish, idolize, respect, worship **8** treasure **9** reverence

veneration 3 awe **5** honor **6** esteem, homage **7** respect, worship **9** adoration, reverence **10** admiration **11** hero worship

venery 3 sex **4** game, prey **5** chase **7** hunting

venesection 10 phlebotomy

Venetian boat: **7** gondola *boatman:* **9** gondolier *product:* **5** glass **9** glassware *ruler:* **4** doge *school:* **6** Titian **7** Bellini, Tiepolo **8** Veronese **9** Giorgione **10** Tintoretto *street:* **5** canal *suburb:* **6** Murano

Venezuela capital: **7** Caracas *city:* **8** Valencia **9** Maracaibo **12** Barquisimeto *island:* **9** Margarita *lake:* **8** Valencia **9** Maracaibo *language:* **7** Spanish *monetary unit:* **7** bolívar *mountain, range:* **5** Andes **6** Parima (Serra, Sierra) **7** Bolívar (Pico) **9** Pacaraima **11** Pico Bolívar, Serra Parima **12** Sierra Parima *neighbor:* **6** Brazil, Guyana **8** Colombia *peninsula:* **9** Paraguaná *river:* **7** Orinoco *sea:* **9** Caribbean *waterfall:* **10** Angel Falls

Venezuelan herdsman: **7** llanero *liberator:* **7** Bolívar (Simón) *people:* **5** Carib **6** Timote

vengeance 6 payoff **7** payback, redress, revenge **8** reprisal, revanche **9** repayment **10** punishment **11** retaliation, retribution

vengeful 8 punitive **10** vindictive **11** retaliatory

venial 5 minor **7** trivial **8** harmless, trifling **9** allowable, excusable, tolerable **10** condonable, forgivable, pardonable, remissible, remittable **13** insignificant

Venice of the East 7 Bangkok, Udaipur

Venice of the North 6 Bruges, Brugge **9** Amsterdam, Stockholm **12** St. Petersburg

Veni, Creator ____ 8 Spiritus

venison 4 deer

veni, vidi, ____ 4 vici

venom 4 bane, hate **5** spite **6** malice, poison, rancor **7** ill will, vitriol **8** embitter **9** contagion, malignity, virulence **11** malevolence

venomous 5 toxic **6** deadly, malign, poison **7** baneful, malefic, noxious **8** spiteful, viperish, viperous, virulent **9** malicious, malignant, poisonous **10** malevolent, pernicious **12** vituperative

vent 3 air **4** emit, flue, hole, pipe, pour, slit **5** burst, expel, issue, loose, utter, voice **6** broach, nozzle, outlet **7** chimney, exhaust, express, give off, opening, orifice, release, take out, unleash, volcano **8** breather, fumarole, spiracle **9** discharge **11** black smoker

venter 3 gut **5** belly **6** paunch **7** abdomen, stomach

ventilate 3 air **5** state, utter **6** aerate, expose **7** discuss, express **9** advertise, broadcast, circulate, verbalize **11** investigate

ventral area 7 abdomen, stomach

ventricle 6 cavity **7** chamber

ventriloquist 9 performer **11** entertainer *companion:* **5** dummy *famous:* **6** Bergen (Edgar)

venture 3 bet, try **4** dare, face, feat, gest, risk **5** brave, peril, stake, wager **6** chance, expose, gamble, hazard **7** attempt, daresay, emprise, exploit **8** endanger, jeopardy, long shot, make bold **9** challenge, crapshoot, speculate **10** enterprise **11** speculation, undertaking

venturesome 4 bold, rash **5** brave **6** daring **8** reckless **9** audacious, daredevil, foolhardy **11** adventurous, temerarious

venue 4 site **5** arena, forum, place, scene **6** locale, outlet **7** setting **8** locality

Venus 6 planet, Vesper **7** daystar, Lucifer **8** Hesperus *husband:* **6** Vulcan *son:* **4** Amor **5** Cupid **6** Aeneas (see also **Aphrodite**)

Venus de ____ 4 Milo

____ vera 4 aloe

veracious 4 just, true **5** exact, frank, right, valid **6** candid, honest **7** correct, factual, sincere **8** accurate, truthful

veracity 4 fact **5** truth **6** candor **7** honesty **8** accuracy, trueness **9** actuality, exactness **11** correctness **12** truthfulness

veranda 5 lanai, porch, stoop **6** piazza **7** gallery, portico

verb *auxiliary:* **3** are, can, did, had, has, may, was **4** have, must, were, will, word **5** could, might, shall, would **6** should *form:* **6** active, gerund **7** passive **10** infinitive, participle *kind:* **10** transitive **12** intransitive *linking:* **6** copula *mood:* **8** optative **10** imperative, indicative **11** subjunctive *tense:* **4** past **6** aorist, future **7** perfect, present **9** predicate **10** pluperfect

verbal 4 oral **5** wordy **6** gerund, spoken **7** literal **9** unwritten **10** infinitive, participle, rhetorical **11** word-for-word

verbalism 4 term **6** phrase **7** wording **8** phras-

ing **9** prolixity, windiness, wordiness **11** phraseology

verbalization 4 talk **6** speech **8** speaking **9** discourse, utterance **12** articulation, vocalization

verbalize 3 air, say **4** talk **5** speak, state, utter, voice, write **6** broach **7** express **8** bloviate, vocalize **9** ventilate

verbatim 5 exact **6** direct **7** exactly, literal, precise **8** directly **9** literally, literatim, precisely **10** accurately **11** word-for-word

verbiage 4 talk **6** phrase **7** diction, wording **8** parlance, phrasing, pleonasm **9** wordiness **10** redundancy **11** phraseology

verbose 5 gassy, windy, wordy **6** prolix **7** diffuse **9** garrulous, redundant, talkative **10** loquacious, pleonastic **11** tautologous

verbosity 9 prolixity, windiness, wordiness **10** redundancy

verboten 5 taboo **6** banned **7** illegal **8** outlawed **9** forbidden **10** prohibited

verdant 4 lush **5** green, leafy, naive **6** grassy, unripe

verdict 6 assize, ruling **7** finding, opinion **8** decision, judgment **9** judgement

Verdi opera 4 Aïda **6** Ernani, Oberto, Otello **7** Nabucco **8** Don Carlo, Falstaff, Lombardi (I), Traviata (La) **9** Don Carlos, Rigoletto, Trovatore (Il) **15** Simon Boccanegra

verdure 7 foliage **8** greenery **9** greenness **10** vegetation

verge 3 hem, lip, rim **4** abut, cusp, edge, sink **5** bound, brink, skirt, staff, touch **6** adjoin, border, fringe, margin **7** selvage **8** approach, shoulder **9** threshold **10** borderline

veridical see **veracious**

verifiable 4 true **6** proven **7** certain **8** provable **9** undoubted

verification 5 proof **10** validation **11** attestation **12** confirmation **13** corroboration

verify 4 aver, test **5** check, prove, vouch **6** attest, settle **7** bear out, confirm **8** document, validate **9** establish, fact-check **11** corroborate, demonstrate **12** authenticate, substantiate

verily 5 truly **6** indeed **7** in truth **9** assuredly, certainly **11** confidently, undoubtedly

veritable 4 real, true **6** actual **7** factual, genuine **8** bona fide **9** authentic, undoubted **10** sure-enough **11** indubitable

verity 5 truth **6** gospel, truism **7** honesty, reality **9** actuality **12** truthfulness

vermiform 8 wormlike

vermilion 3 red

vermin 4 lice, mice, pest, rats, scum **5** fleas, pests, trash **7** bedbugs, varmint

Vermont *capital:* **10** Montpelier *city:* **5** Barre,

Stowe **7** Rutland **10** Burlington *college, university:* **7** Norwich **8** Marlboro **10** Bennington, Middlebury *mountain, range:* **5** Green **9** Mansfield *nickname:* **13** Green Mountain (State) *river:* **11** Connecticut *state bird:* **12** hermit thrush *state flower:* **9** red clover *state tree:* **10** sugar maple

vernacular 4 cant **5** argot, idiom, lingo, slang **6** common, jargon, patois, patter, speech, tongue, vulgar **7** dialect, vulgate **8** language **9** dialectal **10** colloquial **12** mother tongue

vernal 5 fresh, green **6** spring **8** youthful **10** springlike

Verne, Jules *character:* **4** Fogg (Phileas), Nemo (Captain) **12** Passepartout *submarine:* **8** Nautilus *work:* **16** Mysterious Island (The) **21** From the Earth to the Moon **26** Around the World in Eighty Days **28** Journey to the Center of the Earth

versant see **conversant**

versatile 5 handy **6** adroit, facile **7** protean **8** variable **9** all-around, competent, many-sided **10** changeable **11** well-rounded **12** ambidextrous

verse 3 lay, ode, poem, rune **5** lyric, poesy, rhyme **6** ballad, jingle, poetry, sonnet, stanza **7** passage **8** acquaint **11** composition, familiarize *amateurish:* **8** doggerel *analysis:* **8** scansion *four-line:* **8** quatrain *free:* **5** blank **8** unrhymed *humorous:* **8** limerick *six-line:* **6** sestet *three-line:* **6** tercet *two-line:* **7** couplet *writer:* **4** poet

versed 6 adept **6** au fait **7** abreast, skilled, veteran **8** familiar, informed, seasoned **9** au courant, competent, practiced **10** acquainted **11** experienced **13** knowledgeable

versifier 4 bard, poet **6** rhymer **9** poetaster, rhymester, sonneteer

version 4 copy **5** draft, model **6** flavor, remake **7** account, edition, reading, variant **8** revision **9** iteration, narrative, redaction, rendition, rewording **10** adaptation, paraphrase **11** arrangement, description, incarnation, restatement, translation

versus 4 anti **6** contra **7** against, vis-à-vis **11** over against

vertebra 7 segment *kind:* **6** dorsal, lumbar, sacral **8** cervical, thoracic **9** coccygeal

vertebrae 4 back **5** spine **6** coccyx, rachis, sacrum **8** backbone, tailbone **12** spinal column

vertebrate 6 animal *characteristic:* **5** spine **7** cranium **12** spinal column *kind:* **4** bird, fish, frog **6** mammal **7** reptile **9** amphibian

vertex 3 cap, top **4** acme, apex, peak **5** crest, crown **6** apogee, summit, tip-top, zenith

vertical 5 erect, plumb, sheer, steep **7** upright **8** straight **10** lengthwise, straight-up **13** perpendicular

vertiginous 5 dizzy, giddy, woozy **6** fickle, rotary **11** light-headed

vertigo 6 megrim **9** dizziness, giddiness

verve 3 pep, vim, zip **4** brio, dash, élan, fire, life, zest, zing **5** flair, gusto, moxie, oomph, style, vigor **6** bounce, energy, esprit, spirit, spring **7** panache **8** vitality, vivacity **10** enthusiasm, liveliness **13** sprightliness

very 3 too **4** bare, mere, most, much, pure, real, same, true **5** exact, ideal, model, plain, quite, sheer, super, truly, utter **6** actual, ever so, highly, hugely, mighty, really, simple **7** awfully, genuine, greatly, notably, perfect, precise, special **8** absolute, actually, bona fide, selfsame, terribly **9** authentic, decidedly, extremely, genuinely, identical, undoubted **10** absolutely, particular **11** exceedingly *French:* **4** très *German:* **4** sehr *Italian:* **5** assai, molto *Scottish:* **3** gey *Spanish:* **3** muy

vesicle 3 sac **4** cell, cyst **5** bulla **6** cavity **7** blister, vacuole

Vespasian's son 5 Titus

vespertilion 7 bat-like

vespers 8 evensong

_____ **Vespucci 7** Amerigo

vessel 3 can, cup, jar, pan, pot, tub, urn **4** boat, bowl, cask, drum, duct, ewer, olla, pail, ship, tank, tube, vase, vein **5** canal, churn, craft, cruse **6** artery, barrel, bottle, bucket, censer, firkin, flagon, kettle, krater, pottle **7** cresset, pitcher **8** crucible **9** container **10** receptacle, watercraft *Arab:* **4** dhow *combining form:* **3** vas **4** angi, vaso **5** angio *drinking:* **3** cup, mug **4** toby **5** flask, glass, gourd, stein, stoup **6** goblet, seidel **7** tankard, tumbler *Indian:* **4** lota **5** lotah *Scottish:* **6** quaich, quaigh

vest 6 weskit **9** waistcoat

Vesta see **Hestia**

vestal 4 pure **6** chaste, virgin **8** celibate, virginal, virtuous

vestibule 5 entry, foyer, lobby **6** cavity **7** hallway, narthex, passage **8** anteroom, entrance, entryway **10** antechapel **11** antechamber

vestige 4 echo **5** dregs (plural), relic, scrap, stump, trace, track **6** shadow **7** memento, remains, remnant **8** leftover **9** remainder **10** hide or hair **11** hide nor hair

vestment 3 alb **4** cope, garb, gown, robe **5** amice, cotta, dress, fanon, habit, orale, stole, tunic **6** attire, rochet **7** apparel, cassock, garment, maniple, pallium, tunicle **8** chasuble, cincture, clothing, covering, dalmatic, parament, surplice *ancient Hebrew:* 5 ephod 11 breastplate

vestry 6 closet 8 sacristy 9 sacrarium

vesture 4 robe 6 clothe 7 apparel, garment 8 clothing 10 habiliment

Vesuvius 7 volcano

vet 5 check 6 go over, review 7 analyze, examine, inspect 8 appraise, check out, evaluate, look over 10 old soldier

vetch 3 ers 4 herb, tare 6 legume *type:* 4 milk (vetch) 5 crown (vetch), hairy (vetch)

veteran 4 ex-GI 5 adept 6 expert, master 7 old hand, skilled 8 old-timer, warhorse 9 practiced, shellback 10 past master 11 experienced

veto 2 ax 3 axe, nix 4 kill, void 5 quash 6 defeat, forbid, refuse, reject 7 decline, nullify 8 abrogate, disallow, negative, prohibit 9 blackball 10 disapprove 11 prohibition 12 interdiction

vex 3 bug, irk 4 fret, gall, itch, roil 5 annoy, chafe, gripe, harry, rowel, tease, worry 6 badger, baffle, bother, harass, harrow, nettle, pester, plague, puzzle, rankle, ruffle 7 chagrin, torment, trouble 8 bullyrag, distress, irritate

vexation 4 fret, sore 5 chafe, trial 6 bother 7 problem, torment 8 distress, headache 9 annoyance, troubling 10 affliction, harassment, irritation 11 aggravation, bedevilment, provocation

vexatious 5 pesky 7 prickly 8 annoying, tiresome 9 troublous 10 bothersome, irritating 11 distressing, troublesome 12 exasperating

vexed 6 sticky, touchy 7 debated, weighty 8 ticklish 9 difficult, discussed, troubling

vexing 5 tough 7 irksome 8 annoying 9 difficult, harassing, upsetting 10 bothersome, irritating 11 distressing, troublesome

via 3 per 4 over, with 5 along 7 by way of, through 9 by means of

viable 6 doable 7 capable 8 feasible, possible, workable 11 practicable, sustainable

vial 6 ampule 7 ampoule

viands 4 eats, fare, feed, food, grub 7 aliment, edibles, vittles 8 victuals 9 provender 10 provisions 11 comestibles

vibrant 5 alive, vital, vivid 6 bright, lively, punchy 7 ringing 8 resonant 9 consonant, pulsating 10 resounding 11 oscillating 12 effervescent

vibrate 3 jar 4 ring 5 quake, shake, swing, throb, waver 6 quiver, shimmy, thrill, tremor 7 flutter, pulsate 8 undulate 9 fluctuate, oscillate, vacillate

vibration 4 aura 5 quake, shake, trill 6 motion, quaver, quiver, shimmy, spirit, tremor 7 flutter, shaking 8 fremitus, wavering 9 emanation, trembling 11 fluctuation, oscillation, vacillation

vicar 6 pastor, priest 8 minister, reverend 9 clergyman

Vicar of Wakefield, The *author:* 9 Goldsmith (Oliver) *character:* 8 Primrose

vice 3 sin 4 evil, flaw 5 crime, fault 6 defect 7 devilry, failing, frailty, offense, scandal 8 iniquity 9 deformity, depravity, indecency 10 corruption, debauchery, immorality, perversion, wickedness 11 shortcoming

vice-president 4 veep 6 deputy 7 officer 9 executive *American:* 4 Burr (Aaron), Bush (George), Ford (Gerald), Gore (Albert), King (William) 5 Adams (John), Agnew (Spiro), Biden (Joseph), Dawes (Charles), Gerry (Elbridge), Nixon (Richard), Tyler (John) 6 Arthur (Chester), Cheney (Richard), Colfax (Schuyler), Curtis (Charles), Dallas (George), Garner (John Nance), Hamlin (Hannibal), Hobart (Garret), Morton (Levi), Quayle (Dan), Truman (Harry), Wilson (Woodrow) 7 Barkley (Alben), Calhoun (John Caldwell), Clinton (George), Johnson (Andrew, Lyndon Baines, Richard Mentor), Mondale (Walter), Sherman (James Schoolcraft), Wallace (Henry), Wheeler (William) 8 Coolidge (Calvin), Fillmore (Millard), Humphrey (Hubert Horatio), Marshall (Thomas), Tompkins (Daniel), Van Buren (Martin) 9 Fairbanks (Charles), Hendricks (Thomas), Jefferson (Thomas), Roosevelt (Theodore), Stevenson (Adlai) 11 Rockefeller (Nelson) 12 Breckinridge (John)

viceroy 5 nabob 6 exarch, satrap 7 khedive 8 alderman, governor 9 butterfly 11 stadtholder

vice versa 10 conversely 12 contrariwise

vicinity 4 area, nabe 5 range 6 extent, locale, region, shadow 7 suburbs 8 ballpark, district, environs, locality, nearness, precinct 9 closeness, magnitude, proximity 12 neighborhood

vicious 4 evil, mean, vile 5 cruel 6 fierce, malign, savage, sinful, wicked 7 brutish, corrupt, hateful, immoral, noxious, violent 8 depraved, horrible, perverse, spiteful 9 barbarous, ferocious, malicious, malignant, monstrous, nefarious, reprobate 10 degenerate, flagitious, iniquitous, malevolent, villainous, vindictive

vicissitude 5 rigor, trial 6 chance, change 7 weather 8 hardship, mutation, reversal 9 adversity, mischance 10 affliction, difficulty, misfortune, mutability **11** fluctuation, permutation, progression, tribulation

victim 4 butt, dupe, gull, mark, prey **5** chump, patsy **6** pigeon, martyr, quarry, sucker **7** fall guy **8** casualty, fatality, offering, underdog **9** sacrifice

victimize 4 dupe, fool, gull, hoax **5** cheat, cozen, trick **6** prey on **7** deceive, swindle **8** flimflam, hoodwink **9** bamboozle, sacrifice **11** hornswoggle

victor 5 champ **6** top dog, winner **7** subduer **8** champion **9** conqueror **10** vanquisher

Victorian 4 prim **6** prissy, stuffy **7** prudish **8** priggish **11** puritanical, straitlaced **12** old-fashioned

Victoria, Queen *family:* **7** Hanover *father:* **6** Edward *husband:* **6** Albert *prime minister:* **8** Disraeli (Benjamin) **9** Gladstone (William), Melbourne (Lord) *son:* **6** Edward

victory 3 win **4** rout **5** sweep **6** defeat **7** mastery, success, triumph **8** conquest, walkaway, walkover **10** overcoming **11** superiority *costly:* **7** Pyrrhic *easy:* **4** romp **7** runaway **8** cakewalk, walkaway *monument:* **4** arch **13** Arc de Triomphe *reward:* **6** spoils *sign:* **3** vee *symbol:* **4** flag **6** laurel, wreath

Victory author 6 Conrad (Joseph)

victuals 4 chow, eats, feed, food, grub, prog **6** viands **7** edibles, vittles **9** provender **10** provisions **11** comestibles

_____ **Vidal 4** Gore

videlicet 3 viz **5** to wit **6** namely, that is **8** scilicet **11** that is to say

video game 4 Doom, Myst **6** Tetris **7** SimCity **10** Donkey Kong **12** Mortal Kombat *maker:* **3** THQ **4** Sega **5** Atari, Namco, Raven, Shaba, Z-Axis **6** Capcom, Konami **7** Ubisoft, Vivendi **8** Luxoflux, Nintendo, Treyarch, Williams **9** Neversoft **10** Activision, Square Enix

vie 3 pit **5** match **6** oppose, strive **7** compete, contend, contest, counter **8** struggle

Viennese *city hall:* **7** Rathaus *family:* **8** Habsburg, Hapsburg *palace:* **7** Hofburg *park:* **6** Prater *river:* **6** Danube

Vietnam *capital:* **5** Hanoi *city:* **3** Hue **6** Da Nang, Saigon **8** Haiphong **13** Ho Chi Minh City *delta:* **6** Mekong *gulf:* **6** Tonkin **8** Thailand *monetary unit:* **4** dong *mountain:* **8** Fan-si-pan *neighbor:* **4** Laos **5** China **8** Cambodia **9** Kampuchea *river:* **3** Red **6** Mekong *sea:* **10** South China

Vietnamese New Year 3 Tet

view 3 eye, see **4** espy, look, plan, scan **5** scene, sight, vista, watch **6** behold, belief, look at, notice, notion, regard, review, survey **7** close-up, examine, inspect, lookout, observe, opinion, outlook, picture, scenery, vantage **8** judgment, panorama, perceive, prospect, scrutiny, snapshot **10** conviction, inspection, scrutinize **11** contemplate, examination

viewer 7 witness **8** looker-on, onlooker **9** bystander, spectator **10** eyewitness

viewing instrument 5 glass, scope **6** binocs **7** glasses **9** telescope **10** binoculars, microscope **12** field glasses *combining form:* **5** scope

viewpoint 3 eye **5** angle, slant, stand **6** stance **7** outlook **8** attitude, position **9** direction **11** perspective

vigil 4 wake **5** watch **7** lookout, prayers **9** devotions **10** deathwatch **11** wakefulness **12** surveillance, watch and ward

vigilance 5 watch **9** alertness **12** surveillance, watchfulness

vigilant 4 keen, wary **5** alert, awake, aware, chary, sharp **7** careful, jealous, on guard **8** cautious, open-eyed, watchful **9** attentive, sharp-eyed, wide-awake

vignette 5 scene **6** sketch **7** glimpse, picture **8** ornament

vigor 3 pep, vim, zip **4** brio, push, snap, tuck **5** ardor, drive, force, gusto, moxie, oomph **6** energy, mettle, muscle, spirit, starch **7** potency **8** dynamism, strength, tonicity, virility, vitality **9** hardihood, lustiness, puissance **10** get-up-and-go, robustness, sturdiness

vigorous 5 brisk, hardy, lusty, stout, tough, vital **6** active, hearty, lively, potent, robust, strong, sturdy, virile **7** dashing, driving, dynamic, healthy **8** athletic, forceful, muscular, powerful, spirited, youthful **9** energetic, strenuous **10** mettlesome, red-blooded

Viking see **Norse**

vile 4 base, evil, foul, mean, ugly **5** gross, nasty, slimy **6** filthy, horrid, sordid, vulgar, wicked **7** low-down, noisome, obscene, squalid **8** depraved, wretched **9** abhorrent, loathsome, obnoxious, offensive, perverted, repugnant, repulsive, revolting **10** despicable, disgusting **12** contemptible

vilify 5 abuse, libel, smear **6** assail, attack, berate, defame, malign **7** asperse, run down, slander, spatter, traduce **8** denounce, tear down **9** denigrate, disparage **10** calumniate

villa 5 dacha, manor **6** estate, quinta **7** château, mansion **9** residence

village 4 burg, town **5** bourg, thorp **6** hamlet **7** townlet *African:* **4** dorp **5** kraal *Indian:* **6** pueblo *Japanese:* **4** mura *Jewish:* **6** shtetl *Malay:* **7** kampong *Russian:* **3** mir

Village Blacksmith author 10 Longfellow (Henry Wadsworth)

villain 4 boor, heel, ogre **5** demon, devil, heavy, knave, rogue **6** bad guy, rascal, sinner **7** lowlife **8** antihero, criminal, evildoer, offender, scalawag **9** character, miscreant, reprobate, scoundrel **10** blackguard, malefactor *classic:* **4** Iago **5** Judas (Iscariot) **6** Brutus (Marcus Junius) **8** Quisling (Vidkun)

villainous 4 evil **6** rotten, wicked **7** corrupt, debased, heinous, vicious **8** depraved, wretched **9** atrocious, felonious, miscreant, nefarious **10** detestable, diabolical, flagitious, iniquitous, perfidious, traitorous **11** treacherous

villainy 4 vice **5** crime **8** evilness **9** depravity, treachery, turpitude **10** corruption, wickedness

villein 7 peasant **8** villager

villenage 4 yoke **6** tenure, thrall **7** bondage, serfdom **9** servitude, thralldom

vim 3 zip **4** brio, dash, élan, gimp, zing **5** gusto, oomph, verve, vigor **6** bounce, energy, esprit, spirit **7** vinegar **9** animation **10** enthusiasm, razzmatazz

____ **vincit omnia 4** Amor

vinculum 3 tie **4** bond, knot, link, yoke **5** nexus **8** ligament, ligature

vindicable 7 tenable **9** excusable **10** condonable, defendable, defensible, pardonable **11** justifiable, warrantable

vindicate 4 free **5** clear, guard, prove, right **6** acquit, avenge, defend, excuse, refute, shield, uphold, verify **7** absolve, bear out, confirm, deliver, justify, redress, revenge, support, warrant **8** maintain **9** exculpate, exonerate, safeguard **11** corroborate **12** substantiate

vindictive 5 catty, nasty **6** malign **7** hateful, hurtful, vicious **8** punitive, spiteful, vengeful, venomous **9** malicious, malignant, poisonous

vine 3 aka, hop, ivy, iyo, pea **5** grape, kudzu, liana, liane, maile, plant **6** maypop **7** chayote, climber, creeper **8** catbrier, clematis **11** bittersweet *Asian:* **6** pikake *East Indian:* **4** soma

vinegar 3 pep, vim **6** liquid **8** ill humor, sourness **9** condiment **12** preservative *relating to:* **10** acetic acid *steep in:* **6** pickle

vinegarish 4 sour **6** bitter, cranky, ornery **7** bearish, waspish **8** snappish **9** crotchety, irascible **12** cantankerous, cross-grained, disagreeable

Vinegar Joe 8 Stilwell (Joseph)

vineyard *French:* **3** cru **7** château, domaine

Vinland discoverer 4 Leif (Ericsson, Eriksson) **12** Leif Ericsson, Leif Eriksson

vintage 3 age, old **4** crop, wine **5** yield **7** antique, classic, harvest **8** outdated **9** classical **10** antiquated **12** old-fashioned

Viola *brother:* **9** Sebastian *husband:* **6** Orsino *play:* **12** Twelfth Night

viola da ____ **5** gamba

violate 4 rape **5** break, wrong **6** breach, defile, offend, ravish **7** disturb, outrage, profane, traduce **8** fracture, infringe, trespass **9** desecrate, disregard **10** contravene, transgress

violation 4 foul, rape **5** break, crime, wrong **6** breach, injury **7** offense, outrage, perjury, scandal **8** trespass **9** blasphemy, injustice, sacrilege **10** illegality, infraction, ravishment **11** desecration, disturbance, misdemeanor, profanation **12** encroachment, infringement, interruption **13** contravention, transgression

violence 4 fury, riot **5** clash **6** frenzy, mayhem **7** assault, outrage, rampage **8** foul play, savagery **9** onslaught **10** distortion, roughhouse

violent 5 cruel, harsh, rabid **6** fierce, raging, savage, stormy **7** berserk, furious, intense, vicious **8** slam-bang, vehement **9** explosive, ferocious **10** hellacious **11** acrimonious, destructive

violet 5 mauve **6** purple **8** amethyst, lavender **10** heliotrope

violin 6 fiddle **10** instrument *kind:* **5** Amati, Strad **8** Guarneri **10** Guarnerius, Stradivari **12** Stradivarius *part:* **3** bow, nut, peg **4** neck **6** bridge, scroll, string **8** chin rest **9** tailpiece **10** soundboard **11** fingerboard *precursor:* **5** rebec **6** rebeck

violinist *American:* **4** Hahn (Hilary) **5** Elman (Mischa), Fodor (Eugene), Ricci (Ruggiero), Stern (Isaac) **6** Midori, Powell (Maud) **7** Heifetz (Jascha), Menuhin (Yehudi) **8** Kreisler (Fritz), Milstein (Nathan) **9** Zimbalist (Efrem) *Belgian:* **5** Ysaÿe (Eugene) **8** Grumiaux (Arthur) *Czech:* **3** Suk (Josef) *Dutch:* **4** Rieu (André) *English:* **7** Kennedy (Nigel), Menuhin (Yehudi) *French:* **9** Grappelli (Stéphane) **12** Francescatti (Zino) *German:* **6** Mutter (Anne-Sophie) *Hungarian:* **4** Auer (Leopold) **7** Joachim (Joseph), Szigeti (Joseph) *Israeli:* **6** Shaham (Gil) **7** Perlman (Itzhak) **8** Zukerman (Pinchas) *Italian:* **6** Viotti (Giovanni Battista) **7** Corelli (Arcangelo), Vivaldi (Antonio) **8** Paganini (Niccolo) **9** Geminiani (Francesco) *Japanese:* **6** Midori (Goto) *Korean:* **5** Chang (Sarah) *Latvian:* **6** Kremer (Gidon) *Roma-*

nian: 6 Enescu (George) *Russian:* **8** Oistrakh (David, Igor)

violin maker 4 Salò (Gasparo da) **5** Amati (Andrea, Antonio, Girolamo, Nicolo) **7** Maggini (Giovanni Paolo), Stainer (Jacob) **8** Guarneri (Andrea, del Gesù, Giuseppe, Pietro) **10** Guarnerius (Andrea, Giuseppe, Pietro), Stradivari (Antonio, Francesco, Omobono) **12** Stradivarius (Antonio, Francesco, Omobono)

VIP 3 CEO **4** BMOC, lion **5** celeb, mogul, nabob **6** big gun, biggie, bigwig, fat cat, honcho **7** big shot, notable, someone **8** big wheel, luminary, mandarin, somebody **9** big cheese, celebrity, dignitary **10** panjandrum **13** high-muck-a-muck

viper 3 asp **5** adder, snake **7** serpent **10** bushmaster, copperhead, fer-de-lance **11** rattlesnake **13** water moccasin

virago 3 hag **5** harpy, scold, shrew, vixen **6** amazon, dragon, gorgon, ogress **8** battle-ax, fishwife, harridan, Xantippe **9** battle-axe, termagant, Xanthippe

Virgil 4 poet **5** guide **6** orator **8** cicerone *epic:* **6** Aeneid *hero:* **6** Aeneas *poems:* **8** Eclogues, Georgics

virgin 3 new **4** pure **5** first, fresh, unwed **6** chaste, intact, maiden, modest, unused, vestal **7** initial **8** celibate, innocent, primeval, pristine, spotless **9** abstinent, undefiled, unmarried, unspoiled, unsullied, untouched **10** immaculate

virginal 4 pure **5** fresh **6** chaste, intact, maiden, spinet **8** pristine, virtuous **9** undefiled, unspoiled, unsullied, untouched

Virgin Goddess 5 Diana **6** Hestia **7** Artemis

Virginia *capital:* **8** Richmond *city:* **7** Norfolk, Roanoke **10** Alexandria **11** Newport News **13** Virginia Beach *college, university:* **3** VMI **7** Hampton **10** Sweet Briar **11** George Mason, Old Dominion **12** James Madison **13** Randolph-Macon **14** William and Mary *historical site:* **10** Monticello **11** Mount Vernon **12** Williamsburg *mountain, range:* **6** Rogers **9** Blue Ridge *nickname:* **11** Old Dominion *river:* **5** James **7** Potomac **10** Shenandoah *state bird:* **8** cardinal *state flower:* **7** dogwood (American) *state tree:* **7** dogwood (American)

Virginian, The *author:* **6** Wister (Owen) *character:* **7** Trampas

Virgin Island 5 Peter **6** Norman, St. John **7** Anegada, St. Croix, Tortola **8** St. Thomas

Virgin Islands (U.S.) *capital:* **15** Charlotte Amalie *island:* **6** St. John **7** St. Croix **8** St. Thomas *location:* **10** West Indies *territory of:* **12** United States

Virgin Islands, British *capital:* **8** Road Town *island:* **5** Peter **6** Norman **7** Anegada, Tortola **11** Jost Van Dyke, Virgin Gorda *location:* **10** West Indies

virginity 6 purity **8** celibacy, chastity **10** chasteness, maidenhead, maidenhood

Virgin Queen 9 Elizabeth

Virgo star 5 Spica

virgule 5 comma, slant, slash **7** solidus **8** diagonal

viridity 5 green **7** naïveté **9** freshness, greenness, innocence

virile 4 male **5** macho, manly **6** manful, potent, robust **7** manlike **8** forceful, vigorous **9** energetic, masculine

virtual 5 moral, tacit **7** de facto **8** implicit **9** essential, practical **10** electronic **11** fundamental

virtuality 4 core, pith, soul **5** being, juice, stuff **6** effect, marrow, nature **7** essence, makings **8** quiddity **9** substance **10** capability **12** essentiality, quintessence, potentiality

virtually 4 nigh **6** all but, almost, fairly, nearly, next to **7** morally **8** as good as, in effect, well-nigh **9** basically, in essence, literally **10** implicitly **11** effectively, essentially, practically **13** approximately, fundamentally, substantially

virtue 5 merit, power, right, trait, valor, value, vigor, worth **7** courage, feature, potency, probity, quality **8** chastity, goodness, morality, strength **9** attribute, character, puissance, rectitude, rightness **10** excellence, excellency, perfection **11** uprightness *cardinal:* **4** hope, love **5** faith **7** charity, justice **8** prudence **9** fortitude **10** temperance

virtuosic 5 showy **6** expert, flashy **7** hotshot, skilled **9** brilliant, masterful **10** consummate, prodigious **12** razzle-dazzle

virtuoso 4 whiz **6** expert, master, savant, wizard, wonder **7** artiste, hotshot, maestro, prodigy **10** past master, wunderkind

virtuous 4 good, pure **5** moral, noble, pious, right **6** chaste, decent, modest, proper **7** ethical, sinless **8** innocent, spotless **9** blameless, faultless, guiltless, righteous, unsullied, untainted **10** inculpable, moralistic **11** respectable, right-minded, untarnished

virulent 5 harsh, toxic **6** biting, bitter, malign, poison **7** cutting, hateful, hostile, noxious **8** scathing, spiteful, venomous **9** malicious, malignant, pestilent, poisonous, rancorous, vitriolic **10** pathogenic

virus 3 bug **8** pathogen **9** contagion, infection

vis 5 force, might, power

visage 3 mug, pan 4 cast, face, look, mien, phiz, puss 6 aspect, kisser 8 features 9 semblance 10 expression 11 countenance

vis-à-vis 4 date 6 escort, facing, toward, versus 7 against 8 fronting, opposite, together 9 tête-à-tête 10 compared to, face-to-face 11 counterpart

visceral 3 gut 4 deep 5 inner 8 internal, intimate 9 intuitive 10 intestinal 11 instinctive, instinctual

viscid see **viscous**

viscount 4 lord, peer 8 nobleman

viscous 4 limy, ropy 5 gluey, gooey, gummy, limey, slimy, thick 9 glutinous, semifluid 10 gelatinous 12 mucilaginous

vise 5 clamp, screw 7 squeeze

Vishnu 4 Hari *avatar:* 4 Rama 5 Kurma 6 Buddha, Matsya, Vamena, Varaha 7 Krishna 9 Narasinha *consort:* 3 Sri 4 Shri 7 Lakshmi *home:* 4 Meru

visible 6 patent 7 obvious 8 apparent, viewable 9 available, well-known 10 detectable, observable 11 conspicuous, discernible, macroscopic, perceivable, perceptible 12 recognizable

Visigoth *conquest:* 4 Rome *king:* 6 Alaric

vision 3 eye 5 dream, fancy, image, sense, sight 6 beauty, seeing 7 concept, fantasy, feature, picture, specter 8 daydream, eyesight, phantasm, presence, prophecy 9 foresight, nightmare 10 apparition, perception, phenomenon, revelation 13 manifestation *combining form:* 4 opto 5 opsis *deceptive:* 6 mirage *relating to:* 5 optic 6 visual 7 optical

visionary 4 seer 5 ideal, lofty, noble 6 unreal 7 blue-sky, dreamer, utopian 8 fanciful, idealist, illusory, quixotic, romantic 9 ambitious, ideologue, imaginary 10 abstracted, daydreamer, idealistic, starry-eyed 11 impractical

visionless 5 blind

visit 3 gam, see 4 call, chat, stay, talk, tour 5 pop in, run in 6 call on, come by, drop by, drop in, look in, look up, stay at, stop by, stop in 7 force on, sojourn 8 come over, converse, stay with, stopover 10 social call

visitation 3 woe 4 wake 5 cross, trial 6 misery, ordeal, plague 8 calamity 9 martyrdom 10 affliction 11 tribulation

visitor 5 alien, guest 6 caller, drop-in 7 company, invitee 8 stranger, visitant 9 transient 10 houseguest

visor 4 bill, mask 6 domino 8 eyeshade, disguise, face mask, sunshade

vista 4 view 5 scene, sight 7 lookout, outlook 8 panorama, prospect 9 landscape 11 perspective

visual 5 optic 6 ocular 7 graphic, optical, seeable 8 viewable 9 pictorial 11 discernible, perceivable, perceptible

visualize 3 see 4 view 5 fancy, image 6 call up 7 feature, imagine, picture 8 conceive, envisage, envision 9 conjure up

vital 4 dire 5 alive 6 lively, living, mortal, urgent 7 animate, crucial, pivotal 8 animated, cardinal, critical, decisive, integral, pressing, required, vigorous 9 essential, important, necessary, requisite 10 imperative, red-blooded 11 fundamental, life-or-death 12 invigorating 13 indispensable

vitality see **vigor**

vitalize 5 liven 6 arouse, excite, infuse, perk up, spirit, vivify 7 animate, enliven, quicken 8 energize 9 encourage, galvanize, stimulate 10 invigorate

vitals see **viscera**

vitamin 6 biotin, niacin 7 choline, folacin, retinal, retinol 8 thiamine 9 carnitine, cobalamin, folic acid 10 calciferol, pyridoxine, riboflavin, tocopherol 12 ascorbic acid

Vita Nuova author 5 Dante (Alighieri)

vitelline 5 yolky 6 yellow

vitiate 3 mar 4 harm, soil, undo 5 annul, spoil, sully, taint 6 damage, debase, defile, impair, negate 7 blemish, corrupt, debauch, deprave, nullify, pervert, tarnish 8 abrogate 9 undermine 10 bastardize, demoralize, invalidate

vitreous 6 glassy

vitriol 4 acid, bile 5 spite, venom 6 malice, rancor 7 sulfate 8 acrimony 9 virulence 12 sulfuric acid

vitriolic 4 acid 5 acrid 7 acerbic, caustic, cutting, mordant 8 scathing, stinging, virulent 9 rancorous, truculent

vituperate 3 rag 4 lash, rail, rant, rate 5 abuse, baste, curse, scold, score 6 berate, malign, revile, scorch 7 asperse, bawl out, chew out, condemn, cuss out, upbraid 8 lambaste 9 castigate 10 tongue-lash

vituperation 5 abuse 6 rebuke 7 censure, obloquy, reproof 8 scolding 9 contumely, invective 10 scurrility 11 fulmination, mudslinging 12 billingsgate 13 tongue-lashing

vituperative 7 abusive, railing, scurril 8 scathing, scolding, scurrile, venomous, viperish 9 invective 10 censorious, scurrilous 11 opprobrious 12 contumelious

vivace 5 brisk 6 lively 8 animated, spirited

vivacious 3 gay 4 airy, pert 5 perky, spicy, sunny, zesty 6 bouncy, breezy, bubbly, jaunty, lively, sparky 7 buoyant, chipper 8 animated, pixieish, spirited **9** ebullient, sprightly **12** effervescent, high-spirited

vivacity see **verve**

Vivaldi epithet 9 Red Priest (the)

____ **vivant 3** bon

vivarium 9 terrarium

viva voce 4 oral **6** orally, spoken **11** word-of-mouth

viverrid 5 civet, fossa, genet **7** linsang

vivid 5 alive, sharp **6** bright, garish, lively, punchy, visual **7** graphic, intense, vibrant **8** animated, colorful, eloquent, lifelike **9** chromatic, pictorial **10** expressive **11** picturesque

vivify 5 liven, renew **6** excite, infuse, kindle, revive **7** animate, enliven, quicken, refresh, restore **9** stimulate

vixen 3 fox, nag **5** harpy, scold, shrew **6** ogress, virago **8** fishwife, harridan, Xantippe **9** termagant, Xanthippe

viz 5 to wit **6** namely, that is **8** scilicet **9** videlicet **12** in other words

vizard 4 face, mask **5** guise, visor **6** domino **8** disguise

vocabulary 4 cant **5** argot, lingo, slang, words **6** jargon, patois **7** lexicon **8** glossary **9** word-hoard **10** vernacular **11** terminology

vocal 4 oral **5** blunt, frank **6** phonic, spoken, voiced **7** uttered **8** eloquent **9** outspoken **10** articulate, expressive, free-spoken

vocalic 5 vowel

vocalist 4 diva **6** belter, canary, singer **7** crooner, warbler, yodeler **8** minstrel, songbird **9** balladeer, chanteuse, chorister **10** cantatrice, prima donna

vocalization 4 song **5** voice **6** speech **7** diction **8** speaking **9** utterance **11** enunciation **12** articulation **13** pronunciation

vocalize 3 air, hem **4** sing, talk **5** chant, croon, speak, state, utter, voice **6** warble **7** express **9** enunciate, pronounce

vocal organ 6 larynx **8** voice box *bird:* **6** syrinx

vocation 3 art, job **4** call, work **5** craft, trade **6** career, métier **7** calling, mission, pursuit **8** business, lifework **10** employment, handicraft, occupation, profession

vociferate 3 bay, cry **4** bark, bray, call, roar, yawp, yell **5** shout **6** bellow, clamor, holler **7** thunder

vociferous 4 loud **5** noisy **6** shrill **7** blatant, clamant, raucous **8** strident **9** clamorous **11** openmouthed **12** obstreperous

vodka *brand:* **5** Stoli **7** Absolut **8** Smirnoff **11** Stolichnaya *source:* **3** rye **4** corn **5** wheat **6** barley, potato

vogue 3 cry, fad, ton **4** chic, mode, pose, rage **5** craze, favor, furor, style, trend **6** furore **7** fashion **10** dernier cri, popularity **11** stylishness

voice 3 put, say **4** part, talk, tell, vent **5** say-so, sound, speak, state, utter **6** assert, choice, medium, singer, speech **7** declare, express, opinion, present **8** vocalize **9** condition, enunciate, formulate, pronounce, statement, utterance, verbalize **10** articulate, expression, instrument *female:* **4** alto **5** mezzo **7** soprano **9** contralto *high:* **5** tenor **7** soprano **8** falsetto *in grammar:* **6** active **7** passive *Latin:* **3** vox *male:* **4** bass **5** tenor **8** baritone *quality:* **5** pitch **6** timbre *quiet:* **7** whisper *relating to:* **5** vocal **8** phonetic *without:* **4** dumb, mute

voice box 6 larynx

voiced 4 oral **5** vocal **6** sonant, spoken **7** uttered **8** phonated **9** expressed

voiceless 3 mum **4** dumb, mute, surd **6** silent **8** breathed **12** inarticulate

void 3 gap, nix **4** emit, hole, idle, lack, null, undo **5** abyss, annul, blank, clear, empty, inane, quash **6** bereft, cancel, cavity, hollow, negate, remove, vacant, vacate, vacuum **7** absence, give off, negated, nullify, rescind, reverse, vacuity, vacuous **8** abrogate, deserted, evacuate **9** black hole, discharge, eliminate, emptiness **10** extinguish **11** nothingness

voilà 4 ta-da **5** ta-dah, there

volant 4 fast, spry, yare **5** agile, fleet, quick, zippy **6** flying, lively, nimble **9** dexterous, sprightly

volar 6 palmar

volatile 5 flaky **6** fickle, flakey, flying, lively **7** erratic, essence, flighty **8** fleeting, fugitive, skittery, skittish, unstable, variable, volcanic **9** ephemeral, explosive, fugacious, mercurial, momentary, transient **10** capricious, changeable, evanescent, inconstant, short-lived, transitory **11** impermanent **13** temperamental

volatility 10 fickleness **11** flightiness, inconstancy, instability **13** changeability

volcanic 7 violent **8** volatile **9** explosive *crater:* **4** maar *explosion:* **8** eruption *glass:* **8** obsidian *matter:* **3** ash **4** lava, tufa, tuff **5** magma **6** scoria *mound:* **4** cone *passage:* **6** throat **7** conduit *vent:* **8** fumarole **9** solfatara

volcano 4 hill, vent **8** mountain *Alaska:* **6** Katmai (Mount) **8** Wrangell (Mount) **9** Aniakchak (Crater) *Andes:* **5** Omate **12** Huaina Putina *Antarctica:* **6** Erebus (Mount) *Azores:* **4** Alto (Pico) *California:* **6** Lassen (Peak) *Canaries:* **5** Teide (Pico de), Teyde (Pico de) **8** Tenerife (Pico de) *Co-*

lombia: 5 Huila (Nevado del), Pasto 6 Purace 7 Galeras *Costa Rica:* 4 Poás 5 Barba, Irazú *Ecuador:* 6 Sangay 8 Antisana, Cotopaxi *extinct:* 4 Popa (Mount) 5 Iriga, Kenya (Mount) 8 Mauna Kea 9 Haleakala (Crater) *Guatemala:* 4 Agua 5 Fuego 7 Atitlán *Hawaii:* 7 Kilauea 8 Mauna Kea, Mauna Loa *Honshu:* 4 Nasu 5 Asama, Azuma 6 Bandai 8 Nasudake 9 Asamayama *Iceland:* 5 Askja, Hecla, Hekla *Indonesia:* 3 Awu (Gunung) 5 Agung (Gunung) 7 Tambora (Gunung) *island:* 5 Thera, Thira 8 Krakatau, Krakatoa, Santorin 9 Santorini *Italy:* 8 Vesuvius 9 Stromboli *Iwo Jima:* 9 Suribachi (Mount) *Japan:* 3 Aso 5 Unzen 6 Asosan *Java:* 4 Gede (Gunung) 5 Bromo, Gedeh (Gunung), Kelud (Gunung), Salak (Gunung) *Madeira:* 5 Ruivo (Pico) *Martinique:* 5 Pelée (Mount) *Mexico:* 6 Colima 7 Orizaba 9 Paricutín 12 Popocatepetl *mud:* 5 salse *New Zealand:* 7 Ruapehu (Mount) 9 Ngauruhoe, Tongariro *Peru:* 5 Misti (El) *Philippines:* 3 Apo (Mount) 4 Taal 5 Mayon (Mount) 8 Pinatubo (Mount) *Sicily:* 4 Etna *Solomons:* 5 Balbi *South America:* 5 Lanín, Maipo, Maipu *Sumatra:* 5 Dempo (Gunung) 7 Kerinci 8 Kerintji *type:* 6 shield 10 cinder cone *Washington:* 11 Saint Helens (Mount) *West Indies:* 9 Soufrière

_____ **volente** 3 Deo

volition 4 will 6 choice, desire, intent, option 8 decision, election 9 selection 10 preference

volley 4 hail, shot 5 burst, round, salvo, storm 6 return, shower 7 barrage 8 drumfire 9 broadside, cannonade, discharge, fusillade

volplane 5 glide

Volpone 3 Fox (The) *author:* 6 Jonson (Ben) *servant:* 5 Mosca

Volsung *grandson:* 6 Sigurd 9 Siegfried *great-grandfather:* 4 Odin *son:* 7 Sigmund

voltage 5 power 6 energy 9 intensity

Voltaire *drama:* 5 Zaïre 6 Alzire, Brutus, Mèrope, Oedipe 7 Mahomet 8 Tancrède *novel:* 5 Zadig 7 Candide *real name:* 6 Arouet (François Marie)

volte-face 5 U-turn 8 flip-flop, reversal, turnover 9 about-face, inversion, turnabout 10 switcheroo 13 change of heart

voluble 4 glib 5 gabby, talky, windy 6 chatty, fluent, mouthy, prolix 7 verbose 8 effusive, vocative 9 garrulous, talkative 10 longwinded, loquacious

volume 4 body, book, bulk, mass, size, tome 5 album, flood, folio, space 6 amount, scroll 7 content 8 capacity, loudness, quantity 9 aggregate 12 displacement

voluminous 4 full 5 bulky 6 legion, prolix 7 copious 8 numerous, prolific 9 capacious 10 convoluted 13 multitudinous

Volumnia's son 10 Coriolanus

voluntary 4 free 7 willful, willing, witting 8 elective, freewill, optional 10 autonomous, deliberate, volitional 11 independent, intentional, spontaneous 13 discretionary

volunteer 5 offer 6 enlist, join up, sign up 7 present, propose, suggest *hospital:* 12 candy striper

Volunteer State 9 Tennessee

voluptuous 4 sexy 5 ample, buxom 6 wanton 7 languid, sensual 8 luscious, sensuous 9 bodacious, luxurious 10 curvaceous

volute 5 helix, shell 6 scroll, spiral 7 mollusc, mollusk 8 curlicue

vomit 3 gag 4 barf, cast, gush, hurl, lose, puke, spew, toss 5 expel, retch 6 spit up 7 bring up, throw up, upchuck 8 disgorge 11 regurgitate

vomiting 6 emesis

Vonnegut work 9 Galapagos, Timequake 10 Cat's Cradle, Hocus Pocus 11 Player Piano 13 Sirens of Titan (The) 18 Slaughterhouse Five 20 Breakfast of Champions 22 Happy Birthday Wanda June

voodoo 3 hex 4 jinx, juju, mojo 5 charm, magic, spell, vodun 6 amulet, whammy 7 bewitch, enchant, sorcery 8 ensorcel, wizardry 9 ensorcell 10 hocus-pocus, mumbo jumbo, necromancy, witchcraft 11 abracadabra, implausible, unrealistic *relative:* 5 obeah 8 santeria 9 Candomblé

voracious 4 avid 5 eager 6 ardent, greedy, hungry 7 piggish, starved 8 edacious, famished, ravenous, starving 9 rapacious 10 gluttonous, insatiable, omnivorous, quenchless

vortex 4 eddy, gyre 5 swirl 7 tornado 9 hurricane, maelstrom, whirlpool, whirlwind 11 tourbillion

votary 3 bug, fan, nut 4 buff 5 lover 6 addict, zealot 7 admirer, apostle, devotee, groupie, habitué 8 adherent, advocate, believer, disciple, follower 9 worshiper 10 aficionado, enthusiast, worshipper

vote 3 opt 4 poll 5 elect, judge, offer 6 ballot, choice, choose, decide, ratify, select, ticket 7 adjudge, declare, endorse, express, opinion, propose, suggest, verdict 8 election, suffrage 9 franchise 10 expression *affirmative:* 3 aye, nod, yea, yes 6 placet *kind:* 5 proxy, straw, voice 6 secret 7 write-in 8 absentee 10 plebiscite, referendum *negative:* 2 no 3 nay *right to:* 8 suffrage 9 franchise

votive 8 grateful 10 devotional

vouch 5 prove **6** affirm, assert, assure, attest, uphold, verify **7** certify, confirm, support, witness **8** accredit **9** guarantee **11** corroborate **12** substantiate

voucher 3 IOU **4** chit **5** proof **6** coupon, surety **7** receipt **9** affidavit, indenture **10** credential **11** certificate **13** authorization

vouchsafe 4 give **5** award, favor, grant **6** accord, bestow, confer, oblige **7** concede, furnish

vow 4 aver, oath, word **5** swear, troth **6** assert, attest, pledge, plight **7** confirm, declare, promise, warrant **8** covenant **9** assertion, guarantee **10** obligation **11** declaration

vowel 6 letter, symbol **11** speech sound *kind:* **4** high, long **5** glide, schwa, short **9** diphthong **11** monophthong *omission:* **7** aphesis **11** contraction *variation:* **6** ablaut, umlaut

voyage 4 sail, trek, trip **5** jaunt **6** cruise, junket, outing, travel **7** journey, odyssey, set sail **8** traverse **9** excursion **10** expedition, pilgrimage

voyeur 6 peeper **10** peeping Tom

Vronski's lover 12 Anna Karenina

Vulcan see **Hephaestus**

vulgar 3 low, raw **4** base, lewd, loud, rude, vile **5** crass, crude, gaudy, gross, rough, showy, tacky **6** coarse, earthy, flashy, garish, ribald, sordid, tawdry **7** chintzy, kitschy, lowbred, lowbrow, obscene, profane, uncouth **8** churlish, improper, indecent, off-color, unseemly **9** barbarous, graceless, low-minded, offensive, tasteless, unrefined **10** indecorous, indelicate, scurrilous, unpolished, vernacular **11** pretentious

vulgate 10 vernacular

Vulgate translator 6 Jerome

vulnerability 8 exposure, soft spot, weakness **10** underbelly **12** Achilles' heel

vulnerable 4 open, weak **6** liable **7** exposed **10** assailable **11** susceptible

vulnerary 4 balm **5** salve, tonic **7** healing, unguent **8** curative, ointment, remedial, salutary, sanative **9** medicinal, wholesome **10** salubrious **11** restorative, therapeutic **12** healthgiving

vulpine 3 sly **4** foxy, wily **5** slick **6** artful, astute, crafty, shrewd, tricky **7** cunning, foxlike **8** guileful

vulture 4 bird **6** condor **11** lammergeier, lammergeyer *food:* **7** carrion *relative:* **4** hawk **5** eagle **6** falcon **7** buzzard

vulturine 8 ravenous **9** predatory, rapacious, raptorial **10** predaceous, predacious, scavenging

W

wacky 3 fey, mad **4** daft, nuts **5** batty, daffy, crazy, flaky, kooky, loony, loopy, silly **6** absurd, fruity, insane, screwy **7** bonkers, cracked, foolish, idiotic, lunatic, offbeat **8** crackers, demented **9** eccentric **10** irrational **11** harebrained **12** preposterous

wad 3 gob, jam **4** chaw, cram, lump, mint, pile, plug, quid, roll, swab **5** chunk, stuff **6** boodle, bundle, packet, pellet **7** fortune **8** bankroll

waddle 6 toddle

waddy 4 club, cosh **6** cowboy, cudgel **7** rustler **8** bludgeon

wade 4 ford, plod **5** labor **6** drudge, plodge, trudge *into:* **5** set to **6** attack, plunge, tackle **9** undertake

wadi 3 bed **4** wash **5** gully **6** arroyo, coulee, course, ravine **9** streambed **10** depression **11** watercourse

wafer 4 chip, disk, host **5** matzo, obley, slice **6** matzoh **7** cracker

waffle 4 yo-yo **5** tripe, waver **6** dither, drivel, seesaw **7** blather **8** flip-flop **9** fluctuate, vacillate **10** equivocate

waft 4 flag, gust, puff, waif, wave **5** carry, drift, float, hover **7** pennant

wag 3 bob, nod, wit **4** card, lash, wave **5** clown, cutup, joker, shake, swing, whisk **6** kidder, switch, twitch, waddle **8** brandish, comedian, funnyman, jokester

wage 3 fee, pay **6** income, reward, salary **7** carry on, payment, stipend **8** earnings, pittance, receipts **9** emolument **10** recompense **12** compensation, remuneration

wager 3 bet, lay, pot **4** ante, game, risk **5** stake **6** chance, gamble, hazard **7** venture

waggery 3 gag **4** jest, joke, prank, sport **7** devilry, kidding, roguery **8** deviltry, drollery, mischief **10** impishness, pleasantry **11** roguishness **12** sportiveness **13** practical joke

waggish 4 arch, pert **5** antic, comic, droll, saucy, witty **6** impish, jocose **7** comical, jocular, playful, puckish, roguish **8** humorous, prankish, sportive **9** facetious **10** frolicsome **11** mischievous

waggle 3 bob **4** reel, sway

Wagner, Richard *birthplace:* **7** Leipzig *father-in-law:* **5** Liszt (Franz) *festival site:* **8** Bayreuth *opera:* **4** Ring **6** Rienzi **7** Walküre (Die) **8** Parsifal **9** Lohengrin, Rheingold (Das), Siegfried **10** Die Walküre, Tannhäuser **12** Das Rheingold **13** Meistersinger (Die) **14** Flying Dutchman (The) **15** Götterdämmerung **16** Tristan und Isolde **17** Ring of the Nibelung (The) *patron:* **6** Ludwig *recurring theme:* **9** leitmotif, leitmotiv *wife:* **5** Minna **6** Cosima

wagon 3 van **4** cart, dray, tram, trek, wain **7** caravan, coaster, hayrack **9** Conestoga

wahoo 3 ono **8** mackerel **9** winged elm **11** burning bush

waif 5 gamin, stray **6** gamine, orphan, urchin **8** wanderer **9** foundling **10** ragamuffin **11** guttersnipe

wail 3 bay, cry **4** bawl, blub, fuss, howl, keen, weep, yowl **5** mourn, whine **6** bemoan, lament, plaint, repine **7** blubber, ululate **8** complain **9** complaint **11** lamentation

wain 5 wagon **9** Big Dipper

wainscot 4 dado

waistband 3 obi **4** belt, sash **6** girdle **8** ceinture, cincture **10** cummerbund

waistcoat 4 vest **5** gilet **6** jerkin, weskit

wait 4 bide, idle, lurk, stay **5** abide, dally, delay, serve, tarry, watch **6** expect, hold on, linger, remain **8** hang fire, mark time, sit tight **10** anticipate **11** stick around

waiter 4 tray **6** carhop, garçon, salver, server **7** servant **9** attendant

Waiting for ___ 5 Godot, Lefty

wait on 4 tend **5** serve **6** attend, tend to **7** care for, cater to **9** look after

waive 4 cede, stay **5** allow, defer, delay, forgo, table, yield **6** give up, hold up, put off, shelve **7** abandon, concede, dismiss, hold off, suspend **8** hand over, hold over, postpone **9** surrender **10** relinquish

wake 4 path, stir, wash **5** alert, arise, get up, rally, rouse, track, vigil, watch **6** arouse, bestir, excite, kindle, stir up **7** roll out **8** activate, backwash **9** aftermath, stimulate

wakeful 5 alert **8** restless, vigilant **9** insomniac, sleepless

waken see **wake**

Walden author 7 Thoreau (Henry David)

wale 3 rib **4** bend, welt **5** brace, ridge **6** strake

Wales *capital:* **7** Cardiff *city:* **6** Bangor **7** Newport, Swansea **8** St. David's *island:* **8** Anglesey *mountain:* **7** Snowdon *patron saint:* **5** David *river:* **3** Dee *strait:* **5** Menai *symbol:* **4** leek **6** dragon **8** daffodil (see also **Cymric**)

walk 3 pad **4** gait, hike, hoof, pace, path, plod, roam, slog, step, trip **5** alley, amble, clump, mince, paseo, stave, strut, stump, trail, tramp, tread, troop **6** hoof it, prance, ramble, sashay, stride, stroll, toddle, trudge, waddle, wander **7** saunter, shamble, shuffle, stumble, swagger, traipse **8** ambulate, traverse **9** promenade **11** base on balls, perambulate, peregrinate

walkaway 4 romp, rout

walking shorts 8 Bermudas

walking stick 4 cane **5** staff **6** crutch, insect **7** phasmid, whangee

walk out 5 leave **6** strike

walk out on 5 leave **6** desert **7** abandon, forsake

Walküre composer 6 Wagner (Richard)

walkway 4 path **7** passage **9** promenade

wall 3 bar, hem **4** side, stop **5** block, close, fence, hedge **6** immure **7** barrier, close in, enclose **8** blockade, surround **9** barricade, enclosure, roadblock, structure *bearing:* **7** support *hanging:* **8** tapestry *painting:* **5** mural **6** fresco *protective:* **7** parapet, rampart *top of:* **6** coping

wallaby 8 kangaroo

wallet 5 funds **6** folder **8** billfold **9** accessory, resources **10** pocketbook

Wallis and Futuna Islands *capital:* **7** Matautu *island:* **4** Uvéa *territory of:* **6** France

wallop 3 bop, hit **4** bang, bash, beat, belt, blow, boil, bust, clip, drub, lick, pelt, slam, slug, sock, whip, whop, whup **5** baste, paste, pound, punch, smack, whack **6** buffet, pummel, thrash, thwack **7** shellac, trounce **8** lambaste

walloping 4 huge **5** giant **7** immense, mammoth, monster **8** colossal, enormous, gigantic, smashing **10** gargantuan, impressive, incredible, prodigious

wallow 4 bask, roll **5** enjoy, revel **6** billow, welter **7** delight, indulge **9** luxuriate

Wall Street debut 3 IPO

___ Walpole 4 Hugh **6** Horace

___ Walton 3 Sam **5** Izaak

waltz 5 dance, valse

Waltz King 7 Strauss (Johann)

Wampanoag chief 9 Massasoit, Metacomet **10** King Philip

wampum 4 peag **5** beads, money **6** shells

wan 3 dim **4** ashy, gray, pale, waxy, weak, worn **5** ashen, faint, livid, lurid, pasty, waxen **6** anemic, doughy, feeble, infirm, pallid, peaked, sallow, sickly **7** ghastly, languid **8** blanched **9** bloodless, colorless, washed-out **10** cadaverous, white-faced

wand 3 rod **4** pole, tube **5** baton, staff

wander 3 bat, bum, gad **4** mill, roam, rove, swan **5** amble, dally, drift, float, gypsy, mooch, prowl, range, stray, tramp **6** ramble, stroll **7** deviate, digress, diverge, maunder, meander, saunter, traipse **8** divagate, straggle, vagabond **9** expatiate, gallivant **10** kick around

wanderer 4 waif **5** gypsy, nomad, rover, stray **7** pilgrim, vagrant **8** runabout, vagabond

wandering 7 erratic, migrant, nomadic, vagrant **8** vagabond **9** itinerant, migratory, walkabout, wayfaring **10** roundabout **11** peripatetic

wane 3 dim, ebb **4** fail, fall **5** abate, let up **6** lessen, recede, reduce, relent, shrink, weaken **7** decline, dwindle, slacken, subside **8** decrease, diminish, moderate, slack off, taper off

wangle 6 scheme **7** finagle, wheedle **8** inveigle, scrounge **10** manipulate

wannabe 5 clone **7** also-ran, copycat, hopeful, wishful **8** apparent, aspiring, desiring, desirous **9** ambitious, look-alike, potential

want 4 lack, like, need, void, wish **5** covet, crave, fault **6** dearth, desire, penury **7** absence, poverty, require **8** exigency **9** indigence, necessity, neediness, privation **10** deficiency, desiderate, inadequacy, scantiness **11** destitution, requirement **13** insufficiency

wanting 4 away, less, sans **5** minus, scant, short **6** absent, scanty, scarce **7** lacking, missing, without **9** deficient **10** inadequate, incomplete **12** insufficient

wanton 4 doxy, jade, lewd, minx, rank, slut **5** bawdy, cruel, hussy, loose, tramp, trull, wench **6** coquet, floozy, harlot, lavish, trifle, unruly **7** baggage, cyprian, immoral, jezebel, lustful, obscene, Paphian, sensual, trollop, wayward **8** inhumane, pitiless, ruthless, slattern, spiteful, sportive, strumpet **9** dissolute, luxuriant, malicious, merciless **10** gratuitous, lascivious, malevolent, outrageous, prostitute **11** extravagant, mischievous, uncalled-for

wapiti 3 elk **4** stag **7** red deer

war 4 feud, odds **5** fight **6** battle, combat, strife **7** contest **8** conflict, struggle, variance **9** hostility **10** antagonism **11** competition

German: **5** Krieg **10** blitzkrieg *god:* **3** Tiu, Tyr **4** Ares, Mars, Odin **5** Woden, Wotan *goddess:* **4** Enyo **5** Anath **6** Inanna, Ishtar **7** Bellona *Latin:* **6** bellum *Muslim:* **5** jehad, jihad *relating to:* **7** martial

War and Peace *author:* **7** Tolstoy (Leo) *character:* **6** Andrey (Prince), Pierre (Bezukhov) **7** Natasha (Rostova) *composer:* **9** Prokofiev (Sergey)

warble 4 sing **5** carol, chirp, trill, tweet **6** gadfly, maggot, quaver **7** descant, melisma, twitter

warbler 4 bird **6** singer **7** kinglet **8** songster **9** blackpoll **11** gnatcatcher *European:* **10** chiffchaff

____ **Warbucks 5** Daddy

war casualties group 3 DAV

war cry 5 motto **6** slogan *Greek:* **5** alala *Japanese:* **6** banzai

ward 4 care **5** aegis, stave **6** barrio, charge **7** custody, defense, keeping **8** district, division, precinct, security **9** bishopric **10** protection **11** safekeeping **12** guardianship

warden 6 jailer, keeper, regent **7** provost **8** governor, guardian, official **9** castellan, constable, custodian, protector **10** commandant, supervisor

ward off 5 avert, parry, rebut, repel **6** divert **7** deflect **8** turn away **9** forestall

wardrobe 5 trunk **6** closet **7** apparel, armoire, clothes **8** clothing **9** garderobe **12** clothespress *assistant:* **7** dresser

warehouse 4 stow **5** depot, lodge, stock, store **7** confine, deposit, shelter, storage, stowage **8** building **9** stockroom, storeroom **10** depository, repository **11** accommodate *oriental:* **6** godown

wares 4 line **5** goods, stock **9** vendibles **11** commodities, marketables, merchandise

warfare 6 battle, combat, strife **8** conflict, struggle **10** operations **11** hostilities *type:* **4** germ **10** trench **10** biological

warhorse 4 hack **5** steed **7** charger, courser, veteran **8** chestnut, standard

warlike 7 hawkish, martial **8** militant, military **9** bellicose, combative, truculent **10** aggressive, pugnacious **11** belligerent

warlock 3 wiz **4** mage **5** magus **6** wizard **8** conjurer, conjuror, magician, satanist, sorcerer **9** diabolist, enchanter **11** necromancer

warm 4 bask, heat, kind **5** angry, fresh **6** ardent, genial, heated, heat up, loving, reheat, secure, tender **7** affable, cordial, excited, fervent, sincere **8** friendly, gracious, spirited **9** heartfelt **10** passionate, responsive **11** kindhearted, sympathetic **12** affectionate, enthusiastic, wholehearted **13** compassionate *air:* **7** thermal

warmed-over 5 banal, stale, tired, trite **6** old-hat **7** clichéd **8** shopworn, timeworn **9** hackneyed

warmhearted 4 kind **6** benign, kindly, loving, tender **7** cordial **8** generous **9** benignant, unselfish **10** benevolent **11** magnanimous, sympathetic **12** affectionate **13** compassionate

warmth 4 glow, heat **7** comfort **8** fondness **9** affection **10** cordiality

warmup 5 run-up **6** lead-in, opener **7** kickoff, preface, prelude, preview **8** overture, preamble, prologue **9** countdown **11** preliminary **12** introduction

warn 3 tip **4** clew, clue **5** alert **6** advise, inform, notify, tip off **7** apprise, caution, counsel **8** admonish

warning 3 tip **4** hint **5** alarm, alert **6** caveat, notice, signal, tip-off **7** caution, counsel, summons **8** monition, monitory **10** admonition, cautionary **12** admonishment *legal:* **6** caveat

War of the Worlds author 5 Wells (H. G.)

warp 4 base, bend, cast, kink, rope, wind **5** color, curve, twist **6** buckle, debase, deform, wrench **7** confuse, contort, corrupt, deflect, distort, pervert, torture, vitiate **10** bastardize **12** misrepresent

warrant 4 pawn, writ **5** proof, prove, token **6** affirm, assert, assure, attest, avouch, ensure, ground, insure, pledge, secure **7** certify, contend, declare, justify, precept **8** guaranty, maintain, mittimus, sanction, security **9** assurance, authority, authorize, guarantee **10** foundation **11** certificate **12** confirmation **13** justification

warranty 4 bail, bond **6** surety **8** covenant, security **9** guarantee

warren 4 maze **7** network, rabbits **8** tenement

Warren novel 14 All the King's Men

warrior 2 GI **4** hero **7** battler, fighter, soldier **8** champion **9** combatant **10** serviceman *female:* **6** Amazon *Japanese:* **5** ronin **7** samurai *princess:* **4** Xena **7** Lawless (Lucy)

Warsaw castle: **5** Zamek *river:* **7** Vistula

wart 4 flaw **6** defect, growth **7** blemish, verruca **11** excrescence

wary 5 alert, cagey, canny, chary, leery **7** careful, dubious, guarded, mindful **8** cautious, skittish, vigilant, watchful **10** suspicious **11** circumspect, distrustful

wash 3 lap, pan, tub **4** hose, lave, suds, wadi **5** bathe, clean, creek, douse, drift, float, flush, gully, marsh, scrub, slosh, swill **6** drench, shower, sluice, splash **7** cleanse,

coating, launder, laundry, shampoo, suffuse **8** backwash

washed-out 4 beat **5** all in, faded, spent, tired, weary **6** bushed, effete, sapped, used-up, wasted **7** drained **8** depleted **9** exhausted

washed-up 4 beat, done **5** kaput, spent **6** done in **7** also-ran, defunct, done for, through **8** finished

washing 4 bath **6** lavage **7** laundry **8** ablution, lavation *ceremonial:* **6** lavabo

Washington capital: **7** Olympia *city:* **6** Tacoma **7** Seattle, Spokane **9** Vancouver **10** Walla Walla *college, university:* **7** Gonzaga, Whitman **9** Evergreen *dam:* **11** Grand Coulee *mountain, range:* **7** Cascade, Olympic, Rainier **8** St. Helens *nickname:* **9** Evergreen (State) *river:* **6** Yakima **8** Columbia *state bird:* **9** goldfinch *state flower:* **12** rhododendron *state tree:* **7** hemlock

Washington, D.C., designer 7 L'Enfant (Pierre-Charles)

Washington, George home: **11** Mount Vernon *wife:* **6** Martha

Washington Square author 5 James (Henry)

wasp 5 mason **6** digger, hornet, vespid **8** braconid **9** ichneumon, mud dauber **12** yellow jacket

waspish 5 testy **6** snappy, snarky, snippy, touchy **7** peevish, vespine **8** petulant, snappish, vinegary **9** crotchety, fractious, irritable, querulous **10** vinegarish **12** cantankerous, cross-grained

wassail 5 binge, carol, drink, revel, spree, toast **6** bender **7** carouse, revelry, roister **8** carousal, drinking

Wasserstein play 15 Heidi Chronicles (The) **17** Sisters Rosenzweig (The)

waste 4 arid, fail, kill, loss, ruin, sack, wild **5** empty, offal, scrap, trash **6** barren, damage, debris, desert, devour, litter, ravage, refuse, sewage, shrink, weaken **7** badland, consume, despoil, destroy, fritter, garbage, pillage, plunder, rubbish **8** decrease, desolate, emaciate, enfeeble, misspend, prodigal, spoilage, squander, wear away, wildland **9** devastate, dissipate, excrement, sweepings, throw away **10** desolation, wilderness **11** prodigality **12** extravagance, extravagancy *maker:* **5** haste *time:* **5** dally **6** dawdle, footle, piddle, trifle

waste away 4 fade, fail **6** molder, shrink **7** atrophy, decline, dwindle, shrivel **10** degenerate

wasted 3 lit **4** high **5** drunk, gaunt **6** peaked, sickly, stoned **7** elapsed, ravaged **8** skeletal

9 emaciated 10 cadaverous, skeletonic 11 intoxicated

wasteful 6 lavish **8** prodigal **9** throwaway **10** profligate, thriftless, uneconomic **11** extravagant, improvident, inefficient, spendthrift

wastefulness 6 excess **10** lavishness **11** prodigality **12** extravagance, immoderation

wasteland 4 wild **5** heath **6** barren **10** desolation, wilderness

Waste Land author 5 Eliot (T. S.)

wastrel 3 rip **4** rake, roué **7** rounder, spender **8** prodigal **9** fritterer, libertine **10** dissipater, high roller, ne'er-do-well, profligate, squanderer **11** scattergood, spendthrift

watch 3 eye, see, spy **4** bide, look, mind, tend, tout, wait, wake, ward **5** guard, shift, vigil **6** attend, follow, look at, notice, sentry **7** care for, lookout, monitor, observe, surveil **8** bulletin, eagle eye, scrutiny, sentinel, watchman **9** attention, timepiece, vigilance **10** duty period, observance **11** chronometer, observation **12** surveillance *chain:* **3** fob *maker:* **10** horologist

watchdog 5 guard **6** keeper **8** Cerberus, guardian **9** custodian, protector

watcher 6 viewer **7** guarder, lookout **8** beholder, follower, guardian, observer, onlooker **9** spectator

watchful 4 wary **5** alert, chary **7** on guard, wakeful **8** cautious, vigilant **9** attentive, observant, sleepless, wide-awake **10** unsleeping *Scottish:* **5** tenty **6** tentie

watchman 5 guard, scout **6** patrol, picket, sentry, warder **7** lookout **8** sentinel

watch out 6 beware **8** take care

watchtower 6 turret **7** lookout **8** barbican, bartizan **10** lighthouse

watchword 3 cry **5** motto **6** mantra, parole, signal, slogan **8** password **9** principle **10** shibboleth **11** catchphrase, countersign

water 4 hose, soak, thin, tide **5** drink, fluid, spray **6** dilute, liquid, supply **7** moisten **8** irrigate, moisture, snowmelt, sprinkle **10** excellence **13** amniotic fluid *body:* **3** bay, sea **4** gulf, lake, pool **5** ocean **6** lagoon, strait **9** reservoir *combining form:* **4** aqui, aquo, hydr **5** hydro *French:* **3** eau *goddess:* **4** Nina **7** Anahita, Anaitis *Latin:* **4** aqua *Spanish:* **4** agua

water buffalo 4 arna **5** bovid **7** carabao *female:* **5** arnee

water clock 9 clepsydra

water closet 2 WC **3** loo **4** head, john **5** privy **6** toilet **7** latrine **8** bathroom, lavatory

watercourse 4 dike, duct **5** bayou, canal, ditch **6** arroyo **7** channel, conduit **8** aqueduct, headrace, tailrace **9** streambed

water cow 6 dugong **7** manatee

watered-down 5 washy **6** dilute **7** diluted

waterfall 5 chute, sault, shoot **7** cascade **8** cataract *Brazil:* **6** Iguaçú (Falls), Iguazú (Falls) *California:* **8** Yosemite (Falls) *Canada:* **5** Grand (Falls) **8** Takkakaw **9** Churchill (Falls) *Canada-U.S.:* **7** Niagara (Falls) *Congo:* **6** Boyoma (Falls) **7** Stanley (Falls) *former Nile:* **4** Owen (Falls) **5** Ripon (Falls) *Kentucky:* **10** Cumberland (Falls) *New Zealand:* **10** Sutherland (Falls) *Niagara:* **8** American, Canadian **9** Horseshoe *Norway:* **6** Rjukan (Falls) *Oregon:* **9** Multnomah (Falls) *South Africa:* **6** Tugela (Falls) *Snake River:* **4** Twin (Falls) **8** Shoshone (Falls) *Venezuela:* **5** Angel (Falls) *Washington:* **10** Snoqualmie (Falls) *world's highest:* **5** Angel (Falls) *Wyoming:* **11** Yellowstone (Falls) *Zambezi River:* **8** Victoria (Falls)

water finder 6 dowser **11** divining rod

waterfront 8 seacoast **9** lakeshore, riverside

water hole 5 oasis

watering hole 3 bar, pub **4** café **5** oasis **6** lounge, nitery, resort, saloon, tavern **7** barroom, cabaret, gin mill, taproom **9** nightclub, nightspot, roadhouse **10** supper club **11** rathskeller

waterless 3 dry **4** arid, sere **7** bone-dry, parched **8** droughty **9** anhydrous **10** dehydrated

waterlog 8 saturate

waterloo 4 ruin **6** defeat **7** failure **8** disaster, downfall

water nymph 3 nix **4** lily **5** naiad, nixie **6** mayfly, Nereid **7** Oceanid **9** dragonfly

water oscillation 6 seiche

water pipe 4 bong **5** spout **6** hookah **8** narghile, nargileh **12** hubble-bubble

water plant 7 aquatic, seaweed **8** duckweed, wild rice **9** arrowhead, tape grass **10** hydrophyte, manna grass **11** bladderwort

water rat 6 nutria

watershed 6 crisis, divide **12** turning point

water spirit 3 nix **5** nixie, nymph **6** sprite, undine

water tank 7 cistern

watery 4 pale, thin, weak **5** banal, bland, vapid, washy **6** dilute, serous **7** diluted, insipid

wattle 4 gill, grid, jowl **5** frame **8** caruncle **9** framework, interlace **10** interweave

wattle and ____ 4 daub

wave 3 wag **4** flag, flap **5** heave, ridge, surge, sweep, swell **6** comber, influx, marcel, motion, period, ripple, signal, waggle **7** breaker, dismiss, flutter, gesture, upsurge **8**

activity, brandish, flourish, undulate **9** disregard *large:* **7** tsunami

waver 4 reel, sway **5** swing, weave **6** dither, falter, quaver, quiver, teeter, totter, wobble **7** flicker, stagger, whiffle **8** hesitate, undulate **9** oscillate, vacillate **12** shilly-shally

wavering 4 weak **5** shake, shaky **6** unsure, wobbly **7** halting **8** doubtful, insecure, to-and-fro, unstable **9** equivocal, faltering, fluctuant, hesitancy, undecided, vibration, whiffling **10** hesitating, hesitation, indecision, irresolute **11** fluctuating, vacillating, vacillation **12** irresolution, shilly-shally

Waverley novels 6 Rob Roy **7** Ivanhoe **10** Kenilworth **14** Quentin Durward *author:* **5** Scott (Walter)

wavy 4 ondé, undé **7** rolling **8** rippling, swelling **9** fluctuant **10** undulating **11** fluctuating

wavy pattern 5 moiré **8** squiggle **10** undulation **11** crenulation

wax 4 come, grow, rise **5** boost, build, mount **6** become, expand, record **7** augment, enlarge **8** heighten, increase, multiply, paraffin, simonize **9** secretion, substance *Chinese:* **4** pela

waxen 3 wan **4** ashy, pale **5** ashen, livid **6** pallid, smooth **7** pliable **8** blanched, moldable **9** colorless

way 3 ilk **4** door, kind, mode, much, path, road, sort, type, very **5** entry, habit, means, order, route, state, style, usage **6** access, artery, action, avenue, course, custom, degree, manner, method, street **7** ability, fashion, feature, ingress, opening, outcome, respect **8** distance, entrance, practice **9** boulevard, condition, direction, procedure, technique **11** opportunity, possibility **12** thoroughfare

wayfarer 4 hobo **5** gipsy, gypsy, hiker, nomad, rover, tramp **7** rambler **8** traveler, vagabond **9** itinerant, journeyer, traveller

wayfaring 6 roving **7** nomadic, vagrant **8** vagabond **9** itinerant, traveling, wandering **10** travelling **11** peripatetic **13** perambulatory

waylay 4 jump **5** brace **6** ambush, attack **8** surprise **9** bushwhack, still-hunt

Wayne's World *actor:* **5** Myers (Mike) **6** Carvey (Dana) *character:* **5** Garth, Wayne

Way of All Flesh author 6 Butler (Samuel)

Way of the World author 8 Congreve (William)

wayward 5 balky **6** fickle, unruly **7** froward, restive, vagrant, willful **8** contrary, perverse, untoward **9** whimsical **10** capricious, headstrong **11** intractable, wrongheaded **12** ungovernable **13** unpredictable

we *French:* **4** nous *German:* **3** wir *Italian:* **3** noi *Spanish:* **8** nosotros

weak 3 dim, wan **4** puny, soft, thin **5** faint, frail, shaky, timid **6** dilute, feeble, flimsy, infirm, sickly, unsure, watery, wobbly **7** brittle, diluted, fragile, rickety, spindly, tenuous, unsound **8** decrepit, delicate, helpless, impotent, inferior, insecure, timorous, unstable, wavering **9** deficient, enfeebled, inaudible, powerless, spineless, uncertain **10** improbable, inadequate, unreliable, unstressed **11** debilitated, implausible, ineffective, ineffectual, vacillating, watered-down **12** unconvincing, undependable **13** insubstantial, unsubstantial

weaken 3 lag, sap **4** fail, flag, thin, wane **5** abate **6** damage, dilute, impair, lessen, reduce, soften **7** corrode, decline, disable, dwindle, subvert, unbrace **8** enervate, enfeeble, moderate **9** attenuate, grind down, honeycomb, undermine **10** debilitate, demoralize, invalidate

weak-kneed 5 timid **6** wobbly **7** gutless **8** cowardly, wavering **9** faltering, uncertain, whiffling **10** irresolute **11** lily-livered, vacillating **12** fainthearted, shilly-shally **13** pusillanimous

weakling 4 wimp, wuss **5** mouse, sissy **7** doormat, milksop, sad sack **8** pushover **9** jellyfish **10** namby-pamby **11** milquetoast, mollycoddle **12** invertebrate

weakness 4 flaw, hole, vice **5** crack, fault, taste **6** defect, desire, liking, relish **7** failing, frailty **8** appetite, debility, fondness, soft spot **9** infirmity **10** feebleness **11** decrepitude, shortcoming **12** Achilles' heel

weal 4 welt **5** ridge **7** welfare **9** well-being

weald 5 woods **6** forest **8** woodland **10** timberland, wilderness

wealth 5 goods, worth **6** assets, estate, mammon, plenty, riches **7** capital, fortune **8** holdings, opulence, property **9** abundance, affluence, profusion, resources **11** possessions

Wealth of Nations author 5 Smith (Adam)

wealthy 4 rich **5** flush **6** loaded **7** moneyed, opulent, well-off **8** affluent, well-to-do **9** well-fixed **10** prosperous, well-heeled **12** silk-stocking

wean 4 free, part **5** alien **6** detach **8** accustom, estrange, separate

weapon 3 bow, gun **4** bill, bolo, bomb, club, dart, dirk, mace, nuke, pike, shiv **5** A-bomb, arrow, H-bomb, knife, lance, prick, rifle, saber, sabre, sling, spear, steel, sword **6** dagger, Magnum, musket, pistol, poleax, rapier, rocket **7** bazooka, broadax, car bomb, carbine, firearm, gisarme, halberd, handgun, javelin, machete, missile, shotgun, sidearm, stun gun, torpedo, war club **8** battle-ax, bludgeon, broadaxe, catapult, crossbow, death ray, nerve gas, nunchaku, partisan, partizan, petronel, revolver, spontoon, tomahawk **9** battle-axe, blackjack, boomerang, derringer, slingshot **10** atomic bomb, machine gun, projectile **11** blunderbuss, depth charge, nuclear bomb **12** quarterstaff **13** brass knuckles

weapons 4 arms **7** arsenal, battery **8** ordnance **9** armaments, artillery, munitions **13** armamentarium

wear 3 rub **4** fray, tire **5** chafe, dress, erode, grind **6** abrade, attire, endure, impair **7** corrode, exhibit, fatigue, fashion **8** abrasion, clothing *and tear:* **12** depreciation *thin:* **4** fray **5** chafe **6** tatter **7** hackney

wear down 5 drain, erode, grind **6** abrade, weaken **7** corrode, degrade, exhaust, fatigue

weariness 5 ennui **7** boredom, fatigue, languor **8** lassitude **9** lethargy **10** enervation, exhaustion **12** taedium vitae

wearing 6 taxing, tiring, trying **9** difficult, fatiguing

wearisome see **tiresome**

wear out 3 fag **4** bust, do in, fray, poop, tire **5** drain **6** efface, tucker **7** consume, deplete, exhaust, frazzle **8** overstay

weary 4 beat, jade, limp, tire, worn **5** drain, jaded, spent, tired **6** bushed, done in, pooped, tucker, wasted **7** drained, fatigue, worn-out **8** dog-tired, fatigued, tiresome **9** apathetic

weasand 6 gullet, throat **7** trachea **8** windpipe **9** esophagus

weasel 5 dodge, evade, hedge, slink, sneak, stoat **6** ermine, escape, ferret, mammal **7** sneaker **8** sidestep **9** pussyfoot **10** equivocate *Scottish:* **8** whittret

weather 4 rain **5** storm **6** bear up, endure, expose **7** climate, ride out, undergo **9** withstand *forecasting:* **11** meteorology

weathercock 4 vane

weathered 8 hardened, seasoned, tempered

weave 4 cane, lawn, leno, spin, sway **5** braid, cloth, lurch, twine, waver **6** careen, fabric, pleach, raddle, wobble, zigzag **7** pattern, stagger, textile, texture **8** contrive **9** interlace **10** crisscross, intertwine

weaver 4 loom **7** Arachne, webster

web 3 net **4** mesh, vane **5** snare, snarl **6** enmesh, fabric, tangle **7** ensnare, netting, network **8** entangle **10** enmeshment **12** entanglement

Weber opera 6 Oberon **9** Euryanthe **10** Freischütz (Der)

____ **Webster 4** Noah **6** Daniel

Web vending 5 e-tail **9** e-commerce

wed 4 join, link, mate, yoke **5** hitch, marry, merge, unite **6** splice **7** combine, conjoin, connect, espouse **10** tie the knot

wedded 7 marital, nuptial **8** conjugal, hymeneal **9** connubial **11** matrimonial

wedding 5 union **6** bridal **7** spousal **8** espousal, marriage, nuptials *words:* **3** I do

wedding anniversary *fifteenth:* **7** crystal *fifth:* **6** wooden *fiftieth:* **6** golden *first:* **5** paper *seventy-fifth:* **7** diamond *tenth:* **3** tin *twentieth:* **5** china *twenty-fifth:* **6** silver

wedge 4 shim **5** chock, stuff **8** golf club, golf shot, keystone **10** force apart

wedge-shaped 7 cuneate **8** cottered, sphenoid **9** cuneiform *mark:* **5** caret

wedlock 4 knot, yoke **8** espousal, marriage **9** matrimony **11** conjugality **12** connubiality

wee 4 tiny **5** bitsy, bitty, early, small, teeny **6** little, minute, teensy **9** itty-bitty, miniature **10** diminutive, teeny-weeny **11** Lilliputian, little bitty **12** teensy-weensy

weed 4 dock, tare **5** chess, clear, plant **6** cockle, darnel, dodder, nettle, remove **7** burdock, burseed, ragweed, ruderal **8** amaranth, charlock, purslane **9** chickweed, cocklebur, dandelion, knotgrass, marijuana, poison ivy, poison oak, stickseed **10** cheatgrass, lady's thumb, sow thistle *biblical:* **4** tare *European:* **6** spurry **7** spurrey *killer:* **8** paraquat **9** herbicide *Western:* **4** loco

weedy 4 lean, thin **5** lanky **6** skinny **7** scrawny, stringy, willowy **8** untended **9** overgrown

week 6 period **8** hebdomad *two weeks:* **9** fortnight

weep 3 cry, sob **4** drip, moan, ooze, tear, wail **5** bleed, exude, sweat **6** lament **7** blubber, dribble, trickle **8** transude

weepy 5 misty, moist, teary **7** tearful **10** lachrymose

weevil 7 billbug **8** curculio

weft 3 web **4** pick, woof, yarn **6** fabric, thread

weigh 3 way **4** heft, rate, tare **5** count, judge, scale, study **6** burden, ponder **7** balance, measure, oppress, perpend **8** appraise, bear down, consider, evaluate, militate **11** contemplate

weigh down 4 load **5** press **6** burden, sadden **7** depress, oppress **8** encumber **10** discourage, overburden

weight 3 tax **4** heft, lade, load, mass, onus, task **5** class, force, power **6** amount, assign, burden, charge, credit, import, moment, saddle **7** oppress, potency, quality **8** encumber, poundage, pressure, prestige, quantity **9** authority, influence, magnitude **10** corpulence, importance **11** consequence **12** significance *allowance:* **4** tare *apothecary:* **4** dram **5** grain, pound **7** scruple *Asian:* **4** tael **5** catty *gem:* **5** carat *measure of:* **3** fun, kin, kip, oke, tan, tod, ton, vis, yin **4** dram, gram, mina, rotl **5** grain, libra, ounce, picul, pound **7** long ton, scruple **8** kilogram, short ton **9** metric ton *system:* **3** net **4** troy **6** metric **10** apothecary **11** avoirdupois

weightiness 4 pith **6** import, moment **7** dignity, gravity **9** heaviness, magnitude, solemnity **10** importance **11** consequence, massiveness **12** significance **13** momentousness

weight lifting term 4 curl, pull, push **5** clean, press, shrug, squat **6** snatch **8** deadlift **12** clean and jerk

weightlifter 4 Kono (Tommy), Tang (Gonghong) **5** Dimas (Pyrros), Mutlu (Halil) **6** Weller (Ronny) **7** Krastev (Antonio) **8** Alexeyev (Vasily), Pechalov (Nikolay) **9** Chemerkin (Andrei), Reza Zadeh (Hossein), Taranenko (Leonid) **10** Schemansky (Norbert)

weighty 3 fat **5** grave, gross, heavy, hefty, obese, sober, staid **6** fleshy, portly, sedate, severe, solemn, somber **7** massive, serious, telling **8** cumbrous, grievous, powerful **9** corpulent, effective, important, momentous, ponderous **10** burdensome, convincing, cumbersome **11** significant, substantial **12** considerable **13** consequential

weir 3 dam **5** stank

weird 3 odd **5** eerie, queer **6** creepy, freaky, spooky **7** bizarre, curious, oddball, strange, uncanny **8** freakish, peculiar, singular, sinister **9** eccentric, fantastic, unearthly **10** mysterious **11** inscrutable **12** supernatural **13** preternatural

weirdo 4 geek, kook, loon **5** freak **7** nutcase, oddball **8** crackpot **9** eccentric, screwball

welcome 4 hail **5** cheer, greet, hello, howdy **6** accept, invite, salute **7** embrace, invited, receive **8** greeting, pleasant, pleasing **9** agreeable, favorable, reception **10** gratifying, hospitable **11** hospitality, pleasurable

weld 4 bond, fuse, join **5** braze, joint, merge, unite **6** solder

welfare 3 aid **4** dole, help, weal **5** pogey **6** health, relief, succor **7** benefit, fortune, success, support **8** interest **9** advantage, happiness, well-being **10** assistance, commonweal, prosperity

welkin 3 sky **5** ether, vault **6** heaven **7** heavens **8** empyrean **9** firmament

well 3 far, fit, pit **4** easy, emit, hale, hole, pool, rise, sane **5** amply, clear, cured, fully, quite, shaft, sound, truly **6** easily, freely, healed, indeed, justly, kindly, likely, nicely, origin, rather, really, source, spring, wholly **7** clearly, healthy, perhaps, readily, rightly **8** entirely, expertly, pleasing, possibly, probably, properly, sensibly, smoothly, suitably **9** advisable, correctly, desirable, elegantly, favorably, fittingly, fortunate, perfectly, wholesome

well-being 4 weal **6** health **7** welfare **8** thriving **9** happiness **10** prosperity

well-bred 6 urbane **7** genteel, refined **8** cultured, highborn, polished **9** civilized, patrician **10** cultivated **11** blue-blooded, gentlemanly

well-built 4 buff **5** hunky, solid **8** muscular **9** strapping

well-developed 5 curvy **7** fulsome, rounded, shapely **8** advanced **9** Junoesque **10** curvaceous

well-disposed 7 amiable **8** friendly **9** favorable, receptive **11** sympathetic **13** understanding

Welles movie 5 Trial (The) **7** Macbeth, Othello **8** Jane Eyre, Stranger (The), Third Man (The) **11** Citizen Kane, Touch of Evil **15** Journey into Fear **16** Chimes at Midnight, Lady from Shanghai (The) **20** Magnificent Ambersons (The)

well-favored 4 fair **5** bonny **6** comely, lovely, pretty **7** winsome **8** gorgeous, handsome **9** beauteous, beautiful **10** attractive **11** good-looking

well-fixed see **well-to-do**

well-founded 5 sound, valid **6** cogent **8** rational **9** justified **10** convincing

well-groomed 4 neat, snug, tidy, trig, trim **5** natty, smart **6** dapper, snappy, spiffy, spruce, sprucy **7** orderly **8** clean-cut **9** shipshape

well-heeled see **well-to-do**

Wellington 4 duke **7** general **8** Iron Duke *horse:* **10** Copenhagen *original name:* **9** Wellesley (Arthur) *victory:* **7** Vitoria **8** Talavera, Waterloo **9** Salamanca

well-known 5 famed, noted **6** famous **7** bigname, eminent, popular **8** renowned **9** notorious, prominent **10** celebrated **11** illustrious

well-liked 7 beloved, favored, popular **8** favorite **9** cherished, preferred

well-mannered 5 civil, suave **6** poised, polite, proper, urbane **7** genteel, tactful **9** courteous **10** diplomatic

well-nigh 6 all but, almost, fairly, nearly, next to **8** as good as **9** just about, virtually **11** essentially, practically

well-off see **well-to-do**

well-paying 7 gainful **9** lucrative, rewarding **10** profitable, worthwhile **11** moneymaking **12** advantageous, remunerative ´

Wells novel 11 Time Machine (The) **12** Invisible Man (The) **14** War of the Worlds (The)

wellspring 4 font, root **5** fount **6** origin, source **7** genesis **8** fountain **10** provenance **11** provenience **12** fountainhead

well-thought-of 6 valued, worthy **7** admired, reputed **9** estimable, reputable **10** creditable **11** respectable

well-timed 6 timely **7** apropos, fitting, timeous **9** favorable, opportune **10** auspicious, felicitous, fortuitous, propitious, seasonable

well-to-do 4 rich **5** flush **6** loaded, monied **7** moneyed, upscale, wealthy **8** affluent **10** prosperous **11** comfortable

well-turned 4 trim **5** plump **7** rounded, shapely **10** curvaceous, felicitous, Rubenesque, statuesque **11** clean-limbed

well-worn 5 banal, musty, stale, stock, tired, trite **6** frayed, old-hat, shabby **7** clichéd **8** bromidic, cobwebby, dog-eared, overused **9** hackneyed **10** threadbare **11** commonplace, stereotyped

Welsh see **Cymric**

welsh 5 dodge **6** renege, resile **7** back out, default

welt 4 blow, edge, seam, wale, weal **5** ridge, wheal, whelk **6** insert

welter 4 coil, moil, toss **5** chaos, churn, steep, surge **6** flurry, hassle, hubbub, jumble, lather, ruckus, seethe, thrash, wallow, writhe **7** ferment, turmoil **8** disorder **9** confusion

_____ **Welty 6** Eudora

wen 4 bleb, cyst **5** blain **6** growth **7** vesicle **11** excrescence

wench 3 gal **4** girl, jade, lass, maid, minx, miss, puss, slut, tart **5** hussy, nymph, tramp, trull, whore, woman **6** damsel, gamine, harlot, hoyden, lassie, maiden, wanton **7** jezebel, servant, trollop **8** slattern, strumpet

wend 3 hie **4** fare, pass **6** direct, push on, repair, travel **7** journey, proceed

werewolf 9 loup-garou **11** lycanthrope

Werther's beloved 5 Lotte **9** Charlotte

Wesleyan 9 Methodist

West 8 Occident

western 5 oater **9** Hesperian **10** horse opera, occidental *hemisphere:* **8** Americas, New World

Western novelist 4 Grey (Zane), Ross (Dana

Fuller) **5** Brand (Max), Faust (Frederick), Short (Luke) **6** Judson (E. Z. C.), L'Amour (Louis), Patten (Lewis), Wister (Owen) **7** Guthrie (A. B.), Leonard (Elmore) **8** Buntline (Ned), McMurtry (Larry)

West Indies *country:* **4** Cuba **5** Haiti **7** Bahamas, Grenada, Jamaica **8** Barbados, Dominica **10** Guadeloupe, Martinique, Puerto Rico, Saint Lucia **17** Dominican Republic *island group:* **6** Virgin (Islands) **7** Bahamas, Leeward (Islands) **8** Antilles (Greater, Lesser), Windward (Islands)

West Point *father of:* **6** Thayer (Sylvanus) *freshman:* **5** plebe *student:* **5** cadet

West Side Story *composer:* **9** Bernstein (Leonard) *heroine:* **5** Maria *lyricist:* **8** Sondheim (Stephen)

West Virginia *capital:* **10** Charleston *city:* **8** Wheeling **10** Huntington *mountain:* **10** Spruce Knob *nickname:* **8** Mountain (State) *river:* **4** Ohio *state bird:* **8** cardinal *state flower:* **12** rhododendron *state tree:* **10** sugar maple

west wind see at **wind**

wet 3 sop **4** damp, dank, rain, soak, wash, weak **5** douse, drown, drunk, humid, moist, rainy, soggy, soppy, souse, water **6** dampen, drench, soaked, sodden, soused, sweaty, watery **7** moisten, raining, soaking, sopping **8** drenched, dripping, humidify, irrigate, moisture, saturate, slippery **9** saturated, spineless *combining form:* **4** hygr **5** hygro

wet blanket 6 grinch **7** killjoy **8** sourpuss **9** pessimist **10** spoilsport **11** party pooper

wether 4 goat **5** sheep

wetland 3 bog, fen **4** mire, quag **5** marsh, swamp **6** morass, muskeg, slough

whack 3 bat, hit, pop, try **4** bash, belt, biff, blow, chop, cuff, kill, pelt, shot, sock, stab, wham, whap, whop **5** crack, punch, smack, smash **6** attack, defeat, murder, strike, wallop **7** bump off **8** knock off, lambaste *up:* **4** part **5** divvy, split **6** divide **7** portion **9** apportion

whale 3 hit **4** beat, cete, flog, hide, lash, whip **5** giant **6** defeat, strike, stripe, thrash **7** mammoth **8** cetacean, behemoth **9** leviathan **10** flagellate *arctic:* **7** bowhead *group:* **3** gam, pod *killer:* **4** orca *kind:* **3** sei **4** blue **5** right, sperm **6** baleen, beluga, killer **7** narwhal, rorqual **8** cachalot *novel:* **8** Moby Dick *toothed:* **5** pilot (whale) **9** blackfish *white:* **4** huso *young:* **4** calf

whalebone 9 scrimshaw

wham 3 hit **4** bang, beat, blow, boom, clap, slam **5** blast, burst, crack, crash, smash, whack **6** impact, propel, strike **7** explode

whammy 3 hex, zap **4** jinx, juju **5** curse, spell **6** hoodoo, voodoo **7** evil eye

wharf 4 dock, pier, quay **5** jetty, levee

Wharton novel 10 Buccaneers (The), Ethan Frome **12** House of Mirth (The) **14** Age of Innocence (The) **18** Custom of the Country (The)

whatever 5 at all **9** in any case

whatnot 7 étagère

wheal 4 lump, welt **5** ridge, whelk

wheat 4 crop **5** emmer, flour, grain, grass, spelt **6** cereal **7** einkorn *beard:* **3** awn *beat:* **6** thresh *chaff:* **4** bran *crushed:* **6** bulgur *disease:* **4** rust, smut *type:* **4** club **5** durum

wheedle 3 con **4** coax **5** cozen **6** cajole, entice, seduce **7** blarney, flatter **8** blandish, inveigle, scrounge, soft-soap **9** sweet-talk

wheel 3 VIP **4** auto, gyre, move, reel, spin, turn **5** cycle, drive, motor, pilot, pivot, round, whirl **6** bigwig, circle, gyrate, league, rotate, totter, travel **7** big shot, circuit, revolve **8** rotation **9** about-face, volteface *part:* **3** hub, rim **4** tire **5** felly, spoke *shaft:* **4** axle *spoke:* **6** radius *toothed:* **3** cog **4** gear

wheeze 3 saw, yuk **4** gasp, hiss, joke, puff, rasp **5** adage, cough **6** saying **7** proverb, whistle **8** chestnut, rhonchus

whelk 4 wale, weal, welt **5** wheal

whelm 4 bury, sink **5** cover, drown, flood, swamp **6** deluge, engulf **8** bear down, inundate, overbear, overcome, submerge **9** devastate

whelp 3 cub, kid, pup **4** bear **5** child, puppy **9** youngster

whereas 5 since, while **6** seeing, though **7** howbeit **8** although **11** considering

wherefore 3 why **4** thus **5** proof **6** ground, reason, whence **8** argument **11** explanation

wherewithal 5 funds, means, money **9** resources

wherry 4 boat **5** barge, scull **7** lighter, rowboat

whet 4 edge, goad, hone **5** drink, rally, rouse, waken **6** arouse, awaken, excite, kindle **7** sharpen, starter **8** aperitif **9** appetizer, challenge, stimulate **10** incitement **11** hors d'oeuvre

whiff 3 fan **4** blow, gust, hint, puff, waft **5** expel, smoke, tinge, trace **6** breath, exhale, inhale **7** soupçon, whisper **9** strikeout **10** indication, inhalation

whiffet 6 nobody, squirt **9** nonentity

whiffle 4 blow, gust, puff **5** waver **6** dither, falter **9** fluctuate, vacillate **12** shilly-shally

while 4 pass, time, when **5** spell **6** albeit, mo-

ment, though **7** howbeit, stretch, whereas **8** although, as long as, so long as

whilom 4 past **6** bygone, former **7** onetime, quondam **8** formerly, previous, sometime **9** erstwhile

whim 3 bee **4** idea, kink **5** dream, fancy, freak, humor **6** maggot, megrim, notion, vagary **7** caprice, capstan, conceit, thought **8** crotchet

whimper 3 cry **4** fret, mewl, pule, wail **5** bleat, whine **6** snivel

whimsical 4 iffy, zany **5** ditsy, ditzy, droll, fancy, flaky **6** chancy, fickle, fitful, flakes, quirky, random **7** erratic, flighty, mutable, puckish, wayward **8** fanciful, freakish, volatile **9** eccentric, impulsive, mercurial, pixilated, screwball, uncertain, vagarious **10** capricious, pixillated **13** unpredictable

whimsy 3 bee **4** play **5** dream, fancy, freak, humor **6** levity, maggot, megrim, notion, vagary **7** caprice, conceit, fantasy **9** capriccio, frivolity

whim-wham 4 dido **5** curio, fancy, frill **6** bauble, gewgaw, ruffle, trifle **7** bibelot, flounce, trinket, whatnot **8** furbelow, gimcrack, kickshaw **9** objet d'art **10** knickknack

whine 3 cry **4** cant, fret, fuss, kick, moan, pule, wail **5** bleat, gripe **6** grouse, repine, snivel, whinge, yammer **7** grumble, snuffle, whimper **8** complain **9** bellyache

whinny 5 neigh **6** nicker **7** whicker

whiny 5 fussy **7** fretful, grouchy, peevish **8** petulant **9** irritable, querulous

whip 3 cut, hem, set, tan **4** beat, cane, crop, dash, flog, hide, jerk, lash, lick, pull, rout, wind, wrap **5** abuse, mop up, quirt, spank, sting, whale, whisk **6** defeat, lather, snatch, strike, stroke, subdue, switch, thrash, urge on **7** agitate, dessert, provoke, rawhide, shellac, trounce, utensil **8** coachman, lambaste, overcome, vanquish **9** instigate, overwhelm **10** flagellate **13** cat-o'-nine-tails *braided:* **10** blacksnake

whippersnapper see **whiffet**

whipping boy 4 goat **5** patsy **7** fall guy **9** scapegoat

whippy 6 supple **7** elastic, springy **8** flexible **9** resilient

whir 3 fly, hum **4** burr, buzz, whiz **5** chirr, churr, drone, whizz **7** revolve, vibrate **9** bombinate

whirl 3 ado, gig, pop, try **4** eddy, flit, fuss, gyre, moil, reel, shot, spin, stab, stir, swim, turn, veer **5** hurry, pivot, swirl, whack, wheel **6** bustle, circle, gyrate, hassle, hubbub, pother, rotate **7** circuit, dervish, tur-

moil 8 ballyhoo, gyration, rotation **9** commotion, pirouette **10** revolution

whirligig 4 gyre, spin **6** beetle, gyrate **8** carousel **9** pirouette **12** merry-go-round

whirlpool 3 ado **4** eddy, fuss **6** bustle, flurry, furore, tumult, vortex **7** turmoil **8** vortices (plural) **9** commotion, maelstrom *bath:* **6** hot tub **7** Jacuzzi

whirlwind 2 oe **4** rush, stir, to-do **5** hasty, spout, swift **6** bustle **7** cyclone, tornado, twister, typhoon **8** headlong **9** commotion, dust devil, dust storm, hurricane **10** waterspout **11** tourbillion

whish 4 fizz, hiss **6** fizzle **8** sibilate

whisk 3 mix, nip, wag, zip **4** beat, flit, whip **5** broom, brush, fluff, hurry, speed **6** switch

whisker 4 hair **7** bristle **8** filament, vibrissa **9** outrigger **11** hairbreadth

whiskered 5 hairy **6** pilose **7** bearded, bristly, hirsute **8** stubbled, unshaven

whiskers 5 beard **6** goatee **7** stubble, weepers **8** bristles **9** burnsides, peach fuzz, sideburns **11** dundrearies, muttonchops

whiskey 3 rye **6** liquor, Scotch **7** alcohol, bourbon *with beer chaser:* **11** boilermaker

whisper 4 buzz, hint, hiss, whiz **5** rumor, shade, tinge, touch, trace, whiff **6** breath, gossip, murmur, mutter **8** sibilate, susurrus **9** suspicion, undertone **11** susurration

whist 4 game, hush **5** quiet, still **6** silent **9** noiseless, soundless

whistle 4 pipe, toot **5** flute, whiff **6** signal, tootle, wheeze

whistle-stop 5 stump **8** campaign, politick **9** barnstorm **11** electioneer

whit 3 bit, fig, jot, rap **4** atom, damn, hoot, iota, mite **5** crumb, scrap, shred, speck, whoop **7** dribble, modicum, smidgen **8** molecule, particle

white 4 pure **5** cream, ivory, livid, milky, snowy **6** albino, blanch, bleach, pallid **7** silvery **9** colorless *combining form:* **4** leuc, leuk **5** leuco, leuko *egg's:* **5** glair **6** glaire **7** albumen

White novel 12 Stuart Little **13** Charlotte's Web

white cliffs of _____ 5 Dover

White Fang author 6 London (Jack)

White House *designer:* 5 Hoban (James) *first occupant:* **5** Adams (Abigail, John)

white lightning 5 hooch **7** bootleg, whiskey **9** moonshine **10** bathtub gin **11** mountain dew

whiten 4 fade, pale **5** frost **6** blanch, bleach, blench **8** etiolate **10** decolorize

white plague 2 TB **8** phthisis **11** consumption **12** tuberculosis

whitewash 6 parget **7** cover up **9** gloss over, gloze over, sugarcoat

whither 5 where **7** whereto **9** whereunto

whiting 3 cod **4** hake **10** silver hake

Whitman work 13 Leaves of Grass

Whitsunday 9 Pentecost

Whittier poem 9 Snow-Bound **10** Maud Muller **11** Barefoot Boy **16** Barbara Frietchie

whittle 3 hew **4** chip, form, fret, pare, trim **5** carve, shape, shave, skive **6** reduce, sculpt **8** diminish

whiz 3 fly, hum, zip **4** buzz, flit, hiss, zoom **5** hurry, speed, swish, whirl **6** expert, fizzle, genius, phenom, rotate, whoosh **8** virtuoso **10** wunderkind

whoa 3 hey **4** slow, stop **6** hold up

whole 3 all, fit, sum **4** full, hale, sane **5** sound, total, uncut, unity **6** entire, entity, healed, intact, system, unhurt **7** healthy, perfect, plenary **8** complete, entirely, entirety, flawless, restored, totality, unbroken, unmarred *combining form:* **3** hol, pan **4** holo

wholehearted 6 ardent **7** devoted, earnest, fervent, sincere **8** bona fide **9** committed, heartfelt, steadfast, unfeigned **10** passionate, unwavering **11** impassioned **12** enthusiastic **13** unquestioning

whole-hog 6 all-out, gung-ho **8** complete, thorough **9** full-scale **11** straight-out **13** thoroughgoing

wholeness 7 oneness **8** entirety, totality **9** integrity, soundness **10** intactness, perfection

whole note 9 semibreve

whole number 5 digit **6** cipher **7** integer, numeral

wholesome 3 fit **4** good, hale, safe, sane, well **5** right, sound **6** benign **7** healthy **8** hygienic, salutary **9** favorable, healthful **10** beneficial, salubrious

wholly 3 all **4** only **6** in toto, singly, solely, purely **7** totally **8** entirely **10** altogether, completely **11** exclusively

whomp 3 hit **4** beat, drub, slap, whip, whup **5** crash, thump **6** crunch, strike, thrash, wallop **7** clobber, shellac, trounce **8** lambaste

whomp up 4 stir **5** rouse, spark **6** arouse, excite, foment

whoopee 3 fun **5** revel, yahoo **6** gaiety, hoopla, hooray, yippee **7** jollity, revelry, wassail, whoopla **8** hilarity **9** festivity, high jinks, merriment **10** hurly-burly **11** merrymaking

whoopla see **hoopla**

whop 3 bat, bop **4** bash, beat, biff, blow, drub, lick, sock **5** baste, pound, smack, thump, whack **6** batter, buffet, defeat, hammer, pummel, strike, thrash, thwack, wallop **7** trounce **8** lambaste

whopper 3 lie **4** lulu **5** beaut, doozy, whale **6** doozie **8** knockout, tall tale **9** humdinger

whopping 4 huge, vast **6** mighty **7** amazing, immense, massive **8** colossal, enormous, gigantic, whacking **9** bodacious, humongous, monstrous **10** gargantuan, incredible, prodigious **13** extraordinary

whorl 4 coil, eddy, turn **5** swirl **6** spiral

why 5 cause **6** enigma, motive, puzzle, reason, riddle **7** mystery, problem, what for **9** conundrum, rationale, therefore, wherefore **10** puzzlement **11** explanation

wicked 4 evil, mean, very, vile **5** awful, black, wrong **6** fierce, malign, sinful, unholy **7** corrupt, hateful, heinous, immoral, naughty, ungodly, vicious **8** depraved, devilish, fiendish **9** atrocious, barbarous, dangerous, extremely, hazardous, injurious, malicious, malignant, nefarious **10** iniquitous, malevolent, outrageous **11** treacherous

wickedness 3 sin **4** evil, vice **7** devilry **8** enormity, iniquity, satanism **9** depravity **10** corruption, immorality **12** devilishness, fiendishness

wicker 4 twig **5** osier, withe **6** branch

wicket 4 arch, door, gate, hoop **6** window
sticky: **3** fix, jam **4** knot **7** toughie **9** conundrum, tight spot

wide 4 vast **5** broad, fully **8** extended, spacious, straying, sweeping **9** deviating, expansive, extensive, inclusive **10** completely **13** comprehensive

widen 4 ream **6** dilate, expand, extend, open up, spread **7** broaden, distend, enlarge

widespread 4 rife, vast **6** common **7** current, general, popular, rampant, regnant **8** far-flung **9** extensive, pervasive, prevalent **10** far-ranging, ubiquitous

widget 5 gismo, gizmo **6** device, dingus, doodad, gadget, hickey, jigger **7** gimmick, whatsit **9** doohickey, thingummy **11** contraption, thingamabob, thingamajig, thingumajig

width 4 gape, kerf, span **5** depth, range **6** spread **7** breadth **9** extension

wield 3 use **5** exert **6** handle **7** control **8** brandish, exercise **10** manipulate *the gavel:* **7** preside

wiener 3 dog **5** frank **6** hot dog **7** sausage **11** frankfurter **13** Vienna sausage

Wiesel work 4 Dawn **5** Night **8** Fifth Son (The) **9** Testament (The)

wife 3 Mrs. **4** mate **5** bride, woman **6** female, matron, missis, missus, spouse **7** consort,

partner **8** helpmate, helpmeet *Latin:* **4** uxor *of a rajah:* **4** rani **5** ranee

wifely 7 uxorial

wig 3 jaw, rap, rug **4** flip, rail, rate **5** chide, freak, scold **6** berate, peruke, rebuke, revile, toupee **7** bawl out, chew out, reproof, upbraid **8** postiche, reproach **9** hairpiece, reprimand **10** tongue-lash

wiggle 4 jerk **5** shake, twist **6** fidget, squirm, writhe *Scottish:* **5** hotch

wight 3 man **5** human **6** animal, mortal, person **7** critter **8** creature **10** human being, individual

wild 3 mad **4** fast **5** crazy **6** barren, raging, savage, stormy, unruly **7** erratic, frantic, furious, natural, untamed, vicious **8** barbaric, blustery, desolate, frenetic, frenzied, reckless **9** barbarian, barbarous, delirious, fantastic, turbulent, wasteland **10** incautious, outlandish **11** extravagant, intractable, sensational, tempestuous, uncivilized, uninhabited **12** preposterous, uncontrolled, uncultivated, ungovernable, unmanageable **13** irresponsible, undisciplined

wild ass 5 kiang **6** onager

wildcat 4 eyra, lynx **6** ocelot, strike **10** jaguarundi

Wild Duck author 5 Ibsen (Henrik)

wildebeest 3 gnu

wilderness 4 bush **5** heath, waste **6** barren, desert **9** backlands, wasteland **10** hinterland **11** backcountry

Wilder play 7 Our Town **10** Matchmaker (The) **14** Skin of Our Teeth (The)

wild-eyed 6 raving **7** blue-sky, radical **9** visionary

wile 4 ploy, ruse, vamp **5** charm, feint, guile, trick **6** allure, deceit, entice, gambit **7** attract, beguile, bewitch, chicane, cunning, enchant, gimmick **8** artifice, inveigle, maneuver, trickery **9** captivate, chicanery, fascinate, magnetize, stratagem **10** subterfuge

wiliness 5 guile **7** cunning

will 4 like, wish **5** cause, elect, leave, order **6** choice, choose, decree, desire, direct, intend, intent, liking, option, ordain, please **7** bequest, consent, control, passion, purpose **8** appetite, bequeath, pleasure, volition **9** intention, testament **10** discipline **11** disposition, inclination, self-control **13** determination, self-restraint *addition:* **7** codicil *maker:* **8** testator **9** testatrix *without:* **9** intestate

willful 5 heady **6** dogged, mulish, ornery, unruly **7** froward, wayward **8** perverse, stubborn **9** obstinate, pigheaded, voluntary **10** deliberate, hardheaded, headstrong, purposeful, self-willed **11** intentional, intractable, wrongheaded **12** contumacious, pertinacious, ungovernable

Williams play 10 Camino Real, Rose Tattoo (The) **14** Glass Menagerie (The), Summer and Smoke **16** Cat on a Hot Tin Roof, Night of the Iguana (The), Sweet Bird of Youth **18** Suddenly Last Summer **20** Streetcar Named Desire (A)

William Tell *canton:* **3** Uri *composer:* **7** Rossini (Gioacchino)

willies 6 creeps, shakes **7** jimjams, jitters, shivers **9** whim-whams **10** goose bumps **13** heebie-jeebies

willing 3 apt **4** fain, game, glad, open **5** prone, ready **6** minded **7** forward, witting **8** amenable, disposed, inclined, obliging, unforced **9** agreeable, compliant, favorable, receptive, voluntary **10** deliberate, volitional **11** intentional, predisposed

williwaw 4 gust, wind **5** blast **8** outburst, paroxysm **9** commotion

will-o'-the-wisp 7 fantasy, figment, phantom **8** daydream, delusion **11** ignis fatuus

willow 5 osier, salix **6** sallow **10** cricket bat *flower cluster:* **6** catkin *kind:* **5** crack, pussy, white **6** basket **7** weeping *Virginia:* **4** Itea

willowy 4 tall **5** lithe **6** pliant, supple, svelte **7** lissome, pliable, slender **8** graceful

Wilson play 6 Fences **11** Piano Lesson (The) **12** Talley's Folly **13** Hot l Baltimore (The) **20** Ma Rainey's Black Bottom

wilt 3 sag **4** swag **5** droop, dry up, wizen **6** wither **7** shrivel **8** languish

wily 3 sly **4** cagy, foxy **5** cagey, canny, slick **6** artful, astute, clever, crafty, shrewd, tricky **7** cunning, devious, vulpine **8** guileful, scheming **10** serpentine

wimble 4 bore **5** auger, borer, brace, drill **6** gimlet

Wimbledon's game 6 tennis

wimp 4 nerd, wuss **5** sissy **6** weenie **7** doormat, nebbish **9** jellyfish **11** milquetoast

wimple 4 bend, veil, wrap **5** cover, curve **6** ripple *wearer:* **3** nun

wimp out 6 beg off, cave in, give in **8** back down

wimpy 4 lame, puny, weak **5** dinky, inept, timid **6** craven, feeble **7** gutless **8** cowardly, feckless, impotent, pathetic **9** spineless **10** namby-pamby, wishy-washy **11** ineffective, ineffectual

win 3 get **4** beat, earn, gain, kayo **5** reach, score **6** attain, defeat, obtain, secure **7** achieve, acquire, conquer, procure, produce, realize, succeed, success, triumph,

victory **8** conquest, persuade **9** influence **10** accomplish *over:* **6** disarm, induce **8** convince, persuade, talk into **9** prevail on

wince 5 cower, quail, start **6** blanch, blench, cringe, flinch, recoil, shrink **7** squinch

wind 3 air, dry, fan, gas **4** bend, blow, clue, coil, curl, gale, gird, gust, haul, hint, reel, rest, talk, turn, warp, wrap **5** cover, crank, curve, force, hoist, raise, sound, spool, twine, twist **6** breath, breeze, circle, enlace, girdle, notion, zephyr **7** enclose, entwine, envelop, inkling, involve, monsoon, nothing, tighten **8** easterly, encircle, entangle, surround, tendency, westerly **9** direction, idle words, influence, insinuate **10** indication, intimation, suggestion *Adriatic:* **4** bora *cold:* **4** bora **7** mistral, pampero **8** williwaw *combining form:* **4** anem **5** anemo, venti, vento *gentle:* **6** breeze, zephyr *god:* **6** Boreas (north) **8** Favonius, Zephyrus (west) *hot:* **6** simoom **7** sirocco **8** scirocco *instrument:* **4** vane **10** anemometer **11** weather vane *into:* **8** aweather *measure of speed:* **4** knot *Mediterranean:* **4** bora **7** sirocco **8** levanter, libeccio, scirocco *scale:* **8** Beaufort *stormy:* **4** gale **7** cyclone, tornado, twister **9** hurricane **11** northeaster *warm:* **4** föhn **5** foehn **7** chinook

windbag 6 gabber **7** blabber **8** bigmouth, blowhard, braggart

windfall 4 boon, gain **5** break **7** jackpot **8** fortuity

winding 4 curl, kink **5** snaky **6** spiral **7** coiling, curving, devious, sinuous **8** flexuous, indirect, tortuous, twisting **9** meandrous **10** circuitous, convoluted, meandering, roundabout, serpentine **11** anfractuous **12** labyrinthine

wind instrument 3 sax **4** horn, oboe, pipe, tuba **5** flute, shawm **6** cornet **7** bagpipe, bassoon, panpipe, piccolo, sackbut, trumpet **8** bagpipes, clarinet, crumhorn, recorder, trombone **9** krummhorn, saxophone **10** cor anglais, flugelhorn, French horn, sousaphone **11** English horn

windmill 4 spin **5** wheel **7** machine *fighter:* **10** Don Quixote

window 3 eye **4** pane **7** opening **8** aperture, casement, jalousie *cover:* **5** blind **7** curtain, shutter *French:* **7** fenêtre *over a door:* **7** transom **8** fanlight *part:* **4** pane, sash, sill **5** frame *projecting:* **3** bay **5** oriel *roof's:* **6** dormer **7** lucarne **8** skylight *round:* **5** oxeye *Scottish:* **7** winnock *ship's:* **4** port **8** porthole

windpipe 7 trachea *combining form:* **6** trache **7** tracheo

windrow 4 bank, heap, hill, mass, pile **5** mound, ridge, stack

wind up 3 end **4** halt **5** close **6** finish, settle **8** complete, conclude **9** terminate

windup 3 end **5** close **6** ending, finale, finish **9** backswing **10** completion, conclusion **11** termination

windy 4 airy **5** blowy, gassy, gusty, inane, tumid, wordy **6** breezy, prolix, stormy, turgid **7** diffuse, orotund, pompous, verbose **8** blustery, inflated **9** bombastic, overblown **11** tempestuous **13** grandiloquent, unsubstantial

wine 4 vino **5** drink, juice **8** beverage *aromatized:* **8** vermouth **9** hippocras *beverage:* **5** negus, punch **6** bishop, cooler **7** sangria **8** sangaree, spritzer **9** hippocras *bottle:* **6** fiasco, magnum **8** decanter, jeroboam **10** methuselah *cabinet:* **8** cellaret *cask:* **3** tun, vat **4** butt, pipe *cellar:* **6** bodega *combining form:* **3** eno, oen **4** oeno *discoverer:* **4** Noah *distillate:* **6** brandy, cognac *dry:* **3** sec **4** brut *flavor:* **4** mull *fortified:* **4** port **5** Tokay **6** Malaga, Muscat, sherry **7** Madeira, marsala, oloroso **8** muscatel *fragrance:* **4** nose **7** bouquet *lover:* **9** oenophile **11** oenophilist *maker:* **7** vintner **8** vigneron **10** winegrower **13** viticulturist *merchant:* **7** vintner *pink:* **4** rosé **5** blush *red:* **4** port **5** Gamay, Macon, Medoc, Rioja **6** Barolo, Beaune, claret, merlot, Shiraz **7** Chianti **8** Bordeaux, Burgundy, cabernet, Sancerre **9** Lambrusco, Pinot Noir, St. Emilion, zinfandel **10** Beaujolais, Sangiovese **11** Petite Sirah **12** Valpolicella *region:* **3** Ahr **4** Asti, Cuzo, Jura, Nahe, Napa, Saar, Toro **5** Baden, Douro, Jerez, Loire, Mosel, Pfalz, Rhône, Ruwer **6** Alsace, Sonoma, Veneto **7** Mendoza, Tuscany **8** Bordeaux, Burgundy, Rheingau **9** Champagne **10** Napa Valley **11** Finger Lakes, Rheinhessen *relating to:* **6** vinous *residue:* **4** marc *rice:* **4** sake *richness:* **4** body *sediment:* **4** lees **5** dregs *shop:* **6** bistro, bodega, tavern *sparkling:* **4** Asti **7** Vouvray **8** cold duck, sparkler, Spumante **9** champagne, Lambrusco *specialist:* **9** enologist **10** oenologist *spiced:* **5** negus **6** mulled (wine) **9** hippocras *steward:* **9** sommelier *study of:* **7** enology **8** oenology *sweet:* **4** port **5** Tokay **6** canary, Malaga, muscat **7** Catawba, Madeira, malmsey, marsala, oloroso, Vouvray **8** Malvasia, muscatel, sauterne **9** Sauternes **11** scuppernong *sweeten:* **4** mull *vessel:* **7** chalice *white:* **4** hock **5** Rhine, Soave **7** Catawba, Chablis, Moselle, Orvieto, Vouvray **8** Bordeaux, muscadet, Riesling, Semillon, vermouth **9** champagne, Hermitage, Meursault, pinot gris **10** chardonnay, Montrachet **11** Chenin Blanc, pinot grigio, scuppernong **13** liebfraumilch **14** sauvignon blanc *year:* **7** vintage

wing 3 ala, arm, ell, fly **4** sail, unit, vane **5** annex, flank, fleet, pinna, wound **6** flight **7** airfoil, faction, flanker, section **9** appendage, expansion, extension, improvise *combining form:* **3** ali **4** pter **5** ptero *relating to:* **4** alar **5** alary

wingding 4 bash, fete, gala **5** binge, party **7** blowout, shindig **9** festivity

winged 5 alate, fleet, rapid, swift **7** soaring **8** elevated *deity:* **4** Amor, Eros, Nike **5** Cupid **6** Hermes **7** Mercury *horse:* **7** Pegasus *monster:* **5** harpy

wingless 8 apterous

winglike 4 alar **5** alary *part:* **3** ala **4** alae (plural)

wink 3 bat, nap **5** flash, jiffy, shake, trice **6** moment, second, signal **7** connive, flicker, instant, twinkle **9** nictitate, twinkling **11** split second

winner 3 ace **4** lulu **5** beaut, doozy **6** doozie, top dog, victor **7** success **8** champion **9** conqueror, humdinger **11** titleholder

Winnie-the-Pooh *author:* **5** Milne (A. A.) *character:* **3** Roo **5** Kanga **6** Eeyore, Piglet, Tigger

winning 8 charming, engaging, pleasing **9** agreeable **10** delightful, successful, triumphant, victorious **11** captivating **13** prepossessing

winnow 3 fan **4** blow, cull, pare, sift, sort **6** delete, filter, narrow, reduce, remove, screen, select **8** separate

winsome 5 sweet **6** dulcet, lovely **8** charming, cheerful, engaging, pleasing **9** easygoing **12** lighthearted

winter 6 season **9** hibernate *French:* **5** hiver *Spanish:* **8** invierno

Winter's Tale, A *author:* **11** Shakespeare (William) *character:* **7** Camillo, Leontes, Paulina, Perdita **8** Florizel, Hermione **9** Antigonus, Autolycus, Polixenes

wintry 3 icy **4** cold **5** bleak, hoary, nippy, snowy **6** frigid, frosty **8** chilling, freezing, hibernal **12** bone-chilling

wipe 3 dry, rub **4** swab **5** towel, whisk **6** napkin, smudge, sponge **8** squeegee

wipe out 4 rout **5** crash, erase, smear, sweep **6** efface **7** blot out, destroy, expunge **8** decimate **9** eradicate, extirpate **10** annihilate, obliterate

wipeout 4 fall, rout **5** crash **8** drubbing **11** destruction **12** annihilation

wire 3 rod **4** cord, line, send **5** cable, metal **6** thread **7** message **8** meshwork, telegram **9** cablegram, telegraph **10** finish line *measure:* **3** mil **5** gauge

wiry 4 lean, ropy **6** sinewy, supple **7** fibrous, stringy

Wisconsin *capital:* **7** Madison *city:* **6** Racine **7** Kenosha **8** Green Bay **9** Milwaukee *college, university:* **5** Ripon **6** Beloit **9** Marquette *lake:* **7** Mendota *motto:* **7** Forward *nickname:* **6** Badger (State) *peninsula:* **4** Door *river:* **7** St. Croix **9** Menominee, Wisconsin **11** Mississippi *state bird:* **5** robin *state flower:* **6** violet *state tree:* **10** sugar maple

wisdom 5 sense **7** insight, science **8** judgment, learning, sagacity, sageness, sapience **9** good sense, knowledge **10** horse sense **11** common sense, information

wise 4 sage **5** brash, cagey, canny, cocky, fresh, nervy, sassy **6** astute, cheeky, crafty, fill in, inform, notify, shrewd, sophic **7** gnostic, knowing, politic, prudent, sapient **8** discreet, flippant, impudent, insolent, sensible, tactical **9** advisable, expedient, judicious, sagacious, scholarly **10** discerning, insightful, perceptive, thoughtful **11** foresighted, impertinent, intelligent, smart-alecky **13** contemplative, knowledgeable, perspicacious *old man:* **6** Nestor *person:* **4** sage **6** savant **7** scholar

wiseacre see **wise guy**

wisecrack 3 dig, gag **4** barb, gibe, jape, jest, joke, quip **5** sally **6** zinger **9** witticism

wise guy 6 smarty **7** mobster **8** gangster, smart-ass **9** know-it-all, swellhead **10** smart aleck **11** smarty-pants, wisenheimer

wise man 4 guru, sage **5** magus **6** Nestor, savant

Wise Men see **Magi**

wish 3 bid **4** care, goal, like, long, lust, want **5** covet, crave, fancy, foist, order, yearn **6** desire, impose **7** request **10** desiderate

wishbone 7 furcula

wishful 5 eager **7** anxious, hopeful, longing **8** desirous

wishy-washy 4 lame, weak **5** banal, bland, vapid, wimpy **6** jejune, watery **7** insipid, languid **10** namby-pamby **11** ineffective, ineffectual **13** characterless

wisp 3 bit **5** shred, strip, trace **6** sliver, snatch, streak **7** smidgen, snippet **8** fragment **9** scintilla

wispy 4 slim **5** frail **6** flimsy, slight **7** slender, tenuous **8** fleeting, nebulous **10** evanescent

Wister novel 9 Virginian (The)

wistful 3 sad **6** dreamy, triste **7** longing, pensive **8** yearning **9** nostalgic **10** melancholy

wit 3 wag **5** brain, comic, droll, humor, irony, joker **6** banter, esprit, jester, reason, satire, wisdom **7** farceur, punster **8** banterer, comedian, funnyman, judgment, humorist, jokester, quipster, repartee **9** alertness, ingenuity, intellect **10** cleverness, persiflage

witch 3 hag, hex **5** crone, dowse, spell **6** voodoo, Wiccan **7** charmer **8** magician, sorcerer **9** sorceress **11** enchantress *companion:* **3** cat *group:* **5** coven *male:* **6** wizard **7** warlock *meeting:* **6** sabbat **7** sabbath *town:* **5** Endor *vehicle:* **5** broom

witchcraft 5 magic, wicca **6** hoodoo, voodoo **7** devilry, hexerei, sorcery **8** wizardry **9** diablerie, sortilege, voodooism **10** black magic, hocus-pocus, mumbo jumbo, necromancy **11** abracadabra, thaumaturgy

witch hazel 5 shrub **6** lotion

witchy 6 Wiccan **7** magical **8** wizardly **9** sorcerous **11** necromantic **12** thaumaturgic

with 3 for, per, pro, via **4** over, upon **5** about **6** having **7** against, by way of, through **8** as well as **9** by means of, in favor of **10** by virtue of *French:* **4** avec *German:* **3** mit *Italian, Spanish:* **3** con *Latin:* **3** cum

withal 3 too, yet **4** also **5** still **6** as well, though **7** besides, howbeit, however **8** after all, moreover **11** furthermore, nonetheless **12** additionally, nevertheless

withdraw 4 exit, quit **5** demit, leave, unsay **6** depart, bow out, call in, cash in, desert, detach, recall, recant, recede, recoil, retire, secede, shrink **7** back out, drop out, pull out, retract, retreat, scratch, take off, take out **8** back down, evacuate, fall back, pull away, push back, separate, take back, turn away **9** disengage, stand down **10** disconnect, give ground

withdrawal 4 exit **6** exodus **7** exiting, pullout, removal, retreat **9** departure **10** alienation, detachment, retirement, retraction, revocation

withdrawn 4 cool **5** aloof **6** casual, remote **7** distant, removed **8** detached, isolated, reserved, retiring, solitary **9** incurious, unaffable, uncurious **10** unsociable **11** indifferent, introverted, standoffish, unconcerned, unexpansive **12** uninterested, unresponsive

wither 3 age, dry **4** fade, sear, wilt **5** dry up, parch, quail, wizen **6** scorch **7** mummify, shrivel

withered 4 sere **7** sapless **8** shrunken, wrinkled **9** shriveled

withhold 4 deny **5** check **6** deduct, detain, refuse, retain **7** abstain, deprive, forbear, inhibit, refrain, reserve **8** restrain, subtract **9** constrain

within 4 into **5** among **6** inside **7** indoors, inwards **8** enclosed, interior, inwardly **10** inner place *prefix:* **3** ent **4** endo, ento **5** infra, intra, intro

with-it 6 modern, modish, trendy **7** à la mode, current, faddish, stylish **8** up-to-date **9** au courant **11** fashionable **12** contemporary

without 4 less, open, past, sans **5** minus **6** absent **7** lacking, open air, outside, wanting **8** outdoors **10** externally, out-of-doors *Latin:* **4** sine

with respect to 2 re **4** as to, in re **5** as for **7** apropos **8** touching **9** as regards, regarding **10** concerning

withstand 4 bear, buck, defy **5** fight, repel **6** endure, oppose, resist, suffer **7** hold off, survive, sustain **8** tolerate, traverse

withy 4 twig **5** osier **6** branch, willow **8** flexible **9** resilient

witless 3 mad **4** daft, nuts **5** crazy, daffy, dotty, nutty, silly **6** insane, simple, stupid **7** asinine, cracked, foolish, idiotic **8** demented, deranged, mindless **9** bedlamite, brainless, senseless **10** weak-minded, unbalanced

witlessness 5 folly **6** idiocy, lunacy **7** inanity **8** insanity **9** absurdity, stupidity

witness 3 see **4** note, sign, view **5** proof, vouch **6** attest, depone, depose, notice, viewer **7** bear out, confirm, betoken, certify, testify, watcher **8** attester, beholder, deponent, evidence, looker-on, observer, onlooker **9** bystander, spectator, testament, testifier, testimony **11** affirmation, attestation, corroborate, testimonial **12** confirmation

witticism 3 dig, gag, mot **4** gibe, jape, jest, jibe, joke, quip **5** crack, sally **6** bon mot **8** one-liner, repartee **9** throwaway, wisecrack

witting 5 aware **7** knowing, willful **8** sensible, sentient **9** cognizant, conscious, voluntary **10** deliberate **11** intentional

witty 5 funny **6** clever, jocose **7** amusing, jocular **8** humorous **9** facetious **13** scintillating

wiz 3 ace **5** adept, fiend **6** artist, expert, phenom **7** artiste **8** virtuoso

wizard 3 ace **4** mage **5** adept, druid, fiend, magus **6** expert, phenom **7** warlock **8** conjurer, magician, sorcerer, virtuoso **9** enchanter **10** past master **11** necromancer, thaumaturge **13** thaumaturgist

wizardly 5 magic **6** mystic, witchy **7** magical **9** sorcerous **10** mysterious **11** necromantic **12** thaumaturgic

Wizard of Menlo Park 6 Edison (Thomas Alva)

Wizard of Oz *author:* **4** Baum (L. Frank) *character:* **6** Tin Man **7** Dorothy **9** Scarecrow **11** Tin Woodsman **12** Cowardly Lion *dog:* **4** Toto

wizardry 5 magic **6** voodoo **7** sorcery **8** witchery **9** diablerie, sortilege **10** black magic, necromancy, witchcraft **11** bewitchment, conjuration, enchantment

wizen 3 dry **4** sere, wilt **5** dry up **6** shrink, wither **7** dried-up, shrivel, wrinkle

wizened 4 aged, sere **5** dried **6** shrunk **7** pinched **8** shrunken, withered, wrinkled

wobble 4 reel, rock, sway **5** quake, shake, waver, weave **6** dither, falter, quaver, teeter, totter **7** stagger, stumble, tremble **8** nutation **9** vacillate

wobbly 4 weak **5** rocky, shaky **6** unsure **7** rackety, rickety **8** insecure, rachitic, unstable, unsteady, wavering **9** faltering, teetering, tottering **10** nutational **11** vacillating

Wodehouse, P. G. *castle:* **9** Blandings *character:* **6** Bertie (Wooster), Gussie (Fink-Nottle), Jeeves, Psmith **7** Wooster (Bertie) **8** Emsworth (Lord), Mulliner (Mr.) **10** Threepwood (Clarence, Freddie) **12** Lord Emsworth *club:* **6** Drones

Woden see **Odin**

woe 3 rue **4** bale, bane, care **5** grief **6** misery, regret, sorrow **7** anguish, sadness, trouble **8** calamity **9** heartache **10** affliction, heartbreak **11** lamentation, unhappiness **12** wretchedness

woebegone 3 low, sad **4** blue, down, worn **6** shabby **7** doleful, forlorn, ruthful **8** dejected, dolorous, downcast, wretched **9** depressed, miserable, sorrowful **10** despondent, melancholy **11** crestfallen, downhearted, low-spirited

woeful 3 sad **5** heavy, sorry **6** dismal, rueful, tragic, triste **7** ruthful **8** dejected, dolorous, downcast, grievous, mournful, stricken, tortured, wretched **9** afflicted, aggrieved, depressed, heartsick, miserable, plaintive, sorrowful **10** deplorable, lamentable, lugubrious, melancholy **11** distressing, downhearted, low-spirited **12** disconsolate

wolf 4 bolt, lobo, rake, roué **5** canid **6** canine, coyote, devour, gobble, masher **7** Don Juan, poverty **8** Casanova, lothario **10** starvation *genus:* **5** Canis *group:* **4** pack *young:* **5** whelp

Wolfe novel 17 Look Homeward Angel, Of Time and the River **18** You Can't Go Home Again **20** Bonfire of the Vanities (The)

wolfish 4 wild **5** cruel, feral **6** fierce, lupine,

savage **7** bestial, brutish, vicious **9** ferocious

wolverine *European:* **7** glutton *genus:* **4** Gulo

Wolverine State 8 Michigan

woman 4 dame, lady **5** madam **6** female, matron **8** mistress **10** girlfriend *attractive:* **5** belle, vixen **6** beauty, eyeful, looker **7** stunner **8** knockout *combining form:* **4** gyny **5** gynec **6** gynaec, gyneco, gynous **7** gynaeco *courageous:* **7** heroine *dignified:* **6** matron **7** dowager **10** grande dame *dowdy:* **5** frump *English:* **6** milady *first, biblical:* **3** Eve *first, mythological:* **7** Pandora *French:* **5** femme *German:* **4** Frau **8** Fräulein *Hawaiian:* **6** wahine *Indian:* **5** squaw *Italian:* **5** donna **7** signora *old:* **3** hag **4** dame **5** crone **6** beldam, carlin, gammer, granny *Polynesian:* **6** wahine *pregnant:* **7** gravida *resembling:* **8** gynecoid *royal:* **5** queen **8** princess *sailor:* **4** Wave *servant:* **4** maid *soldier:* **3** Wac *Spanish:* **4** doña **5** mujer **6** señora *strong:* **6** amazon, virago *surfer:* **6** wahine *unmarried:* **4** miss **6** maiden **8** spinster *young:* **4** girl, lass **6** lassie, maiden **7** ingenue

womanize 4 wolf **9** gallivant, philander **10** fool around, mess around

womanizer 4 rake, roué, stud, wolf **6** masher **7** Don Juan, gallant, playboy **8** Casanova, lothario **9** ladies' man, mack daddy **10** ladykiller **11** philanderer

womb 6 uterus *combining form:* **6** hyster **7** hystero

women *hatred of:* **8** misogyny *organization of:* **3** DAR, NOW **8** sorority *seclusion of:* **6** purdah

wonder 3 awe **4** muse **5** doubt **6** marvel **7** dubiety, miracle, portent, prodigy **8** mistrust, question **9** amazement, speculate, suspicion **10** admiration, skepticism **12** astonishment

wonderful 4 keen **5** grand, great, nifty, super, swell **6** divine, groovy, peachy, spiffy **7** amazing, strange, too much, topping **8** dynamite, fabulous, glorious, spiffing, terrific **9** admirable, excellent, marvelous, wunderbar **10** astounding, delightful, miraculous, out-of-sight, stupendous **11** astonishing, outstanding

wondrous 6 mystic **7** amazing, awesome, strange **9** marvelous **10** astounding, formidable, miraculous, portentous, prodigious, remarkable, stupendous, surprising **11** astonishing, spectacular **13** extraordinary

wonk 4 dork, geek, nerd, swot **5** dweeb, grind

wonky 4 awry **5** geeky, nerdy, shaky **7** bookish **8** unsteady

wont 3 apt **4** used **5** habit, usage **6** custom,

manner **8** accustom, habitude, inclined, practice **10** accustomed, consuetude

wonted 5 usual **7** routine **8** habitual, ordinary **9** customary **10** accustomed

woo 3 sue **5** court **6** pursue **7** address, entreat

wood 5 weald **6** forest, lumber, timber **8** golf club *combining form:* **3** xyl **4** lign, xylo **5** ligni, ligno *decayed:* **4** punk *eater:* **7** termite *for burning:* **5** fagot **6** tinder **8** kindling *fragrant:* **5** cedar *golf:* **6** driver *hard:* **3** ash, elm, oak **4** ebon, rata, teak **5** aalii, alder, aspen, beech, birch, ebony, maple **6** cherry, poplar, walnut **7** hickory **8** chestnut, hornbeam, ironwood, mahogany, sycamore *imperfection:* **4** knot **5** gnarl *light:* **5** balsa **6** corkwood *made of:* **5** treen *measure:* **4** cord **5** stere *pattern in:* **5** grain **6** figure *product:* **3** tar **5** paper **10** turpentine *soft:* **3** fir, yew **4** pine **5** cedar, larch **6** spruce **7** cypress, hemlock, redwood

wood alcohol 6 methyl **8** carbinol, methanol

woodchuck 6 marmot **9** groundhog

wood coal 7 lignite

wooded 5 bosky, treed **6** sylvan **8** forested, timbered

wooden 5 rigid, stiff **6** clumsy **7** awkward, stilted **8** ligneous **10** inflexible

wooden shoe 4 clog **5** sabot

woodland 5 copse, taiga, weald **6** forest, pinery **7** coppice *deity:* **3** Pan **4** faun **5** satyr **6** Faunus **7** silenus

wood nymph 5 dryad

woodpecker 4 bird **7** flicker, wryneck **9** sapsucker *genus:* **5** Picus *kind:* **5** downy, green, hairy **8** imperial, pileated **9** redheaded **11** ivory-billed

woodsman 6 logger **8** forester **10** bushranger

wood sorrel 3 oca **6** oxalis **8** shamrock **9** carambola

woodsy 6 rustic, sylvan

woodwind 3 sax **4** oboe, reed **5** flute, shawm **7** bassoon, piccolo **8** clarinet **9** saxophone **10** cor anglais, instrument **11** English horn **13** contrabassoon

woodworker 9 carpenter **12** cabinetmaker

woody 8 ligneous **12** station wagon

wooer 4 beau **5** lover, spark, swain **6** suitor **7** admirer, gallant, sparker

woof 4 bark, crow, weft, yarn **5** boast, weave **6** fabric, thread **7** texture

wool 3 fur **4** coat, hair **6** fabric, fleece *cut:* **5** shear *fabric:* **4** felt **5** baize, crepe, serge, tweed **6** covert, duffel, duffle, kersey, mohair, poplin, shoddy, velour **7** flannel, worsted **8** cashmere, chenille **9** gabardine **10** broadcloth *fat:* **7** lanolin *kind:* **4** hogg **6** angora, hogget, virgin *low-quality:* **5** mungo **6**

shoddy *musk-ox:* 6 qiviut *process:* 7 carding *short fiber:* 4 noil *source:* 4 goat, lamb 5 camel, llama, sheep 6 alpaca

Woolf, Virginia *home:* 10 Bloomsbury *husband:* 7 Leonard *novel:* 5 Waves (The), Years (The) 7 Orlando 11 Mrs. Dalloway 13 Room of One's Own (A) 15 To the Lighthouse

woolly 5 fuzzy, hairy, nappy 6 fleecy, shaggy 7 hirsute

woozy 4 hazy, sick, weak 5 dazed, dizzy, faint, fuzzy, muzzy, vague 6 addled, blurry, groggy, punchy 8 confused 9 slaphappy 11 light-headed

word 3 vow 4 oath, term 5 logos 6 pledge 7 promise 8 locution 9 utterance 10 expression *connective:* 11 conjunction *group:* 6 clause, phrase 8 sentence *last:* 4 Amen *misused:* 8 malaprop 11 malapropism *naming:* 4 noun *new:* 7 coinage 9 neologism *of action:* 4 verb *of honor:* 4 oath 7 promise *origin:* 9 etymology *part:* 8 syllable *root:* 6 etymon *scrambled:* 7 anagram *shortened:* 11 contraction 12 abbreviation *square:* 10 palindrome *ultimatum:* 4 else *with opposite meaning:* 7 antonym *with same meaning:* 7 synonym *with same pronunciation:* 7 homonym 9 homophone *with same spelling:* 7 homonym 9 homograph

wordbook 5 vocab 7 lexicon 8 glossary 9 thesaurus 10 dictionary, vocabulary

word-for-word 7 literal 8 ad verbum, verbally, verbatim

wordiness 8 verbiage 9 logorrhea, prolixity, verbosity 10 bloviation

word-of-mouth 4 oral 6 spoken, verbal 8 viva voce 9 unwritten

Wordsworth, William *friend:* 9 Coleridge (Samuel T.) *poem:* 7 Prelude (The) *sister:* 7 Dorothy

wordy 5 windy 6 prolix, verbal 7 diffuse, verbose 9 dictional, garrulous, iterative, redundant, vocabular 10 long-winded, logorrheic, loquacious, rhetorical

work 3 act, fix, job, run, use 4 duty, line, opus, task, tend, till, toil 5 chore, craft, drive, forge, grind, guide, labor, shape, solve, sweat, trade 6 effect, effort, métier, result, strain, strive 7 arrange, calling, control, fashion, operate, perform, product, provoke, pursuit, resolve, travail 8 activity, business, contrive, drudgery, exertion, function, vocation 10 assignment, employment, occupation, profession *unit:* 3 erg 5 joule

workaday 5 plain, usual 7 mundane, prosaic, routine 8 ordinary 9 quotidian 11 commonplace

worker 4 doer, hand, serf 5 prole 6 toiler, wallah 7 artisan, laborer 8 employee, mechanic, operator 9 operative 11 proletarian *fellow:* 7 comrade, partner 9 colleague *group:* 4 crew, gang 5 artel, shift, staff, union *hard:* 5 slave 6 beaver, drudge *insect:* 3 ant, bee 4 wasp 7 termite *itinerant:* 6 boomer 7 migrant *unskilled:* 4 peon 7 jackleg, laborer

working 4 busy, live 6 active, useful, viable 7 dynamic, engaged, running 8 employed, occupied 9 operative 11 functioning *not:* 5 kaput 6 broken

work out 3 fix 5 solve, train 6 devise, settle 7 arrange, develop, resolve 8 exercise

workout 4 test 5 drill 8 exercise, practice 10 daily dozen

work over 4 beat, redo 5 scrag, study 6 beat up, mess up, redraw, rehash, revamp, revise 7 examine, redraft, restyle, rewrite, rough up 9 manhandle

workroom 3 lab 4 shop 6 studio 7 atelier 10 laboratory

Works and Days author 6 Hesiod

world 5 class, earth, globe, realm 6 career, cosmos, nature, planet, public, sphere, system 7 kingdom, society 8 creation, division, everyone, renowned, universe 9 human race, macrocosm, microcosm 13 distinguished *combining form:* 4 cosm 5 cosmo

worldly 5 blasé 6 carnal, earthy, urbane 7 earthly, fleshly, mundane, profane, secular, sensual, terrene 8 material, telluric, temporal 9 sublunary 11 terrestrial 12 cosmopolitan 13 sophisticated

worldly-wise 12 cosmopolitan 13 sophisticated

World Series winner *1990:* 4 Reds *1991:* 5 Twins *1992, 1993:* 8 Blue Jays *1995:* 6 Braves *1996, 1998, 1999, 2000:* 7 Yankees *1997, 2003:* 7 Marlins *2001:* 12 Diamondbacks *2002:* 6 Angels *2004:* 6 Red Sox *2005:* 8 White Sox *2006:* 9 Cardinals *2007:6* Red Sox *2008:8* Phillies *2009:7* Yankees *2010:6* Giants

World War I *battle:* 5 Aisne, Marne, Somme, Ypres 6 Isonzo, Verdun 7 Jutland 9 Caporetto 10 Tannenberg 11 Dardanelles *battle line:* 9 Siegfried *general:* 4 Foch (Ferdinand), Haig (Douglas) 6 Joffre (Joseph), Pétain (Philippe) 7 Allenby (Edmund) 8 Pershing (John) 10 Hindenburg (Paul von), Ludendorff (Erich) *hero:* 4 York (Alvin) 8 Red Baron (The) 10 Richthofen (Manfred von) 12 Rickenbacker (Eddie) *treaty:* 10 Versailles

World War II *admiral:* 6 Dönitz (Karl), Halsey (William "Bull"), Nimitz (Chester), Nimitz

(Chester) **8** Yamamoto (Isoroku) *alliance:* **4** Axis **6** Allies *battle:* **4** St.-Lô **5** Anzio, Bulge **6** Bataan, Midway, Tarawa, Warsaw **7** Britain, Iwo Jima, Okinawa, Saint-Lô **8** Coral Sea, Normandy **9** El Alamein, Leyte Gulf **10** Stalingrad **11** Guadalcanal *general:***4** Jodl (Alfred), Tojo (Hideki) **5** Clark (Mark) **6** Arnold (Hap), Keitel (Wilhelm), Patton (George), Rommel (Erwin), Zhukov (Georgy) **7** Bradley (Omar) **8** Marshall (George) **9** MacArthur (Douglas), Rundstedt (Gerd von) **10** Eisenhower (Dwight David), Kesselring (Albert), Montgomery (Bernard) *hero:* **6** Murphy (Audie) *journalist:* **4** Pyle (Ernie) *weapon:* **5** A-bomb **6** rocket **8** buzz bomb

world-weary 5 blasé, jaded **7** cynical **9** apathetic, exhausted

worldwide 6 cosmic, global **8** catholic **9** planetary, universal **10** ecumenical **12** cosmopolitan

worm 3 cad, cur **4** grub, lout **5** borer, creep, fluke, leech, louse, screw, treat **6** edge in, maggot, no-good, squirm, thread, wiggle, wretch, writhe **7** extract, triclad, wriggle **8** helminth, nematode, squiggle **9** planarium, trematode *African:* **3** Loa *marine:* **6** nereid **7** annelid, tubifex *parasitic:* **5** fluke, leech **7** ascarid, ascaris, cestode, filaria **8** helminth, trichina **9** strongyle

worn 3 old, wan **4** aged, beat **5** drawn, jaded, tatty, tired, weary **6** eroded, frayed, ragged, shabby **7** haggard **8** fatigued **9** woebegone **10** threadbare

worn-out 4 beat **5** all in, spent, tired, weary **6** bleary, bushed, ragged, used-up **7** drained, run-down **8** decrepit, depleted, fatigued, overused **9** exhausted, worm-eaten **10** broken-down, threadbare, tumbledown **11** debilitated, dilapidated

worried 6 afraid, on edge **7** anxious, nervous **8** bothered, distrait, troubled **9** concerned, tormented **10** distracted, distraught, distressed

worry 3 nag, try, vex **4** care, fret, fuss, gnaw, goad, pain, stew, test **5** angst, annoy, beset, shake, tease, trial, upset **6** assail, attack, bother, harass, needle, pester, plague, pull at, unease **7** afflict, anguish, anxiety, concern, disturb, oppress, torment, trouble **8** aggrieve, distress, irritate **9** agitation, annoyance, misgiving

worrywart 7 fusspot **9** Cassandra, doomsayer, pessimist **10** fussbudget

worse 8 inferior

worsen 4 sink **7** decline **10** degenerate **11** deteriorate

worship 4 love **5** adore, honor **6** admire, dote on, homage, revere **7** idolize, lionize, liturgy, respect **8** devotion, idolatry, venerate **9** adoration, affection, reverence **10** admiration, veneration *object of:* **3** god **4** icon, idol *place of:* **5** altar **6** church, mosque, shrine, temple **9** cathedral, synagogue **10** tabernacle

worshipper 3 fan **6** votary **7** admirer, devotee **8** adherent, believer, disciple **10** enthusiast

worsted 4 yarn **5** stuff **6** caddis, fabric **7** cheviot, etamine, flannel, lasting **8** shalloon **9** bombazine, sharkskin **10** broadcloth

worth 4 rate **5** merit, price, value **6** regard, riches, wealth **7** caliber, calibre, fortune, quality, stature **9** resources, substance, valuation **10** excellence

worthless 4 vain **6** futile, no-good, otiose **7** inutile **8** nugatory **9** no-account

worthwhile 6 paying **7** gainful **9** estimable, honorable, lucrative **10** profitable, well-paying

worthy 4 good **5** noble **8** laudable, standout **9** admirable, deserving, desirable, estimable, honorable **10** acceptable, creditable **11** commendable, meritorious

Wotan see **Odin**

Wouk novel 10 Winds of War (The) **11** Caine Mutiny (The)

would-be 7 hopeful, wishful **8** apparent, aspiring, desiring, desirous **9** ambitious, potential

wound 3 cut **4** blow, harm, hurt, pain, rift **6** damage, injure, injury, insult, lesion, trauma **8** lacerate **10** laceration *sign:* **4** scab, scar **5** blood **7** blister

wow 3 hit **4** boff, grab **5** amaze, boffo, smash **6** dazzle **7** astound, impress, success **8** bedazzle

Wozzeck composer 4 Berg (Alban)

wrack 4 kelp, raze, ruin **5** smash, total **7** destroy, flotsam, remnant, seaweed **8** decimate, demolish, shambles, wreckage **11** destruction

wraith 5 ghost, shade, spook **6** double, shadow, spirit **7** phantom, specter, spectre **8** phantasm **10** apparition

wrangle 3 row **4** spar, spat, tiff **5** argue, brawl, fight, scrap **6** bicker, fracas, haggle, hassle **7** brabble, dispute, fall out, finagle, quarrel, quibble **8** squabble **11** altercation

wrangler 6 cowboy **8** buckaroo **9** ranch hand

wrap 3 fur **4** bind, cape, cere, coat, roll **5** cloak, drape, shawl, stole **6** bundle, clothe, enfold, invest, jacket, mantle, muffle, parcel, shroud, swathe **7** bandage, blanket, conceal, dress up, embrace, enclose, engross, envelop, involve, package, swaddle **8** bundle up, enshroud

wrapped up 4 deep **6** intent **7** engaged **8** absorbed, consumed, immersed **9** engrossed **11** preoccupied

wrapper 5 cover **6** jacket **10** dust jacket **12** dressing gown

wrap up 6 muffle **8** close out, complete, conclude **9** summarize

wrap-up 4 coda **5** close **6** capper, closer, finale, report **7** closing **8** epilogue **9** summation **10** denouement

wrath 3 ire **4** fury, rage **5** anger **6** choler **8** ferocity **9** vengeance **10** punishment **11** retribution

wrathful 3 mad **5** angry, irate **6** heated, raging **7** enraged, furious **8** choleric, incensed, inflamed **10** infuriated

wreak 5 cause, exact, visit **6** effect, impose **7** inflict

wreath 3 bay, lei **5** crown **6** anadem, laurel **7** chaplet, circlet, coronal, coronet, garland, laurels

wreathe 4 coil, curl, wind **5** twine, twist **6** spiral **7** entwine **9** corkscrew **10** interweave

wreck 4 do in, heap, hulk, raze, ruin **5** beach, crack, crash, cream, smash, total, trash **6** beater, damage, jalopy, junker, pileup, ravage, strand **7** clunker, crack-up, destroy, scuttle, smashup, torpedo **8** decimate, demolish **9** vandalize

wreckage 5 wrack **6** debris **7** flotsam **8** detritus, shambles **11** destruction

wrecker 8 salvager, tow truck

wrench 4 jerk, pull, rack, tool, turn, warp, yank **5** force, twist, wrest, wring **6** change, injure, injury, snatch, socket, sprain, strain **7** disable, distort, pervert, squeeze **8** distress, twisting *kind:* **6** monkey **7** ratchet

wrest 4 rend, rive **5** exact, twist, wring **6** elicit, extort, snatch, wrench **7** extract, squeeze

wrestle 6 combat, strain, strive, tussle **7** contend, grapple, scuffle **8** struggle

wrestling *champion:* **4** Ladd (Ernie), Race (Harley) **5** Gagne (Verne), Hogan (Hulk), Studd (Big John) **7** Ventura (Jesse) **8** Kowalski (Killer) **9** Slaughter (Sgt.) **13** André the Giant *hold:* **4** lock **6** nelson **8** headlock, scissors *kind:* **4** sumo *term:* **3** pin **4** fall **5** throw **8** takedown

wretch 3 cur, dog **4** scum, toad, worm **5** devil, knave, louse, rogue, skunk, snake **6** rascal, rotter **7** caitiff, hangdog, lowlife, outcast, rat fink, stinker, villain **8** scalawag, stinkard **9** scoundrel **10** blackguard, sleazeball **11** rapscallion

wretched 3 low, sad **4** base, foul, mean, vile **6** abject, dismal, horrid, scurvy, sordid, woeful **7** abysmal, doleful, forlorn, ignoble,

ruthful, servile, squalid, unhappy **8** dejected, dolorous, hopeless, inferior **9** afflicted, execrable, miserable, sorrowful **10** despairing, despicable, deplorable

wretchedness 3 woe **6** misery **7** anguish **8** distress

wriggle 4 worm **5** slink **6** squirm, writhe

Wright, Richard *character:* **6** Bigger (Thomas) *novel:* **8** Black Boy **9** Native Son

wring 3 wry **5** choke, exact, screw, twist, wrest **6** extort, squirm, wrench, writhe **7** afflict, draw out, extract, squeeze, torment *the neck:* **5** scrag

wringing-wet 5 soppy **6** soaked, sodden, soused **7** soaking, sopping **8** drenched, dripping **9** saturated

wrinkle 4 fold, ruck, ruga, seam **5** crimp, crisp, plica, ridge, wizen **6** cockle, crease, furrow, pucker, rumple **7** crumple, scrunch, shrivel **9** corrugate, crow's-foot, worry line **11** corrugation

wrinkled 5 lined **6** rugose, rumply **7** creased **8** puckered, rugulose

wrist 5 joint **6** carpus *bone:* **6** carpal, hamate **8** pisiform

writ 5 brief, order **6** assize, capias, decree, elegit, extent **7** mandate, process, summons, warrant **8** detainer, document, mandamus, mittimus, praecipe, replevin, subpoena **9** execution **10** attachment, certiorari, court order, injunction **11** fieri facias, scire facias, supersedeas **12** habeas corpus, venire facias

write 3 ink, jot, pen **4** note **5** chalk, draft, print, score, spell **6** answer, author, byline, draw up, indite, ordain, pencil, record, scrawl, scribe **7** compose, dissert, engross, fire off, put down, scratch, set down **8** inscribe, scribble, spell out **9** autograph, transpose **10** correspond

write down 4 note **6** record, reduce **10** transcribe

write off 6 cancel **7** dismiss, expense **8** amortize, discount **9** eliminate **10** depreciate

write-off 4 debt, loss **7** expense **8** donation **9** allowance, deduction, reduction

writer 4 poet **6** author, penman, scribe **8** composer, novelist **9** scribbler, wordsmith *bad:* **4** hack (see also **author**)

write-up 5 blurb, story **7** account, article

writhe 4 curl, worm **5** twist **6** squirm, suffer, wallow, welter, wiggle, wrench **7** agonize, contort, distort, wriggle **8** convolve, squiggle

writing 4 book, hand, note **5** essay, paper, print, prose, style, words **6** letter, notice, record, script **8** document, longhand **10** literature, penmanship **11** calligraphy, composition, inscription *character:* **6** letter **9**

cuneiform **10** hieroglyph *combining form:* **4** gram **6** grapho, graphy *for the blind:* **7** braille *instrument:* **3** pen **5** chalk, quill **6** pencil, stylus *sacred:* **5** Bible, Koran, Quran **6** Talmud, Tantra **9** scripture *surface:* **5** board, paper, slate **6** scroll **9** parchment

wrong 3 bad, ill, off, sin **4** awry, evil, harm, hurt, tort **5** abuse, amiss, badly, crime, false, inapt, unfit **6** afield, astray, injure, injury, malign, offend, sinful, unfair, unjust, untrue **7** defraud, immoral, oppress, outrage, violate **8** aggrieve, ill-treat, improper, inequity, iniquity, mistaken, opposite **9** erroneous, grievance, incorrect, injustice, misguided, unethical, violation

wrongdoer 5 felon **6** sinner **8** criminal, offender **9** miscreant, reprobate **10** accomplice, delinquent, malefactor **12** transgressor

wrongdoing 3 sin **4** evil **5** crime **7** misdeed, offense **8** iniquity **10** misconduct **11** malefaction, malfeasance, misbehavior

wrongful 6 unjust, unfair **7** illegal, illicit, lawless **8** criminal, improper, unlawful **12** illegitimate

wrongheaded 6 mulish **7** froward **8** contrary, perverse **9** obstinate

wrought 4 made **6** formed, shaped, worked **7** created **8** finished, hammered **9** decorated, fashioned *up:* **7** excited, stirred

wry 4 bent **5** askew, twist, wrest **6** ironic, wrench **7** crooked, twisted **8** humorous, sardonic

wryneck 10 woodpecker **11** torticollis

wurst 8 sausage

Wuthering Heights *author:* **6** Brontë (Emily) *character:* **5** Cathy **9** Catherine **10** Heathcliff *family:* **6** Linton **8** Earnshaw

Wycliffite 7 Lollard

Wyoming *capital:* **8** Cheyenne *city:* **6** Casper **7** Laramie *mountain, range:* **5** Rocky **7** Gannett (Peak) **9** Wind River **10** Grand Teton *nickname:* **8** Equality (State) *river:* **5** Green, Snake **6** Powder **7** Bighorn *state bird:* **10** meadowlark *state flower:* **16** Indian paintbrush *state tree:* **10** cottonwood

X

x 3 chi, ten **4** kiss **5** annul, cross, erase, error, times, wrong **6** cancel, delete, efface **7** mistake, unknown **8** abscissa **9** signature

Xanthippe 3 nag **5** scold, shrew **6** nagger **9** termagant *husband:* **8** Socrates

xenon *symbol* **2** Xe

Xenophon *work* **8** Anabasis **9** Cyropedia, Hellenica

xerophyte 6 cactus

Xerxes *crossing site:* **10** Hellespont *defeat:* **7** Plataea, Salamis *father:* **6** Darius *kingdom:* **6** Persia *mother:* **6** Atossa *victory:* **11** Thermopylae

Xmas 4 Noel, yule **8** Nativity, yuletide

X-ray *discoverer:* **8** Roentgen (Wilhelm) *science:* **9** radiology

xylophone *relative* **7** marimba **9** xylorimba **10** vibraphone

Y

yacht 4 race, sail **6** cruise **7** cruiser **8** sailboat **12** cabin cruiser

yahoo 3 hun, yay **4** boor, clod, dolt, hood, lout, punk, thug **5** brute, chuff, churl, clown, rough, rowdy, tough **6** hoorah, hooray, hurrah, savage, terror, vandal, yippie **7** buffoon, bumpkin, hoodlum, ruffian, toughie **8** bullyboy, hooligan **9** roughneck **10** clodhopper

Yahweh 3 God **6** Adonai, Elohim **7** Jehovah

yak 2 ox 3 gab, jaw 4 blab, chat 5 clack, prate
6 babble, gabble, jabber, natter, yammer 7
blabber, blather, chatter, palaver, prattle 11
confabulate
Yale student 3 Eli
Yalta participant 6 Stalin (Joseph) 9
Churchill (Winston), Roosevelt (Franklin
Delano)
yam 4 taro 7 boniato 11 sweet potato
yammer 3 cry 4 bawl, crab, fuss, moan, wail,
yawp, yell 5 bleat, gripe, whine 6 babble,
bellow, clamor, gabble, grouch, grouse, jabber, natter, snivel, squawk 7 blather, prattle,
whimper 8 complain 9 bellyache, caterwaul
yank 3 tug 4 grab, jerk, pull, tear 5 hoick 6
snatch, wrench 7 extract
yap 3 gab 4 bark, hick 5 mouth, prate 6 babble, bowwow, gabble, jabber, natter, rustic,
yammer 7 blather, bumpkin, chatter, hayseed, prattle 9 hillbilly 10 clodhopper
yard 3 pen 4 herd, quad, spar, unit 5 court,
garth, glass 6 length 7 grounds, measure 9
curtilage, enclosure 10 playground, quadrangle five and one-half: 3 rod part of: 4
foot two hundred and twenty: 7 furlong
yardstick 4 norm, test 5 basis, gauge, model
7 measure, pattern 8 paradigm, standard 9
barometer, benchmark, criterion, guideline
10 touchstone
yare 4 deft, spry 5 agile, brisk, handy, lithe,
quick, ready, zippy 6 lively, nimble, volant
7 lissome 9 sprightly
yarn 4 tale, talk 5 fiber, story 6 caddis, cotton, crewel, strand, thread 7 account, cad-
dice 8 anecdote, tall tale 9 adventure,
narration, narrative ball of: 4 clew coil: 5
skein 6 skeane cotton: 10 candlewick for
fastening a sail: 6 roband metallic: 6 tinsel
woolen: 6 crewel 7 worsted 8 shetland
yaw 4 rock, swag, veer 5 lurch 6 swerve 7 deviate 9 alternate, deviation 10 deflection
yawn 3 gap 4 bore, gape 5 ennui 6 cavity, tedium 7 boredom, bromide 10 dullsville
yawning 4 deep 5 agape 6 gaping 7 abyssal 9
cavernous
yawp 3 bay, cry, nag 4 bark, bawl, beef, crab,
fuss, gape, wail 5 bleat, gripe 6 clamor, outcry, squall, squawk, yammer 8 complain 9
bellyache
yaws 9 frambesia
yclept 5 named 6 called
yea 3 aye, too 4 also, amen, even, more, okay
5 truly 6 agreed, assent, as well, indeed, really, verily 7 besides, granted 8 likewise,
moreover, positive 9 certainly 10 definitely
11 affirmation, affirmative 12 additionally
yeanling 3 kid 4 lamb

year 4 time 5 cycle 6 period academic division: 4 term 7 quarter, session 8 semester 9
trimester French: 5 année kind: 4 leap 5 solar 6 fiscal 8 academic, calendar, sidereal
Latin: 5 annus Scottish: 7 towmond Spanish: 3 año
yearbook 5 annal 6 annual 7 almanac
yearling 4 colt, foal 5 filly
Yearling, The author: 8 Rawlings (Marjorie
Kinnan) character: 4 Jody fawn: 4 Flag
yearly 6 annual 8 annually
yearn 4 ache, burn, itch, long, lust, pant,
pine, sigh, wish 5 dream, spoil 6 hanker,
hunger, thirst
yearning 4 wish 5 ardor, drive, eager 6 desire, thirst 7 craving, wistful 8 appetite 10
aspiration
years 3 age, era five: 7 lustrum 12 quinquen-
nial, quinquennium four: 11 quadrennial,
quadrennium one hundred: 7 century 9
centenary 10 centennial one thousand: 10
millennium ten: 6 decade 9 decennial, decennium three: 9 triennial, triennium two:
8 biennial, biennium
yeast 4 barm, foam, suds 5 froth, spume 6
lather, leaven 7 ferment
yeasty 5 dizzy, giddy, light 6 frothy 7 flighty
8 immature, restless, seething 9 exuberant,
frivolous, unsettled 11 light-headed
Yeats, William Butler beloved: 9 Maud
Gonne birthplace: 6 Dublin play: 7 Deirdre
9 Herne's Egg (The) 16 Countess Cathleen
(The) poetry: 5 Tower (The) 12 Second
Coming (The) 16 Wild Swans at Coole
(The) 18 Sailing to Byzantium theater: 5
Abbey
yegg 5 thief 6 robber 7 burglar 8 picklock 11
safecracker
yell 3 cry 4 bawl, call, howl, roar, wail 5
cheer, hallo, hollo, shout, whoop 6 bellow,
clamor, holler, outcry, scream, shriek,
squall 10 vociferate
yellow 3 age 4 buff, mean, weak, yolk 5 amber, blond, color, lemon, straw, tawny, topaz 6 canary, coward, craven, flaxen,
golden, sallow 7 citrine, gutless, ignoble,
jasmine, mustard, saffron 8 cowardly, discolor 9 dastardly, jaundiced, spunkless 11
sensational 12 dishonorable 13 pusillanimous brownish: 3 dun 5 amber, ocher dye:
7 annatto greenish: 5 olive 6 acacia 10
chartreuse
yellowhammer 5 finch 7 bunting, flicker
yelp 3 cry, yap 4 bark 6 outcry, squeal
Yemen capital: 4 Sana 5 Sanaa city: 4 Aden 5
Ta'izz desert: 10 Rub' al-Khali gulf: 4
Aden island: 7 Socotra island group: 7 Ka-

maran *language:* 6 Arabic *monetary unit:* 4 rial *neighbor:* 4 Oman 11 Saudi Arabia *peninsula:* 7 Arabian *sea:* 3 Red 7 Arabian

yen 4 ache, itch, long, lust, pine, sigh, urge 5 taste, yearn 6 desire, hanker, hunger, thirst 7 craving, longing, passion 8 appetite, yearning 9 hankering

yeoman 5 clerk 6 farmer 7 freeman 8 retainer 9 attendant, beefeater, landowner 10 freeholder 11 homesteader

yeomanly 5 loyal 6 sturdy 8 faithful

Yerby *novel* 13 Foxes of Harrow (The)

yes 3 aye, yea, yeh, yep, yup 4 okay, yeah 5 agree 6 agreed, assent, gladly 7 consent, exactly 8 all right 9 assuredly, certainly, willingly 11 affirmation, affirmative, undoubtedly *French:* 3 oui *German:* 2 ja *Italian:* 2 si *Russian:* 2 da *Spanish:* 2 si

yeshiva 6 school 8 seminary

yes-man 5 toady 6 lap dog, minion, stooge 7 spaniel 8 groveler, truckler 9 flatterer, sycophant 10 bootlicker 13 apple-polisher

yesterday 4 past, yore 8 recently 10 recent time *French:* 4 hier *Spanish:* 4 ayer

yesteryear 4 past, yore 7 history 8 foretime, lang syne 12 auld lang syne

yet 3 but, too 4 also, even, more, only, save 5 so far, still 6 as well, though, withal 7 besides, earlier, finally, howbeit, however, someday, thus far 8 after all, hitherto, moreover, sometime 10 eventually, ultimately 11 furthermore, nonetheless, still and all 12 additionally, nevertheless

Yevtushenko *poem* 7 Babi Yar, Baby Yar

Ygerne see Igraine

Yiddish *bit:* 5 shtik 6 shtick 7 schtick *bargain:* 7 metziah *bore:*6 nudnik 7 nudmick *burst:* 5 plotz *cash:* 6 mezuma *celebration:* 6 simcha *comment:* 6 kibitz 7 kibbitz *converse:* 7 shmooze 8 schmooze *craziness:* 8 meshugas, mishegas *crazy:* 7 meshuga 8 meshugge *crazy person:* 11 meshuggener *drag:* 5 shlep 6 schlep, shlepp 7 schlepp *fool:* 10 shmendrick *go away:* 7 gay avek *go to sleep:* 10 gay shlafen *grandpa:* 5 zayde *gripe:* 6 kvetch *knickknack:* 9 tchotchke *long story:* 8 megillah *loser:* 6 nebish *man of integrity:* 6 mensch *matchmaker:* 8 shadchen *meddler:* 5 yenta *money:* 4 gelt *munch:* 4 nosh *nerve, gall:* 7 chutzpa 8 chutzpah *pleasure, pride:* 6 noches *rejoice:* 5 kvell *subhuman:* 5 golem *unlucky person:* 9 shlemazel

yield 3 bow, net, pay 4 bear, bend, cave, cede, crop, earn, fold 5 defer, grant, waive 6 accede, bounty, buckle, comply, impart, output, profit, relent, render, resign, return,

reward, submit, supply, tender 7 abandon, bring in, concede, consent, deliver, furnish, harvest, produce, product, proffer, provide, revenue, succumb 8 abdicate, collapse, generate, hand over 9 acquiesce, surrender 10 bring forth, capitulate, production, relinquish

yielding 4 soft 6 docile, pliant, supple 7 bearing, passive, pliable 8 flexible 9 adaptable, malleable, tractable 10 manageable, productive, submissive 11 acquiescent, unresistant

yikes 3 gee, wow 4 gosh, uh-oh

yin and ____ 4 yang

yip 3 cry 4 bark, yelp

yippee 3 yay 6 hoorah, hooray, hurrah, hurray 10 hallelujah

yoga posture 5 asana

yoke 3 bar, tie, wed 4 bond, join, link, pair, span, team 5 clamp, frame, hitch, marry, unite 6 attach, couple, inspan 7 bondage, connect, control, harness, peonage, serfdom, slavery 8 marriage 9 servitude 10 crosspiece, oppression *combining form:* 3 zyg 4 zygo *part:* 5 oxbow

yokel 3 oaf, yap 4 boor, clod, hick, rube 5 churl, swain 6 rustic 7 bucolic, bumpkin, hayseed 9 chawbacon, hillbilly 10 clodhopper, countryman

yolk 4 food 6 yellow

yon see yonder

yonder 5 there 7 farther, further, thither 8 outlying

yore 3 old 7 history 8 foretime, lang syne 9 antiquity, yesterday 10 yesteryear

you 2 ye 3 one 4 thee, thou *French:* 2 tu 4 vous *German:* 2 du 3 Sie *Spanish:* 2 tu 5 usted 7 ustedes

young 3 fry, new 4 baby, tyro 5 brood, fresh, green 6 babies, callow, infant, junior, litter, tender, unripe 7 untried 8 childish, immature, juvenile, unformed, youthful 9 unfledged 10 unfinished, unseasoned 11 unpracticed 13 inexperienced *animal:* 3 cub, fry, kid, kit, pup 4 calf, colt, fawn, foal, joey 5 puppy 6 kitten, heifer, piglet *bird:* 5 chick 7 gosling *bring forth:* 3 ean 4 yean *hare:* 7 leveret *sheep, goat:* 4 lamb 8 yeanling

younger 6 junior

youngster 3 boy, cub, kid, lad, tad, tot 4 girl, lass, tike, tyke 5 chick, child 6 moppet, shaver, squirt 8 juvenile 9 fledgling

your 3 thy

youth 3 lad 5 prime 6 period, spring 8 juvenile, preadult, teenager 9 stripling 10 adolescent, springtide, springtime 12 inexperience *ancient Greek:* 6 ephebe 7 ephebus *goddess of:* 4 Hebe *mythological:*

6 Adonis, Apollo, Icarus 8 Ganymede *time of:* 9 salad days

youthful 5 fresh, green, young 6 boyish, callow, maiden, unripe 7 puerile 8 immature, juvenile, virginal 9 beardless, unfledged

yowl 3 bay, cry 4 bawl, howl, wail 6 scream, squall, squeal 7 ululate 9 caterwaul

yucca 7 cassava 9 bear grass

Yugoslav leader 4 Tito (Josip Broz)

Yukon *bay:* 9 Mackenzie *capital:* 10 Whitehorse *city:* 6 Dawson *mountain:* 5 Logan *river:* 5 Yukon 8 Klondike

yule 4 Noel, Xmas 8 Nativity 9 Christmas 13 Christmastide

Z

Zambia *capital:* 6 Lusaka *city:* 5 Kitwe, Ndola 11 Livingstone *lake:* 5 Mweru 9 Bangweulu 10 Tanganyika *monetary unit:* 6 kwacha *mountain range:* 8 Muchinga *neighbor:* 5 Congo 6 Angola, Malawi 7 Namibia 8 Tanzania, Zimbabwe 10 Mozambique *river:* 5 Kafue 7 Luangwa, Zambezi *waterfall:* 13 Victoria Falls

zany 3 nut, wag 4 card, fool, kook 5 antic, campy, clown, comic, crazy, cutup, dotty, goofy, idiot, joker, kooky, loony, nutty, wacky 6 jester, madcap 7 buffoon, farceur, half-wit 8 clowning, clownish, comedian, funnyman, jokester 9 harlequin, prankster, screwball, simpleton, trickster 11 merry-andrew

zap 3 hit 4 blow, kill, nuke 5 blast, snuff 6 attack 7 destroy, wipe out 8 dissolve 9 eliminate, irradiate, liquidate 10 annihilate

Zauberflöte composer 6 Mozart (Wolfgang Amadeus)

zeal 4 brio, fire, zest 5 ardor, drive, mania 6 desire, energy, esprit, fervor, spirit 7 avidity, passion, urgency 8 devotion, dynamism, keenness 9 eagerness, intensity, vehemence 10 enthusiasm, fanaticism, fierceness

zealot 3 bug, fan, nut 4 buff 5 fiend, freak 6 maniac, votary 7 devotee, fanatic, sectary 8 partisan 10 aficionado, enthusiast 12 true believer

zealous 4 avid, keen 5 afire, eager, fiery, fired, nutty, rabid 6 ardent, fervid, gung-ho 7 devoted, fanatic, fervent 8 frenetic, obsessed, wild-eyed 9 dedicated, fanatical, possessed 10 passionate 11 impassioned 12 enthusiastic

zebra 6 equine 7 referee 9 crosswalk *extinct:* 6 quagga *type:* 6 Grevy's 8 mountain 9 Burchell's

zebu 4 oxen

Zebulun 9 lost tribe *brother:* 4 Levi 5 Judah 6 Simeon *father:* 5 Jacob *mother:* 4 Leah

zecchino 6 sequin

Zechariah 7 prophet

Zedekiah 9 Mattaniah *father:* 6 Josiah

zenana 5 harem, serai 8 seraglio

zenith 3 top 4 acme, apex, peak 6 apogee, height, summit, vertex 8 capstone, pinnacle 11 culmination 12 highest point *opposite:* 5 nadir

Zenobia *husband:* 9 Odenathus *kingdom:* 7 Palmyra

Zeno follower 5 Stoic

Zephaniah 7 prophet 9 Sophonias

zephyr 6 breeze 8 west wind

Zephyrus *father:* 8 Astraeus *mother:* 3 Eos 6 Aurora

zeppelin 5 blimp 7 airship 9 dirigible

zero 2 oh 3 aim, nil, nix, zip 4 love, nada, none, null, void 5 aught, nadir, zilch 6 cipher, naught, nobody 7 nothing, nullity 8 goose egg 9 nonentity

zest 4 élan, peel, tang, zeal 5 gusto, taste 6 flavor, relish 7 delight, passion, sparkle 8 appetite, piquancy, pleasure 9 eagerness, enjoyment 10 enthusiasm

zesty 4 racy, tart 5 brisk, sharp, spicy, tangy 6 biting, lively, savory, snappy 7 peppery, piquant, pungent 8 exciting, poignant, seasoned, spirited 9 flavorful

Zetes *brother:* 6 Calais *father:* 6 Boreas *mother:* 8 Orithyia *slayer:* 8 Heracles, Hercules

Zethus *brother:* 7 Amphion *father:* 4 Zeus 7 Jupiter *mother:* 7 Antiope

Zeus 7 Jupiter *brother:* 5 Hades 8 Poseidon *daughter:* 3 Ate 4 Hebe 5 Helen 6 Athena 7 Artemis 9 Aphrodite 10 Persephone, Proserpina *father:* 6 Cronus *home:* 7 Olympus

(Mt.) *lover:* 4 Leda, Leto, Maia 5 Danaë, Dione, Metis 6 Aegina, Europa, Latona, Semele, Themis 7 Alcmene, Antiope, Demeter 8 Callisto, Eurynome *mother:* 4 Rhea *nurse:* 9 Almathaea *oracle:* 6 Dodona *shield:* 5 aegis *sister:* 4 Hera, Juno *son:* 4 Ares 5 Arcas, Argus, Minos 6 Aeacus, Apollo, Hermes, Zethus 7 Amphion, Perseus 8 Dionysus, Heracles, Hercules, Sarpedon, Tantalus *tree:* 3 oak *wife:* 4 Hera, Juno *weapon:* 11 thunderbolt

zigzag 4 tack, turn 5 angle, crank, weave 6 jagged 7 chevron 8 flexuous, indirect, serrated *course:* 6 slalom

zilch 3 nil, zip 4 nada, zero 5 aught, squat 6 cipher, diddly, naught, nobody 7 nothing, nullity 8 goose egg 9 nonentity 11 diddly-squat

Zimbabwe *capital:* 6 Harare *city:* 5 Gweru 6 Kwekwe, Mutare 8 Bulawayo, Maxvingo 11 Chitungwiza *dictator:* 6 Mugabe (Robert) *ethnic group:* 5 Shona 7 Ndebele *former name:* 8 Rhodesia *lake:* 6 Kariba *language:* 5 Bantu *neighbor:* 6 Zambia 8 Botswana 10 Mozambique 11 South Africa *river:* 4 Sabi 7 Limpopo, Zambezi *waterfall:* 13 Victoria Falls

zinc 7 element *ingot:* 7 spelter *ore:* 6 blende 10 sphalerite *symbol:* 2 Zn

zing 3 pan, pep, rap, vim, zap, zip 4 brio, dash, élan, slam, snap, zeal 5 ardor, flair, oomph, verve, vigor 6 energy, esprit, fervor, spirit 7 panache, passion, sparkle 8 dynamism, vitality 9 animation, eagerness 10 ebullience, enthusiasm

zinger 3 dig 4 barb, gibe, jibe, slam 6 retort 7 riposte

Zion 5 bliss 6 heaven, Israel 7 Elysium 8 eternity, paradise 12 New Jerusalem, promised land

Zionist *American:* 5 Szold (Henrietta) *English:* 7 Sokolow (Nahum) 8 Zangwill (Israel) *German:* 6 Nordau (Max Simon) *Hungarian:* 5 Herzl (Theodor) *Israeli:* 5 Buber (Martin) 8 Weizmann (Chaim)

zip 3 fly, nil, nix, pep, run, vim 4 brio, dash, hiss, rush, nada, snap, tear, whiz, zero, zest, zing, zoom 5 drive, gusto, hurry, oomph, speed, squat, whisk, zilch 6 bustle, energy, hasten, hustle 7 nothing 8 vitality 10 excitement, liveliness 11 diddly-squat

zippy 4 keen, spry, yare 5 agile, alert, brisk, peppy, quick, ready 6 lively, nimble, snappy, speedy 7 dynamic 8 spirited 9 sprightly

zircon 6 jargon 7 jargoon, mineral *variety:* 7 jacinth 8 hyacinth

zirconium *symbol* 2 Zr

zit 6 pimple

zither 10 instrument *Chinese:* 3 kin 4 ch'in *Japanese:* 4 koto *relative:* 8 autoharp, dulcimer

zodiac sign 3 Leo (the Lion) 5 Aries (the Ram), Libra (the Balance, the Scales), Virgo (the Virgin) 6 Cancer (the Crab), Gemini (the Twins), Pisces (the Fishes), Taurus (the Bull) 7 Scorpio (the Scorpion) 8 Aquarius (the Water Bearer) 9 Capricorn (the Goat) 11 Sagittarius (the Archer)

Zola work 4 Nana 7 J'accuse 8 Drunkard (The), Germinal 9 La Débâcle 10 L'Assommoir 13 Thérèse Raquin

zombie 5 robot 8 cocktail 9 automaton

zone 4 area, band, belt 5 layer, tract 6 region, sector 7 portion, quarter, section, segment, stretch 8 district, division, encircle, surround 9 partition, territory

zonked 4 high 5 dazed, doped, drunk, tight 6 ripped, stoned 7 drugged, drunken, smashed 8 hopped-up, tripping, turned on, wiped out 9 spaced-out, strung out, stupefied 10 inebriated, tripped out 11 intoxicated

zoologist *American:* 5 Clark (Eugenie), Hyatt (Alpheus) 6 Carson (Rachel), Fossey (Dian), Osborn (Henry Fairfield), Yerkes (Robert) 7 Agassiz (Alexander), Ditmars (Raymond), Merriam (Clinton) 8 Hornaday (William) *Austrian:* 6 Frisch (Karl von) *British:* 6 Darwin (Charles), Huxley (Julian, Thomas) 7 Goodall (Jane), Medawar (Peter) 9 Lankester (Edwin) *Dutch:* 10 Swammerdam (Jan) *French:* 6 Buffon (G.-L. Leclerc), Cuvier (Georges) *German:* 7 Haeckel (Ernst) *Norwegian:* 6 Nansen (Fridtjof) *South African:* 5 Broom (Robert) *Swedish:* 8 Linnaeus (Carolus)

zoom 3 hum, zip 4 buzz, dash, whiz, zero 5 focus, speed, whizz 6 streak 7 shoot up 9 skyrocket

zoophyte 5 coral 6 sponge 8 bryozoan 9 gorgonian 10 sea anemone

Zoroastrian *demon:* 4 deva *god:* 10 Ahura Mazda *sacred writings:* 6 Avesta

zounds 3 gad 4 egad 8 gadzooks 11 odd's bodkins

zucchetto 7 calotte 8 skullcap

zwieback 5 toast 7 biscuit

zygomatic bone 5 malar 9 cheekbone

zygote 4 cell 6 oocyst